Cultural Studies
An Anthology

Edited by Michael Ryan

Associate Editor Hanna Musiol

Blackwell
Publishing

BLACKWELL PUBLISHING

350 Main Street, Malden, MA 02148-5020, USA
9600 Garsington Road, Oxford OX4 2DQ, UK
550 Swanston Street, Carlton, Victoria 3053, Australia

First published 2008 by Blackwell Publishing Ltd

1   2008

Library of Congress Cataloging-in-Publication Data is available for this book

ISBN: 978-1-4051-4576-3 (hardback)
ISBN: 978-1-4051-4577-0 (paperback)

A catalogue record for this title is available from the British Library.

Set in 10.5 on 12.5 pt Ehrhardt
by SNP Best-set Typesetter Ltd., Hong Kong
Printed and bound in Singapore
by Markono Print Media Pte Ltd

The publisher's policy is to use permanent paper from mills that operate a sustainable forestry policy, and which has been manufactured from pulp processed using acid-free and elementary chlorine-free practices. Furthermore, the publisher ensures that the text paper and cover board used have met acceptable environmental accreditation standards.

For further information on
Blackwell Publishing, visit our website at
www.blackwellpublishing.com

For Iris Marion Young
friend, comrade

Cultural Studies

For Iris Marion Young
friend, comrade

Contents

Contents

Preface

Cultural Studies is a new field at the university level. It emerged in the 1950s amongst British literary scholars with an interest in the study of television, the news media, and what they called the "popular arts," and it has since grown to include a wide range of disciplines from Sociology, Communications, and Anthropology to Music, Geography, Literature, Education, and Film. That rapid development is reflective of economic, technological, and social changes that have made the media central to human existence as well as of advances in the methods of the cultural sciences since the 1960s such as Structuralism[1] and Post-Structuralism[2] which have made possible more complex understandings of culture.

The emergence in the West of commercialized mass culture in the nineteenth century in the form of dance halls, dime novels, and daily newspapers and in the twentieth century in the form of film, television, and mass market magazines provoked an interest in how culture functions in human society. Anthropologists began studying culture considered as a way of life in the nineteenth century. They were interested in the symbols, rituals, and practices of "primitive" cultures. In the early twentieth century, sociologists began to apply the same methods and ideas to modern societies. They became interested in cultural institutions such as fashion as well as in the cultural dimension of politics – the way charisma functions in political leadership, for example. The experience of fascism inspired sociologists associated with the Frankfurt School to study the influence of commercialized mass culture such as film and popular literature on people's political beliefs and behavior. Even seemingly meaningless movies are important, they felt, because they shape people's understandings of and actions in the world.

This early work in Cultural Studies noted that culture plays an important role in forming our identities, constructing our perceptions of the world around us, and providing formats for social action that lend meaning to our activities. A significant advance in the study of culture occurred in the mid-twentieth century. Students of Structuralism such as Roland Barthes pointed out that culture is semiotic; it operates like linguistics in that it is a signifying system. When we consume cars, we not only acquire a physical object; we also acquire a sign that signifies to others who we are and what our economic status is. A revived interest in Marxism in the late twentieth century added another dimension to the study of culture. Marxist cultural scholars argued that culture is an instrument of economic power. Media corporations promote attitudes, assumptions, and ideas appropriate to the capitalist economic system of which they are a part. Other Marxist scholars pointed out that culture provides ways of dissenting from the corporate-run economic order.

Culture has always had two meanings. First, culture is a way of life specific to a particular community. The culture of white, upper-class teens in an American suburb is quite distinct from the culture of patriarchal shepherd communities in mountain villages in Uzbekhistan. The styles of speech, the moral assumptions, the gender identities, and the political outlooks will all be measurably different. Culture in this sense consists of the forms of thought, speech, and action as well as the rituals, institutions, and protocols of a particular community. They distinguish that community from others around it, and they express and reproduce settled understandings that allow a particular society to function. When a cultural community shares a sense that ostentation is inappropriate, for example, those with wealth in the community will not rub it in others' faces by driving expensive cars. The culture will enforce a certain restraint in dress, habitation, and the like through gestures of approval or disapproval. Not all national communities are homogeneous, however. When national or geographic communities consist of diverse social sub-groups, the relations between the dominant culture and the sub-groups can be vexed. A classic contemporary case is that of Muslims in France who wish to wear traditional Islamic dress in public settings where the norms of the dominant culture prevail.

Second, culture is the deliberate design of signifying materials into meaningful artifacts. Culture in this sense consists of events and objects such as movies, television shows, dance concerts, rap songs, web postings, and the like that mean something because we share codes that determine that a sound or image or action will be meaningful in a certain way in a particular context or situation. Cultural production does not simply replicate codes, however; it is also, quite obviously, creative and dissonant. It changes the configuration of symbols, narratives, and understandings of the world in which we live. Artists change how people think, feel, and act by changing the symbols, the narratives, and the styles in which they think, feel, and act. Such change is on-going, and one way of understanding the nexus between the two meanings of culture is to say that the production of new cultural events and objects such as rap songs and movies is constantly contending with culture defined as a shared understanding of the world. If culture in one sense allows us to perceive and value the same things, culture in the second sense allows us to produce new perceptions and values that differ from the dominant culture. Supposedly "tasteless" American sexual comedies of the *American Pie* variety, for example, erode old moral assumptions and make possible new styles of identity for young men and women. They take issue with a previously dominant understanding of young female sexuality especially as deviant or abnormal if it is active and precocious.

Cultural Studies is distinguished as an academic undertaking by its willingness to foreground the political dimensions of our lives. It notices, for example, that ownership is power, power is control, and control is frequently exercised through culture. Culture is much more than entertainment. It is the software program of human life. Who controls cultural production is an important issue, therefore, because culture not only reflects reality; it also produces it. By making certain understandings of the world dominant, cultural producers, especially those with control over mass markets in television, film, music, and journalism, shape how people think, feel, and act in the world. How we act depends on what is in our minds – what images and stories and metaphors we use for understanding the world. It makes an enormous difference, for example, whether those fighting the United States around the world are perceived through the metaphor of "terrorism" (which transfers an action into an identity) or perceived as "Islamic fundamentalist radicals angry at the military presence of the United States in the Muslim Holy Land and at US support for Israel's occupation of Palestine" (which is less of a metaphor and which would require a more painstaking media representation than one is likely to find on, say, Fox News). If they are perceived through the metaphor of terrorism, then we are more likely to be easily mobilized by political leaders to engage in military action against them, but if the alternative, more complex understanding were disseminated widely, then the virtue of such military action would become more debatable.

Cultural Studies also emphasizes the way culture can be used to resist control. Rap artists in the early 1990s, for example, sought to shift dominant media perceptions of young African-Americans that portrayed them as violent, drug-addicted gangsters. Songs such as "The Nigga You Love to Hate" challenged the dominant media perspective and gave expression to thoughts and feelings that were found nowhere in the news media. Such cultural works made it possible to think about the lives of African-American youth in more complex terms than were possible or likely in media dominated by people with little experience of and little sympathy for the lives of young African-Americans. Cultural resistance is important, therefore, because one's identity is in part determined by how one is treated by others. If the prevailing image of your social group in a culture is negative, the likelihood that you will be mistreated increases. Cultural production is an important way of challenging and rectifying dominant misrepresentations.

Cultural Studies draws attention to the fabricated character of much of what we take to be "reality." The power of those who control a society culturally, economically, politically, and socially is best secured by the pretense that the projection of their values, choices, assumptions, and ideals into the world constitutes "reality." But if one notices, as Cultural Studies does, the cultural character of this reality, the fact that it is a product of choices, projections, and fabrications, then it ceases to have such a hold on us. For example, the drug of choice for wealthy white men – alcohol – is portrayed in western culture as a harmless diversion even though it kills, and an entire culture of taste has arisen around such cultural fetishes as French wine. The drugs of choice for sub-groups whose more painful experience of economic deprivation makes more potent sedatives attractive – heroin, crack cocaine, methamphetamines – are illegal, and the dominant culture portrays them as signs of moral deviancy. This cultural strategy of portraying others as deviant helps secure the legitimacy of one's own economic power and social status. One will appear more "moral," and as a result, one's access, by virtue of economic power, to political power will appear justified.

Culture thus produces a particular reality by fabricating a distinction between the morally acceptable and the morally deviant. But if one begins to think of those realities as being cultural, they become less real. Dominant cultural values (such as those that make a desire for alcohol seem natural and a desire for heroin seem depraved) suddenly seem questionable and contingent. They do not rest on a natural foundation that assures that one's beliefs and assumptions about drugs are justifiable because true. They rest instead on a political choice that expresses a dominant group's preferences. It has no natural ground; it is instead a cultural fabrication.

It is more than a little disturbing to think that most of what goes on in our minds is the result of such fabrications. When we value something or prefer something or decide something or feel something strongly, we would prefer to be acting on our own. But usually we are not. Usually, we are merely voicing our culture. And "our" culture often is other people's decisions about what should be valued in our particular world. Such values generally serve those people's interests and assure their social, economic, and political power. Most of those values seem so normal and natural that is difficult for us even to see them as constructs or fabrications. In western societies, we get so used to seeing mostly white men in positions of economic, social, and political power, for example, that we cease to think it is in fact abnormal and deviant. We get so used to treating one dangerous and often fatal drug as normal and others as deviant that we do not notice how irrational that moral scheme is.

It helps to go to the historical past or to isolated contemporary societies that exist in a kind of historical past to get a better sense of how contingent reality can be. In one New Guinea culture, young girls are expected to perform oral sex on older men for a period of time as part of their ritualized passage into adulthood. Similarly, in ancient Athens, boys were expected to perform oral sex for older men for an extended period of time before they were treated as adults and accepted into the community. In each culture, the practice was considered normal. No doubt, all the young men and women involved thought so as well.

Now imagine that we are all in one way or another like those young men and women. We all think and feel and act on the basis of assumptions that come from our culture and that appear perfectly normal, morally right, and natural – but that are in fact quite weird and that benefit those with power over us: like spending most of our lives working like busy little drone ants so that a small group of people can become very rich off our labors and enjoy themselves quite a bit at our expense; or killing angry young Arab men for objecting to our stationing of an army in their backyard so that oil will continue to flow to fuel an economy run by people willing to commit murder to preserve their economic power; or treating heroin as depraved while binging, often fatally, on "normal" alcohol; or behaving like belligerent, domineering animals in supposedly civilized business settings; or believing that the outcome of cultural rituals such as sports are incredibly important when two hundred years from now they will be meaningless.

Cultural Studies encourages us to think about these things in a critical and self-conscious fashion. It asks us to step back from the culture in which we are immersed and to view it critically and analytically. Once one does that, one begins to see that most of what is considered to be reality is in fact debatable and questionable because it is the product of choices and fabrications. Alcohol versus heroin a no-brainer? It's only so because you aren't thinking enough. Cultural Studies places us all in the position of the character in *The Matrix* who is offered a choice between a red pill and a blue pill, waking up to cultural fabrication or staying asleep in the real world.

Michael Ryan
Stonington
July 2007

Notes

1. Structuralism is a school of thought that assumes that linguistics provides a model for understanding other systems of meaning such as culture. In a Structuralist understanding, such events as a fashion show or such objects as cars are "signifiers" whose meaning is determined by their relations with other signifiers. Signifiers acquire meaning by their difference from other signifiers, just as the meanings or signifieds they refer to have an identity of their own only as they differentiate from other meanings. Systems of meaning are complete unto themselves and do not depend on the reference of sign to thing or object. Rather, meaning is entirely determined within the signifying system. A bright red Porsche Carrera, for example, is little different from other cars in a material sense; it has the same engine, the same transmission, etc. But it signifies a different meaning – luxury, wealth, social power, a particular kind of adventurous personality, etc. That meaning only makes sense if there are other adjacent meanings from which it differs – the hum-drum middle-class values of someone who drives a dull brown Honda Civic, for example. The Honda Civic may have a better engine, transmission, etc., and may be better in a material or real sense. But as a signifier within a system of meaningful relations between terms in which meaning is generated entirely by the relations of difference between the signifiers within the system, the Honda, despite its being a better, more reliable car in a material sense, is a lesser semiotic or signifying object. It signifies comparatively less wealth, prestige, status, social power, etc.
2. Post-Structuralism is usually said to begin with the work of Jacques Derrida in the late 1960s. If Structuralists such as Roland Barthes studied the way systems of meaning attach to material things such as fashion shows or cooking and eating, so that a sense of cultural order develops on top of nature, Derrida was interested in the way all our systems of meaning impose order on an inherently amorphous world of signifying material. It is possible to take apart or deconstruct any system of order or of meaning by noticing how it arises on top of and necessarily represses an inherent disorder in its elements. For example, if language is, as Structuralism claims, a system of differences in which no term has an identity apart from its differences from all other terms in the linguistic system, then at no point is there a fulcrum of stability on which one can construct a well-founded order of meaning. Everything differs from everything else. There is no moment that transcends or steps outside of this flow of differentiation. Everything is inherently unstable and contingent. All our decisions as to what is meaningful are just that – decisions, rather than expressions of an order inherent in nature.

Acknowledgments to Sources

The editor and publisher gratefully acknowledge the permission granted to reproduce the copyright material in this book:

Every effort has been made to trace copyright holders and to obtain their permission for the use of copyright material. The publisher apologizes for any errors or omissions in the above list and would be grateful to be notified of any corrections that should be incorporated in future reprints or editions of this book.

Chapter 1   Michele Hilmes, "Battle of Global Paradigms," originally published as "Who We Are, Who We Are Not: Battle of Global Paradigms," pp. 53–73 from *Planet TV: A Global Television Reader*, ed. L. Parks and S. Kumar (New York: New York University Press). © 2003 by New York University. Reprinted with permission from the author and New York University Press.

Chapter 2   David Hesmondhalgh, "Ownership, Organisation, and Cultural Work," pp. 134–54 from *The Cultural Industries* (London, Sage Publications). © 2002 by David Hesmondhalgh. Reprinted with permission from the author and Sage Publications Ltd.

Chapter 3   Robert McChesney, "The World Wide Web and the Corporate Media System," originally published as "So much for the magic of technology and the free market: The World Wide Web and the corporate media system," pp. 5–35 from *The World Wide Web and Contemporary Media Theory*, ed. A. Herman and T. Swiss (New York: Routledge). © 2000 by Routledge. Reproduced with permission from the author and Routledge, a division of Taylor & Francis Group.

Chapter 4   Alison Beale, "Identifying a Policy Hierarchy: Communication Policy, Media Industries, and Globalization," pp. 78–89 from *Global Cultures: Media, Arts, Policy and Globalization*, ed. D. Crane, N. Kawashima and K. Nawasaki (New York: Routledge). © 2002 by Routledge. Reproduced with permission from the author and Routledge, a division of Taylor & Francis Group.

Chapter 5   Imre Szeman, "The Rhetoric of Culture: Some Notes on Magazines, Canadian Culture and Globalization," pp. 212–30 from *Journal of Canadian Studies*, vol. 35, no. 3. © 2000 by Journal of Canadian Studies. Reprinted with permission from Journal of Canadian Studies.

Chapter 6   Don Mitchell, "Metaphors to Live By: Landscapes as Systems of Social Reproduction," pp. 120–44 from *Cultural Geography: A Critical Introduction* (Malden, MA: Blackwell). © 2000 by Donald Mitchell. Reprinted with permission from Blackwell Publishing.

Chapter 7   Tony Bennett, "Hegemony, Ideology, Pleasure: Blackpool," pp. 135–54 from *Popular Culture and Social Relations*, ed. T. Bennett, C. Mercer and J. Woollacott (Milton Keynes and Philadelphia: Open University Press). © 1986 by Tony Bennett. Reprinted with permission from the author.

Chapter 8   Mike Davis, "City of Quartz: Excavating the Future in Los Angeles," pp. 223–40, 261–2 from *City of Quartz: Excavating the Future in Los Angeles* (London: Verso). © 1990 by Verso. Reprinted with permission from Verso.

Chapter 9   Geraldine Pratt, "Grids of Difference: Place and Identity Formation," pp. 26–48 from *Cities of Difference*, ed. R. Finger and J. M. Jacobs (New York and London: Guilford Press). © 1998 by The Guilford Press. Reprinted with permission from Guilford Publications, Inc.

Chapter 10   Ackbar Abbas, "Cosmopolitan De-scriptions: Shanghai and Hong Kong," pp. 772–6, 777–83, 785–6 from *Public Culture*, Vol. 12, no. 3. © 2000 by Duke University Press. All rights reserved. Used by permission of the publisher.

Chapter 11   Kathleen C. Stewart, "An Occupied Place," pp. 137–64 from *Senses of Place*, ed. S. Feld and K. Basso (Santa Fe, NM: School of American Research Press). © 1996 by the School of American Research, Santa Fe, USA. Reprinted with permission from the School for American Research.

Chapter 12   Judith Butler, "Bodily Inscriptions, Performative Subversions," pp. 103–15 from *The Judith Butler Reader*, ed. S. Salih and J. Butler (Malden, MA: Blackwell). Selected from "Subversive Bodily Acts," *Gender Trouble: Feminism and the Subversion of Identity* (New York: Routledge, 1990), pp. 163–80, 215–16. © 1990 by Judith Butler. Reproduced by permission of the author and Routledge, a division of Taylor & Francis Group.

Chapter 13   Linda McDowell and Gillian Court, "Missing Subjects: Gender and Sexuality in Merchant Banking," pp. 229–51 from *Economic Geography*, vol. 70, no. 3 © 1994 by Economic Geography. Reprinted with permission from Clark University.

Chapter 14   Barbara Creed, "Horror and the Monstrous-Feminine: An Imaginary Abjection," pp. 44–70 from *Screen*, vol. 27, no. 1. © 1986 by Screen. Reprinted with permission from the author and Screen.

Chapter 15   Mark McClelland, "Japanese Queerscapes: Global/Local Intersections on the Internet", pp. 52–69 from *Mobile Cultures: New Media in Queer Asia*, ed. C. Berry, F. Martin and A. Yue (Durham, NC: Duke University

Press). © 2003 by Duke University Press. All rights reserved. Used by permission of the publisher.

Chapter 16   Lisa Duke, "Get Real! Cultural Relevance and Resistance to the Mediated Feminine Ideal," originally published as "'Get Real!' Relevance and Resistance to the Mediated Feminine Ideal," pp. 211–33 from *Psychology & Marketing*, vol. 19, no. 2. © 2002 by John Wiley & Sons, Inc. Reprinted with permission from John Wiley & Sons, Inc.

Chapter 17   Karl Marx and Friedrich Engels, "The German Ideology," pp. 39–40 from *The Marx-Engels Reader 2e*, ed. Robert C. Tucker (New York: W. W. Norton & Company). © 1978, 1972 by W. W. Norton & Company, Inc. Used by permission of W. W. Norton & Company, Inc.

Chapter 18   Louis Althusser, "Ideology," originally published as "Theory, Theoretical Practice and Theoretical Formation: Ideology and Ideological Struggle," pp. 1–42 from *Philosophy and the Spontaneous Philosophy of the Scientists & Other Essays* (London and New York: Verso). © 1990 by Verso. Reprinted with permission from Verso.

Chapter 19   John Fiske, "Interpellation," originally published as "British Cultural Studies and Television," pp. 284–326 from *Channels of Discourse, Reassembled*, ed. R. C. Allen (Chapel Hill and London: University of North Carolina Press). © 1992 by The University of North Carolina Press. Used by permission of the publisher.

Chapter 20   Pun Ngai, "Becoming Dagongmei: Politics of Identity and Difference in Reform China," pp. 1–18 from *The China Journal*, no. 42, July. © 1999 by The China Journal. Reprinted with permission from The China Journal.

Chapter 21   Teun van Dijk, "The Ideology and Discourse of Modern Racism," pp. 277–93 from *Ideology: A Multidisciplinary Approach* (London: Sage Publications Ltd). © 1998 by Teun A. van Dijk. Reprinted with permission from the author and Sage Publications Ltd.

Chapter 22   Sohail H. Hashmi, "9/11 and the Jihad Tradition," pp. 149–64 from *Terror, Culture, Politics: Rethinking 9/11*, ed. D. J. Sherman and T. Nardin (Bloomington: Indiana University Press). © 2006 by Daniel J. Sherman and Terry Nardin. Reprinted with permission from Indiana University Press.

Chapter 23   Margaret Morse, "An Ontology of Everyday Distraction: The Freeway, the Mall and Television, pp. 99–124, 226–32 from *Virtualities: Television, Media Art, and Cyberculture* (Bloomington, Indiana University Press). © 1990 by Margaret Morse. Reprinted with permission from Indiana University Press.

Chapter 24   Ann Burlein, "Nichemarketing the Apocalypse: Violence as Hard-Sell," pp. 75–115 from *Lift High the Cross: Where White Supremacy and the Christian Right Converge* (Durham, NC and London: Duke University Press). © 2002 by Duke University Press. All rights reserved. Used by permission of the publisher.

Chapter 25   Kenneth Burke, "The Rhetoric of Hitler's 'Battle'," pp. 191–220 from *The Philosophy of Literary Form: Studies in Symbolic Action* (Baton Rouge:

Chapter 26   John D. H. Downing, "Public Speech, Dance, Jokes, and Song," pp. 105–18 from *Radical Media: Rebellious Communication and Social Movements* (Thousand Oaks, CA and London: Sage Publications). © 2001 by Sage Publications, Inc. Reprinted by permission of Sage Publications, Inc.

Chapter 27   Mark Hulsether, "Thinking About the End of the World with Conservative Protestants," pp. 190–9 from *Religion, Culture and Politics in the Twentieth-Century United States* (Edinburgh: Edinburgh University Press). © 2007 by Mark Hulsether. Reprinted with permission from Edinburgh University Press, www.eup.ed.ac.uk, and Columbia University Press.

Chapter 28   Jayson Harsin, "The Rumor Bomb: American Mediated Politics as Pure War." An earlier, longer version of this article appeared as "The Rumor Bomb: Theorizing the Convergence of New and Old Trends in Mediated US Politics" in *Southern Review: Communication, Politics & Culture*, vol. 39, no. 1. © 2006 by J. Harsin. Reprinted with permission from the author.

Chapter 29   George Kamberelis, and Greg Dimitriadis, "Talkin' Tupac: Speech Genres and the Mediation of Cultural Knowledge," pp. 119–50 from *Sound Identities: Popular Music and the Cultural Politics of Education*, ed. C. McCarthy, G. Hudak, S. Miklauc and P. Saukko (New York: Peter Lang). © 1999. Reprinted with permission from Peter Lang Publishing.

Chapter 30   Richard Lewontin, Steven Rose and Leon Kamin, "What is Race," originally published as "IQ: The Rank Ordering of the World," pp. 119–29, 298 from *Not in Our Genes: Biology, Ideology, and Human Nature* (New York, Pantheon Books). © 1984 by R. C. Lewontin, Steven Rose and Leon J. Kamin. Used by permission of the authors and Pantheon Books, a division of Random House, Inc.

Chapter 31   Paul Gilroy, "The Crisis of 'Race' and Raciology," pp. 11–41; 49–53 from *Against Race: Imagining Political Culture Beyond the Color Line* (Cambridge, MA, Belknap Press of Harvard University Press). © 2000 by Paul Gilroy. *Against Race* was published in the UK under the title *Between Camps: Nations, Culture and the Allure of Race 2e* (London: Routledge, 2004). Reprinted with permission from the author and Harvard University Press.

Chapter 32   Sherene Razack, "What Is to Be Gained by Looking White People in the Eye? Culture, Race, and Gender in Cases of Sexual Violence," pp. 894–923 from *Signs: Journal of Women in Culture and Society*, vol. 19, no. 4. © 1994 by The University of Chicago. Reprinted by permission of the University of Chicago Press.

Chapter 33   Grant Farred, "Fiaca and Veron-ismo: Race and Silence in Argentine Football," pp. 47–61 from *Leisure Studies*, vol 23, no. 1. © 2004 by Taylor

& Francis Ltd. Reprinted with permission from the publisher (Taylor & Francis Ltd, http://www.tandf.co.uk/journals).

Chapter 34   Dick Hebdige, "*Subculture: The Meaning of Style*," pp. 130–42 from *The Subcultures Reader*, ed. K. Gelder and S. Thornton (New York: Routledge). © 1979 by Dick Hebdige. Reprinted with permission from Taylor & Francis Books UK.

Chapter 35   Paul Hodkinson, "The Goth Scene and (Sub)Cultural Substance," pp. 135–47 from *After Subculture: Critical Studies in Contemporary Youth Culture*, ed. A. Bennett and K. Kahn-Harris (New York: Palgrave Macmillan). © 2004. Reprinted with permission from Palgrave Macmillan.

Chapter 36   Pamela J. Tracy, "'Why Don't You Act Your Color?': Preteen Girls, Identity, and Popular Music," pp. 45–52 from *Race/Gender/Media: Considering Diversity Across Audiences, Content and Producers*, ed. R. A. Lind (Boston, MA: Pearson, Allyn & Bacon, 2004). © 2004 by Pearson.

Chapter 37   Marcos Becquer and José Gatti, "Elements of Vogue," pp. 445–53 from *The Subcultures Reader*, ed. K. Gelder and S. Thornton (New York: Routledge). © 1997 by M. Becquer and J. Gatti. Reprinted with permission from the authors.

Chapter 38   Simon Reynolds, "In Our Angelhood: Rave as Counterculture and Spiritual Revolution," pp. 239–48 from *Generation Ecstasy: Into the World of Techno and Rave* (Boston, MA: Little Brown). © 1999 by Routledge Publishing, Inc. Reprinted with permission from Routledge Publishing, Inc.

Chapter 39   Ben Chappell, "Lowrider Style: Cultural Politics and the Poetics of Scale," © 2007 by Ben Chappell. Reprinted with permission from the author. Some material from this essay appeared in an earlier form in pp. 100–20 in the volume *Technicolor: Race, Technology, and Everyday Life*, ed. A. Nelson, T. Linh and A. Hines (New York University Press, 2001).

Chapter 40   Stephen Duncombe, "Purity and Danger," pp. 141–53; 163–73 from *Notes from the Underground: Zines and the Politics of Alternative Culture* (New York and London: Verso). © 1997 by Stephen Duncombe. Reprinted with permission from Verso.

Chapter 41   Mike Featherstone, "Perspectives on Consumer Culture," pp. 5–22 from *Sociology*, vol. 24, no. 1 (Sage Publications). © 1990 by BSA Publications Ltd. Reprinted with permission from Sage Publications Ltd.

Chapter 42   Roland Barthes, "Mythologies," pp. 81–3 from *Literary Theory: An Anthology*, ed. J. Rivkin and M. Ryan (Malden, MA: Blackwell, 1998). Orig. pp. 36–8 and 114–17 from *Mythologie*, trans A. Lavers (New York: Hill & Wang, 1972). Translation copyright © 1972 by Jonathan Cape Ltd. Reprinted with permission from Hill & Wang, a division of Farrar, Straus and Giroux, LLC, and the Random House Group Ltd.

Chapter 43   Elizabeth Niederer and Rainer Winter, "Fashion, Culture and the Construction of Identity", newly written for this volume. © 2008 by Blackwell Publishing Ltd.

Chapter 44 Sze Tsung Leong, ". . . And then there was shopping," pp. 129–35 from *The Harvard Design School Guide to Shopping*, ed. C. J. Chung, J. Inaba, R. Koolhaas and S. T. Leong (Cambridge, MA: Harvard Design School). © 2001 by Harvard Design School. Reprinted with permission from Taschen GmbH.

Chapter 45 Douglas B. Holt, "Does Cultural Capital Structure American Consumption?" pp. 1–25 from *Journal of Consumer Research*, vol. 25. © 1998 by Journal of Consumer Research, Inc. Reprinted with permission from the University of Chicago Press.

Chapter 46 Sharon Zukin, "Julia Learns to Shop," pp. 35–43 and 282–3 from *Point of Purchase: How Shopping Changed American Culture* (New York: Routledge). © 2003 by Routledge Publishing, Inc. Reprinted with permission from Routledge Publishing, Inc.

Chapter 47 Angela McRobbie, "Fashion as a Culture Industry," pp. 253–63 from *Fashion Cultures, Theories, Explorations, and Analysis*, ed. S. Bruzzi and P. C. Gibson (London and New York: Routledge). © 2000 by Angela McRobbie. Reprinted with permission from the author.

Chapter 48 Paul Smith, "Tommy Hilfiger in the Age of Mass Customization," pp. 249–62 from *No Sweat: Fashion, Free Trade, and the Rights of Garment Workers*, ed. A. Ross (New York and London: Verso). © 1997. Reprinted with permission from Verso.

Chapter 49 Andy Opel, "Constructing Purity: Bottled Water and the Commodification of Nature," pp. 67–76 from *Journal of American Culture*, vol. 22, no. 4 (winter). © 1999 by Journal of American Culture. Reprinted with permission from Blackwell Publishing.

Chapter 50 Gayle Wald, "Just a Girl? Rock Music, Feminism, and the Cultural Construction of Female Youth," pp. 585–610 from *Signs: Journal of Women in Culture and Society*, vol. 23, no. 3. © 1998 by The University of Chicago. Reprinted with permission from the University of Chicago Press.

Chapter 51 John Collins, "Some Anti-Hegemonic Aspects of African Popular Music," pp. 185–94 from *Rockin' the Boat: Mass Music and Mass Movements*, ed. R. Garofalo (Boston, MA: South End Press). © 1992 by Reebee Garofalo. Reprinted with permission from South End Press.

Chapter 52 Marcus Breen, "Desert Dreams, Media, and Interventions in Reality: Australian Aboriginal Music," pp. 149–70 from *Rockin' the Boat: Mass Music and Mass Movements*, ed. R. Garofalo (Boston, MA: South End Press). © 1992 by Reebee Garofalo. Reprinted with permission from South End Press.

Chapter 53 Anahid Kassabian, "Ubiquitous Listening," pp. 131–42 from *Popular Music Studies*, ed. D. Hesmondhalgh and K. Negus (London, Arnold). © 2002 by Arnold. Reproduced by permission of Edward Arnold (Publishers) Ltd.

Chapter 54 Charity Marsh and Melissa West, "The Nature/Technology Binary Opposition Dismantled in the Music of Madonna and Björk," pp. 182–203 from *Music and Technoculture*; ed. R. T. A. Lysoff and L. C. Gay, Jr

(Middletown, CT: Wesleyan University Press). © 2003 by Rene T. A. Lysoff and Leslie C. Gay. Reprinted with permission from Wesleyan University Press. www.wesleyan.edu/wespress.

Chapter 55   Will Straw, "Characterizing Rock Music Culture: The Case of Heavy Metal," pp. 97–110 from *On Record: Rock, Pop, and the Written Word*, ed. S. Frith and A. Goodwin (New York: Pantheon Books). © 1990 by Will Straw. Reprinted with permission from the author.

Chapter 56   Murray Forman, M. (2000) "'Represent': Race, Space and Place in Rap Music" pp. 65–90 from *Popular Music*, vol. 19, no. 1. © 2000 by Cambridge University Press. Reprinted with permission from the author and publisher.

Chapter 57   Stuart Hall, "Encoding, Decoding," pp. 129–38 from *Culture, Media, Language*, ed. S. Hall, D. Hobson, A. Lowe and P. Willis. This chapter is an edited extract from "Encoding and Decoding Television Discourse," *CCCS Stencilled Paper*, 7 (Birmingham: CCCS, 1973). © 1980 by Stuart Hall. Reprinted with permission from the author.

Chapter 58   John Hartley, "Heliography: Journalism and the Visualization of Truth," pp. 140–63 and 229–30 from *The Politics of Pictures: the Creation of Public in the Age of Popular Media* (New York: Routledge). © 1992 by John Hartley. Reprinted with permission from Taylor & Francis Books UK.

Chapter 59   Stuart Allan, "The Cultural Politics of News Discourse," pp. 77–97 from *News Culture*, 2e. (Buckingham, Open University Press). © 2004 Stuart Allan. Reprinted with permission from the Open University Press.

Chapter 60   Justin Lewis, Karin Wahl-Jorgensen and Sanna Inthorn, "Images of Citizenship on Television News: Constructing a Passive Public," pp. 153–64 from *Journalism Studies*, vol. 5, no. 2. © 2004 by Taylor & Francis Ltd. Reprinted with permission from the publisher (Taylor & Francis Ltd, http://www.tandf.co.uk/journals).

Chapter 61   Alice Crawford, "*Unheimlich* Maneuver: Self-Image and Indentificatory Practice in Virtual Reality Environments," pp. 237–55 from *Eloquent Images: Word and Image in the Age of New Media*. ed. M. E. Hocks, and M. R. Kendrick (Cambridge, MA: MIT Press). © 2003 by Massachusetts Institute of Technology. Reprinted with permission from the MIT Press.

Chapter 62   Astrid Deuber-Mankowsky, "The Phenomenon of Lara Croft," pp. 1–5, 7–12 & 91–2 from *Lara Croft: Cyber Heroine*, trans D. J. Bonfiglio (Minneapolis: University of Minnesota Press). © 2005. Reprinted with permission from University of Minnesota Press.

Chapter 63   David Howard, "From the Missile Gap To The Culture Gap: Modernism In The Fallout From Sputnik," pp. 61–72 from *The Writing on the Cloud: American Culture Confronts the Atomic Bomb*, ed. A. M. Scott and C. D. Geist (Lanham MD: University Press of America). © 1997. Reprinted with permission from the University Press of America.

Chapter 64   Ian Gordon, "Nostalgia, Myth, and Ideology: Vision of Superman at the End of the 'American century'," pp. 177–93 from *Comics & Ideology*, ed.

M. P. McCallister, E. H. Sewell and I. Gordon (New York: Peter Lang Publishing). © 2001. Reprinted with permission from Peter Lang Publishing.

Chapter 65 Kaja Silverman, "Camera and Eye," pp. 125–37 and 242–5 (notes) from *The Gaze Threshold of the Visible World*. (New York, Routledge). First appeared in 1993 as "What is a Camera?, or History in the Field of Vision" in *Discourse*, vol. 15, no. 3. © 1993 by *Discourse*. Reprinted with permission from Wayne State University Press.

Chapter 66 Russell J. A. Kilbourn, "Re-writing 'Reality': Reading the Matrix," pp. 1–19 from *Canadian Journal of Film Studies/Revue canadienne d'études cinématographiques*, vol. 9, no. 2. © 2000. Reprinted with permission from the Canadian Journal of Film Studies/Revue canadienne d'études cinématographiques.

Chapter 67 Gina Marchetti, "Jackie Chan and the Black Connection," pp. 137–58 from *Keyframes: Popular Cinema and Cultural Studies*, ed. M. Tinkcomm and A. Villiarejo (London and New York: Routledge). © 2001 by Gina Marchetti. Reprinted with permission from the author.

Chapter 68 Sue Thornham and Tony Purvis, "Stories and Meanings," pp. 29–44 and 183 (notes), and 188–204 (relevant refs) from *Television Drama* (London: Palgrave Macmiillan). © 2005. Reprinted with permission from Palgrave Macmillan.

Chapter 69 Nick Couldry, "Teaching Us to Fake It: The Ritualized Norms of Television 'Reality' Games," pp. 57–74 from *Reality TV: Remaking Television Culture*, ed. S. Murray and L. Ouellette (New York: New York University Press). © 2004 by New York University. Reprinted with permission of the author and New York University Press.

Chapter 70 David Morley, "Theories of Consumption in Media Studies," pp. 296–313, 324–8 (relevant refs) from *Acknowledging Consumption: A Review of New Studies*, ed. D. Miller (New York: Routledge). © 1995 by D. Morley. Reprinted with permission from the author.

Chapter 71 Janice Radway, "Reading the Romance," pp. 1042–9 from *Literary Theory: An Anthology*, ed. J. Rivkin and M. Ryan (Malden, MA: Blackwell); pp. 209–22 and 256 from Conclusion *Reading the Romance: Women, Patriarchy and Popular Literature* (Chapel Hill: University of North Carolina Press, 1984). © 1984, new introduction © 1991 by the University of North Carolina Press. Used by permission of the publisher.

Chapter 72 P. David Marshall, "The Cinematic Apparatus and the Construction of the Film Celebrity," pp. 90–118 & 263–9 (relevant notes) from *Celebrity and Power: Fame in Contemporary Culture* (Minneapolis and London: University of Minnesota Press). © 1997 by the Regents of the University of Minnesota. Reprinted with permission from University of Minnesota Press.

Chapter 73 Matt Hills, "Fan Cultures between 'Fantasy' and Reality," pp. 90–114, 190–2 from *Fan Cultures* (London and New York: Routledge). © 2002 by Matt Hills. Reprinted with permission from Taylor & Francis Books UK.

Chapter 74   John Frow, "Is Elvis a God? Cult, Culture, and 'Questions of Method'," pp. 197–210 from *International Journal of Cultural Studies*, vol. 1, no. 2. © 1998 by Sage Publications. Reprinted with permission from Sage Publications Ltd.

Chapter 75   Mark Seltzer, "Serial Killing for Beginners," pp. 1–25 from *Serial Killers: Death and Life in America's Wound Culture* (New York and London: Routledge). © 1998 by Routledge. Reprinted with permission from Taylor & Francis Groups, LLC.

Chapter 76   Ian Baucom, "The Riot of Englishness: Migrancy, Nomadism, and the Redemption of the Nation," pp. 190–218 and 242–3 (notes) from *Out of Place: Englishness, Empire, and the Locations of Identity*. (Princeton, NJ: Princeton University Press). © 1999 by Princeton University Press. Reprinted with permission from Princeton University Press.

Chapter 77   Anna Lowenhaupt Tsing, "The Economy of Appearances," originally published as "Inside the Economy of Appearances," pp. 55–77, 279–83 (notes and references) 114–44 from *Public Culture*, vol. 12. © 2000 by Duke University Press. All right reserved. Used by permission of the publisher.

Chapter 78   Jo Ellen Fair, *Francophonie* and the National Airwaves: A History of Television in Senegal," pp. 189–210 from *Planet TV: A Global Television Reader*, ed. L. Parks and S. Kumar (New York: New York University Press). © 2003 by New York University. Reprinted by permission of the author and New York University Press.

Chapter 79   Koichi Iwabuchi, "Discrepant Intimacy: Popular Culture Flows in East Asia," pp. 19–36 from *Asian Media Studies*, ed. J. Erni and S. H. Chua (Malden, MA: Blackwell). First appeared as "Becoming Culturally Proximate: A/scent of Japanese Idol Dramas in Taiwan," pp. 54–74 from *Asian Media Productions*, ed. B. Moeran (London, Curzon, 2001) and as "Nostalgia for Asian Modernities: Media Consumption of 'Asia'," in *Japan Positions: East Asia Cultures Critique*, vol. 10, no. 3 (2002). The chapter is also a condensed version of some chapters from (2002) *Recentring Globalization: Popular Culture and Japanese Transnationalism* (Durham, NC: Duke University Press). © 2005 by Blackwell Publishing Ltd. Reprinted by permission from Blackwell Publishing.

Chapter 80   Greg Dimitriadis and Cameron McCarthy, "Contemporary Approaches to the Arts," originally published as part of "Imagination, Education and the Search for Possible Futures," pp. 18–35 from *Reading and Teaching the Postcolonial: From Baldwin to Basquiat and Beyond* (New York: Teachers College Press, Columbia University). © 2001 by Teachers College, Columbia University. All rights reserved. Reprinted with permission from Teachers College Press.

Chapter 81   Chua Beng Huat, "Conceptualizing East Asian Popular Culture," pp. 200–221 from *Inter-Asia Cultural Studies*, vol. 5, no. 2. © 2004 by Taylor & Francis Ltd. Reprinted with permission from the publisher (Taylor & Francis Ltd, http://www.tandf.co.uk/journals).

I
Policy and Industry

1

Policy and Industry

1

Battle of the Global Paradigms

Michele Hilmes*

Across the globe the medium of broadcasting, in its early decades and indeed throughout its history, is associated strongly with the project of national identity formation. There are many reasons for this. Primarily, and not of course coincidentally, broadcasting's development corresponded with the crucial period of nationalism that followed the transgressions and disruptions of World War I, not only in Europe and the United States but in former colonial nations as they began to define and fight for an identity separate from their occupying powers. Just as radio had played a large part in the war effort itself, and with the bias toward military control of the medium that had to be supported or resisted once the conflict ended, so radio would be deployed in the ongoing process of redefining and reinforcing national boundaries.

Yet it is, paradoxically, the ability of radio to *transcend* the normal geographical borders of nations that mandated its nationalized structures of control. As Valeria Camporesi points out, "the international vocation of radio could only be restrained by means of political and economic agreements enforced by national governments."[1] Thus, here is one fundamental irony of radio, and later television: that a medium uniquely suited for crossing borders, transcending national boundaries, and permeating all strata of international culture should be so essentially linked to the tightest form of institutional control known to twentieth-century media.

This sort of irony has its flip side: finally, here was a medium that the state *could* control. Unlike books, newspapers, magazines, and films, which despite occasional attempts at licensing or censorship remained stubbornly resistant to the constraining ministrations of the state, broadcasting seemed to present the perfect excuse for the state to step in. Its necessary use of the electromagnetic spectrum, requiring allocation decisions; its expensive and tightly patented technology; the requirement that users go out and buy newly available specialized equipment, which could then be monitored and controlled, even licensed – all of these factors gave, in most countries, an opening for a level of state intervention only made acceptable by the mystification and ignorance about radio's eventual uses still prevalent in the early 1920s. During a time in which *internal* disruptions of unified national identity (renegotiations of social power around

* Originally published as "Who We Are, Who We Are Not: Battle of Global Paradigms," pp. 53–73 from *Planet TV: A Global Television Reader*, ed. L. Parks and S. Kumar (New York: New York University Press). © 2003 by New York University. Reprinted with permission from the author and New York University Press.

gender, class, and race/ethnicity) became as important as *external* threats, it did not take long for most countries to see the advantage in a nationally owned, nationally run, or at least nationally chartered system of radio broadcasting that could unite the country in a simultaneous, controlled address simply impossible before, as well as protect its culture from airborne invasions from without. Far more effectively than any one newspaper, magazine, publishing house, or film studio, broadcasting became "the nation's voice" in countries across the globe. The project of defining "who we are, who we are not" – always a task that involves internal as well as external negotiations of identity – thus became a worldwide endeavor through the timely introduction of broadcasting technology in the second decade of the twentieth century.[2]

In this global nationalizing project, one dominant duality comes into play: a "battle of the paradigms" between two of the earliest and most prominent systems to establish themselves. One nation after another observed the privately owned, competitive commercial system of the United States and the state-chartered, public service monopoly of Great Britain and used their examples to craft local solutions. As this dualistic modeling extended across the globe in the 1920s and 1930s, more often than not it was the United States that came out the loser both rhetorically and practically. The vast majority of European countries installed some form of the noncommercial public service system modeled after the BBC, as did colonial nations, where such systems were often imposed by occupying powers. Often such systems were seen as the only defense against not only direct American influence but also the uncontrolled outbreak of popular culture – and oppositional national ideologies and identities – that a commercial system might provoke or encourage, as local elites moved to keep this new medium firmly under centralized control.

In Finland, for example – along with the other Scandinavian countries – an initial period of experimentation with privately owned stations ceded quickly to a conscious emulation of the British model, since "public service broadcasting would have an important role in fostering patriotism in the newly independent state."[3] In Germany private investment was allowed alongside the Lander, or regional, stations, until Hitler's government took control in 1932. After the war, a national state-run network worked in tandem with regionally owned stations, supported by a combination of advertising revenues and license fees. Italy's system was similar. France allowed a certain number of commercial radio stations to operate alongside the dominant state channel before World War II, but shut all but the state system down during the war and maintained the state system alone until the 1970s. Colonial nations such as India, South Africa, Rhodesia, and Egypt relied on the state-owned networks installed by their colonial governments, sometimes in addition to commercial stations, until well after movements for independence.[4] Throughout, as a Finnish broadcasting historian puts it, "the BBC held a pre-eminent position among the major national broadcasting companies."[5]

The introduction of television worked to challenge the dominance of state monopolies in many cases, including Great Britain itself. (Conversely, in the United States, the new possibilities represented by television reawoke the moribund reform movement, leading to increased pressure for educational and public service broadcasting.) By this time, both the United States and Britain had become active in recruiting other nations to their respective visions of media organization. In Israel, whose formative years relied on government-controlled radio vital to its precarious self-definition and defense, television threatened to introduce unwelcome instability. The Israeli government fought off American attempts to institute a commercial television system by relying on British help in establishing a state-controlled organization.[6] In South America, within the US sphere of influence, US networks actively invested in private broadcasting companies from the 1940s on, weakening state systems.[7] During the Cold War era, US government agencies explicitly recruited the broadcasting industry into its expansionist plans, linking commercial television with democratic ideology and actively promoting its spread and growth (and not coincidentally opening up new American markets in the process). Susan Smulyan recounts the interesting example of occupied Japan, where after the war the United States confronted the contradictions in its easy equation of marketplace economics with democratic systems. While promoting a commercial, audience-research-based, pluralistic approach to broadcasting content, the occupying administration could not afford to permit truly alternative viewpoints to filter in to its hegemonic retelling of the "truth" of Japan's role in the war. A state-controlled, public service system worked better to accomplish American ideological goals.[8]

No other countries made more frequent and productive use of this contrast than the United States and Great Britain themselves. Historians of British broadcasting, from Briggs to Scannell and Cardiff, agree that comparison with the United States runs as a continuous constitutive undercurrent throughout the period in which the British Broadcasting Company and later the British Broadcasting Corporation were founded.[9] In the report of the Crawford Committee, which in 1926 formed the British Broadcasting Corporation divested of its traces of private ownership and made a state-authorized and funded entity, the negative example of the United States became a key support for the BBC's emerging public monopoly structure: "It is agreed that the United States system of free and uncontrolled transmission and reception is unsuited to this country, and that Broadcasting must accordingly remain a monopoly – in other words that the whole organisation must be controlled by a single authority."[10] Correspondingly, the figure of Great Britain appears frequently in the background of American radio history, emerging into prominence at certain crucial moments. In the heat of the debates of the early 1930s leading up to the ratification of the Communications Act of 1934, for example, the Federal Radio Commission itself echoed the familiar duality:

> This system is one which is based entirely upon the use of radio broadcasting stations for advertising purposes. It is a highly competitive system and is carried on by private enterprise. There is but one other system – the European system. That system is governmental. Under that system, broadcasting is conducted by the government or by some company chartered by the government. There is no practical medium between the two systems. It is either the American system or the European system.[11]

As we will see, it was no secret that it was the British system that provided the basic model for "the European system." I argue that this pattern of mutual projection and comparison was not simply strategic but determinant: if either system had not existed, the other would have had to invent it. From the earliest moments – 1920 onward – the United States and the United Kingdom regarded each other across the Atlantic with an intense and selective scrutiny that provided ammunition for supporters of both systems. On both sides, publications and debates comparing the British system with that of the United States appeared frequently during radio's first decade, and would at various times subsequently shape public policy and engage nationwide deliberations.[12]

This history of mutual interdependence deserves a more lengthy study than I can give it here. The ways Great Britain and the United States defined, defended, and discursively constructed their competing systems had repercussions across the globe. It is worth taking a look at some of the foundational moments of this opposition in order to pick apart some of the basic assumptions, shortcomings, idiosyncrasies, and methods of deployment that underlie both commercial and public service broadcasting, as defined by their two dominant supporters during highly formative years. Comparative histories of this sort, though rarely undertaken, can provide a useful tool for deconstructing features of national institutions regarded as simply "natural" and to question "commonsense" knowledge about their structure and effects.[13] For the purposes of this chapter I will lightly skim over three significant episodes that demonstrate the practical effects of this mutual project of discursive construction of "who we are, who we are not" at a national level. I will focus primarily on the threat of "Americanization" to the public service system, as this is the dominant trend worldwide. The first episode involves the use of the concept of "American chaos" by British policy makers in the early 1920s, leading to the formation of the British Broadcasting Corporation in 1926 and the development of its influential public service model. I argue that projection of fear of the popular onto the specter of "American chaos" allowed the BBC in its early years to avoid some hard questions about the limited "public" nature of the British system. This created key elisions that would become fundamental to the elitist Reithian philosophy of "uplift" and service, not only in Great Britain but in many other nations as well. The second traces the flap created in 1933 when the US National Association of Broadcasters (NAB), attempting to fight off broadcast reform at home, did so by publishing a highly one-sided rebuttal of the British system in the most prejudicial rhetoric available. Here we can see the philosophy of "marketplace democracy" emerging, in a historically specific form that would be used, over and over, to justify the weakness of public broadcasting in the United States and the aggressive recruitment of other nations into the commercial system. Finally, having briefly focused on US networks' attempts in the 1930s to adopt BBC-derived programming strategies in order to defuse calls for reform, I will look at the ways the BBC at first distanced itself from, then adapted to, the "American" influence toward popular programming, consistent scheduling, and audience measurement. I will close with some reflections on the nature of the "public sphere" created under public service and commercial systems, with gender as the focus.

American Chaos

In Britain as in the United States, some of radio's earliest and most eager proponents were radio equipment manufacturers, who pressed in both countries for permission to set up stations and begin to market radio sets. In 1922 the British Post Office, under whose jurisdiction radio fell, entered into complex negotiations with the dominant radio interests in the United Kingdom. Records of these meetings reveal a slowly emerging compromise between the dominant company, Marconi, and its competitors to devise a means by which Marconi patents could be used but an effective Marconi monopoly could be avoided. It was not a nascent notion of public service to the nation, but rather Marconi head Godfrey Isaac's insistence that his company's cooperation depended on a noncommercial system (backed by the powerful Newspaper Proprietors' Association, which feared competition for advertising dollars) that finally broke the deadlock. The British Broadcasting Company was established in October 1922 as a consortium of manufacturers, pooling their patents to further radio development in the United Kingdom, jointly setting up noncommercial stations that would not compete with each other.

In the winter of 1921 the Post Office had dispatched its assistant secretary, F. J. Brown, to the United States to observe how the Americans were handling the radio situation. He embarked on a tour of the country over several months, and attended the first of the US Radio Conferences convened by Herbert Hoover in January 1922. Brown, characterized by Briggs as "one of the leading figures in the history of broadcasting," exerted considerable influence on the eventual establishment of the BBC.[14] In the spring of 1923 his testimony before the Sykes Committee – convened to reauthorize the British Broadcasting Company – proved crucial in its deliberations. It is in Brown's reports and testimony that the strategic use of the concept of "American chaos" first appears. The goal of avoiding American chaos becomes the primary rationale for discouraging private ownership of radio in Britain and a way of avoiding discussion of the self-interested agendas of the radio companies and newspaper publishers in the process. Interestingly, in the light of what came later, Brown stresses that "The Post Office held that it was essential that there should be no monopoly" in British broadcasting, referring at this point to the danger of Marconi's dominant position.[15] He is questioned on this point by a member of Parliament, Mr. Trevelyan, who states, "There is no monopoly there [in America], and there are a large number of Broadcasting companies. That is how I come to question . . . why the Post Office here has set itself, apparently, to adopt an entirely different system from the American, whether it was because of the failure, in their view, of the American?" Brown answers, "Yes, it was. The American system was leading to chaos, it was doing so already while I was there, and because of that chaos Mr. Hoover called a Committee of Officials and Manufacturers . . . with the view of arriving at some agreed scheme for preventing that chaos."[16] Here he has managed to use the term "chaos" linked to the United States three times in a single sentence; obviously this is a crucial point. In the absence of any overtly expressed public service function for radio, the concept of "American chaos" stands in for a host of considerations and agendas that the BPO at this point felt it more expedient to conceal.[17] This construction becomes a central one; it is echoed in the statement by Lord Gainford later in the proceedings: "Within six months we have achieved more than America did in two years, and have avoided the chaos which exists in the USA."[18] Or, as a BBC official statement summarized at the beginning of the Sykes Committee deliberations: "The initiative which led to the formation of the Company came from the Post Office. They knew that, if the American chaos were to be avoided, one broadcasting authority was essential."[19] And this broadcasting authority must be the state, not a commercial company or consortium.

What was this "chaos"? Though it is true that little regulation affected the growing numbers of experimental broadcasting stations springing up across the United States during this period, by 1922 large corporations such as Westinghouse and AT&T had begun to establish stations in the larger cities. With a well-tuned set it was possible to receive a variety of distinct signals in most locations, and various groups such as the American Radio Relay League had organized to produce codes, standards, and even "silent nights" so that distant signals could be received. In January 1922 the Interstate Commerce Commission had installed a system of licensing that divided broadcasters into A and B stations, with the B license and its more favorable and less crowded wave-length reserved for more established stations that followed certain restrictions.[20] This brought a considerable diminishment of voices to the spectrum. Even F. J. Brown was forced to concede that the chaos was not really observable in most places on a level of daily listening:

Q: (Mr. Eccles) Did you listen in at all?
A: (Brown) Yes, what I head was fairly good and was not interrupted.
Q: (Mr. Eccles) What I heard was fairly good; I was wondering whether the chaos might not have been exaggerated?
A: (Brown) It may have been exaggerated.[21]

But it is not on the literal technical level that the notion of "chaos" functioned in the British debates. Rather, it was the sheer *uncontrolled* potential of radio in and of itself, along with the dominance in the United States of commercial sales pitches and their attendant appeal to the unmitigated popular, that created a perception of unruliness and disorder. The BPO shifts its stance from wishing to *avoid* a monopoly to establishing a state-owned monopoly within a span of three short years, motivated by a need for control over this developing medium that the notion of "American chaos" came to symbolize, however inaccurately. Later, in a famous phrase, John Reith would attribute all the social good his public service system had managed to accomplish to precisely "the brute force of monopoly."

The crucial missing term here, of course, is "commercial." A state monopoly became the only way of avoiding a commercial broadcasting system, which, whether dominated by culturally suspect Marconi interests or permitting uncontrolled competition, threatened all parties involved. Not only would it compete for advertising revenues with the powerful newspaper industry, it would open the doors to the kind of populist access so readily observable in the United States. Advertising meant catering to popular – meaning middle- to lower-class, hence unauthorized – tastes and interests, as the press and film industry already did. Further, there is a sense that emerges from the debates at this time that Marconi, while a British company, was not truly one of "us" and that leaving such a vital national project as broadcasting in these slightly disreputable hands simply would not do.[22] That racial and class concerns underlay the decision making, in Britain as in most countries, can be seen in a speech given in 1926 by Prime Minister Baldwin in celebration of the BBC's first years of service.

> In the same way, it is too early yet to say what the influence on civilisation of the moving picture may be, but I confess that there is one aspect of it upon which I look with the gravest apprehension, and that is the effect of the commoner type of film, as representing the white races, when represented to the coloured races of this world, (Hear, hear). I need say no more on that subject except this, that in my view the whole progress of civilisation in this world is bound up with the capacity that the white races have, and will have, to help the rest of the world to advance, and if their power to do that be impeded by false ideas of what the white races stand for, it may well be that their efforts will not only fail, but that the conception of the white races generated in the hearts of the coloured races throughout the world may be an initial step in the downfall of those white races themselves. *I have ventured to say these things to you because we all felt here how different have been these past four wonderful years in the development of this great gift of science to mankind; how different from what they might have been had those in charge of them been actuated merely by mercenary and "get rich quick" motives.* (Cheers).[23] (emphasis added)

Here Baldwin explicitly links commercial culture and its "get rich quick" ethos to the destabilization of existing social hierarchies, and congratulates the BBC for adopting a system designed to keep threatening influences under control. Implicit is the argument that a commercial broadcasting system would have thrown open the airwaves to the disruption of the dominant cultural order.

The close connection of this discourse with the threat posed by an "Americanized" system is clearly articulated in another speech by Reith:

> In the beginning we were to some extent guided by the example of America. I do not mean that America indicated the path, but rather that America showed us what pitfalls to avoid; we learnt from her experience. Broadcasting in America was well under way, with a two years' start, when the service was first inaugurated in Great Britain, and it was soon common knowledge that the lack of control in America was resulting in a chaotic confusion. . . . Britain, as I say, benefitted by America's example, and a centrally controlled system of broadcasting stations was the result.[24]

In the context of the overall debate it is very clear that "American chaos" has come to stand in for "commercial competition" and its attendant "social unruliness" as a rationale for a unified system under centralized state-appointed control. Broadcasting in Britain would not be thrown open to individual or commercial entrepreneurship, as in the United States, but would be carefully controlled to limit the intrusion of "chaotic" voices from social groups and classes whose interests might clash with the maintenance of the existing social order and stability. This first and crucial displacement onto American practices of an unresolved tension at home – a "public" service open only to a very small and highly elite segment of the population – would be written into the very charter of the British Broadcasting Corporation by the Crawford Committee in 1926. This would help to justify the transformation of the commercially based Company into the government-chartered Corporation, and the rest, as they say, is history.

However, during the late 1920s and early 1930s the meaning of "American chaos" shifted in a significant way: emerging from behind its implied screen of technical or administrative disorder, it could now nominate more overtly the cultural disarray posed by American radio. It is possible that it was discourse on the American side of the equation, employed to help commercial broadcasters win their war over educational radio claims in the early 1930s, that pushed British commentators into a more inclusive condemnation of American practices. Certainly the National Association of Broadcasters was the first to throw down the gauntlet.

British Quality

As Robert McChesney has convincingly described, the early 1930s, before the passage of the Communications Act of 1934, represent one of the few times in US history that the commercial basis of US broadcasting was called into serious and effective question.[25] The efforts of educational broadcasters to secure public funding and reserve frequencies for a type of public service broadcasting that was evolving in Great Britain (and other countries) brought the topic of the structure and financing of the American system into question in a way never previously undertaken. US broadcasters recognized this threat, and McChesney details the many tactics employed to defeat the scattered and underfunded league of education stations.

One tactic was to emphasize the public service that the major networks claimed to perform, modeled after the BBC. A sudden outpouring of symphonies, public affairs, and serious dramatic programs wafted over the American airwaves from 1933 to 1938, as broadcasters first promised to pull up their socks and then had to follow through, however briefly. Most of these efforts drew on a particular definition of "quality" programming taken from observation of BBC practices, and were (at first, at least) offered on a sustaining (nonsponsored) basis. NBC hired Arturo Toscanini to direct the NBC Symphony Orchestra, patterned after the BBC orchestra. Adaptations of literary and stage works, an area that the BBC had developed strongly, were emphasized in programs like the *Mercury Theatre of the Air*, the *Columbia Workshop*, and *Everyman's Theater*. Certain well-respected "radio auteurs" were given a freer hand than ordinarily, such as Orson Welles, Arch Oboler, and Norman Corwin, adopting the more authorial approach to drama that the BBC emphasized. Continuity acceptance departments were established at both major networks to provide some form of centralized control over the unruliness of programs created by sponsors and their agencies. The separation of women's programs into the separate but unequal daytime schedule helped to distance the "quality" pretensions of nighttime programming from the more overtly commercial, feminized daytime.

A particular aspect of network public image polishing involved renewing and reinvigorating links with the BBC itself. In 1933 NBC appointed an official representative to the BBC, Fred Bate; in the same year CBS employed Cesar Saerchinger, an American journalist already based in London, in a similar capacity. The BBC responded in 1935 by hiring Felix Greene as their man in New York – where he would play a much more vital role in advising the Canadian system than he did in the United States. These young men were meant to serve primarily as goodwill ambassadors, though they also worked at arranging various kinds of trans-Atlantic broadcasts and in facilitating guest performances on each other's outlets.[26]

Meantime, the head of the NBC, Merlyn Aylesworth, and John Reith of the BBC had developed a cordial and even personal friendship based on frequent, polite correspondence and a cross-Atlantic visit or two. Their letters, housed in the Wisconsin NBC papers, show an increasingly if somewhat affectedly intimate tone, especially on Aylesworth's part. They address each other as "My dear Merlyn" and "Dear Sir John" and Aylesworth signs off, "Affectionately yours." Reith visits Aylesworth at his home in the autumn of 1933, following up a 1931 visit made by Aylesworth to Britain. Aylesworth informs Reith in a letter written in December 1933 that "we all consider you as a part of our family" (which he copied to General Sarnoff).[27] Just a few weeks later the family was looking a bit dysfunctional.

The crisis in relations between the BBC and NBC arose as a part of the larger battle over commercial versus public service broadcasting. As one of their more effective volleys in the public opinion war, educational radio supporters persuaded the High School Debating League of the United States to take on as the subject of 1933's national debate competition the topic "Resolved: That the United States Should Adopt the Essential Features of the British System of Radio Control and Operation." This resulted in a flood of articles and publications on both sides of the issue, culminating in a 191-page pamphlet assembled by the National Association of Broadcasters entitled *Broadcasting in the United States*. It consisted of a thirty-two-page, highly complimentary description of "American Radio," with charts and graphs enumerating the many hours of high-quality sustaining and commercial broadcasting purportedly put out by American networks and stations, followed by a twenty-six-page denunciation of the British system called "The American vs. the British System of Radio Control." Similar to the British use of "American chaos," these two NAB-authored pieces made heavy use of the tactic of praising the US system by denigrating the British:

> American radio is the most competitive in the whole world. Hundreds of local stations are forever looking for local entertainment talent. The two competing "chains" are forever trying to develop new competitive entertainment stars. Additionally the advertisers, in multitudes, are forever competitively flinging new entertainment stars into the radio firmament. You have to take the volcanic dust of their advertising convulsions along with the stars; but you get the stars. You get them because each of these competitors has to stay awake. . . . The British Broadcasting Corporation does not have to stay awake. It doesn't even begin broadcasting – for instance – till after ten o'clock in the morning, on week days; and on Sundays, till recently, it didn't begin broadcasting till three o'clock in the afternoon. And then, on Sundays, it always laid off and did no broadcasting from six-thirty to eight in the evening. It can afford to rest. It knows that no rival will broadcast while it's sleeping. And it takes a sort of social revolution to wake it up.[28]

Here American initiative and "wide awakeness," all based on commercial competition, are contrasted with British complacency and sleepiness, with an underlying attribution of elitism that only a "social revolution" could shake free. This native American vitality was then linked to innate characteristics of the United States as a nation in contrast to England:

> It must be remembered that not only is Great Britain a small country, but that on the whole, its population possesses similar traits of mind and character – similar viewpoints and interests. There is not the marked diversity in racial, cultural, social and economic backgrounds which one finds in the United States. Each part of the country has priceless cultural heritages of its own, which color its viewpoint, and affect many of the radio programs it desires. Likewise the many races which have gone to make up our nation have a right to programs ministering to their racial consciousness, for each of them have brought something of great value to the evolution of the American character.[29]

Or, to put it another way,

> The nervously-active American is never in a mood to take educational punishment. You *must* interest him – or he quickly tunes you out. This characteristic is in only slightly lesser degree fundamental to any discussion of listener reaction in any country. It is the rule and the law and the testament upon which every successful broadcast structure is based. It is the risk, for instance, that Sir John Reith runs in Britain when he avowedly gives his public what he believes it is good for it to have.[30]

Here a liberal-pluralist concept of America's racial background is contrasted to Britain's homogeneity – this in a country that effectively barred African Americans from the airwaves and had made *Amos 'n' Andy* its most popular show. Education is termed "punishment" and commercial competition becomes practically a biblical mandate. After this diatribe, the pamphlet offers a compilation of various articles and talks about the competing paradigms by US broadcasting spokesmen. This section included a collection of mostly critical responses to the BBC from the British press compiled by Major Joseph Travis of London, in the preface to which it is asserted, "the great mass of radio listeners, realizing that the BBC is a monopoly and can do as it pleases (which impression is given in most of the addresses and articles by BBC officials), have decided that it is a waste of time and money to send their criticisms to either the BBC or the press."[31] It concluded its most vehemently argued section, the reprint of a speech by news commentator William Hard, with the rhetorical flourish:

> I hold up to you the superior scholarship, the superior good taste, the superior urbanity of the British broadcasting system. It is all that can be said for it in comparison with ours. I hold it up to you and I ask you: Will you for that bribe surrender what America has given to you in your inherent passion for all feasible liberty of utterance? Will you for that bribe surrender all your chances of free expression on the whole American air to the autocratic determination of one selected citizen? If so, vote British. If not, vote American.[32]

Here John Reith himself has become the devil incarnate, with a suspect and autocratic "superiority" his only defense. The American Revolution is being fought again, this time in the air. The pamphlet appeared in early January 1934 and hit London like a bomb. On January 10 an urgent telegraph from NBC's Fred Bate in London to Merlyn Aylesworth breathlessly wailed,

> DEEPEST RESENTMENT HERE NAB PUBLICATION EVEN REACHING CON-SIDERATION SEVERING RELATIONS STOP FEEL ADVISABLE YOU CBS DEFINE ATTITUDE TOWARD STATEMENT SURE TO BE CHALLENGED STOP FAILURE ADVISE ME PUBLICATION IN TIME OR PROVIDE COPY RESULTED MOST EMBARASSING SITUATION TODAY STOP. . . . SUGGEST LINE OF ACTION STOP SITUATION TENSE.[33]

A frantic, and rather humorous in retrospect, exchange of telegrams and letters ensues. Aylesworth attempts to reassure Bate and Reith, by downplaying the NAB as a fractious bunch of small-time station owners, as opposed to the big network guardians of more enlightened culture. Reith expresses his dismay, pointing out that many members of the reform opposition had lobbied for a BBC endorsement of their views, which the BBC had honorably rebuffed, only to be insulted in this way. Aylesworth again reassures Reith, at great length and with considerable disingenuousness, considering the strength of the reform movement in the United States: "We consider the whole matter of little importance in this country and just a lot of fun between school children who have a good time debating the subjects."[34]

NBC was obviously trying to have it both ways during this period, at once rigorously defending commercial broadcasting against any thought of a public service system in the United States, while simultaneously attempting to get credit for supporting and exemplifying the "high culture" goals of just such a system. It also displaced onto "Britishness" the whole concept of broadcast reform, projecting undesirable "foreign" attributes onto those who objected to commercial radio's narrow limits. It limited the reformist agenda to a definition of "public service" that was eminently criticizable in American terms: elitist, focusing on high culture and formal education, and above all British. This effectively obscured well-founded and more radical criticisms of the commercial system made by the reform movement at home, such as the lack of political debate on the airwaves, the concentration of station ownership in mainstream commercial hands, corporate America's ability to keep anticorporate views off the air, and censorious network practices.

The "American" Popular

Though this episode blew over without marked incident – including any change to the American system of broadcasting, as the commercial broadcasters received just about every concession they wanted from Congress – it does mark a transition to the next stage of US/BBC relations. Beginning in the late 1920s, the threat of American "chaos" would be detached from the regulatory situation and rearticulated to a different, though related, set of concerns. Or, more accurately, the underlying fear of allowing private industry (i.e., Marconi) to dominate radio was allowed to emerge from behind its mask of Americanization into prominence once the danger of Marconi was safely defused. By the late 1920s, commercialism itself, and the cultural chaos it engendered, could be openly denounced as a threat to all that was good in British broadcasting, and once again the American model stood the BBC in good stead. In contrast to the United States, where as early as 1922 the commercial broadcaster was regarded by the powers that be as uniquely capable of serving the public, in Great Britain "national" interests become constructed as specifically opposed to economic interests. Sir William Mitchell-Thompson, Post Master General, justified continued funding of the BBC before Parliament in these terms:

> There were . . . at the head of the British Broadcasting Company men not merely of great organising and technical ability but men with vision, men with high purpose, men with wide outlook, *men who looked at the problem not from the trade angle but from the national angle*. . . . They set broadcasting upon a plane of high ideals, and they based it on a broad conception of their duty to the public and to public morality.[35] (emphasis added)

The man that Sir Mitchell-Thompson most had in mind was doubtless the imposing head of the BBC since 1922, John Reith. Reith's best-known statement of his views comes from his 1924 account of the BBC's early years, *Broadcast over Britain*.

> As we conceive it, our responsibility is to carry into the greatest possible number of homes everything that is best in every department of human knowledge, endeavour, and achievement, and to avoid the things which are, or may be, hurtful. It is occasionally indicated to us that we are apparently setting out to give the public what we think they need – and not what they want, but few know what they want, and very few what they need. . . . In any case it is better to over-estimate the mentality of the public, than to under-estimate it.[36]

Reith's task of uplift was made immensely easier by frequent and unfavorable contrast with US radio programming, usually emphasizing the influence of the system of commercial broadcasting and the cultural chaos it brought in its wake. This is a tradition that begins very early, even by those who fundamentally admired American radio culture. Describing the United States in 1924, A. R. Burrows writes, "It mattered not whether one station overlapped another in wave-length or in hours of transmission, or whether the performance of a classical masterpiece was followed by an appeal on behalf of somebody's soap or pickles. It was all part of a new game."[37] Yet another British visitor to the United States in 1927, Peter Eckersley, observed of NBC's programs,

> Some of the concerts were good, but the majority suffered through commercialism, and to our ears would sound extremely crude. For example, I heard an announcement that a particular hour was to be the "Brightness Hour," brightness means smiles, smiles means white teeth, teeth will be whiter if you use X tooth paste, the manufacturers of which are responsible for the program. In other cases the advertisement is less crude.[38]

A 1929 editorial in *Radio Times*, the BBC-published (and advertising-supported) program magazine, put it even more strongly:

In America, the ether is racked and torn with competing broadcasting stations filling the air with advertising matter. . . . In America, even the wireless reception of a Beethoven Symphony cannot be free from association with someone's chewing gum or pills. In England, the tired worker who has been all day shouted at and advertised to in his newspaper, on the hoardings, in train or omnibus, may settle down to his evening's wireless entertainment with the feeling that at last he is free from the necessity to listen to someone who has something to sell.[39]

"Chaos" becomes articulated to the rampant spread of commercial mass culture, with its "crude" and "vulgar" and above all "American" manifestations. Another *Radio Times* opinion piece concludes,

The thoughtful listener will come away with the double impression that, while American radio has startling vitality in its method of presentation, its material, which largely consist of songs of the jazz order sung by artists of the genus "crooner," is, to British ears at least, confined within a rut of lowering and monotonous sentimentality . . . much that this vitality contributes to radio on that side of the Atlantic would be termed "vulgar" on this.[40]

That there are class and gender biases to these characterizations is not hard to discern. The undisciplined, feminized "mass" audience, indulging its own low, vulgar, sentimental, or crude tastes, became decisively associated with Americanness. And the devils goading them on were commercial culture and its handmaiden, advertising. The BBC increasingly came to see itself as the last best hope in Britain for the preservation of cultural standards somehow free from the taint of trade and populism. Yet with a system that collected license fees from the entire public, in a regressive structure that taxed the working classes as much as the upper classes, it could not entirely dismiss the claims that popular tastes and preferences made on broadcasting service. Better to convince oneself that the less welcome aspects of popular taste were not truly "British," but stemmed from American influence, and as such were permissible to resist.

Programmers began to resist the increasing intrusion of "American" elements into BBC programs, even as irresistible pressure to adopt more popular practices built up in the early to mid-1930s. In 1936 Cecil Graves, director of programming at the BBC, expressed his displeasure toward a new variety program called *Follow the Sun*:

What depressed me much more than all of this was the fact that it was another example of trying to introduce American methods and American phraseology into our broadcasting . . . . I notice it creeping in in various directions. . . . Such expressions as "we bring to you," "We offer you," etc. are examples, but it goes deeper than this and is noticeable in the form used as well as in the actual words. There is no demand for this kind of thing and we certainly don't want to create one. We are perfectly capable of producing first-class shows with first-class presentation without apeing American models.[41]

A responding memo from Peter Eckersley, generally an advocate of the popular expansion of BBC programming, shows the range of opinion on the subject.

I ventilated the matter of Americanisation, as you wished, at Programme Board this morning. . . . Coatman, as was to be expected, was violently opposed to any form of Americanisation in our programmes. . . . He speaks of America as a country completely composed of barbarians, and it would do him a lot of good to go over there and see that there are plenty of things that they do just as well as we do here and that they have their own cultural ideals.[42]

Despite such attitudes, in the late 1930s certain "American style" programs were introduced to popular acclaim and became a cherished part of the BBC schedule. One of the first was the comedy/variety show *Band Wagon*, followed by the long-running *It's That Man Again*, described by its own producer as "An English version of the Burns and Allen show."[43] The British comedian Mabel Constanduros, having heard the radio serial *One Man's Family* while on a visit to the United States, adapted it into the first British comedy serial, *The English Family Robinson*, in 1937, which led to the long-running *Mrs. Dale's Diary*.[44] Of course, though these popular British programs might have drawn some inspiration from American models, as Valeria Camporesi points out, their deeper roots lay squarely in British traditions of popular culture, adapted to the new radio medium. Had the early management of the BBC not set its face so resolutely against more popular forms of expression, no doubt a British popular radio tradition would have emerged much earlier.

One of the most influential practices adopted by the BBC after the example of the United States, however, may well be the simple concept of regularly scheduled programming, which we now take almost wholly for granted as simply inherent to radio: that a program appear weekly, or daily, on a regular day at a regular time. This practice, called "fixed point" scheduling, was deplored as American and actively opposed by the early BBC since it worked against the British conception of the proper mode of broadcast listening. Program lengths were less standardized than in the United States. What US broadcasters referred to negatively as "dead air" was considered entirely appropriate on BBC schedules; and the listener was expected to seek out desired programs and make a point of being available to listen to them, in contrast to the deplored "tap listener." By the mid-to late 1930s, however, fixed point scheduling had become more prevalent, based largely on what the BBC had begun to learn about the needs and wants of the public it served.

Which Public, Whose Service?

Here I turn to a consideration of the BBC's conception of its audience, the listening public that the BBC had been created to serve, a conception increasingly under fire as the 1930s progressed.[45] As has been noted, the early BBC viewed its audience from the top down, defining the "universal access" so key to public service concepts as the ability to *receive programs*, not to *participate* in decisions about what types of programming might be desirable or appropriate.[46] The BBC, as seen in the Reith quote above, had always held that audience research on any organized scale was not only impractical but actually undesirable. The point of broadcasting was to offer the public something above their own taste, "to lead, not to follow." It might seem contradictory that a broadcasting service created expressly to serve the public, funded by contributions paid directly by the public, would be so unconcerned about the opinions and characteristics of that public as to resist even regular surveys or opinion polls. And as early as 1930 the contradiction between planning broadcasting as a public service and the only very vague and tenuous connection most broadcasters had with the public had begun to seriously concern at least a few British broadcasters. Yet once again, audience survey methods were linked to commercial, American practices, making it easier to reject the entire notion. A move to initiate an audience measurement service, as was done extensively in the United States by this time, was launched not surprisingly by those in charge of the more popular forms of programming: Val Gielgud, head of Drama, in particular, urged that some kind of analysis be done. In a memo to the top BBC directors in 1930, he spoke frankly:

> I cannot help feeling more and more strongly that we are fundamentally ignorant as to how our various programmes are received, and what is their relative popularity. It must be a source of considerable disquiet to many people besides myself to think that it is quite possible that a very great deal of money and time and effort may be expended on broadcasting into a void. . . . I do not suggest that popular opinion is or should be the last word as to whether our programmes are or are not good and should or should not be continued in any particular form.[47]

Charles Siepmann, director of Talks (later to move to the United States, where he would contribute heavily to the FCC's stringent "Blue Book"), replied,

> Gielgud's memorandum interests me very much. I know exactly what he feels, and share his view that some alteration in our present system of measuring the reaction of the public is required. I do not share his view on the democratic issues. However complete and effective any survey we launch might be, I should still be convinced that our policy and programme building should be based first and last upon our own conviction as to what should and should not be broadcast.[48]

This distrust of public opinion and the ways it might be used underlay even the eventual establishment of a Listener's Bureau in 1936. Once again, study of the American system produced mixed reviews: American measurement methods might be emulated for their sophisticated techniques, but should never substitute for the judgment of the professional broadcasters of the BBC. This unwillingness to cater to the interests of the listening public and the insistence on the goal of uplifting and improving it seem to have produced one feature of British broadcasting that stands in great contrast to the American experience: the virtual exclusion of women from the masculinized public sphere created by the early BBC, as well as from significant participation in production and authorship. This would not change until the advent of war suddenly provoked a more urgent need to reach the wider public, if need be on their own terms.

   It cannot be said that the BBC refused to recognize any differences in taste and program preference in its audience. Class and region were assumed to be important categories affecting radio listening habits, but gender almost never so, particularly when it came to entertainment. Survey after survey, during the early years of measurement, concentrate on class and region, and occasionally on age, but leave gender out as a category of analysis. In contrast, by the mid-1930s American daytime radio hours were filled with programs designed specifically for the frequently surveyed female audience, largely because of their much-vaunted consumer power. By no coincidence were those the parts of the day seen as most heavily, and deplorably, commercial. Such programming as the daily serials or "soap operas," talk shows, instructional programs, and musical formats, all directed primarily toward a female audience and mindful of women's interests, tastes, and concerns, arguably developed a new kind of feminized public sphere within radio's dominantly masculine address.[49] Female producers, writers, and actors found ample outlet for their talents, and introduced some of the most innovative and lasting forms that shaped American broadcasting. Though confined, until the war years, to the "women's ghetto" of the daytime, radio's feminized "subaltern counterpublic" sphere allowed for considerable expression and debate of controversial (and often "vulgar") topics, such as feminine sexuality, home versus career, family relationships, and forms of women's knowledge.[50] These expressions were certainly trammeled by the limitations of commercial sponsors' narrow interests, but a surprising diversity of voices based on program ownership and control developed in daytime. Entrepreneurs like Mary Margaret McBride developed their own programs, sought out their own advertisers, and determined the content of their shows, buying time on local stations and national networks. This limited the extent to which a dominantly masculine superstructure of decision makers could exercise control over feminine discourse.

In the United Kingdom such a feminine sphere was very slow to develop. In 1935 the BBC decided to turn its attention to a complete revision of program policy, with special emphasis on the daytime, an area that had been largely neglected. At no time in the study is the daytime audience of women even identified, much less deemed worthy of special programming consideration.[51] While some of the "talks" programming during the day addressed issues thought to be of special interest to women, such as cooking and child rearing, the notion of entertainment specially geared to the female audience remained undeveloped. The same applies to histories of British broadcasting: neither Briggs nor any other historian to date has made women's programs or the female audience during these early decades a subject of study. In the summaries of programming done by the BBC yearbook each year from 1929 until the late 1940s, women's programming is not even a recognized category.

Not until audience research had been under way for several years did the revelation that women's interests in programs differed from men's have much effect on BBC practices. The necessity of recruiting women into the war effort led to the first real attempts to create shows of varied content that appealed to women – and to treat them with the same respect as other programs and schedule them at times convenient for women to listen, By then, producers could use audience listening figures to bolster their arguments that the programs were popular and effective. Here it seems clear that the articulation of audience research to American-style commercialism had a distinctly negative impact on the ability of the British public service system to serve all members of its public equally well. The same could be said for class-based tastes and interests: the working and lower middle classes paid the vast bulk of the license fees that supported broadcasting, but their own tastes, concerns, and habits – like those of women – were considered by the BBC's early directors as matters only for discouragement, correction, and uplift – if they were considered at all. In the United States the "chaos" of the commercial system allowed market power (that possessed by white, middle-class women, in particular) to disrupt the social control that powerful broadcasters and regulators could exercise over the scope and content of programming. In the more homogenized and centralized system of Great Britain, social power combined with state power to present a formidable barrier to participation by members of subordinate classes, without the potential for disruption presented by "chaotic" competition and commercialism. This would begin to change rapidly during the war years and after the introduction of commercial television in the mid-1950s. On the other hand, American television would soon enter its most tightly controlled and restrictive decades, under the influence of restrictive regulation and the new system of network, rather than sponsor, production of programming.

Conclusion

We can see in these debates that both countries used the example of the other as a containment device: to limit the options available to a duality of extremes, in which differences were emphasized, similarities usually played down, and specific aspects enlarged to suit the strategic interests of each. In the United States, denigration of the BBC as a "government monopoly" producing "dull and sleepy" programming for a "superior elite" masked the dominance of the US system by large corporations in fact serving some very similar functions. The major networks' two-faced role helped to narrow and defuse the reform movement, pushing it in an elite direction based on highbrow notions of "quality" programming, and away from more meaningful, radical changes. In the United Kingdom, very real threats of American industrial domination were reified into an effective and long-lasting system of projection of American "chaos," catering to the "vulgar (feminized) masses" and producing "sentimental, sensational" programming that "would never work in England." Under this cover could be swept the domestic threats of class, gender, and racial disorder and the imposition of control by cultural and economic elites. This distinction runs throughout the experience of both countries. Yet it should not be forgotten that strong currents ran against the dominant in each case: a sizable minority in each country actively lobbied for adoption of resistant elements of the other's broadcasting structure and habits, with the backing of not inconsiderable economic and institutional power.

In fact, much mutual influence marked the development of both systems, in the United States culminating in the public broadcasting system finally installed in the late 1960s; in Britain culminating in the introduction of commercial television in the 1950s and of local radio in the 1970s. The vital dualism developed in broadcasting's earliest decades shows no signs of abating, and indeed has spread across the globe, where "Americanness" is often employed to denote those elements of the popular that dominant local powers would like to repress (particularly in the area of gender), and defenses of "quality" programs draw on BBC-derived notions of artistic integrity, anti-commercialism, and cultural uplift.[52] As new technologies break through the artificial barriers of broadcast nationalism, they often come attached to commercial economics that do not fall under the control of local elites and powers. An infusion of "chaos," often articulated with Western, and specifically American, programs and organizations, prompts the development of competing commercial broadcasting stations and networks, and disrupts state broadcasting monopolies. Some evidence indicates that, in many countries, women in particular have used this disruption of prevalent social norms to break with repressive local hierarchies and envision new roles and new aspirations.[53] On the other hand, such commercialized media often primarily empower the affluent, educated classes that can afford them, leaving the rest of the population with an impoverished alternative. The Western values that they bring may be useful to local populations in some ways, but may import problems as well. The debate over the value of preserving some aspects of a public service system, now on the defensive in many countries, takes on new urgency – not least in the United States.

However, this essay shows that the terms of the traditional public service/commercial opposition should not be taken at face value, If we are to defend public service broadcasting effectively in this era of challenge and breakdown, it might be well to ask Stuart Hall's question "which public, whose service?" We may have to acknowledge that highly elitist and repressive agendas can be concealed in a too-quick condemnation of those admittedly mixed offerings that a commercial system brings. On the other hand, commercial broadcasting often conceals as restrictive a system of representation and information behind a cover of inclusion, in which members of the "public" are defined primarily as consumers – which has both positive and negative aspects – and have even less chance of intervention by public debate.[54] Neither the Lord Reiths nor the Rupert Murdochs of this world deserve the final say on the shape of this increasingly vital medium, and it is my hope that this reconsideration of the uses of national identity might help to clarify the terms of the debate.

Notes

Abbreviations:

BBC WAC: British Broadcasting Corporation Written Archives Center, Caversham Park, UK

NBC: National Broadcasting Company collection, Wisconsin State Historical Society, Madison, WI, USA

1. Valeria Camporesi, "Mass Culture and the Defense of National Traditions: The BBC and American Broadcasting, 1922–1954" (PhD diss, European University Institute, Florence 1993), 3. I am grateful for the existence of this groundbreaking work, and have used it frequently to point the way to relevant documents and publications.
2. For further discussion of the aspects of internal national identity formation that took place in the United States during the 1920s through the 1940s, see Michele Hilmes, *Radio Voices* (Minneapolis: University of Minnesota Press, 1997).

3. Eino Lyytinen, "The Foundation of Yleisradio, the Finnish Broadcasting Company, and the Early Years of Radio in Prewar Finland," in Rauno Enden, ed. *Yleisradio, 1926–1996: A History of Broadcasting in Finland* (Helsinki: Yleisradio 1996), 16.

4. The public service/commercial duality did not always work in total opposition. In Russia, China, Japan, and other countries where authoritarian governments held sway, centralized state systems sometimes combined commercialism with state control – operating for-profit stations supported by advertising, with profits going to the government. And Australia and Canada provide examples of productive – and highly contentious – combinations of public service and commercial broadcasting stations operating side by side.

5. Lyytinen, "Foundation of Yleisdradio," 19.

6. Tasha Oren, "A Clenched Fist and an Open Palm: Israeli National Culture, Media Policy, and the Struggle over Television" (PhD diss, University of Wisconsin–Madison, 1999).

7. James Schwoch, *The American Radio Industry and Its Latin American Activities, 1900–1939* (Urbana: University of Illinois Press, 1990).

8. Susan Smulyan, "Now It Can Be Told: American Influence on Japanese Radio during the Occupation," in Michele Hilmes and Jason Loviglio, eds., *Radio Reader: Essays in the Cultural History of American Radio* (London: Routledge, 2001).

9. See Asa Briggs, *The Birth of Broadcasting*, vol. 1 (London: Oxford University Press, 1961), 58–68; Paddy Scannell and David Cardiff, *A Social History of British Broadcasting*, vol I *1922–1939* (London: Basil Blackwell, 1991); also R. H. Coase, *British Broadcasting: A Study in Monopoly* (London: Longman's Green, 1950), 8–23.

10. "Report of the Broadcasting Committee 1925 (Crawford Committee)," Cmd. 2599, R4/31/1, BBC WAC.

11. Federal Radio Commission, "Broadcasters Urged to Study Problems of Radio Advertising," *United States Daily*, 22 December 1931, VI, 2391–2.

12. For recent examples, see Michael Tracey, *The Decline and Fall of Public Service Broadcasting* (New York: Oxford University Press, 1998), Krishan Kumar, "Public Service Broadcasting and the Public Interest," in Cohn McCabe and Olivia Stewart, eds., *The BBC and Public Service Broadcasting* (Manchester: Manchester University Press, 1986), 46–61; Wilf Stevenson, "Introduction," in Wilf Stevenson, ed., *All Our Futures: The Changing Role and Purpose of the BBC* (London: BFI Publishing, 1993), 1–22.

13. See Kate Lacey, "Radio and Political Transition: Public Service, Propaganda and Promotional Culture," in Hilmes and Loviglio, *Radio Reader*.

14. Briggs, *Birth of Broadcasting*, 94.

15. "Testimony of Mr. F. J. Brown, C.B., C.B.E., Assistant Secretary, General Post Office," R4/64/1, Sykes Committee – Minutes of 2nd Meeting – 2 May 1923, 38–39, BBC WAC.

16. Ibid., 36–7.

17. Though the most common overt articulation of "chaos" was with the technical situation of radio (the necessity to control frequency use to avoid interference), this argument was never made very effectively. Coase demonstrates not only that it was spurious (which would have been readily revealed if anyone had cared to make a more than cursory examination of the US situation), but also that it was frequently elided with *administrative* chaos. He notes that if it had been true, it would have been a preemptive argument in favor of monopoly; the fact that so many others were needed indicates its use as a smokescreen.

18. "Lord Gainford's Statement," 31 July 1923, R4/67/1, Sykes Committee – Precis of Evidence – 1923, BBC WAC.

19. "Broadcasting Question: Official Statement by BBC," 14 April 1923, C038/2, British Broadcasting Company – License and Agreement (1923) File 2 – Feb, 1923–July 1926,

BBC WAC. The "historical fact" of "American chaos" lives on in many more recent works: see the BBC's historical Web page for a definition of early US radio as "unregulated" (http://www.bbc.co.uk/thenandnow/history/1920s-1.shtml).

20. Hilmes, *Radio Voices*, 22.
21. "Testimony of Mr. F. J. Brown," 46–7.
22. The fact that the two second-largest companies had significant American investment could not have made the situation any simpler.
23. "Speech Given by Reith 16 December 1926, Dinner in honor of Prime Minister and retiring directors of the Company and Governors-designate of the British Broadcasting Company," p. 8, R44/540/2, Publicity – Speeches and Articles by Managing Director – Reith, Sir John – 1925–26, BBC WAC.
24. John Reith, speech, n.t., n.d., 4–5, R44/540/2, Publicity – speeches and Articles by Managing Director – Reith, Sir John – 1925–26, BBC WAC.
25. Robert W. McChesney, *Telecommunications, Mass Media, and Democracy* (New York: Oxford University Press, 1993).
26. See, on the NBC end, box 34, folder 52, BBC – 1935, and similar files in subsequent years. By 1937 Greene had made himself unpopular around the halls of NBC and CBS due to his general disdain for US broadcasting culture (box 52, folder 27, BBC – Felix Greene – 1937), At the BBC WAC, see the E1/113 group, "Countries – America – American Representative of the BBC." Cesar Saerchinger wrote a book about his experiences, called *Hello America! Radio Adventures in Europe* (Boston: Houghton Mifflin, 1938). In February 1934 NBC assigned two employees to prepare a detailed comparison of the BBC and NBC organizational structures. Box 24, folder 25, Correspondence – BBC – Jan–Aug, 1934, NBC.
27. See box 16, folder 26, Correspondence – BBC (1926–27), NBC.
28. NAB, "William Hard Has a Few Words to Say," in *Broadcasting in the United States* (Washington, DC: NAB Press, 1933), 95.
29. NAB, "American Radio," in *Broadcasting in the United States*, 48.
30. Ibid., 18.
31. Ibid., 114.
32. Ibid., 113.
33. Telegram from Fred Bate to Merlyn Aylesworth, 140 Jan, 1934, box 24, folder 25, NBC.
34. See box 24, folder 25, Correspondence BBC-Jan–Aug 1934, NBC.
35. Testimony before Parliament by Sir William Mitchell-Thompson, V199, Hansard Commons Deb 5s, c1573–1650, 15 November. 1926, BBC WAC.
36. John Reith, *Broadcast over Britain* (London: Hoddard and Stoughton 1924), 34.
37. Arthur R. Burrows, *The Story of Broadcasting* (London: Cassell, 1924), 55.
38. P. P. Eckersley, "American Radio Broadcasting," 1927, p. 1, E15/57, BBC WAC.
39. "Financial Broadcasting: 'Realism' and Reality," *Radio Times*, 21 June 1929, 610–11.
40. "The Big Broadcast," *Radio Times*, 17 February 1933, 383.
41. Memo from CGG (Cecil Graves) to Peter Eckersley and Erik Maschwitz, "Follow the Sun: Broadcast of First Night," 5 February 1936, R34/918/1, Policy – Vaudeville and Variety – File 1 – 1926 – August 1929, BBC WAC.
42. Memo from Peter Eckersley to Cecil Graves, 7 February 1936, R34/918/1, Policy – Vaudeville and Variety – File 1 – 1926–August 1929, BBC WAC.
43. Asa Briggs, *The Golden Age of Wireless* (London: Oxford University Press, 1965), 118.
44. These programs met with quite a bit of in-house opposition due to their popular emphasis, particularly the serial drama directed toward women. See R19/779/1, Entertainment – "Mrs. Dale's Diary" 1947–1951, especially memos from Val Gielgud, BBC WAC.

45. The title of this section comes from Stuart Hall, "Which Public, Whose Service?" in Stevenson, *All Our Futures*.

46. See Richard Collins, *From Satellite to Single Market* (New York: Routledge, 1998), esp. 51–74, for a thoroughgoing critique of this definition of Habermassian "access."

47. Memo from Mr. Gielgud to DP through ADP, "Listeners' Reactions to Programmes," 12 May 1930, R44/23/1 Publicity – Audience Research – File 1 – 1930–33 BBC WAC.

48. Memo from Mr. C. A. Siepmann to Director of Programmes, 26 May 1930, R44/23/1, Publicity – Audience Research – File 1 – 1930–33, BBC WAC.

49. See Hilmes, *Radio Voices*, chaps. 4 and 5.

50. Here I invoke Habermassian notions of the public sphere, as critiqued by Fraser, Negt and Kluge, Landes, McLaughlin, and others. It is surprising that, in the hundreds of articles that have appeared using public sphere theory to support and defend public service broadcasting systems, so few apply gender as a category of analysis to the BBC, though Kate Lacey makes the case compellingly in *Feminine Frequencies: Gender, German Radio, and the Public Sphere* (Ann Arbor: University of Michigan Press, 1996). See Nancy Fraser, "Rethinking the Public Sphere: A Critique of Actually Existing Democracy," in Craig Calhoun, ed., *Habermas and the Public Sphere* (Cambridge: MIT Press 1992), 108–42; Oskar Negt and Alexander Kluge, *The Public Sphere and Experience* (Minneapolis: University of Minnesota Press, 1993) Joan, Landes, "The Public and the Private Sphere: A Feminist Reconsideration," in J. Meehan, ed., *Feminists Read Habermas* (New York: Routledge, 1995), 91–116; Lisa McLaughlin, "Feminism, the Public Sphere, Media and Democracy," *Media, Culture and Society* 15, no. 3 (1993): 599–620.

51. See Memo from E. R. Appleton, "Revision of Programmes," 17 December 1935, R34/874/2, BBC WAC.

52. For an extended grappling with this question, see Sakae Ishikawa, ed., *Quality Assessment of Television* (Luton: University of Luton Press, 1996).

53. See, for instance, Michael Curtin, "Feminine Desire in the Age of Satellite TV," *Journal of Communication* 49, no. 2 (spring 1999): 55–70; Bodil Folke Frederiksen, "Popular Culture, Gender Relations and the Democratization of Everyday Life in Kenya," *Journal of Southern African Studies* 26, no. 2 (June 2000): 209–25; and Szu-Ping Lin, "Prime Time Television Drama and Taiwanese Women" (Ph.D. diss. University of Wisconsin–Madison, 2000).

54. Irene Costera Meijer, "Advertising Citizenship: An Essay on the Performative Power of Consumer Culture," *Media, Culture and Society* 20, no. 2 (1998): 235–49.

2

Ownership, Organisation, and Cultural Work

*David Hesmondhalgh**

Changes in government policy created a new business environment for cultural-industry corporations, for cultural workers, and for consumers from the late 1980s onwards. In short, marketisation helped to create a situation in which the cultural industries became an increasingly important sector for business investment. In response to the Long Downturn of the 1970s and 1980s, private corporations in the advanced industrial world began to intensify the longer-term shift in investment away from extractive and transformative sectors, and towards service industries, including the cultural industries. But at the same time, businesses of all kinds were going through a long phase of organisational innovation and restructuring. How did these changes affect the cultural industries?

The first part of the chapter provides evidence of the considerable growth in size and scope of large cultural-industry corporations. It examines trends in the strategies of these corporations, including conglomeration and vertical integration. What have been the effects of the growth in size and power of the largest cultural-industry corporations on cultural production and on society?

Changes in ownership and corporate strategy tell us only a certain amount about the environments in which creative work takes place, about the way in which cultural industry owners and executives attempt the difficult business of managing and marketing creativity. Even in the complex professional era, as large corporations began to dominate cultural production, much cultural work was nevertheless based on a certain amount of operational autonomy for creative workers and managers. So in the second part of the chapter, I turn to questions of organisation and control. To what extent were the organisational features associated with the complex professional era of cultural production radically altered? Here I address the question: have the rewards and working conditions of symbol creators – and indeed other workers in the cultural industries – improved during this time? To what extent has creative autonomy been expanded or diminished over the last 20 years? What changes have there been in the extent to which creative workers within the cultural industries get to determine how their work will be edited, promoted, circulated?

Ownership and Corporate Structure: The Big Get Bigger

One of the most important transitions from the market professional era of cultural production to the complex professional era involved the increasing presence of large corporations in cultural markets. This trend has intensified in the 1980s and 1990s. There has been a massive growth in the size and scope of cultural-industry corporations. A small number of transnational corporations have enormous power. I will begin by outlining the growth and current scope of these corporations before dealing in more detail with two vital aspects of corporate strategy – conglomeration and integration – and how these strategies have changed over the last 20 years.

The growth in size and the conglomeration of cultural-industry companies were part of a long-term trend in mergers and acquisitions in all industries that quickened during the 1980s in response to the Long Downturn. There were 4,900 mergers in the USA between 1968 and 1973, and this number increased in the 1970s and 1980s. There were over 3,300 corporate acquisitions in 1986 alone (Greco, 1995: 229–30). This was the period of marketisation in US broadcasting policy and two of the three great US broadcasting networks (CBS and NBC) changed hands in huge deals in 1985–6.

Following the Wall Street Crash of October 1987, the US House of Representatives eliminated certain tax breaks that encouraged acquisitions; as a result, mergers of all kinds substantially decreased in the USA in the following years (Greco, 1995: 230) though this move did not put an end to spectacular international mergers. Consumer electronics company Sony purchased CBS Records in 1988 (US$2 billion) and Columbia Pictures Entertainment (US$3.4 billion) in 1989. Time-Life and Warner Communications merged in 1989, in the form of a 'friendly' US$14.9 billion buy-out by Time-Life. Then, after the brief hiatus of the late 1980s, the 1990s saw a huge explosion of mergers in industry as a whole. For example, 1997 saw the highest ever figures for US mergers and acquisitions up to that point: US$912 billion worth of deals (*Business Week*, 30 March 1998: 47). This was echoed in the cultural industries. According to Greco (1996: 5), there were 557 reported media business acquisitions between 1990 and 1995, only just short of the entire total of such deals between 1960 and 1989. Particularly significant have been two waves of mega-acquisitions, in 1994–5 and in 1999–2000. See Table 2.1 for details of other major cultural-industry mergers and acquisitions in the 1990s.

There is another important context for the growth of cultural-industry corporations in the late 1990s. The US economy began to boom from 1995 onwards; finally, the Long Downturn seemed to be in reverse. There was rapid growth of gross domestic product, labour productivity and investment. Even real wages went up. This boom led to what Robert Brenner (2000: 5) has called 'the greatest financial bubble in American history', as equity prices lost touch with reality, and household, corporate and financial debt all reached record levels, leading to an explosion of consumption. As a result of the boom, and of mergers and acquisitions in the cultural industries, a situation had arisen by the late 1990s whereby a small group of corporations were clear leaders in terms of the revenues they gained from global cultural-industry markets.

Table 2.1 Some major cultural-industry mergers and acquisitions

Date	Acquiring firm	Acquired firm (new name in brackets)	Price US$ billions*	Strategic motivation
1994	Viacom	Paramount Comms*	8.0	Conglomeration across publishing, film, broadcasting, cable, theme parks
1994	Viacom	Blockbuster	8.5	Distribution control
1995	Disney	Capital Cities/ABC	19	Vertical integration and control of content creation
1995	Time Warner	Turner Broadcasting	7.4	Vertical integration and conglomeration/synergy
1995	Seagram	MCA (Universal)	5.7	General conglomerate moves into diversified media
1995	Westinghouse	CBS	5.4	General conglomerate moves into broadcasting
1998	AT&T**	TCI (including Liberty Media)*	48***	Telecoms-media convergence
1998	Seagram	PolyGram	10.6	Recording market share plus European film interests
1999	Carlton**	United*	8.0***	Merger of major European media groups
1999	Viacom	CBS	22	Media conglomerate consolidates broadcasting power
2000	Vivendi	Seagram/Universal	35	Very diversified European leisure conglomerate diversifies further
2000	AOL**	Time-Warner** (AOL Time-Warner)	128***	Internet service provider merges with media conglomerate

Notes: * Prices and values are based on reports at the time that the merger or acquisition was announced, except for AOL Time-Warner, which was evaluated at US$350 billion in January 2000, when the merger was first reported, but at US$128 billion, when the merger was finally approved by the US regulatory body, the Federal Communications Commission. The fall in value reflected the fall in share values over the year, as internet and new media hype subsided.
** indicates a merger.
*** indicates evaluation of new merged company rather than price.

The Big Six:

AOL Time-Warner
Walt Disney
Viacom
Vivendi Universal
Bertelsmann
News Corp.

The names and organisational structures of these companies change regularly, as further mergers, acquisitions and sell-offs take place, or are put on hold by regulators.

Below the first tier of six vast cultural-industry corporations listed, each with annual revenues of over US$10 billion, sits a 'second tier' (Herman and McChesney, 1997: 53) of regional giants, consisting in 1999 and 2000 of 42 companies with revenues in excess of one billion dollars per year from media and cultural operations. Apart from three Latin American companies and one Australian concern, all are based in either North America, Europe or Japan. Some of these companies have ambitions to join the elite club of cultural-industry mega-corporations, such as Comcast (US, primarily cable) and German group Kirch. Collectively, the Big 48 have an enormous impact on the cultural-industry landscape, in terms of policy lobbying, and in terms of the standards they set for what constitutes standard practice in the cultural industries. Concentrating only on the largest six corporations can distract attention from the huge importance of these 48 corporations. It is the Big 48 we should focus on to get a real sense of the expanded role of large corporations within the cultural industries.

Even below these two tiers of global giants, there are many other companies, exerting a sizeable influence on particular markets. A report by Zenith consultants (cited by Sánchez-Tabernero et al., 1993: 100) usefully classifies the biggest cultural-industry companies into the following categories:

- Companies dominant in one cultural industry in one country
- Companies influencing one cultural industry across several countries
- Companies having interests across more than one cultural industry in one country
- Companies with interests in more than one cultural industry internationally.

Nearly all the cultural-industry corporations in the Big 48 are in one or more of the first three categories. With conglomeration and internationalisation, more and more companies are entering, or moving into, the final category.

How Central Are the Cultural Industries in Global Business?

The figures involved in mergers and acquisitions, and the now massive size of revenues accruing to the biggest cultural-industry companies, reflect the increasing centrality of the cultural industries in global business. However, we should not make the leap made by some commentators (e.g., Lash and Urry, 1994: Chapter 5) and suggest that the cultural industries form a 'new core' to global business. Cultural-industry corporations are becoming much bigger, but they still have a long way to go to match the largest corporations in the world.

In terms of market valuation, the AOL–Warner deal of 2000 was the biggest merger of any kind of all time. Surely this is evidence that converged media and computer companies represent a new core? In fact, such figures need to be interpreted carefully. The size of the AOL–Warner deal is closer to the hugely-inflated telecommunications mergers of the late 1990s which took place in the wake of the pro-convergence 1996 Telecommunications Act. And even in the new climate of the 1990s, following years of spectacular internal growth and mergers, corporations primarily based on cultural-industry business were still dwarfed in terms of the most relevant indicators by other kinds of corporation. Table 2.2 shows the biggest corporations with significant cultural-industry interests, along with their rank in the *Fortune* magazine list of the biggest 500 companies in the world by revenue in the year 2000. As is clear from the table, even the very biggest cultural-industry corporations – that is, corporations that gain most of their revenues from cultural-industry operations – are dwarfed by the biggest corporations in the world. These corporations are automobile giants (GM, number three in the 2001 Global 500; Ford, number four and Daimler-Chrysler five, Toyota at ten), oil companies such as Exxon Mobil (number one) and Royal Dutch/Shell (six) and BP (seven), retail giants (Wal-Mart, at two) and general conglomerates (Mitsui, at eleven).

These figures should put into perspective the growth of the largest cultural-industry corporations.[1] It may be that in the wake of convergence hype, cultural-industry companies will merge into vast telecommunications conglomerates – as was the case with AT&T's media holdings, for example – or even internet service providers (such as AOL). But these trends have not yet been established firmly enough to warrant the description 'convergence'. What is more, even where such mergers and acquisitions take place, cultural-industry corporations will operate as separate divisions, just as they already do now, within vast consumer-electronic corporations (Sony) and general conglomerates (Vivendi).

Nevertheless, we should not forget the essential fact: the increasing presence of vast companies in the cultural industries. This has important implications. These corporations are able to mobilise massive lobbying powers and can put tremendous pressure on governments not to put into place legislation and regulation which goes against their interests as profit-making companies. This often works against the public interest. The growth of large corporations also affects prevailing conceptions of how to carry out the management of creativity. The biggest firms often tend to be the most prestigious, and set the standard by which other businesses carry out their work, with important implications for conditions of cultural work.

Changing Strategies 1: Conglomeration

An important feature of the complex professional era from the 1960s onwards was conglomeration. This has continued into the 1980s and 1990s but corporate strategy

Table 2.2 The largest corporations with cultural-industry interests

Ranking	Company	Revenue in US$ billions
1	Exxon Mobil (No media interests – included for sake of comparison.)	210.4
8	General Electric This extremely diverse conglomerate owns the US TV network NBC, but this is only one of 21 divisions.	129.9
30	Sony Has five main divisions: consumer electronics, games, music (Sony Music Entertainment), films (Columbia Tristar), and insurance. Consumer electronics accounts for most of its sales.	66.1
91	Vivendi Based in France, centres its business on 'environmental services', such as water, energy, waste management, transport, construction and property. Prior to its purchase of Universal Music Group from Seagram (1999 revenues: US$11.784 billion, 418th in Global 500), its ownership of Canal Plus made it one of the most important players in the European media market. The acquisition gives it the biggest music company in the world plus Universal's film interests, but its other interests still considerably outweigh its media concerns.	38.6
(103)	*AOL Time Warner* The biggest cultural-industry corporation in the world, when this is defined as a corporation where most of the revenues come from cultural-industry concerns. The merger was completed in early 2001. Because the merger was underway throughout 2000, the company is not listed in the 2001 Global 500, but its combined revenues would put it at 103rd on the list.	
174	*Walt Disney*	25.4
201	Microsoft Included for the sake of comparison here. It is building up many alliances with cultural-industry companies. While it is one of the most highly-valued companies in the world, and has very high profit returns on its revenues, it is important to realise that its revenues are still dwarfed by older corporations.	23.0
245	*Viacom*	20.0
299	*Bertelsmann*	16.6
371	*News Corporation* Note that this ranking underestimates the influence of News Corporation mogul, Rupert Murdoch. Another company of which he has main control, *BSkyB*, is a major player in European digital and satellite television, but reports its figures separately (ranking 24th on the Variety 50, with US$3.2 billion of revenue for 2000).	14.1

Notes: italics indicate that most of the company's revenues come from cultural-industry interests.

Source: The *Fortune* Global 500 list for 2001, based on annual reports 2000/2001.

with regard to conglomeration has changed in important ways. The recent fashion
has generally been to build a portfolio of *related* industries, whereas in the 1960s and
1970s the trend was for non-cultural-industry conglomerates to buy into the cultural
industries.

One of the ways in which the Long Downturn of the 1970s and 1980s forced a
rethinking of the way businesses operated was that there was an increasing emphasis on
the notion of 'synergy'. This was originally a medical term: it referred to the way that
two elements (such as two drugs, or two muscles) might work together to produce a
result greater than the sum of the two parts. The idea behind the metaphor was that
the different parts of a corporation should relate to each other in such a manner as to
provide cross-promotion and cross-selling opportunities, so that sales would exceed
what was possible from two separate divisions. As the popularity of such ideas spread
from business schools and management gurus and into corporations, conglomerates
began to specialise again, but not on one activity, as in the pre-diversification era of the
early twentieth century, but on a set of related ones.[2]

The form of conglomeration that received the most publicity in the late 1980s was
the purchase of media producers by consumer electronics companies: so-called hard-
ware/software synergy.[3] Sony's purchases of CBS Records and Columbia Pictures
Entertainment in 1988 and 1989 respectively were widely assumed to represent the
future shape of cultural-industry corporations. The idea was that Sony would be able
to use prestigious American rock music and cinema to help persuade consumers to buy
new consumer technologies, such as the mini-disc. Other significant purchases in the
late 1980s were based on very different strategies, such as general conglomerate General
Electric's purchase of NBC. However, it was the acquisitions by Japanese corporations,
such as the Japanese conglomerate Matsushita's acquisition of MCA Records in 1990,
which received most attention: they fed recession-fuelled fears on the part of US businesses about a loss of global economic domination.

But by the mid-1990s, such hardware/software synergies were widely viewed as a
failure. Some commentators have explained this apparent failure by referring to the
different production cultures needed to produce consumer electronics on the one hand,
and music/films/TV programmes on the other. Some of these accounts are convincing
(Negus, 1997) but some press versions of this view bordered on racism: the implication
was that the Japanese were incapable of producing entertainment; they could only
produce efficient machines. When hardware/software mergers were deemed to be a
failure, the electronics companies began to sell off their media properties, and to form
alliances and joint ventures with media producers on particular projects.

There is no fundamental reason why mergers, as opposed to alliances and joint ventures, between electronics companies and media producers will not return to fashion.
But the 1990s were dominated by three more tenacious forms of synergy-based cultural-
industry conglomerate. (The following typology is adapted from a study by consultants
Booz, Allen & Hamilton, summarised by Sánchez-Tabernero et al., 1993: 94.) The first
was the *media conglomerate*, based almost entirely around a set of core media interests
(for example, News Corporation). The media are also important for the second category,
the *leisure conglomerate*, but take their place alongside other leisure interests, such as
hotels and theme parks (for example, Disney). From the mid-1990s onwards, however,

a third type of cultural–industry conglomerate was becoming increasingly significant as a potential model: the *information / communication corporation* (perhaps best symbolised by AT&T's 1998 takeover of cable group TCI, including the Liberty Media Group). Media, telecommunications and computer corporations have been merging and acquiring each other, in anticipation of further convergence between these markets.

The marketisation of broadcasting has been absolutely crucial in the formation of all three types of conglomerate. For marketisation meant that many new cultural–industry sectors, including radio, plus terrestrial, cable, satellite and digital television, became available as targets of purchase and investment for conglomerates wishing to extend their portfolios, as governments removed restrictions on market concentration and cross-media ownership and as the cultural industries therefore came to be perceived as major new growth areas for business.

Conglomeration clearly entails an increase in the scope and power of individual cultural–industry corporations, in that the same corporation can have stakes in many different forms of communication. Fewer companies therefore come to dominate the cultural industries as a whole. This has an effect on the lobbying power of the corporations, and on their general influence on the way in which cultural production is carried out. Internal dissent amongst the major conglomerates is less likely, as they decrease in number. It undoubtedly allows the corporations to cross-promote their products (whether texts or other commodities). This in turn reinforces the power of the oligopolies dominating the cultural industries. Some also assert that conglomeration leads to diminished diversity and quality – but there are real problems surrounding the evidence for this.

Changing Strategies 2: Vertical Integration

The imperative towards vertical integration is strong in the cultural industries, because of the vital importance of circulation. This in turn derives from the need to control relationships with fickle audiences, and the need to create artificial scarcity for public goods. That is why so many of the key industries have been dominated by an oligopoly of vertically integrated companies. However, as with conglomeration, vertical integration strategies are subject to change; and there are signs of partial disintegration in some industries, and new forms of integration.

Whereas in the late 1980s commentators thought that Sony would be the archetypal cultural–industry corporation, in the 1990s the future seemed to be represented by Disney. For the success of Disney in the 1990s was based on an understanding of the importance of intellectual property: that the cultural industries increasingly operate around the ownership of rights to films, TV programmes, songs, brands. By circulating these symbols across many different media, characters, icons and narratives become increasingly present in public consciousness. New characters and icons can be launched through intensive cross-promotion. Crucial to this strategy though has been vertical integration. Disney not only owns a remarkable back catalogue of films and recordings, its theme parks, hotels, and so on, it also has its own television network and cable channel (it has had its own international distribution company, Buena Vista, for decades).

With its purchase of Capital Cities/ABC in 1995, Disney became one of the largest cultural-industry companies in the world. But it was not just the size of the corporation that made this significant event, it was also the perception that Disney had understood the nature of the new cultural industries: that combining ownership of content and distribution was the way forward. In its list of the biggest media companies (by turn-over) in 1998–9, *Screen Digest* (July 1999: 176) noted that 'the top companies are all highly diversified – vertically and horizontally integrated'.

We must be cautious about portraying developments in the cultural industries as a steady advance of vertical integration. By 2001, analysts were speculating that Disney's fortunes were in reverse, after the poor performance of the blockbuster film *Pearl Harbor*. There has been plenty of movement in the last 20 years *away* from vertical integration. One of the major organisational forms of the early complex professional era, public service television, represented a striking example of vertical integration in the public interest, justified on the grounds that it ensured a coherent schedule of entertainment and information for national citizens. Many of the public service mono-polies had programme-makers of all kinds, technical and creative, on permanent con-tracts, made programmes, controlled broadcasting distribution and some even made the television sets. In the 1990s, however, there was a boom in independent television production across much of the world, driven mainly by two processes: public service corporations dealt with budget cuts by subcontracting production; and policy-makers wanted to encourage growth in the independent sector by measures such as setting quotas of how much production had to be outsourced. This led many commentators to talk of a new era of post-Fordist television, involving flexible working arrangements and networks of interdependent firms, rather than monolithic organisations (Lash and Urry, 1994: Chapter 5; see Robins and Cornford, 1992 for a more sceptical account). Whether this resulted in greater creative autonomy for programme makers is another matter. We shall return to the issue of whether independent production has allowed greater autonomy for symbol creators later in this chapter.

The trend in the US audiovisual industries has been towards vertical integration. It is ironic that while classical public service television permitted vertical integration, the US system, associated with a more market-oriented approach to cultural production, aimed at discouraging it. With marketisation, the disintegration amongst European broadcasters has been reversed in the USA. One of the main ways in which US policy-makers sought to control the mighty power of the networks was to restrict vertical integration by limiting how many local stations the networks could own. And from the early 1960s on, the broadcasters bought nearly all of their TV and radio programmes in packages from independent production companies, such as MTM (which made *The Mary Tyler Moore Show* and *Hill Street Blues*) and Lorimar (*Dallas, Knots Landing*) (see Sterling and Kittross, 1990: 559–63). Some Hollywood studios acted as 'independent' producers in this system, most notably Warner Bros. In the late 1990s, all this changed. The networks were increasingly part of the same media and leisure conglomerates as the major Hollywood studios, and consequently turned to these sibling companies for most of their productions. Those networks not owned by studio-owning conglomerates followed suit, as the studios gained in prestige. According to a report cited by McChesney (1999: 21), the six Hollywood major studios produced 37 out of 46 new prime-time shows scheduled for the Fall/Autumn of 1998. Such integration was apparent further downstream too. Not only were companies such as Columbia (that is, Sony) buying up cinemas, but the studios were now owned by the same companies that owned the other major outlets for films: broadcast and cable television, plus video hire networks. Disney owned ABC, plus numerous cable networks; News Corporation owned Fox and had launched a new television network of the same name in the mid-1980s; Viacom owned Paramount Studios and the fledgling network UPN and in 1999 bought CBS, one of the big three networks; Time-Warner dominated cable networks, and through its purchase of Ted Turner's company TNT in 1997, owned the key cable channels. Even here, in the case of the USA, such transformations cannot be portrayed as an entirely new era of vertical integration. The integration of Hollywood studios with television networks represented a return to the strategies Hollywood used during the classic studio era, from the 1920s to the 1950s. The recording industry also shows high levels of vertical integration. For decades, the major companies have owned pressing and distribution, as well as contracting musicians to them. However, the majors have rarely attempted to own retail outlets, in part because of the complexity and multiplicity of the market for music. What is more, the relationship with independent production is more complex in the music industry than in any other industry (see the section on small companies, below).

Vertical integration is best seen not as a constant process, whereby companies get more and more vertically integrated over time, but as something historically variable across different industries. Changes in government policy, the arrival of new technologies and new business fashions can all bring about shifts towards or away from vertical integration.

Market Concentration and its Limitations

The issue of market concentration has been central to work on the cultural industries in liberal-pluralist communication studies and in political economy approaches to culture. Chapter 2 noted high levels of market concentration in the cultural industries but pointed out that, in some cases, the arrival of corporations in new markets actually reduced the level of market concentration. Good, historically comparative statistics on market concentration are hard to find. Instead, we have to rely on snapshots of particular times, and these need to be treated with caution.

What have been the effects of conglomeration on corporate domination of cultural markets? Ben Bagdikian (2000) provides something of an indication of the effects of such conglomeration in terms of general cultural market concentration. For the first edition of his book *The Media Monopoly*, Bagdikian compiled an apparently unpublished list of the dominant media firms in the US market in 1983 in the following industries: newspapers, magazines, television, book publishing, motion pictures. For each industry, he worked down the lists of dominant companies, counting how many companies it took to account for more than 50 per cent of market share (measured in different ways for different media). He then added the figures together and calculated a total of 50 dominant corporations across the media as a whole.

Bagdikian has repeated the exercise for every subsequent edition of his book, and in the most recent edition (Bagdikian, 2000: xx–xxi) summarises the results.

1983 – 50
1987 – 29
1990 – 23
1997 – 10
2000 – 6

This is a crude method of measuring overall cultural-industry concentration and conglomeration, but it draws attention to the increasing size and scope of the biggest corporations, and their increasing tendency to work across all the different cultural industries.

Writing about the USA, McChesney (1999: 17–18) provides a number of examples of concentration in recent years, with some historical comparison:

- In 1997, the six largest film studios dominated over 90 per cent of US box office revenues and produced 132 out of the 148 films to receive wide distribution.
- The five largest music groups account for over 87 per cent of the US market.
- In cable, which was once a market without significant oligopoly control, according to McChesney, six cable companies had effective monopoly control over local markets across 80 per cent of the USA by 1998.
- Four radio chains controlled one-third of the radio industry's annual revenues of US$13.6 billion (though in fact some would say that this does not suggest a particularly high concentration ratio compared with most industries of comparable size).
- In 1985, the 12 largest theatre (that is, cinema exhibition) companies in the USA controlled 25 per cent of the screens; by 1998, that figure was 61 per cent.
- Between 1992 and 1998, the share of books sold by independent booksellers fell from 42 per cent to 20 per cent, as Barnes and Noble entered the market.

The accumulation of evidence suggests an irresistible tide sweeping the cultural industries towards ever-greater levels of market concentration. But much depends on the historical framework we decide to examine. Radio became more concentrated in the light of the 1996 US Telecommunications Act, but it was still much less concentrated than in the days of network control; in 1945, 95 per cent of all radio stations were affiliated with one or more of the four national networks (Sterling and Kittross, 1990: 260). And concentration levels in cinema exhibition are still relatively low compared with other industries, and certainly compared with the days when the major studios owned them, that is, prior to 1948, when government antitrust action resulted in the studios selling off their cinema interests.

As for new industries such as cable, there is bound to be a process of oligopolisation as such industries mature and as smaller firms are snaffled up by those aiming to increase market share. That's capitalism. This is not to be complacent about existing levels of market concentration. But such statistics do not prove, in themselves, the existence of long-term processes of *increased* concentration in US markets. Market concentration

Table 2.3 Media concentration in Western Europe

Country	Circulation share of top five publishing companies	Circulation share of top five newspaper titles	Audience market share of top two TV channels
Austria	45	69	68
Belgium (fr)	77	55	47
Belgium (fl)	–	–	58
Denmark	50	49	78
Finland	42	39	71
France	–	–	60
Germany	–	23	31
Ireland	–		60
Italy	–	–	47
Luxembourg	100	–	–
The Netherlands	95	–	39
Norway	53	38	80
Portugal	55	91	88
Spain	–	–	51
Sweden	49	33	55
Switzerland (d)	–	–	45
Switzerland (fr)	–	–	49
UK	95	–	68

Source: Meier and Trappel, 1998: 51, based on EC statistical sources.

levels are high across all industries – but even in the wider economy, there is evidence that market concentration does not always go up in advanced industrial economies as a whole.[4]

What about European figures? In their study of media concentration in Europe, Meier and Trappel (1998: 51) provide some figures on concentration based on European Union sources (see Table 2.3). They suggest very high levels of concentration in book publishing, newspapers and television. But again these are non-historical and, given that in many countries television was entirely dominated by one or two channels until the 1980s, there may even be significant reductions of concentration, at least in the terms used here.

Sánchez-Tabernero et al. (1993: 102) compiled statistics comparing the market share of the two largest daily newspaper groups in 1975 and 1990 across 17 European countries (see Table 2.4). Even here, however, the trends were mixed across the 15 countries where figures were available. Five recorded significant increases; four small increases; three large decreases and three small decreases. This certainly does not point to a Europe-wide trend towards significant market concentration in this cultural industry though, as Sánchez-Tabernero et al. point out, their figures do not capture regional trends within countries. In some countries, such as the Netherlands, fewer and fewer cities had more than one newspaper.[5]

My concern here is primarily with the difficulties of proving that levels of market concentration have substantially increased in the cultural industries since the late 1970s.

Table 2.4 Changes in newspaper market concentration

Country	1975 (%)	1990 (%)
Austria	55	68
Belgium (fl)	26	59
Belgium (fr)	52*	68
Switzerland	20	21
Germany	35**	29
Denmark	38	48
Spain	24	29
Finland	26	39
France	15	35
UK	53	58
Greece	61	36
Ireland	n/a	75
Italy	n/a	32
Netherlands	36	35
Norway	48	45
Portugal	60[1]	30
Sweden	30	31
Turkey	46	34

The figures refer to the share of circulation held by the two largest newspaper groups.
* estimate.
** 1976 figures.
Source: Sánchez-Tabernero et al., 1993: 102, reporting European Institute for the Media figures.

But economists find it difficult to agree on any reliable measure of market concentration even in the same period (see Iosifides, 1997), leaving aside the difficulties of historical comparison. One issue amongst many others, for example, is whether different divisions of the same corporation, which at least in principle compete with each other, should be counted as competitors.[6] Even more difficult to prove via reliable statistics is that increased levels of market concentration lead to reduced levels of diversity of output.

   None of this is to deny the importance of the presence of large corporations in cultural markets. Indeed, it is on this particular point that analysis should focus, rather than on the red herring of market concentration. The case for increased corporate control cannot be made via analysis of market concentration figures in quite such a clear-cut way as some writers would have us believe, through a rhetorical piling-up of statistics. Processes of conglomeration and integration, and the increasing size and scope of the largest cultural-industry corporations, are more important. These require separate treatment.

The Continuing Presence of Small Companies

Independent producers proliferated – and became important to debates about cultural production – even as large corporations became dominant in the cultural industries in the middle of the twentieth century. As cultural corporations have become bigger and more dominant, small companies have continued to boom in number. According to one analyst, 80 per cent of the Hollywood film industry is made up of companies with four employees or fewer (Jack Kyser, cited by Magder and Burston, 2002). Even during the period when the book industry was involved in successive waves of mergers and acquisitions, the number of book companies active in the USA increased from 993 in 1960 to 2,298 in 1987, according to Department of Commerce figures (Greco, 1996: 234).

The continued importance of small companies can partly be explained by the fact that the conception stage of texts remains small-scale and relatively inexpensive, and still takes place in relatively autonomous conditions. But there are other factors, more specific to the 1980–2000 period, accounting for the still-prevalent role of small companies.

- The onset of new media technologies brought about by the combined factors of government marketisation policy and intensified business interest in leisure and culture: This has created new types of cultural industry, and before industries 'mature', there is often more room for manoeuvre for independents. Key examples of such independent-friendly new cultural industries over the last 20 years are computer games, multimedia production (for example, educational CD-ROMs) and website design. But the introduction of new technologies is also a product of, and in turn a cause of, a proliferation of new sub-sectors within longer-established industries. For example, as live performance by successful rock acts has become more and more important, from the 1970s onwards, a host of new companies have sprung up providing technical and other forms of support, including amplification specialists, but also lighting and set designers, and so on.
- The rise of a discourse of entrepreneurialism in the economy as a whole (Keat and Abercrombie, 1991): There has been increasing emphasis since the 1970s on the value of 'going it alone', separately from large bureaucratic organisations. This has not only made people willing to set up their own businesses, but it has made large businesses more willing to interact with them.
- As culture has become recognised as a valid form of profit making, banks have become much more prepared to lend venture capital to small and medium-sized cultural businesses.
- As we have seen, industries such as television, dominated by vertically-integrated companies, have seen some disintegration. This has not only brought about an independent production sector, it has also created many ancillary and technical support companies, from film and television catering specialists to companies that rent out editing suites and personnel.
- There has been an increasing emphasis in cultural-industry companies on marketing. So there are also scores of design studios, independent advertising agencies and so on aimed at servicing companies that are increasingly willing to pay more to market their goods and services. What is more, actors, performers and other symbol creators can subsidise their other work, which they may feel is their 'real' work, by operating in these sectors. This has always happened, but now more than ever.

Accounts that focus on conglomeration, integration and the increasing size of the cultural-industry corporations (such as many accounts from the Schiller–McChesney tradition) often understate the importance of small companies. Such companies may account for small levels of market share, but they are important in terms of the numbers of people they employ, and in terms of their potential to foster – or at least act as a conduit for – innovation. This, along with other factors, has meant a strong ethical and aesthetic premium has been placed on institutional independence.

This is particularly apparent in the film industry and in the recording industry. Crucial in many music genres has been a discourse of independence amongst musicians, fans and journalists. This has allowed independent record companies, in some exceptional cases, to serve as the centre of commercial networks which form something of an alternative to prevailing systems of cultural production and consumption. For Jason Toynbee, the particular importance attached to independent production in popular music derives from a longstanding history of 'institutional autonomy' (Toynbee, 2000: 19–25) in popular music-making, which cuts against the efforts of large companies to make profits out of music. This derives from the dispersed, decentralised nature of music-making. Institutional autonomy means that not only do companies cede control of production to musicians (as in all cultural industries); there is also a tendency towards 'spatially dispersed production in small units' (rock groups, swing bands) and 'a strong continuity between production and consumption' in musical subcultures (Toynbee, 2000: 1). Audiences and performers come together in 'proto-markets', which are only partially commodified, and where there is a great deal of resentment towards the industry and 'selling out'. The possibility of institutional autonomy and the high value attached to it in musical subcultures means that spaces have been created where alternative arrangements for the management and marketing of creativity can be tried out. I discuss an important example of such an 'alternative' dynamic later in this chapter.

Interdependence, Interfirm Networks and Alliances

Small companies, then, not only continue to exist; they are multiplying. However, there is a vital caveat, already referred to in passing in the above discussion of independent record companies. A key change in the cultural industries in the years since the 1970s has been that small and large companies are increasingly interdependent: they are involved in complex networks of licensing, financing and distribution.

One of the most important ways in which corporations have changed their organisational structures, in nearly all major areas of business, is that they increasingly subcontract to small and medium-sized firms. These smaller firms are potentially more dynamic and able to innovate; but they are increasingly involved in close relationships with the corporations that subcontract to them. This is true too of the cultural industries.

Such webs of interdependence are not entirely new in the cultural industries. In the film industry, as the Hollywood corporations lost their control over production in the 1950s, new independent production companies entered the market to cater for specialist products, but the Hollywood studios acted as distributors and financiers of independently-produced films (see Aksoy and Robins, 1992). Even in an era in the recording industry when 'majors' and 'independents' were seen by fans, musicians and critics as polar opposites, in truth they were often linked in licensing, financing and distribution deals. Such arrangements, whereby small and large companies form inter-dependent webs, became increasingly prevalent in the 1980s and extended into new areas of the cultural industries, most significantly in European broadcasting, where traditionally production had been handled 'in house' by large state and public service broadcasters (Robins and Cornford, 1992).

There are rewards for both corporations and small companies in such systems of interfirm networking. For the corporations, acting as distributors and financiers of independent producers is an extension of what they already do, in acting as distribu-tors and financiers of their own semiautonomous divisions. A large multi-divisional corporation might get a lower cut of revenues from a text produced by an independent company than from the sales of a text created within one of their own divisions, but the arrangement means that they can get independent companies to bear some of the risks associated with the difficult business of managing symbolic creativity. What is more, symbol creators might well *feel* as though they are more autonomous of commercial pressures, especially in cultural industries where there is a mistrust of corporate bureaucracies.

This makes interdependence sound very rosy. However, in the eyes of many, increas-ing levels of interdependence in the cultural industries mean the end of an era when independents could provide an alternative to the majors: another sign of corporate takeover. And many forms of interfirm networking involve links between very large companies in different industries, and increasingly in different sectors. These involve strategic alliances between corporations, not as in traditional cartel arrangements, but on the basis of specific projects. Such 'alliance capitalism' has been a feature of a very wide range of businesses over the last 20 years. It is especially relevant, says Castells (1996: 162–4), in high-tech sectors, where research and development costs are enor-mously expensive. For Castells, the self-sufficient corporation is increasingly a thing of the past.

While cultural-industry companies compete with each other, at the same time, they operate complex webs of joint ventures and ownership. Auletta (1997: 225) lists a number of reasons for such alliances with potential rivals:

- To avoid competition
- To save money and share risks
- To buy a seat on a rival's board
- To create a safety net, as technological innovation makes for increasing uncertainty
- To make links with foreign companies to avoid 'arousing the ire of local governments'.

The interconnections amongst the six biggest cultural-industry corporations and the 'second tier' of the Big 48 are almost impossible to encapsulate neatly. One of the best attempts to capture the complexity of links between different corporations was printed

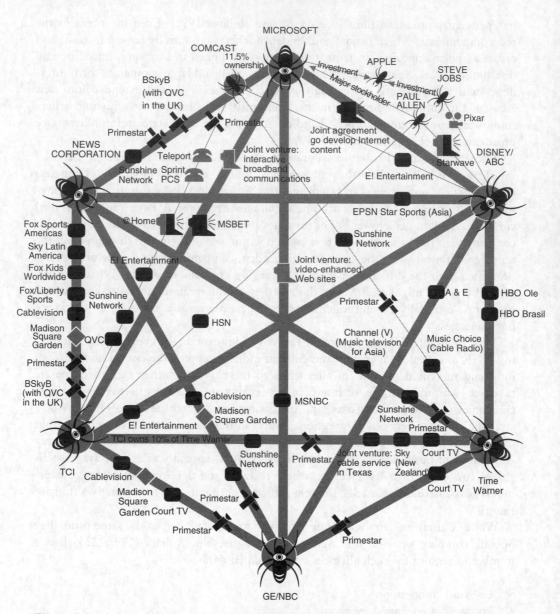

Figure 2.1 A web of collaboration. This diagram, reproduced from a 1997 edition of *The New Yorker*, illustrates the many complex connections existing at the time between a number of companies in the cultural-industry and IT business (Auletta, 1997: 227)

by *The New Yorker* in 1997 (see Figure 2.1). It shows the 'web of collaboration' between six of the most powerful cultural-industry corporations in the world at the time, plus Microsoft, and lists some of the many joint ventures between them. In the rapidly-changing world of the cultural industries, this diagram is already a historical document; but it gives a good sense of how closely intermeshed the major companies are, in terms of joint ventures and ownership. Auletta (1997) describes such links as an American version of keiretsu – the 'ancient Japanese custom of co-opting the competition' through creating structures of collaboration with rivals; a system of 'co-opetition' (Murdock, 2000: 48, quoting *The Financial Times*) rather than competition. As Auletta (1997: 226) suggests, such alliances have implications for texts. As more and more companies become tied to one another, will their journalists cover controversial stories about other companies in the web? Without question, it helps to reinforce the economic power of the biggest corporations. Such alliances have been further encouraged by speculation about future convergence of the telecommunications, computers and cultural industries.[7]

Notes

1. Historical comparison of the relative size of the largest cultural-industry corporations is difficult. Companies based on 'services' were only included in the *Fortune* 500 and Global 500 from 1995 onwards.
2. Very diverse general conglomerates continue to be a feature of the South East Asian business landscape right up to the time of writing. The struggles of, for example, Korean general conglomerates such as Daewoo may or may not affirm European and North American commitment to synergy-based diversification. Some North American general conglomerates such as General Electric thrived in the late 1990s.
3. Such hardware/software synergies were not unprecedented by any means: the Dutch consumer electronics group Philips had its own record division (PolyGram) for decades until it sold it to Seagram in 1995. And the US networks were founded on such synergies: NBC was part of the communications conglomerate RCA, which made radio equipment.
4. Ghemawat and Ghadar (2000) arguing against global megamergers as a business strategy, present evidence to show declining global concentration levels in automobiles, oil and other key industries, including even high-tech industries. Systematic comparisons of market concentration in the cultural industries with levels elsewhere are extremely rare. Murdock and Golding (1977) is a rare and obviously outdated exception.
5. Sánchez-Tabernero et al.'s market share statistics for radio and television are also ambiguous. They show that private companies were becoming involved in these markets but do not provide evidence of significant market concentration.
6. Christianen (1995: 89–91) argues that concentration in the music industry should take account of different record company divisions as separate entities, so that all the different labels under each conglomerate's control would be counted separately, because they are in internal competition with each other. This would make concentration figures much lower, and would help account for the greater diversity of product that followed from some periods of apparent market concentration.
7. See Herman and McChesney (1997: 56–8) and Murdock (2000: 47–51) for further discussion of such alliances.

References

Aksoy, Asu & Kevin Robins (1992). Hollywood for the 21st Century: Global Competition for Critical Mass in Image Markets. *Cambridge Journal of Economics* 16, pp. 1–22.

Auletta, Ken (1997). American Keiretsu. *The New Yorker*, October 20 and 27, pp. 225–7.

Bagdikian, Ben H. (2000). *The Media Monopoly*, 6th edn. Boston: Beacon Press.

Brenner, Robert (2000). The Boom and the Bubble. *New Left Review* II 6, pp. 5–43.

Castells, Manuel (1996). *The Rise of the Network Society*. Oxford: Blackwell.

Christianen, Michael (1995). Cycles in Symbol Production? A New Model to Explain Concentration, Diversity and Innovation in the Music Industry. *Popular Music* 14(1), pp. 55–94.

Davis, Howard & Richard Scase (2000). *Managing Creativity*. Buckingham and Philadelphia: Open University Press.

Greco, Albert N. (1995). Mergers and Acquisitions in the US Book Industry, 1960–89. In: Philip G. Altbach & Edith S. Hoshino (eds.), *International Book Publishing: An Encyclopedia*, pp. 229–42. New York and London: Garland Publishing.

Greco, Albert N. (1996). Shaping the Future: Mergers, Acquisitions, and the US Publishing, Communications, and Mass Media, Industries, 1990–1995. *Publishing Research Quarterly* 12(3), pp. 5–16.

Herman, Edward S. & Robert W. McChesney (1997). *The Global Media*. London: Cassell.

Iosifides, Petros (1997). Methods of Measuring Media Concentration. *Media, Culture and Society* 19, pp. 643–63.

Keat, Russell & Nicholas Abercrombie (eds.) (1991). *Enterprise Culture*. London: Routledge.

Lash, Scott & John Urry (1994). *Economies of Signs and Space*. London: Sage.

Magder, Ted & Jonathan Burston (2002). Whose Hollywood? Changing Forms and Relations inside the North American Entertainment Economy. In: Vincent Mosco & Dan Schiller (eds.), *Continental Integration for Cybercapitalism*. New York: Rowan and Littlefield.

McChesney, Robert W. (1999). *Rich Media, Poor Democracy*. Urbana and Chicago, Illinois: University of Illinois Press.

Meier, Werner A. & Josef Trappel (1998). Media Concentration and the Public Interest. In: Denis McQuail & Karen Siune (eds.), *Media Policy*, pp. 38–59. London: Sage.

Murdock, Graham (2000). Digital Futures: European Television in the Age of Convergence. In: Jan Wieten, Graham Murdock & Peter Dahlgren (eds.), *Television Across Europe*, pp. 35–57. London: Sage.

Murdock, Graham & Peter Golding (1977). Capitalism, Communication and Class Relations. In: James Curran, Michael Gurevitch & Janet Wollacott (eds.), *Mass Communication and Society*, pp. 12–43. London: Edward Arnold, in association with The Open University Press.

Negus, Keith (1997). The Production of Culture. In: Paul du Gay (ed.), *Production of Culture/Cultures of Production*, pp. 67–118. Milton Keynes: The Open University/Sage.

Robins, Kevin & James Cornford (1992). What Is "Flexible" about Independent Producers? *Screen* 33(2), pp. 190–200.

Sańchez-Tabernero, Alfonso, Alison Denton, Pierre-Yves Lochon, Philippe Mounier & Runar Woldt (1993). *Media Concentration in Europe*. Dusseldorf: The European Institute for the Media.

Sterling, Christopher H. & John M. Kittross (1990). *Stay Tuned*. Belmont, California: Wadsworth Publishing Company.

Toynbee, Jason (2000). *Making Popular Music*. London: Arnold.

3

The World Wide Web and the Corporate Media System

*Robert McChesney**

Much contemporary literature discusses the starkly antidemocratic implications and trajectory of the contemporary media system (McChesney, 1999). Dominated by a handful of massive firms, advertisers, and their billionaire owners, the system is spinning in a hyper-commercial frenzy with little trace of public service. In conjunction with this crystallization of the corporate media system in the late 1990s, a theory has emerged asserting that we have no reason to be concerned about concentrated corporate control and the hypercommercialization of media. This claim is that the World Wide Web, or, more broadly, digital communication networks, will set us free. This is hardly an unprecedented argument: every major new electronic media technology in this century – from film, AM radio, short-wave radio, and facsimile broadcasting to FM radio, terrestrial television, cable, and satellite broadcasting – has spawned similar utopian notions. In each case, to varying degrees, visionaries told us how these new magical technologies would crush the existing monopolies over media, culture, and knowledge and open the way for a more egalitarian and just social order. But the World Wide Web is qualitatively the most radical and sweeping of these new communication technologies, and the claims about it top earlier technological visions by a wide margin.

The claims for what the Web will do to media and communication are no less sweeping. "The Internet is wildly underestimated," Nicholas Negroponte, media lab director at the Massachusetts Institute of Technology, states. "It will grow to be the enabling technology of all media – TV, radio, magazines and so on" (quoted in Lohr, 1998b: A11). As the argument goes, if everything is in the process of becoming digital, if anyone can produce a site at minimal cost, and if that site can be accessed worldwide via the Web, it is only a matter of time (e.g., expansion of bandwidth, improvement of software) before the media giants find themselves swamped by countless high-quality competitors. Their monopolies will be crushed. John Perry Barlow, in a memorable comment from 1996, dismissed concerns about media mergers and concentration. The big media firms, Barlow noted, are "merely rearranging deck chairs on the Titanic." The "iceberg," he submitted, would be the World Wide Web, with its five hundred million channels

* Originally published as "So much for the magic of technology and the free market: The World Wide Web and the corporate media system," pp. 5–35 from *The World Wide Web and Contemporary Media Theory*, ed. A. Herman and T. Swiss (New York: Routledge). © 2000 by Routledge. Reproduced with permission form the author and Routledge, a division of Taylor & Francis Group.

(cited in Herman and McChesney, 1997: 107). As one *New York Times* correspondent put it in 1998, "To hear Andy Grove [CEO of Intel] and Reed Hundt [former chair of the Federal Communications Commission] talk, the media industry is about where the horse-and-buggy business was when Henry Ford first cranked up the assembly line" (Landler, 1998: sec. 3, D.9).

In this chapter I try to untangle the claims, even the mythology, about the World Wide Web from the observable record, though this is not an easy task. For one thing, the Web is a quite remarkable and complex phenomenon that cannot be categorized by any previous medium's experience. It is two-way mass communication; it uses the soon-to-be-universal digital binary code; it is global; and it is quite unclear how, exactly, it is or can be regulated. In addition, the World Wide Web is changing at a historically unprecedented rate. Any attempt at prediction during such tumultuous times is nearly impossible; something written about the Web as recently as 1992 or 1993 has about as much currency in 2000 as discourses on the War of the Roses do for understanding contemporary European military policy. But I believe enough has happened in cyberspace that we can begin to get a sense of the Web's overarching trajectory, and a sense of what the range of probable outcomes might be.

While it is no doubt true that the World Wide Web will be part of massive social changes, I do not share the optimism of the George Gilders, Newt Gingriches, and Nicholas Negropontes.[1] Much discussion of the Web is premised upon whether one has a utopian or dystopian, optimistic or pessimistic view of technology and social change. In short, is one a technological determinist, and is that determinism of the utopian or Luddite variety? These are interesting debates but, conducted in isolation from social factors, they are not especially productive. The Web utopianism of Negroponte and others is based not just on a belief in the magic of technology, but, more important, on a belief in capitalism as a fair, rational, and democratic mechanism that I find mythological. It is when technological utopianism or determinism are combined with a view of capitalism as benign and natural that we get a genuinely heady ideological brew. So it is true that the Web is changing the nature of our media landscape radically. As Barry Diller, builder of the Fox television network and a legendary corporate media seer, put it in December 1997, "We're at the very early stages of the most radical transformation of everything we hear, see, know" ("All Together Now," 1997: 14). What I wish to examine in this chapter, specifically, is if these changes will pave the way for a qualitatively different media culture and society or if the corporate commercial system will merely don a new set of clothing.

The Mythology of the Free Market

One of the striking characteristics of the World Wide Web is that there has been virtually no public debate over how it should develop; a consensus of "experts" simply decided that it should be turned over to the market. Indeed, the antidemocratic nature of Web policy making is explained or defended on very simple grounds: the Web is to be and should be regulated by the free market. This is the most rational, fair, and democratic regulatory mechanism ever known to humanity, so by all rights it should be automatically applied to any and all areas of social life where profit can be found. No debate is necessary to establish the market as the reigning regulatory mechanism, because the market naturally assumes that role unless the government intervenes and prevents the market from working its magic. Indeed, by this logic, any public debate over Web policy can only be counterproductive, because it could only lead us away from a profit-driven system. Public meddling would allow unproductive bureaucrats to interfere with productive market players.

Combining the market with the Web, we are told, will allow entrepreneurs to compete as never before, offering wonderful new products at ever lower prices. It will provide a virtual cornucopia of choices for consumers, and empower people all over the world in a manner previously unimaginable. Enterprise will blossom as the multitudes become online entrepreneurs. It will be a capitalist Valhalla. Nowhere will the cyber-market revolution be more apparent than in the realm of media and communication. When anyone can put something up on the Web, the argument goes, and when the Web effectively converges with television, the value of having a television or cable network will approach zero. Eventually the control of any distribution network will be of no value as all media convert to digital formats. Production studios, too, will have less leverage as the market will be opened to innumerable new players. Even governments will, in the end, find its power untamable (McHugh, 1997).

As a consequence, the likely result of the digital revolution will be the withering – perhaps even the outright elimination – of the media giants and a flowering of a competitive commercial media marketplace the likes of which have never been seen. Indeed, the rise of the Web threatens not only the market power of the media giants but also the very survival of the telecommunication and computer software giants (see Gilder, 1994).

It is ironic that as the claims about the genius of the market have grown in conventional discourse over the past two decades, the need to provide empirical evidence for the claims has declined. The market has assumed mythological status, becoming a religious totem to which all must pledge allegiance or face expulsion to the margins. The mythology of the market is so widely embraced to some extent because it has some elements of truth. It is formally a voluntary mechanism, without direct coercion, and it permits an element of consumer choice. But the main reason it has vaulted to the top of the ideological totem pole is because it serves the interests of the most dominant elements of our society. And the free market mythology harms few if any powerful interests, so it goes increasingly unchallenged. As this mythology of the free market is the foundation of almost the entire case for the lack of any public debate on the course – and therefore for the privatization and commercialization – of the Web, it demands very careful scrutiny.

The claim that the market is a fair, just, and rational allocator of goods and services is premised on the notion that the market is based on competition. This competition constantly forces all economic actors to produce the highest-quality product for the lowest possible price, and it rewards those who work the hardest and the most efficiently (see Friedman, 1962). Therefore, these new technologies will permit hungry entrepreneurs to enter markets, slay corporate dinosaurs, lower prices, improve products, and generally do good things for humanity. And just when these newly successful entrepreneurs are riding high on the hog, along will come some plucky upstart (probably with a new technology) to teach them a lesson and work the magic of competition yet again. This is the sort of pabulum that is served up to those Americans who lack significant investments in the economy. It provides an attractive image for the way our economy works – making it seem downright fair and rational – but it has little to do with how the economy actually operates. Corporate executives will even invoke this rhetoric in dealing with Congress or the public and, at a certain level, they may even believe it. Yet their actions speak louder than words.

The truth is that for those atop our economy the key to success is based in large part on eliminating competition.[2] I am being somewhat facetious, because in the end capitalism is indeed a war of one against all, since every capitalist is in competition with all others. But competition is also something successful capitalists (the kind that remain capitalists) learn to avoid like the plague. The less competition a firm has, the less risk it faces and the more profitable it tends to be. All investors and firms rationally desire to be in as monopolistic a position as possible. In general, most markets in the United States in the twentieth century have gravitated not to monopoly status, but to oligopolistic status. This means that a small handful of firms – ranging from two or three to as many as a dozen or so – thoroughly dominate the market's output and maintain barriers to entry that effectively keep new market entrants at bay, despite the sort of profitability that Milton Friedman tells us would create competition. In pricing and output, oligopolistic markets are far closer to being monopolistic markets than they are the competitive markets described in capitalist folklore.

To be sure, despite all this concentration these firms still compete – but not in the manner the mythology suggests. As one business writer put it, "Companies in some industries seem to do everything to win customers, apart from cutting prices" (Martin, 1998: 10). Advertising, for example, arises to become a primary means of competition in oligopolistic markets. It provides a way to protect or expand market share without engaging in profit-threatening price competition. On occasion, foreign competition, economic crisis, new technologies, or some other factor may break down a stable oligopoly and lead to a reshuffling of the deck and a change in the cast of corporate characters. But the end result will almost always be some sort of stable oligopoly; otherwise, no sane capitalist would participate. Yet even the notion of oligopoly is insufficient: widespread conglomeration, along with pronounced involvement by the largest financial institutions in corporate affairs, has reduced the level of autonomy in distinct industries, bringing a degree of instability – if not much more direct competition – to the system. Rather then concentrate on specific oligopolistic industries, then, it is perhaps better to recognize the economy as being increasingly dominated by the few hundred largest firms. This certainly is the best context for understanding developments in media and communication.

So how should we expect the World Wide Web to develop in this model of the free market? Exactly as it has so far. Despite now having the technological capacity to compete, the largest firms are extremely reticent about entering new markets and forcing their way into existing and highly lucrative communication markets. Thus the local telephone companies have tended to avoid providing pay television over their wires, and the cable companies have avoided providing telephone services over their lines. This is no conspiracy. There have been a few, and will no doubt be more, attempts by these firms and others to cross over and compete in new markets. But it will be done selectively, usually targeting affluent markets that are far more attractive to these firms (Mehta, 1998). Most important, no existing giant will attempt to enter another market unless they are reasonably certain that they will have a chance to win their own monopoly, or at least have a large chunk of a stable oligopoly with significant barriers to entry. A less risky option for these firms, rather than venturing on entrepreneurial kamikaze missions into enemy territory, is to merge to get larger so they have much more armor as they enter competitive battle, or to protect themselves from outside attack. Short of mergers, the other prudent course is to establish joint ventures with prospective competitors in order to reduce potential competition and risk. In short, the rational behavior is to attempt to reduce the threat of competition as much as possible, and then to engage in as little direct competition as can be managed. When capitalism is viewed in this light, Barlow's "iceberg" thesis is considerably less plausible. After all, the corporate media giants have significant weapons in their arsenal not only to confront but also to shape the new technologies. Moreover, once we have a realistic understanding of how capitalism operates, we can see why the dominant corporate media firms, rather than shrinking, are in fact growing rapidly in the United States and worldwide. In the United States, the media industry is growing much faster than the overall economy, and experienced, for the first time since the 1980s, double-digit growth in the consecutive years 1997 and 1998 (Mermigas, 1997; Cardona, 1997).

But what about new firms? Will they provide the competitive impetus the giants rationally attempt to avoid? In general, new firms are ill-equipped to challenge giant firms in oligopolistic markets due to entry barriers. The role of small firms in the classic scenario is to conduct the research, development, and experimentation that large firms deem insufficiently profitable, then, when a small firm finds a lucrative new avenue, it sells out to an existing giant. Some of the impetus for technological innovation comes from these small firms, eager to find a new niche in which they can grow away from the shadows of the corporate giants in existing industries. It is in times of technological upheaval, as now, with the World Wide Web and digital communication, that brand new industries are being formed and there is an opportunity for new giants to emerge.

It is safe to say that some new communications giants will be established during the coming years, much as Microsoft attained gigantic status during the eighties and nineties. But most of the great new fortunes will be made by start-up firms who develop a profitable idea and then sell out to one of the existing giants. (Witness Microsoft, which spent over $2 billion between 1994 and 1997 to purchase or take a stake in some fifty communication companies.) Indeed, this is conceded to be the explicit goal of nearly all the start-up Web and telecommunications firms, who are founded with the premise of an "exit scenario" through their sale to a giant (Colonna, 1998). As a Web stock-market manager put it in 1998, Web company stock prices were "driven by speculation about who will be the next company to get snapped up by a much bigger company from another medium as a way of buying their way on to the World Wide Web" (Gilpin, 1998: 7). Hence, the traditional function of start-up firms is still the rule. For every new Microsoft, there will be one thousand WebTVs or Starwaves, small technology firms that sell out to media and communications giants in deals that make their largest shareholders rich beyond their wildest dreams. And for every WebTV or Starwave, there are thousands more companies that go belly up.

What should be clear is that this market system may "work" in the sense that goods and services are produced and consumed, but it is by no means fair in any social, political, or ethical sense of the term. Existing corporations have tremendous advantages over start-up firms. They use their power to limit the ability of new firms to enter the fray, to limit output and keep prices higher. Yet the unfairness extends beyond the lack of competitive markets. In participating as capitalists, wealthy individuals have tremendous advantages over poor or middle-class individuals, who have almost no chance at all. Thus, a tremendous amount of talent simply never gets an opportunity to develop and contribute to the economy. It is unremarkable that "sell-made" billionaires like Bill Gates, Ted Turner, Michael Eisner, Rupert Murdoch, and Sumner Redstone all come from privileged backgrounds. And, on the "demand" side of the market, power is determined by how much money an individual has; it is a case of one dollar, one vote rather than one person, one vote. In this sense, then, the political system to which the market is most similar is the limited suffrage days of pre-twentieth-century democracies, when propertyless adults could not vote and their interests were studiously ignored.

In truth, this is what a defense of the market system, in terms of fairness, boils down to: new firms can start and they can become giants, and to do so they probably have to do something quite remarkable, or be very lucky. All it means is that the system holds open the slightest possibility of a nonwealthy person becoming a multimillionaire, that success is extremely difficult to attain in this manner, and that the hope of being rich will drive countless people to their wits' end.

There are a couple of other aspects of capitalism that do not comport to the mythology. First, when free-market mythologists criticize the heavy hand of government, what they really mean by *heavy hand* is that government might actually represent the interests of the citizenry versus those of business. When governments spend billions subsidizing industries or advocating the interests of business, not a peep is heard about the evils of "big government." Government policies play a decisive role in assisting corporate profitability and dominance in numerous industries, not the least of which is communications. Most of the communications industry associated with the technology revolution – particularly the Web – grew directly out of government subsidies. Indeed, at one point fully 85 percent of research and development in the US electronics industry was subsidized by the federal government, although the eventual profits accrued to private firms (T. Chomsky, 1994). The free distribution of publicly owned electromagnetic spectrum to US radio and television companies has been one of the greatest gifts of public properly in history, valued as high as $100 billion. Moreover, it is entirely misleading to submit that in this neoliberal, promarket era of "deregulation" the government is playing a smaller role than in earlier times. In fact, the government role is as large as ever, at least during this formative stage of digital communication systems. Extremely crucial decisions about the Web and digital communication are being considered and will be implemented in the next few years, effectively determining the course of the US media and communication system for at least a generation, perhaps longer.

The exact manner in which the World Wide Web and digital communication develop will be determined by technological specifications, as well as by who controls the commercial digital industry (Harmon, 1998). The government will be singularly responsible for these activities, and what it does and who it favors will go a long way toward determining which firms and which sectors get the inside track. What is different from earlier times is that under "deregulation" there is no pretense that the government should represent the public interest vis-à-vis commercial interests. The government is supposed to expedite commercial domination, which, as a result, should serve the public interest.

Understanding the crucial importance of the government undercuts also the myth that the market exists "naturally," independent of the government, blindly rewarding the most efficient performers. Government policies are instrumental in determining who the winners will and will not be, and those policies are often derived in an anti-democratic and corrupt manner. More broadly, the notion that capitalism is a natural "default" economic or regulatory system for the human race, and can only be messed with by meddling governments or trade unions does not comport at all to the world as we know it. That is, although the establishment of capitalism was a remarkable historical accomplishment, capitalism as an economic system, based on the centrality of investment in pursuit of maximum profit, only developed in a small corner of the world after centuries of social transformation. It required massive changes in morals, laws, religions, politics, culture, and "human nature," not to mention economics. A recent indication of the absurdity of capitalism being humanity's default system comes from postcommunist Eastern Europe, where the attempt to let capitalism develop "naturally" has been nothing short of a disaster in all but a few central European nations where the market had made strong inroads prior to communism.

Another flaw in the mythology of the free market is that it posits that market-driven activities always generate the optimum and most rational social outcome. To some extent this argument for market is based on the almost nonexistent competitive model; in economic theory the degree of market concentration that exists across the economy undermines the claims for producing rational and socially optimal results. But this flaw is much deeper than that, and would even apply in mythological free markets. The simple truth is that markets often produce highly destructive and irrational results (Kuttner, 1997). On the one hand, what is rational for individual investors can easily produce negative results when undertaken by many investors. For example, it is rational for an investor to withdraw an investment during a recession, since the chances for profit are small or nil. But if many investors take this same rational step, they may well turn the recession into a depression in which everyone loses. The economic collapse of many so-called tiger economies of East Asia in 1998 highlights this aspect of markets to a painful degree.

On the other hand, markets produce what are called "externalities." These are the unintended social consequences of markets that are set up to reward individual pursuit of utility and, most important, profit. To put it bluntly, in their pursuit of profits there are things capitalists do that have important effects, but these capitalists do not care – cannot care – because these effects do not alter their bottom lines. Some externalities can be positive, such as when a corporation builds an especially beautiful office building or factory. It receives no material benefit from those in the community who enjoy gazing at the structure, but the community clearly gains. Most externalities are negative, however, such as air pollution. Unless public policy interferes with the market there is no incentive within the market to address the problem. For extreme examples of this phenomenon, one need only travel to cities like Santiago, Chile, or New Delhi, India, where unregulated markets have produced air that is nearly unbreathable, and where the market "solution" is to have the wealthy move to the high-priced areas with the least amounts of pollution.

The media system produces clear externalities. On the positive side, media can produce educational and civic effects through their operations, though the benefits will not accrue to media owners. The negative side of media externalities is well-cataloged. In their pursuit of profit, media firms produce vast quantities of violent fare, subject children to a systematic commercial carpetbombing, and produce a journalism that hardly meets the communication needs of the citizenry. The costs of the effects of this media fare are borne by all of society. Democratic media policy making, then, should systematically attempt to create a system that produces a greater number of positive externalities and the smallest number of negative externalities.

Yet media externalities are not simply the result of the market; they also result from how the market interacts with new technologies, or from the technologies themselves. In the case of television, for example – regardless of its content per se – when it became ubiquitous and dominant, it changed the way people socialized and interacted. It led, for better or (in my view) for worse, to greater social isolation. All communication technologies have unanticipated and unintended effects, and one function of policy making is to understand them so that we may avoid or minimize the undesirable ones. The digitalization and computerization of our society are going to transform us radically, yet even those closely associated with these developments express concern about the possibility of a severe deterioration of the human experience as a result of the information revolution. As one observer notes, "Very few of us – only the high priests – really understand the new technologies, and these are surely the people least qualified to make policy decisions about them" (Charbeneau, 1995: 28–9).

For every argument extolling the "virtual community" and the liberatory aspects of cyberspace, it seems every bit as plausible to reach dystopian, or at least troubling, conclusions. Is it really so wonderful or necessary to be attached to a communications network at all times? Is it such a wonderful environment to be on city streets where everyone is talking into little cell phones? Is sitting in front of a computer or digital television for hours per day really such a great thing for humans to do, even if it is "interactive"? Why not look at the Web as a process that encourages the isolation, atomization, and marginalization of people in society? In fact, cannot the ability of people to create their own "community" in cyberspace have the effect of terminating a community in the general sense? In a class-stratified, commercially oriented society like the United States, can't the information highway have the effect of simply making it possible for the well-to-do to bypass any contact with the balance of society altogether? These are precisely the types of questions that need to be addressed and answered in communication policy making, and precisely the types of questions in which the market has no interest. We should look – and think – before we leap.

The Hunt for the Killer Application

In this "whoever makes the most money wins" environment, the pursuit of Web riches is conducted by a host of other media and nonmedia firms, all of whom act both out of a desire for more profit and out of a fear of being outflanked by their competitors if they do not proceed aggressively. The crucial factor in the World Wide Web's becoming ubiquitous and dominant will be the expansion of broadband capability to the bulk of the population, the ability, that is, of having material flow as quickly online – even as fast as the speed of light – as signals travel on television. When that happens, the Web may well become a vast converged communication machine, eliminating traditional distinctions between communication and media sectors as everything goes digital. The president of NBC News, Andy Lack, predicts that it will be at least the year 2008 until full-motion video – television as we know it – is widely available in US homes via the Web, and others tend to think it could take longer than that (Snoddy, 1997a; Sandberg, 1998). But firms do not have the luxury of sitting back and waiting for that moment: those who will dominate cyberspace in the future will be determined well before the era of widespread broadband access.

The late 1990s, accordingly, has seen a flood of investment to Web-related enterprises (Karlgaard, 1998). "It may seem as if the two year old Internet industry is mounting a takeover of corporate America," the *Financial Times* noted in 1998, "The reality is more like a merger" (Denton, 1998a: 6). Huge sums have been squandered already, and more will certainly be lost in the future as firms seek out the "killer application" that will define the World Wide Web as a commercial medium. But by the end of the 1990s the dust is beginning to settle and some inkling of how great wealth can be generated by the Web is becoming ever more clear. And as the formal policy is to let the market rule, wherever the most money can be found is how the Web will develop.

The two most important corporate sectors regarding the Web are telecommunications and computers. Each of these sectors is more immediately threatened by the World Wide Web than are the dominant media firms. In the case of the seven or eight massive telecommunication firms that dominate the US telephone industry, the Web poses a threat to its very existence. The new technology of Internet protocol (IP) telephony threatens to open the way to vastly less expensive communication and the possibility of newfound competition (Higgins, 1998; "All Together Now," 1997; Taylor, 1998). The telecommunications giant Sprint has gone so far as to revamp its entire network to operate by IP standards (Waters, 1998b, 1998a). More important, the very notion of voice telephony is in the process of being superseded by the digital data networks that send voice as only a small portion of its data delivery. In this sense, the big telecommunications firms may appear like giant dinosaurs made irrelevant by the Web.

Yet the giant telecommunications firms have a few distinct assets with which to play. First, they already have wires into people's businesses and homes and these wires are suitable for carrying Web traffic. Second, the World Wide Web "backbone" of fiber-optic trunk lines is owned by several of the largest US telecommunications firms, including WorldCom-MCI, AT&T, GTE, and Sprint (Yang, 1998). These factors make the telecommunication firms ideally suited to become Internet service providers

(ISPs) to business and consumers, already an area with a proven market (C. Warner, 1998). Indeed, with the entry of the large telecommunication companies into the ISP sector, the *Financial Times* wrote that the "Internet small fry" were "on the road to oblivion." It added: "The situation is very much like the PC market 10 years ago where a lot of smaller PC dealers went out of business" (Poynder, 1998: 12).

With regard to being an ISP, as in other facets of telecommunication, size means a great deal for establishing a competitive advantage. Hence, the dominant trend in the late 1990s has been a wave of massive mergers among the largest telecommunications firms, not only in the United States but globally. The second asset these firms enjoy is a great deal of cash flow, which permits them to engage in more aggressive acquisitions than perhaps any other Web-related firms. The consensus of opinion in the business community is that early in the twenty-first century as few as four to six firms will dominate the entirety of global telecommunications.[3]

The other major contender in providing Web access is the cable television industry; in the United States that means the five or six companies that have monopolies over more than 80 percent of the nation. By the summer of 1998 the Federal Communications Commission (FCC) effectively abandoned the notion that the ISP market could ever be remotely competitive. It granted the regional Bell companies the right to restrict the use of their wires to their own ISP services, rather than make them available to all users at a fair price. By doing so, the FCC hopes to encourage at least two viable ISP services – one telephone based, the other cable based – in each market, rather than have it become a monopoly (Schiesel, 1998a).

Whether or not the ISP industry becomes a killer application remains to be seen, but is certainly shaping up as possibly becoming a highly lucrative aspect of the emerging digital communications networks. The key to great Web wealth may be whether the ISPs can mimic what the US cable companies did (which was to demand partial ownership of cable TV channels if those same channels wanted access to their systems, while simultaneously launching their own channels), and use their control over the crucial Web wires as a means to get a piece of the commercial action that transpires over their systems. This is an issue I will turn to shortly with the discussion of portals. In the meantime, that these firms will dominate the wires providing Internet service is regarded as a good thing in the business press: if these telecommunications giants can put "internet economics on a commercial basis," as one *Financial Times* writer noted, it might lead to "higher user costs," but it would also lead to the Web's more rapid commercial development, which is more important (Kehoe, 1998a: 14).

One of the striking features of having Web access provided by the private sector is that the notion of universal service to the entire population is and must be sacrificed to the needs of the market. The most money is made by pitching high quality service to the affluent who can afford it, and who are most attractive to advertisers. As TCI founder John Malone has put it, the best way to conduct the Web access business is to offer "tiered" service, with high-speed access for the affluent and business, on down to slow Web access for those who cannot afford (Coleman, 1998). In 1998 the average US Internet user had an income that was double the national average, and there was little reason to expect that to change quickly (Webber, 1998). The fees expected for high-speed Internet access in the twenty-first century would exclude all but half of the US population (Hansell, 1998b). The greatest disparity is between African Americans and white Americans, where the difference goes well beyond what one would expect from economic factors alone (Quick, 1998a).

Computer firms, too, are threatened by the World Wide Web. None more than Microsoft, which stands to see its lucrative monopoly on stand-alone computer software eliminated by the rise of digital computer networks. Since recognizing the threat in 1995, Microsoft has used all of its market power and wealth to see that it not be out-flanked on the Web, and that it have a finger (or hand) in the pie of any emerging killer application. Microsoft is a partner with TCI in its digital cable TV operation (Mermigas, 1998d); it also has its own WebTV, connecting TV sets to the Web through tele-phone lines – and that technology may in the end prove superior. In addition, Microsoft has a play in each of the two routes that are competing to establish high-speed Web access to the consumer personal computer market (Crockett, McWilliams, Jackson, and Elstrom, 1998). Through its 11 percent stake in Comcast, Microsoft has a piece of @Home, the cable modem ISP run by the major cable companies. It also is a partner with Intel, GTE, and the "baby Bell" regional phone companies in the venture to offer high-speed Internet access via telephone lines (Takahashi and Mehta, 1998; Schiesel, 1998b), and has a 10 percent stake in Time Warner's Road Runner cable modem service (Bank and Cauley, 1998).

Microsoft has major horses in virtually every route that could lead to a commercially viable consumer-oriented World Wide Web, including its Internet Explorer Web browser, the Microsoft Network online service, and its joint venture with NBC, the website-cable TV MSNBC (Hamm, Cortese, and Garland, 1998). Most observers expect that a key determinant in who profits will be who wins the struggle to set the standards for streaming audio and video at high speeds across the Internet. A number of companies are competing on these standards, including Real Networks, in which Microsoft has a 10 percent stake (Wheelwright, 1998b). Yet Microsoft has little to fear: as the *New York Times* noted in 1998, the company "now owns all or part of each of these companies" (Gleick, 1998: 18).

Microsoft's ravenous appetite for dominating the Web attracted the attention of the US Justice Department, which advanced an antitrust case against it in 1998 and 1999. The first ruling was not in Microsoft's favor, and the ultimate result is very much up in the air (Hof, 1998; Kehoe and Wolfe, 1998). Microsoft built up an impres-sive lobbying army in 1997 and 1998 to prevent any future problems in Washington, DC. In classic fashion, it doled out money to any candidates who might have any say over its activities in Congress, Republicans and Democrats alike (Wayne, 1998). And despite Microsoft's having to jump some hurdles with regulators, Paine Webber's chief investment strategist stated in 1998 that Microsoft's strategy would pay off. The company had established a "dominant position across the entire Information Age spectrum," he noted, making Microsoft "the leading beneficiary of convergence" (Mermigas, 1998b: 18).

But the really important corporate activity, as the Microsoft example suggests, is not understood by looking at firms in isolation, or even at sectors as a whole, but rather by looking at the interaction of firms with those of other sectors. Although digital conver-gence is only just beginning, and there remain important distinctions among computer, telecommunications, and media companies, a striking business convergence has emerged due to the Web. This takes the forms of mergers and acquisitions, equity joint ventures with two or more partners on specific projects, and long-term exclusive strategic alliances between two firms. On the one hand, his convergence is due to the desire to limit risk by linking up with potential competitors or swallowing them. Following the logic of Richard Nixon's memorable adage, it is better to have your enemy inside pissing out rather than outside pissing in. On the other hand, this convergence is explained by the inability of a telecommunications, computer, or media firm to provide a comprehensive Web service.

So ironically, the most striking feature of digital communication may well be not that it has opened up competition in communication markets, but that it has made it vastly easier, attractive, and necessary for firms to consolidate and strike alliances across the media, telecommunications, and computer sectors. In the late 1990s there were a series of mergers between large telecommunications and computer equipment companies, due to the growth of the Internet (Kehoe, 1998b). Almost all the media giants have entered into joint ventures or strategic alliances with the largest telecommunications and software firms. Time Warner is connected to several of the US regional (Bell) telephone giants, as well as to AT&T and Oracle; it has a major joint venture with US West. Disney, likewise, is connected to several major US telecommunications companies, as well as to America Online. News Corp. is partially owned by MCI WorldCom and has a joint venture with British Telecom.[4] The media firms most directly implicated in this convergence are the cable companies, since their wires are arguably the best suited of the existing choices. As noted above, Comcast is partially owned by Microsoft, while Microsoft cofounder Paul Allen purchased Marcus Cable in 1998, but the truly seminal deal was AT&T's $48 billion purchase of cable giant TCI in 1998. The key to the deal was the linking of TCI's wires to the home with AT&T's trunkline fiber-optic system. The point will be to offer "one-stop shopping" to home consumers of local and long-distance telephony, cable television, and high-speed Internet access via cable modems (Mermigas, 1998a; Goldblatt, 1998). Through TCI's Liberty Media, AT&T will now have interests in a large stable of media assets. Criticism of the deal is mostly that it is premature, not improper.

Business analysts expect more mergers among phone, cable, and media companies, a "scramble to control the information pipeline into people's homes." "One way or another," Merrill Lynch's media analyst stated in 1998, cable companies "are going to be affiliated with phone companies. There's going to be consolidation in this industry" (Pope, 1998: B1). In due course the global media oligopoly may become a much broader global communication oligopoly, dominated by a small number of massive conglomerates with a myriad of joint ventures linking all the players to each other. In the battle between the World Wide Web's ballyhooed "decentralizing" bias and the market's tendency toward concentration, the market is winning.

But where, exactly, are the killer applications to justify the expense of some of these acquisitions and joint ventures? By the end of the 1990s the market began to crystallize around two commercial Internet applications. The most important is electronic commerce, using the World Wide Web to buy and sell products. In addition to being interactive, the Web permits marketers to generate a superior profile of a user's past purchases and interests through examining the "cookie" file in a user's Web browser, among other things (Quick, 1998b). At the low end, one 1998 study predicts that US and European spending online will reach $16 billion by 2002 (Hollinger, 1998). Using broader criteria, other studies by private groups and the US government forecast electronic commerce at a whopping $300 billion by 2002 (Green, Cortese, Judge, and Hof, 1998b, 1998a). By all accounts electronic commerce is becoming the future of retailing and commerce, and the US government calls it the foundation of the "emerging digital economy" (Ingersoll, 1998: A3). It seems clearly a historic world phenomenon, lacking only improvements in Internet security before it becomes the standard for commerce (Maddox, 1998a). And as electronic commerce becomes the rule, it will push those not online to get connected.

Yet how do the communications giants benefit from electronic commerce, unless they sell their own products? After all, aren't these transactions simply between buyer and seller? This leads to the second "killer application" for the World Wide Web: portals. Portals refer to Internet services that people "use to start their treks through cyberspace." They bring order to the Web experience. More than browser software or the standard ISP, portals organize the entire Web experience and provide a "search" mechanism to bring Web material to users as effortlessly as possible. If successful, a portal can provide a "home base" for an Internet user, which he need never leave. "Portals are transforming the internet from a chaotic collection of thousands of websites into something more manageable and familiar for consumers and investors," the *Financial Times* notes, "by capturing large audiences and establishing themselves as the primary internet 'channels'" (Parkes and Kehoe, 1998: 7). "The search engines have become to the World Wide Web what Windows is to the computer desktop," a technology investment banker stated in 1998. Even if portals never reach that lofty perch, something like them looks to be the immediate direction for the Web. (Already, the battle for dominating the portal market for digital television – that is, providing the channel guide that will serve as the first home page for viewers – has come down to a slugfest between TCI and News Corp. on one side and a firm allied with NBC and Microsoft on the other [Littleton, 1998: 21]).

The archetype of the portal is America Online (AOL), an ISP that did $2.5 billion in business in 1998. AOL provides an "Internet on training wheels," with e-mail, chat rooms, and banks of operators to answer any questions users might have. With eleven million subscribers, AOL accounts for 40 percent of all online traffic, and 60 percent of home use (Gunther, 1998: 69–80). Fully 80 percent of AOL users never venture beyond AOL's sites ("Ma Bell Convenience Store," 1998). AOL has also shown the way to Web riches, and not only through the monthly access fees it charges its subscribers. In addition, AOL is "drawing advertisers, who sense a mass market taking shape" (Green, Hof, and Judge, 1998: 162). Even more important, it uses its hold on such a huge section of the Web population to extract fees from firms that want to do commerce on AOL (Snyder, 1998a). In just one of scores of deals, for example, the company will receive $12 million plus a share of revenues over four years for giving The Fragrance Center a prominent display on AOL (Lewis, Waters, and Kehoe, 1998). Nor is AOL alone; other providers like Excite! and Yahoo attract massive audiences as well, and each of them is trying to offer full service similar to that provided by AOL

(Green, Hof, and Judge, 1998). This ratchets up the cost of selling wares electronically, with all that that suggests about how competitive digital capitalism is going to be. "Launching an E-commerce site without a portal partner," one investment analyst noted, "is like opening a retail store in the desert. Sure, it's cheap, but does anybody stop there?" (Gurley, 1998: 226).

AT&T, through @Home, intends to take dead aim at the portal market. "The telcos and cable companies are coming after AOL's customers," a Forrester Research analyst stated (Gunther, 1998: 80). AT&T executives have stated that it does not want @Home to be a traditional ISP, offering "dumb-pipes" that others like AOL and Yahoo use to get rich (B. Warner, 1998: 21). "It is clear," the *New York Times* wrote, "that whoever controls the front door that people use to start their Internet surfing – a "portal" in industry jargon – will control the biggest share of advertising and shopping revenues" (Hansell, 1998d: C4). In 1998, Microsoft introduced "start.com," a portal that would provide personalized data collection, web-searching, and email for customers (Lohr, 1998b; Swisher, 1998). This might prove to be Microsoft's best bet in becoming the web's gatekeeper (Sacharow, 1998e). What is clear is that telecommunications, media, and computer firms each have something to contribute to a viable portal, so many more mergers and acquisitions will take place before the market stabilizes. Analysts forecast a "long and brutal war" over control of the portal industry, with estimates for the final number of viable firms ranging from two or three at the low end to four or five at the high end (Hansell, 1998a: C3).

The World Wide Web and the Media Giants

Media firms and media industries are directly involved in both electronic commerce and the establishment of viable commercial portals. Yet these are best regarded as parts of a broader series of moves, in addition to digital television, made by media firms to extend their empires to cyberspace. "For traditional media companies," the *New York Times* correctly notes, "the digital age poses genuine danger" (Landler, 1998: 1). The great fear for the media firms is that the Web will breed a new generation of commercial competitors who take advantage of the medium's relatively minuscule production and distribution costs. And its greatest fear is that the broadband Web will lead to an entirely new media regime that makes the corporate media giants irrelevant and obsolete. It remains to be seen exactly where the Web and/or any other digital communication network will fit into the global media landscape ten or twenty years down the road. As Time Warner CEO Gerald Levin has put it, it is "not clear where you make money on it" (Landler, 1998: 9); but even if the Web takes a long time to develop as a commercial medium, it is already taking up some of the time that people formerly devoted to traditional media (Richtel, 1998). Media firms have responded accordingly, leaving nothing to chance; since the early 1990s they have been establishing an online presence so that as the Internet develops, they will not get boxed out of the digital system.

Most of the Web activities of the traditional media firms have been money losers, and some have been outright disasters. Time Warner's Pathfinder website, for example, began in 1994 with visions of conquering the Web, only to produce a "black hole" for the firm's balance sheet (Wolff, 1998: 16). Likewise, the New Century Network, a website consisting of 140 newspapers run by nine of the largest newspaper chains was such a fiasco that it was shut down in 1998 (Dugan, 1998). But none of the media firms has lost its resolve to be a factor in, or even to dominate, cyberspace. As one media executive put it, in Internet business, "losses appear to be the key to the future" (Wolff, 1998: 18). This is one of the distinguishing characteristics of media firms as they approach the World Wide Web in comparison to entrepreneurs who want to use the Web to become media content providers: the media firms have a very long time frame in mind, and very deep pockets; they simply cannot afford to abandon ship.

By the end of the 1990s, all major media have significant Web activities. The media firms use their websites, at the very least, to stimulate interest in the traditional media fare. This is seen as a relatively inexpensive way to expand sales ("Times Web Site Ends Fee for Foreign Users," 1998). Some media firms duplicate their traditional publications or even broadcast their radio and television signals over the Net – accompanied by the commercials, of course (Wheelwright, 1998a; Tedesco, 1998b). The newspaper industry has rebounded from the New Century Network debacle, and has a number of sites designed to capture classified advertising dollars as they go online (Barron, 1998; Sacharow, 1998a; Brooker, 1998), but most media firms are going beyond this. Viacom has extensive websites for its MTV and Nickelodeon cable TV channels, for example, the point of which is to produce "online synergies" ("MTV Emphasizes Online Synergy," 1998; McConville, 1998). These synergies can be found by providing an interactive component and by adding an editorial dimension beyond what is found in traditional fare, but the main way in which websites produce synergies is by offering electronic commerce options for products related to their sites (Jensen, 1998). Several other commercial websites have incorporated Internet shopping directly into their editorial fare. As one media executive notes, Web publishers "have to think like merchandisers" (Snyder, 1998d: 30). Electronic commerce is now seen as a significant revenue stream for media websites; all in all, the similarity between digital television and what is happening on the Web is striking (Ross, 1998b).

Indeed, by the end of the 1990s the possibility of new Web content providers emerging to slay the traditional media appears more farfetched than ever before. In 1998 there was a massive shakeout in the online media industry, as smaller players could not remain afloat. Forrester Research estimated that the cost of an "average-content" website increased threefold to $3.1 million by 1998, and would double again by 2000 (Denton, 1998b). "While the big names are establishing themselves on the Internet," the *Economist* wrote in 1998, "the content sites that have grown organically out of the new medium are suffering" ("Brands Bite Back," 1998: 78). Even a firm with the resources of Microsoft flopped in its attempt to become an online content provider, abolishing its operation in early 1998. "It's a fair comment to say that entertainment on the Internet did not pan out as expected," said a Microsoft executive (Karon, 1998: 3). As telecommunications and computer firms work to develop Web content, they now turn to partnerships with the corporate media giants.

We can now see that those who forecast that the media giants would smash into the World Wide Web "iceberg" exaggerated the power of technology and failed to grasp the manner in which markets actually work. In addition to having deep pockets and a lengthy time, the media giants enjoy five other distinct advantages over those who might intrude into their territory. First, they have digital programming from their other ventures that they can plug into the Web at little extra cost. This in itself is a huge advantage over firms that have to create original content from scratch. Second, to generate an audience, they can and do promote their websites incessantly on their traditional media holdings; thus bringing their audiences to their sites on the Web. By 1998, it was argued that the only way a Web content provider could generate users was by buying advertising time in the media giants' traditional media; otherwise, a website would get lost among the millions of other Web locations. As the editor-in-chief of MSNBC on the Web has put it, linking the website to the existing media activity "is the crux of what we are talking about; it will help set us apart in a crowded market" (J. Brown, 1998: 96). "Offline branding," a trade publication observed, "is also key to generating traffic" (Riedman, 1998a: 18). It is the leading media "brands" that have been the first to charge subscription fees for their Web offerings; indeed, they may be the only firms for which this is even an alternative (Taylor 1997; Pogrebin, 1998).

Third, as advertising develops on the Web, the media giants are poised to seize most of these revenues. Online advertising amounted to $900 million in 1997, and some expect it to reach $5 billion by the year 2000. It is worth noting that this will still be no more than 3 percent of all US ad spending that year, suggesting again how long a path it will be to an era of Web dominance (Maddox, 1998b; Hall, 1998; Green, Hof, and Judge, 1998). The media giants have long and close relationships with the advertising industry, and work closely with them to make Web advertising viable (C. Ross, 1998a; Mand, 1998a, 1998b; Riedman, 1998b). The evidence suggests that in the commercialized Web, advertisers will have increased leverage over content, in the same manner their influence has increased in television in the 1990s ("Web Becomes a Viable Channel," 1997). A common form of Web advertising is "sponsorships," whereby for a flat sum ranging from $100,000 to $1 million annually, "the advertiser, its agency and the host Web network work together to develop advertorials" (O'Connell, 1998: B1, B6). The media giants also have another concrete advantage in their dealings with major advertisers: they can and do arrange to have them agree to do a portion of their business on their Web.

Fourth, as the possessors of the hottest "brands," the media firms have the leverage to get premier location from browser software makers and portals (Orwall, 1997b). Microsoft Internet Explorer offers 250 highlighted channels, the "plum positions" belonging to Disney and Time Warner, and similar arrangements are taking place with Netscape and Pointcast (Bank, 1999: B6; "Microsoft to Feature 250 Content Channels In New Web Browser," 1997, B3). Fifth – and this relates to their deep pockets – the media giants are aggressive investors in start-up Web media companies. Approximately one-half the venture capital for Web content start-up companies comes from established media firms.[5] The Tribune Company, for example, owns stakes in fifteen Web companies, including the portals AOL, Excite!, and the women-targeted iVillage ("Tribune Company," 1998). If some new company shows commercial promise, the media giants will be poised to capitalize upon, not be buried by, that promise.

In this context, the nature of emerging Web content makes sense. "The expansion in channel capacity seems to promise a sumptuous groaning board," TV critic Les

Brown wrote, "but in reality it's just going to be a lot more of the same hamburger (L. Brown, 1998: 10). By the end of the 1990s the World Wide Web was seen as offering media firms "new synergy," whereby media firms offered enhanced websites based on their traditional media brands chock full of commercial applications such as electronic commerce (Caruso, 1998: C3). The most popular areas for Web content are similar to those of the traditional commercial media, and, for the reasons just mentioned, they are dominated by the usual corporate suspects. Viacom's MTV is squaring off with GE's NBC, AT&T's TCI, and *Rolling Stone* to, as one of them put it, "own the mind share for music." Each website is "slavishly reporting recording industry news and gossip," all to become at least one of the "default destinations for people interested in music on the Web." The stakes are high: Forrester Research estimates that online music sales, concert ticket sales, and music-related merchandise sales could reach $2.8 billion by 2002 (Reilly, 1998: B1).

The greatest war for market share is with regard to sports websites, where Disney's ESPN, News Corp.'s Fox, GE and Microsoft's MSNBC, Time Warner's CNNSI, and CBS's Sports Line are in pitched battle. Sports are seen as the key to media growth on the Web; advertisers, for one, understand the market and want to reach it. In addition, sports websites are beginning to generate the huge audiences that advertisers like (Grover, 1998). To compete for the Web sports market, it is mandatory to have a major television network that can constantly promote the website. One Forrester Research survey found that 50 percent of respondents visited a sports website as a direct result of its being mentioned during a sports broadcast. Indeed, 33 percent said they visited a Web sports site while watching a sports event on TV (Snyder, 1998c). The media giants also routinely bring their largest advertisers to their sports websites as part of package deals between advertisers and the firm's television properties (Snyder, 1998b). Media giants can also use their resources to purchase exclusive Web rights from major sports leagues, as Disney has with the NFL (Tedesco, 1998c). And, as with music sites, sports offer all sorts of electronic commerce possibilities (Gellatly, 1998).

We might want to ponder what all of this means for the nature of journalism on the Web. This is really a fundamental issue; if the Web fails to produce a higher caliber of journalism and stimulate public understanding and activity, the claim that it is a boon for democracy is severely weakened. Many have chronicled the deplorable state of commercial journalism at the hands of the media giants.[6] There is little reason to expect a journalistic renaissance online. At present the trend for online journalism is to accentuate the worst synergistic and profit-hungry attributes of commercial journalism, with its emphasis on trivia, celebrities, and consumer news. One observer characterized the news offerings on AOL, drawn from all the commercial media giants, as less a "marketplace of ideas" than "a shopping mall of notions" (Solomon, 1998).

This does not mean that there are no considerable advantages or differences between the emerging digital world and what preceded it. Even if the Web becomes primarily a commercial medium for electronic commerce, e-mail, and commercial news and entertainment fare, it will also be a haven for all sorts of interactive activities that never existed in the past. In particular, the Web's openness permits a plethora of voices to speak and be heard worldwide at relatively minimal expense. This is indeed a communications revolution, and one that is being taken advantage of by countless social and political organizations that heretofore were marginalized (Quick, 1997). In 1998, for example, the global and largely secretive negotiations for a Multilateral Agreement on Investment (MAI) were undercut when a flurry of Web communication created a groundswell of popular opposition. The MAI was barely covered in the commercial media, and to the extent that it was the coverage was favorable to a global bill of rights for investors and corporations (N. Chomsky, 1998). Yet this point should not be exaggerated. As a rule, journalism is not something that can be undertaken piecemeal by amateurs working in their spare time. It is best done by people who make a living at it, and who have training, experience, and resources. Journalism also requires institutional support (from commercial and governmental attack) to survive and prosper. Corporate media giants have failed miserably to provide a viable journalism, and as they dominate journalism online there is no reason to expect anything different. In this context, it should be no surprise that the leading product of Web journalism is none other than Matt Drudge, who, as *The Economist* puts it, "spares himself the drudgery of fact-checking" ("The Press in Spin Cycle," 1998: 35).

Another way to grasp the corporate media approach to cyberspace is to look at the activities of the two largest media firms, Time Warner and Disney. Time Warner produces nearly 200 websites, all of which are designed to provide what it terms an "advertiser-friendly environment," and it aggressively promotes its websites to its audiences through its existing media (Landler, 1998: 9; Freeman, 1998). Its CNN website is now available in Swedish, with other languages to follow (Jakobsen, 1997; Galetto, 1997). The company uses its websites to go after the youth market, to attract sports fans, and to provide entertainment content similar to that of its "old" media (Griffith, 1998; Shaw, 1997). It established a major website focused on 1998 World Cup soccer in order to attract global attention to its Web activities (Elliott, 1998). The success of the World Cup website led Time Warner to "go ahead with more ad-supported non-US Internet projects." As a Time Warner executive stated, "We've had hits originating from 92 countries with their own Internet suffixes. . . . We now want to take things we learned from this and move on" (Koranteng, 1998: 20). Also in 1998, Time Warner began to develop entertainment content explicitly geared for the Web, in anticipation of a broadband future (Maddox, 1998c); the company is bringing advertisers aboard with long-term contracts and giving them equity interest in some projects (Sharkey, 1997). Its most developed relationship with advertisers is the ParentTime website venture it has with Procter and Gamble (Riedman, 1997).

Disney's vision of the digital future also sees a major role for advertising. "With a click of a remote-control button," ABC president Preston Padden enthused in 1997, "customers will be able to tell us if they want a free sample of a new headache remedy or wish to test-drive a new car" (Pope, 1998: B5). Disney has been as aggressive in cyberspace as Time Warner and the other media giants have; in 1997, as part of a "blitz by Disney to establish Internet beachheads for many of its products," it launched a subscription site for its Daily Blast children's website, available exclusively on the Microsoft Network (Orwall, 1997a: B4). In 1998 Disney announced that it was extending its conception of advertising to see that Web commerce was more directly "integrated into Disney's site." Its first major deal was with Barnes and Noble, granting the bookseller exclusive right to sell books across all Disney websites. Disney not only gets a percentage of sales, but it also gets free promotion of its wares in Barnes and Noble stores and on the Barnes and Noble website. According to Disney, the two sites that offered the most promise for commercial synergy were its ESPN Internet Ventures and ABCNews.com (Sacharow, 1998b: 22). Disney's ultimate online aim, as the president of Disney's Starwave website producer stated, is "to create the destination which contains everything someone could want. . . . It's the brand power that we have" (Sacharow, 1997: 48).

But establishing hegemony over any new media rivals on the Web still does not mean that cyberspace will prove particularly lucrative; one could argue it proves the opposite. Time Warner, for example, was exultant that it sold enough online advertising to cover nearly 50 percent of its online unit's budget for 1998. For a small start-up venture, this would spell death (Freeman, 1998). This is where we return to our point of departure for this section, to electronic commerce and portals, the two prospective killer applications on the Web. What is the relationship of the media firms to these two phenomena?

With regard to electronic commerce, media firms stand to be major players because a significant amount of what is being sold are media products. It also casts the future of traditional media retailers – bookstores, music stores, video rental stores – in a shadowy light. The way as shown by the rapid emergence of Amazon.com, the online bookseller; its market value in 1998 was greater than the combined market values of Barnes and Noble and Borders, the two chains that dominate US bookselling (Karlgaard, 1998). Selling music online is by all accounts expected to be one of the next great arenas for electronic commerce. In 1998, online music sales totaled $87 million; in 2005 they are projected to reach some $4 billion (Rawsthorn, 1998c). The key factor, from the industry's perspective, is to work on laws and technologies to prevent copyright infringement (Chervokas, 1998; Bulkeley, 1998b). By 2005 or so, people will have the music downloaded directly to their computers, rather than mailed to their home, which should increase sales exponentially (Rawsthorn, 1998b). Before selling out to Seagram in 1998, music superpower PolyGram established a board-level panel to assess how the Web was changing the essential nature of selling music (Goldsmith, 1998).

Selling music online will probably be the strongest direct threat to an existing media industry. The market power of the five firms that dominate global music is based largely on their extensive distribution networks; with electronic distribution those networks cease to matter. The production of music in and of itself is not a particularly expensive undertaking. On the surface, one might ask what function the music companies fulfill as distribution goes online (Pareles, 1998). (When bandwidth expands, in a decade or so, and movies can be distributed directly online as well, the media giants will face less threat there because the capital costs of filmmaking are significantly higher, and their distribution networks will remain important because the role of big screen theater exhibition should not change.) The challenge for the music giants – Bertelsmann, Sony, Seagram, Time Warner, and EMI – will be to parlay their existing market strength, during the next decade or so while they still have it, into online market power. They are already in negotiation with Internet service providers and portals to grease the wheels for selling their wares in a privileged manner online (Rawsthorn, 1998a). They combine this with their large promotional budgets to try to establish barriers to entry that can survive the World Wide Web (Siklos, 1998). The big five might be able to use these factors to keep start-ups at bay, but media giants like Disney, News Corp., and Viacom – with their own significant market power online and promotional budgets – should find themselves in a position to expand their music activities if they wish to do so.

Some media giants have incorporated electronic commerce directly into the heart of their planning for the future. GE's NBC, following the trail it is blazing in television, has established Giftseeker, an online shopping website. NBC will incorporate Giftseeker directly into its television advertising sales, so that clients will integrate their NBC advertising with Giftseeker exposure (Ross, 1998c). Bertelsmann and Sony, the third- and sixth-largest global media firms, respectively, are not only wed to electronic commerce, but they have downplayed owning digital television channels and systems, making the development of the Web a main strategic focus (Studemann, 1997). Sony, for example, is a major investor in NextLevel, the firm that already dominates the hardware market for the crucial digital TV set-top boxes (Calley, 1998). Sony is looking to finally capitalize upon synergies between its consumer electronic activities and its media holdings; it hopes to build the home-entertainment systems that are ideal for downloading Sony music, movies, and games (Kunii, Brull, Burrows, and Baig, 1998). Bertelsmann plans to become the leading global Web retailer of music and books (Sacharow, 1998d). One Bertelsmann publishing executive stated, "Our goal is, quite simply, to eventually offer online all books, from all publishers, in all languages" (Nix, 1998: 7).

It is with portals that the media giants are making the greatest inroads. Portals, in effect, are pretty much media companies, and that is how they see themselves. "Any media company is leveraging their relationship with their audience. Period. End of discussion," an AOL executive said. "You build the audience, you figure out how to extract value. . . . We have a very big ability to control the flow of our audience" (Gunther, 1998: 79–80). GE's NBC led the media foray into portals with its purchase of Snap and partial interest in Snap creator CNET in June 1988 (Hansell, 1998b). Disney followed the NBC deal almost immediately by purchasing 43 percent of the portal InfoSeek with an option to take controlling interest. The head of Disney's Internet Group called the deal "mission-critical" to Disney's future growth (Parkes and Kehoe, 1998: 7). "The game is to end up with something bigger and better than AOL," said an ABC executive (Tedesco, 1998a: 15). Observers expect the other media giants to purchase their own portals if they are not turned off by the high prices. The remaining independent portals are eager either to get purchased by media giants or to work closely with them (Mermigas, 1998c; Scism and Swisher, 1998). "The Internet media business," the *New York Times* wrote, "is expected to follow the pattern of cable television, where entrepreneurs created CNN, ESPN and MTV and were later bought out by Time Warner Inc., Disney and Viacom Inc. respectively" (Lohr, 1998a: A11). Whether or not media giants come to own portals outright, they almost certainly will be major players in all of them.

It may turn out, as a few Web experts suggest, that portals will prove to have been a flash in the pan (Sacharow, 1998c). As the president of InfoSeek has put it, "The Internet's still in the Stone Age" (Tedesco, 1998a: 15). Yet however it develops, the following comment from the president of Time, Inc. seems fairly accurate: "I believe the electronic revolution is simply one new form of communications that will find its place in the food chain of communications and will not displace or replace anything that already exists, just as television did not replace radio, just as cable did not replace network television, just as the VCR did not replace the movie theatres" (Snoddy, 1997b: 7). The evidence so far suggests that media giants will be able to draw the Web into their existing empires. While the Web is in many ways revolutionizing the way we lead our lives, it is a revolution that does not appear to include changing the identity and nature of those in power.

Conclusion

Based on current trends, this much can be concluded about the World Wide Web: despite its much-ballyhooed "openness" to the extent that it becomes a viable mass medium, it will likely be dominated by the usual corporate suspects. Certainly a few new commercial content players will emerge, but the evidence suggests that the content of the digital communications world will appear quite similar to that of the predigital commercial media world (Bulkeley, 1998a). In some ways the Web has even extended commercial synergies and the role of advertising and selling writ large to new dimensions. This does not mean that the World Wide Web will not be a major part in reconfiguring the way we lead our lives; it almost certainly will. Some aspects of these changes will probably be beneficial whereas others may be detrimental.

Nor does this mean that there will not be a vibrant, exciting, and important noncommercial citizen sector in cyberspace open to all who veer off the beaten path. For activists of all political stripes, the Web increasingly plays a central role in their organizing and educational activities. But we should not extrapolate from this sector that this is the overriding trajectory of cyberspace; it isn't. The capacity to establish websites is not the same as the capacity to dominate a culture or a society. In a less dubious political environment, the Web could be put to far greater democratic use than it is or likely will be in the foreseeable future. But the key point is simply that those who think that technology can produce a viable democratic public sphere by itself where policy has failed to do so are deluding themselves. And the dominant forces in cyberspace are producing the exact type of depoliticized culture that some Web utopians claimed that technology would slay. Indeed, a main function of noncommercial Web activities in the coming years may well be ideological: if one doesn't like what is predominantly available, the argument will go, she should shut up and start her own website or visit any one of the millions of obscure sites. It is not a political issue.

Aside from the notion of Web content per se, the notion that the Web is a democratic medium – that it will remain or become available to the public on anything close to egalitarian terms – seems dubious at best. A market-driven digital communications system seems just as likely to widen class divisions as it is to narrow them. In the eighteenth century, Thomas Paine wrote, "The contrast of affluence and wretchedness continually meeting and offending the eye, is like dead and living bodies chained together." In the digital age, however, the affluent can increasingly construct a world where the wretched are unchained and out of sight – a communications world similar to the gated residential communities to which so many millions of affluent Americans have fled (Turow, 1997; Parkes, 1997). A viable democracy depends upon minimal social inequality and a sense that an individual's welfare is determined in large part by the welfare of the general community. Unfortunately, the media system, and digital communication in particular – can accentuate the antidemocratic tendencies of the broader political economy (Dahl, 1989; Christiano, 1996).

Notes

1. For a discussion of the new "wired" house, see Schonfeld (1998).
2. For discussions of the imperative to eliminate competition, see Engler (1995) and Sweezy (1981) especially ch. 2, appendix B, "Competition and Monopoly."
3. See Herman and McChesney (1997), ch. 4.
4. See Herman and McChesney (1997), chs. 3 and 4, and Flaherty (1997).
5. This is drawn from Herman and McChesney (1997), ch. 4.
6. For a discussion see McChesney (1999), chs. 1 and 2.

References

"All Together Now" (1997). *Electronic Media*, December 15, p. 14.

Bank, D. (1999). Microsoft May Face Battle Over "Content". *Wall Street Journal*, February 13, B6.

Bank, D. & L. Cauley (1998). Microsoft, Compaq Make Net-Access Bet. *Wall Street Journal*, June 16, A3.

Barron, K. (1998). Bill Gates Wants Our Business. *Forbes*, April 6, pp. 46–7.

"Brands Bite Back" (1998). *Economist*, March 21, p. 78.

Brooker, K. (1998). Papers Lose Tweedy Tude, Find Black Ink. *Fortune*, June 8, pp. 36–7.

Brown, J. (1998). MSNBC on the Net Ready to Play Ball. *Electronic Media*, January 19, p. 96.

Brown, L. (1998). Market Forces Killed the Media Dream. *Television Business International*, April, p. 10.

Bulkeley, W. (1998a). Radio Stations Make Waves on the Web. *Wall Street Journal*, July 23, B1, B5.

Bulkeley, W. (1998b). Sound Off. *Wall Street Journal*, June 15, R24.

Calley, L. (1998). Sony Plans to Purchase a 5 percent Stake in NextLevel. *Wall Street Journal*, January 5, A3.

Cardona, M. (1997). Media Industry Grows Faster Than GDP: Veronis. *Advertising Age*, November 3, p. 16.

Caruso, D. (1998). If It Embraces Everything from CD's to Films, It Must Be the New Synergy. *New York Times*, July 20, C3.

Charbeneau, T. (1995). Dangerous Assumptions. *Toward Freedom* 43(7), pp. 28–9.

Chervokas, J. (1998). Internet CD Copying Tests Music Industry. *New York Times*, April 6, C3.

Chomsky, N. (1998). Hordes of Vigilantes. *Z Magazine*, July/August, pp. 51–4.

Chomsky, T. (1994). *World Orders Old and New*. New York: Columbia University Press.

Christiano, T. (1996). *The Rule of the Many*. Boulder, CO: Westview Press.

Coleman, P. (1998). Malone Proposes In-tier-net. *Broadcasting and Cable*, June 15, p. 53.

Colonna, J. (1998). For Internet Stocks, the Fall of Overvalued Companies Can Hurt Strong Companies as Well. *New York Times*, June 1, C5.

Crockett, R., G. McWilliams, S. Jackson & P. Elstrom (1998). Warp Speed Ahead. *Business Week*, February 16, pp. 80–3.

Dahl, R. (1989). *Democracy and Its Critics*. New Haven, CT: Yale University Press.

Dennett, D. (1991). *Consciousness Explained*. Hammondsworth, UK: Penguin.

Denton, N. (1998a). Mainstream.com. *Financial Times*, January 3–4, p. 6.

Denton, N. (1998b). Online Media Face Heavy Job Losses. *Financial Times*, March 12, p. 6.

Dugan, J. (1998). New-Media Meltdown. *Business Week*, March 23, pp. 70–1.

Elliott, S. (1998). A Big World Wide Web Site by Time Inc. New Media Is Devoted to the 1998 Soccer World Cup. *New York Times*, June 4, C12.

Engler, A. (1995). *Apostles of Greed: Capitalism and the Myth of the Individual in the Market*. London: Pluto Press.

Flaherty, N. (1997). Diving In at the Deep End. *Cable and Satellite Europe*, March, pp. 61, 63.

Freeman, L. (1998). Led by Warner, Animation Leads Syndicators to Web. *Advertising Age*, January 19, s10.

Friedman, M. (1962). *Capitalism and Freedom*. Chicago: University of Chicago Press.

Galetto, M. (1997). CNN Spots Online Gold and Starts Speaking Swedish. *Electronic Media*, March 17, p. 28.

Gellatly, A. (1998). Online Crowd-Pleasers. *Financial Times*, June 10, p. 24.

Gilder, G. (1994). *Life after Television*. New York: W. W. Norton.

Gilpin, K. (1998). Thinking Rationally as the Web Goes Wild. *New York Times*, July 12, p. 7.

Gleick, J. (1998). Control Freaks. *New York Times Magazine*, July 19, p. 18.

Goldblatt, H. (1998). AT&T's Costly Game of Catch-Up. *Fortune*, July 20, pp. 25–6.

Goldsmith, C. (1998). PolyGram Establishes Panel to Focus on Internet Effects, Posts Profit Growth. *Wall Street Journal*, February 12, B6.

Green, H., R. Hof & P. Judge (1998). Vying to Be More Than a Site for More Eyes. *Business Week*, May 18, p. 162.

Green, H., A. Cortese, P. Judge & R. Hof (1998a). The Click Here' Economy. *Business Week*, June 22, p. 124.

Green, H., A. Cortese, P. Judge & R. Hof (1998b). Click Here for Wacky Valuations. *Business Week*, July 20, pp. 32–4.

Griffith, V. (1998). Get Them While They're Young. *Financial Times*, January 5, p. 19.

Grover, R. (1998). Online Sports: Cyber Fans Are Roaring. *Business Week*, June 1, p. 155.

Gunther, M. (1998). The Internet Is Mr. Case's Neighborhood. *Fortune*, March 30, pp. 69–80.

Gurley, J. (1998). The Soaring Cost of E-Commerce. *Fortune*, August 3, p. 226.

Hall, L. (1998). Web Ads Changing Online Business. *Electronic Media*, March 23, p. 16.

Hamm, S., A. Cortese & S. Garland (1998). Microsoft's Future. *Business Week*, January 19, 58–68.

Hansell, S. (1998a). Disney Will Invest in a Web Gateway. *New York Times*, June 2, C3.

Hansell, S. (1998b). Hooking Up the Nation. *New York Times*, June 25, C5.

Hansell, S. (1998c). The Battle for Internet Supremacy Is Shifting to the Companies That Sell Connections to Users. *New York Times*, June 29, C4.

Harmon, A. (1998). Technology to Let Engineers Filter the Web and Judge Content. *New York Times*, January 19, C1, C4.

Herman, E. & R. McChesney (1997). *The Global Media: The New Missionaries of Corporate Capitalism*. London: Cassell.

Higgins, J. (1998). IP Telephony: Does AT&T Have Its Number? *Broadcasting & Cable*, July 8, pp. 36–8.

Hof, R. (1998). How Sweet It Is (Again) for Chairman Bill. *Business Week*, July 6, p. 31.

Hollinger, P. (1998). Internet Shopping Set to Soar in Next Four Years. *Financial Times*, January 27, p. 5.

Ingersoll, B. (1998). Internet Spurs US Growth, Cuts Inflation. *Wall Street Journal*, April 16, A3.

Jakobsen, L. (1997). CNN Interactive in Swedish. *Cable & Satellite Express*, March 20, p. 8.

Jensen, J. (1998). Columbia Tristar Teen TV Show Adds Interactive. *Advertising Age*, July 13, 27.

Karlgaard, R. (1998). The Web Is Recession-Proof. *Wall Street Journal*, July 14, A18.

Karon, P. (1998). Online Entertainment Crashes. *Variety*, May 4–10, p. 3.

Kehoe, L. (1998a). Internet Plumber Needed. *Financial Times*, June 17, p. 12.

Kehoe, L. (1998b). The End of the Free Ride. *Financial Times*, July 1, p. 14.

Kehoe, L. & R. Wolfe (1998). System on Line: Ruling Clears Microsoft's Way to Market. *Financial Times*, June 25, p. 4.

Koranteng, J. (1998). Times Inc. New Media Explores Outside US. *Ad Age International*, June 29, p. 20.

Kunii, I., S. Brull, P. Burrows & E. Baig (1998). The Games Sony Plays. *Business Week*, June 15, pp. 128–30.

Kuttner, R. (1997). *Everything for Sale: The Virtues and Limits of Markets*. New York: Alfred A. Knopf.

Landler, M. (1998). From Gurus to Sitting Ducks. *New York Times*, January 11, sec. 3, pp. 1, 9.

Lewis, W., R. Waters & L. Kehoe (1998). AOL Shares Leap as Group Rebuffs AT&T. *Financial Times*, June 18, p. 20.

Littleton, C. (1998). Channel Scrollers Become High Rollers. *Variety*, July 20–6, p. 21.

Lohr, S. (1998a). Microsoft Will Soon Offer Peek at New-Media Strategy. *New York Times*, February 2, C5.

Lohr, S. (1998b). Media Convergence. *New York Times*, June 29, A11.

"Ma Bell Convenience Store" (1998). *Economist*, June 27, pp. 61–2.

Maddox, K. (1998a). Forrester Study Says Users Ready for E-Commerce. *Advertising Age*, March 23, p. 34.

Maddox, K. (1998b). Rapid Growth Online. *Electronic Media*, April 6, p. 10.

Maddox, K. (1998c). Warner Bros. Develops New Web Content Model. *Advertising Age*, June 22, p. 8.

Mand, A. (1998a). Beyond Hits and Clicks. *Mediaweek*, March 30, pp. 48, 52.

Martin, P. (1998). The Merger Police. *Financial Times*, March 12, p. 10.

McChesney, R. (1999). *Rich Media, Poor Democracy: Communication Politics, History, and Scholarship in Dubious Times*. Urbana: University of Illinois Press.

McConville, J. (1998). New Nick Web Site Not Just for Kids. *Electronic Media*, March 16, p. 18.

McHugh, J. (1997). Politics for the Really Cool. *Forbes*, September 8, pp. 172–92.

Mehta, S. (1998). US West Is Set to Offer TV Programming and Internet Access over Phone Lines. *Wall Street Journal*, April 20, B6.

Mermigas, D. (1997). Strong Media Forecast for '98. *Electronic Media*, November 3, p. 31.

Mermigas, D. (1998a). TCI Goes Digital with Microsoft. *Electronic Media*, January 19, pp. 3, 119.

Mermigas, D. (1998b). New Media Takes on the Old. *Electronic Media*, May 11, pp. 28–9.

Mermigas, D. (1998c). Avoiding the Web's Pitfalls. *Electronic Media*, May 18, p. 18.

Mermigas, D. (1998d). Analysts Adding Up AT&T–TCI Deal. *Electronic Media*, July 6, pp. 3, 25.

"Microsoft to Feature 250 Content Channels in New Web Browser" (1997). *Wall Street Journal*, July 15, B3.

"MTV Emphasizes Online Synergy" (1998). *Broadcasting and Cable*, June 22, p. 59.

Nakamura, L. (1998). After/Images of Identity: Gender, Technology, and Identity. Unpublished manuscript from speech given at "Disciplining Deviance" Conference, Duke University, October 4.

Negroponte, N. (1995). *Being Digital*. New York: Alfred A. Knopf.

Nix, J. (1998). Bertelsmann to Sell Books on the Internet. *Variety*, March 2–8, p. 7.

O'Connell, V. (1998). Soap and Diaper Makers Pitch to Masses of Web Women. *Wall Street Journal*, July 20, B1, B6.

Orwall, B. (1997a). On-Line Service by Disney's ABC Unit Will Be Promoted by AOL, Netscape. *Wall Street Journal*, April 4, A5.

Orwall, B. (1997b). Disney Blitzes Cyberspace with "Daily Blast" Service. *Wall Street Journal*, July 28, B4.

Pareles, J. (1998). Records and CD's? How Quaint. *New York Times*, July 16, B1, B6.

Parkes, C. (1997). The Birth of Enclave Man. *Financial Times*, September 20–1, p. 7.

Parkes, C. & L. Kehoe (1998). Mickey Wants Us All Online. *Financial Times*, June 20–1, p. 7.

Pogrebin, R. (1998). For $19.95, Slate Sees Who Its Friends Are. *New York Times*, March 30, C1, C7.

Pope, K. (1998). Telecom World Is Wondering: "Who's Next?" *Wall Street Journal*, June 25, B1.

Poynder, R. (1998). Internet Small Fry on the Road to Oblivion. *Financial Times*, April 29, p. 12.

Quick, R. (1997). The Crusaders. *Wall Street Journal*, December 8, R6.

Quick, R. (1998a). Internet Contains a Racial Divide on Access and Use, Study Shows. *Wall Street Journal*, April 27, B6.

Quick, R. (1998b). On-Line Groups Are Offering Up Privacy Plans. *Wall Street Journal*, June 22, B3.

Rawsthorn, A. (1998a). Digital Music On-Line for Cable TV Customers. *Financial Times*, January 20, p. 2.

Rawsthorn, A. (1998b). Discord over On-Line Music Royalties. *Financial Times*, January 21, p. 8.

Rawsthorn, A. (1998c). Internet Sales Could Become Key to the Music Industry. *Financial Times*, June 2, p. 18.

Reilly, P. (1998). Web Publishers Wage War for Music Scoops. *Wall Street Journal*, April 15, B1.

Richtel, M. (1998). Survey Finds TV Is Major Casualty of New Surfing. *New York Time*, July 16, D3.

Riedman, P. (1997). ParentTime 1st Channel for PointCast. *Advertising Age*, August 18, p. 19.

Riedman, P. (1998a). P&G Plans Pivotal Ad Forum about Net. *Advertising Age*, May 11, 4.

Riedman, P. (1998b). Cyber Brands Spread the Word with Off-Line Ads. *Advertising Age*, July 6, p. 18.

Ross, C. (1998a). Broadband Kicks Open Internet Door for Cable. *Advertising Age*, April 13, s6, s23.

Ross, C. (1998b). NBC Opens On-Line Revenues Stream. *Advertising Age*, June 1, p. 2.

Ross, C. (1998c). Hachette Looks for On-Line Profits with Outside Help. *Advertising Age*, June 29, p. 50.

Sacharow, A. (1997). Star Power. *Adweek*, May 5, p. 48.

Sacharow, A. (1998a). Disney-B&N Deal Signals Shift in Online Sales Business. *Mediaweek*, February 2, p. 22.

Sacharow, A. (1998b). Wolf at the Portal? *Mediaweek*, February 9, p. 47.

Sacharow, A. (1998c). After Divorce, Online Newspapers Regroup. *Mediaweek*, March 16, p. 31.

Sacharow, A. (1998d). Rhapsody in BMG: Music Service Expands Online. *Mediaweek*, April 13, p. 34.

Sacharow, A. (1998e). NBC Opens Door to Its Portal Strategy with CNET's Snap. *Mediaweek*, June 15, p. 33.

Sandberg, J. (1998). It Isn't Entertainment That Makes the Web Shine; It's Dull Data. *Wall Street Journal*, July 20, A1, A6.

Schiesel, S. (1998a). Venture Promises Far Faster Speeds for Internet Data. *New York Times*, January 20, A1, C7.

Schiesel, S. (1998b). F.C.C. May Act to Aid Home Internal Access. *New York Times*, July 17, C1, C3.

Schonfeld, E. (1998). The Network in Your House. *Fortune*, August 3, pp. 125–8.

Scism, L. & K. Swisher (1998). Internet Firms Heat Up on News of Interest by Media Companies. *Wall Street Journal*, June 19, C1, C2.

Sharkey, B. (1997). Warner's Web. *IQ*, August 18, pp. 10–14.

Shaw, Russell (1997). CNN/SI Challenges ESPN Site. *Electronic Media*, July 21, pp. 20, 32.

Siklos, R. (1998). Can Record Labels Get Back Their Rhythm? *Business Week*, July 27, pp. 52–3.

Snoddy, R. (1997a). Programmer Turned Publisher. *Financial Times*, June 9, p. 7.

Snoddy, R. (1997b). Chronicle of a Death Foretold. *Financial Times*, August 18, p. 7.

Snyder, B. (1998a). Web Publishers Morph into On-Line Retailers. *Advertising Age*, February 9, p. 30.

Snyder, B. (1998b). AOL's Partners Put Up Millions, Wait for Payoff. *Advertising Age*, April 20, p. 30.

Snyder, B. (1998c). Sport Web Sites Rely on Strength of TV Networks. *Advertising Age*, May 11, pp. 46, 50.

Snyder, B. (1998d). AT&T Inks $120 Mil Package at Disney. *Advertising Age*, June 29, pp. 1, 52.

Solomon, N. (1998). Motherhood, Apple Pie, Computers. *Eugene Register-Guard*, June 12, A2.

Studemann F. (1997). Online and on Top. *Financial Time*, November 18, Germany section, p. 9.

Sweezy, P. M. (1981). *Four Lectures on Marxism*. New York: Monthly Review Press.

Swisher, K. (1998). Microsoft Readies New Home Page for the Internet. *Wall Street Journal*, February 3, B5.

Takahashi, D. & S. Mehta (1998). Bells Push a Modem Standard to Rival Cable's. *Wall Street Journal*, January 21, B6.

Taylor, P. (1997). Publishers to Charge Web Users. *Financial Time*, December 29, p. 11.

Taylor, P. (1998). Big Shake-Up for Telecom Suppliers. *Financial Times*, May 6, IT supplement, p. 1.

Tedesco, R. (1998a). NFL Keeps ESPN Game Plan. *Broadcasting and Cable*, June 1, p. 37.

Tedesco, R. (1998b). Disney Stakes Big "Net Claim with Infoseek". *Broadcasting and Cable*, June 15, p. 15.

Tedesco, R. (1998c). N2K Links with Disney, ABC Radio. *Broadcasting and Cable*, July 8, p. 46.

"The Press in Spin Cycle" (1998). *Economist*, June 20, p. 35.

"Times Web Site Ends Fee for Foreign Users" (1998). *New York Times*, July 15, C6.

"Tribune Company" (1997). *Goldman Sachs Investment Research*, May 14, p. 27.

Turow, J. (1997). *Breaking Up America*. Chicago: University of Chicago Press.

Warner, B. (1998). Online Sprawl. *IQ*, May 25, p. 21.

Warner. C. (1998). Dialing for ISP Dollars. *Mediaweek*, June 1, pp. 30, 32.

Waters, R. (1998a). Sprint Lean Needs Firm Landing. *Financial Times*, June 2, p. 18.

Waters, R. (1998b). Sprint Remodels Network to Adapt to Internet Age. *Financial Times*, June 3, p. 15.

Wayne, L. (1998). Inside Beltway, Microsoft Sheds Its Image as Outsider. *New York Times*, May 20, C4.

"Web Becomes a Viable Channel" (1997). *Advertising Age*, December 22, p. 21.

Webber, T. (1998). Who, What, Where: Putting the Internet in Perspective. *Wall Street Journal*, April 16, B12.

Wheelwright, G. (1998a). Upheavals for the Broadcasting World. *Financial Times*, May 6, IT section, p. 5.

Wheelwright, G. (1998b). Tap into the Sound of the Superhighway. *Financial Times*, June 2, p. 11.

Wolff, M. (1998). Burn Rate. *Advertising Age*, June 8, pp. 1, 16, 18.

Yang, C. (1998). How the Internet Works: All You Need to Know. *Business Week*, July 20, pp. 58–60.

4

Identifying a Policy Hierarchy: Communication Policy, Media Industries, and Globalization

Alison Beale*

In the course of international trade negotiations since World War II, a cultural exemption to liberalized trade has been a regular demand from many participating countries. This chapter considers the cultural exemption strategy, most recently manifested in the failed negotiation of the Multilateral Agreement on Investment (MAI) in 1998 and again in the 1999 World Trade Organization (WTO) talks. I argue that the language of an exemption for culture masks the issues at the heart of the relationship between national cultural policies and international markets. National and regional trade negotiators claim a principled base in their responsibility for "public goods" such as universal access to telephony and telecommunications and for citizens' rights to cultural diversity and development. But this responsibility conflicts with others. The concerns of the national governments and the world-regional markets such as the European Union (EU) represented by the negotiators have been to ensure the flow of capital through the electronic paths of the information highway, and to expand investment in ICTs (information and communication technologies). Not far behind these goals is securing advantage for domestically based cultural industries including television, to which ICTs are increasingly linked via cross-ownership and investment, and technological convergence.

In terms of national priorities, therefore, there is a hierarchy in which policies for the arts and heritage come third after information technology and cultural industries policies. In a related ranking, the public interest, public good, diversity, cultural rights, and cultural development – to list the major citizenship-related concepts much cited but effectively ignored in the context of international trade – come a distant second to the market rationalization euphemized as "consumer sovereignty."

The Cultural Exemption: Europe

The cultural exemption originates in European, especially French, resistance to the increasingly one-way flow of trade with the United States in film after World War II, an irritant ever since aggressive American moves to export film began in the 1920s. Two features of this background should be underscored. First, there is the historic importance of secondary markets in providing the high return on investment upon which Hollywood and, after it, the television and recorded music industries have come to depend. These markets have been part and parcel of the long-standing international structure of American cultural industries. Second, these industries have benefited from extensive diplomatic and trade intervention on the part of the American government. During the 1920s, for example, "American films seized over 50 percent of the market in a number of European countries and over 80 percent in Britain and Italy," even as screen quotas were introduced (Nowell-Smith 1998:3). With the assistance of the US Department of State and American embassies in Europe, most of this protective legislation was withdrawn by 1945 (Bernier 1998:109). As one commentator has noted "there is evidence of a concerted strategy between the American government and the Motion Picture Export Association of America (MPAA) to promote the export of American movies not only as earners of foreign currency but as bearers of the American flag" (Nowell-Smith 1998:7). This is pursued to such an extent that the MPAA has the reputation of being "the little State Department" (Wasko 1995:166).

In the post–World War II years European promotion of the film industry and intra-European co-production (instigated by Jean Monnet, the "father" of the European Union) culminated in a series of co-production agreements between European countries, as well as the Blum-Byrnes Agreement regulating competition between the French and American film industries (Nowell-Smith 1998:8). But the American critic Victoria De Grazia has argued against seeing these developments as a successful blending of national interest and pan-European interest. Rather, she argues that there has been a slippage between nationalism and Europeanism at several key junctures in the European cinema; in the Nazi era, in the economic boom of the 1960s, and currently within the new borders and among the diversifying populations of Europe. Despite the problematic nature of this ideological framework for defending a European culture, in the long run it has won legitimacy for national cinema as "a veritable monument to high culture" especially in France (De Grazia 1998:21). Though British cinema is in a somewhat different position, it is art cinemas, rather than commercial cinemas, that are regarded as emblems of the nation and of Europe.

As later developments in the European Union were to prove, commercially oriented cultural products, co-production agreements with the United States that side-stepped "European" interests, and the growing broadcasting and new media technology sectors exacerbated existing differences between countries and cultural sectors. The "cultural exemption" was until recently based on a common cultural front concealing ineffective policy and conflict among European nations in their attempts to join forces against Hollywood. The ambivalence about American influence in such countries as France and Britain, given the participation of European artists and companies in the newer cultural industries of popular music and television, leads to accusations of hypocrisy from American skeptics when Europeans continue to argue for a cultural high ground as the basis for imposing limits on American products (De Grazia 1998; Pells 1997).

The unification of the European Union has not come about through the consolidation of a European audiovisual or cultural space, but through firm foundations built for the

European audiovisual and information technology sectors as part of economic integration in the 1980s (Beale 1999a; Humphreys 1996; Raboy 1999). As Caroline Pauwels (1991) has demonstrated, far from being built on "consumer sovereignty" in any meaningful sense, these foundations have been laid using this catchphrase as publicity rather than as the object of policy (p. 71). Private interests brought forward by both national and pan-European representation, rather than national or European citizens' interests, have been the key factors in developing the European telecommunications sector. One analysis concludes, "EU telecommunications policy would not have proceeded so far, so fast, without a significant policy shift among the member states themselves: from polarization between 'liberalizers' and 'protectionists' towards a new liberalizing consensus" (Humphreys and Simpson 1996:118).

Meanwhile, at the Uruguay Round of the General Agreement on Tariffs and Trade (GATT) talks in 1986, the first in the sequence of liberalizing trade agreements this chapter is concerned with, European countries obtained a complete exclusion of audiovisual and cultural goods. Janet Wasko (1995) has called the US cultural defeat at the Uruguay Round "a remake of scenes already played out" (p. 165), but one could argue that, in addition, it was a sideshow. The cultural exemption not only masked the historic differences among European countries and among private interests within their borders; it drew attention away from other routes to economic integration and cultural globalization that were fast developing in telecommunications and ICTs (Winseck 1997; Raboy 1996).

The Cultural Exemption: Canada

"Cultural sovereignty," the key to the MAI debate over culture, is a phrase which has accumulated layered meanings during the history of Canadian cultural policies. Its origins are in the establishment of the CBC/Radio Canada as a cultural defense system against American transborder radio. Through the public broadcaster an ideological association was formed between cultural sovereignty and the public sector, according to the rationale of "the state or the United Stats." The Canadian state was legitimized in compensating for market failure, reaching a geographically dispersed population, and assuring the coverage of Canadian news and representation of the regions. Following demands for public funding for the film and publishing industries in the 1960s, cultural sovereignty also came to mean public support for Canadian cultural industries, whose existence as providers of Canadian content and Canadian jobs was argued to be essential to providing the glue holding the Canadian polity together. Today, cultural sovereignty is used to represent the idea of cultural sovereignty as national security. Public investment in computer-mediated communication is defended on the basis of cultural sovereignty, because computer networks, innovation, and expertise underpin communications and economic production and must be provided in order to guarantee Canada's continued prosperity and political integrity (Menzies 1998).

Canadian researchers reviewing the history of Canadian cultural policy argue that cultural sovereignty thus became, first, a cultural industries policy (which has also industrialized the organization and subsidy of the arts and heritage) (Beale 1997) and, second, a rationale for significant public support for computer-mediated communication. At the same time, spending on public broadcasting, for example, has decreased (Babe 1996). This analysis suggests to some researchers that opening up cultural policy to economic arguments has been a Pandora's box that results in economic considerations taking priority over cultural ones (Godard 1998). A different argument links the triumph of the economic rationale to the centrality of public spending on communication technology in Canada (Dowler 1996). And another view suggests that in the Canadian context some form of economic rationale – market failure – has always been present, and that the cultural industries model has been a success, contributing to continuing demands for both public investment in and protection for Canadian cultural industries and market expansion in order for Canada-based companies to remain competitive. This argument gives qualified support to the North American Free Trade Agreement (NAFTA) (Dorland 1996) but it also raises the issue of how policy measures are unequal in their impact across cultural industries, and across cultural industries, the arts, and heritage.

By the time of the negotiation of the Free Trade Agreement between Canada and the United States in 1988, Canada was the most important secondary market for cultural exports from the United States. Today, far from being significantly controlled in Canada: "Foreign products or firms account for more than 90 per cent of the drama on English-language television, 81 per cent of consumer magazines on Canadian newsstands, 79 per cent of the revenue for recorded music, and close to 95 per cent of annual screen time at Canadian theatres" (Magder 1999:12). This is despite Canadian controls on investment, and content requirements for television and radio that have not yet been altered by free trade in culture.

Free trade with the United States and Mexico has been the goal of the Canadian business elite and government since the 1980s. Its advocates gave Canadians (who in repeated opinion polls tend not to support free trade, yet vote for governments that do) repeated assurances that the cultural sector, employment standards, the universal public health-care system, and other institutions and regulatory powers of the federal government would not be affected by such agreements. NAFTA (1993) featured a cultural exemption clause for cultural industries. The trade-off was that the exemption is subject to the "notwithstanding" clause which specifies in Article 2005 that "a party" can retaliate with measures of "equivalent commercial effect" and do so using sectors unrelated to culture. Commentators questioned the agreement on both sides of the border. The Canadian cultural community pointed out the vulnerability of Canadian interests to potential retaliation. In the US Congress, the original FTA bill had specified that future administrations would have to seek elimination of the cultural exemption.

After NAFTA came into force, retaliation against Canadian exercise of cultural sovereignty occurred in several high-profile cases. The most famous of these is the landmark *Sports Illustrated* case, that magazine being one of the Canadian "editions" of American publications (US editorial content packaged in Canada with Canadian advertising) on whose Canadian advertising the federal government imposed an excise tax of 80 percent. The purpose of the tax, of course, was to encourage advertisers to spend their dollars in such Canadian magazines as *MacLean's* (the largest-circulation news magazine) and *Chatelaine* (the largest-circulation homemakers magazine). In 1997 a

ruling by the World Trade Organization determined that Canada would have to withdraw the tax, a ruling described by Ted Magder (1999) as "a stunning victory for the
United States" (p. 12). Eventually a negotiated settlement was reached between Canada
and the United States which compromised on some of the more severe implications of
the ruling for Canada. However, the Canadian government also lost the right to provide
postal subsidies for Canadian magazines, which it had been doing since the nineteenth
century (Magder 1999). It later introduced some support measures in the form of grants
for Canadian publications, but these were not expected to make up for a projected loss
of up to 40 percent of Canadian magazine titles over the next few years as a result of
the WTO ruling.

Globalization: Victims or Partners?

Before going on to look at the Multilateral Agreement on Investment, the most recent
site of confrontation over the exemption of culture from trade rules, it is important to
point out two possible interpretations of the direction of national cultural policies since
the 1980s. The *Sports Illustrated* case, for example, appears to suggest that international
trade rules as enforced by the GATT, the WTO, and the International Chamber of
Commerce are responsible for destroying the ability of national governments to act on
behalf of national interests in culture. Even where cultural exemptions are in place,
countries are obliged to bring their treatment of national and nonnational cultural
enterprises into line in order to avoid internationally sanctioned trade retaliation in other
sectors. The result is like libel "chill": it leads to the "voluntary" forfeit of national
cultural sovereignty in anticipation of such retaliation.

But a second interpretation would argue that national governments and economic
unions such as the EU have played a role in the creation of free trade, in which bringing
their national cultural subsidies and institutions into line and reconfiguring the regulation of broadcasting and information technology sectors at the ministerial level have
played a substantial part. I share this view and would argue that a singular national or
world-regional cultural interest may now be seen for the fiction it is. It is principally
national "champions," cultural enterprises that have consolidated their market share
since the 1970s, information technology firms, and exporters of programming that
benefit from Canadian trade rules, and which in Europe have benefited from the information society policies of the EU. During the 1970s and 1980s Canada invested in the
production side of film and television, and concentrated its attention on exportable
cultural goods rather than in the more visibly "subsidized" cultural goods consumed at
home, such as the performing arts. It also imposed Canadian content quotas in television
and radio, which were particularly effective in supporting the recorded music industry.
But like the major US and British players, Canadian television producers have found
their greatest success outside Canada, to the extent that Canada is now the third highest
exporter of television programming in the world.

One of the less obvious features of the *Sports Illustrated* case was that a major beneficiary of Canadian tax on advertising in non-Canadian magazines has been Rogers Communications, Canada's largest cable operator, which owns MacLean-Hunter, the largest

English-language magazine group, and its Quebec cable counterpart, Telemedia. Are the business interests of such consortia with their huge market share the equivalent of national cultural interest, or of public interest?

Like other countries, the United States has imposed foreign investment limits in the media and broadcasting areas and has reserved the right to administer direct grants, tax incentives, and other forms of subsidy (Wasko 1995). In a manner consistent with this historic stance, the United States was one of the countries to reserve the right to maintain foreign investment restrictions in the media and broadcasting sectors at the 1998 MAI negotiations. Nonetheless it has always been the US trade negotiators' contention that culture is a tradable commodity like any other. Canadian policy analysts disagree, as indicated in the following quote:

> We are obviously confronted here with a longstanding conflict about what could be termed, for lack of a better expression, the specificity of cultural products envisaged from an international trade perspective. The main actors are few and well-defined. Essentially the request for a totally free and open market in cultural products comes from the United States, while the proponents of some form of cultural exception are to be found in Europe, more particularly in France, and in Canada. (Bernier 1998:110–11)

American commercial law analysts stress the importance of extending conventions on copyright as a means of expanding trade in intellectual property, the key to prosperity. They argue that expanding the recognition of copyright will ultimately be more rewarding to producers than continued national cultural exemptions (Strong 1993:123). What is interesting about this argument is that it assumes the reason for national cultural exemptions to be the protection of national cultural producers. This, rather than cultural sovereignty or a national cultural interest, is clearly the historic US position.

And of course, it may be the Canadian position as well. In the backroom parlance of trade negotiations, Americans seem to have got Canada's number as far as the commitment of our government to a cultural rather than commercial defense of Canadian cultural industries is concerned. An American analyst inquired of the 1994 merger of Rogers Communications and MacLean-Hunter: "Are Canadians protecting their culture or their economy?" (Lehman 1997:211). A defender of Canadian cultural big business, borrowing a line from the national anthem, countered, "'We cannot protect our own turf unless there is someone out there big enough to stand on guard for thee'" (p. 211).

The MAI and the Cultural Exemption

The impetus to set up the Multilateral Agreement on Investment came from the US trade representative to the Organization for Economic Cooperation and Development (OECD), from the EU within the WTO, from enthusiastic national governments such as Canada and the financial sector. Negotiations were initiated in 1995, but stalled in 1998. The reason for the MAI's failure was not the lack of consensus on a cultural exemption but disagreement on a number of matters related to the unprecedented scope of the proposed agreement. The MAI's key characteristic was that it was comprehensive; for the first time an international trade agreement was to *include* all sectors not specifically *excluded*.

The MAI was therefore widely described as a Bill of Rights for investors. A major feature was that foreign companies were to receive "national treatment." This meant that any national subsidies in the form of direct payments or tax relief, investment tax credits, content regulations, and so on were to apply equally to national and foreign companies. There were to be no controls on profit repatriation. Most significant was a rule mandating that countries could not apply environmental, minimum wage, or regional or sectoral development controls that could be shown to impair a rate of profit similar to that in the home country of the investor or multinational. This indirect but substantial threat would force member countries to "harmonize" legislation in these areas to the lowest common denominator. The big stick approach to forcing harmonization extended to the speculative realm of potential threats to potential investments. A complaint could be brought against a signatory country that its laws inhibited potential profit taking from potential investors, and they could choose the venue in which to have such complaints adjudicated.

Prior to the 1998 MAI discussions, countries appeared to adopt several strategies toward trade in culture, suggesting various analyses of the effects the agreement might have on culture and different strategies to manage such effects. A majority of countries did not submit position papers that voiced reservations which directly affected culture. The common reason given for not doing so was that they were waiting to see whether a general exemption on culture was accepted. A few countries did submit reservations for the cultural industries, principally the right to maintain foreign investment restrictions: these included the United States, Italy, Turkey, the United Kingdom, and the Netherlands. Australia, Spain, Korea, and Mexico also submitted lists of specific reservations related to broadcasting, film, and book publishing.

Canada, Australia, and Turkey were the only countries to specifically state their assumption that there would be a *general agreement for the cultural industries* (my emphasis). France, in addition, submitted the first draft of a general exemption for "cultural diversity." It is notable that many of the countries that did not support a general exclusion for culture are home to the top audiovisual companies in the world. These countries include the United States, Japan, Germany, the United Kingdom, and the Netherlands.

The riotous World Trade Organization meeting of late 1999 in Seattle picked up some of the same agendas but did not attempt to do so in the umbrella fashion that had alarmed not only opponents but cautious supporters of free trade. Intellectual copyright was a major item on the table, but by then a cultural exemption was not.

The Diversity Strategy

After the failure of the MAI negotiations, several countries, notably France and Canada, began to pursue a concerted strategy for a cultural exemption in future trade talks. The Canadian minister for heritage, the Honorable Sheila Copps, led a group of 22 culture ministers who had first met in Sweden in 1998 at a United Nations Educational, Scientific, and Cultural Organization (UNESCO) Intergovernmental Conference on Cultural Policies for Development. They met in Canada in June 1998 and in September 1999 in Mexico. They called themselves the International Network on Cultural Policy and included Armenia, Brazil, Britain, Canada, China, Egypt, France, Hungary, Malaysia, Mexico, Sweden, and Ukraine, as well as a parallel organization of cultural nongovernmental organizations from these countries.

The work of this group drew on the French-initiated strategy of identifying uncontrolled global trade in culture as a threat to cultural diversity. It was supported by a well-advanced UNESCO program of cultural development that had linked cultural diversity to rights to education and freedom of expression and to the human rights of minorities. The same UNESCO initiative, the "World Decade on Cultural Development" that had culminated in the report *Our Creative Diversity* (World Commission on Culture and Development 1996) also viewed cultural diversity as a potential resource to be exploited for the benefit of cultural copyright holders – the minorities whose cultural rights it was concerned with (Beale 1999b:452–54). The Council of Europe is now carrying out a related Transversal Study on Cultural Policy and Cultural Diversity, with partners from non-European countries including Canada (Baeker 2000).

The rhetoric of the cultural exemption has evolved from defending national modernities to commercializing local hybridities. The Canadian government and UNESCO are cases in point. Since the 1960s the Canadian government's language and its action have shifted from a protectionist emphasis on Canadian cultural sovereignty and the uniqueness of the Canadian way of life to marketing hybridized Canadian cultural production to both domestic and international markets. This was clearly the agenda of the Canadian government as early as a 1994 foreign policy review highlighting such divergent exports and emblems of Canada as the works of Celine Dion and Michael Ondaatje (Beale 1997).

Diversity is tied to a human-rights agenda that arose in the concept of cultural development. But the means of protecting diversity are cultural sustainability, which may mean self-exploitation in the commodification, branding, copyrighting, and marketing of, especially, minority cultures. The World Commission on Cultural Development, treading carefully to avoid transgressing the principle of national cultural sovereignty, came up with a program to protect cultural diversity against what it implies is global Americanization, to be guaranteed by national governments, international human rights conventions, and through the marketing of intellectual property produced in minority cultures (World Commission on Cultural Development 1996). The capacity of intellectual copyright regimes to be enforced for the benefit of creators rather than owners and distributors remains to be seen.

The Council of Europe's study of cultural diversity appears to have more potential for identifying the ways in which states and international human-rights and trade regimes can come to terms with the complex societies of immigrants that most nations have become, which will entail establishing cultural policy on a footing very different from the nationalist modernism that characterizes so many policies (Baeker 2000). Notwithstanding this advance, the pursuit of diversity meantime provides countries such as France and Canada with a moral high ground that national interest does not provide. It is intended to be an irrefutable proposition that diversity is best secured through trade protections for cultural industries.

And this is where the private sector comes back in. Enthusiastic support for a strategy of cultural diversity has come from a surprising source in Canada, the Cultural Industries Sectoral Advisory Group on International Trade, or SAGIT. In a report to the minister of trade in early 1999, these leaders of the film, broadcasting, and cable industries, including the aforementioned Rogers Cable and MacLean-Hunter, advocated "a new international instrument that sets out rules on what kinds of domestic regulations can be used to promote and protect cultural diversity" (Scoffield 1999). These monopolists, some of whom have fought Canadian content regulation, others of whom tailor their production of Canadian television programs to international markets, see the writing on the wall and know an opportunity when it presents itself.

In theory, the ground that unites advocates for minority cultures and for cultural hybridity with cultural entrepreneurs is the provision of entertainment for diverse populations ill served by national public media, mainstream press and periodicals, and Eurocentric cultural institutions. The researchers involved in the Council of Europe study, and in the diversity initiatives of the Canadian Department of Heritage have identified informal diasporic and some genre and audience hybridizing initiated by private broadcasters as evidence of the potential for innovative approaches to audiences. They also note, however, that the national framework may not be the most appropriate or realistic one in which to pursue this audience development strategy (Baeker 2000). Diversity may be a comfortable strategy for lobbies such as the Sectoral Advisory Group on International Trade (SAGIT) because it comes without specific performance requirements to guarantee diversity. But the real divergence between these companies and proponents of cultural diversity arises where, for example, audiences or publics of particular minorities are too small or scattered to attract private investment or advertisers. Ultimately, what the SAGIT lobby in Canada and other private companies outside the United States hope for is that they will be protected as exemplars of "local" cultures and providers for diverse audiences. This should be seen for what it is: an opportunity to gain business advantage rather than a commitment either to traditional national cultural sovereignty or to cultural diversity.

Conclusion

The role of national governments (including the United States) in cultural globalization and of the private and public interests to which they respond is a difficult issue that has been neglected. The developmental gap between a cultural theory of globalization and a theory of the role of cultural *policy* in globalization is explored in Jan Nederveen Pieterse's formulation of globalization as cultural hybridization. Taking the analysis beyond postmodern identity politics, Nederveen Pieterse (1995) argues that "What globalization means in structural terms . . . is *the increase in the available modes* of *organization:* transnational, international, macro-regional, municipal, local . . . criss-crossed by functional networks of corporations, international organizations and nongovernmental organizations" (p. 50). While this deeper perspective on the structural foundations of hybrid culture is welcome, Nederveen Pieterse concludes that "essentialism will remain strategic as a mobilisational device as long as the units of nation, state, region, civilization, ethnicity remain strategic." We can see this essentialism strategically alive in the SAGIT report above.

But if some consider the national interest, national culture, or the public sphere as a national space to be among the essentialist concepts still strategically significant, I would argue not only that they are unraveling in the face of cultural hybridization, but that their strategic significance and their mobilizing capacity is and has historically been highly unstable and contextual. By this I mean, first, that it is important to consider whether mobilization in support of "national culture" is a politically necessary posture in many states, unless to conceal the role of the state in further market integration.

Second, it is crucial to note the variability of cultural policy language depending on the context in which it is deployed. Diversity is a concept much bandied about in management discourse, but until recently, at least, it has been in the public sector rather than the private that job equity has been addressed. In the private sector lateral structures, informal work environments, and job mobility are elements of a diversity strategy that is to some extent responsive to the local sites of multinational corporations, enabling them to describe themselves as culturally diverse.

The delinking of communications and information technology networks from the traditional marriage of national public and private sectors and their reemergence as the foundation for global markets is a reality whose fallout on national policies for broadcasting and for the arts and heritage is still being accounted for. In Europe and in Canada, as I have discussed elsewhere (Beale 1999a, 1999b), the relocation of decision-making about the ICT sector to trade and finance ministries and intragovernmental bodies has established a hierarchy in which the information technology and communications framework is isolated from accountability.

Marc Raboy (1999) has argued that we must move cultural policy advocacy beyond the national setting, because of the uncoupling of cultural production and distribution networks from nation-states. The oligopoly of information technology companies has become the focus of civil society movements seeking to protect the public resources of communication. The question then, as Raboy puts it, is what meaningful role national governments can play in developing a "socially progressive global regulatory framework for mass media, information, and communication technologies" (p. 305)? Similarly, how well will the multistranded strategy of cultural diversity as conducted by national governments represent the cultural interests of citizens of countries all over the world as economic and political integration proceed?

References

Babe, R. (1996). Economics and Information: Toward a New (and More Sustainable) World-View. *Canadian Journal of Communication* 21, pp. 161–78.

Baeker, G. (2000). Cultural Policy and Cultural Diversity in Canada. Unpublished Report for the Council of Europe Study on Cultural Policy and Cultural Diversity.

Beale, A. (1997). Subjects, Citizens or Consumers? Changing Concepts of Citizenship in Canadian Cultural Policy. In: A. Seager, L. Evenden, R. Lorimer & R. Mathews (eds.), *Alternative Frontiers: Voices from the Mountain West*, pp. 51–65. Montreal: Association for Canadian Studies.

Beale, A. (1999a). Development and *Désetatisation*: Cultural Policy in the European Union. *MIA/Culture and Policy* 90, pp. 91–105.

Beale, A. (1999b). From "Sophie's Choice" to Consumer Choice: Framing Gender in Cultural Policy. *Media, Culture and Society* 21, pp. 435–58.

Bernier, I. (1998). Cultural Goods and Services in International Trade Law. In: D. Browne (ed.), *The Culture/Trade Quandary: Canada's Policy Options*, pp. 108–54. Ottawa: Centre for Trade Policy and Law.

Burgelman, J.-C. (1999). The Future of the Welfare State and its Challenges for Communication Policy. In: A. Calabrese & J.-C. Burgelman (eds.), *Communication, Citizenship and Social Policy: Rethinking the Limits of the Welfare State*, pp. 125–36. Lanham, MD: Rowman and Littlefield.

De Grazia, V. (1998). European Cinema and the Idea of Europe (1925–1995). In: G. Nowell-Smith & S. Ricci (eds.), *Hollywood and Europe: Economics, Culture, National Identity 1945–1995*, pp. 19–33. London: British Film Institute.

Dorland, M. (ed.) (1996). *The Cultural Industries in Canada: Problems, Policies and Prospects*. Toronto: James Lorimer and Co.

Dowler, K. (1996). The Cultural Industries Policy Apparatus. In: M. Dorland (ed.), *The Cultural Industries in Canada: Problems, Policies and Prospects*, pp. 138–56. Toronto: James Lorimer and Co.

Godard, B. (1998). Feminist Speculations on Value: Culture in the Age of Downsizing. In: A. Beale & A. Van Den Bosch (eds.), *Ghosts in the Machine: Women and Cultural Policy in Canada and Australia*, pp. 43–76. Toronto: Garamond.

Humphreys, P. (1996). *Mass Media and Media Policy in Western Europe*. Manchester: Manchester University Press.

Humphreys, P. & S. Simpson (1996). European Telecommunications and Globalization. In: P. Gunnet (ed.), *Globalisation and Public Policy*, pp. 105–24. Cheltenham, UK and Brookfield, US: Edward Elgar.

Lehman, A. (1997). The Canadian Cultural Exemption Clause and the fight to maintain an identity. *Syracuse Journal of International Law and Commerce* 23, pp. 187–218.

Magder, T. (1999). Going Global. *Canadian Forum*, August, pp. 11–16.

Menzies, H. (1998). Challenging Capitalism in Cyberspace: the Information Highway, the Postindustrial Economy, and People. In: R. W. McChesney, E. M. Wood & J. B. Poster (eds.), *Capitalism and the Information Age: The Political Economy of the Global Communication Revolution*, pp. 87–98. New York: Monthly Review Press.

Nederveen Pieterse, J. (1995). Globalization as Hybridization. In: M. Featherstone, S. Lash & R. Robertson (eds.), *Global Modernities*, pp. 45–68. Thousand Oaks, CA: Sage.

Nowell-Smith, G. (1998). Introduction. In: C. Nowell-Smith & S. Ricci (eds.), *Hollywood and Europe: Economics, Culture, National Identity 1945–1995*, pp. 1–19. London: British Film Institute.

Pauwels, C. (1999). From Citizenship to Consumer Sovereignty: the Paradigm Shift in European Audiovisual Policy. In: A. Calabrese & J.-C. Burgelman (eds.), *Communication, Citizenship and Social Policy: Rethinking the Limits of the Welfare State*, pp. 65–76. Lanham MD: Rowman and Littlefield.

Pells, R. H. (1997). *Not Like Us: How Europeans Have Loved, Hated, and Transformed American Culture since World War II*. New York: Basic Books.

Raboy, M. (1996). Cultural Sovereignty, Public Participation and Democratization of the Public Sphere: the Canadian Debate on the New Information Infrastructure. *Communications and Strategies* 21 (1st quarter), pp. 51–77.

Raboy, M. (1999). Communication Policy and Globalization as a Social Project. In: A. Calabrese & J.-C. Burgelman (eds.), *Communication, Citizenship and Social Policy: Rethinking the Limits of the Welfare State*, pp. 293–310. Lanham, MD: Rowman and Littlefield.

Scoffield, H. (1999). Ottawa Urged to Push for Global Culture Accord, *Globe and Mail*. Toronto, February 18.

Strong, S. (1993). Banning the Cultural Exclusion: Free Trade and Copyrighted Goods. *Duke Journal of Comparative and International Law* 4, pp. 93–123.

Wasko, J. (1995). Jurassic Park and the GATT: Hollywood and European Update. In: F. Corcoran & P. Preston (eds.), *Democracy and Communication in the New Europe: Change and Continuity in East and West*, pp. 157–71. Cresskill, NJ: Hampton Press.

Winseck, D. (1997). Contradictions in the Democratization of International Communication. *Media, Culture and Society* 19, pp. 219–46.

World Commission on Culture and Development (1996). *Our Creative Diversity*. Paris: UNESCO.

5

The Rhetoric of Culture: Some Notes on Magazines, Canadian Culture, and Globalization

*Imre Szeman**

The fallout from two rulings against Canada by the World Trade Organization (WTO) made headlines on the same day in *The Globe and Mail* (Honey, Scoffield). The WTO's interim ruling against the Canadian auto pact in October 1999 was in the news again a year later when the final ruling was made concerning the date on which the pact would be eliminated in its entirety (Scoffield). As of 19 February 2001, the auto pact will expire, and with it a vision of economic nationalism that seems to many to be out of step with the times. At the same time, the Heritage ministry announced details of its Canadian Magazine Fund, a "$150-million olive branch extended to magazine publishers to lessen the competitive blow from US-based publications" (Honey R3). The fund was first announced in conjunction with the passage of an amended and toothless Bill C-55 in 1999, which was itself a response to an earlier ruling by the WTO on Canada's national magazine policy.

In the case of the auto pact, the federal government seems to be largely untroubled by the WTO ruling and is ready to let the pact die with little opposition. Industry Minister John Manley suggested that "the importance of the auto pact has been significantly reduced over recent years. . . . What we've built is a sector that is very strong, and is far exceeding the auto pact minimums" (qtd. in McKinnon and Kennan B9). When it comes to magazines and periodicals, however, the government appears much more committed to supporting and defending the Canadian industry against the threat of foreign competition. The short-term outlook is unfavourable: while the Canadian Magazine Fund is intended to help make the industry much stronger, Chris McDermott, manager of periodical and publishing programmes for the Department of Canadian Heritage, nevertheless admits that at best it "may just help the industry stay where they're at" (qtd. in Honey R3).

The different governmental responses to these two legal decisions may seem to rest merely on the economic strength of one sector (automobiles) in comparison to another (magazines). In the absence of adequate legislative protections it seems clear that Canadian magazines will require continued financial support from the government if they

*Pp. 212–30 from *Journal of Canadian Studies*, vol. 35, no. 3. © 2000 by Journal of Canadian Studies. Reprinted with permission from Journal of Canadian Studies.

are to continue publishing. But there is clearly more to the actions taken by the Heritage ministry in setting up the magazine fund than support for an economically threatened industry. That the fund is being administered by the Heritage ministry and not by Industry Canada suggests more than financial concern. What is at issue in the defence of the magazine industry is, of course, the continued existence of Canadian *culture*, at least insofar as it is expressed through and represented in magazines and periodicals.

In the context of recent disputes over magazine policy in Canada, I would like to explore what it means to continue to defend – in terms of public policy, but also as a general political stance – a specifically national culture in the era of globalization. I am less concerned with whether the nation or nation-state remains a viable political or conceptual unit in the context of globalization – whether, that is, the *national* part of "national culture" has been disturbed or displaced by globalization.[1] Rather, I would like to consider whether the concept of culture itself effectively carries with it those other ideas and ideals (political, economic and social) that are so often associated with national culture and with the idea of national cultural differences. One reason for defending the cultural industries in Canada – besides, that is, their importance to the overall economy[2] – is that we think culture is bound up with our values and our distinctive way of life, expressed empirically through governmental policies and programmes and abstractly in Canadian visions of the social good. To lose control over our cultural industries, whose creations and representations help produce and reproduce these values and this distinctiveness, seems to imply a loss of this way of life. I would like to argue, however, that the focus on culture as a trope or symbol of these other (often vaguely felt rather than clearly articulated) values actually impedes our understanding of Canada's place in globalization and its position within broader structures of global power. I have chosen to examine this issue in the context of the recent struggles over Canadian magazine policy because some of the difficulties of protecting a national culture in the era of globalization are expressed in a particularly heightened form here – again, not because the nation is powerless to defend its culture in the face of rulings by international bodies like the WTO, but because the defence of culture through the defence of the magazine industry reveals paradoxes and contradictions that it is important for us to unravel at this time. In the context of Bill C-55, there are two questions I would like to ask. First, why do we still imagine that there is a need for a national culture? Second, what role do we imagine that magazines play in producing or maintaining such a culture, and what does this tell us about national culture today?

Before I address these questions, I want to review shifts in magazine policy in Canada over the past several decades. While there is a long history of governmental involvement with and concern over the magazine industry in Canada (Vipond 60–66, Desbarats), the most recent disputes over magazine policy have their origin in the early 1960s. In 1961, the Royal Commission on Publications (the O'Leary Commission) was charged with examining the health of the Canadian magazine industry. The commission found that, unsurprisingly, the health of the Canadian industry was directly linked to competition from American magazines. The O'Leary Commission first drew attention to the danger posed by the distribution of "split runs" of American magazines in Canada. Split runs combine the editorial content of a magazine's parent issue – an issue of *Time* magazine, for example, produced for distribution in the United States – with advertising solicited from Canadian companies to replace any ads directed to an American audience. Because split runs involve no new or additional editorial costs, American magazines are able to sell advertising in Canada at a substantially discounted rate that Canadian magazines cannot possibly match, which correspondingly poses a direct threat to an industry that depends almost entirely on advertising to generate revenue and profits.

To rectify this situation, the O'Leary Commission recommended that the Canadian federal government develop policies intended to discourage the entry of split runs into Canada. Legislation introducing tax penalties and other measures intended to dissuade Canadian companies from advertising in non-Canadian publications was passed in April 1965. But the changes in income tax law did not apply to foreign magazines that had been printed and published – even in part – in Canada before 1965. As a result, two of the most successful American magazines, *Time* and *Reader's Digest*, were in effect made "honorary Canadian citizens and provided . . . with a customs wall that prevented the entry of new foreign competitors" (Magder 12). This exemption paved the way for the introduction by Time Inc. of *Sports Illustrated (SI) Canada* in 1993, a move that marked the beginning of the end for Canada's ability to protect its domestic magazine industry and that led, finally, to the passage into law of the revised version of Bill C-55 in 1999.

Bill C-55 is the Canadian government's response to the 1997 ruling by the WTO against the policies then in place to safeguard the Canadian magazine industry. In June 1996, following *SI Canada's* use of the exemption granted Time Inc. in 1965 to circumvent Tariff Code 9958 and other policy mechanisms intended to ensure that Canadian advertising dollars were spent on Canadian magazines, the federal government tabled new legislation against split runs. That new legislation, called Bill C-103, was passed before the end of that year. By June 1997, the WTO dispute panel had made a ruling against Bill C-103 that rendered all Canada's existing magazine policies null and void.[3] The recent attempt to replace the policies disallowed under the General Agreement on Tariffs amid Trade (GATT) by the WTO with yet another new set of legislative protections had almost the very opposite effect: in 1999, Bill C-55 legally opened the Canadian market to American split-run magazines. Initially, Bill C-55 was designed to circumvent the WTO ruling by making it illegal for Canadian companies to buy ads in split-run magazines. While the entry of split runs into the Canadian magazine market thus would not be prohibited outright, it would have been made unfeasible by undermining the rationale for producing split runs in the first place. In the winter of 1999, the US threatened economic reprisals against the Canadian export of steel, textiles, wood products and plastics, sectors that constitute $4 billion in annual trade (Morton [1999], Fraser and McKenna [1999]). The threat resulted in the creation of a "compromise" version of Bill C-55: American magazines may solicit 12 per cent of their ad content from Canadian advertisers without having to add *any* original Canadian editorial content. In other words, split runs, long the bane of the Canadian magazine sector, have become legitimated in Canadian law. The amount of Canadian ad content permissible in American split-run magazines is set to increase to 18 per cent within three years. This is significant: 18 per cent of the ad space in the 13 major American "women's service" magazines – *RedBook, Cosmopolitan*, and so on – amounts to 3,400 pages. By comparison, the *total* advertising space of the seven major Canadian magazines in the same category is 4,800 pages (Milner and Fraser B1).

Even given the federal government's recent announcement of the Canadian Magazine Fund, it seems all but certain that Bill C-55 will have dire implications for the Canadian magazine industry: more split runs means less ad revenue for Canadian magazine companies already working with slim profit margins, which means that it is very likely that several magazines will cease publication. The threat posed by Bill C-55 to Canadian magazines depends on the nature of each magazine. Most threatened are those with a clear profit motive – general interest magazines like *Maclean's* and lifestyle magazines such as *Flare* – rather than literary or intellectual magazines – *Brick*, *Borderlines*, *Matrix* – which have a minimal commercial agenda. More generally, the WTO ruling points to difficulties in future attempts to protect Canadian culture in the age of globalization. These legal difficulties compound other problems introduced by new technologies, which are already being faced by the Canadian Radio-Television and Telecommunications Commission as it struggles to work out a way of patrolling national borders with respect to the Internet.[4] Heritage Minister Sheila Copps has made various attempts to defend the concept of national culture on the international stage, for example, through Canada's involvement with the International Network of Ministers Responsible for Culture and its commitment to UNESCO's Stockholm Action Plan on national culture. But it seems that Canada's long-standing commitment to the legal protection of national cultural industries is in jeopardy – that is, if Canada retains a commitment to new international juridico-economic agreements like the General Agreement on Tariffs amid Trade (GATT).

Why do we still imagine a need for a national culture? And what do magazines have to do with producing and maintaining this culture? The implications of the WTO ruling against Canadian magazine policy seem like a genuine cause for concern. Outside corporate boardrooms, it is difficult to find support for the decline of national cultures and the ascension of a global culture articulated through and around commodity consumption; very few of us would be happy to allow Canadian culture to become part of what Benjamin Barber has described as "McWorld" without a fight, even if we might suspect that we are already well on our way there, If we consider national culture to be synonymous with the persistence and existence of cultural difference (too often imagined as being a good in itself), Canada's commitment to this new international system of juridico-economic agreements seems to be pointing us in this direction. But are things really so simple?

In Canada, the commitment to the defence and protection of a national culture has always been tied to broader political beliefs and positions. If there remains continuing widespread agreement on the function and necessity of Canadian cultural policy (except by the editorial board of the *National Post*), it is because we think a cultural policy can preserve what has been destroyed in the United States: genuine democracy in the public sphere and a public culture that is not wholly determined by the logic of the free market. This is the potential difference between Canada and the United States elaborated by George Grant, who identified the United States with a destructive modernity that produced " a way of life based on the principle that the most important activity is profit-making" (47).

Grant's identification of Canada and particularly of the activities of the Canadian state with the production of an anti-capitalist and anti-modern space (mirrored in Marshall McLuhan's descriptions of Canada as a "counter-environment") has remained an essential underlying component of contemporary critical considerations of the fate of Canadian culture. For example, in her supple and sophisticated examination of the dynamics of nationalism, the nation-state and culture in Canada, Jody Berland draws many of the same conclusion as Grant. She sees the recent attacks on government support of culture as "part of a systematic process of redefining subjects – legally, discursively, politically – as consumers in a particular marketplace niche whose own cultural endeavours must find a strategic place in the ever-expanding landscape of continental and global culture" (47). Berland believes it is important to defend the government's role in culture, despite any suspicions critics might have about the activities of the state and the parochial character of the nation. Similarly, Joyce Zemans argues that there is a link between a strong Canadian cultural identity and the possibility of a democratic, public space of "real sharing and exchange – a space for the Canadian imagination" (119). She adds, "[A] coherent cultural policy will continue to position the promotion of cultural identity as a key goal of government policy and a strategy for achieving national well-being" (119). I am not suggesting that every discussion of culture in Canada continues to see the link between nation and culture as essential. Recently, for example, Himani Bannerji has drawn attention to the potentially dangerous or exclusionary aspects of cultural nationalism, and Robert Chodos, Rae Murphy and Eric Hamovitch have pointed out that while "in Canada, cultural nationalists have tended to see the nation-state as an instrument of resistance to McWorld, arguing that state agencies such as the Canadian Broadcasting Corporation, the National Film Board and the Canada Council, have played key roles in keeping the country distinct . . . it is equally possible to see the nation-state as an agent of McWorld" (159–60). But the more common position still remains the one articulated by James Laxer who, in his attack on the uncritical acceptance of the "globalization myth" by Canadian business and political élites, laments the loss of "certain social values that distinguish us from Americans" (94) in a manner that echoes Grant's lament some three decades earlier.

The national boundaries of Canada have often been associated with the larger ontological, ethical and epistemological boundaries between what might be characterized as the destructive forces of capitalist modernity and the compassionate, democratic and anti-imperialist values that exist beyond capitalism. These values are imagined as existing in Canadian institutions and individuals; they emerge out of Canada's particular historical situation and circumstances. Similarly, Canadian culture in all its forms – from popular culture (pop music, sports and television) to high culture (literature, ballet and classical music) – has often been imagined as positioned against the crude market values articulated in the various cultural forms that together make up the American McWorld. Barbara Godard, for instance, has argued that the intervention of the Canadian government into the cultural sector through such agencies as the Canada Council created a situation in Canada in which "no longer dependent on the market place of the metropole, artists could create more freely for the Canadian public" (101). Certainly, if one examines the arguments put forward by the Canadian and American governments to the WTO in their dispute over the magazine industry, it is difficult *not* to see culture, if not the nation, as the boundary between a compassionate society and one defined by pure capitalist rationality. In making its case that Canadian magazines and American split runs were not "like products," and so not governed by GATT, the Canadian government argued:

> Magazines are distinct from ordinary articles of trade. Magazines are intended, by their very nature, for intellectual consumption as opposed to physical use (like a bicycle) or physical consumption (like food). It follows that the intellectual content of a cultural good such as a magazine must be considered its prime characteristic. . . . Editorial material developed for the Canadian market reflects a Canadian perspective and contains specific information of interest to Canadians. The content is qualitatively different from editorial material copied from foreign publications. What has been said of the essential properties of magazines is equally applicable to their end-use. The end-use of a magazine in not simply reading: it is transmission and acquisition of specific information. (WTO para 3.61, 3.63)

In the United States, a magazine is defined very differently:

> The type, texture, color, thickness, and even the perfume of the paper can be important factors to market appeal. The dimensions of a magazine, the manner in which its pages are bound, the typesetting, and the appearance of the ink, can also be significant. The type, appearance, and frequency of advertisements may be a factor in a consumer's purchasing decisions as well. All of these attributes – including editorial content – combine to form an *overall package*. . . . For the Canadian and US magazine industries, editorial content generally represents substantially less than 20 percent of the cost of producing a consumer magazine. (WTO para 3.78)

On the surface, this bald statement of hard facts confirms the worst suspicions of Canadians about the values of their neighbours to the south. It is hard not to see the American response as both self-interested and deliberately obtuse about the cultural dimension of magazines outlined by the Canadian government. This seems to be a clear case of the American government's desire to expand its global cultural interests – economic and ideological – through the establishment of "the principle that culture is a commodity" (Carr 29). It would not be hard, on the other hand, to see in the Canadian argument a claim about the essential nation-building function of magazines that is similar in form to the claims made by Benedict Anderson on behalf of the novel and the newspaper. At this point, everything seems to be falling into a predictable pattern that permits, on the one hand, anxious hand-wringing over what could happen to Canada and its unique culture and value systems, and on the other, a celebration about what Canada has managed to accomplish culturally against great odds. At precisely this point, I want to stop and push things in a more uncomfortable direction. It is not just the relevance of national culture as a conceptual category that is at issue in Bill C-55. We need to answer the second question I introduced earlier: what is it that makes *magazines* so important to the cultural life of the nation? What would we lose by losing our Canadian magazines – that is, magazines produced in Canada by Canadians largely for a Canadian audience? This question seems so self-evident that one wonders why I need even articulate it: magazines are one dimension of a healthy national culture, and culture is – in the words of Victor Rabinovitch, the former assistant deputy minister of-cultural development – "at the heart of what makes a community unique. Through language, customs, values, and lifestyles, it is possible for communities to differentiate themselves, express their identities and create a sense of uniqueness and belonging that is central to human comfort and security" (219).[5]

I remind you it is magazines like *Flare* and *Maclean's*, rather than small-circulation periodicals like *Matrix* and *Brick*, the federal government was hoping to help. Small magazines with specialized Canadian audiences are least likely to lose advertising dollars to split runs. Small presses that might run ads for Canadian novels or poetry collections in *Brick* would be unlikely to shift to *People Canada*, even if advertising space was offered at a substantially discounted rate. It is a different matter with *Maclean's*, of course, and this is reflected in the terms of the Canadian Magazine Fund, which devotes the overwhelming majority of its support to magazines with more than $60,000 in advertising revenue (Honey R3). It is easy to imagine how the entry of split runs of *Newsweek* or *US News* and *World Report* would affect the extremely slim profit margins *Maclean's* subsists on as a result of going head-to-head with the Canadian version of *Time*. The loss of a magazine like *Maclean's* would certainly mean a reduction of the amount of Canadian news information available in the weekly news format. But whether this is of real significance to the greater cause of Canadian culture or Canadian national-ism is a different question. The effect of magazine legislation on *Brick* as opposed to *Maclean's* further highlights the importance of category that is seldom discussed in relation to Canadian magazine policy: *audience*. Small magazine audiences are not likely to "switch' to split runs of American small magazines, which for precisely this reason are unlikely candidates for split runs, which makes it pointless for *advertisers* to make the switch.[6] On the other hand, a magazine like *Maclean's* seems to be more or less equivalent to – or *convertible* with – all of the other news weeklies on the market; adver-tisers imagine they will be able to address the same market with, say, *Newsweek Canada* as they would through *Maclean's*, but at a sizeable discount. This possibility of "con-vertibility," of an audience seeing one commodity as much like the other, is important to our understanding of the true cultural significance of at least one segment of the magazines circulated in Canada today.

Magazines are complicated bearers of national culture and of cultural difference. The Canadian argument to the WTO panel stressed that the prime characteristic of a maga-zine was its content – a content that, if produced for the Canadian market, "reflects a Canadian perspective and contains specific information of interest to Canadians." One could challenge the logic of this assertion, or at least suggest that it assumes all things produced in Canada and for Canadians necessarily reflect their perspective (which appears here in the singular, as if there was just one Canadian perspective to be reflected). Of course, not all content is equal. Most news stories *Maclean's* publishes would never make it into an American-based news weekly. But *Maclean's* also publishes international news stories, celebrity puff pieces and features on social trends, technology and business similar to those found in *Time* or *Newsweek*. If we accept Anderson's claims about the function of "print capitalism" in relation to nationalism, that is, that cultural technologies like the novel and the newspaper helped to produce the nation by creating a shared, imagined social space that could overcome the distances of real space, it certainly seems that a loss of capacity (that is, content) in printed information about Canada would lead to a diminishment of national ties across space. At the same time, it is important not to point out that magazines are somewhat different than these other national cultural print technologies since they originate at a different point in the history of the nation than the newspaper. In North America, the magazine industry began at the end of the nineteenth century within the first true nationally distributed mass magazines, *Ladies Home Journal* and *Munsey's Magazine*. Richard Ohmann identifies the explosion of mass circulation magazines between 1885 and 1900 not with the production of the American national culture *per se*, but with a particular form of it: a national *mass* culture, which was organized along very different lines than the nascent national culture that immediately preceded it.

With this in mind, we must consider what the Canadian government never discusses in its presentation to the WTO: the relationship between a magazine's content and its form, and the effect of this relationship on the role of magazines in producing and fostering Canadian national culture.

What Walter Benjamin once suggested about newspapers seems to me to be equally applicable to magazines – if not directly, then at least by means of a homology. For Benjamin, newspapers were essentially, that is, *formally* related to a certain vision of modernity and the modern subject. The intention of the newspaper is not to help the reader "assimilate the information it supplies as part of his own experience . . . its intention is just the opposite, and it is achieved: to isolate what happens from the realm in which it could affect the experience of the reader. The principles of journalistic information (freshness of the news, brevity, comprehensibility, and, above all, lack of connection between individual news items) contribute as much to this as does the make-up of the pages and the paper's style" (158–9). As ephemeral commodities that entice consumers by offering them perpetual "newness" newspapers, magazines and other forms of media embody certain "cultural" values and ideologies *irrespective* of the particularities of their content. This is not to say that content is secondary to form; instead, form and content must always be seen as dialectically intertwined, and it is possible to speak about them separately only for heuristic purposes. But it is not to suggest that it is not just the potential flood of split runs into a limited market for advertising dollars that threatens the ability of a magazine like *Maclean's* to define and defend something uniquely Canadian. Rather, the weekly news magazine format *already* suggests a framing and approach to news events that is similar to other, foreign (American) magazines. Most contemporary media forms already embody cultural values and ideologies – those of a capitalist modernity often, though incorrectly, associated with America in particular – and thus the defence of the magazine industry on cultural grounds is problematic, to say the least.

Maurice Charland has made a similar point in his discussion of Canada's "technological nationalism," which he describes as a nationalism that "ties Canadian identity, not to its people, but to their mediation through technology" (197). Echoing Benjamin's identification in the newspaper of a certain mode of capitalist modernity that is expressed through its very form, Charland notes that technological nationalism promises a liberal state in which technology would be a natural medium for the development of the *polis*. This vision of the nation is bankrupt, however, because it provides no substance or commonality for the *polis* except communication itself. As a consequence, technological nationalism's (anglophone) Canada has no defence against the power and seduction of the American cultural industry or, indeed, of the technological experience. (198)

The limitations of an overt attention to nationalist "content" at the expense of an understanding of the importance of nationalist "form" (or its lack) constituted in many ways the theme of Grant's work on Canadian nationalism. Given that magazines are first and foremost cultural *commodities*, one might have expected this limitation to become abundantly clear in the recent struggles over Canadian magazine policy. After all, magazines require protection in Canada due precisely to their form: they are cultural objects that require advertising for their very existence, and not just because advertising offers the financial support that makes the publication of a magazine's content possible. It is a mistake to see a magazine's content as completely divorced from the advertising that makes it possible. If Ohmann places magazines at the birth of twentieth-century mass culture – a mass consumer culture in which culture is made for profit – it is because they were among the first artefacts to blur the distinctions between form and content in a way recognizable in our own experience of mass culture. The success of *Munsey's Magazine* at the end of the nineteenth century was based on "a formula of elegant simplicity: identify a large audience that is not hereditarily affluent or elite, but that is getting on well enough, and that has cultural aspiration; give it what it wants; build a huge circulation; sell lots of advertising space at rates based on that circulation; sell the magazine at a price *below* the cost of production, and make your profit on ads" (Ohmann 25). Form and content overlap in the audience's cultural aspirations, which are addressed by advertising as much as by the articles in the magazine. Very early on, magazines explicitly targeted key demographic groups with considerable spending power (for example, middle-class and affluent women), thus ensuring the overlap of form and content – the content that spoke to these groups also dictated the advertisers who would spend money to have their products appear in the magazine. But such an overlap became even more pronounced in magazines such as *Godey's Lady's Book*, which "latched onto a central ideology of that time – progress – in a version tailored to the advancement of women [and] took up the cause of labor-saving devices like the sewing machine, anesthesia, women doctors, exercise and education for women" (27). The cultural aspirations and desires reflected in the articles were seen as consummated through the purchase of the advertised objects accompanying them. Magazines contain a unique marriage of content that is simultaneously a form of advertising and advertising that is also content. This marriage makes magazines the cultural objects they are. It is important, of course, to emphasize that content is not finally reducible to form, or vice versa. At the same time, the recent explosion of "lifestyle" magazines as varied as *Wallpaper, Shift, Outside* and *Sony Style* indicates the dangers of seeing magazines as defined by an intellectual content whose relationship to cultural form is perhaps only coincidental in the end. The cultural significance of magazines lies not in the printed text collected between its covers, but in what the existence of such a cultural form suggests about the relationship between culture and economics in a society like ours.

Magazines require policy protection in Canada due to their form: they are able to deliver content *only* if they can deliver a targeted consumer audience to advertisers at a cost acceptable to the latter. Perhaps for the wrong reasons, the US Trade Representatives' understanding of what magazines are is thus closer to the truth than the understanding of the Canadian government. Magazines *are* commodities; they are, furthermore, commodities that perform a specific kind of cultural work – they reinforce and legitimize both capitalism and commodity culture. The US Trade Representatives' definition of a magazine focusses on a magazine's appearance – its look and feel – and precludes the possibility of reflecting on the cultural work magazines do and their status as exemplary objects of mass commodity culture. I am not suggesting that the American definition should be accepted at face value, but that it should not be rejected outright in favour of a Canadian argument that too simply links culture with content.

The federal government's support of the magazine industry as a way of supporting Canadian culture is problematic. This holds true for the support of Canadian culture generally – from what Anderson might describe as "print-capitalism" to the media forms Charland associates with "technological nationalism." Discussions of Canadian culture and its relationship to Canadian social and political values concentrate on content to the exclusion of form. These discussions fail to take into account the degree to which, at a certain base or structural level, these values are not entirely distinct from a capitalist modernity chiefly expressed in American society.

It is still important to consider the content of Canadian cultural forms, even if such an emphasis has led to an insistence on the production of a narrow, overdetermined definition of "Canadianness," especially in film and television production (Rukszto). It is equally important, however, to consider the forms themselves. It is probably no longer very useful – empirically or conceptually – to think about any of the products of Canadian culture as somehow different in kind – again, different *formally* – from those created by American cultural industries. Are certain kinds of artistic or literary productions excluded from this general rule? This seems questionable. Critics have challenged the idea repeatedly over the past century. Michael Denning has suggested that "all culture is mass culture under capitalism" and that "there is no mass culture *out there*; it is the very element all breathe" (258, 267).[7] Whatever else it might be, the fact that our culture is "Canadian" does not make it immune from capitalism or from capitalism's general regime of the commodification of culture.

In Canada, we tend to view the nation as that which alone can make culture "cultural," in the way Rabinovitch defines the term, and which can also produce a culture that is not linked to capitalist rationality in any way. There is indeed a sense in most versions of cultural nationalism (as reflected earlier in Barbara Godard's comments) that genuine culture and art can only be produced outside the market, which is why only the nation-state can secure and ensure the production of culture in Canada. But when the nation – both as a theoretical concept and as a nation-state that creates cultural policies – marks the boundary between what might be described as *cultural use value* and *cultural exchange value*, great misunderstandings about the role of culture and the nation inevitably arise. After all, what would we really lose by losing sense of our

Canadian magazines? In some cases, very little: *Flare* would be no great loss. If *Maclean's* disappeared, we might end up with less news from Moose Jaw, which would be a shame, and there would certainly be fewer jobs for Canadians in the magazine industry, which is also a loss. But I do not think the disappearance of *Maclean's* would mean the loss of some essential cultural component we could not do without. Or rather: what we sometimes take as culture – those political and social values we might want to fight for, which stand in opposition to the general regime of commodification and the erosion of social programmes – are not tied to magazines in particular or other forms of mass culture generally. Indeed, the association of these values with culture might obscure the real things that need to be articulated and struggled over, especially now.

I do not mean to suggest there should be no governmental cultural policies or that the government should not invest in cultural production in Canada. Government investment is essential, not to bolster an ultimately exclusionary national culture that we would be lost without, but because culture is a sector of the economy that is threatened by the more favourable economies of scale possessed by our southern neighbours. If we view the question as an economic rather than a cultural issue, we change the terms of the debate. For example, cultural producers will no longer be expected to justify themselves in terms of their contribution to some greater idea of Canadian culture. And, given the global market for the creation of cultural "content" for export, such an argument is more likely to catch the attention of governments that are committed to the notion of national culture in documents but not in realized policies.

Nor am I suggesting that cultural politics are subordinate to "real" politics. In her defence of a left politics that is also a cultural politics, Judith Butler points to the recent disturbing recourse among thinkers on the left as much as on the right to "an apparently stable distinction between material and cultural life [that] is clearly the resurgence of a theoretical anachronism, one that discounts the contributions to Marxist theory since Althusser's displacement of the base-superstructure model, as well as various forms of cultural materialism – for instance, Raymond Williams, Stuart Hall, Gayatri Chakravorty Spivak" (36). Butler is right: an attempt to make a distinction between material and cultural life is problematic. With respect to *national* culture, however, an emphasis on the defence of culture reproduces an ideological distinctions between material and cultural life at the same time it claims to be breaking it down. The defence of culture in Canada is premised on culture's intimate connection to the material realities of social life and economics. The connection certainly exists, though it is different than what we usually imagine. By emphasizing the importance of culture to Canadian material life, we tend to produce a vision of culture that is idealized and which passes over Canadian culture's modern, capitalist, commercial character. So while we should not abandon cultural politics for the supposed pragmatism of "real" politics – an argument made by Todd Gitlin and Richard Rorty in the American context – we need to understand more thoroughly the exact nature of the politics articulated by our claims on behalf of national culture.

Cultural nationalism desires a space in which culture cannot be so easily reduced to its contemporary commodity status. The ultimate goal of a national culture (or so it seems) is to create a culture distinguished by its lack of economic instrumentality – in other words, by its distance from the market, what Pierre Bourdieu characterizes as its "cynical subordination to demand" (*Rules* 142). Why, however, is the achievement of this goal linked to the space of the nation? It is one thing to argue for the necessity and importance of *national* culture and another to suggest that there is an absolute value to having a culture that is not determined by the dictates of the market. In the Canadian situation, the two arguments have been collapsed into one, creating false problems and false demands. It is not really a national culture we need or desire. As long as we articulate our desires for a *different* form of culture as a *national* form of culture, our political struggle will seem futile in the face of a globalization that sweeps over all established national and cultural boundaries. The fact of globalization should show us that the struggle we have imagined as a *national* one is an *international* one: culture globally shares a common enemy, which in Canada long ago appeared in the guise of American popular culture. Our enemy is contemporary neoliberalism, an order that "erects into defining standards for all practices, and thus into ideal rules, the regularities of the economic world abandoned to its own logic: the law of the market, the law of the strongest" (Bourdieu, "Reasoned" 125). The success of global neoliberalism is premised on its ability to make its logic unassailable and unquestionable by connecting it to progress, reason and science in a way that has relegated "progressive thought and action to archaic status." (125). Zygmunt Bauman recently suggested that we are living through a period in which "the 'public' has been emptied of its own separate content; it has been left with no agenda of its own – it is now but an agglomeration of private troubles, worries and problems" (65). Instead of worrying about what might happen to Canadian culture in the era of globalization, we should focus on the recovery of our sense of the public, which decades of neoliberalism has dissolved. Combating neoliberalism will require a collective international effort. It will require the excavation of desires that lay buried in cultural nationalism. We must bring these desires to the fore, reframe them as political demands for a culture and a way of life in which everything has not been reduced to the laws of the market. This will mean the end of *national culture* as we think of it now. It does not mean the end of the political struggle associated with cultural nationalism. We must clarify our goals and decide where to direct our energies.

In the rulings I described at the beginning of this paper, what is at issue is not the preservation of national sovereignty but the political and social values connected with cultural decision-making. Canada's relationship to neoliberal capitalism remains conflicted. On the one hand, the Canadian government has willingly entered into agreements such as the GATT and the North American Free Trade Agreement, which implies an acceptance of a reigning global neoliberal order defined by "policies and processes whereby a relative handful of private interests are permitted to control as much as possible of social life in order to maximize their personal profit" (McChesney 1). On the other hand, the reaction to Bill C-55 suggests discomfort with the acceptance of the neoliberal order. To describe this discomfort as "cultural" ultimately confuses things, making it seem as if the two rulings (one about magazines, the other about cars) are about different things, when they are about the same thing: the kind of world we want. Are Canadians committed to the values and logic of the free market? Or does the free market challenge social policies and programmes that are the result of a different vision of the ends of society and government? One way to answer this question is to reframe it by placing both sides of it on the same register, that is, to point out that the auto pact is as much an issue of culture as magazines, even if autos do not fall under the domain of the Heritage ministry. How can this be? We must recognize "that economics itself is a discourse, that the economy is always articulated, in complex ways, by cultural practices" (Grossberg 17). Thus cultural practices are important sites of struggle and resistance. The reverse is also true – cultural practices are articulated by and through the economy. In this context, the willingness of the federal government to allow the auto pact to expire does not reflect only the current success of the auto industry in Canada: it also points to a burgeoning acceptance of the culture of neoliberalism; the concerted defence of culture, narrowly defined, often obscures and elides that acceptance.

Notes

1. The nation continues to be a force in global politics and economics, if perhaps in a different way than before. For instance, if there now exists a "whole series of global juridico-economic bodies, such as GATT [General Agreement on Tariffs and Trade], the World Trade Organization, the World Bank, and the IMF [International Monetary Fund]" (Hardt and Negri 336), it is only because nation-states actively established them. The power of these bodies comes from the willingness of nation-states to apply appropriate moral, legal, economic and military pressure on other nation-states.

2. Without exception, policy documents on the importance of Canadian culture stress its expanding role in the Canadian economy. See, for instance, Canada Heritage, *The Road to Success: Report of the Feature Film Advisory Committee* (Hull: Minister of Public Works and Government Services, 1999) and The Cultural Industries Sectoral Advisory Group of International Trade, *New Strategies for Culture and Trade: Canadian Culture in a Global World* (Available at: http://www.infoexport.gc.ca/trade-culture/menu-e.asp).

3. For an exceptional overview of the Canadian government's reaction to *SI Canada* and a detailed examination of the successive stages of the WTO assessment of the dispute between Canada and the United States, see Magder.

4. *The Globe and Mail* business columnist Eric Reguly suggested that "Monday, Jan. 10, will probably go down in history as the day the Canadian culture died" (B9). On this day, America Online, the world's biggest Internet company, announced its $160 billion (US) takeover of Time Warner, the world's biggest media company. The implication is that Canadian culture cannot possibly withstand the broadcasting and narrowcasting power of such a behemoth of American culture.

5. The general theme of Rabinovitch's definition of culture is commonly found in government documents, as well. In general, public policy statements treat culture in extremely idealist terms, which replicate the Romantic links between culture and nation forged by Herder and other early theorists of the nation. See, for example, the definition of culture articulated recently by Clifford Lincoln, chair of the Standing Committee on Canadian Heritage. He writes: "Perhaps this is the magic of culture: that indefinable essence and quality which permeates each of our lives in one way or another, which lifts us beyond the routine and the mundane into another world of creativity, of beauty and of visual and aural fulfilment – which defines the senses" (1). One effect of making culture "magical" is to make it immaterial and unaffected by politics and economics. Such apparently "natural" definitions are clearly ideological.

6. I should point out that things are not as rosy for small magazines as I suggest here. One of the important elements of Canadian magazine policy has been its provision of postal subsidies that substantially reduce their mailing costs. When these subsidies are threatened, the survival of the small magazines is also threatened.
7. Having said this, I take Susan Hegeman's point that "it is difficult to generalize about the conceptual relationship between 'culture' and totality" (56).

References

Anderson, Benedict (1991). *Imagined Communities*, Rev. ed. New York: Verso.

Bannerji, Himani (2000). *The Dark Side of the Nation: Essays in Multiculturalism, Nationalism and Gender*. Toronto: Canadian Scholars Press.

Barber, Benjamin R (1996). *Jihad vs. McWorld: How Globalism and Tribalism Are Reshaping the World*. New York: Ballantine.

Bauman, Zygmunt (1999). *In Search of Politics*. Stanford: Stanford University Press.

Benjamin, Walter (1968). *Illuminations*, trans. Harry Zohn. New York: Shocken Books.

Berland, Jody (1997). Politics after Nationalism, Culture after "Culture". *Canadian Review of American Studies* 27(3), pp. 35–50.

Bourdieu, Pierre (1996). *The Rules of Art: Genesis and Structure of the Literary Field*, trans. Susan Emanuel. Stanford: Stanford University Press.

Bourdieu, Pierre (1998). A Reasoned Utopia and Economic Fatalism. *New Left Review* 227, pp. 125–30.

Butler, Judith (1998). Merely Cultural. *New Left Review* 227, pp. 33–44.

Canada. Department of Canadian Heritage (1999). *The Road to Success: Report of the Feature Film Advisory Committee*. Ottawa: Minister of Public Works and Government Services Canada.

Canada. Department of Canadian Heritage (2000). Report of the Cultural Industries Sectoral Advisory Group of International Trade. *New Strategies for Culture and Trade: Canadian Culture in a Global World*. October 12, at http://www.infoexport.gc.ca/trade-culture/menu-e.asp

Carr, Graham (1991). Trade Liberalization and the Political Economy of Culture: An International Perspective on the FTA. *Canadian-American Public Policy* 6.

Charland, Maurice (1986). Technological Nationalism. *Canadian Journal of Political and Social Theory* 10(1–2), pp. 196–220.

Chodos, Robert, Rae Murphy & Eric Hamovitch (1993). *Canada and the Global Economy: Alternatives to the Corporate Strategy for Globalization*. Toronto: Lorimer.

Denning, Michael (1991). The End of Mass Culture. In: James Naremore & Patrick Bratlinger (eds.), *Modernity and Mass Culture*, pp. 253–68. Bloomington: Indiana University Press.

Desbarats, Peter (1995). The Special Role of Magazines in the History of Canadian Mass Media and National Development. In: Benjamin D. Singer (ed.), *Communications and Canadian Society*, pp. 72–88. Toronto: Nelson Canada.

Fraser, Graham & Borrie McKenna (1999). US plots 4-sector trade war. *The Globe and Mail*, January 12, B1.

Gitlin, Todd (1995). *The Twilight of Our Common Dreams: Why America is Wracked by Culture Wars*. New York: Metropolitan Books.

Godard, Barbara (1995). Writing on the Wall. *Border/Lines* 38–39, pp. 100–2.

Grant, George (1970). *Lament for a Nation: The Defeat of Canadian Nationalism.* Toronto: McClelland & Stewart.

Grossberg, Lawrence (1999). Speculations and Articulations of Globalization. *Polygraph* 11, pp. 11–48.

Hardt, Michael & Antonio Negri (2000). *Empire.* Cambridge: Harvard University Press.

Hegeman, Susan (1997). Imagining Totality: Rhetorics of and versus "Culture". *Common Knowledge* 6(3), pp. 51–72.

Hobsbawn, Eric (1990). *Nations and Nationalism Since 1780.* Cambridge: Cambridge University Press.

Honey, Kim (2000). The $150-million Prescription: Ottawa Is about to Hand Out Some Serious Money in a Bid to Defend Canada's Magazine Industry Against American Imports. *The Globe and Mail*, October 4, R3.

Laxer, James (1993). *False God: How the Globalization Myth Has Impoverished Canada.* Toronto: Lester Publishing Ltd.

Lincoln, Clifford (1999). "Foreword" to *A Sense of Place – A Sense of Being: The Evolving Role of the Federal Government in Support of Culture in Canada*, pp. 1–2. Ninth Report. Standing Committee on Canadian Heritage, June.

McChesney, Robert (2000). Introduction to *Profit Over People*, by Noam Chomsky, pp. 7–16. New York: Seven Stories Press.

Magder, Ted (1998). Franchising the Candy Store: Split-Run Magazines and a Now International Regime for Trade in Culture. *Canadian-American Public Policy* 34, pp. 1–72.

McKinnon, Mark & Greg Keenan (2000). Historic Auto Pact to Die in February: US Big Three Tariff Exemption Will End. *The Globe and Mail*, October 5, B1, 9.

McLuhan, Marshall. Epilogue: Canada as Counter-Environment. *The Global Village: Transformations in World Life and Media in the 21st Century*, pp. 147–66. New York: Oxford University Press.

Milner, Brian & Graham Fraser (1999). US Magazines Poised to Pounce. *The Globe and Mail*, May 27, B1.

Morton, Peter (1999). US Targets Steel, Textiles as Trade Rift Intensifies. *National Post*, January 12, Al, 2.

Ohmann, Richard (1996). *Selling Culture: Magazines, Markets, and Class at the Turn of the Century.* New York: Verso.

Purvis, Andrew (1999). Look Who's on the Marquee: Canadian Art And Artists Are Beating a Path to the World's Door as the Country Becomes a Powerhouse of Cultural Exports. *Time* (Canada), August 9, pp. 49–57.

Rabinovitch, Victor (1999). Method and Success in Canada's Cultural Policies. *Queen's Quarterly* 106(2), pp. 217–31.

Reguly, Eric (2000). AOL's Giant Reach Makes CRTC Superfluous. *The Globe and Mail*, January 15, B9.

Robbins, Bruce (1998). Part 1: Actually Existing Cosmopolitanism. Introduction. In: Pheng Cheah & Bruce Robbins (eds.), *Cosmopolitics: Thinking and Feeling Beyond the Nation*, pp. 1–19. Minneapolis: University of Minnesota Press.

Rorty, Richard (1998). *Achieving Our Country: Leftist Thought in 20th-Century America.* Cambridge: Harvard University Press.

Rukszto, Katarzyna (1997). Up for Sale: The Commodification of Canadian Culture. *Fuse Magazine* 20(4), pp. 7–11.

Scoffield, Heather (1999). WTO Sets Auto Pact Deadline. *The Globe and Mail*, October 4, B1.

Vipond, Mary (1989). *The Mass Media in Canada*, Revised edition. Toronto: Lorimer.

Walton, Dawn (1999). Buoyant Auto Industry Shifting up a Gear, *The Globe and Mail*, June 15, B16.

World Trade Organization (1997). Canada–Certain Measures Concerning Periodicals. Dispute Resolution Panel Report WT/DS31/R, March 14.

Zemans, Joyce (1997). Canadian Cultural Policy in a Globalized World. *Canadian Review of American Studies* 27(3), pp. 111–25.

II

Place, Space, Geography

6

Metaphors to Live By: Landscapes as Systems of Social Reproduction

Don Mitchell*

This chapter examines the ways that we apprehend, take meaning from, and ultimately consume in and through landscapes. It also explores the reason why apprehending and taking meaning from landscapes is socially important. Richard Peet (1996: 23) puts the issue this way:

> Because landscapes are partly natural, their signs are frequently long lasting, and because landscapes are the homes of women and men, they are particularly suited to the ideological task of framing the social imaginary. By recreating landscapes, filling them with signs carrying ideological messages, images are formed of past and future "realities," patterns of meaning created and changed, and, thereby, control exerted over the everyday behavior of the people who call these manufactured places their natural, historic homes; this applies to people of all classes.

"Framing the social imaginary": by this Peet means that landscapes, through the accretion of meanings over time, come to define how people think about a place (and how they think about their place in that place), how they behave in it, and how they expect others to behave. The landscape is, in this sense, "read" by its inhabitants and visitors, so as to divine the messages encoded in its signs.

For some, the fact that landscapes are meaning*ful* in this sense implies that they give off to the world a "spirit" or a "sense of place" – a *genius loci*. Such a *genius loci*, as Loukaki (1997) shows in the case of the Sacred Rock of the Acropolis in Athens, is tightly bound up in the creation, perpetuation, and transformation of myth, while myth itself is made "permanent" – or at least less vulnerable to change – by its association with landscapes. As Loukaki (1997: 325) cautions, however, it is equally clear that there is never a "single universal, unchanging truth or authenticity of *genius loci*" in any place. The key methodological issue then – and one of paramount importance for those of us who want to understand the relationship between the production of culture and the production of landscape – is the ways in which the intentional meanings of the builders of a landscape clash with the myriad other meanings that may be attributed to or derived

*Pp. 120–44 from D. Mitchell, *Culture Geography: A Critical Introduction* (Malden, MA: Blackwell). © 2000 by Donald Mitchell. Reprinted with permission from Blackwell Publishing.

from a landscape by its "users," Given that meaning is always a product of struggle between "producers" and various "users" of landscape, it should be apparent, however, that just because landscapes can take on multiple meanings, that does not thereby mean that all meanings are created equal. For in any contest over meaning, the key issue will always be one of power. It makes little sense to argue, as Peter Jackson (1989: 177) has done, that for any landscape, "there are potentially as many ways of seeing as there are eyes to see," because, in a world riven by relations of power, that potentiality will simply never be fulfilled. The objective is to see precisely how such potentiality is always and everywhere thwarted (and therefore how meaning is controlled).

Metaphors to Live By

The degree to which landscapes are *made* (by hands and minds) and represented (by particular people and classes, and through the accretion of history and myth) indicates that landscapes are in some very important senses "authored." Hence landscape can be understood to be a kind of text (see Meinig 1979; Duncan 1990; Barnes and Duncan 1992; Duncan and Ley 1993). In fact, it seems clear that Carl Sauer himself labored under this metaphor, if subconsciously, in his landscape methodology. For what was his objective but to "read" the landscape for evidence of the culture that made it? If the reading metaphor was implicit in Sauer, it was made explicit in the 1970s by, among others, geographer Peirce Lewis (1979), in his article "Axioms for Reading the Landscape." Lewis (1979: 12) argued that a landscape was in many regards like a book – but a particular kind of book. "Our human landscape is our unwitting autobiography, reflecting our tastes, our values, our aspirations, and even our fears, in tangible form." Yet, for all his interest in how to read a landscape, and in what the book of landscape represents, Lewis seemed little interested in problematizing how landscapes were, so to speak, written. Rather, the process seems in Lewis's telling to be somewhat akin to "automatic writing," wherein the pen of the author is guided by some mysterious force larger than the author her- or himself. The author is merely a channel or medium. Thus the key word, "unwitting." Moreover, what was written was itself a reflection of a unitary consensus culture, as far as Lewis was concerned. He was quite explicit: "culture is a *whole* – a unity – like an iceberg with many tips protruding above the surface of the water. Each tip looks like a different iceberg; but each is in fact part of the same object" (Lewis 1979: 19). As we have already seen, such a conception of culture is hardly realistic – a point which Lewis (1979: 12) recognizes in a roundabout way when he concedes that reading a landscape is far harder than reading a book; it is more like reading a "book whose pages are missing, torn, and smudged; a book whose copy has been edited and re-edited by people with illegible handwriting." "Culture," obviously, is a product and process of struggle. How else do the "pages" of the landscape get torn and rewritten?

A unitary notion of culture as an "author" – and hence such an easily reconstructed *single* meaning of landscape such as Lewis posits – is too simplistic. James Duncan and Nancy Duncan (1988), therefore, have sought over the past decade to problematize this notion of reading. Their argument is that the text metaphor needs to be deepened.

James Duncan (1990: 4–5) has argued, for example, that by "accepting landscapes as texts, broadly defined, we are led to examine a number of issues which have hitherto been ignored" in geography. First, we need to examine "how landscapes encode information." Second, one must understand, through an analysis of relations of power, *how* differently situated people are *able* to read landscapes. This is no easy task, since "in order to answer these questions we must go beyond a consideration of the formal semiotic or tropological properties of the landscape as a system of communication, to see the landscape in relation to both structured political practices and individual intentions."

Drawing on the post-structuralist theories of Roland Barthes (among others), Duncan and Duncan (1988) argue that reading a landscape is the province both of "experts" (like themselves) and of ordinary people as they go about their everyday lives. The text metaphor is thus not something to be approached only intellectually. Rather "reading the landscape" is something we all *do*, day in and day out. Writing with Trevor Barnes, James Duncan argues that texts "should . . . be seen as signifying practices that are read, not passively, but as it were, rewritten as they are read." More pointedly, "this expanded notion of texts . . . sees them as constitutive of reality rather than mimicking it – in other words, as cultural practices of signification rather than as referential duplications" (Barnes and Duncan 1992: 5). This notion rides on the idea of "intertextuality," an idea that "implies that the context of any text is other texts" (Duncan 1990: 4). These "other texts" in turn include everything from texts as we normally understand the term (books, legal documents, scripts, etc.) on through to "other cultural productions such as paintings, maps and landscapes, as well as social, economic and political institutions" (Barnes and Duncan 1992: 5). Everything, then, is a text, ready to be decoded, read for meanings, and rewritten in our everyday cultural practices. We are all cultural "readers" – a way of understanding landscape considerably more "active" and anarchic than that presented, for example, in my discussion of Johnstown and the controversies over establishing *the* proper meaning for its landscape.

By employing the text metaphor, geographers such as Duncan and Duncan place themselves right at the center of some of the strongest currents of contemporary cultural studies, currents that argue it is impossible to ascribe to a text anything like a stable and universal meaning. For many cultural theorists it is simply the case that we live in a world of texts, a world defined by a degree of "intertextuality," where, because any text of which we are a part necessarily refers to other texts, and because we make our way in the world by reading, often quite intelligently, sometimes rather subversively, it is both unwise and impossible to seek to discover "a" or "the" meaning of a text. The text metaphor is important, therefore, because it suggests that hegemonic productions – including landscapes – are always undermined by alternative individual and collective readings. In fact, it is the very act of *reading* that *authors*. Reading itself is the productive force of meaning. The "meanings" implicit in a cultural text like landscape are therefore "multiple and positional, . . . there are many ways of seeing and reading the landscape" (McDowell 1994: 163). Landscape is a system of *signs*, signs that themselves may very well be unstable and open to revision.

Yet the discussions of Johnstown, Chinatown, Sacré-Coeur, and the politics of representation in the previous chapter indicate some shortcomings of this metaphor.

Among other things, landscape, by its very representational nature, is designed (on the ground *and* in other media, like painting) to present a single *true* perspective, and even if this is ideological and therefore partial and open to alternative readings, it is nonetheless the case that meaning is backed up by powers that cannot and should not be reduced to the status of "text." The power of property ownership, supported by the police and the military power of the state, which is so central to the construction of landscapes, is hardly something that can be adequately undermined by subversive readings and mere meaning-construction (no matter how important these practices may in fact be). What is landscape, after all, but an *imposition* of power: power made concrete in the bricks, mortar, stones, tar, and lumber of a city, town, village, or rural setting – or on canvas or photo-stock.

We may, in fact, read landscapes all the time, and we may certainly construct all manner of meanings out of them. But unless we are willing to ignore both the ideological nature and material power of "culture" and landscape, such readings make a weak foundation for political action. While it "is possible, indeed normal, to decipher or decode space," as the French Marxist Henri Lefebvre (1991: 160) argues, the further assumption that *because* we decode, all there *is to do* is to decode, "cheerfully commandeer[s] social space and physical space and reduce[s] them to an epistemological (mental) space" (1991: 61). That is, such a move transfers the weight of social action from material practice to mental exercise. It furthers the erasure of the non-textual, non-linguistic practices at work in making a landscape. Landscapes, as with other nonverbal practices and activities, are "characterized by a spatiality that is in fact irreducible to the mental realm," according to Lefebvre (1991: 62). Further, "to underestimate, ignore and diminish space amounts to the overestimation of texts, written matter, and writing systems, along with the readable and the visible, to the point of assigning to these a monopoly on intelligibility." In short, the textual metaphor runs the risk of reducing the lived and experienced to merely the thought.

In partial recognition of this problem geographers have sought other metaphors which perhaps better explain the lived nature of landscapes. Unlike the metaphor of text, the metaphors of "theater," "stage," or "set" within and upon which the spectacle of life plays out – as tragedy, to be sure, but just as much as comedy – suggests a realm of action and social practice that is more than just the mental exercise of reading. Most simply, "landscapes provide a stage for human action, and, like a theatre set, their own part in the drama varies from that of an entirely discreet unobserved presence to playing a highly visible role in the performance" (Cosgrove 1993: 1). In that sense, the metaphor of theater suggests a further metaphor: that landscapes are live stages for the spectacle of life. Theories of spectacle are gaining prominence in geography and other cultural studies fields (they all rely to one degree or another on Guy Debord's [1994] aphoristic manifesto, *The Society of the Spectacle*). Like landscape, "spectacle" was an important term in Renaissance Europe, where it "could mean simple display, but also something to wonder at, thus touching mystery. It could take on the sense of a mirror through which truth which cannot be stated directly may be seen reflected and perhaps distorted, and it could mean an aid to vision as in the still-uncommon corrective lenses" (Daniels and Cosgrove 1993: 58). The important point, however, is that a spectacle is something experienced, acted in, lived. But it is a lived relation of a special sort. The very notion of "spectacle" implies something orchestrated, something designed. So if we live out the spectacle of landscape then it is certainly quite plausible that we do so under someone else's direction. This same limitation plagues the theater metaphor too. While we all may be actors in the drama of landscape, it is also often the case that someone else writes the script. Our movements, our experiences, perhaps even our emotions, are to one degree or another scripted for us by and in the landscape.

Yet the very purpose of "landscape" – as theater, as spectacle, as a text in which we engage in our "own" readings – is often precisely to mask the relationships of control that govern the production of landscape (and, to continue the theater metaphor, the productions taking place in the landscape). How many of us actively seek out the conditions under which the shopping district or mall we frequent was made and is maintained? How often do we wonder about the conditions under which toil the carpenters, janitors, bookkeepers (and all the rest who make that landscape possible)? The "lived-relations" of landscape that the spectacle metaphor points to, while not to be minimized in their own right, are also part of a process that maintains the *illusion* of landscapes as seamless zones of pleasure: pleasure in the view that landscape affords, and pleasure in the stage for activity that it provides. The point, then, is not at all that the metaphors of text, theater, and spectacle are somehow wrong – indeed, it can be quite rightly claimed that these are metaphors we literally live by – rather, it is to understand the limitations of those metaphors, and to see how any metaphor that helps us understand some aspect of the world hides as much as it reveals. Landscapes, through their aesthetization of space, may very well be texts, and they may often be texts that revel in depictions of the good life, but they are also, always, physical concretizations of power, power that the landscape itself often works quite hard to fetishize as something else altogether. Nowhere is this clearer than in the way that landscape becomes a stage – and perhaps also a text – for the construction and maintenance of unequal relations of gender.

Gendered Landscapes

Obviously, it is not just nationalism or class relations that are propped up through landscape representation. So too are relations of gender, sexuality, and race represented, reinforced, euphemized, fetishized, and naturalized in the landscape. To focus just on gender, and as Janice Monk (1992: 124–6) shows, nearly every monument to be found in the public landscape codifies and reinforces – often quite subtly, sometimes rather blatantly – the masculinist, patriarchal power that tries so hard to determine the shape and structure of the world. At one level, women are strikingly absent from public monuments and memorials. In Australia, for example, of more than 2,000 memorials to participation in World War I, only three (one small local memorial and two major memorials in Sydney and Melbourne) depict any women at all. In the two large memorials, "you have to look hard" to see women, according to Ken Inglis who made a study of them (cited in Monk 1992: 125). In Washington, DC, as late as 1986 only four women were portrayed in all the outdoor monuments (Gross and Rojas 1986, cited in Monk 1992: 124).

At a different level, when women *are* depicted in statues, monuments, or representational painting they are often highly idealized – and unlikely. Think of the numerous French images of fighting "maidens," breasts bared, as they defend the barricades in Paris (cf. Wilson 1991). "[E]ven if executed with a high degree of naturalism," according to Marina Warner (1985: 28, quoted in Monk 1992: 126), "female figures representing an ideal or abstraction hardly ever interact with real, individual women. Devices distinguish them: improbable nudity, heroic scale, wings, unlikely attributes." So while depictions of women at one level are absolutely unrealistic – fighting bare-breasted or sprouting wings at critical moments are not everyday behaviors – they are at another quite realistic: they accurately represent societal, clearly masculinist *ideals* and *ideologies* about women, ideals and ideologies designed precisely to keep women in their place.

And what kind of place is that? Feminist scholars have shown that built landscapes – the landscapes of homes, parks, shopping districts, and public squares – are remarkable in their desire to confine and control women. Take, as only one example, the development of the suburban landscape. To start with, few better examples of how landscapes are always a mix of representation and built form can be found, as nearly every history of suburbia points out. But what does this mix of representation and form *mean*? And what does it *do*?

From the outset, suburbia *as a landscape* is inseparable from suburbia *as a gendered space*. In his insightful history, Robert Fishman (1987) traces the suburban residential landscape to a desire for the separation of work and home that developed among the bourgeoisie of eighteenth-century London. This desire was not innocent of gender. Quite the contrary, it was closely wrapped up in changing conceptions of femininity and masculinity. In pre-modern London – a city so closely packed it is now almost inconceivable (from center to open fields was about a one-half mile radius) – and even after London began to greatly expand in the seventeenth century, rich and poor lived cheek-by-jowl, often in the same buildings. Work was rarely separated from residence: the "identity of work and home was the basic building block of eighteenth century urban ecology" (p. 21). To live among the poor meant no loss of status to a member of the bourgeois elite. Indeed, it was often necessary to the successful prosecution of business. The degree to which homes were businesses, and businesses homes, was reflected in a quite different conception of the "family" than we in the suburbanized West have grown accustomed to (and to which our politicians pay no end of homage). Instead, "[e]ven for the wealthy elite of merchants and bankers, the family was not simply (or perhaps even primarily) an emotional unit. It was at least equally an economic unit. . . . Virtually every aspect of family life was permeated by the requirements of the business" (p. 29). The implications for "womanhood" and femininity, as for "manhood" and masculinity, were profound. The importance of the family as an economic unit, according to Fishman (p. 29), was "most clearly seen in the active role played by women in London commercial life. A wife's daily assistance in the shop was vital for smaller businesses, and even the most opulent merchants were careful to give their wives a role sufficiently prominent that they could participate in and understand the source of their income." Such a family/household/business structure was evident in the landscape itself. "The typical merchant's townhouse . . . was surprisingly open to the city. Commercial life flowed freely, so that virtually every room had some business as well as familial function" (p. 29).

Compare that with the common descriptions of women's lot in contemporary suburbia. As early as 1869, middle-class women – and feminist activists – such as Catherine Beecher and Harriet Beecher Stowe argued that women's role in society was as a "spiritual center and efficient manager of the home, which was portrayed as a retreat from the world for the working husband and the centre of domestic harmony" (Monk 1992: 128; see also Hayden 1981, 1984; MacKenzie and Rose 1983; McDowell 1983). This "cult of domesticity" as it has come to be called, defined middle-class femininity at least through the 1950s in the United States, and similar structures of womanhood are still often venerated through some of the characters of popular soap operas in Australia, Britain, and North America. Ideally, modern suburban women guarded the private space of hearth and home, providing a refuge from the public sphere. In all practicality such a role, as it was concretized in the landscapes of suburbia, has meant a spatial isolation of women. It has also implied an incredible "privatization" of space, as various functions of family reproduction – cooking, cleaning, childcare – are incorporated into the interior of the house, and communal strategies for such reproduction are not just downplayed, but actively designed out. They have not remained a live option for most women (or men, for that matter). The landscape of suburbia both reflects and reinforces the atomized "nuclear" family, seeking to make each family fully independent from the society around it. Suburbia thus encourages a strange form of individualism, one that is predicated on isolation – and particularly the isolation of women.

How did we get from the relatively "open" eighteenth-century bourgeois London where women were an essential (if not necessarily equal) part of the life of business, to the nineteenth- and twentieth-century suburbs where women are essentially cloistered in a landscape that works hard to preclude their involvement in anything but the business of familial reproduction? Fishman (p. 35) traces this transition to the development of a new kind of "closed family [that] contradicted the basic principles of the eighteenth century city." Key to the development of the new family (and of women's role in it) was a Protestant sect within the London merchant bourgeoisie known as the Evangelicals. "Members of the Established church but uncertain of its efficacy, the Evangelicals taught that the most secure path to salvation was the beneficent influence of a truly Christian family. Anything that strengthened the emotional ties within the family was therefore holy; anything that weakened the family and its ability to foster true morality was anathema" (p. 35). Hence, the traditional, mixed, urban household of the eighteenth-century London bourgeoisie was seen by Evangelicals as detrimental to morality. A new landscape needed to be created that nurtured and protected both the family and what Evangelical writer William Wilberforce called "the reformation of manners."

Such a landscape, however, was predicated on a particular ideology concerning women, an ideology that set Evangelicals apart from many others in the English middle class of the time. "On the one hand, they gave to women the highest possible role in their system of values: the principal guardian of the Christian home. On the other, they fanatically opposed any role for women outside that sphere" (p. 35). For Wilberforce, "the more favorable disposition to Religion in the female sex" seemed designed "to afford to the married man the means of rendering an active share in the business of life more compatible . . . with the liveliest devotional feelings; that when the husband should return to his family, worn and harassed by worldly cares or professional labors, the wife habitually preserving a warmer and more unimpaired spirit of devotion, than is perhaps consistent with being immersed in the bustle of life, might revive his languid piety" (quoted on p. 36). The city was ill-suited to such an ideology of womanhood, and hence "this contradiction between the city and the Evangelical ideal of the family provided the final impetus for the unprecedented separation of the citizen's home from the city that is the essence of the suburban ideal" (p. 38).

But for this ideal to take hold, Evangelicals (and other like-minded potential suburbanites) had to wed their ideology to a landscape form. For this they drew on the ideal of the country park and manor, with its careful manufacture of aesthetically pleasing "natural" vistas. Fishman traces the development of such a suburban, picturesque landscape ideal as it evolved in the Evangelical settlement of Clapham, about five miles from the center of London. In Clapham, houses were organized around a central common, which the settlers had remade into a "delightful pleasure ground" through careful planting of trees and shrubs in what was considered to be a "naturalistic" style (p. 55). For those who built houses at a distance from the common, the goal was to continue the landscaping style on their own land. "Contemporary drawings" of Clapham, Fishman (p. 55) reports, "show wide tree shaded lawns sweeping up from the common to Palladian houses behind which large gardens and orchards were planted. Each house added its own well maintained greenery to the whole" (see also Cosgrove 1993). Here then is suburbia as we have come to know it: "The true suburban landscape, as seen at Clapham, is a balance of the public and the private. Each property is private, but each contributes to the total landscape of *houses in a park*" (p. 55, original emphasis). But this was a certain kind of public–private compromise. As important as the look of the landscape was its function. The houses at Clapham literally "interiorized" social life and turned it in on the family itself. "The library [in the house] and the garden outside were the Evangelical substitute for all the plays, balls, visits, and coffee houses of London. Here the closed domesticated nuclear family became a reality" (p. 56).

For a large variety of reasons, which Fishman explores in great detail, the landscape innovations signaled by Clapham (which, as he points out, were not unique, but rather exemplary), proved enormously popular – and financially successful. Such a suburbanization not only responded to changing ideologies of the family, but also served a pent-up demand for housing. Just as importantly, the development of suburbia provided an outlet for the investment of newly won capital that the middle classes had at their disposal. Hence, right from the beginning, the suburban landscape was commodified, and a central location for speculation (pp. 62–72). Once the ideal had been established, and once the family had been remade to fit the landscape, even as the landscape was remade to fit the new family, suburbia exploded, becoming, as it were, the *only* option for respectable middle-class life. And this respectability, as we have seen, was predicated on the sequestering of women in the domestic sphere. Definitions of femininity – and of masculinity – were predicated on finding a spatial form that policed the divide between public and private spheres. If landscape is a stage, then it is a stage very clearly structured to move the drama of life in particular – and not at all infinite – directions.

Landscape as Expectation: Aesthetics, Power, and the Good Life

Shopping for signs: the cultural geography of the mall

Suburban landscapes mix public and private spaces in particular and peculiar ways. They create a stage on which gender is performed in a never-ending production. Likewise, shopping malls use peculiar mixes of public and private to create a different sort of stage, a stage for not only the production of identity, but its consumption too. Malls are theaters in which the spectacle of everyday life is given a new and glamorous cast (as any 14-year-old can tell you). But perhaps the text metaphor is the best one for understanding just what a mall is and what it does. Malls are landscapes that are all about signs: they are clearly *meant* to be read. As landscapes, the meaning of malls (and similar spaces like festival marketplaces) seems particularly obvious. Their job is to provide us with an exquisite sense of expectation – the expectation that through the magic of money (or a decent credit line on the Visa), one can transform one's self into anything one pleases, the expectation that one can be as glamorous and desirable as the wares on display and the people who pass by in the corridors. Malls aren't just *about* signs; they are elaborate *systems* of signs. They *are* texts. But as Lefebvre (1991: 160) has noted, "certain spaces produced by capitalist promoters [like many contemporary landscapes] are so laden with signs – signs of well-being, happiness, style, art, riches, power, prosperity, and so on – that not only is their primary meaning (that of profitability) effaced but meaning disappears altogether." What does he mean by this? How can a place, built to be read, in the end be so completely illegible?

When the Park Meadows Mall opened 15 miles south of Denver, Colorado, at the beginning of September, 1996, the media hype could not have been greater. Each of the local television stations sent reporters and camera crews to cover the opening – an opening that they themselves fervently advertised on the news shows for months before the event itself. The week of the opening, newspapers published special supplements, replete with maps of the mall (both interior and exterior) and special features on the wares on display in many of the stores. These features, however, were merely a culmination. A search of electronic indexes by the Denver weekly *Westword* found that between January 1 and September 1, 1996, Colorado newspapers had run 407 stories with the word "Park Meadows" in them ("Off Limits" 1996). The stories in print and electronic media dilated on the size of the mall and its success in attracting top-name "anchor" stores like Dillards and the swank Nordstroms, and they described in breathless detail the design of the interior spaces – spaces that made this, as the corporate owner of the mall (the Hahn Company) avers, not a mall at all, but a "retail resort" Such hype, however, is not at all surprising. Now, at a time when the commodity is everything, and when corporations like Nike and Benetton can so easily make their advertising *news*, it would have been far more surprising if there had been little or no media hype, if the talking heads of the media had *not* rushed to the scene of the opening, if the supposed purveyors of the news had *not* so readily acquiesced in the production of spectacle. If you lived in Colorado or Eastern Wyoming, you did not need to visit the mall to know what it is like, to understand what it is supposed to mean, and why it is so special.

I went anyway. I went to see what a "retail resort" could possibly be. As the press made so clear in its breathless reportage, the interior of the mall is fitted out to look like a ski resort. There are lodgepole pines and Douglas firs studding the hallways, peeled wood beams seem to support the catwalks of the second floor and the roof, and instead of a "food court," the "retail resort" has a "dining hall" meant to resemble the rustic cafeterias of the ski lodges a hundred miles to the west (even so, this dining hall is replete with all the fast-food franchises you would expect: beyond design features, there are no surprises in this mall). In the first months after the mall opened, the temporary main entrance on the west side was through the Eddie Bauer store. Eddie Bauer is one of those stores that sells adventure and travel as fashion, showing how you can be an intrepid, imperialist explorer without ever leaving your range rover (except to step into the mall) – and still look good. The rugged outdoors motif of the mall hits you with a vengeance the moment you enter the Park Meadows Retail Resort.

Once out of Eddie Bauer, and onto the main floor, you are confronted with a miniaturized (but still two-story) mock-up of some of the sandstone rocks that comprise the Red Rocks Amphitheater, 30 miles to the northwest. Red Rocks Amphitheater was constructed to take advantage of spectacular natural rock formations by the Works Progress Administration during the Depression. It is a quite spectacular site, with the stage nestled at the base of massive standing, red stones and the lights of Denver twinkling below. The Park Meadows version was built, by contrast, to specifications laid down by a California design firm and by contractors pouring a specially formulated concrete over a chicken-wire frame. Bronze and pewter squirrels and beavers (rock-climbing beavers!) have been bolted or glued to the surface, and the whole thing, deciding that honoring Red Rocks was not enough, has been turned into a fountain with water cascading down two sides. Every twenty minutes or so, the water turns off, only to be replaced by steam, whether to represent some sort of eruption (which in a presumptively sandstone environment would be fascinating), or just a gee-whiz sort of event for kids and their parents is hard to determine.

This "Red Rocks" fountain occupies the center atrium of the mall. The catwalks of the second floor skirt around it, and indeed provide places for some of the best people-watching in the mall. The facing of these catwalks, about three feet thick, makes a space for a set of murals depicting the mountain and plains scenery of Colorado. Highly stylized paintings represent each of the lines of Katherine Lee Bates's famous anthem "America the Beautiful" (the myth holds that she wrote this on the summit of Colorado's Pike's Peak in 1893, a year of exceptional depression and labor unrest):

> Oh! Beautiful, For spacious skies
> For amber waves of grain
> For purple mountain majesties
> Above the fruited plain.
> America! America!
> God shed His grace on thee
> And crown thy good with brotherhood
> From sea to shining sea.

The central idea – God shed His grace on thee – is centered directly over the main hallway connecting the swank anchor department store Nordstroms to the almost equally swank Dillards. It is hard to miss the meaning: my consumption, your consumption – it is all *ordained*. The signs couldn't be clearer: we have every right to *expect* such a landscape. As Americans, it is a true manifest destiny. And we can do it all in a *park*! It is all so natural!

While the designers of the mall have stuffed it so full of signs reminding us just how natural conspicuous consumption is and should be, they have done so for a reason. Jon Goss (1993; see also Crawford 1992; Hopkins 1990; Morris 1993) has subjected the semiotics of the mall to close scrutiny (as have many others engaged in geography and cultural studies). He has especially taken care to show how, and particularly why, those semiotics are *emplaced* in the space of the mall. For Goss (1993: 20), the mall represents a particularly clear example of "the commodification of reality." He acknowledges that "all human societies . . . recognize a class that mediates between the material and symbolic worlds," but that it is only in recent times that "this class can control both sides of this relation, and that they are able to persuade us that our 'self-concept' as well as social status is defined by the commodity." Moreover, to the degree that our relations are mediated through the commodity, then our relationship to each other is in some senses commodified as well – and in this we often readily acquiesce. We succumb to what Goss (1993: 20) calls the "magic of advertising" in which "the materiality of the commodity" is masked. Most particularly, through our consumption, and through the advertising – in media and in the space of the mall – that accompanies it, the "sign value" of a commodity has not only displaced the commodity's "use-value" but it "*has become* use value" (Goss 1993: 21, citing Haug 1986). Such sign values have a fascinating geography when they are put into circulation in the mall.

In the first place, malls are quite expensive to build. Developers thus engage in extensive market analysis – and special pleading before city councils and county commissions for tax-breaks – before deciding on where to locate a mall. Developers deploy "teams of market researchers, geo-demographers, accountants, asset managers, lawyers, engineers, architects, artists, interior designers, traffic analysts, security consultants, and leasing agents" long before they ever break ground (Goss 1993: 22). Once building begins, of course, numerous contractors, electricians, carpenters, landscapers, iron workers, brick-layers, painters, carpet layers, plumbers and concrete pourers must be employed and coordinated. When the mall opens, the owner-developers need to carefully manage the mix of tenants to "ensur[e] complementarity of retail and service functions" so as to attract the desired mix of consumers. Above all, management does not want to attract "those whose presence might challenge the normality of consumption" by making their working-class, poor, or racial status felt, for example (Goss 1993: 22; see also Goss 1992).

But even attention to such details of retail mix are not enough to make a mall "work." Analysis of consumers' movement patterns have shown that American shoppers typically will not walk more than 600 feet – which provides an outer limit of mall size, unless developers and designers can find a means to *fool* the shoppers into thinking they are not walking as far as they are (Goss 1993: 33; see also Garreau 1991, 117–18). The ultimate fear of mall owners is that customers will *leave*. "Our surveys show," one mall manager remarks, that "the amount of spending is related *directly* to the amount of time spent at centers. . . . *Anything* that can prolong shoppers' visits are [sic] in our best interests overall" (quoted in "Food Courts . . ." 1990, cited in Goss 1993: 22). Hence at Park Meadows – a mall that is really just one long rectangular box – the lower hallway gives the impression of sinuousness: one can never see more than 20 or 30 yards ahead, as the hallway turns slightly back and forth, obstructing long views. What one sees, dead ahead, is instead another enticing store only a few paces away. The hallway thus *seduces* shoppers down its length. Upstairs, one *can* see from one end to the other, but here the catwalks themselves divide and turn, opening to views of the halls below (and that fountain!), and forcing pedestrians to slide from one side of the hallway to the other, constantly bumping into stores they were not intending to visit. Along both corridors, the way is broken by oversized flagstone fireplaces (remember the "resort" theme) surrounded by rustic, slightly plush furniture. I was a little surprised not to find a collection of old paperbacks and battered Scrabble and Trivial Pursuit games filling shelves near these "lounges," presumably left by skier-shoppers who had come before me. The whole essence of Park Meadows is one of invitation, but, masked as it is, it is only an invitation to spend. The fireplaces may speak of sociability, but this is a sociability with a purpose. The shopping mall, Goss (1993: 33) rightly proclaims, "is a machine for shopping." As such, "the built environment is . . . physically persuasive or coercive" (Goss 1993: 31).

So it is finally in this sense that we can understand the comments by Lefebvre with which I opened this section. On the one hand, the mall is a surfeit of signs, each of which, no matter how it may be interpreted by the users of malls, serves to actively hide or mask the mall's function, which is to make money. Or if it doesn't hide that function, then it certainly naturalizes it, such that the "commodification of reality" becomes simply "God-given": "God shed His grace on thee." On the other hand, these signs ultimately become literally meaningless. The space itself is coercive, establishing the limits to life that no amount of subversive reading can undo. Subversive readings are readily accommodated within the structure of the mall itself. As I stood watching "Red Rocks" erupt, a 10-year-old or so boy walked past me in a T-shirt advising us to "Rage Against the Machine." On the back of the tee was a stylized picture of a hand about to unleash a Molotov cocktail. He and his parents were on their way to join the queue at McDonald's in the "dining hall." The mall-as-landscape is indeed quite accommodating: it not only sets our expectations; it fulfills them – a quarter-pounder at a time, no matter how much we may rage against the machine for shopping.

The city as mall: modern capitalism and postmodern urbanism

Jon Goss might now disagree with my interpretation of his research on malls. In a more recent article, Goss (1996) has focused on "festival marketplaces," those historically-themed shopping districts that have become increasingly important parts of the redevelopment schemes of cities throughout the USA, Canada, and Europe. He argues that while much of the scholarly critique of these commodified spaces is correct, it is also too one-sided, because it does not pay enough attention to how these spaces are *used* by those who frequent them. He cites his own epiphany in this regard: he was at the newly opened Aloha Towers Marketplace in Honolulu one day and happened across a gay couple holding hands and watching the sunset. The open expression of homosexuality is certainly not a sanctioned behavior in most public spaces of society, yet here it seemed unremarkable. Goss thus wonders whether the cynicism of academic critics of privatized public spaces like malls and marketplaces is warranted. As spaces open to the public, festival marketplaces are given all manner of readings by their users. And as spaces of sociability such landscapes allow for the *staging* of all kinds of activities, many of which find expression in a way that has nothing to do with the dictates of the commodity or of consumption.

Or do they? Landscapes are *always* a site of struggle, a place for resistance, and a concretization of contest. That is true. But it is also true, as we have already seen, that the whole reason for making a place *into a landscape*, that is, for attempting to emplace the landscape ideal, is precisely to staunch that struggle and to make social relations appear fully natural and timeless. Indeed, we can almost say that to the degree a landscape is contested, it stops being a landscape and becomes something else – a contested space.

To understand this point, it is useful to examine in a bit more detail two contested *ideals* – two ideologies, in fact – that I think are mutually opposed to each other. These ideals, of course, are never fully achieved in practice – the fact that they are continually contested by those holding different ideas assures that. The important issue is thus how the ideals help direct social action and the social production of public space. The first ideal is "landscape" itself, and the important point to think about here is the *privatized* nature of landscape that has marked the ideal right from the beginning (as we have seen). The second is "public space," an ideal just as complex and contradictory as landscape. But here the thing to keep in mind is that the *ideal* of public space is inclusiveness and unmediated interaction. The landscape (in this sense) is commodified through and through – that is part of its *ideal* structure. Public space rejects commodification – that too is part of its *ideal* structure. Landscape is where one recreates – it is literally a *resort* – and where one basks in the leisure of a well-ordered scene. Public space is a space of conflict, of political tussle, of social relations stripped to their barest essentials. A place cannot be both a public space and a landscape, at least not at the same time (even if landscapes are always sights of and for politics, and public spaces are often sights of and for pleasurable recreation).

As Goss (1996) admits, malls and festival marketplaces rarely live up to their billing as public spaces, creating instead a highly controlled environment which functions, as Darrell Crilley (1993: 153) has put it, like a "theater in which a pacified public basks in the grandeur of a carefully orchestrated corporate spectacle." In such landscapes, the intrusion of undesirables – the homeless, the unemployed, or the otherwise threatening – seems to imperil the carefully constructed suspension of disbelief on the part of the "audience" that all theatrical performances (and hence all landscapes) demand.[1] Or perhaps it is a double suspension of disbelief that is at work:

> The power of a landscape does not derive from the fact that it offers itself as a spectacle, but rather from the fact that, as mirror and mirage, it presents any susceptible viewer with an image at once true and false of a creative capacity which the subject (or Ego) is able, during a moment of marvelous self-deception, to claim as his own. A landscape also has

the seductive power of all *pictures,* and this is especially true of an urban landscape – Venice, for example – that can impose itself immediately as a *work.* Whence the archetypal touristic delusion of being a participant in such a work, and of understanding it completely, even though the tourist merely passes through a country or countryside and absorbs its image in a quite passive way. The work in its concrete reality, its products, and the productive activity involved are all thus obscured and indeed consigned to oblivion. (Lefebvre 1991: 189)

Creating a city – or a part of the city, such as a mall or festival marketplace – *as* landscape is therefore important because it restores to the viewer (the tourist, the suburban visitor, or even the city resident) an essential sense of control within a built environment which is instead "controlled," as Johnstown shows so clearly, through the creative, seemingly anarchic destruction of an economy over which they may in fact have very little control. Or more precisely, it provides an illusion of control in a space so highly designed, so carefully composed, so exquisitely "set" by the owners and developers of that space that a visitor's control can only ever be an illusion.

Put another way, the built environment "must be seen as simultaneously dependent and conditioning, outcome and mechanism of the dynamics of investment, production and consumption" (Knox 1993: 3). Yet, at this moment in time, such dynamics of investment, production and consumption must be seen in the context of a "socio-cultural environment in which the emphasis is not on ownership and consumption *per se* but on the possession of particular *combinations* of things and the *style* of consumption" (1993: 18). That is, the landscape must (and does) function as a vast system of *signs*, signs that "advertise" meanings to their consumers – and to those watching them. The recreation of the city *as* landscape works to order all the multitudinous spaces produced through myriad investment, production, and consumption decisions into an understandable whole. "Although urban space is produced and sold in discrete parcels," as Paul Knox (1993: 28) puts it, "it is *marketed* in large packages" (see also Mair 1986). Public spaces are transformed into "mere" signs, symbols of something else, rather than valued in their own right.

A second distinction that sets landscape apart from and against public space is that landscapes, in all their seductiveness, imply another illusion: that which Richard Sennett (1994) identifies as a lack of resistance to our own "lived relations," and to our own will. In fact, more and more, our own will, as well as our own sense of well-being and comfort, seems to depend on a certain "freedom from resistance." As Sennett (1994: 310) explains, "the ability to move anywhere, to move without obstruction, to circulate freely, a freedom greatest in an empty volume" has come to be defined *as* freedom itself in "Western civilization."

> The mechanics of movement has invaded a wide swath of modern experience – experience which treats social, environmental, or personal resistance, with its concomitant frustrations, as somehow unfair and unjust. Ease, comfort, "user-friendliness" in human relations come to appear as guarantees of individual freedom of action.

This ideology of comfort and individual movement as freedom reinforces an "impression of transparency" that works to make the urban landscape knowable by erasing its "products and productive activity." "[R]esistance is a fundamental and necessary experience for the human body," Sennett (1994: 310) concludes: "through feeling resistance, the body is roused to take note of the world in which it lives. This is the secular version of the lesson of exile from the Garden. The body comes to life when coping with difficulty." The irony, of course is that in the hyper-planned urban public spaces of the postmodern city, as in the spaces of the mall, the "impression of transparency" and the ability to move without resistance is made possible only by planning for the careful overall *orchestration* of individuals' movement. Freedom from resistance in built space seems only possible if control over movement is ceded to the planners of malls and public spaces. People become comfortable by giving up their active political *involvement* in space and acquiescing instead in becoming *spectators* of the urban "scene."

This is not a completely new development, however. Sennett (1994: 347) argues that a "public realm filled with moving and spectating individuals [that] no longer represented a political domain" can be traced at least to the city of the nineteenth-century *flâneur* (a sort of traveling spectator – usually male – always viewing and observing, but rarely actively participating in and shaping the urban scene), and probably a lot earlier. It is the curious condition of the modern city, a condition only heightened in the postmodern city, that "one was and is surrounded by life, even if detached from it." And in places like contemporary Greenwich Village (where Sennett lives), "ours is a purely visible agora" (that is, a landscape) where "political occasions do not translate into everyday practice on the streets; they do little, moreover, to compound the multiple cultures of the city into common purposes" (1994: 358). In this regard, the landscape-as-leisure returns with a vengeance, creating a sort of citizenship, according to Sennett, that is *predicated* on the externalization of those deemed "undesirable." Whether this is accomplished through design or through law – both of which are as important to the landscape of the mall and festival marketplace as they are to the city street – is less important than the fact that such exclusions are seen as a wholly desirable aspect of citizenship. Through landscape, politics is fully aestheticized.[2]

The Circulation of Meaning: Landscape as a System of Social Reproduction

We've come a long way, in this chapter, in our discussion of landscape, but we have also come full circle: from the aesthetics and aestheticized politics of landscape painting to the aesthetics and aestheticized politics of the city made over *as* landscape. Both forms of aestheticization – of the built form of landscape and of its representation – were clearly important to the decline and redevelopment of Johnstown. By emphasizing the aesthetics of disaster and industry, Johnstown sought to rejuvenate itself. Inevitably whenever politics – in this case the politics of social control, of racism, and of labor unrest – is aestheticized and made into something to be gawked at, something of that politics is lost: which is exactly the point of making a place into a landscape.

And that points us to the final issue that needs to be explored in our analysis of landscape, an issue that raises again the question of just how it is that landscape functions in society. That is, we need to return for a brief moment to two important and related questions with which we began our discussions of landscape and look at them again now that we have explored many of the varied aspects of the idea and materiality of "landscape." These questions were: What is landscape? And what does, landscape do? We can now give more complete (and slightly differently inflected) answers to these questions.

Landscape and the reproduction of labor and capital

As we have seen, landscape is complex and multifaceted, both a site to be struggled over and an ideology that seeks to govern our lived relations. In this sense we can see the landscape as a "vortex" within which swirl all manner of contests – between classes, over gender structures, around issues of race and ethnicity, over meaning and representation, and over built form and social use. The landscape serves all at once as mediator, integrator, and actor in these struggles. "As a produced object, landscape is like a commodity in which evident, temporarily stable, form masks the facts of its production, and its status as social relation. As both form and symbol, landscape is expected by those who attempt to define its meanings to speak unambiguously for itself" (Mitchell 1996: 30). In this sense, the *form* of the landscape actively incorporates the struggles over it. "Landscape is thus a fragmentation of space *and* a totalization of it. People make sense of their fractured world by seeing it as a whole, by seeking to impose meanings and connections" (1996: 31). We all *do* read the landscape, but we are not all equal in the process of "authoring" it – nor in controlling its meanings. Landscape representations serve precisely to create (or attempt to create) a total and naturalized environment. If the landscape is a text, then it is a very powerful one indeed. And if it is a theater or stage, then it is one in which the director is power itself.[3]

If that is what landscape *is*, then the question arises again as to what it *does*. To answer that question, it is important to remember that despite all the fragmentation, the diversity, the continual ebb, flow, and transformation of social life, we live in a world that *is* a "social totality": there are aspects of social life – political, economic, and cultural aspects – that are global and universal (or at least have pretensions to be so).[4] One of those overarching processes, contested as it undeniably always is, is the drive to accumulate capital – a drive that, as Marx rightly showed long ago, is no respecter of pre-existing social, political, economic, or cultural boundaries, or of pre-existing "ways of life." Yet the accumulation of capital can *only* occur to the degree that it *uses* those pre-existing ways of life and turns them to its own advantage. As Marx (1987: 537) put it, in a statement both admirably simple and exceptionally profound in its implications (implications that Marx himself never fully grasped): the "maintenance and reproduction of the working class is, and ever must be, a necessary condition to the reproduction of capital." On the one hand, Marx (1987: 537) argued that the reproduction of the working class – of labor-power – could be left "safely . . . to the labourer's instinct for self-preservation." On the other hand, he understood (1987: 168) that such a statement was too simple. The reproduction of the working class, he argued, everywhere and always possesses an "historical and moral element," which may appear as a set of "natural" or "necessary wants," but, because it is "historical and moral," is clearly socially constructed. The historical and "moral" development of the working classes in any place – in short, its "culture" – is itself a continual site of struggle. To what degree do workers (whether called working or middle class does not matter) "need," for example, detached houses and cars; to what extent do they "need" wages sufficient for them to become constant consumers? By contrast, when is it "historically" or "morally" "natural" for workers to live in shacks and to subsist on wages of under a dollar a day? And what is the relationship between the places in which these two worlds exist?

Sharon Zukin (1991: 16) argues that landscape "connotes the entire panorama of what we see: both the landscape of the powerful – cathedrals, factories, and skyscrapers – and the subordinate, resistant or expressive vernacular of the powerless – village chapel, shantytowns, and tenements." But note that in this description, Zukin holds the two landscapes spatially separate, seeing the "high culture" of production and symbolic development as disconnected from the powerless integrity of the vernacular. In reality, each sort of landscape *depends* on the other: our ability to consume is predicated on "their" low wages and the miserable conditions that exist elsewhere. Or to use one of Zukin's own examples, the development of a landscape of skyscrapers is a product of social struggle both within and outside them: struggles over the conditions of labor and labor reproduction (who will construct, clean, and staff the buildings? where will these workers live? how will they eat and with whom will they socialize?); struggles over land use (where will urban renewal, and where will gentrification occur? how strong are neighborhood organizations both where the skyscrapers are built and elsewhere in the city? what will the social costs of commuting be – and who will bear them?), and issues of race, gender, and citizenship (who will be allowed in the "public" space of the corporate plazas? how will the value of the buildings be maintained in the face of the changing demographic nature of the city?). Each of these struggles has its obverse in struggles over the nature of the places in which the skyscraper workers will live (city or suburb? small town exurb or downtown tenement?), and in the far-flung places that will provide them their sustenance (the bananas for their cereal, the shoes on their feet, the building materials for their own houses). Indeed, the answer to this second set of struggles will also be answers to the first set – and the chain of connection between and across landscapes is nearly infinite. The production of any landscape requires the constant reproduction of other landscapes in other places. The reproduction of labor-power in one place is impossible without its (always socially different) reproduction in other places.

But within this social totality, there exist important contradictions. At each place in the chain – in the building, maintenance, and staffing of the skyscraper, in the factory making Nikes or the plantation growing bananas, in the shantytowns on the banks of the Rio Grande and Harlem rivers, in the suburban tract homes of Piscataway, New Jersey, or the council houses of Paisley, Scotland – the reproduction of the inequality that makes the whole totality possible is always subject to revolt. If productive landscapes are to be maintained under capitalism (or for that matter, any other political-economic system), then possibilities for revolt must be minimized. This provides marginalized social actors with an important degree of power – indeed an essential degree because their status as a threat must always be neutralized. As a social and obfuscatory mediation, as both an input to and outcome of all these social struggles, landscapes are built as an attempt to insure this neutralization. Like culture, then, the landscape acts as a site of social integration, and therefore of social hegemony. The landscape emerges as a social compromise between threat and domination, between the imposition of social power and the subversion of social order. In turn, the very *form* of landscape results from these interactions and contested impositions. The landscape itself, as a unitary, "solid" form, is therefore a contradiction, held in uneasy truce (unless actively contested at some moment in time). Ongoing and everyday social struggle – along with all the mundane aspects of everyday life itself, like shopping, playing, and working – forms and reforms the landscape. Landscape reifies (at least momentarily) the "natural" social order. And landscape, therefore, becomes the "stage" for the social reproduction of not only labor-power, but society itself.

Yet the reproduction of labor-power remains important. By defining the reified "natural" relations of place, landscape materially affects the equation of surplus value extraction within a region (that is, it greatly affects the conditions under which firms will or will not be profitable). To the degree that social unrest, various social demands, or movements for self-determination or autonomy within a region can be stilled by pressing in on people the "naturalness" of existing social relations, surplus value can be expanded; reproduction is not threatened. If it can be successfully asserted that workers in Johnstown have no choice but to accept declining wages (because the old mills and new pollution requirements drive up costs; or because cheap foreign steel is flooding the market), to the degree that they can be convinced that making their mortgage is their own individual problem despite their employer shutting them out of a job, then to that degree, either in Johnstown itself or more "globally," capital can continue to function. The production of a landscape, by objectifying, rationalizing, and naturalizing what is really social, can have the effect of stopping resistance in its tracks. As *social* values are naturalized in place, they are historically made concrete. If, as David Harvey has argued, the landscapes of capitalism are often a barrier to further accumulation (as with Johnstown) and have to be creatively destroyed (wiping out heavy industry and sanitizing space to make it attractive to tourists, for example), it is also the case that a landscape can become a great facilitator to capital (since it determines the "nature" of labor).

Landscape as a form of regulation

Another way to think about this issue is to understand a landscape (and its constituent components) as part of a system of social regulation. Geographers such as James Duncan and Nancy Duncan (1988) have argued that landscapes should be understood not only as texts, but also as part of "discursive formations." A discourse can be defined a systematic set of statements (written or verbal), or, more generally, of signs (the implicit and explicit messages in any type of text). A "discursive formation" is the regularized, organized, routinized system of signs that exists in any particular time or place (cf. Foucault 1972). Discursive formations are obviously variable, and that is what makes them interesting. A discursive formation is therefore analogous to what could be called a "landscape formation." The important point is that "discursive and landscape formations relate not just to other discourses" – they are not only "intertextual" – "nor to power in general, but to the regulative powers of definite, geo-historical, political and economic social relations" (Peet 1996: 22). Landscapes, Peet (1996, 22) argues, as kinds of discursive formation, are, for particular historical and geographical situations "projector[s] of regulatory power" because they effectively limit the range of possible expression and representation within a discursive formation. As solid, socially powerful signs, they perform the vital function of "social regulation in the interests of class, gender, ethnic, and regional power systems."

The notion of social regulation draws on a body of ideas known as "regulation theory." Developed by French political economists in the 1970s and 1980s, regulation theory argues that rather than market equilibrium, the driving force behind the relative stability of capitalism as a social system is the "mode of regulation." The mode of regulation of any place and time is the constellation of state and civil institutions, coupled with norms and habits that encourage people to act in the general interest of economic stability. Accepting the discipline of wage cuts or interest rate hikes, coupled with religious teachings about frugality and school lessons in self-sacrifice, for example, might encourage workers to save and thereby make pools of capital available for investment in regional industries or services. Conversely, the rise of easy consumer credit, coupled with concerted advertising (and government pronouncement) that equates consumption with the good life, might (as in the 1990s) help smooth over a growing crisis of over-accumulation.[5] In either case, a particular mode of regulation (arrived at through experimentation and social struggle) defines what is known as a particular "regime of accumulation," which is a relatively stable, relatively long-term, system of capital accumulation. Any regime of accumulation is full of contradictions and will eventually become unworkable (as during the worldwide Depression of the 1930s, the Latin American debt crisis of the 1970s and 1980s, or the unfolding Asian economic crisis at the end of the 1990s). When a regime of accumulation collapses, so too does its associated mode of regulation collapse. Instability follows, and new modes of regulation governing new regimes of accumulation must be developed (as with the adoption of Keynesian macroeconomic policies in the wake of the Depression, and the imposition of "structural adjustment" in the wake of the Latin American debt crisis) (Aglietta 1976; Boyer 1990; Lipietz 1986).

Landscape is implicated in this process of regulatory change in two ways. In the first place, as Alan Scott (1988) has argued, a given regime of accumulation, coupled with the usually multiple modes of regulation with which it is associated, tend to bias development in favor of certain industries and against others (as with Johnstown and the decline of heavy manufacturing like steel-making and the rise of services like tourism and insurance-form processing) (see also Storper and Walker 1989). Similarly, the built environment often acts as a refuge for capital in times of crisis (especially crises of over-accumulation) when investment in production makes little sense. The physical landscape is thus often *built* as part of the development of, and eventual solution for, crises in the regime of accumulation (as when new mortgage systems were created in the USA during the Depression to jump-start suburban housing construction) (Harvey 1982). Second, as we have seen, landscapes themselves are a constituent part of the system of norms, habits, and institutions that regulate social life at any given moment. Indeed, landscapes are particularly important ingredients in social regulation because they are places where discourse and material practice meet – where acts of representation (about what constitutes the "good life," for example) and the material acts of living (working, consuming, relaxing) inevitably intersect. This means that landscapes should be understood as "the spatial surfaces of regulatory regimes, intended to frame social imaginaries often in definite, system supportive ways, articulated via discursive means among others, but conjoined expressly with regional and national [and now global] systems of power" (Peet 1996: 37). But such a framing of social imaginaries is always tentative and experimental. No social actor – and certainly no *collective* social actor – can know in advance just the proper mix of discipline and enjoyment, "freedom from resistance," and unpredictable social mixing that will be successful in the job of regulation. And even if they could, there is never any guarantee that they could implement their plans for spatial social regulation flawlessly and without dissent. All they can do is try to create the landscape after the image they find most desirable (Mitchell 1997).

To the degree that a landscape is both a built environment ("the homes of women and men," as Peet put it in the opening paragraphs of this chapter) *and* a system of representation – a system of signs – it is one of the most important sites for struggle over social regulation. In these struggles, Peet concludes (1996: 23), power is maintained through the successful:

> manipulation of the image–making capacity of the socialized subject at that cognitive level where thoughts are colored by mental pictures of reality. This kind of "visualization" is most fully effected when nature and region are employed *as* signs, when the landscapes people trust are invested *with* signs, when social and political markers are taken *for* nature or history in some pure, unadulterated sense.

Landscape is part of a system of social regulation and reproduction because it is *always* an inseparable admixture of material form and discursive sign. The very value of a landscape – in structuring ways of life, in providing a place to live – is precisely this mixture of textuality and materiality.

Conclusion

So, finally, it comes down to this: perhaps "landscape" in all its fascinating complexity is best seen as a force in, and place for, the social reproduction of society. Like "culture," landscape seeks to regularize or naturalize relations between people. Like "culture," then, landscape has a political economy. And while this is not everything, it is vitally important both to how landscapes are produced and to how they function in society. As a site of social reproduction, the landscape is too vital to be left only to the study of the metaphors that guide our understanding of it (as important as those are). Rather, the key point is to see, and attempt to explain (to ourselves and to others) just how it functions – to understand its role in the culture wars that mark our lives, which, while irreducible to questions of political economy, are nonetheless inseparable from such questions. If landscape is a stage then it is a stage for many things: the politics of economic development and the politics of culture to name just two. And if landscape is a text, then it is so *because* of its very materiality – its existence as trees, shrubs, bricks, mortar, paint, canvas, and the pages of a book – not despite that materiality. But for that point to make more sense, it is important at this point to turn away from the explicit consideration of the landscape and to explore more deeply the cultural politics that takes place in and on the landscape, that *depends* on the landscape – and upon which the landscape itself unavoidably depends too for its very shape, meaning, and social function.

Notes

1. This section is adapted from Mitchell (1997).
2. The best analysis of the aestheticization of politics in the realm of cultural production is still Benjamin (1968 [1936]).
3. As we will see below, it is deceptive to speak of "power" in general and universal terms. Power works in and through particular historically- and geographically-specific social formations.
4. The best analyses of the world as a social totality remain Lukács (1971), and Debord (1994). This section draws on Mitchell (1994 and 1996: chapter 1).
5. During the recession of the early 1990s, President George Bush took to media-covered shopping trips in hopes of convincing Americans to spend their way out of economic malaise. It has worked so well that in 1997 1.3 million Americans filed for personal bankruptcy protection (despite low inflation and low unemployment). Total consumer debt in the USA exceeded $1.2 trillion in 1997.

References

Aglietta, M. (1976). *A Theory of Capitalist Regulation*. London: New Left Books.

Barnes, Trevor & James Duncan (1992). Introduction: Writing Worlds. In: Trevor Barnes & James Duncan (eds.), *Writing Worlds: Discourse, Text and Metaphor in the Representation of Landscapes*, pp. 1–17. London: Routledge.

Benjamin, Walter (1968). The Work of Art in the Age of Mechanical Reproduction. In *Illuminations: Essays and Reflections*. New York: Schocken Books, originally published 1936.

Boyer, B. (1990). *The Regulation School: A Critical Introduction*. New York: Columbia University Press.

Cosgrove, Denis (1993). *The Palladian Landscape: Geographical Change and Its Cultural Representations in Sixteenth-Century Italy*. University Park: Pennsylvania State University Press.

Crawford, Margaret (1992). The World in a Shopping Mall. In: M. Sorkin (ed.), *Variations on a Theme Park: The New American City and the End of Public Space*, pp. 3–30. New York: Hill and Wang.

Crilley, Darrell (1993). Megastructures and Urban Change: Aesthetics, Ideology and Design. In: Paul Knox (ed.), *The Restless Urban Landscape*, pp. 127–64. Englewood Cliffs, NJ: Prentice-Hall.

Daniels, Stephen & Denis Cosgrove (1993). Spectacle and Text: Landscape Metaphors in Cultural Geography. In: James Duncan & David Ley (eds.), *Place / Culture / Representation*, pp. 57–77. London: Routledge.

Debord, Guy (1994). *The Society of the Spectacle*, trans. Donald Nicholson-Smith. New York: Zone Books.

Duncan, James (1990). *The City as Text: The Politics of Landscape Interpretation in the Kandyan Kingdom*. Cambridge: Cambridge University Press.

Duncan, James & Nancy Duncan (1988). (Re)Reading the Landscape. *Environment and Planning D: Society and Space* 6, pp. 117–26.

Duncan, James & David Ley (eds.) (1993). *Place / Culture / Representation*. London: Routledge.

During, Simon (ed.) (1993). *The Cultural Studies Reader*. London and New York: Routledge.

Fishman, Robert (1987). *Bourgeois Utopias: The Rise and Fall of Suburbia*. New York: Basic Books.

"Food Courts: Tasty!" (1990). *Stores*, August, pp. 52–4.

Foucault, Michel (1972). *The Archeology of Knowledge*. New York: Harper.

Garreau, Joel (1991). *Edge City: Life on the New Frontier*. New York: Doubleday.

Goss, Jon (1992). Modernity and Postmodernity in the Retail Built Environment. In: K. Anerson & F. Gale (eds.), *Inventing Places*, pp. 159–77. Melbourne: Longman Scientific.

Goss, Jon (1993). The "Magic of the Mall": An Analysis of Form, Function, and Meaning in the Contemporary Retail Built Environment. *Annals of the Association of American Geographers* 83, pp. 18–47.

Goss, Jon (1996). Disquiet on the Waterfront: Reflections on Nostalgia and Utopia in the Urban Archetypes of Festival Marketplaces. *Urban Geography* 17, pp. 221–47.

Gross, S. H. & M. H. Rojas (1986). *But Women Have No History! Images of Women in the Public History of Washington, DC*. St. Louis Park, MN: Glenhurst Publications.

Harvey, David (1979). Monument and Myth. *Annals of the Association of American Geographers* 69, pp. 362–81.

Harvey, David (1982). *The Limits to Capital*. Chicago: University of Chicago Press.

Harvey, David (1989a). *The Condition of Postmodernity: An Enquiry into the Origins of Cultural Change*. Oxford: Blackwell.

Harvey, David (1989b). *The Urban Experience*. Oxford: Blackwell.

Harvey, David (1996). *Justice, Nature, and the Geography of Difference*. Oxford: Blackwell.

Haug, W. F. (1986). *Critique of Commodity Aesthetics*. Minneapolis: University of Minnesota Press.

Hayden, Delores (1981). *The Grand Domestic Revolution: A History of Feminist Designs for American Homes, Neighborhoods and Cities*. Cambridge, MA: MIT Press.

Hayden, Delores (1984). *Redesigning the American Dream: The Future of Housing, Work and Family Life*. New York: W.W. Norton.

Hopkins, Jeffrey (1990). West Edmonton Mall: Landscapes of Myth and Elsewhereness. *Canadian Geographer* 30, pp. 2–17.

Jackson, Peter (1989). *Maps of Meaning: An Introduction to Cultural Geography*. London: Unwin Hyman.

Knox, Paul (1993). Capital, Materials Culture and Socio-Spatial Differentiation. In: Paul Knox (ed.), *The Restless Urban Landscape*, pp. 1–34. Englewood Cliffs, NJ: Prentice Hall.

Lefebvre, Henri (1991). *The Production of Space*, trans. Donald Nichilson-Smith. Oxford: Blackwell.

Lewis, Pierce (1979). Axioms for Reading the Landscape: Some Guide to the American Scene. In: Donald Meinig (ed.), *The Interpretation of Ordinary Landscape: Geographical Essays*, pp. 11–32. New York: Oxford University Press.

Lipietz, Alain (1986). New Tendencies in the International Division of Labor: Regimes of Accumulation and Modes of Regulation. In: Alan Scott & Michael Storper (eds.), *Production, Work, Territory*, pp. 16–40. Boston: Allen and Unwin.

Loukaki, Argyro (1997). Whose *Genius Loci*? Contracting Interpreations of the "Sacred Rock of the Athenian Acropolis". *Annals of the Association of American Geographers* 87, pp. 306–29.

Lukács, Georg (1971). Reification and the Consciousness of the Proletariat. In: *History and Class Consciousness: Studies in Marxist Dialectics*, pp. 83–222. Cambridage, MA: MIT Press.

McDowell, Linda (1983). Towards an Understanding of the Gender Division of Urban Space. *Environment and Planning D: Society and Space* 1, pp. 59–72.

McDowell, Linda (1994). The Transformation of Cultural Geography. In: Derek Gregory, Ron Martin & Granham Smith (eds.), *Human Geography: Society, Space and Social Science*, pp. 146–73. Minneapolis: University of Minnesota Press.

MacKenzie, Suzanne & Rose, Dameries (1983). Industrial Change, the Domestic Economy, and Home Life. In: J. Andreson, S. Duncan & R. Hudson (eds.), *Redundant Space in Cities and Regions*, pp. 155–200. New York: Academic press.

Mair, Andrew (1986). The Homelesses and the Post-industrial City. *Political Geography Quarterly* 5, pp. 351–68.

Marx, Karl (1987). *Capital*, Volume I. New York: International Publishers.

Meinig, Donald (ed.) (1979). *Interpretations of Ordinary Landscapes: Geographic Essays*. New York: Oxford University Press.

Michell, Don (1994). Landscape and Surplus Value: The Making of the Ordinary in Brentwood, California. *Environment and Planning D: Society and Space* 12, pp. 7–30.

Mitchell, Don (1995). There's No Such Thing as Culture: Towards a Reconceptualization of the Idea of Culture in Geography. *Transactions of the Institute of British Geographers* 20, pp. 102–16.

Mitchell, Don (1996). *The Lie of the Land: Migrant Workers and the California Landscape*. Minneapolis: University of Minnesota Press.

Mitchell, Don (1997). The Annihilation of Space By Law: The Roots and Implications of Anti-homeless Laws in the United States. *Antipode* 29, pp. 303–35.

Monk, Janice (1992). Gender in the Landscape: Expressions of Power and Meaning. In: K. Anderson & F. Gale (eds.), *Inventing Places: Studies in Cultural Geography*, pp. 123–38. Melbourne: Longman Cheshire.

Morris, Meaghan (1993). Things to Do with Shopping Centries. In: Simon During (ed.), *The Cultural Studies Reader*, pp. 295–319. London: Routledge.

"Off Limits" (1996). *Westword*, September, pp. 12–18.

Peet, Richard (1996). A Sign Taken for History: Daniels Shays' Memorial in Petersham, Massachusetts. *Annals of the Association of American Geographers* 86, pp. 21–43.

Scott, Alan (1988). *New Industrial Spaces*. London: Pion.

Sennett, Richard (1994). *Flesh and Stone: The Body and the City in Western Civilization*. New York: W.W. Norton.

Storper, Michael & Richard Walker (1989). *The Capitalist Inperative: Territory, Technology and Industrial Growth*. Oxford: Blackwell.

Walker, Richard (1981). A Theory of Suburbanization: Capitalism and the Construction of Urban Space in the United States. In: M. Dear & A. Scott (eds.), *Urbanization and Urban Planning in Capitalist Society*, pp. 383–429. London: Methuen.

Wilson, Elizabeth (1991). *The Sphinx in the City: Urban Life, the Control of Disorder, and Women*. Berkeley: University of California Press.

Zukin, Sharon (1991). *Landscapes of Power: From Detroit to Disney World*. Berkeley: University of California Press.

7

Hegemony, Ideology, Pleasure: Blackpool

Tony Bennett*

When the Eiffel Tower created its furore among the Parisians, Blackpool showed its enterprise by being the first place in the United Kingdom to put up a similar erection! When the Great Wheel at Earl's Court, London, tickled the Cockneys with its novelty, Blackpool was the only town in the United Kingdom to erect one of its own![1]

Thus the 1897 Blackpool Town Guide, typical in its claims to outdo every other town in Britain, the capital city included. In 1924, the standard of comparison Blackpool constructed for itself, only in order to exceed it, was imperial Rome:

> Just south of the Victorian Pier is Blackpool's latest attraction acknowledged by all the swimming authorities to be the largest and finest enclosed open-air swimming bath in the world. We can go the world over and back into the days of the older civilizations, but we cannot find anything more wonderful than this magnificent new bath, not even the Coliseum of Rome in the height of its glory.[2]

Throughout its history as a popular holiday resort, Blackpool has represented itself as a town operating on the very threshhold of modernity, exploring and pushing back the outer limits of progress. The claims, moreover, have typically had a distinctively northern, and especially Lancashire, articulation. Never slow to cock a snook at the metropolis – cockneys being idly tickled by the Great Wheel whilst the people of Blackpool go ahead and build one – Blackpool has, at various times, imaginarily placed itself at the centre of the nation and, even more grandiosely, of the Empire, thus disputing London's claims to preeminence. In this respect, the 'discourse of modernity' which has governed the forms in which Blackpool has represented itself has been connected, at various moments, to a distinctive brand of northern populism, the two jointly forging an image of 'the people of the North' as sharing a no-nonsense, down-to-earth, practical regional spirit, best exemplified in the triumphal achievements of northern industrial capitalists, constructed in opposition to the all-talk, no-action pretensions of the South. A true case of 'second city firsts', Blackpool has, I want to argue, thus furnished the

* Pp. 135–54 from *Popular Culture and Social Relations*, ed. T. Bennett, C. Mercer and J. Woollacott (Milton Keynes and Philadelphia: Open University Press). © 1986 by Tony Bennett. Reprinted with permission from the author.

site for the enunciation of a distinctively regional claim to cultural leadership, albeit one heard only within the confines of northern, and particularly Lancashire, culture.[3] At the same time, this discourse of modernity has also occasionally pointed in other directions, dismantling opposing discourses by articulating their claims to itself. Current publicity posters for the revolution – a loop-the-loop ride at the Pleasure Beach – thus declare: 'Join the Revolution – Only Here at Blackpool's Pleasure Beach'. This not only puts London in its place but is as effective and economical an instance of the containment of oppositional discourses as Marcuse could have ever hoped to find.[4]

My purpose in this essay is to consider the operation of this discourse of modernity and the varying ideologies and sets of values that have been drawn into association with and expressed by means of it at different moments in Blackpool's history. In doing so, I shall be partly concerned with such representational forms as town guides and publicity brochures. However, I shall focus rather more on the popular entertainments which, at different times, have predominated in the town, considering these from the point of view of the discourses embodied in the sedimented forms of their architectural styles or, more pliably, in their characteristic themes and modes of address. My particular concern, in relation to these, will be to elucidate the part that the regimes of pleasure embodied in such popular entertainments – that is, not merely the forms of pleasure on offer but the systems of signs and associated ideologies under which they are constructed and offered as pleasures – play in relation to the processes of hegemony more broadly conceived.

Elements of a History[5]

Although Blackpool has long boasted that it was the world's first working-class holiday resort, it became so very much against its will and better inclinations. The commercial development of the town as a holiday resort dates from the 1790s with the opening of a railway line between Preston and the Fylde coast. Throughout the greater part of the next century, however, Blackpool remained, and struggled hard to remain, a dignified holiday resort catering principally for the respectable middle classes and upper strata of artisan workers from the northern manufacturing towns. The town's political machinery, dominated by local tradesmen catering for this market until more or less the turn of the century, provided the necessary infrastructure (piped water, street lighting, the promenade, etc.), to support the commercial development of recreational facilities within the town. The capital which funded these projects – public and private – came from two main sources. Many ventures, such as the North Pier (1865), were financed by local subscription. Others were capitalized by Lancashire and Yorkshire businessmen. Very little London capital, or, indeed, capital from anywhere outside the northern counties was attracted to Blackpool until towards the end of the century.

The forms of recreation provided in this period, especially from the mid-century on, were of an excessively 'rational' and improving kind. The North Pier, utterly lacking in commercial embellishment, offered little more than the opportunity for dignified perambulation over the ocean. The Winter Gardens (1878) epitomised the town's claims to culture and elegance. Constructed with the declared intention of making Blackpool a major European cultural centre – rivalling London – its opening was cele- brated with a degree of civic pride and pomp that now seems scarcely credible: the mayors of 68 towns were invited to process through the town, led by the Lord Mayor of London in his ceremonial carriage. Whilst, of course, the actual practice may have been different, a Blackpool holiday was both represented and organised as a refined and cultivated affair. John Walton paints the following picture of Blackpool holiday-makers in the period prior to the 1880s:

> Whether they were manufacturers, professional men, shopkeepers, clerks or working men in skilled or supervisory grades, whatever the differences between them in other respects, they generally accepted common standards of propriety and decorum. They gave due weight to the code of moral responsibility which went hand in hand with the pursuit of economic independence, and they sought at least to keep up appearances. The working men among them were self selecting, for only the relatively thrifty and aspiring could afford to come to the seaside for more than the odd day before the great price fall of the late nineteenth century. They saved carefully and spent, according to their lights, 'ratio- nally', on items of long-term practical utility; and they saw their seaside holiday in these terms. They eschewed frivolity or excess, cultivating regular habits and an earnest demean- our. They took their pleasures seriously, and a seaside holiday was the occasion for rest, recuperation and edification. Health was pursued by judicious and carefully-regulated bathing, and by gentle exercise where the medical ozone could be inhaled. Improving recreations were permissible, and the pursuit of 'useful knowledge' was expressed in con- chology and fossil-hunting. Such visitors desired little in the way of commercial entertain- ment, although their preoccupations were reflected in increasingly lavish aquaria and winter gardens at the larger resorts by the 'seventies, and there was a steady demand for concerts, plays and even well-conducted dances. But the main *desiderata* were good natural amenities, quietness and decorum, for there were sensibilities here to be protected.[6]

Respectable middle-class and artisan holiday-makers were not, however, the only people to visit Blackpool during this period. From as early as 1781, when a road was opened up between Preston and Blackpool, agricultural labourers from northern Lancashire had made their way to Blackpool at weekends or on special festivals. In 1840, the opening of a rail link between Preston and Fleetwood put Blackpool within easy day-trip reach of the northern spinning and weaving towns and, from 1842, special excursion trains regularly plied the line, dropping Blackpool passengers off at Poulton until a direct line to Blackpool was opened in 1846. The initial impetus behind the development of excursion trains was largely of a 'rational' and improving kind. Organ- ised by temperance and religious bodies, and sometimes directly by employers, their purpose was to expose the working classes, if only for a day, to the improving physical and moral climate then prevailing in Blackpool. However, where voluntary organisa- tions led, workers' co-operative associations and straightforwardly commercial ventures could follow. By the 1850s, Blackpool was subject to a regular flood of day-trip visitors – as many as 10,000 a day coming in by train alone – both at weekends and in the wakes holidays of the northern industrial towns; that is, virtually right through the summer.[7]

And with the people came tradesmen catering for their tastes in food, drink and popular entertainments. Freak shows, small side-shows and competitions, waxworks, monstrosities, quack medicine, popular dramas, small mechanical rides – such were the popular entertainments which followed the popular classes to Blackpool. Combining elements of both traditional wakes celebrations and the newer urban fairs which, by the mid-nineteenth century, were increasingly taking the place of the former,[8] they also anticipated aspects of the fixed-site mechanical fun-fairs of the 1880s and 1890s. And the primary zone of their operation was the beach, traditionally unregulated land, outside the control of the local political machinery. From mid-century, the organisation of pleasure at Blackpool thus exhibited a Janus face. The improving, civilising recreations aimed at the middle class and upper artisan holiday trade dominated the promenade and town centre whilst the beach was occupied by the messy and variegated sprawl of countless side-shows competing for the working class day-trip market. In effect, both the traditional and newer urban forms of popular recreation, under considerable attack in the inland towns at the time, had been displaced to Blackpool beach where they were able to thrive in an excess of unbridled vulgarity.[9]

Not surprisingly, the citizens of Blackpool, especially those who had invested in the middle-class holiday market, sought to resist and to turn the tide of this working-class invasion which threatened to drive away the respectable trade. The beach, moreover, had become an ideological scandal, an affront of the town's carefully constructed image as the embodiment of a unique blend of respectability, progress and modernity, a triumphal hymn to the hard-headed verve and practicality of the northern bourgeoisie. Initially, an attempt was made to exclude day-trippers by petitioning the railway companies not to run excursion trains to the town. When this failed, attention concentrated on bringing the piers and the beach within the scope of the town's regulatory capacities. In 1868, Central Pier – or, as it was colloquially known, 'the People's Pier' – was opened. Catering specifically for the working-class trade (entry was free and unimpeded compared with the penny entrance fee charged at the North Pier), Central Pier became a major centre for popular entertainments, particularly drinking and dancing, both of which were free from the restrictions prevailing in the town. One of the corporation's first acts, when Blackpool became an incorporated borough in 1876, was to extend its licensing and policing authority to include the piers. The beach, however, was the site of the longest struggle between the 'respectable' and the 'popular' within Blackpool leading, in 1897, to an attempt to prohibit all trading on the beach. The outcry which greeted this forced the corporation to relent to the degree of allowing food and drink stalls to operate on the beach but drawing the line at 'Phrenologists, Quack Doctors, Mock Auctioneers and Cheap-Jacks'.

This attempt to exclude the popular tradition from Blackpool backfired owing to the peculiar structure of land ownership prevailing in the town which enabled showmen evicted from the beach to set up shop in the forecourts of houses on the promenade.[10] Instead of being exiled from the town, popular entertainments deriving from the wakes and urban fairs thus gained a more scandalously prominent position within it, elevated from the beach to the promenade, thus laying the foundations for the Golden Mile – a vast stretch of stalls, side-shows, freak shows, curiosities and the like which dominated Blackpool's frontage south of the Tower until the early 1960s.

This direct attack on the beach, however, was the product of rather different interests and alliances from those which had fuelled earlier attempts to regulate the forms of pleasure permissible in the town. By the 1880s and 1890s, principally as a consequence of the rise in disposable family income in Lancashire's cotton towns, Blackpool was attracting a considerable volume of working-class *holiday,* as distinct from *day-trip,* trade. Population statistics attest to the significance of this period within Blackpool's development. In 1861, Blackpool's resident population was 3,707. By 1891, it had grown to 23,846 and, by 1901, to 47,348. Similarly, the period witnessed a quantum leap in the number of registered landladies – who provided residential and catering facilities geared specifically to the working-class market – from 400 in 1871 to 4,000 in 1911.[11] The middle-class holiday trade declined in the same period, partly because middle-class visitors began to go elsewhere to escape the 'degraded' tone of Blackpool and partly because falling prices brought about a relative reduction in middle-class spending power. The consequent increase in the ratio of working-class to middle-class holiday-makers, and in the relative value of their custom, resulted in the development of a significant entertainment industry aimed at a mass working-class market. The high capital requirements of this industry attracted to Blackpool a new type of entrepreneur and a new breed of impresario. It also, and for the first time, led to a significant amount of London capital, especially from sources associated with the music hall, being invested in the town.

In a useful survey of the development of the seaside towns of north-west Lancashire, Harold Perkin has argued:

> Each resort has its own peculiar history and evolution, but in general the most important factor in determining the social tone was the competition for domination of the resort by large, wealthy residents, hotel keepers and providers of 'genteel' entertainments such as concert halls and bathing establishments; by small property owners, boarding-house keepers and purveyors of cheap amusements; and, later in the century, by large capitalist enterprises, usually financed from outside, providing cheap, spectacular entertainment for a mass public.[12]

By the late nineteenth century, as a consequence of these developments, the terms of the struggle over popular recreations in Blackpool and the patterns of alliance associated with it had changed. No longer one between entrepreneurs catering for the 'respectable' market and small showmen catering for the 'vulgar' tastes of the popular classes, the attack on the latter now came from an alliance between the 'respectable' interests in the town and the new entrepreneurs and impresarios who wished to develop the working-class market, rather than to eliminate or reform it, with this latter group playing very much the active, leading role.

However, this is not to suggest that the terms within which this struggle was conducted were purely commercial in orientation. There were considerable ideological interests at stake, too. Most historians are agreed that the commercially provided forms of mass entertainment which typified the later nineteenth century – the music hall, spectator sports and the popular press, for example – proved considerably more successful in promoting the cultural hegemony of the ruling classes than had earlier attempts at morally reforming the people by promoting the spread of 'rational recreations'. Whilst this is true, the suggestion which sometimes accompanies this argument – that the shift from the one strategy to the other was a shift from a struggle for hegemony conducted by ideological and cultural means to one conducted purely by commercial means – is misleading. The popular entertainments promoted on a highly capitalised basis in the late nineteenth-century embodied a programme of ideological and cultural re-formation just as much as had the earlier 'rational recreations', albeit that the means whereby popular values and attitudes were to be 're-formed' had changed significantly. The 'rational recreations' movements, in seeking both to oppose and repress traditional and developing forms of working-class recreation, had aimed to re-form the popular classes by filling their lives with a different cultural content. The later, commercially provided forms of mass entertainment, by contrast, sought less to oppose the given forms of working-class recreation than to reorder their ideological and cultural articulations. They transformed working-class culture not by taking issue with it as a monolithic entity and seeking to install in its place another monolithic entity (the 'rational' culture of the middle classes) but by breaking it down into its elements – its taste, preferences and characteristic activities – and hooking these and, with them, the people, into an association with hegemonic ideological formations.

At Blackpool the shift from the one strategy to the other was aptly symbolized by the appointment of Billy Holland as manager of the Winter Gardens in 1887. As I have noted, the Winter Gardens were founded with the express ambition of bringing culture to Blackpool. The aim, in the words of a founding shareholder, was to provide 'high class entertainment which no lady or gentleman would object to see'. Within a few years of its opening, however, declining revenues forced the controlling company to sacrifice culture for profit. Billy Holland, earlier a manager of a music hall in the London suburbs where he had gained a certain notoriety for his slogan, 'Come and Spit on Bill Holland's Hundred Guinea Carpet', effectively reversed the Winter Gardens' policy of cultural improvement in implementing, as his catch-phrase, the motto 'Give 'em what they want'.

But, in 'giving 'em what they wanted', such impresarios at the same time transformed the tastes, preferences and practices of the people, inscribing them in new sets of cultural and ideological relations. Virtually all the forms of mass entertainment developed in Blackpool in this period, in catering for the people's tastes also relocated their recreations, wrenching them away from their traditional associations and selectively reconstructing them in an association with new sets of values and ideologies. In the main, two sets of themes predominated. Perhaps most influential initially, imperialist motifs were strongly present in both the architectural styles and characteristic themes of a wide range of popular entertainments; Nigger (*sic*) minstrel shows at the Winter Gardens; the construction of an Indian façade to the South Pier; the 1913 design of the Casino, the main frontispiece to the Pleasure Beach, in the style of an Indian palace, the staging of mock naval battles out at sea including, on one occasion, the mock invasion (successfully repulsed!) of the town by Afghan hordes; penny slot machines which, when activated, depicted white men shooting 'natives': in these ways, the thematics and architecture of pleasure inveigled the pleasure-seeker in relations of complicity with imperialist values and sentiments.

More influential in the longer term, however, was the rearticulation of the discourse of modernity which, initially a complement to the image of respectability the town had constructed for itself, assumed an increasingly brash countenance. In their very material form, many of the popular entertainments developed in this period stood as a triumphant testimony to the powers of northern industrialism. The Tower, the centrepiece of the town's phallic boasting ever since its – as the 1897 Town Guide put it – 'erection' in 1894, displayed the prowess of 'the workshop of the world' in the sphere of pleasure. More generally, the harnessing of machinery for pleasure embodied in the development of mechanical rides – especially, in the early twentieth century, at the Pleasure Beach – constituted a modernization of pleasure which, had it been allowed to, might have spoken for itself as a sufficiently eloquent testimony to the virtues of progress. But it was not allowed to. Persistently, as the increasingly dominant form of hailing in operation at Blackpool, impresarios claimed to be offering 'the latest', 'the most up to the minute' forms of popular entertainment, often 'direct from America'. Dick Hebdige has argued that, throughout the twentieth century, American influence on British popular culture has largely been regarded as a threat to indigenous forms of hegemony and, as such, something which conservative critics have universally deplored and resisted.[13] This has not been true of Blackpool where the discourse of modernity came to assume an increasingly Americanised form, working with the town's previous image rather than against it, resulting in the construction of the town as being in advance of the rest of Britain in anticipating, implementing ahead of its time, America as the very image of the modern. A little America in Lancashire: it was in the terms of this newer and brasher northern populism that the image of Blackpool was re-formed, although less in its official versions of itself than in the commercially provided forms of popular entertainment predominating in the streets.

In order to appreciate the broader cultural significance of these transformations in the forms of Blackpool's self-presentation, however, it is necessary to shift our attention away from Blackpool and toward the characteristics which most specifically distinguished Lancashire working-class culture in the late-nineteenth and early twentieth centuries.

A 'Regional Popular'

In his *Work, Society and Politics,* a study of the culture of the work-place in the Lancashire factory system, Patrick Joyce takes issue with accounts which construe the stability of late nineteenth-century Britain as the result of the 'ideological capture' of a labour aristocracy effected by the promulgation of a bourgeois ethic of respectability. In the case of Lancashire, he argues, such approaches fail to account for the degree to which the vast mass of the proletariat, and not just the upper strata of skilled operatives, was accommodated to the status quo. Moreover, he suggests, they tend to present a one-sided, over-intellectualised picture of the processes whereby hegemony is fought for, won and lost. The labour aristocracy thesis, in the stress it places on the nexus of ideas defined by the terms 'respectability' and 'self-improvement', is a version of what Joyce calls 'ideological hegemony' in which analysis focuses on the degree to which a common stock of ideas is able to mediate the relations between ruling and subordinate classes. Against this view, he argues that the hegemony of the owning classes in mid- to late-nineteenth-century Lancashire was achieved by more distinctively social and cultural means, chiefly attributable to the way the system of factory paternalism – and the dense web of social and cultural relations which radiated out from the factory – permeated the very tissue of daily life for the Lancashire working classes. Their accommodation to the factory system and, through that, to the Lancashire bourgeoisie, he writes, 'occurred not so much at the level of ideas and values, but at the centre of people's daily concerns, in terms of their sense of personal and communal identity'.[14]

Joyce also takes issue with the view, mainly associated with the work of Perry Anderson, that the industrial bourgeoisie failed to become a genuinely hegemonic class in the nineteenth century, sacrificing political power and its ambition to exert intellectual and moral authority over society as a whole to the political and intellectual representatives of the landed classes for the sake of consolidating its economic power.[15] To the contrary, Joyce argues, by the mid-century the Lancashire industrial bourgeoisie had every cause for self-satisfaction and little reason to consider itself merely a poor relation to the élites prevailing at the national level. It had consolidated the basis of its economic power in the factory system and, through the mechanisms of employer paternalism, had established a set of social and cultural relations which yoked working-class life, in all its dimensions, into a close orbit around and dependency on the factory. It wielded effective political power at the local and regional levels via its control over the machinery of local government, and played an increasingly prominent role in civic life, both corporately, through its funding of museums, parks, libraries and the like, and privately, by means of the wide range of cultural activities – sports, brass bands, day-trips to the seaside – supported by individual employers on a voluntary basis. The result, Joyce concludes, was a distictively regional form of hegemony which functioned, on all levels of social and cultural life, to check the political power of the central state apparatuses and to limit the purchase, within Lancashire, of national styles of political, moral and intellectual leadership. Not merely a regional 'exception to the rule', Joyce contends, but one which should induce a more qualified appraisal of the situation prevailing nationally:

> When the mentality of the industrial bourgeoisie in these years is correctly understood, there is cause for looking again at the national scene through the eyes of Marx, and seeing England as the most bourgeois of nations, the industrial bourgeoisie going from strength to strength and consolidating its economic power in political terms despite the aristocratic appearances of national government.[16]

The important point to stress here is that the regional hegemony of the Lancashire bourgeoisie was, to a considerable extent, directly dependent on its displacement of and opposition to the forms of hegemony which prevailed at the national level. It constituted an identifiably distinct system of culturally organized class relationships which, in part, worked because it was constructed against the aristocratic appearances of national government. In gridding the opposition bourgeois-aristocratic onto the opposition North-South so that the latter, regionally organised perception of cultural differences overrode class-based perceptions of cultural differences, it grouped 'the people of the North' into a putatively undifferentiated unity against those of the South.

The history of the forms and organisation of pleasure at Blackpool, and above all of its ideological articulation, lends some degree of support to this contention. The discourse of modernity, varying in form but always the articulating centre of Blackpool's constructed self-image, was most effectively condensed not as an abstracted set of ideas – although it was active in this form, too – but in the sedimented forms of the town's architecture and its pleasures, made concrete, as Gramsci insisted an enduring hegemony must be, at the level of the mundane and the particular, a set of lived ideological relations which the visitor inescapably entered into and breathed in with the ozone. Moreover, at least until recently, it was a discourse which possessed a distinctively regional edge, connected, historically, to the system of employer hegemony Joyce describes by a multitude of strands. It is worth recalling that the typical context in which the northern working classes visited Blackpool was not as individuals or families but as members of work-based communities – moving there in whole streets and towns during wakes weeks, or visiting for a day on the occasion of annual outings which were frequently factory-based and organised and paid for by employers. (Joyce records that the Preston firm of Horrockses and Miller sent 1,570 members of its work-force to Blackpool as early as 1850.) To visit Blackpool, in this context, meant to encounter a discourse that had slipped sideways, uncoupled from its usual association with work and harnessed to the mechanisms and machinery of pleasure. Furthermore, it meant to encounter a discourse that had been, to a degree, delocalised, shorn of its associations with a particular town, a particular industry or a particular employer and given a regional and, by the end of the nineteenth century, a popular voice and presence in contrast to the sombre pretentiousness of, say, Manchester and Liverpool city centres.

Hugh Cunningham has argued that, by the end of the nineteenth century, the people's culture, compared with the hey-day of Chartism, had been massively depoliticized, bolted back into a safely residual niche within the national culture.[17] The history of popular entertainments in Blackpool, whilst exemplifying this tendency, also suggests that it is mistaken to regard the struggle in which ruling groups engage to win the hearts and minds of the people as a unitary one, without contradictions, enunciated exclusively at the national level. The struggle for the popular in Blackpool formed part of a specifically regionally based system of cultural and intellectual leadership constructed in a degree of opposition to that prevailing at the national level. The blended combination of the discourse of modernity and northern populism which, toward the end of the nineteenth century, came to characterise the forms of 'hailing' predominating in Blackpool's popular entertainments worked to dismantle traditional forms of popular recreation more directly linked to and emerging from the popular classes and to substitute in their place commercially provided forms of popular entertainment in which regionally popular traditions and values, particularly those of northern chauvinism, whilst surviving, were also articulated to the cultural claims and pretensions of northern industrial capitalists. In effect, Blackpool and all that it was made to stand for within the regional culture, compacted 'the people of the North' into a unity constructed in an opposition to the metropolitan élites. In this respect, it constituted the site for the operation of a putatively hegemonic discourse – admittedly limited in its reach –

enunciated at a regional level, a 'regional-popular' organised in a relationship of partial opposition to or partial collusion with the national-popular. This is emphatically not to suggest that this contradiction was the site, even remotely, of a significant cultural or ideological 'rupture'. But it is to suggest that regionally specific inflections of the organisation of cultural and ideological class relationships will repay closer attention.

Nor is this to suggest that the discourse of modernity has been the only one in evidence at Blackpool – of which more later – or that it has been unitary in its functioning and effects. To the contrary, it has been profoundly multi-accentual, capable of being inflected in different directions and of articulating different values at different points in time and for different publics. Initially a complement to the aura of respectability which characterised the early development of the resort, the town's motto of progress has consistently retained its responsible, improving, rational connotations. This has been particularly true of the official images of the town put into circulation by the corporation, images which, at times, have assumed positively visionary proportions. One of the clearest examples of this is provided by the 1924 Town Guide in which the discourse of modernity is articulated to a rhetoric of planning to conjure up an image of Blackpool as a future arcadia to be produced by enlightened rulers:

> Blackpool's pioneers, though they were possessed of the virile spirit of 'Progress', which has become the Borough's official motto and very real watchword, did not know the ultimate size of the great city of health and happiness they were well and truly laying. The result was that up to a few years ago Blackpool was practically parkless and singularly devoid of trees, greenery and flowers . . . Blackpool's modern rulers have a vision which they mean to realize. It is that of a vast, beautiful and balanced Borough stretching at least from the borders of Fleetwood to those of Lytham, with parks and trees and broad, airy thoroughfares everywhere, and it is by no means impossible that the whole Fylde coast-line from the Wyre to the Ribble will become one vast health resort under unified government.[18]

However, in its more characteristic forms, as enunciated at street level in the claims and practices of the major entertainments industries operating in the town, the discourse of modernity, at least since the beginning of the twentieth century, has had a more abrasive, more populist edge, undercutting the more outlandish pretensions of the town's civic leaders. It has also, in more recent years, bent that rhetoric back on itself, disconnecting its specifically regional associations, appealing above the heads of the Lancashire bourgeoisie to a broader, more updated vision of progress in its anticipatory Americanisation of pleasure. This has been particularly true of the post-war period. With the decline of the cotton industry, the demise of the factory system and the virtual disappearance of the whole set of social and communal relations associated with it, the themes of modernity and progress – still massively in evidence – have split in their functioning. On the one hand, they have assumed an increasingly self-referential character. In this respect, Blackpool, these days, represents nothing so much as itself – an isolated pool of modernity surrounded by a ravaged industrial hinterland which has singularly failed to keep up with the times. On the other hand, Blackpool increasingly seeks to associate itself with the modernity of an abstracted international capitalism shorn of any specifically regional associations. The role of Lancashire and of Lancashire culture in mediating between and connecting the two, making Blackpool, as representative of Lancashire, by the same token the representative of a modernising capitalism is, these days, and for obvious reasons, conspicuously absent.

Blackpool's bid for modernity, in other words, is nowadays constructed in spite of, rather than because of, its being in Lancashire. Its 'modern' past, increasingly appearing as the product of an antiquated history, constitutes, in this respect, something of a problem in that the town is littered with the archaic relics of earlier, once advanced but now outmoded technologies (the Tower). The pressures which this creates are keenly felt. It is clear from recent Town Guides that, even in its official forms, Blackpool is once again trying to update its image. In an attempt to secure a larger share of the middle-class holiday market, the resort now increasingly represents itself as a cosmopolitan leisure centre – the Las Vegas of the North – whilst simultaneously distancing itself from its traditional Lancastrian and working-class associations. Even the traditional aspects of a Blackpool holiday – such as a stroll along the piers – have been updated (they all have 'super-modern frontages'). At Blackpool, everything is new no matter how old it is.

Text and Performance

The functioning of this discourse of modernity, however, can only be properly understood when placed in the context of the opposing discourses it has worked against and helped to dismantle. The vaunting claims through which it has sought to undermine and rival the cultural centripetalism of the metropolis have constituted merely one of he discourse's cutting edges in this respect. It has also faced in the other direction, operating against the mutated echoes of the carnivalesque, a transgressive discourse embodied in the practices of the popular classes and their preferred entertainments which, from the mid-nineteenth century, has constituted the unofficial Blackpool, the underbelly beneath its constructed image of progress, respectability and modernity.

The spirit of carnival, of course, has never been as strong in Britain as in Europe, particularly France where, as Mikhail Bakhtin has shown, the tradition of popular carnival fuelled the development of Renaissance humanism and where, as Le Roy Ladurie has demonstrated, carnival celebrations could, at times, spill over into directly political forms of social protest.[19] None the less, the carnival tradition in Britain was never entirely vanquished by the 'triumph of Lent'. Christopher Hill has detailed the respects in which the subversive and transgressive aspects of carnival informed the messianic vision of a wide range of radical sects during the English Revolution.[20] Although shorn of any connection with developed political philosophies, elements of the carnivalesque continued to inform the popular festivals which periodically interrupted the annual cycle of agricultural labour in the eighteenth century. In a recent discussion, Douglas Reid has argued that many of the elements of carnival – excessive eating and drinking, the suspension of sexual prohibitions, the subversion and transgression of normal rules of behaviour, the symbolic inversion of dominant ideological values – remained central aspects of the wakes celebrations of early nineteenth-century workers:

'goose-riding', horse-racing, foot-racing in *déshabillé*, all through the main streets of the town, bizarre competition and great feasting, were certainly reversals of everyday norms, even for the chief participants. To most of the crowd the extraordinary concentration of unfamiliar amusements and familiar activities taken to excess must have constituted wakes as 'rituals of disorder'.[21]

This is not to suggest that, in itself, the carnival tradition should be construed as progressive or that rituals of transgression should be counted as oppositional in their own right. Nor did Bakhtin ever advance such a view, although this is often how his work has been appropriated. What Bakhtin celebrated in his study of Rabelais was not the carnival tradition as such but the direction in which that tradition was made to point, the specific way in which its cultural and ideological meaning was inflected, in being articulated to the progressive currents of Renaissance humanism.[22] It was the *fusion* of these two traditions and the new meanings which accrued to the carnivalesque as a consequence, rather than the mere brute fact of carnival, that Bakhtin regarded as valuable. Whereas most theorists of carnival stress only its negative aspects, construing it as merely a compendium of transgressive rituals, Bakhtin placed a quite exceptional emphasis on its positive aspects. The value of excess associated with carnival eating, drinking and sexuality, he argued, formed part of an image of the people as a boundless, unstoppable material force, a vast self-regenerating and undifferentiated body surmounting all obstacles placed in its path. For Bakhtin, the unique significance of the Renaissance consisted in the respects in which the transgressive aspects of carnival were connected to Renaissance criticisms of medieval ideology whilst its positive aspects were simultaneously connected to progressive humanist currents of thought, the body of the people serving as the very image of and prototype for a secular and humanist philosophy of history as a continuously unfolding process of human self-creation. In Rabelais, he argues, 'the destruction of the old picture of the world and the positive construction of a new picture are indissolubly interwoven with each other'.[23]

In sum, Bakhtin's concern was not with carnival but with the *discursive rearticulation* of elements of the carnivalesque in the culture and ideology of the Renaissance. It is thus the *transformative* aspects of Rabelais' work that he constantly stressed: 'Rabelais by no means advocated crude gluttony and drunkenness. But he does affirm the lofty importance of eating and drinking in human life, and strives to justify them ideologically, to make them respectable, to erect a culture for them.'[24] In other contexts, deprived of these specific ideological and cultural articulations, he judged the various elements of the carnivalesque quite censoriously. It is thus that he contrasted the way Rabelais connects the stress placed within carnival on material and bodily processes to a humanist view of the body as a harmonious combination of corporeal and mental functions, to be developed through physical and intellectual exercise, to 'the licentiousness and coarseness of medieval practice'.[25] Similarly, he spoke of the subsequent degeneration of carnival language and its functioning: 'To this very day, the unofficial (male) side of speech reflects a Rabelaisian degree of indecency in it, of words concerning drunkenness and defecation and so forth, but all this is by now clichéd and no longer creative.'[26]

There can be no question, then, of any uncritical celebration of carnival as if the practices which comprised it somehow spoke their own meaning, voicing the authentic spirit of the people independently of the prevailing social and cultural relationships in which they are inscribed. Carnival may be, as Terry Eagleton has suggested, no more than a 'popular blow-off'.[27] It may also be, as Reid makes clear in his discussion of wakes celebrations, connected with customs that are wantonly cruel and sexist. For all that, the residue of the carnivalesque which survived in the nineteenth-century wakes and, later, urban fairs constituted a discourse which refused to be placed, which rejected the subalterned niche preserved for the working classes within bourgeois culture and which effected, however inarticulately and temporarily, a periodic overthrowing, a *bouleverse-ment* of the bourgeois values of 'sobriety, orderliness, "rationality" and the pursuit of progress'.[28] It is for this reason, Reid suggests, that in the late eighteenth and early nineteenth centuries, local élites withdrew their support and patronage from wakes celebrations and, with the backing of the upper strata of skilled artisans, began to hem them in with restrictions. Urban fairs were similarly persecuted in the mid-century only, as Hugh Cunningham observes, to be actively promoted by both central government and local authorities toward the end of the century, presented as an aid rather than a threat to public order. Cunningham advances three reasons for this change. First, the values and norms of showmen changed as they became 'respectable and wealthy entrepeneurs of leisure, patronized by Royalty'.[29] Second, the mechanisation of fairs meant that fairground entertainments were increasingly brought into line with the values of industrial civilization, a testimony to the virtues of progress. Third, and in good part as a consequence of these changes, the habits of fairgoers changed; by the end of the century, he argues, 'fairgoing had become a relatively routine ingredient in an accepted world of leisure' as 'fairs became tolerated, safe, and in due course a subject for nostalgia and revival'.[30]

The struggles surrounding the history of popular recreation in Blackpool rehearsed these more general developments, giving them a peculiarly condensed expression owing to the exceptional concentration of popular entertainments within the town. At the same time, the struggles were more protracted as a consequence of the longer-term and more permanent sites that, first, the beach and, later, the promenade afforded elements of the carnivalesque placed under pressure in the inland towns. As late as the 1930s, Tom Harrison pointed to the general pervasiveness of carnival elements in Blackpool.[31] Indeed, remnants of the carnivalesque can still be found in Blackpool, although they are now exceedingly marginalised, located only within the interstices of the town's pleasure economy – in the back-street shops selling masks, willy-warmers and a whole range of incredible phallic objects – or, in a massively incorporated form, in the multiple references to the world of carnival at the Pleasure Beach, references which keep alive the discourse of carnival only in an always-already recuperated, Disneyfied form.[32] And, as elsewhere, the carnivalesque was opposed and dismantled by a combination of tactics – initially, by means of attempted legal regulation and prohibition and, subsequently, by means of breaking it up into its constituent elements and culturally re-forming those elements, modifying their meaning, by drawing them into the orbit of, and making them complicit with, the discourse of modernity.

The history of the Pleasure Beach illustrates both these processes. Located at the southern edge of the town, the Pleasure Beach occupies what used to be, in the mid-nineteenth century, a gipsy encampment where both resident families and itinerant entertainers offered a variety of traditional entertainments – astrology, fortune-telling, palmistry, phrenology and so on. Mechanical rides were first developed on this site – originally just a vast area of sand stretching back from and continuous with the beach – in the late 1880s. During the same period, the site was also occupied by exhibitions derived from the wakes fairs – peep-shows, fat ladies and the like. Whereas initially the corporation had opposed these developments, it lent its support to two entrepeneurs who, in 1895, bought the tract of land on which these entertainments were located with the express purpose of developing it into an integrated open-air pleasure complex on the model of American amusement parks. At this time, the site was occupied by a jumble of independently owned and operated mechanical rides existing side-by-side with gipsy amusements and side-shows characteristic of the urban fairs of the period. Its transformation into the Pleasure Beach – a huge, walled-in entertainments complex, run as a single entity by a private company still in the hands of the family of one of its co-founders – was accomplished by a variety of strategies, all of which were well in place by the 1930s. Taken together, these resulted in a modernising streamlining of pleasure which early achieved a degree of unity unobtainable elsewhere in Blackpool where the fragmented structure of land ownership permitted – and, to a degree, still permits – the coexistence of different regimes of pleasure.

First, by means of legal powers secured from the corporation, gipsies were prohibited from operating on the site and, by 1910, were finally evicted. This not only made the Pleasure Beach more respectable; it dislodged from the site the traditional Romany entertainments which jarred with the model of pleasure embodied in the importation of increasingly sophisticated mechanical and theme rides from American amusement parks. This has been perhaps the most distinctive of the Pleasure Beach's techniques of modernisation. Beginning with the introduction of dodgems in 1910 – billed as 'The first in Europe direct from America' – the Pleasure Beach has periodically updated itself by importing a series of ride innovations from America, constantly weaving these into its rhetoric of self-representation as offering the biggest, the best, the only one of its kind, the unique, the latest, the most up-to-the-minute range of thrills, spills and popular entertainments. Related to this, independent side-show operators were transformed into concessionaries, allowed to operate on the site (in return for a portion of their take) only if they conformed with the requirements of company policy. This entailed, very early on, the exclusion from the site of all elements of the grotesque and the modernisation of such traditional side-show entertainments as remained. The net result of these tendencies is a peculiar contradiction. The forms of machinery in use at the Pleasure Beach today operate to suspend the normal restraints which hem in and limit the body, but all of this takes place within a system of signs operative in the themes of the rides, their architectural design and the predominant forms of hailing in use which is solidly compacted with an unabashed ideology of progress. The body may be whirled upside down, hurled this way and that by the machinery of the rides, but, in the coding of these pleasures for consumption, the dominant symbolic order remains unwaveringly the right way up.

However, to consider only the discourses embodied in the sedimented forms of the town's major popular entertainments would give a misleadingly one-sided impression of the cultural 'feel' of Blackpool. This is not merely to suggest that there are elements which contradict or differ from the dominant ideological coding of pleasure in the town such as I have described it, although this is true. Paradoxically, contemporary Blackpool is also the site for the enunciation of a simply massive discourse of nostalgia, of a longing for selectively preserved and romanticised pasts, although I would argue that this discourse is ultimately contained within the discourse of modernity in the form of the claims the town makes to be the only holiday resort sufficiently forward-looking to keep the remnants of its past – the Tower and the piers, for example – in good working order. Rather more to the point is the consideration that if, as I have argued, the ideological coding of pleasure at Blackpool has certain textual properties, then, just as is the case with the relations between any text and its readers, so the 'text of pleasure' prevailing at Blackpool does not itself automatically produce or guarantee the way it will be responded to or negotiated by the pleasure-seeker. This is to take issue somewhat with Louis Marin's analysis of Disneyland; or, at least, it is to suggest that it is a model which should not be uncritically extended elsewhere. According to Marin, the system of ideas and values given concrete form in the thematics of Disneyland constitute a 'representation realised in geographical space of the imaginary relationship which the dominant groups of American society maintain with their real conditions of existence or, more precisely, with the real history of the United States and with the space outside of its borders'.[33]

He further contends that the way the geographical space of Disneyland is organised – its division into various sections (Adventureland, Frontierland, Fantasyland, Tomorrowland, Mainstreet USA) and the ordering of the relations between them – constitute a narrative and one, moreover, which entirely constrains the narrative performance (the tour) of the visitor. In order to construct his or her tour into a narrative – a sequence of events with meaning – the visitor is forced to rely on the representations of America and its imaginary history which totally pervade the park as an entirely self-enclosed environment.

> In other words, Disneyland is an example of a *langue* reduced to a univocal code, without *parole*, even though its visitors have the feeling of living a personal and unique adventure on their tour. And since this *langue* is a stereotyped fantasy, the visitor is caught in it, without any opportunity to escape.[34]

Blackpool, even the Pleasure Beach, the most consummate expression of its discourse of modernity, differs from this in at least two respects. First, the town lacks a singular narrative organisation. Unlike Disneyland, it was not constructed in accordance with a preconceived plan but has rather been progressively constructed and selectively reconstructed, in partial and piecemeal fashion, thereby making for a series of discourse clashes and different narrative possibilities at any given point in time. Second, the visitor to Blackpool is not always already narrativised in the manner of the visitor to Disneyland, a subject already placed within Disney ideology, before he or she gets there, by the output of the Disney film industry. In effect, to visit Disneyland is to complete a process of narrativisation inaugurated elsewhere. No such broader narrative system bears on the visitor to Blackpool. Instead, the visitor is able to deploy a wide range of cultural resources in constructing his or her pleasure-route through the, in any case, more uneven and contradictory 'text of pleasure' prevailing in the town. And among these resources are elements of the carnivalesque. For Bakhtin, it is important to recall, carnival was, above all, a practice of the people and its theatre was the street. To the degree that it still exists in Blackpool, the carnivalesque takes this form – the never-ending excess of eating and drinking, the disruption of conventional temporal rhythms, the transgression of normal rules of dress and behaviour by the wearing of funny hats and the like. In themselves, of course, such practices are of no special value or political significance. But they point to a residue, a utopian excess which spills over the ability of the discourse of modernity to frame and contain, interpret and make intelligible the visitor's experience, a residue which could be made to point in fruitful directions.

Tom Harrison recorded that imitation bosses once figured prominently as targets at the Pleasure Beach and noted that there used to be a dummy policeman in a stationary car on the dodgems which had to be removed as the figure became damaged too quickly and too repeatedly. In 1981, street sellers were offering dartboards printed over with a full-face picture of Margaret Thatcher. A couple of years previously, giant Charles ears were the feature of the season. Not much to go on, but pointers as to the ways in which the same set of pleasures might, in being ideologically recoded, give rise to different meanings with different political effects. At least, such an orientation to popular entertainments, seeking to reorder their cultural and ideological articulations and, thereby, to hook popular practices into an association with critical or progressive values is preferable to one which opposes such practices in the name of some higher, abstracted ideal.

Notes

1. Official Town Guide, 1897, p. 33 (I am indebted to Grahame Thompson of the Open University for making copies of Blackpool Town Guides available to me and for pointing out their considerable value and interest).
2. Official Town Guide, 1924, p. 34.
3. Southern visitors are, and always have been, a statistical rarity at Blackpool. An English Tourist Board survey conducted in 1972 revealed that Blackpool relied overwhelmingly on the northern counties, Scotland and, to a lesser extent, the Midlands for its business.
4. See H. Marcuse, *One Dimensional Man: The Ideology of Industrial Society*, Sphere Books, London, 1968.
5. Many of the perspectives in this section are derived from B. Turner and S. Palmer, *The Blackpool Story*, Palmer and Turner, Clevelys, 1981. Unattributed quotations are also taken from this source.
6. J. K. Walton, *The Blackpool Landlady: A Social History*, Manchester University Press, 1978, pp. 137–8.
7. Wakes holidays were derived from rush-bearing festivals, usually held in the summer to celebrate the anniversary of the dedication of a local church. As such, their dates were variable – August in Middleton, June in Oldham. See J. K. Walton and R. Poole, 'The Lancashire Wakes in the Nineteenth Century', in R. D. Storch (ed.), *Popular Culture and Custom in Nineteenth Century England*, Croom Helm, London, 1982.
8. Walton and Poole argue that the decline of traditional wakes celebrations has been exaggerated, but do not dispute that this was the general tendency.

9. For a useful survey of the mid-century attacks on fairs, see H. Cunningham, 'The Metropolitan Fairs: A Case-Study in the Social Control of Leisure', in A. P. Donajgrodzki (ed.), *Social Control in Nineteenth Century Britain*, Croom Helm, London, 1977.

10. J. K. Walton has convincingly argued that many of Blackpool's peculiar characteristics can be attributed to the extremely fragmented structure of land ownership which prevailed in the town from towards the end of the eighteenth century. This enabled small tradesmen to establish themselves in the town in a way that was not possible in Southport, for example, where a much more highly concentrated structure of land ownership facilitated the exclusion of commercial activities which might detract from the 'respectable' tone of the town; see J.K. Walton, 'Residential Amenity, Respectable Morality and the Rise of the Entertainment Industry: The Case of Blackpool, 1860–1914', *Literature and History*, vol. 1, 1975.

11. I am indebted to John Golby of the Open University for these figures.

12. H. J. Perkin, 'The "Social Tone" of Victorian Seaside Resorts in the North-West', *Northern History*, vol. XI, 1975–6.

13. See D. Hebdige, 'Towards a Cartography of Taste, 1935–1962', *Block*, no. 4, 1981

14. P. Joyce, *Work, Society and Politics, The Culture of the Factory in later Victorian England*, Rutgers University Press, New Jersey, 1980, p. xv.

15. See P. Anderson, 'Origins of the Present Crisis', *New Left Review*, no. 23, 1964.

16. P. Joyce, *Work, Society and Politics*, p. 3.

17. See H. Cunningham, 'Class and Leisure in Mid-Victorian England' in B. Waites, T. Bennett and G. Martin (eds), *Popular Culture: Past and Present*, Croom Helm, London, 1982.

18. Official Town Guide, 1924, p. 42.

19. See M. M. Bakhtin, *Rabelais and His World*, MIT Press, Cambridge, Mass. 1968; and E. Le Roy Ladurie, *Carnival in Romans*, George Braziller, New York, 1979.

20. See C. Hill, *The World Turned Upside Down: Radical Ideas During the English Revolution*, Penguin, Harmondsworth, 1975.

21. D. A. Reid 'Interpreting the Festival Calendar: Wakes and Fairs as Carnivals', in R. D. Storch (ed.), *Popular Culture and Custom*, p. 129.

22. For a fuller discussion of this aspect of Bakhtin's work, see T. Bennett, *Formalsim and Marxism*, Methuen, London, 1979, pp. 82–92.

23. M. M. Bakhtin, *The Dialogic Imagination*, University of Texas Press, Austin and London, 1981, p. 169.

24. Ibid., p. 185.

25. Ibid., p. 171.

26. Ibid., p. 238.

27. T. Eagleton, *Walter Benjamin, or Towards a Revolutionary Criticism*, New Left Books, London, 1981, p. 148.

28. D. A. Reid, 'Interpreting the Festival Calendar', p. 125.

29. H. Cunningham, 'Class and Leisure', p. 163.

30. Ibid., p. 164.

31. T. Harrison, 'The Fifty-second Week: Impressions of Blackpool', *The Geographical Magazine*, April, 1938.

32. I have discussed this aspect of the Pleasure Beach elsewhere. See T. Bennett, 'A Thousand and One Troubles: Blackpool Pleasure Beach' in *Formations of Pleasure*, Routledge and Kegan Paul, 1983.

33. L. Marin, 'Disneyland: A Degenerate Utopia', *Glyph* I, p. 54.

34. Ibid., p. 59.

8

City of Quartz: Excavating the Future in Los Angeles

*Mike Davis**

The carefully manicured lawns of Los Angeles's Westside sprout forests of ominous little signs warning: 'Armed Response!' Even richer neighborhoods in the canyons and hillsides isolate themselves behind walls guarded by guntoting private police and state-of-the-art electronic surveillance. Downtown, a publicly-subsidized 'urban renaissance' has raised the nation's largest corporate citadel, segregated from the poor neighborhoods around it by a monumental architectural glacis. In Hollywood, celebrity architect Frank Gehry, renowned for his 'humanism', apotheosizes the siege look in a libary designed to resemble a foreign-legion fort. In the Westlake district and the San Fernando Valley the Los Angeles Police barricade streets and seal off poor neighborhoods as part of their 'war on drugs'. In Watts, developer Alexander Haagen demonstrates his strategy for recolonizing inner-city retail markets: a panopticon shopping mall surrounded by staked metal fences and a substation of the LAPD in a central surveillance tower. Finally on the horizon of the next millennium, an ex-chief of police crusades for an anti-crime 'giant eye' – a gco-synchronous law enforcement satellite – while other cops discreetly tend versions of 'Garden Plot', a hoary but still viable 1960s plan for a law-and-order armageddon.

Welcome to post-liberal Los Angeles, where the defense of luxury lifestyles is translated into a proliferation of new repressions in space and movement, undergirded by the ubiquitous 'armed response'. This obsession with physical security systems, and, collaterally, with the architectural policing of social boundaries, has become a zeitgeist of urban restructuring, a master narrative in the emerging built environment of the 1990s. Yet contemporary urban theory, whether debating the role of electronic technologies in precipitating 'postmodern space', or discussing the dispersion of urban functions across poly-centered metropolitan 'galaxies', has been strangely silent about the militarization of city life so grimly visible at the street level. Hollywood's pop apocalypses and pulp science fiction have been more realistic, and politically perceptive, in representing the programmed hardening of the urban surface in the wake of the social polarizations of the Reagan era. Images of carceral inner cities (*Escape from New York, Running Man*), high-tech police death squads (*Blade Runner*), sentient buildings (*Die*

* Pp. 223–40, 261–2 from M. Davis, *City of Quartz: Excavating the Future in Los Angeles* (London: Verso).

Hard), urban bantustans (*They Live!*), Vietnam-like street wars (*Colors*), and so on, only extrapolate from actually existing trends.

Such dystopian visions grasp the extent to which today's pharaonic scales of residential and commercial security supplant residual hopes for urban reform and social integration. The dire predictions of Richard Nixon's 1969 National Commission on the Causes and Prevention of Violence have been tragically fulfilled: we live in 'fortress cities' brutally divided between 'fortified cells' of affluent society and 'places of terror' where the police battle the criminalized poor.[1] The 'Second Civil War' that began in the long hot summers of the 1960s has been institutionalized into the very structure of urban space. The old liberal paradigm of social control, attempting to balance repression with reform, has long been superseded by a rhetoric of social warfare that calculates the interests of the urban poor and the middle classes as a zero-sum game. In cities like Los Angeles, on the bad edge of postmodernity, one observes an unprecedented tendency to merge urban design, architecture and the police apparatus into a single, comprehensive security effort.

This epochal coalescence has far-reaching consequences for the social relations of the built environment. In the first place, the market provision of 'security' generates its own paranoid demand. 'Security' becomes a positional good defined by income access to private 'protective services' and membership in some hardened residential enclave or restricted suburb, As a prestige symbol – and sometimes as the decisive borderline between the merely well-off and the 'truly rich' – 'security' has less to do with personal safety than with the degree of personal insulation, in residential, work, consumption and travel environments, from 'unsavory' groups and individuals, even crowds in general.

Secondly, as William Whyte has observed of social intercourse in New York, 'fear proves itself'. The social perception of threat becomes a function of the security mobilization itself, not crime rates. Where there is an actual rising arc of street violence, as in Southcentral Los Angeles or Downtown Washington DC, most of the carnage is self-contained within ethnic or class boundaries. Yet white middle-class imagination, absent from any firsthand knowledge of inner-city conditions, magnifies the perceived threat through a demonological lens. Surveys show that Milwaukee suburbanites are just as worried about violent crime as inner-city Washingtonians, despite a twenty-fold difference in relative levels of mayhem. The media, whose function in this arena is to bury and obscure the daily economic violence of the city, ceaselessly throw up spectres of criminal underclasses and psychotic stalkers. Sensationalized accounts of killer youth gangs high on crack and shrilly racist evocations of marauding Willie Hortons foment the moral panics that reinforce and justify urban apartheid.

Moreover, the neo-military syntax of contemporary architecture insinuates violence and conjures imaginary dangers. In many instances the semiotics of so-called 'defensible space' are just about as subtle as a swaggering white cop. Today's upscale, pseudo-public spaces – sumptuary malls, office centers, culture acropolises, and so on – are full of invisible signs warning off the underclass 'Other'. Although architectural critics are usually oblivious to how the built environment contributes to segregation, pariah groups – whether poor Latino families, young Black men, or elderly homeless white females – read the meaning immediately.

The Destruction of Public Space

The universal and ineluctable consequence of this crusade to secure the city is the destruction of accessible public space. The contemporary opprobrium attached to the term 'street person' is in itself a harrowing index of the devaluation of public spaces. To reduce contact with untouchables, urban redevelopment has converted once vital pedestrian streets into traffic sewers and transformed public parks into temporary receptacles for the homeless and wretched. The American city, as many critics have recognized, is being systematically turned inside out – or, rather, outside in. The valorized spaces of the new megastructures and super-malls are concentrated in the center, street frontage is denuded, public activity is sorted into strictly functional compartments, and circulation is internalized in corridors under the gaze of private police.[2]

The privatization of the architectural public realm, moreover, is shadowed by parallel restructurings of electronic space, as heavily policed, pay-access 'information orders', elite data-bases and subscription cable services appropriate parts of the invisible agora. Both processes, of course, mirror the deregulation of the economy and the recession of non-market entitlements. The decline of urban liberalism has been accompanied by the death of what might be called the 'Olmstedian vision' of public space. Frederick Law Olmsted, it will be recalled, was North America's Haussmann, as well as the Father of Central Park. In the wake of Manhattan's 'Commune' of 1863, the great Draft Riot, he conceived public landscapes and parks as social safety-valves, *mixing* classes and ethnicities in common (bourgeois) recreations and enjoyments. As Manfredo Tafuri has shown in his well-known study of Rockefeller Center, the same principle animated the construction of the canonical urban spaces of the La Guardia–Roosevelt era.[3]

This reformist vision of public space – as the emollient of class struggle, if not the bedrock of the American *polis* – is now as obsolete as Keynesian nostrums of full employment. In regard to the 'mixing' of classes, contemporary urban America is more like Victorian England than Walt Whitman's or La Guardia's New York. In Los Angeles, once-upon-a-time a demi-paradise of free beaches, luxurious parks, and 'cruising strips', genuinely democratic space is all but extinct. The Oz-like archipelago of Westside pleasure domes – a continuum of tony malls, arts centers and gourmet strips – is reciprocally dependent upon the social imprisonment of the third-world service proletariat who live in increasingly repressive ghettoes and barrios. In a city of several million yearning immigrants, public amenities are radically shrinking, parks are becoming derelict and beaches more segregated, libraries and playgrounds are closing, youth congregations of ordinary kinds are banned, and the streets are becoming more desolate and dangerous.

Unsurprisingly, as in other American cities, municipal policy has taken its lead from the security offensive and the middle-class demand for increased spatial and social insulation. De facto disinvestment in traditional public space and recreation has supported the shift of fiscal resources to corporate-defined redevelopment priorities. A pliant city government – in this case ironically professing to represent a bi-racial coalition of liberal whites and Blacks – has collaborated in the massive privatization of public space and the subsidization of new, racist enclaves (benignly described as 'urban villages'). Yet most current, giddy discussions of the 'postmodern' scene in Los Angeles neglect entirely these overbearing aspects of counter-urbanization and counter-insurgency. A triumphal gloss – 'urban renaissance', 'city of the future', and so on – is laid over the brutalization of inner-city neighborhoods and the increasing South Africanization of its spatial relations, Even as the walls have come down in Eastern Europe, they are being erected all over Los Angeles.

The observations that follow take as their thesis the existence of this new class war (sometimes a continuation of the race war of the 1960s) at the level of the built environment. Although this is not a comprehensive account, which would require a thorough analysis of economic and political dynamics, these images and instances are meant to convince the reader that urban form is indeed following a repressive function in the political furrows of the Reagan–Bush era, Los Angeles, in its usual prefigurative mode, offers an especially disquieting catalogue of the emergent liaisons between architecture and the American police state.

The Forbidden City

The first militarist of space in Los Angeles was General Otis of the *Times*. Declaring himself at war with labor, he infused his surroundings with an unrelentingly bellicose air:

> He called his home in Los Angeles the Bivouac. Another house was known as the Outpost.
> The *Times* was known as the Fortress. The staff of the paper was the Phalanx. The *Times*
> building itself was more fortress than newspaper plant, there were turrets, battlements,
> sentry boxes. Inside he stored fifty rifles.[4]

A great, menacing bronze eagle was the *Times's* crown; a small, functional cannon was installed on the hood of Otis's touring car to intimidate onlookers. Not surprisingly, this overwrought display of aggression produced a response in kind. On 1 October 1910 the heavily fortified *Times* headquarters – citadel of the open shop on the West Coast – was destroyed in a catastrophic explosion blamed on union saboteurs.

Eighty years later, the spirit of General Otis returned to subtly pervade Los Angeles's new 'postmodern' Downtown: the emerging Pacific Rim financial complex which cascades, in rows of skyscrapers, from Bunker Hill southward along the Figueroa corridor. Redeveloped with public tax increments under the aegis of the powerful and largely unaccountable Community Redevelopment Agency, the Downtown project is one of the largest postwar urban designs in North America. Site assemblage and clearing on a vast scale, with little mobilized opposition, have resurrected land values, upon which big developers and off-shore capital (increasingly Japanese) have planted a series of billion-dollar, block-square megastructures: Crocker Center, the Bonaventure Hotel and Shopping Mall, the World Trade Center, the Broadway Plaza, Arco Center, CitiCorp Plaza, California Plaza, and so on. With historical landscapes erased, with megastructures and superblocks as primary components, and with an increasingly dense and self-contained circulation system, the new financial district is best conceived as a single, demonically self-referential hyperstructure, a Miesian skyscape raised to dementia.

Like similar megalomaniac complexes, tethered to fragmented and desolated Downtowns (for instance, the Renaissance Center in Detroit, the Peachtree and Omni Centers in Atlanta, and so on), Bunker Hill and the Figueroa corridor have provoked a storm of liberal objections against their abuse of scale and composition, their denigration of street landscape, and their confiscation of so much of the vital life activity of the center, now sequestered within subterranean concourses or privatized malls. Sam Hall Kaplan, the crusty urban critic of the *Times*, has been indefatigable in denouncing the anti-pedestrian bias of the new corporate citadel, with its fascist obliteration of street frontage. In his view the superimposition of 'hermetically sealed fortresses' and air-dropped 'pieces of suburbia' has 'dammed the rivers of life' Downtown.[5]

Yet Kaplan's vigorous defense of pedestrian democracy remains grounded in hackneyed liberal complaints about 'bland design' and 'elitist planning practices'. Like most architectural critics, he rails against the oversights of urban design without recognizing the dimension of foresight, of explicit repressive intention, which has its roots in Los Angeles's ancient history of class and race warfare. Indeed, when Downtown's new 'Gold Coast' is viewed en bloc from the standpoint of its interactions with other social areas and landscapes in the central city, the 'fortress effect' emerges, not as an inadvertent failure of design, but as deliberate socio-spatial strategy.

The goals of this strategy maybe summarized as a double repression: to raze all association with Downtown's past and to prevent any articulation with the non-Anglo urbanity of its future. Everywhere on the perimeter of redevelopment this strategy takes the form of a brutal architectural edge or glacis that defines the new Downtown as a citadel vis-à-vis the rest of the central city. Los Angeles is unusual amongst major urban renewal centers in preserving, however negligently, most of its circa 1900–30 Beaux Arts commercial core. At immense public cost, the corporate headquarters and financial district was shifted from the old Broadway-Spring corridor six blocks west to the greenfield site created by destroying the Bunker Hill residential neighborhood. To emphasize the 'security' of the new Downtown, virtually all the traditional pedestrian links to the old center, including the famous Angels' Flight funicular railroad, were removed.

The logic of this entire operation is revealing. In other cities developers might have attempted to articulate the new skyscape and the old, exploiting the latter's extraordinary inventory of theaters and historic buildings to create a gentrified history – a gaslight district, Faneuil Market or Ghiardelli Square – as a support to middle-class residential colonization. But Los Angeles's redevelopers viewed property values in the old Broadway core as irreversibly eroded by the area's very centrality to public transport, and especially by its heavy use by Black and Mexican poor. In the wake of the Watts Rebellion, and the perceived Black threat to crucial nodes of white power (spelled out in lurid detail in the McCone Commission Report), resegregated spatial security became the paramount concern.[6] The Los Angeles Police Department abetted the flight of business from Broadway to the fortified redoubts of Bunker Hill by spreading scare literature typifying Black teenagers as dangerous gang members.[7]

As a result, redevelopment massively reproduced spatial apartheid. The moat of the Harbor Freeway and the regraded palisades of Buner Hill cut off the new financial core from the poor immigrant neighborhoods that surround it on every side. Along the base of California Plaza, Hill Street became a local Berlin Wall separating the publicly subsidized luxury of Bunker Hill from the lifeworld of Broadway, now reclaimed by Latino immigrants as their primary shopping and entertainment street. Because politically connected speculators are now redeveloping the northern end of the Broadway corridor (sometimes known as 'Bunker Hill East'), the CRA is promising to restore pedestrian linkages to the Hill in the 1990s, including the Angels' Flight incline railroad. This, of course, only dramatizes the current bias against accessibility – that is to say, against *any* spatial interaction between old and new, poor and rich, except in the framework of gentrification or recolonization.[8] Although a few white-collars venture into the Grand Central Market – a popular emporium of tropic produce and fresh foods – Latino shoppers or Saturday strollers never circulate in the Gucci precincts above Hill Street. The occasional appearance of a destitute street nomad in Broadway Plaza or in front of the Museum of Contemporary Art sets off a quiet panic; video cameras turn on their mounts and security guards adjust their belts.

Photographs of the old Downtown in its prime show mixed crowds of Anglo, Black and Latino pedestrians of different ages and classes. The contemporary Downtown 'renaissance' is designed to make such heterogeneity virtually impossible. It is intended not just to 'kill the street' as Kaplan fears, but to 'kill the crowd', to eliminate that democratic admixture on the pavements and in the parks that Olmsted believed was America's antidote to European class polarizations. The Downtown hyperstructure – like some Buckminster Fuller post-Holocaust fantasy – is programmed to ensure a seamless continuum of middle-class work, consumption and recreation, without unwonted exposure to Downtown's working-class street environments.[9] Indeed the totalitarian semiotics of ramparts and battlements, reflective glass and elevated pedways, rebukes any affinity or sympathy between different architectural or human orders. As in Otis's fortress *Times* building, this is the archisemiotics of class war.

Lest this seem too extreme, consider *Urban Land* magazine's recent description of the profit-driven formula that across the United States has linked together clustered development, social homogeneity, and a secure 'Downtown image':

How to Overcome Fear of Crime in Downtowns

Create a Dense, Compact, Multifunctional Core Area. A downtown can be designed and developed to make visitors feel that it – or a significant portion of it – is attractive and the type of place that 'respectable people' like themselves tend to frequent . . . A core downtown area that is compact, densely developed and multifunctional will concentrate people, giving them more activities. . . . The activities offered in this core area will determine what 'type' of people will be strolling its sidewalks; locating offices and housing for middle- and upper-income residents in or near the core area can assure a high percentage of 'respectable', law-abiding pedestrians. Such an attractive redeveloped core area would also be large enough to affect the downtown's overall image.[10]

Sadistic Street Environments

This conscious 'hardening' of the city surface against the poor is especially brazen in the Manichaean treatment of Downtown microcosms. In his famous study of the 'social life of small urban spaces', William Whyte makes the point that the quality of any urban environment can be measured, first of all, by whether there are convenient, comfortable places for pedestrians to sit.[11] This maxim has been warmly taken to heart by designers of the high-corporate precincts of Bunker Hill and the emerging 'urban village' of South Park. As part of the city's policy of subsidizing white-collar residential colonization in Downtown, it has spent, or plans to spend, tens of millions of dollars of diverted tax revenue on enticing, 'soft' environments in these areas. Planners envision an opulent complex of squares, fountains, world-class public art, exotic shubbery, and avant-garde street furniture along a Hope Street pedestrian corridor. In the propaganda of official boosters, nothing is taken as a better index of Downtown's 'liveability' than the idyll of office workers and upscale tourists lounging or napping in the terraced gardens of California Plaza, the 'Spanish Steps' or Grand Hope Park.

In stark contrast, a few blocks away, the city is engaged in a merciless struggle to make public facilities and spaces as 'unliveable' as possible for the homeless and the poor. The persistence of thousands of street people on the fringes of Bunker Hill and the Civic Center sours the image of designer Downtown living and betrays the laboriously constructed illusion of a Downtown 'renaissance'. City Hall then retaliates with its own variant of low-intensity warfare.[12]

Although city leaders periodically essay schemes for removing indigents *en masse* – deporting them to a poor farm on the edge of the desert, confining them in camps in the mountains, or, memorably, interning them on a derelict ferry at the Harbor – such 'final solutions' have been blocked by councilmembers fearful of the displacement of the homeless into their districts. Instead the city, self-consciously adopting the idiom of urban cold war, promotes the 'containment' (official term) of the homeless in Skid Row along Fifth Street east of the Broadway, systematically transforming the neighborhood into an outdoor poorhouse. But this containment strategy breeds its own vicious circle of contradiction. By condensing the mass of the desperate and helpless together in such a small space, and denying adequate housing, official policy has transformed Skid Row into probably the most dangerous ten square blocks in the world – ruled by a grisly succession of 'Slashers', 'Night Stalkers' and more ordinary predators.[13] Every night on Skid Row is Friday the 13th, and, unsurprisingly, many of the homeless seek to escape the 'Nickle' during the night at all costs, searching safer niches in other parts of Downtown. The city in turn tightens the noose with increased police harassment and ingenious design deterrents.

One of the most common, but mind-numbing, of these deterrents is the Rapid Transit District's new barrelshaped bus bench that offers a minimal surface for uncomfortable sitting, while making sleeping utterly impossible. Such 'bumproof' benches are being widely introduced on the periphery of Skid Row. Another invention, worthy of the Grand Guignol, is the aggressive deployment of outdoor sprinklers. Several years ago the city opened a 'Skid Row Park' along lower Fifth Street, on a corner of Hell. To ensure that the park was not used for sleeping – that is to say, to guarantee that it was mainly utilized for drug dealing and prostitution – the city installed an elaborate over-head sprinkler system programmed to drench unsuspecting sleepers at random times during the night. The system was immediately copied by some local businessmen in order to drive the homeless away from adjacent public sidewalks. Meanwhile restaurants and markets have responded to the homeless by building ornate enclosures to protect their refuse. Although no one in Los Angeles has yet proposed adding cyanide to the garbage, as happened in Phoenix a few years back, one popular seafood restaurant has spent $12,000 to built the ultimate bag-lady-proof trash cage: made of three-quarter inch steel rod with alloy locks and vicious outturned spikes to safeguard priceless moldering fishheads and stale french fries.

Public toilets, however, are the real Eastern Front of the Downtown war on the poor. Los Angeles, as a matter of deliberate policy, has fewer available public lavatories than any major North American city. On the advice of the LAPD (who actually sit on the design board of at least one major Downtown redevelopment project),[14] the Community Redevelopment Agency bulldozed the remaining public toilet in Skid Row. Agency planners then agonized for months over whether to include a 'free-standing public toilet' in their design for South Park. As CRA Chairman Jim Wood later admitted, the decision not to include the toilet was a 'policy decision and not a design decision'. The CRA Downtown prefers the solution of 'quasi-public restrooms' – meaning toilets in restaurants, art galleries and office buildings – which can be made available to tourists and office workers while being denied to vagrants and other unsuitables.[15] The toiletless no-man's-land east of Hill Street in Downtown is also barren of outside water sources for drinking or washing. A common and troubling sight these days are the homeless men – many of them young Salvadorean refugees – washing in and even drinking from the sewer effluent which flows down the concrete channel of the Los Angeles River on the eastern edge of Downtown.

Where the itineraries of Downtown powerbrokers unavoidably intersect with the habitats of the homeless or the working poor, as in the previously mentioned zone of gentrification along the northern Broadway corridor, extraordinary design precautions are being taken to ensure the physical separation of the different humanities. For instance, the CRA brought in the Los Angeles Police to design '24-hour, state-of-the-art security' for the two new parking structures that serve the Los Angeles *Times* and Ronald Reagan State Office buildings. In contrast to the mean streets outside, the parking structures contain beautifully landscaped lawns or 'microparks', and in one case, a food court and a historical exhibit. Moreover, both structures are designed as 'confidence-building' circulation systems – miniature paradigms of privatization – which allow white-collar workers to walk from car to office, or from car to boutique, with minimum exposure to the public street. The Broadway Spring Center, in particular, which links the Ronald Reagan Building to the proposed 'Grand Central Square' at Third and Broadway, has been warmly praised by architectural critics for adding green-ery and art (a banal bas relief) to parking. It also adds a huge dose of menace – armed guards, locked gates, and security cameras – to scare away the homeless and poor.

The cold war on the streets of Downtown is ever escalating. The police, lobbied by Downtown merchants and developers, have broken up every attempt by the homeless and their allies to create safe havens or self-organized encampments. 'Justiceville', founded by homeless activist Ted Hayes, was roughly dispersed; when its inhabitants attempted to find refuge at Venice Beach, they were arrested at the behest of the local councilperson (a renowned environmentalist) and sent back to the inferno of Skid Row. The city's own brief experiment with legalized camping – a grudging response to a series of exposure deaths in the cold winter of 1987[16] – was ended abruptly after only four months to make way for construction of a transit repair yard. Current policy seems to involve a perverse play upon Zola's famous irony about the 'equal rights' of the rich and the poor to sleep out rough. As the head of the city planning commission explained the official line to incredulous reporters, it is not against the law to sleep on the street per se, 'only to erect any sort of protective shelter'. To enforce this prescription against 'cardboard condos', the LAPD periodically sweep the Nickle, confiscating shelters and other possessions, and arresting resisters. Such cynical repression has turned the majority of the homeless into urban bedouins. They are visible all over Downtown, pushing a few pathetic possessions in purloined shopping carts, always fugitive and in motion, pressed between the official policy of containment and the increasing sadism of Downtown streets.[17]

Frank Gehry as Dirty Harry

If the contemporary search for bourgeois security can be read in the design of bus benches and mega-structures, it is also visible at the level of *auteur*. No recent architect has so ingeniously elaborated the urban security function or so brazenly embraced the resulting *frisson* as Los Angeles's Pritzker Prize laureate, Frank Gehry. As we saw earlier, he has become one of the principal 'imagineers' (in the Disney sense) of the neo-boosterism of 1990s. He is particularly adept as a crossover, not merely between architecture and modern art, but also between older, vaguely radical and contemporary, basically cynical styles. Thus his portfolio is at once a principled repudiation of post-modernism and one of its cleverest sublimations; a nostalgic evocation of revolutionary constructivism and a mercenary celebration of bourgeois-decadent minimalism. These amphibian shifts and paradoxical nuances in Gehry's work sustain a booming cottage industry of Gehry-interpretation, mostly effused with hyperbolic admiration.

Yet Gehry's strongest suit may simply be his straightforward exploitation of rough urban environments, and his blatant incorporation of their harshest edges and detritus as powerful representational elements in his work. Affectionately described by colleagues as an 'old socialist' or 'street-fighter with a heart' much of his most interesting work is utterly unromantic and anti-idealist.[18] Unlike his popular front mentors of the 1940s, Gehry makes little pretense at architectural reformism or 'design for democracy'. He boasts of trying 'to make the best with the reality of things'. With sometimes chilling luminosity, his work clarifies the underlying relations of repression, surveillance and exclusion that characterize the fragmented, paranoid spatiality towards which Los Angeles seems to aspire.

A very early example of Gehry's new urban realism was his 1964 solution of the problem of how to insert high property values and sumptuary spaces into decaying neighborhoods. His Danziger Studio in Hollywood is the pioneer instance of what has become an entire species of Los Angeles 'stealth houses', dissimulating their luxurious qualities with proletarian or gangster façades. The street frontage of the Danziger – on Melrose in the bad old days before its current gourmet-gulch renaissance – was simply a massive gray wall, treated with a rough finish to ensure that it would collect dust from passing traffic and weather into a simulacrum of nearby porn studios and garages. Gehry was explicit in his search for a design that was 'introverted and fortress-like' with the silent aura of a 'dumb box'.[19]

'Dumb boxes' and screen walls form an entire cycle of Gehry's work, ranging from his American School of Dance (1968) to his Gemini G.E.I. (1979), both in Hollywood. His most seminal design, however, was his walled town center for Cochiti Lake, New Mexico (1973): here ice-blue ramparts of awesome severity enclose an entire community (a plan replicated on a smaller scale in the 1976 Jung Institute in Los Angeles). In each of these instances, melodrama is generated by the antithesis between the fortified exteriors, set against 'unappealing neighborhoods' or deserts, and the opulent interiors, open to the sky by clerestories and lightwells. Gehry's walled compounds and cities, in other words, offer powerful metaphors for the retreat from the street and the introversion of space that characterized the design backlash against the urban insurrections of the 1960s.

This problematic was renewed in 1984 in his design of the Loyola Law School located on the western edge of Downtown Los Angeles in the largest Central American barrio in the United States. The inner-city situation of the Loyola campus confronted Gehry with an explicit choice between the risks of creating a genuine public space, extending into the community, or choosing the security of a defensible enclave, as in his previous work. The radical, or simply idealist, architect might have gambled on opening the campus to the adjacent community, giving it some substantive stake in the design. Instead, as an admiring critic explained, Gehry chose a fundamentally neo-conservative design that was:

> open, but not *too open*. The South Instructional Hall and the chapel show solid backs to Olympic Boulevard, and with the anonymous street sides of the Burns Building, form a gateway that is neither forbidding nor overly welcoming. It is simply there, like everything else in the neighborhood.[20]

(This description considerably understates the forbidding qualities of the campus's formidable steel stake fencing, concrete bloc ziggurat, and stark frontage walls.)

But if the Danziger Studio camouflages itself, and the Cochiti Lake and Loyola designs bunch frontage in stern glares, Gehry's baroquely fortified Frances Howard Goldwyn Regional Branch Library in Hollywood (1984) positively taunts potential trespassers 'to make my day'. This is undoubtedly the most menacing library ever built, a bizarre hybrid (on the outside) of dry-docked dreadnought and Gunga Din fort. With its fifteen-foot security walls of stucco-covered concrete block, its anti-graffiti barricades covered in ceramic tile, its sunken entrance protected by ten-foot steel stacks, and its stylized sentry boxes perched precariously on each side, the Goldwyn Library (influenced by Gehry's 1980 high-security design for the US Chancellery in Damascus) projects the same kind of macho exaggeration as Dirty Harry's 44 Magnum.

Predictably, some of Gehry's intoxicated admirers have swooned over this Beirutized structure as 'generous' and 'inviting', 'the old-fashioned kind of library', and so on. They absurdly miss the point.[21] The previous Hollywood Regional Branch Library had been destroyed by arson, and the Samuel Goldwyn Foundation, which endows this collection of filmland memorabilia, was fixated on physical security. Gehry accepted a commission to design a structure that was inherently 'vandalproof'. The curiosity, of course, is his rejection of the low-profile, high-tech security systems that most architects subtly integrate in their blueprints. He chose instead a high-profile, low-tech approach that maximally foregrounds the security functions as motifs of the design. There is no dissimulation of function by form; quite the opposite, Gehry lets it all hang out. How playful or mordantly witty you may find the resulting effect depends on your existential position. The Goldwyn Library relentlessly interpellates a demonic Other (arsonist, graffitist, invader) whom it reflects back on surrounding streets and street people. It coldly saturates its immediate environment, which is seedy but not particularly hostile, with its own arrogant paranoia.

Yet paranoia could be a misnomer, for the adjacent streets are a battleground. Several years ago the Los Angeles *Times* broke the sordid story about how the entertainment conglomerates and a few large landowners, monopolizing land ownership in this part of Hollywood, had managed to capture control of the redevelopment process. Their plan, still the object of controversy, is to use eminent domain and public tax increments to clear the poor (increasingly refugees from Central America) from the streets of Hollywood and reap the huge windfalls from 'upgrading' the region into a glitzy theme-park for international tourism.[22] Within this strategy, the Goldwyn Library – like Gehry's earlier walled compounds – is a kind of architectural fire-base, a beachhead for gentrification. Its soaring, light-filled interiors surrounded by bellicose barricades speak volumes about how public architecture in America is literally being turned inside out, in the service of 'security' and profit.

Notes

1. See National Committee on the Causes and Prevention of Violence, *To Establish Justice, To Ensure Domestic Tranquility (Final Report)*, Washington DC 1969.
2. 'The problems of inversion and introversion in development patterns, and ambiguity in the character of public space created within them, are not unique to new shopping center developments. It is commonplace that the modern city as a whole exhibits a tendency to break down into specialised, single-use precincts – the university campus, the industrial estate, the leisure complex, the housing scheme . . . each governed by internal, esoteric rules of development and implemented by specialist agencies whose terms of reference guarantee that they are familiar with other similar developments across the country, but know almost nothing of the dissimilar precincts which abut their own.' (Barry Maitland, *Shopping Malls: Planning and Design*, London 1985, p. 109.)
3. Cf. Geoffrey Blodgett, 'Frederick Law Olmsted: Landscape Architecture as Conservative Reform', *Journal of American History* 62: 4 (March 1976); and Manfredo Tafuri, 'The Disenchanted Mountain: The Skyscraper and the City', in Giorgio Ciucci, et. al., *The American City*, Cambridge, Mass. 1979.
4. David Halberstam, *The Powers That Be*, New York 1979, p. 102.

5. Los Angeles *Times*, 4 November 1978, X, p. 13. See also Sam Hall Kaplan, *L.A. Follies: A Critical Look at Growth, Politics and Architecture*, Santa Monica 1989.

6. Governor's Commission on the Los Angeles Riots. *Violence in the City – An End or Beginning?*, Los Angeles 1965.

7. In the early 1970s the police circularized members of the Central City Association about an 'imminent gang invasion'. They urged businessmen 'to report to the police the presence of any groups of young Blacks in the area. These are young people between the ages of twelve and eighteen, both boys and girls. One gang wears earrings and the other wears hats. When encountered in groups of more than two they are very dangerous and armed.' (Los Angeles *Times*, 24 December 1972, I, p. 7.)

8. Gentrification in this case is 'Reaganization'. In a complex deal aimed at making the north end of the Broadway corridor an upscaled 'bridge' linking Bunker Hill, the Civic Center and Little Tokyo, the CRA has spent more than $20 million inducing the State to build the 'Ronald Reagan Office Building' a block away from the corner of Third and Broadway, while simultaneously bribing the Union Rescue Mission $6 million to move its homeless clientele out of the neighborhood. The 3,000 civil servants from the Reagan Building are intended as shock troops to gentrify the strategic corner of Third and Broadway, where developer Ira Yellin has received further millions in subsidies from the CRA to transform the three historic structures he owns (the Bradbury Building, Million Dollar Theater and Grand Central Market) into 'Grand Central Square'. The 'Broadway-Spring Center' – discussed in the text – provides 'security in circulation' between the Reagan Building and the Square.

9. In reflecting on the problem of the increasing social distance between the white middle classes and the Black poor, Oscar Newman, the renowned theorist of 'defensible space', argues for the federally ordered dispersion of the poor in the suburban residential landscape. He insists, however, that 'bringing the poor and the black into the fold' (sic) must be conducted 'on a tightly controlled quota basis' that is non-threatening to the middle class and ensures their continuing social dominance. (*Community of Interest*, Garden City 1981, pp. 19–25.) Such 'tightly controlled quotas', of course, are precisely the strategy favored by redevelopment agencies like Los Angeles's as they have been forced to include a small portion of low or very-low income housing in their projected 'urban villages'. It seems inconceivable to Newman, or to these agencies, that the urban working class is capable of sustaining their own decent neighborhoods or having any voice in the definition of public interest. That is why the working poor are always the 'problem', the 'blight' in redevelopment, while the gilded middle classes always represent 'revitalization'.

10. N. David Milder, 'Crime and Downtown Revitalization', in *Urban Land*, September 1987, p. 18.

11. *The Social Life of Small Spaces*, New York 1985.

12. The descriptions that follow draw heavily on the extraordinary photographs of Diego Cardoso, who has spent years documenting Downtown's various street scenes and human habitats.

13. Since crack began to replace cheap wine on Skid Row in the mid 1980s, the homicide rate has jumped to almost 1 per week. A recent backpage *Times* story – 'Well, That's Skid Row' (15 November 1989) – claimed that the homeless have become so 'inured to street violence' that 'the brutal slayings of two people within two blocks of each other the night before drew far less attention than the taping of an episode of the television show, "Beauty and the Beast"'. The article noted, however, the homeless have resorted to a 'buddy system' whereby one sleeps and the other acts as 'spotter' to warn of potential assailants.

14. For example, the LAPD sits on the Design Advisory Board of 'Miracle on Broadway', the publicly funded body attempting to initiate the gentrification of part of the Downtown historic core. (*Downtown News*, 2 January 1989.)

15. Interviews with Skid Row residents; see also Tom Chorneau, 'Quandary Over a Park Restroom', *Downtown News*, 25 August 1986, pp. 1, 4. In other Southern California communities the very hygiene of the poor is being criminalized. New ordinances specifically directed against the homeless outlaw washing oneself in public 'above the elbow'.

16. See 'Cold Snap's Toll at 5 as Its Iciest Night Arrives', *Times*, 29 December 1988.

17. See my '*Chinatown*, Part Two? The Internationalization of Downtown Los Angeles', *New Left Review*, July–August 1987. It is also important to note that, despite the crack epidemic on Skid Row (which has attracted a much younger population of homeless men), there is no drug treatment center or rehabilitation program in the area. Indeed within the city as a whole narcotic therapy funding is being cut while police and prison budgets are soaring.

18. 'Old socialist' quote from architect and 'Gehry Kid' Michael Rotundi of Morphosis; Gehry himself boasts: 'I get my inspiration from the streets. I'm more of a street fighter than a Roman scholar,' (Quoted in Adele Freedman, *Progressive Architecture*, October 1986, p. 99.)

19. The best catalogue of Gehry's work is Peter Arnell and Ted Bickford, eds, *Frank Gehry. Buildings and Projects*, New York 1985. Also cf. Institute of Contemporary Art, *Frank O. Gehry, An Exhibition of Recent Projects*, Boston 1982; and University of Southern California, *Frank Gehry: Selected Works*, Los Angeles 1982.

20. Mildred Friedman, ed., *The Architecture of Frank Gehry*, New York 1986, p. 175.

21. Pilar Viladas, 'Illuminated Manuscripts', *Progressive Architecture*, October 1986, pp. 76, 84.

22. See David Ferrell's articles in the Los Angeles *Times*, 31 August and 16 October 1987. In a letter to the *Times* (16 September 1987) the former Los Angeles Director of Planning, Calvin Hamilton, corroborated that the Hollywood Chamber of Commerce 'dominated and aggressively manipulated for their own purposes the decision process. In most areas of planning concern, in my opinion, they were only interested in maximizing their own profit, not in doing a comprehensive, balanced plan for the improvement and long-term benefit of all the people in Hollywood.'

9

Grids of Difference: Place and Identity Formation

Geraldine Pratt*

When I was taught urban social geography in the 1970s, I learned about the city as a mosaic of social worlds, an exciting array of enclaves in the inner city (ethnic villages, gay ghettos, artist enclaves, elite neighborhoods) ringed by homogeneous middle-class, family-oriented suburbs. Part of my interest in the subject stemmed from the understanding that different areas of the city sustained radically different ways of life. Worlds apart in social terms, they stand as neighbors in space. I am still fascinated by the geographical premise of Tom Wolfe's novel (1987) about New York City, *The Bonfire of the Vanities*: that the space between two freeway ramps divides the Bronx from Park Avenue, and that by missing one turnoff you can emerge into a social world that operates with different codes, where other sets of identities are performed and where your identity is out of place.

With recent theorizing about identity and place, this view of the city now seems outdated. Rather than thinking about identities as solidified around one or two social traits such as ethnicity, or gender, or stage in the life cycle, or sexuality, identities are conceived as a process, as performed, and as unstable. Current theories call attention to the fact that we have multiple and sometimes contradictory subject positions and are sometimes torn between identifications, often moving between identifications in different situations and places. This notion of subjectivity has been articulated by Kathy Ferguson through the metaphor of mobile subjectivities: "I have chosen the term *mobile* rather than *multiple* to avoid the implication of movement from one to another stable resting place, and instead to problematize the contours of the resting one does" (1993, p. 158). "Class," she notes, "like race, gender, erotic identity, 'etc.,' can be crucial but still temporary and shifting resting places for subjects always in motion and in relation" (p. 177).

So too, it has been argued that it is inappropriate to view places as bounded because any boundaries are permeable, the global flows through the local, and the local is always dynamic (Massey, 1994). Moreover, there is a deep suspicion about mapping cultures onto places, because multiple cultures and identities inevitably inhabit a single place (think of the multiple identities performed under the roof of a family home) and a single

*Pp. 26–48 from *Cities of Difference*, ed. R. Finger and J. M. Jacobs (New York and London: Guilford Press). © 1998 by The Guilford Press. Reprinted with permission from Guilford Publications, Inc.

cultural identity is often situated in multiple, interconnected spaces. Gupta and Ferguson (1992) argue against assuming the isomorphism of space, place, and culture. They resist the conventional view that cultures are localized and bounded in space and that cultural difference can be represented through a spatial grid of discrete and separate places. They reject, in other words, a vision of the city as a mosaic of spatially discrete and spatially bounded social worlds.

While convinced of the need to rethink the links between place and identity, many theorists are wary of tendencies simply to invert the isomorphism of place and identity, that is, to conceive of mobile identities as *de*-territorialized. Despite her metaphor, Ferguson herself recognizes (1993, p. 162) that subjectivities do get anchored and that understanding this process requires careful attention to the specifics of geography and particular locales. In this, she anticipates Angelika Bammer's criticism of contemporary writing that universalizes displacement, with the effect of "elaborating a new, post-modernistically hip version of the universal subject" (1994, p. xiii; see also Kaplan, 1987; Morris, 1990; Wolff, 1993). Bammer calls for work that puts "the 'place' [and historical specificity] back into 'displacement'" (p. xiv). Gupta and Ferguson (1992) direct attention to processes of re-(as opposed to de-)territorialization.

This chapter is a partial exercise in thinking within this middle ground, by considering the many and different ways that identities are territorialized in contemporary North American cities and the varying scales at which boundaries are produced. The denial of the reality of boundaries would seem to be a luxury affordable only to those not trapped by them. (The same is probably true for the romanticization of them.) My argument is that borders in space and place are tied up with social boundaries (the formation of identity and its complement, the production of difference) but that there are multiple grids of difference and complex and varied links between place and identity formation. It is important to understand these processes of boundary formation in order to create opportunities for imagined and actual alliances across them.

Identities Are Still Bounded

Accepting that identities are a process, a "project," and a "performance" is compatible with an understanding that a stable identity is reenacted through daily life. In my recent research and writing with Susan Hanson, we have been interested in how particular places not only enable but exact the performance of particular gender, class, and racial identities. We have argued that employers and employees in Worcester, Massachusetts, both intentionally and unintentionally conspire in boundary projects by creating extremely local labor markets within the metropolitan area, which have the effect of enabling and imposing different family and gender relations, as well as class and racial identities, on individuals living in different parts of the city (Hanson & Pratt, 1995). At the extremes of intentionality and containment, employers to the southeast of the city in the Blackstone Valley were rumored to have prevented transportation linkages and improvements in order to maintain control of the local (white, working-class, low-waged) labor supply, while blocking other employers from coming into the region. Less obvious in intent but equal in effect, employers' propensity (in all areas studied) to advertise locally and hire through word of mouth, paired with the local job searches of many employees (especially women and workers in "lower" occupational grades), served to create locally bounded and distinctive labor markets. The fact that so many women, in particular, look for jobs close to home is not a matter of unmediated choice. Women with the heaviest domestic workloads were the most likely to find work close to home; power relations in the home thus played an important role in producing bounded labor markets.

These bounded labor markets make a difference to the identities enacted by women living in different parts of the city. They provide different resources, in terms of types of jobs available, hours and schedules of work, and wages paid for comparable work. Two individual case histories make this point. First, the place-bound restrictions on occupational class identity are illustrated by the case of one woman with whom we spoke in the Blackstone Valley. The Blackstone Valley had few clerical jobs, relative to a middle-class area that we studied. The circumstances of this one woman demonstrate the effects of the limited number of clerical jobs available there. This woman, 50 years old when interviewed in 1989, had migrated to the Blackstone Valley in the late 1960s from England with her husband. She had worked as a clerical worker before migrating and sought this type of work when her husband was laid off in 1970. Given that she had young children and no car, she needed to find work close to home, with "mothers' hours." Like so many women with whom we spoke, she found out about her job through neighborhood contacts – in this case from a woman neighbor who knew of an opening for a clerical job at her own workplace. When computers were brought into her work-place, the woman we interviewed told us that she "couldn't get it" and she was moved into production to work as an assembler. The new job was clearly a demotion, and not only in terms of status: it involved a shift from salary to waged work, and reductions in both pay and benefits. This woman preferred office work and returned, throughout the interview, to her loss of status: "Now I'm on the same level as everyone else at the plant today. I'm just assembly. If a machine is down, I do another [assembly] job." She described her current job as "a bore . . . It's just a paycheck." Of particular interest is this woman's recognition that her present circumstances were in large part dictated by her residential location. When she got a car, she said that "I looked around a little, but the majority of things that interested me, they were mostly around Worcester." Though these jobs were less than 10 miles away, she judged them to be too far and opted to stay (despite her dissatisfaction) in her job as assembler. The reputation of the Blackstone Valley, as home to poorly paid, well-disciplined factory workers, became a reality for this woman.

One gets the same sense of an identity congealing around an individual, in large part because of residential location in a spatially circumscribed labor market, in the case of a woman who had recently migrated from Puerto Rico and was presently living and working in Main South, an inner-city, low-income area of Worcester, home to large numbers of Latino and Vietnamese households. She lived in an area around Piedmont Street, a notorious and stigmatized street in the eyes of middle-class residents of Worcester, and worked in a nearby industrial laundry with many of her neighbors: "About 12 people who work here live where I live. All my good friends [at the laundry] live near me in the building that I'm talking about. I started working, and then cousins came and friends came, and all started working." She characterized her job as "suitable for dogs": the hours were long (a 10-hour day was not unusual) and wages low (in general, firms in Main South paid the lowest wages for comparable work, relative to firms in three other areas that we studied); and she very much wanted to find another job within the year. It is important, however, to note that the preceding quotes are translations of her words in Spanish. This woman lived and worked almost exclusively with Spanish-speaking Worcesterites and, working long hours, her opportunities to learn English were extremely limited. Her low wages minimized opportunities to move to another part of the city (where rents are higher), and yet a number of employers told us that her address alone would disqualify her from a job in their establishment. Again, the qualities and resources of her neighborhood seem to stabilize a poor Puerto Rican identity from which it seems extremely difficult to move away.

Within feminist and postmodernist writing there has been some resistance to the type of narrative that Susan Hanson and I, and many others, have constructed around stabilized identities and bounded places. We do not, however, see bounded places and spatialized identities as natural and static; our point has been to reveal the processes and power relations that produce bounded areas and the implications of these for those who are contained and enact their identities within them. While this provides the rationale for examining the relation between identities and bounded places, the feminist poststructuralist literature constructively sensitizes one to the inevitable partiality of these narratives, in terms of identities of both places and individuals. There is also a danger of missing the relationship between identities formed in different places. As a way of thinking about relationality and fragmented subjectivities, as well as responding to the empirical reality of international migration, a number of feminists (and others) have been drawn to tell stories about movement and identity formation.

Crossing Boundaries and Identity Formation

Writing about her experience of migrating from Romania to the United States, Marianne Hirsch (1994, p. 73) describes a fusion of geography and identity shifts associated with adolescent development:

That is why it is so hard for me to write about the period of transition – my adolescence. My childhood remained in [Romania]. It is in Vienna that I had my first period, my first crush, wear my first stockings, try on lipstick. My first date, my first kiss, my first dances and parties, are all in Providence. That's where I lose my pudginess, grow another two inches (or is it two centimeters?), have my teeth straightened, become a teenager. But which of those changes are due to chronology, which to geography?

In instances where developmental changes are of less obvious significance, the geography of identity shifts is clearer. Feminists writing about 19th-century British travel writers in Africa, for example, have considered how different aspects of identity come to the fore in different contexts (Blunt, 1994; McEwan, 1994; Mills, 1994). Writing about Mary Kingsley, Alison Blunt (1994) describes how she was positioned as a *woman* travel writer in Britain, while her whiteness and class position overran her gender to some extent in West Africa. Ill of health in Britain, Mary Kingsley seemed to abandon these unfortunate trappings of femininity when she resumed her travels: in West Africa (beyond enjoying excellent health!) she moved between masculine and feminine codes of conduct. Other feminists have described how travel has altered their own sense of self, seeing differing aspects of identity and another grid of difference in a new context. Teresa de Lauretis (1988, p. 128) tells of the importance of immigration to the United States for her awareness of ethnic difference: "[My] first (geographical) dis-placement [from Italy to the United States]," she writes, "served as a point of identification for my first experience of cultural difference (difference not as simple distinction, but as hierarchized)." Through traveling to Cuba from the United States, Johnetta Cole (Bateson, 1990, p. 45) describes how she came to understand herself in gendered and not just racialized terms: "There I was," she says, "seeing for the first time the possibility that the race thing was not forever and ever; and then the other ism [sexism] was right up there saying, what about me?"

Along with simply highlighting another grid of difference, travel across boundaries can produce new identities. At an urban scale, bell hooks (1990) has articulated how movement across bounded places can sharpen an oppositional consciousness and in a sense unify an identity politics because societal contradictions and inequities become visible through travel; hooks writes about her experiences growing up in a small Kentucky town, where the railroad tracks divided the residences of African Americans – shacks and unpaved roads – from the town of whites. African Americans would cross those tracks, as service workers, and she argues that it is the recognition of this movement between margin and center – the knowledge and experiences of both separation and connection – that engenders oppositional consciousness (for additional examples from the secondary literature, see Rose, 1993). Moreover, hooks herself envisions a new identity space beyond the old polarities of difference (e.g., black and white) (Soja & Hooper, 1993). In this she resonates with postcolonial theorists such as Bhabha who are searching to articulate "strategies of selfhood – singular or communal – that initiate new signs of identity and innovative sites of collaboration, and contestation" (1994, pp. 1–2). Crossing boundaries figures prominently in his conception of these strategies: "It is in this sense that the boundary becomes the place from which something begins its *presencing*" (Bhabha, 1994, p. 5; emphasis in original).

Bhabha, as do others, historicizes these new subjectivities as a fin de siècle phenomenon and, as a postcolonial theorist, focuses on hybridity beyond grids of racial difference. There is room to explore arguments such as these within other grids of difference and, in a short vignette that follows, I again turn to the work that Susan Hanson and I have done in Worcester, Massachusetts, to experiment with the possibilities of exhausting the polarities of class identities among some groups of women.

In our writing about women's lives in Worcester, Susan Hanson and I have tried to think about how crossing class boundaries might spawn progressive politics among "middle-class" women (Pratt & Hanson, 1988). We start with the observation that there is a spatialization to the fragmentation of many women's identities.[1] The argument builds from the recognition that most women still find work in traditionally female-dominated occupations that tend to have relatively low status, poor benefits, and low remuneration. This means that many women, while living in middle-class households (defined in terms of their partners' jobs[2]) in relatively affluent neighborhoods, work in working-class occupations. As an index of this, using 1980 census data from Worcester and looking only at households in which women and men are employed, in one-quarter of the households in which the male's job is classified as managerial and professional, the woman is employed in a so-called nonskilled white-collar job. This would be a job like telephone operator, cashier, waitress, or retail clerk. One could argue that these women literally move through class locations during the day. At their jobs they are working class, at home they are middle class. For most men in our societies, residential location reinforces work class location; for many women, there is a radical disjuncture between these two class experiences. Of course, the two experiences are nonetheless linked: the working-class status of middle-class wives can be read, in part, as an extension of their subordinated position in the family.

There is something very interesting about the fact that many women live out the fragmentation of this part of their identity both temporally and spatially. The implications of this for exhausting the binary of working- and middle-class identities is intriguing. It may be that contradictions thrown up by multiple-class locations are managed by compartmentalizing different parts of one's life and identity, and that the spatial separation of home and workplace encourages this. Rosemary Pringle (1988), for example, notes that the relations of home and work are lived differently for "middle-class" (to some extent in terms of their own jobs and through their husbands' class standings as managers) and "working-class" Australian secretaries (who tended to be employed in "lower secretarial" jobs and to be married to men in the trades). The former tended to compartmentalize the two parts of their lives more completely: "As far as they were concerned, their home life was not relevant to what they did at work: they assumed a separation" (p. 227). Pringle observed that middle-class women were reluctant to bring their private lives to work – "their 'middle classness' required that they be able to resist intrusions on their 'private' lives" (p. 226) – while working-class secretaries spoke openly and predominantly about their families and social activities. This difference may be tied to attempts on the part of middle-class secretaries to manage their experiences of class disjuncture.

Alternatively, different class locations may disrupt each other, and the fact that many women experience different class locations may have transformative effects.[3] Working women may bring back to their middle-class residential communities a knowledge of a greater range of experiences and needs. This may partially explain the gender gap in electoral politics and women's greater support for social services, which have been noticed in the United States at least since 1980 (Klein, 1984). We get clues of how these gender differences might translate into the transformation of urban places from a large survey conducted in the Greater Vancouver region in 1990 (Hardwick, Torchinsky, & Fallick, 1991). Women were much more likely than were men to support statements such as "Housing developments should contain a variety of income groups"; "The single family house is not essential for a 'true' family life"; or "I like the variety and stimulation one finds in the city." They were less likely to agree with a statement like "Attempting to mix lifestyles in any one part of the city leads to friction." (Unfortunately, differences among women were not pursued.)

My causal scenario for why many women are seemingly more accepting than are men of cultural and architectural diversity is extremely speculative, but – given the potential significance of these patterns for the places in which we live – they are well worth speculating about. I am tracing an argument about how class-based residential segregation, and the fact that many middle-class women track across different class positions during the course of their days, may transform our cities by encouraging the creation of more diversity in place. Movement across class boundaries may find concrete, material expression in our built environments.

Unsettling Generalizations

It would be unwise, however, to overgeneralize the identity effects of crossing boundaries and to settle into new assumptions about isomorphisms between identity and place (e.g., crossing boundaries = new in-between identities). Boundary crossings can also disempower, fragment identity, and protect privilege, and bounded communities may have progressive effects.

In thinking about this I put my ongoing research on domestic workers in Vancouver, British Columbia, in tension with Bhabha's claims about the empowerment of Filipino/a migrants: "In their cultural passage as migrant workers . . . they embody the Benjaminian 'present': that moment blasted out of the continuum of history. Such conditions of cultural displacement and social discrimination – where political survivors become the best historical witnesses – are the grounds on which Frantz Fanon . . . locates an agency of empowerment" (Bhabha, 1994, p. 8).

It is important also to remember that these are the grounds of disempowerment. In Canada, large numbers of women come from the Philippines to work as domestic workers for Canadian families (6,400 entered through the Foreign Domestic Movement Program (now the Live-in Caregiver Program) in 1990 alone (60% of all women who came to Canada through this program in 1990 were Filipinas) (WCDWA, 1993; for details see Bakan & Stasiulis, 1995). In my interviews with nanny agents and government officials in the summer of 1994 it was patently clear that these gatekeepers hold no illusions that Canadians will do this work. One government official who administers the Live-in Caregiver Program through a local employment office put it succinctly: "The reason that we have to bring in [nannies] from abroad is that the occupation is so poorly paid that no one wants to do it." It is arguable, however, that Canadians are cleansed of guilt about hiring "Third World" women to do this work under conditions intolerable to Canadians, on the grounds that Filipinas are using the Live-In Caregiver Program as an immigration strategy: "Filipinos have a very different motivation [compared to European nannies]. . . . [T]hey are coming to immigrate to get citizenship, to bring in their families. They will put up with a lot in order to have a clean record, which makes for a whole other set of problems. But it means that they're likely to stay on the job" (nanny agent). A knowledge that the program enables Filipinas to cross international boundaries offers some justification, then, for labor conditions unacceptable to Canadians (see also Arat-Koc, 1990). So too, it is arguable that spatial separation shields Canadians from the day-to-day reality that many Filipinas have left their own children in the Philippines to care for Canadian families; 29% of the 144 domestic workers interviewed in a survey done under the auspices of the West Coast Domestic Workers' Association (WCDWA) in 1992/93 reported having at least one child in the Philippines (Mikita, 1994). A number of employers whom I have interviewed addressed this issue through a First World/Third World frame and, empathetic with Filipinas in these circumstances, find a comfortable space for themselves in the knowledge that these women are enacting their role of "good mother" by making the sacrifice of leaving their children. One woman whom I interviewed chose to sponsor a Filipina with an infant in the Philippines instead of an older, single Filipina, on the grounds that leaving an infant was a sign of deep maternal love and signaled the capacity to love her [the employer's] Canadian children. Thus, while border crossings may raise Filipinas' consciousness, they also effectively shield Canadians from making connections and/or legitimate social and employment relations that might otherwise raise some discomfort.

The ways in which border crossings can maintain old identity classifications and grids of difference, as well as privilege, are also apparent in an interview that I carried out in the summer of 1995 with parents who employ domestic workers. In writing about just one interview, I sketch the outlines of their childcare history and then "let the tape run" at length in order to unravel some of the complexities that emerge in thinking about identities and places.

This couple lives in a gentrifying inner-city neighborhood, adjacent both to Vancouver's "skid row" and "Chinatown," and home to a good number of Chinese and Vietnamese residents. The couple with whom I spoke were white professionals who owned a home in the area. That identities are crafted from fragmented and often contradictory subject positions was evident from the remarks made by the woman (Teresa), who seemed less comfortable living in her multicultural neighborhood when her children's childcare was involved. They had taken their first child to a day-care center outside the neighborhood, close to Teresa's workplace, until he was 18 months old. Because of a bureaucratic mishap, their child lost his day-care space at this age. This is the point at which the real dilemmas of living in a multicultural neighborhood began to be debated in the household. Teresa first looked into a family day-care arrangement in her neighborhood, run by an Italian woman in her home. She tapped into her multicultural networks to check this out: "I have a friend who is Italian so I asked: 'How does this woman check out?,' wanting as much collateral as possible. 'Can I trust this person with my child?'" The woman was recommended highly, which meant that Teresa "just felt worse after being there": "I went to visit on a very bright sunny snowy morning. The TV was on. The curtains were drawn. There were about six kids all sort of bouncing off each other, in a very bold way." She rejected the day-care arrangement because "the sort of sensory deprivation put me off." She felt that she had exhausted her networks and "advertising was the very last thing that we wanted to do," so her husband (Tom) started to inquire through his networks. Eventually, a friend knew of a "fellow" worker who might want the job: "That's how we met up with the other woman. . . . She brought her own [8-month-old] child to be here. And that situation lasted for about a year and a half [until their next child was born]. And it was a very very good situation."

TERESA: It was great. She came over the first time and she was younger than I had imagined this person should be. But she was mature. Early twenties. Really confident. And energetic and had lots of experience.

TOM: And she and [her daughter] had lovely manners.

TERESA: Both really gentle.

TOM: With her own child and with [their son].

As the discussion about this caregiver progressed, it became clear to me that a norm of similarity was very important to Teresa.

TERESA: We had sort of agreed at the beginning about discipline, and sort of philosophy.

G.P.: How did you agree?

TERESA: I had taken the Parent Effectiveness Training course. I'll show you the book later. But it's very clear about giving kids choices. And preserving self esteem. Let them experience competencies. So I sort of talked to her about the highlights that were important to me in this book. And our philosophy was in common. Just sort of . . . I don't know . . . comfortable with each other. And her spirituality was similar. And all that stuff. And she was pretty well vegetarian. I'm not vegetarian. That's not really important to me. But she had good food choices. She wasn't going to fill the kids up with candy, and chips and pop and stuff, which I could see happening with other baby-sitters. And so that part was important to me as well.

When their second child was born, they had to rearrange childcare.

TERESA: One option that keeps coming up from living in this area, which has a lot of Chinese and Vietnamese people, was that many people have the old Chinese grandmother looking after their kids. The woman across the park who is Caucasian and both her kids have had this older Chinese lady looking after them. . . . But I felt really like I didn't want to do that because I didn't want to have anyone here who I couldn't communicate with.

TOM: I did want it. But we didn't agree.

G.P.: Because you weren't worried so much about . . .?

TOM: No, I felt it would have been a great situation. But it wouldn't have been a great situation if Teresa was worried. So I couldn't pursue it. But I thought that would be great.

G.P.: Because of the language?

TOM: Yes. And being able to stay in the home. And there is a network in the park of grandmothers and kids.

TERESA: The downside is that, while learning Cantonese would be great and learning about another culture, but what I also observe is that the old ladies don't have a lot of energy for stimulating the kids. So on rainy days they are all kind of in front of the television, and behavior is dealt with by either yelling or bribing with candies. So it didn't meet my kind of standards.

G.P.: [Directed toward Tom] So you kind of liked the connectedness of the neighborhood?

TOM: That's one of the reasons why we live here. The neighborhood has a great sense of community. That for me would have just been another way of living that way. But if Teresa wasn't going to be comfortable with it, it wouldn't have worked.

G.P.: And there is a different balance [between you]. Because they are different priorities.

TERESA: Yes.

TOM: Mmmm.

So it becomes evident, in listening to Teresa speak, that although she feels comfortable living in the neighborhood herself, she is less comfortable with cultural difference when it affects her children's care. Eventually, after hiring a Filipina nanny to care for their children in their home, two spaces became available at their son's original day-care center. They accepted those spots, even though this arrangement cost roughly $300 more a month and required car transport. (Tom in particular expressed a commitment to a carless lifestyle and mentioned the sacrifices in this regard that went along with their childcare choice.) It is also interesting to note that a number of middle-class parents in the area transport their children out of the neighborhood for childcare. Teresa estimated that eight children within a two block radius of their home go to their sons' day-care center, a migration precipitated by their enthusiasm for it (as Tom put it, "I think it's just a question of, a sort of snowballing thing"). There is a day-care center in the neighborhood, but it is on Hastings Street (skid row) "and no one wants to use it because it is part of the Hastings traffic" (Teresa). The Hastings Street day-care center undoubtedly is used by some parents in the area (or it would be closed) but seemingly not by middle-class parents in their neighborhood.

There are several aspects of this interview that point to the complexities of theorizing the links between identity formation and place. First, Teresa appears to be divided in relation to her neighborhood – we see the fragmentation of identity in play – and, second, the multicultural neighborhood eventually works for her (and evidently a good number of other white middle-class families) because she is able to cross outside of it in one part of her life (her role as a mother). Her privilege allows her to do this, and being able to do so allows her to enact middle-class child-rearing standards. Further, by taking their children out of the neighborhood, these families possibly reproduce a new generation of social and cultural boundaries among children in the neighborhood. But, third, this interview demonstrates how a geographical boundary can sustain an openness to cultural difference. Tom's acceptance of cultural difference is very much tied to a sense of neighborhood. He embraces the Chinese grandmother option because it is a way of living as part of the community. Further, he was exploring an exchange with a Mandarin-speaking neighbor, offering English instruction in exchange for Mandarin instruction for his children. Tom was much less receptive to the idea of hiring a Filipina caregiver, not because of her cultural identity, but because she was coming from outside their local networks: "I felt less um . . . When we hired [the Filipina caregiver] the whole process of deciding whether to have someone to come in somehow wasn't comfortable. I felt. . . . It's complicated. I felt like we would be passing over our children to some other person who we had no idea about at all. Even with the references, there was part of me saying it didn't feel quite right. . . . I wasn't going to block it, but when the decision was made to put them in [day care], I felt much better."

This makes the simple but critical point that boundaries and a commitment to the local are not necessarily politically regressive. In this instance, they nurtured a willingness to cross boundaries of identity and culture. The boundedness of the local opens possibilities to create relationships across differences. The complexities of place and identities are such that it seems unwise to expect a necessary or uncomplicated relationship between identities and places. It is possible to imagine ideals of community that envelope difference and bounded spaces that foster multicultural ideals. Madan Sarup (1994, p. 103) asks, "At present the norm stresses similarity, but what would happen if the norm changed and if the norm stressed difference? What would happen if there was a recognition of the diversity of subjective positions and cultural identities?" And can we ask, in what spaces might this norm of diversity be practiced?

Multicultural Spaces

Implicit in at least some writing about "decentered," "in-between," "hybridized" identities, and a multiculturalism that exists through a norm of difference is the sense that this identity may find expression within globalized, multicultural cities. So, as an example of "a broadminded acceptance of cosmopolitanism," Gupta and Ferguson quote a "young white reggae fan in the ethnically chaotic neighborhood of Balsall Heath in Birmingham" (1992, p. 10). The geographical identifier is worth noting. As a way of articulating the norm of difference, Iris M. Young imagines the ideal of the nonoppressive city, in which individuals from different social groups enjoy experiencing each others' cultures without the pretense or presumption of belonging to or fully understanding those other cultures: "We witness one another's cultures and functions in such public interaction, without adopting them as our own. The appreciation of ethnic foods or professional musicians, for example, consists in the recognition that these transcend the familiar everyday of my life" (1990, p. 319). Iain Chambers (1994a, 1994b) speculates that the globalization of contemporary cities serves to destabilize the centrality of a single identity:

> The idea of cultural complexity, most sharply on display in the arabesque patterns of the modern metropolis – and that includes Lagos as well as London, Beijing and Buenos Aires – weakens earlier schemata and paradigms, destabilises and decentres previous theories and sociologies. Here the narrow arrow of progressive time is displaced by the open spiral of heterogeneous collaborations and contaminations, and what Edward Said has recently referred to as "atonal ensembles." (1994a, p. 93)

> This encourages me to contemplate living with the responsibility for the always provisional nature of fabricated habitats that are never realized but are always in the process of becoming. In this I begin to learn the art of losing myself (as opposed to merely getting lost) and thereby gain the opportunity of falling through the gap in my consciousness, rationalism and inherited verdicts, to begin learning the languages of silence and a capacity for listening. (1994b, p. 249)

As compelling as this urban imaginary may be, I think that we should be cautious about the freedoms and diversity of actual cities, based on an awareness that boundaries are drawn and redrawn at very fine spatial scales. I rely on a final empirical vignette, from Williams's (1988) ethnography of one block in a racially integrated, rapidly gentrifying inner-city neighborhood in Washington, DC, to make this point. Most of the whites living on the block studied by Williams were relatively recent arrivals. In occupational terms, they are classified as political activist lawyers, environmental activists, university professors, or newspaper reporters. These people bought into the area, in part, because they were attracted by its varied racial composition and an ideal of multi-culturalism. Despite the attractions of racial heterogeneity, the realities of labor market segmentation were translated starkly into the housing market and strict racial segregation persisted: all of the white households owned row houses on the one side of the street, while long-term African American residents lived in rental apartments facing them. Members of neither group had entered the homes of the other.

Williams's analysis of the television-viewing habits of these residents is particularly interesting to me because it demonstrates the process of boundary formation in a multicultural space, and the interplay between material and cultural boundaries. While mass television could be taken as an index of the nationalization and indeed globalization of culture and as a vehicle for crossing boundaries, in fact residents on one side of the street rarely watched the same programs as those on the other. Instead, they watched each other through programs that seriously distorted each other's lives and perpetuated stereotypes of race and urban living. African American women living in the apartments, who did most of the television viewing in their households, watched programs like *Dallas* and *Dynasty*, dramas of wealthy, troubled white families living in large houses. The white homeowners watched what Williams terms gentrified television, programs like *Hill Street Blues* and *St. Elsewhere*. Although these latter programs have been represented as self-conscious attempts to undermine racial and gender stereotypes and to portray urban life in realistic ways, Williams argues that they simply reproduce these stereotypes and a vision of city life as chaotic, violent, and unpredictable, in which liberal, well-intentioned people are vulnerable to attacks from gangs and drug addicts, and where lower-income people live uniformly sordid and violent lives. She sees these programs as "extraordinary urban vehicles for cross-class communication" that "guide assumptions" that the white homeowners make about everyday life. These programs "lead [the homeowners] to interpret and frame ambiguous scenes with more unease, fear, and distrust [than they might otherwise]. These programs thus speak powerfully to the uncertainties of [the] new owners, although a direct connection between watching them and growing more hostile [to their neighbors across the street] might be difficult to prove" (1988, p. 112). Liberal whites are attempting to live in a multicultural place, but the cultural representations that they watch on television portray a dichotomous cultural urban space that then partially structures, through fear and hostility, their relations in their neighborhood, reproducing dichotomized urban places.

The television preferences of the African Americans can be interpreted as a sign of their contradictory status, drawn to the ethics of home ownership but unable to gain entrance to these property relations. Their in-between and contradictory status is apparent in their relations with Latino families within their building. In recent years about a half dozen extended Latino families, refugees from El Salvador, had moved into the apartment building inhabited by African Americans. There was a fair amount of conflict between African American and Latino residents, articulated through their different ideas of how the building should be used. The categories of race and difference were signified and worked through the material use of the building. Many African Americans attributed declining conditions within the building to the presence of Latino families. They were critical of what they perceived to be overcrowding on the part of Latinos, as well as the tendency of Latinos to domesticate semipublic spaces, such as the laundry and halls. As one African American woman put it, "Spanish people use the hall like a porch." In appealing to the management company, African American residents distinguished themselves from Latino families and employed the rhetoric of home ownership, citing their personal morality, concern about the building, and residential stability. Williams writes that "black women tenants argue that by settling in and taking an active moral interest in a building you can act like a homeowner. This ethos then frames the rhetoric through which they demand particular privileges and services" (1988, p. 68). By tying African Americans so closely to the ideals of home ownership, Williams positions them within the same ideological space as the homeowners across the street.

The boundaries on this one street are multiple and drawn in different places in different ideological spaces. Material boundaries (homeowner/renter; different traditions of drawing lines between public and private spaces) underline racial categories. Cultural representations of race reproduce material divisions. I am struck not only by the multitude of boundaries but by the loss of political agency that flows from them. As the deterioration of living conditions, possibly due to disinvestment on the part of the landlord, is interpreted as the consequence of racial difference among tenants, the potential for effective tenant organizing is undermined. As the white residents, whose gentrifying impulse is prompted by the ideals of a type of multiculturalism (bracketing the material consequences of this impulse for their neighbors across the street and the responsibility that they may bear for any disinvestment on the part of the landlord), burrow into the security of their private homes, a vision of urban living that seeks out difference is lost. Sorting through the boundaries and overlapping ideological spaces – seeing the boundaries and points of intersection – is a very preliminary step toward building alliances that might work against the homogenizing forces of gentrification.

One of the points of interest of this case is that, if the residents have any hope of retaining the social and economic diversity of their neighborhood, they will likely have to move beyond "enjoying" difference to actually engaging with it by pursuing a common political project located in space. In this instance, a multicultural space localizes the political project, but it certainly does not ensure a multicultural space of identity formation or political practice.

Conclusions

The last vignettes raise the issues of what we mean by multiculturalism and how ideals of multiculturalism relate to urban space. Shohat and Stam (1994, p. 47) argue that multiculturalism "has become an empty signifier [on to] which diverse groups project their hopes and fears. . . . For us, the word 'multiculturalism' has no essence; it points to a debate." They hope to prod the debate towards a radical critique of power relations, to a multiculturalism that makes connections and decolonizes through reordering and equalizing power relations between communities.

With our long history of studying the ways in which urban space orders grids of social difference, social geographers have much to contribute to this debate, at the very least by continuing to detail the material and cultural boundaries that permeate the city. As Shohat and Stam (1994, p. 358) put it, multiculturalism is not simply "nice": "like a suburban barbecue to which a few token people of color are invited"; it involves seeing and taking responsibility for histories of social and economic inequalities. It seems to me that efforts toward this kind of multicultural "space" are not advanced by representations that conceive of cities as blurred, chaotic, borderless places; these representations of urban space potentially screen hierarchized grids of difference. One must understand the multiple processes of boundary construction in order to disrupt them, in order to build toward multicultural spaces of radical openness and radical politics, what Shohat and Stam (1994, p. 359) term "mutual and reciprocal relativization."

At the same time, processes of border construction and the "reterritorialization" of identity are clearly complex, far more complex than the metaphor of "a mosaic of social worlds" suggests. Through various empirical vignettes I have tried to show how bounded places can stabilize identities or, alternatively, open up the potential for crosscultural communication. Some individuals are contained by places; others move across boundaries and enact different aspects of their identity in different places. Crossing boundaries can have transformative effects or protect the status quo. The most consistent message of this chapter is that the relations between place and identity are complex and variable. There is therefore a persistent need to examine the specificity of these processes, in time and place, and to resist overgeneralizing one set of relations or effects. There is a need to take seriously the historical geography of identity formation.

Acknowledgments

I thank Jennifer Hyndman for her very helpful comments on a draft of this chapter. The two vignettes from Worcester owe much, of course, to a long and productive association with Susan Hanson. The empirical material for the crossing boundaries and multicultural spaces sections of this chapter were first written for a paper ("Travelling Theory and Spatial Metaphors") presented at the Making Worlds: Metaphor and Materiality in the Production of Feminist Texts Conference, sponsored by Southwest Institute for Research on Women (SIROW), at the University of Arizona, Tucson, October 1993. A reworked version of the conference paper appears as "Geographic Metaphors in Feminist Theory" in S. Aiken, A. Brigham, S. Marston, and P. Waterstone (Eds.), *Making Worlds: Metaphor and Materiality in the Production of Feminist Texts*. Tucson: University of Arizona Press, 1997. The research on domestic work has received generous support from the Social Sciences Humanities Research Council (SSHRC Grant No. 5-57335). I thank Trina Bester for her careful transcription of the parent interview.

Notes

1. I do not want to overgeneralize my claims about gender. I, for example, do not experience the class rupture that I describe here.
2. I recognize the difficulties associated with this class positioning (Pratt & Hanson, 1991). I am drawing attention to the fact that many working-class women live in higher-income residential areas because of their husbands' class standing.
3. On the other hand, the politics that result from this disruption may be less "progressive." The multiplicity of class locations inhabited by women in the same occupations may, for example, impede workplace organization. This is precisely what Cho (1985) concludes from her participant observation study of women working at Microtek, Inc., in Silicon Valley. Most of the unskilled assembly jobs at Microtek were filled by women, but – if one takes into consideration the rest of their lives and identities – these women were situated in diverse class circumstances: "One Korean woman worker's husband was a medical doctor, while one American woman's boyfriend was a fabrication operator at a firm in Silicon Valley. . . . In general, a significant number of the married women's husbands had high-income jobs, such as chemical engineering. There were also quite a few single women who had two jobs to meet their living expenses" (pp. 200–201). Cho argues that the diverse cultural and class backgrounds discouraged women from discovering and pursuing their common interests as assembly workers. She reports that many of the married women "never read [their pay-checks] with care" (p. 201) and it was therefore not surprising that it was a single mother who discovered that the company was violating its own regulations by failing to pay overtime.

References

Arat-Koc, S. (1990). Importing Housewives: Non-citizen Domestic Workers and the Crisis of the Domestic Sphere in Canada. In: S. Arat-Koc, M. Luxton & H. Rosenberg (eds.), *Through the Kitchen Window: The Politics of Home and Family*, pp. 81–103. Toronto: Garamond.

Bakan, A. & D. Stasiulis (1995). Making the Match: Domestic Placement Agencies and the Racialization of Women's Household Work. *Signs: Journal of Women in Culture and Society* 20, pp. 303–35.

Bammer, A. (ed.). (1994). *Displacements: Cultural Identities in Question*. Bloomington and Indianapolis: Indiana University Press.

Bateson, M. C. (1990). *Composing a Life*. New York: Plume.

Bhabha, H. (1994). *The Location of Culture*. London and New York: Routledge.

Blunt, A. (1994). *Travel, Gender, and Imperialism: Mary Kingsley and West Africa*. New York: Guilford Press.

Chambers, I. (1994a). *Migrancy Culture Identity*. London and New York: Routledge.

Chambers, I. (1994b). Leaky Habitats and Broken Grammar. In: G. Robertson, M. Mash, L. Tickner, J. Bird, B. Curtis & T. Putnam (eds.), *Travellers' Tales*, pp. 245–9. London and New York: Routledge.

Cho, S. K. (1985). The Labor Process and Capital Mobility: The Limits of the New International Division of Labor. *Politics and Society* 14, pp. 185–222.

de Lauretis, T. (1988). Displacing Hegemonic Discourses: Reflections on Feminist Theory in the 1980s. *Inscriptions* 3(4), pp. 127–44.

Ferguson, K. (1993). *The Man Question: Visions of Subjectivity in Feminist Theory*. Berkeley: University of California Press.

Gupta, A. & J. Ferguson (1992). Beyond "Culture": Space, Identity, and Politics of Difference. *Cultural Anthropology* 7, pp. 6–23.

Hanson, S. & G. Pratt (1995). *Gender, Work, and Space*. London and New York: Routledge.

Hardwick, W., R. Torchinsky & A. Fallick (1991). *Shaping a Livable Vancouver Region: Public Opinion Surveys*, B.C. Geographical Series, No. 48. Vancouver, British Columbia, Canada.

Hirsch, M. (1994). Pictures of a Displaced Girlhood. In: A. Bammer (ed.), *Displacements: Cultural Identities in Question*, pp. 71–89. Bloomington and Indianapolis: Indiana University Press.

Hooks, B. (1990). *Yearning: Race, Gender, and Cultural Politics*. Toronto: Between the Lines.

Kaplan, C. (1987). Deterritorializations: The Rewriting of Home and Exile in Western Feminist Discourse. *Cultural Critique* 6, pp. 187–98.

Klein, E. (1984). *Gender Politics: From Consciousness to Mass Politics*. Cambridge, MA: Harvard University Press.

Massey, D. (1994). *Space, Place and Gender*. Cambridge and Oxford, UK: Polity Press.

McEwan, C. (1994). Encounters with West African Women: Textual Representations of Difference by White Women Abroad. In: A. Blunt & G. Rose (eds.), *Writing Women and Space*, pp. 73–100. New York: Guilford Press.

Mikita, J. (1994). *The Influence of the Canadian State on the Migration of Foreign Domestic Workers to Canada: A Case Study of the Migration of Filipina Nannies to Vancouver, British Columbia*. Unpublished MA thesis, Department of Geography, Simon Fraser University, Burnaby, British Columbia, Canada.

Mills, S. (1994). Knowledge, Gender, and Empire. In: A. Blunt & G. Rose (eds.), *Writing Women and Space*, pp. 29–50. New York: Guilford Press.

Morris, M. (1990). Banality in Cultural Studies. In: P. Mellencamp (ed.), *Logics of Television: Essays in Cultural Criticism*, pp. 14–43. Bloomington: Indiana University Press.

Pratt, G. & S. Hanson (1988). Gender, Class and Space. *Environment and Planning D: Society and Space* 6, pp. 15–35.

Pratt, G. & S. Hanson (1994). Geography and the Construction of Difference. *Gender, Place and Culture* 1, pp. 5–29.

Pringle, R. (1988). *Secretaries Talk*. London and New York: Verso.

Rose, G. (1993). *Feminism and Geography: Disciplinary Discourse and Difference*. Cambridge, UK: Polity Press.

Sarup, M. (1994). Home and Identity. In: G. Robertson, M. Mash, L. Tickner, J. Bird, B. Curtis & T. Putnam (eds.), *Travellers' Tales*, pp. 93–104. London and New York: Routledge.

Shohat, E. & R. Stam (1994). *Unthinking Eurocentricism*. London and New York: Routledge.

Soja, E. & B. Hooper (1993). The Spaces That Difference Makes: Some Notes on the Geographical Margins of the New Cultural Politics. In: M. Keith & S. Pile (eds.), *Place and the Politics of Identity*, pp. 183–205. London and New York: Routledge.

WCDWA (West Coast Domestic Workers' Association) (1993). Supporting Documentation for WCDWA Brief to Employment Standards Act Review Committee. #302, 119 West Pender St., Vancouver, British Columbia, Canada.

Williams, B. (1988). *Upscaling Downtown*. Ithaca, NY: Cornell University Press.

Wolfe, T. (1987). *The Bonfire of the Vanities*. New York: Bantam.

Wolff, J. (1993). On the Road Again: Metaphors of Travel in Cultural Criticism. *Cultural Studies* 7, pp. 224–39.

Young, I. M. (1990). The Ideal of Community and the Politics of Difference. In: L. Nicholson (ed.), *Feminism/Postmodernism*, pp. 300–23. New York: Routledge.

10

Cosmopolitan De-scriptions:
Shanghai and Hong Kong

*Ackbar Abbas**

Cities have historically been the privileged, if not necessarily exclusive, sites for the emergence of the form of life that we call the cosmopolitan. In Shanghai and Hong Kong, in particular, some form of the cosmopolitan did indeed emerge under colonial conditions, and some other form of cosmopolitanism may be developing today. Nevertheless, the description of Shanghai and Hong Kong I give here is not intended to be a straightforward empirical account of what kind of cosmopolitan city each became under colonial rule or what crucial changes each is undergoing as communist China today reasserts itself as a global power. Rather, I direct attention to a certain elusive quality of both cities and to the fact that the most familiar images of these cities do not necessarily describe them best. To put this another way: cosmopolitanism must take place somewhere, in specific sites and situations – even if these places are more and more beginning to resemble those "non-places" that French anthropologist Marc Augé has argued characterise the contemporary city. In a non-place, "one is neither *chez soi* nor *chez les autres*."[1] Like the city, Augé's non-place must be understood not literally, but as paradox: a non-place is far from being nonexistent. Rather, it is a result of excess and overcomplexity, of a limit having been exceeded. Beyond a certain point, there is a blurring and scrambling of signs and an overlapping of spatial and temporal grids, all of which make urban signs and images difficult to read. The overcomplex space of non-places means, among other things, that even the *anomalous* detail may no longer be recognisable as such because it coexists with a swarm of other such details. This means the anomalous is in danger of turning *nondescript*, in much the same way that the more complex the city today, the more it becomes a city without qualities. The cosmopolitan as urban phenomenon is inevitably inscribed in such non-places and paradoxes, raising the question we will have to address at some later point of how it might survive there.

To grapple with the anomalous/nondescript nature of overcomplex spaces, I draw on what Ludwig Wittgenstein called "description" and appropriate it for the analysis of cities.[2] On the one hand, when Wittgenstein writes that "we must do away with all *explanation*, and description alone must take its place," description can be understood

*Pp. 772–6, 777–83, 785–6 from *Public Culture*, Vol. 12, no. 3. © 2000 by Duke University Press. All rights reserved. Used by permission of the publisher.

as a kind of *de-scription*. This means that it is concerned not with knitting together explanations that make smooth connections between disparate series; rather, it welcomes friction – that is, disjuncture – and the mobile, fugitive, fragmentary detail. Wittgenstein writes: "We want to walk: so we need *friction*. Back to the rough ground!" On the other hand, Wittgenstein also insists that what concerns description is "of course, not empirical problems": "And this description gets its light, that is to say its purpose, from the philosophical problems. These are, of course, not empirical problems; they are solved, rather, by looking into the workings of our language, and that in such a way as to make us recognize those workings: in despite of an urge to misunderstand them." For our purposes, what might correspond to "language" is space. As philosophical issues are resolved by looking into the workings of language, so urban issues like cosmopolitanism might be clarified through a critique of space. Like language, space produces "an urge to misunderstand" its workings, an urge that needs to be resisted through de-scription.

What follows, then, is neither a theoretical nor an empirical account, but a description of the cosmopolitan in relation to the spatial history of Shanghai and Hong Kong.

* * *

Shanghai and Hong Kong have always had a special relation to each other, if only through their relationship to the rest of the world. The historical facts about them are well known. Both cities were essentially created by Western colonialism in the aftermath of the Opium Wars: Shanghai as a lucrative treaty port and Hong Kong as a British colony and staging post for trade with China. For better or for worse, the two cities seemed to have been linked at birth, which makes it possible sometimes to read what is tacit in the history of one city in the history of the other. Each developed a form of cosmopolitanism under colonialism. From the outset, Shanghai generated a set of images about itself that contributed to its mystique but that we sometimes think of as merely outlandish or bizarre. Nevertheless, it is these often conflicting and contradictory images that we will need to interrogate. It may be that every city gives itself away in the self-images that it produces; somewhat like dream images that lead us to another history, or like cinema where, as Gilles Deleuze has argued, it is the filmic image that underlies the film narrative and not the other way around.[3]

We can begin with Shanghai, which was historically the senior city. Consider the political anomaly of extraterritoriality. In Shanghai, within the space of a hundred years, the extraterritorial presence of foreigners – British, American, and French, and after 1895, Japanese (to name only the most obvious) – turned the city into the Shanghai of legend, into what J. G. Ballard called "this electric and lurid city more exciting than any other in the world."[4] The existence of the different concessions, each with its own set of extraterritorial laws, meant that internal control of the city always had to be negotiated, often with the triad underworld operating as unofficial arbiters. However, this created less an anarchic city than a polycentric, decentered city controlled by many different hands. For example, the French Settlement used a 110-volt electric system, while the International Settlement used 220 volts! But far from being lawless, the space of Shanghai was subject to constant negotiations, and every initiative was observed

from multiple perspectives. It was the existence of such a negotiated space that helped
Shanghai in the 1920s and 1930s develop its own special brand of cosmopolitan urban
culture: what we might call a cosmopolitanism of extraterritoriality.

The most visible signature of extraterritoriality was in the city's built space, with its
proliferation of different styles of architecture, by turns elegant and kitschy. There were
Tudor-style villas, Spanish-style townhouses, Russian-style churches, and German-style
mansions, along with the internationalism of the buildings on the Bund and, of course,
the Shanghainese lanehouses or Li Long housing complexes, these last also built by
foreign architects with their preconceptions of what vernacular housing should look like.
It was all a question of style imported from elsewhere – a shallow kind of cosmopolitanism, a dream image of Europe more glamorous even than Europe itself at the time; the
whole testifying, it seems, to the domination of the foreign, especially if we remember
the decrepitude of the Chinese section of the city. But, at least in part, this was a deceptive testimony because within this setting something contrary was also happening. It
could be argued, as Leo Ou-fan Lee has done in "Shanghai Modern," that the foreign
presence produced not only new kinds of public and social spaces (such as cinemas,
department stores, coffeehouses, dance halls, parks, and racecourses), but also spaces
that could be *appropriated* by the Chinese themselves and used to construct a Chinese
version of modern cosmopolitan culture. From this point of view, cosmopolitanism in
Shanghai could be understood not as the cultural domination by the foreign but as the
appropriation by the local of "elements of foreign culture to enrich a new national
culture."[5] Lee's persuasive account, rich in fascinating details, is interesting, too, for its
attempt to steer the argument away from too facile "political critiques" of the cosmopolitan as cultural imperialism, towards a more nuanced reading of cultural history.

Still, foreign domination and local appropriation are not necessarily mutually exclusive. For example, it should not be forgotten that Shanghai's strength as a cosmopolitan
city was always based on China's weakness as a nation, As such, there was always an
underlying tension between national culture on the one hand, which could only be
constructed as anticolonial resistance, and Shanghai cosmopolitanism on the other,
Shanghai was always a subtly nonviable city, where splendour and squalor existed side
by side. It was precisely the city's characteristic multivalence – its capacity to be all at
once a space of negotiation, domination, and appropriation – that generated yet another
image, perhaps the most telling of all: the grotesque. This grotesque nature of the city
is captured best in a scene in Ballard's semiautobiographical novel, *Empire of the Sun*,
documenting the last days of old Shanghai. The scene is set outside the Cathay Theater,
at the time the largest cinema in the world. For its showing of *The Hunchback of Notre
Dame*, the management recruited two hundred real-life hunchbacks from the back
streets of Shanghai to form an "honour guard" for the glitterati attending the show! A
grand guignol quality was never far behind the cosmopolitanism of Shanghai.

This grotesque element hints at something quite significant about Shanghai's cosmopolitanism, which could be extended even to the cosmopolitanism of other cities. It
suggests that the cosmopolitan "attitude" in this case consists not in the toleration of
difference but in the necessary cultivation of *indifference*: the hunchbacks were hired
not in the spirit of equal opportunity employment but to create a gross sensation.
Furthermore, to some extent the colonial experience had shattered the innocence of

difference. The end result of having to negotiate a multivalent space that makes so many contrary demands on the individual was the cultivation of indifference and insensitivity to others. Even scandal and outrage could be openly accepted. Indeed, in its time old Shanghai had the reputation of being the most "open" city in the world. It was the one place in China that was free from the control of a debilitated and bureaucratic state apparatus, giving it an air of freedom that drew in both political reformers and intellectuals, both prostitutes and adventurers. The other side of this freedom and openness, however, was a certain isolation – a linkage to the world that went together with a delinkage from the rest of China. There was always something very fragile about Shanghai cosmopolitanism. After 1949, Chinese communism, born in Shanghai, quickly made Shanghai's urban culture no more than a memory.

For a long time, Hong Kong did not develop the kind of cosmopolitan culture that Shanghai exhibited in the 1920s and 1930s, a cosmopolitanism that emerged from the anomalous space of extraterritoriality. Dependency meant that for most of its history, Hong Kong, culturally speaking, was caught in the double bind of divided loyalties. It was politically ambivalent about both Britain and China; ambivalent about what language, English or Chinese, it should master; and confident only about capital. The one moment when it began to rival the cultural vibrancy of Shanghai in the 1930s was during the 1980s and 1990s, after the Joint Declaration announcing the return of Hong Kong to China in 1997: that is, at precisely the moment when Hong Kong felt most vulnerable and dependent. This was the period when more and more people discovered, invented, and rallied behind what they called "Hong Kong culture." This Hong Kong culture was a hothouse plant that appeared at the moment when something was disappearing: a case of love at last sight, a culture of disappearance. In contrast to Shanghai in the 1930s, nationalism was a negative stimulus: one major anxiety was that the internationalism of the port city would be submerged and smothered by its reinscription into the nation. But the anxiety was tempered by a tacit hope that Hong Kong might indeed be a special case. This was what redirected attention back to the city's local peculiarities, in an attempt to reinvent it one last time even as it disappeared. This sense of disappearance as the experience of living through the best and the worst of times was the seminal theme of the New Hong Kong Cinema. If filmmakers like Wong Kar-wai, Stanley Kwan, Ann Hui, and Tsui Hark managed to convey in their films a cosmopolitan sensibility, it was partly by focusing on local issues and settings, but in such a way that the local was dislocated: through the construction of innovative film images and narratives and, above all, through the introduction of the disappearing city as a major protagonist in their films.[6] Hong Kong cosmopolitanism was stimulated then not so much by a space of multivalence – which was the case in 1930s Shanghai – as by a space of disappearance, one effect of which was the transformation of the local into the *translocal* as a result of historical exigencies.

To recapitulate: in Shanghai in the 1920s and 1930s we found a cosmopolitanism of extraterritoriality, and in Hong Kong from the 1980s onward, a cosmopolitanism of dependency, with its thematic of the disappearing city. But what of today and tomorrow? Two events in the 1990s can be considered symptoms that the cultural space these two cities seem destined to cohabit is once again changing. The 1990s saw not only the return of Hong Kong to China as an SAR (Special Administrative Region) but also the economic and cultural reappearance of Shanghai after more than four decades in the political cold. To consider if a new kind of cosmopolitanism is emerging today in Shanghai and Hong Kong, we will first have to consider the changing historical space of these two cities.

Now that Hong Kong is part of China again, there is a lot of speculation about whether Shanghai will replace it as the country's main economic and financial center once the Chinese yuan becomes fully convertible. The mayor of Shanghai, Xu Kuangdi, in a Hong Kong newspaper interview, addressed the issue of Shanghai and Hong Kong as follows: "You don't have to worry about Shanghai replacing Hong Kong; or that because of Hong Kong, Shanghai is not going to become a financial centre. They play different roles. . . . In the future, their relationship will be like two good forwards on a football team. They will pass the ball to each other and both will do their best to score more goals. But they are on the same team – China's national team." In the same interview, he conceded that Hong Kong "is more international than Shanghai. It is a financial centre for Southeast Asia. Not only does it link China with the world, it also serves as a trading market for Southeast Asian countries. Shanghai primarily serves as a link between the mainland and the rest of the world."[7]

Xu's homely image of Shanghai and Hong Kong as two good forwards on the national team is reassuring because as a public statement it understandably minimises whatever tensions might exist between the city, the nation, and the transnational or global. But such tensions do exist. In Hong Kong, for example, these tensions produced a skewing of cultural and political space that could be read in the city's cultural forms, such as its architecture and new cinema. The return of Hong Kong to China threatened to make the former disappear in the sense that the transnational status it had established for itself might be merged and submerged into the national. In Shanghai, because of the different relation of the city to the nation, it is not a question of the city's disappearance but of its reappearance, a reappearance coinciding with China's reinscription, after decades of closure, into the global economy. But Shanghai's "reappearance" is as complexly situated as Hong Kong's culture of disappearance in a space of tensions and skewed images. For example, since the early 1990s Shanghai has been obsessed with a mania for building and urban development, but accompanying it like a shadow is something that at first sight seems rather puzzling: the state's interest in preservation projects. It is within the problematic of tensions between the city, the nation, and the transnational that comparisons between "reappearance" in Shanghai and "disappearance" in Hong Kong can be made and the question of cosmopolitanism can be posed.

Let's take the Shanghai case. Before the early 1990s, there was very little interest among the Shanghainese in the buildings they lived and worked in. If a large part of old Shanghai was preserved, it was by default, because the city had too few resources to embark on major programs of urban restructuring. As late as the early 1990s, visitors to Shanghai often remarked how little Shanghai had changed visually from its pre-1949 days, except to note that a large part of the glitter had gone. However, after Deng Xiaoping's 1992 visit, and within the space of a few years, the Pudong area of Shanghai across the Huangpu River from the Bund has developed into a mini-Manhattan, following Deng's agenda for it: "A new look each year, a transformation in three years." Today, even Hong Kong visitors, blasé about new buildings, are amazed by Shanghai. In a few short years, Shanghai saw the construction of over a thousand skyscrapers, a subway line, a highway overpass ringing the city, another bridge and tunnel across the Huangpu to Pudong, and the urbanization of Pudong itself, how coming into being before our eyes like the speeded-up image of time-lapse film. Interestingly enough, together with this frenzy of building and development – subsidised by the sale of land leases and joint venture capital – the city has shown an interest in preservation, something not specifically recommended by Deng. So far, around 250 buildings have been registered as municipal listed buildings, with another 200 more being considered. This is remarkable enough for us to ask, What, in fact, is happening?

Let me offer the following hypothesis: Preservation in Shanghai is motivated by something quite different from the usual pieties about "cultural heritage," which, given the city's colonial past, can only be ambiguous. It is motivated more by anticipations of a new Shanghai to rival the old than simply by nostalgia for the past. In other words, preservation is something more complex than just a question of the past remembered: in Shanghai, the past allows the present to pursue the future; hence "memory" itself is select and fissured, sometimes indistinguishable from amnesia. This paradox of the past as the future's future also throws a particular light on Shanghai's urban development, which, like preservation, takes on a special quality: Shanghai today is not just a city on the make with the new and brash everywhere – as might be said more aptly of Shenzhen, for example. It is also something more subtle and historically elusive: *the city as remake*, a shot-by-shot reworking of a classic, with the latest technology, a different cast, and a new audience. Not "Back to the Future" but "Forward to the Past." The minor story of preservation in Shanghai gives an important *gloss* – in both senses of the word – to the major story of urban development.

In rapidly developing cities, urban preservation as a rule is either ignored or merely paid lip service. Take the case of Hong Kong, in many ways a role model for Shanghai and other Chinese cities. Yet Hong Kong offers a comparatively straightforward example of the relationship between development and preservation. Though it is true that there are some preserved buildings in this former British colony – the best known being the clock tower of the demolished Hong Kong–Canton Railway Station, now a part of the Hong Kong Cultural Centre Complex; the old Supreme Court building; Western Market; and Flagstaff House, formerly British military headquarters and now a tea museum – on the whole, preservation happens ad hoc, with no systematic plan for municipal preservation comparable to Shanghai's. An interest in Hong Kong and its history, moreover, and hence in preservation, is only a recent phenomenon with origins tied to 1997 and an anxiety that Hong Kong as we knew it might come to an end with the handover. However, such an interest in preservation never proved strong enough to prevent hardnosed development decisions from being made in the market economy of a so-called noninterventionist state, and this circumstance has changed little since Hong Kong became an SAR. By contrast, the twist that Shanghai provides is in opting to develop and, at the same time, preserve at least part of the city, as if deliberately giving the lie to the notion that development and preservation are incompatible. This presents us with enough of anomaly to prompt the question: Precisely what role is preservation meant to play in Shanghai's impending transformation?

To begin with the obvious, the economic importance of preservation cannot be underestimated. Invoking a continuity with a legendary past – no matter how ambiguous that past may have been – enhances the city's attractiveness, gives it historical cachet, and hence equips it to compete for foreign investment and the tourist trade on more favourable terms. The past is a kind of symbolic capital. At the same time, preservation often accompanies the revitalization and gentrification of decaying areas of the city and contributes to urban renewal. But preservation has a third feature peculiar to Shanghai itself: namely, the way the economic role of preservation maps onto the tensions inherent in China's "socialist market economy." Since late 1978, this economy has created a private sector within a socialist state; that is, it has allowed the global into the national. Moreover, the new private sector has consistently outperformed the state in the marketplace, raising questions of to what degree the state is in touch with the new market conditions, Mao had succeeded in curtailing capitalism by establishing the socialist state, just as Europe had ameliorated capitalism's effects through the welfare-democratic state. But that was a bygone capitalism. The new capitalism, global capital, is freshly able to act, constantly outpacing the interventions of the nation-state and making it look heavy-footed.[8]

In this context, the state's interest in preservation, via municipal policy, makes a lot of sense. Not only is preservation well within the competence of the state; it is also a way by which the state can enter the global market through promoting the city's past – that is, through the heritage industry. It is an implicit assertion of the state's involvement in and contribution to the future development of Shanghai – a way of mediating the need of the state for legitimacy and the demand of the private sector for profitability. By a strange twist, the state's interest in preservation is an assertion that it is still a player in the new global game. Hence, the entirely different relation to preservation in Hong Kong and Shanghai: in the one, ad hoc and linked to anxieties about the city's disappearance; in the other, state-planned and related to the city's reappearance as a soi-disant "City of Culture."

The working together of development and preservation in Shanghai suggests that a new problematic is emerging. Something peculiar must be happening if preservation produces not a sense of history but the virtuality of a present that has erased the distinction between old and new – or where local history is another gambit in the game of global capital. Perhaps virtual cities can only look like what Shanghai today looks like, with old and new compressed together in an apocalyptic now. The listed buildings on the Bund and the chaos of skyscrapers in Pudong do not so much confront as complement each other on either side of the Huangpu River; in a sense, both old and new are simply steps in the remake of Shanghai as a City of Culture in the new global space. In such a space, heritage issues can be fused and confused with political and economic interests. And precisely because of this, urban preservation in the global era cannot be seen in isolation from other urban and social phenomena. Links begin to emerge between what at first sight seem to be unrelated social spaces – between, for example, the municipal *preservational* projects such as the old buildings around Yu Yuen Garden, in the old "Chinese city," now turned into a kind of vernacular mall, and the city's much more publicized *developmental* projects of cultural modernization, such as the new Shanghai Museum and the Grand Theater, both in an already modernized Renmin Square. We can see hints of a similar logic of globalism operative in each.

Take the new Shanghai Museum, which was opened in 1996. It is designed to resemble a giant *ting,* an antique Chinese bronze vessel. The obvious visual message here is that in the city's pursuit of modernity, Chinese tradition is not forgotten. But there is also something else. Consider the experience of entering the museum. In the exhibition halls, we find the rare artworks that the museum is famous for expertly displayed: the ancient bronzes, the Sung and Yuan paintings. But what also catches the attention is how ostentatiously *clean* the museum is, not a common experience in Shanghai. There always seem to be some workers polishing the brass on the railings or the marble on the floor. Even the toilets are kept meticulously clean. The dirtier the streets around it, the cleaner the museum. And suddenly you realize that the museum does not think of itself as being part of a local space at all, but as part of a virtual global cultural network. The Shanghai Museum is not just where artworks are being shown in Shanghai; it is also where Shanghai *shows itself off* in its museum, with its image cleaned up and in hopes that the world is looking.

But "globalism" is not without its own aporias and anomalies, For example, something of the tensions in Shanghai's new social space can be felt in one admittedly minor but symptomatic example: the etiquette of mobile phones. For the newly affluent entrepreneurial class, these phones are as much functional tools as symbols of the culture of globalism. It is also this class that, along with foreign visitors, can patronize the expensive and elegant restaurants that are reappearing in Shanghai. One of the most expensive of these is the Continental Room at the Garden Hotel, whose standards of elegance require guests to switch off their mobile phones out of consideration for fellow diners, What seems an unobjectionable policy from one point of view has produced many a contretemps. For these new entrepreneurs, dining at the Garden Hotel and using mobile phones go together. There is no conception that these electronic devices can be in certain social situations sources of irritation for oneself or others. What we find here is an example of transnationalism without a corresponding transnational subject. These new kinds of social embarrassment may not be insignificant in that they are symptoms of how the speeded-up nature of social and cultural life inevitably results in the production of multiple, sometimes conflicting, paradigms confusing for the person who needs to negotiate them.

Of course, it is true that social life since the modern era has always been marked by change and confusion. Cosmopolitanism has been seen as an ability to acquit oneself, to behave well, under difficult cultural situations by juggling with multiple perspectives – even when these perspectives were forced upon us or adopted in indifference. The question is: Are the kinds of changes taking place in Asian cities and elsewhere today forcing upon us situations in which we cannot behave well, because these changes are threatening to destroy the space of cities as we know them and creating cities we do not know? From this point of view, the apparently slight example of the use of mobile phones in "inappropriate" situations now takes on greater weight. Their indiscriminate use in the present case is neither an example of boorishness nor a lack of consideration for others, nor even a transgression of the boundaries of social etiquette. It is, rather, a genuine confusion about where the boundaries are, making both "transgression" and "behaving well" equally problematic.

If the speed of change is creating spaces we do not understand, then one strategy might be to slow things down – to preserve some almost erased concept of civility and respect for otherness in the midst of chaos. This was what the older cosmopolitanisms had strived for. But, it seems to me, such a *conservative* strategy has little space for manoeuvre. One of the most interesting things we can learn from the example of urban preservation in Shanghai today is how it, too, is infused with the spirit of globalism. "Preservation" and "heritage" do not act as brakes against development; in some strange way, they further a developmental agenda. The problem of cosmopolitanism today still remains how we are to negotiate the transnational space that global capital produces.

Clearly, cosmopolitanism can no longer be simply a matter of behaving well or even of an openness to otherness. Otherness lost its innocence as a result of the colonial experience. Even less attractive is the alternative of a brutal embrace of ethnocentric vision, an anticosmopolitanism made more extreme because it exists in the new and charged situation of information and speed. Information does not only dispel bigotry but also disseminates it. Can there be a cosmopolitanism for the global age, and what would it be like?

We might look for an answer in the analysis of the nature of cities today, particularly an analysis of their linkage to the transnational more so than to the national. As the fashion designer Yohji Yamamoto said in Wim Wenders's 1989 film *Notebook on Cities and Clothes*, "I like all big cities. More than Japanese, I feel I'm from Tokyo. . . . Tokyo has no nationality." Large nation-states like the previous Soviet Union have been breaking up, but this is not because some kind of transnational state is coming into being, only a transnational or global space where nation-states are still located. And cities are the locales or nodal points of this transnational space, which exists not in some abstract dimension but in the very specific sites and problem areas of the city. It exists, for example, in the problematic details of heritage and preservation in present-day Shanghai, in the non-places that Augé has pointed to, or in new kinds of social embarrassment that are the result of quickly shifting cultural paradigms. Whether a cosmopolitanism for the global age will emerge depends on our ability to grasp a space, that of the global city, that is always concrete even in its elusiveness. And this involves not so much imagining a transnational state as reimagining the city.

Notes

1. Marc Augé, *A Sense for the Other*, trans. Amy Jacobs (Stanford, CA: Stanford University Press, 1998), 106.
2. All quotations are from paragraphs 107 and 109 of Ludwig Wittgenstein, *Philosophical Investigations*, trans. G. E. M. Anscombe (Oxford: Basil Blackwell, 1974), 46–7.

3. See Gilles Deleuze, *Cinema*, 2 vols., trans. Hugh Tomlinson and Barbara Habberjam (Minneapolis: University of Minnesota Press, 1986–9).
4. J. G. Ballard, *Empire of the Sun* (London: Grafton Books, 1985), 17.
5. Leo Ou-fan Lee, "Shanghai Modern: Reflections on Urban Culture in China in the 1930s," *Public Culture* 11 (1999), 104.
6. See Abbas, "The Erotics of Disappointment," in *Wong Kar-wai*, ed. Jean-Marc Lalanne, David Martinez, Ackbar Abbas, and Jimmy Ngai (Paris: Editions Dis Voir, 1997), 39–81.
7. Xu Kuangdi, interview by Matthew Miller and Foo Choy Peng, *South China Morning Post* (Hong Kong), China Business Review section, 9 July 1998, 8.
8. On these issues, see Ulrich Beck, *What Is Globalization?* (Cambridge: Polity Press, 2000).

11

An Occupied Place

Kathleen C. Stewart*

This chapter evokes the "senses of place" emergent in the doubly occupied landscape of the hills and *hollers* of southern West Virginia. At the end of a long century of occupation by the coal industry – through the economic and cultural destabilizations of cycles of boom and bust, the mass migrations to the cities and returns to the hills, and the final mine closings in the eighties – the hills find themselves reeling in the dizzying, diacritical sensibilities of the local and the transnational, the past and the present, the all-too-real effects of history and an alternate way of life embodied in the very look of *thangs got down*. The impossible dream of a stable home place proliferates within the shock of a threatening surround that has penetrated it to the core. The detritus of history piled high on the local landscape has become central to a sense of place emergent in re-membered ruins and pieced-together fragments.

Far from being a timeless or out-of-the-way place, the local finds itself reeling in the wake of every move and maneuver of the center of things. It continually reconstitutes itself through a ruminative re-entrenchment in local forms and epistemologies. *Things that happen* are re-membered in an incessant, daily narrativization of the accidental, contingent, and phantasmic effects of the industrial and postindustrial order of things. Local *ways of talkin'* and *ways of doin' people* become metacultural markers of a local way of life in distinction to the demonized ways of the cities. As they say in the hills, *thangs are not what they seem*, and everything depends on the prolific creativity of *makin' somethin' of thangs* that happen. The sense of place grows dense with a social imaginary – a fabulation of place contingent on precise modes of sociality and on tense, shifting social deployments of local discourses that give place a tactile, sensate force.[1]

The problem for the ethnography of such a sense of place is how to track its densely textured poetics through its own tense diacritics of center and margin, local and global, past and present without reducing it to the "gist" of things or to the abstract schemas of distant "cause" and encapsulating "explanation." This is a poetics emergent in the daily practices of textualizing *thangs that happen* in precise, mimetic detail that dramatizes rhythms of life, artful turns of phrase, and palpable tensions and desires. It resides

* Pp. 137–64 from *Senses of Place*, ed. S. Feld and K. Basso (Santa Fe, NM: School of American Research Press). © 1996 by the School of American Research, Santa Fe, USA. Reprinted with permission from the School for American Research.

in the labored breathing of all the old men slowly smothering from black lung disease and in all the nervous, restless action of people *runnin' the roads* and *runnin' their mouths* all day. It depends on the dialogic provisionality of things remembered and retold; it begins with things overheard or seen out of the corner of the eye and ends in "truths" lodged in the concrete yet shifting life of signs. *Thangs are not what they seem*, and yet people search for signs of palpable if ephemeral meaning. The sense of place grows more, not less, present and pressing as a social imaginary emerges in talk and signifying action – a network of signs that are scanned and *studied on* and collected like the dense layers of trashed objects that demarcate people's *places* in the hills.

The problem of considering "senses of place," then, is a problem of tracking the force of cultural practices subject to social use and thus filled with moments of tension, digression, displacement, excess, deferral, arrest, contradiction, immanence, and desire. Theorists such as Barthes (1957, 1974, 1975), Bakhtin (1981, 1984, 1986), and Benjamin (1969, 1978) have each in their own way pointed to this excessive and hard-to-grasp quality of cultural productions. For Barthes, there is the relentless "texting" of things coupled with the indeterminacy of "meaning" in the text, the inevitable gaps or slippages in the working of signs coupled with the uncontained excesses of reading. For Bakhtin, there is the radical dialogics of cultural production, the genealogical "meaning" of signs and forms discoverable only in their social and historical usage, and the ungraspable "something more" of genre and voice. Benjamin makes a claim for the redemptive potentiality of images and objects whose meaning is inherently dialectical and politically double-edged.

In such accounts, culture is not an end point or a blueprint for thinking and acting but an order of effects glimpsed in gaps or pauses in the sign where epistemological certainty is arrested by the hard-to-grasp sense of something "more" and "other." The very effort to imagine culture, then, is itself a continuous effort to reopen a space attentive to the forms and moves of cultural production. It takes more than the safe distance of a relativist chant or the effort to debunk stereotypes or to "disprove" myths. It takes more than an artful re-presentation of local voices as if they could "speak for themselves." It takes not less theorizing on the part of ethnography but more, in order to expose the complicity of our own cultural critique-as-usual in obscuring or enclosing the force, tension, and density of cultural imaginations in practice and use.

"Sense of place" in the account that follows refers to the effects of contingency, signifying density, and social location glimpsed at moments of tension, displacement, and deferral. It is written into the West Virginia landscape not as a smooth story that follows the lines of its own progress from beginning to end as a master narrative would but as a collection of fits and starts in the moves of master narrative itself. It is made up of narrativized moments of encounter, shock, description, digression, and lyrical, ruminative aporias that give pause. It dwells in and on the formed particularity of things and the spaces of desire (and dread) they incite in the imagination.

In the effort to re-present, or translate, in an academic context something of the force of the sense of place in the hills, my account finds itself sharply divided between evocation and theoretical exegesis. It performs, rather than obscures, the inescapable problematics of subject and object, power and powerlessness, distance and closeness, form and meaning that are not only central to ethnographic efforts at intercultural speculation but also key to the everyday machinations of cultural poetics and senses of place in the "modern" world. My claim is that it is only in holding open the gaps and tensions in cultural representation itself that we can glimpse an "other" mode of cultural critique that speaks from a "place" of contingency, vulnerability, and felt impact. This, it seems to me, is the significance for "us" of the sense of place and the point of holding open an interpretive space in which to consider it.

In the hills, the sense of place is lodged in precise ways of attending to things. It begins and ends in an incessant compulsion to story things that happen to interrupt the progress of events. It tracks along through an endless process of remembering, retelling, and imagining things. It fixes on a tactile mimesis of decomposing objects and launches itself again and again as a continuous search for redemptive, luminous signs that speak to people and point to the possibility of the "something more" in a culture and a place. In the effort to evoke something of this sensibility, I have used every trick I could imagine to catch the reader up in the dialogic provisionality of its "truths," including dense descriptions with amassed details, direct polemics, re-presented stories, and direct appeals to the reader to "picture" this and "imagine" that.

My story, like the stories I heard in the hills, begins and ends in a process of re-membering, retelling, and re-placing. It began with two years of fieldwork between 1980 and 1982 and continued through a dozen return visits in the years that followed and through the twists and turns of fieldnotes, tape recordings, memories, photographs, phone calls, postcards, letters, telegrams, and professional papers. Over time, it has become a process of long dwelling on things remembered and retold, forgotten and imagined.

In the account that follows, I re-present stories with ethnopoetic notations meant to evoke something of the intensely elaborated cultural poetics of the placed, local speech in the hills (see Derrida 1978; Hymes 1975, 1981, 1985; Tedlock 1972, 1983) and to mimic the effects of poetics in performance (see Bauman 1977, 1986; Bauman and Briggs 1990). I use boldface lettering to indicate emphasis, line breaks to indicate rhythm and pause, and occasional representations of spoken pronunciations to evoke the differences between Appalachian dialect and "Standard English." My interpretive strategy here, of course, is a process of translation both of the oral to the written and of a local (and stigmatized) language to a particular audience for desired effects. It is not in any way an effort to achieve an objective representation of a linguistic reality but is an ideological strategy, informed by Bakhtin's translinguistics (1981; see also Vološinov 1986), that traces forms in their social and political use. It is an effort to evoke some of the density and texture of expressive forms that voice a cultural poetic embedded in a way of life and the politics of its constant subversion and reproduction in the face of national and transnational forces.

To the same end, I use italics to indicate culturally marked local terms or terms that have some marked cultural relevance in their social use. For the sake of textual fluency, most terms are italicized only the first time they appear; for the sake of the critical dif-ference that emerges at moments of interruption and arrested progress, some terms are italicized repeatedly to mark and remember the space of the local sense of place. The sense of place in the hills, as I imagine it, stands as an allegory of an interpretive space or a mode of cultural critique that often finds itself crowded into the margins of the

American imaginary and yet haunts the center of things and reminds it of something it cannot quite grasp.

Digging In

Picture hills so dense, so tightly packed in an overwhelming wildness of green that they are cut only by these cramped, intimate hollers tucked into the steep hillsides like the hollow of a cheek and these winding, dizzying roads that seem somehow tentative, as if always threatening to break off on the edges or collapse and fall to ruins among the weeds and the boulders as so many others have done before them. Picture hillsides so steep that the sun shines down on them for only a few hours a day before passing over the next ridge. Picture hills slashed round and round with the deep gashes of strip mining like a roughly peeled apple, and hilltops literally lopped off by machines the size of ten-story buildings. And these creeks – this ever-audible soundscape to the everyday – that in the spring swell and rage at the bridges and overhanging shacks and leave behind a wake of mud and trash that reaches high into the trees. Picture mountainous heaps of coal slag that catch fire from internal combustion under all the thousands of tons of their own weight and burn for months or years at a time, letting off a black stench of oily smoke. Picture the hills bursting into red and orange flames at all hours of the night – flames likened to the pits of hell. Picture sagging creek banks shored up with tires, rusted trucks, and refrigerators, and picture treacherous slag "dams" holding back lakes of black oily water from the mines. Picture how, when it rains, the men go on watch through the night, climbing the steep hills to peer into the blackness and wonder if the dam will hold.

Picture the tattered remnants of the old coal-mining camps crowded into the hollers, and the way people's places perch precariously on the sides of hills or line the roads with the hills pressed hard against their backs. Some stand freshly painted in yards filled with kitsch figurines and plastic swimming pools. Others bear the faded pastel blues, greens, and yellows they have worn for many years, the paint worn through in places to weathered boards, their porches starkly swept and lined with chairs. Others still are deeply decayed, with broken porches, partially caved-in roofs, broken water pipes gushing out the underside, and relatives' trailers packed tight into their yards for lack of land to rent or buy.[2]

Picture the places way up the hollers in a wilder, more dangerous zone away from the hardtop and neighbors. Here whole compounds may be pieced together with the remains of the old places now long fallen into ruin. A main house may be surrounded by tiny shacks made out of scrap metal and no bigger than a bed, where grown sons or crazy relations stay. There may be an outhouse, a cold cellar, a pump house, chicken coops, a pigsty, and several small gardens. Or there may be only a grassless yard heaped with metals and woods, bits of toys, and dismembered machines. There will be chairs stuck out in the middle of it all – the place where Fred or Jake or Sissy sits – and farther out, encircling the compound, a ring of rusted, disemboweled trucks and cars, a pen filled with baying hounds and, beyond that, the hills themselves where you will come across the graveyards, the orchards, the ruins, the named places, the strip mines, the trucks belly-up, the damp, decayed mattresses, some scattered items of clothing, some campfire sites, some piles of beer cans, some bags of trash . . .

I could tell you how sometimes clumps of coal mud explode into the sink and then the water runs black, or there is no water at all, for the rest of the day. Or how sometimes, when a house falls vacant, it disappears overnight and later reappears as an addition to someone else's place. I could say that houses, like people and things, circulate until they become abstracted into moving forms, that it is their movements and rememberings that seem to matter most.

If I had fifty thousand words in which to describe the life of watched and remembered things in these hills, I would use them, as James Agee did in *Let Us Now Praise Famous Men* (Agee and Evans 1941), to heap detail upon detail so that we might at least imagine an escape from the "you are there" realism of ethnographic description into a surreal space of intensification. Like Agee, I could describe the rooms and rafters, the cracks in the walls, the damp underneaths of the houses where dogs and fleas and other creatures lie, the furniture, the contents of drawers, the smell of coal soot ground into the floors over years and covering the walls with a thin greasy layer, a second-story bedroom ceiling open to the sky where the roof has fallen in, the way gauzy curtains are drawn across the windows so that everything outside can be seen without knowing it is being watched, a poor family of six huddled together on mattresses on the living room floor because that is the only room that gives shelter in the winter.

For Agee, every "thing" he encountered became a sign communicating exploitation, injustice, disappointment, and desire. Writing during the Great Depression, he railed against existing forms of documentary writing in an effort "to open up a passionately ambiguous new space" (Reed 1988:160) beyond any claims to be able to represent such "things" as tenant farmers (or "hillbillies" or "white trash"). He turned his book into a political allegory about relations between "Us" who represent "Them" and Them represented in an attempt to destabilize not just a particular representation of "them" but the very claim to know the "meaning" of such "things" at all. The inevitable failure of representation to capture an absolute "real" meant only a further commitment to the political act of poesis – the continuous effort to imagine what might be called a "cultural real." Escape, he said, is impossible: ruin is our only hope – a complete abandonment to the currents of existence.

In the effort to clear a space in which to imagine a cultural poesis, Agee's writing grew hypergraphic, pushing minutely described things into a space of "mimetic excess" (Taussig 1993) where they were at once naturalized as the real and marked in their very textualization as a cultural construction. Reality and writing seemed to transpose themselves in cultural objects (Reed 1988:161); a cultural poesis seemed to have somehow scripted itself right into the matter of things. The texture of wood on a country church wall appeared "as if it were an earnest description" (Agee and Evans 1941:38). "A chain of truths did actually weave itself and run through: it is their texture that I want to represent, not betray or pretty up into art" (1941:240). He wished he could put bits of wood, fabric, and excrement on the page rather than words. He wished the book could be printed on newsprint so that it would fade and fall apart with use, mimicking the ephemerality of everyday life and cultural meaning.

Picture, then, a place that has given itself over to such "abandonment to the currents of existence." A place, as people would say, "caught between a rock and a hard place" – a home place hardened into a protective cocoon from the threatening life beyond the hills and yet always emptying out as people leave in search of work. A place mired in the abject decay of things left behind, yet vibrant with re-membered presence. A place grown at once tactile and imaginary, at once real and as insubstantial as ghostly traces. A place where place is everything, and yet a family's place is not where they "live" but where they *stay at*, as if the staying has to be marked, like a temporary respite requiring constant vigilance. Imagine how "place" and even "culture" itself could become a space of desire – "a thousand plateaus of intensification" (Deleuze and Guattari 1991).

Imagine the desire to amass such a "place" around you, to dig yourself into it, to occupy it. The porches piled high with couches, chairs, plastic water jugs. The yards filled with broken toys, washing machines, scrap metal and salvaged wood, cars and trucks on blocks or belly-up, being dismembered piece by piece. All the living room walls crowded with pictures of kin who have left and the dead in their coffins, the paintings of the bleeding Sacred Heart of Jesus with the beautiful longing eyes. All the mantels and tabletops covered with *whatnots* and shrines. The newspaper clippings of deaths and strikes. The children's drawings and trophies. The heart-shaped Valentine's Day chocolate boxes saved every year for twenty years and mounted on bedroom walls. All the velveteen tapestries of John L. Lewis, John F. Kennedy, and Elvis.[3]

The Shock of History

Imagine life in a place that was encompassed by the weight of an industry, that was subject to a century of cultural displacements, and that now faces the final collapse of mining and the slow, inexorable emigration of the young. Imagine a history remembered not as the straight line of progress but as a flash of unforgettable images. Remember the *old timey* cabins in the hills, the fires, the women dead in childbirth, the slick company representatives who dropped by the cabins of unsuspecting farmers, stayed for dinner, and casually produced a bag of coins in exchange for parcels of "unused ridgeland" (Eller 1982:54). Remember the company camps that sprang up around mines like someone else's mirage, complete with company scrip, company stores, company doctors, company thugs, company railroads, company schools, company churches, and company baseball teams. Company thugs carried sawed-off shotguns, policing who came and went on the trains. They say the thugs stood sentry in the hills over a camp in the night. You could see their lanterns and that's how you knew they were there. Then the lights would go out and you didn't know. Imagine all the arresting images of strikes, lockouts, house evictions, people put out in the alleys with their stuff all around them and the snow coming down.

> They was a settin' in chairs
> like they was in their own livin' room.
> And that's the truth.
> They had nowhere to go and the snow comin' down right on top of 'm.
> People lived in tents and the babies lay upon the quilts on the ground.

Armed miners holed up on a mountain and the federal government was called in to drop bombs on them from airplanes.

There were the dizzying swings of boom and bust, the mechanization of the mines, the mass migrations of the fifties and sixties, the final boom during the oil crisis of the 1970s, the final mine closings in the eighties, the collapse of the place, the painful hanging on, the unthinkable leavings. Imagine how the place became a migrational space that caught people in the repetition of drifting back and forth from the hills to the cities looking for work (Ardery 1983; Coles 1971; Cunningham 1987; Gitlin and Hollander 1970). How country songs of heartache and displacement became their theme songs. How ecstatic fundamentalism boomed in a performative excess of *signs* of the spirit and dreams of another world beyond. How the place itself drew them back to dig themselves in – "so far in I ain't never comin' out." How the place grew palpable to the remembered senses: the smell of snakes in the air, the sound of slow voices chatting in the yard, the breeze striking the tin pie plates in a garden, the taste of ramps and dandelion greens.

Imagine a place grown intensely local in the face of loss, displacement, exile, and a perpetually deferred desire to return to what was always already lost or still ahead, just beyond reach. Picture how a home place long threatening to dissolve into the sheer shiftiness of history might grow filled with an intense synesthesia of person, sociality, and landscape, how a haunted cultural landscape becomes a dizzying, overcrowded presence. Imagine how people say they *smother* and are hit by waves of *the dizzy* and *the nerves*, how they say they wouldn't "never want to leave." Imagine how they find themselves "caught between a rock and a hard place," re-membering a home place that is always emptying out and backing away from the cold impossibility of the foreign land of the cities "beyond" that remains their only option.

Imagine the need to remember through the constant repetition of images fixed, condensed, studied on, and made visceral, the need to watch, to chronicle, to make something of thangs, the attachment to things that matter, the fascination with objects on which the mind can stare itself out.[4] Remember all the named places in the hills that mark the space of accidents and tragedies. Imagine how people *just set* and talk at the old gas stations and stands – the beat-up old stores on the side of the road that sell daily necessities with long shelf lives like cigarettes, soda pop, candy, cakes, and the canned milk for the endless pots of coffee.[5] Picture how people watch for things that happen and scan for signs. Picture the endless proliferation of stories throughout the day and over the years.

Imagine how an encompassed and contested way of life can grow immanent, how it might be scripted right into the matter of things, how objects and bodies marked by events could become images that twist and turn in the strands of history and sociality and then rise like moons on the horizon – sudden caesuras in which the mind could collect itself by staring itself out on things. Imagine the desire to amass such a place around you, to dig yourself into it, to occupy it . . .

Re-membering Place

Imagine the past and the present as sensed, tactile places that remember and haunt, how the past *just comes* to people out roaming the hills in body or mind. Picture a "real" embodied in the particularity of precise effects – how identity, social history, and a sense of place can all be recounted together in a litany of *places* in the hills, social places, and places on the body. There is the constant recounting of places on the body where life has left its impact – the scars, the locations of pain, the disfigurements, the amputations, the muscles and joints and bones that remember. There are the constant social rituals of placing people – Who are your kin, where do you work, who do you know, where do you stay at, what has happened to you? There is the constant remembering of named places in the hills: the remains of the big white houses of the *operators* (managers) looming over the camps, the worked-out mouths of mines lying dark and gaping on the sides of the hills and, farther in, the chimneys and aging orchards that *remember* a family farm, the graveyards and rusted train tracks and mining tipples that *remember* accidents, strikes, and other "striking" scenes like the prayer services held underground at the start of a shift, when hundreds of miners would crouch in the water under the low ceilings listening to the preaching of death and salvation, the place where the union organizer was shot dead and his blood ran out in the coal dirt and was lost, the strip-mined hill that collapsed in on itself and slid down to cover the Graham family graves, the places of hunts, suicides, murders, and car accidents, of children electrocuted on old mining wires, of fires when the people trapped inside cried out for help while the others stood outside and listened, helpless.

Imagine the watchfulness, the effort to track the workings of a "system" that is "located," if anywhere, in the nervous, shifting, hard-to-follow trajectories of desire. Picture the restlessness, the need to get out and go: all the coming and going, the *running the roads*, the *running their mouths*, the *roaming*, the *trading* – how people literally "keep moving" as if to occupy this place and to fill somehow its overfilled yet emptying space. Then picture all the places where people *just set* – a chair left out in the middle of the kitchen floor or on the porch or in the yard or out in the hills, a favorite stump or rock.

Picture the constant working on things, the dismembering and remembering of things, the strange agency of fashioning aesthetic effects out of things that are always falling apart or are already fallen into decay. Picture how people are always *foolin' with* their places – someone is tearing off his back porch, someone else is building on a bedroom or jacking up a sag, another is building an arbor for her grape vines, and another leaves her coal stove out in the front yard for weeks "for spring cleaning." Bud Caulley had his house half repainted for longer than anyone could remember: "Hit's where he cain't tell whether he likes the old or the new. And tell you the truth, buddy, I cain't either. Can you?"

Picture the proliferation of signs of a local life written tentatively yet persistently onto the landscape. The tiny wooden or cinder-block post offices that bear the names Amigo, Red Jacket, Ruin, Helen, Black Eagle, Viper, Iroquois, Hard Shell, Winding Gulf, Odd, East Gulf, Coal City, Cook Town, Persistence, Lillybrook. The tiny particleboard entrepreneurial shacks with signs that read "BEeR CiGArETs PoP" in huge irregular lettering. The trucks perched on the side of the road selling watermelons or made-in-Mexico velveteen wall hangings of the Last Supper, the Sacred Heart, the rebel flag. Hand-painted road signs – "Please Don't Throw Your Trash Here," "Anteeks," "Eggs For Sale," "WATCH IT: Road Washed Out Up Aways Ahead." Church signs advertising a welcome and a warning: "Sinners Welcome," "Sinners

Apply Within," "Repent, For The Day Is Near." The massive coal trucks rushing around steep curves, their names mounted in bold letters on the grill – "Heaven's Highway," "Good Time Buddy," "Let the Good Times Roll." At one curve, two hand-painted billboards crammed with biblical quotations face each other in a heated debate over how literally to interpret the signs of the "End Times." At another, a hand-painted road sign perched at the top of a treacherous hill offers only the starkly haunting warning: "ETERNITY AHEAD."

Picture people sitting on porches, standing beside fences, clumps of men gathered around benches at the gas station or the stand, how they stare as you pass, keeping track.

Getting Caught

Imagine yourself always already caught in the tense fabulation of story and sociality and surrounded by events you *cain't hep but notice*. Imagine tracking a day in the camps by a constant watching out of the corner of the eye . . .

June 24, 1982. Kitty passes my place to see Sissy about the girls' fighting. Sissy goes to see about Miss Banks, who has had an operation on her knee. Kitty comes to see if I think Sissy's mad at her "for saying anything to her;" Sissy, she says, has been acting funny with her. Anna Mae, out hanging her rugs, yells to Lilly to come out "if you want to" and they stand talking over the fence that joins their places. Kitty, still with me, wonders what they are talking about, "not that it's any a my business." She says they say Anna Mae's daughter has cancer and this leads to stories of the grotesque – cancers, bizarre accidents of mothers rolling over on their sleeping babies, bloody childbirth in the truck on the way to the hospital, babies born with the mark of the beet or the hamburger or the apple that the pregnant mother craved – "looks just like it." We say it's a shame that Kitty's daughter Julie had to find out from the other kids on the school bus that she was adopted, that Kitty should have told her herself. This leads us to talk about the danger of things left unsaid; Mr. Walker in Rhodell shot himself to death because he kept things to himself. I recall the look in his eyes the last time I saw him – at the public auction of his store which he had neglected more and more over the years as his drinking got worse until finally people got tired of sour milk and bugs in their rice and "quit tradin' with him." I bring Sissy her cuttings and we sit out on her porch in the late afternoon sun, dangling our legs over the edge. Sissy says Kitty thinks she was the one who told about Julie being adopted, but she never would – "Ain't nobody's business." We watch the men on evening shift leave out, the men on day shift come in. We can smell Miss Murdock's greens cooking ("She's sa hateful she won't tell nobody where she got em"), Dreama's pork frying ("You reckon Bud's back workin?").

Imagine a vigilant scanning become automatic, relentless, compulsive; people cain't hep but notice. Imagine that passing trucks can be recognized by their distinctive sounds, that their comings and goings are automatically tracked and timed to figure where they have been and how long they have lingered there. Imagine the scanning for signs . . . how everything depends on things overheard, overseen, on the effort to make

somethin' of thangs. Imagine how when someone falls sick or dies the others quite literally miss seein' 'm.

Imagine the *aggravation* that builds when the responsibility to bear witness is drawn
to the task of tracking those who run the roads all day or those who stay holed up out
of sight. How the constant necessity for fluid, relational engagement seizes up into the
sensation of smothering in the face of too much stuff, too much talk, the ever-present
excesses of action and expression, the smothering intensity of being left to study on
thangs. Picture how people, holed up and studyin' on thangs, get *squirrelly* and have to
git out and go.

. . . Picture the restlessness of the young men runnin' the roads day and night until
they run out of gas and money or until they are stopped by the force of accident. Then
picture them, still restless, roaming up and down the holler in their wheelchairs. Picture
Riley Meadows's neighbors, who watched him when he stayed "holed up in there" after
his wife died. "And they say he's got a calendar in there on his wall and every morning
when he gets up he marks an X through another day gone by without her. He counts
the days she's gone." He's gone "mean." He won't talk to anyone. He won't get out
and go. "He'll aggravate you to death." Picture those who watch for Miss Graham when
she drops out of sight for a while. They "figure she's in there a drankin', Hit's just a
matter a time 'fore somethin' happens."

Picture how the hills grow infilled with the excesses of a place reacting to the threat
of a world *got down*. Picture the shifting satisfactions and aggravations of those who sit
on their porches in the gathering dusk to re-collect a barrage of images that have an
impact and leave a trace as the hills come in to darken the sky at the end of the day.
Picture, too, all the old men, slowly smothering with black lung, who dream of going
back up into the hills once more – to a place "far in" where they could just set. More
than once I have been persuaded to take them, pushing their wheelchairs over roots and
wet leaves to a clearing and propping spare oxygen tanks around them.

A Social Imaginary

Picture the place as an intense social imaginary born in the nervous oscillation of loss
and the dream of return and raised in the tense fabulation of a ghostly insubstantiality
that is also a tactile attachment. Picture the enchantments and investments in these hills
as a lost and possible world. Here, sociality is not an afterthought or a "context" that
adds a dimension to meaning after the fact, but a force field that pulls meaning along
in its wake on a twisted path through dread and desire, loyalty and betrayal.

Imagine those moments when the hills abandon themselves to a social imaginary,
when the place becomes a phantasmagoric dream space – a wild zone beyond the pale
filled with things dangerous, tragic, surprising, spectacular, and eccentric. Imagine the
"real" at such moments as a resistant surface scanned by wishes and regrets and dis-
closed by desire – a collection of fantastic fragments and effects through which things
appear obliquely yet powerfully as what they are and what they can be.[6]

. . . They say there are snakes up there and wild young men who lie in wait or come
in the night to rob and maim. Once there were hippies – demon worshippers – who

lived out there under a rock. There are eccentric hermits living on nothing and white trash families filled with incest; there are criminals in stolen car rings drifting back and forth to Chicago and hiding out from the police.

. . . There was the night that Frankie, a Vietnam vet who was rumored to be living under rocks, went on a burning spree that took out five barns and shacks in the hour before dawn while volunteer firefighters raced from one call to the next, unable to keep up with him or to find a trace of him.

. . . There is Eva Mae. Poor, black, and "crazy," she walks the road between Amigo and Rhodell all day long, waving a gun or a butcher knife at any car that tries to stop and give her a ride.

. . . They say people are crazy and there's no telling what they might do. They keep guns loaded by the bed and at the door and shoot at the sound of noises in the night. They say the smell of snakes in the dog days of August is strong enough to make you sick.

Yet the wildness and danger only fan the flames of desire. There are the graveyards to visit, the old orchards to be harvested, the berries and greens to gather if you dare. Old women venture out in packs, salivating over dandelion greens, ramps, and a dozen named varieties of weeds as if they embodied desire itself. Lacy Smith talks of a place up in the hills where a tiny hole opens into a great big room full of Indian things. He and Bud have looked for it but they never could find it again "where the hole is so small."

Danger and promise mark the space of a dream world born of the tense union of contingency and desire, or what is and what could have been. Caught between a rock and a hard place, people cling to the hills as a place of impossible possibility. They say people shouldn't get above their raisin'. They say they would never want to leave. They scavenge and loot. They hunt. They fish. They scavenge wood, they loot coal from the slag heaps at the worked-out mines. They scavenge checks as they scavenge meat – food stamps, social security, black lung, disability, welfare. They carry away booty under cover of darkness.

. . . There was the night that a group of striking miners sitting in the waiting room of the health clinic spun a collective fantasy of how they would scale the big brick walls of Governor Rockefeller's mansion and loot it for all it was worth.

. . . Or the night, like so many others, that some of the young men, caught in the trap of alcoholic roaming, made the trip to Chicago as a bold, spontaneous adventure, drinking all the way. They woke up in the city, in the noise, the traffic; they got lost; there was trouble with the police. Then again a drunken, dreamy night and they found themselves back in the hills, dreaming of losing themselves in a place "way back in" where they could never find their way out again.

There are all the stories of those who have found themselves adrift out in the world beyond the hills and dreamed of return. There was Ray Meadows, stationed in Germany in the seventies, who caught himself staring out the kitchen window at a lone dandelion in the yard and, hillbilly that he was, it was all he could do to keep from *showin' hisself* by running out and plucking it to eat. There was Bobby Lilly, who was too *backward* to get anything to eat on the train coming home from the Korean War and who arrived home so weak from starvation that he fell sick and had to be nursed back to health on a diet of beans and corn pone. There was the day Jimmy Cunningham started back from Baltimore but was stopped by a feeling and turned back. He started out again the next day and made it back all right. "I ain't superstitious. I don't believe in black cats and all that. But a feelin' is somethin' different. A feelin' ain't somethin' you ignore." And one night Helen James had a dream. She dreamed that she was driving away in a big slow luxury car, drifting past beautiful pastoral mountain scenes filled with color and sound. She was coming up over the top of a big hill and she felt something "big" was going to happen. But then there was nothing – the terrifying annihilation of free fall. She woke up smothering. "It makes you not want to go nowhere."

Placed Itineraries

Imagine yourself, then, not in a cleared ethnographic space of explanatory contexts and structures but in a distracted space, moving as if in body from one place to the next and drawn along by digressions that lead into the social imaginary.[7]

> All right now, you know where Miss Banks stays at up there, don't you?
> All right, now, go on down Miss Banks's place past that big ol' bridge where that McKinney boy went over and hit looks like you might go in after 'm if you ain't careful, buddy.
> Yeah BUDDY.
> All right, now, you'll see a bridge what's got one side down and the other side 'bout covered up in briars.
> Keep on 'til you see the Black Eagle post office.
> That's where the snake handlers stay at and Bud says he's skeered to deliver the mail down there where he might put his hand in a mailbox and there's a snake in there.
> I don't guess they get much mail down there, do you?
> All right, now, keep on, keep on, pretty soon you come to that place where they shot up that boy. What was that boy's name?
> You know that one kilt his wife.
> Well, really, I don't believe it was his wife, but they was a livin' together and I don't know what all.
> Well they was in to it and he kilt her right there.
> They said there was blood all over the walls and never could get it out of the carpet because Sissy went down there right after it happened and she told me it was bad.
> All right, now, you know where that old woman stays, there's a washin' machine out front, well it's just past the sign for "free coffee."
> . . . and perty soon you come to a big ol' red colored house up on the hill . . .

Imagine a place constantly rewritten and re-membered, a place where sociality emerges in digressions and culls itself into *big meanings* at moments of shock. Imagine the force of social imagination at work in the desire to mime, to re-member, to participate in the matter of things. To matter. To follow distraction into something like "the heart of things" – of only as a temporary resting place, a place to just set.

Picture how people out roaming in the hills come up against places, and how a memory of inescapable impact just comes. Every time Tammy goes to the river now she "cain't hep but recall that pore man drownded." A young, strong man was swimming out in the river with his friends,

> where it's just over your head even way out.
> And he started to go down.
> Well they tried to hep him and they was all around him but they said hit was just like
>   somethin' was pullin' him down.
> And finally he told em, he said, "you better let me go and y'all get back to the shallow."
> He said "I'm a goin down."
> And they said they could feel him go down their legs, and they felt his hands slide down
>   their legs like he wanted to hold on and then he was gone.
> Honey, that haunts me.
> And it does, too.

Picture how events actively imagined in this way and weighted with social use reverberate beyond the particularities of any account, how "the image contains its own remainder, in the act of the imagination" (Strathern 1991:xxiii). Imagine how meaning, memory, and motive adhere to storied things to become an encountered force that stops people dead in their tracks, effects a gap in understanding, and motivates a search for meaningfulness.

June 4, 1982. Sissy and I walked up Devil's Fork holler. As we passed Amigo 2, stories just came to her of the people and events that once surrounded the now-deserted shacks.[8] The farther we went up the holler, the more our talk drifted into a lyrical, melancholic rumination. At a bridge Sissy recalled the old swimming hole there when the creek was still clean:

> But that was back before they got the commodes in and the govermint come in, told us a
>   septic tank had to be so many feet apart and that's the law.
> Well, all right, now, in 'Migo most a them lots ain't big enough for the law and we tried
>   to tell 'm but you just cain't talk to them people. They said, "You have to have 'm so
>   far apart."
> So people started dumpin' in the creek.
> Honey, I hated to see it where that water was as blue! an' used to we'd swim here, the sun
>   shined down on it, an all us comin' up then, we'd spend all day.

I noticed an overgrown stand of *ramblin' roses* in the middle of an empty field. Sissy said:

> Well, you cain't see it but there's a chimbley other side them blooms, runs right up the
>   far side of 'm, the grass is about covered it now.
> Jake Catlitt, he built that house, big house and it had a stone front to it and them old timey
>   beams and big ol' windas.
> Well, Jake lived in it and then his baby Pete, he lived there too.
> An he'd just got married and they was livin' there and there was another young couple
>   stayin' there with 'em to help pay the bills. There wasn't much work at that time but
>   Jake, he was workin' down at that Joe's service station down Black Eagle and he was off
>   at work.

And the two women were home alone and it was where they didn't know how to make the
  fire in the stove and reckon they got it too hot and they said it musta caught on one of
  them old beams.
Well they run out with the baby, cause one of em had a baby, an pore old Petey, he was
  a comin' back from work, an he seen it and come a runnin' and a hollerin' buddy.
And the Reeds, they stayed right down here, they come on and them other people down
  'Migo 2, they seen the smoke and they come on. Ever'body come a runnin' but there
  weren't nothin' they could do.
The fire bust out a them windas and burned them old timey beams and it tuk that whole
  house, burned it right down to the ground, buddy.
Petey an them went down Viper to stay, and I never did hear what happened to them other
  people.
But that's where them roses bloom 'round that old chimbley. It's a perty place, but it's
  been lonely too long. They oughta get somebody in, come stay out here.

A rambling rose vine entwined around a crumbling chimney "remembers" an old
family farm, the dramatic fire in which the place was lost, and the utopic potential still
clinging to the traces of history. Concrete objects that have decayed into fragments and
traces embody absence and the process of remembering itself; they haunt people. The
deserted place "remembers" and grows lonely.

Imagine how "meaning" can coalesce in the tactility of a cryptic object. How representation occurs as a kind of re-presenting that stimulates and provokes rather than
provides the closure of information, explanation, or code decoded. How people search
for a profundity lurking in appearances. How they find excesses that encode not "a
meaning" per se but the very surplus of meaningfulness vibrating in a remembered
cultural landscape filled with contingency and accident, dread and depression, trauma
and loss, and all those dreams of escape and return.

Imagine a place reverberating with countless accounts like Bud Graham's hunting
story – accounts in which a distracted, everyday chronicling of events is repeatedly
interrupted by "striking" images of places where things have happened. Imagine how
simple itineraries suddenly give themselves over to a striking image, as if arrested by a
space of intensification, and then recover – shifting back to an everyday sensibility but
one that has become infused with the promise of shocking interruption.

Yeah, buddy, I been all over these here heels.
Used to, we'd go up huntin' and them dogs'd run all up Devil's Fork clear up to the old
  Graham place, crost Tommy Creek and way over yonder to Madeline, and them dogs
  a mine was as good coon dogs as you'd ever wanna see and couldn't nobody else's dogs
  catch em and buddy they'd try, too. [laughing]
I remember the time, that Bud Henson fella useta stay down here at 'Miga, awful bad to
  drank.
And one night he was out here a layin' out drunk.
And his dogs got after them dogs a mine, and I said buddy, I said, you better git them
  dogs 'fore they run theirselves t' death.
Well, he said, my dogs can outrun anythang and I said well all right then, I guess you
  know your own dogs and them dogs run all night.
And in the mornin' they was ever' one of em dead.

Well he was tore up.

We hadda go pick up them dogs and brang em on back to 'm and he jest set there an watched em come.

Well we buried em for 'm, right there by that big ol' overhangin' rock looks out over nothin' where that old feller jumped off that time after his boy got kilt in the mines and there was people skeered a that place.

Claimed the old man's h'aint was still up there.

Well I can't say nothin' about that, but we buried them dogs up there.

Yeah boy! them days we hunted coon and rabbit, possum, and just ever'thang, buddy, and we'd brang it on back and skin it, cook it up and we'd eat it.

Anymore, people's got to where they won't eat wild thangs but they're good t' eat.

You have to know how to cook it, is all.

First you let it cool, you have to cool the wildness out of it and then parboil it, and cook it and eat it.

People don't know t' parboil it.

People don't know thangs like 'at anymore.

But I been all over these here heels.

Imagine, once again, the problematics of trying to "picture" such a place in an overview or to name it "in a word" (see Clifford 1983, 1986) – whether as a colonized space (settled, shaped, and finally abandoned by King Coal), an exotic space (filled with alterity), or a dying and degraded space (filled with decay). Picture me as the ethnographer trying to get the story straight.

Picture me, in the length of an afternoon, grilling Riley Hess for an accurate outline of his work history in the mines so that I could help him document his eligibility for black lung benefits. Sifting through a suitcase full of old pay stubs and papers, I tried to reconstruct the requisite twenty years of mining out of his fragmented documentation of a work history of fits and starts and migrations back and forth from one camp to another and from the hills to Detroit and Arizona and back. Riley, sitting with me, grew nervous and digressed from my futile attempts at chronology into stories of dramatic encounters, hilarious failures, and bitterly hard times. I remember the baffled look on his face. And I remember that his stories grew progressively more graphic and imaginary until they had wrenched us (or at least him) into a narrative space that was at once more situated and contingent and yet opened an interpretive, expressive space in which there was more room to maneuver (Chambers 1991).

I bet you didn't know there's hills underground, same as above, a hill's got a inside same way its got a outside.

They're two sided.

And this one time, buddy, I started out and I was a pullin' two hundred and ten cars and ever' one of em loaded up over the top.

I always checked my brakes but I reckon they were wet because they weren't no good a' tall and I didn't know a thang about it.

And at the bottom of one a them hills there's a right smart twist, where the track takes a turn.

And its a low ceilin' and no room on the sides but just for the train to git through.

You have to feel your way through.

You kin loose your head if you stick it out like that Reed boy got kilt.

You gotta keep your head and feel your way through.

Well we started down and we was a goin' perty good, y' know.

And I tried the brakes and honey they weren't nothin' there.

Well I told the brakeman, buddy, we're a runnin' away.

I said find yourself a place and jump off if you can because I knowed we was gonna come off.

Well the brakeman, he was on t'other side and he found hisself a place and he jumped. There wasn't no place on my side and I knowed it.

Well I called the dispatcher and I told him, I said, buddy I'm a runnin' away and I got down inside the engine and let it go.

We hit that ceilin', and buddy, there's coal and steel a flyin'.

We went right into that hill and twenty-eight cars come in after us and they hadda time of it. They hadda take that thang out a there piece by piece where they said it done melted together.

They hadda tear that engine apart to git me outta that thang.

Well they wanted me to go to the hospital and they had the ambulance a waitin' at the mouth and the lights a flashin' but I said huh uh, NO-OOO, now I've had enough, and I got up and went home.

But I never did work no more motorman job no more after that.

Imagine yourself, then, not in the space of the "you are there" realism of flat ethnographic description but in an intensely occupied and imagined space, watching to see what will happen. Imagine the sense of being at home in a place caught between a rock and a hard place – at once protected from a threatening outside world and smothering. The sense of groping along in the midst of a mine field of forces, tracking the traces of earlier impacts. Imagine a subjectivity located not in the power to name and evaluate but in the memory/imagination of events and images that just come and stand as reminders of things uncaptured by any sense of an overarching "order of things." Imagine the desire to relate an impact, the sudden move "to incarnate oneself, to become more determined . . . (the) sudden narrowing of horizon" (Bakhtin 1979:357, as quoted in Todorov 1984:106). Imagine yourself surrounded.

Picture Sissy, who sits on the stoop with her coffee in the early morning watching the blanket of mountain fog rise in floating, ghostly shapes. Picture all the neighbors as they sit on the porches in the evening to watch the hills darken in a ring around the camp.

The Spectacle of Impacts

Imagine the kind of place where, when something happens, people make sense of it not by constructing an explanation of what happened but by offering accounts of its impacts, traces, and signs.

. . . Once there was an underground explosion that shook camps in a radius as wide as thirty miles. No one (but me) was interested in identifying what it "was" – what had "happened" to cause the ground to shake. Instead there was a flurry of talk about its placed effects – in Winding Gulf they said it knocked all the plates off Kitty's shelves;

in East Gulf it knocked old man Graham out of his chair and he's got a place on his arm to show for it; in Helen, it knocked a bucket of coal out of Julie's mommie's hands and spread a blanket of greasy coal soot over her kitchen floor – "seems like she never could git that flo' clean agin' after that." In the end, we have the graphic, culled images of the plates being knocked off the shelves, the "place" on the old man's arm, the spooky, ever-greasy floor.

Another time, in the spring of 1981, a forest fire burned in the hills surrounding Amigo, slowly working its way down to the camp. For days the air was so thick with smoke that all you could see beyond the alleys of the camp were bursts of blue and orange flame. At night the sight was spectacular and people would sit on their porches and comment on its beauty and force and its chilling resemblance to the pits of hell – a world on fire. During the day there was a feeling of aggravation. There were dramatic stories of people going up into the hills to fight the fire and contentious/nostalgic claims of how *used to* a forest fire meant everyone worked day and night to save the farms. Finally, the fire threatened to jump the creek. Its presence grew more pressing and the houses closest to the creek began to steam. The atmosphere in the camp grew more watchful and calm – more satisfied – as the threat of fire grew palpable. All afternoon we carried buckets of water from the creek to throw on the threatened houses and people noticed everything that happened as if out of the corners of their eyes. Later, there were hilarious comments. They were *tickled* by the look of old Miss Henson running back and forth from the creek with a rusty bucket full of holes. They noticed that Bud Smith would walk right by the Graham's place to dump his buckets on some other place where he was still speaking to the people. They noticed how the smoke just seemed to gather round that *no account* hypocritical Preacher Cole, the flames licking at his heels.

In Agee's words, these are moments of "abandonment to the currents of existence." They are moments of what Taussig (1993) calls "mimetic excess," in which an image flashes uncontained, objects and events become spectacles, subjects become spectators and performers in the spectacle, and the act of mimesis, given over to its own excesses, comes into its own as a local mode of interpretation and an epistemological principle. They are moments that enact the cultural poetics of being in place in a place that actively surrounds, impacts, and remembers. They are moments of occupying an always already occupied place.

A Visit(ation)

February 1985 – a visit back. Dreama sat in the living room with picture albums, coffee, cigarettes, and ashtrays spread around her. The TV was on, the beans were on the cookstove, there was a cake in the oven, her rugs were soaking in the ringer washer, she had just washed the floor, and she was on the phone with her sister. There was an awkwardness between us – a space made by my long absence and our inability to *just talk* about neighbors and the camp. She asked if I was still in Michigan and if I liked it there. She said she herself could never leave West Virginia and never would. Then we began with talk about bodies: Opal was eight now and still weighed only forty-two pounds; Gary Lee and Opal got glasses but they broke them right away; it was almost a year before they got them fixed and now the eye doctor said Gary would have to wear them for years instead of for just six months if he had worn them when he first needed them. Dreama had had a hysterectomy after years of hemorrhaging and her organs hanging out down there. Then the endometriosis got so bad that she finally consented to another operation. But they "still didn't git all of it," and now the pain was getting bad again and her stomach was distended as if she were pregnant.

But I won't have another one, I figure they tried twicet and they didn't get it.
Bud's doctor says he'll be dead in a year if he don't quit drankin'. There ain't nothin' wrong with his liver but they say the likker, hit's poisonin' his system.
Ever' day when I come home I look for him to be dead.

The statement is surrounded by smaller statements about livers and modes of death and the places Dreama is coming back from when she "looks for" him to be dead and how "good he is with the kids and don't take nothin from us for his likker" and how

he never has been mean but for the one time when I was big with Sissy and he got into it with me and tuk off with that Birdsong woman.
But he come back.
They fuss at me to throw him out where he dranks s' bad but I couldn't never leave him now, not and leave him all alone.
We get along good. He says he don't wanna die but he says he cain't hep hisself. And you can see how his belly's got. That ain't fat on him, he don't weigh but a hundred twenty pounds. He don't eat nothin'. It's bloat where he's poisoned hisself and he cain't hep it.

Then the talk moved to people leaving the area to find work – talk of displacement and opportunities and broken hearts and broken homes and broken links of communication.

Ricky and Ellen, they went off, and they went down North C'raliny I b'lieve they went to work and they weren't down there no time and she found herself somebody and Ricky, he come on home.
I seen him go up the road yesterday but they say he tuk it awful hard.
But she found herself somebody and Ricky, he come on home.
They say Buster Reed, from up over Graham's store, he's kin to Miss Reed and them, he went down North C'raliny.
Had him a job waitin' for him when he got down there.
And he went to work for that R. J. Reynolds company they got down there.
But he come back when he got him a job on one a them tree farms.
Now he had him a job set up for him to come back to.
I seen him goin' up the road little while back.
Then them Lacy boys and Grahams, they been goin' in and out. But they's just boys, you know, they hitchhike down and back all the time but I ain't heared if they ever found work yet. Seen some of 'm yesterday runnin' up and down the road.
Then there was one a Miss Taylor's daughters, left out for North C'raliny, tuk the kids and all.

But I ain't heared nothin' 'bout her.
Miss Taylor closed up the stand, said nobody wasn't comin' in no more and she had to
    give it up for a while and I hate to see it go.
Well, way it is, you got to go all the way down the Dairy Queen to git your cigarettes.
Buddy, I'm lookin' for the stand to git back up.

In between stories there was the continuous action of noticing the dogs, the beans,
the washing, the creek, and the constant phone calls back and forth tracking people's
whereabouts – "Has Bud got up there to take mommy?" . . . "Well. Ewolt said he seen
him down Iroquois while back . . ."

Mickey Heath from down at Wyco, he went out to some place in Ohia.
They said the rent's $350 a month and that's just rent.
Then you got your lights, and you know that's gotta be high in the city, and you got your
    cookin' gas.
All right. Then there's your phone, there's your cable.
And nothin' left for groceries I don't guess.
Mickey and them, they come on back.
But they already done sold their house, now they ain't got no place.

Her nephew Wes called to give Dreama the plot of the "story" (soap opera) she
missed seeing yesterday.

I didn't git to see it where Bud was a layin' home and he tuk to wantin' to watch the
    cartoons.
Oh! I was s' mad!
Well it's been up over a year and a half he's out a work this time and he's got s' bad to lay
    home and I can't get none a my work done where he tries to get me to set and talk, you
    know.
. . . Well all right.

Dreama's sister called to say Bud got there and left to take their mother to the
doctor's.

Mom's been down awful bad, well she never did get over Hollie.

Bud came in with stories of the parking lot at the doctor's office: ". . . an' I seen Miss
Lavender down at the tracks. Somebody oughtta go see about her." Bud and Dreama's
nephew Dewayne sat at the kitchen table drinking beer and staring at me out of the
corners of their eyes. From time to time one of them would quietly add something to
the talk.
    I told them some stories I had heard the day before. One was of a woman who went
to Ohio and had to take an apartment that had no bathroom (even in the city they have
places without bathrooms) and they had to "rig up somethin'" in the kitchen. Another
was of a woman who had been gone for years and came back to show off her big fancy

car and diamond rings. Then I remembered Jerry Graham's story of how *thangs had got down* in Iroquois and the people were being shipped by bus to the tobacco fields in No'th C'raliny and how those people out there wouldn't even give them water to drink and how the wind came and blew away their trailers and all their stuff and how they lost everything and had to come home and were livin' all piled up like cats and dogs.

Dreama repeated the images after me, and then, after a silence, she launched into a litany of her dead whose pictures hung on the walls – some in coffins, some in uniforms, the ancestors in ancient photographs that she had had colorized. Some were mounted on small wooden shrines. She pointed them out one by one where they hung amid her collection of vibrant, heartrending things – the letters from her people in Michigan and Ohio who had "left out of here," the Sacred Heart of Jesus, pierced and dripping blood. I said how beautiful his eyes were. She said she just loved hearts.

I don't know why, I just always have tuk to 'm.

That there is Liam, he got kilt in the war.

Then Peanut, he drank hisself to death

He was up Cook Town one day, wasn't even drunk they said and they said he just laid his head down, well, they didn't even know he was dead, just thought he kindly seemed to go to sleep, you know.

Peanut just put his head down and died.

Then Sissy, that's the one that hurts the most cause she was special, buddy.

She'd stand up for us, you know, talk up for us if somethin' happened.

She left her inspiration on ever'thang she come near.

Well, Lenny, that's her husband, he'd go cut down trees, you know, and sell the wood where he was outta work.

This time she begged him "Lenny, don't you do it" where it was Sunday.

Sissy told Mommy, she said she had a bad feelin' like somethin' was gonna happen, you know.

But he went and he made her to come with him, he made 'm all to go.

Well first tree he cut, and it started to come down on Sissy's baby where she was a playin' and Sissy jumped to push the baby free and the tree hit come right down on her bust her head all to pieces on the ground.

They said they had to cut her out from under it.

I just never could get over that. . . .

Course you know 'bout Hollie, he was the sweetest thang there ever was and never did hurt nobody.

Thought he was gonna get to go fishin' and Jesus tuk him on.

Bud and Dewayne went out and sat in the truck. The room was nearly dark and the air was heavy with heat and smoke. The next time the phone rang Dreama told Ellen, "Bud and Dewayne are back drankin'." We could hear them playing Waylon Jennings in the driveway.

The kids came in from school and climbed up on us. Dreama said the house was haunted. Bud saw a beautiful woman standing in the doorway staring at him ("like ta skeered him to death"), and once the lid to the washing machine lifted itself all the way up and then slowly lowered itself down.

We all seen it.

Several times they heard people moving around in the rooms upstairs, and there was often a tapping on the back window up there.

Not like they was tryna git in or git out but just tappin', fast.

I ain't seen nothin' since I got saved again but Bud, he sees thangs.

Opal whimpered: "Mommy, you skeered me, you skeered me bad." Dreama explained:

She means that night.

I was a layin' in the bed and I seen Sissy [her dead sister] kindly slide around the corner of the stairs like she'd just come down from upstairs, I could see her like a shadow out the corner of my eye, and she come and stood right there at the foot of the bed and beckoned me to come on, come on, just like that.

Honey, that like to skeered me near to death an' I set up in that bed and screamed and I mean screamed.

I thought she meant come on right then out of this world, you know.

So I made 'm to turn on all the lights and we had t' sleep with all the lights on for the longest time after that happened.

Well, I'd been a dreamin' on her ever' night when she come to me like that. But this here, this weren't no dream b'cause it skeered me too bad to be no dream.

But what skeers me worst is people.

Anymore, it's got to where you don't know what they might try and that glass out in the door, well anybody could just reach in and git the handle and come on in on us.

And the bridge worries me awful bad.

Last week 'nother one a them ties come out and went in the creek an' Opal says she's skeered to try and make it acrost, small as she is, if we lose another one.

Lenny, he won't fix it.

After Sissy, he married Corlee, that's Liam's widda, and they bought this place.

Somethin' happen to that bridge, and we'd be here with no way to git the truck out.

But I just love it out here and I wouldn't never want to leave.

Well, this place is home to me.

Acknowledgment

I would like to thank the School of American Research for its gracious hospitality in hosting the advanced seminar, and Keith Basso and Steven Feld for organizing the seminar, for their endless encouragement, and for their painstaking editing.

Notes

1. The term "social imaginary" as I am using it necessitates extending Anderson's (1983) concept of "imagined communities" beyond metacultural, ideological claims to community into the micropoetics of the density, texture, and force of everyday modes of discourse and sociality.

2. Thirty percent of the people in the counties of southwestern West Virginia live in trailers, because eighty percent of the land is still owned by coal, oil, and gas companies.

3. John L. Lewis was the powerful leader of the United Mine Workers of America in its heyday. JFK visited West Virginia in 1960, focusing national attention on the problems of Appalachia as a "depressed area."

4. In *The Origin of German Tragic Drama* (1977), Walter Benjamin articulates a theory of allegorical thought as a process in which the mind stares itself out on luminous images. In *Mimesis and Alterity* (1993), Michael Taussig traces the politics of this phenomenon in "primitive" mimesis and "magical thought" and its resurgence in contemporary life.

5. The term *stand* derives from the farming days when local merchants would establish stockades or "stands" alongside the road where animals being driven to or from market could be fed and watered and travelers could stay the night. They developed into local trade centers where farmers traded corn and other products for retail goods (Eller 1982:14) and finally became the local version of the urban corner store and the suburban convenience store.

6. See Zizek (1991) for an extensive discussion of relations between desire and a Lacanian sense of "the real."

7. In his article "Tactility and Distraction" (1991), Taussig articulates the need for alternative models of cultural meaning to displace the still dominant inclination to see meaning as mental thought and clearly modeled symbolic code. He introduces what he calls the tactility of meaning and the distractedness of everyday life in contemporary advanced capitalist culture.

8. Amigo was once a collection of four camps stretching up the holler – 'Migo 1, 'Migo 2, 'Migo 3, and "the colored camp."

References

Agee, James & Walker Evans (1941). *Let Us Now Praise Famous Men*. Boston: Houghton Mifflin.

Anderson, Benedict (1983). *Imagined Communities: Reflections on the Origin and Spread of Nationalism*. London: Verso.

Ardery, Julia (ed.) (1983). *Welcome the Traveler Home: Jim Garland's Story of the Kentucky Mountains*. Lexington: University Press of Kentucky.

Bakhtin, Mikhail (1979). *Estetika Slovesnogo Tvorchestya (The Aesthetics of Verbal Creation)*. Moscow: S. G. Bocharov.

Bakhtin, Mikhail (1981). *The Dialogic Imagination*, trans. Caryl Emerson and Michael Holquist. Austin: University of Texas Press.

Bakhtin, Mikhail (1984). *Problems of Dostoevsky's Poetics*, trans. and ed. Caryl Emerson. Minneapolis: University of Minnesota Press.

Bakhtin, Mikhail (1986). *Speech Genres and Other Late Essays*. Austin: University of Texas Press.

Barthes, Roland (1957). *Mythologies*. New York: Hill and Wang.

Barthes, Roland (1974). *S/Z*. New York: Farrar, Straus, and Giroux.

Barthes, Roland (1975). *The Pleasure of the Text*. New York: Hill and Wang.

Bauman, Richard (1977). *Verbal Art as Performance*. Prospect Heights, Illinois: Waveland Press.

Bauman, Richard (1986). *Story, Performance and Event: Contextual Studies in Oral Narrative*. Cambridge: Cambridge University Press.

Bauman, Richard & Charles Briggs (1990). Poetics and Performance as Critical Perspectives on Language and Social Life. *Annual Review of Anthropology* 19, pp. 59–88.

Benjamin, Walter (1969). *Illumination: Essays and Reflections*, trans. Harry Zohn, ed. Hannah Arendt. New York: Schocken Books.

Benjamin, Walter (1977). *The Origin of German Tragic Drama*, trans. John Osborne. London: New Left Books.

Benjamin, Walter (1978). *Reflections: Essays, Aphorisms, Autobiographical Writings*, trans. Edmund Jephcott. New York: Schocken Books.

Chambers, Ross (1991). *Room for Maneuver: Reading (the) Oppositional (in) Narrative*. Chicago: University of Chicago Press.

Clifford, James (1983). Power and Dialogue in Ethnography: Marcel Griaule's Initiation. In: George Stocking (ed.), *Observers Observed: Essays on Ethnographic Fieldwork* (History of Anthropology 1), pp. 121–56. Madison: University of Wisconsin Press.

Clifford, James (1986). On Ethnographic Allegory. In: James Clifford & George E. Marcus (eds.), *Writing Culture: The Poetics and Politics of Ethnography*, pp. 98–121. Berkeley: University of California Press.

Coles, Robert (1971). *Migrants, Sharecroppers, and Mountaineers*. Children of Crisis, Volume 2. Boston: Little, Brown/Atlantic Monthly.

Cunningham, Rodger (1987). *Apples on the Flood: The Southern Mountain Experience*. Knoxville: University of Tennessee Press.

Deleuze, Gilles & Felix Guattari (1991). *A Thousand Plateaus*. Minneapolis: University of Minnesota Press.

Derrida, Jacques (1978). *Writing and Difference*, trans. Alan Bass. Chicago: University of Chicago Press.

Eller, Ronald (1982). *Miners, Millhands, and Mountaineers: Industrialization of the Appalachian South, 1880–1930*. Knoxville: University of Tennessee Press.

Gitlin, Todd & Nancy Hollander (1970). *Uptown: Poor Whites in Chicago*. New York: Harper and Row.

Hymes, Dell (1975). Folklore's Nature and the Sun's Myth. *Journal of American Folklore* 88, pp. 345–69.

Hymes, Dell (1981). *"In Vain I Tried to Tell You": Essays in Native American Ethnopoetics*. Philadelphia: University of Pennsylvania Press.

Hymes, Dell (1985). Language, Memory, and Selective Performance: Cultee's "Salmon's Myth" as Twice Told to Boas. *Journal of American Folklore* 98, pp. 391–434.

Reed, T. V. (1988). Unimagined Existence and the Fiction of the Real: Postmodernist Realism in *Let Us Now Praise Famous Men*. *Representations* 24, pp. 156–75.

Strathern, Marilyn (1991). *Partial Connections*. Savage, Maryland: Rowman and Littlefield.

Taussig, Michael (1991). Tactility and Distraction. *Cultural Anthropology* 6(2), pp. 147–53.

Taussig, Michael (1993). *Mimesis and Alterity: A Particular History of the Senses*. New York: Routledge.

Tedlock, Dennis (1972). On the Translation of Style in Oral Narrative. In: Américo Paredes & Richard Bauman (eds.), *Towards New Perspectives in Folklore*, pp. 114–33. Austin: University of Texas Press.

Tedlock, Dennis (1983). *The Spoken Word and the Word of Interpretation*. Philadelphia: University of Pennsylvania Press.

Todorov, Tzvetan (1984). *Mikhail Bakhtin: The Dialogic Principle*, trans. Wlad Godzich. Minneapolis: University of Minnesota Press.

Vološinov, V. N. (1986). *Marxism and the Philosophy of Language*, trans. Ladislav Matejka & I. R. Titunik. Cambridge, MA: Harvard University Press.

Zizek, Slavoj (1991). *For They Know not What They Do: Enjoyment as a Political Factor*. New York: New Left Books.

III

Gender and Sexuality

12

Bodily Inscriptions, Performative Subversions

*Judith Butler**

"Garbo 'got in drag' whenever she took some heavy glamour part, whenever she melted in or out of a man's arms, whenever she simply let that heavenly-flexed neck . . . bear the weight of her thrown-back head. . . .

How resplendent seems the art of acting! It is all impersonation, whether the sex underneath is true or not."

– Parker Tyler, "The Garbo Image,"
quoted in Esther Newton, *Mother Camp*

Categories of true sex, discrete gender, and specific sexuality have constituted the stable point of reference for a great deal of feminist theory and politics. These constructs of identity serve as the points of epistemic departure from which theory emerges and politics itself is shaped. In the case of feminism, politics is ostensibly shaped to express the interests, the perspectives, of "women." But is there a political shape to "women," as it were, that precedes and prefigures the political elaboration of their interests and epistemic point of view? How is that identity shaped, and is it a political shaping that takes the very morphology and boundary of the sexed body as the ground, surface, or site of cultural inscription? What circumscribes that site as "the female body"? Is "the body" or "the sexed body" the firm foundation on which gender and systems of compulsory sexuality operate? Or is "the body" itself shaped by political forces with strategic interests in keeping that body bounded and constituted by the markers of sex?

The sex/gender distinction and the category of sex itself appear to presuppose a generalization of "the body" that preexists the acquisition of its sexed significance. This "body" often appears to be a passive medium that is signified by an inscription from a cultural source figured as "external" to that body. Any theory of the culturally constructed body, however, ought to question "the body" as a construct of suspect generality when it is figured as a passive and prior to discourse. There are Christian and Cartesian precedents to such views which, prior to the emergence of vitalistic biologies in the nineteenth century, understand "the body" as so much inert matter, signifying nothing or, more specifically, signifying a profane void, the fallen state: deception, sin,

*Pp. 103–15 from *The Judith Butler Reader*, ed. S. Salih and J. Butler (Malden, MA: Blackwell). Selected from "Subversive Bodily Acts," *Gender Trouble: Feminism and the Subversion of Identity* (New York: Routledge, 1990), pp. 163–80, 215–16. © 1990 by Judith Butler. Reproduced by permission of the author and Routledge, a division of Taylor & Francis Group.

the premonitional metaphorics of hell and the eternal feminine. There are many occasions in both Sartre's and Beauvoir's work where "the body" is figured as a mute facticity, anticipating some meaning that can be attributed only by a transcendent consciousness, understood in Cartesian terms as radically immaterial. But what establishes this dualism for us? What separates off "the body" as indifferent to signification, and signification itself as the act of a radically disembodied consciousness or, rather, the act that radically disembodies that consciousness? To what extent is that Cartesian dualism presupposed in phenomenology adapted to the structuralist frame in which mind/ body is redescribed as culture/nature? With respect to gender discourse, to what extent do these problematic dualisms still operate within the very descriptions that are supposed to lead us out of that binarism and its implicit hierarchy? How are the contours of the body clearly marked as the taken-for-granted ground or surface upon which gender significations are inscribed, a mere facticity devoid of value, prior to significance?

Wittig suggests that a culturally specific epistemic *a priori* establishes the naturalness of "sex." But by what enigmatic means has "the body" been accepted as a *prima facie* given that admits of no genealogy? Even within Foucault's essay on the very theme of genealogy, the body is figured as a surface and the scene of a cultural inscription: "the body is the inscribed surface of events."[1] The task of genealogy, he claims, is "to expose a body totally imprinted by history." His sentence continues, however, by referring to the goal of "history" – here clearly understood on the model of Freud's "civilization" – as the "destruction of the body" (148). Forces and impulses with multiple directionalities are precisely that which history both destroys and preserves through the *Entstehung* (historical event) of inscription. As "a volume in perpetual disintegration" (148), the body is always under siege, suffering destruction by the very terms of history. And history is the creation of values and meanings by a signifying practice that requires the subjection of the body. This corporeal destruction is necessary to produce the speaking subject and its significations. This is a body, described through the language of surface and force, weakened through a "single drama" of domination, inscription, and creation (150). This is not the *modus vivendi* of one kind of history rather than another, but is, for Foucault, 'history" (148) in its essential and repressive gesture.

Although Foucault writes, "Nothing in man [*sic*] – not even his body – is sufficiently stable to serve as the basis for self-recognition or for understanding other men [*sic*]" (153), he nevertheless points to the constancy of cultural inscription as a "single drama" that acts on the body. If the creation of values, that historical mode of signification, requires the destruction of the body, much as the instrument of torture in Kafka's "In the Penal Colony" destroys the body on which it writes, then there must be a body prior to that inscription, stable and self-identical, subject to that sacrificial destruction. In a sense, for Foucault, as for Nietzsche, cultural values emerge as the result of an inscription on the body, understood as a medium, indeed, a blank page; in order for this inscription to signify, however, that medium must itself be destroyed – that is, fully transvaluated into a sublimated domain of values. Within the metaphorics of this notion of cultural values is the figure of history as a relentless writing instrument, and the body as the medium which must be destroyed and transfigured in order for "culture" to emerge.

By maintaining a body prior to its cultural inscription, Foucault appears to assume a materiality prior to signification and form. Because this distinction operates as essential to the task of genealogy as he defines it, the distinction itself is precluded as an object of genealogical investigation. Occasionally in his analysis of Herculine, Foucault subscribes to a prediscursive multiplicity of bodily forces that break through the surface of the body to disrupt the regulating practices of cultural coherence imposed upon that body by a power regime, understood as a vicissitude of "history." If the presumption of some kind of precategorial source of disruption is refused, is it still possible to give a genealogical account of the demarcation of the body as such as a signifying practice? This demarcation is not initiated by a reified history or by a subject. This marking is the result of a diffuse and active structuring of the social field. This signifying practice effects a social space for and of the body within certain regulatory grids of intelligibility.

Mary Douglas's *Purity and Danger* suggests that the very contours of "the body" are established through marking that seek to establish specific codes of cultural coherence. Any discourse that establishes the boundaries of the body serves the purpose of instating and naturalizing certain taboos regarding the appropriate limits, postures, and modes of exchange that define what it is that constitutes bodies:

> ideas about separating, purifying, demarcating and punishing transgressions have as their main function to impose system on an inherently untidy experience. It is only by exaggerating the difference between within and without, above and below, male and female, with and against, that a semblance of order is created.[2]

Although Douglas clearly subscribes to a structuralist distinction between an inherently unruly nature and an order imposed by cultural means, the "untidiness" to which she refers can be redescribed as a region of *cultural* unruliness and disorder. Assuming the inevitably binary structure of the nature/culture distinction, Douglas cannot point toward an alternative configuration of culture in which such distinctions become malleable or proliferate beyond the binary frame. Her analysis, however, provides a possible point of departure for understanding the relationship by which social taboos institute and maintain the boundaries of the body as such. Her analysis suggests that what constitutes the limit of the body is never merely material, but that the surface, the skin, is systemically signified by taboos and anticipated transgressions; indeed, the boundaries of the body become, within her analysis, the limits of the social *per se*. A poststructuralist appropriation of her view might well understand the boundaries of the body as the limits of the socially *hegemonic*. In a variety of cultures, she maintains, there are

> pollution powers which inhere in the structure of ideas itself and which punish a symbolic breaking of that which should be joined or joining of that which should be separate. It follows from this that pollution is a type of danger which is not likely to occur except where the lines of structure, cosmic or social, are clearly defined.
>
> A polluting person is always in the wrong. He [*sic*] has developed some wrong condition or simply crossed over some line which should not have been crossed and this displacement unleashes danger for someone.[3]

In a sense, Simon Watney has identified the contemporary construction of "the polluting person" as the person with AIDS in his *Policing Desire: AIDS, Pornography, and the Media*.[4] Not only is the illness figured as the "gay disease," but throughout the media's hysterical and homophobic response to the illness there is a tactical construction of a continuity between the polluted status of the homosexual by virtue of the boundary-trespass that is homosexuality and the disease as a specific modality of homosexual pollution. That the disease is transmitted through the exchange of bodily fluids suggests within the sensationalist graphics of homophobic signifying systems the dangers that permeable bodily boundaries present to the social order as such. Douglas remarks that "the body is a model that can stand for any bounded system. Its boundaries can represent any boundaries which are threatened or precarious."[5] And she asks a question which one might have expected to read in Foucault: "Why should bodily margins be thought to be specifically invested with power and danger?"[6]

Douglas suggests that all social systems are vulnerable at their margins, and that all margins are accordingly considered dangerous. If the body is synecdochal for the social system *per se* or a site in which open systems converge, then any kind of unregulated permeability constitutes a site of pollution and endangerment. Since anal and oral sex among men clearly establishes certain kinds of bodily permeabilities unsanctioned by the hegemonic order, male homosexuality would, within such a hegemonic point of view, constitute a site of danger and pollution, prior to and regardless of the cultural presence of AIDS. Similarly, the "polluted" status of lesbians, regardless of their low-risk status with respect to AIDS, brings into relief the dangers of their bodily exchanges. Significantly, being "outside" the hegemonic order does not signify being "in" a state of filthy and untidy nature. Paradoxically, homosexuality is almost always conceived within the homophobic signifying economy as *both* uncivilized and unnatural.

The construction of stable bodily contours relies upon fixed sites of corporeal permeability and impermeability. Those sexual practices in both homosexual and heterosexual contexts that open surfaces and orifices to erotic signification or close down others effectively reinscribe the boundaries of the body along new cultural lines. Anal sex among men is an example, as is the radical re-membering of the body in Wittig's *The Lesbian Body*. Douglas alludes to "a kind of sex pollution which expresses a desire to keep the body (physical and social) intact,"[7] suggesting that the naturalized notion of "the" body is itself a consequence of taboos that render that body discrete by virtue of its stable boundaries. Further, the rites of passage that govern various bodily orifices presuppose a heterosexual construction of gendered exchange, positions, and erotic possibilities. The deregulation of such exchanges accordingly disrupts the very boundaries that determine what it is to be a body at all. Indeed, the critical inquiry that traces the regulatory practices within which bodily contours are constructed constitutes precisely the genealogy of "the body" in its discreteness that might further radicalize Foucault's theory.[8]

Significantly, Kristeva's discussion of abjection in *Powers of Horror* begins to suggest the uses of this structuralist notion of a boundary-constituting taboo for the purposes of constructing a discrete subject through exclusion.[9] The "abject" designates that which has been expelled from the body, discharged as excrement, literally rendered

"Other." This appears as an expulsion of alien elements, but the alien is effectively established through this expulsion. The construction of the "not-me" as the abject establishes the boundaries of the body which are also the first contours of the subject. Kristeva writes:

> *nausea* makes me balk at that milk cream, separates me from the mother and father who proffer it. "I" want none of that element, sign of their desire; "I" do not want to listen, "I" do not assimilate it, "I" expel it. But since the food is not an "other" for "me," who am only in their desire, I expel *myself*, I spit *myself* out, I abject *myself* within the same motion through which "I" claim to establish myself.[10]

The boundary of the body as well as the distinction between internal and external is established through the ejection and transvaluation of something originally part of identity into a defiling otherness. As Iris Young has suggested in her use of Kristeva to understand sexism, homophobia, and racism, the repudiation of bodies for their sex, sexuality, and/or color is an "expulsion" followed by a "repulsion" that founds and consolidates culturally hegemonic identities along sex/race/sexuality axes of differentiation.[11] Young's appropriation of Kristeva shows how the operation of repulsion can consolidate "identities" founded on the instituting of the "Other" or a set of Others through exclusion and domination. What constitutes through division the "inner" and "outer" worlds of the subject is a border and boundary tenuously maintained for the purposes of social regulation and control. The boundary between the inner and outer is confounded by those excremental passages in which the inner effectively becomes outer, and this excreting function becomes, as it were, the model by which other forms of identity-differentiation are accomplished. In effect, this is the mode by which Others become shit. For inner and outer worlds to remain utterly distinct, the entire surface of the body would have to achieve an impossible impermeability. This sealing of its surfaces would constitute the seamless boundary of the subject; but this enclosure would invariably be exploded by precisely that excremental filth that it fears.

Regardless of the compelling metaphors of the spatial distinctions of inner and outer, they remain linguistic terms that facilitate and articulate a set of fantasies, feared and desired. "Inner" and "outer" make sense only with reference to a mediating boundary that strives for stability. And this stability, this coherence, is determined in large part by cultural orders that sanction the subject and compel its differentiation from the abject. Hence, "inner" and "outer" constitute a binary distinction that stabilizes and consolidates the coherent subject. When that subject is challenged, the meaning and necessity of the terms are subject to displacement. If the "inner world" no longer designates a topos, then the internal fixity of the self and, indeed, the internal locale of gender identity, become similarly suspect. The critical question is not *how* did that identity become *internalized?* as if internalization were a process or a mechanism that might be descriptively reconstructed. Rather, the question is: From what strategic position in public discourse and for what reasons has the trope of interiority and the disjunctive binary of inner/outer taken hold? In what language is "inner space" figured? What kind of figuration is it, and through what figure of the body is it signified? How does a body figure on its surface the very invisibility of its hidden depth?

From Interiority to Gender Performatives

In *Discipline and Punish* Foucault challenges the language of internalization as it operates in the service of the disciplinary regime of the subjection and subjectivation of criminals.[12] Although Foucault objected to what he understood to be the psychoanalytic belief in the "inner" truth of sex in *The History of Sexuality*, he turns to a criticism of the doctrine of internalization for separate purposes in the context of his history of criminology. In a sense, *Discipline and Punish* can be read as Foucault's effort to rewrite Nietzsche's doctrine of internalization in *On the Genealogy of Morals* on the model of *inscription*. In the context of prisoners, Foucault writes, the strategy has been not to enforce a repression of their desires, but to compel their bodies to signify the prohibitive law as their very essence, style, and necessity. That law is not literally internalized, but incorporated, with the consequence that bodies are produced which signify that law on and through the body; there the law is manifest as the essence of their selves, the meaning of their soul, their conscience, the law of their desire. In effect, the law is at once fully manifest and fully latent, for it never appears as external to the bodies it subjects and subjectivates. Foucault writes:

> It would be wrong to say that the soul is an illusion, or an ideological effect. On the contrary, it exists, it has a reality, it is produced permanently *around*, *on*, *within*, the body by the functioning of a power that is exercised on those that are punished. (my emphasis)[13]

The figure of the interior soul understood as "within" the body is signified through its inscription *on* the body, even though its primary mode of signification is through its very absence, its potent invisibility. The effect of a structuring inner space is produced through the signification of a body as a vital and sacred enclosure. The soul is precisely what the body lacks; hence, the body presents itself as a signifying lack. That lack which *is* the body signifies the soul as that which cannot show. In this sense, then, the soul is a surface signification that contests and displaces the inner/outer distinction itself, a figure of interior psychic space inscribed *on* the body as a social signification that perpetually renounces itself as such. In Foucault's terms, the soul is not imprisoned by or within the body, as some Christian imagery would suggest, but "the soul is the prison of the body."[14]

The redescription of intrapsychic processes in terms of the surface politics of the body implies a corollary redescription of gender as the disciplinary production of the figures of fantasy through the play of presence and absence on the body's surface, the construction of the gendered body through a series of exclusions and denials, signifying absences. But what determines the manifest and latent text of the body politic? What is the prohibitive law that generates the corporeal stylization of gender, the fantasied and fantastic figuration of the body? We have already considered the incest taboo and the prior taboo against homosexuality as the generative moments of gender identity, the prohibitions that produce identity along the culturally intelligible grids of an idealized and compulsory heterosexuality. That disciplinary production of gender effects a false stabilization of gender in the interests of the heterosexual construction and regulation of sexuality within the reproductive domain. The construction of coherence conceals the gender discontinuities that run rampant within heterosexual, bisexual, and gay and lesbian contexts in which gender does not necessarily follow from sex, and desire, or sexuality generally, does not seem to follow from gender – indeed, where none of these dimensions of significant corporeality express or reflect one another. When the disorganization and disaggregation of the field of bodies disrupt the regulatory fiction of heterosexual coherence, it seems that the expressive model loses its descriptive force. That regulatory ideal is then exposed as a norm and a fiction that disguises itself as a developmental law regulating the sexual field that it purports to describe.

According to the understanding of identification as an enacted fantasy or incorporation, however, it is clear that coherence is desired, wished for, idealized, and that this idealization is an effect of a corporeal signification. In other words, acts, gestures, and desire produce the effect of an internal core or substance, but produce this *on the surface* of the body, through the play of signifying absences that suggest, but never reveal, the organizing principle of identity as a cause. Such acts, gestures, enactments, generally construed, are *performative* in the sense that the essence or identity that they otherwise purport to express are *fabrications* manufactured and sustained through corporeal signs and other discursive means. That the gendered body is performative suggests that it has no ontological status apart from the various acts which constitute its reality. This also suggests that if that reality is fabricated as an interior essence, that very interiority is an effect and function of a decidedly public and social discourse, the public regulation of fantasy through the surface politics of the body, the gender border control that differentiates inner from outer, and so institutes the "integrity" of the subject. In other words, acts and gestures, articulated and enacted desires create the illusion of an interior and organizing gender core, an illusion discursively maintained for the purposes of the regulation of sexuality within the obligatory frame of reproductive heterosexuality. If the "cause" of desire, gesture, and act can be localized within the "self" of the actor, then the political regulations and disciplinary practices which produce that ostensibly coherent gender are effectively displaced from view. The displacement of a political and discursive origin of gender identity onto a psychological "core" precludes an analysis of the political constitution of the gendered subject and its fabricated notions about the ineffable interiority of its sex or of its true identity.

If the inner truth of gender is a fabrication and if a true gender is a fantasy instituted and inscribed on the surface of bodies, then it seems that genders can be neither true nor false, but are only produced as the truth effects of a discourse of primary and stable identity. In *Mother Camp: Female Impersonators in America*, anthropologist Esther Newton suggests that the structure of impersonation reveals one of the key fabricating mechanisms through which the social construction of gender takes place.[15] I would suggest as well that drag fully subverts the distinction between inner and outer psychic space and effectively mocks both the expressive model of gender and the notion of a true gender identity. Newton writes:

> At its most complex, [drag] is a double inversion that says, "appearance is an illusion." Drag says [Newton's curious personification] "my 'outside' appearance is feminine, but my essence 'inside' [the body] is masculine." At the same time it symbolizes the opposite

inversion; "my appearance 'outside' [my body, my gender] is masculine but my essence 'inside' [myself] is feminine."[16]

Both claims to truth contradict one another and so displace the entire enactment of gender significations from the discourse of truth and falsity.

The notion of an original or primary gender identity is often parodied within the cultural practices of drag, cross-dressing, and the sexual stylization of butch/femme identities. Within feminist theory, such parodic identities have been understood to be either degrading to women, in the case of drag and cross-dressing, or an uncritical appropriation of sex-role stereotyping from within the practice of heterosexuality, especially in the case of butch/femme lesbian identities. But the relation between the "imitation" and the "original" is, I think, more complicated than that critique generally allows. Moreover, it gives us a clue to the way in which the relationship between primary identification – that is, the original meanings accorded to gender – and subsequent gender experience might be reframed. The performance of drag plays upon the distinction between the anatomy of the performer and the gender that is being performed. But we are actually in the presence of three contingent dimensions of significant corporeality: anatomical sex, gender identity, and gender performance. If the anatomy of the performer is already distinct from the gender of the performer, and both of those are distinct from the gender of the performance, then the performance suggests a dissonance not only between sex and performance, but sex and gender, and gender and performance. As much as drag creates a unified picture of "woman" (what its critics often oppose), it also reveals the distinctness of those aspects of gendered experience which are falsely naturalized as a unity through the regulatory fiction of heterosexual coherence. *In imitating gender, drag implicitly reveals the imitative structure of gender itself – as well as its contingency.* Indeed, part of the pleasure, he giddiness of the performance is in the recognition of a radical contingency in the relation between sex and gender in the face of cultural configurations of causal unities that are regularly assumed to be natural and necessary. In the place of the law of heterosexual coherence, we see sex and gender denaturalized by means of a performance which avows their distinctness and dramatizes the cultural mechanism of their fabricated unity.

The notion of gender parody defended here does not assume that there is an original which such parodic identities imitate. Indeed, the parody is *of* the very notion of an original; just as the psychoanalytic notion of gender identification is constituted by a fantasy of a fantasy, the transfiguration of an Other who is always already a "figure" in that double sense, so gender parody reveals that the original identity after which gender fashions itself is an imitation without an origin. To be more precise, it is a production which, in effect – that is, in its effect – postures as an imitation. This perpetual displacement constitutes a fluidity of identities that suggests an openness to resignification and recontextualization; parodic proliferation deprives hegemonic culture and its critics of the claim to naturalized or essentialist gender identities. Although the gender meanings taken up in these parodic styles are clearly part of hegemonic, misogynist culture, they are nevertheless denaturalized and mobilized through their parodic recontextualization. As imitations which effectively displace the meaning of the original, they imitate the myth of originality itself. In the place of an original identification which serves as a determining cause, gender identity might be reconceived as a personal/cultural history of received meanings subject to a set of imitative practices which refer laterally to other imitations and which, jointly, construct the illusion of a primary and interior gendered self or parody the mechanism of that construction.

According to Fredric Jameson's "Postmodernism and Consumer Society," the imitation that mocks the notion of an original is characteristic of pastiche rather than parody:

> Pastiche is, like parody, the imitation of a peculiar or unique style, the wearing of a stylistic mask, speech in a dead language: but it is a neutral practice of mimicry, without parody's ulterior motive, without the satirical impulse, without laughter, without that still latent feeling that there exists something *normal* compared to which what is being imitated is rather comic. Pastiche is blank parody, parody that has lost it humor.[17]

The loss of the sense of "the normal," however, can be its own occasion for laughter, especially when "the normal," "the original" is revealed to be a copy, and an inevitably failed one, an ideal that no one *can* embody. In this sense, laughter emerges in the realization that all along the original was derived.

Parody by itself is not subversive, and there must be a way to understand what makes certain kinds of parodic repetitions effectively disruptive, truly troubling, and which repetitions become domesticated and recirculated as instruments of cultural hegemony. A typology of actions would clearly not suffice, for parodic displacement, indeed, parodic laughter, depends on a context and reception in which subversive confusions can be fostered. What performance where will invert the inner/outer distinction and compel a radical rethinking of the psychological presuppositions of gender identity and sexuality? What performance where will compel a reconsideration of the *place* and stability of the masculine and the feminine? And what kind of gender performance will enact and reveal the performativity of gender itself in a way that destabilizes the naturalized categories of identity and desire.

If the body is not a "being," but a variable boundary, a surface whose permeability is politically regulated, a signifying practice within cultural field of gender hierarchy and compulsory heterosexuality, then what language is left for understanding this corporeal enactment, gender, that constitutes its "interior" signification on its surface? Sartre would perhaps have called this act "a style of being," Foucault, "a stylistics of existence." And in my earlier reading of Beauvoir, I suggest that gendered bodies are so many "styles of the flesh." These styles all never fully self-styled, for styles have a history, and those histories condition and limit the possibilities. Consider gender, for instance, as *a corporeal style*, an "act," as it were, which is both intentional and performative, where "*performative*" suggests a dramatic and contingent construction of meaning.

Wittig understands gender as the workings of "sex," where "sex" is an obligatory injunction for the body to become a cultural sign, to materialize itself in obedience to a historically delimited possibility, and to do this, not once or twice, but as a sustained and repeated corporeal project. The notion of a "project," however, suggests the originating force of a radical will, and because gender is a project which has cultural survival as its end, the term *strategy* better suggests the situation of duress under which gender performance always and variously occurs. Hence, as a strategy of survival within compulsory systems, gender is a performance with clearly punitive consequences. Discrete genders are part of what "humanizes" individuals within contemporary culture; indeed, we regularly punish those who fail to do their gender right. Because there is neither an "essence" that gender expresses or externalizes nor an objective ideal to which gender aspires, and because gender is not a fact, the various acts of gender create the idea of gender, and without those acts, there would be no gender at all. Gender is, thus, a construction that regularly conceals its genesis; the tacit collective agreement to perform, produce, and sustain discrete and polar genders as cultural fictions is obscured by the credibility of those productions – and the punishments that attend not agreeing to believe in them; the construction "compels" our belief in its necessity and naturalness. The historical possibilities materialized through various corporeal styles are nothing other than those punitively regulated cultural fictions alternately embodied and deflected under duress.

Consider that a sedimentation of gender norms produces the peculiar phenomenon of a "natural sex" or a "real woman" or any number of prevalent and compelling social fictions, and that this is a sedimentation that over time has produced a set of corporeal styles which, in reified form, appear as the natural configuration of bodies into sexes existing in a binary relation to one another. If these styles are enacted, and if they produce the coherent gendered subjects who pose as their originators, what kind of performance might reveal this ostensible "cause" to be an "effect"?

In what senses, then, is gender an act? As in other ritual social dramas, the action of gender requires a performance that is *repeated*. This repetition is at once a reenactment and reexperiencing of a set of meanings already socially established; and it is the mundane and ritualized form of their legitimation.[18] Although there are individual bodies that enact these significations by becoming stylized into gendered modes, this "action" is a public action. There are temporal and collective dimensions to these actions, and their public character is not inconsequential; indeed, the performance is effected with the strategic aim of maintaining gender within its binary frame – an aim that cannot be attributed to a subject, but, rather, must be understood to found and consolidate the subject.

Gender ought not to be construed as a stable identity or locus of agency from which various acts follow; rather, gender is an identity tenuously constituted in time, instituted in an exterior space through a *stylized repetition of acts*. The effect of gender is produced through the stylization of the body and, hence, must be understood as the mundane way in which bodily gestures, movements, and styles of various kinds constitute the illusion of an abiding gendered self. This formulation moves the conception of gender off the ground of a substantial model of identity to one that requires a conception of gender as a constituted *social temporality*. Significantly, if gender is instituted through acts which are internally discontinuous, then the *appearance of substance* is precisely that, a constructed identity, a performative accomplishment which the mundane social audience, including the actors themselves, come to believe and to perform in the mode of belief. Gender is also a norm that can never be fully internalized; "the internal" is a surface signification, and gender norms are finally phantasmatic, impossible to embody. If the ground of gender identity is the stylized repetition of acts through time and not a seemingly seamless identity, then the spatial metaphor of a "ground" will be displaced and revealed as a stylized configuration, indeed, a gendered corporealization of time. The abiding gendered self will then be shown to be structured by repeated acts that seek to approximate the ideal of a substantial ground of identity, but which, in their occasional *dis*continuity, reveal the temporal and contingent groundlessness of this "ground." The possibilities of gender transformation are to be found precisely in the arbitrary relation between such acts, in the possibility of a failure to repeat, a de-formity, or a parodic repetition that exposes the phantasmatic effect of abiding identity as a politically tenuous construction.

If gender attributes, however, are not expressive but performative, then these attributes effectively constitute the identity they are said to express or reveal. The distinction between expression and performativeness is crucial. If gender attributes and acts, the various ways in which a body shows or produces its cultural signification, are performative, then there is no preexisting identity by which an act or attribute might be measured; there would be no true or false, real or distorted acts of gender, and the postulation of a true gender identity would be revealed as a regulatory fiction. That gender reality is created through sustained social performances means that the very notions of an essential sex and a true or abiding masculinity or femininity are also constituted as part of the strategy that conceals gender's performative character and the performative possibilities for proliferating gender configurations outside the restricting frames of masculinist domination and compulsory heterosexuality.

Genders can be neither true nor false, neither real nor apparent, neither original nor derived. As credible bearers of those attributes, however, genders can also be rendered thoroughly and radically *incredible*.

Notes

1. Michel Foucault, "Nietzsche, Genealogy, History," in *Language, Counter-Memory, Practice: Selected Essays and Interviews*, trans. Donald F. Bouchard and Sherry Simon, ed. Donald F. Bouchard (Ithaca, NY: Cornell University Press, 1977), p. 148. References in the text are to this essay.
2. Mary Douglas, *Purity and Danger* (London, Boston, and Henley: Routledge and Kegan Paul, 1969), p. 4.
3. Ibid., p. 113.
4. Simon Watney, *Policing Desire: AIDS, Pornography, and the Media* (Minneapolis: University of Minnesota Press, 1988).
5. Douglas, *Purity and Danger*, p. 115.
6. Ibid., p. 121.
7. Ibid., p. 140.
8. Foucault's essay "A Preface to Transgression" (in *Language, Counter-Memory Practice*) does provide an interesting juxtaposition with Douglas's notion of body boundaries constituted by incest taboos. Originally written in honor of Georges Bataille, this essay explores

in part the metaphorical "dirt" of transgressive pleasures and the association of the forbidden orifice with the dirt-covered tomb. See pp. 46–8.

9. Kristeva discusses Mary Douglas's work in a short section of *Powers of Horror: An Essay on Abjection*, trans. Leon Roudiez (New York: Columbia University Press, 1982), originally published as *Pouvoirs de l'horreur* (Paris: Éditions de Seuil, 1980). Assimilating Douglas's insights to her own reformulation of Lacan, Kristeva writes, "Defilement is what is jettisoned from the *symbolic system*. It is what escapes that social rationality, that logical order on which a social aggregate is based, which then becomes differentiated from a temporary agglomeration of individuals and, in short, constitutes a *classification system* or a *structure*" (p. 65).

10. Ibid., p. 3.

11. Iris Marion Young, "Abjection and Oppression: Dynamics of Unconscious Racism, Sexism, and Homophobia," paper presented at the Society of Phenomenology and Existential Philosophy Meetings, Northwestern University, 1988. In *Crises in Continental Philosophy*, ed. Arleen B. Dallery and Charles E. Scott with Holley Roberts (Albany: SUNY Press, 1990), pp. 201–14.

12. Parts of the following discussion were published in two different contexts, in my "Gender Trouble, Feminist Theory, and Psychoanalytic Discourse," in *Feminism/Postmodernism*, ed. Linda J. Nicholson (New York: Routledge, 1989) and "Performative Acts and Gender Constitution: An Essay in Phenomenology and Feminist Theory," *Theatre Journal*, 20, no. 3, Winter 1988.

13. Michel Foucault, *Discipline and Punish: the Birth of the Prison*, trans. Alan Sheridan (New York: Vintage, 1979), p. 29.

14. Ibid., p. 30.

15. See the chapter "Role Models" in Esther Newton, *Mother Camp: Female Impersonators in America* (Chicago: University of Chicago Press, 1972).

16. Ibid., p. 103.

17. Fredric Jameson, "Postmodernism and Consumer Society," in *The Anti-Aesthetic: Essays on Postmodern Culture*, ed. Hal Foster (Port Townsend, WA.: Bay Press, 1983), p. 114.

18. See Victor Turner, *Dramas, Fields and Metaphors* (Ithaca: Cornell University Press, 1974). See also Clifford Geertz, "Blurred Genres: The Refiguration of Thought," *in Local Knowledge, Further Essays in Interpretive Anthropology* (New York: Basic Books, 1983).

13

Missing Subjects: Gender, Power, and Sexuality in Merchant Banking[1]

Linda McDowell and Gillian Court*

The economic structure of advanced industrial nations in the postwar decades has undergone fundamental changes, as the long debate among geographers about its nature and spatial form attests. Probably the most significant change has been the shift to a service-based economy, such that more than two-thirds of all waged workers in countries like the United States and the United Kingdom are now employed in service occupations. Associated with this transition has been a far-reaching transformation in the gender division of labor. The feminization of the labor force has been profound, particularly in the last decade. In Great Britain, for example, no less than eight out of ten new jobs created in the 1980s have been for women. While parts of the service sector have long been recognized as a feminized job ghetto, increasingly these "new" occupations rely on the marketing of attributes conventionally associated with the "natural" attributes of femininity – sociability, caring, and, indeed, servicing – which are marketed as an integral part of the product for sale (Hochschild 1983; Jenson 1989; Leidner 1991).

One consequence of the expansion of the service sector, however, is that increasing numbers of men are also employed in these jobs, which Leidner (1991) has termed interactive service occupations, in which personal bodily attributes and character traits are a significant part of the job. These jobs involve selling the worker as part of the overall service. As Leidner argues, "these jobs differ from other types of work in that the distinctions among product, work process, and worker are blurred or non-existent, since the quality of the interaction may itself be part of the service offered" (1991, 155). These jobs, she argues, "have several distinctive features that make them especially revealing for the investigation of the interrelation of work, gender and identity as . . . workers' identities are not incidental to the work but are an integral part of it. Interactive jobs make use of workers' looks, personalities, and emotions, as well as their physical and intellectual capacities, sometimes forcing them to manipulate their identities more self-consciously than do workers in other kinds of jobs" (Leidner 1991, 155–56).

As these jobs are increasingly central to the economy, and will no doubt become even more significant (Christopherson 1989; Sayer & Walker 1992; Smith, Knights, &

* Pp. 229–51 from *Economic Geography*, vol. 70, no. 3. © 1994 by Economic Geography. Reprinted with permission from Clark University.

Willmott 1991), a set of new and interesting questions is posed for economic geographers interested in the causes and consequences of new social and spatial divisions of labor. New questions arise, for example, about the structure of spatial divisions. Women's labor market participation is less geographically distinct than men's. Occupational specialization is not associated with geographic region to the same degree. New patterns of north-south divisions may then develop with feminization. In particular, it seems clear that a new set of issues about subjectivity and gendered identities should become central to economic geography. We should begin to consider how the characteristics of service sector jobs are connected to the gendered attributes of workers and how this varies across space and time. Are the familiar patterns of sex segregation in the labor market being restructured and, if so, how and to whose advantage (McDowell 1991)? How do jobs become gendered in the first place? What flexibility is there in this process? And how is the gender encodement of tasks achieved and maintained or contested and challenged? While some of these questions have been addressed with reference to manufacturing, only a few studies have raised similar questions in relation to the expansion of service sector occupations in advanced economies. In the main, these studies have focused on the bottom end of the sector, on what might perhaps be termed "servicing" occupations, such as secretarial work (Pringle 1989), selling fast food (Crang 1992; Gabriel 1988; Leidner 1991), and selling insurance (Leidner 1991; Knights & Morgan 1991; Morgan & Knights 1991). Little investigation has been carried out of the ways in which the construction and manipulation of gendered identities have been important in the expansion of that set of high-powered, high-status occupations, particularly in the financial services sector, that have been portrayed as the epitome of success in 1980s Britain and North America. This paper focuses on a subset of such occupations: high-status employment within merchant banking.

In the 1980s in Britain, the financial services sector was one of the most rapidly expanding employment sectors. Retail and merchant banking, broking, insurance, and associated legal services all exhibited record growth rates. Financial services thus outperformed virtually all sectors of the economy, with annual growth rates exceeding 7 percent in the boom years of the mid-1980s. The spatially concentrated growth of the wholesale banking sector, in particular, in the South East of England was a key element in the restructuring of the space economy that occurred during the decade and significantly deepened the north–south divide (Court & McDowell 1993; Thrift & Leyshon 1992; Peck 1993). Unprecedented rates of growth took place, for example, in the traditional area for banking, the Square Mile in the City of London, where in the mid-1980s employment growth occurred at rates eight times faster than those of any other small area in the United Kingdom.

This expansion of financial services throughout the 1980s has had a profound effect not only on the occupational structure of the City of London but also on its built environment (Pryke 1991). There has been a huge boom in new construction and renovation (Zukin 1991), not only of office buildings but also of spaces for recreation, play, and pleasure. In areas like the new Broadgate development, for example, the developers have carefully constructed a total landscape of work and leisure: a new global landscape of financial power complete with upmarket restaurants, the obligatory atrium or two, a circular open space for staging spectacles, and plenty of outdoor statuary.

In a stimulating collection of papers, Budd and Whimster (1992) argue that the globalization of financial services, their dominance in a small area of London, and the
construction of new spaces of work and play have effected an "interpenetration of areas
of life previously separated by hierarchies and boundaries," allowing "a repatterning of
personality, lifestyle, neighborhoods and the metropolis" (p. 3). This interpenetration
results in a blurring of the boundaries of work and pleasure and in new notions of the
ideal worker. Social and cultural aspects of the construction of work are becoming
increasingly important. Hence, Budd and Whimster argue, greater attention must be
paid to the cultural aspects of current economic restructuring. Sayer and Walker (1992)
develop related arguments when they suggest the theoretical centrality of the social
division of labor for geographic analysis. The new social division of labor, they argue,
extends over a vast geographic scale to "encompass new sectors, new jobs and new ways
of working" (Sayer & Walker 1992, 2). This complex division of labor, in their view, is
"an active force in social ordering, economic development and the lived experience of
the participant (1992, 1), thus placing questions of daily experience and the social
identity of workers on the geographic agenda. They also suggest that one of the
most important aspects of these new divisions and new ways of working is the growing
numbers of women entering waged labor in an array of occupations. They argue that
this feminization of the labor force is at the heart of new questions about the service
economy, and yet, as Sayer and Walker recognize, "scholars have barely begun to grasp
this nettle" (1992, 103, fn.).

The purpose of this paper is to grasp the nettle and examine a set of questions about
men and women's lived experience at work, looking at ways in which economic geographers might begin to focus on cultural aspects of economic change in investigating
the social construction of labor power and its gendered attributes. While a considerable
set of questions arising from feminization demand investigation – from regional variations in growth rates to the impact of women's labor force entry on spatial patterns of
demand for housing and other consumer goods – this paper will focus on social practices
within the workplace itself. Our aim is to uncover the ways in which gendered identities
are constructed at work to produce and reproduce the worker as a subject. We argue
that not only are everyday social relations in the workplace imbued with notions of
power and domination in a general sense, but also that particular ideas about sexuality
are key mechanisms in the maintenance of women's occupational segregation. So far,
the significance of the construction of gender identities at work – the development of
particular versions of masculinity and femininity appropriate to success in particular
occupations – has been neglected by geographers.

Approaches to the Analysis of Occupational Segregation

While the worker who stalks the pages of the conventional economic geography texts
and monographs is no longer a disembodied being without sex or class attributes,
unlocated in family or community structures, workers do appear to enter the labor
market with their gender attributes firmly established (Scott and Storper 1986; Storper
and Walker 1989). Perhaps somewhat paradoxically, major responsibility for inserting

the social characteristics of labor into economic geographies lies with the left critique of the individualism of neoclassical location theorists. Not surprisingly, given their theoretical orientation, work within this school tended to pay greater attention to class relations than to gender relations (Christopherson 1989; Women and Geography Study Group 1984; McDowell 1991). Gender differences were not, however, neglected in the new economic geography. Massey's innovative text, *Spatial Divisions of Labour* (1984), for example, demonstrated women's significance as a reserve army of labor in the rounds of economic restructuring that redrew the British space economy in the 1970s and early 1980s. Massey argued that new jobs for women were attracted to both the old industrial regions, previously dominated by male-employing heavy industries, and to rural areas, where women previously worked on a casual or temporary basis, often in family businesses, because women were a reserve of cheap "green" labor. In a similar way, the significance of female labor in international restructuring and locational change was regarded as a major explanatory factor in the New International Division of Labor school. In this work, women also were theorized as reserves of "green" labor, attractive to newly mobile capital in search of higher rates of profit than had become possible in the advanced industrial nations (Frobel, Heinrichs, & Kreye 1980).

While the divisions of labor approaches implicitly drew on feminist analyses of how women's domestic responsibilities were part of the explanation for their construction as a reserve army, they paid less attention to the reasons why women were drawn into a particular narrow range of occupations as the labor market became increasingly feminized. In these studies, women's occupational segregation was noted rather than explained. There has been an explosion of work, however, that has attempted to theorize women's subordinate position in the labor market. Feminist scholars working within a broad Marxist church have developed theories of patriarchy as a system that either parallels capitalism, drawing on Marxist notions of exploitation, or as an inseparable part of the capitalist mode of production (Beechey 1977; Hartmann 1979; Vogel 1983; Walby 1986, 1991). (These theories are designated, respectively, the dual and single systems approaches.) Indeed, it is this stream of explicitly feminist work that has closest links with the divisions of labor school. Others have worked within alternative frameworks to address the particular issue of women's occupational segregation. For example, economists have variously drawn on human capital theory (Mincer 1962) and dual and segmented labor market theory (Barron & Norris 1976; Rubery 1980) to explain women's relegation to lowly positions in the labor market.[2]

As well as abstract theorizing and aggregate-scale analyses about women's labor market position, the last 20 years have seen many smaller-scale, more qualitative analyses of women's subordinate position in the labor market. A growing number of case studies, mainly but not exclusively in the manufacturing sector and widely separated in time and space, have begun to shed light on a wide and varied range of social practices on the "shopfloor" that act as obstacles to women's advancement (Bradley 1989; Cockburn 1993, 1991; Game & Pringle 1984; Kessler-Harris 1982; Milkman 1987; Pringle 1989; Westwood 1984). While most of these case studies have been undertaken by scholars outside geography, geographers have not neglected women's occupational segregation in local labor markets. Their contribution to the growing literature has, hardly surprisingly, focused on a specifically spatial explanation for its persistence. The major emphasis in the geographic work has been on women's restricted journeys to work in comparison with men's as an important factor in reproducing women's inferior labor market position (Hanson & Johnston 1985; Johnston-Anumonwo 1988; Villeneuve & Rose 1988). Pratt and Hanson's huge study of women in the Worcester, Massachusetts labor market has been particularly influential in drawing the attention of geographers to the significance of gender divisions. In several papers drawing on this study (Hanson & Pratt 1988, 1991; Pratt & Hanson 1988, 1991a, 1991b, 1994), they have focused in detail on the question of why the segregation of women within a relatively narrow range of occupations within the Worcester labor market is so persistent. In particular, they have extended our knowledge of the role of residential location and the process of gender differences in job search behavior in the maintenance of occupational sex segregation. While critical of the notions of human capital theory – that women's occupational choices reflect rational allocation decisions within the household – they "agree with the human capital theory's emphasis on women's domestic labor as a major source of occupational segregation" (Pratt & Hanson 1991a, 149).

What many geographers have not yet explored, however, is the social construction of occupations themselves as gendered. In their work, they tend to represent occupations as empty slots to be filled and workers as already socially constituted men and women with fixed gender attributes. Thus, although Hanson and Pratt, for example, are interested in why women end up in particular jobs in certain areas of their case study area, they do not explore why these particular jobs are jobs for women. For most geographers, the focus of analysis has been on explanations of why women enter particular sectors or certain occupations in the labor market in growing numbers, rather than on the logically preceding question of how these occupational ghettos arise. The gendering of jobs and workers has been taken for granted. As Scott (1988, 47) has argued, "if we write the history of women's work by gathering data that describe the activities, needs, interests, and culture of 'women workers,' we leave in place the naturalized contrast and reify a fixed categorical difference between women and men. We start the story, in other words, too late, by uncritically accepting a gendered category (the woman worker') that itself needs investigation because its meaning is relative to its history."

Thus the process of *occupational sex typing* (or better, *stereotyping*), as distinct from occupational segregation, tends to be taken for granted. But jobs are not gender-neutral; rather, they are created as appropriate for either men or women. Jobs and occupations themselves, and the set of social practices that constitute them, are constructed so as to embody socially sanctioned but *variable* characteristics of masculinity and femininity. This association is apparently self-evident in the analysis of classically "masculine" occupations; consider, for example, the heroic struggle and camaraderie involved in male heavy manual labor compared with the characteristics of feminized occupations such as secretarial work, although even these have changed their gender associations over the century (Bradley 1989).

Sexing Jobs

Suggesting that many studies of occupational segregation have neglected the processes by which jobs become gendered, that they have focused on occupational segregation rather than on occupational sex stereotyping, is not to imply that they have ignored the association of, for example, skill designation with gender or the embodiment of gender attributes in job definitions and workplace practices. This clearly is not so. A large body of work has revealed how the supposedly natural attributes of femininity (for example, docility, dexterity, or "caring") have been set up in opposition to masculine attributes to organize and reorganize labor processes and to reward workers differentially on the basis of gender (see, for example, Beechey & Perkins 1987; Cockburn 1983; Crompton & Jones 1984; Crompton & Sanderson 1990; Milkman 1987; Phillips & Taylor 1980; Walby 1986).

Little attention has been paid, however, to the ways in which new jobs are stereotyped initially and to the ways in which everyday social practices reaffirm or challenge these gender attributions over time. Formal organizational structures and informal workplace practices are not gender-neutral but are saturated with gendered meanings and practices that construct gendered subjectivities at work. Indeed, Pratt and Hanson have recently argued for an exploration of gendered subjectivities, suggesting that "women's subjectivity is structured partially at home, within the family household, and partially at work, but the actual dynamics of these processes lie unexplored. For men, we assume a simpler formula: their subjectivity is shaped through their work experience" (Pratt & Hanson 1991a, 245). While we disagree with their assumption about men's subjectivity, we concur with them in their suggestion that geographers explore the construction of gendered subjectivities at work.

Transforming Gender Relations in the New Service Economy?

Clearly, then, a question needs to be asked about how jobs become gendered and what relations of power and domination maintain or transform these gender associations. How, in a period of rapid economic transformation like the 1980s, when a range of new service sector jobs became dominant, was gender encodement established? Among those "top-end" service sector jobs in financial services, in the wide range of managerial and white-collar service sector jobs that have become an increasingly important part of the labor market in recent years, the association with gender is much less apparent than in the "old" jobs or in many of the expanding "bottom-end" servicing jobs (Filby 1992). These high-status occupations would seem not to embody gendered attributes, not to require those "natural" gendered characteristics, be they strength or docility, but to be gender-neutral and so, theoretically, open to suitably qualified applicants of either sex.

Connell (1987) has suggested that in periods of rapid change, what he calls the gender regime or gender order may be disrupted. He maintains that the history of gender relations is an uneven, or lumpy, one, in which hegemonic notions of masculinity and femininity may be suddenly transformed. Further, Connell points to the workplace as one of the crucial milieux in which gendered subjectivities are constructed. As he argues, contrasting and competing femininities within and between different milieux are common. In a period of rapid economic change it may be that gendered identities in the home and the workplace are being transformed and disrupted.

McDowell (1991) has suggested that part of the "flexible" restructuring strategies of contemporary economic change has been the creation of specifically "female" or feminized jobs. Women's growing labor force participation has not been solely a *consequence* of the expansion of jobs particularly suited to them (in the service sector or the caring professions or in part-time employment) but also part of the deliberate creation of particular job categories and working practices to draw women in as cheap labor. It therefore seems that the gendering, and possibly the regendering, of occupations may be an important strategy in economic restructuring and labor market change, although how widespread and explicit a management strategy this is remains to be ascertained. Although a number of geographers have begun to investigate aspects of the relationship between the feminization of the labor market and economic restructuring (Christopherson 1989; Villeneuve & Rose 1988), few geographers have yet directly addressed questions about power and domination and the ways in which gendered social practices in everyday social relations are part of the production and renegotiation of sex segregation. A number of scholars in other disciplines have proved a helpful stimulus to our own theorizing about the sort of ways in which occupational gendering is accomplished and regendering occurs. Therefore, before turning to the details of our own empirical work, we briefly outline some of this literature.

Gendered Organizations: Sexing and Resexing Jobs

An important stimulus for our own work on the construction and maintenance of gendered occupations in the financial services came from within organization theory, especially from recent studies that have drawn attention to the ubiquity of sexuality in organizational processes and the ways in which it is related to the structures of power (Acker 1990; Hearn & Parkin 1987; Pringle 1989). This work develops a very different notion of organizations and firms from that which is conventional within economic geography. Sexuality in these studies is defined as a socially constructed set of processes that includes patterns of desire, fantasy, pleasure, and self-image. Hence it is not restricted solely, nor indeed mainly, to sexual relations and the associated policy implications around the issue of sexual harassment. Rather the focus is on power and domination and the way in which assumptions about gender-appropriate behavior and sexuality as broadly defined influence management practices and the everyday social relations between workers,

Dominant notions of sexuality in contemporary Western culture are based on a set of gendered power relations in which men's dominance over women is expressed and re-created. Images of hostility and domination, including fantasies of humiliation and revenge, have been shown to be a central part of masculine sexual identity. (A cursory glance at the images of women used in advertising or in many popular films should bring home the validity of this assertion.) As Stoller (1979, 94) has argued, central to the construction of sexuality in discourse, symbolism, and in social practice is an image of the phallus as "aggressive, unfettered, unsympathetic, humiliating." Recent work on organizational structures in a range of industries has begun to demonstrate the centrality of this image in everyday social relations and in interactions in many workplaces. It is a particularly significant image in the world of merchant banking, as we demonstrate below.

The growing recognition of the ways in which male sexuality structures organizational practices counters commonly held views that sexuality at work is a defining characteristic of *women* workers. According to Acker (1990, 139), organizations' "gendered nature is partly masked through obscuring the embodied nature of work. Abstract jobs and hierarchies . . . assume a disembodied and universal worker. This worker is actually a man: men's bodies, sexuality and relationships to procreation and waged work are subsumed in the image of the worker. Images of men's bodies and masculinity pervade organisational processes, marginalising women and contributing to the maintenance of gender segregation in organizations." Pringle (1989), in her study of the relationships between secretaries and bosses, made a similar observation, noting that the association between masculinity and rationality allowed male sexuality to remain invisible yet dominant, positioning women as the inferior "other" at work.

Epidermalizing the World

In her stimulating book, *Justice and the Politics of Difference*, Young (1990) has also singled out aspects of embodiment as a key element in the structure of oppression in contemporary capitalist societies. Like Acker, she too focuses on deviations from the contemporary hegemonic version of an idealized body, which is not only male but also slim and light-skinned. This idealization establishes as "the other" not only women but also people of color and those who are not the perfect shape or size. Young also emphasizes the significance of lived social experience in the maintenance of oppression through what she calls cultural imperialism and violence.

> Much of the oppressive experience of cultural imperialism occurs in mundane contexts of interaction – in the gestures, speech, tone of voice, movement and reactions of others. Pulses of attraction and aversion modulate all interactions, with specific consequences for experience of the body. When the dominant culture defines some groups as different, as the Other, the members of those groups are imprisoned in their bodies. Dominant discourse defines them in terms of bodily characteristics, and constructs those bodies as ugly, dirty, defiled, impure, contaminated or sick. (Young 1990, 123)

The net result is what Young refers to as "epidermalizing the world," or the "scaling of bodies." As Young explains, this epidermalization is a particularly significant part of the explanation of women's inferior position:

> Women's oppression [is] clearly structured by the interactive dynamics of desire, the pulses of attraction and aversion, and people's experiences of bodies and embodiment. While a certain cultural space is reserved for revering feminine beauty and desirability, in part that very cameo ideal renders most women drab, ugly, loathsome, or fearful bodies. (Young 1990, 123)

Gender Performance and Regulatory Fictions

Both Young and Butler, in her stimulating analysis of the acquisition of gendered identities, *Gender Trouble* (1990), draw on Foucauldian notions to show how dominant discourses construct some groups as ugly or degenerate bodies in contrast to the purity or respectability of neutral or rational subjects. Butler extends these ideas to suggest that gendered identities are multiple and fluid, indeed that gender itself is an imitative structure and is contingent. In her view gender is a parody, a disciplinary production, a fabrication, or a performance, and so is open to resignification and recontextualization. This idea of a gender performance is particularly helpful in understanding the construction and maintenance of gender identities and gendered power relations in the workplace.

A number of examples should suffice to demonstrate the general relevance of this argument. As Acker suggested, women may have to become honorary men to be successful. Others, including Pringle (1989) in her study of secretaries, have pointed out the limited number of roles or performances available to women working in subordinate occupations. Pringle (1989, 3) distinguished "wives, mothers, spinster aunts, mistresses and femme fatales" in her work. Davidson and Cooper (1992), in their study of women in management positions, *Shattering the Glass Ceiling*, argued that the available scripts, what Butler termed "regulatory fictions," are restricted to the earth mother, the pet, the seductress, and the honorary man. We might add the bitch or the ball breaker, a male designation of professional women rather than a role that women themselves actively embrace.

Doing Gender on the Job: Male Performance

This idea of gender as performance is not, however, restricted to women. Interactive service work demands a performance of men, too. Leidner (1991), in her fine study of the fast food industry and door-to-door insurance selling, demonstrated the ways in which employees in these industries reconciled the work they did with a gendered identity they could accept. She showed how low-status, often demeaning work was imbued with socially defined masculine attributes in ways that excluded women, reinforced male power, and reconstructed the work as heroic, even glorious, for the men who did it. The insurance selling example makes her point most clearly.

At first sight it might seem that selling insurance on the doorstep – cold calling, as it is known in the trade – is a job that might draw on quintessentially feminine attributes. It involves the presentation of self as pleasant, sympathetic, and non-threatening, a congenial attitude, eagerness to please, and an ability to talk people into doing something they might not want to do. As Leidner argues, "deferential behavior and forced amiability are often associated with servility. . . . Such behavior is not easy to reconcile with the autonomy and assertiveness that are considered central to 'acting like a man'" (1991, 165). Leidner found, however, that the insurance sales force that she interviewed was almost entirely male and that these men were able to interpret their jobs as congruent with proper gender encodement. They emphasized the "manly" parts of the job and stressed control of their clients rather than deference to them. "They assigned a heroic character to the job, framing interactions with customers as contests of will. To succeed, they emphasized, required determination, aggressiveness, persistence and stoicism" (Leidner 1991, 166). The men interviewed regarded women as lacking "the killer instinct" needed to succeed, to control, win, or conquer a customer – language that, as Leidner points out, resembles the sexual seduction of an initially unwilling partner. This language of power and seduction also saturates very different types of work in high-status financial services occupations in the City of London, as we shall demonstrate.

A second study of insurance selling carried out by Morgan and Knights (1991) demonstrates Butler's argument that gender identities are regulatory fictions. In their study, Morgan and Knights were able to reveal not only the alternative scripts available to men at work but also how senior management were able to play off different versions of masculinity against each other in order to feminize insurance selling. In a conflict between the "macho" masculinity of the insurance sales force – similar to Leidner's example – and the old-fashioned patriarchal or paternalistic masculinity of bank managers, the male sales force was eliminated and insurance selling was transferred to female bank tellers operating within the bank premises. The eventual outcome of the restructuring was a reduction in overall salary costs, increased profits, and "a salesforce firmly under the patriarchal gaze of professional bankers, fixed within a particular part of the bank's new career structure and non-threatening in terms of salary, status and inter-personal relationships to the bank managers" (Morgan & Knights 1991, 191). For individual women, the reorganization opened up more interesting jobs, greater autonomy, and possible career mobility, even though the overall impact was relatively limited for women as a group. Women with skills and ambition could be directed into selling, leaving the traditional male management career path unthreatened. Whereas the male sales force lost and women made limited gains, career managers came out of the restructuring process unscathed, indeed in an even stronger position. As Morgan and Knights suggest, "one could almost say that one group of men are using women in order to defeat another group of men – not, after all, the first time that has been done!" (1991, 196).

Management and corporate strategy thus play a central role in the construction of gendered identities in the workplace. Organizations invent and reproduce cultural images of gender, and, through recruitment strategies, job classifications, and the regulation of workplace behavior, they create occupations that embody gendered images of the people who should occupy them. These images are not always stable: they are sometimes challenged by workers who are excluded and, on occasion, reshaped by management as part of the restructuring process or as a way of expanding the pool of potential recruits to an occupation. On a daily basis, relations of power and domination and the ways in which these are associated with men, male bodies, and masculine performances play a central role in the subordination of women. These work practices are imbued with gendered meanings, which play a crucial part in the construction of a gendered subjectivity in the workplace. It was these processes that we set out to investigate in a study of merchant banking in the City of London in the early 1990s.

Sexing City Jobs: Masculinity and Femininity in Merchant Banking

The financial services sector has been a significant element of employment growth in advanced industrial economies throughout the 1980s (Court & McDowell 1993; Thrift & Leyshon 1992). It has been particularly important in the major metropolises (Castells 1989; Sassen 1991), where it has had an important impact on social practices and local communities (Budd & Whimster 1992; Sassen 1991) as well as on the structure of the urban economy and the surrounding regions. The professional occupations in this sector require educational credentials for entry – credentials that women are acquiring in growing numbers – as well as particular class attributes (Crompton & Sanderson 1990) associated with the cultural capital acquired in certain schools and universities. The more routine functions in financial services have long been a feminized ghetto (Crompton & Jones 1984). Interesting questions about the intersection of class, status, and gender in recruitment and promotion strategies as the merchant banking sector expanded throughout the 1980s are thus raised.

The expansion of financial service occupations in the 1980s was, at the time, seen as the hallmark of success of the Thatcherite social and economic revolution. The overblown rhetoric of the time, celebrating the success of the City, is remarkable for its sexualized language. Thus, for example, the period immediately following the 1986 Financial Services Act is referred to as "big bang," identified as a sexual metaphor by Stanley (1992). The performance of the sector in the late 1980s, and of the players within it, are commonly portrayed in sexual terms, and the participants are seen as embodying the most glorious of macho-masculine attributes. Thus, reflecting on the 1980s in a "quality" British newspaper, a company director described the atmosphere in the City in the following terms:

> In the City the Eighties were one long hard on, everybody had the horn – every thrusting merchant banker; every double-dealing broker; every hard-nosed limp-dicked lawyer (yes, even they could get it up) – and they weren't too fussy who they screwed. Clients came. Clients went. Here today and screwed tomorrow. . . . And was all this frenzy about reshaping British business? Forget it. Size! Who could pull off the biggest deals? Who could command the biggest fees? Who had the biggest cock in town? That's what it was all about. (Moore 1992, 34)

During these boom years, merchant banking and associated City occupations represented the apotheosis of success, power, glamor, and, above all, a certain type of masculinity that Thrift and Leyshon (1992) have summed up in the catch phrase "sexy greedy." They point out that these jobs have caught the popular imagination as the essence of the 1980s yuppie life-style. Thus, in Britain, *Serious Money* (a play), "Capital City" (a television series), and *Nice Work* (David Lodge's novel and television spin-off) captured the same ethos (protagonist Gordon Gekko's greed is good) as the US film *Wall Street* portrayed. This film has attracted the attention of cultural theorist Norman Denzin (1990). In his astute portrayal of *Wall Street* as a conventional morality play, in which seduction and fall precede a redemption in which old-fashioned virtues triumph, he is alert to the significance of familial imagery – especially the contrasted images of the rule of the father. He is less sensitive, however, to the ways in which power in this "sexy greedy" genre embody masculinity. While Thrift, Leyshon, and Daniels (1987) are less oblivious to the embodiment of masculinity in these occupations, they too pay little attention to the ways in which such jobs are gendered, of how everyday social practices and workplace cultures construct and re-create images of the ideal worker as male. The general association of money with seduction and desire has also been noted by Harvey, who argues that "money, as the supreme representation of power in capitalist society, itself becomes the object of lust, greed and desire" (1989, 102).

Cultural Capital/Capital Culture

In order to investigate the construction of gendered subjectivities in the new high-status occupations in the financial services sector – the brokers, analysts, market makers, salespersons who seemed the embodiment of Thatcherite virtues in the 1980s – we carried out detailed interviews with male and female professional and clerical workers in a number of merchant banks in the City of London.[3] First, however, we collected basic descriptive statistics about the merchant banking work force by means of a short postal survey of all 360 merchant banks with postal addresses in the City of London and its environs. The results indicated that, despite the expansion of well-paid opportunities within merchant banking over the decade, male domination of the City has barely changed (Budd & Whimster 1992; Pryke 1991; Thrift & Leyshon 1992). As Table 13.1 indicates, women, although not absent from the world of banking, are far more

Table 13.1   The Gender Division of Occupations in Merchant Banks, 1992

Occupational category	Men (%)	Women (%)
Directors, strategic managers	17	3
Treasury/investment specialists	17	5
Business specialists	13	6
IT specialists	8	5
Other support specialists	4	7
Professionals (lawyers, etc.)	3	1
Graduate and other trainees	2	2
Clerical staff	32	70
Other (messengers, drivers, etc.)	4	1
Total numbers	13,212	9,283

Source: Authors' survey of merchant banks in Greater London, of which 80% were in the City. *N* = 166.

Note: Our results compare with the Census of Employment, where 45% of employees in financial service occupations in the City of London were women. Unlike women in retail banking, virtually all women in merchant banking are employed full-time – 98% in the case of our survey.

likely to be concentrated in feminized occupations, especially clerical and secretarial work, and in the lower tiers of the "professional" occupations. But even at the highest tiers of merchant banks, there is a small number of women. Women are on the board of directors, for example, in two or three City banks, although many remain all-male bastions at this level. In general, however, women occupy a small proportion of senior positions in most areas of financial services. The only occupation where their representation is significant at senior levels is in personnel services and human resources departments, where the "female" attributes of caring for others give them a "natural" advantage.

It might be argued that financial services jobs in the City – in the world of high finance and the trading floor in particular – represent all that is socially defined as masculine. The cultural capital and associated social characteristics traditionally valued by City bankers – private sector schooling, a good university, the right accent and class background – still dominate recruitment and selection practices for professional positions, especially in corporate finance, despite some relaxation of these criteria in recent decades. Masculinity seems an almost inevitable corollary of these attributes. From our in-depth interviews, in which we collected the educational and occupational history of our informants, it is possible to establish the extent to which the "right" schools and universities are still dominant. Among the 50 respondents in professional occupations whom we interviewed in depth, almost half (48 percent) had been educated either at Oxford or Cambridge or at one of five other elite universities (Bristol, Durham, Exeter, London, and Trinity College Dublin). The percentage rose to 63 in the most traditional, or "blue-blooded," bank in our sample.

An interesting difference emerged from the analysis of employees' educational and class backgrounds between men in the corporate finance divisions and men employed in dealing and trading occupations. The cultural capital possessed by these men varied. Dealers were less likely to have degrees, having entered the banking profession usually at the age of 18. As we delved deeper into their everyday workplace practices and behaviors, we found that these educational differences were mirrored by two contrasting versions of masculinity. Both male and female respondents remarked on the differences between them. As one of our respondents, a senior woman in corporate finance, suggested, in a remark that is representative of a range of comments that we recorded: "There's a cultural divide between them, between traders and what I might call small 'e' executives." A male respondent in his mid-20s, himself a product of one of the most prestigious private boys' schools in Great Britain and Trinity College Cambridge, was able to define this divide more clearly for us:

> In corporate finance, the social background of people is quite narrow – Oxbridge, Bristol, Exeter[4] – so that gives a certain social division immediately. By contrast, the trading floor is very different. Much more sort of, as they say these days, yahoo, where they tend to be recruited at 18, straight from school, highly numerate, amazingly quick minds. They spend a couple of years in the back office and then go on to the trading floor. With regard to social group, the trading floor's one end and the rest of the bank the other.

Yet another respondent commented that the qualification for trading was "raw basic intelligence."

Dual Masculinities in Merchant Banking

Interesting parallels exist between our findings and those of Morgan and Knights (1991) in their work on the retail banking sector. In both cases, one or another version of a twofold social construction of masculinity was adopted by male employees. In the upper echelons of corporate finance the valued masculinity more closely reflected the staid and sober paternalism of managers in the retail banking sector, whereas in the heady world of sales and trading the male culture that is established valorizes a more macho masculinity of "guts," "iron balls," and the "killer instinct" necessary to overcome clients' resistance, to make sales, and to conclude deals. It is this latter version of masculinity that has become more dominant in media representations of City life in the 1980s. It also appears to have become a more dominant way of behaving in City institutions during the 1980s, particularly since deregulation, as expanded opportunities enabled men from a wider range of class backgrounds to enter the City. In popular parlance, a category of men known in London as "barrow boys" gained well-paid employment. This trend, in the words of a representative of a more traditional masculinity, stems from a time when "American practices" began to dominate social exchange in the City (City Lives Project 1990). "A gentleman's word" and trust between men who knew each other socially, often from their schooldays, was replaced by more formal rules of exchange, as well as by opportunities to break them. The 1980s, in Britain and in the United States, certainly seem to have been distinguished by a number of scandals, by insider trading, malpractice, and other problems.

Macho masculinity

An indication of "American" practices and the type of attitudes and behavior that define what we have termed "macho masculinity" in US-owned institutions may be gained from Lewis's book *Liar's Poker* (1989). This is a racy account of his own experience as a salesman for Salomon Brothers in New York and London during the mid-1980s. The extent to which a particular construction of macho masculinity based on notions of power, seduction, and domination structured everyday social practices is clearly revealed in his text. This masculinity clearly operated to exclude women from key positions by emphasizing bodily "otherness." Lewis documented the construction of a male culture and camaraderie in Salomon's that was something between the worlds of a boys' private school and a street gang. The imagery of the trading floor was that of "a jungle of chest-pounding males": "a trader is a savage and a great trader a great savage" (p. 20). Alternatively, investment banking in the United States "is a war fought mainly between North East private school graduates" (p. 29). The most telling sexual imagery at Salomon's, reflecting Stoller's view of the phallus, is in the designation of successful salesmen:

> A new employee, once he reached the trading floor, was handed a pair of telephones. He went on line almost immediately. If he could make millions of dollars come out of those phones, he became that most revered of all species: a Big Swinging Dick . . . nothing in the jungle got in the way of a Big Swinging Dick . . . that was the prize we coveted . . .

everyone wanted to be a Big Swinging Dick, even the women. Big Swinging Dickettes. (Lewis 1989, 42–3)

Not surprisingly, however, the "Dickette" seemed to be more a mythical than actual figure in Lewis's book. It is recognized that the culture of the trading floor is inimical to women. Thus, in New York some of the larger financial institutions, including Merrill Lynch, Morgan Stanley, Bear Sterns, Prudential Securities, First Boston, and Salomon Brothers, have introduced policies to counter the "locker room humor" and other sexist social practices on trading floors in order to make it easier to retain well-qualified women recruits (*Independent on Sunday*, 17 November 1991).

In London, as our interviews revealed, the world of trading and selling was similarly constructed. As many of our respondents, both men and women, noted, the atmosphere in the dealing rooms and on the trading floors is masculine. One respondent suggested that "foreign exchange has always been the lads' floor . . . they kick a paper football round the office and things like that." Another reported that "they throw the secretary's soft toys around and make sexist remarks when they mess about," and a third remarked on her own exclusion because "it's all a good laugh with the lads and then go out and be sleazy together."

Sexual metaphor was commonly used to describe the "thrill of conquest" in concluding a deal, or "consummating a deal," as one of our interviewees put it. Everyday social relations habitually included ribald language, sexualized "horseplay," and a degree of sexual harassment of women. Thus, it was reported to us that "in one room, they had a blow-up woman they used to throw around and things like that." And, as another of our respondents wryly concluded, in this part of banking "I think the worse men behave, the faster they get promoted; obviously the same does not apply to women." Another commented that "the bolshiest people make the most money."

The atmosphere in the dealing rooms makes it hard for women, perhaps unused to such vigorous or unruly social relations at work, to survive. As one respondent suggested, "I think when you start you are at a bit of a disadvantage because you are not used to shouting down phones at men and giving people orders and being really tough."

A small number of women whom we interviewed had experienced unwelcome sexual advances from both colleagues and clients. Most women, however, regarded the sexual innuendo and repartee that was commonplace in the banks, especially among traders, analysts, and the sales force, as generally good natured and not directed either at them or at any individual in particular. As one respondent, an analyst in a merchant bank, reported, "there is harassment of women as a group, but not of women individually." She was able to ignore the foul language, blue jokes, and posters on the trading floor (and to "take it like a man"?). Indeed, several of the small number of women working in this area whom we interviewed emphasized that their male colleagues saw them as "one of the boys." They explained to us that one of the reasons why the excessively masculinist behavior did not get too far out of hand was because of the underlying relations of interdependence that bind analysts, traders, and salesmen (usually men) together as a team. Another respondent, who had found the harassment more intimidating, especially when directed at her (with comments about her underwear, for example), also commented on how the ties of interdependence that bound people together enabled her to dismiss unwelcome attention. This woman, a dealer, suggested that "brokers will try and sort of score with you," but "if it is a broker, you can just tell them to piss off because basically they need you to get the money."

One striking fact about the ribaldry and sexual innuendo was its overwhelmingly heterosexual nature. As Lewis argued about Salomon's, "the firm tolerated sexual harassment but not sexual deviance' (1989, 57). Gay men, along with women, whether straight or lesbian, were marginalized. In our interviews we also found an overwhelming emphasis on heterosexual discourse and practices. As a female dealer commented about her co-workers, "most of them are completely homophobic." Although she was aware of a single gay man in her department, he kept his sexual preferences hidden from his male co-workers.

Traditional masculinity

In the corporate finance divisions, an alternative male gender performance was dominant. Among the bank directors, treasury specialists, managers, and directors in capital development divisions, a different set of social attributes and acceptable behaviors was valued. Here, we found the more traditional image of bankers preeminent. The right school and university, the correct accent and tailor were important, and the "old boy network" operated in recruitment and mentoring practices. In one of the banks in our survey, a long-established, "blue-blooded," family-owned bank, there were continuing links between a number of schools and Cambridge colleges and the bank. In probing interviews with personnel in the human resources departments at three banks, as well as with specialist employees, we became forcibly aware of the repeated insistence on the importance of "fit" – a notion that our respondents found hard to define but could clearly recognize. The following quotation, ironically from a respondent who felt her lack of fit quite keenly, sums up the valued set of desirable social attitudes: "I'm not interested in beagles, I don't want a wine cellar, I'm not interested in horse trials, it doesn't matter to me who wins Wimbledon, if I go to the opera it doesn't have to be Glyndebourne because I go to listen to the music."

A significant number of our male respondents (over half of them) who conformed to a variant of what we might term "formal" or "traditional" masculinity, quite self-consciously referred to their work as a performance. A commonly used phrase, for example, was "we are selling ourselves, as well as a product," and many of them discussed, unprompted, the sort of image that they tried to create. They were aware of the strong social restrictions around dress codes (no brown suits or shoes, for example) and the limited extent to which deviations were permitted. A female respondent commented on her male colleagues' responses to a visiting stockbroker:

> Now there's a chap in the stock broking arm who's very . . . sort of fairly rustic . . . I mean he's a lovely man but to say he's rustic is probably the best way of putting it . . . he always wears brown everything and they all tease him . . . you can't wear brown for heaven's sake . . . coming into a merchant bank with brown shoes on . . . outrageous and you've got a polyester tie, God, you can't have a polyester tie, you've got to have a silk tie.

Another deviation that is not sanctioned: "Someone wore short sleeves instead of long ones with cuff links and he's been, I mean, berated so many times for not having a proper shirt on . . . you see, there's all these codes."

Further, men in management or supervisory roles reported on the ways in which they operated sanctions on the appearance and behavior of their junior colleagues. A middle rank manager, an assistant director in the corporate finance division, indicated the element of control of appearance: "I often tell people, in a nice way, if I can, to get their hair cut, or to buy a deodorant. I may advise them where to buy their shirts, not to wear a Marks and Spencer's suit but to buy something a bit better."

The same man, albeit reluctantly, confirmed Young's contention about the significance of "scaling bodies" as a mechanism of exclusion. The men whom we interviewed, in particular those between age 25 and perhaps the early 40s, were noticeably similar in appearance. They were all white (in the whole sample we interviewed only one person of color, a London-born woman of Asian origin), mostly tall, and not significantly overweight. When questioned about this, this respondent, rather shamefacedly, confessed to having recently interviewed, and rejected, an overweight male applicant, who, he claimed, by his appearance did not present a sufficiently serious image of the bank. It also became clear from questioning a range of respondents that the use of headhunters to recruit at senior levels perpetuated the common mold; in the words of a director, "these firms know the sort of person that we want, they know who would fit in."

Multiple Femininities

What about women? Are they able to "fit in" to the world of corporate finance by becoming Acker's honorary men? Clearly, in most parts of a merchant bank, apart from the dealing and trading areas, being "one of the boys" would be the wrong script. For the majority of female employees, in fact, this question was not appropriate; they worked in female-dominated occupations and in areas of the bank where their investment in a particular version of femininity was taken for granted, both by the women themselves and by their male colleagues, or, more usually, male superiors. Thus, for example, for the secretaries we interviewed, the adoption of a masculinized role or performance was not an option.

Foucault's analysis of the way in which subjectivity is constituted through different disciplinary mechanisms, by techniques of surveillance, and by power-knowledge strategies so that we discipline ourselves is a helpful way of understanding women's investment in their sense of self as feminine, even when their participation in that set of power relations rationally seems to be disadvantageous. For secretaries, all of whom were women, being female was part of the job. A wide range of social practices reinforced the association of femininity with inferior status. The very layout of space in merchant banks, the size of rooms, the way in which they are partitioned, the organization of entrances and exits, the informal separation of workers by status and gender that we so clearly observed in the dining room and in open public spaces outside the banks, creates and reinforces gendered subjectivities and their relationship to power and status (Colomina 1992; Spain 1992). For the secretarial staff, the fact that they were female was not an issue in everyday social interaction in the workplace, as their own gender, social behavior, and the gender of the job coincided. There are, as Pringle (1989) has shown, however, a number of alternative femininities available to secretarial staff that structure the boss – secretary relationship in particular ways. The "mother," "mistress or office wife," or "dolly bird" models are available, and the selection of one often depends on the age of the secretary and her physical appearance. The particular stereotype also influences the range of tasks that a secretary is routinely expected to perform.

The Honorary Male – Or Not?

The relationship between a female body and lack of power is, of course, part of the reason why women have been forced to act as if they were men to achieve success. For women in senior positions in merchant banks, their gender and appearance is at odds with the masculinist nature of the occupation that they fill and the tasks they perform. Similarly, the masculine ethos that dominates everyday interactions in merchant banking, perhaps especially on the trading floor and in the dealing rooms, constructs women as "the other." Thus, a common option that many women take at work in order to minimize their difference is to become "an honorary man" (Acker 1990), adopting masculinist norms and behavior and, often, a variant of the male business dress. Many of our respondents explained their strategy in similar terms: "I always wear a suit. I like to look as male as I can, or at least neutral." For these women who adopted a variant of male dress, one of the reasons was not only to ape men, but also to differentiate themselves from the secretarial staff.

> I wear these men's shirts; I mean they are ladies, they are made for ladies at a men's tailors; and you should wear a jacket, women should wear jackets unless you want to be associated with a secretary, that's one of the rules, you have to wear something quite subtle, black or navy or grey, don't wear loud or garish things or they'll spot you, they'll say, ooh, like your outfit or things like that.

Noticeably, however, it was the younger and more junior women among our female respondents who attempted to pose as men, or at least present themselves as neutral bodies. "I tend to wear sort of rather boring frumpy things because I felt initially there was less of a distinction between me and the men and I wouldn't be noticed as a girl. I don't know why I do it now."

The analysis of our interviews with women working in the most senior positions, however, revealed that the honorary man was not the only performance on offer. For women, like men, more than one gender role was appropriate. Women bankers were also able to choose between different regulatory fictions at work. Indeed, it was suggested to us by most of the senior women we interviewed that playing male was in fact an undesirable option that could not be sustained. As one woman who had "made it" to director level remarked about the masculine strategy she had originally adopted, "Over the years I've come to the conclusion why should I try to be a little man? I'm not a little man. It's not going to work. I'll never be a man as well as a man is." As feminist theorists Threadgold and Cranny-Francis have pointed out, "masculine and feminine behaviours have different personal and social significances when acted out by male and female subjects. What is valorized in patriarchy is not masculinity but male masculinity" (1990, 31).

There are strategies of resistance, however, to the dominance of masculinity and its association with power. It became evident that there are ways in which femininity might be constructed as an advantage in the workplace. A number of our respondents who had achieved seniority argued that they were able to use and play on their femininity to achieve visibility. And, further, that the availability of multiple images of femininity might be used to advantage by women bankers. One woman was very clear about the ways in which she might, by her appearance, conform to, reinforce, or challenge the view that her clients and colleagues held of her as a woman, depending on the circumstances. In response to a question about how she presented herself, she replied:

> It depends who I'm going to be seeing. Sometimes I'll choose the "executive bimbo" look; at other times, like today when I've got to make a cold call, it's easiest if I look as if I'll blend into the background. I think this (a plain but very smart tailored blue dress) looks tremendously, you know, professional. No statement about me at all. Don't look at me, look at these papers I'm talking to you about. But I wear high heels too, so I'm 6 feet tall when I stand up. And I think that commands some small sense of 'well, I'd probably better listen to her, at least for a little while.' I do sometimes dress quite consciously because you've got to have some fun in life, and sometimes wearing a leather skirt to work is just fun because you know they can't cope with it.

The parallels between this quotation and Judith Williamson's (1992) reflections on her own sense of self in her introduction to the work of the feminist photographer, Cindy Sherman, are striking.

> When I rummage through my wardrobe in the morning I am not merely faced with a choice of what to wear. I am faced with a choice of images: the difference between a smart suit and a pair of overalls, a leather skirt and a cotton frock, is not just one of fabric and style but one of identity. You know perfectly well that you will be seen differently for the whole day, depending on what you put on; you will appear as a particular type of woman with one particular identity which excludes others. The black leather skirt rather rules out girlish innocence, oily overalls tend to exclude sophistication, ditto smart suit and radical feminism. Often I have wished I could put them on all together, or appear simultaneously in every possible outfit, just to say, Fuck you, for thinking any one of these is me. But also, See, I can be all of them. (Williamson 1992, 222)

Another woman who was also a "high flyer" had also thought about the image she presented and deliberately changed it, deciding that she would no longer dress as an honorary man.

> One of the things that I have changed in my career is . . . well at first I thought you should buy suits that look like men's suits, that are just slightly tailored to be for women and you should wear your hair back in a bun and look terribly professional. . . . I guess the way I

present myself and the way I like to work has changed a lot. I like to laugh a lot. Some of the guys wouldn't necessarily feel it was good to laugh in a meeting but I do and I get away with it all right. And I try to be more feminine too – or I don't try, I just try to be the way I am rather than the way someone else is. I find it works really well. I've never had anyone object to me coming to a meeting and in many cases I've had people say to me it's really nice to be working with a woman.

We noticed, however, that many of (the tiny number of) these senior women were not English. This "double outsider" status seemed to give them a freedom to break prescribed norms of expected social behavior, particularly with clients.

I have a real advantage. Since I'm American nobody has any particular idea of what I should be like or they expect me to be a little bit loud. I can say something naff or ask a question that is indiscreet or things like that and it's not out of character for what people expect an American to do. And they don't mind if an American woman is in a business role. American women don't stay at home necessarily and their wife isn't an American woman so they don't compare me to her.

Another respondent, from one of the former colonies, was also able to play the outrageous "wild colonial girl" and behave in meetings in ways that challenged conventional norms. We must emphasize, however, that these women were a minority, seemingly secure in their own version(s) of femininity and in their careers. It is hard to conclude whether their femininity was a cause or a consequence of their success or to what extent these women felt that another self – a different them – was visible outside the workplace. Similar findings about the adoption of a parody femininity by women in high-status professional occupations have, however, been documented by Watson (1992) in her study of the professional civil service in England and by Pringle (1993) in her comparison of women medical consultants in Australia and Great Britain.

Masquerade?

The consequences of these games, of a masquerade at work, of the adoption of a masculinized version of femininity by some women and a deliberately feminine version by others as a workplace strategy, are important for women's sense of self. The French feminist theorist Irigaray (1985) has written about womanliness or femininity in similar terms to those Butler uses. Thus she has defined femininity as a mask or a performance, describing the mimicry that she sees as constitutive of feminine subjectivity as a masquerade of femininity in which a woman loses herself by playing on her femininity.

In a provocative paper, originally published in 1929 but recently influential again, Joan Riviere (1986) documents the implications for women who take on a masculine identity in order to compete in the professions. She suggests that women who take on a masculine identity may also put on "a mask of womanliness" or masquerade in a feminine guise in order to "avert anxiety and the retribution feared from men" (p. 35). Thus, in Riviere's case notes about a woman university lecturer, it is suggested that she copes with her male colleagues by being flippant or frivolous, that "she has to treat the situation of displaying her masculinity to men as a 'game', as something not real, as a 'joke'" (p. 39).

Although we have not yet explored these ideas in the context of merchant banking, they seem a potential way forward in exploring why so many women do not achieve the really powerful positions. There are also fruitful lines of comparison between women who parody masculinity and those who parody femininity. Something more is at work than seeing women as straightforwardly oppressed by the structures of power and practices of representation. Rather it is important to begin to explore "the problem of the investments that subjects have in complying with the practices of representation" (Threadgold & Cranny-Francis 1990, 7). As Coward (1984) has asked, "What is the lure of these discourses which causes us to take up and inhabit the female position?" It also seems clear from our results that there is no single female position, but rather a range of performances open to subjects who are women, and that these performances have different implications for success in the world of waged labor. Important questions about embodiment and performance remain to be raised. Thus we argue that the processes of being and becoming a woman (or a man) in the world of waged work should not be ignored by geographers, especially in the context of the shift toward service sector employment and a feminized labor force. As Threadgold and Cranny-Francis have pointed out, "the feminist story that rewrites the liberal humanist and capitalist narrative of individualism sees subjectivities, too, as a function of their discursive and bodily histories in a signifying network of meaning and representation" (1990, 3).

The Tyranny of Time

In recommending a "cultural turn" – the investigation of lived experience in Sayer and Walker's (1992) terms – we are not suggesting that representational practices and discursive strategies are a sufficient explanation of women's inferior position in the labor force. Significant material practices continue to affect women's attachment to the labor force. In our case study, perhaps the most obvious factor that hindered the combination of work and domestic life – for men, of course, as well as for women – was evidence of a highly developed Protestant work ethic. The average number of hours worked per day by respondents in professional positions was between 10 and 12, and respondents in secretarial and support or back office professions (e.g., personnel, advertising, accountancy) also endorsed the hard-working ethos of the banks, Although the respondents in these latter occupations were less likely to work beyond 6:00 p.m. on a regular basis, when an urgent deal was under way it was common for them to work long hours. In the corporate finance occupations, individuals at all levels and in all positions expected to work through the night when business was brisk, sometimes for several days at a stretch. It was the dealing professionals, however, who regularly worked the longest hours.

It is common practice for analysts, dealers, and traders to be at their desks at 8:00 a.m. and to remain for long hours. The advent of electronic communications between the exchanges of London, New York, and Tokyo has played a significant role in extending working hours for traders and analysts. Lewis (1989, 41) suggested that the best analysts "lost their will to live normal lives. They gave themselves entirely over to their employers and worked around the clock. They rarely slept and often looked ill; the better they became at the job, the nearer they appeared to death." Or, as one of our respondents commented about the senior dealers in her department: "You think they are dead to look at them." The business climate of 1992 is different from the frantic years of the mid-1980s, and yet it is clear that very long hours continue to be the norm rather than the exception in this sector of banking.

The general expectation that people will spend long hours in the workplace clearly makes life difficult for those with parental obligations. Women with small children were the exception rather than the norm, and none of the banks in which we interviewed had established and accepted schemes to facilitate women returning after childbirth. Part-time work was possible but had to be individually negotiated, and we found some evidence in one of the banks that a woman who had recently taken an option of part-time work as an analyst was regarded by other women as not pulling her weight.

As we found, long hours are not restricted to analysts and traders but are common throughout the world of merchant banking, making career advancement difficult for women with young children. Frances Heaton, whom we did not interview, is director general of the Takeover Panel and one of the small number of women who has penetrated to the highest levels of corporate finance. Reflecting on her career in an article entitled "Mistress of the Square Mile" (surely not inadvertent sexual imagery?) in *The Observer* (19 January 1992, 31), she argued that "corporate finance is a hopeless job for a woman with young children. It was an unhappy time for the family since I never knew what time I was getting home, pressured from long and unpredictable hours . . . people are worked into the ground. There is a heavy load with a lot of mental pressure. It is also physically demanding."

Conclusions

We have attempted to indicate some of the directions that work on the sexual division of labor might take in the future. As service sector occupations expand in advanced industrial societies, questions about the construction of subjectivity at work will become increasingly important. The lines between the worker and the product are blurred in jobs in which a personal relationship is part of the product. A fruitful line of further research might therefore explore the relationships between economic restructuring, changes in competitive conditions, and the social construction of occupations, including their gendering. At a large geographic scale, in the context of the general shift toward a low-wage, feminized economy in both Britain and the United States, the social construction of occupations clearly has immense consequences.

At a smaller spatial scale, it is apparent that masculine and feminine subjectivities are both constructed and changed within the workplace. Particular gender identities are embedded in everyday social practices and in what we might term occupational cultures. This recognition enables a more complex notion of the significance of sexual identity and gender relations in the workplace to be developed and so moves away from static notions of men and women seeking slots in an already gender-differentiated labor market. It also opens up space to investigate the ways in which men and women are able to resist the apparent gender appropriateness of particular occupations and realign them in ways that more closely match their own sense of self. Thus the apparently "female" attributes of certain occupations are able to be reinterpreted by male workers to embody socially designated attributes of masculinity, and vice versa. Here, perhaps, geographers might reach outside their disciplinary boundaries and ask broader questions about economic restructuring, which involves not only struggles over the gendering of new jobs but also the reallocation of existing occupations in a period of intense economic change.

Notes

1. This work is part of a larger program of five related research projects on economic restructuring in South East England that is being carried out at the Open University and Cambridge University, funded by the Economic and Social Research Council. This paper draws on the project on women's work and social polarization in the financial services sector, grant number R 000 23 3006.

    We should like to thank Susan Hanson for her fine editing, which ensured that our own voices appeared in the text; and, in the absence of a wife each, Hazel Christie and Suzy Reimer for help with child care when most needed.

2. For a useful summary of the different approaches to women's labor market segregation, see Dex (1985).

3. This research has a number of parts: (1) a quantitative postal questionnaire survey of all the British and foreign banks in the City (360 in total); (2) a statistical analysis of the personnel data of the merchant-banking arm of a large retail bank; and (3) detailed in-depth taped interviews at three merchant banks, one attached to one of the major clearing banks and two other British-owned merchant banks. In this part of the study matched samples of men and women, wherever possible, in a range of occupations throughout the job hierarchy were interviewed. The final element consisted of smaller numbers of interviews in a range of British- and foreign-owned banks to gain an indicative view of differences in working practices in this range of institutions. In all, 78 interviews have been undertaken. For obvious reasons none of these banks may be identified. All aspects of the case study work are now complete. The postal survey is complete (response rate 46%) and analyzed, as are the personnel data. The interview results presented here are based on an initial analysis of the transcripts from the 78 taped interviews.

4. All are high-status universities with a high proportion of students from private schools.

References

Acker, J. (1990). Hierarchies, Jobs, Bodies: A Theory of Gendered Organisation. *Gender and Society* 4, pp. 139–58.

Barron, R. & G. Norris (1976). Sexual Divisions and the Dual Labour Market. In: D. Barker & S. Allen (eds.), *Dependence and Exploitation in Work and Marriage*, pp. 47–69. London: Longmans.

Beechey, V. (1977). Some Notes on Female Wage Labour in Capitalist Production. *Capital and Class* 3, pp. 45–66.

Beechey, V. & T. Perkins (1987). *A Matter of Hours: Women, Part-Time Work and the Labour Market*. Oxford: Polity Press.

Bradley, H. (1989). *Men's Work: Women's Work*. Oxford: Polity Press.

Budd, L. & S. Whimster (eds.) (1992). *Global Finance and Urban Living: A Study of Metropolitan Change*. London: Routledge.

Butler, J. (1990). *Gender Trouble: Feminism and the Subversion of Identity*. London: Routledge.

Castells, M. (1989). *The Informational City: Information Technology, Economic Restructuring and the Urban-Regional Process*. Oxford: Basil Blackwell.

Christopherson, S. (1989). Flexibility in the US Service Economy and the Emerging Spatial Division of Labour. *Transactions of the Institute of British Geographers* 14, pp. 131–43.

City Lives Project (1989–92). Unpublished Interviews with Key Decision Makers in the City of London, National Sound Archives, London SW7.

Cockburn, C. (1983). *Brothers: Male Dominance and Technological Change*. London: Pluto Press.

Cockburn, C. (1993). *In the Way of Women: Men's Resistance to Sex Equality in Organizations*. Basingstoke: Macmillan.

Colomina, B. (1992). The Split Wall: Domestic Voyeurism. In: B. Colomina (ed.), *Sexuality and Space*, pp. 73–130. Princeton, NJ: Princeton Architectural Press.

Connell, R. W. (1987). *Gender and Power*. Cambridge: Polity Press.

Court, C. & L. McDowell (1993). Serious Trouble?: Financial Services and Structural Change. Working Paper No. 3, the South East Research Programme, The Open University and Cambridge University. (Available from Faculty of Social Sciences, The Open University, Milton Keynes, MK7 6AA.)

Coward, R. (1984). *Female Desire. Women's Sexuality Today*. London: Granada Publishing.

Crang, P. (1992). A New Service Society? On the Geographies of Service Employment. Ph.D. thesis, University of Cambridge.

Crompton, R. & G. Jones (1984). *White Collar Proletariat*. London: Macmillan.

Crompton, R. & K. Sanderson (1990). *Gendered Jobs and Social Change*. London: Unwin Hyman.

Davidson, M. & C. Cooper (1992). *Shattering the Glass Ceiling: The Woman Manager*. London: Paul Chapman.

Denzin, N. (1990). Reading "Wall Street": Postmodern Contradictions in the American Social Structure. In: B. S. Turner (ed.), *Theories of Modernity and Postmodernity*, pp. 31–44. London: Sage.

Dex, S. (1985). *The Sexual Division of Work*. Brighton: Wheatsheaf.

Filby, M. P. (1992). "The Figures, the Personality and the Bums": Service Work and Sexuality. *Work, Employment and Society* 6, pp. 23–42.

Frobel, F., J. Heinrichs & O. Kreye (1980). *The New International Division of Labour*. Cambridge: Cambridge University Press.

Gabriel, Y. (1988). *Working Lives in Catering*. London: Routledge.

Game, A. & R. Pringle (1984). *Gender at Work*. London: Pluto Press.

Hanson, S. & I. Johnston (1985). Gender Differences in Work Length Trip: Explanations and Implications. *Urban Geography* 6, pp. 193–219.

Hanson, S. & G. Pratt (1988). Spatial Dimensions of the Gender Division of Labor in a Local Labor Market. *Urban Geography* 9, pp. 180–202.

Hanson, S. & G. Pratt (1991). Job Search and the Occupational Segregation of Women. *Annals of the Association of American Geographers* 81, pp. 229–53.

Hartmann, H. (1979). Capitalism, Patriarchy and Job Segregation by Sex. In: Z. Eisenstein (ed.), *Capitalist Patriarchy and the Case for Socialist Feminism*, pp. 206–47. New York: Monthly Review Press.

Harvey, D. (1989). *The Condition of Postmodernity*. Oxford: Basil Blackwell.

Hearn, J. & P. W. Parkin (1987). *Sex at Work*. Brighton: Wheatsheaf.

Hochschild, A. (1983). *The Managed Heart: Commercialization of Human Feeling*. Berkeley: University of California Press.

Irigaray, L. (1985). *The Sex Which Is Not One*, trans. Catherine Porter with Caroline Burke. Ithaca, NY: Cornell University Press.

Jenson, J. (1989). The Talents of Women and the Skills of Men: Flexible Specialisation and Women. In: S. Wood (ed.), *The Transformation of Work*, pp. 141–55. London: Unwin Hyman.

Johnston-Anumonwo, I. (1988). The Journey to Work and Occupational Segregation. *Urban Geography* 9, pp. 138–54.

Kessler-Harris, A. (1982). *Out to Work: A History of Wage-Earning Women in the United States*. Oxford: Oxford University Press.

Knights, D. & G. Morgan (1991). Selling Oneself: Subjectivity and the Labour Process in the Sale of Life Insurance. In: C. Smith, D. Knights & H. Willmott (eds.), *White Collar Work: The Non-manual Labour Process*. London: Macmillan.

Leidner, R. (1991). Selling Hamburgers, Selling Insurance: Gender, Work and Identity. *Gander and Society* 5, pp. 154–77.

Lewis, M. (1989). *Liar's Poker: Two Cities, True Greed*. London: Hodder and Stoughton.

McDowell, L. (1991). Life without Father and Ford: The New Gender Order of Postfordism. *Transactions of the Institute of British Geographers* 16, pp. 400–19.

Massey, D. (1984). *Spatial Divisions of Labour*. London: Macmillan.

Milkman, R. (1987). *Gender at Work: The Dynamics of Job Segregation by Sex during World War II*. Chicago: University of Chicago Press.

Mincer, J. (1962). Labor Force Participation of Married Women: A Study of Labor Supply. In: *Aspects of Labour Economics*, National Bureau of Economic Research. Princeton, NJ: Princeton University Press.

Moore, A. (1992). My Pact with the Devil. *Weekend Guardian*, August 15–16, p. 34.

Morgan, G. & D. Knights (1991). Gendering Jobs: Corporate Strategy, Mangerial Control and the Dynamics of Job Segregation. *Work, Employment and Society* 5, pp. 181–200.

Peck, J. (1993). End of Great Divide as South-East Is Dragged into the Jobless Mire. *Guardian*, April 1, p. 11.

Phillips, A. & B. Taylor (1980). Sex and Skill: Notes Towards a Feminist Economics. *Feminist Review* 6, pp. 79–88.

Pratt, G. & S. Hanson (1988). Gender, Class and Space. *Environment and Planning D: Society and Space* 6, pp. 16–35.

Pratt, G. & S. Hanson (1991a). Time, Space and the Occupational Segregation of Women: A Critique of Human Capital Theory. *Geoforum* 22, pp. 149–58.

Pratt, G. & S. Hanson (1991b). On Theoretical Subtlety, Gender, Class, and Space: A Reply to Huxley and Winchester. *Environment and Planning D: Society and Space* 9, pp. 241–6.

Pratt, G. & S. Hanson (1994). Human Geography and the Construction of Difference. *Gender, Place and Culture* 1, pp. 5–30.

Pringle, R. (1989). *Secretaries Talk*. London: Verso.

Pringle, R. (1993). Femininity and Performance in the Medical Profession. Paper presented at the Newnham Geographical Society, Newnham College in Cambridge, February.

Pryke, M. (1991). An International City Going "Global": Spatial Change in the City of London. *Environment and Planning D: Society and Space* 9, pp. 197–220.

Riviere, J. (1986). Womanliness as a Masquerade. In: V. Burgin, J. Donald & C. Kaplan (eds.), *Formations of Fantasy*, pp. 35–45. London: Methuen.

Rubery, J. (1980). Structured Labour Markets, Worker Organisation and Low Pay. In: A. Amsden (ed.), *The Economics of Women and Work*. Harmondsworth: Penguin.

Sassen, S. (1991). *The Global City: New York, London and Tokyo*. Princeton, NJ: Princeton University Press.

Sayer, A. & D. Walker (1992). *The New Social Economy: Reworking the Division of Labour*. Oxford: Basil Blackwell.

Scott, J. (1988). Deconstructing Equality versus Difference: Or, the Uses of Post-Structuralist Theory for Feminism. *Feminist Studies* 14, pp. 33–50.

Scott, A. & M. Storper (1986). *Production, Work and Territory: The Geographical Anatomy of Industrial Capitalism*. London: Allen and Unwin.

Smith, C., D. Knights & H. Willmott (eds.) (1991). *White Collar Work: The Non-Manual Labour Process*. London: Macmillan.

Spain, D. (1992). *Gendered Spaces*. London: University of North Carolina Press.

Stanley, C. (1992). Cultural Contradictions in the Legitimation of Market Practice: Paradox in the Regulation of the City. In: L. Budd & S. Whimster (eds.), *Global Finance and Urban Living*, pp. 142–70. London: Routledge.

Stoller, R. (1979). *Sexual Excitement: The Dynamics of Erotic Life*. New York: Pantheon.

Storper, M. & R. Walker (1989). *The Capitalist Imperative: Territory, Technology and Industrial Growth*. Oxford: Basil Blackwell.

Threadgold, T. & A. Cranny-Francis (1990). *Feminine, Masculine and Representation*. London: Allen and Unwin.

Thrift, N. & A. Leyshon (1992). In the Wake of Money: The City of London and the Accumulation of Value. In: L. Budd & S. Whimster (eds.), *Global Finance and Urban Living*, pp. 282–311. London: Routledge.

Thrift, N., A. Leyshon & P. Daniels (1987). "Sexy Greedy": The New International Financial System, the City of London and the South East of England. Working Papers in Producer Services No. 7, University of Bristol and University of London.

Villeneuve, P. & D. Rose (1988). Gender and the Separation of Employment from Home in Metropolitan Montreal, 1971–1981. *Urban Geography* 9, pp. 155–79.

Vogel, L. (1983). *Marxism and the Oppression of Women*. London: Pluto Press.

Walby, S. (1986). *Patriarchy at Work*. Cambridge: Polity Press.

Walby, S. (1991). *Theorising Patriarchy*. Oxford: Basil Blackwell.

Watson, S. (1992). Is Sir Humphrey Dead? The Changing Culture of the Civil Service. Working Paper No. 103, School of Advanced Urban Studies, University of Bristol.

Westwood, S. (1984). *All Day, Every Day*. London: Pluto Press.

Williamson, J. (1992). Images of "Woman": The Photography of Cindy Sherman. In: H. Crowley & S. Himmelweit (eds.), *Knowing Women: Feminism and Knowledge*, pp. 222–34. Cambridge: Polity Press.

Women and Geography Study Group (1984). *Gender and Geography*. London: Hutchinson.

Young, I. M. (1990). *Justice and the Politics of Difference*. Princeton, NJ: Princeton University Press.

Zukin, S. (1991). *Landscapes of Power: From Detroit to Disney Land*. Berkeley and Los Angeles: University of California Press.

14

Horror and the Monstrous-Feminine: An Imaginary Abjection

*Barbara Creed**

Horror and Abjection

Mother is not herself today.
– Norman Bates, *Psycho*

All human societies have a conception of the monstrous-feminine, of what it is about woman that is shocking, terrifying, horrific, abject. "Probably no male human being is spared the terrifying shock of threatened castration at the sight of the female genitals," Freud wrote in his paper "Fetishism" in 1927.[1] Joseph Campbell, in his book *Primitive Mythology*, noted that "there is a motif occurring in certain primitive mythologies, as well as in modern surrealist painting and neurotic dream, which is known to folklore as 'the toothed vagina' – the vagina that castrates. And a counterpart, the other way, is the so-called 'phallic mother,' a motif perfectly illustrated in the long fingers and nose of the witch."[2] Classical mythology also was populated with gendered monsters, many of which were female. The Medusa, with her "evil eye," head of writhing serpents, and lolling tongue, was queen of the pantheon of female monsters; men unfortunate enough to look at her were turned immediately to stone.

It is not by accident that Freud linked the sight of the Medusa to the equally horrifying sight of the mother's genitals, for the concept of the monstrous-feminine, as constructed within and by a patriarchal and phallocentric ideology, is related intimately to the problem of sexual difference and castration. In 1922 he argued that the "Medusa's head takes the place of a representation of the female genitals."[3] If we accept Freud's interpretation, we can see that the Perseus myth is mediated by a narrative about the *difference* of female sexuality as a difference which is grounded in monstrousness and which invokes castration anxiety in the male spectator. "The sight of the Medusa's head makes the spectator stiff with terror, turns him to stone."[4] The irony of this was not lost on Freud, who pointed out that becoming stiff also means having an erection. "Thus in the original situation it offers consolation to the spectator: he is still in possession of a penis, and the stiffening reassures him of the fact."[5] One wonders if the experience

*Pp. 44–70 from *Screen*, vol. 27, no. 1. © 1986 by Screen. Reprinted with permission from the author and Screen.

of horror – of viewing the horror film – causes similar alterations in the body of the male spectator. And what of other phrases that apply to both male and female viewers – phrases such as "It scared the shit out of me"; "It made me feel sick"; "It gave me the creeps"? What is the relationship between physical states, bodily wastes (even if metaphoric ones), and the horrific – in particular, the monstrous-feminine?

Julia Kristeva's *Powers of Horror* provides us with a preliminary hypothesis for an analysis of these questions. Although this study is concerned with literature, it nevertheless suggests a way of situating the monstrous-feminine in the horror film in relation to the maternal figure and what Kristeva terms "abjection," that which does not "respect borders, positions, rules," that which "disturbs identity, system, order."[6] In general terms, Kristeva is attempting to explore the different ways in which abjection, as a source of horror, works within patriarchal societies as a means of separating the human from the nonhuman and the fully constituted subject from the partially formed subject. Ritual becomes a means by which societies both renew their initial contact with the abject element and then exclude that element.

Through ritual, the demarcation lines between human and nonhuman are drawn up anew and presumably made all the stronger for that process. One of the key figures of abjection is the mother who becomes an abject at that moment when the child rejects her for the father who represents the symbolic order. The problem with Kristeva's theory, particularly for feminists, is that she never makes clear her position on the oppression of women. Her theory moves uneasily between explanation of, and justification for, the formation of human societies based on the subordination of women.

Kristeva grounds her theory of the maternal in the abject, tracing its changing definitions from the period of the pagan or mother-goddess religions to the time of Judaic monotheism and to its culmination in Christianity. She deals with abjection in the following forms: as a rite of defilement in paganism; as a biblical abomination, a taboo, in Judaism; and as self-defilement, an interiorization, in Christianity. Kristeva, however, does not situate abjection solely within a ritual or religious context. She argues that it is "rooted historically (in the history of religions) and subjectively (in the structuration of the subject's identity), in the cathexis of maternal function – mother, woman, reproduction" (p. 91). Kristeva's central interest, however, lies with the structuring of subjectivity within and by the processes of abjectivity in which the subject is spoken by the abject through both religious and cultural discourses, that is, through the subject's position within the practices of the rite as well as within language.

> But the question for the analyst-semiologist is to know how far one can analyze ritual impurity. The historian of religion stops soon: the critically impure is that which is based on a natural "loathing." The anthropologist goes further: there is nothing "loathsome" in itself; the loathsome is that which disobeys classification rules peculiar to the given symbolic system. But as far as I am concerned, I keep asking questions. . . . Are there no subjective structurations that, within the organization of each speaking being, correspond to this or that symbolic-social system and represent, if not stages, at least *types* of subjectivity and society? Types that would be defined, in the last analysis, according to the subject's position in language . . . ? (p. 92)

A full examination of this theory is outside the scope of this article; I propose to draw mainly on Kristeva's discussion of abjection in its construction in the human subject in relation to her notions of (a) the "border" and (b) the mother-child relationship. At crucial points, I shall also refer to her writing on the abject in relation to religious discourses. This area cannot be ignored, for what becomes apparent in reading her work is that definitions of the monstrous as constructed in the modern horror text are grounded in ancient religious and historical notions of abjection – particularly in relation to the following religious "abominations": sexual immorality and perversions; corporeal alteration, decay, and death; human sacrifice; murder; the corpse; bodily wastes; the feminine body; and incest.

The place of the abject is "the place where meaning collapses" (p. 2), the place where "I" am not. The abject threatens life; it must be "radically excluded" (p. 2) from the place of the living subject, propelled away from the body and deposited on the other side of an imaginary border which separates the self from that which threatens the self. Kristeva quotes Bataille: "Abjection . . . is merely the inability to assume with sufficient strength the imperative act of excluding abject things (and that act establishes the foundations of collective existence)" (p. 56). Although the subject must exclude the abject, it must, nevertheless, be tolerated, for that which threatens to destroy life also helps to define life. Further, the activity of exclusion is necessary to guarantee that the subject take up his or her proper place in relation to the symbolic.

> To each ego its object, to each superego its abject. It is not the white expanse or slack boredom of repression, not the translations and transformations of desire that wrench bodies, nights and discourse; rather it is a brutish suffering that "I" puts up with, sublime and devastated, for "I" deposits it to the father's account (*verse au pere – pere-version*): I endure it, for I imagine such is the desire of the other. . . . On the edge of nonexistence and hallucination, of a reality that, if I acknowledge it, annihilates me. There, abject and abjection are my safeguards. The primers of my culture. (p. 2)

The abject can be experienced in various ways, one of which relates to biological bodily functions, the other of which has been inscribed in a symbolic (religious) economy. For instance, Kristeva claims that food loathing is "perhaps the most elementary and archaic form of abjection" (p. 2). Food, however, becomes abject only if it signifies a border "between two distinct entities or territories" (p. 75). Kristeva describes how, for her, the skin on the top of milk, which is offered to her by her father and mother, is a "sign of their desire," a sign separating her world from their world, a sign which she does not want. "But since the food is not an 'other' for 'me,' who am only in their desire, I expel *myself*, I spit *myself* out, I abject *myself* within the same motion through which 'I' claim to establish *myself*" (p. 3). Dietary prohibitions are, of course, central to Judaism. Kristeva argues that these are directly related to the prohibition of incests; she argues this not just because this position is supported by psychoanalytic discourse and structural anthropology but also because "the biblical text, as it proceeds, comes back, at the intensive moments of its demonstration and expansion, to that mytheme of the archaic relation to the mother" (p. 106).

The ultimate in abjection is the corpse. The body protects itself from bodily wastes such as feces, blood, urine, and pus by ejecting these substances just as it expels food that, for whatever reason, the subject finds loathsome. The body extricates itself from them and from the place where they fall, so that it might continue to live.

> Such wastes drop so that I might live, until, from loss to loss, nothing remains in me and my entire body falls beyond the limit – *cadere*, cadaver. If dung signifies the other side of the border, the place where I am not and which permits me to be, the corpse, the most sickening of wastes, is a border that has encroached upon everything. It is no longer I who expel. "I" is expelled. (pp. 3–4)

Within the biblical context, the corpse is also utterly abject. It signifies one of the most basic forms of pollution – the body without a soul. As a form of waste it represents the opposite of the spiritual, the religious symbolic: "Corpse fanciers, unconscious worshippers of a soulless body, are thus preeminent representatives of inimical religions, identified by their murderous cults. The priceless debt to great mother nature, from which the prohibitions of Yah-wistic speech separates us, is concealed in such pagan cults" (p. 109).

In relation to the horror film, it is relevant to note that several of the most popular horrific figures are "bodies without souls" (the vampire), the "living corpse" (the zombie), and the corpse-eater (the ghoul). Here the horror film constructs and confronts us with the fascinating, seductive aspect of abjection. What is also interesting is that such ancient figures of abjection as the vampire, the ghoul, the zombie, and the witch (one of whose many crimes was that she used corpses for her rites of magic) continue to provide some of the most compelling images of horror in the modern cinema. The werewolf, whose body signifies a collapse of the boundaries between human and animal, also belongs to this category.

Abjection also occurs where the individual fails to respect the law and where the individual is a hypocrite, a liar, a traitor: "Any crime, because it draws attention to the fragility of the law, is abject, but premeditated crime, cunning murder, hypocritical revenge are even more so because they heighten the display of such fragility. He who denies morality is not abject; there can be grandeur in amorality. . . . Abjection, on the other hand, is immoral, sinister, scheming, and shady" (p. 4). Thus, abject things are those which highlight the "fragility of the law" and which exist on the other side of the border that separates out the living subject from that which threatens its extinction. But abjection is not something of which the subject can ever feel free – it is always there, beckoning the self to take up its place, the place where meaning collapses. The subject, constructed in and through language, through a desire for meaning, is also spoken by the abject, the place of meaninglessness – thus, the subject is constantly beset by abjection which fascinates desire but which must be repelled for fear of self-annihilation. The crucial point is that abjection is always ambiguous. Like Bataille, Kristeva emphasizes the attraction, as well as the horror, of the undifferentiated:

> We may call it a border; abjection is above all ambiguity. Because, while releasing a hold, it does not radically cut off the subject from what threatens it – on the contrary, abjection acknowledges it to be in perpetual danger. But also because abjection itself is a composite of judgement and affect, of condemnation and yearning, of signs and drives. Abjection preserves what existed in the archaism of pre-objectal relationship. . . . (pp. 9–10)

To the extent that abjection works on the sociocultural arena, the horror film would appear to be, in at least three ways, an illustration of the work of abjection. First, the horror film abounds in images of abjection, foremost of which is the corpse, whole and mutilated, followed by an array of bodily wastes such as blood, vomit, saliva, sweat, tears, and putrifying flesh. In terms of Kristeva's notion of the border, when we say such-and-such a horror film "made me sick" or "scared the shit out of me,"[7] we are actually foregrounding that specific horror film as a "work of abjection" or "abjection at work" – in both a literal and metaphoric sense. Viewing the horror film signifies a desire not only for perverse pleasure (confronting sickening, horrific images, being filled with terror/desire for the undifferentiated) but also a desire, having taken pleasure in perversity, to throw up, throw out, eject the abject (from the safety of the spectator's seat).

Second, there is, of course, a sense in which the concept of a border is central to the construction of the monstrous in the horror film; that which crosses or threatens to cross the "border" is abject. Although the specific nature of the border changes from film to film, the function of the monstrous remains the same: to bring about an encounter between the symbolic order and that which threatens its stability. In some horror films the monstrous is produced at the border between human and inhuman, man and beast (*Dr. Jekyll and Mr. Hyde* [1931, 1941], *Creature from the Black Lagoon* [1954], *King Kong* [1933]); in others the border is between the normal and the supernatural, good and evil (*Carrie* [1976], *The Exorcist* [1973], *The Omen* [1976], *Rosemary's Baby* [1968]); or the monstrous is produced at the border which separates those who take up their proper gender roles from those who do not (*Psycho* [1960], *Dressed to Kill* [1980], *Reflection of Fear* [1971]); or the border is between normal and abnormal sexual desire (*Cruising* [1980], *The Hunger* [1983], *Cat People* [1942, 1982]).

In relation to the construction of the abject within religious discourses, it is interesting to note that various subgenres of the horror film seem to correspond to religious categories of abjection. For instance, blood as a religious abomination becomes a form of abjection in the "splatter" movie (*The Texas Chainsaw Massacre* [1974]); cannibalism, another religious abomination, is central to the "meat" movie (*Night of the Living Dead* [1968], *The Hills Have Eyes* [1977]); the corpse as abomination becomes the abject of ghoul and zombie movies (*The Evil Dead* [1982]; *Zombie Flesheaters* [1979]); blood as a taboo object within religion is central to the vampire film (*The Hunger*) as well as the horror film in general (*Bloodsucking Freaks* [a.k.a. *The Incredible Torture Show*, 1976]); human sacrifice as a religious abomination is constructed as the abject of virtually all horror films; and bodily disfigurement as a religious abomination is also central to the slash movie, particularly those in which woman is slashed, the mark a sign of her "difference," her impurity (*Dressed to Kill, Psycho*).

The Abject Mother

The third way in which the horror film illustrates the work of abjection refers to the construction of the maternal figure as abject. Kristeva argues that all individuals experience abjection at the time of their earliest attempts to break away from the mother.

She sees the mother–child relation as one marked by conflict: the child struggles to break free but the mother is reluctant to release it. Because of the "instability of the symbolic function" in relation to this most crucial area – "the prohibition placed on the maternal body (as a defense against autoeroticism and incest taboo)" (p. 14) – Kristeva argues that the maternal body becomes a site of conflicting desires. "Here, drives hold sway and constitute a strange space that I shall name, after Plato (*Timeus*, 48–53), a *chora*, a receptacle" (p. 14). The position of the child is rendered even more unstable because, while the mother retains a close hold over the child, it can serve to authenticate her existence – an existence which needs validation because of her problematic relation to the symbolic realm.

> It is a violent, clumsy breaking away, with the constant risk of falling back under the sway of a power as securing as it is stifling. The difficulty the mother has in acknowledging (or being acknowledged by) the symbolic realm – in other words, the problems she has with the phallus that her father or husband stands for – is not such as to help the future subject leave the natural mansion. (p. 13)

In the child's attempt to break away, the mother becomes an abject; thus, in this context, where the child struggles to become a separate subject, abjection becomes *"a precondition of narcissism"* (p. 13). Once again we can see abjection at work in the horror text where the child struggles to break away from the mother, representative of the archaic maternal figure, in a context in which the father is invariably absent (*Psycho, Carrie, The Birds* [1963]). In these films, the maternal figure is constructed as the monstrous-feminine. By refusing to relinquish her hold on her child, she prevents it from taking up its proper place in relation to the Symbolic. Partly consumed by the desire to remain locked in a blissful relationship with the mother and partly terrified of separation, the child finds it easy to succumb to the comforting pleasure of the dyadic relationship. Kristeva argues that a whole area of religion has assumed the function of tackling this danger:

> This is precisely where we encounter the rituals of defilement and their derivatives, which, based on the feeling of abjection and all converging on the maternal, attempt to symbolize the other threat to the subject: that of being swamped by the dual relationship, thereby risking the loss not of a part (castration) but of the totality of his living being. The function of these religious rituals is to ward off the subject's fear of his very own identity sinking irretrievably into the mother. (p. 64)

How, then, are prohibitions against contact with the mother enacted and enforced? In answering this question, Kristeva links the universal practices of rituals of defilement to the mother. She argues that within the practices of all rituals of defilement, polluting objects fall into two categories: excremental, which threatens identity from the outside, and menstrual, which threatens from within.

> Excrement and its equivalent (decay, infection, disease, corpse, etc.) stand for the danger to identity that comes from without: the ego threatened by the non-ego, society threatened by its outside, life by death. Menstrual blood, on the contrary, stands for the danger issuing

from within identity (social or sexual); it threatens the relationship between the sexes
within a social aggregate and, through internalization, the identity of each sex in the face
of sexual difference. (p. 71)

Both categories of polluting objects relate to the mother: the relation of menstrual blood
is self-evident; the association of excremental objects with the maternal figure is brought
about because of the mother's role in sphincteral training. Here Kristeva argues that
the subject's first contact with "authority" is with the maternal authority when the child
learns, through interaction with the mother, about its body: the shape of the body, the
clean and unclean, the proper and improper areas of the body. Kristeva refers to this
process as a "primal mapping of the body" that she calls "semiotic." She distinguishes
between maternal "authority" and "paternal laws": "Maternal authority is the trustee
of that mapping of the self's clean and proper body; it is distinguished from paternal
laws within which, with the phallic phase and acquisition of language, the destiny of
man will take shape" (p. 72). In her discussion of rituals of defilement in relation to the
Indian caste system, Kristeva draws a distinction between the maternal authority and
paternal law. She argues that the period of the "mapping of the self's clean and proper
body" is characterized by the exercise of "authority without guilt," a time when there
is a "fusion between mother and nature." However, the symbolic ushers in a "totally
different universe of socially signifying performances where embarrassment, shame,
guilt, desire etc. come into play – the order of the phallus." In the Indian context, these
two worlds exist harmoniously side by side because of the working of defilement rites.
Here Kristeva is referring to the practice of public defecation in India. She quotes
V. S. Naipaul, who says that no one ever mentions "in speech or in books, those squat-
ting figures, because, quite simply, no one sees them." Kristeva argues that this split
between the world of the mother (a universe without shame) and the world of the father
(a universe of shame) would, in other social contexts, produce psychosis; in India
it finds a "perfect socialization": "This may be because the setting up of the rite of
defilement takes on the function of the hyphen, the virgule, allowing the two universes
of *filth* and *prohibition* to brush lightly against each other without necessarily being
identified as such, as *object* and as *law*" (p. 74).

Images of blood, vomit, pus, shit, and so forth, are central to our culturally/socially
constructed notions of the horrific. They signify a split between two orders: the maternal authority and the law of the father. On the one hand, these images of bodily wastes
threaten a subject that is already constituted, in relation to the symbolic, as "whole and
proper." Consequently, they fill the subject – both the protagonist in the text and the
spectator in the cinema – with disgust and loathing. On the other hand, they also point
back to a time when a "fusion between mother and nature" existed; when bodily wastes,
while set apart from the body, were not seen as objects of embarrassment and shame.
Their presence in the horror film may evoke a response of disgust from the audience,
situated as it is within the symbolic, but at a more archaic level the representation of
bodily wastes may evoke pleasure in breaking the taboo of filth – sometimes described
as a pleasure in perversity – and a pleasure in returning to that time when the mother-
child relationship was marked by an untrammeled pleasure in "playing" with the body
and its wastes.

The modern horror film often "plays" with its audience, saturating it with scenes of blood and gore, deliberately pointing to the fragility of the symbolic order in the domain of the body which never ceases to signal the repressed world of the mother. This is particularly evident in *The Exorcist*, where the world of the symbolic, represented by the priest-as-father, and the world of the presymbolic, represented by woman aligned with the devil, clashes head on in scenes where the foulness of woman is signified by her putrid, filthy body covered in blood, urine, excrement, and bile. Significantly, a pubescent girl about to menstruate played the woman who is possessed – in one scene blood from her wounded genitals mingles with menstrual blood to provide one of the film's key images of horror. In *Carrie*, the film's most monstrous act occurs when the couple are drenched in pig's blood, which symbolizes menstrual blood – women are referred to in the film as "pigs," women "bleed like pigs," and the pig's blood runs down Carrie's body at a moment of intense pleasure, just as her own menstrual blood runs down her legs during a similar pleasurable moment when she enjoys her body in the shower. Here women's blood and pig's blood flow together, signifying horror, shame, and humiliation. In this film, however, the mother speaks for the symbolic, identifying with an order that has defined women's sexuality as the source of all evil and menstruation as the sign of sin. The horror film's obsession with blood, particularly the bleeding body of woman, where her body is transformed into the "gaping wound," suggests that castration anxiety is a central concern of the horror film – particularly the slasher subgenre. Woman's body is slashed and mutilated, not only to signify her own castrated state, but also the possibility of castration for the male. In the guise of a "madman" he enacts on her body the one act he most fears for himself, transforming her entire body into a bleeding wound.

Kristeva's semiotic posits a preverbal dimension of language that relates to sounds and tone and to direct expression of the drives and physical contact with the maternal figure: "it is dependent upon meaning, but in a way that is not that of *linguistic* signs nor of the *symbolic* order they found" (p. 72). With the subject's entry into the symbolic, which separates the child from the mother, the maternal figure and the authority she signifies are repressed. Kristeva argues that it is the function of defilement rites, particularly those relating to menstrual and excremental objects, to point to the "boundary" between the maternal semiotic authority and the paternal symbolic law:

> Through language and within highly hierarchical religious institutions, man hallucinates partial "objects" – witnesses to an archaic differentiation of the body on its way toward ego identity, which is also sexual identity. The *defilement* from which ritual protects us is neither sign nor matter. Within the rite that extracts it from repression and depraved desire, defilement is the translinguistic spoor of the most archaic boundaries of the self's clean and proper body. In that sense, if it is a jettisoned object, it is so from the mother. . . . By means of the symbolic institution of ritual, that is to say, by means of a system of ritual exclusions, the partial-object consequently becomes *scription* – an inscription of limits, an emphasis placed not on the (paternal) Law but on (maternal) Authority through the very signifying order. (p. 73)

Kristeva argues that, historically, it has been the function of religion to purify the abject but with the disintegration of these "historical forms" of religion, the work of purification now rests solely with "that catharsis par excellence called art" (p. 17).

> In a world in which the Other has collapsed, the aesthetic task – a descent into the founda-
> tions of the symbolic construct – amounts to retracing the fragile limits of the speaking
> being, closest to its dawn, to the bottomless "primacy" constituted by primal repression.
> Through that experience, which is nevertheless managed by the Other, "subject" and
> "object" push each other away, confront each other, collapse, and start again – inseparable,
> contaminated, condemned, at the boundary of what is assimilable, thinkable: abject.
> (p. 18)

This, I would argue, is also the central ideological project of the popular horror film – purification of the abject through a "descent into the foundations of the symbolic construct." In this way, the horror film brings about a confrontation with the abject (the corpse, bodily wastes, the monstrous-feminine) in order, finally, to eject the abject and redraw the boundaries between the human and nonhuman. As a form of modern defilement rite, the horror film works to separate out the symbolic order from all that threatens its stability, particularly the mother and all that her universe signifies. In Kristeva's terms, this means separating out the maternal authority from paternal law.

As mentioned earlier, the central problem with Kristeva's theory is that it can be read in a prescriptive rather than a descriptive sense. This problem is rendered more acute by the fact that, although Kristeva distinguishes between the maternal and paternal figures when she speaks of the subject who is being constituted, she never distinguishes between the child as male or female. Obviously, the female child's experience of the semiotic *chora* must be different from the male's experience in relation to the way it is spoken to, handled, and so on. For the mother is already constituted as a gendered subject living within a patriarchal order and thus aware of the differences between the "masculine" and the "feminine" in relation to questions of desire. Thus, the mother might relate to a male child with a more acute sense of pride and pleasure. It is also possible that the child, depending on its gender, might find it more or less difficult to reject the mother for the father. Kristeva does not consider any of these issues. Nor does she distinguish between the relation of the adult male and female subject to rituals of defilement – for instance, menstruation taboos, where one imagines notions of the gendered subject would be of crucial importance. How, for instance, do women relate to rites of defilement such as menstruation rites, which reflect so negatively on them? How do women within a specific cultural group see themselves in relation to taboos that construct their procreative functions as abject? Is it possible to intervene in the social construction of woman as abject? Or is the subject's relationship to the processes of abjectivity, as they are constructed within subjectivity and language, completely unchangeable? Is the abjection of women a precondition for the continuation of sociality? Kristeva never asks questions of this order. Consequently her theory of abjection could be interpreted as an apology for the establishment of sociality at the cost of women's equality. If, however, we read it as descriptive, as one attempting to explain the origins of patriarchal culture, then it provides us with an extremely useful hypothesis for an investigation of the representation of women in the horror film.[8]

Alien and the Primal Scene

The science fiction horror film *Alien* (1979) is a complex representation of the monstrous-feminine in terms of the maternal figure as perceived within a patriarchal ideology. She is there in the text's scenarios of the primal scene, of birth and death; she is there in her many guises as the treacherous mother, the oral sadistic mother, the mother as primordial abyss; and she is there in the film's images of blood, of the all-devouring vagina, the toothed vagina, the vagina as Pandora's box; and finally she is there in the chameleon figure of the alien, the monster as fetish object of and for the mother. But it is the archaic mother, the reproductive/generative mother, who haunts the mise-en-scène of the film's first section, with its emphasis on different representations of the primal scene.

According to Freud, every child either watches its parents in the act of sexual intercourse or has fantasies about that act – fantasies that relate to the problem of origins. Freud left open the question of the cause of the fantasy but suggested that it may initially be aroused by "an observation of the sexual intercourse of animals."[9] In his study of "the Wolf Man," Freud argued that the child did not initially observe the parents in the act of sexual intercourse but rather witnessed the copulation of animals whose behavior the child then displaced onto the parents. In situations where the child actually witnesses sexual intercourse between its parents, Freud argued that all children arrive at the same conclusion: "They adopt what may be called a *sadistic view of coition*."[10] If the child perceives the primal scene as a monstrous act – whether in reality or fantasy – it may fantasize animals or mythical creatures as taking part in the scenario. Possibly the many mythological stories in which humans copulate with animals and other creatures (Europa and Zeus, Leda and the Swan) are reworkings of the primal scene narrative. The Sphinx, with her lion's body and woman's face, is an interesting figure in this context. Freud suggested that the Riddle of the Sphinx was probably a distorted version of the great riddle that faces all children – Where do babies come from? An extreme form of the primal fantasy is that of "observing parental intercourse while one is still an unborn baby in the womb."[11]

One of the major concerns of the science fiction horror film (*Alien, The Thing* [1951, 1982], *Invasion of the Body Snatchers* [1956, 1978], *Altered States* [1980]) is the reworking of the primal scene in relation to the representation of other forms of copulation and procreation. *Alien* presents various representations of the primal scene. Behind each of these lurks the figure of the archaic mother, that is, the image of the mother in her generative function – the mother as the origin of all life. This archaic figure is somewhat different from the mother of the semiotic *chora* posed by Kristeva in that the latter is the pre-Oedipal mother who exists in relation to the family and the symbolic order. The concept of the parthenogenic, archaic mother adds another dimension to the maternal figure and presents us with a new way of understanding how patriarchal ideology works to deny the "difference" of woman in her cinematic representation.

The first birth scene occurs in *Alien* at the beginning, where the camera/spectator explores the inner space of the mother-ship whose life support system is a computer aptly named "Mother." This exploratory sequence of the inner body of the Mother culminates with a long tracking shot down one of the corridors which leads to a womblike chamber where the crew of seven are woken up from their protracted sleep by Mother's voice monitoring a call for help from a nearby planet. The seven astronauts emerge slowly from their sleep pods in what amounts to a rebirthing scene that is marked by a fresh, antiseptic atmosphere. In outer space, birth is a well-controlled, clean, painless affair. There is no blood, trauma, or terror. This scene could be interpreted as a primal fantasy in which the human subject is born fully developed – even copulation is redundant.

The second representation of the primal scene takes place when three of the crew enter the body of the unknown spaceship through a "vaginal" opening: the ship is shaped like a horseshoe, its curved sides like two long legs spread apart at the entrance. They travel along a corridor that seems to be made of a combination of inorganic and organic material – as if the inner space of this ship were alive. Compared to the atmosphere of the *Nostromo*, however, this ship is dark, dank, and mysterious. A ghostly light glimmers, and the sounds of their movements echo throughout the caverns. In the first chamber, the three explorers find a huge alien life form that appears to have been dead for a long time. Its bones are bent outward as if it exploded from the inside. One of the trio, Kane, is lowered down a shaft into the gigantic womblike chamber in which rows of eggs are hatching. Kane approaches one of the eggs; as he touches it with his gloved hand, it opens out, revealing a mass of pulsating flesh. Suddenly the monstrous thing inside leaps up and attaches itself to Kane's helmet, its tail penetrating Kane's mouth in order to fertilize itself inside his stomach. Despite the warnings of Ripley, Kane is taken back on board the *Nostromo* where the alien rapidly completes its gestation processes inside Kane.

This representation of the primal scene recalls Freud's reference to an extreme primal-scene fantasy in which the subject imagines traveling back inside the womb to watch her or his parents having sexual intercourse, perhaps to watch her or his own conception. Here three astronauts explore the gigantic, cavernous, malevolent womb of the mother. Two members of the group watch the enactment of the primal scene in which Kane is violated in an act of phallic penetration – by the father or phallic mother? Kane himself is guilty of the strongest transgression; he actually peers into the egg/womb in order to investigate its mysteries. In so doing, he becomes a part of the primal scene, taking up the place of the mother, the one who is penetrated, the one who bears the offspring of the union. The primal scene is represented as violent and monstrous (the union is between human and alien), and is mediated by the question of incestuous desire. All restagings of the primal scene raise the question of incest, as the beloved parent (usually the mother) is with a rival. The first birth scene, in which the astronauts emerge from their sleep pods, could be viewed as representation of incestuous desire par excellence: the father is completely absent; here the mother is sole parent and sole life support.

From this forbidden union, the monstrous creature is born. But man, not woman, is the "mother," and Kane dies in agony as the alien gnaws its way through his stomach.

The birth of the alien from Kane's stomach plays on what Freud described as a common misunderstanding that many children have about birth: that the mother is somehow impregnated through the mouth – she may eat a special food – and the baby grows in her stomach from which it is also born. Here we have a third version of the primal scene.

A further version of the primal scene – almost a convention of the science fiction film[12] – occurs when smaller crafts or bodies are ejected from the mother ship into outer space, although the ejected body sometimes remains attached to the mother ship by a long lifeline or umbilical cord. This scene is presented in two separate ways: when Kane's body, wrapped in a white shroud, is ejected from the mother ship; and when the small space capsule, in which Ripley is trying to escape from the alien, is expelled from the under-belly of the mother ship. In the former, the "mother's" body has become hostile; it contains the alien whose one purpose is to kill and devour all of Mother's children. In the latter birth scene the living infant is ejected from the malevolent body of the "mother" to avoid destruction; in this scenario, the "mother's" body explodes at the moment of giving birth.

Although the "mother" as a figure does not appear in these sequences – nor indeed in the entire film – her presence forms a vast backdrop for the enactment of all the events. She is there in the images of birth, the representations of the primal scene, the womblike imagery, the long winding tunnels leading to inner chambers, the rows of hatching eggs, the body of the mother ship, the voice of the life-support system, and the birth of the alien. She is the generative mother, the pre-phallic mother, the being who exists prior to knowledge of the phallus.

Alien and the Monstrous-Feminine

In explaining his difficulty in uncovering the role of the mother in the early development of infants, Freud complained of the almost "prehistoric" remoteness of this "Minoan-Mycenaean" stage: "Everything in the sphere of this first attachment to the mother seemed to me so difficult to grasp in analysis – so grey with age and shadowy and almost impossible to revivify – that it was as if it had succumbed to an especially inexorable repression."[13] Just as the Oedipus complex tends to hide the pre-Oedipal phase in Freudian theory, the figure of the father, in the Lacanian rewriting of Freud, obscures the mother-child relationship of the imaginary. In contrast to the maternal figure of the Lacanian imaginary, Kristeva posits another dimension to the mother – she is associated with the preverbal or the semiotic and as such tends to disrupt the symbolic order.[14]

I think it is possible to open up the mother question still further and posit an even more archaic maternal figure, to go back to mythological narratives of the generative, parthenogenetic mother – that archaic figure who gives birth to all living things. She exists in the mythology of all human cultures as the mother-goddess who alone created the heavens and earth. In China she was known as Nu Kwa, in Mexico as Coatlicue, in Greece as Gaia (literally meaning "earth"), and in Sumer as Nammu. In "Moses and Monotheism," Freud attempted to account for the historical existence of the great mother-goddesses: "It is likely that the mother-goddesses originated at the time of the curtailment of the matriarchy, as a compensation for the slight upon the mothers. The male deities appear first as sons beside the great mothers and only later clearly assume the features of father-figures. These male gods of polytheism reflect the conditions during the patriarchal age."[15] Freud proposed that human society developed through stages from patriarchy to matriarchy and finally back to patriarchy. During the first, primitive people lived in small hordes, each one dominated by a jealous, powerful father who possessed all the females of the group. One day the sons, who had been banished to the outskirts of the group, overthrew the father – whose body they devoured – in order to secure his power and to take his women for themselves. Overcome by guilt, they later attempted to revoke the deed by setting up a totem as a substitute for the father and by renouncing the women whom they had liberated. The sons were forced to give up the women, whom they all wanted to possess, in order to preserve the group, which otherwise would have been destroyed as the sons fought among themselves. In "Totem and Taboo," Freud suggests that here "the germ of the institution of matriarchy" may have originated.[16] Eventually, however, this new form of social organization, constructed upon the taboo against murder and incest, was replaced by the reestablishment of a patriarchal order. He pointed out that the sons had "thus created out of their filial sense of guilt the two fundamental taboos of totemism, which for that very reason inevitably corresponded to the two repressed wishes of the Oedipus complex."[17]

Freud's account of the origins of patriarchal civilization is generally regarded as mythical. Lévi-Strauss points out that it is "a fair account not of the beginnings of civilization, but of its present state" in that it expresses "in symbolical form an inveterate fantasy" – the desire to murder the father and possess the mother.[18] In her discussion of "Totem and Taboo," Kristeva argues that a "strange slippage" (p. 56) has taken place in that, although Freud points out that morality is founded on the taboos of murder and incest, his argument concentrates on the first to the virtual exclusion of the latter. Yet, Kristeva argues, the "woman – or mother – image haunts a large part of that book and keeps shaping its background" (p. 57). She poses the question:

> Could the sacred be, whatever its variants, a two-sided formation? One aspect founded by murder and the social bond made up of a murderer's guilt-ridden atonement, with all the projective mechanisms and obsessive rituals that accompany it; and another aspect, like a lining, more secret and invisible, non-representable, oriented toward those uncertain spaces of unstable identity, toward the fragility – both threatening and fusional – of the archaic dyad, toward the non-separation of subject/object, on which language has no hold but one woven of fright and repulsion? (pp. 57–8)

From the above, it is clear that the figure of the mother in both the history of human sociality and in the history of the individual subject poses immense problems. Freud attempts to account for the existence of the mother-goddess figure by posing a matriarchal period in historical times while admitting that everything to do with the "first attachment to the mother" is deeply repressed – "grey with age and shadowy and almost impossible to revivify." Nowhere does he attempt to specify the nature of this matriarchal period and its implications for his own psychoanalytical theory, specifically his theory of the Oedipus complex, which, as Lacan points out, "can only appear in a patriarchal form in the institution of the family."[19] Kristeva criticizes Freud for failing to deal adequately with incest and the mother questions while using the same mystifying language to refer to the mother; the other aspect of the sacred is "like a lining," "secret and invisible," "non-representable." In his rereading of Freud, Lacan mystifies the figure of woman even further: "the woman is not-all, there is always something with her which eludes discourse."[20] Further, all three writers conflate the archaic mother with the mother of the dyadic and triadic relationship. They refer to her as a "shadowy" figure (Freud); as "non-representable" (Kristeva); as the "abyss of the female organ from which all life comes forth" (Lacan),[21] then make no clear attempt to distinguish this aspect of the maternal imago from the protective/suffocating mother of the pre-Oedipal or the mother as object of sexual jealousy and desire as she is represented in the Oedipal configuration.

The maternal figure constructed within and by the writings of Freud, Lacan, and Kristeva is inevitably the mother of the dyadic or triadic relationship, although the latter figure is more prominent. Even when she is represented as the mother of the imaginary, of the dyadic relationship, she is still constructed as the pre-Oedipal mother – that is, as a figure about to "take up a place" in the symbolic, as a figure always in relation to the father, the representative of the phallus. Without her "lack," he cannot signify its opposite – lack of a lack or presence. But if we posit a more archaic dimension to the mother – the mother as originating womb – we can at least begin to talk about the maternal figure as *outside* the patriarchal family constellation. In this context, the mother-goddess narratives can be read as primal-scene narratives in which the mother is the sole parent. She is also the subject, not the object, of narrativity.

For instance, in the Spider Woman myth of the North American Indians, there was only the Spider Woman, who spun the universe into existence and then created two daughters from whom all life flowed. She is also the Thought Woman or Wise Woman who knows the secrets of the universe. Within the Oedipus narrative, however, she becomes the Sphinx, who also knows the answers to the secret life, but here her situation has been changed. She is no longer the subject of the narrative; she has become the object of the narrative of the male hero. After he has solved her riddle, she will destroy herself. The Sphinx is an ambiguous figure; she knows the secret of life and is thereby linked to the mother-goddess, but her name, which is derived from "sphincter," suggests she is the mother of toilet training, the pre-Oedipal mother who must be repudiated by the son so that he can take up his proper place in the symbolic. It is interesting that Oedipus has always been seen to have committed two horrific crimes: patricide and incest. But his encounter with the Sphinx, which leads to her death, suggests he is also responsible for another horrific crime – that of matricide. For the Sphinx, like the Medusa, is a mother-goddess figure; they are both variants of the same mythological mother who gave birth to all life. Lévi-Strauss has argued that a major issue in the Oedipus myth is the problem of whether man is born from woman. This myth is also central to *Alien*: "Although the problem obviously cannot be solved, the Oedipus myth provides a kind of logical tool which relates the original problem – born from one or born from two? – to the derivative problem: born from different or born from same?"[22]

The Medusa, whose head signifies, according to Freud, the female genitals in their terrifying aspect, also represents the procreative function of woman. The blood that flows from her severed head gives birth to Pegasus and Chrysaor. Although Neptune is supposed to be the father, the nature of the birth once again suggests the partheno-genetic mother. Teresa de Lauretis argues that "to say that narrative is the production of Oedipus is to say that each reader – male or female – is constrained and defined within the two positions of a sexual difference thus conceived: male-hero-human, on the side of the subject; and female-obstacle-boundary-space, on the other."[23] If we apply her definition to narratives that deal specifically with the archaic mother – such as the Oedipus and Perseus myths – we can see that the "obstacle" relates specifically to the question of origins and is an attempt to repudiate the idea of woman as the source of life, woman as sole parent, woman as archaic mother.

Roger Dadoun, also referring to this archaic maternal figure, describes her as

> . . . a maternal thing situated on this side of good and evil, on this side of all organized form, on this side of all events – a totalizing, oceanic mother, a "mysterious and profound unity," arousing in the subject the anguish of fusion and of dissolution; the mother prior to the uncovering of the essential *béance* [gap], of the *pas-de-phallus* [absence of the phallus], the mother who is pure fantasm, in the sense that she is posed as an omnipresent and all-powerful totality, an absolute being, only in the intuition – she does not have a phallus – which deposes her. . . .[24]

Dadoun places emphasis on her "totalizing, oceanic" presence. I would stress her archaism in relation to her generative powers – the mother who gives birth all by herself, the original parent, the godhead of all fertility, and the origin of procreation. What is most interesting about the mythological figure of woman as the source of all life (a role taken over by the male god of monotheistic religions) is that, within patriarchal signifying practices, particularly the horror film, she is reconstructed and represented as a *negative* figure, one associated with the dread of the generative mother seen only as the abyss, the monstrous vagina, the origin of all life threatening to reabsorb what it once birthed. Kristeva also represents her in this negative light: "Fear of the uncontrollable generative mother repels me from the body; I give up cannibalism because abjection (of the mother) leads me toward respect for the body of the other, my fellow man, my brother" (pp. 78–9).

In this context it is interesting to note that Freud linked the womb to the *unheimlich*, the uncanny:

> It often happens that neurotic men declare that they feel that there is something uncanny about the female genital organs. This *unheimlich* place, however, is the entrance to the former *Heim* [home] of all human beings, to the place where each one of us lived once upon a time and in the beginning. There is a joke saying that "Love is home-sicknesses"; and whenever a man dreams of a place or a country and says to himself, while he is still dreaming: "this place is familiar to me, I've been here before," we may interpret the place as being his mother's genitals or her body.[25]

Freud also supported, and elaborated upon, Schelling's definition of the uncanny as "something which ought to have remained hidden but has come to light."²⁶ In horror films such as *Alien*, we are given a representation of the female genitals and the womb as uncanny – horrific objects of dread and fascination. Unlike the mythological mother narratives, here the archaic mother, like the Sphinx and the Medusa, is seen only in a negative light. But the central characteristic of the archaic mother is her total dedication to the generative, procreative principle. She is outside morality and the law. Ash's eulogy to the alien is a description of this mother: "I admire its purity; a survivor unclouded by conscience, remorse or delusions of morality."

Clearly, it is difficult to separate out completely the figure of the archaic mother, as defined above, from other aspects of the maternal figure – the maternal authority of Kristeva's semiotic, the mother of Lacan's imaginary, the phallic woman, the castrated woman. While the different figures signify quite separate things about the monstrous – feminine, as constructed in the horror film, each one is also only part of the whole – a different aspect of the maternal figure. At times the horrific nature of the monstrous-feminine is totally dependent on the merging together of all aspects of the maternal figure into one – the horrifying image of woman as archaic mother, phallic woman, and castrated body represented as a single figure within the horror film. However, the archaic mother is clearly present in two distinct ways in the horror film.

First, the archaic mother – constructed as a negative force – is represented in her phantasmagoric aspects in many horror texts, particularly the science fiction horror film. We see her as the gaping, cannibalistic bird's mouth in *The Giant Claw* (1957); the terrifying spider of *The Incredible Shrinking Man* (1957); the toothed vagina/womb of *Jaws* (1975); and the fleshy, pulsating womb of *The Thing* and *Poltergeist* (1982). What is common to all of these images of horror is the voracious maw, the mysterious black hole that signifies female genitalia as a monstrous sign threatening to give birth to equally horrific offspring as well as threatening to incorporate everything in its path. This is the generative archaic mother, constructed within patriarchal ideology as the primeval "black hole." This, of course, is also the hole that is opened up by the absence of the penis, the horrifying sight of the mother's genitals – proof that castration can occur.

However, in the texts cited above, the emphasis is not on castration; rather it is the gestating, all-devouring womb of the archaic mother that generates the horror. Nor are these images of the womb constructed in relation to the penis of the father. Unlike the female genitalia, the womb cannot be constructed as a "lack" in relation to the penis. The womb is not the site of castration anxiety. Rather, the womb signifies "fullness" or "emptiness" but always it is its *own point of reference*. This is why we need to posit a more archaic dimension to the mother. For the concept of the archaic mother allows for a notion of the feminine that does not depend for its definition on a concept of the masculine. The term "archaic mother" signifies woman as sexual difference. In contrast, the maternal figure of the pre-Oedipal is always represented in relation to the penis – the phallic mother who later becomes the castrated mother. Significantly, there is an attempt in *Alien* to appropriate the procreative function of the mother, to represent a man giving birth, to deny the mother as signifier of sexual difference – but here birth can exist only as the other face of death.

Second, the archaic mother is present in all horror films as the blackness of extinction – death. The desires and fears invoked by the image of the archaic mother, as a force that threatens to reincorporate what it once gave birth to, are always there in the horror text – all-pervasive, all-encompassing – because of the constant presence of death. The desire to return to the original oneness of things, to return to the mother/womb, is primarily a desire for nondifferentiation. If, as Georges Bataille argues, life signifies discontinuity and separateness, and death signifies continuity and nondifferentiation,[27] then the desire for and attraction of death suggests also a desire to return to the state of original oneness with the mother. As this desire to merge occurs after differentiation – that is, after the subject has developed as separate, autonomous self – then it is experienced as a form of psychic death. In this sense, the confrontation with death, as represented in the horror film, gives rise to a terror of self-disintegration, of losing one's self or ego – often represented cinematically by a screen that becomes black, signifying the obliteration of self, the self of the protagonist in the film and the spectator in the cinema. This has important consequences for the positioning of the spectator in the cinema.

One of the most interesting structures operating in the screen-spectator relationship relates to the sight/site of the monstrous within the horror text. In contrast to the conventional viewing structures working within other variants of the classic text, the horror film does not constantly work to suture the spectator into the viewing processes. Instead, an unusual phenomenon arises whereby the suturing processes are momentarily undone while the horrific image on the screen challenges the viewer to run the risk of continuing to look. Here I refer to those moments in the horror film when the spectator, unable to stand the images of horror unfolding, is forced to look away, to not-look, to look anywhere but at the screen. Strategies of identification are temporarily broken, as the spectator is constructed in the place of horror, the place where the sight/site can no longer be endured, the place where pleasure in looking is transformed into pain and the spectator is punished for his or her voyeuristic desires. Perhaps this should be referred to as a *fifth* look operating alongside the other "looks" that have been theorized in relation to the screen-spectator relationship.[28]

Confronted by the sight of the monstrous, the viewing subject is put into crisis. Boundaries, designed to keep the abject at bay, threaten to disintegrate, collapse. According to Lacan, the self is constituted in a process which he called the "mirror phase," in which the child perceives its own body as a unified whole in an image it receives from outside itself. Thus, the concept of identity is a structure that depends on identification with another. Identity is an imaginary construct, formed in a state of alienation, grounded in misrecognition. Because the self is constructed on an illusion, Lacan argues that it is always in danger of regressing:

> Here we see the ego, in its essential resistance to the elusive process of Becoming, to the variations of Desire. This illusion of unity, in which a human being is always looking forward to self-mastery, entails a constant danger of sliding back again into the chaos from which he started; it hangs over the abyss of a dizzy Assent in which one can perhaps see the very essence of Anxiety.[29]

The horror film puts the viewing subject's sense of a unified self into crisis, specifically in those moments when the image on the screen becomes too threatening or horrific to watch, when the abject threatens to draw the viewing subject to the place "where meaning collapses," the place of death. By not-looking, the spectator is able momentarily to withdraw identification from the image on the screen in order to reconstruct the boundary between self and screen and reconstitute the self that is threatened with disintegration. This process of reconstitution of the self is reaffirmed by the conventional ending of the horror narrative in which the monster is usually "named" and destroyed.[30]

Fear of losing oneself and one's boundaries is made more acute in a society which values boundaries over continuity and separateness over sameness. Given that death is represented in the horror film as a threat to the self's boundaries, symbolized by the threat of the monster, death images are most likely to cause the spectator to look away, to not-look. Because the archaic mother is closely associated with death in its negative aspects, her presence is marked negatively within the project of the horror film. Both signify a monstrous obliteration of the self and both are linked to the demonic. Again Kristeva presents a negative image of the maternal figure in her relationship to death: "What is the demoniacal – an inescapable, repulsive, and yet nurtured abomination? The fantasy of an archaic force, on the near side of separation, unconscious, tempting us to the point of losing our differences, our speech, our life; to the point of aphasia, decay, opprobrium, and death?" (p. 107).

Alien collapses the image of the threatening archaic mother, signifying woman as "difference," into the more recognized figure of the pre-Oedipal mother.[31] This occurs in relation to two images of the monstrous-feminine: the oral-sadistic mother and the phallic mother. Kane's transgressive disturbance of the egg/womb initiates a transformation of its latent aggressivity into an active, phallic enemy. The horror then played out can be read in relation to Kristeva's concept of the semiotic *chora*. As discussed earlier, Kristeva argues that the maternal body becomes the site of conflicting desires (the semiotic *chora*). These desires are constantly staged and restaged in the workings of the horror narrative where the subject is left alone, usually in a strange, hostile place, and forced to confront an unnameable terror, the monster. The monster represents both the subject's fears of being alone, of being separate from the mother, and the threat of annihilation – often through reincorporation. As oral-sadistic mother, the monster threatens to reabsorb the child she once nurtured. Thus, the monster, like the abject, is ambiguous; it both repels and attracts.

In *Alien*, each of the crew members comes face to face with the alien in a scene whose mise-en-scène is coded to suggest a monstrous, malevolent maternal figure. They watch with fascinated horror as the baby alien gnaws its way through Kane's stomach; Dallas, the captain, encounters the alien after he has crawled along the ship's enclosed, womblike air ducts; and the other three members are cannibalized in a frenzy of blood in scenes that emphasize the alien's huge razor-sharp teeth, signifying the monstrous oral-sadistic mother. Apart from the scene of Kane's death, all the death sequences occur in dimly lit, enclosed, threatening spaces reminiscent of the giant hatchery where Kane first encounters the pulsating egg. In these death sequences the terror of being abandoned is matched only by the fear of reincorporation. This scenario, which enacts the conflicting desires at play in the semiotic *chora*, is staged within the body of the mother-ship, the vessel that the space travelers initially trust, until Mother herself is revealed as a treacherous figure programmed to sacrifice the lives of the crew in the interests of the company.

The other face of the monstrous-feminine in *Alien* is the phallic mother. Freud argued that the male child could either accept the threat of castration, thus ending the Oedipus complex, or disavow it. The latter response requires him to mitigate his horror at the sight of the mother's genitals – proof that castration can occur – with a fetish object that substitutes for her missing penis. For him, she is still the phallic mother, the penis-woman. In "Medusa's Head" Freud argued that the head with its hair of writhing snakes represents the terrifying genitals of the mother, but that this head also functions as a fetish object: "The hair upon the Medusa's head is frequently represented in works of art in the form of snakes, and these once again are derived from the castration complex. It is a remarkable fact that, however frightening they may be in themselves, they nevertheless serve actually as a mitigation of horror, for they replace the penis, the absence of which is the cause of horror."[32] Freud noted that a display of the female genitals makes a woman "unapproachable and repels all sexual desires." He refers to the section in Rabelais which relates "how the Devil took flight when the woman showed him her vulva."[33] Perseus' solution is to look only at a reflection, a mirror image of her genitals. As with patriarchal ideology, his shield reflects an "altered" representation, a vision robbed of its threatening aspects. The full difference of the mother is denied; she is constructed as other, displayed before the gaze of the conquering male hero, then destroyed.[34] The price paid is the destruction of sexual heterogeneity and repression of the maternal signifier. The fetishization of the mother's genitals could occur in those texts where the maternal figure is represented in her phantasmagoric aspects as the gaping, voracious vagina/womb. Do aspects of these images work to mitigate the horror by offering a substitute for the penis?

Roger Dadoun argues very convincingly that the Dracula variant of the vampire movie is "an illustration of the work of the fetish function":[35]

> . . . against the primitive identification with the mother, a phallus; against the anguish of psychotic break-down, sexuality; against spatio-temporal disorganization, a ritual – and this is what is fabricated, we could say, on the positive slopes of fetishism, a sexualized phallic object, it is as rigid and impressive as it is fragile and threatened, where we will perhaps have the pleasure of recognizing one of the familiar figures of horror film, Count Dracula.[36]

Dadoun argues that the archaic mother exists as a "non-presence . . . signifying an extremely archaic mode of presence."[37] Signs of the archaic mother in the Dracula film are the small, enclosed village; the pathway through the forest that leads like an umbilical cord to the castle; the central place of enclosure with its winding stairways, spider-webs, dark vaults, worm-eaten staircases, dust, and damp earth – "all elements which come back to the *imago* of the bad archaic mother."[38] At the center of this, Dracula himself materializes. With his black cape, pointed teeth, rigid body – carried "like an erect phallus" – piercing eyes, and "penetrating look,"[39] he is the fetish form, "a substitute of the maternal phallus."[40]

It is clear, nevertheless, since the threat comes from the absent maternal phallus, that the principal defense is sex. The vampire, markedly fascinated by the maternal *pas-de-phallus* and identifying himself with the archaic mother for lack of having a phallus, becomes phallus; he transfers a default of *having* to the plan of an illusory *being*.[41]

As he emerges in Dadoun's argument, the Dracula figure is very much acting on behalf of the mother – he desires to be the phallus for the mother. When he is finally penetrated by the stake, his heart is "revealed as hollow, a gash, or a gaping wound – it is castration made flesh, blood and *béance* [absence] . . . ."[42] However, it is possible that we could theorize fetishism differently by asking: For whom is the fetish-object a fetish? The male or female subject? In general, the fetishist is usually assumed to be male, although Freud did allow that female fetishism was a possibility.[43] The notion of female fetishism is much neglected, although it is present in various patriarchal discourses.

Mary Kelly argues that "it would be a mistake to confine women to the realm of repression, excluding the possibility, for example, of female fetishism":

When Freud describes castration fears for the woman, this imaginary scenario takes the form of losing her loved objects, especially her children; the child is going to grow up, leave her, reject her, perhaps die. In order to delay, disavow that separation she has already in a way acknowledged, the woman tends to fetishise the child: by dressing him up, by continuing to feed him no matter how old he gets, or simply by having another "little one."[44]

In *The Interpretation of Dreams*, Freud discusses the way in which the doubling of a penis symbol indicates an attempt to stave off castration anxieties.[45] Juliet Mitchell refers to doubling as a sign of a female castration complex: "We can see the significance of this for women, as dreams of repeated number of children – 'little ones' – are given the same import."[46] In this context, female fetishism represents an attempt by the female subject to continue to "have" the phallus, to take up a "positive" place in relation to the symbolic.

Female fetishism is clearly represented within many horror texts – as instances of patriarchal signifying practices – but only in relation to male fears and anxieties about women and the question What do women want? (*The Birds, Cat People, Alien, The Thing*). Women as yet do not speak their own "fetishistic" desires within the popular cinema – if, indeed, women have such desires. The notion of female fetishism is represented in *Alien* in the figure of the monster. The creature is the mother's phallus, attributed to the maternal figure by a phallocentric ideology terrified at the thought that women might desire to have the phallus. The monster as fetish object is not there to meet the desires of the male fetishist, but rather to signify the monstrousness of woman's desire to have the phallus.

In *Alien* the monstrous creature is constructed as the phallus of the negative mother. The image of the archaic mother – threatening because it signifies woman as difference rather than constructed as opposition – is, once again, collapsed into the figure of the pre-Oedipal mother. By relocating the figure of woman within an Oedipal scenario, her image can be recuperated and controlled. The womb, even if represented negatively, is a greater threat than the mother's phallus. As phallic mother, woman is again represented as monstrous. What is horrific is her desire to cling to her offspring in order to continue to "have the phallus." Her monstrous desire is concretized in the figure of the alien, the creature whose deadly mission is represented as the same as that of the archaic mother – to reincorporate and destroy all life.

If we consider *Alien* in the light of a theory of female fetishism, then the chameleon nature of the alien begins to make sense. Its changing appearance represents a form of doubling or multiplication of the phallus, pointing to the mother's desire to stave off her castration. The alien is the mother's phallus, a fact made perfectly clear in the birth scene when the infant alien rises from Kane's stomach and holds itself erect, glaring angrily around the room, before screeching off into the depths of the ship. But the alien is more than a phallus; it is also coded as a toothed vagina, the monstrous-feminine as the cannibalistic mother. A large part of the ideological project of *Alien* is the representation of the maternal fetish object as an "alien" or foreign shape. This is why the body of the heroine becomes so important at the end of the film.

Much has been written about the final scene, in which Ripley (Sigourney Weaver) undresses before the camera, on the grounds that its voyeurism undermines her role as successful heroine. A great deal has also been written about the cat. Why does she rescue the cat and thereby risk her life, and the lives of Parker and Lambert, when she has previously been so careful about quarantine regulations? Again, satisfactory answers to these questions are provided by a phallocentric concept of female fetishism. Compared to the horrific sight of the alien as fetish object of the monstrous-feminine, Ripley's body is pleasurable and reassuring to look at. She signifies the "acceptable" form and shape of woman. In a sense the monstrousness of woman, represented by Mother as betrayer (the computer/life-support system) and Mother as the uncontrollable, generative, cannibalistic mother (the alien), is controlled through the display of woman as reassuring and pleasurable sign. The image of the cat functions in the same way; it signifies an acceptable, and in this context, a reassuring fetish object for the "normal" woman.[47] Thus, Ripley holds the cat to her, stroking it as if it were her "baby," her "little one." Finally, Ripley enters her sleep pod, assuming a virginal repose. The nightmare is over and we are returned to the opening sequence of the film where birth was a pristine affair. The final sequence works, not only to dispose of the alien, but also to repress the nightmare image of the monstrous-feminine, constructed as a sign of abjection within the text's patriarchal discourses.

Kristeva's theory of abjection, if viewed as description rather than prescription, provides a productive hypothesis for an analysis of the monstrous-feminine in the horror film.[48] If we posit a more archaic dimension to the mother, we can see how this figure, as well as Kristeva's maternal authority of the semiotic, are both constructed as figures of abjection within the signifying practices of the horror film. We can see its ideological project as an attempt to shore up the symbolic order by constructing the feminine as an imaginary other that must be repressed and controlled in order to secure and protect the social order. Thus, the horror film stages and restages a constant repudiation of the maternal figure.

But the feminine is not a monstrous sign *per se*; rather, it is constructed as such within a patriarchal discourse that reveals a great deal about male desires and fears but tells us nothing about feminine desire in relation to the horrific. When Norman Bates remarked to Marion Crane in *Psycho* that "Mother is not herself today," he was dead right. Mother wasn't herself. She was someone else – her son Norman.

Notes

1. Sigmund Freud, "Fetishism," in *On Sexuality*, Pelican Freud Library, vol. 7 (1977; reprint, Harmondsworth: Penguin, 1981), p. 354.
2. Joseph Campbell, *The Masks of God: Primitive Mythology* (New York: Penguin, 1969), p. 73.
3. Sigmund Freud, "Medusa's Head," in *The Standard Edition of the Complete Works of Sigmund Freud*, ed. and trans. James Strachey (London: Hogarth Press, 1964), 18: 273–274.
4. Ibid., p. 273.
5. Ibid.
6. Julia Kristeva, *Powers of Horror: An Essay on Abjection* (New York: Columbia University Press, 1982), p. 4. Subsequent references are cited parenthetically in the text.
7. For a discussion of the way in which the modern horror film works upon its audience, see Philip Brophy, "Horrality – the Textuality of Contemporary Horror Films," *Screen* 27, no. 1 (January–February 1986): 2–13.
8. For a critique of *Powers of Horror*, see Jennifer Stone, "The Horrors of Power: A Critique of Kristeva," in *The Politics of Theory*, ed. F. Barker et al. (Colchester: University of Essex, 1983), pp. 38–48.
9. Sigmund Freud, "From the History of an Infantile Neurosis," in *Case Histories II*, Pelican Freud Library, vol. 9 (1979; reprint, Harmondsworth: Penguin, 1981), p. 294.
10. Sigmund Freud, "On the Sexual Theories of Children," in *On Sexuality*, Pelican Freud Library, vol. 7 (1977; reprint, Harmondsworth: Penguin, 1981), p. 198.
11. Sigmund Freud, "The Paths to the Formation of Symptoms," in *Introductory Lectures on Psychoanalysis*, Pelican Freud Library, vol. 1 (1973; reprint, Harmondsworth: Penguin, 1981), p. 417.
12. Daniel Dervin argues that this structure does deserve the status of a convention. For a detailed discussion of the primal-scene fantasy in various film genres, see his "Primal Conditions and Conventions: The Genres of Comedy and Science Fiction," *Film/Psychology Review* 4, no. 1 (Winter–Spring 1980): 115–147.
13. Sigmund Freud, "Female Sexuality," in *On Sexuality*, Pelican Freud Library, vol. 7 (1977; reprint, Harmondsworth: Penguin, 1981) p. 373.
14. For a discussion of the relation between the "semiotic" and the Lacanian "imaginary," see Jane Gallop, *The Daughter's Seduction: Feminism and Psychoanalysis* (Ithaca, N.Y.: Cornell University Press, 1983), pp. 124–125.
15. Sigmund Freud, "Moses and Monotheism," in *Standard Edition*, 23: 83.
16. Sigmund Freud, "Totem and Taboo," in *The Origins of Religion*, Pelican Freud Library, vol. 13 (Harmondsworth, Penguin, 1985), p. 206.
17. Ibid., p. 205.
18. Quoted in Georges Bataille, *Death and Sensuality: A Study of Eroticism and the Taboo* (New York: Walker and Co., 1962), p. 200.
19. Quoted in Anthony Wilden, ed. and trans., *The Language of Self* (Baltimore: Johns Hopkins University Press, 1970), p. 126.

20. Quoted in Stephen Heath, "Difference," *Screen* 19, no. 3 (Autumn 1978): 59.

21. Quoted in ibid., p. 54.

22. Claude Lévi-Strauss, *Structural Anthropology*, trans. C. Jacobson and B. G. Schoepf (New York: Doubleday, 1976), p. 212.

23. Teresa de Lauretis, *Alice Doesn't: Feminism, Semiotics, Cinema* (Bloomington: Indiana University Press, 1984), p. 121.

24. Roger Dadoun, "Fetishism in the Horror Film," *Enclitic* 1, no. 2 (1977): 55–56.

25. Sigmund Freud, "The Uncanny," in *Standard Edition*, 17: 245.

26. Ibid., p. 225.

27. Bataille, *Death and Sensuality*.

28. For a discussion of cinema and the structures of the "look," see Paul Willemen, "Letter to John," *Screen* 21, no. 2 (Summer 1980): 53–66.

29. Jacques Lacan, "Some Reflections on the Ego," *International Journal of Psychoanalysis* 34 (1953): 15.

30. For a discussion of the relationship between the female spectator, structures of looking, and the horror film, see Linda Williams, "When the Woman Looks," in Barry Grant (ed.), *The Dread of Difference* (University of Texas Press, 1996).

31. Dadoun refers to a similar process when he speaks of the displacement of the large "omni present mother" into the small "occulted mother." "Fetishism in the Horror Film," p. 55.

32. Sigmund Freud, "Medusa's Head," p. 105.

33. Ibid., p. 106.

34. For a fascinating discussion of the place of woman as monster in the Oedipal narrative, see de Lauretis, *Alice Doesn't*, chap. 5.

35. Dadoun, "Fetishism in the Horror Film," p. 40.

36. Ibid., p. 42.

37. Ibid., p. 53.

38. Ibid., p. 64.

39. Ibid., p. 57.

40. Ibid., p. 56.

41. Ibid., pp. 59–60.

42. Ibid., p. 60.

43. Sigmund Freud, "An Outline of Psychoanalysis," *Standard Edition*, 23: 202: "This abnormality, which may be counted as one of the perversions, is, as is well known, based on the patient (who is *almost always* male) not recognizing the fact that females have no penis" (my emphasis).

44. Mary Kelly, "Woman-Desire-Image," *Desire* (London: Institute of Contemporary Arts, 1984), p. 31.

45. Sigmund Freud, *The Interpretation of Dreams*, Pelican Freud Library, vol. 4 (1976; reprint, Harmondsworth: Penguin, 1982).

46. Juliet Mitchell, *Psychoanalysis and Feminism* (Harmondsworth: Penguin, 1974), p. 84.

47. The double bird images of Hitchcock's *The Birds* (1963) function in the same way: the love birds signify an "acceptable" fetish, the death birds a fetish of the monstrous woman.

48. For an analysis of the horror film as a "return of the repressed," see Robin Wood, "Return of the Repressed," *Film Comment* 14, no. 4 (July–August 1978): 25–32; and "Neglected Nightmares," *Film Comment* 16, no. 2 (March–April 1980): 24–32.

15

Japanese Queerscapes: Global/Local Intersections on the Internet

*Mark McClelland**

Although Japan was slow to reform its telecommunications industry so as to facilitate widespread Internet access, Japanese is now the third most widely used language on the Net after English and Chinese. In 1998 the number of characters used on Japan's 18 million Web sites was already in excess of the total number of printed characters in all Japanese newspapers and magazines published in a year.[1] However, unlike English, Japanese is not an international language and, as Gottlieb points out, the difficulty of learning to read Japanese for non-Japanese means that, "in the case of the Japanese script, geographical location remains very much a predictor of social practice and preference."[2] Despite the potentially "global" reach of the Internet, material written in Japanese is generally accessible only to Japanese people themselves, and so far practically no research exists in English on the ways the Internet is being used in Japan. This essay looks at two "queer" uses of the Internet by two very different Japanese subcultures and suggests ways that the use of the Internet in Japan troubles the rhetoric of globalization that has so far characterized much research on Internet use in Western societies.

I have chosen to focus on two Internet realms, Japanese women's YAOI sites and *nyūhāfu* (newhalf) sites, because of their potential to subvert Western classifications of sexual identity. For instance, YAOI is an acronym made up of the first letters of the phrase *YAma-nashi* (no climax), *Ochi-nashi* (no point), and *Imi-nashi* (no meaning); it describes a genre of Japanese women's fiction/art dedicated to graphic descriptions of "boy love" (sex between boys and young men). There are nearly as many sites featuring boy love created by straight Japanese women as there are sites produced by gay men about homosexuality, and their audience is almost entirely made up of schoolgirls and young women. Nyūhāfu, on the other hand, is a term used to describe transgendered men who work in the sex and entertainment industry. Newhalf are not transsexual, even though some of them do undergo sex-change surgery, but many of them understand themselves to be a distinct "intermediate sex" and seek out and accept their role as entertainers. Newhalf sites are often run by transvestite/transsexual cabarets and bars and serve to promote the bars as well as offer a space for the entertainers working there

*Pp. 52–69 from *Mobile Cultures: New Media in Queer Asia*, ed. C. Berry, F. Martin and A. Yue (Durham, NC: Duke University Press). © 2003 by Duke University Press. All rights reserved. Used by permission of the publisher.

to discourse about who they are. The political correctness that so often accompanies discussion of homosexuality, transgenderism, and transexualism in English is here largely absent.[3]

These domains are extremely extensive and well organized, with most of the sites being linked together in Web rings that acknowledge a sense of common content and identity. Many site owners are known to each other, and links carry the casual browser from one site to another along pathways established by friendship and common interest. They therefore have some sense of community about them in that they offer a space for like-minded individuals to come together and relax. It is therefore easier to generalize about these sites than about the more diverse sites with "gay" content aimed at gay men.[4] Also, these sites are interesting for being largely "about" sexual interactions between biologically male bodies but not being written or produced by or for gay men. Much queer theory, although gesturing at inclusiveness, tends to become a description of distinctively gay male issues and concerns. In looking at (straight) women's YAOI fiction and the Newhalf Network, the association of male–male sex and gay men can itself be "queer(i)ed." Most important, though, I think that these sites stretch the parameters of the English term *queer*, which attempts to be as inclusive as possible, and shows its limitations. Queer, it would seem, is not so much about content as about political positioning. It is an attitude;[5] where that attitude is missing, as it is on both the YAOI and newhalf sites, it seems unlikely that any sense of community can be created because neither of these realms sets out to self-consciously "oppose" heteronormative discourse or practices. They offer, not an alternative to the constricting regime of compulsory heterosexuality, but a respite from it. This is the underlying assumption behind Japanese society's often cited "tolerance" of nonnormative sexuality: that it is always circumscribed by heteronormative discourses and institutions.[6]

Women's YAOI Fiction on the Internet

Japanese women have long been avid consumers of popular entertainers who would seem to disrupt sexual and gender boundaries while at the same time being committed to normative gender performances in their daily lives. In the early modern period, *onnagata* (female-role players) in the kabuki theater were popular role models for many townswomen, who followed the fashions pioneered by men performing as women on stage.[7] Later, in the Taishō period (1912–1927), the *otokoyaku* (male-role performers) in the all-woman Takarazuka Revue became national celebrities to their all-female audience. Both kabuki and the Takarazuka continue to be popular today and gender play on the Japanese screen and stage is still widespread.[8] But perhaps the most intriguing evidence for Japanese women's fascination with transgender/homosexuality occurs in girls' comics (*shōjo manga*) featuring stories of "boy love" (*shōnen'ai*).

Romantic stories about "male love" (*nanshoku*) have a long tradition in Japan, usually focusing on the attraction between a priest or samurai lover (*nenja*) and his acolyte (*chigo*) or page (*wakashū*).[9] However, these early stories were written by men for an anticipated male audience; women *manga* artists and writers did not begin to feature love stories between "beautiful boys" (*bishōnen*) until the early 1970s. These early romances, aptly described as *Bildungsroman* by Midori Matsui, were long and beautifully crafted tales, often set in private boys' schools in the past century.[10] Some manga, however, used figures from Japan's past, such as Yamagishi Ryoko's *Emperor of the Land of the Rising Sun* (1980–1984) about the eighth-century Prince Shōtoku. Schodt describes the manga as "One of the most popular girls' stories of all time [which] depicts a revered founder of Japan as a scheming, cross-dressing homosexual with psychic powers."[11]

In the early 1980s, amateur women manga artists began to create their own boy-love comics and fictions and circulate them at *komiketto* (comic markets) held all over Japan.[12] As well as original works, these women also produced "parodies" (*parodi*) and "fanzines" (*dōjinshi*) based on mainstream boys' manga. Like Western "slash fiction" writers, the authors took heterosexual, heteronormative narratives and "queered" them by imagining sexual relationships between the male characters. These amateur manga tended to focus on the sex and contained less well-crafted stories, leading to the acronym YAOI, as described above. The sexually explicit nature of many of these stories is made clear in another suggested derivation for the acronym YAOI: *YAmete, Oshiri ga Itai!* (Stop, my ass hurts!). Demand for these privately produced texts was such that mainstream publishers began to sign up the most talented of their creators and make them commercially available. The YAOI manga are now big business and hundreds of new titles are released each year. One of the earliest boy-love monthly magazines was *June* (pronounced ju-neh), first published in 1978. In 1995, *June* was still being published, now in a three-hundred-page bimonthly format and with a circulation of between 80,000 and 100,000.[13] *June* was so successful in pioneering a new style in boy-love stories that the term *June-mono* (June things) now refers to boy-love stories in general. Many other boy-love manga followed *June's* lead, and there are now so many YAOI titles, and such is Japanese women's interest in them, that special editions of general manga and animation magazines often bring out boy-love specials. For instance, the February 1999 issue of *Pafu*, describing itself as a "Boy's Love Special," contained synopses and illustrations from a wide variety of boy-love comics organized according to genre, including sexual love.

As with Western slash fiction writers, the advent of the Internet provided a new forum for women writers and artists to distribute and popularize their work, and the Japanese Net contains several thousand sites created by women celebrating the love between "beautiful boys." The strict division of labor in many Japanese companies between the male career-track regular employees and the noncareer female "office ladies" has resulted in word processing and data input being gendered as women's work; many women thus develop computing skills superior to their male colleagues'. Furthermore, the fact that much routine computing work is contracted out to women in the home is indirectly facilitating women's access to the Internet.[14] Recent statistics indicate that women are the majority of new Internet users and that they access the Net primarily for entertainment and not business.[15] The various structural features of Japan's employment system that disenfranchise women may in fact be supporting their access to the Internet, and, because most women work in noncareer positions, they have greater time to devote to their hobbies than do men.

A search for YAOI on Yahoo Japan (June 2000) produced 557 individual Web pages as well as two links sites: *Creative Girls' Home* and *Yaoi Intelligence Agency*.[16] *Creative Girls'* had 801 sites listed, all connected in some way with "YAOI, boys' love (*bōizurabu*), and *June*," whereas *Yaoi Intelligence* provided a choice of 43 different categories of "*June* and boys' love" pages. These included 543 "original," 400 "same-character," 225 "games" (where players role-play as boys), 140 "parody," 98 "novels," 90 "adult," and 81 "SM." Despite the fact that all the sites on *Creative Girls'* are in Japanese (sites in English and are not allowed to join), T'Mei, the Ringmaster, provides a brief English introduction. She stresses that the illustrations must not be stolen for reproduction on other pages, commenting, "Do not presume that we will never notice your sneaking in and stealing our works, for there are many ways to detect your shameful acts." To stop "foreigners" from accessing and taking images for use on their own sites, a few Japanese sites have introduced password protection. In these instances, the Web page owner simply posts a message on the site's entrance page stating, "In order to stop foreigners entering and stealing our illustrations, we have introduced a password," which is usually followed by an explanation of what the password is. Here the use of the Japanese language itself is a kind of code that is expected to keep foreigners out. There seem to be two reasons behind this precaution: as mentioned above, some foreign site owners have been stealing images and reproducing them on their own sites without due recognition; however, other Japanese site owners have complained that their sites are being linked to "unpleasant" (*iyarashii*) foreign sites that, in this instance, probably refers to child pornography.

The number of boy-love sites is so large that it is difficult to make generalizations about them. Some consist only of illustrations, either created by the site owner herself or by her guest, friends, or members of the "circle" to which she belongs; other sites are exclusively text-based, consisting of *shōsetsu* (short stories). Most sites, however, contain a mixture of the two and other material, often including a profile of the site owner; her diary, where she details what she has been reading or doing; a guest slot, where she features the work of a friend; and a BBS where browsers can comment on the site or offer news or information relating to new publications. A brief description of the sites' contents is listed on their Web links entry. For instance, *Yaoi a laboratory* describes itself as dedicated to commercial YAOI stories, containing criticism and ranking of the work of YAOI writers; *I'm on your side* (subtitled *Boys or Guys Love OK*) is an interactive game based on the male students of a fictional university and high school that share the same campus; *Catnap* is dedicated to love stories centering on the members of boy band L'Arc en Ciel and also features illustrations and manga; and *Sadistic* contains original stories about men in their twenties with an emphasis on SM and hard sex.[17]

That an exclusively female audience is anticipated for this material is made clear on the entrance page to most sites. The creator of *Sadistic*, for instance, states, "I recommend that men and people who do not understand YAOI should proceed no further; I welcome women over the age of 18" (but no age check is given). *Catnap's* author writes that her site is "basically for women," continuing, "If you don't like YAOI or don't know what it is, please leave quickly." Despite the common assumption that women are more interested in romance and relationships than sex, many of the illustrations and stories contain graphic sexual scenarios. One story on *Sadistic* involves a 15-year-old boy who seduces his 22-year-old neighbor. Although his family moves away from the area soon after, the boy has been so deeply impressed by his first sexual experience that he is unable to forget the older man, and the writer describes a number of scenes in which the boy masturbates while day dreaming about the touch of his first lover's lips and hands: "As I lay in bed I began to think of Toshiaki and my hand naturally stretched down to my groin. Oh, oh . . . I can imagine that big, firm hand on my body . . . imagine him looking at me. Oh, oh, Toshiaki! To be clasped to that breast . . . to be kissed by those lips is a dream. I love you Toshiaki. To be together with him is to dream. I . . . love . . . you. Oh! My sperm should flow along with his . . . he should hear my cries . . . With sticky white liquid on my fingers, I stare into space . . ."

As he grows older he begins to sleep with women in a vain attempt to recreate the intensity of his first sexual encounter. These graphically described sex scenes become increasingly bizarre. At one stage, he is asked by a female partner whether he has ever experienced anal sex (i.e., anally penetrated a woman), in response to which he muses, "Is it a lie to say this is my first time when last time it was with a man?" And although he penetrates the woman and "his body convulsing . . . spat sperm out into a condom," his thoughts are once more with his first love. Afterward he thinks to himself, "Today, as always, it wasn't especially pleasant. It feels like all I have done is ejaculated. [I feel] more or less empty . . . let's face it, it's impossible with anyone but him . . ." This story line, mixing heterosexual and homosexual encounters and focusing on sexual acts unusual for women such as anal intercourse, has parallels in "ladies comics," again written by and for women, that emphasize sex. As Schodt says of these comics, they "would make American and European feminists wince" because they depict "a woman seducing a son's very young friend, a woman becoming a molester of men on a subway, and women characters who apparently enjoy gang rapes [and] sodomy."[18] However, although sexually graphic, the sex in many YAOI stories does not itself seem to be the "point" but is used to underline the centrality of the characters' feelings. As I have argued elsewhere, this differentiates Japanese women's "homosexual" narratives from those characteristic of Japan's gay press.[19]

Because YAOI is primarily about sex between "beautiful boys" (*bishōnen*) and "beautiful men" (*biseinen*) it confounds Western conventions that stigmatize the sexual representation of children.[20] These stories and illustrations that imagine sexual interaction between men and young boys are known as *shōtakon* (Shōtaro Complex, Shōtaro being the boy hero, always dressed in short pants, of a popular 1960s animation show entitled *Tetsujin 28-go* in Japan and released in the US as *Gigantor*, a term created by YAOI writers and modeled on the loanword *rorikon* (the well-known Lolita Complex). In Western societies it is hard to imagine sexual scenarios more transgressive than transgenerational homosexual acts between adult men and pubescent boys, and yet this is a central trope in women's YAOI. This differentiates YAOI from Western slash fiction that imagines sexual interaction between the *adult* male stars of TV shows such as *Star Trek* or the *X Files* and is a clear example of the cultural relativity of sexual values.[21] Despite the fact that women and children are often assumed to be the primary "victims" of pornography, YAOI is a pornographic genre created by women about (male) children and is considered innocuous enough that it appears in comics commercially produced for an audience of schoolgirls, young women, and housewives. Schoolgirls and house-wives are not normally considered a "queer" constituency, and yet their interest in graphic homosexual love stories involving boys troubles Anglo-American assumptions about the synchronicity of "sexual identity" and sexual fantasy.

Japan's Newhalf Net

Japan has a long tradition of transgendered men offering sexual services to gender-normative men. In the Tokugawa period (1600–1867), transgendered prostitutes (*kagema*), who were often affiliated with kabuki theaters, would offer their services to male members of the audience.[22] In the Taishō (1912–1927) and early Shōwa (1927–1989) periods this role seems to have been taken over by *okama*, a slang term for the buttocks that, when applied to male homosexuals, means something like the English "queen." In the 1960s and 1970s, the term *geiboi* (gay boy) referred to cross-dressing male hustlers, and *gei* (gay) still carries transgender connotations today.[23] Giving fixed content to any Japanese terminology dealing with sexual- or gender-nonconformist individuals is problematic and producing English-language equivalents almost impossible.[24]

Nyūhāfu is particularly difficult to translate, partly because its meaning in Japanese is ambiguous. The term was first popularized in Japan in the early 1980s due to the success of Matsubara Rumiko, a male-to-female transgendered model and singer. In 1981 she issued an album of songs entitled *Newhalf* and the next year published a photo collection.[25] Newhalf, along with gay boy and Mr Lady (*Mr redi*), became one of the many terms used in the media to refer to transgendered men working in the entertainment industry. Since the legalization of sex-change operations in Japan in 1998 and the resulting resurgence of media interest in transgender identities, newhalf has established itself as the most popular term for male-to-female transgenders. Several books, such as *Deciding to Be a Newhalf and Living Like "Myself,"* have been published since 1998, but the variety of identities expressed by individuals using the newhalf label is such that it is impossible to fix its meaning.[26]

On the surface, it would seem that newhalf refers to individuals who, in English, would probably be described as transsexual, but definitions of newhalf in the Japanese media contradict this. For instance, one definition in a sex industry guidebook defines newhalf as "male homosexuals who have had a sex-change operation."[27] The common-sense assumption that newhalf are male homosexuals (*dansei dōseiaisha*) is also clear from an article in the popular magazine *Da Vinchi*, which describes them as "male homo-sexuals who have 'come out,' undergone a sex change and work in the sex industry."[28] This definition is problematic, as most newhalf who introduce themselves on the Inter-net would not see themselves as male homosexuals but a distinct "intermediate sex" (*chūsei*); some newhalf take hormones, some have silicon implants, and some have their male genitalia removed, but by no means all undergo sex-change operations. Newhalf do, however, tend to work in the entertainment industry in some capacity or other; therefore, newhalf is better understood as an occupational category rather than a sexual orientation.[29] The interviews in *Deciding to Be a Newhalf* support this; several of the newhalf sex workers interviewed cite commercial concerns as reasons for undertaking specific transgender practices. For instance, Cherry expresses affection for her "nicely shaped penis" because her clients often request that she penetrate them.[30] However, other newhalf in the collection say that they decided to have their penis removed and an artificial vagina created so that they could avoid being asked to provide either active or passive anal sex. For some newhalf, then, decisions about how to transgender their body are taken with their livelihood in mind and not out of any desire to make their exterior body correspond to an interior sense of gender identity. Newhalf therefore share many similarities with transgendered men in other societies who also seek out work in the prostitution world, such as the *travesti* of South America, who Cornwall points out are "neither . . . 'transvestite[s]' nor . . . 'transsexual[s],' as defined in Western terms."[31] Newhalf also share similarities with the *bakla* of the Philippines, and some Philippine male-to-female transgendered prostitutes enter Japan on "entertainer" visas to seek out jobs in the sex trade.[32]

Newhalf can be understood as a site of identity. However, it is an identity based on occupation, because being a newhalf in Japan is not seen as a part-time activity, whereas simply cross-dressing as a woman is.[33] The newhalf in *Deciding to Be a Newhalf* speak of themselves as "professionals." It is true that newhalf have "come out" in that they transgender the body in very obvious ways, often taking hormones or obtaining breasts through silicon implants. A newhalf is therefore very different from a man who simply likes to cross-dress (*josō*), (although the Internet also provides easy access to information on clubs and bars that offer professional stylists who help their male guests create the most attractive female persona). However, the association of newhalf with the sex and entertainment industry makes the conceptualization of newhalf as a political identity problematic, as newhalf often present themselves as offering a service for men either as "hostesses" in clubs, cabarets, or bars, or as "escorts" and "companions." They very much locate themselves in the entertainment sphere. When offering sexual services, newhalf tend to stress their *intersexual* status by pointing out their firsthand knowledge of male anatomy and their ability to offer increased sexual pleasure to straight men. Unlike biological women, newhalf "understand" straight men's desires because they are believed to share them.

Many newhalf sites are hosted by clubs, bars, cabarets, and escort agencies and provide both information about the venue and the services on offer as well as an opportunity for the newhalf employees to introduce themselves and discourse about what being a newhalf means. Many sites also include BBS and chat rooms where a variety of individuals can write in with their questions and remarks. Like Japanese media in general, these sites contain a wide variety of levels and genres, from graphic sex talk and pornographic pictures to more sophisticated reflections on "how to sex," personal biographies and experiences of newhalf employees and visitors, and snore general news. They are not simply business sites but "realms" offering a great deal of information, entertainment, and sexual titillation. Two typical sites are *Newhalf Health Aventure* and *Virtual Gaybar Elizabeth*.[34] The latter is an information-based site, although the emphasis is very much on entertainment. It is a very colorful, well-designed, and interactive site; as visitors browse through the many pages on offer, they are treated to a synthesized rendition of *Phantom of the Opera*. Misaki, the Web mistress, greets the visitor with the phrase "On a cold day get warm by imagining Misaki's naked body. What? You've got an erection . . . Well, there's nothing I can do about that." But the intended audience of the site is not exclusively male. For instance, one page is for women who like to have newhalf friends; as Misaki points out, "Some women seem to like men who are like women [*onna ni chikai otoko*]." This includes sexual interest too, for many of the women writing in to the page inquire about whether newhalf are interested in having sex with women – Misaki says some are – and how they might go about doing this. As Misaki, who is sexually interested in both men and women, writes, "Basically I have a woman's heart but there still remains about 10 percent inside me which could be called 'male.'" Although not confrontational in an Anglo-American sense, Misaki does discuss "identity politics" when s/he argues that "some people might think I want to live as a woman; I don't, I want to live as myself [*watshi toshite ikitai*]."

Newhalf Health Aventure (*Nyūhāfu herusu abanchūru*) is basically a salon offering sex. "Health" (*herusu*) in Japanese is short for "health massage," just one of the euphemisms developed in the 1980s to disguise the real business of prostitution taking place in massage parlors.[35] *Health Aventure* is upfront about the services offered by its newhalf employees, stating, "We, the newhalf at *Aventure*, try to ensure that all our customers feel satisfied and secure so that [they can experience] enjoyable sex by using our hearts, bodies, skills and magic. We respectfully wait for your visit from the bottom of our hearts. Credit cards accepted." Immediately below are the club's telephone number and a chart detailing the "courses" (*kōsu*) on offer, their duration, and price. These include the basic "health" course, which lasts 30 minutes and involves "kissing, fellatio, etc., but anal fuck (AF) and reverse anal fuck (*gyaku* AF) are not included." This is followed by the 60-minute "regular," which can include AF. The "long regular" is the same as the above but lasts for 90 minutes. The "optional course" includes "soft SM, dressing up as a woman [*josō*] and lesbian play [*rezupurei*]."[36] The "king course" involves two newhalf playmates, and the "Cindarclla course" enables a customer to cross-dress in the club's clothes and then go out on a date with one of the newhalf hostesses. For busy businessmen, lunchtime courses arc offered Monday to Friday between 12:00 p.m. and 4:00 p.m. at a reduced rate.

The main purpose of *Aventure's* home page is to advertise its services, and each of the newhalf "companions" working for the club is profiled.[37] This information includes pictures, age, blood group, star sign, anatomical details such as whether they have breasts and if so whether silicon or the result of hormones, and the current state of their genitalia. Also detailed are the sexual acts the newhalf will or can perform. This kind of description sounds extremely clinical, but the Web page manages to offer this information, to borrow a phrase, "in the best possible taste," employing the exquisitely polite Japanese that is characteristic of highly trained professionals working in the service industry. Being offered a "reverse anal fuck" in the same language a five-star hotel waiter might offer a napkin makes for disorienting reading to my English mind, but because the sex industry is a relatively expensive service industry, the same linguistic rules apply. As Kondo comments, "Awareness of complex social positioning is an *inescapable* element of any utterance in Japanese, for it is *utterly impossible* to form a sentence without *also* commenting on the relationship between oneself and one's interlocutor."[38] This applies equally to the relationship between the purveyors of sexual fantasy and their clients.

There are several hundred newhalf sites from all over Japan, most of which offer, to some degree or other, sexual services. Not all are hosted by large institutions such as *Aventure*; for instance, *Home Delivery Newhalf System* is the home page of Momo and Sakura, who provide the following sexual services either at a client's home or hotel room: kissing, fellatio, vibrator, anal sex, reverse anal sex, and SM play.[39] Momo and Sakura are clearly in partnership together (they offer "double play"), and their Web site, like that of *Aventure*, is very clear about what services are on offer and how much they cost. Other sites are more circumspect and offer newhalf the chance to post their pictures and describe the kind of acts they will perform but without detailing fees. *Newhalf Net* has a short, text-based iMode feature for those using a mobile phone to surf the Net. This contains brief five-line biographies of newhalf, their preferred sexual acts, telephone numbers, and email addresses.

Other sites listed on the Newhalf Net, such as *TV's Forum Japan*, that at first glance might seem to be more information-oriented, on further inspection also primarily deliver "entertainment" of a sexual nature.[40] For instance, *TV's Forum* describes itself as "a place where people who love women's underwear can get together" and features pictures of men posing in a variety of women's underwear as well as stories detailing their sexual exploits involving partners of both sexes. As with most newhalf sites, email addresses are given and viewers are encouraged to write and make dates to "play."

As frequently occurs in Japanese sex industry discourse, identities, terminologies, and practices blur and become confused. The ruling paradigm for sex industry participation is "play" (*asobi/purei*), and, as with any game, the rules can be bent or broken, especially if the client is prepared to pay more. Japan's noninterventionist legislation regarding private sexual practice has enabled the Internet to offer a cornucopia of erotic entertainment where there is surely something on offer for people of all persuasions. None of the sites I have discussed are password-protected, and none I attempted to enter required proof of age; although sometimes the question "Are you over 18?" was posted on the first page, the browser had only to click in the affirmative to enter.

Conclusion

The two Internet realms discussed, women's YAOI sites and the Newhalf Net, trouble the parameters of even a term like queer, which seeks to be inclusive of all sexualities that fall outside "mainstream" heterosexuality and the discourse attempting to tie sex to reproduction within the family. Schoolgirls as a constituency are not generally considered queer, yet their interest in homosexual love stories between young boys clearly falls outside the parameters of what would be considered acceptable in Anglophone societies. Newhalf, too, in their acceptance of the space made available to them in Japan's sex industry and their self-promotion as an "intermediate sex" better able to satisfy the sexual demands of (straight) men because of their privileged understanding of male anatomy, trouble the political associations of queer and make it seem unlikely that newhalf could be included in an umbrella category of groups as diverse in their interests as gay men, lesbians, and those Japanese individuals who understand themselves to be transsexual in the English connotation of this term.

As outlined above, neither YAOI nor the newhalf phenomenon represents a radically new departure in Japan's sexual culture. The Internet has not enabled the emergence of a new type of sexual discourse but simply allowed greater access to sexual images, narratives, and practices; it has made them more popular and more readily available. Whereas previously a schoolgirl would have had to attend a komiketto to purchase her favorite YAOI manga, paying large sums of money on transport, entrance fees, and hard copies of the comics, she can now access her favorites sites from the privacy of her bedroom, download images to keep, and even upload her own art and stories. Similarly, a man (or woman) with an interest in transgendered men who previously would have had to journey to the red light districts of Japan's major cities to meet and converse with newhalf is now able to enter this realm through the Internet. It is possible to download images of one's favorite newhalf, read about her doings in her diary, send her email, or chat with her live. It is possible to make sexual assignations or simply organize a date while saving money by cutting out the expensive fees charged by clubs and cabarets for making introductions. A man can even download information about several different newhalf on his mobile phone and then make a date to meet one of them during his lunch hour or stop off before his long commute home at one of the love hotels built near many train interchange stations.

In making more easily accessible the variety of sexual discourses, representations, and practices that have long been a part of Japan's popular culture, it is unlikely that the Internet is, by itself, going to encourage the increasing politicization of sexuality so long as Internet use is understood as a form of entertainment. Just as the video recorder and cable TV have brought pornography into the domestic sphere, the Internet,[41] too, is further blurring the boundaries between the private home and the commercial sex scene, or indeed the office and the world of sexual entertainment.[42]

So far, the Japanese government's reluctance to regulate sexual expression on the Internet has meant that it is in Japanese, not English, that the widest range of sexual representations and services are freely available. These diverse realms that confound Anglo-American understandings of pornography, sexual identity, and the correspondence between sexual identity and sexual fantasy have been protected from the disapproving Western gaze by the inaccessibility of the Japanese language. There are signs, however, that especially with regard to child pornography (four-fifths of which is said to originate in Japan) Western nations are putting pressure on Japan through international conventions to begin the process of Internet regulation.[43] Thus, although sexual sites on the Japanese Internet, so long as they are inscribed in the discourse of "entertainment," are unlikely to become politicized, the availability of material disapproved of in more censorious Western nations is itself likely to become a political issue.

Notes

Translations are my own unless otherwise noted.
1. Nanette Gottlieb, *Word Processing Technology in Japan: Kanji and the Keyboard* (Richmond, U.K.: Curzon Press, 2000), 182.
2. Gottlieb, 200.

3. "Political correctness" has yet to make it to Japan. For instance, the "lesbian and bi women's forum" *Bibian*, 7 June 2000, <http://www.silkroad.ne.jp/bibian> (7 June 2000), which contains sexuality information and chat rooms for women, opens with a bare-breasted and provocatively clad blonde woman, seemingly scanned in from the pages of *Playboy*. Interestingly, this site is pioneering the adoption of the term *bian* (from *rezubian*) as an alternative to *rezu*, which is associated with women performers in male pornography, and is a further example of how Western borrowings like "newhalf" are invested with specifically Japanese meanings.

4. For a discussion of how gay men use the Internet in Japan, see Mark McLelland, "Out and About on Japan's Gay Net," *Convergence* 6, no. 3 (2000): 16–33.

5. "Queer" developed in the late 1980s as a new adversarial site of identity for individuals who felt "lesbian" and "gay" to be too limiting and exclusionary of other sexual minorities such as bisexuals, transsexuals, and sex workers. It is used in this sense in Michelangelo Signorile's *Queer in America: Sex, the Media and the Closets of Power* (New York: Anchor, 1994). However, with the integration of queer theory into the academy and the increasing commodification of queer cultures, much of its confrontational force has been lost. As Morton comments, queer is now often used to mean "the embracing of the latest fashion over an older, square style by the hip youth generation." Donald Morton, "Birth of the Cyberqueer," in *Cybersexualities: A Reader on Feminist Theory, Cyborgs and Cyberspace*, ed. Jenny Wolmark (Edinburgh: Edinburgh University Press, 1999), 295. Neither the school-girl readers of YAOI nor newhalf sex workers are queer in either of the above senses. However, queer in the lifestyle sense has now entered Japanese through the magazine *Queer Japan* (first published 2000). Volume 2 (June 2000) is dedicated to "salarymen doing queer" and focuses on lifestyle and culture. It is too soon to judge whether this new departure in Japanese gay media will be successful.

6. Sharon Chalmers, "Lesbian (In)visibility and Social Policy in Japanese Society," in *Gender and Public Policy in Japan*, ed. Vera Machie (London: Routledge, forthcoming).

7. Liza Dalby, *Kimono: Fashioning Culture* (New Haven: Yale University Press, 1993), 275.

8. Mark McLelland, *Male Homosexuality in Modern Japan: Cultural Myths and Social Realities* (Richmond, U.K.: Curzon Press, 2000), chap. 3, 43–60.

9. Tsuneo Watanabe and Jun'ichi Iwata, *The Love of the Samurai: A Thousand Years of Japanese Homosexuality* (London: Gay Men's Press, 1989); Gary Leupp, *Male Colors: The Construction of Homosexuality in Tokugawa Japan* (Berkeley: University of California Press, 1995).

10. Midori Matsui, "Little Girls Were Little Boys: Displaced Femininity in the Representation of Homosexuality in Japanese Girls' Comics," in *Feminism and the Politics of Difference*. ed. S. Gunew and A. Yeatman (Boulder, CO: Westview Press, 1993), 178.

11. Frederik Schodt, *Dreamland Japan: Writings on Modern Manga* (Berkeley: Stone Bridge Press, 1996), 182.

12. Sharon Kinsella, "Japanese Subcultures in the 1990s: Otaku and the Amateur Manga Movement," *Journal of Japanese Studies* 24, no. 2 (1998): 289–316.

13. Schodt, 120.

14. *Wall Street Journal*, "Your Career Matters: Net Lets Japanese Women Join Work Force at Home," February 29, 2000, B1.

15. Gottlieb, 181.

16. *Creative Girls' Home*, 15 September 1998, <http://www.lunatique.org/yaoi> (5 June 2000); *Yaoi Intelligence Agency*, 2000, <http://www.may.sakura.ne.jp/~yia/se/> (5 June 2000).

17. *Yaoi a laboratory*, 16 June 2000, <http://www.lilac.cc/~maco/> (16 June 2000); *I'm on Your Side*, 1 March 2000, <http://www.bridge.ne.jp/~pbem/DEMO/SIDE.html> (16 June 2000); *Catnap*, 14 June 2000, <http://www.people.or.jp/~asagi/catnap/> (14 June 2000); *Sadistic*, 14 June 2000, <http://www.2.networks.ne.jp/~foo/SDSTC/> (14 June 2000).

18. Schodt, 125.

19. Mark McLelland, "No Climax, No Point, No Meaning? Japanese Women's Boy-Love Sites on the Internet," *Journal of Communication Inquiry* 24, no. 3 (2000): 274–94.

20. Despite the fact that 15 percent of the 150 pornographic Internet sites sampled by Mehta and Plaza contained images of children, they report, "We never came across an image depicting a sexual act between an adult and a child/adolescent, or acts between children," which suggests that these images are very rare on the American USENET system. But, such images are, of course, ubiquitous on Japanese YAOI sites. Michael Mehta and Dwayne Plaza, "Pornography in Cyberspace: An Exploration of What's in USENET," in *Culture of the Internet*, ed. Sara Kiesler (Mahwah, NJ: Erlbaum, 1997), 64.

21. For a discussion of slash fiction, see Mirna Cicioni, "Male Pair-Bonds and Female Desire in Fan Slash Writing," in *Theorizing Fandom: Fans, Subculture and Identity*, ed. C. Harris and A. Alexander (Cresskill, NJ: Hampton, 1998), 153–78; Constance Penley, "Feminism, Psychoanalysis and the Study of Popular Culture," in *Cultural Studies*, ed. Lawrence Grossberg, Cary Nelson, and Paula A. Treichler (New York: Routledge, 1992), 479–500; Henry Jenkins III, *Textual Poachers: Television Fans and Participatory Culture* (New York: Routledge, 1992).

22. Leupp, 72.

23. *Geiboi* is used in this sense in Matsumoto Toshio's movie *Bara no sōretsu* (Funeral procession of roses, 1969). Shot in a semidocumentary style, the film documents Tokyo's late 1960s gay bar (*geibā*) scene and stars the famous transvestite actor Peter, who is now one of Japanese television's top hostesses.

24. For a discussion of terms relating to gender nonconformist individuals in Japan, see McLelland, *Male Homosexuality in Modern Japan*, 7–12.

25. Rumiko Miyazaki, *Watashi wa toransujendā* [I am transgendered], (Tokyo: Neoraifu, 2000), 202.

26. Anri Komatsu, *Nyūhāfu ga kimeta "watash" rashii ikikata* [Deciding to be a newhalf and live like myself], (Tokyo: KK Ronguserāzu, 2000).

27. Altbooks, *SEX no arukikata: Tōkyō fūzoku kanzen gaido* [How to find your way around Tokyo's sex scene: A complete guide], (Tokyo: Mediawākusu, 1998), 167.

28. *Da Vinchi*, "Sei wo koeta hito bito wo rikai suru hito koto yōgo kaisetsu" (An explanation of terms for people who have gone beyond their sex), March 1999.

29. As described later, some newhalf offer services for men, women, and men dressed as women.

30. Komatsu, 128.

31. Andrea Cornwall, "Gendered Identities and Gender Ambiguity among *Travestis* in Salvador, Brazil," in *Dislocating Masculinity: Comparative Ethnographies*, ed. A. Cornwall and N. Lindisfarne (London: Routledge, 1994), 114.

32. *The Sex Warriors and the Samurai*, prod. Parminder Vir, dir. Nick Deocampo, 25 min., Formation Films Production for Channel Four, 1995, videocassette.

33. Being an *okama* or effeminate homosexual (rather like the English term "drag queen") can also be seen as a part-time activity. See my discussion of the okama farmer who works on his farm during the day and at night serves as a hostess in a bar (McLelland, *Male Homosexuality in Modern Japan*, 48).

34. *Aventure*, 14 February 2000, <http://www.newhalf.co.jp/> (1 July 2000); *Virtual Gaybar Elizabeth*, 27 January 1999, <http://homepage1.nifty.com/Newhalf/index.html> (5 July 2000).

35. For a discussion of Japan's sex trade, see Peter Constantine, *Japan's Sex Trade: A Journey through Japan's Erotic Subcultures* (Tokyo: Tuttle, 1993); and Altbooks.

36. In this context, *rezupurei* refers to a cross-dressed male client pretending to be a lesbian.

37. Although counters advertising the number of hits can be unreliable, it would seem that *Aventure* is popular, having attracted 82,002 hits between 14 February and 30 May 2000. On 29 May alone, it attracted 1,145 visitors.

38. Dorinne Kondo, *Crafting Selves: Power, Gender, and Discourses of Identity in a Japanese Workplace* (Chicago: University of Chicago Press, 1990), 31.

39. *Home Delivery Newhalf* System, September 1998, <http://members.xoom.com/_XMCM/newhalf/eigyou.html> (15 July 2000).

40. *TV's Forum Japan*, 17 July 2000. <http://www.geocities.com/WestHollyWood/Village/9111> (17 July 2000).

41. The mobile phone is another technology disrupting the traditional distinction between the desexualized domestic sphere and the world of commercial sex. It is used by gay men who live with their parents (or wives or partners) to negotiate their sexual relationships (see McLelland, *Male Homosexuality in Modern Japan*, 212–14) and by schoolgirl prostitutes who call into "telephone clubs" where potential clients wait to receive their calls. See Takarajima, *Ura Tōkyō kankō* [Backstreet Tokyo sightseeing] (Tokyo: Takarajimasha, 1998), 54–55; "Clueless in Tokyo: Schoolgirls Exchange Sexual Talk for Money to Buy Designer Clothes," *The Economist* 339, no. 7969 (June 8, 1996): 66.

42. I had to obtain a letter from the University of Queensland explicitly granting me exemption from a university statute forbidding the use of office computers for the viewing of pornographic images in order to complete the research for this chapter.

43. "Japan's Shame: Lawmakers are finally pushing legislation to help end the country's dubious distinction as the world's main source of child pornography," *Time International* 153, no. 5 (April 19, 1999): 34.

16

Get Real! Cultural Relevance and Resistance to the Mediated Feminine Ideal

Lisa Duke*

Bocock (2000) has noted that "consumption, in late twentieth-century western forms of capitalism, may be seen . . . as a social and cultural process involving cultural signs and symbols, not simply as an economic, utilitarian process" (p. 3). One example of consumption as a social and cultural process is the way in which the fashion/beauty media instill in women and girls a desire for the products and services they see portrayed on countless screens and pages (Budgeon, 1994). The most popular magazines targeted to American girls, that is, *Teen*, *YM*, and *Seventeen*, are filled with advertising and editorial touting the latest personal care products, cosmetics, fashions, exercise programs, and weight-loss systems. Teen magazines inform or remind readers of the newest products and looks available on the beauty market and instruct girls on the value and proper use of these goods (see Evans, Rutberg, Sather, & Turner, 1991). The advertising for these products and services is presented in a most favorable environment, with text that presents the consumption of fashion/beauty products as a natural part of being female, integral to achieving an ideal version of femininity, and key to a girl's social success (see Budgeon, 1994, p. 64). Critics of the teen-magazine genre have claimed the "fashion discourses" that are the mainstay of these publications "indoctrinate consumers into an ideology of consumption . . . immers[ing] consumers' self-perceptions in cultural meanings and social ideals that foster depthless, materialistic outlooks, and a perpetual state of dissatisfaction over one's current lifestyle and physical appearance" (Thompson & Haytko, 1997, p. 16).

In what is perhaps the first, most influential textual analysis of a magazine targeted to girls (the British publication, *Jackie!*), McRobbie (1978) identified "codes of femininity" that she argued were incorporated into the text to "shape the consent of the readers to a set of particular values" (p. 2); among these were codes of romance, personal and domestic life, fashion and beauty, and pop music (p. 36). McRobbie argued that these codes were the essential elements of scripts the magazine provided for girls to use in the exercise of their everyday lives. All girls were presumed to have identical interests and an equal need and desire for such scripts. In a content analysis of American teen magazines 15 years later, Evans et al. (1991) came to a similar conclusion: "Articles and

*Originally published as "'Get Real!' Relevance and Resistance to the Mediated Feminine Ideal,'", pp. 211–33 from *Psychology & Marketing*, vol. 19, no. 2. © 2002 by John Wiley & Sons, Inc. Reprinted with permission from John Wiley & Sons, Inc.

advertisements mutually reinforced an underlying value that the road to happiness is attracting males for a successful heterosexual life by way of physical beautification" (p. 110).

Media critics have routinely maintained that the magazines' pressure on girls to "make up and slim down" is unhealthy and ostensibly unavoidable; the implication has been that this pressure is keenly felt by all girls and the effects are strong (e.g., Currie, 1996). Further, Jackson and Kelly (1991) have claimed that the effects of mediated standards of beauty might be even more detrimental to Black females, who are "under-represented and/or portrayed differently than are White females" (p. 68). However, there is a growing literature that indicates that African American girls may be more resistant to messages regarding ideal beauty as it is routinely presented by mainstream media (Duke, 2000; Frisby, 2000; Milkie, 1999). Likewise, African American girls may be less persuaded by marketing efforts that leverage selling messages against these images and ideals.

This research examines the links between text as a consumption object, identity, and meaning making. Our analysis addresses Englis's (1994) observation that "researchers have done little to understand how ideals of beauty are culturally encoded, how these ideals are internalized by consumers . . . or how the ideals propagated in mass media affect consumers' acquisitions of products and services designed to attain these looks" (p. 49). Although the literature is rife with explorations of how adolescents use consumption as a way of expressing identity, this research addresses a gap in the literature on audiences of fashion/beauty media by introducing themes of opposition and anti-consumption that have not previously been explored. These findings are part of a longitudinal study initiated in 1994, on how White and African American adolescent girls interpret and use the material in the top teen magazines: *Teen, Seventeen, YM* (Duke, 2000).[1] This study inquires into the way a particular audience's interpretive frame enables them to critique and distance themselves from selected aspects of a consumption object with which they regularly engage.

African American Readers of Teen Fashion/Beauty Texts

Teen magazines are an impressive force in the print world. In a national ranking of 300 top US magazines (ranked by estimated gross revenue), *Seventeen* ranked 4th, *YM* was 77th, and *'Teen* 88th (*Advertising Age*, June 12, 2000, pp. s4–s6). All three magazines posted growth of total revenues from 3–7.4% in '98–'99, and each of the publications has paid circulations in excess of 2,000,000. Of the 14 million girls between the ages of 12 and 19 in the United States, it is estimated that over half read *Seventeen* (1997 MRI Teenmark).

African American girls make up a substantial percentage of the audience for the top three mainstream teen magazines. *Seventeen* reaches 44% of "ethnic females 12–19" (defined as African American, other race, or from a Spanish-speaking household); *'Teen* and *YM* each reach 34% of these same girls. African American girls ages 12–19 make up the single largest non-White group of readers – they comprise, on average, about 12% of the readership for each of the three major teen titles (Source for all: 1997 MRI

Teenmark). The 1997 MRI TwelvePlus notes that although only 12% of people over the age of 12 identify themselves as Black, 16% of *Seventeen*'s readers do, meaning that magazine draws a greater percentage of African American readers than are represented in the population.

Content analyses of mainstream magazines, including but not exclusively fashion magazines, show that African Americans have had gradually increasing representation in the text and advertisements (Bowen & Schmid, 1997; Stevenson & Stevenson, 1988; Zinkhan, Qualls, & Biswas, 1990). However, the Black representation in mainstream magazines lags behind the percentage of Blacks in the population (Atkin, 1992). One study of fashion advertising found African American women represented in just 2.4% of ads in magazines whose subscribers were 15% Black (Jackson & Kelly, 1991, p. 69). Among the explanations offered most often for scant minority representation in mainstream magazines and the use of minority models who closely mimic the Anglo/ American ideal are marketers' fears that the larger contingent of White consumers may not identify with and therefore may not buy products represented by people of color (Gitlin, 1983) Also, marketers may believe they more effectively reach minority markets by placing advertising in media vehicles specifically intended for minorities (Bowen & Schmid, 1997). Critical theorists argue that the real issue at stake is the continued control and subordination of Blacks, who are positioned through media texts and images as a group responsible for and deserving of their relative social powerlessness (Bourne, 1990; Ukadike, 1990).

If teen magazines imply any girl can be beautiful and socially successful with their help, what does the relative absence of Black girls say – that mediated ideals of femininity do not apply to them? How do African American girls negotiate those messages?

The culturally situated, adolescent media audience and racial identity theory

Because of researchers' focus on White youth, the unique adolescent experience of African American girls has seldom been addressed (Smith, 1982). "The net result has been . . . that little attention has been given to either how a Black girl perceives herself as a female or how she is perceived by others as a female" (p. 262). In fact, race has profound implications for studies of what it means to be an American female; it is one of the most important indicators of girls' self-image. Prendergast, Zdep, and Sepulveda (1974) found that Black girls rated themselves consistently higher than White girls did on several dimensions of self-esteem (e.g., being good looking, being athletically adept). These results have been supported by later studies, which have found that African American girls rate their overall attractiveness much higher than White girls (Parker, Nichter, Nichter, & Vuckovic, 1995). Smith (1982) has noted, ". . . Despite the evidence that Black girls and women are faced with the prospects of being devalued by both Black and the general White society in favor of White women, Black females have been able to maintain a positive sense of self against what appear to be overwhelming odds" (p. 281).

Bell-Scott and McKenry (1986) have argued that African Americans do not turn to the larger society to meet their esteem needs. Rather, it is the African American family and community that give their youth the emotional sustenance needed to maintain esteem. The role of families – in particular, mothers – in nurturing the Black adolescent female's self-esteem is evident in the literature (Duke, 2000; Leeds, 1994). In a theme that recurs throughout the literature on how Black girls negotiate demands of all-pervasive, White-dominated fashion and beauty texts, a supportive minority culture successfully mitigates the more damaging messages of the society at large.

Helms (1995) posits a five-stage process of racial identity development through which members of racially oppressed groups progress: Preencounter, encounter, immersion/emersion, internalization, and integrative awareness. Although not specifically formulated to address Black females, Helms's model provides a context in which to consider African American adolescents' responses to popular media.

In the preencounter stage, girls have not engaged in significant racial identity work. Acknowledgement of race and racial differences is suppressed or at least, unexamined – girls may engage in "idealization of the dominant White world view" (Helms, 1995, p. 20). In the encounter stage, girls might be expected to express ambivalence toward their racial group and their membership in it, until some event, usually in adolescence, triggers an exploration of the meaning of racial identity and a girl's relationship to it (Phinney & Rosenthal, 1992, p. 150). In the immersion/emersion stage, girls engage mentally and emotionally in their identity work – to celebrate "Blackness," usually in opposition to Whites. Girls immerse themselves in a Black world, and judge other Blacks on how authentically African American they are, based on their conformity to stereotypic Black characteristics. Emersion involves the gradual development of a unique Black identity. In the next stage, internalization, a girl's racial identity becomes solidified and blended with her personal identity – she finds security in her racial group membership and becomes committed to it. Finally, in the stage of integrative awareness, girls "value their own collective identities as well as empathize and collaborate with members of other oppressed groups" (Helms, 1995, p. 186). Phinney and Chavira (1992) have demonstrated that significant progress along the racial identity continuum occurs between the ages of 16 and 19. Differences in racial identity development may have a profound effect on the ways Black girls accept, negotiate, disregard, or overlook media content regarding beauty, fashion, and other modes of feminine self-presentation.

Methods and Procedures

Although the mainstream media's underrepresentation and stereotypical presentation of racial minorities is frequently addressed in the literature, few studies inquire into the ways minority audiences negotiate and, in many cases, resist the dominant culture's mediated ideals. This study illustrates how minority purchase of products such as teen magazines can precipitate consumer resistance and critique rather than embrace of Eurocentric ideals of femininity that drive the beauty industry. Thus, in this case, *consumption* is conceptualized not only as purchase, but acceptance of and aspiration to the ideals employed by the beauty industry to sell goods and services, for example, a thin body type, European American facial features, a preference for a made-up appearance. Conversely, anticonsumption is rejection, subversion, or negotiation of those same ideals, although such a critique does not preclude purchase of the vehicle for conveying these ideals.

This article is part of a longitudinal study that uses in-depth interviews to trace the magazine interpretations of girls as they age from early to late adolescence. The data discussed in this article are drawn from a group of 16 African American girls – eight in early adolescence, ages 12–14, and eight who are 17 and 18, and ten White girls, ages 16–18. Participants are from middle-class suburbs of Atlanta, Savannah, and Chicago, and were chosen via the snowball method after the researcher met a core group of girls through acquaintances.

After agreeing to participate in this study, girls were provided with money to purchase a teen magazine, which they were asked to read before their scheduled interviews. The teen magazine of a girl's choice was used as a stimulus device during the interview, a technique called autodriving. Autodriving requires that participants be provided with photographs, music, text, or video as prompts for their interpretations (McCracken, 1988, p. 36). Through the use of this technique, girls were able to provide more vivid interpretations of the text and often used the magazine to strengthen descriptions of their reading experiences.

Interviews began with a grand-tour question (Crabtree & Miller, 1992, p. 81), "Tell me, and show me, how you read this magazine." This allowed the participant to talk at length, with the magazine serving as a prompt. Although an interview guide was used in initial exchanges with participants, the conversation was allowed to flow naturally and the guide was referred to only to ensure all the issues had been covered.

Interpretive data can never be said to describe an objective reality outside each participant's experience of it, as it is communicated to and interpreted through the researcher. Although all interpretations have been verified by the participants, certain aspects of the analysis, such as the precise language of themes and ways of linking certain data, result from the researcher's socially situated frames of reference as a middle-class, White, female academic. This study was designed with built-in checks on the researcher's interpretations. First, girls verified the researcher's interpretations postinterview, that is, through member checks. Second, several of the African American girls participated in a focus group lead by a moderator of the same race, a 21-year-old female college student. The group setting was important because, as Steiner (1991) has noted, "It is the group, in its own communication, that publicly challenges preferred readings, uncovering hidden structures . . . and naturalized ideological operations" (p. 331). Six of eight girls in the older African American group agreed to participate; five of those six actually attended. Girls were provided with dinner in return for their participation in the focus group.

During the focus group, questions from individual interviews were rephrased and asked again for verification. The focus group also provided an opportunity for feedback on results from a partial, preliminary analysis and to clarify points girls made during their individual interviews.

Analysis

After transcribing tapes of participant interviews, the Lincoln and Guba (1985) method of categorizing data was used to establish emergent themes and organizing constructs. Transcripts were examined for instances of language, descriptions of content, particular uses of text, and units of information (Lincoln & Guba, 1985, p. 344) to be grouped into categories (e.g., identity formation, self-expression through artifice). With the use of a variation of the Lincoln and Guba representation (p. 347) of constant comparison (Glaser & Strauss, 1967), units were examined individually and sorted into sets that were subsequently labeled with the abstract functions that unified them. Next, function categories were analyzed to see if they contained substantially more units from girls of one racial group. All data were categorized or else judged to be irrelevant or so atypical as not to be thematically viable. Analysis was complete when categories were saturated with compelling data instances, emergent patterns and regularities were identified, and it was determined that additional analysis would not contribute significantly to the findings (Lincoln & Guba, 1985, p. 350).

Findings

How girls read

Girls read the same teen magazine differently as they age, and, eventually, many "graduate" to reading women's service and adult fashion magazines. But even at the time of girls' peak interest, early adolescence, reading a teen magazine is, for the most part, an activity to fill in time between important activities. For most girls in this study, most of the time, the teen magazine was an abiding companion in times of boredom, entertaining their eyes and minds on long car trips and during interminable study halls. They turned pages to the magazine in time to music on the radio, or with eyes that shifted steadily from written page to television screen and back again. Girls read in the bathroom, in school classrooms, and, more often than not, in their bedrooms before nodding off to sleep.

Often, girls read in tandem with some other activity that did not require their full attention, like talking on the phone. They seldom read the whole magazine at one sitting, nor did they even read entire stories or articles, especially if they had to turn a page to do so. Girls read in stages, usually scanning the magazine first for brightly colored pictures or the headlines of particularly relevant articles. Later, they would return to the magazines to revisit images and articles they found compelling. Girls described keeping the magazines for years, picking them up several times over great spans of time, seeing new things each time they read.

Magazines build loyalty with their readers by presenting the same kinds of material, in a similar form, month after month. This consistency engages the novice, but irritates the more worldly wise. Older girls identified formulae in the text not evident to younger girls. The predictability of the content initially lends authority to the ideas and concepts common to all the major teen titles. These texts speak in one voice about girls and their

place in the world. As girls become familiar with the content and format of teen magazines, it becomes less pressing to examine each issue closely; one blends into another,
with the same ads, with different pictures of the same kind of girl, worrying over
the same issues, pursuing the same kinds of boys. At some point, around age 17, the
lessons of teen magazines have been embraced or ignored, but they have certainly been
learned.

Race matters: reading in black and white

Kenya, 13 (on teen magazine fashions): I don't know anybody who would wear this.
Interviewer: How about the makeup? . . .
Kenya: I don't wear makeup.
Interviewer: Okay. And how about the shampoo and stuff like that?
Kenya: Un uh. 'Cause . . . my beautician washes my hair.

The big three teen magazines, *'Teen, Seventeen,* and *YM,* position themselves in the
market as magazines for Everygirl – regardless of race. But Black girls seemed to understand that in this category, every girl was White – White models, White products, a
White perspective. It is tangible evidence of Willis's (1992) observation that, ". . . in a
sexist society, it's impossible to take one's femaleness for granted; in a racist society,
Whiteness is simply generic humanness, entirely unremarkable" (p. 101). White dominance is naturalized, an accepted and unspoken truth of mainstream media
consumption.

Black girls detected bias in almost every aspect of the text: the images, the products
featured, the behaviors portrayed, the topics covered. The breadth of the magazines'
bias remained invisible to White girls, but was all too clear to many Black girls – the
mainstream teen magazine ignores or overlooks their most fundamental concerns and
interests as African Americans:

Tonya, 17: And I was looking at (the calendar page) because . . . wanted to see if
they mentioned anything about . . . African American History Month. And it
didn't. So, I flipped on. . . . They're limiting their scope . . . just including silly
little things and not things that are relevant to the outside world.

Although older White girls recognized relatively few models of color in teen magazines, they argued that somehow this was less important than that the text was appropriate for all girls. The dearth of minority images was attributed to demands of the
market ("Black girls don't read these magazines") and oversight ("There are usually a
lot more pictures of Black girls – this is not a good issue"). White girls had no conception of how the text might change to reflect more closely the needs and concerns of
Black girls; they were unaware that the world created in teen magazines was seen by
older Black girls as a White one. The inclusion of more pictures of people of color would
make the magazines' treatment of all girls equal in White girls' minds.

Younger Black girls, too, were generally less aware of the bias older Black girls
detected; this may be due to their greater desire to fit in to the dominant picture and

be addressed as a teen girl rather than a Black teen girl, as predicted by racial identity theory. Older Black girls were more interested in being recognized as African Americans. Such recognition would go beyond a superficial inclusion of more photos of people of color; girls also noted the absence of text that addressed their unique experiences, perspectives, and needs as Black people:

> *Nicole, 17 (from focus group):* Some stuff is universal. But then there's the makeup and stuff you can't relate to, and it's like, you know, we live in a White world. . . . I try not to think about stuff like that, but basically, yeah, it is.

Cultural relevance: the real vs. the ideal

Relevance, as the term has been used in studies of media interpretations, has been defined as "how viewers' subjectivities and the text come together in specific moments of interpreting the text" (Cohen, 1991, p. 443). Relevance has been proposed as a key concept in studies that focus on the way life circumstances (e.g., race, social class, or sexual orientation) of an audience segment helps structure meaning that audience takes from the media (Cohen, 1991; Lind, 1996; Morley, 1980).

One of the ways an audience member can express whether a media message is relevant is through discussion of how realistic or unrealistic the message seems. However, the reality of media messages has been shown to mean different things to different audience segments. One group may interpret *real* to mean that mediated representations and situations closely reflect their lived experience. However, when an audience has no experience upon which to judge the reality of the media representations, the representation itself can set expectations of that reality. For example, when one social group aspires to the life-style of another, the realism of the media's portrayal of the desired life-style may be given more credence (Englis, 1995).

What media audiences mean by real media content shifts according to medium as well as the social and cultural contexts from which an audience operates. African American girls in this study noted a bifurcation between what they deem real and the images and situations in teen magazines. Black girls' statements about the magazine centered around desiring to see more of the real and realistic, whereas the text was often said to focus on inaccurate, unbelievable, or exaggerated ideals of femininity. Real content was what many African American girls looked and yearned for in the text – a way of thinking about and seeing the world consistent with their experience as members of a particular minority culture. For example, some of the girls saw the problem pages, with letters from girls looking for answers they could find nowhere else, as more real than other kinds of content:

> *Shawn, 17:* "Sex and Body Talk." . . . The cool thing about that is that people are asking real questions in here . . . Like people who are scared to ask questions to other people and you can find the answer in the magazine. I always look at that.

Few other kinds of content were described as real. In fact, Black girls consistently criticized teen magazines for departures from what they thought of as real. *Not real* was seen as expected content oriented to Anglo/Americans. It was material that presented a literally monochrome picture of youth, without nuance, texture, and color:

> *Kira, 17 (from focus group):* I know it's a majority White clientele, but (the magazine) goes to all types of people and it's not realistic these days to have a whole magazine full of White people and the token Black girl . . . 'Cause they know that more than only White people subscribe to this magazine. They just get one Black person – you have no Latinos, no Asian Americans, nothing. Stupid.

Not real were formulaic stories with predictable endings that came too soon and too easily:

> *Tonya, 17:* [This is a story about] the girl who's . . . gonna be on this Lifetime Special . . . "Fifteen and Pregnant." . . . I just wanted to see how they portrayed it . . .
>
> *Interviewer:* Do you have any friends that are pregnant or were pregnant?
>
> *Tonya:* Yeah . . . they're just as immature now as when they got pregnant. I can see [the Lifetime Special] . . . making her have this transformation, like she's this woman now and knows all.

Not real was presenting minor setbacks as tragedies, written from a perspective that routinely put relatively simple problems center stage:

> *Interviewer:* Did anything in "Romance" pertain to you?
>
> *Shelly, 17:* No, it was actually corny. . . . She had tryouts, everybody thought she made it, but she didn't. Her boyfriend brought her roses. Her family took her shopping. I'm thinking, "Oh, this isn't reality. I know that wouldn't happen to me." . . . My family would be like – "Go get a job now!"

Not real was not affordable to the typical middle-class girl:

> *Focus Group Voice 1:* You wish you had the money to buy all this stuff.
>
> *Voice 2:* . . . Or if you do buy them, where are you going to wear them?

Not real was assuming an image that was perhaps socially advantageous, but directly opposed to the real you or the you others have come to know. For example, by taking on a new, more mainstream persona, singer/actress Courtney Love was seen by one Black girl as abandoning a core group of people with whom she had been strongly associated – an alliance based strongly on contrary aesthetic and cultural ideals. She also saw that the result of Love's transformation was fawning encouragement and idealization by the media:

> *Nicole, 17:* Courtney Love . . . she's all over every fashion magazine . . . how she is so beautiful and wonderful. . . . I feel like if this was her, she would have been that way all along . . . Because she's not Cindy Crawford or anything. She's the lead singer for Hole . . . A pure grunge person like herself walking around in pastel

colors and high heel, strappy shoes? . . . If I was like a hardcore fan, I probably wouldn't listen to her music anymore. . . . You'd be like "No, she used to be like me, jeans and a T-shirt. Now look."

Not real was the way the fashion and beauty industry (mis)understands or (mis)represents itself as serving all women. Not real was only showing Black women at the extreme ends of the color continuum and then placing those women in culturally incongruent places, situations, and product endorsements:

Nicole, 17: I just don't think Black people use Paul Mitchell myself, so that (ad featuring a Black model) is just a lie. My God, . . . Paul Mitchell would ruin my hair.

Not real was a recurring group of unfamiliar yet purportedly famous, beautiful, but disconcertingly homogeneous faces:

Tonya, 17: I like reading the magazine, but it doesn't have any African American or Hispanic or Asian models. . . . So even though I like reading it, sometimes I can't relate to all the things that they put inside. They could make it more realistic, with more culture.

Not real was the magazines' propensity to make interaction with boys seem intimidating or, at the very least, uncomfortable. It was magazines' implication that spending time with a boy is the most important thing a girl can do:

Tonya, 17: The theme of it (fashion spread) was the girl met a guy at some beach house and suddenly things got a lot more interesting. Like she couldn't just have a good time with her family or be realistic . . .
Interviewer: How would you have shot it if it were your spread? . . .
Tonya: . . . Not necessarily having to have some guy involved . . . they make it seem like boys are oxygen . . . like you have to have a guy to be a teenager.

Whereas White girls occasionally mentioned that models in the magazines were artificially made up and therefore not real, Black girls regularly commented on the lack of realism in multiple aspects of the magazine, In short, unrealistic material was that which ran contrary to African American girls' culturally situated viewpoint.

These results pose an interesting counterpoint to the findings of Press (1991), who found that the concept of television program realism was an important point of difference between the interpretations of working- and middle-class women. While middle-class women enjoyed the unrealistic, fantastical nature of many programs and were critical of the way shows portrayed the middle-class, suburban life-style; working-class women found more to criticize in the former and much to admire in the latter. The material working-class women saw as realistic often portrayed an idealized image of middle-class existence. Press has said, "These pictures come to constitute a normative vision of reality that may influence viewers' interpretations of their own experience, and certainly influences viewers' ideas about what typical American life is and ought to be like" (p. 102). The working-class women saw the ideal as an enviable state; they longed for a better reality, one different from their own, but still close enough to seem attainable.

Most African American girls in this study, particularly older girls, did *not* defer to the magazines' authority in defining their femininity, which was strongly influenced by culture and frequently defined in direct opposition to the mediated ideal. In general, African American girls felt White magazine models who were very thin or made up were not attractive; that diet products and cosmetics were not essential or even desirable for Black girls to look their best. In their eyes, personality, attitude, character, and style were the primary elements of real beauty (see Duke, 2000, and Parker et al., 1995). African American girls were aware of but did not accept the preferred reading, that is, the reading intended by the texts' producers. Nor did they find the unrealistic nature of the text particularly pleasurable as fantasy material.

The realism the African American girls spoke of was not the difference between the real and the imagined. After all, most girls, Black and White, recognize that mediated images routinely alter reality. White girls often spoke of wanting to see more real girls in their magazines – girls who did not look like models. But they usually passed over the occasional image of real girls in the text. White girls knew to say reality is better, but their eyes led them back to the ideal – a reality only for the limited few who work hard enough for the look. Englis (1995) has argued that, "for many who aspire to this quasi-mythical lifestyle," advertising fantasy can be perceived as real (p. 14). However, in contrast to this fantasy-inspired longing and the working-class women in Press (1991), who aspired to a mediated vision of reality, African American girls compared the fictional work to their real-world experience and not only denied the veracity of the ideal, but *preferred their reality* to it.

A new class of beauty

Within the pages of the magazine, girls saw three distinctly different classes of models. Rated on a continuum of inaccessibility, the super-model is at the top – older than other females in the magazine, heavily made up and retouched to present an almost otherworldly beauty, usually seen only in pages financed by major national advertisers. Well-known singers, actresses, and other performers may also fall into this category. They were women the girls knew by name and by reputation; girls saw some of them on multiple pages in every magazine, every month, for years. The frequency with which this handful of women appear make their images indelible in the minds of girls – every girl in the study knew who Tyra and Claudia and Cindy are, what they look like from head to toe, and even details of their personal lives. These are the models with most power to influence how nonreaders view the ideal, because they cut across magazines and media; their images are ubiquitous.

Next on the continuum are the fresh new faces, the lesser known advertising models and models appearing in the magazines' editorial sections. These girls appear younger than the supermodels and they work in relative anonymity. Although they are seldom seen in successive magazines, they seemed vaguely similar to girls who say they all look the same. The magazines seek to personalize some of these models by offering information about them, but girls seemed most interested in learning their ages. To many of the girls in this study, Black and White, these models were a departure from supermodels in that they are more like Everygirl: beautiful, but not exceptionally so. However, most Black girls paid very little attention to the appearance of models. For example, Kira was a reticent reader; she only looked at *Seventeen* because her fashion and beauty magazine of choice, *YSB* (oriented to young, single, black girls), was no longer being published. Kira never commented on the models. When asked about the White model wearing a bathing suit she liked, she said, "I didn't even notice her." She turned great clumps of pages when she came to the articles containing beauty advice. "Yeah, because, to tell you the truth, they have nothing to do with me. 'Cause I don't have that kind of hair, so I have no use to look at them."

In 1994, these two levels of models – well-known supermodels and celebrities and anonymous professional models – dominated the pages of teen magazines. Virtually none of these were women of color, but the few who appeared were said by Black participants to conform closely to Anglo/American beauty standards. In recent years, however, the magazines have introduced a new level of model: real girls who, though attractive, find their ways into magazines because of their style and accomplishments and because they exemplify a particular regional appeal. Last on the continuum from supermodel to nonmodel, and closest to the reader, these girls are most frequently seen in "School Zone," a recurring *Seventeen* feature in which students from a specific high school are highlighted for their unique styles. This feature was intriguing to most participants in this study – Black and White – because School Zone was populated with girls who were real (in contrast to fake professional models) and diverse.

Black girls looked at the real girls in features like School Zone and saw people like themselves and their friends. They liked what they saw. If she could be anyone in the magazine, Tonya, an African American girl, said she would not choose a model but a girl in the School Zone feature because "she seems pretty cool." With features like School Zone, girls were given the chance to look beyond appearance to know more about the faces on the pages – where the featured teens live, what they think, how they coexist with others different from themselves. School Zone teens are often pictured naturally, in groups of friends, in actual school settings. Girls seemed to be attracted to this feature, its models, and their presentations because they are so distinctly different from the typical magazine fare.

For example, Shawn, a Black girl, prided herself on being able to blend with different groups of students at her school. When she read, she sought out *Seventeen*'s School Zone feature with black-and-white photos of real best friends from different schools across the country. She said she would like her best friends to be featured in a story. She pointed to people who are physically dissimilar with particular interest, "I think that they have totally different personalities and it's cool they go together."

School Zone was influential on a number of levels, not least as a source of fashion ideas. The clothes worn in this section are chosen not by advertisers and magazine stylists, but by teens. Girls seemed to be able to tell the difference. Another Black girl, Faith, was drawn to the School Zone feature because, "All that other stuff (fashions) . . . it don't look like something I would wear. And much of this stuff . . . looks okay."

School Zone gave girls an opportunity to see how teens in other parts of the country and world negotiate some of the same appearance and personal style issues with which they struggle. School Zone was one of the most favorably mentioned features in all the magazines, but it is but a small part of a single title. The use of real girls in teen magazines gave the text greater relevance to the African American girls in this study, even when the real girls were White. Black girls consistently responded favorably to images that reflected the naturalism and greater variety of facial features and body types that they embrace as beautiful.

Reading against the mainstream: why girls persist

With the exception of the rare feature like School Zone, Black girls were excluded from mainstream teen magazines in a number of ways – looking past a bevy of White models to the text, Black girls still failed to see representation of their lives or the lives of the majority of Black people. Black girls saw advertised products and ways of interrelating as race specific. Even characters in a story were ascribed a race based on cultural clues: One girl said she knew a story was about a White woman because it was about adoption and she did not know many Black people who adopt babies. The same girl noted that certain clothing brands mentioned in the text were White brands. Even girls whose lives were comfortably middle-class identified the affluent lifestyles portrayed in fashion/beauty magazines as "White":

Nicole, 17: . . . Black people in general, they don't buy Gucci pants . . . They buy what's affordable . . . I'm sure like Oprah probably is like that . . . but not like the average Black woman.

For comparison, a copy of an all-Black teen magazine, *Sisters In Style*, was introduced during the interviews. Although some of the Black girls responded favorably to the publication, especially to the boys it featured, an equal number rated the magazine negatively or said it was not for them. Older girls took issue with what they saw as the shoddy production values and shallow content of *Sisters in Style*. Tonya, 17, who defined herself as a reader, was unimpressed by the magazine. "At least with *Seventeen* . . . you go into a little depth." *Sisters In Style*, she says, "is a lot of pictures, very little words." At the postinterview focus group, even Kira, 17, who initially favored the all-Black publication, questioned its quality standards: "I need more than pretty pictures of (male music star). At least, *Seventeen*, you've got a variety of things you can read about. I wouldn't spend my money for some pictures and maybe two articles." Nicole, 17, also disliked that the publication was printed on a low-quality stock that made for poor photographic reproduction; in addition, she objected to the magazine's idealization of young Black girls lacking the sophistication she exemplified and sought:

Nicole, 17: The little Black teenagers they have in there just look cheesy . . . I'm not like that! . . . They're the little Black girls with the braids and little funky haircuts . . . Or they're still in the baggy pants . . . It's like you look at that and think,

"Hmm, I'm a young Black teenage person and that's how I'm supposed to look." And you don't think about what *you* like anymore. It's based on what you see. And . . . I don't want to be like that.

Most African American girls in this study were generally dissatisfied with being segregated into a niche magazine audience. Over and over, Black girls stressed their desire for greater inclusion in the well-produced, widely available teen magazines read by the majority of teen girls. But they also expressed a desire to include more people of all ethnic and racial backgrounds in mainstream publications. When asked what they might include if they edited a magazine just for Black girls, African American participants frequently rejected the notion that their magazine should serve an exclusive target:

Melissa, 13: I wouldn't make a magazine just for Black girls . . . It would have an equal amount of Black and White people . . . All different kinds of colors . . . Asian guys and Black guys and White guys.

To achieve fairer representation, Black girls say magazines need to consider not only the color of the models they use, but also editorial and advertising. The Black girls in this study want greater diversity in the types of beauty products teen magazines feature, the images of success they portray, and the breadth of cultural experience they address.

Discussion

Englis (1995) has noted marketers' tendency to "assume all consumers are attracted by alluring images of young, urban upscale Caucasian success" (p. 16) and has underscored the need for research that focuses on the marketing implications of consumers' group memberships. Instead of viewing fashion/beauty texts like teen magazines as concretized blocks of meaning, Fiske has preferred Altman's (1986) conception of the text as a menu, from which the audience selects items and creates meanings relevant to their social and cultural perspectives; "the meanings and pleasures that are eventually produced are determined by the social allegiances of the person engaged in it, not by any preferential or possessive activity of the text itself" (Fiske, 1988, p. 248). Participants in this study exemplify this view; in some instances, they demonstrated their agency through "partial consumption," that is, they took from teen magazines the material they judged to be truly "generic," or that meshed with their views as African Americans. Black girls in this study also routinely assumed an anticonsumption attitude by ignoring or negatively critiquing material that they felt reflected an unalloyed Anglo/American focus and an ideology of *White* femininity. Indeed, critique of the limited and idealized presentations of femininity in mainstream teen magazines constituted a large part of Black girls' interpretative act.

The middle-class African American girls in this study make up what Fish (1980) would call an "interpretive community" in that, by virtue of their membership in a marginalized group, they voiced similar interpretations of much of the material in mainstream teen magazines. Although these girls did not speak as a univocal mass, they did share assumptions about the nature and purpose of the text and developed strategies for constructing meanings that differ from the audience majority. Although the African American girls in this study read mainstream teen magazines regularly, they did not engage the texts as fully as did White girls, for simple reasons: They did not see their values in the magazines. They did not see products they can use. Their tastes and attitudes were watered down or ignored. Their family and friends were nominally visible. They did not see *themselves*. And yet, teen magazines claim African American girls as part of their target audience and these girls represent a significant percentage of the readership.

This seeming contradiction can be explained by viewing teen-magazine consumption as a series of acts – and by understanding that partial acts of consumption may be consistent with a reader's desire to critique the text. Because teen magazines are frequently used by girls for identity work, the potential for consumption occurs on three levels: (a) readers can consume the text (read) and concomitantly, (b) aspects of the dominant society's conception of femininity and beauty contained therein (ideological indoctrination), with the text-producer's ultimate goal of (c) creating in girls the desire to complete their consumption task in the marketplace (ideologically driven purchase behavior). African American girls regularly circumvented this consumption cycle; their partial consumption of mainstream teen magazines, through text purchase and reading, did not usually lead to attitudes or behavior that would complete the consumption act in the larger marketplace. Instead, purchase and use of the magazines was frequently a precursor to Black girls' expression of anticonsumption attitudes regarding the texts' fundamental premises. Especially for older Black girls, a primary gratification for reading these magazines was not aspiration to, but critique of, the ideals reflected in the text. Thus, these girls gain a greater sense of solidarity with other Black girls and affirm the value of a more inclusive African American beauty culture. In this sense, then, mainstream teen magazines are more than mere commodities – "they are goods to think with, goods to speak with" (Fiske, 1989, p. 30); what is said and thought, however, may be diametrically opposed to the text producer's preferred reading, depending on the cultural context of the reader.

In mainstream teen magazines, White girls are presented with material that largely reflects, reinforces, or amplifies their individual and cultural ideals. Black girls, on the other hand, recognize that the bulk of material in these magazines conflicts with the interests and ideals of most African Americans. When girls in this study noticed a disparity between their lived reality and the reality presented in teen magazines, they typically moved toward resolution of this difference in one of two ways: White girls were more likely to adjust their sense of reality in order to accommodate ideas and images presented in teen magazines. For example, one White participant commented that real teenage girls didn't look like the models in *Seventeen*. A few moments later, she reversed herself, saying some girls *must* look like the models, "People are born like that . . . they don't all get pimples." The feminine ideal presented in mainstream teen magazines is just close enough to White girls' reality to appear attainable – all a girl need do is master the diet, exercise, fashion, and makeup regimens promoted by the magazines. Pursuit of excellence in these four areas of appearance enhancement frequently enticed White girls into the marketplace in search of the newest and best tools available for replicating the feminine ideal presented in the text. Month after month, White girls who buy into the ritual of beautification through consumption end up back at the table of contents of their favorite teen magazine, seeking the latest information on beauty by the book.

African American girls are not oblivious to beauty standards; they do, for example, enjoy fashion, purchase hair products, and have their nails done, as do many White girls. However, African American girls were far less likely to embrace the idea perpetuated by teen magazines that beauty can be bought; they resisted the notion that a girl's attractiveness, her social standing, her very identity, are inextricably linked with commodity consumption (Agger, 1992, and Pringle, 1983, cited in Duke & Kreshel, 1998, p. 50). For example, most African American girls in this study used no cosmetics and saw no need for them. In mainstream fashion/beauty texts, White girls see and strive for "better" versions of themselves. For the Black girls, however, exclusion from these publications seemed to bolster anticonsumption attitudes, leading them to reject the magazines' central premise that their looks, their lives, their reality, could be improved if they conformed more closely to the mediated feminine ideal.

Black girls easily perceived the teen magazines they read as targeting White girls – however, they were able to take what was useful from the text nonetheless. As one African American girl pointed out, "Just because it's a White magazine doesn't necessarily make it a bad magazine." Black girls' response to exclusion was simply to continue reading until they found material to which they could relate – as Bobo (1995) has noted, "we have learned to ferret out the beneficial and put up blinders against the rest" (p. 55). Unlike White girls, who frequently consume teen magazines in search of transformation, African American girls sought information, for example, about social issues, relationships, and health. Material such as issue-oriented features (e.g., on abortion or drug use), some of the fashion articles, problem pages, horoscopes, quizzes, and venues where readers share their most embarrassing moments were of interest to girls of all races, but Black girls were interested in little else teen magazines had to offer.

This study demonstrates the power of interpretive communities to resist the dominant culture's "generic" consumer appeals. Indeed, Fiske (1989) has argued "semiotic resistance" – one example of which is African American girls' denigration of Eurocentric beauty messages in mainstream teen magazines as *not real* – "results from the desire for the subordinate to exert control over the meanings of their lives" (p. 10). Thus, the Black girls in this study derived a sense of power and indeed, pleasure, from critiquing beauty images that did not reflect their ideals. Rather than subvert their identities to an unattainable mediated standard, they used the text to help consolidate self- and racial identities. Through critical use of the fashion/beauty discourse, "the sense of 'who I am' is constantly defined and redefined through perceived contrasts to others" (Thompson & Haytko, 1997, p. 20).

Because interpretive communities foster a collective consciousness that can challenge the status quo (Davis & Gandy, 1999), for example, White beauty ideals, Helms' (1995) racial identity model merits further exploration as the possible mechanism by which this consciousness is formed, and for insights it may provide into minority audiences' responses to particular images, issues, and marketing propositions. In this study, younger African American girls (ages 13 and 14) did not consciously engage the text with as strong a racial orientation as older girls (ages 17 and 18). They did not seem as conscious of the racial bias older African American girls said was inherent in the magazines. Older Black girls consistently self-identified positively and in opposition to "White" standards; for example, several girls commented on the overemphasis they believed White girls and teen magazines put on looks and male/female relationships, and declared that Black girls were too sensible to act similarly.

Media critics who worry that texts such as teen magazines present girls with a false sense of reality and unrealistic ideals need to qualify their statements. Asking which girls and whose reality may lead to new avenues of inquiry as researchers continue to explore how patterns of consumption are used to differentiate groups and mark social boundaries (Englis, 1995).

This research suggests that the gatekeepers of fashion/beauty texts like teen magazines are trailing the desires of a growing constituency of consumers for more culturally authentic media representations. However, as marketers focus more on audience differences rather than similarities, for example, utilizing more niche or one-to-one marketing efforts, "the prospects for monolithic [social] control are weakened" (Rotzoll, Haefner, & Hall, 1996, p. 82). For example, as the beauty industry's marketing efforts become more authentically inclusive, narrowly defined, ethnocentric ideals of feminine behavior and beauty will have less influence on *all* women.

McRobbie (1994) has observed:

The long overdue but increasing visibility of Black and Asian models in fashion magazines allows for . . . processes of projection and identification. But this cannot be as an exclusive one-to-one relationship between the text and reader. It is not simply a question of looking at the images. Instead, circulating images have to be considered as potentially extending the shared cultures of femininity. (p. 190)

This comment suggests a number of questions: How does the discourse of femininity change once idealized beauty is no longer the exclusive domain of the White woman? Alternatively, how might girls' understandings of race and racial identity change as a result of out-group images and/or perspectives being accorded in-group status by the media? At the textual level, will the material purported to represent girls of color begin to do so in an authentic and egalitarian manner, or will it continue to be distorted to more closely reflect the values and attitudes of the larger market of White consumers? Even if minority girls judge teen magazine images of girls of color as inauthentic, what might the long-term effect of exposure be – greater assimilation into the dominant view, passive resistance, or ongoing anticonsumption and ideological opposition? These are questions that can only be addressed by more research that accommodates the culturally situated responses of girls, and by researchers who approach participants as active, engaged members of increasingly challenging markets.

Note

1. Participants are described as African American or Black, interchangeably, or White, as participants used these terms.

References

Agger, B. (1992). *Cultural Studies as Critical Theory*. London: Falmer.

Altman, R. (1986). Television/Sound. In: T. Modleski (ed.), *Studies in Entertainment: Critical Approaches to Mass Culture*, pp. 39–54. Bloomington: Indiana University Press.

Atkin, D. (1992). An Analysis of Television Series with Minority-Lead Characters. *Critical Studies in Mass Communication* 9, pp. 337–50.

Bell-Scott, P. & P. C. McKenry (1986). Black Adolescents and Their Families. In: G. K. Leigh & G. W. Peterson (eds.), *Adolescents in Families*, pp. 410–32. Mason, OH: South-Western Publishing.

Bobo, J. (1995). The Color Purple: Black Women as Cultural Readers. In: G. Dines & J. M. Humez (eds.), *Gender, Race, and Class in Media: A Text Reader*. Thousand Oaks, CA: Sage.

Bocock, R. (2000). *Consumption*. New York: Routledge.

Bourne, S. C. (1990). The African American Image in American Cinema. *Black Scholar* 21, pp. 12–19.

Bowen, L. & J. Schmid (1997). Minority Presence and Portrayal in Mainstream Magazine Advertising: An Update. *Journalism and Mass Communication Quarterly* 74, pp. 134–46.

Budgeon, S. (1994). Fashion Magazine Advertising: Constructing 'Femininity' in the 'Post-feminist' Era. In: L. Manca & A. Manca (eds.), *Gender and Utopia in Advertising: A Critical Reader*. Lisle, IL: Precopian Press.

Cohen, J. (1991). The 'Relevance' of Cultural Identity in Audiences' Interpretations of Mass Media. *Critical Studies in Mass Communication* 8, pp. 442–54.

Crabtree, B. F. & W. L. Miller (1992). *Doing Qualitative Research*. Newbury Park, CA: Sage.

Currie, D. H. (1996). Decoding Femininity: Advertisements and Their Teenage Readers. *Gender and Society* 11, pp. 453–78.

Davis, J. L. & O. H. Gandy (1999). Racial Identity and Media Orientation. *Journal of Black Studies* 29, pp. 367–71.

Duke, L. L. (2000). Black in a Blonde World: Race and Girls' Interpretations of the Feminine Idea in Teen Magazines. *Journalism and Mass Communication Quarterly* 77, pp. 367–92.

Duke, L. L. & P. Kreshel (1998). Negotiating Femininity: Girls in Early Adolescence Read Teen Magazines. *Journal of Communication Inquiry* 22, pp. 48–71.

Englis, B. G. (1994). Beauty before the Eyes of Beholders: The Cultural Encoding of Beauty Types in Magazine Advertising and Music Television. *Journal of Advertising* 23, pp. 49–65.

Englis, B. G. (1995). To Be or Not to Be: Lifestyle Imagery, Reference Groups, and the Clustering of America. *Journal of Advertising* 24, pp. 13–16.

Evans, E. D., J. Rutberg, C. Sather & C. Turner (1991). Content Analysis of Contemporary Teen Magazines for Adolescent Females. *Youth and Society* 23, pp. 99–120.

Fish, S. (1980). *Is There a Text in This Class? The Authority of Interpretive Communities*. Cambridge, MA: Harvard University Press.

Fiske, J. (1988). Critical Response: Meaningful Moments. *Critical Studies in Mass Communication* 5, pp. 246–50.

Fiske, J. (1989). *Reading the Popular*. Boston: Unwin Hyman.

Frisby, C. M. (2000). Black Like Me: How Idealized Images of Caucasian Women Affect Body Esteem and Mood States of African American Females. Paper presented at the Association for Education in Journalism and Mass Communication, Phoenix.

Gitlin, T. (1983). *Inside Prime Time*. New York: Pantheon.

Glaser, B. G. & A. L. Strauss (1967). *Discovery of Grounded Theory: Strategies for Qualitative Research*. Chicago: Aldine De Gruyter.

Helms, J. E. (1995). An Update of Helms's White and People of Color Racial Identity Models. In: J. G. Ponterotto, J. M. Casas, L. A. Suzuki & C. M. Alexander (eds.), *Handbook of Multicultural Counseling*. Thousand Oaks, CA: Sage.

Jackson, L. A. & S. K. Kelly (1991). The Frequency and Portrayal of Black Females in Fashion Advertisements. *Journal of Black Psychology* 18, pp. 67–70.

Leeds, M. (1994). Young African American Women and the Language of Beauty. In: K. I. Callaghan (ed.), *Ideals of Feminine Beauty: Philosophical, Social and Cultural Dimensions*. Westport, CT: Greenwood Press.

Lincoln, Y. S. & E. G. Guba (1985). *Naturalistic Inquiry*. Newbury Park: Sage.

Lind, R. A. (1996). Diverse Interpretations: The 'Relevance' of Race in the Construction of Meaning in, and the Evaluation of, a Television News Story. *Howard Journal of Communications* 7, pp. 53–74.

McCracken, G. D. (1988). *The Long Interview*. Newbury Park, CA: Sage.

McRobbie, A. (1978). *Jackie!: An Ideology of Adolescent Femininity*. Birmingham: Centre for Contemporary Cultural Studies.

McRobbie, A. (1994). *Postmodernism and Popular Culture*. London: Routledge.

Milkie, M. A. (1999). Social Comparisons, Reflected Appraisals, and Mass Media: The Impact of Pervasive Beauty Images on Black and White Girls' Self-Concepts. *Social Psychology Quarterly* 62, pp. 190–2.

Morley, D. (1980). *The 'Nationwide' Audience: Structure and Decoding*. British Film Institute Monograph, p. 11.

Parker, S., M. Nichter, M. Nichter & N. Vuckovic (1995). Body Image and Weight Concerns among African American and White Adolescent Females: Differences that Make a Difference. *Human Organization* 54, pp. 103–14.

Phinney, J. S. & V. Chavira (1992). Ethnic Identity and Self-Esteem: An Exploratory Longitudinal Study. *Journal of Adolescence* 15, pp. 271–81.

Phinney, J. S. & D. A. Rosenthal (1992). Ethnic Identity in Adolescence: Process, Context, and Outcome. In: G. R. Adams, T. P. Gullotta & R. Montmayor (eds.), *Adolescent Identity Formation*. Newbury Park, CA: Sage.

Prendergast, P., S. M. Zdep & P. Sepulveda (1974). Self Image among a National Probability Sample of Girls. *Child Study Journal* 4, pp. 103–14.

Press, A. (1991). *Women Watching Television*. Philadelphia: University of Pennsylvania Press.

Pringle, R. (1983). Women and Consumer Capitalism. In: C. V. Bladock & B. Cass (eds.), *Women, Social Welfare and the State in Australia*, pp. 85–103.

Rotzoll, K. B., J. E. Haefner & S. R. Hall (1996). *Advertising in Contemporary Society*. Urbana: University of Illinois Press.

Smith, E. J. (1982). The Black Female Adolescent: A Review of the Educational, Career and Psychological Literature. *Psychology of Women Quarterly* 6, pp. 261–88.

Steiner, L. (1991). Oppositional Decoding as an Act of Resistance. In: R. Avery & D. Eason (eds.), *Critical Perspectives on Media and Society*. New York: Guilford.

Stevenson, T. H. & W. J. Stevenson (1988). A Longitudinal Study of Blacks in Magazine Advertising: 1946–1986. In: *Proceedings of the Annual Meeting of the Southern Marketing Association*, pp. 75–8. Carbondale, IL: Southern Marketing Association.

Thompson, C. J. & D. L. Haytko (1997). Speaking of Fashion: Consumers' Uses of Fashion Discourses and the Appropriation of Countervailing Cultural Meanings. *Journal of Consumer Research* 24, pp. 15–28.

Ukadike, N. K. (1990). Western Film Images of Africa: Genealogy of an Ideological Formulation. *Black Scholar* 21, pp. 30–48.

Willis, E. (1992). *No More Nice Girls: Countercultural Essays*. Hanover: Wesleyan University Press.

Zinkhan, G. M., W. J. Quails & A. Biswas (1990). The Use of Blacks in Magazine and Television Advertising: 1946–1986. *Journalism Quarterly* 67, pp. 547–53.

IV

Ideologies

17

The German Ideology

Karl Marx and Friedrich Engels*

The Ruling Class and the Ruling Ideas:
How the Hegelian Conception of the Domination
of the Spirit in History Arose

The ideas of the ruling class are in every epoch the ruling ideas: i.e., the class which is the ruling *material* force of society is at the same time its ruling *intellectual* force. The class which has the means of material production at its disposal, consequently also controls the means of mental production, so that the ideas of those who lack the means of mental production are on the whole subject to it. The ruling ideas are nothing more than the ideal expression of the dominant material relations, the dominant material relations grasped as ideas; hence of the relations which make the one class the ruling one, therefore, the ideas of its dominance. The individuals composing the ruling class possess among other things consciousness, and therefore think. Insofar, therefore, as they rule as a class and determine the extent and compass of an historical epoch, it is self-evident that they do this in its whole range, hence among other things rule also as thinkers, as producers of ideas, and regulate the production and distribution of the ideas of their age: thus their ideas are the ruling ideas of the epoch. For instance, in an age and in a country where royal power, aristocracy and bourgeoisie are contending for domination and where, therefore, domination is shared, the doctrine of the separation of powers proves to be the dominant idea and is expressed as an 'eternal law'.

The division of labour, which we already saw above as one of the chief forces of history up till now, manifests itself also in the ruling class as the division of mental and material labour, so that inside this class one part appears as the thinkers of the class (its active, conceptive ideologists, who make the formation of the illusions of the class about itself their chief source of livelihood), while the others' attitude to these ideas and illusions is more passive and receptive, because they are in reality the active members of this class and have less time to make up illusions and ideas about themselves. Within

*Originally published as pp. 39–40 from *The Marx-Engels Reader 2e*, ed. Robert C. Tucker (New York: W. W. Norton & Company). © 1978, 1972 by W. W. Norton & Company, Inc. Used by permission of W. W. Norton & Company, Inc.

this class this cleavage can even develop into a certain opposition and hostility between the two parts, but whenever a practical collision occurs in which the class itself is endangered they automatically vanish, in which case there also vanishes the appearance of the ruling ideas being not the ideas of the ruling class and having a power distinct from the power of this class. The existence of revolutionary ideas in a particular period presupposes the existence of a revolutionary class; about the premises of the latter sufficient has already been said above.

If now in considering the course of history we detach the ideas of the ruling class from the ruling class itself and attribute to them an independent existence, if we confine ourselves to saying that these or those ideas were dominant at a given time, without bothering ourselves about the conditions of production and the producers of these ideas, if we thus ignore the individuals and world conditions which are the source of the ideas, then we can say, for instance, that during the time the aristocracy was dominant, the concepts honour, loyalty, etc., were dominant, during the dominance of the bourgeoisie the concepts freedom, equality, etc. The ruling class itself on the whole imagines this to be so. This conception of history, which is common to all historians, particularly since the eighteenth century, will necessarily come up against the phenomenon at ever more abstract ideas hold sway, i.e., ideas which increasingly take on the form of universality. For each new class which puts itself in the place of one ruling before it is compelled, merely in order to carry through its aim, to present its interest as the common interest of all the members of society, that is, expressed in ideal form: it has to give its ideas the form of universality, and present them as the only rational, universally valid ones. The class making a revolution comes forward from the very start, if only because it is opposed to a *class*, not as a class but as the representative of the whole of society, as the whole mass of society confronting the one ruling class.[1] It can do this because initially its interest really is as yet mostly connected with the common interest of all other non-ruling classes, because under the pressure of hitherto existing conditions its interest has not yet been able to develop as the particular interest of a particular class. Its victory, therefore, benefits also many individuals of other classes which are not winning a dominant position, but only insofar as it now enables these individuals to raise themselves into the ruling class. When the French bourgeoisie overthrew the rule of the aristocracy, it thereby made it possible for many proletarians to raise themselves above the proletariat, but only insofar as they became bourgeois. Every new class, therefore, achieves domination only on a broader basis than that of the class ruling previously; on the other hand the opposition of the non-ruling class to the new ruling class then develops all the more sharply and profoundly. Both these things determine the fact that the struggle to be waged against this new ruling class, in its turn, has as its aim a more decisive and more radical negation of the previous conditions of society than all previous classes which sought to rule could have.

This whole appearance, that the rule of a certain class is only the rule of certain ideas, comes to a natural end, of course, as soon as class rule in general ceases to be the form in which society is organised, that is to say, as soon as it is no longer necessary to represent a particular interest as general or the 'general interest' as ruling.

Note

1. Universality corresponds to: (1) the class versus the estate; (2) the competition, world intercourse etc.; (3) the great numerical strength of the ruling class; (4) the illusion of the *common* interests (in the beginning this illusion is true); (5) the delusion of the ideologists and the division of labour.

18

Ideology

Louis Althusser*

Marx showed that every social formation constitutes an 'organic totality', comprised of three essential 'levels': the economy, politics, and *ideology* – or '*forms of social consciousness*'. The ideological 'level', then, represents an objective reality, indispensable to the existence of a social formation – an objective reality: that is, a reality independent of the subjectivity of the individuals who are subject to it, even whilst it concerns these individuals themselves; this is why Marx used the expression 'forms of social consciousness'. How does the objective reality and social function of *ideology* present itself?

In a given society, people participate in *economic* production whose mechanisms and effects are determined by the *structure of the relations of production*; people participate in *political* activity whose mechanisms and effects are governed by the *structure of class relations* (the *class struggle*, law and the State). These same people participate in other activities – religious, moral, philosophical, etc. – either in an active manner, through conscious practice, or in a passive and mechanical manner, through reflexes, judgements, attitudes, etc. These last activities constitute *ideological activity*; they are sustained by voluntary or involuntary, conscious or unconscious, adherence to an ensemble of representations and beliefs – religious, moral, legal, political, aesthetic, philosophical, etc. – which constitute what is called the 'level' of *ideology*.

Ideological *representations* concern nature and society, the very world in which men live; they concern the life of men, their relations to nature, to society, to the social order, to other men and to their own activities, including economic and political practice. Yet these representations are not *true knowledges* of the world they represent. They may contain some *elements* of knowledge, but they are always integrated into, and subject to, a total *system* of such representations, a system that is, in principle, orientated and distorted, a system dominated by a *false conception* of the world or of the domain of objects under consideration. In fact, in their real practice, be it economic or political, people are effectively determined by *objective structures* (relations of production, political class relations); their practice convinces them of the *existence* of this reality, makes them perceive *certain objective effects* of the action of these structures, but conceals the essence of these structures from them. They cannot, through their mere practice, attain *true*

*Originally published as L. Althusser, "Theory, Theoretical Practice and Theoretical Formation: Ideology and Ideological Struggle," pp. 1–42 from *Philosophy and the Spontaneous Philosophy of the Scientists & Other Essays* (London and New York: Verso). © 1990 by Verso. Reprinted with permission from Verso.

knowledge of these structures, of either the economic or political reality in whose mechanism they nevertheless play a definite role. This knowledge of the *mechanism of economic and political structures* can derive only from *another practice*, distinct from immediate economic or political practice, *scientific practice* – in the same way that knowledge of the laws of nature cannot be the product of simple technical practice and perception, which provide only empirical observations and technical formulae, but is, on the contrary, the product of specific practices – *scientific practices* –distinct from immediate practices. None the less, men and women, who do not have knowledge of the political, economic and social realities in which they have to live, act and perform the tasks assigned them by the division of labour, cannot live without being guided by some *representation* of their world and their relations to this world.

In the first instance men and women find this representation readymade at birth, existing in society itself, just as they find – pre-existing them – the relations of production and political relations in which they will have to live. Just as they are born 'economic animals' and 'political animals', it might be said that men and women are born 'ideological animals'. It is as if people, in order to exist as conscious, active social beings in the society that conditions all their existence, needed to possess a certain *representation* of their world, a representation which may remain largely unconscious or, on the contrary, be more or less conscious and thought out. Thus, ideology appears as a certain '*representation of the world*' which relates men and women to their conditions of existence, and to each other, in the division of their tasks and the equality or inequality of their lot. From primitive societies – where classes did not exist – onwards, the existence of this *bond* can be observed, and it is not by chance that the first form of this ideology, the reality of this bond, is to be found in *religion* ('bond' is one of the possible etymologies of the word *religion*). In a class society, ideology serves not only to help people live their own conditions of existence, to perform heir assigned tasks, but also to 'bear' their condition – either the poverty of the exploitation of which they are the victims, or the exorbitant privilege of the power and wealth of which they are the beneficiaries.

The representations of ideology thus consciously or unconsciously accompany all the acts of individuals, all their activity, and all their relations – like so many landmarks and reference points, laden with prohibitions, permissions, obligations, submissions and hopes. If one represents society according to Marx's classic metaphor – as an edifice, a building, where a juridico-political *superstructure* rests upon the infrastructure of economic foundations – ideology must be accorded a very particular place. In order to understand its kind of effectivity, it must be situated in the *superstructure* and assigned a relative autonomy vis-à-vis law and the State; but at the same time, to understand its most general form of presence, ideology must be thought of as sliding into all the parts of the edifice, and considered as a distinctive kind of *cement* that assures the adjustment and cohesion of men in their roles, their functions and their social relations.

In fact, ideology permeates all man's activities, including his economic and political practice; it is present in attitudes towards work, towards the agents of production, towards the constraints of production, in the idea that the worker has of the mechanism of production; it is present in political judgements and attitudes – cynicism, clear conscience, resignation or revolt, etc.; it governs the conduct of individuals in families and their behaviour towards others, their attitude towards nature, their judgement on the 'meaning of life' in general, their different cults (God, the prince, the State, etc.). Ideology is so much present in all the acts and deeds of individuals that it is *indistinguishable from their 'lived experience'*, and every unmediated analysis of the 'lived' is profoundly marked by the themes of ideological obviousness. When he thinks he is dealing with pure, naked perception of reality itself, or a pure practice, the individual (and the empiricist philosopher) is, in truth, dealing with an impure perception and practice, marked by the invisible structures of ideology; since he does not *perceive* ideology, he takes his perception of things and of the world as the perception of 'things themselves', without realizing that this perception is given him only in the veil of unsuspected forms of ideology.

This is the first essential characteristic of ideology: like all social realities, it is intelligible only through its *structure*. Ideology comprises representations, images, signs, etc., but these elements considered in isolation from each other, do not compose ideology. It is their *systematicity*, their *mode of arrangement and combination*, that gives them their meaning; it is their *structure* that determines their meaning and function. The *structure* and mechanisms of ideology are no more immediately *visible* to the people subjected to them than the *structure* of the relations of production, and the mechanisms of economic life produced by it, are visible to the agents of production. They do not perceive the ideology of their representation of the world *as ideology*; they do not *know* either its structure or its mechanisms. They *practise* their ideology (as one says a believer practises his religion), they do not know it. It is because it is determined by its *structure* that the reality of ideology exceeds all the forms in which it is subjectively lived by this or that individual; it is for this reason that it is irreducible to the individual forms in which it is lived; it is for this reason that *it can be the object of an objective study*. It is for this reason that we can speak of the nature and function of ideology, and study it.

Now a study of ideology reveals some remarkable characteristics.

1.   We notice, first of all, that the term *ideology* covers a reality which – while diffused throughout the body of society – is divisible into distinct areas, into *specific regions*, centred on several different themes. Thus, in our societies, the domain of ideology in general can be divided into relatively autonomous regions: religious ideology, moral ideology, juridical ideology, political ideology, aesthetic ideology, philosophical ideology. Historically, these regions have not always existed in these distinct forms; they only appeared gradually. It is to be expected that certain regions will disappear, or be combined with others, in the course of the development of socialism and Communism, and that those which remain will participate in the internal redivisions of the general domain of ideology. It is also important to remark that, depending upon the historical period (that is, the mode of production), and within identical modes of production, according to the different social formations in existence, and also, as we shall see, the different social classes, this or that *region of ideology* dominates the others in the general domain of ideology. This explains, for example, the remarks of Marx and Engels on the dominant influence of religious ideology in all the movements of peasant revolt from the fourteenth to the eighteenth centuries, and even in certain early forms of the

working-class movement; or, indeed, Marx's remark (which was not in jest) that the French have a head for politics, the English for economics, and the Germans for philosophy – a significant remark for understanding certain problems specific to the working-class traditions in these different countries. The same kind of observations might be made regarding the importance of religion in certain liberation movements in former colonial countries, or in the resistance of Blacks to white racism in the United States. Knowledge of the different regions within ideology, knowledge of the *dominant ideological region* (whether religious, political, juridical, or moral), is of prime importance for the strategy and tactics of ideological struggle.

2.   We note as well another essential characteristic of ideology. In each of these regions, ideology, which always has a determinate structure, can exist *in more or less diffuse or unthought forms, or, contrariwise, in more or less conscious, reflected, and explicitly systematized forms – theoretical forms*. We know that a religious ideology can exist with rules, rites, etc., but without a systematic theology; the advent of theology represents a degree of theoretical systematization of religious ideology. The same goes for moral, political, aesthetic ideology, etc.; they can exist in an untheorized, unsystematized form, as customs, trends, tastes, etc., or, on the contrary, in a systematized and reflected form: ideological moral theory, ideological political theory, etc. The highest form of the theorization of ideology is *philosophy*, which is very important, since it constitutes the laboratory of *theoretical abstraction*, born of ideology, but itself treated as theory. It is as a theoretical laboratory that philosophical ideology has played, and still plays, a very significant role in the birth of the sciences, and in their development. We have seen that Marx did not abolish philosophy; by a revolution in the domain of philosophy he transformed its nature, rid it of the ideological heritage hindering it and made of it a scientific discipline – thus giving it incomparable means with which to play its role as the theory of real scientific practice. At the same time, we must be aware that – with the exception of philosophy *in the strict sense* – ideology, in each of its domains, is irreducible to its *theoretical* expression, which is generally accessible only to a small number of people; it exists in the masses in a theoretically unreflected form, which prevails over its theorized form.

3.   Once we have situated ideology as a whole, once we have marked out its different regions, identified the region that dominates the others, and come to know the different forms (theorized and untheorized) in which it exists, a decisive step remains to be taken in order to understand the ultimate meaning of ideology: *the meaning of its social function*. This can be brought out only if we understand ideology, with Marx, as an element of the *superstructure* of society, and the essence of this element of the superstructure in its relation with the *structure of the whole* of society. Thus, it can be seen that the function of ideology in class societies is intelligible only on the basis of the existence of social classes. In a classless society, as in a class society, ideology has the function of assuring the *bond* among people in the totality of the forms of their existence, the *relation* of individuals to their tasks assigned by the social structure. In a class society, this function is *dominated* by the form taken by the division of labour in distributing people into

antagonistic classes. It can then be seen that ideology is destined to assure the cohesion of the relations of men and women to each other, and of people to their tasks, in the general structure of class exploitation, which thus prevails over all other relations.

Ideology is thus destined, *above all*, to assure the domination of one class over others, and the economic exploitation that maintains its pre-eminence, by making the exploited accept their condition as based on the will of God, 'nature', moral 'duty', etc. But ideology is not only a 'beautiful lie' invented by the exploiters to dupe the exploited and keep them marginalized; it also helps *individuals of the dominant class* to recognize themselves as dominant class subjects, to accept the domination they exercise over the exploited as 'willed by God', as fixed by 'nature', or as assigned by a moral 'duty'. Thus, it likewise serves them as a bond of social cohesion which helps them *act as members of the same class*, the class of exploiters. The 'beautiful lie' of ideology thus has a double usage: it works on the consciousness of the exploited to make them accept their condition as 'natural'; it also works on the consciousness of members of the dominant class to allow them to exercise their exploitation and domination as 'natural'.

4.   Here we touch on the decisive point which, in class societies, is at the origin of the *falsity* of ideological *representation*. In class societies, ideology is a representation of the real, but necessarily distorted, because necessarily biased and tendentious – tendentious because its aim is not to provide men with *objective knowledge* of the social system in which they live but, on the contrary, to give them a mystified representation of this social system in order to keep them in their 'place' in the system of class exploitation. Of course, it would also be necessary to pose the problem of the function of ideology in a classless society – and it would be resolved by showing that the deformation of ideology is socially necessary as a function of the nature of the social whole itself, as a function (to be more precise) of *its determination by its structure*, which renders it – as a social whole – opaque to the individuals who occupy a place in society determined by this structure. The opacity of the social structure necessarily renders *mythic* that representation of the world which is indispensable for social cohesion. In class societies this first function of ideology remains, but is dominated by the new social function imposed by the *existence of class division*, which takes ideology far from the former function.

If we want to be exhaustive, if we want to take account of these two principles of necessary deformation, we must say that in a class society, ideology is necessarily deforming and mystifying, both because it is produced as deforming by the opacity of the determination of society by its structure and because it is produced as deforming by the existence of class division. It is necessary to come to this point to understand why ideology, as representation of the world and of society, is, by strict necessity, a *deforming and mystifying* representation of the reality in which men and women have to live, a representation destined to make men and women accept the place and role that the structure of this society imposes upon them, in their *immediate* consciousness and behaviour. We understand, by this, that ideological representation imparts a certain '*representation*' of reality, that it makes *allusion* to the real in a certain way, but that at the same time it bestows only an *illusion* on reality. We also understand that ideology gives men a certain 'knowledge' of their world, or rather allows them to 'recognize' themselves in their world, gives them a certain 'recognition'; but at the same time ideology only introduces them to its *misrecognition*. *Allusion-illusion* or *recognition-misrecognition* – such is ideology from the perspective of its relation to the real.

It will now be understood why every science, when it is born, has to break from the mystified-mystifying representation of ideology; and why ideology, in its *allusive-illusory* function, can survive science, since its object is not knowledge but a social and objective misrecognition of the real. It will also be understood that in its social function science cannot replace ideology, contrary to what the *philosophes* of the Enlightenment believed, seeing only illusion (or error) in ideology without seeing its *allusion* to the real, without seeing in it the social function of the initially disconcerting – but essential – couple: *illusion* and *allusion*, recognition and misrecognition.

5. An important remark concerning class societies must be added. If in its totality ideology expresses a representation of the real destined to sanction a regime of class exploitation and domination, it can also give rise, in certain circumstances, to the expression of the *protest of the exploited classes* against their own exploitation. This is why we must now specify that ideology is not only divided into regions, but also *divided into tendencies* within its own social existence. Marx showed that 'the ruling ideas of each age have ever been the ideas of its ruling class'. This simple phrase puts us on the path to understanding that just as there are dominant and dominated classes in society, so too there are dominant and dominated ideologies. Within ideology in general, we thus observe the existence of *different ideological tendencies* that express the 'representations' of the different social classes. This is the sense in which we speak of bourgeois ideology, petty-bourgeois ideology, or proletarian ideology. But we should not lose sight of the fact that in the case of the capitalist mode of production these petty-bourgeois and proletarian ideologies remain *subordinate* ideologies, and that in them – even in the protests of the exploited – it is always the ideas of the dominant class (or bourgeois ideology) which get the upper hand. This scientific truth is of prime importance for understanding the history of the working-class movement and the practice of Communists. What do we mean when we say, with Marx, that bourgeois ideology dominates other ideologies, and in particular working-class ideology? We mean that working-class protest against exploitation expresses itself *within the very structure of the dominant bourgeois ideology*, within its *system*, and in large part with its representations and terms of reference. We mean, for example, that the ideology of working-class protest 'naturally' expresses itself in the form of bourgeois law and morality.

The whole history of utopian socialism and trade-union reformism attests to this. The pressure of bourgeois ideology is such, and bourgeois ideology is so exclusively the provider of raw ideological material (frames of thought, systems of reference), *that the working class cannot, by its own resources, radically liberate itself from bourgeois ideology*; at best, the working class can express its protest and its aspirations by using certain elements of bourgeois ideology, but it remains the prisoner of that ideology, held in its dominant structure. For 'spontaneous' working-class ideology to transform itself to the point of freeing itself from bourgeois ideology it must *receive, from without, the help of science*; it must transform itself under the influence of a new element, radically distinct from ideology: science. The fundamental Leninist thesis of the 'importation' of Marxist science into the working-class movement is thus not an arbitrary thesis or the description of an 'accident' of history; it is founded in necessity, in the nature of ideology itself, and in the absolute limits of the natural development of the 'spontaneous' ideology of the working class.

Very schematically summarized, these are the specific characteristics of ideology.

19

Interpellation

*John Fiske**

For Althusser, ideology is not a static set of ideas imposed upon the subordinate by the dominant classes but rather a dynamic process constantly reproduced and reconstituted in practice – that is, in the ways that people think, act, and understand themselves and their relationship to society.[1] He rejects the old idea that the economic base of society determines the entire cultural superstructure. He replaces this base/superstructure model with his theory of overdetermination, which not only allows the superstructure to influence the base but also products a model of the relationship between ideology and culture that is not determined solely by economic relations. At the heart of this theory is the notion of ideological state apparatuses (ISAs), by which he means social institutions such as the family, the educational system, language, the media, the political system, and so on. These institutions produce in people the tendency to behave and think in socially acceptable ways (as opposed to repressive state apparatuses such as the police force or the law, which coerce people into behaving according to the social norms). The social norms, or that which is socially acceptable, are of course neither neutral nor objective; they have developed in the interests of those with social power, and they work to maintain their sites of power by naturalizing them into the common-sense – the only – social positions for power. Social norms are ideologically slanted in favor of a particular class or group of classes but are accepted as natural by other classes, even when the interests of those other classes are directly opposed by the ideology reproduced by living life according to those norms.

Social norms are realized in the day-to-day workings of the ideological state appara-tuses. Each one of these institutions is "relatively autonomous," according to Althusser, and there are no overt connections between it and any of the others – the legal system is not explicitly connected to the school system nor to the media, for example – yet they all perform similar ideological work. They are all patriarchal; they are all con-cerned with the getting and keeping of wealth and possessions; and they all endorse individualism and competition between individuals. But the most significant feature of ISAs is that they all present themselves as socially neutral, as not favoring one particular class over any other. Each presents itself as a principled institutionalization of equality: the law, the media, and education all claim, loudly and often, to treat all individuals

* Originally published as "British Cultural Studies and Television," pp. 284–326 from *Channels of Discourse, Reassembled*, ed. R. C. Allen (Chapel Hill and London: University of North Carolina Press). © 1992 by the University of North Carolina Press. Used by permission of the publisher.

equally and fairly. The fact that the norms used to define equality and fairness are those derived from the interests of the white, male, middle classes is more or less adequately disguised by these claims of principle, though feminists and those working for racial and class harmony may claim that this disguise can be torn off with relative ease.

Althusser's theory of overdetermination explains this congruence between the "relatively autonomous" institutions by looking not to their roots in a common, determining economic base but to an overdetermining network of ideological interrelationships among all of them. The institutions appear autonomous only at the official level of stated policy, though the belief in this "autonomy" is essential for their ideological work. At the unstated level of ideology, however, each institution is related to all the others by an unspoken web of ideological interconnections, so that the operation of any one of them is "overdetermined" by its complex, invisible network of interrelationships with all the others. Thus the educational system, for example, cannot tell a story about the nature of the individual different from those told by the legal system, the political system, the family, and so on.

Ideology is not, then, a static set of ideas through which we view the world but a dynamic social practice, constantly in process, constantly reproducing itself in the ordinary workings of these apparatuses. It also works at the micro-level of the individual. To understand this we need to replace the idea of the individual with that of the subject. The individual is produced by nature, the subject by culture. Theories of the individual concentrate on differences between people and explain these differences as natural. Theories of the subject, on the other hand, concentrate on people's common experiences in a society as being the most productive way of explaining who (we think) we are. Althusser believes that we are all constituted as subjects-in-ideology by the ISAs, that the ideological norms naturalized in their practices constitute not only the sense of the world for us, but also our sense of ourselves, our sense of identity, and our sense of our relations to other people and to society in general. Thus we are each of us constituted as a subject in, and subject to, ideology. The subject, therefore, is a social construction, not a natural one. A biological female can have a masculine subjectivity (that is, she can make sense of the world and of her self and her place in, that world through patriarchal ideology). Similarly, a black person can have a white subjectivity and a member of the working classes a middle-class one.

The ideological theory of the subject differs in emphasis, though not fundamentally, from that developed in psychoanalysis by placing greater emphasis on social and historical conditions, particularly those of class. Althusser drew upon Freudian theory to develop his idea of the subject. As Ann Kaplan notes, feminists too have used psychoanalytic theory, though much more sophisticatedly, to theorize the gendered subject. This gendered subject is more rooted in psychological processes, the ideological subject of Althusser in historical and social ones.

But both theories stress the role played by the media and language in this constant construction of the subject, by which we mean the constant reproduction of ideology in people. Althusser uses the words *interpellation* and *hailing* to describe this work of the media. These terms derive from the idea that any language, whether it be verbal, visual, tactile, or whatever, is part of social relations and that in communicating with someone we are reproducing social relationships.

In communicating with people, our first job is to "hail" them, almost as if hailing a cab. To answer, they have to recognize that it is to them, and not to someone else, that we are talking. This recognition derives from signs, carried in our language, of whom we think they are. We will hail a child differently from an adult, a male differently from a female, someone whose status is lower than ours differently from someone in a higher social position. In responding to our hail, the addressees recognize the social position our language has constructed, and if their response is cooperative, they adopt this same position. Hailing is the process by which language identifies and constructs a social position for the addressee. Interpellation is the larger process whereby language constructs social relations for both parties in an act of communication and thus locates them in the broader map of social relations in general.

Hailing is obviously crucial at the start of a "conversation," though its ideological work continues throughout. Look, for instance, at the opening statements of the anchor and reporter on a US network news report in April 1991:

Anchor: There is growing concern tonight about the possible economic impact that a nationwide railroad strike set for midnight tonight poses. The unions and the railroads remain deadlocked. Wyatt Andrews brings us up to date on what President Bush and Congress may do about it

Reporter: By morning 230,000 rail workers might not be working on the railroad and the strike threatens millions of Americans. Just as thousands of commuters may find no train leaving the station beginning tonight at midnight.

The word *strike* hails us as anti-union, for "striking" is constructed as a negative action by labor unions that "threatens" the nation. By ascribing responsibility to the unions, the word hides the fact that management plays some role, possibly even a greater one, in the dispute. The report opposes the unions not to management plays but to "the railroads" and thus excludes the unions from them. This exclusion of the unions from the railroads allows the unspoken management to become synonymous with them, and ideology continues its work by constructing the railroads not as an industry but as a national resource and so uses them as a metonym for the nation and, by extension, of "us." Recognizing ourselves in the national "us" interpellated here, we participate in the work of ideology by adopting the anti-union, subject position proposed for us. This is subject-as-ideology is developed as the item progresses:

Passenger A: Gas, miles, time. The highways are going to be packed. Not much we can do, though.

Passenger B: I'm going to stay home. I've got an office in my home and I'm going to just stay there and work.

Reporter: But the commuter inconvenience is nothing compared to the impact on freight trains. Up to half a million industrial jobs may be at stake. Whether it's cars in the heartland or chemicals in Kansas City, the railroads still carry more freight than either trucks or airplanes, meaning that the strike would threaten the heart of industrial America in the heart of this recession.

Railroad Official: If we don't get this strike settled quickly a lot more people are going to be out of work, a lot more product is not going to be shipped and this economy's recovery is going to be set back immensely.

Reporter: Negotiations meanwhile seem to be at bedrock bottom, on wages, on health care, and the number of workers per train. Both sides even late today were on opposite tracks. The unions complain the railroads blocked raises and stone-walled the negotiations for three years. The railroads accuse the unions of protecting legions of workers who essentially do nothing.

Railroad Offical: The issue with our union is between who works and who watches. That's the issue of whether we have excess people in the cab who don't have anything to do.

The national "we" is constructed as hard-working producers at the personal level by the passengers and at the industrial level by the reporter. The repeated use of the "heart" metaphor not only makes "America" into a living, breathing body (like the one "we" inhabit), but it constructs the unions as a potentially lethal disease, if not a stiletto-wielding assassin! The railroad official continues to conflate "the railroads" (by which he means "the management") with the national subject of the hard-working producer.

So far, the dispute has been cast solely in terms of the bad effects the unions have upon this national "us," and only in the reporter's next segment do we receive a hint that there are causes of the dispute that may both justify it and implicate management in it. These hints are left floating, so we have no way of assessing the reasonableness of the wage claims, for instance. The generalized terms – "on wages, on health care, on the number of workers per train" – contrast with the concrete realities of 230,000 unionists not working and of the million of Americans, thousands of commuters, and up to half a million jobs that are threatened. We might like to think about the ideological practice of not allowing the unions to speak for themselves "live," but of putting their case into the words of the reporter management "us." Unionists would not, for instance, describe their negotiating opponents as "the railroads," nor would they categorize their arguments as mere "complaints" while according management's the stronger status of "accusations."

The news item concludes by continuing the ideological practice that by now seems so natural and familiar:

Reporter: What exactly happens in the morning? If you are a commuter, check locally. Some Amtrak and commuter trains will be operating and some of the unions say they will strike only freight lines and not passenger trains. In Washington, watch Capitol Hill. Tomorrow President Bush is likely to ask Congress to impose a solution: the move, the unions say, plays right into the railroads' hands. The unions have all along warned the railroads would stall the negotiations and force tonight's strike all in the snug belief that Congress would bail then out.

As Mimi White points out . . . this view of ideology as a process constantly at work, constructing people as subjects in an ideology that always serves the interests of the dominant classes, found powerful theoretical support in Gramsci's theory of hegemony. Originally, *hegemony* referred to the way that one nation could exert ideological and social, rather than military or coercive, power over another. However, cultural theorists tend to use the term to describe the process by which a dominant class wins the willing consent of the subordinate classes to the system that ensures their subordination. This consent must be constantly won and rewon, for people's material social experience constantly reminds them of the disadvantages of subordination and thus poses a constant threat to the dominant class. Like Althusser's theory of ideology, hegemony does not denote a static power relationship but a constant process of struggle in which the big guns belong to the side of those with social power, but in which victory does not denote a static power relationship but a constant process of struggle in which the big guns belong to the side of those with social power, but in which victory does not necessarily go to the big guns – or, at least, in which that victory is not necessarily total. Indeed, the theory of hegemony foregrounds the notion of ideological struggle much more than does Althusser's ideological theory, which at times tends to imply that the power of ideology and the ISAs to from the subject in ways that suit the interests of the dominant class is almost irresistible. Hegemony, on the other hand, posits a constant contradiction between ideology and the social experience of the subordinate that makes this interface into an inevitable site of ideological struggle. In hegemonic theory, ideology is constantly up against forces of resistance. Consequently it is engaged in a constant struggle not just to extend its power but to hold on to the territory it has already colonized.

Note

1. Louis Althusser, "Ideology and Ideological State Apparatuses," in *Lenin and Philosophy and Other Essays* (London; New Left Books, 1971), pp. 127–86.

20

Becoming Dagongmei: Politics of Identities and Differences

*Pun Ngai**

Dagongmei, the working daughter, is a newly embodied social identity emerging in contemporary China, produced to meet the changing socioeconomic relations of the country and the needs of capital. A new identity has been crafted, accompanied by a new ethics of self, which is inscribed on young rural female bodies when they enter into a particular set of production relations, experiencing the process of proletarianization and alienation.[1] At first glance, this construct looks inevitably to be a disciplinary project that works with homogeneous and reactive forces to interpellate the self with a modern worker identity. With insights from Dorinne Kondo's *Crafting Selves* (1990, 16), a disciplinary project on identity, which implies unity and fusion, often goes together with a fragmentation of the self. The process of constituting an identity is imbued with a politics of difference that offers a vivid configuration of self and identity in everyday life struggles situated in particular moments and occasions. This politics of difference highlights a heterogeneous, incoherent, fluid, and conflict-laden process of identity-making on specific bodies in distinct situations.

In this chapter I describe the process as it builds a social identity; I look both from the side of power and the side of the subject, and I examine regulatory and identificatory practices inside and outside the workplace. Dagongmei is a specific ethics of self, construed at the particular moment when private and transnational capital emerged in post–Mao China. As a condensed identity, dagongmei reveals the story of how a state socialist system gives way to the capitalist global economy and how capitalist practices depend entirely on a complex web of regulations, and on class, rural-urban differences, kin and ethnic networks, and sexual relations.[2] In particular, I will look at a play of difference in the process of producing the subject dagongmei in the workplace, and how social and historical differences along the lines of social status, class, and gender differences regulate a work hierarchy that, in turn, is reinforced by a workplace distinction system in terms of work position, wage and bonus, accommodation, and even work clothing. Along with the politics of difference, I also highlight a politics of discourse in which we see how disciplinary production deploys the art of metaphor, the power of language, and the politics of othering and differentiating in crafting a new identity, that

*Pp. 1–18 from *The China Journal*, no. 42, July. © 1999 by The China Journal. Reprinted with permission from The China Journal.

of dagongmei. The "manufacture" of identity involves both the politics of discourse and the politics of difference.

By writing on the politics of difference I do not intend to look at the inherent fragmentation of the psychological self in its signification process of becoming a subject. Rather I locate a play of difference in the process of creating the subject dagongmei in the larger field of social and cultural meanings embedded in a rapidly reconfiguring Chinese society. I highlight the social and historical differences in the self-internalization of the new identity of dagongmei as it appears in the significatory chain and strives to emerge into the symbolic world. At the core of the regulatory and identificatory practices in urban and industrial China, there is a politics of difference that establishes a violent hierarchy between the rural and the urban, the northerner and the southerner, and the male and the female. In the workplace I was informed by this politics, and it let me see and experience how regional, kin, and ethnic differences were imagineered in crafting the identity of dagongmei.

As a newly coined term dagongmei embraces multilayered meanings and denotes a new kind of labor relationship fundamentally different from that of Mao's period. *Dagong* means "working for the boss" or "selling labor," thereby connoting commodification and capitalist exchange of labor for wages (Lee 1998). It is a new concept that contrasts with the history of Chinese socialism. Labor, especially alienated labor, supposedly emancipated for more than thirty years, is again sold to capitalists, this time under the auspices of the state machine. In contrast to the term gongren, or worker, which carried the highest status in the socialist rhetoric of Mao's day, the new word dagong signifies a lesser identity – that of a hired hand – in a new context shaped by the rise of market factors in labor relations and hierarchy. Mei means younger sister; it denotes not merely gender but also marital status – mei indicates single, unmarried, and younger (in contrast to *jie*, older sister), and thus mei often signifies a lower status. Dagongmei therefore implies an inferior working identity inscribed with capitalist labor relations and sexual relations.

The term dagongmei, paradoxically, did not necessarily carry a negative sense for the young rural girls themselves; rather, it provided new identities and new senses of the self to be acquired once they worked inside a global factory. Self-subjectivization was crucial to the power of capital that needed willing labor. As Foucault (1994, 81–2) has said, the project of political technology or governmentality is at the same time a project of selfsubjectivization. It is fascinating to see how these two conflicting forces converge and contrast in manufacturing consent and identity in the workplace, and how these contestations can be understood within the larger dynamics of Chinese society that highlight shifting hegemony, values, and social forces in the postsocialist period.

A Fumbled Identity: My First Day on the Shop Floor

At 6:00 a.m. in late autumn 1996 I awoke while my dormitory roommates were still sleeping. I was a bit excited because after two weeks of reading company archives and other documents in the general office at the Meteor electronics factory, I was finally going out to work on the assembly line. In order to look like a factory girl, I bought T-shirts, jeans, and shoes in a local market in the Nanshan district. I also had my hair curled – at the suggestion of Tall Ling, the director's secretary. Arriving a bit early at the factory, I saw Jun from the personnel department eating breakfast at a small food shop just opposite the factory building. "You don't need to hurry," Jun said, "I know you are going to work on the shop floor today." With a smile, she added that today, in my new clothes, I looked like a factory worker. "Without your glasses, you are our double."

Jun led me to the department of general affairs where I signed some paperwork and received my factory uniform: two sets of blue overalls, a blue cap, a pair of white gloves, and a pair of slippers. Blue was the color that designated the production department. Before I went upstairs to the shop floor, I changed my clothes in the washroom. Jun was still with me and she laughed at my appearance. I somehow felt that although I was in overalls, my image was awkward and my newly assumed identity had not crystallized. Jun brought me to assembly line B on the fourth floor. It was about 8:00 a.m. Except for some echoes of machine sounds, silence reigned on the whole shop floor. I was shocked, not by the silence but because the moment I appeared on the shop floor everyone stared at me. With my heart throbbing, I wondered, did my appearance in my overalls look bizarre? Didn't I look like a dagongmei? Was I not expected to work on the shop floor? He-chuan, the foreman of line B, looked at me as if he were expecting me, and he was the only one to welcome me. He led me to my seat on the middle of the line, a position on the screwing station, and asked me to sit down. I did as he asked, knowing that all gazes still fell on my body – a body unfit for an identity.

My identity as an ethnographer, albeit ambiguous and unstable, was certainly too reified for me to adapt to a new identity. Time after time I wondered and asked myself: Was I anything like a factory girl? I knew all the workers could never acknowledge my appearance as a dagongmei, even if in the end they accepted me as someone who worked with them. My past identities did become diluted and ambiguous as time went on, and I found myself totally lost in the industrial world, toiling twelve hours each day without knowing what was going on in the outside "civilized" world. Yet I still dared not ask the question of whether or not I was a dagongmei. People treated me differently on the shop floor, which reminded me of my past identities. No one, not even myself, was able to inscribe on me the proper identity of dagongmei. Indeed, from the beginning the production machine had no interest in incorporating me; I was left alone.

Different Fate, Different Identity: Meifang's Coming

The fate of my coworker Meifang greatly contrasted with my fate. The production machine held a strong desire to turn Meifang into a dagongmei, a modern female worker. So did Meifang herself. None of us was born to be a worker, especially those like Meifang who were born to be "peasants." Granting oneself an identity that could find no residue – no cause and effect and no justification in biological factors or any born-to-be attributes – involved particularly sophisticated techniques and strategies of power. Internalization, on the other hand, required further meandering, painful, and even perverted ways of technologizing the self.

The day that Meifang started she was brought to a seat opposite me. Unlike my training period, she was given serious warnings and strict instructions before she could start working. Bailan, our line leader, first checked her overalls, cap, and gloves, and then told her to have her hair neatly tied up and completely covered by her work cap: "Make sure not a single string of hair falls on the desk, the chair, or the floor. Short hair is easily dropped in the product and can't be easily noticed. Your fingernails should be trimmed, otherwise the gloves will tear and cause flecks on the product," Bailan said.

Then Meifang was instructed to wear a static electricity belt on her wrist to prevent her body's static from interfering with the electronic products. She was also given a metal recorder and told to tap it before she put the product onto the conveyor belt: "You should never forget to tap it. The recorder not only counts how much work you do, but also the amount that the entire line produces. All the numbers from each recorder should be the same at the end. You should not make any mistake," Bailan said, and then started to teach Meifang her assigned task.

I noticed immediately a basic difference in the way the management treated Meifang and me. He-chuan had told me to take care of my fingers and not to be hurt by the screwdriver, whereas Bailan told Meifang to take care of the driver and not let it get worn. Moreover, it took me a week to understand that Meifang was hired to supplement my work because management thought I could not keep up with the work pace and that it was likely that I would occasionally leave the line for other reasons.

Meifang was given on-the-job training for a three-month probation period before she was granted a work contract for one year, which was the practice for all newcomers. In our work process, four miniature screws and two even smaller ones were used to attach a main board to two outer cases. Picking up screws from the box and putting them in the appropriate positions required nimble fingers and a quick hand; otherwise one might pick up more than one screw at the same time because they easily stuck to the fingers, and they easily could be lost. But this was not the difficult part – the element that required the greatest skill was handling the electric screwdriver. The amount of force necessary mattered most: different sizes of screws or the same sizes in different positions involved different amounts of force. Too much force would result in small cracks in the case; too little force and the screw might tilt and require repositioning. It took me three days to become adept at the work process.

Although Meifang took nearly as long as I to learn the work process, a few days later she was able to work much faster. But she was silent all the time. Even after working for two weeks she still often just nodded and smiled at me and then went back to work, "She seems unhappy. She doesn't utter a word for a whole day. How odd!" my coworker Fatso gossiped to me at lunch one day. What kept Meifang quiet? What worried her when other workers relaxed and fell into laughter from time to time? Was a fairly fit body to do the job still not good enough for her?

Indeed, a fairly fit body was not enough because it was not complete; it was unsatisfactory to both the production machine and the workers themselves. For survival in a modern factory one needed something more, something fundamental to one's sense of

self. Meifang was unhappy and I was uncomfortable. There was something we felt
lacking and this lack was unarticulated. We were both capable of doing the work but
we were not well equipped to be workers, dagongmei, who strived to live in a modern
industrial space.

If it is correct to say, as do Gilles Deleuze and Félix Guattari (1984, 28), that the
creation of lack is a function of the market economy, the art of the dominant class, and
that it is deliberately created, organized, and produced in and through social production,
then we need to know how this primary fear of lack in Meifang, as well as in others like
her, is produced and how they are induced to live with it. Dagongmei as a cultural-
symbolic artifact contains a set of reactive forces that try to homogenize human activities
and senses of self that should be plural, fluid, and fragmentary. The process of homogenization is a process of exclusion and displacement, which produces anxiety, inflicts
pain, and drives individuals to integrate into the collective will of the hegemonic
construct.

To Be a Worker: The Politics of Rural–Urban Difference

The politics of labor identity in China is linked not only to the project of industrialization but also to a distinctive spatial rural-urban dichotomy. The rural space could only
nurture peasants and the urban space workers. Three decades of Chinese socialist
history did not imagine a modernization project but rather a curtain between rural and
urban and thus between peasants and workers. Chinese socialist beings were born to
have an identity not from biology but from locality, and by their locality were designated
either urban or rural. Mao's industrialization required the extraction of rural resources
to support the urban establishment; rigid plans for rural and urban development; and
thus a strict control on individual status and identity (Solinger 1999). The art of naming
and classification thus was central to Mao's politics; the hukou system of registration
was one such creation. Deng's industrial development and ways of realizing the market
economy, on the other hand, demanded not only raw material but also human power
from the rural areas, which is why Meifang and millions of other rural women were
needed as dagongmei.

Among the 550 workers in the Meteor factory in early 1996, only eleven held an
urban hukou; all of the rest came from rural villages or rural towns all over the country
and were listed as peasants in the official registry classification. These migrants were
born in rural areas, and as such they were not workers but had already been named as
peasants. Yet they were needed as laborers. This time the state socialist machine, burdened by its past history, was powerless to regear itself and it gave way to the capitalist
machine. The identity of the dagongmei echoed a relationship to the urban, to capital,
but not to the state. There was, and there had to be, new models of workers in the new
era. The machine of capital thus felt free to reterritorialize the urban-rural boundaries
and to mimic the politics of naming and exclusion.

At first newcomers like Meifang were not considered by Meteor management to be
qualified workers but rather workers to be. Even after they had worked for a few months
in the factory, young women were often still considered to be from the country. They

were easily identifiable not because of their lack of skill or speed at work but because of their appearance and their inappropriate behavior in the industrial space. They often looked fresh and quiet, and although they wore T-shirts and jeans they did not put on face powder or lipstick and their jeans were a bit out of style. Their main pastime – knitting – further imparted a distinctly rural image. Still, not only did the production machine aim to transform them into dagongmei, modern working daughters, but the girls themselves also aimed for this goal.

I always kept my work pace as slow as possible to ensure that every piece I produced was of good quality. I was afraid that any defect for which I was responsible would cause my coworkers, especially Meifang, to be reprimanded. Still, mistakes could not be avoided. In the late afternoon of Meifang's fifth day, still within her training period, I became very drowsy and hoped that someone would start talking. Our foreman, He-chuan, holding a route-finder, suddenly showed up in front of Meifang and yelled, "What the hell are you doing? You are going to spoil this casing. Such a big scratch here (he pointed to the case of the route finder). Did you learn something by heart? You know you are not ploughing a furrow, don't you? These products are very expensive, you couldn't pay for it even if you worked in the fields for a year. *Cushou cujiao!* (Rough hands, rough feet)." Then he turned his eyes to me, and showing embarrassment, added, "These village girls are always like that, difficult to teach."

He-chuan left. I saw Meifang's face grow flushed and her eyes fill with tears. I was angry at He-chuan's sudden and irresponsible reproach: he had not tried to determine who had caused the scratch before shouting at Meifang. But then I understood that he actually could never know who was responsible. He just came to the most likely target, shouting so that all of us doing the same work process could hear and share the responsibility. In shouting to express his authority. He-chuan was in effect defeating himself, showing that he could not totally control the labor process. But his language had another function. It produced a surplus value that the disciplinary power did not expect: helping to craft the identity of dagongmei. The metaphor he used – ploughing a furrow – signified the low value placed on farm work and hence a lesser working identity. Such metaphors were invoked time and time again on the shop floor: to make a scratch on the case is like ploughing a furrow on the land, and thus one is a peasant, not a worker. But even though one is only a peasant, one should behave like a worker.

In the metaphor that He-chuan used in his reprimand, he did not mean to imply that working in the factory was like farming on the land, but he could not escape the same paradox: industrial work was not agricultural work, but in some sense it might still be like it. Otherwise how could the metaphor be effective? Invoking the metaphor did show the contradictory nature of the discourse, but it never wasted energy. By juxtaposing farming and industrial work in this way, a hierarchy of values was reinforced in which factory work occupied a higher rank. A gap was produced, a void that allowed power to produce abject subjects.

Meifang was not the only girl subject to this kind of reprimand and the power of language. Every day on the shop floor I heard discriminatory language directed toward the workers. The Cantonese term *xiangxiamei* (village girl) was often used to depreciate the status of the women from rural areas. Phrases like "xiangxiamei, you know nothing except farming," "xiangxiamei, what else can you understand? Learn the rules and behave in a civilized way," "a xiangxiamei is always like a xiangxiamei, cushou cujiao," and "xiangxiamei can never be taught! [They are] foolish and stupid" were frequently heard in the workplace, especially when a male foreman or line leader came to criticize or scold the workers. The metaphorical meanings hidden in these daily usages were the great contrasts between the body and the space: unfit xiangxiamei living incompatibly in the modern industrial world. On the one hand, were the stupid, uneducated, and uncivilized rustic women whose labor was cheap and despised. On the other hand, was the modern technology of the factory, whose products were valuable and exported internationally. Intense anxiety was aroused by such remarks, making some people feel lacking, unfit, or not properly suited to the life of the factory. Women like Meifang felt frustrated for not living up to the demands of a modern world and for not being modern themselves.

Shop floor conversations, arguments, and reprimands always served to remind Meifang and other recent hires of their past identities as peasants. "Cushou cujiao" was the physical stigma of the person as a peasant, whereas xiangxiamei was the abject identity that had to be polished and upgraded. It took me quite a long time to understand why Meifang was not happy. To avoid being discriminated against one had to try hard to change oneself, Self-technologizing, as Foucault (1988) said, is the core of power and a product of modern subjectivity. To make war with one's past identity was for the sake of establishing a new identity; to cut the umbilical cord of one's past life was to create a base for building up a new self. Industrial work was desired not only for the wages but for the new identity and the new sense of life that it created. The imagined peasantness of cushou cujiao was the constitutive outside, or the negative otherness of the new identity. Without mirroring and then negating one's past identity it was difficult to make a new life.

One chilly evening in spring 1996 I had a chance to talk to Meifang in her dormitory. At first she remained timid and kept her head low. I tried hard to start a conversation by asking general questions about where she was from, how old she was, and how many siblings she had. She told me she was from a village in the north of Hunan Province and then gave me a few details about her family situation. Then, without warning, she started crying. I was upset by seeing the tears flowing down her face.

"I really want to go back home."

"Why? You work so well in the factory."

"I don't know, I miss my home. I feel that I don't fit in the workplace."

"But why? You are not working slower than the other people."

"I don't know why. I just feel I don't fit here. I feel I'm too different from the others. Next month after I get my wage, I'll leave."

The month passed, however, and Meifang did not leave.

Later she told me, "Life is hard here, but if others can stand it, why not me?" Moreover, Meifang had started to go out with other workers on their days off, and at night she listened to Cantonese popular music with them. She bought more current fashions and she asked me to help her buy hair shampoo, facial cleaner, and a lipstick from Hong Kong. Buying cosmetics was one of the ways I did favors for the workers, although not without a sense of guilt over introducing more commodified goods to them.

The Admonition Meeting

Our line had a fifteen-minute "admonition meeting" (*xun dao hui*) every Wednesday at 4:30 p.m. A few minutes before it started, Bailan, the line leader, would stop the line in preparation for speeches by members of the personnel and production departments. Tin, the production department assistant manager, always came. If there were serious production problems, the department manager himself, Mr. Wu, would show up. Tin was a university graduate in his early thirties and had worked at the Meteor plant for over four years. In the eyes of the line women, he was a sharp and capable figure of urban background. We also sometimes thought he was attractive, if he was in a good mood. He was urbane and educated; in a world of few men, he was often a target of fantasy.

One Wednesday Meifang and I were musing about what would happen at the afternoon admonition meeting. At 4:30 Ying, from personnel, along with Tin, He-chuan, and Bailan appeared, and all the line workers, except me, were asked to queue up in front of the line. I was told to stay in my seat. Again I felt like an outsider; time and time again I found that the production machine had no intention of disciplining me. On this day Ying wore a three-piece outfit with a skirt and looked like an urban career woman. At Meteor, she was classified as clerical staff. Her status, wage, fringe benefits, and living conditions were all different from the line workers. In a managerial tone, she stated:

> This week a worker was caught punching another worker's timecard in her absence. This is a serious violation and we reserve the right to dismiss her at once. There is no excuse for anybody to clock on for best friends or fellow villagers. The helper will be punished more seriously than the one who asked for help. In the factory one should be responsible for oneself only. If you are so used to helping each other in the village, remember that now you are in the factory. . . .
>
> The company inspected the workers' dormitory on Monday. Production tools, such as scissors and adhesive tape, were found in two workers' bunks. Although they are not expensive things, these are acts of theft. In accordance with the factory regulations, these two workers each have been fined 50 yuan. Again, we consider these serious offenses. If they violate the rules again, these two workers will be dismissed immediately.
>
> During the inspection, I found cartons that had been brought out by the workers to make benches in their rooms. I emphasize that workers are not permitted to bring any production materials outside the factory gate, even if they are waste. Waste is not your property, it belongs to the company. You have no right to use it. To put it seriously, I can treat that as stealing too. Your habit of taking waste back home should be changed. Let me repeat, you are working now in the factory; the bad habits you bring from the country should be given up. No spitting on the floor, and keep your bunk and room clean.

Ying's speech did not surprise anybody; it was the usual stuff. The workers simply stood quietly, some showing no interest in listening. Information circulated among workers through gossip and rumors, not through this kind of formal address. All the shop floor workers already knew who had been caught clocking on for another worker and who was fined for possession of company materials. The common feeling toward the workers who were caught was that they were "unlucky." Meifang kept her head low and did not look at Ying. But Ying's words had their function. Even if she could not uphold the factory regulations and impose them on the workers, she nevertheless could sometimes put into words the nature of peasantness. *Huxiang bangzhu* – helping each other – was perceived to be an attribute of village life that had to be given up to live in an industrial world. Workers were to be responsible for themselves alone: the production machine wanted isolated individuals only. Industrial women were to learn to compete with each other and not help each other.[3]

Stealing, too, was often taken to be a bad habit common to country people. Ying and other staff of urban origin often warned me not to leave valuable things in the dormitory. Workers were not allowed to bring bags into the workplace. All workers were inspected going in or out of the gate because each one was considered a potential thief. Bad characteristics of human nature like stealing were thought to be nurtured in rural areas. The notion of private property thus became a complicated issue for the peasant workers. They were told to give up sharing resources and were even taught to despise the practice because sharing was related to stealing, as in the repeated emphasis that factory waste products were company property that workers must not take away to reuse. The logic of capitalist practice needed to win out against any noncapitalist reasoning in order to assert its hegemony. To gain the power, to win the battle, all other lifestyles I had to be destroyed.

Tin's speech focused more on the production target and work discipline on the line. He said that our line had more rejects than the other lines, which negatively affected production speed. He reminded us not to talk while working and said that everybody should be more attentive. Next Monday, Western customers from Europe were scheduled to visit the company, and he told us to behave ourselves: "Everybody should wash their overalls on the weekend. We don't want the customers to see a speck of dirt on your body or in the workplace. No one is allowed to leave his or her work seat until the end of the tour. Materials and cartons should be well allocated and labeled. Company policy is to show we have a completely modern and well-trained work force and a technologically advanced factory." Workers were asked for cooperation. It seemed that a sense of belonging to the company and a sense of self-esteem as a modern worker were to be articulated in front of the foreign customers.

At dinner the women on our line discussed the speeches. They accepted much of what Tin said, but they laughed at Ying. She had at least ten nicknames, such as "Miss Canton," "tall mei," "bossy cat," and "chicken." Posing as a "modern lady," she was less an admired figure than a target of jeers and innuendoes. She was often mocked behind her back, when tone and attitudes were mimicked and made fun of. Immediately after her sudden inspection of the shop floor, laughter would erupt and rough language would spread down the line: "The bossy cat dresses up so nice. What is she going to do tonight? Flirt with men?" or, "Miss Canton really thinks she is Miss Canton. I can't stand the way she walks." As a figure standing for modernity and urbanity, Ying was seen to be on the side of management and capital. It was a negative image, and not one the women workers wanted to imitate.

Inventing Local, Kin, and Ethnic Identity and Inequality

The politics of difference and othering in crafting subjects are further complicated by the intertwining of local, kin, and ethnic relations in the workplace. Women workers were not merely identified and classified as urban or rural people, but also more specifically by region and ethnic group (Lee 1998). In the Meteor factory, one-third of the women were from villages or towns in Guangdong Province. These Guangdong women were linguistically and regionally divided according to whether they came from Cantonese-dialect areas, Chaozhou-dialect areas, or Hakka areas (only two of the women workers were Shenzhen locals). The remaining two-thirds of the total female labor force came from other provinces across China and were, both inside and outside the factory, referred to as *Waisheng ren* (provincial outsiders). They were commonly nicknamed by province of origin: Sichuan mei, Hunan mei, Hubei mei, or simply Bei mei (northern girls); whereas women from Guangdong Province were called Chaozhou mei, Canton mei, and Hakka mei. These were all common terms used in the workplace to identify individuals, especially in daily language when workers addressed each other.

The identification of a person according to region or ethnicity embodies a sense of spatial inequality far more subtle than the rural-urban disparity. Where one is from and one's dialect foretells one's status and wealth, and thus one's bargaining power and position in the workplace hierarchy. The rural-urban distinction, as a soil for nurturing differences, is deliberately divided into finely stratified hierarchies through its intersection with locality and with kin-ethnic identities.[4]

The most common question in the workplace, which was often used to start a conversation or make friends with strangers, was "Ni shi shenme difang ren?" (literally, "A person of what *difang* [place] are you?"). Difficult to paraphrase, it carries a much richer meaning than the English phrase "Where are you from?" *Di* means the place, the locality, while *fang* embodies a cultural meaning of *di*, connoting specific kin and ethnic relationships. Thus the question asks not only where you are from, but also what is your kin-ethnic identity and which local dialect do you use. In daily conversations workers in the Meteor plant seldom directly asked each other their names but rather asked about affiliation to local and kin-ethnic groups. With few exceptions, workers were grouped into different locality or kin-ethnic enclaves, and were enmeshed in different networks of obligation and authority in the workplace.

Regional and kin-ethnic networks were often manipulated by the production machine to create a division of labor and job hierarchies. In the Meteor factory all of the important and supervisory positions were to some extent affected by local and kin-ethnic power. A line leader was chosen not only for her work capabilities but also for her network affiliations and prestige among the workers.

Siu Wah, the line leader of line C, told me that the control of everyday operations on the shop floor was not as easy as it might appear. It involved the cooperation and consent of every worker in each seat. For a rush order, the work pace had to be increased, which required the women's cooperation. Thus, the most reliable workers were from one's own kin group and area, and the best thing to do was to enlarge one's own group. Such enlargement thus was the most important political way for dominant groups to maintain their status or for weaker groups to struggle for enhancement of their position. The weakest groups were the outsiders to the province, especially those from north China, who were often called Waisheng mei or Bei mei. They were forced to take jobs packing or soldering, the drudge work. Competition for "good jobs" was a daily occurrence on the shop floor, and workers relied on local or kin-ethnic power for these job negotiations.

The Meteor management skillfully made use of local and kin-ethnic relations to facilitate production efficiency and profit maximization, and to facilitate the control of workers. Locals and kin were considered responsible for each other's performance. In cases where unskilled new workers were hired on a relative's recommendation, the relatives often served as trainers, which saved the management time and money. Sometimes kin were made to take responsibility for those newcomers who did not conform to factory discipline or violated some of the basic rules of workers' behavior.[5] The workers were afraid that if their recommendation proved unsuitable, they would not have another chance to introduce a kin or a friend and their own reputations would be affected as well. This self-disciplining within localistic and kin-ethnic circles heightened the efficiency of labor control, and to a certain extent enforced the submissiveness of the female workers.

Regional and kin-ethnic differences among workers were further exaggerated, invented, and manipulated to divide and rank the workforce. A work hierarchy was developed along the lines of the imagined cultural traits of each individual. The director of Meteor, Mr. Zhou, said that in his ten years of work experience in Shenzhen, he had developed a particular knowledge about each kin-ethnic and locality group. He believed that different groups had different sorts of personalities and work capacities that were suitable for different kinds of jobs. His imagination, or invention, of their traits shaped the hierarchy of the labor force inside the factory. For example, he viewed the Chaozhou mei as submissive and attentive but clever, and thus suitable for accounting and personnel work. The Hakka mei were shy and reticent but industrious. They were good listeners and good followers, and so after training they were fit for midlevel management such as foremen or line leader. Zhou said the Hakka mei were often seen by other employers in Shenzhen to be inferior to the Cantonese, but he himself thought they were better because the Cantonese had more choices for upward mobility and so were not as loyal as Hakkas. At Meteor, most of the supervisor and line leader positions were filled by Hakka and Chaozhou people, while almost all of the Waisheng mei were on the production line.

The Waisheng mei, those from outside the province, were eager to show off their capabilities, Zhou said, given that the local government and local people discriminated against them in job hiring, promotion, and right of residence. Zhou thought that the Hubei mei were better than the Hunan mei because poor regions made for hard workers. Hubei mei were considered good operatives – they were dexterous and willing to work hard. Certainly it was obvious that they had less bargaining power, especially because they were only a small group in the workplace.[6]

The manipulation of kin-ethnic groups was further complicated by the production machine's use of them against each other to prevent labor resistance. Mr. Wu, the production manager, said that although local groups seemed to dominate in certain positions, he would not let them totally control any part of the work process. Locality groups placed on the same production line were easier to control and train, but he would insert an individual from another group as a counterweight. Wu said he did not trust these groups because they had many tricks and they could resist at any time by collective illness and slowdowns. In line B where I worked there were twenty-one workers, including eight from Chaozhou, five from Hakka areas, three from Sichuan, three from Hunan, and one from Guizhou. Our line leader, Bailan, was from Chaozhou. Bailan tried to keep a balance between each group and rarely showed preference for any particular group, but in times of difficulty or for rush orders she relied on her own locals, the Chaozhou mei, to help her. In daily conversations Cantonese and Mandarin were the two dialects most often used in our line as official languages, but when Bailan asked for help from her locals she would use the Chaozhou dialect. Distrust among groups was serious. Communication was not only hindered by different dialects but also by the constructed bias and discrimination from the production machine. A divided workforce was created as locality and kin-ethnic relations were mapped out and reinforced to shape a hierarchy of jobs and to facilitate labor control.

The Wage System and Differentiation

The divisions in the workforce were further enacted and codified by the wage system. Excluding the Hong Kong managers, positions such as those occupied by He-chuan, Ying, or Bailan received the highest salaries. The wage system was central to the production and reproduction of workplace life because it was the most obvious and crucial mechanism in playing out the politics of difference and differentiation. Conspicuously organized on a hierarchical basis, the wage system contributed to a kaleidoscope of power and status along lines of locality, kin-ethnicity, and gender. The wage system at Meteor was very complicated because it simultaneously deployed various payment methods, like monthly pay, daily pay, hourly pay, overtime work pay, and production bonuses. The pay one received spoke for one's status and identity and was self-explanatory, although the exact amounts were confidential.

Daily talk about wages was, however, frequent in the workplace and would mount when payday approached. Despite the policy on wage confidentiality, most of the workers actually knew each other's salary, either through their own networks or through rumor. The incomes of the five Hong Kong managers were in amounts often beyond workers' imaginations, but could be judged by the managers' daily expenditures (such as frequent eating out in the restaurant or calling taxi services) as somewhere in the range of fifteen to twenty times that of local managerial staff. Most of the mainland Chinese workers showed no interest in comparing their wages with the Hong Kong managers, because they were, in effect, from another world. All of the office and supervisory staff members above the grade of line leader were paid at a monthly rate. These urban people or college degree holders earned a monthly income in a range between 1,000 and 1,500 yuan. Envied by the majority of workers who were paid a mixture of hourly rate, overtime rate, and production bonus, these office and supervisory staff members enjoyed a privileged position with a stable income and good prospects. They were also housed in a different type of dormitory that usually was composed of units with cooking and water facilities. Of these positions the dagongmei could only dream, as they knew their rural and education background inscribed on them a different fate.

The line operators and manual workers were generally paid at an hourly rate. In 1996, normal working hours in the daytime were paid in renminbi, at a rate of RMB 2.4 per hour. Overtime work at night was paid in Hong Kong dollars at $3.6 per hour. Such wage practices induced these workers to work as long as possible at night for overtime work pay. If they did not work overtime, their wages could be as low as 300 yuan, and such amounts in Shenzhen could only support their daily basic expenditures on food, rent, and clothing. A lunchbox meal cost 2 yuan, and dinner at a food store could reach as high as 5 yuan. The price of a pair of jeans varied from RMB 20 to RMB 50 at the local market. The company charged each worker fifty yuan monthly for staying in the factory dormitory. "We all hate night work, but it is the only way to earn Hong Kong dollars and the money," the line women on the shop floor often said to me.[7] With overtime pay and the production bonus the line workers could have an average pay of around 500 to 600 yuan a month. Some workers told me that they moved to the Meteor plant because of its abundant overtime work paid in Hong Kong dollars, which accounted for up to one-third of the line workers' wages.

Besides overtime pay, the line workers received a bonus share that made up about one-fourth of their monthly wages. These bonus shares often were the most contested terrain in the payment system because they induced favoritism and clientalistic networks on the shop floor. The amount of production bonus received by each line worker was determined by his or her line leader based on an assessment of individual performance and productivity. The workers often complained to me that the assessment of the bonus was not "scientific" because it was subjective and hence it was hard to challenge the assessment scheme. The common understanding was whoever has a relative as the line leader gets a "good bonus," and such an arrangement was crucial to safeguarding one's salary. Power struggles along locality and kin-ethnicity lines were waged on these concrete monetary rewards. From the perspective of the line leaders, these production bonuses provided her or him room for manipulating line workers' consent and cooperation, especially when meeting rush orders.

The wage system for paying the line leaders was the most complicated one. It was based on neither monthly pay nor hourly rate but rather was directly linked to the line's productivity, and was composed of a mixture of a basic salary and the median income of the workers on the specific line. The basic salary of the line leaders ranged from 400 to 600 yuan, and by adding the median income of the line's workers, the leaders' wages were often double those of the workers'. A line leader at Meteor could earn as much as the supervisory staff if his or her line performed well.

This system induced line leaders to raise the productivity of their lines as high as possible. Struggles to be line leader were intense in the workplace. Capability was a necessary but not sufficient factor for promotion to line leader. Work experience and strong workers' support, usually along lines of locality and kinship, were another must. Three line leaders, from Canton, Chaozhou, and Sichuan, respectively, were friendly toward me. All of them had been working at Meteor for over three years and had been promoted to the position from line worker. Each had a "big sister" image that was supported by strong kin-ethnic networks in the workplace. One night my line leader,

Bailan, invited me to her room to have soup, and I noticed that she was provided with better dormitory conditions than were the line workers. The line operators' or basic workers' room were shared by eight persons, while Bailan's room was shared only by four. All dormitory rooms had one toilet and one balcony for hanging washed clothes, but Bailan's room also had a TV set, which was collectively owned by the roommates. A higher wage, plus a better living environment, all contributed to the workplace hierarchy.

Daily Prejudice and Accommodation

In general, workers entering the factory were preinscribed with a local or ethnic identity that dictated a set of invented cultural traits and a presumed work capability. They also were judged by their dialect and accent, both within the factory premises and outside. At work, cultural traits were manipulated and mixed up with economic interests, and thus individual workers were snared into a hierarchy and then a conflict among themselves. Privileged groups such as the Cantonese and Chaozhou internalized the management's favoritism by mirroring a model image and living up to that invention. The abject groups, especially the Waisheng ren, resisted management's derogatory images of them either by working hard to show their industriousness and looking for chances to show their capabilities or, alternatively, by adopting the stereotypes imposed on them. Everyday tactics were fluid and strategic, and on different occasions individuals would react differently. The following passage is taken from my field notes, recording a complaint by a Sichuan worker:

10 April 1996: Li Ting's Anger

At about 11 p.m. I'd finished taking a bath and looked around to join in on some women's talk before going to bed. I passed Li Ting's room, and noticed she was angry with her roommate Yue, a Cantonese woman. On fire, Li Ting shouted, "Don't think yourself extraordinary for being a Cantonese! You always bully people." Yue did not argue back but ran off to the other room. I calmed down Li Ting and asked her what happened. She said, still angry: "This woman always runs wild and does whatever she wants to do. She never considers others and she looks down on people. I can't stand her any longer. Because she's a Cantonese, she thinks she's big. She broke my bowl, and has no intention of buying me another. Instead she said my stuff blocked her way . . . She never cleans the room but always criticizes others for making the room dirty and always thinks that Waisheng ren are much dirtier than any other people.

Different local or ethnic groups in the workplace seldom made friends across their boundaries, and the distrust was worsened by the lack of spare time to communicate with each other. Daily conflicts escalated due to the tight space and rushed time, aggravated by the mutual creation of negative images toward each other. In the eyes of Cantonese or Chaozhou groups, Waisheng mei were often portrayed as uncivilized persons and as much lazier and dirtier. Waisheng mei, who although poorer were often better educated than the Guangdong people, regarded the Cantonese as rude, proud, crafty, and never to be trusted. "These are the people who tread on my feet and remind me daily that I am a lesser human," was the common feeling of Waisheng mei toward the Cantonese. At work, Waisheng mei were allocated work at the bottom of the job hierarchy. In daily life they were excluded and bullied. Mutual exclusion based on a construct of local and ethnic elements into a "personhood" was arbitrary and violent.

Language and Identity: The Cantonization of the Workplace

The struggle over rural, urban, regional, and ethnic identities was further exacerbated by the struggle over languages, specifically the politics of dialects in the workplace. Language is a system of differences produced and reproduced in a spider web of social differences, hierarchies, and distinctions that construe social reality.[8] The struggle over legitimate language, as Bourdieu (1991, 52–4) notes, is highly political because it encompasses a struggle over identity, status, and power. The politics of identity is enmeshed in a politics of language. It matters what dialect one speaks, and with what accent. In the factory a hierarchy of dialects was deployed in a "language war" that was linked to the struggle over work position, resources, and power.

This language war was launched in the workplace in different arenas and was aimed at different goals. First, it involved the rivalry between Mandarin and Cantonese. Mandarin is the official language in China and is politically superior, but in much of Guangdong it has lost its legitimacy. The subordination of the national official language to the local dialect is due in part to the fact that the importance of state power in regulating social life has given way to local market forces. The war between the two languages does not merely reflect the intense combat between the state and the market machines in regulating social life but also makes it and shapes it. In the workplace Mandarin is still commonly used, but it is no longer endowed with power, superiority, or a hegemonic position. Cantonese, on the other hand, as the commercial language has the upper hand in shaping the workplace hierarchy. Although the members of the factory's upper management are from Hong Kong, those in middle management are mostly Cantonese speakers from cities like Guangzhou, Zhongshan, and Shunde. The managerial language thus is Cantonese, which was normally used in managerial meetings, in passing orders from a higher level to a lower level, and in daily encounters among those in positions of management and supervision.

A command of Cantonese, then, was a must for climbing the hierarchical ladder. It improved the chance for promotion, because in Cantonese one could not only converse better with superiors but also be part of the same habitus and the same expressive style, and thus be more readily assimilated into managerial culture. Mr. Zhou and the four Hong Kong managers never uttered a word in Mandarin. Even when they knew that an individual's Cantonese was poor, they still insisted on using it. For them Cantonese was cultural capital: it was a symbol of superior status and identity that helped them to exercise their authority more effectively. This power of language was neither invisible nor silently exerted on individuals but rather was explicitly demonstrated. Subordinates who were not native speakers yet learned to speak Cantonese fluently were appreciated and had a better chance of promotion. Those who did not know Cantonese had to bear the costs in misunderstandings with superiors or others, and the anxiety that such misunderstandings created. If one did not want to remain at the bottom of the work hierarchy, one was induced to learn Cantonese, or at least to understand enough to survive in the workplace.

Although the language war had resulted in a victory for the commercial language of Cantonese, there was still defiance and transgression from time and time. Tensions were particularly acute when a Mandarin speaker in a high position in the workplace came into contact with a Cantonese speaker, notably in the case of communications between the engineering and production departments. The staff in the production department, both Cantonese speakers and non-Cantonese speakers, were totally assimilated to Cantonese. The engineers and technicians in the engineering department, however, were mainly university graduates from northern cities and exhibited a rather unyielding attitude to Cantonese. For them, accurate Mandarin, with a Beijing accent, was still an emblem of their credentials, status, and self-dignity, and these young male professionals persisted in using Mandarin even though they all could understand Cantonese. Interesting encounters were found when the engineers spoke to the staff in production department; one side spoke in Mandarin, consciously maintaining the superiority of the national language drawn from its political capital, and the other side persisted in speaking Cantonese as the official language in this workplace and the local industrial world. Needless to say, both sides understood each other well, and neither was willing to give in.

Communication on the production lines was more complicated, although the tensions were somewhat less acute. When the line leaders reported to their supervisors they usually spoke in Cantonese. But when they talked to the women on the line they preferred to use Mandarin when speaking to Waisheng workers. Most of the line leaders were not native speakers of Cantonese; some were from Chaozhou, some from Hakka. For them, both Mandarin and Cantonese were foreign languages and they used each in appropriate situations. There were exceptions, however. San, the leader of line D, was from Hunan; she had been promoted to her position after working for more than four years on the production line. She seldom spoke in Cantonese to supervisors or to other line leaders. As a tough and capable figure in the workplace, San had been promoted to the position not because she could assimilate herself to the managerial culture or because of any particular relationship with the upper management, but rather solely because of her work capability and her rigid discipline. She was one of the most disliked people in the workplace; she was never softspoken to women on the line and she often reprimanded workers loudly in Mandarin. They, in turn, often made fun of her, particularly the Cantonese-speaking workers. They mimicked her Mandarin speech and tones, drawing attention to her "unmanagerial" language to undermine her status and authority.

Intrigued by San's persistence in talking in Mandarin, one day I asked her, "San, why do you always speak in Mandarin? You know Cantonese, don't you?" She replied, "I can't help but speak Mandarin. I don't know why. I knew Cantonese after one year of working in Shenzhen. But I don't want to speak in Cantonese unless I am forced to. Probably I don't like the Cantonese. They are always too proud; they think they are rich, so everyone should use their dialect." But San was idiosyncratic; she was an exceptional case of resistance to the dominant language. The majority in the workplace were busy at, and induced into, the play of language politics.

The second dimension of the language war was the internal conflict within the Cantonese dialect. The language machine was not satisfied at creating a hierarchy based simply on the differentiation between Mandarin and Cantonese; rather a more subtle struggle was built on the internal divisions within Cantonese itself. The Cantonese spoken in the workplace was further differentiated into different styles and accents, such as Hong Kong Cantonese, Guangzhou Cantonese, Hakka Cantonese (rural Cantonese), and Guangxi Cantonese. Accents were the embodied stigma of cultural capital, inscribed with a hierarchical access not only to covert power but also to overt institutionalized power. The more one could mimic Hong Kong and Guangzhou Cantonese, the more one was granted status and authority in the workplace. Indeed, it was clearly noticeable that the higher the managerial hierarchy, the more Hong Kong or Guangzhou Cantonese was spoken. The assistant managers and the supervisors were fluent in Hong Kong Cantonese because they were often in contact with the Hong Kong managers, most of whom were native Guangzhou Cantonese. The foremen and line leaders had learned Guangzhou Cantonese because they often communicated with their Cantonese superiors. Different accents of Cantonese endowed people with different cultural capital, and thus affected their bargaining power in fighting for a higher work position and negotiating a new identity. If workers did not make an effort to change accents and instead stuck to rural Cantonese, then no matter how superior they might feel to the Mandarin or other dialect speakers, they were still at the bottom of the internal hierarchy.

Yiping, a Guangdong Hakka, was the receptionist and phone operator when I started at the Meteor factory. She was a friendly, pretty girl who had been promoted from the production line to the counter. But after her one-month probation period she was moved back to the line again. "She can never pronounce Lin and Ling accurately, nor can she hear any difference between the sounds. She always connects the phone line to the wrong person," Ling, the secretary in the general office grumbled to me. "She is a Hakka from a rural area and she can't speak Cantonese properly. What's more, she doesn't know how to handle unwelcome phone calls and people." Ling spoke proper Hong Kong Cantonese, despite the fact that she was a Chaozhou person.

One night I found Yiping in the dormitory, listening to Hong Kong Cantonese popular songs. She was still hurt by her demotion and she planned to leave for home: "I don't want to work here, they made me feel inferior. If they don't give me a chance, I will go elsewhere." But in fact, knowing that her Hakka Cantonese accent counted against her, Yiping tried hard to change herself. She took every chance to talk to me, hoping that I could inculcate in her a more urbane and highly valued Cantonese. Listening to Cantonese songs was another favorite way to learn Cantonese, and she often sang loudly.

On the passage to becoming dagongmei, self-technologizing was complete when one dreamed, desired, and determined to live up to the hegemonic mode of life – to acquire a modern identity and to command a superior dialect of Cantonese. To become dagongmei, one had to change not only the "bad" habitus of one's lifestyle but also one's dialect. The price of symbolic power was great, and there was no choice but to scramble for it. Language was, as Bourdieu (1991, 52) has said, a hidden political mythology prophesying, coding, and legitimating a system of social differences. The play of difference is highly political. Rural life was imagined as an alterity so that it could be undervalued. For a rural being to become an urban industrial subject, he or she had to be divided from the totality of her or his past life – habitus, disposition, accent, and identity. The rural world had to be imagined as a deficient reality that could not give birth to complete human beings or modern subjects. First, the capitalist machine invented the rural beings as incomplete, as "lacking." Then the rural beings thought and saw themselves as such. There is a process of double displacement at work here. As stated by Huck Gutman: "Deficient reality is transformed into the imaginary and the imaginary is superimposed upon the real in such fashion that the imaginary transforms, takes over, becomes, the real" (1988, 112). Thus the real is not impossible; it is simply more and more artificial (Deleuze & Guattari 1984, 34).

Dagongmei, as a new social body, thus contains multiple reactionary forces that work to produce a homogenous sense of self that is nevertheless fragmentary, fluid, and entangled. Becoming dagongmei is a dual process of displacement and replacement that produces anxiety, uncertainty, and pain for individuals in their daily struggles, and drives them toward a self-technologizing project, helping to accomplish a hegemonic construct. Selves are not inherently fragmentary but are socially negated and divided in order to give birth to a new subject. The workplace here is not merely a microcosm of the dual society at large, but part of the process of production and reproduction of an increasingly polarized society. It is through the everyday practices of such an environment that the politics of identification by which the production machine could command the microphysics of power over the self were governed. The production machine, in making use of existing social relations, simply reproduced itself as one part of the system at the same time that it built the system. The factory regime itself was not a pyramid of power hierarchies but rather a kaleidoscope of power and hierarchies created by weaving together identities of gender, kin-ethnic ties, and rural–urban disparity.

Notes

1. For a comparable situation, see Kondo 1990.
2. For historical studies on Chinese workers that highlight the importance of locality, kin-ethnic ties, and gender in the process of making the Chinese working class in the early twentieth century, see Honig 1968; Hershatter 1986; and Perry 1993.
3. Helping others to clock in was a regular practice in the Meteor workplace. Sometimes workers needed extra time for activities such as sending money back home. The post office was only open during the day and most of the workers had to sacrifice their lunch time to go there. Moreover, long queues were expected at lunch time, so they got back to the factory late. Thus other workers would step in if they saw their kin or fellow villagers were not back in time.

4. For more on these hierarchies, see Honig 1986; Hershatter 1986; and Perry 1993.
5. On the disciplinary and regulatory role of kin, see Hareven 1982.
6. No doubt there were heterogeneous views among different employers in Shenzhen toward local and kin-ethnic peculiarities, and it is always dangerous to draw any generalizations. But my study of the Meteor plant relates a valuable story about how the regional and kin-ethnic cultural traits were imagined, articulated, and then lived out in a specific workplace and how they had a great impact on the job positions and mobility of workers.
7. I was the only one in the workplace who did not get paid. I refused to receive a wage from the company, but traded it in return for some rest on Sundays.
8. I do not hold the Saussurian perspective in which language is viewed as an internal linguistic structure based on a system of difference. Rather I follow Bourdieu's (1991) line that the difference is social.

References

Bourdieu, Pierre (1991). *Language and Symbolic Power*. London: Polity Press.

Deleuze, Gilles & Félix Guattari (1984). *Anti-Oedipus: Capitalism and Schizophrenia*. London: Athlone.

Foucault, Michel (1986). Of Other Spaces. *Diacritics* 16, pp. 22–7.

Foucault, Michel (1988). Technologies of the Self. In: Luther H. Martin, Huck Gutman & Patrick H. Hutton (eds.), *Technologies of the Self*. London: Tavistock.

Foucault, Michel (1994). *Ethics: Subjectivity and Truth*, ed. Paul Rabinow. London: Penguin.

Foucault, Michel (1997). *The Essential Works of Michel Foucault, 1854–1984*, Volume 1, ed. Paul Rabinow.

Gutman, Huck (1988). Rousseau's Confessions: A Technology of the Self. In: Luther H. Martin, Huck Gutman & Patrick H. Hutton (eds.), *Technologies of the Self*. London: Tavistock.

Hareven, Tamara K. (1982). *Family Time and Industrial Time: The Relationship between the Family and Work in a New England Industrial Community*. Cambridge: Cambridge University Press.

Hershatter, Gail (1986). *The Workers of Tianjin, 1900–1949*. Stanford: Stanford University Press.

Honig, Emily (1986). *Sisters and Strangers: Women in the Shanghai Cotton Mills, 1919–1949*. Stanford: Stanford University Press.

Kondo, Dorinne K. (1990). *Crafting Selves: Power, Gender, and Discourse of Identity in a Japanese Workplace*. Chicago: University of Chicago Press.

Lee, Ching Kwan (1998). *Gender and the South China Miracle: Two Worlds of Factory Women*. Berkeley: University of California Press.

Perry, Elizabeth J. (1993). *Shanghai on Strike: The Politics of Chinese Labor*. Stanford: Stanford University Press.

Solinger, Dorothy J. (1999). *Contesting Citizenship in Urban China*. Berkeley: University of California Press.

21

The Ideology and Discourse of Modern Racism

*Teun van Dijk**

A Concrete Example

This chapter examines in some detail the ideology and discourse as expressed in a recent book: *The End of Racism: Principles for a Multiracial Society*, by Dinesh D'Souza (1995). Also in some of his other books, for example on multiculturalism, D'Souza has made himself a vociferous spokesman of the New Right in the USA, and a staunch defender of conservative ideas. Indeed, we might call D'Souza one of the main 'ideologues' of contemporary conservative ideologies in the USA.

In the *End of Racism* D'Souza deals with what he sees as a 'civilizational crisis' in the USA, and focuses on what he consistently calls the 'pathologies' which, according to him, characterize the African American community in general, and the black 'under-class' in particular (in my analysis, words in my running text actually used by D'Souza will be indicated by double quotation marks). Given the size of this book (724 pages), this is no mere ideological tract. On the contrary, D'Souza has set himself the task of writing a broadly documented study of the ethnic and racial situation in the USA. An endorsement by George M. Frederickson in *The New York Review of Books*, printed on the cover, says: 'The most thorough, intelligent, and well-informed presentation of the case against liberal race policies that has yet appeared.'

Thus, D'Souza deals with what he sees as the breakdown of the 'liberal hope' of race relations in the USA, the origins of racism, slavery, the rise of liberal anti-racism, the civil rights movement, Eurocentrism and Afrocentrism, the IQ debate, finally culminating in an apocalyptic vision of the 'pathologies' of black culture. In many respects, this book may be seen as the ideological foundation of a conservative programme of race relations in the USA. Since D'Souza is a scholar attached to the conservative think tank of the American Enterprise Institute, we may conclude that his book does not merely express a personal opinion, but also has a powerful institutional backing. Contemporary ideologies are often produced and reproduced by such ideological institutions.

Given his right-wing radicalism in ethnic–racial matters, D'Souza has been severely criticized, and accused of racism (in the introduction to the second edition of the book

*Pp. 277–93 from T. A. van Dijk, *Ideology: A Multidisciplinary Approach* (London: Sage Publications Ltd).
© 1998 by Teun A. van Dijk. Reprinted with permission from the author and Sage Publications Ltd.

he discusses and rejects such critique). After having examined his theses and evidence in detail, and analysed the discursive formulation of his underlying ideologies, I have come to the conclusion, with others, that this book indeed articulates a special form of 'cultural racism', celebrating white, Western cultural and civilizational hegemony, and especially problematizing and attacking African-American culture. As is also clear from much of the literature on 'modern racism', most forms of racism are no longer biologically based, but take a more 'acceptable' form as cultural racism: others are not vilified for what they are, but for what they do and think. More generally, D'Souza defends ideas that are sometimes called 'symbolic racism': a forceful rejection of any form of affirmative action, a strong repudiation of egalitarian values, problematization of blacks, blaming the victim, and so on.[1] Indeed, he even proposes the repeal of the Civil Rights Act of 1964 (p. 544), and he favours 'rational discrimination' in the private sphere.

Our Ideological and Social Enemies and Us

Given their multiple group memberships, individuals may acquire and personally adapt several ideologies or ideology fragments. This means that D'Souza's book is not merely an expression of conservatism and modern racism, but a personal combination of these and other ideologies, attitudes, beliefs, values, models and other social and personal representations.

Yet, where he expresses positions and opinions that seem to be widely shared, at least among conservatives, in the USA (and also in Europe), we may assume that he is not merely writing as an individual, but also as a member of several ideological communities. At the end of his book, thus, he explicitly aligns himself with other 'cultural conservatives' (p. 521). His opinions about multiculturalism, affirmative action, the inner city ghettos and related topics are widely shared by other conservatives in the USA. Hence, abstracting from more personal views, we may read and analyse his book as a formulation of group ideologies.[2]

The ideological enemy

Ideologies are often formulated, explicitly or implicitly, as attacks against ideological opponents or enemies. Anti-Communism has been the most prominent example, especially in the USA, of this kind of anti-ideology. In D'Souza's book, this ideological enemy is what he calls 'cultural relativism', whose major tenet is that all cultures are equal, and that we should not assume any value hierarchy between different cultures. D'Souza traces this tendency to early twentieth century anthropology, and especially to Franz Boas and his students.

Throughout his book, cultural relativism is frequently blamed for virtually all ills of US society, and especially as the ideological source of contemporary 'anti-racist' policies and practices in the USA:

[1] [The main problem is] Liberal anti-racism. By asserting the equality of all cultures, cultural relativism prevents liberals from dealing with the nation's contemporary crisis –

a civilizational breakdown that affects all groups, but is especially concentrated among the black underclass. (p. 24)

[2]   Fundamental liberal principles are being sacrificed at the altar of cultural relativism. In its fanatical commitment to the relativist ideology of group equality, liberalism is inexorably destroying itself. (p. 530).

[3]   Relativism has become a kind of virus, attacking the immune systems of institutional legitimacy and public decency. (p. 532)

As these examples also show, the reference to liberalism as an ideological orientation is at least ambiguous. On the one hand, the specific US sense of politically or culturally 'progressive' may be meant by it, as in example 1, whereas D'Souza himself does not deny his allegiance to the original, philosophical-political meaning of the term, as in example 2. We may therefore expect that the ideological conflict presented in his book will be articulated in starkly polarized terms, where all They think is inherently bad, and all We think is inherently good. The rhetoric and lexical style of these examples expresses this ideological polarization, as is shown in the use of metaphors from the domain of health ('virus', 'immune system') in 3 and from traditional religion ('sacrificed on the altar of'), as well as by the use of hyperboles ('civilizational breakdown') in example 1. The rhetorical contrast in 3 suggests that there is a struggle between Us and Them. *They* are enemies who 'attack' us, and We defend – as an 'immune system' – legitimacy and decency in the USA. Framed in those terms, the ideological debate turns into a fierce struggle between Good and Evil, as was also the case in classical anti-communism until the Reagan era.

The social enemy

D'Souza and his fellow cultural conservatives not only have an intellectual, ideological enemy, but also a social one, namely, African-Americans. Although, as we shall see in more detail below, he emphasizes that his animosity is not directed against blacks as a 'race', but rather against African-American culture, his special focus on blacks can hardly hide the fact that he is not merely fighting a cultural war. It is this reason why in his book, and its underlying ideology, 'culture' and 'ethnicity' represent the respectable mask behind which (acknowledged) ethnocentrism mingles with various brands of modern racism. Although much of his fury targets the black 'underclass' and its social 'pathologies', he often forgets this specification and problematizes the whole black 'culture', which he sees as coherent and associated with all African-Americans in the USA.

This is a very anti-black book. If D'Souza had more generally been worried by the 'breakdown of civilization', as he so hyperbolically calls the present 'crisis' in the USA, he could have targeted many other social or cultural groups. With many of the same arguments and examples, he could also have focused on Latinos, on Native Americans, on the 'dependent' white underclass, on all unmarried mothers, all criminals, or all minorities who profit of affirmative action. He does not. He specifically singles out blacks, and his extremely biased, if not racist, judgements barely leave another conclusion than that these are his real social enemies:

[4]   The last few decades have witnessed nothing less than a breakdown of civilization within the African-American community. The breakdown is characterized by extremely high rates of criminal activity, by the normalization of illegitimacy, by the predominance of single-parent families, by high levels of addiction to alcohol and drugs, by a parasitic reliance on government provision, by a hostility to academic achievement, and by a scarcity of independent enterprises. (p. 477)

This quote sums up D'Souza's major points of resentment against the African-American community. Indeed, he does not speak here of a (relatively small) section of this community, but of the community as a whole. Where many others would talk of 'social problems' of some inner-city areas, D'Souza's view is more apocalyptic. He sees 'nothing less than a breakdown of civilization'. In many places of his book, he explicitly speaks of African-Americans as a 'threat' not only to themselves but to the whole society:

[5]   The conspicuous pathologies of blacks are the product of catastrophic cultural change that poses a threat both to the African-American community and to society as a whole. (p. 478)

Whereas conservatives before had communists as the major internal as well as external enemy, this kind of socio-political paranoia now targets blacks. In order to emphasize the 'pathologies' of blacks, the Asian community in the USA is held up as the good example, an example that at the same time serves as a strategic argument against those who might see racism in D'Souza's attacks against blacks:

[6]   By proving that upward mobility and social acceptance do not depend on the absence of racially distinguishing features, Asians have unwittingly yet powerfully challenged the attribution of minority failure to discrimination by the majority. Many liberals are having trouble providing a full answer to the awkward question: 'Why can't an African-American be more like an Asian?'

One might easily explain this racial divide-and-rule principle by the fact that D'Souza himself is an example of the Asian success story (he is from India), but there are few other traces of his Asian (or Indian) allegiances in the book. He does not speak for immigrants or minorities at all. On the contrary, as is true of many conservative immigrants, he completely identifies with Western civilization, and the dominant white majority which, obviously, could not have a more persuasive spokesman when it comes to attacking multiculturalism and affirmative action: who is more credible in attacking the others than one of them? As may be expected, conservative blacks and other people of colour in the USA are extensively celebrated and promoted, and have full access to the media and other ideological institutions, especially when they serve as 'useful idiots' and sustain the dominant consensus of the white elites.

Obviously, such groups and group relations need to be located in the more complex, socio-political and intellectual framework of US society. Thus, among the ideological enemies (the 'relativists' or the 'Boasians' – from Franz Boas, famous US anthropologist) he further identifies most liberal (progressive) scholars, politicians and journalists, proponents of civil rights and affirmative action, anti-racists, and all those whom he portrays as condoning or having vested interests in the continuation of 'black pathologies'. One stylistic ploy in the derogation of his ideological enemies is to call them 'activists', including professors whose opinions he dislikes. In passing he also includes some other target groups and ideologies of conservative scorn:

[7]   . . . activists draw heavily on leftist movements such as Marxism, deconstructionism, and anticolonial or Third World scholarship. (p. 345)

[8]   . . . solutions [of African-American scholar Cornell West] are a quixotic combination of watered-down Marxism, radical feminism, and homosexual rights advocacy, none of which offers any realistic hope for ameliorating black pathologies. (p. 520)

In sum, although not the main target of his ire, his ideological enemies stretch far along the social horizon, and include all progressive, alternative or otherwise non-mainstream groups and the institutions associated with them.

Us

Whereas there is little ambiguity about who his enemies are, who are *We* in this polarized representation of the civilizational conflict? As usual in this kind of discourse, *We* are largely implicit and presupposed, and in need of much less identification. In a large part of this book on the 'breakdown of civilization', *We* are simply all civilized people. More specifically, also in the historical sections of the book, *We* are those (mostly Europeans) who invented 'Western' civilization. Within the context of the USA, *We* may variously be all non-blacks, or whites, or all those opposed to multi-culturalism, affirmative action and state interference.

Whereas his positive descriptions of all these different We-groups with which D'Souza identifies leave no doubt about his allegiances, his closest ideological reference group comprises what he calls the 'cultural conservatives':

[9]   The only people who are seriously confronting black cultural deficiencies and offering constructive proposals for dealing with them are members of a group we can call the reformers. Many of them are conservatives. . . . (p. 521)

They are the ones who, at the end of the book, have 'understood' the seriousness of the 'civilizational breakdown' in the African-American community, and have made proposals to amend it. Quite predictably, D'Souza includes a group of conservative blacks among their ranks, and does not seem fazed by the inconsistencies such a selection engenders when he at the same time lambasts the entire African-American community. Apparently, and as always, there are exceptions, and those are Our friends.

Since ideologies articulate within and between groups, we now have the first elements of the social framework that sustains D'Souza's ideologies. We know his enemies and we know his friends, and we know that he serves as the ideologue for these friends, and as the ideal opponent of his enemies.

The Conflict and the 'Crisis'

Ideological struggles are rooted in real political, social or economic conflicts. They do not merely involve arbitrary groups, but involve group relations of power, dominance or competition. At stake is access to scarce social resources, both material as well as symbolic ones. The conflict that serves as the background for the ideological struggle in which D'Souza takes part involves both 'race' and class, and especially focuses on the relations between the white majority and the African-American minority in the USA.

As is also obvious from the historical chapters of his book, this conflict has a long history: European world exploration and colonization, the enslavement of Africans by Europeans (and Arabs), the plantation economy in the rural South, abolition, the emergence of scientific racism, the Jim Crow laws, racial segregation, the civil rights movement, the end of formal segregation and official racism, affirmative action, large scale immigration from Asia and Latin America, multiculturalism in education, and finally the conservative backlash of which D'Souza's book is a salient example.

Despite their 'real' socio-economic backgrounds, conflicts are socio-political constructs, which are defined differently by the various groups involved in them, depending on their ideological orientation, group goals and interests, as well as the everyday experiences of their members. Ongoing socio-political conflicts such as that of race relations in the USA are characterized not only by the many structural properties of social inequality and occasional reform. They also know a series of 'crises', which are also defined by shared mental representations of (and hence differently interpreted by) groups in conflict. A crisis may occur when one of the participant groups enhances its political, economic or ideological dominance and oppression or when the dominated group engages in explicit forms of resistance. Thus the conservative backlash that coincided with conservative Reagonomics and the victory of neo-liberalism in the 1980s and 1990s, is one of such crises. This crisis in turn found its ideological motivation in the reaction against the (modest) political and economic gains of African-Americans that resulted from another crisis, namely, the civil rights movement and the social government policies of the 1960s and 1970s.

The social and political function of D'Souza's book should be defined against this general background of race relations, politics and policies in the USA, but draws its rhetorical relevance and persuasiveness especially from a self-defined 'civilizational crisis'. That is, structural properties of US society (such as poverty, especially in the black ghettos or overall socio-cultural changes) are interpreted and presented as a major threat. Once defined as 'catastrophic', such a perceived threat demands urgent action and policy, and D'Souza's book provides the ideological principles for such a 'multiracial society', as its subtitle specifies. We have seen that just talking of (well-known) 'problems' will not do in such a rhetorical book. Hence such social problems need to be magnified to a disaster of major proportions, as also the frequently hyperbolic style of D'Souza shows:

[10] . . . the nation's contemporary crisis – a civilizational breakdown that affects all groups . . . (p. 24)

[11] . . . a deterioration of basic civilizational norms in the ghetto. (p. 241)

[12] The conspicuous pathologies of blacks are the product of catastrophic cultural change that poses a threat both to the African–American community and to society as a whole. (p. 478)

[13] For many whites the criminal and irresponsible black underclass represents a revival of barbarism in the midst of Western civilization. (p. 527)

In other words, we do not merely have a conflict between two groups, whites and blacks, in the USA, but a momentous struggle, namely, that between (white) 'civilization' and (black) 'barbarism'. And, as may be expected, D'Souza is the hero who has taken on the Herculean task of fighting the forces of barbarism, as also the Greek heroes defended their civilizations against the barbarian foreigners. D'Souza explicitly refers to the Greek history of 'Western civilization' and democracy, as an example which, until today, deserves emulation, including 'rational', ethnocentric discrimination of the barbarian others. Thus, his struggle is not just one that tries to safeguard the interests and privileges of the dominant, white middle class, but more grandly presents itself as a valiant defence of Western civilization against the onslaught of a 'rainbow' coalition of blacks, immigrants, leftists, gays, lesbians, multiculturalists, Boasian relativists and others who threaten the status quo. In that respect, D'Souza and his book, and the ideologies he defines, are quite coherently conservative and ethnocentric. Let us now try to reconstruct these ideologies and other social representations from his book and then examine in some more detail their persuasive discursive manifestations.

Reconstructing Ideologies

Recall that ideologies, defined as basic social representations of groups, should not be identified with their discursive expression. Indeed, the relation between ideologies and discourse may be very indirect – usually, more specific beliefs from social attitudes and from personal models of events show up in text and talk, further modified by the constraints of context models of speakers and writers. That is, more often than not, ideological beliefs need to be inferred, hypothetically reconstructed, from actual discourse, for instance by comparison with repeated (contextually different) discourses of other group members. Since we only have one (large) text here, such comparisons can only be made within the book itself, as well as with those texts or examples the author refers to and agrees with. Moreover, in typical ideological treatises of this kind, the very formulation of the 'principles' involved may be close to the underlying ideologies because D'Souza does not tell many concrete stories, but argues at a general, abstract level. Moreover the overall, contextual purpose of the book is to attack what he sees as a threatening ideology (cultural relativism) and to promote another, which he does not name explicitly, although he aligns himself with what he calls 'cultural conservatism'.

As may be expected from a book that deals with various political, social, economic and cultural issues, also D'Souza's book manifests several, related ideologies, depending on his respective identifications with different groups or communities, as explained above: Western, white, middle-class, male, heterosexual, professional, conservative elites. However, D'Souza focuses on his main ideological and social enemies, namely, the cultural relativists and African-Americans. Also class is a salient dimension, as is obvious from his special wrath against the black 'underclass'. His frequent generalizations show, however, that he takes the whole black community as a metonymic (*totum pro parte*) representation of the black poor.

In sum, we may expect four types of ideology here, those of race–ethnicity, class, culture and politics, and an overall 'meta-ideology' organizing these, namely, that of conservatism. It is this over-arching conservative ideology that establishes coherence and numerous links between the beliefs in the respective ideologies. For instance, where D'Souza defends socio-political, neo-liberal beliefs about limited state intervention, we may expect racialized beliefs about African-American dependency on the state in general, and about black welfare mothers in particular. And where his cultural ideologies defend the uniqueness and hegemony of Western civilization, we may expect both the class and race ideologies to feature beliefs about the 'barbarism' of the underclass. The same cultural ideologies may be connected to ideological beliefs about the 'bankruptcy' of relativist multiculturalism, whereas conservative–liberal individualism emphasizes the importance of personal merit against group-based, collective affirmative action. Similarly, the conservative ideology of law and order will be 'racialized' in this case in the evaluation of 'black crime'. Many other such cross-linkages between main ideologies and specific attitudes may be reconstructed from this book.

As we shall see in more detail below, such an ideological complex will be brought to bear in the central attitude that provides the basis and the title of this book, namely, that contrary to what is maintained by blacks and their liberal white supporters, the USA is not (or at least no longer) a racist country. It is this denial of racism which constitutes one of the core attitudes of modern elite racism. Disguised by what is defined as a 'culture war' between liberal relativists and conservative cultural supremacists, we thus discover the continuation of the ongoing 'race war' that has characterized the 'American dilemma' for centuries. Indeed, the book's subtitle advocates a 'multiracial' society, but the contents of the book show that the supremacy of the dominant white 'race' should not be challenged. 'Rational discrimination' is a 'natural' right of this dominant ethnic group:

[14]   The Greeks were ethnocentric, they showed a preference for their own. Such tribalism they would have regarded as natural, and indeed we now know that it is universal. In some situations an instinctive ethnocentrism is inevitable, as when one's society is under external attacks and one must rally to its defence. (p. 533)

We see here at work one of the most prominent devices of the ideological legitimation of inequality, namely, that such a situation is 'natural' and hence 'universal'. At the same time, such a passage shows another device in the representation of the others, namely, how outgroups are constructed as enemies against whose 'external attacks' we must 'naturally' defend ourselves. Thus, racism is not only made respectable, while natural, but also a patriotic duty of whites in the 'culture war' and the 'civilizational crisis' (p. 535).

After this brief overall characterization of the various ideologies involved, let us now examine some of their contents and structures.

Conservatism

It was argued, above, that 'conservatism' it not so much a (group) ideology, but rather an overarching, meta-ideology that organizes other ideologies. For instance, applied to neo-liberal ideologies in the realm of the political economy, conservative ideologies typically advocate a limited role of the state (or government) in the market. Similarly, when applied to cultural ideologies, conservative meta-principles may take two complimentary variants: limited state intervention in some cultural domains (education, media, religion), or active state intervention, for example through tough legislation, in the domains that are seen to threaten the moral order (family values, sexuality, multiculturalism). And finally, when applied to racial or ethnic ideologies, conservatism will similarly allow (condone or not strictly police) various forms of discrimination, as the right of each person or ethnic group to 'prefer one's own'.

Values   As all ideologies, also conservative meta-ideologies are based on a selection and combination of values drawn from a cultural commonground. D'Souza for instance positively refers to the following values (of which the ideological, attitudinal and discursive constructions will be examined below):

- freedom
- personal merit
- discipline
- prudence
- moderation
- responsibility
- self-restraint
- hard work
- authority
- order
- decency
- elitism
- non-permissiveness.

Such an ideological selection of rather general cultural values usually also involves a set of counter-values when the ideology is brought to bear in an ideological struggle with ideological opponents. Thus, these values are selected and emphasized especially against (certain variants of) those of egalitarian, progressive liberalism: equality, social responsibility, social support, moral freedom, cultural relativism, freedom from oppression, representativeness, anti-authoritarianism, permissiveness, creativity, self-critique, progress, democracy, and so on.

Given these values and their counterparts, some of the conservative ideological beliefs defended by D'Souza in his book are the following.

1   The social and civilizational status quo is being threatened.
2   The state should not interfere where it does not belong.
3   Social programmes to help the poor are counterproductive.
4   People should be judged individually by their own achievements.
5   Inequality has individual not social causes.
6   People have duties, and not only rights.
7   A coherent society does not allow multiple cultures or worldviews.
8   There are natural inequalities between (groups of) people.
9   Society must be characterized by law and order.
10   All individuals should take initiative and pursue excellence.
11   Children shall be born in wedlock.
12   All people must work.

These ideological principles are not always directly formulated in the *End of Racism*, but especially appear in the negative evaluation of the ideologies and attitudes of D'Souza's enemies, for example in favour of state intervention in the ghetto, welfare, affirmative action, social responsibility of business companies, social disadvantage, the legitimacy of single mothers or other family structures, decent jobs, equal group representation, equal outcomes, and so on.

As suggested before, these conservative values and ideological beliefs will appear to be manifested in more specific group ideologies and attitudes. Indeed, some of the ideological beliefs mentioned above might even be omitted because they are domain- or group-specific general beliefs. Thus, the freedom from state intervention in fact implies that the state should also not be (very) active in the social domains, for example with social programmes for the poor or the elderly. Similarly, the opposition to 'illegitimacy' of children or to unmarried mothers, is of course a further specification of overall conservative beliefs about family values.

Ethnocentrism/modern racism

Although conservatism is the overarching ideological framework that organizes the social and cultural beliefs in *The End of Racism*, ethnocentric modern racism is its specific ideological core. This conclusion may be rather ironical given the title of D'Souza's book, but within the framework of our elite theory of racism, such denials are paramount in all forms of modern racism. Hence D'Souza's rage against anti-racists, his systematic mitigations of the continued relevance of 'race' in the USA, and his alleged 'ignorance' of widespread discrimination against of African-Americans in virtually all social domains. For the same ideological reasons he attacks civil rights 'activists', those who plead for (or see no alternative for) affirmative action, and those he sees as using racism as an excuse for own failure and 'civilizational breakdown'.

As group ideologies, ethnocentrism and modern racism feature the following basic beliefs about the own group, namely (white) Westerners, and its relations to other groups. Most of these ideological principles are based on the core value of (cultural if not natural) inequality between groups.

1   Our Western culture is superior.
2   Ethnocentrism is natural and sometimes inevitable.
3   Discrimination may be rational.
4   The USA is not and should not be a multicultural society.
5   Cultural assimilation of culturally deviant groups is necessary.
6   We are tolerant.
7   The USA is not a racist society. / We are not racists.

Related to these ideological self-representations is the, polarized, negative representation of the others: first the liberal cultural relativists, for example in terms of the following beliefs.

1   They think that all cultures are equally valuable.
2   They advocate multiculturalism.
3   They criticize Western civilization.
4   They accuse us of colonialism and racism.
5   They want proportional representation of ethnic minorities.

The second main enemy, the social opponents, are blacks, African-Americans, and more generally all non-Westerners in the book. They are variously described on the basis of the following ideological beliefs.

1   They are primitive, uncivilized, barbarians.
2   African-American pathologies are cultural.
3   They are culturally deviant.
4   They break the law.
5   They tend to be criminal.
6   Their culture(s) are stagnant.
7   They depend on the state.
8   They take no initiative.
9   They are promiscuous.
10 They are not striving for excellence.
11 They use racism as an excuse for own failure.

In other words, negative other-presentations deriving from ethnocentric and racist ideologies are often articulated around the attribution of violations of our basic values and ideological principles. Thus, where we are tolerant, anti-racism is intolerant; where we value personal merit and discipline, they lack such values; where we are decent they are promiscuous, where we work hard, they are too lazy to work, and so on.

Ideological structures

On the basis of repeated general propositions in D'Souza's book, a number of beliefs were selected that are general enough to be included in the conservative meta-ideology and the ideologies of cultural racism or ethnocentrism. It was, however, argued that ideologies probably have some kind of internal organization, for instance a schematic structure of fixed categories. Such a schema would be relevant each time people need to acquire or change an ideology, for instance when they become new members of a social group. Searching for a format for such a schema, I assumed that given the close link between group ideology and the self-representation of the group, a group schema modelled on the fundamental societal co-ordinates of the group would be a good candidate. The question now is whether the ideological propositions inferred from de D'Souza's book can be validly assigned to such a schema.

Thus, if we have to design a framework for the ideologies of racism and ethnocentrism, we may propose the following (simplified) structure:

* *Membership criteria* – only members of our own culture, ethnic group 'race' or nation;
* *Activities* – discriminate others;
* *Goals* – exclusion, segregation or assimilation of others;
* *Values* – natural inequality, cultural homogeneity;
* *Societal position: relation to other groups* – we (our culture) are (is) superior to the others;
* *Resources* – Western civilization, (political and economic) power, whiteness.

Obviously, since group self-schemata are usually (though not always) positive, and 'racism' is culturally and socially sanctioned, at least officially, most people who share this schema will not describe themselves as 'racists', but for instance as nationalists. Recall that the group schema and its categories will feature those fundamental group beliefs that define the identity as well as the basic interests of the group. When these interests are under threat, they will most energetically be defended, or when lost they will be reclaimed.

This is also the case for D'Souza's book. Thus the membership criteria category defines who does or may belong to Us, and hence the others are defined by racists or ethnocentrists as foreigners, aliens, immigrants, outsiders, and so on. The activities of the members should be geared towards the realization of the essential group goal, which is basically to keep others out or down, or if that is impossible to fully assimilate them (in this case culturally). These aims are the basis of the negative evaluations in the attitude of multiculturalism, as we shall see below.

The basic value of ethnocentrism and racism is to emphasize 'natural' inequality between groups, against the egalitarians and the relativists. It is not surprising that such a value only serves the interests of those who are dominant, and therefore, in the societal position category, we find the fundamental definition of Our position, namely, that We are superior to Them (i.e. Our civilization, culture, knowledge, etc., is better than Theirs).

Since dominant group position and reproduction need resources, the crucial resource in a racist ideology is the symbolic power of being part of (Western) civilization and of being white, that is, the very criteria of their membership of their own group. Given the fundamental nature of resources for group power and reproduction, these are the ideological interests that will be defended most forcefully. This is indeed the case in D'Souza's book, wherein the repeatedly expressed concern is that (Western) civilization is breaking down, that other cultures may get the upper hand, and that Our (Western, white, male, middle-class, etc.) group and its interests may lose power.

The societal position category in the ideological schema typically features a relation to other groups, in this case obviously the group(s) that are the very target of racist or ethnocentric groups, namely, foreigners, immigrants, aliens, minorities, and so on, especially those of another culture and/or appearance ('race'). Given the relationship of superiority involved here, the other-group schema associated to this self-schema typically will feature those categories and beliefs that are opposed to those for our own group.

Their membership category (as defined by Us) is, say, 'being black', or as D'Souza's insists, 'having a coherent black culture'. It is also here that the 'essential' evaluation of the others is being represented, namely, as being primitive, uncivilized, barbarians, lacking initiative, being promiscuous, and so forth.

Their (negative) activities may be ideologically summarized as 'They violate all our norms' (are criminals, push drugs, get illegitimate children, don't want to work, accuse us of racism, etc.). Their goal is represented, for example, as equal rights, multiculturalism and an equal economic share. Their values are all those opposed to Ours: egalitarianism, relativism, permissiveness, dependency on state, disrespectfulness of order and authority, indecency, and so on. Their position is represented on the one hand as (culturally) inferior, and on the other hand as a threat to our culture, civilization and other resources; moreover, they accuse us of racism and intolerance. Since the other group is hardly powerful, few resources will be attributed to them, and the point is precisely to make sure that they will not get access to our resources, or their resources (such as their own culture) will be negatively valued, as is the case, as we shall see, for the attitude about Afrocentrism.

These basic ideological group schemas for Us and Them will then be further detailed for specific social domains in a number of more detailed attitudes about specific groups, for example about African-Americans, or about Us (whites, etc.) in the USA, and for specific issues, such as racism, multiculturalism or affirmative action, as I shall spell out below.

Note, finally, that I did not attempt to schematize the list of conservative basic beliefs, since conservatism is not a specific group ideology, but rather a meta-ideology that organizes some basic principles of other group ideologies. The typical conservative beliefs (about state intervention, individualism, law and order, family structure, etc.) are in fact all specifications of fundamental conservative values. Thus freedom is defined as freedom from state intervention, and personal merit is inconsistent with social welfare, decency prohibits illegitimate children, and so on. If we would have to define conservatives as a 'group' we might say that it is constituted precisely by the category of its values (against progressives). That is, the identity, actions, goals, position and resources of conservatives all focus on the realization of those values. It is in this way that the meta-ideology of conservatism constrains other (group) ideologies, such as those of racists, or professors, or business people, for whom the conservative value system will have different applications depending on the interests and specific group goals of these groups.

Attitudes

Theoretically, ideologies control and organize more specific attitudes. Thus, whereas basic ethnocentric and racist ideologies represent the overall properties of Us (Westerners, whites) and Them (non-Westerners, blacks), attitudes feature more specific social beliefs, such as prejudices, about specific outgroups. Thus, African-Americans are further represented as follows.

1 They are the cause of the breakdown of civilization.
2 They have one coherent (black) culture.
3 (Poor) blacks have scandalous pathologies:
   • excessive reliance on government;
   • conspirational paranoia about racism;
   • resistance to academic achievement;
   • celebration of the criminal;
   • normalization of illegitimacy;
   • single-parent families.
4 Their pathologies are due to African-American culture.
5 Their culture is functionally inadequate.
6 They are themselves racist:
   • they have an ideology of black supremacy.
7 They are violent and criminal.
8 They abuse drugs.
9 They have an expensive lifestyle (they are 'flashy').
10 They may have lower intelligence.
11 They have fewer skills.
12 They have no mores.
13 They celebrate or condone broken families.
14 They do not adapt to the dominant (Our) culture.
15 They do not take responsibility.
16 They have paranoia about racism.
17 Their middle class has an unfounded black rage.
18 They are weak in developing businesses.
19 They repudiate standard English.
20 They celebrate the 'Bad Nigger'.
21 They dress in conspicuous clothes.
22 They use obscene language.
23 They do not want to work.
24 They are not punctual.

25 They do not respect matrimony.
26 They cause the bastardization of America.
27 Their intellectuals refuse to criticize underclass pathologies.

These beliefs may be further organized in a more structured schema of which, however, the overall principle is again clear: the others (here the blacks) are represented as our negative mirror image – literally as our dark side. Whatever values and principles We share, They don't have them.

The core concepts organizing these beliefs are *difference*, *deviation* and *threat*, applied in all social domains, for example those of culture in general, habits, language, dress, work ethic, family values, character, tolerance, modesty, industriousness, individual merit and achievement, and so on. That is, their cultural mores are not only different from ours, but they also deviate from our norms and laws, and ultimately, their cultural deviance as well as their aggression, crime and other behaviour are a threat to Us and the whole nation, including themselves. Note that within the attitudinal representation of African-Americans, we also encounter some specific beliefs about black subgroups, such as black intellectuals, women or the 'underclass'.

Often, however, the text is not that specific, so that many negative attributes ascribed to a relatively small group of young men in the ghettos are in fact generalized towards the whole group. It is this (over)generalization that is one of the hallmarks of racism: they are all alike. Although D'Souza recalls (without much conviction) that 'it is not in their genes', and that he therefore cannot be called a racist, the distinction between African-American 'culture' and 'race' is very subtle in his argument, and often non-existent. Indeed, most blacks would see his very negative and aggressive stereotyping as little more than a form of racist derogation hiding behind a thin veil of cultural critique.

In his rejection of racism as the cause of the deplorable social condition of the African-American community, D'Souza has no other option than to blame the victims themselves (a strategy he energetically denies and even attacks as one of the criticized forms of anti-racism). That is, he focuses on 'black pathologies' and sees these as a 'civilizational breakdown', as discussed above. Hence the blacks, and no other group or organization, are the cause of the 'catastrophe' that is threatening 'Us' in the USA.

More sober analysts of the socio-political situation in the USA (and elsewhere in the world) would probably wonder why D'Souza's rhetoric focuses on just those 'pathologies' and why these should constitute something as dramatic as a 'civilizational break-down' and a 'threat' to the whole nation. Since when is welfare, when no jobs are available, a pathological form of 'parasitic reliance'? If so, most of the Western European welfare systems would not be an object of envy. And what about single-parent families? These are increasingly normal in many parts of the world, especially in highly developed nations, such as those in Scandinavia, where up to around 40 per cent of mothers are not married. What we have here, obviously, is a socio-cultural difference, and hardly a pathology, and even less something as apocalyptic as the 'bastardization of America' as D'Souza so delicately describes black families. And how would D'Souza's black conservative friends who are prominent professors (as well as all other blacks with an academic degree) interpret his conclusion that African-Americans are 'hostile' to achievement? Surely, there are other, more fundamental, social and economic problems in the USA, such as the poverty of many millions of families and children.

What is important for my analysis, however, is not so much a critical challenge of D'Souza's work (many others have done that already) but a demonstration of how values, ideologies and attitudes influence the definition and evaluation of the social situation. Where many see poverty, racism, marginalization and many other social ills in the USA, D'Souza's ideology has blinded him to such realities. On the contrary, in a grand movement of reversal he blames the victims of this situation. Even a well-founded analysis of US society, not only by blacks, is thus claimed to be pathological. Hence, we see how different ideologies may lead to opposed assessments of the 'facts'.

Notes

1. For 'symbolic' racism and related forms of 'modern', 'everyday,' or 'new' racism, see, for example, Barker (1981); Dovidio and Gaertner (1986); Essed (1991). For (the permanence of) racism in the USA, see also Bell (1992); Doob (1993); Feagin and Sikes (1994); Feagin and Vera (1995); Powell (1993). For a bibliography, see Weinberg (1990).
2. For studies of neo-conservatism and the New Right, see Bennett (1990); Kroes (1984); Levitas (1986).

References

Barker, M. (1981). *The New Racism*. London: Junction Books.
Bell, D. A. (1992). *Faces at the Bottom of the Well: The Permanence of Racism*. New York: Basic Books.
Bennett, D. H. (1990). *The Party of Fear: From Nativist Movements to the New Right in American History*. New York: Vintage Books.
Doob, C. B. (1993). *Racism: An American Cauldron*. New York: HarperCollins.
Dovidio, J. F. & S. L. Gaertner (eds.) (1986). *Prejudice, Discrimination, and Racism*. Orlando, FL: Academic Press.
D'Souza, D. (1992). *Illiberal Education: The Politics of Sex and Race on Campus*. New York: Vintage Books.
D'Souza, D. (1995). *The End of Racism: Principles for a Multiracial Society*. New York: Free Press.
Essed, P. J. M. (1991). *Understanding Everyday Racism: An Interdisciplinary Theory*. Newbury Park, CA: Sage.
Feagin, J. R. & M. P. Sikes (1994). *Living with Racism: The Black Middle-Class Experience*. Boston, MA: Beacon.
Feagin, J. & H. Vera (1995). *White Racism*. London: Routledge.
Kroes, R. (1984). *Neo-Conservatism, Its Emergence in the USA and Europe*. Amsterdam: Free University Press.
Levitas, R. (ed.) (1986). *The Ideology of the New Right*. Cambridge: Polity.
Powell, T. (1993). *The Persistence of Racism in America*. Paterson, NJ: Littlefield Adams Quality Paperbacks.
Weinberg, M. (1990). *Racism in the United States: A Comprehensive Classified Bibliography*. New York: Greenwood.

22

9/11 and the Jihad Tradition

Sohail H. Hashmi*

We're told that they were zealots fueled by religious fervor . . . religious fervor . . . and if you live to be a thousand years old will that make any sense to you? Will that make any goddamn sense?
 – David Letterman, Late Show with David Letterman, September 17, 2001

Soon after the 9/11 attacks, we learned a great deal about how the nineteen hijackers plotted, trained for, and executed their mission. We were given personal histories of many of the men: their family backgrounds, their education, their travels, the mosques they attended. But we still know relatively little about why they felt compelled to kill thousands of people and to die doing so. The clearest glimpse of their psychology comes from a handwritten note in Arabic, identical copies of which were found in the luggage of two of the hijackers and in the rubble of the World Trade Center. The note contains instructions on how to prepare mentally for the attack, instructions laced with Islamic justifications and exhortations.[1]

Many, if not all, of the nineteen hijackers were undoubtedly motivated by "religious fervor." They died because they were convinced they were waging jihad. But saying this doesn't really clarify the question of motives any more than claiming that someone died for "love of country," for "honor," for "justice" – or any other abstraction. The hijackers' religious fervor can be unpacked into a number of more tangible *potential* motivations. As the foot soldiers of al-Qaida, they may have been content to let Osama bin Laden and other al-Qaida leaders enunciate their grievances for them. Indeed, given the declarations of bin Laden and his lieutenants in the years preceding the 9/11 attack, the nineteen terrorists may have felt their cause needed no further elaboration.

Bin Laden and his supporters continually invoke the jihad tradition. They do so, I believe, not only to gain public support among Muslims, but from the fervent belief that they are authentic interpreters of jihad. By claiming to act according to the strictures of jihad, they invite a response from their opponents, not because such arguments are likely to sway the terrorists, but simply in order to show how their arguments are unrepresentative of the broad mainstream of the tradition. And indeed their many

*Pp. 149–64 from *Terror, Culture, Politics: Rethinking 9/11*, ed. D. J. Sherman and T. Nardin (Bloomington: Indiana University Press). © 2006 by Daniel J. Sherman and Terry Nardin. Reprinted with permission from Indiana University Press.

Muslim and non-Muslim opponents have vigorously disputed al-Qaida's interpretations of jihad. Too often, however, those who criticize al-Qaida's actions have settled for general denunciations such as the claims that these terrorists and other militant Muslim groups have "nothing to do with Islam," or that they have "hijacked Islam," or at the least that they distort the jihad tradition within Islam. I argue in this chapter that al-Qaida is in fact not especially radical when we confine our attention to its stated grievances or goals. But it is on the fringes of the jihad tradition when we shift our attention to the means it employs to realize its objectives. Al-Qaida, like many terrorist groups that have preceded it, seems to have embraced the idea that "the ends justify the means," and with it the logic of total war. This repudiation of limits on the means to one's ends puts al-Qaida's war outside the jihad tradition. For as in the Western just war tradition, the Islamic ethical discourse on war has historically separated two broad, related, *but morally independent* sets of questions: Under what circumstances or for what ends is war justified? And, once war has begun, how may fighting be properly conducted?

The Question of Ends

The jihad tradition emerged and began to evolve during the lifetime of the prophet Muhammad himself. For the first thirteen years of his prophetic mission (610–622 CE), while he was in Mecca, Muhammad refused to engage in any form of violence in response to the opposition and persecution that he and the earliest Muslims faced at the hands of the polytheist Meccans. Jihad during the Meccan period of Islam's development was an inward "struggle," as the word literally means, aimed at morally developing the character of individual Muslims. One Qur'anic verse from this period advises Muslims to "listen not to the unbelievers, but strive [*jahada*] against them with it [the Qur'an] with the utmost effort" (25:52). In dealing with belligerent non-Muslims, the Prophet taught nonviolent resistance.

If the Prophet had died or been killed in Mecca, Islam might have evolved along lines similar to those of early Christianity, as an otherworldly and generally pacifist sect devoid of political ambitions in this world. But the fusing of religion and politics that occurred in Christianity some three centuries after Christ occurred in Islam within the lifetime of the Prophet. In the year 622, Muhammad and most of his followers relocated from Mecca to Medina. It is in Medina that the Islamic community became a state, and where there is a state, there is sure to be, as Max Weber emphasized, violence or the threat of violence.[2]

In Medina, the jihad struggle acquired a military aspect. This development is marked in a number of Qur'anic verses. The first verse to be revealed on this topic gives permission to Muslims to defend themselves with force if they are attacked by their enemies: "To those against whom war is made, permission is given [to fight back], because they are wronged. And surely God is most powerful in their support" (22:39). A subsequent series of verses makes such self-defense a requirement for the faithful: "Fight in the cause of God those who fight you" (2:190). The justification for the resort to violence given here is that "tumult and oppression [*fitna*] are worse than killing [*qatl*]"

(2:191). Finally, after nearly eight years of warfare between the Muslims and an array of enemies, the Qur'an seems to enjoin a war of conversion against the remaining polytheist Arab tribes: "But when the forbidden months are past, then fight and slay the polytheists [*mushrikin*] wherever you find them. Seize them, besiege them, and lie in wait for them using every stratagem. But if they repent, and establish regular prayers, and practice regular charity, then open the way for them. For God is most forgiving, most merciful" (9:5). For all others, including Christians and Jews, the Qur'an seems to sanction a war of conquest aimed at political subjugation if not religious conversion: "Fight those who do not believe in God or the Last Day, nor hold forbidden that which has been forbidden by God and his Messenger, nor acknowledge the religion of truth, from among those who have been given the Book, until they pay the poll-tax [*jizya*] with willing submission, having been subdued" (9:29).

Following the Prophet's death in 632, the Islamic state spread rapidly through military conquest of the Arabian Peninsula and large parts of the Byzantine Empire and through the overthrow of the Sassanid Empire. The Islamic faith spread much more gradually through the teaching and example of missionaries and merchants. At the same time, Muslim scholars began to formulate Islamic laws of war, focusing on the Medinan notion of armed jihad while neglecting the nonviolence of the Meccan period. Thus jihad acquired a predominantly military connotation in the law books of Islam. It was left mainly to Islamic mystics, the Sufis, to emphasize the nonviolent, spiritual aspects of jihad, as in the famous tradition (*hadith*) ascribed to the Prophet, who, returning from a military engagement, told his supporters that they had left the lesser jihad only to enter the greater jihad, the one waged within one's own soul.[3]

Muslim legal theory divided wars against non-Muslims into two categories: first, defensive fighting to repulse aggression against Muslim lands (*dar al-Islam*); and second, the struggle to expand *dar al-Islam* by reducing the territory of the infidels (*dar al-narb*). Both types of struggle justified killing, although in the second type (which we may call the expansionist jihad), killing was permitted only as the final stage in a hierarchy of options to be offered the enemy: first, that they accept Islam; second, that they accept Islamic sovereignty and agree to *dhimmi* (protected) status, which accorded them a great deal of communal autonomy; and finally, that if they refused the other two options, they were to be given fair warning and fought. The goal of the Islamic state in fighting non-Muslims was to bring them under Islamic sovereignty, not to convert them, at least not through military means. Conversion to Islam, the theory assumed, would occur naturally as the conquered peoples were exposed to the principles of Islam. The theory also allowed the Muslim ruler to conclude truces with non-Muslim powers if he deemed such agreements to be in the Muslims' interests.

The legal theory of an expansionist jihad remained just that, a theory, for many centuries; indeed, the theory itself may have been formulated during the second, third, and fourth Islamic centuries (eighth to tenth centuries CE) to revive the spirit of Islamic expansionism that had animated the explosive growth of the first century. The idea of expansionist jihad was resuscitated by the Ottoman Turks during the fifteenth and sixteenth centuries CE, only to fade again in the seventeenth. With the advent of European imperialism in the nineteenth century, the discourse of defensive jihad became dominant among Muslim peoples throughout Africa and Asia.

Among the vast majority of modern Muslim scholars, the only appropriate type of jihad is held to be the defensive kind. Some reject completely any expansionist aspect to jihad, arguing that the classical jurists had misinterpreted the Qur'an and the Prophet's teachings to justify it. Others hold that while it may have been historically justified in the seventh or eighth centuries CE, the modern division of the world into nation-states that agree to abide by international law has made wars of religion obsolete and morally unjustified.

Where do Osama bin Laden and his supporters fit in this tradition? They have been characterized as extremists lurking on the fringes of Islamic thought. But in terms of the justifications for jihad, al-Qaida's statements are not radical; they are in fact quite pedestrian. Bin Laden and his supporters, like the vast majority of Islamic activists for the past two centuries, appeal to the notion of defensive jihad.

The first major statement of al-Qaida's grievances and goals came in August 1996 in a lengthy, rambling manifesto published in the London-based Arabic newspaper *al-Quds al-ʿArabi*. The statement was later translated into English and posted on the Internet in October 1996 by the Committee for the Defense of Legitimate Rights, a Saudi dissident group with ties to bin Laden's organization. The "Ladenese Epistle: Declaration of War (Parts I–III)," as the document was dubbed, charges the "Zionist-Crusader alliance and their collaborators" with waging a war against Muslims all over the world. Muslims are being persecuted, robbed of their land and possessions, and massacred in Palestine, Kashmir, the Philippines, Eritrea, Chechnya, and other places, all while the United States and its allies, under the cover of the "iniquitous" United Nations, block means of assistance for them. "The latest and the greatest of these aggressions . . . is the occupation of the land of the two holy places – the foundation of the house of Islam, the place of the revelation, the source of the message and the place of the noble Kʿaba, the *qibla* [direction of prayer] of all Muslims – by the armies of the American Crusaders and their allies."[4]

Much of the statement focuses on the Muslim allies of the "American Crusaders," namely, the Saudi regime that let American troops into the kingdom in 1990 during the Gulf War. King Fahd had justified his decision to allow US troops on Saudi soil by promising that they would leave in a few months, as soon as the exigency under which they had arrived had passed. Yet, the statement observes, "today it is seven years since their arrival and the regime is not able to move them out of the country." Instead, the regime has rebuffed appeals from the ʿ*ulama*, jailed religious dissidents, and continued to issue false proclamations regarding American intentions in Saudi Arabia.[5]

By doing nothing to expel the American "occupiers," the statement alleges, the current Saudi leaders continue a pattern established by the founder of the kingdom, ʿAbd al-ʿAziz, who permitted, under British urging, the loss of Palestine. Now his son, Fahd, has committed the ultimate betrayal of the Muslim community (*umma*) by calling a "Christian army to defend the regime. The crusaders were permitted to be in the land of the two holy places [i.e., Mecca and Medina]. . . . The country was widely opened from the north to the south and from the east to the west for the crusaders. The land was filled with military bases of the USA and the allies. The regime became unable to keep control without the help of these bases." When the Saudi rulers permitted the violation of the sanctity of the Arabian Peninsula, the statement charges, they had in effect renounced their Islamic identity and joined forces with the infidels (*kufr*).[6]

The 1996 statement received very little attention at the time, and even after the 9/11 attacks it was neglected in public commentary on al-Qaida's motivations. Attention after 9/11 was instead focused on a subsequent declaration, the World Islamic Front's proclamation of "Jihad against Jews and Crusaders," published in *al-Quds al-ʿArabi* on February 23, 1998. This second document was a much terser statement than the 1996 Ladenese Epistle, and it cannot be fully understood without the earlier statement. Even the 1998 statement went generally unnoticed, however, until it was resurrected on various websites after the 9/11 attacks.[7]

The proclamation of jihad lists three "crimes and sins committed by the Americans" that amount to "a clear declaration of war on God, his messenger, and Muslims." The first is the offense discussed at length in the 1996 statement: the American "occupation" of the most sacred of Islamic lands, the Arabian Peninsula. With rhetorical flourish, the statement begins: "The Arabian Peninsula has never – since God made it flat, created its deserts, and encircled it with seas – been stormed by any forces like the crusader armies spreading in it like locusts, eating its riches and wiping out its plantations." The United States is not only plundering the peninsula's riches, it is "dictating to its rulers, humiliating its people, terrorizing its neighbors, and turning its bases . . . into a spearhead through which to fight the neighboring Muslim peoples."

The second "crime" of the United States is its continued blockade and sporadic military attacks on Iraq, "despite the great devastation inflicted on the Iraqi people by the Crusader–Zionist alliance, and despite the huge number of those killed, which has exceeded one million." The statement is careful to emphasize the harm done to the Iraqi people; no mention is made of the regime of the Iraqi dictator, Saddam Hussein, which was generally reviled by militant Islamic groups as an irreligious tyranny.

The third transgression is American support for Israel and Israel's occupation of Jerusalem and repression of the Palestinians. After the 9/11 attacks, many commentators made much of the fact that support for Israel came third on this list, and that this fact signified that the Israeli–Palestinian conflict did not figure prominently in al-Qaida's motivations. We were told repeatedly that mention of Israeli occupation of Palestinian territories was nothing but a cynical ploy by bin Laden to win Muslim support. While it is true that the US presence in the Arabian Peninsula seems to be al-Qaida's principal grievance, as stated explicitly both in 1996 and in 1998, it would be a mistake to discount the importance of the Israeli–Palestinian conflict. Clearly, bin Laden and his supporters seek to tap widespread Muslim hostility to US policies in that conflict. But those who charge opportunism on the part of bin Laden neglect to mention that the Israeli occupation of Jerusalem figured prominently in the 1996 statement as well. Moreover, they fail to appreciate the depth of Muslim feelings on this issue. The perception that the United States provides carte blanche support to Israel as it occupies Jerusalem and large tracts of the West Bank and Gaza, that American weapons are used in the suppression of the Palestinian *intifada*, that the United States frequently shields Israel from UN criticism in the Security Council – all while the sanctions against Iraq remained in place for a decade after the Gulf War – sparks the rawest emotional responses. These complaints do not need to be first on the list. They require no elaboration in the 1998 declaration. They are immediately understood by the statement's intended Muslim audience. As long as the conflict in Israel and the Palestinian territories continues, militant Muslim groups worldwide will exploit this issue to attack the United States. Bin Laden admitted as much in an October 21, 2001, interview with a correspondent from the Qatar-based television network al-Jazeera. In response to the correspondent's observation that bin Laden had shifted his emphasis in the interview to Palestine rather than the American presence in Saudi Arabia, bin Laden responded, "Sometimes we find the right elements to push for one cause more than the other. Last year's blessed *intifada* helped us to push more for the Palestinian issue. This push helps the other cause. Attacking America helps the cause of Palestine and vice versa. No conflict between the two; on the contrary, one serves the other."[8]

The 1998 statement concludes that because the United States and its allies, including its so-called Muslim allies, have declared war on Islam, true Muslims have no choice but to wage a defensive jihad. Bin Laden is careful in all his statements to invoke the notion of defensive jihad, not just because self-defense is the timeworn justification for most acts of violence, but also because it provides a number of important Islamic grounds for bin Laden's particular war. In a defensive jihad, various restraints imposed on the expansionist jihad are relaxed. All able-bodied Muslims, male and female, are required as an individual obligation to rush to the defense of the Muslim victims. If some Muslims are not close to the fighting and they cannot travel to the battlefield, they are required to assist the Muslim defenders in other ways. Requirements relating to proper authority – that is, who may declare and under whose leadership the jihad may be fought – become more ambiguous. If the leaders of the Islamic state are incapable or unwilling to lead the defensive struggle, other Muslims must assume this responsibility. And finally, the normal constraints on how Muslims may fight to repulse the aggression are loosened under claims of necessity. Just how much latitude Muslim fighters have in a defensive jihad will be discussed in the next section.

If we accept the 1996 and the 1998 declarations as articulating the ideas that motivate Osama bin Laden and his supporters – and I find no reason to deny that they do – then there is nothing at all remarkable about their arguments. Like the militant Islamic groups that preceded them, they selectively quote from the Qur'an to establish the religious basis for their defensive jihad, but they are driven by the same sort of anti-imperialism that motivates other religious and nonreligious groups in the Middle East and around the world. In other words, the driving force behind their acts of violence is far more political and mundane than it is theological or sacred.

The understanding of jihad involved here is not that characteristic of the period of Arab expansion in the seventh and eighth centuries or the Ottoman Turkish expansion of the fifteenth and sixteenth centuries, but one formed over the past two centuries as Muslims struggled to resist Western expansion. In the nineteenth and early twentieth centuries, the aggressor nations would have been identified as the British, the French, and the Russians. Since the end of World War II, the United States has increasingly occupied this position, and of course all the more so as it became the guardian of the Persian Gulf during the late 1980s and 1990s. While the United States was establishing a direct military presence in the Persian Gulf for the first time in its history, many of the men who would emerge as al-Qaida's leaders were fighting the Soviets in

Afghanistan. Driving one superpower from the region, in their view, was the prelude to the battle against the second.

Members of al-Qaida may (and probably do) harbor an existential hatred for the values and culture of the West ("they hate us because they resent our freedom and envy our wealth," we were told by a number of pundits and politicians after 9/11), but that is not what drove nineteen young men to hijack and crash airplanes into buildings. Al-Qaida's recruits may view themselves as the vanguard of an ideological movement that will ultimately overturn the societies of the rich and powerful West, but their words and actions indicate they are astute enough to realize this is a remote possibility. In the minds of the 9/11 hijackers, the attack upon New York and Washington, DC, was a continuation of the same war al-Qaida had waged in Nairobi and Dar es Salaam (where it bombed the American embassies) and in Aden (where it bombed the USS *Cole*). The hijackers died with the hope that they were helping to drive the United States out of Muslim states and thereby to weaken the Muslim governments the United States supports and which al-Qaida is determined to overthrow.

The grievances articulated by al-Qaida are hardly unique to it or in any way remarkable. The charge that Crusaders (i.e., Christians) and Zionists, in league with nominal Muslim leaders of the various Muslim states, are engaged in a campaign to weaken, humiliate, and exterminate Muslims, that they will repress by any means the legitimate demands of Muslim peoples for the establishment of an Islamic state – all of this has been heard many times before.

What is remarkable about al-Qaida is that it has declared its war against the United States directly and that it is willing to take this war to American soil. Before al-Qaida, American citizens and American interests were targeted by militant Islamic groups, but generally within Muslim countries and as a means of destabilizing the real targets, the Muslim governments the militants were battling. The 1996 declaration reversed this emphasis: "Everyone agrees that the situation cannot be rectified (the shadow cannot be straightened when its source, the rod, is not straight) unless the root of the problem is tackled. Hence it is essential to hit the main enemy who divided the *umma* into small countries and pushed it, for the last few decades, into a state of confusion."[9] "Straightening the rod" means, as the 1998 statement declared, attacking "Americans and their allies . . . in order to liberate the al-Aqsa Mosque and the holy mosque [in Mecca] from their grip, and in Order for their armies to move out of all the lands of Islam, defeated and unable to threaten any Muslim."[10]

As in all propaganda, the 1996 and 1998 declarations of war against the United States and its allies contain many distortions and half-truths. The US military presence in the Arabian Peninsula hardly amounts to an American occupation of the sanctuaries of Mecca and Medina. A concerted Western campaign to destroy Islam and to exterminate Muslims in a latter-day crusade is of course nonsense. Those who subscribe to this view have a hard time explaining why NATO intervened on behalf of the Muslims of Kosovo. But as in all effective propaganda, the two statements from al-Qaida identify and exploit many latent Muslim grievances. Chief among them are hostility to the perceived double standard in American dealings with Israel as compared with Muslim countries, and the support the United States lends to repressive governments throughout the Muslim world, while proclaiming its commitment to democracy and human rights. By declaring that it is willing to take on the world's greatest power in order to redress widely felt injustices, al-Qaida garners the support of many ordinary Muslims.

The Question of Means

Many Muslims share al-Qaida's stated objectives, and they accept the argument that the goals warrant the use of all means necessary to achieve them, including terrorism. But most Muslims, as polls have repeatedly shown, do not support terrorist methods even though they may sympathize with al-Qaida's goals. With respect to means, bin Laden and his supporters are indeed on the fringes of Islamic thought.

The conduct of Muslim armies has been an important concern of the jihad tradition from its very origins. In one of the first verses discussing war in self-defense, the Qur'an states, "Fight in God's cause against those who wage war against you, but do not transgress limits, for God loves not the transgressors" (2:190). The "limits" are enumerated in various statements of the Prophet and the first four caliphs. According to authoritative traditions, whenever the Prophet sent out a military force, he would instruct its commander to adhere to certain restraints, including giving fair notice of attack and sparing women and children.[11] The Prophet's immediate successors continued this practice, as is indicated by the "ten commands" of the first caliph, Abu Bakr:

> Do not act treacherously; do not act disloyally; do not act neglectfully. Do not mutilate; do not kill little children or old men, or women; do not cut off the heads of the palm-trees or burn them; do not cut down the fruit trees; do not slaughter a sheep or a cow or a camel, except for food. You will pass by people who devote their lives in cloisters; leave them and their devotions alone. You will come upon people who bring you platters in which are various sorts of food; if you eat any of it, mention the name of God over it.

Clearly, then, the Qur'an and the actions of the Prophet and his successors established the principles of discrimination between combatants and noncombatants and of limited warfare, Later jurists devoted considerable attention to elaborating just who qualified as a noncombatant and what tactics were permissible against combatants. The consensus was that those who traditionally do not take part in fighting, especially women, children, the old, and the infirm, are never legitimate targets. Jihad can never be "total war," in which unnecessarily cruel or excessive means of destruction are used against the enemy.

Modern Muslim scholars have continued to develop these principles. One of the most important contributions comes from the Syrian scholar Wahba al-Zuhayli, who writes:

> Islamic law does not characterize all of the enemy population as combatants. The combatants include all those who prepare themselves for fighting, either directly or indirectly. . . . As for the civilians who are at peace and devote themselves to work that is neutral in terms of [militarily] assisting the enemy . . . none of these are termed as combatants whose

blood may be shed with impunity. On this point, Islamic law and international law converge.[12]

Like the vast majority of Muslim ethicists, Zuhayli rules out the possibility of collective responsibility, that all citizens belonging to a perceived foe are somehow responsible for their state's actions. Zuhayli also echoes the overwhelming consensus of modern scholars that Islamic ethics is consistent with the basic principles of international humanitarian law, including the Geneva Convention and its related protocols, that makes the deliberate targeting of noncombatants and the terrorizing of civilian populations a war crime.[13]

In their 1996 declaration of war, bin Laden and his supporters had very little to say on how they would wage their fight. They did acknowledge that "due to the imbalance of power between our armed forces and the enemy forces, a suitable means of fighting must be adopted, i.e., using fast-moving light forces that work under complete secrecy." In addition, the statement goes to great lengths to glorify the particular type of guerrilla operation that al-Qaida was adopting: the suicide bombing.[14]

The radical break with the centuries-old jihad tradition comes at the end of the 1998 statement. In the part described as a *fatwa*, or legal edict, bin Laden and his co-signers declare, "The ruling to kill the Americans and their allies – civilians and military – is an individual duty for every Muslim who can do it in any country in which it is possible to do it."[15] Ever since this statement was released, bin Laden has been challenged by various interviewers to justify on Islamic grounds his endorsement of killing civilians. The most detailed defense by bin Laden of which I am aware came in an October 21, 2001, interview with al-Jazeera television correspondent Tayseer Alouni. The exchange is worth reproducing at some length.

> *OBL:* The killing of innocent civilians, as America and some intellectuals claim, is really very strange talk. Who said that our children and civilians are not innocent and that shedding their blood is justified? That it is lesser in degree? When we kill their innocents, the entire world from east to west screams at us, and America rallies its allies, agents, and the sons of its agents. Who said that our blood is not blood, but theirs is? . . . .
>
> *Alouni:* So what you are saying is that this is a type of reciprocal treatment. They kill our innocents, so we kill their innocents.
>
> *OBL:* So we kill their innocents, and I say it is permissible in law and intellectually, because those who spoke on this matter spoke from a juridical perspective.
>
> *Alouni:* What is their position?
>
> *OBL:* That it is not permissible. They spoke of evidence that the Messenger of God forbade the killing of women and children. This is true.
>
> *Alouni:* This is exactly what I'm asking about.
>
> *OBL:* However, this prohibition of the killing of children and innocents is not absolute. It is not absolute. There are other texts that restrict it.
>
> I agree that the Prophet Muhammad forbade the killing of babies and women. That is true, but this is not absolute. There is a saying, "If the infidels killed women and children on purpose, we shouldn't shy away from treating them in the

same way to stop them from doing it again." The men that God helped [attack, on September 11] did not intend to kill babies; they intended to destroy the strongest military power in the world, to attack the Pentagon that houses more than 64,000 employees, a military center that houses the strength and the military intelligence.

Alouni: How about the twin towers?

OBL: The towers are an economic power and not a children's school. Those that were there are men that supported the biggest economic power in the world. They have to review their books. We will do as they do. If they kill our women and our innocent people, we will kill their women and their innocent people until they stop.

In his November 7, 2001, interview with Pakistani journalist Hamid Mir, bin Laden expanded on his notion of the collective responsibility, and hence the collective vulnerability, of all Americans: "The American people should remember that they pay taxes to their government, they elect their president, their government manufactures arms and gives them to Israel and Israel uses them to massacre Palestinians. The American Congress endorses all government measures and this proves that the entire America is responsible for the atrocities perpetrated against Muslims. The entire America, they elect the Congress."[16]

As for the Muslims who are killed in al-Qaida's attacks, if they are killed in non-Muslim countries, "the Islamic Shar'ia says Muslims should not live in the land of the infidels for long." If they are killed in Muslim countries, al-Qaida fighters are to be excused for their deaths because when "an enemy occupies a Muslim territory and uses common people as human shields, then it is permitted to attack that enemy."[17] So, according to bin Laden's statements, in the name of retaliation, the civilians killed are either not innocents or they are collateral damage.

Throughout Islamic history, various groups have given extreme interpretations to Qur'anic verses and Prophetic traditions to justify their violent actions. Some of the most notorious include the Khawarij of the seventh and eighth centuries, the Assassins of the twelfth century, and the Wahhabis of the nineteenth century. Their justifications went against the weight of the jihad tradition, and they were treated as extremists by the mainstream Muslims of their times. Some observers describe al-Qaida as falling within the same pattern of disaffected, marginalized Muslim sects. There are many points of comparison: Like the Khawarij, those organized under the banner of al-Qaida have no compunction about killing indiscriminately. Like the Assassins, their fighters are trained to die in the process of killing their opponents. Like the Wahhabis, they are convinced that the Muslim societies around them are steeped in false understandings of Islam, and that they, the only true Muslims, must violently purge Muslim societies of their un-Islamic notions. Indeed, al-Qaida seems to have achieved a full amalgam of all the distinctive traits of the previous groups.

The comparison between al-Qaida and earlier extremist groups should not be taken too far, however. Certainly, it is too much of a stretch to trace a genealogy of "Islamic terrorism" that begins with the Khawarij or the Assassins and then continues through the Wahhabis to al-Qaida today. Al-Qaida's terrorism is rationalized with Islamic justifications, but it falls within a history of modern terrorism that has little to do with Islam. What is missing from the genealogy above are the historical antecedents of modern terrorism in the Middle East, which include the activities of radical Jewish groups in Palestine during the 1940s, the Arab and the European parties to the Algerian liberation struggle of the 1950s, and the Palestine Liberation Organization of the 1970s. These movements perfected such terrorist methods as bombing civilian buildings, assassinating leaders, and hijacking civilian airliners. Contemporary Muslim terrorists have their roots as much in this violent legacy inspired by European revolutionaries, anarchists, and nihilists as in earlier Muslim extremism.

But bin Laden and his supporters quote the Qur'an and not the Communist Manifesto, the prophet Muhammad and not Trotsky. It is necessary therefore to address their justifications from within the tradition they invoke. Many points could be discussed, but I will focus here on only two of the most salient issues raised by al-Qaida's methods: the justification of targeting civilians and of suicide attacks.

Bin Laden defends the targeting of civilians primarily on the basis of reciprocity. The United States and its allies are killing Muslim civilians around the world, so it is justifiable for al-Qaida to respond by attacking American civilians. In his October 21, 2001, interview, bin Laden cites two Muslim "authorities" who, he claims, provide Islamic justification for targeting civilians.[18] Neither of the men he mentions is a well-known legal scholar, however. In other statements, bin Laden has alluded only vaguely to "principles of jurisprudence" that support his position. As for the vast majority of *'ulama* who have condemned his terrorism, bin Laden, like all extremists before him, categorically rejects their authority: "The fatwa of any official *'alim* [singular of *ulama*] has no value for me. History is full of such *ulama* who justify *riba* [usury], who justify the occupation of Palestine by the Jews, who justify the presence of American troops around Haramain Sharifain [the two sanctuaries of Mecca and Medina]. These people support the infidels for their personal gain. The true *ulama* support the jihad against America."[19] Because he claims to be waging a defensive jihad against a ruthless, unprincipled opponent, bin Laden views the normal restraints applicable to Muslim fighters as being suspended: "If inciting people to do that [defend themselves] is terrorism, and if killing those who kill our sons is terrorism, then let history witness that we are terrorists."[20]

Leaving aside the merits of bin Laden's contention that he is in fact waging a defensive jihad against an unprincipled enemy, his assertion that Islamic ethics or jurisprudence permit indiscriminate warfare is untenable. The jihad tradition cannot be interpreted as endorsing the principle that in the name of retaliation or reciprocity, any and all tactics are permissible. Muslim extremists selectively quote such Qur'anic verses as "If then anyone transgresses the prohibition against you, transgress you likewise against him" (2:194), and "Fight the polytheists all together (*kaffatan*) as they fight you all together" (9:36) to justify their terrorism. Not only do they fail to take into account the historical circumstances surrounding these verses, they also fail to consider that both verses conclude with the line: "But know that God is with those who are mindful of God's limits (*al-muttaqin*)."

The jihad tradition relaxes restrictions on the weapons or methods of warfare in the face of military necessity, but never the principle that civilians are not to be directly targeted. This prohibition of attacks on noncombatants is defended as a rule derived from the Qur'an and the Prophet's *hadiths*. Even bin Laden on occasion acknowledges this rule, as in his November 7, 2001, interview: "The September 11 attacks were not targeted at women and children. The real targets were America's icons of military and economic power."[21] Yet this claim is obviously disingenuous; hijacking civilian airliners and crashing them into the Twin Towers when they were known to hold thousands of civilians makes human beings and not buildings "the real targets."

So, to meet this objection, bin Laden and his supporters fall back on the notion of reciprocity. Suffice it to say in response that retaliation in kind was a pagan Arab practice (and even then one limited by notions of chivalric honor) that was forbidden by the Prophet as a fundamental part of his reform of Arab martial values. The urge to revive the practice resurfaced during the rule of Abu Bakr (632–34 CE). One account relates that Byzantine forces routinely decapitated Muslim prisoners, and so Muslim commanders ordered a similar execution of Byzantine prisoners. When Abu Bakr learned of the practice, he ordered its immediate cessation. The Muslim commanders then protested that they were merely answering the enemy with his own methods. To which Abu Bakr is reported to have asked, "Are the Byzantines our teachers?"[22]

Bin Laden's second justification for al-Qaida's methods is that they are "martyrdom operations." This characterization rationalizes the specific tactic now favored by Islamic militants around the world: suicide attacks. Muslim extremists certainly did not invent or perfect this technique; one needs only recall the Japanese kamikaze pilots and the Tamil Tigers, who deployed the young, individual suicide bomber with devastating effect in India and Sri Lanka. But beginning with Hezbollah's suicide attacks in Lebanon against Israeli, American, and other targets, Muslim terrorists have employed it with such frequency that it will now forever be connected in the minds of many with "jihad." Muslim groups employ this tactic because it is the most effective weapon in the arsenal of the weak. But they also justify this tactic as a form of martyrdom, as if the deliberate taking of one's life in war has always been an accepted part of the jihad tradition.

The fact is that it is not an accepted part of the jihad tradition. Suicide in general is strongly condemned in Islamic teachings, and as a result it is rare in Muslim societies.[23] The response of Muslim groups employing suicide as a tactic, and of many Muslims who support them, is that the fighter who blows himself or herself up in attacking the enemy is not committing suicide but performing an act of self-sacrifice (martyrdom) similar to that of any soldier who marches into the face of certain death. Indeed, the line between combat and suicide is often fine and easily crossed. This is especially true when soldiers of a badly outnumbered and outgunned army fight a superior force rather than retreat or surrender. Americans still celebrate as heroic such suicidal ventures as the defense of the Alamo, Pickett's charge at the battle of Gettysburg, and Custer's last stand. Similarly, Muslims commemorate many a doomed struggle, most fervently the stand against all odds by the Prophet's grandson Husayn at Karbala in 680 CE.

But there is a distinct difference between Husayn's defense of himself and his family at Karbala and what young men and women do today with the idea that they are earning paradise through jihad. The difference has to do not only with the targets involved, as discussed above, but the very act by which innocent people are killed. The *mujahid* (one who wages jihad) goes into battle with the intention to fight and *to live*, but with the conviction that if he should die, it is because God wills it. The suicide bombers who crash airplanes or trucks packed with explosives into buildings perform their deeds with the intention *to die*, justifying their deaths as acts of self-sacrifice.

One *hadith* from the Prophet, out of the many that mention suicide, relates directly to the actions of the suicide bombers:

> There was a man who fought more bravely than all the Muslims on behalf of the Muslims in a battle in the company of the Prophet. The Prophet looked at him and said, "If anyone would like to see a man from the people of the Fire [i.e., hell], let him look at this man." On that, one of the Muslims followed him, and he was in that state [that is, fighting fiercely] until he was wounded, and then he hastened to end his life by placing his sword between his breasts [and pressed it with great force] until it came out between his shoulders. Then the man [who was watching that person] went quickly to the Prophet and said, "I testify that you are God's Messenger!" The Prophet asked him, "Why do you say that?" He said, "You said about so-and-so, 'If anyone would like to see a man from the people of the Fire, he should look at him.' He fought more bravely than all of us on behalf of the Muslims, but I knew that he would not die as a Muslim [martyr]. So when he got wounded, he hastened to die and committed suicide."[24]

The person who pulls the trigger of an explosives belt wrapped around his or her body is committing suicide as surely as the man who falls upon his own sword.

Morality and Terrorism

Some readers may question the point of subjecting the statements and actions of terrorists to moral scrutiny. Doesn't the internal logic of terrorism itself defy any moral justification? Isn't the terrorists' goal to commit such atrocities that they demoralize their victims or induce retaliatory action that garners active support from otherwise uncommitted sympathizers? Or, as some American officials argued after 9/11, doesn't responding to the terrorists' stated grievances only legitimize their methods?

My response is threefold: First, on the intellectual level, the misappropriation of the Qur'an and *hadith* to defend terrorism must be shown for what it is: a distortion of the jihad tradition. The distortion is so complete that today Muslims and non-Muslims regularly call groups like al-Qaida "jihadis," when in fact their methods do not conform to the basic principles of jihad. The time has come for the majority of Muslims who understand jihad as a just war, in which terrorism has no place, to reclaim this concept from the extremists.

Second, on a practical level, the religious arguments of the terrorists must be answered by others from within the same tradition or else the terrorist groups will continue to attract followers. Osama bin Laden and his supporters may be completely impervious to counterarguments or moral discourse of any sort. But unless we conclude that all those who join al-Qaida or other extremist Muslim groups are pathologically homicidal or suicidal or both, there is a need to answer their ideas with other ideas. Perhaps if enough Muslims undertake this mission and sustain it with principled arguments long enough, a few young men or women who would otherwise join the ranks of the terrorists would turn away from them.[25] Even one individual so diverted would be justification enough for responding to the terrorists.

My third response is offered with the long-term fight against terrorism and America's relations with the Muslim world in mind. The support al-Qaida garners from ordinary Muslims comes from a confusion between ends and means. Because many Muslims around the world feel deeply that the world order created and dominated by the West, and the United States in particular, is inimical to their interests, they are willing to embrace any means necessary to reverse the situation – or at least to teach their alleged oppressors a lesson. Curiously, the same confusion of ends and means is apparent in the pronouncements of American leaders who declare that because of the brutal means al-Qaida uses, it seeks to reach "maximal" goals, including the destruction of the West or the imposition of its vision of Islam all over the world. Invoking such apocalyptic ends serves quite conveniently to bolster the position of those who claim there is no point at all in addressing al-Qaida's stated grievances.

Al-Qaida's conflation of ends and means is fundamentally incompatible with the jihad tradition as it has evolved for centuries. But we turn a deaf ear to al-Qaida's arguments at our own peril. To examine and to respond to the arguments is in no way to legitimize them. Taking a close look in particular at the grievances articulated by al-Qaida is in no way tantamount to "giving in" to or "sympathizing" with the terrorists. The surest way to bolster Muslim support for the terrorists is to ignore the causes from which terrorism springs and the justifications given to rationalize it. In the end, if we are to win the war against terrorism, we must prosecute the war on all fronts: military, political, economic – and moral.

Notes

1. For the text of this note, see http://www.fbi.gov/pressrel/pressre101/letter.htm (December 14, 2001); and http://more.abcnews.go.com/sections/world/DailyNews/attaletter_1.html (December 14, 2001).

2. Max Weber, "Politics as a Vocation," in *From Max Weber: Essays in Sociology*, ed. and trans. Hans H. Gerth and C. Wright Mills (New York: Oxford University Press, 1946), 78.

3. This *hadith* is not found in any of the six canonical *hadith* collections and appears to have been introduced by Sufis in the ninth century. Over the course of Islamic history, its authenticity has been challenged by Muslim scholars eager to emphasize the military, and not purely spiritual, dimensions of jihad. Regardless of its authenticity, it is now so widely quoted by Muslims that one could argue it has become normative to Islamic tradition.

4. "Ladenese Epistle: Declaration of War (Parts I–III)," part I, 1–2, at http://www.washingtonpost.com/ac2/wp-dyn/A4342–2001Sep21 (September 28, 2001).

5. "Ladenese Epistle," II: 2–3.

6. Ibid. For further details on the sanctity of the Arabian Peninsula in Islamic tradition, see Sohail H. Hashmi, "Moral Communities and Political Boundaries: Islamic Perspectives," in *States, Nations, and Borders: The Ethics of Making Boundaries*, ed. Allen Buchanan and Margaret Moore (New York: Cambridge University Press, 2003), 186–94.

7. One notable exception is Bernard Lewis's analysis, "License to Kill: Osama bin Laden's Declaration of Jihad," *Foreign Affairs* 77:6 (November/December 1998): 14–19.

8. "Transcript of bin Laden's October Interview," 4, at http://www.cnn.com/2002/WORLD/asiapcf/south/02/05/binladen.transcript (November 18, 2003).

9. "Ladenese Epistle," I:6.

10. "Jihad against Jews and Crusaders," 2, at http://www.washingtonpost.com/ac2/wp-dyn/A4993–2001Sep21 (September 28, 2001).

11. A representative sample of Prophetic statements on restrictions in fighting is available in Muhammad ibn ʿAbdallah, Khatib al-Tabrizi, *Mishkat al-Masabih*, trans. Mawlana Fazlul Karim (New Delhi: Islamic Book Service, 1988), 2:387–89.

12. Wahba al-Zuhayli, *Athar al-harb fi al-fiqh al-Islami: Dirasa muqarana* (Damascus: Dar al-Fikr, 1981), 503.

13. For more on contemporary Muslim views on legitimate means of waging war, see Muhammad Abu Zahra, *Concept of War in Islam,* trans. Muhammad al-Hady and Taha Omar (Cairo: Ministry of Waqf, 1961); Yadh ben Ashoor, *Islam and International Humanitarian Law* (Geneva: International Committee of the Red Cross, 1980); Karima Bennoune, "As-Salamu ʿAlaykum? Humanitarian Law in Islamic Jurisprudence," *Michigan Journal of International Law* 15 (Winter 1994): 605–43; and Sohail H. Hashmi, "Saving and Taking Life in War: Three Modern Muslim Views," in *The Islamic Ethics of Life: Abortion, War, and Euthanasia,* ed. Jonathan E. Brockopp (Columbia: University of South Carolina Press, 2003), 129–54.

14. "Ladenese Epistle," II:4ff.

15. "Jihad against Jews and Crusaders," 2.

16. "Osama Claims He Has Nukes," *Dawn* (Karachi), November 10, 2001, 1, at http://www.dawn.com/2001/11/10/top1.htm (January 2, 2004).

17. Ibid.

18. The two men bin Laden mentions are Sami Zai of Pakistan and Abdullah bin Ohkmah al-Shehebi of Saudi Arabia. "Transcript of bin Laden's October Interview," 4.

19. "Osama Claims He has Nukes," 1.

20. "Transcript of bin Laden's October Interview," 1.

21. "Osama Claims He Has Nukes," 1.

22. ʿArif Abu ʿId, *al-ʿAlaqat al-kharijiyya fi dawlat al-khilafa* (Kuwait: Dar al-Arqam, 1983), 222, relates this account and discusses many other issues relating to reciprocity in Islamic jurisprudence.

23. See Jonathan E. Brockopp, "The 'Good Death' in Islamic Theology and Law," in *The Islamic Ethics of Life: Abortion, War, and Euthanasia,* 177–93.

24. Narrated by Bukhari, *Sahih al-Bukhari,* bk. 77 (Divine Will, *al-Qadar*), no. 604.

25. Most reputable Muslim scholars condemned the 9/11 attacks as unjustifiable terrorism. But many of the same scholars have supported Palestinian suicide bombings in Israel as legitimate resistance to occupation. See Haim Malka "Must Innocents Die? The Islamic Debate over Suicide Attacks," *Middle East Quarterly* 10:2 (Spring 2003): 19–28, at http://www.meforum.org/article/530(January 2, 2004). Terrorism cannot be condoned under any circumstances within the jihad tradition, as I have argued in this chapter. Making exceptions in the Palestinian case only undermines the condemnation of terrorism in other cases.

23

An Ontology of Everyday Distraction: The Freeway, the Mall, and Television

Margaret Morse*

Thus television turns out to be related to the motor car and the aeroplane as a means of transport for the mind.

– Rudolf Arnheim

This chapter articulates an intuition that has been expressed from time to time in critical literature – that television is similar or related to other, particular modes of transportation and exchange in everyday life. The investigation of the subjective and formal bases of this intuition is limited here to the built environments of freeways and malls.[1] Television and its analogs, the freeway and the mall, are conceptualized as a nexus of interdependent two- and three-dimensional cultural forms which don't so much *look* alike as observe similar principles of construction and operation. These shadows or inverse aspects of the work world are forms of communication that also function interdependently.

Freeways, malls, and television are the locus of virtualization or an attenuated *fiction effect*, that is, a partial loss of touch with the here-and-now, dubbed here as *distraction*. This semifiction effect is akin to but not identical with split-belief – knowing a representation is not real, but nevertheless momentarily closing off the here-and-now and sinking into another world – promoted within the apparatuses of the theater, the cinema, and the novel. Its difference lies primarily in that it involves two or more objects and levels of attention and the copresence of two or more different, even contradictory, metapsychological effects, Ultimately, distraction is related to the expression of two planes of language represented simultaneously or alternately, the plane of the subject in a here-and-now, or *discourse*, and the plane of an absent or nonperson in another time, elsewhere, or story.

However, beyond the invocation of an *elsewhere* and a "spacing out" or partial absence of mind described here, many aspects of "distraction" are left to the imagination or to later treatment: a review of the rich field of the iconography of automobiles, freeways, malls, and television,[2] an account for the shifting relations between mastery and

* Originally published as "An Ontology of Everyday Distraction: The Freeway, the Mall and Television," pp. 99–124, 226–32 from M. Morse, *Virtualities: Television, Media Art, and Cyberculture* (Bloomington, Indiana University Press). © 1990 by Margaret Morse. Reprinted with permission from Indiana University Press.

bondage and the feelings of pleasure and boredom involved in their use, and the ambiguous value the analogs of television enjoy in our culture – each in its own way being considered a "vast wasteland" and a waste of time as well as a devotion allied with the American dream.

The preconditions of distraction are postulated in the phenomenon of "mobile privatization," and the general features that promote his divided state of mind are described as "the phantasmagoria of the interior." Furthermore, freeways, malls, and television are posed as interrelated and mutually reinforcing systems organized in a way which allows for "liquidity," the exchange of values between different ontological levels and otherwise incommensurable facets of life, for example, between two and three dimensions, among language, images, and the built environment, and among the economic, societal, and symbolic realms of our culture.

Television is a key element of these exchanges and transformations, not only because it invests images with exchange-value, but also because it models exchange itself, both as an apparatus which includes the viewer virtually in discourse and via representations of constant shifts through various ontological levels, subjective relations, and fields of reference. The dualism of *passage* and *segmentation* which is part of the freeway, mall, and televisual realms is discussed more theoretically in relation to *discourse* and *story*.

There is nothing discrete about television, for its very nature is to annex pretelevisual culture and leisure time to itself, This chapter seeks, in broad strokes, to situate television as a cultural form in a larger sociocultural context of everyday life. This speculative project draws explicitly and tacitly on previous works of synthesis to support its premises, for example Raymond Williams's relation of broadcasting to the changing social context of mobile privatization in which it developed; Walter Benjamin's *Passagen-Werk* or arcade project of research on the genealogy of commodity fetishism in the nineteenth century in glass- and steel-enclosed shopping arcades, dioramas, and such exhibition halls as the Crystal Palace; and Mikhail Bakhtin's notion of the *chronotope* or unit of space/time that oscillates between literary representation and the spatiotemporal experience of everyday life. The archetypal chronotope, the *road*, for instance, invites comparison with the *freeway*, as does Benjamin's conception of the *arcade* with the *mall*.

Michel de Certeau's *The Practice of Everyday Life* is an inspiration to the basic premise of interchangeability between signs and objects described here. Noting that "in modern Athens, the vehicles of mass transportation are called *metaphorai*" (115),[3] de Certeau articulates concepts of language and narrative with such forms of everyday life as architecture, transportation, and food. His vision of liberation from formal determination, surveillance, and control is based on the distinction between language and society as formal systems versus language as it is enunciated or as a social form enacted in practice at any one time. This distinction is expressed spatially, for example, as the difference between *place*, a proper, stable, and distinct location, and *space*, composed of intersections of mobile elements, taking into consideration vectors of direction, velocities, and time variables. He concludes that "space is a practiced place," a geometry of the street redefined and made habitable by walkers (117).

De Certeau's vision of liberation via enunciative practices bears the marks of its conception in another time and place, that is in a pre-mall, pre-freeway and largely print-literate, pretelevisual world. In the meantime, in the United States at least, the very nature of the street and pedestrian activity as well as the predominant modes and media for linguistic communication have changed. However, the notion of praxis as enunciation, be it linguistic, pedestrian, or other which evades pre-determined paths and escapes from literal reality into an *elsewhere* and to other levels of conscious-ness is, as we shall see, one fully congruent with the operation of malls, or for that matter, freeways and television. Indeed, *distraction* is based upon the representation of *space* within *place* (in which, as we shall see, space becomes displaced, a *nonspace*) and the inclusion of (for de Certeau, liberating) *elsewheres* and *elsewhens* in the here-and-now.

Thus, de Certeau's very means of escape are now designed into the geometries of everyday life, and his figurative practices of enunciation ("making do," "walking in the city," or "reading as poaching") are modeled in representation itself. Could de Certeau have imagined, as; he wrote on walking as an evasive strategy of self-empowerment, that there would one day be videocassettes which demonstrate how to "power" walk? This investigation takes stock of this new cultural environment.

To contour this new terrain is less to map postmodernity than to explain why a map per se is virtually impossible to construct. For the level of iconicity shared by television and its analogs is one of common preconditions and principles of articulation rather than one of resemblance in shape or the boundedness of contiguous or even specifiable locations in space. Rather these analogs share the *nonspace* and the simultaneous tem-poralities of *distraction*.

Derealized Space

The late twentieth century has witnessed the growing dominance of a differently con-stituted kind of space, virtuality or a *nonspace* of both experience and representation, an *elsewhere* that inhabits the everyday. Nonspace is not mysterious or strange to us, but rather the very haunt for creatures of habit. Practices and skills which can be performed semiautomatically in a distracted state – like driving, shopping, or television-watching – are the barely acknowledged ground of everyday experience. This ground is without locus, a partially derealized realm from which a new quotidian fiction emanates.

Nonspace is a ground within which communication as a flow of values between and among two and three dimensions and between virtuality and actuality – indeed, an uncanny oscillation between life and death – can "take place." One finds the quintes-sential descriptions of nonspace in the postwar generation which was first to explore suburbia. Tony Smith's description of a car ride along a newly constructed section of the New Jersey Turnpike at night (quoted in Hobbs 14) expressed a formative experi-ence of *elsewhere* out of which grew (in the 1960s) the conception of environmental art by artists like Robert Smithson. With earthworks such as *Spiral Jetty*, Smithson under-mined the object-hood and the locus in space of his sculpture, lost somewhere between documentation in a gallery or museum and an inaccessible referent somewhere else. Robert Hobbs explains Smithson's nonsite and non-space sculptures as a profound assessment of mid-twentieth-century experience:

In an era of rootlessness, massive reordering of the landscape, large-scale temporary buildings, and media implosion, he viewed people's essential apprehension of the world as a
rejection of it. Vicariousness, projection to some other place by rejecting where one actually
is, has become a dominant mid-twentieth-century means of dealing with the world. Making
the nonsite (which brings together nonseeing and nonspace under one rubric) a primary
determinant of his aesthetic forms, Smithson emphasized ways people nonperceive.
(15–16)

Later descriptions of nonspace (for example Baudrillard's notion of simulation) also
emphasize it as a focus of derealization. Baudrillard conceives of simulation as a loss of
referential anchorage to the world or the insecurity of denotation as it applies primarily
to objects, whereas his own spatial allusions to *networks*, inert *masses*, and *black holes* lay
claim to a kind of poetic scientificity. But this mixed metaphor in "The Ecstasy of
Communication" is the vehicle which conveys the full complexity of his conceptualization of spatiality in postmodernity: "The vehicle now becomes a kind of capsule, its
dashboard the brain, the surrounding landscape unfolding like a televised screen (instead
of a live-in projectile as it was before)."[4] The interiors of the home television viewing
space, the automobile, the space capsule, and the computer are ultimately associated
with the interiority of the human mind. The image of the exterior world from these
interiors is no longer a "Western window" onto reality, but for Baudrillard, the dubious
vision of television.

In his popular and playful ontology of the shopping mall, *The Malling of America*,
William Severini Kowinski goes even further, calling the mall a "TV you walk around
in." Here the mode of locomotion is different, but the interiority (not just exterior
vision) of the viewer is equated with television itself: "The mall is television, [in terms
of] people's perceptions of space and reality, the elements that persuade people to
suspend their disbelief" (71). These spatial comparisons depend on a common experience of some degree of fictitiousness within their (un)realities. The implication is that
television epitomizes a new ontology of the everyday: vast realms of the somewhat-less-
than-real to which significant amounts of free time (unpaid leisure, the shadow of work)
are devoted on a routine, cyclical basis. The features of this derealized or *nonspace* are
shared by freeway, mall, and television alike.

The first distinguishing feature of nonspace is its dreamlike *displacement* or separation
from its surroundings. Freeways are displaced in that they do not lie earthbound and
contiguous to their surroundings so much as they float above or below the horizon. The
freeway disengaged from its immediate context is "a bridge over the barriers of both
social and natural geography," offering as well "a continued shelter from engagement
with ghetto areas" (Kevin Lynch, quoted in Brodsly 39–40). In Kevin Lynch's famous
study of cognitive maps of the city, from the point of view of the streets, the freeway
is almost invisible, "not felt to be 'in' the rest of the city" (quoted in Brodsly 31). Similarly, from the subjective point of view of a driver or passenger experiencing motion
blur, the city isn't visible either except at times as a distant miniature seen from a
freeway which is usually also physically depressed or elevated from its surroundings or
shielded by its own greenbelt. To paraphrase Charles Kuralt, the freeway is what makes
it possible to drive coast to coast and never see anything. In fact, the freeway divides

the world in two, into what David Brodsly calls "local" and "metropolitan" (24) orientations. These also denote two realities: the one, heterogeneous and static; the other, homogeneous and mobile. The passage between them can be accompanied by a shock, a moment of "severe disorientation" (Brodsly 24).

Furthermore, the process of displacement is a prelude to condensation. The freeway not only represents transportation from the city in the suburbs, but it is also a greenbelt and an escape "from the world of stucco into an urban preserve of open space and greenery" (Brodsly 49). Suburbia is itself an attempt via serial production to give everyman and everywife the advantages of a city at the edge of the natural world. Thus, the suburbs are "a living polemic against both the large industrial metropolis and the provincial small town," which nonetheless manage to "maintain the facade of a garden patch of urban villages, a metropolitan small town, without ever compromising the anonymity that is a hallmark of city life" (Brodsly 33, 45).[5] Freeways and the suburbs they serve are thus examples of the "garden in the machine," which provides mass society with a pastoral aesthetic and rhetoric.

Malls are similarly "completely separated from the rest of the world," Kowinski calls this separation "the first and most essential secret of the shopping mall":

> It was its own world, pulled out of time and space, but not only by windowless walls and a roof, or by the neutral zone of the parking lot between it and the highway, the asphalt moat around the magic castle. It was enclosed in an even more profound sense – and certainly more than other mere buildings – because all these elements, and others, psychologically separated it from the outside and created the special domain within its embrace. It's meant to be its own special world with its own rules and reality. (60)

The mall is a spatial condensation near a node where freeways intersect, serving a certain temporal radius; it is "a city, indeed a world in miniature."[6] Shops that are four-fifths of normal size[7] are linked together within a vast and usually enclosed, multileveled atrium or hail, devoted solely to the pedestrian consumer (albeit served by autos and trucks).[8] A regional center saturated by chain stores which turns its back on local shops,[9] the mall is the paradoxical promise of adventure on the road within an idyll of Main Street in a small town before the age of the automobile (see Graham and Hurst).[10]

The mall is not only enclosed, Kowinski adds, but it is protected from exposure to the natural and public world through unobtrusive but central control. This private surveillance escapes the kind of sharp vigilance in the light of democratic values to which it would be subject in the public world: we do not expect the consumer to possess the same kinds of rights or responsibilities as the citizen. Shopping malls are essentially governed by market planners (that is, by a fairly limited pool of mall entrepreneurs, builders, owners, and managers) and market forces. Each mall is carefully situated and designed in terms of its architecture; the "retail drama" of its syntax of shops and types of commodities, promotions, and advertising conveys a unified image that attracts some parts of the surrounding population and discourages others.

Consumers of all ages (but probably not all social conditions) come together to recreate the lost community of the street and the agora now under the private management of the arcade. The courts of foot traffic allow consumers and "mall rats" (nonconsuming loiterers) to intermingle in an attenuated and controlled version of a crowded street. Thus the mall retains elements of the milling crowd, but as a private space in which anonymous individuals, preferably ones with particular demographic characteristics, gather en masse. So the paroxysms of release from individuality via bodily contact described by Elias Canetti in *Crowds and Power* are unlikely; the street celebrated by Bakhtin as a place of festival which erases boundaries between self and other is scarcely imaginable.[11]

Rather than a site of "contamination," the mall is a place to shore up the boundaries of the self via commodities which beckon with the promise of perfection from beyond the glass or gleam of the threshold in brightly lit shops. These commodities with roles in retail drama have a somewhat dreamlike quality even in terms of their use-value, for they are less often connected with labor or the small necessities of life (for example, needles and thread, nails and hammers, seed and fertilizer, and so forth) than linked to leisure and a designer lifestyle (note the category shift of pots and pans, now that cooking is linked to luxury living). Rather, the preferred commodities of retail drama are "lost objects," the very things a subject desires to complete or perfect his or her self-image. And, rather than being unique, these objects are mass-produced, the very ones to be seen advertised on television, in print, and on display beyond the glass.

Television is likewise premised upon private reception in an environment isolated from events "out there," which determine the conditions of life outside the home. John Ellis has described this practice as the "double distance" of television's complicity with the viewer against an "outside world" represented as "hostile or bizarre," and the viewer's delegation of "his or her look to the TV itself."[12] Both means of distancing constitute "the opposition 'inside/outside', which insulates the viewer from events seen by TV" (169).[13]

But this division of the world is complicated by the reconstruction of an idealized version of the older forms of transport, social, and media communication within the very enclosures from which they are excluded. The past inscribed within the present is constructed *as past* through this very act of separation; a local and heterogeneous world beyond continues to exist but with fading resources, a phantom from an anterior world. This interior duality has symbolic dimensions as well: oppositions between country and city, nature and culture, sovereign individual and social subject are neutralized only to be reconstituted within nonspace in a multilayered compromise formation, a utopian realm of *both/and* in the midst of *neither/nor*.

This process of displacement from context is also one of dislocation. In a quite literal, physical sense, freeways, malls, or television are not truly "places." That is, they cannot be localized within the geometrical grids that orient the American city and countryside.

As Brodsly explains in his essay on the LA freeway, a freeway is not a place but a *vector* (25–26);[14] even its name or number is a direction rather than a location. Channels of motion dedicated solely to one-way, high-velocity travel, freeways are largely experienced as "in-betweens," other than as places where one enjoys the full reality of a point of departure or a destination. And magnitude on the freeway is popularly measured in minutes rather than miles. Yet, within that waste of time spent in-between, usually alone and isolated within an iron bubble, a miniature idyll with its own controlled climate and selected sound is created. In this intensely private space, lifted out of the social world, the driver is subject, more real and present to him- or herself than the miniatures or the patterns of lights beyond the glass, or farther yet, beyond the freeway.

Television is also dislocated, insofar as it consists of two-dimensional images dispersed onto screens in nearly every home in the United States, displaying messages transmitted everywhere and nowhere in particular. Television is also a vast relay and retrieval system for audiovisual material of uncertain origin and date which can be served up instantaneously by satellite and cable as well as broadcast transmission and videocassette. Other two-dimensional media including newspapers and periodicals (the prime example being the hybrid satellite/print production of *USA Today*, that appeared briefly as a television magazine program as well) are increasingly identified less with the specific location(s) from which they emanate (insofar as that can be ascertained) and more with a range or area of distribution they "cover" – indeed, mass-circulation media have constituted the "nation" as a symbolic system of common associations as well as a legal and political creation. The freeway and the mall provide the greatest evidence and manifestation of a homogeneous, material culture, just as television is the main source of shared images (visual and acoustic). There is also a "national" weather within these enclosed spaces of mall and home and auto – the even temperature of the comfort zone.[15]

Nonspace is not only a literal "nonplace," it is also *disengaged* from the paramount orientation to reality – the here-and-now of face-to-face contact. Such encounter with the other is prevented by walls of steel, concrete, and stucco in a life fragmented into enclosed, miniature worlds. As Brodsly explains: "Metropolitan life suggests the disintegration in space and time of individual's various dwelling places. Often living in 'communities without propinquity', the individual metropolitan must somehow confront the task of reintegrating his or her environment. . . . One does not dwell in the metropolis; one passes through it between dwelling places" (2). This task of reintegrating a social world of separated, dislocated realms is accomplished by means of an internal dualism, of *passage* amid the *segmentation* of glass, screens, and thresholds. Thus, each form of communication becomes a *mise-en-abyme*, a recursive structure in which a nested or embedded representation reproduces or duplicates important aspects of the primary world within which it is enclosed.[16]

The freeway, for instance, is divided into a realm of passage, both over the outside world and from inside an idyllic, intensely private, steel-enclosed world of relative safety. At the same time, the sociality with the outside world that has become physically impossible inside the automobile is recreated via radio, compact disc, and tape.

Television is similarly derealized as communication; that is, the primacy of discourse in television representation is not anchored as enunciation in a paramount reality of community, propinquity, and discursive exchange. While every act of enunciation disengages an utterance from the subject, space, and time of the act of enunciation (see Greimas and Courtés),[17] television – with its temporal and spatial separation of interlocutors into a one-way, largely recorded transmission – is *doubly disengaged*. Hence televisual utterances waver uncertainly in reality status. However, the primary levels of "interface" with the viewing audience of television are those televisual utterances which represent direct engagement or address oriented proxemically on face-to-face discourse, that is, the discursive level of presenters, hosts, and spokespersons. The discursive plane of television includes all sorts of unrelated, nonprogram material from ads, logos, IDs, and public service announcements, to promotions and lead-ins, as well as the discursive segments within programs themselves, from openers and titles to presentational segments. This primary plane of discourse seems to be an overarching presumption of television representation even when it isn't directly on-screen, and. it builds the framework of television flow as a whole.[18]

Further acts of internal disengagement install second- and third-level segments as units of narrative (disengaged) or dialogue (engaged) within the primary discursive plane of the television utterance. However, the nesting order of disengagement does matter, for Greimas notes that the effect is different when dialogue is included in narration rather than when narrative is included in dialogue. In the former situation, predominant in the novel, for example, dialogue is referentialized, that is, given a spatiotemporal locus (however fictive) by the narration; in the latter situation, predominant in US televisual representation, narration is dereferentialized, that is, lifted out of a spatiotemporal context (however real) into a symbolic or affective realm. That is to say, even in nonfiction genres such as the news, the dominant reference point of the utterance will be a simulacrum of an ultimately fictitious situation of enunciation rather than a world outside.

Metapsychological Effects of Privatization

In "Paris: Capital of the Nineteenth Century," Walter Benjamin anticipated the everyday world to come and discovered the roots of nonspace in the phenomenon of *privacy* and enclosure. Indeed, the nineteenth-century arcades of Milan served as a direct model for the contemporary American mall.[19] While *privatization* has largely been conceived as an economic and political term,[20] it appears to have metapsychological effects associated with its derealized surroundings – the postmodern development of what Benjamin called the "phantasmagoria of the interior," a mixture of levels of consciousness and objects of attention. The process of distancing the worker from the workplace and the enclosure of domestic life in the home, separated from its social surroundings, allowed a compensatory realm of fantasy to flourish, a conglomeration of exotic remnants in which new and old are intermingled. This phantasmagoria of the interior broke with the immediate present in favor of a primal past and the dream of the epoch to come. However, the twentieth-century phantasmagoria idealizes not the primal but the immediate past, and is an agent responsible for its decay. And the utopia or dystopia which these forms anticipate seems less a vision of a future earth transformed for good or ill than a hermetic way of life liberated from earth itself.

The temporal world is also lifted out of history in favor of cyclic repetitions less determined by than modeled secondarily on daily and seasonal cycles of the sun, the stages of life, and the passage of generations. As labor is more and more liberated from solar and circadian rhythms, cycles of commuting, shopping, and viewing become shiftable as well. Television program schedules are "intricately woven into the fabric of our routine daily activities" (Moores 23), because they are organized by the same division of labor outside and inside the family which recruits the daily commuter and the recreational shopper. And it is the demands of labor itself that may produce a state of mind and body which is best compensated within the comfort zone.

Time is largely experienced as duration on the freeway, a "drive time" guided by graphics in Helvetica, connoting a clean, homogeneous or unmarked publicness and a vague temporality from the 1960s on (Savan). Continuity with the past is represented largely in terms of automobile model and year. Similarly, within the mall (as in Disneyland, McDonald's and other realms of privately owned mass culture), decay or the fact of time itself has been banished from cycles of destruction and regeneration via a scrupulous cleanliness and constant renewal of worn parts.

On television, duration of viewing time is also the prime experience of temporality. The work of time itself as decay is seldom represented in images of the human body or everyday life. Nor is the past so much remembered via narrative as it is rerun or embedded as archival images within contemporary, discursive presentation. Even the image quality of the past – records of grainy black and white – is gradually undergoing electronic revision to meet today's expectations. The phantasmagoria of television and its analogs is thus less to be imagined as escape to flickering shadows in the cave than as a productive force that shapes spatiotemporal and psychic relations to the realities it constitutes. The state of mind promoted within the realms of nonspace can be described as *distraction*.

Distraction as a dual state of mind depends on an incomplete process of spatial and temporal separation and interiorization. The automobile, for instance, is connected to the world outside via the very glass and steel which enclose the driver. However, the dualism of outside/inside within these separate realms means that a connection with "outside" drifts between a "real" outside and an idealized representation.

A sheet of glass alone is enough to provide a degree of disengagement from the world beyond the pane. Add to this the play of light which appears to be part of the *mise-en-scène* of the mall, the freeway, and television – the world beyond the glass glows more brightly than the darker passages and seats we occupy. Beyond its glow, even the "real" world seen through a clear glass windshield, shop window, or screen has a way of being psychically colored and fetishized by the very glass which reveals it; the green glasses of the inhabitants of the Emerald City of Oz are a mythic expression of this vitreous transformation.[21]

However, green visions promote a state of mind that remains somewhere between Oz and Kansas, or between regression to the primal scene and a commercial transaction: because mental life on the freeway, in the marketplace, and at home is linked to very real consequences for life, limb, and pocketbook, it requires vigilance while it also allows for and even promotes automatisms and "spacing out." "Being carried away" to a full-blown world of fantasy is not in order – but the "vegging out" of the couch potato is a well-publicized phenomenon. Malls and freeways also can induce a state of distraction: for example, the very design and intentions of the mall taken to extreme can induce what the "cosmallogist" Kowinski diagnoses as the "zombie effect" (floating for hours, a loss of a sense of time and place) which he diagnoses as a copresence of contradictory states of excitement enhanced to the point of overstimulation mixed with relaxation descending into confusion and torpor (339). In discussing the habit of driving Brodsly calls "detached involvement" (47) an awareness of the outside environment mixed with that of an intensely private world within the interior of the automobile. Noting that the automobile is one of the few controlled environments for meditation in our culture, he describes how even the temporal link with the outside world may fade: "Perhaps no aspect of the freeway experience is more characteristic than the sudden realization that you have no memory of the past ten minutes of your trip" (41).[22]

In his mythological investigations of everyday life, Roland Barthes made the subjective experience of driving a metaphor for the operation of mythology itself. In "Myth Today," he turned from analysis of objects and scenes like the "cathedral-like" "New Citroën" to the practice of driving as an alternation between two objects of attention:

> If I am in a car and I look at the scenery through the window, I can at will focus on the scenery or on the windowpane. At one moment I grasp the presence of the glass and the distance of the landscape; at another, on the contrary, the transparency of the glass and the depth of the landscape; but the result of this alternation is constant: the glass is at once present and empty to me, and the landscape unreal and full. (123)

For Barthes, this constant alternation constitutes a spatial category of a continuous *elsewhere* which is his model for the alibi of myth. If we were to expand Barthes's metaphor of semiotics and driving with concepts of discourse, the alternation of which he wrote would also be one which shifts between planes of language and subjectivity. That is, the awareness of a subject would shift between a here-and-now in the interior of the automobile and awareness of a world elsewhere beyond the glass (in which the interior is also lightly reflected) through which the subject speeds. But because the interior of the auto is disconnected and set in the midst of a new kind of theater of derealized space, the experience of what is normally the paramount reality – the experience of self-awareness in a here-and-now – becomes one of unanchored mobility. This mobile subject in the midst of *elsewhere* is a cultural novum and the model for a new kind of fiction effect, a fiction of presence unbound and uncircumscribed by the fourth wall, without a 180° line to separate the world of the imaginary and the subjunctive from the commonplace.

The freeway provides the most obvious examples of *mobile subjectivity*:

> Each [freeway] exit ramp offers a different visual as well as kinesthetic sensation. The interchange is like a mobile in a situation where the observer is the moving object. It is the experience of an effortlessly choreographed dance, with each car both performing and observing the total movement and the freeway architecture providing the carefully integrated setting. (Brodsly 50)

Yet from the observer/moving object's point of view, this mobility is a paradoxical feeling of stasis and motion. In *nonspace*, the body in motion is no longer a kinesthetic key to reality, for at the wheel of the automobile or of remote control engaged in small motor movements which have become highly skilled and automatic, it explores space as an inert mass, technically or electronically empowered with virtual or actual speed.

Indeed, what we experience is not an erasure, circumvention, or fragmentation of the body, but its investment with a second and more powerful skin within which a core remains secure, intact, and at rest in a vortex of speed.

Of course, mobility is a multifaceted and paradoxical concept per se, with many fields of reference: from displacement from one location to another to the freedom of movement which is symbolically equated with social mobility, to the feelings of pleasure in effortless flight which has roots in infancy, to the fundamental psychic link of motion with causality and subjecthood first described by Aristotle. But mobility also suggests the opposite of subjecthood, the freely displaceable and substitutable part, machine or human, which enables mass production and a consequent standardization brought to the social as well as economic realm. *Nonspace* engages all of these possibilities.[23]

Motion is not only paradoxical, it is also relative. Safe within the halls of consumption, the body may stroll with half a mind in leisurely indirection. But the shops passed in review are themselves a kind of high-speed transport, the displacement of goods produced in mass quantities in unknown elsewheres into temporal simultaneity and spatial condensation. And on the freeway as well as the airplane, a new and paradoxical experience of motion has evolved: on one hand, the relative motion of an enclosed space beyond which the world passes in high-speed review; or inversely, the dynamic sensation of movement itself experienced by a relatively inert body traversing the world at high speed.[24] At least before the advent of the simultaneous and multiple perspectives of cubism, motion in Western representation was usually confined to the world of the story beyond the glass, stationary or moving images presented for the eyes of a stationary (and one-eyed) subject. A "bubble" of subjective here-and-now strolling or speeding about in the midst of elsewhere is one of the features that constitute new, semifictitious realms of the everyday.

Of course, any mobility experienced by the television viewer is virtual, a "range" or displaced realm constituted by vectors, a transportation of the mind in two dimensions. Our *idyll*, or self-sufficient and bounded place, is the space in front of the TV set, what Baudrillard calls "an archaic envelope" ("Ecstasy" 129). Yet Baudrillard thinks bodies left on the couch are "simply superfluous, basically useless," "deserted and condemned," like the immense countryside deserted by urbanization. But these couch bodies are also travelers, responding in a checked, kinetic way to the virtual experiences of motion we are offered as subjects or view in objects passing our screens.[25] Television also offers the road in the midst of the idyll, reconstituting a virtual world of face-to-face relationships shared between viewer and television personalities displaced or teleported from elsewhere in the process, a fiction of the paramount reality of discourse. Thus *discourse* or represented acts of enunciation can be understood as a container for both the viewer and the personalities of television which provides protection from a world thereby constituted as beyond and elsewhere.

Discursive segments also constitute a plane of passage between the shows, items, and stories embedded within the plane. Sometimes *passages* are even marked as such via the motion of subjects who can speak as if directly to us, the viewers within the televisual representation. For instance, the syndicated yet local program, *Evening Magazine*, often showed its local hosts in motion, walking as they introduced unrelated, packaged stories (produced at many different stations) to the viewer.[26] While this practice seems strange and gratuitous, it is quite simply a visual realization of the virtual power of language as a means of transport. The use of movement as passage marker is echoed, for instance, in the work of visual anthropologists Worth and Adair,[27] who, in trying to understand the films they had incited members of the Navajo tribe to make, concluded that "almost all the films made by the Navajos portray what to members of our culture seems to be an inordinate amount of walking" (144). Worth and Adair concluded that for the Navajo, walking itself was an event and "a kind of punctuation to separate activities" (148). On television, such marking may also be represented in far more minimal than spectacular ways, for example, spatially via shifts of an on-screen subject in body orientation and eyeline or verbally via the use of discursive shifters. Thus the overall discursive framework of televisual representation, including the use of hosts and presenters of all kinds, provides a means of passing between object-worlds, be they stories provided for entertainment or fantasies which surround commodities, in a way which virtually includes the viewer.

In *Visible Fictions*, John Ellis determined that the *segment* is the basic unit of television (in opposition to or modification of Raymond Williams's notion of flow).[28] The basic dualism of televisual representation opts for neither concept alone but helps to explain why, despite its segmentation into unrelated items, television is not commonly perceived as fragmented, but rather experienced as unified and contained. Nor is that coherence achieved simply by virtue of "flow" or the juxtaposition of items on the same plane of discourse. The duality of *passage* and *segmentation* in physical as well as represented space is related in turn to the dual planes of language, the engaged discourse of a subject in passage, and the disengagement of stories from the here-and-now of the subject.

The separate segments that disengage from discursive passages are recursive or embedded "hypodiegetic worlds" (McHale 113) at one level removed from the frame of passage. Segments with widely disparate topics in contrasting expressive moods from the tragic or the comic to the trivial or traumatic can be united via discourse into flow. Other sub- or "hypo" levels of narration can appear within any one discursive or narrative segment – three, for instance, are typical of news reports (115). Thus television discourse typically consists of "stacks" of recursive levels which are usually quite different in look and "flavor." These stacks are also signified at different spatial and temporal removes from the viewer and have different kinds of contents. Thus a shift of discursive level is also a shift of ontological levels, that is, to a different status in relation to reality. Television formats then amount to particular ways of conceptualizing and organizing "stacks" of worlds as a hierarchy of realities and relationships to the viewer.

Formally, shifting from one televisual segment to another may be a shift in the hierarchy of discourse – but shifts and passages between levels can also occur within segments. For instance, there is a category of television segment, including advertisements, logos, and rock videos (see my "Rock Video"), the *raison d'être* of which is to engage the viewer with a sign, image, or commodity by means of a represented passage through a whole range of discursive and ontological levels. Such segments are *condensations* of what are ordinarily dispersed in syntactic alternations of discursive segments with embedded stories or fantasies.

Furthermore, televisual representations may include several layers in the same visual field *simultaneously*. An obvious example is the image of the narrating news anchor against "world" wallpaper and over-the-shoulder news windows. Like television, freeways and malls provide similar examples of multiple worlds condensed into one visual field: for example, the automobile windshield is not merely glass and image of the world into which one speeds, but also a mirror reflection of the driver and passengers; a rear-view mirror provides a window of where one has been as well as side views of landscape unfolding and distorted by speed.

The representation of the copresence of multiple worlds in different modes[29] on the television screen is achieved via division of the visual field into areas or via the representation of stacked planes which can be tumbled or squeezed and which, in virtual terms, advance toward and retreat from the visual field of the viewer. Discursive planes are differentiated from embedded object-worlds via *axes*: changes of scale along the z-axis of spatial depth indicate a proxemic logic of the shared space of conversation with the viewer. In contrast, embedded stories are oriented around x- and y-axes, actually or virtually by means of the field/reverse field of filmic continuity editing. The primary logic of alternation in television segments is then not that of suture of the story-world, as in filmic fictions,[30] but rather of communication with a spectator in various degrees of "nearness." The constant reframings in and out along the z-axis of depth which David Antin saw as part of the television form apparently do have a function as links with a spectator rather than as inexplicable or gratuitous reframings of a spatially continuous, diegetic world. Even in fictional worlds beyond the plane of discourse, a relation to the z-axis of discursive relations with the viewer can be discerned. For example, in her discussion of soap operas on television, Sandy Flitterman notes the lack of continuity editing and the practice of alternating framing of characters in a two-shot as nearer to and farther from the viewer (200). This practice can be explained historically by the television studio situation of live editing by means of switching between two cameras. But it can also be explained as part of a proxemic logic of relations with the spectator which pervades even fictional worlds.

What is ultimately at stake in this insistent relation to the viewer is a site of exchange. For the representation of mixed and simultaneous worlds is deeply allied with the cultural function of television in symbolically linking incommensurabilities of all sorts – the system of goods or commodities and the economic relations it orders, the sexual-matrimonial system which orders sociality, and the symbolic order of language, including images, symbols, and the spoken and written word. If television itself is a great storehouse for tokens of all these cultural systems, exchange-values are created by their juxtaposition, but even more by means of passages through them, in which television programming offers many different itineraries from which to choose.

The viewer as mobile subject has remote control over trajectories and channels plus power to take the off-ramp and leave the zone of televisual space. However, the television viewer who enters a car to go shopping, or even to work, hasn't left *nonspace* behind – these realms are variations thereof. (For this reason "home shopping" channels represent less the interaction of television with the world than a "short circuit" of communication and growing withdrawal into enclosed systems.)

Thus the realm of *nonspace* is divided again via the play of motion and stillness organized by passages and thresholds to the worlds behind the glass, by a *mise-en-scène* of light and darkness, and by proxemic indicators of nearness and distance within an unanchored situation. This very mobility allows what could be a profoundly disorienting and fragmented experience of life to act as a powerful means of reunifying the flow of time and space into a virtual here-and-now of a communal world. Voices and images offer community to a disengaged and enclosed world of the home, the automobile, and the mall. A banished, paramount reality is recreated as a phantom within elsewhere. The result may be the "secular communion"[31] of the freeway, the shared passages of the mall, or parasociality in relation to television personalities. Thus the institutions of mobile privatization restore a vision of the world from which they are disengaged and which they have largely displaced.

A Nexus of Exchange Between Economic, Social, and Symbolic Systems

Realms of everyday experience – the freeway, the shopping mall, and television – are part of a sociohistorical nexus of institutions which grew together into their present-day structure and national scope after World War II. Transportation, broadcasting, and retailing displaced the earlier sociocultural forms of modernity such as the railroad, the movies, and the shop windows along a brightly lit boulevard (Williams 26).[32] These earlier forms of modernity were in themselves means of surveillance and control. Like the cinema, the railroad is an odd experience of immobile motility, virtual and actual, in which spatiality retains a semipublic nature.

Institutions of communication after World War II intensified processes of privatization and massification which had begun far earlier. Private life in the postwar era presumed a significant amount of leisure or discretionary time and "an apparently self-sufficient family home" which "carried, as a consequence, an imperative need for new kinds of contact" (Williams 27). Raymond Williams pointed out the paradox which the notion of "mass" communications hides – the increasing functional isolation and spatial segmentation of individuals and families into private worlds which are then mediated into larger and larger entities by new forms of communication.

In the United States, the paradox of mass culture and social isolation is even more acute, for to a far greater extent, the public airwaves, rights-of-way, and places of assemblage have been given over to private ownership or use and to market forces. Perhaps because the principles of mobile privatization are congruent with widely and deeply held American values of the good life along with dreams of social mobility which hold that ideal attainable for all, the choice of the private automobile over public conveyances, for instance, "seems to reflect an overwhelmingly popular consensus rarely matched by social movements, and it flourishes because it continues to serve that general will" (Brodsly 36). The principles of mobile privatization guided the creation of systems of transport and social communication that promise liberty in the midst of sociality, privacy amongst community, and an autonomy of protected selfhood nourished by its environment.

What the institutions of mobile privatization then represent are a means of social integration and control which can dispense with the need for any "central" or panoptical position of surveillance, visible display of force, or school of discipline, because they are fully congruent with the values of individualism and hedonistic pleasure, as well as desires for social recognition and dreams of community. Furthermore, the practices of driving, shopping, and television viewing are dreams become habit.

Take, for instance, the perception of freedom and self-determination experienced by the driver of the automobile in comparison with that public mode of transport, the train. An automobile driver, Otto Julius Bierbaum, exclaimed in 1902:

> The railway just transports you – and that's the immediate contrary to traveling. Traveling means utmost free activity, the train however condemns you to passivity. Traveling is getting rid of the rules. But the railway squeezes you into a time-table, makes you a prison of all kinds of rules, and locks you into a cage that you are not supposed to leave and not even to unlock whenever you want. . . . Who considers that traveling may as well call a march in review a stroll. (Quoted in Sachs 3–4)[33]

The automobile represents an apparent freedom from the lockstep of a public time-schedule as well as "the complete subversion of the traditional sanctuary of the public realm – the street," so that merely driving a private automobile can be understood as a ritual expression of national faith: "Every time we merge with traffic we join our community in a wordless creed: belief in individual freedom, in a technological liberation from place and circumstance, in a democracy of personal mobility. When we are stuck in rush-hour traffic the freeway's greatest frustration is that it belies its promise" (Brodsly 5). This faith in mobility sustains cultural homogeneity rather than diversity; and paradoxically, the feelings associated with vast improvements in the freedom of motion are in lockstep with submission to demands for greater conformity.

A common faith in freedom of movement and of choice among commodities, destinations, and channels sustains the institutions of mobile privatization. They are the realms of answered prayers, embodiments of dearly held beliefs and phantoms of desire become commonplace, a field of action constituted by the automatisms and chains of associations which make up vast networks in the symbolic system of our culture. Constraints built on these chains of associated ideas are owned, not imposed, and require very little surveillance. As an early theorist of representational punishment cited by Foucault in *Discipline and Punish* explained:

> This link [between ideas] is all the stronger in that we do not know of what it is made and we believe it to be our own work; despair and time eat away the bonds of iron and steel, but they are powerless against the habitual union of ideas, they can only tighten it still more; and on the soft fibres of the brain is founded the unshakable base of the soundest of Empires. (103)

The empire of the habitual is the matrix of mental and social life, made of mundane opportunities and choices and composed of practices conducted half-aware, which assemble one's very personhood. What is new in contemporary life are not these institutions of mobile privatization per se, but the interpenetration of layer upon layer of built environment and representation, the formative and derivative, the imaginary and mundane. Embodying values as neither here nor there, both present and absent, they are ideal expressions of the *zones* of ontological uncertainty, expressions of both Kansas and Oz.[34]

Although we may perceive no alternative, no one forces people to watch television or to drive, particularly on the freeway, or to go to the mall or to buy anything on display there or on television. But few indeed resist. One prescription for an aesthetic mode of resistance to consumer culture requires the passerby to remain bewitched on this side of the window, glass, or mirror, poised at the moment between perfection and lack, never cashing in desire for the disappointments of fulfillment.[35] But aesthetic resistance depends on an older disposition of the subject in relation to the spectacle of an imaginary world framed and discrete behind the glass. The cycle of consumption in a "highway comfort" culture is designed for maximum mobility and circulation of a consumer inside the imaginary world of images and objects. One of the successes of this system of inter-relations is on one hand, the liquidity of images, objects, and commodities, and on the other, the ease with which the subject passes from one role to another – driver; passerby, and consumer – each requiring a different mode of attention and psychic investment in objects.

Such *convertibility* between these various systems of communication and exchange is necessary; freeways, malls, and television are not merely similar in form, they are systems constructed to interact in mutually reinforcing ways.[36] Each institution is a kind of sociocultural distribution and feedback system for the others: television (most obvi-ously as mass-audience, network broadcasts) serves as the nationwide distribution system for symbols in anticipation and reinforcement of a national culture presented not only as desirable but as already realized somewhere else. The mall is a displacement and the enclosure of the walkable street and a collective site in which to cash in the promises of the commodities seen on television. The freeway is the manifestation of personal mobility at its most literal, its radius a lifeline that makes the consumption style of suburban living and shopping economically feasible as well as logistically pos-sible. The auto on the freeway is a juncture between television and mall, a "home" and commodity fetish on wheels. Convertibility between systems means that values can be exchanged whether they are expressed as commodity objects or images, in two or three dimensions or in gigantic or miniature scale.

Just as the mall is a miniature suburbia, a figure of desire become literal and three-dimensional, the television box is a quintessential miniature, both as copy *and* prototype. Even in its gigantic form, the large screen projection, it is no bigger than a picture window or an alternative to wallpaper. Bachelard explains how miniaturization is an attempt to master and control the world, which one can then enter in one's imagination by making oneself very small (148–82). This *miniaturization* is responsible for the feel-ings of safety linked with malls, freeways, and television, what Susan Stewart in *On Longing* termed "feminization," as opposed to a "masculine" metaphor of the gigantic as abstract authority of the state in collective and public life. Miniaturization is a process of interiorization, enclosure, and perfection, one in which the temporal dimensions of narrative or history are transformed into spatial ones, a plenitude of description of seemingly endless details. This contraction of the world which expands the personal serves a process of commodification as well, the transformation of action into exchange, nature into marketplace, history into collection and property. The realm of the gigantic and exaggerated in public life, a collective body in pieces, has been shrunk into a perfect whole. Kowinski describes the technique of miniaturizing the shops and concessions in theme parks and malls as designed to evoke the nostalgic feelings the adult has when visiting the world of childhood, the once vast seen as tiny. The incomprehensible then comes near, no longer too far away or too foreboding: the distant and the exotic are sought in order to collapse them into proximity and approximation with the self.

However, once within the miniature, the universe looms endless, just as the stars shine through Benjamin's glass-topped arcades of nineteenth-century Paris. How are malls, freeways, and television as miniatures compatible with representation of the universal and the social? In *Learning from Las Vegas* Robert Venturi described a new kind of monumentality which began with the Las Vegas strip cut off from the surrounding desert and concluded within the darkened and low-ceilinged casinos, spotted with islands of activity, from glowing tables to garden oases. Rather than the tall and imposing, like the skyscraper as upended panopticon and symbol of coercive or (via reflective glass) impenetrable power, the new monumentality is long and low, without discernible edges or ends or secure locus in place, rather like mirages lifted above the grids of homes, shops, and offices. Indeed, the very lack of panoptical positions afforded within the wings and cubbyholes of the typical mall is responsible for its sense of endlessness and a sense of disorientation within it. The freeway is "long and lowness" incarnate, but it also offers "kinks in the road" beyond which one can anticipate the unknown, in which accident and death can lurk, as a prime source of the monumental within a highly controlled, otherwise predictable system. "Kinks in the road" on television are temporal in order, possibilities of irruption of the unexpected in a plot or a schedule within an endlessness of parallel worlds which go on whether switched on or not, whether we watch or not, a world which is a primary reference in daily conversation, which we may or may not be equipped to enter.

In principle, miniatures like the mall are conceptual units which are invertible: that is, a mall can be lifted off the page, a scale model can be shrunk or expanded and plunked down in a nowhere that is anywhere that suitable freeway access and (usually upscale) demographics prevail. This liquidity is certainly one of the secrets of commodity culture, allowing signs and images to become realized as objects of desire and also to circulate freely between different levels of reality. One still "unnatural" and hence disconcerting feature of postmodernity is the presence of glowing signifiers of desire realized in the midst of everyday life – images magnified into monuments (for example, Michel de Certeau speaks of New York skyscrapers as "letters") or the big world shrunk down to the miniature size of a theme park or a mall. This invertibility between language and reality, that is, world-to-image-to-world fit, is inherent in the performative aspect of language, or in the capacity to declare worlds into existence within designated and proper boundaries. But those boundaries now extend to cover much of everyday experience: perhaps never before has it been so opportune or so feasible to realize a symbol or idea dramatically in 3-D. This expansion of the performative, making the actual virtual and the virtual actual, is behind the most recognizable features of postmodernity as theorized in Boorstein's culture of the image and "pseudo-events," in Callois's description of an undecidable state between the animate and inanimate,[37] and in Baudrillard's "simulations." Beyond liquid worlds that readily convert into one another, we are now undergoing a process of gradual convergence of the analogy of television with television itself. In the mall, not only can television screens be found in department stores and passages, but the mall as an architectural form has begun to sprout "video walls." On the freeway, we can soon anticipate the appearance of the virtual video screen or "head-up display" that will float in a driver's field of vision like a freeway sign (Duensing 3).[38] It seems that soon one will have to speak of one great machine.

Conclusion

The nonspace of privatized mobility is not neutral ground. It is rather the result of the dominance of one set of values over other values held a little less dear. Those other values, loosely allied with the "public sphere," are represented but not included in a way which gives them substance. The dominance of the values linked with mobile privatization is also the result of a misunderstanding. Ideas in the marketplace, that is, words and images as markers of economic and social exchange, are not the same thing as the free marketplace of ideas; and correlatively, consumers are not the same thing as subjects of discourse. Broadcast and narrowcast ratings and cassette sales figures, for instance, are the measure of the first kind of marketplace, the pure exchange-value of language and images. To the extent that the stock of ideas is determined by pure exchange-value, the marketplace of ideas is diminished. (Deregulation and dismantling of obligation to a "public," however defined, are perhaps better understood as a "depublication" of transport, social, and media communication, the legal and regulatory surface of the general phenomenon of privatization discussed here.) To strengthen the second kind of values – those related to discursive exchange among subjects, community, and a shared commitment to the just as well as the good life – requires foundation work. First, a widely held sense of the difference between the market value and the discursive value of ideas must be established. Then, recognizing the extent and scope of an attenuated fiction effect in everyday life – an effect now largely unappreciated or considered trivial and hence subject to little vigilance – might already be a step toward bringing distraction within a controlled, psychic economy of disavowal. For distraction both motivates and promotes the "liquidity" of words and images in economic exchange by undermining a sense of different levels of reality and of incommensurable difference among them.

However, the analysis of the situation advanced here suggests how difficult such a project has become. First, the means of advancing such notions are largely restricted to those very venues of privatization and distraction which work against them. Furthermore, older concepts of liberation in everyday life based on "escape attempts" (see Cohen and Taylor) and figurative practices are no longer viable in a built environment that is already evidence of dreamwork in the service of particular kinds of commerce, communication, and exchange. Indeed, older notions of the public realm and of paramount reality have been largely undermined, and a return to a pretelevisual world of politics, the street, or marketplace is unlikely.

Not that there is nothing outside of the built environment of freeways, malls, and television. There is indeed a heterogeneous world of local values; the decaying world of the city and town left beyond the enclosures is also becoming a gentrified and lively realm of privilege and experimentation. Because the realms of privatization present a facade of self-sufficiency and self-determination, means of change are easier to imagine as coming from those realms outside than from within. Thus a prime strategy that has been devised for changing television is one of penetration of these enclosed worlds with other public and private voices.[39] What is ultimately at stake in puncturing everyday enclosures for low-intensity dreams are the rights and responsibilities of subjects in the public realm, a once gigantic, now shrunken terrain to be reclaimed from everyday life.

However, when included within television, the public and private worlds outside are distanced ontologically under several other layers of representation. That is why inclusion in representation per se is not enough to open the television apparatus out into the public world – for the privileged sites of subjectivity on television are first, those allotted to the enunciation of televisual utterances and the interests those utterances serve; and second, to those subjects in passage represented in the utterance, shifting between a relation to the viewer and relations to embedded object-worlds. That is, the very formats and conventions that have evolved in US televisual representation work against dialogue with the "other," the excluded outsiders. Or the past and otherness are included by proxy in a way that blunts the sense of an outside and of other possible worlds.

Furthermore, even the embedded narratives or dramatic segments under the plane of discourse are not conducive to the representation of change, either formally or at the level of social content. Narrative that embraces change, heterogeneity, and historical reach is undermined at a global level by the underlying serial organization of televisual representation per se: the notion of a linear sequence with a beginning, a middle, and an end, in which "something happens," is limited to the microlevel of the segment. The spatiotemporal organization of narrative on television can be compared with Bakhtin's analysis of the "road" chronotope in Greek romance. That is, the road was not a place where a change from one state or condition to another could occur – it was rather an obstacle course which merely delayed the eventual reunion of two characters who were destined to be lovers. These characters neither change, nor develop, nor age in a journey governed solely by fortuitous incident. Like the romance, television narrative often manages to combine a sense of passage with an ultimately static situation. Like itineraries in the mall or the freeway, these stories are highly segmented enchainments that have largely given up any pretense of development. The itineraries of viewing will always pass by representations of cultural goods of various kinds, over and over, but the system of combination seems impervious to change.

So when the dominant principles of alternation on television work against both the narrative process of change in characters and a rhetorical process of argumentation, how can they then challenge or encourage change in the mind of the viewer? Differentiation by means of lifestyle and disposable income must be distinguished from the differences between subjects in "local" and "heterogeneous" outside realms. That is why the proliferating venues for ever more demographically segmented audiences for audio-visual representation bode well only if they also bring about formats that allow for the entry of new subjects from the outer world at the primary level of discourse. However, considering that this primary level of discourse is itself a fictional representation of discourse and part of a process that transforms outsiders automatically into insiders, the problem of representing discourse is one of degree. At best one can present a some-what more intersubjective fiction of discourse and an only somewhat different kind of celebrity and momentary fame.

Yet, models of "penetration" and discursive exchange are necessary and useful pre-cisely because the power relations of mobile privatization are the conventional expres-sion of a kind of legal and social fiction based on widely held values. Changes in shared fictions, values, and beliefs occur over the long term, slowly and incrementally, not merely because once-shared values are discredited or may be no longer viable, but because alternative values and their constituencies have labored to mark themselves in discourse. I believe the criticism of television can serve cultural change where it keeps such long-term goals in mind.

Notes

1. Rudolf Arnheim's mention of the "aeroplane" along with the "motor car" suggests another analog of television in the airport, in the experience of flying, and in the air transportation network (164, also quoted in Rath 199). This investigation is primarily concerned with consumption and everyday experience. Because flying is not as everyday an experience as driving and shopping and because it is imbricated directly in corporate as well as military and surveillance uses of images (for example, Paul Virilio's *War and Cinema*), the airplane as analog of television is left to exploration elsewhere.

   The mass-circulation periodical which preceded television, the magazine in print, is another obvious and important analog of television. The magazine format and the "magazine concept" were discussed in the paper on which this chapter is based, given at the Conference on Television at the Center for Twentieth Century Studies in 1988.

2. Todd Gitlin's discussion of the iconographic function of the automobile in the program "Miami Vice" and its juxtaposed ads exemplifies this kind of analysis. For a general descrip-tion of the iconography of automobiles, the title essay of Marshall McLuhan's *The Mechani-cal Bride* remains among the most insightful in making the link between technology and sexuality, the automobile and the female body as a love machine with replaceable parts. Stephen Bayley's *Sex, Drink, and Fast Cars* is a more recent monograph on the subject which notes pleasures of all kinds connected with the automobile, from kinesthetic/visceral and aesthetic to the sadomasochistic and death-driven. Bayley emphasizes the masculinity of that iconography. The difference between the two conceptions of automotive gender may be negotiated via the distinction between an interior womblike comfort zone versus the exterior, between driver and driven, the auto-woman as object of mastery and status display. Malls, on the other hand, are a predominantly female domain, as papers by Ann Friedberg and Meaghan Morris demonstrate and develop, while the gender of the television even in terms of the machine itself is divided in ways related to division of labor in the home and workforce.

3. The projects of synthesis drawn on here also have in common their work against the terror imposed by theory or intellectual discourse as well as the terror of the state. By returning to an earlier rich and highly validated cultural period at the cusp of the development of commodity culture, Benjamin's long-term view circumvents some of the immediate intellectual prejudices of his age which might foreclose the capacity to analyze cultural forms in the broadest sense. Bakhtin's appreciation of heterogeneity and the mixture of different voices in culture is designed to validate difference and make heard suppressed and otherwise voiceless parts of the social world. He developed the concept of the *chronotope* (see esp. the essay "Forms of Time and of the Chronotope in the Novel") in an age in which intellectuals sought tools for circumventing a closed discourse with concepts which reached into the manifestations of daily life in representation for reminders of what is not included in it. Compare other work which turns to the common, the everyday, and the "real" in the 1930s and 1940s in the context of economic failure and the exposure of discourses of the "word" as tools of institutional power. The relations of class to culture that Williams studied formed the intellectual framework against and within which he articulated his ideas. Michel de Certeau's project of evasion and transformation of dominant and predetermined forms of everyday life can also be seen as an attempt to poke holes in a hermetic, structuralist notion of language as well as to find possibilities for liberation in the everyday.

4. E. Ann Kaplan cites Baudrillard's automobile metaphor in relation to a McLuhanian comparison of hot and cold media in *Rocking around the Clock* 50–51.

5. Brodsly is here writing of Los Angeles. The same dream is in force today, despite smog and congestion. "The sustaining dream of most Southern Californians is to not live in, or even near, a city. Just as when millions of young families flocked to the small farming town on the fringes of a burgeoning Los Angeles after World War II, today people are seeking economically and socially homogeneous suburban neighborhoods. In short, they're looking for a comfortable small-town atmosphere within commuting distance of a big city, an almost idyllic place to watch the kids, the grass, the real estate values and the equity grow while they pursue the American dream" (Sam Hall Kaplan 28). The author explains that today people who look at computer screens all day do not want tract housing, but rather accept higher density in order to attain a "village atmosphere." Despite what is sometimes considered an infrastructure nearing the point of defeat and random outbreaks of freeway frustration into violence, surveys of Los Angeles commuters suggest surprising equanimity and even satisfaction with their lot.

6. "On both sides of these passages, which obtain their light from above, there are arrayed the most elegant shops, so that such an arcade is a city, indeed a world, in miniature" – *Illustrated Paris Guide*, cited by Walter Benjamin in "Paris: Capital of the Nineteenth Century" (165).

7. Modeled directly on buildings in theme parks such as Disneyland, which was itself modeled on Disney's hometown of Marceline, Missouri. Kowinski 67, reviewing the work of Richard Francaviglia.

8. The typical layout of a mall includes two fully enclosed levels, a central court, and side courts, with one or more department stores or "anchors" at either end, and about one hundred shops, services, and eating places. The interior typically mixes elements associated with exterior and interior design. The Urban Land Institute defines a mall as "a group of architecturally unified commercial establishments built on a site which is planned, developed, owned and managed as an operating unit. . . . Design, temperature, lighting, merchandise, and events are all planned according to unifying principles" (see Kowinski 60).

9. The difference between the two is not merely size and ownership but every facet of public relations, marketing, and retailing (see DePalma 1).

10. Graham and Hurst note that corporate atriums are "parallel forms to the suburban shopping malls" which evidence the same tensions: "The urban corporate atrium is an attempt to smooth over contradictions between environmental decay and technological progress. As a miniutopian retreat from the stresses of city life it revokes the old notion of a 'garden' as an idealized landscape (the return to a preurban Eden), attempting to reconnect it to the idea of technology as an aid to man." The authors conclude that because these atriums are largely separate from the fabric of the city, they represent exclusive enclaves which do not serve democratic values or the maintenance of community (71).

11. A recent application of the *chronotype* to film noir by Vivian Sobchack in "'Lounge Time'" suggests the importance of the semipublic *loungetime* as an idyllic contrast to the road for rootless postwar sexual-social relationships. Today's homeless and displaced people find public lounge space with difficulty, for it has been rededicated to driving and paying customers and linked to commercial sightlines.

12. For an interpretation of pleasure and the home reception of the news related to this very distancing from the world, see Stam 23–43.

13. Joshua Meyerowitz discusses displacement in the figurative sense as a loss of the sense of place in the social hierarchy in *No Sense of Place*. He argues that because televisual representation has provided a view of the "backstage" of adulthood and masculinity, as well as political power, the dominant positions in the social hierarchy have been essentially demystified for children, women, and the citizen. His observations about the "public-public" nature of events such as the press conference "that are carried beyond the time-space frame by electronic media, and therefore are accessible to almost anyone" (287), are plausible as applied to representation before it is mediated by the television apparatus. Here it is argued that the realm of controlled production and privatized reception as a framework within which such "public-publicness" is embedded has significant consequences not only for the representation itself but also for the metapsychology of its reception. Notions such as "nonspace" allow the imaginary aspects of Meyerowitz's unifying and leveling process to be conceptualized.

14. In many cities, the freeway once acted as a kind of container or beltway around the city, eventually to become surrounded by suburbia. However, wherever the freeway may be drawn on the map, it is not really "located" in the grid of streets over or under which it extends, nor is it accessible without specially designed transitions, which are, as Lynch pointed out, not always easy to locate from the street.

15. The effects of an imaginary unity are not restricted to "nationhood," but can extend to smaller and greater units. See, for instance, Rath on the counternational effect of the broadcast transmission area in German-speaking countries.

    Andrew Ross describes how the weather acts as an ideology, a means of naturalizing the social, and a way of explaining "an otherwise apparently contingent world of events" ("Work" 123). Note that Ross is discussing the weather outside the venues discussed here – the world without comfort control beyond the window or glass. The "ideology" of the national weather inside is a more truly "lived relation" to the relations of production for most Americans. Meanwhile, the vagaries of traffic and the speed of travel to work, the beach, or the mall as impeded by accidents and contingencies, are most often considered and treated as if they were a force of nature like the weather "outside" of which Ross speaks.

16. Brian McHale provides an explanation of the *mise-en-abyme* and its importance for postmodernist literary fiction in expressions of ontological uncertainty (124–28).

17. The engaged utterance is a simulacrum of the situation of enunciation, that is, *discourse*. The disengaged utterance is story. Note that subject, space, and time can be engaged or disengaged separately rather than en masse.

18.   "Flow" here is not the pure juxtaposition of unrelated segments that Raymond Williams
      found so fascinating in television. It is rather the result of proposing a model hierarchy
      among segments, in a way related to Nick Browne's notion of the "supertext," but con-
      ceived in terms of discourse and including other discursive material on a par with com-
      mercials. At some primary level, though, Williams's pure and unreconstructed flow
      undeniably plays a role in television reception. See also Turner in "Frame."
19.   Kowinski, in "The Mall as City Suburban," describes the motivation for building the first
      mall as providing needed opportunities for face-to-face contact among the isolated environ-
      ments of cars, housing, and office. Victor Gruen modeled the first covered mall in the
      United States, Southdale Center in Edina, Minnesota, on covered pedestrian arcades,
      especially the Galleria Vittorio Emanuel in Milan in 1956 (Kowinski 119). The large depart-
      ment stores of Europe were in turn modeled on the garden city in such ideal realizations
      as the Crystal Palace.
20.   Public and private are complex and historically shifting notions. While Jürgen Habermas
      is the best-known contemporary philosopher of the disappearance of the public realm, this
      concern has a long tradition in the United States in the struggle between market forces and
      democratic values for dominance of areas of life. Hannah Arendt's *The Human Condition*
      traces the changing practices and concepts regarding *privacy* from the Greeks through the
      Romantic period and is the most generally helpful on the concept.
21.   See Culver, whose enlightening link between Frank Baum's *Emerald City of Oz* and the
      growth of commodity display in shop windows is tied to a model of discrete fiction and
      identification rather than the utterly different disposition of the spectator "inside" the glass
      which characterizes the most sophisticated development of consumer culture. Culver's
      main question can guide any investigation of the institutions of consumption: why is it that
      Americans so willingly and apparently knowingly seek out and accept bogus substitutes,
      paper symbols, and commodity objects they know are inadequate to fulfill their needs, not
      to mention their desires? Culver presumes this occurs as an act of will – rather than in a
      state of distraction.
22.   Spaulding Gray's "L.A., the Other" features a "real" story told by a woman who suddenly
      finds herself traveling in the opposite direction on the freeway miles from where she was
      last aware of her relative position. She interprets this lapse as an intervention in her life by
      beings from outer space. Such experiences of "spacing out" are viewed here as endemic
      rather than otherworldly.
23.   I might add that this experience of motility and subjectivity is divided differently by gender,
      much as David Morley has described the power relations around the dial and the remote
      control around the family television – the wife and mother decides what to watch only when
      no one else is there. Just so, the experience of driving is gendered. As his future bride said
      to Sonny Crockett in an episode of the 1987–88 season's "Miami Vice," "I'll bet no woman
      has driven your testosterone."
24.   See the chapter "Speed" in Stephen Kern's *The Culture of Time and Space 1880–1918* for
      a discussion of the distinction between relative and absolute (subjectively intuited) motion.
      Note also that *nonspace* is not at all Kern's "empty space" or the void. Paul Virilio's medita-
      tions on the relation between speed and power of a coercive or military nature are only
      peripherally related to the "private" speed developed here.
25.   See Freud on jokes and body responses to "too much" and "too little" in *Jokes and the
      Unconscious*.
26.   The two local hosts of the show address the home viewer directly across the heads of name-
      less other people, as if they were in a bubble of space which could exchange talk and looks
      with our home-viewing space, while an objectively closer realm in front of them remains

an otherwise distant and unrelated diegetic world. This bubble of subjectivity can also be found in other televisual genres such as logos and rock videos. What seems to be at stake are two things: the end of a "line" or fourth wall which divides representational realms, and the notion of a mobile rather than stationary or positioned spectator and/or presenter, able to roam and cross the barriers between multiple worlds at will. The constant alternation of static settings with "driving" segments in "Miami Vice" is an inverse example of the process embedded within story, marking the interiorized subjectivity or "true" self "under cover," also reflected in music and conversation.

27. "For the Navajo, walking was an important event in and of itself and not just a way of getting somewhere. We expected the filmmakers to cut out most of the walking footage – but they didn't. It was the least discarded footage" (Worth and Adair 146). "In reading the Navajo myths and stories later we were struck by how, in most Navajo myths, the narrator spends much of his time describing the walking, the landscape, and the places he passes, telling only briefly what to 'us' are plot lines" (147).

28. See 120–21 and 140–41, and generally his discussion of television, Ellis does not relate "segmentalization" to the development of spot advertising, whereas it could be argued that the struggle for control of the enunciation which led to spot advertising is served by segmentation, that is, an argument of consequences not from particular events but from techniques of power.

29. These include mixtures of pictorial systems, two- and three-dimensional images, symbols, and the written word in a single image as well as different planes of language. Worth and Adair considered it odd that the Navajos made photos with layouts of painted words to "try out ideas" and that they linked clips of symbolic events without concern for spatio-temporal continuity. However, layouts of painted words would be quite compatible with contemporary televisual representation.

30. Especially in regard to fiction films on television, such an alternation of story and discourse is perceived as interruption by all sorts of extraneous material and an incessant disruption of the psychological mechanism of disavowal that Beverly Houston explained in "Viewing Television."

Segmentation imposed on continuity editing is a mismatch of principles of coherence and dramatic unity of character, plot and setting, and editing, as well as conditions of viewing which promote fairly concentrated attention, and identification can only suffer thereby. What is interruption from the point of embedded fictions is more likely to be perceived as passage among segments and engagement with the viewer in discursive genres. Nonetheless, ads have retained the sense of being foreign bodies in flow at least since the advent of spot advertising in the mid-1950s, whereas when sponsors controlled programming the shift of subjects of discourse was smoother.

31. "It is hardly an exaggeration to call the freeway experience," as Joan Didion does, "the only secular communion Los Angeles has" (quoted in Brodsly 36–37).

32. The boulevard is discussed at length in Berman; street lighting in Schivelbusch.

33. Sachs goes on to explain how the symbolic value of the auto is undermined as soon as it becomes generally accessible and how it actually generates social inequalities.

34. See McHale, esp. 43–58. McHale proposes that the shift in dominance from epistemological to ontological questions is the primary distinguishing feature of postmodernism. The *zone* is a concept with a prior history in nineteenth-century Paris suburbs.

35. "In short, Dorothy loves the mechanism which turns display into a narrative of desire and enables her to experience the pastoral idyll vicariously. . . . She desires the figure that represents desire, recognizing in that image her own capacity for infinite desire" (Culver 112–13).

36. Kowinski stresses the chain of relationships: "The shopping mall completed the link between the highway and television; once the department stores and the national chains and franchises were inside, just about anything advertised on the tube could be found at the mall, The mall provided the perfect and complementary organization for the national replicated and uniform outlets of the Highway Comfort Culture. The mall, too, was national, and it was also replicated and uniform in management as well as appearance – the chains knew what to expect just about everywhere. They could slip easily into any mall; one size fits all" (51).

37. Denis Hollier calls Caillois's essay on the praying mantis in *Le myth et l'homme* the first to deal with the issue of simulation (76–77).

38. Duensing describes the technology patented by Jay Schiffman of Auto Vision Associates in Ferndale, Michigan. The virtual television is resisted for safety reasons, but its gradual acceptance is anticipated as a process comparable with the pioneering of the car radio by Bill Lear in 1929. What kind of programming the virtual television will display is discussed largely in terms of safety and attention. The process of looking at the virtual screen while driving is described in terms of "time sharing."

39. Avenues for images and voices which might represent subjects other than network representatives, advertisers, and celebrities, that is, members of a general public, or for that matter other private voices remain few: independent productions, the lowly public service announcement, cable community access programming, private networks for exchanging videocassettes, and computer networks. The growing segmentation of what was once broadcasting into cable channels and superstations supported by satellite as well as the videocassette is an opportunity for heterogeneous voices to enter into representation – but only if the discursive practices developed in network television are themselves changed. Venues of "publicness" that range from PBS and C-SPAN to Paper Tiger and Captain Midnight merit separate discussion as to how each contributes as a model of entry into the realms of distraction.

References

Antin, David (1990). Video: The Distinctive Features of the Medium. In: John G. Hanhardt (ed.), *Video Culture: A Critical Investigation*, pp. 147–66. Rochester: Visual Studies Workshop.

Arendt, Hannah (1974). *The Human Condition.* Chicago: University of Chicago Press.

Arnheim, Rudolf (1979). *Rundfunk als Hörkunst.* Munich: Hanser.

Bachelard, Gaston (1969). *The Poetics of Space*, trans. Maria Jolas. Boston: Beacon.

Bakhtin, Mikhail (1981). *The Dialogic Imagination: Four Essays*, trans. Caryl Emerson & Michael Holquist (ed.), Michael Holquist. Austin: University of Texas Press.

Baudrillard, Jean (1983). The Ecstasy of Communication. In: Hal Foster (ed.), *The Anti-aesthetic: Essays on Postmodern Culture*, pp. 126–34. Port Townsend, Wash.: Bay P.

Bayley, Stephen (1986). *Sex, Drink, and Fast Cars: The Creation and Consumption of Images.* London: Boston Faber.

Benjamin, Walter (1983). *Das Passagen-Werk*, Rolf Tiedemann (ed.), Frankfurt am Main: Suhrkamp.

Benjamin, Walter (1969). Paris: Capital of the Nineteenth Century. In: Hannah Arendt (ed.), *Illuminations*, trans. H. Zohn, New York: Shocken.

Berman, Marshall (1982). *All That Is Solid Melts into Air: The Experience of Modernity.* New York: Simon.

Brodsly, David (1981). *L. A. Freeway: An Appreciative Essay.* Berkeley: University of California Press.

Caillois, Roger (1972). *Le mythe et l'homme.* [c.1938] Paris: Gallimard.

Canetti, Elias (1973). *Crowds and Power.* New York: Viking.

Cohen, Stanley & Laurie Taylor (1978). *Escape Attempts: The Theory and Practice of Resistance to Everyday Life.* London: Penguin.

Culver, Stuart (1988). What Manikins Want: *The Wonder World of Oz* and *The Art of Decorating Dry Goods Windows. Representations* 21, pp. 97–116.

de Certeau, Michel (1984). *The Practice of Everyday Life*, trans. Steven F. Rendall. Berkeley and Los Angeles: University of California Press.

DePalma, Anthony (1987). The Malling of Main Street. *The New York Times*, April 19, Business 1.

Duensing, Edward S. (1989). Television on the Move: In-Car Video Screen Small but Critics Question Safety. *Los Angeles Times*, September 11, p. II–3.

Ellis, John (1982). *Visible Fictions: Cinema, Television, Video.* London: Routledge & Kegan Paul.

Flitterman, Sandy (1987). Psychoanalysis, Film, and Television. In: Robert Allen (ed.), *Channels of Discourse*, p. 200. Chapel Hill: University of North Carolina Press.

Foucault, Michel (1979). *Discipline and Punish: The Birth of the Prison*, trans. Alan Sheridan. New York: Vintage.

Freud, Sigmund (1963). *Jokes and the Unconscious*, trans. James Strachey. New York: Norton.

Gitlin, Todd (1986). Car Commercials and *Miami Vice*: "We Build Excitement." In: Todd Gitlin (ed.), *Watching Television: A Pantheon Guide to Popular Culture*, pp. 136–61. New York: Pantheon.

Graham, Dan & Robin Hurst (1987). Corporate Arcadias. *Artforum*, December, pp. 68–74.

Greimas, A. J. & J. Courtés (1982). *Semiotics and Language: An Analytical Dictionary*, trans. Larry Christ et al. Bloomington: Indiana University Press.

Hobbs, Robert (1981). Introduction. *Robert Smithson: Sculpture.* Ithaca, NY: Cornell University Press.

Hollier, Denis (1988). The Word of God: "I am Dead." *October* 44, pp. 76–7.

Houston, Beverly (1984). The Metapsychology of Endless Consumption. *Quarterly Review of Film Studies* 9(3), pp. 183–95.

Kaplan, E. Ann (1987). *Rocking around the Clock: Music, Television, Postmodernism and Consumer Culture.* New York: Methuen.

Kaplan, Sam Hall (1988). The New Suburbia. *Los Angeles Times Magazine*, September 16, p. 28.

Kern, Stephen (1983). *The Culture of Time and Space 1880–1918.* Cambridge, MA: Harvard University Press.

Kowinski, William Severini (1985). *The Malling of America: An Inside Look at the Great Consumer Paradise.* New York: William Morrow.

McHale, Brian (1987). *Postmodernist Fiction.* New York: Methuen.

McLuhan, Marshall (1967). *The Mechanical Bride: Folklore of Industrial Man.* Boston: Beacon.

Meyerowitz, Joshua (1985). *No Sense of Place: The Impact of Electronic Media on Social Behavior.* New York: Oxford University Press.

Moores, Shaun (1988). "The Box on the Dresser": Memories of Early Radio and Everyday Life. *Media Culture and Society* 10, p. 23.

Morris, Meaghan (1992). Great Moments in Social Climbing: King Kong and the Human Fly. In: Beatriz Colomina (ed.), *Sexuality and Space*, pp. 1–51. New York: Princeton Architectural Press.

Morse, Margaret (1991). Rock Video: Synchronizing Rock Music and Television. In: Leah R. Vande Berg & Lawrence A. Wenner (eds.), *Television Criticism: Approaches and Applications*, pp. 289–312. White Plains, NY: Longman.

Rath, Claus-Dieter (1985). The Invisible Network: Television as an Institution in Everyday Life. In: Phillip Drummond & Richard Paterson (eds.), *Television in Transition: Papers from the First International Television Studies Conference*, pp. 199–204. London: British Film Institute.

Ross, Andrew (1987–88). The Work of Nature in the Age of Electronic Emission. *Social Text* 18, pp. 116–28.

Sachs, Wolfgang (unpublished). Are Energy-Intensive Life-Images Fading? The Cultural Meaning of the Automobile in Transition.

Savan, Leslie (1978). This Typeface is Changing Your Life. In: James Monaco (ed.), *Media Culture: Television, Radio, Records, Books, Magazines, Newspapers, Movies*, pp. 223–34. New York: Dell.

Schivelbusch, Wolfgang (1988). *Disenchanted Night: The Industrialization of Light in the Nineteenth Century*, trans. Angela Davies. Berkeley: University of California Press.

Sobchack, Vivian (forthcoming). "Lounge Time": Post-war Crises and the Chronotope of Film Noir. In: Nick Browne (ed.), *Refiguring American Film Genres: History and Theory*. Berkeley: University of California Press.

Stam, Robert. Television News and Its Spectator. In: E. Ann Kaplan (ed.), *Regarding Television*, pp. 23–43.

Stewart, Susan (1984). *On Longing: Narratives of the Miniature, the Gigantic, the Souvenir, the Collection*. Baltimore: Johns Hopkins University Press.

Turner, Victor (1977). Frame, Flow and Reflection: Ritual and Drama as Public Liminality. In: Michel Benamou & Charles Carameilo (eds.), *Performance in Postmodern Culture*, pp. 33–55. Madison: Coda.

Venturi, Robert, Denise Scott Brown & Steven Izenour (1972/1977). *Learning from Las Vegas: The Forgotten Symbolism of Architectural Form*. Cambridge, MA: MIT Press.

Virilio, Paul (1989). *War and Cinema: The Logistics of Perception*. London: Verso.

Williams, Raymond (1975/1992). *Television: Technology and Cultural Form*. New York: Shocken; Rpt. Hanover, NH: University Press of New England.

Worth, Sol & John Adair (1975). *Through Navajo Eyes: An Exploration in Film Communication and Anthropology*. Bloomington: Indiana University Press.

Nichemarketing the Apocalypse:
Violence as Hard-Sell

*Ann Burlein**

Analysts see Christian Identity today as a movement shaped, and even divided, by two choices. Should adherents withdraw from a mainstream they see as hopelessly corrupt? Or should adherents selectively engage with the mainstream to create conditions appropriate for the kingdom?[1] Rather than being lived as abstract either/ors, such choices constitute crossroads where people find themselves again and again: Is this not how commitments are made, politicization happens, and a life is lived?

Much, then, depends on how leaders imagine this crossroads over time. When Christian Identity believers wage spiritual warfare against "the powers, principalities and world rulers of this present darkness" (Ephesians 6:12), to what extent do they envision their fight as literal and to what extent metaphorical? How do they imagine the human and the divine to connect? Do believers pledge themselves to act as the spark that ignites the cleansing fire of divine vengeance that will usher in the kingdom now? Or do believers pledge to preserve their identity, submitting to the powers that be to continue performing the truth of the remnant in the face of this darkening age?

These questions lie at the heart of Christian Identity. I find them unsettling. For when politics is war by other means (as Foucault argued), religion can become the ultimate power fantasy. In calling religion a power fantasy, I am not dismissing religion. Dismissal assumes a reductive understanding of both power and fantasy. My life has taught me the opposite: it matters how we imagine power. Such imaginings are part of why people do religion. How to keep hope alive in a world filled with suffering, suffering that is – let us have the courage to say it – unendurable? And when do hopes become your worst fear, a form of violence that you must let die? For what is it, really, to hold an elusive and invisible something as that which is most real in the face of a visible reality that does not see your ultimate concern?

Negotiating this gap lies at the heart of apocalypticism. I mean apocalypticism not just in the strict sense of Christians who believe in a literal end to time, but in the more secular sense, too, of an apocalyptic sensibility that dreams of a new and better world to be reborn at the end of this vale of tears, however these tears be caused.[2]

In negotiating this gap, desire emerges as a complicating factor. According to Lacan, what desire wants is to run, not complete, its course. The object of desire is deferred even as it is sought, precisely so that one can seek and reseek perpetually.[3] Thus, even such a movement as Christian Identity, which revels in overt expressions of hatred and openly desires to vanquish its enemies, does not, cannot, offer a straightforward economy of desire. Instead, violence operates in Christian Identity as a pole of attraction precisely because – and to the extent that – it is also denied.

I find such reflections unsettling because they locate Christian Identity in the terrain between reality and fantasy. Reality and fantasy are distinguishable: you can tell, sometimes, that what you are doing is fantasy if only because therein lies its appeal (think of day-dreaming). Yet, though distinct, reality and fantasy are not clearly so. The "real" world crosses into fantasy and fantasy crosses into the real, producing self-fulfilling prophecies of all sorts.

In this chapter, I explore these questions by focusing on Pete Peters's life course as a Christian Identity minister. Pete and Cheri Peters embraced Christian Identity just when a significant minority of its leaders began advocating the use of force to effect revolutionary change – and just when Robert Mathews began The Order to walk that talk. Mathews's project ended in his death, as well as a federal crackdown that culminated in a movementwide sedition trial.[4] Emerging as leaders in this context, the Peterses began their career by engaging in various mainstreaming projects. This chapter focuses on the mainstreaming projects that Pete Peters set into motion in 1988. In the first two sections, I explore the power fantasies that informed these attempts. In the third section, I investigate how Peters's understanding of spiritual warfare changed through interacting with the mainstream. This change happened because Peters's commitment to mainstreaming arises from a power fantasy that has nothing to do with accommodating to the mainstream. When his mainstreaming efforts do not effect the expected results, rather than question his belief in God as Law, he denounces mainstreaming – including his belief in the Constitution as a divinely authored text that links the human and the divine – as idolatry. Pushed to rework his understanding of spiritual warfare, Peters intensifies his identification with violence.

Peters's life course provides the chapter's overarching plotline. But his commitments do not take shape in a vacuum. Thus, the second section also explores how convergences have recently emerged between Christian Identity and the Christian right. Both ministries offer a politics of the body – both the individual body envisioned as a Temple of the Holy Spirit and the national body politic envisioned as God's Temple – in need of cleansing. Thus, both Peters and Dobson call Christians to articulate people's concern for their children into the romance of male protectionism by invoking the same biblical image. In this dangerous and deceitful age, the story goes, men must protect the innocence of their families by taking this country back from secular humanists, who have been surreptitiously reprogramming the sexual and gender mores of young people through pop culture since the 1960s as part of a conspiracy to annihilate all memory of Christianity from the national body politic.

Along with imagining masculinity, the Right's body politics also imagines a social world: the boundaries of belonging that enable people to feel at home in that imagined community we call the nation. This late modern version of the masculine romance uses apocalypse as a crucible to fuse the boundaries of the masculine body with the boundaries of the national body politic, resurrecting masculinity, the morality of power, and national identity – and thereby closing the gap between what is and what ought to be.

At the Heart of Mainstreaming Lies a Body Fantasy: *Remnant Resolves*

The text that best illustrates Peters's early efforts at mainstreaming is a pamphlet entitled *Remnant Resolves*. During Scriptures for America's (SFA's) July 1988 Family Bible Camp, members felt "spiritually burdened" by "the need and the desire to see Biblical principles of government once again established in our nation"; SFA wrote *Remnant Resolves* as a first step toward realizing this dream so that "the fight of our Forefathers against tyranny may not have been in vain."[5]

In its preamble, *Remnant Resolves* sets forth a classic creation mythology of religious nationalism. God made the United States as a nation whose nature *is* the Bible and created its citizens as a people whose nature *is* the First Amendment: "We recognize that our purpose on the earth is to worship God and enjoy Him forever, and that the highest form of worship is obedience to His Law" (*RR*, 3). This vision is illustrated on the pamphlet's cover, on which a large heavenly hand, surrounded by light, reaches down with a scroll entitled *Remnant Resolves* that spills over a tiny map of the North American continent. God's hand is big, the scroll is bigger, and the land mass is dwarfed by them both. Religious and political freedom are envisioned as a hierarchical chain of authority in which obedient submission to God's overpowering hand empowers Christians to be the visible representatives of that invisible hand: Phineas, the High Priest, who runs his spear through the coupling bodies of an interethnic pair. Given this vision, it is impossible to classify Peters's mainstreaming efforts as either religion or politics. When God is law and human freedom lies in religious obedience, spirituality requires execution in the world.

The first section of *Remnant Resolves* delineates what, then, one must do to build this vision. The most fundamental building block, according to the pamphlet, is self-government. Yet self-government does not mean democracy. According to *Remnant Resolves*, any government in which men *make* law enshrines human hubris as a collective King George. Instead, *Remnant Resolves* promotes biblically correct government in which (white Christian) men *administer* laws given by God (*RR*, 5–6).

Scriptures for America does not shrink from the corollary. Civil government that punishes good and protects evil is counterfeit authority, and "Christians have the right, indeed, the undeniable duty to resist this tyranny" in favor of executing biblical law. The text specifically enjoins substituting charity for welfare, preventing Jews from holding office, using a gun to defend "life, family, liberty and property," and repudiating sexual sins such as abortion, interracial marriage, and homosexuality (*RR*, 6).

Here *Remnant Resolves* reiterates an argument made earlier by Peters in *Authority: Resistance or Obedience? The Key to the Kingdom*: "The authority the scripture speaks of[6] comes from God, does His will, i.e. executes His law, punishes evildoers, and gives no cause to fear to those who do good. *It is not* a governing authority that would protect homosexuals, forbid Bibles and Jesus in school, finance and promote the murder of babies in the womb, slaughter our youth in unconstitutional no-win wars [Vietnam], forbid Christian parents from giving their children a Christian education, forbid travel without a license, deny the first fruits of our labors [income tax], feed those who will not work, require a number to exist [Social Security], etc."[7]

Peters's pamphlet refutes a reconfiguration of the Christian Identity movement that arose after the 1985 sedition trials as Christian Identity leaders such as Dan Gayman pulled back from advocating violence, interpreting Romans 13 as mandating submission to the state in all but the most extreme emergencies.[8] In contrast, in a sermon entitled "Sedition and the Old Time Religion" (which echoed the analysis of Cheri Peters in her documentary on the sedition trials entitled *Sedition . . . U.S.S.A. Style*), Peters argued that Christians owe their deepest allegiance not to the state – that is communism – but to Christ their King as free men.[9] Peters calls this freedom "the Old Time Religion," which he defines by quoting James 1:27: "This is the true and undefiled religion in the sight of our God and Father, to visit orphans in their distress, and to keep oneself unstained by the world." Acknowledging that liberal churches interpret James as calling Christians to build orphanages, Peters castigates social Gospellers for refusing to address the cause of the orphan's plight. In Peters's view, it is the government that creates orphans and widows through no-win wars in foreign lands like Vietnam as well as through social programs like abortion and welfare. Obeying such ungodly authority, Peters declares, closes the door in God's face. In contrast, active resistance opens the door to God's kingdom now.[10] In this religious imaginary, the coming of the kingdom hinges on whether humans open or close the door.

In keeping with this view, Peters uses nostalgia (in this case, for the Old Time Religion) to represent a fundamentally antidemocratic stance as populist and empowering. Likewise, SFA models *Remnant Resolves* after resolutions made by colonial committees of correspondence. This nostalgic mimicry invents a transmission history in which *Remnant Resolves* forms the most recent link in a chain that extends from the Constitution to the Articles of Confederation, the Declaration of Independence, the Declaration of Rights drawn up by the First Continental Congress, the Fairfax Resolves – all the way back to the early covenants made by the Puritans.

In so doing, SFA inserts *Remnant Resolves* into a wider political and hermeneutic sensibility called Christian Constitutionalism. This sensibility interprets the Bible alongside legal documents like the Constitution and the Declaration of Independence as equivalent Scriptures: the Bible is read as law and legal documents are read as God's inspired Word. Christian Constitutionalism includes not just white supremacists like Peters but also Christian Patriots, tax protestors, and militia members, most of whom would not identify with white supremacy. It also includes large segments of the Christian right, particularly those influenced by Christian Reconstructionism, a movement whose calls for reconstructing the United States according to biblical law have exerted influence far beyond its small number of card-carrying members.

Christian Constitutionalism fabricates an alternative legal tradition that is also a religious tradition of sacred texts. Yet, for all its nostalgia, this "invented tradition" is intensely antitraditionalist.[11] It rejects all traditions of hermeneutics as man-made systems that corrupt God's meaning. Constitutionalists "fundamentalize" historical documents as well as their authors, reading any and all references to the Bible or God as evidence that America's forefathers founded an explicitly Christian republic – even when these references are metaphorical and even when uttered by deists.

Constitutional fundamentalists invent traditions for their opponents as well. Sociologists Jeffrey Hadden and Anthony Schupe suggest that the whole notion of secular humanism hinges on a literalist reading of the 1961 Supreme Court case *Torcaso v. Watkins.*[12] This case declared it unconstitutional for a state (in this case, Maryland) to require citizens (here Torcaso, who was appointed public notary) to swear an oath affirming belief in God. Justice Hugo Black wrote a brief footnote in which he opined: "Among religions in this country which do not teach what would generally be considered a belief in the existence of God are Buddhism, Taoism, Ethical Culture, Secular Humanism, and others."[13] According to historian Martin Marty, "A new name for a non-existent denomination was born full-blown from the mind of one justice."[14] Decontextualized and repeated in newsletters, radio shows, and publishing houses, secular humanism became "real" by this re-citing.

Likewise, Constitutionalist claims that the income tax was unconstitutionally ratified, for example, are cited and re-cited in legal clinics, lectures, radio broadcasts, computer bulletin boards, and independently published books. Circular citation within these alternative communication networks produces a simulated web that endows such claims with the effects of truth for those who stand within these communities.

Radicalizing the stream: may the government take warning

Entering into and redirecting these circles of citation is why SFA wrote *Remnant Resolves*. The first half of the pamphlet delineates the building blocks for establishing Christ's Lordship over the nation; the second half formulates a plan for "mass distribution with the goal of getting them read into the Congressional record."[15] Urging individuals to file the pamphlet at their county courthouse (which many deem the highest level of legitimate government), SFA reasoned that once *Remnant Resolves* became a matter of public record, various Patriot groups across the country could appeal to it as precedent when filing liens or setting up common-law courts.[16]

Remnant Resolves was also intended to put federal authorities on notice. In March 1989, Peters and five other Christian Identity leaders took the pamphlet to Washington, DC, where they claim to have lobbied sixty congressional officials, speaking in particular against gun control. The trip concluded on March 24 with a public reading of *Remnant Resolves* on the steps of the Capitol at high noon on Good Friday, the traditional day and time of Jesus' crucifixion.

Setting the public reading of *Remnant Resolves* in the context of sacred time indicates that Peters's mainstreaming attempts do not arise from a willingness to work within the system. Instead, when Peters sees the capital city, he remembers Acts 17:16–23, in which Paul points to an altar that the Greeks had dedicated "to an unknown God" and says, "What therefore you worship in ignorance, this I proclaim to you."[17] Peters goes to DC as a prophet who denounces the nation for mistaking these stone buildings and the state power they memorialize for the God whose mighty arm made America possible. He warns that war can be averted *if* the government heeds *Remnant Resolves:* "The authorities in King George III's government, as well as the King himself, made a grave error in not listening to and taking seriously these resolves. It is our prayer the same tragic mistake will not occur again."[18] This prophetic proclamation is a relation of force. Peters delivers an ultimatum. Yet, a relation of force is a relation; it is conditional on the hearer's response. Peters focuses not on the fact that the only acceptable response to an ultimatum is capitulation, but on his vulnerability in this relation. Will they hear?

May Christians take warning: trumping the Christian right

How ought the nation to respond? Peters's model is biblical: cleanse the Temple. This model is one that Peters shares with the Christian right: James Dobson explicitly patterned his Focus on the Family ministry after this biblical image. The image of cleansing the nation as God's Temple appears in the Bible as a response to the threat posed by the Assyrian Empire, which destroyed the Northern Kingdom of Israel in 722 BCE and which invaded the Southern Kingdom a few years later during Hezekiah's reign but was repulsed at its capital, Jerusalem. Like much in the Hebrew Bible, the image recurs. Its first appearance describes the reforms instituted by King Hezekiah; its second appearance describes similar reforms (re)instituted by King Josiah. Dobson models Focus on the Family on the reforms of Hezekiah (narrated in 2 Kings 18); SFA models its *Remnant Resolves* on the reforms of Josiah (narrated in 2 Kings 22–23 and 2 Chronicles 34–35).

Josiah became king as Assyria was disintegrating. Sensing a power vacuum, Josiah rejected his predecessors' pro-Assyrian policy of "cultural cosmopolitanism" and promoted nationalism by encouraging worship of Yahweh.[19] The Bible represents Josiah's policies as carrying out covenant promises that Israel had made long ago and forgotten. These promises were found in a mysterious "book of the law" (assumed since the time of Jerome to be some version of Deuteronomy) that was discovered in the Temple during Josiah's reign. Several biblical scholars have suggested that this mysterious book of the law was not so much found as planted – not an original text but a pretext for Josiah's reforms.[20]

Homi Bhabha has suggested that nations are narrations.[21] Here, the Bible (re)creates the nation of ancient Israel through narrating a story of religious return. The nation had forgotten its God, lost its book of the law. Its antidote was to remember. Thus, Josiah commanded the law book to be read publicly in a covenant ceremony that (re)committed the nation to Yahweh and to his house, the Jerusalem Temple. This commitment was (re)produced by removing "foreign" symbols from the Jerusalem Temple and destroying local places of worship (the high places that dotted the countryside) where the fertility deities of the populace and indigenous Canaanites were honored either in place of Yahweh or in a syncretistic form alongside Yahweh.

Josiah's reforms used religious remembrance as a technology of power to construct national identity at the level of bodily ego. According to philosopher Etienne Balibar, such embodied memories enable people to live the nation's political boundaries as "a projection and protection of an internal collective personality," and thereby inhabit the abstract entity of "Israel" as "home."[22] Yet there is a price for such empowerment: Josiah produces a sense of belonging inside the nation by casting indigenous religious practices as outside the nation.

Modeled after Josiah's reforms, *Remnant Resolves* rejects the cultural cosmopolitanism of the "New World Order." Instead, it warns that if Congress does not return to the nation's original creation order, Christian men are resolved to do it for them. Also like Josiah, Peters stages a public reading of *Remnant Resolves* on the Capitol steps at the moment of Christ's salvific death for the sins of his people. This staging reenacts the covenant: Jesus' death holds out the promise of forgiveness and redemption: if "my people who are called by my name humble themselves and pray and seek my face and turn from their wicked ways, then I will hear from heaven, will forgive their sin, and heal their land" (2 Chronicles 7:14). Thus, like Josiah, Peters positions religion as the vanishing point where state power crosses into the psyche to produce national identity – having been called by God's name. And Peters does so, like Josiah, by stigmatizing both "aliens" and his competitors.

In the newsletter describing SFA's DC trip, Peters distinguished SFA's "standing in the gates" (the gates were the public gathering places in walled biblical cities) from "Christians [who] have been playing church, saving souls, building fun parks, etc., allowing the gates (local, state and nation) to go to hell."[23] Peters castigates the Christian right for proclaiming, "If we make him the Lord and king of all, then he will heal this land" and yet defining the culture war as "a battle with a spiritual Satan. . . . It amazes me that they are willing to take on the devil, but if some devil in a three piece suit from the IRS or the BATF knocks on their door you will see just how brave they are."[24]

In contrast, Peters insists that Christian men neither withdraw from culture (as fundamentalists did after the 1920s Scopes trial), nor talk about a "big tent" (as Ralph Reed once did), nor counsel followers to avoid appealing to biblical authority (as Dobson's Focus on the Family does). Whereas Dobson urges followers to become politically involved because "Christians are citizens too," Peters insists that "Christians are ambassadors of Christ and ambassadors go to heads of state."[25] Exempt from the laws of the land where they reside, such ambassadors proclaim their king: "The God you worship in ignorance I now reveal to you!"

In this spirit, *Remnant Resolves* concludes by quoting 2 Chronicles 7:14. As the last words of Peters's public reading, this verse rings out from the Temple Mount over this land like the Liberty Bell. With this act, SFA uses memory as a political technology to appropriate a key text of the Christian right. Eight years earlier, when the Christian right had come to D.C. for its April 1980 Washington for Jesus rally, its leaders chose 2 Chronicles 7:14 as their theme text. According to political scientist Matthew Moen, "The importance of that Bible verse to the Christian Right transcends 'Washington for Jesus.' It has really been the movement's statement of purpose: to turn an immoral United States toward God so that He might forgive her and rebuild her glory. Recognizing the significance of that passage, Stan Hastey [of the Baptist Joint Committee on Public Affairs] labeled it 'the controlling text of the religious right.'"[26]

Remnant Resolves' appropriation of 2 Chronicles is not just any appropriation, because this divine promise is not just any promise. Second Chronicles 7 narrates the primordial moment to which both Josiah and Hezekiah staged a "return." After King Solomon dedicated the Jerusalem Temple, Yahweh appeared to him in a dream, reiterated the covenant he had made with Solomon's father, David, and declared that because he has chosen the Temple for himself, if "my people who are called by my name . . . turn from their wicked ways, then I will hear from heaven, will forgive their sin, and heal their land" (2 Chronicles 7:14). By concluding *Remnant Resolves* with this verse, SPA annexes the Christian right's articulation of the verse – simply takes it over as if the verse were a plot of land to be conquered and colonized, claimed for Christian Identity.

Concluding with 2 Chronicles 7:14 suggests that *Remnant Resolves,* like Josiah's lost-found book of the law, is performative. More pretext than text, it fantasizes the Bible as a repository of divine power that believers can tap into by mimetically reenacting covenant promises like 2 Chronicles 7:14. All the remnant need do is "add faith and stir and the true King, God and Savior becomes real to us."[27] If the nation heeds its warning and follows the blueprint outlined in *Remnant Resolves,* then the United States will get the real thing: a literal kingdom where Jesus is king and Christian men are empowered to represent that overpowering Hand. Delivering on this promise literally is Peters's goal and therefore his brand name.

The Paramilitary Romance and Nichemarketing

Real nations love Jesus

From this hostile competition, one might assume that Peters shuns the Christian right. Indeed, Peters at first dismissed Christian Reconstructionism as "fully saturated by Jews."[28] Yet over the years, Peters has quoted increasingly from Rousas Rushdoony and Gary DeMar, as well as Peter Marshall and David Barton.[29] Peters envisions this relationship in gendered terms: before people can eat the strong meat of the Word, he says, they must be given (mother's) milk.[30] The gender metaphor expresses the central paradox of mainstreaming: Peters seeks to move Christian Identity mainstream, but he does so in hopes of moving the mainstream right.

For example, in a 1993 sermon celebrating July 4 (delivered after sharing a stage with Barton), Peters urges Barton to go one step further: "When you start investigating the Christian roots of this country, you cannot help but come face to face with the reality of the racial roots of this country. . . . Those men who are going back and discovering our Christian roots had better, if they've got the Spirit of God upon them, be honest. They were not only Christian, but they were one race of people and in the Constitution they made known that they were concerned about one group of people."[31]

Peters portrays white supremacy as the foregone conclusion of returning to the nation's religious roots: "Be honest." Yet such links are never automatic. After the Oklahoma City bombing, for example, many militia leaders professed openness to all races and creeds. Although some of these protestations were about damage control, some were genuine: the militia movement is not monolithic.[32] Yet many Constitutionalists do distinguish between "sovereign citizens," whose rights stem from the divinely inspired "organic" Constitution (defined as the original Constitution and the Bill of Rights), and "14th Amendment citizens," whose rights stem from manmade additions.

In this invented tradition, women and people of color became citizens by virtue of the federal government and therefore must obey its laws. In contrast, white men became citizens by virtue of divine decree; hence when a white man destroys his driver's license, marriage certificate, and social security card, he reactivates his sovereign status and need no longer obey the federal government.

The Christian right also distinguishes rights given by God from rights created by secular humanist elites. Instead of distinguishing sovereign from amended citizens, however, the Christian right distinguishes civil from special rights. Although the details of these invented traditions differ, both set into motion the cultural silences that swirl around race and sexuality to create "others" whose unruly bodies can then be cast outside the sacred circle of citizenship. Cultural critic Alisa Solomon explains:

> Through its various attacks – on gays, immigrants, African Americans – the Right insists on "deserving" citizens who must demonstrate their worthiness of constitutional protections. The rhetorical tropes aimed at exclusion of these "aliens" and "cheats" are almost interchangeably applied to all three groups. Queers, for example, are derided in the same terms as the "welfare queen," who is, of course, always figured as black. Both are depicted as sexually incontinent, immoral beings who try to trick the state out of scarce resources. "Special rights," forged in the cauldron of antigay initiatives, became an instrumental phrase in the restructuring of "welfare as we know it." . . . What's more, the welfare reform effort relied, in turn, on the increasingly mainstream disdain for public spending of any sort – a view made popular by the Right's relentless assault on the National Endowment for the Arts. . . . [In sum,] anyone whose sexuality cannot be maritally contained – homosexuals and unwed mothers most of all – are cast out from civil protections, and in the Right's fantasy, from citizenry itself.[33]

Thus, whereas it is important to recognize the diverse attitudes among Christian Constitutionalists regarding racism, it is equally important not to get lost amid these feedback loops. After all, the Founding Fathers did not just happen to be silent on the inalienable rights of other races. Benjamin Franklin brought to the Constitutional Convention a strong resolution against the slave trade written by the Pennsylvania Abolition Society; the resolution stayed in his pocket.[34] The result of this and similar silences was a Constitution that, though founded on overt protestations of "no taxation without representation," defined political representation through coded language combining "agendas for individual freedom" with "mechanisms of devastating racial oppression."[35] Hence, W. E. B. Du Bois argued in *Black Reconstruction* that any constitutionalism that idealizes literal fidelity to the founders' original intent cannot break free of the racial violence at the nation's origin. How much less capable of breaking free is a sensibility that idealizes the Constitution as God's plan for this nation.

As did their models, the biblical kings Josiah and Hezekiah, both Dobson and Peters use "traditional religion" as an image. Its invocation of the past signifies the pleasure of protest and passion. Thus, calls for religious return have less in common with the desire to return to a bygone age (à la the Amish) and more with Coca-Cola's marketing campaign, in which the company resurrected its original contour bottle (introduced in 1916 to differentiate Coke from the competition) to "unleash the power of nostalgia."[36] Long ago, there was a nation inspired by God and infused with a preordained potency, whose power was lost to unseen conspirators. The appeal of this fantasy lies not in the past but in its future promise. All one need do is recapture that stolen, forgotten self and the nation will rise again.

This is why pointing out contradictions in the Right's countermemories does not bring the Right tumbling down like a house of cards. Emptiness is key to how this image appeals. "It is precisely through such displacement," argues theorist Slavoj Žižek, "that desire is constituted." Žižek explains:

> The element that holds together a given community cannot be reduced to a point of sym-
> bolic identification: the bond linking its members always implies a shared relationship
> toward a Thing, toward Enjoyment incarnated. This relationship towards the Thing,
> structured by means of fantasies, is what is at stake when we speak of the menace to our
> "way of life" presented by the Other. . . . This Nation-Thing is determined by a set of
> contradictory properties. It appears to us as "our Thing" (perhaps we could say *cosa
> nostra*), as something accessible only to us, as something "they," the others, cannot grasp,
> but which is nonetheless constantly menaced by "them." It appears as what gives plenitude
> and vivacity to our life, and yet the only way we can determine it is by resorting to differ-
> ent versions of an empty tautology: all we can say about it is, ultimately, that the Thing
> is "itself," "the real Thing," "what it is really about," and so on. . . . The structure here
> is the same as that of the Holy Spirit in Christianity. The Holy Spirit *is* the community
> of believers in which Christ lives after His death; to believe in Him is to believe in belief
> itself – to believe that I'm not alone, that I'm a member of the community of believers. . . . In
> other words, the whole meaning of the Thing consists in the fact that "it means something"
> to people.[37]

I suggest that this paradox of desire – the emptiness of the Nation Thing as envisioned on the screen of communication technologies – explains what Michael Barkun
describes as the *irony* of recent convergences between Christian Identity and the Christian right. Whereas in the late 1980s, "the radical right was an isolated, insular subculture, detached from and shunned by the larger society;" by the 1990s things had
changed. In his epilogue updating *Religion and the Racist Right: The Origins of the
Christian Identity Movement,* Barkun observes:

> The circumstantial ties between the [Oklahoma City] bombing and the radical right should
> have definitively de-legitimized the radical right. But instead of reinforcing its pariah
> status, the bombing helped move it toward the mainstream, supplying it with the kind of
> media access it never previously enjoyed and attributing to it a power about which it had
> only fantasized. Such media access, in a time of rising anti-government sentiment, has
> opened new recruiting possibilities, while the attribution of power has made the fringe
> right an increasingly attractive prize for some mainstream politicians to covet.[38]

Barkun attributes this change to three "bridging mechanisms." First, militias now
provide "transition points" so that "rather than shift abruptly from 'normal' to 'abnormal' politics, one can move by stages." Second, Christian Identity repackaged its racism
as antigovernment politics. Finally, its conspiratorial sensibility has proliferated into
evangelical Protestantism and the New Age movement (as Barkun notes) but also, and

more important (I contend), into a social sector that Barkun does not consider: main-stream pop culture.[39]

Communications technologies have created a new beast: "the mass-mediated human, whose sense of space and time, whose emotional repertoires and deepest motivations cannot be extricated from what has emanated through the airwaves."[40] Through their pioneering use of mass communications technologies, both Peters and Dobson use the biblical image of the nation/body as God's Temple to reconstruct the emotional rep-ertoires and motivations through which people do the Nation Thing. This image reart-iculates mainstream hopes and fears – hopes and fears that find their primary articulation in popular culture and, specifically, in the paramilitary romance that emerged in the 1970s and 1980s in response to challenges associated with the 1960s.

A key challenge of that era was Vietnam, which many (mostly white) Americans experienced as a crisis in the masculinity of the American soldier and, by extension, in the nation. The United States had lost, in the eyes of American racial consciousness, to an effeminate inferior race from the technologically backward Third World.[41] In response, military and political leaders narrated a cultural memory that denied defeat. By insisting that the nation had lost because of its "self-imposed restraint," these leaders set about repairing belief in national and technological supremacy by remasculinizing the nation.[42]

This official memory had a popular counterpart, which sociologist William Gibson calls the "New War" genre. Throughout the 1970s and 1980s, Hollywood produced action-adventure blockbusters (such as *Dirty Harry* and *Rambo*) by the score. Men's fiction (consider Reagan's favorite author, Tom Clancy, whose Jack Ryan series includes *The Hunt for Red October* and *Patriot Games*) also proliferated, with some twenty to forty series released each year. In 1975, former Green Beret commander Robert Brown founded *Soldier of Fortune* as a magazine for "the independent warrior who must step in to fill the dangerous void created by America's failure in Vietnam." Brown sold up to 185,000 copies per issue to readers who were college-educated, married, and spent $1,000 annually on firearms and accessories, which were hyped through a complex interplay of nostalgia (marketing a .45, for example, as an "affordable legend") and fantasy (so that buying Rambo's weapon was promoted as a way to make Rambo, or the myth of masculinity that his knife embodied, real). Alongside the popularity of military-style automatic firearms went new recreation possibilities, including combat training schools, firing ranges, and paintball.[43]

Gibson traces the popularity of this New War genre to the fact that "mobilization for war had been a constant part of American life since the beginning of WWII in 1941. . . . The long cold war against communism had for decades been presented not as a manageable conflict with a socioeconomic system that differed from Western democracy and capitalism, but rather as a holy war against the presence of the devil in the modern world."[44] Thus, apocalypticism has long provided a stage for the formation of national and masculine identity, as well as their interimbrication (using one to prop up the other to avoid acknowledging that this emperor has no clothes). Given such intimate and lengthy training in apocalypse as identity, when faced with loss at home and abroad in the aftermath of the 1960s, "white men," Gibson suggests, "began to dream, to fantasize remaking the world and returning to an imaginary golden age, a time before Vietnam, before feminism, before civil rights," before deindustrialization and downsizing of all kinds.[45]

Whereas traditional war movies and Westerns, which faded out after Vietnam, tended to engender identifications with law enforcement or the military, the New War hero is paramilitary. Birthed into warriorship by the loss of his wife and children (who die, usually because the government lacked the courage to keep its promise of protection), the New War hero fights alone or with a small band of outlaw warriors. An old war hero like James Bond found female agents in his bed only to win them over so that they want him warm and alive; paramilitary warriors find Black Widow women whose embrace leads to death – theirs or his.[46] The old war hero derived his martial prowess from his moral character and therefore needed nothing more than conventional weapons; the paramilitary warrior derives his power from customized weaponry that functions as a signature extension of his hard body/phallus.[47]

Intense and phantasmatic weaponry is necessary for an age in which the masculine style of a John Wayne seems embarrassingly naïve. Vietnam revealed the virtuous war depicted by Westerns and WWII movies to be an illusion. No longer could one simply ignore the gap between men and Real Men. Hence, the paramilitary warrior divests himself of the phallus – but only to reclaim it as most truly his own, in part through fetishized weaponry and in part through vivid marks of male self-torture (as in the case of John J. "what you call hell he calls home" Rambo). The fantasy that the paramilitary romance offers is that male pain purifies power, rendering it once again legitimate, moral, innocent, even wise. In this version of the romance of male protectionism, white men rise up like a phoenix from the ashes of victimization, sufficiently strong to take action and take control, restoring this nation to its original state: God's holy Temple.[48]

Perhaps the most extreme white supremacist rearticulation of the paramilitary romance, Louis Beam's strategy of "leaderless resistance," comes right out of the New War genre. In response to the increasing government crackdown stimulated by the terrorism of The Order, Beam advocated that white supremacists form independent paramilitary cells (in contrast to the top-down military model of the Klan, which enables lawyers like Morris Dees to sue organizations as corporations responsible for the illegal acts of their members). Like Rambo, Beam had fought in Vietnam; when he returned stateside, Beam "took the war back home."[49] As leader of the Texas branch of David Duke's Knights of the Ku Klux Klan, Beam formed paramilitary units that in 1981 intimidated Vietnamese shrimp fishermen in Galveston Bay.[50]

Yet, in the 1980s, white supremacists were not alone in forming their identities in terms of the paramilitary romance: rather than declaring a War on Poverty, Reagan declared a War on Drug Dealers and supported the Nicaraguan Contras. Likewise, in his analysis of the 1992 standoff at Ruby Ridge between Christian Identity believer Randy Weaver and federal authorities seeking Weaver's arrest (an event that, along with Waco, catalyzed the militia movement), sociologist James Aho attributes the escalation of this standoff, which lasted ten days and took the lives of three people, to the fact that all four major protagonists trained in paramilitarism with Special Forces. Weaver dropped out of community college in 1968 to join the army, where he was assigned to the Green Berets. Although he never went to Vietnam, he became an expert in field engineering and the M-14 rifle. William Degan, who died at Ruby Ridge, served as an armed infantryman in Vietnam. After the war, he put his skills to use in the Special Operations Group of the US Marshal Service. Degan had been given the task of delivering Weaver's subpoena, along with fellow federal marshal Jack Cluff. Cluff had been an army helicopter gun crew chief in Vietnam from 1968 to 1969, providing air support for a Green Beret unit that was training Cambodian soldiers, for which he earned twenty-six medals. Bo Gritz (the Populist Party leader who negotiated Weaver down from the mountain, thanks in part to a letter of introduction from Pete Peters), served as an intelligence officer and reconnaissance chief for a Green Beret unit in Vietnam from 1968 to 1969. According to Aho, Gritz was the most decorated Green Beret in Vietnam. After the war, he commanded US Special Forces in Latin America and later headed "special activities" for the US Army General Staff at the Pentagon. In 1983, he led the original mission to Laos to rescue American POWS whom Gritz believed were abandoned by the federal government as part of its effort to cover up CIA involvement in cocaine trafficking as a way to fund its covert counterinsurgency efforts. Writes Aho: "It was Gritz himself who served as role model for the bluff and swagger man-of-action who in the face of government corruption and indifference seizes the day in the movie thrillers *Uncommon Valor, Missing in Action,* and *Rambo: First Blood Part II.* Bo Gritz is not merely a product of American paramilitary culture; he is its archetype."[51] Is it surprising, then, Aho asks, that the two sides played into, and played out, each other's worst fears and fantasies? Both were acting the same script.

Gibson suggests that a similar set of values informed those he interviewed at *Soldier of Fortune*'s annual conferences from 1985 to 1987. He writes:

> Being *active* – in contrast to the passivity of the general population – was a key value to the conventioneers. As active men, they considered themselves *responsible* for their own welfare and that of their families. A former US Army Special Forces instructor who now ran a "Base Operational School" in Mesa, Arizona, praised his clients as "normal blue-collar and white-collar people who don't think the federal government is going to take care of them in a stressful time." A Hawaiian aircraft mechanic and member of an Army National Guard Unit spoke more personally: "We feel that it may come a time when it's up to the head of the household to take care of his family. On this planet, there are guys who are doers and guys who are watchers."[52]

Gibson's interviews reveal explicit attempts by white supremacists to recruit *Soldier of Fortune* readers. The magazine's advertising manager routinely discarded potential ads that contained the words "KKK" and "Nazi," eventually discarding ads containing the word "Christian" as well. But the manager's method was not foolproof. In 1981, William Pierce, founder of the neo-Nazi organization The National Vanguard and author of *The Turner Diaries,* bought the magazine's mailing list and sent copies of his catalogue to subscribers.[53] Gibson suggests that the magazine's readers were a "natural" constituency for white supremacists, who needed merely to link the *Soldier of Fortune*'s existing anticommunist ideology – with its well-grooved articulation between national freedom and male protectionism – with the anti-Semitic identification of communism with Judaism. Yet getting individuals to make that link is not automatic. Indeed, the advertising manager at *Soldier of Fortune* learned he had slipped up when outraged subscribers called in protest.

Increasingly, as Barkun notes, militias provide a bridge for people to transition step by step. The militia manual *Citizen Soldier* by Robert Bradley (sold by Peters) features a colonial militiaman on its cover and promises advice on "How to protect your home, family and freedom when the government can't." Convinced that federal fiscal policies concerning the national debt and social programs will result in national insolvency, Bradley warns that when the government becomes unable to fund welfare, inner cities will erupt in racial and ethnic unrest just as Los Angeles erupted after the Simi Valley verdict (aided and abetted by white liberals seeking to install socialism). Bradley counsels people to be prepared by forming a neighborhood watch from which they can recruit potential militia members.

Bradley forms his apocalyptic imaginary on a racialized national topography: white suburban homes versus dark inner cities. Unrest in post-WWII prophecy novels often coupled racialized images of social disintegration in inner cities with portraits of corrupt government officials luring the people into slumber.[54]

As the following case study demonstrates, because Dobson's radio audience extends well beyond the narrow confines of prophecy circles, Dobson rarely invokes biblical apocalypse overtly. Yet, when he is at his most adamant about identifying his ministry with "the defense of righteousness," he is at his most apocalyptic. For example, in a 1993 newsletter to constituents, Dobson recounts how he learned that "our mission in support of righteousness must be offensive in nature, not merely defensive," when he and his wife Shirley were touring "the Holy Land." Standing "among archaeological digs and ancient battlegrounds," James and Shirley Dobson see: "Their world, like ours, was divided between God's Kingdom and the domain of Satan." On the western shore of the Sea of Galilee lived the devout Jews to whom Jesus preached, and on the other side lived "the Canaanites whom Joshua had driven out of the [*sic*] Israel and who practiced the Greek form of fertility cults . . . [including] the ancient worship of Baal, the god of nature – lightning and thunder." Faced with this geography, what did Jesus do? Dobson recalls Mark 4:35–5:13, in which Jesus, when he and his disciples were in a boat on the Sea of Galilee, rowed "directly toward the forbidden world." Dobson concludes: "Jesus did not remain in the safety of the Western territory. He constantly sought out evil and confronted it head-on."

Similarly, visiting a cave at Ceasarea Phillipi (identified as a center for Baal worship) reminds Dobson of a biblical passage that is also set there: Matthew 16:13–16. In this passage, Jesus asks his disciples who they think he is and Peter responds, "You are the Messiah, the Son of the Living God." Dobson comments:

> Then Jesus said something very important to our understanding: "And I say unto thee, That Thou art Peter, and upon this rock I will build my church; and the gates of hell shall not prevail against it" (Matthew 16:18). I have always interpreted that reference to the "gates of hell" as a defensive statement. In other words, I presumed Jesus was assuring us believers that we would not be overcome by the forces of evil. But look at the wording again. When Jesus spoke of "the gates," He referred to the entrance of a walled city – a fortress. We would all agree that a fortress is not an offensive weapon – it is a defensive

structure. "Gates" do not attack anyone. They are designed to protect those who are huddled within. Jesus was not telling the disciples that the church would somehow survive Satan's assault. He was assuring us the enemy would not prevail against *our* onslaught! We are to take the Good News directly into his territory and penetrate the stronghold of wickedness. This is accomplished not with the weapons of war but with the powerful force of love and persuasion.[55]

As the next case study shows, Dobson's primary identification is with sentimentality. Hence he eschews military arms to take up arms of another kind: the force of love and persuasion. Yet, identifying with sentimentality does not lead Dobson to confine his mission, stated as "preserving the Bible-based family," to defensive warfare. Instead, he maps the biblical text onto an apocalyptic geography that divides the world into the Christian West and the Baal-worshipping rest and thereby transforms talk of crucifixion – a self-sacrifice – into orders to lift high the cross and launch an offensive assault.

The paradox of hard-sell style: how to keep the hate you find

This shared orientation within the apocalyptic imaginary of the paramilitary romance does not mean that Peters and Dobson, or the white supremacist and the Christian right, are identical. Both Peters and Dobson insist on the necessity of engaging with the mainstream offensively, but Peters identifies with the bravado of Clint "make-my-day" Eastwood, whereas Dobson sounds more like Arnold Schwartzenegger in *Kindergarten Cop*, learning that a real man would rather be a head of the household than a paramilitary warrior. As indicated by my earlier reading of *Remnant Resolves'* appropriation of 2 Chronicles 7:14, I interpret these competing identifications as nichemarketing.

Nichemarketing explains the paradoxical nature of Peters's mainstreaming projects. Rather than indicating his willingness to work within the system, Peters practices mainstreaming to speak the silences that lie at the heart of how America does the Nation Thing – and to speak these silences even better than *Soldier of Fortune* or Rambo; even better than Special Forces, the Reagan administration, or Christian Constitutionalism; even better than the softer version of male "headship" promoted by the Christian right. Yet, as we've seen, performing silences requires ideological work: the work of memory, the work of marketing.

Immediately following SFA's stint with *Remnant Resolves* at the Capitol, Peters and three associates attended a pastor conference held by Bill Gothard because "some in our midst are coming up with false teachings and perversions of Romans 13, advocating blind obedience to the State and I discovered they were getting this material from Bill Gothard."[56] While lunching with Baptist ministers after Gothard's first lecture, Peters inquired about the assault rifle ban Congress was then debating in response to the 1989 Stockton killings (in which Patrick Purdy, a fan of the New War genre, used a military-style assault weapon to attack a schoolyard of Southeast Asian children). Asked Peters: "'Gentlemen, if House Bill 669 passes, it could mean the confiscation of our weapons. If it does pass, are you going to tell your congregation to obey the civil authorities and turn them in?' There was no answer until finally one preacher, with a lowered head and voice said, 'I'm not turning mine in.' [Peters's associate] Brother Weiland, who was sitting next to me said, 'That's not what he asked.' Then, after a few moments of silence the preacher said, 'I would probably tell them *not* to turn them in.'"[57]

Encouraged, Peters accompanied his newsletter with a pamphlet entitled *Everything You Wanted to Know (and Preachers Were Afraid to Tell You) about Gun Control*. Denouncing "pietistic so-called Christians" for whom freedom means only freedom from sin, Peters quotes Luke 22:35–36 ("Let him who has no sword sell his robe and buy one") and explains: "The sword of that day *was a lethal weapon*, equivalent in our time to a pistol, a rifle, a machine gun and, yes, an assault rifle."[58] Arguing that "the phony churches and preachers of our day have caused our warrior types to feel archaic, unneeded, and less than Christian," Peters does not merely accuse the religious establishment of failing to preserve the faith. As he sees it, "America's decline and weakening can be attributed to the switch from a (strong, logical, masculine) Bible-based Christianity to a (weak, emotional, illogical, feminine) non-Biblical *Judeo*-Christianity."[59] When the church is a Christian's greatest enemy, the extremity of the times mandates extreme tactics.[60] In Peters's conclusion, the Ol' Time Religion meets the "active" man of the paramilitary romance: "*know you need your gun to protect yourself against government* should it ever become a de facto, out-of-control, unGodly, law perverting, oppressive system. The bigger issue is not hunter's rights or defense against criminals but the Government itself. To some brainwashed, apathetic people this statement may sound bizarre, even frightening, but the writings and teachings of our forefathers show it is not new. . . . The citizens who hold onto their guns with a vise-like grip become a caution and warning light to any oppressive government and a statement they are ready to do their duty if need be."[61]

Peters was not alone in interpreting federal gun control legislation responding to the 1989 Stockton killings as the first step in a state-run communist conspiracy. Within the various overlapping subcultures of gun enthusiasts, many gun owners read the Second Amendment as a sacred covenant. This countermemory champions the right to bear arms as enabling the colonists to beat the British and their descendants to defeat the Indians. Explains Gibson: "From this religious or mythological perspective, the semi-automatic combat rifle came to symbolize the entire American creation myth, and gun control in turn represented an abridgement of God's covenant by the forces of evil."[62] As Peters puts it,

> Our people have a law written on their hearts (Hebrews 8:10) which seems to tell them to hold on to their guns. . . . Not only are our public enemies trying to disarm the people, but you can nearly anticipate another public massacre (like in Stockton, California) which would enhance their effort. Almost as a natural reaction, groups of people are arousing and making countering moves. We report on this on page 26 of this newsletter and have reprinted an anonymous mailing recently sent to us. Isaiah 52:1–2 will happen.[63]

The anonymous mailing to which Peters refers came from the Patrick Henry cell of the Constitutional Militia of America. The "natural reaction" he celebrates is what we now know as the militia movement.[64]

Thus, even Peters, whose mode of leadership is primarily pastoral, speaks violence loud and proud. Even after the Oklahoma City bombing – or perhaps especially in light of the "ironical" way the bombing moved Christian Identity mainstream – Peters wears his identification with the radical right as proof of his authenticity. Echoing the popular country song that croons "I was country before country was cool," Peters proclaims, "I was Identity before Identity was cool."[65] His analogy casts the Christian right as the numerous cross-over country music artists who have appropriated country music for material gain, removing country from its roots and softening it beyond recognition.

It would be a mistake, however, to read nichemarketing at face value. After a decade interviewing white supremacists, psychologist Raphael Ezekiel describes leaders' deployment of violence as theater: a structure of feeling in which leaders perform "the almost-unspoken possibility . . . that makes the organization visible and that draws members." Ezekiel reads leaders' invocations of violence as command performances whose terms and limits are influenced by the constituents leaders seek to recruit, mobilize, and retain. Whereas most constituents have no wish either to go to jail for their beliefs or even to harm some nonwhite person, followers are attracted by the thrill implicit in the threat of violence, in being involved with "something serious." As a result, leaders must balance "giving members a sense that they are running a risk and making members fearful." Likewise, although both the proverbial loose cannon and the organized terrorist cell are disavowed by leaders, they provide "the vital infusion of *violence as possibility*" necessary for the movement's reputation and aura.[66] Hence Scott Appleby calls calculated ambiguity regarding violence "a hallmark of the discourse of religious extremists."[67]

As indicated by *Everything You Always Wanted to Know (and Preachers Were Afraid to Tell You) about Gun Control*, Peters is not averse to taking violence as his not quite unspoken subtext, akin to sex. This pamphlet champions militias. Yet in the same breath, Peters eschews offensive violence, containing militias within the mainstreaming philosophy of *Remnant Resolves* by representing armed citizens as "a caution and a warning light," a.k.a. deterrence. Likewise, in *The Bible: Handbook for Survivalists, Racists, Tax Protestors, Militants and Right-wing Extremists*, after citing biblical precedents for these practices, Peters qualifies: "It is not the purpose of this writing to promote or advocate violence, but rather to stir a Christian people to such a stance that none would dare provoke violence."[68]

At the same time that Peters eschews armed insurrection, he dreams of white Christian men who stand sufficiently tall and whose style is sufficiently militant to intimidate others, including federal authorities, into backing down for fear that physical violence will break out. This is a power fantasy: to be so threatening that one need not use force to get what one wants. It is also a fantasy about bearing the marks of a mystical destiny, made visible in race and gender, that compels others to submit. And it is above all a dream of an impossible kind of fullness. Peters projects an ideal body image whose boundaries coincide with those of the national body politic. On the one hand, this fullness is secured by a fantasy of God the Great Geneticist who writes his law on white hearts. On the other hand, this fullness is secured by a constitutionalist countermemory that reveres the gun as this Law's visible manifestation (much as Rambo's trademark knife bridges the gap between real men and Real men).

In keeping with this desire to have his cake and eat it too, Peters denounces violent confrontation with the government at the present time as foolish – both for the long-term survival of the movement and for Peters himself, who can be held legally responsible. Decrying the Oklahoma City bombing as instigated by the government to justify persecuting the Patriot movement, Peters established a litmus test: anyone who insists on waging offensive physical warfare is either a fool, he warns, or (more likely) an agent provocateur.[69] Such protestations are sincere. They are also, and equally, about maintaining multiple layers of deniability. And they are no less about keeping hope alive through a hard sell in which violence is the image that lures.

Precisely because violence functions as fantasy and lure, violence must also be held at bay – close, but not too close. When it comes to violence, white supremacist desire, precisely because it is desire, insists on having it both ways: identifying with violence as a fantasized possibility that is perpetually deferred precisely so that members can keep on desiring.[70]

Like desire, mainstreaming is paradoxical. The Oklahoma City bombing mainstreamed Christian Identity in ways *Remnant Resolves* did not. And Peters's efforts to mainstream Christian Identity while moving the mainstream right move Peters as well. For if mainstreaming works by rearticulating cultural vectors – the racism at the heart of Christian Constitutionalism, the apocalyptic masculinity engendered by the paramilitary romance – then the cultural vectors that Peters strives to respin can also move him to places he did not intend to go.

An End to Mainstreaming: Forget Our American Forefathers!

In 1988, when Pete and Cheri Peters returned home from the summer Bible Camp at which SFA wrote *Remnant Resolves*, the nearby university town of Fort Collins, Colorado, was embroiled in controversy. The Town Council was considering an ordinance banning discrimination against gays and lesbians in housing and employment. After holding hearings that drew about 350 people, the Council put the ordinance to popular vote in the upcoming November election.[71]

Representing himself to the press as just another "conservative minister" (in the words of the *Denver Post*), Peters denounced the ordinance in several radio sermons, which he advertised in local papers: "Will Fort Collins Become the Choice City for Sexual Perverts? Should Christians Ever Obey Such an Ordinance? Should society consider sodomy, which is called a crime against nature in common law, a class one felony? Tune in this Sunday and next!"[72]

Peters even hosted Dobson associate Rev. David Noebel from Colorado Springs, whom Peters billed as having "the courage to speak out" with "shocking facts" about "the other side of the so-called alternate life style called homosexuality."[73] A John Bircher until 1987, Noebel's commitment to antigay politics stems from his work with Billy Hargis, head of the Anti-Communist Crusade. In 1965 Hargis appointed Noebel head of The Summit, a summer school in Manitou Springs, Colorado, that prepares teens to resist the communist forces (allegedly) dominating colleges and pop culture.[74] In 1974 it was discovered that Hargis had had sexual relations with students, including several men. Three years later, Noebel published *The Homosexual Revolution*, which he dedicated to Anita Bryant in praise of her antigay campaign in Florida. Adopting the stance of male protector, Noebel proclaimed it time for "Christian leadership" to speak out lest people wonder why a woman and mother was heading this battle.[75] Throughout the book Noebel constructs his authority by portraying himself as a "veteran" who has seen "the horrors of youth seduction by expert male homosexuals, who skillfully initiate their victims into a world of absolute vileness and degradation."[76] Noebel's "veteran-ness" was crucial in the formation of Colorado for Family Values (the group that successfully sponsored Amendment 2, the statewide ballot initiative that prohibited including sexual orientation in antidiscrimination legislation), which developed out of a meeting of Noebel, Tony Marco, and Kevin Tebedo in the basement of Pulpit Rock Church in Colorado Springs when Noebel was guest teaching a Sunday school class.[77]

Claiming that homosexuality is "fast becoming America's number 1 social issue," *The Homosexual Revolution* warns, "Overnight, homosexuality has mushroomed into a menacing abomination. Sodomites by the millions have come out of the closet – defiant, militant, organized – clamoring for 'rights' and respectability." Noebel encloses the word rights in quotes, for "in fact, homosexuals want not simply equal treatment before the law, but, rather, preferred treatment. Not only do they want to enjoy their lifestyles privately, but also they want to demonstrate those same deviant lifestyles publicly." Noebel's fear of flaunting demonstrates that the issue at stake in distinguishing "special" from civil rights is not the actual existence of gay people but our social existence: who gets to give us a name, who must feel shame.[78]

As indicated by his dedication, title, and "veteran" identification, Noebel's organizing narrative is the paramilitary romance. Consider his chapter "The Politics of Homosexuality," whose epigraph observes that "homosexuality is an affliction the KGB delights to discover." Noebel's object lesson is Great Britain, which, after WWI, experienced a "culture of rebellion" that openly accepted homosexuality. As a result (Noebel claims), when England was first confronted with Hitler, the nation adopted a posture of appeasement. Citing Carter's pledge during his presidential campaign to separate his personal religious beliefs against homosexuality from his political life, Noebel warns that the United States after Vietnam

> . . . stands before the Communist enemy much like England stood before the Nazi enemy. If we make homosexuality as respectable as England did in the twenties and thirties, we surely will be swept away with the previous nations of the world who believed they could defile the laws of God.
>
> The hour is late. We must publicly and privately stand for spiritual and moral values as revealed by God in the Bible and stand resolutely against the homosexual revolution or we, too, will die.[79]

Drawing on the antigay campaigns of the McCarthy era, Noebel represents homosexuality as "a kind of national death wish" that seeks to "change the natural order created by God Himself."[80] Thus Noebel (and, as I shall soon show, Peters as well) casts homosexuality as a rejection of God's Law on a bodily level. Noebel reads this physical rejection as the outward sign of an inner rejection of God's grace (a satanic sacrament, if you will). Such spiritual death is national in scope, for not only is the body the Temple of the Holy Spirit, but the nation, too, is God's holy Temple. Behind the open acceptance of homosexuality, then, Noebel sees a communist plot designed to take over the nation from within (or behind) by separating church from state. This theocratic countermemory uses popular prejudices regarding homosexuality to link people into a theocratic populism. Its populism, however, derives not from a commitment to democracy but from a fusion of anticommunism with a particular way of imagining the body. This fusion engenders presumptions of a God-given natural law, which Noebel converts into the political necessity of fusing God's Law with the law of the land – "or we, too, will die."[81]

The power of this threat is not literal but imaginary. In our society, homosexuality does mark destruction – not of the national body politic but of the imagined body through which one acquires intelligibility and social existence: "I will be destroyed if I love in that way."[82] A child enters into "the family" by undergoing prohibitions: one identifies with whites, not blacks; one is male, not female, and thus desires women, not men. Writes Judith Butler:

> Becoming a "man" within this logic requires repudiating femininity as a precondition of the heterosexualization of desire and its fundamental ambivalence. If a man becomes heterosexual by repudiating the feminine, where could that repudiation live except in an identification which his heterosexual career seeks to deny? Indeed, the desire for the feminine is marked by that repudiation: he wants the woman he would never be. He wouldn't be caught dead being her: therefore he wants her. She is his repudiated identification (a repudiation he sustains as at once identification and the object of his desire). One of the most anxious aims of his desire will be to elaborate the difference between him and her, and he will seek to discover and install proof of that difference. . . . That refusal to desire, that sacrifice of desire under the force of prohibition, will incorporate homosexuality as an identification with masculinity. But this masculinity will be haunted by the love it cannot grieve.[83]

Hence the paramilitary identification of the new war hero, who must prove/perform his masculinity repeatedly by repudiating those loves the culture cannot grieve. As Linda Kintz observes, "Metaphorically, an apocalyptic national crisis is often figured in terms that suggest sodomy, in which the enemy sneaks up from behind or attempts to penetrate the hero's armored safety. . . . The hero must thus always fight on two fronts, against both the enemy and the establishment. In this world, liberalism is heavily coded as a sign not only of duplicity and moral corruption but of cowardice and character defects as well."[84]

Drawing on mainstream stereotypes of gays and lesbians as narcissistic and immature, this way of imagining the body casts homosexuality as the very epitome of sin or hubris: the glorification of "I want" in defiance of God's creation order. As Peters puts it in "Sodomites Seduce City Council": "Who said they were worthy of death? God. Turn to Leviticus 20:13 if you don't believe me. . . . God is setting up laws for society [that] are perfect and just. . . . We come along [saying], 'We've found a better solution, God. We don't know why you were so hard and so unjust.' . . . We've got this false theology that says we've got a better way to deal with this: pass an ordinance that says we can't discriminate. I think Leviticus 20:13 is pretty discriminatory. So sit back Christians and do nothing. The next time they will outlaw Leviticus 20:13. . . . They will keep going until they destroy every vestige of Christian values."[85] To keep chaos at bay and shore up physical and national defenses, Real men must submit to no one – except that large hand, surrounded by light, that descends from the heavens holding a scroll: *Remnant Resolves*. Through this projected male body/ego, the assertion of "male headship" is converted into an experience of submission.

Peters follows this championing of a literal reading of Leviticus 20, his brand name, by quoting Christian Reconstructionist Rousas Rushdoony to the effect that the state, while professing neutrality to religion, has established a new religion: secular humanism. He warns, "Any revival of Christian strength will thus precipitate major conflict because it will threaten the humanist establishment." For Peters, God's law constitutes a sort of genetic tinder, encoded on the hearts of white Christians, so that all one needs is a catalyzing spark and men will be Real men once again. A side of Peters welcomes this threat:

> I pray that they [the Town Council] recognize the seriousness of the decision that lies before them. This puts the Christian who believes in protecting the Christian lifestyle called the Way in the position of being criminal. It will eventually, and I'm not advocating this, but I'm gonna tell you what happens, if men keep passing laws like this it will eventually lead to death. . . . Eventually some man is gonna follow the law that is written on his heart and there's already some of them out there. Not necessarily in the churches – the churches run 'em off – they're in the bars. But they know what the just punishment is for homosexuality. And if one of these days a homosexual is going to try to recruit one of their kids they're gonna stand up for the laws of God.[86]

Arguing in large part against the cold war, Edward Steichen's 1950s photo exhibit *The Family of Man* captioned a series of pictures depicting heterosexual couples from around the globe with the phrase "We two make a multitude." In the hands of Noebel and Peters, this hope becomes a fear. Gays and lesbians cannot reproduce so they must recruit – your children.[87] This bodily imaginary sanctions prejudice as the "natural" instinct to protect one's children.

In contrast to Peters's overt championing of the violence of Leviticus 20, Noebel explicitly disclaims any hatred of, or desire to discriminate against, gays and lesbians.[88] Yet identifying homosexuality as the epitome of sin underlies both his claim to "love the sinner but hate the sin" as well as his selection of homosexuality from a biblical list of sins as the sin most worthy of censure. Formed within the 1950s anticommunist Old Right, Noebel warns, "Not only will homosexuality characterize the end-time as it characterized the end-time of Sodom, but the anti-Christ himself could well be a homosexual. . . . Is it any wonder that some people already are writing about an international coterie of homosexual activity vying for political power?"[89]

Likewise, in its Amendment 2 campaign, Colorado for Family Values (CFV) sought to distance itself from the overt hatred of leaders like Peters. The group sponsored a "No Room for Hatred" campaign with the motto "Rather than scorn: hope for homosexuals" and ads offering referral to DoveTail, an ex-gay ministry.[90] The group also sponsored campaign ads featuring people of color claiming: "Sexual orientation is not an underprivileged class needing protection. It is a powerful special interest group" and "A 'Yes' vote on Amendment Two will maintain the integrity of true minority protections by not allowing sexual orientation protected status." These ads affirmed the racism implicit in identifying civil rights as "special help" given to those who, in the words of Tony Marco, "need an extra leg up" while simultaneously positioning the Right in the position of the protector.[91]

In the election action seminar and kit that CFV marketed to groups interested in installing similar antigay amendments in their state constitutions, CFV Communications Specialist Mark Olsen argued that the uniqueness of "The CFV Philosophical Model" consists in the way it deliberately transvalued "the D word," as when people say it is good to be a discriminating shopper. According to Olsen, "When I say to discriminate is to choose, and just because some people choose on the wrong basis doesn't mean you take away all rights to choose, heads nod. People understand that. Yes the word discrimination has some really ugly baggage [unintelligible] into it from the civil rights fights of the 1960s, but it's not permanent."[92] Olsen tells the story of Bob Smith, who "loved to tell jokes about homosexuality. He got a good gut laugh out of it. He understood there was something abnormal. But he was adamantly opposed to Amendment 2 as homophobic and wrong to discriminate. He's got something in his gut and something down here in his heart about how a person's supposed to vote, but there's no communication in between. It's a no-man's land, created by our opposition." Drawing on C. S. Lewis, Olsen argues that Bob Smith has become "a man without a chest." The special rights rhetoric of CFV, however, "built a bridge, a lifeline, over that no-man's land. I think this is where swing voters are at. They know something is wrong with homosexuality in their gut but they don't think they can vote for it [Amendment 2]." Olsen notes a similar "syndrome" regarding abortion: people whose religious beliefs oppose abortion feel they have no right to impose purely personal dogma on others. Rebuts Olsen:

> But revulsion to homosexuality is something the Holy Spirit put there and very little amount of political rhetoric [on the part of gay rights advocates] is going to change that. . . . People *want* to support us. . . . But they won't on the basis of morality and revulsion alone in today's climate with the kind of rhetoric that is being aimed at us by the opposition. It's a very important part of American and especially the Western ethic: "I don't agree with you, but I don't want society to mistreat you." That's what homosexuals have played on. People don't like homosexuality, but it's wrong to discriminate. The fallacy in there is unaddressed: the issue of discrimination. We need to tell people that opposing militant homosexuality is the height of fairness. It prevents mistreatment. . . . We didn't omit moral objections and revulsions – we gave people a way to access all of them. . . . You can take a really inflammatory and provocative fact and you won't lose those elements but you'll gain a lot more if you put it in context and document that fact. . . . There are some facts that we presented that do make people want to hate. They make people want to pick up a gun. The fact is, we said: Facts don't hate, they just are. . . . Our campaign did go into the emotional, the visceral, people's gut level feelings about homosexuality. But by placing them in a common sense, rational context, we told the voters it was OK to consider them in their voting discussions.

Added Will Perkins: "This approach gave people hard-nose, real life objective reasons for voting how they felt."[93]

Olsen dramatizes these "real-life reasons" in his "docu-novel" *Refuge*, which narrates the paramilitary romance in an antigay key. *Refuge* tells the story of Vern Yates, a software specialist with a "hip Christian aesthetic," who opposed Amendment 2 as discriminatory only to lose his family to a liberal government gone out of control. Vern finds himself in an America at the beck and call of militant gay activists whose calls for "tolerance" and "equal rights" mask an aggressive plan to smash "the strangle-hold of Judeo-Christian dogma" by convincing social services to take conservative children from their parents (saving them from homophobic indoctrination) and forcing its true believers into hiding in the Colorado mountains, where they are tracked by an HIV-positive butch dyke named Sonya. Olsen concludes his antigay apocalypse with this warning: "To those of us following these trends, the picture of America shown by *Refuge* seems entirely possible – if her citizens don't stand up and contend for their rights. . . . So, please get involved. Let's keep this book a work of fiction. Let's keep it from becoming an awful prophecy of life to come in America."[94]

Seen in terms of a bodily imaginary in which gays and lesbians reject God's most basic law of procreation, antigay politics can function as a bridge between the theocratic Right (be it Christian Identity or Christian Reconstructionism) and sections of the Right that eschew the antidemocratic sentiments implicit in theocracy (although, as we shall soon see, this bridge is neither logically necessary nor sociologically automatic.) What makes this bridge possible is the Christian Constitutionalist identification of Christianity as the sole source of this nation's health, strength, and success. The Right engenders credibility for the Christian Constitutionalist identification of Christianity as the source of the nation's strength and success by articulating its ideological claims of supremacy "in those places where things are felt before they are thought or believed," in people's most intimate memories of familiarity and familiality – fused as these memories often are with biblical memories and images, whose cadences and possibilities articulate with unspeakable hopes and fears.[95] From a fantasy about sexuality and the body, to the Christian Constitutionalist identification of Christianity as the sole source of the nation's health and strength, to theocracy: from the body, to the national body politic, to the Church as "the community of believers in which Christ lives after death" – thus does apocalypse fuse fears for children/the future into the paramilitary romance of men protecting their own by cleansing the national body.

Peters himself acknowledges using this issue to reinvigorate his ministry – both internally ("recharging his batteries" when he was feeling dry for sermon material) and externally (drawing public attention).[96] My sense is that Peters saw opposing the ordinance as a no-brainer, a mainstreaming opportunity for which he expected little opposition. In the short term, this was true: when the issue was put to popular vote, 56.8 percent of the votes cast opposed expanding antidiscrimination protections to include sexual orientation.[97]

During the campaign, Peters's church never filed as a political action committee, mostly (I believe) because Peters does not see himself as part of "the system." In response, the Colorado Attorney General sued the church for failure to file a contributions and expenditures report as required by the Colorado Campaign Reform Act.

When notified by the Larimer County Clerk of his election code violation, Peters asked: "As an ambassador of Jesus Christ, a Christian pastor and evangelist with Holy instructions to, among other things, proclaim the word of God, how and when did I and my labors as a Christian pastor fall under your jurisdiction?"[98] Working within the framework outlined in *Remnant Resolves*, he proclaimed: "When the LaPorte Church of Christ publicly opposed the sin of homosexuality and the promotion of that sin by the Fort Collins City Council, it was doing so out of the worship of Christ." Hence he refused to hire a lawyer, claiming Jesus Christ was the church's lawyer: "When the Pastor of the LaPorte Church of Christ appears in court he has done so in the presence of two or three Christian witnesses[;] thus Jesus Christ, the church's counselor is present and Christ through His spirit has and will give counsel."[99] In a move that proved controversial in the Christian Patriot movement, Peters decided to "just stand on the word of God" in his legal briefs.[100] Working within the fundamentalist hermeneutic of constitutionalism, Peters invoked Public Law 97–280, in which Congress declared 1983 "The Year of the Bible," claiming that this declaration put the government on record acknowledging the Bible as law.[101]

Thus, in his court briefs, Peters represented himself as simply quoting the government back to itself. Drawing on the common (although false) interpretation of the Founding Fathers as suspicious of strong government, Peters argued that insofar as the court was originally established "to serve as a check and balance" on state power, the court must "instruct the state to let the church be."[102] Instead, the court sided with the state, and in May 1993, after the fine had exceeded $10,000, the state seized the church and auctioned its contents.[103]

Peters's response can be read as a classic case of the authoritarian personality, but his stubborn insistence can also be read as image creation: Peters's version of Coke's contour bottle "recognizable the world over without trace of brand identification."[104] Indeed, representing his court battle as an issue of religious liberty enabled him to cross over into media networks of the Christian right. James Kennedy's *The Coral Ridge Hour* featured Peters on a show entitled "Taking Liberties: The Betrayal of Our Heritage," which concluded its account of Peters's court battle with these words: "What has happened to the LaPorte Church of Christ is not an isolated incident. Indeed, there is a concerted effort to strip away our religious liberties in this country. . . . Today in America liberty for Christians is at risk." The program's only reference to Peters's white supremacist beliefs was indecipherable: "Although many Christians would disagree with some aspects of Pastor Peters's theology [which remained unspecified], most would agree with his resolve to stand for his faith."[105]

A similar silence surrounded Peters's appearance on *Keystone On the Line*, a cable TV talk show on the evangelical Keystone Inspirational Network. The program's host introduced Peters as "this fantastic man who stood up in this day and age," noting later that, "If there was ever someone who was speaking out in these last days, Pete, it is certainly you. And I believe we need more John Bunyans just like you."[106] This guest appearance launched Peters's own cable TV show on the evangelical network, called *Truth for the Times*.

Moreover, image creation is not just for others. Faced with defeat, rather than abandoning his ultimate concern and acknowledging that God's genetic law never gets sparked as it should, Peters turns "aggression toward the ideal and its unfulfill-ability . . . inward, and this self-aggression becomes the primary structure of conscience. . . . Oddly, the psyche's moralism appears to be an index of its own thwarted grief and illegible rage."[107]

Thus, when the court denied his appeal on April 6, 1992, Peters upped his ante, writing a pamphlet whose cover proclaimed *Death Penalty for Homosexuals Is Prescribed in the Bible*. He told reporters that the fine had inspired him to counterattack the gay and lesbian community.[108] His pamphlet also attacked Amendment 2, which was up for statewide vote the following fall. The pamphlet denounces "lukewarm, cowardly, goody goody, praise the Lord, Judeo-Christians" for campaigning against special rights for gays and lesbians while supporting civil rights: "Now the historical record shows, forty years ago, the family values in America would never allow homosexuals to have free speech, free assembly, safety, etc., and thus, the homosexual was afraid to come out of the closet. Now lukewarm Judeo-Christians consider it family values to allow them to do so. Such values are not Bible values, for the Bible allows those who continue in the sin of homosexuality, no such rights."[109] In contrast, Peters insists, "*Law by its Very Nature is Intolerant and Discriminatory*" insofar as lawbreakers suffer the consequences of their actions: "This is particularly true concerning the subject of homosexuality where young people are led to believe they can make up their own law, that is, choose their own sexual preference. They are not being told that there is the existing Law of their Creator, God, that is not to be disobeyed without grave consequences" (*Death Penalty*, 3; emphasis in original).

Like Noebel, Peters means "grave" literally. Citing research from Paul Cameron's (discredited) Family Research Institute, Peters notes that homosexuality brings disease, serial murders, and "the death of the family name or lineage" (*Death Penalty*, 8).[110] "Yet, homosexuals do not mind promoting their lifestyle, which is, in reality, to promote the death penalty" (7). Framed through the paramilitary romance, homosexuality means their death or yours: "After all, the Bible says not only is the homosexual worthy of the death penalty, but also those who give approval to it [homosexuality]" (8). Lest God's people also be judged worthy of death, the nation must be cleansed: "When the people of the land repent, they demand that just that be done [that the nation be cleansed], revival takes place, and consequently a healing of the land" (9).

As in *Remnant Resolves*, quoting 2 Chronicles 7:14 is a way to trump the Christian right. Peters proposes a counteramendment – no lukewarm Amendment 2 but "the real thing." Noting that twenty-five states already have sodomy laws, Peters urges Christians to campaign "state by state (as the homosexuals have done)" for a law that would make the death penalty mandatory for gays and lesbians (*Death Penalty*, 7). He frames his proposal as a prophetic ultimatum: "History shows, however, that it is just a matter of time before courageous men rise up and do what unrighteous government refuses to do. . . . There will be far less death and suffering if society simply enforces Sodomy Criminal laws in every state in the union according to His righteous, existing Law. The facts of this writing show it can and should be done. Pray Christians take the initiative and do so lest a worst judgement of death befalls us as a nation" (25).

Although the plot of this fantasy is familiar (thus did Peters conclude *Remnant Resolves* and respond to the assault rifle ban), something crucial has changed. Before his court battle, Peters tempered representations of violence with the belief that Christian men can performatively invoke the kingdom by catalyzing the law written genetically on the hearts of the white race and recorded in its Constitution. Thus, although Peters had recommended this same counteramendment in 1988 while opposing the Fort Collins ordinance, at that time he tempered talk of the death penalty with qualifiers: "I don't believe in vigilantism."[111] Likewise, when Christian Identity adherents in Shelby, North Carolina, were accused of killing five gay men in 1987 to "avenge Yahweh on homosexuals," Peters testified in court that the adherents' Christian Identity beliefs, far from indicating motivation for the crime, actually proved their innocence. He reasoned that Christian Identity teaches that the execution of gays and lesbians must come not from vigilantes, but from the government. When God's law is enforced by vigilantes it is delegitimated.[112] Obviously, one cannot take such statements at face value. But neither am I willing to dismiss them as hypocrisy or expediency. Peters believed that if he sparked the divine law genetically encoded on white hearts and established in the Constitution, God's kingdom would come.

In Peters's 1992 death penalty pamphlet, disclaimers and rejections of vigilante action disappear. Disillusioned regarding the possibility of speaking to the state's "true nature," he shifts from advocating civic intolerance (the use of legal force or legitimate violence against "outsiders") to permitting violent intolerance (the use of illegal force against the "outsider").[113] Peters still hedges his talk of executing gays and lesbians with prayer that Christians take legal initiatives. Committed to long-term white supremacist organizing, he is not about to become Order founder Robert Mathews. Instead, he reimagines the connection between the human and the divine: the Constitution no longer does the trick.

As indicated by its dedication, the primary target of Peters's *Death Penalty* pamphlet is former Green Beret and Rambo model Bo Gritz, who in 1992 was running for president on the Populist Party ticket.[114] When speaking to Christian Identity ministers during his campaign, Gritz refused to endorse capital punishment for gays and lesbians.[115] In *Death Penalty*, Peters accuses Gritz of blasphemy for claiming to stand on God's Law as the source of the nation's strength while affirming the "live and let live" individualism that is such a common point of Western regional identification.[116] Peters's denunciation of Gritz was divisive, something he did not do lightly. His usual mode of operation, although something at which he has had little success, is to try to bring the fragmentary and fractious Right together.[117] Not this time. Arguing against Gritz, however, also pushed Peters to rethink his own commitment to Christian Constitutionalism:

> Earlier I spoke of an individual who was running for high office. That individual took the position that although he did not agree with homosexuality, he felt that if two people were consenting adults, then this is America, and they have a right of choice. Does that sound familiar? He is not alone. That is the type of thinking that is prevalent today. . . . In this country, we do not call it Baalism, we call it Constitutionalism. . . . We have forsaken the commandments of the Lord, and we have followed the Baals, but we do not see ourselves as Baal worshippers. We see ourselves as tolerant, Constitutionalists, Christians and conservatives. Those Constitutionalists who take this position consider themselves Christians

who are upholding Christian values. What have they *really* done? They have simply repeated the actions of their forefathers in the wilderness.[118]

The wilderness in question is not the North American West, but the wilderness of the Dead Sea into which the biblical Hebrews escaped from slavery to worship their god. Here Peters rereads that moment on which "The Greatest Love Story Never Told" turned: at the foot of Mount Sinai, just when Moses is pledging the nation's troth to keep God's covenant, the people ask Aaron to make a golden calf (which symbolized the Canaanite god Baal). Comments Peters: "They were not worshipping the calf any more than we worship the donkey or the elephant that represents our political parties" (*Baal*, 53). Likewise, when the white race came to America, they fought to be free, thanked God – and then held a Convention that replaced God's law with the rule of the people and erected another golden calf: the Constitution.

Peters includes himself in his indictment: "Since the time of the Constitutional Convention, we have had preacher after preacher, and I am one of them, who has said that the framers of this Constitution were men of God, Christian men" (*Baal*, 69). Now, however, he denounces the invented traditions of Christian Constitutionalism as just that: invented. The Constitution, he charges, does not mention Christ or God's Word; it allows for homosexuality, abortion, usury, and people of other races to rule over whites. Hinting at distinctions between First- and Fourteenth-Amendment citizens, Peters asks: *"Have you ever known a sacred or divinely inspired document that needed to be amended?* . . . If we return to some of the moorings that our American forefathers gave us, we have gained nothing. I say, let us take the initiative now. Let us go forward and surpass those men. They were good men, but there is nothing in the Scriptures that says we cannot be better men. Forget our American forefathers" (73, 69; emphasis added).

Whereas Peters went to DC with *Remnant Resolves* delighting in the power of his performance as a man giving warning, now he denounces this mainstreaming strategy as idolatry. Catherine Wessinger analyzes Christian Constitutionalists as practicing a kind of magic that seeks to "appropriate the enemy's power by imitating their actions and their use of words possessing power."[119] Whereas Peters once trusted the courts, as guardians of the divinely ordained Constitution, to protect him, when his court briefs fail to produce the desired result, he concludes – not that God's law is not written genetically on the hearts of the white race – but that the state is a myth whose power is created by people in their imaginations, when really "it is like the Wizard of Oz, they are just pudgy little men, and who should be afraid of whom?" (*Baal*, 3).

Peters's battle with the state of Colorado illustrates the self-fulfilling prophecy that haunts apocalyptic movements. This includes millennial movements that eschew violent confrontation, for even disengagement can lead to conflict. Indeed, given "the complex network of laws and regulations that governs a modern society, whether in regulation of firearms, tax payments, or the treatment of children [much less election laws]," Barkun contends that such conflicts are inevitable.[120] Peters's reflections seem to agree with Barkun's assessment, although he draws different conclusions. Said theoretically, Peters concludes that his fight is with the specifically modern form of power that accompanied the rise of the nation-state: biopower. As Peters puts it:

Baal is regarded as "owner." Have you ever thought about the idea that someone owns you? Does the company store or the corporation you work for own you? . . . As for me, I belong to God and it bothers me that some state god has decided that I am one of his resources. . . . *We did not recognize at the time that was a religious battle we were fighting. Our battle against the creeping takeover of socialism, and their use of subsidies, grants, tax exemptions, Social Security, public (government) schools, welfare, all loosely termed the New Deal and now the New World Order, is a religious battle"* (*Baal*, 22–3; emphasis added).

Having long derided the Christian right for mistaking "the powers, principalities and world-forces of this present darkness" as *spiritual* Satans, Peters emerges from his battle with the state deriding Christian Constitutionalists and militias for waging a *political* battle. Thus does Peters claim the other side of his brand name.

Certainly, Peters has always insisted that those who fight only for the Constitution fight in vain. For example, in the SFA newsletter promoting the then-emergent phenomenon of militias, Peters prefaced his reprint of a flier from the Constitutional Militia with the following reminder: "Note: It has no appeals to Jesus Christ, the source of all liberty, truth and freedom."[121] Yet, whereas before, Peters appended notes, after his court battle, which he credits with "helping me focus on the issue of submission," he avows, "I have been guilty of thinking that before we tear something down, we should find a replacement. It is like telling God we will go through the Red Sea, but not until He tells us where to find food on the other side. . . . Someone will say, 'Well, if we do not have the Constitution, what can we do?' Let us go forward and find out. Maybe God has it all under control after all, and if we just begin doing our part, that kingdom will emerge" (*Baal*, 18, 63, 79).

Whereas Dan Gayman responded to the federal crackdown on the supremacist constellation in the early 1980s by urging followers to submit to authority, Peters cites the vision of the biblical book Daniel, in which a stone crushes a statue that represents state power. "What happens when you make that choice for God?" Peters asks. "The Kingdom begins to come into existence, and it begins to crush the Baals. The Kingdom is that stone that is cut out of the mountain without hands. That stone is being cut by those who refuse to be ruled over by tyrants and those who call out for their King. Let us choose Him as our King, as our Lawgiver and as our Judge, and He will save us" (*Baal*, 117). As Peters puts it, just as people told the Wright brothers "Man can't fly," so people say "You can't see the Kingdom now." Oh, yes, we can, Peters avows. If Israel had a Kingdom before, Israel can have a Kingdom again – if she dares to renew and cleanse herself. Even if you don't completely believe, Peters promises, if you begin to comprehend that the Kingdom is now, "then in one or two generations our children will see the streets of gold in that great City." For when I deny "His presence and His reigning right here and now. . . I have denied the Kingdom to my children" (158–9).

Peters gives up on mainstreaming as performatively invoking the Kingdom. Much of that strategy seems to have been about enjoyment: projecting a body image, standing tall, stepping into the impossible fullness of a body image that is projected outward into a world. Mainstreaming for Peters was about putting your body on the line and acquiring the fullness of self that you know you really are.

Peters loses that. But he doesn't give up on his belief. Nor does he grieve. Instead, he redoubles his belief in God's Law by internalizing it, thereby keeping his desire alive through fabricating an interior world. Having lost the Constitution as the link between humans and the divine, Peters still dreams of being the spark that re-fuses – only now, the stage on which he seeks to performatively invoke God's kingdom is first and foremost spiritual: an even more radical version of human belief, shorn of this-worldly supports. In place of the fullness of performing one's masculine body as identical with the national body, Peters offers a future body: the children. This new understanding of spiritual warfare heightens the tension between fantasy and reality, rather than lessening it.

When this chapter began I noted that one thing religion does is help people negotiate the gap between ideals, the way the world ought to be, and reality, the accidental, happenstance, and uncontrollable way the world is. Although religion can be hyped in ways that facilitate an active refusal to acknowledge the existence of its own phantoms, it can also be used to confront precisely those problems that are so structurally deep and collectively embedded that they defy any attempt at a quick fix. Much depends on how power is imagined.

Peters's career as a Christian Identity leader illustrates the ambivalence of the desire for the sacred. Religion can facilitate catharsis by articulating losses and failures into a structure of disavowal that resolutely forgets its failures and disowns the violence at its origin. Yet religion can also empower people to confront these losses and failures in the hope of transvaluing conditions of absolute impossibility into conditions for possible action. The key to such a transvaluation is developing the willingness to remember and actively avow the loss and violence that runs through memories and histories.

Notes

1. Jeffrey Kaplan, "Christian Identity," in *Encyclopedia of White Power*, ed. Jeffrey Kaplan (Lanham, MD: Rowman and Littlefield, 2000), 53, and *Radical Religion in America* (Syracuse: Syracuse University Press, 1997), 54.

2. Philip Lamy, "Secularizing the Millennium," in *Millennium, Messiahs, and Mayhem*, ed. Thomas Robbins and Susan Palmer (New York: Routledge, 1997), 93–117. This gap between the real and the "really" real is why religion is so frequently involved with violence, an involvement that even the most militant believers in nonviolence do not escape. Writes historian R. Scott Appleby: "Both the extremist and the peacemaker are militants. Both types go to extremes of self-sacrifice in devotion to the sacred. . . . In these ways they distinguish themselves from people not motivated by religious commitments – and the vast middle ground of believers". *The Ambivalence of the Sacred* (Lanham, MD: Rowman and Littlefield, 2000), 11.

3. Elizabeth Grosz, *Jacques Lacan: A Feminist Introduction* (New York: Routledge, 1990), 64–7.

4. Jeffrey Kaplan, "The Context of American Millenarian Revolutionary Theology," *Terrorism and Political Violence* 5, no. 1 (spring 1993): 54.

5. SFA, *Remnant Resolves* (LaPorte, CO: SFA, 1989), 1–3; hereafter cited in text as *RR*.

6. The text is Romans 13: "Every person must submit to the supreme authorities. There is no authority but by act of God, and the existing authorities are constituted by him; consequently anyone who rebels against authority is resisting a divine institution, and those who so resist have only themselves to thank for the punishment they receive."

7. Pete Peters, *Authority: Resistance or Obedience? The Door to the Kingdom* (LaPorte, CO: SFA, n.d.), 8.

8. See Jeffrey Kaplan's analysis of Dan Gayman, head of the Church of Israel in Schell City, Missouri, in "The Context of American Millenarian Revolutionary Theology," 53–4, and *Radical Religion in America*, 56–7.

9. Pete Peters, *Sedition and the Old Time Religion* (LaPorte, CO: SFA, n.d.), 19; distributed in pamphlet form with SFA's March 1988 newsletter.

10. Peters's more "radical" message has attracted followers of Dan Gayman who are frustrated by Gayman's increasing withdrawal in the name of Romans 13. See Jeffrey Kaplan and Leonard Weinberg, *The Emergence of a Euro-American Radical Right* (New Brunswick, NJ: Rutgers University Press, 1998), 140.

11. Sadik Al-Azm, "Islamic Fundamentalism Reconsidered: A Critical Outline, Part II," *South Asia Bulletin* 14, no. 1 (1994): 95; Michael Barkun, *Religion and the Racist Right* (Chapel Hill: University of North Carolina Press, 1994), 284–7.

12. Jeffrey Hadden and Anthony Schupe, *Televangelism* (New York: Holt, 1988), 65.

13. Ibid., citing Martin Marty, *Context* 17, no. 19 (1 November 1985): 1.

14. Ibid.

15. Pete Peters, newsletter, vol. 1, no. 2 (LaPorte, CO: SFA, 1988).

16. Write Kaplan and Weinberg: "Common law courts are pseudo-judicial bodies that issue bogus liens, arrest warrants and various fake judicial rulings. They are intended to harass real judges, county recorders, other public officials and private citizens who stand in the freemen's way in one fashion or another. . . . The most spectacular of these 'courts' was the Freemen/Justus Township in Jordan Montana, a ranch where some 2 dozen freemen claimed immunity to American law and held federal authorities at bay for over a month before surrendering" (*Euro-American Right*, 73, 72). For a brief review of events in Jordan, plus an excerpt from one of the teaching texts the Freemen used, see Ted Daniels, *A Doomsday Reader* (New York: New York University Press, 1999), 176–98. On the Freemen generally, see Catherine Wessinger, *How the Millennium Comes Violently* (Chappaqua, NY: Seven Bridges, 2000), 158–217.

17. Pete Peters, newsletter, vol. 3 (LaPorte, CO: SFA, 1989), 11–12.

18. SFA, *Our Forefathers' Resolves* (LaPorte, CO: SFA, n.d.), 1.

19. Norman Gottwald, *The Hebrew Bible* (Philadelphia: Fortress, 1985), 370.

20. Indeed, some biblical scholars argue that the Bible's account of the monarchic period is itself more pretext than text, a narrative told from the perspective of later political struggles that were retrojected into Israel's past. In this reading, talking about Assyria, the first Temple, and the monarchy are ways of talking about Persia, the second Temple, and the elite ambition to resist Persian imperial domination.

21. Homi Bhabha, ed., *Nation and Narration* (New York: Routledge, 1990).

22. Etienne Balibar, "The Nation Form: History and Ideology," in *Race, Nation, Class*, ed. Etienne Balibar and Immanuel Wallerstein, trans. Chris Turner (New York: Verso, 1991), 93, 95.

23. Peters, newsletter, vol. 3, 13.

24. Pete Peters, *Baal Worship* (LaPorte, CO: SFA, 1995), 23.

25. Peters, newsletter, vol. 3, 14.

26. Matthew Moen, *The Christian Right and Congress* (Tuscaloosa: University of Alabama Press, 1989), 37–8. This verse plays a key role in the National Day of Prayer headed by James Dobson's wife, Shirley.

27. Pete Peters, newsletter, vol. 2 (LaPorte, CO: SFA, 1992), 4.

28. Pete Peters, newsletter (LaPorte, CO: SFA, February 1988), 2.

29. Barton is Reconstructionism's most well-known popularizer. In September 1992, Dobson interviewed Barton on his radio show and sold his videotape arguing that separation of church and state is a myth disseminated by secular humanists. Dobson rebroadcast the Barton interview on 2 May 1996, the National Day of Prayer: Dobson, "Our Spiritual Heritage (Mr. David Barton)' CS 744/8923 (1992; Colorado Springs: FOF, 1996). Barton's books were highly influential for early versions of Focus on the Family's public policy seminars.

30. Pete Peters, "Never-Ending Last Days?" newsletter, vol. 3 (LaPorte, CO: SFA, 1995).

31. Pete Peters, "The Spirit of the Lord, Part II, Liberty in America," sermon cassette (LaPorte, CO: SFA, July 1993).

32. Michael Barkun, *Religion and the Racist Right*, rev. ed. (Chapel Hill: University of North Carolina Press, 1997), 281–4.

33. Alisa Solomon, "Nothing Special: The Specious Attack on Civil Rights," in *Dangerous Liaisons*, ed. Eric Brandt (New York: New Press, 1999), 65–6.

34. John Hope Franklin, "The Moral Legacy of the Founding Fathers," in *Race and History* (Baton Rouge: Louisiana State University Press, 1989), 159.

35. Toni Morrison, *Playing in the Dark* (Cambridge, MA: Harvard University Press, 1992), 6, xiii. Also see Gayatri Chakravorty Spivak, "Constitutions and Culture Studies," *Yale Journal of Law and Humanities* 2, no. 1 (winter 1990): 136; Robin Blackburn, *The Overthrow of Colonial Slavery* 1776–1848 (London: Verso, 1988), 123–4.

36. Roberto C. Goizueta, *The Coca-Cola Company* 1994 *Annual Report* (Atlanta: Coca-Cola Company, 1995), 17; available from The Coca-Cola Company, P.O. Drawer 1734, Atlanta, GA 30301.

37. Slavoj Žižek, "Eastern Europe's Republics of Gilead," in *Dimensions of Radical Democracy*, ed. Chantal Mouffe (New York: Verso, 1992), 200, 194–6.

38. Barkun, *Racist Right*, rev. ed., 290.

39. Ibid., 289–90.

40. Susan Douglas, *Listening In* (New York: Random House, 1999), 5.

41. Susan Jeffords, *The Remasculinization of America* (Bloomington: Indiana University Press, 1989).

42. Ibid., 44, referring to Richard Nixon, *No More Vietnams* (New York: Arbor House, 1985).

43. William Gibson, *Warrior Dreams* (New York: Hill and Wang, 1994), 7, 148, 236–40, and "Is the Apocalypse Coming? Paramilitary Culture after the Cold War," in *The Year 2000*, ed. Charles Strozier and Michael Flynn (New York: Free Press, 1997), 181–2.

44. Gibson, "Is the Apocalypse Coming?" 182.

45. Ibid., 180.

46. Gibson, *Warrior Dreams*, 57.

47. Ibid., 236–40.

48. David Savran, *Taking It Like a Man* (Princeton, NJ: Princeton University Press, 1998), 202, 5, 197–206. Savran sets the New War hero's reinvigoration of masculinity through victimization within a broader context that includes Robert Bly's followers searching for the Wild Man within as well as the spiritual male advancing toward the New Age. For

analysis of how these dynamics also limit the vision of Vietnam films whose message is antiwar, see Marita Sturken, *Tangled Memories* (Berkeley: University of California Press, 1997). For the argument that the legacy of rooting male bonding in the shared experience of oppression in South Asia eviscerates the vision of racial reconciliation offered by buddy films such as *Lethal Weapon* and *Grand Canyon*, reiterating racism in ways that work against interracial dialogue and encounter, see Hazel Carby, *Race Men* (Cambridge, MA: Harvard University Press, 1998), 170–83.

49. Louis Beam, "Vietnam: Bringing It on Home," in *Essays of a Klansman* (Hayden Lake, ID: AKIA, 1983), 35–41, cited in James Aho, *This Thing of Darkness* (Seattle: University of Washington Press, 1994), 191, n. 8.

50. James Ridgeway, *Blood in the Face* (New York: Thunder's Mouth, 1990), 87, 102. For an analysis of Beam's white supremacist involvement, see "Louis Beam," in Kaplan, *Encyclopedia of White Power*, 17–23. For a genealogy of Beam's notion of leaderless resistance, see Kaplan, "Leaderless Resistance," in *Encyclopedia of White Power*, 173–85.

51. Aho, *This Thing of Darkness*, 54–8, 60–5.

52. Gibson, *Warrior Dreams*, 160–1.

53. Ibid., 212–13.

54. Paul Boyer, *When Time Shall Be No More* (Cambridge, MA: Harvard University Press, 1992), 258–60.

55. James Dobson, newsletter (Colorado Springs: FOF, August 1993).

56. Peters, newsletter, vol. 3, 22. During the 1960s and 1970s, Gothard's seminars were the most popular source of family advice among fundamentalists. See Susan Harding, *The Book of Jerry Falwell* (Princeton, NJ: Princeton University Press, 2000), 171. At the time of the seminar Peters attended, Gothard was directing the Institute in Basic Youth Conflicts. According to *Christianity Today:* "Essentially, he uses Scriptures to teach that everyone is under authority, and that the chief authority, God, deals with people through various structures and channels of authority: family, church, business and government" ("Bill Gothard Steps Down During Institute Shakeup," *Christianity Today*, 8 August 1990, 46–7).

57. Peters, newsletter, vol. 3, 23. At SFA's next Family Bible Camp, Peters was filmed addressing biblical teachings on gun control. Individual campers were then filmed speaking directly to their congresspersons, asking them to listen to Peters's message because he represented their views. The constituent's personal message was spliced at the head of Peters's more general message, the constituent signed a letter to the congressperson, and the package was mailed to Washington. See Pete Peters, "Congressional Video Outreach," newsletter, vol. 4 (LaPorte, CO: SFA, 1989), 20.

58. Pete Peters, *Everything You Wanted to Know (and Preachers Were Afraid to Tell You) about Gun Control* (LaPorte, CO: SFA, n.d.), 20.

59. Pete Peters, *Strength of a Hero* (LaPorte, CO: SFA, December 1989), 2–3.

60. Appleby, *The Ambivalence of the Sacred*, 90.

61. Peters, *Everything You Wanted to Know*, 20.

62. Gibson, "Is the Apocalypse Coming?", 185.

63. Peters, newsletter, vol. 3, 2; Pete Peters, newsletter, vol. 2 (LaPorte, CO: SFA, 1990), 2. The theme verse of *America the Conquered*, Isaiah 52:1–2, promises that Israel will shake itself up from the dust and loose the chains around its neck: "It only takes a remnant . . . *for a strange phenomenon* exists in this end time captivity that has never existed before, NEVER HAVE SLAVES BEEN SO WELL ARMED": Peters, *America the Conquered* (1991; LaPorte, CO: SFA 1993), 214; emphasis in original.

64. The militia movement is usually dated several years after this newsletter, for the movement is typically understood as responding to Ruby Ridge (August 1992) and Waco (February 1993). Certainly, it was the latter events, occurring in the media eye, which led to a proliferation of citizen militias.

65. Pete Peters, "The Planting of Spirits: Introduction to 1996 Summer Bible Camp," sermon cassette 787 (LaPorte, CO: SFA, n.d.).

66. Raphael Ezekiel, *The Racist Mind* (New York: Viking, 1995), xxx, 62, xxxi.

67. Appleby, *The Ambivalence of the Sacred*, 94–5.

68. Pete Peters, *The Bible: Handbook for Survivalists, Racists, Tax Protestors, Militants and Right-wing Extremists* (LaPorte, CO: SFA, n.d.), 12.

69. Peters responded in the same way to The Order. Whereas he declared its rank and file innocent (except for charges of racketeering), he denounced Order leader Bob Mathews as a government operative who tricked his followers by claiming to be forming a revolutionary movement: Peters, newsletter (LaPorte, CO: SFA, December–January 1988), 3.

70. Jacqueline Rose, *Why War? Psychoanalysis, Politics and the Return to Melanie Klein* (Cambridge, England: Blackwell, 1993), 64.

71. Judy Harrington, "Gays in Fort Collins Back Anti-Discrimination Law," *Denver Post*, 8 June 1988, sec. B, p. 4; "Votes on Rights for Gays Likely in Fort Collins," *Denver Post*, 1 August 1988, sec. B, p. 5; "Fort Collins Voters to Decide Gay Rights Issue," *Denver Post*, 4 August 1988, sec. B, p. 5.

72. Pete Peters, newsletter, vol. 5 (LaPorte, CO: SFA, 1988), 4. "Opposition to the law was spearheaded by a conservative minister in nearby LaPorte, and the issue was fought largely in the city's churches": "Fort Collins Rights Law Losing," *Denver Post*, 9 November 1988, sec. GAA.

73. Exhibit 1 of *LaPorte Church of Christ's Brief to the Colorado Court of Appeals in "Meyer v. LaPorte Church of Christ,"* distributed with newsletter (LaPorte, CO: SFA, 1991), n.p.

74. Noebel's influence on Dobson has been quite direct.

75. David Noebel, *The Homosexual Revolution* (Tulsa, OK: American Christian College Press, 1977), 19. Noebel's response of male headship was mirrored by Cheri Peters after the Fort Collins campaign. Moved by the sight of her "sweet shy" teenage daughter speaking at a City Council meeting in contrast to the many outspoken lesbians in attendance, Cheri Peters concluded, "I want to propose to our City Council that we eliminate women from serving in a position God never intended for them to be in, and never allow anyone but a white Christian male to make decisions in our town!": Cheri Peters, newsletter, vol. 5 (LaPorte, CO: SFA, 1988), 24–5.

76. Noebel, *Homosexual Revolution*, 15.

77. William Martin, *With God on Our Side* (New York: Broadway Books, 1996), 345–8; Ward Harkavy "Original Sin," *Westword*, 8–14 September 1988, pp. 13–14, 16–28; Tom Morton "The Summit," *Colorado Springs Telegraph*, 1 July 1990, sec. F, pp. 1, 4–5. For a less abbreviated account of CFV's origins that gives greater room to the role initially played by women, see Stephen Bransford, *Gay Politics vs. Colorado and America: The Inside Story of Amendment Two* (Cascade, CO: Sardis, 1994), 12–27.

78. Noebel, *The Homosexual Revolution*, 36, 54–5, 26, 49.

79. Ibid., 118–19.

80. Ibid., 28, 143–56. For analysis of 1950s antigay campaigns, see Jennifer Terry, *An American Obsession* (Chicago: University of Chicago Press, 1999), 329–52.

81. Noebel, *The Homosexual Revolution*, 27–8.

82. Judith Butler, *The Psychic Life of Power* (Stanford: Stanford University Press, 1997), 27.

83. Ibid., 137–8.

84. Linda Kintz, *Between Jesus and the Market* (Durham, NC: Duke University Press, 1997), 247.

85. Peters, "Sodomites Seduce City Council," sermon cassette tape 280 (LaPorte, CO: SFA, n.d.). Also see Peters, *Baal Worship*, 136. For discussion of the association of homosexuality with narcissism more generally, see Kath Weston, *Families We Choose* (New York: Columbia University Press, 1991), 156.

86. Peters, "Sodomites Seduce City Council."

87. Noebel, *The Homosexual Revolution*, 63.

88. Ibid., 20.

89. Ibid., 134.

90. Within CFV, there was considerable debate about the degree of distance desirable. For an account of the controversy regarding this particular strategy, see John Gallagher and Chris Bull, *Perfect Enemies* (New York: Crown, 1996), 109–11; Michael Booth, "Amendment Two Architect Hits CFV for Tactics," *Denver Post*, 9 March 1993, sec. A, pp. 1, 10. DoveTail ministries was founded by Joyce Marco, wife of CFV cofounder Tony Marco; she has a lesbian daughter. Tony Marco claims to have left CFV due to the organization's willingness to use materials that defamed and degraded gays and lesbians (personal letter from Tony Marco to Tony Ogden, head of Equal Protection Only Coalition, 25 November 1991, in possession of the author).

91. CFV campaign materials in possession of the author.

92. CFV, model notebook, tape 6.

93. CFV, model notebook, tape 3. Likewise, in the special message delivered at this seminar by James Ryle, pastor of the Boulder Valley Vineyard Church, Ryle declared: "Satan was the original homosexual in that he was created for the express purpose of taking all the praise and worship of creation and giving it unto God through his incredible endowments. . . . Somewhere in there he took it [the worship of creation] and turned it onto himself and began making love to himself and he became in that act homosexual. That is why he takes the musicians, the artists, the craftsmen, the entertainers." Ryle goes on to dream of a world where creativity was not "perverted": "Can you imagine the music that would fill the air? Can you imagine the art that would adorn our houses? Can you imagine the movies that we would see? Can you imagine the books that we would read? Can you imagine the plays that would be put on, the unfolding drama of redemption?" (CFV, model notebook, tape 6).

94. Mark Olsen, *Refuge* (Cascade, CO: Sardis Press, 1996), 120, 165, 191.

95. Kintz, *Between Jesus and the Market*, 235.

96. Peters, "Sodomites Seduce City Council." The church is thought to have spent about $1,000 on the campaign: "LaPorte Church Ordeal with the Law Over," *Colorado Christian News*, June 1993, p. 4.

97. UPI, 9 November 1988, NEXIS, accessed 29 July 1993.

98. Exhibit 4 in *LaPorte Church of Christ's Brief* (booklet distributed by SFA in lieu of a newsletter, 1991), n.p. This booklet collects the various legal documents produced during this process.

99. Exhibit 7, *LaPorte Church of Christ's Brief*, n.p.

100. Peters, "Our TV Debut," cassette tape (LaPorte, CO: SFA, n.d.).

101. Peters, *LaPorte Church of Christ's Brief*, n.p.

102. Peters, Exhibit 10, *LaPorte Church of Christ's Brief*, n.p. Garry Wills argues against the myth that the Founding Fathers' distrust of strong central government led them to institute a government of "checks and balances" in *A Necessary Evil* (New York: Simon and Schuster, 1999), especially the chapters "Checking Efficiency" and "Co-equal Branches," 71–90.

103. "LaPorte Church Ordeal with Law Over," p. 4.

104. For this authoritarian personality reading, see Kaplan, *Radical Religion in America*, 7.

105. D. James Kennedy, "Taking Liberty: The Betrayal of Our Heritage," videotape in possession of the author.

106. Peters, "Our TV Debut."

107. Butler, *The Psychic Life of Power*, 142, 183.

108. Associated Press, "Gays See Pamphlet as Threat: Pastor Defends Flier as His Response to Fine," *Rocky Mountain News*, 6 May 1992, regional ed., local sec., p. 7, NEXIS, accessed 29 July 1993.

109. Pete Peters, *Intolerance of, Discrimination against, and the Death Penalty for Homosexuals Is Prescribed in the Bible* (LaPorte, CO: SFA, April 1992), iii–iv; hereafter cited in text as *Death Penalty*.

110. For Cameron, see Jean Hardisty, *Mobilizing Resentment* (Boston: Beacon, 1999), 102.

111. Peters recounts his first – failed – proposal in "Sodomites Seduce City Council." Arguing with the clergy coalition that if Christians continue fighting (as they usually do) in a defensive posture they will lose to homosexuals "step after step, city after city, state after state, child after child. We've got to start taking aggressive action with as much guts as they have." Peters tried to persuade them to propose a counterordinance – "I'm not taking about vigilante action, I don't believe in it" – according to which if a court of law found someone guilty of sodomy, that person would be treated as a murderer subject to a felony charge and execution if convicted. The clergy coalition did not bite.

112. North Carolinians Against Racist and Religious Violence [NCARRV], "White Patriots Indicted for Shelby Mass Murder," newsletter, vol. 7 (Durham: NCARRV, spring 1988), 1–4; Center for Democratic Renewal [CDR], update (Atlanta, GA: CDR, 29 May 1989).

113. Appleby, *The Ambivalence of the Sacred*, 15, quoting David Little, "Religious Militancy" in *Managing Global Chaos*, ed. Chester Crocker and Fen Hampson (Washington, DC: US Institute of Peace, 1996), 79–81.

114. Begun in 1984 by Willis Carto, head of the Liberty Lobby, the Populist Party sought to mainstream white supremacy through electoral campaigns (including running David Duke for president in 1988). See Sara Diamond, *Roads to Dominion* (New York: Guilford, 1995), 260–5.

115. The dedication begins "To politicians running for office or attempting to stay in office who are more concerned for God's vote than man's and His Laws than man's" and goes on to pray that "my Colonel friend . . . and all Christian soldiers be mindful of the need to be obedient to our Great Commander and Master, the Lord Jesus Christ, and uphold His orders concerning homosexuality" (Peters, *Death Penalty*, n.p.).

116. Peters, *Baal Worship*, 26.

117. Kaplan, *Radical Religion*, 6–7, and "Pete Peters," in *The Encyclopedia of White Power*, 241.

118. Peters, *Baal Worship*, 68–9; hereafter cited in text as *Baal*.

119. Wessinger, *How the Millennium Comes Violently*, 169, 160.

120. Barkun, *Racist Right*, 252.

121. Pete Peters, newsletter, vol. 2 (LaPorte, CO: SFA, 1990), 2.

V

Rhetoric and Discourse

25

The Rhetoric of Hitler's "Battle"

Kenneth Burke*

The appearance of *Mein Kampf* in unexpurgated translation has called forth far too many vandalistic comments. There are other ways of burning books than on the pyre – and the favorite method of the hasty reviewer is to deprive himself and his readers by inattention. I maintain that it is thoroughly vandalistic for the reviewer to content himself with the mere inflicting of a few symbolic wounds upon this book and its author, of an intensity varying with the resources of the reviewer and the time at his disposal. Hitler's "Battle" is exasperating, even nauseating; yet the fact remains: If the reviewer but knocks off a few adverse attitudinizings and calls it a day, with a guaranty in advance that his article will have a favorable reception among the decent members of our population, he is contributing more to our gratification than to our enlightenment.

Here is the testament of a man who swung a great people into his wake. Let us watch it carefully; and let us watch it, not merely to discover some grounds for prophesying what political move is to follow Munich, and what move to follow that move, etc.; let us try also to discover what kind of "medicine" this medicine-man has concocted, that we may know, with greater accuracy, exactly what to guard against, if we are to forestall the concocting of similar medicine in America.

Already, in many quarters of our country, we are "beyond" the stage where we are being saved from Nazism by our *virtues*. And fascist integration is being staved off, rather, by the *conflicts among our vices*. Our vices cannot get together in a grand united front of prejudices; and the result of this frustration, if or until they succeed in surmounting it, speaks, as the Bible might say, "in the name of" democracy. Hitler found a panacea, a "cure for what ails you," a "snakeoil," that made such sinister unifying possible within his own nation. And he was helpful enough to put his cards face up on the table, that we might examine his hands. Let us, then, for God's sake, examine them. This book is the well of Nazi magic; crude magic, but effective. A people trained in pragmatism should want to inspect this magic.

*Pp. 191–220 from K. Burke, *The Philosophy of Literary Form: Studies in Symbolic Action* (Baton Rouge: Louisiana State University Press). © 1941, 1967 by Louisiana State University Press. 3e © 1973 by The Regents of the University of California. Reprinted with permission from the University of California Press.

1

Every movement that would recruit its followers from among many discordant and divergent bands, must have some spot towards which all roads lead. Each man may get there in his own way, but it must be the one unifying center of reference for all. Hitler considered this matter carefully, and decided that this center must be not merely a centralizing hub of *ideas,* but a mecca geographically located, towards which all eyes could turn at the appointed hours of prayer (or, in this case, the appointed hours of prayer-in-reverse, the hours of vituperation). So he selected Munich, as the *materialization* of his unifying panacea. As he puts it:

> The geo-political importance of a center of a movement cannot be overrated. Only the presence of such a center and of a place, bathed in the magic of a Mecca or a Rome, can at length give a movement that force which is rooted in the inner unity and in the recognition of a hand that represents this unity.

If a movement must have its Rome, it must also have its devil. For as Russell pointed out years ago, an important ingredient of unity in the Middle Ages (an ingredient that long did its unifying work despite the many factors driving towards disunity) was the symbol of a *common enemy,* the Prince of Evil himself. Men who can unite on nothing else can unite on the basis of a foe shared by all. Hitler himself states the case very succinctly:

> As a whole, and at all times, the efficiency of the truly national leader consists primarily in preventing the division of the attention of a people, and always in concentrating it on a single enemy. The more uniformly the fighting will of a people is put into action, the greater will be the magnetic force of the movement and the more powerful the impetus of the blow. It is part of the genius of a great leader to make adversaries of different fields appear as always belonging to one category only, because to weak and unstable characters the knowledge that there are various enemies will lead only too easily to incipient doubts as to their own cause.
>
> As soon as the wavering masses find themselves confronted with too many enemies, objectivity at once steps in, and the question is raised whether actually all the others are wrong and their own nation or their own movement alone is right.
>
> Also with this comes the first paralysis of their own strength. Therefore, a number of essentially different enemies must always be regarded as one in such a way that in the opinion of the mass of one's own adherents the war is being waged against one enemy alone. This strengthens the belief in one's own cause and increases one's bitterness against the attacker.

As everyone knows, this policy was exemplified in his selection of an "international" devil, the "international Jew" (the Prince was international, universal, "catholic"). This *materialization* of a religious pattern is, I think, one terrifically effective weapon of propaganda in a period where religion has been progressively weakened by many centuries of capitalist materialism. You need but go back to the sermonizing of centuries to be reminded that religion had a powerful enemy long before organized atheism came upon the scene. Religion is based upon the "prosperity of poverty," upon the use of ways for converting our sufferings and handicaps into a good – but capitalism is based upon the prosperity of acquisitions, the only scheme of value, in fact, by which its pro-liferating store of gadgets could be sold, assuming for the moment that capitalism had not got so drastically in its own way that it can't sell its gadgets even after it has trained people to feel that human dignity, the "higher standard of living," could be attained only by their vast private accumulation.

So, we have, as unifying step No. 1, the international devil materialized, in the visible, point-to-able form of people with a certain kind of "blood," a burlesque of contemporary neo-positivism's ideal of meaning, which insists upon a *material* reference.

Once Hitler has thus essentialized his enemy, all "proof" henceforth is automatic. If you point out the enormous amount of evidence to show that the Jewish worker is at odds with the "international Jew stock exchange capitalist," Hitler replies with one hundred per cent regularity: That is one more indication of the cunning with which the "Jewish plot" is being engineered. Or would you point to "Aryans" who do the same as his conspiratorial Jews? Very well; that is proof that the "Aryan" has been "seduced" by the Jew.

The sexual symbolism that runs through Hitler's book, lying in wait to draw upon the responses of contemporary sexual values, is easily characterized: Germany in disper-sion is the "dehorned Siegfried." The masses are "feminine." As such, they desire to be led by a dominating male. This male, as orator, woos them – and, when he has won them, he commands them. The rival male, the villainous Jew, would on the contrary "seduce" them. If he succeeds, he poisons their blood by intermingling with them. Whereupon, by purely associative connections of ideas, we are moved into attacks upon syphilis, prostitution, incest, and other similar misfortunes, which are introduced as a kind of "musical" argument when he is on the subject of "blood-poisoning" by inter-marriage or, in its "spiritual" equivalent, by the infection of "Jewish" ideas, such as democracy.[1]

The "medicinal" appeal of the Jew as scapegoat operates from another angle. The middle class contains, within the mind of each member, a duality: its members simul-taneously have a cult of money and a detestation of this cult. When capitalism is going well, this conflict is left more or less in abeyance. But when capitalism is balked, it comes to the fore. Hence, there is "medicine" for the "Aryan" members of the middle class in the projective device of the scapegoat, whereby the "bad" features can be allocated to the "devil," and one can "respect himself" by a distinction between "good" capitalism and "bad" capitalism, with those of a different lodge being the vessels of the "bad" capitalism. It is doubtless the "relief" of this solution that spared Hitler the necessity of explaining just how the "Jewish plot" was to work out. Nowhere does this book, which is so full of war plans, make the slightest attempt to explain the steps whereby the triumph of "Jewish Bolshevism," which destroys *all* finance, will be the triumph of *"Jewish"* finance. Hitler well knows the point at which his "elucidations" should rely upon the lurid alone.

The question arises, in those trying to gauge Hitler: Was his selection of the Jew, as his unifying devil-function, a purely calculating act? Despite the quotation I have already given, I believe that it was *not*. The vigor with which he utilized it, I think, derives from a much more complex state of affairs. It seems that, when Hitler went to Vienna, in a state close to total poverty, he genuinely suffered. He lived among the impoverished; and he describes his misery at the spectacle. He was *sensitive* to it; and his way of manifesting this sensitiveness impresses me that he is, at this point, wholly genuine, as with his wincing at the broken family relationships caused by alcoholism, which he in turn relates to impoverishment. During this time he began his attempts at political theorizing; and his disturbance was considerably increased by the skill with which Marxists tied him into knots. One passage in particular gives you reason, reading between the lines, to believe that the dialecticians of the class struggle, in their skill at blasting his muddled speculations, put him into a state of uncertainty that was finally "solved" by rage:

> The more I argued with them, the more I got to know their dialectics. First they counted on the ignorance of their adversary; then, when there was no way out, they themselves pretended stupidity. If all this was of no avail, they refused to understand or they changed the subject when driven into a corner; they brought up truisms, but they immediately transferred their acceptance to quite different subjects, and, if attacked again, they gave way and pretended to know nothing exactly. Wherever one attacked one of these prophets, one's hands seized slimy jelly; it slipped through one's fingers only to collect again in the next moment. If one smote one of them so thoroughly that, with the bystanders watching, he could but agree, and if one thus thought he had advanced at least one step, one was greatly astonished the following day. The Jew did not in the least remember the day before, he continued to talk in the same old strain as if nothing had happened, and if indignantly confronted, he pretended to be astonished and could not remember anything except that his assertions had already been proved true the day before.
>
> Often I was stunned.
>
> One did not know what to admire more: their glibness of tongue or their skill in lying.
>
> I gradually began to hate them.

At this point, I think, he is tracing the *spontaneous* rise of his anti–Semitism. He tells how, once he had discovered the "cause" of the misery about him, he could *confront it*. Where he had had to avert his eyes, he could now *positively welcome* the scene. Here his drastic structure of *acceptance* was being formed. He tells of the "internal happiness" that descended upon him.

> This was the time in which the greatest change I was ever to experience took place in me.
>
> From a feeble cosmopolite I turned into a fanatical anti–Semite

and thence we move, by one of those associational tricks which he brings forth at all strategic moments, into a vision of the end of the world – out of which in turn he emerges with his slogan: "I am acting in the sense of the Almighty Creator: *By warding off Jews I am fighting for the Lord's work*" (italics his).

He talks of this transition as a period of "double life," a struggle of "reason" and "reality" against his "heart."[2] It was as "bitter" as it was "blissful." And finally, it was "reason" that won! Which prompts us to note that those who attack Hitlerism as a cult of the irrational should emend their statements to this extent: irrational it is, but it is carried on under the *slogan* of "Reason." Similarly, his cult of war is developed "in the name of" humility, love, and peace. Judged on a quantitative basis, Hitler's book certainly falls under the classification of hate. Its venom is everywhere, its charity is sparse. But the rationalized family tree for this hate situates it in "Aryan love." Some deep-probing German poets, whose work adumbrated the Nazi movement, did gravitate towards thinking *in the name of* war, irrationality, and hate. But Hitler was not among them. After all, when it is so easy to draw a doctrine of war out of a doctrine of peace, why should the astute politician do otherwise, particularly when Hitler has slung together his doctrines, without the slightest effort at logical symmetry? Furthermore, Church thinking always got to its wars in Hitler's "sounder" manner; and the patterns of Hitler's thought are a bastardized or caricatured version of religious thought.

I spoke of Hitler's fury at the dialectics of those who opposed him when his structure was in the stage of scaffolding. From this we may move to another tremendously important aspect of his theory: his attack upon the *parliamentary*. For it is again, I submit, an important aspect of his medicine, in its function as medicine for him personally and as medicine for those who were later to identify themselves with him.

There is a "problem" in the parliament – and nowhere was this problem more acutely in evidence than in the pre-war Vienna that was to serve as Hitler's political schooling. For the parliament, at its best, is a "babel" of voices. There is the wrangle of men representing interests lying awkwardly on the bias across one another, sometimes opposing, sometimes vaguely divergent. Morton Prince's psychiatric study of "Miss Beauchamp," the case of a woman split into several sub-personalities at odds with one another, variously combining under hypnosis, and frequently in turmoil, is the allegory of a democracy fallen upon evil days. The parliament of the Habsburg Empire just prior to its collapse was an especially drastic instance of such disruption, such vocal diaspora, with movements that would reduce one to a disintegrated mass of fragments if he attempted to encompass the totality of its discordancies. So Hitler, suffering under the alienation of poverty and confusion, yearning for some integrative core, came to take this parliament as the basic symbol of all that he would move away from. He damned the tottering Habsburg Empire as a "State of Nationalities." The many conflicting voices of the spokesmen of the many political blocs arose from the fact that various separationist movements of a nationalistic sort had arisen within a Catholic imperial structure formed prior to the nationalistic emphasis and slowly breaking apart under its development. So, you had this Babel of voices; and, by the method of associative mergers, *using ideas as imagery,* it became tied up, in the Hitler rhetoric, with "Babylon," Vienna as the city of poverty, prostitution, immorality, coalitions, half-measures, incest, democracy (i.e., majority rule leading to "lack of personal responsibility"), death, internationalism, seduction, and anything else of thumbs-down sort the associative enterprise cared to add on this side of the balance.

Hitler's way of treating the parliamentary babel, I am sorry to say, was at one important point not much different from that of the customary editorial in our own newspapers. Every conflict among the parliamentary spokesmen represents a corresponding conflict among the material interests of the groups for whom they are speaking. But Hitler did not discuss the babel from this angle. He discussed it on a purely *symptomatic* basis. The strategy of our orthodox press, in thus ridiculing the cacophonous verbal output of Congress, is obvious: by thus centering attack upon the *symptoms* of business conflict, as they reveal themselves on the dial of political wrangling, and leaving the underlying cause, the business conflicts themselves, out of the case, they can gratify the very public they would otherwise alienate: namely, the businessmen who are the activating members of their reading public. Hitler, however, went them one better. For not only did he stress the purely *symptomatic* attack here. He proceeded to search for the "cause." And this "cause," of course, he derived from his medicine, his racial theory by which he could give a noneconomic interpretation of a phenomenon economically engendered.

Here again is where Hitler's corrupt use of religious patterns comes to the fore. Church thought, being primarily concerned with matters of the "personality," with problems of moral betterment, naturally, and I think rightly, stresses as a necessary feature, the act of will upon the part of the individual. Hence its resistance to a purely "environmental" account of human ills. Hence its emphasis upon the "person." Hence its proneness to seek a noneconomic explanation of economic phenomena. Hitler's proposal of a non-economic "cause" for the disturbances thus had much to recommend it from this angle. And, as a matter of fact, it was Lueger's Christian-Social Party in Vienna that taught Hitler the tactics of tying up a program of social betterment with an anti-Semitic "unifier." The two parties that he carefully studied at that time were this Catholic faction and Schoenerer's Pan-German group. And his analysis of their attainments and shortcomings, from the standpoint of demagogic efficacy, is an extremely astute piece of work, revealing how carefully this man used the current situation in Vienna as an experimental laboratory for the maturing of his plans.

His unification device, we may summarize, had the following important features:

1. *Inborn dignity*. In both religious and humanistic patterns of thought, a "natural born" dignity of man is stressed. And this categorical dignity is considered to be an attribute of *all* men, if they will but avail themselves of it, by right thinking and right living. But Hitler gives this ennobling attitude an ominous twist by his theories of race and nation, whereby the "Aryan" is elevated above all others by the innate endowment of his blood, while other "races," in particular Jews and Negroes, are innately inferior. This sinister secularized revision of Christian theology thus puts the sense of dignity upon a fighting basis, requiring the conquest of "inferior races." After the defeat of Germany in the World War, there were especially strong emotional needs that this compensatory doctrine of an *inborn* superiority could gratify.

2. *Projection device*. The "curative" process that comes with the ability to hand over one's ills to a scapegoat, thereby getting purification by dissociation. This was especially medicinal, since the sense of frustration leads to a self-questioning. Hence if one can hand over his infirmities to a vessel, or "cause," outside the self, one can battle an external enemy instead of battling an enemy within. And the greater one's internal inadequacies, the greater the amount of evils one can load upon the back of "the enemy." This device is furthermore given a semblance of reason because the individual properly realizes that he is not alone responsible for his condition. There *are* inimical factors in the scene itself. And he wants to have

them "placed," preferably in a way that would require a minimum change in the ways of thinking to which he had been accustomed. This was especially appealing to the middle class, who were encouraged to feel that they could conduct their businesses without any basic change whatever, once the businessmen of a different "race" were eliminated.

3. *Symbolic rebirth.* Another aspect of the two features already noted. The projective device of the scapegoat, coupled with the Hitlerite doctrine of inborn racial superiority, provides its followers with a "positive" view of life. They can again get the feel of *moving forward,* towards a *goal* (a promissory feature of which Hitler makes much). In Hitler, as the group's prophet, such rebirth involved a symbolic change of lineage. Here, above all, we see Hitler giving a malign twist to a benign aspect of Christian thought. For whereas the Pope, in the familistic pattern of thought basic to the Church, stated that the Hebrew prophets were the *spiritual ancestors* of Christianity, Hitler uses this same mode of thinking in reverse. He renounces this "ancestry" in a "materialistic" way by voting himself and the members of his lodge a different "blood stream" from that of the Jews.

4. *Commercial use.* Hitler obviously here had something to sell – and it was but a question of time until he sold it (i.e., got financial backers for his movement). For it provided a *noneconomic interpretation of economic ills.* As such, it served with maximum efficiency in deflecting the attention from the economic factors involved in modern conflict; hence by attacking "Jew finance" instead of *finance,* it could stimulate an enthusiastic movement that left "Aryan" finance in control.

Never once, throughout his book, does Hitler deviate from the above formula. Invariably, he ends his diatribes against contemporary economic ills by a shift into an insistence that we must get to the "true" cause, which is centered in "race." The "Aryan" is "constructive"; the Jew is "destructive"; and the "Aryan," to continue his *construction,* must *destroy* the Jewish *destruction.* The Aryan, as the vessel of *love,* must *hate* the Jewish *hate.*

Perhaps the most enterprising use of his method is in his chapter, "The Causes of the Collapse," where he refuses to consider Germany's plight as in any basic way connected with the consequences of war. Economic factors, he insists, are "only of second or even third importance," but "political, ethical-moral, as well as factors of blood and race, are of the first importance." His rhetorical steps are especially interesting here, in that he begins by seeming to flout the national susceptibilities: "The military defeat of the German people is not an undeserved catastrophe, but rather a deserved punishment by eternal retribution." He then proceeds to present the military collapse as but a "consequence of moral poisoning, visible to all, the consequence of a decrease in the instinct of self-preservation . . . which had already begun to undermine the foundations of the people and the Reich many years before." This moral decay derived from "a sin against the blood and the degradation of the race," so its innerness was an outerness after all: the Jew, who thereupon gets saddled with a vast amalgamation of evils, among them being capitalism, democracy, pacifism, journalism, poor housing, modernism, big cities, loss of religion, half measures, ill health, and weakness of the monarch.

2

Hitler had here another important psychological ingredient to play upon. If a State is in economic collapse (and his theories, tentatively taking shape in the pre-war Vienna, were but developed with greater efficiency in post-war Munich), you cannot possibly derive dignity from economic stability. Dignity must come first – and if you possess it, and implement it, from it may follow its economic counterpart. There is much justice to this line of reasoning, so far as it goes. A people in collapse, suffering under economic frustration and the defeat of nationalistic aspirations, with the very midrib of their integrative efforts (the army) in a state of dispersion, have little other than some "spiritual" basis to which they could refer their nationalistic dignity. Hence, the categorical dignity of superior race was a perfect recipe for the situation. It was "spiritual" in so far as it was "above" crude economic "interests," but it was "materialized" at the psychologically "right" spot in that "the enemy" was something you could *see*.

Furthermore, you had the desire for unity, such as a discussion of class conflict, on the basis of conflicting interests, could not satisfy. The yearning for unity is so great that people are always willing to meet you halfway if you will give it to them by fiat, by flat statement, regardless of the facts. Hence, Hitler consistently refused to consider internal political conflict on the basis of conflicting interests. Here again, he could draw upon a religious pattern, by insisting upon a *personal* statement of the relation between classes, the relation between leaders and followers, each group in its way fulfilling the same commonalty of interests, as the soldiers and captains of an army share a common interest in victory. People so dislike the idea of internal division that, where there is a real internal division, their dislike can easily be turned against the man or group who would so much as *name* it, let alone proposing to act upon it. Their natural and justified resentment against internal division itself, is turned against the diagnostician who states it as a *fact*. This diagnostician, it is felt, is the *cause* of the disunity he named.

Cutting in from another angle, therefore, we note how two sets of equations were built up, with Hitler combining or coalescing *ideas* the way a poet combines or coalesces *images*. On the one side, were the ideas, or images, of disunity, centering in the parliamentary wrangle of the Habsburg "State of Nationalities." This was offered as the antithesis of German nationality, which was presented in the curative imagery of unity, focused upon the glories of the Prussian Reich, with its mecca now moved to "folkish" Vienna. For though Hitler at first attacked the many "folkish" movements, with their hankerings after a kind of Wagnerian mythology of Germanic origins, he subsequently took "folkish" as a basic word by which to conjure. It was, after all, another non-economic basis of reference. At first we find him objecting to "those who drift about with the word 'folkish' on their caps," and asserting that "such a Babel of opinions cannot serve as the basis of a political fighting movement." But later he seems to have realized, as he well should, that its vagueness was a major point in its favor. So it was incorporated in the grand coalition of his ideational imagery, or imagistic ideation; and Chapter XI ends with the vision of "a State which represents not a mechanism of economic considerations and interests, alien to the people, but a folkish organism."

So, as against the disunity equations, already listed briefly in our discussion of his attacks upon the parliamentary, we get a contrary purifying set; the wrangle of the parliamentary is to be stilled by the giving of *one* voice to the whole people, this to be the "inner voice" of Hitler, made uniform throughout the German boundaries, as leader and people were completely identified with each other. In sum: Hitler's inner voice, equals leader-people identification, equals unity, equals Reich, equals the mecca of Munich, equals plow, equals sword, equals work, equals war, equals army as midrib, equals responsibility (the personal responsibility of the absolute ruler), equals sacrifice, equals the theory of "German democracy" (the free popular choice of the leader, who then accepts the responsibility, and demands absolute obedience in exchange for his sacrifice), equals love (with the masses as feminine), equals idealism, equals obedience to nature, equals race, nation.[3]

And, of course, the two keystones of these opposite equations were Aryan "heroism" and "sacrifice" vs. Jewish "cunning" and "arrogance." Here again we get an astounding caricature of religious thought. For Hitler presents the concept of "Aryan" superiority, of all ways, in terms of "Aryan humility." This "humility" is extracted by a very delicate process that requires, I am afraid, considerable "good will" on the part of the reader who would follow it.

The Church, we may recall, had proclaimed an integral relationship between Divine Law and Natural Law. Natural Law was the expression of the Will of God. Thus, in the middle age, it was a result of natural law, working through tradition, that some people were serfs and other people nobles. And every good member of the Church was "obedient" to this law. Everybody resigned himself to it. Hence, the serf resigned himself to his poverty, and the noble resigned himself to his riches. The monarch resigned himself to his position as representative of the people. And at times the Churchmen resigned themselves to the need of trying to represent the people instead. And the pattern was made symmetrical by the consideration that each traditional "right" had its corresponding "obligations." Similarly, the Aryan doctrine is a doctrine of resignation, hence of humility. It is in accordance with the laws of nature that the "Aryan blood" is superior to all other bloods. Also, the "law of the survival of the fittest" is God's law, working through natural law. Hence, if the Aryan blood has been vested with the awful responsibility of its inborn superiority, the bearers of this "culture-creating" blood must resign themselves to struggle in behalf of its triumph. Otherwise, the laws of God have been disobeyed, with human decadence as a result. We must fight, he says, in order to "deserve to be alive." The Aryan "obeys" nature. It is only "Jewish arrogance" that thinks of "conquering" nature by democratic ideals of equality.

This picture has some nice distinctions worth following. The major virtue of the Aryan race was its instinct for self-preservation (in obedience to natural law). But the major vice of the Jew was his instinct for self-preservation; for, if he did not have this instinct to a maximum degree, he would not be the "perfect" enemy – that is, he wouldn't be strong enough to account for the ubiquitousness and omnipotence of his conspiracy in destroying the world to become its master.

How, then, are we to distinguish between the benign instinct of self-preservation at the roots of Aryanism, and the malign instinct of self-preservation at the roots of Semitism? We shall distinguish thus: The Aryan self-preservation is based upon *sacrifice*, the sacrifice of the individual to the group, hence, militarism, army discipline, and one big company union. But Jewish self-preservation is based upon individualism, which attains its cunning ends by the exploitation of peace. How, then, can such arrant individualists concoct the world-wide plot? By the help of their "herd instinct." By their sheer "herd instinct" individualists can band together for a common end. They have no real solidarity, but unite opportunistically to seduce the Aryan. Still, that brings up another technical problem. For we have been hearing much about the importance of the *person*. We have been told how, by the "law of the survival of the fittest," there is a sifting of people on the basis of their individual capacities. We even have a special chapter of pure Aryanism: "The Strong Man is Mightiest Alone." Hence, another distinction is necessary: The Jew represents individualism; the Aryan represents "super-individualism."

I had thought, when coming upon the "Strong Man is Mightiest Alone" chapter, that I was going to find Hitler at his weakest. Instead, I found him at his strongest. (I am not referring to *quality*, but to *demagogic effectiveness*.) For the chapter is not at all, as you might infer from the title, done in a "rise of Adolph Hitler" manner. Instead, it deals with the Nazis' gradual absorption of the many disrelated "folkish" groups. And it is managed throughout by means of a spontaneous identification between leader and people. Hence, the Strong Man's "aloneness" is presented as a *public* attribute, in terms of tactics for the struggle against the *Party's* dismemberment under the pressure of rival saviors. There is no explicit talk of Hitler at all. And it is simply *taken for granted* that *his* leadership is the norm, and all other leaderships the abnorm. There is no "philosophy of the superman," in Nietzschean cast. Instead, Hitler's blandishments so integrate leader and people, commingling them so inextricably, that the politician does not even present himself as candidate. Somehow, the battle is over already, the decision has been made. "German democracy" has chosen. And the deployments of politics are, you might say, the chartings of Hitler's private mind translated into the vocabulary of nationalistic events. He says *what he thought* in terms of *what parties did*.

Here, I think, we see the distinguishing quality of Hitler's method as an instrument of persuasion, with reference to the question whether Hitler is sincere or deliberate, whether his vision of the omnipotent conspirator has the drastic honesty of paranoia or the sheer shrewdness of a demagogue trained in *Realpolitik* of the Machiavellian sort.[4] Must we choose? Or may we not, rather, replace the "either – or" with a "both – and"? Have we not by now offered grounds enough for our contention that Hitler's sinister powers of persuasion derive from the fact that he spontaneously evolved his "cure-all" in response to inner necessities?

3

So much, then, was "spontaneous." It was further channelized into the anti-Semitic pattern by the incentives he derived from the Catholic Christian-Social Party in Vienna itself. Add, now, the step into *criticism*. Not criticism in the "parliamentary" sense of doubt, of hearkening to the opposition and attempting to mature a policy in the light of counter-policies; but the "unified" kind of criticism that simply seeks for conscious ways of making one's position more "efficient," more thoroughly itself. This is the kind of criticism at which Hitler was an adept. As a result, he could *spontaneously* turn to a scapegoat mechanism, and he could, by conscious planning, perfect the symmetry of the solution towards which he had spontaneously turned.

This is the meaning of Hitler's diatribes against "objectivity." "Objectivity" is interference-criticism. What Hitler wanted was the kind of criticism that would be a pure and simple coefficient of power, enabling him to go most effectively in the direction he had chosen. And the "inner voice" of which he speaks would henceforth dictate to him the greatest amount of realism, as regards the tactics of efficiency. For instance, having decided that the masses required certainty, and simple certainty, quite as he did himself, he later worked out a 25-point program as the platform of his National Socialist German Workers Party. And he resolutely refused to change one single item in this program, even for purposes of "improvement." He felt that the *fixity* of the platform was more important for propagandistic purposes than any revision of his slogans could be, even though the revisions in themselves had much to be said in their favor. The astounding thing is that, although such an attitude gave good cause to doubt the Hitlerite promises, he could explicitly explain his tactics in his book and still employ them without loss of effectiveness.[5]

Hitler also tells of his technique in speaking, once the Nazi party had become effectively organized, and had its army of guards, or bouncers, to maltreat hecklers and throw them from the hall. He would, he recounts, fill his speech with *provocative* remarks, whereat his bouncers would promptly swoop down in flying formation, with swinging fists, upon anyone whom these provocative remarks provoked to answer. The efficiency of Hitlerism is the efficiency of the one voice, implemented throughout a total organization. The trinity of government which he finally offers is: *popularity* of the leader, *force* to back the popularity, and popularity and force maintained together long enough to become backed by a *tradition*. Is such thinking spontaneous or deliberate – or is it not rather both?[6]

Freud has given us a succinct paragraph that bears upon the spontaneous aspect of Hitler's persecution mania. (A persecution mania, I should add, different from the pure product in that it was constructed of *public* materials; all the ingredients Hitler stirred into his brew were already rife, with spokesmen and bands of followers, before Hitler "took them over." Both the pre-war and post-war periods were dotted with saviors, of nationalistic and "folkish" cast. This proliferation was analogous to the swarm of barter schemes and currency-tinkering that burst loose upon the United States after the crash of 1929. Also, the commercial availability of Hitler's politics was, in a low sense of the term, a *public* qualification, removing it from the realm of "pure" paranoia, where the sufferer develops a wholly *private* structure of interpretations.)

I cite from *Totem and Taboo*:

> Another trait in the attitude of primitive races towards their rulers recalls a mechanism which is universally present in mental disturbances, and is openly revealed in the so-called delusions of persecution. Here the importance of a particular person is extraordinarily heightened and his omnipotence is raised to the improbable in order to make it easier to attribute to him responsibility for everything painful which happens to the patient. Savages really do not act differently towards their rulers when they ascribe to them power over

rain and shine, wind and weather, and then dethrone them or kill them because nature has disappointed their expectation of a good hunt or a ripe harvest. The prototype which the paranoiac reconstructs in his persecution mania is found in the relation of the child to its father. Such omnipotence is regularly attributed to the father in the imagination of the son, and distrust of the father has been shown to be intimately connected with the heightened esteem for him. When a paranoiac names a person of his acquaintance as his "persecutor," he thereby elevates him to the paternal succession and brings him under conditions which enable him to make him responsible for all the misfortune which he experiences.

I have already proposed my modifications of this account when discussing the symbolic change of lineage connected with Hitler's project of a "new way of life." Hitler is symbolically changing from the "spiritual ancestry" of the Hebrew prophets to the "superior" ancestry of "Aryanism," and has given his story a kind of bastardized modernization, along the lines of naturalistic, materialistic "science," by his fiction of the special "blood-stream." He is voting himself a new identity (something contrary to the wrangles of the Habsburg Babylon, a soothing national unity); whereupon the vessels of the old identity become a "bad" father, i.e., the persecutor. It is not hard to see how, as his enmity becomes implemented by the backing of an organization, the rôle of "persecutor" is transformed into the rôle of persecuted, as he sets out with his like-minded band to "destroy the destroyer."

Were Hitler simply a poet, he might have written a work with an anti-Semitic turn, and let it go at that. But Hitler, who began as a student of painting, and later shifted to architecture, himself treats his political activities as an extension of his artistic ambitions. He remained, in his own eyes, an "architect," building a "folkish" State that was to match, in political materials, the "folkish" architecture of Munich.

We might consider the matter this way (still trying, that is, to make precise the relationship between the drastically sincere and the deliberately scheming): Do we not know of many authors who seem, as they turn from the rôle of citizen to the rôle of spokesman, to leave one room and enter another? Or who has not, on occasion, talked with a man in private conversation, and then been almost startled at the transformation this man undergoes when addressing a public audience? And I know persons today, who shift between the writing of items in the class of academic, philosophic speculation to items of political pamphleteering, and whose entire style and method changes with this change of rôle. In their academic manner, they are cautious, painstaking, eager to present all significant aspects of the case they are considering; but when they turn to political pamphleteering, they hammer forth with vituperation, they systematically misrepresent the position of their opponent, they go into a kind of political trance, in which, during its throes, they throb like a locomotive; and behold, a moment later, the mediumistic state is abandoned, and they are the most moderate of men.

Now, one will find few pages in Hitler that one could call "moderate." But there are many pages in which he gauges resistances and opportunities with the "rationality" of a skilled advertising man planning a new sales campaign. Politics, he says, must be sold like soap – and soap is not sold in a trance. But he did have the experience of his trance, in the "exaltation" of his anti-Semitism. And later, as he became a successful orator (he insists that revolutions are made solely by the power of the spoken word), he had this "poetic" rôle to draw upon, plus the great relief it provided as a way of slipping from the burden of logical analysis into the pure "spirituality" of vituperative prophecy. What more natural, therefore, than that a man so insistent upon unification would integrate this mood with less ecstatic moments, particularly when he had found the followers and the backers that put a price, both spiritual and material, upon such unification?

Once this happy "unity" is under way, one has a "logic" for the development of a method. One knows when to "spiritualize" a material issue, and when to "materialize" a spiritual one. Thus, when it is a matter of materialistic interests that cause a conflict between employer and employee, Hitler here disdainfully shifts to a high moral plane. He is "above" such low concerns. Everything becomes a matter of "sacrifices" and "personality." It becomes crass to treat employers and employees as different *classes* with a corresponding difference in the classification of their interests. Instead, relations between employer and employee must be on the "personal" basis of leader and follower, and "whatever may have a divisive effect in national life should be given a unifying effect through the army." When talking of national rivalries, however, he makes a very shrewd materialistic gauging of Britain and France with relation to Germany. France, he says, desires the "Balkanization of Germany" (i.e., its breakup into separationist movements – the "disunity" theme again) in order to maintain commercial hegemony on the continent. But Britain desires the "Balkanization of *Europe*," hence would favor a fairly strong and unified Germany, to use as a counter-weight against French hegemony. *German* nationality, however, is unified by the *spiritual* quality of Aryanism (that would produce the national organization via the Party) while this in turn is *materialized* in the myth of the blood-stream.

What are we to learn from Hitler's book? For one thing, I believe that he has shown, to a very disturbing degree, the power of endless repetition. Every circular advertising a Nazi meeting had, at the bottom, two slogans: "Jews not admitted" and "War victims free." And the substance of Nazi propaganda was built about these two "complementary" themes. He describes the power of spectacle; insists that mass meetings are the fundamental way of giving the individual the sense of being protectively surrounded by a movement, the sense of "community." He also drops one wise hint that I wish the American authorities would take in treating Nazi gatherings. He says that the presence of a special Nazi guard, in Nazi uniforms, was of great importance in building up, among the followers, a tendency to place the center of authority in the Nazi party. I believe that we should take him at his word here, but use the advice in reverse, by insisting that, where Nazi meetings are to be permitted, they be policed by the authorities alone, and that uniformed Nazi guards to enforce the law be prohibited.

And is it possible that an equally important feature of appeal was not so much in the repetitiousness per se, but in the fact that, by means of it, Hitler provided a "world view" for people who had previously seen the world but piecemeal? Did not much of his lure derive, once more, from the *bad* filling of a *good* need? Are not those who insist upon a purely *planless* working of the market asking people to accept far too slovenly a scheme of human purpose, a slovenly scheme that can be accepted so long as it operates with a fair degree of satisfaction, but becomes abhorrent to the victims of its disarray? Are they not then psychologically ready for a rationale, *any* rationale, if it but offer them some specious "universal" explanation? Hence, I doubt whether the appeal was in the sloganizing element alone (particularly as even slogans can only be hammered home, in speech after speech, and two or three hours at a stretch, by endless variations on the themes). And Hitler himself somewhat justifies my interpretation by laying so much stress upon the *half-measures* of the middle-class politicians, and the contrasting *certainty* of his own methods. He was not offering people a *rival* world view; rather, he was offering a world view to people who had no other to pit against it.

As for the basic Nazi trick: the "curative" unification by a fictitious devil-function, gradually made convincing by the sloganizing repetitiousness of standard advertising technique – the opposition must be as unwearying in the attack upon it. It may well be that people, in their human frailty, require an enemy as well as a goal. Very well: Hitlerism itself has provided us with such an enemy – and the clear example of its operation is guaranty that we have, in him and all he stands for, no purely fictitious "devil-function" made to look like a world menace by rhetorical blandishments, but a reality whose ominousness is clarified by the record of its conduct to date. In selecting his brand of doctrine as our "scapegoat," and in tracking down its equivalents in America, we shall be at the very center of accuracy. The Nazis themselves have made the task of clarification easier. Add to them Japan and Italy, and you have *case histories* of fascism for those who might find it more difficult to approach an understanding of its imperialistic drives by a vigorously economic explanation.

But above all, I believe, we must make it apparent that Hitler appeals by relying upon a bastardization of fundamentally religious patterns of thought. In this, if properly presented, there is no slight to religion. There is nothing in religion proper that requires a fascist state. There is much in religion, when misused, that does lead to a fascist state. There is a Latin proverb, *Corruptio optimi pessima*, "the corruption of the best is the worst." And it is the corruptors of religion who are a major menace to the world today, in giving the profound patterns of religious thought a crude and sinister distortion.

Our job, then, our anti-Hitler Battle, is to find all available ways of making the Hitlerite distortions of religion apparent, in order that politicians of his kind in America be unable to perform a similar swindle. The desire for unity is genuine and admirable. The desire for national unity, in the present state of the world, is genuine and admirable. But this unity, if attained on a deceptive basis, by emotional trickeries that shift our criticism from the accurate locus of our trouble, is no unity at all. For, even if we are among those who happen to be "Aryans," we solve no problems even for ourselves by such solutions, since the factors pressing towards calamity remain. Thus, in Germany, after all the upheaval, we see nothing beyond a drive for ever more and more upheaval, precisely because the "new way of life" was no new way, but the dismally oldest way of sheer deception – hence, after all the "change," the factors driving towards unrest are left intact, and even strengthened. True, the Germans had the resentment of a lost war to increase their susceptibility to Hitler's rhetoric. But in a wider sense, it has repeatedly been observed, the whole world lost the War – and the accumulating ills of the capitalist order were but accelerated in their movements towards confusion. Hence, here too there are the resentments that go with frustration of men's ability to work and earn. At that point a certain kind of industrial or financial monopolist may, annoyed by the contrary voices of our parliament, wish for the momentary peace of one voice, amplified by social organizations, with all the others not merely quieted, but given the quietus. So he might, under Nazi promptings, be tempted to back a group of gangsters who, on becoming the political rulers of the state, would protect him against the necessary demands of the workers. His gangsters, then, would be his insurance against his workers. But who would be his insurance against his gangsters?

Notes

1. Hitler also strongly insists upon the total identification between leader and people. Thus, in wooing the people, he would in a roundabout way be wooing himself. The thought might suggest how the Führer, dominating the feminine masses by his diction, would have an incentive to remain unmarried.

2. Other aspects of the career symbolism: Hitler's book begins: "Today I consider it my good fortune that Fate designated Braunau on the Inn as the place of my birth. For this small town is situated on the border between those two German States, the reunion of which seems, at least to us of the younger generation, a task to be furthered with every means our lives long," an indication of his "transitional" mind, what Wordsworth might have called the "borderer." He neglects to give the date of his birth, 1889, which is supplied by the editors. Again there is a certain "correctness" here, as Hitler was not "born" until many years later – but he does give the exact date of his war wounds, which were indeed formative. During his early years in Vienna and Munich, he foregoes protest, on the grounds that he is "nameless." And when his party is finally organized and effective, he stresses the fact that his "nameless" period is over (i.e., he has shaped himself an identity). When reading in an earlier passage of his book some generalizations to the effect that one should not crystallize his political views until he is thirty, I made a note: "See what Hitler does at thirty." I felt sure that, though such generalizations may be dubious as applied to people as a whole, they must, given the Hitler type of mind (with his complete identification between himself and his followers), be valid statements about himself. One *should* do what he *did*. The hunch was verified: about the age of thirty Hitler, in a group of seven, began working with the party that was to conquer Germany. I trace these steps particularly because I believe that the orator who has a strong sense of his own "rebirth" has this to draw upon when persuading his audiences that his is offering them the way to a "new life." However, I see no categorical objection to this attitude; its menace derives solely from the values in which it is exemplified. They may be wholesome or unwholesome. If they are unwholesome, but backed by conviction, the basic sincerity of the conviction acts as a sound virtue to reinforce a vice – and this combination is the most disastrous one that a people can encounter in a demagogue.

3. One could carry out the equations further, on both the disunity and unity side. In the aesthetic field, for instance, we have expressionism on the thumbs-down side, as against aesthetic hygiene on the thumbs-up side. This again is a particularly ironic moment in Hitler's strategy. For the expressionist movement was unquestionably a symptom of unhealthiness. It reflected the increasing alienation that went with the movement towards world war and the disorganization after the world war. It was "lost," vague in identity, a drastically accurate reflection of the response to material confusion, a pathetic attempt by sincere artists to make their wretchedness bearable at least to the extent that comes of giving it expression. And it attained its height during the period of wild inflation, when the capitalist world, which bases its morality of work and savings upon the soundness of its money structure, had this last prop of stability removed. The anguish, in short, reflected precisely the kind of disruption that made people *ripe* for a Hitler. It was the antecedent in a phrase of

which Hitlerism was the consequent. But by thundering against this *symptom* he could gain persuasiveness, though attacking the very *foreshadowings of himself.*

4. I should not want to use the word "Machiavellian," however, without offering a kind of apology to Machiavelli. It seems to me that Machiavelli's *Prince* has more to be said in extenuation than is usually said of it. Machiavelli's strategy, as I see it, was something like this: He accepted the values of the Renaissance rule as a *fact.* That is: whether you like these values or not, they were there and operating, and it was useless to try persuading the ambitious ruler to adopt other values, such as those of the Church. These men believed in the cult of material power, and they had the power to implement their beliefs. With so much as "the given," could anything in the way of benefits for the people be salvaged? Machiavelli evolved a typical "Machiavellian" argument in favor of popular benefits, on the basis of the prince's own scheme of values. That is: the ruler, to attain the maximum strength, requires the backing of the populace. That this backing be as effective as possible, the populace should be made as strong as possible. And that the populace be as strong as possible, they should be well treated. Their gratitude would further repay itself in the form of increased loyalty.

   It was Machiavelli's hope that, for this roundabout project, he would be rewarded with a well-paying office in the prince's administrative bureaucracy.

5. On this point Hitler reasons as follows: "Here, too, one can learn from the Catholic Church. Although its structure of doctrines in many instances collides, quite unnecessarily, with exact science and research, yet it is unwilling to sacrifice even one little syllable of its dogmas. It has rightly recognized that its resistibility does not lie in a more or less great adjustment to the scientific results of the moment, which in reality are always changing, but rather in a strict adherence to dogmas, once laid down, which alone give the entire structure the character of creed. Today, therefore, the Catholic Church stands firmer than ever. One can prophesy that in the same measure in which the appearances flee, the Church itself, as the resting pole in the flight of appearances, will gain more and more blind adherence."

6. Hitler also paid great attention to the conditions under which political oratory is most effective. He sums up thus:

   "All these cases involve encroachments upon man's freedom of will. This applies, of course, most of all to meetings to which people with a contrary orientation of will are coming, and who now have to be won for new intentions. It seems that in the morning and even during the day men's will power revolts with highest energy against an attempt at being forced under another's will and another's opinion. In the evening, however, they succumb more easily to the dominating force of a stronger will. For truly every such meeting presents a wrestling match between two opposed forces. The superior oratorical talent of a domineering apostolic nature will now succeed more easily in winning for the new will people who themselves have in turn experienced a weakening of their force of resistance in the most natural way, than people who still have full command of the energies of their minds and their will power.

   "The same purpose serves also the artificially created and yet mysterious dusk of the Catholic churches, the burning candles, incense, censers, etc."

26

Public Speech, Dance, Jokes, and Song

John D. H. Downing*

The most accessible and most fundamental mode of radical expression is speech for public purposes (i.e., even if clandestine, uttered within one or more publics) and, not least, ironic and satirical speech. Close to it are dance and song. The instances below, including the "high-art" poem *Requiem*, exemplify, notably, the rebellious strands in popular culture and the importance of nonmedia networks in alternative public spheres. Many, particularly aspects of German labor movement songs, also exemplify the typically impure, irretrievably mixed character of oppositional expression. At the same time, Benjamin's aura, the interactive aesthetics of radical communication, is evidenced at almost every turn. Last, many of the illustrations below are drawn from radical cultural expression in the face of a repressive power structure, from New World slavery to Stalinism and military dictatorships, including masculinist cultures that strictly regiment women.

Moroccan Women Street Traders

Deborah Kapchan's (1996) study of Moroccan women market traders nicely introduces us to some of the fundamentals, in this case, the subtle but powerful erosion of patriarchal codes, in a way reminiscent of Scott's (1985, 1990) analysis of everyday resistance.

Let us begin with context. In 1980s Morocco, for women to act as traders in the public marketplaces rather than as shoppers was a very new phenomenon, unknown 20 years earlier. How, then, did these women communicate in public to casual passers-by, generally unrelated to them, males as well as females? How did they manage to assert themselves, to be insistent in calling shoppers' notice to the merits of their wares, and yet stay unsanctioned, remaining within – while simultaneously stretching the bounds of – what was considered acceptable for women?

Kapchan (1996) presents a detailed analysis of their selling patterns that evinces an impressive capacity to negotiate and erode patriarchal codes without sparking a

*Pp. 105–18 from J. D. H. Downing, *Radical Media: Rebellious Communication and Social Movements* (Thousand Oaks, CA and London: Sage Publications). © 2001 by Sage Publications, Inc. Reprinted by permission of Sage Publications, Inc.

damaging condemnation or retribution. One of these market women, trading in herbal medications, actually spoke out loud in the marketplace about male impotence and sexual intercourse. But to legitimate her candor to her largely male audience, she wove into her speech reference to sayings in the *Qur'an* or familiar proverbs and aphorisms, which established her piety. Statements such as "God bless the parents" normally required a repetition from the hearers, so that inclusion of the statement and its answering echo were also ways of bringing the hearers along with her. She might even affect extra piety, saying "I didn't hear you all say, 'God bless the parents,'" and they would feel duty-bound to repeat the saying more loudly (Kapchan, 1996, pp. 103–37).

A different example comes from a conversation in which a male customer was insistently trying to bargain a woman trader down. He told her he would go buy the item from the store (where prices were rarely negotiable), and she responded, "Well, offer a price, sir, and buy. It's not shameful. We're just like the store. What's the matter with us [women vendors]? Aren't we all Muslims?" "No, no," he replied, "we're all Muslims, one people" (Kapchan, 1996, p. 58).

What she was doing here, Kapchan explains, was to respond to his dismissive comment on her female trader status – stores were still owned by men – by pulling him into agreeing with a pious statement, one generally used in Moroccan conversation to call for harmony between Arab and Berber men. She extended it to apply to male-female relations, as a way of pressuring him into a degree of respect for her and continuing the negotiation on her terms.

Here were subtly subversive communications, bending the limits of the possible for women, gradually altering the contours of Moroccan women's freedom of public expression. They involved no expense, no collective organization, only the elaboration and deployment of rhetorical skills in conversation, sometimes very finely tuned, and the necessary degree of emotional determination not to be inhibited from self-assertion. Yet, these are the communicative stances from which radical alternative media are ultimately derived and with which they interact.

A related example is offered by various kinds of verbal humor, not particularly as expressed by professional stand-up comedians, but rather in everyday situations. Humor is multifaceted, and so, it is important not to infer it is always beneficial or always subversive.[1] Nonetheless, in many situations, humorous comments or actual jokes directed against employers, against bureaucrats, against clergy, against hypocritical and corrupt authorities, against colonial invaders, against racially defined superiors, serve to puncture the pretensions of those on high and to reduce the legitimacy of their authority. The more these comments and jokes diffuse out along conversational networks, the more purchase they achieve. Women's ironic discussions among themselves of males constitute a universal example of subversive speech communication. Once more, in the strictly gender-segregated cultures of North Africa, both the flat rooftops in cities, where washing is hung out, and the women's bathhouse are locations where only women congregate and thus where this freer talk is possible, a kind of women's alternative public sphere (cf. Fraser, 1993). The Moroccan market women made ample use of humorous comment. But there are many further examples, some cited later in this section under the heading of satirical cartoons and political pornography.[2]

Rabelais and the Marketplace

A notable example comes from Mikhail Bakhtin (1984), who in his now famous book about 16th-century French writer François Rabelais addressed the way in which Rabelais' notoriously raunchy novel, *Gargantua and Pantagruel*, focused so much attention on its characters' belching, farting, urinating, defecating, sexual release and proclivities. He argued that Rabelais had reproduced the standard speech of the town or village marketplace, a language far removed from the stilted purities of the court, the intelligentsia, or the clergy, a language full of vitality and force, far more vibrant than "correct speech." Bakhtin[3] proposed that particularly underlying Rabelais' novel was the deep folk tradition of many, many centuries that addressed hierarchy, power, repression, and fear, with mocking laughter:

> Laughter . . . was not only a victory over mystic terror of God, but also a victory over the awe inspired by the forces of nature, and most of all over the oppression and guilt related to all that was consecrated and forbidden. . . . It was the defeat of divine and human power, of authoritarian commandments and prohibitions, of death and punishment after death, hell. . . . Through this victory laughter clarified man's consciousness and gave him a new outlook on life. This truth was ephemeral; it was followed by the fears and oppressions of everyday life, but from these brief moments another unofficial truth emerged, truth about the world. (Bakhtin, 1984, pp. 90–1)

The collective expression of this irreverent laughter in late medieval Europe was confined to locations such as the town and village markets and intermittent carnival festivities and fairs, which were quite frequent throughout the year. Common days for such festivals included Shrove Tuesday and the feast of Corpus Christi. Perhaps the most extreme instance was All Fools' Day, when all the solemnities of religion and authority were ritually inverted and mocked. Excrement was used instead of incense in the mock mass in the church, and priests riding in carts tossed dung at passers-by. Men and women cross-dressed, and kitchen utensils were pressed into use as musical instruments.

In contrast to the rollicking forms of subversive communication reviewed by Bakhtin, Fabré (1994) notes the much more sober public speech at annual African American festivals in the 19th century:

> African Americans . . . were using the power of the imagination to invent, visualize, and represent themselves in roles they had always desired. . . . Feasts . . . marked the passage from various forms of subordination and enslavement to a "season" of change which could ultimately bring complete emancipation and liberation. (p. 75)

There would be "fairs, parades, picnics, banquets, and dances . . . the ringing of bells, burning of powder, display of banners" (p. 85).

Besides this prefiguration of the future, there was also a rehearsal of key moments in the recent past of Africans in the Americas. The mnemonic aspect of radical communication, as we will see again and again, beginning with the Mothers of the Plaza de

Mayo, the poem *Requiem*, and African American dance in this chapter, is one of its critically important aspects. One such festival was the Fourth of July, when the wider ideals of 1776 could be restated but when black insurrectionist Nat Turner's attempted slave rebellion was also memorialized. Not only Turner: Crispus Attucks in Massachusetts; in Baltimore, the Haitian revolution; a local leader of the Underground Railroad known popularly as Jerry Rescue in Syracuse. Another such festival in New York and Philadelphia was January 1, used in the early 19th century to celebrate the 1808 legal end to the right of US citizens to buy new slaves from Africa. At that point in US history, it was both a sign of change and a push to still further change that such events came to be part of the open public sphere rather than clandestine.

Radical speech events of these kinds – to recompose Habermas's (1987[1984]) terminology in favor of something perhaps less precise, but certainly less aseptic – are sometimes downplayed as brief and harmless safety-valve occasions, helping to stabilize an unjust social order. James C. Scott (1990, pp. 178–81) takes important issue with this view. He suggests that even when these communicative events are sponsored from on high, the fact that elites want them to act as a safety valve does not mean that they do so. He notes how often elites are preoccupied with the potential for serious disturbances in connection with such festivals. Scott's observation also reminds us how we need constantly to steer between dismissing radical communication as trivial and overstating its impact. Furthermore, the time frame over which we assess the question of radical media impact is also decisive in assessing it accurately.

Mothers of the Plaza de Mayo

A further example, this time of radical public speech in demonstrations,[4] and especially of their relation to keeping political memory alive, is provided by Susana Kaiser's (1993) study of the communication strategies of the Mothers of the Plaza de Mayo.[5] This was a group of mothers and grandmothers among the very few who publicly protested the systematic tortures, murders, and disappearances perpetrated by the Argentinian military junta of 1976 to 1982. Any form of opposition at that time, however mild, brought the risk of being defined as subversive, which in the junta's language meant being officially marked out for bestial repression. As many as 30,000 citizens may well have perished in this process. The media were silent, "normality" reigned, if the junta and the media could be believed, and protest virtually evaporated.

The Mothers, regardless, met every Thursday in the Plaza de Mayo and demonstrated, wearing diapers as head scarves to communicate graphically their own maternal identities and the absolute legitimacy of their questions about their own disappeared children. They held aloft placards with enlarged photos of their children, including their names and the last date they were seen alive. The Mothers continued, too, year after year, even after 1982, when the junta had collapsed, and when the political class wanted nothing more than to turn the page and forget the atrocities – when the Mothers were written off in many quarters as just a bunch of crazy obsessive old women.

Finally, however, some 15 years after the junta had fallen, a few individuals formerly involved in the repression began to come forward and confess to some of the crimes committed. In due course, some mainstream media began to address the issue, sometimes poorly, but at long last, it was on the public agenda. Some of those responsible were indicted for kidnaping; they and others were the object of angry denunciations in the streets and restaurants when they were spotted and of *escraches*, demonstrations outside their houses, to the point where they were barely able to circulate, a virtual form of citizens' house arrest (Kaiser, 2000).

Finally, in 1998–99, some of the most vicious members of the former junta found themselves jailed despite the amnesty that was supposed to ensure their impunity, on the ground that they had ordered the kidnaping of children, namely, the infants of those they had executed, some born in their torture cells. Kidnapping was a crime not covered under the amnesty. And, then, in Chile in 1999, some of their counterparts from the Pinochet dictatorship, who had the same blood on their hands, found themselves in jail on the same charge, while Pinochet himself was detained under house arrest in Britain facing extradition to Spain under European Union human rights law. The crazy old women's communication strategy had flowered.

Keeping political memory alive, therefore, was at the very center of the Mothers' message and successful strategy. It is important to note how their public speech also took nationalist, religious, and military themes and used them in a form of *détournement* against the ruling powers. At the time of the Malvinas/Falklands war, when the junta desperately sought to prop up its popularity by retaking the islands from Britain, the Mothers chanted in the square, "The Malvinas are Argentine – and so are our children!" They spoke in public in other ways, for example, kneeling at the altar rail and before the priest delivered the communion wafer to them, announcing out loud for all to hear: "I accept this Host in the name of [X.Y.], my daughter, who was last seen alive on the [day/month/year]." Given the Argentine Catholic hierarchy's deep complicity with the junta's crimes, such public statements were a communication against church and state alike. Once the captain of a detachment sent to scare them out of the square told his troops to train their rifles on the Mothers and rapped out "Take aim!" A number of the Mothers spontaneously shouted back "Fire!" – with their colossal courage rendering his terror tactics threadbare.[6]

Clandestine speech and networking have also been of great political importance in many repressive situations. Let us examine some further examples from African American history and one from 20th-century Russian history.

Networks Among African American Mariners

Bolster (1997) has described how African American mariners played a very significant radical communication network role in the period before and during the Civil War:

> Voyaging between the West Indies, Europe, and the American mainland enabled enslaved seamen to observe the Atlantic political economy from a variety of vantage points, to subvert their masters' discipline, and to open plantation society to outside influences . . . situated on vessels connecting all corners of the Atlantic world, black seafaring men

were newsmongers central to the formation of black America and a multidimensional racial identity. They broadcast accounts from Blacks' perspectives regarding the Haitian Revolution, the movements to abolish the slave trade and emancipate slaves, and the debate over decolonization that centered on the question of whether people of color would remain in the United States. (pp. 26, 36)

Bolster similarly notes how the first six black autobiographies published in English before 1800, each of them an opening salvo in the media war against slavery, were written by sailors. One of the main slave rebellions in the United States was led by Denmark Vesey, also a former mariner.

A further example of the mixture between oral and media modes of radical communication networks is offered by African American David Walker's *Appeal to the Colored Citizens of the World*, published in Boston in 1829. This pamphlet, a devastating attack on Africans' enslavement, was considered pivotal in the antislavery campaign by a whole chain of leading African American activists of the 19th and 20th centuries, including Frederick Douglass, Maria Stewart, and W. E. B. DuBois, as well as William Lloyd Garrison (Hinks, 1997, pp. 112–15).

In this case, we see an absorbing instance of media/network interplay. The pamphlet found its way to Savannah, Richmond, Wilmington, Charleston, and New Orleans as a result of a network of individual distributors, the initial links in the chain being coastal mariners (both black and white). From there, the copies fanned out through urban freedmen and -women, mobile nonplantation slaves such as riverine mariners, preachers, (including some white Methodists), and runaways in some of the marshy coastal regions of the South where small Maroon communities persisted. Plantation slaves, who generally could not read because learning to do so risked brutal punishment, had it read to them despite the surveillance of their masters (Hinks, 1997, pp. 116–72). As a result of the Georgia plantocracy's panic, which recognized the pivotal role played by mariners in this communication network, the legislature put a 40-day quarantine on all ships with black sailors aboard that docked in Georgia ports (Bolster, 1997, pp. 197–8).[7]

Poets of the Stalin Era

As our final example of radical speech communication in conditions of extreme repression and its potential power despite the huge odds against it, let us consider how the leading Russian poet, Anna Akhmatova, at the depth of Stalin's terror, composed her long poem *Requiem*. Several pages long, it was about her son's jailing and the terror imposed by Stalin, but she never wrote it down in case it should be found and used against her or him. Instead, she had a series of closely trusted friends each memorize one portion in case she should herself be liquidated. Astoundingly, its impact gradually overflowed from the tiny, brave circle in which it was first committed to memory. Over the years, *Requiem*[8] became a powerful talismanic statement, committed to memory in its entirety by many as a flame of determination to withstand and survive the Stalin regime's monstrous repression.

Communication in Dance

We switch now to consider dance and the body as a mnemonic communication instrument subverting a strategy of cultural extinction. It is perhaps hard for many people to think of dance as a mode of communication. If they reflect on it at all, they think of dance as something people do at parties to relax and get sexy, or as art (= classical European ballet). How can dance be communication when no words are spoken, and sometimes no music is played?

These responses are littered with hidden assumptions. We see the assumption that percussion has to involve drums and probably even that drums are percussion, not music. We see the assumption that art is one thing, communication another. We see the assumption that body language is not communication. We see the assumption that pleasure and relaxation and sexual expression are not enmeshed with art.

Dance, among African Americans during the centuries of their enslavement, was a particular kind of alternative medium of communication. Sometimes performed for the slave holders but also performed clandestinely,[9] it was for many reasons a particularly important form of communication. It constituted the continuation of a culture denied, a culture that over the centuries drew further and further away, but which, even after African languages had been banned and then nearly forgotten, spoke of a time before enslavement. It was the bodily celebration of a different era, before the totalitarian unfreedom of the Americas. It was an enactment of political memory.

This leads to a second point, namely, the mode of dance traditional within African cultures, where the body's fulcrum when dancing is the hips, unlike European dancing, where the fulcrum is generally the sternum. Abrahams (1992, pp. 94–5) notes that African dancing also embraced patting one's body; snapping one's fingers; clapping one's hands; using one's feet as percussive instruments; involving hips, legs, arms, and hands, sometimes operating separately from each other according to different counter-rhythms and cross-rhythms. Each part of the body also held a symbolic meaning. This represented an intensely powerful mnemonic expression because it engaged the entire person, demanding all the body's and all the mind's attention. And, needless perhaps to underscore, African dancing's aesthetics were powerfully interactive. There was no gulf between performers and audience, except the plantation masters, on the occasions they demanded a show.

Third, because the laws said the enslaved Africans' bodies were owned by the plantocracy, this expression of their own body culture represented a certain reclamation of their being. Their bodies were moving to their own pace and demands, not the slave driver's. Having, often, to perform traditional dance at the planters' festivities obviously cut into this self-assertion, but from contemporary accounts, it would seem that many Africans could retain their sense of validation and excitement and were able not to be engulfed in alienation at being part of a "command performance."

After the Civil War and Emancipation, Tera Hunter (1997, pp. 168–86) has noted, dance continued to be important. Urban dance halls became very popular among working class African Americans, despite being denounced as immoral by both the white authorities and the emerging black professional class. In the black neighborhoods of Atlanta, dance was to be found everywhere, at picnics, house parties, and especially in some of the churches. Music and dance styles were similar in both secular and religious settings, a reality abundantly evident in the entire history of blues, soul, gospel, and other African American musical genres. Dancing in religious services, however, was deemed by polite society, black as well as white, to be on a par with the city dance halls. Nevertheless, Hunter writes,

> The blues and dance were developed with a fierce sense of irreverence – the will to be unencumbered by any artistic, moral or social obligations, demands or interests external to the community which blues and dance were created to serve. . . . The feelings of self-empowerment and transcendence emanating from the blues and dance were evident. . . . The complex rhythmic structure and driving propulsive action endowed participants with the feeling of metaphysical transcendence, of being able to overcome or alter the obstacles of daily life. (pp. 183–4)

Dance in this context, then, during slavery and afterward, was a form of communication principally directed within the community, not as a communication from the community to those outside it. Radical communication may direct itself to strengthening those to whom it is addressed, to validating their dignity and renewing their cultural identity (Rodríguez, in Dunning 2001). It need not necessarily be a programmatic or propaganda endeavor, nor need it be a protest framed explicitly against those in power.

Song

Song has been another familiar alternative medium. In Soviet Russia, both guitar poetry and rock music played an important role from the 1960s onward. But we could equally cite the political street ballads of 18th-century Paris or London, African American work songs and religious songs, the history of blues music, the role of *nueva canción* in Latin America in the 1960s and later, the *rembetiko* music generated in the 1920s by Greek refugees from Turkey, the Mexican and Mexican American *corridos*, protest songs of the labor movement in Germany and elsewhere, antiwar songs from the Vietnam war era, antinuclear lyrics, reggae, punk, rap, and many other instances.[10]

Here, I will focus on just two: the blues and song in the German labor movement around the turn of the 20th century.

The blues provide another opportunity to consider religious elements in radical media, and another illustration of time's importance in assessing radical media impact. The linkages between religious and secular expression in the blues were always extremely tight (cf. Barlow, 1999; Harris, 1992; Keil, 1966; Levine, 1977, pp. 190–297; Sobel, 1979).[11] Patently, the melodies, stylistic elements, sometimes the instrumentation, and most certainly the intensity of expression and feeling all bear testimony to this truth. The point is that even in secular versions, the existential intensity of the musical expression derives in significant measure from its spiritual connotations – even, I would suggest, when the lyrics are not merely secular but also somewhere between sexually suggestive and downright bawdy. For while the preacher might wish to sanitize the devil's best lyrics, his satanic majesty's best tunes often found their way straight into the gospel churches' hymns.[12]

The fundamental point is that there was a huge communicative charge to the musical sound, in principle almost independent of the lyrics. This is one of the hardest, most elusive elements to describe or discuss in music, and yet, most everyone will admit its centrality. Harris (1992) cites Thomas Dorsey[13]:

> Blues were really born shortly after slaves were free, and they were sung the way singers felt inside. They were just let out of slavery or put out, or went out. . . . They poured out their souls in their songs . . . blues is a digging, picking, pricking at the very depth of your mental environment and the feelings of your heart . . . It's got to be that old low-down moan and the low-down feeling; you got to have feeling. (p. 98)

Thus, over time, gospel blues voiced the wrenching decades of slavery, of sharecropping, of Jim Crow, of lives uprooted in the urban North, of relentless racism, and of life's more everyday trials and tribulations. They also searched for consolation by acknowledging the American nightmare and by fastening on to anciently rooted modes of generating hope through the expression of spiritual anguish. For a while in the 1960s, this music was often judged defeatist and passive by black political activists, and, indeed, as blues music at about that time embraced the electric guitar and heavier percussion and branched out into fusion with newer forms of rock music, it spoke a more directly assertive and defiant message.

In a sense, this argument about the blues was about whether radical media should be directly defiant or should help people handle defeat so that they can accumulate the strength to fight another decade. The time frame for judging the roles of radical alternative media shows itself once again as an important dimension in judging radical media's impact.

The German song example nicely illustrates the issue of *mestizaje* in popular culture and the frequent difficulty in identifying in what senses its strands can be termed oppositional. In Germany from the 1840s onward, song anthologies with a labor dimension were published, but explicitly socialist songbooks only began to emerge in the 1860s (Lidtke, 1985, pp. 102–35). There may have been no less than 250 such song-books published between 1870 and 1914, reflecting the dramatic and seemingly inexorable growth of the German Social Democratic Party,[14] a growth that, as Lidtke demonstrates in considerable detail, brought with it a mass of cultural activities, daily newspapers, women's newspapers, quarterly theoretical journals, workers' festivals, poetry and drama clubs, and all kinds of study programs. The German party was the envy of similar parties across the world at the time, many of which could only marvel at its numbers, organization, and presence throughout every aspect of working class life.

Songs were to be found in two basic categories: the standard political songs, which could be sung at a variety of occasions and whose wording was set, and the strike songs, which might have had a common core but whose wording was changed to suit the specifics of the occasion. Some traditional songs were included, but not if they had nationalistic or religious lyrics. Sometimes, however, if these were easily replaceable by, for instance, references to freedom, then these changes were made in the text. Lidtke (1985) notes that "the labor movement was a singing movement" (p. 108) and that workers who had never read a word of the Marxist classics had probably often sung such songs in company with others in the movement's clubs. He suggests that

> in song, and especially in group singing, one simultaneously enjoyed the companionship of other people, expressed some ideological tendencies (often vague, to be sure), and could also find gratification by participating in simple artistic performances. Songs encourage an infinite repetition of ideas, and for that reason consciousness can be more deeply affected by song texts than by speeches that are heard once. . . . Words and phrases that seem trivial when judged by the standards of high theory may nonetheless take on considerable meaning when understood as part of an informal matrix of sentiments and aspirations. (pp. 108, 114)

At the same time, Lidtke draws attention to some rather mixed dimensions of song in the German labor movement. The lyrics were typically written for, not by, workers themselves, and addressed them in exhortation. The actual melodies were often well-known tunes to patriotic songs, such as *Deutschland, Deutschland Über Alles*. Even though the Social Democrats changed the words, and even though in the 19th century the song was patriotic rather than imperialist – Germany "before" everything rather than "over" everything – the tune still carried a hegemonic referent. And last, these songs did not change very much over the decades in response to changing trends in society. To that extent, Lidtke (1985) suggests, those singing them "declared not so much *what* they believed, but *that* they believed and that they *belonged*" (p. 135).

The songs did not then, probably, carry the racination of the blues or their depth of sentiment. They were an assertion of pride in workers' place in and contribution to society, a rejection of their exclusion from political power at the official level nationally – but they were not necessarily an expression of either their own deepest yearnings or of a clearly defined political agenda that could become hegemonic over time.

Notes

1. See Charles Husband's (1988) important essay on racist humor.
2. See, too, the extended discussion of enslaved African Americans' humor in Levine (1977, pp. 298–366).
3. In Stalin's Soviet Union, his book was itself a veiled denunciation of the stifling status quo.
4. The street demonstration is frequently written off as a passé form of radical communication and only effective if picked up by mainstream media – indeed, to be an artificial media event. Writing shortly after the tremendous impact of the demonstrations against the World Trade Organization in Seattle, Washington, in November 1999, this "higher political cynicism" looks distinctly threadbare (www.speakeasy.org/citizen). Favre (1999), in a valuable sociological analysis of the demonstration, notes among other things that the police are required to report on all demonstrations to the civil authorities, meaning that media inattention has no correlation with whether or not a message is delivered to the power structure. The police habit of publicly under-estimating the numbers at demonstrations does not mean they do so in private communications as well.

5. May Square, in the center of Buenos Aires, with the president's official palace at one end.

6. Shooting down unarmed mothers in Argentina's main square would hardly have hushed up the regime's crimes, nationally or internationally.

7. Another fascinating example of clandestine speech and political organizing is provided by Tera Hunter's (1997) study of African American laundrywomen in Atlanta in the decades following the Civil War (pp. 67–8, 74–97). They secretly organized as the Washing Society and called a strike in July 1881, tactically timed for 2 to 3 months before the International Cotton Exposition, the first-ever world's fair in the Southern states. It was the largest and most wounding of all the strikes in Atlanta in those years and led to many later forms of self-help and self-defense network organizing.

8. English translations of the poem, neither of them entirely satisfactory but still useful, are in both the W. W. Norton and the Penguin Books editions of selections from Akhmatova's works. For poems as radical alternative communication, see Alan Bold (1970), *Penguin Anthology Of Socialist Verse*. See, too, Cronyn, McKane, and Watts (1995), as well as African American and antiwar poetry broadsides of the 1960s (Sullivan, 1997, pp. 27–87) and John Brentlinger's (1995, pp. 197–214) absorbing and sensitive account of the politics and practice of poetry during the Sandinista period in Nicaragua.

9. There was a tradition of "steal aways" at night for the Africans to celebrate and continue their cultures. The sound would be contained by holding a large inverted cooking pot up above the heads of the speakers and singers.

10. See, for example, *Blues in the Mississippi Night* (1946/1990); *Greek-Oriental Rebetica* (1991); Limón (1992); Marcus (1989); Mattern (1991); Potash (1997); Seeger (1992).

11. This is not to say that African American religious expression was musically homogeneous. Harris (1992) devotes much of his study to the transition process in the 1920s whereby respectable, mass-attendance northern churches gradually shed their leaderships' deeply held assumption (cf. Tera Hunter) that blues music was culturally retrograde and morally suspect. The same supercilious attitude was evident at the posh dance clubs, although it was a standing joke that people with that attitude who attended rent parties where blues were played would pretty soon drop their propriety and start to throw down, too.

12. This is not unique to African American culture. Some of Johann Sebastian Bach's most famous religious chorale melodies are versions of tunes with originally quite spicy lyrics. The hybrid quality of which we spoke in Part I takes many, many forms.

13. A pivotal figure in the development of gospel blues (not to be confused with Tommy Dorsey, the music tycoon portrayed in the film *The Godfather* as terrified by the Mafia's slaughter of his favorite racehorse into releasing the young Sinatra from his contract).

14. At that point in time, the standard designation of a Marxist-inspired workers' party. It was the German party's majority endorsement of the move to war in 1914, leading to over 4 years' of mass slaughter of the working class – German, French, British, American, Russian, to name only some – that poses one of the harshest questions as to how effective are radical media and oppositional culture.

References

Abrahams, R. D. (1992). *Singing the Master: The Emergence of African American Culture in the Plantation South*. New York: Pantheon.

Bakhtin, M. M. (1984). *Rabelais and His World*. Bloomington: Indiana University Press.

Barlow, W. (1999). *Voice Over: The Making of Black Radio.* Philadelphia: Temple University Press.

Bold, A. (ed.) (1970). *The Penguin Book of Socialist Verse.* Harmondsworth, UK: Penguin.

Bolster, W. J. (1997). *Black Jacks: African American Seamen in the Age of Sail.* Cambridge, MA: Harvard University Press.

Brentlinger, J. (1995). *The Best of What We Are: Reflections on the Nicaraguan Revolution.* Amherst: University of Massachusetts Press.

Cronyn, H., R. McKane & S. Watts (eds.) (1995). *Voices of Conscience: Poetry from Oppression.* North Shields, UK: Iron Press.

Dunning, J. D. H. (ed.) (2001). *Radical Media.* Thousand Oaks, CA: Sage.

Fabré, Geneviève (1994). African American Commemorative Celebrations in the Nineteenth Century. In: G. Fabré & R. O'Meally (eds.), *History and Memory in African American Culture,* pp. 72–91. New York: Oxford University Press.

Favre, P. (1999). Les Manifestations De Rue Entre Espace Privé Et Espace Publique. In: B. François & E. Neveu (eds.), *Espaces Publiques Mosaïques: Acteurs, Arènes Et Rhètoriques Des Débats Publics Contemporains,* pp. 135–52. Rennes: Presses Universitaires de Rennes.

Fraser, N. (1993). Rethinking the Public Sphere: A Contribution to the Critique of Actually Existing Democracy. In: C. Calhoun (ed.), *Habermas and the Public Sphere,* pp. 109–42. Cambridge, MA: MIT Press.

Habermas, J. (1987 [1984]). *The Theory of Communicative Action.* Boston, MA: Beacon.

Harris, M. W. (1992). *The Rise of the Gospel Blues: The Music of Thomas Andrew Dorsey in the Urban Church.* New York: Oxford University Press.

Hinks, P. B. (1997). *To Awaken My Afflicted Brethren: David Walker and the Problem of Antebellum Slave Resistance.* University Park: Pennsylvania State University Press.

Hunter, T. (1997). *To Joy My Freedom: Southern Black Women's Lives and Labors after the Civil War.* Cambridge, MA: Harvard University Press.

Husband, C. (1988). Racist Humour and Racist Ideology in British Television, or I Laughed Till You Cried. In: C. Powell & G. E. C. Paton (eds.), *Humour in Society: Resistance and Control,* pp. 149–78. London: Macmillan.

Kaiser, S. M. (1993). The Madwomen Memory Mothers of the Plaza de Mayo. Master's Thesis, Film and Media Studies Department, Hunter College, City University of New York.

Kaiser, S. M. (2000). The Torturer Next Door: Challenging Impunity in Post-dictatorial Argentina. Paper Delivered at the International Communication Association Conference, Acapulco, Mexico, June.

Kapchan, D. (1996). *Gender on the Market: Moroccan Women and the Revoicing of Tradition.* Philadelphia: University of Pennsylvania Press.

Keil, C. (1966). *Urban Blues.* Chicago: University of Chicago Press.

Levine, L. W. (1977). *Black Culture and Black Consciousness: Afro-American Folk Thought from Slavery to Freedom.* New York: Oxford University Press.

Lidtke, V. (1985). *The Alternative Culture: Socialist Labor in Imperial Germany.* New York: Oxford University Press.

Limón, J. E. (1992). *Mexican Ballads, Chicano Poems: History and Influence in Mexican-American Social Poetry.* Berkeley: University of California Press.

Marcus, G. (1989). *Lipstick Traces: A Secret History of the Twentieth Century.* Cambridge, MA: Harvard University Press.

Mattern, M. (1991). Popular Music and Redemocratization in Santiago, Chile. *Studies in Latin American Popular Culture* 10, pp. 101–13.

Potash, C. (ed.) (1997). *Reggae, Rasta, Revolution: Jamaican Music from Ska to Dub.* New York: Schirmer.

Potel, J.-Y. (1982). *The Promise of Solidarnosc.* New York: Praeger.

Rodríguez, C. (2001). *Fissures in the Mediascape: A Comparative Analysis of Citizens' Media.* Cresskill, NY: Hampton Press.

Scott, J. C. (1985). *Weapons of the Weak: Everyday Forms of Peasant Resistance.* New Haven, CT: Yale University Press.

Scott, J. C. (1990). *Domination and the Arts of Resistance: Hidden Transcripts.* New Haven, CT: Yale University Press.

Seeger, P. (1992). *American Industrial Ballads* (Smithsonian/Folkways Recordings). Cambridge, MA: Rounder Records.

Sobel, M. (1979). *Trabelin' on: The Slave Journey to an Afro-Baptist Faith.* Westport, CT: Greenwood.

Sullivan, J. D. (1997). *On the Walls and in the Streets: American Poetry Broadsides from the 1960s.* Urbana: University of Illinois Press.

Thinking about the End of the World with Conservative Protestants

Mark Hulsether*

At least three things are clear about evangelical end-times speculation. One is that it is a major phenomenon. During the 1970s, Hal Lindsey's *The Late Great Planet Earth* sold twenty-eight million copies, making it the top-selling non-fiction book of the decade – yet its success was dwarfed by the twelve-volume, multi-media juggernaut of the *Left Behind* series, written by Jerry Jenkins and NCR leader Tim LaHaye. Dozens of variations on the same plot are available as films, novels, sermons, and Bible study tapes; some of these break through to mainstream theaters and marketing behemoths like Wal-Mart, while others circulate through churches and Christian bookstores. One scholar tried to estimate the number of Christians who are 'deeply preoccupied' with the end-times, 'place [this] at the center' of their worldview, and believe that God has 'a specific, detailed, plan for history's last days.' By this definition, he found eight million prophecy believers out of an evangelical sub-culture of fifty million.[1] However, this leaves aside people who are concerned about the end-times as just one interest among others within a broad evangelical worldview. We might define prophecy belief so that it blends seamlessly into US culture at large. Where does it end when twenty-five per cent of US citizens think that the Bible predicted the attacks of 9/11, sixty-two per cent have no doubt that Jesus will return, and eighty-five per cent accept the Bible as divinely inspired? Can interest in films like *Matrix Revolutions* (2003) and *End of Days* (1999) – both with apocalyptic scenarios and heroes who are crucified somewhat like Christ – be disentangled from end-times prophecy belief?

Second, certain basics about the tradition are straightforward. End-times belief is part of the evangelical sub-culture. It stands in a long tradition of interpreting apocalyptic texts of the Hebrew Bible like the book of Daniel and similar Christian texts such as the book of Revelation and the thirteenth chapter of Mark. Christians have commented on these texts throughout history; for example, Puritans drew on this tradition when they spoke about building a Kingdom of God in America. In the nineteenth century, writers like Cyrus Scofield (author of the *Scofield Reference Bible*) reworked the tradition into the theory of dispensational premillennialism. As discussed above, dispensationalists interpret the Bible by breaking it into stages, including current and

*Pp. 190–9 from M. Hulsether, *Religion, Culture and Politics in the Twentieth-Century United States* (Edinburgh: Edinburgh University Press). © 2007 by Mark Hulsether. Reprinted with permission from Edinburgh University Press, www.eup.ed.ac.uk, and Columbia University Press.

future stages that they see as foretold in prophecy. Premillennialists believe that Jesus will return before a thousand-year period at the end of time called the millennium, which they expect to begin soon in the context of a global crisis. End-times believers map standard plot elements from apocalyptic texts – for example, the rapture of believers and rise of an anti-Christ with marks like the number 666 — onto current events. Whereas most scholars see apocalyptic texts as comments on struggles during the years when they were written — especially persecution of Jews and Christians by Greeks and Romans — end-times believers see these texts as predicting the future and seek one-to-one correspondences with current political events. For example, a mysterious enemy called Gog in the book of Ezekiel became associated with scenarios of the Soviet Union attacking Israel, and one Biblical literalist managed to translate the Hebrew word for 'bow and arrow' as 'missile launcher.'[2]

All of the following people have been identified as the anti-Christ in end-times discourse: King George III, several Popes, Adolph Hitler, John Kennedy, Henry Kissinger, Sun Myung Moon, and Ronald Reagan. Marks of the Beast include the Stamp Act during the Revolutionary War, the blue eagle logo of the National Recovery Administration in the New Deal era, and a birthmark on the face of Soviet leader Mikhail Gorbachev during the Cold War. In every generation since the book of Daniel was written, prophecy writers have piled up evidence that their interpretive scenarios have flawlessly predicted all events up the moment when they are writing – then concluded with an appeal to readers to trust them about the future.[3] Through such methods, believers comment on current events and express their hopes and fears about the future. For example, they currently worry that the anti-Christ is planning a global system to control people using implanted computer bar codes. Since 1948 they have often voiced concern about Israel – both support for Israeli policy and the expectation that most Jews will be punished for rejecting Christ. One evangelist used a computer analysis of the Bible to discern that Palestinian leader Yasser Arafat was in league with the anti-Christ. Coded messages could be uncovered if, for example, one read the book of Daniel backward and counted every seventh letter. Through such a method, the preacher discovered the words 'Arafat shake hands'; he felt that this revealed the futility of peace negotiations that were underway at the time.[4]

A third feature of end-times discourse is implicit in what we have already said – it includes a sense of embattlement or persecution that focuses the discontent of ordinary people against people they perceive as enemies. It can mobilize dissent toward many political ends. Even the elite authors of end-times novels are examples of this phenomenon when their fears of the anti-Christ merge with fears of corporate globalization or domination by secular liberals. However, we can discover a wider range of dissent if we expand the discussion. Rastafarian musician Bob Marley might be considered an end-times prophecy believer, and much hip-hop is bursting with apocalyptic images.[5] More important for US evangelicals is the blend of end-times ideas and populism. For example, let us return to Huey Long. Long deserves some of his reputation as anti-democratic; after all, he was a successful Louisiana politician during an era when there was no route to power that did not involve corruption and ruthless political tactics. In this context, Long used Biblical rhetoric to focus the anger of his working-class supporters against southern elites, rather than against the northern elites and local blacks who were often targets of kindred politicians. The 1995 film *Kingfish* captures some of the complexities. Overall, this film reflects the common interpretation of Long as little more than a proto-fascist demagogue. However, in one scene he presents his plan to increase taxes on the rich as an example of 'God's law' and denounces his enemies by quoting a prophetic text: 'Break up the concentration of wealth in this country and redistribute it according to the Lord's plan. For if you do not, listen: "Go to now, ye rich men. Weep and howl for the miseries that shall come upon you"!'[6]

With these three points to orient our discussion, the point to underscore is the ambiguity of end-times politics. Scholars disagree whether the discourse encourages fatalism. Many argue that it breeds cynicism and complacency about efforts at social reform. Premillennialists tend to be downbeat about the prospects for humans doing God's will on earth, at least compared with those who expect progress toward the millennium within history; they feel that modern society is more like a Babylon to shun than a kingdom of God to build. In this view, Jesus needs to come back and clean up the mess made by humans before the kingdom of God can come. Trying to reform Babylon makes no sense. What does make sense is to flee, preferably to a place with a nice view of God destroying one's enemies.

However, many scholars overstress this fatalistic interpretation. There is no contradiction – in fact there are logical affinities – between actively working toward one's goals and believing that God is fighting on one's side to guarantee an inevitable victory. The rise of Dominion theology dramatizes the worldliness of many prophecy believers. Radical Dominionists want to reconstruct US law along strict Biblical lines (thus their other name, Reconstructionists); some of them literally stockpile arms that they expect to use in a coming war with the anti-Christ. Moderate Dominionists (including many NCR leaders) shift their stress away from a goal of separating from Babylon toward a goal of redeeming it; one of their mottos is the Bible verse, 'Occupy Until I Come.'[7] Either way, they attack premillennialists for timidity and otherworldliness. One measure of their growing strength is the behavior of heroes in end-times novels since the 1970s. Earlier heroes were often passive victims awaiting rescue by God, whereas today's heroes (such as the fighters in *Left Behind*'s Tribulation Force) are bold, confident, and technologically savvy. Moreover, even classic forms of premillennialism have optimistic aspects. One scholar speaks of a contrast between liberal Protestant optimism that is like a flashlight dimly illuminating a future landscape, and premillennial optimism that concentrates its utopian hopes on a vision of heaven, like a flashlight held close to a page.[8]

Whether end-times beliefs focus dissent in fatalistic or optimistic ways, their political impact remains fluid. Suppose that a passenger sitting next to you on a plane is reading *Left Behind*. Suppose she notices you reading this book and says to you conspiratorially, 'The Bible teaches that we must fight God's enemies – don't you agree?' What does she mean? Clearly there is room for alarm about what this question might imply for people in the network of militias, paramilitary cells, and churches of the far right. *The Turner Diaries* was a favorite book of Timothy McVeigh, the Christian terrorist who bombed the Oklahoma City Federal Building. It describes how a disciplined group can (as McVeigh did) blow up a building with a truck bomb using agricultural fertilizer. This is among the milder episodes in the book, which reads as a how-to manual for starting your own terrorist cell. Its heroes escalate the conflict to nuclear war using bombs they obtain by taking over a military base. Their plans are guided by 'The Book,' which assures them that 'We are truly the instruments of God in the fulfillment of His Grand Design.' In their liberated zone they lynch 55,000 race traitors, including many identified as 'faculty members from the nearby UCLA campus.' The hero comments: 'As the war of extermination [that is, the clean-up operations after the nuclear attack] wore on, millions of soft, city-bred, brainwashed, Whites gradually began reclaiming their manhood. The rest died.'[9]

The Turner Diaries takes its vision of establishing order and rolling back gains of the civil rights movement to cartooonish extremes. Often it returns to images of black rapists who threaten white sexual purity; the book opens with an attack that at first seems to be an example of this threat, although it turns out to be a government goon squad confiscating white people's guns (in this version of reality blacks collude with the police and are never harassed by them). The heroes execute 'pulpit prostitutes' who compromise with Republican leaders; they complain that 'the Jewish takeover of the Christian churches . . . [is] virtually complete.' That is, they condemn NCR leaders for inadequate commitment to Dominion theology and excessive support for Israel. Such support is anathema for the splinter of the far right called the Christian Identity movement, which teaches that the true identity of the Bible's chosen people is Anglo-Saxon and that Jews are the 'spawn of Satan.'[10]

Almost everyone would consider such ideas noxious. However, it is equally clear that other forms of end-times belief are fairly innocuous. One preacher saw a rise in overdue library books as a sign of Christ's imminent return. Your airline companion may be reading *Left Behind* with no more political agenda than passengers who are reading Stephen King novels or watching *The X-Files* as their in-flight movie. Consider the end-times believers who watched *The PTL Club*, a television show hosted by Jim and Tammy Faye Bakker in the 1980s. PTL stands for 'Praise the Lord' and 'People That Love.' The Bakkers' show was a Christian version of *Oprah*, and their empire included an amusement park called Heritage USA that was a Christian version of Disneyland. Like many of their viewers, Jim and Tammy were raised in a Pentecostal sub-culture that taught them to shun 'the world' – not attend movies, not to use make-up, and so on. However, by their heyday they modeled for their viewers how to use Pentecostal teachings about God's blessing to blend seamlessly into a world of middle-class consumerism. They represent a classic case of what we earlier called Pentecostal pragmatism as opposed to primitivism. Jim told his viewers not simply to ask God for a Cadillac, but to tell God the exact color it should be.[11]

Unfortunately PTL took this to such extremes – for example, using donations to buy an air-conditioned doghouse, a yacht, and a pet giraffe – that it provoked a backlash. Like many other evangelists, Bakker used a seed-faith fundraising approach. That is, he taught that anyone who made a gift to God could expect this seed to grow into a yield of material blessings. In effect, donating to PTL was partly like offering a hopeful prayer, but also like investing in lucrative stock. Bakker pushed this model so hard that the lines blurred between asking viewers to support a program they valued (as National Public Radio does during pledge drives), inviting viewers to invest in PTL through seed-faith gifts, and making fraudulent guarantees of future vacations at Heritage USA in apartments that PTL promised to build with the donations. We might compare his vision to the promises of future growth made – on a larger scale – by Enron Corporation. Just as Enron's financial house of cards collapsed, so did PTL's, and the question arose whose fault it was – the company's for making promises it could not keep or investors' for believing these promises. Jim Bakker wound up in jail, and today Tammy Faye is better known among college students for appearing on an MTV reality show than for her work on PTL. One of the few people who benefited from PTL's debacle was Falwell. He gained control of PTL by presenting himself as a father figure who could put its house in order, and wound up appropriating its communications satellite.

The point we must grasp is that both Tammy Faye and Timothy McVeigh are part of end-times discourse. When Tammy appeared on television after PTL's collapse and sang, 'When Life Gives You a Lemon, Start Making Lemonade,' her song included a line about 'being pruned by God's blade.'[12] Fans could recognize this line as Biblical prophetic motif and recall how PTL had talked about Christ's return along with vacations at Heritage USA. But in this case, if end-times theology is supposed to be other-worldly and defined by a sense of fighting God's enemies – then exactly what did PTL viewers fight, other than a sense that they were not yet as comfortable as Tammy in the world of consumerism? If an evangelical sub-culture is supposed to be defined by its distance from and embattlement with dominant culture, doesn't the boundary of the PTL sub-culture appear less like the perimeter of a paramilitary compound and more like a wave that ripples off and disappears somewhere near a shopping mall?

In light of this range of meanings, the question arises: where do the heavy-hitters of end-times discourse like LaHaye and Robertson fall on this continuum, and how do ordinary readers in pews and airplanes interpret them? To begin, it is clear that some sectors of the NCR shade into the less radical parts of the extreme right. This does not mean that *The Turner Diaries* reveals the pure essence of prophecy that will naturally ripen into action for serious believers; NCR leaders worked hard to distance themselves from it. Nevertheless – approaching this question from the far right looking toward the center – the same far-right network that produced McVeigh also produced the former KKK leader David Duke, who won the Republican nomination and fifty-five per cent of the white vote for governor of Louisiana in the 1990s. Approaching from the NCR establishment looking right, Robertson's book, *The New World Order*, recycled key arguments from the *Protocols of the Elders of Zion*, albeit with fewer Jews and more New Agers in its conspiracy. Written shortly after the fall of the Soviet Union when George Bush, Sr., spoke about building a new world order, Robertson stated that Bush's participation in the Trilateral Commission and his co-operation with the United Nations in the Persian Gulf War were part of a Satanic conspiracy to institute 'an occult-inspired world socialist dictatorship.' For his part, LaHaye is a major NCR leader who has stated that public schools teach youth to be 'anti-God, anti-moral, anti-family, anti-free enterprise, and anti-American'; he blames ruling 'educrats' controlled by a web that includes the National Endowment for the Humanities, the Trilateral Commission, and the Illuminati.[13]

It is also clear that prophetic scenarios reinforce isolationism and unilateralism – as well as nationalism, although only insofar as government leaders are seen as Biblically sound. In books like *Left Behind*, when US leaders capitulate to the anti-Christ, the duty of believers is to disobey them, even to the extent of treason and armed resistance. In Robertson's *End of the Age* – a book that restated the themes of *New World Order* in a novel with a similar plot – a heroic Christian general lies to the President and secedes from the US with several nuclear bases. With God's help, he battles a world government headquartered in Iraq that worships the Hindu 'demon' Shiva.[14] End-times books teach that cosmic history depends on faithful disciples – especially, although not exclusively from the US – refusing to co-operate with the United Nations. As one scholar summarizes, within end-times discourse 'treaties, alliances, and participation in the UN all pave the way for the coming of the anti-Christ . . . [who] unites the world to form a One World Government.'[15] He promises peace – thus duping ignorant people like the head of a seminary portrayed in *End of the Age* who says that the anti-Christ represents everything that liberal Christians had expected in the Messiah. However, once the anti-Christ gains power, he tries to kill everyone who will not worship him. In most versions of the plot, believers escape the tribulation by being raptured before it starts. However, *Left Behind* is an exception to this rule, and we have seen how believers debate whether to stockpile arms for fighting in the tribulation. The plot always ends with Jesus returning to win a cosmic battle, either by turning the tide in a war fought by Christians or fighting the war himself.

It is difficult to assess the political impact of end-times prophecy compared with other factors. Clearly it plays some role in shaping public attitudes. At a minimum it inflects the climate of discussion and helps to block roads not taken, especially in US policies toward Israel. At times it has been part of high-level discussions. Reagan's end-times beliefs were a factor in his ideas about the Cold War and the support he garnered from the NCR. Robertson is prominent in Republican politics. George W. Bush has made many religiously inflected comments about the Iraq war. He spoke of a crusade against radical Islam after the attacks of 11 September 2001, and he continues to speak about a global war between good and evil in a way that implies a contrast between Western Christian values and much of the Muslim World. Whether or not Bush actually stated that 'God told me to strike at al-Qaeda and I struck them, and then he instructed me to strike at Saddam, which I did' (either this report or Bush's denial of it is a lie) he made it clear to advisors that he felt 'God put me here' to pursue his Middle East policies.[16]

Bush's comments are in dialogue with the sixty per cent of US citizens who say that they expect Biblical prophecies to come true and the twenty-five per cent who say that the Bible predicted the attacks of 9/11.[17] Recall how we discussed the relation between the Puritan ethic and the rise of capitalism; neither caused the other, but the two reinforced each other. Likewise, end-times belief – with its nationalism, self-righteousness, dualism, and possible fatalism – does not shape US foreign policy by itself. Nor is it merely a reflection of deeper processes in US policies, for example, in the anti-Christs it targets in any given year. The point is that together they form a mutually reinforcing world-view that powerfully motivates believers and is difficult to refute in conventional rational terms.

A key interpretive problem, however, is that the continuum of end-times belief does not simply run from McVeigh through Robertson to Bush – it keeps running to the center and all the way through Huey Long to Bob Marley on the left. Moreover, people traveling this route can get sidetracked at the mall with Tammy Faye anywhere along the way. End-times beliefs can be compartmentalized, fade into the mix of other concerns, or become diluted. We have noted that apocalyptic theology dovetailed with anti-Communism in Billy Graham's sermons. At the same time as we take Graham's melding of the Cold War and the Bible with the utmost seriousness – if Graham made people more fatalistic about the question of whether nuclear war was inevitable, what issue could be more weighty? – we might also notice that by the 1980s the supermarket tabloid *Weekly World News* published a story about Graham's end-times book, *Approaching Hoofbeats*. Although this story was full of easily corroborated facts about the book, it ran it alongside another story about an asteroid that (according to the tabloid's 'reporter') was the literal location of hell and would probably crash into the earth in the year 2000. Another article in the same issue, receiving equal billing with Graham, was entitled 'Shoplifter Stuffs 4–lb. Frozen Chicken Down Her Bra . . . Then Passes Out from the Cold.'[18]

The point I am trying to accent is that end-times believers fight God's enemies in many ways, from the chillingly political to the utterly trivial and many points in between. Most evangelical sermons are closer to Tammy Faye than to Timothy McVeigh, especially by the time that they filter down to supermarket lines. What we don't know, and can't know without case-by-case investigation, is how this plays out in the interplay between authors like LaHaye and his readers. To what extent does imagining oneself fighting God's enemies represent a utopian critique of capitalism, to what extent a distraction from social issues, and to what extent a death wish? What would it mean to someone who watched *Left Behind* during the same week that she also watched *The Matrix*, worked at a minimum wage job, talked to her lesbian cousin, was sexually harassed, took offense when her pastor said that her Pakistani co-worker was going to hell, and danced to R.E.M.'s song, 'It's the end of the world as we know it, and I feel fine'? How would this all fit together, pull apart, or co-exist in separate compartments? We do not have good answers to such questions. We need to inquire further about this issue.

Notes

1. Paul Boyer, *When Time Shall Be No More: Prophecy Belief in Modern American Culture* (Cambridge MA: Harvard University Press, 1992), ix. Some paragraphs in this section are adapted from my review essay on Boyer, 'It's the end of the world as we know it,' *American Quarterly* vol. 48, no. 2 (1996), 375–84. See also Bruce Forbes and Jeanne Kilde eds, *Rapture, Revelation and the End Times* (New York: Palgrave Macmillan, 2004).
2. Boyer, *When Time Shall Be No More*, 133.
3. Boyer, *When Time Shall Be No More*; Dwight Wilson, *Armageddon Now! The Premillennarian Response to Russia and Israel Since 1917* (Grand Rapids: Baker Book House, 1977).
4. Local religious broadcast on channel 99, Knoxville, Tennessee cable television, 3/16/97.
5. On alternative uses of apocalyptic see Peter Linebaugh, "Jubilating: or, how the Atlantic working class used the Biblical jubilee against capitalism, with some success," *Radical History Review* no. 50 (1991), 143–82 and Wojcik, *End of the World as We Know It*.

6. *Kingfish: the Story of Huey Long* (Turner Pictures Worldwide, 1995.) For Long's own words, see his 1934 pamphlet, *Share Our Wealth* (Indian Mills, WV, 1980).

7. Diamond, *Roads to Dominion*. The text quoted is Luke 19:13 (King James Version). The context for these words is a story about a master – typically interpreted as Jesus – who gives his servants money and a command with a disputed meaning; the *New Revised Standard Version* translates it as 'Do business with these until I come back.'

8. Boyer, *When Time Shall Be No More*, 319; Heather Hendershott, *Shaking the World for Jesus: Media and Conservative Evangelical Culture* (Chicago: University of Chicago Press, 2004), 176–209.

9. Andrew MacDonald, *The Turner Diaries* (2nd edn) (copyright William Pierce, 1978; Hillsboro, WV: National Vanguard Books, 1995), 71, 160–1, 207.

10. MacDonald, *Turner Diaries*, 64. For more on these issues see Michael Barkun, *Religion and the Racist Right* (revised edn) (Chapel Hill: University of North Carolina Press, 1997).

11. Frances Fitzgerald, 'Jim and Tammy,' *New Yorker*, 4/23/90, 45–87. For more in this vein see Carol Flake, *Redemptorama: Culture, Politics, and the New Evangelicalism* (New York: Penguin, 1984).

12. Tammy Faye Messner (her name after remarriage) on *The Shirley Show*, video recording in author's possession, n/d, ca. 1994.

13. Pat Robertson, *The New World Order* (Dallas: Word Publishing, 1991), 92; for a critique see Michael Lind, 'Rev. Robertson's Grand International Conspiracy Theory,' *New York Review of Books* (2/2/95), 21–5. LaHaye quoted in Bivins, *Fracture of Good Order*, 95.

14. Pat Robertson, *The End of the Age: a Novel* (Dallas: Word Publishing, 1996). His conflation of Muslims and Hindus, like a related conflation of New Agers and secular rationalists in *New World Order*, is an extreme example of the evangelical tendency to divide the world into two basic camps – Christians versus everyone else.

15. Amy Johnson Frykholm, in Forbes and Kilde, *Rapture, Revelation and the End Times*, 169.

16. Melani McAlister, *Epic Encounters: Culture, Media, and US Interests in the Middle East, 1945–2000* (Berkeley: University of California Press, 2001). See also Garry Wills, *Reagan's America* (New York, Penguin: 1988) and Rogin, *Ronald Reagan, the Movie*. Bush quote reported by Mahmoud Abbas and cited in Kaplan, *With God on Their Side*, 9; Seymour Hersh, 'Up in the Air,' *New Yorker* 12/5/05, 43. Bush later distanced himself from the crusade remark, since it worked at cross-purposes with a stress on universal values of freedom that can be shared by Muslims who support global capitalism and Western-style democracy.

17. 2002 Time/CNN poll cited in Bill Moyers, 'Environmental Armageddon,' accessed at *http://www.beliefnet.com/story/161/story_16143_1.html*.

18. Graham, *Approaching Hoofbeats: the Four Horsemen of the Apocalypse* (New York: Avon, 1985); *Weekly World News*, 4/15/79, 2–3, 8–9, and 21.

28

The Rumor Bomb:
American Mediated Politics
as Pure War

*Jayson Harsin**

"Saddam Hussein has longstanding, direct and continuing ties to terrorist networks . . . Iraq has sent bomb-making and document forgery experts to work with al Qaeda. Iraq has also provided al Qaeda with chemical and biological weapons training." American president George W. Bush made this well-circulated statement on February 8, 2003. Over a year later, in June 2004, Chief Weapons Inspector David Kay stated, "We simply didn't find any evidence of extensive links with Al Qaeda, or for that matter any real links at all" (Kranish & Bender 2004). Yet the Bush administration continued to launch and the news media continued to circulate softer variations on Bush's original strong claim of "longstanding, direct and continuing ties." As recently as March 2005, polls showed that over half of all Americans still believed Saddam Hussein had WMD before the US invasion of Iraq, while 60 percent still believed Hussein played a role in aiding Al Qaeda with 9/11.[1]

Regardless of the veracity of claims, belief persists. The relationship between tenuous claims, their circulation, and the appearance and persistence of belief points to a common strategy in contemporary American political practice – the rumor bomb. In this essay I examine several key transformations in mediated American political discourse that encourage the use of rumor as a privileged communication strategy and that promise its efficacy. Changing institutional news values, communication technologies, and political public relations (PR) strategies have converged to produce a profoundly vexing relationship between rumor and verification, which is exploited by politicians with anti-deliberative aims of managing belief.

The strategic use and (sometimes) careless circulation of rumor characterizes the current climate of American media and politics,[2] the effects of which are often discussed in isolation in literature on the beleaguered American public sphere, new market pressures and changing news values in news media, and the banality of rumor's success in war situations. But these phenomena must be viewed together in a theory of convergence and conjuncture if we are to better explain the turn to rumor from the position of production, mediation, circulation, and reception, where it may reinforce already

* An earlier, longer version of this chapter appeared as "The Rumor Bomb: Theorizing the Convergence of New and Old Trends in Mediated US Politics" in *Southern Review: Communication, Politics & Culture*, vol. 39, no. 1. © 2006 by J. Harsin. Reprinted with permission from the author.

held beliefs, produce new ones, or simply reinforce a paralyzing cynicism about a mediated democratic spectacle.

While war communication, especially in the form of propaganda, has traditionally had clear goals of producing belief, consent and behavior, it is usually assumed to be categorically different from peacetime democratic political communication practices. At least since Periclean Athens, democracy has been theorized as a political form characterized by open political debate. Deliberate distortions, intimidation, exclusion, and discourse reduced to emotional appeals results in paranoia have been regarded as destabilizing if not destructive to the political culture of democracy itself.[3] *Pure War*, however, creates an overarching culture structured by indefinite potential exterior threat(s). For fifty years this was the Cold War. Today the Bush administration's agenda (from communication to policy initiatives such as the Patriot Act) in the War on Terror has been deterritorialized as an information war directed at US citizens as well as Iraqis, Arab nations, and global citizens (Bolton 2006; Shehata 2002; Kurtz 2003; Marshall 2003). In this fight the Bush administration uses a rhetorical device common in any war – rumor. Yet they use it as a form of propaganda for domestic as well as war issues. Such communication practice is the most exaggerated form of a kind of anti-politics where war and peacetime communication practices have imploded.[4] In a climate where verification is in crisis and disorientation is the structure of feeling due to the "information superhighway" and virtual reality, information accidents can happen (Virilio 2000a). But some information bombs are not accidents. Rumor becomes useful and dangerous.

What Is a Rumor?

As I use the term,[5] rumor includes one or more of the following characteristics: (i) a crisis of verification; (ii) the need to eliminate public uncertainty and restore social stability; (iii) a condition of political anxiety and be used to transfer anxiety and uncertainty onto an opponent; and while it may include interpersonal communication, it is most characterized by highly developed electronically mediated societies where news travels fast.

First, a crisis of verification is perhaps the most salient and politically dangerous aspect of rumor. Berenson (1952) defines rumor as a kind of persuasive message involving a proposition that lacks "secure standards of evidence" (Pendleton 1998). What, then, is the difference between a rumor and a lie? Lies are untrue statements, whether the speaker knows it or not.

Secondly, rumor use aims to reduce or augment public anxiety. As I am using the term, rumor "relates to a situation about which there is some uncertainty and a felt need to reduce that uncertainty" (Pendleton 1998, 71). However, when rumor is launched, it does not eliminate anxiety and uncertainty through logical refutations and consoling presentations of evidence. It simply eliminates the feeling of anxiety and uncertainty by transferring it to a new object (often a scapegoat), or by using strategically ambiguous language that may dupe uncritical audiences with the appearance of certainty and reliability.

Thirdly, the rumor bomb is characterized by Speed and Electronically Mediated Societies. While rumor is not a novel political strategy, its ability to spread rapidly has accelerated its reach, use, and power. Rumor in the nineteenth century existed, but lacked widespread accessible technologies to circulate quickly and broadly. Today the uncertainty caused by a crisis in gatekeeping, itself stemming from market pressures to entertain and to report quickly for scoops, gives rumor a unique circulatory power and thus opportunity to be exploited by political PR.

Three Convergent Factors Explaining Rumor Bombs

Three major phenomena have converged into a highly formative conjuncture for political communication and the use of rumor:

1) changing news values and newsgathering practices influenced by new communication technologies and increasing concentration of news organization ownership;
2) increasing influence of PR on political communication, especially executive branch information and news management; and
3) the influence of war communication strategies on so-called democratic political communication, resulting in an anti-deliberative politics or a spectacle of democratic politics.

News media market and newsgathering practices

Changes in news media market and institutional codes of newsgathering can be divided into four sub-groups: concentration, values, speed, and secrecy.

First, corporate mergers have increased the pressures toward speed and expanding viewer- and readerships, and the demand for ever-increasing profit. The phenomena of horizontal and vertical media convergences and strategies of synergy have helped blur the boundaries between news and entertainment. Entertainment and tabloid reporting have long been characterized by rumors. Thus, the traditional codes of ethics and standards of newsgathering are more frequently bowing to the dictates of profit in a market where "serious" and "soft" news categories are less clearly demarcated. Briefly, I will note some major reasons why contemporary media market pressures produce conditions of news gathering and presentation practices favorable to rumor.

The first important explanation of rumor explosion in news today can be attributed to cuts in staff and financial resources for investigation and editing. In fact, "routine placement of PR messages as news is likely to accelerate as corporate mergers combine more media companies under common ownership" (Bennett 2003, 175). The importance of political PR in rumor launching and circulation is well-illustrated by recent stories about the Bush administration's use of "fake news" video releases, staged press conference questions, and the use of "fake reporters." (Rich 2005).

Secondly, this cost-cutting is combined with the market drive for speed in a news world operating in real-time. The explosion of digital cable, satellite, and the internet in the late 1980s and early 1990s produced a more fiercely competitive news market, in which events could be covered as they happened. Pressures of speed and real-time reporting sometimes end up in unattributed sources, speculations, and rumor circulation (Thussu 2003, 121; Seib 2004, 14). Philip Seib adds, "News organizations are more susceptible to such manipulation when desire for speed outweighs concern about verification". According to David Bohrman, CNN White House Bureau Chief, "The media is doing the fact-checking it can. . . . [but] more sources seem to be stepping up to speak who haven't spoken in the past, and the (news) cycle on cable news is so fast, it's immediate" (Deggans 2004). Bohrman calls this under-factchecked new journalism the "journalism of assertion," in which "some media outlets simply report charges and let the audiences sort it all out" (ibid.). Yet the effect of the internet is not just a faster traditional news media with laxer editing standards and gatekeeping. The internet is also increasingly the *source* of traditional media's news.

If the internet is a factor contributing to dwindling audiences for traditional news media (press and network TV),[6] it is also increasingly playing an agenda-setting role for traditional news media, Some political communication scholars trace the trend to the influence of Matt Drudge's blog-like *Drudge Report*, which broke the Clinton–Lewinsky affair before traditional elite news media followed suit (Paletz 2002, 78; Bennett 2003, 8). Blogs and email have played an increasingly powerful agenda-setting role (sometimes an alternative agenda to the mainstream news organizations and sometimes an inter-media agenda-setting) vis à vis traditional news organizations. Their influence is attributed to their speed and low cost, both of which the traditional news organizations imitate,

But this inter-media agenda setting has also favored the circulation of rumor. The inter-media agenda setting power of the internet does not by any means result in the inclusion of counter-public views and voices but may equally circulate any number of internet-based lies and rumors. The February 2004 rumor that John Kerry, while married, had an affair with an intern in her '20s illustrates the point (Gitlin 2004). It happened that the Drudge Report, then Rupert Murdoch's London-based *Sun* and *The Times*, had posted on their websites a claim that Kerry had had an affair with an intern. Soon the *Wall Street Journal* website had followed suit. While other major newspapers had avoided the story, on February 13 CNN featured a discussion on what the media should do about the accusations. In that discussion, commentator Jeff Greenfield claimed that it didn't matter whether the mainstream traditional media tried to play gatekeeper, because the internet age had dissolved such gates (Gitlin 2004). The problem, Gitlin notes, is that there was no evidence that anything in the story was true. "Three days later, the woman in question issued this statement: 'I have never had a relationship with Senator Kerry, and the rumors in the press are completely false'" (ibid.).

In addition, numerous incidents of plagiarism and the conflation of fact and fiction in American journalism serve as further evidence of a crisis of verification and a news culture that is an easy target for rumor bombs. In 2003, *New York Times* reporter Jayson Blair was found to have plagiarized significant parts of several stories and faked quotes in others. A year later, *USA Today* reporter Jack Kelly was discovered to have significantly fabricated parts of many stones over a 10-year period (Morrison 2004). These examples combined with rumor infiltrations of the media agenda create a gnawing sense of uncertainty for consumers of information on websites, in e-mails, on TV, on the radio and in newspapers and magazines. They are a product of the collapsing authority for agenda-setting and gatekeeping displaced into the internet, an information culture characterized above all by speed and change. The Project for Excellence in American Journalism's annual report for 2005, "The State of the News Media," emphasizes that a major new trend in "models of journalism" is "toward those that are faster, looser, and cheaper" (Project for Excellence in Journalism 2005, overview).

The issue of the inter-news media agenda setting here – what people find interesting or newsworthy on the internet – also raises the issue of how entertainment values have become increasingly important in the news business. As briefly mentioned above, trends of tabloidization and infotainment have crept into traditional news media as a way to retain viewers and deliver them to lucrative advertisers. Tabloid and entertainment trends have been growing in mainstream American news throughout the late twentieth century (after an attempt to professionalize journalism and turn it away from tabloidism in the 1920s), but most recently with the fragmentation of a mass audience due to the explosion of cable, the internet, and less and less interest in traditional news generally, such organizations' content has been driven closer to other entertainment genres. As noted ten years ago, MBAs are ruling the newsrooms with a different set of values and institutional goals than before (Underwood 1995).[7] Some editors and publishers are openly declaring a market crisis for newspapers and a desire to simply give customers/readers whatever they want. In a recent interview with the *Online Journalism Review*, former *San Francisco Chronicle* Vice-president Bob Cauthorn blamed the financial hardships of newspapers on the reporters and editors whom, he believes, "insulate themselves from the public," are not "aligned" with their readers, and instead believe their readers aren't smart enough to determine what sort of news product they want. Speaking of trends toward celebrity news and "trash," Cauthorn proclaims, "If that's what readers want, great. Serve the reader (LaFontaine 2005). Such views are also represented in journalism's most prestigious professional training grounds.[8] Not only does the uni-dimensional reduction of journalism to marketing raise serious questions for journalism's relationship to democracy; it also suggests how news values of entertainment and profit are a breeding ground for rumor.

To embrace tabloid news values is already to embrace and encourage rumor and scandal in general. Tabloid news doesn't aspire to fact-based journalism and values of objectivity. It seeks to be entertaining. It is no surprise then that with tabloid market trends one should find an accompanying pervasiveness of rumor (Bennett 2003, 33; Kovach & Rosenstiel 1999).

But in addition to new market and inter-media pressures is it possible to see the problem of rumor as rooted more deeply in the very foundations of journalistic professional culture – in its dependence on official sources. An overdependence on official, possibly manipulative sources is certainly a problem that critics of American professional journalism have long noted (Bennett 2003, 125) and plays a role in the convergence of forces that have produced the rumor bomb. The dependence on official sources goes hand in hand with news management and growing PR strategies in political communication over the long twentieth century, which will be addressed shortly.[9]

These concerns with belief and news market trends have brought us inevitably to the domain of politics and PR. Thus, while a consideration of new market pressures and journalistic norms helps explain the proliferation of rumor, especially in American news media today, it needs to be viewed in relation to at least two other major factors with which it importantly converges. The second factor in this convergence is PR.

Increasing influence of PR on political communication

The technocratization of American mediated politics is encouraged by long-term media market trends discussed above, which converged with a new kind of managerial rhetoric or the PR-ification of political discourse in the late-twentieth-century US. A managerial political communication style has been developing since the early twentieth century, and more specific PR-managed politics have emerged since the Eisenhower years (Maarek 1995, 11; Sproule 1988). With the rise of mass electronic media in the twentieth century and an elite desire to direct a national political agenda came an increasing executive dependence on ever larger White House staffs for communication management purposes (Perloff 1998, 28–30).[10] The need for strategic communication on the model of PR cor responds to the twentieth century growth of executive power, a phenomenon described as "the rhetorical presidency" and "going public" (Kernell 1997; Tulis 1987). Beginning with Theodore Roosevelt, presidents increasingly played a more powerful role in setting a policy agenda by going around Congress, directly to the American people through planned public events and careful management of the news media. They hoped to influence public opinion which in turn would pressure the legislative branch to respond to public opinion accordingly. Ironically, the persuasive power of the executive branch increased as democracy was being expanded to African-Americans, women, and the poor. The response to the anxiety of democracy was, in political communication, PR. The urge to control and manage the belief of a mass citizenry really started to develop as a serious project in the years directly after World War I, based on the success of the government propaganda apparatus the Committee on Public Information. Returning from war propagandizing, founding father of PR Edward Bernays wrote that propaganda was a new power and form of cultural government that must be used by elites to "organize habits and opinions of the masses" in the name of democracy (1928, 47).

In 1927, looking back at the period since WWI, the young scholar of propaganda Harold Lasswell wrote that attempts to manage popular belief through the manipulation of "'significant symbols, or . . . by stories, rumours, reports, pictures and other forms of social communication' had become routine" (in Ewen 1996, 174). The "social and political implications of this development were profound." Lasswell further observed that "widespread 'discussion about the ways and means of controlling public opinion . . . testifies to the collapse of the traditional species of democratic romanticism and to the rise of the dictatorial habit of mind'" (ibid). From this moment we note the increasing colonization of American politics by war-conceived PR/propaganda practices in league with the executive branch, and we also note the ongoing lamentations about the decline of public debate and rise of public apathy toward public affairs.

While the White House increasingly tried to produce a kind of PR staff to help manage the media and set the public agenda, it was only in the 1950s that presidents and their opponents regularly began to use PR firms to sell their agendas (Maarek 1995, 11). This trend increased through the 1960s. By the time Carter took the presidency in 1976, his strategist Pat Caddell wrote a memo that argued, "In devising a strategy for the Administration, it is important to recognize we cannot successfully separate politics and government. . . . It is my thesis that governing with public approval requires a continuing political campaign" (Grann 2004). However this trend of news management and PR choreography has reached its apex with the Bush II. "By 2000," David Grann wrote in the *New Yorker*, "the strategists who had once advised a candidate solely during a campaign had moved into the White House" (Grann 2004). Not only are campaign tactics normalized for governing but the communication tactics are themselves institutionally influenced by the twenty-four hour cable and internet news cycle. The welcoming news environment for fakes and propaganda was recently emphasized in the flap over the Bush administration's use of PR firms whose fake news in video news releases were sent to television stations who aired them as if they were stories by independent journalists (www.prwatch.org/node/3790). There is ever greater pressure to set news and public agendas and respond to and spin actually existing agendas. Furthermore, the Bush II administration's ability to launch rumors has especially been strengthened by an astute reading of the post-9/11 conjuncture that enables a cultural project of secrecy and unaccountability/mystery.

Two major methods of news management in combination with other PR tactics (slogans, pseudo-events, obfuscation, spin, polling) are leaks and secrecy. As mentioned earlier, leaks can be strategic on the part of he government's disciplined communication apparatus, which may farm out rumor launching to front groups, or they may leak out of the communication apparatus due to dissent within the ranks. Tabloidesque "leaks" such as the 2003 claim that John Kerry was "French-looking" and the more recent Valerie Plame leak were engineered by high-ranking members of the administration as kinds of Information Bombs, designed to channel public attention, attack opponents, and control the media and public agenda.

Secrecy, sometimes discussed as control of source access, has long been a method of managing the press and perceptions of politics. Indeed, as mentioned earlier, it is at the core of ongoing critiques of twentieth-century fact-based, objective journalism, suggesting that journalists, especially in corporate profit-driven news, can not attain independence from sources. The control of access has been perfected by each succeeding executive administration and other areas of the government and business (Robertson 2005). In an article on the Bush administration's news control in *American Journalism Review* on-line, Lori Robertson wrote: "A rigid approach to staying on message and a clampdown on access for reporters and the public have been increasingly used by the executive branch, a trend that began to take shape during the Reagan administration, if not earlier. The current Bush administration has shown that the method can be perfected, with little to no downside for the White House" (February/March 2005). Such a disciplined propaganda apparatus has major implications for mediated democratic politics. The latter becomes a carefully choreographed spectacle, all the more successful under the aegis of security.

One need not be nostalgic for a time when an unbridled watchdog press and a full participatory democracy existed (of course they have not) to note clear differences in the way US political discourse has been practiced and covered by news media from the nineteenth century to the present. Indeed, the great irony may be that with the increasing enfranchisement of more parts of the population (the poor, African Americans, women), the more exclusive, irrational, trivial, emotional and visual mediated public discourse has become in its production and circulation.

What have been the results of increasing political PR in mediated American political discourse combined with changing news market pressures and values? I will briefly rehearse some of these well-known qualities of a structurally dilapidated American mediated political discourse. According to Kathleen Jamieson's widely read account (1988), contemporary public address is perhaps most characterized by its mediated time-compression.

Today news media select and present soundbites, cropping and re-assembling larger discourses and arguments. Likewise, politicians have adapted their mode of address to the technology that mediates, transforms, and circulates it. In the past people were allowed to consider speeches and arguments in their entirety. Speeches were also reprinted in newspapers and aired on early radio in their entirety. Today political strategists produce slogans in hopes of getting them picked up as soundbites for news. From 1968 to 1988, the average TV news soundbite afforded presidential candidates dropped from 42 seconds to 10 seconds. Even lower in 2000 (Paletz 2002, 223; Jamieson 1988, 8). A similar story of time-compression applies to the recent history of political ads. In 1948, one-half-hour radio blocks were the norm; in 1956, five minutes on TV; by the 1970s, one minute on TV. Today, the norm is 15–30 seconds on TV (Jamieson 1988, 9–10; Paletz 2002, 229).

The overall style of political communication has thus changed according to the convergence of many pressures. Politicians used to go through the history of an issue, addressing proposed alternatives. Such attention to history and engagement with opposing views is rare. Furthermore, politicians and advocates used to use dramatization and emotion more to accompany rational argumentation; today audiences of political speech often get little else but dramatization, assertions, and strategic, branded visual associations. In the past, key terms used to be defined (such as "weapons of mass destruction" or freedom). Today, glittering generalities dominate. Playing into the new media values for drama and scandal, name-calling (*ad hominem*) is more common than addressing opponents' arguments.

Thus, says Jamieson, audiences are often left with the likelihood of simply embracing positions that are already theirs, or they may embrace a politician and his/her claims out of blind partisan loyalty (Jamieson 1988, 10–12; Swanson 2004, 50–1). Many of these developments that Jamieson outlines are the result of advocates and politicians adapting to new media business values, structures, and news gathering practices on which the circulation of public address depends. To better ensure news will publicize well-crafted messages, political actors have increasingly depended on PR professionals to design speech strategy.

These trends help explain both the news coverage of the rumors discussed above and why the Bush administration would use them, which also explains how many Bush voters and viewers of Fox news were left to blindly follow their party's suggestions or to choose what were simple reiterations of their own beliefs, justified or not. But these are trends in American news media as a business and in audiences in American culture that have been complicit if not wholly active in the process and in the way American politics has responded to them. Scholars like Ewen (1996) have identified the rise of a "dictatorial habit of mind" in the PR-politics nexus of the 1920s and J. Michael Sproule has referred to the same phenomena as characterizing a turn from individual political rhetoric aimed at influencing reflective, agonistic publics to the new "managerial rhetoric" that continues today, where speakers are indices of larger institutions whose goal is to shape and control public opinion and behavior. But this was not simply a business phenomenon and we would be missing part of the rumor and belief production factors convergence if we didn't turn to the influence of military communication agendas.

Militarization of political communication practices

The style of political communication that has become dominant in the last ten years in the US is most closely modeled on traditional war propaganda style and information management, which as Lasswell observed, developed out of WW I (Sproule 1997, 33; Cook 1998, 52; Cutlip, Center, & Broom 2000, 123–4).

The present-day control of source access, the use of press and video releases, surrogate speakers, dramatization and message coordination, as well as coercion, all form a sophisticated media management apparatus that mirrors war communications apparatuses such as the US World War I Committee on Public Information (CPI).[11] The CPI bombarded local media markets with official press releases that "stayed on message" (111). They launched releases by mail and telegraph 24 hours a day. Trying to cater to news values, they also syndicated their own human interest stories to appeal to a range of news and entertainment readers. Just as the CPI tried to manage the unpredictable immigrant populations by making contacts with over 600 foreign language newspapers and publishing in nineteen languages, today the White House Office of Communications sends satellite interviews to niche media markets. While the CPI used newsreels and Hollywood talent to boost support for the war, contemporary White House and Defense Department PR uses video releases and issue ads (to say nothing of the Defense Department's ongoing relationship with Hollywood and the video game industry). In the CPI, Director George Creel noted that 'people do not live by bread alone; they live mostly by catch phrases' (112); today Communications staff labor to provide the news with catchy slogans that will be repeated ad nauseum. Ewen notes the CPI abandoned "fact-oriented journalism" for a type of political persuasion more akin to advertising, relying on emotional appeals and a "language of images" (Ewen 1996, 113); Jamieson notes that political discourse today is characterized by hyper-dramatization, hyper-visualization, "hit and run" name-calling and assertions without support. Would we be remiss to begin thinking about mediated US public discourse from the perspective of war and government techniques of population control as much as from the perspectives of market logics and consumer tastes? These trends appear to have started after WW I and, with the convergence of factors described above, have reached their closest state of similarity in the present. It is here that we see recent uses of rumor for what they are – information control strategies, aimed at producing consent, belief in or cynical paralysis towards larger policies positioned in a state of *Pure War*.

By viewing these characteristics of war communication in convergence with US cultural and political developments in governmentality, we can start to see a general anti-democratic tendency of US government communication practices in the service of technocratic population control. This means that it is in error to consider contemporary American politics as mainly about debating issues that will set an agenda for public policy. Equally, it is in error to conduct analyses of American news media and their treatment of politics as if they were somehow detached observers and/or watchdogs critical to the debate and vigilance necessary for robust democracy. Rather, the militarization of communication practices, in league with technological and market change, has resulted in the erosion of these journalistic aspirations that were once considered necessary for robust democracy. In their absence, rumor bombs are effectively planted in news networks, exploding into ever wider rings of circulation.

Rumor, Branding, and Postmodern Belief

What is the relationship of these converging factors in news, political PR, and military communication style to belief and consent? While all of these forces explain how contemporary polities are ripe for rumor production and how news media are especially ripe for rumor circulation, one should add that rumor in mainstream traditional news media tends to go through a process of launching, circulation, and then correction (Sterne 2003). Correction may not at all interrupt durable attachments to belief; nor does it necessarily issue from the rumor's original source. Often this process can take many years. In the 1991 Gulf War the rumor that Iraqi soldiers had ripped Kuwaiti babies out of hospital incubators and left them strewn about the floor like firewood, as President Bush Sr. said several times, was only revealed to be a PR stunt after the war (Jowett 1993, 286). The same is true of WMD and Iraq–al Qaeda links. The problem, again, in terms of public belief is that once the rumor is launched many people appear to become quite attached to it and resistant to corrections, or it may reinforce already existing desires, beliefs, and fantasies.[12]

Political communication today is heir to the technocratic opinion management of Bernays and Lippman in the 1920s and Goebbels in the 1930s and 1940s (themselves heirs to Plato's philosopher king and his noble lie). Today the idea of political PR and anti-deliberative news management in a media culture of warp speed is to produce a virtual dromomaniacal citizen subject; the mind can not stop to evaluate evidence because the parade of images and emotional appeals will not give it time or space. Its aim is to move. This style of communication contains its own anti-deliberative motive. In this context where news implodes with entertainment and propaganda and deliberative citizenship fades as a distant memory, a new consumerist citizenship unfolds as a spectacle of deliberative democracy. Fundamental changes in political communication practice as branding find a public-relations-driven politics poised to use rumor as the contemporary weapon of choix for tapping emotions and constructing short-lived attachments.

Paul Virilio's (1997) theory of *Pure War* further contextualizes these convergences.

Conclusion: Pure War, Anti-Deliberation, and the Politicization of Speed

Virilio's three typologies of war in Western history help us see that US-mediated political discourse has existed within a condition of *Pure War* since WW II. Furthermore, it helps us understand that institutional norms of political communication generally (orchestrated by PR), and especially executive branch communication strategies, aim to annihilate debate and public deliberation by discursive and extra-discursive means, through control of access to sources, leaking of false or unverifiable information, produced in a climate of secrecy and authorized by appeals to public security. These conditions produce a spectacle of deliberative democracy.[13]

According to Virilio's typologies of war (1997), war was once a tactical activity that took place outside the city walls or moats, where armies fought it out, but in which civilian life went about its business without becoming completely subordinate to belligerent activities. This period gave way to a period of Total War, characterized by a new subordination of all social life during wartime. Economic and industrial activities were subordinated to war efforts and civilians were enlisted to supply its logistical demands. However, the advent of the arms race and nuclear weapons from WW II on initiates a new period of constant preparation for war and actual war-making, sometimes distant and covert. Here the major differences between peace-time culture and war time culture implode. And perhaps most importantly, *Pure War* is marked by information war and population control once exclusively directed at a foreign enemy and now also redirected back onto the domestic population. It is the domestic population now that must first be controlled in order to perpetuate the state of *Pure War* which demands that humans devote their lives to the economic and moral initiatives of the war at the expense of investment in social welfare and public goods.

Unsurprisingly, the turn to *Pure War* does not bode well for democratic public life and its requisite communication practices. Virilio begins to speak pessimistically of a "transpolitics," the end of politics. Indeed, the dominance of speed in market-driven news coverage, political communication and its effects in anti-deliberation aims to make politics, like war, automated. Thus, Virilio writes, "Behind the libertarian propaganda for a *direct (live) democracy*, capable of renovating party-based *representative democracy*, the ideology of an *automatic democracy* is being put in place, in which the absence of deliberation would be compensated by a 'social automatism' similar to that found in opinion polls or the measurement of TV audience ratings" (Virilio 2000b, 109). Virilio's practical response is that those who witness this tyranny of speed must politicize it.

Though Virilio's *Pure War* (1997) has a conspiratorial ring to it (the very existence of the Project for a New American Century [PNAC] would seem to free Virilio from X-files comparisons), the communication aspects of *Pure War* have indeed become institutionalized in American politics and government. In many ways, from the Committee on Public Information to the vision of technocratic democracy, we may see resonances of Virilio's thinking. With the Cold War's culture of *Pure War,* its propaganda apparatus, and its disastrous effects for a more open public discourse (see Whitfield 1990), one can see evidence of the kind of endocolonization of which Virilio speaks.

Now with the War on Terror, democratic public life appears more jeopardized than ever. *Pure War* and information bombs (of which the rumor bomb is a type) create a confused, anxious citizenry.

Rumor, one of the distinguishing features of contemporary American mediated politics is a theoretical portal into new thinking about new political and social relations. The recent pervasiveness of rumor in mediated American public discourse is at the vexing convergence of new news market logics and resultant news gathering values and practices; and a century old process of technocratizing American public life, which itself is closely tied up with techniques and initiatives of total and *Pure War*. In *Pure War*, enemies are deterritorialized, including Iraqis and Americans. In a culture of *Pure War* that produces local rumors and global tremors, it isn't only the 28,000–31,000 Iraqi civilians that have died since the US-led coalition invaded Iraq in the name of freedom; many Americans are captivated, over 16,600 are wounded, and over 2,300 of them are now dead . . . Or so it is rumored.[14]

Notes

1. http://abcnews.go.com/Politics/PollVault/story?id=582744&page=2
2. While the political use of rumor has not been well studied in the present (most attention going to its close relative, spin), the singular catylsts that have been identified as productive of rumor – speed, entertainment news values, and political PR – have been identified as international news and politics trends the most advanced forms of which are American (Swanson 2004, 50–53; Thussu 2003; Seib 2004; Blumler & Gurevich (1995). However, none so far has proposed or demonstrated how rumor use and circulation is facilitated by this convergence of factors.
3. I am referring especially to the speech of Diodotus in Thucydides section "the Mytilenean Debate" (1954). Discussion of the type of discourse that is necessary for functional democracy is broad. See Kellner (no date); Benhabib 1996; Gans 2003.
4. As Virilio says, information bombs have become the supreme accident of the present. Real-time interaction is to information today what radioactivity was to energy in the epoch marked by the atomic bomb and its deterrence. Orson Welles' "War of the Worlds" is an exemplary information bomb.
5. The concept's definition is up for grabs. The scholarship on rumor across sociology, psychology, and communication studies agrees on very little (Berenson 1952; Pendleton 1998; Bordia & Difonzo 2004).
6. See Pew Internet and American Life Project (2004, pt. 2).
7. For a critique of this commercialization of news and some of its institutional values from the position of democratic theory, see Gans (2003).
8. See Janet Castro's Public Lecture at the American University of Paris, "International Perspectives and the One-minute News Cycle," September 19, 2005.
9. Recently, the unquestioning use of "fake news" video releases, which are actually PR fakes originating in the Executive branch, by mainstream news is telling. See www.prwatch.org/tazonomy/term/120/9.
10. See Tebbel and Watts (1985, 330–5).
11. This comparison is not meant to be exhaustive. There are a potentially huge number of comparisons and influences one could make by looking at case studies of war and news (Knightley 2004), but for economy's sake, I am focusing here on the CPI in WW I.

12. Evidence for this comes from a recent study that was conducted one month prior to the 2004 American presidential election. The study was conducted by the University of Maryland's Program on International Policy Attitudes/Knowledge Networks in October 2004. All further references to this study correspond to the following website: http://www.pipa. org/OnlineReports/Pres_Election_04/html/new_10_21_04.html.

13. Virilio speaks about the intentions of such "politics" and its strategies of communication/control. But I would stress how much easier this is accomplished with the cultural sensibilities encouraged by speedy new media technologies and the difficulty of finding/forging space-time for deliberation. Thus, politicians who are rhetorically savvy, in classical rhetorical fashion, assess the situation and often respond to it successfully with the *arme de choix*, rumor.

14. Figures from October, 2005 (http://icasualties.org/oif/, www.iraqbodycount.net/).

References

Barber, Benjamin, Kevin Mattson & John Peterson (1997). The State of Electronically Enhanced Democracy: A Report of the Walt Whitman Center. November, online at www.rutgers.edu/markle.htm (accessed October 4, 2004).

Baudrillard, Jean (1988). Simulacra and Simulations. In: M. Poster (ed.), *Jean Baudrillard, Selected Writings*. Stanford: Stanford University Press.

Benhabib, Seyla (ed.) (1996). *Democracy and Difference. Contesting the Boundaries of Political*. Princeton, NJ: Princeton University Press.

Bennett, Lance (2003). *News, the Future of an Illusion*. London: Longman.

Blumler, J. & M. Gurevich (1995). *The Crisis of Public Communication*. London and New York: Routledge.

Bernays, Edward (1928). *Propaganda*. New York: Horace Liveright, Inc.

Bernays, Edward (1955). *The Engineering of Consent*. Norman, OK: University of Oklahoma.

Berenson, Bernard (1952). *Rumor and Reflection*. New York: Simon and Schuster.

Bolton, Alexander (2006). Senate GOP Plans Iraq PR Blitz. Monday, January 9, online at http://thehill.com/thehill/export/TheHill/News/Frontpage/010406/iraq.html

Bordia, Prashant & Nicholas Difonzo (2004). Problem Solving in Social Interactions on the Internet: Rumor as Cognition. *Social Psychology Quarterly* 67(1), pp. 33–49.

Campbell, Karlyn & Kathleen Hall Jamieson (1990). *Deeds Done in Words*. Chicago: University of Chicago Press.

Condit, Celeste (1989). The Rhetorical Limits of Polysemy. *Critical Studies in Mass Communication* 6, pp. 103–22.

Cook, Timothy (1998). *Governing with the News*. Chicago: University of Chicago Press.

Cutlip, Scott, Allen Center & Glen Broom (2000). *Effective Public Relations*, 8th edn. Upper Saddle River, NJ: Prentice-Hall.

Deggans, Eric (2004). The Truth Is Out There. *St. Petersburg Times*, September 19, 2004, online at www.sptimes.com (accessed October 1, 2005).

Ewen, Stuart (1996). *PR: A Social History of Spin*. New York: Basic Books.

Gans, Herbert J. (2003). *Democracy and the News*. New York and London: Oxford University Press.

Gilboa, Eytan (2005). The CNN Effect: The Search for an International Relations Theory of Communication. *Political Communication* 22, pp. 27–34.

Gitlin, Todd (2004). Lying about Kerry. *Free Democracy*, online at www.freedemocracy.com (accessed February 21, 2005).

Grann, David (2004). Mark Halperin and the Transformation of the Washington Establishment. *New Yorker*, October 18, 2004, online at www.newyorker.com/fact/content/?041025fa_fact

Horrigan, John, Kelly Garrett & Paul Resnick (2004). The Internet and Democratic Debate: Wired Americans Hear more Points of View about Candidates and Key Issues than Other Citizens. They Are Not Using the Internet to Screen out Ideas with Which They Disagree. Pew Internet and American Life Project at www.pewinternet.org/pdfs/PIP Political Info Report, pdf

Jamieson, Kathleen Hall (1988). *Eloquence in the Electronic Age*. New York: Oxford University Press.

Jowett, Garth (1993). Propaganda and the Gulf War. *Critical Studies in Mass Communication* 10(3), pp. 286–301.

Kellner, Douglas (n.d.). Habermas, the Public Sphere, and Democracy: A Critical Intervention, online at http://www.gseis.ucla.edu/faculty/kellner/papers/habermas.htm (accessed January 9, 2006).

Kernell, Samuel (1997). *Going Public: New Strategies in Presidential Leadership*. Washington, DC: CQ Press.

Knightley, Philip (2004). *The First Casualty*. Baltimore: Johns Hopkins University Press.

Kovach, Bill & Tom Rosenstiel (1999). *Warp Speed: America in the Age of Mixed Media*. New York: The Century Foundation.

Kranish, Michael & Bryan Bender (2004). Bush Backs Cheney on Assertion Linking Hussein, Al Qaeda. *Boston Globe*, June 16, 2004, online at www.boston.com/news/nation/washington/articles/2004/06/16/bush_backs_cheney_on_assertion_linking_hussein_al_qaeda/ (accessed February 3, 2005).

Kurtz, Howard (2003). For the News Leak, a Long If Not Honorable History. *Washington Post*, October 6, 2003, at www.lexisnexis.com (accessed October 4, 2004).

La Fontaine, David (2005). Old-School Community Journalism Shows: It's a Wonderful "Light," August 25, 2005, at www.ojr.org/ojr/stories/050825lafontaine/ (accessed October 6, 2005).

Lippman, Walter (1922/1963). Public Opinion. *The Essential Lippman*, pp. 102–4. New York: Random House.

Maarek, Phillip (1995). *Political Marketing*. London, John Libbey.

Maltese, John (1992). *Spin Control*. Chapel Hill: University of North Carolina.

Marshall, Joshua Micah (2003). The Postmodern President. *Washington Monthly* 35(9), at www.epnet.com (Academic Search Premier) (accessed November 5, 2003).

Morrison, Blake (2004). Ex-USA Today Reporter Faked Major Stories. *USA Today*, March 19, 2004, at www.usatoday.com/news/2004-03-18-2004-03-18_kelleymain_x.htm (accessed February 2, 2004).

Paletz, David L. (2002). *The Media in American Politics*. New York: Longman.

Pendleton, S. C. (1998). Rumor Research Revisited and Expanded. *Language & Communication* 18, pp. 69–86.

Perloff, Richard (1998). *Political Communication*. Mahweh, NJ: Lawrence Erlbaum.

Project for Excellence in Journalism (2005). Five Major Trends, online at www.stateofthemedia.org (accessed September 28, 2005).

Rich, Frank (2005). When Real News Debunks Fake News. *International Herald Tribune*, February 19.

Robertson, Lori (2005). In Control. *American Journalism Review*, February/March, at www.ajr.com (accessed December 1, 2005).

Schell, Orville (2005). Introduction. *Now They Tell Us*. New York: New York Review of Books.

Seib, Philip (2004). *Beyond the Front Lines: How the News Media Cover a World Shaped by War*. New York: Palgrave.

Shehata, Samer (2002). Why Bush's Middle East Propaganda Campaign Won't Work. *Salon.com*, July 12, 2002, online at www.salon.com/news/feature/2002/07/12/propaganda/index_np.html

Sproule, J. Michael (1988). The New Managerial Rhetoric. *Quarterly Journal of Speech*.

Sproule, J. Michael (1997). *Propaganda and Democracy*. New York: Cambridge University Press.

Sterne, Jonathon (2003). Notes toward the Next Media War. *Bad Subjects*, Issue 64, online at http://bad.eserver.org/issues/2003/64/sterne.html (accessed March 1, 2005).

Swanson, David (2004). Transnational Trends in Political Communication: Conventional Views and New Realities. In: Esser Frank & Barbara Pfetsch (eds.), *Comparing Political Communication*, pp. 45–63. Cambridge: Cambridge University Press.

Tebbel, J. & S. M. Watts (1985). *The Press and the Presidency*. New York: Oxford University Press.

Thussu, Daya (2003). War, Infotainment and 24/7 News. In: D. Thussu (ed.), *War and the Media*, pp. 117–32. London: Sage.

Tulis, Jeffrey (1987). *The Rhetorical Presidency*. Princeton, NJ: Princeton University Press.

Underwood, Doug (1995). *When MBA's Rule the Newsroom*. New York: Columbia University Press.

Virilio, Paul (1986). *Speed and Politics*. New York: Semiotexte.

Virilio, Paul (1997). *Pure War*. New York: Semiotexte.

Virilio, Paul (1999). *The Politics of the Very Worst*. New York: Semiotexte.

Virilio, Paul (2000a). *The Information Bomb*. London: Verso.

Virilio, Paul (2000b). *War and Cinema*. London: Verso.

Whitfield, Stephen J. (1990). *The Culture of the Cold War*. Baltimore: Johns Hopkins University Press.

29

Talkin' Tupac: Speech Genres and the Mediation of Cultural Knowledge

George Kamberelis and Greg Dimitriadis*

Much recent work within cultural studies, communication studies, cultural psychology, and anthropology has retheorized liberal-humanist notions of knowledge and identity, demonstrating that both are more provisional, politically contested, historically unfinished, and inventive than previously imagined (e.g., Bhabha, 1994; Clifford, 1988; Grossberg, 1992; Hall, 1996; Markus & Kitayama, 1991; McCarthy, 1998). These theorists have argued, quite convincingly, that knowledges and identities are constructed/ produced in specific historical-social-cultural sites through the appropriation of specific discourses and practices salient within those sites (Bourdieu, 1990). Central to these appropriation processes is their mediation by speech genres, which are conventionalized and codified patterns of discourse. From this perspective, an articulation of theories of discourse with theories of speech genres provides a productive theoretical framework for empirical investigations of how young people construct social and cultural knowledges and identities on complex, uneven, and shifting discursive landscapes (Dimitriadis & Kamberelis, 1997). More specifically, examining how young people appropriate and transform specific speech genres as they think and talk about the culture(s) they inhabit provides important understandings about how these genres enable and constrain their efforts to reproduce and resist the power arrangements that constitute their lives and to construct social knowledges and identities within these arrangements.

In this chapter, we focus on one group of youth – urban African American middle school children – and we examine some of the discursive tactics they used to construct their cultural knowledges and identities on fast-moving and sometimes violent social and cultural terrains. More specifically, we map how these adolescents deployed an adaptation of the "television talk show" genre to discuss the life and death of rap star Tupac Shakur. Importantly, we began our study of these young people focused on their investments in rap music and rap artists, hoping to understand the complexities and nuances of their musical tastes and dispositions, as well as how these tastes and dispositions contributed to their identity construction processes. Our interest in speech genres (and the television talk show genre more specifically) emerged during the course of the study because it was such a salient dimension of our participants' everyday talk and

*Pp. 119–50 from *Sound Identities: Popular Music and the Cultural Politics of Education*, ed. C. McCarthy, G. Hudak, S. Miklauc and P. Saukko (New York: Peter Lang). © 1999. Reprinted with permission from Peter Lang Publishing.

patterns of social interaction. As the study progressed, rap music and rap culture became less a primary research focus and more an arena for the study of local discursive tactics and their effects on children's processes of knowledge and identity construction.

The primary argument promoted in this chapter is that appropriating the television talk show genre to frame their understanding and communication about Tupac's life and death resulted in certain epistemological and practical possibilities and constraints. Specifically, this speech genre seemed to afford discussions of complex and subtle personal and interpersonal issues more readily than it did discussions of analogous economic, social, and political issues. Indeed, the primary focus of talk among our research participants centered on a series of conflicts that occurred between Tupac and fellow rapper, Biggie Smalls. This intense and almost exclusive focus helped constitute the field of "possible selves" and "possible worlds" (Bruner, 1986) that were visible to these young people within this situated activity. Before saying more about the empirical dimensions of our work, we will elaborate on our theoretical understandings of identities, discourses, and genres.

Theoretical Framework: Identities, Discourses, and Genres

Identities

Theorists of race, class, and gender have argued recently that these social categories are less "essential" than they are "positional" (Alcoff, 1988; Appadurai, 1996; Bhabha, 1994; Grossberg, 1992; Rosaldo, 1989). Raced, classed, or gendered identities involve positioning oneself at the intersection of various identity axes within a changing historical context of identity markers. From this perspective, being black or Latina or working class or female (or various combinations of these and other social categories) is to take up a position within a moving historical context, to choose how to interpret this position, and to imagine how to alter the context that made such positioning available in the first place. This way of thinking about identity seems to avoid reducing agency to the intentions of a homunculus while also escaping antihumanist assaults on the very notion of agency by reconceptualizing identity as the activity of positioning oneself within (and against) existing social and cultural networks and ideologies. Instead, identities are recognized as multiple, complex, porous, and shifting sets of positionings, attachments, and identifications through which individuals and collectives understand who they are and how they are expected to act across a range of diverse social and cultural landscapes (Hall, 1996).

According to Foucault's notion of power/knowledge, people invariably construct racial, class, and gender identities in ways that partially reproduce the power matrices of specific historical–social–cultural hegemonies. As Gramsci (1971), Fairclough (1992), Foucault (1990), and others have shown, people also resist such power matrices through the discursive construction of their positions within those matrices. In short, identities (and the meanings assigned to them) are actively constructed through specific social practices and not merely discovered or passively assumed. These local identities constitute compromises or articulations between resistance and accommodation to larger social formations and their concomitant practices and ideologies. Identities, then, are always tentative and partially unstable because they are continually constructed within particular configurations of discursive and material practices that are themselves constantly constituting and reconstituting themselves.

Discourses and the power/knowledge nexus

Foucault (1972, 1979, 1990) was fundamentally interested in the power of discourse to produce social formations, as well as how discourses define, construct, and position individuals within those formations. According to Foucault, discourses "systematically form the objects of which they speak" (1972, p. 49). Such forms of social production occur by constructing "truths" about both the natural and social worlds, which eventually become received or taken-for-granted definitions and categories. Drawing largely upon the work of Foucault, Fiske (1996) noted that discourses provide a "social formation . . . with ways of thinking and talking about areas of social experience that are central in its life" (p. 7). Different discourses provide different interpretive lenses for constituting reality, lenses which are selectively brought to bear upon particularly salient social experiences. Some discourses dominate others at particular historical moments, and some are more powerful and more durable than others. Culture itself, according to Fiske, can be conceived as a "river of discourses" (p. 7). Such discourses "are deep, powerful currents carrying meanings of race, of gender and sexuality, of class and age" (p. 7), and individuals often embrace them in uncritical ways. Yet Fiske himself pointed out that there are limits to the "river" metaphor.

> The naturalness of a river can imply an inevitability in flow and counterflows, can reduce media events to tourist spectacles that people watch from a safe distance . . . and can reduce or even eliminate political intervention, social agency, and discursive struggle (pp. 7–8).

We want to suggest that some of these problems with reduction can be avoided by focusing on moment-to-moment discursive practices as mediated by speech genres. Speech genres, as we note below, mediate between the macrolevel discourses and microlevel practices that constitute the engines of both social reproduction and social change.

Speech genres

Bakhtin (1986) defined speech genres as discursive forms that organize utterances into coherent ensembles of structures and practices. A speech genre

> is not a form of language, but a typical form of utterance; as such the genre also includes a typical kind of expression that adheres in it. . . . [Speech] genres correspond to typical situations of speech communication, typical themes, and consequently, also to particular contacts between the *meanings* of words and actual concrete reality under certain typical circumstances (p. 87).

Bakhtin went on to argue that all utterances are constructed not from individual words but from speech genres:

> We speak only in definite speech genres, that is, all our utterances have definite and relatively stable typical *forms of construction of the whole*. Our repertoire of oral (and written) speech genres is rich. We use them confidently and skillfully *in practice*, and it is quite possible for us not even to suspect their existence *in theory* (p. 78).

Although Bakhtin posited speech genres as the fundamental templates and building blocks of discourse, he was careful not to represent them as static or ossified structures, but ones that are continually reconstituted within new contexts and in the hands of new users. "A genre lives in the present," he noted, "but always remembers its past" (1984, p. 104).

As such, genres are historically and ideologically saturated "aggregate[s] of the means for seeing and conceptualizing reality" (Bakhtin & Medvedev, 1985, p. 137). Genres are indexical, signaling the ideologies, norms, values, and social ontologies of the communities of practice in which they typically function. Indeed, it was central to Bakhtin's theory of genres that the thematic and stylistic construction of texts embody ideological values rooted in socio-cultural-historical contexts (Bakhtin & Medvedev, 1985, p. 21). No elements of texts are pure form; texts are also populated with ideological intentions or value orientations. In the appropriation of genres, then, people also appropriate these ideologies as obvious and familiar, as horizons against which their actions and the actions of others make sense.

Bakhtin's discussion of how speech genres mediate identity practices and the social discourses within which they are embedded provides a particularly powerful framework for describing the particular discursive practices through which the urban African American youth with whom we have been working construct their social knowledges and identities. Such a theoretical framework helps demonstrate precisely how these young people take up certain subject positions through the enactment of certain speech genres. Central here is an examination of what typified forms of discourse (i.e., speech genres) young people deploy when discussing events that are salient to their lives and constitutive of their identities. This articulation of speech and event provides insights into what kinds of knowledges are enabled (and constrained) by what kinds of discursive practices and frames, as well as what kinds of frames are preferred for understanding what kind of experiences. The durability or resiliency of certain kinds of knowledge will thus be located (at least in part) in the durability of speech genres and/or the durable ways in which they are taken up.

Conversationalization and Popular Media Discourses

It is necessary to situate any cultural analysis both historically and culturally, and our analysis depends upon understanding one of the strongest trends in contemporary American culture (and various other cultures as well), the trend toward "conversationalized" discourse. According to Fairclough (1992, 1995) public discourse has tended to take on an increasingly conversational character. Affected by this tendency are not only printed media and advertising but also official documents such as employment applications and insurance forms, radio and television programs, formal government reports and academic texts. Among the more salient discursive features that characterize discourse as conversational are utterances replete with affective verbs (e.g., feel, love, want); the use of the present tense to relate past events (e.g., and he tells me, "I'll be back"); an abundance of reported speech, colloquial lexicons and idioms; a proportionally large number of personal (and often inclusive) pronouns; many oral discourse markers (e.g., oh well, yeah, like, really); dense intertextual links to the public media and other forms of popular culture such as song lyrics or advertising slogans; and thematic content that might be considered private such as sexual affairs and financial dealings.

A cursory historical analysis of media communication in almost any domain of public interchange would show that the boundary between "news" and "entertainment" has become increasingly fuzzy during the past several decades (and perhaps even longer). This trend, for example, is evidenced in tabloids such as the *National Enquirer*, in television news magazines such as *A Current Affair*, in reportage of special events such as the Olympics, and even in the "official" news programs of network television. In relation to this historical trend, Fairclough (1992) provides microlevel analyses of more personal/informal forms of discourse within the public sphere across a number of different texts, including university advertisements, television shows, and newspaper headlines. For example, he shows how newspapers routinely represent the voices of powerful individuals or social forces in informal or colloquial ways, using a headline from the *Daily Mirror* to support his claim: "Di's Butler Bows Out . . . in Sneakers!" He points out that "the voice of the royal butler . . . is a popular speech voice, both in the direct discourse representation . . . and in the attributed use of 'sneakers'" (pp. 111–12). Princess Diana, in turn, becomes "Di," and she is described as "'nice,' 'ordinary,' 'down to earth,' and 'natural'" (p. 112). In the very commercial context of this newspaper, information about the royal family revolves around personal and personalized issues and concerns. This personalization is instantiated in the texts themselves, which are markedly colloquial.

Fairclough notes that the use of more informal language in public texts is indicative of two tendencies: "the tendency of public affairs media to become increasingly conversationalized" and "its tendency to move increasingly in the direction of entertainment – to become more 'marketized'" (Fairclough, 1995, p. 10). As market forces overtake media such as records, radio, and television, they become more personal or conversational. Quite often, efforts to render news and information more informal and approachable are deemed democratic. More people have access to news and other public information because media events are "brought to the level" of the average citizen. However, such "marketization undermines the media as a public sphere" as well (p. 13). As a particular manifestation of liberal-pluralist ideologies, conversationalized public discourse renders the meanings of social and political events and issues in terms of individual agency and everyday social practice. "There is a diversion of attention and energy from political and social issues which helps to insulate existing relations of power and domination from serious challenge" (p. 13). Conversationalized discourses routinely collapse personal and political issues, quite often reducing conflict to individual differences, which can ultimately be resolved by individuals through dialogue. Additionally, conversationalized public discourse blurs the line between information and entertainment and between public and private. Among other things, this blurring functions to render commodified possible selves and worlds durably real. It also encourages bringing issues traditionally considered to be private into the public sphere for discussion and evaluation. This point will be amplified below in our discussion of the television talk show genre.

Conversationalized discourses are realized and sustained in and through a number of different speech and activity genres. Two of these are particularly relevant for our purposes here. First is the emergence of the popular/psychologized public icon in rap, an idiom that had earlier been the locus of more collective, party- or event-oriented activities (Dimitriadis, 1996). Tupac Shakur was such an icon, and the struggle between his "positive" pro-black side and his "negative" "gangsta" side was as important to his very public career as his music. Second is the emergence of popular television talk shows in the mid 1980s. Shows such as *Phil Donahue*, *Oprah Winfrey*, *Ricki Lake*, *Jenny Jones*, and *Geraldo* encourage their guests to voice – and increasingly often, to fight over – interpersonal concerns and issues with the goal of resolving them through talk.

Rap and the psychologized hero

Recent trajectories in rap music seem linked constitutively to the emergence of conversationalized discourses. Indeed, hip hop began as a largely party-oriented music, almost entirely dependent upon face-to-face action and interaction. The musical event itself was more important than any particular verbal or vocal text that might occur in it and later be lifted out for reproduction and marketing. Loose collectives such as The Sugarhill Gang and The Furious Five traded verses in live interactive settings, all with the primary goal of getting live crowds involved in an unfolding event. As rap grew in popularity, however, the individual icon and the self-contained vocal text became increasingly important. The first such figure or character type was "the gangsta." Gangsta rappers, including Dr. Dre, Ice Cube, and Ice-T, told first-person (often three-part) narratives which relayed their criminal exploits in explicit and thrilling detail. These gangstas became the most visible and important part of hip hop culture during the late 1980s as rap became wildly successful in recorded commodity form.

In large measure, the gangsta was a larger-than-life character or figure whose exploits existed at the surface of exaggerated violence and brutality. During the early to mid 1990s, however, more personal and more complex portraits of these figures began to emerge. Most importantly, rappers like The Geto Boys, Biggie Smalls, and Tupac Shakur "psychologized" the gangsta type, adorning their stories with disturbing personal and psychological insights. The goal was no longer only to present a violent snapshot of gangsta life, but to help us understand what was happening "inside" the figure of the hero. Biggie Smalls (or Notorious B.I.G.), for example, framed his debut album *Ready to Die* as an aural/musical biography, beginning with his birth and ending with his suicide. Smalls thus used his biography to contextualize his music, blurring the line between the personal and the public, between information and entertainment.

This album was not only intended to get dance crowds dancing (as in early hip hop), or to relate violent exploits (as in gangsta rap), but also to give us a peek into Biggie Smalls' psyche – his motivations, desires, and feelings as explicated in deeply psychological narratives.

Tupac Shakur is another prime example of the psychologized rap hero. His biography is a crucial part of his public image, and the details of his life, which are talked about on record and off, have become almost legendary. In a key example, the song "Dear Mama" chronicles his early life in explicit detail, including his lack of a father, his reliance on his mother, her use of crack cocaine, and his turn toward crime. Again, Tupac goes beyond a two-dimensional sketch of his life to present a complex, deeply structured, and highly textured portrait of it. In weaving together the narrative of his mother and her struggles, he simultaneously constructs an "account" that functions to justify or explain the choices he made (Buttny, 1993).

Tupac's self-revelations often position him at the nexus of complex and seemingly conflicting social forces. In fact, "Dear Mama's" personal narrative is made all the more poignant by the widely known fact that Shakur's mother, Afeni Shakur, was a famous Black Panther – one of the Panther 21 who were arrested for allegedly attempting to orchestrate a series of bombings in New York City. According to popular accounts, Tupac inherited much of her militant black-power world view. These accounts emphasize, for example, the fact that Tupac has a black panther tattooed on his arm and the fact that a number of his songs depict or celebrate the struggles of black people (e.g., "White Man'z World" and "Keep Ya Head Up"). To a large extent, Tupac is heralded as a contemporary bearer of 1960s-inspired black nationalist attitudes and sentiments.

Yet Tupac is as much gangsta as revolutionary. He was involved in a number of shootings (including one with two off-duty police officers); he was sentenced for up to four-and-one-half years in prison for sexual abuse; he was almost fatally injured in an assassination attempt and robbery; and he ultimately was murdered in a drive-by shooting. Much of his music reflects this gangsta lifestyle, as evidenced, most especially, on *All Eyez On Me*, which was recorded on the Death Row Records label (see, for example, "Ambitionz az a Ridah," "2 of Amerikaz Most Wanted," and "Can't C Me"). Many interviews and news stories on Tupac have stressed his complex and divided soul, pointing out how his internal struggles between "good" (fighting for black rights) and "evil" (his uncritical gangsta posturing) were central to his music, which, again, ran the gamut from the more "positive" to the wildly "negative." *Rap Pages*, for example, subtitled their December, 1996 tribute to Tupac "Exploring the Many Sides of Tupac Shakur" and included a feature article entitled "Loving Tupac: The Life and Death of a Complicated Man."

Many rappers, such as Biggie Smalls and Tupac, have become near-mythic public figures whose personal struggles were and are an integral part of their music. This fact was set into high relief in the feud that erupted between Tupac (and his record label, Death Row Records) and Biggie Smalls (and his label, Bad Boy Records). The history of this feud is complex. According to Tupac, he and Biggie had been friends early on in their careers. In 1994, however, Tupac was ambushed and shot while heading to a recording studio to meet Smalls. He was shot five times but survived. Although the shooting was never solved, Tupac publicly accused Biggie Smalls of setting him up. A number of seemingly related and popularly disseminated incidents followed. A friend of Suge Knight (head of Death Row Records) was killed at a party, and Knight blamed Puff Daddy (head of Bad Boy Records) for the murder. An entourage of Death Row Records' members then threatened Biggie Smalls at an industry award party, brandishing guns. Finally, Suge Knight, reputedly associated with the LA-based gang, the Bloods, was rumored to have threatened Puff Daddy's life.

These real-life events overlap and blur into events chronicled on a number of recorded singles released by these two artists. Biggie Smalls, for example, released the caustic "Who Shot Ya?" in 1995 as a b-side to the hit "Big Poppa." This single plays off the phrase "Who Shot Ya?" presumably alluding to Tupac's earlier and apparently unsolved shooting. Thus, Tupac is the private audience targeted by this ostensibly public message. Lines such as "Cash rules everything around me/ Two Gloc 9s for any mother fucker whispering about mines" abound in this track, along with various threats and boasts by Biggie and Puff (e.g., "Didn't I tell you not to fuck with me! . . . Can't talk with a gun in your mouth?").

Tupac, in turn, released his scalding "Hit 'Em Up" in 1996 in which he viciously attacked both Smalls and Junior Mafia (Smalls' group; his protégés). This track explores in explicit detail the personal falling out between Tupac and Biggie. Tupac begins the track by saying "That's why I fucked your bitch, you fat mother fucker," an allusion to the rumor that he slept with Biggie's wife, R&B singer Faith Evans. Faith has denied the claim but, as we will note later, it has gained factual status within the popular imagination. Tupac goes on, during the course of this track, to threaten Tupac, Junior Mafia, and all of Bad Boy Records with attacks grounded in their personal histories. At one point, Tupac raps about their early friendship, "Biggie, remember when I used to let you sleep on the couch?" Yet, as he raps, "now it's all about Versace? You copy my style/ Five shots couldn't drop me/ I took it and smiled." According to Tupac, Smalls returned his friendship by trying to imitate Tupac's musical style (which revolved around the expensive tastes of the "playa" lifestyle, as evinced in the reference to Versace), and eventually orchestrating his attempted assassination.

This particular conflict demonstrates how the line between what artists portray through their lyrics and what happened in real life gets blurred. This blurring is in no small measure related to the tendency within the rap music industry in the early nineties to foreground the inner lives, experiences, and conflicts of its artists – artists who are portrayed as mythic figures with complexly explicated biographies. Equally important for our argument, this particular moment in hip hop's history seems constitutively linked to more global cultural imperatives marked by a tremendous increase in conversational or personalized discourses in the public sphere.

Television talk shows

A primary function of contemporary broadcast media is to render information or news more informal and entertaining. Rap, with its alternative stress on reality ("we're like reporters") and entertainment ("we're like actors"), is entirely linked to this move. Fairclough argues that television talk shows are particularly salient, even exaggerated, generic forms of these conversationalized discourses. For example, he notes that Oprah

Winfrey – who addresses a wide range of topics on her wildly successful hour-long talk show – is an "accomplished performer" who is "witty, humorous," and has a "winning smile." Her warm and open demeanor serves to construct her as "an ordinary person sharing the lifeworld of people in the studio and home audiences" (Fairclough, 1995, p. 142). Yet, Fairclough also emphasizes that Oprah Winfrey provides more than entertainment alone for her audience. Oprah "is also at times a moralist and educator, directly addressing viewers on the themes of the programme" (p. 142). Like many talk show hosts, she is both teacherly and friendly, peddling information in an entertaining and informal manner. Indeed, commercially successful venues such as *Oprah Winfrey* effectively link seemingly personal interactions between and among participants with educational and moralistic discourses, helping to present news or information in an easily digestible form. Perhaps more cynically, the television talk show is a kind of "suburban" genre that functions to domesticate a turbulent social world in its fascination with multiple and contradictory forms of titillation (McCarthy, 1998). As a polysemic discursive practice that blurs public and private, news and entertainment, and underclass, working-class, and middle-class sensibilities, the television talk show is an exaggerated and almost caricatured embodiment – and thus a particularly potent exemplar – of the general trend toward conversationalized public discourse.

Drawing on the work of Fairclough, Janice Peck has called attention to the fact that the therapeutic imperatives so important for talk shows foreground conversation and "communication" as primary ways to resolve disputes that might otherwise be located outside the individual and within larger social structures or cultural frames:

> The programs' personalization strategies, parasociality, and therapeutic framework organize social conflict within narratives of individual and interpersonal dysfunction. Within those confines, all problems seem to be amenable to therapeutic intervention – to treatment via the "talking cure". . . . Therapeutic discourse translates the political into the psychological – problems are personal (or familial) and have no origin or target outside of one's own psychic process (Peck, 1995, pp. 75–6).

Ricki Lake is one of the most popular talk show figures to enact such a translation. As Lake herself notes, "Being in therapy and talking about my own problems and being able to communicate honestly has affected my work" (quoted in Star Talker, 1994, p. 57). Although violent conflicts between participants – "high-decibel confrontations that draw hoots and cheers from the studio audience" (Zoglin, 1995, p. 77) – are often characteristic of these shows, the ability to talk through problems is valorized as one of their most important messages. The discourse that occurs on *Ricki Lake* and similar shows locates what could be constructed as social or political issues or problems in and within individual psychological processes. These talk shows personalize issues and make all news entertainment as well. Although this effort to make news accessible as entertainment is, in many ways, democratic, Fairclough notes that it also functions to naturalize dominant ideologies by constructing a cultural imaginary about social relations that renders them less asymmetrical and more benign than they really are. Talk shows and similar media venues promote the idea that because we are all the same underneath, we can talk across and outside of our social positionings.

In relation to this point, Bakhtin's notion of dialogism is particularly useful for understanding precisely how self and other are constituted through the appropriation and redeployment of popular cultural resources. By dialogic, Bakhtin meant not only that people use language to engage in dialogue but, more importantly, that any stretch of discourse (e.g., phrase, utterance, text) tastes of the past texts and discourses from which it was constructed. Ongoing social discourse is always constructed from multiple intersecting languages and systems of meaning drawn from various local, social, and cultural environments. From a dialogic perspective, certain social and historical conditions partially determine what meanings can and cannot be assigned to utterances within particular discursive contexts. Yet, individuals exercise historical forms of agency in the ways that they appropriate, use, and transform extant forms of discourse. Moreover, some historical conditions (and their concomitant discourses) index the real and ward off critique more powerfully and pervasively than others. Thus, the precise articulations between the durability and transformability of social discourses and the concrete possibilities for individual agency are always empirical problems.

Thinking about the speech of an individual as dialogic rather than as originating from the speaker is critical for explaining how people represent themselves in what Clifford (1988) referred to as a "diversity of idioms." It affords insight into how the power of social formations both enables and constrains the various self-constructions they attempt by enacting various speech genres. Key questions in this regard include the kinds of genres people have access to, which ones they prefer, and which ones they deploy comfortably and competently. These are the questions that guided our investigation of how one group of urban African American youth worked to construct their identities, social relations, and visions of the world around them as they "talked through" their understanding of the life and death of perhaps their most important cultural hero, Tupac Shakur.

Youth Heralding the Psychologized Rap icon in and through the Television Talk Show Genre

The empirical work that we report here was conducted as part of a larger program of community service and research at a local youth-based community center. The participants were 10- to 12-year-old African American children. Although most were boys, several girls also participated. Some children participated on a routine basis; others participated only occasionally. Although most children attended the center daily, our formal meetings with them were conducted once a week. During these meetings, we talked about, wrote about, listened to, and watched videos related to various forms of black vernacular culture, including gospel, blues, jazz, soul, and rap. Participants in the program committed to various short-term projects such as publishing a newsletter. These projects grew out of participants' interests and included listening to, reading articles about, watching music videos and documentaries about, and writing about figures such as Mahalia Jackson, B.B. King, Snoop Doggy Dogg, and Tupac Shakur. When not working on specific projects, these young people engaged in more open-ended discussions focusing on artifacts suggested by members of the group. Most of these discussions were tape recorded. Segments of these tapes were transcribed and used as prompts for future group discussions and as material for generating written products. These written products allowed the children to extend and deepen their discussions, to put momentary closure on their work together, and to create tangible products for public consumption.

The particular project that we focus on in this chapter came out of a series of open-ended, child-initiated, and child-led discussions about Tupac Shakur. Since Tupac had died less than a week before we began this project, he had been a constant focus of discussion. Indeed, we discussed his life during the first six project sessions. During the seventh session, we suggested working on a written project together, perhaps a tribute to Shakur. We elicited or suggested a number of different kinds of texts that the members of the group might write including biographies, music reviews, movie reviews, personal reflections, and essays. We encouraged the children to use tape recorders as they generated ideas for their texts (either alone or in small groups). Their recordings functioned both as data for us and as props for subsequent texts and performances that the children created.

The "talk show" genre as a key frame for organizing talk about Tupac emerged in the discussion session after we introduced the idea of producing some kind of tribute to Tupac. Several children launched into a lively discussion about Tupac and his recent album (under the pseudonym Makaveli), *The Don Killuminati*. During this discussion, Kris (a pseudonym, as are all other participant names) talked about the introduction to the song "To Live and Die in L.A.," which is a skit framed as a question–and–answer session from a fictitious radio "call-in" show called *Street Science*. On this track, the female host of the show begins and a male caller responds:

> *Host: Street Science*, you're on the air. What do you feel when you hear a record like Tupac's new one?
> *Caller:* I love Tupac's new record.
> *Host:* Right, but don't you feel like that creates tension between East and West? He's talking about killing people. "I had sex with your wife." Not in those words. But he's talking about, "I wanna see you deceased."

Kris's reaccented version of this exchange, which embodied the speakers' intonations almost perfectly, was "Biggie Smalls, how do you feel, how Tupac been saying, he had sex with your wife?" Laughing, Lakisha pitched in the comment, "but not in those words." Still laughing, she added, "You ain't dead yet? You still talking? Roaches!" Interestingly, Lakisha's utterance indexed another skit from the same album. This skit precedes the song, "Bomb First," in which Tupac calls himself a "bad boy killer." The skit is framed as a news report about Tupac's new album and the East–West conflict that constitutes much of the thematic material of the album. In the context of this fictitious news report, Tupac yells, "You niggas still fucking talking? You niggas still breathing? Fucking Roaches!"

Kris's and Lakisha's performative exchange emerged spontaneously and produced the discursive context within which many subsequent talk show interactions took place. For example, directly following this exchange, three other young people took recorders, separated themselves from the group, and produced talk shows. In all of these shows, both the primary thematic material and the talk show frame were appropriated by our participants as devices for talking about their knowledge of and affiliation with Tupac Shakur and the cultural world in which his life and work was embedded.

Because the television talk show genre had not come up in our brainstorming sessions, we were a bit surprised that the children fastened onto it so intently (and intensively). We were even more surprised that this genre remained so central to their work on the Tupac anthology. Once the talk show format was introduced, it was appropriated consistently and pervasively in a majority of the work sessions that occurred during the subsequent five weeks. In all but a single week, at least one child or group chose to produce a talk show no matter what kind of text we asked them to produce (and we specifically asked them to produce facsimiles of a real news report, a biography, and a rap song).

As we mentioned earlier, the use of this speech genre seemed to have concrete effects on how our young participants framed the events they reported. This was not particularly surprising since a primary function of speech genres is to fuse form, thematic content, and practice (Kamberelis, 1995). One concrete effect of deploying the television talk show genre was that the thematic content that the children foregrounded in their dialogic discussions and projects were ones that are typically foregrounded in media coverage of rap artists (and other pop culture icons), most of which are highly personal and psychological. More specifically, the children constantly gravitated toward discussions about Tupac's murder, including his betrayal by Biggie Smalls and his conflict with Biggie over Biggie's wife, Faith. These topics dominated both formal discussions and informal conversation among peers and between peers and adults during the months that both preceded and followed Tupac's murder.

In most of the remainder of this chapter, we demonstrate some of the ways that these youth fused the dialogic talk show format with psychologized content from the world of rap music in their discursive practices. We do this by analyzing segments of transcripts from two of the talk shows that different children or groups of children created and performed. Importantly, there was considerable thematic and stylistic overlap across the many different talk shows produced by various children. For example, all of the talk shows showcased the privileging of affective and conflict-laden discourse and the power of talk to resolve the conflicts. However, each show was also unique in the particular themes that it foregrounded, the particular speech genres that it laminated onto the television talk show genre, and the particular ways that it fashioned the fusion of conversationalized discourse and psychologized social facts. For example, the first transcript that we analyze embodied a fusion of these two discursive features with exceptionally rich intertextual links to the lyrical content of certain rap songs and albums, as well as the myths that grew up around them. Within the second transcript we analyze, these two features were woven together with confessional discourse, which Foucault (1979, 1990) has argued is a particularly powerful normalizing technology of the self. Through our analyses of these two transcripts, we hope to show some of the ways in which the television talk show genre both enabled and constrained children's efforts to construct social knowledges and identities.

On the first day of the sessions devoted to the Tupac anthology, Kris and Rufus created and performed the first full-blown television talk show. As they performed their show, several other boys and girls pitched in comments from the audience rim. A segment of the transcript from this performance appears below:

R: Biggie Smalls, how do you feel what Tupac did to you?

K: Well, I'm, I ain't sweatin' it really because, all he's saying is ain't nuttin' but a joke to me.

R: Tupac, how do you feel? (*Voice deepens as he enacts Tupac's response*) Man, you stole my lyrics, my jewelry, so I stole your wife, you big fat mug (*Laughter*).

K: Well, nigga you wanna sport with my wife, ooh, cause I ain't even like that old girl anyway. She wasn't a little girl. You played your own self nigga, 'cause I don't like her, and you can have her nigga, 'cause I got more money than you do. That's why I'm gonna have Junior Mafia and them smoke your punk tail.

R: Oh, Junior Mafia ain't gonna do nothin'. Now, now, you all gonna try to smoke me. Then I'm gonna fake my death, and West Side gonna come on y'all and shoot y'all up (*Sound effects*). Now, what you gotta say about that? Huh? Wanna square? Wanna square? Huh?

[Section omitted where Kris and Rufus stop recording and regroup]

K: (*Voice shifts back to that of talk show host*) Back to me men, back to me please. Stop the arguing, all right.

R: (*Aside*) Back to Biggie.

K: Back to Biggie now. Biggie Smalls, how do you feel, about, Tupac saying that he want you d- deceased, dead? He said he gonna get his West Coast on you. He said he had his West Coast in the back. So (*Pause*)

R: (*Whispered prompt*) How do you feel?

K: How do you feel?

R: Well, I can kill any of them niggas anyway, 'cause guess what? I got my North Coast and South Coast on y'all niggas.

This performance is interesting both thematically and interactionally because it foregrounds key personal and interpersonal events in Tupac's and Biggie Smalls's lives. Rufus (who is playing Tupac) says "you stole my lyrics, my jewelry, so I stole your wife, you big fat mug." This utterance indexes a number of accusations made by Tupac in his single "Hit 'Em Up," where he charges that Biggie stole his style and his jewelry (during the shooting mentioned earlier), and that he ultimately got revenge by sleeping with Biggie Smalls' wife, Faith. Rufus also seems to index this single when he refers to "West Side!," a phrase that gets repeated in the song.

When asked to create a text that has something to do with Tupac Shakur, Rufus and Kris chose to take the psychologized struggle between Tupac and Biggie that is the thematic content of this single and re-situate it within the interactional frame of the television talk show (Bakhtin, 1981; Kamberelis & Scott, 1992). This fusion of psychologized thematic content, the dialogic format of the talk show genre, and the quotidian practices of "street talk" is quite predictable from the theoretical perspectives offered by Fairclough and Peck. It is also very important in terms of the kinds of knowledge it enables and constrains about these folk heroes and the wider world in which they operate. A closer look at some of the discursive features used by Rufus and Kris will bring this point into relief.

Many of the features that both Fairclough and Peck have argued are central elements of contemporary broadcast culture (especially insofar as this culture is embodied in television talk shows) are embedded in this constructed dialogue. For example, the interaction is framed by Rufus in terms of "feelings." He begins by asking, "Biggie Smalls, how do you feel what Tupac did to you?" He then asks a similar question of Tupac, "Tupac, how do you feel?" Importantly, this line of questioning, including its wording, thematic focus, and syntax, mirrors the line of questioning Kris first broached when attempting to mimic the introduction to the Tupac song, "To Live and Die in L.A." Although Rufus's version of it is different both from the original version and Kris's version, both foreground feelings. As we demonstrated above, the version from the album is directed to a radio listener and focuses on the new Tupac album – "What do you feel when you hear a record like Tupac's new one?" Kris appropriated this feeling-focused question and redeployed it in relation to the conflict between Tupac and Biggie, which had been so much a part of their talk for several weeks: "Biggie Smalls, how do you feel, how Tupac been saying, he had sex with your wife," to which Lakisha added, "but not in those words," which is a near-verbatim appropriation from the dialogue of the album's introductory skit.

Importantly, these kinds of "therapeutic" questions are relatively uncommon in much rap music, which tends to focus on physically impenetrable male characters. Yet, there is some overlap here between the kinds of issues treated in talk shows and the kinds of issues central to rap music, especially recent variants of this musical form. Interpersonal conflict and its resolution, for example, tend to be foregrounded in both media forms, albeit somewhat differently. Talk show discourse focuses on "therapeutic" solutions, which are "formulated around intimate, revelatory conversation" (Peck, 1995, p. 61). The goal of such discourse is to restore to good health the "individual psyche" through open communication and speech about feelings (p. 60). In contrast, conflict in much rap music often includes yelling, screaming, and physical confrontation, which is deployed rhetorically to build tension, sometimes almost to the breaking point. The goal of these conflict-resolution tactics is not usually therapeutic restoration, at least insofar as such restoration has been normalized within "mainstream" society. When conflicts are resolved, they are typically resolved through physical violence. Gangsta rap is a key example of this tendency.

The articulation of these partially incommensurable conflict-resolution strategies in the dialogue created by Kris and Rufus is very interesting. Kris (acting as a talk show host) asks Rufus (acting as Tupac) to express his feelings about his conflict with Biggie, positing faith – at least provisionally – in the ability of open communication to resolve it. However, this provisional faith is continually disrupted when they threaten to break into a fight. Interestingly though, these disruptions are often smoothed over by sliding back into the discourse of the television talk show genre. For example, role-playing the parts of Tupac and Biggie, Kris and Rufus almost come to blows. First Kris says, "That's why I'm gonna have Junior Mafia and them smoke your punk tail." Rufus replies with:

Now, now, you all gonna try to smoke me. Then I'm gonna fake my death, and West Side gonna come on y'all and shoot y'all up (*Sound effects*). Now, what you gotta say about that? Huh? Wanna square? Wanna square? Huh?

Kris restores order by assuming the interviewer role once again, "Back to me, men, back to me, please. Stop the arguing, all right." Once order is restored, Kris reinvokes the feelings-centered dialogue of the television talk show, "Biggie Smalls, how do you feel, about, Tupac saying that he want you d- deceased, dead?" In short, the eruption of conflict and the escalation of emotion are contained with a performative and discursive frame that privileges personal feelings and open communication about these feelings.

This general communication pattern, which blends television talk show discourse with the discourse of rap and revolves around psychological/interpersonal issues of rap artists, was central both to media coverage of the real life conflict between Tupac and Biggie over Faith Evans and in the talk of our young participants. The claim that Tupac slept with Biggie's wife as a form of revenge was a recurring motif throughout their interactions. Recall that we discussed this fact in relation to the mock television talk show created and performed by Kris and Rufus. It was also the central motif of a mock television talk show created and performed by John a week later. In this show, he played three different characters (talk show host, Faith Evans, and Biggie Smalls), the latter two of whom were brought together to "work on" their conflict in the controlled space of national television and under the arbitration of the show's host. As John performed various roles, he switched voices, postures, and seating positions. Marco and Rufus pitched in snippets of dialogue, comments, and questions from their audience positions. As the performance emerged, all three boys seemed to contribute to each other's knowledge and construction of relevant facts and events:

> J: (*Playing talk show host*) All right. What is this with you and Biggie Smalls getting
>   into it over Faith? (*Long pause*)
>   (*Pause and some background noise, perhaps coordinating an answer*)
> J: (*Whisper*) All right, let's get back. (*Pause*)
> M: Right, you know, I tried to get hooked up with, I (*Indecipherable*). Who is
>   Faith?
> J: (*Laughter*) Forget it. We'll bring in a magazine.
> R: (*Laughter*) I'll bring in the magazine. I'll bring a picture of her.
> J: (*Playing talk show host again*) Ladies and gentlemen, bring out Faith!
>   (*Playing Faith and enacting a high-pitched voice*) Oh, thank you, thank you.
>   (*Playing talk show host*) Faith, did you have a relationship with Biggie Smalls?
>   (*Playing Faith*) John, yes I did.
>   (*Playing talk show host*) Faith, did you love Biggie Smalls?
> R: John, yes I did.
> J: (*Playing Faith*) No, I didn't.
>   (*Playing talk show host*) Faith, (*Background commotion and laughter*) Faith, did you
>   ever make love to Tupac?
> R: (*Playing Faith*) Yes, I did.

> J: (*Playing Faith*) John, yes.
> (*Playing talk show host*) How did you make Notorious Big feel?
> R: (*Playing Faith*) Sad, mad, very, very (*Pause*)
> J: (*Playing Faith*) I don't know, John. I can't answer that.
> [*Transcript continues with an interview of Biggie Smalls*]

Playing the role of talk show host, John opens this monologue by explicitly positing Faith as the nexus of the conflict between Tupac and Biggie when he asks, "What is this with you and Biggie Smalls getting into it over Faith?" This is important because the conflict between the two men was very complicated, involving many factors including the exchange (legitimate or otherwise) of economic, cultural, and symbolic capital within the music industry. Indeed, the conflict began (as noted above) with an attempted robbery in New York City, during which Tupac reputedly lost $40,000 worth of jewelry. According to Tupac, Biggie knew this robbery would happen and told him nothing about it. Although it is easy to see how their conflict could be reduced to "getting into it over Faith," it is important to note that there are many equally plausible alternatives. Why not, for example, attribute the conflict to the prevalence of rampant materialism, the increase of black-on-black crime, the victimization of women, or the extremes of social Darwinist thinking? Given these (and other) plausible alternatives, the fact that John (and others) selected a personal and intimate subject (i.e., the exchange of sexual capital in the context of romantic betrayal) as the major reason for the conflict between Tupac and Biggie is both interesting and important to our argument. This selection seems related in no trivial way to the ideological constraints of the television talk show genre that John chose as the discursive format for rehearsing and exploring his knowledge about Tupac. This genre affords or encourages conversationalized discourse such as emotional, intimate, and self-revelatory questions. As a cursory survey of these kinds of shows would reveal, they typically feature subjects that involve "painful relationship problems, the kind everyone can relate to" (Zoglin 1995, p. 77). And conversely, such shows tend to steer people away from discourse about macro-economic, social, and cultural explanations for human and social problems.

In addition to foregrounding interpersonal relationships, intimate subjects, and feelings, John's monologue embodies a "confessional" quality. For example, he asks Faith to reveal the details of her relationship with both Biggie and Tupac (i.e., Did she sleep with Tupac? Did she ever really love Biggie?). As Foucault and others have noted, the "confession" is a primary technological apparatus of bio-power through which individuals are made into subjects:

> The confession is a ritual of discourse in which the speaking subject is also the subject of the statement; it is also a ritual that unfolds within a power relationship, for one does not confess without the presence (or virtual presence) of a partner who is not simply the interlocutor but the authority who requires the confession, prescribes, and appreciates it, and intervenes in order to judge, punish, forgive, console, and reconcile (Foucault, 1990, pp. 61–2).

Foucault's explanation of how oppressive or restrictive forms of power are reproduced through the enactment of the confession is particularly helpful for understanding how subjects are produced within discursive regimes such as the television talk show. Whenever the confession is enacted – and this is usually in particular discursive sites such as the ones highlighted by Foucault (schools, churches, prisons, therapy sessions, etc.) – the subject of the discourse is simultaneously constituted by it and subjected to it. Things are yet more complex than this, however. Because confession is multifunctional and because confessing is experienced as "personal," it tends to render brute and restrictive forces of power as nonexistent or benevolent. This is especially true in the late twentieth century since, as Fairclough has noted, the confession has become more widespread and more public due to the increasing presence and power of the media. This is particularly relevant for our purposes in this chapter because "the compulsion to delve into and talk about oneself, and especially one's sexuality, in an ever widening set of social locations . . . . appears on the face of it to be a liberating resistance to objectifying bio-power" (Fairclough, 1992, p. 53).

From this perspective, the act of confession seems to transform the confessee. It "exonerates, redeems, and purifies him [sic]; it unburdens him [sic] of his wrongs, liberates him [sic], and promises him [sic] salvation" (Foucault, 1990, p. 62). However, according to Foucault and many of his followers, this sense of freedom and resistance is an illusion. In reality, confession draws more of the person ever so subtly into extant networks of power (Fairclough, 1992; Foucault, 1990). With its semblance of agency, confession constitutes a marvelous technology of the self, a paramount instance of bio-power at work.

The discourse of television talk shows, with its privileging of affect, creates a context ripe for confession. One typically does not probe affective domains (e.g., loss, guilt, shame, sin) for sport but to excavate and exonerate the negativity and heaviness associated with such feelings through talk. So, the purpose of asking questions such as "How did you make Notorious Big feel?" is to help addressees confess their sins, hear the confessions of others, renew themselves, and move forward with their lives.

Like other features of the discourse of contemporary media, its confessional quality contributes to the translation of economic, social, and political questions into personal ones. And because confession is an instrument of disciplinary bio-power, confessing feels like a liberating experience, not a restrictive one. Yet, as Peck noted, the material function of confession is to reproduce extant arrangements of power. Within the discursive frameworks created by John (as well as by Kris and Rufus earlier), Tupac, Biggie, and Faith are constrained by the requirements of the television talk show genre. They must play according to a set of rules that, ironically, constitutes an effective technology of disciplinary power.

Discussion and Conclusions

The examples of discourse that we analyzed were highly representative of the thematic content and style of much of the talk that the children engaged in throughout the many weeks during which we discussed the life and death of Tupac Shakur. The preponderance of this talk seemed to focus on the role of Faith Evans in the ongoing set of disputes between Tupac and Biggie Smalls, and the form of this talk resembled the conversationalized discourse of the television talk show, wherein "talking about feelings" is posited as a primary discursive means through which to resolve such disputes. Importantly, the discourse requirements of the television talk show genre (as well as contemporary broadcast media discourse more broadly conceived) encourage the use of psychologized iconic discourses, which promote liberal-humanist ideologies of individual agency, intention, and choice.

Among other things, our findings underscore the fact that understanding young people's access to, preferences for, and competences with different forms of talk is essential to understanding how they come to understand cultural events that are salient within their lives. Because they are primary carriers of ideologies, different speech genres enable and constrain different kinds and degrees of cultural knowledge (Fairclough, 1992; Hymes, 1996; Kamberelis, 1995). Thus, understanding how young people appropriate and deploy the various speech genres that are available and/or salient in their lives is crucial for understanding how they reproduce and/or disrupt dominant cultural discourses. As we noted at the beginning of this chapter, popular culture provides many of the discourses (and speech genres) in which and through which young people constitute both their personal and cultural identities and their knowledge about the world. What speech genres young people gravitate toward and how these genres are rearticulated within their microlevel speaking practices are fundamental both to the reproduction and disruption of cultural discourses and to children's ongoing processes of identity production. Thus, understanding how specific speech genres enable and constrain how young people talk about their lives and their worlds is crucial for understanding the trajectories of their "thinking" and "acting" (Fairclough, 1992; Fiske, 1996; Kamberelis, 1995; Wertsch, 1991).

As we demonstrated through our analyses, one speech genre that seemed particularly compelling for the young people in our study was the television talk show genre. We are not claiming, however, that this genre is a singularly important one for young people. Whether or not such a claim could be supported would require a much more ambitious study than the one we conducted. Among other things, it would require comparisons across a number of different speaking genres, a range of discursive settings, a large number of participants, and an extended time span. Our claim is much more modest and may be summarized as follows: the young people in our study did, in fact, repeatedly choose to deploy the television talk show genre to discuss the life and death of Tupac Shakur, and this genre had concrete discursive effects on how they constructed and positioned themselves in relation to these issues and events.

To understand why these patterns were so salient in our data requires some understanding of the wider set of discursive practices that are common currency within the lives of many urban African American youth. In the many different formal discussions, informal conversations, and observations that we have conducted in the community in which our study took place, we have found that television talk shows have a tremendous appeal to a wide range of audiences across a wide range of ages. We have also found that personalized and conversationalized discourse and the psychologization of social issues are extremely common discursive practices among the people who constitute these audiences. We will elaborate on each of these issues, focusing first on the conversationalization of public discourse.

During a discussion that focused on the viewing practices of our participants and their family members, it became clear that television talk shows were a staple of family entertainment. For example, *Ricki Lake* and *Jenny Jones* were mentioned repeatedly as favorite shows by many of our participants. Interestingly, both of these shows seem to be targeted at younger audiences in comparison with shows like *Oprah Winfrey* and *Maury Povich*, which are targeted at older viewers. Moreover, shows like *Ricki Lake* and *Jenny Jones* tend to showcase more extreme examples of the kinds of animated interpersonal conflicts that we have discussed throughout this chapter, a fact that was not lost on our young viewers. Rufus, for example, noted that "the best one is *Ricki Lake* and *Jenny Craig* [*Jenny Jones*]." He continued, "it's funny, they be start fighting and stuff; it be looking funny; . . . they be doin' cat fights, them girls." Later in the conversation he added that he found it more enjoyable to watch shows filled with arguing and fighting than shows where the guests "just be talking." That this preference was pervasive and durable for most of our participants was reinforced many times when we viewed television shows and films with them. Almost without exception, they were riveted to the screen during intense action scenes. In contrast, they lost interest and began to talk among themselves (often about issues unrelated to the show or film) during scenes that involved mostly talk or narration.

The viewing practices of our participants were also closely linked to their family lives and social lives. Many young people told us that they watched these television talk shows with members of their families. Marco, for example, said, "Everyday after school, I see my grandma watchin' it, and I sit down and lay on the couch and I start watchin' it, and he [his brother] come in and start watchin' it. And then it be me, him, and my grandma." Indeed, we got the impression from various discussions that our participants' viewing practices were intensely social.

Our discussion of television talk shows also led to discussions of other kinds of television shows that our participants watched. For example, during one discussion of *Ricki Lake*, Marco brought up another show, *The Love Connection*. Mention of this show prompted Rufus to share his recollection of a particular episode in which a man refused to pay for gas needed while on a date. Rufus broke into laughter as he told us, "She dumped him!" Although television shows like *The Love Connection* differ from television talk shows in many respects, both types of shows foreground overtly conversationalized discourses, focus largely on personal issues and interpersonal conflicts, and encourage confessional discourse. Extreme interpersonal conflict is also central to another set of media events commonly consumed by our young participants – professional wrestling. Indeed, watching and talking about professional wrestling was a very popular "sport" among them. The television at the community center where they "hung out" was almost always tuned to professional wrestling when it was being broadcast; most of our participants had accumulated a rich body of knowledge about the spectacle; and most engaged in fairly frequent discussions about particular contestants, emphasizing their idiosyncratic personalities, their antics, and their recent contests. Like rap music and many of the "events" featured on television talk shows, professional wrestling features violent conflicts between and among highly stylized and psychologized individual icons. These characters typically engage in complex psychodramas, and their actual matches are interspersed with interviews and antics that heighten their interpersonal conflicts. Wrestling is indeed embedded within its own mythological narratives with definable characters who engage in both physical and psychological drama. As such, wrestling is another key, albeit paradoxical, example of the tendency toward "conversationalized" discourses within the contemporary broadcast media.

These findings about the broader reception practices of our participants, their friends, and their families reinforce our general argument that there is a certain discursive reciprocity between their viewing practices and the "forms of talk" with which they are most comfortable and most competent. This reciprocity suggests that understanding the forms and functions of certain speech genres is essential to understanding the productive (and restrictive) articulations between young people's consumption practices (e.g., viewing, reading, listening) and their production practices (e.g., speaking, arguing, performing).

We turn now to the psychologization of social and political issues. We have already shown that our participants tended to provide psychological explanations for social and political problems and events. We also noted that this tendency is central to the discourse of the television talk show genre, which we argued is a particularly powerful instance of the trend toward conversationalization within the contemporary broadcast media more broadly conceived. Indeed, during the very first discussion in which we discussed Tupac's death and before any mention of *Ricki Lake*, one participant, Latrice, commented that Biggie didn't have anything to do with Tupac's murder because Faith wasn't "worth all of that." In making this assertion, Latrice implicitly attributed Faith Evans as the primary source of the conflict between the two men, and she justified her claim about why Biggie did not murder Tupac with the warrant that Faith was not attractive enough to motivate a murder. During this discussion, Lakisha and John brought up the single "Hit 'Em Up," which is presumably about Tupac's affair with Faith. As we mentioned in our earlier analyses, this single became a common "prop" around which many subsequent discussions and performances were staged. Predominant themes that were played out included the presumed fact that Tupac let Biggie sleep on his couch when he [Biggie] was down and out, that Biggie had stolen some of Tupac's jewelry (during the robbery), that this act had caused animosity between the two men, and that Tupac slept with Faith as an act of revenge.

We witnessed numerous other interactions and performances during which these young people constructed the facts of Tupac's life and death in a highly psychologized way. Almost exclusively, they linked the murder to the conflict between Tupac and Biggie, and they foregrounded personal and interpersonal issues gleaned from albums, videos, news reports, fanzines, and so on to flesh out the motives of the actors involved. For example, when asked why Tupac chose to target Faith to get back at Biggie for his robbery, Rufus volunteered, "like that's what he likeded the most. And like Tupac likeded his jewelry the most and Biggie Smalls likeded his wife the most." When asked what he thought about Tupac's revenge tactics, Rufus replied "he [Biggie] shouldn't have stole his rhymes, shouldn't stole none of that junk. He stole his jewelry." Rufus also located some of the agency for these events in Faith, noting that she had been unfaithful to Biggie because she liked Tupac more, a claim that added yet another layer of psychologized explanation to the narrative that Rufus constructed to account for the conflict between Tupac and Biggie.

To summarize much of what we have already said, both the thematic content and the form of our participants' talk about Tupac's murder were modeled after the television talk show genre, at least in large measure. We concluded from this tendency that the television talk show genre (and the discourses of contemporary broadcast media more broadly conceived) were discourses with which our participants had tremendous familiarity and fluency. We also suggested that understanding how young people construct themselves and their worlds requires excavating locally specific linkages among societal discourses, consumption or reception practices, and microlevel speaking practices (especially in relation to speech genres), and we provided modest empirical support for this claim. As the primary vehicles of societal discourses, speech genres are discursive "combinations of specific blindnesses and insights. Each is adapted to conceptualizing some aspects of reality better than others" (Morson & Emerson, 1990, p. 276). Or as Burke so astutely noted many years ago, all discursive frames constitute "terministic screens," which are at once reflections, selections, and deflections of reality (Burke, 1966, p. 45). Thus, fastening onto the television talk show genre both enabled and constrained the ways that the young people in our study processed the complex events in the world of rap that so captivated their attention. For example, it seemed that certain structural social and political facts and implications relevant to Tupac's life and death were elided when the television talk show genre became the primary lens through which these facts and implications were viewed, even though this speech genre is socially potent and discursively complex. If we are right here, it is incumbent upon us to imagine how and why these issues were not constructed otherwise. In relation to this point, Charlie Braxton wrote:

> In the absence of absolute truth about the murder of Tupac Shakur, many people attempt to fill the void by proposing countless theories as to who may have killed him and why. Theories range from the plausible to the straight up imbecilic, but very few, if any, examine the critical socio-political issues that ultimately led to the conditions surrounding Shakur's death (1997, p. 97).

We have suggested all along that, in their appropriation of the discourses and discourse formats of the contemporary broadcast media, our participants avoided asking certain kinds of questions and generating certain kinds of explanations. More specifically, they tended to avoid wider social and political questions and explanations in favor of personal and psychological ones, which have "no origin or target outside of one's own psychic process" (Peck, 1995, p. 76). The restricted set of questions and explanations that resulted from these specific appropriation practices made visible some kinds of knowledges and rendered others relatively invisible. Framed as they were within the discourses of contemporary broadcast media, a certain inevitability plagued their accounts of the controversy between Tupac and Biggie. At the heart of the conflict were two individual personalities with strong wills, idiosyncratic compulsions, individual desires, and specific sets of goals. Given this construction, the two most salient solutions available to Biggie and Tupac were to fight it out or to talk it over – or perhaps to fight it out and then talk it over. This kind of resolution is not necessarily a bad thing. Indeed, many, including us, would argue that it is the best of these options. Whether or not this is true is irrelevant to our argument, however. What is relevant is that the conversationalization and psychologicalization of the conflict between Tupac and Biggie suppressed the possibility of generating economic, social, and political explanations for the conflict and, therefore, the envisagement of more structural kinds of resolutions.

This fact indexes some larger issues about the relations among discourses, communicative practices, and knowledge. What people actually do with language in concrete acts of communication has important implications for how they understand and explain public events, as well as how they, themselves, act. This nexus turns on issues of public access to cultural resources. How people come to understand themselves and their worlds depends in no small measure upon what kinds of access they have to what kinds of discursive frames within the public sphere, because these frames are fundamental to appraising and evaluating social reality. Moreover, specific ways of speaking and ways of knowing are embedded within wider social practices, such as television watching. Like the "confession," engaging in these speaking practices interpellates people into specific subject positions wherein they are both subjects of and subjected to certain ways of processing the world – ways that are good for some things and not so good for others (e.g., Hymes, 1996).

Several implications follow from this assertion. First, we need to understand more fully how and why society makes readily available certain cultural resources and not others. In relation to this point, might viewing social events with the possibilities made available through the lenses of different genres help young people become more astute social critics? With respect to the data that we analyzed in this chapter, for example, what knowledges might have been constructed had our participants resisted "common sense" choices about what genres were most appropriate to discuss Tupac's life and death, processed these events through a variety of generic lenses, and compared the results of doing so? Finally, might such interpretive practices have promoted more open and critical stances toward the constitutive relations between language and reality?

To conclude, we would like to make two summary points – one that is theoretical/ methodological and one that is empirical. The work we have presented in this chapter suggests the power of theorizing and investigating speech genres as primary mediators between societal discourses and everyday social practices. Speech genres are the instruments deployed by young people as they actively construct their social knowledges and identities in the context of specific sociocultural practices. Moreover and more importantly, they are also instruments that are differentially available to young people, depending upon a whole set of contingent microsociological and macrosociological factors. Though often theorized, empirical research is necessary to understand more fully the constitutive linkages among discourses, knowledges, and identities, and how speech genres mediate their coconstitution.

Although we ventured into this empirical terrain, we emerged with claims that are both tentative and modest. We found that the genres that the young people in our study gravitated toward and trafficked in (as well as the speech events within which they were embedded) are ones that have been popularized recently within the contemporary public media industries. Although these genres allowed children to construct fairly complex psychological understandings and explanations, they rendered invisible (or at least eclipsed) more global and more structural social and political understandings and explanations. More research of the sort we have conducted is necessary to map more precisely how specific speech genres enable and constrain young people's efforts to reproduce and resist the power arrangements that constitute their lives and to construct social knowledges and identities within these arrangements.

References

Alcoff, L. (1988). Cultural Feminism versus Post-structuralism: The Identity Crisis in Feminist Theory. *Signs: Journal of Women and Culture* 13(3), pp. 405–36.

Appadurai, A. (1996). *Modernity at Large*. Minneapolis: University of Minnesota Press.

Bakhtin, M. M. (1981). *The Dialogic Imagination*, trans. C. Emerson & M. Holquist. Austin: University of Texas Press.

Bakhtin, M. M. (1984). *Problems of Dostoevsky's Poetics*, trans. C. Emerson. Minneapolis: University of Minnesota Press.

Bakhtin, M. M. (1986). *Speech Genres and Other Late Essays*, trans. V. W. McGee. Austin: University of Texas Press.

Bakhtin, M. M. & P. N. Medvedev (1985). *The Formal Method in Literary Scholarship: A Critical Introduction to Sociological Poetics*, trans. A. J. Werhle. Cambridge, MA: Harvard University Press.

Bhabha, H. K. (1994). *The Location of Culture: Literature Related to Politics*. London: Routledge.

Bourdieu, P. (1990). *The Logic of Practice*. Stanford, CA: Stanford University Press.

Braxton, C. (1997). Who Killed Tupac Shakur? In: M. Datcher & K. Alexander (eds.), *Tough Love: The Life and Death of Tupac Shakur*, pp. 97–100. Alexandria, VA: Alexander Publishing Group.

Bruner, J. S. (1986). *Actual Minds, Possible Worlds*. Cambridge, MA: Harvard University Press.

Burke, K. (1966). Terministic Screens. In: *Language as Symbolic Action: Essays on Life, Literature, and Method*, pp. 44–62. Berkeley: University of California Press.

Buttny, R. (1993). *Social Accountability in Communication*. London: Sage.

Clifford, J. (1988). *The Predicament of Culture: Twentieth Century Ethnography, Literature, and Art*. Cambridge, MA: Harvard University Press.

Dimitriadis, G. (1996). Hip Hop: From Live Performance to Mediated Narrative. *Popular Music* 15(2), pp. 179–94.

Dimitriadis, G. & G. Kamberelis (1997). Shifting Terrains: Mapping Education within a Global Landscape. *The Annals of the American Academy of Political and Social Science* 551, pp. 137–50.

Fairclough, N. (1992). *Discourse and Social Change*. Cambridge: Polity Press.

Fairclough, N. (1995). *Media Discourse*. London: Edward Arnold.

Fiske, J. (1996). *Media Matters*. Minneapolis: University of Minnesota Press.

Foucault, M. (1972). *The Archaeology of Knowledge and the Discourse on Language*, trans. A. M. Sheridan Smith. New York: Pantheon Books.

Foucault, M. (1979). *Discipline and Punish: The Birth of the Prison*, trans. A. Sheridan. New York: Vintage Books.

Foucault, M. (1990). *The History of Sexuality. Volume 1: An Introduction*, trans. A. Sheridan. New York: Vintage Books.

Gramsci, A. (1971). *Selections from the Prison Notebooks of Antonio Gramsci*, trans. and ed. Q. Hoare & G. N. Smith. New York: International Publishers.

Grossberg, L. (1992). *We Gotta Get Out of This Place: Popular Conservatism and Postmodern Culture*. New York: Routledge.

Hall, S. (1996). Who Needs "Identity"? In: S. Hall & P. du Gay (eds.), *Questions of Cultural Identity*, pp. 1–17. London: Sage.

Hymes, D. (1996). *Ethnography, Linguistics, Narrative Inequality*. London: Taylor & Francis.

Kamberelis, G. (1995). Genre as Institutionally Informed Social Practice. *Journal of Contemporary Legal Issues 6*, pp. 115–71.

Kamberelis, G. & K. D. Scott (1992). Other People's Voices: The Coarticulation of Texts and Subjectivities. *Linguistics and Education 4*, pp. 359–403.

Markus, H. & S. Kitayama (1991). Culture and the Self: Implications for Cognition, Emotion, and Motivation. *Psychological Review* 98(2), pp. 224–53.

McCarthy, C. (1998). *The Uses of Culture: Education and the Limits of Ethnic Affiliation*. New York: Routledge.

Morson, G. S. & C. Emerson (1990). *Mikhail Bakhtin: Creation of a Prosaics*. Stanford, CA: Stanford University Press.

Peck, J. (1995). TV Talk Shows as Therapeutic Discourse: The Ideological Labor of the Televised Talking Cure. *Communication Theory* 5(1), pp. 58–81.

Rosaldo, R. (1989). *Culture and Truth: The Remaking of Social Analysis*. Boston: Beacon Press.

Star Talker. (1994). *Broadcasting and Cable* 124, December 12, pp. 56–7.

Wertsch, J. V. (1991). *Voices of the Mind: A Sociocultural Approach to Mediated Action*. Cambridge, MA: Harvard University Press.

Zoglin, R. (1995). Talking Trash. *Time*, January 30, pp. 77–8.

VI

Ethnicity

30

What Is Race?

Richard Lewontin, Steven Rose, and Leon Kamin*

Before we can sensibly evaluate claims of genetic differences in IQ performance between races, we need to look at the very concept of race itself: What is really known about genetic differences between what are conventionally thought of as human races?

Until the mid-nineteenth century, "race" was a fuzzy concept that included a number of kinds of relationships. Sometimes it meant the whole species, as "the human race"; sometimes a nation or tribe, as "the race of Englishmen"; and sometimes merely a family, as "He is the last of his race." About all that held these notions together was that members of a "race" were related by ties of kinship and that their shared characteristics were somehow passed from generation to generation. With the rise to popularity of Darwin's theory of evolution, biologists soon began to use the concept of "race" in a quite different but no more ultimately consistent way. It simply came to mean "kind," an identifiably different form of organism within a species. So there were light-bellied and dark-bellied "races" of mice, or banded- or unbanded-shell "races" of snails. But defining "races" simply as observable kinds produced two curious contradictions, First, members of different "races" often existed side by side within a population. There might be twenty-five different "races" of beetles, all members of the same species, living side by side in the same local population. Second, brothers and sisters might be members of two different races, since the characters that differentiated races were sometimes influenced by alternative forms of a single gene. So a female mouse of the light-bellied "race" could produce offspring of both light-bellied and dark-bellied races, depending on her mate. Obviously there was no limit to the number of "races" that could be described within a species, depending on the whim of the observer.

Around 1940, biologists, under the influence of discoveries in population genetics, made a major change in their understanding of race. Experiments on the genetics of organisms taken from natural populations made it clear that there was a great deal of genetic variation between individuals even in the same family, not to speak of the same population. Many of the "races" of animals previously described and named were simply alternative hereditary forms that could appear within a family. Different local geographic populations did not differ from each other absolutely, but only in the relative

* Originally published as "IQ: The Rank Ordering of the World," pp. 119–29, 298 from R. C. Lewontin et al., *Not in Our Genes: Biology, Ideology, and Human Nature* (New York, Pantheon Books). © 1984 by R. C. Lewontin, Steven Rose and Leon J. Kamin. Used by permission of the authors and Pantheon Books, a division of Random House, Inc.

frequency of different characters. So, in human blood groups, some individuals were type A, some type B, some AB, and some O. No population was exclusively of one blood type. The difference between African, Asian, and European populations was only in the proportion of the four kinds. These findings led to the concept of "geographical race" as a population of varying individuals, freely mating among each other but different in average proportions of various genes from other populations. Any local random breeding population that was even slightly different in the proportion of different gene forms from other populations was a geographical race.

This new view of race had two powerful effects. First, no individual could be regarded as a "typical" member of a race. Textbooks of anthropology would often show photographs of "typical" Australian aborigines, tropical Africans, Japanese, etc., listing as many as fifty or a hundred "races," each with its typical example. Once it was recognized that every population was highly variable and differed largely in average proportions of different forms from other populations, the concept of the "type specimen" became meaningless. The second consequence of the new view of race was that since every population differs slightly from every other one on the average, all local interbreeding populations are "races," so race really loses its significance as a concept. The Kikuyu of East Africa differ from the Japanese in gene frequencies, but they also differ from their neighbors, the Masai, and, although the extent of the differences might be less in one case than in the other, it is only a matter of degree. This means that the *social* and *historical* definitions of race that put the two East African tribes in the same "race" but put the Japanese in a different "race" were biologically arbitrary. How much difference in the frequencies of A, B, AB, and O blood groups does one require before deciding it is large enough to declare two local populations are in separate "races"?

The change in point of view among biologists had an eventual effect on anthropology in that about 30 years ago textbooks began to play down the whole issue of defining races, but the changes in academic views have had little effect on everyday consciousness of race. We still speak casually of Africans as one race, Europeans as another, Asians as another, using distinctions that correspond to our everyday impressions. No one would mistake a Masai for a Japanese or either for a Finn. Despite variation from individual to individual within these groups, the differences between groups in skin color, hair form, and some facial features make them clearly different. What racists do is to take these evident differences and claim that they demonstrate major genetic separation between "races." Is there any truth in this assertion? Are the differences in skin color and hair form that we use to distinguish races in our everyday experience typical of the genetic differentiation between groups, or are they for some reason unusual?

We must remember that we are conditioned to observe precisely those features and that our ability to distinguish individuals as opposed to types is an artifact of our upbringing. We have no difficulty at all in telling individuals apart in our own group, but "they" all look alike. The question is, if we could look at a random sample of different genes, not biased by our socialization, how much difference would there be between major geographical groups, say between Africans and Australian aborigines, as opposed to the differences between individuals within these groups? It is, in fact, possible to answer that question.

During the last forty years, using the techniques of immunology and of protein chemistry, geneticists have identified a large number of human genes that code for specific enzymes and other proteins. Very large numbers of individuals from all over the world have been tested to determine their genetic constitution with respect to such proteins since only a small sample of blood is needed to make these determinations. About 150 different genetically coded proteins have been examined, and the results are very illuminating for our understanding of human genetic variation.

It turns out that 75 percent of the different kinds of proteins are identical in all individuals tested, regardless of population, with the exception of an occasional rare mutation. These so-called *monomorphic* proteins are common to all human beings of all races; the species is essentially uniform with respect to the genes that code them. The other 25 percent, however, are *polymorphic* proteins. That is, there exist two or more alternative forms of the protein, coded by alternative forms of a gene, that are common but at varying frequencies in our species. We can use these polymorphic genes to ask how much difference there is between populations, as compared with the difference between individuals within populations.

An example of a highly polymorphic gene is the one that determines the ABO blood type. There are three alternative forms of the gene, which we will symbolize by A, B, and O, and every population in the world is characterized by some particular mixture proportions of the three. For example, Belgians have about 26 percent A and 6 percent B; the remaining 68 percent is O. Among Pygmies of the Congo, the proportions are 23 percent A, 22 percent B, and 55 percent O. The frequencies can be depicted as a triangular diagram, as shown in Figure 30.1. Each point represents a population, and the proportion of each gene form can be read as the perpendicular distance from the point to the appropriate side of the triangle. As the figure shows, all human populations are clustered fairly close together in one part of the frequency space. There are no populations, for example, with very high B and very low A and O (lower right-hand corner). The figure also shows that populations that belong to what we call major "races" in our everyday usage do not cluster together. The dashed lines have been put around populations that are similar in ABO frequencies, but these do not mark off racial groups. For example, the cluster made up of populations 2, 8, 10, 13, and 20 include an African, three Asian, and one European population.

A major finding from the study of such polymorphic genes is that none of these genes perfectly discriminates one "racial" group from another. That is, there is no gene known that is 100 percent of one form in one race and 100 percent of a different form in some other race, Reciprocally, some genes that are very variable from individual to individual show no average difference at all between major races. Table 30.1 shows the three polymorphic genes that are most different between "races" and the three that are most similar among the "races." The first column gives the name of the protein or blood group, and the second column gives the symbols of the alternative forms (*alleles*) of the gene that is varying. As the table shows, there are big differences in relative frequencies of the alleles of the Duffy, Rhesus, and P blood groups from "race" to "race," and there may be an allele like Fy^b that is found only in one group, but no group is "pure" for any genes. In contrast, the Auberger, Xg, and Secretor proteins are very polymorphic within each "race," but the differences between groups is very small. It must be

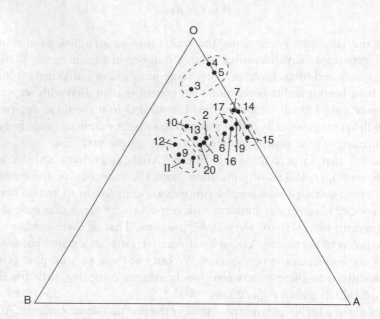

Figure 30.1 A triallelic diagram of the ABO blood group allele frequencies for human populations. Each point represents a population: the perpendicular distances from the point to the sides represent the allele frequencies as indicated in the small triangle. Populations 1–3 are African, 4–7 are American Indians, 8–13 are Asians, 14–15 are Australian aborigines, and 16–20 are Europeans. Dashed lines enclose arbitrary classes with similar gene frequencies, which do not correspond to the "racial" classes. (Jacquard, 1970.)

Table 30.1 Examples of extreme differentiation and close similarity in blood-group allele frequencies in three racial groups

Gene	Allele	POPULATION: Caucasoid	Negroid	Mongoloid
Duffy	Fy	0.0300	0.9393	0.0985
	Fy^a	0.4208	0.0607	0.9015
	Fy^b	0.5492	0.0000	0.0000
Rhesus	R_0	0.0186	0.7395	0.0409
	R_1	0.4036	0.0256	0.7591
	R_2	0.1670	0.0427	0.1951
	r	0.3820	0.1184	0.0049
	r'	0.0049	0.0707	0.0000
	Others	0.0239	0.0021	0.0000
P	P_1	0.5161	0.8911	0.1677
	P_2	0.4839	0.1089	0.8323
Auberger	Au^a	0.6213	0.6419	–
	Au	0.3787	0.3581	–
Xg	Xg^a	0.67	0.55	0.54
	Xg	0.33	0.45	0.46
Secretor	Se	0.5233	0.5727	
	se	0.4767	0.4273	

Source: From a summary provided in L. L. Cavalli-Storza and W. F. Bodmer, *The Genetics of Human Populations* (San Francisco: Freeman, 1971), pp. 724–31. See this source for information on other loci and for data sources.

Table 30.2   Allelic frequencies at seven polymorphic loci in Europeans and black Africans

Locus	EUROPEANS: Allele 1	Allele 2	Allele 3	AFRICANS: Allele 1	Allele 2	Allele 3
Red cell acid phosphatase	0.36	0.60	0.04	0.17	0.83	0.00
Phospho-glucomutase 1	0.77	0.23	0.00	0.79	0.21	0.00
Phospho-glucomutase-3	0.74	0.26	0.00	0.37	0.63	0.00
Adenylate kinase	0.95	0.05	0.00	1.00	0.00	0.00
Peptidase A	0.76	0.00	0.24	0.90	0.10	0.00
Peptidase D	0.99	0.01	0.00	0.95	0.03	0.02
Adenosine deaminase	0.94	0.06	0.00	0.97	0.03	0.00

Source: R. C. Lewontin, *The Genetic Basis of Evolutionary Change* (New York: Columbia Univ. Press, 1974). Adapted from H. Harris, *The Principles of Human Biochemical Genetics* (Amsterdam and London: North-Holland, 1970).

remembered that 75 percent of known genes in humans do not vary at all, but are totally monomorphic throughout the species.

Rather than picking out the genes that are the most different or the most similar between groups, what do we see if we pick genes at random? Table 30.2 shows the outcome of such a random sample. Seven enzymes known to be polymorphic were tested in a group of Europeans and Africans (actually black Londoners who had come from West Africa and white Londoners). In this random sample of genes there is a remarkable similarity between groups. With the exception of phosphoglucomutase-3, for which there is a reversal between groups, the most common form of each gene in Africans is the same form as for the Europeans, and the proportions themselves are very close. Such a result would lead us to conclude that the genetic difference between blacks and whites is negligible as compared with the polymorphism within each group.

The kind of question asked in Table 30.2 can in fact be asked in a very general way for large numbers of populations for about twenty genes that have been widely studied all over the world. Suppose we measure the variation among humans for some particular gene by the probability that a gene taken from one individual is a different alternative form (allele) than that taken from another individual at random from the human species as a whole. We can then ask how much less variation there would be if we chose the two individuals from the same "race." The difference between the variation over the whole species and the variation within a "race" would measure the proportion of all human variation that is accounted for by racial differences. In like manner we could ask how much of the variation within a "race" is accounted for by differences between tribes or nations that belong to the same "race," as opposed to the variation between individuals within the same tribe or nation. In this way we can divide the totality of human genetic variation into a portion between individuals within populations, between local populations within major "races," and between major "races." That calculation has been carried out independently by three different groups of geneticists using slightly different data and somewhat different statistical methods but with the identical result. Of all human genetic variation known for enzymes and other proteins, where it has been possible to actually count up the frequencies of different forms of the genes and so get an objective estimate of genetic variation, 85 percent turns out to be between individuals within the same local population, tribe, or nation; a further 8 percent is between tribes or nations within a major "race"; and the remaining 7 percent is between major "races." That means that the genetic variation between one Spaniard and another, or between one Masai and another, is 85 percent of all human genetic variation, while only 15 percent is accounted for by breaking people up into groups. If everyone on earth became extinct except for the Kikuyu of East Africa, about 85 percent of all human variability would still be present in the reconstituted species. A few gene forms would be lost – like the Fy^b allele of the Duffy blood group that is known only in European, or the Diego blood factor known only in American Indians – but little else would be changed.

The reader will have noticed that to carry out the calculation of partitioning variation between "races," some method must have been used for assigning each nation or tribe to a "race." The problem of what one means by a "race" comes out forcibly when making such assignments. Are the Hungarians European? They certainly *look* like Europeans, yet they (like the Finns) speak a language that is totally unrelated to European languages and belongs to the Turkic family of languages from Central Asia. And what about the modern-day Turks? Are they Europeans, or should they be lumped with the Mongoloids? And then there are the Urdu- and Hindi-speaking people of India. They are the descendants of a mixture of Aryan invaders from the north, the Persians from the west, and the Vedic tribes of the Indian subcontinent. One solution is to make them a separate race. Even the Australian aborigines, who have often been put to one side as a separate race, mixed with Papuans and with Polynesian immigrants from the Pacific well before Europeans arrived. No group is more hybrid in its origin than the present-day Europeans, who are a mixture of Huns, Ostrogoths, and Vandals from the east, Arabs from the south, and Indo-Europeans from the Caucasus, In practice, "racial" categories are established that correspond to major skin color groups, and all the borderline cases are distributed among these or made into new races according to the whim of the scientist. But it turns out not to matter much how the groups are assigned, because the differences between major "racial" categories, no matter how defined, turn out to be small, Human "racial" differentiation is, indeed, only skin deep. Any use of racial categories must take its justifications from some other source than biology. The remarkable feature of human evolution and history has been the very small degree of divergence between geographical populations as compared with the genetic variation among individuals.

IQ Differences Between Groups

The only way to answer the question of genetic differences in IQ between groups would be to study adoption across racial and class boundaries. Such studies are not easy to find, but the several that have been done all give the same result. In the study by Tizard[1] of black, white, and mixed-parentage children in English residential nurseries, using three preschool tests of mental performance, the differences were not larger than could be expected from statistical variations, due to chance; but, taken at face value, blacks and mixed-parentage children did *better* than whites. Another relevant case is the comparison of the children of black and of white US soldiers and German mothers who were left behind to be raised in Germany when their fathers returned home after the Occupation. Again, there is a small difference favoring the black children. Two studies comparing the amount of white ancestry of black children with their IQ scores found no correlation, On the other hand, a study of black children adopted by white families showed a much higher IQ than for children in the general population, but within these adoptees, children of two black parents performed less well than when one of the biological parents was black and one white.[2] In fact, this is the sum total of evidence on genetic differences between blacks and whites that makes any effort at all to separate the genetic from the social.

Like all the studies of the heritability of IQ, these five have more or less serious methodological problems, and no positive conclusions can be reached using them. The point is not that they prove a genetical identity between races, which they certainly do not, but that there is no evidence for any genetic difference in IQ score. The first four studies, the only ones then available, were reviewed in a report that was meant to be the final judicious word from the American social science establishment, "Race Differences in Intelligence," under the auspices of the Social Sciences Research Council's Committee on Biological Bases of Social Behavior.[3] It is characteristic of the deep ideological commitment of American social science to a hereditarian point of view that the results were characterized as showing that

> Observed average differences in the scores of members of different US racial–ethnic groups on intellectual ability tests probably reflect in part inadequacies and biases in the tests themselves, in part differences in environmental conditions among the groups, and in part genetic differences among the groups. . . . A rather wide range of positions concerning the relative weight to be given to the three factors can reasonably be taken on the basis of the current evidence, and a sensible person's position might well differ for different abilities, for different groups, and different tests.

Precisely how a "sensible person" could reasonably take the position that the observed difference between US racial–ethnic groups is partly genetic, on the basis of the evidence presented, we are not told. Nor is it revealed by this disingenuous summary that, where differences were seen in those observations, they were in favor of *blacks*.

The evidence on cross-class adoptions is sparse. In one sense, adoption in general is cross-class because adopting parents as a group are richer, better educated, and older than the biological parents; and, as we have seen, adopted children have significantly raised IQs.

The study conducted in France by Schiff et al.,[4] however, was designed especially to test the effect of class. The investigators located thirty-two children who had been born to lower-working-class parents, but who had been adopted before six months of age by upper-middle-class (or above) parents. They also located twenty *biological* siblings of the same children. These siblings had been reared by their own working-class mothers. Thus, the two groups of siblings were genetically equivalent but had experienced quite different sorts of environments. The adopted children, by school age, had an average IQ of 111, 16 points higher than that of their stay-at-home siblings. Perhaps more important, 56 percent of the stay-at-homes had failed at least one year in the French school system, compared to only 13 percent of the adopted children.

We should recall that the title of the article by A. R. Jensen that rekindled interest in the heritability and fixity of IQ was "How Much Can We Boost IQ and Scholastic Achievement?" The answer, from cross-racial and cross-class adoption studies, seems unambiguous: As much as social organization will allow. It is not biology that stands in our way.

Notes

1. B. Tizard, "IQ and Race," *Nature* 247(1974): 316.
2. S. Scarr-Salapatek and R. A. Weinberg, "IQ Test Performance of Black Children Adopted by White Families," *American Psychologist* 31 (1976): 726–39.
3. J. Loehlin, G. Lindzey, and J. Spuhler, *Race Differences in Intelligence* (San Francisco: Freeman, 1975).
4. Schiff et al., "How Much *Could* We Boost Scholastic Achievement" *Cognition* 12(2), September 1982: 165–96.

31

The Crisis of "Race" and Raciology

Paul Gilroy*

It is indeed the case that human social and political organization is a reflection of our biological being, for, after all, we are material biological objects developing under the influence of the interaction of our genes with the external world. It is certainly not the case that our biology is irrelevant to social organization. The question is, what part of our biology is relevant?

Richard Lewontin

A genuine revolution of values means in the final analysis that our loyalties must become ecumenical rather than sectional. Every nation must now develop an overriding loyalty to mankind as a whole in order to preserve the best in their individual societies.

Martin Luther King, Jr.

It is impossible to deny that we are living through a profound transformation in the way the idea of "race" is understood and acted upon. Underlying it there is another, possibly deeper, problem that arises from the changing mechanisms that govern how racial differences are seen, how they appear to us and prompt specific identities. Together, these historic conditions have disrupted the observance of "race" and created a crisis for raciology, the lore that brings the virtual realities of "race" to dismal and destructive life.

Any opportunities for positive change that arise from this crisis are circumscribed by the enduring effects of past catastrophe. Raciology has saturated the discourses in which it circulates. It cannot be readily re-signified or de-signified, and to imagine that its dangerous meanings can be easily re-articulated into benign, democratic forms would be to exaggerate the power of critical and oppositional interests. In contrast, the creative acts involved in destroying raciology and transcending "race" are more than warranted by the goal of authentic democracy to which they point. The political will to liberate humankind from race-thinking must be complemented by precise historical reasons why these attempts are worth making. The first task is to suggest that the demise of

* Pp. 11–41; 49–53 from P. Gilroy, *Against Race: Imagining Political Culture Beyond the Color Line* (Cambridge, MA, Belknap Press of Harvard University Press). © 2000 by Paul Gilroy. *Against Race* was published in the UK under the title *Between Camps: Nations, Culture and the Allure of Race 2e* (London: Routledge, 2004). Reprinted with permission from the author and Harvard University Press.

"race" is not something to be feared. Even this may be a hard argument to win. On the one hand, the beneficiaries of racial hierarchy do not want to give up their privileges. On the other hand, people who have been subordinated by race-thinking and its distinctive social structures (not all of which come tidily color-coded) have for centuries employed the concepts and categories of their rulers, owners, and persecutors to resist the destiny that "race" has allocated to them and to dissent from the lowly value it placed upon their lives. Under the most difficult of conditions and from imperfect materials that they surely would not have selected if they had been able to choose, these oppressed groups have built complex traditions of politics, ethics, identity, and culture. The currency of "race" has marginalized these traditions from official histories of modernity and relegated them to the backwaters of the primitive and the prepolitical. They have involved elaborate, improvised constructions that have the primary function of absorbing and deflecting abuse. But they have gone far beyond merely affording protection and reversed the polarities of insult, brutality, and contempt, which are unexpectedly turned into important sources of solidarity, joy, and collective strength. When ideas of racial particularity are inverted in this defensive manner so that they provide sources of pride rather than shame and humiliation, they become difficult to relinquish. For many racialized populations, "race" and the hard-won, oppositional identities it supports are not to be lightly or prematurely given up.

These groups will need to be persuaded very carefully that there is something worthwhile to be gained from a deliberate renunciation of "race" as the basis for belonging to one another and acting in concert. They will have to be reassured that the dramatic gestures involved in turning against racial observance can be accomplished without violating the precious forms of solidarity and community that have been created by their protracted subordination along racial lines, The idea that action against racial hierarchies can proceed more effectively when it has been purged of any lingering respect for the idea of "race" is one of the most persuasive cards in this political and ethical suit.

Historians, sociologists, and theorists of politics have not always appreciated the significance of these sometimes-hidden, modern countercultures formed by long and brutal experiences of racialized subordination through slavery and colonialism and since. The minor, dissident traditions that have been constituted against the odds amid suffering and dispossession have been overlooked by the ignorant and the indifferent as well as the actively hostile. Some initiates, who should certainly know better, have even rejected and despised these formations as insufficiently respectable, noble, or pure. Nonetheless, vernacular cultures and the stubborn social movements that were built upon their strengths and tactics have contributed important moral and political resources to modern struggles in pursuit of freedom, democracy, and justice.[1] Their powerful influences have left their imprint on an increasingly globalized popular culture. Originally tempered by the ghastly extremities of racial slavery, these dissident cultures remained strong and supple long after the formalities of emancipation, but they are now in decline and their prospects cannot be good. They are already being transformed beyond recognition by the uneven effects of globalization and planetary commerce in blackness.

Where the dangers represented by this historic decline have been recognized, the defense of communal interests has often mobilized the fantasy of a frozen culture, of arrested cultural development. Particularity can be maintained and communal interests protected if they are fixed in their most authentic and glorious postures of resistance. This understandable but inadequate response to the prospect of losing one's identity reduces cultural traditions to the simple process of invariant repetition. It has helped to secure deeply conservative notions that supply real comfort in dismal times but do little justice either to the fortitude and the improvisational skills of the slaves and their embattled descendants or to the complexities of contemporary cultural life.

We need to understand the appeal of the idea of tradition in this context. Where it is understood as little more than a closed list of rigid rules that can be applied consciously without interpretation or attention to particular historical conditions, it is a ready alibi for authoritarianism rather than a sign of cultural viability or ethical confidence. Indeed, the defense of tradition on these grounds can, as we shall see, open a door to ultraconservative forms of political culture and social regulation.

In identifying these problems and moving beyond them, I shall try to show that the comfort zone created in the fading aura of those wonderful cultures of dissidence is already shrinking and that the cultures themselves are not as strong, complex, or effective as they once were. They do still occasionally flicker into spectacular life, urging desperate people to stand up for their rights and giving them a potent political and moral language with which to do it. However, there is no reason to suppose that they will be able to withstand all the destructive effects of globalization and localization, let alone the corrosive power of substantive political disagreements that have arisen over the nature of black particularity and its significance relative to other contending identity-claims: religion, sexuality, generation, gender, and so on.

The dissident traditions inaugurated by the struggle against slavery, a struggle for recognition as human rather than chattel, agent and person rather than object, have already been changed by translocal forces, both political and economic, that bear heavily on the symbolic currency of "race." This situation is another fundamental part of the crisis of raciology. It provides further inducements to recognize that the current disruption of race-thinking presents an important opportunity. There is here a chance to break away from the dangerous and destructive patterns that were established when the rational absurdity of "race" was elevated into an essential concept and endowed with a unique power to both determine history and explain its selective unfolding.

If we are tempted to be too celebratory in assessing the positive possibilities created by these changes in race-thinking and the resulting confusion that has enveloped raciology, we need only remind ourselves that the effects of racial discourses have become more unpredictable as the quality of their claims upon the world have become more desperate. This is a delicate situation, and "race" remains fissile material.

A Crisis of Raciology

Any inventory of the elements that constitute this crisis of raciology must make special mention of the rise of gene-oriented or genomic constructions of "race." Their distance from the older versions of race-thinking that were produced in the eighteenth and nineteenth centuries underlines that the meaning of racial difference is itself being changed as the relationship between human beings and nature is reconstructed by the impact of the DNA revolution and of the technological developments that have energized it.² This chapter is premised upon the idea that we must try to take possession of that profound transformation and somehow set it to work against the tainted logic that produced it. In other words, the argument here unfolds from the basic idea that this crisis of "race" and representation, of politics and ethics, offers a welcome cue to free ourselves from the bonds of all raciology in a novel and ambitious abolitionist project.

The pursuit of liberation from "race" is an especially urgent matter for those peoples who, like modern blacks in the period after transatlantic slavery, were assigned an inferior position in the enduring hierarchies that raciology creates. However, this opportunity is not theirs alone. There are very good reasons why it should be enthusiastically embraced by others whose antipathy to race-thinking can be defined, not so much by the way it has subordinated them, but because in endowing them with the alchemical magic of racial mastery, it has distorted and delimited their experiences and consciousness in other ways. They may not have been animalized, reified, or exterminated, but they too have suffered something by being deprived of their individuality, their humanity, and thus alienated from species life. Black and white are bonded together by the mechanisms of "race" that estrange them from each other and amputate their common humanity. Frantz Fanon, the Martiniqean psychiatrist and anticolonial activist whose work frames these concerns, observed this dismal cycle through its effects on the lives of men: "the Negro enslaved by his inferiority, the white man enslaved by his superiority alike behave in accordance with a neurotic orientation."³ Dr. Martin Luther King, Jr., another influential pathologist of "race," whose work counterpoints Fanon's own, was fond of pointing out that race-thinking has the capacity to make its beneficiaries inhuman even as it deprives its victims of their humanity.⁴

Here, drawing implicitly upon the combined legacies of King and Fanon, his sometime interlocutor, a rather different, postracial and postanthropological version of what it means to be human might begin to take shape. If this radically nonracial humanism is to be placed upon more stable foundations than those provided by King's open-minded and consistent Christianity or Fanon's phenomenological, existential, and psychoanalytic interests, it must be distinguished from earlier, less satisfactory attempts to refigure humankind. Its attempt at a comprehensive break from those traditions of reflection is signaled fundamentally by a refusal to be articulated exclusively in the male gender. From this angle, the precious, patient processes that culminate in community and democracy do not exist only in the fraternal patterns that have proved so durable and so attractive to so many. The ideal of fraternity need no longer compromise or embarrass the noble dreams of liberty and equality. This willfully ungendered humanism is not reducible to demands for equality between men and women or even for reciprocity between the sexes. Those revolutionary ideas are already alive and at large in the world. They can be complemented by a change of the conceptual scale on which essential human attributes are being calculated.

This change, in turn, entails the abolition of what is conventionally thought of as sexual division. Minor differences become essentially irrelevant. The forms of narcissism they support need not retain their grip upon the world. If that aim seems to be an unduly utopian or radical aspiration, we would do well to recall the important practical example of these principles currently being pursued by the military organizations of the overdeveloped world. Forced by recruitment shortfalls and other demographic changes to accept the possibility that women are just as physically capable of front-line combat duties as their male counterparts, these organizations have undertaken a partial but nonetheless significant de-masculinization of soldiery. While Demi Moore was being incarnated as GI Jane, Western military organizations were conducting a number of technical studies of exactly how the female body can be modified by exercise and training so that its physical potential for military activities can be optimized. Scientists at Britain's Ministry of Defence Research Agency have, for example, outlined a form of basic training, cryptically known as "personnel selection standards," for their new female recruits. The British Army has emphasized that it cannot eliminate intrinsic physical differences such as hip size and varying proportions of fat and muscle; however, "initial results from the new training regime have, on average, added 2 lbs more muscle while removing 6 lbs of fat." One British officer said: "Brute strength is not a great part of military life in the 1990s."[5] Comparable strategies are also being revealed on the other side of scarcity in the underdeveloped parts of the planet. The active and enthusiastic contribution of women to the genocide of Tutsi and the killing of Hutu political opponents that took place in Rwanda during 1994 provides one warning against any desire to celebrate these changes as inherently progressive.[6]

Perhaps, pending the eventual sublation of governmental militarism, the ideal of military genderlessness can enhance our understanding of moral and civic agency. As a sign of transition, it hints at a universality that can exist in less belligerent forms. There need be no concessions to the flight from embodiment that has been associated with the consolidation of abstract, modern individuality.[7] Here, the constraints of bodily existence (being in the world) are admitted and even welcomed, though there is a strong inducement to see and value them differently as sources of identification and empathy. The recurrence of pain, disease, humiliation and loss of dignity, grief, and care for those one loves can all contribute to an abstract sense of a human similarity powerful enough to make solidarities based on cultural particularity appear suddenly trivial.[8]

Some other features of this pragmatic, planetary humanism can be tentatively enumerated. Though most political philosophers who consider these questions have ignored this possibility or failed to recognize its truly subversive force, I would suggest that a certain distinctiveness might also be seen to emerge though the deliberate and self-conscious renunciation of "race" as a means to categorize and divide humankind. This radically nonracial humanism exhibits a primary concern with the forms of human dignity that race-thinking strips away. Its counteranthropological and sometimes misanthropic orientation is most powerfully articulated where it has been accompanied by a belated return to consideration of the chronic tragedy, vulnerability, and frailty that have defined our species in the melancholic art of diverse poetic figures from Leopardi and Nietzsche to Esther Phillips and Donny Hathaway. Its signature is provided by a grim determination to make that predicament of fundamentally fragile, corporeal existence into the key to a version of humanism that contradicts the triumphal tones of the anthropological discourses that were enthusiastically supportive of race-thinking in earlier, imperial times.

   This is not the humanism of existentialists and phenomenologists, short-sighted Protestants or complacent scientists. Indeed, mindful of raciological associations between past humanisms and the idea of progress, this humanism is as unfriendly toward the idea of "race" as it is ambivalent about claims to identify progress that do not take the de-civilizing effects of continuing racial division into account. I want to show that important insights can be acquired by systematically returning to the history of struggles over the limits of humanity in which the idea of "race" has been especially prominent. This humanism is conceived explicitly as a response to the sufferings that raciology has wrought. The most valuable resources for its elaboration derive from a principled, cross-cultural approach to the history and literature of extreme situations in which the boundaries of what it means to be human were being negotiated and tested minute by minute, day by day. These studies of the inhumanity inspired by and associated with the idea of "race" are not, of course, confined to slavery or the brutal forms of segregation that followed it. They have arisen from numerous episodes in colonial history and from the genocidal activities that have proved to be raciology's finest, triumphant hours. They are especially worthwhile, not because the suffering of the victims of extreme evil offers easy lessons for the redemption of the more fortunate; indeed, we cannot know what acute ethical insights the victims of race-thinking may have taken with them in death. The victims of these terrors are necessarily mute, and if there are any survivors, they will be beset by guilt, shame, and unbearably painful and unreliable memories. They will not be the best guides to the moral and political lessons involved in histories of pointless suffering, but they may still be able to yield important insight into the moral dilemmas of the present. We should therefore pay attention to the doubts that the most eloquent and perceptive survivors of systematic inhumanity have thrown on the value of their own testimony. We must be alert to its unspoken conventions and genres, for there are tacit rules governing the expectations of the reading publics that have formed around these painful, moving words and texts.

   However, in an unprecedented situation in which ambivalence reigns and general laws of ethical conduct are difficult to frame, this legacy of bearing witness should not be spurned as a distraction from the laborious tasks of documentation and historical reconstruction. It is far better to make this dubious testimony our compass and to seek our bearings in the words of witnesses than to try vainly to orient ourselves with the unreliable charts supplied by covertly race-coded liberal or even socialist humanisms, which, if they did not steer us into this lost position, have offered very few ideas about how we might extricate ourselves from it and find ourselves again without the benefit of racial categories or racial lore.

Genes and Bodies in Consumer Culture

The contemporary focus on the largely hidden potency of genes promotes a fundamental change of scale in the perception and comprehension of the human body. This change is not an automatic product of only the most recent scientific developments and needs to be connected to an understanding of techno-science, particularly biotechnology, over a longer period of time. Its impact upon the status of old, that is, essentially eighteenth-century, racial typologies has been inexcusably neglected by most writers on "race."

The tragic story of Henrietta Lacks, an African-American mother of five from Baltimore who died of cervical cancer at the age of thirty-one in October 1951, can provide important orientation as we move away from the biopolitics of "race" and toward its nano-politics. Cells taken without consent from Lacks's body by Dr. George Gey, a cell biologist at the Johns Hopkins Hospital, were grown in tissue culture and have been used since then in countless scientific experiments all over the world. The cell-line extracted from her cancer, now known as HeLa, was the first human tumor cell-line to be cultivated. It had a number of unusual properties. The unprecedentedly virulent cells grew rapidly and proliferated, invading adjacent cultures and combining unexpectedly with other organisms in the labs where they were in use.[9] They were soon being marketed as a "research organism" and have proved to be an indispensable tool in the burgeoning biotech industry.

The Lacks case raises important issues about when material of this type extracted from a body can be considered human tissue and the point at which it is to be identified alternatively as a form of property that belongs, not to the person in whose body it began, but to the commercial interests involved in selling it for private profit. The story of HeLa cells is also instructive for the confusion that was created when enzymes that suggested Mrs. Lacks's "blackness" revealed themselves, confounding and perplexing researchers who had assumed her "whiteness" or had, more importantly, failed to think raciologically about her legacy or their own research. This episode can be used to mark the point at which an important threshold in thinking about "race" was crossed. The message conveyed by commerce in HeLa cells exceeds even the old familiar tale in which black patients have sometimes been abused and manipulated by the white doctors employed to treat them. It would appear that race-defying cells, the body's smallest vital component, have become absolutely central to controversies over the limit and character of species life.

At the risk of sounding too anthropocentric, I would suggest that the cultivation of cells outside the body for commercial and other purposes is an epoch-making shift that requires a comprehensive rethinking of the ways we understand and analyze our vulnerable humanity. Like the speculative manipulation of genetic material between various species that has followed it with unpredictable and possibly dangerous results for all human beings, this change suggests a wholly new set of boundaries within which humanity will take shape. The "engineering" of transgenic animals and plants, some of which have supposedly benefited from the insertion of human genes into their DNA, is a related phenomenon that has also been the subject of intense debate about its potentially catastrophic consequences. The international and therefore necessarily "transracial" trade in internal organs and other body parts for transplant, sometimes obtained by dubious means, is another pertinent development. The challenges that have arisen from the manipulation and commerce in all aspects of human fertility, including the vividly contentious issue of whether mothers of one "race" might perversely choose to bear babies of another, represent yet another key change, while a number of recent attempts to patent or hold copyright in organisms, cells, and other elements of life itself would be the final sign that we have to adjust our conceptions of life and our mutable human nature.[10]

All these changes impact upon how "race" is understood. Awareness of the indissoluble unity of all life at the level of genetic materials leads to a stronger sense of the particularity of our species as a whole, as well as to new anxieties that its character is being fundamentally and irrevocably altered. With these symptomatic developments in mind, it is difficult to resist the conclusion that this biotechnological revolution demands a change in our understanding of "race," species, embodiment, and human specificity. In other words, it asks that we reconceptualize our relationship to ourselves, our species, our nature, and the idea of life. We need to ask, for example, whether there should be any place in this new paradigm of life for the idea of specifically *racial* differences.

The well-known and surprisingly popular portrait of human beings as an essentially irrelevant transitory medium for the dynamic agency of their supposedly selfish genes is not the only morally and politically objectionable consequence of emergent, genomic orthodoxy. It, too, has fundamental implications for the coherence of the idea of "race" and its relationship to the increasingly complex patterns of natural variation that will no doubt be revealed in a geographically distributed species and the endlessly varying but fundamentally similar individuals who compose it. The specification of significant differences can only be calculated within specific scales, what the physicist Ilya Prigogine calls "domains of validity."[11] Sadly, however much common sense and popular comprehension of "race" lag behind these developments, they do not mean that ideas of "race" based upon immediate appearance have become instantly redundant, acquiring a residual status that contrasts sharply with the conspicuous power they enjoyed previously in the ages of colonial empires, mass migration, and mass extermination.

As actively de-politicized consumer culture has taken hold, the world of racialized appearances has become invested with another magic. This comes courtesy of developments like the proliferation of ever-cheaper cosmetic surgery and the routine computer enhancement and modification of visual images. These changes, which build upon a long history of technical procedures for producing and accentuating racial differences on film,[12] undermine more than the integrity of raciological representation. They interact with other processes that have added a conspicuous premium to today's planetary traffic in the imagery of blackness. Layer upon layer of easily commodified exotica have culminated in a racialized glamour and contributed an extra cachet to some degree of nonspecific, somatic difference. The perfect faces on billboards and screens and in magazines are no longer exclusively white, but as they lose that uniformity we are being pressed to consider and appreciate exactly what they have become, where they fit in the old hierarchy that is being erased, and what illicit combination of those familiar racial types combined to produce that particular look, that exotic style, or that transgressive stance. The stimulating pattern of this hyper-visibility supplies the signature of a corporate multiculturalism in which some degree of visible difference from an implicit white norm may be highly prized as a sign of timeliness, vitality, inclusivity, and global reach.

A whole new crop of black models, stylists, photographers, and now, thanks to the good offices of Spike Lee, a black advertising agency, have contributed to this change of climate in the meaning of racialized signs, symbols, and bodies. The stardom of prominent iconic figures like Tyson Beckford, Tyra Banks, and, of course, Lee himself supplements the superhuman personalities and conspicuous physical attributes of the latest heroic wave of black athletes who built connections to the emerging planetary market in leisure, fitness, and sports products. In that domain, blackness has proved to be a substantial asset. What Fanon, pondering the iconic stardom of Joe Louis and Jesse Owens, called "the cycle of the biological"[13] was initiated with the mythic figure of The Negro: either unthinkingly lithe and athletic or constitutionally disposed to be lethargic and lazy. That modern cycle may also be thought of as terminating in the space of black metaphysicality. Zygmunt Bauman has argued that the primal scene of postmodern social life in the overdeveloped world is being staged in a distinctive private relation to one's own corporeality, through a disciplinary custodianship that can be specified as the idea of the body "as task."[14] This has unexpected consequences where the ideal of physical prowess, to which blacks were given a special title in exchange for their disassociation from the mind, assumes an enhanced significance.

It is best to be absolutely clear that the ubiquity and prominence currently accorded to exceptionally beautiful and glamorous but nonetheless racialized bodies do nothing to change the everyday forms of racial hierarchy. The historic associations of blackness with infrahumanity, brutality, crime, idleness, excessive threatening fertility, and so on remain undisturbed. But the appearance of a rich visual culture that allows blackness to be beautiful also feeds a fundamental lack of confidence in the power of the body to hold the boundaries of racial difference in place. It creates anxiety about the older racial hierarchies that made that revolutionary idea of black beauty oxymoronic, just as it requires us to forget the political movement that made its acknowledgment imperative. It is as though these images of nonwhite beauty, grace, and style somehow make the matter of "race" secondary, particularly when they are lit, filtered, textured, and toned in ways that challenge the increasingly baffled observer's sense of where racial boundaries might fall. In this anxious setting, new hatreds are created not by the ruthless enforcement of stable racial categories but from a disturbing inability to maintain them. Conforming enthusiastically to wider social patterns, the surface of black bodies must now be tattooed, pierced, and branded if they are to disclose the deepest, most compelling truths of the privatized ontology within. The words "Thug Life" famously inked onto the eloquent torso of the late Tupac Shakur, like the hexagrams, Oriental characters, cartoon pictures, and other devices sported by a host of stars – Treach, Foxy Brown, and Dennis Rodman, to name only three – conform to this trend and have the additional significance of showing the world how far from the color black these muscled black bodies really are.

It should be clear that the shape-shifting and phenotype-modifying antics that abound in the world of black popular culture did not culminate in the strange case of Michael Jackson.[15] His physical transformation of himself ushered in this new phase of creative possibilities. Playful mut(il)ation did not contradict either his affirmation of an African-American heritage or his well-publicized distaste for Africa itself. Similar patterns enjoy a far more insidious afterlife in the antics of the legions of models, athletes, and performers whose beauty and strength have contributed to the postmodern translation of blackness from a badge of insult into an increasingly powerful but still very limited signifier of prestige. The ongoing activities of this group in the worlds of television, music, sports, fashion, entertainment, and, above all, advertising supply further proof that as far as "race" is concerned, what you see is not necessarily what you get.

All these developments stem from and contribute to the same uncertainties over "race." They help to call the self-evident, obvious authority of familiar racialized appearances, of common-sense racial typologies, into question. Bodies may still be the most significant determinants in fixing the social optics of "race,"[16] but black bodies are now being seen – figured and imaged – differently. Thanks to Adobe Photoshop® and similar image-processing technologies, skin tones can be more readily manipulated than the indelibly marked musculatures that sell the sweated and branded products of Tommy Hilfiger, Calvin Klein, Timberland, and Guess in the glossy pages of over-ground publications like *Vibe* and *The Source* that trade widely in aspects of black culture but are not primarily addressed to any black reading public. This crisis has ensured that racialized bodies represented as objects – objects among other objects – are never going to be enough to guarantee that racial differences remain what they were when everyone on both sides of the line between white and colored knew what "race" was supposed to be.

These timely occurrences should be placed in the context of the leveling forces of placeless development and commercial planetarization. The meaning and status of racial categories are becoming even more uncertain now that substantial linguistic and cultural differences are being flattened out by the pressures of a global market. Where cultural continuity or overlap is recognized between different racialized groups, the smallest cultural nuances provide a major means of differentiation. Once the course of the main-stream is diverted through marginal, underexploited cultural territory, an emphasis on culture can readily displace previous attention to the receding certainties of "race." In these conditions, the relationship between cultural differences and racial particularity gets complex and fraught. Culture, no less than Mrs. Lacks's valuable cells, becomes akin to a form of property attached to the history and traditions of a particular group and regulated by anyone who dares to speak in its name. This can produce some odd conflicts over the assignment of fragments that resist all disciplinary powers. One small illustration springs to mind from the workings of the British political system. Much to the disgust of the Labour Party's black members of Parliament, Bernie Grant and Paul Boateng, who wanted to place it in other political traditions, some of Bob Marley's music was employed as the curtain raiser for a fringe meeting of the European Movement (UK) at the 1996 Conservative Party conference. The person responsible for this grave affront to Marley's inherent socialism was Sir Teddy Taylor, an eccentric, Euro-skeptic but reggae-loving right-winger who explained to the media that he "thought the song ["Three Little Birds"] summed up the Tory policy on Europe."[17]

The emphasis on culture as a form of property to be owned rather than lived char-acterizes the anxieties of the moment. It compounds rather than resolves the problems arising from associating "race" with embodied or somatic variation. Indeed, we must be alert to circumstances in which the body is reinvested with the power to arbitrate in the assignment of cultures to peoples. The bodies of a culture's practitioners can be called upon to supply the proof of where that culture fits in the inevitable hierarchy of value. The body may also provide the preeminent basis on which that culture is to be ethnically assigned. The body circulates uneasily through contemporary discussions of how one knows the group to which one belongs and of what it takes to be recognized as belonging to such a collectivity. Differences within particular groups proliferate along the obvious axes of division: gender, age, sexuality, region, class, wealth, and health. They challenge the unanimity of racialized collectivities. Exactly what, in cultural terms, it takes to belong, and, more importantly, what it takes to be recognized as belonging, begin to look very uncertain. However dissimilar individual bodies are, the compelling idea of common, racially indicative bodily characteristics offers a welcome short-cut into the favored forms of solidarity and connection, even if they are effectively denied by divergent patterns in life chances and everyday experience.

Even more pernicious symptoms of the crisis of raciology are all around us. They are more pronounced in Europe now that the racial sciences are no longer muted by the memories of their active complicity in the genocide of European Jews. The special moral and political climate that arose in the aftermath of National Socialism and the deaths of millions was a transitory phenomenon. It has receded with the living memory of those frightful events. The Nazi period constitutes the most profound moral and temporal rupture in the history of the twentieth century and the pretensions of its modern civilization. Remembering it has been integral to the politics of "race" for more than fifty years, but a further cultural and ethical transition represented by war-crimes trials, financial reparations, and a host of national apologies is irreversibly under way. It aims to place this raciological catastrophe securely in an irrecoverable past, what Jean Améry called "the cold storage of history," designed more to be cited or passed en route to other happier destinations rather than deliberately summoned up, inhabited, or mourned in an open-ended manner. Official restitution promotes a sense of closure and may be welcomed as a sign that justice has been belatedly done, but it may also undercut the active capacity to remember and set the prophylactic powers of memory to work against future evils. The effects of trauma may be modified if not moderated by the passage of time. They are also vulnerable to the provision of various forms of compensation: substantive and vacuous, formal and informal, material and symbolic.

This is not a straightforward conflict between a culturally sanctioned public obligation to remember and a private desire to forget the unforgettable. The manner, style, and mood of collective remembrance are absolutely critical issues, and the memory of racial slavery in the New World is not the only history of suffering to have been belittled by the power of corrosive or trivializing commemoration. One small example suffices here. The slaves in Steven Spielberg's courtroom drama *Amistad* arrive at their Cuban auction block fresh from the horrors of the Middle Passage. They are buffed: apparently fit and gleaming with robust good health. They enjoy the worked-out and pumped-up musculature that can only be acquired through the happy rigors of a postmodern gym routine. Against the grain of white supremacy's indifference and denial, the Middle Passage has been deliberately and provocatively recovered, but it is rendered in an impossible and deeply contentious manner that offers only the consolation of tears in place of more challenging and imaginative connections. It may be that those coveted abdominal muscles are now deemed to be an essential pre-condition for identifying with the superhuman figures of heroes like Spielberg's Joseph Cinqué.[18]

There has never been spontaneous consensus over how to commemorate and memorialize histories of suffering. Significant discrepancies have been apparent, for example, between the ways that African Americans and Ghanaians have approached the conservation of fortified sites of slave-trading activity that have recently become places of pilgrimage and cultural tourism for some of the more affluent daughters and sons of the Atlantic diaspora.[19] In the very same moment that these sharp divisions have appeared inside what we were once urged to see as a single "racial" group, a torrent of images of casual death and conflict have been transmitted instantaneously from all over the African continent. For some, these dismal reports have ushered in nostalgia for the orderly world of colonial empires and threatened to make savagery something that occurs exclusively beyond the fortified borders of the new Europe. Through genocide in Rwanda and slaughter in Congo and Burundi, civil strife in Liberia, Sierra Leone, and Nigeria, corruption and violence in Kenya, Uganda, Sudan, and Mozambique, government by terror has been associated once again with infrahuman blackness reconstituted in the "half-devil, half-child" patterns favored by older colonial mentalities.[20] Attempts to emphasize that many of the architects of mass killing in Rwanda and Bosnia were educated to the highest standards of the Western humanities have not achieved the same prominence.[21] Placing some of them on trial for war crimes or for the genocidal activities involved in their crimes against humanity has raised more difficult questions about the specificity and uniqueness of earlier mass killing and the central place of the "race-thinking" that has recurrently been featured as a means to justify more recent episodes.[22]

Interestingly, the important work of South Africa's Truth Commission has mobilized a version of the history of Apartheid that accentuates its political affinities as well as its concrete historical connections to the criminal governance of the Nazi period.[23] With these connections underlined, Apartheid's elaborate theories of cultural and tribal difference can be swiftly reduced to the bare bones of raciology that originally warranted them and dispatched Broederbond commissioners back to Europe during the 1930s in pursuit of an appropriate ethnic content for the ideal white culture that was being actively invented.[24]

An even blend of those deceptively bland terms "ethnicity" and "culture" has emerged as the main element in the discourse of differentiation that is struggling to supersede crude appeals to "race" by asserting the power of tribal affiliations. These timely notions circulate in more specialized language, but any sense that they bring greater precision into the task of social division is misleading. The culturalist approach still runs the risk of naturalizing and normalizing hatred and brutality by presenting them as inevitable consequences of illegitimate attempts to mix and amalgamate primordially incompatible groups that wiser, worldlier, more authentically colonial government would have kept apart or left to meet only in the marketplace. The unfolding of recent postcolonial history has sent out a less nostalgic and more challenging message: if the status of "race" can be transformed even in South Africa, the one place on earth where its salience for politics and government could not be denied, the one location where state-sponsored racial identities were openly and positively conducted into the core of a modern civic culture and social relations, then surely it could be changed anywhere. If it is as mutable as that, what then does racial identity comprise?

The widespread appearance of forms of ultranationalist race-thinking that are not easily classified as either biologistic or cultural but which seem to bear the significant imprint of past fascism is another dimension to the crisis of raciology. In Britain, today's patriotic neo-fascists are still undone by the memory of the 1939–45 war, torn between their contradictory appeals to the figures of Churchill on one side and Hitler on the other. The French Front Nationale has included a full complement of Holocaust deniers and apologists for colonial brutality, but it also managed to stand black and Jewish candidates in the elections of May 1997. The most prominent of these, Hugette Fatna, the organization's secretary for France's overseas territories, proudly declaimed, "I'm black and proud of it . . . I'm a free woman, and I accept my difference,"[25] as though democratic denunciations of her then leader, Jean-Marie Le Pen, as a racist, required her to deny it. In other places, the loquacious veterans of Apartheid's death squads have protested at length that, speaking personally, they are not themselves inclined to antiblack racism. The Italian-born Belgian broadcaster Georges Ruggiu faces a trial for crimes against humanity as a result of being arrested and charged with complicity in the 1994 genocide of Tutsis. His inflammatory programs on Radio Mille Collines famously compared the Hutu assault to the French Revolution. Thus, in their genocidal confrontation with the African proxies of "Anglo-Saxon" geo-political ambition, the francophone killers seemed to have imagined themselves as an extension of the French nation to which they were bound. Gérard Prunier has described this as "the Fashoda syndrome."[26]

The advocates of these unsettling varieties of racialized politics have been forced to become fluent in the technical, anthropologic language of ethnicity and culture. Their opinions are also likely to be leavened with mechanistic determinism and neurotic hyper-patriotism. Nonetheless, these obvious ties to past raciologies should not be allowed to obscure the fact that the language produced by this crisis of race-thinking differs from its predecessors. When facing these new phenomena, what we used to be able to call an antiracist opposition must involve more than merely establishing the secret lineage that associates these contemporary groups with their radically evil, authentically fascist antecedents. What Primo Levi, with characteristic precision, referred to as "the silent Nazi diaspora" continues to go about its strategic work, but soon, mobilizing the fragmentary memories of Hitlerism will not be enough to embarrass its activists, never mind defeat them. Nazism and other related versions of populist ultranationalism have found new adherents and, more worryingly, new bands of imitators in all sorts of unlikely locations. The glamour of that particular political style and its utopian charge will be explored later on. They, too, have increased as emotional, psychological, and historical distance from the events of the Third Reich has grown.

All these factors contribute to a situation in which there are diminishing moral or political inhibitions against once more invoking "race" as a primary means of sorting people into hierarchies and erecting unbridgeable chasms around their discrete collective identities. Why, then, describe this situation as a crisis of raciology rather than its crowning glory? It is a crisis because the idea of "race" has lost much of its common-sense credibility, because the elaborate cultural and ideological work that goes into producing and reproducing it is more visible than ever before, because it has been stripped of its moral and intellectual integrity, and because there is a chance to prevent its rehabilitation. Prompted by the impact of genomics, "race," as it has been defined in the past, has also become vulnerable to the claims of a much more elaborate, less deterministic biology. It is therefore all the more disappointing that much influential recent work in this area loses its nerve in the final furlong and opts to remain ambiguous about whether the idea of "race" can survive a critical revision of the relationship between human beings and their constantly shifting social nature.[27]

Whether it is articulated in the more specialized tongues of biological science and pseudo-science or in a vernacular idiom of culture and common sense, the term "race" conjures up a peculiarly resistant variety of natural difference. It stands outside of, and in opposition to, most attempts to render it secondary to the overwhelming sameness that overdetermines social relationships between people and continually betrays the tragic predicaments of their common species life. The undervalued power of this crushingly obvious, almost banal human sameness, so close and basically invariant that it regularly passes unremarked upon, also confirms that the crisis of raciological reasoning presents an important opportunity where it points toward the possibility of leaving "race" behind, of setting aside its disabling use as we move out of the time in which it could have been expected to make sense.

There is a danger that this argument will be read as nothing more than a rather old-fashioned plea for disabusing ourselves of the destructive delusions of racism. Injunctions of that kind have been a recurrent feature of some liberal, religious, socialist, and fascist pronouncements on these matters since the term "race" was first coined. While I value that political pedigree, I want to try to be clear about exactly where this line of thought departs from its noble precursors in those traditions that have contributed so extensively to the ideas and the practice of antiracism. All the earlier arguments conform to the same basic architecture. They posit the particular, singular, and specific against the general, universal, and transcendent that they value more highly. In contrast, the approach I favor attempts to break up these unhappy couples. It has less to say about the unanswerable force of claims to singularity and particularity that have fueled ethnic absolutism. Instead, it directs attention toward the other side of these simultaneous equations. We should, it suggests, become concerned once again with the notion of the human into which reluctant specificity has been repeatedly invited to dissolve itself. My position recognizes that these invitations would be more plausible and attractive if we could only confront rather than evade the comprehensive manner in which previous incarnations of exclusionary humanity were tailored to racializing codes and qualified by the operation of colonial and imperial power. In other words, the alternative version of humanism that is cautiously being proposed here simply cannot be reached via any retreat into the lofty habits and unamended assumptions of liberal thinking, particularly about juridical rights and sovereign entitlements. This is because these very resources have been tainted by a history in which they were not able to withstand the biopolitical power of the race-thinking that compromised their boldest and best ambitions. Their resulting failures, silences, lapses, and evasions must become central. They can be reinterpreted as symptoms of a struggle over the boundaries of humanity and then contribute to a counterhistory that leads up to the rough-hewn doorway through which any alternative conception of the human must pass. This can only be attained after a wholesale reckoning with the idea of "race" and with the history of raciology's destructive claims upon the very best of modernity's hopes and resources. A restoration of political culture is the evasive goal of these operations.

Another curious and perplexing effect of the crisis of raciology is a situation in which some widely divergent political interests have been able to collaborate in retaining the concept and reinvesting it with explanatory power. Strange alliances and opportunistic connections have been constructed in the name of ethnic purity and the related demand that unbridgeable cultural differences be identified and respected. This desire to cling on to "race" and go on stubbornly and unimaginatively seeing the world on the distinctive scales that it has specified makes for odd political associations as well as for less formal connections between raciological thinkers of various hues. In doing battle against all of them and their common desire to retain and reinflate the concept so that it becomes, once again, a central political and historical reference point, we must be very clear about the dimensions of this moment and the significant discrepancies that have arisen between different local settings. We should recognize that "race" has been given a variety of accents. Problems of compatibility and translation have been multiplied by the globalization of culture in which local codes may have to fight against the encroachments of corporate multiculturalism if they are to retain their historic authority and explanatory power. For example, America's distinctive patterns of color consciousness may not be anything other than a fetter on the development of the planetary market in health, fitness, leisure, and sports products mentioned above. Certain common features, like the odd prestige attached to the metaphysical value of whiteness, do recur and continue to travel well, but they too will be vulnerable to the long-term effects of this crisis. Some distinctive local patterns undoubtedly persist, but their anachronistic longevity compounds the problem. Where communication becomes instantaneous, the crisis of racial meaning is further enhanced by the way attachments to the idea of "race" develop unevenly and remain primarily associated with the context of overdevelopment.

We cannot remind ourselves too often that the concept of "race" as it is used in common-sense, everyday language to signify connectedness and common characteristics in relation to type and descent is a relatively recent and absolutely modern invention. Though it would be foolish to suggest that evil, brutality, and terror commence with the arrival of scientific racism toward the end of the eighteenth century, it would also be wrong to overlook the significance of that moment as a break point in the development of modern thinking about humanity and its nature. Even prescientific versions of the logic of "race" multiplied the opportunities for their adherents to do evil freely and justify it to themselves and to others. That problem was compounded once confused and unsystematic race-thinking aspired to become something more coherent, rational, and authoritative. This threshold is important because it identifies the junction point of "race" with both rationality and nationality. It is the beginning of a period in which deference toward science, scientists, and scientific discourses around "race" began to create new possibilities and orchestrate new varieties of knowledge and power centered on the body, what Foucault identifies as "political anatomy."

The story of how this change was influenced by imperatives of colonial trade and government and shaped by growing imperial consciousness, how it was endorsed and then challenged by the developing science of anthropology, discredited by the catastrophic consequences of racial science, silenced by the aftereffects of Nazi genocide only to gain another commanding voice in the wake of Watson and Crick, is a familiar one. But the most recent phases in this process – which we have already seen in not simply and straighforwardly reducible to the resurgence of biological explantions – have not been understood adequately.

Beyond the New Racism

Some years ago, a loose group of scholars in which the English philosopher Martin Barker was especially influential began, in recognition of changed patterns in the way the discourse of racial difference was employed in politics, to speak about the emergence of what they called a New Racism. This racism was defined by its strong culturalist and nationalist inclinations. Whereas in the past raciology had been arrogant in its imperial certainty that biology was both destiny and hierarchy, this persuasive new variant was openly uncomfortable with the idea that "race" could be biologically based. Consciousness of "race" was seen instead as closely linked to the idea of nationality. Authentic, historic nations had discrete cultural fillings. Their precious homogeneity endowed them with great strength and prestige. Where large "indigestible" chunks of alien settlement had taken place, all manner of dangers were apparent. Conflict was visible, above all, along cultural lines. Of course, these regrettably transplanted aliens were not identified as inferior, less worthy, or less admirable than their "hosts." They may not have been infrahuman, but they were certainly out of place. The social, economic, and political problems that had followed their mistaken importation could only be solved by restoring the symmetry and stability that flowed from putting them back where they belonged. Nature, history, and geopolities dictated that people should cleave to their own kind and be most comfortable in the environments that matched their distinctive cultural and therefore national modes of being in the world. Mythic versions of cultural ecology were invented to rationalize the lives of these discrete national and racial identities. The Germans became a people in their forests, whereas the British were a nation whose seafaring activity shaped their essential inner character. In all cases, fragments of self-evident truth nourished the fantasies of blood and belonging,[28] which in turn demanded an elaborate geopolitical cartography of nationality.[29]

The culturalist arguments of the New Racism enjoy a lingering residual appeal. Similar patterns appeared in a number of different settings. They were evident in Britain, where cultural difference rather than biological hierarchy emerged as the core substance of the nation's postcolonial racial problems. They were audible in the United States, where five great raciocultural agglomerations (Asians, blacks, Hispanics, whites, and Native Americans) appeared and took on many of the fateful characteristics associated with eighteenth-century racial groups; and they were evident also in parts of Europe where conflicts between migrant workers and their resentful hosts were rearticulated as the grander cultural and religious opposition between Christian universalism and resurgent Islamic fundamentalism.

The historic role of these culturalist notions in the consolidation and development of Apartheid in South Africa ought to be obvious. The wider shifts from biology to culture, from species to ethnos, from rigid, predictable hierarchy toward the different perils represented by a cultural alterity that was as fascinating as it was contaminating were all to some extent pre-figured in the constitution of the Apartheid system. Whether or not these forms of power and authority were broadly representative of colonial governance in general cannot be settled here.[30] The pernicious fiction of separate but equal identities based in discrete homelands was an important marker of a change in which the idea of contending national and ethnic traditions was employed to legitimate and rationalize the move from natural to cultural hierarchies. This shift was not, of course, an absolute change. Nature and culture may have functioned as neatly exclusive poles in the models of early modern thought, but as the organic overtones of the word "culture" reveal, the boundaries between them have always been porous. The New Racism endorsed the annexation of the idea of natural difference by the claims of mutually exclusive, national cultures that now stood opposed to one another. In the political geometry of nation-states, culture was offset not by nature but by other cultures. What seems new about the New Racism, twenty years after this insight was first employed, is not so much the tell-tale emphasis on culture that was its intellectual hallmark but the way its ideologues refined the old opposites – nature and culture, biology and history – into a new synthesis: a bioculturalism that, as Barker had pointed out, drew its deterministic energy from the intellectual resources supplied by sociobiology.[31]

When this point is made, it is always necessary to emphasize that there are many subtle shadings between the biological and the cultural and that the culturalist versions of racial discourse – though superficially more benign than the cruder force of biological "race" theory – are no less vicious or brutal for those on the receiving end of the cruelties and terrors they promote. With these important qualifications in mind, it is better to say that the starting point of this book is that the era of that New Racism is emphatically over. This should not be interpreted as a suggestion that we are therefore traveling back toward some older, more familiar version of biological determinism. To be sure, a genomic reworking of biology has reemerged to supply the dominant pessimistic motifs in talk about "race," but the mere presence of what is better understood as a post-biological perspective does not confirm my diagnosis. There are several new versions of determinism abroad. They place and use the human body in a number of contrasting ways. The impatient manner in which other, less mechanistic, varieties of social and historical explanation are silenced by genomics betrays the transfiguration of biologic into something unanticipated: a nonwholistic micromechanism in which organisms are to be engineered, tooled, and spliced and human life takes on qualities associated with the dead, menacing, but compliant world of machines.

This change of perspective demonstrates that today's raciology is no longer confined to the cognitive and perceptual habits of political anatomy. It has been drawn by technological and conceptual changes toward ever-smaller scales. Thus what appears to be the *re*birth of biologism is not in fact the resurgence of older colonial and imperial codes that accentuated hierarchy rather than simple difference but part of a bigger contemporary transformation in the ways that people conceptualize the relationship between nature, culture, and society, between their freedom and their human agency. The status of "race" is inevitably transformed by this. Yes, we are once again in a period in which social and cultural differences are being coded according to the rules of a biological discourse, but it cannot be emphasized enough that this latest raciological regime differs from its predecessors. We must not approach it as though it represents a retreat behind the culturalist ambitions of the old, that is, the New, Racism. It is a distinctive phenomenon that needs to be apprehended and countered as such. "Race" can no longer be ossified, and, as may have been anticipated, it is the gene-centeredness of this discourse that defines its deterministic approach to human action in general and the formation of racial groups in particular.[32]

The history of scientific writing about "races" has involved a long and meandering sequence of discourses on physical morphology. Bones, skulls, hair, lips, noses, eyes, feet, genitals, and other somatic markers of "race" have a special place in the discursive regimes that produced the truth of "race" and repeatedly discovered it lodged in and on the body. The historian of science Londa Schiebinger has demonstrated how the study of bodily components and zones first helped to focus the racializing gaze, to invest it with real scientific authority and to bring "race" into being in strongly gendered forms while simultaneously producing an understanding of gender and sex that saturated the interconnected discourses of "race," nation, and species.[33] The textbooks of classical, eighteenth-century raciology were studded with images. Their argumentation proceeded swiftly from illustration to illustration. The enduring power of the best-known visual material – depictions of Caucasian and Nordic heads or of the various skulls to be measured, drawn, and classified – was more than an ironic counterpoint to the inscription of respectable racial science. It raises the interesting possibility that cognition of "race" was never an exclusively linguistic process and involved from its inception a distinctive visual and optical imaginary. The sheer plenitude of racialized images and icons communicates something profound about the forms of difference these discourses summoned into being. Racial differences were discovered and confirmed in fragmentary selections of physical characteristics. Because the combination of phenotypes chosen to identify a "race" so actively generated the chosen racial categories, antiraciological thinking was soon alerted to the way that particular criteria varied within the selected groups as well as between them. My concern here is not with the well-known history of those necessarily doomed attempts to produce coherent racial categories by picking representative combinations of certain phenotypes: lips, jaws, hair texture, eye-color, and so on. It is far more interesting that this race-producing activity required a synthesis of logos with icon, of formal scientific rationality with something else – something visual and aesthetic in both senses of that slippery word. Together they resulted in a specific relationship to, and mode of observing, the body.[34] They fixed upon a certain variety of perception that favored particular representational scales and could only follow on from the isolation, quantification, and homogenization of vision. Foucault is the most famous explorer of the epistemological consequences that accompanied the institutionalization of this anthropological gaze and its "autonomization of sight."[35]

Whether the distinguishing marks, organs, and features were discovered on the external surface of the body or were thought to dwell somewhere inside it where the hidden properties of racially differentiated blood, bone, and sinew were imagined to regulate social and cultural manifestations, the modern idea of race favored a specific representational scale and operated within the strictest of perceptual limits. We can call that distinctive ratio the scale of comparative anatomy. The idea of "race" leaked quite rapidly from the lofty confines where that scale was first codified and calibrated, but it always worked best in conjunction with those ways of looking, enumerating, dissecting, and evaluating. Abstract and metaphysical, "race" defined and consolidated its accidental typologies. In moving toward the empirical and the concrete, it (re-)produced a set of methods, regulated a certain aesthetics,[36] and quietly delimited the field in which color-coded ethics would operate. The most compelling truths of political anatomy were produced "performatively" from the hat that raciological science provided, like so many startled rabbits in front of an eager, noisy crowd. The idea of "race" enjoyed its greatest power to link metaphysics and scientific technology under those conditions. Reinforced by belief in separate and opposing national cultures, it would later inspire the colonial anthropologies that succeeded the earliest versions of scientific raciology. Our situation is demonstrably different. The call of racial being has been weakened by another technological and communicative revolution, by the idea that the body is nothing more than an incidental moment in the transmission of code and information, by its openness to the new imaging technologies, and by the loss of mortality as a horizon against which life is to be lived.

Blackness can now signify vital prestige rather than abjection in a global infotainment telesector where the living residues of slave societies and the parochial traces of American racial conflict must yield to different imperatives deriving from the planetarization of profit and the cultivation of new markets far from the memory of bondage. In 1815 Cuvier, who would eventually dissect her, commissioned melancholy portraits of Saartjie Baartman depicted from several angles in a peculiarly empty landscape by Léon de Wailly. Almost two centuries later, a different encounter with the limits of black humanity has been provided by the dubious pleasures of the animated movie *Space Jam*. Baartman's earth-bound infrahumanity has been replaced by the larger-than-life presence of a godly Michael Jordan, who collaborates in a bright extraterrestrial pas de deux with Bugs Bunny – the reductio ad absurdum of African trickster tale telling. When Jordan takes wing to persuade us that a black man can fly, can we agree that the eighteenth-century perceptual regimes that first gave us "race" have been superseded along with many of their epistemological and metaphysical pretensions? Now that the microscopic has yielded so comprehensively to the molecular, I want to ask whether these outmoded representational and observational conventions have been left behind. This would mean that much of the contemporary discourse animating "races" and producing racialized consciousness is an anachronistic, even a vestigial, phenomenon. Screens rather than lenses now mediate the pursuit of bodily truths. This is a potent sign that "race" should be approached as an afterimage – a lingering effect of looking too casually into the damaging glare emanating from colonial conflicts at home and abroad.

Disregarding for a moment the obvious dangers represented by contemporary eugenic ambitions, which neither employ the word "eugenic" nor coincide with divisions derived from the old racial categories, I want to argue that the perceptual and observational habits that have been associated with the consolidation of today's nanoscience might also facilitate the development of an emphatically postracial humanism. Genomics may send out the signal to reify "race" as code and information, but there is a sense in which it also points unintentionally toward "race's" overcoming. This cannot be a single, bold act of creativity, a triumphant, once-and-for-all negation. It must be more like a gradual withering away arising from growing irrelevancy. At the smaller than microscopic scales that open up the body for scrutiny today, "race" becomes less meaningful, compelling, or salient to the basic tasks of healing and protecting ourselves. We have a chance, then, to recognize the anachronistic condition of the idea of "race" as a basis upon which human beings are distinguished and ranked. We can draw an extra measure of courage from the fact that proponents of the idea of "races" are further than ever from being able to answer the basic question that has confounded them since the dawn of raciology: if "race" is a useful way of classifying people, then how many "races" are there? It is rare nowadays to encounter talk of a "Mongoloid race."

We have already had to appreciate that it may coincide with the political desires of some people inside the imagined community of a racialized group to proceed on the basis of given or automatic unanimity and to approach their own "race" as a single, undifferentiated magnitude bound together not by the superficialities of history or language, religion or conquest, but by some underlying, essential similarity coded in their bodies. Here, of course, science and the everyday world of racial, I would prefer to say *racializing*, talk, part company and mysticism and occultism take over. The political language used to describe and justify these models of belonging has also been partially updated. Notions of the essential unity of particular "races" have similarly moved on with the times, sometimes acquiring a New Age gloss and a matching therapeutic language. We will see that these "essentialist" and "primordialist" outlooks have become all the more vicious by virtue of the wounds they have acquired as the idea of a fundamental, shared identity has been challenged by the appearance of sharp intraracial conflicts.

In the overdeveloped world, de-industrialization and brutal economic differentiation have complicated this situation still further. Everywhere, struggles arising from family, gender, and sexuality have also been dearly visible within the same groups that used to be identified as unitary racial communities. The impact of these factors of division has been intensified by shifts that have occurred in the relationship between "race" and the principle of nationality. The latter has lost some of its appeal and much of its complexity because it has been assimilated too swiftly either to the idea of closed, exclusive racialized cultures or to the biological determinisms that reduce behavior, sociality, and common interests to information inscribed in cells or arrangements of molecules.

As far as black political cultures are concerned, in the period after emancipation, essentialist approaches to building solidarity and synchronized communal mobilization have often relied upon the effects of racial hierarchy to supply the binding agent that could in turn precipitate national consciousness. Routine experiences of oppression, repression, and abuse – however widespread – could not be transferred into the political arena from which blacks were barred. Instead they became the basis for dissident cultures and an alternative public world. Togetherness produced under these conditions was inherently unreliable. Its instability added to the attractiveness of the authoritarian solutions that offered shortcuts to solidarity, especially where everyday consciousness of racial difference fell short of the models of nationhood that had been borrowed wholesale from the Europe-centered history of the dominant group. Where the political chemistry of nation, race, and culture came together to produce these alarming results,

the rebirth of fascist thinking and the reappearance of stern, uniformed political movements was not far away, as we shall see. These developments have not always been
marked by the convenient emblems shamelessly borne by fascisms in the past.

Ecology, Ethics, and Racial Observance

The word "ecology" was coined in 1866 by Ernst Haeckl, the German disciple of
Darwin and Lamarck who would become known for his zoology and his ultranationalist
critique of the dysgenic effects of Western civilization.[37] The elaboration of the term in
the development of racial science before and during Nazi rule should be acknowledged
before it can be engaged here. It can be connected in profound ways to the notions of
Lebensraum (living-space) that figured in but were not created by the racist population
policies and agricultural and scientific planning of the Nazi period.[38] What can only be
called "ecological sensibilities" have an elaborate role in the geo-organic, biopolitical,
and governmental theories of the German geographers Friedrich Ratzel and Karl Haus-
hofer and the early-twentieth-century Swedish geopolitician Rudolf Kjellén.[39] These
writers supplied important conceptual resources to Nazi racial science, helping it to
conceptualize the state as an organism and to specify the necessary connections between
the nation and its dwelling area. We invest differently in this approach as a result of
having to face its historic associations with that raciology, as well as Hitlerism and
sundry other attempts to deduce the ideal form of government from organic analogies.[40]
Today, building self-consciously on attempts by the botanist Sir Alfred George Tansley
to theorize the ecosystem via patterned interaction between organisms and habitats in
the widest possible sense, an even more complex sense of interactivity governing relations between human beings and their environments has been prompted by the more
acute critics of genetic determinism. A refined ecological perspective complements
those critiques with a complex, chaotic, and resolutely nonreductive organicism. This
confounds mechanistic notions of cause and effect and objects loudly to the reduction
of individual human particularity to the "maps" of its DNA sequences. Richard
Lewontin spoke from the critical perspective he describes as a "reverse Lamarckian
position" when he emphasized that

> it takes more than DNA to make a living organism . . . the organism does not compute
> itself from its DNA. A Living organism at any moment in its life is the unique consequence
> of a developmental history that results from interaction of and determination by internal
> and external forces. The external forces, what we usually think of as "environment," are
> themselves partly a consequence of the activities of the organism itself as it produces and
> consumes the conditions of its own existence. Organisms do not find the world in which
> they develop. They make it. Reciprocally, the internal forces are not autonomous, but
> act in response to the external. Part of the internal chemical machinery of a cell is only
> manufactured when external conditions demand it . . . Nor is "internal" identical with
> "genetic."[41]

A similar sensitivity to the complexity of these interactive processes can be useful when
we move from focusing on the immediate environments in which individual organisms

exist and turn instead to the ecological conditions in which relations between agents/ actors are staged. This attention to intersubjectivity can be supplemented by yet another idea. It is drawn from Frantz Fanon's phenomenological study of "epidermalized" embodiment and directly inspired by his bitter Hegelian discovery that the curse of racial domination is the condition, not of being black, but of being black in relation to the white.[42] The ontological complexities of the black predicament that Fanon uncovered in the workings of colonial power are no longer, if they ever were, exclusively confined to those contested locations. Indeed, the political and cultural changes I have described as part of the crisis of "race" have carried into the core of contemporary concerns the same anxieties about the basis upon which races exist. I am suggesting that the only appropriate response to this uncertainty is to demand liberation not from white supremacy alone, however urgently that is required, but from all racializing and raciological thought, from racialized seeing, racialized thinking, and racialized thinking about thinking. There is one other overriding issue associated with these utopian aspirations. However reluctant we may feel to take the step of renouncing "race" as part of an attempt to bring political culture back to life, this course must be considered because it seems to represent the only *ethical* response to the conspicuous wrongs that raciologies continue to solicit and sanction.

Making this ethical point has an additional significance. Students of "race" have not always been sufficiently alive to the ethical dimensions of our own practice, particularly when analyzing the recurrent association between raciology and evil. This overdue reform of our own thinking has become imperative as the memory of the Nazi genocide has ceased to form the constellation under which we work. The deliberate wholesale renunciation of "race" proposed here even views the appearance of an alternative, metaphysical humanism premised on face-to-face relations between different actors – beings of equal worth – as preferable to the problems of inhumanity that raciology creates. If this metaphysics ultimately acquires a religious cast, as in the very different cases presented by the more philosophical writings of Martin Luther King, Jr., on one hand and the work of the philosopher Emmanuel Levinas on the other, it can be rescued from the worst excesses of idealism if only it is recognized as incorporating a provocative attempt to reactivate political sensibilities so that they flow outside the patterns set for them in a world of fortified nation-states and antagonistic ethnic groups. The spaces in which "races" come to life are a field from which political interaction has been banished. It is usually replaced by enthusiasm for the cheapest pseudo-solidarities: forms of connection that are imagined to arise effortlessly from shared phenotypes, cultures, and bio-nationalities. This is a period in which the easy invocation of "race" supplies regular confirmation of the retreat of political activity, defined here not as statecraft but as the exercise of power in a reasoned public culture capable of simultaneously promoting both self and social development. If we choose the testing route I favor, toward the evasive goal of multicultural democracy, the rehabilitation of politics requires bold and expansive gestures. The demand for liberation from "race" becomes still more eloquent in the special context provided by this ethical and political project. It becomes an essential prerequisite if we are to give effective answers to the pathological problems represented by genomic racism, the glamour of sameness, and the eugenic projects currently nurtured by their confluence.

Our foundational question should be this: Where do these changes leave the idea of racial difference, particularly when it cannot be readily correlated with complex genetic variation? Current wisdom seems to suggest that up to six pairs of genes are implicated in the outcome of skin "color." They do not constitute a single switch.

Several years ago Stephen Lawrence, a young black man, was brutally murdered by several young white men at a bus stop in South East London. His tragic death was but one fatality in a sequence of racial attacks that had been perpetrated in the same area. Two others, Rolan Adams and Rohit Duggal, had been killed in comparable circumstances, but it was the Lawrence murder that became a landmark in the politics of "race" in Britain.[43]

The whole story of political action around these and other similar deaths cannot be recapitulated here. For these limited purposes, it is enough to say that a small but dynamic movement grew up around these terrible tragedies and that the actions of the bereaved families and their various groups of supporters took place both inside and outside the formal institutions of government, publicity, and legislation. Tactical actions were intended to project anger, amplify grief, win support, change consciousness, and raise money for legal fees. Political initiatives included a demand for the justice that had been effectively denied when police, courts, and prosecutors refused to act with speed and diligence against the attackers. They also encompassed a demand for sympathy for the plight of the families in their loss and their sadness that has left a substantial mark on the life of our nation. These actions articulated a further sequence of supplementary demands: for recognition of the seriousness of the offense and for acknowledgment of the humanity of the victims and the distinctively unwholesome nature of the brutal offenses that had left them to die on the pavement while their blood drained away. A government-sponsored judicial inquiry into Lawrence's murder and the way the police and the criminal justice system had responded to it raised the disturbing issue that "institutional racism" had conditioned the workings of Britain's government agencies.

Although most aspects of the forbiddingly complex case of Stephen Lawrence cannot be explored here, that does not mean they have been forgotten. There are also solid moral and political reasons why that bitter episode and the events that followed it should not be used as illustrative material on the way toward a more general and inevitably speculative argument about the nature of racial categories and the limits of racialized explanation. Nevertheless, that is what I wish to do.

The British National Party – an openly neo-fascist group – had been very active in the area where Stephen Lawrence was murdered. Their national headquarters was close to the spot where he died, and it was not surprising that the group's presence in the neighborhood and its possible role in legitimating white supremacist terror there became the focus of political activity directed toward the police and the local state. In the names of antifascism and antiracism, activists demanded that the party's well-fortified headquarters be shut down. There were tactical divisions within the campaign as to how this might be achieved. One group favored localized direct action, another preferred to pursue more familiar patterns of protest. Rather than march against the bunker, they chose to make their public demands in the central area of the city where government buildings are located and where the media would attend. Another, local demonstration was held outside the fortified building. This action was animated by the suggestion that if the authorities were unable to move against the group and their headquarters (which had become powerful symbols of the malevolent forces of racism and fascism), antiracist demonstrators would do so. This demonstration, held on Saturday, October 16, 1993, pitted a large number of protesters against a considerable formation of police in riot gear that had been deployed to protect the neo-fascists from the wrath of the antiracists.

The details of the violence that followed are interesting but not essential to the points being explored here. As a result of the physical confrontation between these groups, forty-one demonstrators were injured. Nineteen police officers were treated for their injuries, and four of them spent the night in the hospital. Conflict over the behavior of the marchers erupted after the event. This was something more than the routine cycle of mutual denunciation. In particular, the police claimed that antiracist marchers had singled out black officers and made them special targets for hostility and attack. One of these policemen, deployed by his superiors in defense of the rights of an organization that does not recognize him as belonging to the national community or upholding its laws, was Constable Leslie Turner. Turner said he had been attacked because he was black. He told the newspapers, "It was white demonstrators. There were no black people there that I could see. They singled me out as being a traitor." Whatever his thoughts to the contrary, it is possible that Officer Turner's plight might well have been worse if there had been larger numbers of black protesters around that day. On the scale of human suffering that ends with brutal murder, his experiences are slight, even trivial. His story of victimage may even have been fabricated to win new legitimacy for a dubious police operation. But I want to proceed as if, almost irrespective of what really happened, there was indeed a measure of truth in what he said about that demonstration. What if he *was* attacked as a traitor? What kind of traitor would he have been? What if he *was* assaulted by angry people on the basis that by being a black police officer he had somehow violated the political position that they imagined to match his uniformed black body? What is the currency of what are sometimes called "coconut," "choc-ice," or "oreo cookie" ontologies with their strict and pernicious divisions between "inside" and "outside"? What if the mob was not alive to the irony of his being deployed in defense of the local neo-Nazis? What if they, too, succumbed to the vicious logic of race-thinking?

I am telling this tale here in order to conjure up some of the substantive problems lodged in the way people conceptualize and act upon racial difference. If dedicated antiracist and antifascist activists remain wedded to the most basic mythologies and morphologies of racial difference, what chance do the rest of us have to escape its allure? If the brutal simplicity of racial typology remains alive even in the most deliberate and assertive of antifascist gestures, then perhaps critical, avowedly "anti-essentialist" intellectuals are asking too much when we inquire about the renunciation of "race," or when we aspire to polychromatic and multiethnic utopias in which the color of skin makes no more difference than the color of eyes or hair. It would probably be inappropriate to assume too much common ground between this readership and those anti-Nazi demonstrators. But it is not illegitimate to inquire into where professional and academic interests might resonate in this narrative. Have we, too, become complicit in the reification of racial difference? What has happened to the antiracist assumptions that governed our scholarly activities in previous times? Have they been beaten back by the gains of postbiological determinism, which is claiming the right to account for human behavior back from the social sciences? This argument should not be misunderstood. It seeks to initiate a period of reflection and clarification about our intellectual, ethical, and political projects in the critical scholarship of "races" and raciologies.

I am alive to all the ironies of my position. I understand that taking antipathy toward "race" beyond the unstable equilibrium represented by my liberal use of scare quotes might be viewed as a betrayal of those groups whose oppositional, legal, and even democratic claims have come to rest on identities and solidarities forged at great cost from the categories given to them by their oppressors. But to renounce "race" for analytical purposes is not to judge all appeals to it in the profane world of political cultures as formally equivalent. Less defensively, I think that our perilous predicament, in the midst of a political and technological sea-change that somehow strengthens ethnic absolutism and primordialism, demands a radical and dramatic response. This must step away from the pious ritual in which we always agree that "race" is invented but are then required to defer to its embeddedness in the world and to accept that the demand for justice requires us nevertheless innocently to enter the political arenas it helps to mark out.

Simply to raise these issues may be to violate a tacit scholarly agreement. The link between antiracist practice and intellectual work in this area is certainly not what it was twenty years ago, and yet there are precious few reflections on the changes signaled along the road that leads through municipal antiracism and beyond it into the barren terrain where work on "race" is overshadowed by privatized, corporate multiculturalism and cultures of simulation in which racial alterity has acquired an important commercial value. This just might be a suitable time to break the foundational oscillation between biology and culture, to open the closed circuit that analyses of what we used to call the New Racism have become. It will be more fruitful in future to trace the history of racial metaphysics – or rather of a metaphysical raciology – as an underlying precondition for various versions of determinism: biological, nationalistic, cultural, and now, genomic.

It has become commonplace to remark that, however noble, the idea of antiracism does not communicate any positive or affirmative notes. What, after all, are antiracists in favor of? What are we committed to and how does it connect with the necessary moment of negativity that defines our political hopes? There are difficulties in framing those objectives, utopian and otherwise. I see this as another small symptom of the larger, chronic condition involved in the crisis of "race" and attempts to escape it by refiguring humanism. The history of racism is a narrative in which the congruency of micro- and macrocosm has been disrupted at the point of their analogical intersection: the human body. The order of active differentiation that gets called "race" may be modernity's most pernicious signature. It articulates reason and unreason. It knits together science and superstition. Its specious ontologies are anything but spontaneous and natural. They should be awarded no immunity from prosecution amid the reveries of reflexivity and the comfortable forms of inertia induced by capitulation to the lazy essentialisms that postmodern sages inform us we cannot escape.

Notes

1. C. Peter Ripley et al., eds., *The Black Abolitionist Papers* (University of North Carolina Press, 1985), 4 vols.

2. "The fact that the development of computer technology, with its demands on information theory, has occurred contemporaneously with the growth of molecular biology has not merely provided the physical technology, in instrumentation and computing power, without which the dramatic advances of the decades since the 1960s would not have been possible. It has also given the organising metaphors within which the data was analysed and the theories created." Steven Rose, *Lifelines* (Penguin, 1997), p. 120.

3. Frantz Fanon, *Black Skin, White Masks*, trans. Charles Lam (Markman, Pluto Press, 1986 [1952]), p. 60.

4. Martin Luther King, Jr., *Where Do We Go from Here: Chaos or Community?* (Harper and Row, 1967), p. 53.

5. "Recent tests at the US Army Research Institute of Environmental Medicine in Massachusetts showed that 78% of women who underwent similar training qualified for 'very heavy' military jobs." Hugh McManners, "Army Sets Out to Banish Better Breed of Woman," *Sunday Times*, March 17, 1996.

6. African Rights, *Rwanda Not So Innocent: When Women Become Killers* (1975).

7. Carole Pateman, *The Disorder of Women* (Stanford University Press, 1989), esp. chapter 2.

8. Richard Rorty, "Cruelty and Solidarity," in *Contingency, Irony and Solidarity* (Cambridge University Press, 1989).

9. Beverley Merz, "Whose Cells Are They, Anyway?" *American Medical News* (March 23–30, 1990), pp. 7–8; "Modern Times: The Way of All Flesh," BBC 2 Television, March 19, 1997.

10. Jeremy Rifkin, *The Bio-Tech Century: Harnessing the Gene and Re-Making the World* (Tarcher Putnam, 1998).

11. Ilya Prigogine, *The End of Certainty: Time, Chaos and the New Laws of Nature* (Free Press, 1997), p. 29.

12. Richard Dyer, *White* (Routledge, 1997), chapter 3.

13. Fanon, *Black Skin, White Masks*, p. 161.

14. "Bodily fitness as the supreme goal, meant to be pursued, yet never reached, by means of self-coercion, is bound to be forever shot through with anxiety seeking an outlet, but generating a constantly growing demand for ever new yet untested outlets. I propose that this product of the 'privatisation' of the body and of the agencies of social production of the body is the 'primal scene' of postmodern ambivalence. It lends postmodern culture its unheard-of energy, an inner compulsion to be on the move. It is also a crucial cause, perhaps the prime cause, of its inbuilt tendency to instant ageing." Zygmunt Bauman, *Life in Fragments* (Polity Press, 1995), p. 119.

15. Donna Haraway, *Modest_Witness@Second_Millennium.FemaleMan©_Meets OncoMouse™: Feminism and Technoscience* (Routledge, 1997) p. 262.

16. "The glances of the other fixed me there, in the sense in which a chemical solution is fixed by a dye." Fanon, *Black Skin, White Masks*, p. 109.

17. *The Voice*, issue 724 (October 15, 1996).

18. Howard Jones, *Mutiny on the Amistad* (Oxford University Press, 1987).

19. Stephen Buckley, "Heritage Battle Rages at Slavery's Sacred Sites," *Guardian* (August 1, 1995).

20. "The trouble with the NPFL is that, in baffle, they may capture a street corner, but then they go for a beer, and when they come back they're surprised to find that they've lost it again," Lemuel Potty told reporters in Monrovia. "They're rubbish, but at least they're better than their rivals the Krahn. They go into battle wearing women's wigs, necklaces and rubber overcoats." Potty, a National Patriotic Front of Liberia (NPFL) sympathizer who owned a nightclub in the Mamba Point district, was describing the civil war raging in his country which has so far killed over 150,000 people. "I'm not saying that the war isn't going full pelt. There are quite a few dead people lying around in the streets, but actually the gunmen are far more interested in looting luxury goods than killing each other. Shops selling trainers were the first to be looted, but they also like robbing tailors' shops. The NPFL wear brightly coloured sailors' life vests, or T shirts they've looted from the Save The Children Fund. Their basic look is ghetto rap musician. You can always spot them because they all wear blue berets, stolen from the Army and Navystore, but the Krahn are more flamboyant. One Krahn fighter dresses in wellington boots and a woman's head scarf, and calls himself Lieutenant Colonel Double Trouble. They do the real fighting in the countryside. When they come to Monrovia they don't really come to fight. They come to shop." *Eastern Express*, April 24, 1996.

21. Michael Chege, the director of African Studies at the University of Florida, has repeatedly drawn attention to the role of elite academics in formulating the genocidal doctrines implemented in Rwanda. See Tim Cornwell's "Rwandan Scholars Conspired," *Times Higher Education Supplement* (February 28, 1997). The suicide of Nikola Koljevic, prolific Shakespearean scholar, ideologue of "ethnic cleansing," and prime architect of the destruction of Sarajevo, raises similar issues in a different setting. See Janine di Giovanni's article "The Cleanser" in *Guardian Weekend* (March 1, 1997).

22. As I write, only two men, Jean-Paul Akayesu and Jean Kambanda, have been found guilty for their roles in the mass killing.

23. Kader Asmal et al., *Reconciliation through Truth: A Reckoning with Apartheid's Criminal Governance* (James Currey, 1997). See also Patrick J. Furlong, *Between Crown and Swastika: The Impact of the Radical Right on the Afrikaner Nationalist Movement in the Fascist Era* (Wesleyan, New England, 1991); and Carlos Santiago Nino, *Radical Evil on Trial* (Yale University Press, 1996).

24. June Goodwin and Ben Schiff, *Heart of Whiteness: Afrikaners Face Black Rule in the New South Africa* (Scribner, 1995), p. 177.

25. Jonathan Steele, "National Effrontery," *Guardian* (May 24, 1997).

26. Gérard Prunier, *The Rwanda Crisis: History of Genocide* (Columbia University Press, 1995), pp. 103–106.

27. Marek Kohn's *The Race Gallery: The Return of Racial Science* (Cape, 1995) and John Hoberman's *Darwin's Athletes: How Sport Has Damaged Black America and Preserved the Myth of Race* (Houghton Mifflin, 1997) are two important books that against much of the momentum of their own arguments remain determined to hold on to the idea of racial science.

28. Martin Thorn, *Republics, Nations and Tribes* (Verso, 1995).

29. Guntram Hennik Herb, *Under the Map of Germany: Nationalism and Propaganda, 1918–1945* (Routledge, 1997); Jeremy Black, *Maps and History* (Yale University Press, 1997), especially chapter 4.

30. Mahmood Mamdani, *Citizen and Subject* (Princeton University Press, 1997).

31. Martin Barker, *The New Racism* (Junction Books, 1980).

32. Steven Rose, *Lifelines: Biology, Freedom, Determinism* (Penguin Books, 1997).

33. Londa Schiebinger, *Nature's Body: Gender in the Making of Modern Science* (Beacon Press, 1993).

34. Martin Kemp, "Temples of the Body and Temples of the Cosmos: Vision and Visualization in the Vesalian and Copernican Revolutions," in Brian S. Baigrie, ed., *Picturing Knowledge: Historical and Philosophical Problems Concerning the Use of Art in Science* (University of Toronto Press, 1996), pp. 40–85.

35. Jonathan Crary, *Techniques of the Observer: On Vision and Modernity in the Nineteenth Century* (MIT Press, 1992).

36. Alex Potts, *Flesh and the Ideal: Winckelmann and the Origins of Art History* (Yale University Press, 1994), esp. sections IV and V.

37. Howard Kaye points out that Haeckl's *Welträtsel*, a treatise of "national socialism in support of racial community," sold more than 300,000 copies between 1900 and 1914. Howard Kaye, *The Social Meaning of Modern Biology* (Yale University Press, 1986), p. 38.

38. Mechtild Rössler, "'Area Research' and 'Spatial Planning' from the Weimar Republic to the German Federal Republic: Creating a Society with a Spatial Order under National Socialism," in Monika Renneberg and Mark Walker, eds., *Science, Technology and National Socialism* (Cambridge University Press, 1994), pp. 126–38.

39. Sven Holdar, "The Ideal State and the Power of Geography: The Life-Work of Rudolf Kjellén," *Political Geography* 11 (1992), pp. 307–23; Herb, *Under the Map of Germany*.

40. Anna Barmwell, *The History of Ecology in the Twentieth Century* (Yale University Press, 1989), p. 50.

41. Richard Lewontin, *The Doctrine of DNA: Biology as Ideology* (Penguin Books, 1991), pp. 63–4.

42. Fanon, *Black Skin, White Masks*, p. 110.

43. Sir William Macpherson of Cluny, "A Report into the Death of Stephen Lawrence" (Her Majesty's Stationery Office, 1999).

32

What Is to Be Gained by Looking White People in the Eye? Culture, Race, and Gender in Cases of Sexual Violence

*Sherene Razack**

Was it just that old race thing that had thrown her off when her eyes met Grace's? Her neighbour Wilma's father said he'd never in his adult life looked a white person in the eye. He'd grown up in the days when such an act very often ended in a black person's charred body swinging from a tree. For many years, Blanche worried that it was fear which sometimes made her reluctant to meet white people's eyes, particularly on days when she had the lonelies or the unspecified blues. She'd come to understand that her desire was to avoid pain, a pain so old, so deep, its memory was carried not in her mind, but in her bones. Some days she simply didn't want to look into the eyes of people raised to hate, disdain, or fear anyone who looked like her.

NEELY 1992, 111

Conversations about Culture

"I had a Vietnamese doctor who wouldn't look me in the eye when we discussed the risks of amniocentesis," a woman says to me angrily at a Christmas party and wonders whether or not the doctor ought to be compelled to put aside his cultural peculiarities in the interests of his white, Western patients. Eye contact, a perennial favorite as a marker of the perils associated with cross-cultural encounters, is a popular topic these days. A Crown attorney's book on the cultural attributes of his Aboriginal clients garners praise, particularly for his description of how Aboriginal men's failure to look judges in the eye is a mark of respect rather than an admission of guilt (Ross 1992).[1] In academe, professors are reportedly "going for the judicial jugular," subjecting judicial decisions on Aboriginal issues to scrutiny and itemizing the "difficulties courts face as they are called to sit in judgment of another culture and, in the case of land claims, another time" (MacQueen 1992, A4). The controversy over culture, and specifically

* Pp. 894–923 from *Signs: Journal of Women in Culture and Society*, vol. 19, no. 4. © 1994 by The University of Chicago. Reprinted by permission of the University of Chicago Press.

over the cultural bias of the judiciary, has also emerged in the context of sexual violence against Aboriginal women and women of color, although Aboriginal women more often have been at the center of the debate.[2] In his opening submission to the court in a sexual assault case involving a sixty-three-year-old Roman Catholic bishop and young Aboriginal girls under his charge at a residential school thirty years ago, a Crown prosecutor proposed to build his case of nonconsent on a bedrock of culture.[3] Referring to the role of the expert witness he intended to call to testify, an anthropologist specializing in Aboriginal culture, the Crown argued: "The purpose of [Dr. Van Dyke's] evidence is to put into context what these witnesses mean when they say, 'I did it because he told me to do it.' That is an indication of a reflection of their cultural background, the way they perceive this individual" (*R. v. O'Connor* 1992, 16). Yet, culture used in service of proving the nonconsent of young Aboriginal girls who have been sexually assaulted is highly unusual. Far more typical is culture used as a defense of the accused when the accused is of Aboriginal or non-Anglo-Saxon origin.

The cultural contexts of victims of violence and their attackers have also interested black and Aboriginal feminist researchers and women's advocacy groups, but in this context there is likely to be more of an awareness of the dilemmas and contradictions that surface whenever cultural considerations are taken into account. For instance, feminist service providers to immigrant women have stressed the need to understand how culture shapes refugee and immigrant women's experiences of and responses to violence (Rafiq 1991). Activists also note, however, that in a racist society any discussion of culture and violence in immigrant communities can be interpreted by white society as "another sign of backwardness" (Thobani 1993, 12). That is, violence in immigrant communities is viewed as a cultural attribute rather than a product of male domination. In the face of racism, it has sometimes not made sense for feminists working in the context of violence against women in immigrant and Aboriginal communities to talk about culture at all. When women from nondominant groups talk about culture (among whom I count myself), we are often assumed by others to be articulating a false dichotomy between culture and gender; in articulating our difference, we inadvertently also confirm our relegation to the margins. Culture talk is clearly a double-edged sword. It packages difference as inferiority and obscures gender-based domination within communities, yet cultural considerations are important for contextualizing oppressed groups' claims for justice, for improving their access to services, and for requiring dominant groups to examine the invisible cultural advantages they enjoy.

This article is an attempt to examine the uses to which culture is put in the courts when the issue is violence against racialized women.[4] It is equally an attempt to explore the risks of talking culture for women of color and Aboriginal women. We need to ask, Can we move the discussion about culture from cultural modes of making eye contact to what is to be gained and lost by looking white people in the eye? Both within their communities and outside of them, the risks racialized women encounter when they talk about culture in the context of sexual violence are manifested on several levels. First, many cultural communities understand culture and community in ways that reflect and leave unchallenged male privilege. Indeed, the notion of culture that has perhaps the widest currency among both dominant and subordinate groups is one whereby culture is taken to mean values, beliefs, knowledge, and customs that exist in a timeless and unchangeable vacuum outside of patriarchy, racism, imperialism, and colonialism. Viewed this way, culture maintains "a superautonomy that reduces all facets of social experience to issues of culture" (Calmore 1992, 2185). Second, racialized women who bring sexual violence to the attention of white society risk exacerbating the racism directed at both men and women in their communities; we risk, in other words, deracializing our gender and being viewed as traitors, women without community. These risks are particularly acute when, as so often happens, it is the dominant group who controls the interpretation of what it means to take culture into account.

When the terrain is sexual violence, racism and sexism intersect in particularly nasty ways to produce profound marginalization. In using the pronoun *we*, I do not want to claim, however, that as a woman of color I experience this to the same degree or incur the same risks as do Aboriginal women in Canada in talking culture. For each group, the risks are different and, more important, their need to talk about culture in spite of these risks emerges out of different histories and present-day realities. Aboriginal women often confront sexual violence in a context in which several generations have been victims of sexual violence. There is, too, a legacy of harsh socioeconomic realities. The continued denial of sovereignty and the Canadian government's consistent refusal to honor treaties and resolve land claims are profound injustices. Further, the categories *Aboriginal women* and *women of color* clearly are not homogeneous. What I would suggest we share is the fact that both women of color and Aboriginal women are obliged to talk about culture and violence within the context of white supremacy, a context in which racism and sexism and their intersections are denied. Both groups of women, therefore, in talking about their cultural specificities, run the risk, in different ways, of being granted some cultural differences but only at the expense of acknowledging their experience of sexual and racial violence. Culture becomes the framework used by white society to preempt both racism and sexism in a process that I refer to as culturalization. The risks of talking culture require us to exercise great caution whenever cultural considerations enter legal discourse or discussions about access to services. In working through the risks and in identifying how cultural considerations often work in the service of dominant groups. I hope to explore how Aboriginal women and women of color might talk about the specificities of their cultural experiences without risking a denial of the realities of violence, racism, and sexism in their lives.

The Culturalization of Racism

Contemporary discussion about culture and violence takes place within the context of modern racism, a racism distinguished from its nineteenth-century counterpart by the vigor with which it is consistently denied. In its modern form, overt racism, which rests on the notion of biologically based inferiority, coexists with a more covert practice of domination encoded in the assumption of cultural or acquired inferiority. The culturalization of racism, whereby black inferiority is attributed to "cultural deficiency, social inadequacy, and technological underdevelopment," thrives in a social climate that is officially pluralist (Essed 1991, 14; Calmore 1992, 2131). We speak more of cultural and ethnic differences and less of race and class exploitation and oppression. The concept of culturalized racism is important, it seems to me, for three reasons. First, it highlights a major feature of how modern racism works: its covert operations. Second, it explains why denial is so central to how racism works. To quote Philomena Essed, "There are two levels at which racism as ideology operates: at the level of daily actions and their interpretations and at another level in the refusal to take responsibility for it" (Essed 1991, 44). If we live in a tolerant and pluralistic society in which the fiction of equality within ethnic diversity is maintained, then we need not accept responsibility for racism. We can conveniently forget our racist past and feel secure in the knowledge that at least the residential schools are closed. Like the Dutch society Essed writes about, whose newspapers put the word *racism* in quotation marks, Canadians are outraged when racism, particularly indirect racism, is named, as it is not supposed to exist. What is denied is that "whites regularly idealise and favour themselves as a group" (Essed 1991, 43). Thus, there can sometimes be a more or less general rejection of overt racism and at the same time "an increasing reluctance to see race as a fundamental determinant of white privilege and black poverty" (Essed 1991, 30). Third, a "declaration of faith in a plural, diverse society," comments Homi Bhabha, serves as an effective defense "against the real, subversive demands that the articulation of cultural difference – the empowering of minorities – makes upon democratic pluralism" (Bhabha 1992, 235). Cultural differences are used to explain oppression; if these differences could somehow be taken into account, oppression would disappear. According to this logic, as Arthur Brittan and Mary Maynard noted in *Sexism, Racism, and Oppression,* power is subsumed under culture, and oppression is reduced to a symbolic construction in which there are no real live oppressors who benefit materially and no real oppressed people to liberate (Brittan & Maynard 1984, 19). In effect, minorities are invited to keep their culture but enjoy no greater access to power and resources.

In the context of law, because democratic pluralism means, to borrow Bhabha's aphorism, that "multiculturalism must be seen to be done, as noisily and publicly as possible," white judges are being urged to be culturally sensitive (Bhabha 1992, 232). Judges begin to practice what Dwight Greene has described for the American context as a kind of "pluralistic ignorance": "Mostly affluent white males talking among themselves about what are the reasonable choices for poor people of color to be making in situations virtually none of the judges have ever been in" (cited in Calmore 1992, 2136). In Canada, white judges have been discussing Aboriginal culture and its relevance to the sentencing of Aboriginal males convicted of sexual assault, among other offenses. At least three judicial education programs have been undertaken to "sensitize" judges to issues of cultural diversity among immigrant as well as Aboriginal communities (projects conceived of as entirely separate from gender sensitivity training, thereby rendering racialized women invisible). Sensitivity in this context means learning how to read culturally specific behavior in the courtroom setting. When it is the behavior of generic women (read white) that must be translated, sensitivity includes such things as understanding that a victim of a sexual assault may giggle on the witness stand not to express her agreement with the sexual assault but rather to convey her discomfort (Tyler 1992). For women of color and Aboriginal women who are sexually assaulted, cultural sensitivity, as I shall show below, can be about both victims and offenders unable to make eye contact. In the context of the latter, sensitivity is often about the culturalization of rape: how cultural and historical specificities explain and excuse the violence men direct at women. Culture, working in tandem with judicial tendencies to minimize the harm of rape, then becomes a mitigating factor in the sentencing of Aboriginal and minority men convicted of sexual assault.

The Culturalization of Sexism

Culture as a defense: Aboriginal offenders

In cases of sexual assault when victims and their attackers are of the same race, it is often assumed that it is gender and not race that is the meaningful factor at work influencing how rape is "scripted" in court (Marcus 1992, 392). Yet, as Kristin Bumiller has pointed out, rape trials are most often about fallen angels who must prove their innocence in contributing to their fall from grace. The emphasis in a rape trial on the victim's purity "reinforces the presumption that punishing violent men is justified to the extent that women are worthy of trust and protection" (Bumiller 1991, 97). Racialized women, however, are considered inherently less innocent and worthy than white women, and the classic rape in legal discourse is the rape of a white woman. The rape script is thus inevitably raced whether it involves intraracial or interracial rape. The criminal justice system, Jennifer Wriggins argues, takes less seriously the rape of black women either by black men or white men (Wriggins 1983, 121).[5] Examples from the Canadian context of Aboriginal offenders, while they show that male judges continue to minimize the harm of sexual assault, also confirm that race never absents itself from the rape script. Rather, racial and cultural differences and the implication that colonization has had a devastating impact on Aboriginal men all contribute to making invisible the harm that is done to Aboriginal women who are sexually assaulted. Additionally, viewing Aboriginal men as dysfunctional (and not, e.g., oppressed) indirectly serves to confirm the superiority of white men.

In Margo Nightingale's study of Aboriginal women in sixty-seven cases of sexual assault, Canada's history of colonization pervades the legal environment just as extensively as do historical and social attitudes toward women, and it becomes impossible to untangle which factor is contributing most to lenient sentencing of Aboriginal males accused of sexual assault (Nightingale 1991). For instance, Nightingale notes that the stereotype of the drunken Indian still operates to ensure that alcohol abuse is viewed as more significant for Aboriginal than for white offenders. What is interesting, however, is the gendered response to this stereotype. For an Aboriginal man accused of rape, alcohol abuse can be seen as a mitigating factor, sometimes a root cause of the violence against women. For an Aboriginal woman who is raped, however, intoxication becomes a form of victim blaming. A woman who has passed out, Nightingale notes, is often considered to have suffered less of a violation, and the number of victims who are passed out is greatly exaggerated.[6] Similarly, the ostracism that might be suffered by a woman who complains of rape in an isolated northern community is not noticed while the suffering a male offender might experience in a jail far from home where no one speaks his language has occasionally been taken into account.

Just what are the statements that flag race and gender coming together under the banner of culture to diminish the reality of sexual assault and its impact on Aboriginal women? Nightingale identified perhaps the most notorious Canadian case to date to illustrate the combination of gender and cultural bias in sexual assault sentencing. In *R. v. Curley, Nagmalik, and Issigaitok*, a sentence of seven days was meted out to three Inuit men found guilty of having intercourse with a female under the age of fourteen. Relying on his experience in the Eastern Arctic, Judge Bourassa considered the culture of the accused men and was especially lenient on the basis that, according to his information, in Inuit culture, a young woman is deemed ready for intercourse upon menstruation. An assumed cultural difference was also used to bolster the defense's argument that the accused men were ignorant of Canadian law on sexual assault. On appeal, cultural considerations continued to shape the rape script by eclipsing the realities of the violence done to the young girl. Although the sentence was increased to reflect the view that ignorance of the law was no excuse, there was no effort made to determine if the victim had in fact suffered great harm (Nightingale 1991, 92–4).[7]

Similar cultural considerations have arisen in cases where the defense has argued for a community-based treatment program as an alternative to prison. In *R. v. Naqitarvik*, the same Judge Bourassa accepted the community-based solution on the basis that the community's unique cultural methods of dealing with sexual assault (in this instance a healing circle) had a significant role to play in healing the offender. On appeal, the issues once again revolved around culture as the court elected to impose a stiffer sentence on the basis that the community-based program was no more than a counseling program and that, further, "the witnesses in this case do not describe a culture markedly different than that in the rest of Canada. Rather, the incident itself arose as the victim and her sister played music on a modern player for which there was an electric cord," an indication in the court's eyes that Inuit culture was sufficiently modern that it could not be characterized as different from the mainstream (Nightingale 1991, 92–3).

Judges, and the lawyers who argue the cases before them, can work with a notion of cultural difference as inferiority but recognize, at the same time, the damaging impact of colonization (at least in sexual assault cases if not in land claims where such recognition would have a bearing on the restitution of land); that is, they sometimes display a willingness to consider the history of colonization and its present-day effects as mitigating factors in the sentencing of Aboriginal males.[8] One reads in decisions, for instance, some empathy for sexual offenders who come from "the worst Indian reserve in the province" (*R. v. T.* 1989, 8). In *R. v. Whitecap and Whitecap*, the very difficult social and economic conditions on the Red Earth Indian reserve are noted (*R. v. Whitecap [R. T.] and Whitecap [D. M.]* 1989); in *R. v. Okkuatsiak*, the offender is described as a victim of the economic conditions in Nain (*R. v. Okkuatsiak* 1987, 234). Judges also note in their decisions the vicious cycle of sexual abuse that began with residential schools (*R. v. J. [E.]* 1991). What is absent here is any acknowledgment of the impact of this history of colonization and its present-day legacy on Aboriginal women as the victims of sexual assault. This is how gender and race conflate to produce an absence of the realities of Aboriginal women.

At the time of Nightingale's study, few Aboriginal women had written of the cultural bias of the judiciary in cases of sexual assault involving Aboriginal men, perhaps wary, as Nightingale speculates, that such a critique would only serve to further criminalize Aboriginal men and leave Aboriginal women open to the charge of race treason, very much as Anita Hill was during her testimony regarding Clarence Thomas. Since then, Teressa Nahanee, a member of the Squamish Indian Nation, has strongly protested the gender bias of Northern judges. Reviewing both reported and unreported decisions in the sentencing of Inuit males accused of sexual assault during the period 1984–89, Nahanee concluded, as did Nightingale, that lenient sentencing of Inuit males cannot be defended on the basis of cultural sensitivity: "This (lenient sentencing] is simply a process whereby white patriarchs bond with brown patriarchs in justice administration. The northern judiciary keep Inuit male sex offenders in the North by accepting cultural defenses put forward by Inuit males accused in rape cases. Inuit women claim the 'culture' defined in this sentencing process does not represent 'Inuit modern culture,' or traditional practices. It is culture defined by flown-in, southern, white anthropologists who take a text-book approach to culture" (Nahanee 1992, 5). Indeed, Pauktuutit, the Inuit Women's Association of Canada, as Nahanee reports, has launched a constitutional challenge of sentencing decisions on the basis that lenient sentencing of Inuit males in sexual assault cases interferes with the right to security of the person and the right of equal protection and benefit of the law of Inuit women (Nahanee 1992, 3). Along the same lines as Nightingale (and the evidence uncovered in my own research), Nahanee elaborates on how race is confused with culture and comes to be used as a mitigating factor in the sentencing of Inuit male offenders. Instead of using the "reasonable man" standard, she writes, the Northern court "has invented a fictional Inuit man": "He can be many things. He can be a high-ranking public official, raised 'traditionally,' a family man, with no criminal record for whom the crime is unpremeditated. Or, he is not well educated, under the influence of alcohol, unemployed, with no previous record. No matter what elements of the fiction are used, he is Inuit [sic] and he will not be sentenced to more than two years less a day" (Nahanee 1992, 34).

  Both Nightingale and Nahanee have rightly focused on cases in which cultural sensitivity rested on a highly gendered, unsophisticated view of culture and, I would add, on a gendered view of the impact of colonization. My own research into cases of sexual assault has confirmed their conclusions.[9] Recently, however, some judges have been more careful of the gendered consequences of viewing rape through the lens of race and/or culture as well as history. For example, in *R. v. M. (G. O.)*, the court noted: "The seriousness of the offence does not vary in accordance with the colour of the skin of the victim, her cultural background or the place of her residence" (*R. v. M. [G. O.]* 1990, 81); in *R. v. Ritchie*, it is noted that sexual assault "is not acceptable in society whether it be within the Indian society or the general society" (*R. v. Ritchie* 1988, 1). There is an emerging awareness of the dangers of relying on culture as a mitigating circumstance. In *R. v. J. (H.)*, this use of culture is specifically refuted: "There have been instances when Canadian judges were persuaded to bend the rules too far in favour of offenders from Native communities or disadvantaged backgrounds. When that happens a form of injustice results; specific victims and members of the public generally are given cause to believe that the justice system has failed to protect them. . . . H. J. cannot properly be portrayed as a naive young man who should only be pitied and not condemned. He is not a 'child of the forest'" (*R. v. J. [H.]* 1990, 3). If Aboriginal offenders are no longer "children of the forest," the dangers for Aboriginal women of deficient and clumsy attempts on the part of legal players in the justice system to interpret culture and history remain nonetheless. It continues to be primarily white male judges and lawyers with little or no knowledge of history or anthropology who interpret Aboriginal culture and its relevance to the court. Wrapped in a cloak of sensitivity to cultural differences and recognition of the consequences of colonization, the anthropologizing of sexual assault continues to have gendered overtones and to maintain white supremacy as securely as in days of more overt racism and sexism.

Eye contact and the cultural differences approach

In 1989, a Crown attorney with extensive experience prosecuting Native offenders in the North wrote an article on how cultural bias affects the sentencing of Native accused men. Two years later, the article became a book. In *Dancing with a Ghost*, Rupert Ross begins from the standpoint of cultural sensitivity, urging lawyers and judges to critically examine their own cultural assumptions and advising them to do their best to discover Aboriginal realities and truths (Ross 1992, 2). Ross explains with an example: "I have learned, to my chagrin, that in some northern reserve communities looking another straight in the eye is taken as a deliberate sign of disrespect for their rule is that you look inferiors straight in the eye" (Ross 1992, 2). He then goes on to elaborate how such cultural differences have an impact on sentencing. Significantly, Ross is responding to his perception that sentencing of Native offenders has been too harsh and at variance with the wishes of Aboriginal communities themselves. His identification of cultural differences, then, is intended to avoid this outcome. Largely anecdotal, Ross's commentary serves to highlight where cultural interpretation through white male eyes can take us in the area of sexual assault.

Ross intends to make an argument for community-based justice and for lenient or nonexistent jail terms, an outcome he considers justifiable if it can be shown that Aboriginal communities both desire it and can offer protection to the community. The first part of this argument, that Aboriginal communities desire this outcome, relies on anecdotes of the victims themselves. A teenage rape victim refuses to testify, Ross reports, because she believes that her assailant has paid enough of a penalty while waiting for the case to come to trial (Ross 1992, 2). Another victim of abuse by an assailant described as dangerous also refuses to testify and Ross opines in such cases "that it is more than fear or embarrassment at work: I suspect instead that it is perceived as ethically wrong to say hostile, critical, implicitly angry things about someone in their presence. . . . In our ignorance, we have failed to admit the possibility that there might be rules other than ours to which they regularly display allegiance, an allegiance all the more striking because it is exercised in defiance of our insistent pressures to the contrary" (Ross 1992, 4). Ross feels certain that Aboriginal communities do not want violent, abusive men punished but instead healed and forgiven. Describing the sentencing of a young man who had beaten his wife in an alcoholic rage, Ross compares his own position that such an offense required a jail term as a deterrent to that of the men and women of the community. Aware perhaps that he might well be criticized for a gender-blind account of community, Ross notes that, while the community leaders asking that the young man remain in the community were all male, the courtroom was jammed with women. As he speculates, "Each of those ladies knew that when his jail term was over he would come back. If he came back feeling reviled by the women of the village, his problems with women would only grow worse. If, in contrast, they demonstrated their forgiveness, their support and their waiting welcome, the opposite result might occur. In their view, while jail sentences might on occasion be necessary for the protection of all, the person who has to pay that price should not be cut off from community affection and support. To do so would only put the community further at risk" (Ross 1992, 6). Finally, to support his speculation that Aboriginal women endorse community sanctions as an alternative to jail, Ross cites the 1989 report by the Ontario Native Women's Association (which he mistakenly dates 1990) that recommends the establishment of healing houses for women, children, and abusers (Ontario Native Women's Association 1989).

While it would be wrong to overdramatize the impact of Ross's cultural interpretations or to fail to note that he himself warned that his comments were restricted to isolated Aboriginal communities of his experience in Northern Ontario, his comments have been taken up by the chief judge of the Yukon territories, Heino Lilles, and reflect the approaches taken in some recent sexual assault cases in the North. Judge Lilles's own theorizing about cultural bias is noteworthy not only because of his position in the justice system and his involvement in various judicial education programs but because, like Ross's, his statements are accompanied by an acknowledgment that Aboriginal communities are highly disadvantaged communities. These interpretations are not, in other words, overtly racist; rather, they are presented as culturally sensitive, even anti-racist initiatives (Lilles 1990, 1992).[10]

Like Rupert Ross, Chief Justice Heino Lilles has spent some of his professional life within the context of Northern justice and hence has had ample opportunity to see how harshly the criminal justice system has dealt with Native offenders, a situation he attributes to two principal factors: "The social and economic poverty in which many Natives live, and a subtle, unintentional but persistent discrimination by the decision makers in the criminal justice system" (Lilles 1990, 330). If players in the judicial system can do little about poverty, they can certainly address discrimination, and it is to this end that Judge Lilles writes about culture and cultural bias. Decision makers in the justice system in the North, including police, lawyers, and judges, come from a cultural, social, and economic background different from that of the majority of persons in the communities where they serve, notes Judge Lilles. Such individuals are unintentionally biased; that it is to say, they may possess "an inclination, bent, or predisposition to make decisions a certain way, based on the sum total of the individual's own cultural and social experiences" (Lilles 1990, 343). Put this way, the problems of Northern justice originate in poverty as well as in a "misinterpretation" of cultural differences (Lilles 1990, 330). Admitting that it is difficult to generalize about Aboriginal values (but apparently not so difficult to do so about white culture), Judge Lilles nevertheless proceeds to rely on a chart comparing the value systems of Aboriginal peoples and non-Aboriginal peoples and to suggest how these differing values enter into judicial proceedings.[11] The question of eye contact surfaces once again, and Lilles, relying on Ross, notes that the justice system often unnecessarily criminalizes and labels young Aboriginal people because of the assumption (based on their alleged tendency not to make eye contact) that they are unreliable, remorseless, and uncooperative (Lilles 1990, 341).

It is important to note that under the umbrella of cross-cultural sensitivity Judge Lilles includes a number of practices that do not originate in culture but rather in the material practices of Northern justice. Thus, Crown prosecutors prosecute more readily because they are unwilling to overrule the police; police charge more readily; the level of policing is 200–300 percent greater than in other jurisdictions; few support services exist as alternatives to jail. All these factors contribute to a scenario that is explained away by poverty and misunderstandings of cross-cultural encounters. Significantly, the word *racism* does not occur throughout Lilles's article. If cultural differences and poverty are the source of the problems of Northern justice, then Aboriginal and community-based justice in which, presumably, cross-cultural concerns disappear, is at least one important strategy toward greater justice.[12] It is precisely this option that is now being considered in the disposition of some sexual assault cases and in two recent cases in which Judge Lilles presided, although, significantly, it is a white judge who is in the position of deciding what a community-based disposition should be.

Healing Offenders

Culture as a defense and the pursuit of a "culturally relevant disposition" in the case of *R. v. P. (J. A.)* revolved around the Aboriginal concept of healing, an approach to justice described in the *Report of the Aboriginal Justice Inquiry of Manitoba* as follows:

> The underlying philosophy in Aboriginal societies in dealing with crime was the resolution of disputes, the healing of wounds and the restoration of social harmony. It might mean an expression of regret for the injury done by the offender or by members of the offender's clan. It might mean the presentation of gifts or payment of some kind. It might even mean the forfeiture of the offender's life. But the matter was considered finished once the offence was recognized and dealt with by both the offender and the offended. Atonement and the restoration of harmony were the goals – not punishment. (*Report of the Aboriginal Justice Inquiry* 1991, 27)

P. pleaded guilty to sexually assaulting his two daughters and a foster child over the course of several years. The assaults began when each of the girls reached the age of thirteen years. The defense urged the court to adopt a community-based disposition in lieu of a period of incarceration (normally a two-year minimum and a maximum of life imprisonment for sexual intercourse with a minor). Notwithstanding the serious breach of trust involved, Judge Lilles agreed to the community-based disposition on the basis of three factors, each of which bears examination for how culture, community, and colonization can be used to compete with and ultimately prevail over gender-based harm. First, the chief (on behalf of the five clan elders) supported P.'s bid for a community-based disposition. As described by Judge Lilles in his decision and later in an article, the chief spoke in some detail about the community's efforts to recover from the devastating effects of colonization and in particular the Alaskan highway, which passed through the community in 1942. Alcohol, sexual abuse at residential schools and in homes, and the breakdown of the traditional community structure resulted, in the chief's words, in a "time of great cultural downfall" (*R. v. P. [J. A.]* 1991, 305). The community's response was to break the cycle of abuse through a healing circle in which both victims and offenders would come forward for treatment and rehabilitation. Also testifying on P.'s behalf were a number of witnesses, including one of his daughters and his wife who supported the call for a community solution already in place in the community in the form of a weekly collective counseling session. A third factor in P.'s favor was the fact that he had been a leader in bringing Native culture back to the community and possessed, in the eyes of the judge, "the potential to be a future leader in the Teslin community" (*R. v. P. [J. A.]* 1991, 315). Aware that his decision was likely to attract censure, Judge Lilles accepted the community alternative, as does Rupert Ross, on the basis that a community disposition can be "hard time" and even more difficult for the offender than a term of imprisonment. As he elaborates, "In this case I heard evidence about the humiliation which accompanies disclosure of an offence like this in a community the size of Teslin. 'First one must deal with the shock and then the dismay on your neighbour's faces. One must live with the daily humiliation, and at the same time seek forgiveness not just from the victims, but from the community as a whole,' For in a Native culture, a real harm has been done to everyone. A community disposition continues that humiliation, at least until full forgiveness has been achieved" (*R. v. P. [J. A.]* 1991, 317). Culture and community remain in this decision unexamined and ungendered while the subtext of colonialism (never named as racism and thus a legacy of the past and not part of the present) informs white judicial cultural sensitivities.

It is mainly within remote, Northern communities that culturally relevant sentencing has occurred. In the Northwest Territories, there is, as Judge Lilles is concerned to note, "an exceptionally harsh system of justice" with an imprisonment rate of 790 per 100,000 population as compared to 112.7 for the rest of Canada and 426 per 100,000 for the United States (Lilles 1992, 330). Arguably, such an environment demands that alternatives to incarceration be explored. At the very least they demand that we examine the root causes of the problems apparent in the judicial system. In this context, it seems sensible to explore, as Judge Lilles has advised, the potential of probation reviews as a means of monitoring whether or not community-based dispositions are working. What is worrying is the offender-centered features of this approach, the almost entirely male cast of spokespersons for the community, the denial of racism as a key factor affecting the treatment of all Aboriginal peoples, and sexism in Aboriginal women's lives. Of concern, too, is the failure to question whether what may be appropriate for a small Aboriginal community of 300 may be transposed to altogether different contexts.

Lilles's decision in *R. v. P. (J. A.)* has not to my knowledge drawn public criticism but another decision of Judge Lilles, also involving sexual assault and healing, has. The connections between *R. v. P (J. A.)* (1991) and *R. v. Hoyt* (1991) are instructive in that cultural considerations in the former appear in the latter despite significant differences in context. Between 1965 and 1971, John Hoyt, a white probation officer in White-horse (the capital of the Northwest Territories, population 60,000) who also served as a volunteer assisting Native youth, molested three minors of Aboriginal origin whom he supervised on a camping trip and whom he counseled and befriended. In view of Hoyt's early guilty plea, over forty letters of reference, the devastating impact on Hoyt's family, and a remorseful offender who would like to assist his victims in their "healing," Judge Lilles imposed a fine of $2,000 per victim. While he did not ultimately accept the defense's suggestions that Mr. Hoyt contribute to the community by "researching alternatives in sentencing for sexual abuse cases, assist the authorities in developing badly needed programming for sexual offenders, assist the Native community, while allowing him to facilitate the healing process for himself and his victims," Judge Lilles did concede that such suggestions were "very attractive" (*R. v. Hoyt* 1991, 17). The Court of Appeal in January 1992 dismissed an appeal by the Crown that the sentence was too light (*R. v. Hoyt* 1992).

The Lilles decision in *Hoyt* did draw criticism from the Yukon Association for the Prevention of Community and Family Violence. As the authors of the response argued, Judge Lilles gave no weight to the one victim who testified about the harm done to him and presumed on the weakest of evidence that there was no risk of recidivism, notwithstanding the testimony by Mr. Hoyt's psychologist that the accused's understanding of the consequences of his behavior for his victims was limited. Finally, on the judge's attraction to the defense's proposal of community work, the authors state their association's response bluntly: "To be crass, one wonders if the criminal offence of arson qualifies one for the position of fire marshall" (Forde, Pasquali, and Peterson 1991, 7).

Judge Lilles's decisions may simply be illustrative of a more generalized tendency to dispense offender-centered rather than victim-centered justice in cases of sexual assault, but what is interesting about the *P. (J. A.)* and *Hoyt* decisions is the extent to which they reflect the judge's acceptance of community-based dispositions and of healing in particular, concepts that are intended to reflect his sensitivity to the social and economic conditions of Aboriginal communities in the North, to their history of colonialism, and to specific cultural differences. That Judge Lilles is himself a white man and that Hoyt, a white probation officer, is one of those players in the justice system whom Judge Lilles earlier identified in his article as likely to possess cultural biases, seems not to have altered the strategy or encouraged a cautious interpretation of cultural considerations. The victims, in this case Aboriginal boys, also were not considered in the eager acceptance of community-based justice.

Judges dispensing justice in Canada's North are confronted with the vulnerability of Aboriginal children in the North. There are many cases involving pedophiles who are also authority figures, a heritage of colonialism that surfaces in the rape of a sister by a brother who was himself raped as a child by a white authority figure, high suicide rates among young people, and extensive alcohol abuse *(R. v. J. [E.]* 1991; *R. v. Roach* 1987; *R. v. Kowch* 1989; *R. v. Vaneden* 1988). Judges must thread their way through culture and history in order to determine who is offender and who is victim. In this context there are only victims, but they are certainly not all equally placed. While a few decisions do not constitute a trend, *Hoyt* and *P. (J. A.)* and others nevertheless suggest that judging in this context demands more careful attention to the meaning of community, history, and culture. As the Yukon Association for the Prevention of Community and Family Violence noted in the case of Mr. Hoyt, his standing in the community might look very different if one took the perspectives of the victims into account (Forde, Pasquali, and Peterson 1991, 7).

Between a Rock and a Hard Place: Aboriginal Women's Responses to Sexual Violence

Community has not been a safe place for women, and Aboriginal women have not failed to note this. The Ontario Native Women's Association's study on violence confirmed what many earlier studies had noted: the level of violence directed against women and children in Aboriginal communities and families was much higher than for non-Aboriginal populations. Eighty-four percent of the respondents to their survey thought that family violence occurs in their communities, and 24 percent personally knew of cases of family violence that had led to death, most frequently of women (Ontario Native Women's Association 1989, 3). Indeed, male violence was one reason why the Native Women's Association of Canada (NWAC) went to court in 1991 for the right to sit at the table during the constitutional talks on Aboriginal self-government. Arguing that their exclusion from the table posed a grave threat to Aboriginal women, NWAC explained to the court the basis for its fears: "Why are we so worried as women? . . . We have a disproportionately high rate of child sexual abuse and incest. We have wife battering, gang rapes, drug and alcohol abuse and every kind of perversion imaginable has been imported into our lives. The development of programs, services, and policies for handling domestic violence has been placed in the hands of men. Has it resulted in a reduction of this kind of violence? Is a woman or a child safe in their own home in an Aboriginal community? The statistics show this is not the case" (*Native Women's Association of Canada*, applicants' memorandum 1992, 14). As Federal Court of Appeal Judge Mahoney stated in his reasons for judgment allowing the claim of NWAC, while there are Aboriginal women who hold executive positions on their national organizations, notably Rosemary Kuptana of the Inuit Tapirsat, who did sit at the Constitutional table, the "record suggests that some 'nations' . . . will continue to opt for male domination" (*Native Women's Association of Canada*, reasons 1992, 7).

Confronting male domination within Aboriginal communities has required an understanding of how white domination of Aboriginal communities has contributed to the causes and extent of male violence. As the Ontario Native Women's Association stressed in their report on violence, Aboriginal people do not have self-government and are regulated in much of their everyday affairs through the federal government. This continuing colonization and the devastating impact of past domination are the contexts in which Aboriginal family violence must be examined (Ontario Native Women's Association 1989, 23). Unlike judicial consideration of colonization, however, Aboriginal women stress the contemporary dimensions of colonization and its impact on both men and women. Aware of racism but equally concerned about the violence inflicted on women and children, respondents to the Ontario Native Women's Association's provincewide study on Aboriginal family violence were emphatic that they did not condone violence and wanted it stopped: 82 percent of respondents wanted their abusers charged even though they also expressed a fear of the wider implications of involving Canadian police in Aboriginal family disputes. The association's report emphasizes healing of all members of the family but solidly maintains, "Of course, the needs and safety of the abused woman and children are more urgent at first" (Ontario Native Women's Association 1989, 50). Its recommendations reflect this priority, referring first of all to the need to provide services and healing lodges for women and children who are victims of violence and second to treatment programs for batterers.

In other reports by Aboriginal women on family violence, it is clear that the twin realities of racism and violence inform the analysis of strategies. In Alberta, the author of a report on abused Aboriginal women notes that for "too many Aboriginal women the inability of Aboriginal communities to protect her and her children from abuse means the only option is to relocate outside the community" (Courtrille 1991, 23). Victimized in their own communities and victimized outside of it, even in shelters, such Aboriginal women do indeed find themselves between a rock and a hard place: either violence or the double victimization and harsh reality of being without community and family. Their insistence that culture is an issue when dealing with violence springs from an acknowledgment of this predicament. In the Northwest Territories, the Status of Women Council has also been clear that women's relationship to community is fraught with contradictions. The council's report on violence identifies as problematic community denial of abuse, alcohol used as an excuse for violent behavior, and the fact that "some of our worst abusers may be community leaders" (Northwest Territories Status of Women Council 1990b, 26–7). In a subsequent brief to the Judicial Inquiry into the Conduct of Territorial Court Judge R. M. Bourassa endorsed the position taken by Teressa Nahanee, noting that "reference to cultural considerations may be prejudicial to the delivery of justice to a particular culturally-defined group of victims" (Northwest Territories Status of Women Council 1990b, 11). Finally, in *Voices of Aboriginal Women: Aboriginal Women Speak Out about Violence*, a booklet published by the Canadian Council on Social Development and the Native Women's Association of Canada, Aboriginal women once again make clear why they prefer an approach to violence that is community-centered and focused on healing: "Most of the Aboriginal victims of family violence are women and children and the offenders are men. The Aboriginal victims must deal with the offender or be subject to exile outside the community, from their home, far from close relatives. It is important to realise that the victims and members of the family are victimized again by the system because they must leave their home and community. Aboriginal women feel that it is the offender that is most in need of help to break the cycle of violence, but is the most ignored. But the women do not want to give up their right to safety. So the logical approach is to intervene and take the offender away from home" (Canadian Council on Social Development and Native Women's Association of Canada 1991, 25–6). The dilemma that Aboriginal women face in being forced to choose between their personal safety and community was expressly acknowledged in the *Report of the Aboriginal Justice Inquiry of Manitoba*. Acknowledging the submission of Professor Emma Laroque on the issue of violence against Aboriginal women, Justices Hamilton and Sinclair concluded succinctly, "What they [Aboriginal women] are forced to run to is often as bad as what they had to run from. Why they feel they have to leave is a matter worthy of comment" (*Report of the Aboriginal Justice*

Inquiry of Manitoba 1991, 485). Drawing on submissions made to the Inquiry by Aboriginal women, the two commissioners describe in considerable detail the specific strategies necessary for the protection of Aboriginal women and conclude with a discussion of healing and Aboriginal women:

> As the victims of childhood sexual abuse and adult domestic violence, they have borne the brunt of the breakdown of social controls within Aboriginal societies. There was substantial support for an entirely new system, to break the cycle of abuse and to restore Aboriginal methods of healing designed to return balance to the community, rather than punish the offender. . . . We recommend that women be involved in the implementation of our recommendations, and that they be represented on the various administrative bodies that will become necessary. While the role of Aboriginal women in Aboriginal society is not well understood in non-Aboriginal circles, we have been told, and accept, that a resumption of their traditional roles is the key to putting an end to Aboriginal female mistreatment. The immediate need is for Aboriginal women to begin to heal from the decades of denigration they have experienced. But the ultimate objective is to encourage and assist Aboriginal women to regain and occupy their rightful place as equal partners in Aboriginal society. (*Report of the Aboriginal Justice Inquiry of Manitoba* 1991, *507*)

Responses such as this speak of healing and community but also speak of the safety of women and of equality; they are different in a significant way from the forgiving approach noted by Ross and Lilles because they attempt to come to terms with women's realities at the intersection of racism and sexism.

White judges and lawyers seeking neat culturally sensitive, ungendered solutions to justice have not often stopped to question their authority to interpret Aboriginal culture, history, and contemporary reality. Self-reflexivity has been entirely absent from discussions of culture and the courts. Talal Asad's point that "'cultural translation' is inevitably enmeshed in conditions of power – professional, national, international" would suggest that Canadian courts must begin with the *contemporary* fact of white supremacy in and out of the courtroom and not simply get by with a passing reference to its history and hazy references to contemporary cultural biases and social conditions (Asad 1986, 163). There are, however, perils in calling for an interrogation of notions of culture in a legal context. Clearly, women and children who are victims of violence do not stand in relation to culture as do their assailants. We will need to ask, as Leila Abu-Lughod did about the Bedouin communities she studied, how cultural responses work to sustain the power differences within groups, such as the difference in status between men and women (Abu-Lughod 1991, 162). This does not then become a dichotomy between culture and gender but an interrogation into how culture is gendered and gender is culturalized. A second, equally compelling issue is that a discussion about culture may well displace an inquiry into domination: "Culture is the essential tool for making other. As a professional discourse that elaborates on the meaning of culture in order to account for, explain, and understand cultural difference, anthropology also helps construct, produce and maintain it. Anthropological discourse gives cultural difference (and the separation between groups of people it implies) the air of the self-evident" (Abu-Lughod 1991, 143). It is not difference that is feared, Cherrie Moraga notes, but similarity. The oppressor fears "he will discover in himself the same aches, the same longings as those of the people he has shitted on . . . he fears he will have to change his life once he has seen himself in the bodies of the people he has called different" (Moraga 1992, 26). The eagerness with which theories of cultural difference are taken up in the justice system while racism and sexism remain unnamed is a reminder that culture is treacherous ground to travel. The two cases that follow illustrate this danger.

Kitty Nowdlok-Reynolds and Donald Marshall: Culture or Racism?

The case of Kitty Nowdlok-Reynolds, an Inuk woman brutally raped by an Inuk man, provides one example of how little culture can have to do with the way Aboriginal women who are victims of violence are treated in the justice system (Royal Canadian Mounted Police Public Complaints Commission 1992). Following the arrest of her attacker, Kitty Nowdlok-Reynolds moved from the North to Vancouver as she had prearranged before her attack. The police failed to get a statement prior to her leaving, and after a series of inept police bureaucratic maneuvers, Crown counsel sought and obtained a warrant for her arrest in order to compel her attendance in court in the Northwest Territories, two thousand miles away. The warrant was executed and Nowdlok-Reynolds was taken in handcuffs, jailed for five days, and escorted from Vancouver to Edmonton to Yellowknife, and then back to Edmonton to Toronto to Ottawa and finally to Iqaluit, Northwest Territories. Uninformed of her rights, kept in five jails, denied showers, and ultimately transported to the courtroom in the same vehicle as her attacker, Nowdlok-Reynolds was eventually released, and arrangements were made for her to fly unescorted to Vancouver, whereupon she was left to find her way home at one in the morning. As the commissioners appointed to hear her complaint concluded, Kitty Nowdluk-Reynolds was the victim of a brutal rape and the victim of the criminal justice system: we "may be pardoned," they opined, "for wondering which victimizing incident had the greater effect, the sexual attack on June 7, 1990 or the treatment accorded to her by the criminal justice system" (Royal Canadian Mounted Police Public Complaints Commission 1992, 47). The commissioners noted the practices and policies of the criminal justice system that focus on the accused and fail to respond to the needs and rights of the victims. They also identified bureaucratic and individual incompetence. As at no time could it be clearly established that the police were overtly racist or sexist, the commissioners did not acknowledge that racism was an important factor in how Kitty Nowdluk-Reynolds was treated.[13] In response to Nowdluk-Reynolds's assessment that at least one constable exhibited a prejudicial attitude to her because she was Inuk, the commissioners suggested that all new police recruits receive cross-cultural training. The report does not consider what enables police officers to exhibit the callousness they did to an Aboriginal victim of a brutal rape. Such a question would have required the commissioners to delve deeper into the social context of Aboriginal/white relations in order to reveal how racism produced responses to Kitty Nowdluk-Reynolds. Yet, even if the question of what causes such callousness cannot be answered, we must at least ask what sustains it. Either we conclude that police are generally insensitive to this degree (for the commission clearly established police insensitivity) or we face the fact that together Kitty Nowdluk-Reynolds's race and gender produced specific police responses. A knowledge of Inuit culture, even knowledge that took into account gender, would hardly have altered these responses to her.

When it was established that Donald Marshall, a Mi'kmaq, was imprisoned for eleven years for a murder he did not commit, an inquiry into the Nova Scotia justice system forced a naming of what remained unnamed in the case of Kitty Nowdluk-Reynolds: racism. Here, too, as Aboriginal and white commentators noted, the difficulties around naming and describing racism were manifest throughout the inquiry. For example, as James Youngblood "Sakej" Henderson pointed out, "race was perceived as an essential quality that marks a person's identity" (Henderson 1992, 37). Racism could only consist of overt, intentional acts (of which there were ample examples); systemic racism and "the hazy line between racism and incompetence and negligence" remained unexamined as it did in the Nowdluk-Reynolds inquiry (Henderson 1992, 41). The end result, as Joy Mannette argues, was that, notwithstanding testimony of an overtly racist nature from police, judges, and lawyers, Donald Marshall was deemed to have lost eleven years of his life in jail due to "human fallibility, in the guise of individual incompetence, which caused the apparent systemic breakdown" (Mannette 1992, 65).

In the face of such a widespread denial of racism in the justice system, culture had an interesting role to play in the Marshall inquiry. Minority voices were included in the inquiry, for example in the form of testimony from a white psychiatrist as to what happens when Mi'kmaq people encounter the judicial process, testimony that resembled the kind of cultural information with which Ross and Judge Lilles were working, namely, the tendency of Aboriginal witnesses to remain aloof and uncommunicative when testifying in court (Mannette 1992, 68). Instead of helping to contextualize the responses in court of Aboriginal witnesses, Mannette suggests that such testimony psychologized what might be better characterized as an institutional problem: Donald Marshall's cultural unease with the entire judicial process. She maintains that the distinct and non-Western configuration of Mi'kmaq society remained unacknowledged and its distinctiveness disappeared under the banner of cultural diversity: "Mi'kmaq world view emerges in the Marshall Inquiry, then, as an excluded, not preferred interpretative framework within a dominant ethnic hegemonic order" (Mannette 1992, 72). Mannette has identified, in this argument, a major risk that is taken whenever culture and not racism becomes the focal point: the answer to the "problem" becomes one of inclusion, most often through the device of cultural sensitivity and by extension, cross-cultural training. At no time is the justice system examined for the ways in which it is organized to the cultural advantage of the dominant group.

Risks for Immigrant Women

As in the case of Donald Marshall, when immigrant women plead for cultural considerations to be taken into account, they can very quickly find themselves backed into a multicultural corner. As Homi Bhabha commented (in reference to the exoneration of Clarence Thomas from the charge of sexual harassment of Anita Hill), "Suddenly, lip service is paid to the representation of the marginalized. A traditional rhetoric of cultural authenticity is produced on behalf of the 'common culture' from the very mouths of minorities. A centralizing, homogeneous mode of social authority is derived from an ever-ready reference to cultural 'otherness'" (Bhabha 1992, 235). The culturalization of racism, whereby minorities are seen as culturally inferior, makes any foray into cultural difference risky. Attempts by women of color to draw the connections between racism, sexism, and violence have sometimes floundered in the wake of these powerful currents of racism. How will the story of rape from within one's own cultural group be heard by the dominant group when, as Yasmin Jiwani concluded from her study of South Asians in the media, South Asian women, "whether muslim, hindu or sikh," are portrayed "as victims trapped in the patriarchal mould of the east" (Jiwani 1992, 14)? Muslim, Hindu, and Sikh men confirm handily the superiority of Western men (and not incidentally, the right of Western men to eradicate them in the Gulf War) in this scenario. Indeed, as Jiwani recounts, responses from white women to articles on Muslim women and the veil included the sentiment that, in comparison to Eastern women, Western women should consider their own men "as gems of enlightenment and kindness" (Jiwani 1992, 14).

Culture as a defense used by men of color has been rejected by Canadian courts, for example, in *R. v. Betancur* (1985) when the offender, of Colombian origin, attempted to argue that his cultural background explains how he might have misinterpreted the behavior of the victim. However, Canadian judges have also accepted a cultural defense from men of a non-Anglo-Saxon background, relying in some instances on testimony from psychiatrists about the connection between rape and a "cultural and perverse lifestyle" (*R. v. E. G.* 1987, 379), Judicial comments include, in *R. v. S. (D. D.)* that a culturally based "absolute patriarchy" explained the offender's character and tendency to dominate his wife; and in *R. v. L. (K.)* the accused's and the victim's South Vietnamese cultural backgrounds sanctioned "a pathological relationship" of physical abuse by the male and passive acquiescence of the women *(R. v. S. [D. D.]* 1988, *15; R. v. L. [K.]* 1989, 3). Culture, when it is taken into account, usually reinforces the dominant group's superiority, as when a male of Polish origin who is found guilty of sexual assault is described sympathetically by the court as being a new immigrant "perhaps unfamiliar with Canadian social mores or the rules of social interaction" (*R. v. Drozdkik* 1988, 5).

Although women of color, like Aboriginal women, have consistently named patriarchal violence within the context of racism and the histories of colonialism and imperialism, the second part of the message is unlikely to be heard as strongly as the first. Women of color have often found it necessary, for instance, to distance themselves from the culturalization of violence while arguing at the same time for culturally sensitive services for women who have been victims of silence. Thus the Coalition of Immigrant and Visible Minority Women of British Columbia states in its report to the British Columbia Task Force on Family Violence that "no culture condones violence" (Jaffer 1992, 204). A study done by African women in Toronto observes that culture is a "cocoon in which people, especially men, hide and use to oppress others" (Musisi & Muktar 1992, 22). An Ontario study of the needs of culturally diverse assaulted women makes equally clear that "contrary to the prevalent stereotypes about the cultural acceptance of violence against women in non-Western countries, there is no tolerance for violence anywhere." This study also affirms unequivocally: "The contexts in which women experience abuse by their partners must be taken into account if abuse is to be understood and adequate services provided. Women's experiences in their home countries, their approach to community, their encounter with racism, sexism, and classism in the dominant culture, are part of these contexts" (Mahboubeh 1991, 5).

Immigrant women have described their problems around violence as one of equality of access and the services to assist survivors of violence as suitable only to the needs of Anglo-Saxon and/or French-Canadian women (Rafiq 1991, 12). From this point of departure, cross-cultural service delivery becomes the goal for service providers of the dominant groups. Yet rarely is it noted that majority group members usually know very little about the impact of racism on the lives of the racialized women they serve. For instance, a handbook for service providers working with immigrant women includes a chapter on culture that begins with the notion that "it is just a gap in awareness that we need to fill in order to improve the quality of our service" (Coutinho 1991, 49). Although racism is mentioned and the author cautions that ethnocultural factors should not be confused with broader societal factors, the practical steps she suggests to improve cross-cultural service delivery emphasizes learning about behavioral differences such as eye contact and a variety of "cultural cues" that identify a person's cultural identity. Culture is once again taken to encompass a specific set of readily identifiable values, practices, and responses that characterize all the members of a particular group. More important, those who use broad generalizations about various cultures (nonrationality, stress on spiritual grace rather than material comfort, etc.) reveal an enormous potential to stereotype and rank cultures according to racist assumptions. The popularity of cross-cultural awareness sessions, in which service providers of the dominant group learn about cultural cues from charts that categorize the values of various cultures indicate that, while little has shifted in terms of who provides service and how those services are provided, immigrant women's demands for equality of access can be absorbed handily by a smattering of stereotypes acquired by white service providers and legal professionals in the name of cross-cultural sensitivity.

Culture as an Oppositional Weapon

The risks of talking culture are immense. What is too easily denied and suppressed in this discussion is power. Reflecting on the problems of anthropologists in doing cross-cultural representation, Thomas McCarthy comments, "Good intentions and literary inventions alone cannot compensate for massive inequalities in the conditions of communications. The crisis of cross-cultural representation could be resolved in the end only through cross-cultural communications that were actually, rather than virtually, decentered and multivocal, that is, only through the actual empowerment of 'others' to participate as equal partners in the conversation of humankind" (McCarthy 1992, 645). Massive inequalities in the conditions of communications require us to pay attention, in McCarthy's words, to text consumption as well as text production. While cultural considerations may be intended to promote sensitivity, dominant groups too readily adopt the cultural differences approach, relieved not to have to confront the realities of racism and sexism. The challenge is therefore how to reduce these massive inequalities in communication so that racialized women can speak as well as be heard as they intended, without risking further marginalization.

Cross-cultural sensitivity training will be of little use unless it is pursued in the context of the greater empowerment of the subordinate group. The project of working across cultures must, for a start, include an acknowledgment of contemporary relations of domination and how they are lived. For example, the cross-cultural training endorsed by the Aboriginal Justice Inquiry of Manitoba includes not only matters relating to Aboriginal culture but also issues of discrimination and profiles of the enormous socio-economic injustice that is contemporary Aboriginal reality. More important, cross-cultural training is pursued alongside of self-determination and the creation of a separate Aboriginal justice system. For our part, immigrant women such as myself, who are not faced with the issues of land claims and sovereignty, must watch out instead for the ethnicization of our concerns. Legal professionals and service providers must come from our own communities. While it may be worthwhile to communicate cultural differences to members of the dominant group, we also ought never to forget how rooted such differences are in our histories of racial oppression. In exploring what Euro-American nurses need to know about their African-American clients, Evelyn L. Barbee suggests that a priority has to be understanding "the consequences of Euro-American patriarchy" and the role that racism plays in supporting the abuse. Specifically, she cites Ashbury's six factors that influence battered African-American women seeking help: the number of shelters available in African-American communities; the amount and nature of a friend and family support system; social isolation experienced in a society dominated by Euro-Americans; reluctance to expose an African-American man as a batterer because he is more vulnerable than a white man; internalized media stereotypes of African-American women; and concern for endangering her relationship when there are so few African-American men available (Barbee 1992).

Cultural considerations might be effectively deployed if they remain grounded in the realities of domination. In the courtroom, the cultural background of racialized women can be used to explain the structural constraints of our lives. For example, in seeking to have the court admit an anthropologist as an expert on Aboriginal culture in the rape trial of Bishop Hubert Patrick O'Connor (accused of raping several of his Aboriginal pupils), the Crown prosecutor argued as follows: "Dr. Van Dyke is simply going to tell us, tell the court something about general widely applicable attributes of, we call it not necessarily Native culture, but traditional culture. The witnesses are going to say, they're not going to say, 'I came from a traditional culture'; they're going to tell the court, 'When I came to school I didn't speak English, and this is what happened to me and this is how I dressed differently and I ate different food. . . .' Dr. Van Dyke is going to say that that creates a certain relationship between the dominant culture and the subordinate culture, and whether that's of any value to the court or not is for the court, my lord" (*R. v. O'Connor*, 1992, 33). It will not be easy, however, to talk about culture and domination in the same breath. In the trial above, the judge raised a host of objections to such testimony, which we might expect. Evincing some irritation that the expert would in fact be telling the court what to think and how to assess the evidence, Justice

Thackray wondered how he could be expected to move from generalizations about Aboriginal communities to the specific complainant (*R. v. O'Connor*, 1992, 16). He also complained about the impending prospect of being given a seminar on social issues in a forum in which one was not appropriate (*R. v. O'Connor*, 1992, 18). Finally, the charges against Bishop O'Connor were stayed after the Crown failed to comply with earlier orders to disclose to the defense notes and tapes of interviews with the four complainants and the files of therapists and other medical personnel. The Crown's appeal of the decision to stay charges will bring the issue of access to women confidential medical records to the fore, and groups representing Aboriginal women, women with disabilities, the Women's Legal Education and Action Fund, and the Canadian Mental Health Association who have been granted intervenor status will argue, among other things, that mandatory disclosure of private communications with medical professionals will have the effect of deterring victims of sexual assault from seeking treatment (R. v. O'Connor and Aboriginal Women's Council, Canadian Association of Sexual Assault Centres, Disabled Women's Network Canada, the Women's Legal Education and Action Fund, and the Canadian Mental Health Association 1993). To fully contextualize the lives of women and children who are sexually assaulted, feminists working in law take a risk that information is likely to be used against women and children as much as for them. In talking about culture and domination, therefore, while we will have to stand on firm ground and stay away from broad unsubstantiated generalizations about cultural values and practices, we will also have to be careful in how we choose to describe specific practices of domination against racialized women. There can be no casual, unreflective use of culture in the courts.

Notes

1. Crown attorneys refer to lawyers representing the state in federal jurisdiction.
2. The Aboriginal people of Canada include Indian, Metis, and Inuit people. *Indian* typically refers to Aboriginal people entitled to be registered as Indians (Status Indians) according to the Indian Act of Canada, although there are many people of Indian ancestry not entitled to register under the Act for a variety of reasons; *Metis* refers to Aboriginal people of mixed blood, and *Inuit* refers to Aboriginal people known formerly as Eskimos. The word *Native* is also used to refer to Indian, Metis, and Inuit people.
3. In Canada, many Aboriginal children were forcibly removed from their homes and taken away to residential schools run by the Catholic church. Allegations of rampant sexual and physical abuse are increasingly common, and many cases have been proven.
4. I have used the term *racialized women* to refer to women whose ethnicity, as indicated by skin color, accent, religion, and other visible markers, denotes that they are of non-Anglo-Saxon, non-French origin. In the eyes of the two dominant groups, such women are raced.
5. Wriggins argues that rape will continue to be treated in the criminal justice system in a racist manner as long as society is racist. Black men convicted of raping white women will continue to be punished more severely than when black women are the victims (135–40).
6. There are obviously parallels here to how intoxicated non-Aboriginal victims of sexual assault are treated, but I would argue that the pervasiveness of the stereotype of the drunken

Indian ensures that, for the judiciary and for society, Aboriginal women's intoxication offsets the harm of sexual assault.

7. Note that consent is not an issue in the case of rape of a girl under fourteen years of age.

8. It has been suggested that Judge Bourassa's original attraction to a community disposition in *R. v. Naqitarvik* stemmed in fact from his special concern for the survival of a small and fragile Arctic Inuit community (Bell 1991, 37).

9. Twenty-nine cases prior to 1989 and ten cases from 1989 to 1992 confirm Nightingale's conclusions on sexual assault cases in predominantly Northern jurisdictions.

10. Note that the word *disadvantaged* implies that the problem is one of bad luck. There is thus no agent of domination, whereas to say *oppressed* implies that oppressors exist.

11. A chart of Native and white value systems is popular not only among judges in their training sessions but is also used by some sexual assault centers in their recent bid to understand cultural differences. One handout used by the Hamilton Sexual Assault Centre correctly attributes the original description of Native values to Justice Thomas Berger 1977, 1:93–9. The Berger report was highly influential and remains a frequently cited description of Native culture.

12. Ideas for Aboriginal justice systems and community-based initiatives have been advanced for some time in Canada, particularly by Aboriginal communities themselves. Most recently, the Law Reform Commission has cautiously endorsed the idea. While the commission is careful to explore potential difficulties, gender-based concerns are not among these (Law Reform Commission of Canada 1991, 16–23). A public inquiry into the administration of justice for Aboriginal people in Manitoba concluded more strongly that a separate Aboriginal justice system was required but stressed also that Aboriginal self-government and the settlement of land claims were necessary steps before justice could be served. The concerns of Aboriginal women are addressed in this report (*Report of the Aboriginal Justice Inquiry of Manitoba* 1991, 639–74).

13. The suggestion that we should presume that racism exists in such a context unless disproven has been strenuously resisted in the Canadian context. A report prepared for the Ontario Human Rights Commission that suggested that, because racism is the norm, the tendency to assume an accuser is not racist skews the process of investigation was relected out of hand by the attorney general, Marion Boyd. Boyd told reporters that this amounted to tampering with an investigation (Mackie & Abbate 1993).

References

Abu-Lughod, Leila (1991). Writing against Culture. In: Richard Fox (ed.), *Recapturing Anthropology*, pp. 137–62. Santa Fe: School of American Research Press.

Asad, Talal (1986). The Concept of Cultural Translation in British Social Anthropology. In: James Clifford & George E. Marcus (eds.), *Writing Culture: The Poetics and Politics of Ethnography*, pp. 141–64. Berkeley and Los Angeles: University of California Press.

Barbee, Evelyn L. (1992). Ethnicity and Woman Abuse in the United States. In: Carolyn Sampselle (ed.), *Violence against Women: Nursing Research, Education and Practice Issues*, pp. 153–65. New York: Hemisphere.

Bell, Jim (1991). The Violating of Kitty Nowdluk. *Arctic Circle*, July/August, pp. 32–8.

Berger, Thomas (1977). *Northern Frontier, Northern Homeland: The Report of the Mackenzie Valley Pipeline Inquiry*. Ottawa: Supply and Services Canada.

Bhabha, Homi (1992). A Good Judge of Character: Men, Metaphors, and the Common Culture. In: Toni Morrison (ed.), *Race-ing Justice, En-gendering Power: Essays on Anita Hill, Clarence Thomas, and the Construction of Social Reality*, pp. 232–50. New York: Pantheon.

Brittan, Arthur & Mary Maynard (1984). *Sexism, Racism, and Oppression*. Oxford: Blackwell.

Bumiller, Kristin (1991). Fallen Angels: The Representation of Violence against Women in Legal Culture. In: M. A. Fineman & N. S. Thomadsen (eds.), *At the Boundaries of Law*, pp. 95–112. New York: Routledge.

Calmore, John O. (1992). Critical Race Theory, Archie Shepp, and Fire Music: Securing an Authentic Intellectual Life in a Multicultural World. *Southern California Law Review* 65(5), pp. 2129–30.

Canadian Council on Social Development and Native Women's Association of Canada (1991). *Voice of Aboriginal Women: Aboriginal Women Speak Out about Violence*. Ottawa: Canadian Council on Social Development.

Courtrille, Lorraine (1991). *Abused Aboriginal Women in Alberta: The Story of Two Types of Victimization*. Edmonton: Misener-Margetts Women's Resource Centre.

Coutinho, Tereza (1991). Culture. In: Rafiq 1991, pp. 49–64.

Essed, Philomena (1991). *Understanding Everyday Racism: An Interdisciplinary Theory*. Newbury Park, CA: Sage.

Forde, Jan, Paula Pasquali & Alexis Peterson (1991). A Victim-Centred Approach. *Yukon News*, July 12, pp. 7–9.

Henderson, James Youngblood "Sakej" (1992). The Marshall Inquiry: A View of the Legal Consciousness. In: Joy Manette (ed.), *Elusive Justice*, pp. 35–62. Halifax: Fernwood.

Jaffer, Mobina (1992). *Is Anyone Listening? Report of the British Columbia Task Force on Family Violence*. Vancouver.

Jiwani, Yasmin (1992). To Be and Not to Be: South Asians as Victims and Oppressors in the *Vancouver Sun. Sanvad* 5(45), pp. 13–15.

Law Reform Commission of Canada (1991). *Report No. 34 on Aboriginal Peoples and Criminal Justice*. Ottawa: Law Reform Commission of Canada.

Lilles, Heino (1990). Some Problems in the Administration of Justice in Remote and Isolated Communities. *Queen's Law Journal* 15, pp. 327–44.

Lilles, Heino (1992). A Plea for More Human Values in Our Justice System. *Queen's Law Journal* 17, pp. 328–49.

McCarthy, Thomas (1992). Doing the Right Thing in Cross-Cultural Representation. *Ethics* 102(3), pp. 635–49.

Mackie, Richard & Gay Abbate (1993). Boyd Rejects Human Rights Report on Racism. *Globe and Mail*, July 15, A14.

MacQueen, Ken (1992). Academia Goes for the Judicial Jugular. *Toronto Star*, December 18, A4.

Mahboubeh, Katirai (1991). *Assessing the Needs of Alternative Services for Culturally Diverse Assaulted Women*. Hamilton, ON: Interval House of Hamilton-Wentworth.

Mannette, Joy (1992). The Social Construction of Ethnic Containments: The Royal Commission on the Donald Marshall Jr. Prosecution. In: Joy Manette (ed.), *Elusive Justice*, pp. 63–78. Halifax: Fernwood.

Marcus, Sharon (1992). Fighting Bodies, Fighting Words: A Theory and Politics of Rape Prevention. In: Judith Butler & Joan W. Scott (eds.), *Feminists Theorize the Political*, pp. 385–403. New York: Routledge.

Moraga, Cherrie (1992). La Guera. In: Margaret L. Andersen & Patricia Hill Collins (eds.), *Race, Class and Gender: An Anthology*, pp. 20–7. Belmont, CA: Wadsworth.

Musisi, Nakanyike & Fakiha Muktar (1992). *Exploratory Research: Wife Assault in Metropolitan Toronto's African Immigrant and Refugee Community.* Toronto: Canadian African Newcomer Aid Centre of Toronto.

Nahanee, Teressa (1992). Sex and Race in Inuit Rape Cases: Judicial Discretion and the Charter. Unpublished typescript in possession of the author.

Native Women's Association of Canada and Her Majesty the Queen, Reasons for Judgment (1992). Fed. C.A., June 11, Mahoney, J. A.

Native Women's Association of Canada, Gail Stacey-Moore and Sharon McIvor and Her Majesty the Queen, The Right Honourable Brian Mulroney and the Right Honourable Joe Clark in RE the Referendum Act, Applicants' Memorandum of Fact and Law in the Fed. Ct. (Trial Division), September 18, 1992, file No. T 2283–92.

Neely, Barbara (1992). *Blanche on the Lam.* New York: Penguin.

Nightingale, Margo (1991). Judicial Attitudes and Differential Treatment: Native Women in Sexual Assault Cases. *Ottawa Law Review* 23(1), pp. 71–98.

Northwest Territories Status of Women Council (1990a). Open Letter to Madame Justice Conrad. June 18.

Northwest Territories Status of Women Council (1990b). *We Must Take Care of Each Other: Women Talk about Abuse.*

Ontario Native Women's Association (1989). *Report on Aboriginal Family Violence.* Thunder Bay, ON.

R. v. Betancur. Dist. Ct. (Ont.) (1985). December 20, Reasons for Sentence, Weiller, J., file no. LSA 362.

R. v. Drozdkik. County Ct. (B.C.) (1988). March 31, Reasons for Sentence, Boyd, J., file no. CC870536.

R. v. E. G. C.A. (Ont.) (1987). *Ontario Appeal Cases* 20, p. 379.

R. v. Hoyt. C.A. (Yukon) (1992). January 17, Oral Reasons for Judgment, Taqqert, Lambert, and Hollinrake.

R. v. Hoyt. Terr. Ct. (Yukon) (1991). July 18, Reasons for Sentence, Lilies, C.J.T.C.

R. v. J. (E.). S.C. (Yukon) (1991). March 15, Judgment Delivered Orally, Madison, J., file no. 90–06337.

R. v. J. (H.). Pr,C. (B.C.) (1990). January 17, Reasons for Sentence, Barrett, J., file no, 1095FC.

R. v. Kowch. S.C. (Yukon) (1989). March 20, file no. 87-4661.

R. v. L. (K.). P.C. (Man.) (1989). September 18, Reasons for Sentence, Meyers, J.

R. v. M. (G.O.). S.C. (NWT) (1990). *Canadian Criminal Cases* 54(3d), p. 81.

R. v. Moses (1992). Terr. Ct. (Yukon). *Canadian Criminal Cases* 71(3d), pp. 347–85.

R. v. O'Connor. S.C. (B.C.) (1992). December 2, 1992, Excerpts of Proceedings at Trial.

R. v. O'Connor and Aboriginal Women's Council, Canadian Association of Sexual Assault Centres, Disabled Women's Network Canada, the Women's Legal Education and Action Fund, and the Canadian Mental Health Association. C.A. (B.C.) (1993). June 30, Written Reasons for Judgment of Application for Iritervenor Status, Taylor, J. A., Wood, J. A., Hoolinrake, J. A., Rowles, J. A. & Prowse, J. A., concurring.

R. v. Okkuatsiak (1987). *Nfld. & P.E.I.R.* 65, p. 233.

R. v. P. (J.A.) (1991). 6 C.R. (4th) 126. *R. v. P. (J.A.). Northwest Territories Reports* [1991].

R. v. Ritchie. County Ct. (B.C.) (1988). March 2, Reasons for Sentence. Houghton, C.C.J., file no. CC39/87.

R. v. Roach. S.C. (Yukon) (1987). December 8, file no. 523.87.

R. v. S. (D.D.). Prov. Ct, (Ont.) (1988). November 2, Reasons for Sentence, Lang-don, J.

R. v. T. (J.J.). C. A. (Sask.) (1989). April 26, Judgment Delivered Orally, Tallis, J. A., Vancise & Gerwing, J. A., concurring.

R. v. Vaneden. Terr. Ct. (Yukon) (1988). February 1, Reasons for Sentence, Ilnicki, J. R. v. Whitecap (R.T.) and Whitecap (D.M.). C.A. (Sask.) (1989). January 5, Judgment Delivered Orally, Gerwing, J. A., Tallis, J. A., concurring. Wakeling, J. A., in dissent.

Rafiq, Fauzia (ed.) (1991). *Toward Equal Access: A Handbook for Service Providers Working with Survivors of Wife Assault*. Ottawa: Immigrant and Visible Minority Women against Abuse.

"Report of the Aboriginal Justice Inquiry of Manitoba. Vol. 1. The Justice System and Aboriginal People" (1991). Winnipeg: Queen's Printer.

Ross, Rupert (1992). *Dancing with a Ghost: Exploring Indian Reality*. Markham, ON: Octopus.

Royal Canadian Mounted Police Public Complaints Commission (1992). *Public Hearing into the Complaint of Kitty Nowdluk-Reynolds: Commission Report*. Allan Williams, Q. C., S. Jane Evans, Lazarus Arreak, Vancouver.

Thobani, Sunera (1993). There Is a War on Women. A Desh Pradesh Workshop. *Rungh: A South Asian Quarterly of Culture, Comment and Criticism* 1(1&2), p. 12.

Tyler, Tracey (1992). Are Judges Guilty of Gender Bias? The Jury's Out. *Toronto Star*, December 2, A1, A17.

Wriggins, Jennifer (1983). Rape, Racism, and the Law. *Harvard Women's Law Journal* 6, pp. 103–41.

33

Fiaca and Veron–ismo: Race and Silence in Argentine Football

*Grant Farred**

Introduction

On the main highway leading from the airport into downtown Buenos Aires, a few miles before you reach the famous Avenida de Julio, the main street that goes through the heart of the city, there is a 20-storey high apartment complex. Emblazoned on it is a mural of Juan Sebastian Veron; before and after the disastrous 2002 Football World Cup campaign an Argentine national hero (Veron's return to the Argentine team, as well as the retention of heavily criticized coach Marcelo Bielsa, represents that rare sporting instance in which inglorious athletic failure is afforded the opportunity for rehabilitation by the national media). The image on that building in 'Baires', as the city is commonly referred to by the local inhabitants, is a salient one, both because of who Veron is and who he is not.

The mural is a signal accomplishment for the former Manchester United midfielder. It is surprising that in a nation that loves forwards, especially wayward, inspirational ones, here the Argentine capital chose to honour a midfielder. Moreover, Veron is a player who hails from the hinterland, his attachment to Buenos Aires is only secondary, a product of his brief stint with the city's most robustly supported club, Boca Juniors. In recent Argentine footballing history, the pantheon of national icons is dominated by forwards. The inaugural figure in this lineage is Mario Kempes, the prolific goalscorer with the flowing black locks who was instrumental in Argentina's victory in 1978. In that World Cup, the Dutch 'total footbal' philosophy – nurtured over two unsuccessful World Cups, 1974 (Germany) and 1978, replete as it was with all its erudition, artistry and sophistry – could not match Kempes' exploits upfront.

Kempes was supported, when Argentina won that first World Cup, by the disciplined goalkeeping of Jaime Filol and a defence well marshalled by the imperious center-back and captain, Daniel Passarella. In 1986, as England goalkeeper Peter Shilton needs no reminding, there was the goalscoring wizardry of Diego Maradona, one of Juan Veron's heroes and the greatest Argentine player ever – or, some would simply say, the greatest player ever. In the 1986 tournament, hosted by Mexico, Maradona's

* Pp. 47–61 from *Leisure Studies*, vol. 23, no. 1. © 2004 by Taylor & Francis Ltd. Reprinted with permission from the publisher (Taylor & Francis Ltd, http://www.tandf.co.uk/journals).

controversial 'hand of god' became the hand that lifted the World Cup trophy. Since Maradona's descent into drugs and infamy Argentina has produced strikers such as (the substance-abusing) Claudio Caniggia and Gabriel 'Batigol' Batistuta (an explosive marksman given to inexplicable outbursts and peripatetic tendencies, a player who has moved, it seems, too often from one prominent Italian club – Fiorentina, Roma, Inter – to another); Caniggia and Batistuta are, each in their own way, the very definition of prolificacy and waywardness. By virtue of being a midfielder alone, Veron's mural represents an emblematic moment in Argentine footballing culture.

Born and raised in a lower-middle-class family in El Mondogno, an area of La Plata, some 60 miles from Buenos Aires (only a province away but a world removed from the cosmopolitanism of the capital). Juan Sebastian is the son of footballer Juan Ramon Veron. Politically astute and aware of his nation's class stratifications. Veron grasped the import of the crisis that has wracked Argentina since 2001, Veron was especially conscious of the effects of the economic crisis on the national psyche in the aftermath of the inglorious Argentine failure at World Cup 2002. In Argentina, he remarked: 'we've always had what we would call the middle class, as well as the rich and the poor. However the middle class was gradually becoming part of the poorer class in Argentina' (Raphael, 2003). The footballer from the La Plata 'hinterland' had become, in the process of his own diasporization in Europe (and Britain), a cosmopolitan critic of Argentine national politics with acute consciousness of how vulnerable his society was to the workings of the global economy. Concerned about the stability of and security in his country, he hinted to a journalist that he is 'not sure about living in Argentina again'.

Like his father, the younger Veron played for the local club, Estudiantes. In the 1960s Juan Ramon was a talented forward nicknamed 'Bruja'. Juan Ramon was called the 'Witch' in part because of his hooked nose, a feature the younger Veron has inherited. The older Veron also earned his nickname because of the 'magic' in his boots, a characteristic for which the midfielder son is not quite as renowned. 'Seba', as the English commentators have dubbed Juan Sebastian, began his career with the team from La Plata at the tender age of 5. Ever attuned to the history of their clubs, Estudiantes, known as 'Los Diablos Rojos' (the 'Red Devils', a moniker they share with his former club, England's Manchester United) to their fans, bequeathed the father's sobriquet to the son. Estudiantes called the younger Veron 'La Brujita', the 'Little Witch'. Like father, like son.

Except, of course, that 'Seba' boasts a footballing résumé markedly more successful than his father's. After spending his early professional years, from 1993 to 1996, with his local club. Veron moved from Estudiantes to Boca Juniors of Buenos Aires where he played briefly with his idol Maradona (Boca is arguably the club most closely identified with the Argentine capital's working class; much more so than either River Plate or Racing, the other major clubs from Buenos Aires). Soon afterwards, with only 17 appearances for Boca, he was signed by Sampdoria of Italy's Serie A. He was with the Genoan club for two seasons before moving to Parma, winning a couple of trophies there, and then on to Lazio of Rome where he was warmly adopted by the 'tifosi', the rabid fans in the Italian capital.

Notoriously fascist and racist (they 'taunt rivals Roma with a banner reading "Black team, Jewish supporters"' (Hill, 2001a; see also Podaliri & Balestri, 1998), the 'tifosi' welcomed Veron's silky passing skills. The habitually intolerant Lazio fans did not, conveniently, pay too much attention to their midfielder's race (motivated, presumably, by footballing expedience and their own complex conception of race). The 'tifosi's' mis-recognition – or non-recognition – of Veron as 'black' may be explained in terms of regional origin. While he may not be physiogomically 'white', he was identified as 'Latin' (or even more narrowly, as 'Argentinian'), presumable to distinguish him racially from the identifiably 'black' players who hail from Africa or other parts of the ersthwhile European empire – such as the black Frenchman Lilian Thuram or Dutchman Edgar Davids, both of Juventus.

Described as an Argentine with some Italian ancestry, Veron possesses an Italian passport. Just prior to his move to Old Trafford, Veron was among a group of Argentine players involved in a controversy surrounding the veracity of his passport – holding a 'metropolitan' passport in addition to his national one enables him to play in Europe as an EU citizen. In the midst of the 2001 scandal, 'La Brujita' joined Manchester United where he revealed himself to be only an adequate midfielder, ranking well behind the black Frenchman Patrick Viera (of Arsenal, a player who fled the racism of Serie A, where he was a bit-performer for Juventus) and Englishman Steven Gerrard (Liverpool). Widely viewed as an under-achiever in England, Veron has frequently been linked with a return to Italy, especially to Lazio where he is still venerated. Instead, in the summer of 2003, he chose London's Chelsea.

It was clear from Argentina's World Cup plans that coach Marcelo Bielsa was going to run – to borrow basketball terminology – every one of his team's plays through Veron. National skipper Roberto Ayala's injury was, to cast this turn of events cynically, fortunate for him because Veron had already been installed as the de facto captain by the Argentine public and the media. With Ayala sidelined, Veron assumed the armband and the official role of team pivot. No one, it seemed, touched the ball without looking for Veron, no matter how well or how badly he was positioned. As no Argentine fan needs reminding, that strategy failed miserably, in part because Veron was not accustomed to a system that centralized him without allowing him to play his natural game. Veron built his reputation as creative midfielder, not as the Gerrard or Viera-like forager who could win the ball, but as the central player who was always available in space and able to hit raking, incisive passes and more than capable of scoring long-range goals.

In spite of his struggles with Manchester United that eventually led to his transfer to Chelsea in August 2003. Veron is still considered one of the preeminent modern midfielders, the powerful link man who can play off the strikers and regularly unleash the crisp shot on goal. But he failed miserably at the World Cup 2002. By Argentina's final game of the tournament. Veron's ignominy was complete as the gifted young Pablo Aimar of Spain's Valencia replaced him as the Argentine playmaker. 'Seba' gracefully took his place on the bench and, even when he did come on minutes from the end of Argentina's final game against Sweden, he looked a forlorn figure. Veron was aimless, adrift in a team that had been designed for him.

There were moments in that final game, punctuated as it was by a pathos that rarely articulates itself on the football field or even in relation to the game, when Veron's fate recalled that of the talented black English winger John Barnes. Brilliant in his play for his club Liverpool. Barnes was expected to carry a mediocre England team for two

World Cups after a breathtaking goal in 1984 at the Maracana stadium against Brazil. Just as Barnes was criticized for his 'poor' displays for the national team by the English press, Veron became, in that moment, yet another talented 'black' player who was labelled a club level powerhouse but a failure in the international arena.

The invocation of Barnes, however, is at once a resonant, ideologically inefficacious, and an athletically inaccurate way of characterizing Veron. Both Barnes and Veron have been deemed internationally sub-par, however inaccurate the evaluation may be – Veron certainly dazzled in moments at the World Cup 1998 when he put the England midfield to the sword, while Barnes never set the stage alight in his two appearances (Mexico 1986 and Italia 1990). Unlike Veron, Barnes was a massive success as a club player, supreme in his ability to stand out in the great Liverpool sides of the 1980s, an accomplishment that seems likely to elude the Argentine. However, Barnes and Veron differ most in terms of their articulation around matters of race: Veron is silent where Barnes is eloquently forthright (they are also different in relation to the issue of nationalism, since Barnes has always stood disjunctively in relation to his – black – Englishness while Veron embraces his Argentineness unquestioningly). As Barnes made clear throughout his career and with a compelling erudition in the opening lines of his autobiography, he has always been a self-consciously black player:

> Short of size and breath, the policeman kept about twenty yards behind me, trailing me for all his worth. As I continued my way through the streets of London, I knew what was going through the policeman's mind. He was convinced this black boy was heading down Wigmore Place intent on burglary . . . Being followed after dark by the police became part of my life . . . I had to turn down Wigmore Place – I lived there. (Barnes, 1999, p. 1)

A consciousness of racism was integral to Barnes's life (Hill, 2001b) while, Veron, on the other hand, is symptomatic of Argentine society: race is a subject that Argentines almost never address. More precisely, it is not that race represents an impermissible discourse but that it constitutes a political complex that lies beyond the purview of Argentine consciousness. Metaphorized as the Buenos Aires vernacular, race is *fiaca*. The absence of a racially conscious discourse marks a retreat from the politics of race. *Fiaca* represents the circumscription of the everyday economies of racial politics as it obtains in the rest of Latin America and the post-colonial world.

On Sunday afternoons, 'Portenos' (as the residents of Buenos Aires are known) engage in a social practice dubbed '*fiaca*.' After lunch they leave their homes and inhabit public spaces, many of them spacious green parks on a waterfront dotted with boats. *Fiaca*, however, marks less a withdrawal from the mundane into the pleasurable than it does a disengagement with the political. *Fiaca* is the act of ideological retreat. Temporally, it takes place in that limited, imagined, moment between intense domesticity, the most important meal of the week and its social accoutrement, and the resumption of labour – the mythical, almost Fordist work week, since this is a nation where many citizens do work on Sundays. This paper will use *fiaca* as a metaphor to discourse broadly about how race, the historic silences that mark Argentine history and culture, the paradigm of post-coloniality, and how this Latin American – or Southern Cone, to be more specific – nation's self-imaginings can be read off the body of the black footballer.

This paper posits Juan Sebastian Veron as a black footballer, although he will neither speak nor acknowledge his own racial Otherness, in order to critique the wider cultural politics of race in contemporary Argentina; or, the absence of a politics of race. Veron figures here as a Barthesian 'double articulation': he, and more precisely, his body, in its palimpsestic ideological enunciations (the racialized, often against its own representation of itself, Latin body that is subjected to post-colonial scrutiny), 'speaks' both as cultural icon and multiply inscribed political text, Veron is read here as sports star, the national icon that, like all celebrities, resonates beyond, speaks for, and is appropriated (and expropriated) by constituencies well beyond his own cultural terrain, the Argentine and international football field. However, in order to 'doubly articulate' Veron as the enunciation of *fiaca* this paper will, especially in the following section, outline the paradigm that produced the footballer, and only rarely invoking him, in order to understand his contextual grounding. Explicating his context will enable an extrapolation of and from the conditions that influenced Veron, the construction of the midfielder as a metaphoric Argentine who originates but stands removed from Latin America; the Argentine who is racially disjunctive from the nation but ideologically representative of it.

This paper attributes Veron, by ironically invoking one of the most iconic figures in Argentine history, Juan Peron, as a cultural corollary to *fiaca*, the quality of 'Veronismo'; the capacity not to incite to radical social transformation, as 'Peronismo' did in post-War Argentina, but to maintain the silence around potentially disruptive ideological and historical issues. 'Veron-ismo' is defined as the non-articulation of race, racial difference or racism in Argentine sport and the broader society. Mindful of the scholarship of Archetti, Alabarces and Romero on Argentine sport, (see Archetti, 1994; Archetti & Romero, 1994; Alabarces, 1999; Alabarces et al., 2001) this paper addresses race, an issue largely neglected by these thinkers. For them, identity, masculinity, violence and nation are the key concerns.

In order to centralize race within Argentine cultural discourse, Veron is located here as representative, at the very least, 'evocative,' in current sports sociology terminology (Richardson, 2000, p. 5), of the overburdened conjuncture of race, racism, (national) difference, post-coloniality and historic silences (and silencings) in his national community. He is positioned directly in relation to (and sometimes as metonymic of) his nation so that Veron stands as more than simply a case study (though he is that, too, in moments) of the footballer that will not claim a racialized identity, even as he establishes himself as thoughtful critic of the Argentine nation-al.

Race is not an issue that Veron takes up at all, not in his native Argentina, not in the cauldron of football racism perpetrated by the supporters of Roman clubs such as Lazio, nor in an England where there is, because of the history of racist abuse and the recent success of black players, a heightened awareness of racism. Veron, the diasporic cosmopolitan, grapples with cultural difference, and its concomitant politics, in the Southern Cone and Europe, but he has remained impervious to racial articulation. Raced discourse is, within this discussion of him, made to 'double' back on his aporetic articulations. Racial reticence, 'Veronismo', is, rather, symptomatic of the Argentine predilection for silence/silencing. Veron is the footballer, the a/symptomatic body, whose cultural persona provokes, indeed, makes possible, crucial questions about his society: why does Veron, and Argentine society, silence his racial identity? Why does race constitute the racially unspeakable for so many Argentine constituencies?

Argentine Exceptionalism

As other Latin American societies will colloquially testify, Argentina has always thought of itself not only as different from the rest of the continent, but as not being of the continent at all. Argentina, in Latin folklore, is the South American country where the inhabitants speak Spanish but think in Italian, and identify with Europe. Buenos Aires is less, as popular parlance would have it, the Paris of Latin America than it, subliminally, imagines itself as being psychically at one with the capitals of Europe. Its residents, especially the 'Portenos,' live imaginatively in Paris, if only at a geographical remove. Argentina is, in the terms of this paper, in the relationship of the *fiaca* to its context. It signifies nothing so much as a deliberate disengagement from the rest of the continent – it is in Latin America but not of it. Argentina stands, in this way, as the refutation of Marxist historicism: in and for Argentina, context – the physical place that is inhabited – means nothing, or very little, at all.

This Latin American society may value and appreciate 'Latin' football skills but there is nothing of the Samba about the Argentine style of play. This is the team of the tango: emphatic defensive thrust followed by an equally emphatic, choreographed parry, occasionally interspersed with moments of individual brilliance and improvization. Forwards from Kempes to Caniggia may be venerated, but the success of its teams is built on a sturdy, almost militaristic defense. Daniel Pasarella, captain of the 1978 World Cup team was not, coincidentally, a military man, the player who best represented the glum authority and ruthless efficiency of the military dictatorship. Kempes, Ossie Ardiles, and the flamboyant Ricky Villa apart, the 1978 team had nothing of the resistant spirit of the *desaparecidos* ('*las madres do los desaparecidos*', those mothers protesting the 'Dirty War'[1] that was being waged even as the World Cup was being hosted and won by Argentina) about them. Pasarella's was a team of disciplined conformists, inadvertently (whether they liked it or not) the *generalisimo's* team that defeated the stylized brilliance of Johan Cruyff's Dutch masters. In a telling reversal of roles, the 1978 Argentina team played like a stereotypically efficient European side, while the Dutch – with their intricate, crisp passing and capacity to dribble and retain the ball – had very much the spirit of the inspired Latin team about them.

If Argentina thinks of itself as different from, not paradigmatically or ideologically a part of Latin America, it is in large measure because it conceives of itself as an outdated, imperialist Europe (Rock, 1987; Shumway, 1991). Which is to say, Argentina conceives of itself not as contemporary post-modernist, multiracial, racially and culturally hybrid Europe, the types of places where Veron. Batistuta and Aimar currently ply their trade (frequently on European passports), but as the Europe of the nineteenth-century colonialist project. Argentina's national self-image is, ideologically, deeply rooted in the nineteenth century. This 'long epoch' or the 'long duree' marks the moment when Argentina won its independence (1810) and the grand decades, 1852 to

1890, which saw the formation of the nation-state; the nineteenth century was also a period that saw massive European investment (especially by Britain). Well into the first half of the twentieth century Argentina, in a relationship only interrupted by the economic collapse of the 1930s, 'flourished as an informal component of the British Empire – smirkingly referred to as the 'sixth dominion' by British diplomats' (Rock, 2002, p. 60).

Centuries after being colonized, trading and culturally aligning with various European powers (from Spain to Italy to England), and huge-scale immigration by Europeans, in Argentina's national imaginary, its identity is white, an identity that Veron can be said to have assumed. Not in the problematic sense offered by contemporary theorists of whiteness where Euro-American roots are ontologically challenged, but in a nineteenth century imperial sense where whiteness is posited in relation to Otherness. With its historic attachment to Europe, Argentina conceives of itself as white because it is High Cultured, literate, and racially distinct from its Latin neighbours. Like so many understandings of the national self, Argentina's self-perception turns upon negation. Both in the sense that it prides itself upon *not* being the Other, and in that it distances its (national) self from the social, cultural, and racial 'lacks' of other South American countries. In relation to Latin America, Argentina thinks (of which residues remain despite the current crisis, made all the more evident by the strong showing by the reactionary Carlos Menem before he was defeated by Nestor Kirchner in the 2003 elections) itself more economically prosperous, more culturally advanced; it regards its infrastructure as more sophisticated, its education system more developed, and its national literature (in which the venerated figure of Jorge Luis Borges plays a seminal role)[2] more rich, complex and recognized in European capitals.

Argentine imperviousness to the demands of the continental local (and that of the local national) and to racial difference may stem from the 'lack' of its own indigenous populace which has, in Latin societies from Bolivia to Ecuador to Brazil, compelled attention to the issue. The capacity of the indigenous population to make its leadership accountable as native constituencies in the Andean nations have struggled to do – to offer the autochthonous as a viable ideological alternative and a pressing political concern – is absent in Argentine society. Without this kind of historically rooted internal pressure, deprived by its own violences of a 'local' counterpoint, Argentina has remained both largely insulated and, in the national imaginary, racially distinct from the rest of the continent. Argentina is not like any of its Southern Cone or Latin American neighbours: Argentina is not Chile, Argentina is not Peru, Argentina is not Uruguay.

Black Brazil

Most importantly, Argentina is not Brazil. For the best part of a century, Argentina has defined itself against its northern neighbour Brazil. Especially in terms of race, Argentines conceive of themselves as superior to Brazilians. When Argentina plays Brazil, the stakes are immeasurably high. In Veron's terms, these matches are a 'clasica,' a contest in which it is not only two countries, much like an India-Pakistan cricket test, engaged in high-intensity athletic warfare, but two cultures in competition. Argentina-Brazil football matches dramatize the multi-layered contestation between two sets of values, two conflicting national identities, and two antagonistic definitions and perceptions of Latin America. In these ideologically overdetermined 'clasicas', Argentine commentators, with no fear of censorship or approbation from their networks or their viewers, refer to the Brazilian players as 'macacos', monkeys. The 'macacos' designation functions as a Darwinian trope that dignifies Brazilian racial inferiority.

Through naming the Brazilians 'macacos', Argentina marks its opponents as belonging to an earlier, less developed civilization, invoking a racial typology that has through centuries of Orientalist discourse been associated with Africans or people of African descent. Africans, as colonized and decolonized subjects, in their native continent and in the diaspora, have long been dubbed 'macacos' or apes, ascribing to black subjects an inherent intellectual underdevelopment – blacks are innately simian and backward. The Argentine commentators are assigning to Brazilians a place as the racialized natives of the Conradian 'jungle', or, the rain forest, to make the topographical metaphor more geographically appropriate. The Brazilians stand in symbolic contradistinction to Argentines, who (continue to, however, precariously) trace their genealogies to Europe, be it north or south.

With the strong historical, physical and cultural presence of Africa in Brazil, blackness has been integrated – if not always immunized from denigration – into this Latin society. With the syncretization of faiths, the blending of Roman Catholicism with Africanist religious practices such as Candomble, Umbanda ('white' or beneficent magic) and Macumba ('black' magic), the borrowing of musical influences from Africa, Europe and the Americas, with the powerfully, residually, psychic relationship between West Africa and Brazil, blackness is a long established part of the Brazilian identity. Brazil's play has, since football travelled north from the Pampas (courtesy of British colonialism) to the land of the Sugar Loaf, been marked by the kind of flair, inventiveness, and freedom of expression admired the world over. Like the black cricketers of the Caribbean who bat and bowl with flair and ingenuity, Brazilian football is identified as charismatic, flamboyant and artistic.

Nowhere is the desire to emulate the Brazilian style stronger than in Africa, where one-time African Footballer of the Year was named Abedi 'Pele', after the Brazilian legend himself. 'Pele' may have started out as Abedi's nickname, but it soon branded him, and symbolically linked Africa to Brazil. Abedi's ambition was iconic, and fortunately his skills were sufficient so that the self-branding never became an embarrassment. For blacks in the diaspora and the continent alike, Brazil is the footballing motherlode: the site/side of origin, the Mecca of the game. While Brazilians are increasingly practicing their trade in Europe (and now, increasingly, in Japan's J-League), for decades black players from abroad have journeyed to Latin America to play there.

In Africa and Latin American societies that identify themselves as black, football functions as a reverse, and benign, cultural Middle Passage. Brazil's skill, flair and footballing vision, as well as its passion for playing the game with *joie de vivre*, is the diaspora's gift to the motherland. It is for this reason that Brazil's triumphs are celebrated the post-colonial world over as culturally racialized, 'black' victories. The triumph not only of the subaltern, but the triumph of a 'black' style, the articulate expression of samba way of playing sport – ever mindful, of course, of the stereotypes that attach to such forms of cultural articulation. It is for this reason that the Argentines, where freedom of cultural expression is so frequently absent (although the technical expertise and defensive organization is respected) could never serve as a model for Africa of the post-colonial world. There is nothing 'black' about the way Argentina plays, Diego Maradona's inspirational talents apart.

The Racially Unmixed

Unlike the inveterately mixed Brazilians (although they undoubtedly have their own racial hierarchization where whiteness is similarly valorized), with their commingling of African, and European heritage, Argentina's national fiction is founded upon the notion of racial purity. Argentina imagines its population to be constituted out of a blend of Europeanness – its citizens trace their roots to Italy, Spain, Germany and England. This is a problematic national imagining that reflects a crucial element of the Argentine identity. It is a nation where, with the exception of courageous groups of dissenters (such as the 'Mothers of the Disappeared', also known as the '*las madres de plaza de Mayo*' who opposed Argentina's 'Dirty War')[3] and now, President Kirchner, apart, historically, the populace has shown itself able to disengage from the atrocities of the past and the present. The history and the legacy of the dictatorships, the memory of the 'disappeared,' the genocide committed against the native subjects who once inhabited the now largely unpeopled province of Patagonia, those horrific events remain insufficiently addressed in Argentine society – it remains to be seen how successful Krichner's efforts at national psychic interrogation will be. Those memories are glossed only rarely in public discourse, they are more likely to be glossed over, ignored, silenced into an unspeakable history.

Similarly with race, Argentina can imagine itself to be putatively white, modernist European because it has never really accounted for the multiple traumas of its past. The Argentine nation can lay claim to whiteness because Otherness, the 'macacos' quotient, if you will, was exterminated without a substantive public recording or engagement with that past. The silence around Patagonia and the 'disappeared' (which is less considerable), the horrors committed historically against internal constituencies, marks a key instance of *fiaca*, a moment of collective national forgetting, illustrating disturbingly how the practice of *fiaca* functions.[4]

Key to the conversation about silence (and race and the repression of political memory) is the national non- or misrecognition of 'La Brujita', the enactment of 'Veron-ismo'. Physionogmically, Veron looks more 'Brazilian' than he does 'Argentine'. Even though, of course, Brazil has always had players who look identifiably white, such as the midfielder Juninho and the goalkeeper Marcos on the World Cup winning 2002 team. In complexion Veron resembles the Brazilian captain Cafu, he is maybe a shade lighter than the midfielder Gilberto.

As the racist discourse is deployed, however, Veron's difference – he does not look, physically, like any of his teammates, his darkness stands out in relation to their physiognomic whiteness – marks a crucial moment of 'Veron-ismo': the ideological and rhetorical forgetting, the paradigmatic refusal to produce a racialized discourse that attends to Veron's racial salience. Football commentators, the national press and Argentines in general, never comment on his racial difference. 'Veron-ismo' enables the recuperation of the black athletic body from racialized hybridity through the (silent) workings of Argentine national identity, through the discourses that have no vocabulary for public utterance. It is Veron's Argentine-ness that insulates him from racial epithets, it is his national citizenship that immunizes him from the Brazilian taint of the racially impure. It is, however, a visual spectacle so burdened with the ideology of racism that it implicitly emphasizes the contingency and complexity of both racist discourse and national identity. It is not simply that Argentine society is so adept at marking and demeaning 'foreign' blackness, but that 'Veron-ismo' is resilient in its refusal to see difference amongst its own national subjects.

Veron represents the racial pathologization of blackness, the tendency toward *fiaca*, strategic and deliberate disengagement, of the Argentine nation, with its own, unrecognizable Others. It is precisely because of his blackness, its public unspeakability, and his historic silence about it, that Veron is transformed into a signal figure. In his case, 'Veron-ismo' facilitates self-misrecognition: the overwriting of blackness by interpellative Argentine whiteness. The denial of blackness represents not only the repression of a discourse but the very ontology of Argentine-ness. Through the non-acknowledgement of his difference, 'Veron-isma' iterates itself as the cultural/athletic equivalent of *fiaca*. The nation that will not fully engage political atrocity or historic genocide will, similarly, not speak its Otherness as a discourse of intra-national difference. If the recognizably, identifiably, black subject – at the very least, the racially hybrid subject – does not mark himself as black, does not enunciate his difference, then the Argentine nation can unproblematically construct itself as not only imaginatively, but substantively, white. The nation can emblazon itself as publicly white on an apartment building in a black body because there is no counter-narrative available.

It is only in the moniker of 'La Brujita', the 'Witch', that the merest inkling of discomfiture within the paradigm of 'Veron-ismo' can be discerned. In the popular imaginary (especially of the literary variety, from children's stories to canonical texts such as *The Crucible*) the 'Witch' functions as a force of non-sociability, of transgression, a portent of social upheaval, a condition which Argentines have lived with all too intimately in the uncertain, desperate economic times that marked the post-2001 crisis. In Veron's case however, the pejorative connotations of the 'Witch' is evacuated, the insidious nature of this linguistic symbol is diluted through genealogy and diminutivization – the son's moniker carries no threat because it derives from the father's physiognomy. Because of the distinct footballing lineage of 'La Brujita,' Veron is represented as native, and non-threatening, to the nation. The 'Little Witch' has not only been domesticated, it has also been inserted as the figurehead of and for the dominant national cultural practice, rendered familiar (and, familial, in the sense that the nation imaginatively constructs itself as 'family'), integrated into whiteness and out of difference.

'Veron-ismo,' the rendering of Veron as not so much putatively but ideologically white marks the transcendence of Althusser's project of interpellation. It is not that Veron has been hailed or addressed into 'whiteness', rather, he has not needed to be interpellated: that is the ultimate triumph of the Argentine nation's racial/racist discourse. Veron, no matter his racial composition, is by ideological default always white in the Argentine public imaginary. This marks yet another articulation of Argentine exceptionalism (it is so different from the rest of Latin America that its own intra-racial differences need never be publicly, or even privately, spoken), lending Argentina a signality in Latin American discourse where blackness, in the form of both the native population (Bolivia, Ecuador, Brazil) and the progeny of enslaved Africans (Brazil, Venezeula), is acknowledged, compels the project of nation-building through racial difference.

In Argentina, interpellation exceeds and liquidates itself when it is no longer necessary to do the work of socio-political subject construction: when the subject is ontologized as white, when the very essence of the black subject – the black being – can unproblematically be construed as whiteness. When 'whiteness' simply is. In Veron's case, whiteness can instinctively, viscerally, be read off not his body, but his shirt, at once eviscerating the body and reifying the national shirt. The powder blue and white stripes of his Argentine national jersey is, symptomatically, the most powerful enunciation of 'Veron-isma'; the national cultural uniform is all that is required to mark him as not Brazilian. On the football field, more than any other venue, Argentina is not Brazil because it's players are all paradigmatically white. Argentina is not Brazil because its national team players are not, in the self-conception of its populace, racially mixed.

The Argentine nation is raced white because the sources of difference have either been erased or not acknowledged. So authoritative is Argentine national marking that Veron can not only be presumed the best qualified to lead the nation (as in the opening two matches of the World Cup), but he can do so without having his difference remarked upon. What the national disengagement with race represents, in Veron's case, is how in Argentina difference is not so much transcended as ideologically invalidated. Consequently, 'La Brujita' has not comprehended the salience of his own mural. The image of Veron stands out, but who he is visually – racially – cannot, will not, be afforded the same opportunity. 'Veron-ismo' means that he does not need to understand how, or, in fact, that he stands out. The Argentine subject is afforded whiteness inexorably. Veron's whiteness is integral to his ontology, there is nothing of the Fanonian 'black skin, white mask' about him because to be Argentine is to be white.[5] In contradistinction, of course, to Argentina's relationship to the rest of Latin America, where to be other than Argentine is to be inveterately Other.

Resisting the Post-Colonial

It is for this reason that post-colonial discourse, which enjoys such currency in contemporary European and North American critical discourse, has thus far had little if any purchase in Argentine thinking. The post-colonial is a concept, a historical experience, founded upon race: the oppression, exploitation, and liquidation of black and brown bodies; the resistance of those communities to European colonialism and the eventual liberation of Africa, Asia and the Caribbean from white European rule. More importantly, post-colonial theory of the last fifteen or twenty years has turned its attention as much to the colonial past and its deleterious effects as to the issue of how the black post-colonial subject has reconstructed the metropolis. London, Paris, Amsterdam, Berlin and Stockholm have over the last four decades been demographically, ideologically and culturally transformed by the post-colonial chickens who came 'home' to roost – and in the process remade the metropolitan coop.

As much as Argentina constructs itself as philosophically and epistemologically 'European,' it is at the post-colonial conjuncture where this displaced Latin American nation locates itself disjunctively in relation to the metropolis. This is the point at which Argentina disarticulates itself from imperial Europe, the post-modern post-colonial, as literary figures from Gabriel Garcia Marquez to Salman Rushdie make clear, is inconceivable without the problematic of difference. Post-colonial theory cannot gain a foothold in Argentine thinking because it is predicated upon the discourse of race, and racial difference, and the complications and unattainability of pure racial identity. In an Argentine society that understands itself as cosmopolitan, the post-colonial, and, ironically, Europe, the very origin of its epistemologies has to be rejected in part because the very conditions that transformed Europe, migrancy, gastarbeiters, the process of racial and cultural hybridization, are now increasingly manifesting themselves in Argentina. Economic migrants from Chile, Peru, Paraguay, Uruguay and, of course, neighbouring Brazil, and Africans from places as far away as Lagos, Nigeria who hawk in the markets of Buenos Aires, have been steadily making their way into Argentina and transforming the society. Implicitly with and explicitly without its consent, Argentina is being diasporized into post-coloniality and a concomitant blackness.

Independent for almost two hundred years, Argentina is now resisting post-coloniality. It will not allow the discourse of race public utterance because, paradoxically, that will not only mark its passage to post-coloniality, but will also align Argentina with a post-modern Europe and integrate it more fully, economically and culturally into Latin America. In order to become post-colonial Argentina has to, in a cultural sense, return itself to its geographical context. It has to, à la Marx, come home. Anachronistic mis-identification with Europe has to be resisted at this historical juncture because the metropolis is no longer distinct from the Latin American periphery.

Rio and London, home to the samba and the somber respectively, have at this moment more in common than Buenos Aires and Paris. Argentine exceptionalism becomes, through this rejection of the metropolis, the extreme(ly) abject condition. Conjointly, *fiaca* and 'Veron-ismo' demonstrates the process by which the erstwhile secondary (Argentina) becomes the primary (Europe) through excessive, outdated attachment to philosophical modalities and it also makes clear why the point of origin has to be rejected because it is no longer conceptually compatible. Most importantly, it reveals the epistemological fallacy and the cost of post-imperial Argentina exceeding post-colonial Europe in terms of its adherence to the paradigm of modernity. This is the height of Argentina's proclivity for *fiaca*. Argentina becomes, through this gesture, not so much nostalgic – for an imperial Europe – but fixated in both its fealty to a (modernist) mode of being and its resistance to recognizing its philosophical and historic anachronism.

In rejecting post-coloniality, Argentina disconnects itself from where it is. Historically alienated from Latin America, Argentina has now taken its distance and removed itself, in fundamental ways, from Europe. Geographically dislocated, conceptually and psychically displaced, Argentina reveals itself to be philosophically anachronistic – it belongs to an outdated notion of Europe inimitable to Europe itself. Philosophically, psychically and physically isolated at the far end of the South American continent, Argentina now has to rethink its relation to both Europe and its Latin neighbours.

Conclusion

All too often Argentina has turned in on itself in order to secure the verities and epistemological foundations of an earlier era, insisting upon claiming a past that was itself racially hybrid. The Argentine nation is fictionalizing itself once again, except that this time it is a fiction that has no currency outside of its borders; powerful and resilient though that fiction may be, it cannot postpone indefinitely a national interrogation into the purchase of 'whiteness' and exceptionalism within Argentina's borders. It is, as is to be expected in a moment of economic crisis (Rock, 2002, p. 60)[6] and social upheaval (when a cultural practice such as football is overly burdened with restoring internationally 'pride' in the ravaged national self), for this very reason that Veron has to be so resolutely rendered white: football is the most popular sport in the country, like it is in all of Latin and Central America, and it is in this public, international forum that the nation's self-representation must be most steadfast even as it is in danger of becoming ontologically uncertain.

If blackness has no public Argentine voice, even when the body itself is black, then the nation's whiteness cannot be drawn into question. If the moment of *fiaca*, the interregnum between independence and post-coloniality can be extended indefinitely, then through 'Veron-ismo' the engagement with the discourse of race can be further postponed. In this extended ideological interstices, Veron's signality can be reduced to an empty cultural signifier. For as long as *fiaca* remains the dominant made of racial politics as silencing, then 'La Brujita' from La Plata is simply the outstanding midfielder, the footballer who transformed his nation's perceptions of midfielders, affording them an iconic status once only lavished upon strikers. As long as *fiaca* is the preeminent form of racial discourse, it will not matter that Veron is eventually displaced (or complemented, as seems increasingly likely) by Aimar, who in any case has all the flair – and those flowing, unkempt, rock star-like locks – of a forward. Except, of course, if Veron's visage is able to exceed itself and 'Veron-isma' is interrogated.

Veron has to be disengaged from his talents and understood as a politicized visuality, as an affront to the nation, not as a confirmation of its powerfully incorporative sense of itself. His personage has to be de-lineated from his father's, a player during a different Argentine moment, but one not without its own post- (and inter-) Peronista silences. Veron has to be seen, metaphorically, if not literally (though the revealed black body at the end of the game exchanging shirts with the opposition can function as a visceral maker of different from his teammates), without the national jersey. The once iconic midfielder must be rehabilitated, not as a footballer, but as the subject of the nation's black unconscious. He must be made to stand outside the Argentine nation so that the nation might be capable of seeing itself as something other/Other than what it knows.

Argentina has to understand itself constitutively, not cumulatively, which is to say, it has to see itself as aporetic, racially disrupted, rather than continuous, racially homogenous. The silence around racial discourse has to become generative rather than an uninterrupted articulation of *fiaca*. Argentina must be made to look toward and engage Brazil and Ecuador and Bolivia and Chile. Most significantly, it must be made to work toward interrogating the silences of the past and the present. Argentina is a nation that has already taken too much of a discursive and ideological *fiaca* from race.

Acknowledgements

This paper is dedicated to Walter Mignolo and Pablo Wright. To Walter: Reluctant Argentine, universalist intellectual who gave me the opportunity to engage Buenos Aires. To Pablo Wright and his family for providing a first-hand experience of *fiaca* in 2001.

Notes

1. The Argentine president, Nestor Kirchner, has made the issue of the 'disappeared' a cornerstone of his policy Himself imprisoned by the military junta, he intends to establish a commission to investigate the death squads and to uncover, in so far as it is possible, those responsible for the murder of activists from that era: he has also proposed revoking immunity legislation which protects government officials from the period who were involved in the death of Argentine citizens. Kirchner's policy signals a major break, especially with his one time presidential rival. Carlos Menem in contemporary Argentine history with his preparedness to subject the Argentine past to public scrutiny.
2. Jorge Luis Borges (1899–1986) is considered the most Argentine of writers. Born in Buenos Aires, Borges learned to speak English before Spanish; he lived in Geneva as a teenager, acquiring not only a BA at the College of Geneva but also proficiency in French and German. Borges is heralded as the definitive Argentine author because his work, though rooted in and rotited through his native city, was influenced by European fiction and demonstrated the kind of universality associated with metropolitan artists. Borges is presumed to have produced an *oeuvre* that gave articulate voice to Argentine modernity as well as initiating the Latin American genre of 'fantastic realism'.
3. The notorious 'Dirty War', waged by successive military juntas between 1974 and 1983, has been written about extensively, both within and outside Argentine. See, for example, Taylor (1997), Partnoy (1986) and Verbisky (1996). U2's album. 'The Joshua Tree', also popularized this struggle with their song 'Mothers of the Disappeared'.
4. It is necessary to briefly explain that this critique of Argentine 'exceptionalism' is not unaware of how the 'mark of whiteness' enunciates itself form Mexico City to Medellin, from Santiago to Sao Paulo, from Quito to Caracas, often finding complex articulations on the football fired. In Chile, Uruguay and Venezuela, to mention just three, the all too often unengaged question of the post-colonial stirs but often unlike in Argentina, confronted by, and therefore contained by, the nativist and statist visions of these societies. But many Latin American countries, Brazil included – the nation that has never had a person of colour as a heard of state – the elite, the bourgeoisie, and the intellectual left – mediate their relationship to their own black subalterns and Europe with anxious, even envious glances in the direction of Buenos Aries.

5. Veron may claim, through the tattoo on his arm, Che Guevera as his hero, but there is nothing of the political or cultural radical about him. Much like the mural's racial salience is lost in and because of the workings of Argentine nation-alist discourse, so the Che tattoo functions as little more than an adornment of the black body.
6. See also Perry Anderson's essay, which primarily addresses the succession of 'Lula' as Brazilian president, but which touches on, in key moments, the current Argentine crisis in *The London Review of Books*, 18 December 2002.

References

Alabarces, P. (1999). Post–Modern Times: Identities and Violence in Argentine Football. In: G. Armstrong & R. Ginlianotti (eds.), *Football Cultures and Identities*, pp. 77–85. Basingstoke: Macmillan.

Alabarces, P., R. Coelho & J. Sanguinetti (2001). Treacheries and Traditions in Argentinian Football Styles: The Story of Estudiantes de La Plata. In: G. Armstrong & R. Giulianotti (eds.), *Fear and Loathing in World Football*, pp. 237–50. Oxford: Berg.

Archetti, E. (1994). Argentina and the World Cup: In Search of National Identity. In: J. Sugden & A. Tomlinson (eds.), *Hosts and Champions: Soccer Cultures, National Identities and the USA World Cup*, pp. 37–63. Aldershot: Ashgate.

Archetti, E. & A. Romero (1994). Death and Violence in Argentinian Football. In: R. Giulianotti, N. Bonney & M. Hepworth (eds.), *Football, Violence and Social Identity*, pp. 37–72. London: Routledge.

Barnes, J. (1999). *John Barnes: The Autobiography*. London: Healine.

Hill, D. (2001a). Football's Black Past Is Not yet History. *The Guardian*, July 7.

Hill, D. (2001b). *Out of His Skin: The John Barnes Phenomenon*. London: WSC Books.

Partnoy, A. (1986). *The Little School: Tales of Disappearance and Survival*. Pittsburgh, PA: Cleis Press.

Podaliri, C. & C. Balestri (1998). The *Ultras*, Racism and Football Culture in Italy. In: A. Brown (ed.), *Fanatics! Power, Identity and Fandom in Football*, pp. 88–100. New York: Routledge.

Raphael, A. (2003). Home Thoughts. *The Observer Sport Monthly*, March, No. 37, p. 42.

Richardson, L. (2000). New Practices in Writing Qualitative Research. *Sociology of Sport Journal* 17(1), pp. 5–20.

Rock, D. (1987). *Argentina 1517–1987: From Spanish Colonization to Alfonsin*. Berkeley: University of California Press.

Rock, D. (2002). Racking Argentina. *New Left Review*, September/October 17, pp. 55–86.

Shumway, N. (1991). *The Invention of Argentina*. Berkeley: University of California Press.

Taylor, D. (1997). *Disappearing Acts: Spectacles of Gender and Nationalism in Argentina's Dirty War*. Durham, NC: Duke University Press.

Verbisky, H. (1996). *The Flight: Confessions of an Argentine Dirty Warrior*. New York: The New Press.

VII

Identity, Lifestyle, Subculture

34

Subculture: The Meaning of Style

*Dick Hebdige**

Subculture: The Unnatural Break

Subcultures represent 'noise' (as opposed to sound): interference in the orderly sequence which leads from real events and phenomena to their representation in the media. We should therefore not underestimate the signifying power of the spectacular subculture not only as a metaphor for potential anarchy 'out there' but as an actual mechanism of semantic disorder: a kind of temporary blockage in the system of representation. . . .

Violation of the authorized codes through which the social world is organized and experienced have considerable power to provoke and disturb. They are generally condemned, in Mary Douglas' words (1967), as 'contrary to holiness' and Levi-Strauss has noted how, in certain primitive myths, the mispronunciation of words and the misuse of language are classified along with incest as horrendous aberrations capable of 'unleashing storm and tempest' (Levi-Strauss 1969). Similarly, spectacular subcultures express forbidden contents (consciousness of class, consciousness of difference) in forbidden forms (transgressions of sartorial and behavioural codes, law breaking, etc.). They are profane articulations, and they are often and significantly defined as 'unnatural'. . . . no doubt, the breaking of rules is confused with the 'absence of rules' which, according to Levi-Strauss (1969), 'seems to provide the surest criteria for distinguishing a natural from a cultural process'. Certainly, the official reaction to the punk subculture, particularly to the Sex Pistols' use of 'foul language' on television and record, and to the vomiting and spitting incidents at Heathrow Airport, would seem to indicate that these basic taboos are no less deeply sedimented in contemporary British society.

Two Forms of Incorporation

Has not this society, glutted with aestheticism, already integrated former romanticisms, surrealism, existentialism and even Marxism to a point? It has, indeed, through trade, in

*Pp. 130–42 from *The Subcultures Reader*, ed. K. Gelder and S. Thornton (New York: Routledge). © 1979 by Dick Hebdige. Reprinted with permission from Taylor & Francis Books UK.

the form of commodities. That which yesterday was reviled today becomes cultural consumer-goods, consumption thus engulfs what was intended to give meaning and direction. (Lefebvre 1971)

. . . The emergence of a spectacular subculture is invariably accompanied by a wave of hysteria in the press. This hysteria is typically ambivalent: it fluctuates between dread and fascination, outrage and amusement. Shock and horror headlines dominate the front page (e.g. 'Rotten Razored', *Daily Mirror*, 28 June 1977) while, inside, the editorials positively bristle with 'serious' commentary and the centrespreads or supplements contain delirious accounts of the latest fads and rituals (see, for example, *Observer* colour supplements 30 January, 10 July 1977, 12 February 1978). Style in particular provokes a double response: it is alternately celebrated (in the fashion page) and ridiculed or reviled (in those articles which define subcultures as social problems). . . .

As the subculture begins to strike its own eminently marketable pose, as its vocabulary (both visual and verbal) becomes more and more familiar, so the referential context to which it can be most conveniently assigned is made increasingly apparent. Eventually, the mods, the punks, the glitter rockers can be incorporated, brought back into line, located on the preferred 'map of problematic social reality' (Geertz 1964) at the point where boys in lipstick are 'just kids dressing up', where girls in rubber dresses are 'daughters just like yours'. . . . The media, as Stuart Hall (1977) has argued, not only record resistance, they 'situate it within the dominant framework of meanings' and those young people who choose to inhabit a spectacular youth culture are simultaneously *returned*, as they are represented on TV and in the newspapers, to the place where common sense would have them fit (as 'animals' certainly, but also 'in the family', 'out of work', 'up to date', etc.). It is through this continual process of recuperation that the fractured order is repaired and the subculture incorporated as a diverting spectacle within the dominant mythology from which it in part emanates: as 'folk devil', as Other, as Enemy. The process of recuperation takes two characteristic forms:

1   the conversation of subcultural signs (dress, music, etc.) into mass-produced objects (i.e. the commodity form)
2   the 'labelling' and re-definition of deviant behaviour by dominant groups – the police, the media, the judiciary (i.e. the ideological form).

The commodity form

The first has been comprehensively handled by both journalists and academics. The relationship between the spectacular subculture and the various industries which service and exploit it is notoriously ambiguous. After all, such a subculture is concerned first and foremost with consumption. It operates exclusively in the leisure sphere. . . . It communicates through commodities even if the meaning attached to those commodities are purposefully distorted or overthrown. It is therefore difficult in this case to maintain any absolute distinction between commercial exploitation on the one hand and creativity/originality on the other, even though these categories are emphatically opposed in the value systems of most subcultures. Indeed, the creation and diffusion of new styles is inextricably bound up with the process of production, publicity and packaging which must inevitably lead to the defusion of the subculture's subversive power – both mod and punk innovations fed back directly into high fashion and mainstream fashion. . . .

. . . As soon as the original innovations which signify 'subculture' are translated into commodities and made generally available, they become 'frozen'. Once removed from their private contexts by the small entrepreneurs and big fashion interests who produce them on a mass scale, they become codified, made comprehensible, rendered at once public property and profitable merchandise. In this way, the two forms of incorporation (the semantic/ideological and the 'real'/commercial) can be said to converge on the commodity form. Youth cultural styles may begin by issuing symbolic challenges, but they must inevitably end by establishing new sets of conventions; by creating new commodities, new industries or rejuvenating old ones (think of the boost punk must have given haberdashery!). This occurs irrespective of the subculture's political orientation: the macrobiotic restaurants, craft shops and 'antique markets' of the hippie era were easily converted into punk boutiques and record shops. It also happens irrespective of the startling content of the style: punk clothing and insignia could be bought mail-order by the summer of 1977, and in September of that year *Cosmopolitan* ran a review of Zandra Rhodes' latest collection of couture follies which consisted entirely of variations on the punk theme. Models smouldered beneath mountains of safety pins and plastic (the pins were jewelled, the 'plastic' wet-look satin) and the accompanying article ended with an aphorism – 'To shock is chic' – which presaged the subculture's imminent demise.

The ideological form

The second form of incorporation – the ideological – has been most adequately treated by those sociologists who operate a transactional model of deviant behaviour. For example, Stan Cohen has described in detail how one particular moral panic (surrounding the mod–rocker conflict of the mid-60s) was launched and sustained (Cohen 1972). Although this type of analysis can often provide an extremely sophisticated explanation of why spectacular subcultures consistently provoke such hysterical outbursts, it tends too overlook the subtler mechanisms through which potentially threatening phenomena are handled and contained. As the use of the term 'folk devil' suggests, rather too much weight tends to be given to the sensational excesses of the tabloid press at the expense of the ambiguous reactions which are, after all, more typical. As we have seen, the way in which subcultures are represented in the media makes them both more *and less* exotic than they actually are. They are seen to contain both dangerous aliens and boisterous kids, wild animals and wayward pets. Roland Barthes furnishes a key to the paradox in his description of 'identification' – one of the seven rhetorical figures which, according to Barthes, distinguish the meta-language of bourgeois mythology. He characterizes the petit-bourgeois as a person '. . . unable to imagine the other . . . the other is a scandal which threatens his existence' (Barthes 1972).

Two basic strategies have been evolved for dealing with this threat. First, the Other can be trivialized, naturalized, domesticated. Here, the difference is simply denied

('Otherness is reduced to sameness'). Alternatively, the Other can be transformed into meaningless exotica, a 'pure object, a spectacle, a clown' (Barthes 1972). In this case, the difference is consigned to a place beyond analysis. Spectacular subcultures are continually being defined in precisely these terms. Soccer hooligans, for example, are typically placed beyond 'the bounds of common decency' and are classified as 'animals'. . . . On the other hand, the punks tended to be resituated by the press in the family, perhaps because members of the subculture deliberately obscured their origins, refused the family and willingly played the part of folk devil, presenting themselves as pure objects, as villainous clowns. Certainly, like every other youth culture, punk was perceived as a threat to the family. Occasionally this threat was represented in literal terms. For example, the *Daily Mirror* (1 August 1977) carried a photograph of a child lying in the road after a punk–ted confrontation under the headline 'Victim of the Punk Rock Punch-up: the Boy Who Fell Foul of the Mob'. In this case, punk's threat to the family was made 'real' (that could be my child!) through the ideological framing of photographic evidence which is popularly regarded as unproblematic.

None the less, on other occasions, the opposite line was taken. For whatever reason, the inevitable glut of articles gleefully denouncing the latest punk outage was counterbalanced by an equal number of items devoted to the small details of punk family life. For instance, the 15 October 1977 issue of *Woman's Own* carried an article entitled 'Punks and Mothers' which stressed the classless, fancy dress aspects of punk. Photographs depicting punks with smiling mothers, reclining next to the family pool, playing with the family dog, were placed above a text which dwelt on the ordinariness of individual punks: 'It's not as rocky horror as it appears' . . . 'punk can be a family affair' . . . 'punks as it happens are non-political', and, most insidiously, albeit accurately, 'Johnny Rotten is as big a household name as Hughie Green'. Throughout the summer of 1977, the *People* and the *News of the World* ran items on punk babies, punk brothers, and punk–ted weddings. All these articles served to minimize the Otherness so stridently proclaimed in punk style, and defined the subculture in precisely those terms which it sought most vehemently to resist and deny. . . .

Style as Intentional Communication

. . . The cycle leading from opposition to defusion, from resistance to incorporation encloses each successive subculture. We have seen how the media and the market fit into this cycle. We must now turn to the subculture itself to consider exactly how and what subcultural style communicates. Two questions must be asked which together present us with something of a paradox: how does a subculture make sense to its members? How is it made to signify disorder? To answer these questions we must define the meaning of style more precisely. . . .

Umberto Eco writes, 'not only the expressly intended communicative object . . . but every object may be viewed . . . as a sign' (Eco 1973). For instance, the conventional outfits worn by the average man and woman in the street are chosen within the constraints of finance, 'taste', preference, etc. And these choices are undoubtedly significant. Each ensemble has its place in an internal system of differences – the conventional modes of sartorial discourse – which fit a corresponding set of socially prescribed roles and options. These choices contain a whole range of messages which are transmitted through the finely graded distinctions of a number of interlocking sets – class and status, self-image and attractiveness, etc. Ultimately, if nothing else, they are expressive of 'normality' as opposed to 'deviance' (i.e. they are distinguished by their relative invisibility, their appropriateness, their 'naturalness'). However, the intentional communication is of a different order. It stands apart – a visible construction, a loaded choice. It directs attention to itself; it gives itself to be read.

This is what distinguishes the visual ensembles of spectacular subcultures from those favoured in the surrounding culture(s). They are *obviously* fabricated (even the mods, precariously placed between the worlds of the straight and the deviant, finally declared themselves different when they gathered in groups outside dance halls and on sea fronts). They *display* their own codes (e.g. the punk's ripped T-shirt) or at least demonstrate that codes are there to be used and abused (e.g. they have been thought about rather than thrown together). In this they go against the grain of a mainstream culture whose principal defining characteristic, according to Barthes, is a tendency to masquerade as nature, to substitute 'normalized' for historical forms, to translate the reality of the world into an image of the world which in turn presents itself as if composed according to 'the evident laws of the natural order' (Barthes 1972). . . .

Style as *Bricolage*

. . . The subcultures with which we have been dealing share a common feature apart from the fact that they are all predominantly working class. They are, as we have seen, cultures of conspicuous consumption – even when, as with the skinheads and the punks, certain types of consumption are conspicuously refused – the it is through the distinctive rituals of consumption, through style, that the subculture at once reveals its 'secret' identity and communicates its forbidden meanings. It is basically the way in which commodities are *used* in subculture which marks the subculture off from more orthodox cultural formations.

Discoveries made in the field of anthropology are helpful here. In particular, the concept of *bricolage* can be used to explain how subcultural styles are constructed. In *The Savage Mind* Levi-Strauss shows how the magical modes utilized by primitive peoples (superstition, sorcery, myth) can be seen as implicitly coherent, though explicitly bewildering, systems of connection between things which perfectly equip their users to 'think' their own world. These magical systems of connection have a common feature: they are capable of infinite extension because basic elements can be used in a variety of improvised combinations to generate new meanings within them. *Bricolage* has thus been described as a 'science of the concrete' in a recent definition which clarifies the original anthropological meaning of the term:

[Bricolage] refers to the means by which the non-literate, non-technical mind of so-called 'primitive' man responds to the world around him. The process involves a 'science of the concrete' (as opposed to our 'civilised' science of the 'abstract') which far from lacking logic, in fact carefully and precisely orders, classifies and arranges into structures the *minutiae* of the physical world in all their profusion by means of a 'logic' which is not our own. The structures, 'improvised' or made up (these are rough translations of the process of *bricoler*) as *ad hoc* responses to an environment, then serve to establish homologies and analogies between the ordering of nature and that of society, and so satisfactorily 'explain' the world and make it able to be lived in. (Hawkes 1977)

The implications of the structured improvisations of *bricolage* for a theory of spectacular subculture as a system of communication have already been explored. for instance, John Clarke has stressed the way in which prominent forms of discourse (particularly fashion) are radically adapted, subverted and extended by the subcultural *bricoleur*:

> Together, object and meaning constitute a sign, and, within any one culture, such signs are assembled, repeatedly, into characteristic forms of discourse. However, when the bricoleur re-locates the significant object in a different position within that discourse, using the same overall repertoire of signs, or when that object is placed within a different total ensemble, a new discourse is constituted, a different message conveyed. (Clarke 1975)

In this way the teddy boy's theft and transformation of the Edwardian style revived in the early 1950s by Savile Row for wealthy young men about town can be construed as an act of *bricolage*. Similarly, the mods could be said to be functioning as *bricoleurs* when they appropriated another range of commodities by placing them in a symbolic ensemble which served to erase or subvert their original straight meanings. Thus pills medically prescribed for the treatment of neuroses were used as ends-in-themselves, and the motor scooter, originally an ultra-respectable means of transport, was turned into a menacing symbol of group solidarity. In the same improvisatory manner, metal combs, honed to a razor-like sharpness, turned narcissism into an offensive weapon. Union jacks were emblazoned on the backs of grubby parka anoraks or cut up and converted into smartly tailored jackets. More subtly, the conventional insignia of the business world – the suit, collar and tie, short hair, etc. – were stripped of their original connotations – efficiency, ambition, compliance with authority – and transformed into 'empty' fetishes, objects to be desired, fondled and valued in their own right.

At the risk of sounding melodramatic, we could use Umberto Eco's phrase 'semiotic guerrilla warfare' (Eco 1972) to describe these subversive practices. The war may be conducted at a level beneath the consciousness of the individual members of a spectacular subculture (though the subculture is still, at another level, an intentional communication . . .) but with the emergence of such a group, 'war – and it is Surrealism's war – is declared on a world of surfaces' (Annette Michelson, quoted Lippard 1970).

The radical aesthetic practices of Dada and Surrealism – dream work, collage, 'ready mades', etc. – are certainly relevant here. . . . The subcultural *bricoleur*, like the 'author' of a surrealist collage, typically 'juxtaposes two apparently incompatible realities [i.e. "flag": "jacket"; "hole": "teeshirt": "comb": "weapon"] on an apparently unsuitable scale . . . and . . . it is there that the explosive junction occurs' (Ernst 1948). Punk exemplifies most clearly the subcultural uses of these anarchic modes. It too attempted through 'perturbation and deformation' to disrupt and reorganize meaning. It, too, sought the 'explosive junction'. . . . Like Duchamp's 'ready mades' – manufactured objects which qualified as art because he chose to call them such, the most unremarkable and inappropriate items – a pin, a plastic clothes peg, a television component, a razor blade, a tampon – could be brought within the province of punk (un)fashion. Anything within or without reason could be turned into part of what Vivien Westwood called 'confrontation dressing' so long as the rupture between 'natural' and constructed context was clearly visible (i.e. the rule would seem to be: if the cap doesn't fit, wear it). . . .

Style as Homology

The punk subculture . . . signified chaos at every level, but this was only possible because the style itself was so thoroughly ordered. The chaos cohered as a meaningful whole. We can now attempt to solve this paradox by referring to another concept originally employed by Levi-Strauss: homology.

Paul Willis (1978) first applied the term 'homology' to subculture in his study of hippies and motor-bike boys using it to describe the symbolic fit between the values and life-styles of a group, its subjective experience and the musical forms it uses to express or reinforce its focal concerns. In *Profane Culture*, Willis shows how, contrary to the popular myth which presents subcultures as lawless forms, the internal structure of any particular subculture is characterized by an extreme orderliness: each part is organically related to other parts and it is through the fit between them that the subcultural member makes sense of the world. For instance, it was the homology between an alternative value system ('Tune in, turn on, drop out'), hallucogenic drugs and acid rock which made the hippy culture cohere as a 'whole way of life' for individual hippies. In *Resistance Through Rituals* Clarke *et al.* crossed the concepts of homology and *bricolage* to provide a systematic explanation of why a particular subcultural style should appeal to a particular group of people. The authors asked the question: 'What specifically does a subcultural style signify to the members of the subculture themselves?'

The answer was that the appropriated objects reassembled in the distinctive subcultural ensembles were 'made to reflect, express and resonate . . . aspects of group life' (Clarke *et al.*, 1975). The objects chosen were, either intrinsically or in their adapted forms, homologous with the focal concerns, activites, group structure and collective self-image of the subculture. They were 'objects in which (the subcultural members) could see their central values held and reflected' (Clarke *et al.*, 1975). . . .

The punks would certainly seem to bear out this thesis. The subculture was nothing if not consistent. There was a homological relation between the trashy cut-up clothes and spiky hair, the pogo and amphetamines, the spitting, the vomiting, the format of the fanzines, the insurrectionary poses and the 'soulless', frantically driven music. The punks wore clothes which were the sartorial equivalent of swear words, and they swore as they dressed – with calculated effect, lacing obscenities into record notes and publicity releases, interviews and love songs. Clothed in chaos, they produced Noise in the calmly orchestrated Crisis of everyday life in the late 1970s – a noise which made (no)sense in exactly the same way and to exactly the same extent as a piece of *avant-garde* music. If we were to write an epitaph for the punk subculture, we could do no better than repeat Poly Styrene's famous dictum: 'Oh Bondage, Up Yours!', or somewhat more concisely: the forbidden is permitted, but by the same token, nothing, not even these forbidden signifiers (bondage, safety pins, chains, hair-dye, etc.) is sacred and fixed.

This absence of permanently sacred signifiers (icons) creates problems for the semiotician. How can we discern any positive values reflected in objects which were chosen only to be discarded? For instance, we can say that the early punk ensembles gestured towards the signified's 'modernity' and 'working-classness'. The safety pins and bin liners signified a relative material poverty which was either directly experienced and exaggerated or sympathetically assumed, and which in turn was made to stand for the spiritual paucity of everyday life. In order words, the safety pins, etc. 'enacted' that transition from real to symbolic scarcity which Paul Piccone (1969) has described as the movement from 'empty stomachs' to 'empty spirits – and therefore an empty life notwithstanding the chrome and the plastic . . . of the life style of bourgeois society'.

We could go further and say that even if the poverty was being parodied, the wit was undeniably barbed; that beneath the clownish make-up there lurked the unaccepted and disfigured face of capitalism; that beyond the horror circus antics a divided and unequal society was being eloquently condemned. However, if we were to go further still and describe punk music as the 'sound of the Westway' or the pogo as the 'high-rise leap', or to talk of bondage as reflecting the narrow options of working-class youth, we would be treading on less certain ground. Such readings are both too literal and too conjectural. They are extrapolations from the subculture's own prodigious rhetoric, and rhetoric is not self-explanatory: it may say what it means but it does not necessarily 'mean' what it 'says'. In order words, it is opaque: its categories are part of its publicity. . . .

To reconstruct the true text of the punk subculture, to trace the source of its subversive practices, we must first isolate the 'generative set' responsible for the subculture's exotic displays. Certain semiotic facts are undeniable. The punk subculture like every other youth culture, was constituted in a series of spectacular transformations of a whole range of commodities, values, common-sense attitudes, etc. It was through these adapted forms that certain sections of predominantly working-class youth were able to restate their opposition to dominant values and institutions. However, when we attempt to close in on specific items, we immediately encounter problems. What, for instance, was the swastika being used to signify?

We can see how the symbol was made available to the punks (via Bowie and Lou Reed's 'Berlin' phase). Moreover, it clearly reflected the punks' interest in a decadent and evil Germany – a Germany which had 'no future'. It evoked a period redolent with a powerful mythology. Conventionally, as far as the British were concerned, the swastika signified 'enemy'. None the less, in punk usage, the symbol lost its 'natural' meaning – fascism. The punks were not generally sympathetic to the parties of the extreme right. On the contrary, . . . the conflict with the resurrected teddy boys and the widespread support for the anti-fascist movement (e.g. the Rock against Racism campaign) seem to indicate that the punk subculture grew up partly as an antithetical response to the re-emergence of racism in the mid-1970s. We must resort, then, to the most obvious of explanations – that the swastika was worn because it was guaranteed to shock. (A punk asked by *Time Out* (17–23 December 1977) why she wore a swastika, replied: 'Punks just like to be hated'.) This represented more than a simple inversion or inflection of the ordinary meanings attached to an object. The signifier (swastika) had been wilfully detached from the concept (Nazism) it conventionally signified, and although it had been re-positioned (as 'Berlin') within an alternative subcultural context, its primary value and appeal derived precisely from its lack of meaning: from its potential for deceit. It was exploited as an empty effect. We are forced to the conclusion that the central value 'held and reflected' in the swastika was the communicated absence of any such identifiable values. Ultimately, the symbol was as 'dumb' as the rage it provoked. The key to punk style remains elusive. Instead of arriving at the point where we can begin to make sense of the style, we have reached the very place where meaning itself evaporates.

Style as Signifying Practice

We are surrounded by emptiness but it is an emptiness filled with signs.
Lefebvre 1971

It would seem that those approaches to subculture based upon a traditional semiotics (a semiotics which begins which some notion of the 'message' – of a combination of elements referring unanimously to a fixed number of signifieds) fail to provide us with a 'way in' to the difficult and contradictory text of punk style. Any attempt at extracting a final set of meanings from the seemingly endless, often apparently random, play of signifiers in evidence here seems doomed to failure.

And yet, over the years, a branch of semiotics has emerged which deals precisely with this problem. Here the simple notion of reading as the revelation of a fixed number of concealed meanings is discarded in favour of the idea of *polysemy* whereby each text is seen to generate a potentially infinite range of meanings. Attention is consequently directed towards that point – or more precisely, that level – in any given text where the principle of meaning itself seems most in doubt. Such an approach lays less stress on the primacy of structure and system in language ('langue'), and more upon the *position* of the speaking subject in discourse ('parole'). It is concerned with the *process* of meaning–construction rather than with the final product. . . .

Julia Kristeva's work on signification seems particularly useful. In *La Révolution du Langage Poétique* (1974, trans. 1984) she explores the subversive possibilities within language through a study of French symbolist poetry, and points to 'poetic language' as the 'place where the social code is destroyed and renewed' (Kristeva 1984). She counts as 'radical' those signifying practices which negate and disturb syntax . . . and which therefore serve to erode the concept of 'actantial position' upon which the whole 'Symbolic Order' is seen to rest.[1]

Two of Kristeva's interests seem to coincide with our own: the creation of subordinate groups through *positioning in language* (Kristeva is especially interested in women), and the disruption of the process through which such positioning is habitually achieved.

In addition, the general idea of signifying practice (which she defines as 'the setting in place and cutting through or traversing of a system of signs') can help us to rethink in a more subtle and complex way the relations not only between marginal and mainstream cultural formations but between the various subcultural styles themselves. For instance, we have seen how all subcultural style is based on a practice which has much in common with the 'radical' collage aesthetic of surrealism and we shall be seeing how different styles represent different signifying practices. Beyond this I shall be arguing that the signifying practices embodied in punk were 'radical' in Kristeva's sense: that they gestured towards a 'nowhere' and actively *sought* to remain silent, illegible.

We can now look more closely at the relationship between experience, expression and signification in subculture; at the whole question of style and our reading of style. To return to our example, we have seen how the punk style fitted together homologically precisely through its lack of fit (hole:teeshirt::spitting:applause::bin-liner:garment::anarchy:order) – by its refusal to cohere round a readily identifiable set of central values. It cohered, instead, *elliptically* through a chain of conspicuous absences. It was characterized by its unlocatedness – its blankness – and in this it can be contrasted with the skinhead style.

Whereas the skinheads theorized and fetishized their class position, in order to effect a 'magical' return to an imagined past, the punks dislocated themselves from the parent culture and were positioned instead on the outside: beyond the comprehension of the average (wo)man in the street in a science fiction future. They played up their Otherness, 'happening' on the world as aliens, inscrutable. Though punk rituals, accents and objects were deliberately used to signify working-classness, the exact origins of individual punks were disguised or symbolically disfigured by the make-up, masks and aliases which seem to have been used, like Breton's art, as ploys 'to escape the principle of identity'.

This working-classness therefore tended to retain, *even in practice, even in its concretized forms*, the dimensions of an idea. It was abstract, disembodied, decontextualized. Bereft of the necessary details – a name, a home, a history – it refused to make sense, to be grounded, 'read back' to its origins. It stood in violent contradiction to that other great punk signifier – sexual 'kinkiness'. The two forms of deviance – social and sexual – were juxtaposed to give an impression of multiple warping which was guaranteed to disconcert the most liberal of observers, to challenge the glib assertions of sociologists no matter how radical. In this way, although the punks referred continually to the realities of school, work, family and class, these references only made sense at one remove: they were passed through the fractured circuitry of punk style and re-presented as 'noise', disturbance, entropy.

In other words, although the punks self-consciously mirrored what Paul Piccone (1969) calls the 'pre-categorical realities' of bourgeois society – inequality, powerlessness, alienation – this was only possible because punk style had made a decisive break not only with the parent culture but with its own *location in experience*. This break was both inscribed and re-enacted in the signifying practices embodied in punk style. The punk ensembles, for instance, did not so much magically resolve experienced contradictions as *represent* the experience of contradiction itself in the form of visual puns (bondage, the ripped tee-shirt, etc.). Thus while it is true that the symbolic objects in punk style (the safety pins, the pogo, the ECT hairstyles) were made to form a "unity" with the group's relations, situations, experience' (Clarke *et al.*, 1975), this unity was at once 'ruptural' and 'expressive', or more precisely it expressed itself through rupture.

This is not to say, of course, that all punks were equally aware of the disjunction between experience and signification upon which the whole style was ultimately based. The style no doubt made sense for the first wave of self-conscious innovators at a level which remained inaccessible to those who became punks after the subculture had surfaced and been publicized. Punk is not unique in this: the distinction between originals and hangers-on is always a significant one in subculture. Indeed, it is frequently verbalized (plastic punks or safety-pin people, burrhead rastas or rasta bandwagon, weekend hippies, etc, versus the 'authentic' people. For instance, the mods had an intricate system of classification whereby the 'faces' and 'stylists' who made up the original coterie were defined against the unimaginative majority – the pedestrian 'kids' and 'scooter boys' who were accused of trivializing and coarsening the precious mod style. What is more, different youths bring different degrees of commitment to a subculture. It can represent a major dimension in people's lives – an axis erected in the face of the family around which a secret and immaculate identity can be made to cohere – or it can be a slight distraction, a bit of light relief from the monotonous but none the less paramount realities of school, home and work. It can be used as a means of escape, of total detachment from the surrounding terrain, or as a way of fitting back in to it and settling down after a week-end or evening spent letting off steam. In most cases it is used, as Phil Cohen suggests, magically to achieve both ends. However, despite these individual differences, the members of a subculture must share a common language. And if a style is really to catch on, if it is to become genuinely popular, it must say the right things in the right way at the right time. It must anticipate or encapsulate a mood, a moment. It must embody a sensibility, and the sensibility which punk style embodied was essentially dislocated, ironic and self-aware. . . .

Note

1. The 'symbolic order' to which I have referred throughout should not be confused with Kristeva's 'Symbolic Order' which is used in a sense derived specifically from Lacanian psychoanalysis. I use the term merely to designate the apparent unity of the dominant ideological discourse in play at any one time.

References

Barthes, R. (1972). *Mythologies*. London: Paladin.

Clark, J. (1976). The Skinheads and Magical Recovery of Working Class Community. In: Hall, S. *et al.* (eds.), *Resistance Through Rituals*. London: Hutchinson.

Cohen, A. (1955). *Delinquent Boys: The Culture of the Gang*. London: Free Press.

Douglas, M. (1967). *Purity and Danger*. London: Penguin.

Eco, U. (1973). Social Life as a Sign System. In: Robey, D. (ed.), *Structuralism: The Wolfson College Lectures 1972*. London: Cape.

Geertz, C. (1964). Ideology as a Cultural System. In: Apter, D. E. (ed.), *Ideology and Discontent*. London: Free Press.

Hall, S. (1977). Culture, the Media and the "Ideological Effect". In: Curran, J. *et al.* (eds.), *Mass Communication and Society*. London: Arnold.

Hawkes, T. (1977). *Structuralism and Semiotics*. London: Methuen.

Kristeva, J. (1974). *La revolution du langage poetique*. Paris: Seuil.

Lefebvre, H. (1971). *Everyday Life in the Modern World*. London: Allen Lane.

Levi-Strauss, C. (1969). *The Elementary Structures of Kinship*. London: Eure & Spottiswood.

Lippard, L. (ed.) (1970). *Surrealists on Art*. London: Spectrum.

Picconne, P. (1969). From Youth Culture to Political Praxis. *Radical America*, 15 November.

Willis, P. (1978). *Profane Culture*. London: Routledge & Kegan Paul.

35

The Goth Scene and (Sub)Cultural Substance

Paul Hodkinson*

The practice of recounting and rejecting subcultural theory has possibly never been more popular than it is now among those who study contemporary popular cultural identities. In particular, the neo-Marxist adaptation of the term by Birmingham University's former Centre for Contemporary Cultural Studies (CCCS) regularly takes extensive criticism at conferences and seminars on the subject, either for being flawed from the start, or merely being out-of-date in a twenty-first-century society saturated by media and commerce. The rejection of the CCCS's particular version of subcultural theory has also prompted some calls for the abandonment of the term 'subculture' itself which, among other things, is deemed to be unable to capture the essential fluidity of contemporary lifestyle patterns (see Bennett, 1999). This chapter aims to contribute to such discussions in relation to ethnographic research on a music and style grouping known to its participants as the goth scene.[1]

By way of background information, 'goth' emerged in the early 1980s, when a number of bands and their fans merged elements of punk, glam rock and early New Romantic into what became a 'dark', androgynous style of music and fashion. The music, from then until the time of writing, has often been characterized by sinister or sombre sounds and lyrics, while the style has been dominated consistently by black hair and clothing, as well as the tendency for both females and males to wear distinct styles of make-up. During the mid- to late-1980s, the goth scene gained a relatively high media profile, something exemplified by the relative success of bands such as The Sisters of Mercy, The Cure and The Mission in single and album sales charts. From the beginning of the 1990s, however, the record industry and the media lost interest in the dark sounds and styles associated with goth. Since this time, in spite of the emergence of high profile artists such as Marilyn Manson, and the use of elements of goth style by occasional emerging strands of Indie or Metal, a distinct, small-scale and relatively bounded goth scene has survived and developed in and beyond Britain, predominantly outside the realms of mass media and commerce.

From 1996 to 2000, I conducted extensive ethnographic research focused on the British goth scene, a project whose full findings and conclusions are recounted in greater detail elsewhere (Hodkinson, 2002). This chapter seeks to provide a brief illustration

* Pp. 137–47 from *After Subculture: Critical Studies in Contemporary Youth Culture*, ed. A. Bennett and K. Kahn-Harris (New York: Palgrave Macmillan). © 2004. Reprinted with permission from Palgrave Macmillan.

of some of the ways that analysis of this case study might inform debates around the future of subcultural theory. While initially we shall see that the example of the goth scene can be used to illustrate some of the problems of the CCCS's perspective, it will be suggested subsequently that the relatively clear, bounded form taken by the group does not fit happily with the emphasis on cultural fluidity often found in the work of those who propose the abandonment of the notion of subculture. For this reason, I have suggested that groupings such as the goth scene may be conceptualized most usefully by using a reworked notion of subculture, which replaces some of the problematic elements of the CCCS's own adaptation of the term with a general emphasis on what I have termed *cultural substance*, a relative quality that can be contrasted with cultural fluidity, and which might be identified primarily through evidence of group distinctiveness, identity, commitment and autonomy (Hodkinson, 2002).

The Goth Scene and Objections to the CCCS

One of the most notable objections to CCCS theory is that its focus on youth subcultures as fixed and bounded symbolic structures had the effect of under-emphasizing internal diversity and instability at the same time as failing to account sufficiently for the flows of differentially committed young people across group boundaries (Clarke, 1981; Bennett, 1999). Providing a degree of support for the criticism, my research on the goth scene certainly revealed some individual movement into and out of the grouping, as well as instances of contact between its members and the participants of certain other music scenes – for example, at some mixed alternative or rock-based events. There was also some variation in the levels of commitment among insiders themselves. By way of example, some individuals exhibited an extreme goth-orientated appearance virtually every time they left their home, while others only spent a significant amount of time getting 'gothed up' when they went out to particular pubs or nightclubs. Equally, the goth style itself, rather than being static and simple, entailed a degree of dynamism and diversity, as well as drawing on and overlapping in particular ways with various other styles. This is partially because, in order to earn the respect of their peers, individuals usually sought to develop their own individual 'version' of the goth style rather than to look exactly the same as one another. Indeed, looking too similar to another goth was sometimes liable to be frowned upon as evidence of lack of individual creativity. One of my interviewees explained that, after an initial period of conformity, goths would gradually develop their own individual look through drawing on a variety of influences:

> *Brian:* There's very rarely two people look exactly the same . . . you take things from everywhere – from different types of looks and different people that you see and stuff, and you just make it your own.

Consistent with the emphasis on instances of internal diversity, some other respondents suggested that, as well as individual variations, the goth scene could in fact be divided into identifiable sub-styles:

   Martin:　You get the Sisters [reference to band, The Sisters of Mercy] goths and the
      cobwebby goths, or cyber goths . . . and then if you're like us you're stuck in the
      middle.

While we shall see later that, in the final analysis, they were not overwhelming in the
case of the goth scene, such elements of diversity do reinforce the case that theorists
should beware of over-simplifying the value systems of music and style groupings.

   The case of the goth scene provided more emphatic support for criticisms of the way
in which CCCS theorists essentialized the groupings on which they focused, by 'revealing' underlying collective meanings or functions through semiological analysis of subcultural style (see Cohen, 1972; Hebdige, 1979). This is important because, in spite of
the intense criticism CCCS theory has received on this score (for example, Clarke, 1981;
Bennett, 1999; Muggleton, 2000), the general premise that the aesthetic details of particular styles might directly represent and hence reveal particular shared structural circumstances, psychological features or political statements remains influential. Indeed,
on many occasions during the process of my own research on the goth scene, colleagues
suggested greater emphasis on an analytical interpretation of the distinctive spectacular
styles in question. My response was, and is, that reliance on external semiological analysis would construct more than it would reveal. Without necessarily wishing to endorse
David Muggleton's rather uncritical subjectivist approach to subcultural research, it is
clear that his call for at least some degree of 'fit' between theoretical explanations and
subjective realities is worthy of support (Muggleton, 2000, p. 14).

   What was revealed by my research approach – which combined data from critical
participant observation with the stated views of numerous participants – was the falla-
ciousness of any notion that the meanings behind the goth scene might in some way
have been imprinted neatly in the style its members exhibited. There was little evidence
of any distinct shared *raison d'être* embedded within the clothing, music and lifestyle
practices of participants. Individuals varied considerably in their views as to what the
goth scene was and what it meant, and many suggested that their dark, sometimes
ghostly, appearance represented something of a red herring for those seeking to under
stand their experiences, motivations and meanings. Some respondents to a questionnaire I administered specifically rejected 'common-sense' suggestions that their dark
clothes and music reflected any kind of morbid character or outlook, preferring to
describe their involvement as a means of enjoying themselves through a celebration of
preferred looks and sounds. Here are a few examples:

   Questionnaire:　In your own words, please explain, what is the goth scene all about?
   Donna:　Having fun, getting dressed up and getting drunk.
   Pete:　Rejoicing in a high spirited view of the darker side of life. . . .
   Jonny:　Wearing black clothes, loads of make-up and bouncing to funky music.
   Samantha:　It's about dressing up in your best stuff, socialising and making new
      friends and listening to great music.

A final clear point of divergence between the goth scene and CCCS theory concerns
the extent to which the former was directly and positively constructed, and facilitated

by media and commerce, something that coheres with existing doubts as to the contemporary relevance of Hebdige's notion that conscious packaging and marketing only became associated with subcultural styles some time *after* the groupings had emerged creatively and spontaneously as a response of working-class youth to structural contradictions (Hebdige, 1979, p. 96). As with Thornton's findings on club culture (1995, pp. 122–62), it was clear that the music media alongside both small and large-scale record companies, played a considerable role, both in the initial crystallisation and the subsequent multinational popularity of the goth scene during the 1980s. A number of older respondents to a questionnaire I conducted at a goth festival specifically cited niche and mass media as being responsible for their initial discovery of, and recruitment to, the goth scene:

> *Questionnaire:* Please give details about what or who got you into the goth scene.
> *Dave:* Seeing Sisters of Mercy on TOTP [Top of the Pops] and Mission on radio.
> *Sara:* Heard a song by the Cure on television – bought the album, and albums by related bands, then discovered the clothes.
> *Rhian:* 'The Tube' [TV programme] . . . and hearing John Peel's radio programme.

Although such medium- and large-scale media coverage evaporated somewhat from the beginning of the 1990s, media and commercial players remained crucial, from well-known labels releasing occasional retrospective compilation CDs, to the expanding phenomenon of small-scale independent companies marketing specialist commodities, often via goth fanzines or websites. Essentially, the goth scene, rather than symbolically subverting capitalism, functioned as a highly specialist consumer grouping whose participants required a variety of media outlets and businesses in order to learn about and purchase the commodities that made them collectively distinctive. While such consumption sometimes did involve the creative appropriation of everyday goods along the lines described by Hebdige (1979, pp. 104–5), music and clothes collections also contained items that were produced and marketed explicitly towards goths. It was clear, more generally, that involvement with the goth scene would be better understood as a particular form of consumer choice influenced by a variety of factors, rather than any kind of spontaneous reaction to structural positionings. In particular, the goth scene was not consistent with the notion of subculture as any form of working-class struggle, symbolic or otherwise. Although it recruited from a mixture of backgrounds, research revealed a middle-class bias in the social make-up of the grouping and, more important, a general tendency for participation in the goth scene to eclipse rather than to reflect or express structural affiliations.

Even from the relatively brief examples provided here, I hope it is clear that it would not be appropriate to attempt to explain the goth scene by means of an unreconstructed version of CCCS subcultural theory. In particular, the extent of the links with media and commerce, and the lack of any absolute meaning, function or class identity signified by the style would invalidate use of the structuralist slant placed on the notion of subculture by the Birmingham theorists. While this much is relatively clear, however, the question as to what might be the most informative, valuable and, above all, accurate alternative way to theorize groupings such as the goth scene in the early twenty-first century, is rather less easy to answer. In the next section we shall examine the case of those whose solution is not only to abandon the writings of the CCCS, but also to avoid, and to try to replace, the notion of subculture itself.

Alternatives to Subculture

The most prominent argument of those who seek removal of the notion of subculture from academic vocabulary is that it will always imply too fixed, inflexible and simplistic a state of affairs to enable us to understand the complexity of contemporary cultural lifestyles. Whether regarded as long-term characteristics 'rooted in the sensibilities of post-war music consumers' (Bennett, 1999, p. 610), or a symptom of late-twentieth-century cultural developments (Jameson, 1982, 1991; Chambers, 1985; Muggleton, 2000), fluidity and multiplicity are often deemed to be the primary feature of contemporary youth culture, and indeed consumer lifestyles more generally. Rather than being centred around mutually exclusive subcultures, it is argued that identities are assembled through ever-changing individualized selections from an ever-expanding range of commercial artefacts, practices and identities on offer to all (Polhemus, 1997). While incompatibility with such complexity is the primary and most often cited reason for the abandonment of the notion of subculture, Bennett is equally concerned that the term is losing its value as an interpretive device because, in the wake of CCCS's particular explanations, it is used increasingly, by both academics and journalists, as a descriptor for all manner of different cultural formations in a rather vague and ill-defined fashion (Bennett, 1999, p. 603).

Unfortunately, the considerable consensus on the need to avoid the notion of subculture as it stands does not appear to have been replicated when it conies to the question of alternative ways of conceptualizing the kinds of collective practices and identities to whom it might previously have been applied. A seemingly expanding plethora of differing concepts have emerged which, whether they were originally intended as direct responses to subcultural theory or not, appear to encompass, or at least to include, those cultural formations for whom, until recently, subculture might have been used. Among others, these include *neo-tribe* (Bauman, 1992; Maffesoli, 1996; Bennett, 1999); *lifestyle* (Jenkins, 1983; Shields, 1992; Chaney, 1996); *scene* (Straw, 1991); *postmodern subculture* (Muggleton, 2000) and *bünde* (Hetherington, 1998). There is not room in this relatively short contribution to elaborate extensively on all the individual discussions and justifications for these different terms; suffice it to say that they are often highly compelling and sometimes display notable differences of emphasis.

Notwithstanding individual nuances of explanation or purpose, the key concern for this chapter is that the authors concerned appear relatively united in wishing to focus attention upon loosely-knit transitory forms of culture and on multi-affiliated and ephemeral individual identities and practices. In so doing, they distance themselves – sometimes directly – from the connotations of fixed and clearly bounded groupings or communities which tend to have been invoked by the notion of subculture. Bennett, for example, regards Maffesoli's notion of neo-tribe as preferable to subculture because of its ability to capture 'the shifting nature of youth's musical and stylistic preferences and the essential fluidity of youth cultural groups' (Bennett, 1999, p. 614). Meanwhile, Muggleton, by invoking the notion of postmodern subculture, emphasizes that the celebration of liminal individual identities and styles is more important to contemporary youth than collective labels or styles (Muggleton, 2000).

In spite of the potential value of some of their individual contributions, the sheer number of terms on offer to us here, and the extent to which they appear to overlap with one another, has a rather confusing overall effect. While the existing tendency for imprecise references to subculture certainly *is* problematic, it is not clear that this apparently ever-expanding array of alternatives brings any greater clarity. While in some cases theorists have distinguished their favoured replacement term clearly from the notion of subculture itself, fewer words have been expended clarifying the similarities and differences between each of the 'alternatives' on offer – or, indeed, justifying the use of one rather than another. As a result, the empirical circumstances in which one should utilize the term 'neo-tribe', for example, rather than 'scene', 'bünde' or 'lifestyle', are less than clear. The potential for confusion can be illustrated by Rob Shields' contributions to his own edited collection *Lifestyle Shopping,* which, in spite of their overall value, are afflicted by what comes across as a somewhat interchangeable use of tribe, bünde, lifestyle and even subculture (Shields, 1992).

Aside from such problems of definition and overlap, a more substantive difficulty shared by the various 'alternatives' cited here is that their common orientation towards an emphasis on fluidity and cross-fertilization may lead to an over-generalized sense of the prevalence of these characteristics. While such features *do* appear to characterize overwhelmingly some contemporary cultural patterns, the current enthusiasm for emphasizing them across the board carries the danger either of misrepresenting or excluding from analysis any collectivities whose empirical reality fails to fit the picture. While there may ultimately be a valuable role for one or more of the 'alternatives' described thus far, it remains necessary to find a way of conceptualizing those elective groupings which, in spite of diverging significantly from the specifics of the CCCS's explanations, may in the final analysis remain less notable for their fluidity than their levels of what may be termed cultural substance.

(Sub)Cultural Substance

Essentially, I mean cultural substance, here, as the relative inverse of the more frequently used notion of fluidity. Therefore, rather than being predominantly characterized by movement and overlap, an elective grouping characterized by significant levels of cultural substance, I suggest, will be relatively stable and bounded in form. Elsewhere, I have elaborated upon this through the use of four indicators that might be applied to groupings in order to assess their level of substance: a *consistent distinctiveness* in group values and tastes, a strong sense of *shared identity,* practical *commitment* among participants, and a significant degree of *autonomy* in the facilitation and operation of the group (Hodkinson, 2002, pp. 28–33). While none of these relative characteristics is particularly revolutionary or unfamiliar the hope is that, collectively, they might act as useful yardsticks in the analysis of contemporary consumer culture, for differentiating predominantly fluid elective amalgamations from those displaying greater levels of substance. While the former may be conceptualized using terminology such as that discussed above (if suitably clarified), my suggestion is that the latter – cultural substance – may form the basis for a much-needed reworking and clarification of the notion of subculture (ibid.).

Importantly, while we have illustrated a number of specific problems with the CCCS's neo-Marxist version of subculture, these need not (and ought not to) lead to the abandonment of the term that the Birmingham theorists took up. There is simply no requirement that all the minutiae of that particular adaptation should stand as integral and irremovable components in the definition and use of subculture, now or in the future. In its general usage, the notion of subculture tends to be associated more often with particular substantive types of elective community than with specifics such as class contradictions, symbolic resistance and the like. And such an interpretation, if properly clarified in the ways I have suggested, in fact reflects consistently present (if over-essentialized) definitional traits of subculture which can be found beneath the specifics of the CCCS and its predecessors. Therefore, while there are radical differences with respect to precise explanations, the notion of subculture – whether in its CCCS guise, or that of the earlier writings of Chicago School sociologists such as Albert Cohen (1955) – has been used consistently to infer groupings with distinct sets of values, defiant collective identities, commitment and dependency among participants, and at least some degree of autonomy from the rest of society. Through the notion of cultural substance as defined here, I hope to have extracted such common themes as relative rather than essentialized qualities, and hence clarified existing connotations so as to retain the notion of subculture as a valuable interpretive device. In illustration of its possible relevance, we now return to our case study.

It has already been established that the goth scene did not have a single underlying meaning or function as well as that it was wholly implicated with media and commerce, and largely middle-class. It has also been emphasized that the grouping exhibited examples of diversity, movement and change. In spite of the importance of such indications of fluidity, however, the conceptualization of the goth scene using a term such as neo-tribe, scene or lifestyle would have risked over-emphasizing such features. It will become clear in the following paragraphs that inevitable instances of heterogeneity and dynamism, such as those described earlier, were more than a little overshadowed by the significant levels of (sub)cultural substance exhibited by the group in respect of the four indicators outlined in the proposed reworking of subculture above.

Blending in and standing out

In spite of the already-described absence of directly symbolized functions or meanings, as well as the presence of notable elements of diversity and dynamism, there remained an overall *consistent distinctiveness* to the range of ideals and tastes exhibited by goths. Although participants themselves sometimes preferred to talk about their 'individuality' rather than the features they shared with their peers, critical participant observation emphasized that internal differences usually took the form of creative, yet subtle variations and additions rather than the sort of diversity that would undermine group boundaries significantly.

Furthermore, although there *were* some indications of different identifiable sub-styles within the goth scene, the similarities and overlaps between them tended ultimately to outweigh their differences from one another. The collective distinctiveness of the goth style as a whole was illustrated on a daily basis by the ease with which goths were recognized, both by one another and by many outsiders to the group.

The clothing, music and other stylistic artefacts which goths selected, adapted and created tended to reflect two key stylistic themes that were relatively consistent from place to place and year to year. First, a general emphasis on 'darkness' predominated, most obviously in the predominance of the colour black, the deep vocals and gloomy lyrics that pervaded much goth music, and the overt visual references to horror fiction such as vampires, bats, crosses and so on. Second, the display of particular types of femininity by both sexes was a theme that tended to cut across elements of diversity and change. Examples included unisex preferences for particular styles of makeup and significant amounts of mesh, fishnet, lace and PVC clothing. In addition to the significance of these two distinctive themes, there was a take-up by goths of selected artefacts associated with a variety of other music scenes, including Extreme Metal, Indie, New Romantic and dance. Crucially, while diverse in terms of their sources, the particular items likely to be appropriated and the way they were utilized as part of an overall goth assemblage were often relatively consistent and predictable. While they were certainly important features, then, diversity, change and overlap came across as being less significant, in the case of the goth scene, than the overall tendency for goths to blend in with one another and to stand out collectively from those outside the group.

Drawing boundaries of identity

In respect of the subjective perceptions and feelings of participants themselves regarding group membership, Muggleton has pointed out that a lack of clear collective alignment might indicate a fluid or postmodern sensibility (2000, pp. 52–3). The goth scene, though, was characterized by a particularly strong consciousness of group *identity*, and one that tended to cut across any perceived internal differences or subgroups. In spite of a reluctance towards overt self-labelling among some of those I interviewed, the majority displayed very clear feelings of belonging to the goth scene as a whole. In a number of cases, respondents were perfectly happy to describe themselves explicitly as 'a goth', as in this example:

> *Joe:* I dress in black and I'm a goth because that's what I do, I dress in black and I'm a goth – end of story.

Meanwhile, those more reluctant to pigeonhole themselves quite so explicitly tended to talk happily about the extent of their involvement in the goth scene and, crucially, to align themselves alongside others whom they regarded as goths. Notably, there was a clear sense that this shared identity transcended the boundaries of place, with numerous respondents emphasizing a close sense of commonality with goths they didn't know in faraway towns and countries. This *translocal* sense of identity often came out most strongly in the form of expressions of distinction from equally consistent conceptions of 'trendies', a perceived homogenous mainstream grouping who were not only disliked because of the verbal and physical threat to goths that they were felt to pose, but also as a result of the perceived superficiality of their tastes. For the following interviewee, standing apart from the norm was a key aspect of participating in the goth scene:

Keith: I think it's a backlash against the media and general Tom, Dick and Harry. You know, just general low quality, shitty clubs. It's a rejection of that kind of thing – you do feel different.

The strength and consistency of such notions of insiders and outsiders, like the consistency of goths' tastes, seemed not to fit comfortably with an emphasis on fluidity. The following extract illustrates effectively the general sense I gained that involvement with the goth scene tended to be a highly significant component in the sense-of-self of participants:

Tanya: I don't really think about that really, because it is just *me* now.
Susan: I think it is really important.
Tanya: Yeah, it must be very important.
Susan: It's how you are. The way you dress, the music you listen to influences . . . other things.
Tanya: I know it's really sad, but [when I went to] Carlisle I just couldn't cope with it because there was no goth scene, I just couldn't cope with it! I had to go back home because I just felt all lost. There were two other goths, maybe three, and guess what – we all sat together! It was purely because we were goths and there were no others so we just suddenly sort of joined.

"Eating, sleeping and breathing" goth?

We have already seen that levels of subcultural commitment did vary, to some extent, from one goth to another. However, consistent with the aforementioned strong subjective sense of affiliation, average levels of practical immersion in the goth scene among its participants were extremely high. Without accounting for *all* their socializing, consumer habits or media use, goth-orientated artefacts, activities and individuals often seemed to dominate. The following estimation about friendships within the subculture was in fact on the conservative side compared with many I received:

Tom: Probably on a close friends level there's about 60 per cent [goths]. On the acquaintances it would probably tip up to about 80 or 90 per cent because of the amount I travel about to other clubs and stuff.

Particular subcultural commitment was also demonstrated by the fact that many goths, like Tom, regularly travelled considerable distances to attend subcultural events, something often induced by the desire to meet up with existing goth friends or to make new ones. In addition, a number of goths had sufficient investment in the grouping to combine cultural preferences with a career, by progressing from being general participants to become specialist producers, organizers and entrepreneurs. Although there certainly were individuals who moved in and out of the goth scene in a relatively short space of time, the norm was for those who became fully involved to stay involved for a significant period. The friendships, status and sense of belonging which was usually experienced by newcomers who embraced the cultural tastes of the group sufficiently, tended to function as a stimulus for the concentration and continuation of their involvement. Although many withdrew a little with the onset of full-time adult responsibilities, increasing numbers remained involved into and well beyond their mid-twenties, Therefore, while few literally 'ate, breathed and slept goth', the levels of group commitment exhibited by most participants would not have been captured by notions such as neo-tribe, which imply a more fickle sensibility.

Self-Sufficient and Self-Contained?

The importance to the goth scene of media and commerce already mentioned above would clearly make it misleading to present the grouping as being entirely independent or authentic. However, the degree to which the grouping was reliant on specialist operations and services run by participants themselves makes the notion of *relative autonomy* a potentially useful one. Central to the ongoing development and survival of the late 1990s British goth scene, then, were small-scale genre-specific retailers and record labels run by goth enthusiasts. Furthermore, a plethora of semi-commercial or entirely voluntary activities, from organizing gigs to giving out promotional flyers, played a key part in the goth infrastructure. Such volunteers and part-time entrepreneurs often found my questions about whether they made a profit a source of hilarity, and were at pains to emphasize personal enthusiasm for the goth scene as their primary motivation.

Equally, while larger-scale media had played an important part in the construction and initial popularity of goth, the late 1990s scene in Britain received relatively sparse media coverage outside a DIY network of flyers, fanzines, websites and online forums produced by, and for, insiders. In particular, the Internet had become a crucial resource. A wealth of specialist goth websites and discussion forums produced by and for goths formed something of a specialist sub-network on the Internet, providing information and interaction. While very much implicated in media and consumer capitalism, then, the goth scene was relatively self-sufficient in terms of the involvement of its own participants as cultural producers, and relatively self-contained in the sense that specialist events, media and retailers reduced contact between goths and those outside their grouping.

Conclusion

What has been illustrated here is that, while it did not fit with the specifics of the neo-Marxist explanations provided by CCCS theory, the late 1990s British goth scene would not have been described accurately by a term that would have emphasized fluidity and cross-fertilization above all else, While we have seen that the grouping did exhibit certain indications of movement, dynamism and flux, it is clear that these did not prevent it from retaining a relatively substantive overall form. Most notably, the relatively high levels of consistent distinctiveness, identity, commitment and autonomy I have described cohere with the notion of cultural substance as outlined here and prompted my conceptualization of the goth scene, both in this chapter and elsewhere (Hodkinson, 2002) using a reworked notion of subculture.

Note

1. It should be noted that, in referring to the goth *scene*, I merely replicate the non-academic way in which goths themselves referred to their grouping. Unlike some theorists (Straw, 1991; Harris, 2000), I do not intend the term *scene* as a theoretical or interpretive device.

References

Bauman, Z. (1992). Survival as a Social Construct. *Theory, Culture and Society* 9(1), pp. 1–36.

Bennett, A. (1999). Subcultures or Neo-Tribes?: Rethinking the Relationship Between Youth, Style and Musical Taste. *Sociology* 33(3), pp. 599–617.

Chambers, I. (1985). *Urban Rhythms: Pop Music and Popular Culture*. London: Macmillan.

Chaney, D. (1996). *Lifestyles*. London: Routledge.

Clarke, G. (1981). Defending Ski-Jumpers: A Critique of Theories of Youth Subcultures. In: S. Frith & A. Goodwin (eds.) (1990), *On Record: Rock, Pop and the Written Word*. London: Routledge.

Cohen, A. (1955). *Delinquent Boys: The Culture of the Gang*. London: Collier-Macmillan.

Cohen, P. (1972). Subcultural Conflict and Working Class Community. *Working Papers in Cultural Studies* 2, pp. 5–70.

Hebdige, D. (1979). *Subculture: The Meaning of Style*. London: Routledge.

Hetherington, K. (1998b). *Expressions of Identity: Space, Performance, Politics*. London: Sage.

Hodkinson, P. (2002). *Goth: Identity, Style and Subculture*. Oxford: Berg.

Jameson, F. (1982). Postmodernism and Consumer Society. In: H. Foster (ed.) (1985), *Postmodern Culture*. London: Photo Press.

Jameson, F. (1991). *Postmodernism or the Cultural Logic of Late Capitalism*. London: Verso.

Jenkins, R. (1983). *Lads, Citizens and Ordinary Kids: Working Class Youth Lifestyles in Belfast*. London: Routledge & Kegan Paul.

Maffesoli, M. (1996). *The Time of the Tribes: The Decline of Individualism in Mass Society*, trans. D. Smith. London: Sage.

Muggleton, D. (2000). *Inside Subculture: The Postmodern Meaning of Style*. Oxford: Berg.

Polhemus, T. (1997). In the Supermarket of Style. In: S. Redhead, D. Wynne & J. O'Connor (eds.), *The Clubcultures Reader: Readings in Popular Cultural Studies*. Oxford: Basil Blackwell.

Shank, B. (1994). *Dissonant Identities: The Rock "n" Roll Scene in Austin, Texas*. Hanover, NH: University Press of New England.

Shields, R. (1992). Spaces for the Subject of Consumption. In: R. Shields (ed.), *Lifestyle Shopping: The Subject of Consumption*. London: Routledge.

Straw, W. (1991). Systems of Articulation, Logics of Change: Communities and Scenes in Popular Music. *Cultural Studies* 5(3), pp. 368–88.

Thornton, S. (1995). *Club Cultures: Music, Media and Subcultural Capital*. Cambridge: Polity Press.

36

"Why Don't You Act Your Color?": Preteen Girls, Identity, and Popular Music

Pamela J. Tracy*

> **Emily:** *They, like, listen to this kind of music [R&B, hip-hop, rap] and we listen to it sometimes. Once I was singing a song and I was singing "The Thong Song" and Vanecia and Teresa were like, "Emily, you're not Black, why do you act like a Black person?"*
>
> **Vanecia:** *When we do this [pretend to be TLC] and stuff, we do dance clubs and all of that other junk and then Emily, she goes, "okay, like you know" and she be acting all Black and all hard like this [Vanecia is snapping her fingers and moving her head back and forth] . . . And I be like "Emily, don't be acting our color, act your color." And, she's like "okay, then whatever." And, then on the next day she be acting our color and I tell her again and she gets real smart with me and we get into fights . . . What I'm trying to say is I can't see why White people don't act White, Black people act Black.*

After spending several months with Emily and Vanecia and their fourth-grade classmates (I'll call them the Central girls) it became apparent that popular music was omnipresent and integral to their everyday lives. More specifically, as illustrated in the quotes above, listening, dancing, and singing to music meant more than entertainment. When they talked about popular music, sang and danced in the school lunchroom and on the playground, and acted out Destiny's Child and TLC in their bedrooms and basements, these girls communicated not only pleasure, but also their racial and gendered identities. The type of music they listened to, how they listened to this music, and who they listened with mattered in terms of how they organized their friendships, how they expressed their identities, and how they negotiated their place in their social and culture worlds. The girls' frustrations with each other and their struggles to understand what it means to "act your color" are an important part of their experience with popular music.

I argue that when they engaged with music, the Central girls constructed a sense of self and other that was tied to contextual conditions (e.g., where they were and who they were with), their understandings of social and cultural relations, and their interpretation of what it means to be "me" and "you." Of course, this reading doesn't tell

*Pp. 45–52 from *Race/Gender/Media: Considering Diversity Across Audiences, Content and Producers*, ed. R. A. Lind (Boston, MA: Pearson, Allyn & Bacon, 2004). © 2004 by Pearson.

the whole story. While the girls negotiated their own identities when engaging with music in the lunch room and/or in their dance groups, dominant racial and gendered belief systems continued to affect their ways of seeing and being with others in other school and home-based contexts.

I conducted research with the Central girls at their urban elementary school in a large midwestern city. The participants were fourth-grade girls ranging in age from 9 to 11 years old. In terms of race and ethnicity, five girls including Emily and April described themselves as White/Caucasian, five girls including Tracey named themselves African American/Black, Teresa said that she was African American/ American Indian/White, one girl described herself as American Indian/White, one said that she was Malaysian, and Maria named herself Hawaiian. I spent approximately ten months and on average three to four days a week with the girls in their school. In addition to individual and peer group interviewing, administering questionnaires, and asking the girls to keep a media journal, I observed and participated regularly during recess, lunch, free time, literature, dance, and art classes. I also participated in a school-wide roller-skating party, clean-up event, read-a-thon, and spring concert. During all of these events, I took notes, asked the girls questions, and participated in their activities.

Before I begin, I want to briefly highlight the theoretical assumptions that guide my interpretations of the Central girls' popular music experiences. Cultural studies audience scholars are interested in understanding how people make sense of media and how media experiences affect everyday life. This scholarship is grounded in the assumption that media and popular culture experiences are important socialization practices that both negatively and positively influence how we construct a sense of self and others. While media and popular culture texts (e.g., movies, TV shows, songs, and fashion) are understood as potentially powerful influences, these scholars argue that audiences actively construct meaning when they interpret media images, sounds, and forms. In fact, sometimes people use media products to construct identities, to resist authority, and to build knowledge.

Nevertheless, meaning construction is understood to be a social process influenced by a variety of contextual conditions including audiences' day to day interactions with others, societal belief systems, economic relations, cultural experiences, other media texts, and familial practices. Some of these social practices, such as working, schooling, and advertising, function ideologically. That is, they work to create belief systems that are taken for granted as "the way things are." These belief systems, more often than not, serve to privilege some people and ways of being over others. For example, the Central girls frequently made connections between their everyday experiences with boys and the music lyrics about heterosexual dating. As they interpreted the texts they reflected on their direct knowledge about relationships. At the same time, many of the lyrics referenced sexual relations that the girls described as "about older girls" and "stuff we don't know about." Despite the fact that they had no direct experience, they accepted the lyrical messages – messages privileging heterosexuality and warning them about boys/men – as valid and important for future reference. In doing so, they relied on social and cultural belief systems about heterosexual relationships and particular gender behaviors to interpret media content.

In terms of research, a variety of scholars emphasize the value of ethnographic study for investigating how audiences engage with media (see, for example, Ang, 1996 and Bennett, 2000). Ethnographic research allows us to understand how the construction of meaning depends on a variety of social relations, practices, and situations. Through observation, participation, and interviewing, we can gain a better understanding of how day-to-day interactions and different contexts affect media experiences. In reference to the Central girls' study, the ethnographic methods I used enabled a closer investigation into their popular music experiences particularly in terms of understanding more fully how they enacted their identities. By spending more time with them and expressing my interest in their lives, we were able to create some space for discussing difficult and seemingly taboo topics.

In addition to valuing context and the social aspect of media use, cultural studies scholars also focus on the process of identity construction. Feminist scholars argue that identity (or how we understand and enact a sense of self and other) is "communicated" and "practiced" rather than predetermined by race, gender, class, age, sexuality, ability, and ethnicity. For example, Vanecia, one of the Central girls, defines herself as an African American/Black and "half White" girl. She explained that "when I am with my mom's family, they are White, I feel different than when I am with my dad's family." As you will read later, Vanecia identified quite strongly with other African American/Black girls when they talked about Whites listening to hip-hop and "acting Black," and, at other moments, she danced to this music with her White friends. How she understands her place in her social and cultural world is complicated and enriched by her many multiple and layered identities. Vanecia's interpretations of her immediate experiences, what might be required of her at any given moment, and her readings of larger social and ideological systems such as media influence the ways she communicates her identities. If we were to judge Vanecia based on her skin color or gender alone we would most likely make assumptions that don't fully represent her day-to-day experiences.

In reference to their popular music experiences, the Central girls communicated their identities in a variety of ways. For example, the girls listened to particular types of music because they identified with certain lyrics, rhythms, and related fashion and dance styles – their lived experiences were reflected in the music form and content. Some girls listened to learn more about what "will happen in the future," projecting ahead to a particular way of being a woman. Heather listened to Macy Gray because she liked the music, but also because she wanted to communicate that she had different tastes than her classmates and, more importantly, that she was different than others. Maria listened to TLC because she felt that the song *UnPretty* and its message about "being yourself and not listening to others" verified her beliefs. And some of the girls sang and danced to certain genres during lunchtime because this communicated that they knew the music, which helped them achieve a certain social status.

In addition, as the girls and boys listened, danced, and sang to particular songs, others around them were constructing perceptions about them. Because Kathleen, a White girl, didn't like rap or hip-hop, she was described as being "all that" or thinking that she was better than others. Conversely, when Marcus, an African American boy, listened to rap music with "cussing" in it, he was constructed as a potential troublemaker. The Central girls' experiences illustrate the relationship between music and identity and highlight that identity is simultaneously how we communicate a sense of self to others and how we are constructed by the world around us.

Emily, April, and Maria on "Acting Black'

During their peer group interview, this group of girls discussed why they felt that African American girls might connect to Destiny's Child music more than they (read: non-Black girls) did. This discussion slowly evolved into several stories about their experiences with being told to "act their own color."

Emily: They [African American/Black girls], like, listen to this kind of music [R&B, hip-hop] and we [non-Black girls] listen to it sometimes. Once I was singing a song and I was singing "The Thong Song" and Vanecia and Teresa were like, "Emily, you're not Black, why do you act like a Black person?"

April: Like a lot of Black people like White things and White people never say anything bad about Black people. . . .

Emily: Yeah. We all like Britney Spears. . . .

Maria: Like at my birthday party. . . . Remember at my birthday party, Chelsea just started dancing and Shaquilla and Vanecia were playing together and they just went, "Oh no, you're White, Chelsea. Listen to something else."

Pam: Does this affect your friendships?

Maria: Kind of.

Maria: Me, Emily, and April don't even listen to some of the music around them when we want to because we are their friends.

Emily: We know what they are going to say. . . .

Maria: Yeah.

Pam: What kind of music? Like Destiny's Child?

Maria: Like even Destiny's Child they go, like Shaquilla goes, "Oh, no, don't do that."

Emily: Me and April were singing it once and she's like "No Emily, no April."

Maria: And Tiffany, remember when they said that about Tiffany. They're not Tiffany's friend even though last year Shaquilla and them were Tiffany's friend. They're not her friend this year because they think she acts like she's Black.

Tracey, Vanecia, and Teresa on "Acting Black"

While they were discussing how they came to know poppin' (a dance move), Teresa, Tracey, and Vanecia started making fun of the boys in their class who have tried to make this move. In doing so, they told stories about one White boy, Kyle, who tried to "act Black." This conversation led to a more serious discussion about their frustrations with White girls who sang and danced in particular ways that, according to this trio, mirrored Black dance and communication styles. First, they explained that they liked to form dance groups during recess to act out their favorite singers, particularly TLC.

Pam: Okay, the other girls that you do this with, Shaquilla, Emily, April, Maria . . . you do the same thing. They say who [which singer] they are. . . .

Vanecia: They say who they are. When we do this and stuff, we do clubs and all of that other junk and then Emily, she goes, "okay like you know" and she be acting all Black and all hard like [Vanecia is snapping her fingers and moving her head back and forth] this no offense, Tracey [I think she said this because she knows they are Tracey's friends], but she acting all Black and hard and other things like that. And I be like, "Emily, no," and she be like, "oh no," and sometimes I be playing with her and I be acting like I'm a different color. . . .

Tracey: And then she go out and get a attitude.

Vanecia: I say, "Emily, don't be acting our color, act your color." And she's like, "okay then whatever." And then on the next day she be acting our color and I tell her again and she gets real smart with me and we get into fights. . . . I end up punching her and she end up running off crying and they end up coming back punching me back and I end up . . .

Pam: What bothers you about Emily acting your color?

Teresa: Cause it's like . . .

Tracey: It's annoying . . .

Vanecia: Well, what I'm trying to say is I can't see why White people act White, Black people act Black, it would be fine.

Teresa: I know. When White people try to act like Black people, it seems like they're not happy with their own color. Or when they try to be like Black . . .

Vanecia: So people will let them fit in.

Pam: So you do listen to this song with other girls. What happens when you are listening to it and Emily is trying to act Black, do you still keep on listening to it? Do you stop?

Vanecia: I listen to it and I tell her to stop.

Teresa: I know, because it gets on my nerves when she tries to act like Black people. Because it's like, why can't they just be happy with their color? Don't try to be like other people. If you don't fit into something, just let somebody know. . . .

Friendship Histories

During the interviews, both groups of girls were very passionate about how they each conceptualized the relationship between music and identities. At those moments when they wanted to communicate racial unity, Vanecia, Teresa, and Tracey established a firm connection between skin color and who can listen to particular musical genres. However, the concepts of "acting Black" or more broadly, "acting your color" continued to be more complex when enacted in everyday life. In this case, cross-cultural friendship histories and gendered relationships significantly affected how girls performed and thought about racial identifies. For example, Kyle, a middle-class White boy who doesn't "act his color," represented for these girls (Teresa, Vanecia, Tracey, and Maria) the most visible "acting Black" case. They spoke frequently about Kyle's attempts to act like his Black friend Nate. According to Teresa, "Kyle tries to be a Black boy . . . listening to our music and saying, 'hey, what's up my homie' . . . this is annoying and I tell him to stop." While it "annoyed" Teresa, she also explained that she doesn't think it bothered Nate because he and Kyle have been friends for a long time. Maria and Emily also made the same assessment. Tracey made the comment that "yo, those are my sisters" indicating that while she didn't like them "acting Black," Emily, April, and Maria were her friends. Emily's comment that it was hard to talk about "acting your own color" because "one of her best friends is African American" may also indicate the ways in which friendship histories complicate these identity conflicts. Friendship histories in relationship to racial identities were important in terms of understanding how both girls and boys negotiated their differences.

Gendered Allegiances

Girls' accusations about "acting your color" reveal only part of their musical story. While racial alliances were forged at these moments, on other occasions, girls publicly relied on each other in their journey to "get the boys out of their face." Their gendered allegiance in this quest was evident in their collaborative attempts to make sure "their music" (not the boy's music) was played during lunch and free time in the classroom. In their mutual attempts to unite, Tracey, Vanecia, Teresa, Maria, Emily, and April formed a dancing/singing group.

> We do it outside on the playground. We can't find no hangout, but the one hangout is over here in a small corner we really like, when we get over there if it's cold or when we get over there, like, anyone will bring snacks for our group. . . . The teachers don't know about the group. . . . We make up our own songs . . . and we only let boys who are nice to us be in the group.

While they occasionally let boys in, they did so only if the boys would let them be the leaders. According to Tracey . . .

> Like Mark, he's the boy you have to watch out for. Like all the girls we're controlling him . . . we have to work hard to keep him away from the girls. We got him in check.

This girl-dominated group provided an opportunity for them to act out their favorite singers and bands, and "to teach other girls who don't know how to dance our moves that we learned . . . so that others won't make fun of them." In addition, they often engaged in public scrutiny of boys who made fun of their music especially when these same boys sang and danced to TLC and N*Sync at other times. Their connections to each other through their shared gendered experiences with boys reveals the necessarily unfixed nature of identity.

The Central girls also used their music to build and maintain their friendship. Tracy described the ways in which popular music helped her to "make up" with other girls after a playground fight. She explained:

Like we were mad because we were outside and everything went wrong. Then during lunch, someone will go up and ask Isabella and Pete [teachers] to turn on Destiny's Child. So they play it and all the girls [who have been fighting] they like get back together once they get back in the class . . . because right when they say the words . . . you can picture your group together . . . when you get together, it makes you end up happy and makes you want to dance and stuff like that."

In this context, after a fight and in the lunchroom – a space that they associated with listening to "their music", the meaning of Destiny's Child's music and the relationship once established between genre and identity changed. For these girls, their relationships and the context of their interactions and engagement with music mattered in terms of how they expressed who they were and how they perceived others. While their racial and gendered identities were always present, these girls shifted their identification with others, at times, based on the exigency of the moment. The girls' experiences illustrate that identities are enacted, that we actively communicate who we are and use media to do so, and that our media consumption is always tied to social and cultural issues.

References

Ang, I. (1996). Ethnography and Radical Contextualism in Audience Studies. In: J. Hay L. Grossberg & E. Wartella (eds.), *The Audience and Its Landscape*, pp. 247–64. Boulder, CO: Westview Press.

Bennett, A. (2000). *Popular Music and Youth Culture: Music, Identity, Place*. New York: St. Martin's Press.

Williams, L. (2000). Commentary: Whites' Entertainment Is Black's Irritainment. *New Pittsburgh Courier*, 91(76), A6.

37

Elements of Vogue

*Marcos Becquer and José Gatti**

Vogueing – the dance fad, the (sub)cultural practice – is not the *object* of this [chapter]; rather, it designates a knowledge practice contiguous to our own. As such, our concern is not to define vogueing, but to elaborate upon the relations among some of the discourses implicated in it as a performance. The various representations of vogueing in recent film and video, particularly Jennie Livingston's *Paris Is Burning* [1990], but also Madonna's *Vogue* [1990] and Marlon Riggs' *Tongues Untied* [1989], among others, enable our elaboration not so much because they unproblematically reflect vogueing, but because they initiate their own discourses (theorisations) of it. Thus, they provide the occasion for a critique which marks vogueing as a site of intersection for the categories of race, class, gender, and sexuality.

Vogueing can be briefly described as a dance which is practised both casually, at gathering places like the pier in Greenwich Village (shown in *Tongues Untied*), nightclubs and even subway cars; and more formally, at events called balls (shown in *Paris Is Burning*) where it serves as a means of challenge between deferent 'houses' (or 'gangs') of poor, young black and hispanic gays. At balls, voguers compete for 'realness' in such categories as, e.g., 'banjee-realness', 'executive-realness', 'high fashion Parisian', 'luscious body-realness', and even 'butch queen first time in drag at a ball'. As deciphered by Willie Ninja, a voguer featured in some of the above-mentioned films and videos, vogueing brings together poses from the magazine of the same name, breakdancing moves, and gestures represented in Egyptian hieroglyphics. Vogueing, then, *articulates*, in a particular form, discursive practices usually associated with diverse social, historical and ethnic contexts. By 'articulation', here, we mean a practice which both speaks and links a set of elements whose historically shifting identities are modified in the process of being articulated (see Laclau and Mouffe 1985: 105).

Recent works dealing with identity politics have deployed the concept of hybridity in an effort to foreground the non-essentiality of composite articulations like vogueing. These works are involved in a critical project which would contest, through the celebration and radicalization of the hybrid, essentialist notions of ethnic and cultural identity. Few if any of these works, however, have directly addressed or critiqued the ideological baggage with which hybridity comes equipped.

*Pp. 445–53 from *The Subcultures Reader*, ed. K. Gelder and S. Thornton (New York: Routledge). © 1997 by M. Becquer and J. Gatti. Reprinted with permission from the authors.

Etymologically linked to animal husbandry and agriculture, for instance, hybridity may, and often does, still presuppose the 'pure' origin of elements – that is, their fixed, essential identities – prior to their hybridization. As one of the definitions found in *Webster's Dictionary* clarifies, a hybrid is 'an offspring of two animals or plants of different races, breeds, varieties, species, or genera.' Hence hybridity may not imply the erasure of essentialism in the hybridized 'offspring' as much as it might merely temporarily defer such essentialism onto parents which have been discreetly classified into 'static, homogeneous' categories.

Moreover, this more or less straightforward reference to parents and offspring threatens to reinforce the ultimate essentialism of sexual(ity) difference, even as it might highlight the heterogeneity of ethnic and cultural identity. In this sense, hybridity harbors the danger of contributing to the hegemony of the heterosexist metaphor which also informs numerous, oft-cited theories of the natural and of material relations. The specific logic implicit here, that two contrasting entities 'come' together to produce a third, masquerades as both universal and transhistorical. It is akin to what Foucault has called 'the meagre logic of contradiction', an Aristotelian notion that has enjoyed special prominence since the nineteenth century, and of which he finds evidence in 'the sterilising constraints of the dialectic' (Foucault 1980: 143–4). Indeed, such logic can be seen to naturalize not only dominant, teleological conceptions of progress and evolution (which are also germane to eugenicist notions of ethnic and cultural purity), but also totalizing and reductive accounts of the mechanisms of struggle which privilege conflicts as *the* means of change. The prevalence of theories of historical development and social transformation informed by such logic no doubt plays a role in the maintenance of the current hierarchical forms of subjectivity.

Thus, while we do not reject conflict as a form of struggle, we question its privileged epistemological status in the presently dominant regime of truth. It is our contention that the power relations implicit in vogueing exceed autotelic logics of contradiction and synthesis, and challenge the hegemony such hetero-logics enjoy. Indeed, considering the subject position(alitie)s occupied by vogueing's (sub)cultural practitioners, and the ones they embrace (and critique, but don't simply contradict) as they traverse sexualities, genders, races and classes in performance, we feel the demand for more nuanced understandings of resistance processes and strategies. Here lies the importance of vogueing (and similar articulations) to the project of thinking struggle.

As a politico-aesthetic characterisation of articulatory discourses such as vogueing, the concept of *syncretism* may prove more suggestive than hybridity. Though the two terms have often been used interchangeably, we would like to stress some important differences between them. The etymology of syncretism points to the tactical articulation of different elements, exemplified in Plutarch by the communities of ancient Crete which, despite their differences, joined to face a common enemy. Thus, syncretism foregrounds the political – rather than the (un)natural – paradigm of articulation and identity, a paradigm under which the factional inhabitants of Crete, rather than forming a homogeneous whole, compose a heterogeneous front of distinct communities in altered relations to each other. As such, the discursive alignment implicit in syncretism remains contingent to relations of power and subject to change according to historical specificity; the elements united in it are denied any a priori 'necessary belongingness', and are precluded any sense of an originary fixity both to their identities and to their relations. In this manner, syncretism designates articulation as a politicized and discontinuous mode of becoming. It entails the 'formal' coexistence of components whose precarious (i.e., partial as opposed to impartial) identities are mutually modified in their encounter, yet whose distinguishing differences, as such, are not dissolved or elided in these modifications, but strategically reconstituted in an ongoing war of position.

In so far as syncretism thus testifies to its elements' permeable boundaries, the political and methodological efficacy of strict relations of contradiction/complementarity between identities presumed fixed (as in, say, dominant models of heterosexuality and/or objectivist dialectics – often functioning as undergirding structures for subordinations in the social) can be radically questioned. It is this implicit relational challenge that most dramatically distinguishes syncretism from hybridity. . . .

It has been significantly due to an ethnography nostalgic for ever-fleeting cultural and ethnic 'purity' that syncretism has gained a derogatory weight, distancing it from its etymology. The ideological effects of this operation, by which the technologies of (post)colonialism have emptied the concept of its political content in a rhetorical manoeuvre casting alignment and resistance as contradiction, are made evident in the present dictionary definitions of syncretism: 'flagrant compromise in religion or philosophy; eclecticism that is illogical or leads to inconsistency; uncritical acceptance'.

In the African diaspora, [for example,] the responses to such colonialist distortions are varied. On the one hand, there have been some attempts to propose alternatives to syncretism as an analytical tool. To mention but a recent one, Brazilian scholar Muniz Sodré offers the concept of 'plasticity' as one of the distinctive features of West African religious and cultural systems, which has kept them open to dialogic interaction. This plasticity, Sodré suggests, has been 'used as a resource by an Africanist continuum in exile' for both survival and adaptation (Sodré 1989: 99; our translation). On the other hand, a vast diasporic literature (as well as filmography) has also appropriated syncretism by simply casting aside the standards of authenticity and charges of (illogical, primitive) contradiction that mark its use by colonialist ethnography. While we maintain the designation of cultural and/or religious practices, like the ones previously mentioned, as 'syncretic', we argue here for a repoliticization of the concept – which may be accomplished not only by retracing the word's etymology, but also by problematizing its historical deployment.

Hence, we propose a reinscription of the contact between, for example, European and African symbolic systems in syncretic articulations, not as contradictory but as *antagonistic*, i.e., in relations which are animated by the partial presence of the other within the self, such that the differential identity of each term is at once enabled and prevented from full constitution. These relations, which, depending on the configurations of power in contingent historical conditions, may or may not crystallize into oppositionalities, exist both horizontally (in equivalential alignments among diverse groups united in struggle, as in the Cretan example) as well as vertically (in dominant/subaltern confrontations, as in colonialism). Antagonistic relations, then, indicate the limits of absolutist conceptions of culture based upon a closed system of unalloyed, hetero-topic differences, and thereby expand the logics of struggle.

Syncretic relations are, in this sense, traversed by a double movement of both alliance and critique. Syncretism involves neither 'flagrant compromise' (ultimately a transposition of the logic of contradiction to a quantitative transaction), nor 'uncritical acceptance' (i.e., pluralist inclusion), but rather a process which articulates elements in a manner that modifies their intelligibility and transforms their combinatory spaces. The Egyptian hieroglyphics, for example, identified by Willie Ninja as one element of vogue, can be seen as an assertion of the heritage claimed by Africanism in the diaspora. Indeed, the paraphernalia that surrounds the voguers interviewed in *Paris Is Burning* often includes gilded Egyptian heads – reminders of a proud African past, as well as indices of non-white standards of beauty. At the same time, however, this aesthetic appropriation also connects vogueing with the (white) gay tradition of self-display through the 'exotic', i.e., through what is literally out of visibility. Michael Moon, for instance, suggests that Orientalist narratives, in which Western/male supremacy represses the (over)sensual Orientals, have had a special resonance for gay audiences subjected to homophobic oppression; the flamboyant re-enactment of these narratives has enabled gays, in turn, to stage performances of political resistance. Jack Smith's films, particularly *Flaming Creatures*, are examples for Moon of this type of re-appropriation which, he writes, 'fueled innumerable small- and large-scale eruptions of queer rebellion . . .' (Moon 1989: 54). Thus, two discourses apparently separate (and often considered 'opposed') are syncretized in vogueing: those of Africanist and of gay struggles. These elements engage, to use Clyde Taylor's expression, in an 'epistemological underground' (Taylor 1989: 102), where oppositional knowledges, dispersed in a field in which the effect of domination both disjoins and subordinates them in historically specific yet continuous ways, nonetheless find structuring connections and challenge hegemony.

Through breakdancing, vogueing establishes another such connection: that of black and hispanic gays with the hip hop culture, that emerged in the South Bronx in the 1970s. Writing about the hip hop movement 'Zulu Nation', Dick Hebdige sees it as 'rapped in a tradition which valorizes verbal and physical dexterity', and that is 'overtly pledged to the sublimation of fight into dance, of conflict into contest, of desperation into style and a sense of self respect' (Hebdige 1988: 216). This description, which uncannily recalls the spirit of the balls, aligns hip hop and vogueing with an African diasporic tradition that includes limbo dance contests in the West Indies and the martial art of *capoeira* in Brazil. Vogueing, however, multiplies the fronts of struggle in alignment by repositioning breakdancing within an emergent history of black and hispanic *gay* pride, thereby critiquing certain (hetero)sexist currents within hip hop. Thus, the syncretic articulation is shown to entail not simply the destruc(tura)tion nor the unqualified acceptance of preceding discourses, but their (re)structuration.

Similar antagonistic tensions and affinities also obtain between voguers and the attitudes of fashion. In *Paris Is Burning*, pre-op transsexual Venus Extravaganza can be seen to underscore tensions with fashion magazines' essentialist representations of woman, by foregrounding the constructed character of her own womanness in performance. At the same time, however, Venus' plans of stardom (as a fashion model) and/or 'normalcy' (as a suburban housewife) also reinforce her affinities with 'the multiplication of persons in a single being which', according to Roland Barthes, 'is always considered by Fashion as an index of [woman's] power' (Barthes 1983: 256–7). In this double movement, then, Venus 'deforms' dominant representations of woman-as-essence, as she re-moulds the concept of woman into what may be called woman-as-positionality. Venus is thus articulated to 'woman' in a manner which modifies both the elements articulated – concept of woman, Venus's own subjectivity – and the discourses in which they are now (and were previously) positioned.

Thus, the syncretization of, e.g., Egyptian hieroglyphics, breakdancing moves and fashion magazine poses demonstrates how sexuality, gender, class and race are (re)posited in vogueing. A space is thereby opened where different discursive formations can strategically figure unsuspected alignments of significations which, nonetheless, remain distinct.

In this sense, we may revise popular accounts of vogueing's relations with the media. Both *Paris Is Burning* and Madonna's *Vogue*, rather narcissistically (in as far as the media, here, assumes the importance of its own impact), accentuate the 'influence' of the media on voguers. The Hollywood icon medley in Madonna's video, typified by the line 'Rita Hayworth gave good face', hails vogueing as the next step in a continuing line of utopian glamour (epitomized by Madonna herself?), but glosses its positions in the traditions of resistance, outside of Hollywood and camp, to which we have referred. *Paris Is Burning*, on the other hand, presents voguers as subjects who, though duped by media ideology, more or less unwittingly subvert it in the momentary euphoria of carnivalesque inversion. . . .

If the media interpellates them as consumers, voguers antagonize such identificatory hailing by means of performances that defy the limits and the strictures of that address. It is, for instance, not necessarily their identities as consumers (nor, for that matter, as representatives of the 'real lives' of the other) but as *stars* (and the mobility between such discursive constructions) that are both enabled and prevented in voguers' relations with the media in its present organization. Their posed articulation thus demands the radical, structural change of both the media and voguers' interpellated, marginalized subjectivities. The engagement of vogueing in the politics of representation in this sense exceeds the cut-and-dry terms of a reductive dialectic, where opposing poles (and the quantity of their influence) would be clearly fixed and identified. Voguers' confrontations with the media are instead marked by the *shifting* limits of their own *agency* in a process *overdetermined* by historical circumstances. Less informed by the fatalism of cooptation than the discourse of influence would insinuate, voguers' simultaneous critique and embrace of the media is played out in a struggle over appropriation.

The stress on influence in *Paris Is Burning*, then (despite its sympathetic portrayals), might well be read as symptomatic of, as Kobena Mercer writes in another context, 'an underlying anxiety to pin down and categorize a practice that upsets and disrupts fixed expectations and normative assumptions' (Mercer 1988: 51); in other words, as an integral part of the film's very ambition to normatively 'explain' vogueing. In order to accomplish its explanatory mission, *Paris Is Burning* institutes a pedagogical relationship with its audience, a relationship indexed in the film by a univocal system of questions and answers that attempts to translate voguers' rich and creative vocabulary. The word 'reading', to take just one example, is flashed in white letters upon a black screen as voguers are summoned to provide an accurate definition. Here, the ideological tenets grounding the film's pedagogical operation (starkly inscribed in the very black-and-whiteness of the gaphic images) can be seen not only to presuppose an audience uninformed about vogueing, but also to circumscribe the critical dissemination of the terms' significations. . . . By (re)encoding a system of self-same differences as its interpretive grid, *Paris Is Burning* in effect delimits the ideological terrain upon which vogueing may operate. As a competent ethnographic primer, the film establishes a structural gap between 'the (fixed) world of voguers' and 'the (fixed) audience', a gap supposedly bridged by a civilising filmmaking, always in search of exotic, authentic phenomena.

It is in this sense that 'influence' and its companion other, 'cooptation', acquire an additional function: that of distinguishing an authentic vogueing from one corrupted by commercialization, This logic turns one voguer's statement, that the balls are no longer what they used to be, into a piece of evidence used to reassure us that *Paris Is Burning* has itself 'captured' the real vogueing at its height – a strategy of validation retroactively further underscored at the film's very beginning, when a character's voice-over announces that the film is about 'the ball circuit and the gay people that are involved in it'. Yet, the idea of authenticity, as we have suggested, is problematized by vogueing itself as a syncretic practice. We might consider, in this sense, Madonna's *Vogue* video less a cooptation (or corruption) than a rearticulation of vogueing, a rearticulation that is not necessarily juxtaposed to the 'authenticity' of vogueing as a subcultural practice, but that is prompted by vogueing as a knowledge practice which produces identity as mobile and unfixed.

Still, the rhetoric of authenticity in *Paris Is Burning* serves to replace any sustained effort towards authorial self-reflexivity, and instead enthrones the *authority* of experience. Indeed, it is precisely upon the basis of the experiential – an epistemological category which dissimulates its own appeals to arbitrarily structured forms of (re)cognition by naturalizing them as immediate presence – that *Paris Is Burning* is, as Livingstone herself declares, 'giving you definitions . . . It's taking forms that you are used to and doing something else to them' (Livingstone 1991). Hence, the film ultimately interprets the knowledge voguers practice, that 'something else', by relegating – and thus containing – it to certain subject position(alitie)s, i.e., to a certain race, gender, sexual orientation and class, and 'their experience'. Not surprisingly, then, voguers are depicted as grotesque embodiments of contradiction (and not antagonism) as they 'playfully reverse' existing power/identity hierarchies. At the expense of its syncretic reconfigurations of the real, vogueing remains fixed in a semiotic realm of differential relations so acquiescent to the dictates of a facile multiculturalism. It becomes just another instance (or moment) in a chain of rationalization which operates in terms of clearly identifiable and stable oppositions (say, black/white, poor/rich, gay/straight, female/male, etc), and which signifies, multiplies and hierarchizes difference by 'explaining' it in terms of closed, arrested categories. An entire heterogeneous community (voguers walk not only as, say, 'Virginia Slims Girls', but also as homeboys, soldiers, executives, students, etc.) is in this sense grouped into a unified, homogeneous Other, housed under the rubric of 'their experience' and fixed in an unproblematized sequence of absolute differences.

In *Tongues Untied*, on the other hand, rather than the experiential being deployed to 'explain' vogueing, it is vogueing that is recruited to redefine the experiential. Marlon

Riggs' appearance in the (auto)biographical narrative of *Tongues Untied* reflexively foregrounds the experiential as a construct which, rather than homogenizing an 'authentic(ated)' black gay identity, diversifies black gay discourses. Thus his statement that '[*Tongues Untied*] crosses many boundaries of genre' indexically illustrates what, for him, is an important part of the video's message, 'that the way to break loose of the schizophrenia in trying to define identity is to realize that you are many things within one person' (Simmons 1991: 191, 193). Indeed, the vogueing sequence (along with many others in the video's constitutive 'digressions') works to render identity heterogeneous. By re-introducing the collective into the filmic discourse, vogueing here challenges the univocality which often accompanies common understandings of the experiential. However, as a syncretic articulation, vogueing can be seen to radicalize even the search for a definite –albeit heterogeneous – black gay identity. By emphasizing the inconclu siveness of the self in antagonism, vogueing *interrupts* the very coherence of the experiential which informs the collective 'I' constructed in *Tongues Untied*.

By 'interruption' here, we mean a practice which critically separates and (re)opens the closed structures into which existing discursive configurations have ossified. As it syncretizes elements in performance, vogueing effectively literalizes interruption in the form of the pose. In Craig Owens' psychoanalytic account of it, the pose stands in an aggressive relation to (the desire of) power (Owens 1985). It inscribes the phallic com- pulsion to halt the 'dance of signs' and (re)produce significations; it also dramatizes, through its very artificiality, the untenability of this desire for stasis in the movement of history. It is in this sense that interruption can be understood as a point of dislocation between the subject and the structure that supposedly contains it. Thus the pose becomes a form of resistance to the evil eye (Lacan's *fascinum*) of the subject– structures that would immobilize it in the chain of significations.

In Madonna's video this resistant pose – encapsulated in the otherizing ethnography of *Paris Is Burning* and emergent in the stroboscopic lyricism of *Tongues Untied* – is given a new, (de)politicized character. It becomes a (star) vehicle of escape to the polymorphous perversity of an idealized, universally available dance floor where, as the lyrics go, 'it makes no difference if you're black or white, if you're a boy or a girl'. Madonna thus defines the very *topos* of multiculturalism as a place where antago- nisms would be erased and struggles rendered superfluous. It is in this indifferent space, underwritten by what Ernesto Laclau calls the violence of the universal (Laclau 1990: xi), that objective differential identities expand indefinitely. Here we discover a crucial link between *Paris Is Burning* and Madonna's *Vogue*, between realism and escap- ism; both are synecdochic of the prevailing constructions of the multicultural. They fetishize an objectified other and/or subsume her under a myth of equality. Both partake in the production of newness, a process which purports to keep us up-to-date as it continually adds on novelties to a relational system that absorbs them; both contain vogueing beneath the pluralist umbrella of hipness. Conceiving of knowledge in quan- titative terms, this safely heterogeneous yet hegemonic multiculturalism excludes nothing.

What is ignored in this process, however, is the status of desire which, in our own interruptive (rather than interpretive) reading of vogueing, continually reassesses dif- ferences in qualitative terms. In this sense, voguers can be seen to pose desire itself as a form of counter-hegemonic knowledge. Understood as a syncretic articulation, vogueing explores the possible within the existing. By embracing, critiquing and restructuring, e.g., ethnicity, gayness, gender, class, etc., it intervenes in sovereign discursive structures – like the experiential and the authentic – which would reduce its elements to immanent moments of a naturalized system of differences and which vogueing 'reads' as inadequate to its reconfigurations of the real. Interrupting the closure of identities and of their relations, vogueing's syncretisms propose new possibilities of struggle.

References

Barthes, Roland (1983). *The Fashion System*, New York: Farrar Strauss & Giroux.

Foucault, Michel (1980). *Power/Knowledge: Selected Interviews and Other Writings 1972–1977*, New York: Pantheon.

Hebdige, Dick (1988). *Hiding in the Light*, London: Routledge.

Laclau Ernesto (1990). *New Reflections on the Revolution of Our Time*, London: Verso.

Laclau, Ernesto & Mouffe, Chantal (1985). *Hegemony and Social Strategy: Towards a Radical Democratic Politics*, London: Verso.

Livingstone, Jennie (1991). 'Paris is Burning', *Outweek* 94.

Mercer, Kobena (1988). 'Diaspora Culture and the Dialogic Imagination: the Aesthetics of Black Independent Film in Britain', In: Mbye B. Chain & Claire Andrade-Watkins (eds.), *Blackframes: Critical Perspectives on Black Independent Cinema*, Cambridge, MA: MIT Press.

Moon, Michael (1989). 'Flaming Closets', *October* 51.

Owens, Craig (1985) 'Posing', in *Difference: On Representation and Sexuality*, New York: New Museum of Contemporary Art.

Simmons, Ron (1991). '*Tongues Untied:* An Interview with Marlon Riggs', in Essex Hemphill (ed.), *Brother to Brother*, Boston: Alyson Publications.

Sodré, Muniz (1989). *O Terreiro e a Cidade*, Petropolis: Vbzes.

Taylor, Clyde (1989). 'Black Cinema in the Post-Aesthetic Era', In: Jim Pines & Paul Willemen (eds.), *Questions of Third Cinema*, London: BFI Publishing.

38

In Our Angelhood: Rave as Counterculture and Spiritual Revolution

Simon Reynolds*

By the mid-nineties, the British media had woken up to the fact that the nation contained two societies: the traditional leisure culture of alcohol and entertainment (spectator sports, TV) versus the more participatory, effusive culture of all night dancing and
Ecstasy. The clash between old Britain and young Britain was dramatized to hilarious
effect in an episode of *Inspector Morse* entitled "Cherubim and Seraphics." The plot
concerns a series of mysterious teenage deaths that appear to be connected to a new
drug called Seraphic. Despite its overt "just say no" slant, the episode mostly works as
an exhilarating advert for Ecstasy culture. (*Literally*, insofar as Morse's remark to his
detective partner – "it's a rave, Lewis!" – was sampled and used by a pirate station.)

This collision of old and new Englands reaches its peak when the detective duo arrive
at the stately home where a rave called Cherub is taking place. Morse drones on about
the noble history of the building; inside, the kids have transformed it into a future
wonderland. Sure, the crooked lab researcher responsible for the Seraphic drug gets his
comeuppance. But the episode ends by allowing the sixteen-year-old girlfriend of one
Seraphic casualty to utter a paean to Ecstasy: "You love everyone in the world, you
want to touch everyone." And it transpires that the teenagers didn't kill themselves
because the drug unbalanced their minds; rather, having glimpsed heaven on earth, they
decided that returning to reality would be a comedown. Who wouldn't want to give E
a try after that? And who would possibly side with decrepit Morse, with his booze and
classical music CDs, against the shiny happy people of Generation E?

This episode of *Inspector Morse* signaled a dawning awareness in the media that recreational drug culture had become firmly installed in Britain during the early nineties
and was now omnipresent almost to the point of banality. Every weekend, anywhere
from half a million to two million people under the age of thirty-five were using psychedelics and stimulants. This geographically dispersed but spiritually connected
network of Love-Ins, Freak-Outs, and All-Night Raves constituted a weekly Woodstock
(or rather Woodstock and Altamont rolled into one, given that Ecstasy's dark side was
starting to reveal itself). The question, then, is this: Has rave proved itself a form of

* Pp. 239–48 from S. Reynolds, *Generation Ecstasy: Into the World of Techno and Rave* (Boston, MA: Little
Brown). © 1999 by Routledge Publishing, Inc. Reprinted with permission from Routledge Publishing,
Inc.

mass bohemia, or is it merely a futuristic update of traditional youth leisure, where the fun-crazed weekend redeems the drudgery of the working week? What are the politics of Ecstasy culture?

Among Ecstasy's social effects, the most obvious is the way it has utterly transformed youth leisure in Britain and Europe. Because alcohol muddies the MDMA high, rave culture rapidly developed an antialcohol taboo. It could be argued that Ecstasy's net effect has actually been to save lives, by reducing the number of alcohol-fueled fights and drunk-driving fatalities.

Like alcohol, Ecstasy removes inhibitions. But because it also diminishes aggression (including sexual aggression), E has had the salutary effect of transforming the night-club from a "cattle market" and combat zone into a place where women come into their own and men are too busy dancing and bonding with their mates to get into fights. These benign side effects spilled outside clubland: with football fans turning onto E and house, by 1991–2 soccer hooliganism in Britain was at its lowest level in five years.

Generally speaking, Ecstasy seems to promote tolerance. One of the delights of the rave scene at its height was the way it allowed for mingling across lines of class, race, and sexual preference. MDMA rid club culture of its cliqueishness and stylistic sectarianism; hence drug culture researcher Sheila Henderson's phrase "luvdup and de-elited." Rave's explosive impact in the UK, compared to its slower dissemination in America, may have something to do with the fact that Britain remains one of the most rigidly class-stratified counties in the Western world. Perhaps the drug simply wasn't as *needed* in America as it was in the UK. For in many ways, MDMA is an antidote to the English disease: reserve, inhibition, emotional constipation, class consciousness.

Yet for all the rhetoric of spiritual revolution and counterculture, it remains a moot point whether Ecstasy's effects have spilled outside the domain of leisure. From early on, commentators noted that the controlled hedonism of the MDMA experience is much more compatible with a basically normal, conformist lifestyle than other drugs. Norman Zinberg called it "the yuppie psychedelic"; others have compared it to a "mini-vacation," an intense burst of "quality time." In his essay "The Ecstasy of Disappearance," Antonio Melechi uses the historical origins of rave in Ibiza as the foundation for a theory of rave as a form of *internal tourism:* a holiday from everyday life and from your everyday self. At the big one-shot raves, some kids spend – on drinks, drugs, souvenir merchandise, travel – as much as they would on a short vacation. Rejecting the idea that this is simply escapism, a safety valve for the tensions generated by capitalist work patterns, Melechi argues that rave supersedes the old model of subcultural activity as resistance through rituals. Where earlier style-terrorist subcultures like mod and punk were exhibitionist, a kick in the eye of straight society, rave is a form of collective disappearance, an investment in pleasure that shouldn't be written off as mere retreat or disengagement.

Melechi's theory of rave – as neither subversive nor conformist but more than both – appeals to the believer in me. From a more dispassionate perspective, though, rave appears more like a new twist on a very old idea. There is actually a striking continuity in the work hard/play hard structure of working-class leisure, from the mods' sixty-hour weekends and Northern Soul's speed-freak stylists, to disco's Saturday-night fever dreams and jazz-funk's All-Dayers and Soul Weekends. When I listen to the Easybeats' 1967 Aussie-mod anthem "Friday on My Mind," I'm stunned by the way the lyrics – a thrilling anatomy of the working-class weekender lifecycle of drudgery, anticipation, and explosive release – still resonate. Thirty years on, we're no nearer to overhauling the work/leisure structures of industrial society. Instead, all that rage and frustration is vented through going mental on the weekend ("Tonight, I'll spend my bread/ Tonight, I'll lose my head"), helped along by a capsule or three of instant euphoria.

From the Summer of Love rhetoric of the early UK acid house evangelists to San Francisco's cyberdelic community, from the neopaganism of Spiral Tribe to the transcendentalism of the Megatripolis/GoaTrance scene, rave has also been home to another "politics of Ecstasy," one much closer to the original intent behind Timothy Leary's phrase. Ecstasy has been embraced as one element of a bourgeois-bohemian version of rave, in which the music-drugs-technology nexus is fused with spirituality and vague hippy-punk-anarcho politics to form a nineties would-be counterculture.

The fact that the same drug can be at the core of two different "politics of ecstasy" – raving as safety valve versus raving as opting out – can be traced back to the double nature of MDMA as a *psychedelic amphetamine*. The psychedelic component of the experience lends itself to utopianism and an at least implicit critique of the way things are. Amphetamine, though, does not have a reputation as a consciousness-raising chemical. While they popped as many pills as other strata of society, the hippies regarded amphetamine as a straight person's drug: after all, it was still legal and being prescribed in vast amounts to tired housewives, overworked businessmen, dieters, and students cramming for exams. Amphetamine's ego-boosting and productivity-raising effects ran totally counter to the psychedelic creed of selfless surrender, indolence, and Zen passivity. So when the spread of methamphetamine poisoned Haight-Ashbury's love-and-peace vibe, the counterculture responded with the "speed kills" campaign. The hippies' hostility toward amphetamine is one reason the punks embraced the chemical.

In their 1975 classic *The Speed Culture: Amphetamine Use and Abuse in America*, Lester Grinspoon and Peter Hedblom draw an invidious comparison between marijuana and amphetamine, arguing that pot smoking instills values that run counter to capitalist norms, while amphetamine amplifies all the competitive, aggressive, and solipsistic tendencies of Western industrial life. Terence McKenna, an evangelist for Gaia-given plant psychedelics like magic mushrooms, classes amphetamine as one of the "dominator drugs," alongside cocaine and caffeine.

Chemically programmed into MDMA is a sort of less-is-more effect: what starts out as an empathy enhancer degenerates, with repeated use, into little more than amphetamine, at least in terms of its effects. When MDMA's warm glow cools through overuse, ravers often turn to the cheaper, more reliable amphetamine. Both these syndromes – excessive intake of E, the use of amphetamine as substitute – explain the tendency of rave subcultures to mutate into speed-freak scenes after a couple of years.

From all this we might conclude that when the amphetamine component of the MDMA experience comes to the fore, rave culture loses much of its "progressive" edge. At one end of the class spectrum are the working-class weekender scenes, where MDMA is used in tandem with amphetamine and the subcultural raison d'être is limited and ultimately conformist: stimulants are used to provide energy and delay the need for sleep, to intensify and maximize leisure time. At the other, more bohemian end of rave culture, MDMA is used in tandem with LSD and other consciousness-raising hallucinogens, as part of a subcultural project of turning on, tuning in, and dropping out.

But the picture is a bit more complicated than this. LSD is widely used in working-class rave scenes, although arguably in ways that break with the Timothy Leary/Terence McKenna model of enlightenment through altered states. Hallucinogens appeal as another form of teenage kicks, a way of making the world into a cartoon or video game. (Hence brands of acid blotter like Super Mario and Power Rangers.) And amphetamine, in high doses or with prolonged use, can have its own hallucinatory and delusory effects. Like MDMA, speed makes perceptions more vivid; its effect of hyperacousia can escalate into full-blown auditory hallucinations. The sensory flood can seem visionary, pregnant with portent. Serious speed freaks often have a sense of clairvoyance and gnosis, feel plugged into occult power sources, believe they alone can perceive secret patterns and conspiracies.

Nonetheless, there is a tension in rave culture between consciousness raising and consciousness razing, between middle-class technopagans for whom MDMA is just one chemical in the pharmacopoeia of a spiritual revolution and weekenders for whom E is just another tool for "obliviating" the boredom of workaday life. This class-based divide has quite a history. Witness the snobbish dismay of highbrow hallucinogen fiends like R. Gordon Wasson, who wrote about his psilocybin visions for *Life* magazine in 1957, only to be appalled when thrill-seeking "riff-raff" promptly descended on the magic mushroom fields of Mexico, or worse, turned to its synthetic equivalent, LSD. Wasson refused to use the pop culture term "psychedelic," preferring the more ungainly and overtly transcendentalist "entheogen" (a substance that puts you in touch with the divine). Such linguistic games and terminological niceties often seem like the only way that intellectuals can distinguish their "discriminating" use of drugs from the heedless hedonism of the masses.

Wasson's writings are one of the sources for John Moore's brilliant 1988 monograph *Anarchy & Ecstasy: Visions of Halcyon Days*. Using shreds of historical evidence, Moore imaginatively reconstructs prehistoric pagan rites dedicated to Gaia worship; he argues for the contemporary revival of these "Eversion Mysteries," insisting that a ritualized, mystical encounter with Chaos (what he calls "bewilderness") is an essential component of any truly vital anarchistic politics.

Anarchy & Ecstasy, written in the mid-eighties, reads like a prophecy and program for rave culture. Crucial preparations for the Mystery rites include fasting and sleep deprivation, in order to break down "inner resistances" and facilitate possession by the "sacred wilderness." The rites themselves consist of mass chanting, dancing ("enraptured abandonment to a syncopated musical beat" that "flings aside rigidities, be they postural, behavioral or characterological"), and the administering of hallucinogenic drugs in order that "each of the senses and faculties [be] sensitized to fever pitch prior to derangement into a liberatingly integrative synaesthesia." The worshippers are led into murky, mazelike caverns, whose darkness is illuminated only by "mandalas and visual images."

All this sounds very like any number of clubs with their multiple levels and corridors decorated with psychotropic imagery. As for the "hierophants" with their intoxicating poisons, this could be the dealers touting "E's and trips." Moore's description of the peak of Mystery rites also sounds very like the effect of MDMA: "The initiate becomes androgynous, unconcerned with the artificial distinctions of gender. . . . Encountering total saturation, individuals transcend their ego boundaries and their mortality in successive waves of ecstasy."

Hardly surprising, then, that organized religion has noticed the way rave culture provides "the youth of today" with an experience of collective communion and transcendence. Just as the early Church coopted heathen rituals, there have been attempts to *rejuvenate* Christianity by incorporating elements of the rave experience: dancing, lights, mass fervor, demonstrative and emotional behavior. Most (in)famous of these was the Nine O'clock Service in Sheffield, the brainchild of "rave vicar" Chris Brain, whose innovations were greeted with keen interest and approval on the part of the Anglican hierarchy until it was discovered that the reverend was loving some of his female parishioners a little too much. Despite this embarrassment, rave-style worship has spread to other cities in the UK, such as Gloucester and Bradford (where the Cathedral holds services called Eternity). There have also been a number of attempts to lure lost and confused youth into the Christian fold via drug-and-alcohol-free rave nights: Club X in Bath (organized by Billy Graham's Youth for Christ) and Bliss (a Bournemouth night started by the Pioneer Network).

None of these quasi-rave clubs administer Ecstasy as a holy sacrament. But perhaps they should, for if any drug induces a state of soul that approximates the Christian ideal – overflowing with trust and goodwill to all men – then surely it's MDMA. While rave behavior is a little outré for the staid Church of England, it chimes in nicely with the more ecstatic and gesturally demonstrative strains of Christianity. Indeed, Moby, techno's most visible and outspoken Christian, claims that "the first rave was when the Ark of Covenant was brought into Jerusalem, and King David went out and danced like crazy and tore off all his clothes."

But the rave experience probably has more in common with the goals and techniques of Zen Buddhism: the emptying out of meaning via mantric repetition; nirvana as the paradox of the full void. Nicholas Saunders's *E Is For Ecstasy* quotes a Rinzai Zen monk who approves of raving as a form of active meditation, of being "truly in the moment and not in your head." Later in Saunders's book, there's an extract from an Ecstasy memoir in which the anonymous author describes the peculiar, depthless quality of the MDMA experience: "There's no inside"; "I was empty. I seemed to have become pure presence." At its most intense, the Ecstasy rush resembles the kundalini energy that yoga seeks to awaken: "liquid fire" that infuses the nervous system and leaves the consciousness "aglow with light."

What makes rave culture so ripe for religiosity is the "spirituality" of the Ecstasy experience: its sense of access to a wonderful secret that can be understood only by direct, unmediated experience, and the way it releases an outflow of all-embracing but peculiarly asexual love. Clearly the most interesting and "subversive" attributes of the MDMA experience, these aspects are also what makes rave fraught with a latent nihilism.

If one word crystallizes this ambivalence at the heart of the rave experience, it's "intransitive" – insofar as the music and the culture lack an objective or object. Rave

culture has no goal beyond its own propagation; it is about the celebration of celebration, about an intensity without pretext or context. Hence the urgent "nonsense" of
MCs at raves and on pirate radio. Witness the following Index FM phone-in session
on Christmas Eve 1992, with its strange combination of semantic impoverishment and
extreme affective charge.

MC 1: Sounds of the Dominator, Index FM. And it's getting busy tonight, London.
    Rrrrrrush!!! 'Ello mate?
Caller 1 (giggly, very out-of-it): 'Ello, London, I'd like to give a big shout out to the
    Car Park posse, yeah? There's my friend, my brother, Eli, and there's my friend
    over there called Anthony, and he's, like, smasher, he's hard –
MC 1: Like you, mate!
CALLER 1: Innit, of course!
MC 1: You sound wrecked –
CALLER 1: Yeah, I'm *totally* wrecked, mate –
    [*UPROAR*, chants of "Oi, oi! Oi, oi!"]
CALLER 1: My bruvva my bruvva my bruvva my bruvva my bruvva –
MC 1: Make some noise!
CALLER 1: Believe you me, mate, 'ardkore you know the score!
MC 1: Respect, mate! 'Ardkore noise!
CALLER 1: Oi, can you gimme gimme gimme "Confusion," mate? 2 Bad Mice.
MC 1 (getting emotional, close to tears): Yeah, we'll sort that one out for you. Last
    caller, we're gonna have to go. Respect going out to you, mate! Hold it down, last
    caller, *rude boy* FOR YEEEEAAARS! Believe me, send this one out to you, last
    caller! From the Dominator! Send this one out to you, mate. You're *a bad boy*,
    BELIEF!!! 90–3, the Index, comin' on strong, *belief!!!*
MC 2: Don't forget, people – New Year's Eve, Index FM are going to be throwing
    a free rave in conjunction with UAC Promotions. *Rrrrrave, rrrrrave!!!!* Three
    mental floors of mayhem, lasers, lights, all the works – you know the score.
MC 1 (gasping feyly): Oh goshhhh!!! Keep the pagers *rushing!* Come and *go.
    OOOOOOH goshhhhh!!* We're comin' on, we're comin on strong, *believe . . .*
    Deeper! Deeper into the groove. . . . Yeah, London Town, we've got another
    caller, wants to go live!
CALLER 2 (sounding rehearsed): Hi, I wanna a big shout to all Gathall Crew, all
    Brockley crew, Pascal, Bassline, Smasher. . . . We're in the house and we're
    rocking, *you be shocking*, for '92, mate!!
MC 1: Believe it, mate!
CALLER 2: 'ARD-*KORE*, you *know* the score!!!
MC 1: Where you coming from, mate?
CALLER 2: South London, mate.
MC 1: Wicked. Shout to the South London crew. Respect! Index! Yeah, London,
    you're in tune to the live line, Index FM, *runnin' t'ings in London right 'bout now.*
    The one and only.

Rapt then and now by phone-in sessions like this one, by the listeners' fervent saluta-
tions and the MCs' invocations, I'm struck by the crusading zeal and intransitive nature

of the utterances: "Rushing!," "Buzzin' hard!," "Get busy!," "Come alive, London!," "Let's go!," "Time to get hyper, helter-skelter!," "Hardcore's firing!," and, especially prominent in the Index-at-Xmas session, the near-gnostic exhortation "Belief!"

Gnosis is the esoteric knowledge of spiritual truth that various pre-Christian and early Christian cults believed could be apprehended directly only by the initiate, a truth that cannot be mediated or explained in words. In rave, catchphrases like "hardcore, you know the score" or "you know the key" are code for the secret knowledge to which only "the headstrong people" are privy. And this is *drug knowledge,* the physically felt intensities induced by Ecstasy, amphetamine, and the rest of the pharmacopoeia. The MC's role, as master of the sacra-*mental* ceremonies, is ceaselessly to reiterate that secret without ever translating it. The MC is an encryptor, a potent inclusion/exclusion device – for if you're not down with the program, you'll never know what that idiot is raving about.

The transcript of the Index-at-Xmas exchange can't convey the electricity of every-one in the studio coming up on their Es at the same time, of the NRG currents pulsing across the cellular-phone ether from kids buzzing at home. Listening to pirate phone-in sessions like this, I felt there was a feedback loop of ever-escalating exultation switching back and forth between the station and the raving "massive" at home. The whole sub-culture resembled a giant mechanism designed to generate fervor without aim.

The rave and the pirate radio show (the "rave on the air") are exemplary real-world manifestations of two influential theoretical models, Hakim Bey's "temporary autono-mous zone" (TAZ) and Gilles Deleuze and Felix Guattari's "desiring machine." The feedback loop of the phone-in sessions makes me think of Hakim Bey's vision of the TAZ as a temporary "power surge" against normality, as opposed to a doomed attempt at permanent revolution. A power surge is what it feels like – like being plugged into the national electrical grid. The audience is galvanized, shocked out of the living death of normality: "Come alive, London!" The combination of the DJ's interminable meta-music flow and the MC's variations on a small set of themes has the effect of abolishing narrative in favor of a thousand plateaus of crescendo. Again and again, the DJ and the MC affirm "we're here, we're now, this is the place to be, you and I are *we*." This radical immediacy fits Hakim Bey's anarcho-mystical creed of "immediatism," so named to indicate its antagonism to all forms of mediated, passivity-inducing leisure and culture.

The rave also corresponds to Deleuze and Guattari's model of the "desiring machine": a decentered, nonhierarchical assemblage of people and technology characterized by flow-without-goal and expression-without-meaning. The rave works as an intensifica-tion machine, generating a series of heightened here-and-nows – sonically, by the music's repetitive loops, and visually, by lights, lasers, and above all the strobe (whose freeze-frame effect creates a concatenated sequence of ultravivid tableaux).

Just as a rave can't function without ravers, similarly the "desiring machine" depends on its human components – what Deleuze and Guattari call the "body-without-organs." The opposite of the organism – which is oriented around survival and reproduction – the body-without-organs is composed out of all the potentials in the human nervous system for pleasure and sensation without purpose: the sterile bliss of perverse sexuality, drug experiences, play, dancing, and so forth. In the rave context, the desiring machine and the body-without-organs are fueled by the same energy source: MDMA. Plugged into the sound system, charged up on E, the raver's body-without-organs simply buzzes, bloated with unemployable energy: a feeling of "arrested orgasm" captured in pirate MC ejaculations like "oooooh gosh!"

Described by Deleuze and Guattari as "a continuous, self-vibrating region of intensities whose development avoids any orientation toward a culmination point or external end," the body-without-organs is an update of Freud's notion of polymorphous perversity: a diffuse eroticism that's connected to the non-genital, nonorgasmic sensuality of the pre-Oedipal infant. The body-without-organs also echoes age-old mystical goals: Zen's Uncarved Block, a blissful, inchoate flux preceding individuation and gender; the "translucent" or "subtle body," angelic and androgynous, whose resurrection was sought by the gnostics and alchemists.

In *Omens of Millennium* – a book about the contemporary resurgence of gnostic preoccupations with angels and near-death experiences – Harold Bloom argues: "To be drugged by the embrace of nature into what we call most natural in us, our sleepiness and our sexual desires, is at once a pleasant and an unhappy fate, since what remains immortal in us is both androgynous and sleepless." MDMA, an "unnatural" designer drug whose effects are antiaphrodisiac and insomniac, might be a synthetic shortcut to recovering our angelhood. I remember one time on E enjoying a radical sensation of being without gender, a feeling of docility and angelic gentleness so novel and exquisite I could only express it clumsily: "I feel really *effeminate.*" The subliminal hormonal "hum" of masculinity was suddenly silenced.

Such sensations of sexual indifference have everything to do with MDMA's removal of aggression, especially sexual aggression. E's reputation as the "love drug" has more to do with cuddles than copulation, sentimentality than secretions. E is notorious for making erection difficult and male orgasm virtually impossible; women fare rather better, although one female therapist suggests that on Ecstasy "the particular organization and particular focusing of the body and the psychic energy necessary to achieve orgasm [is] . . . very difficult." Despite this, MDMA still has a reputation as an aphrodisiac – partly because it enhances touch, and partly because affection, intimacy, and physical tenderness are, for many people, inextricably entangled and conflated with sexual desire.

Unaware of Ecstasy's effects, many early commentators were quick to ascribe the curiously chaste vibe at raves to a post-AIDS retreat from adult sexuality. But one of the most radically novel and arguably subversive aspects of rave culture is precisely that it's the first youth subculture that's *not* based on the notion that sex is transgressive. Rejecting all that tired sixties rhetoric of sexual liberation, and recoiling from our sexsaturated pop culture, rave locates bliss in prepubescent childhood. Hence the garish colors and baggy clothing, the backpacks and satchels, the lollipops and pacifiers and teddy bears – even the fairground sideshows. It's intriguing that a drug originally designed as an appetite suppressant should have this effect. Anorexia has long been diagnosed as a refusal of adult sexual maturity and all its accompanying hassles. Ecstasy doesn't negate the body, it intensifies the pleasure of physical expression while completely emptying out the sexual content of dance. For men, the drug/music interface acts to de-phallicize the body and open it up to enraptured, abandoned, "effeminate" gestures. But removing the heterosexist impulse can mean that women are rendered dispensable. As with that earlier speed-freak scene, the mods (who dressed sharp and posed to impress their mates, not to lure a mate), there's a homosocial aura to many rave and club scenes. Hence the autoerotic/autistic quality to rave dance. Recent converts to raving often express the sentiment "it's better than sex."

The samples that feature in much rave music – orgasmic whimpers and sighs, soul diva beseechings – induce a feverish state of *intransitive amorousness*. The ecstatic female vocals don't signify a desirable/desirous woman, but (as in gay disco) a hypergasmic rapture that the male identifies with and aspires toward. The "you" or "it" in vocal samples refers not to a person but a sensation. With E, the full-on raver lifestyle means literally falling in love every weekend, then (with the inevitable midweek crash) having your heart broken. Millions of kids across the globe are riding this emotional roller coaster. Always looking ahead to their next tryst with E, addicted to love, in love with . . . nothing?

In her memoir *Nobody Nowhere*, the autistic Donna Williams describes how as a child she would withdraw from a threatening reality into a private preverbal dream-space of ultravivid color and rhythmic pulsations; she could be transfixed for hours by iridescent motes in the air that only she could perceive. With its dazzling psychotropic lights, its sonic pulses, rave culture is arguably a form of *collective autism*. The rave is utopia in its original etymological sense: a nowhere/nowhen wonderland.

So perhaps the best classification for Ecstasy is "utopiate," R. Blum's term for LSD. The Ecstasy experience can be like heaven on Earth. Because it's not a hallucinogen but a sensation intensifier, MDMA actually makes the world seem *realer;* the drug also feels like it's bringing out the "real you," freed from all the neurosis instilled by a sick society. But "utopiate" contains the word "opiate," as in "religion is the opium of the people." A sacrament in that secular religion called "rave," Ecstasy can just as easily be a counterrevolutionary force as it can fuel a hunger for change. For it's too tempting to take the easy option: simply repeating the experience, installing yourself permanently in rave's virtual reality pleasuredome.

Lowrider Style:
Cultural Politics and
the Poetics of Scale

Ben Chappell*

Lowriders are customized cars marked by such adornments as elaborate lacquer paint jobs, murals, luxurious interiors, colored lighting accents, and custom wheel rims and tires. Mechanical modifications of a lowrider can include cutting the suspension springs to make the car ride low, and installing hydraulic lifts over the wheels to allow the driver to raise and drop the car at will. As ethnographers of lowriders have pointed out, lowrider style is a means of working-class, Mexican-American cultural production.[1] As such, lowriders *privilege* marginalized racial, cultural, and locational identities (cf. Rose 1994), and in doing so, offer a challenge to the hegemonies implicit in terms such as "minority" (see Laguerre 1999; Villa 2000). Thus even when it is not explicitly "political" or "resistant," lowrider style is a tacitly oppositional form of expression (Chambers 1991), making lowriders a site of debate, contestation, and struggle.[2] Parents and teachers warn children to scorn lowrider style as a form of "gang culture" while television and film directors depict the style in ways that reinforce that association, while paradoxically appropriating it in advertising or entertainments like the "reality?" TV show "Pimp my Ride." Meanwhile, stories of being pulled over by police officers are ubiquitous among lowriders; police also break up informal lowrider gatherings, sometimes using force to shut down popular cruising strips like Whittier Boulevard in Los Angeles (see Rodríguez 1991).

My purpose in this essay is not merely to argue that lowriders are oppositional – that point has been adequately made in much of the previous lowrider scholarship. What I want to discuss is how this political valence is constructed. Specifically, I will argue that lowrider style employs a material poetics which challenges conventions of scale in material culture that are also embedded in social relations of domination and alterity. That is, in the way that they relate to cultural associations with miniature and gigantic scales of objects, lowriders engage and critique the power relations of the status quo on the field of signification, thus contributing to a lowrider aesthetic that has dangerous, thrilling, and identifying connotations. In what follows, I will first relate two lowrider car-

*© 2007 by Ben Chappell. Reprinted with permission from the author. Some material from this essay appeared in an earlier form in pp. 100–20 in the volume *Technicolor: Race, Technology, and Everyday Life*, ed. A. Nelson, T. Linh and A. Hines (New York University Press, 2001).

show genres of display – showing and hopping – to the miniature and the gigantic. I also will demonstrate that the material poetics which lowriders practice contest conventional cultural "narratives" even while deploying them in order to effect what Ramón Saldívar has termed a "dialectic of difference" (1990) in the construction of Chicano/Chicana identities, forming an oppositional, hybrid cultural practice.

The terms of my analysis are provided by Susan Stewart's rich work *On Longing* (1993). Addressing a wide range of "texts," from folklore, public display events, and literature to objects like model railroads and dollhouses, Stewart uncovers themes of scale and position in Western culture: inside/outside, large/small, etc. Beginning with Aristotle, she shows how scale – the size and degree of things – plays a key and problematical role in the construction of aesthetics and reference points of "taste," "culture," and so on.[3] Thus to play with the scale of things is to play with conventions and thereby to address the social relations and "powers of authority" that make things conventional. Stewart constantly reminds us that there is no "miniature" in nature. It takes culture to mark some things as normal, others as too small, and still others as excessively large – and "Western culture" has risen to the task. Despite being identified with an "Other" in the United States, lowriders are a part of the history of "the West," to which the United States has been both heir and innovator, and which is the object of Stewart's study. The conventions that are at stake in Stewart's work are also in effect on the streets where lowriders cruise.

The minority identity which lowriders privilege most is Mexican American, working class, and urban. This identity group is one party in the situation I am calling oppositional. In the other corner, a behemoth with many names: José Davíd Saldívar calls it "Anglocentric hegemony" (1997:37); José Limón names "Anglos," being careful to insist on quotation marks (1994:6); and Manuel Peña refers to "mainstream, American middle-class, 'Anglo-conformity' culture" (1985:117). All of these terms reference a historic social position of privilege, incorporating normative aesthetic and scalar discourses as well as the hegemonic or coercive means of enforcing them (see also Lipsitz [1998] and many other sources on "Whiteness"). It is an anthropology of this "dominant culture" and its discontents that Stewart contributes to an understanding of lowriders.

My view on lowrider cars is based on an ongoing ethnographic project in Texas that I initiated by attending my first lowrider car show in 1997.[4] I also draw on the small but rich body of scholarly literature on lowriding. The preeminent ethnographer of lowrider culture was the late Brenda Jo Bright. In her dissertation and publications, Bright situates lowriders within the problematic of popular culture in late modernity, as a translocal expressive practice associated with a particular identity group and implicated in social conflicts characteristic of racialized, capitalist, American society. Bright discusses the way that lowriders serve as highly personalized forms of expression within a larger cultural framework, how they represent various kinds of mobility in a world of truncated options for Chicanos, and how they interact with other popular idioms, such as hip-hop music, films, and comics.[5] Much of Bright's work, like other research and journalism on lowriding, centered on car shows as public "display events" in which lowrider style is in its most heightened, elaborated material form (Abrahams 1981).

Objects of Desire: The Miniature on Display

While there is significant variation among lowrider car shows, there are two broad categories of events at most: the show-car events and the hopping events. Shows take place in parks, fair grounds, convention centers or other semi-public (but bounded) spaces. Show cars are displayed in their designated spots within the show grounds, and are evaluated by appointed judges or audience ballot. Prizes are awarded in several categories, bringing trophies and sometimes cash. Show cars sport the most expensive and elaborate murals, often ten or more coats of multicolored, lacquer paint, interiors decorated with crushed velvet on every possible surface, and accessories such as televisions, chandeliers, fountains, and bars. The car's body may be modified to such an extreme that drivers opt not to drive it and risk accident, but instead deliver the car to the show grounds on a trailer (official rules at *Lowrider Magazine*-sanctioned events mandate that the car be drivable). To build a show car is an expensive undertaking, with the most famous cars requiring tens of thousands of dollars and years of work. For those who are excluded by age or income from car competition, subgenres of lowrider model cars and lowrider bikes have also emerged, with display competitions in their own right.

Those familiar with Stewart's work may already begin to see a relationship. Among the "modes of signification" which she discusses, the miniature and the gigantic form a dialectical pair. She considers the miniature as "a metaphor for the interior space and time of the bourgeois subject' (1993:xi), while "[i]n contrast to the still and perfect universe of the miniature, the gigantic represents the order and disorder of historical forces" (1993:86). Stewart finds the miniature to be perfectly expressed in the interior space of the adult hobbyist's dollhouse. This object is a material narrative of desire for secured boundaries and ordered perfection, characteristic of bourgeois consumption and a cultivated distance from alienated, physical labor. At first glance, the miniature can be found at a lowrider car show in the model cars and lowrider bikes which are miniature versions of lowrider cars, but the full-sized cars themselves, when decorated for show, also suggest miniature luxury dwelling spaces – a mansion stuffed into a car. While show car accessories cost a lot, they are cheap compared with real mansions – thus, like a hobby dollhouse, a customized lowrider interior shows the dominant motifs of wealth and nostalgia, but in less expensive form. In both cases the signifiers, miniature objects, are more affordable than their signifieds, life-sized luxury items. Moreover, as Stewart puts it, "Use value is transformed into display value here" (1993:61–2), and the miniaturized thing is aestheticized into an object of desire.

The desire narrated by the miniaturized mansion-space of a show lowrider is multivectored and diverse. It is often manifested as nostalgia. The miniature is "nostalgic in a fundamental sense" for Stewart, and nostalgia is a narrative of desire *par excellence*, often exemplifying how such narratives can be more about their subjects than their objects. By constructing desire for times and places which exist only in narrative, nostalgia speaks to the present time and the present in space, even as it attempts a narrative negation of the present. In this attempt, nostalgia also negates history, freezing and miniaturizing the people and places it narrates. In the case of bourgeois hobby miniatures, nostalgia often references preindustrial production and artisanship – an example is a miniature antique chair. In preindustrial times, such a chair would have been made by hand; now that mode of production is obsolete or esoteric enough to make the real thing unaffordable for most consumers – but hobbyists can perform nostalgia for the preindustrial by reproducing a miniature chair for a dollhouse.

Similarly, lowriders join industrial objects with craft, endowing them with new significance. With reference to Mexican–American history, the investment of a car with symbolic value and manual labor (as well as folk mechanical engineering) with prestige is a posture of resistance to what Carlos Velez-Ibañez has termed a "commodity identity" that labels Mexican Americans as "cheap labor" (1997). When a car is modified, the surplus value that is extracted in industrial labor is being reclaimed in artisanal labor. This contrast would position lowriders within a less-alienated domain of labor – a folkloric or symbolic mode of production (see Flores 1995:149,152), a labor of love.[6] Therefore, as I will elaborate below, the working-class associations of lowriding are complicated by this deployment of the miniature. Or perhaps the reverse is true.

Gender is also contested in the lowrider scene. In lowrider magazines, which often feature female models in bikini swimsuits posing in front of cars, lowriders are presented as the objects of a specific kind of male, heterosexual desire. In these cases, women's bodies are used as ornaments for the magazine and the cars it depicts. This has been controversial within the Mexican–American community, as is clear in the letters section of virtually every issue of *Lowrider Magazine (LRM)*. Women also contest this association by building and driving lowriders themselves, though they do not always find fault with the models explicitly. LRM recently published an issue devoted to the "Ladies of Lowriding," in which pictorial features juxtapose two female roles: that of the innovative mechanic and customizer, and the ornamental model. The contested gender politics of lowriding is a rich subject for investigation and critique. Since my focus here is on the scalar dynamics of the cars themselves, and in the interest of space, I will only pause to suggest that the dynamics of scale I address are very much at work in the negotiation of gender boundaries and even the customization of human bodies for display.[7]

The Gigantic: Hopping Boundaries

A separate, designated space within the same car show is the venue of the hopping competition. These events rely on a technology which, since the 1960s, has particularly distinguished lowriders from all other genres of car modification: the hydraulic suspension. Drawing power from arrays of car batteries in the trunk and controlled by "switches," the hydraulic system allows the driver to lower the car or lift it to a less conspicuous height at the chance encounter with traffic police; one can also engage the hydraulic lifts installed over each wheel in order to make the car bounce on its tires, and even dance. Two hopping events are standard, with many variations. The basic car hop is a competition to achieve sheer height by engaging the hydraulics rhythmically so that the maximum "bounce to the ounce" is achieved. Judges carefully measure the car hop with large rulers, and the highest bounce wins.

The car dance is a more free-form competitive event with an emphasis on skilled performance, similar in some ways to figure skating or trick skateboarding. As in the car hop, the driver stands outside the car, holding the hydraulic switches. Music plays, and he or she attempts to keep the car in constant motion for a set time (e.g. 90 seconds), going through a repertoire of movements that may involve sending the entire car flying off the ground like a bucking bull. Danger is at a premium here. Scores are based in part upon crowd response, and going to extremes is rewarded. The hydraulics may get overworked and start to burn out. At a car dance I attended in south Texas, the winner drove his machine past the limit, keeping the purple Nissan dancing as a steel suspension spring snapped, smoke began to pour out of the trunk, his partner hovered nearby with a fire extinguisher, and the crowd went wild.

If show car interiors represent the miniature in a lowrider show, the hopping events offer a clear juxtaposition of the gigantic. While the miniature is a scale of consumption from the point of view of the spectator, the gigantic is that of being consumed, cut down to size, or potentially crushed, any of which seem like a real possibility in the presence of an enormous, bouncing car. Batteries, hydraulics, and springs assert motion and power against the still perfection of the show cars, as the hopping car violates even the law of gravity. The gigantic is precisely what the carefully crafted boundaries of the miniature guard against, and demonstrates the kind of transgression Bakhtin (1984) identified as being in a "carnivalesque" mode.[8]

And yet, this transgression is not completely at odds with the show cars' aesthetic. Alongside the concern for "correctness of design" and the effort to make everything just so, which lowriders also perform in their verbal evaluations of cars as being "tight," "clean," or as having "class," there is a pronounced ambivalence at work. The colors of a lowrider, for example, are not the subdued "tints and nuances" which Baudrillard found in "bourgeois objects" (1996), similar to what Stewart paraphrases as "the moral refusal of color" (1993:29). And the signs of consumption are often excessive by bourgeois standards, to an extent that might be called baroque (indeed, it has been: see Griffith 1989; cf. Wolfe 1965; Hebdige 1988). Who spends $20,000 on a car that they do not plan to drive, anyway? Like the miniature books which Stewart describes as being dense in their textuality, lowriders heap detail upon detail, becoming materially and semiotically verbose. They become gigantic in their multiplied significance, even if they begin as "normal" sized cars. These interior spaces spill over into exteriority. They lean toward a narrative that Bakhtin found in the carnivalesque core of popular culture: the grotesque. Bakhtin writes: "Contrary to modern canons, the grotesque body is not separate from the rest of the world, it is not a closed, completed unit; it is unfinished, outgrows itself, transgresses its own limits . . . the emphasis is on the apertures or the convexities, or on various ramifications and offshoots" (1984:26). This overflowing significance is dramatized in the lowrider car with hood, trunk, and doors thrown open to spectators' gazes, and with chrome, gold-plate and even crushed velvet decorating not only the car's interior but the engine. By accumulating display value in excess, lowriders both occupy and exceed the space of the miniature.

Again, class alignment is clearly being complicated here as well as scale. The bourgeois nostalgia that emerges for Stewart in hobbyists' dollhouses and in texts such as pastoral poems miniaturizes the European peasantry and the lower classes as timeless, devoid of history, picturesque, and most importantly, distant. Yet lowrider interiors are not nostalgic for a pastoral life so much as they are for a modern-industrial form of affluence. They narrate a longing not for a moment inevitably lost in time, and consigned to memory, but rather for resources placed out of reach by the failure of a promised American class mobility to deliver. The wealth displayed in a lowrider show car is a simulation of riches, a kind of parody of the American dream. Like model trains, which to Stewart index leisure and the privilege of erasing the act of labor, lowrider handiwork is a sign of leisure, but it is leisure wrenched out of evenings and weekends, from the rare and valuable moments "off work." To amend a phrase from Mary Douglas (1984), then, the consumer culture of a lowrider is consumption "out of place": while it mimics the miniaturizing of bourgeois leisure practices and displays the financial resources that grant purchasing power, it also violates the norms of taste which usually describe boundaries between classes (see Bourdieu 1984).

Displays of Difference

It would seem by now that in a confrontation between the miniature and the gigantic at a lowrider show, the gigantic is winning out. In this event, the lowrider show could be construed as a modern carnival, a popular space of resistance and liberation from the suffocating regime of bourgeois white supremacy. But the picture again is complicated. The entire car show usually takes place within a bounded space, and to enter, one often must pay an admission fee and pass police or other guards. In a car show, the gigantic expressions of lowrider style are confined, interiorized, and miniaturized with respect to the larger outside world. Stewart notes a similar ambivalence, emphasizing that the gigantic always has at least two possible forms. Giving the impression of being all-encompassing, the gigantic can also represent the landscape or the monument, signifying place, irresistible power, and the right to narrate official history – a domain. It can be deployed officially in parades, corporation-sponsored events, civic celebrations, and media representations, referencing the power and reach of the state or the bank. But at a lowrider show, the official, monumental side of the gigantic never entirely erases the carnivalesque "underbelly" – thus the association with an "Other" population and the "wrong" parts of town continue to make lowriders dangerous signs. At a car show in San Antonio, a welcome speech by the mayor was met with polite applause. When a member of a community arts organization got up and proclaimed lowriders to be "mobile art from the barrio," though, the crowd broke into loud cheers and raised their "plaques" (car club names sculpted out of chromed metal) above their heads. This moment provided a clear juxtaposition of claims: the official presence of the mayor lent a token, general respectability, but the crowd's most enthusiastic identification was apparently with *local* associations.

There is an important place in Mexican-American memory for signs of affluence and consumption that are discomfiting to those traditionally invested in the imposed order of the miniature. The lowrider gigantic can serve to outsiders as "a symbol of surplus and licentiousness, of overabundance and unlimited consumption" (Stewart 1993:80), even as it signifies "style" or "class" to lowriders themselves. In this, lowriders find a precedent in the zoot-suit-wearing *pachuco* of war-time Los Angeles. *Pachucos* provide one of the most important images in lowrider iconography: murals painted on lowrider cars often feature zoot-suiters prominently, the logo of *Lowrider* magazine is a stylized *pachuco* face, and zoot-suit modeling has been a common activity in the history of low-rider shows. At a Texas lowrider show early in my fieldwork, a high-school Ballet Folklorico dance group performed in zoot suits, dramatizing in one piece the 1943 attacks on *mexicano pachucos* by Anglo servicemen known as the "Zoot Suit Riots." These figures present a nostalgia for the energetic defiance of youth and an emergent Chicano consciousness, but also a particular articulation of identity, style, and cultural politics.

In the 1940s, the perceived dandyism of the zoot-suiters was an affront to a nation in the grip of total war – for example, while "proper" citizens were making austere adjustments to their wardrobes to comply with the rationing of materials, the zoot suit required an abundance of fabric, more than its share. More importantly, the zoot suit marked bodies already deemed "Other" by a racial order in an aggressive gesture of independence (Sanchez-Tranquilino and Tagg 1992). During the Zoot Suit Riots, Anglo sailors, incensed by the *pachucos'* apparent disregard for the war effort and resis-tance to cultural assimilation, attacked Chicanos in zoot suits on sight, beating them and stripping some naked before leaving them in the street while the police stood idly by (Acuña 1981:326–7; see also Mazón 1984).

As an ambivalent figure, alien to received notions of both Mexican and "American" culture, the *pachuco* has posed a challenge to theorists of Mexicano identity in the United States. Infamously, Mexican intellectual Octavio Paz (1961) depicts the pachuco as a perpetual adolescent, caught between two possible "adult" national identities, and refusing to commit to either one in a state of arrested development. This adolescent image is also adopted by Mazón (1984) in his psycho-history, the only book-length treatment of the Riots, albeit with more political acumen. More recently, however, the ambivalence of identity which is expressed in popular styles like that of the *pachuco* (as well as the lowrider) has been treated not as developmentally pathological, but more as indicative of a particular social quandary in which subjects find themselves caught and which is translated from the experience of social conflict and racism into expressive culture and an active cultural politics (Paredes 1993; Limón 1994:91–2). In particular, the logic of "refusal" (see Hebdige 1979) may be read as part of the immanently critical "doubleness" which some critics have identified in the particular experience of Western modernity associated with "minority" status (Gilroy 1993; Bhabha 1990).

Analysis of "minority" popular cultural practices thus calls for a logic of ambivalence. Identifying narratives of the miniature and the gigantic gives us a view to the struggles over meaning which occur in lowriding, but the significance of lowriders is not depen-dent exclusively on one or another. It is precisely the close proximity of both in lowrider expression which challenges the Western–modern order of things. The Nissan which won the car dance mentioned earlier had a crushed-velvet interior, thus employing both miniature and gigantic modes. Lowriders signify from a semiotic borderlands, confus-ing categories: they are mobile yet metonymical of particular neighborhoods; they express both working-class pride and aspirations to middle-class consumption; they carefully define boundaries around a highly elaborated interior space, then proceed to move as though boundaries did not exist. Lowriders thus defy definition in the terms of a society and history in which Anglos have claimed dominance, constructiiig a poetics of a "significant Other," similar to that found by some critics in Chicano literature: a "Chicano phantasmatic, mediating between higher and lower worlds" (Saldívar 1997:66).

As such, lowriders are hybrids of multiple influences, but as Néstor García Canclini (1995) notes, a hybrid culture is not of necessity syncretic – the crucible never successfully melds the diverse elements of lowrider identity together into a finished alloy. Rather, lowrider identity is the site of perpetual contestation on how to draw generic boundaries around the style, how to ascribe cultural authority, how to define the group. Who are the lowriders? Who should they be? What is appropriate expressive action in lowriding? To whom does it belong? Who is a star and who a sellout? These questions are negotiated in moments of selective engagement and refusal of dominant structures, in flashes of both opposition and complicity (Hutcheon 2002; Pérez-Torres 1994) with symbolic convention as well as with the regulation of place and movement. Attention to scale does not offer complete or simple answers to these questions, but as Stewart points out, "If authority is invested in domains such as the marketplace, the university, or the state, it is necessary that exaggeration, fantasy, and fictiveness in general be socially placed within the domains of anti- and nonauthority." Thus material "narratives" which confront power as signs that stretch the boundaries of scale indicate an oppositional poetics at work.

Notes

1. The argument presented in this essay also appeared in different form in Chappell 2001. For an introduction to lowrider scholarship, see also Bright (1994, 1995, 1997, 1998, 2000), Chappell (1998, 1999, 2002, 2003, in press), as well as Beck (1980), Best (2006), Gradante (1982, 1985), Griffith (1989), Lowrider (2003), Mendoza (2000), Plascencia (1983), Stone (1990), Vigil (1991). In addition to studies devoted to the topic, lowriding turns up to greater or lesser extents within scholarship on hip-hop (Cross 1994; Ro 1996), urban space (Rojas 1995), the rhetoric of public culture (Cintron 1997), and gang studies (Vigil 1988), to cite only a few examples.

2. Chambers's notion of the "oppositional" refers to those cultural interventions that, while working sometimes within the structures of domination themselves, exploit the "cracks" in power in order to make space and "room to maneuver" (cf. Hall 1981; de Certeau 1984; Hutcheon 2002). Without capturing Chambers's nuanced work entirely, this approach to cultural politics can be understood to move from models of large-scale political change to the contestation of everyday life (though his work focuses on narrative), from strategy to tactics (Sandoval 2000), from an emphasis on production to consumption (Hebdige 1988), and from a discourse of political purity to one of more "contaminated" political action (cf. K. Stewart 1991).

3. These reference points appear in many other studies as well, such as in Bourdieu's discussion of how the small and big mouths of speakers can gesture toward particular social positions (1991), or in the work of Bakhtin, cited below.

4. The most intensive fieldwork took place in 1999–2001, comprising my participation in lowrider cruising in Austin, Texas and attendance at car shows in other cities, such as Houston

and San Antonio. The ethnographic project is ongoing, and as been generously funded by the Wenner–Gren Foundation for Ethnographic Research (grant #6600), the University of Texas at Austin, Bridgewater College, and the Mednick Fellowship of the Virginia Foundation for Independent Colleges.

5. In addition to the scholarship cited above, documentation of lowriding in print includes articles in the popular media (West 1976; Trillin 1978), and an ample literature produced by participants in lowrider style themselves, in *Lowrider Magazine*, as well as numerous regional and national publications such as *Orlie's Lowriding, Vajito*, and others (see especially Penland 1997 and 2003). The online "virtual boulevard" cruised by lowriders is growing, as is evinced by sites such as www.layitlow.com. Additional popular and middlebrow accounts of lowriding include exhibition catalogs and other art books (Parsons, Padilla, and Arellano 1999; C. Sandoval 2000; Donnelly 2000; San Diego Automotive Museum 2006), technical how-to guides (Ferreira 1990; Hamilton 1996); and even a kind of *testimonio* on the police repression of lowriding in Los Angeles (Rodríguez 1991).

6. For a class-based discussions of car customization in general, see Borhek (1989) and Watkins (1991). This is a complex issue, as both mobility and middle-class status has traditionally been associated with car ownership in America (Flink 1988), though as in other contexts, the car is also a site of pleasure, semiotic authority, and a kind of agency, albeit a far from unproblematic one (Gilroy 2001). Yet the status of urban Chicanos in American imaginaries as "probably deviant" (Moore 1985) marks lowrider styles of consumption as "Other." For example, a comment I regularly hear when discussing my research is that elaborate car decoration in urban contexts suggests "drug money." Within the context of an urban neighborhood, however, such a vehicle can also demonstrate the purchasing power of a steady job, and can motivate the driver to avoid "gang" encounters that can be hazardous to the meticulously painted and chromed car (see Bright 1997).

7. A more detailed account of one contesation of gender within lowriding can be read in Chappell 2001, and many more regularly appear in the pages of *LRM*. See also the chapter "Ladies of Lowriding" in Penland's history (2003).

8. On Bakhtin and carnivalesque transgression, see, e.g., Limón (1995: ch. 6), and Stallybrass & White (1986).

References

Abrahams, Roger D. (1981). Shouting Match at the Border: The Folklore of Display Events. In: Richard Bauman & Roger D. Abrahams (eds.), *And Other Neighborly Names: Social Process and Cultural Image in Texas Folklore*, pp. 303–322. Austin: University of Texas Press.

Acuña, Rodolfo (1981). *Occupied America: A History of Chicanos*. 2nd edition. New York: Harper & Row.

Bakhtin, Mikhail (1984). *Rabelais and His World*, trans. Hélène Iswolsky. Bloomington: Indiana University Press.

Baudrillard, Jean (1996). *The System of Objects*, trans. James Benedict. New York: Verso.

Beck, Peggy V. (1980). The Low Riders. Folk Art and Emergent Nationalism. *Native Arts/West*. Oct. 1(4), pp. 25–7.

Best, Amy (2006). *Fast Cars, Cool Rides: The Accelerating World of Youth and Their Cars*. New York: New York University Press.

Bhabha, Homi K. (1990). Introduction: Narrating the Nation. In: Homi K. Bhabha (ed.), *Nation and Narration*, pp. 1–8. London: Routledge.

Borhek, J. T. (1989). Rods, Choppers, and Restorations: The Modification and Recreation of Production Motor Vehicles in America. *Journal of Popular Culture* 22(4), pp. 97–107.

Bourdieu, Pierre (1984). *Distinction: A Social Critique of the Judgement of Taste*, trans. Richard Nice. Cambridge MA: Harvard University Press.

Bourdieu, Pierre (1991). *Language and Symbolic Power*, trans. John Thompson and Gino Raymond. Maiden, MA: Blackwell.

Bright, Brenda Jo. (1994). Mexican American Lowriders: An Anthropological Approach to Popular Culture. Ph.D. diss., Department of Anthropology, Rice University.

Bright, Brenda Jo. (1995). Remappings: Los Angeles Low Riders. In: Brenda Jo Bright & Liza Bakewell (eds.), *Looking High and Low: Art and Cultural Identity*, pp. 89–123. Tucson: University of Arizona Press.

Bright, Brenda Jo. (1997). Nightmares in the New Metropolis: The Cinematic Poetics of Low Riders. *Studies in Latin American Popular Culture*, 16, pp. 13–29.

Bright, Brenda Jo. (1998). "Heart Like a Car": Hispano/Chicano Culture in Northern New Mexico. *American Ethnologist* 25(4), pp. 583–609.

Bright, Brenda (2002). Lowriders. In: *Customized: Art Inspired by Hot Rods, Low Riders and American Car Culture*. Catalog of an exhibition held at the Institute of Contemporary Art, Boston. New York: Henry N. Abrahams.

Chambers, Ross (1991). *Room for Maneuver: Reading (the) Oppositional (in) Narrative*. Chicago: University of Chicago Press.

Chappell, Ben (1998). Making Identity with Music and Cars: Lowriders and Hip-hop as Urban Chicano Performance. M.A. report. Center for Intercultural Studies in Folklore and Ethnomusicology, Department of Anthropology, University of Texas at Austin.

Chappell, Ben (1999). Is a Lowrider Postmodern? Hybridity, Ambivalence, and Critique in Urban Expressive Culture. *Text, Practice, Performance* 1, pp. 35–52.

Chappell, Ben (2001). "Take a Little Trip with Me": Lowriding and the Poetics of Scale. In: Alondra Nelson & Thuy Linh N. Tu (eds.), with Alicia Headlam Hines, *Technicolor: Race, Technology, and Daily Life*, pp. 100–20. New York: New York University Press.

Chappell, Ben (2002). Mexican American Lowriders: Postmodernism as Popular Practice. In: Thomas Doerfler & Claudia Globisch (eds.), *Postmodern Practices: Beiträdge zu einer Vergehenden Epoche*, pp. 229–45. Münster, Germany: LIT Pub.

Chappell, Ben (2003). Lowrider Space: A Critical Encounter of Knowledges. PhD diss., Américo Paredes Center for Cultural Studies, Department of Anthropology, University of Texas at Austin.

Chappell, Ben (In press). Lowrider Cruising Spaces. In: Anja Bandau & Marc Priewe (eds.), *Mobile Crossings: Representations of Chicana/o Cultures*, pp. 51–62. Trier, Germany: WVT.

Cintron, Ralph (1997). *Angel's Town: Chero Ways, Gang Life, and the Rhetorics of the Everyday*. Boston: Beacon Press.

Cross, Brian (1994). *It's Not About a Salary – Rap, Race, and Resistance in Los Angeles*. London: Verso.

de Certeau, Michel (1984). *The Practice of Everyday Life*, trans. Steven Rendall. Berkeley: University of California Press.

Donnelly, Nora, (ed.) (2000). *Customized: Art Inspired by Hot Rods, Low Riders and American Car Culture*. Exhibition Catalog, Institute of Contemporary Art, Boston. New York: Henry N. Abrams.

Douglas, Mary (1984). *Purity and Danger: An Analysis of the Concepts of Pollution and Taboo*. London: Routledge.

Ferreira, David (1990). *Blue Magic Can Happen*. Hayward, CA: Vida Vision.

Flink, James (1988). *The Automotive Age*. Cambridge, MA: MIT Press.

Flores, Richard (1995). *Los Pastores: History and Performance in the Mexican Shepherd's Play of South Texas*. Washington, DC: Smithsonian Institution Press.

García Canclini, Néstor (1995). *Hybrid Cultures: Strategies for Entering and Leaving Modernity*, trans. Christopher L. Chiappari & Silvia L. López Minneapolis: University of Minnesota Press.

Gilroy, Paul (1993). *The Black Atlantic: Modernity and Double Consciousness*. Cambridge, MA: Harvard University Press.

Gilroy, Paul (2001). Driving While Black. In: Daniel Miller (ed.), *Car Cultures*, pp. 81–104. London: Berg.

Gradante, William (1982). Low and Slow, Mean and Clean. *Natural History* 91(4), pp. 28–39.

Gradante, William (1985). Art Among the Low Riders. In: Abernathy F. E. (ed.), *Folk Art in Texas*. Dallas: Southern Methodist University Press.

Griffith, James (1989). Mexican American Folk Art. In: *From the Inside Out*, pp. 52–9. San Francisco: Mexican Museum.

Hall, Stuart (1981). Notes on Deconstructing "the Popular." In: Raphael Samuel (ed.), *People's History and Socialist Theory*. pp. 227–40. London: Routledge & Kegan Paul.

Hamilton, Frank (1996). *How to Build a Lowrider*. North Branh, Minnesota: Cartech.

Hebdige, Dick (1979). *Subculture: The Meaning of Style*. London: Methuen.

Hebdige, Dick (1988). Hiding in the Light: On Images and Things. London: Comedia.

Hutcheon, Linda (2002). *Politics of Postmodernsim*, 2nd ed. London: Routledge.

Laguerre, Michel (1999). *Minoritized Space: An Inquiry into the Spatial Order of Things*. Berkeley: Institute of Governmental Studies Press.

Limón, José E. (1994). *Dancing with the Devil: Society and Cultural Poetics in Mexican-American South Texas*. Madison: University of Wisconsin Press.

Lipsitz, George (1998). *The Possessive Investment in Whiteness: How White People Profit from Identity Politics*. Philadelphia: Temple University Press.

Lowrider: An American Cultural Tradition (2003). Smithsonian Institution virtual gallery. http://latino.si.edu/virtualgallery/Lowrider/Enter_LR.html. Accessed March 7, 2006.

Mazón, Mauricio (1984). *The Zoot-Suit Riots: The Psychology of Symbolic Annihilation* Austin: University of Texas Press.

Mendoza, Ruben (2000). Cruising Art and Culture in Aztlan: Lowriding in the Mexican American Southwest. In: Lomeli F. A. & K. Ikas (eds.), *US Latino Literatures and Cultures: Transnational Perspectives*, pp. 3–36. Hiedelberg, Germany: Universitatsverlag C. Winter.

Moore, Joan (1985). Isolation and Stigmatization in the Development of an Underclass: The Case of Chicano Gangs in East Los Angeles. *Social Problems* 33(1), pp. 1–12.

Parsons, Jack, Carmella Padilla & Juan Estevan Arellano (1999). *Low 'n Slow: Lowriding in New Mexico*. Santa Fe: Museum of New Mexico Press.

Paredes, Américo (1993). The Problem of Identity in a Changing Culture: Popular Expressions of Culture Conflict Along the Lower Rio Grande Border. In: Richard Bauman, (ed.), *Folklore and Culture on the Texas-Mexican Border*, pp. 19–47. Austin: CMAS Books (University of Texas Press).

Paz, Octavio (1961). *The Labyrinth of Solitude: Life and Thought in Mexico*, trans. Lysander Kemp. New York: Grove.

Penland, Paige R. (1997). The History of Lowrider Magazine: What a Long, Low Trip it's Been. *Lowrider Magazine* (January) 19(1), pp. 74–82.

Penland, Paige R. (2003). *Lowrider: History, Pride, Culture*. Osceola, WI: Motorbooks, International. Electronic document: www.lowridermagazine.com/historybook. Accessed Feb. 27, 2006.

Peña, Manuel (1985). *The Texas-Mexican Conjunto: History of a Working-Class Music*. Austin: University of Texas Press.

Pérez-Torres, Raphael (1994). Nomads and Migrants: Negotiating a Multicultural Postmodernism. *Cultural Critique* 26 (Winter 1993–4), pp. 161–89.

Plascencia, Luis F. B. (1983). Low Riding in the Southwest: Cultural Symbols in the Mexican Community. In: Mario T. García, et al. (eds.), *History, Culture and Society: Chicano Studies in the 1980s*, pp. 141–75. Ypsilanti, Michigan: Bilingual Press (National Association for Chicano Studies).

Ro, Ronin (1996). *Gangsta: Merchandizing the Rhymes of Violence.* New York: St. Martin's Press.

Rodríguez, Roberto (1997). *Justice: A Question of Race.* Tempe, AZ: Bilingual Review Press.

Rojas, James (1995). The Latino Landscape of East Los Angeles. NACLA Report on the Americas XXVIII (January/February) (4), pp. 32–7.

Rose, Tricia (1994). *Black Noise.* Hanover, NH: University Press of New England (Wesleyan).

Saldívar, José David (1997). *Border Matters: Remapping American Cultural Studies.* Berkeley: University of California Press.

Saldívar, Ramón (1990). *Chicano Narrative: The Dialectics of Difference.* Madison: University of Wisconsin Press.

Sanchez-Tanquilino, Marcos & John Tagg (1992). The Pachuco's Flayed Hide: Mobility, Identity, and Buenas Garas. In: Lawrence Grossberg, Cary Nelson & Paula Treichler (eds.), *Cultural Studies*, pp. 556–66. London: Routledge.

San Diego Automotive Museum (2006). Bajito y Suavecito: Lowriders of Southern Califronia. Exhibition January 27-March 27.

Sandoval, Chela (2000). *Methodology of the Oppressed.* Minneapolis: University of Minnesota Press.

Sandoval, Denise (2000). *Arte y Estlio: The Lowriding Tradition.* Los Angeles: Petersen Automotive Museum.

Stallybrass, Peter & Allon White (1986). *The Poetics and Politics of Transgression.* Ithaca, NY: Cornell University Press.

Stewart, Kathleen (1991). On the Politics of Cultural Theory: A Case for "Contaminated" Cultural Critique. *Social Research* 58(2), pp. 395–412.

Stewart, Susan (1993). *On Longing: Narratives of the Miniature, the Gigantic, the Souvenir, the Collection.* Durham: Duke University Press.

Stone, Micheal C. (1990). "Bajito y Suavecito": Low Riding and the "Class" of Class. *Studies in Latin American Popular Culture* 9, pp. 85–126.

Trillin, Calvin (1978). Our Far-flung Correspondents: Low and Slow, Mean and Clean. *New Yorker* (July 10) 54(21), pp. 70–4.

Vélez-Ibañez, Carlos (1997). *Border Visions: Mexican Cultures of the Southwest United States.* Tucson: Arizona University Press.

Villa, Raül Homero (2000). *Barrio Logos: Space and Place in Urban Chicano Literature and Culture.* Austin: University of Texas Press.

Vigil, James Diego (1988). *Barrio Gangs: Street Life and Identity in Southern California.* Austin: University of Texas Press.

Vigil, James Diego (1991). Car Charros: Cruising and Lowriding in the Barrios of East Los Angeles. *Latino Studies Journal* 2(2), pp. 71–9.

Watkins, Evan (1991). "For the Time Being, Forever": Social Position and the Art of Automobile Maintenance. *Boundary* 2 18(2), pp. 150–65.

West, Ted (1976). Scenes From a Revolution: Low and Slow. *Car and Driver* (August), pp. 47–51.

Wolfe, Tom (1965). *The Kandy-Kolored Tangerine-Flake Streamline Baby.* New York: Pocket Books.

40

Purity and Danger

Stephen Duncombe*

I don't know why your office felt compelled to send a letter to us, but I can guess that one of two things is happening

#1 You are completely unaware of the nature of the DIY (do it yourself) punk/ hardcore thing. It hates your company and all that it stands for. If you do obtain a tape from any of the bands therein, the odds are high that many of the songs would be about how you suck, MTV sucks, corporate exploitation of underground culture sucks, etc.

or #2 You are completely aware that many bands want to "make it big". . . . Sony Music Entertainment Inc. is looking for artists to flesh out their "alternative" roster. You're offering stardom in the guise of "getting your message to a larger audience" and "better distribution." You think you'll get someone to bite.

If situation #1 applies, I almost feel sorry for you. The fact that this DIY guide exists is proof positive that you are not needed. . . .

If your reasoning followed #2, welcome; you have probably made a wise advertising decision. You will probably get plenty of "punk/HC" bands who want to be next year's "alternative" heroes. . . .

Fuck you very much.

> Reply to a Sony A&R (talent) scout from the editors of
> Book Your Own Fuckin' Life[1]

Underground culture and the zines that speak for it are products of an attempt to create an authentic, nonalienating culture. But this culture, like all bohemias before it, is produced within a larger, alienating society. Between this alternative culture and the mainstream society, lines are continually drawn: our world and theirs, integrity and selling out, purity and danger. This division is not merely the product of immature paranoia. At the root of underground culture is its separation from the dominant society – its very existence stems from this negation. And, as the letter from the editors of *Book Your Own Fuckin' Life* illustrates, these dividing lines are also based on a realistic assessment of the threat posed by living in a commercialized society in which all culture – especially

*Pp. 141–53; 163–73 from *Notes from the Underground: Zines and the Politics of Alternative Culture* (New York and London: Verso). © 1997 by Stephen Duncombe. Reprinted with permission from Verso.

rebellious culture – is gobbled up, turned on its head, and used as an affirmation of the very thing it was opposed to. The underground is filled with people who have heard the Beatles' song "Revolution" and Gil Scott-Heron's "The Revolution Will Not Be Televised" used to sell Nike shoes. They know of zines funded by corporations. They listened and learned: raise the drawbridge, barricade yourself within, keep yelling no. Adopt a will-toward-smallness in the hopes that you will be too insignificant a morsel for the rapacious jaws of marketing to devour. Keep yourself safe, keep yourself pure.

But they also understand the costs of purity. The stifling ghettoization that ensures that the messages and critiques of the underground stay within the narrow confines of a homogeneous elect. The rules of the underground that become as constraining as any rules on the outside. The inability to live a total life, always being split between the work you do for money and the creation you do for pleasure. The provincialism of bohemia.

For much of the early life of zines this conflict was muted. After all, to whom could you sell out? Who was interested in an obscure culture that celebrated losers? But with the mainstream discovery and celebration of zines and the underground, the struggle between purity and danger was pushed to the fore.

Ironically, even as this divide threatens to tear the cultural world of zines apart, it also holds it together. For as anthropologist Mary Douglas points out, the ideas of "purity and danger" function in many societies as an organizing principle, instilling order in an otherwise chaotic world. Because the world of zines values individualism so highly and disdains rules so profoundly, this sort of conflict offers a locus around which the zine community can define itself. But whereas Douglas argues that the divisions are often arbitrary, I believe that in the world of zines they are not. The debate in the zine world around purity and danger is a natural outgrowth of the difficulties encountered in attempting to create an alternative community within a society that seems to thrive on its discontents.[2] Threatened by their enemy's embrace, zinesters devise strategies for survival.

Reluctant Subjects

As I was slyly switching the Kinko's counter with my personal one, I was surrounded by a bunch of Ravers. "No way, Cometbus*! I read about that in* Details *magazine," they said. . . . "It wasn't my fault," I grumbled.*

Aaron, Cometbus[3]

Most zine writers are less than thrilled that their culture and craft have been "discovered" by the mainstream media. This is not too astonishing; after all, it is in reaction to the negative qualities of the mainstream media that zine culture was created. *Temp Slave's* Keffo reprints a letter he sent to *Time* magazine in response to its feature on zines, arguing that as much as he was interested in the subject matter of the article, "TIME failed to mention the best reason for zine publishing. Simply put, TIME and all the other major media sources are boring and irrelevant. The 'American Century' is over and so is TIME."[4] While Keffo's prognosis may be a bit premature, his point is clear: zines are the antithesis of the major media.

As mentioned previously, there is also great distrust in the zine world of how the major media will represent them when they do come knocking. After a *New York Times* reporter leaves numerous messages on his answering machine, Doug, editor of *Pathetic Life*, ruminates in his zine as to why he won't return the calls. "A little publicity would be nice," he admits:

> If I had a few hundred subscribers I wouldn't have to hand out fliers [advertising department store sales and the like on the street]. . . . But I have my doubts about the entire field of big-time journalism. I've been reading the daily papers for as long as I can remember . . . and one thing I've always noticed is that when a particular article concerns something I know about, it always includes an error or two.

Besides disliking the *New York Times* as an "especially scummy newspaper," Doug fears that "if I cooperated 100%, sent back issues and answered every question, the article would still spell my name wrong, forget to mention the zine's address, and no doubt misinterpret my psychosis." Besides, he concludes, they'll never run the article.[5] Doug was wrong about the *New York Times* not running the article, and they included his zine even without an interview, but he was right on other points. They didn't print his address, and they reduced the multidimensional personality that comes out in his perzine into a caricature of a lonely, yet "quirky," fat slob.[6]

"I was made to look like a lonely, punk cartoon from the suburbs," complains *NO LONGER A FANzine* publisher Joe Gervasi about his portrayal in a *Details* magazine article, even though "neither my 'zine nor what I told [the reporter] should have had him believing this."[7] Zine writers contacted by the commercial media were finding out that the media were not really interested in them, but were creating a package of what they thought that zine writers represented. For example, CNN once used zines to illustrate a "war" going on between generations, even though none of the zine writers interviewed on air said anything to this effect.[8]

Blue Persuasion's Aaron Lee tells of a local Kentucky TV news crew coming to visit him for a "human interest" story as "apparently, the guy with the Biggest Ball of String in Lexington was out of town." Poking around a local magazine store looking at zines, the reporter only perked up after coming across *Teenage Gang Debs*. "'You mean it's a *whole magazine* about the *Brady Bunch?*' she gasped. You'd think she just found the cure for cancer. . . . I made a mental note to cancel my subscription." When the reporter finally got around to seeing Aaron's own zine, "the first thing she flipped to was good ol' Jerry Butler, with his dick in a turkey carcass." "A week later," Aaron reports, "the piece of shit aired with any glimpse of yours truly edited out. Which allowed for two minutes of *Teenage Gang Debs* coverage, and two minutes of [the proprietor of the magazine store] gushing 'zines are cool.'"[9] Apparently cool people are interested in the Brady Bunch, not human/animal copulation.

Faced with this selective representation some zine writers simply decide not to cooperate with the mainstream media at all. *"Every day there's some fucking mainstream magazine, paper or TV show that I hear is covering Riot Grrrl,"* screams Ananda in *Riot Grrrl* 8. And all of them, she says, invariably show "us as this item, this quaint new marketable 'discovery' of a fashion or music trend." "*USA Today* said we like to 'sport leg hair' . . . [in] *Melody Maker* we'll look like we're only about punk music. [In] *Newsweek* . . . we're only about looking weird and . . . worship[ing] Madonna and *Sassy* Magazine." What angers Ananda the most is that "riot grrrl is about destroying boundaries . . . but these mags make us look like we're one 'thing'." This codification is opposed to what she sees as the conversation and debate about definitions that takes place in the exchange of zines. Her advice: "Feel free to say *No* if someone from the media makes an 'offer' to you. But if you do go along with it, please only represent yourself."[10] This media blackout became "official" policy for Riot Grrrls.

While some in the zine world decide it's destructive to talk to a mainstream media that they don't respect and that doesn't respect them, others, in the zine tradition of sabotage, feed them misinformation. Dishwasher Pete has repeatedly declined interviews with the mainstream media. But when asked to appear as a guest on the "Late Night with David Letterman" show in summer 1995, he agreed. Knowing, however, that nobody at the show had any idea what he looked like, he had them fly in an old friend from California to impersonate him. I spent an amusing evening sitting with the real Pete and a bunch of other zine writers watching the faux Pete answer questions about his quest to wash dishes across the nation (and nearly light the TV host on fire with a demonstration of his burning hand trick).[11]

Another episode, which became better known, involved Megan Jasper, a sales rep at Seattle's Caroline Records, who fed a *New York Times* reporter bogus lingo for a "Grunge Lexicon" that accompanied the paper's feature story on the success of grunge music and style. Amazingly, the reporter actually believed that such phrases as "swingin' on the flippity-flop" (hanging out) and terms like "cob nobbler" (loser) were authentic subcultural "code."[12] The real joke, however, may be on the underground. For as Tom Frank, editor of the journal primarily responsible for spreading the news of the grunge hoax, pointed out, it really didn't matter if the lingo was authentic or not.[13] The *New York Times* got what it wanted: a story on the newest hip trend, the voice of the new generation.[14]

Because zines are so small and "underground," and because the mainstream media are so powerful and their reach is so immense, it really doesn't matter whether the underground talks to the mainstream media or not, whether it tries to level with them or feed them lies. The mass media will print or broadcast what they like, and to millions of people across the United States, their spin on the underground and their take on zines will be the only representation available. "I have a lot of problems with media infiltration of 'underground culture,'" zine editor Missy Lavalee writes, "because the media distorts it terribly, but then people see the media version, adopt it themselves, and then the underground culture ends up being exactly how the media portrayed it."[15] Missy is right. I wouldn't be surprised if somewhere out there in the USA, a young, alienated kid, looking for a culture to call his or her own, is asking some others if they plan on "swingin' on the flippity-flop" tonight.

Irony

The sun beams down on a brand new day
No more welfare tax to nay

> Unsightly slums gone up in flashing light
> Jobless millions whisked away
> At last we have more room to play
> All systems go to kill the poor tonight
> Gonna
> Kill kill kill
> Kill the poor
> Kill the poor. . . . Tonight
>
> Dead Kennedys

For adherents of a culture that puts a high value on authenticity, zine writers use irony as a rhetorical device with puzzling frequency. The punk zine *No Longer a Fanzine* prints a comic by Kyle Baker, "God Bless Alternative Rock,"[16] which praises "the idea of featuring bands of longhaired white guys with no shirts and big muscles! [because] It's so alternative." In the broader underground, the biggest hits of the seminal American political punk band, the Dead Kennedys, included songs such as "Kill the Poor," which proposed killing poor people with a neutron bomb as a way to rid society of poverty while leaving valuable real estate intact.[17]

Authenticity, as I've argued earlier, is an ideal of the underground to be "true" to the "real" self. Zines, therefore, are best when, to use Lionel Trilling's definition, they demonstrate "a congruence between avowal and actual feeling."[18] Yet again and again, in the pages of zines or in the lyrics of punk rock or alternative music, irony creeps in. Irony is the opposite of authenticity. Where the ideal of the latter is to chart as short and straight a path between what one believes and what one expresses, irony succeeds when it does the opposite: when one's expression is the antithesis of what one really feels. Kyle despises the mainstreaming of "alternative rock," the Dead Kennedys side with the poor against the rich, yet their words say the opposite. What explains this?

Unlike an affirmative assertion, irony depends for its meaning entirely on context and on a knowing audience. Outside its original setting and translated for an uninitiated audience, it makes no sense. This is its value. For those in the cultural underground, using irony is a pragmatic response to a commercial culture that eats up any positive statement, strips it of its original meaning and context, and reproduces and disseminates it as an affirmation of its own message of consumption. No key is needed to unlock the meaning of and disseminate an "authentic" message to a mass audience – the link between message and intent is clear. But a cultural combination is needed to liberate the meaning of irony. Just try selling Nikes with the Dead Kennedys' "Kill the Poor." Irony is one of the ways that zinesters keep the vultures off their culture.

It also provides a perch for zine writers to stand on and do their own picking. Using the dominant culture's language and symbols but altering their meanings allows for a certain amount of control over that language and those symbols. As Mikhail Bakhtin writes, "The satirist whose laughter is negative places himself above the object of his mockery."[19] Irony is a secret laugh at ol' massa without him knowing. It allows the zine writer to dominate, if only in laughter, the dominant culture.

Irony also demands an active engagement with its audience, and this fits well with zinesters' ideals of an active engagement with culture. Given clues only to what the author *doesn't* think, the reader deciphering an ironic statement has to use his or her imagination to figure out what the author does believe. The reader helps create the message. And as it takes at least two – with a shared meaning system – to make effective irony, this form of humor reinforces community. While irony functions to disconnect the underground from the dominant society, it also functions to *connect* those in the underground to one another. There are those who are "in the know" and "get it," and those who aren't and don't. In a virtual community such as the zine world in which there are no explicit rules or strong bonds holding it together, irony – or more accurately, the shared meaning system upon which irony depends – acts as a sort of glue holding together an otherwise disjunct group of individuals.

But boundaries of inclusion are necessarily also boundaries of exclusion, and irony reinforces the ghettoization of the underground. Not only are the marketing creeps locked out, but as the irony gets thicker and thicker and the references become more and more obscure, so is anybody new. "You're either on the bus, or you're off the bus," Tom Wolfe wrote about an earlier tribe of bohemians, and if you're off the bus – not understanding the mores and codes of subcultural meaning – it's very hard to find a way to get on in the first place.[20]

There is also another price paid for the irony that holds this community together and keeps outsiders out. Irony is negative. I don't mean this in a touchy-feely sense of "bad vibes" and all that, but in the way I've explained before. Irony can only work as negation of an already existing culture which it uses as a reference point. This relationship is complex, but the problem is simple: irony renders the underground's role and its zine voice, that of a parasite. While criticizing the dominant culture obiquely through irony, the underground reaffirms its dependency on it.

Irony is not cynicism and a resigned acceptance of the way things are. It holds out the ideal that there might be something else on the other side of the reality it lampoons, and then leaves what that might be up to the reader. It's playful and fun. It's my preferred voice when I write for zines. Yet I sometimes fear that irony also keeps the underground forever living in a dominant world that it can see through, with ironic vision, but never escape.

Besides, the article of faith that critical irony cannot be co-opted by the commercial culture is a shaky one. Exactly how shaky was demonstrated in 1996 when Nike, the master of this game, added the song "Search and Destroy" to its sneaker ad lineup. The song, written in the early seventies by draft-dodging punk pioneer Iggy Stooge (aka Iggy Pop), was originally a mock celebration of the Vietnam War and American testosterone-driven culture. Reborn and stripped of any ironic message, "Search and Destroy" is now the soundtrack to a testosterone-driven basketball game and marketing strategy. I suppose it's only a matter of time until "Kill the Poor" sells Nikes too, most likely providing the musical backdrop to a scene of Nike-wearing ghetto kids playing aggressive b-ball.

Originality

Locust. A small white cardboard box, painted black inside, with a large (3″) dead locust glued to the inside cover and a cassette tape glued to the bottom.
"*zine*" in the Factsheet Five *Collection, New York State Library*[21]

Originality is highly prized in the zine world, finding its expression in the immense breadth of topics that zines cover and the idiosyncratic forms they take. As part of the libertarian belief that each individual is entirely unique, the ideal that each individual's creation should be unique naturally follows. Creation becomes testimony to a person's originality.

This is one of the wonderful traits of zines. Freed from having to address either a mass audience or a profitable niche market, zine writers explore and express their individuality. Brett Sonnenschein creates *Roulez,* "the newsletter for and about the serious Miles Bornes player," expressing his devotion to the game and his eagerness to trade and share it with nonplaying zine writers.[22] *Murtaugh* is a zine that brings together the unlikely pair of punk rock and baseball. Why? Because these are the things that interest its editor Spike Vrusho.[23] Or meet the Renaissance-person editor of *Gamma-Ray Universe* who explains that "this zine is about thinking in new ways. . . . *Music* is one of the avenues that leads me to this goal, *scientific research* is another."[24] In each case the originality of the zine is a byproduct of the originality of the author, and the zine illustrates his or her desire to be "true to self" in their creation.

But how to explain *Poor Doggie,* a zine made up of stories of pet dogs and their demise? It turns out that the author was at one time a pet-cemetery employee, but I don't really believe that this zine – however original – is an expression of the editor's authentic self. Something else is going on here. Like the shock value of punk rock, *Poor Doggie* is the product of an attempt to create something – anything – that has not already been manufactured by the commercial culture industry and, moreover, will be difficult for it to co-opt. As Aaron of *Blue Persuasion* found out, it takes very little for the mass media to understand and use a zine that celebrates nostalgia for pop culture as *Teenage Gang Debs* does; it's more difficult for them to assimilate a picture of a man having intercourse with a turkey carcass, or stories about dead dogs.[25]

It's also hard to assimilate things that barely make sense. It's a stretch to imagine anyone co-opting a list of "What's in the bag?" a feature in *Exformation* that lists pennies, flies, wadded-up tissue, and other refuse left in a bag.[26] Or *Feh*, odd comix illustrating stories with neither rhyme nor reason.[27] Or, for that matter, an article in *Hell Bound* on "How to turn your bread into fertile dirt" by leaving it sealed in a bag for a month.[28]

Part of this bizarre zine content is pure Dadaist nonsensical fun: *Feh* comix, in the words of their creator Sam Andreeff are "not supposed to make any sense."[29] But equally part of this urge to create nonsense is the zine writer's desire to invent something "new" in an age where everything seems to have been done, bought up and sold out already. "Been there, done that," as the copy to a popular soda advertisement runs. As I've discussed earlier, one of the ways zinesters create something new is to personalize what they are writing about, another is to strive towards the novel. And completely novel, I must admit, is *Eleventh Pin*, a zine that consists solely of pictures of a solitary bowling pin in different settings.[30] Or Donald Busky simply making up his own national and international news in his zine, *The Weird News*.[31]

In the editorial of his first issue of *Beer Frame*, Paul Lukas explains his choice of such items as mousetraps and foot-measuring devices to write about: "If you're searching for another recitation of how cool it is to read *Hate,* listen to Pavement, or drink on Ludlow Street, please look elsewhere – *the whole world knows about that stuff already.*"[32]

Hate is an underground comic that has become popular with a wide audience; Pavement is a band once in the "obscurity-is-next-to-godliness" club that has suffered the same fate; and Ludlow Street in the Lower East Side of New York features a string of "cool" bars now frequented by the suburban "bridge and tunnel" crowd.[33] All these things have been "discovered." Paul, by contrast, writes about admittedly banal things that no one has ever given much thought to, justifying his picks by arguing that he "wasn't interested in doing just another version of something that had already been done before."[34]

Even zines themselves are suspect, now that they've become too well known. Paul, like other zine writers I've talked to recently, is shying away from calling *Beer Frame* a zine. Just because it's a "zine," Paul explains, "You'll get the people who think it's really great. Like 'Oh, wow. It's really groovy that you do this. I think it's really amazing'. . . . They don't even care whether it's good or bad . . . and I don't want that sort of unconditional approval."[35]

As the underground is discovered, virgin ground needs to be unearthed. The internal logic of the zine world, which values originality as an expression of authenticity, and the external forces of a commercial culture continually discovering and assimilating facets of the underground together drive a perpetual raising of the stakes. In the free-wheeling, image-swapping, postmodern information economy, it is genuinely difficult to set anything apart as novel for long, since its very novelty becomes its selling point. After just a few issues, Paul Lukas parlayed *Beer Frame's* originality into a syndicated column in alternative newsweeklies, then a column in the glossy *New York* magazine, and finally into a commercial book. But the quest for the original is continually undertaken. On the Lower East Side, some young squatter punks – or "crusties" as they're called – tattoo their faces, forever drawing a distinction between themselves and the bourgeoisie (or at least until it becomes next year's hit fashion). And zines such as *Murder Can Be Fun, Answer Me!*, and *Dead Star: for John Wayne Gacy*, celebrate mass murderers as the ultimate un-cooptables, positing pure evil as the only purity left.[36]

In this continual striving for originality, meaning is sometimes a casualty. While I find *Beer Frame's* hidden histories of everyday objects fascinating, and really enjoy the humor that went into pictures of bowling pins in *Eleventh Pin*, it is hard to get excited about *Big Fish: Special Hat Size Issue*, a zine comprising handwritten "hat sizes of some of the major poets in America."[37] Such zines fetishize originality. No longer is the choice of unique subject matter an authentic expression of an individual; instead, it becomes the manifestation of a hollow concept: originality for originality's sake. This hollow originality is a common enough occurrence in the underground publishing world to warrant a comic by Shannon Wheeler poking fun at it, drawing an "original" comic of drawing an original comic.[38]

Originality is important in the creative expression of an individual, but it loses something when it's not coupled with a critical discernment of worth.[39] Even though the zine tendency to strive toward the original originates in reaction against commercial culture's colonization, zine writers can easily end up replicating the very same consumerist logic: in with the new and out with the old, a celebration of this year's model without any judgment of value. When this happens, originality becomes banality.

In addition, the constant raising of stakes to set off a world undiscovered, unsullied, and pure, results in closing down the expanse of community. I'm reminded of John Foster's "Three Days in the Life of a Loser" cited earlier, in which he writes of his "attempt to present a facade of cool" by "talk[ing] about records so obscure that nobody present has heard of them."[40] Following the ultimate illogic of underground originality, the price of being truly cool is to risk talking to yourself about absolutely nothing.

Opening Up or Selling Out?

> He's the one
> Who likes all our pretty songs
> And he likes to sing along
> And he likes to shoot his gun
> But he knows not what it means
> Knows not what it means . . .
>   Kurt Cobain, singer/
>   songwriter of Nirvana, 1991[41]

"I'm sure you've heard the debate about is it really a good thing that Nirvana has done what they've done," asks Dan Werle, editor of *Manumission*, referring to the fact that the band signed to a major label and appeared on MTV.

> First with the skeptical analysis: it's horrible, it's disgusting, they're just corporate whores, and they've got no purpose whatsoever now. But perhaps someone – I grew up in the middle of Iowa – is watching a Nirvana video . . . and they see someone wearing a Bad Brains T-shirt and then look at Bad Brains and say . . . What were Bad Brains all about? And they look back at '79 . . . and the whole other list of bands that came out of that. Then it seems that maybe it's not so bad.[42]

This, once again, is the conundrum facing the underground: is it preferable to proselytize the good news – even via the commercial culture industry – or to stay small and pure and avoid "selling out."

For some zine producers the choice is clear. Mike Gunderloy told me of diehard science fiction zine purists, who years before the discovery and marketing of zine culture, refused to have anything to do with *Factsheet Five* because in addition to trading, Mike also made it available at newsstands for a cover price – in their eyes an unforgivable betrayal of the pure trade ethic.

Others – subcultural entrepreneurs I call them – use their zines and zine experience as a stepping stone to launch themselves or their zines into the commercial media world. Reporting in the *Village Voice* on a zine show held in one of the – already discovered – bars on Ludlow Street, where a disproportionate number of slickly published "zines" were displayed, Julia Chaplin writes that "several of the more upwardly mobile publishers admit that their zines are essentially disguised resumes they mail out to prospective employers."[43] Underscoring this new relationship between mainstream and underground cultural worlds, *Factsheet Five* ran a series of articles in a recent issue on how to sell your writing and market your zine commercially under the barely ironic collective headline: "How To Sell Out!"[44] In the post–discovery age, zines can be the path from being a loser to becoming a winner.[45]

For others, the choice to enter into the mainstream cultural world is one of more complex means and ends. Roxxie, who has transformed her lesbian sports zine *Girljock* into a glossy magazine complete with an Absolut vodka advertisement on the back of one issue, talked to me about one of the reasons she has pushed to expand her zine's reach through commercial channels. "I suppose it's my wish that teenage girls will have more options for themselves as they're growing up," she explains. "And so if you're, say, a very isolated teenager somewhere in the midwest, hopefully there might be a place where you might be able to . . . run into something like *Girljock*."[46]

Being a lesbian teenager is tough any place, but stuck in a provincial area where you have no peers or role models, it can be devastating. As Roxxie points out, "the suicide rate for lesbian and gay teens is alarmingly high . . . . [as is] the chance that they'll be drug addicts or alcoholics." A publication like *Girljock* "normalizes" lesbians who like sports. It tells young lesbians that they're not sick and not alone, as zines like *Homocore* did for gay punk rockers. But gay punks, because of their interest in punk rock, can easily find out about *Homocore* from an ad in *Maximumrocknroll* or a review in another zine. They are already hooked into the underground world that gives them access to this material. Teenage lesbian jocks are not. For them, it may be what's in the sports section of the magazine racks at the B. Dalton's in the local mall, or nothing. By printing on multicolor slick paper and with a production run of 10,000 financed by corporate advertising, Roxxie got *Girljock* accepted by two national distributors who sell widely outside the hipster record and bookstores that traditionally carry zines. Roxxie "sold out" in the hope that a teenage girljock, shopping in a mall someplace, is finding *Girljock* next to *Sports Illustrated* and realizing – perhaps for the first time – that she is not alone.[47]

Like it or not, most people's access to culture and media is limited to mainstream channels. When underground culture is discovered, these channels pipe the exotic world of bohemia out to the masses. But, as Dan points out above, the stream does not flow only one way. The mass media can also serve as reverse conduits back into alternative culture. A couple years ago I received a letter from a young woman named Kate Wolfe requesting my zine. When I later asked her how she had found out about my zine, she replied: "I guess I'm a newcomer to the whole zine scene. I was reading *Sassy* magazine one day and every month they have something called 'Zine of the Month' . . . Then I heard about *Factsheet Five* which was filled with zillions of zany zines. I must have sent away for 200 of them." Mine was one. Through a decidedly commercial medium, Kate had discovered the world of zines.[48]

However, even without zines going slick or appearing in *Sassy*, commercial access to them is spreading. The Tower chain, under the guidance of zine enthusiast Doug Biggert, sells more than 500 different zines through its bookstores and record outlets. While Biggert argues that the profit Tower makes on zines is minimal compared to that garnered from more commercial products, he still admits, "We've already sold over a million dollars worth of zines . . . and sales are always increasing."[49] Dwarfing the few underground bookstores, and not bound by the conservatism of the few remaining independents, Tower Books – until recently – had by far the widest selection of zines in my home city of New York.

All of this bodes well for the expansion of the world of zines – but it has its costs as well. Part of the power of the self-published press was its very obscurity, and the culture that arose out of this near invisibility. "It's nice to have wide distribution," Kevin Pyle, another one of the editors of *World War III*, explains.

> But I remember back when I was going to school in Kansas in 1986 and there was *nothing*. But then one person had seen *WWIII* and so we'd send off, or we'd get *Factsheet Five*. There was a certain network . . . a whole community involved in a world that is not being sold to you by big corporations. I think [this] has certain advantages to it. You become a part of something . . . [it] has an air of conspiracy.[50]

What Kevin illustrates is the importance of the context in which the message of underground culture is received. The meaning of zines has always been embedded in the lived experience of alternative culture. "In order to find out about them, you have to become part of the culture," one zine writer comments, "which is what makes them different than anything."[51] In discovering zines through personal connections, trading a zine in a network, you become, as Kevin says, "part of something . . . an air of conspiracy." In buying a zine at Tower Books the alternative message of zines as part of a community who "entertain themselves" is entirely lost. You are simply part of the consuming public.

The context of reception is particularly important in the case of zines since – as I've argued before – their politics reside less in what they say and more in what they are: repositories of nonalienated creation and media for nonalienating communication. This becomes clear when the zine gospel is spread through nonzine means. Mike Gunderloy's and Cari Goldberg Janice's commercial book *The World of Zines* begins with the encouraging advice: "Everyone can be a producer! That's the underlying message of the zine world."[52] But the very form through which they communicate this message argues against them. Professionally produced, bankrolled by a multinational corporation, distributed and sold in commercial bookstores, *The World of Zines* sends a clear but quite different message: Everybody can *not* be a producer.

This danger is inherent in any underground creation utilizing the ways and means of the commercial culture industry. Recently I was sent "The *Curio* Manifesto," a prospectus for a publication "part glossy, part zine . . . [that] will combine the traditional magazine format with the best of the zine world for a nationwide audience." Regardless of the creator's – no doubt good – intentions, she misses the point of zines entirely. "The best of the zine world" has always resided in the form of zines and the context of their distribution. Even if *Curio* does contain the words and artwork of zinesters, to sell a slick magazine, with a 50,000 circulation and a "corporate soul to foot our print bill," undermines the entire purpose and significance of zines.[53]

As the underground is discovered, paths toward wider distribution and contact are opened up to alternative cultural creators. Whether for reasons of personal gain or public concern, zine writers and other underground creators use these paths. And while the message contained in the content of zines is spread farther and wider than ever before, the radical participatory cultural message of zines is simultaneously muted. The popularity of zines concerns many zine writers, the issue surfacing in the increasing use of the term "sellout" tossed across the pages of zines, and the denial of the charge of "selling out" in others. ("Don't worry, we haven't *sold out*," begins Seth Friedman's editorial in *Factsheet Five*, 55.)[54] While the accusation of "selling out" is sometimes just an elitist defense of the pure, bohemian ghetto, it's not always so simple. Rather, given the manner in which the opening up of the zine world is taking place, the concern that in the process of popularization the real message of zines – as an alternative to the consumer cultural world – will get lost is a valid one. To many in the underground the idea of a nation of people reading zines is great, but not if they know not what they mean.

By Fire or Ice

Teenage angst has paid off well
Now I'm bored and old . . .
Kurt Cobain, 1993[55]

On April 7, 1994, twenty-seven years old and at the height of his career, Kurt Cobain stuck a shotgun in his mouth and blew his head off. "I told him not to join that stupid club," his mother was quoted as saying after his death, referring to the pantheon of rock stars who had killed themselves: Elvis Presley, Jimi Hendrix, Janis Joplin, Jim Morrison. But Kurt hadn't joined *that* club. Those rock stars had killed themselves more or less accidentally, enjoying the fruits of their fame. The lead singer for Nirvana killed himself on purpose, *because* of his fame – intensely uncomfortable with his popularity and status as a rock star. In his suicide note, he wrote that he no longer enjoyed playing; "sometimes I feel as if I should have a punch-in time clock before I walk out on stage," and "the worst crime I can think of would be to pull people off by faking it and pretending as if I'm having a hundred percent fun." "So remember," Kurt ended his note, borrowing a line from original grunge rocker Neil Young singing about former Sex Pistol – now Mountain Dew soda pitchman – Johnny Rotten, "it's better to burn out than to fade away."[56] It's better to die pure than to live corrupted.

"Kurt didn't commit suicide," Scott Munroe writes in *Chairs Missing*, "he was murdered. Murdered by a corporate music industry unwilling to treat musicians as people and not 'product.'"[57] Kurt Cobain was suffering from a heroin addiction, a rocky relationship, and the sensitive rage that made his songs so hauntingly beautiful, but Scott is at least partially right: it was Kurt's discomfort with the demands of the corporate music industry and his fear that he was "faking it" that filled his suicide note. But what also killed him was the underground culture from which he came: a culture that divided the world into polar opposites: our world and theirs, integrity and selling out, purity and danger. Caught between the demands of the commercial music industry for popularity and the underground call for authenticity, Kurt killed himself, entering the only airtight bohemia.

Playing out a tradition of bohemian elitism, as well as pragmatically responding to a culture industry that feeds off innovation and dissent, the underground has learned to worship purity and obscurity. This is part of its romance, but it is also its tragic flaw.

For this will-toward-smallness also wills the culture toward insignificance, and, through attrition, decimation. And after all, what's the point of an alternative culture if it can't sustain enough people to function as an alternative?

Dissatisfied with the constraints of this self-ghettoization, others attempt to break out. But the only coherent cultural/political apparatus that has the sort of reach necessary to spread the news to those outside the underground networks is the corporate culture industry. Bereft of other options, it's here that people turn. The result is that underground culture is sold as style. Stripped of their meaning, zines are an empty husk. A concept is marketed rather than a culture experienced.

Stunted in the darkness or burned up in the light: there is no clear path between the two, but there are explorations. One is to create independent distribution services that can mediate between the zine producers, zine readers, and at times, large commercial outlets. Blacklist Mailorder, a project of *Maximumrocknroll*, is a volunteer-run mailorder operation that distributes both music and zines with a minimal markup price.[58] Riot Grrrl Press reproduces, lists, and circulates *Riot Grrrl* and other women-centered zines.[59] Wow Cool, started by zine writers Mark Arsenault and Josh Petrin, distributes zines, comix, books – printed matter of the underground.[60] These services and many others began as a way to address the problems that distributing through the mainstream culture networks posed.

While these subcultural institutions help extend the scope of zines and underground culture without resorting to mainstream collaboration, they are not without their own difficulties. The prospective reader or listener still has to be "in the know" even to find out that these services exist. Once found they can open up a wide world that allows the bypassing of commercial outlets, but first that world has to be discovered. In addition, distribution services, whatever their intent, eradicate the networking aspect that is so important to the zine world. As Marc of Wow Cool readily concedes: "I really do think the best way to get zines is either through the mail from the individual or from the person who actually does it." Running Wow Cool, Marc sees that the personal aspect of zine culture is a casualty. After *Cometbus*, 30, was reviewed in *Sassy*, he says, "We must have gotten a couple hundred orders . . . and except for the occasional 'Oh, I love Aaron,' and then the four or five people who actually wrote letters, most of them were: 'Send me a *Cometbus* #30. Here's my dollarfifty' and not interested in the interaction part."[61]

That personal exchange becomes a casualty of even subcultural distribution services is partly a matter of size. As I discussed earlier in terms of zine production, increase in size limits the sort of personal touch and control over the process that a zine producer can have. As they've come to be featured in the mainstream media, even zine purists like Dishwasher Pete and Aaron Cometbus have begun swapping their zines for others only selectively. Losing money trading two hundred and fifty zines is one thing, but the percentage on five thousand is another. The decline in trading in the zine world, however, is more widespread than this explanation accounts for. Even after castigating any and all panels that broached the politics of zine commercialization, Chip Rowe, reporting in *Factsheet Five* on the 1994 Chicago Underground Press Conference, admits to being saddened by what he sees as the death of a zine tradition. "I notice lately that more and more of the listings in *Factsheet Five* have "no trade" listed. Are zine editors, including myself, guilty of losing sight of what it was all about in the first place?"[62]

Perhaps. As the zine world has grown and rubbed shoulders with the mainstream, some of the practices of the latter have rubbed off. When zinesters set up institutions that spread the underground, they also invariably end up contributing to the status quo separation between cultural production and consumption.[63] "Remember the main purpose of this is to promote dialogue and help girls have access to each other's voices," May and Erika write in the front of their *Riot Grrrl Press* catalog. "It would truly bum me out if this turned into a commodification of 'girl zines' where if you have the cash you have access."[64] These women worry because they know it will happen; their catalog, while expanding access, will also increase the distance between producers and consumers. Likewise, the zinesters who set up distribution services and the like, while helping the "alternative culture invest in itself," as Scott Cunningham puts it, are faced with the inevitable intrusion of the bottom line on a living culture. Wow Cool's Marc Arsenault ruefully understands the ethical conflict of acting as middleman for the underground: "This private moment on paper, but I'm supposed to make a buck off of it."[65] But what can the underground do? It seems that any attempt to give it secure footing and a more expansive reach results in its betrayal.

In response, anarchist theorist and zinester Hakim Bey (aka Peter Lanborn Wilson) counsels the rejection of underground stability. He concludes that direct confrontation with mainstream society – a "Spook capable of smothering every spark in an ectoplasm of information" – is futile. The power of the modern corporate culture state can soak up anything it encounters, transforming discontents into affirmations. The solution then is to disappear. This is the strategy of the TAZ or Temporary Autonomous Zone. As Bey explains:

> Its greatest strength lies in its invisibility – the State cannot recognize it because History has no definition of it. As soon as the TAZ is named (represented, mediated), it must vanish, it *will* vanish, leaving behind it an empty husk, only to spring up again somewhere else, once again invisible because undefinable in terms of the Spectacle.

The only way opposition can survive, according to Bey, is to become "a guerrilla operation which liberates an area (of land, of time, of imagination) and then dissolves itself to reform elsewhere/elsewhen, *before* the State can crush it" – or, more likely, before the consumer market can co-opt it.[66]

When confronted with the modern threat of capitalist co-optation (and the disappointment of so-called "revolutionary" police states), celebrating temporality seems to make sense, and some zine writers embrace the idea of TAZ. "My revolution starts today," the editor of *Forever & a Day* writes. "My revolution started yesterday, and the day before and the day before that. I will begin the whole thing over again tomorrow." Fearing that the underground "revolution" has now become "an advertising campaign," the editor goes on: "I will find it necessary to revolt against the revolution."[67]

Permanent revolution: an old line of Leon Trotsky. But "rebellion" is the term that Bey prefers, and it's more accurate. For the TAZ, as he recognizes, is a "counsel of despair."[68] As a strategy for survival it cedes permanent victory to the opposition, reveling in its own frailty and impermanence. Given the history of bohemia this appears practical advice, but it's also lethal. Like an individual who upon losing his or her memory has no sense of self, a community without continuity ceases to function as a community at all. This may be why zine writer Mickey Z, after a very TAZ-like rant in his *Reality Manifesto*, concludes, "Individual liberation is all we can hope for and that is what you must challenge yourself to pursue."[69]

The underground strategies of building up underground institutions of dissemination, or, conversely, celebrating the continual destruction of such institutions, are both honest attempts to chart a course between bohemian isolation and capitulation to the mainstream. But they are both problematic. This isn't because of any lack of will or intelligence on the part of their supporters, but because they are attempting to patch over conflicts inherent in the project of creating an alternative culture that rebels against but resides within the belly of the beast.

In the discussions that followed Kurt Cobain's suicide, I frequently heard people ask why, if he was so tortured over having "sold out," didn't he just give away his millions to help finance alternative institutions? Or why didn't he just go off and live on an island if he didn't want to pretend to enjoy playing to a mass audience? Maybe he didn't do either because the underground culture in which he was embedded doesn't have a viable vocabulary for considering such options. Within the ideological parameters of the underground there was no way for him to reconcile his commercial popularity with his commitment to an alternative vision of how culture and society should be. What I've outlined above are beginnings of building solutions – but only beginnings and ones fraught with difficulty at that. By and large, the underground culture's identity is tethered to the two poles of purity and danger, with both placed firmly in the dominant society. It is a conflict that gives this culture its passion, and, ironically, gave Kurt Cobain's music the same.

Falling Out of Favor

The underground culture is not the only culture with contradictions; the culture of capitalism is also riven in two. True, the market celebrates novelty and change, as the promiscuity of the commodity demands a libertarian culture. But just as this aspect is often not acknowledged, the other side of capitalism should not be forgotten. If profits are to be made and inequality is to be enforced, there must be order. And order requires a culturally conservative milieu.

While the mainstream media were fawning over "quirky" zines such as Brady Bunch fanzine *Teenage Gang Debs*, the state of Florida was busy prosecuting 24-year-old Mike Diana on three counts of publishing, distributing, and advertising obscene material: his comix zine *Boiled Angel*. Admittedly *Boiled Angel* is a far cry from the cloying suburban values celebrated in the Brady Bunch, but with a circulation of three hundred copies, the charges against it and Mike were not about stopping a porno czar from profiting from exploitation, but about policing what is and what is not acceptable cultural expression.

The punishment meted out was severe. Convicted on all three counts in a trial where zine and comix writers testified for the defense, Mike was sentenced in February 1994 to three years' probation and ordered to pay a $3,000 fine, $50 a month in probation fees, and a $1,200 court-mandated psychiatric examination. He has to attend and pay for a journalism class ("so I can become a serious journalist," Mike laughs), do eight hours a week of community service, and keep his full-time job as a convenience store clerk. During his three years of probation, Mike can have no contact with minors, nor is he allowed to draw anything that might be considered obscene – even for his own enjoyment. And to enforce this last restriction, a probation officer can enter Mike's apartment at any time to check on what he is drawing.[70] With lawyers paid for by the Comic Book Legal Defense Fund, Mike appealed the decision but lost again, a Florida Circuit Court judge upholding the decision. *Boiled Angel* would not be the last zine noticed by the law. One year after Mike's initial trial, both the owner and the manager of an independent bookstore in Bellingham, WA, were arrested and charged with "felony distribution of lewd material for profit." The item in question was the latest issue of Jim and Debbie Goad's zine *Answer Me!*[71]

Such clumsy acts of repression, of course, only served to spread the news of the two zines in question, in the process gaining them ironclad subversive credentials. The publicity generated by Mike Diana's case familiarized his name to everyone in the zine world and to First Amendment activists outside, while attracting still others interested in publishing comic books of Mike's drawings. Similarly, the legal repression of *Answer Me!* helped keep it on *Factsheet Five*'s list of top ten zines and made it Chicago's Qvimby Qveer Store's number-one-selling zine of 1995. As much as conspiracy-minded zine writers may fear (and secretly desire) the spectre of jackbooted thugs snatching away their zines, it won't be repression that forces zines out of the light and back underground . . . it will be lack of interest.

"Why is our voice suddenly being heard?" *Emit*'s editor Mole asks rhetorically. "Big corporations take notice when social climates change because they can market an attitude or a movement and convert it into a trend." The problem for the culture industry is that something is inevitably lost in translation. As Mole continues, "They take culture and sell it back to us in a glossy package, neglecting content but pushing style until it fizzles out as nothing more than a passing fad."[72] At that point it's time for the culture vultures to move on.

The mining of the underground is so passé that the editors of *Dirt*, the zine financed by Time-Warner, ran a page that parades their compromised corporate status: "We know damn well what we're doing by printing this faux fanzine. How dumb do you think we are. Hell. We got paid to do this."[73] The selling of the underground is so complete that *Time* magazine printed a – quite perceptive – feature story on the phenomenon, pointing out that "in its infinite pliancy, capitalism proved itself well suited to absorb whatever it was in hip that might fascinate consumers, while discarding the uncomfortable parts."[74] *Time*'s doppelgänger, *Emit*, had pointed it out a year earlier, but said it no better. Meanwhile MTV produced a short video clip on the issue of alternative rockers "Selling Out," demonstrating that even the discussion of selling out had sold out.[75] And the Coca-Cola Company's OK Cola, after a brief test marketing, was shelved. Perhaps disappointed that the underground is not as pure and authentic as it once was, perhaps merely in search of something new, the culture industry has moved on.

By 1995, the *New York Times* was celebrating the return of "normal" rock stars who perform with "no displays of angst, no cryptic lyrics, no resentment of a growing audience," professional musicians who "represent the return of the well-adjusted and congenial to the rock world."[76] A year later, Judith McGrath, president of MTV, confided to the *New York Times* that "The us-versus-them thing seems to be disappearing. [Young] people are more complacent."[77] And writing on the world of fashion and teen buying patterns, *Business Week* reported that "grunge is going out and Fifth Avenue is cool again."[78] Alienation, rebellion, underground culture, and zines are last week's story.

This doesn't mean that zines are finished, perhaps they are just moving back underground. "If the 'zine world' disappeared tomorrow it wouldn't really affect me," says Dishwasher Pete. "I'll still be doing what I'm doing."[79] And so will untold numbers of others who existed before the discovery of the underground, and will continue long after zines have been forgotten.

Notes

1. Exchange of letters reprinted in *Maximumrocknroll* and Underdog Records' *Book Your Own Fuckin' Life: Do-It-Yourself Resource Guide*, 2, 1993, Chicago, IL, back cover.
2. Mary Douglas, *Purity and Danger: An Analysis of the Concepts of Pollution and Taboo* (London: Ark, 1966).
3. Aaron, *Cometbus*, 31, Spring 1994, San Francisco, CA, p. 56.
4. Keffo, *Temp Slave*, 4, 1995(?), Madison, WI, p. 9.
5. Doug, *Pathetic Life*, April 1995, II, San Francisco, CA, p. 1.
6. J. Peder Zane, "Now, the Magazine of 'Me,'" *New York Times*, May 14, 1995, p. E4.
7. Joseph A. Gervasi, "Introduction," *NO LONGER A FANzine*, 4, 1994, Blackwood, NJ, no page.
8. CNN, "Boom or Bust," rebroadcast, July 2, 1995.
9. Aaron Lee, "Aaron to the Media: Shove It!" *Blue Persuasion*, 4, 1994, Lexington, KY, p. 3.
10. Ananda, *Riot Grrrl*, 8, 1992(?), Washington, DC, no page.
11. Late Night with David Letterman, CBS, June 27, 1995.
12. Rick Marin, "Grunge: A Success Story," *New York Times*, November 15, 1992, sec. 9, p. 1.
13. Tom Frank in *The Baffler*, 4, 1992, Chicago, IL.
14. "Cultural jamming" is what critic Mark Dery calls this underground sabotage that feeds off a medium that "accepts photo ops and buzz words as meaningful discourse.' Ironically, or perhaps tellingly, Dery's best writing on the practice of "cultural jamming" appeared in the "Styles" pages of the paper of record – media sabotage as the new hip style? Mark Dery, "The Merry Pranksters and the Art of the Hoax," *New York Times*, December 23, 1990, p. H1.
15. Missy Lavalee, personal correspondence, January 19, 1993.
16. Kyle Baker, *NO LONGER A FANzine*, 3, 1993, Blackwood, NJ, no page.
17. Dead Kennedys, "Kill the Poor," *Fresh Fruit for Rotting Vegetables*, IRS Records, 1981.

18. Lionel Trilling, *Sincerity and Authenticity* (Cambridge MA: Harvard University Press, 1972), p. 2.

19. Mikhail Bakhtin, *Rabelais and His World* (Bloomington: Indiana University Press, 1936/1984).

20. The bohemian tribe was Ken Kesey's "Merry Pranksters"; the book is Tom Wolfe, *The Electric Kool-Aid Acid Test* (New York: Farrar, Strauss and Giroux, 1968).

21. Vortext Publications, *Locust*, no date, Seattle, WA FS₅–NYSL).

22. Brett Sonnenschein, *Roulez*, vol. 1, no. 2, Summer 1993, Jersey City, NJ. Brett traded *Roulez* for a copy of one of my zines through *Factsheet Five*.

23. Spike Vrusho, *Murtaugh*, 10, 1993(?), Brooklyn, NY.

24. *Gamma-Ray Universe*, no. 00–1, 1994(?), Ithaca, NY, no page. Emphasis mine.

25. *Poor Doggie*, no date, Cambridge, MA (FS₅–NYSL).

26. T.L., "What's in the Bag?" *Exformation*, 2, 1994, Brooklyn, NY, p. 14.

27. Sam Andreeff, *Feh*, 1990s, Toronto, Ontario.

28. Jennifer Beard et al., *Hell bound*, 7, June 17, 1993, Olympia, WA, p. 40.

29. *Feh*, Toronto, Ontario; Sam Andreeff, personal correspondence, March 11, 1994.

30. Phil Snyder and Cyclone Publications, *Eleventh Pin*, 2, 1991, Dayton, OH.

31. Donald F. Busky, *The Weird News*, 12, Winter 1992, Philadelphia, PA.

32. Paul Lukas, *Beer Frame*, 1, 1994(?), Brooklyn, NY, p. 2.

33. "Obscurity-is-next-to-godliness" is a term used to describe Pavement by David Sprague, in "Pavement's Meandering Path to Mainstream Listeners," *Long Island Newsday*, sec. 2, p. 49.

34. Paul Lukas, telephone interview, February 13, 1994.

35. Paul Lukas, telephone interview, February 13, 1994.

36. Jim and Debbie Goad, *Answer Me!*, LA, CA, early 1990s; Johnny Marr, *Murder Can Be Fun*, San Francisco, CA, late 1980s; Future Tense Publishing, *Dead Star: For John Wayne Gacy*, 4, Portland, OR, 1994.

37. Sparrow, "Letters," *Factsheet Five*, 32, 1989, Rensselaer, NY, p. 102.

38. Shannon Wheeler, *Reactor*, 6, 1993, Chicago, IL, p. 44. Shannon has also done comix for *Factsheet Five*.

39. Charles Taylor calls this criterion "horizons of significance." *The Ethics of Authenticity* (Cambridge, MA: Harvard University Press, 1991) pp. 35–7.

40. John Foster, "Three Days in the Life of a Loser," *Ched*, 2, October 28, 1993, Portland OR, no page.

41. Nirvana, "In Bloom," *Nevermind*, 1991, Geffen Records.

42. Dan Werle, telephone interview, December 15, 1993.

43. Julia Chaplin, "Zine and Heard," *Village Voice*, July 30, 1996, p. 6.

44. Amelia G, "A Place for Pus: How to Submit Work That Gets Printed"; Steve O'Keefe, "Shut Up and Write"; Seth Maxwell Malice, "Buy This Ad," *Factsheet Five*, 54, December 1994, San Francisco, CA, pp. 114–17.

45. Underground culture can be a sort of farm league for the corporate culture industry. Styles and products germinate underground, have time to dig in their roots, and then, when beginning to flower, they are plucked by big business. "In allowing small-scale and relatively independent activity to continue to exist in cultural work," media critic Herb Schiller explains, "the big cultural firms insure a constant supply of talent and creativity that otherwise might be ignored or even suffocated in their own bureaucratized, symbol-making factories. The 'independents' are continually tapped to replenish exhausted creative energies in the cultural conglomerates."

46. *Girljock*, 10, 1993, San Francisco, CA.

47. Roxxie, telephone interview, June 23, 1994.
48. Kate Wolfe, personal correspondence, November 1993.
49. Cited in Jeremy Mindich, "Soapbox Samurai," *Details*, August 1993, p. 99; also telephone interview with Doug Biggert, October 4, 1993.
50. Kevin Pyle, panel discussion with editors of *WWIII*, October 6, 1993, Exit Art, New York City.
51. Arielle Greenberg, personal interview, August 25, 1993, New York City.
52. Mike Gunderloy and Cari Goldberg Janice, *The World of Zines* (New York: Penguin, 1992), p. 3.
53. M. Teresa Lawrence, "The *Curio* Manifesto," received August 15, 1995. *Curio*'s mailing list comes from *Factsheet Five*.
54. R. Seth Friedman, *Factsheet Five*, 55, March 1995, San Francisco, CA, p. 3.
55. Nirvana, "Serve the Servants," *In Utero*, Geffen Records, 1993.
56. Cited in "A Cry In the Dark," *Rolling Stone*, June 2, 1994, p. 40.
57. Scott Munroe, *Chairs Missing*, April 1994, Stratford, CT, no page.
58. Listed in *Maximumrocknroll*, 63, August 1988, San Francisco, no page.
59. *Riot Grrrl Press*, September–November, 1994(?), Washington, DC.
60. *Wow Cool*, Winter 1994 Catalog, Berkeley, CA.
61. Marc Arsenault, telephone interview, December 14, 1993.
62. Chip Rowe, "Chicago Fun Times," *Factsheet Five*, 53, October 1994, San Francisco, p. 126.
63. Scott Cunningham, among others, drew my attention to this point. Personal interview, September 1, 1993, New York City.
64. May and Erika, *Riot Grrrl Press* catalog, July (1993?), Arlington, VA, no page.
65. Marc Arsenault, telephone interview, December 14, 1993.
66. Hakim Bey, *TAZ* (Brooklyn: Autonomedia, 1985), pp. 100–101; also Peter Lanborn Wilson (aka Hakim Bey), talk at the Libertarian Book Club, April 17, 1995.
67. Anon. *Forever & a Day*, 7, 1993(?), Seattle, WA, no page.
68. Bey, p. 100.
69. Mickey Z, *The Reality Manifesto* (Baltimore: Apathy Press Poets, 1983), no page.
70. Mike Diana, telephone interview, May 13, 1994.
71. Jeff Koyen, "Arrest Me!" *Crank*, 4. 1995, New York City. The issue of *Answer Me!* dealt, in usual Goad fashion, with the issue of rape.
72. Mole, "Whine & Cheez," *Emit*, 1, November–December, 1993, North Vancouver, BC, p. 12.
73. *Dirt*, 51, 1994(?), no page.
74. Richard Lacayo, "Is Anyone Hip?" *Time*, August 8, 1994, p. 52.
75. The interview clip was with Trent Reznor of Nine Inch Nails. Predictably, the interview was edited in such a way as to juxtapose the elitist underground against the populist free market. No mention was made of profit or corporate control.
76. Neil Strauss, "They're Normal. And Rock Stars?" review of Hootie and the Blowfish, *New York Times*, June 22, 1995, p. C13.
77. Quoted in Neil Strauss, "For Record Industry, All Signs Are Gloomy," *New York Times*, December 4, 1996, pp. A1, C14.
78. David Leonhardt, "Like Totally Big Spenders," *Business Week*, June 3, 1996, p. 8.
79. Dishwasher Pete, personal interview, June 21, 1995, New York City.

VIII

Consumer Culture and
Fashion Studies

41

Theories of Consumer Culture

*Mike Featherstone**

This chapter identifies three main perspectives on consumer culture. First is the view that consumer culture is premised upon the expansion of capitalist commodity production which has given rise to a vast accumulation of material culture in the form of consumer goods and sites for purchase and consumption. This has resulted in the growing salience of leisure and consumption activities in contemporary Western societies which, although greeted as leading to greater egalitarianism and individual freedom by some, is regarded by others as increasing the capacity for ideological manipulation and 'seductive' containment of the population from some alternative set of 'better' social relations. Second, there is the more strictly sociological view, that the satisfaction derived from goods relates to their socially structured access in a zero sum game in which satisfaction and status depend upon displaying and sustaining differences within conditions of inflation. The focus here is upon the different ways in which people use goods in order to create social bonds or distinctions. Third, there is the question of the emotional pleasures of consumption, the dreams and desires which become celebrated in consumer cultural imagery and particular sites of consumption which variously generate direct bodily excitement and aesthetic pleasures.

This chapter argues that it is important to focus on the question of the growing prominence of the *culture* of consumption and not merely regard consumption as derived unproblematically from production. The current phase of over-supply of symbolic goods in contemporary Western societies and the tendencies towards cultural disorder and de-classification (which some label as postmodernism) is therefore bringing cultural questions to the fore and has wider implications for our conceptualization of the relationship between culture, economy and society. This has also led to an increasing interest in conceptualizing questions of desire and pleasure, the emotional and aesthetic satisfactions derived from consumer experiences, not merely in terms of some logic of psychological manipulation. Rather sociology should seek to move beyond the negative evaluation of consumer pleasures inherited from mass culture theory. We should endeavour to account for these emergent tendencies in a more detached sociological manner, which should not merely entail a reverse populist celebration of mass pleasures and cultural disorder.

*Pp. 5–22 from *Sociology*, vol. 24, no. 1 (Sage Publications). © 1990 by BSA Publications Ltd. Reprinted with permission from Sage Publications Ltd.

The Production of Consumption

If from the perspectives of classical economics the object of all production is consumption, with individuals maximizing their satisfactions through purchasing from an ever-expanding range of goods, then from the perspective of some twentieth-century neo-Marxists this development is regarded as producing greater opportunities for controlled and manipulated consumption. The expansion of capitalist production, especially after the boost received from scientific management and 'Fordism' around the turn of the century, it is held, necessitated the construction of new markets and the 'education' of publics to become consumers through advertising and other media (Ewen, 1976). This approach, traceable back to Lukács's (1971) Marx–Weber synthesis with his theory of reification, has been developed most prominently in the writings of Horkheimer and Adorno (1972), Marcuse (1964) and Lefebvre (1971). Horkheimer and Adorno, for example, argue that the same commodity logic and instrumental rationality manifest in the sphere of production is noticeable in the sphere of consumption. Leisure time pursuits, the arts and culture in general become filtered through the culture industry; reception becomes dictated by exchange value as the higher purposes and values of culture succumb to the logic of the production process and the market. Traditional forms of association in the family and private life as well as the promise of happiness and fulfilment, the 'yearning for a totally different other' which the best products of high culture strove for, are presented as yielding to an atomized, manipulated mass who participate in an *ersatz* mass-produced commodity culture targeted at the lowest common denominator.

From this perspective it could, for example, be argued that the accumulation of goods has resulted in the triumph of exchange-value, that the instrumental rational calculation of all aspects of life becomes possible in which all essential differences, cultural traditions and qualities become transformed into quantities. Yet while this utilization of capital logic can account for the progressive calculability and destruction of residues of traditional culture and high culture – in the sense that the logic of capitalist modernization is such to make 'all that is solid melt into air' – there is the problem of the 'new' culture, the culture of capitalist modernity. Is it to be merely a culture of exchange value and instrumental rational calculation – something which might be referred to as a 'non-culture' or a 'post-culture'? This is one tendency within the work of the Frankfurt School, but there is another. Adorno, for example, speaks of how, once the dominance of exchange-value has managed to obliterate the memory of the original use-value of goods, the commodity becomes free to take up a secondary or *ersatz* use-value (Rose, 1978: 25). Commodities hence become free to take on a wide range of cultural associations and illusions. Advertising in particular is able to exploit this and attach images of romance, exotica, desire, beauty, fulfilment, communality, scientific progress and the good life to mundane consumer goods such as soap, washing machines, motor cars and alcoholic drinks.

A similar emphasis upon the relentless logic of the commodity is to be found in the work of Jean Baudrillard who also draws upon the commodification theory of Lukács (1971) and Lefebvre (1971) to reach similar conclusions to Adorno. The major addition to Baudrillard's (1970) theory is to draw on semiology to argue that consumption entails the active manipulation of signs. This becomes central to late capitalist society where sign and commodity have come together to produce the 'commodity-sign'. The autonomy of the signifier, through, for example, the manipulation of signs in the media and advertising, means that signs are able to float free from objects and are available for use in a multiplicity of associative relations. Baudrillard's semiological development of commodity logic, entails for some an idealistic deflection of Marx's theory and movement from a materialist emphasis to a cultural emphasis (Preteceille and Terrail, 1985). This becomes more noticeable in Baudrillard's (1983a, 1983b) later writings where the emphasis shifts from production to reproduction, to the endless reduplication of signs, images and simulations through the media which effaces the distinction between the image and reality. Hence the consumer society becomes essentially cultural as social life becomes deregulated and social relationships become more variable and less structured by stable norms. The overproduction of signs and reproduction of images and simulations leads to a loss of stable meaning, and an aestheticization of reality in which the masses become fascinated by the endless flow of bizarre juxtapositions which takes the viewer beyond stable sense.

This is the postmodern, 'depthless culture' of which Jameson (1984a, 1984b) speaks. Jameson's conception of postmodern culture is strongly influenced by Baudrillard's work (see Jameson, 1979). He also sees postmodern culture as the culture of the consumer society, the post-World War Two stage of late capitalism. In this society culture is given a new significance through the saturation of signs and messages to the extent that 'everything in social life can be said to have become cultural' (Jameson 1984a: 87). This 'liquefaction of signs and images' is also held to entail an effacement of the distinction between high and mass culture (Jameson, 1984b: 112): an acceptance of the equal validity of Las Vegas strip pop culture, alongside 'serious' high culture. At this point we should note the assumption that the immanent logic of the consumer capitalist society leads towards postmodernism. We will return to this question later to discuss images, desires and the aesthetic dimension of consumer culture.

It is clear that the production of consumption approach has difficulty in addressing the actual practices and experiences of consumption. The Frankfurt School's tendency to regard the culture industries as producing a homogeneous mass culture which threatens individuality and creativity has been criticized for its elitism and inability to examine actual processes of consumption which reveal complex differentiated audience responses and uses of goods (Swingewood, 1977; Gellner, 1979; B.S. Turner, 1988; Stauth and Turner, 1988).

Modes of Consumption

If it is possible to claim the operation of a 'capital logic' deriving from production, it may also be possible to claim a 'consumption logic' which points to the socially structured ways in which goods are used to demarcate social relationships. To speak of the consumption of goods immediately hides the wide range of goods which are consumed or purchased when more and more aspects of free time (which includes everyday routine maintenance activities as well as leisure) are mediated by the purchase of commodities. It also hides the need to differentiate between consumer durables (goods we use in maintenance and leisure, for example refrigerators, cars, hi-fis, cameras) and consumer non-durables (food, drink, clothing, body-care products) and the shift over time in the proportion of income spent on each sector (Hirshman, 1982: ch. 2; Leiss, Kline & Jhally, 1986: 260). We also need to pay attention to the ways in which some goods can move in and out of commodity status and the different length of life enjoyed by commodities as they move from production to consumption. Food and drink usually have a short life, although this is not always the case; for example a bottle of vintage port may enjoy a prestige and exclusivity which means that it is never actually consumed (opened and drunk), although it may be consumed symbolically (gazed at, dreamt about, talked about, photographed, and handled) in various ways which produce a great deal of satisfaction. It is in this sense that we can refer to the *doubly* symbolic aspect of goods in contemporary Western societies: symbolism is not only evident in the design and imagery of the production and marketing processes, the symbolic associations of goods may be utilized and renegotiated to emphasize differences in lifestyle which demarcate social relationships (Leiss, 1978: 19).

In some cases the object of purchasing may be to gain prestige through high exchange value (the price of the bottle of port is constantly mentioned), especially the case within societies where the aristocracy and old rich have been forced to yield power to the new rich (for example Veblen's 'conspicuous consumption'). The opposite situation can also be envisaged in which a former commodity becomes stripped of its commodity status. Hence gifts and inherited objects may become decommodified on reception and become literally 'priceless' (in the sense that it is extreme bad taste to consider selling them or to attempt to fix a price upon them) in their ability to symbolize intense personal relationships and their capacity to invoke memories of loved ones (Rochberg-Halton, 1986: 176). Art objects, or objects produced for ritual, and hence given a particular symbolic charge, tend often to be ones excluded from exchange, or not permitted to remain in the commodity status for long. At the same time their professed sacred status and denial of the profane market and commodity exchange may paradoxically raise their value. Their lack of availability and 'pricelessness' raises their price and desirability. For example, Willis' (1978) description of the way bike boys make sacred the original '78' records of Buddy Holly and Elvis Presley and refuse to use compilation albums which may have better reproduction, illustrates this process of the decommodification of a mass object.

Hence while there is the capacity for commodities to break down social barriers, to dissolve the long-established links between persons and things, there is also the countertendency, the movement towards decommodification, to restrict, control and channel the exchange of goods. In some societies stable status systems are protected and reproduced by restricting possibilities for exchange, or for the supply of new goods. In other societies there is an ever-changing supply of commodities which gives the illusion of complete changeability of goods and unrestricted access to them; yet here, legitimate *taste*, knowledge of the principles of classification, hierarchy and appropriateness is restricted, as is the case in fashion systems. An intermediate stage would be *sumptuary* laws, which act as consumption-regulating devices, prescribing which groups can consume which goods and wear types of clothing in a context where a previous stable status system is under strong threat from a major upsurge in the number and availability of commodities – the case in late pre-modern Europe (Appadurai, 1986: 25).

In contemporary Western societies the tendency is towards the second case mentioned, with an ever-changing flow of commodities making the problem of reading the status or rank of the bearer of the commodities more complex. It is in this context that taste, the discriminatory judgement, the knowledge or culture capital, which enables particular groups or categories of people to understand and classify new goods appropriately and how to use them, becomes important. Here we can turn to the work of Bourdieu (1984) and Douglas and Isherwood (1980) who examine the ways goods are used to mark social differences and act as communicators.

Douglas and Isherwood's (1980) work is particularly important in this respect because of their emphasis on the way in which goods are used to draw the lines of social relationships. Our enjoyment of goods, they argue, is only partly related to their physical consumption, being also crucially linked to their use as markers; we enjoy, for example, sharing the names of goods with others (the sports fan or the wine connoisseur). In addition the mastery of the cultural person entails a seemingly 'natural' mastery not only of information (the autodidact 'memory man') but also of how to use and consume appropriately and with natural ease in every situation. In this sense the consumption of high cultural goods (art, novels, opera, philosophy) must be related to the ways in which other more mundane cultural goods (clothing, food, drink, leisure pursuits) are handled and consumed, and high culture must be inscribed into the same social space as everyday cultural consumption. In Douglas and Isherwood's (1980: 176ff) discussion consumption classes are defined in relation to the consumption of three sets of goods: a staple set corresponding to the primary production sector (for example food); a technology set corresponding to the secondary production sector (travel and consumer's capital equipment); and an information set corresponding to tertiary production (information goods, education, arts, cultural and leisure pursuits). At the lower end of the social structure the poor are restricted to the staple set and have more time on their hands, while those in the top consumption class not only require a higher level of earnings, but also a competence in judging information goods and services in order to provide the feedback necessary from consumption to employment, which becomes itself a qualification for employment. This entails a lifelong investment in cultural and symbolic capital and in time invested in maintaining consumption activities. Douglas and Isherwood (1980: 180) also remind us that ethnographic evidence suggests that the competition to acquire goods in the information class generates high admission barriers and effective techniques of exclusion.

The phasing, duration and intensity of time invested in acquiring competences for handling information, goods, and services as well as the day-to-day practice, conservation and maintenance of these competences, is, as Halbwachs reminds us, a useful criterion of social class. Our use of time in consumption practices conforms to our class habitus and therefore conveys an accurate idea of our class status (see the discussion of Halbwachs in Preteceille & Terrail, 1985: 23). This points us towards the need for detailed time-budget research (see for example Gershuny & Jones, 1987). Such research, however, rarely incorporates, or is incorporated into, a theoretical framework drawing attention to patterns of investment over the life course which make such class-related differentiation of time use possible. The chances, for example, of encountering and making sense (that is, knowing how to enjoy and/or use the information in conversational practices) of a Godard film, the pile of bricks in the Tate Gallery, a book by Pynchon or Derrida, reflect different long-term investments in informational acquisition and cultural capital.

Such research has, however, been carried out in detail by Pierre Bourdieu and his associates (Bourdieu et al., 1965; Bourdieu & Passeron, 1990; Bourdieu, 1984). For Bourdieu (1984) 'taste classifies and classifies the classifier'. Consumption and lifestyle preferences involve discriminatory judgements which at the same time identify and render classifiable our own particular judgement of taste to others. Particular constellations of taste, consumption preferences and lifestyle practices are associated with specific occupation and class fractions, making it possible to map out the universe of taste and lifestyle with its structured oppositions and finely graded distinctions which operate within a particular society at a particular point in history. One important factor influencing the use of marker goods within capitalist societies is that the rate of production of new goods means that the struggle to obtain 'positional goods' (Hirsch, 1976), goods which define social status in the upper reaches of society, is a relative one. The constant supply of new, fashionably desirable goods, or the usurpation of existing marker goods by lower groups, produces a paperchase effect in which those above will have to invest in new (informational) goods in order to reestablish the original social distance.

In this context knowledge becomes important: knowledge of new goods, their social and cultural value, and how to use them appropriately. This is particularly the case with aspiring groups who adopt a learning mode towards consumption and the cultivation of a lifestyle. It is for groups such as the new middle class, the new working class and the new rich or upper class, that the consumer-culture magazines, newspapers, books, television and radio programmes which stress self-improvement, self-development, personal transformation, how to manage property, relationships and ambition, how to construct a fulfilling lifestyle, are most relevant. Here one may find most frequently the self-consciousness of the autodidact who is concerned to convey the appropriate and legitimate signals through his/her consumption activities. This may be particularly the case with the group Bourdieu (1984) refers to as 'the new cultural intermediaries', those in media, design, fashion, advertising, and 'para' intellectual information occupations, whose jobs entail performing services and the production, marketing and dissemination of symbolic goods. Given conditions of an increasing supply of symbolic goods (Touraine, 1985), demand grows for cultural specialists and intermediaries who have the capacity to ransack various traditions and cultures in order to produce new symbolic goods, and in addition provide the necessary interpretations on their use. Their habitus, dispositions and lifestyle preferences are such that they identify with artists and intellectuals, yet under conditions of the de-monopolization of artistic and intellectual commodity enclaves they have the apparent contradictory interests of sustaining the prestige and cultural capital of these enclaves, while at the same time popularizing and making them more accessible to wider audiences.

It should be apparent that the problems of inflation produced by an oversupply and rapid circulation of symbolic goods and consumer commodities have the danger of threatening the readability of goods used as signs of social status. Within the context of the erosion of the bounded state-society as part of a process of the globalization of markets and culture, it may be more difficult to stabilize appropriate marker goods. This would threaten the cultural logic of differences in which taste in cultural and consumer goods and lifestyle activities are held to be oppositionally structured (see the chart in which they are mapped out in Bourdieu, 1984: 128–9). This threat of disorder to the field or system would exist even if one accepted the premise derived from structuralism that culture itself is subject to a differential logic of opposition. To detect and establish such structured oppositions that enable groups to use symbolic goods to establish differences, would thus work best in relatively stable, closed and integrated societies, in which the leakages and potential disorder from reading goods through inappropriate codes is restricted. There is the further question of whether there are relatively stable sets of classificatory principles and dispositions, that is, the habitus, which are socially recognizable and operate to establish the boundaries between groups. The examples of cultural disorder, the overwhelming flood of signs and images which Baudrillard (1983a) argues is pushing us beyond the social, are usually taken from the media with television, rock videos and MTV (music television) cited as examples of pastiche, eclectic mixing of codes, bizarre juxtapositions and unchained signifiers which defy meaning and readability.

On the other hand if one 'descends' to the everyday practices of embodied persons held together in webs of interdependencies and power balances with other people, it can be argued that the need to glean clues and information about the other's power potential, status and social standing by reading the other person's demeanour will continue. The different styles and labels of fashionable clothing and goods, however much they are subject to change, imitation and copying, are one such set of clues which are used in the act of classifying others. Yet as Bourdieu (1984) reminds us with his concept of symbolic capital, the signs of the dispositions and classificatory schemes which betray one's origins and trajectory through life are also manifest in body shape, size, weight, stance, walk, demeanour, tone of voice, style of speaking, sense of ease or discomfort with one's body, etc. Hence culture is incorporated, and it is not just a question of what clothes are worn, but how they are worn. Advice books on manners, taste and etiquette from Erasmus down to Nancy Mitford's 'U' and Non 'U', only impress their subjects with the need to naturalize dispositions and manners, to be completely at home with them as second nature, and also make clear that this entails the capacity to spot imposters. In this sense the newly arrived, the autodidact, will unavoidably give away signs of the burden of attainment and incompleteness of his/her cultural competence. Hence the new rich who may adopt conspicuous consumption strategies are recognizable and assigned their place in the social space. Their cultural practices are always in danger of being dismissed as vulgar and tasteless by the established upper class, aristocracy and those 'rich in cultural capital'.

We therefore need to consider the pressures which threaten to produce an oversupply of cultural and consumer goods and relate this to more general processes of cultural declassification (DiMaggio, 1987). We also need to consider those pressures which could act towards the deformation of habitus, the locus of taste and classificatory choices. It may be that there are different modes of identity, and habitus formation and deformation emerging which make the significance of taste and lifestyle choice more blurred – if not throughout the social structure, at least within certain sectors, for instance the young and fractions of the middle class. We have also to consider that the much-talked-about cultural ferment and disorder, often labelled postmodernism, may not be the result of a total absence of controls, a genuine disorder, but merely point to a more deeply embedded integrative principle. Hence there may be 'rules of disorder' which act to permit more easily controlled swings – between order and disorder, status consciousness and the play of fantasy and desire, emotional control and de-control, instrumental calculation and hedonism – which were formerly threatening to the imperative to uphold a consistent identity structure and deny transgressions.

Consuming Dreams, Images and Pleasure

As Raymond Williams (1976: 68) points out, one of the earliest uses of the term consume meant 'to destroy, to use up, to waste, to exhaust'. In this sense, consumption as waste, excess and spending represents a paradoxical presence within the productionist emphasis of capitalist and state socialist societies which must somehow be controlled and channelled. The notion of economic value as linked to scarcity, and the promise that the discipline and sacrifices necessitated by the drive to accumulate within the production process will lead to the eventual overcoming of scarcity, as consumer needs and pleasures are met, has been a strong cultural image and motivating force within capitalist and socialist societies alike. At the same time within the middle class, and especially among traditional economic specialists, we have the persistence of the notion of disciplined hard work, the 'inner worldly ascetic conduct' celebrated in nineteenth-century 'self-help' individualism and later twentieth-century Thatcherism. Here consumption is an auxiliary to work, and retains many of the displaced orientations from production. It is presented as orderly, respectable and conserving: old or traditional petit bourgeois values which sit uneasily alongside new petit bourgeois notions of leisure as creative play, 'narcissistic' emotional exploration and relationship building (cf. Bell's, 1976, discussion of the paradox of modern consumer societies: to be a 'Puritan by day and a playboy by night'). This fraction within the new middle class, the cultural specialists and intermediaries we have already referred to (which also includes those from the counterculture who have survived from the 1960s and those who have taken up elements of their cultural imagery in different contexts), represents a disturbing group to the old petit bourgeois virtues and the cultural mission of Thatcherism. This is because they have the capacity to broaden and question the prevalent notions of consumption, to circulate images of consumption suggesting alternative pleasures and desires, consumption as excess, waste and disorder. This occurs within a society where, as we have emphasized, a good deal of production is targeted at consumption, leisure and services and where there is the increasing salience of the production of symbolic goods, images and information. It is therefore more difficult to harness the productive efforts of this expanding group of cultural specialists and intermediaries to the production of a particularly narrow message of traditional petit bourgeois virtues and cultural order.

From this perspective we should pay attention to the persistence, displacements and transformation of the notion of culture as waste, squandering and excess. According to Bataille's (1988; Millot, 1988: 681ff) notion of general economy, economic production should not be linked to scarcity, but to *excess*. In effect the aim of production becomes destruction, and the key problem becomes what to do with *la part maudite*, the accursed share, the excess of energy translated into an excess of product and goods, a process of growth which reaches its limits in entropy and anomie. To control growth effectively and manage the surplus the only solution is to destroy or squander the excess in the form of games, religion, art, wars, death. This is carried out through gifts, potlatch, consumption tournaments, carnivals and conspicuous consumption. According to Bataille, capitalist societies attempt to channel the *part maudite* into full economic growth, to produce growth without end. Yet it can be argued that on a number of levels there are losses and leakages which persist, and, in terms of the argument just mentioned, capitalism also produces (one is tempted to follow the post-modernist rhetoric and say 'overproduces') images and sites of consumption which endorse the pleasures of excess. Those images and sites also favour blurring of the boundary between art and everyday life. Hence we need to investigate: (1) the persistence within consumer culture of elements of the pre-industrial carnivalesque tradition; (2) the transformation and displacement of the carnivalesque, into media images, design, advertising, rock videos, the cinema; (3) the persistence and transformation of elements of the carnivalesque within certain sites of consumption: holiday resorts, sports stadia, theme parks, department stores and shopping centres; (4) its displacement and incorporation into conspicuous consumption by states and corporations, either in the form of 'prestige' spectacles for wider publics, and/or privileged upper management and officialdom.

In contrast to those, largely late-nineteenth-century theories, inspired by notions of the rationalization, commodification and modernization of culture, which exhibit a nostalgic *Kulturpessimismus*, it is important to emphasize the tradition within popular culture of transgression, protest, the carnivalesque and liminal excesses (Easton et al., 1988). The popular tradition of carnivals, fairs and festivals provided symbolic inversions and transgressions of the official 'civilized' culture and favoured excitement, uncontrolled emotions and the direct and vulgar grotesque bodily pleasures of fattening food, intoxicating drink and sexual promiscuity (Bakhtin, 1968; Stallybrass and White, 1986). These were *liminal* spaces, in which the everyday world was turned upside down and in which the tabooed and fantastic were possible, in which impossible dreams could be expressed. The liminal, according to Victor Turner (1969; see also Martin, 1981: ch. 3), points to the emphasis within these essentially delimited transitional or threshold phases upon *anti-structure* and *communitas*, the generation of a sense of unmediated community, emotional fusion and ecstatic oneness. It should be apparent that these enclaved liminal moments of ordered disorder were not completely integrated by the state or the emerging consumer culture industries and 'civilizing processes' in eighteenth- and nineteenth-century Britain.

To take the example of fairs: fairs have long held a dual role as local markets and as sites of pleasure. They were not only sites where commodities were exchanged; they entailed the display of exotic and strange commodities from various parts of the world in a festive atmosphere (see Stallybrass and White, 1986). Like the experience of the city, fairs offered spectacular imagery, bizarre juxtapositions, confusions of boundaries and an immersion in a *mêlée* of strange sounds, motions, images, people, animals and things. For those people, especially in the middle classes, who were developing bodily and emotional controls as part of civilizing processes (Elias, 1978, 1982), sites of cultural disorder such as fairs, the city, the slum, the seaside resort, become the source of fascination, longing and nostalgia (Mercer, 1983; Shields, 1990). In a displaced form this became a central theme in art, literature and popular entertainment such as the music hall (Bailey, 1986). It can also be argued that those institutions which came to dominate the urban market-place, the department stores (Chaney, 1983; R.H. Williams, 1982) plus the new national and international exhibitions (Bennett, 1988), both developed in the second half of the nineteenth century, and other twentieth-century sites such as theme parks (Urry, 1988), provided sites of ordered disorder which summoned up elements of the carnivalesque tradition in their displays, imagery and simulations of exotic locations and lavish spectacles.

For Walter Benjamin (1982) the new department stores and arcades, which emerged in Paris and subsequently other large cities from the mid nineteenth century onwards, were effectively 'dream worlds'. The vast phantasmagoria of commodities on display, constantly renewed as part of the capitalist and modernist drive for novelty, was the source of dream images which summoned up associations and half-forgotten illusions – Benjamin referred to them as *allegories*. Here Benjamin uses the term allegory not to point to the unity or coherence of the doubly-coded message which is occluded, as in traditional allegories such as *Pilgrim's Progress*, but to the way a stable hierarchically ordered meaning is dissolved and the allegory points only to kaleidoscopic fragments which resist any coherent notion of what it stands for (see Wolin, 1982: Spencer, 1985). In this aestheticized commodity world the department stores, arcades, trams, trains, streets and fabric of buildings and the goods on display, as well as the people who stroll through these spaces, summon up half-forgotten dreams, as the curiosity and memory of the stroller is fed by the ever-changing landscape in which objects appear divorced from their context and subject to mysterious connections which are read on the surface of things. The everyday life of the big cities becomes aestheticized. The new industrial processes provided the opportunity for art to shift into industry, which saw an expansion of occupations in advertising, marketing, industrial design and commercial display to produce the new aestheticized urban landscape (Buck-Morss, 1983). The growth of the mass media in the twentieth century with the proliferation of photographic images heightened the tendencies of which Benjamin talks. Indeed the unacknowledged impact of Benjamin's theory can be detected in some of the theorizations of postmodernism, such as those by Baudrillard (1983a) and Jameson (1984a, 1984b). Here the emphasis is on immediacies, intensities, sensory overload, disorientation, the *mêlée* or liquefaction of signs and images, the mixing of codes, the unchained or floating signifiers of the postmodern 'depthless' consumer culture where art and reality have switched places in an 'aesthetic hallucination of the real'. Clearly these qualities cannot be claimed to be unique to postmodernism and have a much longer genealogy, suggesting continuities between the modern and postmodern, and indeed, the pre-modern.

There is a strong populist strand in the writings of Benjamin which is usually contrasted to the alleged elitism of Horkheimer and Adorno. Benjamin emphasized the utopian, or positive moment in the mass produced consumer commodities which liberated creativity from art and allowed it to migrate into the multiplicity of mass produced everyday objects (the influence of surrealism on Benjamin's theoretical framework is evident here). This celebration of the aesthetic potential of mass culture and the aestheticized perceptions of the people who stroll through the urban spaces of the large cities has been taken up by commentators who emphasize the transgressive and playful potential of postmodernism (Hebdige, 1988; Chambers, 1986, 1987). Here the perceptions of Benjamin and Baudrillard are accepted to point to the enhanced role of culture in contemporary Western cities, increasingly centres not only of everyday consumption but also of a wider range of symbolic goods and experiences produced by the culture industries (the arts, entertainment, tourism, heritage sectors). Within these 'postmodern cities' (Harvey, 1988) people are held to engage in a complex sign play which resonates with the proliferation of signs in the built environment and urban fabric. The contemporary urban *flâneurs*, or strollers, play with and celebrate the artificiality, randomness and superficiality of the fantastic *mélange* of fictions and strange values which are to be found in the fashions and popular cultures of cities (Chambers, 1987; Calefato, 1988). It is also argued that this represents a movement beyond individualism with a heightened emphasis upon the affectual and empathy, a new 'aesthetic paradigm' in which masses of people come together temporarily in fluid 'postmodern tribes' (Maffesoli, 1988).

While there is a strong emphasis in such writings upon the sensory overload, the aesthetic immersion, dreamlike perceptions of de-centred subjects, in which people open themselves up to a wider range of sensations and emotional experiences, it is important to stress that this does not represent the eclipse of controls. It needs discipline and control to stroll through goods on display, to look and not snatch, to move casually without interrupting the flow, to gaze with controlled enthusiasm and a blasé outlook, to observe others without being seen, to tolerate the close proximity of bodies without feeling threatened. It also requires the capacity to manage swings between intense involvement and more distanced aesthetic detachment. In short to move through urban spaces, or to experience the spectacles of the theme park and heritage museums, demands a 'controlled de-control of the emotions' (Wouters, 1986). The imagery may summon up pleasure, excitement, the carnivalesque and disorder, yet to experience them requires self-control and for those who lack such control there lurks in the background surveillance by security guards and remote-control cameras.

These tendencies towards the aestheticization of everyday life relate to the distinction between high and mass culture. A dual movement has suggested the collapse of some of the boundaries between art and everyday life and the erosion of the special protected status of art as an enclaved commodity. In the first place there is the migration of art into industrial design, advertising, and associated symbolic and image production industries we have mentioned. Secondly, there has been the internal *avant-gardiste* dynamic within the arts which, in the form of Dada and surrealism in the 1920s (Bürger, 1984) and in the form of postmodernism in the 1960s, sought to show that any everyday object could be aestheticized. The 1960s Pop Art and postmodernism entail a focus upon everyday commodities as art (Warhol's Campbell's soup cans), an ironic playing back of consumer culture on itself, and an antimuseum and academy stance in performance and body art. The expansion of the art market and increase in working artists and ancillary occupations, especially in metropolitan centres, plus the use of art as a vehicle for public relations by large corporations and the state, have resulted in significant changes in the artist's role (see Zukin, 1982).

It has been argued that it is no longer useful to speak of an artistic *avant-garde* in the sense of a group of artists who reject both popular culture and the middle-class lifestyle (Crane, 1987). While the artist's lifestyle may still have an attractive romantic ambience for those engaged in the gentrification of inner city areas and for members of the middle class in general who increasingly value the role of culture in lifestyle construction (Zukin, 1988), many artists have relinquished their commitment to high culture and *avant-gardisme* and have adopted an increasingly open attitude towards consumer culture and now show a willingness to truck with other cultural intermediaries, image-makers, audiences and publics. Hence, with the parallel processes of the expansion of the role of art within consumer culture and the deformation of enclaved art with its separate prestige structure and lifestyle, a blurring of *genres* and the tendencies towards the deconstruction of symbolic hierarchies has occurred. This entails a pluralistic stance towards the variability of taste, a process of cultural de-classification which has undermined the basis of high culture–mass culture distinctions. It is in this context that we get not just scepticism towards advertising's effectiveness, in that its capacity to persuade people to purchase new products – or indoctrinate – is questioned (Schudson, 1986), but a celebration of its aesthetic pedigree. Design and advertising thus not only become confused with art, but are celebrated and museumified as art. As Stephen Bayley (1979: 10) remarks 'industrial design is the art of the twentieth century' (quoted in Forty, 1986: 7).

The attractions of the romantic-bohemian lifestyle with the artist presented as an expressive rebel and stylistic hero has been a strong theme, particularly with respect to popular and rock music, in Britain in the post-war era. Frith and Horne (1987) document this particular injection of art into popular culture which also helped to deconstruct the distinction between high and popular culture. In addition it can be seen as furthering the process of a controlled de-control of the emotions we have spoken of, with jazz, blues, rock and black music presented as forms of direct emotional expression which were regarded as both more pleasurable, involved and authentic by predominantly young audiences, and as dangerously threatening, uncontrolled, 'devil's music' to predominantly older, adult audiences used to more controlled and formal patterns of public behaviour and emotional restraint (Stratton, 1989). Yet there is also a sense in which, despite the popularity of artistic lifestyles and the various neo-dandyist transformations of making life a work of art, this project implies a degree of integration and unity of purpose which is becoming increasingly obsolete, despite the compelling nature of some of the symbols of these lifestyles. There is less interest in constructing a coherent style than in playing with, and expanding, the range of familiar styles. The term style suggests coherence and hierarchical ordering of elements, some inner form and expressiveness (Schapiro, 1961). It has often been argued by twentieth-century commentators that our age lacks a distinctive style. Simmel (1978), for example, refers to the age of 'no style' and Malraux (1967) remarked that our culture is 'a museum without walls' (see Roberts, 1988), perceptions which become heightened in postmodernism with its emphasis upon pastiche, 'retro', the collapse of symbolic hierarchies, and the playback of cultures.

A similar argument can be made with reference to the term lifestyle, that the tendency within consumer culture is to present lifestyles as no longer requiring inner coherence. The new cultural intermediaries, an expanding faction within the new middle class, therefore, while well disposed to the lifestyle of artists and cultural specialists, do not seek to promote a single lifestyle, but rather to cater for and expand the range of styles and lifestyles available to audiences and consumers.

Conclusion

In his book *All Consuming Images*, Stuart Ewen (1988) discusses an advertisement for Nieman-Marcus, a fashionable US department store, which seemingly combines a unity of opposites. It juxtaposes two photographs of the same woman. The first presents an image of an upper-class woman dressed in Parisian *haute couture*; the text beneath the image stresses that *attitude* is 'disposition with regard to people', 'wearing the correct thing at the correct hour', 'exactly sized', 'a mode', 'dressing to please someone else', 'evaluation', 'strolling the avenue'. The second photograph is of a brooding Semitic woman dressed in a Palestinian scarf and desert caftan. In graffiti style typeface the text emphasizes that *latitude* is 'freedom from narrow restrictions', 'changing the structure of a garment when the mood hits', 'whatever feels comfortable', 'a mood', 'dressing to please yourself', 'evolution', 'loving the street life'. Within contemporary culture women and men are asked not to choose, but to incorporate both options. To regard their dress and consumer goods as communicators, as 'symbols of class status' (Goffman, 1951), demands appropriate conduct and demeanour on the part of the wearer/user in order to further the visible classification of the social world into categories of persons. In this sense, within consumer culture there still persist prestige economies, with scarce goods demanding considerable investment in time, money and knowledge to attain and handle appropriately. Such goods can be read and used to classify the status of their bearer. At the same time consumer culture uses images, signs and symbolic goods which summon up dreams, desires and fantasies which suggest romantic authenticity and emotional fulfilment in narcissistically pleasing oneself, instead of others. Contemporary consumer culture seems to be widening the range of contexts and situations in which such behaviour is deemed appropriate and acceptable. It is, therefore, not a question of a choice between these two options presented as alternatives; rather it is *both*. Today's consumer culture represents neither a lapse of control nor the institution of more rigid controls, but rather their underpinning by a flexible underlying generative structure which can both handle formal control and de-control and facilitate an easy change of gears between them.

Bibliography

Appadurai, A. (1986). Introduction. In: A. Appadurai (ed.), *The Social Life of Things*. Cambridge: Cambridge University Press.

Bailey, P. (1986). *Music Hall: The Business of Pleasure*. Milton Keynes: Open University Press.

Bakhtin, M. M. (1968). *Rabelais and His World*. Cambridge, MA: MIT Press.

Bataille, G. (1988). *The Accursed Share*, Volume 1. New York: Zone Books.

Baudrillard, J. (1970). *La Société de consommation*. Paris: Gallimard.

Baudrillard, J. (1983a). *Simulations*. New York: Semiotext(e).

Baudrillard, J. (1983b). *In the Shadow of the Silent Majorities*. New York: Semiotext(e).

Bayley. S. (1979). *In Good Shape*. London.

Bell, D. (1976). *The Cultural Contradictions of Capitalism*. London: Heinemann.

Benjamin, W. (1982). *Das Passagen-Werk*, 2 vols, ed. R. Tiedermann. Frankfurt: Suhrkamp.

Bennett, T. (1988). The Exhibitionary Complex. *New Formations* 4.

Bourdieu, P. (1984). *Distinction: A Social Critique of the Judgement of Taste*, trans. R. Nice. London: Routledge & Kegan Paul.

Bourdieu, P., L. Boltanski, R. Castel & J. C. Chamboredon (1965). *Un Art moyen*. Paris: Minuit.

Bourdieu, P. & J. C. Passeron (1990). *Reproduction in Education, Society and Culture*. 2nd edn (1st edn, 1977). London: Sage.

Buck-Morss, S. (1983). Benjamin's *Passagen-Werk*. *New German Critique*, p. 29.

Bürger, P. (1984). *Theory of the Avant-Garde*. Manchester: Manchester University Press.

Calefato, P. (1988). Fashion, the Passage, the Body. *Cultural Studies* 2(2).

Campbell, C. (1987). *The Romantic Ethic and the Spirit of Modern Consumerism*. Oxford: Basil Blackwell.

Chambers, I. (1986). *Popular Culture: The Metropolitan Experience*. London: Methuen.

Chambers, I. (1987). Maps for the Metropolis: A Possible Guide to the Postmodern. *Cultural Studies* 1(1).

Chaney, D. (1983). The Department Store as a Cultural Form. *Theory, Culture & Society* 1(3).

Crane, D. (1987). *The Transformation of the Avant-Garde*. Chicago: Chicago University Press.

Denzin, N. (1984). *On Understanding Emotion*. San Francisco: Jossey-Bass.

DiMaggio, P. (1987). Classification in Art. *American Sociological Review* 52(4).

Douglas, M. & B. Isherwood (1980). *The World of Goods*. Harmondsworth: Penguin.

Easton, S., A. Hawkins, S. Laing & H. Walker (1988). *Disorder and Discipline*: *Popular Culture from 1550 to the Present*. London: Temple Smith.

Elias, N. (1978). *The Civilizing Process*. Volume I: *The History of Manners*. Oxford: Basil Blackwell.

Elias, N. (1982). *The Civilizing Process*. Volume II: *State Formation and Civilization*. Oxford: Basil Blackwell.

Elias, N. (1987). On Human Beings and their Emotions. *Theory, Culture & Society* 4(2–3).

Ewen, S. (1976). *Captains of Consciousness: Advertising and the Social Roots of the Consumer Culture*. New York: McGraw-Hill.

Ewen, S. (1988). *All Consuming Images*. New York: Basic Books.

Ewen, S. & E. Ewen (1982). *Channels of Desire*. New York: McGraw-Hill.

Forty, A. (1986). *Objects of Desire*. London: Thames and Hudson.

Frith, S. & H. Horne (1987). *Art into Pop*. London: Methuen.

Gellner, E. (1979). The Social Roots of Egalitarianism. *Dialectics and Humanism*, p. 4.

Gershuny, J. & S. Jones (1987). The Changing Work/Leisure Balance in Britain: 1961–1984. In: J. Horne, D. Jary & A. Tomlinson (eds.), *Sport, Leisure and Social Relations*. London: Routledge & Kegan Paul.

Goffman, E. (1951). Systems of Class Status. *British Journal of Sociology*, p. 2.

Habermas, J. (1984). *Theory of Communicative Action*, Volume I. London: Heinemann.

Habermas, J. (1987). *Theory of Communicative Action*, Volume II. Oxford: Polity Press.

Harvey, D. (1988). Voodoo Cities. *New Statesman and Society*, September 30.

Hebdige, D. (1988). *Hiding in the Light*. London: Routledge & Kegan Paul.

Hirsch, F. (1976). *The Social Limits to Growth*. Cambridge, MA: Harvard University Press.

Hirshman, A. (1982). *Shifting Involvements*. Oxford: Basil Blackwell.

Hochschild. A. (1983). *The Managed Heart*. Berkeley: California University Press.

Horkheimer, M. & T. Adorno (1972). *Dialectic of Enlightenment*. New York: Herder & Herder.

Jameson, F. (1979). Reification and Utopia in Mass Culture. *Social Text* 1(l).

Jameson, F. (1984a). Postmodernism: Or the Cultural Logic of Late Capitalism. *New Left Review*, 146.

Jameson, F. (1984b). Postmodernism and the Consumer Society. In: H. Foster (ed.), *Postmodern Culture*. London: Pluto Press.

Lefebvre, H. (1971). *Everyday Life in the Modern World*. London: Allen Lane.

Leiss, W. (1978). *The Limits to Satisfaction*. London: Marion Boyars.

Leiss, W., S. Kline & S. Jhally (1986). *Social Communication in Advertising*. New York: Macmillan.

Liebersohn, H. (1988). *Fate and Utopia in German Sociology*. Cambridge, MA: MIT Press.

Lowenthal, L. (1961). *Literature, Popular Culture and Society*. Palo Alto, CA: Pacific Books.

Lukács, G. (1971). *History and Class Consciousness*, trans. R. Livingstone. London: Merlin Press.

Maffesoli, M. (1988). Affectual Postmodernism and the Megapolis. *Threshold IV* 1.

Malraux, A. (1967). *Museum without Walls*. London.

Marcuse, H. (1964). *One Dimensional Man*. London: Routledge & Kegan Paul.

Martin, B. (1981). *A Sociology of Contemporary Cultural Change*. Oxford: Basil Blackwell.

Mercer, C. (1983). A Poverty of Desire: Pleasure and Popular Politics. In: T. Bennett, et al. (eds.), *Formations of Pleasure*. London: Routledge & Kegan Paul.

Millot, B. (1988). Symbol, Desire and Power. *Theory, Culture & Society* 5(4).

Preteceille, E. & J. P. Terrail (1985). *Capitalism, Consumption and Needs*. Oxford: Basil Blackwell.

Roberts, D. (1988). Beyond Progress: The Museum and Montage. *Theory, Culture & Society* 5(2–3).

Rochberg-Halton, E. (1986). *Meaning and Modernity*. Chicago: Chicago University Press.

Rose, G. (1978). *The Melancholy Science: An Introduction to the Thought of Theodor W. Adorno*. London: Macmillan.

Schapiro, M. (1961). Style. In: M. Phillipson (ed.), *Aesthetics Today*. London: Meridian Books.

Schudson, M. (1986). *Advertising: The Uneasy Persuasion*. New York: Harper.

Shields. R. (1990). "The System of Pleasure": Liminality and the Carnivalesque in Brighton. *Theory, Culture & Society* 7(l).

Simmel, G. (1978). *The Philosophy of Money*, trans. T. Bottomore & D. Frisby. London: Routledge & Kegan Paul.

Spencer, L. (1985). Allegory in the World of the Commodity: The Importance of Central Park. *New German Critique*, p. 34.

Stallybrass, P. & A. White (1986). *The Politics and Poetics of Transgression*. London: Methuen.

Stauth, G. & B. S. Turner (1988). Nostalgia, Postmodernism and the Critique of Mass Culture. *Theory, Culture & Society* 5(2–3).

Stratton, J. (1989). Postmodernism and Popular Music. *Theory, Culture & Society* 6(1).

Swingewood, A. (1977). *The Myth of Mass Culture*. London: Macmillan.

Touraine, A. (1985). An Introduction to the Study of Social Movements. *Social Research* 52(4).

Turner, B. S. (1988). *Status*. Milton Keynes: Open University Press.

Turner, V. W. (1969). *The Ritual Process: Structure and Anti-structure*. London: Allen Lane.

Urry, J. (1988). Cultural Change and Contemporary Holiday-Making. *Theory, Culture & Society* 5(1).

Williams, R. (1976). *Keywords*. London: Fontana.

Williams, R. H. (1982). *Dream Worlds: Mass Consumption in Late Nineteenth Century France*. Berkeley: California University Press.

Williamson, J. (1986). *Consuming Passions*. London: Marion Boyars.

Willis, P. (1978). *Profane Culture*. London: Routledge & Kegan Paul.

Wolin, R. (1982). *Walter Benjamin: An Aesthetic of Redemption*. New York: Columbia University Press.

Wouters, C. (1986). Formalization and Informalization: Changing Tension Balances in Civilizing Processes. *Theory, Culture & Society* 3(2).

Wouters, C. (1989). The Sociology of Emotions and Flight Attendants: Hochschild's *Managed Heart*. *Theory, Culture & Society* 6(2).

Zukin, S. (1982). Art in the arms of power. *Theory and Society* 11.

Zukin, S. (1988). *Loft Living*, 2nd edn. London: Hutchinson/Radius.

42

Mythologies

*Roland Barthes**

In myth, we find again the tri-dimensional pattern which I have just described: the signifier, the signified and the sign. But myth is a peculiar system, in that it is constructed from a semiological chain which existed before it: it *is a second-order semiological system*. That which is a sign (namely the associative total of a concept and an image) in the first system, becomes a mere signifier in the second. We must here recall that the materials of mythical speech (the language itself, photography, painting, posters, rituals, objects, etc.), however different at the start, are reduced to a pure signifying function as soon as they are caught by myth. Myth sees in them only the same raw material; their unity is that they all come down to the status of a mere language. Whether it deals with alphabetical or pictorial writing, myth wants to see in them only a sum of signs, a global sign, the final term of a first semiological chain. And it is precisely this final term which will become the first term of the greater system which it builds and of which it is only a part. Everything happens as if myth shifted the formal system of the first significations sideways. As this lateral shift is essential for the analysis of myth, I shall represent it as shown in figure 42.1, it being understood, of course, that the spatialization of the pattern is here only a metaphor.

It can be seen that in myth there are two semiological systems, one of which is staggered in relation to the other: a linguistic system, the language (or the modes of representation which are assimilated to it), which I shall call the *language-object*, because it is the language which myth gets hold of in order to build its own system; and myth itself, which I shall call *metalanguage*, because it is a second language, *in which* one speaks about the first. When he reflects on a metalanguage, the semiologist no longer needs to ask himself questions about the composition of the language-object, he no longer has to take into account the details of the linguistic schema; he will only need to know its total term, or global sign, and only inasmuch as this term lends itself to myth. This is why the semiologist is entitled to treat in the same way writing and pictures: what he retains from them is the fact that they are both *signs*, that they both reach the threshold of myth endowed with the same signifying function, that they constitute, one just as much as the other, a language-object.

* Pp. 81–3 from *Literary Theory: An Anthology*, ed. J. Rivkin and M. Ryan (Malden, MA: Blackwell, 1998). Previously published as pp. 36–8 and 114–17 from *Mythologie*, trans A. Lavers (New York: Hill & Wang, 1972). Translation copyright © 1972 by Jonathan Cape Ltd. Reprinted with permission from Hill & Wang, a division of Farrar, Straus and Giroux, LLC, and the Random House Group Ltd.

Figure 42.1

It is now time to give one or two examples of mythical speech. I shall borrow the first from an observation by Valéry.[1] I am a pupil in the second form in a French *lycée*. I open my Latin grammar, and I read a sentence, borrowed from Aesop or Phaedrus: *quia ego nominor leo.* I stop and think. There is something ambiguous about this statement: on the one hand, the words in it do have a simple meaning: *because my name is lion.* And on the other hand, the sentence is evidently there in order to signify something else to me. Inasmuch as it is addressed to me, a pupil in the second form, it tells me clearly: I am a grammatical example meant to illustrate the rule about the agreement of the predicate. I am even forced to realize that the sentence in no way *signifies* its meaning to me, that it tries very little to tell me something about the lion and what sort of name he has; its true and fundamental signification is to impose itself on me as the presence of a certain agreement of the predicate. I conclude that I am faced with a particular, greater, semiological system, since it is co-extensive with the language: there is, indeed, a signifier, but this signifier is itself formed by a sum of signs, it is in itself a first semiological system (*my name is lion*). Thereafter, the formal pattern is correctly unfolded: there is a signified (*I am a grammatical example*) and there is a global signification, which is none other than the correlation of the signifier and the signified; for neither the naming of the lion nor the grammatical example are given separately.

And here is now another example: I am at the barber's, and a copy of *Paris-Match* is offered to me. On the cover, a young Negro in a French uniform is saluting, with his eyes uplifted, probably fixed on a fold of the tricolour. All this is the *meaning* of the picture. But, whether naively or not, I see very well what it signifies to me: that France is a great Empire, that all her sons, without any colour discrimination, faithfully serve under her flag, and that there is no better answer to the detractors of an alleged colonialism than the zeal shown by this Negro in serving his so-called oppressors. I am therefore again faced with a greater semiological system: there is a signifier, itself already formed with a previous system (*a black soldier is giving the French salute*); there is a signified (it is here a purposeful mixture of Frenchness and militariness); finally, there is a presence of the signified through the signifier.

Before tackling the analysis of each term of the mythical system, one must agree on terminology. We now know that the signifier can be looked at, in myth, from two points of view: as the final term of the linguistic system, or as the first term of the mythical system. We therefore need two names. On the plane of language, that is, as the final term of the first system, I shall call the signifier: *meaning* (*my name is lion*, *a Negro is giving the French salute*); on the plane of myth, I shall call it: *form.* In the case of the signified, no ambiguity is possible: we shall retain the name *concept*. The third term is the correlation of the first two: in the linguistic system, it is the *sign*; but it is not possible to use this word again without ambiguity, since in myth (and this is the chief peculiarity of the latter), the signifier is already formed by the *signs* of the language. I shall call the third term of myth the *signification*. This word is here all the better justified since myth has in fact a double function: it points out and it notifies, it makes us understand something and it imposes it on us. . . .

Soap-Powders and Detergents

The first World Detergent Congress (Paris, September 1954) had the effect of authorizing the world to yield to *Omo* euphoria: not only do detergents have no harmful effect on the skin, but they can even perhaps save miners from silicosis. These products have been in the last few years the object of such massive advertising that they now belong to a region of French daily life which the various types of psycho-analysis would do well to pay some attention to if they wish to keep up to date. One could then usefully contrast the psycho-analysis of purifying fluids (chlorinated, for example) with that of soap-powders (*Lux*, *Persil*) or that of detergents (*Omo*). The relations between the evil and the cure, between dirt and a given product, are very different in each case.

Chlorinated fluids, for instance, have always been experienced as a sort of liquid fire, the action of which must be carefully estimated, otherwise the object itself would be affected, 'burnt'. The implicit legend of this type of product rests on the idea of a violent, abrasive modification of matter: the connotations are of a chemical or mutilating type: the product 'kills' the dirt. Powders, on the contrary, are separating agents: their ideal role is to liberate the object from its circumstantial imperfection: dirt is 'forced out' and no longer killed; in the *Omo* imagery, dirt is a diminutive enemy, stunted and black, which takes to its heels from the fine immaculate linen at the sole threat of the judgment of *Omo*. Products based on chlorine and ammonia are without doubt the representatives of a kind of absolute fire, a saviour but a blind one. Powders, on the contrary, are selective, they push, they drive dirt through the texture of the object, their function is keeping public order not making war. This distinction has ethnographic correlatives: the chemical fluid is an extension of the washerwoman's movements when she beats the clothes, while powders rather replace those of the housewife pressing and rolling the washing against a sloping board.

But even in the category of powders, one must in addition oppose against advertisements based on psychology those based on psycho-analysis (I use this word without reference to any specific school). '*Persil* Whiteness' for instance, bases its prestige on the evidence of a result; it calls into play vanity, a social concern with appearances, by offering for comparison two objects, one of which is *whiter than* the other. Advertisements for *Omo* also indicate the effect of the product (and in superlative fashion, incidentally), but they chiefly reveal its mode of action; in doing so, they involve the consumer in a kind of direct experience of the substance, make him the accomplice of a liberation rather than the mere beneficiary of a result; matter here is endowed with value-bearing states.

Omo uses two of these, which are rather novel in the category of detergents: the deep and the foamy. To say that *Omo* cleans in depth (see the Cinéma-Publicité advertisement) is to assume that linen is deep, which no one had previously thought, and this unquestionably results in exalting it, by establishing it as an object favourable to those obscure tendencies to enfold and caress which are found in every human body. As for foam, it is well known that it signifies luxury. To begin with, it appears to lack any usefulness; then, its abundant, easy, almost infinite proliferation allows one to suppose there is in the substance from which it issues a vigorous germ, a healthy and powerful essence, a great wealth of active elements in a small original volume. Finally, it gratifies in the consumer a tendency to imagine matter as something airy, with which contact is effected in a mode both light and vertical, which is sought after like that of happiness either in the gustatory category (*foie gras, entremets,* wines), in that of clothing (muslin, tulle), or that of soaps (film-star in her bath). Foam can even be the sign of a certain spirituality, inasmuch as the spirit has the reputation of being able to make something out of nothing, a large surface of effects out of a small volume of causes (creams have a very different 'psychoanalytical' meaning, of a soothing kind: they suppress wrinkles, pain, smarting, etc.). What matters is the art of having disguised the abrasive function of the detergent under the delicious image of a substance at once deep and airy which can govern the molecular order of the material without damaging it. A euphoria, incidentally, which must not make us forget that there is one plane on which *Persil* and *Omo* are one and the same: the plane of the Anglo-Dutch trust *Unilever.*

Note

1. *Tel Quel* II, p. 191.

43

Fashion, Culture, and the Construction of Identity

Elizabeth Niederer & Rainer Winter

Introduction

In writing about the meaning of fashion in our everyday lives, it has become obvious that this aspect, more so than most other dimensions of culture, expresses the moment and circumstances in which we are living. Nevertheless, fashion studies are, in traditional scientific discourse, still not considered a relevant field of research, but are instead regarded as a devalued and inferior social science discipline.

The term "fashion" has many different meanings in our everyday speech. It is used simultaneously for clothing, garment, apparel, style or a special look, but also for accessories such as shoes, handbags, sunglasses or jewellery, hairstyles and make-up. To be "in fashion" means performing specific fashion behaviors and living according to various practices, which can be meaningful and sense making (Craik 1993). People are able to express themselves and their individuality through their dressing up. But fashion should not only be considered as a source of inspiration and empowerment. Some fashionable beauty and body-makeover practices like dieting, fitness, aerobic exercises, plastic surgery and cosmetics are effectively used to control the body and may be examined in the sense of the French philosopher Michel Foucault's (1975) idea of a "disciplinary power."

When it comes to analyzing fashion in the academic field, theorists always start from the viewpoint of their own discipline. For this reason the phenomenon of fashion has to be explained in multidisciplinary terms and out of varied perspectives – for example those of the social sciences, art history, economics, anthropology or psychology. Each approach has its own demands, but only in associating the different characteristics, constructions, and aspects can distinctive contributions to a new theory of fashion be unfolded. Joanne Entwistle (2000) argues that a study of dress and fashion "must acknowledge the connections between production and consumption, considering the relationship between different agencies, institutions, individuals and practices" (2000: 3).

This chapter attempts to connect these disciplines to a critical and creative concept of fashion, constituting "the Cycle of Fashion in Cultural Studies." The approach is deduced from the model of the Circuit of Culture, which was developed by a group of scholars around Stuart Hall (du Gay et al. 1997; Hall 1997).

The transdisciplinary project of Cultural Studies has, ever since its origin, been closely connected with the goal of establishing the issues that arise in everyday and popular culture as objects of research. The discipline deals with everyday changes of meaning, attitude and value-orientation; with the development of productive and creative life–world potentials; with a critique of power structures; with moments of self-empowerment which may be short and fleeting, but formative and influential nonetheless (Winter 2001). Popular culture is understood as a self-evident aspect of modern and postmodern life, as a familiar "horizon of experience" and as a medium for the creation of personal life. It is through popular media and cultural resources (that is to say, through images, symbols discourses, stories, clothes, accessories etc.) that many people specify their identities, form their political opinions, and, collectively, create a common culture. A new pervasive global culture also is based upon such resources. However, popular culture is not only a medium to be used for a symbolic integration into prevailing conditions; it is also a form of counter-power – an area in which the interests of marginalized and subordinated people can find adequate expression. For Cultural Studies, culture is an embattled field in which several competing social groups battle for the implementation of their claims, interests, and ideologies. In doing so, these groups are interested in cultural transformation rather than the reproduction of prevailing conditions. From the perspective of Cultural Studies, culture is not to be equated with objects, nor is it reduced to the artifacts produced and distributed by specialized institutions. Instead, the focus is on the creative production process of culture; on the circulation of meanings and energies; on the mobility and opportunities of everyday life; on the development of the creative aspects of culture as well as on the creation of a common culture. It is not the finished cultural object, but the productivity of a reception process and the potential creativity of the ensuing moments, which determine the research interests of Cultural Studies.

Cultural Studies analysis deals with particular forms of popular culture and media matters such as pop and rock music, TV, cinema or literature. The field of fashion is often neglected, although fashion is framed by popular culture and communicated through mass media. Contemporary power relations shape the production and representation of fashion as much as the way we dress up in our everyday lives. This chapter invites us to reconceive Fashion Studies from a Cultural Studies perspective, focusing on the cultural, social, and political aspects of postmodern society and how they can be changed. In the tradition of Cultural Studies we shall explore the force of fashion in the areas of media conflict, culture and power. The key idea here is that fashion as a cultural phenomenon must be seen in the context of design, production, distribution, consumption and identity.

Culture is Fashion is Change

The genesis of dress starts with "the first adornments of the Upper Paleolithic" (Cannon 1998: 23), but this hardly resembled what we call fashion today. In the ancient world tradition was the main formative force and cultural changes and novelties diffused very slowly (for further information see Crane 1999). Evidences about clothes and garments of this time come from artistic representations such as rock paintings, tomb reliefs, papyrus paintings or sculptures. René Koenig (1988) describes the first diffusions of fashionable garments in prehistoric primitive cultures and in the leading archaic civilizations of Egypt, Greek and Rome, but also in India and in the Middle and Far East. He suggests that already in ancient times fashion was subject to cultural change, which was accompanied by countless practical inventions and discoveries. This "slowness of fashion" (ibid. 17) was the signature of fashion in ancient Rome and Greece. In Egypt, where the pharaoh ruled the country with a hierarchical structure of society, fashion "served an important function in the display of status" (Tortorra 2005: 53).[1] Through all the history of humankind fashion relics have been used as a way to reconstruct the history and cultural manners of a period and the particular state of art at the time; fashion has been throughout more than a way to cover the body from a natural sense of shame or to protect it from inclement weather.[2]

Fashion and its particular symbols and icons are still working in a similar way today, communicating nonverbal cultural and social ascriptions such as class, gender, education, lifestyle affinities, and political affiliations. For example the evolution from men in togas to women in sportswear involves many different cultural velocities of diffusion: the involvement of women in public sporting events from around 1910 created a demand for ladies sportswear fashions; Coco Chanel invented the traditional "jumper" or "sweater", still popular today, out of jersey, a material which suited "the more active lives led by women during wartime" (de la Haye 2005: 249).

In the same way the evolutionary history of blue jeans shows the close connection between fashion trends and social and political issues. Originally worn at the beginning of the twentieth century as functional and sturdy working trousers by American farmers and gold-miners, jeans in the 1950s became a fashionable and provocative way for teenagers and young adults to rebel against establishment and conformity and the restrictions of their own parents. Jeans became a "powerful symbol of anti-establishment ideals around the world" (Botkin 2005: 274). Ten years later, in the 1960s, blue jeans were already a part of the hippie movement, and "the wearing of jeans was both a political and a social statement and the baby boomers embraced the aesthetic of customized decorated denim" (ibid.). Since then the jeans industry has increased rapidly and become a profitable branch of fashion on its own with many new brand marks. Today nearly every *haute couture* designer has his or her own jeans fashion line (e.g. Versace Jeans Couture, Christian Dior Jeans, Armani Jeans). Wearing jeans is no longer an act of resistance, because everybody loves "blue heaven" (US *Vogue*, May 2006: 295). Beyond basic blue jeans, denim material is used for fashion items such as bags, hats, belts, shoes or for home decoration. We agree with Fiske that "we cannot define a jeans wearer by any of the major social category systems – gender, class, race, age, nation, religion, education" (1989: 1). Fiske provides, in *The Jeaning of America* (1989), an example of how the wearing of jeans extends across a complete spectrum of unfixed meanings and points out that "this semiotic richness of jeans means that they cannot have a single defined meaning, but they are a resource bank of potential meanings" (ibid.: 5). The presented interaction between fashion, politics and cultural change is fascinating and demonstrates how constructing, regimenting and meaningful fashion is in our every-day lives.

Culture is on this conception understood, according to Raymond Williams (1958), as a "whole way of life". This definition makes it obvious that fashion and style cannot be left out when we are talking about culture, although one can remain with the other, monolithic position that fashion has only facile concerns, is a trivial pursuit and that serious scientific minds are not required to deal with these issues. Cultural Studies reviews these hypothetical terms of high culture and its traditional categories, and makes the effort to collapse the boundaries in establishing a new understanding of culture, which reflects all the social areas in which we act. Willis et al. (1990) remarked:

> We are all cultural producers in some way and some kind in our everyday lives. It is still often denied or made invisible in many of our official attitudes and practices, in our formal lives and communications. But the necessary symbolic work and symbolic creativity of common culture are now all around us. (1990: 128)

Our approach therefore is to understand fashion as a part of popular culture. Storey (1993) discusses several ways of defining popular culture and explains that in speaking of this culture we have to contrast it with all other forms, such as mass culture, high culture, working-class culture, folk culture, etc. in order to reveal in "the definition of popular culture a specific theoretical and political inflection" (ibid.: 17). According to Storey (ibid.: 17–19), popular-culture aspects of fashion may be located in the following areas:

1. Fashion is integrated and powerful in people's everyday lives. Following Barnard (1996) we act on the assumption that "fashion and clothing are some of the ways . . . in which the social order is experienced, explored, communicated and reproduced (1996: 36).
2. Fashion is used by subcultures but also by upper-class representatives and celebrities to make distinctions through a symbolic use of style. Hebdige (1979) characterizes the style elements of subcultures on the margins like rockers, skinheads and punks and their symbolic objects, such as lavatory chains and safety pins, which were borrowed from other contexts.
3. Fashion is part of mass culture, a commercial good produced by the global fashion industry, which is an important part of the culture industry of the twenty-first century. Angela McRobbie (1998; 1999; 2000) emphasizes the consumptionist and feminist perspective of fashion that are missing, in her view, from many works in Cultural Studies.
4. Fashion satisfies the desire for collectivity. Simmel writes in his famous and seminal article "Fashion", published in 1904, about the longing to be an individual and yet to imitate others at the same time, which is an effect of the social differentiation of modern society.
5. Fashion provides "the people" with a voice. Some groups use fashion as a tool of expression, to protest against social standards and signalize difference (e.g. Che Guevara caps, military camouflage pants, emblems of royalty). At first sight the

style of different labels appears uniform, but a closer look reveals individual signs of symbolic creativity and inimitable art.

6. Fashion unfolds power and various forms of resistance. Fashion theory can be used to explore conflicts involving class, race, gender, religion, and sexual preference – all of which are cultural issues of politics, consumption and identity.

According to Roland Barthes and his development of a semiological approach, unfolded in *The Fashion System* (1984), fashion has to be understood as a way to communicate within a system of institutions, organizations, groups and conventions. Barthes's analysis describes his idea of "written fashion" and the two types of meanings (denotation and connotation) within the fashion system.

Contemplating all these basic terms we have to insist that fashion is polysemic and capable of deconstructing surfaces. People use fashion as a nonverbal way to communicate through symbols, which generate meaning in their everyday lives (Barnard 1996). Individuals or groups make commitments (cultural, social and political) through dressing up in specific forms. In respecting someone's desire to create his/her own look as an opportunity for empowerment, we also approve the power of fashion and enable the criticism of neoliberal industry strategies and the dreadful conditions of production, which should not be forgotten.

The Cycle of Fashion in Cultural Studies

The examination of various fashion theories out of heterogeneous disciplines makes it obvious that a single theory cannot reveal all that fashion means as a social phenomenon. Central theoretical discourses of fashion are:

1. The Trickle-Down Theory. This assumes that fashion originates in the upper class and diffuses to the other classes through their ambition to imitate, and that it reveals by this means hierarchical class distinctions. As soon as a specific type of style has reached the lower class echelons, the upper class is creating a new style (Veblen 1953 [1899]; Spencer 1897; Simmel 1957 [1904]). This theory of fashion is widely used and has often been refreshed and modernized. McCracken (1988) rearticulates it and refers to the gender aspect missing in the theory's original formulation.

2. The Trickle-Across Theory. Here fashion is seen as moving horizontally between groups of similar social levels. King (1963) reviews Veblen and Simmel in arguing that every social group has its own opinion leaders to imitate. Blumer (1968) argues from a position within both theories, pointing out that fashion is a "continuing pattern of change in which certain social forms enjoy temporary acceptance and respectability only to be replaced by others more abreast of the times" (1968: 341–2). Significant fashion emerges from the lower socio-economic classes as the upper class, and is picked up by both equally.

3. The Trickle-Up Theory. This is the most recent approach to examining the meaning of fashion and incorporates the approaches considered in points 1 and 2 above. In this theory, fashion emerges from the street and "bubbles up" to the

upper-income groups. Coco Chanel was the first designer to take advantage of this; her design ideas originated in the streets, because she wanted women to feel comfortable and chic at the same time. "Chanel's attitude was always complex and she related dress to the circumstances in which it was to be worn" (Steele 1992: 125).

4. The criticism following the tradition of Marx. Fashion is a part of the political economy and changes of fashion are profit-driven. This kind of account can be connected with issues of production and regulation. Indeed, every significant point within the "cycle of fashion" is related to ideology and the hegemony of popular culture, raising the question, how can fashion be regarded as trivial and "intellectually disenfranchised" (Barnard 1996)?

From the beginning it was the aspiration of British Cultural Studies to establish transdisciplinarity in research projects with high intellectual claims. Grossberg (1997) highlights the need for Cultural Studies to explore political alternatives as they evolve in popular culture. Following Hall's model of the "circuit of culture" (1997) we attempt here to rebuild the "cycle of fashion"[3] from a Cultural Studies perspective. Our aim is to provide the basis of a theoretical framework to analyse the different stages in the meaning-making process of fashion, and also provide the context.

The process of fashion production is often neglected in fashion studies. The fashion industry in fact not only produces clothes and garments, but also the idea of specific styles based on desire. Fashion designers view themselves as productive artists, composing works of art in the form of shape, colour, fabric, and trimmings. They get their inspiration from everyday life on the streets, in films, and from technology. Usually they are trained in design schools.[4] Coco Chanel is again an exception, since she has no education in fashion design and did not master dressmaking. Nevertheless, she became one of the most important designers of all time, because she had an incomparable feeling for colour, cut, fit, and a creative autonomy to recognize what people need in a particular age. In this spirit she once said: "Fashion is not something that exists in dresses only. Fashion is in the sky, in the street, fashion has to do with ideas, the way we live, what is happening" (http://library.thinkquest.org/04oc/00327/main.html). This artistic perspective is both essential and romantic, which leads to the idea that fashion designers are a special kind of artist, who decide through the rituals of creating styles what is en vogue.

The other side of production concerns assignments after the fashion design aspect is complete: the spreading of the industry to Asia (particularly China, India, Pakistan, Korea, Sri Lanka, Indoniesia and Bangladesh), global trade and manufacturing in low-wage countries, whose economic future is closely connected to the fashion sector. Our attention is directed to the economic process of producing textiles and apparel, to where and under what conditions fashion labels are producing their garments, to the complexities of trade policies and the political circumstances and structures in Asian countries, and to how these grievances can be changed. In revealing the machinations of the fashion industries as harsh working conditions in "sweatshops"[5] in the United States and Asia, new alternatives can be implemented. In the cause of social justice the anti-sweatshop movement (see www.coopamerica.org/programs/sweatshops) needs to be supported in order to raise awareness as a social issue of the existence of sweatshops, child labour and other exploitative practices. Naomi Klein (2000) denounces in her book *No Logo!* the strategies of global industries such as Gap, Nike, Benetton, Calvin Klein, Levi's, and Ralph Lauren. Paul Smith demonstrates their political background:

> At the heart of this convergence of anticorporate activism and research is the recognition that corporations are much more than purveyors of the products we all want; they are also the most powerful political forces of our time. . . . So although the media often describe campaigns like the one against Nike as "consumer boycotts", that tells only part of the story. It is more accurate to describe them as political campaigns that use consumer goods as readily accessible targets, as public-relations levers and as popular-education tools. (Klein 2000: 140)

Unequal power relations caused by economic factors and politics are a major issue in the field of Cultural Studies. The politics of the textile and apparel trade and its outgrowth, such as the resurgence of sweatshops in the United States, are part of the neo-liberal, market-governance project. It is vital to recognize the importance of the different contexts within the fashion production system. In addition to designers and factory workers, the field of production contains many other components, such as wholesalers, vendors, marketing experts, sales people, models, celebrities, journalists, and the consumer. Stone (1999) gives four levels of the fashion industry:

- textile production
- design and manufacturing
- wholesale and retail trade
- auxiliary, which connects the other levels through various media (fashion magazines, fashion shows on TV, fashion websites, etc.).

Even without emphasizing the intersections between them, each component is essential, and leads to the meaning of fashion in our everyday lives, but these cannot be considered properly in this chapter. Our main focus is the importance of a transdisciplinary approach to examining fashion. Thus du Gay et al. (1997) note that culture and economics are "hybrids" intersecting in a "cultural economy" (1997: 2), which produces meaning through "economic" or "cultural" practices (ibid.: 4), which demonstrates how fashion lifts distinctions, and confirms du Gay's idea of a cultural system existing around every commodity. To understand fashion and dress in everyday life it is necessary to explore further the fields of culture, production, and politics; the relation between fashion and identity.

Importantly, Fine and Leopold (1993) establish a connection between production and consumption in thinking about socio-economic contexts. The authors assume in their consideration that consumers have several identities, depending on class, race, gender, education, location, nationality, ethnicity, community and so on, which can be unfolded in a list of identifying settings:

> High or low involvement, arousal, attitude, affect, attributes, intention, reaction, learning, satisfaction, expectation, atmospherics, environment, context, convenience, memory,

familiarity, judgement, choice, impulse, generics, cues, status, brand, impression, class, time, age, inference, endorsement, stereotypes, community, socialisation, norms, knowledge, lifestyle, enthusiasm, materialism, culture, self-perception, routinisation, stimulus, sentiment, role-playing, psychographics, mood, encoding, focus, situation, adaptivity, opinion, leadership, imagination, variety, scripts, vividness, disconfirmation, precipiation, persuasion, reinforcement, reminder, seducation, aesthetics, humour, etc. (1993: 9)

After discussing culture and the production of fashion and clothes, we come finally to the question of the significance of identity in the "cycle of fashion." What do clothes say about a person? What do they say about that person's body image? What do our clothes say about who we are or who we think we are? How does the way we dress communicate messages about our identity?

Identity is a discursive field, actively created and negotiated in anticipated approbation of others, as Hall (1990) makes clear:

> Identity is not as transparent or unproblematic as we think. Perhaps instead of thinking of identity as an already accomplished fact, which the new cultural practices then represent, we should instead think of identity as a "production", which is never complete, always in process, and always consituted within, not outside, representation. (1990: 22)

According to this argument identities can be articulated and twisted on the outside through fashion and changing styles.[6] Mendes (2000: 41) explains: "Call it fashion, costume, or dress, what we wear and how we decorate ourselves tells the world who we are." Through actively managing our appearance we create our own look and construct various images of the self; identity construction can thus be understood from a Cultural Studies perspective as a product of social discourses.

Willis et al.'s (1990) description of identity concerning fashion concretizes these general points in his studies of youth in the following way:

> Clothes, style and fashion have long been recognized as key elements in young people's expression, exploration and making of their own individual and collective identities. They remain among the most visible forms of symbolic cultural creativity and informal artistry in people's lives in our common culture. . . . Clothes are also a crucial medium for grounded aesthetics in which young people express and explore their own specific individual identities. Young people learn about their inner selves partly by developing their outer image through clothes. They use style in their symbolic work to express and develop their understanding of themselves as unique persons, to signify who they are, and who they think they are. (1990: 85–9)

Many scholars have inherited this conceptualization in their theories about fashion. Thus Scott (2005) recasts in her findings the feminist debate around fashion, by exploring the contexts of advertising and everyday life. Men are very often not in a position to determine what is stylish or not, unless they are designers. Mostly it is women who write fashion and beauty articles and create beauty advertisements, and they are raising in that way the voice of the oppressed themselves. It is important to notice that Wilson (1992) and Church Gibson (2000) argue from a "third wave" feminist perspective, reviewing the reductionist feminist approaches. Their central theme is that fashion and dress encourage the male gaze, nevertheless recognizing "the very real social problems and ideological tensions [which] should be central to any feminist study of fashion (Church Gibson 2000: 360). Different feminist notions about fashion and shopping are also made by Morris (1993) in her empirical research about cultural production and women's actions in shopping malls, and she reasons:

> A shopping centre is a "place" combining an extreme project of general "planning" competence (efforts at total unification, total management) with an intense degree of aberrance and diversity in local performance. It is also a "place" consecrated to timelessness and stasis (no clocks, perfect weather) yet lived and celebrated, lived and loathed, in intimately historic terms: for some as ruptural event (catastrophic or Edenic) in the social experience of a community, for others as the enduring scene (as the cinema once was, and the home still may be) of all the changes, fluctuations, and repetitions of the passing of everyday life. (1993: 306)

Fashion-ology

The intention articulated through the term "fashion-ology" (borrowed from Kawamura 2005) is to establish a transdisciplinary theory of fashion, which treats fashion as a powerful example in favour of the "cycle of culture". The considerable theoretical discussion in this field establishes cultural production (Bourdieu 1993) as the grounding requirement for understanding the meaning of fashion. The methodological measures to research fashion and dress have to be subjected to the aim of Cultural Studies to consider major questions and issues, and therefore must match with the aim to institute new methods within the problem under consideration. The central meaning of fashion in identity construction in the global arena of the twenty-first century should make fashion studies an important field of research in Cultural Studies.

Notes

1. The history of dress is not the main issue of this chapter. The appearance and meaning of prehistoric fashion has been observed by Tortorra & Eubank (1989) and by Barber (1994).
2. According to Fluegel (1959) protection, modesty and decoration are the main functions of clothing. The concept of "protection" is the shielding of the body from physical, social and emotional hazards.
3. The "cycle of fashion" describes variations and phases of changing styles in fashion. The term is used by marketing specialists, fashion journalists and designers to describe the fast-moving and temporary nature of the *zeitgeist*.
4. Numerous design schools have been established around the world in the last hundred years. One of the best-established ones is the Fashion Institute of Technology (FIT) in New York City. See www.fitnyc.edu/html/dynamic.html.
5. The term *sweatshop* derives from any kind of "sweating" production or labour in the production of commercial goods.

6. The theoretical relationship between fashion and the self is profoundly discussed by Finkelstein (1991).

References

Barber, Elizabeth W. (1994). Women's Work: The First 20,000 Years: Women, Cloth, and Society in Early Times. New York/London: W.W. Norton & Co.

Barnard, Malcolm (1996). Fashion as Communication. London: Routledge.

Barthes, Roland (1984). The Fashion System. New York: Hill & Wang.

Blumer, Herbert (1968). Fashion. In: David L. Sills (ed.), International Encyclopedia of Social Sciences, pp. 341–5. New York: Free Press.

Botkin, Marie (2005). Jeans. In: Valerie Steele (ed.), Encyclopedia of Clothing and Fashion, Volume 2, pp. 272–7. Detroit: Charles Scribner's Sons.

Bourdieu, Pierre (1993). The Field of Cultural Production. Essays on Art and Literature. New York: Columbia University Press.

Brenninkmayer, Ingrid (1962). The Sociology of Fashion. Cologne: Oplander.

Cannon, Aubrey (1998). The Cultural and Historical Contexts of Fashion. In: Anne Brydon & Sandra Niessen (eds.), Consuming Fashion. Adorning the Transnational Body, pp. 23–38. Oxford/New York: Berg.

Curch Gibson, Pamela (2000). Redressing the Balance: Patriarchy, Postmodernism and Feminism. In: Stella Bruzzi & Pamela Church Gibson (eds.), Fashion Cultures. Theories, Explorations and Analysis, pp. 349–63. London: Routledge.

Craik, Jennifer (1993). Cultural Studies in Fashion. London/New York: Routledge.

Crane, Diana (1999). Diffusion Models and Fashion. A Reassessment. Annals of the American Academy of Political and Social Science 566, pp. 13–24.

De la Haye, Amy (2005). Chanel, Gabrielle (Coco). In: Valerie Steele (ed.), Encyclopedia of Clothing and Fashion, Volume 2, pp. 249–54. Detroit: Charles Scribner's Sons.

Du Gay, Paul, et al. (eds.) (1997). Doing Cultural Studies: The Story of the Sony Walkman. London: Sage/Open University.

Entwistle, Joanne (2000). The Fashioned Body: Fashion, Dress and Modern Social Theory. Cambridge: Polity Press.

Fine, Ben & Ellen Leopold (1993). The World of Consumption. London: Routledge.

Finkelstein, Joanne (1991). The Fashioned Self. Oxford: Polity Press.

Fiske, John (1989). Understanding Popular Culture. Boston: Unwin Hyman.

Fluegel, John Carl (1959). The Psychology of Clothes. London: Hogarth Press.

Foucault, Michel (1975). Discipline and Punish: The Birth of the Prison. New York: Random House.

Grossberg, Lawrence (1997). Introduction: Re-placing the Popular. In: Dancing in Spite of Myself. Essays on Popular Culture, pp. 1–26. Durham, NC: Duke University Press.

Hall, Stuart (1990). Cultural Identity and Diaspora. In: Jonathan Rutherford (ed.), Identity: Community, Culture and Difference, pp. 222–37. London. Lawrence & Wishart.

Hall, Stuart (ed.) (1997). Representation: Cultural Representations and Signifying Practices. London: Sage/Open University.

Hebdige, Dick (1979). Subculture: The Meaning of Style. London: Routledge.

Kawamura, Yunyja (2005). Fashion-ology: An Introduction to Fashion Studies. Oxford & New York: Berg.

King, Charles W. (1963). Fashion Adaption. A Rebuttal to the "Trickle-Down" Theory. In: Stephen A. Greyser (ed.), Toward Scientific Marketing, pp. 108–25. Chicago: American Marketing Association.

Klein, Naomi (2000). No Logo! Taking Aim at the Brand Bullies, online at http://www. sozialistische-klassiker.org/Klein/klein01.pdf (accessed June 25, 2006).

Koenig, René (1988). Menschheit auf dem Laufsteg. Die Mode im Zivilisationsprozeß. Frankfurt/ Main & Berlin: Ullstein.

McCracken, Grant (1988). Culture and Consumption. New Approaches to the Symbolic Character of Consumer Goods and Activities. Bloomington: Indiana University Press.

Mendes, Valerie (2001). Introduction. The Fashion of Fashion. In: Cathy Newman (ed.), Fashion, pp. 28–35. Washington, DC: National Geographic Society.

McRobbie, Angela (1998). British Fashion Design: Rag Trade or Image Industry? London: Routledge.

McRobbie, Angela (1999). In the Culture Society: Art, Fashion and Popular. London: Routledge.

McRobbie, Angela (2000). Fashion as a Culture Industry. In: Stella Bruzzi & Pamela Church Gibson (eds.), Fashion Cultures. Theories, Explorations and Analysis, pp. 253–64. London: Routledge.

Morris, Meaghan (1993). Things to Do with Shopping Centres. In: Simon During (ed.), The Cultural Studies Reader, pp. 391–409. London: Routledge.

Scott, Linda M. (2005). Fresh Lipstick. Redressing Fashion and Feminism. New York: Palgrave Macmillan.

Simmel, Georg (1957 [1904]). Fashion. International Quarterly 10(1), pp. 130–55.

Spencer, Herbert (1897). Principles of Sociology, Volume 2, Part 1. New York: D. Appleton.

Steele, Valerie (1992). Chanel in Context. In: Juliet Ash & Elizabeth Wilson (eds.), Chic Thrills. A Fashion Reader, pp. 118–26. London: Pandora Press.

Stone, Elaine (1999). The Dynamics of Fashion. New York: Fairchild Publications.

Storey, John (1993). A Introductory Guide to Cultural Theory and Popular Culture. Hemel Hempstead, UK: Harvester Wheatsheaf.

Tortorra, Phyllis (2005). Ancient World: History of Dress. In: Valerie Steele (ed.), Encyclopedia of Clothing and Fashion, Volume 2, pp. 51–9. Detroit: Charles Scribner's Sons.

Tortorra, Phyllis G. & Keith Eubank (1989). A Survey of Historic Costume. New York: Fairchild Publications.

Veblen, Thorstein (1953). Theory of the Leisure Class. New York: Mentor Books.

Williams, Raymond (1958). Culture and Society. New York: Columbia University Press.

Willis, Paul, et al. (1990). Common Culture: Symbolic Work at Play in the Everyday Cultures of the Young. Milton Keynes: Open University Press.

Wilson, Elizabeth (1992). Fashion and the Postmodern Body. In: Juliet Ash & Elizabeth Wilson (eds.), Chic Thrills. A Fashion Reader, pp. 3–24. London: Pandora Press.

Winter, Rainer (2001). Die Kunst des Eigensinns. Cultural Studies als Kritik an der Macht. Weilerswist: Velbrück Wissenschaft.

US Vogue, May 2006, p. 295. Website: http://library.thinkquest.org/04oct/00327/main.html (June 25, 2006).

44

.... And Then There Was Shopping

Sze Tsung Leong*

Not only is shopping melting into everything, but everything is melting into shopping. Through successive waves of expansion – each more extensive and pervasive than the previous – shopping has methodically encroached on a widening spectrum of territories so that it is now, arguably, the defining activity of public life. Why has it become such a basic aspect of our existence? Because it is synonymous with perhaps the most significant and fundamental development to give form to modern life: the unfettered growth and acceptance of the market economy as the dominant global standard. Shopping is the medium by which the market has solidified its grip on our spaces, buildings, cities, activities, and lives. It is the material outcome of the degree to which the market economy has shaped our surroundings, and ultimately ourselves.

Scope

Few activities unite us as human beings in the way shopping does. Apart from housing and work, no other program compares in sheer quantity. In the United States, shops outnumber churches, synagogues, and temples by 3.6 times, primary and secondary schools by 10.3 times, universities by 252.9 times, hospitals, clinics, and doctor's offices by 14.6 times, public airports by 178.4 times, libraries by 25.2 times and museums by 242.1 times.[1] In the United Kingdom, the relationship is even more disproportionate, with 8.7 times more shops than churches and 2,174 times more shops than universities. In Japan, shops outnumber museums by 1,429 times, while in Singapore, they outnumber museums by 6,770 times.

Shopping also overwhelms other activities by attracting more people. While not everyone makes it past secondary school (82.1 percent in the US), attends university (23.9 percent in the US[2] and 30 percent in the UK), goes to church (44 percent in the US and 11.5 percent in Europe), or has been to a museum or to a hospital recently, who has not shopped in some way or another – at the mall, market, downtown, through mail order, or online?

* Pp. 129–35 from *The Harvard Design School Guide to Shopping*, ed. C. J. Chung, J. Inaba, R. Koolhaas and S. T. Leong (Cambridge, MA: Harvard Design School). © 2001 by Harvard Design School. Reprinted with permission from Taschen GmbH.

Shopping also takes up more space. In the United States, shopping accounts for the majority – 25 percent – of the built area of nonresidential construction, followed by 15 percent for education and 14 percent for offices. Hospitals account for 6 percent and other public structures such as government buildings and museums account for 5 percent.

And it claims a greater percentage of the workforce than any other field. In the United States, 17 percent of working Americans are employed in the retail trade. The manufacturing industries employ 16.4 percent, while public administration employs 4.7 percent, hospitals 4 percent, schools 5.2 percent, colleges and universities 2.2 percent, and social services 2.5 percent.[3] By mere virtue of proportion, shopping has become inescapable.

Crisis and Evolution

Yet even though shopping is such an inherent part of daily life and even though it overwhelms other activities in number and in scale, it is also the most unstable, most short-lived, and most vulnerable to the threat of decline and obsolescence.

Unlike programs such as schools, universities, and churches, where participation is secured by continuous enrollment, or hospitals, where attendance is ensured by basic human need, there is no guaranteed frequency or density of use for shopping. Because shopping is so dependent on external factors – the economy, trends, or even the weather – attendance can fluctuate drastically in monthly or even hourly cycles.

Most institutions have played a historically stable role within the city, whether because of their general acceptance as indispensable organizations or because of the civic apparatuses that have ensured their existence. Shopping, on the other hand, is continually being reinvented, reformulated, and reshaped to keep up with the most subtle changes in society. No other program has seen so many new concepts and new configurations designed to follow shifts in cultural tastes and in social and urban patterns.

The innumerable forms that shopping has taken throughout history attest to the way shopping has had to invent new techniques to make itself accessible and appealing to the public. While the marketplace and the individual shop have endured as forms that have followed the development of civilization, other forms have taken shape to reflect the changing relationship of humans to material goods and to the city. Because shopping is so intimately tied to the shifting desires of the market, and because its survival is premised on tapping into and sustaining the public's attention, these forms are always facing the threat of obsolescence. Shopping, rather than being a stable urban building block, is best described in terms of cycles, births, declines, and measured in terms of life spans.

Precisely out of this desperation to survive, shopping has found the means to expand by closely monitoring and exploiting the conditions of and fluctuations in its milieu. Shopping has reached its current state through three stages of expansion since the rise of middle-class culture in the nineteenth century; these stages have not only allowed shopping to move into new realms, but have also produced some of the most significant changes in the way the built environment is used and understood.

Mechanics and Expansion into Physical Space

Mechanical inventions allowed for the first stage of expansion in modern shopping environments: physical size. At the end of the nineteenth century, technology not only offered a way to create a desire for material goods by packaging them within an aura of optimized living, it also enabled the new scales of spaces needed to accommodate and display the multiplying number of consumer products.

During the most active period of technological invention in shopping spaces, at the end of the nineteenth and the beginning of the twentieth centuries, technology did not simply coincide with the rapid escalation of consumer culture, it abetted and promoted it. Shopping could make itself relevant to the consumer by providing enhanced environments whose seductions and unprecedented comforts would prove irresistible to the populace. Because technology offered to make the relationship between the consumer and consumerism more convenient and frictionless, and because its acceptance was relatively uncontested, shopping could sponsor the radical alteration of the built environment to receive and induce consumer activity.

With each new invention, new realms became available to shopping. The skylight enabled the arcades, by allowing the interiors of city blocks to be opened to the public and by creating protected environments for nurturing consumerism. The sidewalk liberated the street to the incursion of growing quantities of shopping, by encouraging a leisurely and appealing mode of pedestrian activity. Air conditioning freed new depths of interior space to shopping, by wrapping the consumer in comfortable environments. The escalator gave the shopper a means to traverse without effort the increasing heights of commercial buildings, by putting all levels on the same, easily accessible plane.

Program and Expansion into Human Activity

Yet even though shopping environments were progressively enlarging through mechanical means, they were also becoming more short-lived, as new forms would replace older forms with greater frequency. The arcades were the principal form of Western shopping for about one hundred thirty years, before they were overshadowed by the controlled environments and the seductive spectacle of the department store. The department store, in turn, has taken about a hundred years to mature and level off. But it has only taken fifty years for the suburban shopping center to become the dominant form of consumer activity, to transform significantly the physical makeup of the city, and finally to decline as a result of shopper boredom. The latest concepts, big boxes, warehouse stores, and category killers – representing the apogee in scale for the individual store – have only been around for ten years yet are already being abandoned for the next permutation.

Recently, shopping has reached the limits of physical expansion. In the most commercialized countries, shopping space is fast achieving saturation point. With the accelerated proliferation of malls and warehouse clubs, and with their imminent decline, the possibility for expansion through mechanical enhancement has been exhausted. Air conditioning is beginning to encounter the limits of deep interior space and the escalator has already exploited every possibility of connecting levels into a continuous plane.

To sustain the necessary measure of consumer activity, shopping has had to find new ways to survive. Two simultaneous developments have sparked a radical transformation in the way that shopping might further expand. The first has been the recognition that the very factor that allowed such forms as the shopping mall, big box, and category killer to grow so rapidly and become so successful – size – was also causing their decline. Shoppers were simply being intimidated by the immensity of these shopping spaces. The unprecedented size of these new forms also made other forms of shopping obsolete, thus limiting the range of possibilities and creating a homogeneous and undifferentiated field of shopping that was quickly exhausting the interest of the public.

The second development has been the redefinition of the institution as a result of privatization. The civic and social structures that guaranteed the continued existence of institutions such as museums, airports, churches, schools, and even the city have slowly been dismantled. With governments no longer able or willing to support these institutions, financial support has shifted from a public to a private responsibility. The institution, left to its own resources, has confronted the same conditions as shopping: the instabilities of the market, the loss of consumer interest, the threat of obsolescence. As a result, the institution has had to become like shopping, and shopping has found a way to expand by colonizing the institution.

Shopping appeals to the institution because it offers an immediate means of survival, as it is seen as an almost automatic magnet for revenue and activity. It is also appealing because, being so susceptible to decline, it is always anticipating the next crisis, always looking for different forms in which to present itself anew to the consumer and thereby gain a few more years of life. As a program inherently equipped for change and flexibility in the face of uncertainty, shopping now suits the institution.

The institution appeals to shopping because it opens up new opportunities for reaching the public, whether overtly or covertly. Presently, shopping is expanding into every program imaginable: airports, churches, train stations, museums, military bases, casinos, theme parks, libraries, schools, universities, hospitals. Airports and malls are starting to look indistinguishable. The experience of the museum is becoming increasingly seamless with that of the department store. Even the city is being configured according to the mall and becoming increasingly reminiscent of the suburbs.

Will shopping once and for all debunk the notion of the institution? As much as we may deny or refuse it, shopping has become one of the only means by which we experience public life. In many cases, it determines, sustains, and often defines what it means to be an institution or even a city. Creating a diffuse smoothness between previously distinct entities, shopping has enveloped, permeated, and invaded all human activity.

Information and Expansion into Everything Else

We have yet to realize the full effects of the third major expansion of the modern shopping environment. To sustain consumer activity, shopping is launching a vast network of information technology designed to understand, in as much detail as possible, all the factors that influence people to shop. Realms that we once thought protected are becoming available to commercial scrutiny. Our movements, incomes, purchasing patterns, likes and dislikes are being coded and analyzed through credit cards, smart cards, and other tracking devices, in the hopes of increasing purchasing activity.

Information now represents the means by which shopping can continue its expansion. How much we spend, how much we make, how much we owe, where we live, where we travel, where we work, how well and where we've been educated, where we go shopping and how often, what books we read, what movies we like, what sports we play, what we own, what we don't have and don't yet know we need represent a fraction of the information retailers can mobilize to better target and entice us as consumers. Through this new wave of technological inventions, shopping is spreading into virtually all areas of our lives.

So even if shopping is constantly facing crisis and decline, it is also being constantly (and artificially) reinvented, reinterpreted, refashioned, reborn, rechanneled, and repackaged. What allows this is an apparatus – a survival mechanism – that can seize on any technique for squeezing out a pathway toward life: modulation, constant change, camouflage, mutation, predation, sabotage, parasitism, surveillance. As markets become more volatile, consumers become more fickle, capital becomes more fluid, information becomes more accessible, and as technology gets more sophisticated, so do the modulations of shopping acquire more reach, more agility, and more speed. After shops have become limitless in size, after shopping has overtaken all activities, and after all aspects of our lives have been quantified and analyzed, shopping will still find another vehicle by which to survive and expand.

In the end, there will be little else for us to do but shop.

Notes

1. Calculated from Statistical Abstract of the United States, 120th ed. (2000).
2. New York Times Almanac (1999), 362.
3. Statistical Abstract of the United States, table 653.

45

Does Cultural Capital Structure American Consumption?

Douglas B. Holt*

Although consumption has, throughout history, served as a consequential site for the reproduction of social class boundaries, the particular characteristics of consumption that are socially consecrated and, hence, used to demarcate these boundaries have been configured in myriad ways. For example, elite lifestyles have been characterized by a rigid, formal interactional style and understated simplicity (the gentry of the eighteenth century), extravagant, fashion-conscious public sociability (high society in "the Gilded Age" of the late nineteenth century), informal social clubbiness (the new upper-middle class of the early twentieth century), and cultural refinement (the highbrow taste of urban elites in the twentieth century; see Collins 1975, pp. 187–211). But, many academics and critics now claim that in postmodern consumer societies, the United States in particular, consumption patterns no longer act to structure social classes. The massive proliferation of cultural meanings and the fragmentation of unitary identities, two primary traits of postmodern culture, have shattered straightforward correspondences between social categories and consumption patterns. So we find conservative, individualist arguments typical of marketing and economics (e.g., Schouten & McAlexander 1995), liberal sociological arguments (e.g., Halle 1993), and radical postmodern arguments (Baudrillard 1981), all inveighing that consumption patterns are no longer consequential to class reproduction. In such societies, critical analysis of the reproduction of social class through consumption has become an increasingly treacherous interpretive exercise. Analyses that seek out such patterns are often dismissed as essentialist or worse. But is it true that social class is no longer produced through distinctive patterns of consumption? Or, alternatively, is this relationship occluded when old theorizing is used to analyze a new social formation?

Pierre Bourdieu's (1984) theory of cultural capital and taste offers the most comprehensive and influential attempt to develop a theoretical framework to plumb the social patterning of consumption in an increasingly mystified social world. Yet this theory has received a chilly reception in the United States, routinely subject to both theoretical critique and empirical refutation. This study is motivated by the premise that these criticisms have misconstrued Bourdieu's research and so have not explored fully the

*Pp. 1–25 from *Journal of Consumer Research*, vol. 25. © 1998 by Journal of Consumer Research, Inc. Reprinted with permission from the University of Chicago Press.

potential usefulness of the theory for disentangling the relationship between class and consumption in contemporary postmodern societies.

Distinguishing Bourdieu

Max Weber (1978) coined the term "social class" to capture the idea that, in addition to the economic resources described by Marx, hierarchical social strata are also expressed and reproduced through "styles of life" that vary in their honorific value. Societies segregate into different reputational groupings based not only on economic position, but also on noneconomic criteria such as morals, culture, and lifestyle that are sustained because people tend to interact with their social peers. American social class strata were first analyzed in Veblen's (1970 [1899]) bombastic essays about the leisure class, Simmel's (1957 [1904]) theory of trickle-down status imitation, and in the Lynds' studies of "Middletown," but it is the approach developed by W. Lloyd Warner and his associates in a series of widely publicized studies of the stratification of small American cities following World War II that has dominated consumer research for more than 30 years (Coleman 1983; Coleman & Rainwater 1978; Rainwater et al. 1959; Warner et al. 1949). Notwithstanding a variety of incisive critiques, the Warnerian approach offers an important formulation of the relationship between social class and lifestyle that is foundational for the advances made by Bourdieu. Yet the advantages of Bourdieu's theory relative to Warner have never been foregrounded, likely because Warner's social Darwinist presuppositions are directly at odds with Bourdieu's (1984) critical view of consumption patterns as a consequential site of class reproduction.

Warner's anthropological approach

The Warnerian approach to social class describes the primary social strata within a community by mapping the relative amount of respect and deference accorded to each group. The primary Warnerian method, evaluated participation, requires ethnographic interviews with a stratified random sample of the population of a town or small city. The interview is structured to allow informants to express specific criteria used to judge the reputation of fellow townspeople. This approach yielded a multidimensional conception of status: reputation is influenced by a wide range of moral, aesthetic, intellectual, educational, religious, ethnic, and personal behaviors for which hierarchical judgments can be formed. Like Veblen, Simmel, and the Lynds before him, Warner finds that consumer behaviors (e.g., "the 'right' kind of house, the 'right' neighborhood, the 'right' furniture"), are among the most important expressions of particular status positions in a community (Warner et al. 1949, p. 23). In addition, institutional affiliations (churches, clubs, political organizations) and neighborhoods are used to make judgments. These data are interpreted relationally to build the status hierarchy operating in each town. Because ethnographic studies using evaluated participation are prohibitively expensive to administer, Warnerian status studies since the 1950s have relied instead on surrogate measures such as the Index of Status Characteristics (Warner et al. 1949), the Index of Social Position (Hollingshead & Redlich 1959), or the Computerized Status Index (Coleman 1983), which are derived from survey measures of occupation, income, neighborhood, and house type.

There is still much to value in Warner's conception of status. In particular, its structuralist emphasis on relational differences in collective understandings of social position is an important but largely unacknowledged precursor to recent American sociological studies of the symbolic boundaries that sustain social hierarchies (e.g., Lamont 1992). However, in sociology, the Warnerian approach was long ago discredited owing to its narrow functionalist presuppositions that deny the interplay between cultural, economic, and political resources in the construction of social classes (Bendix & Lipset 1951; Gordon 1963; Pfautz & Duncan 1950). Beyond this metatheoretic problem, two specific conceptual lacunae become evident when Warner's approach is compared with Bourdieu's theory.

Conflating dimensions of social class

Warner's community studies provide extensive empirical support for Weber's multidimensional conception of social class: collective understandings of reputation are formed on the basis of criteria such as consumption patterns, economic position, morals, and educational attainment.[1] Yet, Warnerian research never isolates and investigates the relationships between these dimensions. Without so doing, it is impossible to understand the distinctive contributions of consumption to social class. Instead, consumption is an untheorized covariate. Warner argues that each status group develops, like a society in microcosm, a unique way of life; the consumer goods and activities that classes adopt are arbitrary. Any good or activity can be used as a means of maintaining in-group solidarity and excluding status inferiors. So he does not offer a coherent theory describing the conditions leading to status group formation, how these differences structure tastes, and why they are relatively durable over time. This lack of specification decreases the usefulness of Warner's approach since it offers no explanation for the elective affinities between particular groups and particular consumption patterns. One example of this theoretical black box is the debate in marketing concerning the relative explanatory power of income and social class in predicting consumption patterns (see Schaninger [1981] for a review). Consistent findings that social class measures capture more variance than income alone never broach the central theoretical question underlying demonstrations of covariation: If factors other than income influence stratified consumption patterns, what are they and how do they work?

Object signification

For Warner, American social classes are organized in a manner analogous to the social structure of small, isolated, preindustrial societies of classic anthropological ethnographies – *"Gemeinshaft"* communities bound by affiliative ties within strong, interpenetrating social networks. Thus, his method emphasizes descriptions of peoples' networks of friends, acquaintances, and organizational affiliations. This view of social organization motivates Warner's incipient theory of status-based consumption patterns. Similar to Veblen, Simmel, and the Lynds, Warner views consumption objects as positional markers reinforcing status boundaries. In this emulationist model, elites are engaged in a continual game with those below in which elite consumption patterns are universally valorized, and thus lower-class groups attempt to emulate them, leading elites to defend the distinctiveness of their consumption through pecuniary symbolism (Veblen), stylistic innovation (Simmel), and activities bounded by closed social networks (Warner).

This view of social class is an anachronism built upon a Rockwellian image of small town life that represents a minuscule and declining fraction of the contemporary United States (in contradistinction to Warner's famous aphorism, "To study Jonesville is to study America"). Although status judgments based on the goods one owns and the activities in which one participates have merit for describing small, isolated, relatively immobile populations, they are of little value for most of the population in an era of transnational consumer capitalism. Status construction now must contend with the tremendous geographic mobility of American professionals and managers, the privatization of social life, the proliferation of media and travel, and the anonymity of urban environments, all of which have impersonalized the "other" whom one views as social references (Collins 1981; DiMaggio 1987; Dimaggio & Mohr 1985; Meyrowitz 1985). With interactional groups multiplying and in constant flux, it becomes exceedingly difficult to develop stable consensus goods that represent the group.

In addition, Warner's object signification approach implies a highly strategized conception of consumption: people learn about, acquire, and experience consumption objects as status markers. Yet cultural consumer research has demonstrated repeatedly that consumption patterns can never be explained primarily by recourse to theories based on a view of consumption as instrumental or strategic action. Consuming is significantly an autotelic activity in which tastes are formed around the desires for and pleasures gained from particular goods and activities relative to others; so, to be empirically compelling, a theory describing differences in consumption across groups must explain these differences in terms of tastes, pleasures, and desires rather than strategic action.

Bourdieu's theory of tastes

Across a diverse range of substantive studies, Pierre Bourdieu has synthesized Weberian, Marxist, Durkheimian, and phenomenological traditions to argue for a model of social organization, the generative mechanism for which is competition for various types of capital within social fields. In *Distinction* (Bourdieu 1984), arguably the most important application of this grand theoretical project, Bourdieu describes how these various capitals operate in the social fields of consumption. I first review briefly Bourdieu's key concepts and then discuss how the theory addresses the limitations of Warnerian social class research.[2]

Bourdieu argues that social life can be conceived as a multidimensional status game in which people draw on three different types of resources (what he terms economic, cultural, and social capital) to compete for status (what he terms "symbolic capital"). Distinct from economic capital (financial resources) and social capital (relationships, organizational affiliations, networks), cultural capital consists of a set of socially rare and distinctive tastes, skills, knowledge, and practices. Cultural capital entails what Gouldner (1979) has called a "culture of critical discourse": a set of decontextualized understandings, developed through a reflexive, problematizing, expansionist orientation to meaning in the world, that are readily recontextualized across new settings (as opposed to knowledge of specific facts; see Hannerz 1990), Cultural capital exists in three primary forms: embodied as implicit practical knowledges, skills, and dispositions; objectified in cultural objects; and institutionalized in official degrees and diplomas that certify the existence of the embodied form. Cultural capital is fostered in an overdetermined manner in the social milieu of cultural elites: upbringing in families with well-educated parents whose occupations require cultural skills, interaction with peers from similar families, high levels of formal education at institutions that attract other cultural elites studying areas that emphasize critical abstract thinking and communication over the acquisition of particularized trade skills and knowledges, and then refinement and reinforcement in occupations that emphasize symbolic production. These innumerable, diverse, yet redundant, experiences particular to cultural elites become subjectively embodied as ways of feeling, thinking, and acting through the generative social psychological structure that Bourdieu terms the "habitus." The habitus is an abstracted, transposable system of schema that both classifies the world and structures action. Bourdieu emphasizes that the contents of the habitus are largely presuppositional rather than discursive and that the habitus structures actions through a process of creative typification to particular situations. In its subjective embodied form, cultural capital is a key element of the habitus.

Like other capital resources, cultural capital exists only as it is articulated in particular institutional domains. According to Bourdieu (as well as many other theorists of modernity), the social world consists of many distinctive, relatively autonomous, but similarly structured (i.e., "homologous") fields such as politics, the arts, religion, education, and business. Fields are the key arenas in which actors compete for placement in the social hierarchy through acquisition of the statuses distinctive to the field. Thus, cultural capital takes on a distinctive form in each field: for example, in the academic field, cultural capital takes the form of intellectual brilliance, research competence, and detailed expertise that is embodied in presentations, teaching, and informal interactions, objectified in journal articles and books, and institutionalized in prestigious university degrees and society fellowships. In *Distinction*, Bourdieu documents how cultural capital is enacted in fields of consumption, not only the arts but also food, interior decor, clothing, popular culture, hobbies, and sport. Although cultural capital is articulated in all social fields as an important status resource, it operates in consumption fields through a particular conversion into tastes and consumption practices.

Unlike economic theories of markets in which people are conceived as strategic actors, in Bourdieu's theory, resources that are valued in fields of consumption are naturalized and mystified in the habitus as tastes and consumption practices. The habitus organizes how one classifies the universe of consumption objects to which one is exposed, constructing desire toward consecrated objects and disgust toward objects that are not valued in the field, The manifestation of the structuring capabilities of the habitus as tastes and consumption practices across many categories of goods and activities results in the construction of a distinctive set of consumption patterns, a lifestyle ("manifested preferences") that both expresses and serves to reproduce the habitus. Within the field of consumption, tastes and their expression as lifestyles are stratified on the basis of the objective social conditions that structure the habitus. Thus, the field of consumption is stratified so that there exist different lifestyles organized by class position. (To continue the academic field example, the same stratified patterns can be discerned in the desired qualities for faculty members at elite "research" schools, "balanced" schools, "teaching" schools, and community colleges.)

Isolating cultural capital, tastes, and consumption fields

Bourdieu argues that it is critical to distinguish between the different types of statuses that accrue in different fields: consumption is a particular status game that must be analyzed in isolation rather than lumped together with work, religion, education, and politics as Warner does. In addition, compared with Warner's conflation of the different bases of social class, a key contribution of Bourdieu's theory is that it effectively disaggregates the key dimensions of taste and explains their unique contribution to social reproduction. Economic capital is inscribed in consumption fields as tastes and consumption practices organized around the exchange value of consumption objects. Like Veblen's pecuniary distinctions, consumption objects can symbolize differences in economic resources of the consumer. But, whereas economic capital is expressed through consuming goods and activities of material scarcity and inputed luxury, cultural capital is expressed through consuming via aesthetic and interactional styles that fit with cultural elite sensibilities and that are socially scarce.

Taste as practice

Warner and Bourdieu both argue that status is expressed and reproduced through implicit evaluations in everyday social interactions. However, for Warner, these interactions occur within heavily sedimented social networks and formal organizations such as leisure and service clubs and religious groups. This allowed him to assume, like Veblen, the Lynds, and Simmel before him, that elites evolve a distinctive constellation of consumption objects that express their status position. Public signaling of these consensus goods affirms one's social position.

Significantly, Bourdieu offers a theory of social class consonant with social relations in advanced capitalist societies. Downplaying public displays of status symbols, Bourdieu emphasizes that status is continually reproduced as an unintended consequence of social interaction because all interactions necessarily are classifying practices; that is, micropolitical acts of status claiming in which individuals constantly negotiate their reputational positions (see also Collins 1981; Goffman 1967). Crucial to this process is the expression of cultural capital embodied in consumer actions. Rather than accruing distinction from pecuniary rarity or from elite consensus, Bourdieu argues that cultural capital secures the respect of others through the consumption of objects that are ideationally difficult and so can only be consumed by those few who have acquired the ability to do so. To take an example that Bourdieu might use were he to study the contemporary United States, when someone details Milos Forman's directorial prowess in *The People vs. Larry Flynt* to a friend over dinner (or, conversely, offers a damning harangue of Forman as an unrepentant proselytizer of the dominant gender ideology), this discussion not only recreates the experiential delight that the movie provided but also serves as a claim to particular resources (here, knowledge of directorial styles in movies and the ability to carefully analyze these characteristics) that act as reputational currency. Such actions are perceived not as explicit class markers but as bases for whom one is attracted to and admires, whom one finds uninteresting or does not understand, or whom one finds unimpressive and so seeks to avoid. Thus, status boundaries are reproduced simply through expressing one's tastes.

In addition to this embodied form, Bourdieu argues that cultural capital also becomes objectified in consumption objects. At first blush, this idea appears to parallel the object signification approach since consumption objects serve as signals of status in both. However, with objectified cultural capital, the stratificatory power of cultural objects results not from group consensus or economic scarcity but from the inferred cultural aptitude of the consumers of the object. In other words, cultural objects such as the high arts that require significant cultural capital to understand and appreciate properly imply that their consumers apply distinctive practices and so serve as surrogate representations of these practices. A foundational premise of Bourdieu's theory, then, is that categories of cultural goods and activities vary in the level of cultural capital required to consume them successfully (i.e., to fully enjoy the act of consuming).

Recovering Bourdieu's theory of tastes from its critics

Cultural sociologists have vigorously debated the applicability of Bourdieu's theory to the contemporary United States for over a decade. Although early research offered modest support, influential recent studies have challenged its usefulness for explaining how social reproduction works in the contemporary United States (Erikson 1996; Gartman 1991; Halle 1993; Lamont 1992). I argue that two crucial flaws in operationalizing tastes limit the credibility of these refutations (see Holt [1997a] for a more detailed version of this argument):

Forms of taste
Quantitative empirical studies of Bourdieu's theory routinely operationalize tastes only in their objectified form – preferences for particular categories, genres, or types of cultural objects. Exemplary studies of this type such as those conducted by Paul DiMaggio (1987; DiMaggio & Mohr 1985; DiMaggio & Ostrower 1990; DiMaggio & Useem 1978) and Richard Peterson (Hughes & Peterson 1983; Peterson & DiMaggio 1975; Peterson & Simkus 1992) use large-scale surveys that are analyzed through regression and factor analyses. The obvious advantage to measuring only objectified tastes is that there are large databases available and this type of data is compatible with sophisticated statistical analysis.

But operationalizing Bourdieu's theory in terms of preferences for cultural objects has become problematic, regardless of whether these objects are conceived as Warnerian consensus goods or as Bourdieuian objectified cultural capital. The utility of goods as consensus class markers has weakened substantially owing to a variety of widely noted historical shifts. Technological advances have led to the wide accessibility of goods, travel, and media by all but the poor (Bell 1976). Innovative styles and designs now diffuse rapidly between haute and mass markets, and between core and periphery states, thus dissolving lags that once allowed for stylistic leadership. From a different vantage point, theorists of postmodernity such as Jean Baudrillard, Jean-Francois Lyotard, and Fredric Jameson have argued that a defining characteristic of advanced capitalist societies is the massive overproduction of commodity signs. This proliferation of signs leads to an anarchic welter of consumer symbols that are not readily assimilated by social groups in any coherent way. This argument is supported by sociological research demonstrating a high degree of overlap in consumer preferences across social categories (e.g., Bourdieu 1984; Peterson & Simkus 1992). In postmodern cultures, it is increasingly difficult to infer status directly from consumption objects, as the object signification approach requires.

Historical changes are also draining the symbolic potency of objectified cultural capital. The postmodern condition is characterized by the breakdown of the hierarchy distinguishing legitimate (or high) culture from mass (or low) culture (Foster 1985; Frow 1995; Huyssen 1986; Jameson 1991). Many of the distinguishing traits of mass culture, such as seriality and mass reproduction, have now become central concerns of the art world, and many popular cultural forms from comic books to rock music to celebrities to television programs are produced and consumed using increasingly complex and esoteric formal lexicons that parallel modern art (Gamson 1994; Jenkins 1992). The objectified form of cultural capital becomes less effective in such a world since it depends on cultural categories and genres for which necessary levels of cultural competence are immanent and vary significantly. Objectified cultural capital can operate effectively only within a stable cultural hierarchy. Thus, as cultural hierarchies have dramatically blurred in advanced capitalist societies, objectified cultural capital has become a relatively weak mechanism for exclusionary class boundaries.

I suggest, then, that the cultural capital requirements necessary to consume successfully particular consumption objects today pose few constraints. Objects no longer serve as accurate representations of consumer practices; rather, they allow a wide variety of consumption styles. But this increasing semiotic malleability does not imply that cultural capital differences in consumption no longer signify. Rather, class differences in American consumption have gone underground; no longer easily identified with the goods consumed, distinction is becoming more and more a matter of practice. As popular goods become aestheticized and as elite goods become "massified" (Peterson & DiMaggio 1975) the objectified form of cultural capital has in large part been supplanted by the embodied form. Given the deteriorating classificatory power of objectified tastes, cultural elites in advanced capitalist societies now attempt to secure distinction by adapting their consumption practices to accentuate the embodied form.

Emphasizing embodied tastes leads to a different style of consuming than in previous eras. In fields organized by a hierarchy of objectified tastes, consumption practices emphasize knowing about and consuming the appropriate goods (e.g., Bourdieu uses Mondrian paintings and Bach concertos as measures). However, for fields in which there is great overlap in the objects consumed, to consume in a rare, distinguished manner requires that one consume the same categories in a manner inaccessible to those with less cultural capital (see Bourdieu's [1984, p. 282] description of the lifestyles of cultural producers). In other words, to express distinction through embodied tastes leads cultural elites to emphasize the distinctiveness of consumption practices themselves, apart from the cultural contents to which they are applied.

Contents of taste

Although not always clear in *Distinction*, it appears that Bourdieu, his supporters, and his critics all now agree that the particular cultural objects in which cultural capital is invested are conventions that are differentially configured across sociohistorical settings (Calhoun et al. 1993; Joppke 1986; Lamont 1992; Lamont & Lareau 1988).[3] It is unlikely, then, that the cultural objects Bourdieu describes as resources for the expression of exclusionary tastes in 1960s Parisian society will operate similarly in other sociohistorical settings. Rather than a nomothetic theory, Bourdieu's theory is a set of sensitizing propositions concerning the relations between social conditions, taste, fields of consumption, and social reproduction that must be specified in each application to account for their particular configuration.

American refutations of Bourdieu's theory (Erikson [1996]; Hall [1992]; Halle [1993]; and Lamont [1992] are the most significant) have, with few exceptions, operationalized elite taste using the same variables as Bourdieu. These studies evaluate whether the particular articulation of cultural capital in Parisian society of the 1960s, objectified primarily in the legitimate arts and embodied in formal aesthetic appreciation, applies to the contemporary United States. These critics echo a claim that is well documented in historical, demographic, and humanist writings (see, e.g., Huyssen 1986), that the fine arts are much less popular among cultural elites in the United States. Only a small fraction of the American population, cultural producers and a small coterie of insiders from the urban upper class, are knowledgeable fine arts consumers of the type Bourdieu describes as predominant in middle-class circles in France. Art history is not currently a regular part of academic training or informal family socialization in the United States, Bourdieu's two primary channels for cultural capital accumulation. And, as sociological studies of genre preferences report, those with high cultural capital are the most ardent consumers of mass culture (DiMaggio & Useem 1978; Peterson & Simkus 1992). Thus, critics conclude that since the high arts play only a peripheral role in the lives of cultural elites, Bourdieu's theory has little explanatory value in the contemporary United States (Erikson 1996; Halle 1993; Lamont 1992).

The flaw in this argument is that the arts constitute only a small fraction of the universe of consumption fields that can be leveraged for social reproduction. By focusing exclusively on art, these studies give short shrift to the activities that American cultural elites expend the vast majority of their nonwork energies pursuing, such as food, interior decor, vacations, fashion, sports, reading, hobbies, and socializing. These fields should be central to empirical studies of Bourdieu's theory in the contemporary United States since tastes serve as a resource for social reproduction only in fields in which cultural elites have invested the requisite time and psychic energy to convert their generic cultural capital assets to particular field-specific cultural capitals.

Methods

I used this reformulation of Bourdieu, specified to account for the sociohistorical context of the contemporary United States by emphasizing mass consumption practices, to guide the design of an interpretive study. The goal of the study is to explore whether variation in cultural capital resources leads to systematic differences in tastes and consumption practices for mass cultural categories. In so doing, I respond to Lamont's call for a detailed mapping of how cultural capital currently operates in the United States (Lamont 1992; Lamont & Lareau 1988). I began with a sample of 50 informants from the vicinity of State College, a small city in rural central Pennsylvania dominated by Penn State University, who were randomly selected from the phone book (about 20 percent response rate). From this group, I compare 10 informants in the top quintile of cultural capital resources (whom I will refer to as "HCCs") to 10 informants whose cultural capital resources are in the lowest quintile (hereafter "LCCs").[4] I view this comparison as a conservative evaluation of Bourdieu's theory since the most significant class differences in cultural-capital-structured taste are found in large urban areas, where the new class (Gouldner 1979) of symbolic manipulators is larger and more cosmopolitan (Lamont 1992) and where there exist many urban subcultures of cultural producers that are more distinctive than the new class populations of suburban, exurban, and rural locations (Crane 1992). While LCCs are all from the local area and so express certain regional particularities in their tastes, the HCCs have lived across the country and the world, so their upbringing and education is similar to other HCCs in the United States.

Informants, all adult permanent residents of the county, were randomly selected from the local phone book, contacted by phone, and offered $20 to participate in an in-home interview. Although more women than men agreed to be interviewed, I compared the male and female informants and did not find any differences on the dimensions of taste reported below (DiMaggio & Mohr [1985] report similar findings). Following prior research (Halle 1993; Lamont 1992; Rainwater et al. 1959; Warner et al. 1949), in-home ethnographic interviews were used to collect data. The interviews lasted an average of one hour and forty minutes, and ranged from one to three hours. The interviews were transcribed into about 950 single-spaced pages of text. In addition to these transcripts, the data examined in the analysis also included details observed in the homes and a demographic questionnaire.

The two groups were constructed on the basis of cultural capital resources. According to Bourdieu and his American interlocutors, cultural capital resources are accumulated in three primary sites of acculturation: family upbringing, formal education, and occupational culture (Bourdieu 1984; DiMaggio & Unseem 1978; Lamont 1992; Peterson & Simkus 1992). The cultural capital rating scheme for this study uses all three of these antecedents, equally weighted. Family upbringing is measured in terms of father's education and occupation, because the father's status dominated family status when these informants were young. Five categories were created for each dimension (5 = high resources for cultural capital accumulation, 1 = low resources for cultural capital accumulation), guided by previous work that has calibrated differences in American education and occupation with differences in cultural capital (see Lamont 1992; Peterson & Simkus 1992). The 10 HCC informants are roughly equivalent to Gouldner's (1979) "New Class": all have at least bachelor's degrees and work in professional, technical, and managerial jobs. Most come from families in which the parents are college educated. In contrast, the 10 LCC informants are from a working-class background: they have at most a high school education, do manual labor or service/clerical work if they have jobs, and come from families where the father has at most a high school education (usually less) and did manual labor.[5]

The goal of the data collection was to elicit detailed descriptions of people's tastes and consumption practices across a variety of popular cultural categories prevalent in the contemporary United States – food, clothing, home decor and furnishings, music, television, movies, reading, socializing, vacations, sports, and hobbies. I developed an interview guide to elicit people's understandings and evaluations of different consumption objects, and the ways in which they consume their choices. Within each category, questions probed for detailed preferences and recountings of particular episodes across a variety of situations and time periods (e.g., for eating: breakfast, lunch, dinner, and snacks; at home vs. take-out, or eat-in restaurants; with family vs. alone; weeknights vs. weekends; before vs. after having children; special meals) to elicit as much detail as possible. Follow-up questions probed key emic terms that emerged in these descriptions.

In the next section, I describe six systematic differences in tastes and consumption practices between HCCs and LCCs that are structured by differences in social conditions. Like all social patterns, these dimensions are significant tendencies rather than orthogonal characteristics of the two groups.

Materiality and Taste

A central contention in *Distinction* is that tastes are structured through continuities in interactions with material culture. The LCCs are acculturated in a social milieu in which they engage continually the material rigors of everyday life (e.g., paying monthly utility bills, keeping the car running, saving money to visit relatives) and so the ability to manage these material constraints becomes a primary value. The tastes of LCCs are organized to appreciate that which is functional or practical – the taste of necessity (Bourdieu 1984, p. 177). Goods and activities are valued for their embodiment of the practical: virtuoso skills that achieve utilitarian ends evoke praise, cultural texts that realistically capture personal experiences are appreciated, corporeal pleasures take precedence.

In contrast, HCCs are acculturated in a social milieu in which they seldom encounter material difficulties and in which their education emphasizes abstracted discussion of ideas and pleasures removed from the material world. For HCCs, the material value of cultural objects is taken for granted: instead taste becomes a realm of self-expression, a means of constructing subjectivity. The tastes of HCCs express this distance from necessity, a distanced, formal gaze and a playful attitude that often takes the material value of cultural objects for granted.

This fundamental distinction in relationship to material culture underlies three important dimensions of taste and consumption practice that distinguish LCC and HCC informants across many of the categories discussed in the interviews: material versus formal aesthetics, referential versus critical appreciation, and materialism versus idealism.

Material versus formal aesthetics

For categories that are an important and a routine part of everyday life such as furniture, food, and clothing, LCC tastes are organized by a desire for pragmatic solutions to basic requirements. The LCC informants express concern for the utilitarian characteristics of their house and its furnishings; they must be comfortable, functional, durable, and easy to care for:

Interviewer: What kind of decor do you like in your house?

Katie (LCC): I like comfort. And things that people don't have to be afraid of when they come in the house, that they have to take off their shoes. Like the dark carpet that you don't have to worry about. I used to have a dark carpet, but the lighter carpet is easier to clean than the dark carpet. The dark carpet shows every little lint and this can go for a week without having to vacuum. I think we go for comfort more than anything else. We each have our own couch, as you see. Now if I had a larger room, I'd have more rocking chairs or another chair. . . . And if I had another house I'd build a larger kitchen. I'd have a rocking chair in the kitchen and I would have it more comfortable in the kitchen.

Interviewer: When you're setting up your house, what kinds of things do you like?

Betsy (LCC): Well, wood, We both like . . . well, we have a lot of wood.

Interviewer: When you say you like wood, what about it? Just any furniture that's made with wood you prefer?

Betsy (LCC): Yes, that's basically what we do. When we go for a piece of furniture, like when we were looking for a recliner, because I knew it was going to be used a lot, I said I want wood and he agreed because you get kids or company or what-ever and they're always going to go for the recliner and, of course, they're not always going to have their arms clean or whatever. I said that's basically what always wore out on mom's furniture because of all the kids. You know, it's just one of those things. I mean you wear out the arms of the furniture. I said, "I want wood." So we basically always go for wood because it's more durable and you just polish it and you know it's going to last. I mean it's not like cloth.

Although material characteristics dominate LCC tastes for interior and furniture, three informants do mention particular styles: two favor a country look, which uses colonial furniture, calico prints, and handmade crafts decorating walls and tables, while one is redecorating her house in Victorian antiques and decor. However, unlike HCCs, LCCs do not invoke a discourse of style to talk about these decorative preferences. Instead, they describe their tastes in terms of the traditions in which they have been raised, which makes their choices comfortable and reassuring.

The HCCs often share LCC material requirements for home interiors; comfort and durability are still important. But rather than dominant dimensions of their taste, material characteristics are baseline criteria; choices between materially satisfactory options are based on formal aesthetic qualities. The HCCs view their homes as canvasses upon which they express their aesthetic sensibilities. Interiors need to be visually appealing, to provide the appropriate experiential properties. Decorating is a highly personalized and personalizing activity that is an aesthetic expression of the cultivated sensibilities of the decorator:

Kathryn (HCC): I like choosing things and fitting things together, and bringing a few things from my old life into the new one, and putting them there as a reminder of where you came from. . . . Houses should be a background and they shouldn't interrupt. They shouldn't make people look at them rather than the people in them. . . . [when decorating] The main thing is not to draw attention to what we're going to do. . . . That's my philosophy, and anything that's glaring or ostentatious or says its important is out the window to me. I don't like something that is built to impress.

Interviewer: Tell me about the changes you've made to the house.

John (HCC): Well, this house was a disaster. I hadn't done anything to it in almost 30 years. It's almost a shrink question. I decided to get my life in order. And part of getting my life in order, now that I have the intellectual energy to do so after [he had recently taken early retirement]. . . . You know, when I'm not working it's amazing how much intellectual energy you have and it's all for you. I realized that my surroundings had to be harmonious and sympathetic and supportive and all of that.

Similarly, preferred clothes of LCC informants are durable, comfortable, reasonably priced, well fitted, and, for clothes that will be seen by others, conforming to role norms (i.e., they are appropriate "work clothes" or "church clothes"). A common reference point that illuminates this materialist idea of desirable clothing is that many of the LCC women but none of the HCC women raise (with no prompting) the option of making clothes as a relevant baseline to evaluate store-bought clothing:

Interviewer: What kind of clothes do you like?

Heather (LCC): Stuff that will last. I don't really like to go with what's fashionable, necessarily, just for the sake of being fashionable. I like to be comfortable.

Interviewer: What kinds of clothes are comfortable?

Heather (LCC): Knits, something, you know, that's comfortable. To work, I wear sneakers and knit pants and t-shirts, you know, that type of stuff cause you didn't know when you were going to have to have to be holding somebody on the floor or whatever (she's a teacher's assistant]. For church and stuff, I wear skirts and sweaters or a blouse or whatever, or if we're going somewhere, I like to dress, not necessarily overdress, but to be dressed nice and be comfortable. . . . I' m just as happy getting something at K-Mart or Wal-Mart or even T J Maxx or something like that, but to go to Messes or Brooks or, you know, some place really expensive, what I consider is really expensive. I find it difficult to spend thirtysome dollars on a shirt, or, you know, $50 or $60 on a skirt when I could go out and buy the material if I have the time to make it for a lot less.

In contrast, HCCs express tastes similar to those applied to decor; they expect material quality as a given and so tastes are structured by particular ideas of what is fashionable:

Kathryn (HCC): I do not like clothes that draw attention to themselves. . . . But, I'm wearing more bright-colored clothes than I used to, because my first husband didn't like me to draw attention to myself so I was dressed in very pale colors. But now, I think partly in reaction to that, I will buy clothes that are more brightly colored if I like them. . . . I don't like clothes that are covered with – I call them "suburban clothes" – they are made of very synthetic fabrics and they have lots of gold on them, and buttons that shine a lot. They look kind of as if they're shouting.

When HCCs do talk of economical choices, these are couched as less desirable outcomes forced by budgetary constraints (i.e., driven by economic capital) rather than as acculturated desires:

Interviewer: How about clothing, what types of clothes do you like?
Denise (HCC): What kind of clothes do I like – it's different from what kind of clothes I can afford. I like well-made, well-tailored clothes that have absolutely luxurious fabrics. However, I have been buying a lot of stuff from L. L. Bean because it's durable and I like gorgeous colors and all those kind of things.
Interviewer: When you say tailored. . . . What kind of styles?
Denise (HCC): I don't like really trendy looking clothes that you're not going to be able to wear next week. I'm trying to think of a look, you know Chanel?

Some HCCs prefer "functional" clothing, but this term has a very different meaning for HCCs than for LCCs. Functional, for HCCs, is a distinctive aesthetic based on parsimonious design and utilitarian construction similar to the functionalism of high modern architecture and design. "Function," rather than a pragmatic solution to everyday needs, is inverted by HCCs into form through an aesthetic opposition to the frivolity of "fashion."

John (HCC): Today I'm buying practical clothes. That is to say they're mostly cotton. They're all washable. Mostly they don't require ironing because I got tired of ironing. . . . I look for – now when I'm buying clothing – I really don't care what the current style is anymore. You know, if it has good design it will always be in style. And I also tend to look for things which probably are more expensive but which I know will be more durable.
Interviewer: Are there any particular clothing styles that you like?
John: Yeah. I guess the best way to say it would be styles that are functional and designed to be worn by human bodies as they are; as opposed to designed to be worn only standing up at cocktail parties or the races or, you know, as soon as you sit down you know it was a mistake.

Critical versus referential reception of cultural texts

Habitus-structured orientations toward material culture also organize distinctive styles of consuming mass cultural texts such as books, television, film, and music. Applying a formal interpretive lens, HCCs read popular entertainment as entertaining fictions that are potentially edifying but that do not reflect directly the empirical world (i.e., what Liebes and Katz [1990] term "critical" interpretations).

Interviewer: Why did you like *Rain Man* so much? Why is that on your list?

Sharon (HCC): Partly because I thought the dynamics between Dustin Hoffman and Tom Cruise was really entertaining and because Dustin Hoffman did such a good job in that role.

Interviewer: When you say just that Dustin Hoffman was really good, what do you mean by that?

Sharon: I found it amazing. . . . When you watch a string of movies – like I've seen most of the Tom Cruise movies – to me most of his roles it's Tom Cruise, not the character that he becomes, even though he does a really pretty decent job, more decent than a lot of actors do. But you're still very aware of who the actor is and in him I see a lot of the same very subtle mannerisms that he brings to every role probably without even realizing it. And I've seen Dustin Hoffman in other things and to me in that movie he became the person he was portraying where your mind. . . . you didn't even think of the fact that you'd seen him in how many other shows or movies because you were into the character. I like it when an actor and actress can do that. I think it's rare.

The LCCs, in contrast, tend to interpret cultural texts from a referential perspective: they read these texts as more or less realistic depictions of the world that are potentially relevant to their own lives (see Press 1991). Because LCCs apply the classificatory system used in everyday life to cultural texts, they are attracted to programs and movies they feel are "real" and to music that speaks directly to their life situation.

Interviewer: What did you like about *Sleepless in Seattle*?

David (LCC): It has a good ending and it's realistic. Yeah, in a way, realistic. In a way it's kind of far out because, you know, there's a tremendous amount of money spent in phone calls and transportation back and forth and that bothered me all during the movie, you know, who can afford that? You know, maybe these people in their positions can. I'm never going to be in that position where I can afford that kind of . . . but, you know, if I could, I would probably get involved with somebody with that. If I had the money to do it, you know.

The LCCs' referential interpretations lead them to dislike programs, movies, and music whose characters, plots, and lyrics confict with their worldview or remind them of disturbing past experiences:

Interviewer: Do you like Steven Spielberg movies?

Betsy (LCC): We liked *E.T.* I haven't seen the one [*Schindler's List*]. Because I'm not in. . . . I know it's all real, as far as what happened to the people, but I can't get into these . . . even when they have them on A&E like when they're showing how the concentration camps were and things like that. But this movie, everyone

I've talked to at work said the same thing as even what the critics are saying that
he really did a good job showing exactly what happened to these people for real.
I talked to a couple of people that seen the movie: "You have to see the movie."
Well, I can't watch that kind of movie. I know it's real and I know this happened
to these people, but I can't get into those kind of movies.

Interviewer: What kind of movies do you like?

Lynn (LCC): I like the more romantic ones. I try to steer away from the ones that
people die of anything, like any diseases or anything like that. . . . Because my
mom died of cancer in 1981 so I usually try to stay away from those.

Some HCCs also dislike and actively avoid scenes with graphic violence, but they
see a tension between the use of violence in a fictional art form and their visceral reactions to it and so do not reject disturbing scenes categorically. For example, like Betsy
above, Sue (HCC) has avoided seeing *Schindler's List* because of its graphic depiction
of genocide, but her rationale for doing so is quite different. Betsy wouldn't think of
seeing *Schindler's List* because the horrific scenes of concentration camps are an extremely
disturbing reality – she calls it "too real" – one that is too painful to voluntarily expose
oneself to. Sue, in contrast, knows that she also will have an intense emotional response
to *Schindler's List* but is conflicted about seeing it because she perceives the movie as
an artistic statement about an important event rather than just "reality."

Materialism versus idealism

Because LCCs are acculturated in materially constrained environments, the good life
is often cast in terms of having an abundance of things one likes and having things that
are popularly understood as luxurious (Bourdieu 1984, p. 177). These materialist tastes
are particularly influential in preferences for housing, food, and vacations. The LCC
informants grew up and currently live in relatively small living spaces – apartments,
trailers, and bungalows. So these informants value uniformly a large living space and
large yards and have pursued these goals to the limits of their financial resources.

Heather (LCC): Well it's kinda weird how we settled on this house. We weren't
looking to buy a house cause we had the house in [town near college], but it was
really, really small. Really small. I mean, our bedroom, you walked sideways
around the bed. It was small. . . . [Seeing the new house for the first time] First
word out – "Wow!" And we walked in and "Whoa!" 'cause it's really big.

I asked Heather if their old house was a Victorian since the town has a large Victorian
housing stock. She nods and continues to talk about the advantages of the floor plan in
the new house. In contrast, HCCs Anna and Rebecca do not evaluate old versus new
houses in terms of size. Instead they emphasize the charm and character of historic
houses that new houses lack. Other LCC informants who have the money to do so
(Ruth, Betsy, Susan) have also moved to larger houses on bigger pieces of property
away from neighbors, while others without the necessary income dream of doing so
("any house out of town where I have some space").

The LCCs with higher incomes consistently express preferences for consumption objects that are indicative of luxury and material abundance: Ruth and her husband own one Mercedes coupe and are shopping for more of these, they have recently acquired numerous antiques, and they enjoy dining regularly at the most expensive restaurant in the county. She tells a story about a birthday party she threw for her husband at this restaurant where they paid for dinner for a large group of friends. Similarly, Lisa and her husband recently dined at an expensive French restaurant, and she professes a desire to own a BMW someday, while Susan and her husband took up yachting on Cheseapeake Bay four years ago and have recently upgraded to a sailboat that can sleep seven people comfortably.

Desirable vacation destinations also reveal a yearning for abundance and luxury. For three of the LCCs an ocean cruise is the ideal vacation, and they speak excitedly about the cruises they have taken, describing the cornucopia of dining and social activities (Nancy: "If you're bored on a cruise, it's your own fault"). Cruises are an ideal expression of LCC materialist tastes because they are popularly constructed as luxurious and they promote an abundance of activities, food, and drink. Another LCC informant spoke in similar terms about her vacations to Poconos resorts:

> *Lisa (LCC):* [Poconos resorts] have all kinds of activities. . . . The next year we went to a different place and got the room with the pool in your own room and that place had horseback riding and carriage rides and it had a shooting range. . . . You pay like $400 a night and it's most of your meals and entertainment, mostly all the activities they had.

Many LCC informants cannot afford these objects of luxury and abundance, yet they too express a yearning for abundance and luxury within the universe of consumption objects that is economically feasible. Among LCCs, restaurants that serve buffet style are consensus favorites – the contemporary American equivalent of the French working-class meals characterized by "plenty" and "freedom" (Bourdieu 1984, p. 194):

> *David (LCC):* Well, generally when I go out to eat, I'm sitting there thinking, "If I was at home I could fix this, a bigger portion for a whole lot less money than what I'm paying here." It destroys the whole thing, because I'm thinking so much about how much. . . . they're making a bloody fortune off me for, you know. . . . where a buffet, you know, I'm in the driver's seat kind of you know. I know up front how much it's going to cost me and I can eat as much as I want. If I go away hungry it's my fault, you know.
>
> *Kate (LCC):* Of late, we've been going over to Milroy for seafood. Every Friday night they have a buffet. . . . They have crab legs, shrimp, all kinds of fish deep fried, with clams that are deep fried. Along with ham, chicken, beef. You have your beverage and delicious homemade dessert and soft ice cream for $6.95. . . . I wish you could see people eat those crab legs. They bring them out on trays and the minute they bring them to the salad bar, everyone rushes to get them.
>
> *Ruth (LCC):* At the Hotel Edison – it's a family-style that has chicken, turkey, or ham that you can pick; there's filling, and there's lettuce with that, Jell-O salad,

dessert, and coffee, all for like $10, you get all this food, as much as you want, they keep bringing it out, plus waffles. That's why it's his favorite thing to eat is to go there and have waffles.

In contrast, through informal and formal humanistic education, HCCs learn to emphasize and value metaphysical aspects of life. They emphasize the subjective production of experience through creative, contemplative, aestheticized, abstracted engagement with the world rather than brute encounters with an empirical reality. Material abundance and luxury are crass forms of consumption because they are antithetical to the ethereal life of the mind. Since HCCs have been raised with few material constraints, they experience material deprivation differently than LCCs. Material paucity is often astheticized, similar to functionalist design, into an ascetic style by HCCs (cf. Bourdieu 1984, p. 196). This said, it should also be noted that HCCs are at least as willing to make material acquisitions, often spending large amounts of money in so doing, provided that the good or activity supplies (or, at least, can be rationalized or imagined to supply) desired metaphysical experiences.

Materialism and idealism, then, refer to the cultural understandings that are inscribed in consumption practices rather than the quantities and physical characteristics of consumption objects. The HCCs are able to consume luxurious and scarce goods while at the same time negating connotations of waste, ostentation, and extravagance through tastes that assign value based on the ability of the good to facilitate metaphysical experience. In contrast, LCCs value abundance and luxury because these objects, with material and symbolic attributes far beyond what they understand as appropriate "use value," signify a seldom-experienced distance from material needs. For example, although HCCs tend to have higher incomes, they live in smaller houses than the economically secure LCCs, have smaller yards, and place little value on house size. Charles, whose yearly income is over $100,000, lives in a small ramshackle bungalow in a middle-class town; John lives in a tiny row house in the historic district of another nearby town; Kathryn, whose family income is nearly $100,000, lives in a nondescript townhouse with well-worn furniture. Sue and Margaret have both recently purchased smaller houses that are more manageable and livable than previous ones. This sense of material frugality is evinced throughout the day-to-day lives of this group. For example, Kathryn emphasizes several times that, because she was brought up in England during the war, she is very careful about her spending and is incensed when food is wasted. Though designer clothes very much appeal to her, she would never buy these items at full price, nor would she buy something that requires dry cleaning. Charles is a vegetarian whose standard lunch is some type of cooked grain (corn, wheat, barley, or oats) or soybeans with dried fruit and skim milk, and then some fruit or Jell-O for dessert. For dinner, he has rice, either plain or with some tomatoes or vegetables. Later in the evening, he eats raw vegetables, and he eats apples throughout the course of the day. He carries a briefcase and wears a leather jacket that he has owned for over 40 years.

Unlike the higher-income LCCs, HCCs never emphasize the extravagance of restaurants as a quality influencing their favorite places to dine. Rather, they use extravagance to contrast with their own tastes, which favor cuisines from other countries, often the peasant variety, eclecticism (interesting foods), artisanry, and casual atmospherics rather than the pretense associated with status-oriented restaurants. Since State College offers little in the way of such restaurants, HCCs expressed little interest in local dining. For example, Margaret denies the material symbolism of expensive restaurants connoting luxury and elegance and instead judges them on their ability to deliver experientially. Since none of the restaurants in the area deliver to her expectations, she occasionally dines at family-style restaurants but usually cooks at home. Similarly, Denise and her family usually go out for pizza and would only go to one of the expensive French restaurants "if one of my sons graduates from medical school or something." Kathryn occasionally takes out-of-town visitors to this restaurant but prefers a local salad bar because she is always watching her figure. Anna and her husband tried a "nice" restaurant near their home, found the food atrocious, and, so, they prefer going out for "bar food" instead.

Work and Taste

Another central premise of cultural capital theory is that class reproduction occurs through acculturation in particular skills and dispositions required for occupational success (Willis 1977). These cultural capital assets not only allow for occupational success but also become valorized as ends in themselves and so serve as a currency to accrue status in the parallel symbolic economy of consumption (Bourdieu 1984; Collins 1975; DiMaggio 1987).

HCC careers are characterized by an emphasis on symbolic analysis, the necessity to synthesize and manipulate information, to understand and respond to new situations, to innovate rather than follow rote instructions. Structured by an ideology of meritocracy and entrepreneurialism, these knowledge-driven occupations place a premium on professional autonomy, peer competition, and the pursuit of an ever-changing knowledge base needed to maintain leverage in the labor market. Further, in the contemporary United States, HCC employment is characterized by a highly mobile national labor market for professional positions that requires frequent integration into new social networks with heterogeneous interests and values (DiMaggio 1987), structuring a cosmopolitan sensibility among HCCs (Hannerz 1990; Merton 1957). In sum, the labor market conditions experienced by contemporary American HCCs structures their tastes, through the habitus, to emphasize cosmopolitanism, individuality, and self-actualization.

In contrast, LCCs participate in a local labor market for highly routinized jobs (Leidner 1993). Work is a job, rarely a career. While many LCC informants like their jobs, particularly because of the social outlet they provide, and express pride in what they do, they also describe the tasks they are asked to perform as mundane, providing little intellectual or creative challenge. Instead, working-class jobs are characterized by rote application of technique, high levels of surveillance, and a low emphasis on creativity and problem solving. Consumption by LCCs, then, is often constructed in opposition to rather than contiguous with work, pursuing experiences more exciting and fulfilling than work provides (Halle 1984; Rubin 1976). This orientation results in consumption practices that have a more autotelic cast compared with the instrumental, achievement orientation of HCCs. There is little sense of a competitive job market in which improving skills is critical in maintaining labor market leverage. Rather than individual achievement, working-class positions emphasize local communal mores (such as found in collective workplace practices to resist managerial control; see Burawoy 1979). The work of LCCs, then, structures tastes that emphasize the local, the autotelic, and the collective (cf. Rainwater et al. 1959).

Cosmopolitan versus local

The HCCs understand their social world to be much more expansive than do the LCCs. All of the HCC informants have lived in other states and five in other countries. They travel routinely throughout the United States and overseas to visit friends and family, for business, and for vacations. In contrast, only two of the LCC informants have lived outside the state in which they currently reside, they rarely travel outside of the mid-eastern states, and rarely mention friends or family outside the immediate vicinity:

Lynn (LCC): I like State College because you're within an hour of everything here, or two hours if you want to go to Harrisburg, a mall, or something like that.
Interviewer: Do you take vacations?
Lynn: Usually, I'll go to my grandparents [in the county] and cook dinner and go out to eat. During the school year usually the days I take off there is something going on at her school – chaperoned a field trip. I don't take a whole lot of days off.
Interviewer: Any other places?
Lynn: Yeah, a little bit, especially during the summer we usually go out to all the little carnivals [around the county].

The HCCs talk frequently about the trade-offs of moving to a rural college town, comparing the physical beauty and peaceful way of life to the lack of cultural resources and demographic diversity. Some feel that the balance attained by a university town is just right, but many feel that they have made a significant lifestyle sacrifice because of the paucity of cultural resources. Because HCCs construct their reference groups on a national and even international basis, a common issue is how to maintain these relationships while living in a small isolated community. For example, Kathryn regularly invites out-of-town friends from Washington, Philadelphia, and New York to stay "out in the country," and these friends reciprocate by putting her up in the city in order to get needed exposure to city life. Charles spends several months of the year visiting friends in Europe and the western United States. Margaret chose weaving as an avocation because it did not require her to become too invested in the local community: it had to "be moveable, to be portable, because I knew that it was likely that we'd be moving around a lot. And I needed something that I could take with me, that I wouldn't feel resentful because I had to pick up and leave something there I had invested time and energy in."

Tastes for news offer another informative example since what one considers relevant news depends on the breadth of the perceived social world in which one lives. The LCCs strongly favor the local newspaper because it covers the nexus that concerns them: they read the local section, obituaries, and local sports. The HCCs view the local newspaper as a poorly written and parochial substitute for big-city papers. For example, Anna uses hunting articles featured in the local newspaper as a synecdoche standing for the parochial LCC mores that she disdains:

> *Interviewer:* Why do you choose to subscribe to the [New York] *Times* as opposed to local newspapers?
>
> *Anna (HCC):* Well, we subscribed to the local newspaper and we stopped our subscription for I guess two major reasons. One is we were sick of seeing the dead animals that hunters have caught on the front page during hunting season. In color, yeah, the bears. And two is we were. . . . we felt that a lot of the editorials were really very. . . . I just think very conservative and I just wasn't . . . when they withheld "Doonesbury." . . . that was kind of the final blow.

Exoticism

The most powerful expression of the cosmopolitan–local opposition in the realm of tastes is through perceptions of and desires for the exotic – consumption objects far removed conceptually from what is considered to be normative within a category. Both HCCs and LCCs enjoy variety in their consumption to a greater or lesser extent, but they differ in their subjective understandings of what constitutes variety. What is exotic for LCCs is mundane for HCCs, and what is exotic for HCCs is unfathomable or repugnant for LCCs. And, while LCCs find comfort in objects that are familiar, HCCs seek out and desire exotic consumption objects.

Discussing food, LCCs offer conventional choices as their favorites for both home-cooked meals and restaurant meals, voicing uncertainty about or disdain toward more exotic choices. For example, while many HCCs eat Chinese food as a regular part of their diet and so do not use this cuisine as a signifier of exoticism, LCCs understand Chinese cuisine as exotic and so tend to avoid it. They rarely cook Chinese at home, they order Chinese dishes conservatively at restaurants by always choosing the same dish or often choosing dishes most similar to American food such as sweet-and-sour pork, and some avoid it completely: "I'll walk past a Chinese restaurant in State College and the smell of walking past it about gags me" (David).

The HCCs, however, frequently emphasize preferences for what they consider to be exotic foods. For example, Ronald asserts his distinctive tastes by describing a business trip to France where he enjoyed dishes that Americans generally consider inedible:

> *Interviewer:* Were there any dishes that you really liked when you were [in France]?
>
> *Ronald (HCC):* I guess the morel mushrooms were the part that I remember the most because they had them on practically everything and they're really great. I also had some very good horsemeat of all things. . . . It was a specialty of the house. It was a tenderloin where they . . . one of these thick French sauces on it. It was really great. . . . I've also been known to eat brains. If those are done properly by a French chef, they can be very good.

Similar differences were evident in entertainment choices as well. For whites who live outside of urban areas, one of the most culturally distant populations imaginable is the predominantly African-American ghetto. How informants position their tastes in regard to urban African-American cultural forms such as rap music, then, is revealing. The LCCs either adamantly dislike or express bewilderment about rap:

Interviewer: How about rap?

Lisa (LCC): No, that's one thing I don't like.

Interviewer: Why don't you like it?

Lisa: I don't know, I just never did, I just think it's silly, these people are talking or whatever you call it, rapping, I call it weird. Any fool can do that, that's my opinion of it when it came out.

Susan (LCC): I like all kinds of music. Classical . . . rap I hate. I shouldn't say I like all, because I do not like rap.

Interviewer: What don't you like about rap?

Susan: I can't understand it half the time. It's too noisy. Too confusing. I just don't like it. The beat. . . . I don't like the talking all the time.

Among HCCs, however, showing respect for and interest in rap expresses cosmopolitan tastes – the tastes of a person whose social world is not only geographically but also racially and economically inclusive:

Interviewer: What do you think of rap music?

Sue (HCC): What little I know about it, is that I think it's the kind of music that's really kind of neat. I like the beat of it. It's very unique culturally. But some of the rap music that is on the radio, I don't care for some of it. But I don't want to denounce all of rap music because of the actions of a few. I think there is a place for it.

Interviewer: So you just heard a little of it here?

Sue: Yeah. Even like some of Sister Souljah and some of those things. I've seen some on MTV. Every so often I'll turn it on. And, as I said, I think it's . . . it seems to have a lot of potential. I know it's very popular among African-Americans and expresses their culture. But I don't like the violence of some of it. And what appalls me about some of the rap music is that it's done by African-Americans but it really degrades, particularly African-American women.

Interviewer: When you say you think it has a lot of potential, what . . . ?

Sue: Well, it's . . . because I think it expresses emotion. I think the rhythm of it and the rhyming to it, is that you can get a lot of . . . what am I trying to say? The music kind of expresses what the words are trying to say. Because of that staccato beat to it. And that's what I find attractive about it. But it's what some of the words are saying that I don't like.

Consumer subjectivity as individuality versus local identity

Cultural historians and critics argue persuasively that the pursuit of individuality through consumption is a central characteristic of advanced capitalist (often "consumer") societies, the United States in particular (Baudrillard 1981; Ewen & Ewen 1992 [1982]; Jameson 1991). This characterization aptly describes HCCs, but is inaccurate for LCCs. Daniel Miller's (1987) conception of the relationship between consumption and subjectivity provides a framework that can be used to explain this difference. The process of consumption allows people to reappropriate meanings that have become objectified in consumption objects through mass production. In highly differentiated, monetized societies dominated by the proliferation and fragmentation of objectified culture (i.e., meanings inscribed in objects found in the public world such as material goods, services, places, media, architecture, etc.), this process of appropriation becomes increasingly problematic. So practical strategies evolve to allow for the construction of subjectivity through consumption.

Although consumer subjectivity is problematic for both HCCs and LCCs, they pursue different strategies to overcome this tension. Consumption practices always simultaneously express the contradictory tendencies of individual distinction and social affiliation, but HCCs and LCCs differentially inflect this dialectic. For LCCs, consumer subjectivity is produced through passionate and routinized participation in particular consumption activities. In most cases these subjectivities are explicitly collective, positioning one within an idioculture of other participants in the locality.

In contrast, given their cosmopolitan social milieu and their equation of subjectivity with individuality, consumer subjectivity for HCCs requires constructing what is perceived to be a unique, original style through consumption objects. The HCCs experience the potential for homogenization of commodity goods to a far greater extent than do LCCs and, thus, are far more energetic in their attempts to individuate their consumption. To express an individualistic sense of subjectivity through consumption is inherently contradictory in an era in which most goods are mass produced and experiences are mass consumed (see Clarke 1993; Holt 1995; Miller 1987), yet HCCs attempt to produce individual subjectivity through authenticity and connoisseurship.

Authenticity
The HCCs locate subjectivity in what they perceive to be authentic goods, artisanal rather than mass produced, and auratic experiences that are perceived as removed from, and so minimally contaminated by, the commodity form. The HCCs tend to disavow mass culture even when mass-produced goods are of high quality, and they camouflage their use of mass-produced goods when using them is unavoidable. John expresses this perspective explicitly in describing a particular plate that has captured his imagination:

Interviewer: What really interests you about this type of pottery right now?
John (HCC): Well, it's very beautiful. It has . . . first of all, I guess good art pottery
   is probably part of the arts and crafts movement. It's not mass produced. Most of
   it is not machine made. It has individuality. There isn't very much of it, relative
   to something like say to Roseville or some of the later potteries where they stamped
   out millions of them, you know . . . I think that our culture is to homogenize
   people. Homogenize their taste. And I think that, you know, you have subdivisions
   that are full of houses that all have vinyl siding and if you look at it in the right

light, they all have a bulge in where they didn't do it right. They'll never be any different color. It will never weather. There's the sameness that I find really – I don't know – it's suffocating. I mean you go into shopping malls, you go into one shopping mall and it seems like every other shopping mall.

Similarly, Kathryn decorates her home with one-of-a-kind artisanal objects, which she views as personally meaningful, rather than mass-produced goods, which express exchange value:

Kathryn (HCC): Things that matter to me are things that remind me of things, rather than things that have their own intrinsic value. In other words, I'd rather put something on the wall that was painted by a friend . . . than something an interior designer had just written up. . . . So I'd never hire an interior designer because I can't imagine living in someone else's stage set, you know.

She approaches her clothing in the same way, hunting through Washington, DC, thrift stores, out-of-town friends' hand-me-downs, even deceased people's clothing, in order to find articles that are unique and so more personalizable in relation to mass-merchandised fashion. Decommodified authenticity is taken to the extreme by Charles, who completely dismisses all of mass culture and, hence, professes complete ignorance of it. When asked about his favorite movies, he has a hard time recalling the last time he's seen one and, out of desperation, dredges up *Casablanca* as his favorite. He never watches television so he does not know of *Roseanne*, and he has barely heard of Madonna or Michael Jackson. Rather, he repeatedly redirects my questions to discussions of his own creations and those of his friends (such as the pieces of art he has scattered about his living room).

The desires of HCCs for decommodified authenticity are also prevalent in vacation preferences. Those LCCs who can afford to take a vacation uniformly favor popular destinations such as Disney World, Sea World, Atlantic City, and the beaches of New Jersey and Delaware. They also tend to prefer trips where the activities are planned by others and highly routinized (ocean cruises, "all-in-one" bus and plane tours, theme parks). In contrast, HCCs dislike and so tend to avoid what they perceive to be mass-produced (and, so, artificial) tourist activities and, instead, wherever they are, engage in a tourist style that seeks the "authentic" experience that is found through exploration and happenstance rather than routinized and popular activities (cf. MacCannell 1976). The authentic is achieved when one actually enters the "world" of a different social milieu, rather than gazing at it from outside:

Kathryn (HCC): When traveling, I go to see friends who know their way around. Two of my friends were artists from down in Manhattan, so we go and see them and eat with them. And it's sort of weird vegetarian restaurants in SoHo you know. . . . So we look for those things. Or we go and see another friend who's in theater and we eat at a Chinese restaurant he knows. We go and see people who know their way around. . . . If we go to Philadelphia, we stay with my sister and we go with them to their lives, which is kind of rather "Mainline." You know, sort of snooty, the Ivy League type. And that's fun for a change, too. And so we see friends and family and go with them into their lives.

The HCCs on occasion "do" popular tourist destinations such as Fisherman's Wharf in San Francisco. But their understanding of these activities – they defensively admit to doing so and suggest that these activities are frivolous compared with other more interesting experiences on the trip – expresses their interests in authentic, decommodified experiences in contrast with LCCs who view these same activities as highlights.

Country music provides another site for invoking tastes for decommodified authentic cultural objects versus the popular. Country music is sharply divided into "traditional" and "contemporary" genres (see Peterson 1978). The most popular radio station in the area plays contemporary country, while the traditional variant (which is usually understood to include bluegrass, swing, and Appalachian "old time" music as well as the "hard" country music of the 1950s–1970s exemplified by Hank Williams, Merle Haggard, and George Jones) is much less popular, played occasionally on the local National Public Radio (NPR) station and in live performances at some clubs in the area. For LCCs, traditional country music is the music they grew up with, a style that, except for the eldest informants, they now view as old-fashioned and backward. All but one who likes country, then, invokes the distinction between this style of country – often describing it as "twangy" and critically stereotyping the lyrical content (Heather: "The guy talks about his dog dying") – and "new" or "contemporary" country. The LCCs strongly prefer the latter because it is has a modern sensibility with lyrics that aptly express their self-understandings. The three HCCs who express a preference for country, however, have little interest in contemporary country. Instead they favor bluegrass and other much less popular traditional styles that are described as original, unique varieties of American music, rather than a music genre that speaks to their lives. (These different tastes for country also provide another example of LCC's referential vs. HCC's critical interpretations of cultural texts described above.)

Connoisseurship
While authenticity involves avoiding contact with mass culture, connoisseurship involves reconfiguring mass cultural objects. Applying a highly nuanced, often idiosyncratic approach to understand, evaluate, and appreciate consumption objects, connoisseurs accentuate aspects of the consumption object that are ignored by other consumers. Thus, personal style is expressed through consumption practice even if the object itself is widely consumed. This stylistic practice necessitates the development of finely grained vocabularies to tease out ever more detailed nuances within a category, the expression of opinionated and often eclectic evaluations of alternatives, and the ability to engage in passionate appreciation of consumption objects meeting one's calculus of "quality" within a category.

All HCCs have at least one category for which they have developed the requisite knowledge and interest of a connoisseur and many have several such categories. John, a quintessential connoisseur, expresses such tastes for virtually every topic in the interview. We spend about 20 minutes talking about oriental rugs, touring his house to admire and evaluate the dozen or so rugs spread throughout. He waxes enthusiastically about their qualities, such as the use of vegetable dye, that make a rug beautiful rather than ordinary.

> *John (HCC):* By the way, these are all vegetable dyes as opposed to aniline dye, which is another level of sophistication that I've worked my way up to. I've reached the point where when I see something that's done with aniline dyes, I don't like it any more. . . . I mean this is a new Turkish carpet (points to a rug), but they're once again using vegetable dyes. Well . . . I know we're running out of time but I want to show you something. Now is that (points to another rug) bad color or is that bad color?
>
> *Interviewer:* It's different.
>
> *John:* This is a very nice rug. But this is aniline dye and that's vegetable dye. And it says it all right there.

Similarly, Sue approaches going out to eat as a connoisseur. She purposely accumulates specialized knowledge about cuisines and restaurants that she uses to construct a distinctive style, leveraged as important interactional resource to interact with her HCC friends.

> *Sue (HCC):* I really like going out to a good meal and having a glass of wine and making an event out of eating. And that's true when I travel, too. I'm one of these people. . . . I research restaurants when I travel and I pick out restaurants in various areas where I'm going if they have good reputations because when I travel I think food is as important as the sights I see. You know, I can skimp on a hotel, but I don't want to skimp on good food. And maybe it's because my lifestyle is so hectic that I enjoy being waited on. But that's something that I really do enjoy doing.
>
> *Interviewer:* When you say it's like an event for you, what do you mean by that?
>
> *Sue:* Well, it's something I look forward to. It's something I find relaxing. I have . . . I love eating. I mean talk to my friends at work. I mean, you know, I have a reputation for loving to eat. And I do, I love to try new and different foods. With the exception of insects and octopus, there's very few things I don't like to eat. So . . . I tell you, to me that's a very important recreational activity.

In addition to the application of detailed knowledge and the accompanying enthusiasm these minutiae bring forth, eclecticism is, in addition to an expression of cosmopolitanism, an important dimension of connoisseurship. Eclecticism allows connoisseurs to construct distinctive tastes in categories in which the use of conventional goods is difficult to avoid because choices are largely constrained to a limited range of mass-produced goods. In categories such as interior decor, clothing, and food, in which consuming often requires combinations of goods (e.g., furniture and decorative items are combined to set up a living room or a bedroom, clothes are combined into an outfit, foods are combined into a meal), eclecticism can take the form of combinatorial inventiveness. For example, while LCCs always offer normative combinations when asked about what they prepare for "special meals" (e.g., turkey dinner "with all the fixings" such as stuffing, potatoes, a green vegetable, gravy, and cranberry sauce), HCC connoisseurs break down these conventions. For example, Kathryn's special meal is an intercontinental pastiche bearing no resemblance to normative combinations (all the more individualized due to the exotic components):

Interviewer: What would you prepare for a special meal?

Kathryn (HCC): Start with a cold soup like vichyssoise or gazpacho, my husband makes a spicy Jamaican chicken with rice, or maybe trout sauced with red wine base with Cointreau, and make a big salad with bitter greens, and a different dessert such as a great big souffle or something like that. We have wine with meals and my husband makes planter's punch.

The same pattern is also evident in discussion of interior decor. Whereas the LCCs who express design preferences favor conventional styles of "country" or "Victorian," HCCs explicitly disavow following a style that is widely adhered to and, instead, talk about how they mix and match to create their own personal look.

For reception-oriented categories such as reading, television and movies, and music, people cannot actively combine different consumption objects, so eclecticism takes a different form: instead of eclectic combinations, connoisseurs express eclectic tastes by crossing or subverting institutionalized genre boundaries. The LCCs typically identify their movie tastes (e.g., "drama" or "action/adventure") their reading choices (e.g., "historical romance"), and music tastes ("contemporary country") using a popularly constructed genre distinction. Compare this to John, who describes his music tastes as beginning in high school with chamber music (for which he continues to prefer to listen to particular recordings on record rather than compact disc), moving on to the Statler Brothers, George Harrison, folk music by artists such as Pete Seeger and the Weavers, Gilbert and Sullivan, the Beach Boys, and "lots of Vivaldi; lots and lots and lots and lots and lots and lots of Vivaldi."

The HCCs' regard for connoisseurship is also evident when they discuss those categories in which they have not invested the resources to develop fine-grained tastes. For these, they evaluate their actions against a connoisseur standard and discuss, apologetically or defensively, their relative neglect:

Interviewer: What are some of your favorite meals generally?

Rebecca (HCC): Okay. Well, this will be a real short section of your interview. I'm not a person who is picky about food. I'm not a person who can tell you necessarily what the ingredients in something are. I'm not a cook. I'm able to cook when I have to. But it's not a priority for me. I can eat the same thing every day, you know.

In contrast, because LCC subjectivity is local and collective, consumer subjectivity depends on community acknowledgment of particular tastes and practices. Rather than seek out authentic decommodified goods and apply idiosyncratic tastes to mass goods, LCC subjectivity parallels the role of insider core members of consumer subcultures (Schouten & McAlexander 1995): they develop the requisite knowledge, skills, and social capital within a particular activity that then become key resources for the construction of subjectivity by self and others. For example, Nancy and her husband started a folk dancing club and spend most of their free time organizing events, going to dance practices, and socializing with some of the members who have become very close friends. From the interview, it is clear that she thinks of herself, first and foremost, as a folk dancer; it is through this avocation that she attains much of her subjective sense of self. Yet, she does not claim this as a distinctive identity. Instead, her sense of self vested in this avocation is a communal one, located in sharing great enthusiasm and development of skills with like-minded others. This is a particularly powerful source of identity for Nancy, not because she has carved out a qualitatively distinctive style, but because, through her devotion, she is located at the nucleus of this local group. Likewise, Katie and her husband have played cards with the same group of six or eight friends two or three times per week for many years. Card playing has become a central constitutive element of Katie's identity, one that exists only to the extent that it is jointly constructed with local others.

Because for LCCs subjectivity does not require asserting individuality in relation to mass culture or normative local tastes, there is no contradiction between subjectivity, mass consumer goods, and the conventions of mass culture. In fact, mass goods and conventions often provide useful resources from which a local identity is constructed. For example, Heather prides herself on wearing clothes with a nautical theme, which she will buy whenever she comes across such clothing at a local department store. Even when describing individuated consumption objects, LCCs rarely camouflage their use of mass-produced objects:

> *Interviewer:* What are some of your favorite meals for dinner?
> *Lynn (LCC):* I like my chicken broccoli casserole.
> *Interviewer:* How do you make that?
> *Lynn:* You just put everything in a casserole pan, cut up your cooked chicken and your cooked vegetables and you can use mixed vegetables and potatoes, and you have a thing of broccoli soup and one thing of broccoli and one broccoli cheese and just throw that in with milk and put it in the oven for 15 minutes and cut out biscuits that come in a round metal can, cut them up and put them on the top and then throw it back in until it's brown. It's pretty good and it's real easy.

Since LCCs do not participate in social worlds in which subjectivity is constructed through individuated consumption, they seldom use the connoisseur's vocabulary of expertise and passion to talk about their preferences. Interview questions that HCCs use as opportunities to express fine-grained sensibilities provoke terse responses from LCCs, who understand these questions to ask for trivial expressions of preference rather than as an invitation for a consumerist performance. For example, Joseph has an impressive collection of 19 rifles hanging on his living-room wall. When I inquire about the guns, Joseph makes clear that he is not so much interested in talking about different models and styles of guns to express connoisseur tastes (he would add "almost anything" for the right price) as he is in telling stories about acquiring and using the guns, such as trading with a friend for a gun, hunting deer and wild turkey with friends, and teaching his sons how to hunt, which invest the guns with particularized local meanings.

Ruth's description of her antiques is particularly poignant in this regard. Through much determination and sacrifice over the last 20 years, Ruth and her husband have raised their income to the upper strata of the State College area. Now that they have reached this position, they are engaged in a project to evolve their lifestyle to match their economic position. Yet, even though Ruth lives in a nice neighborhood, has acquired a large collection of antiques, and entertains expensively, she does not convey an HCC style because she has not acquired the performative means to do so. Although most of her free time over the past five years has been devoted to antiquing, she has not developed the vocabulary of appreciation and evaluation to convey this interest as does an HCC connoisseur such as John:

Interviewer: How did you get into [antiques]?

Ruth (LCC): I always liked antiques, but I never had them. I would go to garage sales. I mean, like 10 years ago, when I was buying stuff at auctions and putting it in the garage, and after the children went and I said "We're gonna re-do the house." And so I started getting, I decided I was gonna do it. And I like Victorian and country and . . . so I went to the garage and started pulling these things out and then it just, I would buy more. (laughs)

Interviewer: You just got more, more involved in it?

Ruth: Yeah.

Interviewer: And so how'd you find out about where all this stuff is, and which pieces you wanted?

Ruth: Oh, just. . . . If I like it, I buy it. I mean, I, I look. Every weekend I look. (laughs) I made some purchases last weekend. In State College at a garage sale that picture for $35.

Interviewer: What, what do you like about the picture?

Ruth: Oh, I just like. . . . It just has personality. Something like a . . . different than new things. (laughs). . . . Plus if it gives you a little more . . . a homey feeling, I think. I don't know, maybe it's my age. (both laugh) This sofa here, I paid $22 for it. But I ended up reupholstering it. It costs me like $700 to refinish it, so, still in all $722. Where can you get a sofa like that?

Interviewer: Are there certain types of things you're looking for?

Ruth: I like Victorian things [pause] I have country things in my kitchen. [pause] But, I just keep looking. [pause] If it appeals to me, we buy it.

Instead of describing her antiques in connoisseur terms, she reverts to pragmatic evaluations (e.g., good prices). Throughout the interview, she is uncomfortable making any strong and specific evaluative claims about the qualities of her antiques compared to others; she just likes them. The interview was uncomfortable for both parties because we both understood that some of my questions encouraged her to express connoisseur tastes and that she was not able to respond as an HCC person might. She quickly became conscious of this inability and felt uncomfortable; likewise, I understood that my questions put her in an uncomfortable position because she had trouble responding as she wanted to, which made me feel uncomfortable.

By comparison, for HCCs, evaluating consumption objects is a primary, sometimes even dominant aspect of consuming. Thus, in many HCC interviews the mention of even the most mundane of consumption objects (e.g., water!) led, with little prompting, to lengthy soliloquies elaborating in great detail the prized and disliked qualities within a category. In these interviews, I was often left with the impression that a primary attraction of many consumption objects is that they serve as resources for very detailed and opinionated conversations about the relative merits of different goods within a category. For HCCs, the interview itself was clearly an enjoyable experience since it closely paralleled this style of consuming.

Leisure as self-actualization versus autotelic sociality

The HCCs place tremendous stock in self-actualizing experiences. So, while opposed to material abundance, experiential abundance is highly valued. The HCCs evince an orientation toward leisure that mirrors their approach to work: they seek out diverse, educational, informative experiences that allow them to achieve competence, acquire knowledge, and express themselves creatively (see Lamont 1992). This is not to argue that HCCs understand leisure as an instrumental pursuit but, rather, that the intrinsic satisfactions of leisure accrue from learning, achieving, and creating. For example, Rebecca is a history buff who has pursued this interest in a prototypically American HCC style. Following other family members, she joined the Daughters of the American Revolution (DAR), where she has risen through the ranks and now gives dozens of history lectures every year to DAR chapters around the state, does her own history research, and plans to write a book. Margaret offers a different example of the same phenomenon: rather than complement her work, she has constructed her leisure to substitute for the primary characteristics of HCC work that she has forgone. Educated at an elite university, she acknowledges considerable ambivalence in her "choice" to be a housewife and mother in order to support her husband's academic career. But she is adamant in framing her primary avocation, weaving, as equivalent to a profession: "I do a lot of weaving. It's basically what I did instead of a job." She attends conferences, subscribes to numerous publications, participates in a study group to keep up-to-date on new techniques and styles, maintains an informal network of weavers with whom she shares such information, and constantly strives to improve her skills and her ability to create new patterns:

Margaret (HCC): I'm basically a student. I mean, I see myself that way. I do a lot of exploratory weaving. I gamble on certain challenges. Try new things. Win some, lose some . . . There are a couple of ways of approaching weaving. One of them is to get into an area and push it. . . . The "pick-up" is specifically an area that I have really pushed both in terms of the design, in terms of the materials used, and in the technique that you use to do it. Previous to that, I spent about two years doing coverlet structures, where I was doing a lot of research and talking to people that had old drafts. And working out various kinds of structures. . . . So I would take these structures and rework them. Taking an idea and manipulating it.

Like HCCs, LCCs also participate in many hobbies in which they apply skills they have learned and further hone these skills. Yet, whereas HCCs understand these hobbies as reflections of and means to accumulate valued skills and knowledge, and as a site for achievement, LCCs emphasize their autotelic aspects – the intrinsic enjoyment that results from the knowledgeable application of skills and talents with others who also enjoy the activity. For example, Joseph enjoys talking on his citizen's band radio, not primarily because it allows him to advance skills or express creative talents, but because it provides an interesting and routinized form of social interaction:

Interviewer: How about hobbies? What would you consider to be your hobby?

Joseph (LCC): I like my CB. I have a citizen's band radio.

Interviewer: So what do you do with it? Do you have a home unit here?

Joseph: Yeah, it's up in my radio home, yeah. I have a home unit. Oh, I talk everywhere on it. I talk to people all over on it.

Interviewer: How much time a week do you spend talking on your . . .

Joseph: Four hours a day or something like that, you know. Off and on. It depends on what kind of . . . like if you got too much static in the air, you just can't hear nothing. It's just all noise. But then when it's . . . like when you got skip. That's people you know . . . say people down in Georgia talking. That's called skip. They're skipping up here. And then when you can get into them, you can sit and talk to them.

Interviewer: Why is that more fun?

Joseph: Well, it just makes contact. You know, it's making contact just to see how far you can get out. And to see . . . it's more or less like . . . I don't know. What would you say, a long distance friend or something like that you know. To see if you can actually . . . you don't realize how many people is out there on them radios. Oh, there are like millions. It's just a challenge to see if you can get back to them, you know, some other date. But when I do, I keep a log of . . . with their call number and the state and what time it is and what channel it was on and the climate outside, the weather. So, you know, I guess it makes a lot of determination the weather and that.

An example that draws out the distinctiveness of HCC and LCC leisure practices is the consumption of nature. In part because of the locale of the study, both HCCs and LCCs engage in extensive consumption of nature – participating in activities such as gardening, hunting, fishing, and hiking. However, HCC and LCC nature consumption differs considerably. The HCCs use nature as a resource that allows them to express their creative abilities:

Sue (HCC): Yeah, I like working in the yard. I find it creative and I also find it relaxing . . . I don't cut the grass. We have some guys that come and do that. And they do some of the heavy trimming too. I do everything else.

Interviewer: Why do you like working in the yard?

Sue: There's just something nice about planting something and watching it grow. You know, it's just – especially if you work with flowers or perennials and trying to arrange things and work with colors. Because particularly when you work with perennials you have something permanent. They come back year after year. And I really enjoy working with perennials.

Interviewer: So what do you try and do when you say you're planting them and working with colors?

Sue: It's kind of like redecorating a house. About two years ago one fall, I decided to redecorate my yard and I dug up all of my perennials and I split them and I moved them all over the yard. Then in the spring they all came up and I got to see the yard look very different.

Margaret (HCC): This is the most exciting place we've lived in that respect. Because this basically was our yard. It was basically my yard to design. And I did. To a large extent there was some stuff here which we left when I looked around. But basically, I designed the beds, designed what went into them. Chose my plants, and filled it up.

Whereas HCCs use nature primarily as a site for the expression of individual creativity and achievement, LCCs tend to commune with rather than express themselves through nature. This communion is often social, "communitas" in Durkheim's terminology. Describing their annual Canadian fishing trip, Katie is adamant that her practice is essentially "being in" nature, no more: "What I like about fishing is just sitting next to the stream, and watching the stream. It's really relaxing." Similarly, Lynn takes regular drives in the country, which she enjoys as a holistic experiential treat. Betsy and her husband have a trailer in a trailer park out in the country where they go every summer weekend to "watch the grass grow." Joseph delights in the experiential qualities of his hunting trips, describing the peacefulness of being out by himself in the woods, interacting with animals:

Interviewer: What do you like about hunting?

Joseph (HCC): Deer hunting, I like to sit and hear the deer sneaking up, you know. Turkey, I like to hear them call, you know, when you call. I like to hear them call and how they work into you and how you work them in. But most of all, I like the way that you can just sit back and it gives you a peace of mind, you know, you can do a lot of thinking and there's nobody there to waken you up except for the turkey or the deer, you know. It's just relaxing out in the woods. You get closer to God out there, too.

HCCs and LCCs consume nature differently because they value different dimensions of the experience. For LCCs the value of leisure inheres primarily in the experience itself and the use of this experience as a social resource, while for HCCs leisure is valued, like other commodities, as a resource that allows for individual expression and personal achievement.

Discussion

Contemporary American ideology holds that tastes are individualized and disinterested. "Be your own dog!" the Red Dog beer ad shouts. But tastes are never innocent of social consequences. To be "cultured" is a potent social advantage in American society, providing access to desirable education, occupations, social networks, and spouses. Conversely, to grow up in conditions that deny the accumulation of cultural capital leads to exclusion from these privileged social circles and condescension and demands of deference from elites, a form of "symbolic violence" (Bourdieu 1984) that is rarely acknowledged because tastes are understood as idiosyncratic choices.

Buttressing this ideology, academic scholarship has often interpreted the oft-noted decline in the potency of consensus markers of class position as a democratic leveling of consumption into class-neutral lifestyles. From the perspective of Warnerian social class theory, the 20 interviews reported here would likely confirm this assertion. I find, like many other studies, that LCCs consume many of the same goods and participate in many of the same activities as HCCs. In fact, supposed consensus symbols of the middle class are sometimes mentioned more often by LCCs: the only two people who enjoy watching golf are from this group, as is the only person who wants to see an opera.

But, in advanced capitalist countries, overlap in the purchase of goods and participation in activities across classes does not necessarily imply the absence of class patterning of consumption (Holt 1997b). Using a reformulated version of Bourdieu's theory of cultural capital and taste that emphasizes the boundary marking capabilities of mass consumption practices, I demonstrate that consumption patterns do vary by cultural capital across a variety of dimensions. I detail six dimensions of taste and consumption practice that distinguish HCCs from LCCs: material versus formal aesthetics, referential versus critical appreciation, materialism versus idealism, local versus cosmopolitan taste, consumer subjectivity as local identity versus individuality, and leisure as self-actualization versus autotelic sociality.

These six dimensions suggest an extension of the most important empirical finding supporting Bourdieu's theory: that HCC "omnivores" tend to like and actively consume a much broader range of both popular and high entertainments than LCC "univores" (DiMaggio & Useem 1978; Peterson & Simkus 1992; Wilensky 1964). Sociologists have argued that since HCCs must interact successfully in heterogeneous social milieus, and since consumption serves as a primary interactional resource for such interaction, they tend to have more diverse tastes (DiMaggio 1987). I also find that HCCs consume a wider variety of genres and styles than do LCCs, but the explanation that these differences are driven by omnivorous versus univorous tastes glosses over a more complex phenomenon. Rather than tastes for diversity, these findings suggest that omnivore consumption is structured by a confluence of tastes – cosmopolitanism, self-actualizing leisure, exoticism, decommodification, connoisseurship – all of which contribute to diverse consumption patterns. In other words, these findings suggest that the widely used concepts of "omnivore" and "univore" tastes conflate more specific dimensions of consumer tastes and practices that covary.

Materialism as a class practice

In consumer research, materialism has been defined as a value or trait characterizing those who use possessions to attain happiness and status (Belk 1985; Richins & Dawson 1992). In order to conceptualize materialism within the worldview of personality psychology, this literature extracts the term from the everyday social situations in which it is deployed and reconstitutes it as an idealist, individualist analytic construct. Such an approach cannot produce a theory of materialism that explains what we observe in everyday life: What are the conditions that have produced materialism as a potent cultural term and dominant practice? And what are the social consequences of its practice?

A defining characteristic of modern capitalist societies is that human relationships are transmogrified into the symbolic qualities of goods produced for sale, what Marx called "commodity fetishism." The competitive dynamics of advanced capitalism have led to the ever expanding colonization by marketplace semiotics of experiences that have historically been enacted in social domains other than commodified material culture (e.g., consider religion, health, family relationships). The experiences of social life that create and sustain human subjectivity, such as love, prestige, security, fear, happiness, joy, and anticipation, are increasingly reconstituted as "benefits" in the world of commodities. Rather than material mediators of culture (as McCracken [1986] would have it), consumer goods now sit at the cultural epicenter. Postmodern consumer society is the logical culmination of this migration of meanings and values from relationships with people to relationships with market goods and spectacles.

Materialism is one important mode in which social identities are constructed through interaction with the marketplace. To understand materialism requires understanding who consumes in a materialist style, who uses the term "materialist" to characterize whom, and the social consequences that result from these practices. Reflecting their workplace ethos and relative advantage in the status marketplace, people whose capital volume is strongly weighted toward economic rather than cultural capital tend to consume using a materialist style of consumption. For economic elites, this means pursuing the newest fashions, the latest technologies, the most luxurious, pampering products and services. For the majority with relatively small and declining incomes, living in a society that so emphasizes material satisfactions constructs relative material deprivation as an intense lack, and, thus, their tastes are structured around attaining glimpses or simulacra of elite comforts.

But, with materialism as the dominant status game, how are cultural elites to distinguish themselves? The only option, structurally speaking, is to develop a set of tastes in opposition to materialism: consuming that emphasizes the metaphysical over the material – idealism – is prestigious currency in the cultural sphere. Hence, HCCs have constructed "materialist" as a pejorative term – synonymous with "showy," "ostentatious," "gaudy," and "unrefined" – to denigrate the practices of people whose tastes are formed by economic capital.

It is a misnomer, then, to equate materialism with status seeking. Materialists are no more (or less) interested in prestige than HCC idealists. Instead, they seek to acquire prestige in a particular status game (materialism) structured around particular practices (acquiring goods and participating in activities that are inscribed with economic symbolism: luxury, leisure, pampering, extravagance). From the perspective of HCCs, those who participate in this mode of status consumption seem particularly desperate to win prestige from their consumption. But, as I demonstrate in this study, cultural elites have their own set of exclusionary practices in which they invert materialism to affirm their societal position. Thus, psychometric scales that isolate materialism as a vulgar form of status claiming, while leaving uninterred the status claims embodied in the practices of cultural elites, serve to reinforce rather than challenge the exclusionary class boundaries erected by HCC consumption. Idealists are also inveterate status seekers who are just as capable of selfishness as materialists.

But what about the societal and environmental consequences of materialism? It is important to disentangle the socially beneficial aspects of idealism from its use as a pernicious symbolic boundary. To do so, we need to recognize that cultural elites are in a privileged position to pursue alternatives to materialism both because they typically are socialized in environments free of material scarcity and also because they reap prestige from idealist practices. Psychometric scales can be useful in weeding the negative social consequences of idealist consumption from its enormous positive possibilities, but they need to be informed by a social reflexivity that acknowledges that values, and social effects, are built into these measures. For example, to understand and ameliorate environmental degradation rather than perpetuate class boundaries, materialism research needs to examine the relationship between materialist and idealist consumption practices and the amount of material resources expended and pollution generated. I am not convinced that idealist consumption is necessarily more environment-friendly than materialist consumption. One can abhor the idea that happiness and identity can be derived through objects and still mail order an abundance of experience-facilitating goods that overload dumps with packaging materials. And, alternatively, one can be extremely materialistic as measured by psychometric scales yet consume many fewer material resources than those who profess to be idealist, as the status condensed in a single pair of Nikes worn by poor African–American urban teens attests.

Decommodification as a class practice

Cultural studies of consumption practice often describe how consumers physically and symbolically transform branded goods as they coproduce collective, family, and individual meanings (see, e.g., Miller 1987). Recently, Levy (1996) has challenged Wallendorf and Arnould's contribution to this literature in which they describe how people decommodify branded goods to make "from scratch" Thanksgiving dinners. Outlining the orthodox marketing position, Levy argues that brands, because they are differentiated through the marketing mix, are already decommodified. Brands offer a diverse plethora of images and personalities, Levy argues, that individuals selectively combine to express a unique identity. Thus, securing subjectivity through consumption of the brand identities offered in the marketplace is a seamless process in which we all engage without tension or contradiction.

Levy's perspective mirrors the ideology of consumer society, one proffered by marketers but enacted only problematically by consumers. Wallendorf and Arnould's discussion of decommodification does not address the degree to which marketed goods are differentiated from generic products, as Levy would have it, but with the difficulties that people have in making use of the images and identities offered in the marketplace in constructing a personal sense of self. The foundational axiom of consumer society is that individual subjectivities are sustained by consuming products that carry, and thus bestow through consumption, distinctive identities (Horkheimer & Adorno 1972). But its continued expansion has yielded a cultural contradiction that is central to the current postmodern cultural condition: as marketed meanings proliferate exponentially and circulate at an accelerated rate, their semiotic potency, their vitality as "real" lived meanings that can be tapped through consumption, is sapped. Decommodification is one process through which people attempt to resolve this contradiction.

I argue that decommodification has become an important resource used in consumer societies to form class boundaries. The HCCs experience this contradiction of post-modern culture more intensely than the LCCs because individualized subjectivity is so central to their habitus. The LCCs more readily accept the marketized meanings of branded products, but, in contrast to Levy's arguments, this is precisely because they are less concerned with the brand's claims to impart particularized subjectivities. Instead, they treat brands much as economists theorize, as signals of functional utility and economic scarcity. The HCCs, however, often seek to avoid market-constructed images because they view these subjectivities as contrived. The problematic for HCCs becomes how to distinguish one's consumption in a world in which market offerings have in some sense tainted the possible alternatives. One strategy is to leave the marketplace altogether or at least to consume in a manner that disguises the mass market.

This finding helps to explain the growing success of marketers who position products targeted to HCCs as authentic (as opposed to mass-produced). A good example is the recent popularity of hand-crafted microbrews among HCCs, which are understood as an artisanal product in comparison to megalithic brands such as Budweiser. Major brewers have responded both by feigning smallness and craft production to capture part of this market as well constructing a defensive counter-positioning as a macrobrew that opposes elite HCC tastes. Similarly, persistent opposition to Wal-Mart stores can be read as a class-marked debate. The HCCs, with access to and influence over the media, oppose Wal-Mart in favor of small, locally owned shops in the downtown areas of towns and small cities, while working-class LCCs are enthusiastic about Wal-Mart's presence, if the chain's market success in merchandising to this group is any indication. HCCs have strong feelings about small owner-operated local retail stores that sell artisanal hard-to-find goods. Such stores, often found in boutique shopping districts in gentrified areas of cities, are perceived as offering a decommodified retail experience that allows for individuation. Of course, these stores are just as implicated in the exchange nexus, but, in terms of signification, their relationship to commodity and mass culture is less apparent. If Levy was correct that brands are seamless "extensions of identity," then we would not expect to witness these marketplace phenomena.

The class organization of aesthetic experience

Critical theorists of both modern and postmodern persuasions have claimed that social structures (e.g., social groups based on categories such as gender, ethnicity, and class; institutions such as religion, education, and the family) have become of negligible importance in organizing cultural activity. Frankfurt School theorists argued that in late capitalist societies, mass cultural products are used to obscure true class differences (Horkheimer & Adorno 1972). The culture industries train consumers of different classes to consume similar products in a similar passive, stupifying manner. Genre and brand differences are assumed to be superficial, since the underlying consumption practices are the same for mass consumption. Postmodernists (e.g., Baudrillard 1981) see the same superficiality but conceive of the consumption experience in a much more producerly vocabulary. Instead of assuming that industrialists structure consumption to disguise class relations, postmodernists place the determinative power in the declassifying effects of postmodern culture. No longer influenced by traditional social structures, consumers play with free-floating signifiers to continually reconstruct themselves using whatever imagery they find pleasurable (Featherstone 1991; Kellner 1989; Lyotard 1984). Both argue that consumption practices are no longer shaped significantly by social class. However, their description of the predominant style of consumption in advanced capitalist societies could not be more different. Critical theorists describe consumers who engage in the passive reception of lowest-common-denominator entertainment, a numbing rather than self-actualizing, affect-laden rather than thought-provoking, activity. Postmodern theorists describe consumers pursuing a highly stylized, aesthetic project, using the whirlwind resources of consumer culture to fabricate idiosyncratic meanings.

This study suggests that neither version accurately describes contemporary American consumption. Instead of a macrohistorical condition, it appears that each theory is describing, in an overzealous, exaggerated manner, a particular class lifestyle. Postmodern theorists describe, not a general condition of postmodernity, but a critical aspect of HCC lifestyle in advanced capitalist societies. The pursuit of individual style in the face of pervasive homogenizing forces is problematic only for HCCs for whom originality and authenticity is a highly valued mark of distinction in their social milieu. The LCCs do not encounter this problem, since they pursue lifestyles in a less individuated manner that neither precludes commodities nor demands unique identities. The phenomenon that postmodern theorists interpret as indicative of the ultimate separation between the cultural and the social is actually a potent cultural cue distinguishing HCCs from LCCs. One might speculate that postmodern theorists are embedded so deeply in the HCC habitus that they are unable to muster the requisite sociological reflexivity to note that the ability to playfully aestheticize a wide range of consumption objects is esteemed, and so has become naturalized, in their social circles, but not in those of lower social classes. As evidence, consider that Lyotard (1984, p. 76) describes eclecticism, conceptualized much the same as in this study, as a general characteristic of the contemporary postmodern condition, rather than as a significant characteristic of the HCC experience of postmodernity. Similarly, critical theorists draw upon their backgrounds as leading cultural producers as a baseline to group all those with less aestheticized practices together. Their class-centric lens does not provide them with the interpretive sensitivity to locate more subtle differences in class consumption. To promulgate their preferred view, they fall back on a model of object signification, correctly observing that objects of popular culture are increasingly distributed across all classes but ignoring that different classes can use the same popular cultural objects as resources for different lifestyles.

Future research

While this study demonstrates that, when modified to account for sociohistorical context, Bourdieu's theory can be used to excavate social class differences in contemporary American consumption, several important lacunae remain. First, the theory suggests that consumption practices are used as a basis for affiliation and distinction in everyday interaction and so serve to perpetuate social stratification. This study provides only partial evidence describing how these tastes are used in everyday life (based on how tastes were used to interact with the upper-middle-class interviewer and through occasional evaluations of others' tastes in the interviews). Field research is needed to investigate directly the micropolitics of consumption.

Second, this study focuses solely on cultural capital, setting aside two other important issues in Bourdieu's theory: the composition of capital (i.e., the percentage of capital that is economic versus cultural) and the trajectory of capital (i.e., the increases and declines in capital volume through one's lifetime and intergenerational transfer of capital). In *Distinction*, Bourdieu analyzes both economic and cultural capital, discussing the difficult processes whereby one form is converted into the other. Adding analysis of capital composition structured by occupation and income would add considerable complexity and explanatory power to this typology. Similarly, it is important to consider how consumption patterns are shaped by trajectory. For example, a person raised in a high-cultural-capital family who drops out of college to practice a trade is likely to be a quite different consumer than a person raised in a low-cultural-capital family, is the first generation to attend college, and has embarked on a middle-level management career, even though their cultural capital resources are, quantitatively, about the same.

Third, for reasons of tractability and exposition, this study divides the cultural capital continuum into five discrete levels and then focuses on the top and bottom quintiles of cultural capital resources in a small city. Such a study leaves out other important class positions deserving of study: the middle three quintiles, where there tends to be more mobility than either in the high or low groups; the poor who live outside the formal economy and whom Bourdieu does not consider in his theory; and urban cultural producers who would rank even higher than the HCCs in this study and, based on previous research, are likely to have distinctive consumption practices of their own.

Fourth, this study examines social class differences apart from other important social categories such as gender and race. Yet, since W. E. B. DuBois' s seminal writings on race and class, social theorists have sought to understand the complex interpenetration of these categories (see Hall [1992] for a sophisticated recent example). For example, an interesting extension of this study would be to explore how class and gender interact. If American women tend to exhibit an "ethic of care" in their consumption practices (Thompson [1996] shows this is so for professional women), this would suggest that gendered tastes are congruent with class tastes for LCC women since both emphasize the use of consumption as a resource to foster local communal ties. For HCC women, in contrast, class and gendered tastes would be in conflict since gendered tastes emphasize a collective orientation while HCC tastes emphasize an individuating consumption style.

And fifth, to pursue further the empirical study of status and consumption requires investigation of the specific configuration of the field of consumption across sociohistorical settings. For example, comparing these American findings to the field of consumption in Japan where consumers face semiotic pluralism similar to the contemporary United States (Tobin 1992), yet where collectivist forms of identity may hinder stylistic strategies based upon individuation, would provide additional insight into how Bourdieu's theory adapts to different sociohistorical fields. In addition, this study takes a presentist "snapshot" approach to map the contents of cultural capital. Such an approach tends to naturalize these contents, imputing that they are a permanent, unchangeable feature of the American consumer landscape. But clearly, to have an effect, these categories must be continually reasserted. In everyday life these tastes are not only performed but also variously contested. To properly situate these categories, then, would require a genealogy, much as Foucault has done with modern sexuality, to chart their emerging and continued dominance in relation to other possible but silent alternatives.

Notes

1. Compare Warner's findings to imperialist interpretations in consumer research asserting that lifestyle and social class are synonomous (Levy 1966; Myers & Gutman 1974).
2. It is impossible to do justice to Bourdieu's theory, complexly articulated over many dozens of studies over more than 30 years, in a short review. Instead I briefly summarize the key concepts that pertain specifically to Bourdieu's work on social reproduction linking cultural capital to the field of consumption, and then highlight those aspects of the theory that distinguish it from Warner. Interested readers are encouraged to read *Distinction* and supporting theoretical statements that outline Bourdieu's project, such as Bourdieu & Wacquant (1992) and Bourdieu (1977).
3. Bourdieu's broad theoretical statements support the contemporary interpretation, yet he often makes ahistorical generalizations about the superordinate status of the high arts as a locus for high cultural capital consumption. In *Distinction*, Bourdieu encourages the latter reading because, in his intensive effort to isolate and describe synchronic differences in formal qualities of taste that vary with cultural capital, he does not execute a fully cultural analysis in which social differences in meanings of those objects consumed, and their sociohistorical genesis, also become a focus of investigation (Calhoun 1993; Gartman 1991).
4. I selected the terms "HCC" and "LCC" to connote a hierarchy of tastes and, thus, of social and moral value. The terms are not intended to denigrate LCCs. Just the opposite: by illuminating hierarchies that are smoothed over in everyday life, I hope to defuse their exclusionary power.
5. Empirical assessments of Bourdieu's theory typically compare two or more social class groupings as I do here. However, many studies use measures of social class to group informants that conflict directly with Bourdieu's formulation. For example, Halle (1993) uses Warnerian measures of income and and neighborhood measures that necessarily conflate economic and social capital with cultural capital, while Erikson (1996) uses Erik Olin Wright's class measures, which are primarily measures of economic capital. I follow Bourdieu's theory more carefully in distinguishing the three socialization agents that are considered central in developing cultural capital resources (for a detailed discussion, see Holt [1997a]). Most

studies do not measure all three sources of cultural capital acculturation. The occupation scale is adapted from Peterson and Simkus (1992), and arguments relating occupation and cultural capital are found in Collins (1975). The education scale is adapted from Bourdieu (1984) and Lamont (1992), calibrating the scale downward for parents given the tremendous status inflation in education over the past several decades (Bourdieu 1984). Although the two resulting groups of informants approximately resemble the upper-middle "New Class" of symbolic manipulators, who derive labor market leverage primarily from cultural capital assets, and the working class, whose social conditions rarely facilitate cultural capital formation, they are not identical. A significant percentage of the middle class with upwardly mobile trajectories out of the working class, particularly those who have entered managerial and entrepreneurial occupations that emphasize economic capital, will still have low cultural capital resources. Similarly, newly minted New Class members whose parents were working class and who were the first in their families to attend college do not typically have the highest level of cultural capital resources. Alternatively, a growing number of HCCs (though none in this sample), such as urban artists, have working-class jobs.

References

Baudrillard, Jean (1981). *Towards a Critique of the Political Economy of the Sign*. St. Louis, MO: Telos.

Belk, Russell (1985). Materialism: Trait Aspects of Living in the Material World. *Journal of Consumer Research*, December 12, pp. 265–80.

Belk, Russell, Melanie Wallendorf & John F. Sherry, Jr. (1989). The Sacred and Profane in Consumer Behavior: Theodicy on the Odyssey. *Journal of Consumer Research*, June 16, pp. 1–38.

Bell, Daniel (1976). *The Cultural Contradictions of Capitalism*. New York: Basic Books.

Bendix, Reinhard & Seymour Martin Lipset (1951). Social Status and Social Structure: A Reexamination of Data and Interpretations. *British Journal of Sociology*, June 2, pp. 150–68; September, pp. 230–54.

Bourdieu, Pierre (1977). *Outline of a Theory of Practice*. Cambridge: Cambridge University Press.

Bourdieu, Pierre (1984). *Distinction: A Social Critique of the Judgement of Taste*. Cambridge, MA: Harvard University Press.

Bourdieu, Pierre & Loic Wacquant (1992). *An Invitation to Reflexive Sociology*. Chicago: University of Chicago Press.

Burawoy, Michael (1979). *Manufacturing Consent: Changes in the Labor Process under Monopoly Capitalism*. Chicago: University of Chicago Press.

Calhoun, Craig (1993). Habitus, Field, and Capital: The Question of Historical Specificity. In: Craig Calhoun, et al. (eds.), *Bourdieu: Critical Perspectives*, pp. 61–88. Chicago: University of Chicago Press.

Calhoun, Craig, Edward LiPuma & Moishe Postone (eds.) (1993). *Bourdieu: Critical Perspectives*. Chicago: University of Chicago Press.

Clarke, John (1993). *New Times and Old Enemies: Essays on Cultural Studies and America*. London: HarperCollins Academic.

Coleman, Richard P. (1983). The Continuing Significance of Social Class to Marketing. *Journal of Consumer Research*, December 10, pp. 265–80.

Coleman, Richard P. & Lee Rainwater (1978). *Social Standing in America*. New York: Basic Books.

Collins, Randall (1975). *Conflict Sociology*. New York: Academic Press.

Collins, Randall (1981). On the Microfoundations of Macrosociology. *American Journal of Sociology* 86(5), pp. 984–1014.

Crane, Diane (1992). *The Production of Culture: Media and the Urban Arts*. Newbury Park, CA: Sage.

DiMaggio, Paul (1987). Classification in Art. *American Sociological Review*, August (52), pp. 440–55.

DiMaggio, Paul & John Mohr (1985). Cultural Capital, Educational Attainment, and Marital Selection. *American Journal of Sociology*, May (90), pp. 1231–61.

DiMaggio, Paul & Francie Ostrower (1990). Participation in the Arts by Black and White Americans. *Social Forces*, March (68), pp. 753–78.

DiMaggio, Paul & Michael Useem (1978). Social Class and Arts Consumption: The Origins and Consequences of Class Differences in Exposure to the Arts in America. *Theory and Society*, March 5, pp. 141–61.

Erikson, Bonnie H. (1996). Culture, Class, and Connections. *American Journal of Sociology* 102(1), pp. 217–51.

Ewen, Stuart & Elizabeth Ewen (1992 [1982]). *Channels of Desire: Mass Images and the Shaping of American Consciousness*. Minneapolis: University of Minnesota Press.

Featherstone, Mike (1991). *Consumer Culture and Postmodernism*. Newbury Park, CA: Sage.

Foster, Hal (ed.) (1985). *The Anti-Aesthetic*. Port Townsend, WA: Bay.

Frow, John (1995). *Cultural Studies and Cultural Value*. New York: Oxford University Press.

Gamson, Joshua (1994). *Claims to Fame: Celebrity in Contemporary America*. Berkeley and Los Angeles: University of California Press.

Gartman, David (1991). Culture as Class Socialization or Mass Reification: A Critique of Bourdieu's *Distinction*. *American Journal of Sociology*, September (97), pp. 421–47.

Goffman, Erving (1967). *Interaction Ritual: Essays on Face-to-Face Behavior*. New York: Pantheon.

Gordon, Milton (1963). *Social Class in American Sociology*. New York: McGraw-Hill.

Gouldner, Alvin (1979). *The Future of the Intellectuals and the Rise of the New Class*. London: Macmillan.

Hall, John R. (1992). The Capital(s) of Cultures: A Nonholistic Approach to Status Situations, Class, Gender, and Ethnicity. In: Michele Lamont & Marcel Fournier (eds.), *Cultivating Differences: Symbolic Boundaries and the Making of Inequality*, pp. 257–85. Chicago: University of Chicago Press.

Halle, David (1984). *America's Working Man*. Chicago: University of Chicago Press.

Halle, David (1993). *Inside Culture: Art and Class in the American Home*. Chicago: University of Chicago Press.

Hannerz, Ulf (1990). Cosmopolitans and Locals in World Culture. *Theory, Culture, and Society* 7, pp. 237–51.

Hollingshead, A. B. & F. Redlich (1959). *Social Class and Mental Illness*. New York: Wiley.

Holt, Douglas B. (1995). How Consumers Consume: A Typology of Consumption Practices. *Journal of Consumer Research*, June 22, pp. 1–16.

Holt, Douglas B. (1997a). Distinction in America? Recovering Bourdieu's Theory of Tastes from Its Critics. *Poetics* 25, pp. 93–120.

Holt, Douglas B. (1997b). Poststructuralist Lifestyle Analysis; Conceptualizing the Social Patterning of Consumption in Post-modernity. *Journal of Consumer Research*, March 23, pp. 326–50.

Horkheimer, Max & Theodor Adorno (1972 [1944]). *Dialectic of Enlightenment*. New York: Herder & Herder.

Hughes, Michael & Richard Peterson (1983). Isolating Cultural Choice Patterns in the US Population. *American Behavioral Scientist* 26, pp. 459–78.

Huyssen, Andreas (1986). *After the Great Divide: Modernism, Mass Culture, Postmodernism*. Bloomington: Indiana University Press.

Jameson, Fredric (1991). *Postmodernism, or The Cultural Logic of Late Capitalism*. Durham, NC: Duke University Press.

Jenkins, Henry (1992). *Textual Poachers: Television Fans and Participatory Culture*. New York: Routledge.

Joppke, Christian (1986). The Cultural Dimension of Class Formation and Class Struggle: On the Social Theory of Pierre Bourdieu. *Berkeley Journal of Sociology* 31, pp. 53–78.

Kellner, Douglas (1989). *Jean Baudrillard: From Marxism to Postmodernism and Beyond*. Stanford, CA: Stanford University Press.

Lamont, Michele (1992). *Money, Morals, and Manners: The Culture of the French and American Upper-Middle Class*. Chicago: University of Chicago Press.

Lamont, Michele & Annette Lareau (1988). Cultural Capital: Allusions, Gaps, and Glissandos in Recent Theoretical Developments. *Sociological Theory* 6(2), pp. 153–68.

Leidner, Robin (1993). *Fast Food, Fast Talk: Service Work and the Routinization of Everyday Life*. Berkeley and Los Angeles: University of California Press.

Levy, Sidney (1966). Social Class and Consumer Behavior. In: Joseph Newman (ed.), *On Knowing the Consumer*, pp. 146–60. New York: Wiley.

Levy, Sidney (1996). Stalking the Amphisbaena. *Journal of Consumer Research*, December 23, pp. 163–76.

Liebes, Tamar & Elihu Katz (1990). *The Export of Meaning: Cross-Cultural Readings of "Dallas."* New York: Oxford University Press.

Lynd, Robert & Helen Lynd (1956 [1929]). *Middletown: A Study in Modern American Culture*. New York: Harvest.

Lyotard, Jean-Francois (1984). *The Postmodern Condition*. Minneapolis: University of Minnesota Press.

MacCannell, Dean (1976). *The Tourist: A New Theory of the Leisure Class*. New York: Schocken.

McCracken, Grant (1986). Culture and Consumption: A Theoretical Account of the Structure and Movement of the Cultural Meaning of Consumer Goods. *Journal of Consumer Research*, June 13, pp. 71–84.

Merton, Robert (1957). *Social Theory and Social Structure*. Glencoe, IL: Free Press.

Meyrowitz, Joshua (1985). *No Sense of Place: The Impact of Electronic Media on Social Behavior*. New York: Oxford University Press.

Miller, Daniel (1987). *Material Culture and Mass Consumption*. New York: Basil Blackwell.

Myers, James & Jonathan Gutman (1974). Life Style: The Essence of Social Class. In: William Wells (ed.), *Life Style and Psychographics*, pp. 235–56. Chicago: American Marketing Association.

Peterson, Richard (1978). The Production of Cultural Change: The Case of Contemporary Country Music. *Social Research* 45, pp. 292–314.

Peterson, Richard & Paul DiMaggio (1975). From Region to Class, the Changing Locus of Country Music: A Test of the Massification Hypothesis. *Social Forces* 53, pp. 497–506.

Peterson, Richard & Albert Simkus (1992). How Musical Tastes Mark Occupational Status Groups. In: Michele Lamont & Marcel Fournier (eds.), *Cultivating Differences*, pp. 152–86. Chicago: University of Chicago Press.

Pfautz, Harold & Otis Dudley Duncan (1950). A Critical Evaluation of Warner's Work in Community Stratification. *American Sociological Review*, April 15, pp. 205–15.

Press, Andrea (1991). *Women Watching Television: Gender, Class, and Generation in the American Television Experience*. Philadelphia: University of Pennsylvania Press.

Rainwater, Lee, Richard Coleman & Gerald Handel (1959). *Workingman's Wife: Her Personality, World, and Lifestyle*. New York: Oceana.

Richins, Marsha & Scott Dawson (1992). A Consumer Values Orientation for Materialism and Its Measurement: Scale Development and Validation. *Journal of Consumer Research*, December 19, pp. 303–16.

Rubin, Lillian Breslow (1976). *Worlds of Pain*. New York: Basic Books.

Schaninger, Charles (1981). Social Class versus Income Revisited: An Empirical Investigation. *Journal of Marketing Research*, May 18, pp. 192–208.

Schouten, John W. & James H. McAlexander (1995). Subcultures of Consumption: An Ethnography of the New Bikers. *Journal of Consumer Research*, June 22, pp. 43–61.

Simmel, Georg (1957 [1904]). Fashion. *American Journal of Sociology*, May (62), pp. 541–58.

Thompson, Craig J. (1996). Caring Consumers: Gendered Consumption Meanings and the Juggling Lifestyle. *Journal of Consumer Research*, March 22, pp. 388–407.

Tobin, Joseph J. (ed.) (1992). *Re-Made in Japan: Everyday Life and Consumer Taste in a Changing Society*. New Haven, CT: Yale University Press.

Veblen, Thorstein (1970 [1899]). *The Theory of the Leisure Class*. London: Unwin.

Wallendorf, Melanie & Eric Arnould (1991). We Gather Together: Consumption Rituals of Thanksgiving Day. *Journal of Consumer Research*, June 18, pp. 13–31.

Warner, W. Lloyd, Marsha Meeker & Kenneth Eells (1949). *Social Class in America: The Evaluation of Status*. New York: Harper Torchbooks.

Weber, Max (1978). *Economy and Society*. Berkeley: University of California Press.

Wilensky, Harold (1964). Mass Society and Mass Culture. *American Sociological Review* 29(2), pp. 173–97.

Willis, Paul (1977). *Learning to Labor: How Working Class Kids Get Working Class Jobs*. New York: Columbia University Press.

46

Julia Learns to Shop

Sharon Zukin*

Just Divorced. Gone Shopping.
Headline on feature story,
New York Times, 2001

Learning to shop is more demanding than figuring out what things to buy. The most important part of shopping is learning to steer your way between what you desire and what you know is right. In New York, where the display of status items is inescapable, just thinking about these things creates a bond among strangers – and is a constant source of guilt and frustration.

I'm sitting in the halfway of my daughter's music school in Greenwich Village one Saturday morning, when the voice of Julia, a piano teacher, breaks into my thoughts. "*I know that bag*," I hear her say.

I raise my head. Could Julia be speaking to me? I look around and see that she is, in fact, staring at my purse.

But why? Julia has never spoken to me before. My purse is one of those subtle Italian handbags, whose manufacturer expanded the business from a little leather shop in Vicenza to an international chain of luxury goods boutiques. Until recently, when they were bought by a multinational conglomerate of luxury brands, the company refused to put a logo on their products. They said their work was so distinctive, it didn't need a logo. This makes them, in short, a noteworthy unbrand – unlike, say, Louis Vuitton, whose logo has been replicated so often by factories in Hong Kong and Taiwan that, several years ago, to the dismay of the LVMH company, almost every New York City schoolgirl carried a knockoff, light brown backpack, with those initials printed in dark brown, on her shoulders.

But why would Julia, of all people, be interested in my plain brown purse? For years I have seen her around the music school, always wearing a T-shirt and jeans. She's sharp and funny and serious about music. She should be talking about Mozart, not about Italian leather bags.

Yet Julia has interrupted her conversation with a violin student's father because she does want to talk about Italian handbags. She doesn't want to tell me she *likes* my bag;

*Pp. 35–43 and 282–3 from S. Zukin, *Point of Purchase: How Shopping Changed American Culture* (New York: Routledge). © 2003 by Routledge Publishing, Inc. Reprinted with permission from Routledge Publishing, Inc.

she wants to tell me she *recognizes* it. She wants to tell me she knows how much it costs and where you can buy it and *what it is*: an expensive Italian purse that deliberately, self-consciously, carries no brand logo. She wants to have a conversation – the first real conversation I have ever had with her – about this bag. Julia wants to tell me she appreciates my purse because she is a shopper.

She begins by lecturing the boy's father about my bag – although he shows only the mildest trace of interest. She tells him the bag is expensive and explains how the company's branding strategy plays up the absence of a logo; she mentions the company's boutique on Madison Avenue.

I manage to stammer that I got the purse as a gift.

But Julia is on a roll. Despite her casual outfits, she is a connoisseur of bags and shoes. Though she cannot afford to buy from Prada or Fendi, she knows what their products look like and describes how they feel when you hold their buttery soft leather in your hands. She knows which of their styles fit her and which don't. She knows the differences between the straps on their backpacks.

Julia tells us she also knows a lot about gemstone earrings. She knows how they are made and recognizes little differences in their design. "I know these things," she says, and smiles at us both shyly and proudly.

Despite my interest in shopping, I don't really know what a Prada bag looks like, and I don't pay much attention to jewelry. Since Julia doesn't earn a lot of money as a music teacher and usually runs around in a T-shirt and jeans, I wonder how she knows about these things. Maybe she reads *Vogue* or watches fashion shows on cable television.

No, Julia knows about these things because she shops. "When I travel," she says, "I always check out the expensive jewelry stores." She doesn't buy anything in these stores, she says; this is a different kind of shopping. Like many of us, she shops because she wants to do "research" on the products.

Julia will go into a store and look carefully at the array of merchandise, noting the styles, craftsmanship, and prices, and then file that information in the back of her mind for future use. Maybe she'll find a cheaper version of one of these products in another shop or an outlet store. Maybe she'll find a knockoff or a slightly different style. At least, she'll have a reference point for comparison shopping – for judging whether a cheaper product in another store is truly a bargain.

Even if she doesn't use this information for buying something, the research is useful for sizing up strangers or people whom she meets; she can categorize them by the products they wear. This woman's a Fendi, that one's a JanSport. This one paid more for a Kipling backpack so she could have the little stuffed animal on the key chain; that one paid more for the chic dark colors of a Tumi. Julia can also use the information to fuel a conversation – the kind of conversation about goods and stores that has become commonplace these days, among both friends and strangers.

The first time I realized these conversations were becoming so common was back in the eighties. Russell Baker, an op-ed page columnist for the *New York Times*, wrote a humorous essay about dinner party conversations that focused on the food rather than on political topics. Not only did people compliment the food, they talked at length about the origins of the dishes, the quality of the ingredients, and the stores where you could buy them. As they ate a dish, they reminisced about where they had eaten such a dish before, how much it had cost them, and where you could procure the best version of that dish – which often happened to be in Provence or Tuscany. Baker poked fun of these conversations because they allowed people to avoid serious political discussion. Since then, however, writers from Tom Wolfe to Robert Frank and David Brooks have ridiculed these concerns as a new form of status consumption – a rebirth of the drive to display luxury goods that Thorstein Veblen criticized at the turn of the twentieth century. Brooks and other writers blame the middle-aged hedonism of baby boomers, especially those of liberal political views, as well as the youthful narcissism of yuppies. But neither age nor political beliefs can explain the cultural sea change to an aesthetic pleasure in consumer goods that Americans had never acknowledged so frankly. Since I was writing about cuisine at the time, I thought that changing attitudes toward food consumption reflected the growing influence of food writers and chefs. Listening to Julia, however, I realized that this shift really reflects the growing influence of shopping.[1]

Shopping isn't just a process of *acquiring* goods and services – it's a lifelong process of *learning about* them. And the faster these products change, the more we have to keep up with the changes by shopping. What we know about products, their prices, and where to get them provides us with news and conversation when we run out of things to say about work or school, and when political events are too depressing to consider. Shopping also gives us a common frame of reference for checking each other out: look at the way middle-class parents ask where your children go to school, or teenagers ask each other where they bought their jeans. Since we often shop, we always know something about shopping; and when we talk about shopping – in contrast to talking about work or politics – our opinions seem to count. We're not just complaining, although we do plenty of that, too. By talking about our responses to goods, we're explaining the topic that ultimately interests us most: ourselves.

Or is it only in the status-conscious big city that conversation turns to shopping? "It's New York," Julia says. "In Syracuse, they don't care whether you're carrying a Prada bag or JanSport or anything else."

But I wonder whether this is true. *Vogue* publishes articles about where celebrities of the fashion world shop, complete with the stores' addresses and phone numbers. Celebrity endorsements by athletes are big news. Almost every website carries information about products, in addition to advertisements, throughout the world.

"I think we all pay attention to those things these days," I say.

Then the boy's father enters the conversation. "I pay attention, " he says. I look into his face to see whether he is joking.

"I see whether someone looks like an 'L. L. Bean person,'" he explains, "not whether they're cool, but whether I'd like to be friends with them."

He isn't joking. He actually believes in the sociologists' idea of a "taste community": you're not only what you eat, you're what your friends eat, too. The French sociologist Pierre Bourdieu developed this idea in the eighties, around the same time that Russell Baker noticed his friends in New York talking about different types of olive oil. Bourdieu had seen that Parisians, who have always waxed philosophic about cuisine and fashion, were making new distinctions between people based on whether they showed different preferences, or tastes, for goods. Unlike the usual explanation of individual tastes, Bourdieu theorized that tastes are clustered together by social class – or, more precisely, by social status. High-status people are likely to eat thin slices of whole-grain bread, while peasants buy baguettes. The main exception is the distinctive, "high-end" tastes of people who are highly educated but not enormously wealthy – in other words, the very people who want to talk about the olive oil would likely be Pierre Bourdieu's and Russell Baker's friends. Like Baker, Bourdieu was curious about the new visibility of these people – the more affluent professionals and intellectuals. He was interested in how the used the quirkiness of their tastes to set new fashions, offsetting the power of the upper class and traditional elites. These issues became important to both consumer culture and the economy as the upper middle class and their pundits grew more affluent, and also more influential, during the eighties, in Europe as well as in the United States.[2]

With Julia, however, we're not dealing with affluent tastes defined by *acquiring* goods. We're dealing with affluent tastes acquired by merely *shopping* for goods. By going into stores, reading about goods, and talking about them, shoppers like Julia accumulate cultural capital. Like economic capital, cultural capital is a resource of privileged social groups. As Bourdieu describes it, people derive cultural capital from education and from experience within a privileged milieu. Yet Julia's cultural capital – not her musical knowledge but her familiarity with expensive consumer goods – comes from the seemingly democratic process of shopping.

Though very few people can afford to buy real Prada bags, anyone can acquire familiarity with them by shopping – by the vicarious consumption that we do when we flip through the fashion magazines, and by the direct participation we do by visiting stores, examining the merchandise, and feeling the goods. Shopping through a store's displays permits us to develop knowledge about goods without acquiring the goods themselves. We can even become fans of some goods and critics of others without committing ourselves to spending any money. Shopping gives us the proximate experience with goods we need to make true distinctions. We can tell whether someone is carrying a real Prada bag or only a fake. We don't do this because we're snobs . . . but because we're truly interested in the aesthetic quality of the things themselves.

Indeed, just then Julia says there are "snobs" who pay attention to such matters. She has a friend who doesn't like a certain store "where they sell Mandarina Duck bags" – another Italian brand – because the salesman in there was nice to her only when she wore Ralph Lauren sunglasses. "It's not the people who can buy the most expensive bags who care whether someone is wearing a real Gucci bag," she says. "It's the others, who shouldn't be spending money on it, who care." So Julia thinks of herself as a moralist. Just because she shops doesn't mean she's a snob.

"You know, I come from a totally different background," she says, "where these things weren't important. My family were immigrants and socialists. When I was growing up, T-shirts didn't have designers' names on them. I don't really like all this." And she smiles again – this time, more shyly than proudly.

Julia experiences a conflict many shoppers feel – a conflict between shopping to supply her needs, as her parents brought her up, and shopping to acquire social status and cultural capital, which is the kind of shopping that has become more popular since the eighties. Though Thorstein Veblen pointed out the prevalence of status shopping in the early 1900s, it was limited, at that time, to the small segment of the population that had financial security and lived in some degree of comfort. Status shopping began to be more widespread with the growth of the middle class after World War II. It became more influential in the sixties when the spending habits of rich people and celebrities began to be widely publicized in the print media and on television. At the same time, the large numbers of women who began to work outside the home and pursue their own careers anxiously sought badges of their new distinction. A broad public for status shopping formed, consisting of the traditional upper-class matrons whom Veblen had depicted as status shoppers, the nonworking, suburban housewives who tried to "keep up with the Joneses," and the working women who wanted to keep up with their peers at work and had more financial leeway in making spending decisions.[3]

Women are not the only status shoppers. Men have always considered their social status when shopping for the big purchases – cars and houses. In the 1960s, however, men, especially unmarried men and gay men, took a bigger role in making decisions about the clothes they wore and the food they ate – decisions that used to be left to wives and mothers. As many men became more interested in style, shopping provided them with new cultural capital. These social changes did not necessarily persuade consumers to buy more. But they did encourage people to approach shopping with more interest – and with more anxiety about making the right choices.[4]

Beginning in the late 1960s, a mass public of consumers was surrounded by the new social space of designer boutiques and discount stores, the cultural labels of branded goods, and a booming literature of product reviews and shopping guides. The influx of products, stores, and texts created a complex, and occasionally overwhelming, culture. Shoppers responded by neither rejecting the whole idea of consumption nor becoming, as many authors would have it, baby-boomer snobs. Instead, shoppers learned to use shopping as an opportunity to do research on goods – and gain cultural capital.

Like Julia, many of us can't afford to buy the things we would like to have. Through magazines, television, and books, we gain cultural capital by vicarious consumption. Looking at goods in stores or on the Internet, reading reviews, and talking about them train us, as they have trained Julia, to appreciate their subtle differences. And once we have developed a fine eye for differences among the goods, we can make distinctions among the people who use them. This is a different approach to shopping from the early years of mass consumption, when most mass market products were homogeneous and most people didn't spend so much time thinking about them. If we're over forty, or if we learned to shop *before* the sixties, we sense a change in ourselves – a contradiction, if you will – with which we're not completely at ease.

"My mother was a good shopper," says Catherine, a woman in her late fifties who lives in Toronto, one of a number of middle-class shoppers I have talked to recently about shopping.[5] "But shopping was different in those days. I grew up in an affluent family, but even so, you shopped for essentials. You probably got one good outfit a year, or maybe two, if you grew. In those days [the fifties], we wore skirts to school, and a skirt would last you four years. You just kept letting the hem down. You might get a new blouse if you got bigger on top. So you'd have three outfits and one for the weekends – jeans and maybe a flannel shirt. It was right after the War, but my parents had come through the Depression, and it affects their mentality – and yours."

Marian, a New Yorker of Catherine's age, has similar memories of shopping. She grew up in a small town in Maine, "My favorite store as a child was the five-and-dime," she says. "I still like five-and-dimes. They're junky places that have everything, and there's always one or two neat things you can find. There were comic books, penny candy . . . so it was all affordable." Like many men and women over forty, Marian remembers an older bargain culture that predates the discount superstore. She remembers when a bargain was about buying less rather than buying more.

"My mother never shopped for me," Marian continues. "I always wore hand-me-downs from my older sister. I wore hand-me-downs until the eighth grade when, thank God, my sister went away. My mother wasn't into shopping for clothes, period. But I remember once she bought us matching dresses. She brought them all the way from Boston. Mine was blue, and my sister's was yellow, and I thought that was pretty neat! I wore my new dress, and when I grew up, I wore my sister's."

Now, however, Marian lives in Manhattan, and she likes the social diversity of her neighborhood. "I like the fact that you have brownstones and projects in the same block," she says, "with a bodega in between." She appreciates that the Korean grocers who have bought most of the bodegas stay open all night: "the neighborhood is safer." But she also likes "the big, suburban grocery stores," especially on Long Island, where she has a vacation home, and the new superstores in Manhattan – "The Gap, Bed Bath & Beyond, T. J. Maxx. . . . I don't have to go more than three blocks to buy anything."

Marian straddles two worlds: those of the more affluent and the less affluent shopper. She has moved from wearing hand-me-down dresses and shopping in the five-and-dime to owning a second home near the ocean on Long Island. Despite being upwardly mobile, however, she doesn't feel comfortable in exclusive stores. Once, when Marian and a friend went into Tiffany, on Fifth Avenue, the two women felt awkward and out of place, especially since they "were only wearing trenchcoats." Marian prefers shopping at K-Mart, a big discount store on Long Island, where rich home-owners shop alongside working-class local people, and you can buy both soda and garden supplies: "I'm more comfortable there than in those exclusive places where you have to spend a lot of money."

Marian, Catherine, and Julia are not shopaholics. They were raised in plain, middle-class families. But shopping is important to them: it provides them with pleasure, variety, convenience, and a taste of living beyond their financial means. Yet shopping also plunges them into a state of conflict. They're not sure they should like having a lot of things, and they feel under pressure because they can't afford to buy everything anyway.

Notes

1. Conversations about the food: Russell Baker, "Worse than Gluttony." *New York Times*, January 4, 1986, and Sharon Zukin, *Landscapes of Power: From Detroit to Disney World*

(Berkeley and Los Angeles: University of California Press, 1991), 202–15. Status consumption: Thorstein Veblen, *The Theory of the Leisure Class (1899)*, in *The Portable Veblen*, ed. Max Lerner (New York: Viking, 1948), 53 – 214; cf. David Brooks, *Bobos in Paradise* (New York: Simon and Schuster, 2000).

2. Tastes of the upper middle class: for Bourdieu, these people were less the "affluent" than "intellectuals," or "the dominated part of the dominating class." See Pierre Bourdieu, *Distinction: A Social Critique of the Judgement of Taste*, trans. Richard Nice (Cambridge: Harvard University Press, 1984).

3. Status shopping: Veblen, *Theory of the Leisure Class.* "Keeping up with the Joneses": Vance Packard, *The Status Seekers* (New York: McKay, 1959).

4. Men became more interested in style: on how more frequent changes in men's fashions encouraged style consciousness, see Thomas Frank, *The Conquest of Cool: Business Culture, Counterculture, and the Rise of Hip Consumerism* (Chicago: University of Chicago Press, 1997); on how style consciousness played out in London, especially among gay men, see Frank Mort, *Cultures of Consumption: Masculinities and Social Space in Late Twentieth Century Britain* (London: Routledge, 1992); on how the social space of a store changed over time to attract male shoppers, see Gail Reekie, "Changes in the Adamless Eden: The Spatial and Sexual Transformation of a Brisbane Department Store 1930–90," *Lifestyle Shopping: The Subject of Consumption*, ed. Rob Shields (London and New York: Routledge, 1992), 170–94.

5. A woman in her late fifties: in this chapter, I draw on a small number of interviews with middle-class shoppers in New York City and Toronto conducted by my research assistant Jennifer Smith Maguire and on two focus groups that I conducted in Brooklyn with working-class black and Latino teenagers and mothers. I have provided all the respondents with pseudonyms and changed details by which they could be identified.

47

Fashion as a Culture Industry

*Angela McRobbie**

When the new Labour government came to power in May 1997, there were few signs that the culture industries would so quickly be propelled to the political centre-stage as representing the great hope for economic recovery and job creation as well as the symbol of a modernised Britain. Granted, Tony Blair had expressed his desire to overturn John Major's traditional and nostalgic image of Britain, the land of spinsters on bicycles and warm beer. Instead the UK was to become a 'young country' (Blair 1996). It was ripe for social change, and young people were the key agents for bringing about this social transformation. But this did not suggest the wholesale endorsement of the culture industries which followed the election of the new government. The Cool Britannia episode, a media and politics publicity jamboree to promote UK creative talent inter-nationally, at once marked the start of the government's bid to turn British-made culture into global commodity and the extent to which such media-led initiatives could so easily rebound. The photo-opportunities at No 10 Downing Street with pop star Noel Gallagher and his wife Meg Matthews were an accident waiting to happen. As soon as government attempted to prove its 'cool' credentials, the unruly 'youth' felt called upon to dissociate themselves from such endeavours. It was reminiscent of the would-be trendy teacher attempting to show his talents on the floor at the school disco and the floor quickly emptying as pupils exchange embarrassed glances and decide to sit this one out. Some months later when actress Emma Thompson was called upon to be a mentor and role model for young women, she acted in exactly the same way. No way, she ungratefully replied, she'd much rather be identified with the bad girls.

But since then, though with less socialising with musicians, fashion designers and celebrities, the emphasis on the culture industries have continued to grow. Minister of Culture Chris Smith claimed in the annual report of the Creative Industries Task Force that more than one million people were now employed in the sector. The new so-called guru to Tony Blair, economist and journalist Charles Leadbeater has talked about the future Hollywoodisation of the UK labour market (Leadbeater 1999). He was referring to the process by which many scripts are written but only a few make it into production. Leadbeater wanted young British 'cultural entrepreneurs' to adopt a more resilient

*Pp. 253–63 from *Fashion Cultures, Theories, Explorations, and Analysis*, ed. S. Bruzzi and P. C. Gibson (London and New York: Routledge). © 2000 by Angela McRobbie. Reprinted with permission from the author.

approach, where failure in one venture becomes an incentive to succeed in the next. At the same time, up and down the country, local councillors discuss 'cultural regeneration'. In de-industrialised regions the prospect of attracting some artists with the lure of cheap studio space is the most desirable of outcomes for policy-makers. It creates interesting stories for the press, it holds the promise of gallery owners and more mainstream media companies moving in and with these the whole panoply of coffee shops, bars and restaurants, i.e. the 'Shoreditch effect'. Such high hopes are not wholly restricted to urban areas; one recent report in the *Guardian* described an attempt to encourage creative and artistic skills among the nation's farming and agricultural community, as they too face the same threat to their livelihoods as did industrial workers twenty years ago (Gibbons 1999).

The new centrality of the arts and culture is now evident almost on a daily basis, from the grand opening of the Tate Modern (May 11, 2000) to the ongoing debates about what art works should be displayed on the 'vacant plinth' on Trafalgar Square. Indeed on BBC2's *Newsnight* programme (May 12, 2000) an architect argued for the whole of the Trafalgar Square space to become a traffic-free site for public art. There is almost a sense of national euphoria as art becomes a topic of discussion not just for the few but for the people as a whole, as Blair put it when asked his thoughts on the opening of Tate Modern. Art critics have become the most called upon experts to give their opinions and explain to this public the thinking behind conceptual art. But it is not just art that attracts this kind of news coverage. The media also report on a regular basis on the numbers of young authors, many still in their teens, signed up by publishers offering huge advances on the basis of a half-finished manuscript. Stories of writers like J. K. Rowling moving from 'rags to riches' as a single parent writing her world bestsellers (the Harry Potter series) on a notepad in Edinburgh cafés while her baby slept in her pushchair have become commonplace. Such swings in fortune have led sociologists to comment on the new lottery-style cultural labour market as evidence of the 'chaos of reward' (Young 1999) or else as a windfall of 'easy money' (Beck 1999). This kind of success is also presented as evidence of the new meritocracy, with many talented young artists and writers and designers coming from poor or working-class backgrounds (Damien Hirst and Tracey Emin are usually offered as examples). British film-making has also been the focus of enormous attention, resulting in the recent setting up of a new Film Council led by film-director Alan Parker with a governmental brief to support scripts which have popular box-office appeal.

The recent successes of British-produced cultural forms has led some commentators like Leadbeater to celebrate the possibility in the UK of a new, more open society where 'everyone has a chance to make it'. One of his models of success is fashion designer Alexander McQueen whom he describes as an East End boy with no formal qualifications. In fact McQueen studied for a Masters at Central St Martin's College of Art and Design. Leadbeater's error is indicative of his desire to insist on the way in which traditional barriers have been broken down, allowing talent to shine through. In fact the success stories of UK-trained fashion designers have been relatively restricted to Stella McCartney, John Galliano and McQueen, with Vivienne Westwood achieving status as a kind of national icon. In the final section of this chapter I shall consider the issues which make it more difficult for fashion designers to sustain both recognition and success in significant numbers and the questions that fashion as a culture industry poses for governmental policy. I shall also argue that fashion design increasingly finds itself forced into re-definition as 'fine art fashion' in order to attract the kind of media attention needed to create names and generate contracts. The new climate for working as a fashion designer in the UK following the high rate of failure and bankruptcy in the mid-1990s has forced a change in practice for most young designers which I will describe in greater length later in this chapter.

It is noticeable, however, that the various articles and essays which have appeared in the last few months on the new prominence of the culture industries have had little or nothing to say about the experience of those working in this labour market, be it fashion or fine art. Instead the focus has been on broader issues, including the idea of 'cultural governance' as marking a new kind of political strategy. Valentine, for example, has described the way in which culture and the arts have been defined as socially beneficial, as healthy for the nation, even a better way of encouraging social inclusion (Valentine 2000). The work of the '*yBas*' (young British artists), British fashion designers and others have been packaged and exported abroad by the British Council as a sign of the vitality of contemporary British culture and, as Valentine also puts it, as 'interesting' in an ethnographic sense. Valentine's list could be extended, with the BBC Radio World Service regularly commenting on and describing this new cultural field for its listeners across the world (May 13, 2000). This argument is implicitly Foucauldian with culture in a dispersed and positive sense marking a new modality of power, one that operates through appeals to the social body to enjoy and find pleasure in these practices. Other commentators have seen in New Labour's culture policies a cruder attempt to put the arts in the service of 'social goals and political aims'. The arts are thereby disciplined, re-cast not as a sphere for dissent but as a 'command culture' to achieve social inclusion and community (Brighton 1999). McGuigan suggests that, drawing on Raymond Williams, the new culture industries operate for government as 'display' (McGuigan 1998). They have been utilised by Blair to achieve a 'governmental project of national aggrandisement'.

As far as I can ascertain, there have only been two less critical assessments of New Labour's cultural policies. Simon Frith correctly draws attention to Chris Smith's background in the municipal politics of the 1980s and his endorsement of the Comedia work of that time which recognised the future of culture as industry, commodity and also as 'way of life' (Frith 2000). This, argues Frith, contributes to Smith's current vision for culture as participative, non-elitist, a field to which more people must have access and also a popular phenomenon. This is an entirely different view of culture from that of the Tories. Likewise even though Liz Greenhalgh recognises the attempt to subject the arts and culture to the language of business and new managerialism, none the less the kind of work initiated by the GLC in the 1980s which addressed issues including audiences and distribution of cultural goods and services are now also central to New Labour's vision of widening participation (Greenhalgh 1998). This is highly ironic in that the GLC is demonised by New Labour as one of the main causes of the electoral failure of the Labour Party through the 1980s. Greenhalgh reminds us that one of the persons behind these GLC policies, Geoff Mulgan, is now himself a policy advisor to the PM. In many ways it was the radically left-wing GLC which reinvented the term 'culture industries' to refer to the small businesses that provided different kinds of cultural expression from those found in the multinationally owned record companies, film and television corporations and big high street fashion retailers.

It is also the case that it was the GLC which first established 'fashion centres' in London to enable lesser-known designers, especially those from ethnic groups, to work in subsidised spaces alongside machinists and to create a more viable design sector less associated with sweatshop wages and exploited immigrant labour. Greenhalgh points out that much of the investment and resources behind the current government's support for the culture industries actually comes from the public purse. Thus it could be argued (though Greenhalgh does not pursue her analysis this far) that despite all the rhetoric about public–private partnerships (and, I would add, despite the flow of funds from corporate sponsors to young British artists), the infrastructure of support for the new culture industries comes from the public sector. The high cost of training in the art schools and universities, 'the use of public funds for large-scale cultural facilities in city regeneration [and] the public promotion of cultural activity abroad' (Greenhalgh 2000), all of these suggest that New Labour is in fact implementing the same policies as those spearheaded by the GLC and also by radical city councils in Sheffield and elsewhere during the long Thatcher years, but this time 'by stealth'. These are left-wing policies reconfigured to maintain the support of Middle England through the emphasis on wealth and success and on the 'Hollywood effect' embodied by the new Film Council.

I would propose that in fact there are two things happening simultaneously, and represented in the different personas of the PM and the Minister of Culture. The former endorses the model of culture and the arts as a source for moral and spiritual regeneration and also for creating better citizens. The latter, in contrast, recognises the existence of cultural inequalities and the domination of culture by the large multinationals and the stranglehold it operates over alternative or independent production, hence the recognition of cultural diversity. But the Minister of Culture is also party, at least as far as public statements are concerned, to the new euphoria about successful cultural entrepreneurs. When I asked him as a participant in a round table discussion (Royal Television Society, February 2000) to comment on the fact that as my research on fashion designers showed, not all cultural entrepreneurs were high wage-earners and in fact most of them were barely scraping a living, unable to take a holiday, never mind take time off to have children, he replied with three short points. First, that it was not the role of government to provide the kinds of support I was suggesting in relation to new forms of social insurance. Second, that government was providing business start-up funding and advice. Third, that these young cultural workers do this work 'because they love it, and they know what they are letting themselves in for'. This raises a final point. Does the money currently being directed towards encouraging cultural regeneration in run-down areas such as Deptford in South-East London find its way to alleviating the real difficulties faced by young creative workers to sustain themselves on the longer term, or is this support more about creating part-time or semi-employment for a wider range of culture intermediaries whose role is managerial, administrative and thus 'supportive' of the artists and designers? Is it also about creating jobs for people who will train the artists on how to present a better business plan, and if so, is this culture industry as employment policy? The answer to this has to be yes. These are presented as enjoyable jobs, close to the media and arts and thus sharing in the glamour and in the limelight. They are typically part-time 'portfolio' jobs, which are often undertaken on a freelance basis. Under such conditions the worker takes on full responsibility for his or her own insurance and other costs, thus lessening the burden to the 'contractor'. By this means the entire cultural labour market comes to be a fragile web, loosely held together, buoyed up by a network of semi-independent producers and contractors all engaged in short-term projects and for whom the juggling of two or three jobs at the same time makes it difficult for them to plan more than six months in advance. The question of policy then, is how will these new occupations turn out, not in the distant future, but simply in the next few years? To what extent can the 'opaque futures' described by Giddens (1997) be a sustainable working reality for so many people?

Working in Fashion Design

The manuscript for my study of the career pathways of young British fashion designers was being completed in the months following the election of New Labour (McRobbie 1998). Indeed, it was only in the course of doing the research and interviewing the designers that policy began to strike me as important. The questions that informed the work in its initial stages were far removed from the world of government and policy. Let me briefly rehearse some of those questions. First, there was the appearance from the mid-1980s onwards of a cultural phenomenon which seemed unique to the UK; the rise of the art-school-trained fashion designer, whose work belonged neither to the haute couture world of the European fashion houses nor to the fashion end of the high street, nor was it simply an expression of the street or youth subcultures.

My instinct was that the art schools, as peculiarly British institutions, played a major role in producing this new kind of creative person. But alongside this hunch which I duly explored both historically and sociologically, was another set of questions. Fashion design, apart from the handful of male stars, was a resolutely feminised field. And despite all the media attention it received from the mid-1980s onwards, it was possible to detect a lack of confidence about how it placed itself and understood itself in the hierarchy of the arts and culture. There was a defensiveness and an anxiety about insisting on the relevance of traditional fine art values and vocabularies. The available language for discussing fashion design, and the criteria for excellence were seemingly under-developed, assertive, somehow unconvincing. In journalism it seemed to be simply a matter of proclaiming this or that designer a genius, and adopting a kind of 'auteur' approach, with different fashion moments, periods or epochs, understood in terms of the distinctive style of range of acclaimed designers. There was very little engaged criticism, or outright disagreement. Fashion design appeared to be a conflict-free zone, both in academic terms and in the wider world of journalistic commentary. This is not to suggest that there was not a substantial and extremely rich body of scholarship in fashion history and in contemporary debates about fashion and consumption, and fashion and the body. But what was entirely lacking was a debate about, let us say, the status of John Galliano and the meaning or value of his work. Why had he achieved such prominence? What was it that marked his work out as so special? Was the success and the acclaim justified? Was the work idea-based and conceptual in the manner of Damien Hirst? Is it the case that the UK fashion designers have been playing with the same kind of ideas and utilising the same kind of self-promotional strategies for years before the *yBas* suddenly came to the attention of the world media?

There was a gender dynamic in fashion's collective lack of confidence. The male designers flamboyantly cut through this by casting themselves almost as dramatists, as masters of spectacle, as theatre directors. This was a bid to disconnect fashion from its lesser status in the art schools where, as the historical research showed, it had to struggle to attain degree status and thus the respect and recognition of the fine artists who ran most of the art schools. To them fashion remained associated with a range of less elevated practices, with dressmaking, with the decorative arts, with embroidery and overall with the degraded field of the feminine. In the book (McRobbie 1998) I describe the various stages which marked fashion's ascendancy, and in particular the role of pioneering women fashion academics from Muriel Pemberton to Madge Garland to Lydia Kemeny. I argue that it was particularly important for fashion design to dissociate itself from the dressmaking tradition and also from manufacture, since the latter carried unwelcome connotations of the 'rag trade'. In short, fashion had to look upwards. It had to assert its leading figures as comparable to great artists and designers in the European tradition. It had to be able to locate itself within modernism and then post-modernism, writing its history to fit with the existing trajectory of art and design history. In actual fact, despite all these efforts, the eventual recognition came more from a pragmatic realisation that the art school sector had to demonstrate a connectedness with the changing world of commercial culture, and it was decided that fashion could be the envoy of change. The emergence, from the mid-1960s, of popular culture as a serious subject for debate outside the art schools, including the attention being paid to fashion photography in the new colour supplements, and the wider more sociological interest in fashion designer-retailers like Mary Quant and the Biba store, gradually won round the principals and vice-chancellors.

I was proposing that a sociological and cultural studies approach might be able to offer better insight into fashion as a cultural practice, fashion as something more than the possession of unique insight, vision, talent or even genius. After all, the limitations of this vocabulary were increasingly apparent to designers who were finding themselves described in euphoric terms one season, and completely ignored by the press the next. There was recognition of the disparity between receiving pages of publicity, even becoming household names while struggling to make ends meet, and existing on a virtually non-existent salary. This called for greater understanding of the various intermediary processes which 'created the creator' (Bourdieu 1993). Could the self-representational strategies of the designers as seen on the catwalks (the work, the collection) be better understood as the result of the deployment and orchestration of a series of design practices which, in turn, were gleaned through the repertoire of available fashion discourses? Thus Galliano's trademark style is one that 'plunders history'. He is famous for staging a particular historical moment not by producing costume drama but by exaggerating or distorting the period piece to give it some degree of visual intensity or even brilliance – what Sally Brampton described as 'lyricism' (Brampton 1996).

Was it the case that the excitement which accompanied the emergence of a new fashion design star could be traced through a series of precise promotional strategies involving fashion editors, fashion writers, fashion buyers (who need something avant-garde to liven up a window display) as well as an array of stylists, photographers, models and friends from college, all of whom might be said to constitute a 'network'? These ideas led me to trace design practice back to the distinctive pedagogies with which the designers, as students, had been familiar. And sure enough what I found was great emphasis on networking, on gaining experience by working for nothing as a student as a way of making contacts. Likewise, the importance of achieving a distinctive style with a noticeable 'signature' is as much a way of attracting the attention of the media, and thus of getting work, as it is a mark of design talent or integrity. I also wanted to under-stand how the designers navigated their way through the fashion business once they had graduated, and how they perceived their own design practice. These kinds of ques-tions, about how they got set up in business, what kind of turnover they needed to keep going, how they managed to meet deadlines and ensure that orders were finished in time to get them shipped off to the US, all of this meant that the study became a work of sociological demystification.

It was the rhythms of their working days, the patterns which gradually built up across the experience of all of those I interviewed, and the extent to which they attempted to reconcile an inner desire to retain a commitment to imagination and vision with the requirements of packaging, branding and marketing their names and labels, which provided the backbone of the study. Romantically they saw themselves as led by inspira-tion, ideas, intuition and dreams; practically though, knew they had to sell a look and a combination of ideas. With skill they deployed the right kind of art vocabulary as a means of branding their own work. This was also a way of locating their work in an ideal retail environment. If a designer described her work in a press release statement or in an interview as 'evoking memories of Matisse', this pointed not only to the kind of customer she had in mind but also the kind of store she hoped would buy her range. Slowly it became clear that fashion design was a multi-layered practice combining design and drawing skills with a much broader range of activities. It was also apparent that the designers I interviewed, despite being well known and having received a good deal of publicity, were in fact working on very small budgets. None of them had really managed to move into the global marketplace, most operated with annual turnovers of less than 1.5 m, and all had either experienced or come close to bankruptcy.

What role did this work of sociological demystification play? What was the point of bringing fashion down to earth by inspecting its less glamorous practices? I argued in *British Fashion Design* that many elements of the present system were anachronistic and detrimental to the long-term success of the sector. As a feminist I was interested in the energy and enthusiasm with which these young women pursued their careers, but it was also apparent that the culture of the fashion design sector, in particular its resistance to opening itself up to self-scrutiny and to promoting wider debate about its internal politics and organisation, made it more difficult for them to succeed. For example, its model of success hinged round the notion of competitive individualism. There was also a rigid hierarchy and whole set of rituals of deference and authority in relation to the high-powered fashion leaders, the key journalists who were able to make or break careers, the 'prima donna' designers who had made it to the top, the carelessness in regard to ensuring good working practices, and basically the existence of a non-democratic culture which allowed snobbishness and elitism to prevail.

In the above respects the fashion designers actually have a lot to learn from their fine art counterparts, especially the infamous *yBas*, whose collaborative and mutually supportive strategies were what made it possible for them to produce their own shows, pull their resources to attract the right kind of publicity, and demonstrate a kind of public loyalty to each other by helping out in each other's shows (McRobbie 1999). While the outcome was also a new celebrity culture of artists on a scale unknown, none the less there was a rejection of authority, hierarchy and tradition. There was also a repudiation of the snobbish patrician values associated with fine art: the 'Sensation' exhibition as almost all commentators pointed out, was anti-elitist, even populist in its overall presentation. Art had become 'ordinary' while fashion design was still aspiring to being 'extraordinary'. Most of the designers I interviewed described feeling isolated and cut off from any opportunities for collaboration. Despite the existence of the 'networks' which functioned more as a means of keeping in touch, there was an expressed need for some form of association which as yet did not exist. No single designer I interviewed had any experience of the kind of group support which has served the *yBas* so well.

But it was also the case that the distance their training had encouraged them to stake from the manufacturing end of fashion design, for fear of being mistaken for a dressmaker or rag trade manufacturer, also did them little good. By having so little hands-on knowledge of the process of production, they were often financially exploited by the middlemen. Often they were over-charged or else discovered too late that their orders were put to the back of the queue when more lucrative ones came in from bigger companies. Beholden to these middlemen, who took charge of the production and farmed out the work on a sub-contractual basis to very low-paid workers, there was little the designers could do when a late delivered order was then cancelled by a big retailer. It was the designers who paid the costs and this practice alone accounted for the majority of bankruptcies. In short, I recommended that the designers get their hands dirty by visiting the factories, learning about production and even finding new ways of sharing facilities with other designers and also pooling manufacturing costs by bringing in direct labour on better wages rather than on relying on exploitative chains.

Finally I argued that it was also important to challenge the rigid and conservative practices of the fashion press. They wielded their power arbitrarily and also drew up a strict agenda about what were and what were not 'fashion stories'. Socialising with the top designers as part of a whole glamorous and international fashion circuit, gratefully receiving all sorts of fashion freebies, and fearful of being left out in the cold for filing a poor review, fashion journalists rarely step out of line. It has been a marked feature of recent news stories about racism and sexual exploitation inside the fashion industry that they have been written by news journalists. The fashion world quickly closes ranks as soon as questions about sweatshops, the employment of under-age children or the widespread existence of racist attitudes are aired in public. This too marks it out as inward-looking, politically conservative, and seemingly unwilling to engage in public debate about its own internal organisation and reluctant to adapt to the place which fashion could play as a major culture industry.

Looking to the Future

There were a number of problems which the young designers faced on an almost daily basis. There was no doubt that there existed an enormous disparity between the high levels of talent and commitment and the ensuing publicity the whole sector received, and the fragile, indeed shabby infrastructure which saw bankruptcy if not as a norm or a rite of passage, then at least as part of the cycle of expectations. This places fashion design in the realm of what the sociologist Ulrich Beck calls 'risk work' (Beck 1992). But need it be so risky, I asked? Need the future be so opaque for these highly trained designers? Is there not an element of fatalism in the theorists of the new world of work which actually lets the government and others off the hook? It did not seem, as I completed the book, so unrealistic to search for better ways of supporting graduate designers after they left college and, given the huge investment already made in their education and training, to make some provisions available to them in the early years. This could take at least two inter-connected forms: access to a series of fashion design and production units or centres which in turn might be in partnerships with art schools and colleges. These would provide on a subsidised basis, expensive high-tech equipment, production facilities as well as shared publicity and promotional resources, business and other training, and also space to work and space to show the work. Equally important might be the ethos of collectivity and sharing, so that the rather vacuous idea of the network becomes something more than just a series of names and telephone numbers.

There are two further issues that needed addressing. First, there was the seeming inability of all the designers I interviewed who were 'independents' and working on a relatively small scale (i.e. employing less than twenty people, selling collections to up to a dozen retail outlets) successfully to break into foreign markets and to consolidate that presence on a long-term basis. Second there was the question of their own personal economies, which showed how narrow their margins were, how easily a bout of illness or a family crisis could destroy the entire business. These remain of central importance three years on. While the first of these issues calls for more serious debate about the viability of small-scale designers surviving in a global market, the second inevitably raises the question of how the career pathways of freelance and self-employed creative workers will be sustainable not just into middle age but also into old age. It might be imagined that this would be the stuff of the Creative Industries Task Force, but sadly not. The two key figures from the fashion world who have played an advisory role are Paul Smith and Caroline Coates. These are both highly knowledgeable and experienced people, but there are not many others who have developed such commitment to policy and to improving the fashion sector as a place of work. The British Fashion Council clearly has a role to play, but so far this has been disappointing, restricted to fund-raising for London Fashion Week and otherwise supporting business startup programmes.

Nor does there seem to be evidence of the 'joined-up thinking' so encouraged by New Labour. The DTI sees the fashion design sector as small fish, the DfEE is more concerned with (yet again) start-up programmes (and graduate designers are not necessarily a priority) and the Creative Industries Task Force has been dominated by film and popular music. Fashion has no lobbyists as loud and outspoken as Alan McGee (former owner of Creation Records), or indeed Lord Puttnam. In short, fashion does not do itself credit on the political front, despite the valuable efforts of its two key representatives. At present fashion experts claim that the newly recommended pathway for young designers is actually working better. That is, instead of being encouraged into going it alone in the early years, a new model is emerging. This sees the majority of graduates going for more sensible jobs in industry in the hope of gaining experience and setting up alone at some point in the future. But will this ever happen, and is it fair to train students to think of themselves as designers only to then encourage them on graduation to get experience with BHS? And is it not the case that the early years after graduation are the best time to explore talent and imagination more fully? If it doesn't happen then, maybe it never will. This recommendation is therefore politically safe, seemingly sensible but ultimately self-defeating. British fashion design is renowned for its uniqueness, adventurousness and creativity. If this is stifled as soon as the students leave college, then that reputation will be lost. The other solution is that the chain store will step in, offering contracts to 'star' designers to produce collections under their own labels but for the mass-market. So far Top Shop has pioneered this with most success, but as I point out (McRobbie 1998), this can be a short-term fix. Come a recession or even simply a downturn in sales and the contract can be ended. What is more, to win such a contract in the first place the designer has to have a 'name', a 'label' and a reputation. How can this be achieved if the early years are to be spent playing safe and working for a large company? Of course, many graduates will want to opt for this route in any case; the fashion industry is big and important enough to absorb trained designers in many roles. But there is a danger of this becoming the official pathway and of thus either throwing the baby out with the bathwater, or else of adopting an 'I told you so' mentality when the ambitious designers come up against difficulties.

In conclusion there seems to be a real and urgent need for the fashion design sector as creative industry to be addressed in more depth and with greater seriousness at every level. But this requires that the fashion world shows itself willing not to turn away from the field of political economy but towards it. It has to become more 'socialised'. This also has to start early, indeed in training. The ethos of art for art's sake is of little help when people's working lives are at stake. The crudely promotional and collaborative strategies learnt by the *yBas* have at the very least improved the annual incomes of young artists in Britain for the first time in recent history. Granted those at the top now can command stratospheric amounts for their work, but there has been a trickle-down, and the artists have themselves become more aware of what it takes to keep a budget ticking over. Perhaps there is also another lesson here. We may be asking too much of designers to train them as artists (in the mode of 'fine art fashion'), and then expect them to make their way in a global market dominated by cheap suppliers and companies now able to 'translate' the look from the catwalk on to the rails at Kookai within a couple of weeks. Why not let them work as artist-designers who have shows in the same way as Damien Hirst *et al.* do? And why not also invite them to apply for Arts Council, British Council, Lottery and whatever other funding is available, including designer-in-residence posts, and then to eradicate the elitism and snobbery for once and for all, to encourage them to think of what they do as not 'extraordinary' but as 'ordinary'? As Damien Hirst has said on may occasions, 'I'm no genius' (quoted in Frith 2000).

References

Beck, U. (1992). *Risk Society: Towards a New Modernity*. London: Sage.

Beck U. (1999). Die Zukunft Oder the Political Economy of Uncertainty. Lecture delivered at the LSE, London, February.

Blair, Rt Hon P. M. (1996). *New Britain: My Vision for a Young Country*. London: Fourth Estate.

Bourdieu, P. (1993). *The Field of Cultural Production*. Cambridge: Polity Press.

Brampton, S. (1996). Flight of Fantasy. *Guardian*, weekend edn, February 2.

Brighton, A. (1999). Towards a Command Culture: New Labour's Cultural Policy and Soviet Socialist Realism. *Critical Quarterly* 41(3), pp. 24–36.

"Creative Industries Mapping" (1998). London: Department of Media, Culture and Sport.

Frith, S. (2000). Mr Smith Draws a Map. *Critical Quarterly* 41(2), pp. 3–8.

Gibbons, F. (1999). Old Macdonald Had a Vision. *Guardian*, Saturday review, July 24, p. 5.

Giddens, A. (1997). Runaway Worlds. Lecture delivered at Runaway Worlds Conference at the ICA, London, February.

Greenhalgh, L. (1998). From Arts Policy to Creative Economy. *Media International Australia*, May (87), pp. 84–94.

Leadbeater, C. (1999). *Living on Thin Air: The New Economy*. London: Viking.

McGuigan, J. (1998). National Government and the Cultural Public Sphere. *Media International Australia*, May (87), pp. 68–83.

McRobbie, A. (1998). *British Fashion Design: Rag Trade or Image Industry?* London and New York: Routledge.

McRobbie, A. (1999). *In the Culture Society*. London and New York: Routledge.

Valentine, J. (2000). Creative Britain. *Critical Quarterly*, Spring, 41(1), pp. 9–17.

Young, J. (1999). *The Exclusive Society*. London: Sage.

48

Tommy Hilfiger in the Age of
Mass Customization

Paul Smith*

The June 1995 issue of *Bobbin*, a garment industry trade journal, contained interviews with a number of high-ranking executives from the top forty apparel companies in the US. Each was asked to make some predictions about the industry and the challenges facing it in the run-up to the millennium. Of the primary concerns these industry leaders expressed, the first related to the organization of labor: they were clear about the need for continued downsizing, particularly within the domestic side of manufacturing. The second related to product development – they saw the need, in essence, to speed up the industry's process of product design, manufacture, and distribution in order to satisfy the ever changing and accelerating demands of retail outlets and their customers.[1]

These two areas of concern reflect the bipolar nature of the industry in the 1990s and in the era of the so-called globalization of economic processes. On the one hand, the "global" economy, dominated by Northern nations, is in the process of shifting the place of production to the South or the Third World, with the aim of reducing the costs of variable capital; in other words, core labor is being located on the periphery. On the other hand, or simultaneously, the place of consumption – and, of course, capital concentration – becomes ever more centralized in the North itself, opening up new channels of product distribution, marketing, and retailing.

In terms of the disposition of world labor power, then, this is a moment of redefinition, or of the search for a renewed vitality in capitalist rates of profit, and it is coincident with the tendency to abandon the old liberal productivist economic order and move toward the ideal, or the fantasy, of global capitalism. For the Northern "developed" nations, this shift has already subvented the rapid expansion and intensification of the means of consumption in the 1980s and '90s, provoking cultural changes and challenges as well as political and economic ones. The economic shape of the last two decades, especially here in the US, has been relatively clear in that respect: a downward turn in productive capital and a rise in the importance of financial capital have had the cultural effect of installing what can only be called a revolution in consumerism. For the garment industry, this revolution has had special relevance. The industry has responded by

*Pp. 249–62 from *No Sweat: Fashion, Free Trade, and the Rights of Garment Workers*, ed. A. Ross (New York and London: Verso). © 1997. Reprinted with permission from Verso.

developing mass designer fashion, extending and expanding the role of mass-produced clothing, affecting all kinds of cultural arenas and encouraging the construction of cultural identifies by way of apparel choices. However, it is open to question whether the industry is in fact responding to cultural demand or whether it is producing that demand as a way of itself responding to the changing conditions of global capitalism. Much of the pressure on apparel companies to refunction their production, to contract it out and offshore it, or simply to sweat it in the domestic workplace, derives from a perceived functioning of the domestic market which is said to be more highly competitive than ever and to be driven by the demands of retail companies – especially department stores – which are themselves responding to straitened domestic circumstances.

Apparel manufacturers have argued that this cranking up is driven by retailers alone. The fact that the tendency is equally bound up with the manufacturers' own continual offshoring of labor, in response to globalization trends, is too often downplayed. Northern apparel producers have to compete with Southern labor, but they can scarcely do so in terms of simple cost – the social conditions and the consumerist nature of Northern societies cannot countenance a drop in wages sufficient to compete. Thus, other modes or areas of competitive advantage have to be found, and these tend to concentrate around the acceleration of sales and, therefore, the speeding up of product development and change. So, for example, the California project Garment 2000, a corporation and union cooperative exercise, specifically suggests that, "We can't compete with the foreign market on labor rates, so we're going for another niche – an accelerated turnaround time for garment production."[2] The possibility of such accelerated turnaround and delivery, provoked by the international labor conditions of the industry, has its effect then in the consumer markets of the North. The retail industry and the apparel companies themselves adjust to this acceleration with speedier fashion cycles and merchandise availability. In any case, apparel companies find themselves in a position where they have to create a demand for the ever more transient commodities in the retail space.

The companies themselves call this process "mass customization," according to a recent lengthy survey of industry practice in the *Daily News Record*.[3] Mass customization entails a number of components that are, if not relatively new for the industry, at least of increasingly central importance. The imperatives of mass customization boil down to three essentials: greater product variety in stores, higher turnover, and lower and better managed inventories. Success in each area depends upon increased cooperation between apparel companies and their retailing outlets. As one executive notes, "Retail partnership is more critical than ever before. We have to share information about the consumer." Such sharing is by now heavily dependent on the use of new information technologies, or what the industry calls "data mining." "We're heavily into Electronic Data Interchange," another executive explains. EDI helps increase the speed and flexibility of merchandise sourcing, the flow and distribution of goods, and their replenishment and inventorization. In general the industry is now seeking to cut down the time between retailers' orders and warehouse shipment. Some manufacturers now accelerate these processes even more by shipping pre-priced goods, which can be put on display with minimal checking by in-store workers.

EDI has a second essential function, that of enabling research into the habits of consumers – both groups and individuals. One company claims that, as a result of data mining, "On a daily basis, we know 75 percent of what is sold, down to the lot and size." Such statistics are used to "anticipate" consumer trends and to fine-tune inventory control, but also to contribute to what the industry euphemistically calls "consumer communications," a term that exceeds the traditional sense of advertising. Companies now expect to engage in "an ongoing dialog with the consumer" – a "dialog" encouraged by means of a whole array of mechanisms, from 800 phonelines, Internet communications and Web sites, to in-store surveys and special event sponsorship (both in and out of stores), in addition to the more familiar use of visual and print media advertising.

Tommy Hilfiger's clothing company, TOM Inc., has been among the leading exponents in this intensified process of mass customization over the last few years. Indeed, Hilfiger clothing can be seen as an extreme case of how the idea of mass designer fashion operates. Mass designer fashion is a specific formation within the industry; it is not equivalent to traditional haute couture (which is often dependent upon highly artisanal means of production and is still somewhat outside the circuits of globalizing capital that nurture the mass clothing industry). Nor is mass designer fashion equivalent to standard garment production (which relies on reordering of staple and relatively stable goods season after season). Mass designer fashion is that peculiar formation which occurs within this nexus of the globalizing economy and the concomitant expansion of the means of consumption. Almost by definition it demands the capture of ever wider segments of the mass market at the same time as it needs to maintain familiar standards of product differentiation between brands, and offer frequent variation. Thus Hilfiger's relative importance and visibility in this context is in part a result of an ongoing strategy which has put his company in a position to cover just about all segments of the clothing market, but which also marks the products as identifiable and unique (the familiar Hilfiger logo and red-white-and-blue designs), offering appreciably variable "looks" or themes from season to season and year to year. While older companies like Levi Strauss, Timberland, or even Ralph Lauren have been slow in entering the mass designer fashion stakes – some being particularly wary of attempting to enter ethnically or racially identified areas of consumer culture – and while many other companies have been content with their long established market niches and hierarchies of market segmentation, the story of Hilfiger's company is just the opposite.

Beginning with a line of preppie-looking, clean-cut, and conservative sportswear (similar to that offered by the Gap, but somewhat more expensive), Hilfiger set out in the early 1990s to compete against department store staple lines like Ralph Lauren and Liz Claiborne with essentially Young Republican clothing. In the course of only a few years, this basically khaki, crew, and button-down WASP style, while remaining a constant theme in Hilfiger collections, has been submitted to variations which were intended to bring the product closer to hip hop style: bolder colors, bigger and baggier styles, more hoods and cords, and more prominence for logos and the Hilfiger name. These variations on a house-in-the-Hamptons theme opened up the doorway to black consumers, and Hilfiger's status is often closely linked to his popularity among African Americans. But at the same time, that market has clearly been only one focus for Hilfiger's ambitions, set on maintaining and expanding markets among nonblack consumers, and continually multiplying the range of products offered. In addition to hip hop styles, Hilfiger now sells golf wear, casual sportswear, jeans, sleepwear, underwear, spectacles, fragrances, and even telephone beepers. Tommy has recently moved into women's wear, and offers a women's cologne to go with the popular men's line. Not content with crossing all these areas of the mass market, Hilfiger seems currently to be conducting a foray into more classic designer markets with high-fashion shows, marked by his appearance at the British fashion shows in 1996 and by the introduction of a line of brightly colored men's wear that was clearly his attempt to become more of a haute couture designer.

Hilfiger's success has been quite astounding since the initial public offering of TOM in 1992. The company now has over 850 in-store department store sales points in the US. In addition, there are now almost fifty Hilfiger specialty stores across the country, a figure that has almost doubled in the course of two years. The company's annual report in early 1996 showed that revenue in the last quarter of 1995 was over $130 million, a 47 percent increase over the previous year. The company's cost for goods sold was less than $72 million, leaving more than $58 million in gross profits – a rate of more than 80 percent. The sound financial health of the company ensures its regular appearance on stockbrokers' to-buy lists, even though share prices keep rising. Early in 1995, the small consortium of TOM's original investors – which had bought the company from Mohan Murjani in the late 1980s – sold their remaining TOM stock for over $50 million, after a year in which the value of the stock had increased by 106 percent. Hilfiger himself was one of this small group, of course, and after his profit-taking he remained as an employee of the company, drawing more than $6 million a year in salary.

The economic success of TOM is explicable largely because the company has led the way in many aspects of mass customization. Hilfiger still does not have (so far as I'm aware) a Web site, or other of the mechanisms that apparel companies now routinely use. But TOM's corporate strategies have been ahead of those of many of its competitors, stressing the acceleration of product delivery, new forms of retailing partnership, innovative EDI usage for inventories and customer tracking, and of course, the speedy and timely introduction of new lines and redesigned goods, assuring consumers a wide range of product choices (something which Hilfiger himself sees as crucial in provoking and expanding demand).

TOM has been especially willing – again, leading the field – to engage in what is now the standard industry practice of licensing. TOM has licensing agreements with some of the world's major clothing companies. This network of links has been methodically and aggressively built up in just the last few years: Pepe plc for jeans; Stride Rite for shoes, Liberty Optical for eyewear, Estée Lauder for fragrance, Russell–Newman for shirts, Jockey for underwear; and so on. While licensing agreements probably have little impact on consumer consciousness, one advantage they have for a company like TOM is that they offer the borrowed cachet of known and respected manufacturers. This is all-important in negotiating sales points with department stores and generally in testifying to the quality of TOM products. Most of TOM's retailing partnerships are with department stores, and in 1995 about 70 percent of Hilfiger's products were sold at those venues. Added to TOM's strategies for speeding up product design, delivery, and turnover; licensing helps ensure access to what is still the principal channel for clothing sales in the US, where 65 percent of all clothing is sold by only thirty-five companies, the majority of which are chain retailers with department stores in malls and urban spaces all across the country.

One reason why the department stores are crucial for mass designer fashion is that many of them are located in the very malls where teenagers proverbially hang out. But perhaps a more important reason is that most big department stores offer their own credit cards which are relatively easy to obtain even if the consumer has low income or a bad credit rating. The industry standard is to offer such cards on the spot with only minimal credit checking and with an initial credit line (usually somewhere between $250 and $750, a relatively low risk for stores) that would encourage the purchase of, say, one complete outfit which would then be paid off over a period of about a year. Naturally, consumers pay heavily for this privilege, since interest rates on department store cards are typically about 21 percent per annum, almost 5 percent higher than the average US credit card rate. However, this cost does not seem to deter those who can access these credit lines. In both Britain and the US, clothing purchases constitute a huge part of consumer credit spending. A measure of the importance of this phenomenon is that the all-time record monthly credit spending in Britain – £6.9 billion in June 1996 – "was due in large part to clothing purchases."[4] US credit card debt in this era of the expansion of the means of consumption passed the $1 trillion mark late in 1995 and has continued to climb ever since. The peak production of this sea of debt occurs not at the Christmas holiday season, but rather at the "back-to-school" season when, according to the American Express Retail Index, a majority of US parents expect to spend an average of $363 per child, and a goodly proportion of that spending will be done on credit cards. The same report suggests that Hilfiger clothing would account for 5 percent of all back-to-school purchases.[5] In this respect, it's quite clear how TOM's strategies intersect with the expansion of the means of consumption.

Where the nexus of consumer-retailer-manufacturer is always most apparent, however, is in the area of advertising. Although TOM, as I've already said, has not explored the area of "consumer communications" quite so thoroughly as companies like Levi Strauss or retailers like Carson Pirie Scott, Hilfiger's exploitation of advertising media has been both thorough and path-breaking. Perhaps the most prominent feature of Hilfiger's strategy in this realm has been the use of high-visibility consumers. In a way that has still not been copied by many other apparel companies (Nike being an important exception), Hilfiger has always ensured that his clothing is found on celebrity bodies. In the last few year his clothing has been publicly displayed by sports figures like Don Nelson, coach of the New York Knicks, popular musicians such as Michael Jackson and the women of TLC, and by black male models like Tyson Beckford. In a series of 1994 spots on the music cable channel, VH1, Hilfiger tried to keep tabs on a more mainstream audience too, featuring performers like Tori Amos and Phil Collins. Any of these celebrities is, of course, a trendsetter, whose mostly urban image is intended to then become desirable in the shopping meccas of suburban malls.

Most important, Hilfiger clothes have been sported by a whole succession of African-American rap musicians. The story of Hilfiger seeing Grand Puba in the street wearing his clothes and inviting him to wear Hilfiger in public appearances is perhaps apocryphal, but it does speak to the general strategy that Hilfiger has adopted in relation to garnering a huge clientele among African Americans. Frequently donated Hilfiger outfits for use in performances and music videos, rappers have functioned as conduits of approval and authorization – authenticity, perhaps – for this white business attempting to sell what are essentially white styles to black consumers. In that sense, Hilfiger has used prominent African Americans in ways that, while they are often less formalized and contractual than the relationship between, say, Nike and Michael Jordan or PepsiCo and Michael Jackson, essentially serve the same purpose.

A certain rank of black sportspeople and entertainment figures (usually men) act as what I call a "regulatory elite" in US black culture. These are people who, earning millions of dollars a year in the face of the chronic and systematic immiseration and devastation of black communities in the US, are elevated to the status of cultural icons and are taken to bear virtually the whole burden of representing blackness in the culture. Even though the bill for the rewards collected by this regulatory elite are footed by predominantly white capital, their cultural significance stems from being venerated as bearers of black identity (by both blacks and whites, most likely – by whites wishfully thinking that racial divisions could be elided by their presence; by blacks, wishfully thinking that the status and spoils of someone like Michael Jordan are not eccentric).

Some of the force of this mechanism of regulation could be seen on display, of course, after the O. J. Simpson trial in 1995, when the not-guilty verdict was greeted by African Americans as a triumph for their race. A less spectacular or public instance, narrated by Darcy Frey in his book about black basketball hopefuls, *The Last Shot*, gives another insight into the workings of this system. Frey tells a story of trying to interview some promising young basketball players in the Coney Island projects, only to be told by their parents that he must pay large sums of money for the privilege.[6] The point, of course (and indeed, the point of Frey's whole book), is that within this one black community, the system whereby the regulatory elite is established is known and used as one of few possible ways of escaping the projects. Frey goes on to tell how the superstar elite is formed, beginning with the injection into the black community of money and inducements by sportswear manufacturers like Nike and by the white-run National Basketball Association (NBA), while the majority of the community remains in poverty, bound by totally limited expectations and possibilities. It is in this sense that the strange system of tokenizing black stardom can be described as regulatory.

And yet it is no simple matter in US culture to criticize this black regulatory elite, since it carries such a burden of African-American identity. It does, of course, become easier to criticize when someone so prominent as Michael Jordan shrugs off the ethical and political problems in his sponsorship relation with Nike and its Third World labor practices. Called to answer for the contradiction of his position, Jordan simply suggested that he could trust Nike "to do the right thing."[7] But for the most part, and as Jordan in fact demonstrates, the system does its work, and the African-American stars can count on there being little concern about the cultural and financial gap between them and the African Americans who are called upon to be their loyal and admiring audience.

For Hilfiger's company, the deployment of rappers like Grand Puba and Snoop Doggy Dogg in extended "consumer communications" has constituted a crucial part of the process of mass customization and has enabled a deliberate and thoroughgoing entry into the black youth market. It is, however, just one such component, and its efficacy depends absolutely on Hilfiger's coordinated effort in other areas of mass customization. The effectiveness of TOM's assault on this particular segment of the market is a function of the successful implementation of industry-wide strategies which have to be seen in conjunction with capital's tendency to outsource labor, to cut the costs of variable capital, and to expand the means of consumption in Northern markets. According to TOM's 1995 annual report, the five places where most Hilfiger clothing is made are Hong Kong, Sri Lanka, Macao, Indonesia, and Montebello, California. In that light, when Hilfiger gives away clothes to rappers, or establishes a loose professional alliance with African Americans like Def Jam boss Russell Simmons (also the owner of Phat Farm clothing company), or hires Kidada Jones (daughter of record tycoon Quincey Jones) to appear in his ads, these are in a sense epiphenomenal activities. What is crucial is the political and economic circuits in which they have their effects. Similarly, when black kids wear TOM merchandise, adopting the clothes and accessories and the Tommy logo as signs not just of fashionability but even of racial authenticity, they are doing more than just establishing a cultural identity and communality. Equally, they are placing themselves in a particular relation to political-economic circuits for which the possibility of their consuming in this way is one of capitalism's central desiderata or imperatives at this juncture when capital is dreaming of globalizing itself.

Of course, not all of Hilfiger's desired consumer audience and clientele is necessarily content with the spectacle of so many black males devotedly sporting Hilfiger clothing and willy-nilly directing African-American dollars into the Hilfiger coffers. One of the most vibrant forums on the Internet where the issues of fashion consumption are discussed is the "chat-room" of Streetsound,[8] a wildly energetic and mind-boggling torrent of opinion, most of which seems to be submitted by African-American men. Hilfiger's clothing and the operations of his company are perennial topics – a testament in itself to the central role his fashions play right now in black culture. But even though Hilfiger merchandise appears to enjoy support and patronage in towns from coast to coast, there are some dissenting voices.

The most common opposition to Hilfiger on this site appears to be an objection to the very principle of black patronage of white business. One such posting will give the flavor of many similar ones:

> Y'all are nothing but Tommy's wench. Some of you do not even have enough money to support the people who put on the jams (the place where you show how real you are and get your new bitch). Yet you spend your last fucking dollar to support some yout' in New York who doesn't give a fuck about give a flying fuck about you. Y'all are real stupid!!!

Such objections are both common and powerful – especially when seen as versions of how black identity might be safeguarded while rejecting the regulatory means put into place by white capitalism, and they echo longstanding debates within black culture. But obviously, they fall short of making connections between cultural and economic processes in the era of global capitalism and the age of mass customization.

This can be seen in an even starker light if we consider the nature of many of the advertisements for Hilfiger merchandise that appear in popular magazines. The principal motif in nearly all of them is the American flag. For instance, in Hilfiger's

1996 campaign for his new line of jeans, the American flag is spread out behind the figure of Kidada Jones, or is apparently the pillow for Ivanka Trump's pouting face. The American theme is even more overt – in the sense that it is verbal as much as visual – in ads for Hilfiger fragrances. The men's fragrance, Tommy, is now advertised under the slogan, "the real american fragrance" (after the first few advertising rounds, when it was called "the new american fragrance"), while the ads for the women's perfume, Tommy Girl, call it "a declaration of independence."

In the double context of, on the one hand, increasingly internationalized economic processes (where core labor is zoned to the periphery), and on the other hand, rampant mass customization (with its production of regulated subcultural identities in the North), TOM's use of this American-national motif is utterly symptomatic. The display of the US flag and the appeal to American identity obscure both the international and the subnational processes that are at stake in the political–economic and cultural formations of this our new world order. Another way of putting this is to say that the US national motif precisely names the power which presides over a division between the zoned labor of the South and massified consumption in the North and confirms that division as an opposition of interests.

These US nationalist emblems in TOM do have the unintended consequence of highlighting some of the complexities and difficult issues that are involved in thinking through the politics of the present situation. What we might call "production activists" in the North sometimes have a limited view of the way labor issues relate to the processes of consumption in the North, and often seem reluctant to address the fact that capitalism deliberately sets off the Northern consumer's "right" to forge cultural identity through consumption against the economic and social rights of core labor. But it is in everyone's interest to challenge such an imposed opposition between the interests of core labor and the interests of massified consumers.

There are, that is, potential benefits in stressing the fact that international labor issues are inextricably tied to the current expansion of the means of consumption in the North. A sharper understanding of the cultural consequences of mass customization might allow production activists to more effectively address those cultural constituencies whose interests are routinely represented as disjunct from the interests of laborers in the periphery. By the same token, cultural activists and organizers, especially within minority communities in the North, might perhaps be able to intensify their opposition to the international aspect of economic processes in the recognition that these are what underpin – indeed, regulate – contemporary forms of cultural identity.

Not that anyone would claim that such recognitions would immediately bring to a halt capital's double-headed movement – the international reorganization of labor power and the expansion of the means of consumption. But they might help produce a bit more anger.

Notes

1. "Top 40 Focus," *Bobbin* (June 1996).
2. "No Need to Trade in Conscience for Affordable Clothing," *San Francisco Chronicle*, July 21, 1996.

3. All the quotes in this and the following paragraph are from the various executives interviewed, and all information has been "mined" from the account of the interviews in "Views from the Top," *Daily News Record*, May 29, 1996.
4. "June Spend on Cards Hits 6.9 bn," *Electronic Telegraph*, July 29, 1996.
5. PR Newswire, August 7, 1996.
6. Darcy Frey, *The Last Shot* (Boston: Houghton Mifflin, 1994).
7. Quoted from CNN Headline News Channel, July 17, 1996.
8. Streetsound's board can be accessed on <<http://streetsound.clever.net/style/fashhiphop.html>>. It is worth keeping in mind here that the Internet itself, however much its advocates (myself included) want to think of it as a means toward a certain cultural freedom and even resistance, is also at the same time part of the expansion of the means of consumption that I've been referring to.

Constructing Purity: Bottled Water and the Commodification of Nature

*Andy Opel**

Growing up in the '70s, I remember the dusty gallon jugs of water in the produce section of the supermarket. I remember wondering why people would buy water when they could turn on the tap for seemingly limitless fresh water. From the layer of dust on those jugs it was clear not many people did, except in emergencies, snowstorms, hurricanes, and the like. Twenty-five years later, stores have entire aisles of bottled water with shiny labels, six-packs, "fresh," "natural," "spring." Again I find myself wondering, why are people *buying* water from the store? And now, today, people are not paying 50 cents a gallon for a milk jug of distilled water, they are paying a dollar a pint, or $8.00 a gallon. In many cases people are paying several times the price of gasoline, three times the price of milk, and almost the same price as coffee, juice, and soft drinks. In many stores, there are now as many brands of water as there are beer (*Bottled*). We see these waters in almost every food store in this country and we see people carrying the bottles around schools, offices, sporting events, and on the street. When we ask for water at a restaurant, we are now confronted with the question, "What kind?" The varieties of brands and styles has turned water into a chemistry lesson: "micro-filtered," "reverse-osmosis," "ozonated," "oxygenated," "mineral enhanced," "hydration drinks."

The proliferation of bottled waters raises a number of questions. What cultural changes have occurred to facilitate this explosion of bottled water? What are the political and economic conditions of water in the global marketplace of the '90s? How does branded, corporately marketed water affect the use and perception of public water supplies? How is the notion of purity constructed and what images are used to signify nature within the labels of bottled water? These are some of the questions I hope to address in this essay. By connecting corporate constructions of purity with marketing strategies, we will see the power of the sign in the commodification of nature.

The Political Economy of Bottled Water

The four elements have been commodities for a long time. Matches and later BIC disposable lighters gave us one of the great expansions of the commodification of fire, and

* Pp. 67–76 from *Journal of American Culture*, vol. 22, no. 4 (winter). © 1999 by Journal of American Culture. Reprinted with permission from Blackwell Publishing.

potting soil – corporate earth – has been packaged for some time. Water and air, more urgently necessary for life, have remained relatively absent from the ever-expanding commercial marketplace until recently. How these elements become commodified and the impact of this commodification pose powerful questions for the larger society. What is the condition of our democratic society when corporations become the guardian of something as essential as water and access to that water becomes a matter of free-market capitalism?

The political economy behind the growth of bottled waters reveals a major incentive to market something so simple, yet so essential as water: profit. In 1981, bottled water consumption represented 1.8% of the US Liquid Consumption Trends and by 1997, that number rose to 6.9%. This translates to 3.9 billion dollars in bottled water sales in 1997 (*Bottled*). Of the almost 4 billion dollars, 1.1 billion is from individualized bottled water sales. The industry draws a distinction between the larger, five gallon jugs distributed to water coolers in offices and homes and the smaller "premium" packaged bottles. For our purposes, we will be looking at the latter. The top five leading brands, based on 1997 dollar sales, are as follows:

1.   *Poland Spring* $297.9 million 7.6% market share
2.   *Arrowhead* 265.7 million 6.8% market share
3.   *Evian* 185.0 million 4.7% market share
4.   *Sparkletts* 183.9 million 4.7% market share
5.   *Hinckley & Schmitt* 123.1 million 3.1% market share (*Bottled*)

Some of these names have become very familiar and their parent companies are also familiar, with *Poland Spring, Arrowhead, Perrier*, and eight smaller brands all owned by Nestlé (Lenzner). Before we look more closely at the economics of the industry, it is worth examining the larger context of the recent history of our public water supplies.

During the recent period of bottled water proliferation, there were a number of public health scares involving drinking water. In 1993, Milwaukee experienced a water-borne outbreak of Cryptosporidium that caused 69 deaths and an estimated 400,000 people to become sick with flu-like symptoms (Kummer 41). A year later, in Washington DC, a filtration system failure caused "elevated turbidity" and an increase in diarrhea illness. These incidents, along with dozens of other scares around the country, appear to have added to a climate of distrust toward our public water supplies. Water quality varies dramatically from one region of the country to another. In the Midwest, agriculture has tainted much of the fresh water with traces of herbicides and pesticides, leaving people little choice but to turn to bottled water. In other areas, water is scarce or tastes bad because of mineral content. Although public drinking water quality may have declined in some parts of the country, the US Environmental Protection Agency (EPA) defends the safety of public water and maintains strict standards for all public drinking water.

In spite of government protection, some people have chosen to put their money into corporate purity instead of calling on their public officials to use tax dollars to address the public water supply. This impulse parallels the rise of neo-liberalism during this same period, trumpeting the virtues of the marketplace while demonizing government as an inefficient, ineffectual bureaucracy. The intersection of politics and economics in this instance created a multi-billion-dollar-a-year industry, moving perception and money away from government and into the private sector. We have heard few howls for cleaning our public water supplies, rather the sound of cash registers as the daily pints of premium water begin to add up to a new annual water bill of hundreds of dollars for more and more people.

The bottled water industry trade associations do not hesitate to capitalize on the tension between the public and the private. Their website states:

> Even the very delivery system that brings our tap water from the reservoir to our glass has been found to contain lead, copper, radon and a potpourri of other contaminants that can cause everything from severe headaches to cancer. Our long standing belief that American tap water is safe to drink may no longer hold water.

There is no conspiracy here, only the industry's desire to spread doubt about public water safety to boost sales of their "safe" water. What they don't say is most people pay less than $10.00/kilogallon (1000 gallons or 1 cent a gallon) for public water as opposed to the $6–8.00 per gallon price of the bottled waters. In some cases, the bottled water turns out to be tap water with a label. The beverage industry has been able to capitalize on high profile problems in any one of the more than 170,000 municipal water supplies while using that water to market as bottled water. Carol Browner, the E.P.A. administrator said, "We want the public to understand that standards set for municipal drinking water supplies are mandatory, and are monitored, and tested more often than for bottled water" (Kummer 8). Although the government supplies the water in some cases, and sets the standards in all cases, the industry uses public fears about public water while profiting from the protections they serve to undermine. The public investment in clean public water becomes a private resource for the bottlers. The International Bottled Water Association (IWBA) promotes the safety of bottled water through their website.

> Most bottled water comes from natural sources like springs or wells that originate from deep within the earth. These protected sources are inspected, tested and certified by the state or country of origin to be of sanitary quality. These bottled waters do not come from surface water sources where certain types of organisms, such as Cryptosporidium, are found.
>
> Some bottled water comes from treated municipal supplies. All IBWA member companies that use municipal sources employ processing methods, such as reverse osmosis, micron filtration and distillation and/or ozonation to remove microbiological and chemical contaminants, including Cryptosporidium, and to ensure the water is of high quality.

This statement reveals the two-pronged strategy of the beverage industry: establish the purity of their sources while raising the fears of contaminated public drinking waters. It also reveals the beginning of the corporate construction of purity: "natural" water coming from "deep within the earth."

Industry predictions remain bullish on water. "Bottled water consumption in the United States is growing faster than consumption of beer, soft drinks, or fruit juices.

The increase is attributed to health concerns of the aging baby-boom generation and the public's fears about the safety of tap water" ("Hoping"). And when it comes to water, there hasn't been a product with this much markup value in a long time. William O'Donnell, president of San Pellegrino USA, said, "People are willing to pay $3 for a cappuccino coffee, sometimes more than once a day. So why not pay $1.50 for water?" A large bottle of Pellegrino wholesales for $1 and sells for $6.25 in restaurants in New York City (Lenzner). Unlike coffee, water is essential and attractive to everyone. This combination is part of the success behind the marketing. The combination of health, weight loss and purity, with fears about public water, has been an overwhelming success for the bottlers. In addition to high markups, the bottled water industry enjoys extremely low costs for the product itself. Estimates range from $.0125 to $.06 cents per gallon of water depending on the distance between the source, the bottling facility, and the consumers (*Bottled*). From 6 cents a gallon to 6 dollars a liter is an impressive markup, enough to get the attention of every large food corporation in the world.

Water has gotten the attention of some of the biggest transnational corporations. PepsiCo entered the bottled water market in 1994, but started TV ads for its Aquafina brand in 1998. Using the tag line "Pure water, No Additives, No Attitude," Pepsi hopes to make Aquafina a mid-priced brand, countering brands like *Evian* in the upscale market (Cuneo Kramer). A product as simple as water has become a true test of branding. With little to distinguish the products themselves, marketers are relying on image, cost, and product placement to distinguish themselves.

From a theoretical perspective, Jean Baudrillard uses earlier definitions of commodities to explain the significance of symbols on commodities today. Marx defined a commodity as having two values: a use value and an exchange value. For example, a shoe has a use, to protect your feet. It also has a value in relation to other things (i.e., shirts, food, hats) with which it might be exchanged. Baudrillard updates this concept by saying a third element has been added, and that is the element of the sign or sign exchange value. An example of sign exchange value would be the Nike swoosh on a sneaker, making a shoe symbolically more valuable (and literally more expensive) without significantly altering the shoe itself. The values imbedded in these symbols are said to determine the value of the commodity. Baudrillard argues that the primacy of the sign has altered the traditional configuration of capitalism. "Traditionally, 'capital only had to produce goods; consumption ran by itself.' Today it is necessary to produce consumers, to produce demand, and this production is infinitely more costly than that of the goods" (Lukes 348). Nike shoes are a good example. With Third World production of the goods, the cost to produce the shoe is small compared to the promotion fees paid to Michael Jordan and the ad campaigns designed to connect the swoosh with Jordan's talent.

Applying this idea to bottled water, we see the cost of the product (water) to be small in comparison with the advertising and marketing campaigns. The symbols attached to the water become the primary cost to the producer. The "best" symbolic constructions of purity coupled with production and distribution create the best-selling water. The choice of symbols, how they are deployed, and how they are received are all connected to larger societal relations to nature as a social and political concern. The labels become a site where the sign exchange value of this commodity is maintained and reproduced.

Another sign of the proliferation of bottled water is McDonald's addition of bottled water to their menu earlier this year: "Seeking to tap into the fast-growing market for bottled water, burger giant McDonald's Corp. has quietly rolled out its own brand into some 1,500 restaurants . . . the bottle has a low-key label with the McDonald's logo" (Lukes 348). The trade journal notes that Coca-Cola, the supplier of McDonald's fountain drinks, has yet to enter the bottled water market and sees no immediate threat to their sales from the introduction of bottled water. This test marketing of water with fast food creates an interesting contradiction between the "purity" of the water on the one hand and the high fat, high salt, genetically engineered potatoes and rainforest beef that make up the rest of the meal.

The case of bottled water is part of a larger process of the commodification of nature within a capitalist, commodity culture. This "new" supermarket item exists at an intersection of consumerism and environmental issues, with corporations creating the environmental images and then reaping the profit of those representations. Dr. John Foster writes about the political economy of the environment and says that, "in order to halt, or even significantly slow down the rate of environmental deterioration, capitalist commodity society will have to give way to environmental necessity" (130). Here Foster is referring to the unsustainable rate of consumption of many of the planet's resources, including fresh water. In the case of bottled water, what we see is an increase in the resources used to distribute a readily available, local product. The packaging, labeling, advertising, transporting, and cooling of bottled waters create extensive hidden environmental costs in what may appear a benign, "pure and natural" drink. Another irony is that the petroleum companies that supply the oil to make the plastic bottles and the plastics companies who make the bottles are major contributors to the pollution and depletion of fresh groundwater, as are the transportation systems employed to get waters across the oceans and continents. The act of purchasing premium water thus becomes an act of contributing to the pollution of someone else's water. "One of the basic contradictions of the capitalist economy," according to radical philosopher Istvan Meszaros, "is that it cannot separate *advance* from *destruction*, nor *progress* from *waste*, however catastrophic the results" (qtd. in Foster 133). Bottled water can be seen by the consumer as *progress*, offering a safe, healthy alternative to a world of carbonated sugar waters, while at the same time these consumers may not see the hidden environmental costs of their purchase.

These environmental costs extend beyond the products themselves, and into public policy. With an increased reliance on bottled water by the middle class, there is the possibility of less urgency to confront the declining quality in public water supplies. And although consumers are assured by the idea of the purity of French alpine water, they may not stop to question the quality of the water in their ice cubes, soft drinks, beer and wine and any number of other hidden sources of tap water consumed every day. "In studies of advertising, the pervasive use of the natural to sell products has come in for little critical examination, perhaps because nature seems to live outside the important, contentious terms of race and gender" (Davis 10).

By closely examining corporate constructions of nature, we can see the marketplace as a site of political struggle. Consumer goods, particularly necessities like food and water, take on increased significance because of their prevalence in people's lives. Toby

Smith in *The Myth of Green Marketing* writes: "The topic of everyday, domestic consumption is important for at least three major reasons. First, it is the prime mover of resources through the ecosystem. Second, it is the source of aggregate demand in the marketplace. Third, it has potential to be a site of ecological political resistance" (159). Bottled waters fall into the first two categories, though they have yet to elicit any significant political resistance. Why we have not seen any resistance is an important question, and in part, is connected to the way these waters have been marketed. Through the skillful use of language and image, bottled waters have come to be associated with health, fitness, purity and "the natural." This has been accomplished through advertising campaigns and product labeling.

Constructing Purity: The Labels of Bottled Water

The words and images used to situate bottled waters in the marketplace are part of the capitalist commodity economy that supplies goods with symbolic exchange value and social meanings. These meanings, created within corporate structures, are laden with ideology and designed to create need while serving a growing market segment. Advertisements convey not only descriptions of the product, but values and *meanings* about how the product fits in a social context:

> As part of the culture industry, advertising constitutes an apparatus for *reframing meanings* in order to add value to products. Ads arrange, organize and steer *meanings* into signs that can be inscribed on products – always geared to transferring the value of one meaning system on another. In this way, advertising comprises a system of commodity-sign production designed to enhance the exchange value of commodities, by differentiating the meanings associated with each commodity. (Goldman 5)

Ads and labels then become a way of adding symbolic value to products, and the symbolic is then translated into material value. People are willing to pay more money for a product based on the images inscribed on the product through advertising. In the case of bottled water, the inscription of meaning is vital because there is so little difference between the products.

> "Packaging really sells the product experience," says Joe Kornick (partner at Chicago design firm Kornick Lindsey). "Nothing is more true in relation to water because of the difficulty in discerning taste. Instead of a ho-hum experience, the package can make it a great experience. It satisfies the rational and emotional needs of consumers." ("Bottled Water" 7)

The industry is well aware of the importance of the symbol and the label. At the 8th Annual Toast of the Tap: International Water Tasting & Competition, held in February 1998 in Berkeley Springs, West Virginia, in addition to awards for taste, a new category for bottled water packaging was established. The first-place winner, [Earth.sub.2]O, conveys with its label "the natural image of our pure, clean spring," said Brad Bevens, marketing manager for [Earth.sub.2]O. Alaska Ice Age won second place "with its dramatic 3-D glacier scene" ("Bottled Water" 8). With little to differentiate the waters, the industry has recognized a major element in the commodification process and rewarded those with the "best" packaging. For this reason, we will look closely at the symbols many of the leaders in the industry have chosen and attempt to reveal some of the meanings conveyed through those symbols.

Nature is an underlying theme on many of the bottled water labels. Nature has a long history as an advertising tool. How nature is presented can be revealing about the relationship between our current culture and the natural world. In *Decoding Advertisements*, Judith Williamson wrote:

> There have been periods in the history of our society when artificial was not a pejorative word as it is today; and when "natural" did not have the bundle of positive connotations which characterize it now. . . . This change in society's view of "the natural" no doubt stems from a change in material conditions – the importance of "the natural" increases directly in proportion as society's distance from nature is increased, through technological development. (124)

Williamson proposed that when a culture is removed from nature, nature becomes a symbol upon which cultural meanings can be imprinted. What is socially accepted becomes "natural" and the unaccepted, "unnatural." In the case of water, corporations are using this ability to imprint their cultural images onto nature (water), constructing new meanings of purity, detached from the nature that at one time provided the purity now re-created through the manufacturing process.

With the number of brands of bottled waters exceeding 900, it is beyond the scope of this essay to examine all or even most of them. Instead, I will look at some of the brands with large market shares, as well as some of the smaller brands with more limited distribution. I will look closely at individual labels and groups of labels to note themes and contrasts. While there are magazine ads, TV commercials, and company websites, I will focus on the labels because the label is the place where every consumer interacts with the product, choosing one product over another, and carrying those images with them out of the store. Labels and advertisements are different and serve different functions, yet the labels serve a powerful identification function in the case of bottled water and are the most prevalent source of brand image for many consumers.

Poland Spring had the largest share of the market in 1997, selling almost $300 million worth of water. The label used to sell all this water is predominantly green, with a picture of a central mountain framed by two smaller peaks and a river flowing toward the viewer. The mountain scene is circled by a tan ring, marked to appear as if it is wooden, with the words, "natural spring water" on the bottom half of the circle and the top obscured by the words "*Poland Spring*," with the word "Spring" being about half again as large as the word "Poland." Below "Spring" are the words, "since 1845." The words "From Maine" appear to the upper right of the picture.

As mentioned earlier, *Poland Spring* is a subsidiary of Nestlé, the company whose methods of marketing infant formula in the Third World were criticized for effectively making new mothers dependent on their products. Water is not so easily forced upon customers. The *Poland Spring* label appeals to another level of dependence. The construction of purity in this label is based on three distinct areas: geography, geology, and history. These themes recur across many bottled water labels on the shelf.

Poland Spring invokes the geography of the state of Maine. Maine is located within a particular physical place and a cultural space. While Maine is the physical place where the source of *Poland Spring* rises to the surface, it is also a locator in the construction of purity. As a cultural space, Maine is often associated with a resort area for the rich and famous, Kennebunkport, and presidential vacations, picturesque fishing towns, and lobster boats. At the same time, Maine the place has a history where rivers were dammed at the turn of the century to power mills. The near extinction of Atlantic salmon runs and the proliferation of paper mills evidence the human impact on Maine's water systems. The physical place of Maine has seen large tracts of pine clear cut for the timber and paper mills. Textile and paper mills relied on the consistent flow of the rivers to carry their effluent to the sea. The EPA reports, "Dioxin in fish tissue is the most significant problem in major rivers" (US), where dioxin is a major by-product of the industrial paper-making process. The ability of the cultural to mask the physical realities of history and geography becomes the tool of the corporation. To do the work of constructing purity out of an impure world, the corporation enlists myth and image, ancient story forms and the current popularity of nostalgia for the past.

The geology of the mountain becomes a second anchor for *Poland Spring*. The snow on the mountain is patterned like a glacier, but since there are no glaciers in Maine, the pattern may be from the trails of a ski resort. Because this is supposed to be spring water, the image of snow/glacier melt is incongruous. This is not spring water, but the image of last winter's snowfall. This snowfall, like much of the precipitation in the Northeast, is laden with the refuse of Midwest power plants. Acid rain, heavy metals, and a whole host of particulates drift in from the west, literally raining down on the place called Maine. The water that has caused a major die-off of high altitude conifers and is raising the pH level of lakes in Maine, is not what people want to pay eight dollars a gallon for.

Finally, the *Poland Spring* label invokes history, building on the nostalgia established by the cultural image of Maine. By using the phrase "Since 1845," *Poland Spring* can be seen as privileging the past. One reading of this would be to assume the water in the store today is very old water, having been entombed and protected from the ravages of modernism. The slogan gives the impression that the spring has been producing the same water, from the same pool of untainted reserves, for a century and a half. In a world where DDT has spread throughout the food chain, groundwater is likely to reflect the changes wrought by industrialism. It is hard to imagine a spring untouched by the industrial revolution, yet the pictures on the label help to create just that image. Another reading might be that the company is trustworthy because they have sold water for almost 150 years. A good track record becomes the signifier of trust, as if the company could prevent the downstream and downwind accumulation of a century's ecological excesses. In either case, history legitimates the product and with the help of nostalgia, reconnects the past to the present, bypassing the intervening years of industrialization.

Poland Spring also has text on the label, identifying the town where the spring is located and where the water is bottled. A trademarked slogan, "What it means to be from Maine," precedes a brief statement about the water. This slogan invokes the cultural space of Maine, allowing non-Maine-iacs to purchase a piece of nostalgic past, from the corporation that owns the trademark rights, of course. "To be from Maine," becomes something for sale, something desired by someone "from New Jersey." Below this slogan is a paragraph which begins, "*Poland Spring* is a real place, nestled deep in the woods of Maine." By emphasizing that this is not a Hollywood fabrication, this is a real place, the label calls on authenticity to verify the purity of the water. This "reality" is contrasted with the images that separate the real from the ideal. As we know, a "real" place has people, activity, commerce, roads, industry, neighboring towns, etc., none of which are pictured on this label. A real place is also related to other places, upstream, downwind, bedroom community, workers' ghetto, or Superfund site. Although this wording evokes authenticity, the reality of *Poland Spring* has been a source of debate.

In 1993, the State of North Carolina Department of Agriculture ordered *Poland Spring* and seven other brands off store shelves for "false and deceptive labeling." The state contended that the companies were selling "well" water as "spring" water (McCarroll). In North Carolina, "spring water" is defined as water that flows naturally to the earth's surface and is drawn off there. Bottlers contend that artesian water, water drawn through bore holes, is essentially the same and the bore holes allow faster, cheaper access. The Food and Drug Administration (FDA) did a review of this issue and concluded by defining "spring water,"

> as water that is derived from an underground formation from which water flows naturally to the surface of the earth. FDA has also decided to provide that "spring water" may be collected below the earth's surface through a bore hole. (Food 61)

The report said water drawn from a bore hole must meet the same standards as the spring water that is coming to the earth's surface. Any change in water quality would then preclude the bore-hole water from being called spring water. With this sleight of hand, the FDA allowed *Poland Spring* to retain the word "spring" even though the water is pumped to the surface as with any artesian well. This government regulation of the terminology of bottled waters adds to the power of the language used in these labels. As people believe strict definitions have been applied, terms like "spring water" and "natural" become sanctioned by the state. Yet, ironically, this is the same state, and the same set of regulations, that governs the public water supply that the public is growing to distrust. Unlike the term "spring water," the FDA has failed to define "natural" and instead relies on an "informal policy" that relies on standards like "minimal processing" with "nothing artificial or synthetic" added (Food 95). Although some states have adopted more specific standards, most defer to the FDA for consistency and trade reasons.

Mountain, or geologic imagery can be found on many bottled water labels. A survey of supermarkets in the Research Triangle region of North Carolina found *Evian*, *Volvic*, *Crystal Geyser*, *Aberfoyle Springs*, *Grayson*, and *Triton* all used mountain pictures or graphics as a central part of the label. These mountains are all snow capped and rugged with no trace of human or animal life, natural alpine areas raised above the polluted world of man and beast. These desolate winter images depict a rare place on our planet, a place where very few beings live, and where man only visits. Although mountains are often associated in the United States with places of retreat for the middle and upper classes, mountains are also isolating, difficult to traverse, and often the site of ecological assault. Mountains are the top of the watershed, and the actions within and upon them are carried downstream. From mining to logging, ranching to million, mountains worldwide and the rivers that run down them carry the scars of human activity. While many people do not live in the harsh world above the treeline, history has shown that from the Rockies to the Urals, people have spent enough time there to leave a scar.

To look at the *Crystal Geyser* label, you might think the water comes from the Alps or maybe the Canadian Rockies. Huge peaks sweep across the label, blanketed in snow, well above treeline. These are not just snowcapped mountains; the snow descends to the base, looking like the Himalayas in winter. A closer look reveals a small insert on the side of the label that describes the source of this water: the Blue Ridge Mountains of Tennessee. A green forested area in the foreground is labeled "source," a green mountainous area in the mid-ground is the "Cherokee National Forest," and some blue-tinted, snow-capped peaks in the background are the "Blue Ridge Mountains." Though the southern Appalachians are beautiful, there is only a short time each winter when some are snow-capped. At 6,684 feet, Mount Mitchell, the highest peak in the Blue Ridge and the highest peak in the continental United States east of the Mississippi, barely exhibits a clear treeline. The small trees at the top of most of the southern Appalachian peaks have been heavily damaged by acid rain drifting in from Tennessee and the Midwest, but this label makes it look like Tennessee might soon be hosting the Winter Olympics. The words "Alpine Spring Water" appear in the middle of the label beneath the name *Crystal Geyser*. "Alpine" is defined as: "of or pertaining to high mountains; living and growing on mountains above timberline, Latin *Alpinus*, of the Alps" (Morris). This geologic image then connects to a geographic image of European purity, linking mountains in the United States with the mountains of Europe. This serves a cultural function as well as a marketing function, since *Evian* water imported from France is one of *Crystal Geyser*'s main competitors.

The number three brand in 1997, *Evian* is in many ways synonymous with bottled water. This water travels across the Atlantic to reach the US consumer, bringing with it the images of the culture and sophistication of France. The *Evian* label uses a pastel color scheme, bright red lowercase letters for the word "*Evian*," and blue and white mountains across the top. The blue words across the bottom read, "Natural Spring Water From the French Alps." On the one-liter bottle, mountain-like shapes are sculpted into the plastic near the top and curving lines ring the bottom. The simplicity of the label is a central component of the symbolism. Mountains rise above the letters, above the works of men, disconnected from the ground. The absence of human, animal, or plant forms tells us this water is not connected to the systems we are a part of. Judith Williamson comments: "One of the most obvious ways you are invited to enter the ad is by filling in the absence" (77). Ads are not only the images presented, but the relation of those images to what is not re-presented. The viewer is then asked to fill in the meaning, and in this case, *Evian* invites you to escape the cyclical connections of water, evaporation, and rain. The mountains on the label are separated from the other text and color by a broad band of white, giving the appearance of floating above the crowded, polluted world of people and machines.

The airbrush look is replicated, though in a different color scheme, on the *Volvic* Spring Water label, also from France. These airbrushed mountains again invoke purity through the image of the absence of life, of the uninhabitable. Jagged peaks, disconnected from the ground, piercing the clouds, claim a purity through coldness. The glacial snowpack becomes the source, white and clean, deposited by the heavens. Though the labels read, "spring water," the images are of cold, clean snow, purified through inaccessibility. Spring water, on the other hand, comes from the ground, and in many cases is pumped out by industrial machines. The conflict between the purity of the alpine regions untouched by human hands and the reality of the human presence required to extract the water, bottle it, and bring it to market, is hidden in these images.

The connection between the geologic images of the mountains and the geographic images of place is repeated across a number of brand labels. *Volvic* uses mountain imagery yet, unlike *Evian*, articulates place and process on the label. A small picture of rolling green mountains is paired with a paragraph describing the Auvergne region of France, the supposed source of the Clairvic Spring where the water is bottled. The paragraph reads:

> In a protected natural park in the Auvergne region of France, *Volvic* Natural Spring Water filters through layers of ancient volcanic rock, resulting in its low mineral content, perfect balance, and high purity.

Thus we see the combination of history, geology, and geography, where the *ancient mountains* within a *French* natural (not national) park produce purity. Although the idea of a natural park may appear odd to some, with *park* referencing a human designation for space and *natural* implying a lack of human intervention, the Dannon Group, the corporation that bottles this water, apparently finds no conflict in the phrase. In contrast to the images of snow and purity through freezing, *Volvic* invokes the heat and power of the volcano to purify its water. From France to Canada to the United States, *place* figures prominently in water bottled lables. Mountains and rural areas, vacation spots or cultural landmarks, most labels locate the source and attempt to connect that source with purity while disconnecting that source from the world we drive our cars in, dispose of our garbage in, and flush our toilets in.

One brand whose label has expanded the role of the historical is *Le Bleu*. Though the name invokes France, this is an American product based in North Carolina with no source or bottling location identified. The image on the front of the label is of a man driving a cart drawn by two horses. The text reads, "Ultra Pure Drinking Water, Distilled Pure, Light and Refreshing." *Le Bleu* has a lengthy paragraph on the back label connecting the past to the present.

> The historical painting "Blue Ridge Water Wagon" symbolizes how once, finding pure, clean water was easy. When the air was clean, nature did a perfect job of making fresh pure water. The sun evaporated water from lakes streams, and oceans, then winds blew it

to the mountains where it condensed into rain and snow. Now, we can duplicate this purity nature once so freely gave us. We go 5 steps beyond mother nature before the water ever enters the bottle. We steam distill our water, then perform additional purification *through our patent pending purification process.*

One reading of this label moves us from the lost natural purity of the past, to the present where people have improved on nature, creating a new standard for purity. This new purity created by humans is also licensed by humans, with *Le Bleu* patenting, and thus owning, the process of purification once ubiquitous to the world we inhabit. The corporation becomes a site where natural processes are "improved upon" and appropriated for profit. "Mother nature" is personified, and presented as no longer able to do the job she once did. No reason is given for this, though the reference to "once so freely gave us" could imply that mother nature is no longer "giving." The wording implies that the reason for this lies with nature, not with people. It then becomes necessary for people to come in and improve upon nature's processes, creating the image of people acting to overcome the weakness or shortcomings of nature.

Man's improvement of water is a theme on a number of bottled waters. Two brands in particular exhibit this theme: Extreme Water H_3O Sport and Life O_2 Super Oxygenated Water. These brands draw on the idea that water is a central component of health, and by altering the water, man has made it more healthy. Extreme Water H_3O Sport uses bright colors in a jagged pattern as a design, dropping any overt reference to place or time. A side panel gives the source location in small print – Ontario, Canada – and adds the phrase, "Supercharged with ozone for additional purity." The back panel is a coupon for $24 off a visit to Busch Gardens and Water Country USA in Williamsburg, Virginia. The label makes no claims about the reality of an extra hydrogen atom added to H_2O (which refers to 2 hydrogen atoms attached to one oxygen atom and is the usual symbol for the molecular structure of water). By claiming to be "extreme water," and raising the number from 2 to 3, the label implies the creation of a new, highly purified water. While the text tells us the water is supercharged with ozone, O_3 is the chemical symbol for ozone. The label might be more accurate with a symbol H_2O_3, though this may begin to exceed widespread understanding of chemistry. With humans as the new agent of water creation, it makes sense that "extreme water" would be consumed in an environment constructed by humans: a theme park like Busch Gardens.

Life O_2, another improvement on the natural, claims to have 700% more oxygen than other bottled waters. Again, the label is a graphic, omitting any overt reference to place or time. The emphasis is on the science, the work of man. A side panel tells us,

> Discover The Oxygen Difference! Life O_2 is infused with extraordinary levels of pure atmospheric oxygen using our patented Superoxygenation process. This technology can produce more than seven times (700%) the amount of oxygen found in other bottled waters and beverages.

Again there is a tension between the natural and the technological. "Atmospheric oxygen" is added, invoking the idea of natural, fresh air, yet this is accomplished through a patented process, reliant on the uniquely owned and controlled machines of the corporation. The chemical symbol is used again, this time just the symbol for oxygen, O_2. The "sports cap" nipple is sealed with plastic labeled "Oxy-Loc" though the visible perforations reveal the lack of any airtight seal by this plastic. This nipple, which is common on many brands of bottled water, can be read as a corporate nipple, replacing mother nature as the source of life-sustaining water. This label conveys an image of the corporation as able to chemically alter a basic element of life, improve it, and make it available to everyone with a dollar to spend. In the waters marketed as sports drinks, nature is replaced by the chemist, refining and purifying one of the four basic elements.

Chemical symbols on bottled water labels are not the only place science has intersected with this consumer phenomenon. Scientists are now considering the potential effects of the consumption of bottled waters, which lack the tooth decay prevention of fluoride added to most municipal water supplies. A recent newspaper lead read:

> Parents hoping to give their children a healthy boost by switching from tap to bottled water may be doing more harm than good. That's the word from dentists who worry that bottled water isn't fortified with fluoride, the mineral primarily responsible for preventing tooth decay. (Hicks)

A new conflict has been created between a previous public project to create better water and a new corporate product that claims greater purity through patented processes. This conflict can be seen as embodying the tension between the fears surrounding public water supplies and the corporate desire to exploit those fears and sell repackaged tap water. Purity then becomes a site of cultural struggle, with public and private entities vying for the ability to inscribe water (nature) with their cultural identifications. Although this is part of the commodification process, the struggle between health and purity adds a new dimension, pitting competing notions of well-being against one another.

Conclusion

Bottled water has become a major influence in the beverage industry. The availability of safe, cold water as an alternative to caffeinated, carbonated, sugary drinks appeals to many consumers for reasons ranging from health to fitness, diet to convenience. These water products are packaged in diverse ways, emphasizing history, geology, and geography, patented processes and pristine sources as legitimators of purity. The labels use a variety of text and images to attempt to convey purity through culturally recognizable symbols. Many of these images mask the connections between human activity and the natural world, presenting instead images of water isolated from the effects of the modern industrialized world.

At the same time, it is this industrialization which has so severely limited the supplies of clean drinking water worldwide, and is the necessary agent to allow for the production and distribution of specialty waters to a consumer society. This process of production and distribution of non-local water further impacts the global water supplies through the environmental costs of extraction, packaging (manufacturing and disposal), transportation, and maintenance (refrigeration and storage) of the bottled water. Although the lure of safe, corporate-sanctioned water appears to be a healthy beverage alternative, the environmental and social impacts have yet to be seen. As people become accustomed to paying $8 a gallon and having water filters in their homes, negative changes in the public water supplies may raise fewer concerns or a less vocal response. With something so essential to life as water, the thought of stratified levels of purity raises significant questions about the benefits of corporately controlled water supplies. If access to safe drinking water becomes a matter of access to the income and privileges of the middle class, a large portion of our population may succumb to the dangers of unsafe water. Regardless of dire predictions, the current commodification of water has raised the cost of water for everyone – water that in many cases has been purified with tax dollars and repackaged with corporate images. Revealing these images for the advertisements they are is one step toward reclaiming the natural and understanding the commodification process.

References

"Bottled Water Is a Packaged Deal" (1998). *Beverage Industry* 89(4), p. 7.

The Bottled Water Web (1998). Online at www.bottledwaterweb.com (accessed September 29, 1998).

Cuneo Kramer, Alice Z. (1998). Aquafina Takes the Middle vs. Upscale Water Brands: Pepsi-Cola's Midpriced Entry Readies First TV Effort. *Advertising Age* 69(25), p. 12.

Davis, Susan G. (1997). *Spectacular Nature: Corporate Culture and the Sea World Experience.* Berkeley: University of California Press.

Food and Drug Administration, Deptartment of Health and Human Services (1995). 21 CFR Parts 103, 129, 165, and 184 Docket No. 88P-00301 RIN 0910–AA11.

Foster, John Bellamy (1994). *The Vulnerable Planet: A Short Economic History of the Environment.* New York: Monthly Review.

Goldman, Robert (1992). *Reading Ads Socially.* London: Routledge.

Hicks, Joyce Clark (1998). Tap into Fluoride for Kids' Teeth. *News and Observer*, November 26, pp. El, 3.

Hoping to Cash in on Liquid Assets (1998). *Nation's Business* 86(10), p. 74.

International Bottled Water Association Home Page (1998). Online at www.bottledwater.org/facts/crypto.html (accessed November 1998).

Kummer, Corby (1998). Carried Away. *New York Times Magazine*, p. 38.

Lenzner, Robert (1997). A Monster Beverage Event. *Forbes* 160(9), p. 64.

Lukes, Timothy W. (1991). Power and Politics in Hyperreality. *Social Science Journal* 28(3).

McCarroll, Thomas (1993). Testing the Waters. *Time* 141,17, 54(1).

Morris, William (ed.) (1981). *American Heritage Dictionary.* Boston: Houghton Mifflin.

Smith, Toby M. (1998). *The Myth of Green Marketing: Tending Our Goats at the Edge of Apocalypse.* Toronto: University of Toronto Press.

US Environmental Protection Agency. *Maine Water Quality*, online at www.epa.gov/ow/resources/9698/me.html (accessed November 1998).

Williamson, Judith (1978). *Decoding Advertisements: Ideology and Meaning in Advertising.* London: Marion Boyers.

IX

Music

50

Just a Girl? Rock Music, Feminism, and the Cultural Construction of Female Youth

Gayle Wald*

Cause I'm just a girl, little ol'me
Don't let me out of your sight
I'm just a girl, all pretty and petite
So don't let me have any rights.
Oh, I've had it up to here!
— No Doubt, "Just a Girl"

Gwen is someone that girls
can look up to and feel like they
know. She is very Everygirl.
— Tony Kanal, No
Doubt bassist[1]

It would have been difficult to tune in to a US Top 40 radio station for very long during summer and fall 1996 without hearing at least one iteration of "Just a Girl," the catchy breakthrough single that propelled the neo-ska band No Doubt to a position as one of the year's top-selling rock acts. "Just a Girl" not only earned No Doubt commercial visibility, it also established twenty-seven-year-old Gwen Stefani, the band's charismatic lead singer, as the latest in a series of female rock musicians to have attracted widespread commercial visibility as well as a loyal following of young female fans. Sporting a bared midriff, retro platinum hair, and a conspicuously made-up face (which often included an Indian *bindi* ornamenting her forehead), Stefani quickly established a reputation as a skillful and dynamic live performer who put on energetic, no-holds-barred shows. Stefani's performance of "Just a Girl" at a 1996 Seattle concert – one variation of an act she was still performing in summer 1997 – provides a memorable illustration. At first prostrating herself on the stage and repeating the phrase "I'm just a girl" in an infantile, whimpering voice, she then abruptly shifts gears, jumping up, railing "Fuck you, I'm a girl!" at the delighted audience (at least half of whom were young women), and exuberantly launching into the remainder of the song.[2]

*Pp. 585–610 from *Signs: Journal of Women in Culture and Society*, vol. 23, no. 3. © 1998 by The University of Chicago. Reprinted with permission from the University of Chicago Press.

Stefani's dramatic staging of disparate modes of femininity exemplifies her adept manipulation of rock spectacle in the tradition of female rockers such as Siouxsie Sioux, Grace Jones, Poly Styrene (of X-Ray Spex), Annie Lennox, Courtney Love, and Madonna. More significantly, her performance of "Just a Girl" exemplifies a trend that since the early 1990s has gained increasing prominence within rock music cultures: female musicians' strategic performance of "girlhood" and their deliberate cultivation of various "girlish" identities in their music, style, and stage acts. The performance of girlhood by contemporary female rockers encompasses a wide range of musical and artistic practices by women within, outside of, and on the margins of the corporate mainstream: from singer-songwriter Lisa Loeb's championing of female nerdiness and cultivation of childlike vocals; to the independent Canadian band Cub's repertoire of songs about childhood, played in an offbeat, deliberately lo-fi manner; to Courtney Love's infamous "kinderwhore" costume of a torn and ill-fitting baby-doll dress and smudged red lipstick; to the phenomenal and global popularity of the Spice Girls, the seemingly omnipresent all-female Britpop studio group that updates the manufactured glitziness of the "girl groups" of the 1960s while promoting a playful, if equivocally feminist, notion of "girl power."[3] Such calculated and, in Love's case, deliberately sexually provocative performances of girlish femininity draw on the mid-1980s precedents set by Madonna (especially around the time of her work in Susan Seidelman's 1985 film *Desperately Seeking Susan*) and Cindy Lauper, whose 1984 hit "Girls Just Want to Have Fun" is revised and updated in No Doubt's "Just a Girl." These earlier pop-rock icons – significantly, the first women in rock to attract the kind of devoted following of young female fans usually associated with male rock stars[4] – set the stage for performers like Stefani, who has attracted her own following of fourteen-year-old "Gwennabes" who clamor backstage at No Doubt shows hoping to get a glimpse of their idol. Following in the footsteps of their progenitors Lauper and Madonna, performers such as Stefani and Alanis Morissette have discovered in acting "like a girl" new ways of promoting the cultural visibility of women within rock music. At the same time, the music industry has discovered in these female stars (each with her own carefully cultivated star persona) new ways to sell its products to young female consumers (i.e., "real" girls).

This chapter examines contemporary female rock musicians' representations of girls, girlhood, and "girl culture" – popular cultural practices that have a corollary in the emergence of what I call, "girl studies" – a subgenre of recent academic feminist scholarship that constructs girlhood as a separate, exceptional, and/or pivotal phase in female identity formation.[5] As evidenced by "Just a Girl," the song that, not incidentally, propelled Gwen Stefani to her position as female rock icon, the performance of girlhood, although by no means a homogeneous or universal enterprise, can now be said to constitute a new cultural dominant within the musical practice of women in rock. This is particularly the case among white women "alternative" rockers, who draw on practices pioneered in the early 1990s in independent music. In this realm, female artists have ventured to celebrate girlhood as a means of fostering female youth subculture and of constructing narratives that subvert patriarchal discourse within traditionally male rock subcultures.[6] The "girlishness" so conspicuously on display among these contemporary women rockers demands attention, not only because it signals the emergence of new, "alternative" female rock subjectivities (revising earlier genre-specific models such as the rock chick, the singer-songwriter, or the diva), but because in so doing, it conveys various assumptions about (white) women's visibility within popular youth/music culture, signposting the incorporation – indeed, the commercial preeminence – of ironic, postmodern modes of gender performance. My interest in this essay is neither to celebrate nor to denigrate the girl as a new modality of female rock performance, but rather to argue that the emergence of the "girl" signals an important moment of contradiction within contemporary youth/music cultures. In the example offered by Stefani, the strategy of appropriating girlhood, like the word "girl" itself, signifies ambiguously: as a mode of culturally voiced resistance to patriarchal femininity; as a token of a sort of "gestural feminism" that is complicit with the trivialization, marginalization, and eroticization of women within rock music cultures; and as an expression of postmodern "gender trouble" that potentially recuperates girlhood in universalizing, ethnocentric terms. For one, even as the song's lyrics redefine girl in a rhetorical or sarcastic manner, Stefani's girlishly feminine persona – and her very commercial popularity, tied as it is to her performance of gender – potentially furthers the notion that within patriarchal society women acquire attention, approval, and authority to the degree that they are willing to act like children. Moreover, just as "Just a Girl" plays cleverly with the codes of good girl/bad girl femininity, so Stefani's performance is carefully calibrated to display elements of "transgressive" femininity (without abandoning the principle that a female rock musician's "pretty face" is the ultimate source of her commercial popularity and, therefore, cultural authority). Indeed, Stefani's performance evinces the possibility that the recuperation of girlhood may not, in and of itself, be incompatible with the relentless eroticization of women's bodies within corporate rock (a contradiction embodied in Stefani's look as a kind of punk Marilyn Monroe); in other words, that female rockers can play at being girls, and even mock the conventions of patriarchal girlhood, while remaining sexy and/or retaining "the charm of passivity."[7] The point here is not merely that "girlish innocence" sells records, but that Stefani's sarcastic discourse of helpless, innocent girlhood simultaneously functions as a strategy of feminism and a strategy of commerce (where feminism and commerce exist in a complex and shifting, rather than a simple and binary, relation to one another). Staged within the very corporate institutions that are agents of dominant discourses that divest women of cultural power, Stefani's performance of infantile, girlish femininity may be symbolically, if not actually, redundant.

As the foregoing analysis of "Just a Girl" is meant to suggest, seemingly transgressive gender play within contemporary rock music cultures often "fronts" for far less transgressive codings and recodings of racialized and nationalized identities. At its worst, such recuperation of girlhood has been staged in terms that equate girlness with whiteness.[8] For Stefani, in particular, playing with the signifiers of girlhood is tacitly a strategy of bolstering white racial authority – indeed, of bracing precisely that cultural power that authorizes her to engage in the parodic mimicry of gender norms without social penalty. In such a way, "Just a Girl" accentuates Stefani's gender transgression – her position as a girl lead singer – while minimizing the visibility of another, more salient aspect of her performance – her negotiation of ska, Jamaica's first urban pop style and No Doubt's primary musical influence (by way of English "rude boys" and 2-toners). Indeed, Stefani's pogo-inspired dance style and her display of raw, raucous energy are themselves hallmarks of ska performance reframed within the context of outrageous, uninhibited, and confident white female alternative rock performance. In this scenario, Stefani's self-conscious "innocence," "helplessness," and "charm" are not only crucial to her critical disarticulation of girlhood from its meaning within patriarchal discourse; they also enable her to naturalize national, and racial, identity. In focusing attention on gender performance as a privileged site and source on political oppositionality, in other words, critical questions of national, cultural, and racial appropriation can be made to disappear under the sign of transgressive gender performance.

This instance of how a contemporary female rock icon's appropriation of girlhood can mask other, related kinds of appropriation recalls Madonna's appropriation of styles associated with black gay drag performance in her hit song and video "Vogue," a song calculated to display Madonna's own transgressive gender/sexual identity. More recently, the emergence of the "girl" as a newly privileged mode of white femininity within alternative rock coincides with the appearance of the white male "loser" (e.g., Beck, Billy Corgan of Smashing Pumpkins, and Kurt Cobain of Nirvana), whose performances of abject or disempowered masculinity work to recuperate white racial authority even as they circulate within an ostensibly self-critical performative economy of "whiteness."[9] Such observations necessitate a rethinking of what Coco Fusco calls "the postmodernist celebration of appropriation";[10] at the very least, that is, an acknowledgment of the need to draw critical distinctions between the feminist refusal of patriarchal discourse and performances that circulate the signs of refusal while actually expressing complicity with patriarchal discourse. As Fusco writes, it is imperative that we "cease fetishizing the gesture of crossing as inherently transgressive, so that we can develop a language that accounts for who is crossing, and that can analyze the significance of each act."[11]

Fusco's insight is crucial for specifying and localizing the political efficacy of what Ernesto Laclau terms "disarticulation-rearticulation," or the process of symbolic struggle through which social groups reformulate dominant codes as a means of negotiating political-cultural agency.[12] Such a practice of critical reappropriation is frequently invoked in discussions of how various subaltern populations discover a means of actively confronting and resisting marginalization in the ironic repossession of signs otherwise meant to enforce marginality. Feminist-marxist critic Laura Kipnis, following Laclau, explains this process as one in which "raw materials can be appropriated and transformed by oppositional forces in order to express antagonisms and resistance to dominant discourses."[13] And yet it is clear in the case of Stefani's sarcastic send-up of "girl," a word that in the context of rock music cultures often signifies not female youthfulness, but female disempowerment, (i.e., patriarchal condescension toward and trivialization of women), that such disarticulation-rearticulation does little to uncouple hegemonic girlhood from something more akin to the brasher and insubordinate "Fuck you, I'm a girl!"

Fusco's argument additionally insists on an interrogation of the links between the cultural practices of contemporary female rockers and various racially and culturally specific assumptions about girlhood. Acquiring its meaning, like the signifier woman, within the context of specific discursive regimes, girlhood is not a universal component of female experience; rather, the term implies very specific practices and discourses about female sexuality, women's cultural-political agency, and women's social location. Likewise, the various contemporary narratives of girlhood produced and disseminated within US rock music cultures are formed within the terms of very particular struggles for social and cultural agency. Moreover, and as revealed by the contrast between the actual maturity and/or musical expertise of the performers in question and the youthfulness of their primary audiences, these struggles to specify and potentially even radicalize girlhood are inseparable from late capitalism's desire for new, youthful markets.

What, then, is the relation between feminism and strategies of representing girlhood within US rock music cultures? Especially in the last decade of the twentieth century, notable for the advent of an artistically self-assured and cannily enterprising generation of highly visible women rock artists, can the strategic "reversion" to girlhood work as a strategy for feminism, or for producing feminist girls? Given the contradictions embodied in Stefani's "Just a Girl," to what degree is the appropriation of girlhood, as a strategy particularly associated with white women's rock performance, also a strategy of performing race – of racializing girlhood itself? How might female rock performers who occupy a different relation to hegemonic girlhood construct different narratives of girlhood?

In the following pages I investigate these questions in more detail and as they pertain to two specific groups of performers: first, the young women in independent rock known as Riot Grrrls, who in the early 1990s initiated their own ongoing "girl-style revolution," and, second, Shonen Knife and Cibo Matto, two Japanese all-female bands that have attracted small but significant US followings, particularly among indie rock aficionados.[14] In so doing, I rely primarily on a critical analysis of the acts, images, music, and lyrics that these women produce, as well as on the public, mediated narratives that circulate (in the print media, on the Internet, in fanzines, on MTV, or in hearsay) around the music and the performers. As my opening story about Gwen Stefani suggests, the contradictions that characterize the use of the girl as a mode of cultural resistance within female rock performance are not necessarily experienced as such by the consumers of this music, who may be more or less receptive, depending on the context and the particularities of their own social locations, to the limitations (political, ideological, and even aesthetic) that such contradiction imposes on a straightforwardly celebratory narrative of such performance. From the standpoint of a certain girl consumer forbidden from using the F-word at school or at home, for example, Stefani's profane mockery of/revelry in girlness may have an air of transgression, danger, or defiance (against parental and school authority, against gendered bourgeois standards and expectations) that is far less salient to another girl consumer (potentially of the same class, national, regional, and ethnic/racial background) more inclined to see Stefani's performance as *merely* playful, without the substance that would mark it as authentically transgressive. The instability of the strategic reappropriation of girlhood is mirrored and reproduced, in other words, in the very instability of the "meanings" that consumers construe from performers who play the "girl" or who attempt to signify "girlness" in an ironic or parodic fashion.

On the other hand, and as the following discussion is meant to illustrate, the ethnocentrism that characterizes certain appropriations of girlhood *is* played out at the level of production, where female musicians operate within very differently racialized spheres of girlhood. While the example of Riot Grrrl raises specific questions about the relation between ideology and independent modes of cultural production, as well as about the potential instrumentality of girlhood to a feminist critique of the corporate music industry, the case of Japanese women bands illustrates how women who are marginalized by dominant narratives of race and gender (understood as mutually constitutive discourses) negotiate their own parodic or complicit counternarratives. Insofar as media representations of Japanese women rockers recapitulate familiar stereotypes of Asian femininity, giving rise to images of Japanese female artists as *ideally* "girlish" and "innocent" (a portrayal that is not necessarily at odds with representations of "exotic" Asian female sexualities), these artists produce distinct narratives that deny girlhood the status of universality and that instead engage the cultural and racial specificity of hegemonic girlhood. These observations have relevance, moreover, to the ways that girlhood is recuperated – or not – within the varied musical and performance practices of African American women, including popular young female performers such as Da Brat, Lil' Kim, Foxy Brown, and Brandy (as well as, perhaps, an earlier incarnation of the group TLC), some of whom (e.g., Brandy) have worked to project an air of girlish "innocence" in their music, videos, lyrics, and performance, and others of whom (e.g., Foxy Brown) have aggressively marketed their "youthful" sexuality, sometimes by pretending to be younger than they really are.[15]

My argument about the ambiguous political effects of "acting like a girl" – either as a strategy for progressive, antiracist feminism or a means of fostering the careers and the creativity of young female popular musicians – is informed by my own fan/consumer practices, as well as by my status as a relatively young white female academic. The issues I discuss here are particularly germane to my own discovery, around 1992, of the loud, fast, and unapologetically "angry" music associated with the predominantly white middle-class women in and around the Riot Grrrl movement. This musical subculture not only provided me new aural and kinesthetic pleasures, but it also encouraged me to begin writing about contemporary music culture as part of my professional practice. It is therefore with an investment simultaneously political, professional, and personal that I approach the question of how girlhood has been appropriated and coded – not, that is, to trash some of the very music and musical practices that have afforded me pleasure, but to strike a cautious and critical tone about them. Although they often are constructed as mutually exclusive in cultural studies analysis, aesthetic pleasures are indissolubly linked to ethico-political critique and hence to the practices inspired and mediated through such critique. This essay is thus not an exercise in critiquing pleasure, but is rather a critique of the production of pleasure through gendered and racialized narratives that signify as "new," transgressive, or otherwise exemplary.

Six years before Gwen Stefani and No Doubt burst onto Top 40 radio and MTV, a small group of young women musicians active in and around the punk music scenes in Washington, DC, and Olympia, Washington, produced a two-page manifesto calling for a feminist revolution within independent rock – what they touted under the slogan "Revolution Girl-Style Now." At the time, members of the bands Bratmobile and Bikini Kill, the independent women rockers at the forefront of this movement, coined the term

Riot Grrrl as a means of signposting their snarling defiance of punk's longstanding (although hardly monolithic) traditions of misogyny and homophobia, as well as the racism and sexism within the corporate music industry. Together with other women active in various punk scenes (such as the related, albeit separate, movement of lesbians in "homocore" music, including the all-female band Tribe 8), they have not only consistently advocated the creation of all-female or predominantly female bands, but they have also emphasized women's ownership of record labels and their control over cultural representation. This last goal has been fostered by myriad Riot Grrrl-affiliated or girl-positive fanzines (such as *Girl Germs* and *Riot Grrrl*), inexpensively produced publications that circulate through feminist bookstores, independent music retailers, networks of friends, and word-of-mouth subscriptions and that explicitly envision women's fan activity as a legitimate and authentic form of cultural production.

For the young, predominantly middle-class white women who have participated in Riot Grrrl subculture, reveling in "girliness" constitutes an aesthetic and political response to dominant representations of female sexuality produced by the corporate music industry, as well as a strategy of realizing women's agency as cultural producers within independent rock. By highlighting girl themes in their music, lyrics, dress, iconography, 'zines, and the like, performers such as Cub, Tiger Trap, Heavens to Betsy, and Bikini Kill have attempted to produce a representational space for female rock performers that is, in effect, off-limits to patriarchal authority, in a manner akin to the way that girls' clubs are off-limits to boys. Such an emphasis on girliness has enabled these women performers to preempt the sexually objectifying gaze of corporate rock culture, which tends to market women's sexual desirability at the expense of promoting their music or their legitimacy as artists. Riot Grrrls's emphasis on forms of girl solidarity has important practical implications as well. For example, Riot Grrrl advocacy of all-women or predominantly women bands originates not in a belief in the aesthetic superiority or in the "authentic" oppositionality of such groups, but in the practical recognition that rock ideology (e.g., the equation of rock guitar-playing with phallic mastery) has dissuaded many young women from learning to play "male" instruments. Similarly, although it was widely derided by male punk rock aficionados as "separatist," the Riot Grrrl practice of reserving the mosh pit (the area directly in front of the stage) for girls stemmed from a desire to rethink the social organization of space within rock clubs and other music venues.

A look at one aspect of Riot Grrrl artistic practice – the carefully designed sleeves of seven-inch records – reveals that for these women in indie rock, resistance to patriarchal discourse takes the form of a rearticulation of girlhood that emphasizes play, fun, innocence, and girl solidarity. The silk-screened sleeve of a 1993 Bratmobile/Tiger Trap split seven-inch (i.e., a seven-inch record that includes one track from one band on each side) on the San Francisco-based label Four-Letter Words features a rudimentarily drawn image of a smiling girl doing a handstand (taken from Kotex tampon advertisements circa 1968), while a Bratmobile/Heavens to Betsy seven-inch released at about the same time features a photograph of the bared midriffs of two young women wearing hip-hugger jeans and tank tops, each sporting the name of a band on her stomach. Many of the images on Riot Grrrl fanzines and record sleeves use childhood photographs of band members to similar effect, as on the sleeve of the "Babies and

Bunnies" seven-inch record by the Frumpies, a Riot Grrrl group combining members of Bikini Kill and Bratmobile recording on the Olympia, washington-based Kill Rock Stars label. The cover of a 1993 Cub seven-inch titled "Hot Dog Day" (Mint Records) intimates themes of girl solidarity and budding queer sexuality by picturing a silver necklace dangling a charm that depicts two smiling girl figures holding hands.

The relentless cuteness of these representations, which might be merely sentimentalizing or idealizing under other circumstances, signifies ironically within the context of punk youth music subcultures, where "youth" is more likely to be associated with aggression, violence, and crisis, and where youth and youthfulness are frequently conflated with boyhood. Similarly, while nostalgia for an imagined past might be merely reactionary in another context (e.g., in debates over multiculturalism and in the much-touted claim that Americans have forsaken a previous commitment to civic virtue), in the context of Riot Grrrl performance these images of playful and happy girlhood are attempts at self-consciously idealizing representation. Such a recuperative iconography of girlhood contrasts – markedly, in some cases – with the music itself, which regularly explores themes of incest, the violence of heteronormative beauty culture, and the patriarchal infantilization and sexualization of girls: in short, themes that conjure not a *lost* innocence, a fall from childhood grace, but an innocence that was not owned or enjoyed, a grace that was denied.[16] The performance of nostalgia complicates and extends the Riot Grrrl performance of righteous outrage at patriarchal abuse; in other words, invoking a yearned-for innocence and lightheartedness that retroactively rewrite the script of childhood.

Yet such idealized representations of girlhood, while undeniably pleasurable and therapeutic, are of uncertain practical or strategic value as a feminist realpolitik, particularly outside the context of popular youth/music culture. At the very least, the nostalgia that characterizes many of these representations lends itself to the production of problematically dystopian, or postlapsarian, narratives of adult female sexualities. Indeed, one of the paradoxes of this nostalgic appropriation of (imagined) girlhood is that it primarily responds to the music industry's infantilizing representation of *adult* female sexuality, as well as to rock music's particular legacy of imagining women's contributions in sexual terms (e.g., women as groupies, sexual sideshows, rock chicks, or boy toys).[17] It is telling, for example, that media coverage of Riot Grrrl – which reached its peak virtually simultaneously with the music, around 1992 or 1993 – focused primarily on the display of anger, "fallenness," or aggressivity rather than cuteness, innocence, or girlish passivity, not only because the Riot Grrrl name itself emphasized girlhood "with an angry 'grrrowl,'" as the *New York Times* put it, but also because these were already familiar tropes from an earlier incarnation of punk music in the 1970s.[18] The strategic reversion to girlhood not only rests on an ability to imagine girlhood outside of patriarchal representation, it also presumes cultural entitlement to "womanly" subjectivity.

The self-conscious performance of nostalgia by Riot Grrrls underscores the culturally constructed nature of women's and girls' access to the public sphere. Such an observation, as I have already suggested, has important implications for the transportability, across socially determined lines of difference, of the Riot Grrrl strategy of reappropriating girlhood to construct alternative (i.e., nonpatriarchal) modes of visibility for women in independent rock. In short, such a deliberate performance assumes a subject for whom girlishness precludes, or is in conflict with, cultural agency. But what of women whose modes of access to, and mobility within, the public sphere depend on their supposed embodiment of a girlish ideal?

The examples of the Osaka-based trio Shonen Knife and the New York-based duo Cibo Matto, Japanese female bands that have attracted small but significant followings among US indie rock audiences, provide telling illustrations of the manner in which Asian women, whose visibility within US culture is often predicated on their acquiescence to orientalist stereotypes, have had to negotiate the terrain of US youth and music cultures differently than have their (primarily white) Riot Grrrl counterparts. In the United States, where Japanese rock musicians (whose music has become increasingly visible since the mid-1980s) are often regarded with a mixture of "sincere" musical interest and objectifying, ethnocentric curiosity, the recurring portrayal of Japanese women bands as interesting novelty acts, cartoonish amateurs, and/or embodiments of western patriarchal fantasies of "cute" Asian femininity presents particular challenges for understanding how evocations of girlhood overlap with discourses of race, gender, and nation in US popular music culture. In contrast to Riot Grrrl bands, whose reappropriations of girlhood are part of a broader effort to harness rock's oppositional energy for feminist critique, Japanese women rockers have negotiated (i.e., resisted, appropriated, or otherwise engaged) a feminist cultural politics from within the context of Western patriarchal discourses that insist on positioning them as the exotic representatives of an idealized girlish femininity.

A look at the portrayal of Shonen Knife in the independent and corporate music media illustrates this point. Formed by two sisters, Naoko and Atsuko Yamano, and their friend and schoolmate Michie Nakatani, Shonen Knife was unknown in the United States until 1985, when the Olympia, Washington-based K Records (also known for promoting Riot Grrrl work) released *Burning Farm*, previously a Japanese recording, on cassette.[19] Two independent releases, *Pretty Little Baka Guy/Live in Japan* (Gasatanka/Rockville 1990) and *Shonen Knife* (Gasatanka/Giant 1990) followed, but it wasn't until the band's 1992 major-label debut, *Let's Knife* (Virgin), featuring the remakes of earlier songs, some recorded for the first time in English, that Shonen Knife won significant airplay on college radio and a coveted opportunity to accompany Nirvana on tour. The immediate, enthusiastic embrace of Shonen Knife in the mid-1980s by indie rock luminaries such as Kim Gordon and Thurston Moore of Sonic Youth is often explained in terms of the band's kitschy punk/pop sound and its trademark parodic "twisting" of icons of American and Japanese commodity culture. Named for a brand of pocket knives (perhaps as a way of encapsulating a succinct critique of patriarchal masculinity?), Shonen Knife readily appealed to US indie rockers, who admired the band's pomo way of blurring the boundaries between advertising jingles and "serious" punk/pop (a practice evident in songs such as "Tortoise Brand Pot Cleaner's Theme").

Despite such affinities, the women in Shonen Knife have repeatedly been portrayed in exoticizing and infantilizing terms, as demonstrated by the liner notes to a late 1980s indie-rock tribute album of Shonen Knife covers, titled *Every Band Has a Shonen Knife*

Who Loves Them (in ironic reference to an album of Yoko Ono covers, despite the fact that Shonen Knife had no apparent connection to the most famous of all Japanese women rock artists in the United States). Here, band members are described in frankly patronizing language: "They are happy people and love what they are doing. . . . They are humble, kind people who do not realize that they are the most important band of our time."[20] Variations on this basic theme abound in later representations, where the band is often cited for sporting "cute" accents – a "lite" version of the more overt and aggressive racism of an infamous *Esquire* magazine article about Ono titled "John Rennon's Excrusive Groupie."[21] "Mostly [Shonen Knife] sing in their native tongue," writes *Rolling Stone*, "but what needs no translation is how their awkward humility mixes with their irrepressible vivacity."[22] The band fares no better in *Melody Maker*, where they are described as the "orient's answer to the Shangri-la's," a phrase that tellingly conjures nostalgia for the manufactured sexual innocence of Phil Spector-managed 1960-era girl groups.[23] One music journalist, in a description that conflates infantilizing images of Asian women's sexuality with stereotypes of female musical incompetence, has asserted that the band's fans like Shonen Knife because "they're little, lots of fun and can't really play."[24] Most tellingly, perhaps, in publicity materials for their 1993 album *Rock Animals*, Virgin Records (which in 1996 released, with very little fanfare, an album of "rarities, curiosities and live tracks" titled *The Birds and the B-Sides*) explicitly distinguishes Shonen Knife's "simplicity," "charismatic innocence," and musical charm from the restive, confrontational femininity of their US indie rock counterparts. These "Ronettes-meets-the-Ramones," gushes the press release, "are definitely not cut from the same battered cloth as their Riot Grrrl and flannel shirted colleagues."

Such a binary opposition pitting Shonen Knife, a charming and adorable Japanese novelty act with musical roots in the classic 1960s girl groups, against unfeminine, unkempt Riot Grrrls provides insight into the work performed by racialized representations of Asian femininity, as well as the specificity of the Riot Grrrl reappropriation of girlhood. For example, because she was widely perceived as having "stolen" John Lennon from his first wife, Cynthia Lennon, and perhaps because of her affiliation with the highly cerebral New York-based avant-garde and noise-rock scenes, Yoko Ono was subjected to a very different set of images: masculinized and desexualized, cast (along with her music) as impenetrable and inscrutable, intimidating and unpredictable, she was portrayed in a manner that recalls earlier, World War II-era stereotypes. By contrast, the major-label marketing of Japanese women bands such as Shonen Knife and Cibo Matto emphasizes girlishness as a way of establishing that these performers will be "fun" – that is, amusing, clever, and entertaining – for US consumers.[25]

While Riot Grrrls have been able to reappropriate girlhood as a part of their political and musical practice, Japanese women bands have had to negotiate an unreconstructed, unironic version of the term "girl" that circulates within US discourses of Asian femininity. As the above examples make plain, the media representations of Shonen Knife (and, more recently, of Cibo Matto) have tended to reinscribe their lack of cultural agency rather than explore their artistic practices as a potential source of such agency. In fact, however, both Shonen Knife and Cibo Matto have produced feminist work that counters dominant notions of a priori girlish Asian femininity, revealing how these notions are shot through with racialized sexism. For example, Shonen Knife's "Twist Barbie," an upbeat pop/rock song that is probably their best-known work among US audiences, articulates an ambiguous relation to European ideals of femininity through the image of a Barbie doll: "Blue eyes, blond hair / Tight body, long legs / She's very smart / She can dance well. . . . O, sexy girl!" This initially humorous parody of Barbie as a miniature and synthetic "embodiment" of ideal European womanhood (a parody that imputes stereotypes of girlish femininity to US white women) is punctuated, later in the song, by the phrase "I wanna be Twist Barbie" – words that potentially express a more ambiguous relation to Western beauty culture and that cleverly play off of the notion of the "wannabe," a means by which young women articulate their subjectivity through their consumption of popular culture. "Twist Barbie" is noteworthy, too, insofar as it expresses US–Japanese trade relations through the figure of a doll marketed to girls. The trope of a toy is perhaps not incidental, since Shonen Knife themselves are imaginatively "toying" with Barbie as a twisted and impossible ideal of (Western) femininity – the word twist here referring both to a popular dance and to the band's own cultural practice, which twists the signs of Western commodity culture. "Twist Barbie" conjures a specific mode of girls' leisure within US commodity culture (the activity of playing with Barbie dolls) to critique a culturally specific expression of patriarchal femininity. The song suggests that women can toy with ideals of femininity themselves as artificial (i.e., as unnatural or nonessential) as the Barbie doll.

This is not to say that a song such as "Twist Barbie" cannot also abet US stereotypes of "cute" or "innocent" Asian femininity: indeed, the deadpan enthusiasm with which Shonen Knife plays and sings "Twist Barbie," on record and in live performance, suggests that they are less critical of a European, Barbie-type ideal than an analysis of their lyrics might imply. The balance of *Shonen Knife* (the 1990 US release that features the first of several English-language versions of "Twist Barbie") is taken up with songs that, in English translation at least, seem to toe the line between parody and complicity. The album's cover art contributes photographs that support this reading of a fundamental ambivalence in Shonen Knife's self-representation: one features what looks like a snapshot of the band members taken when they were schoolgirls, and a second depicts the trio primping for the camera, wearing white dresses festooned with small multicolored bows. (The only element that distinguishes this second photograph is its backdrop: a graffiti-filled wall hints that the photograph may have been taken backstage at a show.)

The title and the cover art of *Viva! La Woman*, Cibo Matto's critically acclaimed 1996 debut album on the Warner Brothers label, illustrate how musicians Yuka Honda and Miho Hatori (who first met in Manhattan) frame their cultural-political agency quite differently. Musically, there is little that connects Shonen Knife's straightforward pop/rock with Cibo Matto's intricate sound, which relies heavily on sampling technologies to produce what one critic describes as "an enticing cross-cultural fusion that mixes bossa nova, hip hop, jazz, African drumming and disco . . . over which Hatori gleefully chants, screams, wails and raps in English, French and Japanese."[26] As their name (Italian for "crazy food") suggests, hybridity is a central theme of Cibo Matto's artistic practice: not only the hybridity that originates in the global circulation of popular youth/music culture, but the hybridity that marks Honda's and Hatori's own "hybrid" locations as Japanese-born New Yorkers whose music draws inspiration from white artists' interpretations of African American hip hop. The duo fosters an image of cosmopolitan sophistication that is distinct from Shonen Knife's (calculated?) image of playful, good girl simplicity. Such a notion is reinforced by the dada quality of the duo's lyrics and the cool, technologically hip image they project in live performance, during which Honda nonchalantly inserts floppy disks into a computer-synthesizer while Hatori sings.

A band photograph from *Viva! La Woman* depicts the musicians as denizens of a high-tech playground: dressed in sequins, Honda (posed on a bicycle) and Hatori appear surrounded by turntables, tape recorders, synthesizers, musical instruments, and, most conspicuously, skateboards, while various other figures (producers? engineers?) busy themselves in the background. As such an image implies, sampling and dubbing technologies, as well as synthesizers that filter and/or distort Hatori's "natural" vocals, afford Cibo Matto a variegated and intricate musical "voice." Cultural agency for these women performers is not staged primarily within the terms of the paradigm offered by US Riot Grrrls, or even within the ambiguously complicit/parodic economy of signification modeled by Shonen Knife. Rather, they demonstrate how the appropriation of girlhood may at times conflict with women's cultural agency.

In their 1995 book *The Sex Revolts*, Simon Reynolds and Joy Press claim that US alternative rock, increasingly focused on "gender tourism" as a source of its rebellion and therefore its identity formation, has witnessed a corresponding decline in the significance of race to its musical and cultural practice.[27] (Although I am appropriating Reynolds and Press's language here, I want to distance myself from their use of the phrase "rock rebellion," a term that is not only potentially condescending but also explicitly masculinist.) According to *The Sex Revolts*, the emergence of "alternative" music (actually a fully corporatized *style* that is, by and large, an object of derision for indie rockers) in the early 1980s is pivotal, marking the end of an era during which black sources served as the primary inspiration for white cultural innovation, and heralding a new era in which the performance of gender, not race, is paramount. If rock cultures were once conceived as, alternatively, a meeting place and a battleground between black and white identities – a cultural sphere where white and black youths violated social taboos against "race mixing" and where white youths fashioned dissident identities according to the models offered by black musicians and black musical culture – these cultures are nowadays more concerned, as Reynolds and Press argue, with the production of new gendered subjectivities that are less apparently marked by dominant discourses of race.

My own analysis of the representation of Shonen Knife and Cibo Matto belies this relatively simplistic thesis, which in turn belies the inevitable interarticulation of racism and sexism. Here, too, I want to register the disturbing resonance of the phrase "gender tourism" in Reynolds and Press's text with "sex tourism," and to note that while it implies the fluidity of gender identifications in rock performance, the term "gender tourism" in this context actually reinscribes the stability of gender in explicitly neo-colonialism terms, where (white) men are the explorers and (Japanese) women the colony to be explored. The analogy is not too farfetched, given the argument I have been developing about the cultural construction of girlhood and girl culture within rock music. Indeed, one of the points of my analysis of contemporary rock cultures has been to show that "girlhood," far from signifying a universal, biologically grounded condition of female experience, instead implies a relation to agency, visibility, and history that emerges within a particular discursive context. The different counternarratives of girlhood produced by a Riot Grrl band like Bikini Kill and a Japanese band like Shonen Knife occupy different antagonistic relations to hegemonic girlhood, whose meaning is itself unstable. The fact that these different narratives take root in very different cultural contexts suggests that we cannot assume the portability of contemporary white US women rockers' critical discourse of girlhood and their advocacy of girl culture.

By way of concluding, then, I want to explore some implications of these themes outside of the specific context of rock music. An anecdote about my own relation to work on girl culture provides a starting point. This essay was inadvertently inspired by a presentation about Riot Grrrls that I gave as part of an academic job talk at New York University several years ago. At the end of my talk, one audience member asked me whether such work on female youth/music culture – and perhaps here he was also implicitly referencing my advocacy of Riot Grrrl as a noteworthy development within punk and postpunk musics – tacitly shifted the emphasis of, or even supplanted, women's studies (and the various critiques integral to its practical interventions within the academy) with something he provocatively termed "girl studies." My answer at the time was something like, "What's wrong with girl studies?"; a response that was calculated (inasmuch as I had time to calculate) to legitimize girls and their specific cultural formations (something integral to the Riot Grrrl project) as well as to authorize my own work on girls/grrrls. I admit, too, that as a candidate performing in front of various tenured faculty and curious graduate students, I felt at that moment like something of a girl. I argued then, as I would now, that research into the discourses of girlhood is crucial if we want to understand how contemporary female performers and their audiences have attempted to create avenues of feminist agency within traditionally masculinist popular forms.

I couldn't then anticipate how resonant this brief and admittedly superficial exchange about the status of "girl studies" would later seem in light of the emergence both of a popular psychological literature of girlhood (which depicts girlhood as a period of crisis in female subjectivity), and of a burgeoning academic subfield of the cultural studies of girls. My own reading of Shonen Knife's playful mimicry of a Barbie-esque ideal of femininity is in tacit dialogue with recent feminist studies that use Barbie as an important cultural text. In such work, Barbie bears the inscription of various overlapping and sometimes contradictory ideologies of race, gender, class, and nation.[28] The "new Barbie studies," particularly when undertaken from queer feminist perspectives, uses this most ubiquitous and notorious symbol of ideal femininity to explore and critique girls' appropriations of patriarchal commodity culture, suggesting that such appropriations may be important to their identity formation. This essay represents my own analogous reading of young women rock musicians' feminist appropriations of hegemonic girlhood, based on the related notion that youth music provides an important cultural venue for the articulation and rearticulation of youthful subjectivities.

And yet some of the limitations of this intellectual project, if not of the very notion that girlhood can be unproblematically reclaimed for feminism or for feminist cultural practices, are also implicit in this reading of the cultural construction of girlhood within rock music. It is noteworthy that "Just a Girl" peaked in popularity at about the same time that Madonna and Courtney Love, two of the female rock performers most associated with the cultural subversion of girlhood, chose to "grow up," at least in terms of their public performance of gender: Madonna through her very public staging of motherhood and her role as Evita in the film version of the famous Andrew Lloyd Webber musical; Love through her starring role in the movie *The People vs. Larry Flynt* and her highly publicized beauty/fashion makeover. There is something predictably depressing, too, about the global popularity of the Spice Girls, who have appropriated the spunky defiance associated with English Riot Grrrls in a patently opportunistic fashion. Particularly within the context of the global struggle for women's rights, it is clear that girlhood cannot yet be spoken of as a universal right or property of women. Moreover, even work that eschews girlhood as the universalizing complement of very particular constructions of human biological development can end up essentializing girlhood as a necessary phase within the life cycle imagined by global capitalism. Rock music cultures, especially the cultures of independent rock, provide crucial sites within which young women can negotiate their own representations of girlhood in varying degrees of opposition to, or collaboration with, hegemonic narratives. As the foregoing analysis of various contemporary female rockers suggests, however, women – especially those who benefit from their privileged national, racial, or economic status – will need to stay alert to the necessity of interrogating, in an ongoing and self-critical fashion, the conditions that govern their access to social and cultural agency. If I am sounding a note of particular urgency, it is because I believe that youth music cultures continue to offer girls important sources of emotional sanctuary and acts as vital outlets for the expression of rage and pleasure, frustration and hope.

Coda

Looking back, 1997 appears to have ranked as *both* the Year of the Girl or the Year of the Woman – or at least this is the "split" conclusion readers of the two leading rock magazines, *Rolling Stone* and *Spin*, might have drawn after consulting each magazine's November special issue devoted to coverage of female rock musicians. Set to coincide with the thirtieth anniversary of the magazine's founding, the *Rolling Stone* special issue features a memorable cover photograph of Courtney Love, Tina Turner, and Madonna collectively hamming it up for the camera, behind a headline that announces "Women of Rock." Unusually heavy with advertisements, even by *Rolling Stone* standards, the issue features a thirty-thousand-word "anecdotal history of women and rock" by veteran rock critic Gerri Hershey, as well as brief interviews (all conducted by female journalists) with twenty-eight women musicians, from Ruth Brown and Yoko Ono to Joan Jett, Me'Shell Ndegeocello, Liz Phair, and Ani DiFranco. Although it was the commercial power of contemporary women musicians such as Mariah Carey, Jewel, and Fiona Apple that apparently first inspired *Rolling Stone*'s editorial board to devote its thirtieth anniversary issue to women of/and rock, the issue highlights many of the current generation's forebears (Hershey's long piece, for example, begins by tracing the influence of female blues singers such as Ma Rainey on rock's first acknowledged female superstar, Janis Joplin). Consistent with *Rolling Stone*'s credo of rock music as "legitimate news and history" (as founding editor Jann Wenner puts it), "Women of Rock" has the feel and heft of a women's literature anthology or a "greatest hits" boxed set: there, together with the "backstage history" of the music, are careful profiles of the genre's canonical figures.

If *Rolling Stone*'s "Women of Rock" issue is shaped by self-consciousness about its status as the "granddaddy" of contemporary popular music magazines, *Spin*'s "The Girl Issue" seems to reflect its own industry position as a youthful upstart seeking to upstage its established, if graying, competitor. "The Girl Issue" not only eschews encyclopedic leanings of "Women of Rock," but its coverage weighs it heavily in favor of the new, the young, … and the "girl." If *Rolling Stone*'s cover suggests three "generations" of women rock musicians, *Spin*'s cover contrastingly features a close-up of the slightly pouty face of twenty-year-old singer-songwriter Fiona Apple, who only two months earlier had received MTV's award for best new artist. Inside the magazine there are articles about "girl power," women fashion designers, and women's/wymyn's music festivals, as well as a compendium of icons to "girl culture" that heavily favors a "riot grrrl" sensibility.

As I've tried to allude to in these brief descriptions, *Rolling Stone*'s and *Spin*'s disparate presentations of women/girls in/and/of rock depends, in large part, on the relative positioning of the magazines within the corporate music press and with respect to the different market demographics that each targets. Yet it nevertheless may be possible to draw tentative conclusions based on each magazine's representation of female performers within the context of rock's history as well as its "futures." While "Women of Rock" highlights the "coming of age" of female rock performers, as well as of rock music itself (as underscored by its choice of cover models: a postmakeover Love, a postpregnancy Madonna, and Turner, a woman notable for having been dubbed rock's "godmother"), "The Girl Issue" is most notable for its "postmodern" refusal to historicize ("girls," as the cover copy implies, are known by first names only: "Alanis, Ani, Gwen, Xena, Chloe, Chelsea, Daria . . ."). Whereas "Women of Rock" emphasizes the contributions of African American women, including blues singers, R&B artists, disco divas, and contemporary rappers, "The Girl Issue" is noticeably silent on the subject of girls who are not also white, with the exception of athletes in the WNBA.

In the coincidence of "Women of Rock" and "The Girl Issue" one might infer a certain gendered generational struggle within rock music journalism, in which *Spin*, in order to differentiate itself from an aging, patriarchal forebear, deploys the "girl" not only to win over a young female readership, but to signify its rejection of the very musical and cultural values that seemingly render it necessary, even at this late date, once again to showcase the "contributions" of female musicians to rock music cultures. While the celebration of the "girl" in such an instance might signify a rejection of a certain patriarchal discourse that trivializes women's participation within rock music even as it extols it, there is also the danger – as evidenced by *Spin*'s own contents – that such a critique recuperates gender in terms that quite literally invisiblize the very issues of race and ethnicity which, as *Rolling Stone* demonstrates, are crucial to an understanding (or at the very least to an accurate recounting) of rock as a musical/cultural practice. There is little doubt that the cultural apparatus of rock music (here including both the recording industry and professional rock journalism) has proven notoriously unfriendly, even hostile, to women performers. On the other hand, and as the *Spin* special issue suggests, playing "the girl" may not always be as "innocent" as it sometimes looks.

Notes

1. Kanal refers here to No Doubt's lead singer Gwen Stefani (quoted in Alona Wartofsky, "Girl without a Doubt," *Washington Post*, June 15, 1997, G1.)
2. This description is based on an account by Jonathan Bernstein ("Get Happy," *Spin*, November 1996, 52). In a performance in Worcester, Massachusetts, Stefani got the boys in the audience to sing, "I'm Just a Girl" and then instructed the girls to chant, "Fuck you! I'm a girl!" (Wartofsky, "Girl without a Doubt," G1.)
3. Barry Walters, "Alreadybe," *Village Voice* 42, no. 7 (1997): 69. I can add little to what already has been said and written about the Spice Girls's decidedly cynical appropriation and recirculation of "girl power" (the "girls" here including the late Princess of Wales and even Margaret Thatcher) as a record industry commodity. As a friend of mine succinctly and appropriately put it, "the Spice Girls are a text that already has been written." Two aspects of the Spice Girls's success story remain interesting, however: first, the fact that the Spice Girls phenomenon, from the start, has been accompanied by the anti-Spice Girls backlash (interested browsers of the Web, for example, can find sites with titles such as "Spice Girls Suck Club" and "Spice Shack of Blasphemy"); and, second, that for all that the Spice Girls represent an obviously "cosmetic" feminism evacuated of commitment to combating patriarchy, the anti-Spice Girls movement seems to have given license to people to use the group's commercial success to voice antifeminist, even misogynist, sentiments. Many of the anti-Spice Girls Web sites exemplify this tendency to conflate disdain for the group's musical production (i.e., disdain for musical commodities) with disdain for women, generally speaking. This latter aspect of the anti-Spice Girls backlash seems particularly insidious given the tendency to elide female subjectivity not only with consumption but with the commodity form itself.
4. Lisa Lewis, *Gender Politics and MTV* (Philadelphia: Temple University Press, 1990), 10.
5. "Girl studies" emerges not only from fields such as psychology, with its longstanding interest in human social and psychic development, but also from newer fields such as cultural studies, which has its own traditions (by way of Birmingham and the Centre for Contemporary Cultural Studies) of analyzing "youth" and the politics of youth subcultures (particularly working-class, predominantly male youth subcultures). The popularity and visibility of the "girl" within popular youth/music cultures, combined with renewed interest in forms of violence/trauma that primarily affect girls (e.g., incest, eating disorders, self-mutilation or "cutting") may have had the effect of spurring academic interest in studying the specific cultural formations and cultural practices of girls. At the time when I began thinking about this essay, for example, a number of other calls for papers and/or book chapters on this topic were circulating. This essay might be said to constitute my own ambivalent and critical venture into girl studies, a subject I return to later.
6. "Alternative" rock is often defined in terms of an aesthetic that disavows, or evinces critical mistrust of, earlier rock subjectivities as well as the music industry itself (see Eric Weisbard

and Craig Marks, eds. *Spin: Alternative Record Guide* (New York: Vintage Books, 1995, vii). And yet "alternative" is also, for my purposes, a corporate demographic and a new set of industry practices spurred by the discovery that independent labels could effectively serve as major-label A&R departments, according to the logic of outsourcing.

7. Simone de Beauvoir, *The Second Sex*, trans. H. M. Parshley (New York: Vintage, 1989), 337.

8. The conclusions of this paper were brought home by the commercially successful Lilith Fair concert tour in 1998, which, although touted by organizer Sarah McLachlan as a "celebration of women in music," in fact primarily functioned as a celebration of white female singer-songwriters, despite the participation of performers such as Missy Elliot and Erykah Badu. The corporate and independent press made much of the Lilith Fair's demonstration that a music festival organized around "women's voices" could draw ticket sales and support a roster of appearances at medium-sized arenas throughout the United States, although very few writers ever noticed that this "Galapalooza," as *Time* put it, was also a universalizing recuperation of white women's music/performance as *women's* music/performance.

9. Of late there has been a great deal written about the "loser." For two good accounts, see Fred Pfeil, *White Guys: Studies in Postmodern Domination and Difference* (New York: Verso, 1995).

10. Coco Fusco, *English is Broken Here: Notes on Cultural Fusion in the Americas* (New York: New Press, 1995), 70.

11. Fusco, 76. There is, of course, an impressive body of scholarship that probes the notion of "appropriation" specifically within the context of US popular music cultures.

12. Ernesto Laclau, "Metaphor and Social Antagonisms," in *Marxism and the Interpretation of Culture*, ed. Cary Nelson and Lawrence Grossberg (Urbana: University of Illinois Press, 1998); and Laura Kipnis, *Ecstasy Unlimited* (Minneapolis: University of Minnesota Press, 1993), 17.

13. Kipnis, *Ecstasy*, 16.

14. "Independent rock" (or "indie rock") is a common term that refers not to a musical aesthetic but to the means of production of the music under discussion.

15. These women's performances underscore the way that girlhood is both denied to, and reinterpreted within the context of, African American women, whose use of the term "girl" as a mode of address suggests a vernacular tradition of such reinterpretation/reappropriation as well.

16. For specific examples, see Gottlieb and Wald, "Smells Like Teen Spirit: Riot Girls Revolution, and Women in Independent Rock." In Andrew Ross and Tricia Rosa (eds.), *Microphone Friends* (New York: Routledge, 1994), 250–74.

17. Angela McRobbie, *Feminism and Youth Culture* (Boston: Unwin Hyman, 1991), 25.

18. See Ann Japenga, "Punk's Girl Groups Are Putting the Self Back in Self-Esteem," *New York Times*, November 15, 1992, 30.

19. According to indie rock lore, the band was first "discovered" by Calvin Johnson, a member of the lo-fi, punk minimalist band Beat Happening, cofounder of the Olympia, Washington-based K record label, and promoter of the idea of an "international pop underground."

20. Weisbard and Marks, Spin Alternative Record Guide 355.

21. Gillian Gaar, *She's a Rebel: The History of Women in Rock & Roll* (Seattle: Seal Press, 1992), 231.

22. Chuck Eddy, "Shonen Knife," *Rolling Stone* 586 (1990): 91.

Gayle Wald

23. Everett True, "Shonen Knife: Blade in Japan," *Melody Maker* 67, no. 49 (1992): 38–39.

24. Stud Brother, "Ninja Wobble," *Melody Maker* 68, no. 47 (1994): 6–7.

25. Such infantilizing images of Japanese women rockers are, of course, merely the benign complement to a more overtly and aggressively racist neocolonial portraiture of Asian femininity. The most flagrant example of this sort of representation comes from an "All-Japan" issue of the punk 'zine *Maximumrocknroll* – an issue ostensibly devoted to defining a shared political-cultural sensibility among US and Japanese indie rockers. In this issue, a regular contributor muses about "nubile Nipponese lovelies" and "all these hot-looking Japanese girl bands" (Shonen Knife gets specific mention), while speculating that as a "species," "Oriental girls" (and here he includes Asian American women) have "Mongolian eyelids" that resemble vulvae, and that this explains "the source of their attractiveness" "Making New Friends with Rev. Norb," *Maximumrocknroll*, 1994, n.p.

26. Kathy Silberger, "Eats Meets West: Cibo Matto's Cross-Cultural Cuisine-Art," *Option* 68 (1996): 61.

27. Simon Reynolds and Joy Press, *The Sex Revolts: Gender Rebellion and Rock'n'Roll* (Cambridge: Harvard University Press, 1995).

28. See, for example, Lucinda Ebersole and Richard Peabody, eds., *Mondo Barbie* (New York: St. Martin's Press, 1993); M. G. Lord, *Forever Barbie: The Unauthorized Biography of a Real Doll* (New York: Morrow, 1994); and Erica Rand, *Barbie's Queer Accessories* (Durham: Duke University Press, 1995).

51

Some Anti-Hegemonic Aspects of African Popular Music

John Collins*

There are many differing views held by social and developmental scientists on the role of popular culture, art, and music in relation to the expression and consolidation of social power. Some see it as a medium through which a central social group controls society; indeed, the structural-functionalists (pre-war British social anthropologists, Talcott Parsons, and others) saw all art and music, not just the popular variety, as part of a tension-managing mechanism regulating the values and "needs" of society. Opposed to these "consensus" models are the "conflict" ones; but these too treat popular culture as an ideological tool used by the ruling class or group to hold power or hegemony. For instance, the Marxist-influenced "Frankfurt School" of pre-war Germany was hostile to popular culture, seeing it as a form of instant gratification that helps create "false consciousness" and what Herbert Marcuse called the "repressive tolerance" of the ruling class.

However, the Italian Marxist Antonio Gramsci, who coined the word "hegemony,"[1] opposed his contemporaries of the Frankfurt School in treating popular culture as an anti-hegemonic or "people's art" that could potentially threaten the ruling class, whose hegemony was never permanent. Gramsci's ideas have never been very influential, and today many writers consider popular culture to have a dual aspect, for besides being hegemonic and associated with social and bureaucratic control, it can also be anti-hegemonic, decentralizing, and individualistic – what Hans Magnus Ensenburger calls "repressive" and "emancipatory,"[2] C. W. E. Bigsby "epithanic" and "apocalyptic,"[3] and James Carey "centripetal" and "centrifugal."[4] Raymond Williams also notes this double aspect when he distinguishes between popular culture which is "developed by the people or by the majority of the people to express their own meanings and values"[5] and mass culture (which incorporates areas of popular culture) which is "developed for people by an internal or external group, imbedded in them by a range imbedded in them by a range of processes from repressive imposition to commercial saturation."[6]

The recent history of African popular music throws light on the anti-hegemonic side of popular culture, for Africa has been faced with the hegemony of the colonial

*Pp. 185–94 from *Rockin' the Boat: Mass Music and Mass Movements*, ed. R. Garofalo (Boston, MA: South End Press). © 1992 by Reebee Garofalo. Reprinted with permission from South End Press.

and neo-colonial powers, and some local popular musicians have attempted to over-come the resulting "cultural imperialism" in various ways, three of which will be discussed here in some detail. First, African popular musicians have "indigenized" their music; second, they have utilized the black music of the New World; and third, they have continued the African tradition of using music to voice protest and social conflict.

The Indigenization of Acculturated African Popular Music

It should first be noted that modernization in Africa does not necessarily imply "cultural imperialization," as an indigenous culture may actually employ external influences for its own purposes, by first imitating and then assimilating them into its own cultural experience. This process has been noted by the writers James Lull,[7] D. Marks,[8] and Paul Rutten[9] to apply even to the popular music of European countries undergoing Anglo-Americanization. And this is also one of the conclusions in Wallis and Malm's book[10] on the popular music industry of 12 small countries (including East African ones) being affected by Western multinationals; for this process of "transculturation," as they call it, besides leading to the formation of a standardized music reflecting Anglo-American culture, also includes the catalytic influence this imported culture has in generating a thriving indigenous music scene. Likewise, David Coplan's work on the black South African popular music scene[11] also demonstrates this double hegemonic/anti-hegemonic aspect of acculturation, which he connects with Western domination on the one hand and the struggle for African cultural autonomy, retrenchment, and indigenization on the other.

The indigenization itself of modern African popular music can be linked to three factors: the geographical diffusion of Western ideas, the cultural tenacity of traditional music, and the emergence of nationalism. And turning first to the indigenization resulting from geographical spread, which may occur when an acculturated music develops in cities, or in the coastal ports where there was the first contact with Europeans, and then spreads into the rural hinterland becoming de-acculturated as it does so. An example of this is the progressive Africanization of coastal brass-band music, such as the late 19th-century West African *adaha* music, which in the 1930s influenced the local Akan recreational music called *konkomba* or *konkoma*.[12] Another example is the East African *beni* music of the local African "askari" troops of World War I, which turned into the Kalela "tribal" dance of the 1930s and 1940s.[13] The geographical factor also applies when an acculturated popular music develops in one African country and then spreads into other African countries where it creates secondary local varieties. For instance, Zairean rumba-influenced "Congo Jazz" spread into Tanzania during the 1960s where it became the "Swahili Jazz" of the mid-seventies.

Indigenization also can take place when an African popular music "re-models"[14] a tenacious traditional genre. It can happen in traditional rural villages, which was the case when the brass band-influenced *konkomba* music, mentioned above, affected the traditional recreational music of the Ewe people of Ghana and Togo during the 1950s – becoming a neo-traditional drum and dance style known as *Borborbor*. Remodeling may also occur in towns where there are large numbers of new rural migrants or where there is a strong "residual" performance style[15] that has "[survived] from the past and [is] available to be re-worked to form new styles."[16] Another example from Ghana is the neo-traditional dance style known as *kpanlogo* which grew up in the mid-1960s through the impact of acculturated highlife music on the traditional recreational music of the Ga people.[17]

The indigenization of popular music is also related to the growth of African nationalism – both of the pre- and post-independence variety. The early nationalist movement began partly as a result of a change in European colonial policy in the late 19th century. Up to the middle of that century it had been policy to foster the growth of a Europeanized African class, but later, with the "scramble for Africa," the Berlin Conference of 1885, and the discovery of quinine (enabling white traders to settle in malarial areas), the Westernized African elite and merchant princes became a threat to late imperial expansion. At the same time, "scientific racism" was concocted and Africa was depicted as a "Dark Continent" with no history. Consequently, African nations were ideologically demoted to "tribes," and there grew up an intense imperial hatred of the African elite whom racists believed disguised their natural "inferior" condition under a thin veneer of European dress, customs, and art forms. For instance, in Nigeria, up to the 1880s the black elite replicated European dramatic, literary, and musical forms through such organizations as Friends of the Academy,[18] the Lagos Philharmonic Society,[19] and the Handel Festival.[20] However, the increasing colonial institutional racism and progressive exclusion of the African elite from administrative jobs and the economic sections they had previously dominated led to an African "united opposition from 1897 to 1915,"[21] and the "nationalist generation."[22] Similarly, in late 19th-century South Africa, when the African imitation of Western culture "failed to achieve major gains in autonomy, contrary tendencies towards cultural retrenchment emerged . . . leading to a heightened sense of cultural nationalism."[23] The musical consequences of this were the Africanization of hymns by separatist Christian churches, such as the United Native African Church of Nigeria (established in 1891) and the Nazarite Faith of South Africa (established in 1911), and the use of traditional music by the African elite. For instance, Yoruba music "played an important role in the labyrinthian maneuvers of the nationalists of the 1920s and 1930s."[24]

Since independence in Africa, this indigenization and national cultural revival has become even more important – and even government policy. Some examples are Tanzania, where President Nyere banned foreign pop music on national radio in 1973, and the following year set up the Ministry of National Culture and Youth "which encouraged dance-bands to compose music that supported the policies of the party and the government."[25] And when Guinea gained independence in 1958, President Sekou Toure expelled French musicians and supported local groups like Bembeya Jazz and Les Ballets Africain.[26] In a similar vein, during Zaire's "Authenticité" campaign of the early 1970s, President Mobutu ordered all local musicians to use their African rather than their European names;[27] for instance, the famous *soukous* or "Congo Jazz" artists Franco and Rochereau became known as Luamba Makiadi and Tabu Ley respectively. Likewise, Ghana's Dr. Nkrumah attempted in the late 1950s to change the name "highlife" to an indigenous one, *osibisaaba*,[28] although in this he was unsuccessful due to resistance from local musicians. Indeed, this search for African identity has spilled beyond national borders in the form of Pan African festivals such as those held in Dakar in 1966, Algeria in 1969, and Nigeria in 1977.

The Musical Influence on Africa of the Black Diaspora

The black music of the New World has and is playing a part in the African pursuit of autonomy and identity, and this influence can be traced as far back as to the introduction of Jamaican *gumbey* or *gombe* music to West Africa in the 1830s[29] and the syncopated brass-band music of West Indian regimental bands stationed there from the mid-19th century,[30] followed first in South Africa[31] and then West Africa[32] by a craze for black minstrelsy and ragtime music. This influence from the black Americas, however, occurred later in Central Africa, where the rumba became popular from the inter-war period, and last of all in East Africa where local popular dance music arose after World War II "primarily from influences not of 'European' but of Afro-American origin."[33]

In fact the black American influence on Africa, both musically and non-musically, has both enhanced and hindered colonial and Anglo-American domination. On the hegemonic side, West Indian troops were used by the colonialists, as were West Indian and African American missionaries. And some of the first African elites who introduced Western ways were the descendants of freed slaves. These include the Krios (Creoles) of Freetown, Sierra Leone, who were returned from North America from the 1790s onward, and the Americo-Liberian elite who were returned from the 1820s by the American Colonisation Society; and the West African Brazilian elite who came from South America from the 1840s, bringing with them Afro-Brazilian Calunga and Carata masquerades[34] and the samba drum.[35]

The anti-hegemonic effect of this influence from the black diaspora is noted by David Coplan, who relates it to "African urban cultural adaption and identity";[36] he also adds that some of the black American Christian missionaries, such as Bishop Turner,[37] actually helped the black South African nationalist cause. Similarly, some of the first African nationalist ideas were introduced to Africa by African American and black Caribbean writers such as Edmund Blyden, Aimé Cesaire, Marcus Garvey, George Padmore, W. E. B. DuBois, and others. Music has also been involved as African musicians have partially been able to by-pass or short-circuit white "cultural imperialism" through the selective borrowing and incorporation of ideas from the black part of the spectrum of imported Western popular performing arts. Some early examples are the catalytic effect of West Indian regimental brass band musicians who played calypsos as well as martial music and made an impact on the *adaha* variety of highlife;[38] the Brazilian influence on early *juju* music, for instance the small square *samba* drum;[39] the impact of the *rumba* on "Congo jazz"; and of ragtime and jazz on the growth of South African popular music.[40]

Since the 1950s and 1960s many black American musicians who play jazz, samba, soul, reggae, rastafarian, and other "roots" music have been inspired by the message of black power, black pride, and the African heritage; indeed many have visited Africa, including James Brown, Jimmy Cliff, Bob Marley, Max Roach, Tina Turner, Randy Weston, and Gilberto Gil, to name a few. This in turn has contributed to black African cultural autonomy, for paradoxically, in copying these black American artists, Africans are being turned toward their own resources, which in recent years has led to the creative explosion of numerous African "pop" styles, such as Afro-rock (e.g., Ghana's Osibisa), Afrobeat (e.g., Nigeria's Fela Anikulapo-Kuti), and Afro-reggae (e.g., Côte D'Ivoire's Alpha Blondy). This imported black American influence has also encouraged the exploration of local roots by contemporary African musicians which has resulted in such music styles as the Ga "cultural" music since the 1970s and the *mbalax* music of Youssou N'Dour of Senegal in the 1980s.

The major reason for this long-term selective African preference for the black rather than the white music of the New World is due to their similarities in socio-historical experience and music. For, as noted by various writers on social and musical change, similarities between interacting cultures provide "cultural analogues" that enhance acculturation[41] and create a familiarity or shared environment that fosters "co-orientation"[42] – or what Luke Uche, in his study of the Nigerian popular music industry, calls "cultural triangulation."[43]

Coplan notes the first type of socio-historical similarity, or shared environment, when he states that "the appeal of black American performance styles in South Africa derives from a comparable experience of two peoples under white domination"[44] – that is, "colonialism" in Africa and the old "Jim Crow" laws in the United States. Since the 1950s, the similarities remain, but are different; for there has been the success of black civil rights in the United States and independence in the Caribbean and Africa.

The musical similarities or analogues between Africa and the black Americas stem largely from the fact that millions of African slaves were taken to the New World during the black diaspora, taking their culture and music with them. And this has remained, either in transmuted form or – particularly in South America and the Caribbean – more or less intact. However, even in Protestant North America, where the suppression of African culture was more thorough, there is much musicological evidence of African retentions in the blues, jazz, and many other types of music. (See writers such as Melville Herskovitz,[45] Rudi Blesh,[46] Richard Waterman,[47] LeRoi Jones,[48] and Paul Oliver.[49])

The other half of the story, the return of black New World performing arts to Africa, has not been so well documented as has the study of African retentions in the Americas. Nevertheless, most writers on African popular music have noted this imported black influence, and, according to John Storm Roberts, "there is no mystery about why the different Afro-American styles were influential in different parts of Africa. In West Africa and the Congo, Cuban music was returning with interest something that had largely come from there anyway, so there was a most natural affinity."[50] Indeed, because the Cuban rumba and other black New World dance music coming into Africa are partially of African origin, this trans-Atlantic cycle of music leaving Africa during the diaspora and then returning can be treated as a form of cultural "feedback." In short, what was taken from Africa to the Americas in the days of slavery has, in various transmuted forms, been reclaimed by Africa in the 20th century.

Popular Music and the African Tradition of Protest and Social Conflict

African popular music is also anti-hegemonic, by carrying on the tradition of using music to express group conflict within the context of social change. The old European image of traditional Africa and its music as only geared to social cohesion and static equilibrium is in fact an ideological concept – like "primitive" and "tribes" – created by colonialists who wanted passive subjects without their own history.

But far from static, modern historians are now stressing the dynamic aspects of pre-colonial Africa; and as the Ghanaian musicologist J. H. K. Nketia states in connection with traditional Akan dance-music styles, "the creation of new musical types is encouraged in African societies."[51] And these traditional styles have often been associated with social tension. Male and female age-sets and secret societies would sometimes demonstrate conflict with the older generation through musical ridicule, for instance by the masked dancer of the Poro secret society of the Mende people of Sierra Leone;[52] and the Akan warrior of Asafo Companies could literally drum a despotic chief or elder out of town. Indeed, the talking drums were actually employed in warfare, which is one of the reasons why the traditional drums of the African slaves were banned in the New World. Then there were songs and rhymes of mutual insult, such as the *tshikona* dance and musical duel of the Venda people of the Transvaal,[53] a tradition carried through to the New World as African American "dozens"[54] and the *picongs* of the Trinidadian calypso "tent wars."[55]

One specific way in which the dynamic musical tradition has been used in modern Africa is in the struggle against colonialism; and just as the vernacular hymns of the African elite played a part in the nationalist movement, so too did the popular music of the masses. In East Africa, the inter-war clash between the Beni supporters and the missionaries was because Beni tried to "capture and use European symbols,"[56] and the hostility of the colonialists to *beni*, with its drill-like dances and uniformed ranks of performers, was because they thought it was subversive – and, in fact, *beni* did play a role in the 1935 copperbelt strike. Just after World War II, the *gombe* bands of the multi-ethnic youth associations of Côte D'Ivoire were absorbed in the nationalist movement.[57] In Ghana, "John Brown's Body" (a black American Civil War song) was adapted by the nationalists to criticize the British imprisonment of Kwame Nkrumah,[58] and on his release the Akan highlife musician E. K. Nyame welcomed him with the song *"Onim Deefo Kukudurufu* Kwame Nkrumah" (Honorable Man and Hero Kwame Nkrumah).[59] In addition, nationalist sentiments were voiced by some local comic opera songs and plays, such as Ghana's Axim Trio's plays "Nkrumah Will Never Die,"[60] and the Nigerian Hubert Ogunde's play "Strike and Hunger," about the 1945 Nigerian general strike.[61] More recent are the revolutionary *chimurenga* songs of the mid-1970s guerrilla war against the Smith regime in Zimbabwe[62] and the anti-apartheid songs of exiled popular South African musicians such as Miriam Makeba, Hugh Masakela, Dudu Pukwana, and Dollar Brand (Abdullah Ibrahim).

Popular music also has a bearing on social stratification and is particularly identified with the poorer layers of society, as popular musicians in Africa usually come from "intermediate"[63] levels of society such as newly urbanized rural migrants, semi-skilled workers, "laborers, messengers, drivers, railroad men, sailors and clerks."[64] Popular music styles also symbolically help create, amongst both players and audience, shared perceptions of group boundaries and social distance. One of the earliest studies of this phenomenon was of the *kalela* dance of young men in the southern African copperbelt region, carried out in the 1950s by Clyde Mitchell, who considered it to be "an analogue or metaphor for the essential patterns of urban social relations"[65] and connected to modern class distinctions; as the *kalela* was only played and danced by lower class "miners, domestic servants and 'lorry boys.'"[66]

Some popular musicians also make a protest on behalf of the poor and downtrodden, one of the most well-known being Nigeria's Fela Anikulapo-Kuti, whose open political defiance of his government has often gotten him into trouble – for instance, his controversial 1976 album *Zombie* that mocked the military mentality, and later releases such as *V.I.P.* or *Vagabonds In Power* and *Coffin for Head of State*. However, usually in African music, political protest against those in power is not direct but oblique – for instance, in the form of animal parables such as the Ghanaian African Brothers Band's highlife song of the late 1960s, "Ebi Te Yie, Ebi Nte Yie" or "Some Sit Well, Whilst Others Do Not."[67] This song is about a group of animals sitting around a fire (i.e. the national cake), with the smaller animals protesting that the larger ones are hogging all the warmth (i.e. wealth). The title of the song has entered into common Akan parlance, a language in which previously there had been no indigenous word or concept for social strata based on wealth and class. However, according to N. K. Asante-Darko and Sjaak van der Geest, there are two ways in which a highlife song can become political; it "may be intended by the composer, or the public may give it a secret political meaning";[68] – that is, the songs are semiotically given a new "signification"[69] or "handled" in a different way.[70] A Ghanaian example is the 1964 song "Agyima Mansa" by Dr. Gyasi and his Noble Kings highlife guitar band, about the ghost of a mother lamenting the plight of her children. The song was banned from the radio as President Nkrumah believed (although Dr. Gyasi denied it) that the song was secretly being used to criticize his regime – "Mother Ghana" lamenting the plight of her population.[71]

Another protest tradition carried through into popular music in Africa is the expression of new ideas of youth and the conflicts they may have with each other and with the older generation. For instance, the Ambas Deda ethnic union of modernizing Temme immigrant youths in Freetown, Sierra Leone often clashed with the Temme elders.[72] Then the Ghanaian *kpanlogo* music of the mid-1960s, mentioned previously, was created by Ga youths and initially frowned upon by the elders as indecent, and indeed, there was an attempt to ban the *kpanlogo* dance by the Ghana Arts Council, until President Nkrumah himself intervened in the matter in 1965 and patronized a display of *kpanlogo* groups at the stadium at Black Star Square in Accra.[73] In Central Africa the Zaiko Langa Langa guitar band, which was formed in 1970 and, first associated with juvenile delinquents, became a focus of the Zairean youth culture. Since then many bands have modeled themselves on it and there is fierce competition amongst them as to who is the leader of youth fashion.

In recent years women musicians, who have been largely excluded from popular music development in Africa, have been struggling for prominence, one of the first being South Africa's Miriam Makeba, who became a professional dance-band singer in 1954. The feminization of popular music began later in West and Central Africa, partly inspired by Makeba and partly by foreign (including black) artists. According to Dr. Omibiyi-Obidike, "by the middle of the 1970s a generation of Nigerian female pop artists had emerged and had started making their mark on the Nigerian music scene,"[74] although there was male opposition to this development, as expressed, for example, in the 1973 Nigerian highlife song by Godwin Omogbewa called "Man on Top."[75] Likewise, since the 1970s women have entered the Ghanaian concert party (local comic opera) business which previously only employed female impersonators; this process began in the early 1960s, when President Nkrumah set up the Workers Brigade Band and Concert Party that employed both actors and actresses. Although Ghanaian highlife has been a "mainly male affair,"[76] through the separatist church choirs that since the late 1970s have begun playing "gospel highlife," women are finally playing guitar-band music. Previously the guitar was always associated in West Africa with palm-wine bars and drunkeness, and so was put out of bounds to women performers by their parents and families.

Finally, it should be added that African musicians today are able to fight for their rights through organizing themselves into trade unions, the first of these being the Nigerian Union of Musicians formed in 1958, the Ghana National Entertainments Association set up in 1960, and the Musicians Union founded in 1961.[77] Both these Ghanaian Unions were dissolved after the 1966 anti-Kwame Nkrumah coup due to the unions' link with Nkrumah's Convention People's Party. However, in 1974 a single unified Musicians Union of Ghana (MUSIGA) was formed to replace them. In short, the tradition of African performers expressing political, social, generational, gender, and organizational conflict and protest has been carried through into the modern context.

To summarize, 20th century African popular performers have found three ways of circumnavigating the problem of "cultural imperialism" and producing a viable contemporary art form in touch with the common person. These are through the progressive Africanization or de-acculturation of genres that were initially modeled on foreign ones, by the creative use of the black dance-music "feedback" from the New World, and by continuing the old African tradition of protest music. Moreover, all these three ways of regaining autonomy have become more important and more self-conscious in postwar times, with the climate of indigenization and cultural awareness in the new independent African nations, and the search for the African "roots" by black performers in the New World.

Notes

1. Antonio Gramsci, *Selections from Prison Notebooks.* London: Lawrence and Wisehart, 1971.
2. Hans Magnus Ensenburger, *The Consciousness Industry.* New York: Seabury Press, 1974.
3. C. W. E. Bigsby, Ed., *The Politics of Popular Culture.* London: Edward Arnold, 1976.
4. James Carey, "A Cultural Approach to Communication." *Communication,* 2. 1975. pp. 1–22.

5. Raymond Williams, "On High and Popular Culture." *The New Republic.* November 23, 1974. p. 15.

6. Ibid.

7. James Lull, Ed., *Popular Music and Edducation.* Beverly Hills: Sage Publications, 1987.

8. D. Marks, "Pop and Folk as a Going Concern for Sociological Research." *International Review of the Aesthetics and Sociology of Music*, 14. 1983. pp. 93–8.

9. Paul Rutten, "Youth and Music in the Netherlands." Paper presented at the International Association for Mass Communications Research, Prague, 1984.

10. Roger Wallis and Krister Maim, *Big Sounds from Small Peoples: The Music Industry in Small Countries.* London: Constable, 1984.

11. David Coplan, "The Urbanization of African Music: Some Theoretical Observations," in Richard Middleton and David Horn, Eds., *Popular Music 2.* Cambridge: Cambridge University Press, 1982. Also by Coplan on South Africa is *In Township Tonight.* South Africa: Ravan Press, 1985.

12. E. J. Collins, *Music Makers of West Africa.* Washington, DC: Three Continents Press, 1985.

13. T. O. Ranger, *Dance and Society in East Africa.* Heinemann Educational Books, 1975. pp. 116–17.

14. J. H. K. Nketia, "Observations on the Study of Popular Music in Africa." Paper presented at the Conference of the International Association for the Study of Popular Music (IASPM), Accra, Ghana, August 1987. p. 12.

15. A term used by Raymond Williams in *Marxism and Literature.* Oxford University Press, 1977; and also by Angelika and Charles Keii in "In Search of Polka Happiness," *Cultural Correspondence*, 14. 1977.

16. John Szwed, "Afro-American Musical Adaptation," in N. B. Whitten Jr. and J. Szwed, Eds., *American Anthropology: Contemporary Perspectives.* New York: Free Press, 1970. pp. 219–28: 226.

17. E. J. Collins, "The Man Who Made Traditional Music." *West Africa Magazine.* London, December 19–26, 1983. p. 2946.

18. Leonard Lynn. *The Growth of Entertainment of Non-African Origin in Lagos from 1860–1920.* Masters Thesis. University of Ibadan, 1967.

19. E. J. Collins and Paul Richards, "Popular Music in West Africa: Suggestions for an Interpretive Framework," in Simon Frith, Ed., *World Music, Politics and Social Change.* New York: University of Manchester Press, 1989. pp. 12–46.

20. M. J. C. Echeruo, "Concert and Theatre in Late 19th Century Lagos, Nigeria." *Magazine* (Lagos). September 1972. pp. 68–74.

21. P. D. Cole. *Modem and Traditional Elites in the Politics of Lagos* and *Modem and Traditional Elites in Late 19th Century Lagos.* Cambridge: Cambridge University Press, 1975.

22. J. S. Coleman, *Nigeria: Background to Nationalism.* Berkeley: University of California Press, 1960.

23. Coplan, 1985. p. 235.

24. Christopher Waterman, *Juju: The Historical Development, Socio-Economic Organization and Communicative Function of a West African Popular Music.* Ph.D. Thesis. University of Illinois, 1986. p. 72.

25. Phillip Donne, "Music forms in Tanzania and their Socio-Economic Base." *Jipemoyo*, No. 3, and *Transactions of the Finnish Anthropological Society*, No. 9. 1980. pp. 88–97.

26. From a UNESCO report, "Cultural Policy in the Revolutionary People's Republic Guinea," published by the Guinea Ministry of Education and Culture, 1979. pp. 80–3.

27. Graham Ewen, *Luamba Franco and Thirty Years of O. K. Jazz*. London: Off the Record Press, 1986. p. 45.

28. E. J. Collins, *E. T. Mensah, The King of Highlife*. London: Off the Record Press, 1986. p. 45.

29. Flemming, Harrev, "Goumbe and the Development of Krio Popular Music in Freetown, Sierra Leone." Paper presented at the Fourth International conference of IASPM, Accra, Ghana, August 1987.

30. A. A. Mensah, "Jazz, the Round Trip." *Jazzforschung*, Volume 3, No. 4. 1971. p. 2.

31. This is mentioned by both David Coplan (1985) and Veit Erlmann, "A Feeling of Prejudice: Orpheus McAdoo and the Virginia Jubilee Singers in South Africa 1890–1898." *Journal of Southern African Studies*, Volume 14, No. 3. April 1988. pp. 331–50.

32. E. J. Collins, "Jazz Feedback to Africa." *American Music*, Volume 5, No. 2. Summer 1987.

33. Gerhard Kubick, "Neo-Traditional Popular Music in East Africa since 1945," in Richard Middleton and David Horn, Eds., *Popular Music*. Cambridge: Cambridge University Press, 1981. p. 86.

34. Afolabi Alajo-Brown, *Juju Music: A Study of its Social History and Styles*. Pittsburgh: Pittsburgh University Press, 1985.

35. Waterman, 1986.

36. Coplan, 1982. p. 123.

37. Coplan, 1985. pp. 42, 79.

38. A. A. Mensah, "Highlife." Unpublished manuscript.

39. Waterman, 1986.

40. Coplan, 1982 and 1987.

41. The idea of cultural analogues occurs in several writings: in Alan P. Merriam's "The Use of Music in the Study of the Problem of Acculturation." *American Anthroplogist*, No. 57. 1955. pp. 28–54; in Richard A. Waterman's "African Influences in the Music of the Americas," in Sol Tax, Ed., *Acculturation in the Americas*. Chicago: University of Chicago Press, 1952; and in Waterman, 1986. p. 28.

42. Theodor Newcomer, "An Approach to the Study of the Communicative Act." *Psychological Review*, No. 60. 1953. pp. 393–404.

43. Luke Uche, "Imperialism Revisited." *Media Education Journal*, No. 6. 1987. pp. 30–3.

44. Coplan, 1985. p. 3.

45. Melville J. Herskovitz, *The Anthropology of the American Negro*. New York: Columbia University Press, 1930.

46. Rudi Blesh, *African Retentions in Jazz*. New York: Cassell Publications, 1949.

47. Waterman, 1952.

48. LeRoi Jones (Amiri Baraka), *Blues People: Negro Music in White America*. New York: William Morrow, 1963.

49. Paul Oliver, *The Savannah Syncopators*. London: Vista Publications, 1970.

50. John Storm Roberts, *Black Music of Two Worlds*. New York: William Morrow, 1974. p. 245.

51. J. H. K. Nketia, *Folk Songs of Ghana*. Accra: Ghana University Press, 1973. p. 66.

52. K. Little, *The Mende of Sierra Leone*. London: Routledge and Kegan Paul, 1987.

53. John Blacking, "The Value of Music in Human Experience." *The Yearbook of the International Folk Music Council*, No. 1. 1969. pp. 33–71.

54. Grace Sims, "Inversion in Black Communication," in T. Kochman, Ed., *Rappin' and Stylin' Out*. University of Illinois Press, 1972. pp. 152–9.

55. Keith Warner, *The Trinidad Calypso*. London: Heinemann Educational Books, 1982. p. 13.
56. Ranger, 1975. p. 166.
57. K. Little, *West African Urbanisation, a Study of Voluntary Associations in Social Change*. Cambridge: Cambridge University Press, 1970.
58. N. Sithole, *African Nationalism*. Oxford: Oxford University Press, 1970.
59. Collins, 1986. p. 6.
60. E. J. Collins, "Comic Opera in Ghana." *African Arts*, Volume 9, No. 2. January 1976. pp. 50–7.
61. Ebun Clark and Herbert Ogunde, *The Making of Nigerian Theatre*. Oxford: Oxford University Press, 1979.
62. Fred Zindi, *Roots Rocking in Zimbabwe*. Harare: Mambo Press, 1985.
63. Waterman, 1986. p. 4.
64. Roberts, 1974. p. 254.
65. Ranger, 1975. p. 3.
66. Ibid. p. 113.
67. Collins, 1986. p. 6.
68. Sjaak Van der Geest and Nimrod Asante-Darko, "The Political Meaning of Highlife Songs in Ghana." *African Studies Review*, Volume 5, No. 1. 1982.
69. Roland Barthes, *Elements of Semiology*. London: Jonathan Cape, 1967.
70. Stuart Hall, "The Rediscovery of Ideology: Return of the Repressed in Media Studies," in M. Gurevitch, et al., Eds., *Culture, Society and Media*. London: Methuen, 1982.
71. Collins, 1986. p. 6.
72. W. Banton, *West African City: A Study of Tribal Life in Freetown*. Oxford: University Press, 1957.
73. Collins, 1983. p. 2946.
74. Mosumola Omibiyi-Obidike, 'Women in Popular Music in Africa." Paper presented at the Fourth International Conference of IASPM, Accra, Ghana, August 1987. p. 7.
75. Collins, 1987. p. 7.
76. Sjaak Van der Geest and Nimrod Asante-Darko, "Men and Women in Ghanaian Highlife Songs," in Christine Oppong, Ed., *Female and Male in West Africa*. London: George Allen and Unwin, 1983. pp. 242–55.
77. Collins, 1985.

52

Desert Dreams, Media, and Interventions in Reality: Australian Aboriginal Music

*Marcus Breen**

"Black boy black boy the color of your skin is your pride and joy"
Coloured Stone

Somewhere in the vast desert regions of Central Australia a small group of Aborigines sit around a cassette player, listening to the gentle country and western tones of a song by the Areyonga Desert Tigers. There's a concentration and sincerity here, as the sun beats down on people whose ancestors may have roamed this island continent 60,000 years ago. Incredibly, in the 1990s, they sit under a eucalyptus tree listening to "AIDS It's a Killer," a song with a special message about the virus that has caused serious concern among Australia's natives. The image is a potent symbol of how an ancient culture coexists in an uneasy alliance with the late 20th century, where a modern disease is challenged through the use of equally modern hi-fidelity technology. AIDS itself is a further symbol within this narrative, and in keeping with the history of Australia's Aborigines, it is more cruel than white media readings of AIDS would suggest. The disease, it seems, could be passed on to Aborigines through their sacred initiation ceremonies, where stone tools are used to make incisions and male circumcision is practiced at the onset of adolescence. Just as cruelly, the disease could circulate through the population through heterosexual relations. Everyday life for the subaltern of the Australian continent becomes a risk in itself. AIDS could wipe out Australia's Aborigines, thereby annihilating an entire civilization that just managed to survive the ravages of European settlement that began in 1788.

While stopping the spread of the AIDS virus is important for the survival of Aborigines, getting information to them about the disease is essential. "AIDS It's a Killer" is one practical means of communication, a fitting example of how Aboriginal music has a cultural and social value that goes to the heart of explaining contemporary Aboriginal society and its place in Australia.

Equally instructive and perhaps more relevant to North Americans, is the song "Munjana." The song grew out of the publicity surrounding the James Savage court

*Pp. 149–70 from *Rockin' the Boat: Mass Music and Mass Movements*, ed. R. Garofalo (Boston, MA: South End Press). © 1992 by Reebee Garofalo. Reprinted with permission from South End Press.

case in Florida. Aboriginal James Savage was sentenced to death on January 24, 1990 for murder. He was born in Australia, but, under a perverse and racist program instituted by federal law in the 1930s, he was one of thousands of Aboriginal children who were sent away from their families to white homes and schools to be educated and socialized in an appropriately white manner. His trial and the circumstances of his life opened up to scrutiny the history of white oppression against black Australia. Aboriginal singer Archie Roach described this case in "Munjana," his most stirring song yet. It sounded the pain in a hollow echo of despair – a lonely man grasping for life in the face of an alien death sentence.

> Hello Russell this is your mother calling
> Please forgive me I can't stop the tears from falling
> You come from this land and sun above
> And always remember the strength of your mother's love.

Lyrically, the song mixed the intensity of maternal love with the deep-seated love of the open land, which is a permanent and challenging subtext of the Aboriginal experience that appears in much of their music.

Roach reinforced the agony of enforced isolation from the black family with "Took the Children Away," which unequivocally articulated black Australia's pain, while challenging white assumptions about black rights and progress toward equality. "Took the Children Away" almost reached the Top Forty charts in Australia late in 1990, opening up a new era of Aboriginal involvement within the mainstream music establishment. That Roach himself had experienced this appalling government policy, surviving it to sing about it, made the song more poignant still:

> You took the children away
> The children away
> Breaking their mother's heart
> Tearing us all apart
> Took them away.

Aboriginal music is making rapid headway into the Australian musical mainstream as well as serving Aboriginal people themselves. It is an exciting and challenging development involving remarkable determination and experimentation from Aboriginal musicians, activists, and bureaucrats. The history of Aboriginal music and its political economy show its fundamental role within Aboriginal life. Now, representations of that life are being transported into the life of white Australia, upsetting the balance of white prejudice and apathy in a country whose attitude towards its natives has been likened to attitudes frequently associated with South Africa. A uniquely Australian form of black power has created the conditions to advance the Aboriginal cause for justice through contemporary music.

That Aboriginal music is becoming a popular medium in Australia is remarkable. Hardly ten years ago, descriptions of Aboriginal music were restricted to the exotic droning sound of the *didgeridu* (a hollowed-out stick, about the thickness of an upper arm, through which air is blown in a deep vibrating, rhythmic manner), clapping sticks, and chants of desert Aborigines. Their lives, it seemed, were dependent on white missionaries and government handouts. Alternatively, there were a few male country music singers and some remarkable women's church-style choirs. And yet it was always the exotic traditional Aboriginal music that captured the imagination of Australia and the world. In many ways the 1880 perspective of the Norwegian explorer Carl Lumholtz became the prominent white view of Aborigines, with its implied Victorian moralism: "The Australian natives are gay and happy, but their song is rather melancholy and in excellent harmony with the sombre nature of Australia. It awakened feelings of sadness in me when I heard it from the solemn gum-tree forest, accompanied by the monotonous clatter of the two wooden weapons."[1] This view married the high-minded European patronage of the "happy native" to the nostalgic, yet uncertain feelings about the vast Australian eucalyptus forests of the coastal regions and unexplored deserts of the center of the continent. It was an unequivocally generous view compared to that expressed by Baldwin Spencer in 1899, who described Aboriginal ritual, with its inextricably linked song and dance, as "eminently crude and savage . . . performed by naked howling savages."[2]

If the male explorers had views that reproduced their predetermined middle class European priorities, their anthropology was accurate for its day, in describing the antipodean experience of native song and dance. Their reports, and dozens like them, expressed consternation at the disorientation a meeting with Aborigines brought. These views predominated, seeping through school textbooks, media reports and representations of Aborigines, so that entire generations of white Australians thought of Aborigines as savages, or in some way inferior and useful only as entertainment – either as shooting targets, sexual objects (Aboriginal women were known as "black velvet," which became a nationally specific, derogatory racist term), or providing exotic song and dance.

While sympathetic academics, like G.H. Strehlow and Jeremy Beckett, introduced a liberal anthropology into a sympathetic sector of Australian academic life from the late 1950s, the vast bulk of Australians treated Aborigines as exceptions to daily life until the 1970s, when a new generation of academics and an activist Aboriginal black rights movement surfaced. The most important feature of the liberal academics' work was a commitment to comprehend Aboriginal life on its own terms and explain it sympathetically. While this may seem as patronizing as some of the earlier descriptions of Aboriginal life, it was an important milestone, simply because it recognized the culture of the Aboriginal people as worthy. More importantly, when examined, it was clear that Aboriginal civilization was mediated by song and dance. This was a major anthropological break-through which demanded attention.

A.M. Ellis identified some of the main features of traditional song from two tribes of the central and southern parts of Australia, the Pitjantjatara and the Aranda. He identified the relationship song has to the Aboriginal view of personal and social relations to the land, where ancestral beings traveled across the land, giving it physical and moral shape as they went. This is known as the Dreaming.

Song is held by these people to be of great power in influencing non-musical events and that if performed correctly in all essential details it will enable performers to draw on supernatural powers left within the soil by the powers during the dreaming. This power may be used for evil as well as good, for which reason the teaching of songs is very strictly controlled. Only the eldest and wisest men know the most potent songs. Song thus is used as a means of social control, in that miscreants are sung about as well as talented hunters and the like, for legal and moral codes are perpetuated in the songs and they also serve to educate children morally and socially.[3]

Comments like this have clarified the intensity of song within everyday Aboriginal culture, while forming the basis for some questionable interest in the exotica of Aboriginal life, often from people with the best intentions. A recent example came from the pen of English writer Bruce Chatwin, who created a lyrically rich, but substantially misleading interpretation of traditional Aboriginal song-culture in his book *The Songlines*. For example, he used Eurocentric reference points to explain his experience of Aboriginal music, serving to deny the music its remarkable place in a unique system of belief: "What makes Aboriginal song so hard to appreciate is the endless accumulations of detail. Yet even a superficial reader can get a glimpse of a moral universe – as moral as the New Testament in which the structures of kinship reach out to all living men, to all his fellow creatures, and to the rivers, the rocks and the trees."[4] Contextualizing Aboriginal song by referring to New Testament morality reproduced 200 years of colonial values and represented the failure of most contemporary intellectuals to grasp the fact that a new or different conceptual and social apparatus is necessary to describe Australian Aborigines and their music.

The really important work that championed Aboriginal music came from Catherine Ellis, who brought none of the male aggression of either the explorer or the careerist academic and writer to her work. Together with her husband she studied Aboriginal culture and the role of Aboriginal song. Her conviction that Aboriginal music provided a new way of seeing Aborigines was the subject of an important book that opened up new avenues for music educators.[5]

> Through song, the unwritten history of the people and the laws of the community are taught and maintained; the entire physical and spiritual development of the individual is nurtured; the well being of the group is protected; supplies of food and water are ensured through musical communication with the spiritual powers; love of homeland is poured out for all to share; illnesses are cured; news is passed from one group to another.[6]

Modern Musical Development

Song stands as the director of cultural traffic within traditional Aboriginal culture. In the prematerialist world of Aboriginal society, song had a uniquely affirming role, objectifying existence and individuality to create an "essential power," namely the "human sense."[7] In this society, "universal communalism" meant that 500 different groups of Aborigines shared their territories and special meanings with one another.[8] But what about Aboriginal culture since the arrival of European civilization and in the present? What of the political economy of making music and of singing songs in the context of capitalist relations as opposed to preindustrial relations? The transformation from traditional "essentialist" readings to the dynamic contemporary is important at a number of levels. Aboriginal music no longer exists in one society, whether at a regional or national level. In the late 1980s and into the 1990s it is part of the flux of musical and cultural life of an entire country and planet. The cultural baggage of modern life – radio, television, film clips, and the cross fertilization of the media – no longer allow discrete cultural formations to comfortably exist isolated from those around them.

But it would be equally inadequate to reject the history of traditional Aboriginal life, in the face of the present. If there is any context in which history forms a particularly strong linkage between one generation and another, it is in societies where ancient values still resonate. Urban Aborigines in towns and cities of Australia as well as isolated rural Aborigines still share the ancient values of the Dreamtime and its values. At one level this may be axiomatic. But in advanced, postindustrial societies like Australia and North America, where the frontier ethic has overwhelmed the old with endlessly reproducible mythologies of newness, it is easy to forget that the values of the old still have a place. The history of degradation and abuse is absolutely necessary for an understanding of contemporary Aboriginal life and music. This history includes details like the successful 1967 national referendum to get white Australia to agree to change the Federal Constitution to allow Aborigines to be treated as Australians for census taking! It is necessary to explain the basic statistical facts of Aboriginal existence in the 1990s, to avoid a gross and unintended misrepresentation of Aboriginal numerical and cultural significance within Australia. According to the 1986 Australian Census there are 206,104 people who consider themselves Aborigines, while 21,514 consider themselves Torres Strait Islanders, making a total of 227,645, or 1.43 percent of the total Australian population of nearly 17 million, in 1986. (Aborigines and Torres Strait Islanders are lumped together in a rough ethnic mix, with far-northern Aborigines bearing some cultural resemblance to the Islanders, although Islanders are really Melanesian).

While these statistics may surprise some people who have believed that the substantial publicity Aboriginal people have generated reflected their vast numbers (as opposed to, say, North American Indians), clearly this is not the case. Indeed, the low numerical strength of Aborigines, combined with their isolation from the major coastal cities of Melbourne, Sydney, and Brisbane, means that their living conditions have often been like those of people in the underdeveloped world. For example, in 1984, the Task Force on Aboriginal and Islander Broadcasting and Communications, working from within the federal government's Department of Aboriginal Affairs, noted: "Aborigines are the most disadvantaged major segment of Australian society with respect to access to communications and the social and economic benefits which they provide."[9] Numerous other studies have noted that Aborigines are equally disadvantaged at every other social level – health, education, child care, and employment – while in 1991, the World Council of Churches noted the following:

> The impact of racism by Australians on Aboriginal people in this nation is not just horrific but genocidal, and must be addressed . . . We saw that the social conditions among Aboriginal communities are deplorable. We saw that the Government has not responded meaningfully to those conditions. We heard from the people their sense of frustration and alienation about a lack of meaningful control over their lives.[10]

This reality hits home when the vastness of the Australian continent and Aboriginal life upon it is understood as taking place largely outside the central population centers. About 70 percent of the Australian continent is considered "remote" and the population density is less than one person per ten square kilometers. Aboriginal representation in remote Australia accounts for about 14 percent of the region's population.[11] Equally, though, it would be wrong to characterize Aboriginal life in that mistaken colonial and idealized manner, as being restricted to one form (tribal or nomadic) or location (urban or rural). The same principle applies to the music. The range and scope of contemporary Aboriginal culture and musical expression stretches back to ancient times and forward through the 1990s. The diversity of the music is remarkable, with traditional music thriving among some desert communities, while newer forms of electric music also find a place, merging in a friendly relationship of support that unites rock with folk, pop with tribal, the joyous with the absolutely desolate.

Traditional music, as we have seen in the statements from E.M. and Catherine Ellis, encapsulated the entire Aboriginal value system. In various regions of Australia the musics differ, but there are some general attributes. Aboriginal tribal music is primarily vocal, with some purely instrumental forms: *didgeridu* solos in the north and songless sacred (non-Christian) performances in Central Australia, where dramatic acts are accorded reverent silence, broken only by the beating together of boomerangs or a stone shield on the hard earth. Most tribal instruments are percussive and continue this beating method. The instruments vary from hand clapping, body slapping, hitting paired boomerangs, thumping the ground with a stick, stamping while dancing, and striking long sticks together. Remarkable and unique instruments like the bullroarer are also used. This is a piece of wood attached to a long piece of twine that is spun in a circular motion above the head, with the air pressure on the wood creating a deep resonant roaring sound.[12] Singing has an important place in all this.

But to early settlers this was heathen mumbo-jumbo. These people and their music needed civilizing and as in many parts of the world in the early 19th century, Christian missionaries saw themselves as the purveyors of civilizing, Christian values. Settler-missionaries in Central Australia spent a considerable amount of time belittling Aboriginal culture while introducing Christian and European values. One of the major features of their proselytizing was the teaching of Biblical beliefs through hymns which were most frequently performed by choirs. "Christian mission music" directly challenged Aboriginal music and values.[13] The two systems – Aboriginal tribal nomad and European settler – especially where Aborigines were "settled" on mission stations, did not collide; European ways simply consumed the Aboriginal. The ammunition used at the forefront of their conversion from "heathenism" to Christianity and modernity was the song. There is no doubt that song, especially the hymn, in the religious and church context is the primary signifier for conversion to Christian belief.[14]

While Christian mission music may have been the main force of traditional cultural annihilation, white settlers were not only missionaries, but large cattle and sheep station or ranch owners, who made (and still make) claims to Aboriginal land. This is the same land which, according to Dreamtime mythology, is sacred and the subject of the song-lines. Nineteenth century settlers introduced other forms of music which had a further impact on Aborigines, including: formal music training, bush folk culture, and the commercial music of touring shows. In the latter category, black minstrel shows were popular in country towns and cities, with Aboriginal performers singing "plantation songs" and Stephen Foster tunes like "The Old Folks at Home" and "Swanee River," which in their turn became part of the bush ballad tradition.[15] The bush ballad style is derived from American hillbilly, together with English, Irish, and Scottish folk songs, and the Australian colonial storytelling of progressive polemicist poets, such as Henry Lawson and Banjo Patterson, who reflected an earnest populism, often reflecting class antagonism with a distinctive narrative progression. As a musical style it comfortably fit into preexisting Aboriginal song and dance styles of Dreamtime story-telling. This mix of styles and influences is present in most conventional rock and roll songs, and is a style that has made its presence felt in contemporary Aboriginal music.

Gum leaf players also performed for black and white audiences, playing versions of the grand old North American popular songs and a few Australian tunes – some of them home grown. (The gum or eucalyptus leaf is played by holding it between the hands and up to the mouth and blowing air across it to make it vibrate. After the *didgeridu* and the bull roarer, it is probably Australia's greatest musical invention.) The introduction of radio in the 1930s brought its own style of cultural transformation, with the gradual development of solo Aboriginal singers in the Jimmy Rogers tradition, mixing hillbilly, folk, country and western, country blues, and yodeling.[16] Jimmy Little was the best-known exponent of this style from the 1960s on, singing "Telephone to Glory," a song straight out of the fundamentalist Baptist repertoire. This was followed by considerable interest in Elvis Presley and a strong passion for Kris Kristofferson (especially "Me and Bobby McGee") and Charley Pride songs. The relevance of this country-folk-rock combination is spelled out by Doug Petherick: "This ability of country and western to celebrate brawls, booze, and the low life on one hand and revival style religion on the other, sometimes in the same writer and even in the same song, has been a strong attraction for Aboriginal listeners."[17] This style of music, building on the bush ballad, is the prominent genre used today. Importantly, too, as with the world music movement in general, with which Aboriginal music has sometimes been associated, "the grain of the voice" has been an important factor in challenging recording, artistic, and commercial conventions.[18] It achieves this "challenging" mode because Aboriginal English sounds harsher, less refined, more nasal, even flatter, than European English. This difference in sound (a linguistic distinction, in fact) adds to the impact of the subject matter of many Aboriginal songs, which cannot avoid dealing with the daily hardship and history of abuse suffered by Australia's natives, illustrated by Archie Roach's "Took the Children Away," as noted earlier.

In recent Australian history, the musics described above permeated the Aboriginal community. Traditional Aboriginal music survived but had to give way to the transforming power of modern form and content. What the missionaries and settlers began, technology and the march of modernizing society took over. It needs to be said, however, that despite these considerable changes Aboriginal music often managed to retain the spiritual sense of place and history, of dignity and purpose. It is significant that despite the transformations of Aboriginal music, community values and an intense connection with the land and the Dreaming distinguishes Aboriginal music from all other music in Australia. Aboriginal behavior based on unique notions of time, space, and non-materiality has never sat comfortably with Europeans, but it can be argued that those values and attitudes have become a part of the easy-going, relaxed Australian lifestyle. These elements have been reinforced since the 1970s, as Aboriginal pride and black consciousness have grown. Popular music changed Aboriginal music and culture, but Aborigines and their music undoubtedly challenged prevailing capitalist relations in European Australia as well. Their music reflected values that were not determined by Judeo-Christian beliefs and the work ethic.

Real and dramatic changes to Aboriginal music, combined with modest victories for Aboriginal people in general, had to wait until the 1970s and an Australian "black power" that saw how improvements could be gained by making use of the opportunities progressive governments made available. Black power in Australia had a major role to play in advancing the cause of popular musical development. In the first instance, traditional Aboriginal values were necessary for Aboriginal identity and survival. Secondly, traditional values which were conveyed most forcefully in music and dance could be conveyed using contemporary musical forms that had broad appeal. The 1970s ushered in this dramatic cultural and political development that is finding its feet in the 1990s.

Changing with Reformist Government

In the early 1970s a wave of optimism rode an unprecedented surge of enthusiasm for political change in Australia. The result was the election of the first federal Australian Labor Party (ALP) government in 23 years. A generation of reactionary government ended and, with it, the excesses that Australia's isolation from the rest of the world could bring. The cultural, economic, and political elite was horrified by its loss of power. Its disregard for the underprivileged (which included the Vietnamese) was effectively screened from most Australians who believed in the petty bourgeois suburban home-owning dream of existence that is so effectively marketed by capitalist establishments. In this scheme, Aborigines were not on the agenda. The election of Gough Whitlam as prime minister in 1972 turned Australia on its head. Youth culture, minorities, and Aborigines became part of the new Australia. "It's Time" was the slogan of the ALP for the 1972 election, and indeed it was. Empowerment was the key, and so a series of gradual reforms were introduced into Australia, one of which was to give Aborigines a greater say in their own lives and future, in particular by introducing legislation that would usher in a new era of land rights. The very act of trusting Aborigines with self-management (loosely defined) and control over their own land (land rights) and money was little short of revolutionary. Aboriginal life and Australia itself would never be the same again.

In 1971 Adelaide University opened the Center for Aboriginal Studies in Music (CASM), with Cath Ellis appearing there as a main player in the preservation and promotion of Aboriginal music. While arguably too much emphasis was placed on conventional musical skills at CASM, such as learning musical notation and classical instruments, tribal elders were also used to pass on musical traditions in the relevant (sacred) context. A new generation of musicians developed skills that made them a professional musician class within the Aboriginal community. This was a further major change. Formal education replaced traditional tribal ways, while the traditional and spiritual values were maintained.

Toward the end of the Whitlam ALP government in 1975 – it was sacked under questionable circumstances by Queen Elizabeth's representative, the governor-general, with unproven assistance by the CIA – public radio was introduced as one of its final acts of defiance against the establishment. This single act opened up communication "from within" communities, rather than "from above," and ushered in "a significant cultural, economic and political break with the media status quo."[19] It provided all sorts of possibilities, including the promotion of Australian independent music and, as part of that scene, Aboriginal music. Other media then expanded and flourished, including an ethnic television station within the Special Broadcasting Service (SBS – which began as a foreign language radio station). Minorities had a voice of sorts. Although the voices were not mainstream, they could be heard simply by tuning in a radio or a television set. Culturally, it meant that for consumers, music could be more than Top Forty, because a different radio format was available. In the 1970s the political implications these changes brought were untried, but they provided a significant stepping stone for the advancement of Aboriginal music and the further advancement of Australian society as a whole.

In 1980, after a period of consolidation, Aborigines had made considerable social and cultural progress, with unlikely assistance from the conservative government of Malcolm Fraser, who allowed the bureaucracy to continue its support of Aboriginal programs established under Whitlam. Of course, much of the developmental work undertaken in these years could only flourish under a reformist government, and so it was that what had been Aboriginal activism in relation to the single issue of land rights during the 1970s became a vast series of activities with the election of the Hawke Labor government in 1983. The floodgates were opened and music was the bearer of the news and the means of articulating ideas and issues that needed to find a concentrated form.

While there is skepticism with governments around the globe, there is no doubt that reformist governments can and do have a major role to play in creating liberal democracies where institutions of state, even bureaucracies, act as "educators" in a Gramscian sense, to facilitate governance.[20] This is an important sub-theme to the discussion of contemporary Aboriginal music because the history of Australia's natives has brought federal and state governments face to face with the most difficult social and political question consistently facing the nation: What about the Aborigines? Developments in Aboriginal music have moved in tandem with the election of reformist governments and the modernization and liberalization of Australian society. These early changes, which led to the establishment of unfriendly bureaucracies for Aborigines, occurred through the activism of older Aborigines like Pastor Doug Nicholls, poet Cath Walker, administrator Charles Perkins, and, in the 1980s, Gary Foley. These people, along with activist Europeans like H.C. "Nugget" Coombes and Professor Fred Hollows, created a uniquely Australian Black Power Movement that could only succeed in its early days with a groundswell of white support for Australia's natives, that made Aboriginal rights and dignity a major platform of the ALP. But it was always black Australians who began marching in city streets in the early 1970s to bring attention to their struggles for rights.

Aborigines, with the help of sympathetic Europeans, created a black power that reflected the easy-going style of Australia. This was not the black power of African Americans like Angela Davis or the Black Panthers, but a brand that used collective support networks to conduct peaceful demonstrations that often generated enormous amounts of unintended publicity, due to the aggressive attempts of the police to break up the demonstrations. As Aborigines became more experienced at political campaigns, they began to more effectively target certain events, such as the Commonwealth Games in Brisbane in 1982, when Aborigines attracted attention from (British) Commonwealth countries to the plight of Aboriginal people. As the issues came into increasingly stark relief through these demonstrations, governments could not fail to take heed. White guilt affected conservative and liberal middle classes alike, so the relatively quiet Black Power Movement in Australia could make demands of state and federal governments. It was remarkable that from the early 1980s, all Australian governments at least paid lip service to the needs of Aborigines.

Real experience, of course, was another thing altogether. As late as December 17, 1990, Robert Tickner, then Federal Minister for Aborignal Affairs in the Hawke Labor Government, had to admit that Aboriginal health was still at a third world level, particularly in isolated communities. At the end of 1990, infant mortality among Aborigines was three times higher than among European Australians, the death rate four times higher, and hospitalization five times higher. The "solution" to these problems in the 1990s was a decision to disburse federal funds of $230 million for water, sanitation, housing, and roads to Aboriginal communities. Nevertheless, the abysmal treatment of Aborigines continues. Reform is never fast enough. History is always there, insistently pressing against the present, reminding people that life has extreme demands. Music conveys this reality more effectively for Aborigines than any formal "political" campaign. For this reason, it is impossible to separate recent developments in Aboriginal music from progressive federal labor government support for Aboriginal people.

Aboriginal Popular Music in the 1980s

In the 1980s, the vast and mostly unhappy history of Aboriginal people began to appear in music. Until this time, Christian mission music, the bush ballad styles, the music hall, and male singer–guitarists had been an entertainment sideshow for Europeans to add to the list of other available exotic and traditional musics. Indeed, for most white Australians their only experience of Aboriginal music was in the late 1960s, when Lionel Rose, former world bantamweight boxing champion and Aboriginal sportsman, had a hit with "I Thank You." Written by white former pop star and entrepreneur, Johnny Young, the song was a sentimental blast of indulgence that avoided politics of either a personal or social nature. Despite the radical changes sweeping the world to the accompaniment of popular music in the late 1960s, Lionel Rose was to remain an alien black man – a boxer, a solo guitar-playing Aborigine – playing entertainer in the bush ballad tradition perhaps, but never a polemicist or politician.

The 1970s were an important period of consolidation. The 1980s saw a substantial change. Young Aborigines, buoyed by the 1979 visit to Australia of Bob Marley, began to see music as a form of black celebration and resistance. Popular music, especially in Adelaide, the capital city with the largest per capita Aboriginal population, took on a new meaning. Music became an overt vehicle for political use. "Music as a utilitarian vehicle" could summarize the Aboriginal vision of the early 1980s. The Aboriginal use of popular music no longer allowed the cultural and anthropological indulgences of the exotic desert people and their tribal musics to be filed somewhere in the background of the European experience of Australia. There was no strange language or instrumentation to isolate the black person's experience from that of the European. Popular music brought the contemporary and historical experience of Aboriginal people into the open. "Rock and roll," as it was experienced through Bob Marley, created a groundswell of interest in the use of the electric band format. The everyday – for Aboriginal people, the pressing political and social issues that most affected them – could be displayed using the rock band medium.

For many European Australians locked into the middle-class urban lifestyle of the cities, the first suggestion that something fundamental had changed in Aboriginal music was the film *Wrong Side of the Road*. Released in 1982, it showed Us Mob and No Fixed Address, two Aboriginal bands on tour. Their music was bursting with politically charged lyrics, while the sound – from the grain of the voices to the slightly awkward reggae-rock – was unlike anything else; unfamiliar, disorienting, and inspiring. It promised a new form of musical expression while opening political issues to public debate that were previously relegated to the serious and frequently disempowered realm of state politics. Of special note and something of a theme for musical progressives in the 1980s was the No Fixed Address song "We Have Survived":

> We have survived the white man's world
> And the horror and torment of it all
> We have survived the white man's world
> And you know you can't change that.

Soon after No Fixed Address and Us Mob began making waves, it became clear that a subculture of well-established Aboriginal musicians existed. Kuckles, with Jimmi Chi, came from Broome in far northwest Western Australia, singing protest music, arguing against uranium mining and for land rights. Chi's best known song, "Brand New Day," was written in 1975 "on the back of a truck during a demonstration against the Court Government (in Western Australia) for allowing mining on (Aboriginal) sacred sites."[21] A rough reggae, the original recording of the song uses a harsh, parodying voice that nervously expresses the Aboriginal plight. Somewhat similar in sound to West Indian singers like The Jolly Boys or Joseph Spence, its appeal comes from its lack of insistence compared to pop's demands. The song maintains its potency 15 years later, forming the basis for the first Aboriginal rock musical, *Bran Nu Dae*. The musical was performed at the Perth Festival in 1990 and is continuing to move around the country, attracting attention with its unflattering and disturbing view of Aboriginal life, as the title song shows:

> Here I live in this tin shack
> Nothing here worth coming back
> To drunken fights and awful sights
> People drunk 'most every night.

The history of "Brand New Day," as a song and as the basis for the musical, provides a model for other recent developments in Aboriginal popular music. Those musicians who saw potential in popular musical forms in the 1970s and made music in that decade created the foundation for those looking to advance the Aboriginal cause through music in the 1980s. In a similar sense, it took 15 years for the urgency of a song written with bold conviction in the back of a pick-up truck to gestate into a fully fledged musical, performed at a festival of the arts. (The question of whether this is a means of actually denying the popular its power, by incorporating it into the bourgeois buildings and cultural domains of middle-class consumers, is a matter that cannot be dismissed. The gulf between popular music's insistent demands and the red carpets of concert halls is vast, difficult to measure, and full of contradictions.) But survival, staying alive, and being part of the struggle for the long run, cliche-ridden as that may sound, is part of the process that Aboriginal performers have had to undertake.

Aboriginal songwriters and bands with intentions of instituting political change could achieve nothing without media support. While SBS, the Australian Broadcasting Corporation, and public radio could do something to publicize the music and issues through music, the mainstream was obsessed with classic hits radio and the Top Forty format that slavishly pursued *Billboard* prescriptions. In the total scheme of things, Aboriginal music has almost never seriously reached into this domain. It has, however, followed the historical process that was established by people like Jimmy Chi and members of No Fixed Address. Putting the media in place was the next step.

Media Conjunctions

Various projects have assisted the promotion of the music and its propagation through broadcasting. Undoubtedly the single most important Aborignal media institution in the country is the Central Australian Aboriginal Media Association (CAAMA). CAAMA in the 1990s is the fulfillment of the political ideals for change that manifested themselves during the Whitlam government from 1972 to 1975. It is an Aboriginal organization, controlled and run by Aborigines under the Aboriginal Councils and Associations Act of 1976. All members of CAAMA must be Aboriginal. A governing committee of at least 12 people is elected from the membership. Established in 1980, with assistance from various federal government departments, CAAMA blossomed through public radio, with a license to provide music to Aboriginal people. This was achieved by applying to the Australian Broadcasting Tribunal for a license to broadcast a particular style of music and programing. Under the Australian system, a frequency allocation is made by the Tribunal after a successful application, with reviews every three or five years by the Tribunal to assess whether the station is in fact meeting its license obligations. The problem for CAAMA was not so much the incredible boldness of applying for and receiving a license to broadcast, as it was filling the air time with appropriate music.

Aboriginal music existed; it was just a matter of finding it and putting it on the air. This was a lot more difficult than it first appeared. To start with, CAAMA was based in Alice Springs, the major city in Central Australia. Intensely isolated, Alice Springs was and is a focus for Aborigines from Central and South Australia. CAAMA's original voluntary workers in the 1980s saw the opportunities public radio access provided for minorities, especially Aborigines, who, in isolated communities in Central Australia, deserved news and information as well as culturally relevant material that would promote their survival and a sense of purpose and empowerment. That ideal has grown and flourished. CAAMA Music, the most recent extension of CAAMA as a media center, is part of the Australian independent music scene and "the Aboriginal recording label of Australia."[22] CAAMA was and probably remains not so much an overt expression of black power as another necessary and practical part of the Aboriginal survival process.

In order to achieve their goals of broadcasting contemporary Aboriginal music, the CAAMA workers had to find musicians from obscure towns and settlements whose only experience of music was performing to other Aborigines. With AM radio station 8CCC at their disposal, CAAMA had an obligation to broadcast Aboriginal music for Aboriginal people six hours each day in three Aboriginal languages and in English. But the recordings were almost nonexistent, except for ethnomusicological recordings of traditional musics and the solo male bush balladeers with a predominantly sentimental style. According to Rodney Gooch, "There was very little Aboriginal music to use on the Aboriginal radio station, so we brought in a lot of people who could sing."[23] The process of recording these people began in a dilapidated two-track studio, and the first CAAMA cassettes were released late in 1980. They featured the bands Colored Stone and Warumpi Band, and solo male performers – Bob Randal, Isaac Yama, and Herbiee Lawton – who brought varying levels of community intensity to their work. "The framework for the label was simply Aboriginal music for Aboriginal people."[24] It was music about the Aboriginal experience using country music and early rock, while somewhere in the background the vastness of a virtually uninhabited desert beat like a heart.

After the first releases, a cassette featuring Kuckles appeared, bringing the music of *Bran Nu Dae* into circulation. The cassette, not vinyl, is important to the CAAMA story. In the first instance, the music was recorded to be broadcast on the radio station to fulfill Aboriginal programing obligations. The circulation of the music for private and other consumption became increasingly significant. In the extensive desert sands of Central Australia, the only way to sensibly circulate the music was on cassette. Vinyl albums and record players were impractical and had none of the portability of battery-powered cassette players. At the end of 1990, thirty-one cassettes were listed in the CAAMA Music Catalogue, with just one recording released on an alternative format, the compact disc.

The move to CD is the next important step in this CAAMA story, reflecting substantial leaps by Aboriginal music into the political and social life of white Australia. A 1990 agreement between Polygram Records Australia and CAAMA to distribute selected

CAAMA recordings represents a significant move to make this music accessible to the average Australian, where before its distribution was restricted to mail order and a handful of selected, sympathetic retail outlets. Among the material being distributed is the CD sampler titled *From the Bush*. There is also a collection of tracks about AIDS sung by Aboriginal bands, *How could I Know* (referred to at the start of this article); a selection about alcohol abuse, *Wama Wanti: Drink Little Bit*; a compilation about living conditions in a Central Australian region *Uwankara Palyanku Kanyinijaku* (UPK); together with five other cassettes by newly recorded Aboriginal bands. This move by Polygram brings Aboriginal music and the political cause further into the foreground of Australian and international life.

CAAMA has undoubtedly played a significant role in advancing the cause of Aboriginal music, first among Aboriginal Australians and more recently among European Australians, using music as a political weapon in the long-term struggle of Aboriginal people for dignity, respect, and land rights claims. Alternatively, for Aboriginal people themselves, taking the music to them in desert settlements brought information and political education where before, there was none, or very little. The CAAMA Catalogue puts it best:

> The past decade has witnessed stunning growth in the development of this music, a fact appreciated more with an understanding of the circumstances under which the music is produced. It is less likely that songs are written in an idyllic outstation setting and more likely that rough fringe camps, ravaged communities and town life is the wellspring of this music. It is no accident that the rise of contemporary Aboriginal Music coincides with the growth of the Central Australian Aboriginal Media Association. Beginning in 1980, the fundamental objectives contained in the CAAMA charter were to provide full media services to its peoples. Arresting cultural disintegration through the broadcast of educational material in language and song demands a basic prerequisite in the form of recording facilities. The CAAMA Studios have recorded a massive amount of material by the Aboriginal composers and musicians of this country. The point of expression for these works is through 8KIN-FM Radio, the regional broadcast service operated through CAAMA.

Arguments that suggest that the media is a "legitimizing agent" that denies the true social and political value of a cultural or social activity by native peoples have been used against media creations like CAAMA.[25] In the case of Aboriginal Australians, the primary focus of CAAMA – namely, to provide music and information for Aborigines – has served to legitimize Aborigines, rather than denigrate their culture. Certainly, the existence of the media among them challenges and changes Aboriginal life and values, but it is more significant in advancing their basic living conditions. Aboriginal media also helps Aborigines to organize themselves. The Australian government's current inquiry into black deaths in custody, launched in the late 1980s and still running early into 1991, happened as a result of well-organized media campaigns in the mid-1980s.

CAAMA began with three volunteer staff, a radio license, and a commitment to the cause of Aboriginal music. Now it is known as the CAAMA Group, an Aboriginal Arts and Crafts business which includes a television production company, and is a major shareholder in Imparja Television which was established along commercial lines in 1988. Imparja Television operates from the CAAMA base in Alice Springs, providing programs via satellite to the Northern Territory and South Australia under the Remote Commercial Television Service (RCTS) agreement. Its formation and subsequent successful license application was controversial, but served to reinforce the need for a voice for Aboriginal people. It was also timely, albeit late. In 1954, a Commonwealth Royal Commission on Television in Australia concluded that the provision of television to rural and remote Australia was necessary, but an economic problem. This is still the case, although the extension of access to television for people in remote Australia had to come through use of the AUSSAT satellite.[26] Buying time on the satellite has nearly bankrupted Imparja. Nevertheless, the satellite, which serves about 300,000 people, most of whom are Aborigines, has played an important role in promoting Aboriginal music to Aboriginals. Moreover, developing skills, like film clip making (as well as radio programing), forms a further developmental stage in advancing Aboriginal interests in the media through a cultural seepage, whereby the sheer existence of Aboriginal "product" cannot go unnoticed by mainstream media programers indefinitely. "Serious" political campaigns and cultural agendas by reformist governments and activists find their place in advancing the voices of Aborigines by funding and supporting indigenous media organizations.

It is also important to note that satellite technology has a function and power that cannot be easily compared with a single radio station. For example, the transglobal nature of satellite technology "fundamentally challenges functions of the nation state and its agents in administering and negotiating communications, information, economic and social orders."[27] It also reinvests power. Satellites give governments, especially those of developing countries, and minority and indigenous groups a chance "to redress the immense power and strategic know-how of transnational corporations. Access to good quality information is critical to these processes."[28]

Public access models of communication, not to mention various forms of democracy, are based on some implementation of these processes. The empowerment of minorities has been a facet of advanced contemporary countries, which has unintentionally been aided and abetted by communication transnationals whose quest forever larger markets has seen their tentacles reach into otherwise remote corners of civilizations – from the slums to the jungles to the deserts. While they reach into these places, bringing sounds, pictures, ideas, and information from their preferred massed suburban audiences of relatively willing consumers, a reversal also takes place. The pictures and sounds of poverty, notions of the non-consumer lifestyles of native peoples, and unconventional behavior challenge the modes of life of the idealized target consumer audience. As Freda Murphy, chairperson of CAAMA's board, said in 1987: "We cannot remain on the fringes of communication, as well as the fringes of town, forever."[29]

Postmodern discourse has indicated some of these articulations, yet often overlooked the multilayered, mutually inclusive, and dependant relationship between idealized target audiences and sources of information. One changes the other, in a dynamic osmosis. In doing so, it is possible for the minority to receive power and influence through the media over and above its numerical strength relative to the majority population or audience. There is, of course, no guarantee of this happening and an equal chance that a complete loss of the intended message will occur through its submersion into mainstream media activity. The osmosis theory demands, however, that at least a mutual, increasing interdependency between the mainstream and the periphery will occur. In the context of electronic media, music, and video in the 1990s, emotional and intellectual cues can be generated to act almost automatically for the idealized target consumer audience, building on the political black power campaigns that are inextricably linked to Aboriginal music. European audiences can respond sympathetically to the information and intellectual and emotional challenges put to them by Aboriginal music.

For CAAMA and Imparja, music provided the original vehicle for the development of both the radio and television outlets. Assisted by federal government funding, CAAMA organized itself to fulfill the needs of remote area Aborigines, first through a radio station, then cassette tapes, and finally a television station. The work of North American anthropologist Eric Michaels cannot go unmentioned here. Michaels identified the imperatives of community functions in the use of television by Aborigines in his book *The Aboriginal Invention of Television in Central Australia*.[30] Michaels championed the reconstruction of the medium, especially the video camera and recorder as used by Aborigines, as an act of monumental transformation and empowerment, suggesting that "Aboriginal cultural rights" would lead to "local, low power community television," which could, when implemented, "avert the cultural catastrophes of language loss and social disorganization in a region where economics and ecology have limited European colonialism."[31]

In a similar way, Imparja Television "made important allowances for local community control of incoming satellite television signals as well as fostering the development of production capacity at the same level."[32] This theme reappeared when the Federal Court upheld the decision of the Australian Broadcasting Tribunal to grant the RCTS license for the Northern Territory and South Australia to Imparja, after the decision was contested by Television Capricornia, the competitor for the license. The Tribunal thought that Imparja was preferable (to Television Capricornia) because of the nature and quality of its services, its responsiveness to the community and its ability to satisfy the needs of that community.[33]

This community function of Aboriginal media is recognized at an Australian federal government level as well. A statement by the former Minister for Transport and Communication, Kim C. Beazley on September 28, 1990 detailed the extension of public broadcasting licenses, with the aim of seeing 200 public radio licenses spread across the country, with Aborigines receiving special mention. The minister's statement said that "the Government continued to give a high priority to establishment of Aboriginal radio services. Special interest public radio license applications will be invited for Perth, Townsville, Kununurra, Broome and Fitzroy Crossing and community licenses to be made available at Katherine and Nhulunbuy will serve to increase Aboriginal radio programming in those areas."[34]

While Alice Springs has seen a proliferation of activity centered around CAAMA, other regional developments have also taken place. Once again, Jimmy Chi has a place here. In 1985–6, he was involved in the formation of the Broome Musicians' Aboriginal Corporation. (He was also involved in establishing the Aboriginal Rehabilitation Center, for people with alcohol problems.) Of the musicians' corporation Chi said: "We started that up to get something happening up here, to make musicians more aware of what they can do . . . music keeps people together in the community framework."[35]

The ultimate manifestation of media in the context of the community nature of Aboriginal society was the introduction, in 1987, of the Broadcasting for Remote Aboriginal Communities Scheme (BRACS). Once again, it is a program developed by sympathetic bureaucrats in Canberra and further indicates the significant conjunctions between government, policy, activism, and cultural production in creating Aborignal music. BRACS has several important characteristics. It is small scale and designed to be operated on a community basis by all community members and to transmit over short distances. BRACS communities will be able to produce their own video and radio programs or make use of AUSSAT programs.[36] Together with CAAMA there are now four other Aboriginal regional media organizations producing programs for radio and in some cases video programs for broadcast in remote areas. They are: the Western Australian Aboriginal Media Association (WAAMA), the Top End Aboriginal Bush Broadcasting Association (TEABBA), the Townsville and Aboriginal Islander Media Association (TAIMA), and the Torres Strait Islander and Aboriginal Media Association (TSIAMA).[37]

Gains in advancing the Aboriginal cause outside the Aboriginal community have been made by well-organized campaigns constructed by Aboriginal and European activists to bring the sounds and concerns of the people into the mainstream. Perhaps the best known of these efforts was Midnight Oil's *Diesel and Dust* album of 1988. That album and a subsequent tour attracted attention to the subject of Aboriginal land rights on a worldwide scale. The tour of the US by Midnight Oil, accompanied by Aboriginal band, Yothu Yindi provided a useful propaganda tool for Aboriginal Australians overseas, just as Scrap Metal, an Aboriginal band from Broome was able to propagandize Australian audiences when they toured with Midnight Oil in Australia in 1988. Yothu Yindi has maintained its commitment to the Aboriginal cause, with the release on February 11, 1991 of a single titled "Treaty." Recorded with the assistance of two important European Australian singer/songwriters, Paul Kelly and (Midnight Oil's) Peter Garrett, it was written with the intention of gaining commercial radio airplay in Australia, and to draw attention to the need for a treaty between black and white Australia. The involvement of Kelly and Garrett suggests that committed activists are very much still a part of the process of advancing the Aboriginal cause through music. (It must be emphasized that these are particular examples from an increasingly diverse and active Aboriginal music sector within Australian rock music.)

Australia's independent record sector has always taken up the challenge of breaking new music before the major record companies take the music to a grand, possibly international scale. That is the case with Aboriginal music. Sydney-based Larrikin Records released Key Carmody's groundbreaking Dylanesque *Pillars of Society* in 1990. Carmody, from Brisbane, spent a large part of the 1980s studying at Queensland University, and finished the decade preparing a doctorate on colonial history and the treatment of his people. His songs reflect the earnest intellect and radical vigor his academic training has given him, while his hard-headed poetic style maintains the tradition of narrative bush ballad morality. For its part, Australia's largest independent label and the second-largest independent in the world, Mushroom Records, launched a new specialist label called Aurora for Archie Roach's debut *Charcoal Lane*. Mushroom, the rock label, also has Yothu Yindi in its catalogue.

Building Bridges was a special development linked to major record companies. As a project it involved concerts featuring Aboriginal and non-Aboriginal musicians performing together in Sydney. The result was a double LP released through CBS, late in 1988. In some ways it was a gratuitous effort, with many of the white performers on the release having no ongoing record of involvement with Aborigines or progressive causes, unlike Peter Garrett or Paul Kelly, although members of Crowded House are well known for their support of Aborigines. For many of the artists appearing on *Building Bridges*, it was a "free kick" release with an opportunity to win publicity points and community good will. Building Bridges was, however, usefully exploited when the Australian Broadcasting Corporation Television broadcast a half-hour extract of the concert in January 1991, with a simulcast on the ABC youth radio network Triple Jay. Other majors have signed Aboriginal acts, including BMG signing Colored Stone – one of the first CAAMA cassette bands. BMG plans to release the Colored Stone back catalogue on CD in 1991. The move to the majors fosters a sense of confidence among Aborigines and a challenge to the potential isolation they often experience in their outback communities. It also promises to bring the music into the main arena of distribution and radio airplay.

Play Loud Play Long, the annual Aboriginal rock music festival in Darwin, Australia's northern capital city, ran for two consecutive years in 1988–89. It provided a further focus for the music and the people to get together to celebrate their identity in music, In 1990, the Aboriginal rock music festival was organized at a more local level in smaller outback towns, Other events, like the Barunga Sports and Cultural Festival near Katherine in the Northern Territory, bring an array of Aboriginal bands and performers together for cultural enrichment and an opportunity to exchange and develop ideas. Solo male performers like Archie Roach, Key Carmody, Jimmy Chi, and Bob Randal make increasingly profound personal statements about the treatment of their people and their own experiences as black Australians. Press and media reporting, as part of the publicity drive to sell the recordings, occasionally reaches the front pages of newspapers and achieves high profiles in other media.

The appearance of recordings "in the language" makes the issue more challenging for white Australians. The rejection of English as the first language of communication incorporates an implicit rejection of European civilization. This challenge to the mainstream of contemporary Australian life is further on the fringes of popular music culture than Aboriginal music being sung in English. Songs and music "in the language" are becoming more prevalent, as people in remote areas grow confident, recording the songs they have created in ancient languages. Aboriginal rock bands singing "in the language" are also filtering through, and CAAMA has several tapes available, but Australian media, being rabidly Anglophone, will probably never play Aboriginal recordings in tribal languages. Public radio, ABC, and SBS will be and are the exception.

Observant readers will have noticed the absence of any reference to women. The Mills Sisters, from Thursday Island, are the exception. They sing melodious trios in a Hawaiian style. Nevertheless, there are very few Aboriginal women working in bands or as solo artists. Aboriginal culture appears to have a lot to do with this, although it can only be assumed that Aboriginal women will become more active. At the end of the 1980s, women could be most readily heard in small choirs, singing Christian hymns and country music favorites. The influence of the Christian missionaries lingers on in remarkable and ironic ways, reinforcing the collective female solidarity that was an important part of tribal life. CAAMA has released a collection of choirs, which features church hymns and secular tunes like "Bobby McGee."

Aboriginal music is part of the ongoing struggle by Aboriginal people for recognition and dignity. Its development has been a gradual process, steeped, as it must be, in the history of Aboriginal civilization and their decimation at the hands of European settlers. As Archie Roach put it when talking about his music: "In Victoria they almost succeeded in destroying the Aboriginal people. The languages have been lost and a lot of the traditions and rituals have gone. A lot of the old fellas (men) know it but won't talk about it because years ago they were punished by the authorities for talking about it. But the spiritual values are still there. That's what I'd rather get across to people. If the spirit dies nothing else is going to be much use,"[38] This may be a long way from a eucalyptus tree in the middle of Australia's central desert, and yet Aboriginal music is helping Aborigines survive the evils that could kill them, while giving them a purpose and a strength to carry on, drawing on ties with the land and spirits that could benefit everybody. Aboriginal music is also giving an increasing number of non-Aboriginal Australians a chance to hear the Aboriginal voice and history first hand. As their polemic becomes part of the world's increasingly competent progressive political movements, they will find their rightful place in the corpus of the world's popular music.

Notes

1. Carl Lumholtz, *Among Cannibals*. Canberra: Australian National University Press, 1980. p. 173.
2. T. G. H. Strehlow, *Songs of Central Australia*. Sydney: Angus and Robertson, 1971. p. 7.
3. Cited in Trevor Jones, "The Traditional Music of the Australian Aborigines," in Elizabeth May, Ed., *Music of Many Cultures: An Introduction*. Berkeley: University of California Press, 1962. p. 162.
4. Bruce Chatwin, *The Songlines*. London: Pan Books, 1988. p. 79.
5. Cath Ellis, *Aboriginal Music: Cross-Cultural Experience from South Australia*. Brisbane: University of Queensland Press, 1985. p. 17.
6. Ibid. p. 17.
7. Karl Marx, "The Origins of Art: Historical Development of the Artistic Sense," in Karl Marx and Fredrick Engels, *On Literature and Art*. Moscow: Progress Publishers, 1976. pp. 126–8.
8. Eric Willmot, "Australia: The Last Experiment." *St. Mark's Review*. December 1978. pp. 23–7.
9. Christina Spurgeon, "Challenging Technological Determinism: Aborigines, Aussat and Remote Australia," in Helen Wilson, Ed., *Australian Communications and the Public Sphere: Essays in Memory of Bill Bonney*. Melbourne: Macmillan, 1989. p. 30.
10. Ibid. p. 31; Mark Brolly, "Church Deplores 'Genocide' of Aborigines." *The Age*. February 5, 1991. p. 3.
11. Spurgeon, in Wilson, 1989. p. 30.
12. Guy Tustall, participating author in Marcus Breen, Ed., *Our Place, Our Music, Aboriginal Music: Australian Popular Music in Perspective*, Volume 2. Canberra: Aboriginal Studies Press, 1989, p. 7.

13. Chester Schultz, participating author in Breen, 1989. p. 15. The destruction of traditional cultures by Christian missionaries as part of a process of "culturation" and modernization is a familiar story to people who know the history of colonization. It has been seen in a pernicious form in recent years with the Christianization of Central and South American Indians by the fundamentalist Protestant interdenominational organization Wycliffe Bible Translators (Summer Institute of Linguistics).

14. Marcus Breen, "Fundamentalist Music: the Popular Impulse," in Marcus Breen, Ed., *Missing in Action: Australian Popular Music in Perspective*, Volume 1. Melbourne: Verbal Graphics, 1987. p. 14.

15. Schultz, in Breen, 1989. p. 15; Eric Watson, "Country Music: The Voice of Rural Australia," in Breen, 1987. pp. 48–77.

16. Schultz, in Breen, 1989. p. 25.

17. Doug Petherick, participating author in Breen, 1989. p. 29.

18. Dave Laing, "The Grain of Punk: An Analysis of the Lyrics," in Angela McRobbie, Ed., *Zoot Suits and Second Hand Dresses: An Anthology of Fashion and Music*, London: Macmillan, 1989, pp. 74–102.

19. Steve Warne, "Beyond the Echoes: A Look at Public Radio," in Breen, 1987. p. 170.

20. Tony Bennett, "The Political Rationality of the Museum," *Continuum*, Volume 3, No. 1. 1990. pp. 35–55.

21. Marcus Breen, "Writing Songs to Inspire a Brand New Day." *Sunday Herald*. September 10, 1989.

22. CAAMA. Catalogue, 1990. A mix of Aboriginal media workers and trainees, assisted by two or three specialist Europeans (media lawyers and technical personnel) has always been the trademark of CAAMA from the early days to the present. Aboriginal members through the CAAMA Board have ultimate control over the station and its affiliates.

23. Marcus Breen, "Desert Rhythms Fulfill an Aboriginal Dream." *Herald*. August 9, 1988.

24. Ibid.

25. Liora Salter, "Two Directions on a One Way Street: Old and New Approaches in Media Analysis in Two Decades." *Studies in Communication*, No. 1. 1980. pp. 85–117.

26. Sam Paltridge, "Australian Remote Television Services." Centre for International Research on Communication and Information Technologies, Policy Research Paper, No. 8. October 1990.

27. Spurgeon, in Wilson, 1989. p. 28.

28. Ibid.

29. Louise Bellamy, "Black and White TV from the Heart." *The Age*. October 22, 1987.

30. Eric Michaels, *Aboriginal Invention of Television in Central Australia 1982–1986*. Canberra: Aboriginal Studies Press, 1986.

31. Tim Rowse, "Review of Aboriginal Invention of Television in Central Australia 1982–86." *Oceania*, Volume 57, No. 4. June 1987. pp. 316–17.

32. Spurgeon, in Wilson, 1989, p. 43.

33. *Communication Update*, 21. Communication Law Centre, Sydney. 1987.

34. Department of Transport and Communication Press Release. September 28, 1990.

35. Breen, "Writing Songs to Inspire a Brand New Day." 1989.

36. Helen Molnar, "The Broadcasting for Remote Areas Community Scheme: Small vs Big Media." *Media Information Australia*, No 58. November 1990. pp. 147–54.

37. Ibid.

38. Marcus Breen, "Black Gold," *Sunday Herald*. November 25, 1990.

53

Ubiquitous Listening

*Anahid Kassabian**

Music Not Chosen

I have always been drawn to studying the engagements of music and subjectivities. I find that intersection of text, psyches and social relations particularly intriguing when the texts in question are sequences of music neither chosen by their listeners nor actively listened to in any recognizable sense. This body of music includes, of course, film and television music, but also music on phones, music in stores, music in video games, music for audio books, music in parking garages, and so on. A quotation in Jonathan Sterne's 'Sounds Like the Mall of America' confirmed my suspicion about the music: we hear more of it per capita than any other music.

The 21 October 2000 issue of *The Economist* had a graph showing annual world production of data, expressed in terabytes. According to researchers at UC Berkeley's School of Information Systems and Management, about 2.5 billion CDs were shipped in 1999. Music CD production far outstrips newspapers, periodicals, books and cinema. And most of the music is being heard often, if not most often, as a secondary activity.

Music to Follow You from Room to Room

By most reckonings, this is a trend that will continue to increase for some time to come. One mark of that might be Bill Gates' ideas for the 'house of the future'. All residents would have unique microelectronic beacons that would identify their wearers to the house. Based on your stored profile, then,

> Lights would automatically come on when you came home . . . Portable touch pads would control everything from the TV sets to the temperature and the lights, which would brighten or dim to fit the occasion or to match the outdoor light . . . Speakers would be hidden beneath the wallpaper to allow music to follow you from room to room. (cnn.com, 2000)

*Pp. 131–42 from *Popular Music Studies*, ed. D. Hesmondhalgh and K. Negus (London, Arnold). © 2002 by Arnold. Reproduced by permission of Edward Arnold (Publishers) Ltd.

The Cisco Internet Home Briefing Center imagines a similar musical environment:

> Music also seems to have no boundaries with access to any collection, available in virtually
> any room of the house through streaming audio. A Digital Jukebox or Internet Radio
> eliminates the limitations of local radio, and can output music, sports and news from
> around the world. (Cisco Internet Home Briefing Center, 'Entertainment')

These ideas are among the most basic and least radical in the field known as ubiquitous computing, or ubicomp. First articulated in the late 1980s by Mark Weiser of Xerox PARC (Weiser, 1991; Gibbs, 2000), ubicomp has become a very active field of research. It is concerned with 'smart rooms' and 'smart clothes', with the seamless integration of information and entertainment computing into everyday environments. This would be akin to the penetration of words, or reading, in everyday life. Texts were first centrally located in, for example, monasteries and libraries; next, books and periodicals were distributed to individual owners; now, words are almost always in our field of vision, on labels, bookshelves, files, etc. Written language is ubiquitous, seamlessly integrated into our environments.

From the perspective, for example, of the Broadband Residential Laboratory built by Georgia Tech last year, these 'stereo-piping tricks of "smart" homes . . . [are] just a starting point' (as quoted in Gibbs, 2000). Their Aware Home has several audio and video input and output devices in each room, and several outlets and jacks in each wall. The MIT Media Lab, as Sandy Pentland has said, has gone in a different direction. They have 'moved from a focus on smart rooms to an emphasis on smart clothes' (Pentland, 2000: 821) because smart clothes offer possibilities that smart rooms do not, such as mobility and individuality. For example, the Affective Computing Research Group 'has built a wearable "DJ" that tries to select music based on a feature of the user's mood' as indicated by skin conductivity data collected by the wearable computer (Picard, 2000: 716).

What Do We Know About Most of The Music We Hear?

Music scholarship across the disciplines is utterly unprepared to think about such practices. As it stands, there are few studies of the music that follows us from room to room, variously called programmed music, background music, environmental music, business music, functional music (Gifford, 1995; Bottum, 2000). One landmark study is Joseph Lanza's book *Elevator Music* (1995) which is first of all a history of music in public space, and, second, a defense of the intramusical features that were part of elevator music in its prime: lush strings, absence of brass and percussion, consonant harmonic language, etc. The book is an invaluable resource, and it makes some fascinating arguments; for example, Lanza suggests that elevator music became the quintessential twentieth-century music because it focused, as did much of the century's technologies, on environmental control.

Sterne takes another tack. Commoditized music, Sterne argues, has become 'a form of architecture – a way of organizing space in commercial settings' (Sterne, 1997: 23).

Not only does the soundscape of the mall predict and depend on barely audible, anonymous background music of the 'Muzak' type, but it also shapes the very space itself.
The boundaries between store and hallway are acoustically defined by the different
music played in each space:

> To get anywhere in the Mall of America, one must pass through music and through changes
> in musical sound. As it territorializes, music gives the subdivided acoustical space a contour,
> offering an opportunity for its listeners to experience space in a particular way. (31)

For Sterne, the issue is one of reification – music has become a commodity relation that
supplants relations between people and that presupposes listener response.

In 'Adequate Modes of Listening', Ola Stockfelt (1997) argues that modes of listening develop in relation to particular genres – he calls these 'genre-normative modes of
listening' – and the style itself develops in relation to its listening situation. He says:

> Each style of music . . . is shaped in close relation to a few environments. In each genre,
> a few environments, a few situations of listening, make up the constitutive elements in this
> genre . . . The opera house and the concert hall as environments are as much integral and
> fundamental parts of the musical *genres* 'opera' and 'symphony' as are the purely intramu-
> sical means of style. (136)

In Stockfelt's argument, modes of listening, listening situation, and musical style coproduce each other. In terms of background music, this helps explain the musical
parameters we all know. What Stockfelt calls 'dishearkening' has produced a particular
set of practices for arranging background music. There is a focus on moments of pleasant 'snapshot listening' rather than development over time, and a focus on comforting
timbres (legato strings) over vivid ones (brass).

None of these studies, however, can cope with the ubicomp world proposed by Xerox
PARC and the MIT Media Lab, nor even with some already existing soundscapes.
Prevailing scholarly notions of listening subjectivity and agency, even in the most inno-
vative works, will not account for the music we wake up to.

Where Did This Music Come From?

> I lead a happy life. Every day I wake in the best of all possible moods and dance my way
> around the room as I get dressed. Then, while I prepare a pleasant breakfast in my tiny
> kitchen, several happy bluebirds land on my windowsill and twitter cheerfully. Outside,
> a tall man in coat-and-tails tips his hat and bids me good-day. A halfdozen scruffy children
> chase a hoop down the street, shouting gleefully. One of them cries out, 'Mornin'
> mister!'
>
>   Ah yes, life is wonderful when you live in a musical from the fifties. Now, perhaps
> you're wondering, 'How could this possibly be true?' Well, I have the unspeakable good
> fortune to live directly behind my local supermarket and each morning I wake up to a
> careful selection of merry tunes which easily penetrate my thin walls to rouse me from my
> slumber. (Schafer, website, 'The Sound of Muzak')

Thus does Tokyo resident Own Schafer begin his eloquent, elegant think-piece about Muzak. Sedimented here is a trace of one of functional music's siblings, i.e. film music and musical theater. To tell functional music's history, one might begin with music hail, or even earlier. Another trace could be followed to radio, and from there to music in salons and gazebos. Or from workplace music to work music and chants. Strangely, these remain untold histories of the omnipresence of music in contemporary life in industrialized settings.

Two histories *are* told – an industrial one and a critical one. The former begins with General George Owen Squier, chief of the US Army Signal Corps and creator of Wired Radio, the company now called Muzak. This history, best represented by Joseph Lanza's book (1995) and Bill Gifford's (1995) *FEED* feature 'They're Playing Our Song', continues through shifts in technologies and markets, to Muzak's 'stimulus progression' patents, to the 1988 merger with small foreground music provider Yesco (Gifford, 1995: 3, 2) and the rise of competitors AEI and 3M.

The other documented history is a counter-history, a story of how a music came into being that could be confused with functional music, but is of course nothing like it ambient music. That history begins with Erik Satie's experiments in the teens and twenties with *musique d'ameublement* (furniture music), soars through John Cage's emphases on environmental sound and on process, and leads inevitably to Brian Eno, from whose mind all contemporary ambient music has sprung. (For versions of this story, see any of the scores of ambient websites.)

This history goes to great pains to distinguish ambient from background music on the grounds of its available modes of listening. As musician/fan Malcolm Humes put it in a 1995 on-line essay:

> Eno . . . tried to create music that could be actively or passively listened to. Something that could shift imperceptibly between a background texture to something triggering a sudden zoom into the music to reflect on a repetition, a subtle variation, perhaps a slight shift in color or mood. (http://music.hyperreal.org/epsilon/info/humes_notes.html)

What is important to defenders of the ambient faith is its availability to both foreground and background listening. But since the mid to late 1980s, background music *has become* foreground music. In the language of the industry, background music is what we call 'elevator music', and foreground music is work by original artists. While background music has all but disappeared, you can now hear everyone from Miriam Makeba to the Moody Blues to Madonna to Moby in some public setting or other and quite possibly all of them at your local Starbucks.

Foreground music seems to make talking about music in public spaces impossible – and perhaps it should be. Certainly there is a several-decades-long history of debate about the dissolution of public space and the public sphere. As Japanese cultural critic Mihoko Tamaoki has argued in her work on coffee houses, Starbucks transforms customers into not a public, but an audience. Moreover, she argues (Tamaoki, unpublished manuscript):

> Starbucks now constitutes a 'meta-media' operation. It stands at once in the traditional media role, as an outlet for both content and advertising. At the same time, it is actually

selling the products therein advertised. And these, in turn, are themselves media products: music for Starbucks listeners.

This is Starbucks' genius as a music label; it is a meta-media operation that produces its own market for its own product all at once, in what once might have been public space. But if we focus too closely on the distribution of recordings, we will not fully address the problems foreground music poses to contemporary listening.

How Do We Listen to Foreground Music?

If one attends to discourse about music in business environments, it has hardly registered the change from background to foreground. By and large, most people talk about music in business environments as annoying and bad, and it is rare indeed to hear anyone talk about music in these settings as music they listen to intentionally elsewhere, even though that seems an obvious connection to make. The reason, I want to argue, is that they are not discussing music, but rather a mode of listening about which most of us are at best ambivalent, thanks in no small part to the disciplining of music in the western academy.

In the wake of Foucault, critiques of music's disciplinary practices have been well argued. We have discussed canon formations, architecture and training; we have argued about analysis and we have talked about transcription. We have talked at length about the expert listening held in such high regard by Adorno and so carefully cultivated by Western art music institutions such as the academy and symphony orchestras. It is perhaps primary among the forces that produce and reproduce the canonical European and North American repertoire. But in all these discussions we have not taken our own collective insights quite seriously enough. Logically, if expert, concentrated, structural listening produces the canon, do not other modes of listening produce and reproduce other repertoires?

This is, I believe, Stockfelt's most important point. Through changes in the arrangement of Mozart's G-minor 40th symphony, he argues, different settings, different sets of musical features, and different modes of listening are co-productive. Text, context and reception create each other in mutual, simultaneous and historically grounded processes. But as foreground music programming has increased, this combination or mutual dependence seems less and less consistent or predictable. When *anything* can be foreground music, does it still make sense to talk about a mode of listening? And if so, what is its relationship to questions of genre?

Do We Hear or Listen?

One possibility is to think of this most disdained activity as hearing rather than listening. This idea appears repeatedly, including in the sales literature of programmed music companies. But the distinction poses some interesting problems. In Webster's each term is defined by the other:

hear vt

to perceive (sounds) by the ear; to receive an impression of through the auditory nerves of the ear; as, to *hear* a voice; to *hear* words.

O friends! I *hear* the tread of nimble feet. – Milton.

to listen to and consider; specifically, (a) to take notice of; pay attention to; as, *hear* this piece of news; (b) to listen to officially; give a formal hearing to; as, he will *hear* your lessons now; (c) to conduct an examination or hearing of (a law case, etc.); try; (d) to consent to; grant; as, he *heard* my entreaty; (e) to be a member of the audience at or of (an opera, radio broadcast, lecture, etc.); (f) to permit to speak; as I cannot *hear* you now. To be informed of; to be told; to learn. (1983: 836)

hear vi

to be able to perceive sound; as, he is deaf, he cannot *hear*.

to listen; to attend; as, he *hears* with solicitude. To be told; to receive by report; as, so I *hear*. (1983: 836)

listen vi

to make a conscious effort to hear; to attend closely so as to hear.

to give heed; take advice; as, to *listen* to warning. (1983: 1055)

One obvious problem with the distinction is the circularity of the definitions, but that is, as we know, in the nature of language. That notwithstanding, we could probably agree that hearing is somehow more passive than listening, and that consuming background music is passive. Certainly everyone – from Adorno to Muzak – seems to think so.

The connotation of passivity in the term 'hearing' is precisely why I prefer 'listening'. To the extent that 'hearing' is understood as passive, it implies the conversion of sound waves into electrochemical stimuli (that is, transmission along nerves to the brain) by a discretely embodied unified subject (that is, a human individual). Yet our engagements with programmed music surely extend beyond mere sense perception and, as I will suggest below, mark us as participants in a new form of subjectivity.

Is there, then, a programmed music mode of listening? Here I want to offer an anecdote as a beginning of an answer. Recently, I asked the students in my popular music class to write an essay on a half-hour of radio broadcasting. Ryan Kelly, a member of the New York City Ballet corps de ballet, began his essay by identifying himself as a non-radio listener. He described sitting down to listen to the tape to begin his essay, and ten minutes later finding himself at the kitchen sink washing dishes. This is, of course, only one story, but an eminently recognizable one.

Jay Larkin of Viacom described to me a proto–ubicomp kind of system he had set up – he has speakers under his pillow, so that he can sleep listening to music without disturbing his wife and without the intrusion of headphones. (He also listens to music constantly at work.) Larkin is profoundly articulate about this matter – he thinks of music as an 'anchor', keeping his mind from spinning off in various directions. Parents of children with attention deficit disorder are often advised to put on music while the kids are working for just such purposes.

From its inception, Gifford says, muzak was about focusing attention in this sense. Workers' minds 'were prone to wandering. Muzak sopped up these non-productive thoughts and kept workers focussed on the drudgery at hand' (Gifford, 1995: 2, 2). My babysitter Anett and many of my students leave the radio or MTV on in different rooms, so that they are never without music. They say it fills the house, makes the emptiness less frightening. Muzak's own literature says 'Muzak fills the deadly silence.'

These have always been background music's functions. We learned them from Muzak, and now they are a part of our everyday lives. As Muzak programming manager Steve Ward says:

> It's supposed to fill the air with sort of a warm familiarity, I suppose . . . If you were pushing a cart through a grocery store and all you hear is wheels creaking and crying babies – it would be like a mausoleum. (as quoted in Gifford, 1995: 3, 2)

All these listeners and music programmers and writers share a sense of listening as a constant, grounding, secondary activity, regardless of the specific musical features.

A Ubiquitous Mode of Listening?

Those of us living in industrialized settings (at least) have developed, from the omnipresence of music in our daily lives, a mode of listening dissociated from specific generic characteristics of the music. In this mode, we listen 'alongside' or simultaneously with other activities. It is one vigorous example of the non-linearity of contemporary life. This listening is a new and noteworthy phenomenon, one that has the potential to demand a radical rethinking of our various fields.

I want to propose that we call this mode of listening 'ubiquitous listening' for two reasons. First, it is the ubiquity of listening that has taught us this mode. It is precisely because music is everywhere that Ryan forgot he was doing an assignment and got up to wash the dishes.

Second, it relies on a kind of 'sourcelessness'. Whereas we are accustomed to thinking of most music, like most cultural products, in terms of authorship and location, this music comes from the plants and the walls and, potentially, our clothes. It comes from everywhere and nowhere. Its projection looks to erase its production as much as possible, posing instead as a quality of the environment.

For these reasons, the term 'ubiquitous listening' best describes the phenomenon I am discussing. As has been widely remarked, the development of recording technologies in the twentieth century disarticulated performance space and listening space. You can listen to opera in your bathtub and arena rock while riding the bus. And it is precisely this disarticulation that has made ubiquitous listening possible. Like ubiquitous computing, ubiquitous listening blends into the environment, taking place without calling conscious attention to itself as an activity in itself. It is, rather, ubiquitous and conditional, following us from room to room, building to building, and activity to activity.

However, the idea of ubiquitous listening as perhaps the dominant mode of listening in contemporary life raises another problem: does this mode of listening produce and accede to a set of genre norms?

A Ubiquitous Genre?

Genre comes from Aristotle and is a term from literary theory for the classification of types of text. 'Members of a genre have common characteristics of style and organization and are found in similar cultural settings' (Bothamley, 1993: 228). By those common characteristics, then, members of a genre can be recognized. Across the media, genre has, of course, become a central organizing principle of both production and consumption; as John Hartley puts it: 'genres are agents of ideological closure – they limit the meaning potential of a given text, and they limit the commercial risk of the producer corporations' (Hartley, 1994: 128). In this sense, genres might be understood to discipline reception.

The most widely cited definition of genre in popular music studies, Franco Fabbri's 1982 essay 'A Theory of Musical Genres', sees it as a complex of style or musical features, performance space and performance and fan/listener behavior – less a discipline than a field of activity. Rob Walser's discussion in *Running with the Devil* expands in this direction, combining Jameson's text-based discussion with Bakhtin's 'horizon of expectations': 'Genres are never sui generis; they are developed, sustained, and re-formed by people, who bring a variety of histories and interests to their encounters with generic texts' (Walser, 1993: 27). In this way, a popular music genre is understood to include both shared musical features and audience expectations and practices. In Stockfelt's terms, style, listening and situation are all part of genre-making processes.

In all these discussions of genre, musical features are conceived expansively, reaching beyond pitch, melody, harmony and rhythm to include timbre, vocal inflections and recording techniques. Taken together, a ubiquitous mode of listening and a careful, socially grounded understanding of genre might make the case for a genre called 'ubiquitous music'. It has, as I have argued, a specific mode of listening. It shares certain features of performance space – simultaneity with other activities and a sense of source-lessness. While including an extraordinarily wide range of musical features, it is generally shaped by mono playback, absence of very high and very low frequencies, absence of vocals, and particular attention to volume as a condition of the other simultaneous activities.

The problem is, of course, that ubiquitous music does not depend on texts belonging only to its own genre, but rather welcomes all texts in a pluralist leveling of difference and specificity (which might explain its partiality for adopting world music forms). Perhaps it is a new kind of genre, what we adopting world music forms). Perhaps it is a new kind of genre, what we might tongue firmly in cheek, call a postmodern pastiche para-genre. But more likely, I think, it signals the death knell of genre as a primary organizing axis for popular music activities.

A Ubiquitous Subjectivity?

Unabashedly polemical, this argument is the necessary precursor to a rethinking of how we approach both the study of music and the idea of subjectivity. As more and more kinds of music are played in more and more settings alongside more and more activities, it becomes crucial to develop ways of approaching this phenomenon. As Gifford (1995: 6, 3) puts it:

> Muzak anticipated the way we live our lives today, accompanied by a constant soundtrack of radio, television, video and film . . . Muzak's real significance is that it paved the way for a new ambient culture, a culture that Sensurrounds us with digitized music and pixelated images, endlessly looping screen savers and point-of-purchase interactive displays, occupying all areas of our multitasking minds.

But many analysts insist on continuing to see the music industry in very traditional terms. According to the phenomenal foresight of experts in an *Economist* special supplement on E-entertainment (7 October 2000), for example:

> If the music industry manages to sort out the piracy problem, the internet will become a hugely important source of revenue. The record companies sold their music all over again when the CD came out, and they can now sell it all over again over the internet, again. What is more, they can sell it in more flexible packages to make it more attractive to different kinds of consumers. (32)

What the *Economist's* writers do not say, and apparently do not even think about, are the vast social changes attendant on these new technologies. The same music will be sold yet a third time, in more flexible packages, precisely because it makes it easier to use the music as an environmental technology, conditioning and conditioned by a new kind of subjectivity.

This third selling is a performance of the ubicomp world in the making. Its attendant subjectivity is not individual, not defined by Oedipus or agency or any discrete unity. The listener of this third selling is no mere subject, but rather a part of an always moving ever-present web. S/he is not a listener of a genre first and foremost, but rather a listener *tout court*. Ubiquitous music is cable that networks all of us together, not in some dystopian energy-producing array à la *Matrix*, but in a lumpy deployment of dense nodes of knowledge/power figured by, for example, the SETI@home project. SETI@home uses home computers when they are otherwise idle as a resource for ramping up computer processing power for the Search for Extra-Terrestrial Intelligence project. In this extreme model of distributed computing, each home computer is a little lump or node in an enormous array of computing activity. Likewise, we are each nodes in an enormous array of listening.

There are numerous attempts to describe what I am getting at here, from many different directions – from Xerox PARC to Donna Haraway to Gilles Deleuze. In *Autoaffections: Unconscious Thought in the Age of Teletechnology*, Patricia Clough proposes, as she puts it, 'a new ontological perspective and an unconscious other than the one organized by an oedipal narrative' (Clough, 2000: 20). Throughout, *Autoaffections* works in two genres – academic prose and prose poetry. Not only the chapters, but also the genre shifts themselves are performances of the book's work.

It opens with a prose poem, 'Television: A Sacred Machine'. It is a work of remarkable power, both more beautiful and more clear than what we usually call theory. Clough says:

> My machine has more parts; it has more action,
> Like the action of fingertips attached to ivory keys,
> Playing in between the beats of a metronome's patterning. (22)

The node we usually call 'self' is attached through keys that make hammers hit wires that make sound that attaches to another node, sound disciplined by the metronome machine to attach the nodes in particular ways.

> Still, I was destined by that piano,
> Destined to find myself in attachment to machines. (25)

This attachment is, as I have suggested, the stuff of contemporary science fiction. Cyborgs, matrices, webs, nets – all these dystopias threaten us with the dissolution of the boundaries of our very selves. But they fail to see what Clough hears: that dissolution is already well under way.

What I am proposing is a theory of subjectivity based on ubiquitous music. I think we should call it ubiquitous subjectivity. Like ubiquitous music, parts phase in and out of participation in ubiquitous subjectivity, but it never leaves us – and we never leave it. If that sounds ominous, it is not meant to. It is simply a habit of mind from an earlier notion about our discreteness, and it is time to notice that ubiquitous music and ubiquitous listening have been forging a different subjectivity for quite some time now. Like *Star Trek*'s Borg, we are uncomfortable being unhooked from the background sound of ubiquitous subjectivity, so we turn radios on in empty rooms and put speakers under our pillows. We hang up when a telephone connection is not kept open by sound. We prefer to be connected, need to listen to our connections, cannot breathe without them. We already live a network we insist on thinking of as a dystopian future.

This networked-through-music subjectivity could seem similar to ideas about music and collectivity. As Eisler and Adorno argue in *Composing for the Films* (1947), many anthropologists and writers about music suggest that music operates differently from the oculocentric individual of contemporary Western culture. They say that music listening:

> preserves comparably more traits of long bygone, preindividualistic collectivities . . . This direct relationship to a collectivity, intrinsic in the phenomenon itself, is probably connected with sensations of spatial depth, inclusiveness, and absorption of individuality, which are common to all music. (21)

Other writers do not attribute this collective quality to music per se, but do – quite rightly – note that music is a part of many social formations and practices in different historical and cultural settings.

I am not suggesting that ubiquitous music has reintroduced such a collective identity through music to modern or postmodern societies. Far from it. What I am arguing, rather, is that ubiquitous music has become a form of phatic communication for late capitalism – its purpose is to keep the lines of communication open for that lumpy deployment of dense nodes of knowledge/power we call selves. We are Borg because isolated consciousness – silence – is unpleasurable in the extreme.

As we continue through the second century of the disarticulation of performance and listening, new relations are developing that demand new models and approaches. It is easy to see that the industry is changing. It is perhaps harder to hear the changes in music, in listening and in subjectivity that all of this portends. Yet musics, technologies, science fiction, social relations and subjectivities have been fermenting these changes throughout the twentieth century. At least in the industrialized world, listening to music is ubiquitous, and it forms the network backbone of a new, ubiquitous subjectivity.

References

Bothamley, Jennifer (1993). *Dictionary of Theories*. London, Detroit and Washington, DC: Gale Research Intl. Ltd.

Bottum, J. (2000). The Soundtracking of America. *Atlantic Monthly*, March, online at http://www.theatlantic.com/issues/2000/03/bottum.htm

Cisco Internet Home Briefing Center: 'Entertainment.' http://www.cisco.com/warp/public/779/consumer/internet_home/

Clough, Patricia Ticineto (2000). *Autoaffections: Unconscious Thought in the Age of Teletechnology*. Minneapolis: University of Minnesota Press.

CNN.COM (2000). The House of the Future Is Here Today, online at http://www.cnn.com/2000/TECH/ptech/01/03/future.homes/

Cubitt, Sean (1984). Maybellene: Meaning and the Listening Subject. *Popular Music* 4, pp. 207–24.

The Economist (2000). A Survey of E-Entertainment (special supplement), October 7.

The Economist (2000). Byte Counters: Quantifying Information, October 21.

Eisler, Hanns & Theodor Adorno (1947). *Composing for the Films*. New York: Oxford University Press (reprinted 1994, Athlone Press).

Fabbri, Franco (1982). A Theory of Musical Genres: Two Applications. In: David Horn & Philip Tagg (eds.), *Popular Music Perspectives*. Götheborg and Exeter: International Association for the Study of Popular Music, pp. 52–81.

Fink, Robert, Orchestral Corporate. *ECHO* 2(1), online at http://www.humnet.ucla.edu/humnet/musicology/echo/Volume2-Issue1/fink/fink-article.html

Gibbs, W. Wayt (2000). As We May Live. *Scientific American*, November, online at http://www.sciam.com/2001/1100issue/1100techbusl.html

Gifford, Bill (1995). They're Playing Our Song. *FEED*, at http://www.feedmag.com/95.10gifford/95/10gifford1.html

Hartley, John (1994). Genre. In: Tim O'Sullivan, et al. (eds.), *Key Concepts in Communication and Cultural Studies*, 2nd edn. London and New York: Routledge.

Kassabian, Anahid (2001). *Hearing Film: Tracking Identifications in Contemporary Hollywood Film Music*. New York and London: Routledge.

Kramer, Lawrence (1994). *Music as Cultural Practice, 1800–1900*. Berkeley: University of California Press.

Lanza, Joseph (1995). *Elevator Music: A Surreal History of Muzak, Easy-Listening, and Other Moodsong*. New York: Picador USA.

McClary, Susan (1986). A Musical Dialectic from the Enlightenment: Mozart's Piano Concerto in G Major, K. 453, Movement 2. *Cultural Critique* 4, pp. 129–70.

O'Sullivan, Tim, John Hartley, Danny Saunders et al., (1994). *Key Concepts in Communication and Cultural Studies*, 2nd edn. London and New York: Routledge.

Pentland, A. (2000). It's Alive!. *IBM Systems Journal* 39(3/4), pp. 821–2.

Picard, R. W. (2000). Toward Computers that Recognized and Respond to User Emotion. *IBM Systems Journal* 39(3/4), pp. 705–19.

Schafer, O. The Sound of Muzak. *Tokyo Classified Rant 'n' Rave*. http://www.tokyoclassified. com/tokyorantsravesarchive299/265/tokyorantsravesinc.htm

Schwarz, David (1997). *Listening Subjects: Music, Psychoanalysis, Culture*. Durham, NC: Duke University Press.

Stephenson, Neal (1992). *Snowcrash*. New York: Bantam Spectra.

Sterne, Jonathan (1997). Sounds like the Mall of America: Programmed Music and the Architectonics of Commercial Space. *Ethnomusicology* 41(1), pp. 22–50.

Stockfelt, Ola (1997). Adequate Modes of Listening, trans. A. Kassabian and L. G. Svendsen. In: D. Schwarz & A. Kassabian (eds.), *Keeping Score: Music, Disciplinarity, Culture*. Charlottesville, VA: University Press of Virginia.

Subotnik, Rose Rosengard (1991). *Developing Variations: Style and Ideology in Western Music*. Minneapolis: University of Minnesota Press.

Tomlinson, Gary (1994). *Music in Renaissance Magic: Toward a Historiography of Others*. Chicago: University of Chicago Press.

Walser, Robert (1993). *Running with the Devil: Power, Gender, and Madness in Heavy Metal Music*. Hanover and London: Wesleyan University Press (University Press of New England).

Weiser, Mark (1991). The Computer for the Twenty-First Century. *Scientific American*, September, online at http://www.ubiq.com/hypertext/weiser/SciAmDraft3.html

54

The Nature/Technology Binary Opposition Dismantled in the Music of Madonna and Björk

Charity Marsh & Melissa West*

Within feminist theory there has been an ongoing body of work that speaks to the subject of gender and technology as well as to nature and technology. This latter topic has increased relevance in the music world due to the rising interest in electronica, techno, and hip-hop in the last decade. What is considered "natural" is often thought of as opposed to what is considered "technological." Nevertheless, there are musicians interested in working with technologies without compromising stereotypically "natural" issues such as self-awareness of one's origins. Björk and Madonna are two female artists who have chosen different methods to narrow the culturally constructed division between nature and technology. Through an investigation into the issues surrounding electronica, nature, and culture, as well as appropriate theories regarding them, we will illustrate how Madonna and Björk fuse the two seemingly opposing forces. Analyzing the efforts and successes of Madonna and Björk further establishes a crucial stepping stone in the process of "de-gendering" nature and technology in popular music.

The musical connections between Madonna and Björk date back to 1994. The title song of Madonna's album *Bedtime Stories* was written by Björk, and Madonna's vocal delivery in it unmistakably reveals Björk's influence.[1] In several interviews, each has stated her respect for the other's music. However, despite these nexus points within the popular music community, Madonna and Björk are viewed differently. Madonna is labeled a mega pop star, charting in the Top 40, whereas Björk established herself as a new wave and alternative artist and has moved into the realm of electronica in her solo career. Regardless, however, they share an ability to produce music that includes elements traditionally viewed by many in Western societies as conflicting.

Defining Nature and Technology

The nature/technology dichotomy is in a continual state of flux, and nature and technology are also included within other categories of difference, such as feminine/

*Pp. 182–203 from *Music and Technoculture*, ed. R. T. A. Lysoff and L. C. Gay, Jr (Middletown, CT: Wesleyan University Press). © 2003 by Rene T. A. Lysoff and Leslie C. Gay. Reprinted with permission from Wesleyan University Press. www.wesleyan.edu/wespress.

masculine and subjective/objective. Clearly, within the realm of popular music there has been a general acceptance that some aspects of technology are viewed as more natural than others. Because cultural definitions of nature and technology are fluid, we must define these terms carefully and contextualize them.

In Western society, the categories of nature and technology are socially constructed respectively as feminine and masculine. In the field of electronic music, likewise, there is much discussion of "warm" and "cold" sounds – warm is aligned with the feminine or nature and cold is aligned with the masculine or technology. Another factor particular to Madonna and Björk's music is the dichotomy existing between acoustic (coded as natural) and electronic (coded as technological) sounds. Part of the problem with binary oppositions is the appropriation of the elements that are in alignment with nature by those that fall under the heading of technology. Because women's biological capacity to bear children is considered natural, Madonna problematizes the distinction between nature and technology by bringing motherhood into a technological realm. Björk's connection to nature extends to her homeland, Iceland, and arises from Björk's descriptions of Iceland's geographical and social characteristics.[2]

Although Madonna and Björk have different reasons for, and varying methods of, synthesizing nature and technology, both contribute to the dismantling of the nature/technology dichotomy promoted within the realm of popular music by using electronic technology in a non-traditional manner. This chapter will focus on Madonna and Björk's views of nature and technology through an analysis of two of their later albums, Madonna's *Ray of Light* (1998) and Björk's *Homogenic* (1997). After a discussion of Madonna and Björk's views on electronic music, we will analyze Madonna's track "Nothing Really Matters" and her embracing of motherhood within a technological setting. We will then move to *Homogenic*, examining Björk's mingling of the concept of Iceland with electronica through her music, album art, and stage presentation. Donna Haraway's concept of the cyborg will be used to theorize the manner in which Björk deconstructs the nature/technology dichotomy as well as to call into question Madonna's relationship with technology.

Binary Oppositions

Binary oppositions comprise the culturally defined value system used predominantly in Western society to categorize difference. This system is comprised of a list of components classified as opposing elements; however, in many instances these elements can be understood through a less value laden approach as actually related to one another. The nature/culture dichotomy relies upon the definition of nature as feminine, subjective, and of the earth, whereas culture is defined as masculine, objective, and controlling the earth. At the center of binary oppositions is gender.

There are a number of factors in popular music that perpetuate the masculine/feminine dichotomy.[3] One of the most influential of these is the division between rock (masculine) and pop (feminine). In her article "Out on the Margins: Feminism and the Study of Popular Music," Mavis Bayton suggests that "far greater value [is] placed on rock as 'serious' music, in contrast to the 'light' and seemingly 'feminine' frivolity of pop" (Bayton 1990: 52). Because both rock and pop are "gendered" using these prominent characteristics, pop musicians are more likely to be women while rock musicians are more likely to be men.[4] This promotes the idea that pop music is less important than rock and also perpetuates the myth that women cannot be "serious" musicians.

Culture's appropriation of nature is manifested through technology, a concept that moves beyond physical objects or machines to a system of relationships and exchanges between the machine, its designer(s), and its users (Terry and Calvert 1997: 3). Paul Théberge discusses the idea of control over sound and, subsequently, control over technology in his book *Any Sound You Can Imagine: Making Music/Controlling Technology* (1997). Théberge considers an advertisement where a woman is portrayed as half human, half machine (Théberge: 1997, 123) – the presence of the woman is intended to furnish the "naturalness" considered absent in technology alone. In the male-dominated field of technology, the image of woman as machine not only implies male control of technology but also male control of woman, nature, and sound.

Although feminist theorists have tried "to undo [the binary] oppositions, to revalue their terms, to cast them as contrasts rather than as strict dichotomies, or to negotiate a path that avoids too close an alignment with either side" (Code 1995: 191), many of these dichotomies continue to exist as the popular conception of electronica demonstrates.

Electronica

Electronica reached new heights within the culture of rave and techno music in the 1990s. Because of the innovative uses of technology in electronic music, it is often deemed a "masculine" art form, and this leaves little room for women (Marsh 1999: 17). Nevertheless, Björk has managed to challenge the persistence of these dichotomies in electronica. *Homogenic* is a synthesis of electronic sounds, techno noises, string orchestration, percussion, and her piercing voice. Often on a quest for new sounds, arrangements, and approaches in her music. Björk opposes the common belief that technology is cold and soulless, instead believing it to be warm and sentimental. She equates the way most people see technology with their fear of change. In an interview, Björk stated, "People saying 'techno is cold' is rubbish. Since when do you expect the instruments you work with to deliver soul? You do music with computers and get a cold tune, that's because nobody put soul into it. You don't look at a guitar and say, 'Go on then and do a soulful tune.' You have to put soul into it yourself" (Micallef 1997). The analogy she uses to explain the misconceptions of technology contains first a computer, an example of technology, culture, and the masculine, and second a guitar, which represents nature and the feminine.[5] Adding "soul" to her music is another criteria for Björk's compositional process. Björk is a pop musician who grew up listening to and playing electronic synthesizers in the 1980s. Goodwin suggests that this relationship with the synthesizer for Björk's generation was crucial to a shift in thinking about electronic instruments. He suggests that "the very technology (the synth) that was presumed in the 1970s to remove human intervention and bypass the emotive aspect of music (through its 'coldness') became the source of one of the major aural signs that signifies the 'feel'!" (Goodwin 1990: 265). Through her refusal to hear electronic music as cold and soulless, Björk has upset another of the characteristics that help define electronica as a "masculine" form of music. Björk stresses the tools are not responsible for making the music, rather it is the responsibility of the producer and the performer.

With the album *Ray of Light*, Madonna released her version of electronica, combining traditional pop melodies with an ambient groove. During the promotion of the album, it became clear that Madonna intended to bring something very new to the electronic music genre. "She [Madonna] was quoted on VH1 as saying she'd always been interested in electro/techno music, but felt that it generally lacked emotion. Working with Orbit, she hoped to 'prove that it could be emotional.'" (Rule 1998: 34). Madonna also goes on to say, "My intention was to marry that scene with something personal and intimate. If I have any complaint about so-called electronica, it's the lack of warmth. I like the textures, but sometimes it sounds alienated and cold" (Gunderson 1998). Clearly Madonna felt limited by the current state of electronic music.

> **Do you remember saying in an interview that techno equals death?**
>
> Yes.
>
> **Do you still believe that?**
>
> To a certain extent. There was a type of techno I was listening to that had a real emotional void. But I think it's developed into something else and now there's feeling and warmth to it. You can attach it to humanity and before I couldn't. I couldn't feel anything. (Walters 1998: 74)

The dichotomies of warmth and cold emerge in her words here, alluding to the nature/technology binary opposition. Through this statement, Madonna shows an interest in reducing the distance between the two polarities. As is often the case in her career, it is assumed that the men working with Madonna are responsible for the creative output. Clearly, Madonna does not view the production of her albums in this manner:

> **How do people like William Orbit or Marius DeVries bring warmth to a synthesizer or a machine?**
>
> They don't; I do. They bring the cold, I bring the warmth [laughs]. (ibid.)

By assuming that Madonna does not have a role in the compositional process, this journalist in effect robs her of any agency in the production of *Ray of Light*. Madonna's assertion that she brings warmth to the cold electronic sounds actually embraces the feminine of the feminine/masculine dichotomy, reflecting ecofeminism's celebrations of women's connection with nature. She also disrupts the assumption that technology is purely masculine in popular music.

The Power Relations between Producer and Performer

William Orbit produced Madonna's album, while Björk worked with LEO's Mark Bell to produce *Homogenic*. In order to analyze how Madonna and Björk disrupt major dichotomies through their work, it is necessary to explore the consequences of a musical relationship between a male producer and a female performer. Do the general imbalances of power in male/female relationships of everyday life transfer to the recording studio? In a majority of cases male producers have the advantage in the studio due to the technological aspects of the music-making process.[6] Although the power struggle between producer and performer continues to prevail ill the popular music industry, Björk and Madonna challenge the gender hierarchy by maintaining control on all levels and by participating in every aspect of the creation of their albums.

Madonna's Relationship with Producer William Orbit

William Orbit was the main producer with whom Madonna worked on *Ray of Light*. "[Orbit's] been breaking boundaries in the ambient underground for years. His *Strange Cargo* series laid the groundwork for countless modern electronic artists, and his remix list reads like a who's who of rock and pop" (Rule 1998: 30). Madonna's relationship with Orbit is not a new one. Orbit mixed several of Madonna's singles in the past, including "Justify My Love" (1990), "Erotica" (1992), and "I'll Remember" (1995). With Orbit as producer, one might even doubt Madonna's agency in the production of *Ray of Light*. Keith Grint has an interesting perspective on this issue: "If Foucault is right that truth and power are intimately intertwined, those seeking to change the world might try strategies to *recruit powerful allies* rather than assuming that the quest for revealing 'the truth' will, in and through itself, lead to dramatic changes in levels and forms of social inequality" (Grint and Gill 1995: 71)[7] To these ends Madonna recruited William Orbit, a powerful ally in the technological realm. Madonna's choice of William Orbit in itself represents her creative and active role in achieving an ambient sound. Madonna is often dismissed as having little or no role in the compositional process, yet the choices she makes, from her producers to the sounds she will use, are an integral part of the creative process.[8] On the other hand, Madanna's control over her career is often celebrated. Through Orbit, Madonna is able to change the perception of music and technology, creating her version of electronic music.

Many studies focus on the composition of a piece without looking beyond that to other important aspects of the music. Grint, for example, criticizes feminist studies of technology that only focus on the design and development phases of an artifact's life, as these constructivist studies of technology fail to see women at all (Grint 1995:18). This is an important point to keep in mind while examining Madonna's album. If we were only to look at William Orbit's role as the producer, we would fail to see the influence Madonna had on the production of the album. William Orbit may produce Madonna's album, but the final product bears Madonna's name and ownership. Grint goes on to propose that studies in the realm of technology focus on the impact technology has on women, rather than the ways women impact the uses of technology (Grint 1995: 18). *Keyboard* magazine had this to say about Madonna's role: "Star artists often keep tight control over their producers. When asked how much creative latitude Madonna allowed Orbit in the studio, she told us that 'William had a very long leash, but I was firmly holding on to the end of it.' Her analogy of the process: 'I was the anchor, he was the waves and the ship was our record'" (Rule 1998: 34).[9] When asked exactly what he did for Madonna in the production of the album, Orbit replied, "It ran all the way from complete tracks, really, to just bare bones backing tracks on which she subsequently put her lyrics and melodies" (Rule 1998: 33). Also, Orbit was not the only person that was brought in to work on the album. Marius DeVries helped with the production,[10] Craig Armstrong orchestrated the violin arrangements,[11] and longtime collaborator Patrick Leonard was brought in to assist with both writing and production. The credits for each and every song on the album name Madonna as a producer along with William Orbit, Marius DeVries, and Patrick Leonard, depending on the song.

Madonna is rarely asked compositional questions in interview situations. Contrast this with an article in *Keyboard* magazine that spends several pages outlining Orbit's compositional techniques on (her!) album. This type of media coverage continues to perpetuate the myth that men are in charge of the technology and compositional work.

Björk's Relationship with Her Co-Producers

Over the years Björk has collaborated with a number of producers. In an interview she explains how she only wants to work with musicians who are as strong as her or stronger.[12] Björk already has a solid understanding of electronica and how the technologies work.[13] The fact that Björk is particular about her co-producers illustrates her desire to maintain a high level of control over her albums. She acknowledges her own strength as a musician and will not relinquish control unless she is matched in musical ability.[14] In order to challenge the gender hierarchy, it is important for artists to completely understand the technological processes used to create music. For example, if Björk is unsure of how a piece of equipment works, she searches for the best person to teach her.[15] Björk's musicianship is well respected by many of the prominent producers and musicians in the field of electronica and techno.

Björk's first two albums, *Debut* (1993) and *Post* (1995), were almost entirely collaborative projects. On *Debut* she worked exclusively with Nellee Hooper. He produced or co-produced ten out of the eleven songs. *Post* was more multicollaborative; Björk co-produced two tracks with Graham Massey, two with Tricky, one with Howie Bernstein, one that uses all three of them, one was produced by Hanslang and Reinsfeld, and four were produced by herself. Björk's first two albums "weren't as much solo projects as duets with the producers who had inspired her: Nellee Hooper, Graham Massey, Tricky, Howie B" (Van Meter 1997: 96). Although Björk's first two albums can be considered both solo efforts and "duets," the male producer's involvement lies just below the surface of each. Björk's musicianship always enables her to maintain her identity in a technological realm. In an interview, Evelyn Glennie, a percussionist who plays with Björk, proclaims her awe at Björk's ability to "hang onto her own identity no matter who she collaborates with."[16] When Björk talks about technology she also acknowledges those people from whom she learns. For example, in a documentary segment she explains how Mark Bell taught her how to use a QY20, a type of sampler for capturing noise and changing the pitch. It has over one hundred sounds, and she is able to create many of her tunes on this portable piece of electronic equipment. In an interview, she expressed her comfort with "taking from both masculine and feminine teachers, and [does not] see any problem with blending tales of conquest and nurture, fort-building and daydreaming" (Powers 1997: 339).

Electronic/Acoustic: Madonna's "Nothing Really Matters"

Madonna's recording of "Nothing Really Matters" reveals a merging of nature and technology. Her vocal delivery and other musical features bring a natural element to its electronic underpinnings. It opens with a synthesized instrumental introduction, where the use of the electronic is fore-grounded through timbre (*Ray of Light*, track 6: 0:00–0:19). The first noise the listener hears is the percussive grinding sound of what reminds one of a computer processor. Added to this is a sound that exploits the overtones of the harmonic series.[17] This sound is electronically produced on the album, but it has its origins in a "natural" place – the harmonic series and the abilities of acoustic instruments to create overtones.[18] Accompanying the fluctuating overtones in the harmonic series is a single low string line that begins in an acoustic state and then is electronically distorted. Above all of this, there is a melodic riff, played in the upper range of the keyboard, that continues throughout the song. This sound is never altered or sequenced but always occurs in its original timbre with some melodic exceptions. The fusion of nature and technology clearly takes place on many levels in the instrumental introduction alone: there is the sound of the electronic processor against the natural harmonic overtones, as well as a melodic riff that becomes naturalized through its repetition against the sound of the distorted single low string tone.[19]

With the entrance of Madonna's voice, another natural element is added to the electronic sounds (*Ray of Light*, track 6: 0:19–0:45). Madonna's voice is not electronically manipulated here, the way a lot of sampled voices are on other albums.[20] Her lyrics are also in direct contrast to the typical lyrics in dance music. Most dance music lyrics are made up of short repeated phrases that are electronically manipulated throughout the song. Madonna, on the other hand, sings long, narrative phrases. Her voice tells a story, arguably asserting her authorship. The short lyrical ideas presented by women in dance music of the mid 1990s on the other hand, clearly expose the "control" of the producer/mixer over the woman's voice. Throughout this piece Madonna does not allow electronic sound to interfere with her voice. In the vocal introduction Madonna's phrases rarely coincide with the phrasing of the melodic riff. Also in this section the processing sound of the instrumental introduction fades into the background, subsumed by more discrete pitched material. In the final phrase of the vocal introduction, when Madonna sings, "I'll never be the same, because of you," the natural sound of the voice is played against the technological sounds (*Ray of Light*, track 6: 0:44–0:53). The voice is juxtaposed against an unpitched repeated bass sound that is then played for an extended time while the pitch is electronically changed. In this section the "natural" of the voice is played against the "technological" of the electronic sounds.

The influence of dance music is undeniable in the first statement of the chorus. The use of a rhythmic bass backbeat most clearly makes this connection (*Ray of Light*, track 6: 0:53–1:13). Compared to traditional dance music styles with repeated lyrics and additive phrases. Madonna uses a more narrative approach.[21] The bass riff in Madonna's chorus alone, although electronic, is a very warm, round, fat sound. Although Madonna is influenced by the dance music genre, her approach is clearly very different. In the chorus it is once again important to note that, although there are a lot of electronic sounds, they occur at the end of Madonna's singing lines. The "wonky echo" (*Ray of Light*, track 6: 1:09–1:10) and ascending button sound (*Ray of Light*, track 6: 1:12–1:13), for example, are heard at the end of the chorus, avoiding contact with Madonna's voice.

The final example to be discussed in "Nothing Really Matters" is the instrumental interlude (*Ray of Light*, track 6: 2:55–3:12). The synthesized solo instrument in it sounds first like a xylophone and then a piano, signifying the natural through its associations with acoustic instruments. This solo has an improvised quality about it, like a jazz solo. The associations with jazz and acoustic piano and xylophone conjure up an earlier form of music, one less controlled by technology in the moment of performance.[22] The improvised instrumental section is played out against the electronic rhythmic section.[23] The beat is maintained electronically and thus juxtaposes the instrumental solo in this section. Also against this electronic beat and instrumental solo is Madonna's voice, repeated over and over again, making a humming sound.

Madonna as Mother in the Technological Realm

Madonna also brings nature to technology through the theme of motherhood on *Ray of Light*. The biological capacity to have children has constructed motherhood as a "natural" role for women. Therefore, electronic music has not traditionally celebrated motherhood as one of its themes; as Edna Gunderson states, "Electronic music is the unlikely vehicle carrying *Ray of Light's* somber freight" (Gunderson 1998). Keith Negus illustrates through his example of Sinead O'Connor as a musical mother that the singer-songwriter has traditionally celebrated themes of motherhood with acoustic guitar (Negus 1997: 179, 180). Negus goes on to cite O'Connor's song "three babies," from the album *I do not want what I haven't got* (1989), as an example of her personal confessional style (Negus 1997: 179, 180).

> The confessional tone is very apparent in her song lyrics and arrangements, production techniques and musical textures. The confessional characteristics are signified musically in the use of a restrained, intimate voice, recorded softly and close to the microphone and with little echo and by the repeated use of the first person. It is also signified in the sparsity of many song arrangements – the sense of emptiness and silence which suggests that only the singer (rather than an ensemble) is present. (Negus 1997: 180)

This confessional tone is very different in Madonna's electronic music. She does not use a restrained, intimate voice, recorded softly and close to the microphone. Instead Madonna opts for a strong voice with plenty of reverb and echo. Madonna also turns away from the sparsity of the typical confessional song arrangement by employing many electronic sounds in combination with her themes of motherhood.

Madonna has continually credited her current spiritual plateau to her relationship with her daughter, Lourdes, often suggesting that the album probably would have been very different if she had not become a mother. When asked what influenced *Ray of Light*, Madonna replied, "The birth of my daughter has been a huge influence. It's different to look at life through the eyes of your child, and suddenly you have a whole new respect for life and you kind of get your innocence back" (Morse 1998). There are several songs on *Ray of Light* that reflect Madonna's new role as a mother, including "Nothing Really Matters," "Little Star," and "Mer Girl." Each of these songs makes heavy use of sounds associated with electronica. Madonna states, "There's a song on the album called "Nothing Really Matters," and it is very much inspired by my daughter. It's just realizing that when the day is done the most important thing is loving people and sharing love . . ." (Gardner 1998). The introductory lyrics to "Nothing Really Matters," however, are problematic in terms of recent feminist queries on the issues of motherhood, which suggest that motherhood may not be a completely fulfilling role for all women. Also, by referring to her selfish nature before she had her baby, Madonna perpetuates the unrealistic notion that mothers must be selfless. The lyrics of the chorus reflect Madonna's new role as mother. As listeners we can assume that the "you" she is referring to is Lourdes, as she has stated that "Nothing Really Matters" was inspired by her daughter (Morse 1998).

In the chorus, Madonna extends the role of female nurturer to all people by stating "Love is all we need," making it an all–inclusive emotion. The final verse of the song makes reference to her daughter when she says, "Everything I give you all comes back to me." In this statement she is articulating the rewarding role motherhood has brought to her life.

Clearly, there are both advantages and disadvantages to Madonna's celebration of motherhood. Women's biological capacity for motherhood is seen by ecofeminists as connecting to an innate selflessness born of their responsibility for ensuring continuity of life (Wajcman 1991: 6). Ecofeminists believe that nurturing and caring are essential to the fulfillment of this responsibility (ibid.: 7). Madonna often plays into these themes of nurturing and selflessness in her representation of motherhood. Since the birth of her daughter, Madonna has privileged motherhood over her career, turning down movie roles and publicity opportunities and even canceling a yearlong world tour. From her privileged position as a wealthy and famous white woman, she has the resources to continue a rewarding career while at the same time focusing on her relationship with Lourdes. By combining themes of nature with electronic music, Madonna's music brings nature to technology, blurring the dividing line.

Implementing Iceland with Electronica: Björk's Homogenic

Throughout her solo career Björk has established herself successfully within the realm of electronica. This, in itself, illustrates her powerful presence and "serious" musicianship, according to the assumptions of the genre. Categorizing Björk's music using the binary system is a real challenge. By combining elements of herself and her Icelandic heritage with the technology of electronic music, Björk has created a unique space that blurs the line between nature/culture, feminine/masculine, body/mind, and self/other. She has, in one sense, blurred the dichotomies and developed a new place in popular music.

The music on Björk's album *Homogenic* cannot be analyzed in a vacuum. An analysis of the traditional division between nature and technology must move beyond the music to other sources of evidence. Björk uses everything, from her music, videos, performances, and album art, to her appearances and representations in and by the media, to produce this enigmatic union.

Björk's identity manifests itself through her Icelandic heritage and her music. Two of the main images associated with the feminine aesthetic are isolation and exoticism. Iceland is isolated geographically as well as culturally. Because of this isolation, what appears to be an exotic aura surrounds Björk. When Björk speaks about Iceland, she talks about her roots, the history, the elements, and her family. For her, Iceland is rejuvenating and inspiring. In one interview she claims, "I function in Iceland perfectly, it's got nature, mountains and winds, and I can at any moment have a walk and sing at the top of my voice without anyone finding me weird. But it's still a really modern place. It's a nice *combination of nature and techno*" (Walker 1997).

Björk describes *Homogenic* as minimalist because it is composed with only beat, strings, and the voice. One of the distinguishing features of Björk's music is her vocalization. In many instances the beat is informed by, and the tracks are produced around, her vocals. Not only does her voice represent Western society's understanding of the natural, but she also incorporates various native Icelandic influences, such as the vocal technique, a combination of speech and singing, used to narrate the sagas from the twelfth and thirteenth centuries.

The history of Iceland is vital to Björk's juxtaposition of nature and technology in her music. Because Iceland only gained independence in 1944, its development as a nation was quick. "Out of this sped-up modernization sprang both an almost mythological relationship to nature and a brand-new fixation on technology" (Van Meter 1997: 96). For over seven hundred years Iceland had been a colony of Denmark. The Icelanders were not allowed to sing or dance or play music because of its association with the devil; thus, they became obsessed with storytelling. "The core of Iceland's national culture was its literary heritage, whose main components were the sagas from the 12th and 13th centuries and the romantic and often nationalistic poems of the 19th century, and which included a nationalistic interpretation of Icelandic history" (Young 1993: 2). Njall Sigurason, a folklore specialist, explains how Björk uses her voice in a specific way, like the Old Icelandic choir men. These men used a reciting voice that was a combination of singing and speaking. Björk's adoption of this technique can be heard throughout the album; an excellent example is in "Unravel" (*Homogenic*, track 3: 1:32–2:28).

Analyzing Björk's vocal technique as natural sounding is not difficult. Various distinctive vocal characteristics occur throughout the album, including Björk's primitive-sounding screams, emphasized by a sampled and digitized beat (*Homogenic*, track 9: 1:38–2:28). In this example there is a basic perception of her voice as "natural" and being manipulated by something completely technological. The distortion of the beats and her voice add qualities of hard techno music, yet the methodical rhythm of the voice and the beat also evoke chantlike characteristics.

The *Homogenic* concert stage was designed in a manner that specifically addresses the distinctions between Western perceptions of natural and technological. The stage is divided in half, with the Icelandic string orchestra (representing "nature" or "traditional" music) on one side and live mixer Mark Bell (representing "technology" or "non-traditional" music) on the other. Throughout the concert, Björk moves freely between the two realms, embodying their crucial link. Björk also establishes an Icelandic context and presence by opening the concert with a traditional Icelandic ballad. She proceeds to synthesize the two components throughout the concert and ends on a purely techno level with a remix of "Pluto".[24] Although Björk began the concert with an Icelandic ballad and ended with her most "techno"-sounding composition from the album, the concert does not project a theme of technology consuming nature, rather, the fluidity of her movement between the two realms disrupts the distinction of both, rejecting the idea that one has power over the other.

Some of the techniques that Björk adopts to incorporate Iceland into her electronic soundscape derive from folk music practice and Icelandic stories. In the first track, "Hunter," Björk uses the interval of a fifth continually throughout the work. For example, the cellos play the repeated two-bar motif a fifth apart (*Homogenic*, track 1: 0:00–0:30). Fifths were common in traditional Icelandic folksongs and their use was particularly relevant to performance. Björk explains, "'Hunter' is based on what my grandma told me at Christmas; about two different types of birds. One bird always had the same nest and partner all their lives. The other was always travelling and taking on different partners. At some point there was a conscious decision made to remain a hunter" (Walker 1997). That decision is most important to Björk and her music.

There are also elements of Ravel's *Bolero* in "Hunter." One of the three main sections of the whole song is the Bolero ostinato (*Homogenic*, track 1: 0:00–1:36). The sounds Björk uses to cover the rhythmic pattern from *Bolero* are tightly interwoven. The same beat is repeated continually throughout the piece, with electronic sounds and the strings adding multiple layering. The electronic melody flows with the beat and takes on an "organic" feel – the perceived artificial sound changing to a perceived natural sound (*Homogenic*, track 1: 0:11–0:30). She exaggerates the strings by using sliding notes that are sluggish and slurring, drawing out specific notes similarly to how she draws out syllables with her voice. There is a sequence to her electronic sounds, with each sound taking its turn to weave in and out of the ostinato. The beats throughout the album are simplistic; Björk made "a conscious decision that the beats would be almost naïve, very natural but explosive, like still in the making." She suggests, "This force is Iceland" (Walker 1997).

Multiple Fusions of Nature and Technology: Homogenic Album Art

Another significant medium Björk uses to engage with the nature/technology dichotomy is her album art. The *Homogenic* album cover features a shocking computerized image of Björk on the front in which she appears half-human. She is a hybrid, a human/machine – a cyborg. Her costume is a kimono, made of shiny silver and crimson red. The necklace elongates her neck, making her head seem as though it is not quite attached to her body. Her fingernails are longer than claws but perfectly manicured and polished. The hair is divided on her head into what looks like two large satellite dishes. Her appearance subsumes representations of various cultures. Her dress associates her with the Orient, her necklace with Africa, and her hair with Asia. There is not one line on her face, and her eyes are black and silver. At first glance one may be tempted to suggest that Björk is merely appropriating other cultures. However, she is not; rather, she has created an image of cultural synthesis. The background is silver with little blue flowers. The flowers are representations of nature, whereas the silver alludes to the metallic and to images of technology. The image seems to have caught her in a state of metamorphosis. Perhaps it is here where the fusion of the "nature goddess" with "technology's cyborg" is most evident.

Inside the jacket there appears to be a microscopic vision of a living organism or plant. The shades are deep reds, like blood, and it appears fleshy. This image is fluid and organic, scientific and natural at the same time. But the idea of the microscope changes the vision to a scientific one. The blood is now controlled and gazed upon by the "masculine." When you turn to the backside of the cover, the scene depicted inside is now viewed from a distance. The image is still organic and scientific but, from this distance, the "masculine science" is less oppressive. The background appears similar to that displayed on the front cover. There is a larger image of a flower surrounded by the fluid, which contains a glowing light resembling an entity made of energy. The shape of this design is also reminiscent of the uterus and the womb. Across this light is Björk's trademark initial. The letter "b" is a graphic design that reminds one of hip-hop, techno, and the realm of electronica. This "masculinized" genre is set in an organic image of fluidity. The glowing light represents the creation of something new or perhaps the combination of the "feminine" and the "masculine." Björk's synthesis of nature and electronica is evident even here.

Conclusion

One of the most interesting concepts used to attack the nature/culture dichotomy is Donna Haraway's cyborg theory. In "A Cyborg Manifesto: Science, Technology, and Socialist-Feminism in the Late Twentieth Century," Haraway describes what she calls "an ironic dream of a common language for women in the integrated circuit" (Haraway 1991: 149). The cyborg theory is a theoretical ideology that contains no gender and is thus a better space for women and men to inhabit. Haraway defines a cyborg as a "cybernetic organism, a hybrid of machine and organism, a creature of social reality as well as a creature of fiction. The cyborg is a matter of fiction and lived experience that changes what counts as women's experience in the late twentieth century" (ibid.). It is imperative to remember that "the machine is not an *it* to be animated, worshipped, and dominated. The machine is us, our processes, an aspect of our embodiment" (ibid.:

180). Consequently, technology can be the machine elements that we use to adjust or alter our physical form or appearance.

Haraway's cyborg theory relates to Björk's accomplishments in the music composition, production, and publicity of *Homogenic*. Through a synthesis of natural and technological elements in her music, Björk is able to compose without necessarily adhering to characteristic boundaries. Creating her music in an electronic industry does not preclude her Icelandic heritage from emerging, nor does her electronic music feel void of emotion.[25] Björk, like Haraway, suggests an alternative escape from the oppressive forces of gendered binary oppositions. Björk manages to accomplish this by juxtaposing the elements traditionally considered by Western societies as opposing. Because "the cyborg [or Björk's *Homogenic*] is no longer structured by the polarity of public and private . . . Nature and culture are reworked; the one can no longer be the resource for appropriation or incorporation by the other" (Haraway 1991: 151). Haraway describes the cyborg manifesto as "an argument for *pleasure* in the confusion of boundaries and for *responsibility* in their construction" (ibid.: 150).[26] As the cyborg theory develops, women's pleasure will be developed in the dismantling of the socially constructed categories of gender. The illumination of rigid gender categories initiates the process of freeing women from their subordination. By obscuring the boundaries between nature and technology, Björk disrupts the traditional role of women in popular music. She exposes gender in electronica by both using and moving beyond the stereotypes, challenging the assumptions that are attached to it. As Haraway suggests, "It means both building and destroying [musics], identities, categories, relationships, [and the way we listen]" (ibid.: 181).

By embracing both "organic and technological components" (Haraway 1991: i) in her music, can Madonna be described as inhabiting the cyborg world? Madonna combines motherhood and acoustic sounds (coded as natural) with technological music. The cyborg lives in a community that breaks down the binary of public and private: it "defines a technological polis based partly on a revolution of social relations in the oikos, the household" (Haraway 1991: 151). Blurring the boundaries between public and private through motherhood lessens the strict distinctions for creating a new place; however, Haraway's theory moves beyond this concept. Haraway envisions people occupying a new space, in a new way: as a hybrid "of machine and organism" (Haraway 1991: 150). Despite Madonna combining elements of nature and technology in her music, does she exist in the new space that Haraway alludes to? Through the techniques used to compose the music on *Ray of Light*, Madonna appears to resists the hybridization: Madonna's voice remains relatively free from any radical electronic alteration. Because of Madonna's reputation for maintaining power over all aspects of her work, we believe that Madonna resists being controlled by the machine.

Haraway's utopian world envisions a society removed of all power imbalances: "I do not know of any other time in history when there was a greater need for political unity to confront effectively dominations of race, gender, sexuality and class" (Haraway 1991: 157). For these reasons it is important to problematize Madonna and Björk's cultural positions. Both Madonna and Björk benefit from their dominant position in most of these categories. Presently Madonna suffers from few issues of inequality in these power relations: she is a wealthy white woman, and although she has expressed bisexuality she is primarily playing out the heterosexual role. Björk's privilege also extends to class, sexuality, and race, however she is often regarded as exotic Other because of her Icelandic heritage. Despite their privilege Madonna and Björk still continue to be marginalized as women in the male dominated field of electronica.

Women's experimentation with technology is not entirely new. There are a number of other women who incorporate technological aspects in their music making. Performance artist Laurie Anderson is well known for her relationship with technology. "Only through [abusing and playing with technology] could she have invented her famous tape bow, where a tape loop is bowed across a violin with cassette heads instead of strings" (O'Brien 1995: 150). Recently in R&B and hip hop women have pushed beyond the boundaries of gender stereotypes. Missy Elliot utilizes various technological means to produce her albums. TLC's transition from R&B to hip hop also connects with technological components. In their music videos "She's a Bitch" and "No Scrubs," Missy Elliot and TLC embody futuristic personas through costume and movement. Toronto-based musician Esthero is another artist striving to move beyond gender barriers in electronica. Although these women also experiment with technology in their music, Madonna and Björk are unique because of their synthesis of nature *and* technology. Yet in spite of their success, women musicians are far from the majority in electronic music. Their positions are marginalized in a number of ways: Madonna is often dismissed as somebody flirting with the latest, hottest trend (in this case techno-culture) rather than as a "serious" musician employing technology, and, although Björk composes in the electronica realm, she is often described as a gypsy, child queen, pixie, or a sprite-like enigma,[27] which perpetuates the idea that women are incapable of harnessing technology to compose "legitimate" music.

Feminists have criticized the topics of analytical debate concerning gender and technology, suggesting that only those practices that reinforce or reproduce existing patterns of gender relations are noticed theoretically (Grint and Gill 1995: 17). "While gender and technology have been constructed as macro-actors and shut away into black boxes, we must insist on opening them up for investigation, where the meaning and significance of technology and gender identity are reconsidered in all their variations as they exist for the actors" (ibid.: 44). Through our analysis of Madonna and Björk we have opened the black box of electronic music, exploring the way two women musicians used technology in a nontraditional manner and contributed to the dismantling of the nature/technology dichotomy that exists in popular music. Although working toward similar goals, Madonna and Björk use various methods and inspirations for combining the two poles. Merging electronic production with themes stereotypically assumed to be feminine, Madonna and Björk have initiated the degendering of electronic music. Through a synthesis of nature and technology, these women have carved unique spaces for themselves in the realm of popular music.

Notes

1. Please refer to track 10, "Bedtime Stories," on Madonna's 1994 album *Bedtime Stories*, 0:00–0:40, and track 8, "Possibly Maybe," on Björk's 1995 album *Post*, 0:00–0:50. From

these examples it is evident that Madonna imitates Björk's vocal technique, using an intimate whispering tone. Although neither artist uses a wide melodic range, their timbral inflections are diverse.

2. Björk often promotes Icelandic principles as "natural." Within this context she includes Iceland's history of colonization by Denmark, Icelandic literary tradition, such as its sagas and folklore, and the Icelandic people's connection to weather and survival of extreme climates. Refer to Aston, Micallef, Van Meter and Walker.

3. For example, acoustic musicians are regarded as feminine, while electronic musicians are seen as masculine. The same is true for the singer/songwriter genre.

4. Traditional rock bands with their electric guitar, keyboard, bass, and drums usually have been made up of male musicians, whereas female pop stars are often featured as solo vocalists, rarely playing these instruments.

5. Although, in the recent past the electric guitar has been associated with men in popular music.

6. Advantages including technological knowledge, male authority, studio experience, accesses to technology.

7. Emphasis is our own.

8. Madonna's creative input in her albums and music videos are underestimated by her critics, yet, at the same time, those same critics celebrate her control over the marketing of her image and career.

9. Although Madonna emphasizes her control, her role in the recording studio is still unclear.

10. DeVries has also produced with artists such as Björk and David Bowie.

11. Armstrong has worked with Massive Attack.

12. Walker 1997.

13. Björk began her recording career at the age of twelve and spent several years as a keyboardist and lead singer in the punk band The Sugarcubes. She is well versed in music theory and music production techniques.

14. What is problematic with this statement is Björk's continual use of only male co-producers. However, she has been known to work with women mixers. Of course, a major problem that continues to exist is the exclusion of women producers from the "boys club" at the top of the field, which is maintained through the assumption that men have a better understanding of technology and how it works.

15. Walker 1997. In this section of the documentary Björk explains how she uses a QY20 to write many of her songs. She speaks of its capabilities and how Mark Bell taught her how to use it.

16. Walker 1997. Besides evidence stated on the album cover, including composition, instrumentation, lyrics, and production, the roles of each person in the studio are unknown.

17. The sound referred to can be produced by playing over the main sound of a pitch to produce the harmonic series.

18. Acoustic is coded as natural in this context.

19. One of the ways that electronic music is developed is by sampling phrases or motives. This particular melodic riff is repeated without being sampled.

20. For example, the way Cher's voice is sampled in "Believe" exposes the technological interference. We thank Jennifer DeBoer for pointing this out to us.

21. The narrative approach is less controlled by technology than the short manipulated phrases of dance music, which are controlled by technology.

22. Although jazz musicians use instruments, which could be considered technology, the instruments we refer to here are acoustic. Because jazz music is an older form of music

than electronica, its sounds have become naturalized. Compared to electronica, where technology is exposed in the electronic sounds, jazz has a much more natural quality to it. Also the idea of an improvised solo implies a sense of freedom. The improvised section in the instrumental interlude seems to avoid the control of technology, specifically the electronic bass backbeat that accompanies it, thus aligning it with nature.

23. The improvised solo has the quality of being free from the control of technology since the improvised solo was originally designed in jazz to give the performer a chance to improvise on the melody.

24. Claudio Dell-Aere is another scholar researching Björk who has come to similar conclusions after watching the *Homogenic* concert. We wish to express our gratitude to him for a number of thought-provoking conversations on this topic.

25. Both Iceland and emotion are coded as natural in this context.

26. Italics are the authors'.

27. Refer to Micallef and Reynolds.

References

Print Sources

Aston, Martin (1996). *Björkgraphy*. London: Simon and Schuster.

Bayton, Mavis (1990). How Women Become Musicians. In: Simon Frith & Andrew Goodwin (eds.), *On Record: Rock, Pop and the Written Word*, pp. 238–57. New York: Pantheon Books.

Cockburn, Cynthia (1985). *Machinery of Dominance: Women, Men and Technical Know-How*. Boston: Northeastern University Press.

Code, Lorraine (1995). Must a Feminist Be a Relativist After All? In *Rhetorical Spaces: Essays on Gendered Locations*, pp. 185–207. New York: Routledge.

Derrida, Jacques (1976). *Of Grammatology*, trans. Gayatri Chaleravorty Spivak. Baltimore and London: Johns Hopkins University Press.

Gardner, Elysa (1998). Ray of Light. *Los Angeles Times*, March 1.

Goodwin, Andrew (1990). Sample and Hold: Pop Music in the Digital Age of Reproduction. In: Simon Frith & Andrew Goodwin (eds.), *On Record: Rock, Pop and the Written Word*, pp. 258–73. New York: Pantheon Books.

Grint, Keith & Rosalind Gill (eds.) (1995). *The Gender-Technology Relation: Contemporary Theory and Research*. London: Taylor and Francis.

Gunderson, Edna (1998). Her *Ray of Light* Shines Earnestly in New Direction. *USA Today*, March 3.

Haraway, Donna J. (1991) *Simians, Cyborgs, and Women: The Reinvention of Nature*. New York: Routledge.

Marsh, Charity (1999). *Homogenic*: Björk's Fusion of Goddess and Cyborg. Unpublished essay.

Micallef, Ken (1997). Home Is Where the Heart Is. *Ray Gun*, September.

Morse, Steve (1998). Madonna in the Lotus Position. *Boston Globe*, March 20, C1.

Negus, Keith (1997). Sinead O'Connor – Musical Mother. In: Sheila Whiteley (ed.), *Sexing the Groove: Popular Music and Gender*, pp. 178–91. London: Routledge.

O'Brien, Lucy (1995). *She Bop*. New York: Penguin Books.

Powers, Ann. Bohemian Rhapsodies. In: Barbara O'Dair (ed.), *Trouble Girls: The Rolling Stone Book of Women in Rock*, p. 339. New York: Random House.

Reynolds, Simon (1998). *Generation Ecstasy: Into the World of Techno and Rave Culture*. London: Little, Brown and Company.

Rule, Greg (1998). William Orbit: The Methods and Machinery behind Madonna's *Ray of Light*. *Keyboard*, July, pp. 30–34, 36, 38.

Terry, Jennifer & Melodie Calvert (eds.) (1997). *Processed Lives: Gender and Technology in Everyday Life*. London: Routledge.

Théberge, Paul (1997). *Any Sound You Can Imagine: Making Music/Consuming Technology*. Hanover, NH: University Press of New England.

Thornton, Sarah (1996). *Club Cultures: Music, Media and Subcultural Capital*. Middletown, Conn: Wesleyan University Press.

Van Meter, Jonathan (1997). Björk: Animal? Vegetable? Mineral? *Spin* December 13/9, pp. 93–8.

Wajcman, Judy (1991). *Feminism Confronts Technology*. University Park, PA: Pennsylvania State University Press.

Walters, Barry (1998). Madonna Chooses to Dare. *Spin* April 14/4, pp. 70–6.

Young, Gester Gundmundssohn (1993). *Icelandic Rock Music as a Synthesis of International Trends and National Cultural Inheritance*, pp. 1–48. Sage Publications.

Video

Walker, Christopher, producer and director (1997). *Bravo Profiles: Björk*. South Bank Show. Video recording.

55

Characterizing Rock Music Culture: The Case of Heavy Metal

Will Straw[*]

The decomposition of psychedelic music, in the late 1960s, followed three principal directions. The first of these, in the United States, involved a return to traditional, largely rural musical styles, with the emergence of country rock, of which the stylistic changes in the careers of the Byrds (in 1968) and the Grateful Dead (in 1970) offer examples. In Britain, a second tendency took the form of a very eclectic reinscription of traditional and symphonic musical forms within an electric or electronic rock context, with groups such as King Crimson, Jethro Tull, Genesis, Yes, and Emerson, Lake and Palmer. The third trend, which may be found in both American and British rock music of this period, was toward the heavy metal sound, frequently based in the chord structures of boogie blues, but retaining from psychedelia an emphasis on technological effect and instrumental virtuosity. In groups on the periphery of psychedelia – such as Blue Cheer, the Yardbirds, Iron Butterfly – many of the stylistic traits that would become dominant within heavy metal were already in evidence: the cult of the lead guitarist, the "power trio" and other indices of the emphasis on virtuosity, the "supergroup" phenomena, and the importance in performance of extended solo playing and a disregard for the temporal limits of the pop song. Their coherence into a genre was reinforced, through the 1970s, by the sedimentation of other stylistic attributes (those associated with stage shows, album-cover design, and audience dress and life-style) and by the relatively stable sites of institutional support (radio formats, touring circuits, record industry structures).

Institutions and Industries in the Early 1970s

Heavy metal music came to prominence at a time when institutions associated with the psychedelic period were either disappearing or being assimilated within larger structures as part of widespread changes within the music-related industries. The overriding tendency in these changes was the diminishing role of local entrepreneurs in the processes by which music was developed and disseminated. The end of the meant

[*]Pp. 97–110 from *On Record: Rock, Pop, and the Written Word*, ed. S. Frith and A. Goodwin (New York: Pantheon Books). © 1990 by Will Straw. Reprinted with permission from the author.

the end of free-form radio, a large number of independent record labels, the ballroom performance circuit, and the underground press, all of which had contributed, at least initially, to the high degree of regionalization within psychedelia and associated rock movements.

For many record company analysts, the number of hit-making independent record labels is an index of the degree of "turbulence" within the industry. The modern history of the American recording industry has thus been divided into three epochs: one running from 1940 to 1958, marked by concentration and integration within and between the electronics, recording, and publishing industries; the 1959 to 1969 period, character- ized by the "turbulence" associated with the introduction on a large scale of rock music; and, finally, the period that began in 1970, and that saw the return of oligopoly to the extent that, in 1979, the six largest corporations accounted for 86 percent of *Billboard*'s total "chart action."[1] Two other statistics are worth noting: by the late 1960s, the album had displaced the single as the dominant format in record sales, and during the 1970s, in large part as a result of the overhead costs associated with oligopoly, the break-even point for album sales went from 20,000 to nearly 100,000 copies.

While the oligopolization of the American record industry in the 1970s is undeniable, it is less certain that one can assume the usual production effect, the sequence oligopoly – bureaucracy – conservatism – standardization. Writers such as Paul Hirsch have argued that the "centralization" of decision making in the industries producing cultural "texts" is rarely like that found in other businesses and that entertainment industries more closely resemble the house construction industry, with its organization of produc- tion along craft lines. Within the record industry, horizontal integration has frequently meant assimilating smaller, specialized labels within conglomerates (through purchases or licensing-distribution agreements), such that those involved in the selection and production of music stay in place. The record industry in the 1970s thus relied far more on outside, contracted producers or production companies than it did in the old days of the salaried artist and repertoire director.

The defining characteristic of much rock music production in the early 1970s was, further, its domination by rock elites, by people already established in creative capacities within the industry. The supergroup phenomena of this period is symptomatic of this, as is the fact that most of the leading heavy metal bands (such as Humble Pie) were formed by remnants of groups popular in the 1960s. And many of the country-rock groups and singer-songwriters who achieved high market penetration in the early 1970s had in one capacity or another long been record company employees (for instance Leon Russell, Carole King, and the members of the Eagles).

The implications of this for the American record industry during these years are not obvious. The reliance on industry elites is indicative of industry conservatism insofar as it displaced "street-level" talent-hunting and might be seen as a resistance to innova- tion. However it meant neglect too of the process whereby musicians with local follow- ings and local entrepreneurial support established themselves regionally and proved their financial viability by recording first for minor labels. The majors were now signing acts without this form of market testing (a contributing factor in the increasingly high ratio of unprofitable to profitable records), and the selection and development of talent, the initiation of new styles, was increasingly the responsibility of the established creative personnel. Recording contracts in this period of growth gave artists unprecedented control over the choice of producers and material.

"Centralization" in this context meant, therefore, a *loosening* of divisions of labor. It is clear, for example, that many of those formerly involved in support capacities (song-writers, session musicians, etc.) achieved star status because of the ease with which they could move between divisions or combine the production, composing, and performing functions (just as members of groups now took it for granted that they could record solo albums).[2] Loose role definitions, and the continuing prosperity of performers and the industry as a whole, also encouraged international record production, with, as one of its effects, the free movement of session personnel (and their musical concerns) between Great Britain and North America (Joe Cocker's *Mad Dogs and Englishmen* album and film remains a useful document of this). While the bases for comparison are limited, the American record industry in the 1970s was not unlike the American film industry following the antitrust decisions of the 1940s, which divorced the production and distribution companies from those involved in exhibition: in both cases, one finds a high reliance on licensing agreements between major companies and smaller produc-tion outfits; in both cases, there is a fluidity of movement between roles and a tendency (for financial – often tax-related – reasons) for stars to build corporate entities around themselves and work in a variety of international locales. Much of the rock literature of the mid-to late 1970s, describing industry growth in terms of the co-optation and destruction of the energies unleashed in the 1960s, regards this as exemplifying a process inevitable within mass culture,[3] but it can be argued that the changes are better under-stood as the triumph of craft-production structures. In this regard, the punk critique of early 1970s rock – which focused on its excesses and its eclecticism, on its "empty" virtuosity and self-indulgence rather than on an assumed standardization – was a neces-sary counterweight to the recuperation argument.

The changes that occurred in the programming policies of FM radio stations in the United States and Canada between the late 1960s and mid-1970s are well documented elsewhere, as is the decline of the local underground press.[4] In both cases, rising over-head costs and an increased reliance on large advertising accounts (with record compa nies the prominent spenders) grew out of and furthered the desire – or need – for market expansion. Either way, both radio stations and magazines paid less attention to marginal or regional musical phenomena. The rise of overhead costs and group performance fees were, similarly, the major factor in the replacement of the mid-sized performance circuit by the large arena or stadium, a process that continued throughout the 1970s, until the emergence of punk and new wave reestablished the viability of certain types of small venues.

These developments certainly did lead to standardization on FM radio and in the rock press. Radio playlist consultants, automated stations, and satellite-based networks all became significant elements in the evolution of FM radio throughout the 1970s, and the development of the rock press from local, subculturally based publications to national magazines is evident in the history of *Rolling Stone*, one of the few rock papers to survive. It would be wrong, though, to see these developments as local examples of the general "standardizing" trend. Radio playlist consultants became important because of the eclecticism and sheer bulk of record company product – individual station directors simply didn't have the time or skill to listen to and choose from all this product. At the same time the increasing rigidity of formats was an effect of demographic research into the expansion of the rock audience beyond its traditional youth boundaries – the recession of the 1970s called for a more accurate targeting of listening groups.[5] It was because such targeting remained a minor aspect of record company strategy (except in the most general sense) that it became crucial in shaping the formats of radio stations and magazines, media commercially dependent on the delivery of audiences to advertisers.

Heavy Metal Audiences and the Institutions of Rock

On one level, Led Zeppelin represents the final flowering of the sixties' psychedelic ethic, which casts rock as passive sensory involvement.

Jim Miller[6]

In discussing heavy metal music, and its relationship to rock culture in a wider sense, I am assuming a relative stability of musical style and of institutional structures from 1969–70 until 1974–6. (Near the end of this period, dance-oriented music began to achieve popularity with segments of the white audiences, with a variety of effects on the sites within which music was disseminated, while the gradual acceptance, in the United States and Canada, of British symphonic or progressive rock resulted in a generic cross-fertilization that eroded the stylistic coherence of heavy metal.)

The processes described earlier as leading to the renewed importance of the *national* rock audience also worked to constitute it as a "mass" audience – the media disseminating music or information about it (radio and the press) now relied on national formats rather than on their ties to local communities (or on the popularity of local personalities). These developments made more important an audience segment that had been somewhat disenfranchised by movements within rock in the late 1960s – suburban youth. In the 1970s, it was they who were the principal heavy metal constituency.

In stressing the geographical situation of heavy metal audiences rather than their regional, ethnic, racial, or class basis, I am conscious that the latter have had wider currency in theoretical studies of rock, and it is obvious that race and class are, for example, highly determinant in the audience profile for soul or opera. Nevertheless, for reasons that should become evident, habitation patterns are crucial for the relationship between music, the institutions disseminating it, and life-styles in a more general sense. The hostility of heavy metal audiences to disco in the late 1970s is indicative in this respect; the demographics of disco showed it to be dominated by blacks, Hispanics, gays, and young professionals, who shared little beyond living in inner urban areas.[7] The high degree of interaction between punk/new-wave currents and artistic subcultures in America (when compared with Great Britain) may also be traced in large part to the basis of both in inner urban areas such as New York's Soho; those living elsewhere would have little or no opportunity to experience or become involved in either of these cultures.

Suburban life is incompatible for a number of reasons with regular attendance at clubs where one may hear records or live performers; its main sources of music are radio, retail chain record stores (usually in shopping centers), and occasional large concerts (most frequently in the nearest municipal stadium). These institutions together make up the network by which major-label albums are promoted and sold – and from which music not available on such labels is for the most part excluded.

My argument is not that this institutional network gave major labels a free hand in shaping tastes but that, in conjunction with suburban life-styles, it defined a form of involvement in rock culture, discouraging subcultural activity of the degree associated with disco or punk, for example. Heavy metal culture may be characterized in part by the absence of a strong middle stratum between the listener and the fully professional group. Only in rare cases in the early 1970s could there be found an echelon of local heavy metal bands performing their own material in local venues. What I have referred to as the dominance of music in general by elites, in conjunction with the overall decline in small-scale live performance activity in the early 1970s, worked to block the channels of career advancement characteristic of other musical currents or other periods within rock history. It might also be suggested that the economy of North American suburbs in most cases discourages the sorts of marginality that develop in large inner urban areas and foster musical subcultures. High rents and the absence of enterprises not affiliated with corporate chains mean that venues for dancing or listening to live music are uncommon. If, for the purposes of this discussion, a music-based subculture may be defined as a group whose interaction centers to a high degree on sites of musical consumption, and within which there are complex gradations of professional or semiprofessional involvement in music together with relatively loose barriers between roles (such that all members will be involved, in varying degrees, in collecting, assessing, presenting, and performing music), then heavy metal audiences do not constitute a musical subculture.

The lack of intermediary strata between heavy metal audiences and groups was further determined by another characteristic of the music. Most of the groups that were predominant – Led Zeppelin, Black Sabbath, Uriah Heep, Humble Pie, Deep Purple, and so on – were British. They were instrumental in establishing a major characteristic of North American rock culture in the 1970s: regular, large-scale touring. The dependence of certain British bands on the North American market has become a structural feature of the rock industry, and is quite different in its significance from the periodic "British invasions" of the charts.

The American rock-critical establishment had a negative response to heavy metal, or at least to the form British musicians gave it. This had two effects on the place of heavy metal within rock culture and its discourse. On the one hand, critical dismissal encouraged heavy metal musicians to employ a populist argument, whose main tenet was that critics had lost touch with the tastes of broad sections of the rock audience. On the other hand, this placed critics in the dilemma of how to respond negatively to the music without employing the terms traditionally used to condemn rock overall (sameness, loudness, musical incompetence, etc.) – the critical terms with greater acceptability within rock culture (commercialism, conservatism) were, at least initially, inappropriate. The explicitly sociological or ethnographic bent of critical writing on heavy metal, its attention to the social/political implications of the music, were symptomatic of the cleavages heavy metal had effected within rock discourse.

In the early and mid-1970s, and particularly in *Rolling Stone*, rock criticism adopted more and more of the terms of journalistic film criticism, valorizing generic economy and a performer's links with the archives of American popular music. (The consistent high regard for singers such as Bruce Springsteen, Emmylou Harris, and Tom Waits, for performers like Lou Reed who played self-consciously with rock and roll imagery, stands out in a rereading of *Rolling Stone* from this period.) The emphasis on the individual career or the genre as the context within which records were meaningful accompanied the rise of the "serious" record review. This not only diminished the interest of heavy metal for its own sake, but also made the audience a relatively minor focus of rock criticism, as the latter moved away from the pop-journalistic or countercultural concerns of a few years earlier.

A major characteristic of heavy metal was its consistent noninvocation of rock history or mythology in any self-conscious or genealogical sense. The iconography of heavy metal performances and album covers, and the specific reworking of boogie blues underlying the music, did not suggest the sorts of modalization (that is, ironic relationships to their design principles or retrospective evocation of origins) that country rock, glitter rock, and even disco (with its frequent play upon older motifs of urban nightlife) possessed. As well, there was nothing to indicate that heavy metal listeners were interested in tracing the roots of any musical traits back to periods preceding the emergence of heavy metal. While the terms "rock" and "rock and roll" recur within song lyrics and album titles, this is always in reference to the present of the performance and the energies to be unleashed now, rather than to history or to myth. Any "rebel" or nonconformist imagery in heavy metal may be seen as a function of its masculine, "hard" stances, rather than as a conscious participation in rock's growing self-reflexivity. That the recent neo-punk movements in Anglo-American rock have found much of their constituency within heavy metal audiences is partly due, I suspect, to the redefinition of punk's minimalism as the expression of raw energy.

Equally striking is the almost total lack of hobbyist activity surrounding heavy metal music. Observation suggests that heavy metal listeners rarely become record collectors to a significant extent, that they are not characterized by what might be called "secondary involvement" in music: the hunting down of rare tracks, the reading of music-oriented magazines, the high recognition of record labels or producers. To the extent that a heavy metal "archive" exists, it consists of albums from the 1970s on major labels, kept in print constantly and easily available in chain record stores. There is thus little basis for the presence in heavy metal audiences of complex hierarchies based on knowledge of the music or possession of obscure records, on relationships to opinion leaders as the determinants of tastes and purchases. An infrastructure of importers, specialty stores, and fanzines was almost nonexistent in heavy metal culture during the early 1970s and emerged only in the 1980s, with the recent wave of newer heavy metal groups.

In its distance from both Top 40 pop culture and the mainstream of rock-critical discourse, heavy metal in the early 1970s was the rock genre least characterized by the culture's usual practices of contextualization. It is rarely the case, for example, that heavy metal pieces are presented on the radio for their nostalgic or "oldie" value. Rather, they are presented as existing contemporaneously with recent material, with none of the transitory aspects of Top 40 or setting down in individual careers or generic histories which the rock press and radio bring to bear upon other forms. The specificity of the heavy metal audience, then, lies in: (1) its nonparticipation in the two dominant components of rock culture, the Top 40 succession of hits and hobbyist tendencies associated with record and information collecting; and (2) its difference, nevertheless, from the casual, eclectic audience for transgeneric music (such as that of Carole King or, more recently, Vangelis). It is this coexistence of relatively coherent taste, consumption, and, to a certain extent, life-style with low secondary involvement in rock culture that in the 1970s most strongly distinguished audiences for heavy metal from those for other sorts of rock music.

Heavy Metal Culture: Masculinity and Iconography

On the whole, youth cultures and subcultures tend to be some form of exploration of masculinity.

Mike Brake[8]

That the audience for heavy metal music is heavily male-dominated is generally acknowledged and easily observable, though statistical confirmation of this is based largely on the audiences for album-oriented rock (AQR).[9] Clearly heavy metal performers are almost exclusively male (recent exceptions such as Girlschool being accorded attention most often for their singularity). Is it sufficient, then, to interpret heavy metal's gender significance simply in terms of its "cock rock" iconography?

One problem here is how to reconcile the hypothesis that heavy involvement in rock music – as critic, record collector, reader of the rock press, or performer – is primarily a male pursuit[10] with the observation that these activities are for the most part absent from the most "masculine" of rock audiences, that for heavy metal. The point is that involvement in rock music is simply one among many examples of critieria by which status is assigned within youth peer groups, albeit one that involves a high degree of eroticization of certain stances and attributes.

Within male youth culture (particularly in secondary school or workplaces), a strong investment in archivist or obscurantist forms of knowledge is usually devalued, marginalized as a component of what (in North America, at least) is called "nerd" culture. I would emphasize that this marginalization is not simply directed at intellectual or knowledgeable males; rather, it involves specific relationships between knowledge and the presentation of the physical body. In recent American youth films (such as *The Last American Virgin*), the nerd is stereotyped as unstylishly dressed and successful at school: it is precisely the preoccupation with knowledge that is seen as rendering the boy oblivious to dress, grooming, posture, and social interaction (particularly as related to sexuality).

If, within a typology of male identity patterns, heavy metal listeners are usually in a relationship of polar opposition to "nerds," it is primarily because the former do not regard certain forms of knowledge (particularly those derived from print media) as significant components of masculinity – if the "nerd" is distinguished by his inability to translate knowledge into socially acceptable forms of competence, heavy metal peer groups value competencies demonstrable in social situations exclusively. Interestingly, within rock culture, neither of these groups is seen to partake of what the dominant discourse surrounding rock in the 1970s has regarded as "cool."

"Cool" may be said to involve the eroticization and stylization of knowledge through its assimilation to an imagery of competence. There developed in the 1970s a recognizable genre of rock performance (Lou Reed, Patti Smith, Iggy Pop, even, to a lesser extent, Rod Stewart) based on the integration of street wisdom, a certain ironic distance from rock mythology, and, in some cases, sexual ambiguity (whose dominant significance was as an index of experience) within relatively coherent musical styles and physical stances. The recurrence of black leather and "rebel" postures in the iconography surrounding such music never resulted in its full assimilation in the more masculine tendencies of rock culture, since these motifs overlapped considerably with those of gay culture or involved a significant degree of intellectualization; but in North America, much of the original constituency for punk and new wave included people whose archivist involvement in rock centered on a tradition dominated by the Velvet Underground and East Coast urban rock in general. Many of those in this current (such as Lenny Kaye and Lester Bangs) became important figures within American rock criticism, and it remains the purest example of secondary involvement in rock music becoming a component of a highly stylized subculture. Since the mid-1970s, performers on its fringes have contributed an alternative constellation of male images to those found in heavy metal, one that participates in what rock culture defines as "cool," but that lacks the androgynous aspects of the bohemian underground. Bruce Springsteen, Bob Seger, and John Cougar Mellencamp are American rock performers who have all achieved mainstream AOR success while presenting, as important components of their styles, an archivist relationship to rock music and a tendency to play self-consciously with the mythologies that surround it.

Another rock culture that may be fruitfully compared with heavy metal emerged around British progressive rock (or what is now derisively called "pomp rock"): symphonic groups such as Yes, Genesis, and Emerson, Lake and Palmer. While certain of these groups – for example, King Crimson and ELP – achieved North American success in the early 1970s, others, such as Genesis and Gentle Giant, did not become popular until the middle of the decade. The audiences for this music, like those for heavy metal, were predominantly male; but to a much greater extent than with heavy metal, one can trace complex gradations of involvement in this music, at least until 1975 or so.

Progressive rock fostered secondary involvement among North American listeners for a number of reasons. Both the earlier albums of many of these groups, and records by minor groups within the same genre, were often available only as imports, and the subculture that sprang up thus both spawned, and centered on, import-oriented record stores, fanzines, and the British musical press (the pattern was repeated by latter new wave fans – large numbers of record stores currently marketing postpunk music began by selling progressive rock imports). Interest in British progresive rock was also closely correlated with the frequent reading of, and subcultural involvement in, science fiction (another component of "nerd" culture).[11] These interests overlapped as well with those of audiences for European electronic music and American minimalism, though the more recent alignment of this music and its audiences with trends within postpunk music has obscured these links. Like heavy metal, progressive rock received little critical favor in the American rock press, which tended to regard jazz-rock fusion as the most important of the avant-garde tendencies during this period.

The distinction between heavy metal and progressive rock audiences began to weaken in the middle and late 1970s. American groups that combined features of these two forms emerged and achieved considerable success (Boston, Kansas, Styx, etc.), and this hybrid sound came to be characteristic of album-oriented rock radio. One effect of this was the growing mainstream acceptance of progressive rock in general and decline in the subcultural activity surrounding it.

The convergence of heavy metal and progressive rock audiences is in several respects paradoxical, as is the later penetration of adult contemporary radio formats by heavy metal bands such as Journey. It is tempting to suggest that, despite progressive rock's consistent nonemployment of erotic motifs and heavy metal's aggressive staging of masculine sexuality – and despite the former's aspirations to status as "serious" music and the latter's populist promise of rock in its purest form – both displayed similar forms of opposition to the constraints and concerns of the Top 40 single. While heavy metal is commonly and justifiably perceived as an expression of violent sexuality, many of its most popular manifestations are explorations of nonromantic and nonerotic themes, whose fantastic and "philosophical" components are evidence of heavy metal's links to a continuing drug-based culture and to many of the same remnants of psychedelia that recurred in progressive rock. (Led Zeppelin's song "Stairway to Heaven" is the best-known example of this.)

The major stylistic components of heavy metal iconography may be inventoried as follows: long hair for both performers and audiences; denim jackets and jeans among audience members; smoke bombs as an element of stage performances; marijuana smoking and the taking of depressant drugs (Quaaludes and alcohol, etc.). On album covers: eclecticism at the beginning, but the gradual cohering of an iconography combining satanic imagery and motifs from heroic fantasy illustration, which could be found increasingly too on the backs of jean jackets, automobiles and vans, T-shirts, pinball machines (and, with the later influence of punk, on buttons). The remarkable aspect of traits such as long hair and denim jackets is their persistence and longevity within heavy metal culture long after they had ceased to be fashionable across the wider spectrum of North American youth culture. This itself reflected a decade-long shift whereby the heavy metal look came to acquire connotations of low socioeconomic position. While this might seem incompatible with my characterization of heavy metal audiences as largely suburban – and therefore, presumably, middle class – it would seem that the heavy metal audience, by the early 1980s, consisted to a significant extent of suburban males who did not acquire postsecondary education and who increasingly found that their socioeconomic prospects were not as great as those of their parents.

The iconography prevalent in heavy metal culture may be seen as the development of (1) certain tendencies emergent within psychedelia, which were in part responsible for the popularization of (2) types of fantasy and science fiction literature and illustration, which, in heavy metal iconography, saw their (3) heroic or masculine features emphasized. It is well known, for example, that, within the hippie counterculture, fantasy literature such as Tolkien's *The Lord of the Rings* was widely read and provided motifs for a wide range of poster art, songs, album covers, and so on. In progressive rock of the early 1970s, related themes dominated, and the commercialization (in poster and book form) of the album covers by artists such as Roger Dean testified to the market for this style. In many cases (Jethro Tull, Genesis) fantastic motifs accompanied the musical invocation of early British history or mythology.

However, the most successfully popularized of these styles was the "heroic fantasy" associated with Conan and spinoff fictional characters. From the late 1960s through the 1970s, this form of fiction passed from paperback novel to high-priced illustrated magazine to conventional comic book format to, ultimately, the cinema: each step was evidence of the genre's broadening appeal and entry into mainstream youth culture. By the mid-1970s, the artwork of Frank Frazetta and others associated with the genre was widely merchandised in poster and calender form, and on the covers of heavy metal albums by such groups as Molly Hatchett. Highly masculine (dominated by an imagery of carnage) and mildly pornographic, this illustrative style has cohered around heavy metal music and its paraphernalia.

The satanic imagery associated with heavy metal iconography almost from its inception (by Black Sabbath) grew out of stylistic traits present within psychedelia (such as those found on early Grateful Dead albums), and its convergence with elements of heroic fantasy illustraion came near the middle of the decade. However, it is arguable whether the readership of fantasy literature overlaps significantly with the audience for heavy metal music (though the audience for heroic fantasy films likely does). The readership of *Heavy Metal* magazine, for example, despite its title, includes more fans of progressive rock than of heavy metal, which is to be expected in that both the magazine and these types of music are the centers of subcultural activity. Studies have demonstrated the low involvement of heavy metal audiences in print media and their high movie attendance.[12]

What heavy metal iconography did do was contribute to the development of a 1970s kitsch, to the proliferation of fantasy and satanic imagery as vehicle and pinball arcade decor, as poster art and T-shirt illustration. For the most part, this has meant inscribing a masculine-heroic element within the fantastic or mystical motifs that surrounded psychedelic and, later, progressive rock. These motifs increasingly stood out against the geometrical-minimalist and retro design principles that became widespread within rock music following the emergence of punk and new wave.

Conclusion

Heavy metal is at once the most consistently successful of forms within rock music and the most marginalized within the discourse of institutionalized rock culture. That literary criticism is not regularly unsettled by the popularity of Harlequin romances while American rock culture regards heavy metal as a "problem" is symptomatic of the tension in the 1970s between the ascension of critical discourse on rock music to respectability and the importance to it of a rock populist reading.

Heavy metal in North America provides one of the purest examples of involvement in rock music as an activity subordinate to, rather than determinant of, peer group formation. While involvement in disco or punk may determine people's choices of types and sites of love and friendship (and even the selection of places to live and work), heavy metal – perhaps because of the inaccessibility of the institutions that produce and disseminate it – does not.

For young men, at least, involvement in rock music is perhaps the most useful index of the relationship between knowledge/competence and physical/sexual presence. Despite my concentration on heavy metal, the most male-dominated of rock's forms, and the most blatant in its associations of masculinity with physical violence and power, I regard the 1970s as significant precisely for the ways in which certain types of rock (glitter, punk) accomplished important interventions in sexual politics. That these interventions and their effects were major, while heavy metal remained the most popular form of rock during this decade, is evidence of the complexity and breadth of rock culture.

Notes

1. B. Anderson, P. Hesbacher, K. P. Etzkorn, and R. S. Denisoff, "Hit Record Trends, 1940–77," *Journal of Communications 30*, No. 2 (Spring 1980), p. 41; R. Peterson and D. Berger, "Entrepreneurship in Organizations: evidence from the popular music industry," *Administrative Science Quarterly 16* (1971), pp. 97–107; P. Titus, "The Rise and Fall of the First Album," *New York Rocker* (September 1980), pp. 24–5.

2. It is true that this fluidity of roles was a characteristic as well of early 1960s pop-rock, wherein songwriters such as Goffin and King might write a song and record it under a concocted group name. The crucial difference is that creative activity in the early 1970s was not based on small-scale enterprise and the anonymity of certain roles. Rather, the high level of freelance activity and the critical discourse within the early 1970s resulted in producers sob groups being seen as highly personalized artists, whose work with others was regarded as creative collaboration.

3. See for example S. Chapple and R. Garofalo, *Rock 'n' Roll Is Here to Pay* (Chicago: Nelson-Hall, 1980).

4. Ibid.

5. See H. Mooney, "Twilight of the Age of Aquarius? Popular music in the 1970s," *Popular Music and Society 7* (1980), p. 185.

6. Jim Miller, "Led Zeppelin," in J. Miller (ed.), *The Rolling Stone Illustrated History of Rock and Roll* (New York: Rolling Stone Press/Random House, 1976), p. 306.

7. See P. Fornatele and J. Mills, *Radio in the Television Age* (Woodstock, NY: Overlook Press, 1980), p. 77.

8 M. Brake, *The Sociology of Youth Culture and Youth Subcultures* (London: Routledge & Kegan Paul, 1980), p. vii.

9. See Fornatele and Mills, *Radio*, p. 74.

10. Simon Frith and Angela McRobbie, "Rock and Sexuality," *Screen Education*, No. 29 (Winter 1978/9), p. 8.

11.   The source of the demographic information on science fiction reading and muscial prefer-
      ences is a personal interview with Len Mogel, publisher of *Heavy Metal* magaizine, in July
      1981. The link between subcultural involvement and science fiction and "nerdishness" is
      no more absolute than are the definitions of these attributes, but is based on my reading of
      several hundred science fiction fanzines from this period. The "nerd" quality of a high
      percentage of those involved in science fiction fandom is often readily acknowledged by
      those active therein, and their marginality within youth peer groups has been confirmed in
      sociological examinations of this subculture, such as Fredric Wertham's extremely flawed
      The World of Fanzines.

12.   See G. C. Bruner, "The Association Between Record Purchase Volume and Other Music-
      related Characteristics," *Popular Music and Society 3* (1979), p. 237.

56

'Represent': Race, Space and Place in Rap Music

Murray Forman*

Say somethin' positive, well positive ain't where I live
I live around the corner from West Hell
Two blocks from South Shit and once in a jail cell
The sun never shined on my side of the street, see?

(Naughty By Nature, 'Ghetto Bastard
(Everything's Gonna Be Alright)', 1991, Isba/Tommy Boy Records)

If you're from Compton you know it's the 'hood where it's good

(Compton's Most Wanted,
'Raised in Compton', 1991, Epic/Sony)

Introduction

Hip hop's capacity to circumvent the constraints and limiting social conditions of young Afro-American and Latino youths has been examined and celebrated by cultural critics and scholars in various contexts since its inception in the mid-1970s. For instance, the 8 February 1999 issue of US magazine *Time* featured a cover photo of ex-Fugees and five-time Grammy award winner Lauryn Hill with the accompanying headline 'Hip-Hop Nation: After 20 Years – how it's changed America'. Over the years, however, there has been little attention granted to the implications of hip hop's spatial logics. *Time's* coverage is relatively standard in perceiving the hip hop nation as a historical construct rather than a geo-cultural amalgamation of personages and practices that are spatially dispersed.

Tricia Rose (1994) arguably goes the furthest in introducing a spatial analysis when she details the ways that hip hop continually displays a clever transformative creativity that is endlessly capable of altering the uses of technologies and space. Her specific references to hip hop culture and space stress the importance of the 'postindustrial city'

*Pp. 65–90 from *Popular Music*, vol. 19, no. 1. © 2000 by Cambridge University Press. Reprinted with permission from the author and publisher.

as the central urban influence, 'which provided the context for creative development among hip hop's earliest innovators, shaped their cultural terrain, access to space, materials, and education' (1994, p. 34). As this suggests, the particularities of urban space themselves are subjected to the deconstructive and reconstructive practices of rap artists. Thus, when, in another context, Iain Chambers refers to rap as 'New York's "sound system" . . . sonorial graffiti' with 'the black youth culture of Harlem and the Bronx twisting technology into new cultural shape' (1985, p. 190), he opens the conceptual door onto corresponding strategies that give rise to the radical transformation of the sites where these cultures cohere and converge or the spaces that are reimagined and, importantly, remapped. Rap artists therefore emerge not only as aberrant users of electronic and digital technologies but also as alternative cartographers for what the Samoan-American group Boo Yaa Tribe has referred to in an album title as 'a new funky nation'.

Indeed, there is very little about today's society that is not, at some point, imbued with a spatial character and this is no less true for the emergence and production of spatial categories and identities in rap music and the hip hop cultures of which it is a central component. Rap music presents a case worthy of examination and provides a unique set of contexts for the analyses of public discourses pertaining to youth, race and space. Rap music is one of the main sources within popular culture of a sustained and in-depth examination and analysis of the spatial partitioning of race and the diverse experiences of being young and black in America. It can be observed that space and race figure prominently as organising concepts implicated in the delineation of a vast range of fictional or actually existing social practices which are represented in narrative and lyrical form. In this chapter, I seek to illuminate the central importance of spatiality in the organising principles of value, meaning and practice within hip hop culture. My further intent is to explore the question of how the dynamics of space, place and race get taken up by rap artists as themes and topics and how they are located within a wider range of circulating social discourses. The prioritisation of spatial practices and spatial discourses that form a basis of hip hop culture offers a means through which to view both the *ways* that spaces and places are constructed and the *kinds* of spaces or places that are constructed.

This chapter traces the way in which hip hop's popularity spread from New York to other US cities, most notably Philadelphia and Los Angeles but eventually more geographically marginal cities such as Seattle, and it discusses changes that have taken place in rap production, particularly the rise of artist-owned labels. Such developments encouraged the emergence of distinctive regional rap sounds and styles, as well as strong local allegiances and territorial rivalries, as the identities and careers of rap acts became more closely tied to the city and to its specific neighbourhoods ('hoods) and communities. The chapter examines the effects of all this on the spatial discourse of rap. It points to a gradual shift within rap from a concern with broad, generalised spaces, to the representation of specific named cities and 'hoods (as illustrated by Gansta Rap from the Californian city of Compton which celebrates and glorifies Compton as well as the street warrior and gang rivalry) and the representation of smaller-scale, more narrowly defined and highly detailed places (as illustrated by rap from the North West city of Seattle which has a distinctively local flavour).

Locating Hip Hop

Describing the early stages of rap music's emergence within the hip hop culture for an MTV 'Rap-umentary', Grandmaster Flash, one of the core DJs of the early scene, recalls the spatial distribution of sound systems and crews in metropolitan New York:

> We had territories. It was like, Kool Herc had the west side. Bam had Bronx River. DJ Breakout had way uptown past Gun Hill. Myself, my area was like 138th Street, Cypress Avenue, up to Gun Hill, so that we all had our territories and we all had to respect each other.

The documentary's images embellish Flash's commentary, displaying a computer generated map of the Bronx with coloured sections demarcating each DJ's territory as it is mentioned, graphically separating the enclaves that comprise the main area of operations for the competing sound systems.

This emphasis on territoriality involves more than just a geographical arrangement of cultural workers and the regionalism of cultural practices. It illuminates a particular relationship to space or, more accurately, a relationship to particular places. As Flash conveys it, the sound systems that formed the backbone of the burgeoning hip hop scene were identified by their audiences and followers according to the overlapping influences of personae and turf. The territories were tentatively claimed through the ongoing cultural practices that occurred within their bounds and were reinforced by the circulation of those who recognised and accepted their perimeters. It is not at all insignificant that most of the dominant historical narratives pertaining to the emergence of hip hop (i.e., Hager 1984; Toop 1984) identify a transition from gang-oriented affiliations (formed around protection of turf) to music and break dance affiliations that maintained and, in some cases, intensified the important structuring systems of territoriality.

Flash's reference to the importance of 'respect' is not primarily addressing a respect for the skills or character of his competitors (although, elsewhere (George 1993) he acknowledges this as well). Rather, his notion of respect is related to the geographies that he maps; it is based on the existence of circumscribed domains of authority and dominance that have been established among the various DJs. These geographies are inhabited and bestowed with value; they are understood as lived places and localised sites of significance, as well as being understood within the market logic that includes a product (the music in its various live or recorded forms) and a consumer base (various audience formations). The proprietary discourse also implies, therefore, that even in its infancy hip hop cartography was to some extent shaped by a refined capitalist logic and the existence of distinct market regions. Without sacrificing the basic geographic components of territory, possession and group identity that play such an important role among gang-oriented activities, the representation of New York's urban spaces was substantially revised as hip hop developed.

Clearly, however, the geographical boundaries that Flash describes and which are visually mapped in the documentary were never firm or immovable. They were cultural boundaries that were continually open to negotiation and renegotiation by those who inhabited their terrains and who circulated throughout the city's boroughs. As the main form of musical expression within the hip hop culture, the early DJ sound systems featured a series of practices that linked the music to other mobile practices, such as graffiti art and 'tagging'. Together, these overlapping practices and methods of constructing place-based identities, and of inscribing and enunciating individual and collective presence, created the bonds upon which affiliations were forged within specific social geographies. Hip hop's distinct practices introduced new forms of expression that were contextually linked to conditions in a city comprised of an amalgamation of neighbourhoods and boroughs with their own highly particularised social norms and cultural nuances.

Hip Hop, Space and Place

Rap music takes the city and its multiple spaces as the foundation of its cultural production. In the music and lyrics, the city is an audible presence, explicitly cited and digitally sampled in the reproduction of the aural textures of the urban environment, Since its inception in the mid-to-late 1970s, hip hop culture has always maintained fiercely defended local ties and an in-built element of competition waged through hip hop's cultural forms of rap, breakdancing and graffiti. This competition has traditionally been staged within geographical boundaries that demarcate turf and territory among various crews, cliques, and posses, extending and altering the spatial alliances that had previously cohered under other organisational structures, including but not exclusive to gangs. Today, a more pronounced level of spatial awareness is one of the key factors distinguishing rap and hip hop culture from the many other cultural and subcultural youth formations currently vying for attention.

Throughout its historical evolution, it is evident that there has been a gradually escalating urgency with which minority youth use rap in the deployment of discourses of urban locality or 'place', with the trend accelerating noticeably since 1987–8. With the discursive shift from the spatial abstractions framed by the notion of 'the ghetto' to the more localised and specific discursive construct of 'the 'hood' occurring in 1987–8 (roughly corresponding with the rise and impact of rappers on the US West Coast), there has been an enhanced emphasis on the powerful ties to place that both anchor rap acts to their immediate environments and set them apart from other environments and other 'hoods as well as from other rap acts and their crews which inhabit similarly demarcated spaces.

Commenting in 1988 on rap's 'nationwide' expansions beyond New York's boroughs, Nelson George writes, 'Rap and its Hip Hop musical underpinning is now the national youth music of black America . . . rap's gone national and is in the process of going regional' (George 1992, p. 80). George was right, as rap was rising out of the regions and acts were emerging from the South (Miami-based 2 Live Crew or Houston's The Geto Boys), the Northwest (Seattle's Sir Mix-A-Lot and Kid Sensation), the San Francisco Bay area (Digital Underground, Tupac. Too Short), Los Angeles (Ice T, N.W.A.) and elsewhere. Indeed, the significance of the east–west split within US rap cannot be overstated since it has led to several intense confrontations between artists representing each region and is arguably the single most divisive factor within US hip hop to date. Until the mid-1990s, artists associated with cities in the Midwest or southern states often felt obligated to align themselves with either East or West, or else they attempted to sidestep the issue deftly without alienating audiences and deriding either coast. In the past several years, however, Houston, Atlanta and New Orleans have risen as important rap production centres and have consequently emerged as powerful forces in their own right.

Today, the emphasis is on place, and groups explicitly advertise their home environments with names such as Compton's Most Wanted, Detroit's Most Wanted, the Fifth Ward Boyz, and South Central Cartel, or else they structure their home territory into titles and lyrics, constructing a new internally meaningful hip hop cartography. The explosion of localized production centres and regionally influential producers and artists has drastically altered the hip hop map and production crews have sprung up throughout North America. These producers have also demonstrated a growing tendency to incorporate themselves as localised businesses (often buying or starting companies unrelated to the music industry in their local neighbourhoods, such as auto customising and repair shops) and to employ friends, family members and members of their wider neighbourhoods. Extending Nelson George's observation, it now seems possible to say that rap, having gone regional, is in the process of going local.

The Regional Proliferation of Artist-Owned Record Labels

Reflecting on the intensification of regional rap activity within the US during what might be defined as the genre's 'middle-school' historical period,[1] Nelson George writes that 1987 was 'a harbinger of the increasing quality of non-New York hip hop', citing as evidence the fact that three of the four finalists in the New Music Seminar's DJ Competition were from 'outside the Apple – Philadelphia's Cash Money, Los Angeles's Joe Cooley, and Mr. Mix of Miami's 2 Live Crew' (George 1992, p. 30). In the pages of *Billboard*, he observed that despite New York's indisputable designation as the 'home' of rap, Philadelphia rappers in particular (most notably, DJ Jazzy Jeff and the Fresh Prince) were making inroads on the scene and on the charts, making it 'rap's second city' (George, ibid.). This expansion was facilitated by the emergent trend in the development of artist-owned independent labels and management companies which entered into direct competition with non-artist-owned companies.

After years of bogus contracts, management conflicts, and poor representation, a growing number of artists began dividing their duties between recording or performing, locating and producing new talent, and managing their respective record companies. By forming self-owned labels and publishing companies and establishing themselves as autonomous corporate entities, forward-thinking rap artists were also able to maintain greater creative control over their production while ensuring increased returns on their sales. In a rather excessive discourse, artists spoke of throwing off the corporate shackles of the recording industry as well as invoking the quite separate issues of building something of which one can be proud or being remunerated in a more lucrative manner.

Once several key labels such as Luther Campbell's Skyywalker Records and Eazy-E's Ruthless Records had been established and had proven the viability of the venture, their initiatives were rapidly reproduced as numerous artists followed suit. For many recording artists, to gain wealth and material renumeration for their work suddenly meant learning the production and management side of the industry and exercising entrepreneurial skills as well. As the trend expanded, small artist-owned and operated labels burgeoned and another tier was added to the industry. With the rise of artist-owned labels there was also an increased emphasis on regional and local affiliations and an articulation of pride and loyalty in each label, its artist roster, and the central locale of operation.

Rap is characteristically produced within a system of extremely close-knit local affiliations, forged within particular cultural settings and urban minority youth practices. Yet the developments in the rap industry, whereby production houses or record labels might be identified on the basis of their regional and local zones of operation, are not unique to this current period. For instance, independent 'race record' labels, which targeted blacks in the South and in larger northern urban centres throughout the 1920s and 1930s, flourished in part due to the enhanced mobility of black populations which maintained their affinities for the various regional blues styles. Nelson George's consistent attention to black musical tradition, the music industry's gradual permutations, and rap's growing national influence led him to note in *Billboard* that 'regional music used to be the backbone of black music and – maybe – it will be again' (31 May 1986, p. 23). He recalls black American musical production in the immediate post-World War 2 period when independent labels were dispersed across the nation, recording locally and regionally based artists while servicing the needs of black music consumers within these regional markets.

Examining the history of black popular music in the 1960s and 1970s, the names Motown, Stax, or Philadelphia International Records (PIR) evoke images of composers, producers and musical talent working within very specific studio contexts in Detroit, Memphis, and Philadelphia. The dispersed independent labels and production sites that operated from the 1950s through the 1970s are therefore culturally meaningful and relevant to descriptions of black music of the period as they convey an idea of consistency and identifiable signature sounds or styles. This trend has continued with rap, with more pronounced and explicit connection to specific locales and the articulations of geography, place and identity that sets the genre apart from many of its musical predecessors.

Of the smaller labels that had thrived in the 1950s, 1960s, and 1970s, most disappeared as musical tastes shifted, as economic transitions evolved, or as the industry majors swallowed them or bumped them out of the market by introducing their own specialty labels. Towards the end of the 1980s, the US music industry was no longer even primarily American, with the major parent companies being massive transnational entities with corporate offices based in several countries. Yet, in both rock and rap there was a resurgence of regional production in the mid-to-late 1980s and, with it, the resurgence of regionally distinct styles. In the black music sector these were exemplified by the Minneapolis funk that was a trademark of artists like Prince, The Time, Jimmy Jam and Terry Lewis, or Jesse Johnson; the Washington, DC go-go sound of Chuck Brown,

Redd and the Boys, and especially Trouble Funk; and from Chicago, house music exemplified by DJ Frankie Knuckles. Rap production in New York, Los Angeles and Miami also began to display regionally distinct 'flavours' to a greater extent as individual producers emerged with their own trademark styles and influences. Individual studios such as Chung King in New York also became associated with specific production styles and sounds in rap.

As evidence of the arrival of artist-owned labels in the rap business, in December, 1989, *Billboard* featured advertisements in a special section on rap that illustrated the trend. Among these were ads for Eazy-E's Ruthless Records (Compton, CA), Luther Campbell's Skyywalker Records (Miami, FL), and Ice T's Rhyme Syndicate (South Central LA). Appearing alongside these were advertisements for the established independent rap labels Def Jam, Tommy Boy and Jive as well as ads for the newer 'street' divisions of major labels including Atlantic ('The Strength of the Street'), MCA ('Wanna Rap? MCA Raps. Word!') and Epic ('Epic in Total Control. No Loungin', Just Lampin"). The phenomenon has since evolved to the extent that artist-owned operations have become relatively standard in the industry, existing as influential players alongside the major labels.

As a later entrant, Death Row Records (initiated in 1992 by principal investors Suge Knight and former member of the rap group Niggaz with Attitude (N.W.A.) Dr Dre) flourished through a lucrative co-ownership and distribution alliance with upstart Interscope Records, which was itself half-owned by Time Warner's Atlantic Group. Although a series of misfortunes in 1996–7 decimated the label, it rose to virtual dominance in the rap field between 1992 and 1997 with top-charting releases by Dr Dre, Snoop Doggy Dogg, and Tupac Shakur as well as the soundtrack albums *Deep Cover* (1992) and *Murder Was the Case* (1994). One of the factors that characterised Death Row Records from its inception and which is common to the dozens of artist-owned and operated rap labels to emerge in the late 1980s and early 1990s, however, is an organised structure rooted in localised 'posse' affiliations.

Homeboys and Production Posses

Greg Tate suggests that, 'every successful rap group is a black fraternal organization, a posse' (1992, p. 134). Of the same theme, Tricia Rose writes that 'rappers' emphasis on posses and neighbourhoods has brought the ghetto back into the public consciousness' (1994, p. 11). For Public Enemy's Chuck D, posse formations are a necessary response to the fragmentive effects of capitalism: 'the only way that you exist within that mould is that you have to put together a "posse", or a team to be able to penetrate that structure, that block, that strong as steel structure that no individual can break' (Eure & Spady 1991, p. 330). As each of these commentators suggests, the posse is the fundamental social unit binding a rap act and its production crew together, creating a collective identity that is rooted in place and within which the creative process unfolds. It is not rare for an entire label to be defined along posse lines with the musical talent, the producers and various peripheral associates bonding under the label's banner.

With collective identities being evident as a nascent reference throughout rap's history in group names like The Sugarhill Gang, Doug E. Fresh and the Get Fresh Crew, X-Clan, or the 2 Live Crew, the term 'posse' was later unambiguously adopted by rap artists such as California's South Central Posse or Orlando's DJ Magic Mike, whose crew records under the name 'the Royal Posse'. In virtually all cases, recording acts align themselves within a relatively coherent posse structure, sharing labels and producers, appearing on each other's recordings and touring together.

The term *posse* is defined as a 'strong force or company' (*Concise Oxford Dictionary*, 1985) and for many North Americans it summons notions of lawlessness and frontier justice that were standard thematic elements of Hollywood westerns in the 1940s and 1950s. This is, in fact, the basis of the term as it is applied within rap circles, although its current significance is related more precisely to the ways in which the Jamaican posse culture has over the years adapted the expressive terminology and gangster imagery of the cinema to its own cultural systems. In her illuminating research on the sinister complexities of the Jamaican posse underworld, Laurie Gunst (1995) explains how the posse system grew under the specific economic, political, and cultural conditions of mid-1970s Jamaica, evolving into a stratified and violent gang culture that gained strength through the marijuana, cocaine and crack trade. As she explains, the Jamaican posse system has, since 1980, been transplanted to virtually every major North American city.

The Jamaican posse expansion is important in this context as it coincides almost precisely with the emergence of rap and hip hop in New York's devastated uptown ghetto environments. This connection is strengthened when rap's hybrid origins that were forged in the convergence of Jamaican sound systems and South Bronx funk are considered. The concept of the posse has, through various social mechanisms and discursive overlays, been traced upon many of rap's themes, images, and postures that take the forms of the pimp, hustler, gambler and gangster in the music's various sub-genres that evolved after 1987. Rap has also been influenced by the gangland models provided by the New York mafia and Asian Triad gangs.

Since roughly 1987 hip hop culture has also been influenced by alliances associated with West Coast gang systems. Numerous rap album covers and videos feature artists and their posses representing their gang, their regional affiliations or their local 'hood with elaborate hand gestures. The practice escalated to such an extent that, in an effort to dilute the surging territorial aggression, Black Entertainment Television (BET) passed a rule forbidding explicitly gang-related hand signs on its popular video programmes.

"The 'Hood Took Me Under": Home, Turf and Identity

It is necessary to recognise that the home territory of a rapper or rap group is a testing ground, a place to hone skills and to gain a local reputation. This is accurately portrayed in the 1992 Ernest Dickerson film *Juice* where the expression 'local' is attributed to the young DJ Q, in one instance suggesting community ties and home alliances whereas, in another context, it is summoned as a pejorative term that reflects a lack of success and an inability to mobilise his career beyond the homefront. In interviews and on recordings most rappers refer to their early days, citing the time spent with their 'home boys', writing raps, perfecting their turntable skills, and taking the stage at parties and local clubs or dances (Cross 1993). Their perspective emerges from within the highly localised conditions that they know and the places they inhabit.

As a site of affiliation and circulation, the 'hood provides a setting for particular group interactions which are influential in rap music's evolution. In rap, there is a widespread sense that an act cannot succeed without first gaining approval and support from the crew and the 'hood. Successful acts are expected to maintain connections to the 'hood and to 'keep it real' thematically, rapping about situations, scenes and sites that comprise the lived experience of the 'hood. At issue is the complex question of authenticity as rap posses continually strive to reaffirm their connections to the 'hood in an attempt to mitigate the negative accusations that they have sold out in the event of commercial or crossover success. Charisse Jones has noted a dilemma confronting successful rap artists who suddenly have the economic means to 'get over' and leave the 'hood. As she writes in the *New York Times* (24 September 1995, p. 43), contemporary artists such as Snoop Dogg or Ice T are often criticised for rapping about ghetto poverty and gang aggression while living in posh suburban mansions.

Those who stay in the 'hood generally do so to be closer to friends and family, closer to the posse. While a common rationale for staying in the 'hood is familiarity and family bonds, in numerous cases artists also justify their decisions to stay along a creative rationale, suggesting that the 'hood provides the social contexts and raw resources for their lyrics. Others leave with some regret, suggesting that the 'hood may constitute 'home' but its various tensions and stresses make it an entirely undesirable place to live (this is even more frequent among rappers with children to support and nurture); there is no romanticising real poverty or real danger.

The 'hood is, however, regularly constructed within the discursive frame of the 'home', and the dual process of 'turning the 'hood out' or 'representing' (which involves creating a broader profile for the home territory and its inhabitants while showing respect for the nurture it provides) is now a required practice among hardcore rap acts. The posse is always explicitly acknowledged and individual members are greeted on disk and in live concerts with standard 'shout outs' that frequently cite the streets and localities from which they hail. This continual reference to the important value of social relations based in the 'hood refutes the damning images of an oppressed and joyless underclass that are so prevalent in the media and contemporary social analyses. Rap may frequently portray the nation's gritty urban underside, but its creators also communicate the importance of places and the people that build community within them. In this interpretation, there is an insistent emphasis on support, nurture and community that coexists with the grim representations that generally cohere in the images and discourses of ghetto life.

As in all other popular music forms, 'paying dues' is also part of the process of embarking on a rap music career, and the local networks of support and encouragement, from in-group affiliations to local club and music scenes, are exceedingly important factors in an act's professional development. One way that this is facilitated is through the posse alliances and local connections that form around studios and producers. For example, in describing the production house once headed by DJ Mark, The 45 King, the rap artist Fab 5 Freddy recalls that 'he had this posse called the Flavor Unit out there in New Jersey . . . He has like a Hip Hop training room out there, an incredible environment where even if you weren't good when you came in, you'd get good just being around there' (Nelson & Gonzales 1991, p. xiii). This pattern is replicated in numerous instances and is also exemplified by the production/posse structure of Rap-A-Lot Records in Houston (home to acts such as the Geto Boys, Scarface, Big Mike, Caine, and The Fifth Ward Boyz) where the company was forced to relocate its offices because 'artists were always kicking it there with their posses like it was a club' (*Rap Sheet*, October 1992, p. 18). By coming up through the crew, young promising artists learn the ropes, acquire lessons in craft and showmanship, attain stage or studio experience and exposure and, quite frequently, win record deals based on their apprentice-ships and posse connections.

Few rap scholars (Tricia Rose and Brian Cross being notable exceptions) have paid attention to these formative stages and the slow processes of developing MC and DJ skills. There is, in fact, a trajectory to an artist's development that is seldom accounted for. In practice, artists' lyrics and rhythms must achieve success on the home front first, where the flow, subject matter, style and image must resonate meaningfully among those who share common bonds to place, to the posse and to the 'hood. In this sense, when rappers refer to the 'local flavour', they are identifying the detailed inflections that respond to and reinforce the significance of the music's particular sites of origin and which might be recognised by others elsewhere as being unique, interesting and, ulti-mately, marketable.

The Spatialisation of Production Styles

The posse structures that privilege place and the 'hood can be seen as influential ele-ments in the evolution of new rap artists as well as relevant forces in the emergence of new, regionally definable sounds and discourses about space and place. For example, critics and rappers alike acknowledge the unique qualities of the West Coast G-funk sound which defined a production style that emerged with Dr Dre's work on the *Deep Cover* soundtrack and the release of his 1992 classic *The Chronic* (Death Row/Inter-scope), and arguably reached its apex with the 1994 release of Warren G's *Regulate . . . G Funk Era* (Violator/Rush Associated Labels). Other local artists in this period, such as the Boo Yaa Tribe, Above the Law, Compton's Most Wanted, and DJ Quik, also prominently featured variations on the G-funk sound and reinforced its influence in the industry as an identifiable West coast subgenre. G-funk makes ample use of standard funk grooves by artists including George Clinton, Bootsy Collins, Gap Band, or the late Roger Troutman, and is characterised as being 'laid-back' and sparse, featuring slow beats and longer sample loops. While it was regarded as a regionally distinct sound, it was also often related specifically to Dr Dre's production style and was comparatively categorised by its difference from the more cacophonous East Coast jams (recognisable in the early work of the Bomb Squad, the production crew of the rap act Public Enemy). As Brian Cross (1993) notes, however, the impact of the G-funk style among California rap acts is also related to the extended influence of late 1970s funk music in the Southwest that was a consequence of limited access to independently produced and distributed rap product in the early 1980s, delaying rap's geographic expansion from New York to the Los Angeles area.

Explaining the Bomb Squad's production processes following the release of Public Enemy's *Fear of a Black Planet* (1990, Def Jam), Chuck D describes his production posse's familiarity with various regional styles and tastes and their attempts to integrate the differences into the album's tracks. As he states:

> Rap has different feels and different vibes in different parts of the country. For example, people in New York City don't drive very often, so New York used to be about walking around with your radio. But that doesn't really exist anymore. It became unfashionable because some people were losing their *lives* over them, and also people don't want to carry them, so now it's more like 'Hey, I've got my Walkman'. For that reason, there's a treble type of thing going on; they're not getting much of the bass. So rap music in New York City is a headphone type of thing, whereas in Long Island or Philadelphia . . . it's more of a bass type thing. (Dery 1990, p. 90)

These regional distinctions between the 'beats' are borne out in the example of the Miami production houses of Luther Campbell or Orlando's Magic Mike. In Florida (and to some extent, Georgia) the focus is on the bass – Florida 'booty bass' or 'booty boom' as it has been termed – which offers a deeper, 'phatter', and almost subsonic vibration that stands out as a regionally distinct and authored style. Within US rap culture, artists and fans alike reflect an acute awareness that people in different parts of the country produce and enjoy regional variations on the genre; they experience rap differently, structuring it into their social patterns according to the norms that prevail in a given urban environment. Thus, the regional taste patterns in South Florida are partially influenced by the central phenomenon of car mobility and the practice of stacking multiple 10- or 15-inch bass speakers and powerful sub-woofers into car trunks and truck beds.

Add to these stylistic distinctions the discursive differences within rap from the various regions (i.e., the aforementioned Gangsta Rap from the West Coast crews, the chilling, cold-blooded imagery from Houston's 'Bloody Nickle' crews on Rap-A-Lot Records, or the 'pimp, playa and hustla' themes that are standard among Oakland and San Francisco cliques), the localised posse variations in vocal style and slang, or the site-specific references in rap lyrics to cities, 'hoods, and crews, and a general catalogue of differences in form and content becomes clearly audible. What these elements indicate is that, while the rap posse provides a structured identity for its members, it can also provide a referential value to the production qualities and the sound of the musical product with which it is associated.

Rap's Spatial Discourse

In his enquiry into the cultural resonance and meanings of the term 'the 'hood', Paul Gilroy poses the question, 'how is black life in one 'hood connected to life in others?

Can there be a blackness that connects, articulates, synchronises experiences and histories across the diaspora space?' (1992, p. 308). He criticises the idea of 'nation' that has emerged as an important structuring concept in American hip hop culture (mainly after 1987) and remains sceptical of the value invested in the discourses of 'family' unity (communicated in the rhetoric of black brotherhood and sisterhood) when there is so much territorial antagonism evident in the strands of rap that privilege the spatialities of gang culture and turf affiliation: Gilroy expresses his perplexity with the closed contours that the 'hood represents, suggesting that its inward-turning spatial perspectives inhibit dialogue across divided social territories and cultural zones. He further argues that redemptive attempts to appeal to either the black 'nation', or to the 'family' of internationally dispersed blacks in the rap subgenre known as 'message rap' are ill-conceived and based in a particularly North Americanist viewpoint that harbours its own exclusive and hierarchically stratified biases.

Perhaps more in line with Gilroy's expansive, trans-Atlantic visions of rap's diasporic potential is the track 'Ludi' (1991, Island Records) by the Canadian act the Dream Warriors. Based in Toronto, the group is part of one of the world's largest expatriate Caribbean communities. Like Gilroy's London, Toronto could be seen as an

> important junction point or crossroads on the webbed pathways of black Atlantic political culture. It is revealed to be a place where, by virtue of factors like the informality of racial segregation, the configuration of class relations, the contingency of linguistic convergences, global phenomena such as anti-colonial and emancipationist political formations are still being sustained, reproduced, and amplified. (Gilroy 1992, p. 95)

In mapping a cultural 'crossroads', the song Ludi utilises an early reggae rhythm and a lightly swinging melody (based on a sample of the Jamaican classic 'My Conversation', released in 1968 by The Uniques) that taps into a particularly rich moment in the evolution of the reggae style and revives a well-known Jamaican track while relocating it within the performative contexts of hip hop.

'Ludi' (which refers to a board game) begins with rapper King Lou stating that the song is for his mother – who wants something to dance to – and his extended family to whom he offers the musical sounds of their original home environment. The family to which he refers is not, in the immediate sense, the family of black-identified brothers and sisters that cohere within nationalistic and essentialist discourse but literally his siblings. He then expands his dedication to the wider 'family' of blacks with a comprehensive roll-call of the English and Spanish-speaking Caribbean islands and Africa which inform (but by no means determine) his cultural identity. There is no attempt to privilege an originary African heritage nor is there a nostalgic appeal to the Caribbean heritage. This extensive list recognises Toronto's hybrid Afro-Caribbean community and refers directly to a locally manifested culture of international black traditions (rather than a single tradition of essentialist blackness) within which the Dream Warriors developed as young artists. The song's bridge also reinforces the Caribbean connection by making several references to the turntable practices of Jamaican sound systems that are mainstays throughout internationally dispersed Caribbean communities.

Later in the track, King Lou's cohort, Capital Q, reminds him that 'there are other places than the islands that play Ludi. Why don't you run it down for the people?' Here, employing a distinctly Jamaican DJ 'toaster' dialect, King Lou provides a wider expression of black diasporic identification as he expands his list to include Canada, the UK, and the United States, countries where the Afro-Caribbean presence is the largest and most influential. He concludes by mentioning his international record labels 4th and Broadway and Island Records and, finally, names the influential Toronto-based independent production house, Beat Factory, that first recorded the group. In this last reference to Beat Factory he effectively returns the scale to the local, closing the circle that positions the Dream Warriors within a global/local system of circulation.

There is no simple means of assessing the impact of this expansive global/local perspective but, within Gilroy's innovative theoretical *oeuvre,* the track can be celebrated for the ways in which its musical and lyrical forms reinforce the dispersed geographies of contemporary black cultures without falling victim to the conservative reductions of black essentialism. Without cleaving towards either the rhetorical rigidity of black nationalist Rap or the nihilistic vitriol of gangster rappers ('niggaz with (bad) attitude'), the Dream Warriors present an alternative path. As 'Ludi' illustrates, the group unselfconsciously articulates an evolving hybrid identity informed by transnational migrations that are actively manifested on local grounds.

On the other end of the rap spectrum is the example of artists who mainly operate within a discursive field featuring spatialised themes of intense locality. Whereas the proponents of Message Rap evoke an expanded vision of black America, it is in contrast to the ghettocentric visions of urban black experience that also emerge in the genre, mainly within the lyrics of Gangsta Rap. Despite many shared perspectives on black oppression and systemic injustices, there exists a tension in the interstices between the expansive nationalisms of Message Rap and the more narrowly defined localisms of Gangsta Rap with its core emphasis on 'the 'hood'. This distance is widened in view of the unapologetic claim among numerous studio gangstas who, like the rap artist Ice Cube on the N.W.A. track 'Gangsta, Gangsta' (1988, Ruthless/Priority), claim that 'life ain't nothin' but bitches and money'. The two subgenres are addressing generally common phenomena in their focus on black struggles for empowerment, yet they are deploying spatial discourses and programmes of action that do not fit easily together.

The emergence of an intensified spatial terminology was not a sudden occurrence, but by 1987 when New York's Boogie Down Productions (also known as BDP), featuring rap acts such as KRS-1, Eazy-E, and Ice T broke onto the scene, the privileging of localised experience rapidly acquired an audible resonance. From New York, BDP released 'South Bronx' (1987, B-Boy), a track that aggressively disputes the allegations of various rappers from Queens who, in the aftermath of Run-D.M.C's commercial successes, claimed that they were rap's true innovators. KRS-1's lyrics reaffirm his home turf in the South Bronx borough as the birthplace of hip hop, reinforcing the message in the now-classic chorus with its chant 'South Bronx, the South, South Bronx'.

Giving name to South Bronx locales and to the artists who inhabited them, anchors his testimony. He attempts to prove its dominance by recounting the genre's formative stages with close attention to locally specific and highly particularised details:

> Remember Bronx River, rolling thick
> With Cool DI Red Alert and Chuck Chillout on the mix
> While Afrika Islam was rocking the jams
> And on the other side of town was a kid named Flash
> Patterson and Millbrook projects
> Casanova all over, ya couldn't stop it
> The Nine Lives crew, the Cypress Boys
> The Real Rock steady taking out these toys
> As hard as it looked, as wild as it seemed
>
> I didn't hear a peep from Queen's . . .
> South Bronx, the South South Bronx . . .

The references to people and places provide a specificity that is comparatively absent in Eazy-E's important (but often overlooked) single release 'Boyz-n-The Hood' (1988, Ruthless/Priority) from the same general period. Musically, 'Boyz-n-The-Hood' is considered to have done little to advance the genre aesthetically. Yet, in its uncompromising linguistic turns and startling descriptions of homeboy leisure (involving beer, 'bitches', and violence), it was riveting and offered a new hardcore funky model for masculine identification in hip hop:

> 'Cause the boyz in the hood are always hard
> Come talkin' that trash and we'll pull your card
> Knowin' nothin' in life but to be legit
> Don't quote me boy, 'cause I ain't sayin' shit.

Describing the LP *Eazy-Duz-It* on which the single first appeared, Havelock Nelson and Michael Gonzales explain that it 'overflows with debris from homophobia to misogyny to excessive violence. And yet, anyone who grew up in the project or any Black ghetto knows these extreme attitudes are right on target' (1991, p. 81). Despite such claims to authenticity, however, it is important to ackowledge that the rugged discourses and sensational imagery of violence and poverty are highly selective and are drawn from a range of mundane, less controversial and less marketable urban experiences.

   Eazy-E's 'Boyz-n-The Hood' reflects many of rap's earlier modes of spatial representation that conceive of the ghetto landscape as a generalised abstract construct, as *space*. The introduction of the terminology of the 'hood, however, also adds a localised nuance to the notion of space that conveys a certain proximity, effectively capturing a narrowed sense of *place* through which young thugs and their potential victims move in tandem. Claims to the representation of authentic street life or 'hood reality emerged with sudden frequency following the rise of Eazy-E and N.W.A., who were among the first to communicate detailed images of closely demarcated space in this manner. This suggests that 'reality', authenticity and reduced spatial scales are conceptually linked among those who developed and sustained the spatial discourses of the 'hood. The main contribution of the track 'Boyz-n-The Hood' is ultimately its influence on the popularisation of a new spatial vocabulary that spread throughout hip hop from all regions as artists from the West Coast gained prominence in the field.

By most accounts, the spatial discourse that coheres around the concept of the 'hood emerges in rap by California-based artists with the greatest frequency and force. But in the popular media as well as in academic treatises, the focus on West Coast rap in this period tends to be on the expressions of 'gangsta' violence and masculine aggression to the exclusion or minimisation of prevalent spatial elements. For example, as David Toop writes, 'the first release on Ruthless Records, launched by rapper Eazy-E and producer Dr Dre in 1986, was like a tabloid report from the crime beat fed through a paper shredder' (1991, p. 180). The very term 'gangsta rap' is more concretely concerned with the articulation of criminality than any other attributes that may emerge from its lyrical and visual texts. Having become sedimented in the popular lexicon as the key or trademark term for the subgenre, it is difficult to challenge critically the primacy of criminality and to replace it with a spatiality that precedes the 'gangsta-ism' that saturates the lyrical texts. The criminal activities that are described in gangsta rap's intense lyrical forms are almost always subordinate to the definitions of space and place within which they are set. It is, therefore, the spatialities of the 'hood that constitute the ascendant concept and are ultimately deserving of discursive pre-eminence.

Since rap's invention, it has become somewhat of a convention for the rapper to be placed at the centre of the world, as the subject around which events unfold and who translates topophilia (love of place) or topophobia (fear of place) into lyrics for wider dissemination. This is illustrated in Ice T's 'Intro' track on his debut album *Rhyme Pays* (1987, Rhyme Syndicate/Sire). As an introduction, the track allows Ice T to present his hip hop curriculum vitae which is explicitly defined in spatial terms:

> A child was born in the East one day
> Moved to the West Coast after his parents passed away
> Never understood his fascination with rhymes or beats
> In poetry he was considered elite
> Became a young gangster in the streets of LA
> Lost connections with his true roots far away . . .

The description of a personal exodus embarked upon by the young rapper under conditions of extreme adversity is crucial to the construction of mystique and legend. Describing his entry into LA gang culture and the rap scene in the magazine *Rap Pages*, Ice T identifies cities, neighbourhoods, high schools and housing projects that have meaning to him and to those familiar with these areas:

> I went to a white school in Culver City, and that was chill, but I was livin' in Windsor Hills near Monterey Triangle Park . . . When I got to high school all the kids from my area were gettin' bussed to white schools and I didn't want to go to them schools. So me and a few kids from the hills went to Crenshaw. That's where the gangs were. *(Rap Pages,* October 1991, p. 55)

Here, place is a lens of sorts that mediates one's perspective on social relations. It offers familiarity and it provides the perspectival point from which one gazes upon and evaluates other places, places that are 'other' or foreign to one's own distinctly personal sites of security and stability (no matter how limited these may be). Ice T may be from the East, but he is shaped by Los Angeles and it is the spaces and places of LA that provide the coordinates for his movement and activities.

Ice T (ibid.) goes on to make the distinction between East Coast rap and the emerging LA 'gangsta' style, noting that the latter developed out of a desire to relate incidents and experiences with a more specific sense of place and, subsequently, greater significance to local youths who could recognise the sites and activities described in the lyrics. In this regard, Rap offers a means of describing the view from a preferred 'here', of explaining how things appear in the immediate foreground (the 'hood) and how things seem on the receding horizon (other places).

Adopting a boastful tone and attitude, Ice T also locates his origins in the New Jersey–New York nexus, essentially fixing his own 'roots' in hip hop's cultural motherland. Ice T is in this mode clearly centring himself, building his own profile. In the process, he relates a history that invests supreme value in New York as the first home of hip hop, naturalising his connections to the artform and validating his identity as a tough, adaptive and street-smart LA hustler, the sell-proclaimed 'West Coast M.C. king'. Ice T's references to New York illuminate the spatial hierarchy that existed at the time; the Northeast was still virtually unchallenged as the dominant zone of hip hop cultural activity. Battles among rap's pioneers and upstarts were still being waged on the local, interborough scale in New York although, gradually, New York's monopoly on rap production and innovation was lost as various other sites of production emerged. The rise of the LA rap sound and the massive impact of the gangster themes after 1987 resulted in the first real incursion on New York's dominance. This development had the additional effect of polarising the two regions as the aesthetic distinctions based on lyrical content and rhythmic styles became more defined and audiences began spending their consumer dollars on rap from the nation's 'West side'.

"The West Side is the Best Side": Representing Compton

The West's arrival was heralded by a deluge of recordings that celebrated and glorified the street warrior scenarios of the California cities of South Central Los Angeles (with help from the 1988 Dennis Hopper film *Colors* and Ice T's galvanising title song on the soundtrack), Oakland and, especially, Compton. Starting with N.W.A.'s 'Straight Outta Compton' (1988, Ruthless/Priority), numerous recordings circulated the narrative imagery of vicious gang-oriented activities in Compton, including the tracks 'Raised in Compton' (1991, Epic) and 'Compton 4 Life' (1992, Epic) by the group Compton's Most Wanted, and DJ Quik's 'Born and Raised in Compton' (1991, Profile) or 'Jus Lyke Compton' (1992, Profile). Appearing on the cover of his album *Way 2 Fonky* (1992, Profile), DJ Quik poses alongside a chain-link fence topped with razor wire, sporting a jacket emblazoned with the Compton logo, proudly advertising his home territory. Through these multiple means of signification the city of Compton rapidly gained a notoriety informed by the image of tough and well-armed homeboys and the ongoing deadly conflict between rival gangs operating with a near-total lack of ethics or moral conscience. This last point can be most clearly discerned in the ubiquitous refrain that 'Compton niggaz just don't give a fuck'.

Tricia Rose and Brian Cross situate the rise of Compton-based rap in two quite different frames of understanding. Rose writes that

> during the late 1980s Los Angeles rappers from Compton and Watts, two areas severely paralyzed by the postindustrial economic redistribution, developed a West coast style of rap that narrates experiences and fantasies specific to life as a poor young, black, male subject in Los Angeles. (1994, p. 59)

Her assessment situates the phenomenon of West Coast styles and lyrical forms in an internally based set of socio-economic conditions that are responsive to transitions within a complex convergence of global and local forces, or what Kevin Robins (1991) refers to as 'the global/local nexus'.

Brian Cross locates the rise of Compton's rap scene within a wider and more appropriate cartographic relation to New York and other California locales:

> Hiphop Compton, according to Eazy, was created as a reply to the construction of the South Bronx/Queensbridge nexus in New York. If locally it served notice in the community in which Eazy and Dre sold their Macola-pressed records (not to mention the potential play action on KDAY), nationally, or at least on the East Coast, it was an attempt to figure Los Angeles on the map of hiphop. After the album had gone double platinum Compton would be as well known a city in hiphop as either Queens or the Bronx. (Cross 1993, p. 37)

Refuting Rose's interpretation, the general narrative content of 'Straight Outta Compton' sheds little light on the city or its social byways and does not demonstrate any particular concern with the locality's economics. Its basic function as a geographical backdrop actually follows the same standard constructions of abstract space heard in Grandmaster Flash and the Furious Five's 'New York, New York', recorded five years earlier, or in Eazy-E's solo effort, 'Boyz-n-the-Hood'.

Without detailed spatial descriptions of landmarks and environment, Compton does not emerge as a clearly realised urban space on the N.W.A. track even though it is the group's home town. The California city is instead treated as a bounded civic space that provides both specificity and scale for the communication of a West Coast Rap presence. The group is 'representing' their home territory and the song's release was their bold announcement that the 'boyz' from the 'hoods of Compton were 'stompin'' onto the scene and could not be avoided by anyone who paid attention to developments in the business. The Compton and South Central LA crews were not only serving notice to their neighbouring communities that they were in charge, but they were also serving notice to New York and the entire hip hop nation that the new sound had arrived and the balance of power (forged in a mix of arrogance and inventiveness) had tipped towards the West. This was the beginning of a decade-long antagonism between East and West coast rap that has too frequently proven that the gangster themes comprising the lyrical content are based in more than mere lip service or masculine posturing.

On the track 'Raised in Compton' (1991, Epic/Sony), MC Eiht of the rap group Compton's Most Wanted explicitly racialises the urban spaces of the city, more fully addressing the specificities of its cultural character and providing a further sense of the place that he recognises as his formative home. He reproduces several of the general elements that N.W.A. had already imposed on Compton's representational repertoire, but for him the city also has a personally meaningful history that is manifested in his identity as a gangster turned rapper:

> Compton is the place that I touched down
> I opened my eyes to realize that I was dark brown
> And right there in the ghetto that color costs
> Brothers smothered by the streets meaning we're lost
> I grew up in a place where it was go for your own
> Don't get caught after dark roaming the danger zone
> But it was hell at the age of twelve
> As my Compton black brothers were in and out of jail.

The attempt to historicise his relations to the city and the 'hood makes this track slightly more complex than 'Straight Outta Compton', as MC Eiht's bonds to the localised Compton environment are defined as the product of an evolving growth process, as a child becomes a man. Subjective history, conveyed here in an almost testimonial form, and the experiences of space, together offer relevant insights on the social construction of a gangster attitude or a gang member's *raison d'être*.

George Lipsitz isolates similar tendencies with his focus on the socio-political impor- tance of merging musical and non-musical sources of inspiration and experience among California chicano rock musicians since the 1960s:

> As organic intellectuals chronicling the cultural life of their community, they draw upon street slang, car customizing, clothing styles, and wall murals for inspiration and ideas . . . Their work is intertextual, constantly in dialogue with other forms of cultural expression, and most fully appreciated when located in context. (Lipsitz 1990, p. 153)

Like the California chicano music Lipsitz describes, 'Raised in Compton' explicitly highlights a customised car culture, urban mobility and the sartorial codes of the Compton streets ('T-shirt and khakis'). In its inclusiveness of the minor details that are, in practice, part of the daily norm for many urban black youth in the cities sur- rounding Los Angeles, the song accesses the spatial and racial characteristics of the city of Compton that have influenced and shaped the man that MC Eiht has become. The closely detailed articulation of spatial specifics (place names and site references, etc.) is still lacking but there is also a rich description of some of the social formations that are spatially distributed and which reproduce the forces underlying the black teen gangster ethos with which MC Eiht, and many others, so clearly identify.

Maintaining the gang member's pledge to defend the gang (or the 'set') and the 'hood forever is the theme of MC Eiht's 'Compton 4 Life' (1992, Epic/Sony). This track also offers a personal profile that ties MC Eiht into the neighbourhood environment and inextricably links him with the deeper gang structures that prevail. Mid-point in the track he challenges outsiders to 'throw up your 'hood 'cause it's Compton we're yellin', in a calculated 'turf' statement that is entirely consistent with the structures of spatial otherness that are fundamental to LA gang culture. Eiht and other gangsta rappers enter into the discourses of alienation and social disenfranchisement as a negative factor compelling them towards a criminal life-style. Yet they also expound their own versions of alienating power, drawing on the imagery and codes of the street and entering into a discourse of domination that subjugates women, opposing gang members or those who are perceived as being weaker and thus less than them. Framed in terms of gun violence and human decimation, these expressions are intended to diminish the presence of others who represent other cities and other 'hoods. This is the articulation of control through domination, ghetto style.

Spatial domination and geo-social containment are conceived in the threatening form of 'one time' or 'five-o' (the police) and other gang members, each of whom constitute unavoidable negatives of life in the 'hood. Defeating the enemy forces is the ultimate goal, but in establishing the competitive dynamic, MC Eiht acknowledges that, even in victory, the local streets and the 'hood impose their own kind of incarcerating authority:

> Compton 4 Life
> Compton 4 Life
>
> It's the city where everybody's in prison
> Niggers keep taking shit 'cause ain't nobody givin'
> So another punk fool I must be
> Learn the tricks of the trade from the street
> Exist to put the jack down, ready and willin'
> One more Compton driveby killin'.

There is a brief pause in the rhythm that could be heard as hanging like doom, stilling the song's pace and flow and creating a discomforting gap in the track. When the chorus 'Compton 4 Life' suddenly breaks in with the final echoing syllable, it becomes clear that the title is formed around a double entendre: it is an expression of spatial solidarity and loyalty to the 'hood, yet it also refers to the pronouncement of a life sentence and the apparent hopelessness of eternal imprisonment in the city's streets and alleys.

As 'Straight Outta Compton', 'Raised in Compton' and 'Compton 4 Life' suggest, 'our sensibilities are spatialized' (Keith and Pile, 1993 p. 26). This point is made resonant when considering Compton artist DJ Quik's mobile narrative on the track 'Jus Lyke Compton' (1992, Priority), in which he witnesses and describes the nationwide impact of the Compton mythology, and Bronx-based rapper Tim Dog's defensive articulation of Bronx pride in the lyrical assassinations of N.W.A. and all Compton artists on the track 'Fuck Compton' (1991, Ruffhouse/Columbia). Compton's central significance is maintained through the lyrical representation of activities that are space-bound and which are then discursively traced onto the identities of the rappers who 'claim' Compton as their own. The issue of whether or not the tracks refer back to a consistently verifiable reality is rendered moot by the possibilities they present as textual spaces of representation. Artists discursively locate themselves in an array of images and practices within the texts, constructing a relatively coherent identity out of the urban debris that is evidently a crucial aspect of the Compton they experience.

Despite claims by critics of gangsta rap, such as David Samuels (*New Republic*, 11 November, 1991), or folk musician Michelle Shocked, who suggests that 'Los Angeles as a whole and South Central specifically bear little resemblance to the cartoon landscape – the Zip Coon Toon Town – of gangsta rap' (*Billboard*, 20 June, 1992, p. 6), the subgenre's narrative depictions of spaces and places are absolutely essential to an understanding of the ways that a great number of urban black youths imagine their environments and the ways that they relate those images to their own individual sense of self. The spaces of Compton and other similar black communities that emerge through their work are simultaneously real, imaginary, symbolic and mythical. With this in mind, the question that should be asked is not 'is this real and true', but 'why do so many young black men choose these dystopic images of spatial representation to orient their own places in the world?' By framing the question thus, the undeniable fascination with the grisly mayhem of the lyrical narratives is displaced and one can then embark on a more illuminating interrogation of the socio-spatial sensibilities at work.

Representing the Extreme Local: the Case of Seattle

By the end of the 1980s, Rap artists had provided an assortment of spatial representations of New York and Los Angeles that were both consistent with and divergent from the prevailing image-ideas of those urban centres. Rap artists worked within the dominant representational discourses of 'the city' while agitating against a history of urban representations as they attempted to extend the expressive repertoire and to reconstruct the image-idea of the city as they understood it. This proved to be a formidable challenge since New York and LA exist as urban icons, resonant signs of the modern (New York) and postmodern (LA) city. They are already well defined, the products of a deluge of representational images, narrative constructions and social interactions.

Rap's emergence from city spaces that are comparatively unencumbered by a deep history of representational images, which carry less representational baggage, presents a unique opportunity for lyrical innovators to re-imagine and re-present their cities. As a traditional frontier city and a prominent contemporary regional centre, Seattle might, in this light, be conceived as an *under*represented city that lacks the wealth of representational history common to the larger centres to the South and the East.

In the mid-1980s the Pacific Northwest was, for much of the US, a veritable hinterland known best for its mountains, rivers and forests and as the home of Boeing's corporate and manufacturing headquarters. In the music industry, Jimi Hendrix was perhaps Seattle's most renowned native son, but the city was otherwise not regarded as an important or influential centre for musical production or innovation. The city's profile changed considerably with the rise of Bill Gates's Microsoft corporation in the outlying area and the emergence of the Starbuck's coffee empire and, by 1990, it was also garnering considerable attention as the source of the massively influential (and commercially successful) 'Grunge/Alternative' music scene that spawned bands such as Hole, Nirvana, Pearl Jam, Soundgarden, and the SubPop label. Music has subsequently emerged as an essential element in the construction of Seattle's contemporary image although the industry's rock predilections have not been as favourable to the city's rap and R&B artists.[2]

In the spring of 1986, Seattle rapper Sir Mix-A-Lot's obscure track 'Square Dance Rap' (NastyMix Records) made an entry onto *Billboard* magazine's Hot Black Singles chart. The release failed to advance any radical new aesthetic nor did it make a lasting contribution to the rap form. Its relevance, however, is in its capacity to reflect the diverse regional activity in rap production at that time as artists and labels attempted to establish themselves within the rapidly changing conditions fostering regional and local expansion. Mix-A-Lot's emergence illustrates the fact that rap was being produced in isolated regions and, as the track's chart status suggests, that it was selling in significant volume within regional 'home' markets.

Despite this, an advertisement for Profile Records appearing six years later in *Billboard's* 'Rap '92 Spotlight on Rap' (28 November 1992), portrays the proliferation of industry activity with a cartographic cartoon entitled 'Rap All Over the Map: The Profile States of America'. New York, Chicago, Dallas, St Louis, Vallejo and Los Angeles are all represented with the names of acts and their respective regions and cities of origin. The Pacific Northwest is conspicuously labelled 'uncharted territory', which refers to Profile's inactivity there but which also reproduces the dominant image of the region as a distant and unknown frontier in the view of those from the nation's larger or more centralised rap production sites.

Regardless of the advertisement's centrist biases, the fact that Seattle was at this stage on the charts (and, in hip hop parlance, 'in the house') indicates that rap's consumer base had extended geographically and, moreover, that new and unforeseen sites of production such as Seattle were also being established. In an interesting spatial inversion, Bruce Pavitt, co-founder of the Alternative-oriented SubPop label, actually regarded Seattle's spatial marginality as a positive factor for local musicians, stating that, 'one advantage Seattle has is our geographical isolation. It gave a group of artists a chance to create their own sound, instead of feeling pressured to copy others' (*Billboard*, 18 August 1990, p. 30). Sir Mix-A-Lot slowly solidified his Northwest regional base. His single 'Baby Got Back' reached the number one position on the *Billboard* pop charts, eventually selling double platinum.

Displaying pride in his Northwestern roots, Sir-Mix-A-Lot provides an excellent example of the organisation of spatial images and the deployment of a spatial discourse. In general terms, details that might be overlooked speak volumes about space and place, presenting additional information about the ways that an individual's daily life is influenced by their local environments and conditions. For instance, the standard group photo in the inner sleeve of *Mack Daddy* depicts Mix-A-Lot's Rhyme Cartel posse wearing wet-weather gear consisting of name-brand Gore Tex hats and jackets. This is a totally pragmatic sartorial statement from the moist climate of the Pacific Northwest that remains true to hip hop's style-conscious trends. It displays a geographically particular system of codes conveying regionally significant information that, once again, demonstrates hip hop's capacity to appropriate raw materials or images and to invest them with new values and meanings.

Of all the CD's tracks, 'Seattle Ain't Bullshittin'' is exceptional for the manner in which it communicates a sense of space and place with clarity, sophistication and cartographic detail. Establishing himself on the track as a genuine Seattle 'player', as the original Northwestern 'Mack Daddy' (a term for a top level pimp), Mix-A-Lot bases his claim to local prestige in his persona as a former Seattle hustler who successfully shifted to legitimate enterprises as a musician and businessman. He adopts a purely capitalist discourse of monetary and material accumulation, reproducing the prevailing terms of success and prosperity that conform to both the dominant social values and the value system inherent within the rap industry.

As the title suggests, Seattle is the centrepiece to the track. This is clear from the beginning as Mix-A-Lot and posse member the Attitude Adjuster ad lib over a sparse guitar riff:

> Boy, this is S.E.A.T.O.W.N,, clown (forever)
> Sea Town, Yeah, and that's from the motherfuckin' heart
> So if you ain't down with your hometown
> Step off, punk
> Mix, tell these fakes what the deal is . . .

As the bass and drums are dropped into the track, Mix-A-Lot lyrically locates himself as a product of Seattle's inner-city core known as the CD (or Central District):

> I was raised in the S.E.A. double T. L.E.
> Seattle, home of the CD, nigga
> 19th and, yes, Laborda,
> pimpin' was hard . . .
> It wasn't easy trying to compete with my homies in the CD.

Seattle's Central District is home to a sizeable concentration of black constituents who comprise roughly 10 per cent of Seattle's total population. Mix-A-Lot's portrayal of the CD neighbourhood is not explicitly racialised yet the references to pimping and competition among 'homies in the CD' easily fall into a common, even stereotypical definition of 'the 'hood' that is pervasive throughout rap of the period.

The Attitude Adjuster states at one point that 'it ain't nothing but the real up here in the Northwest', attesting to the hip hop practices and related cultural identities that are evident in Seattle as well as the rest of the nation. Unlike most major American cities, Seattle's black presence does not have a huge defining influence on its urban character: black youths are a socially marginalised constituency within a geographically marginal city. The Attitude Adjuster's pronouncement may suggest a hint of defensiveness but it also gives voice to the region's black hip hop constituency that is, as the subtext implies, just as 'hardcore' as that of other urban centres.

Having established his ghetto credentials, Mix-A-Lot expounds on several spatially oriented scenarios, shifting scale and perspective throughout the track with his descriptions of local, regional and national phenomena:

> So even though a lot of niggas talk shit
> I'm still down for the Northwest when I hit the stage
> Anywhere U.S.A.
> I give Seattle and Tacoma much play
> So here's to the Criminal Nation
> And the young brother Kid Sensation
> I can't forget Maharaji and the Attitude Adjuster
> And the hardcore brothers to the west of Seattle
> Yeah, West Side, High Point dippin' four door rides . . .

Mix-A-Lot adopts the role of Seattle's hip hop ambassador, acknowledging his own national celebrity profile while accepting the responsibilities of 'representing' the Northwest, his record label and posse, and fellow rap artists from 'Sea Town'. Exploiting his access to the wider stage, he elevates the local scene, bringing it into focus and broadcasting, the fact that hip hop is an important element of the Seattle lifestyle for young blacks living there as well.

The perspective shifts again as Mix-A-Lot adopts an intensely localised mode of description, recalling the days when he 'used to cruise around Seward Park', moving out of the bounded territory of the city's Central District that is the posse's home base. Seattle is cartographically delineated here through the explicit naming of streets and civic landmarks that effectively identify the patterned mobility of the crew:

> Let's take a trip to the South End,
> We go west, hit Rainier Ave. and bust left,
> . . . S.E.A. T.O.W.N., yo nigger is back again
> . . . Gettin' back to the hood,
> Me and my boys is up to no good,
> A big line of cars rollin' deep through the South End,
> Made a left on Henderson,
> Clowns talkin' shit in the Southshore parking lot
> Critical Mass is begging to box
> But we keep on going because down the street
> A bunch of freaks in front of Rainier Beach
> Was lookin' at us, they missed that bus
> And they figure they could trust us . . .

With its references to the city's crosstown byways and meeting places, the track successfully communicates an image of the common, 'everyday' leisure practices of the Rhyme Cartel posse while also retaining a privileged local or place-based perspective that resonates with greater meaning for all Seattle or Tacoma audience members. This audience will undoubtedly recognise its own environment and the track will consequently have a different and arguably more intense affective impact among Seattle's listeners and fans. Unlike Compton, which was popularised through a relentless process of reiteration by numerous artists, Seattle is represented much less frequently: 'Seattle Ain't Bullshittin'' is a unique expression of Northwest identity. For example, there is no similar track on the Seattle-based Criminal Nation's *Trouble in the Hood* which was also released in 1992 (NastyMix/Ichiban), although references to the region are sprinkled throughout several tracks and on the liner sleeve one group member sports a Tacoma T-shirt identifying his hometown.

In 1992, the trend towards such closely demarcated spatial parameters was not yet a common characteristic in rap, although it was increasingly becoming a factor in both lyrical and visual representations. Rather than an expression of a narrow social perspective celebrating the local to the exclusion of other wider scales, 'Seattle Ain't Bullshittin'' demonstrates a rather successful method of representing the hometown local 'flavour' on an internationally distributed recording.

Conclusion

Rap music's shift towards a self-produced discourse introducing the 'hood as a new spatial concept delimiting an 'arena of experience' can be weighed against larger trends currently restructuring global and national economies, transforming national and regional workforces, and, often, devastating urban localities. As numerous supporters have suggested, rap emerges as a voice for black and Latino youth which, as a large subset of North America's socially disenfranchised population, is at risk of being lost in the combined transformations of domestic and global economies that are altering North America's urban cultures today. The discourse of space encompassed by the term ''hood' may in this context also be interpreted as a response to conditions of change occurring at a meta-level, far beyond the scale of the local (and the influence of those who inhabit it).

The requirement of maintaining strong local allegiances is a standard practice in hip hop that continues to mystify many critics of the rap genre. It is, therefore, imperative to recognise and understand the processes that are at work and to acknowledge that there are different messages being communicated to listeners who occupy different spaces and places and who identify with space or place according to different values of scale. It is precisely through these detailed image constructions that the abstract spaces of the ghetto are transformed into the more proximate sites of significance or places of the 'hood. Looking beyond the obvious, spatial discourse provides a communicative means through which numerous social systems are framed for consideration. Rap tracks, with their almost obsessive preoccupation with place and locality, are never *solely* about space and place on the local scale. Rather, they also identify and explore the ways in which these spaces and places are inhabited and made meaningful. Struggles and conflicts as well as the positive attachments to place are all represented in the spatial discourses of rap. This is not a display of parochial narrowness but a much more complex and interesting exploration of local practices and their discursive construction in the popular media.

Notes

1.   As an indication of the distinctions between rap and the more encompassing hip hop culture, rap artist KRS-One has said 'rap is something you do, hip-hop is something you live' (quoted

in *The Source*, June 1995, p. 40). Rap is the music of hip hop and its central form of articulation and expression.

2. Addressing the relatively minor industry consideration for Seattle's black artists, Sir Mix-A-Lot's Rhyme Cartel Records released the conspicuously titled *Seattle . . . The Dark Side* in 1993. The cover prominently proclaims that the release 'flips the script. No Grunge . . . just Rap and R&B . . . SeaTown style'.

References

Chambers, Iain (1985). *Urban Rhythms: Pop Music and Popular Culture*. London.

Cross, Brian (1993). *It's Not about a Salary: Rap, Race, and Resistance in Los Angeles*. London.

Dery, Mark (1990). Public Enemy: Confrontation. *Keyboard*, September.

Eure, Joseph & James Spady (eds.) (1991). *Nation Conscious Rap*. New York.

George, Nelson (1992). *Buppies, B-Boys, Baps and Bohos: Notes on Post-Soul Black Culture*. New York.

George, Nelson (1993). Hip-Hop's Founding Fathers Speak the Truth. *The Source*, November.

Gilroy, Paul (1992). It's a Family Affair. In: Gina Dent (ed.), *Black Popular Culture*. Seattle.

Gunst, Laurie (1995). *Born Fi Dead: A Journey Through the Jamaican Posse Underworld*. New York.

Hager, Steve (1984). *Hip Hop: The Illustrated History of Break Dancing, Rap Music, and Graffiti*. New York.

Jones, Charisse (1995). "Still Hangin" in the "Hood: Rappers Who Stay Say Their Strength Is from the Streets." *New York Times*, September 24, pp. 43–6.

Keith, Michael & Steve Pile (eds.) (1993). *Place and the Politics of Identity*. New York.

Lipsitz, George (1990). *Time Passages: Collective Memory and American Popular Culture*. Minneapolis.

Nelson, Havelock & Michael Gonzales (1991). *Bring the Noise: A Guide to Rap Music and Hip Hop Culture*. New York.

Pike, Jeff (1990). At Long Last, Seattle Is Suddenly Hot. *Billboard*, August 18, pp. 30–4.

"Rap Pages" (1991). The World According to Ice-T, October, pp. 54–67.

"Rap Sheet" (1992). The Bloody 5: A Day in the Hood, October, pp. 18–26.

Robins, Kevin (1991). Tradition and Translation: National Culture in Its Global Context. In: John Corner & Sylvia Harvey (eds.), *Enterprise and Heritage: Crosscurrents of National Culture*. New York.

Rose, Tricia (1994). *Black Noise: Rap Music and Black Culture in Contemporary America*. Hanover.

Samuels, David (1991). The Rap on Rap. *New Republic*, November 11.

Shocked, Michelle & Bart Bull (1992). LA Riots: Cartoons vs. Reality. *Billboard*, June 20, p. 6.

"The Source" (1994). Special Issue: Miami Bass, March.

Tate, Greg (1992). Posses in Effect: Ice-T. In: *Flyboy in the Buttermilk: Essays on Contemporary America*. New York.

Toop, David (1984). *The Rap Attack: African Jive to New York Hip Hop*. Boston.

Toop, David (1991). *Rap Attack: African Rap to Global Hip-Hop*. New York.

X

Media Studies

57

Encoding, Decoding

Stuart Hall*

Traditionally, mass-communications research has conceptualized the process of communication in terms of a circulation circuit or loop. This model has been criticized for its linearity – sender/message/receiver – for its concentration on the level of message exchange and for the absence of a structured conception of the different moments as a complex structure of relations. But it is also possible (and useful) to think of this process in terms of a structure produced and sustained through the articulation of linked but distinctive moments – production, circulation, distribution/consumption, reproduction. This would be to think of the process as a 'complex structure in dominance', sustained through the articulation of connected practices, each of which, however, retains its distinctiveness and has its own specific modality, its own forms and conditions of existence.

The 'object' of these practices is meanings and messages in the form of sign-vehicles of a specific kind organized, like any form of communication or language, through the operation of codes within the syntagmatic chain of a discourse. The apparatuses, relations and practices of production thus issue, at a certain moment (the moment of 'production/circulation') in the form of symbolic vehicles constituted within the rules of 'language'. It is in this discursive form that the circulation of the 'product' takes place. The process thus requires, at the production end, its material instruments – its 'means' – as well as its own sets of social (production) relations – the organization and combination of practices within media apparatuses. But it is in the *discursive* form that the circulation of the product takes place, as well as its distribution to different audiences. Once accomplished, the discourse must then be translated – transformed, again – into social practices if the circuit is to be both completed and effective. If no 'meaning' is taken, there can be no 'consumption'. If the meaning is not articulated in practice, it has no effect. The value of this approach is that while each of the moments, in articulation, is necessary to the circuit as a whole, no one moment can fully guarantee the next moment with which it is articulated. Since each has its specific modality and conditions of existence, each can constitute its own break or interruption of the 'passage of forms' on whose continuity the flow of effective production (that is, 'reproduction') depends.

*Pp. 129–38 from *Culture, Media, Language*, ed. S. Hall, D. Hobson, A. Lowe and P. Willis. This chapter is an edited extract from "Encoding and Decoding Television Discourse," *CCCS Stencilled Paper*, 7 (Birmingham: CCCS, 1973). © 1980 by Stuart Hall. Reprinted with permission from the author.

Thus while in no way wanting to limit research to 'following only those leads which emerge from content analysis', we must recognize that the discursive form of the message has a privileged position in the communicative exchange (from the viewpoint of circulation), and that the moments of 'encoding' and 'decoding', though only 'relatively autonomous' in relation to the communicative process as a whole, are *determinate* moments. A 'raw' historical event cannot, *in that form*, be transmitted by, say, a television newscast. Events can only be signified within the aural-visual forms of the televisual discourse. In the moment when a historical event passes under the sign of discourse, it is subject to all the complex formal 'rules' by which language signifies. To put it paradoxically, the event must become a 'story' before it can become a *communicative event*. In that moment the formal sub-rules of discourse are 'in dominance', without, of course, subordinating out of existence the historical event so signified, the social relations in which the rules are set to work or the social and political consequences of the event having been signified in this way. The 'message form' is the necessary 'form of appearance' of the event in its passage from source to receiver. Thus the transposition into and out of the 'message form' (or the mode of symbolic exchange) is not a random 'moment', which we can take up or ignore at our convenience. The 'message form' is a determinate moment; though, at another level, it comprises the surface movements of the communications system only and requires, at another stage, to be integrated into the social relations of the communication process as a whole, of which it forms only a part.

From this general perspective, we may crudely characterize the television communicative process as follows. The institutional structures of broadcasting, with their practices and networks of production, their organized relations and technical infrastructures, are required to produce a programme. Production, here, constructs the message. In one sense, then, the circuit begins here. Of course, the production process is not without its 'discursive' aspect: it, too, is framed throughout by meanings and ideas: knowledge-in-use concerning the routines of production, historically defined technical skills, professional ideologies, institutional knowledge, definitions and assumptions, assumptions about the audience and so on frame the constitution of the programme through this production structure. Further, though the production structures of television originate the television discourse, they do not constitute a closed system. They draw topics, treatments, agendas, events, personnel, images of the audience, 'definitions of the situation' from other sources and other discursive formations within the wider socio-cultural and political structure of which they are a differentiated part. Philip Elliott has expressed this point succinctly, within a more traditional framework, in his discussion of the way in which the audience is both the 'source' and the 'receiver' of the television message. Thus – to borrow Marx's terms – circulation and reception are, indeed, 'moments' of the production process in television and are reincorporated, via a number of skewed and structured 'feedbacks', into the production process itself. The consumption or reception of the television message is thus also itself a 'moment' of the production process in its larger sense, though the latter is 'predominant' because it is the 'point of departure for the realization' of the message. Production and reception of the television message are not, therefore, identical, but they are related: they are differentiated moments within the totality formed by the social relations of the communicative process as a whole.

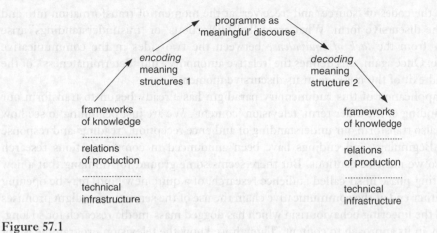

Figure 57.1

At a certain point, however, the broadcasting structures must yield encoded messages in the form of a meaningful discourse. The institution-societal relations of production must pass under the discursive rules of language for its product to be 'realized'. This initiates a further differentiated moment, in which the formal rules of discourse and language are in dominance. Before this message can have an 'effect' (however defined), satisfy a 'need' or be put to a 'use', it must first be appropriated as a meaningful discourse and be meaningfully decoded. It is this set of decoded meanings which 'have an effect', influence, entertain, instruct or persuade, with very complex perceptual, cognitive, emotional, ideological or behavioural consequences. In a 'determinate' moment the structure employs a code and yields a 'message': at another determinate moment the 'message', via its decodings, issues into the structure of social practices. We are now fully aware that this reentry into the practices of audience reception and 'use' cannot be understood in simple behavioural terms. The typical processes identified in positivistic research on isolated elements – effects, uses, 'gratifications' – are themselves framed by structures of understanding, as well as being produced by social and economic relations, which shape their 'realization' at the reception end of the chain and which permit the meanings signified in the discourse to be transposed into practice or consciousness (to acquire social use value or political effectivity).

Clearly, what we have labelled in the diagram (figure 57.1) 'meaning structures 1' and 'meaning structures 2' may not be the same. They do not constitute an 'immediate identity'. The codes of encoding and decoding may not be perfectly symmetrical. The degrees of symmetry – that is, the degrees of 'understanding' and 'misunderstanding' in the communicative exchange – depend on the degrees of symmetry/asymmetry (relations of equivalence) established between the positions of the 'personifications', encoder-producer and decoder-receiver. But this in turn depends on the degrees of identity/non-identity between the codes which perfectly or imperfectly transmit, interrupt or systematically distort what has been transmitted. The lack of fit between the codes has a great deal to do with the structural differences of relation and position between broadcasters and audiences, but it also has something to do with the asymmetry between the codes of 'source' and 'receiver' at the moment of transformation into and out of the discursive form. What are called 'distortions' or 'misunderstandings' arise precisely from the *lack of equivalence* between the two sides in the communicative exchange. Once again, this defines the 'relative autonomy', but 'determinateness', of the entry and exit of the message in its discursive moments.

The application of this rudimentary paradigm has already begun to transform our understanding of the older term, television 'content'. We are just beginning to see how it might also transform our understanding of audience reception, 'reading' and response as well. Beginnings and endings have been announced in communications research before, so we must be cautious. But there seems some ground for thinking that a new and exciting phase in so-called audience research, of a quite new kind, may be opening up. At either end of the communicative chain the use of the semiotic paradigm promises to dispel the lingering behaviourism which has dogged mass-media research for so long, especially in its approach to content. Though we know the television programme is not a behavioural input, like a tap on the knee cap, it seems to have been almost impossible for traditional researchers to conceptualize the communicative process without lapsing into one or other variant of low-flying behaviourism. We know, as Gerbner has remarked, that representations of violence on the TV screen 'are not violence but messages about violence': but we have continued to research the question of violence, for example, as if we were unable to comprehend this epistemological distinction.

The televisual sign is a complex one. It is itself constituted by the combination of two types of discourse, visual and aural. Moreover, it is an iconic sign, in Peirce's terminology, because 'it possesses some of the properties of the thing represented'. This is a point which has led to a great deal of confusion and has provided the site of intense controversy in the study of visual language. Since the visual discourse translates a three-dimensional world into two-dimensional planes, it cannot, of course, *be* the referent or concept it signifies. The dog in the film can bark but it cannot bite! Reality exists outside language, but it is constantly mediated by and through language: and what we can know and say has to be produced in and through discourse. Discursive 'knowledge' is the product not of the transparent representation of the 'real' in language but of the articulation of language on real relations and conditions. Thus there is no intelligible discourse without the operation of a code. Iconic signs are therefore coded signs too – even if the codes here work differently from those of other signs. There is no degree zero in language. Naturalism and 'realism' – the apparent fidelity of the representation to the thing or concept represented – is the result, the effect, of a certain specific articulation of language on the 'real'. It is the result of a discursive practice.

Certain codes may, of course, be so widely distributed in a specific language community or culture, and be learned at so early an age, that they appear not to be constructed – the effect of an articulation between sign and referent – but to be 'naturally' given. Simple visual signs appear to have achieved a 'near-universality' in this sense: though evidence remains that even apparently 'natural' visual codes are culture-specific. However, this does not mean that no codes have intervened; rather, that the codes have been profoundly *naturalized*. The operation of naturalized codes reveals not the transparency and 'naturalness' of language but the depth, the habituation and the near-universality of the codes in use. They produce apparently 'natural' recognitions. This has the (ideological) effect of concealing the practices of coding which are present. But we must not be fooled by appearances. Actually, what naturalized codes demonstrate is the degree of habituation produced when there is a fundamental alignment and reciprocity – an achieved equivalence – between the encoding and decoding sides of an exchange of meanings. The functioning of the codes on the decoding side will frequently assume the status of naturalized perceptions. This leads us to think that the visual sign for 'cow' actually *is* (rather than *represents*) the animal, cow. But if we think of the visual representation of a cow in a manual on animal husbandry – and, even more, of the linguistic sign 'cow' – we can see that both, in different degrees, are *arbitrary* with respect to the concept of the animal they represent. The articulation of an arbitrary sign – whether visual or verbal – with the concept of a referent is the product not of nature but of convention, and the conventionalism of discourses requires the intervention, the support, of codes. Thus Eco has argued that iconic signs 'look like objects in the real world because they reproduce the conditions (that is, the codes) of perception in the viewer'. These 'conditions of perception' are, however, the result of a highly coded, even if virtually unconscious, set of operations – decodings. This is as true of the photographic or televisual image as it is of any other sign. Iconic signs are, however, particularly vulnerable to being 'read' as natural because visual codes of perception are very widely distributed and because this type of sign is less arbitrary than a linguistic sign: the linguistic sign, 'cow', possesses *none* of the properties of the thing represented, whereas the visual sign appears to possess *some* of those properties.

This may help us to clarify a confusion in current linguistic theory and to define precisely how some key terms are being used in this article. Linguistic theory frequently employs the distinction 'denotation' and 'connotation'. The term 'denotation' is widely equated with the literal meaning of a sign: because this literal meaning is almost universally recognized, especially when visual discourse is being employed, 'denotation' has often been confused with a literal transcription of 'reality' in language – and thus with a 'natural sign', one produced without the intervention of a code. 'Connotation', on the other hand, is employed simply to refer to less fixed and therefore more conventionalized and changeable, associative meanings, which clearly vary from instance to instance and therefore must depend on the intervention of codes.

We do *not* use the distinction – denotation/connotation – in this way. From our point of view, the distinction is an *analytic* one only. It is useful, in analysis, to be able to apply a rough rule of thumb which distinguishes those aspects of a sign which appear to be taken, in any language community at any point in time, as its 'literal' meaning (denotation) from the more associative meanings for the sign which it is possible to generate (connotation). But analytic distinctions must not be confused with distinctions in the real world. There will be very few instances in which signs organized in a discourse signify *only* their 'literal' (that is, near-universally consensualized) meaning. In actual discourse most signs will combine both the denotative and the connotative *aspects* (as redefined above). It may, then, be asked why we retain the distinction at all. It is largely a matter of analytic value. It is because signs appear to acquire their full ideological value – appear to be open to articulation with wider ideological discourses and meanings – at the level of their 'associative' meanings (that is, at the connotative level) – for here 'meanings' are *not* apparently fixed in natural perception (that is, they are not fully naturalized), and their fluidity of meaning and association can be more fully exploited and transformed. So it is at the connotative *level* of the sign that situational ideologies alter and transform signification. At this level we can see more clearly the active intervention of ideologies in and on discourse: here, the sign is open to new accentuations and, in Vološinov's terms, enters fully into the struggle over meanings – the class struggle in language. This does not mean that the denotative or 'literal' meaning is outside ideology. Indeed, we could say that its ideological value is strongly *fixed* – because it has become so fully universal and 'natural'. The terms 'denotation' and 'connotation', then, are merely useful analytic tools for distinguishing, in particular contexts, between not the presence/absence of ideology in language but the different levels at which ideologies and discourses intersect.

The level of connotation of the visual sign, of its contextual reference and positioning in different discursive fields of meaning and association, is the point where *already coded* signs intersect with the deep semantic codes of a culture and take on additional, more active ideological dimensions. We might take an example from advertising discourse. Here, too, there is no 'purely denotative', and certainly no 'natural', representation. Every visual sign in advertising connotes a quality, situation, value or inference, which is present as an implication or implied meaning, depending on the connotational positioning. In Barthes's example, the sweater always signifies a 'warm garment' (denotation) and thus the activity/value of 'keeping warm'. But it is also possible, at its more connotative levels, to signify 'the coming of winter' or 'a cold day'. And, in the specialized sub-codes of fashion, sweater may also connote a fashionable style of *haute couture* or, alternatively, an informal style of dress. But set against the right visual background and positioned by the romantic sub-code, it may connote 'long autumn walk in the woods'. Codes of this order clearly contract relations for the sign with the wider universe of ideologies in a society. These codes are the means by which power and ideology are made to signify in particular discourses. They refer signs to the 'maps of meaning' into which any culture is classified; and those 'maps of social reality' have the whole range of social meanings, practices, and usages, power and interest 'written in' to them. The connotative levels of signifiers, Barthes remarked, 'have a close communication with culture, knowledge, history, and it is through them, so to speak, that the environmental world invades the linguistic and semantic system. They are, if you like, the fragments of ideology'.

The so-called denotative *level* of the televisual sign is fixed by certain, very complex (but limited or 'closed') codes. But its connotative *level*, though also bounded, is more open, subject to more active *transformations*, which exploit its polysemic values. Any such already constituted sign is potentially transformable into more than one connotative configuration. Polysemy must not, however, be confused with pluralism. Connotative codes are *not* equal among themselves. Any society/culture tends, with varying degrees of closure, to impose its classifications of the social and cultural and political world. These constitute a *dominant cultural order*, though it is neither univocal nor uncontested. This question of the 'structure of discourses in dominance' is a crucial point. The different areas of social life appear to be mapped out into discursive domains, hierarchically organized into *dominant or preferred meanings*. New, problematic or troubling events, which breach our expectancies and run counter to our 'common-sense constructs', to our 'taken-for-granted' knowledge of social structures, must be assigned to their discursive domains before they can be said to 'make sense'. The most common way of 'mapping' them is to assign the new to some domain or other of the existing 'maps of problematic social reality'. We say *dominant*, not 'determined', because it is always possible to order, classify, assign and decode an event within more than one 'mapping'. But we say 'dominant' because there exists a pattern of 'preferred readings'; and these both have the institutional/political/ideological order imprinted in them and have themselves become institutionalized. The domains of 'preferred meanings' have the whole social order embedded in them as a set of meanings, practices and beliefs: the everyday knowledge of social structures, of 'how things work for all practical purposes in this culture', the rank order of power and interest and the structure of legitimations, limits and sanctions. Thus to clarify a 'misunderstanding' at the connotative level, we must refer, *through* the codes, to the orders of social life, of economic and political power and of ideology. Further, since these mappings are 'structured in dominance' but not closed, the communicative process consists not in the unproblematic assignment of every visual item to its given position within a set of prearranged codes, but of *performative rules* – rules of competence and use, of logics-in-use – which seek actively to *enforce* or *pre-fer* one semantic domain over another and rule items into and out of their appropriate meaning-sets. Formal semiology has too often neglected this practice of *interpretative work*, though this constitutes, in fact, the real relations of broadcast practices in television.

In speaking of *dominant meanings*, then, we are not talking about a one-sided process which governs how all events will be signified. It consists of the 'work' required to enforce, win plausibility for and command as legitimate a *decoding* of the event within the limit of dominant definitions in which it has been connotatively signified. Terni has remarked:

> By the word *reading* we mean not only the capacity to identify and decode a certain number of signs, but also the subjective capacity to put them into a creative relation between themselves and with other signs: a capacity which is, by itself, the condition for a complete awareness of one's total environment.

Our quarrel here is with the notion of 'subjective capacity', as if the referent of a televisional discourse were an objective fact but the interpretative level were an individualized and private matter. Quite the opposite seems to be the case. The televisual practice takes 'objective' (that is, systemic) responsibility precisely for the relations which disparate signs contract with one another in any discursive instance, and thus continually rearranges, delimits and prescribes into what 'awareness of one's total environment' these items are arranged.

This brings us to the question of misunderstandings. Television producers who find their message 'failing to get across' are frequently concerned to straighten out the kinks in the communication chain, thus facilitating the 'effectiveness' of their communication. Much research which claims the objectivity of 'policy-oriented analysis' reproduces this administrative goal by attempting to discover how much of a message the audience recalls and to improve the extent of understanding. No doubt misunderstandings of a literal kind do exist. The viewer does not know the terms employed, cannot follow the complex logic of argument or exposition, is unfamiliar with the language, finds the concepts too alien or difficult or is foxed by the expository narrative. But more often broadcasters are concerned that the audience has failed to take the meaning as they – the broadcasters – intended. What they really mean to say is that viewers are not operating within the 'dominant' or 'preferred' code. Their ideal is 'perfectly transparent communication'. Instead, what they have to confront is 'systematically distorted communication'.

In recent years discrepancies of this kind have usually been explained by reference to 'selective perception'. This is the door via which a residual pluralism evades the compulsions of a highly structured, asymmetrical and non-equivalent process. Of course, there will always be private, individual, variant readings. But 'selective perception' is almost never as selective, random or privatized as the concept suggests. The patterns exhibit, across individual variants, significant clusterings. Any new approach to audience studies will therefore have to begin with a critique of 'selective perception' theory.

It was argued earlier that since there is no necessary correspondence between encoding and decoding, the former can attempt to 'pre-fer' but cannot prescribe or guarantee the latter, which has its own conditions of existence. Unless they are wildly aberrant, encoding will have the effect of constructing some of the limits and parameters within which decodings will operate. If there were no limits, audiences could simply read whatever they liked into any message. No doubt some total misunderstandings of this kind do exist. But the vast range must contain *some* degree of reciprocity between encoding and decoding moments, otherwise we could not speak of an effective communicative exchange at all. Nevertheless, this 'correspondence' is not given but constructed. It is not 'natural' but the product of an articulation between two distinct moments. And the former cannot determine or guarantee, in a simple sense, which decoding codes will be employed. Otherwise communication would be a perfectly equivalent circuit, and every message would be an instance of 'perfectly transparent communication'. We must think, then, of the variant articulations in which encoding/decoding can be combined. To elaborate on this, we offer a hypothetical analysis of some possible decoding positions, in order to reinforce the point of 'no necessary correspondence'.

We identify *three* hypothetical positions from which decodings of a televisual discourse may be constructed. These need to be empirically tested and refined. But the argument that decodings do not follow inevitably from encodings, that they are not identical, reinforces the argument of 'no necessary correspondence'. It also helps to deconstruct the common-sense meaning of 'misunderstanding' in terms of a theory of 'systematically distorted communication'.

The first hypothetical position is that of the *dominant-hegemonic position*. When the viewer takes the connoted meaning from, say, a television newscast or current affairs programme full and straight, and decodes the message in terms of the reference code in which it has been encoded, we might say that the viewer *is operating inside the dominant code*. This is the ideal-typical case of 'perfectly transparent communication' – or as close as we are likely to come to it 'for all practical purposes'. Within this we can distinguish the positions produced by the *professional code*. This is the position (produced by what we perhaps ought to identify as the operation of a 'metacode') which the professional broadcasters assume when encoding a message which has *already* been signified in a hegemonic manner. The professional code is 'relatively independent' of the dominant code, in that it applies criteria and transformational operations of its own, especially those of a technico-practical nature. The professional code, however, operates *within* the 'hegemony' of the dominant code. Indeed, it serves to reproduce the dominant definitions precisely by bracketing their hegemonic quality and operating instead with displaced professional codings which foreground such apparently neutral-technical questions as visual quality, news and presentational values, televisual quality, 'professionalism' and so on. The hegemonic interpretations of, say, the politics of Northern Ireland, or the Chilean *coup* or the Industrial Relations Bill are principally generated by political and military elites: the particular choice of presentational occasions and formats, the selection of personnel, the choice of images, the staging of debates are selected and combined through the operation of the professional code. How the broadcasting professionals are able *both* to operate with 'relatively autonomous' codes of their own *and* to act in such a way as to reproduce (not without contradiction) the hegemonic signification of events is a complex matter which cannot be further spelled out here. It must suffice to say that the professionals are linked with the defining elites not only by the institutional position of broadcasting itself as an 'ideological apparatus', but also by the structure of *access* (that is, the systematic 'over-accessing' of selective elite personnel and their 'definition of the situation' in television). It may even be said that the professional codes serve to reproduce hegemonic definitions specifically by *not overtly* biasing their operations in a dominant direction: ideological reproduction therefore takes place here inadvertently, unconsciously, 'behind men's backs'. Of course, conflicts, contradictions and even misunderstandings regularly arise between the dominant and the professional significations and their signifying agencies.

The second position we would identify is that of the *negotiated code* or position. Majority audiences probably understand quite adequately what has been dominantly defined and professionally signified. The dominant definitions, however, are hegemonic precisely because they represent definitions of situations and events which are 'in dominance (*global*). Dominant definitions connect events, implicitly or explicitly, to grand totalizations, to the great syntagmatic views-of-the-world: they take 'large views' of issues: they relate events to the 'national interest' or to the level of geo-politics, even if they make these connections in truncated, inverted or mystified ways. The definition of a hegemonic viewpoint is (a) that it defines within its terms the mental horizon, the universe, of possible meanings, of a whole sector of relations in a society or culture; and (b) that it carries with it the stamp of legitimacy – it appears coterminous with what is 'natural', 'inevitable', 'taken for granted' about the social order. Decoding within the *negotiated version* contains a mixture of adaptive and oppositional elements: it acknowledges the legitimacy of the hegemonic definitions to make the grand significations (abstract), while, at a more restricted, situational (situated) level, it makes its own ground rules – it operates with exceptions to the rule. It accords the privileged position to the dominant definitions of events while reserving the right to make a more negotiated application to 'local conditions', to its own more *corporate* positions. This negotiated version of the dominant ideology is thus shot through with contradictions, though these are only on certain occasions brought to full visibility. Negotiated codes operate through what we might call particular or situated logics: and these logics are sustained by their differential and unequal relation to the discourses and logics of power. The simplest example of a negotiated code is that which governs the response of a worker to the notion of an Industrial Relations Bill limiting the right to strike or to arguments for a wages freeze. At the level of the 'national interest' economic debate the decoder may adopt the hegemonic definition, agreeing that 'we must all pay ourselves less in order to combat inflation'. This, however, may have little or no relation to his/her willingness to go on strike for better pay and conditions or to oppose the Industrial Relations Bill at the level of shop-floor or union organization. We suspect that the great majority of so-called 'misunderstandings' arise from the contradictions and disjunctures between hegemonic–dominant encodings and negotiated-corporate decodings. It is just these mismatches in the levels which most provoke defining elites and professionals to identify a 'failure in communications'.

Finally, it is possible for a viewer perfectly to understand both the literal and the connotative inflection given by a discourse but to decode the message in a *globally* contrary way. He/she detotalizes the message in the preferred code in order to retotalize the message within some alternative framework of reference. This is the case of the viewer who listens to a debate on the need to limit wages but 'reads' every mention of the 'national interest' as 'class interest'. He/she is operating with what we must call an *oppositional code.* One of the most significant political moments (they also coincide with crisis points within the broadcasting organizations themselves, for obvious reasons) is the point when events which are normally signified and decoded in a negotiated way begin to be given an oppositional reading. Here the 'politics of signification' – the struggle in discourse – is joined.

Note

This chapter reproduces an edited extract from 'Encoding and Decoding in Television Discourse', CCCS Stencilled Paper no. 7.

58

Heliography: Journalism and the Visualization of Truth

*John Hartley**

If there is no history, except through language, and if language . . . is elementally metaphorical, Borges is correct: 'Perhaps universal history is but the history of several metaphors.' Light is only one example of these 'several' fundamental 'metaphors', but what an example! Who will ever dominate it, who will ever pronounce its meaning without first being pronounced by it? What language will ever escape it? . . . If all languages combat within it, modifying only *the same metaphor and choosing the* best *light, Borges . . . is correct again: 'Perhaps universal history is but the history of the* diverse *intonations of several metaphors.'*

Jacques Derrida[1]

Choosing the *Best* Light

Journalism is the art of tele-visualization; it constitutes, then renders visible, distant visions of order. The fundamental test of newsworthiness is disorder – deviation from any supposed steady state – and the most important metaphors of journalistic method, used by journalists themselves to make sense of what they do, are metaphors of sight: eyewitness news, watchdogs, in the spotlight, insight, discovery, revelation – metaphors of bringing to light or looking. The classic *OED* general definition of 'truth' – 'that which exists in fact' – is commonly verified by taking it to refer to 'that which can be seen', even when seeing is itself metaphorical, as in the case of 'seeing' by reading. Thus the founding *medium* of journalism is not the material verbal speech or print of which it is literally made (just as 'the media' are not the material paper and screens upon which news is carried); the medium of journalism is *vision*, seeing what the words say, and not literal sight but imagined; journalists are visionaries of truth, seers of distant order, communicated to their communities by a process of photographic negativization, where the image of order is actually recorded as its own negative, in stories of disorder. Journalism is a philosophical discourse on what Derrida has called the *heliological metaphor.*[2] It is therefore the social practice of heliography.

* Pp. 140–63 and 229–30 from J. Hartley, *The Politics of Pictures: the Creation of Public in the Age of Popular Media* (New York: Routledge). © 1992 by John Hartley. Reprinted with permission from Taylor & Francis Books UK.

It is important to clarify what is going on here, for the process of visualization involves two sense-making moves, which may be parallel but which are certainly moving in opposite directions. Richard Ericson, Patricia Baranek and Janet Chan open their study of news organization, *Visualizing Deviance*, with some observations which help to identify the opposing tendencies in journalism.

First they characterize journalists as 'playing a key role in constituting visions of order, stability and change, and in influencing the control practices that accord with these visions':

> In effect, journalists join with other agents of control as a kind of 'deviance-defining élite', using the news media to provide an ongoing articulation of the proper bounds to behaviour in all organized spheres of life. Moreover, journalists do not merely reflect others' efforts to designate deviance and effect control, but are actively involved themselves as social-control agents. . . . In sum, journalists are central agents in the reproduction of order.[3]

The sense-making component of this process of social visualization and control, it should be noted, is not *reporting*, if by that is meant observation and recording of a thing or event; sense-making is rightly identified by Ericson, Baranek and Chan as 'ongoing articulation of the proper bounds of behaviour'; it is an exercise in disciplining social activity ('organized behaviour'), by means of discourse ('constituting', 'defining', 'articulating'). The social function of journalism has at this general structural level nothing to do with the reality or truth of pre-discursive events in themselves, but with the diegetic world imagined inside reporting; a world verified by constant and militant reference to the real, to be sure, but one in which the real is secondary to the vision, for it is the visualization of order/disorder that is authenticated by reference to actuality, not vice versa. Journalism, in short, makes sense by inventing the real in the image of vision.

Second, this characterization of journalism as a social discourse of disciplinary vision leads to the parallel but contrary observation that truth, as *that which exists in fact*, has already been toppled from its pedestal; journalism seeks verification in *that which can be seen*, but it needs to be understood that what is being verified in such moves is not the truth of factual existence but the plausibility of the discursive vision. The method of journalism, as described by Ericson, Baranek and Chan, draws it in the opposite direction from reporting that which exists in fact at a very great rate of knots:

> Using their sources, journalists offer accounts of reality, their own versions of events as they think they are most appropriately visualized. The object of their accounts is rarely presented for the viewer, listener, or reader to contemplate directly. This is so even in television news, where the pictures are most often of the reporter and his or her sources giving a 'talking head' account. Rarely shown are the documents, behaviours, or other objects that are the subject of the account. And even when they are shown, it is usually to represent indexically or symbolically, rather than iconically.[4]

In other words, the 'reality', whether it be a person, an event (behaviour) or a document, does not mean what it says, at least for the viewer of news. It means: *You can see with your own eyes that I symbolize reality*, because seeing is believing; but what the viewer actually sees is the journalist and his or her account, anchored to reality by visual evidence, which however is not evidence for viewers to read directly (iconically), but to use as verisimilitude (the simulation of truth). Journalists are engaged in producing realist logic of the order of *thus it can be seen that . . .*, but what can be seen is the 'account', the 'version', not the 'reality', even in its textualized form ('documents').

A Real Surprise

Such logic will come as no surprise to students of discourse and textuality, for whom it is axiomatic that reality is a socio-discursive construction, beyond which it is impossible for our sense-making species to go. But these students do not as yet comprise a majority of those who 'contemplate' news as viewers, listeners or readers, even though journalism, using the methods described, now pervades whole populations and entire continents with its visions of order, photo-negativized into stories of disorder. For journalism as a social agency of visualization and control to work, it seems that the vast populations it converts into contemplators of order must not associate truth with *that which exists in fact*, but with *plausible stories*, packed with diegetic visual verisimilitude.

Perhaps the success of this enterprise is historically unsurprising too, for notions of truth as generated by militant nineteenth-century modernist science, presuming that truth exists independently of the observer (but that it can nonetheless be revealed by observation), are not as influential in popular culture as at least one alternative, which finds truth not stranger than fiction but the direct product of fiction. This popular theory of truth is not necessarily 'of' the people, but it does have a long history of being 'for' them. It is in fact a pedagogic strategy developed before the contemporary popular media were technologically or socially established (but after the people who would form the audiences for contemporary media were already being formed by industrialization, urbanization and mass mobility). The literature of popular instruction of the nineteenth-century social engineers, who built bridges of ideology over the yawning chasms between intellectual knowledge and popular reality, used fiction as their mainstay. Here for instance is one of the most prolific of them, R. M. Ballantyne, whose popular *Miscellany* series of cheap books, illustrated with proto-photos, was issued in the 1880s to place 'interesting information' in the hands of those, 'especially the young', who could not otherwise afford access to it. Ballantyne's 'plan' for the *Miscellany* gives this as its general strategy:

> Truth is stranger than fiction, but fiction is a valuable assistant in the development of truth. Both, therefore, shall be used in these volumes. Care will be taken to ensure, as far as possible, that the *facts* stated shall be true, and that the *impressions* given shall be truthful. As all classes, in every age, have proved that tales and stories are the most popular style of literature, each volume of the series . . . will contain a complete tale, the heroes and actors in which, together with the combination of circumstances in which they move, shall be more or less fictitious.[5]

It is worth recording that the volume from which I'm quoting was awarded to its first owner as a 'Reward for Punctual Attendance' by the Sheffield School Board, whose proud device is printed with the date 1870: the year of the Forster Education Act in Britain, which inaugurated free compulsory elementary education for all. So the first generation of literates called into being by universal education were taught that fictitious tales which give a (Hobbesian) *impression* of truth are *in fact* true.

What is really surprising, perhaps, is that the global-social pervasion of journalism in the second half of the twentieth century is using the time-honoured method of visionary storytelling to popularize its epistemological opposite: the ideology of militant nineteenth-century scientific modernism. The heroic eyewitness, out there in the dark continent of reality, piercing the tangled undergrowth of jungly ignorance with the steady eye of the dispassionate observer, is no longer the destiny of scientist explorers like Speke, but of reporters, from top-of-the-range foreign and war correspondents to humble local juniors standing in front of doorways, the visionaries of our times whose stories are authenticated by *being there*, but whose accounts are rendered truthful by, well, faking.

Face Values: Faking, Truth

How can truth result from faking? Late in their study of newsroom culture, Ericson, Baranek and Chan turn to the question of faking in news stories. They suggest that 'fake words' (like 'political terrorism' to describe an *unexplained* bombing incident) are 'required to invest these matters with significance, to make it apparent to common sense that what was being visualized was worth attending to'. Fake words are 'important in filling the gap between a random event in the world and what most people find meaningful'. They continue:

> The need for order, coherence, and unity also motivated other practices commonly referred to in the newsroom as 'fakes'. . . . The term 'fake' within newsroom culture was not used to refer to intentional deception or forging. Rather, it referred to simulation devices, and fictions that would add order, coherence, and unity and thus make their items, segments, and entire newscasts more presentable and plausible.[6]

Such professional fouls are not a fabrication of events to deceive the public; on the contrary they are designed to help public understanding of the world by rendering it meaningful at a structural level, as a whole. Part of the sham actually has nothing to do with the stories as events, but with the presentation of them *as true*:

> Something deeply ingrained in the plausibility structure of newscasts is that the outlet's journalists have been 'everywhere' to cull the news and to produce first-hand accounts of their discoveries. Hence, references are dropped in at appropriate places in the script to the effect that the outlet's journalists have overextended themselves to ensure that they are on-the-scene witnesses of reality for their audiences.[7]

This ideology of eyewitness authenticity is much stronger than the actuality of news-gathering practices. It's a case of form being out of sync with content.

Neither reporters nor their subjects are always where they appear to be. A direct-to-camera stand-up in front of a building is not the same as, but does signify, the reporter's 'being there', the newsworthy event itself presumably unfolding behind his or her back as we watch. Celebrity faces (the current hero-villains of a given tale) are illustrated whenever they are mentioned in a story, using whatever footage is available, which may be months or years old and out of context; the same 15 seconds used night after night in a running story, usually showing the hapless personality endlessly entering or leaving a building or doorway, caught on the cusp between public and private space. Footage is not dated, so news is always 'news', present tense, even when it isn't, The story of a report criticizing police violence against Aborigines is visualized with library footage of an unidentified police/Aboriginal stand-off, in which what is actually shown is an Aborigine striking a police riot shield. Sound effects are added to mute or even still pictures, or conversely a stock shot of a tycoon addressing an AGM is shown mute under a voiceover about a different matter entirely. Editing deftly guides viewers as to what a story means (emotionally, not intellectually). A shot of a war-injured/famished/refugee child is held longer than the information requires, deferred to the 'moment of truth', which is when the close-up victim looks up directly into the camera (at which point several million lumps rise into several million throats, and a proud professional editor can cry 'Gotcha, you sentimental bastards!'). Non-diegetic music and even slow-motion photography are used to emotionalize a homecoming. A single interview with stock-footage cutaways is used to signify a complex event/controversy, while in fact being the visualization of a preconceived news angle commissioned in advance of the event by the news editor of the day. All this is faking, but all the stories thus faked are true.

Meanwhile, as Ericson, Baranek and Chan say, 'good television news has visuals to show what the reporter has visualized in his script' – it is the script, not the event, that is primary. Their example is of a shot of a woman looking up at a burning building with a horrified expression, used to illustrate the truth of the reporter's voiceover: 'relatives waited anxiously for news of the trapped victims'. No doubt they did, but it so happened that the only 'relative' this *particular* woman had in the building was her cat. It doesn't matter; it's the 'truthfulness' of the story, narrated by fictitious devices, that matters. Ericson, Baranek and Chan conclude:

> Editors and producers are compelled to imaginatively construe, alter, and even forgo the facts in order to sustain news as a form of fiction. Concerned as they are with news as theatre, it is impossible for them to 'reflect the essential truth without distortion', or to avoid having 'production techniques . . . distort reality'. . . . The fact of fiction is too central to the news genre for it to be otherwise.[8]

Journalism, then, pervades society with visualizations of order, coherence and unity, which are verified by reference to the eyewitness ideology of newsgathering, and by the ocular proof of visual evidence, but which use that ideology and that evidence in a semiotic struggle between 'random events' and meaningfulness (a struggle which for journalists themselves takes the form of the endless war between picture and soundtrack, sight and sense), in the course of which truth becomes the textual product of fiction, 'theatre' and faking.

It would be easy to conclude that journalism is flawed, making truth claims that are at odds with its ability to deliver; it would be easy to charge journalism with professional hypocrisy or at least wilfull blindness to its own shortcomings. But such a judgmental response to some of the contradictions inherent in journalism:

fake v. truth
fictional form v. factual content
script v. event
narration v. information
emotional response v. dispassionate record
meaningless pictures v. voiceover interpretation
random events v. coherent stories
reports of disorder v. visualized order
picture v. sound

would be playing the same game, trying to resolve the contradictions one way or the other ('should we have raw footage or cooked books?'), preserving a belief in (overvaluing) truth, coherence and order, while stigmatizing (undervaluing) fake, random, disorder. Such a procedure ignores the very obvious characteristic of journalism, which is to hold these oppositions in tension, constantly negotiating a relationship between the two sides, expending really prodigious effort and considerable professional skill on holding the line between them.

Trying to 'decide' *between* these opposites is mere holier than thou self-deception by the critic, and it has at least one general and immediate effect – it limits truth to the coherence/order/eyewitness side of the equation, and denies it to the fake/random/disorder/fiction side. This limitation of truth may explain why journalists are respectful and high-minded about 'facts', which belong to the province of order, but simultaneously cavalier and duplicitous in their use of the very words and pictures that give literalism to their visualizations of order. Unfortunately, it seems that journalists themselves insist on making this ideological binary choice, in order to make sense of, and to be able to continue with, the execution of their social function: to 'provide an ongoing articulation of the proper bounds to behaviour in all organized spheres of life' (Ericson, Baranek and Chan's phrase, quoted p. 141; proclaiming the truthfulness (credibility) of their visions, but hiding both their own presentational fictionality and the world's inchoate chaos. The professional ideology of journalists, in codes of ethics, editorial manifestos and informal reflection, 'chooses' truth. But because of that ideology's binary distinction between imagined facts (sacrosanct) and their actual textual realizations (mere tools and tricks of the trade), the choice is one that restricts truth to facticity, exempting from its sway the very vehicle that conveys it to the public.

To make matters yet more difficult for journalism, even the choice to restrict truth to the domain of facts is no longer such an easy one to make. For facts are not what they used to be.

Two Faces: Janus (Journalism/Science); Twin Peaks (Truth/Communication)

The physical sciences are beginning to theorize, with chaos or catastrophe theory, the possibility of randomness, chance, uncertainty and disorder within the very substance of the universe of things that had previously been imagined as working like clockwork – accurate, interconnected, predictable, reliable, and very well made out of lovely materials. The metaphor is so elegant, in fact, that it takes over; the universe becomes evidence to support the metaphor, transformed into an invention of eighteenth-century rationalist-materialist expansionism, not so much cosmos as chronometer. Meanwhile, certain social, cultural and textual theories (let's call them postmodernist) are beginning to challenge the scientific concept of truth with suggestions that the belief in revelation of truth is as mystical as belief in other kinds of (religious) revelation, that visions of order, coherence and unity are 'totalizing fictions', and that fiction itself, far from being the poor relation of mighty imperial truth, is in fact the characteristic human mechanism for knowledge production, and not just in fairy tales, news or popular miscellanies. The implications of such theories of uncertainty and semiotic productivity are that journalism ought not to be put on trial for being untrue to its own eyewitness ideology; instead it ought to be investigated forensically and historically to see why as a social institution it has maintained for several hundred years the twin but incommensurate commitments to hard, empirical, countable, observable facticity on the one hand, and to fakery, fictionality, tales and 'truthful impressions' on the other.

It is my own hunch that the problem, if it is one, arises out of journalism's twin commitment to truth and communication.

Ever since Newton, science has developed institutionally on the premise that the world is knowable, that observation is the means of knowledge, and that observation will lead not merely to information but to a revelation and understanding of the underlying 'laws' of physics (Newton), of nature (Darwin), and of society (Marx). Journalism is committed to the same metaphysical belief in underlying laws (order), but in addition to this it is committed to generalizing (i.e. making generally available to the general public) these militant scientific realisms (laws of order) through the form of its own methodology of eyewitness visualization; its credibility depends not only on veracity but also on popularity, which in this case doesn't necessarily mean 'well-liked', but does mean 'ubiquitous'.

Journalism, however, actually predates the physical, natural and social sciences as a profession and a discourse, so its twin peaks of truth and popularization are not, historically, mere vulgarized, inverted reflections of a philosophy of knowledge whose summits are found somewhere else (the snow-capped pinnacles of pure science). Historically, in fact, news was classically coterminous with philosophy, being a feature of the same Athenian idleness ('loytering and prating') out of which western philosophy was born.

Interestingly, modern philosophy, arising from the works of Francis Bacon and Thomas Hobbes in the early part of the seventeenth century, is also coterminous with the first English news, permitted by royal licence (though only foreign news) in 1622. In May of that year appeared Nicholas Bourne and Thomas Archer's *Weekely Newes*, and on 15 October *A Relation of the late Occurrents which have happened in Christendom, Nouo 1*, and *A Continuation of the Affaires of the Low Countries, etc., No. 2* were published together by Nathaniel Butter.[9] The professional organization of rationalist materialist science, on the other hand, in the form of the Royal Society, did not occur until after the Restoration, in 1662. (One of the Royal Society's founding members was the prattling sticky-beak gossip John Aubrey, whose *Brief Lives* is a marvel of journalism if not science, and whose antiquarianism, presumably the 'scientific' reason for his membership, was just as founded on tales, speculations, and on reading order into the chaos of evidence, not least through the mechanisms of astrology, as is any journalism.)

No, journalistic truth is not the foundling child of scientific truth, though there may be some evidence for the contrary view; instead, scientific and journalistic knowledge are entangled and mutual, reciprocating methods, epistemologies, personnel and prejudices. But there are differences, chief among which is the orientation of the two professions' *gaze*. The speculum of science is trained on the material world, the speculations of journalism are addressed to the social world. This is not the moment to criticize the implied binarism of such a distinction (that the social world is material, and so on); what's important here is that the epistemological Janus of journalism/science, while being connected, actually does look out in opposite directions. Whereas science as a discourse is addressed to 'knowledge', to other scientists and to action upon the bodies analysed, journalism as a discourse is addressed to 'common sense', to the general public and to action upon society. Science, especially pure science, *must not* communicate directly with the general social formation (its truths, its entire institutional structure, could not survive such an encounter); journalism *must*. That's the difference – communication. But the difference is not separation; january journalism and science are still facets of *knowledge*, which is two-faced. And we all know what that means.

So as the following short history of truth will reveal, the journalistic twin peaks of truth and popularization are just that: twins, not mutually exclusive binaries. Right from the start, visualizations of journalistic truth were concerned not only with its own immanent form but also, and crucially, with its diffusion, and so they were just as concerned with instruction as with information. This concern, although pedagogic, does not visualize the *writer* of journalism as being in possession of the truth, but places the 'moment of truth' at the moment of reading, in the *readership*, who are obliged to work it out for themselves on the basis of the evidence and arguments offered – truth is seen as the result of adversarial forensics. Such a position emphasizes the readership, creating a demand for its enlargement and enlightenment in order to bring the whole of society, not just its literate leadership, into the purview of truth. The job of the journalist in these circumstances is above all to unify, to make common, the community of readers; it's a job of generalization. This enterprise, the creation of the 'common reader', characterizes journalistic theory up until the three revolutions of the eighteenth century, the American, French and Industrial.

A Virgin Birth

Traditionally, seers are blind; they cannot see this sublunary world owing to the intensity of their vision of afar (they have tele-vision). The freedom of the press in the English-speaking world was first promulgated by the blind English visionary poet and political pamphleteer, John Milton, whose *Paradise Lost* is a spatial visualization of the cosmos in verse. His *Areopagitica*, a pamphlet addressed to parliament in 1644 in opposition to the licensing of the press, is the first fully argued case for press freedom. In it, Milton visualizes truth thus:

> Truth indeed came once into the world with her divine Master, and was a perfect shape most glorious to look on: but when he ascended, And his Apostles after hime were laind asleep, then strait arose a wicked race of deceivers, who . . . took the virgin Truth, hewd her lovely form into a thousand pieces, and scatter'd them to the four winds. From that time ever since, the sad friends of Truth, such as durst appear . . . went up and down gathering up limb by limb still as they could find them. We have not found them all, Lords and Commons, nor ever shall doe, till her Masters second comming; he shall bring together every joynt and member, and shall mould them into an immortall feature of lovelines and perfection. Suffer not these licencing prohibitions to stand at every place of opportunity forbidding and disturbing them that continue seeking, that continue to do our obsequies to the torn body of our martyr'd Saint.[10]

Over the torn body of an imagined prelapsarian virgin, this is a strictly visionary view of truth. It neatly solves the philosophical problem of the *incommensurate* nature of different truths (i.e. that scientific, religious, philosophical and poetical truths are different from each other and not interchangeable). It does so by making them dismembered parts of a virgin whose 'body is *homogeneal*, and proportionall',[11] or would be but for the deceivers who have torn it apart. This body will be whole again at the teleological final cause of the second coming. So the seeker for truth, in Milton's view, is one who finds bits of that body and sticks them together. This metaphor of truth as a vulnerable female body simultaneously homogeneous and dissected is the founding metaphor of journalism, producing in turn a methodology that is to go in search of bits which may not even be recognizable when first discovered, proceeding from the known to the unknown in the manner of a jigsaw puzzle, until a more complete picture is pieced together.

What is progressive and modern about Milton's argument is that his metaphor of vision, and his explanation of the incommensurate nature of truths, is both political and indiscriminate; if truth is strewn around in dismembered bits and pieces, who is to say *in advance* what is true and what is not? Milton argues for the 'liberty to know, to utter, and to argue freely according to conscience, above all liberties',[12] which must include the liberty to be wrong. Furthermore, Milton takes this liberty to be general; the licensing of the press is 'an undervaluing and vilifying of the whole Nation', including 'the common people', who are reproached by such regulations because if we be so jealous over them, as that we dare not trust them with an English pamphlet, what do we but censure them for a giddy, vitious, and ungrounded people; in such a sick and weak estate of faith and discretion, as to be able to take nothing down but through the pipe of a licencer.[13]

If licensing be the means to order for printing, says Milton, in what he clearly offers as a *reductio ad absurdum*, then to preserve order 'we must regulat all recreations and pastimes, all that is delightfull to man', including music, song, dancing, eating ('household gluttony'), drinking, clothing, talking ('mixt conversation'), and mixed company ('idle resort').[14] Unfortunately for his *reductio* virtually all of these activities have in fact been regulated, both before and since Milton's time, precisely because governments have displayed a historic distrust for the 'common people', and have sought to regulate their every move, especially moves associated with the ungoverned ('licencious') disposition and display of their bodies.

The alternative for Milton is to preserve order by guarding the freedom to choose: 'for reason is but choosing'.[15] Compulsory virtue is no virtue, and the greatness and strength of the nation, for Milton, is thus to be measured precisely by the amount of 'disputing, reasoning, reading, inventing, discoursing' that 'the people, or the greater part' are taken up with even at times of national danger and war. Freedom to engage in controversy and 'new invention' leads, says Milton, to prosperity, honour and greatness for the nation, while regulation leads back to the state of former ignorance, 'brutish, formall, and slavish'.[16]

But how is such a policy to be implemented? For freedom of the press in this vision is not freedom *from* restraint only, it is freedom *to* seek knowledge. The answer is journalism; it performs the function of preserving order by disseminating to the people the power of choice, which is reason. But without official control and government guidance, how would the people, restored to bodily health by freedom of speech (having been made sick in the first place not by their own giddy viciousness but by the 'pipe of a licencer'), know how to recognize the fragments of truth among the detritus of deception? The method that follows from Milton's model of truth, choice, reason and freedom is still the mainspring of journalism: in order for people to exercise reason there must be alternatives from which to choose, and to make choice itself clearer the alternatives must be as extreme as possible, a requirement that inevitably pushes journalism towards binarism – both sides of the story. Journalistic method is not to describe the world as it is, but to visualize extremes, both positive and negative, visions of disorder, deviations from the line, binary polarities. Without having to determine or define in advance what constitutes order, or what truth's fragmented body looks like, such a method visualizes order and truth negatively by assigning each case or event to one side of a line or the other. By such a method the public can recognize and reconnect for itself the thousand pieces of truth's 'lovely form', a kind of skiamorphic ('shadow-form') silhouette seen not directly, perhaps but in outline, and order can be 'calculated' by triangulating between the various disorders that surround it and thus define its boundary. Journalism thus gives the public something to do; to choose, according to reason, the shape of their own truth.

A Spectator . . .

Appropriately for the art of visualizing order, one of the earliest regular journals was called the *Spectator*. It will serve to show that some of the preoccupations of journalism are very persistent. Number 567 of the *Spectator* for Wednesday, 14 July 1714, for instance, opens with some comments which illuminate both the style of journalism at that time and the relations between journalists and their readership:

> I have received private advice from some of my correspondents, that if I would give my paper a general run, I should take care to season it with scandal. I have indeed observed of late, that few writings sell which are not filled with great names and illustrious titles. . . . A sprinkling of the words 'faction, Frenchman, papist, plunderer,' and the like significant terms, in an Italic character, have also a very good effect upon the eye of the purchaser; not to mention 'scribbler, liar, rogue, rascal, knave, and villain', without which it is impossible to carry on a modern controversy.[17]

Although tongue in cheek, this is an account of what would now be called news values, first among which is audience maximization – giving the paper a 'general run' by making it appeal to 'the eye of the purchaser'. 1714 news values are based on the same tenet as now: bad news is good news. Scandal, elite names, adversarial controversy, accusations of corruption (liar . . . villain) in the same breath as the creation of external enemies (Frenchmen . . . papists), are still the standard visualizations of disorder, served up in what passed for sensationalist style at the time – italic typeface, together with 'the secret virtue of an innuendo' conveyed by dashes, asterisks and etceteras, so that 'the reader casts his eye upon a new book, and, if he finds several letters separated from one another by a dash, he buys it up and peruses it with great satisfaction'.

The following edition of the *Spectator*, No. 568 for Friday 16 July 1714, carries on this theme by relating how such journalism was actually consumed, and by what type of reader:

> I was yesterday in a coffee-house not far from the Royal Exchange, where I observed three persons in close conference over a pipe of tobacco; upon which, having filled one for my own use, I lighted it at the little wax candle that stood between them; and, after having thrown in two or three whiffs amongst them, sat down and made one of the company. I need not tell my reader that lighting a man's pipe at the same candle is looked upon among brother smokers as an overture to conversation and friendship. As we here laid our heads together in a very amicable manner, being entrenched under a cloud of our own raising, I took up the last Spectator [the issue quoted above], and casting my eye over it, 'The Spectator', says I, 'is very witty to-day.'[18]

The wit is in fact a practical joke being played by Mr Spectator for the amusement of his readers; he uses the ensuing conversation to provoke one of his interlocutors, an 'angry politician' with a 'contemptuous manner', into declaring that the asterisks and dashes inserted in the previous day's *Spectator* clearly referred to himself. The moral of this story is that they did not:

At my leaving the coffee-house, I could not forbear reflecting with myself upon that gross tribe of fools who may be termed the over wise, and upon the difficulty of writing any thing in this censorious age which a weak head may not construe into private satire and personal reflection.[19]

In the meantime there are a couple of sociological facts to be gleaned from this pleasant fiction. The journalist addresses his readers as a community united by the etiquette of pipe-smoking in coffee-houses, where it is taken for granted that the *Spectator* is found, and the readership comprises men who are not personally acquainted but who may converse as intimates – that is, men of the same class, a class moreover whose members may expect not only to read the *Spectator* but to appear in it, if only by innuendo, and even if they are fools. This glimpse into the public – private, clubby atmosphere of the then fashionable coffee-houses reveals the first, very upper-crust, home for journalism, where it appears as a discourse on politics, manners, writing and wit, for a readership of leisured gentlemen.

The society visualized by Mr Spectator is by no means archaic. The closed, inward-looking, gentlemanly, mutual contempt of his coffee-house encounter is still familiar, having become a kind of emblem of British 'upperclassness', mythologized for a mass readership in detective thrillers (Wodehouse, Christie), where a civilized but murderous community gathers in some conveniently sequestered stately home or hotel to bump each other off, observed by a Poirot–Marple–Spectator outside/insider who can see, under the polish and politeness, a tribe of fools and a censorious age. The difference is of course that Agatha Christie's society is fully fictional, consumed most avidly by those whose social circumstances render 'high' society a remote fantasy, while Mr Spectator's vision of coffee, pipe and paper pretends not only to reality but also to influence, construing his readers as the very same community of top people that appears in his story. But that apparent difference hides the fact that both of these worlds are rendered visible (real) to the *reader* by the devices of *writing*, which in both cases connect the reader to society by putting into suspenseful narrative the actions and dialogue of an isolated, self-absorbed group of characters, whose deeds and words are not even legible to themselves, let alone to the public, without the help of a spectator–participant. Journalism, in 1714, was already *fictionalizing* the world of affairs, placing itself in a *forensic* relation to society; the 'spectator' is no innocent bystander but an active agent in the *representation* of the imagined public to itself: it actually doesn't matter whether or not the coffee-house conversation reported by Mr Spectator ever took place, or the 'angry politician' ever existed, for their function is precisely representative, and any truth-impression results not from their existential status but from the plausibility of the anecdote in relation to the reader's experience.

. . . in a Fog

News values and the creative spectator–journalist are not the only aspects of journalism to have persisted from the eighteenth century. The stories are pretty much the same too. *Fog's Weekly Journal* of 20 November 1736, for instance, contains five distinct sections: Foreign Affairs, Country News, London, a feature story from a correspondent in Cairo (a lively mixture of history and myth, gossip and speculation), and advertisements, which take up the still customary proportion of the paper, just under 50 per cent. The layout and presentation is unfamiliar, with the feature coming first, the advertisements gathered together at the back, and the stories running on from one to the next without much formal differentiation. There are no pictures (apart from a device calling attention to the largest display advertisement), and the headlines, such as they are, indicate the generic sections of the paper not the content of the ensuing story. But the stories themselves are surprisingly familiar, from the range of topics and subject matter to the content of individual items.

Foreign Affairs comprises a round-up from the major European capitals (and from '*Independant Tartary*'), comprising updates on government business and anecdotes about illustrious individuals. Country News opens with a story which could have come from today's business section:

From *Dublin*, That a Piece of Irish Holland, or Linnen, was bought for 40s. per Yard. *If our foreign Trade could be reduc'd, which is at present so flourishing, and Industry encouraged at Home in numberless Branches of Business, our Wants would be likewise reduced, our Poor better fed, and an Infinity of People better employ'd.*

They're still working on that one. Around the country, the newsworthy stories are: 'That the young Woman in Prison for the Murder of her Child, dash'd her Head against a large Nail, she found in the Dungeon, which pierc'd her Brain and kill'd her'; there's a storm, a fire, an arrest, and, 'from *Exeter* . . . the Loss of Capt. Skinner, with several of his Men, and a Cargo of 20000 1. is confirm'd: And likewise the Convicts, shipp'd at Biddeford for Transportation; but the Thimble-Men from Ilchester Gaol went in another Vessel, which arrived safe.'

From London:

Our Affairs at Home run much in the same Road this Week as the last, Hopkins a Hop Merchant, was attack'd between Tooting and Clapham, by two Footpads, who knock'd him off his Horse, and robb'd him of 16 1. his Watch, Great Coat, Hat and Wig.

They're still working on that one too, though nowadays footpads are called muggers. There are also the usual stories of the dressings-up and doings of the elite: the 'fine Appearance of Nobility, Quality and Gentry' at court; a judicial appointment; a royal birth; an overseas ministerial death. There's a miscellany of news items: the loss to 'Angria the Pyrate' of an East Indiaman and its £100,000 cargo; a proposal to beautify a London square; a summary of the stock market; and juicy titbits from the courts, already a news staple:

A Cause is at Issue in Westminster Hall, between a Gentleman who has dealt much in Beauty, Plaintiff, and a young Lady of particular Virtue, Defendant, on Account of a Mistake concerning three Yards of Lace, of above 20 1. a Yard. The Fair receiv'd it as a Present, but the Gentleman design'd it for a Pair of Ruffles, and has therefore brought his Action of Trouver and Conversion.

It's not quite a case of *plus ça change*, but the treatment, preoccupations and prejudices of these stories are far from alien. This is remarkable not so much because of the passage of time but because of the persistence of journalism as a form of writing despite changes, almost an inversion, in its readership. Journalism still frequently reads like this gentlemanly digest, even though the readership is not now made up of gentlemen, but of those who appear in *Fog's Weekly Journal* only as subjects or outsiders: threatening (footpads), alien (convicts), disreputable (the Lady with Lace virtues), or pitiful (the prison suicide). Not to put too fine a point on it, popular readerships of today are closer in class to these unfortunates than to Hopkins the Hop Merchant, with whom the bewigged and hatted reader of *Fog's Weekly Journal* is being invited to identify. But the language of identification hasn't yet caught up with the democratization of readership; nowadays we're all addressed as if we're tut-tutting gentlemen deploring the criminal tendencies of the population (to which we belong), while joining in the business of the high and mighty (to which we do not).

Duty (and Desire), under Colour of Authority

Within a century of Milton's manifesto, journalism was sufficiently established to be recognizable as a distinct profession, separate from other branches of writing. In the meantime there had been a regicide, an interregnum, a Restoration, a 'Glorious Revolution' and the establishment of the bourgeois liberal parliamentary constitution, not to mention an empire, to which Britain was already sending convicts, and where rumblings were already ominous – the main item of metropolitan news in *Fog's Weekly Journal* for 20 November 1736 is this:

> We hear great Complaints from Carolina of the Georgians, who whether out of Necessity, or a rapacious Desire of what is none of their own, have plunder'd and taken under Colour of Authority, the Goods of lawful Traders in the upper Cherokee Nation, far North of any Part of Georgia Colony.

That problem would not concern the London press or public for very much longer, for the 'Colour of Authority' in the American empire was soon to change its stripe. But the varying fortunes of 'Necessity' v. 'rapacious Desire' were not only of import in the world of public affairs as such, they were of increasing moment within journalism itself as its practitioners struggled to keep up with all this. For the scribblers of Grub Street it was time to put their own house in order, to endow their profession with the respectability of its own code of ethics, its own 'Colour of Authority'.

What better than to plunder the neighbouring colonies of Literature and History? This was done, in 1758 (and republished in 1788), by no less a personage than Dr Samuel Johnson, the archetypal English 'man of letters', professional writer and journalist, codifier of the English language in his *Dictionary*, of critical judgements in his literary writings and conversations, and 'Of the Duty of a Journalist' in this:

> A Journalist is an Historian, not indeed of the highest class, nor of the number of those whose works bestow immortality on others or themselves; yet, like other Historians, he

distributes for a time reputation or infamy, regulates the opinions of the weak, raises hopes and terrors, inflames or allays the violence of the people.[20]

This vision of journalism has two theoretical underpinnings. First, popularization, communication, visualizing deviance: Johnson's journalist performs a series of up/ down operations on presumed but unstated norms or steady-state conditions; the journalist distributes, regulates or raises by over- or undervaluing as appropriate – immortality/time, reputation/infamy, hopes/terrors, allays/inflames. Second, truth: the journalist, like the historian, is subject to law:

> He ought therefore to consider himself as subject at least to the first law of History, the Obligation to tell Truth. The Journalist, indeed, however honest, will frequently deceive, because he will frequently be deceived himself. He is obliged to transmit the earliest intel ligence before he knows how far it may be credited; he relates transactions yet fluctuating in uncertainty; he delivers reports of which he knows not the Authors. It cannot be expected that he should know more than he is told, or that he should not sometimes be hurried down the current of a popular clamour. All that he can do is to consider attentively, and determine impartially; to admit no falsehoods by design, and to retract those which he shall have adopted by mistake.[21]

It's worth remembering that this is 1758, for these 'ethics' sound thoroughly contemporary, with the emphasis on a truth that is far from absolute, but is contingent upon deadlines, flux, uncertainty, lack of authority, unreliable sources, and the demands of demand (popular clamour); in these circumstances, Johnson's idea of the duty of the journalist is also contemporary, resting on the principles of impartiality and retraction.

It seems that some contemporary criticisms of journalists have been around for nearly a quarter of a millenium too, for Johnson goes on to castigate what is now called sensationalism, blaming it in 1758 on the very same causes:

> This is not much to be required, and yet this is more than the writers of news seem to exact from themselves. It must surely sometimes raise indignation to observe with what serenity of confidence they relate on one day, what they know not to be true, because they hope that it will please; and with what shameless tranquility they contradict it on the next day, when they find that it will please no longer; how readily they receive any report that will disgrace our enemies; and how eagerly they accumulate praises upon a name which caprice or accident has made a favourite. They know, by experience, however destitute of reason, that what is desired will be credited without nice examination: they do not therefore always limit their narratives by possibility, but slaughter armies without battles, and conquer countries without invasions.[22]

It's tempting to read this prescient comment in the light of the Gulf and other modern media wars: Panama, Tripoli, Grenada, the Falklands . . . (but I refrain). What's important at this point are the terms Johnson employs to 'oppose' truth, for it is not direct *falsehood* that raises his righteous ire. He opposes truth with *pleasure*, reason with *desire*, making pleasure the opposite of truth, and making reason destitute the moment desire walks in. At one level this is common sense (of which more later), but at another level it is certainly open to question whether truth and pleasure, desire and reason, are mutually exclusive binary oppositions. This was not a problem that troubled Johnson, because he was sure of the answer. The opposition truth/reason v. pleasure/desire convinced him *bodily;* like Hobbes he was able to follow the materialist philosophical method of '*Reade thy selfe*', and what he read included his own considerable desires, which ran to gluttony, sloth and sex, which he recognized but struggled manfully to overcome. Refusing, for instance, an offer regularly to enjoy the backstage entertainments at David Garrick's theatre, he said 'I will never come back. For the white boobies and the silk stockings of your Actresses excite my genitals.'[23]

The Common Reader

Caprice, accident and 'the current of a popular clamour' are all, for Johnson, like sex, self-evidently beyond truth and reason; Johnson, journalism, and science are at one on this. But it's a risky discrimination, for it allows pleasure, desire, clamour, favourites, praise and disgrace to go unanalysed, explicable only as accident and caprice (fate), and it directs attention away from the dynamics of storytelling towards the facticity of information, hopeful, presumably, that narrative can be disciplined ('limited') by something that actually has nothing to do with it ('possibility'). Johnson sets up a form/content binary which valorizes content, but thereby lets form off the hook of reason and analysis.

Journalism is still Johnsonian in this respect. It is interesting to discover that the attributes that Ericson, Baranek and Chan identify as central to journalism's general social project have been isolated as the specific prose style of Johnson himself: Johnsonian prose 'is a use of language designed to give the raw, chaotic, disparate material of human life a quality of generalization, order and cohesion which will render it bearable, controllable, usable'.[24] Samuel Johnson's stature in the eighteenth century was such that his journalism, in the form of periodical essays from the *Rambler* (1750–2), the *Adventurer* (1753) and the *Idler* (1758–60 – to which 'Of the Duty of a Journalist' is a preface), was 'widely and deeply influential'.[25] This was partly because of Johnson's personal stamp; his prowess as a moralist, critic, poet and scholar resulted in the classic literary judgement, expressed here by one of his modern editors, that 'it will not seem excessive to claim that as *man of letters* no one in the English language can stand beside him'.[26] But Johnson's qualities were more than personal:

> The eighteenth century was the first age in which . . . the modern structure of the literary world, with its publishers and their establishments, its periodicals and their editors, all resting on the basis of the great anonymous public which pays for what it reads, was beginning to emerge. The whole structure, in turn, rested on a steady growth in population, urbanization, and literacy.[27]

The good Doctor presided over the invention, establishment and supply of that 'great anonymous public' during the period when it became not only a market, paying for what it read, but also an ideological construct, the naming of which has been credited to Johnson himself: 'Johnson's confidence rested, ultimately, on his faith in the "common reader". He invented the phrase; his age, almost, invented the thing – the anonymous, multitudinous arbiter of taste.'[28]

The anonymous 'common reader', whose judgement is expressed in (and *as*) the market, and for whom truth is thus a commodity or consumer good, is a novelty for Johnson, who nonetheless trusts it – he prefers commercial publication for a market ('learning itself is a trade') to the previous economy of knowledge, namely patronage ('what flattery! what falsehood!'), saying that 'the world always lets a man tell what he thinks, his own way', so under the regime of the common reader a writer 'throws truth among the multitude, and lets them take it as they please'.[29] This is not Edmund Burke's later and much more celebrated 'swinish multitude'; Johnson (himself a provincial of humble family) does not hold his imagined common multitude of readers in contempt, but is content to throw his pearls among them, with commercial journalism as the slingshot of truth, as it were. Boswell says:

> He had, indeed, upon all occasions, a great deference for the general opinion: 'A man (said he) who writes a book, thinks himself wiser or wittier than the rest of mankind; he supposes that he can instruct or amuse them, and the publick to whom he appeals, must, after all, be the judges of his pretensions.'[30]

Johnson is not concerned about the character of the reader (seeing the multitude not as swinish, but as the public). He is more concerned about the quality of writing; journalists should take care that what they throw are in fact pearls. To this end, however, regard for the truth is not enough. Journalists must keep faith with the humblest readers too. Johnson includes as part of the duty of a journalist communication *across* the demographic boundaries of class, gender and specialism, creating a 'common' sense out of restricted knowledges for the common reader, generalizing across the whole of society those visions of order which are the subject of journalism, but doing all this with due regard for the readership as well as the truth:

> A Journalist, above most other men, ought to be acquainted with the lower orders of mankind, that he may be able to judge, what will be plain, and what will be obscure; what will require a comment, and what will be apprehended without explanation. He is to consider himself not as writing to students or statesmen alone, but to women, shopkeepers, and artisans, who have little time to bestow upon mental attainments, but desire, upon easy terms, to know how the world goes; who rises, and who falls; who triumphs, and who is defeated.[31]

Here is a Johnson who has allowed a little ambiguity to creep into his own stern rationalist binarism; here the 'desire, upon easy terms, to know' is not desire *opposed* to reason and truth, but is presented as a reasonable demand by the public, which is itself socially pervasive (in eighteenth-century demographic terms). Johnson is at one with Milton, then, in assigning to the *general* public the power of choice, and in Johnson it is clear that the public means the 'reading public', the 'common reader'.

Already, in 1758, the public, deleted from the political stage by Hobbes, has been reconstituted not only into a fiction imagined by those who address it – the anonymous multitude of common readers – but also into a community, if that's the right word, whose relationship with politics is mediated by journalism. 'How the world goes; who rises, and who falls; who triumphs, and who is defeated' is an apt description of political activity, but here it is not a product of politics as such but the textual product of a kind of journalism which can judge, comment and explain it, in easy terms, to non-specialists, throughout society, through visualizations of disorder (rises/falls, triumphs/defeats). The duty of the journalist was to spread enlightenment throughout society, and with it the heliological metaphor of Enlightenment itself. Journalism has already achieved its contemporary purpose, which can be summarized as the production of 'common' sense.

Notes

1. Jacques Derrida (1978) *Writing and Difference*, trans. Alan Bass, London: Routledge & Kegan Paul, p. 92. The internal quotations are from J.L. Borges, *La Sphère de Pascal.*
2. ibid.
3. Richard V. Ericson, Patricia M. Baranek and Janet B.L. Chan (1987) *Visualizing Deviance: a Study of News Organization*, Milton Keynes: Open University Press, p. 3.
4. ibid., p. 4.
5. R.M. Ballantyne (1882) *Saved by the Lifeboat: a Tale of Wreck and Rescue on the Coast*, London: James Nisbet. This quotation from the introductory note, p. iii.
6. Ericson *et al.*, op. cit., p. 339.
7. ibid.
8. ibid., pp. 340–2.
9. 'Numbering a newspaper', *The Times* (no. 50,000) 25 November 1944.
10. John Milton (1644) 'Areopagitica', in C.A. Patrides (ed.) (1974) *John Milton: Selected Prose*, Harmondsworth: Penguin, pp. 234–5.
11. ibid., p. 236.
12. ibid., p. 241.
13. ibid., pp. 226–7.
14. ibid., pp. 218–19.
15. ibid., p. 220.
16. ibid., pp. 239–41.
17. *The Spectator, Corrected from the Originals . . . by N. Ogle, Esq., in Eight Volumes*, London: Geo. B. Whittaker, 1827; Volume VIII, p. 112.
18. ibid., p. 115.
19. ibid., p. 117.
20. Samuel Johnson (1788), 'Of the Duty of a Journalist' (1758), *The European Magazine, and London Review: Containing the Literature, History, Politics, Arts, Manners & Amusements of the Age* (London: Philological Society of London) XIII: 77–8. Originally published (according to a headnote) as 'the Preface to Payne's Universal Chronicle, in which the Idler originally was printed, in April 1758'.
21. ibid.
22. ibid.
23. Cited in the editor's introduction to Christopher Hibbert (ed.) (1979) *James Boswell: The Life of Johnson*, Harmondsworth: Penguin, p. 25. (The wording differs from the cleaned-up version to be found in the *Life* itself.)

24. Patrick Cruttwell (ed.) (1968) *Samuel Johnson: Selected Writings*, Harmondsworth: Penguin. This quotation from Cruttwell's introduction, p. 21.
25. ibid., p. 22.
26. ibid.
27. ibid., p. 17.
28. ibid., p. 18.
29. From, Johnson's *Journal of* a *Tour to the Hebrides*, cited ibid., p. 17.
30. Hibbert (ed.), op. cit., p. 66.
31. Johnson, 'Of the Duty of a Journalist', op. cit.

59

The Cultural Politics of
News Discourse

Stuart Allen

A senior politician is only ever a sound-bite away from destruction.
(David Mellor, former Conservative government minister)

There is a strong argument that unrelieved coverage of death, crisis and disaster gives a misleading picture of what life is like for most of Britain's citizens most of the time . . . that individual news stories become divorced from proper perspective or context . . . The good news is out there, and the media shouldn't be afraid to report it.

(Martyn Lewis, BBC newsreader)

Journalists are among the pre-eminent story-tellers of modern society. Their news accounts shape in decisive ways our perceptions of the 'world out there' beyond our immediate experience. For many of us, our sense of what is happening in the society around us, what we should know and care about from one day to the next, is largely derived from the news stories they tell. Given that we have to take so much on trust, we rely on news accounts to be faithful representations of reality. We are asked to believe, after all, that truly professional journalists are able to set aside their individual preconceptions, values and opinions in order to depict reality 'as it actually is' to us, their audience. This assumption, deeply inscribed in the methods of 'objective' reporting, encourages us to accept these 'reflections' of reality as the most truthful ones available.

In seeking to render problematic this process of representation, this chapter focuses on how news discourses help to *naturalize* a cultural politics of legitimacy so as to lend justification to modern society's distribution of power and influence. More specifically, it is the extent to which these news discourses effectively *depoliticize* the dominant meanings, values and beliefs associated with these inequalities, and in so doing contribute to their perpetuation, that will be addressed. This chapter thus aims to raise important questions regarding the ways in which the language of news encodifies as 'common sense' a hierarchical series of normative rules by which social life is to be understood.

It will be argued that it is the very *hegemonic* nature of this representational process which needs to be centred for purposes of investigation so as to discern, in turn, how the parameters of 'the public consensus', and with it 'the moral order', are being affirmed, recreated and contested in ideological terms.

Accordingly, the discussion commences with a consideration of the concept of 'hegemony' as it has been taken up by critical researchers analysing the politics of 'common sense'. Attention then turns to newspaper discourse, and later to radio and televisual newscasts, in order to examine a number of the textual strategies in and through which a range of preferred truth-claims about society are inflected as *authoritative, rational* and *appropriate* – and, in this way, potentially *hegemonic*. Such an approach can be shown to provide fresh insights into the means by which news accounts appeal to apparently common-sense renderings of 'reality' ('conventional wisdom', 'received opinion', 'what every reasonable person knows', and so forth) as being self-evidently true. That is to say, it enables the researcher to denaturalize the very naturalness of the ideological rules governing news discourse's representation of 'what can and should be said' about any aspect of social life.

News and Hegemony

For many critical researchers endeavouring to disrupt the seemingly natural tenets of 'common sense' in order to critique them, the concept of 'hegemony' has proven to be highly useful. Most attempts to define the concept attribute its development to Antonio Gramsci, a radical Italian philosopher who died in 1937 after more than a decade in Mussolini's prisons. Very briefly, in his critique of power dynamics in modern societies, Gramsci (1971) describes hegemony as a relation of

> 'spontaneous' consent given by the great masses of the population to the general direction imposed on social life by the dominant fundamental group; this consent is 'historically' caused by the prestige (and consequent confidence) which the dominant group enjoys because of its position and function in the world of production. (Gramsci 1971: 12)

It is this implied distinction between consent and its opposite, coercion, which Gramsci recognizes to be crucial. In the case of the coercive force of ruling groups, he underlines the point that it is the 'apparatus of state coercive power which "legally" enforces discipline on those groups who do not "consent" either actively or passively' (Gramsci 1971: 12). The exercise of this coercive force may involve, for example, the armed forces of the military or the police, courts and prison system to maintain 'law and order'.

This type of coercive control in modern societies is the exception rather than the rule, however, when it comes to organizing public consent. Power, Gramsci argues, is much more commonly exercised over subordinate groups by means of persuasion through 'political and ideological leadership'. It follows that a ruling group is hegemonic only to the degree that it acquires the consent of other groups within its preferred definitions of reality through this type of leadership. In Gramsci's words:

A social group can, and indeed must, already exercise 'leadership' before winning governmental power (this indeed is one of the principal conditions for the winning of such power);
it subsequently becomes dominant when it exercises power, but even if it holds it firmly
in its grasp, it must continue to 'lead' as well. (Gramsci 1971: 57–8)

Subordinate groups are encouraged by the ruling group to negotiate reality within what
are ostensibly the limits of common sense when, in actuality, this common sense is
consistent with dominant norms, values and beliefs. Hegemony is to be conceptualized,
therefore, as a site of ideological struggle over this common sense.

Gramsci's writings on hegemony have proven to be extraordinarily influential for
critical researchers examining the operation of the news media in modern societies.
Three particularly significant (and interrelated) aspects of the cultural dynamics of
hegemony are the following.

First, *hegemony is a lived process*. Hegemonic ideas do not circulate freely in the air
above people's heads; rather, according to Gramsci, they have a material existence in
the cultural practices, activities and rituals of individuals striving to make sense of the
world around them. That is, hegemony is a process embodied in what Williams (1989:
57) aptly describes as 'a lived system of meanings and values', that is, as 'a whole body
of practices and expectations, over the whole of living: our senses and assignments of
energy, our shaping perceptions of ourselves and our world.' It follows that hegemony
constitutes 'a sense of reality for most people in the society' and, as such, is the contradictory terrain upon which the 'lived dominance and subordination' of particular groups
is struggled over in day-to-day cultural practices.

Second, *hegemony is a matter of 'common sense'*. A much broader category than ideology, common sense signifies the uncritical and largely unconscious way of perceiving
and understanding the social world as it organizes habitual daily experience. Gramsci
stresses that common sense, despite the extent to which it is 'inherited from the past
and uncritically absorbed', may be theorized as a complex and disjointed 'infinity of
traces', and as such never simply identical with a class-based ideology. 'Commonsensical' beliefs, far from being fixed or immobile, are in a constant state of renewal: 'new
ideas', as he notes, are always entering daily life and encountering the 'sedimentation'
left behind by this contradictory, ambiguous, 'chaotic aggregate of disparate conceptions' (Gramsci 1971: 422). In critiquing what passes for common sense as 'the residue
of absolutely basic and commonly-agreed, consensual wisdoms', Hall (1977: 325) further
elaborates on this point: 'You cannot learn, through common sense, *how things are*: you
can only discover *where they fit* into the existing scheme of things.'

Third, *hegemony is always contested*. Far from being a totally monolithic system or
structure imposed from above, then, lived hegemony is an active process of negotiation
it can never be taken for granted by the ruling group. In Gramsci's (1971: 348) words,
at stake is 'a cultural battle to transform the popular "mentality" and to diffuse the
philosophical innovations which will demonstrate themselves to be "historically true"
to the extent that they become concretely – i.e. historically and socially – universal.'
Consequently, no one group can maintain its hegemony without adapting to changing
conditions, a dynamic which will likely entail making certain strategic compromises
with the forces which oppose its ideological authority. Dominance is neither invoked

nor accepted in a passive manner; as Williams (1989: 58) points out: 'It has continually to be renewed, recreated, defended, and modified [in relation to] pressures not at all its own.' Hence Gramsci's contention that common sense be theorized as the site upon which the hegemonic rules of practical conduct and norms of moral behaviour are reproduced and – crucially – also challenged and resisted.

Significantly, then, this shift to address the cultural dynamics of hegemony displaces a range of different formulations of 'dominant ideology', most of which hold that news discourse be theorized as concealing or masking the true origins of economic antagonisms, that is, their essential basis in the class struggle. At the same time, this emphasis on the hegemonic imperatives of news discourse allows the critical researcher to avoid the suggestion that the 'effects' of news discourse on its audience be understood simply as a matter of 'false consciousness'. As we shall see, beginning with the next section's discussion of newspaper discourse, an analytical engagement with the cultural dynamics of hegemony provides the researcher with important new insights into how news texts demarcate the limits of 'common sense'.

The Common Sense of Newspaper Discourse

'Journalists believe something is reportable', according to Ericson *et al.*'s (1987: 348) study of Canadian news organizations, 'when they can visualize it in the terms of news discourse.' This process of visualization does not constitute a neutral reflection of 'the world out there'. Rather, it works to reaffirm a hegemonic network of conventionalized rules by which social life is to be interpreted, especially those held to be derivative of 'public opinion' or, at an individual level, 'human nature'. Accordingly, many critical researchers argue that news accounts encourage us to accept as *natural, obvious or commonsensical* certain preferred ways of classifying reality, and that these classifications have far-reaching implications for the cultural reproduction of power relations across society.

In order to develop this line of critique in relation to newspaper discourse, critical researchers have 'borrowed' a range of conceptual tools from various approaches to textual analysis. Particularly influential analyses of newspaper texts have been conducted using, among other methodologies, content analysis, semiotics or semiology, critical linguistics, sociolinguistics and critical discourse analysis (for overviews, see Hartley 1982, 1996; Bell 1991; Fowler 1991; Zelizer 1992; Eldridge 1993; Fairclough 1995; Bell & Garrett 1998). These text-centred approaches provide a basis to break from those forms of analysis which reduce language to a 'neutral' instrument through which 'reality' is expressed. By foregrounding the textual relations of signification, they suggest fascinating new ways to think through Gramsci's theses concerning the lived hegemony of common sense. Moreover, these approaches allow for the opening up of what has become a rather empty assertion, namely that news texts are inherently meaningful, so as to unpack the *naturalness* of the ideological codes implicated in their representations of reality. Thus the notion of 'codification's may be used to specify the means by which the meanings attributed to a text are organized in accordance with certain (usually so *obvious* as to be *taken-for-granted*) rules or conventions.

This is to suggest that a newspaper account, far from simply reflecting the reality of a news event, is actually working to construct a codified definition of what should count as the reality of the event. In order to examine these processes of codification, the specific ways in which a newspaper adopts a preferred language to represent 'the world out there' need to be opened up for analysis. That is to say, it is necessary to identify the means by which a particular newspaper projects its characteristic 'mode of address', its customary way of speaking to its audience, on its pages from one day to the next. Shaping this mode of address, as argued by Hall *et al.* (1978: 60) in *Policing the Crisis*, are a series of imperatives governing how the 'raw materials' of the social world are to be appropriated and transformed into a news account. An event will 'make sense', they argue, only to the extent that it can be situated within 'a range of known social and cultural identifications' or 'maps of meaning' about the social world. Here a key passage by Hall *et al.* (1978) is worth quoting at length:

> The social identification, classification and contextualisation of news events in terms of these background frames of reference is the fundamental process by which the media make the world they report on intelligible to readers and viewers. This process of 'making an event intelligible' is a social process – constituted by a number of specific journalistic practices, which embody (often only implicitly) crucial assumptions about what society is and how it works. One such background assumption is the *consensual* nature of society: the process of *signification* – giving social meanings to events – *both assumes and helps to construct society as a 'consensus'*. We exist as members of one society *because* – it is assumed – we share a common stock of knowledge with our fellow men [and women]: we have access to the same 'maps of meanings'. Not only are we able to manipulate these 'maps of meaning' to understand events, but we have fundamental interests, values and concerns in common, which these maps embody or reflect. (Hall *et al.* 1978: 54–5)

It is this seemingly commonsensical belief that 'the consensus' is 'a basic feature of everyday life' that underpins journalistic efforts to codify unfamiliar, 'problematic' realities into familiar, comprehensible definitions about how the world works.

Of primary importance when distinguishing the newspaper's mode of address is its 'professional sense of the newsworthy', an aspect of its 'social personality' conditioned by various organizational, technical and commercial constraints, as well as by its conception of the likely opinions of its regular readers (its 'target audience'). It follows that individual newspapers, even those sharing a similar outlook, will inflect the same topic differently. As Hall *et al.* (1978) point out:

> The language employed will thus be the *newspaper's own version of the language of the public to whom it is principally addressed*: its version of the rhetoric, imagery and underlying common stock of knowledge which it assumes its audience shares and which thus forms the basis of the reciprocity of producer/reader. (Hall *et al.* 1978: 61)

This form of address, specific to each and every news organization, may thus be advantageously described as the newspaper's distinctive 'public idiom'.

Still, despite the apparent variations in this public language from one title to the next, Hall *et al.* (1978) maintain that it is almost always possible to discern in its usage the 'consensus of values' representing the ideological limits of 'reasonable opinion'. Given that this 'consensus of values' is broadly aligned with the interests of powerful voices which tend to be over-accessed by news organizations, Hall *et al.* (1978) contend that this process of reinflecting a news topic into a variant of public language similarly serves:

> to *translate into a public idiom the statements and viewpoints of the primary definers*. This translation of official viewpoints into a public idiom not only makes the former more 'available' to the uninitiated; it invests them with popular force and resonance, naturalising them within the horizon of understandings of the various publics. (Hall *et al.* 1978: 61)

In this way, then, the definitions, interpretations and inferences of the powerful are embedded, to varying degrees, into the 'everyday' language of the public. Newspapers, as Hall *et al.* (1978: 62) write, ' "take" the language of the public and, on each occasion, return it to them *inflected with dominant and consensual connotations*'.

In order to further critique this process of inflection, then, it is necessary to disrupt the very *naturalness* of the ideological codes embedded in the language of newspaper discourse. Such a line of inquiry will need to elucidate the conventionalized rules, strategies or devices which make it recognizable as a distinct genre of 'purely factual' narrative. In the case of a 'hard' news account, for example, it is possible to show that there are certain prescribed forms of narrative logic associated with the telling of a 'hard' news story which stand in contrast with those of 'soft' news stories (a good journalist, as Bell (1991: 147) observes, 'gets good stories' or 'knows a good story', while a critical news editor asks: 'Is this really a story?' 'Where's the story in this?'). The 'hard' news account is similarly defined in opposition to other types of account, such as 'editorials' or 'leaders' which foreground matters of 'opinion'. This genre of discourse will narrativize the social world in a particular manner, that is, in a way which organizes 'the facts' within a distinctively hierarchical structure based on notions of newsworthiness.

Potential readers of this 'hard' news newspaper account are likely to anticipate that it will provide them with a highly formalized construction of the social world. Formalized, that is, in the sense that the 'hard' news item, whether it appears in a tabloid or broadsheet newspaper, typically reinflects the following elements in distinctive ways:

- *Headline*: represents the principal topic or 'key fact' at stake in the account. To the extent that it is recognized as performing this function by the readers, it is likely to influence their interpretation of the account to follow. In this way, then, it helps to set down the ideological criteria by which the reader is to 'make sense' of what follows.
- *News lead*: typically the opening paragraph or two providing a summary or abstract of the account's essential 'peg' or 'hook' which projects, in turn, 'the story' in a particular direction or 'angle'. The five Ws and H (the who, what, where, when, why and how most pertinent to the event) will likely be in the lead or first paragraph; however, as Keeble (1994: 100) observes, 'the "why" factor is always more problematic.'

- *Narrative order and sequence*: the 'hard' news account almost always follows an 'inverted pyramid style' format. That is, beginning with the news lead, which presents the information deemed to be most 'newsworthy', the account proceeds to structure the remaining details in a descending order of discursive (and usually ideological) significance. By the latter stages of the account, the material being presented could – at least in principle – be dropped without affecting the narrative coherence or sense of the preceding paragraphs. These narrative strategies have become conventionalized to the point that departures from them are likely to disrupt the reader's expectations, yet there is nothing necessary or natural about the rules governing their (in historical terms, rather recent) deployment.
- *Vocabulary*: the regular usage of certain types of stylistic devices, including metaphors, jargon, euphemisms, puns and clichés, tends to characterize a newspaper's 'social personality', as well as its 'professional sense of the newsworthy'. The most marked contrasts are usually between the 'popular', tabloid press and the 'quality', broadsheet titles. In general, the former are usually much more colloquial in vocabulary and emotive in judgement (often to the point of being sensational in tone): 'A vocabulary of emotional arousal', Holland (1983: 85) writes, 'summons laughter, thrills, shocks, desire, on every page of the *Sun*.' The so-called serious newspapers, in contrast, use terms more likely to be regarded as 'un-emotive' or 'dispassionate', and thereby more consistent with an authoritative appeal to objectivity (see also Cameron 1996).
- *Forms of address*: the terms used to refer to, or identify, different news actors indicate a range of important features, including varying degrees of formality ('Tony' versus 'Prime Minister Blair'), the status or power to be attributed to the actor ('monster' or 'fiend' versus 'defendant' or 'alleged perpetrator') or the presumed relationship between the actor and the implied reader of the account (as noted below, made apparent in use of either personalized or impersonalized terms). In the case of the *Sun*, for example, its form of address is personal and direct; as Pursehouse (1991: 98) argues, it 'seeks a relationship with "folks" (not "toffs") and uses a voice of the everyday vernacular and direct "straight talking" to achieve this connection.' The form of address is associated, in turn, with speech of differing degrees of directness, ranging from words reported in quotation marks to those paraphrased by the journalist, thereby raising questions regarding relative truth-value or modality.
- *Transitivity and modality*: the terms chosen by a journalist to represent the relationship between actors and processes, that is, 'who (or what) does what to whom (or what)', are indicative of transitivity. The journalist's transitivity choices can take on an ideological significance, such as where questions of blame or responsibility are raised (see, for example, Clark's (1992) analysis of tabloid news coverage of rape attacks, showing how the victim (e.g. 'no-sex wife') is recurrently blamed for the crime and not her male attacker (e.g. 'hubby'); or Trew's (1979) analysis concerning responsibility for disturbances being attributed to 'strikers' or unions and not employers or the police; see also Fowler 1991; Montgomery 1995). Intertwined with relations of transitivity are those of modality, that is, the ways in which journalists convey judgements concerning the relative truthfulness (or not) of the propositions

they are processing. The apparent 'objectivity' of a news account is enhanced to the extent that modal expressions are minimized, thereby encouraging the reader to believe that the journalist is a dispassionate relayer of facts (as opposed to a subjectively emotive person with opinions).

- *Relations of time*: looking beyond the stated place and time ('dateline') of a news account, it is possible to identify the time structure being imposed via the narrativization of the news event in question. 'Hard' news is a highly perishable commodity which is always in danger of becoming 'out of date'; consequently, such accounts usually contain an explicit temporal reference (such as 'yesterday') in the news lead. In marked contrast with other types of narratives, especially fictional ones, time in the 'hard' news account is typically represented in a nonlinear manner. The account which respects a chronological ordering of the events it describes is a rare exception to a general rule which holds that 'effects' or 'outcomes' are prioritized over 'causes'. 'Perceived news value,' as Bell (1991: 153) writes, 'overturns temporal sequence and imposes an order completely at odds with linear narrative point. It moves backwards and forwards in time, picking out different actions on each cycle.'
- *Relations of space*: interwoven with relations of time are those of space, the latter being represented in a series of ways in the 'hard' news account. Hallin (1986) usefully identifies five typical ways in which journalists refer to geographical locations (see also Brooker-Gross 1985; Chaney 1994). Specifically, place as authority (the 'here' identified in the account is often listed in the dateline; news gathered 'on the scene' is likely to be deemed to have greater credibility); place as actionable information (relatively rare in 'hard' news; much more likely to appear in 'Weekend', travel or real estate sections where readers are looking for such information in order to do something); place as social connection (through its construction of place, a newspaper can give readers a sense of participation in a distant event, thereby acting as a creator of community); place as setting (invitations to 'experience' the event through detailed descriptions of setting appear only infrequently in 'hard' news because they tend to be considered inappropriate for 'objective' reporting); and, finally, place as subject (the ways in which places themselves become 'news' are often ideologically charged, especially at the level of international politics).
- *Implied reader*: journalists construct news account against a backdrop of assumptions about the social world which they expect the readers to share. It follows that the journalist's orientation to the implied reader, or imagined community of readers, necessarily shapes the form and content of the account. Necessarily implicated in this projection of this ideal reader, who may bear little resemblance to the actual living and breathing reader, are an array of ideological presuppositions concerning relations of class, gender, race, ethnicity, sexuality, age and so forth. Brookes and Holbrook (1998) suggest, for example, that British tabloid news coverage of 'mad cow disease' consistently addressed women as housewives and mothers (evidently a typical feature where 'food scares' are concerned: see Fowler 1991, Allan 2002). Personal pronouns are almost always absent in the 'hard' news account, with the exception of the 'I' of an eyewitness or investigative item (this is in sharp contrast to the frequent use of 'we' on the editorial leader page when the newspaper assumes its public voice).

- *Closure*: the achievement of closure with respect to the 'hard' news account is always partial and contingent, that is, it is never fully realized. In narrative terms, the account typically comes to an end abruptly without formal markers signalling closure (in contrast with broadcast news). As noted above, the 'inverted pyramid style' format facilitates the work of the copy-editor, who trims the length of accounts, usually starting from the bottom, in relation to the size of the available 'news hole'. Narrative closure is successful when readers achieve a feeling of completeness, that is, a satisfactory sense that the account has processed an array of facts sufficient to make clear a reasonable and appropriate interpretation of the situation. Thus ideological closure may be said to have been accomplished where readers identify with this dominant interpretation ostensibly encouraged by the account, regarding it to be adequate and factually consistent – for the moment at least – with their personal understanding of the social world.

It is important to note that critical analyses of newspapers, whether tabloid or broadsheet, usually restrict their examinations to the characteristics of the news coverage being generated. This centring of news accounts as the primary focus of inquiry is at the expense of considerations of other forms of content, particularly those types more likely to be seen as mere diversions due to their perceived entertainment value. 'Insofar as acknowledgement is given to entertainment features in the press,' as Curran *et al.* (1980: 288) argue, 'this tends to be grudging and dismissive, as if such content detracts from the central political role and purpose of the press.' As they proceed to point out in their exploration of the non-current affairs sections of newspapers, it is precisely where content is promoted as being 'apolitical' (such as in the realms of human interest as it relates to sport, royalty, celebrities, gossip, competitions, astrology and so forth) that 'ideological significance is most successfully concealed and therefore demands most analysis' (Curran *et al.* 1980: 305). It is also relevant to note that this type of content is regularly disparaged by 'hard' news journalists who are more likely to express concerns over ideology in a different way, namely as a fear that the quality of reporting is being 'dumbed down' by these types of items in the name of boosting circulation figures.

Further studies of 'human interest' or 'soft' news have similarly highlighted how its apparent neutrality reinforces what might be termed the 'dominant political consensus' by encouraging and constraining readers to see events in particular ways. The implications which news coverage of sporting events has for discourses of popular culture, for example, has been the subject of critical attention (see Brookes 2002; Rowe 2004). Similarly, critiques of editorials or 'leaders', feature articles (including 'opposite editorial' or 'op ed' pages or 'backgrounders') and opinion columns have pinpointed a range of issues, including how the inclusion of this 'subjective', 'interpretative' material helps to underwrite the proclaimed 'objectivity' of 'hard' news accounts (see Trew 1979; Love & Morrison 1989; Bell 1991; Fowler 1991; Reah 1998). Cartoons have also been singled out for scrutiny, with several studies assessing how issues concerning, for example, 'the economy' (Emmison & McHoul 1987), national identity (Brookes 1990) and military conflicts (Aulich 1992), among others, have been subject to political caricature (see also Seymour-Ure 1975). Also of interest are 'letters to the editor', not least in terms of how the criteria of inclusion in play delimit the ideological boundaries of *legitimate* or *fair* comment (see Fairclough 1989; Tunstall 1996; Bromley 1998; Wahl-Jorgensen 2002).

Another element of both 'quality' and 'popular' newspapers which similarly deserves more critical attention than it has received to date is the news photograph. Hall (1981: 232–4), in his analysis of news images, suggests that although editors may select a photograph in terms of its formal news values (such as impact, dramatic meaning, unusualness, controversy, and so forth), they are also simultaneously judging how these values will be best treated or 'angled' so as to anchor the intended interpretation for the implied reader. News photographs proclaim the status of being 'literal visual-transcriptions' of the 'real world'; this when, as Hall contends:

> the choice of *this* moment of an event as against that, of *this* person rather than that, of *this* angle rather than any other, indeed, the selection of this photographed incident to represent a whole complex chain of events and meaning, is a highly ideological procedure. But, by appearing literally to reproduce the event as it *really* happened, news photos suppress their selective / interpretive / ideological function. They seek a warrant in that ever pre-given, neutral structure, which is beyond question, beyond interpretation: the 'real world'. (Hall 1981: 241)

News photographs, in this way, help to reinforce the newspaper's larger claim to be 'objective' in its representations of the social world. 'Photography is imbued with the appearance of objectively recorded reality,' writes Banks (1994: 119); 'consequently, editors often seek to use photographs to provide the stamp of objectivity to a news story.'

This appeal to 'objectivity' can be sustained, of course, only to the extent that the reader accepts the photograph as an unmediated image of actual events. What must be denied at all costs, as Taylor (1991: 10) argues, is that news images are 'intricately sewn into the web of rhetoric. They are never outside it, and always lend it the authority of witness' (see also Tagg 1988; Becker 1992; Hartley 1992, 1996; Kress & van Leeuwen 1998). Ostensibly grounded in the 'bedrock of truth', the photograph must naturalize its impossible claim to be making visible 'what really happened' as a neutral, 'historically instantaneous' (Hall 1981) record of reality. This process of naturalization, as Schwartz (1992: 107) maintains, is engendered in and through the conceptual rules or frameworks governing the professional practice of photojournalism: 'Conventions of framing, composition, lighting, and color or tonal value guide the translation of newsworthy subjects into the two-dimensional photographic image.' The array of representational devices employed by the photojournalist need to retain their apparent transparency, she argues, if the source of drama is to be located in the subject itself and not in the strategies invoked by the photographer. In her words: 'Photojournalism, cloaked in its mantle of objectivity, offers the viewer a vision of the world easily consumed and digested, while its naturalism perpetuates its legitimacy as an objective bearer of the news' (Schwartz 1992: 108).

The Language of Radio News

Perhaps the most striking feature of radio as a purveyor of news is the evanescent nature of its language, a quality which arguably accentuates the sense of immediacy already heightened by its mode of address. Radio news is at its best when it is relaying 'breaking stories', that is, news which is 'happening now'. This capacity to 'scoop' or 'first' other news media is one of its primary advantages, while the brevity of its ephemeral reports is a key limitation. In terms of an actual word count, of course, the radio news item typically provides a mere fraction of the information contained, for example, in a newspaper account (see also Crook 1998). Nevertheless, as Crisell (1986) argues, radio provides the listener with an indexical sense of the news, that is, it can provide the voices, sounds, noises and so forth of the 'actuality' of the news event:

> On the radio we hear the noises of the news, or at least the informed view or the eyewitness account 'straight from the horse's mouth' and often on location – outdoors, over the telephone – that newspapers can only *report* in the bland medium of print, a medium bereft of the inflections, hesitations and emphases of the living voice which contribute so largely to meaning, and also less able to evoke the location in which the account was given. (Crisell 1986: 100, original emphasis)

The radio news item, he maintains, declares a direct connection with the listener; it establishes a sense of proximity to the 'world out there' with a degree of vividness impossible to capture in a printed news text.

It is this expressive impact of radio news language which engenders a unique set of issues. Chief among them is the concern that the radio newsworker's choice of descriptive words, together with the use of actuality sounds, will lead to an immoderate degree of persuasive influence being imposed on the listener. The selection and codification of news language, as Leitner (1983: 54) argues, has to be responsive to radio's institutional requirements of 'impartiality' and 'balance': 'Referring to one and the same event with the words *slaughter*, *murder*, *killing* or *assassination*, or to the same group of persons as *terrorists* or *freedom fighters*, may raise questions both of style (appropriateness) and fact.' In his study of BBC radio (and television) news production, Schlesinger (1987: 229–30) cites a corporation memorandum which defines the proper use of terms such as 'guerrillas', 'terrorists', 'raiders', 'gunmen' and 'commandos', in part by explicitly appealing to the newsworker's 'common sense'. In this context, he contends, the concept of 'impartiality' is 'worked out within a framework of socially endowed assumptions about consensus politics, national community and the parliamentary form of conflict-resolution' (Schlesinger 1987: 205).

Also at issue here is how the authoritativeness of this language is linked to the spoken accent associated with its delivery 'on air'. For many listeners in Britain, for example, 'BBC English' is virtually synonymous with received pronunciation or 'RP'. It has long been argued by corporation executives that the 'neutrality' of the newsreader, and with it the prestige of the newscast, is likely to be reinforced through the use of an RP accent (such is also the case, if arguably to a lesser extent, on National Public Radio in the USA). As Crisell (1986) writes:

> On the one hand RP is still commonly regarded as the badge of the well–educated, professionally successful or the socially privileged and therefore as the accent of 'those who know best, the most authoritative'. On the other hand, its universal intelligibility [throughout

> Britain] accords it the status of a 'non-accent': it minimizes the element of idiosyncrasy
> and even of 'personality' in the voice, for which reason the BBC has seldom allowed it to
> be replaced in the delivery of news or official announcements by the regional accents which
> are widely heard elsewhere on the networks. (Crisell 1986: 83)

Implicit to this projection of the newsreader's 'personality' at the level of enunciation, according to Crisell, is its indexical function as a purported guarantee of the 'impersonality' of the larger broadcasting institution (see also Lewis & Booth 1989; Bell 1991; Shingler & Wieringa 1998). That is to say, to the extent that 'editorial bias' is held to be embodied, literally, in the voice of the newsreader, the avowed 'objectivity' of the news organization itself will be preserved.

Related studies of radio interviews, whether occurring in newscasts or current affairs programmes, have similarly generated interesting insights into the characteristic rules or conventions of radio discourse (as have analyses of 'talk' and 'call-in' radio formats; see Hutchby 1991; Scannell 1991; Gibian 1997a, b). Several of these studies have looked beyond the interviewer's posing of questions to examine the communicative strategies she or he is likely to invoke in order to facilitate the interpretation of the interviewee's answers. By keeping the assumed needs of the implied listener in mind at all times, the interviewer manoeuvres to clarify points (often by summarizing, paraphrasing or reinforcing them through repetition) which might otherwise be too complex to be easily grasped. Issues of clarity with regard to style, tone, syntax and diction are directly linked to assumptions about what background knowledge or shared experiences the audience are imagined to possess. Similarly, it is the interviewer who is charged with the responsibility of adjudicating between contending truth-claims, of sorting out 'right' from 'wrong', in broad alignment with the implied listener's 'horizon of expectations' (Bakhtin 1981) *vis-à-vis* the speaking practices deemed appropriate to these factual genres of radio talk.

This line of inquiry is further developed in Fairclough's (1998) analysis of the early weekday morning *Today* programme broadcast on BBC Radio 4, arguably the most influential radio news programme in Britain due to its perceived impact on 'opinion leaders'. He suggests, for example, that interviewers in the course of their interaction with interviewees play a crucial role in rearticulating different discourses together, one implication of which is the reaffirmation of certain protocols of 'conversationalization'. Of particular significance is a 'lifeworld discourse', that is, the presenter's rendition of the 'discourse of ordinary people in ordinary life'. It is this discourse, he argues, which combines with an 'ethos of common sense' to construct, in turn, a basis against which the different viewpoints of the interviewees can be evaluated. This shift away from the 'authority' and 'distance' more traditionally associated with BBC newscasts, Fairclough (1998: 160) maintains, 'appears to be a democratizing move, but it is at the same time an intitutionally controlled democratization: the voices of ordinary people are "ventriloquized" rather than directly heard.'

A close reading of radio interview transcripts can help to identify the types of strategies typically employed by interviewers on programmes such as *Today*. The imposition of orderliness on these interactions, for example, may be shown to be a discursive accomplishment which relies on the cooperation of the interviewee to a remarkable degree. In extending Fairclough's argument concerning this strategic invocation of an ethos of 'common sense' to justify the disciplinary rules regulating these exchanges, it is important to recognize just how fraught these dynamics are with uncertainty, ambiguity and contradiction. Indeed, as Gibian (1997b) observes:

> In the verbal ebb and flow, we're very conscious of who has the floor, who asks the questions, who sets the vocabulary, the tone, the issues; who interrupts, who is silenced or excluded; who gains through the irrational attractions of style, charisma, voice quality, media training; who feels the strong pull of conformity and consensus, the fear of ostracization; and so on. (Gibian 1997b: 139–40)

These seemingly free-flowing 'exchanges' must be contained with in the limits of 'impartiality' if the interviewer's 'neutralistic stance' is to be maintained, a task which requires considerable skill to achieve. Any damage inflicted upon this stance by interviewees, as Greatbatch (1998) contends, would lead to the interviewer being identified with a particular ideological position, a problem which would have to be verbally 'repaired' without delay. In this way, the 'normal bounds of acceptability' which both enable and constrain radio interview interactions are shown to require constant policing to ward off potential threats to their appropriation of 'common sense' (as is similarly the case with televisual interviews; see also Clayman 1991; Harris 1991; Roth 1998).

The Textuality of Television News

The 'moment' of the broadcast news text is clearly a fluid one; its meanings are dispersed in ways which analyses of actual newscasts as static constructs or artefacts cannot adequately address. Turning now to televisual news, of particular interest are the ways in which it seeks to implicate its audience in a specific relationship of spectatorship, ostensibly that of an unseen onlooker or witness. Televisual news claims to provide an up-to-the-minute (now) narrative which, in turn, projects for the viewers a particular place (here) from which they may 'make sense' of the significance of certain 'newsworthy' events for their daily lives. As Hall *et al.* (1976) point out:

> The facts must be arranged, in the course of programming, so as to present an intelligible 'story': hence the process of presentation will reflect the explanations and interpretations which appear most plausible, credible or adequate to the broadcaster, his [or her] editorial team and the expert commentators he [or she] consults. Above all, the known facts of a situation must be translated into intelligible *audio-visual signs, organised as a dscourse*. TV cannot transmit 'raw historical' events as such, to its audiences: it can only transmit pictures of, stories, informative talk or discussion about, the events it selectively treats. (Hall *et al.* 1976: 65)

Accordingly, it is the codified definitions of reality which are regarded as the most 'natural', as the most representative of 'the world out there', that are actually the most ideological.

In order to unpack the conventionalized dynamics of these processes of representation, this section will provide a brief discussion of several pertinent aspects of British televisual newscasts. Specifically, a number of different opening sequences for BBC and ITN newscasts will be examined with an eye to identifying the more pronounced features characteristic of their respective modes of address. This schematic reading is advanced against the current of televisual 'flow' (Williams 1974), so to speak, in order to pinpoint, if in a necessarily partial and highly subjective manner, several conceptual issues for further, more rigorous examination.

Apparent across the range of the different BBC and ITN newscasts under consideration are several shared features:

- *Interruption*: the opening sequence, usually composed of a 15–20 second segment of brightly coloured computer-animated graphics, rapidly unfolds to a sharply ascending piece of theme music (the use of trumpets is typical). Its appearance announces the interruption of the flow of entertainment programming by signalling the imminent threat of potentially distressing information (most news, after all, is 'bad news').
- *Liveness*: the opening sequence helps to establish a sense of urgency and, in this way, anchors a declaration of immediacy for the newscast's larger claim to authoritativeness. The news is coming directly to you 'live'; its coverage of 'breaking news' is happening now (even though most of the content to follow will have been pre-recorded).
- *Time-space*: each of these segments privileges specific formulations of temporality (ticking clocks are used by both the BBC and ITN, which signal the up-to-the-minuteness of the news coverage) conjoined with those of spatiality (images of revolving globes spin to foreground an image of the British nation as defined by geography, in the case of the BBC; while for ITN's *News at Ten*, a London cityscape at night is slowly panned until the camera rests on a close-up of the clockface of the main parliamentary building, the apparent seat of political power).
- *Comprehensiveness*: implicit to this progressively narrowing focal dynamic around time–space is an assertion of the comprehensiveness of the news coverage. The news, having been monitored from around the world, is being presented to 'us' from 'our' national perspective. That is, 'we' are located as an audience within the 'imagined community' (Anderson 991) of the British nation.
- *Professionalism*: the final shot in the succession of graphic sequences (ostensibly sounded by the gong of Big Ben in the case of ITN) brings 'us' into the televisual studio, a pristine place of hard, polished surfaces (connotations of efficiency and objectivity) devoid of everyday, human (subjective) features. A central paradox of broadcast news, as Crisell (1986: 90–1) writes, 'is that if there is one thing more vital to it than a sense of authenticity, of proximity to the events themselves, it is a sense of clear-sighted detachment from them – of this authenticity being mediated through the remote, sterile atmosphere of the studio.'

The camera smoothly glides across the studio floor while, in the case of the *ITN Lunchtime News*, a male voice-over sternly intones: 'From the studios of ITN (.) the news (.)

with Nicholas Owen and Julia Somerville.' Both newsreaders are situated behind a shared desk, calmly organizing their scripts. Serving as a backdrop for them is what appears to be a dimly lit (in cool blue light) newsroom, empty of people but complete with desks, computer equipment, and so forth. Similarly, for the *News at Ten*, as the male voice-over declares: 'From ITN (.) News at Ten (.) with Trevor McDonald', the newsreader appears in shot seated behind a desk, typing on an invisible keyboard with one hand as he collects a loose sheaf of papers with his other one (which is also holding a pen). Whether it is ITN or the BBC, it is the institution behind the newsreader which is responsible for producing the news; it is the very 'impersonality' of the institution which, in ideological terms, is to be preserved and reaffirmed by the 'personality' of the newsreader.

As a result, the mode of address utilized by the respective newsreaders at the outset of the newscast needs to appear to be 'dialogic' (Bakhtin 1981) in its formal appeal to the viewer's attention. This dialogic strategy of co-presence is to be achieved, in part, through the use of direct eye-contact with the camera (and thus with the imagined viewer being discursively inscribed). As Morse (1986: 62) observes, 'the impression of presence is created through the construction of a shared space, the impression of shared time, and signs that the speaking subject is speaking for himself [or herself], sincerely' (see also Hartley & Montgomery 1985; Marriott 1995; Tolson 1996; Morse 1998). The impersonally professional space of the studio is, in this way, personalized in the form of the newsreader who, using a language which establishes these temporal and spatial relations of co-presence with the viewer, reaffirms a sense of shared participation.

Nevertheless, these dialogic relations of co-presence are hierarchically structured. The *direct* address speech of the newsreader (note that the 'accessed voices' will be restricted to *indirect* speech and eye contact) represents the 'news voice' of the network: the newsreader stands in for an institution charged with the responsibility of serving a public interest through the impartiality of its reporting. For this reason, these relations of co-presence need to be organized so as to underwrite the signifiers of facticity and journalistic prestige, as well as those of timeliness and immediacy.

In addition to the steady gaze of expressive eye contact, the visual display of the newsreader's authority is further individualized in terms of 'personality' (white males still predominate), as well as with regard to factors such as clothing (formal) and body language (brisk and measured). This conventionalized appeal to credibility is further enhanced through aural codes of a 'proper' accent (almost always received pronunciation) and tone (solemn and resolute). Such factors, then, not only may help to create the impression of personal integrity and trustworthiness, but also may ratify the authenticity of the newsreader's own commitment to upholding the truth-value of the newscast as being representative of her or his own experience and reliability. Personalized terms of address, such as 'good afternoon' or 'good evening', may similarly work to underscore the human embodiment of news values by newsreaders as they seemingly engage in a conversational discourse with the viewers.

The newsreader or 'news anchor', as Morse (1998: 42) observes, 'is a special kind of star supported by subdued sartorial and acting codes that convey "sincerity"' Taken to an extreme, this can lead to 'Ken and Barbie journalism' where, as van Zoonen (1998) argues, the charge is made that physical attractiveness of the 'anchor team' is taking precedence over their competence as journalists. Also at issue here is the related trend, particularly pronounced in local news, of 'happy talk'. 'As the name suggests,' van Zoonen (1998: 40) writes, 'these are merry little dialogues between the anchors showing how much they like each other and how much they love their audiences.' The main purpose behind 'happy talk', according to her interviews with newsworkers, is 'to "people-ize" the news, as one news editor has put it, and to suggest that journalists and audiences are one big happy family.'

The immediacy of the implied discursive exchange is thus constrained by the need to project a sense of dialogue where there is only the decisive, if inclusionary, voice of the newsreader. As Stam (1983) writes:

> The newscaster's art consists of evoking the cool authority and faultless articulation of the written or memorised text while simultaneously 'naturalising' the written word to restore the appearance of spontaneous communication. Most of the newscast, in fact, consists of this scripted spontaneity: newscasters reading from teleprompters, correspondents reciting hastily-memorised notes, politicians delivering prepared speeches, commercial actors representing their roles. In each case, the appearance of fluency elicits respect while the trappings of spontaneity generate a feeling of unmediated communication. (Stam 1983: 28)

In play are a range of deictic features which anchor the articulation of time ('now', 'at this moment', 'currently', 'as we are speaking', 'ongoing' or 'today') to that of space ('here', 'this is where' or 'at Westminster this morning') such that the hierarchical relationship of identification for the intended viewer is further accentuated.

Contingent upon these relations of co-presence is what has been characterized as the regime of the 'fictive We'. That is, the mode of address employed by the newsreader, by emphasizing the individual and the familiar, encourages the viewer's complicity in upholding the hegemonic frame (see Stam 1983; Morse 1986, 1998; Holland 1987; Doane 1990; Wilson 1993). To the extent that the newsreader is seen to speak not only 'to us', but also 'for us' ('we' are all part of the 'consensus'), then 'we' are defined in opposition to 'them', namely those voices which do not share 'our' interests and thus are transgressive of the codified limits of common sense. As Stam (1983: 29) points out, there needs to be a certain 'calculated ambiguity of expression' if a diverse range of viewers are to identify with the truth-claims on offer: 'The rhetoric of network diplomacy, consequently, favours a kind of oracular understatement, cultivating ambiguity, triggering patent but deniable meanings, encouraging the most diverse groups, with contradictory ideologies and aspirations, to believe that the newscasters are not far from their own beliefs.' As a result, in attempting to authorize a preferred reading of the news event for 'us', the newsreader aims to frame the initial terms by which it is to be interpreted.

The rules of the hegemonic frame, while in principle polysemic (open to any possible interpretation), are typically inflected to encourage a relation of reciprocity between the viewers' and the newsreader's 'personal' sense of 'news values'. The voice-over of the newsreader, in seeking to specify 'what is at issue' in each of the headlined news stories, begins the work of organizing the news event into a preferred narrative structure for us. A brief example of news headlines, in this case from the BBC's *Nine O'Clock News*

Table 59.1

Excerpt 1: BBC *Nine O'Clock News* (with Michael Burke)	
[MB – newsreader] Britain's biggest car plant has been offered a deal to save it from closure	Head and shoulders shot of newsreader; over his right shoulder is a map of UK in Western Europe
thousands of Rover jobs will have to go at Longbridge (.) the rest will have to work more flexibly to give the factory a future	Shot from inside car plant
pleading for Pinochet (.) Chile's foreign minister comes to ask for the dictator's release	Shot of Chile's Foreign Minister on street with police escort
and the birds at risk if a British island joins the space race	Close-up of bird on beach
[opening sequence]	
Good evening (.) Rover car workers . . .	

Excerpt 2: ITN *News at Ten* (with Trevor McDonald)	
[male voice-over] from ITN (.) News at Ten (.) with Trevor McDonald	Opening sequence
[TM – newsreader] Protests tonight as Chile makes Pinochet mercy plea	Shot of Chile's Foreign Minister on street with police escort
unions sacrifice jobs to save Rover plant	Shot from inside car plant
shares plummet as high flying bank chief quits	Shot of bank executive walking through office door
battle of the Brits in tennis' most lucrative tournament	Shot from tennis match
and (.) setting the standard (.) a new approach for night-club bouncers	Shot of night-club bouncer frisking customer outside door
Good evening (.) Chile sent its foreign minister to Britain today . . .	

Note: (.) symbolizes a pause of less than one second.

and ITN's *News at Ten*, broadcast on 27 November 1998 are shown in the excerpts in Table 59.1.

Words are thus aligned with images to affirm, and then reinforce, the interpellative appeals of the news voice and the strategy of visualization: viewers can 'see for them-selves' a range of the elements constitutive of what journalists often call the five Ws and H (who, what, where, when, why and how) of the news lead. Moreover, as Doane (1990: 229) writes, 'the status of the image as indexical truth is not inconsequential – through it the "story" touches the ground of the real.' The extent to which these news headlines are made to 'touch the ground of the real' is thus dependent upon the degree to which hegemonic relations of reciprocity are established such that it is *obvious* to viewers that these are the most significant news events of the day for them to know about, and that it is *self-evident* how they are to be best understood.

Here it is also important not to overlook the larger performative task of these opening sequences for the newscast. That is to say, attention also needs to be directed to their dramatic role in attracting and maintaining the interest of the viewer and, moreover, the sense of reassurance they offer through their very repetition from one weekday to the next (a sharp contrast is provided by the headline of a news bulletin which suddenly 'interrupts' regular programming; see Doane 1990; Harrington 1998). News headlines seek to incorporate the extraordinary into the ordinary; the strangeness of the social world (and hence its potential newsworthiness) is to be mediated within the terms of the familiar. A news event can make sense to the viewers only if they are able to situate it in relation to a range of pre-existing 'maps of meaning' (Hall *et al.* 1978) or forms of cultural knowledge about the nature of society.

The framework of interpretation set down by the news headline thus not only tends to nominate precisely 'what is at issue' and how its significance is to be defined, but also must reaffirm the viewers' sense of what is consequential, or at least relevant, in the context of their daily lives. The language utilized in these opening sequences, both verbal and visual, may therefore be analysed as one way in which the newscast indicates the normative limits of the sense of newsworthiness it attributes to its audience. Clearly, then, once a mode of inquiry elects to seize upon the embeddedness of the newscast in the now and here by prioritizing for critique precisely those elements which are usually ignored in analyses of this type, new aspects of the political struggle over the social relations of signification will be brought to the fore for further exploration.

'The Obvious Facts of the Matter'

Over the course of this chapter's discussion, an attempt has been made to highlight a basis for future research efforts. It is with this aim in mind that I wish to suggest in this closing section that investigations into news discourse may advantageously extend the theoretical trajectory outlined above in a number of substantive ways. To briefly outline one such possibility, I would argue that the concept of hegemony needs to be elaborated much further than it has been to date in journalism studies. Specifically, in a manner which would better enable researchers to account more rigorously for the complex ways in which the news media, as key terrains of the ongoing political struggle over the right to define the 'reality' of public issues, operate to mediate the risks, threats and dangers engendered across the society they purport to describe.

This aim could be realized, in part, by focusing our analyses more directly on the indeterminacies or contradictions (the exceptions to the conventionalized rules) implicated in news discourse's preferred appropriations of 'the world out there'. Here I am suggesting that we need to be much more sensitive to the contingent nature of the representational strategies being used in news discourse. Attempts to demonstrate how these strategies are organized to disallow or 'rule out' alternative inflections of reality should, at the same time, seek to identify the extent to which the same strategies are being challenged, even transgressed, over time. Given that the *naturalization* of any truth-claim is always a matter of degree, it is crucial that analyses recognize the more subtle devices by which common sense has to be continuously revalidated as part of the reportorial performance, and thereby avoid a reliance upon rigid, zero-sum formnulations of hegemony to sustain their theses.

Such an approach may enable us to identify much more precisely the nature of the processes by which this form of media discourse structures the public articulation of truth. Following Williams (1974: 130), who contends that the 'reality of determination is the setting of limits and the exertion of pressures, within which variable social practices are profoundly affected but never necessarily controlled', I would agree with those who argue that a much greater conceptual emphasis needs to be placed on how news conditions what counts as 'truth' in a given instance, and who has the right to define that truth. At the same time, though, equal attention needs to be given to discerning the openings for different audience groups or 'interpretive communities' to potentially recast the terms by which 'truth' is defined in relation to their lived experiences of injustice and inequalities (once again, after Williams, determination is not a single force, but rather an exertion of continuous, but often unpredictable, pressures). Such a shift in focus would mean that research questions posed within a narrowly framed domination–opposition dynamic could be clarified through a much more fundamental interrogation of the very precepts informing the fluid configuration of facticity in the first place.

News discourse could thus be deconstructed not only through a critique of its projection of journalistic distance and 'impartiality', but also by resisting its movement toward closure around common-sense criteria of inclusion and exclusion. It follows that in addition to asking *whose* common sense is being defined by the news account as *factual*, we need to ask: by what representational strategies is the viewer being invited to 'fill in the gaps', or being encouraged to make the *appropriate*, *rational* inferences, in order to reaffirm journalistic procedures for handling contrary facts which are otherwise discrepant to the news frame? In my view, once this 'setting of limits' on the narrativization of meaning has been denaturalized to the point that the politics of its *naturalness* are rendered explicit, analyses may proceed to identify in news discourse the slippages, fissures and silences which together are always threatening to undermine its discursive authority. In other words, this type of research may be able to contribute to the empowerment of those counter-hegemonic voices seeking to contest the truth politics of news discourse, not least by helping to first disrupt and then expand the ideological parameters of 'the obvious facts of the matter'.

Acknowledgements

First published as pp. 77–97 from *News Culture*, 2e. (Buckingham, Open University Press). © 2004 by Stuart Allan. Reprinted with permission from the Open University Press.

References

Allan, S. (2002). *Media, Risk and Science*. Buckingham and Philadelphia: Open University Press.
Allan, S., B. Adam & C. Carter (eds.) (2000). *Environmental Risks and the Media*. London and New York: Routledge.

Anderson, B. (1991). *Imagined Communities*, 2nd edn. London: Verso.

Aulich, J. (1992). Wildlife in the South Atlantic: Graphic Satire, Patriotism and the Fourth Estate. In: J. Aulich (ed.), *Framing the Falklands War*. Buckingham: Open University Press.

Bakhtin, M. (1981). *The Dialogic Imagination*. Austin: University of Texas Press.

Banks, A. (1994). Images Trapped in Two Discourses: Photojournalism Codes and the International News Now. *Journal of Communication Inquiry* 18(1), pp. 118–34.

Becker, K. (1992). Photojournalism and the Tabloid Press. In: P. Dahlgren & C. Sparks (eds.), *Journalism and Popular Culture*. London: Sage.

Bell, A. (1991). *The Language of News Media*. Oxford: Blackwell.

Bell, A. & P. Garrett (eds.) (1998). *Approaches to Media Discourse*. Oxford: Blackwell.

Bromley, M. (1998). 'Watching the Watchdogs?' The Role of Readers' Letters in Calling the Press to Account. In: H. Stephenson & M. Bromley (eds.), *Sex, Lies and Democracy*. London: Longman.

Brooker-Gross, S. R. (1985). The Changing Concept of Place in the News. In: J. Burgess & J. R. Gold (eds.), *Geography, the Media and Popular Culture*. London: Groom Helm.

Brookes, R. (1990). Everything in the Garden Is Lovely: The Representation of National Identity in Sidney Strube's *Daily Express* Cartoons in the 1930s. *Oxford Art Journal* 13(2), pp. 31–43.

Brookes, R. (2002). *Repesenting Sport*. London: Arnold.

Brookes, R. & B. Holbrook (1998). 'Mad Cows and Englishmen': Gender Implications of News Reporting on the British Beef Crisis. In: C. Carter, G. Branston & S. Allan (eds.), *News, Gender and Power*. London: Routledge.

Cameron, D. (1996). Style Policy and Style Politics: A Neglected Aspect of the Language of the News. *Media, Culture and Society* 18(2), pp. 315–33.

Chaney, D. (1994). *The Cultural Turn*. London: Routledge.

Clark, K. (1992). The Linguistics of Blame: Representations of Women in *The Sun's* Reporting of Crimes of Sexual Violence. In: M. Toolan (ed.), *Language, Text and Context*. London: Routledge.

Clayman, S. E. (1991). News Interview Openings: Aspects of Sequential Organization. In: P. Scannell (ed.), *Broadcast Talk*. London: Sage.

Crisell, A. (1986). *Understanding Radio*. London: Mcthuen.

Crook, T. (1998). *International Radio Journalism*. London: Routledge.

Curran, J., A. Douglas & C. Whannel (1980). The Political Economy of the Human Interest Story. In: A. Smith (ed.), *Newspapers and Democracy*. Cambridge, MA: MIT Press.

Doane, M. A. (1990). Information, Crisis, Catastrophe. In: P. Mellencamp (ed.), *Logics of Television: Essays in Cultural Criticism*. London: British Film Institute.

Eldridge, J. (ed.) (1993). *Getting the Message: News, Truth and Power*. London: Routledge.

Emmison, M. & A. McHoul (1987). Drawing on the Economy: Cartoon Discourse and the Production of a Category. *Cultural Studies* 1(1), pp. 93–112.

Ericson, R. V., P. M. Baranek & J. B. L. Chan (1987). *Visualising Deviance: A Study of News Organisations*. Toronto: University of Toronto Press.

Fairclough, N. (1989). *Language and Power*. London: Longman.

Fairclough, N. (1995). *Critical Discourse Analysis*. London: Longman.

Fairclough, N. (1998). Political Discourse in the Media: An Analytical Framework. In: A. Bell & P. Garrett (eds.), *Approaches to Media Discourse*. Oxford: Blackwell.

Fowler, R. (1991). *Language in the News*. London: Routledge.

Gibian, P. (ed.) (1997a). *Mass Culture and Everyday Life*. New York: Routledge.

Gibian, P. (ed.) (1997b). Newspeak Meets Newstalk. In: P. Gibian (ed.), *Mass Culture and Everyday Life*. New York: Routledge.

Gramsci, A. (1971). *Selections from the Prison Notebooks.* New York: International.

Greatbatch, D. (1998). Conversation Analysis: Neutralism in British News Interviews. In: A. Bell & P. Garrett (eds.), *Approaches to Media Discourse.* Oxford: Blackwell.

Hall, S. (1977). Culture, the Media and the 'Ideological Effect.' In: J. Curran, M. Gurevitch & J. Woollacott (eds.), *Mass Communication and Society.* London: Arnold.

Hall, S. (1981). The Determinations of News Photographs. In: S. Cohen & J. Young (eds.), *The Manufacture of News*, rev. edn. London: Constable.

Hall, S., I. Cornell & L. Curti (1976). *The 'Unity' of Current Affairs Television*, working papers in cultural studies. Birmingham: Centre for Contemporary Cultural Studies.

Hall, S., C. Critcher, T. Jefferson, J. Clarke & B. Roberts (1978). *Policing the Crisis: Mugging, the State, and Law and Order.* London: Macmillan.

Hallin, D. C. (1986). *The 'Uncensored War': The Media and Vietnam.* New York: Oxford University Press.

Harrington, C. L. (1998). 'Is Anyone Else Out There Sick of the News?': TV Viewers' Responses to Non-routine News Coverage. *Media, Culture and Society* 20(3), pp. 471–94.

Harris, S. (1991). Evasive Action: How Politicians Respond to Questions in Political Interviews. In: P. Scannell (ed.), *Broadcast Talk.* London: Sage.

Hartley, J. (1982). *Understanding News.* London: Methuen.

Hartley, J. (1992). *The Politics of Pictures: The Creation of the Public in the Age of Popular Media.* London: Routledge.

Hartley, J. (1996). *Popular Reality: Journalism, Modernity, Popular Culture.* London: Arnold.

Hartley, J. & M. Montgomery (1985). Representations and Relations: Ideology and Power in Press and TV News. In: T. A. van Dijk (ed.), *Discourse and Communication.* New York: Walter de Gruyter.

Holland, P. (1983). The Page Three Girl Speaks to Women, too. *Screen* 24(3), pp. 84–102.

Holland, P. (1987). When a Woman Reads the News. In: H. Baehr & C. Dyer (eds.), *Boxed In: Women and Television.* London: Pandora.

Hutchby, I. (1991). The Organization of Talk on Talk Radio. In: P. Scannell (ed.), *Broadcast Talk.* London: Sage.

Keeble, R. (1994). *The Newspapers Handbook.* London: Routledge.

Kress, G. & T. van Leeuwen (1998). Front Pages: (The Critical) Analysis of Newspaper Layout. In: A. Bell & P. Garrett (eds.), *Approaches to Media Discourse.* Oxford: Blackwell.

Leitner, G. (1983). The Social Background of the Language of Radio. In: H. Davis & P. Walton (eds.), *Language, Image, Media.* Oxford: Blackwell.

Lewis, P. M. & J. Booth (1989). *The Invisible Medium.* London: Macmillan.

Love, A. & A. Morrison (1989). Readers' Obligations: An Examination of Some Features of Zimbabwean Newspaper Editorials. *English Language Research Journal* 3, pp. 139–74.

Marriott, S. (1995). Intersubjectivity and Temporal Reference in Television Commentary. *Time and Society* 4(3), pp. 345–64.

Montgomery, M. (1995). *An Introduction to Language and Society.* London: Routledge.

Morse, M. (1986). The Television News Personality and Credibility: Reflections on the News in Transition. In: T. Modleski (ed.), *Studies in Entertainment.* Bloomington: Indiana University Press.

Morse, M. (1998). *Virtualities.* Bloomington: Indiana University Press.

Pursehouse, M. (1991). Looking at *The Sun*: into the Nineties with a Tabloid and Its Readers. *Cultural Studies at Birmingham* 1, pp. 88–133.

Reah, D. (1998). *The Language of Newspapers.* London: Routledge.

Roth, A. L. (1998). Who Makes the News? Descriptions of Television News Interviewees' Public Personae. *Media, Culture and Society* 20(1), pp. 79–107.

Rowe, D. (2004). *Sport, Culture and the Media*, 2nd edn. Maidenhead and New York: Open University Press.

Scannell, P. (ed.) (1991). *Broadcast Talk*. London: Sage.

Schlesinger, P. (1987). *Putting 'Reality' Together BBC News*. London: Methuen.

Schwartz, D. (1992). To Tell the Truth: Codes of Objectivity in Photojournalism. *Communication* 13, pp. 95–109.

Seymour-Ure, C. (1975). How Special Are Cartoonists? *Twentieth Century Studies* 13–14, pp. 6–21.

Shingler, M. & C. Wieringa (1998). *On Air: Methods and Meanings of Radio*. London: Arnold.

Stam, R. (1983). Television News and Its Spectator. In: E. A. Kaplan (ed.) *Regarding Television*. Los Angeles: University Publications of America.

Tagg, J. (1988). *The Burden of Representation: Essays on Photographies and Histories*. London: Macmillan.

Taylor, J. (1991). *War Photography: Realism in the British Press*. London: Routledge.

Tolson, A. (1996). *Mediations: Text and Discourse in Media Studies*. London: Arnold.

Trew, T. (1979). 'What the Papers Say': Linguistic Variation and Ideological Difference. In: R. Fowler, B. Hodge, C. Kress & T. Trew (eds.), *Language and Control*. London: Routledge and Kegan Paul.

Tunstall, J. (1996). *Newspaper Power: The New National Press in Britain*. Oxford: Clarendon.

Van Zoonen, L. (1988). One of the Girls? The Changing Gender of Journalism. In: C. Carter (ed).

Wahl-Jorgensen, K. (2002). Understanding the Conditions for Public Discourse: Four Rules for Selecting Letters to the Editor. *Journalism Studies* 3(1), pp. 69–82.

Williams, R. (1974). *Television: Technology and Cultural Form*. London: Fontana.

Williams, R. (1989). Hegemony and the Selective Tradition. In: S. de Castall, A. Luke & C. Luke (eds.), *Language, Authority and Criticism*. London: Falmer.

Wilson, T. (1993). *Watching Television: Hermeneutics, Reception and Popular Culture*. Cambridge: Polity.

Zelizer, B. (1992). *Covering the Body: The Kennedy Assassination, the Media, and the Shaping of Collective Memory*. Chicago: University of Chicago Press.

Images of Citizenship on Television News: Constructing a Passive Public

*Justin Lewis, Karin Wahl-Jorgensen, and Sanna Inthorn**

Introduction

There has, in recent years, been much concern about low and declining voter turnout in both Britain and the United States. This has been seen as part of a more general decline in civic participation and a decreasing interest in political life (cf. Blumler & Gurevitch, 1995; Buckingham, 2000; Capella & Jamieson, 1997). A number of scholars link the turn away from conventional politics to an absence of places and opportunities for citizens to discuss politics (cf. Eliasoph, 1998; Gamson, 1992; Wahl-Jorgensen, 2002a). As McNair (2000a, p. 197) has put it, "the weight of scholarly opinion . . . harbours . . . a 'pervasive pessimism' concerning the present and future health of the journalism – democracy relationship in societies of the advanced capitalist, liberal-democratic type".

At the same time we have seen declining budgets for domestic and international news amidst widespread accusations of a "dumbing down" in the coverage of public affairs (e.g. Hodgson, 2002; Riddell, 1999). Others, however, have suggested that political journalism continues to fulfil its democratic role (e.g. Blumler, 1999; Brants, 1998; McNair, 2000a) even if the forms it takes are both more varied and more market-oriented. Indeed, Pippa Norris (2000) has argued that political journalism generates a "virtuous circle" of citizen participation. Her research indicates that engaged individuals consume political news, and that this consumption encourages them to become even more politically active and informed as citizens. However, this research, while suggesting that the media are not to blame for all that is rotten in the state of democracy, does not dispute the evidence of a decline in participation in conventional politics.

Our work enters into the debate about the relationship between media and democracy by asking whether the routines and practices of journalism might actually contribute to producing a passive, disengaged citizenry. The news media are, after all, our main source of information about public affairs, so what do they teach us about our fellow citizens? And what do they suggest about the role we should play in a democratic

*Pp. 153–64 from *Journalism Studies*, vol. 5, no. 2. © 2004 by Taylor & Francis Ltd. Reprinted with permission from the publisher (Taylor & Francis Ltd, http://www.tandf.co.uk/journals).

society? In a climate of declining political participation, does the way journalists report the world encourage or discourage citizens to engage with politics and public life? Our focus here is thus on the way the citizen – and public opinion – is *represented* in news media.

Our study assumes that media representations do not merely *reflect* the world but also *construct* our understandings of it (cf. Gieber, 1964). We suggest that representations of citizens, even if they are logical outcomes of time-honoured journalism practices, have ideological significance by shaping the meaning of citizenship. At a more basic level, our study also gets at questions of access and participation in politics through mass media, We agree with McNair (2000b, p. 105) that "the public in a democracy should have opportunities not just to read about, or to watch and listen to the development of political debates as spectators, but to participate directly in them, through channels of access". As Cottle (2000, p. 427) has suggested, whose "voices and viewpoints structure and inform news discourses goes to the heart of democratic views of, and radical concerns about, the news media".

The research presented here draws upon the largest and most comprehensive study of the news media's representation of public opinion and citizenship conducted to date. The study, funded by the British Economic and Social Research Council, looks at television news in both Britain and the United States. The research analysed thousands of news reports in both countries between September 2001 and February 2002, and included *any* reference to public opinion, whether through polls, "vox pops", demonstrations or simply off-the-cuff remarks made about what people think about the world.

The study provides evidence of a troubling pattern of representation, for while there are ample references to citizens and their opinions in television news, the references do not provide an encouraging picture of citizenship. The citizens of our study are passive observers of a world, constructed and defined by those more powerful than themselves. While they are allowed to express basic *emotions* about the world, these representations offer no room for the citizens to express political opinions and offer solutions to problems.

News Media and Citizenship

Despite the crucial role of the media in providing models of citizenship, to date there have been few studies of the subject. Contributions to the field have been made by scholars such as Lewis (2001), Page (1996) and Herbst (1998), who have looked at the news media's use of opinion polls. While these studies give insights into the relationship between media and citizens, there is no research that looks more broadly at how citizen engagement with public affairs is reported.

Media sociologists have long agreed that journalism offers little room for the voices of citizens, and is generally focused on the doings of the powerful (cf. Epstein, 1973; Gans, 1980; Sigal, 1973). Studies of news values (Galtung & Ruge, 1999; Harcup & O'Neill, 2001; Manning, 2001) suggest that the "actions of the elite are, at least usually and in short-term perspective, more consequential than the activities of others" (Galtung & Ruge, 1999, p. 25). Indeed, regular individuals are interesting for the purposes of news coverage primarily when they are victims of crimes or natural disaster. As Cottle (2000, p. 434) observes, "the organization of news is not geared up to the needs of the socially powerless".

The hierarchy of access embedded in dominant news values is not the result of a journalistic conspiracy, but comes out of the practices of newswork; the rationalisations that make, journalism possible (Golding & Elliott, 1999.) Golding and Elliott have suggested that broadcast journalism "is a highly regulated and routine process of manufacturing a cultural product on an electronic production line" (Golding & Elliott, 1999, p. 15). Because of what Merritt has characterised as "the tyranny of space and time" (Merritt, 1995, p. 15), journalism organisations have developed reportorial shortcuts that make it possible for newsworkers to easily gather the information they need. The downside of these shortcuts, however, is that they are heavily biased towards the statements, opinions and interpretations of those whose views are already privileged by society. Tuchman (1978, p. 21) suggests that the institutionalised and centralised beat reporting system is a "news net" that catches the "big fish" or the stories spawned by public relations experts, but lets the little tales of average people slip through the holes. Journalists are quick to point to their own dissatisfaction with these routine practices. Indeed, as Brennen (1995, p. 91) has suggested, the cultural discourse of journalists, captured in newsworkers' fiction writing, implies that although their work was "sometimes exciting and adventurous, the majority of the time it was routine, repetitive, monotonous, dull, and boring".

Our study seeks to move beyond the focus on news values to uncover the ways in which the established routines of journalism *do* allow for regular citizens to appear on television news – as citizens, rather than victims or eyewitnesses.

The Scope of the Study

We analysed a total sample of 5658 television news stories in Britain and the United States. We concentrated our sample on news bulletins with large audiences. In Britain this involved the two early evening broadcasts on BBC and ITV: the BBC News at 6 pm and ITN's Evening News programme at 6.30. In the United States, we examined the three main network news programmes: *ABC World News Tonight, CBS Evening News* and *NBC Nightly News*. The sample originally involved all weekday UK and US television news programmes over a three and a half-month period – chosen in advance – between 30 October 2001 and mid-February 2002. Due to the attack on the World Trade Center and the Pentagon on 11 September, we decided to expand our US news sample back to 12 September (this was not possible with the British sample, for which no archive exists), so that the US sample covered a five-month period.

The fact that the aftermath of the September 11 attacks and the subsequent "war on terrorism" fell within our time frame also allowed us to pay special attention to the way citizens are represented during such a period. The time frame, however, was long enough for normal patterns of news reporting (i.e. without single or unusual events dominating the news) to resume in the second half of our data collection period. We were aware, in our analysis, of the way the post-September 11 period – especially in the United States – might influence the data, and so paid special attention to the consistency of patterns over time and in comparisons between the US and Britain.

Our goal was to analyse *every* reference to citizenship or public opinion, whether implicit or direct. This posed a serious challenge. While overt references to citizens through mechanisms like opinion polls are easy to identify, more subtle inferences about public opinion, such as 'there's a widespread feeling that . . .' are difficult to find without a close reading of every item in a news programme. One of our first tasks was therefore to identify the various ways in which citizens are invoked. To do this, we began with the categories used by Brookes, Lewis and Wahl-Jorgensen in their study of how citizens were represented in the 2001 British General Election (Brookes et al., 2004), and developed and extended those categories to encompass our larger, more varied sample.

If we adopt a fairly inclusive definition of citizenship and public opinion, it becomes clear that references to citizens in the television news media are both a routine and frequent part of the practice of news journalism. Of the 5658 news items we looked at, we found 4398 references to citizen or public opinion (some stories involved several references). During an average week, around 30–40 per cent of stories in both countries made *some* reference to citizens or publics. All the data that follows is, unless stated otherwise, based upon the sample of 4398 references to citizen or public opinion.

In terms of breakdown by country, the US sample consisted of 2880 references (which came from a data set of five months of coverage on three channels, or 15 months of coverage overall), and the UK sample consisted of 1518 references (which came from a data set of three and a half months of coverage on two channels, or seven months of coverage overall). The US sample was larger because it involved three programmes rather than two, and included the period from 12 September to 29 October. The regularity of references to public opinion in the United States and Britain was similar: British news programmes involving 216 references per month of weekday news programmes, and the US 192 references per month of weekday news programmes (a difference that narrows when we consider that US news programmes, while taking a similar half-hour slot, are a little shorter due to the frequency of commercial breaks). We were, of course, interested in exploring any divergence between US and British TV news reporting, although it is worth noting that we discovered far more similarities than differences between the two data sets. This suggests that the *way* news represents citizens is part of a set of well-established journalistic practices that cross national boundaries.

We identified five different ways in which citizens are represented in news:

1. *References to public opinion polls or surveys.* This category identifies the use of polls or surveys about public opinion or citizen behaviour.
2. *Inferences about public opinion.* This category involves statements that *infer* something about public opinion in general, without reference to polling data or other systematic evidence.
3. *Vox pops.* This is the format that allows "ordinary citizens" to appear in news bulletins. This category therefore excludes people interviewed because of their expertise, or people who have merely witnessed an event.

4. *Demonstrators, protesters or other forms of citizen activism.* This involves reference to forms of collective citizen action.
5. *The "some people say" category.* This is a wide-ranging category that refers to a *section* of public opinion without reference to polling data or forms of systematic evidence, and without reference to public opinion in general.

Every category was coded according to the same list of sub-categories, some of the main ones being:

- Who is the *source* of this reference to public opinion (so, for example, is reference to a poll made by a reporter or a politician)? What is the *subject* of this reference to public opinion?
- Which members of the public does this reference to public opinion refer to (so, for example, is a poll of the general public, or of a specific group)?
- What broad political spectrum does this reference to public opinion belong to? This was a complex category, which we discuss in more detail later.
- Is this reference to public opinion "at home" or "abroad"?
- What degree of political engagement is suggested by the reference? This is, again, a complex category which is discussed in more detail later.

When a news story contained more than one reference to public opinion, these were coded individually, allowing us to be precise in our analysis.

Before we discuss our findings, we should note that designing a coherent coding frame was a significant methodological challenge for this project, as references to citizenship and public opinion are often subtle, and do not always include key words. The coding frame was piloted extensively, and repeatedly tested by the three members of the research team to ensure a high level of inter-coder reliability. Most of the material was coded by one main coder, and then tested by the other two members of the research team. On most simple measures (such as the designation or the source of references) agreement between coders was between 90 and 98 per cent. On more complex measures such as the level of citizenship engagement, reliability was initially much lower (around 80 per cent). For this reason, we isolated areas of potential ambiguity, and resolved these each week during project team meetings. While this "collective coding" approach is unorthodox, we felt it appropriate for the most complex forms of measurement. The coding sheet was amended several times during the early stages of the project, and in each case the entire sample was re-coded accordingly, with checks to ensure at least a 90 per cent level of inter-coder reliability.

How Do TV News Journalists Represent Citizens?

It is often assumed that the main form of public or citizen representation in media and public life is the opinion poll (most of the scholarly work on public opinion focuses on polls – see, e.g., Page & Shapiro, 1992; Salmon & Glasser, 1995). In both Britain and the United States the media regularly commission polls, and the polling industry

Table 60.1 Types of reference to public opinion (%)

Type of reference	US television	UK television
Inference to public opinion	42.4	44.3
Vox pops	41.3	38.7
"Some people say"	10.1	13.6
Opinion polls	3.6	1.8
Demonstrations	2.6	1.5

produces a wealth of data about what people think and feel about a wide array of issues. So, for example, a network like CBS News will regularly report on its own polls:

> A CBS News poll out today reflects the growing annoyance. Last month, more than half those sampled were satisfied with government efforts to improve airport security, but that has now plunged to just 37 per cent. Apparently feeling the heat at last, congressional negotiators finally broke a partisan deadlock today and agreed on a common approach. (15 November 2001)

One of our most surprising findings, however, is that the great majority of references to citizen or public opinion *do not involve polls or surveys of any kind*. As Table 60.1 indicates, on US television less than 4 per cent of references to public opinion involve polls, while in Britain it is less than 2 per cent.

While polls have been much criticised for their limitations (e.g. Salmon & Glasser, 1995; Hauser, 1999; Lewis 2001) they remain, for all their contrivances, the *most* systematic form of commonly available evidence we have about what people think about the world. None of the other categories in our study – with the possible exception of demonstrations – requires or involves *any* systematic evidence. Yet all of them *convey an impression* about public opinion. In short, our findings suggest that while television regularly refers to public opinion, it rarely offers any systematic evidence for the claims being made.

This may be partly because journalists are constrained in their reporting of polls – the BBC, for example, has guidelines about the use of polls which do *not* apply to more vague, unsubstantiated claims about public opinion (Brookes et al., 2004). But the reluctance to use polls may also be a function of a tendency to avoid *overt, deliberative* expressions of public opinion – a point we develop later.

The most common references to public opinion are what we have called *inferences* – claims made without reference to supporting evidence. A typical example is this reporter's voiceover on ABC News the day after September 11.

> This morning, though, priorities were being pushed back into place by Americans in no mood to give terrorists the satisfaction of seeing the nation come apart.

While such claims are often plausible as expressions of public opinion (and may be informed by the journalist's reading of opinion polls) they are also impressionistic and involve a degree of poetic licence. It is easy to see, in this context, how a conventional wisdom about public opinion *can* develop with little grounding in empirical evidence, on the basis of beliefs shared within the culture of journalism. This partly explains King and Schudson's (1995) account of how President Reagan was lauded for his popularity despite consistently poor approval ratings in the polling data, and suggests that there may be many more examples of conventional journalistic wisdom contradicting polling data.

We see an even greater degree of poetic licence in the *'some people say'* category, which carries no obligations about representing the weight or character of public opinion. As the following example (about proposals to market the image of the United States) suggests, this is often little more than a linguistic device for *rooting* a body of opinion broadly in the public sphere:

> Charlotte Beers is the new undersecretary of state for public diplomacy. She created advertising campaigns for Head and Shoulders Shampoo, American Express and Uncle Ben's Rice. It is a controversial appointment. Some people believe the US can use the branding principles of advertising to sell a country. Others believe it is naive and superficial. We'll look more closely as the campaign develops. (ABC News, 6 November 2001)

Similarly *"vox pops"*, constituting the second biggest category of references to public opinion, *appear* to provide an impression about public opinion, but they are rarely used in the context of survey data that might suggest how common the views expressed by these "people on the street" actually are. Indeed, the BBC guidelines for the use of vox pops make clear that they are *not* a device intended to indicate the direction or weight of public opinion. Whether viewers understand this is quite another matter: we found *very few* instances when the "unrepresentative" nature of "vox pops" was specified. On the contrary, the place of "vox pops" in a story often creates an *impression* that they represent majority opinion – in this example, to convey the impression of a general frustration with the weather.

> The wild winter storm leaves a blanket of snow and ice unusually deep in the South. From the Gulf Coast of Alabama up to the Carolinas and Virginia, eight inches so far in Raleigh, 10 in Richmond.
> Unidentified woman: "Richmond and the snow drives me bonkers." (NBC News, 3 January 2002)

Examples of *demonstrations* or other forms of citizen activism are the least common form of reference to public opinion on television news – constituting less than 3 per cent of the British sample and less than 2 per cent of the US sample (even though there were a number of public demonstrations held during the period analysed). The most common examples of this in our study were demonstrations around the "war on terrorism" and the bombing of Afghanistan, such as this brief reference on NBC News:

> In Iran, hundreds of thousands filled the streets to show their anger at America on the 23rd anniversary of the Islamic revolution in that country. The crowds were reportedly

much larger than last year because people are upset at President Bush calling Iran part of an axis of evil. (11 February 2002)

In sum, the *most explicit* forms of citizen expression – polls and citizen activism – are by far the *least common* in television coverage, which is more likely to feature vague, impressionistic indicators of public mood or attitude.

Who Speaks About Whom?

It is of little surprise that public opinion at home is considered more newsworthy than public opinion abroad. Indeed, were it not for the presence of a major international story – that of the attacks on the World Trade Center and the Pentagon and the subsequent war in Afghanistan – during this period, the proportions detailed in Table 60.2 would probably be even more slanted towards domestic opinion.

We also see a notable – if predictable – difference between Britain and the United States, with the United States being more inward looking, and British news more likely to take note of public opinion elsewhere. This is, however, rather deceptive, since most of the references on British news to opinion elsewhere focus on the United States, reflecting the dominance of US news in Britain. It is remarkable how few references there are to public opinion in Europe – *especially* in British media (despite the easy availability of data). Indeed, the British broadcasters are a little *less* likely to refer to European opinion than the inward-looking US media. There are, by contrast, almost no empirical measures of opinion world-wide, and yet British TV reporters are more likely to refer vaguely to "world opinion" than to European opinion (even while references to British attitude to Europe are quite common – see Brookes et al., 2004). This suggests that there persists, in the culture of British journalism, an abiding lack of interest in European life.

Those people heard speaking about public opinion are overwhelmingly journalists – the source of 83 per cent of references overall (with similar proportions for the United States and Britain). While politicians may purport to speak for public opinion, they are not often seen doing so on television, the only other significant voice here being domestic "experts" of various kinds (Table 60.3).

If domestic public opinion gets more coverage than public opinion elsewhere, in more than 98 per cent of cases, the *sources* of claims about public opinion are domestic.

Table 60.2 References to public opinion at home and abroad (%)

	At home	Other country	World opinion	Several countries	Europe	Unclear
USA	80.1	16.5	0.7	2.2	0.5	0.1
UK	73.8	24.4	1.1	0.5	0.1	0.0
Total	77.9	19.2	0.9	1.6	0.3	0.0

Table 60.3   Sources for references to public opinion (%)

Anchor/reporter	Politician at home	Expert at home	Military at home	Politician in other country	Expert in other country	Military in other country
83.1	3.9	10.0	0.3	1.4	1.1	0.1

So, even when foreign public opinion makes the news, it is generally conveyed by a domestic expert or reporter.

What emerges here is the degree to which it is common practice for journalists to make claims about public opinion, and to therefore see themselves as speaking for the public or reflecting what people think. This is consistent with journalists' self-understanding which emphasises their role as servants of the public (e.g. Gans, 2003, p. 1). What is less clear is how aware journalists actually *are* of what citizens think and want. Given the lack of evidence used to support claims, the process by which journalists make assumptions about public opinion is clearly a matter that merits scrutiny.

Most studies of journalists' understandings of the public and their opinions provide evidence that journalists have little direct interaction with citizens but rather rely on their own ideas about readers and viewers, constructed within the culture of the newsroom. Gans (1980) found that editors tended routinely to reject feedback in the form of market surveys, letters and phone calls out of a mistrust of statistics *and* of the views represented in these forms of feedback. In their search for audience opinion, editors were much more likely to rely on "known" groups, such as family members, friends or people in their local communities. Similarly, Sumpter's (2000, p. 338) ethnographic case study suggested that journalists construct "imaginary, local readers" who nevertheless "often resembled the interests and demographics of the people in the newsroom". Indeed, Wahl-Jorgensen's (2002b) work on how journalists discuss the people who write letters to the editor suggests that the culture of the newsroom may create a discourse of disdain for the public. All of this indicates that journalists' inferences about public opinion cannot be taken at face value, but should be understood as culturally constructed ideas, built on the basis of what is often feeble evidence.

The Politics of Public Opinion

In modern democracies, public support is used to confer legitimacy upon ideas. We were therefore keen to see how public opinion is represented in ideological terms. Every reference to (or representation of) public opinion was coded in one of four categories: views that could be broadly labelled as on the left, views that could be broadly labelled as on the right, views that indicate a centrist or mixed ideological view, and views that do not indicate any clear ideological preferences.

What is most striking about Tables 60.4 and 60.5 is the degree to which, in both the United States and Britain, citizens are represented as *non-ideological*. In our sample

Table 60.4 How the public is represented in terms of political ideology in US news (%)

	Left wing	Right wing	Mixed	Unclear	Total
Opinion polls	5.9	30.7	0.0	63.4	100
Inferences	0.4	8.4	0.1	91.1	100
Vox pops	1.4	6.4	0.1	92.1	100
Demonstrations	5.3	3.9	1.3	89.5	100
"Some people say"	1.5	7.3	1.1	90.2	100
Whole sample	1.3	8.1	0.2	90.4	100

Table 60.5 How the public is represented in terms of political ideology in UK news (%)

	Left wing	Right wing	Mixed	Unclear	Total
Opinion polls	14.3	14.3	0.0	71.4	100
Inferences	0.1	4.6	0.6	94.7	100
Vox pops	1.4	2.6	0.0	97.4	100
Demonstrations	4.3	8.7	0.0	87.0	100
"Some people say"	0.5	5.3	0.5	93.7	100
Whole sample	0.5	4.2	0.3	95.1	100

overall, 90 per cent of references to public opinion in the United States and 95 per cent of references in Britain expressed no clear ideological leaning. Remarkably, this is even the case with demonstrations. Although they are often associated with the political left, only around 1 in 20 references in our sample overall made this link.

In both countries, "vox pops" seem to be routinely apolitical: thus when citizens are allowed time to speak their minds on the news, 97 per cent in Britain and 92 per cent in the United States are shown saying nothing of any clear political orientation. Even opinion polls – which we often imagine are commissioned to find out what people think about political issues – only suggest support for a politically inflected opinion in 36 per cent of cases in the United States and 29 per cent of cases in Britain.

The range of *apolitical* opinions represented in our sample is enormous, from polls about women's handbags to views about celebrities. And yet, as Table 60.6 indicates, the issues citizens are most often shown (or referred to) expressing themselves about – such as terrorism, crime and transport – are often clearly in the political domain. The apolitical nature of references to public opinion cannot therefore be explained by an excess of human interest or celebrity news – what we see here are citizens being apolitical about manifestly political issues.

The fact that public opinion is seen as steadfastly apolitical on these subjects risks conveying the impression of a citizenry *unable or unwilling to put forward a political view*.

In many cases public expression stops *short* of politics, a realm left to experts and politicians, who are given the freedom to interpret these public expressions as they wish.

Table 60.6 Main topics engaging public opinion (%)

US TV subject	Within country	UK TV subject	Within country
Mood after 11 September	15.9	Health	12.1
Terrorism	10.3	Event in world of sports	7.4
Military attacks on Afghanistan	8.3	Crime	6.3
Anthrax	5.8	Consumption/shopping	5.7
Consumption/shopping	5.3	Military attacks on Afghanistan	5.7
Fear of flying	4.5	Railways	4.9
Economy	3.9	Northern Ireland	3.9

So, for example, a routine report such as the following might be *interpreted* by politicians or parties as support for their economic policies:

> An ABC News poll released today shows consumer confidence holding steady since September 11th. And anecdotal evidence from around the country suggests people are spending again. (ABC News, 2 October 2001)

And even though people themselves *might have* specific and verifiable views about economic policy, this is an issue left for politicians to debate.

There is a sense here that ordinary citizens are almost childlike: they have moods, experiences and emotions, but they are rarely seen making forays into a deliberative public sphere. During coverage of the war on terrorism, for example, we heard a great deal about people's fears, but very little about what they thought about relevant foreign or domestic policy. The following example is fairly typical:

> In America's proud, tall buildings, from the Empire State on Manhattan, now New York City's biggest, to Chicago's Sears Tower, tallest in the country, a feeling that landmarks may not be the safest places to work.
>   Ms Tanya Kukla (Chicago): "Once we go into actual war, I don't want to be near this building at all." (NBC News, 18 September 2001)

Both pro-war and anti-war groups might interpret this woman's reaction in various ways, but what *she* actually thinks about her government going to war remains a mystery. All we know is that she feels nervous. Thus we might say that her reaction, like many others we see, is one of apolitical self-interest.

Similarly, we might hear of people *complaining* about the state of public services – especially in British news – but we will very rarely hear that people want, for example, more public money put into those services – even when polls consistently suggest this is the prevailing opinion.

When citizens *are* heard expressing a view, it tends to be on the right rather than the left – especially in the US media. So, for example, in the following extract the

Table 60.7 Types of citizenship expression and engagement (2244 valid cases)

	Frequency	%
Private individuals speaking about their experience or impressions	666	30
Concern or emotional responses to specific event	408	18
Discussing events, social issues or social groups	663	30
Ranking of concern about an issue	14	0.6
Responses to politicians, parties and party policies	251	11
General appeals to government, corporate world or fellow citizens, with no specific suggestion for action	15	0.6
Suggestions to government, corporate world or fellow citizens, about what should be done	109	5
Other references (celebrity polls, consumer confidence etc.)	120	5
Total	2244	100

impression is conveyed that there is public support in the United States for infringing on civil liberties for the sake of security:

> . . . right now the calls for action are drowning out the second thoughts. As one veteran of World War II put it today, if you have to violate freedom to protect the masses, go ahead and do it. (ABC News, 21 September 2001)

Indeed, the opinion polls featured in US media run more than 5 to 1 in favour of conservative opinions, with no instances of mixed opinions at all. While it could be argued that public opinion in the United States *does* incline to the right rather than the left, a number of careful studies of US public opinion contradict this (e.g. Page & Shapiro, 1992). Moreover, this pattern of bias in US news coverage has been found in previous studies, which suggests that media coverage of public opinion in the United States reflects the centre-right bias of the political class, rather than the more left-leaning inclinations of the public at large (Lewis, 2001).

A number of the left-leaning opinions that were featured on US news followed the Enron scandal, when polls suggested a high degree of support for tighter business regulation:

> Did Enron executives do wrong? Those paying close attention say Yes 78 per cent . . . And nearly as many, 77 per cent, think the executives should not have been allowed to sell their stock while preventing workers from selling theirs. (CBS News, 1 January 2002)

The British TV news media are less inclined to show opinions of *any* political hue, and, in terms of opinion polls, appear to succeed in a remarkable display of balance (with 14.3 per cent of polls on the right and 14.3 per cent on the left). Table 60.7 indicates that. It is in the less systematic articulations of citizen opinion that a small right-wing bias appears to creep in, as in the following example about illegal immigration:

> [the decision not to take the train driver to court is] . . . not going to play particularly well with many people in the South-East constituency who already feel illegal immigrants are getting in too easily . . . and not well with lorry drivers either. (BBC 6 pm News, 4 February 2002)

While this statement is highly plausible, we rarely see similar inferences suggesting a left-leaning body of opinion. Thus we often hear "middle England" invoked as a barrier to progressive policies, and yet there is no progressive equivalent (the part of Britain, for example, that wants to re-nationalise the railways and spend more on health and education, has no moniker in journalistic parlance). The left-leaning inclinations of public opinion on public services might be pertinent, for example, when discussing the privatisation of the railways, which was the sixth most popular topic for invoking public opinion in our British sample. Yet despite clear majority support in polls for bringing the railways back into public ownership (around 60–70 per cent support, according to polls by Mori and ICM), among the dozens of stories on this issue in our sample we found *no* indications that there might be public support for the renationalisation of the railways.

What this suggests is that many British journalists have an instinctive sense that public opinion in Britain tends to be conservative. Since the press in Britain – especially the popular titles – are more likely to lean to the right, it is easy to see where this assumption may come from. So, for example, journalists may well assume that popular right-leaning papers like the *Sun* and the *Daily Mail* are, somehow or other, reflecting their readers' views. Thus it may be that journalists look to the press in Britain rather than to opinion polls as an indicator of the public mood – a gesture that may well reinforce the power of conservative newspaper proprietors to set the news agenda.

Surprisingly, examples of mixed opinion are extremely rare in both countries, the following being one of the few examples indicating ambiguity in public opinion:

> The biggest holdout is Britain, which hasn't adopted the euro, but is watching it very closely. There's a fierce debate here about whether to join the common currency or to keep the strength and sovereignty of the pound, not to mention the picture of the queen. (ITV 6.30 pm News, 10 December 2001)

While this news item does not explicitly tell us who is involved in this debate, there is an implication here that citizens are actually debating a political issue. This is, in terms of TV news coverage, almost unheard of. Citizens may feel, desire or complain, but they do not, on the whole, discuss the merits of political ideas – not, at least, on television news.

Levels of Citizen Engagement

Thus far our findings suggest that the *image of citizens substantively engaged in politics is notable by its absence on TV news.* While public opinion is present on a variety of issues, it is rarely the focus of a news story. The form it takes favours vague, second-hand accounts rather than more explicit expressions (like opinion polls or demonstrations), and it is routinely apolitical.

As these trends began to emerge, we decided to revisit and re-code the data to specifically examine the *degree of political engagement* suggested by each reference. This involved categorising each reference to public opinion in order to identify the *nature* of that opinion: did it involve a statement about people's experience of the world, for example, or did it constitute a more overtly political comment? What we found was that the most common type of citizen representation takes the form of a private individual who speaks (or is referred to speaking) about their *experience*, but who *does not* offer an explicit political opinion – 30 per cent of references overall are in this category. This might typically involve someone complaining about being stuck in a snow storm or being delayed by a late train. What might be *done* about such things is left, in the news story, for others to discuss.

The other main category (also 30 per cent) involves citizens discussing events, social issues or social groups – such as the state of the health service or race relations – but, similarly, without giving any indication of what action should be taken. We might, for example, see a "vox pop" saying that the health service is in a mess, without them saying what might be done about it.

The third most common form of representation (18 per cent of references) is similar, except that it involves people expressing an *emotional* response to a specific event or issue, such as fear or flying or of receiving an anthrax letter. Overall, 78 per cent of all references come in one of these three categories, all of which provide, at most, *commentary* rather than *advocacy*.

What emerges from this analysis is that while politicians are often seen telling us what should be done about the world, *citizens are largely excluded from active participation in such deliberations*. When people *are* shown expressing political views, it is most likely to involve simply giving – or failing to give – consent or support for the policies or actions of political leaders. We are, in other words, shown following rather than leading. Around 11 per cent of references take this form, and include things such as horserace polls, approval ratings, and support for a politician's style or handling of an issue.

Indeed, only around 5 per cent of references to public opinion involve citizens making overt suggestions about what should be done in the world, whether to government, the corporate world or to their fellow citizens. This might involve nothing more elaborate than people saying more public money should be spent to improve public services, that businesses should do more to protect the environment, or that parents should teach their children not to drop litter (*any* such suggestion was coded in this category).

Conclusion: Getting Engaged?

Most broadcasters, policy makers and scholars would agree that television news programmes play a central role in informing citizens in a democratic society. We have discussed what viewers learn about themselves, as citizens, if they take seriously the normative responsibility to keep up with the news. The picture painted by this study provides a rather depressing answer. Citizens are, on the whole, shown as passive observers of the world. While they are seen to have fears, impressions and desires, they do not, apparently, have much to say about what should be done about healthcare, education, the environment, crime, terrorism, economic policy, taxes and public spending, war, peace or any other subject in the public sphere. The world of politics is, in this sense, left to the politicians and the experts.

This is, perhaps, not all that surprising. In terms of traditional news values, the "ordinary citizen" is, almost by definition, generally excluded from news about public affairs. As we have pointed out, most citizens have no authority, celebrity or expertise, and thus have no obvious *place* in a news story, which is mainly reserved for elite sources and opinions. Yet our political system rests, in theory, on what citizens think about the world (e.g. Benhabib, 1994). And the news *is* replete with references to public opinion, whether it is a political commentator speculating in conversation with a news anchor, or "a person on the street" responding to a journalist's questions. The problem is that while these references provide a constant backdrop, they remain remorselessly apolitical. The active citizen, engaged with politics, can be a difficult creature to deal with on a news service committed to impartiality. This is particularly true when public opinion favours clear policy preferences. If a policy is the subject of debate between political parties, showing a majority of citizens clearly taking one side or another makes it more difficult for broadcasters to appear even-handed. This may account for why such issue-based polls are so abundant but so little reported.

But perhaps the most profound obstacle to showing active citizens on television news is the traditional top-down structure of political reporting. Politics on the news is usually about what politicians do, and not necessarily what people want them to do. In the British 2001 election, the issue on which public opinion was most often cited was Europe – even though the same polls showed that most people did *not* regard this as a key issue (Brookes et al., 2004). In short, citizens do not set the agenda.

Is it possible to imagine television news in which citizens not only play a more active role but are seen to do so? While this might involve some radical departures from time-honoured journalistic conventions that perpetuate top-down news coverage, it might also be a pre-requisite for engaging a population increasingly disenchanted with democratic politics.

References

Benhabib, Seyla (1994). Deliberative Rationality and Models of Constitutional Legitimacy. *Constellations* 1, pp. 26–31.

Blumler, Jay (1999). Political Communication Systems All Change: A Response to Kees Brants. *European Journal of Communication* 14, pp. 241–9.

Blumler, Jay & Michael Gurevitch (1995). *The Crisis of Public Communication*. London: Routledge.

Brants, Kees (1998). Who's Afraid of Infotainment? *European Journal of Communication* 13, pp. 315–35.

Brennen, Bonnie (1995). Cultural Discourse of Journalists: The Material Conditions of News-room Labor. In: Hanno Hardt and Bonnie Brennen (eds.), *Newsworkers: Towards a History of the Rank and File*, pp. 75–109. Minneapolis: University of Minnesota Press.

Brookes, Rod, Justin Lewis & Karin Wahl-Jorgensen (2004). The Media Representation of Public Opinion: British Television News Coverage of the 2001 Election. *Media Culture and Society* 26(1), pp. 63–80.

Buckingham, David (2000). *The Making of Citizens*. London: Sage.

Capella, Joseph & Kathleen Hall Jamieson (1997). *Spiral of Cynicism: The Press and the Public Good*. New York: Oxford University Press.

Cottle, Simon (2000). Rethinking News Access. *Journalism Studies* 1(3), pp. 427–48.

Eliasoph, Nina (1998). *Avoiding Politics: How Americans Produce Apathy in Everyday Life*. Cambridge and New York: Cambridge University Press.

Epstein, Edward (1973). *News from Nowhere: Television and the News*. New York: Random House.

Galtung, Johan & Kari Ruge (1999). The Structure of Foreign News. In: Howard Tumber (ed.), *News: A Reader*, pp. 21–31. Oxford: Oxford University Press.

Gamson, William (1992). *Talking Politics*. Cambridge and New York: Cambridge University Press.

Gans, Herbert J. (1980). *Deciding What's News*. London: Constable.

Gans, Herbert J. (2003). *Democracy and the News*. Oxford and New York: Oxford University Press.

Gieber, Walter (1964). News is What Newspapermen Make It. In: Lewis A. Dexter & David M. White (eds.), *People, Society and Mass Communication*. Toronto: Collier-Macmillan.

Golding, Peter & Philip Elliott (1999). Making the News (Excerpt). In: Howard Tumber (ed.), *News: A Reader*, pp. 112–20. Oxford: Oxford University Press.

Harcup, Tony & Deirdre O'Neill (2001). What Is News? Galtung and Ruge Revisited. *Journalism Studies* 2(2), pp. 261–80.

Hauser, Gerard A. (1999). *Vernacular Voices: The Rhetoric of Publics and Public Spheres*. Columbia: University of South Carolina Press.

Herbst, Susan (1998). *Reading Public Opinion*. Chicago: University of Chicago Press.

Hodgson, Jessica (2002). Bell Accuses ITN of Dumbing Down. *Guardian*, February 19.

King, Elliott & Michael Schudson (1995). The Press and the Illusion of Public Opinion. In: Charles Salmon & Theodore L. Glasser (eds.), *Public Opinion and the Communication of Consent*. New York: Guilford Press.

Lewis, Justin (2001). *Constructing Public Opinion: How Elites Do What They Like and Why We Seem to Go Along with It*. New York: Columbia University Press.

Manning, Paul (2001). *News and News Sources: A Critical Introduction*. London: Sage.

McNair, Brian (2000a). Journalism and Democracy: A Millennial Audit. *Journalism Studies* 1(2), pp. 197–211.

McNair, Brian (2000b). *Journalism and Democracy: An Evaluation of the Political Public Sphere*. London: Routledge.

Merritt, Davis (1995). *Public Journalism and Public Life: Why Telling the News is not Enough*. Hillsdale, NJ: Lawrence Erlbaum Associates.

Norris, Pippa (2000). *A Virtuous Circle: Political Communications in Post-industrial Democracies*. New York: Cambridge University Press.

Page, Benjamin (1996). *Who Deliberates? Mass Media in Modern Democracy*. Chicago: University of Chicago Press.

Page, Benjamin & Robert Shapiro (1992). *The Rational Public*. Chicago: University of Chicago Press.

Riddell, Peter (1999). Creche Course. *Guardian*, September 20.

Salmon, Charles & Theodore L. Glasser (eds.) (1995). *Public Opinion and the Communication of Consent*. New York: Guilford Press.

Sigal, Leon V. (1973). *Reporters and Officials: The Organization and Politics of Newsmaking*. Lexington, MA: D. C. Heath.

Sumpter, Randall S. (2000). Daily Newspaper Editors' Audience Construction Routines: A Case Study. *Critical Studies in Media Communication* 17(3), pp. 334–46.

Tuchman, Gaye (1978). *Making News*. New York: Free Press.

Wahl-Jorgensen, Karin (2002a). Coping with the Meaningslessness of Politics: Citizenspeak in the 2001 British General Elections. *Javnost/The Public* 9(3), pp. 65–82.

Wahl-Jorgensen, Karin (2002b). The Construction of the Public in Letters to the Editor: Deliberative Democracy and the Idiom of Insanity. *Journalism* 3(2), pp. 183–204.

61

Unheimlich Maneuver: Self–Image and Identificatory Practice in Virtual Reality Environments

*Alice Crawford**

Werk des Gesichts ist getan
tut nun Herz-Werk
an den Bildern in dir, jenen gefangenen; denn du
überwältigtest sie: aber nun kennst du si nicht.[1]
Rainer Maria Rilke, "Wendung"

We are beings who are looked at, in the spectacle of the world.
Jacques Lacan, *The Four Fundamental Concepts of Psychoanalysis*

As Duke Nukem, Alien Pig-Cop killer and anti-porn crusader, you cruise into the men's room between rounds and contemplate your well-muscled blonde visage in the mirror. Your image gazes lovingly back at you and purrs: "Damn, I look good!" Then, because you are playing the popular first-person-shooter video game, rather than living your own, more pacific life, it's back to the labyrinth to blow the knees off more white slavers from outer space. This moment in *Duke Nukem*, when you are hailed from the screen by what is, in essence, your ideal-ego, which is also the first-person character you've been "inhabiting" through the joystick and, if you're like most video game players, through sitting very close to a rather large television screen, is *unheimlich* in the extreme if one is prone to such sensations. For most players, I imagine, the moment is rather banal. This is, perhaps, just as uncanny, for as we become more accustomed to inhabiting points of view in increasingly immersive simulated environments, it may become commonplace to experience temporary but compelling "self"-identification with characters whose visual characteristics are far removed from one's real-world, embodied attributes.

I begin with an anecdote about this moment in *Duke Nukem* because it carries within it, if we care to tease them out, long strands of questions now under debate in both popular and academic discussions of emergent image-making technologies, most

*Pp. 237–55 from *Eloquent Images: Word and Image in the Age of New Media*. ed. M. E. Hocks, and M. R. Kendrick (Cambridge, MA: MIT Press). © 2003 by Massachusetts Institute of Technology. Reprinted with permission from the MIT Press.

pointedly, questions regarding the nature of the relationship between self-identity and media images. If it is possible to experience a *frisson* of self-(mis)recognition while playing a video game, how far might self-identity be morphed when one is inhabiting a character in a more immersive environment like that of so-called virtual reality (VR)? What would this mean, in terms of relations with ourselves and others?

VR: One Caveat and Three Strains of Speculation

Although the term "virtual reality" has long ago begun to carry with it the whiff of a dead fad, it still serves to pick out a complex (and continually shifting) constellation of technologies and practices actually under development: at its most basic, VR can be described as an array of devices that together form a human-computer interface through which the "spectator" (or better yet, "participant") is immersed in electronically simulated sensory inputs. This immersion works to bring about the sensation of a first-person point of view within an enveloping, artificial environment that can be navigated and manipulated. Howard Rheingold (1991), a popular commentator on the VR phenomenon, describes the VR interface in a refreshingly simple fashion: "Virtual reality is . . . a simulator, but instead of looking at a flat, two-dimensional screen and operating a joystick, the person who experiences VR is surrounded by a three-dimensional computer-generated representation, and is able to move around in the virtual world and see it from different angles, to reach into it, grab it, and reshape it" (17). It is this sort of immersive human–computer interface that will be passing under the label of "VR" here, and it is this sort of interface that offers up such an interesting puzzle in terms of understanding the organization of the human subject in the context of the field of vision, for here the structures of the visual environment in which we recognize ourselves and others are undergoing a rather remarkable reformulation.

Even a cursory glance around popular cultural and the general run of critical responses to the possibilities of identity formation in VR might well give a person the impression that this is largely a disastrous development. Aside from a few pockets of enthusiasm for endless shape shifting, mostly found in sci-fi-ish "lifestyle" magazines such as *Mondo 2000* and *21-C* or in the pages of high postmodernist theory, anxiety is more the norm when it comes to speculations regarding the more powerful, perhaps even intoxicating forms of identification: forms that would be enabled through interaction with increasingly immersive, multisensory interfaces. In response to this anxiety, many critics of the emerging media have joined in a long-standing tradition within media scholarship (inherited from studies of classical narrative cinema, in large part, in which the question of identity/identification looms large). These critics take a decidedly ascetic stance toward the visual images on offer in popular media and prescribe a defensive strategy of rational, dispassionate distanciation from the popular visual. It is suggested that this strategy will, if followed with enough self-discipline and rigor, draw us out of the murky twilight of the visual register and help cure the ills of the body politic.

Although anxiety regarding the role of visuality in constituting the subject has circulated around the technologies of photography, film, and television, the feeling of unease is even more acute for emergent technologies of vision. This is not surprising, really, given that the nature of the encounter with the visual field is notably different in VR than with previous technologically enabled forms of visuality: unprecedented and strange, even *unheimlich*, as I have suggested. In "Supernatural Future," Sean Cubitt (1996) expresses a fairly common understanding of what such an encounter might look like:

> Indeed, the HCI [human-computer interface] seems to be configured around an intensification of the psychic relations formed as identification in cinema, where the dialectic of public and private, of social ritual and intimate fantasy, powers the formation of glamour, returned to the private sphere in the foreshortened space of the domestic television, and now moving to the hunched, one-on-one foetal curl of the body engrossed in the VDU [video display unit], with the promise of ever intensely individuated interfaces in VR. This hyper-individuation works by a similar regression to that evoked by cinema, where the dialectic of identification regresses its audience to the moment of ego formation. In the HCI that regression is carried even further back. (248)

Cubitt is not alone in suggesting that an immersive medium such as VR will not only enable but provoke forms of identification in which the "glamour" (in the oldest sense of the word) of images on screen will work a bewitching spell on our psyches. This leads to Cubitt's scenario of primary narcissism recovered in adulthood, or, as is more commonly proposed, to overidentification with the idealized images of the dominant and dominating culture of standardized media representations.

Such representations include, for example, images like Aryan, hard-bodied Duke Nukem, identification with which would, it is argued, at best strongly interpellate the spectator/participant into bad subject positions, and at worst provoke a psychotic misrecognition of the self as an all-powerful, protean ideal. In pop cultural meditations on VR, examples of such psychotic episodes are a common trope. Consider *Lawnmower Man*, an early and much-cited movie about VR in which a simpleminded handyman is transformed into a powerful VR daemon. Intoxicated with his new powers, he attempts to destroy the world and to take women by force and engages in various other demented endeavors. The movie's tag line, which appeared on the posters, was "God made him simple: Science made him a God." But of course, he wasn't really a God in the end. He just went insane. Even Mark Pesce (1994), the author of VRML (virtual reality modeling language), the code often used to build 3-D Web worlds, has described what seems to be an almost built-in capacity to provoke psychotic moments as the "pathogenic ontology" of VR and warns that VR should be used with caution (29).

Speculation about VR and identity is not, of course, limited to such dire prognostication. There is also a sizable contingent of popular and not so popular critics who are eager (perhaps *all too* eager sometimes) to see the boundaries of the self break down into fluid, polymorphous algorithms in which the mind somehow escapes the "meat" of the body to sail off into the "smooth space" of the matrix. Not surprisingly, some of the most boosterish analysis comes from people working in the fledgling industry of VR and in the margins of the technology press. Take, for example, Jaron Lanier, who has become something of a poster boy for new improved VR identity. Lanier, who worked at the Atari labs during their glory days and was instrumental in developing some proto-VR technologies, can often be found lamenting the fact that our identities are bound by the mundane constraints of the physical world: "We are actually extremely limited. The earlier back into my childhood I remember, the more I remember an internal feeling of an infinite possibility for sensation and perception and form and the frustration of reconciling this with the physical world outside which was very, very fixed, very dull, and very frustrating – really something like a prison" (Lanier, 1999, 242). Lanier and his cohort have suggested that, rather than attempting to establish our identities in the embodied world, we should turn our gaze to the screen, where we can manipulate our self-images endlessly in a virtual world where anything is possible (and nothing is forbidden). When it comes to understanding the way in which subjectivity and the world of visual representation operates, this approach is a through-the-looking-glass twin of the ascetic, even iconoclastic point of view outlined above. On this side of the looking glass, the kind of regressive, narcissistic relationship to the technologies of image making that Cubitt et al. abjure has become a lifestyle objective.

At the same time, a more measured and productive strain of less technophobic literature on the subject is being written by feminist scholars following in the footsteps of Donna Haraway. Haraway, in her practically omnipresent "Manifesto for Cyborgs" (1985), suggested that the blurring of boundaries between human and machine, interior and exterior, self and other might in fact be a change for the better. Human, embodied identity, so the story goes, has too often been the site of gendered, racial, and class oppression. Leave it behind, and more egalitarian prospects open up. Although I am somewhat sympathetic to the appeals of "becoming cyborg" that this tradition of scholarship tends to promote (at least as a theoretical position, if not an actual lifestyle), I am wary of the suggestion that the process of identification needs to break free from its moorings in human embodiment to serve a progressive political agenda. When N. Katherine Hayles (1998) suggests that, in VR, "subjectivity is dispersed throughout the cybernetic circuit . . . the boundaries of self are defined less by the skin than by the feedback loops connecting body and simulation in a techno–bio-integrated circuit" (81), she seems rather sanguine about the prospect. I, on the other hand, cannot help but wonder whether it would not be more productive to keep our focus more firmly on ways in which VR technologies might be used to enhance our embodied intersubjective relations and our relations with our own embodied selves.

To summarize briefly and to simplify a bit, speculation regarding the formation of identity in VR environments tends to be characterized by one of the following assumptions regarding the formation of identity in immersive media environment:

1. Our encounters with VR interface will lead us into a narcissistic regression with psychotic episodes, and this will be bad.
2. Same as 1, only this will be good.
3. VR immersion will disconnect the identificatory process from embodiment, producing mobile, fluid subjectivities that play themselves out primarily "on screen" – in the virtual locales of the interface, rather than in our lives here in the off screen world of fleshly creatures.

On this last perspective narcissism is displaced as central trope, giving way to an under-standing of VR as a place in which fluid ego boundaries become an almost foregone conclusion. Although this final perspective generally avoids a simplistic understanding of identificatory processes, it tends to focus on identification as it is played out in a supposed transition to a posthuman form of subjectivity rather than focusing on how emergent technologies might instead serve to make us more fully human in our lives off screen.

Where Do We Go from Here?

Given how differently each of these scenarios would play out in the socius at large and given all that is at stake, it seems wise to keep in mind the radical futurity of VR, the fact that as a technology and, especially, as a set of cultural practices, VR is under invention at this moment in time and that the manner in which we imagine its uses will be determinative of what it will be. Clearly, we cannot simply look at the arrays of devices and implements, chips and wires, currently in circulation and try to divine what they will do, as if we were reading the future off of goat entrails. As Carolyn Marvin (1988) has convincingly argued, "media are not fixed natural objects; they have no natural edges. They are constructed complexes of habits, beliefs, and procedures embed-ded in elaborate cultural codes of communication" (4). Constant reminders that media are "cultural technologies"[2] are needed to fend off the surging tide of technologically determinist accounts that purport to tell us what we "will" be doing in the future with these contraptions. All of this aside, my argument here is rather simple: that it is not only possible, but likely, that there will be some notable changes in the relationship between the field of vision as it is articulated by emergent image-making technologies and the way the psychic process of identification takes place within this field. Further-more, it is our responsibility at this juncture to imagine tactics for shaping these changes in identificatory practice so that they may serve to liberate us somewhat from the tyranny of dominant modes of idealization in our lives, both on the screen and, most importantly, *away from it*. My suggestions below seek to address some of the drawbacks of the perspectives I have outlined above, particularly the first, "iconoclastic" position, which offers only suspicion regarding the potentialities of visuality and identification in VR environments. The second, "happy narcissist" approach might seem a bit too callow to take very seriously, really, but it does have a fair amount of currency. It also clearly perpetuates a similarly narrow and solipsistic notion of what identification is. The third perspective, that which dreams of the "cyborg-self," tends to focus on the way in which VR encounters might be productive of a cyborg-self that forms its identity not so much in relation to images of the human, but to the machinic and cybernetic. My remarks in the remainder of the chapter will offer a model for understanding sub-jectivity and visuality that attempts to avoid these drawbacks. I make my suggestions as a way of entertaining the possibility that, under the right circumstances, visual prac-tices in the medium of VR might enable new ways of *seeing* and *being seen* that could have a salubrious impact on our lives both on and off the screen, in our not-yet-and-hopefully-never-post-human flesh. A reconsideration of what is entailed in the process

of identification will be productive in amending some oversights the perspectives outlined above.

The Subject of Vision

Although it has become rather commonplace in a number of disciplines to claim that
subjectivity is formed in relation to language and textual practices of representation less
attention has been paid to the mechanisms though which subjectivity arrays it is with
respect to the world of images. What scant attention has been given has, historically,
been dismissive to the point that W.J.T. Mitchell (1991) has characterized the bulk of
speculations regarding the relationship of the visual world to subject formation as
follows:

> Is this subject primarily constituted by language or by imaging? by invisible, spirited
> inward signs, or by visible, tangible, outward gestures? The traditional answer to these
> very traditional questions has been to privilege the linguistic: man is the speaking animal.
> The image is the medium of the subhuman, the savage, the "dumb" animal, the child, the
> woman. (323)

In puzzling out the workings of visuality and identity, it has been difficult to escape the
influence of Jacques Lacan, given the centrality of the question of vision in his writing
and lectures. Though I am sympathetic to Laura Kipnis's (1993) observation that the
feminist romance with Lacan "strongly suggests the Harlequin formula: the hero may
be, on the surface, rude, sexist, and self-absorbed, but it is he alone who knows the
truth of the heroine's desire" (103), it is also the case that Lacanian categories of analysis
offer a rich and resonant vocabulary with which to discuss the formation of subjectivity
in the field of vision, or what Lacan has termed the "Imaginary."

In Lacan we find a treatment of the organization of the human subject in which vision
plays a key role. Most famously, Lacan's (1977) account of the "mirror stage posits the
recognition (or misrecognition) of the image as a reflection of the self as founding
moment in the development of the ego. This moment takes place, so the story goes, in
the infant's encounter with the mirror image of herself, in which she appears as a self-
contained and integrated whole, a moment of (mis) recognition the "situates the ego,
before its social determination, in a fictional direction, which will always remain irreducible for the individual alone" (2). A coherent sense of selfhood, on this account, has its
origin in the apprehension of an image of a human body: the child own. That the illusion of wholeness and self-sufficiency is just that, an illusion, does not change the
primacy of visual relations in this account of the formation of the self.

Furthermore, what resonates here is what Lacan refers to as the "irreducibility' of
self-identification with the image of the body; in the case of the mirror stage narrative,
this image is the indexically motivated sign of the child's own embodied psyche, "indexical" here referring to the fact that the connection between the visual signifier (the
image in the mirror) and the signified (the child's body) is not arbitrary. The image is
related to the subject in this instance as a material trace, in an odd but tangible sense,

of her own, unique fleshly body, a body that moves as she moves and generally responds in a congruent manner with the tactile and kinesthetic sensations that also tell her where she is, and where her boundaries are, etc. I want to emphasize this moment of "irreducibility," which is often overlooked in accounts of identity formation that propose the existence of a fully mobile subject. The connection that is drawn between the mirror image, bodily sensation, and a sense of self, rather than being yet another arbitrary relation open to rearticulation at any moment, is grounded in a synaesthetic moment made possible only through inhabiting a particular set of embodied coordinates. This is quite different from the relation of identity to language, in which the signifier "I," for example, applies as well to me as to you as to anyone else. In the image, there is something more powerfully founding of a stable (if fictive, in a sense) form of identification than the realm of language (Lacan's "symbolic") can offer.

Though it is reasonable to assume that a founding moment of subjectivity occurs in our encounter with a self-image, it would be inappropriate to infer that the way in which the relation with images transpires in further encounters with visuality is uniform. In fact, it seems clear that after this initial encounter, identificatory processes proceed in two starkly different manners. The differences between these two forms of identification are key to understanding how the mechanisms of a self-identity founded in the visual can map quite differently onto intersubjective relations. Reconsidering the distinction between these modes will help in assessing the adequacy of the various accounts of visual identification in VR outlined above.

Narcissistic Identification and the Normative Ego

Identification can be carried out in two radically different modes or, more accurately, *is* carried out in radically different modes at different moments by all of us. The first alternative is graspingly narcissistic, a form of identification that has also been termed "incorporative" or "idiopathic," all of these terms emphasizing the literally self-centered, centripetal nature of this form of identification. In this form of identification the subject attempts to ascribe to itself whatever is deemed desirable in the visual register. It is this narcissistic striving to incorporate all of ideality – "I am the world/I can contain all" – that Cubitt (1996) refers to with respect to VR as "the primary narcissism of 'Her Majesty the baby'" (248), in which the subject's only relation to the visual world is that of an ongoing reflection of her own sweet self. The existence of other subjectivities is of little consequence, if not denied outright, and relations with others take on the form of object relations. This is the same form of identification that, in a psychotic mode, provokes the subject to misrecognize herself as an all-powerful, all-encompassing being. This is an identificatory process that would produce the monadic, self-absorbed shape shifters (and Lawnmower Men) that many critics fear VR will enable.

In this process the normative ego strives desperately to be whole through its insistence on an identification with the ideal and a denial of lank. In *The Threshold of the Visible World*, Kaja Silverman (1996) has mapped out an exhaustive account of the many permutations of identificatory practice in which she usefully describes this incorporative form identification as playing out a psychic insistence on "the principle of an integral self." This principle, she argues, is "tantamount to an inexorable insistence upon sameness" (92) by the ego and is a form of psychic maneuvering of which critics of identification vis-à-vis media images are right to be wary, given its implications for intersubjective relations. The incorporating, narcissistic self not only ascribes inordinate value to itself but maintains an attitude toward other subjectivities that is defensive and even destructive. Silverman describes this attitude as a "hostile or colonizing relation to the realm of the other. Confronted with difference, the ostensibly coherent bodily ego will either reject it as an unacceptable 'mirror,' or reconstitute it in digestible terms" (92).

What is incorporated in narcissistic identification includes only the ideal and is founded upon strong, even murderous abjection, of the nonidealized both in ourselves and within the socius. As Judith Butler (1993) has pointed out with reference to the symbolic realm, the process of identification is in large part a negative process, in which certain identifications are enabled and others foreclosed or disavowed. She rightly emphasizes that the abjection on which self-identification is founded is always a founded mentally social (or antisocial) affair:

> The abject designates . . . precisely those 'unlivable' and 'uninhabitable' zones of social life which are nevertheless densely populated by those who do not enjoy the status of the subject, but whose living under the sign of the 'unlivable' is required to circumscribe the domain of the subject. This zone of uninhabitability will constitute the defining limit of the subject's domain; it will constitute that site of dreaded identification against which – and by virtue of which – the domain of the subject will circumscribe its own claim to autonomy and to life. (3)

On this account, the all-or-nothing drive for wholeness that characterizes narcissistic identification is a constitutive force in relations of domination and exclusion in the realm of intersubjective relations. It is also an invitation to an endless oscillation between self-adoration and self-hatred as the subject momentarily achieves successful identification with the ideal, then inevitably realizes that she cannot quite measure up. The fact that this process is embedded in standardized cultural tropes makes its relation to real, historical structures of inequity even more clear.

In the context of understanding the potential impact of VR on identificatory practices, it is crucial to note that this form of identification operates by constantly parsing out (unconsciously) whom we recognize as subjects and does so along the lines of normative representational codes, the constantly reiterated hierarchies of images that circulate around us, increasingly in electronically mediated forms. All of this in mind, it is clearly wise to be a bit wary of the process of identification vis-à-vis the "popular visual," and it is this narcissistic model that is so often encountered in the more alarmist critiques of VR's potential effects on subject formation. To assume that all identification with idealized visual images takes place under the sign of narcissism, however, ignores the fact that this process is not always and only such a self-centered affair: Although identification with visual ideals opens the door to narcissism and *mis*recognition of the self as all-encompassing, it also opens the door to recognition of the other and makes possible intersubjective relations, which brings us to the second form of identification in question.

Heteropathic/Excorporative Identification

Opposing the narcissistic, incorporative psychic formation is a very different mode of identification variously termed "excorporative" or "heteropathic." In this mode the subject, rather than attempting to see all that is ideal in the visual register as an aspect of an all-consuming self, is capable of appreciating the ideal in others and, more importantly, recognizes the subjectivity of others who do not necessarily fit neatly within the parameters of normative codes of representation. It is with this second, more intersubjectively generous form of identification which Silverman is centrally concerned in her work on what she has called "the cinema of the productive look," a notion that, although not entirely well suited to describing a progressive approach to VR, has certain fundamental similarities to the attitude toward VR as a visual medium that I am suggesting. Silverman emphasizes the multiform nature of ideality as it appears in the process of identification to draw out the possibilities for seeing differently and ascribing value in ways that the normative ego would foreclose. Contrary to the conventional model of identification as a strictly narcissistic affair (the model media critics inherited from studies of classical narrative cinema), Silverman (1996) suggests a model of identification in which, through conscious, collective effort, the idealization that precipitates identification is located in *others,* rather than strictly in the self, and in the traditionally abjected, rather than solely along the lines of normative representational practice:

> [I]deality is the single most powerful inducement for identification; we cans not idealize something without at the same time identifying with it. Idealization is therefore a crucial political tool, which can give us access to a whole range of new psychic relations. However, we cannot decide that we will henceforth idealize differently; that activity is primarily unconscious, and for the most part textually steered. We consequently need aesthetic works which will make it possible for us to idealize, and, so, to identify with bodies we would otherwise repudiate. (2)

What Silverman is pointing to here is an often-overlooked aspect of the process of identification: that an ideal remains a powerless abstraction until it has been psychically affirmed and that the affirmation of ideality is a profoundly intersubjective affair. Without the intersubjective relationship of looking and being looked back at and without being recognized by others as fitting or failing to fit within the parameters of idealized images, the endless procession of images produced by visual media mean nothing either in terms of self-identification or in the classification of others as ideal or abjected. As Silverman puts it, "we can only effect a satisfactory captation when we not only see ourselves, but *feel ourselves being seen* in the shape of a particular image" (57, emphasis added).

VR as a "Theater of the Productive Look"

Although Silverman's "cinema of the productive look" is a strictly filmic affair, the intersubjective aspect of excorporative identification she elaborates is tremendously generative in understanding the liberatory potential of VR experiences. Unlike other visual media, such as photography, television, and film, VR is, at least potentially, a profoundly intersubjective affair. Brenda Laurel, an interface designer and critic, suggests understanding the dynamics of VR as more closely approximating theater than anything else, given that its most interesting and compelling forms will be structured around interactions with other actors *within* the medium itself.

In Lacanian parlance, usually when it is suggested that captation occurs in the moment of "feeling ourselves being seen," the entity referred to as doing the looking is understood to be the strangely disembodied, almost animistic force known as "the gaze." Although the question of the gaze is a fascinating one, I believe we can safely leave it aside here, for it seems clear that captation also occurs with the kind of collective looking that takes place among human subjects. This kind of looking is not the same as the gaze, as a number of recent critics have rightly pointed out. I still argue, however, that the look, when performed collectively, can serve a similar function to the gaze. Namely, it can serve to affirm or deny the subject's self-identification with the ideal and can also, to a much greater extent than theories of the gaze often admit, affect what counts as ideal within the visual realm.

The notion of an *active* idealization should not be misunderstood as a sneaky importation of individual agency vis-à-vis the gaze. It is, on the contrary, a necessarily *collective* endeavor, attempting through the mediation of aesthetic texts and practices to shift the visual terms through which we apprehend the world. Idealization in *this* mode opens up identifications that would otherwise be foreclosed both by the standard representational practices of the dominant culture and by the imperatives of the normative ego. The gazelike function of the collective look has implications for VR as for no other medium: As an intersubjective medium, VR opens up intriguing possibilities for retooling the identificatory process because its immersive and intersubjective characteristics make it possible to experiment with "occupying a subject position that is antithetical to one's psychic formation/self" (Silverman, 1996, 91) in an environment in which one can be "captated" in a psychically powerful fashion, because one is *recognized by others* with whom one is interacting as occupying that subject position.

In this respect VR might potentially serve as a medium for collective experimentation with heteropathic forms of identification. This experimentation would have the capacity to be more affectively powerful than is possible in other electronic media. To illustrate my point here, I'm going to make a narrative leap to some rather famous remarks Lanier has made relating to this issue (though in a quite different context and toward a different end). Speculating about the use of VR as an instrument of self-transformation, Lanier emphasized the ability of VR to simulate "trading eyes" with another person, even swapping nervous and motor systems with another species, in Lanier's example, a lobster: "[t]he interesting thing about being a lobster is that you have extra limbs. . . . We found that by using bits of movement in the elbow and knee and factoring them together through a complex computer function, people easily learned to control those extra limbs. When we challenge our physical self-image, our nervous system responds very quicldy" (quoted in Boddy 1994, 118). Lanier's remarks point out, in a somewhat exaggerated form perhaps, an often overlooked point in discussions of identificatory processes in emerging media, namely, that spectatorship of VR can potentially be quite different from spectatorship vis-à-vis film, television, and photography.

This possibility of inhabiting, temporarily, the visual and physical coordinates of the Other sets the experience apart. One not only imagines oneself in the image of the Other, as in film spectatorship, for example, but *is seen by others* in this guise. Without VR one might feel oneself being "photographed" by many looks as one occupies bodily coordinates radically other than those of one's embodied, off-screen life. The inter-subjectivity of identification in this case would produce a more psychically resonant captation than occurs through other media. Cinema, television, and photography can offer images to idealize or abjure, but they do not incorporate real-time intersubjective relations of looking and being looked at in the way that the VR interface can. In my thinking about this topic, I have been tempted to term these psychically powerful moments of captation-as-other as a form of "ludic psychosis," pointing to the destabiliz-ing effects these moments might have on the normative ego. During captation moments of being recognized as *Other*; the necessity, naturalness, and inevitability of the particu-lar position we normally occupy within the visual register would, I believe be at least *opened* to a radical form of doubt.

Unlike the permanently deranging effects of ongoing psychosis, however, these moments of captation-as-other would be just that: moments. One always has to take the helmet off, jack out, or exit the teledildonic chamber eventually. Even in the case of identification with idealized coordinates, the effects of "degoggling" could, under the right circumstances of collective practice around this medium, have a destabilizing effect on narcissistic forms of bodily identification. One minute you're the Duke, invin-cible and as perfect as only simulated blonde plastic can be, and then the next moment you're, well, you're yourself again. This wrenching removal from the scene of psychic captation in the ideal could, if grounded in an understanding of VR as a theatrical, intersubjective medium, clearly display one's irreducible distance from the array of images of the body that constitute dominant cultural ideals.

Under the right circumstances, such swapping of visual coordinates might allow us to rearticulate cultural standards of corporeal ideality productively by showing up the fictive and essentially arbitrary nature of representational norm and, hence of identity in the imaginary register. As I see it, VR has the potential to bring into question the visual norms by which the gaze sorts us into desirable, undesirable, having and lacking, prized and disprized, and in an affectively powerful fashion. Accordingly, VR might allow us to play with difference in an unprecedented fashion, as it offers unique oppor-tunities for producing visual texts that allow one to be displaced from oneself and facilitating the reading of visual representations "against the grain." In his typically boosterish style, Lanier once said that "VR is the ultimate lack of race or class distinc-tions, or any other form of pretense, since all form is variable" (quoted in Boddy 1994, 118). Now, clearly there is a certain naiveté to such a categorical (and voluntarist) state-ment. The variability of visual form in VR could, however, have some interesting effects, especially in the case of taking on the visual coordinates of culturally disprized "otherness," such as, to take an extreme example, those of the "lobster boy": Grady Stiles Jr., world-class sideshow freak. It would be something *quite* different – structur-ally, qualitatively, affectively – to watch a filmic representation of a culturally disprized body like the lobster boy's and to feel some identification with that subjective position than it would to be in an interactive environment in which you are seen by others as that body: "Look, it's Lobster Boy!" or, "Look, it's that homeless lady!" or "Look, it's Langston Hughes!"

Visually inhabiting a simulated subject position in an immersive, interactive environment is certainly not *identical* to the experience of inhabiting its off-line, embodied counterpart. Therefore, it would be a mistake to argue that to inhabit Langston Hughes's identity in such an environment would allow one to fully know what it would be like to live through that identity in all of its embodied complexity. Nevertheless, this partial inhabitation of the identity of another is a step in an interesting and useful direction, and one that VR could enable in an unprecedented fashion.

By providing an environment in which we can assume various prized and disprized identities in an affectively resonant fashion, VR might allow us to experience more profoundly the arbitrariness of individual location in the "language" of visual representations and the effects of the arbitrary cultural valorization of different bodily images and the abjection of others: male, female, black, white, queer, skinny, fat, poor, freak. It seems possible that these moments, perhaps momentarily, ludically psychotic in their deranging of normal codes of identification, could coax us to acknowledge the abyss that separates and always will separate self-identity from ideality, a relationship that Hal Foster (1996) has rather poignantly characterized as "the gap between imagined and actual body-images that yawns within each of us, the gap of (mis)recognition that we attempt to fill with fashion models and entertainment images every day and every night of our lives" (110). From this perspective, any encounter that would assist us in collectively recognizing culturally idealized representational norms as fictive rather than natural or originary, would be sweet relief.

An Ethics of Spectatorship and Interface Design

Clearly, VR is not an *agape* machine: The technology itself won't inevitably produce destabilizing aesthetic experiences or bring about a radical reconsideration of our normative forms of identification and idealization in the visual register. What is required is an ethic of spectatorship that values such experiences and incorporates entertailment, escapism, and play in a collective search for the good life. (I think here of the ethos of the Cultural Front in the 1930s, a moment in which these elements came together for a brief time without immediately degenerating into arid, joyless pedagogy. On a practical level, there also needs to be a wide array of visual coordinates available for temporary occupation. Currently existing virtual environments, such as they are, are largely commercial spaces designed for shopping, or, at best, commercially created environments such as Habitat, World's Chat, or the wildly popular Sega Dreamcar system. Participants can select a predesigned "avatar" to represent them visually to others but cannot in any meaningful way map out their own visual coordinates and are largely offered innocuous and/or idealized avatars, Kyoko Date–like cutie pies, muscular, lantern-jawed fellows with executive hair, pink bunnies, and the like.

To actualize VR's utopian possibilities, it is important not only that we collectively guide our use of the medium in order to play with something beyond banal ideality. Everyday citizens in the "bitsphere" (as the emerging "public" space of immersive media environments has been described) must also be technically and procedurally capable of downloading their own visual material versus having it dished out entirely be Lucasfilm or Disney and their cohort. As Rheingold (1991) has pointed out, "[a]t the heart of VR is an experience . . . and the problems inherent in creating artificial experiences are older than computers. While MIT and the Defense Department might know a thing or two about spurring new computer technologies, the center of the illusion industry is closer to Hollywood" (46). The design of virtual environments along standard Hollywood lines would, perhaps, offer occasional moments of *unheimlich* (mis)recognition but would clearly not be ideal for forming a contestatory cultural practice within the medium. Fortunately, this is a problem currently being addressed by a number of leading designers of VR environments, including Laurel (1992), who points out that, for virtual environments to have any meaningful variety of subject positions, the authoring tools for these environments probably need to be distributed to the users. The strategy in her view, is "to make the authors of the content also the authors of the structure and the interface" (86), so that the builders of these environments aren't simply appropriating content and putting it into, as she puts it, "White Western" form and structure.

It may be impossible, in the end, to create authoring tools entirely free from cultural bias, but it's a productive ideal to drive toward, even if only asymptotically approachable. If it *does* in fact become possible for anyone with access to a computer to add her visual information to the gallery of avatars on offer, this will not only reorganize the positions of producer and consumer of media images, participant and spectator, but will also allow for visual practices that may better serve as a heuristic for progressive political practice.

Playing with the *Unheimlich*: Ludic Psychosis

In sum, much of the critical work on VR oversimplifies the psychic processes involved in visual identification by emphasizing only the narcissistic and psychotic aspects of a phenomenon that is in fact quite complex and multiform. There has also been little attention given to crucial differences between how VR might inflect the affective experience of images in comparison to other visual media, such as film, television, or photography. With these differences in mind, it seems clear that identification in VR cannot adequately be described by theories of spectatorship developed for earlier media forms. Furthermore, most speculations tend to focus on the on-screen relationship between "spectator" and the interface itself, rather than on intersubjective relations between participants within an environment that must eventually be left behind to return to embodied relations outside the matrix. Finally, as a consequence of this reductive and decontextualized understanding of identification, there have been continued calls for a studied detachment from visual pleasure, an unproductive tactic that serves only to cede the formidable affective power of visual identification to commercial interests. One might say that all three of the perspectives outlined above are fantasies of escape of one sort or another: The "iconoclastic" hopes to escape from the irrationality of the visual register into the relative "sanity" of the symbolic; the "happily narcissistic" hopes to escape the responsibilities of intersubjective relationships by relating primarily to its own inner baby; and the "cyborgian" perspective often seeks to escape from the confines of the fleshly, embodied world altogether. My fantasy, on the other hand, is that we use these emergent technologies to play with the *unheimlich*, this "ludic psychosis," not to escape our bodies "into the matrix" or to participate in narcissistic fantasies of the "I can contain all worlds" variety, and not to embrace a cyborg posthumanism, but rather to periodically estrange ourselves from our accustomed bodily parameters and the confines of the normative ego so that we may return "home to our bodies and to our relations with other embodied creatures like ourselves with greater empathy and within a less tyrannical collective relation to the world of images in which we all must make our way."

Notes

1. "Work of this eyes is done, now/go and do heart's work/on all the images imprisoned within you; for you/overpowered them: but even now you don't know them."
2. For a full definition of "cultural technologies" see Williams 1992.

References

Benjamin, Walter (1968). What Is Epic Theater? In: Hannah Arendt (ed.), *Illuminations*, pp. 147–54. New York: Schocken.

Boddy, William (1994). Archaeologies of the Electronic Vision and the Gendered Spectator. *Screen* 35(2), Summer, pp. 105–22.

Butler, Judith (1993). *Bodies That Matter: On the Discursive Limits of "Sex."* London: Routledge.

Cubitt, Sean (1996). Supernatural Futures: Theses on Digital Aesthetics? In: George Robertson et al. (ed.), *Future Natural: Nature/Science/Culture*, pp. 237–55. London: Routledge.

Foster, Hal (1996). Obscene, Abject, Traumatic. *October* 78(Fall), pp. 107–24.

Haraway, Donna (1985). A Manifesto for Cyborgs: Science, Technology, and Socialist Feminism in the 1980s. *Socialist Review* 80, pp. 65–108.

Hayles, N. Katherine (1998). Virtual Bodies and Flickering Signifiers. *October* 66(Fall), pp. 69–91.

Hayles, N. Katherine (1999). *How We Became Posthuman: Virtual Bodies in Cybernetics, Literature, and Informatics*. Chicago: University of Chicago Press.

Kipnis, Laura (1993). *Ecstasy Unlimited: On Sex, Capital, Gender, and Aesthetics*. Minneapolis: University of Minnesota Press.

Lacan, Jacques (1973). *The Four Fundamental Concepts of Psychoanalysis*, trans. Alan Sheridan. New York: Norton.

Lacan, Jacques (1977). The Mirror Stage as Formative of the Function of the I as Revealed in Psychoanalytic Experience? In: Alan Sheridan (trans. and ed.), *Écrits: A Selection*, pp. 1–7. London: Tavistock.

Lanier, Jaron (1999). Riding the Giant Worm to Saturn: Post-symbolic Communication in Virtual Reality. In: Timothy Druckrey with Ars Electronica (ed.), *Ars Electronica: Facing the Future, A Survey of Two Decades*, pp. 242–3. Cambridge, MA: MIT Press.

Laurel, Brenda (1991). *Computers as Theater*. Menlo Park, CA: Addison-Wesley.

Laurel, Brenda (1992). Brenda Laurel: Lizard Queen? *Mondo 2000* 7, pp. 83–9.

Marvin, Carolyn (1988). *When Old Technologies Were New*. New York: Oxford University Press.

Mitchell, W. J. T. (1991). Iconology and Ideology. In: David B. Downing & Susan Bazargan (ed.), *Image and Ideology in Mode PostModern Discourse*, pp. 321–30. Albany: State University of New York Press.

Mulvey, Laura (1975). Visual Pleasure and Narrative Cinema. *Screen* 16, pp. 7–18.

Pesce, Mark D. (1994). Final Amputation: Pathogenic Ontology in Cyberspace. *SPEL A Journal of Technology and Politics*. Online at: www.hyperreal.org/~mpesFa.html.

Rheingold, Howard (1991). *Virtual Reality*. New York: Simon and Schuster.

Rilke, Rainer Maria (1980). *The Selected Poetry of Rainer Maria Rilke*, trans. Stephen Mitch New York: Vintage.

Silverman, Kaja (1996). *The Threshold of the Visible World*. New York: Routledge.

Springer, Claudia (1991). The Pleasure of the Interface. *Screen* 32(3), pp. 303–23.

Williams, Raymond (1992). *Television, Technology and Cultural Form*. Hanover, NJ: Wesleyan University Press.

The Phenomenon of Lara Croft

Astrid Deuber–Mankowsky[*]

"Lara, your name says a thousand words."

So begins a fan letter to Lara Croft. It is one of many that can be found on the Internet. Of those thousand words the name Lara is supposed to say, the letter's author has found ninety-five. He uses them to compose a love poem, one whose first lines give a vivid impression of what could be called "the phenomenon of Lara Croft":

> Luscious, Likeable, Lovely, Loving, and Loved. Lonely sometimes? A Landmark in computer game history. You speak everyone's Language, a top Lass. You Leap, Lean, and Look, Leaving nothing but empty tombs. Daughter of Lord Henshingley Croft. Adventurous, Adaptable to any surroundings, and Anatomically perfect. An Achiever, Accurate (You never miss!) and heavily Acclaimed by all.[1]

Lara stands for a thousand names, for just as many desires and hopes. Her fans have loved her as they would a star. Indeed, they have loved her more than they would a star, for experiencing Lara in the video game makes possible an intimacy unequaled by the public appearances of music, film, and television celebrities. Lara is not only the beloved; she is also the lover. Yet how can a lover emerge from what my then-fourteen-year-old son described as "pixel porridge"?[2]

In the beginning, Lara Croft was a video game figure like many others. The only things distinguishing the main character of *Tomb Raider* from those of other video games were her sex and improved graphics. Yet soon after its release in November 1996, *Tomb Raider* sales were among the highest on the game market, and Lara Croft gained global fame. She was the first virtual figure to make the transition from the game world into universal media reality. Just months after the game appeared on the market, Lara Croft could be seen on billboards, on television, on magazine covers, in leading game journals, and in various daily newspapers and weekly publications. Young women lent Lara Croft their bodies as her official representatives in the real world, giving interviews and autographs on Lara's behalf and letting themselves be photographed in her trademark attire. Lara appeared at rock concerts, served as a model for fashion designers,

[*] Pp. 1–5, 7–12 & 91–2 from A. Deuber-Mankowsky, *Lara Croft: Cyber Heroine*, trans D. J. Bonfiglio (Minneapolis: University of Minnesota Press). © 2005. Reprinted with permission from University of Minnesota Press.

and promoted products ranging from watches and cars to soft drinks and newspapers. Matching her ubiquity in conventional media was her popularity on the Internet. From June 1997 to May 2002, the *Croft Times*, an online newspaper appearing in several different languages, regularly reported on the Lara cosmos. Thousands of fan sites, online magazines, and chat rooms kept track of her every move. Lara's transmedial presence ultimately earned her the title of "cultural icon" for the new media society.

Along with a presence across different media, the phenomenon of Lara Croft brought with it the ability to mediate among them. Rumors about a planned Hollywood movie started to circulate as early as 1997. In the winter of 1998, Paramount Pictures announced that it had purchased the film rights to *Tomb Raider* and planned to make a multi-hundred-million-dollar trilogy. In the spring of 2000, it was made known that the Oscar-winning actress Angelina Jolie would play the part of Lara Croft. The virtual star was now to be embodied by a real one. When shooting started in August of that year, minute details of the movie's progress were regularly posted on the Internet. The first previews could be downloaded that fall.

What kept this media fever going? What kinds of mechanisms, what kinds of contingencies, what kinds of forces combined to turn a more or less wooden game figure with rudimentary facial expressions into a dream woman and cultural icon?

My work on Lara Croft began in the summer of 1999 during a seminar I held at the Institute for Cultural Studies at Humboldt University in Berlin entitled "Femininity, Representation, and Gender." Lara Croft was one of the subjects we examined while discussing various theories of representation and representation critique. At the time, *Tomb Raider III* was hitting record sales on the global video game market. The German *Lara Croft Magazin* had just appeared, and its first issue featured Lara wearing custom-designed fashions, including a bikini by Gucci.[3] Six months earlier, in a talk at the Social Market Foundation, the British science minister, Lord Sainsbury of Turville, had suggested using Lara Croft as an ambassador for British scientific excellence. According to Sainsbury, Lara Croft was living proof that the United Kingdom stood at the cutting edge of new developments.[4] Around the same time, a columnist for a conservative feminist online publication named Lara as her pick for Republican candidate in the 2000 presidential election.[5] A "Lara for President" campaign subsequently made its way through the media. Later that summer, *Playboy* published nude pictures of a former Lara Croft model for its August 1999 issue. Just as the magazine was being released in the United Kingdom, Core Design, Lara Croft's creator, obtained a court injunction preventing *Playboy* from printing the Lara Croft name and *Tomb Raider* logo alongside the pictures.[6] The company's lawyer claimed that the association with the magazine would tarnish the image of the fictional star. The court ordered *Playboy* to apply stickers blanking out any reference to Lara Croft or *Tomb Raider* on the covers of magazines yet to be distributed.

Instead of offering satisfying answers, my initial attempts at explaining the phenomenon of Lara Croft only raised more and more questions. My search first led me to the economic and political conditions of the computer and video game market. I began to investigate the significance of technical innovations for game success and development, especially in the area of graphics, and examined the relationship between software and hardware, PC and console. In their interactions, these aspects proved to have their own inherent codes and principles, ones that determine not only a game's story line but also its protagonists. In addition, I discovered that links to other media, particularly those to Hollywood cinema and its star industry, played a key role in producing the phenomenon of Lara Croft. Yet all of these together could not explain Lara's particular success. Instead it became progressively clear that filling the explanatory gap would entail directing my attention to the changes to which new media subject our bodily perception and desire. In pursuing these changes, I was led back to the concept of sexual difference. From here the questions guiding my thinking on Lara Croft emerged:

How can analyzing the phenomenon of Lara Croft help us better understand the shifts in meaning currently taking place in the concepts of gender, sex, and sexuality?
Has Lara Croft, at once pinup model and rebellious, man-repelling grrl, overstepped the boundaries between the sexes just as she has those between virtuality and reality?

A Duplicitous Gift

The problem that Lara Croft poses for feminist theory results from precisely those multiple meanings we saw celebrated in the opening line of her admirer's poem: through them Lara has been able to span the gap between men's sexual fantasies and women's longings for supernatural agility. More than merely an object of male desire, Lara Croft became the first positive female role model on the computer game market. She opened up the virtual game world to a whole generation of young women and girls.

The appearance of a heroine in a visual world with so few prompted an editor of a leading German feminist magazine to declare Lara Croft a gift of such importance that women have no choice but to accept her "oversize feminine attributes" as a "necessary tribute to the male world."[7] And indeed, Lara does more than fulfill men's fantasies with her "Oversize feminine attributes" (i.e., those preternaturally large breasts whose origins and alteration have their own narrative in the Lara Croft universe). Women, especially girls, enjoy following the tough adventurer. In her, as many will admit, they feel represented as a woman – a woman who is independent, eager to live life to its fullest, one who is liberated and feels superior to men.

Fostering this image is Lara Croft's biography. Eidos, the multinational corporation responsible for marketing *Tomb Raider*, provided Lara Croft with a blood type (AB–), hobbies (shooting and free climbing), a date of birth (February 14, 1968), parents, an education (private schools in England and Switzerland), a nationality (British), as well as her own childhood. The daughter of the British Lord Henshingley, Lara – so her invented biography goes – grew up in the secure world of the aristocracy, where she received a first-rate education and intensive athletic training. Were it up to her parents, Lara would have married early and started a family befitting her social standing. But a decisive turn of events changes Lara's life. An airplane crash in the Himalayas leaves Lara the only survivor, and she must make her way alone through the mountains for two weeks. It is an experience that puts Lara on the path of becoming the adventurer and tomb raider we know from the computer game: a woman hungry for life, craving freedom and travel, a woman who is independent, self-confident, beautiful, and always taking new risks.[8]

Yet a closer look at this purported gift will show it to be a duplicitous one, for beyond being the object of male and female desire, Lara Croft governs over a hierarchical order of the sexes replete with all the gender stereotypes that feminist theory has been decoding and deconstructing for more than thirty years. Although Lara Croft promotes a process that can be described as at once degendering and medializing the body, this process does not surmount traditional prejudices but reverts to a heterosexual metaphysics of gender. Here we are presented with the paradoxical fact that the leveling of sexual difference and the consolidation of a dualistic order of the sexes are not mutually exclusive. Rather, in a way that is baffling yet logically consistent, each reinforces the other.

The problem with which the phenomenon of Lara Croft confronts us makes one thing clear: if feminist theory is to tackle the difficulties arising from the union of the old media with the new, methodological-critical reflection will be needed. In the face of a universal media society, the field of gender studies is called on to go beyond its traditional boundaries and borrow from the approaches of media theory.

So, for instance, however much Lara Croft serves male and female fantasies of power, she also, in the same breath, transforms all players into gender-neutral "users."[9] That is to say, male and female players are equally bound to the hardware through their desires and fantasies. The sexuality of the user plays a role only insofar as desire is directed toward the medium; once the player begins using the PC or game console, his or her sexuality becomes unimportant. Lara Croft's ability to attract men and women merely satisfies the simple demand that the circle of users increase – a demand she meets with proven artistry. The secret of her appeal to both sexes lies, as the admirer wrote in his fan letter, in her ability to speak "everyone's language." Lara Croft's message awakens the desire of both men and women alike.

Following recent German theorists, I understand media to include "all those material technologies and common forms distributed throughout society whose application determines the collective configuration of perception and experience in our world."[10] Important here is the impact that the technical and material side of media has on perception and communication. The computer is not only a machine or tool; it is also a medium that determines *how* we perceive just as much as *what* we perceive.[11] Any notion of media that remains exclusively oriented to technical aspects cannot sufficiently explain the interaction between the "new media" and their users. We must also consider the concept of the medium from the other side, as it were – from the position of the user.

From this vantage point, we can see that every medium is part of a "sign-event," one that is accompanied by what Slavoj Žižek aptly describes as "the emergence of the pure appearance which cannot be reduced to the simple effect of its bodily causes."[12] That even the technical definition of a computer relies on a nonmaterial sign-event is shown by the expression "virtual machine." By inventing this new terminology, computer scientists wanted to account for the fact that the majority of today's users see the machine component of the computer through the programs of the operating system, while what really happens in the hardware is known only by the engineers.[13] In determining hardware function, the operating system mediates between user program and machine.[14] The computer is, in other words, a medium in the form of a virtual machine, a machine that is accessible only by means of software, that is, signs. It is a medium without a gender, one for which the sexuality of its users is irrelevant.

Lara Croft is a different kind of medium entirely. She speaks everyone's language and her name says, as her fan formulated so well, a thousand words. This makes her into a universal medium of circulation, one that, unlike machines and operating systems, is entitled to a gender. The medium represented by Lara Croft is universal and feminine. The effect of a sign-event, she invites the user to interact with the computer in such a way that the user completely forgets the reality of the machine whose virtualization has already been prepared by the software interposed between user and hardware. As I will argue in more detail, the medium of Lara Croft was not conceived as feminine by accident. The connotations of mediality, representation, and femininity follow a long tradition, one that recurs in the establishment of new media. To analyze the phenomenon of Lara Croft, we will have to look into the question of how the linking of these two media – virtual machine and Lara Croft – came about and what ramifications it has had.

Adhering to the same logic described by Karl Marx in his chapter on the commodity fetish in *Capital*, Lara Croft, like money itself, functions as a medium of circulation erasing all qualitative difference, even sexual difference.[15] To better characterize this medialization of the body, I would first like to distance the concept of sexual difference from any associations it might have with an identity-fixated heterosexuality based solely on gender. Following Judith Butler, I understand sexual difference as an irresolvable question, not a scientific or philosophical object among many, but a place of unrest revealing the limits of epistemological validity.[16] The question of sexual difference aims to interrogate the historical basis of our knowledge and the unquestioned metaphysics of gender it presupposes. According to this metaphysics, the feminine is linked to the body, nature, matter, heteronomy, passivity, and the image, while the masculine is associated with thought (or mind), culture, form, autonomy, activity, and the gaze. The question of sexual difference, beyond its opposition to a gender-based dualism, is concerned with the connections that exist between gender identity, the play with truth, and the foundations of knowledge. The goal is not to define sexual difference better or more precisely, as was once the case, but to maintain it as a place of unrest – a gap through which, as the French philosopher Geneviève Fraisse writes, historicity enters into thought.[17] Sexual difference is not only an irresolvable question, but it also confronts thought itself with its own irresolvability. It cannot, therefore, be subsumed under the well-known and often-criticized distinctions between nature and culture, body and mind.[18] The implications of understanding sexual difference as an irresolvable question for the analysis of Lara Croft will become clear in the course of this book. At this point, I want to stress that the medialization and degendering of the body rewrite the very openness of sexual difference as a hierarchical gender dualism on the abstract level of the binary code. The linkage of these apparently opposing processes testifies to the complexity of the phenomenon of Lara Croft.

Allucquère Rosanne Stone has stressed that the process of degendering that accompanies the virtualization of reality, along with its flip side, the becoming real of virtuality, concerns all users, not just women. As Stone also makes quite clear, it is not a process to be welcomed. While considering what happens to the body when spaces of fantasy are linked globally through the Internet, she points out that "much of the work of cyberspace researchers . . . assumes that the human body is 'meat' – obsolete, as soon as consciousness itself can be uploaded into the network."[19] Separated from wishes, from the intellectual fantasy, even from its own desire, the body is imagined as a piece of dead flesh excluded from the reality of cyberspace. In contrast to the views of many cyberspace researchers, Stone emphasizes that the virtual community has no less a vulnerable origin in the mortal and sexual body, a body that is open to injury, a body that is constituted by a completely different kind of flesh than that which can be subsumed under the category of "meat." With this in mind, Stone writes, "No refigured virtual body, no matter how beautiful, will slow the death of a cyberpunk with AIDS."[20]

Notes

1. Lara Croft's Official Homepage, "Letters to Lara."
2. I would like to thank Roman for helping me with many questions, as well as for patiently introducing me to the video game world. For their encouragement and critical comments, I would also like to thank Ursula Konnertz, Gabriele Dietze, Giaco Schiesser, and Wolf-Dieter Besche.
3. *Lara Croft Magazin*; no. 1 (1999): 27.
4. "License to Thrill."
5. Benson, "Lara Croft for President."
6. Arent, "Game Maker: Lara's No Playmate."
7. Quoted in Vorsatz, "Bitte bleiben Sie dran." [Unless otherwise noted, all translations are my own. – Trans.]
8. Angela McRobbie remarks that Lara Croft's biography "is closer than we may like to think to the boarding school story." See McRobbie, "Coding the Feminine in the 1990s," 6.
9. Sherry Turkle has pointed out that the contemporary notion of "user" didn't appear until the late 1970s, when application programs were first used to help operate personal computers. The programs allowed people to use the computer "without getting involved with the 'guts' of the machine" (*Life on the Screen*, 32–4). While Turkle welcomes the removal of the computer's inner mechanisms from the user's purview as a creation of new space on which to "float, skim, and play" (34), Friedrich Kittler has rightly warned against losing sight of the conditions determined by hardware market development. These conditions could "reduce the contingency or unpredictability of some, but not all, futures by finite degrees" ("Hardware, das unbekannte Wesen," 131).
10. Elsner et al., "Zur Kulturgeschichte der Medien," 163.
11. On the relationship between machine and medium and its history, see Schelhowe, *Das Medium aus der Maschine*.
12. Žižek, *The Plague of Fantasies*, 132.
13. On the consequences of this development and its critique, see Kittler, "Hardware, das unbekannte Wesen," 124.
14. Cf. Mainzer, *Computernetze und virtuelle Realität*, 22.
15. Marx, *Capital*, 115. Here Marx cites the passage from *Timon of Athens* where Timon, having just discovered gold, proclaims, "Come, damned earth, / Thou common whore of mankind." The reliance on sexual difference in Shakespeare's metaphorics is, as Walter Benjamin has shown, likewise no accident. See my "Woman: The Most Precious Loot in the 'Triumph of Allegory,'" 281–303.

16. Butler, "The End of Sexual Difference?" 414–34.
17. Fraisse, *Geschlecht und Moderne*, 28.
18. On Butler's critique of the distinction between sex and gender, see her *Gender Trouble*, 7; as well as my "Geschlecht als philosophische Kategorie," 11–31.
19. Stone, "Will the Real Bodies Please Stand Up?" 94.
20. Ibid.

References

Arent, Lindsey (1999). Game Maker: Lara's No Playmate. *Wired News*, July 15, at www.wired. com/news/culture/0,1284,20762,00.html

Benson, Lynn (1998). Lara Croft for President. *Rightgrrl*! October 30, at www.rightgrrl.com/ l998/laracroft.html

Butler, Judith (1990). *Gender Trouble: Feminism and the Subversion of Identity*. New York: Routledge.

Butler, Judith (2001). The End of Sexual Difference? In: Elisabeth Bronfen & Misha Kavka (eds.), *Feminist Consequences: Theory for the New Century*. New York: Columbia University Press.

Deuber-Mankowsky, Astrid (1998). Geschlecht und Repräsentation: Oder wie das Bild zum Denken komont. *Die Philosophin* 18.

Deuber-Mankowsky, Astrid (2000). Woman: The Most Precious Loot in the "Triumph of Allegory": On the Function and Appearance of Gender Relations in Walter Benjamin's *Passagenwerk*, trans. Dana Hollander. In: Herta Nagl-Decekal & Cornelia Klinger (eds.), *Continental Philosophy in Feminist Perspective: Re-reading the Canon in German*. University Park: Penn State University Press.

Elsner, Monika, et al. (1994). Zur Kulturgeschichte der Medien. In: Klaus Merten, Siegfried J. Schmidt & Siegfried Wischenberg (eds.), *Die Wirklichkeit der Medien: Eine Einführung in die Kommunikationswissenschaft*. Opladen: Westdeutscher Verlag.

Fraisse, Geneviève (1995). *Geschlecht und Moderne: Archäologien der Gleichberechtigung*. Eva Horn (ed.). Frankfurt am Main: Fischer Taschenbuch Verlag.

Kittler, Friedrich (1998). Hardware, Das Unbekannte Wesen. In: Sybille Krämer (ed.), *Medien, Computer, Realität: Wirklichkeitsvorstellungen und Neue Medien*. Frankfurt am Main: Suhrkamp.

Mainzer, Klaus (1999). *Computernetze und virtuelle Realität: Leben in der Wissensgesellschaft*. Berlin: Springer Verlag.

Marx, Karl (1990). *Capital: A Critical Analysis of Capitalist Production*. London 1887. In: Waltraud Falk, et al. (eds.), *Gesamtausgabe*, by Karl Marx and Friedrich Engels, Volume 2.9. Berlin: Dietz Verlag.

McRobbie, Angela (1999). Coding the Feminine in the 1990s. In: Manuela Barth (ed.), *Lara-Croftism*. Munich: Kunstraum München.

Schelhowe, Heidi (1997). *Das Medium aus der Maschine: Zur Metamorphose des Computers*. Frankfurt am Main: Campus Verlag.

Stone, Allucquère Rosanne (2000). Will the Real Bodies Please Stand up? Boundary Stories about Virtual Cultures? In: Jenny Wolmark (ed.), *Cybersexualities: A Reader on Feminist Theory, Cyborgs, and Cyberspace*. Edinburgh: Edinburgh University Press.

Turkle, Sherry (1995). *Life on the Screen: Identity in the Age of the Internet*. New York: Simon and Schuster.

Vorsatz, Marc (1999). Bitte bleiben Sie dran: Cyber-Heldin Lara Croft bringt die Werbung in die PC Spiele. *Tagesspiegel*, April 14.

Žižek, Slavoj (1997). *The Plague of Fantasies*. London: Verso.

XI

Visual Culture

63

From the Missile Gap to the Culture Gap: Modernism in the Fallout from Sputnik

David Howard*

Advance-guard painting in America is Hell-bent for outer space. It has rocketed right out of the realms of common sense and common experience. That does not necessarily make it bad. But it does leave the vast bulk of onlookers earthbound, with mouths agape and eyes reflecting a mixture of puzzlement, vexation and contempt.[1]

To every civilization, at some moment in its existence, the mortal challenge comes. Now Red Russia's dictatorship has thrust such a challenge upon the West. The challenge is not simply military; it is total – intellectual, spiritual, and material. To survive, the free world, led by the United States, must respond in kind. Amid a clamor of alarm and self criticism, America is preparing to shoulder this burden of great historical responsibilities. Technical problems which were long ago the province of isolated specialists have become the concern of a whole citizenry.[2]

In the winter of 1961, during the planning sessions for the Presidential Inauguration of John F. Kennedy in Washington DC, a symbolic changing of the guard was gently being drafted. In addition to the traditional invitations sent to leaders of business and industry, invitations were also sent to poets, painters, and novelists, 155 in total, who were emblematic of a new fusion of art and politics and who were regarded as key figures representing the new "frontiersmen." Writers such as Ernest Hemingway, William Faulkner, and John Steinbeck, playwrights such as Arthur Miller, Thornton Wilder, and Tennessee Williams, artists such as Alexander Calder, Stuart Davis, Mark Rothko and Edward Hopper, and composers such as Paul Hindemith, Igor Stravinsky, and Leonard Bernstein were issued written invitations which stated: "During our forthcoming Administration we hope to seek a productive relationship with our writers, artist, composers, philosophers, scientists and heads of cultural institutions."[3]

The contrast between the cultural attitudes of the Eisenhower and Kennedy Administrations was noted by Presidential Adviser Arthur Schlesinger Jr., who stated in a

*Pp. 61–72 from *The Writing on the Cloud: American Culture Confronts the Atomic Bomb*, ed. A. M. Scott and C. D. Geist (Lanham MD: University Press of America). © 1997. Reprinted with permission from the University Press of America.

speech to the American Federation of Arts in 1962 that, "In the Executive Mansion, where Fred Waring and his Pennsylvanians once played, we now find Isaac Stern, Pablo Casals, Stravinsky, and the Oxford Players."[4] The epitome of this cultural about-face was the appointment of August Heckscher Jr., Director of the Rockefeller-funded Twentieth Century Fund, member of the Art Commission of New York City, and Chairman of the Board of the International Council of the Museum of Modern Art, as the President's special consultant on the arts, charged with drafting the new alliance of culture and state. In striking fashion, high culture and the avant-garde had now migrated from their peripheral haunts of alienated integrity to form the knife edge of Kennedy's "New Frontier."

Yet, a little over one and a half years later, in the hot August of 1962, America's foremost art critic, Clement Greenberg, the intellectual most associated with helping to re-define the relationship and role of the modernist avant-garde in post-war US culture, was anywhere but at the center.[5] Careening over the dusty backroads of the Western Canadian prairies, Greenberg had crossed the frontier separating Canada from the United States, spending ten days and traveling over 3000 kilometers in his mother-in-law's 1956 Dodge. His destination was a small collection of wooden huts on the shores of a remote lake in north central Saskatchewan: Emma Lake, the site of a small summer art camp. Greenberg's arrival on the periphery of North American culture and society, finding in his words a site that was not only marginal to America but actually wrapped in "double obscurity," signals a strategic displacement of the art critic who for many postmodern writers symbolized the tyranny of modernism over less elitist, non-determinist and non-gender-biased forms of visual expression. This period of hegemony exerted by Greenbergian modernism is usually seen by post-modern critics to culminate with the 1965 publication of Greenberg's infamous essay "Modernist Painting," an essay which had actually originally been broadcast by the Voice of America five years previously, in 1960.

If Greenberg's concept of the modernist avant-garde was now to be found flourishing in obscurity on the margins of North American culture, what was the relationship of Greenberg's aesthetic to Kennedy's New Frontier? Was the new cultural formation emerging under the auspices of the New Frontier a new cultural dominant whose pluralism and democratizing sympathies augured in a new period of cultural instrumentalization which continues up to our own era? In order to provide a partial explanation of this cultural dynamic, I argue, it is necessary to return to the darkest days of the Cold War and the launching of Sputnik 1.

On Friday, October 4, 1957, the stunned populace of the United States reeled under the news of the successful launch of the first Soviet transorbital satellite, Sputnik 1. The launch of this satellite, officially baptized "Artificial Traveller Around the Earth," recalled the nightmarish period of national insecurity that followed the successful Japanese attack on Pearl Harbor. Sputnik symbolized a new level of technological and scientific achievement, not to mention an unsurpassed potential for photographic surveillance, all achievements that the United States had previously considered marks of its own unchallenged technological leadership. The Republican presidency of Dwight D. Eisenhower now faced a period of intense public scrutiny seeking to answer the question: "How could the United States have forfeited its leadership in scientific expertise and jeopardized the security of the Free World?" Furthermore, with the visible potential of Soviet technology to breech Fortress America, many US citizens believed nuclear Armageddon was now only minutes away.

These anxieties are reflected in the October 21, 1957 issue of *Life* magazine. The cover photograph displays the planet Earth with three US scientists plotting the orbital trajectory of Sputnik. The scientific specialists appear at a loss, two of them painstakingly examining a large crumpled sheet of mathematical calculations while their colleague maps out the orbit of the satellite. A single orbit is indicated moving around the globe on a North–South axis, sweeping over the two most populous nations of the Earth: linking together the successful communist revolution in the People's Republic of China with the potential communist subversion of the Third World, at that time becoming an increasing focus of the Cold War. Even more ominously, the orbit of Sputnik leads directly to North America, implying that in combination with the successful launch of a Soviet ICBM only two months earlier, North American security was in jeopardy due to the existence of this so-called "missile gap." As one veteran of the Vanguard rocket project stated on the October 21st editorial page: "I think this is the first step toward the unification of the peoples of the world, whether they know it or not."[6] This editorial attributed blame for the calamity to those in the Pentagon and the Eisenhower Administration who "confuse scientific progress with freezer and lipstick output."[7]

Ultimate responsibility fell on the shoulders of President Eisenhower whose photograph within the same issue of *Life* shows a weary president next to a series of photographs representing the latest in space toys and space fashion. The juxtaposition of Soviet technological superiority with a fatigued president and science reduced to a branch of American consumerism pointed a finger of blame towards the debilitating influence of consumerism and mass culture.

Giving further credibility to the Eisenhower Administration's political rivals, statistical estimates of the Soviet Union's lead in the missile gap were published by the mass media in the summer of 1958. According to these figures, beginning in 1959, the Soviet Union's lead in ICBM's would be 100 to 0. Projecting this rate of development, even taking into account concerted American efforts to close the gap, the United States in 1963 would still be considerably behind, with 130 weapons as compared to 2,000 for the Soviet Union.[8] By 1958, Air Force officers and Democratic and liberal Republican congressmen were advocating a missile force in the thousands.

Importantly, however, attention remained fixated on the decadence of American material culture and its undisciplined consumerism that cumulatively was sapping the nation's will to resist. Arthur Schlesinger Jr., author of the 1949 text *The Vital Center* (which helped to redefine American liberalism away from its "soft" associations with social democracy towards a "harder" liberalism that was more business oriented), traced the decline of the United States in the 1950s to the collapse of individual identity in the suburbs with attending consequence of undermining American masculinity. In a 1958 essay entitled, "The Crisis of American Masculinity," Schlesinger cites the homogenizing influence of mass media and its ability to undermine individual creativity and spontaneity as a key to understanding the weakened influence of the United States abroad and the emasculation of the American male at home. What was needed,

according to Schlesinger, foreshadowing Kennedy's call for a New Frontier, was a reclamation of the "American male identity" exemplified by the frontiersman. The recovery of a secure male identity was linked by Schlesinger to three "techniques of liberation,"
one of which included the strategic importance of art in constructing clear gender
boundaries:

> How can masculinity, femininity, or anything else survive in a homogenized world, which
> seeks steadily and benignly to eradicate all differences between the individuals who
> compose it? If we want to have men again in our theatres and our films and our novels –
> we must first have a society which encourages each of its members to have a distinct
> identity.[9]

The assumption that national security, both domestically and externally, relied on a
secure definition of masculine identity was an effective strategy to wield against an
Administration that appeared impotent in the light of Sputnik and that actively undermined secure gender identities by promoting the unrestricted expansion of mass leisure,
as essayist Herbert Gold noted in 1962: "The consumer culture – in which leisure is a
menace to be met by anxious and continual consuming – devours both the masculinity
of men and the femininity of women."[10] The image of the frontiersman promised the
renewal of secure gender and national boundaries by tapping the vigor of the frontier
myth as a bridge to overcoming the missile gap, the culture gap and the crisis of American masculinity. The astronaut would become one tangible symbol of this New Frontiersman in response to the missile gap; certainly the New York modernist artist appeared
logically poised to represent the frontier equivalent in the visual arts. However, at the
core of the pragmatic liberal cultural agenda was a challenging of the very binary
distinctions between the modernists and mass culture that critics, such as Clement
Greenberg, relied upon to justify the survival of the modernist avant-garde.

Between 1939 and 1948, Clement Greenberg had developed his particular variant of
art criticism that had helped to establish the legitimacy of American modernist art in
the post-war period, helping New York and the United States to assume the mantle of
cultural leadership from Paris in the early days of the Cold War. As the art historian
Serge Guilbaut has observed, this process of differentiation from Paris first occurs in
a piece of art criticism written by Greenberg comparing Jackson Pollock and Jean
Dubuffet, published in the *Nation* in February 1947:

> Pollock, like Dubuffet, tends to handle his canvas with an over all evenness; but at this
> moment he seems capable of more variety than the French artist, and able to work with
> riskier elements. . . . Dubuffet's sophistication enables him to "package" his canvases more
> skillfully and pleasingly and achieve greater instantaneous unity, but Pollock, I feel, has
> more to say in the end and is, fundamentally, and almost because he lacks equal charm,
> the more original. Pollock has gone beyond the state where he needs to make his poetry
> explicit in ideographs.
>   He [Pollock] is American and rougher and more brutal, but also completer. In any case
> he is certainly less conservative, less of an easel painter in the traditional sense than
> Dubuffet.[11]

Guilbaut argues that the emphasis on the "vitality, virility, and brutality of the American artist" were signs of "direct, uncorrupted communication that contemporary life demanded," thus ensuring that "American art became the trustee of this new age."[12] The masculine metaphors combined with the individualism of the modern artist indirectly provided a visual corollary of the new liberalism of Arthur Schlesinger Jr. For the first time, Guilbaut notes, the ideology of the avant-garde was becoming reconciled with postwar liberalism.

The post-war triumph of American painting that Greenberg's modernist criticism had helped to cement attains a cultural hegemony within the United States that postmodern critics will argue only becomes dislodged during the mid-1960s. Cultural theorists such as Stephen Conner, in his book *Post-modernist Culture*, argue that Greenberg's dominant position as the avatar of modernism in the United States continues up to the publication of Greenberg's essay "Modernist Painting," mistakenly dated as having been first published in 1965.[13] However, I argue that the alliance of Schlesinger's liberalism and the ideology of Greenberg's modernist avant-garde, that Guilbaut correctly traces to the late 1940s and early 1950s, becomes unraveled between the launch of Sputnik in 1957 and the election of John F. Kennedy in 1960. Greenberg is reluctantly displaced from his position of cultural centrality and consequently reorients his interpretation of modernism towards the margins of North American culture a crucial five years before cultural analysts such as Stephen Conner argue that Greenberg was displaced by an emergent postmodern sensibility.

By the early 1950s, in essays such as "The Plight of Our Culture," Greenberg's optimism for the survival of modernism in a sea of American mass culture was at an all-time high. His hopes for the triumph of a more broadly based modernism are captured in quotations such as the following:

> But can it not be hoped that middlebrow culture will in the course of time be able to transcend itself and rise to a level where it will be no longer middlebrow, but high culture? This hope assumes that the new urban middle classes in America will consolidate and increase their present social and material advantages and, in the process, achieve enough cultivation to support, spontaneously, a much higher level of culture than now. And then, supposedly, we shall see, for the first time in history, high urban culture on a "mass" basis.[14]

As the Canadian art historian John O'Brian has argued, Greenberg was detecting that "the seriousness of work was entering into American categories of leisure. The infusion of unalienated work into play, the argument ran, had the potential to redeem leisure from its emptiness and passivity."[15] Again, as in the late 1940s, the alliance of modernism and the new liberalism of Schlesinger that will help to define Kennedy's New Frontier appear compatible, inoculating American men against the dangerously debilitating and, by implication, feminizing effects of mass culture. Yet in the fallout from Sputnik four years after the publication of Greenberg's "The Plight of Our Culture," Greenberg was being forced to defend modernism from a far more pessimistic and defensive position in relationship to middlebrow culture, reasserting the culture gap between modernism and mass culture as a survival strategy. This would not only distance Greenberg from the emerging liberal agenda on culture but also, I would argue, contribute to the rigidity and ossification of his modernist theory in the 1960s.

By the launch of Sputnik in 1957, the focus of American Cold War policy under President Eisenhower came under increasing attack, especially from a revitalized Democratic party seeking a winning formula for the next presidential race. Between 1957 and the first broadcast of Greenberg's classic statement on modernist formalism, "Modernist Painting," in the spring of 1960, Greenberg's defense of modernism was suddenly immersed in a raging debate that centered on the overlapping concerns of the missile gap and the culture gap. Greenberg's modernism was now increasingly a liability, especially to liberals such as Arthur Schlesinger Jr., as pragmatic liberalism positioned itself to exploit the vulnerability of the Eisenhower Administration and the weakening influence of the "soft" progressive wing of the Democratic party.

In an effort to address the absence of a cultural policy within the Administration, the Director of the Twentieth Century Fund and cultural adviser to Nelson Rockefeller, August Heckscher Jr., was appointed to the President's Commission on National Goals. Heckscher, at the time of the writing of the report, was Chairman of the Board of the International Council of the Museum of Modern Art, indicative of the increasingly important role played by liberals in formulating an increased role for culture, in conjunction with a more aggressive defense policy.

A vital component of the Report on National Goals, ultimately published in 1960, was Heckscher's essay "The Quality of American Culture." The essay opens with a comparative analysis of "Material and Cultural Progress," contrasting the wealth and leisure of the modern United States with the nation's cultural evolution. To Heckscher, the pattern was clear: while the overall material progress of the United States had prospered, culture had lagged behind. Heckscher did not question that some individual artists had been successful but that the success of these few avant-gardists did nothing to close the gap between the huge new middle class of the post-war era and the cultural productions of these few artistic individualists, giving Heckscher "cause for serious uneasiness."[16] Heckscher disparaged intellectuals who, like Greenberg, were critical of mass culture while only offering in its place a reliance on an elitist defense of modernist practices. Likewise, Arthur Schlesinger Jr. unveiled the outline of his new formula for the interaction of culture, business, and government in an article entitled "Notes on a National Cultural Policy," published in the journal *Daedalus* in the spring of 1960. In this article, Schlesinger argued that reliance solely upon private initiative was tainted by its "impotence" to sustain the economic support necessary for a national cultural strategy. Schlesinger avoided, however, the massive government intervention of the New Deal by advocating a limited role for the Federal government in the arts with particular attention to Western European models of government support programs. Recognizing the historical opposition for such government support for the arts, Schlesinger recommended, as an intermediate step, the formation of a Federal Advisory Council of the Arts to explore the avenues for a realignment of social priorities especially between the qualitative and quantitative issues of American daily life.

Kennedy's election in 1960 set in motion a process whereby pragmatic liberal intellectuals could implement their moderate theory concerning the role of culture as a social cement linking high culture to the middle class in order to wean it from its overconsumption of mass culture. As a consequence, the gap separating the cultural positions of Greenberg and the liberal pragmatists widened to the point of rupture. Greenberg's earlier optimism for the flourishing of an urbane modernist culture in the United States was substituted by an increasing pessimism arising from a sense of isolation in the post-Sputnik cultural environment. Greenberg expressed this increasing marginalization from American society in two published articles in 1960 that codified his theoretical stance. "Modernist Painting," first broadcast over the Voice of America, clearly lays out the new ground upon which Greenberg hoped to keep modernist painting moving forward within the momentum of a formalist Kantian aesthetic. The second article entitled "Louis and Noland," published in the May 25, 1960 issue of *Art International*, not only presents examples of the work of two non-New York based painters, the Washington DC artists Morris Louis and Kenneth Noland, as examples of Greenberg's new aesthetic but also suggests his interest, not in the dominance of New York, but in so-called "provincial" environments as vital contexts for the production of modern art.

In outlining his defense of a self-reflexive modern art that would break with the "Tenth Street Touch" of first and second generation abstract expressionist painters, Greenberg advocated an exploration of the formal characteristics of modern painting, "not in order to subvert it, but to entrench it more firmly in its area of competence."[17] Invoking Kant as the first modernist, Greenberg isolated the characteristics of painting according to the criteria of a pure immanent criticism (purity meaning, according to Greenberg, "self definition, and the enterprise of self-criticism in the arts [has become] one of self-definition with a vengeance."[18] While flatness is the term most closely associated with Greenberg's concept of purity, the boundary lines separating immanent critique from contamination with anything external to it enabled Greenberg to play with and disassemble the binary tensions integral to painting as a form of representation. Flatness was not an absolute and, argued Greenberg, "[there] can never be an utter flatness."[19] Sculptural illusion may transgress the "heightened sensitivity of the picture plane," but modernist pictorial illusions of space enabled the viewer to have a new visual experience.[20]

Greenberg's theories of modernist painting expressed in these articles required the viewer to engage with the paintings on their own terms. In works such as Louis' *Saraband*, painted in 1959, and Noland's *Luster*, painted in 1958, the application of thinned oil paint onto areas of unprimed cotton duck asserts the primacy of flatness and opticality while maintaining the visual illusion of depth by the indeterminate way in which the canvas and paint bond. "The effect," states Greenberg in the essay, "Louis and Noland," "conveys a sense not only of colour as somehow disembodied, and therefore more purely optical, but also of colour as a thing that opens and expands the picture plane."[21] The resulting play of surface and depth, the soaking of the pigment into the canvas, also enabled Greenberg to theorize about the visual transcendence of the central painted image by pointing to the illusion of space projected beyond the framing conventions of painting.

Greenberg's promotion of the two Washington abstract painters Louis and Noland as exemplars of his neo-Kantian aesthetic also provides an interesting case study in his self-distancing from the literal and symbolic center of American cultural power. Now

New York, in Greenberg's view, had sunk to new depths of cultural depravity, as indicated in his statement, "Never before in New York has there been so much false and inflated painting and sculpture, never before so many false and inflated reputations."[22] Greenberg saw room for painters to maneuver between provincialism and the so-called cosmopolitanism of the center. For Greenberg, Louis and Noland, by virtue of being 250 miles from the new Babylon of art, had access to the cultural maelstrom of New York without being "subjected as constantly to its pressures to conform as you would be if you lived and worked in New York."[23] In Greenberg's view, Louis and Noland's geographical "isolation" becomes, in this context, an indication of their moral integrity in the face of cultural decay. In response to the pragmatist pursuit of a more pluralist, less hierarchical model of high culture that would hopefully legitimate a reunion of culture with government funding, Greenberg's solution to the plight of culture was a modernist circling of the wagons, jettisoning any lingering Marxist materialism, while retaining the "positivist aspect of the modernist aesthetic."[24] The extent of his pessimism with the center would locate Greenberg, on the eve of the Cuban Missile Crisis in the August of 1962, driving in his mother-in-law's 1956 Dodge across the dusty expanse of the Canadian prairies looking for more examples of integrity in painting on the margins of North American society.

By 1964, Greenberg's daunting reputation as an art critic in North America was undeniable yet, in the spring of that year, three events signaled the increasing irrelevancy of Greenberg's aesthetic for the national cultural agenda. First, Greenberg's efforts to stage a critical reconquest of the art world with his exhibition entitled "Post Painterly Abstraction" at the Los Angeles County Art Museum was an overwhelming disaster, as critics delighted in savaging a now obviously vulnerable Greenberg who dared to promote abstract painting from the margins as the cutting edge of modern art. The exhibition limped through an abbreviated exhibition schedule before expiring in Toronto.[25] Secondly, one month later at the Venice Biennale, Robert Rauschenberg became the first American to be awarded the Grand Prize, winning the honor over the representative of Greenberg's aesthetic, Kenneth Noland.[26]

Rauschenberg's victory signified the triumph of the new pragmatic sensibility: a positive and constructive view of the world that, in the words of the curator of the exhibition Alan R. Solomon, would "not shock" like the earlier modernist avant-garde but actually presented a reveling in "sheer delight". The limited pictorial means of abstract painters such as Noland and Louis were no longer necessary to maintain American cultural leadership abroad and certainly were no longer able or required to function as an avant-garde at home in a land were the boundaries between high and low were blurring if not dissolved entirely. This was reflected in the third blow, as well, when during the planning for the 1964 New York World's Fair, the triumph of American culture was symbolized by Nelson Rockefeller's New York State pavilion, with its pluralist collage of Pop, modernist, and historical painting and the classicizing kitsch of Donald de Lue's sculpture *Rocket Thrower*, a favorite of fair organizer Robert Moses and a throwback to the aesthetic of the 1939 New York World's Fair.[27]

Thus the downfall of Greenberg's pre-eminent position as the key arbiter of American taste in high culture seems, to me at least, to be inextricably linked to the fallout in the aftermath of Sputnik. The fearful image of the threat of Sputnik and

Soviet technology in 1957 on the cover of *Life* magazine symbolizes the impetus of the new liberals to integrate high culture into American life precipitating the rapid collapse of modernism's hegemony and the subsequent emergence of post modernism. As the culture gap between art and American society entered a New Frontier, Greenberg was to find himself displaced on the margins, prowling the bushland of Central Saskatchewan: a frontiersman of another kind.

Notes

1. *Time*, February 20, 1956.
2. *Newsweek*, January 20, 1958.
3. Gary O. Larson, *The Reluctant Patron* (Philadelphia: University of Pennsylvania Press, 1983), 151.
4. Larson, 151.
5. Born in the Bronx in 1909, Greenberg established his reputation as an art critic in the late 1930s. A Trotskyite early in his career, Greenberg was an associate of the New York intelligentsia which included Philip Rahv, Harold Rosenberg, Lionel Abel, and Dwight Macdonald amongst others, and wrote for *Partisan Review, The Nation* and the *Contemporary Jewish Record*. His most important essays from the first phase of his career are "Avant-Garde and Kitsch," published in 1939, and "Towards a Newer Laocoon," from 1940. In the post-war period he is perhaps most notorious as the critic most associated with the triumph of Abstract Expressionism in the United States that helped to establish cultural hegemony for America in the Cold War. Greenberg died on May 7, 1994. For the most complete collection of Greenberg's art criticism see John O'Brian, ed., *Clement Greenberg: The Collected Essays and Criticism*, volumes 1–4, (Chicago: University of Chicago Press, 1986–93).
6. "Common Sense and Sputnik," *Life*, October 21, 1957, 35.
7. "Common Sense and Sputnik," 35.
8. By 1959, the Russian superiority was being downgraded in military intelligence circles. CIA estimates at this time put the United States and the Soviet Union force levels at par, approximately ten missiles per side. However, in order to keep fueling the American defense build-up, estimates for the early 1960s show the persistence of a distinct numerical superiority on the Soviet side: in 1960, approximately 100 missiles to the American 30; and by 1962, 500 missiles to the American estimates of 1–300. For a further discussion of the politics of missile numbers see Roy E. Licklider, "The Missile Gap Controversy" in *Political Science Quarterly* 85 (December 1970): 600–15 and Desmond Ball, *Politics and Force Levels* (Los Angeles: University of California Press, 1980), 3–40.
9. Arthur M. Schlesinger, Jr., *The Politics of Hope* (Boston: Houghton Mifflin Company, 1962), 246.
10. Quoted in Barbara Ehrenreich, *Fear of Falling* (New York: Pantheon Books, 1989), 33–4.
11. Quoted in Serge Guilbaut, "The New Adventures of the Avant-Garde in America," *October* 15 (Winter 1989): 61–78.
12. Guilbaut, 71.
13. Stephen Conner, *Postmodernist Culture: An Introduction to Theories of the Contemporary* (New York and Oxford: Basil Blackwell, 1989), especially pages 81–7.
14. Quoted in John O'Brian, "Introduction," *Clement Greenberg: The Collected Essays and Criticism*, vol. 3, xxix.

15. O'Brian, *Clement Greenberg*, vol. 3, xxx.

16. August Heckscher Jr., "The Quality of American Culture," in *The Report of the President's Commission on National Goals, Goals for America* (New York: Columbia University Press, 1960), 127–46.

17. Clement Greenberg, "Modernist Painting," in Gregory Battcock (ed.), *The New Art* (New York: E.P. Dutton and Company), 67.

18. Greenberg, "Modernist Painting," 68.

19. Greenberg, "Modernist Painting," 73.

20. Greenberg, "Modernist Painting," 73.

21. Clement Greenberg, "Louis and Noland," *Art International*, 4 May 1960, 26–9.

22. Greenberg, "Louis and Noland," 27.

23. Greenberg, "Louis and Noland," 27.

24. Benjamin Buchloh, "Cold War Constructivism" in Serge Guilbaut (ed.) *Reconstructing Modernism: Art in New York, Paris, and Montreal: 1945–1964* (Cambridge: MIT Press, 1990), 244–310.

25. For a discussion of the organization and politics of the 1964 Post Painterly Exhibition see David Howard, "From Emma Lake to Los Angeles: Modernism on the Margins," in John O'Brian, ed., *The Flat Side of the Landscape: The Emma Lake Artists' Workshops* (Saskatoon: Mendel Art Gallery, 1989), 41–9.

26. For a critical examination of the political machinations behind the 1964 Venice Biennale see Laurie J. Monahan, "Cultural Cartography: American Designs at the 1964 Venice Biennale," in Guilbaut, ed., *Reconstructing Modernism*, 369–407.

27. For an analysis of Donald De Lue and the politics of the 1964 New York World's Fair see, Helen A. Harrison, "Art for the Millions, or Art for the Market?" in Helen Harrison et al, *Remembering the Future: The New York World's Fair From 1939 to 1964* (New York: The Queens Museum in conjunction with Rizzoli International Publications, 1989), 137–66.

64

Nostalgia, Myth, and Ideology: Visions of Superman at the End of the "American Century"

Ian Gordon*

Then came, out of nowhere, nostalgia – including nostalgia for things the nostalgia lovers were too young to know.

Friedrich, 1988, p. 72

It is perhaps self-evident that a comic book character that has been in existence for some 60 years owes some of its popularity to nostalgia. Certainly Otto Friedrich in his 1988 *Time* magazine celebration of Superman's 50 years could find no better reason to explain the resurgence of the character's popularity in the late 1970s. But nostalgia never comes out of nowhere.

In the common usage of "nostalgia," many Americans, and indeed others, probably have some wistful memories of Superman, whether from the character's portrayal as a comic book, radio show, comic strip, movie serial, television show, or movie superhero. Some might well have a sentimental yearning for the period in which they first encountered Superman, but few, I venture, would think of themselves as suffering from the disease of homesickness in their thoughts about the character. Labeling the nostalgia for Superman as ideological might suggest a too-easy criticism along the lines of the old joke that Superman, standing for truth and justice on the one hand and the American way on the other, was surely an oxymoron. Nonetheless the nostalgia associated with Superman operates at a number of levels that can be usefully explored to understand the operation of nostalgia as ideology.

There are two facets to the argument that follows. First, I want to argue that Superman connects a wistful nostalgia – nostalgia as homesickness if you will – to a commodity, and in this fashion subjects both longings for the past, and the past itself, to the ideology of the market in which everything can be commodified and sold.

Second, since World War II Superman's owners have explicitly tied the character to "the American Way," which is an ideological construct that among other things unites two seemingly disparate values – individualism and consumerism – with democracy and labels it American. Nostalgia about the character then is inevitably linked to

*Pp. 177–93 from *Comics & Ideology*, ed. M. P. McCallister, E. H. Sewell and I. Gordon (New York: Peter Lang Publishing). © 2001. Reprinted with permission from Peter Lang Publishing.

this notion of America, which gives it a particular ideological cast, possibly more so when the subject of longings is not an American.

Nostalgia and Ideology

The manner in which I use nostalgia and ideology owes much to Clifford Geertz. The heart of the problem is in understanding how "ideologies transform sentiment into significance" (Geertz, 1973, p. 207). Geertz tries to understand this process by examining the stories people tell to and about themselves. Before turlling to such tales, some working definition of nostalgia is necessary. During James Cook's extended voyage in the South Pacific from 1768 to 1771, the men on board his ship developed an acute longing for home, which the ship's surgeon named as a new disease: nostalgia. The term has been much expanded on since, but still retains the notion of a longing for return, a return to a past, to a past that we can never go back to, just as we can never truly return home once having left. In reviewing the widespread critique of nostalgia in the 1960s and 1970s, Christopher Lasch (1984) argued that what is often erased from such evaluations is that while we may not be able to return home, we also carry that home with us in ways that are inescapable. It shapes our present. But, he argued, both nostalgia and anti-nostalgia denied a dependence on the past in daily life, the first by romanticizing the past and the second by demanding life be lived in the here and now. It is also well to remember that Cook's sailors were on a long and difficult voyage in waters dangerous to Europeans, and that a longing for home, far from being pathological, may well have been eminently sensible.

Some theorists have sought to expand the concept of nostalgia beyond the limitations and oppositions Lasch identified. The anthropologist Renato Rosaldo has observed that even as "we valorize innovation" we "yearn for more stable worlds, whether these reside in our own past, in other cultures, or in the conflation of the two" (Rosaldo, 1989, p. 108). Stuart Tannock made the distinction that nostalgia looks to "the past as a stable source of value and meaning" but not necessarily "with the desire for a stable, traditional, and hierarchized society" (1995, p. 455). Concepts of nostalgia have also been used to explain the shaping and performing of postmodern identities in a play of difference and repetition (Frow, 1997, p. 68). This notion has been stretched in a manner whereby nostalgia is linked to the performance of identity as a set of memory structures or grammar through which individuals "invent rhetorical performances of themselves" (Dickinson, 1997, p. 2). Susan Stewart argues nostalgia relies on the process of creating a narrative of the past, which in affect denies the present, and gives the past the whiff of authenticity. This sense of authentic comes from the narrative rather than any a *priori* veracity (Stewart, 1984, p. 23). In effect nostalgia is a construction that also denies the past except as narrative mediation. By examining a narrative then it should be possible to locate the transformation of nostalgic sentiment into significance.

The popularity in Australia in 1994 of the television series *Lois & Clark* (*The New Adventures of Superman*) sparked my initial interest in nostalgia as ideology. In 1994, *Lois & Clark* was a surprise hit in Australia, particularly given that its popularity in the United States was fairly marginal (it ranked third behind CBS and NBC during its

September 12, 1993 network Sunday-night debut on ABC, for instance). In Australia it consistently ranked in the top 10 shows, beating the Ten Network's Commonwealth Games (a sports feast ranking second only to the Olympics) coverage in the ratings, and was poached by the Nine Network from the Seven Network. It would be easy to see the many incarnations of Superman, including this version, simply as a product marketed in different fashions, but the creators of Superman know that it carries meanings beyond its status as a commodity. For instance, Jenette Kahn, president of DC Comics, described Superman in 1983 as "the first god of a new mythology" (Harris, 1990, p. 236). *Lois & Clark's* appeal lay in the way it reworked familiar characters in contemporary settings, which to me relied on a sense of nostalgia.

Mythology

Otto Friedrich asserted in 1988 that it is "one of the odd paradoxes about Superman . . . that while he is a hero of nostalgia, the constant changes in his character keep destroying the qualities that make him an object of nostalgia" (Friedrich, 1988, p. 74). But those changes contribute to the nostalgia about Superman, because the character operates in a mythological dimension, which gives it a form of consistency at a symbolic level. The symbolic resonance of Superman is important in uniting diverse forms, including versions to be discussed later in this chapter as well as the comic book "imaginary tales," which are not held to be part of the main narrative of the Superman comic books but are a sort of apocrypha that further enhances the character's mythological dimension.

Umberto Eco described Superman in a 1972 article as a mythological virtuous archetype locked in a timeless state and thereby never fully consumed by his audience (Eco, 1972). That is, Superman offers infinite possibilities for storytelling focused on virtue, but Superman's virtue is limited and the character's dimensions set by the prevailing social order. Eco's Superman then acts as an instructive tool for what passes as virtue in society, and Superman's popularity at any given time is probably in direct relationship to his creators' success in capturing a dominant mood. In effect, Superman is a product by which we consume virtue. Here it is also worth keeping in mind Claude Levi-Strauss's notion that myth recycles earlier versions of the myth as part of its status (Levi-Strauss, 1968).

Eco's explanation of Superman's status remains convincing because it explains the popularity of different versions of Superman and it touches on the character's position as a consumer durable. Among the numerous earlier incarnations of Superman, four stand out as touchstones in the hero's career. In each version Superman displayed a virtue tied explicitly to his time and locale. The original Superman, who made his debut in *Action Comics* in 1938, molded the entire legend, but in a way that was substantially altered by the second version, which took shape during World War II and tied the character to America's fortunes. Although numerous other versions, including a movie serial and a radio show, intervened between the comic book versions of Superman and the 1950s television show, the TV show is an important third version of Superman because it introduced many of the baby-boomer generation to the hero. It also introduced the important new medium of television to the character's presentation, a medium that continues to influence the portrayal of Superman. The first two entries in the motion picture series starring Christopher Reeve represent a fourth version of Superman, in this case involving both blockbuster action hero and sexually liberated man. Alongside *Lois & Clark*, important later versions of Superman have appeared in two comic book series: *Superman: The Man of Steel* (1986) and *Kingdom Come* (1997). These last three versions have all had to deal in their own way with the character's history. Whether or not one of these versions, or a mixture of parts of these versions, will coalesce into a hallmark of a particular era of the Superman character is not yet clear. The ebbs and flows of the character's development become clearer with the passing of time and the contextualization that history offers.

From the New Deal to the American Way

Both Andrae (1987) and Gordon (1998) have shown that the Superman of the first two years of *Action Comic* was somewhat of a reformist liberal, albeit one given to direct action. In his early years Superman saved a woman mistakenly condemned for murder, confronted a wife beater, prevented the United States from becoming embroiled in a European conflict, destroyed slums to force the government to build better housing (if one considers modern high-rise apartment blocks of the type built for the poor an improvement), tore down a car factory because its shoddy products caused deaths, and fought a corrupt police force. In this version, Superman's virtue was tied to Franklin Roosevelt's New Deal politics, America's 1930s isolationism, and the reality of life in Cleveland where his creators Jerry Siegel and Joe Shuster lived. This somewhat anarchic Superman captured an audience of young fans who probably reveled in his short-cut solutions to social problems and defiance of conventional authority. But this Superman was short-lived.

Beginning in the latter half of 1940, Superman was transformed into a symbol of more general American cultural values in that his individualism was tied to consumerist values. Superman's metamorphosis resulted from the confluence of a morality campaign directed at comic books, Superman's increasing commercial value, and the advent of a heightened patriotism with the growing realization that America would be drawn into the European war. Toward the end of 1940, Superman's publishers, DC Comics, instituted an advisory board of psychologists and child educators in response to a public campaign and legislation against comic books that transgressed public morals. New guidelines for Superman stories prohibited – among other things – the destruction of private property. At the same time Superman himself had become an important piece of private property. DC Comics licensed numerous Superman products, generating over a million dollars of profit in 1940 (Gaines, 1991, passim; Gordon, 1998, pp. 135–7; Kobler, 1941, p. 76).

At first the relationship between the creators of Superman and the commercialism of Superman was strained. DC Comics had purchased all rights to Superman from Siegel and Shuster for $100. Unhappy with their loss of revenue and critical of the company's treatment of them, Siegel and Shuster got a measure of revenge by creating a bitter parody of the marketing of Superman products. In their story, Nick Williams, a shoddy businessman, steals Superman's name to sell a range of goods including bathing suits and automobiles (Siegel & Shuster, 1938). However, by 1941, Siegel and Shuster had negotiated a better deal with DC, probably as part of their arrangement to produce the new comic strip version, whereby they received 5% of all Superman royalties. (Gordon, 1998, p. 135). Thereafter, their Superman stories began to contain plugs for the various products (Siegel & Shuster, 1941).

Myth Making

The commercialization of Superman was in part responsible for the character becoming an American icon. On America's entry into World War II, the defense of the "American Way of Life," which posited the promise of consumer choice in a market of goods as the basis of a democratic society, became an important cry to rally the troops. Countless advertisements sought to mobilize the nation for war by directing consumption into appropriate expenditures that would ensure victory and lay the basis for a post-war democracy of goods. Both the government and advertisers depicted the war as a test of national resolve to curtail expectations to defend and ensure a way of life. Superman with his new respect for authority, his anarchic youthful past, and his iconization as a commodity represented that way of life. The US Army recognized Superman's importance in 1943 and distributed 100,000 copies of the comic book to overseas troops every other month until late 1944, when the practice was discontinued because the comic book was readily available through Post Exchange stores. Shortly after the end of the war, the Superman line of comic books averaged monthly sales of 8,500,000 (Gordon, 1998, p. 149).

Subsequent versions of the character demonstrated this shift of character from iconoclast individualistic liberal reformer to mainstream liberal organizational man. From time to time the producers of Superman found it necessary to address how the commodification of Superman is situated in the Superman mythology. For instance, in the first season of *Lois & Clark*, an episode played with Superman's history as a commodity and drew in part on the 1938 Siegel & Shuster story. In the episode, Clark/Superman struggled to find his true self as his fame resulted in numerous Superman products such as dolls and soft drinks. An agent, straight out of vaudeville, approached Superman with commercial endorsement offers including one to go to Cleveland – an in-joke recognizable to those aware that Jerry Siegel and Joe Shuster created Superman while teenagers living in Cleveland. Eventually Clark/Superman decided that he controlled his own destiny and no manner of commercial product would affect his true self. Nonetheless he agreed to the licensing of his name provided that the profits went to charity.

The different plot devices in the two similar tales highlight an important difference between the 1938 Superman and the 1990s Superman. In the 1938 story the plot is driven by the shoddy business practices of Nick Williams, who seeks to commercialize Superman for his own benefit. The similarity between Siegel and Shuster's loss of their property rights to DC Comics, and Superman's difficulty in controlling the use of his name, makes the story a critique of business practices and a satire of commercialization.

The *Lois & Clark* episode suggested that the producers recognized they must acknowledge, in some way, Superman's status as a commodity. The story is not about commercialization (that is a given) but about a character's true self. The story suggests that we need not be affected by the commodification of everything if we remain true to ourselves. This resolution of the problems of Superman's commercialization was inevitable given that the show was produced by Warner Brothers Television, part of the media conglomerate that acquired DC comics and thereby the Superman trademark in the late 1960s for their licensing value. The outcome also stresses the role of individual over social forces in producing character, in the moral sense, thereby affirming Superman's adherence to individualism, another tenet of the American way. Moreover, the *Lois & Clark* episode retells a story from Superman's history in such a way that the concept of virtue is transformed from a rejection of commercialization to the preservation of individualism. Beyond the issue of commercialization, *Lois & Clark*, and its popularity in Australia, suggests new ways of examining the link between nostalgia, mythology, and commodification.

Probably most Australian viewers of *Lois & Clark* first saw Superman either in the 1950s television show or in the movies starring Christopher Reeve. The television Superman of the 1950s replicated the themes of the World War II comic book Superman and literally wrapped the character in the stars and stripes in the show's opening credits. The show appealed to its primary audience of children, in most part because they shared the secret of Superman's dual identity as Clark Kent. Although Lois Lane had her suspicions, in general she and the show's other adult characters were too slow-witted or blinded by their own preconceptions to recognize Clark and Superman as one and the same. This identification was reinforced by Clark's constant winking asides to the audience. For children, this Superman's most obvious virtue lay in his treatment of them as equals to the exclusion of adults. The undercurrent of attraction and tension between Superman and Lois Lane heightened the sense of audience superiority because we, unlike Lois, knew she already had the regular contact with Superman, albeit in the guise of Clark Kent, that she desired.

For baby-boomer Australians, the 1950s Superman television show provided one of the first contacts with the new medium. If my own experience is anything to go by, the show also acted as a minor flash point in a generational conflict. My parents at best tolerated Superman as the unfortunate but inevitable dross that came with the new medium. For me the show was an escape from the more traditionally educational BBC-derived children's programming. American programs like Superman offered a glimpse of a different society and yet one seemingly in reach of Australians. Superman was *my* show as opposed to my parents' show.

Such anecdotes are the narratives on which nostalgia is often built. That Superman is invoked in anecdotes of childhood adds to the commodity value of Superman as brand name. These sort of narratives may be intensely personal, but the sentiment embedded in them gains significance not only in the repetition of the story but also at a material level when the creators of the narratives live out those sentiments by watching a television show, collecting comic books, or seeing the latest movie.

Let me then add some other anecdotes. A colleague of mine at the University of Southern Queensland remarked that his father, a politicized working–class unionist, had watched the 1950s television Superman and read it through a resistance practice as a satire. For him the show stood for all of the excessive claims America made about itself. An old friend of mine, an art theorist at the Queensland University of Technology, told me that she had not watched the recent *Lois & Clark* series or the 1950s show but had avidly read Superman comics as a child (in the early 1960s) and had seen the movies. A more senior colleague from the University of New South Wales told me that his first contact with the character was through an Australian radio serial in the 1950s, with Leonard Teale, a well-known local actor, as Superman. Likewise, in an account of her Indian childhood the writer Anita Desai cites Superman comic books as an indicator of the diversity of "Anglo-Indian" culture (Desai, 2000). These are very different memories than mine about the character and probably all tinged with a sense of nostalgia. It is important to note, however, that they suggest ways in which the myth can contain different aspects and versions of itself. Such memories also demonstrate how a figure such as Superman can transcend the culture of its creation and become embedded in another.

If baby-boomers remembered Superman fondly and claimed him as their own, the movie version of the late 1970s and early 1980s gave them a chance to relive those memories and introduce their children to the character. The movie Superman retained the essential characteristics of the hero with one important addition. The sexual tension and attraction between Superman and Lois formed an important element of the movies. Most notably, in the second movie Lois and Superman had sexual intercourse, although this required Superman losing, temporarily as it turned out, his super powers. For baby boomers, Superman and Lois Lane's sexual liaison repositioned Superman as a hero of his times. Superman gave up his powers for a sexual relationship, and at the same time fulfilled the fantasy of many fans. But ultimately Superman's destiny is to be super, and so he sacrificed his relationship with Lois to regain his powers and save the world. When he reassumed his Superman status, Lois forgot about their relationship. These incidents took place in the second of the movies. The third in the series had a less serious tone, being closer in feel to the camp 1960s Batman television series. The fourth, released in 1985, took a high moral ground on nuclear weapons and met with a lukewarm reception.

Nostalgic Renderings

Having traced these incarnations of Superman, I want to point to an intersection between mythologizing and nostalgia in the movie and recent television versions of Superman. Mythology allows the hero to appear in different guises and forms and yet remain the hero. Nostalgia contains a sense of loss. So in this particular intersection while the hero is still present, something has been lost. The Superman movies of the early 1980s gave us a symbol from many of our childhoods in a form that legitimized the sexual revolution of the 1960s and 1970s. The sexual congress of Lois and Clark represented no loss of virtue and indeed helped remake and legitimize our concepts of virtue. At the very least, both the sexual revolution and a sexualized Superman represented a destabilization of an established order. Perhaps in the versions of Superman the mythical figure provides the sense of stability and continuity that we nostalgically long for, but the refiguring of the myth allows for human agency on behalf of the character's creators.

The version of Superman displayed in *Lois & Clark* embodies all the above-mentioned versions of Superman. For instance, the series recalls the 1950s television series in numerous ways, including the ongoing sparring between Perry White and Jimmy Olsen, but most notably the inclusion, albeit briefly, of Police Inspector Henderson, a character unsighted in any other version of Superman. Most importantly the show's title indicates that if there is to be a relationship, it will be between Lois and Clark. The movie versions suggested that the only way Superman could consummate a sexual relationship with Lois was to forgo his powers, a non-super Superman being the embodiment of Clark Kent. In the movies Clark was somewhat foppish and Superman, well, a super man. In *Lois & Clark*, Clark is a sensitive young man, but by no means a fop. In the movies the relationship between Superman and Lois threatened his superness, or, if you like, his manness. In the latest television series, Superman's manliness is strengthened and developed through his relationships with Lois and his parents. It is also worth noting that in *Lois & Clark* both the characters were identified as virgins, whereas in the movie versions Lois clearly had a past.

In *Lois & Clark* we can see nostalgia for aspects of the 1950s that were undermined by the sexual revolution. I believe the series allows us a glimpse of how nostalgia can reshape and redirect social values even if through highly commodified mythical forms. The exact way in which this nostalgia plays out and the values expressed through a form such as Superman comes back to human agency. It is not too outrageous to note that there is a world of difference between the 1938 comic book Superman and the 1994 television series Superman, and that that difference in some way can be explained by the difference between two Depression-era teenage boys Siegel and Shuster and the post-feminist women producers of *Lois & Clark*. Les Daniels, the more-or-less official historian of DC Comics, has commented that *Lois & Clark* was mostly about two good-looking people getting it on; a romance novel with pictures (Daniels, 1998, p. 173).

Lois & Clark then captured a certain audience for the Superman character. There are, however, other audiences, and while the superhero–comic-book-buying public may not be the mass audience it once was, having been whittled down to a limited group of adolescent males, comic books are still an important part of the Superman narrative. Since 1986 Superman has been reborn at least twice, and possibly thrice if an "imaginary tale" or an "elseworlds" story (as they are now known) is included, in comic books. In 1985, DC Comics initiated a "Crisis on Infinite Earths" series to celebrate its fiftieth anniversary and in part to give order to its vast array of characters. The outcome of the series wiped the slate clean, and all DC characters began anew.

In a six-part mini-series in 1986, writer/artist John Byrne retold the familiar tale of Superman's origin. His version owed something to the Superman movies that preceded it and laid the basis for the *Lois & Clark* television series that followed. Byrne touched on many of the major themes of Superman, including the commercialism associated with celebrity. In trimming away some of "the barnacles" that DC had attached to Superman, Byrne retained and expanded the role of adoptive parents Martha and Jonathan Kent. In the final episode of the series, Byrne highlighted the immigrant status of Superman, who concludes that America/Earth "gave me all that I am" and "all that matters" (Byrne, 1986). Such a conclusion addressed Superman's history. Although the narrative begins again anew, it also recycles the past allowing the "all that I am" to include the many prior incarnations of the character.

In the introduction to the collected Ballatine Books edition of the series, Byrne wrote of his childhood memories of Superman. Born in England in 1950, Byrne first encountered the character in the 1950s television show and later in black-and-white comic book reprints. For Byrne it was a window into another world.

Byrne saw the task at hand in the series as recreating "Superman as a character more in tune with the needs of the modern comic book audience." He also hopes that his version of the character will inspire some to follow in his footsteps and discover a lifetime's work through the window (Byrne, 1988, n.p.). Byrne's nostalgia about his childhood encounter with Superman, the dreams it inspired, and his eventual arrival in the USA, by way of Canada, suggest that his Superman's "humanity" rests in Byrne's own journey. If that is the case then Byrne's vision of Superman rests on a version of America, or the America of the imagination, as a land of opportunity for immigrants. At the same time, though, Byrne presents Superman's sense of self as deriving from values instilled in him by his parents and a place: America/Kansas/Smallville. The Superman story then also embodies an ideology of assimilation. That this tale was originally sketched by two Jewish teens, Siegel and Shuster, perhaps adds a dimension to this feature, but the important point is how stories told and re-told retain their symbolic features. Superman demonstrates that being American is a state of mind achievable by adopting a set of values. The ideological dimensions of this are multi-variant. Such an ideology might shut off competing notions of what it is to be American, or it might open up a debate on what values are American. On another register, however, this aspect of Superman suggests to his non-US readers that they too can be Americans if they so choose.

The second rebirth of Superman in comic books occurred, according to Les Daniels, as a direct result of DC Comics selling the ABC network on the idea of the *Lois & Clark* show (Daniels, 1998, p. 166). In 1990 the comic book version of Superman had been building to a wedding between Lois Lane and Clark Kent. DC decided to hold off the comic book wedding to coincide with the television series version. Consequently the comic book writers, who were producing four separate comic book titles a month, had to develop a new storyline. The result was the infamous death of Superman in the January 1993 issue of *Superman*, which on the wave of media hype sold some six million copies, many to people who thought they were investing in a collector's item. Superman returned from the dead in a comic book with an October 1993 cover date, and the scheduled wedding eventually took place in late 1996 in both the comic book and the television versions. The hype over the "death" of Superman and the subsequent reaction to his rebirth helped cause a slump in the comic book market, with thousands of direct sale stores closing and revenues that had reached a billion dollars being cut in half (Brodie, 1996). Blaming a gullible press, Daniels suggests in his history of Superman that DC was not directly responsible for this hype, but nonetheless DC fed the demand by reprinting the comic book (Daniels, 1998, pp. 168–9). This crass commercialism may well have undercut the symbolic worth of Superman for the comic book audience, and explains in part the initial low audience numbers for the television show in the United States. In any case, the downturn in the comic book market saw publishers developing many new projects in an attempt to regain lost ground. One of these projects involved a third rebirth of Superman and a significant contribution to the character's mythology based on nostalgia.

The third rebirth occurred in *Kingdom Come*, a special series of four comic books in DC's Elseworlds series. As DC puts it: "In Elseworlds, heroes are taken from their usual settings and put into strange times and places – some that have existed or might have existed, and others that can't, couldn't or shouldn't exist" (*Kingdom Come*, 1997, verso title page). The story strengthened and enhanced the mythological dimensions of Superman by demonstrating the symbolic values at the character's core. The production values of the book, in which the art was painted rather than drawn and colored, indicated the audience and expectations DC had for the book. The series has been gathered together and published as a hardback complete with introduction and an "Apocrypha" section, which suggests that DC takes rather seriously its claims that Superman is a new god. In the superlative-laden introduction, Elliot S! (sic) Maggin writes: "This Is The Iliad . . . this is a story about truth obscured, justice deferred and the American way distorted in the hands of petty semanticists." Here Maggin deliberately evokes the 1950s television show and its phrase "truth, justice and the American way" to stir memories of Superman. Maggin goes on to declare *Kingdom Come*, a message of values and iconography to future generations. *Kingdom Come*, as Maggin states explicitly, is about filling out the values associated with Superman (Maggin, 1997, pp. 6–7).

The story presented in *Kingdom Come* is that of the hero in exile and pretenders occupying his place. That Superman has imposed this exile on himself and that the pretenders are also superheroes is but little matter in the mythological dimensions of the story. But in the economy of comic book production in which a glut of massively muscled gung-ho superheroes and villains (think of the Hulk on steroids) have challenged the market strength of earlier generations of comic book heroes, this aspect of the story can be viewed as yet another level of nostalgia for simple times. In *Kingdom Come* an earlier generation of superheroes has retired, dismayed by Superman abandoning his "never-ending battle." The use of this phrase, also drawn from the 1950s television show and highlighted in bold, drives home the message that the Superman of *Kingdom Come* is an aged version of the 1950s character whose parents and wife have died and who wears the mantle of his "humanity" heavily.

The hero returns from his exile, as inevitably he must in such mythology. His return is triggered when an errant latter-day superhero named Magog carelessly savages a super-powered opponent who, in reaction, manages to attack and "split open" another hero, Captain Atom, resulting in a nuclear explosion. This battle occurs in Kansas, and the entire state becomes a nuclear wasteland as a result of the explosion. In most workings of Superman's origins, Kansas is his boyhood home. After the destruction of Kansas, the remaining superheroes lose all sense of responsibility. The story's choral figure, a preacher, observes this state of affairs, suggesting "now more than ever we need hope!" And then a gust of wind and the words "Look!" "Up in the sky!" – words introduced to the Superman mythos by the late 1930s radio serial – lead to a fullpage panel of Superman. But although he has returned, all is not well because of the rage he contains, which is cued visually by the background of the red S on his costume being black instead of the usual yellow. Humanity, represented by the United Nations Council, is not altogether happy with this return and the realities of power it reveals.

The story builds to a conflict between humanity and superheroes. Superman is deeply conflicted, but retains a moral code: he does not kill. In yet another piece of nostalgia, Superman reminds Batman of when they were the World's Finest team – a reference both to a DC comic that featured team adventures of the two and to their common humanity. When the United Nations seeks to restore order by destroying super humans, who despite Superman's presence threaten humanity through their conflicts, Superman seeks revenge on the UN but is quickly brought back to earth by a reminder of his humanity. In the denouement, Superman dons his Clark Kent glasses, which are not so much a disguise but a reminder of his humanity. In the epilogue, Superman and Wonder Woman announce to Batman that they want him to raise their soon-to-be-born child to ensure his humanity. And in the penultimate panel the three decide that he, or she, will be a "battler for Truth, Justice, and a New American Way."

This equation of the generalities of humanity with the specifics of America might at first seem a slippage brought on by the desire to play with the language of other versions of Superman. But nostalgia and the mythological dimensions of the character drive this desire. The sentiment is transformed into something of significance through the act of retelling the narrative. In this story the authors have strengthened Superman's trust in his humanity, but the very manner of telling the story has reduced humanity to "American." *Kingdom Come* then has the affect of closing off some of the possibilities offered by the nostalgic musings about Superman I recounted earlier in this essay. But of course this is just one version of the character.

Conclusion

Superman is a commodity, a registered trademark, which belongs to the Time Warner conglomerate. He is a product that must be sold to justify the investment in DC Comics. The Six Flags Theme Park's Superman ride that opened in March 1997 underscores the commodity status of the name. Advertised in the words of the 1950s television series, the ride is "faster than a speeding bullet," and "more powerful than a locomotive" – seemingly an outmoded metaphor until one realizes that the ride is literally more powerful, accelerating from zero to 100 miles per hour in 7 seconds and providing 6.5 seconds of weightlessness – but is connected to the comic book character in name only. A new movie version of Superman – Superman *Reborn* – directed by Tim Burton with Nicolas Cage in the title role did not move beyond pre-production, but yet another version of the character was in development. In April 2000 DC Comics announced plans for Stan Lee, the long-time doyen of Marvel Comics, to produce a series of comics for DC under the title *Just Imagine Stan Lee Creating*, starting the lives of many characters, including Superman, from birth. The wire service release notes that Lee recently established his own media company, Stan Lee Media, "to extend his globally recognized brand name . . . to all niche markets of the global popular culture." The wire also notes that Branded Entertainment's Michael Uslan, a producer of Warners' Batman movies, initiated the project ("Superman and Batman Join Forces," 2000). Yet another television version of Superman was announced on September 19, 2000 by The WB Network, which placed a "Teenage Clark Kent Project" into development (Adalian & Schneider, 2000).

Superman demonstrates that aspects of our past can continually be reinvented and *re*-presented to us. That our nostalgia brings with it loaded stories is but one ideological aspect of this reinvention. By tying popular memory to marketable figures, nostalgia has become a way of owning the past. This past owes little to history and is in effect a disembodied commodity. Nostalgia has become the pleasure of consumption.

Note

I wish to acknowledge Brian Musgrove, Charles Shindo and my co-editors who read earlier versions of this chapter. My thanks to Philip Bell and Toni Ross who shared stories about Superman. David Ellison graciously took time away from his own research to present a panel with me at an Australian and New Zealand American Studies Association conference where I presented a much earlier version of this chapter. My thanks to him and the audience.

References

Adalian, J. & M. Schneider (2000). Teen "Superman" Skein Flies to WB. *Variety*, September 25, p. 44.
Andrae, T. (1987). From Menace to Messiah: The History and Historicity of Superman. In: Lazere, D. (ed.), *American Media and Mass Culture: Left Perspectives*, pp. 124–38. Berkeley: University of California Press.
Brodie, I. (1996). A Modern Marvel. *Australian*, November 20, p. 47.
Byrne, J. (1986). The Haunting. *The Man of Steel*, 1(6), December, New York: DC Comics.
Byrne, J. (1988). Superman: A Personal View. In *Superman: The Man of Steel* (n.p.). New York: Ballantine Books.
Daniels, L. (1998). *Superman: The Complete History*. San Francisco: Chronicle Books.
Desai, A. (2000). The Writing Life. *Washington Post Book World*, May 28, p. 8.
Dickinson, G. (1997). Memories for Sale: Nostalgia and the Construction of Identity in Old Pasadena. *Quarterly Journal of Speech* 83(1), pp. 1–27.
Eco, U. (1972). The Myth of Superman. *Diacritics* 2, pp. 14–22.
Friedrich, O. (1988). Up, Up and Away!!!: America's Favorite Hero Turns 50, Ever Changing but Indestructible. *Time*, March 14, pp. 66–73.
Frow, J. (1997). *Time and Commodity Culture*. Oxford: Clarendon Press.
Gaines, J. M. (1991). *Contested Culture: The Image, the Voice, and the Law*. Chapel Hill: University of North Carolina Press.
Geertz, C. (1973). *Interpretation of Cultures: Selected Essays*. New York: Basic Books.
Gordon, I. (1998). *Comic Strips and Consumer Culture, 1890–1945*. Washington, DC: Smithsonian Institution Press.
Harris, N. (1990). *Cultural Excursions: Marketing Appetites and Cultural Tastes in Modern America*. Chicago: University of Chicago Press.

Kobler, J. (1941). Up, Up and Away! The Rise of Superman Inc. *Saturday Evening Post*, June 21, pp. 14–5, 70–8.

Lasch, C. (1984). The Politics of Nostalgia. *Harper's*, November, pp. 65–70.

Levi-Strauss, C. (1968). *Structural Anthropology*. London: Allen Lane.

Maggin, E. S. (1997). Introduction. In: M. Waid & A. Ross (eds.), *Kingdom Come*. New York: DC Comics.

Rosaldo, R. (1989). Imperialist Nostalgia, *Representations* 26(Spring), pp. 107–22.

Siegel, J. & J. Shuster (1938). Superman's Phony Manager. *Action Comics*, 1(6), November. New York: DC Comics.

Siegel, J. & J. Shuster (1941). The City in the Sky. *Action Comics*, 1(42), November. New York: DC Comics.

Stewart, S. (1984). *On Longing: Narratives of the Miniature, the Gigantic, the Souvenir, the Collection*. Baltimore: Johns Hopkins University Press.

Superman and Batman Join Forces with Arch-rival Stan Lee for the Coolest Collaboration on the History of Comic Books (2000). *Business Wire*. Retrieved December 12, 2000, from LEXIS-NEXIS on-line database, April 12.

Tannock, S. (1995). Nostalgia Critique. *Cultural Studies* 9(3), pp. 453–64.

Waid, M. & A. Ross (1997). *Kingdom Come*. New York: DC Comics.

65

Camera and Eye

Kaja Silverman*

It has long been one of the governing assumptions of film theory that the cinema derives in some ultimate sense from the Renaissance, via intervening technologies like the camera obscura, the still camera, and the stereoscope, and that its visual field is defined to a significant degree by the rules and ideology of monocular perspective. Since, within cinema, as within photography, the camera designates the point from which the spectacle is rendered intelligible, the maintenance of the perspectival illusion is assumed to depend upon a smooth meshing of the spectator with that apparatus. Both times that Christian Metz invokes quattrocento painting in *The Imaginary Signifier*, he immediately goes on to speak about the importance of what he calls "primary" identification, or identification with the apparatus.[1] Jean-Louis Baudry also maintains that, within cinema, the ideological effects of perspective depend on identification with the camera.[2] And Stephen Heath explicitly states that "in so far as it is grounded in the photograph, cinema will . . . bring with it monocular perspective, the positioning of the spectator-subject in an identification with the camera as the point of a sure and centrally embracing view."[3]

For both Metz and Baudry, there is a certain inevitability about this identification. Thus, Metz writes that "the spectator can do no other than identify with the camera . . . which has looked before him at what he is now looking at and whose stationing . . . determines the vanishing point" (49). And Baudry represents primary identification as the necessary preliminary to other identificatory relations (295). Significantly, a successful imaginary alignment with the camera is seen a implying not only an access to vision, but an access to a seemingly *invisible* vision; Metz remarks that "the *seen* is all thrust back on to the pure object" (97). The spectator constituted through such an alignment seemingly looks from a vantage outside spectacle. Primary identification also implies a vision which is exterior to time and the body, and which yields an immediate epistemological mastery. Although both Metz and Baudry are quick to denounce this invisible, disembodied, timeless, and all-knowing vision as an ideological construction, they nevertheless see its illusory pleasures as an almost unavoidable feature of the cinematic experience. The viewing subject is constituted in and through this fiction.

*Pp. 125–37 and 242–5 (notes) from K. Silverman, *The Gaze Threshold of the Visible World* (New York, Routledge). First appeared in 1993 as "What is a Camera?, or History in the Field of Vision" in *Discourse*, vol. 15, no. 3. © 1993 by *Discourse*. Reprinted with permission from Wayne State University Press.

Feminist film theory has qualified the claims of Metz and Baudry somewhat by suggesting that classic cinema makes primary identification more available to certain spectators than to others. Laura Mulvey and others have argued that Hollywood not only enforces an equation between "woman" and "spectacle," but effects a closed relay between the camera, male characters, and the male viewer.[4] However, even while showing that the equation of camera and eye is qualified in complex ways by gender, feminist film theory still implicitly assumes that the "ideal" or exemplary" cinematic spectator is constructed through an identification with the camera, and, hence, with transcendent vision.

But the theoreticians of suture articulate a more disjunctive and even antipathetic relation between camera and eye.[5] Spectatorial pleasure, they maintain, depends on the occlusion of the enunciatory point of view, and the seeming boundlessness of the image. But the enunciatory activities of the cinematic text cannot be entirely concealed. Even so simple a device as the implied frame around a given shot can serve as a reminder of those activities. And at the moment that the frame becomes apparent, the viewer realizes that he or she is only seeing a pregiven spectacle, and the *jouissance* of the original relation to the image is lost.

The theorists of suture also thematize the camera as an "Absent One," thereby further emphasizing the distance that separates it from the spectatorial eye. It represents that which is irreducibly Other, that which the subject can never be. Not only does the Absent One occupy a site exterior to the spectator, but it also exercises a coercive force over the spectator's vision. The spectator is consequently, as Hitchcock would say, a "made-to-order-witness."[6]

And although Metz and Baudry insist perhaps more than any other film theorists on the capacity of the eye to accede imaginarily to the place of the camera, there are elements within each of their writings which belie that capacity. As Mary Ann Doane has recently pointed out, the argument advanced by Baudry in "The Apparatus" posits a very different spectator than that assumed by "Ideological Effects of the Basic Cinematographic Apparatus."[7] Whereas the earlier essay presents cinema as an instrument for the perpetuation of the idealist illusion of a transcendental spectator, the later essay stresses the permeability of the boundary separating the spectator from the spectacle. The viewer described by "The Apparatus" is no longer situated at a distinct remove from the image, but is enveloped by it, even undifferentiated from it. Baudry stresses that, at the cinema, as in our dreams, there is "a fusion of the interior with the exterior,"[8] or – to state the case slightly differently – a crossing of the eye over into the field of vision.

And Metz begins the section of *The Imaginary Signifier* titled "The All-Perceiving Subject" with an analogy between cinema and the mirror stage, an analogy which once again calls into question the firm demarcation between spectator and spectacle. Although he subsequently distinguishes this kind of identification from that which the viewer ostensibly forms with respect to the camera, he also stresses that it is only as a result of first passing through the actual mirror stage that the subject can form such an identification (45–9). Primary identification is thus implicitly routed through the image, according to a kind of retroactive logic.

Geoffrey Nowell-Smith suggests that it is not only extra-cinematically that the mirror stage might be said to enable identification with the camera, but within the cinema itself. "So-called secondary identifications," he writes, ". . . tend to break down the pure specularity of the screen/spectator relation in itself and to displace it onto relations which are more properly intra-textual – i.e., relations to the spectator posited from within the image and in the movement from shot to shot."[9] A particularly striking instance of this displacement would seem to be the articulation of shot/reverse shot relationships along the axis of a fictional look, which gives identificatory access to vision from within spectacle and the body. The theoreticians of suture argue that it is only through such specular mediations that the viewer can sustain an identification with the camera.

But within film theory, it is probably Jean-Louis Comolli who has insisted most strenuously on the nonmatch of camera and spectatorial look. "At the very same time that it is thus fascinated and gratified by the multiplicity of scopic instruments which lay a thousand views beneath its gaze," he writes, "the human eye loses its immemorial privilege; the mechanical eye of the photograph machine now sees *in its place*, and in certain aspects with more sureness. The photograph stands as at once the triumph and the grave of the eye. There is a violent decentering of the place of mastery in which since the Renaissance the look had come to reign."[10] Comolli argues that the photograph represents the "triumph" of the eye because it confirms the perspectival laws which have for so long constituted the Western norm of vision – because it shows what we have learned to accept as "reality." It represents the "grave" of the eye because it is cisely than it can, but of doing so autonomously.[11] In this respect, the camera might be said not so much to confirm as to displace human vision from its ostensible locus of mastery.

Jonathan Crary has recently expanded upon and enormously complicated Comolli's argument. In *Techniques of the Observer*, he calls into question perhaps the most fundamental assumption about cinema's visual organization, an assumption which even Comolli does not challenge: the notion that an uninterrupted series of optical devices lead from the camera obscura to the camera. Crary argues convincingly that the nineteenth century witnessed the shift from a "geometrical" to a "physiological" optics.[12]

Techniques of the Observer employs the camera obscura as the privileged example of geometrical optics because, unlike a conventional perspectival construction, it does not prescribe a fixed site for the spectator, but allows a certain degree of physical mobility, thereby fostering the illusion of spectatorial freedom. Since the viewer must physically enter the camera obscura in order to see the images it produces, it also implies "a spatial and temporal simultaneity of human subjectivity and [optical] apparatus" (41), and an emphatic sequestration of the eye from the world (39). It consequently provides a figure not only for a "free sovereign individual" (39), but for a vision which is unburdened by the body, and sharply differentiated from what it sees (55).

While the camera obscura is Crary's primary metaphor for the geometrical optics of the seventeenth and eighteenth centuries, the stereoscope is his emblematic apparatus for the physiological optics which emerged in the nineteenth century, The stereoscope enjoys this status not only because it provides a heterogeneous and planar apprehension of space rather than one which is homogeneous and perspectival, but because it foregrounds the difference between its own principles of organization and those of human vision. The stereoscope contains two images, one of which addresses the left eye and another one which addresses the right. However, the stereoscopic spectator sees neither. Instead, his or her bipolar sensory apparatus conjures forth a fictive image – a composite of the two actual images, with an apparent depth of field. The stereoscope thus positions the spectator in a radically different relation to visual representation than that implied by the camera obscura or perspectival painting.

More is at issue here than the dramatic disjunction of eye and optical apparatus. The stereoscope calls into question the very distinction upon which such mastery relies, the distinction between the look and the object. What the eye sees when peering into the stereoscope is not a specular order from which it is detached, but "an undemarcated terrain on which the distinction between internal sensation and external signs is irrevocably blurred" (24). The stereoscope thus precipitates a referential crisis. This referential crisis has less to do with the displacement of the real by the simulacrum than with a loss of belief in the eye's capacity to see what is "there." Relocated within the "unstable physiology and temporality" of the body (70), human vision no longer serenely surveys and masters a domain from which it imagines itself to be discrete.

Within Crary's argument, the stereoscope is also emblematic of nineteenth-century ways of thinking about the eye in that it is in a sense "about" that organ; it is a direct extension of the discovery that the human subject has binocular rather than monocular vision. *Techniques of the Observer* suggests that from the 1820s on, vision increasingly functioned as the object rather than as the subject of optical knowledge. This investigation of the eye worked to further diminish belief in its supposed objectivity and authority. Not only was a blind spot uncovered at the point at which the optic nerve opens onto the retina (75), but visual apprehension was shown to fluctuate over time (98). Color came to be understood less as an inherent attribute of the object than as an extension of the viewer's physiology (67–71). And the discovery of the afterimage, which feeds directly into cinema, suggested once again that the human eye is capable of a counterfactual perception.

Although the invention of the stereoscope postdates that of the camera, Crary argues that the camera is part of the same epistemological rupture as the stereoscope (5). Photography, like the stereoscope, is "an element of a new and homogeneous terrain of consumption and circulation in which an observer becomes lodged" (13). "Observer" is the term Crary consistently uses to designate a viewer who no longer regards the world from an ostensibly transcendent and mastering vantage point, a viewer whose unreliable and corporeally circumscribed vision locates him or her *within* the field of vision and knowledge. Presumably, then (although he does not argue this case in any specificity), Crary means to suggest that because of its autonomy from the human eye, and its capacity to "see" differently from the latter, photography also dislodges that organ from the seemingly privileged position it occupies within the camera obscura.

Later in *Techniques of the Observer*, Crary proposes that the stereoscope was doomed to extinction because it makes too manifest the disjuncture of camera and look. Photography – and later cinema – prevailed because it maintained earlier pictorial codes, particularly those of perspective, making it an apparent extension of human vision, and resecuring the viewer in a position of visual authority (136). Like Comolli, then, Crary suggests that the photographic image affords the eye an illusory "triumph."

However, there is a strange way in which, even within photography, the mainten-ance of the referential illusion – or the attribution to the image of a "truthful" vision – overtly depends on the isolation of camera from human look. In a crucial passage from early film theory, Andre Bazin suggests that knowledge of the discreteness of camera and human look may be tolerable provided that the photograph seems synony-mous with the "real," since the photograph thereby gives the spectator retroactive access to what he or she would otherwise lack. But, he also maintains that such knowledge may seem at moments the necessary condition for sustaining the belief in the equiva-lence of photograph and referent – that only when the camera is established as being independent of the eye can we trust it. "For the first time," he writes in "The Ontology of the Photographic Image," "between the originating object and its reproduction there intervenes only the instrumentality of a nonliving agent. For the first time an image of the world is formed automatically, without the intervention of man. . . . The objective nature of photography confers upon it a quality of credibility absent from other picture-making . . . we are forced to accept as real the existence of the object reproduced."[13]

And, of course, one of the privileged textual sites out of which cinema might be said to develop is Muybridge's series of sequential photographs of trotting horses, images which were produced precisely to dispel an illusion of the eye – the illusion that a horse in motion always maintains at least one foot on the ground.[14] Here, the camera mani-festly sees what the look cannot. We are thus obliged to consider the possibility that the codes of perspective may survive in cinema and photography without anything approxi-mating the close identification of eye and optical apparatus that was implied in the case of the camera obscura.

The relation between the camera and the human optical organ might now seem less analogous than prosthetic: the camera promises to make good the deficiencies of the eye, and to shore up a distinction which the eye alone cannot sustain – the distinction between vision and spectacle. However, even this formulation suggests that the camera entertains a more benign relation to the eye than is always the case. The camera is often less an instrument to be used than one which uses the human subject; as Crary suggests, the camera is more of a machine than a tool (131). And Vilem Flusser, another recent theorist of the camera, proposes that the photographer is at best a "functionary" of that apparatus.[15]

The concept of the "observer" thus implies not only an embodied and spectacular-ized eye, but one whose operations have been subjected to a complex rationalization – an eye which has been rendered socially productive. "Almost simultaneous with this final dissolution of a transcendent foundation for vision emerges a plurality of means to recode the activity of the eye," Crary writes,

> [means] to regiment it, to heighten its productivity and prevent its distraction. Thus the imperatives of capitalist modernization, while demolishing the field of classical vision, generated techniques for imposing visual attentiveness, rationalizing sensation, and man-aging perception. (24)

In the wake of the camera, the eye can clearly be seen to be the site for the induc-tion of a specific kind of vision, one which is not only socially "useful," but also predetermined. In the next chapter, I will elaborate in considerable detail upon this last point through the category of the "given-to-be-seen."

I have dwelt at such length on *Techniques of the Observer* for three reasons. First, it profoundly problematizes the still-dominant assumptions within film theory that the look – or at least the male look – can be easily aligned with the camera, and that the relation of camera and look always works to the credit of human vision. Second, it provides a very rich and multifaceted account of the actual relation between those two terms. Finally, its discussion of the camera coincides at crucial points with that offered in Harun Farocki's *Bilder der Welt und Inschrift des Krieges*, a film to which I will turn in a few pages.

But even though *Techniques of the Observer* offers invaluable assistance in articulating the relation between the camera and the eye, it omits a crucial term from that equation: the gaze. Crary does not account for the underlying field of vision onto which the camera/eye opposition is mapped. He approaches his topic through such an exclusively historical lens that he fails to discern that the camera derives many of its powers to coerce and define through its metaphoric connection to a term which is much older than it. Indeed, in some larger sense, he neglects to distinguish what is socially and historically relative about the field of vision from what persists beyond one social formation to the next.

Let us now turn to a text about which the opposite could be said, a text for which the visual domain would seem to be absolutely timeless: Lacan's *Four Fundamental Concepts of Psycho-Analysis*. As we will see, Lacan offers a powerful transhistorical model for theorizing the relation of gaze and look. He also uses the camera as a metaphor for the first of those terms. However, he never properly interrogates the relation between camera and gaze, or proposes that it might be central to our present field of vision. Having brought Lacan into the discussion as a way of clarifying what might persist within the visual domain from one epoch to another, I will then be obliged to critique him for ignoring what does not.

The Gaze and the Camera

In *Four Fundamental Concepts of Psycho-Analysis*, Lacan also insists emphatically upon the disjunction of camera and eye, but instead of deploying the camera as an independent optical apparatus, he uses it as a signifier of the gaze. The passage in which he introduces this metaphor locates the subject firmly within spectacle, and attributes to the camera/gaze a constitutive function with respect to him or her: "What determines me, at the most profound level, in the visible, is the gaze that is outside. It is through the gaze that I enter light and it is from the gaze that I receive its effects. Hence it comes about that the gaze is the instrument through which light is embodied, and through which I am *photographed*."[16]

However, although Lacan emphasizes the exteriority of the camera to the look, his use of that apparatus as a metaphor for the gaze works to erase the kinds of historical demarcations drawn by *Techniques of the Observer*. He associates the gaze not with values specific to the last century and a half, but rather with illumination and "the presence

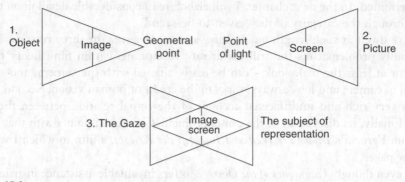

Figure 65.1

of others as such" (91, 84). Within the context of *Four Fundamental Concepts*, the gaze would thus seem to be as old as sociality itself. Even in his deployment of the photographic metaphor, Lacan resists historical periodization. He divides the word "photograph" in half, thereby suggesting that, if the camera is an appropriate metaphor for the gaze, that is because it models or schematizes its objects within light. This is a definition of photography which strips it of most of its apparatic specificity.

Since I have discussed the Lacanian model at considerable length elsewhere,[17] I will reiterate here only its primary features. Lacan elaborates the field of vision through the three diagrams reproduced below in Figure 65.1.

The first diagram represents the preliminary step in Lacan's exhaustive deconstruction of the assumptions behind the system of perspective. In it, the subject is shown looking at an object from the position marked "geometral point." He or she seemingly surveys the world from an invisible, and hence transcendental, position. However, the intervening "image," which coincides with the "screen" in diagram 2, immediately troubles this apparent mastery; the viewer is shown to survey the object not through Alberti's transparent pane of glass, but through the mediation of a third term. He or she can only see the object in the guise of the "image," and can consequently lay claim to none of the epistemological authority implicit in the perspectival model.

Diagram 2 situates the subject at the site marked "picture," and the gaze at that marked "point of light." It thus locates the subject within visibility. It also dramatically separates the gaze from the human eye. Consequently, both the subject-as-spectacle and the subject-as-look are situated outside the gaze. As I suggested earlier, the gaze represents both the point from which light irradiates, and the "presence of others as such" (84). In this second respect, it can perhaps best be understood as the intrusion of the symbolic into the field of vision. The gaze is the "unapprehensible" (83) agency through which we are socially ratified or negated as spectacle. It is Lacan's way of stressing that we depend upon the other not only for our meaning and our desires, but also for our very confirmation of self. To "be" is in effect to "be seen." Once again, a third term mediates between the two ends of the diagram, indicating that the subject is never "photographed" as "himself" or "herself," but always in the shape of what is now designated the "screen."

The last diagram superimposes the second over the first, suggesting that diagram 1 is always circumscribed by diagram 2; even as we look, we are in the "picture," and, so, a "subject of representation." The gaze occupies the site of the "object" in diagram 1, and that of "point of light" in diagram 2. In this double capacity, it is now at an even more emphatic remove from the eye. Indeed, it would seem to "look" back at us from precisely the site of those others whom we attempt to subordinate to our visual scrutiny – to always be where we are not. Once again, the relation between the terms on the left and those on the right is mediated, in this case by something that could be called the "image," the "screen," or the "image/screen," but which I will henceforth designate simply the "screen."

Thus, Lacan provides a transhistorical account not only of the gaze, but also of the entire field of vision, which for him includes the look and the screen. *Four Fundamental Concepts* offers an invaluable corrective to the extreme historical relativism of *Techniques of the Observer*. It suggests that there might be a "deep structure" to the psyche and the socius which is indifferent to many temporal demarcations – something which we might, for instance, designate as "libido" in the case of the psyche and "interrelationship" in the case of the socius. Consequently, certain elements of each may stubbornly persist from one specular regime to another. However, Lacan's model errs too far in the other direction. Its elaboration of the field of vision is finally as untenable in its ahistoricism as one which can acknowledge only historical difference.

I will now attempt to bring together Crary's account of the camera/eye relation with Lacan's account of the gaze/eye relation by advancing a provisional formulation of what is and is not historically variable within the field of vision. I will also attempt to give back to the camera – which Lacan uses as a metaphor for the gaze – some apparatic specificity, and to consider some of the implications of that metaphor. I propose to perform the first of these tasks through a revisionary reading of the paradigm put forward by *Four Fundamental Concepts*, which lends itself in some surprising ways to a historical elaboration. I will undertake the second of these tasks by removing the hyphen from "photo-graph," by taking Lacan's allusion to the camera much more seriously than he intended.

Lacan seems to me correct when he suggests that the gaze and the look are in certain respects ahistorical. If the gaze is to be connected to illumination and "the presence of others as such" – as I agree that it should – then it would seem to represent an inevitable feature of all social existence. Indeed, it would seem to be the registration within the field of vision of the dependence of the social subject upon the Other for his or her own meaning. It is thus necessarily independent of any individual look, and exterior to the subject in its constitutive effects.

As human, the look would seem, by contrast, to be always finite, always embodied, and always within spectacle, although it does not necessarily acknowledge itself as such. Since, as I will argue in the next chapter, the look is a psychic as well as a visual category, it would also seem unavoidably marked by lack. It would consequently seem to be propelled by desire, and to be vulnerable to the lures of the imaginary.

At the same time that I make these concessions to the Lacanian model, I remain convinced that acute variations separate one culture and one epoch from another with respect to at least three dimensions of the field of vision. These variations pertain to how the gaze is apprehended; how the world is perceived; and how the subject experiences his or her visibility. As should be evident, to factor variability into the visual domain at three such crucial sites is to indicate that this domain can assume extremely divergent forms.

I would like to propose that the screen is the site at which social and historial difference enters the field of vision. In *Four Fundamental Concepts*, Lacan elaborates the screen exclusively in terms of the determining role it plays in the visual articulation of the subject. However, in the diagrams included above, it intervenes not just between the gaze and the subject-as-spectacle, but also between the gaze and the subject-as-look, and between the object and the subject-as-look. Since Lacan characterizes the screen as "opaque" (96), it does not merely "open," like a door or a window, onto what it obstructs, but rather substitutes itself for the latter. It must consequently determine how the gaze and the object, as well as the subject, are "seen." But what is the screen?

Although Lacan does not really define this component of the field of vision, he offers a few suggestive remarks about it. In specifying its effects with respect to the subject-as-spectacle, he comments on the possibility open to the latter of manipulating the screen for purposes of intimidation, camouflage, and travesty. He also maintains that it is through the "mediation" of the screen, or "mask," that "the masculine and the feminine meet in the most acute, most intense way" (107). On the basis of these two observations, I some years ago attributed to the screen a representational consistency. However, I elaborated this argument in terms which are quite alien to the intent of *Four Fundamental Concepts*. I attributed to the screen a constitutive role with respect to a series of social categories which do not concern Lacan. "It seems to me crucial that we insist upon the ideological status of the screen by describing it as that culturally generated image or repertoire of images through which subjects are not only constituted, but differentiated in relation to class, race, sexuality, age, and nationality," I wrote in *Male Subjectivity at the Margins* (150).

Now, I would like to put an even greater distance between myself and *Seminar XI*, and define the screen as the conduit through which social and historical variability is introduced not only into the relation of the gaze to the subject-as-spectacle, but also into that of the gaze to the subject-as-look. The screen represents the site at which the gaze is defined for a particular society, and is consequently responsible both for the way in which the inhabitants of that society experience the gaze's effects, and for much of the seeming particularity of that society's visual regime.

I would also like to suggest that Lacan invokes the camera in the context of discussing the gaze not just because the camera, like the gaze, "graphs" with light, but also because the connection between the two terms is so powerfully overdetermined. Indeed, I will go so far as to claim that due to its association with a "true" and "objective vision," the camera has been installed ever since the early nineteenth century as the primary trope through which the Western subject apprehends the gaze. Its elevation to that position has precipitated the crisis in human vision so compellingly documented by Crary, and has worked to foreground the disparity of look and gaze concealed by the camera obscura.

In advancing this formulation, I want both to bring history to the Lacanian paradigm, and to explain how the camera assumes the enormous significance Crary imputes to it.

Not only does the camera work to define the contemporary gaze in certain decisive ways, but the camera derives most of its psychic significance through its alignment with the gaze. When we feel the social gaze focused upon us, we feel photographically "framed." However, the converse is also true: when a real camera is trained upon us, we feel ourselves subjectively constituted, as if the resulting photograph could somehow determine "who" we are.

In claiming that the camera is the primary metaphor for the gaze, I am obliged to complicate enormously the definition which I earlier offered of the screen – to conceptualize it as more than a repertoire of ideologically differentiating images. At the time I was writing *Male Subjectivity at the Margins*, I had already grasped that the screen must work to determine how we experience the gaze, as well as how we are seen. However, my primary concern in theorizing the screen as a mediation between us and the gaze was to find a way of accounting for how the gaze, which is itself unlocalizable and "unapprehensible," has for so long seemed to us masculine. I understood that in order for the gaze to be perceived in this way, the male eye had necessarily to be aligned with the camera. I also saw that the endless subordination of woman-as-spectacle was necessary to the establishment of this alignment. Nevertheless, it did not occur to me to ask the question which now poses itself with a certain urgency: "What is a camera?"

As soon as that question is asked, it becomes evident that it is not enough to suggest that the screen through which we mainly apprehend the gaze is synonymous with the images by means of which a given society articulates authoritative vision. At least since the Renaissance, optical devices have played a central role in determining how the gaze is apprehended, and such devices cannot simply be reduced to a set of images.

The camera is less a machine, or the representation of a machine, than a complex field of relations. Some of these relations are extrinsic to the camera as a technological apparatus, others are intrinsic. Some follow, that is, from its placement within a larger social and historical field, and others stem from its particular representational logic. Crary's remarks about the camera obscura are thus equally applicable to the camera. "What constitutes the camera obscura," he writes,

> Is precisely its multiple identity, its "mixed" status as an epistemological figure within a discursive order *and* an object within an arrangement of cultural practices. The camera obscura is . . . "simultaneously and inseparably a machinic assemblage and an assemblage of enunciation," an object about which something is said and at the same time an object that is used. It is a site at which a discursive formation intersects with material practices. (30–1)

An analysis of the camera both as a representational system and a network of material practices would thus seem the precondition for understanding the primary screen which presently defines the gaze. It would also seem to constitute the necessary first step in a historical conceptualization of the screen.

Harun Farocki's 1988 film, *Bilder der Welt und Inschrift des Krieges (Images of the World and the Inscription of War)* not only offers an extended meditation on the representational logic of the camera, but also conceives of it as an intricate and constantly shifting field of social and technological relations. It is consequently to this text that I will now turn in an attempt to arrive at a clearer understanding of what it means to represent the gaze as a camera. An examination of *Bilder* will help to clarify both the points of continuity and those of discontinuity between that apparatus and earlier visual technologies. It will thus facilitate a further elaboration of the ways in which a fundamentally atemporal gaze is culturally and historically specified.

As we will see, Farocki insists as strenuously as Crary upon the disjunction of camera and eye, and in ways that almost uncannily echo Lacan. Not only does the camera emerge in *Bilder* at a site equivalent to the gaze in *Four Fundamental Concepts*, but human vision is once again situated manifestly within spectacle. But Farocki is not content merely to disassociate camera/gaze and eye, and to establish the placement of the human subject within the purview of that apparatus. He also interrogates another of the camera/gaze's functions – what might be called both its "memorializing" and its "mortifying" effects. Together these two functions serve to define, at least in part, the representational system proper to the gaze. In addition, Farocki scrutinizes the social as well as the psychic field of relations with which the camera is synonymous, and some of the ways in which the social impinges upon the psychic. He looks, that is, at some of the exemplary material practices through which the camera/gaze's disjunction from the eye, the articulating role it plays with respect to human subjectivity, its memorializing function, and its mortifying effect have been historically exploited and discursively specified.

Not surprisingly, gender and race also come into play in *Bilder* in complex ways. Although Farocki reiterates again and again in that text that it is only through the hyperbolic specularization of the female subject that the disjunction between the camera and the male eye can be masked, he also shows how this paradigm can be complicated by other forms of cultural difference. Finally, he attempts to indicate what, if not the domain of the camera/gaze, might be said to represent the province of the look. An analysis of *Bilder* will consequently provide the occasion not only for a further elaboration of how the gaze is figured within the social field, but also for a provisional theorization of the look.

Notes

1. Christian Metz, *The Imaginary Signifier: Psychoanalysis and the Cinema*, trans. Celia Britton, Annwyl Williams, Ben Brewster, and Alfred Guzzetti (Bloomington: Indiana University Press, 1982), pp. 49, 97.
2. Jean-Louis Baudry, "Ideological Effects of the Basic Cinematographic Apparatus," trans. Alan Williams, in *Narrative, Apparatus, Ideology*, ed. Philip Rosen (New York: Columbia University Press, 1986), p. 295.
3. Stephen Heath, *Questions of Cinema* (Bloomington: Indiana University Press, 1981), p. 30.
4. Laura Mulvey, *Visual and Other Pleasures* (Bloomington: Indiana University Press, 1989), pp. 3–26. See also Teresa de Lauretis, *Alice Doesn't: Feminism, Semiotics, Cinema* (Bloomington: Indiana University Press, 1984), pp. 1–36; Linda Williams, "Film Body: An Implantation of Perversions? *Ciné-Tracts*, vol. 3, no. 4 (1981): 19–35; Lucy Fischer, "The

Image of Woman as Image: The Optical Politics of *Dames*," in *Genre: The Musical*, ed. Rick Altman (London: Routledge and Kegan Paul, 1981), pp. 70–84; Sandy Flitterman, "Woman, Desire, and the Look: Feminism and the Enunciative Apparatus in Cinema," *Ciné-Tracts*, vol. 2, no. 1 (1978), pp. 63–68; and Kaja Silverman, *The Subject of Semiotics* (New York: Oxford University Press, 1983), pp. 222–36.

5. The theorists of suture are Jacques-Alain Miller, "Suture (elements of the logic of the signifier)," *Screen*, vol. 18, no. 4 (1977/78): 29–34; Jean-Pierre Oudart, "Notes on Suture," *Screen*, vol. 18, no. 4 (1977/78): 35–47; Stephen Heath, "Notes on Suture? *Screen*, vol. 18, no. 4 (1977/78): 48–76, and "Anato Mo," *Screen*, vol. 17, no. 4 (1976/77): 49–66; Daniel Dayan, "The Tutor-Code of Classical Cinema," *Movies and Methods*, ed. Bill Nichols (Berkeley: University of California Press, 1976), pp. 438–51; and Kaja Silverman, *The Subject of Semiotics*, pp. 194–236.

6. This is how Scotty/Johnny characterizes himself after he discovers that he has been "framed."

7. Mary Ann Doane, *Femmes Fatales: Feminism, Film Theory, Psychoanalysis* (New York: Routledge, 1991), p. 85.

8. Jean-Louis Baudry, "The Apparatus," in *Narrative, Apparatus, Ideology*, p. 311.

9. Geoffrey Nowell-Smith, "A Note on History/Discourse," *Edinburgh 76 Magazine: Psychoanalysis/Cinema/Avant-Garde*, no. 1 (1976): 31.

10. Jean-Louis Comolli, "Machines of the Visible," in *The Cinematic Apparatus*, ed. Teresa de Lauretis and Stephen Heath (New York: St. Martin's Press, 1980), p. 123.

11. Comolli also stresses that the camera exceeds the eye in "Technique and Ideology: Camera, Perspective, Depth of Field," *Film Reader 2* (1977): 135–6.

12. Jonathan Crary, *Techniques of the Observer: On Vision and Modernity in the Nineteenth Century* (Cambridge: MIT Press, 1990), pp. 14–16.

13. André Bazin, *What Is Cinema?* trans. Hugh Gray (Berkeley: University of California Press, 1967), vol. 1, p. 13.

14. For an interesting discussion of Muybridge's photographs and their bearing on the issue of photography's ostensible "realism," see Linda Williams, *Hard Core: Power, Pleasure, and the Frenzy of the Visible* (Berkeley: University of California Press, 1989), pp. 34–48. Mieke Bal launches a fascinating argument against the continuity of Muybridge and cinema in "The Gaze in the Closet," in *Vision in Context*, ed. Teresa Brennan and Martin Jay (forthcoming, Routledge, 1996), although she, too, stresses that Muybridge's photographs show what the eye cannot see.

15. Vilem Flusser, *Towards a Philosophy of Photography* (Gottingen, West Germany: European Photography, 1984), p. 19.

16. Jacques Lacan, *Four Fundamental Concepts of Psycho-Analysis*, trans. Alan Sheridan (New York: Norton, 1978), p. 106.

17. Kaja Silverman, *Male Subjectivity at the Margins* (New York: Routledge, 1992), pp. 125–56.

Re-Writing "Reality": Reading *The Matrix*

*Russell J. A. Kilbourn**

> *"And who are you, Achior, and you hirelings of Ephraim, to prophesy among us as you have done today and tell us not to make war against the people of Israel because their God will defend them? Who is God except Nebuchadnezzar?"*
>
> – Judith 6:2

The purpose of this article is to show how Larry and Andy Wachowski's 1999 film *The Matrix* is neither a mystical tract dressed up in sexy pvc and sunglasses, nor a proto-Baudrillardian allegory.[1] The overarching emphasis is on the necessity of a certain "cultural literacy," whose advantages outweigh its inherent dangers. Given its relative intertextual density and the degree of ironic inversion pervading its structure, balanced against its eye-catching special effects and extreme popularity, *The Matrix* exemplifies this necessity better than most recent cultural texts.

A cursory glance at the many websites spun out of *The Matrix* since its Easter 1999 release – not to mention the first print and online reviews – reveals that much of what could be said has already been said, and gives the impression that *The Matrix* itself isn't saying anything particularly new, either, which is generally true.[2] Cinematographically, the look of the film is often strikingly new – or at least as new as a Gap® khakis commercial once appeared to be.[3] James Poniewozik was the first to formalize the glibly observed reversal of the usual direction of stylistic influence, insofar as the now famous "Swing" and other dance-performance ads utilized the "360-degree freeze-frame effects" some months before the film's release.[4] This reversal of the "normal" direction of cultural influence was soon eclipsed by the film's phenomenal success, however. The stylistic influence of *The Matrix* across the breadth of pop culture in the past year – even since this paper was written – has only increased, especially in film and television advertising.

On the level of the narrative, it is clear that *The Matrix* emerges out of that other matrix, intertextuality, whose apprehension demands the skills necessary for reading and decoding the film's message, which, as I've suggested, is considerably less radical than its appearance might suggest. *The Matrix* self-consciously dramatizes the necessity

*Pp. 1–19 from *Canadian Journal of Film Studies/Revue canadienne d'études cinématographiques*, vol. 9, no. 2. © 2000. Reprinted with permission from the Canadian Journal of Film Studies/Revue canadienne d'études cinématographiques.

of *reading* – the acquisition of a certain "literacy" – balanced against a condition not merely of ideological mystification but of profound epistemological blindness. (I speak of reading and literacy while recognizing the irony that, in the 22nd-century world of *The Matrix*, people do not learn by reading books or computer screens; they simply download the information directly into their brains, as if they were themselves machines).

Read Mercer Stuart draws a telling parallel between the Matrix as "system of control" and Marshall McLuhan's formulation (in *Understanding Media*) of "literacy" as a kind of unavoidable but potentially deadening "matrix": "Literacy remains even now the base and model of all programs of industrial mechanization; but, at the same time, links the minds and senses of its users in the mechanical and fragmentary matrix that is so necessary to the maintenance of mechanical society."[5] This is as good a description as one will find of the "literacy" necessary to living in the contemporary world; and this is precisely the level of literacy which the film's protagonist, Neo (Keanu Reeves), must transcend by learning to read all over again.

The point is that Neo's acquisition of this "second-order" literacy is not only an extension of his initial covert identity as a hacker; even more so it is germane to his ultimate self-affirmation as "the One." Already a hacker when the film opens (and already suspicious that things are not what they seem), Neo's challenge, once he is freed from the Matrix, is to learn to read the code so that he can then "rewrite" it, like the science fiction superhero that he is.

That the Matrix "cannot tell Neo who he is" is evidenced by Agent Smith (Hugo Weaving), who, as Matrix mouthpiece, insists on calling Neo "Mr. Anderson"; while it is Neo himself who insists on the anagramic version of "the One" he is already on the way to becoming. In order to reach this point, however, Neo is confronted with a series of potential narrative bifurcations: choices structuring the narrative and which are only revealed to be false choices once they are made. In other words, in the narrative of *The Matrix*, individual choice and something like an overriding "fate" appear to be two sides of the same coin – "fate" being the pseudonym of narrative inevitability. Thus the question posed by Morpheus (Laurence Fishburne), "Do you believe in fate, Neo?" is already loaded, and Neo's negative response and rationale – that he likes to feel he's "in control of [his] own life" – ironically anticipates the film's central thematic paradox replicated on the formal level.

Throughout the film the act of reading, as "decoding," is thematized, over against the act of writing as "encoding." Just as it exploits the literal self-reflectivity of mirror optics, as well as the oscillation of sleeping and waking, *The Matrix* incorporates a reflexive narrative cursivity in its very structure. This is determined by the foregrounding of the act of narration on the formal level, intradiegetically. There is, for example, Morpheus, for whom time is the enemy, and Agent Smith, who always seems one step ahead ("No, Lieutenant, your men are already dead"; "That is the sound of inevitability, Mr. Anderson," etc.). Then there is the Oracle, who manipulates cause and effect by telling people exactly what they need to hear, exactly when they need to hear it, and whose kitchen motto is the Socratic "Know thyself" (in Latin instead of Greek, however). In different ways, these characters serve to draw attention to the narrative's emphasis on time: it's own temporality (the time of the narrative's unfolding), as well as time thematized, as it is in Alice's Wonderland. And, just as in the Alice books, these two categories of time prove to be inextricable. Narrative time is further complicated through the cinematography, dividing roughly between a realist filmic diegetic temporality, and something the filmmakers have termed "bullet time," where, to literalize the characters' ability to bend and even break the "physical laws" of the Matrix, time is slowed down or compressed in inverse relation to the unrepresentable hyper-velocity of the action at these moments.

"Bullet time" is, in effect, the self-conscious concretizing of a ubiquitous feature of Hollywood cinematic diegesis, in the sense that the narrative point of view, insofar as it is consonant with the placement and movement of the camera, becomes literally "as fast as a speeding bullet," only the bullet has been radically slowed down and brought entirely under the filmmakers' control. This means that, on the formal level – in it's very look and style – the film is from its opening frames at least one step ahead of Thomas Anderson's metamorphosis into Neo, the One who can manipulate time "itself." By the film's conclusion, then, "real time" and the time of the narrative's unfolding are indistinguishable.

It is worth recalling in this context McLuhan's famous definition of the media (in the subtitle to *Understanding Media*: "The Extensions of Man")[6] as prosthetic "extensions" of the human sensorium and central nervous system – a sort of attenuated, materialized echo of St. Augustine's conception of time as an extension of not the senses but the mind.[7] Therefore time (subjective, experiential or phenomenological) could be said to be another "medium" by means of which human experience and understanding of the world is "extended"; time is the medium of not the body or even the senses alone but of mind itself (consciousness). In this respect (the illusion of time's passage) the body follows the mind's lead; thus time is of crucial significance to any narrative, and *The Matrix* is no exception. In fact, the film is exemplary in this regard, foregrounding as it does the central function of time at every level of the story, formal and thematic alike.

Morpheus' role vis-à-vis Neo is as much White Rabbit (ironically) as it is Dante's Virgil, or even John the Baptist. Morpheus' mantra is that time is always against them, they've run out of time, they must act immediately because the agents are on to Neo as the hacker alter-ego of "Thomas Anderson." If Neo is going to realize his potential as "the One," he must be presented with at least the semblance of a choice between his already doubled existence and the answer to the question, "What is the Matrix?" This first section of the film draws extensively on Lewis Carroll's *Alice's Adventures in Wonderland* (1865), and *Through the Looking-Glass* (1871). If not exactly "science fiction," the two *Alice* books present paradigmatic instances of a very tenacious strain of imaginative fiction. In the first case, Alice, in pursuit of the elusive White Rabbit, tumbles down a rabbit hole that leads to Wonderland. In the second, she manages to penetrate the surface of a mirror, passing through to the "Looking-glass House" on the other side:

> "[H]ow nice it would be if we could only get through into Looking-glass House! I'm sure it's got, oh! Such beautiful things in it! Let's pretend there's a way of getting through into it, somehow. . . . Let's pretend the glass has got all soft like gauze, so that we can get

through. Why it's turning into a sort of mist now. I declare! It'll be easy enough to get through –" She was up on the chimney-piece while she said this, though she hardly knew how she had got there: And certainly the glass was beginning to melt away, just like a bright silvery mist.[8]

In both cases, the ending is the same: Alice awakes to discover that the whole thing was just a fantastic dream; a sort of oneiric mushroom trip for children. Insofar as *The Matrix* screenplay borrows from Carroll, it parts company with him on this last point of narrative metaphysics: as Morpheus, the drug-dealing god of dreams, makes clear, there is no going back once you've chosen the red pill and seen for yourself "how deep the rabbit hole goes." (There is a fundamental irony to Morpheus' character in that the function of his namesake, the mythological god of dreams, brother of sleep, is the very opposite: to lead people out of "reality" into the realm of dreams.)

As Agent Smith implies during Neo's interrogation in the first part of the film, choice is about the present moment, poised between past-just-passed and either one future-yet-to-be or another: "One of these lives has a future," Smith explains to Neo. "The other does not." Later, Morpheus recounts the "myth" of the origin of the human's resistance movement: "When the Matrix was first built there was a man born inside that [sic] had the ability to . . . remake the Matrix as he saw fit. It was this man that freed the first of us and taught us the secret of the war; control the Matrix and you control the future." In a sense, this nameless man, whose advent presupposes that of Neo, advocated the power to exchange fate for free will, for choice regarding the future – a future of which it is predetermined (as the Oracle prophesies) nothing will be pre-determined. Once it is too late to go back, Morpheus reveals to Neo that he has been freed from the Matrix to "serve a purpose": the purpose of freeing humankind from serving a purpose.

Neo, for whom nothing is as important as remaining in control of his own life, makes the only possible choice in the above-mentioned scene with Morpheus: the red pill, which is in fact a sort of pharmaceutical "trace program" that facilitates the pinpointing of his body's real location in the endless fields of commodified humans. Before this wrenching, near-death and literal re-birth experience, however, Neo has his own encounter with a mirror, in a scene strongly reminiscent of Jean Cocteau's *Orpheus* (France, 1949) – a cinematic intertext that reminds us of the shadows of death and irrecuperable loss lurking in the background of *The Matrix*, not to mention the visible invisibility of "Orpheus" in "Morpheus." In this crucial scene, the old, cracked mirror's surface yields to Neo's touch; but whereas in the Cocteau film Orpheus passes, like Alice, *through* the mirror into the zone of death or logical inversion on the other side, in *The Matrix* the mirror becomes part of Neo, sticking to his fingers and quickly creeping the length of his arm, engulfing his entire body in its machinic chrome. It is as if the filmmakers wanted to show the subject's assimilation by Baudrillard's simulacrum, effacing the distinction between the subject's organic authenticity and its reflection, as if reality were continuous with the mirror's depthless surface.

But this reading is thwarted by death's intervention as a negative instance of the reality principle. Just as Neo is about to go into cardiac arrest, the trace is completed and down Neo tumbles, through death into a reality worse than death, and then through

a rebirth which is itself a kind of death. (Recall that to remain one's entire life in the
Matrix is a sort of mock-Nietzschean dream [as in *Birth of Tragedy*]: never to be born,
but to live and die in a permanent pre-parturitive state. Of course, this only holds for
the body; the mind spends this time on a permanent holiday, called "life.")

This film's almost parodically literal Lacanian mirror scene departs from *Alice* in the
same gesture of invoking Carroll's narrative. Neo does not pass *through* the looking-glass
but literally merges with it, the "real" and "not-real" becoming momentarily indistinguishable, as if in order to show that what has been taken for real is in fact as illusory
as its cracked and distorted reflection. As Baudrillard might say, the simulacrum is a
mirror that reflects only itself. But Neo's journey does not stop here, and Baudrillard
(like Neo's "residual self-image") is quickly left behind.

Both before and after his "liberation" from the Matrix, Neo – whose point of view
the viewer shares in these scenes – sees himself reflected everywhere: in mirrors, Morpheus' sunglasses, doorknobs, even a spoon. The difference is that the newly awakened
Neo experiences the gradual realization that these reflections are metonyms of the self's
simulacral status in the Matrix (just as they are metaphors of the "authentic"-simulacral
relation obtaining between "reality" and the Matrix in the film's fictional universe).
Apart from the initiatory encounter with the dressing mirror (described above), the
most telling, not to mention the most harrowing, of these multiple specular moments
occurs immediately following Neo's awakening in the pod. He is confronted face-to-face
by the insectile harvesting robot, in whose single metallic "eye" he sees reflected his
own hairless, slimy and barely comprehending visage – as if in complex parody of that
often misquoted line in 1 Corinthians, where the experience of encountering God indirectly is compared to seeing as if in a darkened mirror, and this is in turn contrasted
with a direct encounter, "face-to-face."[9]

Neo meets the cybernetic approximation of his "maker," staring into its eye in which
is reflected only himself, as if to mock him for what neither he nor the viewer yet knows:
that humankind itself is responsible for its own enslavement, having "given birth" to
the AI "singular consciousness" which then "spawned a race of machines." (Stuart
makes a similar point about the film's invocation of 1 Corinthians, reading the scene
of Neo's assimilation by the mirror as a sort of "parable" of this passage, which is a
misrepresentation of both the significance of the scene and the import of St. Paul's
letter).[10]

In this pivotal scene, Neo wakes up in a glowing red oval capsule isomorphically
reminiscent of the red pill that traced his "real world" location. This uterine surrogate
recalls the primary meaning of "matrix" as "womb," which is precisely where people
in the film spend their entire lives, in a state of more-or-less blissful unknowing, unless
"freed" by Morpheus (see Stuart for an alternative discussion of the Matrix as "womb".)[11]
Thus, to be "freed" is to experience birth for the first time, since otherwise people's
lives are living deaths, Freudian nightmares of never leaving the womb at all, with both
mother and father replaced by machines in a technologically updated ironic inversion
of the classic *Frankenstein* scenario. For the "family" of rebellious humans in reality,
the role of the "father" is filled by Morpheus; the role of mother, on the symbolic level,
remains vacant – unless one accords this status to the Matrix itself, which, in terms
of the narrative as a whole, seems an all but inescapable conclusion.[12] The fact remains

– cookie-baking Oracle aside – that "reality" in *The Matrix* is a decidedly patriarchal place, even if the patriarch in question is a super-bad cyber-terrorist in reflective sunglasses and black leather trench coat.

From outside (from the perspective of "reality"), the Matrix looks like streams of data, the tain of the mirror, the coding sequences which determine the 3-D simulacral images and accompanying sensory input that together constitute the "world that has been pulled over [people's] eyes to blind [them] from the truth." But this is not, as in Baudrillard's conception of the simulacrum, the truth that "there is no truth."[13] Rather, the truth the Matrix conceals is that the Matrix is *not* reality; what's worse, reality is still reality. As Baudrillard famously declares,

> Today abstraction is no longer that of the map, the double, the mirror, or the concept. Simulation is no longer that of a territory, a referential being, or a substance. It is the generation by models of a real without origin or reality: a hyperreal. The territory no longer precedes the map, nor does it survive it. It is nevertheless the map that precedes the territory – *precession of simulacra* – that engenders the territory. . . . It is . . . [the] desert of the real itself.[14]

In the film Baudrillard's "desert of the real," as literal absence of the real, is literalized as the presence of the real-as-desert: the sky has been "scorched," and Morpheus' ship, the Nebuchadnezzar, moves through the Wilderness of the sewer-system far underground. The Matrix, as Morpheus says more than once, is a "dreamworld" from which it *is* possible to awake, with the right help – only not, like Alice, back into the familiar comforts of the real. In the film the direction is reversed: a one-way trip out of the simulacrum into a heretofore unknown and singularly uncomfortable reality.

Therefore, to see the code streaming down the monitor screen, as Neo does immediately following his liberation, is to be aware at least of the "constructedness" of the construct – infinitely more desirable than the state of ignorant bliss in which the average denizen of the Matrix lives. And to see the code – as Cypher (Joe Pantoliano) can – as the images it encodes ("blonde, brunette, redhead . . ."), is to occupy an already demystified position: Cypher "de-ciphers" the code. But the real trick, which only Neo ever masters, thereby realizing his potential as "the One," is to turn the whole structure inside out and see the code as code from *within* the Matrix itself. In this sense, then, Neo's trajectory is not simply from subject of experience to subject of knowledge – combined-with-belief-in-self; it is also a movement from subject of narration-as-reader to narrating subject in a way none of the other characters can match. This is why at the film's end Neo becomes the film's narrator, addressing the AI nemesis in a taunting phone call from a pay phone inside the Matrix.

The Matrix as a narrative is, in the end, all about being a narrative; it is "about" the process of its own narration as the emphasis shifts from an allegory of reading to one of writing, from decoding to encoding. But it remains a piece of exemplary narrative fiction by *upholding* rather than compromising or effacing the distinction between the real and the fictional within its own narrative frame, and this is where the Baudrillardians in the audience go astray. The film's reflexive narrative strategies have the very opposite effect from a "laying bare," an exposing of the artifice of the story's fictionality.

They collude, in a seeming paradox, to maintain the illusion or semblance of "fictional reality" demanded by the science-fiction genre. The default position for the viewer is thus the highly pleasurable one of "mystification," as far as the relation between "reality" and Matrix goes, and in terms of the possibility of identification with Neo as hero on a journey of self-discovery.

Neo's final transcendence of the physical "laws" of the Matrix is also an affirmation of the self as the "realest" real thing, which is the very opposite of a mystical self-abnegation. This transcendence is predicated upon the dichotomous structure of the film's fictional world: reality versus the Matrix, and this returns us to a consideration of the status of the Matrix as Baudrillardian third-order simulacrum, which the film-makers themselves seem to want the viewer to believe. Certainly, many commentators have taken the bait, producing reviews and critical articles that bolster this reading.[15]

Baudrillard is not simply referenced in the film; he is *in* the film, in the form of his book, *Simulacra and Simulation*, specifically the chapter "On Nihilism," in the hollowed-out space of which Neo hides his contraband computer disks.[16] But this literal presence of the French theorist's actual book is really a red herring, and does not grant license to read the Matrix as an illustration of a quintessential postmodern "hyper-reality," as a copy without original, no longer predicated on a reality principle. For, if this were the case then there would be nothing *but* the Matrix – no territory, just a map – and its status as "false reality" would be a moot point: it would be a representation of *this* world, to use that language, and to that extent it might be readable as a version of Baudrillard's simulacrum. An attentive reading of Baudrillard, however, demonstrates the fallacious nature of the urge to make the Matrix correspond with the third-order simulacrum, as if the film were in a category of science fiction it is not, whereas in fact it is a throwback to an earlier, pre-cyberpunk science fiction storyline, updated in its particulars – one might say, in its accessories, like cellphones, sunglasses, and personal weaponry – and of course with all the latest special effects.

For all the talk of taking control of the future, the film's visual-stylistic focus is on the present (on up-to-the-minute fashion, music, technology, and "philosophy"), while the overarching ideological orientation of *The Matrix* is backward, toward the past; a nostalgic and utopian perspective, even in its dystopian focalization. (Such "nostalgia" is both evidenced and complicated in the valorization of older, analog telecommunications technology – the "hard line" required to pass from one dimension to another – over the up-to-the-minute digital and cellular technology, which is fetishized all the same, in one of the most egregious pop cultural displays of eating your cake and having it too in recent memory.)[17] But this retroperspective is also evidenced in the structural use of the Old and New Testament intertexts – an allusive matrix exhaustively enumerated by internet zealots of dubious critical objectivity. That this material is there, in the fabric of the film's narrative, is obvious to any culturally literate viewer (for example: that Neo is a "Doubting Thomas," and Mr. Anderson the "son-of-man," or a New Age Messianic hero, an amalgam of Christ and the Neoplatonic "One" – that sort of thing.)[18]

The question is, how do the filmmakers use the doubled biblical narrative of exodus crossed with messianism? And what is the significance of the consequent effect on the film's structure, centred as it is around the distinction between the post-apocalyptic "desert of the real" and the false reality of the Matrix? Between the temptation to continue enjoying (or, indeed, to never leave) the lifelong comforts of the Matrix and the desire to return to a distinctly "human" homeland, not coincidentally named "Zion, the last human city," there exists a sort of reverse-typological relation, where the old and past-tense (the "real") has been "overwritten" by the new and present-tense (the Matrix). And this is revealed as not merely conditioning the Matrix, proving by its persistent existence that the Matrix is false, but also providing the Matrix with its "reality principle" – the very thing whose absolute absence differentiates Baudrillard's simulacrum from its Platonic inspiration.[19]

As Baudrillard remarks in "Simulacra and Science Fiction,"

> The imaginary was the alibi of the real, in a world dominated by the reality principle. Today, it is the real that has become the alibi of the model, in a world controlled by the principle of simulation. And, paradoxically, it is the real that has become our true utopia – but a utopia that is no longer in the realm of the possible, that can only be dreamt of as one would dream of a lost object.[20]

In *The Matrix*, the real remains "real," containing within its dystopian space-time the real utopian no-place of "Zion." The Matrix itself is the dreamworld, the false utopia of a simulated reality. The inevitable nostalgia for this lost and irrecoverable dream-life is embodied in the film by Cypher, who is also, ironically, Baudrillard's spokesman, arguing as he does for the greater "reality" of the Matrix – a position the film, through Morpheus, Neo and the others, militates against. As for the real-world utopian future toward which Morpheus' crew looks with the anticipation of a very secular salvation: it is, quite appropriately, never shown in the film. For Neo the cyber-Messiah (whose advent is a "second coming") the task is to remain inside the Matrix, bending, breaking or even rewriting the rules, hacking traceless paths through the thickets of coded information comprising the dreamworld from which most never awaken.

What is the Matrix? This is the question that drives us, and unfortunately, as Morpheus makes clear, one cannot be told what the Matrix is, one can only be shown. But it can be stated what the Matrix is not: it is *not* an example of Baudrillard's "third-order simulacrum" – the postmodern mode of representation par excellence, which is no longer representation at all, there being no "real" to represent. If anything, the Matrix is an analogue of a much older idea: the second-order simulacrum, an imitation of an imitation, such as Plato designates the shadow images cast on the cave wall in the famous allegory in the *Republic*. And it is precisely because of the persistence, indeed the ubiquity, of these shadows, in the contemporary form of highly influential films like *The Matrix*, that the necessity of a cultural literacy can be seen more clearly than ever.

Notes

1. *The Matrix*, writ. and dir. Larry and Andy Wachowski, 136 min., Warner Bros., 1999, videocassette.
2. A recent "AltaVista" search yielded 178,140 pages with "The Matrix" in the title. The official webpage can still be found at www.whatisthematrix.com/. "Unofficial" but useful

sites abound as well, with "Zion Mainframe–home of the Zion Resistance" (www.geocities. com/Area51/Meteor/3777/matrixmain.html), and "Into the Matrix" (http://www. intothematrix.net/choose.html) as typical examples. The majority of sites are fan-based and highly subjective, and therefore of dubious critical or interpretative value. Often the most interesting of this category are those sites that are also the most ideologically naive. See, for example: "The Matrix as Messiah Movie: The Real Message Encoded Within The Matrix" (http://awesomehouse.com/matrix/parallels.html); or "The Matrix, Dark City, and the [sic] American religious desire," (http://members.aol.com/lyberty5/matrixpaper. html) – both of which seek to reduce the film to a simple, thinly veiled, Christo-messianic allegory. There are also many review sites of the usual widely varying quality, sites devoted to a particular character and/or actor, and so forth. For some of the better initial reviews, see Ray Conlogue, "The matrix: Matrix a retro-stylish disguise for comic-book fun," *Globe and Mail* (31 March 1999); Richard Corliss, "Popular Metaphysics," *Time* (19 April 1999); Roger Ebert, "The Matrix," Chicago *Sun-Times* (March 1999); Dennis Lim, "Grand Allusions," *Village Voice* (7–13 April 1999); Kim Newman, film review, *Sight and Sound* (June 1999).

3. James Poniewozik, "Got Art?," in Salon.com>Media (12 April 1999), 2 (http://salon.com. directory/topics/james_poniewozik/index6.html). Poniewozik offers some examples from contemporary reviews of the film; "'Looks like Men in Black doing a Gap commercial'" – Ottawa Citizen"; "'Directed in . . . 'edgy'-TV-commercial style by Larry and Andy Wachowski'"! – Houston Chronicle" (exclamation marks added by Poniewozik).

4. Ibid.

5. Quoted in Read Mercer Stuart, "Identity in a Paradox [sic] World," [cited 13 March 2000] (www.cleave.com).

6. McLuhan, *Understanding Media: The Extensions of Man* (Cambridge, MA: MIT Press, 1999), 3–4.

7. Saint Augustine, *Confessions*, trans. R. S. Pine-Coffin (Harmondsworth, UK: Penguin Books, 1988). See especially books 10–11.

8. Lewis Carroll, *Alice's Adventures in Wonderland and Through the Looking Glass* (New York: Random House, 1992), 173.

9. 1 Cor. 13:12. *The New Oxford Annotated Bible with the Apocrypha*. Rev. Standard Version. Eds. Herbert G. May and Bruce M. Metzger (New York: Oxford University Press, 1977).

10. Stuart; see note 4.

11. Ibid.

12. This, however, would require a comparison between the film and another Platonic text: the *Timaeus*; specifically Plato's elaboration of the concept of chora. Such a comparison lies beyond the scope of the present essay.

13. Jean Baudrillard, *Simulacra and Simulation*, trans. Sheila Faria Glaser (Ann Arbor: University of Michigan, 1994), 1.

14. Ibid., 1; Baudrillard's emphasis.

15. See, for example: Doug Mann, and Heidi Hochenedel, "Evil Demons, Saviors, and Simulacra in *The Matrix*" (16 February 2000), 11; accessible via the "The Matrix as Messia Movie" site (see Note 2), where it is linked as http://awesomehouse.com/matrix/parallels. html.

16. In the original screenplay, Morpheus actually cites Baudrillard while using the loading construct to bring Neo up to speed historically: "You have been living inside Baudrillard's vision, inside the map, not the territory." (Larry and Andy Wachowski, *The Matrix*, screenplay [n.p., 1996] p. 47). Fortunately, the Wachowskis excised this speech from the film,

suggesting as it does a potential misunderstanding of Baudrillard's central point from the "Precession" essay that there is nothing else other than the simulacrum – that there is in fact no "territory" – a misprision the brothers appear to have moved beyond, with the final edit's more ironic appropriation of Baudrillard, and their own "philosophical" decision to look back to the simulacrum's ultimate source, Plato.

17. See Stuart.
18. See "The Matrix as Messiah Movie," note 2.
19. See Gilles Deleuze, *The Logic of Sense*, trans. Mark Lester with Charles Stivale, ed. Constantin V. Boundas (New York: Columbus University Press, 1990), 253–79.
20. Baudrillard, 123.

Jackie Chan and
the Black Connection

Gina Marchetti*

In his writings on postmodernism, Fredric Jameson is fond of quoting "China," a work by San Francisco based poet Bob Perelman. Jameson describes the creation of the disjointed poem that he uses as an example of the schizophrenic nature of the postmodern condition as follows:

> In the present case, the represented object is not really China after all: what happened was that Perelman came across a book of photographs in a stationery store in Chinatown, a book whose captions and characters obviously remained dead letters (or should one say material signifiers?) to him. The sentences of the poem are *his* captions to those pictures. Their referents are other images, another text, and the "unity" of the poem is not *in* the text at all but outside it in the bound unity of an absent book.[1]

Jameson's encounter with this poem, Perelman's encounter with these photographs in Chinatown, and the present absences, the contradictory feelings of sense and nonsense, totality and fragmentation, unitary address and schizophrenic multiplicity, that both these encounters conjure up parallel the way in which Jackie Chan has been encountered by scholars, fans, and myriad other viewers globally. Jackie Chan seems to be a "material signifier" that may or may not be a "dead letter" to particular viewers. Just as Perelman's "China" represents his own fantasy based on pictures that have other captions in Chinese, Chan seems to represent a "China" that cannot be "translated." Both the Chinese text and the images themselves remain unavailable to those who encounter the poem, and Chan, in his multiple significations and existence as pure image, may be in this same postmodern cultural condition.

In the essay "Global Bodies/Postnationalities: Charles Johnson's Consumer Culture,"[2] Bill Brown analyzes a 1983 short story by Charles Johnson also called "China." In this story, a middle-aged African-American postal worker living in Seattle discovers martial arts by going to see a Hong Kong movie and, inspired, subsequently joins a kung fu school, much to his wife's chagrin. In the essay, Brown looks at Johnson's protagonist's attraction to Chinese culture through kung fu and martial arts movies

*Pp. 137–58 from *Keyframes: Popular Cinema and Culture Studies*, ed. M. Tinkcomm and A. Villliarejo (London and New York: Routledge). © 2001 by Gina Marchetti. Reprinted with permission from the author.

within the context of the American black community. Specifically, Brown traces the connection between African-Americans in the military and the rise in interest in Japanese/Okinawan/Korean martial arts after World War II and the Korean War. He further notes the political connections forged between the civil rights movement and the movement against the war in Vietnam that connected those domestic groups to international solidarity work involving the emergence of Third World interests extending beyond Vietnam to China, Latin America, and Africa. Brown continues to trace these connections in popular culture with the rise of the Hong Kong kung fu film in the black community, reaching its apogee with the phenomenal success of Bruce Lee in the early 1970s.

When Johnson published "China" in 1983, what had been called the "kung fu craze" had quieted. However, the appeal of Hong Kong films in the black community continued. As inner city theaters closed, the African-American audience moved to Chinatown cinemas, and, as these closed, the audience continued to rent or purchase legal and pirated Hong Kong martial arts fare on videocassette.[3] By far the biggest star of the Hong Kong martial arts cinema at that time was Jackie Chan. Chan's visibility in the black community throughout the 1980s and into the 1990s is undeniable. Chan's recognition of his appeal to blacks is also evident. The effacement of this connection with the growth of Chan's popularity outside the African-American community and black viewer-ship worldwide seems noteworthy. Like Perelman's book of photos, blackness serves as a present absence that structures Chan's films.

In the current phase of Chan's career that has catapulted him to stardom in Hollywood, Chan continues to appropriate black culture and use it in his films. Four of his recent films involve Africa, the African diaspora, and/or African-American issues: *Rumble in the Bronx* (1995, recut and released in the United States in 1996), *Mr. Nice Guy* (1997), *Who Am I?* (1998), and *Rush Hour* (1998). In order to attempt to understand Chan's black connection, these films need to be analyzed in relation to transnational consumer culture, postmodernism, postcolonialism, and questions of identity. Chan's relationship to black issues and viewers needs to be addressed, as well as the continuing importance of black culture in films that have crossed over into mainstream theaters with very different audiences.

"We live on the third world from the sun. Number three. Nobody tells us what to do." (Bob Perelman, "China")

In his autobiography, Jackie Chan writes: "The other day, one of my favorite singers, Lionel Richie, came to visit me on the set. Yesterday, Michael Jackson gave me a call."[4] Although Chan includes his encounters with Richie and Jackson as proof of his making it in Hollywood, he says nothing explicitly about the influence of African-American culture in his films or the loyalty of his black fans in his autobiography beyond references to a few black actors (most notably Chris Tucker). His vision of Hollywood, and the American Dream it seems to encapsulate for him, is decidedly white:

I had long watched American films with envy, wishing I had the budgets and resources they boasted with every frame; I'd danced along with Fred Astaire, hummed to Frank

Sinatra and Julie Andrews, laughed at Chaplin and Keaton and Lloyd, the great comics of the silent classics.[5]

Even if he does not acknowledge his black fans in his autobiography and critics who relish the joy of discovery also ignore them, their presence is felt in Chan's films, in his casting choices, locations, themes, and working techniques.

The involvement of the black audience with Hong Kong martial arts films predates Jackie Chan and heralds the rise of Bruce Lee. As Hollywood underwent substantial change owing to the Paramount Decree, television, changing audience demographics, and other factors, and lost its grip on its domestic and international market, the commercial cinemas of the Third World strengthened in India, Mexico, Egypt, and Hong Kong as well as other countries. Italy's spaghetti Westerns and Hong Kong martial arts films, for example, filled the gap in Hollywood's B-movie production.

Always transnational,[6] Hong Kong productions began to cross over from Chinatown cinemas to other "ghetto" theaters. In the case of the United States, Hong Kong provided a cheap product in the form of dubbed martial arts films to inner city cinemas trying to cut costs and develop a new clientele as television and the suburbanization of America eroded the downtown white or racially mixed audience of an earlier generation. In his essay, "The Kung Fu Craze: Hong Kong Cinema's First American Reception," David Desser points out the appeal of the genre to the black audience:

Outside of the blaxploitation genre it largely replaced, kung fu films offered the only nonwhite heroes, men and women, to audiences alienated by mainstream film and often by mainstream culture. This was the genre of the underdog, the underdog of color, often fighting against colonialist enemies, white culture, or the Japanese. The lone, often unarmed combatant fighting a foe with greater economic clout who represented the status quo provides an obvious but nonetheless real connection between kung fu films and black audiences.[7]

The success of films like the dubbed version of *Five Fingers of Death* (1973) transformed not only American popular cinema but Hong Kong cinema as well. The international co-production *Enter the Dragon* (1973) went on to establish what remains the generic baseline to this day. Directed by Hollywood action veteran Robert Clouse,[8] produced and distributed by Warner Bros. and Golden Harvest, the film co-stars Asian-American/Hong Kong star Bruce Lee, ersatz James Bond John Saxon, and African-American martial artist Jim Kelly. The leading role was split three ways to draw in as much of the international action audience as possible from Hong Kong to black America.

Kelly plays Williams, a former soldier who runs a karate academy in the black community. When he arrives in Hong Kong, he verbalizes an immediate solidarity with the impoverished Chinese. Seeing the floating slums in the harbor, he remarks, "ghettoes are the same everywhere; they stink." This moment establishes an immediate link between audiences in Hong Kong and the black ghetto, and it creates an imaginative solidarity that continues to be exploited in action films. For example, this scene is echoed in *Lethal Weapon IV* (1998) when Danny Glover emotionally notes the connection between illegal Chinese immigrants being smuggled in on a boat and the Middle Passage endured by his African ancestors.[9]

Everyone involved in *Enter the Dragon* recognized the importance of Lee's connection to the American martial arts subculture and the crucial import of the popularity of martial arts and Hong Kong film in the black community. Lee knew America well after spending years in the States as a college student, kung fu instructor and competitor, and television personality. He admired black athletes like Mohammed Ali and had several famous black students, most notably Kareem Abdul Jabbar, who fought with his instructor in Lee's last film, *Game of Death* (1978).

Jackie Chan certainly knew what Lee knew. Chan worked as a stuntman on two productions with Lee, *Fists of Fury* (aka *The Big Boss*, 1972) and *Enter the Dragon* (1973), so Chan knew firsthand Lee's formula. Like Lee, Chan refers to black culture in many of his films. In *Police Story* (1985), for example, Chan mimics Michael Jackson's moonwalking in order to get some dog manure off his shoes. In *City Hunter* (1992), Chan break dances and quotes Bruce Lee's fight with Kareem Abdul Jabbar from *Game of Death*. In *Armour of God* (1986), Chan confronts a line of black women martial artists dressed in black leather bustiers, high heels, and black silk stockings, and coiffed with fluffy "Afro" naturals. Chan solidifies his ties to the martial arts subculture and to the American black community by including African-American kung fu practitioner Marcia Chisholm[10] and karate champion Linda Denley[11] in this transnational production.[12]

"It's always time to leave." (Bob Perelman, "China")

Although it appeared new to mainstream American audiences when it opened in 1996, *Rumble in the Bronx* represents a fantasy that has played well in Hong Kong film for decades. As a colony, Hong Kong has been populated by successive generations of immigrants from China or from other places within the diaspora. Jackie Chan's family, for example, came to Hong Kong from Shandong in Mainland China, leaving some family members behind, moved to Australia to work, and maintained connections with Hong Kong through their son Jackie, who could not adjust to life abroad. For most Hong Kong viewers (and many Asian viewers who were not ethnic Chinese), these stories of immigration, economic struggle in a foreign land, racism and brotherhood in an unfamiliar environment struck a responsive chord. Likely, many in the black audience, who also had an intimate understanding of racism, colonialism, and diaspora, could feel that same connection to these narratives.

Given this environment, it is not surprising that Chan sets so many of his films in places other than Hong Kong. In fact, Chan follows the route laid down by the British Empire and the Commonwealth for many within the Chinese diaspora.[13] Of course, scores within the African diaspora know this route or similar ones from the periphery to the center as well. The movement in all these films is from Asia (the Third World) to the West (First World). In *Rumble*, Chan moves from Hong Kong to the Bronx (obviously Canada with the mountains of British Columbia looming in the background of several shots standing in for New York City). *Mr. Nice Guy* takes place in Melbourne, Australia. *Who Am I?* moves from South Africa to Holland, following a Dutch Afrikaner connection, with the jungles of Malaysia (former British colony and one of Chan's and the Hong Kong industry's favorite locations with a roughly 35 percent ethnic Chinese population) opening the film. *Rush Hour* finally delivers Chan to America, and Chan symbolically clings to the United States by hanging on to a Hollywood sign. Chan travels the globe with a purpose, choosing locations where English is spoken, production costs are low, and labor is available. From Vancouver to Melbourne to Johannesburg to Los Angeles, Chan, in his recent films, has worked in locations that would be considered possible sites of relocation for his Hong Kong Chinese audience or familiar places of residence for those in the black diaspora.

> *"The train takes you where it goes."* (Bob Perelman, "China")

In 1992, four white policemen captured on videotape beating a black man, Rodney King, were freed. Violence broke out in Los Angeles, destroying several Asian-owned businesses in the black community. In *Immigrant Acts: On Asian American Cultural Politics*, Lisa Lowe describes the media depiction of these events as follows:

> The dominant US media construction of the Korean Americans in the L.A. crisis has generally reduced and obscured them as "middle men" within US race and class relations, situating them in an intermediary position within capitalist development and suggesting they are more threatened by Blacks than by corporate capitalism.[14]

In *Margins and Mainstreams: Asians in American History and Culture*, Gary Okihiro poses the question, "Is Yellow Black or White?"[15] In fact, there is a long history of Asians serving as "buffers" or "middlemen" between blacks and whites in American and in many colonial situations globally. The Chinese grocer, for example, has played this role in both rural and urban America, and Third World Newreel's documentary *Mississippi Triangle* has explored the triangular nature of race relations in the American South by focusing on several Chinese groceries in the Mississippi Delta.[16] The documentary shows a range of attitudes and feelings among the various communities, from identification across racial lines, kinship, and close relations to misunderstanding, bigotry, and suspicion.

Rumble in the Bronx takes up this feeling of kinship as well as ambivalence. Even the dare-devil Chan would not actually go to the South Bronx to make his film: "I'm no stranger to taking risks, but making a movie on location in the Bronx seemed crazy even to me."[17] The film fashions a vision of the American ghetto that allows for the violent destruction of the Asian grocer as well as the solidification of cross-ethnic affiliations, multicultural understandings, and interracial contact. It flatters the global Asian middle class while not forgetting its debt to the black community frustrated with ghetto life.

Rodney King and the Los Angeles uprising also figure as a present absence in *Rush Hour*. Lee (Jackie Chan), the inspector from Hong Kong, and Carter (Chris Tucker), a police officer in Los Angeles, both have an ambivalent relationship to the American justice system and its relationship to people of color. Obliquely referring to Rodney King and the numerous other instances of black abuse at the hands of the LAPD, Tucker/Carter quips, "This is the LAPD—we're the most hated cops in the free world. My own Mama's ashamed of me. She tells everybody I'm a drug dealer."

Acting as Lee's (and, implicitly, the white viewer's) guide to the black community in Los Angeles, Carter serves as an ambassador of ill will at the outset. In fact, Carter initially appears to be a bigot.[18] He calls Lee a "Chunking cop" and "Mr. Rice A Roni," and he has an argument with a Chinese carryout vender about his "greasy food." When he meets up with the principal Chinese villain at the film's climax, he says, "I've been looking for your sweet and sour chicken ass." The tensions between the Asian and black communities are palpable throughout the film.

> *"I'd rather the stars didn't describe us to each other; I'd rather we do it for ourselves."* (Bob Perelman, "China")

Although an uneasy alliance, the experience of the ghetto links the Chinese with the black community.[19] In *The Star Raft: China's Encounter with Africa*, Philip Snow notes a Chinese exchange student's reaction to Harlem: "It was wrong to criticize them [*hei ren*; literally "black people"], as some people did, for thronging together in ghettoes. She could understand their need to live in poor areas: she was poor herself."[20] Stuart Kaminsky has described Bruce Lee as a "ghetto figure"[21] and described kung fu films as "ghetto myths."[22] In *Kung Fu: Cinema of Vengeance*,[23] Verina Glaessner also talks about the ghetto roots of the genre in the poverty, crime, and social unrest of Hong Kong in the 1960s. The portrait of the Bronx presented in *Rumble* offers nothing in the way of verisimilitude; however, it does offer a certain understanding of the ghetto that seems to strike a responsive chord across races and cultures.

As far as Chan moved away from Bruce Lee and the "ghetto myth," it is interesting that *Rumble in the Bronx* should bring him back full circle with a vehicle that shows a remarkable similarity to *The Way of the Dragon* (1972, aka *The Return of the Dragon*), a film that Lee made before his breakthrough international co-production *Enter the Dragon*, but released worldwide after the latter film proved successful.

> *"Folks straggling along vast stretches of concrete, heading into the plane."* (Bob Perelman, "China")

Rumble's resemblance to this Lee vehicle (one which Lee also directed and wrote) is uncanny. Like *Return*, *Rumble* begins with its protagonist arriving at the airport. In both films, the protagonist is immediately coded as a bumbling foreigner who goes to the West to help with a business problem. These businesses represent Chinese outposts in the wild and violent West, where the Chinese must accommodate themselves to an alien and threatening environment. In both films, flamboyant street thugs (multiracial and multiethnic armed gangs) and avaricious capitalists in well-tailored suits harass the Chinese entrepreneurs. Chan and Lee function to preserve the Chinese presence in the West, while maintaining their own intention to return to Hong Kong.

However, while Lee offers up stylishly dressed black antagonists as part of the Roman milieu in *Return*, Chan actually sets his film in the Bronx and creates out of snippets of Toronto and Vancouver a vision of martial arts multiculturalism in a ghetto environment. Mick LaSalle, a critic for the *San Francisco Chronicle*, asks the following question about the choice of location for *Rumble*:

American discomfort about racial issues puts a squeeze on the film. Keung fights a white street gang in the Bronx, but in the real Bronx a white street gang would have long ago moved to the suburbs. "Rumble" throws Chan into the middle of an unrecognizable, cartoonlike version of America, then makes him look silly by forcing him to take it all too seriously . . . If they wanted neither to film in the Bronx or to tell a real Bronx story, why bother setting the story there?[24]

The answer to this question seems clear. The Bronx provides an imaginative meeting ground for an audience composed of nervous Hong Kong residents, African-Americans, and those within the Asian diaspora. *Rumble* attempts to revive and revitalize Lee's ghetto myth in the aftermath of Rodney King and the Los Angeles crisis.

"The landscape is motorized." (Bob Perelman, "China")

The skyline of New York City punctuates the film, and the Statue of Liberty appears with the World Trade Center towers as the physical emblems of America. The twin promises of freedom and material prosperity through a capitalist market economy thematically frame the film's rather disjointed narrative. New York represents the ideological extremes of a global economy out of control in a way that few other locations do.

As Keung moves from the impressive prosperity of Manhattan to the poverty of the Bronx, *Rumble* continues to rely on internationally known icons. *Fort Apache, the Bronx* (1981) made the South Bronx a global symbol of the crisis of the American inner city, of racial and ethnic tensions, and of the decay of the American Dream. *Rumble* relies on these expectations to play with what the ghetto signifies as well as what ghetto fantasies can promise.

When Keung arrives at his uncle's market in the Bronx, he learns that Uncle Bill (Bill Tung) is literally trying to whitewash the place to prepare to fleece the new buyer, Elaine (Anita Mui). Bill attempts to put his best foot forward, but it is abundantly clear why he wants out of the ghetto as the graffiti reappear and various gangs come in for protection money, shoplifting, and general vandalism.

"Bridges among water." (Bob Perelman, "China")

However, just as the viewer may begin to think Bill is a bigot, a counter-discourse emerges. Bill makes a point of reminding Keung that a white thug killed his father.[25] The grocery functions as a multiracial enterprise. It has a white female cashier, African-American stock clerk, black and white painters, as well as the Asian management. Also, Bill's fiancée, Whitney (Carrie Cain-Sparks), is African-American.

As the wedding of Bill and Whitney symbolizes the marriage of blacks and Asians, *Rumble* carefully creates an image of the ghetto as a place of multiracial and multicultural possibility. Although comedy takes the edge off any uneasiness created by the interracial marriage, Bill and Whitney's wedding devotes screen time to a celebration of black and Asian solidarity. Carrie Cain-Sparks sings a soul-inspired song written by Tim Dang and Nathan Wang, "You Are the One," with black female back-up singers, as she walks down the aisle as Whitney to marry Bill. Later in the sequence, she performs a comic duet in Cantonese with Bill.

Bill and Whitney's interracial marriage points to a significant change from Lee's *Return of the Dragon*. In *Return*, the emphasis was on maintaining a Chinese presence in a hostile environment. *Rumble*, on the other hand, attempts the Chinese facilitation of a transformation of the ghetto into a multiracial and multiethnic community. Clearly, this fantasy has an appeal outside Asian viewership, acknowledging the importance of racial harmony above nationalism, and nodding in the direction of the black audience.

"The sun rises also." (Bob Perelman, "China")

For those who comment on the lack of verisimilitude in the film, the depiction of the gang ranks with the Canadian landscape as one of the most absurd elements in the film. However, Keung's relationship with Tony and his gang provides the structure for the preponderance of the action sequences in *Rumble* and the location of Keung's power over his ghetto environment. Although the reviewer for the *San Francisco Chronicle* misrepresented the gang as entirely white, the gang's leader, Tony (Marc Akerstream), and main henchman, Angelo (Garvin Cross), are white. Indeed, Angelo's bleached white hair and the whiteness of the tattooed buttock emphasize his whiteness as he exposes his rear for Keung to kiss in one of their confrontations.[26] Other members of the gang are Chinese, Hispanic (indicated by the "que pasa" in the New Line version), black, and, possibly, Native American (indicated by buckskin and hairstyle). The importance of the multiculturalism of the gang to Chan's renewed ghetto myth cannot be overemphasized.

Keung embodies all sides of the contradictions that form the foundation of ghetto culture. Like Rodney King, he is a man of color victimized by violent whites. As an Asian storekeeper, he represents the "model minority" victimized by mob violence. Clearly, Chan could not symbolically embody this contradiction if the gang members were black. He would move from representing a ghetto myth to acting as a possible locus of racist sentiment. Keung becomes part of the spectacle of violence against Asians in the American ghetto and survives to show that the "dregs" of American society (who very often, demographically, form the bulk of Chan's young American fans) can be redeemed and drawn into a Greater Chinese[27] vision of solidarity that may even enlighten those outside the Chinese community.

In his essay, "Jackie Chan and the Cultural Dynamics of Global Entertainment," Steve Fore describes Chan's heroic posture as follows:

> In keeping with fundamental principles of the martial arts tradition, he is never the aggressor; he fights in defense of his body, in defense of the social community of which he is a member, and, frequently, in order to demonstrate the superiority of his community's value structure; and (unlike US movie action heroes) he never gloats over a fallen opponent, and may even offer the opponent an opportunity to redeem himself by acceding to the values of Chan's community.[28]

Fore goes on to describe the end to Keung's climactic fight with Tony and his gang. Keung lectures the gang in English (in the New Line version): "Why lower yourself?

Don't you know you're the scum of the earth?" Switching to Cantonese to express himself, Keung continues: "I hope the next time that we meet we won't be fighting each other. Instead we'll be drinking tea together."

The switch to Chinese is significant. Keung offers a positive sign of "Chineseness" in the allusion to the social ritual of tea drinking to the primarily non-Chinese gang members. Like martial arts films over the decades, *Rumble* proffers what is marked as a particularly Chinese path to survival in a hostile environment. If, as Jim Kelley said in *Enter the Dragon*, "ghettoes are the same everywhere," Keung supplies a remedy from a different ghetto (i.e., the slums of Hong Kong) and a different ghetto culture.

"Everyone enjoyed the explosions." (Bob Perelman, "China")

Jackie Chan's starring vehicles in the 1980s and 1990s devote considerable screen time to the destruction of property.[29] The captain in *Rush Hour* seems to speak on behalf of action filmmakers generally when he remarks, 'Every once in a while we've got to let the general public know we can still blow shit up."

Rumble in the Bronx offers this fantasy of destruction of commodities to its viewers. When Keung trashes Tony's hideout, he uses the purloined commodities against the gang, stuffing one hoodlum into a refrigerator crowning another with a television, and manipulating overstuffed chairs, shopping carts, and skis as weapons. A running joke throughout the film involves the destruction of Elaine's market and its contents and the lessening of her will to make it rich with a ghetto enterprise. The store is trashed five times in the narrative. A sign at the entrance saying, "Thank you and come again," hangs ironically over the scenes of destruction and rebuilding.

However, tensions surrounding the positioning of various classes in relation to consumerism and commodities threaten to split the film's viewership. The potential divisions between small business and the working classes and the poor heal quickly with the introduction of White Tiger (Kris Lord). As in many action adventure plots, the principal villain provides a fantasy of capitalism out of control. His riches come from horrific exploitation, violence against the poor and laborers, a disdain for and manipulation of the justice system pointing to the ineffectiveness of police and the government, and a ruthless ability to crush his competition. He establishes himself as a racial threat to multicultural harmony initially through the destruction of his black contacts and their purple Cadillac. White Tiger represents a male, white, bourgeois establishment that immediately alienates virtually all members of the audience, and the villains in *Mr. Nice Guy, Who Am I?*, and *Rush Hour* are virtually identical to him.

"A sister who points to the sky at least once a decade is a good sister." (Bob Perelman, "China")

In addition to the white, male, bourgeois villain, Chan's films also feature African-American and Hispanic/Latina women. Even when most of Chan's opponents are white and his possible love interests generally Asian, Chan manages to include black and Hispanic women in his casts. Sexy opponents as in *Armour of God* or comedic local color as in *Rumble in the Bronx*, these women generally take up a marginal role in the narrative that becomes a central role of potential identification with the fiction for black fans.

Mr. Nice Guy's Lakeisha (Karen McLymont) provides a case in point. Primarily through her name and accent, Lakeisha appears to he African-American. However, the whys and wherefores of how an African-American woman ended up in Melbourne, Australia, as an assistant to a Chinese cook (Jackie, playcd by Jackie Chan) on television remain obscure. She is a black presence in the film, but her history is completely absent. Along with Jackie's Chinese girlfriend, Miki (Miki Lee), and a white Australian female news reporter, Diana (Gabrielle Fitzpatrick), Lakeisha forms part of a multiracial female chorus around Jackie.

On the periphery of the central action of the plot, Lakeisha mainly functions as a physical presence, a thin, colorfully dressed, stylish black woman. Shc providcs an entry into the action for black viewers, and, because of her gender, decorative qualities, and marginality within the narrative, she does not threaten the rest of the audience in any way.

"Run in front of your shadow." (Bob Perelman, "China")

The presence of the black female martial arts adept, like *Mr. Nice Guy's* Lakeisha, puts into play a tension involving questions of racial, gender, and sexual identity in Chan's films. Critics have been divided over whether Chan (and the Hong Kong action genre generally) embodies a remasculinization of castrated, marginalized, colonial/postcolonial subjects or whether he represents a postfeminist androgyny that transcends traditional gender binaries. Yvonne Tasker has commented: "Chan's 'softness' does not consist in a lack of muscularity or an inability to fight, but more in a refusal either to take the male body too seriously or to play the part of Oriental other."[30] Mark Gallagher notes: "Chan's films rely on comic treatments of escape and flight, feminizing his characters while reinscribing his antagonists as caricatures of 'serious masculinity.'"[31] Kwai-Cheung Lo notes this dialectic in play between the representation of Chan in the narrative and in the concluding credit sequences featuring outtakes: "Significantly, it is precisely the outtakes of the flubbed stunts that create the myth of Jackie Chan. Portrayed as a comedian, a common man in the films, Chan becomes a superhero in his outtakes."[32]

The fact that Chan fights along with/against women of color in these films links race and gender together as part of a single problematic. Like black women fighters, the "soft" Chan can represent those doubly marginalized because of their bodies demanding justice through physical action. In contrast to the women fighters, the "hard" Chan symbolizes a dominant masculinity that takes on mythic proportions extratextually through press on his mastery of stunt work.

Lakeisha's presence in *Mr. Nice Guy* also conjures up intertextual associations that may create additional meaning and/or pleasure for some viewers, As the stylish proponent of martial arts, Lakeisha seems to be cast in a mold similar to the blaxploitation heroines of a previous era. Her appearance calls up associations with *Cleopatra Jones* (1973) and *Coffy* (1973), and she alludes to a nostalgia for the Hong Kong martial arts film's twin genre of blaxploitation and female action stars like Pam Grier.

"Pick up the right things." (Bob Perelman, "China")

In "Postmodernism and Consumer Society," Jameson links the "nostalgia film" and "pastiche" as characteristics of postmodernism. A master of both pastiche and nostalgia, Chan self-consciously refers to Hollywood films from all eras in his oeuvre, ranging from Indiana Jones in *Armour of God* (I and II) to the Frank Capra remake of *Pocketful of Miracles/Lady for a Day* in *Mr. Canton and Lady Rose* (1989) and the borrowing from Jean-Claude Van Damme's *Double Impact in Twin Dragons* (1992) as well as his more famous re-creations of Lloyd and Keaton stunts in *Project A* (1983) and *Project A: Part II* (1987). Ramie Tateishi has discussed Jackie Chan's oeuvre in relation to pastiche in his essay, "Jackie Chan and the Re-invention of Tradition."[33] It seems useful to expand on Tateishi's observations and look at Chan's recent work in relation to postmodern aesthetics.[34]

Rumble in the Bronx, *Mr. Nice Guy*, *Who Am I?*, and *Rush Hour* all rely on the pastiche characteristic of the nostalgia film for their aesthetic foundations. As Jameson points out, the nostalgia film does not invoke a sense of an authentic historical moment that may conjure up memories of the past for those who actually lived through that history. Rather, as the postmodern aesthetic announces the "end of history," the nostalgia film relies on knowledge of past styles and mediated images from the mass consumer culture of previous eras to evoke a sense of nostalgia for films, television shows, and the popular culture of the past. Pastiche involves a "blank parody" that relies on direct quotations, literal recreations, and simulations of past media experiences that make no attempt to satirize or offer a political commentary on the earlier historical moment and its relationship to the present.

The invocation of *Return of the Dragon* in *Rumble in the Bronx* has already been discussed, but it is worth noting further that *Rumble* conjures up the kung fu and blaxploitation films of the early 1970s in even more direct ways. In the marketing of *Rumble in the Bronx*, for example, New Line took advantage of the nostalgia for the 1970s circulating within the cinema at that time, most notably through the revival of 1970s style with Afro hairdos, platform shoes, and polyester in Tarantino's *Pulp Fiction* (1994). Kung fu in a ghetto setting seemed to call out for the 1975 funk/disco hit by Carl Douglas, "Kung Fu Fighting," and this song was featured in trailers for the film (even though it is not on the film's soundtrack). Technically, the film also conjures up memories of the earlier Hong Kong martial arts imports through its dubbing.

Similarly, *Rush Hour* is riddled with references to earlier African-American culture, Carter is first introduced in the film dressed as an urban dandy with a black leather coat, earrings, and conspicuous jewelry, driving a sporty black Stingray that seems to complement his outfit. Images of Shaft and Superfly immediately come to mind. Moreover, the coupling of Tucker with Chan recalls the Eddie Murphy/Nick Nolte vehicle *48 Hours* (1982) in which Murphy pays homage to Bruce Lee in a Chinatown alley.

Carter and Lee find common ground with another blast from the past, Edwin Starr's "War," a rock and roll/soul/rhythm and blues crossover hit from 1970. Lee and Carter bond, communicate across linguistic, racial, national, and cultural borders, and reconcile their personal differences through this song that calls for an end to war (most directly the American war in Vietnam). Although Lee is presented as ignorant of

African-American life, he knows "War" by heart and can enunciate every grunt. Similarly, although Carter pleads ignorance of Chinese culture, he clearly knows Hong Kong well enough through its film exports to remark, "You sound like a karate movie." Their bond solidifies through direct references to the "ghetto myth" of the Hong Kong martial arts film that Chan takes up from Bruce Lee by playing a character surnamed Lee.

It is through the two most globally visible aspects of each other's cultures that Lee and Carter can find common ground. Black music and Chinese kung fu share a common cultural currency that circulates transnationally. The Asian and the African diasporas meet in this scene through a recognition of globally circulated images and sounds in the form of mass-mediated consumer culture. Ironically, the capitalism that the fantasy angrily rails against becomes the conduit for the building of these bonds based on familiarity with a song and an image from the ghetto culture of the 1970s.

"Hey guess what? What? I've learned how to talk. Great." (Bob Perelman, "China")

Most critics of the international action film have hypothesized that part of the transnational appeal of the genre comes from the fact it relies on physical spectacle rather than dialogue for its appeal. Given this truism, it is interesting to note that all four of the Chan vehicles under consideration here explicitly deal with language, translation, communication and miscommunication within a polyglot environment. Made within the context of colonial Hong Kong and the Chinese diaspora, the multilingual nature of the films should come as no surprise. They map the frustrations of translations, mistranslations, mispronunciations, and malapropisms that even the most fluent speakers of second and third languages encounter outside their native tongues.

Because of Chris Tucker's background as a verbal comic, *Rush Hour* offers some particularly telling instances of the use and abuse of language. *Rush Hour* was marketed with the following taglines: "The fastest hands in the East meets the biggest mouth in the West," and, "They come from different cultures. But on a case this big, they speak the same language."[35]

The film is book-ended by two pieces of comic repartee. When Carter confronts Lee about hiding his ability to speak English, Lee retorts, "Not being able to speak is not the same as not speaking. You seem as if you like to talk. I like to let people talk who like to talk. It makes it easier to find out how full of shit they are." Carter remains confused, "What the hell did you just say?" At the end of the film, on their way to Hong Kong, Carter surprises Lee with a few words of Mandarin to the stewardess. Solidifying their bond, Lee moves immediately into black argot, "We can hang in my crib – I'll show you my 'hood.'" Lee's command of African-American slang has advanced considerably from an earlier scene in which he gets into a fight with a large bartender when, following Carter's lead, he says with a grin and a pronounced Chinese accent, "What's up, my nigger?" This naïve use of this racial slur also highlights Lee's own crisis of identity in America. Neither black nor white, he represents a vacuum of signification that exists at the center of many of his other starring vehicles.

"Don't forget what your hat and shoes will look like when you are nowhere to be found." (Bob Perelman, "China")

Made a few months after the return of Hong Kong to Chinese sovereignty, *Who Am I?*
uses its amnesiac hero, Jackie/Whoami, as a walking symbol of this postmodern, postcolonial crisis of identity. When Jackie goes to a South African hilltop and screams out
over the vast and uncaring landscape, "Who am I?," it has a particular resonance for
Chan's Hong Kong audience facing the uncertainty of their new identity under the
sovereignty of the People's Republic.[36] In "Muscles and Subjectivity: A Short History
of the Masculine Body in Hong Kong Popular Culture," Kwai-Cheung Lo examine the
bodies of Hong Kong martial arts stars like Jackie Chan as bodies that "occupy an empty
space without any positive content or intrinsic meaning, and their void can only subsequently be filled through the specificity of their particular historical milieu. What they
indicate is only the impossibility of fixed definition."[37] In *Who Am I?*, blackness is used
as a way to explore this identity crisis. In light of Chan's career-long links to the black
community, it seems fitting that he ends up in Africa in this search for identity. In fact,
at the end of the film, Jackie returns to the African village that gave birth to "Whoami"
to search for his "roots."

Who Am I?'s narrative revolves around power dynamics involving the First and the
Third World. In this case, Chan's character is involved in the same racial construct that
exists in *Rumble*. As an Asian, he serves as a racial middleman within multinational
relations between the East and the West, Africa and Europe. His personal identity crisis
parallels the uneasy geopolitical relations that characterize transnational capitalism.
Jackie mediates between the "primitive" world of the black African village and the
sophisticated, cosmopolitan cities of Johannesburg and Rotterdam. He moves from the
skin shacks of the dry African plains to the postmodern glass edifice of one of Europe's
most architecturally daring buildings. He wears the feathers and paint of his adopted
African village, dances in their communal rituals, and is mistaken for an African "native"
on more than one occasion in the film. However, he also commands computer screens,
mobile phones, and state-of-the-art racecars.

Armed in his travels with a fist full of passports and an impressive understanding of
sophisticated technical equipment, Jackie presents an action fantasy version of what
Aihwa Ong has termed "flexible citizenship," a term she uses to refer to "the strategies
and effects of mobile managers, technocrats, and professionals seeking to both circumvent *and* benefit from different nation-state regimes by selecting different sites for
investments, work, and family relocations."[38] He may not know who he is, but Jackie/
Whoami comes out of the Third World able to function in the global arena. He has a
consciousness of the poverty, isolation, and marginality of the Third World coupled
with a Westernized technical education and ability to roam the globe freely. He represents the contradictions of global capitalism and the new politics of race in a transnational consumer society. However, flexible citizenship puts into question fundamental
aspects of identity, and this crisis underlies Chan's screen persona.

"You look great in shorts. And the flag looks great too." (Bob Perelman, "China")

The postmodern emptiness that film critics have noted at the core of the Hong Kong
martial hero may be due to the formation of the figure within a global image industry
honed by the domination of Hollywood and the cultural imperialism of bourgeois

American ideology. Transnational stardom, in many respects, traps Chan. As a conflicted, fragmented, hybrid figure, Chan does not ultimately transcend the powers against which his characters struggle. He is hemmed in by the constraints placed on him as an Asian man, and he seems quite conscious of these limitations as he pokes fun at his own vulnerabilities in his films.

Certainly, this does not represent any new understanding of the racial dynamic within bourgeois, colonial ideology. In many respects, his image seems to echo what W. E. B. Du Bois, at the turn of the previous century, termed "double-consciousness." In *The Souls of Black Folk* (1903), Du Bois states:

> ... in a world which yields him no true self-consciousness, but only lets him see himself through the revelation of the other world. It is a peculiar sensation, this double-consciousness, this sense of always looking at one's self through the eyes of others, of measuring one's soul by the tape of a world that looks on in amused contempt and pity. One ever feels his two-ness, – an American, a Negro; two souls, two thoughts, two unreconciled strivings; two warring ideals in one dark body, whose dogged strength alone keeps it from being torn asunder.[39]

In *Black Skin, White Masks*, Frantz Fanon makes strikingly similar observations about this dualism based on his experiences of being black under French colonialism.[40] The way in which Chan operates in his films parallels the fragmentation and self-consciousness described by Du Bois and Fanon.

Sometimes, Chan's characters represent bodily the forces of colonialism. He plays royal Hong Kong police officers and international spies at the service of Western powers. At other times, he appears to be an emblem of authentic "Chineseness," chauvinistically celebrating the superiority of Chinese culture and the power of Chinese kung fu. Chan's body becomes the place where this racial/colonial battle is played out. He can be comic, pathetic, and awkward, but also potent, heroic, and triumphant.

A mercurial, "flexible citizen," Chan plays many roles in his films that acknowledge and sometimes flatter the white norm. Chan can be the bumbling policeman, the clueless tourist, the "F.O.B." ("fresh off the boat") immigrant, and the unsophisticated, parochial bumpkin. He presents a self-deprecating humor, appreciated by the marginalized, that can also make him less threatening to an empowered audience. When in Africa, he champions the Third World. In the West, he finds acceptance as an entrepreneur or technocrat. He slides between Cantonese, Mandarin, and English, and transcends national borders. Blackness acts as a foil to Chan's pallor and as a support for his color in the racial symbolic in which he operates. The ghetto structures his place within Hollywood's global entertainment environment through the twin genres of blaxploitation and kung fu.

Chan exists somewhere between the two notions of ethnicity Stuart Hall describes, in his influential essay "New Ethnicities," as follows:

> What is involved is the splitting of the notion of ethnicity between, on the one hand the dominant notion which connects it to nation and "race" and on the other hand what I

think is the beginning of a positive conception of the ethnicity of the margins, of the periphery . . . This precisely is the politics of ethnicity predicated on difference and diversity.[41]

Chan effortlessly accommodates himself to the commercial system by navigating a path between nationalism and what Hall calls "diaspora-ization," "the process of unsettling, recombination, hybridization and 'cut-and-mix.'"[42] This process that Hall describes in relation to black culture forges an inextricable link between Chan and experiences of people of color globally. As a "new ethnic," Chan enacts race and ethnicity in a way that goes beyond the borders of Asia, China, or Hong Kong.

"If it tastes good we eat it." (Bob Perelman, "China")

One of the most important contributions of cultural studies in recent years has been its critique of the relationship between postcolonialism and postmodernism currently debated within critical theory. In *The Post-colonial Studies Reader*, the editors, Bill Ashcroft, Gareth Griffiths, and Helen Tiffin, point out: "The intensification of theoretical interest in the post-colonial has coincided with the rise of postmodernism in Western society and this has led to both confusion and overlap between the two."[43] The schizophrenic decentering of the subject has much in common with W. E. B. Du Bois' notion of "double consciousness" as well as Frantz Fanon's description of "black skin" in "white masks." Jameson's description of nostalgia strongly resembles Fanon's discussion of one of the phases in the process of decolonization *in The Wretched of the Earth*.[44] In their essay, "De Margin and De Centre," Isaac Julien and Kobena Mercer note:

> Ethnicity has emerged as a key issue as various "marginal" practices . . . are becoming de-marginalized at a time when "centred" discourses of cultural authority and legitima-tion . . . are becoming increasingly de-centred and destabilized, called into question from within. This scenario . . . has of course already been widely discussed in terms of the characteristic aesthetic and political problems of postmodernism. However, it is ironic that while some of the loudest voices offering commentary have announced nothing less than the "end of representation" or the "end of history", the political possibility of the *end of ethnocentrism* has not been seized upon as a suitably exciting topic for description or inquiry.[45]

Many theorists have argued that postmodernism exists exclusively in the West, and that it only has significance in the East/Third World as an instance of cultural imperialism.[46] Certainly, just as Perelman's "China" haunts Jameson's essays on postmodernism, issues involving race, colonialism, and imperialism disturb postmodern theory. In so many ways, the postmodern condition mimics the postcolonial condition, although "China," and all that it represents, remains on the edges of this theoretical discourse. Its fact, as in the case of Perelman's poem, postmodernist discourse seems to be built on an absence of "China," i.e., the East, the Third World, the postcolonial, the "feminine,"[47] and the racial/ethnic/cultural Other. Although the center of white, bourgeois patriarchy may be vacant, "China" is not present. It remains an absence that shadows the postmodern presence of crisis.[48]

In the films under discussion here, Jackie Chan seems to exemplify that same present absence of race, ethnicity, and nation found in postmodernist theory. He exists at the cusp of the postmodern and the postcolonial, and he can be read as one or the other depending on the circumstances of exhibition and reception.

If examined in this light, the pastiche that characterizes Chan's films can easily be seen in terms of Homi Bhabha's notions of hybridity and mimicsy.[49] He can slip effortlessly between imitations of James Bond, Indiana Jones, and other white masters of global order and Michael Jackson's moon walk or Chris Tucker's version of playing the "dozens." He takes on various racial roles as masks; however, no authentic self is promised behind the persona. Chan turns the image of the Asian cook or houseboy on its head as the polished television chef Jackie in *Mr. Nice Guy*, who can change the kitchen utensils that marked a subordinate status in earlier media images into weapons of ethnic empowerment.[50] However, although Chan may turn ethnic and racial stereotypes on their head and he may mimic the white hero, he does so from a position of uncertainty and questionable power. His deracination frees him in many ways, but limits his legitimacy in other ways. He easily shifts form and position, but, ultimately, accommodates himself to the postmodern condition without much critical footing.

"The people who taught us to count were being very kind." (Bob Perelman, "China")

It is at this stage that it is important to take into account Chan's sudden embrace by the mainstream American public with the success of *Rumble*. Despite earlier failures, New Line Cinema felt that the time was right for the commercial exploitation of Chan in the American market, and the company put considerable time and money (in re-editing, re-dubbing and massively advertising *Rumble*) into this endeavor.[51]

Rumble takes up a postmodern style that operates on familiarity with and a faux nostalgia for Hong Kong kung fu films and biaxploitation films of the 1970s. Tarantino had already revived these genres in films like *Pulp Fiction*, and audiences were primed for films with disjointed narratives, opaque characters, pastiches of earlier formulae, spectacular violence, and vague references to ethnic, racial, and cultural alterity displacing the centrality of white, bourgeois males. *Rumble* struck a responsive chord in a cost-effective manner, and *Rush Hour* followed suit as a low-budget Hollywood vehicle for Chan. Video and limited theatrical release also brought in cash in white middle-class communities for *Mr. Nice Guy, Who Am I?*, and several other Chan vehicles produced by Golden Harvest and picked up for US distribution.

The use of "blackness" as a signifier in each of these vehicles enhances their marketability across various audiences, including white, middle-class, suburbanites who can place Chan within the defined parameters of "multicultural" spectacle found in the Hollywood action genre. In fact, one of the most striking aspects of *Rush Hour* involves the film's relationship to hip-hop/house culture, primarily associated with urban African-American youth, but popular worldwide. Although the film's director, Brett Ratner, a graduate of New York University, came up through the ranks making music videos featuring African-American rap performers like Public Enemy and Wu Tang Clan before directing Chris Tucker in *Money Talks* (1997), contemporary black youth culture takes a back seat in *Rush Hour* to nostalgic evocations of the 1970s. Rap and hip-hop seem to be there and not there in Tucker's banter and in the background music and culture. Although there is an intimate connection between rap and Hong Kong film,[52] this connection exists only on the edges of *Rush Hour*, since perhaps too close an alliance with a subversive subculture would alienate the newly won mainstream American audience.

With *Rush Hour*, Chan has transformed himself into a Hollywood star, without severing his ties to Hong Kong, Japan, and his non-Western fans, by creating a new "ghetto myth" of transnational multiculturalism. His longtime associate Sammo Hung's imitation of the concept of a Chinese policeman paired with an African-American LAPD renegade on network television's *Martial Law* pays tribute to the fundamental popularity of this formula. As an Asian businessman in the United States, Chan represents the new American Dream of "flexible citizenship," and, as an icon, he symbolizes a whitewashing of ghetto culture for global, postmodern consumerism.

"Time to wake up. But better get used to dreams." (Bob Perelman, "China")

In conclusion, Chan seems to appeal to a wide array of viewers because of his ability to link concerns associated with the postcolonial to those connected to the postmodern. Chan's white, middle-class, male, Western fans, who must navigate the uncertainty of identity within the postmodern destabilization of the bourgeois, patriarchal norm, see a fantasy of control over race, gender, and class. The ghetto myth that once appealed primarily to those on the margin now becomes available to those who occupy what used to be the center.

In this regard, Chan's black connection becomes a critical part of this ideological operation. Chan's presence signifies racial difference in a way that seems to allow for transcultural exchanges. He manages the chaos of the ghetto and creates a fantasy in which harmony can be created. Although this harmony is illusory, it has an allure for audiences globally. Chan operates in multiple spheres in which he must appeal to a heterogeneous audience across class, racial, and national borders. He represents a dream of physical empowerment to those in the audience who may be oppressed because of the physical differences of race and gender. He can offer a sort of transcendence to those who may be confined to manual labor by showing that the education of the body through martial arts can bring liberation. Chan manipulates his own identity and can be admired by those who have difficulty mastering a similar fluidity. Like Hong Kong itself, Chan is sometimes Chinese, sometimes colonial, and always transnational. He can be chauvinistic and self-deprecating almost simultaneously. He can make fun of the powerful and identify with the status quo. He represents a postmodern figure of contingency, crisis, and alienation that belies any political certainty alluded to in his films. Ultimately, Chan concretizes contradictions played out globally within the postmodern and the postcolonial conditions, and he manages to profit from the fantasies spurs around racial otherness and the tenacious presence of its absence.

Notes

1. Fredric Jameson, "Postmodernism and Consumer Society," in Hal Foster, ed., *The Anti-Aesthetic: Essays on Postmodern Culture* (Port Townsend, WA: Bay Press, 1983), 123. This poem is quoted in its entirety by Jameson in "Postmodernism and Consumer Society" (121–2) and again in its entirety in a slightly different context in Fredric Jameson, *Postmodernism, or, The Cultural Logic of Late Capitalism* (Durham, NC: Duke University Press, 1991), 28–9. The poem was originally published in *Primer* (Berkeley: This Press, 1978).

2. Bill Brown, "Global Bodies/Postnationalities: Charles Johnson's Consumer Culture," *Representations* 58 (Spring 1997), 24–48. Charles Johnson, "China" (1983) in *The Sorcerer's Apprentice: Tales and Conjurations* (New York: 1987), 61–95.

3. Described by Frances Gateward in "Wong Fei Hong in Da House: Hong Kong Martial Arts Films and Hip Hop Culture," paper presented at Year 2000 and Beyond: History, Technology and Future of Transnational Chinese Film and TV—The Second International Conference on Chinese Cinema, Hong Kong Baptist University, April 20, 2000. Also, this has been my own personal observation of the American Cinema (Chinese owned and operated theater in L'Enfant Plaza in Washington, DC) as well as of the theaters that operated on the North Side in Chicago during the 1980s and New York City's Chinatown theaters during the same period. The clientele at that time was predominantly Chinese, but with a significant percentage of African-American and a lesser percentage of Hispanic and white viewers. I am also familiar with small grocers and merchants in the DC African-American community offering Shaw Brothers and Golden Harvest martial arts films for sale (sometimes under the counter along with X-rated videos).

4. Jackie Chan, *I Am Jackie Chan: My Life in Action*, with Jeff Yang (New York: Ballantine, 1999), 336.

5. Ibid., 253.

6. See Sheldon Lu, "Historical Introduction: Chinese Cinemas (1896–1996) and Transnational Film Studies," in Sheldon Hsiao-peng Lu, ed., *Transnational Chinese Cinemas: Identity, Nationhood, Gender* (Honolulu: University of Hawaii Press, 1997), 1–31.

7. David Desser, "The Kung Fu Craze: Hong Kong Cinema's First American Reception," in Poshek Fu and David Desser, eds, *The Cinema of Hong Kong: History, Arts, Identity* (New York: Cambridge University Press, 2000), 38.

8. Clouse has written about his experiences making the film in Robert Clouse, *The Making of Enter the Dragon* (Burbank: Unique, 1987). Clouse also went on to make *Black Belt Jones* (1974), a film that attempted again to exploit the connections between blaxploitation and the kung fu film. David Desser describes the role Warner Bros. played in marketing both blaxploitation and Hong Kong martial arts films in his essay, "The Kung Fu Craze."

9. This scene was eloquently described by Gayle Wald, "Same Difference: Reading Racial Masculinity in Recent Hong Kong/Hollywood Hybrids," Society for Cinema Studies Conference, Chicago, IL, March 10, 2000.

10. Marcia Chisholm was trained by Dennis Brown, one of the foremost promoters of Chinese martial arts in the Metro Washington, DC, area, known nationally for his annual tournament, the Capitol Classics. According to Master Brown, Marcia Chisholm was and still is a black belt with his school. Email correspondence dated June 13, 2000.

11. Bey Logan, *Hong Kong Action Cinema* (Woodstock, NY: Overlook Press, 1995), 73.

12. Although Chan had worked in the US previously, *Armour of God* represents his first major foray into international location shooting with himself at the helm as director. Shot primarily in Yugoslavia with Europeans in black face to represent African natives, the film is

perhaps best known for nearly occasioning Chan's premature death from a blow to the head during a stunt gone wrong.

13.   On the relationship between the Chinese diaspora and the legacy of European colonialism in Asia, see Lynn Pan, *Sons of the Yellow Emperor: A History of the Chinese Diaspora* (New York: Kodansha International, 1994).

14.   Lisa Lowe, *Immigrant Acts: On Asian American Cultural Politics* (Durham, NC: Duke University Press, 1996), 93–4.

15.   Gary Okihiro, *Margins and Mainstreams: Asians in American History and Culture* (Seattle: University of Washington Press, 1994).

16.   See my essay "Ethnicity, the Cinema, and Cultural Studies," in Lester Friedman, ed., *Unspeakable Images: Ethnicity and the American Cinema* (Urbana: University of Illinois Press, 1991), 277–307. For more on the Mississippi Chinese, see James W. Loewen, *The Mississippi Chinese: Between Black and White* (Prospect Heights, IL: Waveland Press, 1971).

17.   Chan, *I Am Jackie Chan*, 332.

18.   Carter is also presented as being sexist. He makes several smutty remarks to his colleague, Johnson (Elizabeth Pena), about her underwear and her sexual reputation. However, she never quite manages to get her own back in the same way as Lee.

19.   Other scholars have added other things, including religion, spirituality, family obligation, and a constant struggle for survival to this list. See Gateward, "Wong Fei Hong in Da House."

20.   Philip Snow, *The Scar Raft: China's Encounter with Africa* (Ithaca, NY: Cornell University Press, 1988), 211.

21.   Stuart M. Kaminsky in Thomas R. Atkins, ed., *Graphic Violence on the Screen* (New York: Simon and Schuster, 1976), 59.

22.   Attributed to Kaminsky by Peggy Chiao in Chiao Hsiung-Ping, "Bruce Lee: His Influence on the Evolution of the Kung Fu Genre," *Journal of Popular Film and Television* 9 (1) (1981), 3042.

23.   In Verin Glaessner, *Kung Fu: Cinema of Vengeance* (London: Lorrimer, 1974).

24.   Mick LaSalle, "Film Review—Chan Takes a Fall in 'Rumble': Weak Film Might Lose Potential US Viewers," *San Francisco Chronicle*, February 23, 1996.

25.   This information is left out of the re-dubbed version distributed by New Line.

26.   This again harkens back to *Return of the Dragon* in which Chuck Norris's whiteness as Colt, the fighter for hire, is emphasized in the fight he has with Lee in the Roman Colosseum when he takes off his shirt to reveal a hairy chest that proves his undoing when Lee rips the hair off his chest and blows it into the wind with a look of disgust during the battle.

27.   There has been a great deal of controversy in recent years surrounding a constellation of related issues involving Chinese identity in the diaspora, global Chinese ethnic ties, Confucianism, and so-called Asian values. Many of these positions have been put forward by Tu Wei-Ming and can be found outlined in his anthology, *The Living Tree: The Changing Meaning of Being Chinese Today* (Stanford: Stanford University Press, 1994). The concept of "Greater China" has a certain validity; however, when coupled with a resurgence of Confucianism linked with capitalism it takes on a more questionable aspect.

28.   Steve Fore, "Jackie Chan and the Cultural Dynamics of Global Entertainment," in Sheldon Hsiao-peng Lu, ed., *Transitional Chinese Cinemas: Identity, Nationhood, Gender* (Honolulu: University of Hawaii Press, 1997), 255.

29.   I have discussed elsewhere the relationship between working-class film and television fantasy and spectacles of destruction. See Marchetti, "Class, Ideology and Commercial Television: An Analysis of *The A-Team*," in Ian Angus and Sut Jhally, eds, *Cultural Politics*

in Contemporary America (New York: Routledge, 1989), 182–97. For more on class and the action genre, see Chuck Kleinhans, "Class in Action," in David E. James and Rock Berg, eds, *The Hidden Foundation: Cinema and the Question of Class* (Minneapolis: University of Minnesota Press, 1996), 240–63.

30. Yvonne Tasker, "Fists of Fury: Discourses of Race and Masculinity in the Martial Arts Cinema," in Harry Stecopoulos and Michael Uebel, eds, *Race and the Subject of Masculinities* (Durham, NC: Duke University Press, 1997), 334.

31. Mark Gallagher, "Masculinity in Translation: Jackie Chan's Transcultural Star Text," *The Velvet Light Trap* 39 (Spring 1997), 29.

32. Kwai-Cheung Lo, "Muscles and Subjectivity: A Short History of the Masculine Body in Hong Kong Popular Culture," *Camera Obscura* 39 (September 1996), 117.

33. Ramie Tateishi, "Jackie Chan and the Re-invention of Tradition," *Asian Cinema* 10 (1) (Fall 1998), 78–84.

34. For a detailed discussion of postmodernism and contemporary Hong Kong cinema, see Evans Chan, "Postmodernism and Hong Kong Cinema," *Postmodern Culture* 10 (1) (May 2000), http://www.muse.jhu.edu/journals/pmc/v010/10.3 html.

35. Quoted in the *Internet Movie Database*, http://us.imdb.com/Taglines?0120812.

36. Sheldon Lu, "Hong Kong Diaspora Film: From Exile to Wrong Love to Flexible Citizenship and Transnationalism," paper presented at Year 2000 and Beyond: History, Technology and Future of Transnational Chinese Film and TV—The Second International Conference on Chinese Cinema, Hong Kong Baptist University, April 19, 2000.

37. Lo, "Muscles and Subjectivity," 107.

38. Aihwa Ong, *Flexible Citizenship: The Cultural Logics of Transnationality* (Durham, NC: Duke University Press, 1999), 112.

39. W. E. B. Du Bois, *The Souls of Black Folk*, edited by Henry Louis Gates, Jr., and Terri Hume Oliver (New York: Norton, 1999), 11.

40. Frantz Fanon, *Black Skin, White Masks*, translated by Charles Lam Markmann (New York: Grove Press, 1967), 110–11.

41. Stuart Hall, "New Ethnicities," in David Morley and Kuan-Hsing Chen, eds, *Stuart Hall: Critical Dialogues in Cultural Studies* (London: Routledge, 1996), 447.

42. Ibid.

43. Bill Ashcroft, Gareth Griffiths, and Helen Tiffin, eds, *The Post-colonial Studies Reader* (London: Routledge, 1995), 117.

44. Frantz Fanon, *The Wretched of the Earth*, translated by Constance Farrington (New York: Grove, 1963).

45. Isaac Julien and Kobena Mercer, "De Margin and De Centre," in David Morley and Kuan-Hsing Chen, eds, *Stuart Hall: Critical Dialogues in Cultural Studies* (London: Routledge, 1996), 451.

46. This position is summarized in Kuan-Hsing Chen, "Post-Marxism: Between/Beyond Critical Postmodernism," in David Morley and Kuan-Hsing Chen, eds, *Stuart Hall: Critical Dialogues in Cultural Studies* (London: Routledge, 1996), 309–23.

47. Rey Chow and many others have pointed out that the "Orient" occupies a "feminized" space in Western discourse. See Rey Chow, *Woman and Chinese Modernity: The Politics of Reading between East and West* (Minneapolis: University of Minnesota Press, 1991).

48. The best-known critique of Jameson's conception of the Third World can be found in Aijaz Ahmad, "Jameson's Rhetoric of Otherness and the 'National Allegory,'" *Social Text* 17 (Fall 1987), 3–25. See also Jameson's response and an interview with Jameson by Anders Stephanson in the same issue.

49. Homi K. Bhabba, *The Location of Culture* (London: Routledge, 1994).

50. For some provocative thoughts on the Asian cooks that Chan models himself after in *Mr. Nice Guy*, see Phebe Shih Chao, "Gendered Cooking," *Jump Cut* 42 (December 1998), 19–27.

51. The details of Chan's relationship with New Line are outlined in Fore, "Jackie Chan." Later, Miramax picked up some of Chan's other films.

52. Many scholars have examined this connection in detail. See Cynthia Fuchs, "Slicin' Shit Like a Samurai: Hiphop, Martial Arts, and Marketing Styles," paper presented at the Society for Cinema Studies Conference, Chicago, IL, March 10, 2000; Gateward, "Wong Fei Hong in Da House; Grace Wang, "What's Asia Got to Do With It? Asian Sampling in Hip-Hop Culture," paper presented at the Association for Asian American Studies Conference, Tucson, AZ, May 2000.

68

Stories and Meanings

Sue Thornham & Tony Purvis*

2.1 Narrative

Theories of narrative

Narrative concerns the ways in which the *stories* of our culture are put together. The centrality of narrative to the study of culture and society is evidenced in the range of work in which narrative is considered pivotal. Structuralists such as Vladimir Propp, Tvetzan Todorov and Roland Barthes have emphasised the detailed study of narrative structures. Psychoanalytic approaches rely on narratives in order to interpret conscious and, more importantly, unconscious life. In Freudian and Lacanian clinical theory and practice, there is no past or unconscious without the stories which help this past to be understood. In the disciplines of genetics, history and medicine, narratives are associated with the method as well as with the object of research. Because 'narrative is such a fundamental cultural process', John Fiske suggests that 'it is not surprising that television is predominantly narrational in mode' (1987: 128).

Theories of narrative have become central – if often controversial – concerns in historical, political and scientific research. In the work of post-modern theorist and philosopher Jean-François Lyotard (1984), narrative has an *explanatory* function, providing a rationale for macro-global and micro-personal states of affairs. In some theories, gender and sex are understood primarily in relation to narrative. Ken Plummer's account observes how we all tell sexual stories (1995). And poststructuralist theorist Judith Butler sees gender and sex as linked to the conventions and performances of speech acts (1993, 1997). Marxist critic Alex Callinicos acknowledges that there is no sense of history without some form of narrative (1997: 44–76). And in recent postcolonial theory, there are no identities without a story which gives a sense of shape, space and time to the people who embody the identities in question (Homi Bhabha 1990). Narratives, as well as the *rhetoric* of narrative (its imagery, allusions and metaphors) allow the past to be understood (H. White 1975). Narratives can inform versions of the past and have the power to shape how the present might be understood in relation to them.

*Pp. 29–44, 183 (notes), and 188–204 (relevant refs) from S. Thornham and T. Purvis, *Television Drama* (London: Palgrave Macmillan). © 2005. Reprinted with permission from Palgrave Macmillan.

Stories and narratives *show* as well *tell of* the past. Without narrative, history becomes obscure, people less familiar, and space and time less clear. Narrative is not the past, and it does not make the past happen again. The BBC's *Dad's Army* is not the reliving of the Second World War; audiences do not live through the events of romantic-lesbian costume drama *Tipping the Velvet* (2002); and *The Buddha of Suburbia* (1993) is a reflection on, not a replication of, the 1970s. Nevertheless, narratives are the principal means by which the past is made intelligible in the present.

But narrative, because it is a human construction, and because it is something that is central to all social activity (we all tell stories), is also the principal means by which we understand the *present* time. 'Narrative is there', writes Roland Barthes, 'like life itself' (1977: 79). The understanding of the present also involves narrators and narratives. The fact that BBC Radio 4's *Today* is not quite the same as, for example, Radio 1's early-morning news bulletins, suggests that the events of *now* are presented to audiences in packaged and differently narrated (mediated) forms. Although 'live coverage' might give the illusion of seeing the events as they unfold, it is subject to processes of selection, editing, perspective, point of view, camera angle and institutional positioning. Two key dimensions of narrative, the syntagmatic and the paradigmatic,[1] mean that stories are placed in temporal sequences (syntagmatic selections) and located and peopled (paradigmatic selection) according to the demands of the genre and narrative aims. But these selections mean that live TV is never transparent or free of narrative conventions.

The claims of narrative

Before offering a summary of the elements in narrative structures,[2] we can note a number of key claims which have been made about narrative:

1. *Universality:* In 'Introduction to the Structural Analysis of Narrative' (1977), Barthes suggests that narratives are universal, common to all societies, and take many different forms (oral, visual, filmic, televisual, written).
2. *Local and global:* Lyotard (1984) contends that narratives offer subjects and societies accounts of global-international, as well as local-personal states of affairs. Macro-narratives can take the form of explanatory accounts of the world, and micro-narratives can provide individual subjects with a sense of place, purpose, and meaning. But he also suggests that metanarratives or grand explanations of human experience (for example religious accounts) are giving way to a plurality of postmodern micro-narratives (personal voices from the margins).
3. *Structure:* Narratives or stories give a sense of shape to subjects' identities. They provide a sense of a beginning, a middle, an end, with endless junctions in between these three major time points. Yet narrative structures, because they are human constructions, can oversimplify the complexity and plurality of social life. There are only beginnings, middles and ends on the basis of the imposition of narrative, as opposed to natural, conventions.
4. *Identity:* The work of Jacques Lacan, particularly his 'The Function and Field of Speech and Language' (1989 [1977]: 33–125), suggests that it is in language that

human subjects acquire a sense of identity. Although subjects always exceed narratives, language and narrative provide them with the means by which to make sense of identities. Yet the language of narrative can operate to undo identity, exposing its hybrid status.

5. *Diversity and difference:* No one narrative is able to contain the stories which make up a subject's personal, regional, national or international identities. Stuart Hall, drawing on deconstructive criticism, writes that 'identities are constructed through, not outside, difference' (2000: 17).

6. *Space, time and event:* The work of Edmund White (2001) and Michel de Certeau (1984) alludes to the ways metropolitan narratives and fictions give shape to how people live out their identities in space and time. Narratives are interested in the relations between time, space, sequence and causality. Yet narratives mean that events and time zones can be blurred, extended, reduced or ignored.

7. *Politics:* Postcolonial studies (Spivak 1987; Bhabha 1990; Said 1993) suggest that the 'universal' nature of narrative does not mean that stories are universal in their appeal. Some subjects are excluded, either by intention or by convention, from the narration of events. The lives of some are narrated more than the lives of others. Some events are given more prominence in certain narratives than in others.

8. *Form and Fictionality:* Stories are not natural structures so much as they are social constructions which operate in relation to a whole range of narrative strategies. Stories assume a narrator and require a number of devices to take shape. Narratives always tell us about other narratives.

9. *Meaning:* Narratives are one of the principal means by which meanings are articulated. Frank Kermode (1967) writes of the necessity of stories and fiction in the understanding and construction of human cultures. If narratives promise meaning, post-structuralist and deconstructive criticism (Derrida 1978, 1991; Butler 1993, 1997) suggests that within narratives meanings are also *de*constructed; narratives break many of their promises; they remain incomplete; they require readers/viewers to produce meanings.

10. *Context:* The work of Valentin Vološinov (1996 [1929]) and Mikhail Bakhtin (1981, 1986) emphasises that narratives are made meaningful in relation to social, cultural, economic, political and personal situations. Similarly, the spheres of the economic, the public and the cultural are made meaningful in narrative forms. Feminist, as well as reception-based studies, have drawn attention to the importance of text on context, and vice versa.

Forms and structures

Narrative, then, will concern a story and how that story is put together. But, as we have seen, this is not quite as self-evident as it might seem. Who tells the story (its *narrator(s)*) is distinct from the figure who wrote the story (its *author*). Within this basic scheme, further complications emerge. The author writes a story, but the readers and listeners are not the same ones who listen to or read the narrator's story. There will be an *addressee internal* to the narration (a *you* being addressed by the narrator), and an *addressee external* to the narration (an audience or reader), whose identity is never constant. This *literary* model is further complicated when it is mapped onto the study of television. Television does not use narrators as source of the narrative in the same way as novels. First- or third-person narrators in novels are usually more easily identified than their televisual equivalents. So camera angles, shots, sequences, and character perspectives will become important elements to identify in the television drama's narrative. Similarly, authors can be producers, institutions, scriptwriters, authors of a screenplay, and writing teams. Readers are viewers, listeners, audiences and researchers. Finally, if narratives aim at pleasure, as Barthes suggests, then these pleasures, too, are at some point encoded in the television narratives.

As with genre, much of the early work in the study of narrative is indebted to structuralist and formalist perspectives, particularly those associated initially with Ferdinand de Saussure (1974) Vladimir Propp (1968) and Tzvetan Todorov (1975, 1988), and later with Roland Barthes (1977) and Gérard Genette (1980). The more recent of these critics adopt an approach which pays attention to narrative in relation to how stories make *meanings* and how narratives operate to *encode* stories. Moreover, their work is interested in the impact that narrative structures have on the decoding of meaning. Barthes's work set out to highlight the details of the many components of meaning and narrative relations at work in texts. For Barthes, it is the narrative structures that give life and meaning to the text; and it is the text's internal dynamics, between plot, image and sequence, which connect with the text's systems of meaning.

Todorov's work helps us understand the dynamics of narrative structure. He proposes that all narratives operate according to a five-part structure, usefully deployed in the analysis of, for example, television police series, one-off dramas, and television science fiction. Beginning with what he refers to as *equilibrium*, a *disruptive* force destabilises the initial balance. This is followed by a recognition that the disordering event has taken place. Efforts are made at restoration, and a return to a different, as opposed to the same equilibrium, will be evident. This *resolution* indicates that *harmony* is restored. Whilst many genres no longer adhere to such straightforward or ideal structures, it can be seen that conflict and resolution inform many of the plots of popular genres or stories within genres. Much of the pleasure of soaps is their investment in climaxes, delays, deferrals and twists, which come between the beginning and the end of a story-line. Similarly, Vladimir Propp's categorisations of character (heroes, heroines, villains, fathers, helpers, donors, mentors) serve as labels in any schematic analysis of narrative and genre.

Further distinctions, especially those between the *content of the story* and its *shape* or *form*, are made by Vladimir Propp in his *Morphology of the Folk Tale* (1968). Propp dissected and analysed the narratives of Russian folk tales into different morphological functions and spheres of action, and his narratological analysis still stands as a key method in the study of many cultural texts. In addition to the division between the content and shape of a story, Propp considers some key elements of the relations between character and action in narrative. In Propp's model, character is interesting not for the insights it provides into human psychology so much as for its *role* and *function* in initiating and establishing action or event. Whilst Propp's dissection of folk tales has been criticised for its functionalism, the formalism that characterises it is also implicit in the later work of European structuralism.

During the 1960s and 1970s, French structuralist and narratologist Gérard Genette, recasting earlier narratological distinctions, proposed three terms: *histoire* (story), *récit* (text) and *narration*. In the words of Rimmon-Kenan, *story* 'designates the narrated events, abstracted from their disposition in the text and reconstructed in their chrono-logical order' (Rimmon-Kenan 1983: 3). *Text*, on the other hand, is 'spoken or written discourse which undertakes [the story's telling]' (ibid. 1983). In the text, 'events do not necessarily appear in chronological order . . . and all the items of the narrative content are filtered through some prism or perspective (focalizer)' (ibid.). *Narration* refers to 'the act or process of production' (ibid.). What these distinctions emphasise is that a story does not simply exist but is subjected to the formal changes imposed by a narrative (re)ordering of its elements, discussed in the analysis of *Tipping the Velvet* later in this section. Importantly, however, certain questions emerge for television studies: If nar-rative concerns *who* sees and tells the story's action, how is this realised in television?

'What', 'how' and 'who' in narrative

Genette's remains an important study of the analysis of narrative. He draws on a range of genres and shows how the key events of a story may be reordered by *narrative dis-course*. The same story can be narrated in multiple ways so that there is no reason why the narrative discourse must start at the story's 'beginning'. 'Flashback' is a frequent device of television drama. In some popular television narratives (e.g. soaps, comedies), notions of beginnings and ends are problematic, even more so when viewed against the backdrop of television's constant flow. In telling a story, the sequence of the events may be changed, some minor events may be omitted, or the story may be shown from mul-tiple as opposed to singular perspectives. BBC1 soap *EastEnders* famously had a number of versions for a story whose central element was the shooting of Phil Mitchell. The story, that Phil was shot, is not in doubt. *Who* shot him, *who* saw him being shot apart from soap's viewers, and *how* was this information divulged to audiences? These three questions indicate the appeal of narrative in popular drama.

Genette's work stresses the importance of *narrative position*, exploring how events narrated from one perspective are never quite the same when narrated from other posi-tions. As with genre, narrative orderings of stories are never neutral, involving processes such as selection, deselection, cuts and edits. Sarita Malik, for instance, considers ques-tions of selection in relation to the 'racialization of the black subject in television docu-mentary' during the 1960s (2002: 35). Her argument that Black citizens were represented as undesirable neighbours, people who would bring a neighbourhood into disrepute (ibid., 35–55), has important bearing on this current discussion of narrative and narra-tive position. The audience, she writes, 'was encouraged . . . to read "the problem" [Black neighbours] from a White perspective', because the story's positioning was with the white neighbours (ibid., 47). Malik's points emphasise the ways in which audiences may be implicated in the persuasive power of narrative.

These observations can be considered in relation to *Tipping the Velvet* (BBC2: October, 2002; based on the novel of the same name by Sarah Waters)[3]. The story concerns Nan, a young woman who falls in love with Kitty, an emerging music-hall star who is performing in Whitstable. Moving to London with Kitty and her manager, Nan realises that Kitty's feelings for her are not reciprocated. Nan instead finds love on the streets of London, first dressed as a man, and later living as a lesbian. The story as realised by the BBC is costume-based and draws heavily on the formulas and conventions of romance.

The distinctions between what, how and *who* narrates are not just matters of structural detail. Genette's notion of *narrating* is linked to 'who' narrates/tells the narrative. Who sees what happens, and are we invited to share their perspective? 'Who', then, can be thought of initially in terms of either (a) an *omniscient* or all-seeing perspective, or (b) a personal identity whose subjective perspective we share. Who audiences see and who they see *with* in narrative sequences such as those put together in *Tipping the Velvet* is thus of some importance, both in terms of *setting up* and *dismantling* identifications. To identify with an omniscient perspective is to share a different identity and position than if a perspective is limited to the gaze of a single character.

The audience's knowledge of any fictional world is, then, dependent on the telling of a story. Television drama both draws on and adapts the devices associated with written narrative fiction. Strategies such as voice-over, focalisation, montage, jump-cuts and long shots serve as visual replacements for techniques and strategies associated with fictional writing. In *Tipping the Velvet* the sense of an omniscient observer, or someone who can see the flow of the landscape at a glance, is achieved via the *establishing shots*, which present a picture of Whitstable. *Long shots* picture the coastline and more intimate *close-ups* introduce the characters who people this community.

The opening shots of the first episode immediately set up an opposition between this omniscient observer (represented by means of the silent long shots) and the first-person participant narrator (Nan). In order to generate the sense that audiences are accessing the public and the private spheres of Nan's world, the cameras use *eye-line shots*. In narrative fiction, a third-person narrator might represent the views and feelings of two characters in terms of their relations with each other. In television drama, eye-line shots perform the same function. In the opening two music hall scenes of Episode 1, the first shot shows Nan gazing at an object followed by a second shot in which audiences are shown the object of Nan's gaze, in this case Kitty. What is effective about eye-line shots is the way in which the first shot builds up a sense of anticipation and desire, and the second shot reveals the desired object. On the one hand, audiences 'share' Nan's view and subject position, and on the other, they are given the object of her gaze, the *other*. To 'share' Nan's view is not necessarily to agree with her or affirm her position. Rather, it is one of the ways in which television drama allows audiences to access the fictional reality and the dramatic action.

Barthes and the analysis of narratives

In his 'Introduction to the Structural Analysis of Narratives' (1977), Barthes details some of the key sequences and elements involved in the construction and reception of narrative. He makes clear that narrative and discourse, though not reducible to a 'sum of propositions' (1977: 85), are governed by units, rules and grammar (ibid., 82ff.). Like other analysts, he makes a key distinction between *what* happens (story) and *how* the happenings are represented (discourse). His work is considered here under five subdivisions.

1. *Information and action: vital and trivial:* Barthes distinguishes two kinds of action or information in narrative. What he refers to as '*nuclei*' or 'cardinal functions' (ibid., 93) are *essential* pieces of information and action, necessary to the progression of the plot. *Catalysers* are what we might call satellite actions or information, elements which fill the space 'with a host of trivial incidents or descriptions' (ibid., 94). The connections which are built up between nuclei are thus of considerable importance, though what may seem trivial elements should not be dismissed. Consider the key pieces of data surrounding the shooting of Phil Mitchell in *EastEnders* (nuclei) and contrast this with information which, whilst it might not ultimately change the key events, is nevertheless relevant to our understanding and pleasure. Discussion of the narrative along these lines will be concerned with questions of substitution (asking how the action might change if undertaken by another character) and transposition (considering how the action might be viewed if seen through the eyes of another character).

2. *No characters without an action?* In Aristotle's theory of narrative, 'there may be actions without "characters" ... but not characters without an action' (ibid., 104). Like Propp, Barthes considers characters not in terms of psychology but of the function, role or dramatic part they play in relation to narrative and plot actions (106–8). For Barthes, *character and action are inseparable*, the character all the time linked to a 'sphere of actions'. In *Tipping the Velvet*, the action is inseparable from the characters, principally Nan but including her family, her lovers, and how Nan perceives these relations.

3. *Reader–narrative relations:* The third level is narration itself (109). This part of Barthes's work is principally interested in the relations which the text sets up between producer (author, writer) and consumer (reader, viewer, spectator). In this third level of structural analysis, Barthes observes how the author, narrator and characters must not be confused or blurred as one entity. Fictional narratives are not dealing with real people but 'paper beings' (111), understood within the parameters set up by the narrative itself. That said, the world of nineteenth-century London as recreated in *Tipping the Velvet* is understood on the basis of Nan, and on the basis of her credibility as 'real' as opposed to her 'paper' status.

4. *Meanings:* The functions, actions and narration of the story and its discourse are not *outside* of society, even though characters and actions are fictional. 'Narration can only receive its meaning from the world which makes use of it' (115), writes Barthes. No fictional narrative is wholly separate from the realities of the world in which the narrative circulates. And Barthes is in no doubts about the *political* and *ideological* zones in which narratives operate: 'Beyond the narrational level begins the world, other systems (social, economic, ideological) whose terms are no longer simply narratives but elements of a different substance (historical facts, determination, behaviors, etc.)' (115).

5. *Seeing:* In the final section of Barthes's analysis, he discusses the 'system of narrative' (117). The language of narrative serves the purposes of *articulation* (the joining and linking of actions) and *segmentation* (the separation and unlinking of actions). In narrative, he argues, actions and events 'may be separated by a long series of insertions belonging to quite different functional spheres' (119). He refers to this distance as the difference between *logical* and *real* time. Narrative 'does not show, does not imitate', argues Barthes (124). Narrative is not transparent; we do not 'see anything'.

This last observation of Barthes – that we do not 'see' in narrative – might seem odd: television is principally a visual and acoustic medium. However, Barthes's point is important. Television, though a 'visual' medium, does not picture the world in any straightforward sense. Rather, narrative offers meanings, codes and frameworks, and through its language (its systems of signs, images and internal references) narrative, in appearing to point to an external world, offers an interpretation of it. Television drama, then, is one way of 'seeing' the 'truth' of a story, but the story might well have been told as a documentary or as a news item. These problems of realism and reality in television are discussed in the final section of this chapter.

Narrative complexities

Barthes's work sets out to highlight the details of the many components of meaning and narrative relations at work in texts. For Barthes, it is the narrative structures which give life and meaning to the text; and it is the text's internal relations, between plot, image and sequence, which connect with the text's systems of meaning.

Barthes is keen to stress that there is a connection between narrative and meaning on the one hand, and what, on the other hand, is referred to in later sections of *Image-Music-Text* as freedom and *jouissance* ([sexual] *pleasure*). But he stresses that narrative offers a limited freedom (1977: 123). Narrative's dual operations, its enabling and constraining dimensions, are taken up in the early work of Stuart Hall. The work of Hall (1973) and David Morley (1980) expands Barthes's model, showing how meanings encoded by producers are never simply decoded in any one way. Whilst these 'dominant' or preferred readings can never be ignored, there may be other readings which resist, contest or misinterpret the encoders' 'intention' as it is realised in the programme. The programme or narrative is subject to revisions which connect the decoding *context* of viewers with the encoded text.

However, during the period in which Hall and Morley were outlining and expanding their theoretical models, other observations about the function of television programmes reveal a growing concern about the negative impact of narrative. During the 1970s, B. N. Colby and N. M. Peacock (in John Honigman's *Handbook of Social and Cultural Anthropology*, 1973) expressed concerns about the *seductive* power of narrative. 'The subtle and undercover techniques of narrative as art, which do not obviously aim to control, may seduce people into letting their guard down', they write (Honigman 1973: 633). And they suggest that the 'rise of the mass media, which lend themselves more to stories than sermons' (ibid.), may well increase this power. Television's popular narratives are feared, then, for their seductive power: they 'might well assume increasingly important roles in social control' (ibid.).

During the 1980s, concerns about narrative were understood in relation to formulas, rituals and predictability. Sarah Kozloff's essay, 'Narrative Theory and Television' (1992: 67–100), notes some of the trends in American television narratives. She catalogues how the stress on formula and predictability limits narratives. Combined with appealing, pleasant, but standardised characters, functional settings, and narrative strategies which attempt to *naturalise* the discourse, narratives contain few if any surprises. She argues that American television functions like the fairytales analysed by Propp, where subject matter, situations and stereotypical characterisations have a nearly universal appeal (70–7). In the earlier version of her essay, she adds that it seems 'popular cultural forms are more rigidly patterned and formulaic than works of "high art"' (in Allen 1987: 49).[4]

Anxieties about narrative are often related to questions of their effects on audiences, particularly their power to convince audiences of one reality above another. John Corner writes of the 'negative psychological, social, and political consequences often attributed to television narrative form' (1999: 50). He suggests that narrative structure in television 'frequently seduces the viewer into aesthetic relations with what is on screen (e.g. the pleasures of character, of setting, and of action' in ways which 'reduce critical distance' (ibid., 51). Narrative, he suggests, can oversimplify complexity, 'bringing into spurious unity what are more properly regarded as diverse elements of an issue' (ibid.). Finally, he contends that 'certain perspectives on events and circumstances depicted are given an epistemological privileging while others are subordinated, marginalized, or excluded' (ibid.). 'Engagement with the story and its characters entails a degree of alignment, however temporary, with dominant viewpoints' (ibid.).

There is no doubt that narrative is powerful. The mainstream narratives associated with the classic realist text, are often criticised for encouraging audience identification. Commentaries, often by way of letters to newspaper editors, suggest that identification with fictional characters in fiction and popular fantasies reduces 'critical distance': the world of the text, narrative or genre passes itself off as the only version of reality. Narrative can *seem* totalising, and observations about its liberatory potential ignore the ways in which narratives exploit identities. Soap operas, for instance, seem to offer no beginning or end and locate audiences in a permanent present. Despite differences amongst television dramas, standardisation is required because institutions, and not writers, set the terms of how the narrative will be put together for broadcast. Story-lines may be read in the same way, regulated by the form and not the readers or audiences.

The preceding arguments typify some of the criticisms of popular television narrative, and they have informed the research questions of a number of ethnographic studies that have sought to understand the relations between narrative, media form and audiences. Focus in this section, however, is placed on the extent to which the text itself is the site of its own deconstruction. Reader–audience relations are central to any deconstructive practice. Some evidence seems to suggest that texts themselves are never quite as formulaic or as overdetermining as the aforementioned criticism seems to imply.

Ien Ang's *Watching Dallas* (1985) shows how the American soap opera Ang discusses produces not uncritical readers, but ones who see in the television narrative a huge irony, something which opens itself up to mockery, and something which exposes rather than naturalises the workings of American capitalism during the 1980s. All texts can be read ironically, but the responses which Ang received in relation to her work suggest that any preferred reading the _Dallas_ narrative might seem to demand was undercut by the text's implicit irony. Moreover, those groups who expressed 'hatred' for _Dallas_ must surely count among those for whom the narrative was a seduction; the hatred must have been caused by something. If fantasy and narrative, writes Ang, do not 'function in place of, but beside, other dimensions of life (social practice, moral or political consciousness)' (1985: 135), then this seems to imply that texts – of all narrative kinds – are far less seductive and far more _provisional_ in terms of their use, interpretation and circulation than criticism has suggested.[5]

The contradictions of the text (its narrative silences, its absences and its confusions) are discussed in the work of theorist Pierre Macherey (1978). He suggests, like Barthes, that texts are not secret puzzles, which contain final meanings. All texts, because of their very constructed status (in signs, images, visualisations), are read in terms of the permeable nature of these signs and not in terms of the centring hold of the author-producer. In all texts, Macherey argues, there is a 'conflict'. The conflict is not a sign of the text's 'imperfection' so much as it is evidence that the text, contrary to appearances, is 'generated from the incompatibility of several meanings' (1978: 80) What the text leaves unsaid, its 'unconscious', can in the reader's hands generate meanings. Rather than effacing ideology, narrative texts reveal its contradictions.

Television's narratives promote some versions of culture rather than others. Later chapters discuss how gender, race and sexuality have been represented. If we return, however, to Malik's observations about the representation of Black subjects in British documentaries of the 1960s, we can see that whilst they point to the dominant readings of 'race', she is also clear that these were being contested – albeit very slowly – inside and outside the media. The 'media space which Black people could potentially occupy', she writes, 'although highly regulated, had to be regarded as a significant site of struggle' (2002: 50). The television text is not a seamless whole able to _impose_ its narrative so much as it is composed of competing – and often contradictory – elements.

Narrative contradictions

This section concludes with a reading of _Tipping the Velvet_, where consideration is given to the ways in which all narratives set up their own contradictions. Although identification with narrators or characters might seem to offer the key means of entering the fictional world of narrative, the text's own narrative serves to deconstruct its naturalising appeal. Narratives, far from seducing audiences, set up more problems than they appear to solve.

The opening sequences of _Tipping the Velvet_ employ a series of _jump-cuts_, where the editing creates a break so that the time and/or space is discontinuous. Continuity is provided by Nan's voice-over. She appears to prepare audiences for what is to be an intimate account of life in a fishing village. The scene is set for a romantic costume drama. Nan appears to ensure for herself a central place in the drama as its narrator and focaliser, someone with whom the audience will identify. In the opening three minutes, voices, songs, facial images, silences, blurrings of scenes, slow motion and dramatic anticipation establish that the space and time of the narrative are on one level uniquely the possession of Nan. They seem to ensure that it will be through Nan that audiences gain knowledge of this fictional world.

However, Nan and her story are only singular and unique when viewed alongside the multiple other narratives that compete with the story told in *Tipping the Velvet*. Insofar as the period being dramatised is set in the past, then Nan's story is a way of re-viewing and re-thinking this past, and understanding the culture of its subjects. A reading that attends to the text's reworking of the past might be interested in the text's historical accuracy far more than Nan's identity. But how accurate is this past if its central focus is not the nineteenth century but an account of lesbian sexual cultures? The 'accuracy' of the text's historical setting, moreover, is problematised by the impressionistic and surreal style of this BBC romance. The text's accuracy is in part reliant on, but also problematised by Nan. She is not in a position to 'see' everything. In identifying with Nan, audiences must now accept a limited and not a comprehensive insight into this fictional world. *Identification* with Nan also assumes *identifying* with her lesbian desires at some point. Even if this is also a narrative which describes nineteenth-century sexual cultures, is not any perspective a limited one? Identification with Nan on the basis of her views and motivations necessarily entails limitation: she is only *one* character in the narrative.

The drama's initial stress on identity (audiences learn fairly quickly that Nan is 'lesbian')[6] means that the costume-drama genre or historical periodisation might be less important than the sexuality and same-sex passion which the three episodes depict. Apart from anything else, Nan is only ever understood in the intersubjective field upon which the narrative relies. From the outset, this is a narrative which builds up an identity (Nan) only to make identification with her increasingly difficult.

Over-the-shoulder and point-of-view shots seem to ensure that audiences will feel and think from Nan's perspective. When Nan looks out from the carriage to the London buildings and streets, audiences 'see' Nan's view, almost as if looking over her shoulder. But Nan, now fast changing into the 'Tom' of Episode 2, wanders the streets dressed as a man; shots of Nan-Tom walking though London streets are mixed with Nan's voice-over commentary, but this is now a commentary which seems detached from the drama's 'real-time' action. With whom do audiences now identify? Which *characters* (Tom, Nan or the voice-over) seduce the audience? Are we seduced by a *lesbian* or a *rent boy*? Is the seducer finally a seductress, a disembodied voice, or the institution which made the programme?

These questions are not meant to trivialise how narrative identifications occur or to undermine critical work which stresses the degree to which narratives may seek to impose a particular world-view. But they do show how the text itself establishes its own difficulties. As the work of Barthes and Foucault shows, the text's formal features are themselves bound up with ideologies, histories and myths that are never neutral. But the particular inflections and emphases of the text's form (its signifiers) are always unstable, never able to contain a final meaning. Postcolonial theorist Gayatri Spivak, influenced by Marxist, feminist and deconstructive criticism, has suggested that all texts rely on metaphors or connections which also point to the gaps and fissures in the text.

These gaps are as important as the apparent closures to which the text might seem to lead because they take readers and audiences in plural as opposed to singular directions. 'In the process of deciphering a text . . . we come across a word that seems to harbour an unresolvable contradiction', she writes (Spivak 1976: lxxvii). In attempting to locate or fix meaning, Spivak argues, we find only further 'concealment' 'self-transgression' and 'undecidability' (ibid.) Thus in all acts of decoding, audiences attempt to stabilise what a text means on the basis of gaps it leaves. Whilst audiences may exercise determination in the construction of meaning, this is always in relation to a text which is unable to establish its own completion.[7]

Tipping the Velvet, then, can be read as a costume drama, a historical romance, a story about women who love other women, a narrative about a history which has often been hidden from dominant accounts of Victorian Britain, or an account of middle-class and working-class lives in late-nineteenth-century England. Using formalist methods, we can analyse it in terms of story, discourse and narration. Judgements about narrative structures, as Barthes observes, also concern questions of viewer–narrative relations and meaning. Television narratives visualise and construct meanings, and they do so in relation to historical, social and political context. Finally we can note that they also solicit pleasures: of watching, of listening and of understanding. Some of these may function to confirm our sense of our own and society's identity. Others, however, may lead us in very different directions: towards unexpected identifications and unanswered questions.

Notes

1. See Fiske (1987: 128–30).
2. See summaries included in the work of Graeme Burton (2000), Patricia Holland (1997), Nick Lacey (2000) and James Watson (1998).
3. Closer comparisons of form can be achieved by comparing Waters's written text with the BBC version.
4. For a detailed breakdown of Kozloff's model, see Burton (2000: 116–17).
5. See Tony Bennett and Janet Woollacott's *Bond and Beyond* (1987), which considers how popular narrative fiction may or may not have seduced readers and film-goers into thinking that the 'figure of Bond' is 'a popular hero' (1987: 1).
6. 'Lesbian' is itself contentious to the degree that it is primarily a twentieth-century identity category.
7. Worries over agency in any act of reading or viewing are discussed by Nelson (1997: 2–3). However, the text itself can be seen to raise problems which incite agency or acts of interpretation.

References

Allen, R. C. (ed.) (1987). *Channels of Discourse*. London and New York: Routledge.
Ang, I. (1985). *Watching Dallas*. London: Methuen.
Bakhtin, M. M. (1981). *The Dialogic Imagination: Four Essays*, trans. C. Emerson and M. Holquist. Austin: University of Texas Press.

Bakhtin, M. M. (1986). *Speech Genres and Other Late Essays*, trans. V. W. McGee, ed. C. Emerson & M. Holquist. Austin: University of Texas Press.

Barthes, R. (1977). *Image—Music—Text*, trans. S. Heath. London: Fontana.

Bennett, T. & J. Woollacott (1987). *Bond and Beyond*. London: Macmillan.

Bhabha, H. (ed.) (1990). *Nation and Narration*. London: Routledge.

Burton, G. (2000). *Talking Television: An Introduction to the Study of Television*. London: Edward Arnold.

Butler, J. (1993). *Bodies That Matter: On the Discursive Limits of Sex*. New York and London: Routledge.

Butler, J. (1997). *The Psychic Life of Power: Theories in Subjection*. Stanford, CA: Stanford University Press.

Callinicos, A. (1997). *Theories and Narratives: Reflections on the Philosophy of History*. Cambridge: Polity Press.

Corner, J. (1999). *Critical Ideas in Television Studies*. Oxford: Oxford University Press.

De Certeau, M. (1984). *The Practice of Everyday Life*. Berkeley, CA: University of California Press.

Derrida, J. (1978). *Writing and Difference*, trans. A. Bass. London: Routledge & Kegan Paul.

Derrida, J. (1991). 'Différence.' In: P. Kamuf (ed.), *A Derrida Reader: Between the Blinds*. New York: Columbia University Press.

Fiske, J. (1987). *Television Culture*. London: Methuen.

Genette, G. (1980). *Narrative Discourse*. Ithaca, NY: Cornell University Press.

Hall, S. (1973). *Encoding and Decoding in the Television Discourse*, Occasional Paper no. 7. Birmingham: CCCS.

Hall, S. (2000). Who Needs 'Identity'? In: P. du Gay, I. Evans & P. Redman (eds.), *Identity: A Reader*, pp. 15–30. London: Sage.

Holland, P. (1997). *The Television Handbook*. London: Routledge & Kegan Paul.

Honigman, J. (ed.) (1973). *Handbook of Social and Cultural Anthropology*. Chicago, IL: Rand McNally.

Kermode, F. (1967). *The Sense of an Ending: Studies in the Theory of Fiction*. London: Oxford University Press.

Kozloff, S. R. (1992). Narrative Theory and Television. In: R. C. Allen (ed.), *Channels of Discourse, Reassembled*, pp. 67–100. London: Routledge & Kegan Paul.

Lacan, J. (1989). *Écrits: A Selection* [1977], trans. A. Sheridan. London and New York: Routledge.

Lacey, N. (2000). *Narrative and Genre: Key Concepts in Media Studies*. Basingstoke: Palgave Macmillan.

Lyotard, J.-F. (1984). *The Postmodern Condition: A Report on Knowledge*. Manchester: Manchester University Press.

Macherey, P. (1978). *A Theory of Literary Production*. London: Routledge & Kegan Paul.

Malik, S. (2002). *Representing Black Britain: Black and Asian Images on Television*. London: Sage.

Morley, D. (1980). *The "Nationwide" Audience*. London: British Film Institute.

Nelson, R. (1997). *TV Drama in Transition: Forms, Values and Cultural Change*. Basingstoke: Palgrave Macmillan.

Plummer, K. (1995). *Telling Sexual Stories: Power, Change and Social Worlds*. London and New York: Routledge & Kegan Paul.

Propp, V. (1968). *Morphology of the Folktale*. Austin: University of Texas Press.

Rimmon-Kenan, S. (1983). *Narrative Fiction: Contemporary Poetics*. London: Routledge & Kegan Paul.

Said, E. (1993). *Culture and Imperialism*. London: Chatto & Windus.

Saussure de, F. (1974). *Course in General Linguistics*. London: Fontana/Collins.

Spivak, G. C. (1976). Translator's Preface. In: Jacques Derrida, *Of Grammatology*, pp. ix–lxxxvii. Baltimore, MD: Johns Hopkins University Press.

Spivak, G. C. (1987). *In Other Words: Essays in Cultural Politics*. London: Routledge & Kegan Paul.

Todorov, T. (1975). *The Fantastic: A Structural Approach to a Literary Genre*, trans. R. Howard. Ithaca, NY: Cornell University Press.

Todorov, T. (1988). The Typology of Detective Fiction. In: D. Lodge (ed.), *Modern Criticism and Theory: A Reader*, pp. 137–44. New York: Longman.

Vološinov, V. N. (1996). *Marxism and the Philosophy of Language* [1929], trans. L. Matejka and I. T. Titunik. Cambridge, MA and London: Harvard University Press.

Watson, J. (1998). *Media Communication: An Introduction to Theory and Process*. Basingstoke: Palgrave Macmillan.

White, E. (2001). *The Flâneur*. London: Bloomsbury.

White, H. (1975). *Metahistory*. Baltimore, MD: Johns Hopkins University Press.

Teaching Us to Fake It: The Ritualized Norms of Television's "Reality" Games

Nick Couldry*

Whatever its contribution to the overblown claims of semiotics as a general "science" of language, Roland Barthes's analysis of "myth" and its connection to ideology remains useful as a specific tool to understand particular types of media language such as advertising and also that most striking of recent phenomena, reality TV.[1] Myth itself, Ernesto Laclau has argued, is increasingly a requirement of contemporary societies whose divisions and dislocations multiply.[2] If so, reality TV's mythical claim to represent an increasingly complex social space – for example, in the largely entertainment mode of the gamedoc or reality game show – may have significance far beyond the analysis of the television genre. I will make this assertion more precise by considering reality TV's ritual dimensions and their link to certain media-centric norms of social behavior.

The idea underlying reality TV is hardly new. Here is the television anchor who commented on the 1969 Apollo moon touchdown speaking three decades ago: "[Television's] real value is to make people participants in ongoing experiences. Real life is vastly more exciting than synthetic life, and this is real-life drama with audience participation."[3] This notion – and the associated claim of television to present real life – does not disappear in the era of television "plenty," but rather comes under increasing pressure to take new forms.[4] The subgenre of gamedocs on which I will concentrate is a later adaptation to those pressures, succeeding an early wave of docusoaps and television verité in the mid-1990s, and a usbsequent crisis of many docusoaps' documentary authority because of scandals about fake productions – for example, over Carlton TV's documentary *The Connection* (1999), which supposedly uncovered an operation for sumuggling drugs from Colombia, but was alleged by the London *Guardian* to have faked various scenes.[5] But if the gamedoc signifies a shift to a "postdocumentary" television culture, the result is not an abandonment of reality claims but their transformation.[6] As John Corner puts it in regard to the first British series of *Big Brother*, "*Big Brother* operates its claims to the real within a fully managed artificiality, in which almost everything that might be deemed to be true about what people do and say is necessarily and

* Pp. 57–74 from *Reality TV: Remaking Television Culture*, ed. S. Murray and L. Ouellette (New York: New York University Press). © 2004 by New York University. Reprinted with permission of the author and New York University Press.

obviously predicated on the larger contrivance of them being there in front of the camera in the first place."[7]

My interest here is less in the gamedoc as generic form (excellently discussed by Corner), but in the wider social process that gamedocs constitute. At stake in these often much-hyped programs is a whole way of reformulating the media's (not just television's) deep-seated claim to present social reality, to be the "frame" through which we access the reality that matters to us as social beings.[8] in the gamedoc, this involves the promotion of specific norms of behavior to which those who court popularity by living in these shows' constructed spaces must conform.

To get analytic purchase on this complex process, the term "myth" by itself is too blunt. Instead, we need the more precise notions of "ritual" and "ritualization" that can link the television form to the wider issues of authority and governmentality.[9] Most contemporary self-performance can, as Gareth Palmer notes, be interpreted in light of Michel Foucault's theory of governmentality, whereby power is reproduced through norms not just of control but also of expression and self-definition. I want, however, to push further than Palmer does the implications of the fact that in gamedocs, "what develop[s is] not so much a self [as] a *media self*."[10]

What is this media self? What is its social status, and what are its social consequences? To link gamedocs to governmentality is not enough since all contemporary social space is in this sense governed by norms that regulate what is acceptable, meaningful, and pleasurable, and what is not. We need also to ask: Are gamedocs such as *Big Brother* spaces for reflecting on governmentality shared by performers and audiences alike, or spaces for audiences to reflect on governmentality by watching others (the performers) being governed, or finally, a process whereby both performers and audiences are in effect governed through the unreflexive naturalization of particular behavioral norms?[11]

The Ritual Space of the Reality Game Show

What might we mean by the ritual properties of television forms such as the gamedoc?[12]

Ritual action and media form

First, it is important to emphasize that by ritual, I mean more than habitual actions. While much of gamedocs *does* consist of rituals in this commonsense use of the term (as people get up, eat, wash up, chat, and sleep for the cameras), this use adds nothing to the idea of habit. Instead, I am interested in the two more substantive anthropological senses of ritual: as formalized action; and as action (often, but not necessarily formalized) associated with certain transcendent values.

The first sense captures how certain action-patterns are not only repeated but organized in a form or shape that has a meaning over and above any meaning of the actions taken by themselves. So putting a ring on a finger in the context of a wedding signifies the act of marriage, and putting a wafer in a mouth, again in a specific context and not elsewhere, signifies the act of Holy Communion. The leading theorist of ritual, the late Roy Rappaport, defined ritual as "the performance of more or less invariant sequences of formal acts and utterances *not entirely encoded* by the performers" – ritual action, in other words, is always more than it seems.[13] In the second sense of the term, less emphasis is placed on the formality of actions and more on the kinds of values with which those actions are associated. In a line of argument that goes back to the great French sociologist Émile Durkheim's *Elementary Forms of Religious Life*, many have seen in ritual action an affirmation of the values underlying the social bond itself that's more important than its exact formal properties.[14]

When I talk of media rituals, I want to combine aspects of these two senses. From the formal analysis of ritual, I want to take the idea that rituals can reproduce the building blocks of belief without involving any explicit content that is believed. Far from every ritual expressing a hidden essence in which the performers explicitly believe, rituals by their repetitive form reproduce categories and patterns of thought in a way that *bypasses* explicit belief. On the contrary, if made explicit, many of the ideas apparently expressed by ritual might be rejected, or at least called into question; it is their *ritualized* form that enables them to be successfully reproduced without being exposed to questions about their "content." This is useful in understanding how ritual works in relation to media, where quite clearly, there is no explicit credo of shared beliefs about media to which everyone signs up. From the transcendent account of ritual, I want to take the idea that there is an essential link between ritual and certain social values, or at least certain large *claims* about the social. As I have argued elsewhere, there is a striking similarity between the socially oriented values (our sense of what binds us as members of a society) that underlie Durkheim's sociology of religion and the types of claims that media, even now, implicitly make about their power to represent "the social."[15]

Media rituals are actions that reproduce the myth that the media are our privileged access point to social reality, yet they work not through articulated beliefs but the boundaries and category distinctions around which media rituals are organized. Let us adopt the following working definition: media rituals are formalized actions organized around key media-related categories and boundaries whose performances suggest a connection with wider media-related values.[16]

What aspects of the gamedoc process would count as media rituals under this definition? One example would be the "ceremony" developed in the British version of *Big Brother* on each night when a housemate is evicted. Once the result of the week's popular vote has been announced to the inmates by live link from the *Big Brother* studio, the evictee is given one hour exactly to get their baggage ready. With one minute to go, the lead presenter, Davina McColl, walks live from the studio across the barrier to the house. The door to the house is opened and the evictee emerges, clutching belongings, usually to the cheers of supporters in the crowd outside. From the house door, McColl leads the evictee, as they take in the adulation of the crowd, back to the studio for a live interview, where the evictee is asked to reflect on their time in the house.

This weekly pattern has been repeated in each British *Big Brother* series until the series' final week, when the last inmate leaves the house as the winner. In its regularity, we have a clever simulation of other forms of television ceremonial. But it is not the formalization that I have most in mind in calling this a media ritual; rather, it is the way the whole sequence is based around a fundámental boundary between "ordinary person" and "media person" – in other words, around the media-value celebrity.[17] A basic point of *Big Brother* is to enact a transition for each housemate from ordinary person to media person; the eviction ceremony is designed to make that transition seem natural (natural as television event, that is). The "celebrification process" in *Big Brother* is obvious to everyone, both performers and viewers, even though far from transparent in its details and exclusions.[18] But its significance is greater, since underlying the idea that the house-mates become celebrities is another more basic media value: that being in the *Big Brother* house is somehow more significant than being outside the house. In short, mediated reality is somehow "higher" or more significant than nonmediated reality – which as I have maintained elsewhere, is the value that underlies the legitimation of media institutions' general concentration of symbolic power.[19] Kate Lawler, the winner of the third series of *Big Brother* (hereafter BB₃), in her reactions to her final hour in the house, vividly enacted the boundary and hierarchy between media and nonmedia "worlds." She cried and seemed overawed by the transition from the apparently private, though of course intensely mediated world of the *Big Brother* house to the explicitly mediated world outside with its cheering crowds and press flashbulbs. When McColl came to interview her *inside* the house (on the series' final night, the winner gets to be inter-viewed inside the house, where only they have earned the right to stay), Lawler had difficulty speaking. She acted starstruck in front of McColl (who in Britain, is a minor celebrity in her own right because of *Big Brother*). McColl gave Lawler the standard phrase used by fans on meeting their idol: "No, it's me who can't believe I'm sitting here with *you*" (BB₃, 26 July 2002).

At this point, I want to shift the focus to the related concept of ritualization. For it is in the dynamic relationship between the ritual high points of, say, *Big Brother* and the wider process of ritualizing the often banal actions in the *Big Brother* house that we find the best entry-point to the social, not merely textual, process that gamedocs constitute.

Acting "up" for the cameras

Media rituals cannot, any more than rituals in general, be studied in isolation from the larger hinterland of ritualization: that is, the whole gamut of patterns of action, thought, and speech that generate the categories and boundaries on which media rituals are based. It is this hinterland of everyday action that makes the special case of media rituals possible.

As the anthropologist Catherine Bell contends in her study of religious ritual, ritu-alization organizes our movements around space, helps us to experience constructed features of the environment as real, and thereby reproduces the symbolic authority at stake in the categorizations on which ritual draws.[20] The background ritualizations that underlie media rituals work in a similar way, through the organization of all sorts of actions around key media-related categories ("media person/thing/place/world," "liveness," "reality").[21]

The term ritualization is our way of tracing how rituals connect to power; for media rituals, the link in question is to the increasing organization of social life around media centers. Drawing again on Bell, we must study how

the orchestrated construction of power and authority in ritual . . . engage[s] the social body in the objectification of oppositions and the deployment of schemes that effectively reproduce the divisions of the social order. In this objectification lie the resonance of ritual and the consequences of compliance.[22]

In principle, this could lead us from the celebrification rituals of *Big Brother* to the mass of actions whereby all of us contribute to celebrity culture (buying celebrity magazines, for example). But with gamedocs, there is also a tighter link between ritual and ritualization: What are the nine weeks in the *Big Brother* house if not a space of ritualization, where inmates' banal, everyday routines are tested for their appropriateness to a mediated space?

If rituals are naturalized, stable forms for reproducing power relations, ritualization is the much wider process through which the categories underlying those power relations *become* naturalized in action, thought, and words. The raw material of ritualization is much more liable to be destabilized by doubt, reflexivity, and correction. The action in the BB3 house reflected similar instabilities, as various inmates thought about leaving the house voluntarily (see below). A particular focus in BB3 was inmates' mutual accusations of performing to the cameras and the anxious denials that resulted. It could be argued, of course, that all this was part of BB3's developing plot and entertainment value, but we see below how, on the contrary, this issue opened up conflicts among inmates, and between inmates and the show's producers, about the norms of behavior in the house – conflicts that could not be contained within BB3 as a "game."

Gamedocs and real "experience"

One of the words most frequently used by BB3 contestants was "experience": they wanted to make the most of the *Big Brother* experience, they were asked how their experience in the house had gone when they left, and so on. Although hardly a simple word to disentangle, experience connotes something both significant and real, and usually something *more* significant and real than the everyday run of things. But since the conditions of the *Big Brother* house made it exceptional from the start, there was always a tension: Was the *Big Brother* experience significant because it was exceptional, or was it significant because however exceptional it seemed, it showed something important about the underlying continuities of human nature? Such ambiguities are the very stuff of myth in Barthes's sense.[23]

Yet however ambiguous the claims of *Big Brother* and other gamedocs to represent reality, without *some* such claim their status – as shows that make celebrities out of real ordinary people – collapses. Every gamedoc has a specific myth about how it represents the social world. A number of British shows rely on the myth that in the face of extreme physical challenges, especially those requiring team collaboration (however artificially constructed), an important aspect of human reality is shown. This is the myth

underpinning *Survivor* (Canton TV, 2000), an international format less successful in
Britain than *Big Brother*, perhaps because it is less obviously aimed at a stereotypical,
"young" audience (having some middle-aged contestants, and much less emphasis on
celebrity and sex), although arguably the almost comic exoticism of *Survivor's* British
version (with its tribal gatherings and the like) undermines its wider reality claim in any
case.[24]

In *Castaway* 2000, a failed variant on the *Survivor* theme produced for the millennial
year (BBC1, 2000), thirty-five people were put onto Taransay, a deserted island just off
the coast of the Hebridean island of Harris, for one year to see how they would survive.
Taransay is, in fact, in full view of one of the most beautiful beaches in Scotland
(I know because I holiday on Harris myself), so its claim to present a controlled experiment in genuine isolation was strained from the outset. Still, the program's mythical
intent was clear from its opening voice-over:

> *Castaway* 2000 is a unique experiment to discover what happens when a group representa-
> tive of British society today is stranded away from modern life. On the deserted Scottish
> island of Taransay, they'll have a year to decide how to run the community, devise new
> ways of living together, and reflect on what aspects of life are really important in the 21st
> century.[25]

Other recent experiments have sought to mine the old myth of "human nature" even
further. *The Experiment* (BBC2, 2002, with a subsequent US version) offered a reworking by two psychologists of the well-known US 1970s "Prisoner" experiment, which
had pitted two selected groups against each other, one in the role of "guards" and the
other in the role of "prisoners," in order to test how far the former exploited their
artificial authority over the latter. The television program relied both on the myth of
objectivity built into psychological experimentation and the additional myth that
cameras changed nothing significant about the so-called experiment.

The BBC has now produced a further variation on *Castaway* and *Survivor*, sending
a group of selected teenagers to the Borneo jungle. *Serious Jungle* has not been broadcast
as of this writing, but from the producer's comments, it is the youth (and supposed
innocence?) of the contestants that underwrites its claim to truth, refracted through the
fictional model of *Lord of the Flies*: "*Serious Jungle* has a serious point to it, and because
it is focused on children, the viewers will see very clear and honest reactions to their
experiences."[26] At the same time, the organizer of the teenagers' trip showed a touching
faith in the quality of the experiences they would undergo, mixing the myth of television's superior reality with the older one of the encounter with nature:

> For the first time these children will be forging relationships that are no longer about what
> music they like or what trainers they wear. They will change so much during these few
> weeks that going home to their old friends could be quite difficult for them.[27]

In spite of the implied distinction from the youth culture represented by *Big Brother*
here, nowhere is the underlying myth of gamedocs challenged: that there is plausibility
in reading human reality into what transpires in a space made and monitored for
television.

The particular success in Britain of *Big Brother* may derive, in part, from its clever mix of mythical authorities: the suggestion of scientific experiment is there (with "top psychologists" even being given their own show on each Sunday night of BB₃), but also the validating myths of celebrity and popular "interactivity." Popular participation is itself, of course, a useful myth; viewers of *Big Brother*, after all, have no control over its format, the initial choice of participants, the instructions or rules given to participants, the principles of editing, or indeed how the "popular vote" is interpreted to contestants and audience.

None of these contradictions should surprise us. For it is precisely in the oscillation between contingent detail and some broader, mythical value that for the anthropologist Maurice Bloch, echoing Barthes, the power of ritual lies.[28] In Bloch's analysis of Madagascan rituals, the broader value is that of "ancient history" lost in the mists of time; in contemporary societies, no one believes in history in that sense, but the myths of human nature, science, and what Marc Augé has called "the ideology of the present" are powerful substitutes.[29]

The Norms of Reality Performance

There is another myth reproduced through the gamedoc form and its apparently innocent rituals of television celebrity. I say myth, but it is more like a half statement that works largely by *not* being articulated – hence its affinity to ritual. This is the idea that surveillance is a natural mode through which to observe the social world. Few, perhaps, would subscribe explicitly to the will to "omniperception" (as the leading sociologist of surveillance puts it) implied here.[30] Yet by constant media repetition, this notion risks rigidifying into a myth that is fully integrated into our everyday expectations of the social.

The pleasures of surveillance

What are we to make of the idea that to find out about an aspect of social reality, it is natural to set up an "experimental situation" (with or without the endorsement of qualified psychologists), watch what happens when people are either not yet aware of the presence of cameras or are presumed to have forgotten it, and treat the result as "reality"? You might think it hypocritical for a sociologist like myself, who regularly interviews and observes others, to protest so much. But there is an obvious difference between the gamedoc and the normal context for sociological or indeed psychological research: confidentiality. Remember that *The Experiment* was in part designed by two psychologists as a hybrid of the entertainment form and an experimental situation.[31] Never in the recent history of the social and psychological sciences have studies been conducted for a simultaneous *public* audience, unless we return to Jean-Martin Charcot's public demonstrations in the 1870s with hysterics at the Paris Salpêtrière, and also recall the long history of public operations on the living and dead that preceded Charcot. Yet even in that early modern history of public experiment, there is no parallel for experimental subjects being watched in permanently retrievable form by an audience of millions.

The emerging model of surveillance and governance, and the rejuvenated "experimental science" that is parasitic on them, is disturbing. Its implications are greater than the popular legitimation of everyday surveillance, important as that is.[32] For surveillance-entertainment (a cumbersome, but equally accurate name for the gamedoc) has implications for everyday social relations that surveillance focused on criminal activity does not. While the saturation of public space with closed-circuit television is, of course, a matter of concern, the issue is more its effects on the quality of everyone's experience of public space, rather than the effects on how people might perform in front of the visible and invisible cameras – which is precisely why the New York art campaigners the Surveillance Camera Players' *performances* in front of surveillance cameras are striking, as ways of denaturalizing a dimension of public life that we screen out of our consciousness entirely. But in surveillance-entertainment, the impacts on "performance" are surely the *key* issue since its underlying premise is that we can expect *any* everyday activity legitimately to be put under surveillance and monitored for a huge, unknown audience.

What is remarkable is how easy it is to hide this disturbing idea beneath the cloak of ritual. In a six-part series introduced by Britain's Channel Four in 2002 called *Make My Day*, the *Big Brother* format was turned adeptly into a pure entertainment package. The idea of the program was a simple, if alarming extension of the *Candid Camera* format: friends or family nominate someone to the producers to be put under secret surveillance for a day to test their reactions to five challenges; if all are passed, the unwitting contestant wins £5,000 and retrospectively the "benefit" of having "starred" for national television "in her very own game show" (as one episode put it). The "challenges" are simple tests of the subject's ability to act as a person with a "normal" sexual appetite and a "natural" interest in celebrity. Will this young woman let into her house a half-naked man (recruited to match her tastes in men) needing to make an urgent phone call? Yes! – move to stage two. Will the same young woman allow herself to be distracted from getting to work when a member of her favorite pop band approaches her in the street, pretending to be lost and needing help to find his way? Yes! – move to stage three, and so on.

This series attracted little attention, and the predictability of its challenges was surely a weakness. What is interesting, however, is how the unwitting contestants reacted at the end of that day, when its strange events were explained to them by the well-known British celebrity and show narrator Sara Cox.[33] What we saw on the program – and of course, we have no way of knowing how far this was rehearsed or edited – is the contestant delighted, even awestruck, at the revelation, clutching her face, crying out "oh, my God!" and the like. Any later reflections by the contestant on having in effect consented to being submitted to twelve hours of secret filming for national television (including an opening scene in their bedroom) were left to our speculation.

My point is not to moralize about this particular series but to offer it as an example of how easily consent to the process of surveillance before a national audience (even if quite counterintuitive) can be made to seem natural, given the right ritual context. Here are Cox's explanatory words to one contestant:

Hello, it's Sara Cox here. You must be thinking you have had the strangest day of your life. Well it's all because of Channel 4's *Make My Day*. We have been secretly filming you using hidden cameras all day long and we reckon it's about time you got out from under your mother's feet so as a big thank you we would love to give you a deposit on your first flat. . . . I really hope we've made your day.

The program is useful because it is so artless. Here we see quite directly how two positive behavioral norms (one automatically positive – obtaining your own, independent place to live – and the other increasingly constructed as positive in contemporary British culture – showing an interest in celebrity) are combined to make the program's whole sequence of events seem natural and legitimate. (It must also have helped the producers that the "contestant" was living with her mother, who presumably gave legal consent to the presence of cameras in her daughter's bedroom.) Underwriting those norms here is the principle that "media experience" (discovering that the contestant's meetings with celebrities were not just accidental but real – that is, planned specifically by the media for her) automatically trumps "ordinary experience," including any questionable ethical dimensions it may have. This is a social "magic" (in Marcel Mauss's sense): a transformative "principle that eludes examination" that we must nonetheless try to unravel.[34]

The Real (Mediated) Me

BB₃ differed from previous British series of *Big Brother* in its emerging divide between those inmates who were clearly unhappy with the expected norms for behavior in the house and those who broadly accepted them. Even among the latter were a number who were unhappy at times, including the eventual finalists ('[*Big Brother* voice:] How are you feeling, Alex? [Alex:] Um . . . institutionalized").[35] Of the former, two left voluntarily, and another (Sandy, who happened to be the only housemate without fashionable, young looks) remained quiet and isolated for a few weeks before being voted out (as the *Big Brother* voice-over noted on one occasion: "Sandy was the first to go to bed" (cut to Sandy reading a book in bed).[36]

An interesting case was Tim, the only obviously upper-class inmate, a later replacement in the house who never settled. He was not so much withdrawn, like Sandy, as openly complaining at the tasks given to the inmates and the way others played up to the cameras. His complaints (in the program's famous Diary Room) were portrayed by the producers through editing and commentary as those of a moaner, who conveniently, was also discovered to be physically vain when his black hair dye started to show and he was caught on camera shaving his chest in the apparent privacy of his bed.

There was no particular drama to his eviction (on 19 July 2002) since he had made it clear on camera that he was "desperate" to leave the house. The eviction was presented in a hostile manner by McColl before the vote result: "The whole house thinks Tim's going to be out and to be honest the whole of the nation thinks Tim's going to be out." Tim emerged from the house to boos and hisses from the waiting crowd. His live interview was more dramatic; criticized by McColl for "whinging" and his unwillingness to play the *Big Brother* game, Tim responded that he had thought the set tasks "could have been a bit more mature." He was challenged to defend his charge that other inmates were playing up to the cameras:

> *McColl:* On a number of occasions, you talked about performing, other people per-
> forming. What did you mean by that?
>
> *Tim:* The whole time I was in there I was very much myself. I don't think my whole
> personality came out because there wasn't much to stimulate a lot of it . . . but
> there were a lot of people in there who I'm convinced are not like that in their
> normal life . . .
>
> *McColl:* [*interrupting*] Like who?
>
> *Tim:* [*continuing over McColl*]*:* and when I spoke to them one-to-one and you found
> out more about them as a person, that's the side I really liked, but they never
> showed enough of that. As soon as a camera came in or they felt they were being
> watched, they were up and [*mimes clapping to music*] singing and dancing and
> sure the public obviously like it because they get really into it, but . . .
>
> *McColl:* [*interrupting again*] But it's not that it's that. I think that generally some of
> them are quite up, positive people. [*cheering in background from crowd to whom the
> conversation is being relayed outside on large screens*] If you can't perform, physically
> you can't do it, not for seven or eight weeks, you can't do it.
>
> *Tim:* No, there were times when they didn't and they dipped, and that's the times
> you saw them when they weren't acting.
>
> *McColl:* OK, Tim . . . let's move onto something a bit more positive.[37]

There is an unresolvable conflict here between two norms of how to behave in the house: first, to give the public what they are assumed to want ("singing and dancing" [Tim], or being "up positive people" [McColl]), and second, the unobjectionable, but also vague norm of "being yourself." If as an inmate you find the second norm is incompatible with the first, what are you to do? Many inmates betrayed anxiety about whether they had been themselves – for example, Jonny (the eventual runner-up), who asked Jade why his housemates had put him up for eviction more than once and was told it was because "you've studied it, you know what the people on the outside would like."[38] He vehemently denied this, but in his eviction interview on the series' final night (26 July 2002), he failed to resolve the contradiction. When asked by McColl, "Who's the real you?" the melancholy loner smoking by the pool or the comic performer, he responded immediately:

> *Jonny:* The real me's the stupid, idiotic clown, but it takes a lot to get us down to
> the serious, quiet Jonny, but it worked in there.
>
> *McColl:* It stripped you down, did it?
>
> *Jonny:* Yes.

Yet he admitted at another point: "I don't care what anybody says, you're always aware of the cameras, and on the other end of them cameras is your family and your friends who you love." Or take Sophie, a late arrival who appeared unhappy during much of her time in the house, but who (like Jonny) was treated favorably in the show's comments on her performance. What follows is an exchange from her eviction interview (28 June 2002), where McColl asks a standard question, drawing on the idea of media experience being better (or bigger) than ordinary experience.[39] Sophie's answer is ambiguous, however:

> *McColl:* What's it like in that house? . . . I mean it's like a pressure cooker.
> *Sophie:* It is.
> *McColl:* . . . everything's big, feelings are felt stronger, what was it like for you?
> *Sophie:* Um, I felt . . . It's very . . . false in a way. . . . I mean, everyone in he house, . . . they've not got a mask on, but . . .

Here, contemporary media's wide-ranging myth that cameras tell us more about underlying reality because they magnify feelings that are presumed already to exist is directly contradicted. These contradictions matter because they cannot, in principle, be resolved. They are contradictions within the myth that *Big Brother* produces to legitimate itself: on the one hand, it claims to show us the human reality that must come out when ordinary people live for a long time under the cameras; on the other hand, it polices any differences of interpretation about what that reality should be, ruling out any behavior excluded by the production choices it makes and ruling in the so-called positive selves that it presumes the public wants to see and contestants want to display. Once contestants start to doubt the latter reality, as in BB$_3$, there is nowhere for the producers to turn but ritual: rituals of vilification turned on Tim, who posed the most direct threat to the show's norms, or rituals of incorporation, affirming the show's status by including successful inmates in the club of celebrity. Here are McColl's final words on the last night:

> Kate entered the house unknown and now she's taking her first innocent steps into a world of unseen wealth and privilege, . . . offers of casual sex, fame beyond her dreams, and general admiration. . . . I hope you've enjoyed this as much as I have. This has been *Big Brother* 2002. Thank you for watching. Good-bye.

The producers could afford some irony here, of course, in the show's final moments, but not, as we have seen, when the show's myth was directly challenged.[40]

Toward an Ethics of Reality TV

Where has this brief, skeptical tour of the British gamedoc brought us? Clearly, the gamedoc is a generic adaptation of considerable robustness (after all, it no longer carries the docusoap's hostage to fortune, the residual claim to documentary authority), and in the case of the British version of *Big Brother*, great resourcefulness and commercial promise: BB$_3$ was widely reported as having "rescued" Channel Four in the 2002 season.[41]

This chapter's argument, however, has been that our analysis cannot rest with observations on the adaptability of television genres. For *Big Brother* and all gamedocs are *social* processes that take real individuals and submit them to surveillance, analysis, and selective display as means to entertainment and enhanced audience participation. It is this social process, not the program's textual properties, that should be our main focus, and I offered some concepts (myth, ritual, and ritualization) to help us grasp its real and ideological dimensions.

There is, of course, one further step to which the argument needs to be taken, and that is ethics. What are the ethics of surveillance-entertainment? Or perhaps as the first question, where should we stand to get an adequate perspective on the possible ethical dimensions of the social process that gamedocs constitute, both by themselves and in their interface with the rest of social life? Finding that perspective is not easy. Part of the fascination of that oxymoron "reality TV" is its ambiguity, which in the case of *Big Brother* rests on another: between the expressive, almost obsessively self-reflexive individualization that it displays for us ("saturated individualism," as Michel Maffesoli has called it) and the barely accountable "exemplary center" that underwrites (or seeks to underwrite) the plausibility and legitimacy of that display.[42] By exemplary center, I mean the mythical "social center" that media institutions, even as they face unprecedented pressures from the dispersal of media production and consumption, attempt to project: the apparently naturally existing social "world" to which television likes to claim it gives us access.[43] The point is not that we can do without media or that media are exactly the same as other unaccountable forms of governmental or corporate power but rather that we cannot avoid at some point turning to an ethical critique if we are to address how media are transforming, and being transformed by, the social space in which, like it or not, we have to live. This chapter, I hope, has provided some useful starting points for that wider debate.

Notes

1. Roland Barthes, *Mythologies* (London: Paladin, 1972).
2. Ernesto Laclau, *New Reflections on the Revolution of Our Time* (London: Versa, 1990), 67.
3. Cited in Carolyn Marvin, *Blood Sacrifice and the Nation* (Cambridge: Cambridge University Press, 1999), 159.
4. On television "plenty," see John Ellis, *Seeing Things* (London: IB Tauris, 2000).
5. On the early wave of the mid-1900s, see Ib Bondebjerg, "Public Discourse/Private Fascination," *Media Culture and Society* 18 (1996): 27–45; Richard Kilborn, "'How Real Can You Get?' Recent Developments in 'Reality' Television," *European Journal of Communication* 13, no. 2 (1994): 201–18. On the subsequent crisis of many docusoaps, see Caroline Dover, "British Documentary Television Production: Tradition, Change, and 'Crisis' within a Practitioner Community" (Ph.D. diss., University of London, 2001).
6. See John Corner, "Performing the Real: Documentary Diversions," *Television and New Media* 3, no. 3 (August 2002): 255–69.
7. Ibid., 256.
8. Nick Couldry, *The Place of Media Power: Pilgrims and Witnesses of the Media Age* (London: Routledge, 2000); see also Roger Silverstone, "Television, Myth and Culture," in *Media, Myths and Narratives*, ed. James Carey (Newbury Park, CA: Sage, 1988).

9. See Nick Couldry, *Media Rituals: A Critical Approach* (London: Routledge, 2002); and Gareth Palmer, "*Big Brother:* An Experiment in Governance," *Television and New Media* 3, no. 3 (2002): 311–22.

10. Palmer, "*Big Brother,*" 305–6, emphasis added.

11. *Big Brother*, third series (May–July 2002), is my main example.

12. The term "ritual" is a difficult one, and there is no space here to explain in detail its history or my specific use of the term "media rituals" (but see Couldry, *Media Rituals*).

13. Roy Rappaport, *Ritual and Religion in the Making of Humanity* (Cambridge: Cambridge University Press, 1999), 24, emphasis added.

14. Émile Durkheim, *The Elementary Forms of Religious Life*, trans. Karen Fields (1912; reprint, Glencoe, IL.: Free Press, 1995).

15. Couldry, *Media Rituals*.

16. For further background, see ibid., chapters 1–3.

17. See Nick Couldry, "Playing for Celebrity: *Big Brother* as Ritual Event," *Television and New Media* 3, no. 3 (2002): 289.

18. See ibid. For "celebrification process," see Chris Rojek, *Celebrity* (London: Reaktion Books, 2001), 186–87.

19. See Couldry, *The Place of Media Power*, chapter 3.

20. Catherine Bell, *Ritual Theory, Ritual Practice* (New York: Oxford University Press, 1992).

21. On these categories, see Couldry, *Media Rituals*.

22. Bell, *Ritual Theory*, 215.

23. Barthes, *Mythologies*.

24. Interestingly, the *Survivor* prize money is £1 million, compared to *Big Brother's* £70,000 – surprising until you realize that the more successful *Big Brother* contestants have in the past picked up promotional deals, hosted television shows, or issued pop singles.

25. *Castaway* 2000, 25 January 2000.

26. Marshall Corwin, cited in *Observer* 31 March 2002, 15. For more on *Serious Jungle*, see its website: www.bbc.co.uk/talent/jungle.

27. Alex Patterson, cited in *Observer*, 31 March 2002, 15.

28. Maurice Bloch, *Ritual, History, and Power* (London: Athlone Press, 1989), 130.

29. Marc Augé, "Le Stade de l'écran," *Le Monde Diplomatique*, June 2001, 24.

30. David Lyon, *Surveillance Society: Monitoring Everyday Life* (Milton Keynes, Buckingham [England]: Open University Press, 2001), 124–25.

31. Steve Reicher and Alex Haslam, cited in *Guardian*, 3 May 2002, 7.

32. See Mark Andrejevic, "Little Brother Is Watching: The Webcam Subculture and the Digital Enclosure," in *Media/Space*, ed. Nick Couldry and Anna McCarthy (London: Routledge, forthcoming); Couldry, *Media Rituals*, chapter 6; and Palmer, "*Big Brother.*"

33. Cox is host DJ of Radio 1's high-profile early morning show.

34. Cited in Pierre Bourdieu, *The State Nobility* (Cambridge: Polity, 1996), 7.

35. BB3, 17 July 2002.

36. Ibid., 29 May 2002.

37. This and later passages are the author's transcription.

38. BB3, 28 June 2002.

39. See Couldry, *The Place of Media Power*, 113, cf. 47–8.

40. Such irony is often misinterpreted as skepticism or distance, when in fact its effect is just the opposite (Slavoj Žižek, *The Sublime Object of Ideology* [London: Verso, 1989], 32–3; see also Couldry, *The Place of Media Power*, 45).

41.   See, for example, *Guardian*, 27 July 2002, 7.
42.   Michel Maffesoli, *The Time of the Tribes* (London: Sage, 1996), 64. The phrase "exemplary center" is from Clifford Geertz, *Negara: The Theatre State in Nineteenth-Century Bali* (Princeton, NJ: Princeton University Press, 1980), 13.
43.   See Couldry, *Media Rituals*, chapter 3.

XII

Audience, Performance, Celebrity

70

Theories of Consumption in Media Studies

David Morley*

Introduction

The very development of the field of media studies has been premised on an understanding of the centrality of the process of media consumption in contemporary social and cultural developments. Over time (as detailed below) the model of media consumption in play within the field has oscillated between two poles. At one pole there have been models of media consumption which stress the power of the media (or the 'Culture Industries') and correspondingly treat media audiences as relatively passive and powerless, 'victims' of various kinds of media effects. Against this, especially in recent years, a variety of approaches has been developed, which lay more stress on media consumption as an active process, in which audience members are understood not only actively to select from the range of media materials available to them, but also to be active in their different uses, interpretations and 'decodings' of the material which they consume. The development of a model of media consumption which can reconcile the necessary concern with various forms of media power, with a recognition that audiences – or media 'consumers' – cannot adequately be treated as mere dupes or 'victims' of the media, is crucial to the development of the field. Indeed, the debate about this issue has been one of the most contentious within media studies, over the last fifteen to twenty years.

It is in this context that the present chapter is written. This work has also attempted to broaden the frame of media studies, and to move beyond the field's traditional focus (on the effects of television, radio and the press) so as to address the contemporary significance of a fuller range of the new information and commentation technologies, from the point of view of their users, or 'consumers'.

Effects, Uses and Decodings

The history of studies of media consumption can be seen as a series of oscillations between perspectives that have stressed the power of the text (or message) over its

*Pp. 296–313, 324–8 (relevant refs) from *Acknowledging Consumption: A Review of New Studies*, ed. D. Miller (New York: Routledge). © 1995 by D. Morley. Reprinted with permission from the author.

audiences and perspectives that have stressed the barriers 'protecting' the audience from the potential effects of the message. The first position is most obviously represented by the whole tradition of effects studies, mobilising a 'hypodermic' model of media influence, in which the media are seen as have the power to 'inject' their audiences with particular messages, which will cause them to behave in a particular way. This has involved, from the right, perspectives that would see the media causing the breakdown of 'traditional values' and, from the left, perspectives that see the media causing their audience to remain quiescent in political terms, or causing them to inhabit some form of false consciousness.

Interestingly, one finds curious contradictions here. On the one hand, television is accused of reducing its audience to the status of 'zombies' or 'glassy-eyed dupes', who consume a constant diet of predigested junk food, churned out by the media 'sausage factory' and who suffer the anaesthetic affects of this addictive and narcotic substance. However, at the same time as television has been held responsible for causing this kind of somnambulant state of mind (as a result of their viewers' consumption of this 'chewing gum for the eyes'), television has, of course, also been accused of making us *do* all manner of things, most notably in the debates around television and violence – where it has been argued that the viewing of violent television content will cause viewers to go out and commit violent acts. One point of interest here is that these 'television zombies' are always other people. Few people think of their own use of television in this way. It is a theory about what television does to other, more vulnerable people.

One of the most influential versions of this kind of 'hypodermic' theory of media effects was that advanced by Adorno and Horkheimer (1977) along with other members of the Frankfurt School of Social Research. Their 'pessimistic mass society thesis' reflected the breakdown of modern Germany society into fascism, a breakdown that was attributed, in part, to the loosening of traditional ties and structures which were seen as then leaving people more 'atomised' and exposed to external influences, and especially to the pressure of the mass propaganda of powerful leaders, the most effective agency of which was the mass media. This 'pessimistic mass society thesis' stressed the conservative and reconciliatory role of 'mass culture' for the audience. Mass culture suppressed 'potentialities', and denied awareness of contradictions in a 'one-dimensional world'; only art, in fictional and dramatic form, could preserve the qualities of negation and transcendence. Implicit here was a 'hypodermic' model of the media, which were seen as having the power to 'inject' a repressive ideology directly into the consciousness of the masses. The passive role attributed to the media consumers is apparent in the language in which Adorno and Horkheimer develop their argument. Thus, they claim that the 'Culture Industry' has automatic ideological effects on its consumers: 'Under the regime of the Culture Industry . . . the film leaves no room for imagination or reflection on the part of its audience . . . the film forces its victims to equate it directly with reality' (Adorno & Horkheimer 1977: 353–4), and again 'the machine rotates on the spot . . . [and] moves rigorously in the worn grooves of association . . . the product prescribes every reaction. . . . The Culture Industry forces its productions on the public' (ibid.: 361–2).

However, against this overly pessimistic backdrop, the emigration of the leading members of the Frankfurt School (Adorno, Marcuse, Horkheimer) to America during the 1930s led to the development of a specifically 'American' school of research in the 1940s and 1950s. The Frankfurt School's 'pessimistic' thesis, of the link between 'mass society' and fascism, and the role of the media in cementing it, proved unacceptable to American researchers. The 'pessimistic' thesis proposed, they argued, too direct and unmediated an impact by the media on its audiences; it took too far the thesis that all intermediary social structures between leaders/media and the masses had broken down; it didn't accurately reflect the pluralistic nature of American society; it was – to put it shortly – sociologically naïve. Clearly, the media had social effects; these must be examined, researched. But, equally clearly, these effects were neither all-powerful, nor simple, nor even necessarily direct. The nature of this complexity and indirectness also needed to be demonstrated and researched. Thus, in reaction to the Frankfurt School's predilection for critical social theory and qualitative and philosophical analysis, the American researchers developed what began as a quantitative and positivist methodology for empirical radio audience research into the 'Sociology of Mass Persuasion'.

Over the next twenty years, throughout the 1950s and 1960s, the overall effect of this empirically guided 'Sociology of Mass Persuasion' was to produce a much more qualified notion of 'media power', in which media consumers were increasingly recognised to not be completely passive 'victims' of the culture industry. In a review of the field in the early 1970s, Counihan (1973) summarised these developments thus:

> Once upon a time . . . worried commentators imputed a virtual omnipotence to the newly emerging media of mass communication. In the 'Marxist' version . . . the media were seen as entirely manipulated by a shrewd ruling class, in a 'bread and circuses' strategy, to transmit a corrupt culture and neo-fascist values – violence, dehumanised, consumer brain-washing, political passivity, etc. – to the masses. . . . These instruments of persuasion, on the one hand, and the atomised, homogenised, susceptible masses on the other, were conjoined in a simple stimulus–response model. However, as empirical research progressed, survey and experimental methods were used to measure the capacity of the media to change 'attitudes', 'opinions' and 'behaviour'. In turn, the media–audience relationship was found to be not simple and direct, but complex and mediated. 'Effects' could only be gauged by taking account of other factors intervening between the media and the audience member. Further, emphasis shifted from 'what the media do to people' to 'what people do to the media', for audiences were found to 'attend to' and 'receive' media messages in a selective way, to tend to ignore or to subtly reinterpret those messages hostile to their particular viewpoints. Far from possessing autonomous persuasive and other anti-social power, the media were now found to have a more limited and, implicitly, more benign role in society; not changing, but 'reinforcing' prior dispositions, not cultivating 'escapism' or passivity, but capable of satisfying a great diversity of 'uses and gratifications'; not instruments of a levelling of culture, but of its democratisation. (Counihan 1973: 43)

In this passage, Counihan notes the increasing significance, at that time, of a new perspective on media consumption – the 'uses and gratifications' approach, largely associated with the work of the Leicester Centre for Mass Communications Research, in Britain, during the 1960s. Within that perspective, the viewer is credited with an active role, and it is then a question, as Halloran (1970) put it, of looking at what people do with the media rather than what the media do to them. This argument was obviously of great significance in moving the debate forward – to begin to look at the active engagement of the audience with the medium and with the particular television programmes that they might be watching. One key advance, which was developed by the uses and gratifications perspectives was that of the variability of response and interpretation. From this perspective, one can no longer talk about the 'effects' of a message on a homogeneous mass audience, who are all expected to be affected in the same way. However, the limitation is that the 'uses and gratifications' perspective remains individualistic, in so far as differences of response or interpretation are ultimately attributed to individual differences of personality or psychology. Clearly, the uses and gratifications approach does represent a significant advance on effects theory, in so far as it opens up the question of differential interpretation. However, it remains severely limited by its insufficiently sociological or cultural perspective, in so far as everything is reduced to the level of variations of individual psychology.

It was against this background that Stuart Hall's (1973) 'encoding/decoding' model of communication was developed at the Centre for Contemporary Cultural Studies, as an attempt to take forward insights that had emerged within each of these other perspectives. It took, from the effects theorists, the notion that mass communication is a structured activity, in which the institutions that produce the messages do have the power to set agendas, and to define issues. This is to move away from the idea of power of the medium to make a person behave in a certain way (as a direct effect, which is caused by a simple stimulus, provided by the medium) but it is to hold on to a notion of the role of the media in setting agendas and providing cultural categories and frameworks within which members of the culture will tend to operate. The model also attempted to incorporate, from the uses and gratifications perspective, the idea of the active viewer, who makes meaning from the signs and symbols that the media provide. However, it was also designed to take on board, from the work developed within the interpretative and normative paradigms, the concern with the ways in which responses and interpretations are structured and patterned at a level beyond that of individual psychologies. The model was also, critically, informed by semiological perspectives, focusing on the question of how communication works. The key focus was on the realisation that we are, of course, dealing with signs and symbols, which only have meaning within the terms of reference supplied by codes (of one sort or another) which the audience shares, to some greater or lesser extent, with the producers of messages.

The premises of Hall's encoding/decoding model were:

1. The same event can be encoded in more than one way.
2. The message always contains more than one potential 'reading'. Messages propose and prefer certain readings over others, but they can never become wholly closed around one reading: they remain polysemic.
3. Understanding the message is also a problematic practice, however transparent and 'natural' it may seem. Messages encoded one way can always be read in a different way.

In this approach, then, the message is treated neither as a unilateral sign, without ideo-logical 'flux'; nor, as in the uses and gratifications approach, as a disparate sign which can be read any way, according to the psychology of the decoder. Reference can usefully be made here to Volosinov's (1973) distinction between sign and signal, and his argu-ment that structuralist approaches tend to treat the former as if they were the latter – i.e. as if they had fixed meanings. The television message is treated as a complex sign, in which a preferred reading has been inscribed, but which retains the potential, if decoded in a manner different from the way in which it has been encoded, of communicating a different meaning. The message is thus a structured polysemy. It is central to the argu-ment that all meanings do not exist 'equally' in the message: it has been structured in dominance, despite the impossibility of 'total closure' of meaning. Further, the 'pre-ferred reading' is itself part of the message, and can be identified within its linguistic and communicative structure.

Thus, when analysis shifts to the 'moment' of the encoded message itself, the com-municative form and structure can be analysed in terms of what the mechanisms are which prefer one, dominant reading over the other readings; what are the means which the encoder uses to try to 'win the assent of the audience' to his preferred reading of the message.

Before messages can have 'effects' on the audience, they must be decoded. 'Effects' is thus a shorthand and inadequate way of marking the point where audiences differ-entially read and make sense of messages that have been transmitted, and act on those meanings, within the context of their situation and experience. Hall (1973) assumes that there will be no necessary 'fit' or transparency between the encoding and decoding ends of the communication chain. It is precisely this lack of transparency, and its conse-quences for communication, which we need to investigate, Hall claims. Having estab-lished that there is always a possibility of disjunction between the codes of those sending and those receiving messages through the circuit of mass communications, the problem of the 'effects' of communication could now be reformulated, as that of the extent to which decodings take place within the limits of the preferred (or dominant) manner in which the message has been initially encoded. However, the complementary aspect of this problem is that of the extent to which these interpretations, or decodings, also reflect, and are inflected by, the codes and discourses which different sections of the audience inhabit, and the ways in which this is determined by the socially governed distribution of cultural codes between and across different sections of the audience; that is, the range of different decoding strategies and competencies in the audience.

To raise this as a problem for research is already to argue that the meaning produced by the encounter of text and subject cannot be 'read off' straight from 'textual charac-teristics'. From this point of view the text cannot be considered in isolation from its historical conditions of production and consumption: 'What has to be identified is the use to which a particular text is put, its function within a particular conjuncture, in particular institutional spaces, and in relation to particular at audiences' (Neale 1977: 39–40). Thus, the meaning of the text must be thought of in terms of which set of dis-courses it encounters, in any particular set of circumstances – and how this encounter may restructure both the meaning of the text and the discourses that it meets. The meaning of the text will be constructed differently according to the discourses (knowledge, prejudices, resistances) brought to bear on the text by the reader: the crucial factor in this encounter of audience/subject and text will be the range of discourses at the disposal of the audience. Thus social position may set parameters to the range of potential readings, through the structure of access to different codes; certain social positions allow access to wider repertoires of available codes, certain others to narrower ranges.

In short, the encoding/decoding model was designed to provide a synthesis of insights that had come out of a series of different perspectives – communication theory, semiology, sociology and psychology – and to provide an overall model of the communication circuit as it operated in its social context. It was concerned with matters of ideological and cultural power and it was concerned with shifting the ground of debate, so that emphasis moved to the consideration of how it was possible for meaning to be produced. It attempted to develop the argument that we should look not for the meaning of a text, but for the conditions of a practice – i.e. to examine the foundations of communication, but, crucially, to examine those foundations as social and cultural phenomena.

Psychoanalytic Theories of the Audience: *Screen* Theory

The growing influence of feminism during the 1970s led, among other effects, to a revitalisation of interest in psychoanalytic theory, given the centrality of the concern with issues of gender within psychoanalysis. Within media studies, this interest in psychoanalytic theories of the construction of gendered identities was one of the informing principles behind the particular approach to the analysis of the media developed by the journal *Screen*. This British journal was heavily influential for a period in the 1970s.

Screen theory was centrally concerned with the analysis of the effects of cinema (and especially the regressive effects of mainstream, commercial, Hollywood cinema) in 'positioning' the spectator (or subject) of the film, through the way in which the text (by means of camera placement, editing and other formal characteristics) 'fixed' the spectator into a particular kind of 'subject-position', which, it was argued, 'guaranteed' the transmission of a certain kind of 'bourgeois ideology' – of naturalism, realism and verisimilitude.

'*Screen* theory' was largely constituted by a mixing of Lacan's (1977) rereading of Freud, stressing the importance of language in the unconscious, and Althusser's (1971) early formulation of the 'media' as an 'Ideological State Apparatus' (even if operating in the private sphere), which had the principal function of securing the reproduction of the conditions of production by 'interpellating' its subjects (spectators, audiences) within the terms of the 'dominant ideology'. Part of the appeal of this approach, to media scholars, rested in the weight which the theory gave to the ('relatively autonomous') effectivity of language – and of 'texts' (such as films and media products), as having real effects in society. To this extent, the approach was argued to represent a significant advance on previous theories of the media (including traditional Marxism) which had stressed the determination of all superstructural phenomena (such as the media) by the 'real' economic 'base' of the society – thus allowing no space for the conceptualisation of the media themselves as having independent (or at least, in Althusser's terms 'relatively autonomous') effects of their own.

Previous approaches, it was argued, had neglected the analysis of the textual forms and patterns of media products, concentrating instead on the analysis of patterns of ownership and control – on the assumption, crudely put, that once the capitalist ownership of the industry was demonstrated, there was no real need to examine the texts (programmes or films) themselves in detail, as all they would display would be minor variations within the narrow limits dictated by their capitalist owners. Conversely, *Screen* theory focused precisely on the text, and emphasised the need for close analysis of textual/formal patterns – hardly surprisingly, given the background of its major figures (Heath 1977/8; MacCabe 1974) in English studies. However, their arguments, in effect, merely inverted the terms of the sociological/economic forms of determinist theory which they critiqued. Now it was text itself which was the central (if not exclusive) focus of the analysis, on the assumption that since the text 'positioned' the spectator, all that was necessary was the close analysis of texts, from which their 'effects' on their spectators could be automatically deduced, as spectators were bound to take up the 'positions' constructed for them by the text (or film).

The textual determination of *Screen* theory, which its constant emphasis on the 'suturing' (cf. Heath 1977/8) of the spectator, into the predetermined subject position constructed for him or her by the text, thus allocated central place in media analysis to the analysis of the text. As Moores (1993) puts it, 'the aim was to uncover the symbolic mechanisms through which cinematic texts confer subjectivity upon readers, sewing them into the film narrative, through the production of subject positions' (Moores 1993: 13), on the assumption that the spectator (or reading subject) is left with no other option but to 'make . . . the meanings the film makes for him/her' (Heath 1977/8: 58).

Undoubtedly, it was one of the great achievements of *Screen* theory, drawing as it did on psychoanalysis, Marxism and the formal semiotics of Christian Metz (1975), to restore an emphasis to the analysis of texts which had been absent in much previous work. In particular, the insights of psychoanalysis were extremely influential in the development of later feminist work (see pp. 320–1) on the role of the media in the construction of gendered identities and gendered forms of spectatorship (see e.g. Brunsdon 1981; Byars 1991; Gledhill 1988; Mattelart 1984; Modleski 1984).

However, despite the theoretical sophistication of much of the psychoanalytic-based work, in offering a more developed model of text/subject relations it has, until now, contributed little to the empirical study of the audience. This is for the simple reason that those working in this tradition have, on the whole, been content to 'deduce' audience responses from the structure of the text. To this extent, and despite the theoretical advances achieved by this work in other respects, I would argue that the psychoanalytically based work has ultimately mobilised what can be seen as another version of the hypodermic theory of effects – in so far as it is, at least in its initial and fundamental formulations, a universalist theory which attempts to account for the way in which the subject is necessarily positioned by the text. The difficulty, in terms of audience studies, is that this body of work, premised as it is on universalist criteria, finds it difficult to provide the theoretical space within which one can allow for, and then investigate, differential readings, interpretations, or responses on the part of the audience. This is so quite simply because the theory, in effect, tries to explain any specific instance of the text/reader relationship in terms of a universalist theory of the formation of subjects in general.

From within this perspective, emphasis falls on the universal, primarily psychoanalytic processes through which the subject is constituted. The text is then understood as reproducing or replaying this primary positioning, which is then the foundation of any particular reading. My argument would be that, in fact, we need to question the assumption that all specific discursive effects can be reduced to, and explained by, the functioning of a single, universal set of psychic mechanisms – which is rather like a theory of Platonic forms, which find their expression in any particular instance. The key issue is that this form of psychoanalytic theory poses the problem of the politics of the signifier (the struggle over ideology in language) exclusively at the level of the subject, rather than at the intersection between constituted subjects and specific discursive positions – i.e. at the site of interpellation, where the discursive subject is recognised to be operating in interdiscursive space.

In making this argument, I follow Stuart Hall's (1981) critique of the Lacanian perspective. Hall argues that without further work, further specification, the mechanisms of the Oedipus complex in the discourse of Freud and Lacan are universalist, transhistorical and therefore 'essentialist'. To that extent, Hall argues, these concepts in their universalist forms cannot usefully be applied, without further specification and elaboration, to the analysis of historically specific social formations.

This is to attempt to hold on to the distinction between the constitution of the subject as a general (or mythical) moment and the moment when the subject in general is interpellated by the discursive formation of specific societies. That is to insist on the distinction between formation of subjects for language, and the recruitment of specific subjects to the subject positions of discursive formations through the process of interpellation. It is also to move away from the assumption that every specific reading is already determined by the primary structure of subject positions and to insist that these interpellations are not given and absolute but, rather, are conditional and provisional, in so far as the struggle in ideology takes place precisely through the articulation/disarticulation of interpellations. This is to lay stress on the possibility of contradictory interpellations and to emphasise the unstable, provisional and dynamic properties of subject positioning. It is also to recognise that subjects have histories and that past interpellations affect present ones, rather than to 'deduce' subjects from the subject positions offered by the text and to argue that readers are not merely bearers or puppets of their unconscious positions. It is to insist, with Volosinov (1973), on the 'multiaccentuality of the sign', which makes it possible for discourse to become an arena of struggle.

These are, in my view, the main difficulties with much psychoanalytic work in media studies, in so far as it is a theoretical perspective which presumes a unilateral fixing of a position for the reader, imprisoning him or her in its structure, so as to produce a singular and guaranteed effect. The text, of course, may offer the subject specific positions of intelligibility, it may operate to prefer certain readings above others; what it cannot do is to guarantee them – that must always be an empirical question. This is, in part, because the subject that the text encounters is, as Pecheux (1982) has argued, never a 'raw' or 'unacculturated' subject. Readers are always already formed, shaped as subjects, by the ideological discourses that have operated on them prior to their encounter with the text in question.

If we are to theorise the subject of television or film, it has to be theorised in its cultural and historical specificity, an area where psychoanalytic theory is obviously weak. It is only thus that we can move beyond a theory of the subject which has reference only to universal, primary psychoanalytic processes, and only thus that we can allow a space in which on can recognise that the struggle over ideology also takes place at the moment of the encounter of text and subject and is not 'always already' predetermined at the psychoanalytic level.

Facts, Fictions, and Popular Culture

If, in the British context, media studies was reinvigorated in the early 1970s by what Stuart Hall (1982) has characterised as the 'rediscovery of ideology', this 'rediscovery' also led in the first instance to a focus on the analysis of the ideological structure of 'news', (both on television and in the press) and, more generally, to a focus on the analysis of media coverage of politics and, in particular, media coverage of explicitly 'controversial' issues such as industrial and race relations (Glasgow Media Group 1976, 1980).

Some of this work was framed within a more (or less) sophisticated concern with 'bias' (see the work of the Glasgow Media Group, 1976, 1980) while other studies mobilised concepts of ideology derived from the work of Gramsci and Althusser (see e.g. Hall *et al.* 1981). However, while internally differentiated in this respect, much of this work shared two key premises: first, that it was in the field of explicitly political communications that the concern with the reproduction of ideology (and the presumed consequence of the maintenance of social order or 'hegemony') would be most productively focused, and second (partly inscribed in the theoretical model of ideology underpinning the first premise – see Abercrombie *et al.* 1980) that the (ideological) effects of the media could, in effect, be 'deduced' from the analysis of the textual structure of the messages they emitted. To this extent, the media audience was largely absent from these analytical discourses, and the power of the media over their consumers was often taken for granted (Connell 1985).

Both of these premises came to be severely questioned in subsequent years. In the first case, there was a growing recognition of the considerable political significance of a much wider realm of cultural products (partly due to the influence of feminist and antiracist perspectives on the symbolic process of construction of personal and cultural identities), and a consequent concern with the ideological structure of 'entertainment' media, popular fiction and music. In the second place, there was a growing recognition – dating notably from Hall's seminal paper on the 'encoding' and 'decoding' of TV (Hall 1973) – of the complex and contradictory nature of the process of cultural consumption of media products, both within the realm of TV (e.g. Morley 1980) and within the broader field of popular culture (Hebdige 1979, 1988).

From the mid-1970s onwards, researchers within the media/cultural studies traditions in Britain began to explore the political and ideological significance of the structure of media products outside of the 'news' category. These studies focused on issues such as the construction of gender identities in soap opera (Ang 1985; Hobson 1982), the presentation of racial stereotypes in drama and light entertainment (Cohen & Gardner 1984), the political and cultural values embedded in popular fiction and drama (Bennett & Woollacott 1987; McArthur 1981; MacCabe 1981), and the presentation of knowledge itself in quiz shows (Mills & Rice 1982). In Britain much of this work was collected and summarised in the Open University's influential course on 'Popular Culture' (1981). These studies demonstrated that any concern with the influence of the media in the construction of culture needed to operate with a wider and more inclusive definition of the kind of media texts considered to be relevant. In this context, the study of news and explicitly 'political' media products was then seen to be but a small part of the overall field of materials with which media scholars needed to be concerned.

These developments paved the way for the notable boom in studies of media consumption which occurred during the 1980s. To take only the best-known examples, the body of work produced in that period included, *inter alia*, my own study of the 'Nationwide' audience (Morley 1980); Hobson's study of 'Crossroads' viewers; Modleski's (1984) work on women viewers of soap opera; Radway's (1984) study of readers of romance fiction; Ang's (1985) study of 'Dallas' viewers; Fiske's (1987) study of 'Television Culture'; Philo's (1990) and Lewis's (1991) studies of the audience for TV news, and the work of Schroder (1988) and Liebes and Katz (1991) on the consumption of American TV fiction in other cultures. Towards the end of the decade, much of the most important new material on media consumption was collected together in the published proceedings of two major conferences on audience studies: Drummond and Paterson's (1988) collection *Television and its Audience*, bringing together work on audiences presented at the International Television Studies Conference in London in 1986, and Seiter *et al.*'s (1989) collection *Remote Control: Television, Audiences and Cultural Power*, based on the conference of that name held in Tübingen in 1987.

While this work in the field of media consumption was naturally varied in its particular emphases and concerns, a number of threads of continuity can be picked out. Centrally, almost all of this work was concerned to move away from the Frankfurt School's image of the media consumer as a passive dupe of the all-powerful Culture Industry. The emphasis was on media consumers' choices, actions and forms of creativity. Much of the work was influenced by notions of the consumer of popular culture as an active 'bricoleur' – as evinced most sharply in Hebdige's (1979) formulation of how the process of cultural consumption should be understood:

> Popular culture offers a rich iconography, a set of symbols, objects and artefacts, which can be assembled and reassembled by different groups in a literally limitless number of combinations. The meaning of each selection is transformed as individual objects are taken out of their original, historical and cultural contexts and juxtaposed against other objects and signs from other contexts. (Hebdige 1979: 104)

In a similar vein, Fiske (1986) argued that the Culture Industry could not simply express dominant values, otherwise they would be of no interest to subordinate groups. Fiske's argument was that

> Culture is a process of making meanings that people actively participate in: it is not a set of 'preformed' meanings, handed down and imposed on people. . . . The mass produced text can only be made into a popular text by the people, and this transformation occurs when the various subcultures can activate sets of meanings from it, and insert these meanings into their daily cultural experience. (Fiske 1986: 404)

However, this radical stress on the active nature of cultural consumption was not without its critics, and a number of voices soon began to bemoan what they saw as the trend towards a certain 'romanticisation' of the freedom of the media consumer, in the establishment of a new conventional wisdom in this field, in which the question of media power was in danger of being altogether lost sight of. Thus Modleski complained that

> The insight that audiences/consumers are not completely manipulated, but may appropriate mass cultural artefacts for their own purposes has been carried so far that mass culture no longer seems to be a problem at all, for some critics. (Modleski 1986: xi)

Modleski went on to argue that, in their reaction against the Frankfurt School, media scholars, especially those working within a cultural studies perspective, had now entirely lost any critical perspective on popular culture. As she put it:

> If the problem with the Frankfurt School was that its members were too elitist, too far outside the culture they examined, many cultural studies writers today have the opposite problem – they are so concerned not to be 'elitist' that they fall into a mode of populism – immersed in popular culture themselves, half in love with their own subject, they seem unable to achieve the proper critical distance from it, and end up writing apologies for mass culture. (Modleski 1986: xi)

The 'New' Audience Research: Revisionism and Interpretivism

By the end of the 1980s, it certainly seemed that the new conventional wisdom of media studies was a very 'optimistic' one, so far as the position of the media consumer was concerned, and the passively consuming audience seemed to be, definitively, a thing of the past. Some part of this 'optimism' may have been influenced by a certain technological determination – in which it was assumed that technological advances (the video, enabling time-shifting; the remote control, enabling channel-hopping) were empowering the media consumer in important new ways. Thus Erni (1989) argues bluntly that 'in the context of the enormous changes in television technology' (such as the increasing use of VCR technology and the development of 'television-computer-telephone hybrids') audience research work focusing on broadcast television 'becomes somewhat obsolete' (ibid.: 39). In a not dissimilar vein, Lindlof and Meyer (1987) argue that the 'interactive' capacities of recent technological developments fundamentally transform the position of the consumer. As they put it:

> with increasing adoption of technological add-ons for the basic media delivery systems, the messages can be edited, deleted, rescheduled or skipped past, with complete disregard for their original form. The received notion of the mass communications audience has simply little relevance for the reality of mediated communication. (Lindlof & Meyer 1987: 2)

The technological advances are often seen to have transformative (if not utopian) consequences for the TV audience. Thus, in the Italian context, RAI's publicity at one point claimed that:

> The new telematic services, video recorders and video discs . . . will make a more personal use of the medium possible. The user will be able to decide what to watch, when he [*sic*] wants. It will be possible, then, to move beyond that fixed mass audience which has been characteristic of TV's history: everybody will be able to do his [*sic*] own programming. (Quoted in Connell & Curti 1985: 99)

The problem here is that many of these arguments run the danger of abstracting these technologies' intrinsic 'capacities' from the social contexts of their actual use. In understanding such technological developments, we could more usefully follow Bausinger (1984) in his concern with the question of how these technologies are integrated into the structure and routines of domestic life – into what he calls 'the specific semantics of the everyday'. However, it was not only a technologically driven form of optimism that was at stake here: by the late 1980s, it could be argued that the 'optimism' had became central to the model of media consumption which had come to dominate the field. Thus, by 1990, Evans noted that audience work in media studies could largely be characterised by two assumptions: (a) that the audience is active (in a non-trivial sense) and (b) that media content is always 'polysemic' or open to interpretation. The question is, what these assumptions are taken to mean exactly, and what their theoretical and empirical consequences are (cf. Evans 1990).

As noted earlier, Hall's (1973) formulation of the encoding/decoding model had contained, as one of its central features, the concept of the 'preferred reading' (towards which the text attempts to direct its reader), while acknowledging the possibility of alternative negotiated or oppositional readings. The difficulty is that this model has subsequently been quite transformed, to the point where it is often maintained that the majority of audience members routinely modify or deflect any dominant ideology reflected in media content (cf. Fiske 1987), and the concept of a 'preferred reading', or of a 'structured polysemy', drops entirely from view. In this connection I have to confess a personal interest, as I have been puzzled to find some of my own earlier work (cf. Morley 1980) invoked as a theoretical legitimation of various forms of 'active audience theory' (variously labelled as the 'new revisionist' or 'interpretivist' perspective by other critics). For my own part, while I would argue that work such as the *Nationwide Audience* project (along with that of Ang 1985; Liebes & Katz 1991; and Radway 1984) offers counter-evidence to a simple-minded 'dominant ideology' thesis, and demonstrates that any hegemonic discourse is always insecure and incomplete, this should not lead us to abandon concern with the question of, as Martin-Barbero puts is, 'how to understand the texture of hegemony/subalternity, the interlacing of resistance and submission, opposition and complicity' (Martin-Barbero 1988: 462). That was (and remains) precisely the point of studying audience consumption of media texts, a point which now, with the discrediting of some of the more 'romantic' versions of 'active audience theory' is in great danger of being obscured – as demonstrated, for example, by Seaman's (1992) total failure to understand the significance of what he describes as 'pointless populism' in audience studies. This is by no means to deny the existence of problems in contemporary audience theory. I would agree with Corner (1991) that much recent work in this field is marred by a facile insistence on the polysemy of media products, and by an undocumented presumption that forms of interpretive resistance are more widespread than subordination, or the reproduction of dominant meanings (cf. Condit (1989) on the unfortunate current tendency towards an overdrawn emphasis on the 'polysemous' qualities of texts in media studies). To follow that path, as Corner (1991) correctly notes, is to underestimate the force of textual determinacy in the construction of meaning from media products, and not only to romanticise improperly the role of the reader, but to risk falling into a 'complacent relativism, by which the interpretive contribution of the audience is perceived to be of such a scale and range as to render the very idea of media power naïve' (Corner 1991: 281).

In a similar vein to Corner, Curran offers a highly critical account of what he describes as the 'new revisionism' in mass communications research on media audiences. In brief, his charge is that while 'this . . . "revisionism" . . . presents itself as original and innovative [it] . . . is none of these things' (Curran 1990: 135), but rather amounts to 'old pluralist dishes being reheated and presented as new cuisine' (ibid.: 151). The history Curran offers is an informative one, alerting us to the achievements of scholars whose work has been unrecognised or neglected by many (myself included), thus far. However, my contention is that this is a particular history which could not have been written (by Curran or anyone else) fifteen years ago, before the impact of the 'new revisionism' (of which Curran is so critical) transformed our understanding of the field of audience research, and thus transformed our understanding of who and what was important in its history. I would argue that it is precisely this transformation which has allowed a historian such as Curran to go back and reread the history of communications research, in such a way as to give prominence to those whose work can now, with hindsight, be seen to have 'pre-figured' the work of these 'new revisionists'.

According to Blumler *et al.* (1985: 257) the interpretivist focus on the role of the reader in the decoding process 'should be ringing bells with gratificationists . . . because . . . they are the most experienced in dealing with a multiplicity of responses'. Similarly, Rosengren (1985) claims that Radway's (1984) work 'indirectly offers strong validation of the general soundness of uses and gratifications research', and he goes on to claim that 'in her way, Radway has reinvented . . . gratifications research' (Rosengren 1985: 278).

The first question, in this connection, as Schroder (1987) notes, is perhaps whether, rather than constituting evidence of a genuine unity between cultural studies and uses and gratifications perspectives, what we see here, in Blumler *et al.*'s argument is, in fact, a misguided attempt to reduce interpretivist concepts to gratificationist terms. The second (and as Schroder 1987 notes, rather embarrassing) question is why has it required a cultural studies scholar to excavate a lost sociological tradition? The answer that Schroder offers, and with which I for one am inclined to agree, is that in spite of the tributes now paid by Curran *et al.* to those who can, retrospectively, be identified as the forgotten 'pioneers' of qualitative media audience research, 'the fact remains that, until the 1980s, their qualitative work . . . was . . . the victim of a spiral of silence, because they attempted to study what mainstream sociology regarded as unresearchable, i.e. cultural meanings and interpretations' (Schroder 1987: 14).

However, despite my differences with him, concerning the general terms of his critique, I would agree with Curran that recent reception studies, which document audience autonomy and offer optimistic/redemptive readings of mainstream media texts, have often been taken to represent not simply a challenge to a simple 'effects' or 'dominant ideology' model, but rather as, in themselves, documenting the total *absence* of media influence, in the 'semiotic democracy' of postmodern pluralism.

As Curran observes (1990: 148), Fiske's (1986) celebration of a 'semiotic democracy', in which people drawn from a vast shifting range of subcultures and groups construct their own meanings within an autonomous 'cultural economy', is problematic in various respects, but not least because it is readily subsumable within a conservative ideology of sovereign consumer pluralism. The problem with the concept of 'semiotic democracy', as Murdock (1989) notes, is that this model of 'perfect competition' is as 'useless in understanding the workings of the cultural field as it is in economic analysis, since it is obvious that some discourses (like some firms in the market) are backed by greater material resources and promoted by spokespersons with preferential access to the major means of publicity and policymaking' (Murdock 1989: 438). Hence, as Hall argues, to speak of the cultural field is 'to speak of a field of relations structured by power and difference' in which some positions are in dominance, and some are not, though these 'positions are never permanently fixed' (Hall 1989: 57).

Budd, Entman and Steinman argue that work of this kind now routinely assumes that 'people habitually use the content of dominant media against itself, to empower themselves' (Budd *et al.* 1990: 170) so that, in their analysis, the crucial 'message' of much contemporary American cultural studies media work is an optimistic one: 'Whatever the message encoded, decoding comes to the rescue. Media domination is weak and ineffectual, since the people make their own meanings and pleasures' (ibid.: 170) or, put another way, 'we don't need to worry about people watching several hours of TV a day, consuming its images, ads and values. People are already critical, active viewers and listeners, not cultural dopes manipulated by the media' (ibid.: 170). While I would certainly not wish to return to any model of the audience as 'cultural dopes', the point Budd *et al.* make is a serious one, not least because, as they note, this 'affirmative' model does tend then to justify the neglect of all questions concerning the economic, political and ideological forces acting on the construction of texts (cf. Brunsdon 1989), on the (unfounded) assumption that reception is, somehow, the only stage of the communications process that matters, in the end. Apart from anything else, and at the risk of being whimsical, one might say that such an assumption does seem to be a curiously Christian one, in which the sins of the industry (or the message) are somehow seen to be redeemed in the 'after-life' of reception.

One crucial question concerns the significance that is subsequently given to often quite particular, ethnographic accounts of moments of cultural subversion, in the process of media consumption or decoding. Thus, Budd *et al.* note that, in his account of the ways in which Aboriginal Australian children have been shown to reconstruct TV narratives involving blacks, in such a way as to fit with and bolster their own self-conceptions, Fiske (1986) shows a worrying tendency to generalise radically from this (very particular) instance, so that, in his account, this type of 'alternative' response, in quite particular circumstances, is decontextualised and then offered as a model for 'decoding' in general, so that, as Budd *et al.* (1990: 179) put it, 'the part becomes the whole and the exception the rule' (see also Schudson 1987).

While we should not fall back into any form of simplistic textual determinacy, none the less we must also avoid the naïve presumption that texts are completely open, like 'an imaginary shopping mall in which audience members could wander at will, selecting whatever suits them' (Murdock 1989: 236). I would agree with Murdock that the celebration of audience creativity and pleasure can all too easily collude with a system of media power that actually excludes or marginalises most alternative or oppositional voices and perspectives. As Murdock (1989: 236) argues, 'because popular programmes . . . offer a variety of pleasures and can be interpreted in different ways, it does not follow . . . that attempts to maximise the diversity of representations and cultural forms within the system are redundant'.

The equivalence that Newcomb and Hirsch (1987) assert between the producer and consumer of messages, in so far as the television viewer is seen to match the creator (of the programme) in the making of meanings, is in effect a facile one, which ignores De Certeau's (1984) distinction between the strategies of the powerful and the tactics of the weak (or, as Silverstone and I have argued elsewhere (Morley & Silverstone 1990), the difference between having power over a text, and power over the agenda within which that text is constructed and presented). The power of viewers to reinterpret meanings is hardly equivalent to the discursive power of centralised media institutions to construct the texts which the viewer then interprets, and to imagine otherwise is simply foolish. The problem, as Ang (1990: 247) argues, is that while 'audiences may be active, in myriad ways, in using and interpreting media . . . it would be utterly out of perspective to cheerfully equate "active" with "powerful"'.

References

Abercrombie, N., S. Hill & B. Turner (1984). *The Dominant Ideology Thesis*. London: Allen & Unwin.

Adorno, T. & M. Horkheimer (1977). The Culture Industry: Enlightenment as Mass Deception. In: J. Curran, M. Gurevitch & J. Woollacott (eds.), *Mass Communication and Society*. London: Edward Arnold.

Althusser, L. (1971). Ideological State Apparatuses. In: L. Athusser (ed.), *Lenin and Philosophy*. London: New Left Books.

Ang, I. (1985). *Watching "Dallas."* London: Methuen.

Ang, I. (1990). Culture and Communication. *European Journal of Communications* 5(2–3).

Bausinger, H. (1984). Media, Technology and Everyday Life. *Media, Culture and Society* 6(4).

Bennett, T. & J. Woollacott (1987). *Bond and Beyond: The Political Career of a Popular Hero.* London: Macmillan.

Blumler, J., M. Gurevitch & E. Katz (1985). Reaching Out: A Future for Gratifications Research. In: K. Rosengren, et al. (eds.), *Media Gratification Research*. Beverly Hills, CA: Sage.

Brunsdon, C. (1981). Crossroads: Notes on a Soap Opera. *Screen* 22(4).

Brunsdon, C. (1989). Text and Audience. In: E. Seiter, H. Borchers, G. Kreutzner & E.-M. Warth (eds.), *Remote Control*. London: Routledge.

Budd, B., R. Entman & C. Steinman (1990). The Affirmative Character of American Cultural Studies. *Critical Studies in Mass Communications* 7(2).

Byars, J. (1991). *All That Hollywood Allows*. London: Routledge.

Cohen, P. & C. Gardner (eds.) (1984). *It Ain't Half Racist, Mum*. London: Comedia.

Condit, C. (1989). The Rhetorical Limits of Polysemy. *Critical Studies in Mass Communications* 6(2).

Connell, I. (1985). Blaming the Meeja. In: L. Masterman (ed.), *Television Mythologies*. London: Comedia.

Connell, I. & L. Curti (1985). Popular Broadcasting in Italy and Britain. In: P. Drummond & R. Paterson (eds.), *Television in Transition*. London: British Film Institute.

Corner, J. (1991). Meaning, Genre and Context. In: J. Curran & M. Gurevitch (eds.), *Mass Media and Society*. London: Edward Arnold.

Counihan, M. (1973). Orthodoxy, Revisionism and Guerilla Warfare in Mass Communications Research. Mimeo, Centre for Contemporary Cultural Studies, University of Birmingham.

Curran, J. (1990). The "New Revisionism" in Mass Communication Research. *European Journal of Communications* 5(2–3).

De Certeau, M. (1984). *The Practice of Everyday Life*. Berkeley: University of California Press.

Drummond, P. & R. Paterson (1988). *Television and Its Audiences*. London: British Film Institute.

Erni, J. (1989). Where Is the Audience? *Journal of Communication Enquiry* 13(2).

Evans, W. (1990). The Interpretive Turn in Media Research. *Critical Studies in Mass Communication* 7(2).

Fiske, J. (1986). Television: Polysemy and Popularity. *Critical Studies in Mass Communication* 3(1).

Fiske, J. (1987). *Television Culture*. London: Methuen.

Glasgow Media Group (1976). *Bad News*. London: Routledge & Kegan Paul.

Glasgow Media Group (1980). *More Bad News*. London: Routledge & Kegan Paul.

Gledhill, C. (1988). Pleasurable Negotiations. In: E. Pribram (ed.), *Female Spectators*. London: Verso.

Hall, S. (1973). Encoding and Decoding in the TV Discourse. Reprinted in S. Hall, I. Connell & L. Curti (eds.) (1981), *Culture, Media, Language*. London: Hutchinson.

Hall, S. (1981). Theories of Language and Ideology. In: S. Hall, I. Connell & L. Curti (eds.), *Culture, Media, Language*. London: Hutchinson.

Hall, S. (1982). The Rediscovery of Ideology. In: M. Gurevitch, T. Beunett, J. Curran & J. Woollacott (eds.), *Culture, Society and the Media*. London: Methuen.

Hall, S. (1989). Ideology and Communication Theory. In: B. Dervin, L. Grossberg, B. J. O'Keefe & E. Wartella (eds.), *Rethinking Communication*, Volume 2. London: Sage.

Hall, S., I. Connell & L. Curti (1981). The Unity of Current Affairs TV. In: T. Bennett, S. Boyd-Bowman, C. Mercer & J. Wollacott (eds.), *Popular Television and Film*. London: British Film Institute.

Halloran, J. (1970). *The Effects of Television*. London: Panther.

Heath, S. (1977/8). Notes on Suture. *Screen* 18(4).

Hebdige, D. (1979). *Subculture: The Meaning of Style*. London: Methuen.

Hebdige, D. (1988). *Hiding in the Light*. London: Comedia/Routledge.

Hobson, D. (1982). *Crossroads*. London: Methuen.

Lacan, J. (1977). *Ecrits: A Selection*. London: Tavistock.

Lewis, J. (1991). *The Ideological Octopus*. London: Routledge.

Liebes, T. & E. Katz (1991). *The Export of Meaning*. Oxford: Oxford University Press.

Lindlof, T. & T. Meyer (1987). Mediated Communication: The Foundations of Qualitative Research. In: T. Lindlof (ed.), *Natural Audiences*. Norwood, NJ: Ablex.

McArthur, C. (1981). Historical Drama. In: T. Bennett, S. Boyd-Bowman, C. Mercer & J. Woollacott (eds.), *Television and Film*. London: British Film Institute.

MacCabe, C. (1974). Realism and the Cinema. *Screen* 15(2).

MacCabe, C. (1981). Days of Hope. In: T. Bennett, S. Boyd-Bowman, C. Mercer & J. Woollacott (eds.), *Popular Television and Film*. London: British Film Institute.

Martin-Barbero, J. (1988). Communication from Culture. *Media, Culture and Society* 10.

Mattelart, M. (1984). *Women, Media, Crisis*. London: Comedia.

Metz, C. (1975). The Imaginary Signifier. *Screen* 16(2).

Mills, A. & P. Rice (1982). Quizzing the Popular. *Screen Education* 41.

Modleski, T. (1984). *Loving with a Vengeance*. London: Methuen.

Modleski, T. (ed.) (1986). *Studies in Entertainment*. Bloomington: Indiana University Press.

Moores, S. (1993). *Interpreting Audiences*. London: Sage.

Morley, D. (1980). *The Nationwide Audience*. London: British Film Institute.

Morley, D. & R. Silverstone (1990). Domestic Communications: Technologies and Meanings. *Media, Culture and Society* 12(1).

Murdock, G. (1989). Cultural Studies: Missing Links. *Critical Studies in Mass Communication* 6(4).

Neale, S. (1977). Propaganda. *Screen* 18(3).

Newcomb, H. & P. Hirsch (1987). Television as a Cultural Forum. In: W. Rowlands & B. Atkins (eds.), *Interpreting Television*. Newbury Park, CA: Sage.

Open University (1981). *U203: Popular Culture Course*. Milton Keynes: Open University Press.

Pechcux, M. (1982). *Language, Semantics and Ideology*. London: Macmillan.

Philo, G. (1990). *Seeing and Believing*. London: Routledge.

Radway, J. (1984). *Reading the Romance*. Chapel Hill: University of North Carolina Press.

Rosengren, K. (1985). Growth of a Research Tradition. In: K. Rosengren, L. Wenner & P. Palingreen (eds.), *Media Gratifications Research*. Beverley Hills, CA: Sage.

Schiller, H. (1988). The Erosion of National Sovereignty by the World Business System. In: M. Taber (ed.), *The Myth of the Information Revolution*. London: Sage.

Schroder, K. (1987). Convergence of Antagonistic Traditions? *European Journal of Communications* 2.

Schroder, K. (1988). The Pleasure of *Dynasty*. In: P. Drummond & R. Paterson (eds.), *Television and Its Audiences*. London: British Film Institute.

Schudson, M. (1987). The New Validation of Popular Culture. *Critical Studies in Mass Communication* 4(1).

Seaman, W. (1992). Active Audience Theory: Pointless Populism. *Media, Culture and Society* 14.

Seiter, E., H. Borchers, G. Kreutzner & E.-M. Warth (eds.) (1989). *Remote Control*. London: Routledge.

Volosinov, V. (1973). *Marxism and the Philosophy of Language*. New York: Academic Press.

71

Reading the Romance

Janice Radway[*]

Had I looked solely at the act of reading as it is understood by the women themselves, or, alternately, at the covert significance of the romance's narrative structure, I might have been able to provide one clear-cut, sharp-focus image. In the first case, the image would suggest that the act of romance reading is oppositional because it allows the women to refuse momentarily their self-abnegating social role. In the second, the image would imply that the romance's narrative structure embodies a simple recapitulation and recommendation of patriarchy and its constituent social practices and ideologies. However, by looking at the romance-reading behavior of real women through several lenses, each trained on a different component or moment of a process that achieves its meaning and effect over time, each also positioned differently in the sense that one attempts to see the women's experience from within while the other strives to view it from without, this study has consciously chosen to juxtapose multiple views of the complex social interaction between people and texts known as reading. Although I think each view accurately captures one aspect of the phenomenon of romance reading, none can account fully for the actual occurrence or significance of the event as such. In part, this is a function of the complexity inherent in any human action, but it is also the consequence of the fact that culture is both perceptible and hidden, both articulate and covert. Dot and the Smithton women know well both how and why they read romances. Yet at the same time, they also act on cultural assumptions and corollaries not consciously available to them precisely because those givens constitute the very foundation of their social selves, the very possibility of their social action. The multiple perspectives employed here have been adopted, therefore, in the hope that they might help us to comprehend what the women understand themselves to be gaining from the reading of romances while simultaneously revealing how that practice and self-understanding have tacit, unintended effects and implications.

Although it will be impossible, then, to use this conclusion to bring a single, large picture into focus simply because there is no context-free, unmarked position from which to view the activity of romance reading in its entirety, I can perhaps use it to remind the reader of each of the snapshots provided herein, to juxtapose them rapidly

[*] Pp. 1042–9 from *Literary Theory: An Anthology*, ed. J. Rivkin and M. Ryan (Malden, MA: Blackwell); pp. 209–22 and 256 from J. Radway, "Conclusion," *Reading the Romance: Women, Patriarchy and Popular Literature* (Chapel Hill: University of North Carolina Press, 1984). © 1984, new introduction © 1991 by the University of North Carolina Press. Used by permission of the publisher.

in condensed space and time. Such a review will help to underscore the semantic richness and ideological density of the actual process known as romance reading and thus highlight once and for all the complicated nature of the connection between the romance and the culture that has given rise to it.

If we remember that texts are read and that reading itself is an activity carried on by real people in a preconstituted social context, it becomes possible to distinguish *analytically* between the meaning of the act and the meaning of the text as read. This analytic distinction then empowers us to question whether the significance of the act of reading itself might, under some conditions, contradict, undercut, or qualify the significance of producing a particular kind of story. When this methodological distinction is further complicated by an effort to render real readers' comprehension of each of the aspects of the activity as well as the covert significance and consequences underlying both, the possibilities for perceiving conflict and contradiction are increased even more. This is exactly what has resulted from this account of the reading preferences and behavior of Dorothy Evans and the Smithton women.

Ethnographic investigation, for instance, has led to the discovery that Dot and her customers see the act of reading as combative and compensatory. It is combative in the sense that it enables them to refuse the other-directed social role prescribed for them by their position within the institution of marriage. In picking up a book, as they have so eloquently told us, they refuse temporarily their family's otherwise constant demand that they attend to the wants of others even as they act deliberately to do something for their own private pleasure. Their activity is compensatory, then, in that it permits them to focus on themselves and to carve out a solitary space within an arena where their self-interest is usually identified with the interests of others and where they are defined as a public resource to be mined at will by the family. For them, romance reading addresses needs created in them but not met by patriarchal institutions and engendering practices.

It is striking to observe that this partial account of romance reading, which stresses its status as an oppositional or contestative act because the women use it to thwart common cultural expectations and to supply gratification ordinarily ruled out by the way the culture structures their lives, is not far removed from the account of folkloric practices elaborated recently by Luigi-Lombardi-Satriani and José Limon.[1] Although both are concerned only with folkloric behavior and the way indigenous folk performances contest the hegemonic imposition of bourgeois culture on such subordinate groups as "workers, . . . peasants, racial and cultural minorities, and women," their definitions of contestation do not rule out entirely the sort of behavioral activity involving mass culture that I have discovered among the Smithton readers.

Lombardi-Satriani, for instance, argues that the folkloric cultures of subordinate groups may contest or oppose the dominant culture in two distinct ways. On the one hand, folklore may express overtly or metaphorically values that are different from or question those held by the dominant classes. On the other hand, opposition also can occur *because* a folkloric performance exists. Limon adds, however, that it is not the simple fact of a folkloric practice's existence that produces opposition: rather, opposition is effected when that performance "counter-valuates." What he means by counter-valuation is a process of inversion whereby the original socioeconomic limitations and devaluations of a subordinate group are first addressed by the folkloric performance and then transformed within or by it into something of value to the group. If the process is successful, Limon maintains, the performance contests by supplementation. In effect, it simultaneously acknowledges and meets the needs of the subordinate group, which, as the consequence of its subordination, are systematically ignored by the culture's practices and institutions.

When romance reading is examined, then, as an activity that takes place within a specific social context, it becomes evident that this form of behavior both supplements and counter-valuates in Limon's sense. Romance reading supplements the avenues traditionally open to women for emotional gratification by supplying them vicariously with the attention and nurturance they do not get enough of in the round of day-to-day existence. It counter-valuates because the story opposes the female values of love and personal interaction to the male values of competition and public achievement and, at least in ideal romances, demonstrates the triumph of the former over the latter. Romance reading and writing might be seen therefore as a collectively elaborated female ritual through which women explore the consequences of their common social condition as the appendages of men and attempt to imagine a more perfect state where all the needs they so intensely feel and accept as given would be adequately addressed. . . .

By the same token, it should also be pointed out that although romance writing and reading help to create a kind of female community, that community is nonetheless mediated by the distances that characterize mass production and the capitalist organization of storytelling. Because the oppositional act is carried out through the auspices of a book and thus involves the fundamentally private, isolating experience of reading, these women never get together to share either the experience of imaginative opposition, or, perhaps more important, the discontent that gave rise to their need for the romance in the first place. The women join forces only symbolically and in a mediated way in the privacy of their individual homes and in the culturally devalued sphere of leisure activity. They do nothing to challenge their separation from one another brought about by the patriarchal culture's insistence that they never work in the public world to maintain themselves but rather live symbiotically as the property and responsibility of men.

In summary, when the act of romance reading is viewed as it is by the readers themselves, from within a belief system that accepts as given the institutions of heterosexuality and monogamous marriage, it can be conceived as an activity of mild protest and longing for reform necessitated by those institutions' failure to satisfy the emotional needs of women. Reading therefore functions for them as an act of recognition and contestation whereby that failure is first admitted and then partially reversed. Hence, the Smithton readers' claim that romance reading is a "declaration of independence" and a way to say to others, "This is my time, my space. Now leave me alone."

At the same time, however, when viewed from the vantage point of a feminism that would like to see the women's oppositional impulse lead to real social change, romance reading can also be seen as an activity that could potentially disarm that impulse. It might do so because it supplies vicariously those very needs and requirements that might otherwise be formulated as demands in the real world and lead to the potential restructuring of sexual relations. . . .

As I have pointed out, the narrative discourse of the romantic novel is structured in such a way that it yields easily to the reader's most familiar reading strategies. Thus the act of constructing the narrative line is reassuring because the romantic writer's typical discourse leads the reader to make abductions and inferences that are always immediately confirmed. As she assembles the plot, therefore, the reader learns, in addition to what happens next, that *she* knows how to make sense of texts and human action. Although this understanding of the process must he taken into account and attributed to a positive desire to assert the power and capability of the female self, it cannot be overlooked that the fictional world created as its consequence also reinforces traditional female limitations because it validates the dominance of domestic concerns and personal interaction in women's lives. The reader thus engages in an activity that shores up her own sense of her abilities, but she also creates a simulacrum of hcr limited social world within a more glamorous fiction. She therefore inadvertently justifies as natural the very conditions and their emotional consequences to which her reading activity is a response.

Similarly, in looking at the Smithton readers' conscious engagement with the manifest content of the ideal romance, it becomes evident that these women believe themselves to be participating in a story that is as much about the transformation of an inadequate suitor into the perfect lover-protector as it is about the concomitant triumph of a woman. Her triumph consists of her achievement of sexual and emotional maturity while simultaneously securing the complete attention and devotion of this man who, at least on the surface, admits her preeminent claim to his time and interest. The act of constructing the romantic tale thus provides the reader first with an opportunity to protest vicariously at man's initial inability to understand a woman and to treat her with sensitivity. Secondarily, the process enables a woman to achieve a kind of mastery-over her fear of rape because the fantasy evokes her fear and subsequently convinces her that rape is either an illusion or something that she can control easily. Finally, by witnessing and approving of the ideal romantic conclusion, the reader expresses her opposition to the domination of commodity values in her society because she so heartily applauds the heroine's ability to draw thc hcro's attention away from the public world of money and status and to convince him of the primacy of her values and concerns.

It seems apparent, then, that an oppositional moment can be said to characterize even the production of the romantic story if that process is understood as the women themselves conceive it. I have elsewhere called this stage or aspect of the reading process a "utopian" moment,[2] drawing on Fredric Jameson's important argument that every form of mass culture has a dimension "which remains implicitly, and no matter how faintly, negative and critical of the social order from which, as a product and a commodity, it springs."[3] In effect, the vision called into being at the end of the process of romance-reading projects for the reader a utopian state where men are neither cruel nor indifferent, neither preoccupied with the external world nor wary of an intense emotional attachment to a woman. This fantasy also suggests that the safety and protection of traditional marriage will not compromise a woman's autonomy or self-confidence. In sum, the vision reforms those very conditions characterizing the real world that leave so many women and, most probably, the reader herself, longing for affective care, ongoing tenderness, and a strong sense of self-worth. This interpretation of the romance's meaning suggests, then, that the women who seek out ideal novels in order to construct such a vision again and again are reading not out of contentment but out of dissatisfaction, longing, and protest.

Of course, in standing back from this construction of the romance's meaning, once again to assess the implications of its symbolic negation and criticism of the social order, it becomes possible to see that despite the utopian force of the romance's projection, that projection actually leaves unchallenged the very system of social relations whose faults and imperfections gave rise to the romance and which the romance is trying to perfect. The romance manages to do so because its narrative organization prompts the reader to construct covert counter-messages that either undercut or negate the changes projected on an overt level. To begin with, although the narrative story provides the reader with an opportunity to indulge in anger at the initial, offensive behavior of the hero, we must not forget that that anger is later shown to be unwarranted because the hero's indifference or cruelty actually originated in feelings of love. Thus while the experience of reading the tale may be cathartic in the sense that it allows the reader to express in the imagination anger at men that she would otherwise censor or deny, it also suggests to her that such anger as the heroine's is, in reality, unjustified because the offensiveness of the behavior prompting it was simply a function of the heroine's inability to read a man properly. Because the reading process always confirms for the reader that she knows how to read male behavior correctly, it suggests that her anger is unnecessary because her spouse, like the hero, actually loves her deeply, though he may not express it as she might wish. In the end, the romance-reading process gives the reader a strategy for making her present situation more comfortable without substantive reordering of its structure rather than a comprehensive program for reorganizing her life in such a way that all needs might be met. . . .

Little need be said here about the way in which the romance's treatment of rape probably harms romance readers even as it provides them with a sense of power and control over their fear of it. Although their distaste for "out-and-out" violation indicates that these women do not want to be punished or hurt as so many have assumed, their willingness to be convinced that the forced "taking" of a woman by a man who "really" loves her is testimony to her desirability and worth rather than to his power suggests once again that the romance is effectively dealing with some of the consequences of patriarchy without also challenging the hierarchy of control upon which it is based. By examining the whole issue of rape and its effect on the heroine, the romance may provide the reader with the opportunity to explore the consequences of related behavior in her own life, Nonetheless, by suggesting that rape is either a mistake or an expression of uncontrollable desire, it may also give her a false sense of security by showing her how to rationalize violent behavior and thus reconcile her to a set of events and relations that she would be better off changing.

Finally, it must also be noted here that even though the romance underlines the opposition between the values of love and those associated with the competitive pursuit of status and wealth, by perpetuating the exclusive division of the world into the familiar categories of the public and the private, the romance continues to justify the social placement of women that has led to the very discontent that is the source of their desire to read romances. It is true, certainly, that the romance accepts this dichotomy in order to assert subsequently that the commonly devalued personal sphere and the women who dominate it have higher status and the evangelical power to draw the keepers of the public realm away from their worldly interests. Yet despite this proclamation of female superiority, in continuing to relegate women to the arena of domestic, purely personal relations, the romance fails to pose other, more radical questions. In short, it refuses to ask whether female values might be used to "feminize" the public realm or if control over that realm could be shared by women and by men. Because the romance finally leaves unchallenged the male right to the public spheres of work, politics, and power, because it refurbishes the institution of marriage by suggesting how it might be viewed continuously as a courtship, because it represents real female needs within the story and then depicts their satisfaction by traditional heterosexual relations, the romance avoids questioning the institutionalized basis of patriarchal control over women even as it serves as a locus of protest against some of its emotional consequences. . . .

As I have mentioned previously, Dot Evans and the Smithton readers believe very strongly that romance reading changes at least some women. They seem to feel that bad romances especially prompt them to compare their own behavior with that of passive, "namby-pamby" heroines who permit their men to abuse them and push them around. This comparison, they believe, then often leads to greater resolve on the part of the reader who vows never to let her spouse injure her in a similar fashion. Dot and her customers also believe that they learn to assert themselves more effectively as a consequence of their reading because they so often have to defend their choices of material to others and justify their right to pleasure.

Although I have no way of knowing whether this perceived assertiveness is carried over to their interactions with their husbands and families over issues beyond that of how to spend leisure time, the women's self-perceptions should not be ignored if we really do want to understand what women derive from reading romances. Of course, it could be the case that these readers develop assertive techniques in a few restricted areas of their lives and thus do not use their newfound confidence and perceived power to challenge the fundamental hierarchy of control in their marriages. However, it is only fair not to assume this from the beginning in order to guard against the danger of automatically assigning greater weight to the way a real desire for change is channeled by a culture into nonthreatening form than to the desire itself. To do so would be to ignore the limited but nonetheless unmistakable and creative ways in which people resist the deleterious effects of their social situations. . . .

We must not, in short, look only at mass-produced objects themselves on the assumption that they bear all of their significances on their surface, as it were, and reveal them automatically to us. To do so would be to assume either that perceptible, tangible things alone are worth analyzing or that those commodified objects exert such pressure and influence on their consumers that they have no power as individuals to resist or alter the ways in which those objects mean or can be used.

Commodities like mass-produced literary texts are selected, purchased, construed, and used by real people with previously existing needs, desires, intentions, and interpretive strategies. By reinstating those naive individuals and their creative, constructive activities at the heart of our interpretive enterprise, we avoid blinding ourselves to the fact that the essentially human practice of making meaning goes on even in a world increasingly dominated by things and by consumption. In thus recalling the interactive character of operations like reading, we restore time, process, and action to our account of human endeavor and therefore increase the possibility of doing justice to its essential complexity and ambiguity as practice. We also increase our chances of sorting out or articulating the difference between the repressive imposition of ideology and oppositional practices that, though limited in their scope and effect, at least dispute or contest the control of ideological forms.

If we can learn, then, to look at the ways in which various groups appropriate and use the mass-produced art of our culture, I suspect we may well begin to understand that although the ideological power of contemporary cultural forms is enormous, indeed sometimes even frightening, that power is not yet all-pervasive, totally vigilant, or complete. Interstices still exist within the social fabric where opposition is carried on by people who are not satisfied by their place within it or by the restricted material and emotional rewards that accompany it. They therefore attempt to imagine a more perfect social state as a way of countering despair. I think it absolutely essential that we who are committed to social change learn not to overlook this minimal but nonetheless legitimate form of protest. We should seek it out not only to understand its origins and its utopian longing but also to learn how best to encourage it and bring it to fruition. If we do not, we have already conceded the fight and, in the case of the romance at least, admitted the impossibility of creating a world where the vicarious pleasure supplied by its reading would be unnecessary.

Notes

1. Luigi Lombardi-Satriani, "Folklore as Culture of Contestation," *Journal of the Folklore Institute*, pp. 99–121, and José Limon, "Folklore and the Mexican in the United States" (unpublished paper), pp. 1–21.
2. Jan Radway, "The Utopian Impulse in Popular Literature," *American Quarterly* 33 (Summer 1981), pp. 140–62.
3. Fredric Jameson, "Reification and Utopia," *Social Text* 1 (Winter 1979), p. 144.

72

The Cinematic Apparatus and the Construction of the Film Celebrity

*P. David Marshall**

The Audience's Pleasure and Play and the Construction of Significance with Intimacy and Enigma

The relationship that the audience builds with the film celebrity is configured through a tension between the possibility and impossibility of knowing the authentic individual. The various mediated constructions of the film celebrity ensure that whatever intimacy is permitted between the audience and the star is purely at the discursive level. The desire and pleasure are derived from this clear separation of the material reality of the star as living being from the fragments of identity that are manifested in films, interviews, magazines, pinup posters, autographs, and so on. Depending on the level of commitment of the audience member, certain types of fragments or traces of identity are deemed adequate. For some, the characters of the films themselves, which among them construct their own intertextual framework of the celebrity's identity, are quite sufficient. For others, those called fanatics or fans, the materiality of identity must be reinforced through the acquisition of closer representations of existence and identity. The autograph and the pinup poster epitomize the committed fan of a film celebrity. Belonging to a fan club entails an investment into the maintenance of a coherent identity, as members circulate information about the celebrity that for the members establishes a somewhat separate and distinctive episteme concerning the star's true nature. Recent work on fan culture has articulated the relative affective investment that can be part of the cultural experience of the star for the audience. Fandom can actively transform the meaning of stars well beyond the material presented in magazines and newspapers.[1]

In his book on film stars, Morin lists some of the requests that fans have made of their favorite celebrities. Some ask for locks of hair, others for small possessions that will allow the fan to enter the private sphere of the star through the fetish object. Most ask for photographs. Some are driven to ask their favorite stars' advice on their own personal matters.[2] According to Margaret Thorpe, in the 1930s and 1940s a studio typically received up to fifteen thousand fan letters a week. A first-class star would have received directly three hundred letters a week.[3]

The range of audience participation in the construction of the film celebrity sign is wide and varied. Nevertheless, stars possess a general allure in their combination of the everyday and the extraordinary that is modalized through a discourse on intimacy and enigma. The ordinary elements of the film star are important as a marked entrance point for the audience to play with kinds of identity and identification. Since its inception, the film industry has produced stars who have emerged from apparently "normal" backgrounds. The mythology of stardom that has been circulated in the trade literature since Laemmle's Biograph Girl media event is the possibility that anyone can be a star. Because of the sustained focus on external appearance, as opposed to acting ability, the film star appeared to be chosen quite randomly. Merit was secondary to luck and circumstance. In this way, the Hollywood film industry perpetuated a myth of democratic access. The concept of merit and ability was transposed into the language of character and the personal history of the star. Humble beginnings, hard work, and honesty were the extratextual signs of the film celebrity that supported this myth of the democratic art. The extensive discourse on the stars' personal and private lives often was constructed on how fame and fortune could corrupt the ordinary human being housed in the star personality. This theme became one of the central film story lines of a progressively self-reflexive Hollywood. From *42nd Street* to three versions of *A Star Is Born*, Hollywood reinforced its anyone-can-make-it mythology.

In contradistinction to the democratic nature of access, the image of the film star expressed the inaccessibility and extraordinary quality of the celebrity lifestyle. In double senses of the word, the images of wealth were typically *classless*, and in this way were compatible with the democratic ideology that surrounded Hollywood movies, despite their oligopolistic economic structure. The mansions of the movie stars had all the signs of wealth and prestige but none of the cultural capital to reign in the appearance of excess. The swimming pools, with their unique shapes, the immodest and therefore grandiose architecture pillaged from countless traditions without cultural contextualization, and the elaborate grounds and gates were all signs of the nouveau riche, a class excluded from the dominant culture because of its inability to coordinate the signs of wealth. Movie stars' prestige was built on the signs of consumer capitalism, and their decadence and excess were celebrations of the spoils of an ultimate consumer lifestyle. Their wealth, generated through the expansion of leisure as an industry and the entertainment consumer as a widening domain of subjectivity, was cause for celebration – not cultural responsibility.

To use Bourdieu's typology of taste and distinction, the movie star's ostentatious presentation of wealth exemplified an aesthetic that was obvious and overdone. In opposition, those who possessed not only capital but cultural and intellectual capital constructed their distinctive taste in terms of abstraction and distance from these more obvious and overt expressions of wealth.[4]

The power of the film celebrity's aesthetic of wealth and leisure in the twentieth century can not be seen to be static. With its close connection to the construction of consumer lifestyles, the film celebrity's forays into recreational pursuits helped define the parameters of pleasure through consumption for all segments of society. Perhaps the best example of this expansive and proliferating power to influence the entire socius has been the growing centrality of the Hollywood image of the healthy body. Tanned skin had been seen traditionally as evidence of physical labor, specifically farm labor. Although there may have been a bucolic connotation to the image of the tanned and brawny farmhand, it contained no further signification of an easy, leisurely life. To be tanned was evidence that one had engaged in hard work under the sun. Hollywood film stars helped construct a new body aesthetic as they attempted to look healthier under the intense lighting of their film shoots. The activity of suntanning achieved a glamorous connotation because it now indicated one had the time to do virtually nothing but lie in the sun. The film star worked in this domain of breaking down and reconstructing conceptions of distinctions. Thus, certain expensive or class-based outdoor sports, such as yachting and tennis, provided a conduit between these new body images of health and fitness that demanded time and energy in the sun and the other moneyed classes. Leisure and wealth became in the twentieth century associated with having a tan and a well-toned body; however, these new signs, appropriated from the laboring class, had to have been achieved through sports and hobbies, and not work.[5]

The classlessness of film celebrities despite their clear wealth aligned them as a group with their audience. Their wealth, if thought of as an extrapolation of a consumer subjectivity, also aligned them with an ethos fostered in late capitalism. The construction of identity in the domains of consumption as opposed to production made the film star an image of the way in which a lifestyle/identity could be found in the domain of nonwork. The star, then, to borrow from Ewen's study of the development of a general consumer consciousness in the twentieth century through advertising and general business objectives, performed as a "consumption ideal": a representative of the modern way of life.[6] Anyone has access to the goods of the large department stores, and therefore can play in this democratic myth of identity construction through consumption.

The chasm between the type of lifestyle constructed by the film star and that constructed by the audience is continually filled in by the rumors, gossip, and stories that circulate in newspapers and magazines concerning the complex and tragic lives led in Hollywood. In early Hollywood, the reported excesses of lifestyle and success were treated in a disciplinary manner by the press. If one thinks of a film star as a consumption ideal, then failures and tragedies were the results of a consumer lifestyle that was incongruous with the personal roots of the star. Much of the writing of the personal life stories of the stars, particularly the form of gossip writing that focused on failure, emphasized the traps of success. The discourse on film star tragedy, then, was concerned with the reconciliation of the personal and the psychological with the manner and means of consumption. The root cause for the diversion of lifestyle from the person's true nature was the instant success gained by the film star. The disciplinary morals offered by these scandals of the stars for the audience concerned the need to match one's psychological personality with an appropriate lifestyle and consumption identity. The stars represented extreme constructions of lifestyle. The audience member had to work toward some kind of balance. Finally, the audience also learned about the essential human frailties and personality types of these distant stars. Despite their larger-than-life presence on screen, film stars were essentially human and covered the gamut of personality types.

Summary

The film celebrity as a general discourse occupies a central position in the development of the twentieth-century celebrity, and it is for this reason I have provided a rather lengthy genealogy of its formation. Because of cinema's history, covering the entire twentieth century, and because the cinematic apparatus's development and growth coincided with the growth and extension of consumer capitalism, the film celebrity has provided a way in which the discourses of individualism, freedom, and identity have been articulated in modern society. With the film star's relative nonattachment to material forms of production because of his or her work solely in the manufacture of images, the discourse on and about screen stars was particularly concerned with the manner of consumption and the associated construction of lifestyles. The discourse on film celebrities and their consumption was also integrated into a study of personality, character, and general psychological profile. Through various extratextual sources, the celebrities provided the ground for the debate concerning the way in which new patterns of consumption could be organized to fit the innate patterns of personality.

In the rest of this chapter, I examine a contemporary film celebrity in depth to reveal the way in which these various discourses are modalized through a particular celebrity sign. Within the discussion of the intertextual and extratextual elements in the sign/text construction of the celebrity, I develop a typology of celebrity and audience subjectivity as it relates to film.

Tom Cruise: The Construction of a Contemporary Film Celebrity

The channels of knowledge

Tom Cruise is classified by a variety of sources as a movie star. To achieve this status, Cruise articulates through various texts and representations that he possesses certain qualities that are not possessed by others. He exits the realm of the everyday and moves into the representational world of the public sphere. For Cruise, the filmic text, where he performs various roles that are constructed into clear-cut narratives, becomes the primary means by which he becomes identifiable as a recognizable public figure. Surrounding the particular moments of each film release are the intersections of several strategic discourses that work to construct the celebrity quality of the film star. On one level, the agency that represents Tom Cruise, along with the corporation and production company that has produced the film, attempts to promote an organized conception of Tom Cruise that is connected with the specific release of the film. Cruise, then, is both contained by the package of the film and is the package that works to draw the attention of the press to consider the film significant or of interest. The film star works in the arena of publicity that predates the exhibition date of the film.

The origins of film stardom: the physical performer

The specific constructions that are strategically operated in the release of a film can be likened to Richard DeCordova's historical categories of the development of the star persona.[7] In the early twentieth century, audience knowledge about the performers in cinema was limited. Thus, we see the development of monikers that were connected to their performances on screen rather than their real names. Film actors were identified by the audience and the film industry, as mentioned above, through their physical characteristics. We can call this first category of identification, in line with DeCordova's analysis, the *physical performer*: what is identified by industry and audience are the physical characteristics that make him or her unique in the field of film performers. Thus, this is a discourse that emphasizes beauty or lack thereof, the performer's nose, smile, eyes, entire body type. It is an objectification of the performer that is more often than not metonymic; that is, one element/feature represents the entire performer and connects his or her reality from one film to the next. The metonymic process should not be seen as emerging solely from the industry or the audience. The industry attempts to read the public, based on a variety of polling techniques as well as less scientifically and more culturally defined conceptions of beauty and attraction. The historical organization of this pretesting can be captured by the screen test, where a performer is filmed to determine his or her commodity potential and value to the studio. If the test is successful, then the performer is released in a feature film and marketed as a starlet, a rising star. Audience reaction to the new performer is fully tested after the release of his or her first films. A determination of star quality is determined from this rereading of the film's audience, general public reaction, and the associated press coverage of the individual performer.

Cruise as physical performer

In the transformation of DeCordova's categories into an individual celebrity text, one can see that the construction of the physical performer emerges at the beginning of any film celebrity's career. At that point, extratextual knowledge of the actor is limited. Even his or her on-screen presence is often constrained to only moments of screen time – a newcomer is not often the star of his or her early films. Nevertheless, there is a particular quality or group of qualities that become the way in which the actor becomes recognizable as a specific type. When the celebrity is identified in these physical terms, there is the risk that he or she will become typecast, or arrested in the formation of celebrity status and cast in roles based only on some clear-cut stereotypical image/quality.

Tom Cruise's emergence as a film actor and star is first connected to the physicality of his performance. The category with which Cruise was identified, by both industry and audience, was that of youth. In his second film, *Taps* (1981), Cruise, although originally cast for a much smaller part, was able (according to the biographical information made significant when he began to star in films later in his career), because of his apparent innate screen presence, to expand his role into something much larger and more significant. In the film he plays a gungho, arms-obsessed cadet at a military academy. His role presents youth as pure action: unthinking instead of contemplative, assured, confident, and narrow-minded in his choice of actions. His character, David Shawn, is willing to murder and quite willing to die. All of this is done with a certain bravado that is expressed in Cruise's use of his smile and grin, something that has become a trademark in his movement to celebrity status. In terms of the film's character, the smile and the grin indicate the reckless insanity of the personality. It was with this role that Cruise's name moved into the popular press.

Cruise's film debut was also in a film designated specifically for a youth audience. In *Endless Love* (1981), a Franco Zeffirelli-directed film about modern obsessive teenage love, Cruise plays a small role that is not mentioned in any of the reviews. What is significant is his position once again in terms of categories of youth. The film industry worked to establish a legion of youthful stars in the 1980s. Connected with their rise were several coming-of-age films as well as the construction of a group of actors who came to be known through the popular press as the Hollywood brat pack. As a market segment, the youth audience was considered to be the very center of the film industry. The development of films that focused on generational themes, and through those narratives established territory for the elevation of certain young actors to stardom, could be seen as a general industrial strategy. Cruise was part of this organization of the film industry around its principal exhibition market.

In these earliest incarnations, Cruise possesses a character type that is closely aligned with his own physical look. He is a physical performer, and our knowledge of his private world is virtually nonexistent. He is characterized by his engendering young male handsomeness. As well, he must be structured and must structure himself into the construction of filmic youthful maleness. The gendering of his physical presence, then, is carried out in reference to past icons who define what makes a male film star. He is thus engendered into a cultural pattern of representation.

What this means is that Cruise, as a new potential star, is mapped onto the types of male stars that predated his appearance. In the postwar period, the intersection of male and youth has been represented by past stars as confused rebellion. The images of Marlon Brando and James Dean, along with Elvis Presley, established this dominant construction of male youth. No doubt the extratextual elements that revealed aspects of their personal lives also enhanced the images of these stars beyond their filmic type. Generally, however the consistency of character type in their films operates as the primary focus for the rearticulation of filmic maleness in future male stars. Cruise's construction of male "physical performer" must reply to the way in which these past stars exhibited strength and presence. Fundamentally, we can see that Dean, Brando, and even, to a degree, Paul Newman represent the interiorization of male power: there is a repressed fury in their performances that is represented by their brooding character portrayals and their bursts of aggression and violence.

These past film stars, then, operate as icons or archetypes that work to define the organization of new types of stars in their originary or emergent forms as physical performers. Cruise's physical performance must also work in response to the antiheroic male film stars of the 1970s: De Niro, Pacino, and Hoffman.[8] Because of their representations of ethnicity and of the working class and underclass, the designation of heroic qualities to these stars seems a misnomer. Nevertheless, they represent film stars: they are instrumental in the organization of film investment capital, they can demand high payment fees as well as a percentage of box-office revenues, and they are easily and readily recognizable in the public sphere. Tom Cruise's emergence as a physical performer, then, must negotiate these filmic identities to establish a certain continuity in the construction of the male film star and the uniqueness or differentiation of his particular example of the lineage. What this entails for the emerging star is that an attachment to the cultural icons of male representation produced by filmdom must be made evident so that subsequent extension of the icon can be made in the growth of the individual star.

What is interesting is that Cruise's first six films are intensely focused on youth and, more or less, on rebellion. In *The Outsiders* (1983), Cruise is involved in midwestern youth gang encounters between the rich and the poor. In the first film that features Cruise in the lead role, *Losin' It* (1983), a generic low-budget male-oriented teenage sex comedy, the emphasis is on loss of virginity, adventure in Tijuana, and a red convertible sports car. His next two movies establish the clear nature of the physical performer Tom Cruise. In *Risky Business* (1983), Cruise plays an upper-class teenager who plays out his fantasies when his parents go out of town and leave him alone for the first time. Finally, in *All the Right Moves* (1983), Cruise plays a very talented quarterback for a working-class town's high school football team. His success on the field is seen as his way out of the dead-end setting of the steel factory community.

As mentioned above, all of these films provide a unified theme concerning Tom Cruise as performer. All of them emphasize his youth. By implication, this emphasis on youth also emphasizes his youthful body and face. Cruise's screen presence, then, is constructed specifically around his embodiment of male beauty. His confidence in movement is part of this construction. His athletic build becomes another marker of his success as engendered representation of filmic male. Iconically, Cruise is connected to stars who represent the very mainstream of American film beauty. In the tradition of Newman and Redford, Cruise embodies Americanness as opposed to some Other of ethnicity. In terms of appearance, he is neither exotic nor enigmatic.

The emergence of the film celebrity is dependent on this original construction of the physical performer, where the actor is celebrated as a "type." The actor remains relatively anonymous except for these screen images. There is no deepening of the meaning of the actor beyond the screen presentations. However, the screen presentations provide a certain redundancy of image, an overcoding that is directed toward a decoding by the audience of the physical performer's reason for being celebrated, the material that can be used to determine the legitimacy of his elevated public stature.

There is a danger that the process of development of the screen star may be arrested in terms of what I have labeled as the actor as pure physical performer. In such a case, the categorization of "type" overcomes the actor's possibility of creating subjective differences in character portrayals. If the type is replicable by other performers, then the inherent value of the emerging screen star is limited. One can see this operation of the economics of film production in relationship to stardom most starkly in the relatively rapid positioning and replacing of female screen presentations. For example, in the James Bond series of films, there has been a consistency in the actors who have played Bond. Sean Connery became synonymous with the Bond persona through the 1960s, as did Roger Moore in the 1970s and 1980s. In contrast, the women in these films have been constructed to be infinitely replaceable, because the nature of their fame is built entirely on their physical performance. The basis of their physical performance is dependent on their ability to present alluring images of the female body. Although the Bond character clearly represents a "type," the patterning of that type engages an elaboration of performance beyond a clear aesthetic of beauty. Built into the type is a construction of masculine allure that permits a greater degree of action, power, and will. The very legitimate characterization of the many female actors who have appeared in the Bond films as the "Bond girls" underlines the film industry's systematic maintenance of a female stardom stalled and often imprisoned within the confines of the category of the physical performer.

The picture personality

The progression from physical performer to "picture personality" is the principal subject of DeCordova's in-depth analysis of the early history of screen stardom.[9] It is also analogous to the progression of the individual star from clearly formulated representation of "type" on the screen to the substantiation of the character type through the development of a public profile of the actor that is fundamentally extratextual in the contemporary moment. The key difference between the picture personality and the physical performer in the past was that the actor's name, as opposed to the character's name or type, became recognized by the audience and was used to link films together to provide a consistency around the actor's public persona. As DeCordova reveals in his reading of the popular press of the early twentieth century, the first biographical profiles of the screen stars of the 1910s were focused on this link between their screen presence and their personal lives: a homologous private world was established that would not challenge their filmic characters. It is interesting to see in the genealogy of the construction of current film celebrity that the same substantiation occurs as the physical performer begins to be constructed as a public personality. The example of Tom Cruise's transformation is exemplary.

Tom Cruise as picture personality

For Cruise, the line of demarcation between physical performer and recognizable screen personality, which identifies his representation beyond the screen, is drawn with the release of the feature film *Risky Business*.[10] Through this film, Cruise generates a great number of newspaper and magazine articles, not about the film, but about the star. The process of working out the internal nature of Tom Cruise begins. Articles start appearing first in youth-oriented magazines.[11] The film role becomes the basis for determining the real Tom Cruise, as something of a homology is constructed. Cruise, in publicity photos, plays with the image portrayed in the film – his public image becomes conflated with the Ray-Ban sunglasses used extensively by the character. For more mainstream magazines and reviewers, the movie provides the centerpiece for discussion. In these magazines, Cruise is interpreted as representing not only a role, but a generation of youth through his role and his "cool" attitude, best articulated through his use of the Ray-Bans and his relative detachment and distance from indicating the significance of experience. Again there is a conflation of the role with the public world; a connection is made to the resonance of the star's image and deportment in the film and life with the audience segment that has celebrated the film. The image of youth proliferates in other ways, as the look of the star becomes the way in which "Youth" and the interests of youth are represented in various forms of mediated culture.

Critical at this point in the development of the film celebrity is the necessity not to present contradictory evidence concerning the nature of Tom Cruise. His "real" persona is, at this stage, very much connected to that portrayed on the screen. Thus, the elaborate extratextual discourse on Cruise that appears in newspapers and magazines works to bolster the new screen personality. Cruise's own publicists also guard the integrity of the screen persona in an effort to maintain Cruise as a significant and marketable commodity. His commodity status is dependent still on the screen presentation, or what the character on the screen embodies. The production company, the studio, and the star's developing team of publicity agents begin to manage the consistency of the image. In this way, Cruise establishes a new variation on the male film celebrity, one that builds on the previous constructions but provides markers of distinction and differentiation. The form of those distinctions relates to the way in which a new "structure of feeling" envelopes the production of new film celebrities.[12]

This new structure of feeling lends a certain vagueness to the way a new film celebrity emerges. The vagueness relates to the manner in which the audience may interpret this constructed subjectivity embodied in the celebrity as well as the temporality of that construction, where the concrete reality of the celebrity is grounded in the moment. Through his screen image, Cruise has been positioned as part of a new generation of male stardom that has been connected to the way in which youth has rethought their imbrication in the social world. We can see in this formative version of Cruise as a celebrity sign/text that there are certain elements that provide a correlation of Cruise to this new attitude.

Youth – which connoted rebellion in previous film stars – is reconstructed through Cruise: youth is correlated with confidence and savvy. The difference between youth and the adult world in this new configuration is not based principally on challenging the models of success and value in contemporary society, as previous youthful male heroes emphasized; rather, the Cruise persona makes coherent the inherent value of a higher sensitivity to the way in which the system of success works, so that one can use it more effectively to gain personal success. The connection of youth and confidence through Cruise's persona can be characterized as a celebration of personal will, not to transform the system, but to move smoothly through the system to occupy already designated positions of power and influence. Cruise's screen personality has had a certain consistency since 1983. The film texts have worked to reinforce the reconstruction of this new conception of the power of youth, youthful action and agency. It is significant that the character in *Risky Business*, which has been so formative for Cruise's public personality, is depicted as a relatively well-off, probably upper-middle-class teenager. It is the type of image that indicates a clear connection and affinity to forms of cultural and economic capital and the forms of influence they imply. Most of Cruise's subsequent films rarely represent images of the upper classes; but they do present Cruise's characters as embodying the outward features and appearances of wealth as well as clear aspirations to assert their apparent natural right to be part of the wealthy. In most cases the films emphasize the ease with which Cruise can become comfortably successful.

In the filmic texts, this relationship to the ease of success is manifested around either sports/athleticism or the managing of sophisticated technology. In all cases, Cruise is something of a natural, but also a natural risk taker who goes beyond the bounds of the technology or game to demonstrate ultimate human dominance of will. In *All the Right Moves*, Cruise is a high school football hero who, through his sheer talent, can transcend his humble origins. In the enormously successful *Top Gun* (1986), Cruise portrays a character whose nickname is Maverick. He is chosen for an elite fighter squadron because of his capacity to supersede the talents of a technically good pilot. Cruise has not had to work hard to develop this skill; he manifests a natural affinity for handling this technical hardware.

Reinforcements of Cruise's screen personality can be seen in other films. In *The Color of Money* (1986), a more sophisticated film than his earlier vehicles, Cruise plays a naturally gifted pool player who is relatively unaware of the more subtle techniques he could use to win money at the game until he meets an older pool hustler played by Paul Newman. There are a number of layers of meanings in this film, which I will return to later in this chapter. What is significant with reference to the construction of a screen personality is that there is a consistency in the representation of Tom Cruise between *The Color of Money* and his earlier films. The organization of his public persona coheres among these various filmic texts. A particular and idiosyncratic celebrity sign is clearly established that intersects with a given set of values concerning youth, success, and appearance.

Top Gun established the stability of the commodity aspect of Cruise's celebrity sign. It signaled its differentiation from other constructions of stardom that predated Cruise and its clear relationship to a general restructuring of the attitudes of youth and success in the 1980s. It also heralded the power of this particular configuration of screen personality to produce, virtually on its own construction of character, a successful film. Two years following the release of *Top Gun* and *The Color of Money*, Cruise starred in a film that demonstrated his commodity power in the construction of audiences. *Cocktail* (1988), in its opening scenes, seems to provide a narrative continuity for the character, as if this character in this distinct movie has, in fact, emerged like Tom Cruise from *Top Gun*. In the opening sequence, we see Cruise as Brian Flanagan being dropped by his army buddies to catch a bus to "New York": he has completed his army service and is about to go on and achieve fame and fortune in the big city. The Flanagan character in this film never separates from our image of the Cruise star and, in fact, the film – through camera angles, obsessive shots of the Cruise smile and grin, and a celebration of Cruise's body and movement – actively plays and integrates the Cruise screen personality into the meaning of the text. Cruise as Flanagan becomes very quickly a bartending star, which allows him to act within the narrative as the star. The character is thronged by adoring fans in several sequences in the film. These fans, the bar patrons, are predominantly women, and their adulation of Flanagan for his acrobatic bartending skills is connected through the film text to the sexual aura of Cruise as male star. He acknowledges their looks and responds with greater histrionics. His success is further measured in the film by his success in sleeping with women. The women bar patrons in the filmic text represent for the producers of the movie a construction of the form of female adulation perceived to exist in the film audience (the public) for Cruise himself. Through an uncomplicated plot, Cruise's character is constructed as a divided personality, where physical prowess and beauty become separated from the moral integrity of character, The film ends with a reconciliation of the Cruise character, so that his outer beauty is matched by his inner morality and integrity. With this unification, the plot is resolved and Cruise as Flanagan is permitted his version of success: he owns his own bar and possesses his own woman. In terms of a developing screen personality, the meaning of Cruise's celebrity sign is also unified: his physical attractiveness is constructed to be contained by his strength of personality.

Cruise's 1990 film *Days of Thunder* represents the triumph of his "picture personality," or the overcoming of the filmic text with the consistency of his form of public personality/celebrity. The actual filmic text is surrounded with extratextual detail about Cruise and this very personal project. Magazines, in their efforts to anticipate the success of the film at the box office, provide this deepening of the significance of the film before the film's release. These anticipatory stories contain little analysis of the content of the film – the dearth of information ensures that what is discussed coheres with the strategies of the publicity agents and the production company behind the film. In this particular film production, the organization of production is inevitably connected to Tom Cruise's management.

What we find in this reportage is the building of a homology between the film content and the person and personality of Cruise. For instance, we learn that Cruise's interest in auto racing stems from his involvement with actor and professional race car driver Paul Newman during the making of *The Color of Money*.[13] Although this interest is outside any filmic text, it is inside the world of public personalities and celebrities – it is in the realm of public knowledge. *Days of Thunder* works to maintain the coherence of personality on-screen and off-screen. Again, this personality emerges fundamentally in the realm of filmic texts. We also are told that Cruise has indeed become a respectable racer. In several articles, his track time is mentioned as the fastest nonprofessional lap clocked at the track. The truth of the movie text is borne out in the "real" Cruise. Likewise, we are made aware in this extratextual discourse that Cruise is credited with the "story idea." This connection is further substantiated in the film's opening credits.

The extratextual discourse that is coordinated with the release of the film is organized specifically around the star and the star's relationship to the content of the film. Several interviews and features are written on the set. One female writer centers her story on her experiences as a passenger with Cruise in the stock car used in the film. What is being articulated in this story is the proximity of the writer to the "real" Cruise. Although no real interview was conducted, the writer provides evidence for the establishment of the real Cruise personality. Very few words were spoken; instead, there was the evident action and experience of driving at high speed around a track. Cruise, like his filmic characters in most of his previous movies, is a man of action. Words then become extraneous to the experience.[14] This story also provides ample evidence that the film character and Cruise have certain common interests and common characteristics. The separation of the private world of Tom Cruise and the public world of his filmic characters is not constructed. The screen personality predominates in the decoding of the Cruise celebrity sign.

Forms of Transgression: Establishing the Autonomous
Nature of the Film Celebrity Sign

In the intense construction of a screen personality, the star builds, in effect, an over-coded representation of him- or herself. This has a certain utility for the recirculation of the screen personality in future films. With Tom Cruise, we can see this most evidently in films like *Cocktail* and *Days of Thunder*, where he reinvents variations of his previous performances. There continues to be the risk, however, that, as in the category of the physical performer, the screen personality will be arrested in his or her construction of a type, even though that type has been particularized and deepened by the actor into a coherent personality.

The maintenance of celebrity status for the film actor involves what I call transgression. DeCordova asserts that the development of stardom is related to the way in which Hollywood actors of the 1920s became the object of intense search for their meaning and coherence beyond the screen into their private lives. There was a proliferation of extratextual discourse concerning stars' lives and lifestyles, a discourse that began to fill the entertainment pages of newspapers and the motion picture magazines of the period.[15] To a degree, these exposés complemented the characterizations the screen actors represented in their films. There were other tendencies as well; for example, as described in the earlier discussion of the screen apparatus and its construction of stardom, the stars were depicted in all their grandeur. Their mansions and their extravagant lifestyles became objects of intense scrutiny. Their lives, though sometimes presented as ordinary in their rituals, were more regularly represented as quite extraordinary. DeCordova notes that stardom was intimately connected to this heightened scrutiny of the actors' private lives. From that close examination, a whole discourse on their transgressions of the norms of behavior became available to the public. Knowledge of their marriages and their divorces, hints of improper liaisons, and scandals that involved sexual indiscretions were commonplace in the press.[16] Film stars, like their theatrical forebears, began to be examples of how the perversions of wealth led to the breakdown of norms. The extratextual discourse that was intensely involved in mapping and charting the private lives of the stars provided a public discourse on intimacy and a constructed narrative or morality tale that implicitly expressed where the normative center of that discourse should be.

Transgressions that emerged from the search of the private lives of stars could lead to several scenarios for the construction of the film celebrity sign. In the instance of Fatty Arbuckle and his trial for manslaughter after one of his "famous" wild parties, the transgression virtually destroyed his power as a celebrity sign. The scandal represented too large a moral transgression.[17] Reporting on Hollywood life rarely reached this level of normative transgression. More typical in style were reports on affairs of the heart and, if those were impossible or implausible, revealing portraits of the everyday lives of the Hollywood stars. In these cases, the levels of revelation would not destroy any actor's sign as a celebrity. Rather, such reporting would function primarily to enhance actors' independence from their screen images. A common form of discussion of stars concerned how they lead normal lives, and in this way, their lives were in contradiction to their screen personalities' extraordinary lives. Another common area was the development of a discourse that served to deepen the text of the star as glamorous. Gossip columnists and Hollywood reporters for magazines and newspapers would chart the public appearances of the stars at restaurants, premieres, galas, and parties. Elizabeth Taylor's elaborate off-screen life, with marriages and divorces, appearances, charity involvement, and spectacular oscillations in weight and substance abuse, eventually made her completely autonomous as a public personality from her screen roles; indeed, her acting is now virtually forgotten in most articles about her. In all these cases, the actors achieve independence from the ways in which their films have painted them. I describe this transformation as a kind of transgression that builds into the star an autonomous subjectivity.

A second form of transgression must also occur in order for the film celebrity to construct a certain autonomy of his or her cultural sign: the celebrity must break the filmic code of his or her personality. The screen personality must be denaturalized into a code of acting. The roles chosen must break the conventional mold of the specific screen personality. This construction of the autonomous film star through acting is analogous to the historical development in the industry of invoking the code of acting to legitimate the cultural form. Producer Adolph Zukor's Famous Players Company, as discussed above, epitomizes this use of theatrical codes of acting to deepen the cultural significance of the filmic text. Zukor brought in stars of the theater to sell film to a "cultured" audience. In a similar fashion, screen stars, in order to demonstrate that they have abilities that go beyond the limited construction of their screen personalities, work to establish their abilities as actors by playing roles that transgress their previous sign constructions. For example, a comedy star like Robin Williams plays a dramatic role, and thereby works to establish his range as an actor. Female stars such as Farrah Fawcett in *The Burning Bed* and Jessica Lange in *Country* play roles that quite deliberately soil their images of beauty with mutilations of their faces and bodies as a way to transgress their "picture personalities," which have given them little room to maneuver and negotiate. The code of acting serves to deepen the celebrity text by demonstrating that skill and talent are elemental in the actor's fame.

Transgressions are also forms of risk in achieving autonomous status. The original connection to the audience is tampered with and the degree to which the star can transform, the limits within which an extratextual life can be tolerated by an audience, is an unknown. As Richard Dyer has emphasized, the trials and tribulations of an actor such as Judy Garland can reconfigure a new core audience that relates directly to the experiences of tragedy: gay culture's embrace of Garland as misunderstood, as maintaining a false exterior, is now the classic case of how extratextual transgressions can form a committed though differently motivated audience for a particular celebrity.[18]

Tom Cruise as Transgressor

The mode of transgression takes on a number of forms and narratives. For Cruise, as for other film celebrities, this implies an extensive study of his personal life. We begin to find out about the development of the Cruise personality outside of the filmic texts, in the images of mass-circulation magazines and newspapers. Biographical details begin appearing that establish the autonomy of the star personality. We learn that Cruise grew up dyslexic and continues to have difficulty reading scripts. We learn that this disability has led him to be a more determined and focused actor on the set. We are also told that, as he grew up with no father present and only sisters, Cruise is very protective of his family, in a very paternal way. Published profiles of Cruise have mentioned these kinds of private details since his appearances in *The Color of Money* and *Top Gun* in 1986.[19] It is also evident that there is a general lack of information about Tom Cruise. There have been very few interviews, and those few that have been granted have invariably been closely connected to the film project being promoted at that time. Both his agent, Mike Ovitz, and more particularly his public relations manager, Pat Kingsley, have protected Cruise; they conduct one of the most elaborate screening processes used by any Hollywood star before granting any interview.[20] There is also very little merchandise made and promoted that celebrates the star Cruise outside his film roles. For example, there are no posters that work to maintain and concretize Cruise's independent value from his films, In this way, Cruise maintains his aura, the enigmatic quality of the star.

It is only with his most recent work that Cruise's maintenance of image control has been broken. Various celebrity-attended functions, the work of the paparazzi, and gossip columnists, among others, are operating in the space between the film image and the supposed "real" person. He is "caught" by these investigators of public personalities as he leaves special events, restaurants, and film premieres, where the defenses of publicity agents are supposedly lacking. Various magazines and television programs compete in conducting elaborate investigations for the truth of a character, for the way in which they can reveal the intimate realm of the star. The interview, a strategy in which the celebrity maintains apparent control, is often used by the more mainstream and entertainment-oriented press. Magazines such as *People* and *Us* tend to ensure the compliance of the stars on whom they produce feature articles. Such a piece may involve a tour of the inner sanctum of the star: we see the inside of the star's home, or perhaps we are taken on a "typical" day with the star. In a 1990 cover story on Cruise in *Us*, the photos of the interior space of his cavernous living room are artfully done. The rest of the photos are publicity stills from his various movies. The text is an interview that attempts to uncover the authentic Tom Cruise. Part of the questioning attempts to determine the validity of rumors and gossip that have circulated about the star, as a function of the more respectable entertainment magazines is to operate as more legitimate sources of knowledge than the supermarket tabloids. We discover that Cruise's nickname is Laserhead, because of the intensity he can muster for any project. As well, there is a discussion about the importance of his dogs:

Us: They also said that your dog was in therapy.
Cruise: (laughing) My dog?! Get the hell outta here! Are you serious?
Us: Dead serious.
Cruise: Oh my God, give me a break! Where do they get this stuff?
Us: So it's not true?
Cruise: Yeah right, like my dog is sneaking out and going to therapy!
Us: Do you have a dog?

Cruise: I have two golden retrievers. They travel with me wherever I go. They're really good. They're just kinda there and they're always happy to see me. I love them.[21]

A *National Enquirer* article typifies the other type of story about Tom Cruise. With the lack of compliance of the celebrity, the story is seen to be more uncensored, less controlled by the star himself. It is in this story that we discover that Cruise's friends consider him a "womanizer" and that he has, after only a few short months, as the headline proclaims, bought a $200,000 diamond ring for his future bride. The scandal, of course, is that his previous marriage has been so quickly supplanted by his relationship with the costar of his last film, *Days of Thunder*. Accompanying the text is a series of snapshots of Cruise embracing his new love, Nicole Kidman, outside a Hollywood restaurant. In contrast to the pictures appearing in the glossy *Us* feature, these are black–and–white photos, clearly unsolicited by either Cruise or his companion. The *Enquirer* photos allow us entry into the private world of Cruise. This visual entry is enhanced by the inside reports on the difficulty Cruise had in convincing Kidman to marry. There are also secondhand quotes from Cruise, from these inside sources, that further the illusion of intimacy for the reader. For example, "I couldn't be happier. Nicole's a one in a million girl and I knew that if I didn't propose to her, I might lose her to somebody who did. Even though marriage didn't work out with Mimi [Rogers], I love being married. And I know in my heart that Nicole and I are made for each other."[22]

For the current argument, the details of Cruise's personal life are not significant; what is significant is that these various constructions of Cruise that appear in the different presses establish the distinction between Tom Cruise on the screen and Tom Cruise the celebrity. In other words, whether the stories and images are controlled by his personal management team or have emerged out of the heightened presence of his image as a cultural commodity in the selling of magazines, newspapers, and advertising, Cruise's public persona begins to be distinct from his screen persona. This form of autonomous subjectivity is very important for establishing the power of the film star as a distinct cultural commodity that is transferable to other domains, other cultural projects, and can be separated from his past films.

As Brownstein has chronicled, film stars have also worked actively to situate themselves in activities generally unrelated to the film industry. Cruise, along with other stars, has aligned himself with a number of what are described as liberal political positions on the environment and nuclear disarmament.[23] In fact, a whole political consultancy business has developed in Hollywood to aid celebrities in choosing issues with which to become involved. Although Cruise is not a prominent member of the politicized community among film stars, movement into the political sphere generally works to establish the relative independence of any film celebrity. The connection with charities or political campaigns deepens the character profile of the celebrity. Instead of being characterized as simply beautiful, handsome, or a mouthpiece for the screenwriter, the celebrity with a connection to these more serious domains adds the possible connotations of depth, intelligence, and commitment to his or her public persona. The public personality then demonstrates a subjectivity that goes beyond the self to the conception of selflessness and public leadership.

The autonomous Cruise is only partially constructed by these extratextual documents that establish his distinctness from his screen presence. Principally, Cruise has focused on establishing his depth of personality through the code of acting. Cruise's transgression into a form of autonomous subjectivity that bestows upon him a certain economic power in the film industry is modalized through his performing in films that work to shatter his picture personality construction. This can be characterized as acting "against type," which means working against how one is constructed in terms of physical presence, and also acting in what are labeled quality films. In terms of the trajectory toward some level of autonomous stardom, this form of acting transgression follows the construction of a clear film personality. In order for a star to transgress, a clear delineation of his or her screen presence must be firmly in place; thus, Cruise's first film that begins to break the boundaries of his film character, *The Color of Money*, is produced and released several years into his career. The difference in this first transgressing film is quite subtle: although Cruise continues to play the talented and naturally successful character, he is surrounded by an actor and director who are both known to be serious and well respected. Paul Newman, Cruise's costar, is an actor who has a very legitimate and lengthy list of film acting credits. As well, Newman is known to be a "serious" individual who has been involved in a number of liberal political campaigns over the past twenty years. In addition, the film builds on the sediments of Newman's own career and film history: Newman re-creates the character of "Fast Eddie" Felson from the 1961 film *The Hustler*, twenty-five years later. Finally, the director, Martin Scorsese, is the preeminent "quality" American director of the past twenty years. The various layers of meaning that surround Cruise's performance construct the atmosphere for the invocation of the acting code.[24]

With *Rain Man*, a 1988 film, Cruise further constructs a tension between his overcoded screen personality type and the transgression of the type through the discourse of acting. Once again, Cruise is surrounded by quality. Dustin Hoffman, his costar, is an Academy Award winner; he will win a second Oscar for his role in *Rain Man*. Barry Levinson, the director, has produced a series of "thoughtful" and artful comedies. The code of acting is central to the construction of the entire film. Cruise continues to play within the general range of his previously constructed screen personality; however, it is the content of the film that ensures a different reading of Cruise. Hoffman's portrayal of Raymond Babbitt, the autistic brother of Cruise's character, Charlie Babbitt, has been described as "acting non-stop," with Hoffman immersed in the mannerisms of his character.[25] This is the textual detail that becomes the central theme of most reviews of the film in the critical and noncritical movie press. From *People* we are given to understand that Hoffman stayed in character in everyday life in his complete employment of the psychological aspects of the Method form of acting. The *New York Times* labels the film a star vehicle for Hoffman in his continuous quest for the accolades of the Academy. Cruise is carried in this tour de force of the film acting profession. However, Vincent Canby asserts in his *New York Times* review that although Hoffman upstages everyone in the film, Cruise is "the real center. . . . It may be no accident that Charlie (and Mr. Cruise) survived *Rain Man* as well as they do."[26] Cruise, through this film, is working to transform his public image from malleable and predictable male film star to serious actor who chooses very carefully the productions with which he is involved. A new series of connotations become associated with a Cruise film. Because of his newfound capacity as an actor as well as his proven ability to attract other quality actors and directors to any given project, Cruise now becomes a moniker that has a certain guarantee of quality. Within the cultural production of films, the name Cruise develops a brand-name status that not only includes his promise of alluring filmic masculinity, but also is symbolic of serious and quality films. It is in this brand-name status that the star's subjectivity becomes melded with his commodity status. The establishment of brand-name status that represents quality also is a sign of star autonomy. It indicates that the actor has in fact moved to the center of the production and that his or her status may be equivalent to that of the auteur or the producer or both.

Cruise ensures this construction of his autonomous power through his involvement in *Born on the Fourth of July* (1989). It is in this film that Cruise employs the acting code to transgress fully his "naturalized" film persona. Indeed, the very plot of the film is organized around the transformation of an athletic young man into a paraplegic Vietnam veteran. Cruise, in portraying this changed man, also indicates his ability to provide a sense of his own commitment to the code of acting that in its intensity rivals the work of Dustin Hoffman in *Rain Man*. Much of the textual material written about *Born on the Fourth of July* is concerned with Cruise's complete transformation of self in the role: this transformation indicates how deeply he has committed to the character. Often pointed out in background articles is the fact that Cruise, like Hoffman in *Rain Man*, stayed in character to test his believability in everyday life. For Cruise, the success of the test was determined by his unrecognizability as the star "Cruise," to the point that he was treated "like any other wheelchair confined person": he wanted to feel the frustration and anger that would arise from the disability and the inaccessibility of the world to physically handicapped people. To be able to dismantle the star's image in the "real" world is the clear mark of a star able to transgress his or her categorization as star and integrate the professional dimension of serious actor into his or her celebrity and concurrent commodity status.

In the latest stages of Cruise's construction of public subjectivity, one sees the capacity for an indulgent integration of public and private life to be played out in his new films. *Far and Away* (1992), a sweeping gesture by Cruise and director Ron Howard to construct a dramatic Irish/American period piece in the tradition of *Doctor Zhivago*, unites as costars Cruise and his "real" wife, Nicole Kidman. Cruise's autonomous economic power permits the development of such a project; his perceived-to-be-stable audience operates as the risk capital insurance that leads to the film's production and distribution. Cruise is also building a unity between his filmic presence and his "real" life. The romantic dyad so crucial to the Hollywood film is doubly celebrated through this film.[27] Cruise maintains his clear relationship to his constructed picture personality, which, through his new autonomy as star producer, can envelop a version of his private life.

His 1993 releases provide further evidence of his centrality in the organization of Hollywood productions. Both films rely on best-selling novels for their advance publicity and their cultural significance. Cruise manages to merge in these films the integrity of acting performance with the recognizable personality he developed in his 1980s films. As in *The Color of Money*, Cruise costars in *A Few Good Men* (1992) with a major and therefore legitimate screen star in Jack Nicholson. In *The Firm* (1993), Cruise reestablishes his persona as the successful young man destined for further success. In both of these "serious" films, Cruise operates as the connecting fiber from an older generation of audience to a younger generation that happens to be more central to the industrial organization of the film industry.

By far the most interesting of Cruise's transgressions, both within the film text and extratextually, is his 1994 film *Interview with the Vampire*. Cruise's being cast as the star of the film version of Anne Rice's 1976 novel became a source of hysterical controversy. The author herself was outraged that Cruise was to play the Lestat character, but having sold the film rights to the book – and considering Cruise's contractual involvement with the film – there was little Rice could do to remove Cruise. Rice saw the image of Cruise – his essential picture personality as an all-American, wholesome, and youthful star – as antithetical to her character Lestat, a being motivated by homoerotic companionship and baroque bacchanalia in his insistent bloodsucking killing as a vampire. In effect, before it went into production Rice disowned the film publicly, along with countless fans of her books who were equally vocal about the casting of Tom Cruise. Further controversy stirred as Cruise was believed to have eliminated from his character the possibility of explicit homoeroticism in the film (later attributed to Rice's original screenplay and subsequently supplanted and reinserted into the movie by the director, Neil Jordan).[28] With the release of the film, Rice recanted equally publicly, dramatically endorsing the film and its star through an advertisement in *Daily Variety* that was subsequently reprinted by Geffen Pictures in the *New York Times*. In the ad, she said, in part: "I loved the film. I simply loved it. . . . I never dreamed it would turn out this way. . . . The charm and humor, and invincible innocence which I cherish in my beloved hero Lestat are all alive in Tom Cruise's performance."[29] She then went on to thank her readers for their concern about the cast and the production of the film, and attempted to allay their fears and pumped-up desires to boycott the film.

Cruise's star construction in *Interview with the Vampire* provides a wonderful blend of transgression and maintenance. The novel's homoeroticism, though muted, is still found in the film. Also, Cruise as Lestat is not a pleasant character. Cruise thus evokes once again a form of transgression through the code of acting. Yet both he and his costar Brad Pitt are depicted for the most part as beautiful and handsome representations of masculinity, which ultimately facilitates their success at procuring a succession of victims. It is the conflict between Cruise's dominant picture personality and the transgressive nature of the text that produces a massively proliferating discourse about Cruise and his suitability in the press. Cruise's star construction becomes the site upon which a number of fears about norms and sexual morality are activated.

Subsequent to the film's release, Cruise was involved in a number of interviews. The most noteworthy of these took place on Oprah Winfrey's television show, where Cruise, with a goatee and long hair, answered questions from an audience that had just seen the film. The separation from his overcoded image of a clean-cut American star perplexed Oprah's audience. Indeed, the dominant theme was "How could you produce such a dark character and such a dark film? We don't need any more of that." Cruise's response became his defensive mantra throughout the program: while smiling (an appeal to his dominant picture personality), Cruise responded, "It was a vampire movie, and vampires act that way." The homoeroticism was also mentioned by a gay audience member, who thanked Cruise for the film and how it related to his experiences. Cruise, looking appropriately embarrassed, explained that it was acting and that the male companionship made sense for the Lestat character. The postrelease interviews and new image of Cruise produced a deepening of the Cruise persona; that very deepening through both acting and controversy continues to produce the autonomy of Cruise in the public sphere. His face and his actions continue to produce interest and become the nodal point for a wider range of discourses on individuality, sexuality, morality, and, self-reflexively, the celebrity himself.

Conclusion

What must be remembered about these various constructions of a film celebrity is that they are modalized or operationalized in the audience. The film industry, the coterie of personal agents surrounding the star, and the star him- or herself are involved in this active building of a public personality. Integrated into that structure is some measure of the response of a public and then the reformulation of that response (in whatever form) into the further cultural production of the celebrity. The audience, then, for Tom Cruise is not necessarily very involved in the meanings of his public personality. For some in the possible audience, there is an absolute abhorrence of his physical presence. For others, there is mild acceptance of his various constructions of self. The audience then moves in and out of using the film celebrity to represent idealizations of self or alternatively dystopian visions of self and others, or even of allowing the celebrity's public personality to mean nothing at all. The full complexity of the interaction of the audience with the celebrity apparatus is beyond the bounds of this analysis; what can be seen are the outlines of celebrity construction that are actively used by the audience.

The film celebrity emerges from a particular cultural apparatus. In its diverse incarnations, the film celebrity represents the building and dissipation of the aura of personality. The filmic text establishes a distance from the audience. The extratextual domains of magazine interviews, critical readings of the films, television appearances, and so on are attempts at discerning the authentic nature of the film celebrity by offering the audience/public avenues for seeing the individual in a less constructed way. It is important to realize that these other discourses that try to present the "real" film star are in themselves actively playing in the tension between the film celebrity's aura and the existence of the star's private life. The will to knowledge about the star's private and personal domains is coexistent with and dependent on the constructed aura or controlled domain of knowledge provided by the narratives of his or her film texts.

Finally, the film star has been constructed to represent the ultimate independence of the individual in contemporary culture. In the most obvious way, the film star is granted economic power to fabricate a lifestyle of wealth and leisure through the income earned from film releases. In a less obvious way, the film star's private life is chronicled to demonstrate the star's relationship to the normative center of the society. Film stars, collectively and historically, have been granted this normative leeway in the organization of their personal lives. Their lives become the idiosyncratic markers that demonstrate the expansive limits of individual independence in the culture. However, the normative leeway is granted only to those who can actively construct their individual autonomy from other constraining apparatuses. The ultimate film star or celebrity, then, has *individually* transgressed the constructions of public personality that have been placed by the film apparatus and the public. With this status, the film star is constructed to possess a great deal of power to determine his or her own future, film projects, and public image.

Notes

1. For an interesting survey of the work on fandom, see Lisa Lewis (ed.), *Adoring Audience: Fan Culture and Popular Media* (London: Routledge, 1992). Also see Henry Jenkins, *Textual Poachers: Television Fans and Participatory Culture* (London: Routledge, 1992).
2. Morin, *Les Stars*, 75–83.
3. Margaret Thorpe, *America at the Movies*; cited in ibid., 66.
4. See Pierre Bourdieu, "The Aristocracy of Culture," in *Distinction: The Social Critique of the Judgment of Taste* (Cambridge: Harvard University Press, 1984), 11–96.
5. Richard Dyer, *Stars* (London: British Film Institute, 1979), 43–5.
6. See Stuart Ewen, *Captains of Consciousness* (New York: McGraw-Hill, 1976). Ewen speaks of youth as a "consumption ideal," and this idea is integrated successfully into David Buxton's critique of rock stars in *Le Rock: star système et société de consummation* (Grenoble: La Pensée Sauvage, 1985), ch. 3.
7. DeCordova, *Picture Personalities*, 1–23.
8. Walker identifies this group of actors as antiheroes in *Stardom*, ch. 7.
9. Richard DeCordova, *Picture Personalities*, particularly 50–97.
10. *Risky Business* was a profitable film. It earned $30.4 million in box-office revenues in North America alone and was number one on *Variety's* weekly list of box-office leaders on November 23, 1983. It scored particularly well with the young adult demographic. It could also be labeled as Cruise's first film that was a "star vehicle," that is, a movie that showcased his talents. See *Variety*, November 23, 1989, 9; May 11, 1989.
11. Several articles appeared that established the first evidence of Cruise as a recognizable star, including D. Hutchings, "No Wonder Tom Cruise Is Sitting Pretty – Risky Business Has Paid Off in Stardom," *People*, September 5, 1983, 107–8; "Tom Cruise Makes All the Right Moves," *Teen*, December 1983, 54–5; E. Miller; "Tom Cruise: An Actor with Heart," *Seventeen*, February 1984, 63–4. The first article about Cruise to appear in *Rolling Stone*, the magazine most closely associated with youth and young adult culture, was coordinated with the release of *Top Gun*: C. Connolly, "Winging It," *Rolling Stone*, June 19, 1986, 36–8, 89.
12. On the structure of feeling, see Raymond Williams, *The Long Revolution* (Harmondsworth: Penguin, 1965), 64–88.
13. Jeanne Marie Laskas, "Car Crazy: What's Driving Tom Cruise?" *Life*, June 1990, 71. The same detail is repeated in virtually all of the magazine stories published about Cruise and the film before its release.
14. Laskas, "Car Crazy."
15. DeCordova, *Picture Personalities*, 98–105.
16. Ibid., 117–21.

17. Ibid., 125–30.
18. Dyer, *Stars*.
19. "Cruise Guns for the Top: An All-American Kid Wins Over Audiences," *Newsweek*, June 9, 1986, 73.
20. Jennet Conant, "Lestat C'est Moi," *Esquire*, March 1994, 70–6.
21. "Tom Cruise and His Movie Machine," *Us*, August 6, 1990, 25.
22. *National Enquirer*, July 17, 1990, 20.
23. Ronald Brownstein, *The Power and the Glitter: The Hollywood-Washington Connection* (New York: Random House, 1990), 298.
24. Indeed, the various forms of film references in *The Color of Money* ensure that many articles treat the film and the actors in terms of an aesthetic code. The best example of this integration of the film and the actors into a canon of quality can be found in David Ansen, "The Big Hustle," *Newsweek*, October 13, 1986, 68–74.
25. Vincent Canby, "Brotherly Love of Sorts," *New York Times*, December 16, 1988, C12.
26. Ibid.
27. For an in-depth reading of performance and the construction of romantic dyads in films, see Virginia Wright Wexman, *Creating the Couple: Love, Marriage and Hollywood Performance* (Princeton, NJ: Princeton University Press, 1993).
28. See Janet Maslin, "'Paradise Lost' Inspires Meditation on Vampires," *New York Times*, October 28, 1993, C15, C20. See also Conant, "Lestat C'est Moi." A profile of how Cruise was dealing with the negative publicity around the film just prior to its release can be found in Kevin Sessum, "Cruise Speed," *Vanity Fair*, October 1994.
29. Geffen Pictures advertisement, *New York Times*, October 2, 1994, 12. This ad was reprinted in the *Times* from an advertisement in *Daly Variety*, September 23, 1994, headlined "To My Readers: A Personal Statement by Anne Rice Regarding the Motion Picture *Interview with the Vampire*."

73

Fan Cultures between 'Fantasy' and 'Reality'

Matt Hills*

In this chapter I will approach fandom as a form of cultural creativity or 'play' which moves, non-competitively, *across* the usual boundaries and categories of experience rather than being caught up within any particular 'field':

> Play enables the exploration of that tissue boundary between fantasy and reality, between the real and the imagined, between the self and the other. In play we have a license to explore, both our selves and our society. *In play we investigate culture, but we also create it.* (Silverstone 1999: 64, my italics)

My central concern here will be with the broadly emotional experiences of fans. Without the emotional attachments and passions of fans, fan cultures would not exist, but fans and academics often take these attachments for granted or do not place them centre-stage in their explorations of fandom.

In the first section below I will consider non-psychoanalytic versions of fans' affective 'play'; I will then move on to consider how different fan cultures (horror fans; *Star Trek* fans; soap opera fans) have been psychoanalysed by critics. I will develop an approach to fandom – based largely on the work of psychoanalyst Donald Woods Winnicott – which takes into account both the 'structural'/historical dimensions of fan cultures and the 'lived experiences' of fans, without subordinating either one to the other. This will retain and develop my focus on fandom's 'dialectic of value'; I will argue that we cannot focus simply on the fan's experience or on the cultural determinations of fan 'readings' of texts. An approach is needed which preserves space both for the individual fan's psychology and for the cultural 'context' in which fan cultures exist.

Fandom as 'Affective Play'

The question of affect in cultural studies is particularly evident in the ongoing work of Lawrence Grossberg (1988, 1992a, 1992b, also 1997a, 1997b): 'If affect cannot be

*Pp. 90–114, 190–2 from M. Hills, *Fan Cultures* (London and New York: Routledge). © 2002 by Matt Hills. Reprinted with permission from Taylor & Francis Books UK.

"found" in the text or read off its surfaces (any more than meaning can), it is also the case that affect is not something that individuals put into it. Affect is itself articulated in the relations between practices' (1992a: 83). Grossberg's focus on fandom and affect is useful because it promises to overcome the split whereby de Certeauesque theory deals with fan 'interpretation', while non-theoretical understandings of fan 'love' persist alongside this more dense theoretical material (Jenkins 1992; Brooker 2000). Grossberg refuses to leave fan 'affect' outside the scope of theorisation:

> Affect is not the same as either emotions or desires. Affect is closely tied to what we often describe as the feeling of life. You can understand another person's life, but you cannot know how it feels. But feeling, as it functions here, is not a subjective experience. It is a socially constructed domain of cultural effects . . . different affective relations inflect meanings and pleasures in very different ways. Affect is what gives 'colour', 'tone' or 'texture' to our experiences. (Grossberg 1992b: 56–7)

But Grossberg's model of affect lacks 'playful' potential (i.e. movement across boundaries of 'inner' and 'outer', 'real' and 'fantasy') because the boundaries of affect are firmly established. For Grossberg, scrupulously observing the disciplinary norms of cultural studies, there must be no suggestion that feeling is 'subjective'. No one else can get inside the 'colours', 'tones' and 'textures' of my life, but those colours, tones and textures can nevertheless be analysed as 'socially constructed' *effects* that I am subjected to. But if this is so, then my fan investments, passions and attachments are never really 'mine'. Any sense of self is merely inscribed according to cultural rules, and the self is thus seemingly an effect of cultural context and its 'mattering maps' (Grossberg 1992b: 57). Any sense of self experienced and inscribed through fandom can only appear to be false:

> [f]ans . . . circulate and also consume particular types of information as a kind of personal/ collective property. Fan websites present this information in largely standardised formats which are personalised by the individual fan primarily through the interpolation of auto-biographical example . . . [implicitly declaring] this is my site, my contents, . . . my way . . . Fan sites endlessly rewrite from this finite base of factual knowledge, and they do so from the first person. (Hoxter 2000: 174–5, 178)

Clearly the 'first person' is not to be trusted. And yet how is this lived self-inscription any different to the self-inscription which is practised by academics? Cultural studies academics also read a limited number of (canonical) books, and the purpose of a well-turned bibliography is to display one's learning in a 'standardised format'. Just as the fan produces a sense of self through displaying their personalised knowledge, then so too does the academic build up a notion of their work as 'personal/collective'. According to the principle of 'self and other equality', any implied criticism of the fan's 'false' subjectivity must also rebound on the academic's similarly 'false' self-inscriptions. And yet this does not occur; despite academics' and fans' shared 'romanticism' – both are committed to their 'authentic' selves – cultural studies retains the guiding (inter)disciplinary norm of excluding the subjective. At best, this can result in a misrecognition of the emotional processes of the academy, taking us back to a particular imagined academic subjectivity which supposedly transcends the 'subjective'. At worst, this commitment to cultural construction rather than the 'subjective' can actually cut cultural studies off from the lived experiences of those that it seeks to engage with.

The disciplinary importance of warding off the subjective is also testified to in Brian Massumi's (1996) critique of Grossberg's work. Massumi suggests that 'Grossberg slips into an equation between affect and emotion at many points, despite distinguishing them in his definitions' (1996: 237n3). Both Grossberg and Massumi are, in different ways, concerned with establishing that affect can be analysed, and that it is not unstructured, unformed or unobservable in its effects. Both are concerned, in different ways, with separating 'affect' from 'emotion'. For Grossberg, this move establishes the authority of a cultural studies' 'structural' perspective influenced by Deleuzian thought, while for Massumi it legitimates a Deleuzian/Spinozist reading of affect as 'effect'. In part, Massumi's criticism of Grossberg resembles a fan's claim of 'possession' or ownership' over their favoured text, seeking, as it does, to reinstate a more 'correct' or 'proper' reading and thereby laying claim to 'Deleuze [as] . . . the great white hope of a non-Saussurean cultural theory' (Osborne 2000: 46).

Is it possible to avoid wholly reproducing 'common sense' categories (e.g. fans' 'love' for a text) while also respecting the fan's 'affect' as subjective, and therefore as meaningfully 'possessed' by a self? Roy Boyne has recently observed that sociological thought is foundationally committed to the 'denial of the subject', although he notes that 'the subjective moment . . . remains residual and obdurate even after the fiercest dilutions, deprivations and denials to be found within social science' (Boyne 2001: x). If this 'subjective moment' is to be taken seriously without entirely falling back into 'common sense' (see also Blackman & Walkerdine 2001) then this would mean presenting an account of fandom which meets both of the following criteria:

1. It must display continuity with fan experiences (of 'possession' and 'ownership'), and
2. It must re-present these emotional experiences within a consistent theoretical framework.

A number of recent theorists of emotion such as Campbell (1997), Lupton (1998) and Williams (2001) have all sought to move away from the constructivist position which has dominated cultural studies. Each of these theorists has emphasised the importance of 'outlaw emotions' which do not simply reflect culturally constructed categories (Campbell 1997: 162), the extra-discursive and discursive nature of emotions (Lupton 1998: 38), and the sheer 'slipperiness' of emotions: 'Our discourses and constructions of emotion . . . are never simply the end of the matter. . . . The multi-dimensional nature of emotions should . . . be stressed here, "over-spilling" a range of disciplinary borders and boundaries along the way' (Williams 2001: 135).

However, a persistent 'tailoring' of affect to a singular and bounded position has occurred not only in constructivist cultural studies but also in much recent film studies work which has taken up a 'cognitivist' position.[1] Carroll (1990) has offered a summary of the basic assumption driving this work: 'What . . . identifies and individuates given emotional states? Their cognitive elements. Emotions involve not only physical perturbations but beliefs and thoughts about the properties of objects and situations' (1990: 26). This work repeats the boundary-building of Grossberg's constructivist approach, albeit in a different guise. The issue this time is not (structured) affect versus (unstructured) emotion, but is instead affect versus cognition.[2]

The notion of 'affective play' does not simply transgress the ordered accounts offered by different disciplines; it also necessarily transgresses cultural studies' affect/emotion binary by reintroducing the subjective into cultural studies (Campbell 1997; Lupton 1998). And it transgresses cognitive film theory's affect/cognition binary by refusing to view these as useful alternatives (Buckingham 2000: 112; Barbalet 1998: 45). This results in a situation where:

> we need theories that allow for the creation of affective meanings that are new and potentially liberatory. I question whether the notion of oppositional subcultures serves this purpose. . . . [T]hat I must belong to and reflect the values of an oppositional subculture to express outlaw emotions potentially *restricts possibilities for expressing personal significance as it is reflective of the pattern I make of my life and experiences.* (Campbell 1997: 162, my italics)

In short, neither constructivist nor cognitive theories can account for the formation of fan cultures through the expression of 'personal significance'. Sharing the problems of the 'regime of value' examined in chapter 2, any approach which reads affect off from a cultural context implies that affect cannot underpin the generation of new cultural formations and contexts. The fans' 'oppositional subculture' must always precede and culturally support fan interpretation and affect, rather than vice versa. Taking this latter view means considering affect as playful, as capable of 'creating culture' as well as being caught up in it.

What I have already termed the 'dialectic of value' (within which the fans' intensely felt and personal 'possession'/ownership of the text is important) therefore seems to be deflected by Grossberg's framing of 'affect' within a model of cultural construction. For Grossberg, fans' sense of textual 'possession' and 'ownership' can only appear as delusional effects of cultural positioning, as seems to be the case in Hoxter's account of online *Exorcist* fans.

Grossberg's model of affect has perhaps been most usefully extended in Dan Fleming's (1996) study, *Powerplay: Toys as Popular Culture*. Attempting to draw together cultural studies and psychoanalysis Fleming arrives at a view of 'object relational interpellation' (1996: 199) which stresses the non-alignment of different planes of subject-positioning, namely the 'object-relational' and the 'ideological'. He illustrates this notion through the series of *Star Trek: The Next Generation* figures produced by Playmates, considering the extent to which object-relational interpellation may *not* fall into 'ideological interpellation'. Fleming's argument hinges on the child's developmental capacity to 'play the other' through playing with toy characters; it is this playful capacity for fluid identification and self-objectification which the 'adult' is deemed to lack in his or her absorption into more fixed subject positions. Fleming thereby suggests that the hegemonic dominance of the masculine identity of Captain Jean-Luc Picard, which he argues is central to the televised narrative of *ST:TNG*, is unlikely to retain such a centrality within the child's play. Whereas televised narrative opens a space for the other only to close it off again, 'the toys are not the TV series. The child who carries around a little plastic Borg as an object of totemistic attachment is identifying with the monster, the "inhuman", in a way that is never explicitly allowed by the conventions of the TV series' (1996: 201). For Fleming, 'ideological interpellation' implies a fixing of the subject from 'outside'; it is a matter of compliance. 'Object-relational interpella-tion', on the other hand, reserves greater space for the subject in terms of this position-ing being navigated from the 'inside':

> To suggest that some objects hold us enthralled, not just because they are conduits for delivery of an ideological 'summons', a fix, but also because we summon forth from them a function as devices of enthralment, *is to propose a more interested role for the subject than has been allowed in most cultural studies to date* (and evokes the notion from psychoanalytic object-relations theory that pleasure is not an end in itself but a 'signpost' to a meaningful object). (1996: 196, 197, my italics)

The question which then remains is the following: if a 'more interested role for the subject' can seemingly only be introduced by drawing on object-relations psychoanaly-sis, then can this 'subjective move' be developed by moving cultural criticism further towards the principles of psychoanalysis? Given my own call here for a more fully 'subjective' rather than constructivist or 'discourse-determinist' cultural studies,[3] this is a possibility that I will address in the next section.

Psychoanalysing Fan Cultures

It would be a mistake to assume that psychoanalysis can offer up a singular theory of affective play which can then simply be 'applied' to fan cultures.[4] For one thing, there are probably almost as many schools of psychoanalysis as there are fan cultures, and no two psychoanalytic approaches completely share a view of affect. Psychoanalyses of fandom have been thin on the ground, but have tended to predominantly use the work of object-relations theorist Donald Woods Winnicott (Randolph 1991; Stacey 1994; Harrington & Bielby 1995), or the post-Freudians Jean Laplanche and Jean-Bertrand Pontalis (Penley 1992; Creed 1993), with references also being made to Melanie Klein's work (Elliott 1999; Hoxter 2000; see also Stacey 1994 and Dawson 1994).

There has been a confluence of *theoretical* and *ethical* opposition to psychoanalysis within cultural studies. Theoretical opposition focuses on the accusation that psycho-analysis is a transhistorical and universal model of subjectivity (i.e. it fails to be histori-cally sensitive). Ethical opposition focuses on a number of charges. First, it supposes that psychoanalysis is an elitist form of cultural criticism since it claims to be able to 'read' the unconscious of the 'other' (Fiske 1990). Second, it supposes that psychoanaly-sis inherently pathologises fan cultures (i.e. fans are treated as psychologically aberrant or as disturbed in some way). Andrew Tudor, for example, has questioned the specific predominance of psychoanalytic theory in work on horror fiction (and its fans) in just these terms:

> perhaps . . . psychoanalytic theories of horror gain credibility from the widespread belief that horror fans are a peculiar bunch who share a perverse predilection. A taste for horror is a taste for something seemingly abnormal and is therefore deemed to require special explanation in terms of personality features not usually accessible to the casual observer. How could anyone want to be horrified, disgusted even, unless there was some deeply hidden reason of which they were not aware? (Tudor 1997: 446)

However, by considering the psychoanalytic work which has been done on fan cultures I will demonstrate that ethical objections are occasionally misplaced, while theoretical objections can be meaningfully addressed. I will consider Kleinian-influenced work first. Next I will examine work which draws on Laplanche and Pontalis, and finally I will conclude this chapter by considering Winnicottian interpretations of fan culture.[5]

Klein: Containing (Horror) Fans

> [I]n the process of identifying with a celebrity, the fan unleashes a range of fantasies and desires and, through projective identification, transfers personal hopes and dreams onto the celebrity. In doing so, the fan actually experiences desired qualities of the self as being contained by the other, the celebrity. In psychoanalytic terms, this is a kind of splitting: the good or desired parts of the self are put into the other in order to protect this imagined goodness from bad or destructive parts of the self. There is, then, a curious sort of violence intrinsic to fandom. . . . The relation of fan and celebrity is troubled because violence is built into it. (Elliott 1999: 139)

This quote is taken from Anthony Elliott's account of Mark Chapman, the fan who shot and killed John Lennon. Although Elliott is concerned with Chapman's mental health (and justifiably so), his account also implies a number of things about 'fans' more generally. Elliott draws on Melanie Klein's work on the paranoid-schizoid position, as well as referring to 'projective identification'. The latter, as Elliott's account demonstrates, is a psychical process whereby dangerous or disavowed aspects of the self are projected onto somebody else. But this attempt at 'getting rid' of part of the self is not entirely successful, as the self then identifies with what has been cast out:

> Klein follows the bizarre logic of this process to show how the interior which is expelled and located in others is still attached to the self. What is projected is also identified with so that all that has been thrown out returns, and the violence of the expulsion . . . is matched by the violence of the invasion of the self when the bad objects strike back. (Parker 1997: 100)

The 'paranoid-schizoid' position, on the other hand, is a position which is never surmounted in our psychological health, and which we return to in times of stress and anxiety. This is important as it means that the 'paranoid–schizoid' position cannot be linked to some kind of definitive 'developmental' narrative. And if it is never clearly 'left behind' then its functioning cannot be viewed as 'regressive'.

The 'paranoid–schizoid' position involves a 'splitting' of the self into 'good' and 'bad' parts, something which becomes necessary because the goodness of the self cannot be accepted or secured in times of great stress and internal self-division: 'Paranoid-schizoid mechanisms come into action when anxiety is high: they provide a kind of "first aid"; in particular, by separating out goodness from badness, they function to "protect" the goodness' (Segal 1991: 179).

This, like many psychoanalytic accounts, can sound very counter-intuitive: what are these 'bad' and threatened 'good' parts of the self? Surely our 'selves' are not internally torn apart in such violent ways? But object-relations theory is always concerned with how our identities are made up out of 'the relations of the self to external others or "objects"' (Stacey 1994: 228), and therefore how we 'introject' (take inside the self) aspects of others while expelling or 'projecting' out elements of our internal self. This ongoing process of exchange between 'inner' and 'outer' is what characterises any broadly object-relations perspective: the self is always related to, and realised in, a particular environment. These exchanges of self and environment occur, however, at the level of unconscious fantasy: we are not aware of their dynamics. It is this emphasis on identity as a process related to social and cultural others/objects which makes this approach valuable to cultural studies.[6]

Kleinian approaches to fandom have tended to focus on star–fan relationships, as do both Elliott (1999) and Stacey (1994). Elliott deals with the pathology of this relationship by emphasising projective identification, while Stacey emphasises the more 'normal' processes of projection and introjection. And yet Elliott's account does not seem to contain the 'violence' of fandom that it broaches as a topic. Spilling out of the pathological figure of Mark Chapman, Elliott's account implies that 'fandom' (which he contrasts to 'fanaticism') is also marked by a deeply buried violence of idealisation. This 'violence' of fandom seems to slip from detailed psychoanalytic reasoning and towards the stereotype of the 'deranged' fan, causing clinical terms to bleed into a 'common sense' devaluation of fandom. This is one of the key dangers of psychoanalysing fandom; *contra* Elliott's work (in this case, at least), it is important not to allow psychoanalytic readings to 'over-step' their bounds. In short, the use of psychoanalytic interpretation needs to be carefully monitored and contained by the 'analyst'. This 'containment' is important because it should strive to prevent a form of psychoanalytic 'authority' from writing its 'knowledge' over common sense categories. Just as I have observed that narrative and 'common sense' closures in autoethnographies are narcissistic, so too are all types of psychoanalytic closure which are achieved by surreptitiously filtering psychoanalytic expertise through 'common sense'.

Ironically, Kleinian accounts of fandom seem unable to recognise fan culture as anything other than a confirmation of key Kleinian terms. There is little or no creative 'object-relationship', one might mischievously suggest, between a Kleinian critic and their object of study. Instead, the theory concerned is projected onto the object (fan culture), blanketing it without remainder or resistance. This problem is less evident in Stacey (1994) and Dawson (1994), as both of these cultural critics offer astute and related critiques of Kleinian work. Stacey notes that object relations theory remains 'problematically universalistic' (1994: 232); despite its attempts at situating the self in an external environment, this 'environment' is still a psychoanalytic model rather than a sociological version of the 'outside'. Dawson reiterates this criticism, suggesting that Klein's work shows a disregard for the politics of the external world: 'real effects on others . . . are subordinated to a concern for the inner drama' (1994: 45).

This concern with the 'inner drama' is replayed in Julian Hoxter's (2000) Kleinian-influenced account of *Exorcist* fans. Following on from a detailed and intriguing engagement with Kleinian theory (see Hoxter 1998), Hoxter shifts tack to psychoanalyse horror fans rather than horror films. The resulting work is marked by the recurrent problem of psychoanalytic accounts of fan culture: 'common sense' stereotypes of fandom are once again mapped onto and conflated with psychoanalytic conceptual distinctions. 'Expert' accounts therefore reproduce a sense of the aberrant fan who somehow 'lacks' a proper engagement with culture. To be fair, Hoxter is well aware of this possibility. Following on from a specific interpretation of *Exorcist* fans' 'acquisition of fan knowledge' he comments that:

> This is not to suggest for one moment that ordinary film fans – even horror fans – are in some way 'disturbed'. It is rather that in the kind of informational acquisitiveness, in the reification of facts as facts that their websites present, we can ascribe a certain eloquence to the self-regulation of the field of enquiry of cult. (Hoxter 2000: 180)

Unfortunately, it is necessary to distinguish between the logic of Hoxter's account and his claim here. For, having linked these *Exorcist* fans to post-Kleinian accounts of 'intellectual consumption as defence' (2000: 179), Hoxter can hardly then claim that his account lacks implications of pathologisation. He implies that the fans' knowledge is a way of displacing 'a sense of insecurity and anxiety regarding the status of the fan before his object' (2000: 178) rather than a valid expression of learning. There is thus something eternally 'improper' about fan knowledge; this status of 'knowledge as defence' does not seem to apply, for example, to the post-Kleinian critic who is securely contained by his theory. Fan knowledge is supposedly a compensation for a type of powerlessness. This time, however, the fans' powerlessness is related to subjective anxiety rather than to an exclusion from official cultural capital or economic capital.

The issue of containment forms part of Hoxter's argument. He states that 'containment' is an important psychical process because it allows the child to internalise (take in from the maternal other) an ability to process and transform bad feelings into more tolerable states.[7] Hoxter then links this process of projection and introjection to the fans' relationship with *The Exorcist*:

> To express this in Kleinian terms, one would suggest that the fan imbues the film with the function of a kind of knowing container and the spectator's fear is projected with the expectation of a moderated return, enabling the spectator successfully to introject and safely to enjoy the film–as–fiction. (2000: 181)

Hoxter then goes on to conclude that it is 'doubtful whether Internet fan networks currently function as truly receptive containers which can understand and return and therefore strengthen the fan's (infant's) own capacity to contain' (2000: 185). This argument therefore sets up a Kleinian-influenced ideal which the fan culture does not live up to. Hoxter's qualifying statement that this 'is not to suggest that they perform no useful purpose' (*ibid.*) is therefore rather redundant. The fact of the matter is that whatever this 'useful purpose' is defined as, it can only be a 'lesser' function than the idealised strengthening of the fans' own 'containment' of emotional experience. These fans are never viewed as possessing advanced forms of emotional literacy; they are consistently viewed as second-rate, and as failing to measure up to the 'good' objects and demands of post-Kleinian theory. As such, this work corresponds to the second of the ethical objections raised against psychoanalysis: despite explicitly seeking not to, it continues to view fandom as aberrant or, at the very least, as 'deficient'.

Laplanche and Pontalis: Fantasising (Horror and *Star Trek*) Fans

The work of Jean Laplanche and Jean-Bertrand Pontalis has been highly influential in film theory as well as trickling through into work on fan cultures:[8]

> Fantasy, in Laplanche and Pontalis' account, has a number of characteristics which are suggestive for . . . a reworking of psychoanalytic film theory. The first is . . . its existence for the subject across a number of subject positions. 'A father seduces a daughter', then, is the 'summarised version of the seduction fantasy', but the actual structure of the fantasy offers 'a scenario with multiple entries, in which nothing shows whether the subject will be immediately located as daughter; it can as well be fixed as father, or even in the term seduces' (Laplanche and Pontalis 1986: 22–3). Identification in fantasy, then, is shifting, unconfined by boundaries of biological sex, cultural gender or sexual preference. (Thornham 1997: 95)

This loosening of identification in fantasy promised to extricate psychoanalytic film theory from the problems created by seeing identification as rigidiy structured by gender. It provided 'an alternative to [an] emphasis on cinema's power to fix or "position" both the female characters within a narrative and also the female spectator in the cinema' (Donald 1989: 137). Laplanche and Pontalis's work thus held out the promise of more 'mobile' subject positions being taken up in fantasy.

However, a number of factors complicate this celebratory narrative of progress (from 'bad' fixed subject positions to 'good' fluid subject positions). I will consider only one here: the issue of 'primal fantasies' or 'fantasies of origin'. Laplanche and Pontalis argue that there are three, and only three, types of primal fantasy. Each fantasy works, like a myth, to explain the mysterious origins of the subject, and each has its roots in 'childhood theories', in other words, in the child's attempts to account for 'his' existence. These fantasies are therefore structurally limited to the sets of questions which confront the child: 'The originary fantasies are limited in kind to castration, seduction, and the primal scene of coitus between the parents' (Rapaport 1994: 87). Seduction fantasies explain the origin of sexuality (this is mistakenly conceptualised by the child as a kind of intrusion from outside; see also the related criticisms of Laplanche's later theory of the 'primal situation' in Campbell 2000: 8). Primal scene fantasies explain the origin of the individual (the primal scene is often mistaken in a number of ways in childhood theories of sexuality: either sexual intercourse is represented as an act of violence, or the child imagines intercourse and birth to operate through oral and anal mechanisms rather than through genital activity). And castration fantasies 'explain' the origin of sexual difference, again mistakenly since – assuming a one-sex model – the woman's genitals are misrecognised as a 'lack'.

Such a theory becomes incapable of explaining historical and generic 'fantasy', i.e. the fantasies of film and forms of fiction, other than as reworkings of a limited repertoire of 'primal' or 'original/originary' fantasies. As Linda Williams has put it: 'the most difficult work . . . will come in the attempt to relate original fantasies to historical context and specific generic history' (1999: 279).

The difficulties involved in linking original/primal fantasies to media texts as fantasies have arguably been glossed over and potentially wished out of the theoretical frame: 'other questions can be posed and "answered" in fantasy but these [the primal fantasies] are the most basic ones' (Penley 1992: 493; see also Laplanche 1989: 163 for a defence of the primal fantasies as open to 'culturalist' explanation and discussion). Other cultural critics respond to the problem of the primal fantasies by rejecting their structural limitation and adding 'new' primal fantasies (Lebeau 1995: 80–1), and some rely on the very primacy of the 'primal fantasies' to validate and value their area of research:

> The horror film . . . continually draws upon the three primal fantasies . . . in order to construct its scenarios of horror. Like the primal phantasies, horror narratives are particularly concerned with origins: origin of the subject; origin of desire; origin of sexual difference. (Creed 1993: 153; see also the mapping of primal phantasies onto 'body genres' in Williams 1999)

It is also important to note that discussing horror, for example, as especially close to primal fantasies carries an implication for fans of the genre. These fans are supposedly caught up in specific scenes of fantasy, unable to process and transcend childhood theories of sexuality, and unable to adopt the more 'knowing' position of the psychoanalytic theorist. Horror fans are again denied a position of meaningful 'knowledge', supposedly being caught up in the affective 'body genre' of horror (Williams 1999). This ignores horror fans' own construction of a counter-moral dualism which contrasts 'good' fan knowledge to the 'cringing' of the 'bad' non-fan, or non-(true)-fan:

> We understood that when special-effects maestro Tom Savini popped up on-screen as 'third bystander from the left' . . . it was the filmmaker's way of winking at the fans in the audience, to which the correct response was a knowing laugh. I remember forming a fleeting bond with a fellow movie-goer at a screening of *The Fly* . . . when an on-screen doctor preparing to abort Geena Davis' insect foetus turned out to be director David Cronenberg. While everyone else cringed, the two of us chuckled smugly from opposite sides of the auditorium, like ships signalling each other in deep fog. (Kermode 1997: 60)

While (academic-)fans such as Kermode discuss their fan knowledge in terms of genre 'literacy' (1997: 65) and fan 'education' (*ibid.*: 58), in psychoanalytic accounts of the horror genre and (by implication) its fans, any possibility of fan knowledge is at best dismissed as a gendered/ideological construction, and at worst, denied altogether. In contrast to this position, I have so far sought to illustrate the limits to fan knowledge, given that this is contained by fan imagined subjectivities and moral dualisms, and also given that fan knowledge is marked by absences and communal legitimations. But I have also indicated the limits to academic knowledge, which needs to be similarly situated within its own proliferating moral dualisms, absences and communal legitimations. I have suggested that any 'good' psychoanalytic account of fandom – to follow the principle of self–other equality established in the previous chapter – must rebound on academic 'epistemophilia' and hence on academic knowledge/affect. If the 'knowing' fan may be defending aspects of their subjectivity and their tastes, then the same may be true for the 'knowing' critic.

The apparent need to maintain a moral difference or dualism between academic and fan is evident in Penley's psychoanalysis of *Star Trek* fans as 'slash' writers. Slash is a type of fan fiction (or fan art) which depicts male characters such as Captain Kirk and Mr Spock as sexually and romantically involved with one another, while (usually) maintaining that the characters concerned are still 'heterosexual'. Slash writing has also extended to cover female/female slash, although this type of slash has yet to be meaningfully examined psychoanalytically in fan studies.

Slash has, perhaps, been disproportionately focused on by academic writers working on fandom, probably because it offers an example of 'tactical' fan reworking which can be fitted into a de Certeau-derived model. For Penley, psychoanalysis is once again important because the activities of these slash-writing fans seem to resist any other 'logic' of explanation: 'I agree with Lamb and Veith's argument, although I think it helps us more to understand the sociological question of "why Kirk and Spock?" than the perhaps more psychical question of "why two men?"' (Penley 1992: 490–1). But this comparison of explanations is telling: why is the 'psychoanalytic' question purely a matter of gender rather than referring to the actual characters? Can 'Kirk' and 'Spock' not form the objects of psychoanalytic investigation? This must, in some sense, remain a possibility given that Penley wants to emphasise 'the fans' identification with the whole *Star Trek* universe' rather than 'just the characters' (*ibid.*: 491).

Penley also offers the standard justification for using Laplanche and Pontalis (1986 [1968]): their account allows that 'the subject can hold a number of identificatory positions' (1992: 480). The 'complexity' of Laplanche and Pontalis's account is therefore assumed to make sense of the 'complexity' of slash writing and fan identification. But by separating off the issue of 'gender' from the issue of characterisation (Kirk/Spock), albeit temporarily, Penley enacts the same type of splitting that marks Creed's account of the horror film. For Creed surface details (secondary fantasies) are reduced to 'primal' or original fantasies, and for Penley the seemingly incidental (K/S) is subordinated to the essential (slash as male/male). This shift is not absolute; Penley does pay attention to the specificity of K/S and *Star Trek* fandom, and oscillates productively in her own identifications between 'sociologist' and 'psychoanalyst'. Ultimately, Penley's moral dualism is thus distinctive from those offered by Creed and Hoxter. For Penley, the 'good' fans that she identifies with 'show a strongly psychoanalytic understanding of the relation of the unconscious to everyday life' (1992: 491). But these fans are also a 'bad' object. They also trouble Penley by refusing to identify as feminists: 'I cannot tell you how many times during the three slash conventions I have attended that I heard the phrase, "I'm not a feminist, but . . ."' (*ibid.*: 491). This is actually a more intricate moral dualism than those usually inhabited by academic writers. On the axis of psycho-analytic understanding Penley perceives herself and the fans as engaged in a communal activity, while at the level of self-declared politics the fans remain, rather disappoint-ingly for Penley, adrift of her own position, which is nevertheless assumed to be morally superior to the fans'. Burt (1998: 15) does not quite seem to capture the intricacy of Penley's position when he castigates her work for reinstating the academic's superiority over fans. And Michele Barrett certainly misses this intricacy altogether in the following rather bizarre comment:

> It is a shame that the image of *Star Trek* in cultural studies is so coloured by Constance Penley's rather bizarre enthusiasm for the sexual fantasies of a tiny group of fans. As an increasing literature on 'The Metaphysics of Star Trek', 'Star Trek in Myth and Legend', 'Star Trek and History' and so forth demonstrates, there are more serious things to say about this huge phenomenon. (Barrett 1999: 181)

Barrett succeeds in superimposing a new and highly rigid moral dualism onto Penley's work ('serious' versus 'frivolous' work), while simultaneously displaying an apparent ignorance of the fact that 'Penley's' enthusiasm for slash has been shared by many other scholars.[9] Barrett also neglects to consider that her 'more serious' examples are also products of the '*Star Trek* industry' (Westfahl 1996) as well as of 'serious' or 'disinter-ested' reason.

Penley may be overstating her own case when she argues that she has given up 'the righteous rush of the negative critique' (1997: 3), since there is more than a tinge of righteous disappointment in her 1992 conclusions. But the moral dualism enacted by Penley's work does not align psychoanalysis/sociology with academic/fan or knowl-edge/affect. In this case, the academic is both within the space of knowledge and affect, going 'completely ga-ga over this fandom' (1992: 491, *contra* Burt's 1998 reading), as well as working within the spaces of psychoanalysis and sociology. My own disappoint-ment with Penley's disappointment stems from the fact that her work ultimately con-tinues to use a 'psychoanalysis' versus 'sociology' binary to reinstate a moment of 'us' ('good' feminist academics) versus 'them' ('bad' non-feminist-identifying fans). Fans and academics can be united in psychoanalytic alliance (unlike all the previous accounts I have examined here), but they remain sociologically divided. Of course, this division could also be read as a criticism of feminist academics who are too distant from the fans' concerns. But this possibility is foreclosed by the details of Penley's discourse: 'they [the fans] perceive . . . a middle-class feminism that disdains popular culture and believes that pornography degrades women' (1992: 492). The implication is that these fans – caught up in a 'common sense' equation of feminism with anti-populist subjectivities and agendas – misrecognise the fact that feminism is actually what they are doing, and what they should declare themselves in alliance with. Penley's psychoanalytic/sociological split could also be defended as a realist representation: i.e. it simply is the case that fans and academics are socially divided groups and communities. But this (relatively naive) empiricism would neglect the dynamics of any such division, failing to consider how this division is reproduced through the torn halves of fan and academic imagined subjectivities rather than through the fans' ('deficient') inability to perceive the ('objective') superiority of academic accounts.

If I began this examination of psychoanalysis hoping to find a more 'interested' role for the subject, then it has to be noted at this point that this has hardly been forthcoming. Psychoanalytic accounts have generally been tailored to the cut of (ideological) academic arguments and moral dualisms, constantly placing fans as deficient, and constantly decrying the possibilities of fan 'knowledge' in favour of an emphasis on fan affects, emotions or fantasies (which, of course, do not possess the status of 'knowledge'). I have suggested that the splitting of emotion or fantasy from cognition or knowledge forms a typical part of many moral dualisms (and this splitting is indeed shared by academic accounts of academic moral superiority and some fan accounts of fan moral superiority such as Kermode 1997). To find a way out of this particular type of splitting it is necessary to turn to a psychoanalytic model which refuses to prioritise system-building 'knowledge' over emotion, and which refuses to split 'fantasy' from 'reality'. The seeds of such an approach, I will suggest, are given in D. W. Winnicott's account of play.

Winnicott: the 'Little Madnesses' of (Soap Opera) Fans

The first useful convergence between Winnicott's work and fan culture lies in the notion of the 'transitional object': '[t]o get to the idea of playing it is useful to think of the *pre-occupation* that characterises the playing of a young child. The content does not matter. What matters is the near-withdrawal state, akin to the *concentration* of older children and adults' (1971: 60). Within this withdrawn state the child enacts delusions of omnipotence, *assuming rights of control and possession over the object which is paradoxically both created and found*. The most significant feature of the transitional object is that it opens and occupies a 'third area' in the child's experience, belonging neither in the realm of inner and outer reality but being instead a 'resting place for the individual engaged in the perpetual human task of keeping inner and outer reality separate yet interrelated' (1971: 3). Winnicott persistently stresses the continuity which this third space possesses with cultural experience, believing that the initial transitional object is decathected when its creative mediation has spread out over the whole cultural field. Elsewhere this play–culture continuity is presented like so: '[o]ut of . . . transitional phenomena develop much of what we . . . greatly value under the headings of religion and art and also the little madnesses which are legitimate at the moment, according to the prevailing cultural pattern' (1988: 107).

So, the transitional object must always have some kind of physical and intersubjective existence; it cannot be some kind of imagined entity or hallucination. But at the same time, the transitional object forms part of the young child's initial separation of subjective and objective spheres, being the first me and not-me object. It is through the transitional object that the child recognises the existence of a world outside him- or herself. By taking on this role, the child's transitional object opens up a space between internal and external which 'religion and art' will later come to occupy. The transitional object also preserves a crucial contradiction:

> the child jumps from a perceived world to a self-created world. In between there is a need for all kinds of transitional phenomena . . . [where] there is a tacit understanding that no-one will claim that this real thing is a part of the world or that it is created by the infant. It is understood that both these things are true: *the infant created it and the world provided it*. (Winnicott cited in Phillips 1988: 117, my italics)

Harrington and Bielby (1995), in a rather under-cited but major study of soap fans, apply Winnicott's work on the 'transitional object' to this fan culture. Their account is a rich and powerful use of psychoanalysis which refuses to denigrate fan 'knowledge' and which also preserves a sense of the 'personal' significance which favoured texts can hold for their fans. Harrington and Bielby's account therefore meets both the criteria established (in the first part of this chapter) for the psychoanalysis of fan culture. It respects the fans' sense of textual ownership (i.e. it leaves a place for the interested subject rather than reducing this to an effect of social or cultural structure) while also repositioning this 'ownership' within a consistent theoretical position (i.e. it doesn't simply replay 'common sense' accounts of fannish 'love' for a text, despite coming close to this in its accounts of fan 'limerence'). Furthermore, Harrington and Bielby do not replicate some of the tensions and problems in Kleinian and 'fantasy'-based approaches to fan cultures, since their work avoids imputing a 'deficient' lack to the soap fans that they study. So far, so good, *contra* the ethical objections of sociological-cultural studies critics. However, my chief criticism of Harrington and Bielby's work would be that although they move towards avoiding a universal or transhistorical position (the socio-logical-cultural studies 'theoretical' objection to psychoanalysis), they do not sufficiently rework Winnicott's own arguments. Their wholesale 'application' of Winnicottian psychoanalysis leaves their argument stuck with problems which are unresolved in Winnicott's work.

Harrington and Bielby argue that soap fans' pleasure in viewing is usually explained *away* by theoretical accounts; it is viewed as escapism, as identification, as resistance to dominant ideology, and so on (1995: 130). This results in a situation where fans' enjoy-ment is 'rationalised' in academic accounts rather than being explored as an event in and of itself. Harrington and Bielby emphasise that popular culture is experienced by its fans, and that this experience should not be over-rationalised by theory. This argu-ment has also been more recently picked up by Michael Real: 'In the effort to hyper-rationalise culture through theory, we create false hope and a false goal if our theoretical rationality attempts to convert all cultural experience into elite culture or folk culture or some other rationally approved alternative' (2001: 176). In Harrington and Bielby's account, however, it is the notion of 'ludic reading' which both respects the fans' intense pleasure and provides a theoretically consistent interpretation: 'a key form of pleasure is rooted in activities that allow individuals to challenge the boundaries between internal and external realities' (1995: 133). Through affective play, soap opera becomes a 'transitional object' for its fans. Soap texts therefore no longer belong purely in 'external reality', nor are they entirely taken in to the fans' 'internal reality'. Instead these texts can be used creatively by fans to manage tensions between inner and outer worlds. If any one of us became caught up purely in our inner world of fantasy then we would effectively become psychotic; if we had no sense of a vibrant inner world and felt entirely caught up in 'external' reality then, conversely, we would lack a sense of our own uniqueness and our own self (a sense which, I would suggest, is lived and experienced even by sociologists wanting to argue that this is an ideological/constructed effect of social structures). It is therefore of paramount importance for mental health that our inner and outer worlds do not stray too far from one another, and that they are kept separate but also interrelated. That fans are able to use media texts as part of this process does not suggest that these fans cannot tell fantasy from reality. Quite the reverse; it means that while maintaining this awareness fans are able to play with (and across) the boundaries between 'fantasy' and 'reality' (1995: 134). As I have already mentioned, it is also important to realise that this process is ongoing and does not correspond to a childhood activity which adults are somehow not implicated in. All of us, throughout our lives, draw on cultural artefacts as 'transitional objects'.

Roger Silverstone (1994, 1999) has also applied Winnicott's work in television studies and cultural studies. Winnicott's emphasis on the always unfinished task of reality acceptance, and on the continuity between culture and the child's first act of play both lend a considerable degree of legitimacy to this exercise. Problems arise from the fact that Silverstone appears to concede too readily that 'the implication of my argument . . . is that television must offer a regressive experience, if by regressive is understood a return to some earlier phases of an individual's development or to a withdrawal to a dream-like state' (1994: 18). But this concession can only be mistaken given the logic of Silverstone's own borrowings from Winnicott. Regression to infantile identifications cannot find a role within the creative and affective 'play' of the media fan. This is due to the fact that play and its cultural derivatives form part of the 'perpetual human task of keeping inner and outer reality separate but inter-related'. That this project is necessarily and inevitably *an on-going dynamic* means that its manifestations can in no way be tied to implications of blanket regression. Such pathologising inferences stem in part from Silverstone's uneasy oscillation between identifying television *per se* with the transitional object while at the same moment allying it with the 'potential space released by' the child's first transitional object (1994: 13; Silverstone (1999) avoids these problems).

Silverstone (1994) and Harrington and Bielby (1995) both seem to replicate a confusion which is inherent in Winnicott's own account of the transitional object. A distinction needs to be made between the transitional object-proper (an actual physical object which the child both finds and creates, originally through fantasies of destruction) and the cultural field which is said to displace the transitional object through the natural decathexis of the object-proper. But in neither account is such a distinction drawn. Harrington and Bielby differentiate between 'child' and 'adult' experiences of transitional phenomena (1995: 134) but simultaneously collapse this distinction by using the term 'transitional object' to cover each type of play experience. I suspect that this problem occurs as a result of Winnicott's own argument, given its stress on a lived *continuity* in the use of transitional phenomena and its *differentiation* between the transitional object-proper and the 'transitional space' of the cultural field.

Admittedly, Harrington and Bielby devote considerable attention to the cultural contexts within which the 'little madnesses' of different transitional objects can be tolerated:

> What, then, divides what is acceptable as a transitional object from what is unacceptable? . . . [D]imensions of fiction/nonfiction and highbrow/lowbrow intersect in complex ways, making it difficult to reach only one conclusion as to why some forms of play are socially acceptable while others are not. By all accounts, though, soap operas are both lowbrow and fictional. Fans use them as transitional objects, even though it is socially unacceptable to do so. (Harrington & Bielby 1995: 136)

This further complicates their account, as they start to relate Winnicottian theory to systems of cultural value, inter-relating psychoanalytic and cultural explanations of the fan experience. Their argument also begins to relate the fans' experience of playful pleasure to industrial and social-historical contexts: '[industry] changes [such as increased space for viewer letters in commercial fan magazines] break down the barrier between the fictional and the real by fostering an illusion of intimacy between celebrities and fans . . . and create space for this type of play to flourish' (1995: 152). But this specific point is highly problematic: ludic reading is viewed here as something which can be directly encouraged by industry machinations, despite that fact the transitional phenomena are both 'created and found'. This contradiction – which is central to Winnicott's account – is therefore overruled in Harrington and Bielby (1995) by a logic of ideological coercion where 'an illusion of intimacy' is created by TV industry strategies. And this occurs despite the authors' earlier statement that 'ideological' explanations of play and fan pleasure should be avoided. There is a shift in the logical model that Harrington and Bielby use; at moments they remain focused on affective play, but then fall back into a model of theoretical over-rationalisation.

I have suggested that difficulties arise in Silverstone (1994) and Harrington and Bielby (1995) because of both accounts' allegiance to faithfully reproducing or 'applying' Winnicott's work. One of the major problems with Winnicott's narrative is how the movement from the *proper transitional object (pto)* to the objective (or at the least, intersubjective) world of the cultural field might be accomplished. Elizabeth Wright (1987: 96) has criticised the lack of clarity in this move, as has Adam Phillips:

> [U]nlike later and more sophisticated cultural objects, like works of art, the first Transitional Object is essentially idiosyncratic and unshareable. Winnicott, however, never makes clear how the child gets from the private experience to the more communal experience, from a personal teddy bear to a pleasure in reading Dickens. (Phillips 1988: 115)

Or, we might add, from a private experience playing with a *Star Wars* toy figure to a communal pleasure in attending *Star Wars* conventions. And this addition also gives the game away: Phillips's assumption is that 'personal' and 'communal' pleasures will adopt different objects, implying a high/low culture distinction in which 'sophisticated' texts replace 'unshareable' teddy bears. But as I will go on to show, this distinction cannot operate in relation to contemporary *pto*s.

Silverstone is absolutely correct in his statement that 'television will become a transitional object in those circumstances where it is already constantly available or where it is consciously (or semi-consciously) used by the mother-figure as a baby sitter' (1994: 15). Silverstone points out, furthermore, that television also displays the material trustworthiness needed to qualify as a transitional object, because this object must survive the child's fantasised destructions of it. In this carefully delimited sense, then, television *can* act as the *pto* but only insofar as it interacts appropriately with the biography of the child concerned. Television's texts can be used as a child's *pto* but can also be interpreted later by that same child as part of their cultural experience (functioning both as *pto* and as decathected *pto*). The possibility of this biographical continuity between *pto* and cultural experience represents a sociohistorical shift, the significance of which cannot be overstated.

I therefore want to suggest a psychoanalytically-derived definition of fan culture. This definition ties in with the 'dialectic of value' because it views cultural contexts and affective play as inter-linked, rather than reading affect off from a 'determining' cultural context (see Box 73.1).

Box 73.1

A fan culture is formed around any given text when this text has functioned as a *pto* in the biography of a number of individuals; individuals who remain attached to this text by virtue of the fact that it continues to exist as an element of their cultural experience. Unlike the inherently private but also externally objective *pto*, this 'retained' object must negotiate its intensely subjective significance with its intersubjective cultural status. It is this essential tension which marks it out as a *secondary transitional object*. This process illustrates that the *pto*'s movement into the cultural field may not be one of pure diffusion, but may imply a residual kernel or preserved distribution of interest which corresponds to a subjective location of the third space.

The secondary transitional object is therefore always an idiosyncratic localising of Winnicott's 'third space' ('space' which is neither purely internal nor external, being a mediating point between internal and external forces acting on the self). Although the secondary transitional object cannot be 'possessed' in quite the same way as the *pto*, and must therefore be viewed as a communal/intersubjective fact or experience, many fan cultures nevertheless testify to the original creativity of the subject via their idiosyncratic cultural location. In this case, the 'third space' which interests Winnicott cannot be viewed as synonymous with 'culture', religion or art *tout court* but should be perceived instead as a region of 'personalised' culture.

This takes us towards a definition of the secondary transitional object. Such an object can be arrived at in two ways: first, it may be *a transitional object which has not altogether surrendered its affective charge and private significance for the subject, despite having been recontextualised as an intersubjective cultural experience* (whereas the *pto*'s subjective significance does not translate into an intersubjective experience). It is this struggle between intersubjective cultural experience and personal significance which helps to explain fans' seemingly irrational claims of 'ownership' over texts and icons. However, the secondary transitional object may not be a *pto* which has directly been 'retained' by the fan, but may instead be arrived at by virtue of its absorption into the subject's idiosyncratically-localised third space. In this case, the secondary transitional object enters a *cultural repertoire which 'holds' the interest of the fan and constitutes the subject's symbolic project of self.* This helps to explain how fans' interests can be extended and relocated by the contagion of affect, with fan interest being channelled through intertextual networks of texts and icons. The first definition of the secondary transitional object emphasises the psychical processes of early experience, whereas the second definition accepts that subjective 'third space' cannot be reduced entirely to psychical processes, being capable of extension and redefinition according to the objects which are encountered socially and historically by the subject.

Such a revisionist Winnicottian definition poses the related question as to whether all televisual or filmic *pto*s are inevitably retained within the adult's cultural world. I would suggest that matters of generic identification and cultural value could determine whether or not object-relationships are retained, depending on the cultural 'appropriateness' of this retention (in line with aspects of Harrington and Bielby's (1995) discussion).

Attachments to generically-identified 'children's programmes' may not be retained (see Messenger Davies 1989: 179) due to the child's perception that to do so would be inappropriate. This may occur as a matter of parental devaluation of the text, or it may arise through any number of social pressures acting on the child to take heed of these generic markers. Texts which are more likely to be retained would seem to be those which appeal from the very beginning to both children and adults, either through a form of doublecoding or through an emphasis on sociological dislocation/fantasy which can support both child and adult engagements. The generic marking of these programmes is hence sufficiently imprecise so as to permit a fluid combination of adult and child viewer demographics (see Buxton (1990); Spigel & Jenkins (1991); Tulloch & Alvarado (1983); Carpenter (1977); Pearson & Uricchio (eds) (1991)). The 'structural integrity' of many cult texts will therefore tend to support an intergenerational mix of fans (see Taylor (1989) on the intergenerational role of the film *Gone With the Wind* for its female fans; see also Dolan (1996: 11) on the rise of generational identities within culture).

Another issue introduced by the contemporary intersection of 'developmental' biographies and the media is that of the 'quality' of transitional objects which start their cultural lives as manufactured media commodities. While we cannot contrast commodified texts to somehow non-commodified teddy bears, and while the element of commodification may be deemed irrelevant to the child who will always both find and create the *pto* (Winnicott 1971: 104) it may nevertheless be the case that, as Dan Fleming testifies:

To go fast is to forget fast: in the present context this evokes all too clearly the relationship between children and toys today. In writing this book I have been keenly aware of writing about the quickly abandoned. I have seen Transformers or Turtles lying apparently unwanted even while I was struggling to understand their appeal. (Fleming 1996: 198)

What, then, can be the quality of a transitional object which is so quickly seized on and equally quickly decathected and disregarded?

It seems to be the case that many fan cultures, and especially those surrounding cult texts, stand as the precise antithesis to the 'quickly abandoned' Turtles and Transformers. Where the affective relationships of fan culture preserve an attachment which challenges the disposability, pre-programmed obsolescence and contained innovation of the commodity, the readily forgotten 'Mutant Ninja/Hero Turtle' appears to be far more thoroughly integrated within the circuits of capital and consumerism. Indeed, as Alex Geairns, 'Cult TV expert' for the magazine *Infinity* has noted:

> There's . . . one type of TV appreciation which has yet to gain a name. This is when a TV series gains a huge following for a very short time over its run, and is very quickly discarded upon cancellation or conclusion. The usual symptoms of Cult TV appreciation are there – the merchandise, the various art and craft skills, even in some cases the conventions. But the appreciation is not ongoing – it dies with the programme. To be a fully sanctioned cult show, the life of a programme must continue through the fans after its death. (Geairns 1996: 21)

Geairns's suggested label of 'Fad TV' might seem appropriate for the accelerated production–consumption cycle of toy manufacture and transmedia 'synergy'. If the structural integrity of the commodified *pto* is such that it imposes social pressure upon the child to move on to the next object-experience then we might ponder its trustworthiness as a transitional object. For in one sense the commodity *pto* does *not* resist the child's fantasies of destruction: the programmed commodity cannot be trusted (cf. Bettelheim (1978) on the value of the fairytale's trusted repetition). It vanishes at the whims of the culture industry. The structural integrity of the object is hence weakened by the reliance of actual, physical toys on the overarching meta-narrative of an accompanying TV series. Kinder (1991: 35) has pondered 'whether early exposure to television accelerates the process described by D. W. Winnicott of "decathecting transitional objects"', placing the child more rapidly in a situation whereby shared cultural experiences – in the form of commodity 'supersystems' (*ibid.*: 122) – must be acknowledged.

Robert M. Young (1989) presents the argument that contemporary consumption – especially that based around the experience of 'high-tech' – rediscovers the transitional object in adult life, such that a Walkman, a car stereo or in-dwelling earphones can all 'enfold' the consumer in a womb-like protected, trusted and intense space. But Young's introduction of the 'transitional object' into arguments surrounding consumption ignores the difficulties implied by combining processes of consumption and object-relating; difficulties which surface in the idea of 'Fad TV' and in the reality of discarded toys with whom an object-relationship has been broken off according to the psychically colonised rhythms of production and consumption.

Affective play 'creates culture' by forming a new 'tradition' or a set of biographical and historical resources which can be drawn on throughout fans' lives. This produces an enduring affective 'structure' which corresponds to the subject's personalised third space. However, it cannot be absolutely recovered *as a structure* precisely because it can be extended as new cultural objects enter the subject's 'third space' over time and according to a 'logic' of association. Cultural tradition and reproduction hence emerge from the idiomatic location of the space of play within the cultural field. Winnicott is very clear on the attributes which are taken on by this space. Phenomena of the play area take on 'infinite variability, contrasting with the relative stereotypy of phenomena that relate either to personal body functioning or to environmental actuality' (1971: 116). That 'infinite variability' can be produced through play may go a long way towards explaining the apparent fixity and repetition of fans' media consumption. Adam Phillips notes the conscious fixity of interest which fandom represents, although for him this is a problem to be solved rather than a lived experience to be respected:

> Psychoanalysis is the art of making interest out of interest that is stuck or thwarted. It doesn't, in other words, believe that the football fan isn't really interested in football: it believes that he is far more interested in football than he can let himself know . . . [W]e treat the objects of interest as clues, as commas that look like full stops. (Phillips 1998: 14)

Interest may well become 'stuck' – this seems to capture the situation of the cult fan all too well – but does this imply that the fan must he released from their interest? Such an argument replicates the Winnicottian notion of the decathected transitional object, positing a total diffusion of cathexis (and hence the mobility of free-floating interest) as an ideal which is rarely, if ever, reproduced given the actuality of the *pto*'s residue. We are, perhaps, all 'stuck' on something, whether that thing is the dogma of Lacanian lack, sociological antisubjectivism, Deleuzian philosophy, or the dogma of a specific fandom. I would suggest that it is whether or not our 'stuckness' can act as a personal and good enough 'third space' for affective play that is significant, and not whether or not we – or our interests – are 'stuck' *per se*.[10]

Summary

- In this chapter I have argued that it is important to view fans as players in the sense that they become immersed in non-competitive and affective play. I have suggested that what is distinctive about this view of play is that (i) it deals with the emotional attachment of the fan and (ii) it suggests that play is not always caught up in a pre-established 'boundedness' or set of cultural boundaries, but may instead imaginatively create its own set of boundaries and its own auto-'context'.
- I have criticised previous considerations of fan affect for their lack of playfulness; that is, for reducing affect to an effect of pre-existing structures or conventions. Fans, I am suggesting, create the conventions that they attend (to), through subjective and affective play. This opposes my account to many strongly anti-subjective sociological and philosophical currents in cultural studies.

- I then examined a range of psychoanalytic accounts of fan culture, aiming to explore psychoanalysis as a space in which the 'subjective' could be theorised or restored. However, many of these accounts conflicted with the criteria for work on fan cultures which had been set out both in this and the preceding chapter. Kleinian and fantasy-based approaches tended to position fans as 'deficient', thereby recreating an academic moral dualism of 'us' versus 'them'.
- Winnicottian accounts, I have argued, offer the clearest potential for a psychoanalytic interpretation of fan cultures. This is so because Winnicott suggests that our emotional attachments within culture, or 'little madnesses', continue throughout our lives as a way of maintaining mental/psychical health. In this reading, fandom is neither pathologised nor viewed as deficient; instead it can be theorised psychoanalytically as a form of 'good' health. Such an account can also be turned on the figure of the academic, for whom theory and theorists can provide a personal and idiosyncratic 'third space' for play activity. Just as fans create the contexts of their fan cultures, so too do academics create new contexts for future work through the interplay of affective play and 'tradition' (producing academic movements such as 'deconstruction' or even something called 'cultural studies').
- I then concluded by suggesting that Winnicott's work cannot simply be adopted wholesale: to address theoretical charges of universalism it is necessary to introduce a new conceptual distinction between 'proper' and 'secondary' transitional objects.

My reworking of Winnicott in this chapter contributes to a dual-lensed approach which does not view the 'dialectic of value' as resolutely sociological. My use of Winnicott circles around the same 'dialectic of value' of fandom, providing a different perspective on the same cultural and psychical process. In this case, however, my attention has been much more closely and minutely directed towards thinking about fans' 'concentration' on their favoured texts. Through Winnicott's interest in keeping open the question 'did you find this or did you make it?', I have not had to close down the dialectic of value prematurely. Fan cultures, that is to say, are neither rooted in an 'objective' interpretive community or an 'objective' set of texts, but nor are they atomised collections of individuals whose 'subjective' passions and interests happen to overlap. Fan cultures are both found and created, and it is this inescapable tension which supports my use of Winnicott's work, as well as supporting what I have termed the 'dialectic of value' that is enacted by fan cultures.

Notes

1. See, for example, Smith (1995); Grodal (1999); Plantinga and Smith (1999); Freeland (2000); see also Hallam with Marshment (2000: 122–42).
2. I have already suggested that the affect/cognition opposition results in a situation where theorists side 'with' one term 'against' the other and thereby participate in a moral dualism (which also extends along modernist/postmodernist lines). Although it is true to say that 'the difficulty at the heart of emotion theory has been to marry . . . the affective

and the cognitive . . . in some effective and plausible way' (Redding 1999: 2), this difficulty has only been exacerbated by its theoretical transformation into a powerful moral dualism.

3. As Jeanne Randolph has observed: 'It would seem that at some point one must reflect upon these questions subjectively, that one must take advantage of the fact that art and entertainment presuppose a subjective audience' (1991: 56).

4. Compare, for example, the following two claims: 'It is no exaggeration to say that, in psychoanalysis as it is practised today, work on the affects command a large part of our efforts. There is no favourable outcome which does not involve an affective change. We would like to have at our disposal a satisfactory theory of affects, but that is not the case.' (Green 1996: 174). And: 'psychoanalysis is . . . the theory *par excellence* of the affects' (Silverman 1996: 1).

5. Winnicott's work, and that of Christopher Bollas which develops a broadly Winnicottian perspective on aesthetics, has recently moved into favour in areas of cultural studies; see, for example, Elliott (1996); Minsky (1998); Campbell (2000) as well as Bollas (1987, 1989, 1992, 1995, 1999, 2000). I do not have the space here to develop a discussion of Bollas's developments of 'Winnicottian' theory (see Hills 1999), nor to focus on the recent work of Jean Laplanche (1999a, 1999b). However, my own reworking of Winnicottian theory is very much indebted to the work of 'Winnicottians' such as Christopher Bollas and Adam Phillips (1993, 1994, 1995, 1998).

6. It is also worth noting that my own account of moral dualisms, and the many and varied splittings between the 'good' self and the 'bad' other, possesses Kleinian overtones. But the splittings that I have referred to are more-or-less conscious, relating as they do to 'imagined subjectivities'. These 'good' and 'bad' objects are moral precisely because they are available in people's self accounts and self-valuations of 'the good'. Moral dualisms, in short, do not operate through processes of unconscious fantasy, although I would not rule out the possibility that they involve unconscious elements. Moral dualisms are also always socially and culturally located: they depend on cultural concepts of the 'good' (the 'duly trained' good subject) rather than on lived experiences of 'goodness' or 'badness'; again, this indicates that moral dualisms relate to imagined subjectivities, and thus to versions of ourselves that we realise do not correspond to our lived selves, but which are retained because of the cultural value that we can claim as a result. Although the 'goodness' of the self may be threatened at the level of unconscious fantasy, moral dualisms always work to support the consciously 'good' self versus a 'bad' other. By contrast, fans' claims of ownership over texts are often less available in self-accounts, suggesting that fans' implicit sense of ownership is closer to unconscious processes.

7. The psychoanalytic narrative of this process runs as follows: the child's distress is responded to by the mother, who then 'becomes a container for the baby's unbearable experiences' (Segal 1992: 122). The child is then able to introject, take back inside, in fantasy 'the mother with her ability to contain the baby's distress and to make good sense of it' (*ibid.*). Strengthening containment in this way means that the baby is better able to sustain a sense of hope and to deal with emotional frustrations.

8. One of their essays, 'Fantasy and the origins of sexuality', has even been described as 'a cult text among people working on fantasy and culture' (Rose in Fletcher and Stanton 1992: 55).

9. Russ (1985); Lamb and Veith (1986); Bacon-Smith (1992); Jenkins (1992); Penley (1991, 1992); Cicioni (1998); Green, Jenkins and Jenkins (1998); Cumberland (2000).

10. See McDougall (1985: 67) and (1989: 82) for a consideration of 'pathological transitional objects' which lead to addictive rather than affective play, and which McDougall therefore

terms 'transitory objects' because of their fleeting and unsatisfactory ability to allow inner and outer worlds to be inter-related. My argument here is that what might appear to be a form of 'addictive play' among fans is actually affective play. This should not be taken to imply that fandom cannot become 'addictive play' in specific cases, but it remains important to avoid tainting the 'normal' or 'little madnesses' of fandom with grand theoretical assumptions of pathology, as Elliott and Hoxter seem to.

References

Bacon-Smith, C. (1992). *Enterprising Women: Television Fandom and the Creation of Popular Myth*. Philadelphia: University of Pennsylvania Press.

Bacon-Smith, C. & T. Yarborough (1991). Batman: The Ethnography. In: R. E. Pearson & W. Uricchio (eds.), *The Many Lives of the Batman: Critical Approaches to a Superhero and His Media*. London: BFI Publishing.

Barbalet, J. M. (1998). *Emotion, Social Theory and Social Structure*. Cambridge: Cambridge University Press.

Barrett, M. (1999). *Imagination in Theory*. Cambridge: Polity Press.

Bettelheim, B. (1978). *The Uses of Enchantment: The Meaning and Importance of Fairy Tales*. London: Penguin.

Blackman, L. & V. Walkerdine (2001). *Mass Hysteria: Critical Psychology and Media Studies*. London: Palgrave.

Bollas, C. (1987). *The Shadow of the Object: Psychoanalysis of the Unthought Known*. London: Free Association Books.

Bollas, C. (1989). *Forces of Destiny: Psychoanalysis and Human Idiom*. London: Free Association Books.

Bollas, C. (1992). *Being a Character: Psychoanalysis and Self Experience*. London: Routledge.

Bollas, C. (1995). *Cracking Up: The Work of Unconscious Experience*. London: Routledge.

Bollas, C. (1999). *The Mystery of Things*. London: Routledge.

Bollas, C. (2000). *Hysteria*. London: Routledge.

Boyne, R. (2001). *Subject, Society and Culture*. London: Sage.

Brooker, W. (2000). *Batman Unmasked: Analysing a Cultural Icon*. London: Continuum.

Buckingham, D. (2000). *After the Death of Childhood*. Cambridge: Polity Press.

Burt, R. (1998). *Unspeakable Shaxxxspeares*. London: Macmillan.

Buxton, D. (1990). *From the Avengers to Miami Vice: Form and Ideology in Television Series*. Manchester: Manchester University Press.

Campbell, J. (2000). *Arguing with the Phallus*. London: Zed Books.

Campbell, S. (1997). *Interpreting the Personal: Expression and the Formation of Feelings*. Ithaca: Cornell University Press.

Carpenter, H. (1977). *J. R. R. Tolkien: A Biography*. London: George Allen and Unwin.

Carroll, N. (1990). *The Philosophy of Horror or Paradoxes of the Heart*. London: Routledge.

Cicioni, M. (1998). Male Pair-Bonds and Female Desire in Fan Slash Writing. In: C. Harris & A. Alexander (eds.), *Theorizing Fandom: Fans, Subculture and Identity*. Cresskill: Hampton Press.

Creed, B. (1993). *The Monstrous-Feminine*. London: Routledge.

Cumberland, S. (2000). Private Uses of Cyberspace: Women, Desire and Fan Culture, online at http://media-in-transition.mit.edu/articles/cumberland.html (accessed July 20, 2001).

Dawson, G. (1994). *Soldier Heroes*. London: Routledge.

Dolan, M. (1996). *Modern Lives: A Cultural Re-reading of "The Lost Generation."* Indiana: Purdue University Press.

Donald, J. (ed.) (1989). *Fantasy and the Cinema.* London: BFI Publishing.

Elliott, A. (1996). *Subject to Ourselves: Social Theory, Psychoanalysis and Postmodernity.* Cambridge: Policy Press.

Elliott, A. (1999). *The Mourning of John Lennon.* Berkeley: University of California Press.

Fiske, J. (1990). Ethnosemiotics: Some Personal and Theoretical Reflections. *Cultural Studies* 4(1), pp. 85–99.

Fleming, D. (1996). *Powerplay: Toys as Popular Culture.* Manchester: Manchester University Press.

Fletcher, J. & M. Stanton (eds) (1992). *Jean Laplanche: Seduction, Translation, Drives.* London: ICA.

Freeland, C. (2000). *The Naked and the Undead.* Boulder: Westview Press.

Geairns, A. J. (1996). Who Are You Calling a Cult? *Infinity*, Issue 4, November 1996, p. 21.

Green, A. (1996). *On Private Madness.* London: Rebus Press.

Green, S., C. Jenkins & H. Jenkins (1998). Normal Female Interest in Men Bonking: Selections from *The Terra Nostra Underground* and *Strange Bedfellows.* In: C. Harris & A. Alexander (eds.), *Theorizing Fandom: Fans, Subculture and Identity.* Cresskill: Hampton Press.

Grodal, T. (1999). *Moving Pictures.* Oxford: Clarendon Press.

Grossberg, L. (1988). It's a Sin: Politics, Post-modernity and the Popular. In: L. Grossberg, A. Curthoys, T. Fry & P. Patton (eds.), *It's A Sin: Essays on Postmodernism, Politics and Culture.* Sydney: Power Publications.

Grossberg, L. (1992a). *We Gotta Get Out of This Place.* London: Routledge.

Grossberg, L. (1992b). Is There a Fan in the House?: The Affective Sensibility of Fandom. In: L. A. Lewis (ed.), *The Adoring Audience.* London: Routledge.

Grossberg, L. (1997a). *Bringing It All Back Home: Essays on Cultural Studies.* Durham, NC: Duke University Press.

Grossberg, L. (1997b). *Dancing in Spite of Myself: Essays on Popular Culture.* Durham, NC: Duke University Press.

Hallam, J. & M. Marshment (2000). *Realism and Popular Cinema.* Manchester: Manchester University Press.

Harrington, C. L. & D. Bielby (1995). *Soap Fans: Pursuing Pleasure and Making Meaning in Everyday Life.* Philadelphia: Temple University Press.

Hills, M. (1999). The Dialectic of Value: The Sociology and Psychoanalysis of Cult Media. Unpublished PhD dissertation, University of Sussex.

Hoxter, J. (1998). Anna with the Devil Inside: Klein, Argento and "The Stendhal Syndrome". In: A. Black (ed.), *Necronomicon Book Two.* London: Creation Books.

Hoxter, J. (2000). Taking Possession: Cult Learning in *The Exorcist.* In: X. Mendik & C. Harper (eds.), *Unruly Pleasures: The Cult Film and Its Critics.* Guildford: FAB Press.

Jenkins, H. (1992). *Textual Poachers: Television Fans and Participatory Cultures.* London: Routledge.

Kermode, M. (1997). I Was a Teenage Horror Fan: Or, "How I Learned to Stop Worrying and Love Linda Blair". In: M. Barker & J. Petley (eds.), *Ill Effects: The Media/Violence Debate.* London: Routledge.

Kinder, M. (1991). *Playing with Power in Movies, Television and Video Games – From Muppet Babies to Teenage Mutant Ninja Turtles.* Berkeley: University of California Press.

Lamb, P. F. & D. L. Veith (1986). Romantic Myth, Transcendence, and *Star Trek* Zines. In: D. Palumbo (ed.), *Erotic Universe.* New York: Creenwood Press.

Laplanche, J. (1989). *New Foundations for Psychoanalysis.* Oxford: Blackwell.

Laplanche, J. (1999a). *Essays on Otherness*. London: Routledge.

Laplanche, J. (1999b). *The Unconscious and the Id*. London: Rebus.

Laplanche, J. & J.-B. Pontalis (1986). Fantasy and the Origins of Sexuality. In: V. Burgin, J. Donald & C. Kaplan (eds.), *Formations of Fantasy*. London: Methuen (translation first published in *International Journal of Psychoanalysis* 49, 1968).

Lebeau, V. (1995). *Lost Angels: Psychoanalysis and Cinema*. London: Routledge.

Lupton, D. (1998). *The Emotional Self*. London: Sage.

McDougall, J. (1985). *Theatres of the Mind*. London: Free Association Books.

McDougall, J. (1989). *Theatres of the Body*. London: Free Association Books.

Massumi, B. (1996). The Autonomy of Affect. In: P. Patton (ed.), *Deleuze: A Critical Reader*. Oxford: Blackwell.

Messenger Davies, M. (1989). *Television is Good for Your Kids*. London: Hilary Shipman.

Minsky, R. (1998). *Psychoanalysis and Culture*. Cambridge: Polity Press.

Osborne, P. (2000). *Philosophy in Cultural Theory*. London: Routledge.

Parker, I. (1997). *Psychoanalytic Culture*. London: Sage.

Pearson, R. E. & W. Uricchio (eds.) (1991). *The Many Lives of the Batman: Critical Approaches to a Superhero and His Media*. London: BFI Publishing.

Penley, C. (1991). Brownian Motion: Women, Tactics and Technology. In: A. Ross & C. Penley (eds.), *Technoculture*. Minneapolis: University of Minnesota Press.

Penley, C. (1992). Feminism, Psychoanalysis and the Study of Popular Culture. In: L. Grossberg, C. Nelson & P. Treichler (eds.), *Cultural Studies*. London: Routledge.

Penley, C. (1997). *Nasa/Trek: Popular Science and Sex in America*. London: Verso.

Phillips, A. (1988). *Fontana Modern Masters: Winnicott*. London: Fontana.

Phillips, A. (1993). *On Kissing, Tickling and Being Bored: Psychoanalytic Essays on the Unexamined Life*. London: Faber & Faber.

Phillips, A. (1994). *On Flirtation*. London: Faber & Faber.

Phillips, A. (1995). *Terrors and Experts*. London: Faber & Faber.

Phillips, A. (1998). *The Beast in the Nursery*. London: Faber & Faber.

Plantinga, C. & G. M. Smith (eds.) (1999). *Passionate Views: Film, Cognition and Emotion*. Baltimore: Johns Hopkins University Press.

Radway, J. (1987). *Reading the Romance*. London: Verso.

Randolph, J. (1991). *Psychoanalysis and Synchronized Swimming*. Toronto: YYZ Books.

Rapaport, H. (1994). *Between the Sign and the Gaze*. Ithaca, NY: Cornell University Press.

Real, M. R. (1996). *Exploring Media Culture: A Guide*. London: Sage.

Real, M. R. (2001). Cultural Theory in Popular Culture and Media Spectacles. In: J. Lull (ed.), *Culture in the Communication Age*. London: Routledge.

Redding, P. (1999). *The Logic of Affect*. Ithaca, NY: Cornell University Press.

Russ, J. (1985). *Magic Mommas, Trembling Sisters, Puritans and Perverts*. New York: Crossing.

Segal, J. (1992). *Melanie Klein*. London: Sage.

Silverman, K. (1996). *The Threshold of the Visible World*. London: Routledge.

Silverstone, R. (1994). *Television and Everyday Life*. London: Routledge.

Silverstone, R. (1999). *Why Study the Media?* London: Sage.

Smith, M. (1995). *Engaging Characters*. Oxford: Clarendon Press.

Spigel, L. & H. Jenkins (1991). Same Bat Channel, Different Bat Times: Mass Culture and Popular Memory. In: R. E. Pearson & W. Uricchio (eds.), *The Many Lives of the Batman: Critical Approaches to a Superhero and his Media*. London: BFI Publishing.

Stacey, J. (1994). *Star Gazing: Hollywood Cinema and Female Spectatorship*. London: Routledge.

Taylor, H. (1989). *Scarlett's Women: Gone with the Wind and Its Female Fans*. London: Virago Press.

Thornham, S. (1997). *Passionate Detachments*. London: Arnold.

Tudor, A. (1997). Why Horror? The Peculiar Pleasures of a Popular Genre. *Cultural Studies* 11(3), pp. 443–63.

Tulloch, J. & M. Alvarado (1983). *"Doctor Who" The Unfolding Text*. London: Macmillan.

Westfahl, C. (1996). Where No Market Has Gone Before: "The Science Fiction Industry" and the *Star Trek* Industry. *Extrapolation* 37(4), 291–301.

Williams, L. (1999). Film Bodies: Gender, Genre and Excess. In: S. Thornham (ed.), *Feminist Film Theory*. Edinburgh: Edinburgh University Press.

Williams, S. (2001). *Emotion and Social Theory*. London: Sage.

Winnicott, D. W. (1971). *Playing and Reality*. London: Penguin.

Winnicott, D. W. (1988). *Human Nature*. London: Free Association Books.

Wright, E. (1987). *Psychoanalytic Criticism: Theory in Practice*. London: Routledge.

Young, R. M. (1989). Transitional Phenomena: Production and Consumption. In: B. Richards (ed.), *Crises of the Self: Further Essays on Psychoanalysis and Politics*. London: Free Association Books.

Is Elvis a God? Cult, Culture, Questions of Method

*John Frow**

Here are two texts. The first is from 'A Love Letter to Elvis on the Anniversary of his Death, August 16, 1977, by Joni Mabe'; the letter is a collage of verbal text and images of a woman, presumably Joni Mabe herself, photographed in various loving and at times explicitly sexual postures with a life-size plastic Elvis doll, and it serves as a frontispiece to Marcus (1991). The text reads:

Dear Elvis,

You don't know how many times I've dreamt and wished that you were my lover – or father. But you died without a trace of myself ever touching your life. I could have saved you Elvis. We could have found happiness together at Graceland. I know that I could have put your broken self back together. It's as if you could have discovered that sex and religion could be brought together in your feelings for me.

The hurt you carried every day, the passion that dried up with the years, I could have restored. All of those women sapped your spirit and gave you nothing but the simulation of passion. I know the secrets of the Southern night.

I worship you. My sleep is filled with longing for you. I try to make a go of daily life but all else fades before this consuming image of yourself always present in my mind. This image guides me to the places I want to be. I lay here now thinking, agonizing – in other words – masturbating over the impossibility of ever being your slave. Sometimes I feel I've been hypnotized, that I can no longer bear existence without you. Other men in their fleshly selves could never measure up to your perfection. When making love to you in the later years, I still could sense your throbbing manliness. You really touched the woman in me. I no longer know the difference between fact and fantasy. My poisoned spirit cries out for relief, for just one caress to remind me that you really were a man and not a god. If God listened to my prayers you'd be lying beside me now.

No matter who I'm with it's always you. Elvis I have a confession to make. I'm carrying your child. The last Elvis imitator I fucked was carrying your sacred seed. Please send money. Enclosed are the photographs of myself and the earthly messenger you sent.

Love sick for you, baby . . .

Joni Mabe

*Pp. 197–210 from *International Journal of Cultural Studies*, vol. 1, no. 2. © 1998 by Sage Publications. Reprinted with permission from Sage Publications Ltd.

The second text is a story from the *National Examiner*, cited in Fiske (1993), in which Elvis appears to a group of US marines on duty in Saudi Arabia and says to them: 'Don't worry, I'll be watching over you and all your fellow servicemen. I'll act as your guardian angel and be alongside you during the battles to come.'

Let me make two brief points about these texts before I open out to some more general considerations. The first is that their truth status – the utter ambivalence of Joni Mabe's text, where the possibility of irony and parodic mockery in no way affects the emotional intensity of the message, and the irrelevance of the protocols of journalistic verification to supermarket tabloids like the *National Examiner* – is beside the point; they develop fantasies which are carried with equal force in parodies, in pastiches, in fictional narratives, and in the most intimate and personal testimonies of fans. The second point is that these fantasies form part of a thematically coherent and widely diffused corpus of recurrent narratives. Hinerman (1992), for example, reports similar stories of the visitation of those who are troubled or dying by an Elvis who tells them 'I'll be with you', and Marcus (1991: 121–2) indeed argues that 'the identification of Elvis with Jesus has been a secret theme of the Elvis story since 1956'. And what's perhaps most striking about this identification is the ease with which it fits into Christian orthodoxy, even and perhaps especially in the heartland of Southern Baptism.

With these two texts I adumbrate both the concern of this chapter with the religious dimensions of celebrity, and a set of full-blown cliches about the role of apotheosis and the cult of the dead and immortal god in popular culture. For there is nothing that has not already been said a thousand times about the cultic aspects of stardom. In the case of Presley, the central focus has been on the status of Graceland and the Elvis Presley Birthplace in Tupelo as cult centres. Graceland is the object both of everyday pilgrimage and of especially intense commemoration during the vigils of Tribute Week, culminating in the candle-lit procession around Presley's grave on the eve of the anniversary of his death – a ceremony, writes the archaeologist Neil Silberman (1990: 80), directly parallel to the fire rituals associated with ancient solar heroes. Gary Vikan's and Gilbert Rodman's analyses of Graceland as *locus sanctus* similarly point to the votive graffiti and offerings, including elaborate hand-crafted homages such as posterboard collages and box dioramas depicting scenes from Elvis's life (Rodman, 1996: 117; Vikan, 1994); this central site is then repeated in local sites of commemoration – the 'handmade Elvis shrines that can be found on front porches, yards, and roadsides scattered across the rural South' (Rodman, 1996: 175). Other commentators invoke the Aztec sacrificial Sun King whose insignia Elvis wore on his Las Vegas costumes (Kroker et al., n.d.), or point to the communion-like performances by Elvis impersonators in which the white scarves ritually thrown to female fans pass on the bodily traces of the communicant (Fiske, 1993: 116; Spigel, 1990: 181). And Harrison (1992) exhaustively documents every aspect of the Elvis cult in a sustained transposition of a religious vocabulary on to the phenomena of stardom – without, however, ever managing to notice the constitutive role of joking and irony in the reverence paid to Elvis.

A small handful of stars and public figures experiences this adoration that raises them beyond the human plane: in our century, perhaps, in addition to Elvis, Rudolph Valentino, Lenin, Stalin, Hitler, Mao, James Dean, Kurt Cobain, Bruce Lee, Che Guevara, Evita Peron, and that other dead princess whose ghost is now haunting cultural studies. Even the most extreme fame, as in the case of Marilyn Monroe or John Lennon or Pele, falls short of this transsubstantiation that is apotheosis. And yet – and this is my argument – we lack almost completely the intellectual tools to make sense of this process. At best, in what is still in many ways the most interesting analysis of stardom, Edgar Morin elaborates the banal vocabulary of the idol, the pantheon, the cult into an account of the imaginary processes of identification and projection by which the systems of religious worship and fan culture both bring to bear that 'immense affective surge which constitutes the participation of the spectator' (Morin, 1960: 40). But Morin is never sure whether to take the analogy between stars and gods seriously; his ambivalence is nicely summed up in his quotation of Parker Tyler to the effect that the term ' "Anthropomorphic gods . . . must not be taken literally, but it is not merely a manner of speaking" ' (quoted without further attribution in Morin, 1960: 105). Neither a figure nor not a figure, the religious relation exists midway between dead metaphor and a theory which has yet to find itself.

No such caution and no such subtlety afflict the tradition of analysis that, for convenience, I shall call Jungian, and whose noisiest proponent in the field of popular culture is perhaps Camille Paglia. The emphasis here is all on the continuities of a changeless human nature which allow the 'modern cult of celebrity' to reawaken in its audience 'atavistic religious emotions'; the image of Princess Diana thus 'taps into certain deep and powerful strains in our culture, strains that suggest that the ancient archetypes of conventional womanhood are not obsolete but stronger and deeper than ever' (Paglia, 1995: 164), and Elvis becomes the direct inheritor of the 'youth cult' created – single-handedly, it would seem – by Byron (Paglia, 1990: 364). For Greil Marcus, coming from a quite different angle, Elvis is at once an exemplary culture hero, one of those 'pure products of America' who 'go crazy', 'a man who lived with nearly complete access to disaster, all the time' (Marcus, 1991: 6–7), and the bearer thereby of a mystical national theodicy. In him we find 'a presentation, an acting out, a fantasy of what the deepest and most extreme possibilities and dangers of our national identity are'; a mystery is revealed to us, so that 'we gasp. We get it. We feel ennobled and a little scared, or very scared, because we are being shown what we could be, because we realize what we are, and what we are not. We pull back' (Marcus, 1991: 31). Our understanding of him is too small, too human: this is a person who 'appeared on the *Ed Sullivan Show* not as a country boy eager for his big chance but as a man ready to disorder and dismember the culture that from his first moment had tried to dismember him, and that *had failed*'; he was, writes Marcus in a sentence that only an American could have written, 'the first public figure since Jesus that couldn't be ignored by any segment of his civilization, yet that foretold and embodied a new mode of being that would eventually dismantle the very society that was so fascinated by his presence' (Marcus, 1991: 95).

In none of these analyses (and the countless others like them) is there a clear sense of how seriously the concept of the sacred should be taken, and of how the sacred might have come to be caught up with, and indeed produced as a central auratic effect by, the mass-representational systems of film, of rock, and of the theatre of mass politics. More problematically still, these analyses tend to partake of the very religious ethos that they describe: the notion of the charismatic genius and of the atavistic reincarnation each in its own way inscribes itself within an imaginary of ineffable presence. Against this imaginary, let me invoke the dry caution of William James, running a thread between Kant and the epistemologies of Bachelard and Althusser: 'Knowledge about a thing is not the thing itself', says James (1961: 379) to his Scottish audience. 'You remember what Al-Ghazzali told us in the Lecture on Mysticism – that to understand the causes of drunkenness, as a physician understands them, is not to be drunk.'

I propose that the form of apotheosis associated with the modern star system is a phenomenon of a strictly religious order; and in what follows I seek to trace out, very schematically, some of the implications of this proposition for the study both of contemporary religious experience and of systems of mass representation. My aim here is not to undertake such a study; it is to ask what its methodological and disciplinary conditions might be, and in particular to ask whether cultural studies has an appropriate take on these questions.

It is conventional to distinguish between the institutional and doctrinal dimensions of religion and what we might call its *ethos*. Religious affect never floats freely, but the structure to which it is tied need not be that of systematically organized religion. The 20th-century philosophy of religion, largely accepting this distinction, has sought to apprehend the nature of the experience of the sacred through the concept of the *numinous*. In Rudolf Otto's (1958) formulation there are three aspects to that intense experience of presence that he calls the numinous: first, it is understood as a *mysterium*: it is completely other than ourselves, and cannot be translated into the ordinary categories of human thought; nor can this experience be conveyed to someone who has not undergone it. Second, this *mysterium* is *tremendum*: it inspires awe, even terror at the overwhelming power which is revealed in religious experience, and which threatens to annihilate individual consciousness. Third, it is *fascinans*: it exercises an uncanny attraction, and inspires an emotion which is at once like love and like fear or even revulsion.

Otto's influential analysis operates at the highest level of abstraction to isolate an essence of the religious experience, understood as being the shared foundation of all religions. At a lower level of abstraction, a certain tradition of comparative anthropology seeks to understand the sacred not as an experience in itself but as a taxonomic operation which plays a central role in the formation of a religious cosmos. Finally, there are numerous accounts of socially and culturally specific religious formations, describing an enormous range of variations in the techniques and the cognitive frameworks from which particular experiences of the numinous arise – and indeed, that experience is not necessarily a component of all religions. For my purposes it is not necessary to descend to this level of concreteness, although any more detailed analysis of the cult of Elvis would certainly have to take into account, for example, the institutional particularities of Southern Baptism in relation to which it has flourished, its white southern working-class basis, its generational structure, as well as the ways in which it is *not* restricted to or defined by these structures.

For now, let me focus on that intermediate level of abstraction at which, in the classic Durkheimian formulation, the sacred is understood as an empty category defined structurally by nothing but its opposition to the profane (Durkheim, 1915: 38). This opposition then comes to govern a series of further structural relations within the cosmos. Against the homogeneous, amorphous, undifferentiated space of the profane world is set the radical heterogeneity of sacred space, which – 'saturated with being' and with significance (Eliade, 1961: 12) – interrupts it, breaks its flow, opens out on to absolute otherness. Time is similarly heterogeneous: unlike profane time, sacred time is reversible, because 'every religious festival, any liturgical time, represents the actualization of a sacred event that took place in a mythical past, "in the beginning"' (Eliade, 1961: 68–9). But this sheer otherness of the sacred is itself a kind of content; and already in Durkheim it is possible to see the emergence of a positive characterization of the sacred as it divides internally to produce a distinctive ambivalence, an oscillation between repulsion and fascination, dread and desire, the *tremendum* and the *fascinans*. For Durkheim (1915: 411) this takes the form of a division between the pure and the impure, and between beneficence and malevolence, both of which are the object of interdiction: thus 'the pure and the impure are not two separate classes, but two varieties of the same class, which includes all sacred things'. The sacred, as evidenced in its ambiguous latin root *sacer*, designates at once the accursed, the outcast, and the holy, a force which is above all dangerous, contagious, and compelling; it is, in Roger Caillois's words (1959: 21), 'what one cannot approach without dying'.

The sacred is thus a force or a presence, whether anthropomorphized or not, which is conceived non-naturalistically as a suspension or rupture of normal time and space by the uncontrollable outbreak of 'spots' of transcendence. Gods are positioned directly in relation to this force, as the force itself or as emanations of it. Demi-gods and their Christian variant, saints – and we must not be misled by centuries of humanism into believing that the categories of 'god' and of 'human being' are incompatible – mediate between the profane world and its transcendental other.

Demi-gods of the type of Elvis and Diana are intercessionary figures, gods in human form whose presence spans and translates between two worlds. This positioning is clearly apparent in Lynn Spigel's analysis of Elvis impersonators. She writes: 'Religious worship is not just a handy metaphor; . . . the impersonator is often considered a medium who channels the spirit of Elvis, which in turn channels the will of God' (1990: 191). At once a virtuoso performance of resurrection and a ruse, a trick, a game, these halfparodic simulations are, in their odd way, a form of worship. A female Elvis impersonator tells Spigel (1990: 191) that Elvis '"showed a great love for his fans. That's what bonds us all together: the love that he showed for humanity"'. For another fan she interviews, Mae Gutter, Elvis is 'a Christ figure – someone who Gutter believes mediates between heaven and earth and fills his followers with love' (Spigel, 1990: 192). And at the convention of Elvis impersonators that Spigel attends a Hawaian/Swiss impersonator, after singing his song 'He's living' ('He's living in my heart, he's living in my soul'), then invites the audience 'to pray with him for the dead Elvis, imploring us in prayer to thank God "for giving us Elvis and the one true King, Our Lord Jesus Christ"'. The impersonator, says Spigel (1990: 193), has a special relation to the redemptive logic of the Christian sacrament, 'for he or she works as a medium who channels the spirit of a saviour, all the while opening up a public space where people can express their mutual faith in an abstract principle that no one can name'.

Yet this performative evocation of the living presence of the dead King is always just that, an evocation, a repetition, a re-presentation. This is the gist of the argument that McKenzie Wark makes in an attempt to shift the reading of Elvis away from that myth of presence in which both fan culture and most rock criticism are entrapped, and to pose instead the question of the economy of representation within which stardom is constituted. That 'pure moment of original presence in Elvis's music and image', writes Wark (1989: 25–6), does not precede the moment of recording but rather follows it; it is 'an echo, a recording, a remix and edit from the vast palette of reproducible art'. One figure of this causal reversal operated by the mass mediation of sound and image might be the echo effect created for Elvis's voice by Sam Philips by cutting a master tape from two vocal tracks mixed a split-second apart, producing thereby 'a weird, non-architectural, electric space' which is, says Wark (1989: 26),

> the doubled space of recording, sound shadowed by its twin, its echo, the trace of its passage into recording. From the beginning Elvis was lost to this other space of recording totally. His 'live' performances are merely a dissimulation of the real Elvis, the recorded Elvis.

The power that Elvis wielded, and that he himself sought to explain by means of astrology, numerology, and Christian revivalist lore, had a much more mundane origin in a technology of repetition: at once the withdrawal of sound and image from the linear flow of time, and their dissemination in an endless series of copies. The real person of Elvis is always and from the beginning a copied person, the authenticity of which derives from the fact and the extent of copying, of representation, rather than from anything that precedes it. His charismatic force is an effect of

> the modern power of recording, piling up rhythms and images and sounds and stories like so many bones of the body of Elvis, laying them up until they piled up high into the air. . . . Till the time came when Elvis himself became a mere corporeal appendage to so great a body of recording. (Wark, 1989: 27)

To relate the apotheosis of Elvis to an economy of representation seems to me a crucial move. At the same time, Wark sidesteps a number of important questions by setting recording and religion in opposition to each other (this move, I will suggest later, is an almost inevitable one for the modernizing intellectuals who work in cultural studies). The question that I pose instead is this: how is it that a form of religious experience can, under certain circumstances, be so central to the secular culture of mass-recording? But before I broach this question, let me pose three preliminary questions which I hope will take me to the heart of the matter. Why does so much of the cult of Elvis take the form of parody? Why is the Elvis mythology so insistent on his doubleness? And why was his death such a good career move?

Even a quick look at some of the hundreds of Elvis-related websites is enough to convey a sense of his cultural ambivalence. The various lists of Elvis sightings, the speculations on whether and where he is still alive, the conspiracy theories concerning his death, the First Presbyterian Church of Elvis the Divine, the 24-Hour Church of Elvis, the various web-shrines, the list of parallels with the life and teachings of Jesus, the petitions for a national Elvis holiday in the US and for the creation of an Elvis clone, the endless tributes, the 'scientific evidence (in the form of a Masters thesis) that the woman Michael Jackson wed is in fact not Elvis Presley's daughter' (Elvis fans hate Michael Jackson) – all these are either directly parodic or, more usually, an extraordinary mix of mockery and reverence. The King is a joke, an object of ridicule, as much as and indeed precisely to the extent that he is an object of worship and one of the central figures through which American popular culture imagines the relation between the living and the dead. This is to say that the categories of the sacred and the comic are not necessarily antagonistic, and certainly within contemporary popular culture they are inextricably fused, Marcus (1991) gets it precisely right when speaking of the emergence within popular culture of strange new Elvis hybrids: 'Elvis Christ, Elvis Nixon, Elvis Hitler, Elvis *Mishima*, Elvis as godhead, Elvis inhabiting the bodies of serial killers, of saints, fiends. Each was a joke, of course; beneath each joke was bedrock, obsession, delight, fear.'

Nowhere is this ambivalence clearer than in the case of those multipliers of Elvis, the impersonators, estimated at some 3000 in the US alone in 1992, whose performance is at once a take-off, a camp parody of a piece of cultural kitsch (this is why almost all impersonators mime the overweight, white-jumpsuited Elvis of the Las Vegas years rather than the young Elvis) and at the same time a reverential reproduction of that presence that cannot be copied but that can be evoked, alluded to, signified through the very imperfection of the impersonator, where the word 'impersonator' has the sense both of impostor and of one who enters into the person of the dead and resurrected singer.

Impersonation is one aspect of the theme of doubleness that runs through the Elvis narrative. There is the fact that already in 1956 the warm-up act for Elvis's show at the Louisiana Fair Grounds was done by exact replicas who dressed like him and sang his songs (Garber, 1993: 370); and that Elvis is said to have selected the material he would record by listening to impersonators who would give him a sense of how the songs would sound (Goldman, cited in Joyrich, 1993: 88). There are the stories of the faked death, in which the body displayed in the casket is said either to have been a wax dummy, or 'the body of an English look-alike fan who had been invited to Graceland because he was dying of cancer' (Fiske, 1993: 112). And there are the various forms in which Elvis takes on the role of *revenant* – as comeback artist, as phantom hitchhiker, as the man who haunted the rock revolution which he initiated and then sat out. The essence of superstardom, says Garber (1993: 373), may be 'to be simultaneously belated and replicated; not to be there, and to cover up that absence with representations'. For Edgar Morin, speaking of the process of projection in which the star acquires a superhuman status, the double is 'the repository of latent magical powers: every double is a virtual god' (Morin, 1960: 98). But doubling is also the structure of iteration by which the effect of presence is produced in representation, and by which, in the case of mass-recording, an infinite number of identical representations produces a correspondingly magnified effect of presence, the superhuman presence of the star who is at once absent and immortal.

This absence of the recorded star, their presence as recording, is the reason why the worship of stars is a cult of the dead.[1] The image and the recorded sound of Elvis precede his person in the circuit of recognition in which they have their life; he is remembered before he is known, recognized as an ideality in ways that his actual bodily being could never match. The star competes with his ghostly rival, the double that is more real, more authentic, and unchanging for all time. The effect of his death is only that he can now become himself, *tel qu'en lui-même enfin l'éternité le change*: eternity changes him at last into the person he really was.

It is for this reason, as John Castles argues in a remarkable thesis to which this paper is heavily indebted, that the star's biography is always tragic in form: like the hagiography from which it derives,[2] it is structured by premonition – 'James Dean Knew He Had a Date With Death' (Castles, 1993: 152): by a subordination of profane, linear, irreversible time to a temporality in which the moment of death is always given in advance, and in which every gesture, every choice, every session in the Beale St bars, every step towards Sun Studios, is laden with significance. The star is always already dead; by the same token, however, the star lives forever. 'James Dean dies; it is the beginning of his victory over death' (Morin, 1960: 123). Morin thus lists the four phenomena that accompany the star's apotheosis: first, a spontaneous refusal to believe that the star is actually dead; second, legends of their survival and of the fabrication of evidence of death; third, spiritualist notions of the continued existence of the dead among the living – the phantom hitchhiker; and fourth, the development of a cult establishing connections between the living and the immortal dead (Morin, 1960: 132). The final corollary to this argument is that 'living stars . . . are a subset of dead ones' (Castles, 1993: 170). The life of the recording artist and the movie star is realized in reversible and repeatable time; their fullest being is lived here, in what we can recognize as sacred time, time outside of time, the time of circulated representations which transcends and transfigures whatever it is we think of as ordinary life.

The first thing to say about this mechanism, I think, is that it involves a quantitative effect: the 'passages of recorded time' in which stars are constituted are multiplied in time as repetition and in space as replication (Castles, 1993: 47). The star is thus not just a recorded but a disseminated person, not just widely known but widely known to be widely known. 'Every star image is composed of the fact that stars contain in their singular body the gaze of a collectivity' (Castles, 1993: 109), and this is in the first place an arithmetical fact.

But how does this fact of being known to many people then undergo a qualitative change to transform the star from a human being into a nonhuman, a more-than-human being? Let me suggest an answer by way of analogy. Jaynes (1976: 167–72) argues that neolithic representations of the gods always have a greater ratio of eye size to overall facial size (up to 20%) than is found in human beings (about 10%): the gaze of the god is of greater intensity than that of humans. We might remember that one of the things that was held against the young Elvis was his use of eye shadow, artificially enlarging the size of his eyes (Garber, 1993: 367). What this suggests is that the gaze of the god is an intensifier, a manifold which condenses a multiplicity of looks and returns them with increased force to the single fan. That is what is overwhelming – *tremendum* and *fascinans* – about the look of the star, the gaze of the god: this concentration of the energy of the many into a spell-binding focus on the one. My recognition of this look which reflects and magnifies my own is a kind of love, a kind of adoration; Morin (1960: 18) speaks of it as a 'phenomenon of the soul which mingles most intimately our imaginary projection-identifications and our real life', and he points to its ambivalence, the desire of the worshipper to consume his god. Marcus (1991: 202) too notes 'the complex of worship and resentment all fans carry', and the Vermorels' (1992) research into fan cultures reveals the same oscillation, often within the one letter or testimony, between adoration and hatred.

John Castles's metaphor for the construction of the divinity of the star in the returned and intensified gaze is the relation of the performer to the crowd in the ritualized structure of the rock concert. What takes place in this ritual is a mutual constitution of the audience and the star in ecstatic identification: 'When the crowd screams at the appearance of the star they are performing the essential task of making themselves into a crowd which then tumbles down into the star figure who absorbs it and can then give it back or withhold it' (Castles, 1993: 135). This mirror-recognition, in which the crowd alternately loses itself and recomposes itself, then gives way to a third moment in which 'each member of the crowd can then copy the star's embodiment of all of them. The "super-self" made by the crowd is then imaginarily reappropriated, repossessed by each of its moments' (Castles, 1993: 137); each spectator is swollen with the energy and presence they absorb from the star made big by the crowd.

Underlying and enabling this directly specular relation to the crowd, however, is the prior relation of the star to an inchoate 'mass' by way of the recordings which constitute in advance his or her recognizable presence. As Connor (1989: 153) notes, the live concert builds upon an 'inversion of the structural dependence of copies upon originals', by means of technologies of amplification, magnification, and repetition – sound equipment, huge video screens, and the playing of material that is already familiar from recordings. The core of stardom is thus of a semiotic order. The star belongs to a domain constructed by recording and the modes of repetition specific to it which exists outside or beyond ordinary life, profane time; this is the basis for the promise that, in identifying with the star, we too will overcome death.

I said before that the purpose of this chapter is not directly to undertake a study of the relation between systems of mass representation and religious experience, but to ask what the preconditions of such a study might be. My starting point is what I take to be the failure of cultural studies – with rare exceptions – to come to terms with, to theorize in any adequate way, what is perhaps the most important set of popular cultural systems in the contemporary world, religion in both its organized and its disorganized forms. Religion is an embarrassment to us; it's an embarrassment to me, and above all because we Western intellectuals are so deeply committed to the secularization thesis which makes of religion an archaic remnant which ought by now to have withered away. This thesis – never more than a polemical one (Martin, 1969: 16) – is plainly wrong. It is wrong as a matter of fact, both because organized religion is flourishing in many parts of the world, and because religious sentiment – the belief in a cosmic order and in the continuing life of the dead – has migrated into many strange and unexpected places, from New Age trinketry to manga movies and the cult of the famous dead.[3] Indeed, many of these mutant religious forms have precisely to do with the restoration of that intercessionary realm, the 'vast continuity of being between the seen and the unseen' (Berger, 1967: 112), which, on the Weberian thesis, was eliminated by the Protestant naturalization and rationalization of the creation. The secularization thesis is also wrong, however, as a matter of theory, predicated as it is on a logic of historical progression through necessary historical stages culminating in the achieved rationality of a fully secular and fully Western modernity (cf. Graham, 1992: 184–5). We have been told the story of the disenchantment of the world so many times that we have come to believe it, despite all evidence to the contrary.

Let me conclude, then, with three modest observations about the disciplinary and curricular focus of cultural studies. The first is an argument that among the things we need to know about and to teach our students is the history and sociology of religion. It is not possible to do contemporary cultural studies adequately without deep resources of knowledge of other cultures and of the disciplines that study them. The second and corollary argument is that we need to take religion seriously in all of its dimensions because of its cultural centrality in the modern world; and we need to do so without ourselves participating in those religious myths of origin and presence – the myth, for example, of the great star whose charisma is the cause rather than the effect of their fame (Marshall, 1997: 55–6) – which are a constant theoretical temptation in the study of popular culture. Finally, let me make the observation that for many Australians these lessons have come from our increased awareness of Aboriginal spirituality, and our sense both of the need to respect and honour traditional belief systems, and of the tensions between a religious cosmology and the Enlightenment ethos which governs, and which rightly governs, our work. That tension is inescapable, and we cannot pretend not to be subject to it. But this is then also a methodological question: how is it possible for our knowledge to ground itself in a hard-won rationality which must, as a matter of principle, put doubt and sceptical enquiry before faith, and yet at the same time to enter sympathetically into forms of understanding which are quite alien to it, and to do so without condescending to those other knowledges, without seeking to destroy them, and without seeking to deny the forms of desire and will to power which are constitutive of enlightened reason? I don't know, in any schematic way, the answers to these questions; but I do know that it is crucial to the future of our discipline to get them right.

Notes

1. Cf. Wark (1989: 28): by his death Elvis became 'the King of the passage into the better world of recording', into 'recorded culture . . . the cult of the dead'.
2. Vikan (1994: 150) writes of the Elvis *vitae* as speaking 'of a dirt-poor southern boy who rose to fame and glory; of the love of a son for his mother, of humility and generosity, and of superhuman achievement in the face of adversity', as well as of a death which is a martyrdom to and for his fans.
3. Berger (1967: 109), while supporting the notion of a process of secularization, nevertheless allows for the possibility that there may be 'a continuation of more or less traditional motifs of religious consciousness outside their previous institutional contexts'.

References

Berger, Peter (1967). *The Sacred Canopy: Elements of a Sociological Theory of Religion*. New York: Doubleday.

Caillois, Roger (1959). *Man and the Sacred*, trans. Meyer Barash. Glencoe, IL: The Free Press.

Castles, John (1993). The Individual and Stardom. PhD thesis, University of Technology, Sydney.

Connor, Steven (1989). *Postmodernist Culture: An Introduction to Theories of the Contemporary*. Oxford: Basil Blackwell.

Durkheim, Emile (1915). *The Elementary Forms of the Religious Life*, trans. Joseph Ward Swain. London: George Allen & Unwin.

Eliade, Mircea (1961). *The Sacred and the Profane* (1959), trans. Willard R. Trask. New York: Harper & Row.

Fiske, John (1993). *Power Plays, Power Works*. London: Verso.

Garber, Marjorie (1993). *Vested Interests: Cross-Dressing and Cultural Anxiety*. New York: Harper Perennial.

Goldman, Albert (1981). *Elvis*. New York: McGraw.

Graham, Gordon (1992). Religion, Secularization and Modernity. *Philosophy* 67, pp. 183–97.

Harrison, Ted (1992). *Elvis People: The Cult of the King*. London: Fount.

Hinerman, Stephen (1992). "I'll Be Here with You": Fans, Fantasy and the Figure of Elvis. In: Lisa A. Lewis (ed.), *The Adoring Audience: Fan Culture and Popular Media*, pp. 107–34. London: Routledge.

James, William (1961 [1902]). *The Varieties of Religious Experience*. New York: Collier.

Jaynes, Julian (1976). *The Origin of Consciousness in the Breakdown of the Bicameral Mind*. Boston: Houghton Mifflin.

Joyrich, Lynne (1993). Elvisophilia: Knowledge, Pleasure, and the Cult of Elvis. *Differences* 5(1), pp. 73–91.

Kroker, Arthur, Marilouise Kroker & David Cook (eds.). *Panic Encyclopaedia: The Definitive Guide to the Postmodern Scene*, at http://ctech.concordia.ca/krokers/panic.html

Marcus, Greil (1991). *Dead Elvis: A Chronicle of a Cultural Obsession*. New York: Doubleday.

Marshall, David (1997). *Celebrity and Power: Fame in Contemporary Culture*. Minneapolis: University of Minnesota Press.

Martin, David (1969). *The Religious and the Secular: Studies in Secularization*. London: Routledge & Kegan Paul.

Morin, Edgar (1960). *The Stars*, trans. Richard Howard. New York and London: Grove Press and John Calder.

Otto, Rudolph (1958). *The Idea of the Holy* (1923), trans. John W. Harvey. Oxford: Oxford University Press.

Paglia, Camille (1990). *Sexual Personae: Art and Decadence from Nefertiti to Emily Dickinson*. New Haven: Yale University Press.

Paglia, Camille (1995). *Vamps and Tramps: New Essays*. London: Viking.

Rodman, Gilbert (1996). *Elvis after Elvis: The Posthumous Career of a Living Legend*. London: Routledge.

Silberman, Neil Asher (1990). Elvis: The Myth Lives on. *Archaeology* 43(4), p. 80.

Spigel, Lynn (1990). Communicating with the Dead: Elvis as Medium. *Camera Obscura* 23, pp. 176–205.

Vermorel, Fred and July (1992). A Glimpse of the Fan Factory. In: Lisa A. Lewis (ed.), *The Adoring Audience: Fan Culture and Popular Media*, pp. 191–207. London: Routledge.

Vikan, Gary (1994). Graceland as *Locus Sanctus*. In: Geri DePaoli (ed.), *Elvis + Marilyn: 2 × Immortal*, pp. 150–66. New York: Rizzoli.

Wark, McKenzie (1989). Elvis: Listen to the Loss. *Art & Text* 31, pp. 24–8.

75

Serial Killing for Beginners[1]

*Mark Seltzer**

She loved accidents: any mention of an animal run over, a man cut to pieces by a train, was bound to make her rush to the spot.

– Émile Zola, *La Bête humaine* (1890)

Hence the new millenium's passion for standing live witness to things. A whole sub-rosa schedule of public spectation opportunities, "spect-ops," the priceless chance to be part of a live crowd, watching. Thus the Gapers' Blocks at traffic accidents, sewer-gas explosions, muggings . . . people leaving their front doors agape in their rush to get out and mill around and spectate at the circle of impacted waste drawing sober and studious crowds, milling in rings around the impact.

David Foster Wallace, *Infinite Jest* (1996)

Serial killing has its place in a public culture in which addictive violence has become not merely a collective spectacle but one of the crucial sites where private desire and public fantasy cross. The convening of the public around scenes of violence – the rushing to the scene of the accident, the milling around the point of impact – has come to make up a *wound culture*: the public fascination with torn and open bodies and torn and opened persons, a collective gathering around shock, trauma, and the wound.

Serial killing, by all accounts, became a career option at the turn of the century. Serial murder and its representations, for example, have by now largely replaced the Western as the most popular genre-fiction of the body and of bodily violence in our culture. And recent splatterpunk Westerns, such as Cormac MacCarthy's novel *Blood Meridian* or films like Clint Eastwood's *The Unforgiven* or Jim Jarmusch's *Dead Man*, make the case that the Western was really about serial killing all along. But accounting for this style of addictive violence and its fascinations is another story.

What is it about modern culture that makes the type of person called the serial killer possible? The spectacle of the wounded body has, of course, always had its lurid attractions. Nor did the last century invent murder in large numbers or the sex crime. But by 1900 something strange and something new appears on the scene. The wound, for one thing, is by now no longer the mark, the stigmata, of the sacred or heroic: it is the icon, or stigma, of the everyday openness of every body. This is a culture centered on trauma (Greek for wound): a culture of the atrocity exhibition, in which people wear their damage like badges of identity, or fashion accessories. And by 1900 a new kind of person has come into being and into view, one of the superstars of our wound culture: the lust-murderer or stranger-killer or serial killer.

If murder is where bodies and history cross, "senseless" murder is where our most basic senses of the body and society, identity and desire, violence and intimacy, are secured, or brought to crisis. The emergence of the kind of individual called the serial killer is bound up, it will be seen, with a basic shift in our understanding of the individuality of the individual. And this is bound, in turn, to a general mutation in our understanding of both "the criminal" and "the sexual."

First, then, what does it mean for the serial killer to emerge as a species of person? And, second, why has this species of person, and the intimacies of sex and violence, pleasure and power that drive him, become a flash-point in contemporary society? These are some of the large questions I will be taking up in the pages that follow. We can begin to approach them by way of a brief look at a recent change in public policy with regard to the sex offender. This is not a book about the sex offender; nor is the serial killer simply to be located at the extreme end of a continuum of male sexual violence, with the "minor" sex offender at the other. Serial killing has its own logic. But that logic is inseparable from renovated experiences of both sex and crime.

On July 1, 1997, the State of California released a database of nearly 64,000 convicted sex offenders statewide, now available on CD-ROM at county sheriff's offices and larger police departments. "Serious" sex offenders must register with local police each year, and failure to register may count as a "third strike," punishable by life imprisonment. The intent, according to the State Attorney General, is a " 'lifting of the veil of anonymity' shielding sex offenders from their neighbors"; the effect, opponents of the law contend, are "dangerous intrusions into privacy, sweeping a wide array of past offenders into a permanent class of stigmatized, second class citizens." Although targetted at "serious" offenders – "alerting parents and communities to the presence of potentially dangerous people," the broad brush of the law threatens to tar "adults convicted of committing same-sex consensual acts its public," and even public exposure of people convicted of crimes like indecent exposure. The law also imposes penalties on anyone who "misuses the CD-ROM information to commit crimes against sex offenders," who now "may face invasions of privacy or violence by their neighbors." The new California database supplements the earlier establishment of a statewide 900 number adults may call to check on "whether people are registered sex offenders." (The sex-offender 900 number fee is $10.) It moves beyond, at least with respect to its information technologies, the practice of other states, such as Louisiana, where sex offenders must inform neighbors of their presence via postcards.[2]

It is not merely that the protection of privacy and the public's right to know come into conflict in such cases: that the right to privacy gives way to the crime of anonymity, where the sex criminal is concerned. Some of the most severe stress-points in the American nervous system become visible here.[3] Here I want, in very preliminary fashion, to touch on three of them. First, there is the matter of the public/private divide, in all its normalcy and in all its incoherence. The public/private divide is always what is at issue, what trembles, in the sex offense and in responses to it. If this is most evident in the case of pornography – the exposure of sex and fantasy in public, the sex crime, more generally, is routinely experienced in terms of the violent passage of fantasy into act, private desire into public spectacle.

Second, and along the same lines, there is the way in which such crimes are everywhere marked by the "looping" of collective bodies of information and individual desire; and here I refer not simply to the CD-ROMs and 900 numbers that register and locate the sex criminal. Repetitive, compulsive, serial violence, it will be seen, does not exist without this radical entanglement between forms of eroticized violence and mass technologies of registration, identification, and reduplication, forms of copy-catting and simulation.

Third, there is the permanent *branding* of potentially dangerous people: the formation of a permanent class of the stigmatized person, a brand of person, marked and identified for all time by his criminal acts. This enters the law despite the fact that rates of recidivism (that is, the rate at which acts reconfirm identities) are in fact lower for the high-risk offenders required to register themselves than for other groups (about 19% compared to about 22%).[4] The very category of the "potentially dangerous individual" – here, the notion of the sex criminal as a *kind of person* – has by now taken on the self-evident and obdurate banality of common sense. But it is perhaps necessary to recover some of the strangeness of this notion.

During the course of the nineteenth century, there is a radical shift in the understanding of crime, a shift in focus from the criminal act to the character of the actor: the positing of the category of the dangerous individual.[5] And during the course of the nineteenth century, there is a shift in the understanding of desire, a shift in focus from sexual acts to sexual identity: from the vagrancies of sexual desire and sexual relations to a category of person, specified and rendered intelligible by the singular nature of his sexual identity – a social intelligibility and self-intelligibility bound up through and through with the indelible nature of one's sexuality. A kind of act was now a species of person. This twin shift in understanding from act to life form – from the character of acts to the character and identity of the actor – is perfected in the dangerous individual called the sex-criminal.[6]

The serial killer emerges at the dark intersection of all these strands. By the turn of the century, serial killing has become something to do (a lifestyle, or career, or calling) and the serial killer has become something to be (a species of person). The serial killer becomes a type of person, a body, a case history, a childhood, an alien life form. In 1996 in New York City a serial rapist and murderer was arrested who had in his possession a manuscript-in-progress entitled, "How to Be a Successful Serial Killer or Mass Murderer." In the words of the serial killer Henry Lee Lucas, "I'm not one of a kind. There's lots of others out there just like me."[7] Murder by numbers is the work of the individual I describe as the statistical person: the serial killer, that is, is not merely one of an indeterminate number of others but an individual who, in the most radical form, experiences identity, his own and others, as a matter of numbers, kinds, types, and as a matter of simulation and likeness ("just like me").

He is a case history and, perhaps above all on the popular understanding, a childhood. This follows in part from the modern belief that childhood experience forms the adult, the founding premise, for example, of psychoanalysis. It is also the basic premise of a contemporary scene in which public life is everywhere referred back to scenes of an endangered, or dangerous, domesticity or privacy, and not least to the scenes of childhood trauma. Child abuse – wounded as a child, wounding as an adult – is one of the foundational scripts in accounting for the serial killer. It has a sort of a priori status, even when evidence for it is absent. But even where evidence is absent, this is not to say that this governing belief does not loop back on these cases: framing not merely the public intelligibility of the serial killer but also his self-intelligibility.[8]

I will be returning to this script but also to its limits. What counts as abuse, depersonalization, wounding takes strange detours in these cases. Ted Bundy, for example, illegitimate but not physically or sexually abused, described himself as a "very verbal person." He described his mother, in his bizarre, third-person "confessions," entirely in terms of her relation to words and writing: "My mother taught me the English language . . . How many times did she type my papers as I dictated them to her? [She] gave me great verbal skills . . . I could have written them out in shorthand but would dictate things I had left out." His mother, he continued, has "beautiful handwriting, very good vocabulary, but she never *says* anything! She says, 'I love you,' or 'I'm sorry we haven't written. Everything's fine,' or 'We miss you . . . Everything will turn out . . . 'Blah, blah, blah.'"[9]

Persons, for Bundy, were faceless numbers and types: "I mean, there are *so* many people . . . Terrible with names . . . *and* faces. Can't remember faces."[10] That is, persons, faces, names, for this very verbal person, are a defaced and dead language, the dead repetitions and clichés that register intimacy ("I love you") only as a worn quotation, a dictated, typed, stereotyped interiority. In his adolescence, Bundy became what he called a "radio freak," addicted to the public intimacies of talk radio. Awaiting execution, he attributed his acts to "his warping by printed matter that involved violence and sexual violence."[11] Writing, dictation, typing, shorthand, communication technologies, the data stream, pulp fiction and the true crime genre, the mass media and mediatronic intimacy: all traverse these cases, enter into the interiority of this style of violence, from the later nineteenth century on.

Serial Killers makes a case for the significance of experiences such as these, alongside the popular and general modes of "explanation," such as early trauma – explanations that often remain so general, so self-evident, or so transparently tautological that they miss a large part of reality. For what would it look like to experience oneself, through and through, as a type of person? What would it feel like to experience this perpetual looping of information and desire, technology and intimacy, violence and pleasure as one's form of life?

"It is impossible to estimate how many children come of age in violent, loveless homes across the land," one recent encyclopedist of serial violence writes: "If every child produced from a dysfunctional relationship was homicidal, the United States would be one giant charnel house by now."[12] What this study, among many others, describes as "America's murder epidemic," amounts to the positing of a national malady of trauma and violence. Serial killing is thus represented as at once an horrific departure from normalcy and as abnormally normal: wounds to an idealized and intact American culture that is at the same time seen *as* a wound culture. "As the influence of American culture spreads to less developed countries," another popular study of serial killing observes, "the fear is that, unless checked somehow, the disease of serial murder will spread as well."[13] Hence if such crimes "appal the nation," the national landscape itself seems spectral, pathological, unreal: "1.8 million children vanish from home every year. . . . The case of vanishing adults is even more obscure"; the serial killer's "mask of normalcy" means that he "will have developed an uncanny knack for becoming invisible and fading into the background."[14] What this vanishing means and what this fading into the background means are parts of the story I will be telling. Testifying before a Senate committee on motiveless violence, the true crime writer Ann Rule argued that the national distribution of serial murder cases indicates that serial killers "run to the borders" of the country, in a physical expression of their mental extremity.[15] Cases, in fact, tend to cluster in the most populous regions. But this style of explanation – like the notions of a "murder epidemic" (Newton) or "serial murder as an infectious disease" (Norris) – makes visible the tendency to merge the natural and national body, where pathological violence is concerned. This version of a lurid sociobiology is commonplace enough: the body typically is drawn on, lends the weight of its apparent "givenness" to, social and cultural representations. But it is also more than that. It is more than that to the extent that the boundaries between the natural and collective body, private fantasy and public space, intimacy and publicity, are just what are, as we say, "at risk" in the matter of corporeal compulsive violence.

Serial Killers maps the psychotopography of that violence. The first part of this book traces the typical scenes of serial murder and the type of persons who inhabit them. Here I set out the strange form of intimacy – the form of life that I will be calling *stranger-intimacy* – that occupies these scenes. These sites, acts, and figures make up the overlit national landscapes of compulsion, addiction, and violence that define *the pathological public sphere*. In the second chapter of this part, I turn to the ways in which serial sexual violence – its maladies of agency, its addictive relation to mass-produced images and representations, its identification of destruction and possession, its logic of killing for pleasure – depends on an intricate rapport between murder and machine culture. It depends not least on the intimacies between graphic violence and the technologies of registration, recording, and reproduction: the graphomanias of the Second Industrial Revolution. My examples include some of the inaugural writings on lust-killing (among others, Bram, Stoker's *Dracula* and Zola's *La Bête humaine*) and some of the most extraordinary accounts of the inner experience of addiction (from Jack London's *John Barleycorn* to the cybernetics of the self in AA programs).

The chapters that make up the second part of this book are about the formation of the serial killer as the species of person proper to a mass-mediated public culture: *the mass in person*. It is often remarked of the serial killer that "the absence of a sense of self allows the criminal to fade back into society as a common individual."[16] But what sort of violence is incipient in the very notion of "the common individual" in a culture that mandates at the same time that one must "Be Your Self" and "Obey Your Thirst"?

And how does the very banality of this way of thinking about "self" and "society" make the experience of one's everyday openness to collective forces and mass identifications traumatic and insupportable: turn the mandate of "each for each" into the war of "all against all"? The profile of the serial killer – his composite portrait or statistical picture – emerges as the very icon of the mass in person. Crucially, these maladies of self-difference, or self-distinction, are, in the case of the serial killer, immediately translated into violence along the lines of sexual difference: the sex-violence thing and the identity-thing reinforce each other at every point. In this part I draw my examples, first, from the range of official, psychological, and popular accounts of the serial killer; second, from the mass-market genre of bodily violence, pulp fiction (particularly Jim Thompson's novel *The Killer Inside Me*), tracking the popular psychology of the serial murderer pulp fiction sets in place; third, from the technologies of simulation and "lifelikeness" that enter into pornographic violence; and, finally, from the career of Jeffrey Dahmer – a career in which the *splatter codes* of sex and violence, public sex and pathologized privacy, and machine culture's turn of the life-like against life itself take on the most explicit and terminal form.

The third part of the book draws together all these elements, in part by way of one of the most sensational American episodes of serial violence: the 1890s case of the Chicago inventor, entrepreneur, medical practitioner, and serial murderer Herman Webster Mudgett, alias H. H. Holmes. This case, one of the most extensively documented (albeit in documentations that seldom move beyond lurid redescription), sets in place many of the components of serial killing. It spectacularly foregrounds the lethal spaces in which these crimes take place: here, the 100-room "Murder Castle" Holmes constructed and operated. It makes explicit the intimacies of serial violence and machine culture: the strange, prosthetic devices Holmes invented to process his victims, his utter absorption in technologies of writing and communication, his technophilias and graphomanias. Holmes's inventions and self-inventions make him something like an extreme limit-case of the self-made man. Finally, the spectacular character of his crimes registers at every point *the entering of the mass spectacle into the interior of addictive bodily violence*.

The last part of this book centers on America's wound culture: the torn bodies and torn persons about which the crowd gathers. It maps, that is, the wound landscapes of contemporary culture and locates some of its landmarks. Here I pressure the psychoanalytic, and popular, understanding of trauma toward an account of what might be described as the sociality of the wound. And I pressure the popular understanding of the body-machine-image complex toward a different account of what it means to inhabit the pathological public sphere today.

In the concluding pages of this introduction I want less to explain than briefly to exemplify some of the interlaced components in these crimes, and to indicate some of the basic limits in governing accounts of serial killing and its fascinations. Such accounts, on both popular and professional fronts, have in effect dramatized rather than specified such fascinations, hence functioning as something of an antidote to registering their most radical cultural implications. Which is perhaps one indication of the extraordinary complex of concerns – sexual, social, technological, and artistic – that the concept of the serial killer makes visible and draws into relation.

Word Counts and Body Counts

The prototype of the serial killer is, of course, the case of Jack the Ripper, who killed a series of women in 1880s London. This case put in place the popular model of the serial killer as white-male-sadist-performance artist, although such criminals are by no means all white or all male or their victims all women, and although the ritualistic or "artistic" aspect of these crimes means, for the most part, that patterns or "signatures" emerge. That nothing reliable is known about the identity or motives of this London killer is itself a central part of the model: the endless rituals of noncomprehension that continue to surround the kind of person called the serial killer.

Only two things are known for certain about the Ripper case. There was for a time a series of torn and opened bodies of too public women on the public streets (the victims it seems of professional sex in public). And there was a series of more than 300 letters (none authenticated) mailed to the London press, signed Jack the Ripper. In such cases, the boundaries come down between private desire and public life, along with the boundaries between private bodies and the public media. Letters and bodies, word counts and body counts, go together from the inception of serial murder.

Abnormally Normal

Here is something like a personal confession, part of an anonymous letter received by an Ohio newspaper in November 1991:

> I've killed people. . . . Technically I meet the definition of a serial killer (three or more victims with a cooling-off period in between) but I'm an average-looking person with a family, job and home just like yourself. . . . I've thought about getting professional help but how can I ever approach a mental health professional? I can't just blurt out in an interview that I've killed people.[17]

There is by now nothing extraordinary about such communications to the mass media, from the Ripper letters to the letter bomber called Unabom. Nor is there anything extraordinary about the "technical" self-definition of the serial killer that centers this confession, although there is some disagreement about the baseline qualifying number. (The FBI defines serial murder simply "as involving an offender associated with the killing of at least four victims, over a period greater than seventy-two hours.")[18] And the "cooling-off period," distributing the murders serially over time, has come to provide the working distinction between serial and mass murder (with "spree-killing" falling somewhere in between).

But if this is a personal confession, it is also strangely *im*personal, and not merely because the killer's desire to approach the "mental health professional" is just one step from a twelve-step outlook on addictive killing. This is an anonymous letter on several counts. The writer experiences the technical definition of the serial killer as a self-definition: the killer takes the FBI's composite picture or standard "profile" of the serial killer as a self-portrait.

One refrain in coverage of serial killing is just this dead average and look-alike character of the killer. The forensic psychiatrist Helen Morrison, who has done thousands of hours of interviews with serial killers, puts it this way: "These are basically cookie-cutter people, so much alike psychologically I could close my eyes and be talking to any one of them." There is something uncanny about how these killers are so much alike, living composites, how easily they blend in. The serial killer, as one prosecutor of these cases expressed it, is "abnormally normal": "just like you or me."[19]

One of the court psychiatrists in the case of the Milwaukee killer Jeffrey Dahmer remarked about the "chameleon-like" character of the killer: "Dress him in a suit and he looks like 10 other men." In the recent serial killer movie *Virtuosity*, the computer composite of the serial killer comes to life, takes life. In another recent movie, *Copycat*, there is no deeper motive to killing than turning oneself into a copy of someone else. This is the killer as "the devoid" or (to borrow a term from Dennis Cooper's serial killer fantasy novel *Frisk*) as "Mr. Xerox." The serial killer is "citizen X" (the "Russian Ripper" Chikitilo) or "the monochrome man" (the self-description of the London serial killer, Dennis Nilsen, who murdered and dismembered 15 young men in the early 1980s). In his remarkable novel on the abnormal normality of serial killing, *The Minus Man*, Lew McCreary describes the profile of the killer, the minus man, this way: "He looks like a million people."[20]

The Stranger-Killer

Serial killing is also called stranger-killing. The serial killer is always "the stranger beside me" or "everyone's nextdoor neighbor": "average-looking" and "just like yourself." The stranger, in the lonely crowd, is one who is near but also far. *The Stranger Beside Me* is the title of Ann Rule's book on Ted Bundy. Bundy, while a student at the University of Washington – majoring in abnormal psychology, of course – had a work-study job at a suicide prevention and crisis hotline. One of his volunteer coworkers and friends at the hotline was the true crime writer, Rule, a contributor to *True Detective* magazine who had contracted to write a book on the recent "Ted" killings in the Seattle area (that is, on Bundy himself). Her book on the stranger beside her wavers between shock (he couldn't have done it, I *know* him!) and journalistic glee (what luck!).[21]

Ted Bundy himself struck everyone as perfectly *chameleon-like*: it was observed again and again that "he never looked the same from photograph to photograph." Bundy's death-row interviews are endless strings of mass media and pop-academic clichés. The interviews read as if the pages of *Psychology Today* were time-sharing his words, his eyes, his face, his mind. They are spoken in the third person, where he lived. In the words of the serial killer Henry Lee Lucas (who was the loose prototype for the John McNaughton film *Henry: Portrait of a Serial Killer*): "A person was a blank." The complete yielding to nonpersonality is one of the serial killer's signatures, the proper name of the minus man. Or, as Bundy, "a type of nonperson" who was also such a verbal person, expressed it: "Personalized stationery is one of the small but truly necessary luxuries of life."[22]

The Serial Killer Profile

The FBI serial-crime unit attempts to fill in the blank – through its vaunted profiling system and fifteen-page, fill-in-the-blanks Violent Crime and Apprehension Program (VICAP) form – for police reports on repeat crimes. But the profilers have in all been generally ineffectual in tracking down killers. As one ex-agent in serial homicide investigations put it, "I mean, how many serial killer cases has the FBI solved – *if any!*"[23]

But the FBI has managed to put in place something like a job description, a sort of "most wanted" ad. "Serial killers," as one recent sociologist of serial homicide notes, "are influenced by the media as well as by academic psychology, and many make a specific study of earlier offenders."[24] Serial killers make a study of their own kind of person. The Ohio killer-letter writer is only one among many others who had, it turns out, "read many books about serial killers."

The designation of the serial killer as a type of person has had, we have noted, a sort of switchback or looping effect: public knowledge about kinds of people has a way of interacting with the people who are known about and how these people conceive of themselves. Serial-killer, virtual-reality profiles come to life and copy-catting as motive are fictional versions of the "technical definition" of the serial killer lifting itself up by its own bootstraps.

The Copycat Killer

Fact and fiction have a way of changing places here: virtual reality, after all, has its own reality. Robert Ressler, the cofounder of the FBI's Behavioral Science Unit (BSU) who coined the term "serial killer" in the mid-1970s, had two things on his mind at what he called this "naming-event": the British designation, "crimes in series," and "the serial adventures we used to see on Saturday at the movies."[25]

Ressler's story of the profilers, *Whoever Fights Monsters*, carries as its frontispiece a reproduction of William Blake's *Red Dragon*, with this inscription: "For Bob Ressler with best wishes, Francis Dolarhyde and Thomas Harris." Dolarhyde is the fictional serial killer who identifies himself with Blake's Dragon in Harris's novel *Red Dragon*. That novel is the prequel to *Silence of the Lambs*, in which Ressler and his colleague at the BSU, John Douglas, are brought together as the composite for the FBI chief. According to Douglas, in his recent book on the FBI's serial crime unit, *Mindhunter*, "Harris picked up the story while sitting in on our courses at Quantico." Douglas's own recent account of the FBI's serial-crime unit makes clear the FBI's own recourse to fiction and film. "Our antecedents," as he puts it, "actually do go back to crime fiction more than crime fact."[26]

The distinctions between fact and fiction and between bodies and information vanish, along the lines of an identification without reserve. In the early 1980s, Douglas was holding in his head about 150 cases at a time, without active backup and without, as yet, computer backup. The serial killer simulates others and fades into his environment. As the Son of Sam profile expressed it, "He's the kind of guy . . . who probably goes to work everyday. Maybe he does something with statistics. An accountant or a clerk. He just kind of melts into the city scene."[27] The mindhunter works by simulation, too. He works – like Poe's prototype detective, Dupin (one of the crime-fiction sources Douglas cites) – by identifying himself with the killer. He copies the copy, xeroxes Mr. Xerox: "I'm one of them . . . put yourself inside these guys shoes – or in their minds."

The mindhunter identifies with a criminal whose own identity has yielded to an identification with accounts of his kind of person, accounts that, in circular fashion, include the profiler's own. Bodies, identities, and information are drawn into an absolute and violent proximity. In 1983, Douglas relates, the mindhunter's mind exploded from the information overload: "The right side of [the] brain had ruptured . . . in layman's terms, his brain has been fried to a crisp."[28] This is, of course, John Douglas as Johnny Mnemonic. And this begins to intimate how serial killing inhabits the information society, where nothing could be less certain than the line between bodies of information and other kinds of bodies.

The Letter Bomb

There is a standard sense of serial killing as "senseless," as "murder with no apparent motive." And this happens even when the motives are laid out right on the surface. Consider, for example, the serial bomber called UNABOM's 35,000-word manifesto, where the links between word counts and body counts, hacking information and bodies, are clear enough:

> Then in June, the Unabomer sent his 35,000 word diatribe to the Times and the Post. . . . If papers did not print the tract, he warned, he would kill again. . . . That same month he mailed a fatal package bomb to a California timber lobbyist whose body parts had to be collected in 11 separate bags.[29]

Serial killing is "murder by numbers." Information processing and serial killing, computer profiles and torn bodies, feed on each other in these cases:

> Sixteen bombings in 17 years; 23 wounded and maimed, three people dead. . . . Federal agents spent more than $50 million as well as a million work hours . . . agents had developed a vast computer system with 12 million bytes of information.[30]

Serial killing is the form of public violence proper to a machine culture: the era of the Second Industrial Revolution that is also popularly called "the information society" or "digital culture" and might be called the Discourse Network of 2000. In the Network, the unremitting flood of numbers, codes, and letters is popularly seen as replacing real bodies and real persons, threatening to make both obsolete. What it really makes obsolete is the difference between bodies and information. As Norbert Wiener, the founder of cybernetics, put it some time ago, both persons and machines are "communicative organisms." The erosion of the difference between "living beings and inanimate matter" in digital culture means that, as technocrat Wiener blandly put it, "the distinction between material transportation [bodies] and message transportation [information] is not in any theoretical sense permanent or unbridgeable."[31]

The Unabomber sends back this message in the form of the letter bomb. The Unabom Manifesto is nothing but pop-psychology and pop-sociology about the information society. It is a series of clichés, dead words, about being "swamped by the vast volume of material put out by the media": about being assaulted, bombarded, soul-murdered, by bits of information.[32] The psychotic, we know, is one who takes things literally, to the letter. The psycho-killer, the letter bomber, brings numbers and codes and words back to bodies – with a vengeance.

The slogan of the information society is minds without bodies: "More brains – less sweat." Ted Kaczynski – the brilliant mathematician and prolific letter writer – was a boy with a "thin body" who "hung out with the brains." It is as if he had already left his body behind. But then, we are told, "all the brains fooled around with homemade explosives."[33]

The letter bomber is a writer who dreams of words with a direct physical impact. He dreams of words as weapons aimed at bodies: verboballistics. "In order to get our message before the public, *with some chance of making a lasting impression*, we've had to kill people."[34] Bodies and writing come together in the letter bomb and its victims: "All of my fingers were missing two sections . . . My Air Force Academy ring shot six feet through the air and bounced off a wall. The impact was so strong, you could read the word ACADEMY in the plaster."[35] The "signature" letter bomb – the point of impact of bodies, technologies, and words – is the letter bomber's way of reconnecting brains to bodies. Going postal is his way of reconnecting what for him the information society disconnects: private desire and public life. "An intensely private man" who "lunges for publicity": sending his signature bombs through the postal system is his way of writing on the wall.[36]

The Mass in Person

The British serial killer, Dennis Nilsen, arrested in 1983 for the murder of a number of young men, described himself as a "professionally perfect person";[37] he was diagnosed (in a court psychiatrist's forensic psychologese) as suffering from "False Self Syndrome."[38] After an earlier career in the military and as a policeman, he entered the civil service, where he interviewed hundreds of people looking for work (*K* 18). He imagined his career as the killer of a series of anonymous men in the same workaday terms: "If I had been arrested at sixty-five years of age there might have been thousands of bodies behind me" (*K* 19). Imagining arrest for murder at the age of retirement from civil service is to imagine the stranger-intimacies of his public life and the stranger-killings of his private life as two versions of the same thing.

In public service, Nilsen "frankly revelled in the equality that [his] uniform provided" (*K* 57). The uniform served as a sort of social exoskeleton: a social ego, an external "muscle armor that is merely borrowed . . . and fused onto the individual," maintaining his boundaries and identity from without.[39] It formed part of what Nilsen

called his "union principles." Nilsen was an ardent union activist, but his union principles, and his devotion to what he called "the machinery of democracy," went deeper.
He dreamed of a "total natural unity": "My best friends were the sea, sky, rivers,
trees . . . I was at one with the natural environment" (*K* 51, 285). These numberless
"friends" – sea, sky, rivers, trees – are traditional *crowd-symbols*.[40] The dream of a direct
filiation with Nature is the dream of a direct *fusion* with an indistinct mass of others:
the complete fusion with the mass at the expense of the individual that forms the inner
experience of what I will be calling *the mass in person*. The machinery of democracy, for
the mass in person, perfects itself in the dead levelling by which all individual distinctions vanish: "dead people," as the *Badlands* spree killer Charles Starkweather put it,
"are all on the same level."

Nilsen dismembered bodies while blasting Aaron Copland's *Fanfare for the Common
Man* on his personal stereo. (Conversely, Laurie Anderson's prosthetic ballad *O Superman* was another favorite [*K* 9].) As he expressed it: "I want crowds around me to listen
to my solitude" (*K* 246) The killer described the bonfire he made of the bodies he had
taken apart as a return to a total natural unity: "A mixing of flesh in a common flame and
a single unity of ashes . . . a uniform and anonymous corporation cemetery" (*K* 149). He
described his ultimate place in the mass public sphere as a sort of corporate and collective
gathering point: or, more exactly, his final public service was as a mass spectacle of
pathology and abjection. He was a black hole of violation and pollution about which the
contemporary national body gathers, spectates, and discharges itself: in his words, he was
"a national receptacle into which all the nation will urinate" (*K* 175).

Lifelikeness

The public/private divide and its transgressions are crucial, I have begun to suggest,
in cases of serial killing and in instances of sexual violence more generally. Nilsen called
himself "a tragically private person not given to public tears" (*K* 206). For him, among
others, stranger intimacy – what he described as "entertaining strangers" and "killing
for company" – was inseparable from stranger-killing (*K* 184, 85). It provided the
missing point of contact between private desire and public life: "No sex, just a feeling
of oneness" (*K* 124).

Cruising the London scene, Nilsen experienced an anonymous same-sexuality in
terms of "the idea of sex in public" (*K* 124, 87). This feeling of oneness in public sex
made for an experience of homosexuality (same-sexuality) as a radical experience of self-
sameness: same-sexuality and self-sameness referred back to each other at every point.
This violent translation of sexual difference into self difference, sexual sameness into self
sameness, will be taken up in detail in the pages that follow. It is one of the central components in the inner logic of serial killing. On this logic, the killer's disorders of identity
yield to a sheer identification with others. Hence, for Nilsen, "it starts in narcissism and
ends in confusion" (*K* 69). Stranger killing takes the form of a suicide by proxy: "I was
killing myself only but it was always the bystander who died" (*K* 252).[41]

The complete failure of distinction between self and others is yet more complicated.
In this case, among many others, the yielding of identity to identification proceeds by

way of an utter absorption in *technologies of reflection, reduplication, and simulation*. For Nilsen, it involved, above all, a fixation on mirror images of his own made-up body and on the mirroring and photographing and filming of the made-up, taken apart, and arti-factualized bodies of his victims. Nilsen, self-described as a "central camera," was addicted to the lifeless model body, his own and others: to the body made up as corpse. He was addicted to images of what he called the unreflectiveness and "ineffectiveness of a non-personality." The unreflectiveness of a non-personality depended in turn on technologies of modeling and reflection. Mirror-images, "a visually perfect state," constituted, for him, "an unresisting model of life": that is, the visually perfect state of the corpse, the *tableau vivant* of the *nature morte*, of death mimicking life, such that life takes a step backward. (*K* 75, 263). For the serial killer, *lifelikeness* – what I will call the *primary mediation* of the modern body and modern subject, in its technical simulation and reproducibility – substitutes for the imperfection and threat of living life itself. Chameleon-like, the serial killer copies and simulates others; the monochrome man, he melts into place; the minus man, predead, he plays dead and takes life.

Wound Culture

Serial Killers is about forms of public violence in our culture: what these acts and representations of violence look like, why they have emerged as a cultural flashpoint, and how the very idea of "the public" has become inseparable from spectacles of bodily and mass violence. The spectacular public representation of violated bodies, across a burgeoning range of official, academic, and media accounts, in fiction and in film, has come to function as a way of imagining and situating our notions of public, social, and collective identity. Hence these "atrocity exhibitions" indicate something more than a taste for senseless violence. They have come to function as a way of imagining the relations of private bodies and private persons to public spaces. These exhibitions make up the contemporary pathological public sphere, our wound culture.

Mass murder in America has had two popular sites: the fast-food system (The McDonald's Massacre) and the postal system (Going Postal). On these sites systems, numbers, and bodies collide. Personal communications, in the postal system, are the property of the impersonal clerks of the system. David Berkowitz, the mailman/serial killer called the Son of Sam, had a lifetime appointment in that system. He traced his killings to a letter to his father that "stated a devine [sic] mission that I felt was intended for me." A sort of dimestore Schreber (Freud's prototype paranoiac, "soul-murdered" by divine messages), Berkowitz continued to be letter-bombed by demons. They set up in him what one character in the recent film about trauma, machine violence, and virtual reality, *Strange Days*, calls a "switchboard of the soul."

In prison, Berkowitz longed for "more personal freedoms such as keeping a pen in my cell, being able to go out, under guard and mail letters, go to the post office, and have a hotline telephone in my cell that leads directly to Chief of Detectives."[42] In the Belgian serial killer film *Man Bites Dog* (1992), in which the mass media and mass murder foment each other, the psycho-killer Benoit blithely remarks: "I usually start the month with a postman."

The fast-food world, as Lew McCreary describes it in *The Minus Man* – a novel in which the serial killer is a postal worker, too – is a place of stranger-intimacy: "These are the kinds of places where people don't look at each other much, where many come in alone and eat alone. . . . No one could describe anyone they ever saw in such a place who was not crazy and babbling."[43] Or, as Denis Johnson, one of the great communicators of America's contemporary trauma culture, describes it in his novel *Angels*: "the fast-food universe" is a "tiny world half machinery and half meat."[44]

This world of half meat and half machinery is one of the lethal places that make up our wound culture, in which death is theater for the living. The crowd gathered around the fallen body, the wrecked machine, and the wound has become a commonplace in our culture: a version of collective experience that centers the pathological public sphere. The current a-la-modality of trauma – the cliché du jour of the therapeutic society of the nineties – makes this clear enough. So too does the most recent (1996) national election. The election was a contest about trauma and wounds: the shattered and already posthumous war veteran – dead man talking – and the make-love-not-warrior whose tag-line is "I feel your pain."

In the early days of television there was a program called *Queen for a Day*. The premise was this: three unfortunate, over-embodied and under-classed women engaged in a competition in abjection by relating the horror stories of their lives. An audience applause meter determined the outcome of the competition. Coronation and prize – generally laborsaving household appliances, as I remember it – followed. This public spectacle of private exposure has been generalized, of course, as the program of talk radio and confession TV, where the only prize is appearing in the stocks, in the virtual town meeting gathered to witness wounds.

The most popular current television series, *ER*, is pure wound culture: the world, half-meat and half-machinery, in a perpetual state of emergency. *ER* is an endless series of torn and opened bodies and an endless series of emotionally torn and exposed bio-technicians. There are the routine hook-ups of bodies and appliances; trauma and techno-speak; cardiac arrest and broken hearts. These are the spectacles of persons, bodies, and technologies that make up a wound culture and the scenes that make up the pathological public sphere: the scenes, and the culture, in which serial killing finds its place.

Notes

1. The illustrations which formed part of the original version of this chapter have been omitted.
2. Todd S. Purdum, "Registry Laws Tar Sex-Crime Convicts With Broad Brush," *New York Times*, July, 1, 1997, pp. Al, A19.
3. I am here drawing on Michael Taussig, *The Nervous System* (New York: Routledge, 1992).
4. For these numbers, see ibid., p. A19.
5. See Michel Foucault, "The Dangerous Individual," *Michel Foucault: Politics, Philosophy, Culture: Interviews and Other Writings 1977–1984*, trans. Alan Sheridan, et al., ed. Lawrence

D. Kritzman (New York: Routledge, 1988). I will be returning to the notion of the dangerous individual and its implications in the following chapter.

6. The shift from act to species is central to the orbitting of a wide range of contemporary thinking around the problem of *identity*. On this shift and some of its implications, see, for example: Michel Foucault, *The History of Sexuality*, vol. 1 (New York: Pantheon, 1978); Judith Butler, *Gender Trouble: Feminism and the Subversion of Identity* (New York: Routledge, 1990); Wendy Brown, *States of Injury: Power and Freedom in Late Modernity* (Princeton, N.J.: Princeton University Press, 1995); Jonathan Ned Katz, *The Invention of Heterosexuality* (New York: Dutton, 1995).

7. Lucas quoted in Michael Newton, *Serial Slaughter: What's Behind America's Murder Epidemic* (Port Townshend, WA: Loompanics Unlimited, 1992), p. 7.

8. On the modelling of child abuse and the a priori status of trauma more generally, see Ian Hacking, *Rewriting the Soul: Multiple Personality and the Sciences of Memory* (Princeton, N.J.: Princeton University Press, 1995).

9. Bundy quoted in Stephen G. Michaud and Hugh Aynesworth, *Ted Bundy: Conversations with a Killer* (New York: Signet, 1989), p. 7, 10.

10. Ibid., 104.

11. Ibid., pp. 10–11; Ann Rule, *The Stranger Beside Me* (New York: Signet, 1989), p. 495.

12. Newton, *Serial Slaughter*, p. 23.

13. Joel Norris, *Serial Killers* (New York: Anchor Books, 1988), p. 19.

14. Newton, *Serial Slaugher*, p. 23; Norris, *Serial Killers*, pp. 79, 84.

15. Rule, Testimony before the US Senate, July 12, 1983; US Senate Judiciary Committee. *Serial Murders· Hearing on Patterns of Murders Committed by One Person, in Large Numbers with No Apparent Rhyme, Reason, or Motivation.* (Washington, D.C.: US Government Printing Office, 1984).

16. Norris, *Serial Killers*, pp. 40–41.

17. Quoted in Eugene H. Methvin, "The Face of Evil," *National Review*, Jan. 23, 1995, 34.

18. This is the definition adopted, for instance, in Philip Jenkins, *Using Murder: The Social Construction of Serial Homicide* (New York: Aldine de Gruyter, 1994), p. 23.

19. See Helen Morrison, *Serial Killers and Murderers* (Lincolnwood, IL: Publications International, 1991), pp. 7–9, and Methvin, "The Face of Evil," p. 42.

20. Dennis Cooper, *Frisk* (New York: Grove, 1991), p. 53; Lew McCreary, *The Minus Man* (New York: Penguin, 1991), p. 221. On Cooper's *Frisk*, see chapter 6; on McCreary's *The Minus Man*, the concluding part of this study, "Wound Culture."

21. Rule, *The Stranger Beside Me*.

22. Bundy, quoted in Rule, p. 221.

23. Quoted in Ron Rosenbaum, "The FBI's Agent Provocateur," *Vanity Fair* (Apr. 1993), p. 124.

24. Jenkins, *Using Murder*, p. 224.

25. Robert K. Ressler (and Tom Shachtman), *Whoever Fights Monsters* (New York: St. Martin's, 1992), pp. 29–30.

26. John Douglas (and Mark Olshaker), *Mindhunter: Inside the FBI's Elite Serial Crime Unit* (New York: Scribner, 1995), pp. 95, 32.

27. NYPD Commissioner Tim Dowd, quoted in Elliot Leyton, *Hunting Humans: Inside the Minds of Mass Murderers* (New York: Pocket, 1988), p. 174.

28. Douglas, *Mindhunter*, pp. 17, 20.

29. "Probing the Mind of a Killer," *Newsweek*, Apr. 15, 1996: 36–8.

30. "Chasing the Unabomer," *Newsweek* 10 July 1995, 40–3; "Probing the Mind of a Killer," *Newsweek* 15 April 1996, 36, 37; *New York Times* 2 Aug. 1995, pp. A1, A16; *Washington Post* 2 Aug. 1995, pp. A1, A16, A17.

31. Norbert Wiener, *The Human Use of Human Beings: Cybernetics and Society* (Garden City, NJ: Doubleday, 1954), pp. 98, 136.

32. Unabom Manifesto, excerpted in *The New York Times* 2 Aug. 1995, p. A16.

33. "Probing the Mind of a Killer," *Newsweek*, 15 Apr. 1996, p. 34.

34. Unabom Manifesto, excerpted in *The New York Times*, 2 Aug. 1995, p. A16 (my emphasis).

35. John Hauser, "What the Unabomer Did to Me," *Newsweek*, 15 Apr. 1996, p. 40.

36. "Probing the Mind of a Killer," *Newsweek*, 15 Apr. 1996, p. 30.

37. Nilsen, quoted in John Lisners, *House of Horrors* (London: Corgi, 1983), pp. 178, 180.

38. Brian Masters, *Killing for Company: The Story of a Man Addicted to Murder* (New York: Random House, 1993), p. 214; the following quotations are drawn from the Nilsen Papers, (notes and prison journals written by Nilsen in 1983), as excerpted by Masters; hereafter abbreviated *K*.

39. Klaus Theweleit, *Male Bodies: Psychoanalyzing the White Terror*, vol. 2 of *Male Fantasies*, trans. Erica Carter and Chris Turner (Minneapolis: University of Minnesota Press, 1989), pp. 222–3.

40. See Elias Canetti, *Crowds and Power*, trans. Carol Stewart (New York: Noonday Press, 1984), pp. 75–92.

41. Pet-killing is one leg of the "triad" of indicators in the genesis of the serial killer, with bed-wetting and firestarting forming the other two. Nilsen, however, was a devoted pet-keeper. He stated about his pet dog that "her great redeeming feature was that she was not formed in my image," (*K* 163). It is as if the union principles that made for a fusion of all persons in his own image required something to mark the difference between self and other and between persons and nonpersons. The dog's name – Bleep – seems itself a figure for censorship: that is, for the desired, but also insupportable, noncommunication between private desire and public expression.

42. The prison diary of David Berkowitz (1981), as quoted by Leyton, *Hunting Humans*, p. 166.

43. McCreary, *The Minus Man*, pp. 156–7.

44. Denis Johnson, *Angels* (New York: Vintage, 1989), p. 62. Johnson's most recent novel, *Already Dead: A California Gothic* (New York: Harper Collins, 1997), brilliantly inhabits the techno-gothic landscapes, the psychotopographies, of this traumatized, predead, or "already dead" culture.

XIII

Transnationality, Globalization, Post-Coloniality

The Riot of Englishness: Migrancy, Nomadism, and the Redemption of the Nation

Ian Baucom*

How does newness enter the world? Of what fusions, translations, conjoinings is it made?

Salman Rushdie, The Satanic Verses

In its afterlife – which could not be called that if it were not a transformation and a renewal of something living – the original undergoes a change.

Walter Benjamin, Illuminations

The View from the Milk Tin

In the days of his childhood in Trinidad, V. S. Naipaul informs the reader of *The Enigma of Arrival*, the labels on the cans of condensed milk in his kitchen were illustrated with an image of beautiful black-and-white English cows chewing the green grasses of an English down. In the closing pages of the text, Naipaul indicates that wandering the grounds of the country house where he has come to live, he discovers the "original" of that gentle, pastoral image. "Always on a sunny day on this walk, and especially if at the top of the slope some of the cattle stood against the sky, there was a corner of my fantasy in which I felt that some minute, remote yearning – as remote as a flitting, all but forgotten cinema memory from early childhood – had been satisfied, and I was in the original of that condensed-milk label drawing" (331). Settled into the splendid grasses of his pastoral retreat, Naipaul finds that he can turn away from the English present, from the confusions of England's postcoloniality, and, above all, from England's cities. In those cities, he knows that he can discover countless men and women similar to himself, ex-colonial migrants who have come to England to make a new home. He refuses the city because he believes that though so many of its inhabitants share an experience of displacement very much like his own, many do not share his vision of England. Crucially, he discerns that many of his fellow immigrants and

*Pp. 190–218 and 242–3 (notes) from I. Baucom, *Out of Place: Englishness, Empire, and the Locations of Identity*. (Princeton, NJ: Princeton University Press). © 1999 by Princeton University Press. Reprinted with permission from Princeton University Press.

their children refuse to join him in mourning England's death and instead insist on marking the nation's urban expanses as places in which the narratives of empire and Englishness continue to be written. Naipaul does not fail to know that England survives the formal endings of empire. He simply refuses to countenance his knowledge of the nation's continuing transformation. Rejecting an England that dares to outlive imperialism, he codes his refusal as a denial of the metropolis and invents the English country side as the landscape of the past, and the past as the landscape of rest. While Naipaul's attitude is comprehensible, it demands that he blind himself. His rigorous refusals of the city prevent him from recognizing that while England's cities are certainly places in which the nation's cultural identity continues to be refashioned, this does not mean that the inhabitants of the metropolis have betrayed England. As it is the object of this chapter to indicate, the labors of cultural translation by which the nation's urban migrants, among others, have written the text of England's newness can also be read as labors devoted to England's redemption. But in order to understand how the narratives of postcolonial migrancy can generate a reading of England's contemporaneity that identifies the migrant not as England's vandal but as its redeemer, we must turn from the scene of Naipaul's self-imposed exile to those city streets he has declined to gaze upon and to a moment in which Naipaul would assuredly discover England's immigrants, and their children, announcing themselves as the enemies of Englishness.

Scenes of Violence

On the 12th of April, 1981, the Sunday edition of the London *Times* greeted its morning readers with front-page photographs of a bleeding police inspector and a smoke-filled London street littered with bricks and the glass of shattered windows. Above and below these photographs ran banner headlines: "The Bloody Battle of Brixton . . . 114 Police Hurt; Area Sealed Off."[1] By the time London's newspaper readers had unfolded their papers, gazed upon these images, and absorbed the grim statistics of this outbreak of urban violence, the news that *The Times* trumpeted was, however, no longer new. From the evening of Friday, April 10, onward, British television had carried live broadcasts of the riotous spectacle *The Times* was belatedly reporting. Into countless English homes these broadcasts poured the "news" that hundreds, if not thousands, of "youths" had taken to the streets in one of the city's "immigrant" neighborhoods and were "rioting." The publication of volumes of writing would follow these television broadcasts, as diverse scholars, activists, and politicians tried to decide if this was, in fact, what had happened, and labored to determine what it all meant. Unwilling to be left out of this process in which the riot, first reproduced as video, was now produced once again as text, Parliament established a committee to investigate the "disorders." And it is with the report of that committee that I wish to begin my reading of the location of riot in a contemporary discourse of English identity.

In the first sentence of the report that he submitted to Parliament, Lord Scarman, chair of the committee charged with the task of investigating the disorders, indicated that the riot itself was perhaps less significant than the fact that the riot had "happened" on television. "During the weekend of 10–12 April (Friday, Saturday and Sunday)," Lord Scarman noted, "the British people watched with horror and incredulity an instant audio-visual presentation on their television sets of scenes of violence and disorder in their capital city, the like of which had not previously been seen in this century in Britain."[2] Scarman's language is arresting. For it is unclear from his phrasing whether he wishes to suggest that the violence of the riot was unprecedented, or is convinced that this April weekend was epochal because it had gathered the nation in an inspection of televised violence. Whatever he was trying to say, it is clear that in Lord Scarman's mind the horror and incredulity of the "British people" extended not only to what was happening in Brixton but to what was literally taking place in their own homes, on the glass surfaces of their television screens.

If Lord Scarman's nervous obsession with the appearance of the riot on television allegorizes the terror of shattered windows invoked by the photographs on the front page of the *Sunday Times*, and, in thus technologizing the window dividing the watchers from the watched, registers the profound fragility of that glass boundary separating the "British people" from the riotous mob on the street, then his report admits another tear. Turning from the immediate nature of the events in Brixton, Scarman pauses to contemplate a future in which "disorder will become a disease endemic in our society" (2). This identification of riot as a species of contagion invokes a time-honored understanding of the crowd as a social form that reproduces itself through an act of contaminated touching.[3] As his report unfolds, it becomes apparent that Scarman's initial nervousness about the televising of the riot connects not only to the possibility that the television may be a window through which the architectures of Englishness are opened to the crowd's performative disorders, but also to his suspicion that the television screen locates the point of the "British people"'s contact with the contaminations of the rioters. Disorder, he fears, will become endemic precisely because television, rather than acting as a glassy prophylactic against riot, will act as the technological organ of the riot's communication. His fear is not only that certain viewers, watching the violence, will leave their homes to join the rioting. Scarman fears a comprehensive infection of the general populace in which future viewers, impelled by whatever reasons, will abandon their homes, take to the streets, and shatter the image with which he began: the "British people" at home, distinctly separate from the plague in the street. Though he never indicates what might prompt this general, self-cultivated infection, Scarman cannot avoid betraying the suspicion that the "British people" might choose to reproduce themselves as the crowd they have seen because riot carries not only a threat of violence but a promise of pleasure.

But what sort of pleasure does rioting elicit?

Scarman's report indicates that if rioting does produce pleasure, its more dangerous delights are those of observation, not participation; that what is at stake in a reading of the televisual reproductions of rioting are not the immediate gratifications of crowd disturbance but the *affective* delights which attach to the visual consumption of the riotous event. In a recent essay, Brian Massumi (the American translator of Deleuze and Guattari's *A Thousand Plateaus*) has suggested that affect is something like what Paul Fry calls the "ostensive" moment.[4] Affect, he argues, defines a certain vacation from, and of, significance; as an experience of "intensity" it occupies a bewilderingly "happy" moment in which we become aware of the suspension of the structuring economies of meaning:

> Intensity is qualifiable as an emotional state, and that state is static – temporal and narrative noise. It is a state of suspense, potentially of disruption. . . . It is not exactly passivity, because it is filled with motion, vibratory motion, resonation. . . . Much could be gained by integrating the dimension of intensity into cultural theory. *The stakes are the new*. For structure is the place where nothing ever happens, that explanatory heaven in which all eventual permutations are prefigured in a self-consistent set of invariant generative rules. Nothing is prefigured in the event. It is the collapse of structured distinction into intensity, or rules into paradox. . . . *Could it be that it is through the expectant suspension of that suspense that the new emerges?*[5]

1 will not dwell on the ease with which Massumi's description of the affective – as a space of vibratory motion, noise, disruption, and dis-ordering – can be translated into a journalistic description of riot. Instead, I want to address the construction of newness that Massumi derives from this reading of affect, a construction of the new which is implicit in Lord Scarman's description of the Brixton disturbances. For these under-standings of affect and rioting ignore an alternative account of how newness enters the world, an account that permits us to read riot not as the space of the asignificant but as the site of a certain uncertainty, as the expression not merely of a nomadic but of a migrant politics, as the space not only of disruption but also, potentially, of redemption.

In Massumi's account, newness names not only a break from the prison house of meaning but a flight from that economy of expectation which houses events within structures. Because the new is not merely the emergence of the unexpected, but that which we cannot expect to reemerge, it gestures neither to the future nor to the past. A profoundly untimely form of rupture, it neither differs nor defers; it neither translates nor renders itself translatable. A pure performance, a pure uncertainty, a purely are-ferential newness, affect, Massumi insists, "is the system of the inexplicable: emergence, into and against (re)generation . . . unqualified. As such, it is not ownable or recogniz-able, and is thus resistant to critique" (87–8). And it is precisely because of this autono-mous and haughty indifference that Massumi associates affect and newness with pleasure. A perfect amphetamine, the affect-event offers to trip its consumer into the narcotic spaces of a radically deterritorialized newness, to liberate us into the intensity of meaninglessness, to send us on a vacation to the isle of the lotus-eaters. As an affec-tive catalyst of the new, rioting, in such a reading, manifests itself as the nomadic par excellence, as a perfect performance of the deterritorializing war machine.

As a special 1981 issue of the journal *Race and Class* testifies, it would be quite pos-sible to read the Brixton uprisings in such terms. In the concluding essay of the issue, which was published in response to the April events, Paul Gilroy draws attention to those British laws of suspicion – commonly referred to as Sus laws – to which the uprising was in many ways a response. Operating under these laws – which permitted the police to arrest individuals not only for crimes that had been committed but for crimes that the police believed the "suspect" was about to commit, and which further allowed the police to identify large areas of a city as "criminal" and hence to arrest any person found within these contaminated spaces – the Brixton police launched a street campaign on the 7th of April, 1981. By the end of the week, the police had stopped and questioned over a thousand people and had arrested over one hundred. On the evening of Friday, April 10, a group of approximately one hundred black youths surrounded a car in which the police were holding a young man, and released him. The officers in the car radioed for help, sixty policemen, with dogs and riot gear arrived, and a fight ensued. For the next three days Brixton was engulfed in riot. In its April 12 edition, the *Sunday Telegraph* published a comment by a young black man that offered to decode the riot's economy of violence: "It's not against the white community," the man said, "It's against the police. They have treated us like dirt."[6] A reader content with Massumi's Deleuzian theory need read no further. One could conclude with an interpretation of the riot as an event in a nomadic politics that articulates itself as a waging of war upon the state and the state's policing of movement, and with a reading of the rioter as nomad, as one who exists to deterritorialize, to manifest that deliriously vacant new space of which Massumi dreams.

And undoubtedly this is, in some respects, what the uprising signified – or, in Massumi's terms, deliriously failed to signify. But it is worth considering the ways in which these events open themselves to an additional understanding of newness, and, in so doing, permit us to read the moment of urban rioting not as a "black hole" in the time of the imperial afterward, but as a moment in which the affect-event – understood now as a principle of allusive repetition, as a *certain* uncertainty – takes place within a disciplinary structure whose orders and arrangements of meaning the riot re-collects and re-creates (in much the same fashion as the flowing game of cricket visible to C.L.R. James re-creates the disciplinary structures of Englishness). To read it thus is by no means to ignore the comments of the man cited in the *Sunday Telegraph*, but to offer an alternative account of what his words might mean: to insist, first of all, that his words do, in fact, have some meaning, that a battle against the police is a "significant" event, and, second, that a fight *against* something is also, in this context, a fight *for* something. It is to argue that the urban riot manages not merely to vandalize but to reorganize England's spaces of belonging, to introduce newness to the world not simply as a schizophrenic epiphany but, as Rushdie puts it in *The Satanic Verses*, as a process of "fusions, translations, conjoinings" (8). To supplement a nomadological hermeneutic of rioting with such a reading is to reveal that the riot zone is not simply an affect-event but – like the country house, the cricket field, and the Victoria Terminus – one of England's contested spaces of memory, an English *lieu de memoire* refashioned, in this case, by the cultural politics of postcolonial migrancy.

We can begin this alternative reading by noting that the Sus laws were not the only English laws which had a bearing upon the Brixton uprising. During the week of the Brixton riots, Parliament was debating Margaret Thatcher's British Nationality Act, a piece of legislation that, in the succinct words of the *Sunday Times*, "for the first time seeks to define British Citizenship and those who 'belong to Britain' . . . [and] to abolish the historic right of common British citizenship enjoyed by the colonial peoples."[7] As discussed in the introduction to this book, the Nationality Act defined the nation's community of belonging according to the principle of "partiality." To be British, it mandated, one had to trace a line of descent to an ancestor born on the island. In effect, the law thus drew the lines of the nation rather snugly around the boundaries of race and erased the present as a space available for new engenderings of national identity. If the nation must express a relation to its past, the act suggested, then that past is the past of biology, not of history.

The Nationality Act provoked widespread dissent. Labour MPs attacked it relentlessly; Indira Ghandi, whom the prime minister was visiting during the week of the riot, denounced it; and multitudes of Britain's inhabitants protested it in the press, through their elected representatives, and on the street. The Brixton riots, which were in many ways a riot against the police, must also be read in the context of this collective outrage. But in that moment in which riotous protest is directed against a police force whose government has proposed to pass a law that threatens to contract the boundaries of the community of national belonging, the cultural politics of riot shifts from the extranational domain of nomadism to the intranational domain of migrancy. Or, to state the argument rather differently, if riot can be represented as a vehicle of a nomadic politics whose object is to locate the individual outside of the nation-state's space of operation, then it can also be read as the expression of a migrant politics whose object is to *re*position the individual within a national community of belonging. And, in assembling as a crowd to articulate their grievances as *citizens*, the Brixton rioters were acting not only in the name of the nation but in the most English of ways.

In one of his more important essays, E. P. Thompson, drawing on the work of his fellow historian George Rude, has insisted that historians read the English crowd not according to tropes of randomness, madness, treason, or disarray, but within the metaphors of an ordering disorderliness. The English crowd, Thompson suggests, acts to protect a customary body of rights that its members believe to be threatened, customary rights that, crucially, typically enshrine local ways of being, local traditions of organizing the social, the political, and the economic.[8] The particular series of customary rights that the riotous crowd perceives to be threatened and acts to defend is, in some respects, less significant than the crowd's defense of the principle of the local *and* the relation which the crowd establishes between its present time and the time of the nation's past. The English crowd, Thompson argues, appeals to the past, or invents the past, in order to address or erase the depredations of the present, and it does so not that it might vandalize the nation, but in the name of restoring the nation to itself, in the name of re-creating England as a diverse assortment of local communities, local knowledges, and local polities.

And this, according to Paul Gilroy, is precisely the labor of those rioting crowds which, in the summers of 1981 and 1985, took to the streets of Brixton and Handsworth. Stressing that the behavior of these urban crowds was not, as media reports suggested, "anomic [or] irritational" but entirely "purposive" (*"There Ain't No Black in the Union Jack"*, 239), Gilroy argues that the purpose of these rioters was to defend the right of a local community to define its own "particular set of values and norms in everyday life" (234). The riots, in his reading, were a fight *against* the police and *for* a sense of "community" that assumed as its first principle "the strong association of identity and territory" (243). Local knowledges, values, and norms are, on this account, precisely knowledges that derive from the locale; the defense of the one was, Gilroy indicates, the defense of the other. And it was for this reason that in these neighborhoods the flow of riotous protest became a very *spatial* competition, a "competition between the police and the mob for control of the riot-torn area," a competition in which, for Gilroy, the major question to be resolved was whether "local people might gain control over their own neighborhood" (241).

That Gilroy, like most commentators, recollects the Brixton and Handsworth riots precisely as Brixton and Handsworth events, rather than London or Manchester happenings, does not mean that they were not also English events. Rather they can be understood as recent interventions in a very long struggle to define what England is: a unitary, homogeneous, nation ("one, one, one"), or a variegated array of local communities, local dialects, local ways of playing the game ("always two, or three, or fifteen"). Gilroy is clearly no great fan of E. P. Thompson, largely because in some of his political writings, Thompson seems willing to assume the givenness of the category of the nation and to forget, as Gilroy is prompt to remind him, that many Britons "recognize and define themselves primarily in terms of *regional* or *local* tradition" (*"There Ain't No Black in the Union Jack"*, 55, emphasis original), but there is a profound similarity between Gilroy's account of the communitarian politics of the rioters and Thompson's reading of the "moral economy" of the "English" crowd. Gilroy's rioters are not, therefore, the designated "inheritors" of the ideological convictions of Thompson's eighteenth- and nineteenth-century crowds (discursive genealogies rarely produce such simple lines of descent). But in defending the right of the nation's subjects to define themselves as citizens whose primary loyalty is nevertheless to a "regional or local tradition," they re-create one of the country's traditional ways of being English.

This historical irony provides the keynote of Salman Rushdie's response to the Nationality Act in an essay entitled "The New Empire within Britain." Imagining himself to be addressing a primarily white audience, Rushdie informs his readers that, whether they realize it or not, in assaulting the nation's communities of immigrants, the bill has simultaneously assaulted the nation's past.

> This already notorious piece of legislation, expressly designed to deprive black and Asian Britons of their citizenship rights, went through in spite of some, mainly non-white, protests. And because it didn't really affect the position of the whites, you probably didn't realize that one of your most ancient rights, a right you had possessed for nine hundred years, was being stolen from you. This was the right to citizenship by virtue of birth, the *ius soli*, or right of the soil. For nine centuries any child born on British soil was British. Automatically. By right. Not by permission of the state. The nationality act abolished the *ius soli*. From now on citizenship is the gift of government. You were blind, because you believed the Act was aimed at the blacks; and so you sat back and did nothing as Mrs Thatcher stole the birthright of every one of us, black and white, and of our children and grandchildren for ever.[9]

Rushdie is clearly outraged. He is almost as obviously unoriginal in the phrasing of his argument. But if his arguments are a trifle familiar, they are productively so. For Rushdie is here mimicking the outraged voices of England's eighteenth- and early-nineteenth-century crowds, crowds whom, as George Rude argues, most commonly conceived of themselves as defenders of the rights of the "freeborn" Englishman. Their discourse, like Rushdie's here, was the discourse of the *ius soli*; their outrage the outrage of those to whom the rights of the soil had been denied. This echo is not, however, the only chord of repetition that Rushdie strikes. He returns also to that moment in the English past to which generations of English crowds were most willing to return, to an imaginary and ideal past associated with a pre-Norman England. The rights of the soil, Rushdie asserts, are nine centuries old. They are the rights, that is, of an England that predates the invasion of 1066, an England toward which the conservatively utopic crowd was incessantly willing to turn a mournful and nostalgic eye. "One of the most remarkably persistent beliefs of all," Rude notes, "was that perfect 'liberties' had existed under the Saxon Kings and that these had been filched, together with their lands, by the invading Norman knights."[10] Rude traces the persistence of this belief to the Chartist constructions of an English past, to which the radical ideologues of the Charter claimed they were returning the nation. Rushdie's essay marks the strategic survival of that belief into the late twentieth century. More significant, the essay marks the availability of a mythologized English past to a migrant's protest against England's present betrayals of itself.

It is in assuming this role of the defender of the English past that Rushdie, in this essay, is most interesting. By constructing his audience as a body of white Britons, he positions his voice quite carefully. His, apparently, is a voice of protest, a voice of a black and Asian Britain. As the self-announced voice of this community, however, his delight is to surprise his imagined reader by raising his protest both on behalf of his fellow migrants and on behalf of the nation, the national past, and the nation's future. In fastening on the *ius soli*, Rushdie quite carefully repeats one of the basic gestures of English social criticism, the gesture not simply of measuring the present against the past but of calling on the present to submit itself to the past. But he does so in order to reveal that the national past has become the possession not only of the state but of the nation's communities of postcolonial migrants. He does so in order to reveal that England's history is also his, and that the politics of remembrance may as often be oppositional as reactionary.

Homi Bhabha, in a seminal essay on England's postcoloniality, crowd disturbance, and the temporality of the nation, offers some partially consonant insights. In an attempt to understand riot as an element of that "contemporary within culture" with which the custodians of the state are so uncomfortable, Bhabha refers to two memorable images in *Handsworth Songs*, a documentary film shot during the "black uprising" in Handsworth in 1985. "Two memories repeat incessantly to translate the living perplexity of history into the time of migration: the arrival of the ship laden with immigrants from the ex-colonies, just stepping off the boat, always just emerging . . . [the other] image is of the perplexity and power of an emergent peoples, caught in the shot of a dreadlocked rastaman cutting a swathe through a posse of policemen. It is a memory that flashes incessantly through the film."[11] Bhabha's concern in calling our attention to these images is to name the tropes of the performative in the cultural discourse of the nation. The performative is Bhabha's collective name for the contemporary, the emergent, and the time of migration; it is also his word for what Frantz Fanon, in his celebrated essay on national consciousness, called that space of anticolonial struggle, that "zone of occult instability . . . [that] fluctuating movement which the people are just giving shape to" (*The Wretched of the Earth*, 227). This area of fluctuance is the space of cultural self-fashioning out of which, Fanon suggests, the postcolonial nation emerges as an uncertain and perpetual invention. Bhabha glosses this occult performativity as "the prodigious, living principle of the people . . . [the] continual process by which national life is redeemed and signified as a repeating and reproductive process" (297), and then collapses all of this – the performative, the emergent, the time of migration, the redemptive, repetitive, living principle of the people – onto that memorable image of urban riot in which a rastaman is seen "cutting a swathe through a posse of police."

The invocation of this catalog of mutually defined tropes by the image of a dread-locked man battling with the police suggests that we have moved quite a distance from that reading of riot rendered available by Massumi and Deleuze. At the moment in which the rastaman and the police appear in Bhabha's essay, they are linked, Bhabha's argument suggests, not by the rioter's war on the English state, but by his attempts to redeem England from the depredations of its juridical and regulatory institutions. The rioter appears here not as the nation's enemy but as its savior. This move, which is emblematic of the movement that I am attempting to trace from the placement of riot in the nomadic war machine to its location in the cultural politics of migrancy, is enabled by Bhabha's willingness to graft a Benjaminian branch onto Frantz Fanon's discursive tree. Benjamin's Messianic labor of redemption finds articulation, Bhabha suggests, not strictly in an act of remembrance in which the nation is obliged to conform its present to the available memories of the past, but through a difficult Fanonian performance by which the contemporary reveals the nation not as the prisoner of the past but as its liberator. In the image of the redemptive rioter, it is not the past that redeems and disciplines the unruly present, but the riotous present that perpetually gives birth to itself by redeeming the past.

But if we are to follow Bhabha, and to say that the problem of reading the Handsworth or Brixton riots is at least in part the problem of determining what such events remember, then we must ask what past, or pasts, the Brixton riots recollect and performatively redeem. Bhabha, unfortunately, is of limited help here. For, with the makers of the documentary on Handsworth, he can find "no stories in the riots, only the ghosts of other riots" (307). At this moment, as Bhabha identifies uprising as the antirepresentational, as a performative newness that gestures to nothing but itself or manages to invoke itself only as a figure of repetition which never exceeds the specificity of a list of other, earlier, uprisings, his reading of riot approaches Massumi's reading of affect. If there are no stories in the riots, then there are only serial intensities that not only are resistant to critique but offer no commentary on England's postcoloniality.

Bhabha's reading of riot thus places him in only partial agreement with Rude's and E. P. Thompson's readings of the moral economy of the English crowd. The three writers converge on the figure of the crowd as the nation's self-announced redeemer. But redemption is a trope both of salvation and of repetition. And on the issue of what the crowd manages – or purports – to repeat, Bhabha's reading diverges from that of the historians. Rude and Thompson indicate that the desire of previous generations of rioters was not to announce England as mass disorder, or to mark their Englishness by repeating the disorderly behavior of their ancestors, but to disorder the distortions of their contemporaneity to return England to its imaginary self, to mark their English-ness as a threatened England's "true" citizens, guardians, and redeemers. Bhabha's argument suggests that the rioters work to allow England to repeat itself as a riotous affect-event.

The question that arises, then, is whether the contemporary generation of rioters with which Bhabha and Gilroy are most concerned redeem the nation *as* rioters or *through* rioting, whether they announce that England is most itself in its repetitive moments of asignifying disorder, or re-create England through an act of disorderly protest. Do the rioters, in the words that Bhabha borrows from *Handsworth Songs*, recall earlier riots in which there are "no stories"? Or do they, as Gilroy's arguments suggest, remind England of earlier crowds gathered to perform the "story" of their recollective possession of England, and to redeem their local space in the nation's corporate com-munity of belonging? My inclination is clearly toward Gilroy, but it is an inclination that is accompanied by several questions. If the recollective work of riot is referential, must not the Brixton and Handsworth risings refer to something more than the history of English working-class protest? Must they not recollect an additional body of local knowledges, an additional set of "values and norms," an additional series, indeed a *global* series, of cultural vernaculars? Moreover, whatever local knowledges the riots defend, how does this defense of the local, and the locale, differ from the nostalgic celebrations of the local, and the locale, that I have suggested are central to the culture of British imperialism? How can the zone of riot be both a *lieu de memoire* and a space of newness? And finally, to return to the question with which I concluded the previous chapter, if the zone of riot is a space of newness, how can such riotous newness be rendered desir-able? How can it seduce its participants *and* its beholders away from a longing for the fixed, the essential, the unitary?

Permanence and Unsettlement

Answers to all of these questions are contained in the riddle of postcolonial migrancy, and in Rushdie's posing of that riddle in *The Satanic Verses*. But as often as Rushdie, in this text, represents migrancy as a condition of remembering an "English" *and* an-other history, of discovering the nostalgic as the breeding ground of the new, and of learning to surrender the pleasures of the unitary for the love of the multiple, he also indicates that migrancy can entail a rejection of other histories, a denial of newness, and a refusal of multiplicity. He indicates that to understand how migrancy can encompass the former, essentially affirmative gestures, one must investigate, rather than merely dismissing, the latter acts of refusal. He suggests that we must begin at the end, with the migrant's refusal of multiplicity, if we are at last to arrive at the beginning, to re-encounter those other histories, those other locations of identity, those other local knowledges which the migrant is willing to defend – in an act of riot if necessary – and through the defense of which the migrant redeems the nation as a corporate but locally differentiated space of belonging.

If *The Satanic Verses* is, among other things, an anatomy of the condition of postco-lonial migrancy, then the condition of being *among other things* is not only a description of the place of a narrative of migrancy in a text that has not one but many, even too many, stories to tell. It is also, in Rushdie's reading, the ineradicable fact of migrancy itself. Migrancy, he suggests, is the living among other, and other's, things; the inhabiting of not one but many places; the condition of belonging to, or being implicated by, not a single but a multitude of narratives. It is, as Rushdie has it late in the text, a "moving through many stories at once" (457). As Aijaz Ahmad has noted, however, to belong to so many places and so many narratives is to surrender to such an excess of determinations that the migrant ultimately risks belonging nowhere, precisely because he or she "belongs to too many places."[12] Rushdie is quite aware of this, and if he generally renders migrancy visible as the delirium of the multiple, he also represents it as the refusal of multiplicity, as the desire for unity, the longing to inhabit a known and bounded space and to be possessed by a sole and unitary narrative.

It is partially – though only partially – for this reason that Islam assumes such importance in this text. For Islam's governing metaphors, in Rushdie's reading, are metaphors of the one: belonging to the one, confessing the one, and residing in the one. Rushdie understands the promise of Islamic residence that Mahound makes to the people of Jahilia – the promise of inhabiting a settled and unitary space that is as much a historical locale as it is a space in the sacred imaginary – to be a promise in which the postcolonial migrant, whether Muslim or not, wishes to believe.

> The city of Jahilia is built entirely of sand, its structures formed of the desert whence it rises. It is a sight to wonder at: walled, four-gated, the whole of it a miracle worked by its citizens, who have learned the trick of transforming the fine white dune-sand of those forsaken parts – the very stuff of inconstancy, – the quintessence of unsettlement, shifting, treachery, lack-of-form, – and have turned it, by alchemy, into the fabric of their newly invented permanence. These people are a mere three or four generations removed from their nomadic past, when they were as rootless as the dunes, or rather rooted in the knowledge that the journeying itself was home.
>
> Whereas the migrant can do without the journey altogether; it's no more than a necessary evil; the point is to arrive. (94)

For Rushdie, nomadism is the condition of living in a displacement so radical that it ceases to exist. Nomadism is the name for the inhabitation of the journey. If the nomad has a home, it is a home whose rooms are walled by the dislocations of travel. Within the dispersed spaces of the nomadic habitus, the nomad need never leave and never arrives. According to Rushdie, however, for the migrant the point is to arrive. Most specifically, the desire of the migrant is to succeed where the citizens of Jahilia have succeeded, to transform the quintessence of unsettlement into an invented permanence. This yearning for permanence becomes, in fact, less a longing to arrive than a desire to have arrived. It is a wish to be done with the endless business of arriving, a tedium before the infinity of ports to pass through, languages to learn, schools to enter, papers to file, and laws to satisfy. It is a desire to rest, to belong. The politics of migrancy, therefore, may not necessarily be a nationalist politics, but migrancy certainly encompasses a politics of emplacement. This means that for the migrant, as for any other subject, cultural identity can be the product as much of what is forgotten as of what is remembered, that arrival might entail a willed forgetting of unsettlement, a refusal of multiple loyalties, a submission to the seductions of the one.

In *The Satanic Verses*, Rushdie connects this longing to have arrived to the acts of forgetfulness and the labors of redemption. In brief, Saladin Chamcha enacts his longing to arrive as a deliberate, if selective, forgetting of himself in the interest of redeeming himself as English and unitary. Gibreel Farishta, alternatively, marks his arrival through a re-creation, a multiplication of the place to which he has come, in the name of redeeming that place for the English and the erstwhile subjects of empire. The distance between Chamcha and Farishta is in many ways a product of this profound difference of opinion regarding the objects of redemption. For Chamcha, it is the migrant who must be redeemed in order that he, or she, might be reconciled to England. For Farishta, it is England that requires redemption in order that the nation might be reconciled to its migrants.[13] But to say this is to offer a contraction rather than a reading, and in order to understand Rushdie and to trace a return from Chamcha and Farishta to the location of riot in the contemporary narratives of Englishness, one must read the novel.

Saladin Chamcha is, in the fullest sense of Stephen Greenblatt's words, a self-fashioned man. An Indian actor residing in London, he is the product of a meticulous and relentless labor of self-erasure and self-fabrication. Even his name is an invention, or, rather, a censored translation of a given original. Born Salahuddin Chamchawala, he has contracted himself, torn the difficult syllables from his name and offered himself to his English brethren as a word that can be easily pronounced. He is, as the narrator of *The Satanic Verses* describes him, "a creature of *selected* dis-continuities, a *willing* reinvention; his preferred revolt against history being what makes him, in our chosen idiom, 'false'" (427). Chamcha codes his revolt against history as a revolt against India and a revolt against his past. He survives through an act of willed amnesia, a forgetting of his origins, a denial of his dislocatedness. Gayatri Spivak, in an essay on *The Satanic Verses*, has suggested that migrancy is a condition of "turned-awayness."[14] By this she seems to mean that the migrant turns away from the space that he or she now inhabits to remember the abandoned space of "origin," to dwell in remembrance and desire in the cultural landscapes from whence he or she has departed. There are characters in *The Satanic Verses* who live this way. Hind Sufyan, Chamcha's unwilling hostess at the Shandaar B and B and Café, lives in London but turns from it to inhabit the Bangladesh from which her husband has taken her. Surrounded by the subcontinental foods that she cooks and the Hindi and Bengali movies she rents, she dwells in the absence from which she has migrated. Saladin Chamcha, however, has turned the other way. He has turned away from India, away from the landscapes of the past in which he has lived, to a nation that he has adopted and in whose image he longs to reproduce himself.

If, however, as the narrator of the text fleetingly suggests, this marks Chamcha as false, then his falsity is a product not only of what he no longer pretends, even partially, to belong to, but of the falsity of that England which he claims to inhabit and by which he wishes to believe himself redeemed. For Chamcha's England, the England that he imaginatively occupies, is a museum. "Him and his Royal Family," his weary English wife declaims, "you wouldn't believe. Cricket. The Houses of Parliament, the Queen. The place never stopped being a picture postcard to him" (175). Chamcha is punished for his pretense. The England he discovers is a place that refuses to conform to the picturesque renderings of itself. The English actors with whom he works seem intent on betraying their cultural heritage: they guzzle cheap American champagne, dress in Donald Duck T-shirts, and, most horrifically, tart themselves up in Indian garb. This is all thoroughly intolerable to Chamcha, who has made his pilgrimage to England not to discover ersatz versions of the subcontinent or America but to be saved from the accident of his Indian birth by the glories of the English past. "For a man like Saladin Chamcha," the narrator almost pityingly observes, "the debasing of Englishness by the English was a thing too painful to contemplate" (75). Chamcha responds to this debasement as he has responded to India: he turns away, refuses to contemplate what is before him, and surrounds himself with a postcard picture of England. But he is not permitted to continue in this devotional act. Punished once by an England that insists on displaying its hybrid tawdriness, he is punished again by a narrator who deems it time for him to see a little more of the nation he has come to inhabit, explodes the plane in which he is flying, transforms him into a goat-horned devil, and deposits him in an attic room of Muhammad and Hind Sufyan's Shandaar Café.

The Shandaar Café is a multiply inhabited space. It is not only an eatery but a hostel of sorts, a run-down bed-and-breakfast housing recent immigrants to England. Above the ground-floor café, the Sufyans rent out rooms to new arrivals, some of whom have entered the country legally, many of whom have not, and all of whom find that they are not yet done with the wearying business of arriving. Among them these diverse inhabitants define a catalog of migrancy. Six immigrant families, who have qualified for borough-funded temporary housing but have not yet secured the right to permanent residence in England, are, at best, a sort of footnote to that catalog. They are a community in hiding, lodged five to a room, who live less in the Shandaar Café than in the gaps of the Home Office's memory. They live in deferral, not sure whether they wish the government to remember or to forget them, as they await the resolution of their status. These families are, in truth – or at least before the law – not yet migrants. For them the Shandaar Café is not a terminus; it is limbo. They live in anticipation of a moment in which their legal identities will catch up with their bodies, a moment in which their waiting will end and they will have arrived. Ghostly presences in the café, glimpsed only behind the crack of a rapidly shutting door, they are, Rushdie mournfully reflects, "temporary human beings, with little hope of being declared permanent" (264). Trapped in an uncompleted journey between the homes they have left and the new home to which they would come, these thirty wanderers are the frustrated specters of the migrant uncanny. They are the empire's repressed, patiently awaiting permission to return.

Their landlords, however, *have* arrived. Muhammad and Hind Sufyan, and their daughters Mishal and Anahita, have been in England more than a dozen years and have passed through loss and waiting to the accomplishment of licit habitation. The family's response to the permanence of their arrival is not, however, unitary. Edouard Glissant has suggested that there are a variety of cultural strategies available to a transplanted people as they struggle to survive the shock of their displacement. These strategies tend to be organized around the migrant's willingness, or unwillingness, to be changed "into something new, into a new set of possibilities."[15] A desire to resist the new, which is also an investment in "maintaining the old order of values in a new locale," manifests

itself in what Glissant terms the impulse toward "reversion." "Reversion is the obsession with a single origin: one must not alter the absolute state of being. To revert is to
consecrate permanence, to negate contact. Reversion will be recommended by those
who favor single origins" (16). Hind Sufyan is an apostle of reversion. She is, as Glissant's argument suggests, devoted to permanence, but not to the permanence she is
offered in England. To have arrived and settled in London is, for Hind, to be a prisoner
of loss, and she responds to the cultural amputation she has suffered by clutching the
subcontinent to herself with the eager palm of a phantom limb. As Chamcha lives by
his voice, so Hind lives by her hands. But where Chamcha's voice sighs to the cadences
of the King's English, Hind's hands shape and cook the delicacies of Bangladesh. In
her kitchen, she turns away from England and returns to the pantries of her past. When
she is not in her Proustian kitchen, she is before her television, bathing in the video
waters of "an endless supply of Bengali and Hindi movies on VCR through which. . . .
[she can] stay in touch with events in the 'real' world" (250–1). When she is not in her
kitchen or watching television, she is nowhere. She does not go out. We never see
her leave the Shandaar Café, her little Bangladesh in England.

Her teenage daughters, though they live in her house, inhabit another world. They
survive, to follow Glissant a little further, not in reversion but in assimilation. They are
English, and aggressively so, though not as Chamcha is English. Theirs, rather, is the
debased England of his fellow actors and of his manager. They wear scandalously form-
fitting clothing emblazoned with images of "the new Madonna"; cut and dye their hair
in late-punk styles; abominate their mother's cooking; yearn for bangers and mash; trip
the "radical," "crucial," and "Fucking *A*" syllables of a Bethnal Green patois off their
saucily London tongues; and think nothing of the nation in which they were born.
"Bangladesh in't nothing to me," Mishal informs Chamcha, who is horrified to discover
that the girls understand themselves to be, like him, English, "Just some place Dad and
Mum keep banging on about . . . Bungleditch . . . What I call it, anyhow" (259).

Mishal and Anahita force the terrible realization on Chamcha that he and the girls
are the only people in the café who consider themselves "English," and further require
him to recognize that though their respective Englands are radically dissimilar, they are
nevertheless alike in their flirtations with Englishness and their rejections of the suit of
a subcontinental past. Yet the thoroughness with which the girls reject "Bungleditch"
also reveals that the girls are less unlike their mother than they might wish. Anahita
and Mishal's denial of Bangladesh and their wholesale adoption of a working-class
London order of Englishness is not profoundly different from their mother's commitment to the landscape of her youth and her refusal to make contact with the city in
which she finds her body, if not her self. Both mother and daughters, to return to
Glissant's language, are hostages to an obsessive belief in single origins. Both, like
Chamcha in his turn, are resolutely turned away. To survive the shock of their translations, each of these migrants, in their various ways, worships culture as a locale and
deifies one genius loci by forgetting another. Spivak maintains that within such "turned-
awayness," "Rushdie implants the migrant's other desire, the search for roots as far
down as they'll go. The name for this radical rootedness is, most often, religion" (*Outside
in the Teaching Machine*, 223). The various obsessions of Anahita, Mishal, Hind, and
Chamcha imply that if, as Spivak argues, migrancy entails a structure of sacral belief,

then the gods of such a polytheist religion might as often be localities – whether imaginary, experienced, or remembered – as extraterrestrial divinities. Spivak's comment further suggests that the commitment to locality, by which the migrant defines a self through the manipulations of a sentimental economy of refusal and avowal, is a commitment also to the common sacral fantasy of redemption.

An essential sadness, however, attaches to Hind's, Mishal's, Anahita's, and Chamcha's strategies of survival. In a text repeatedly constructed as a narrative of mourning, Rushdie does not hesitate to pour the bitter sorrow of his prose over these four figures. This common sadness suggests that even as the "strategies" of reversion and assimilation are united in their pursuit of a single locality of belonging, they are unified also as failed epistemologies of redemption. Glissant, who is less willing than he should be to recognize the similarity of these modes of living in displacement, *is* quite clear on this point. Both reversion and assimilation fail to save the migrant from the terrors and difficulties of living a life in translation, he argues, because both strategies begin and end with an act of deliberate misrecognition. Rushdie renders this misrecognition manifest as the syllabus of English persons and English things that Hind and Chamcha decline to gaze upon. For Chamcha, the contents of that syllabus of refusal are quite fixed: he will refuse to recognize the existence of anything outside the frame of his postcard England. Or, as he announces to his host at the Shandaar Café, "You're not my people. I've spent half my life trying to get away from you" (253). For Hind, the list of the not-seen is rather less certain. It begins, however, not in aesthetic repugnance but in fear: "They had come into a demon city in which anything could happen, your windows shattered in the middle of the night without any cause, you were knocked over in the street by invisible hands, in the shops you heard such abuse you felt like your ears would drop off but when you turned in the direction of the words you saw only empty air and smiling faces, and every day you heard about this boy, that girl, beaten up by ghosts . . . best thing was to stay home, not go out for so much as to post a letter, stay in, lock the door, say your prayers, and the goblins would (maybe) stay away" (250). But of course neither Hind's goblins nor Chamcha's "people" will stay away. However much they are refused, however resolutely they are turned away from, they reappear. To deny them is to enter a closeted life whose door can at any moment be suddenly, and rudely, opened. To misrecognize the unruly intrusions of the English present or the subcontinental past is not to be redeemed; it is to deny the trauma of a wound.

Within such a denial there is an investment in the redemptive – or at least the preservative – capacities of an act of cultural blasphemy. If it has been the fate of Rushdie's text to be read as an exorbitantly blasphemous artifact, then there is a failure of reading in such understandings of *The Satanic Verses* that extends beyond the tragedies of misreading attaching to the "*Satanic Verses* affair." For while the text expresses more than a little interest in the blasphemous, its primary interest is in suggesting that an act of *cultural* blasphemy is impossible, that cultural codes of belonging can be denied or refashioned but not recanted. This exposure of the impossibilities of blasphemy derives not from the text's demonstration of that familiar dynamic in which blasphemy cannot be spoken of outside a context of belief, or even of that operation in which those artifacts of the sacred that a commodity-centered culture renders merely decorative are resacralized precisely at that shocking moment in which they are dipped in the curiously sanctifying brine of an artist's urine. Rather, they are exposed through Rushdie's manipulation of the economies of memory and forgetting. Rushdie represents cultural blasphemy as a desire to forget and reveals its impossibility at those moments in which his characters, to their horror, learn that if they can fail to remember, they cannot choose to forget.

The yearning to forget is an expression of that form of melancholy which desires to erase the not-wanted, which invokes itself as a naming of the not-wanted, and which, in this act of naming, guarantees that the not-wanted cannot be forgotten. It is a cognitive loop sequence: a commitment to brooding, tantalization, frustration, and failure. In Rushdie's novel, Saladin Chamcha is the most desperate to blaspheme, India is that which he most frequently longs to forget, and India is that which he cannot fail to remember. There is a lesson here for those custodians, fabricators, and readers of national identity who wish to posit the nation as a pure present, to forget its founding violences, or to resist the disciplinary submissions of the nation to a reified anteriority by counseling us to learn how to forget. To believe that the nation, or the subject, can be redeemed through an act of willed forgetting is to deny the difficulties and persistencies of memory in the vain hope that the struggles to belong can be completed without reference to the looming anteriorities of history. It is to commit to the bankrupt areferentiality of a purely performative invention of the present. Ultimately, it means failing to recognize that while blasphemy may be desirable, it is not possible. It is also, Rushdie insistently suggests, to misapprehend the labor of redemption, to believe, with Chamcha, that it is the migrant, or the migrant's procedures of cognition, which must suffer a reinvention, rather than the migrant habitus which must be redeemed.

There is, however, one inmate of the Shandaar Café committed to the redemption of the English habitus through a translative rewriting of England's spaces and discourses of belonging. Jumpy Joshi, who attended an English university with Chamcha but did not besot himself with the liquors of Olde England, is the minor hero of Rushdie's text. Alone among the inhabitants of the Shandaar Café, he refuses to submit to the terrorism of the categorical imperatives of Englishness or Indianness.[16] Alone among the café's community of migrants, Jumpy Joshi insists that to define the migrant subject as that which requires re-formation or redemption under the reified signs of a unitary locality of belonging is to embrace life as a victim of place. Joshi agrees that the migrant is a victim of his or her dislocative emplacements, but argues that to choose to manufacture a life as the emblem of a fetishized place, as Hind, Chamcha, Mishal, and Anahita in their various ways have done, is to *court* the twinned statuses of victim and caricature. It is to make oneself, Rushdie suggests through the voice of Joshi, a prisoner of description, to define the self as an allegory of the described and worshiped place. In the moment of Chamcha's goaty apotheosis, Joshi discovers the inevitable end of a project of migrant desire that begins and ends with the decision to re-form the self. For while Chamcha longs to represent himself as a mannequin of Englishness, the police who discover his postwreck body envision him as an immigrant Satan. And, as Chamcha belatedly discovers, it is the police and not the migrant who add to the powers of description the sanctions of law.

Joshi responds to the plight of his fellows by turning their attention from the costuming of the self to the labor of reconstructing the English habitus. Glissant's word for this is diversion, a trickster strategy that defines itself not as a refusal to see, or as a flight from the horrors of the seen, but as an intentionally skewed way of seeing. To divert England is to devour even the most barbed of English fare, to stew England in the migrant's gastric juices, and to return England to itself as markedly, perhaps aromatically, different. Joshi's politics are less olfactory. He sets out to reform England by rewriting its most exclusionary narratives of belonging. He returns to Enoch Powell's infamous "Rivers of Blood" speech to offer a poetic misreading of the politician's dream of ruin. "Reclaim the metaphor, Jumpy Joshi had told himself. Turn it; make it a thing we can use" (186). Adopting but estranging Powell's metaphor, he revels in the effervescence of blood, tropes the street as capillary effluence, and offers the migrant as England's life-sustaining transfusion. Joshi's tragedy is that while he has an acute understanding of the productive values of an act of cultural misprision, he is a weak poet. When a friend discovers and reads his poetry, he recoils from the banal locutions of his own language and hides his verses. Thereafter they are never read again. They disappear from Rushdie's text, as the Satanic Verses disappear from the Koran. In a fashion, however, Joshi's poetry may be said to reappear in the novel, and to resound on the same tongue that speaks the Koran's censored verses. Gibreel Farishta, who as the Angel Gibreel articulates the Koranic repressed, gives a new voice to Joshi's hidden verses. In his speaking, however, the river of blood is not only a word on the page. It is, as Powell feared, an event in the street, an act of riot.

Tropicalization

Gibreel Farishta, like Chamcha, identifies the experience of migrancy as a labor of redemption. In his reading, however, it is not the migrant who must be redeemed by the spaces that he or she inhabits. Rather, like Jumpy Joshi, Farishta suggests that it is the space of cultural inhabitation which must be redeemed, and the migrant who will act as England's cultural redeemer. If Farishta and Chamcha disagree on this issue, then they differ also in their definitions of who, or rather what, the migrant is, or should be. For Chamcha, the migrant is a multiple personality yearning for perfection and rest in the integrity of the one. For Farishta, who as an actor in India has become famous as the filmic incarnation of a pantheon of gods, identity is polyphony, excess, a moving through many stories at once. More significant, while Chamcha unswervingly believes that for the migrant to "arrive" in England he or she must strip away those signs of cultural alterity which it was the object of the English empire to repress, Farishta delightedly discovers the migrant's arrival in England as a riotous return of the repressed and desires to save England, as the English crowd had so often offered to save the nation, by returning England to the blinked-away landspaces of its elsewhere and its past.

Farishta enters London armed with a text of the city. The text is an atlas, *London A to Z*, a map that Gibreel proposes to use to plot the route of a passage in which he, as the most angelic of wanderers, will mark his transforming presence on the streets and walls of the city. "The atlas in his pocket was his master plan. He would redeem the city square by square. . . . He would redeem this city, Geographer's London, all the way from A to Z" (326). However, in plotting his redemptive approach to the city as an ordered march, square by square, through the gridded spaces of Geographer's London, Gibreel confronts one of those paradoxes that are Rushdie's signature. Gibreel wishes to save the city for multiplicity, for the abundance and superfluity of the thousand and one narratives that are the substance of England's migrant history. He intends to reveal that England is not unitary, that England's spaces of inhabitation are not interrupted or vandalized by the returns of the post-colonial migrant, but that Englishness, as John Ruskin briefly dared to believe, is constituted as an imperfect and perpetually incomplete construction. Through Gibreel's incursive visitation to the city of London, Rushdie labors to free England from the "confining myth of authenticity" to which Saladin Chamcha has submitted, and to redeem England for "eclecticism," uncertainty, mutability (52). But in choosing to plan his redemptive march through the city on the basis of his guidebook's knowledge of the city, Gibreel assumes that the city has awaited his coming. He labors under the conviction that London is, as the Geographer indicates, a fixed and gridded space, a disciplined territory. As he attempts to plot his route through the city, however, he discovers what Ruskin had discovered a century before: that the city itself is migrant, that its streets and squares and alleys have refused to submit to discipline, that it exceeds and frustrates the best intentions of cartography. "The city in its corruption," he learns, "refused to submit to the dominion of the cartographers, changing shape at will and without warning, making it impossible for Gibreel to approach his quest in the systematic manner he would have preferred" (327). To his surprise, Gibreel learns that the city has anticipated his arrival, that it has already begun to divert itself, that it is its own redeeming angel.

This recognition raises a question: if London contains within itself the principle of its own transmutation and redemption, what need is there for Gibreel to proceed? A partial answer to that question lies in the pocket of Gibreel's coat. The simple and confident existence of the map dwelling in that pocket suggests that although London is uncontainably various, it is not officially known as such. Gibreel's labor, then, assumes a familiarly angelic function. His work is not to act but to announce; not to redeem but to broadcast redemption's accomplishment. But this is an incomplete answer and one with which Rushdie is ultimately dissatisfied. For Rushdie's interest, finally, is not in mutability and the eclectic as pure forms, but in what he refers to in *The Satanic Verses* as a "historically validated eclecticism" (52). The problem with the city, as Gibreel discovers it, is that it reveals a passion for the various without regard to variety's content. Rushdie may be a prophet of cultural uncertainty, but he is not a priest of that postmodern cult in which the uncertain emerges as an unnamed god. In this he differs from a critic such as Homi Bhabha who, in wedding the postcolonial to the postmodern, can discover in such events as the Brixton riots no stories, only the ghosts of unspoken earlier stories, in the performative no local significance, only the asignificances of the affect-event.

Rushdie aspires not simply to demonstrate that the narratives of Englishness are narratives of the multiple, but to name at least a fraction of what such multiplicity encompasses. In this regard his response to *Handsworth Songs* is revealing. It is in this film that Bhabha discovers that raging rastaman whom, together with the film's makers, he manages to read as embodying no story – only the ghost of some other story. Rushdie, in reviewing the film, has no patience with such narrative evacuations. The film fails, he suggests, because it gestures toward the "other stories" of the migrant inhabitation of England but refuses to tell them. Indeed, Rushdie argues, the film manages to plot the thousand and one narratives of postcolonial migrancy solely as a unitary narrative of rage and, in doing so, manages to erase the other stories of a contemporary England that a place like Handsworth locates: "It's important, I believe, to tell such stories; to say, this is England. Look at the bright illuminations and fireworks during the Hindu Festival of Lights, Divali. Listen to the Muslim call to prayer, 'Allahu Akbar,' wafting down from the minaret of a Birmingham mosque. Visit the Ethiopian World Federation, which helps Handsworth Rastas 'return' to the land of Ras Tafari. These are English scenes now. English songs."[17] Rushdie's stress is on the Englishness of the scenes he is describing, but it is a stress heightened by his sense of the need to give the multiple ways of being English a local habitation and a name. He appeals to his reader not to look upon the "performative" but to gaze upon the particular and diverse ways in which English identity is rehearsed. He asks that we see the rastaman not simply as the embodiment of a principle of cultural fluctuance but as the carrier of one of those stories – one suggesting that Haile Selassie is now as English as the Festival of Lights or the Book of Common Prayer.

If Rushdie desires to elicit the stories of England's hybridity, then Gibreel Farishta is the servant of that desire. As much as he is an angelic wanderer, Gibreel is a roaming repository of England's narratives. All who come in contact with him surrender to an impulse to reveal themselves, to divulge their tales, to pour their voices into the portals of his semidivine ear. As he wanders through the city of London, he finds himself wandering through a collection of stories whose only connection to one another is that, for all their dissimilarities, they are English. Gibreel influences more than the people he meets: his passing affects the city also. And it is in forcing the city to disclose itself, not simply as multiform, but as a hybrid whose various branches have been grafted from cuts of an imperial tree, that he most fully accomplishes his redemptive work.

Confronted with a metropolis that frustrates his desire for multiplicity not by being singular but by exhibiting itself as generically and blankly mutable, Gibreel resolves to "tropicalize" the city and indulges himself in a contemplation of the consequences of his act. "Gibreel enumerated the benefits of the proposed metamorphosis of London into a tropical city: increased moral definition, institution of a national siesta, development of vivid and expansive patterns of behaviour among the populace, higher quality music . . . better cricketers; higher emphasis on ball control among professional footballers. . . . Religious fervour, political ferment, renewal of interest in the intelligentsia. . . . Spicier food; the use of water as well as paper in English toilets . . ." (354–5). Gibreel's musings on the consequences of his transformation of the English weather indicate that there is more involved in his act of tropicalization than a simple fiddling with meteorological phenomena. In the trope of tropicalization, and in Gibreel's unpacking of that trope, Rushdie finds a way to render the uncanny as the redemptive and to discover a riotous merging of the discourses of migrancy and Englishness. In enumerating his list of "benefits," Gibreel constructs a catalog of cultural difference consonant with Saladin Chamcha's catalog of the refused and the unseen. Spicy food, religious fervor, expansive behavior, and all the other items on this burlesque list are entries in Chamcha's encyclopedia of the Not-English. But they are Not-English in a particular way, for they are the eclectic fragments of the cultures that the English empire collected. They are the metonyms of the Not-England that England occupied, reluctantly abandoned, and now wishes to forget. In Gibreel's tropicalizing proclamation, however, it becomes impossible for England to forget this catalog of alterity – not because Gibreel will magically require spicy foods, religious fervor, and expansive behavior to manifest themselves in London, but because, as always, he will render visible what is already there. Gibreel's real magic is not to rain this catalog of difference upon England but to erase the difference of difference. To tropicalize London is not to make the metropolis a foreign city but to deny the foreignness of these differences to the city, to announce that London is a conurbation of such differences, to reveal that when he speaks of siestas, better cricketers, and the use of water as well as paper in toilets, he speaks of "English scenes."

In tropicalizing London, Gibreel rewrites the cultural cartography of the city. He erases its boundaries and collapses the distinction between the here and the elsewhere. He opens London's gates to that most spectacular return of the repressed, in which the willfully forgotten double appears not as an image of the *unheimlich* but as a coinhabitor of the home. In doing so, in allowing the elsewhere of English history to become coincident with an English locale, Gibreel manages also to answer a question around which much of Rushdie's narrative has been organized. "How does newness come into the world?" the narrator asks in the opening pages of the book; "How is it born? Of what fusions, translations, conjoinings is it made?" (8). The latter questions, which appear simply to clarify the opening query, contain, in fact, the clues to the answer that Gibreel will provide. Newness, it appears, enters the world not as an utter beginning or the manifestation of some pure element never seen before, but as a novel conjoining of what already exists, as transfusion, as the hybridization of the here and the elsewhere, the now and the then. The paradox of newness in this text is that the new is not the negation or opposite of the old or the past but the conjunction of diverse pasts, the overlapping of the histories of the English here and the imperial elsewhere in London's present. This moment of newness, in which the new emerges as the marriage, in the present, of various "English" pasts, is more than similar to that moment of redemption embedded in Benjamin's Messianic time in which the past is collapsed onto and revealed within the now. Newness and redemption are, in Rushdie's text, identical – and both are manifest in Gibreel's act of tropicalization. In returning England's elsewhere to its here, and in collapsing the multiple landscapes of its imperial past onto the metropolitan expanse of its postimperial present, Gibreel has succeeded in redeeming the city. He has brought newness into the world. He has revealed a new way of being English.

And this, of course, is also an old way of being English, and a riotous way of being English. Gibreel boisterously returns England to its pasts and its elsewheres not in order to vandalize the nation but to save England for itself. And this, as I have discussed earlier in this chapter, is the historic work of the rioting English crowd. The crowd's labor, to finally reconcile Bhabha to E. P. Thompson and George Rude, is the labor of a determinate indeterminacy. In its act of riot, the crowd raises its disruptive voice not in the name of disruption but in order to disorder what it perceives to be the distortions of the contemporary; it does so by wedding the present and the here to the – perhaps imaginary – particularities of a displaced past or elsewhere. This suggests that if riot is to be read as a meaningful cultural event, rather than according to tropes of randomness and disarray, then the performative occasion of riot must be seen as writing a *certain* uncertainty onto the spaces of cultural inhabitation. In the eighteenth century, this certain uncertainty can be seen in the moral economy of crowd behavior that led rioting English laborers to spill through the market squares of the island's cities in order to restore the market to a "customary," preindustrial way of operating. In the twentieth century, this ordered disorder can be detected in the riotous demands of a Brixton crowd to reclaim those citizenship privileges of the *ius soil* filched by the 1981 Nationality Bill. Either instance suggests that the crowd, in its moments of "newness," is often the most historically minded of cultural performers – and this is assuredly true of that exuberantly crowdlike actor Gibreel Farishta, whose yearnings for the overseas and displaced spaces of English history manifest themselves in his tropicalizing riot of the English habitus.

Of course, should the crowd's, or Gibreel's, desire become merely a yearning to return to the apparent perfections of the past, then we would be confronting something that is not at all "new." We would then be addressing a discourse or a cultural performative committed yet again to purity, the authentic, and the erasure of the present rather than its productive corruption and hybridization. Since, finally, this is not what I believe is figured in Gibreel's riotous performances, we must, however briefly, turn from his tropicalization of the city to the text's most recognizable scene of crowd disturbance. Toward the end of the novel a riot breaks out in the urban neighborhoods around the Shandaar Café when Uhuru Simba, a black political activist, dies in police custody. The terms by which this riot can be read are apparently familiar. The collective outrage at the death of Simba bespeaks not only anger before an act of police violence but a desire of those black Britons who take to the street to protest his death that he and they be recognized before the law as legitimate inhabitants of the national community, that they be invested with the juridical protections attaching to English civic identity, that their bodies be granted the rights of inviolability which are the privileges of the English body when in the custody of the English state. The riot, in this reading, emerges as an expression of a migrant politics of emplacement, as an insistence that black Britons must be recognized to occupy spaces within the island's towns and cities *and* a legitimate place within the geography of citizenship. Asked what he thought of English civilization, Mahatma Gandhi reportedly once suggested that he thought it would be a good idea. The riot on the streets around the Shandaar Café can be read as an extended gloss on that pithy wisdom, as a demand not that England disband itself, but that it be faithful to its own good idea.

That, of course, is not the only available reading of this event, and Rushdie signals his awareness of the riot's hermeneutic indeterminacy by staging it – as Lord Scarman staged the Brixton disorders – as an event on television. Rushdie represents the riot not from its bewildering ground level but from above, from the recording eye of a helicopter-mounted television camera. Gazing down on the scene, and broadcasting the digitized images of what it observes to the living rooms of an aghast nation, the camera sees this scene: "A man lit by a sun-gun speaks rapidly into a microphone. Behind him there is a disorderment of shadows. But between the reporter and the disordered shadow-lands there stands a wall: men in riot helmets, carrying shields. The reporter speaks gravely; petrolbombs plasticbullets policeinjuries water-cannon looting . . . But the camera sees what he does not say. A camera is a thing easily broken or purloined; its fragility makes it fastidious. A camera requires law, order, the thin blue line. Seeking to preserve itself it remains behind the shielding wall, observing the shadow-lands from afar, and of course from above" (454–5). In surrendering the narrative voice of his text to the recording machinery of the camera, Rushdie reveals the camera's capacity not only to record events but to produce them. More significant, he demonstrates that the camera's electronic eye does not simply observe territory but manufactures a symbolic geography. What the camera sees, and visually disseminates, is not a riot but a bordered space, a realm of order and a terra incognita beyond. It fabricates a cartography of the recognized and the unknown, of the sunlit and the shadowland, of the grave and the disordered. Locating itself exactly at the space of the thin blue line, the camera defines its glassy lens as the limit of civility and vandalism. Standing in for the screens of the viewing audience, the lens of the camera defines the border of the culturally licit. Separating the watchers from the watched, the camera serves also to separate the English viewing public from the denizens of the shadowland beyond.

This reading of the riot is also familiar. As are the failures of the television to separate the watchers from the watched; its simultaneous closing and opening of the houses of the viewing public to the spaces of riot; its tendency at once to render the rioter untouchable and to invite him or her to slip through a video-window into the "nation's" living room. There is, however, at least one more reading of the riot available to us, a reading that attends both to the riot's location in the discourses of migrant emplacement and nomadic deterritorialization, and to its position within the recollective moral economies of the English crowd and the narrative constructions of English "newness." Prior to his death, Uhuru Simba addresses the court in which he is being arraigned in the following words: "Make no mistake . . . we are here to change things. I concede that we ourselves shall be changed; African, Caribbean, Indian, Pakistani, Bangladeshi, Cypriot, Chinese, we are other than we would have been if we had not crossed the oceans, if our mothers and fathers had not crossed the skies in search of work and dignity and a better life for their children. We have been made again: but I say that we will also be the ones to remake this society, to shape it from the bottom to the top. We shall be the hewers of the dead wood and the gardeners of the new" (414). In this unabashedly polemical outburst, Rushdie, through the ventriloquized voice of Simba, comes as close as he will allow himself to a manifesto. Within that manifesto he seeds a trope that is crucial to his project as a novelist and a cultural critic.

In turning to the metaphors of "crossing over," Simba alludes to the metaphors of translation that have become central to attempts to read the postcolonial condition. To be translated is, as Rushdie informs us in *Midnight's Children*, to be borne across. It is also to have been begun again, or, less passively, to begin again. Translation is a belated writing, an act of repetition. But it is also, as Walter Benjamin has taught us, an act of enunciation in which the copy brings into question the authoritative status of the original. It is a moment of cultural production divested of the compulsion to originate, a moment in which beginning is posterior to the begun, in which newness emerges as a reinscription, a cross-inscription, a writing over. Migrancy, Rushdie's narratives repetitively announce, is an act of translation. It is a bearing across of bodies, of narratives, and, as Virgil and Hind Sufyan would instruct us, of household gods. In being borne across, however, the migrant is obligated neither to forget the departed nor to eradicate the arrived at but to transfuse, to conjoin, to translate the one into the other – in the hope of realizing the hyphenated difficulty of the one-another.[18]

This is what Rushdie marks in the tropicalization of London. This is the translative newness toward which so much of the narrative of *The Satanic Verses* tends, and of which Uhuru Simba speaks. But, the troubling question remains, is this what is achieved not in the metaphoric and meteorological riot of tropicalization but in the bloody event of riot on London's streets? The answer must be both yes and no. As the riot flames to its most intense heat and fire consumes the Shandaar Café and claims the lives of Hind and Muhammad Sufyan, Gibreel Farishta stumbles into the pitchy, smoldering mass of the boardinghouse to discover Saladin Chamcha, his bitter adversary, trapped and choking beneath the weight of a fallen timber. As Gibreel contemplates Saladin in this moment of crisis, Rushdie's narrative swings close to the narrative of Forster's *A Passage to India*. Here again, a plot of revenge is offered the counterplot of redemption. And here, once again, a path to redemption, a path from war to friendship, is chosen. In words that are among the most poignant and sentimental of this too frequently mournful text, Rushdie directs his dark angelic instrument: "Gibreel Farishta steps quickly forward, bearing Saladin along the path of forgiveness in the hot night air; so that on a night when the city is at war, a night heavy with enmity and rage, there is this small redeeming victory for love" (468).

Rushdie's invocation of love at this moment serves to remind us that if love is capable of the labors of redemption, then it is also frequently prone to violence. It would be too easy, and ethically too cavalier, to attempt to derive from this imbrication of the discourses of love, violence, and redemption a model of reading that would present the act of riot, whether in the pages of Rushdie's text or on the streets of Brixton, as a simple labor of love. But in allying these three discourses, Rushdie's text's reminds us that it would be equally naive not to see the passions of riot as, in some measure, animated by that outrage which is love. Rushdie's language at this moment not only turns us to the capacities of the loving and the redemptive to commune with the violent but returns us, once more, to the trope of translation. For in this moment in which love and redemption emerge so fully into the open, their accomplishment is guaranteed by an act of bearing across. As Gibreel carries Saladin out of the flames, the two men return to that sky-tumbling moment in which, intertwined in the indeterminacies of being "Gibreelsaladin Farishta Chamcha," they are marked not by their divergencies but by "a fluidity, an indistinctness, at the edges of them" (8). Locked in this moment of embrace, of fusion, of translation into the spaces of one another's arms, the two men join one another as a metonymic miniature of cultural hybridity. If England is ever to be realized as a good idea, it is, Rushdie suggests, in such an utterly hybridized moment of riotous newness and redemption that is "of fusions, translations, conjoinings" made.

But, inevitably, the sentimentality of this moment cannot survive the crisis of its performance. Like Forster's offer of intimacy this moment cannot endure the shock of embrace to dwell in the banalities of the everyday. This is the problem with a reading of riot that attends to its redemptive grounds of possibility. Riot is an exceptional event whose slender victories may never counter-poise its violence. But even could its violence be discounted, and it cannot, the sheer exceptionality of riot limits its translative and redemptive capacities. As long as newness is figured as a performative event that exists only in the brevity of crisis, it can be invoked but not depended on. Rushdie's challenge, finally, is not to render riot synonymous with the redemptions of the new but to find a temporality of the new that is not catastrophic, to discover a time for newness, for translation, for the one-another, which can survive the boredoms of the everyday. He discovers this in the trope of tropicalization. For it is finally weather, and not riot, that visits us each day; weather that washes over us, marks us, and translates our corporeal and cultural physiognomies. It is the English weather that Rushdie will translate into the riotous precipitant of the new.

The Meteorics of Redemption

In order to read Gibreel's tropicalization of London as an act of riot in which the nation is redeemed by recalling its present to a past and an elsewhere, we must return to one of the questions with which this chapter began. We must, that is, examine the ways in which the occasion of riot is also a moment of remembrance. For remembrance, as I began this study by suggesting, and as I have argued throughout this book, is often intimate with forgetting. The experience of remembrance as a simultaneous commitment to forgetting animates the brooding passions of V. S. Naipaul's post-imperial melancholy. It governs the "village green" nostalgia of cricketing discourse, disciplines the practices of imperial tourism, and blinds the visitor to the Victoria Terminus to those "marks of difference" written on that edifice. John Ruskin's calls for national remembrance are invigorated by a similar courting of amnesia. For Ruskin's desire was not simply to redeem England from the depredations of modernity by sub-ordinating the present to the past, but to recall the past in order to erase the present. In either case, he demands that the nation forget its contemporaneity – and particularly its urban contemporaneity – in order that England might be recollectively redeemed. In appealing to the memory of his readers, Rushdie risks marking his tropicalized discourse as a discourse of repetition that yet again refuses the present. But Gibreel's act of riot does not thus obliterate the urban present. For London survives its tropicalization. It survives, however, as something that is both old and new, both here and there. It survives as that which globalizes the locale and localizes the global. In the moment of riot, which is in this sense a less imaginatively violent moment than that for which Ruskin longed, Rushdie tropes the present not as a table of erasure but as an overwritten text.

Yet in the figure of writing over, Rushdie does return to a moment in Ruskin's work, though this is a moment that the Victorian critic, symptomatically, proved himself too willing to forget. In the final pages of his essay on the "Lamp of Memory," Ruskin pauses to consider those flaws and fissures with which time marks the surfaces of the work of architecture. In these wandering superinscriptions traced onto the mnemonic locations of English identity by "the passing waves of humanity" (*Works*, 8:234), Ruskin discovers a "parasitical or engrafted sublimity" (*Works*, 8:238). The sublimity of these "rents" and "fractures" is the sublimity of a meandering, migrant, English history capable of marking the score of its passing onto the stones of the nation's habitus. It is the sublimity of the historical text that is rendered apparent not as a univocal document but as a polytropic artifact. It is the sublimity of a community of belonging that is revealed not as unified and complete but as perpetually in progress. In attending to the marks of history continuously written over, or "engrafted" onto, the space of English belonging, Ruskin fleetingly recognizes that the locations of Englishness are resolutely and repetitively hybridized by the survival of the English past into the moments of its present. Perhaps more significant, Ruskin acknowledges that in order to read England, to trace its character and identity on the surfaces of its built space, one must attend both to the shape of the nation's design and to those "golden stain[s] of time" (*Works*, 8:234) which, in being written over the designed space, render England visible as a space, in Salman Rushdie's words, "of fusions, translations, conjoinings."

But what are those "golden stains of time"? Ruskin equivocates, indicating at one moment that they are the signatures of the "passing waves of humanity," and, at another, that they are the "lines which rain and sun [have] wrought" (*Works*, 8:243). They are, of course, both: the imprints of an English weather that manifests itself at once in fogs, mists, and winds, *and* in the squalls and storms of human lives washing through the island's towns and cities. Most specifically, for my purposes here, these marks of time and weather are the cuts of that tropicalized meteorics which engraft onto the surface of the English metropolis the stains of empire. Spicy foods, better cricketers, the Festival of Lights, and cries of "Allahu Akbar" are the stone-altering dew of England's postwar atmospherics. In coming to England, the migrants from the island kingdom's ex-imperial territories brought not only their bodies but their "weather patterns" and a capacity to weather England's spaces of belonging. In the "tropicalizing" riot that Gibreel Farishta invokes, England's migrants emerge as the sublime principle ensuring that the laid stones of the English habitus continue to live as they re-create and redeem the nation by recalling it to that which it has attempted to displace. With all the island's other subjects, these tellers and makers of English stories flow through the nation's streets, schools, cricket clubs, train stations, houses, and cathedrals not as a shattering of windows but as a weathering storm, cutting their thousand and one inscriptions into the nation's spaces of belonging, marking England's newness, returning overseas histories to the island locale, revealing the nation as a space of "fusions, translations, conjoining."

Notes

1. *The Times* (London), April 12, 1981, 1.
2. The Rt. Hon. Lord Scarman, O.B.E., *The Brixton Disorders: 10–12 April 1981, Report of an Inquiry* (London: Her Majesty's Stationery Office, 1981), 1.
3. See Gustav Le Bon, *The Crowd* (New York: Penguin Books, 1960).
4. See Paul Fry, *A Defense of Poetry: Reflections on the Occasion of Writing* (Stanford: Stanford University Press, 1995).
5. Brian Massumi, "The Autonomy of Affect," *Cultural Critique* 31 (Fall 1985): 86–87 (emphasis added). Massumi derives the notion that the asignifances of the affective elicit pleasure, or happiness, from a series of experiments in cognitive psychology in which a

group of children frustrated a team of researchers by identifying the "saddest" and least coherent of a series of cartoons as the most pleasant. For a full reading of these experiments, see Hertha Sturm, *Emotional Effects of Media: The Work of Hertha Sturm*, ed. Gertrude Joch Robinson (Montreal: McGill University Graduate Program in Communications, 1987), 25–37; and Massumi's comments in "The Autonomy of Affect," 83–5.

6. *Sunday Telegraph* (London), April 12, 1981. Cited in Frances Webber, "Notes and Documents," *Race and Class*, nos. 2/3 (Autumn 1981): 225.

7. *Sunday Times* (London), April, 19, 1981.

8. E. P. Thompson, "The Moral Economy of the English Crowd in the Eighteenth Century," in *Customs in Common* (London: Merlin Press, 1991), 185–258.

9. Salman Rushdie, "The New Empire within Britain," in *Imaginary Homelands*, 136.

10. George Rude, *The Crowd in History, 1730–1848* (New York: John Wiley and Sons, 1964), 230.

11. Homi Bhabha, "DissemiNation, Time, Narrative, and the Margins of the Modern Nation," in *Nation and Narration* (London: Routledge, 1990), 306.

12. Aijaz Ahmad, *In Theory: Classes, Nations, Literatures* (London: Verso, 1992), 127.

13. It could be argued that Farishta's desire is to redeem England in order to reconcile the nation to Islam. If, however, his language is attended to at that moment in which – acting as the vengeful angel of history – he redeems London in riot and fire, it becomes apparent that it is his desire to remake England not in the image of Islam but in the cartoon image of the ex-imperial tropical cultures from which so many of the nation's migrants have come: "Gibreel enumerated the benefits of the proposed metamorphosis of London into a tropical city: increased moral definition, institution of a national siesta, development of vivid and expansive patterns of behaviour among the populace, higher-quality popular music . . . better cricketers; higher emphasis on ball-control among professional footballers, the traditional and soulless English commitment to 'high work-rate' having been rendered obsolete by the heat . . ." (*The Satanic Verses*, 335). This is only a fragment of Gibreel's catalog, to which I will return later in this chapter.

14. Spivak, "Reading the Satanic Verses," in *Outside in the Teaching Machine* (New York, 1993), 223.

15. Edouard Glissant, *Caribbean Discourse: Selected Essays*, trans. J. Michael Dash (Charlottesville: University of Virginia Press, 1989), 14.

16. I borrow this translation of Kantian rhetoric from Gayatri Spivak *Outside*. See her "Three Women's Texts and a Critique of Imperialism," especially 267–8.

17. Salman Rushdie, "Handsworth Songs," in *Imaginary Homelands* (London: Granta, 1991), 117. Rushdie's criticism of the film provoked a round of animated responses that ranged from Stuart Hall's condemnation of the author's "lofty, disdainful," and complacent attitude to Darcus Howe's defense of Rushdie's insistence on intimate and particular acts of narrativization. See *Guardian* (London), January 12, 15, 19, 1987.

18. Or, as Walter Benjamin has it, of discovering that "afterlife" moment in which "the original undergoes a change." See "The Task of the Translator," in *Illuminations* (ed. Hannak Arendt; New York: Harcourt Brace, 1968), 73.

The Economy of Appearances

*Anna Lowenhaupt Tsing**

the unemployed become murderers
        with uniforms and badges of rank
    vast forests are torn apart
It is necessary that I emphasize
        the problem of power
    that tends to turn people into bandits
                            – Pramoedya Ananta Toer, as reworked by Peter Dale Scott,
                                        in "Minding the Darkness"

Scale. Relative or proportionate size or extent.[1]

Indonesia's profile in the international imagination changed completely at the end of the 1990s. From the top of what was called a "miracle," Indonesia fell to the bottom of a "crisis." In the middle of what was portrayed as a timeless political regime, students demonstrated, and, suddenly, the regime was gone. So recently an exemplar of the promise of globalization, overnight Indonesia became the case study of globalization's failures.

The speed of these changes takes one's breath away – and raises important questions about globalization. Under what circumstances are boom and bust intimately related to each other? Might *deregulation* and *cronyism* sometimes name the same thing – but from different moments of investor confidence? Such questions run against the grain of economic expertise about globalization, with its discrimination between good and bad kinds of economic policy. Yet the whiggish acrobatics necessary to show how those very economies celebrated as miracles were simultaneously lurking crises hardly seem to tell the whole story. A less pious attitude toward the market may be necessary to consider the specificities of those political economies, like that of New Order Indonesia, brought into being together with international finance.[2]

This chapter brings us back to the months just before Indonesia so drastically changed, to canoe at the running edge of what turned out to be a waterfall. It concerns

*Originally published as "Inside the Economy of Appearances," pp. 55–77, 279–83 (notes and references) from A. Lowenhaupt Tsing, *Public Culture*, vol. 12. © 2000 by Duke University Press. All rights reserved. Used by permission of the publisher.

a set of incidents that can be imagined as a rehearsal for the Asian financial crisis as well as a minor participant in the international disillusion that led to the Suharto regime's downfall. In 1994, a small Canadian gold prospecting company announced a major find in the forests of Kalimantan. Over the months, the find got bigger and bigger, until it was biggest gold strike in the world, conjuring memories of the Alaskan Klondike and South Africa's Witwatersrand. Thousands of North American investors put their savings in the company called Bre-X. First-time investors and retired people joined financial wizards. Whole towns in western Canada invested (Eisler 1997). The new world of Internet investment blossomed with Bre-X. Meanwhile, Bre-X received continuous coverage in North American newspapers, especially after huge Canadian mining companies and Indonesian officials entered the fray, fighting over the rights to mine Busang, Bre-X's find.[3] The scandal of Indonesian business-as-usual, opened to public scrutiny as corruption, heightened international attention and garnered support for Bre-X. But, in 1997, just when expectation had reached a fevered pitch, Busang was exposed as barren: There was nothing there. Gasps, cries, and lawsuits rose from every corner. The Toronto Stock Exchange changed its rules to avoid more Bre-Xs.[4] Bre-X lawsuits set new international standards.[5] Several years later, Bre-X investors still hoped and complained across the Internet, as they peddled the remains of their experiences: jokes, songs, and stock certificates (as wallpaper, historical document, or irreplaceable art, ready to hang).[6] Meanwhile, Indonesian mining officials and copycat prospecting companies scrambled to free themselves from the Bre-X story, even as they reenacted its scenes, hoping to revive its investor enthusiasm.[7]

The Bre-X story exemplifies popular thinking about the pleasures and dangers of international finance and associated dreams of globalization. The story dramatizes north-south inequalities in the new capitalisms; it celebrates the north's excitement about international investment, and the blight of the south's so-called crony capitalisms: business imagined not quite/not white. Depicting southern leaders as rats fighting for garbage, the story also promises new genres of justice for the northern investor who dares to sue. Finance looks like democracy: The Internet, they say, opens foreign investment to the North American everyman. But the Bre-X story also narrates the perils of the downsized, overcompetitive economy: the sad entrepreneurship of selling worthless stock certificates. As one writer put it, mixing metaphors, "The Bre-X saga will come to be known as the demarcation of the Internet as the weapon of choice for investors" (Zgodzinski 1997).

Most salient to my concerns about the working of global capitalism is the genre convention with which Bre-X started its own story, and by which it was finished off. Bre-X was always a performance, a drama, a conjuring trick, an illusion, whether real gold or only the dream of gold ever existed at Busang. Journalists compared Busang, with its lines of false drilling samples, to a Hollywood set.[8] But it was not just Busang; it was the whole investment process. No one would ever have invested in Bre-X if it had not created a performance, a dramatic exposition of the possibilities of gold.

Performance here is simultaneously economic performance and dramatic performance. The "economy of appearances" I describe depends on the relevance of this pun; the self-conscious making of a spectacle is a necessary aid to gathering investment funds. The dependence on spectacle has not been peculiar to Bre-X and other mining scams:

It is a regular feature of the search for financial capital. Start-up companies must dramatize their dreams in order to attract the capital they need to operate and expand. Junior prospecting companies must exaggerate the possibilities of their mineral finds in order to attract investors so that they might, at some point, find something. This is a requirement of investment-oriented entrepreneurship, and it takes the limelight in those historical moments when capital seeks creativity rather than stable reproduction. In speculative enterprises, profit must be imagined before it can be extracted; the possibility of economic performance must be conjured like a spirit to draw an audience of potential investors. The more spectacular the conjuring, the more possible an investment frenzy. Drama itself can be worth summoning forth.[9] Nor are companies alone in the conjuring business in these times. In order to attract companies, countries, regions, and towns must dramatize their potential as places for investment. Dramatic performance is the prerequisite of their economic performance.

Yet conjuring is always culturally specific, creating a magic show of peculiar meanings, symbols, and practices. The conjuring aspect of finance interrupts our expectations that finance can and has spread everywhere, for it can only spread as far as its own magic. In its dramatic performances, circulating finance reveals itself as both empowered and limited by its cultural specificity.

Contemporary masters of finance claim not only universal appeal but also a global scale of deployment. What are we to make of these globalist claims, with their millennial whispers of a more total and hegemonic world-making than we have ever known? Neither false ideology nor obvious truth, it seems to me that the globalist claims of finance are also a kind of conjuring, a dramatic performance. In these times of heightened attention to the space and scale of human undertakings, economic projects cannot limit themselves to conjuring at different scales – they must conjure the scales themselves. In this sense, a project that makes us imagine globality in order to see how it might succeed is one kind of "scale-making project"; similarly, projects that make us imagine locality, or the space of regions or nations, in order to see their success are also scale-making projects. The scales they conjure come into being in part through the contingent articulations into which they are pushed or stumble. In a world of multiple, divergent claims about scales, including multiple, divergent globalisms, those global worlds that most affect us are those that manage tentatively productive linkages with other scale-making projects.

Analytic tools with which to think about the global picture are still rudimentary. Many ethnographers find ourselves with data about how a few people somewhere react, resist, translate, consume, and from here it is an easy step to invoke distinctions between local reactions and global forces, local consumption and global circulation, local resistance and global structures of capitalism, local translations and the global imagination. I find myself doing it. Yet we know that these dichotomies are unhelpful. They draw us into an imagery in which the global is homogeneous precisely because we oppose it to the heterogeneity we identify as locality. By letting the global appear homogeneous, we open the door to its predictability and evolutionary status as the latest stage in macronarratives. We know the dichotomy between the global blob and local detail isn't helping us. We long to find cultural specificity and contingency within the blob, but we can't figure out how to find it without, once again, picking out locality.

This chapter suggests that we address these dilemmas by giving attention to the making of *scale*. Scale is the spatial dimensionality necessary for a particular kind of view, whether up close or from a distance, microscopic or planetary. I argue that scale is not just a neutral frame for viewing the world; scale must be brought into being: proposed, practiced, and evaded, as well as taken for granted. Scales are claimed and contested in cultural and political projects. A "globalism" is a commitment to the global, and there are multiple, overlapping, and somewhat contradictory globalisims; a "region-alism" is a commitment to the region; and so on. Not all claims and commitments about scale are particularly effective. Links among varied scale-making projects can bring each project vitality and power. The specificity of these articulations and collaborations also limits the spread and play of scale-making projects, promising them only a tentative moment in a particular history. The performative dramas of financial conjuring offer one perspective from which to appreciate the specificity and contingency of particular niches within capitalist scale-making.

One of the chief puzzles of globalist financial conjuring is why it works. We've all seen ads for hamburgers, express mail, or computers bridging cultures across the globe. But it's one thing to offer a stylish picture of diversity, and another thing to figure out how entrepreneurial projects actually manage to affect people who may not pay them any mind. Conjuring is supposed to call up a world more dreamlike and sweeter than anything that exists; magic, rather than unsparing description, calls capital. The puzzle seems deeper the more the material and social worlds to be reshaped and exploited are geographically, culturally, and politically remote from financial conjuring centers. How do the self-consciously glossy and exaggerated virtual worlds conjured by eager collectors of finance become shapers of radically different peoples and places? My frame highlights contingent articulations in which globalist financial conjuring links itself with regional and national scale-making projects, making each succeed wildly – if also partially and tentatively. It seems likely that successfully conjuring the globe is possible, at least now, only in thick collaborations with regional and national conjurings; certainly financial conjuring has been deeply implicated in promises of making regional and national dreams come true.

Globalist conjuring sometimes supports the most bizarre and terrible of national and regional dreams. Certainly this was the case in the Bre-X story. Finance capital became linked with greedy elite dreams of an authoritarian nation-state supported by foreign funds and enterprises; this is a nation-making project I call franchise cronyism to mark the interdependence of corruption and foreign investment. These in turn became linked with migrant dreams of a regional frontier culture in which the rights of previous rural residents could be wiped out entirely to create a Wild West scene of rapid and lawless resource extraction: quick profits, quick exits. To present this rather complicated set of links, I offer a diagram (figure 77.1). Diagrams by their nature are oversimplifications, and this one is certainly no exception. To acknowledge this, I have named each of the three scale-making projects I discuss in a self-consciously joking manner. Yet the play-fulness is also a serious attempt to focus attention on the specificity and process of articulation. Finance capital is a program for *global* hegemony; franchise cronyism is one particular *nation*-making project; frontier culture is an articulation of a *region*. Each is a scale-snaking project with its sights set on a different scale: global, national, and

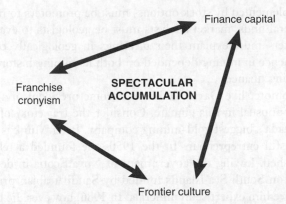

Figure 77.1   F-C Articulations in the Economy of Appearances. This diagram is both serious and a joke

regional. The links among them cross scales and strengthen each project's ability to remake the world. At the same time, none of these three projects is predictable or ubiquitous in the world. Coming together as they did for a moment, they created a great fire. Looking back on them now, we see they didn't create an evolutionary ladder to the stars. Isn't this sense of engagement and contingency what scholars and social commentators most need to bring into view?

"Yes, We Are Still in Business"

Bre-X was the brainchild of a Canadian stock promoter named David Walsh. Walsh dropped out of high school at the end of tenth grade and soon joined a Montreal trust company, rising quickly to become the head of the investment department. After thirteen years, Walsh left to try to form his own trust company. Three unsuccessful years later, he agreed to start an office in Calgary for another firm, only to quit the next year. From then on, Walsh worked to set up his own companies: first, the oil-oriented Bresea Resources Ltd. (named after his sons Brett and Sean), and then, in 1985, Bre-X Minerals Ltd., which from the first aimed to find gold.[10]

Gold mining had become a profitable industry in the 1970s, when the United States ended the Bretton Woods standard of fixed exchange rates, and the price of gold, which had been held constant at $35 per ounce for many years, skyrocketed, hitting $850 per ounce in 1980.[11] Canadian companies rushed to take advantage of the new gold prices by exploring not only in the Canadian West, but around the world. Junior mining exploration companies, whose goal is to find the minerals that can be exploited by major companies, sprouted by the dozens. Toronto became the world's mining finance capital. In 1997, there were 1,225 publicly traded mining companies in Canada, and mining stocks represented 21.5 percent of all trades on the Toronto Stock Exchange (Francis 1997: 24). In this industry, the line between various kinds of expertise is thin: geologists (with salaries supplemented by stock options) must be promoters to raise the money to finance their mineral finds, market analysts must be geologists to evaluate those finds, and stock promoters must explain their offerings in geologically convincing terms. Canadian preeminence in mining depended on both its mining history and its position as a center of mining finance.

For a stock promoter like David Walsh to become president of a gold exploration company was not unusual in this climate. Consider the trajectory of the president of Barrick Gold, Canada's biggest gold-mining company. Peter Munk is a high-flying but not always successful entrepreneur. In the 1950s, he founded a television and hi-fi company that crashed, leaving the government of Nova Scotia in deep debt; he went on to build hotels on South Sea islands funded by Saudi Arabian princes. Nothing in his background gave him expertise in minerals. In 1986, however, he bought a worked-over mine in Nevada. It turned out to be the most profitable gold mine in the world, pushing Munk's company into a leading position (Wells 1996). Peter Munk was "a dreamer who became a king" (Newman 1996). In this context, David Walsh's little enterprise made sense.

In 1988, Walsh listed Bre-X on the Alberta Stock Exchange at 30 Canadian cents per share. His wife Jeanette supported the household by working as a secretary. The family bought on credit, and, over C$200,000 in debt, both David and Jeanette Walsh declared personal bankruptcy in 1992. Bre-X shares sometimes fell as low as two cents; in his 1991 annual report, David Walsh wrote, "Yes, we are still in business." In 1993, however, Walsh pulled together some money for a trip to Indonesia. There he met Dutch-born geologist John Felderhof, who had achieved some fame in identifying the Ok Tedi copper and gold mine in Papua New Guinea in 1967, but suffered hard times in the 1980s. Felderof agreed to help Walsh find gold in Kalimantan and contacted Filipino geologist Michael de Guzman for the project. Filipino geologists had been in great demand in Indonesia because of their experience, education, and regional savvy.[12] De Guzman brought several Filipino associates to the team.[13]

Mining properties were cheap and available in Indonesia in the early 1990s because the Australians, who had come in some ten years before in their own wave of national mining speculation, were trying to get out. Felderhof had worked for some Australian companies and had witnessed the financial boom and bust in which mineral exploration was begun and then abandoned, promising or not. He convinced Walsh to form a partnership with an Indonesian entrepreneur to buy an old Australian claim around the creek called Busang in East Kalimantan, and Walsh raised the money to drill some holes. The results were disappointing, and by December 1993 they were about to close the property. Then, early in 1994, de Guzman struck gold. Walsh was quick and effective in informing investor newsletters and brokerage firms. Felderhof's estimates grew bigger and bigger. In 1993, Bre-X was trading at 51 Canadian cents a share; by May 1996, stocks were trading at C$286.50, accounting for a ten-to-one split. In April, Bre-X had been listed on the Toronto Stock Exchange; in August, the stock was listed in the United States on NASDAQ; in September, it was also listed on the Montreal Stock Exchange. By then the company's market capitalization was over C$6 billion (Goold and Willis 1997: 64–5). Awards started to roll in: Mining Man of the Year for Bre-X President David Walsh; Explorer of the Year for chief geologist John Felderhof. On

March 9 and 10, 1997, Bre-X officers and geologists were feted in awards dinners and ceremonies at the Prospectors and Developers Association of Canada meetings. They were at the height of their success.

Conjuring

On March 19, 1997, Michael de Guzman fell 800 feet from a helicopter into the rainforests of Kalimnantan. Although up to that point he had been considered little more than the Filipino sidekick, at the moment of his death, de Guzman became the company, his face displayed everywhere in the news media over charts of the company's finds and stock prices. If Bre-X had been a big story before, it was truly dramatic now.

Mysteries abounded. A suicide note was found in which de Guzman wrote that he couldn't stand the pain of hepatitis; but he was an optimistic man and in quite good health. What happened to the third man the other Filipino geologists had seen enter the helicopter? Rumors circulated like wildfire. One Philippines scholar confided to me, "When I heard about the watch found in the helicopter, I had to find out what kind it was. When they said 'Rolex,' I knew he was murdered. No Filipino gangster would dispose of his victim without first removing his Rolex." A sign, a trophy. The trouble was, the scene was cluttered with signs, clues, false leads. Wives of de Guzman who knew nothing of each others' existence cropped up everywhere: in Manila, Jakarta, Manado, Samarinda. Rumors circulated that de Guzman had parachuted into Zurich. When a corpse was finally found, the face and much of the body had been devoured by wild pigs. Multiple autopsies failed to establish the identity of the body beyond controversy: Could Bre-X have changed the fingerprint on his employee identity card? Did the dental records match? And where were his geologist friends when it was time for the funeral?[14]

It was at this period, too, that the gold deposit at Busang came to seem just as mysterious. Bre-X had been drilling core samples at Busang since 1993; by 1997, some sites looked like "Swiss cheese" (Hajari 1997). As Busang became famous, industry professionals came to visit. Bre-X President Walsh later complained, "Virtually every mining geologist, analyst went to the site, but I never received one letter or phone call during that whole period that something was amiss over in Indonesia" (*Calgary Sun*, October 12, 1997). The "analysts" Walsh refers to were mining stock analysts, and, indeed, dozens visited the site, each fueling investors' attraction with more glowing reports. But in March 1997, the US company Freeport McMoRan sent their assayors as the "due diligence" element of their agreement to become partners with Bre-X at Busang. Freeport found nothing. Furthermore, they claimed that the kind of gold in Bre-X's samples was inappropriate for the site: It was stream-rounded alluvial gold instead of igneous gold. Bre-X's assay methods were now open to question. Rumors flew of plots and coverups, and the price of Bre-X stocks roller-coasted. Perhaps Freeport was making false claims to take over the property. Perhaps Bob Hasan, an Indonesian partner, was buying up cheap stocks at a bargain-basement price. Why else had he taken out a bank loan to log just in this area, just at this time? Perhaps New York investors were trying to beat out Canadians. The gamble drew stock speculators into the fray and on April

2, the trading was so intense that it closed down the computer system at the Toronto Stock Exchange.[15] On May 3, however, the independent test report arrived. Its finding: *no* economic gold deposit. The ballooning stock swap immediately deflated; Bre-X stocks were officially worthless.[16] Yet what are we to make of the mysteries?

I am not a journalist, and my concern does not involve just which gold miners and which Indonesian government officials and which stock market participants knew about or participated in various conjuring acts. I'm more interested in the art of conjuring itself, as practiced not only by Bre-X officers and employees but also by the analysts, reporters, investors, and regulators who formed their retinue. I am struck by two counterintuitive observations. First, mystery, rumor, and drama did not come to Bre-X at the tail end of its ride; these qualities marked the Bre-X story from its beginnings. Rather than closing Bre-X down, mystery and drama kept Bre-X alive and growing; it was only when an official report stopped the show that the company died. Second, Bre-X is not the only company that has required spectacle to grow. Bre-X seems typical of the junior Canadian mineral exploration companies that it has helped usher into the international spotlight – except, of course, it was more successful at first and later more despised. Junior companies don't have the equipment or capital to take their mining ventures very far. They must make a big splash, first, to attract enough investors to keep prospecting, and, second, to bring in big mining companies to buy out their finds.

One can draw the net wider. The mystery and spectacle Bre-X cultivated is representative of many kinds of companies in which finance capital is the ruling edge of accumulation. Such companies draw investments through drama. And the importance of drama guarantees that it is very difficult to discern companies that have long-term production potential from those that are merely good at being on stage. The charismatic and dramatic attraction of international finance capital was a key feature of Southeast Asian development strategies during the "economic miracle." After the 1997 financial crisis, we were told to distinguish between the real and the fake, but does not the whole design of these accumulation strategies work against our ability to draw this line? As in a beauty contest, artistry and drama are necessary to compete; spectacle and mystery, playing equally across the line of the real and the fake, establish the winning reality of performance.[17]

Bre-X initially attracted investors because of the excitement of the reports coming out about Busang. From the very first, Bre-X was in the news, and journalists constantly wrote about Busang. The success with which Bre-X attracted investors depended on these reports, and particularly on the ways they used and elaborated tropes that brought the Bre-X find into other circulating stories of wealth, power, and fulfillment. Some of these stories were colonial adventure tales: the search for hidden, uncounted riches in remote places. *Maclean's*, a Canadian magazine, wrote: "Two, four, and then maybe six million ounces will be pulled from Busang annually. There has never been an El Dorado like this" (Wells 1997c: 40). Other stories told of frontier independence and the promise of wealth "at the end of a miner's rainbow," as the *New York Times* put it, where "independent-mindedness" led miners to "forbidding jungles" in search of the "century's greatest gold strike" (DePalma 1997: Al). There were stories of science in the service of human innovation. There were stories of war and conquest – "the battle for

Busang" – recalling the French and the United States in Vietnam, and Bre-X became, repeatedly, a "rumble in the jungle," and then, eventually, a "bungle" or a "jumble" in the jungle.[18]

There were also pervasive stories of underdog charisma. After announcing the Busang find, Bre-X had to fight for the rights to mine it. The story of little Bre-X up against the big North American mining companies and the big Indonesian establishment generated an overwhelming response, ushering in Bre-X's greatest period of popular investment. When US ex-President George Bush and Canadian ex-Prime Minister Brian Mulroney put pressure on Jakarta at the request of a big company, Bre-X's David Walsh, with his high school education, his beer belly, and his ineptness, looked like David up against Goliath. He made such a convincing "little guy" that after the scam was exposed, many refused to imagine him responsible. As *Fortune* magazine's reporter wrote, "Even now I have trouble believing that Walsh participated. . . . Walsh looked more like some poor schlemiel who had just won the lottery and couldn't locate his ticket" (Behar 1997: 123).

Stockholders, too, contributed to the stories swirling around Bre-X.[19] Bre-X established an Internet presence early on, with stories posted on their Web site; meanwhile, investors' chat lines buzzed with Bre-X news.[20] The more controversy swirled around Bre-X, the more investors talked and exchanged rumors, extending, too, dreams of wealth, conspiracy theories, reinterpretations of the mining geology and engineering, and romances of unexpected underdog advantage. On the Internet, dramatic presentation was often clearly the point. As one *Silicon Investor* contributor wrote about the Bre-X Internet thread, "The theater is open. The stage is set 24 hours a day. There is always an audience" (Zgodzinski 1997).

One Internet contributor signed herself "Ole49er," reminding readers that the Wild West is never far from discussion of Bre-X. A Canadian share-holder with whom I spoke explained that Canadians were excited about the chance to invest in minerals in Indonesia because of the symbolic importance of mining in Canada as well as a national anxiety about the closing of the frontier. Environmental regulations in Canada, he explained, made it difficult to mine profitably in the last wide open spaces of the Canadian West. Yet those open spaces might be pursued abroad in foreign lands. As a substitute frontier, Bre-X's Kalimantan continued the excitement of the frontier story of Canada's development.

But what of Kalimantan in this story? In the moment of frontier making, financial conjuring runs up against the landscape, but not quite as in its dreams. At this trick in the magic show, an opportunity presents itself to ask about how the magic works, and how it doesn't.

Frontiers

Let me return to the beginning of the Bre-X story, or, at least, *one* beginning, in Kalimantan. A brave man is hacking his way through the jungle, alone and surrounded by disease and danger. There is nothing there but mud, malaria, leeches, hepatitis, and the pervasive loneliness of the jungle trek. But one day . . . he discovers gold!

This is an old story, told not only about Borneo, but about many a jungle or lonely rock cliff. But it is also what the Bre-X miners told the press. According to the *Far Eastern Economic Review* (McBeth 1997: 42–3):

> The story of how Felderhof and de Guzman unearthed Busang's golden secret is the stuff that fables are made of. Mostly it is a human saga – about two quiet, very ordinary men from opposite sides of the world who persevered for years in the face of tropical illnesses and some of the harshest terrain in the world. . . .
>
> Felderhof first landed in Indonesia in 1980. . . . [H]e worked his way from west to east across the centre of the vast Borneo island. . . . Those were hard times. He lived in jungle villages, eating whatever was available, carrying what he needed on his back, and hacking his way through some of the remotest rain forest in Asia.
>
> De Guzman has gone through similar hardships. . . . He's had malaria 14 times since he met up with Felderhof in 1986. . . . Travelling alone, de Guzman took a seven-hour boat ride up the Mahakam River, then trekked 32 kilometers. . . . During a week of old-fashioned prospecting, he recognized a geological setting he had come to know well in the Philippines.

The story has come close to the moment of discovery. The *New York Times* tells that moment succinctly: "1994. Michael de Guzman, a mining geologist, is trekking through the Busang site doing work for Bre-X when a bit of yellow rock on a river bank catches his eye. 'Check it out,' he writes on a plastic strip and tacks it to the rock. His assistant follows with a more detailed analysis and writes: 'Checkmate'" (DePalma 1997: C10).

One might be suspicious of this sudden appearance from nowhere of an assistant, but let's let that pass and move on to the second act in the discovery, the scientific theory that lets the miners know that a glitter of gold might be the tip of an underground hoard. Without science, de Guzman is just a Filipino guy playing with rocks; with science, he is the translator between nature and North American industry.

> Working alone at 3 o'clock one morning, it suddenly became crystal clear [to de Guzman]. Bounding upstairs, he woke Puspos [the assistant] and explained his theory: that Busang, with its dome-like geological structure, lay at a fault-line crossroads. Together on that January morning, the two spent eight hours in "nonstop technical brainstorming." (McBeth 1997: 44)

It is a lovely story, but it bears a very odd relationship to everything else one might want to say about mining in Kalimantan. By the time de Guzman arrived at Busang, foreign prospectors, migrant miners, and local residents had all combed the landscape for gold. Yet his "discovery" story does not reflect the interdependence of his knowledge with that of other miners. Local residents, government regulations, mining camps, churches, markets, bus schedules, army officers, village heads, property disputes: all are missing. The frontier story requires that de Guzman wander alone on an empty landscape.

The story of lonely prospectors making independent discoveries in a remote jungle moved North American investors and stimulated the capital flow that made Bre-X rich.

These images are repeated in the portfolio of every North American prospecting company working in Kalimantan. Consider the exploration of a Canadian prospecting company called International Pursuit, as reported in *Gold Newsletter's Mining Share Focus*. International Pursuit was prospecting in the wake of the Bre-X drama and needed to distance itself from Bre-X. Yet the frontier story is precisely the same. The company has sent its prospectors to the empty, wild landscape of Kalimantan, where, through a combination of luck and science, they stumble on precious metals. They are especially in luck because in late 1997 the devastation brought about by El Niño drought and forest fires had given the landscape some of the wild loneliness of which they dreamed. El Niño, they say, was a godsend because the streams dried up, revealing hidden minerals. "[I]t was as if Mother Nature had lifted a curtain, exposing tie secrets below" (Lundin 1998: 4). Ignoring local residents' hunger, fire damage, smoke inhalation, and displacement, he bragged, "International Pursuit's exploration teams were among the relative few left on the ground" (ibid.).

I first began to think about gold mining because of the spread of desolation and wildness across large swathes of the Kalimantan landscape. A new landscape had developed in resource extraction areas: Quiet scenes of forests, fields, and houses had become wild terrains of danger, urgency, and destruction. The mad rush for gold joined and stimulated mad rushes for logs, birds' nests, incense woods, marble, and even sand.

Three developments were essential to this transformation of the terrain. First, big and small entrepreneurs were interdependent. Transnational companies and transregional migrants from all over Indonesia complemented each other. In mining, big companies have official permits; independent miners are illegal. Independent miners lead company prospectors to the best spots. The companies displace them but then employ them for prospecting. The companies complain about the illegals, blaming them for environmental problems, thus protecting their own reputations. The illegals supply everyday services for the companies. The companies follow the small miners and the small miners cluster around the companies; they become codependents.

Second, nature had to be made into loot, free for all. In the 1980s, logging companies worked hard to extinguish local rights to resources. "This place belongs to Indonesia, not to you," the logging bosses said when residents complained. The military followed and supported their claims, creating an authoritarian lawlessness that made resources free for those who could take them. By the mid-1990s, local residents said, "We still know our customary rights, but no one cares about them." The roads invited migrants. Violence became key to ownership. Swarming miners escalated the terror, the risk, and the urgency of taking everything out, right away.

Third, frontier migrants arrived at the end of long chains of culture and capital. Small miners rarely owned the hydraulic pumps with which they removed topsoil; they contracted them from urban entrepreneurs in profit-sharing arrangements. Often, they subcontracted with local residents, dividing imagined profits even further. Migrants and local residents learned to share cultural practices of entrepreneurship that reached from distant cities deep into the forest. Local residents brought mining activities up the rivers, through their familiar forests, close to home, spreading frontier standards of rapid resource extraction. They have been drawn into the competition and violence of frontier relationships, taking on even the superficial trappings of migrant-oriented subsistence. In these entrepreneurial chains, a spreading frontier culture is created. It is a culture dedicated to the obliteration of local places, local land and resource rights, and local knowledges of flora and fauna. The makeshift camps of the miners proliferate across the landscape, mixing migrants and local residents in an anti-local regionality in which commitment to the local landscape is as useless as the gravel residue left after gold has been picked out and taken away.

Frontier culture is a conjuring act because it creates the wild and spreading regionality of its imagination. It conjures a self-conscious translocalism, committed to the obliteration of local places. Such commitments are themselves distinctive and limited – and thus "local" from another perspective. Yet they break with past localisms in self-conscious regionalism. This is a conjuring of scale, and frontier resource extraction relies on it.

A distinctive feature of this frontier regionality is its magical vision; it asks participants to see a landscape that doesn't exist, at least not yet. It must continually erase old residents' rights to create its wild and empty spaces where *discovering* resources, not stealing them, is possible. To do so, too, it must cover up the conditions of its own production. Consider the contrasts between the features of the story of the frontier that must be told and the frontier conditions I observed: The lone prospector replaces swarming migrants and residents, searching the landscape. The excitement of scientific discovery replaces the violence of expropriation as local resource rights are extinguished and armed gangs enforce their preeminence. The autonomy of the prospector's find replaces the interdependent negotiations of big companies and illegal miners, each leading the other to new sites and trading political and material assets as they form complementary players.[21]

Why does the frontier story have any power at all, considering what it erases? How can it imagine the Kalimantan landscape so wrongly? These *trompe l'oeils* became possible because of national discipline: the violence of the military, which spreads a regional lawlessness; the legal regulations that privileged company rights and profits yet allowed illegal migrants to accumulate in the spreading wildness; the confusion between private entrepreneurship and public office that forged the national government. This is not the only kind of nation-making that can exist. To explore its specificity, it is useful to turn our attention to CoWs.

CoWs

CoWs are Contracts of Work. No mining company can extract minerals in Indonesia without one. Like animals, CoWs come in generations. The first CoW was a much revered and singular ancestor, granted to Louisiana's Freeport McMoRan to mine in West Papua.[22] Succeeding generations of CoWs have become more differentiated, more limited, and more finely detailed.[23] Yet as they develop, they continue to be icons, even fetishes, held up to show the relationship between the Indonesian nation and the world. Ideally, they guarantee that resource extraction activities work in the interests of the Indonesian nation as well as the mining company. They specify the conditions that create mutual benefits shared between the nation and its foreign investors.

CoWs have been magical tools of the national elite. Although merely paper and ink, they conjured a regular income for the Indonesian nation-state. Their terms must be secure and attractive by international standards, or they will not draw capital. But if they meet these standards, they can conjure the funds that allow the nation-state to produce itself as what one might call a "miracle nation": a nation in which foreign funds support the authoritarian rule that keeps the funds safe. I have called this "franchise cronyism." In exchange for supplying the money to support the national leaders who can make the state secure, investors are offered the certainties of the contract, which ensures title to mineral deposits, fixes taxation rates, and permits export of profit.

The CoW guarantees that investors are not working with "dictators." As one Canadian Bre-X investor explained to me, in investing his modest funds he always avoided the countries of dictators. This was the reason the Bre-X investment seemed reasonable. I was confused: What is a dictator? As we talked, I realized that a dictator is a foreign ruler who interferes with Canadian investment. Indonesia's President Suharto was not a dictator, at least before Bre-X. As Bre-X president David Walsh put it, his company – like other Australian and Canadian mining companies in the 1980s and 1990s – targeted Indonesia "by virtue of its geological setting, favorable investment climate and political stability" (Wells 1997c: 42).

Other nations could be and were imagined in Indonesia. Suharto's New Order emerged violently in 1966 from an earlier scene of diverse and competitive programs for making the nation, and from the start the regime depended on the repression of other Indonesian national visions through censorship and militarization. Political quietude was nurtured, too, through internationally sponsored "development," which came to refer to programs of state expansion dedicated to convincing diverse local people of the unified national standards of state power. Through "development," the state conceived a legal framework to claim the nation's resources and make them available for foreign expropriation, thus amassing the materials through which its version of the nation could prosper.

When investment capital began to circulate wildly across national boundaries in the 1980s, the Indonesian elite was ready for it. They beckoned to the mining sector, saying: "There are still vast tracts of unexplored land in Indonesia. For those who dare to venture, Indonesia offers immense possibilities."[24] The Australians came. One Indonesian ex-mining official candidly admitted that these were "irresponsible investments" with "rubbish technology." When the Canadian companies followed in the 1990s, it was more of the same: "It's a repetition of history. It's not really a gold rush. It's rather a stock market rush."[25] Yet the government transformed the stock market rush into a gold rush by offering it regional frontiers in the making. The regime gave the companies Contracts of Work, despite their irresponsibility. The CoWs wrote away local rights. Military men deployed to enforce CoWs felt encouraged to start their own entrepreneurial schemes, creating a model of government in which administrators by definition doubled as entrepreneurs who, supported by kickbacks, freed up resources for investors, including themselves. Civil servants became franchise entrepreneurs too, learning to conjure the miracle nation locally. It was they who sanctioned the mass migration of illegal small loggers and miners that kept the regional economy afloat while bigger investors took out bigger resources and profits. In this escalating mobility and lawlessness, the mysteries of the search for buried treasure became possible. Whether there was gold or not, the economy could grow, spurred on by fabulous dreams.

By the 1990s, the Suharto regime began to take for granted its domestic stability and international support. The work of disguising official kickbacks as sound investment policy seemed already complete. Perhaps this will help to explain how the set performance of the miracle nation could have been allowed to deteriorate into dramatic excess. Drama ultimately embarrassed the Suharto regime, allowing investors to label it corrupt. At the same time, it provided a moment of opportunity for investors, who could maneuver within the new embarrassments of national performance to gain a better position for themselves. No investors did better than Bre-X and its rivals in opening up those dramatic cracks and making them visible on international news screens. However unself-conscious the manipulation, it seems clear that the over-the-top drama of franchise cronyism set off around Bre-X allowed the Bre-X investment bubble to last far longer than it could have otherwise, drawing out the drama from the 1994 announcement of gold to the 1997 death of de Guzman. This drama popularized the Bre-X story, vastly enlarging investment.

In January 1994 Barrick Gold offered to buy a stake in Bre-X. Barrick was involved in an aggressive campaign of acquisitions in an attempt to become the world's biggest gold mining company. As mentioned previously, Barrick's CEO, Peter Munk, was a risk taker who had made his fortune from the lucky purchase of a Nevada mine, which turned out to be a fabulous mother lode. Furthermore, Barrick had targeted Indonesia as a possible site for high-profit, low-cost mining. Bre-X's Busang was just Barrick's kind of buy (Goold and Willis 1997: 99–100).

When Bre-X turned him down, Barrick moved into the cracks of the Indonesian regime, working the connection between greed and vulnerability that their nation-making performances had themselves produced. The high-powered politicians on Barrick's advisory board pressured due minister of mines and energy, and even President Suharto.[26] Barrick then approached the president's daughter Tutut, a tycoon in road construction contracts. Barrick offered her Busang's construction contracts, and she pushed the minister of mines to negotiate a Barrick Bre-X split in which the government would control 10 percent of the mine, Barrick 70 percent, and Bre-X 20 percent. Bre-X was vulnerable because they had begun drilling without a CoW; now the ministry pulled out even their temporary exploration permit to clinch the deal (Wells 1997c).

Bre-X stockholders went wild with anger. In the glare of their dissatisfaction, the drama escalated. Placer Dome, another Canadian company, made a better bid.[27] Meanwhile, Bre-X made a spectacular play by approaching the president's son, Sigit, and offering him 10 percent of the mine plus an eye-catching $1 million per month to push their case. Whether naive, as read at the time, or unimaginably clever, this move took the performance of franchise cronyism to its extreme limits, offering the investment drama a new life. Now Suharto's children were pitted against each other publicly.

Barrick continued to have government support until it gained a new opponent: entrepreneur Bob Hasan, the long-time friend and golfing buddy of the president, and the man who best knew how to mimic foreign investors' ploys to enlarge his own empire. Hasan played the patriot of the miracle nation, arguing passionately that the enrichment and empowerment of national elites is the first principle of national interest. Barrick irritated him by sending in North American politicians, and he railed against their "cow-boyisms," which made Indonesia look helpless under the American thumb.[28] Mean-while, too, he managed to acquire a 50 percent share in Bre-X's Indonesian partner.[29]

The game was almost over when President Suharto asked Bob Hasan to work out a solution for Bre-X, and yet, this too was a moment of momentous drama. Bre-X stock-holders were at the edge of their seats. Activist stockholder George Chorny wrote a public letter to Hasan, reminding him that it was Bre-X that discovered the gold. "It's not any of the guys at Barrick or Placer. It's not the Indonesian government. All the Indonesian government did was to welcome the people of Bre-X to come into their country with open arms to explore this jungle, this desolate jungle in the middle of nowhere" (Wells 1997b). For Chorny, the frontier is always already empty. But Hasan had a different perspective; making the frontier was a national responsibility. Hasan dismissed both Barrick and Placer Dome and brought in the regime's favorite company, Freeport McMoRan. In Hasan's solution, Freeport McMoRan would take 15 percent of the mine and become sole operator; the Indonesian government would take 10 percent; Hasan's companies would take 30 percent; and the remaining 45 percent would remain with Bre-X. Backed into a corner, Bre-X signed gracefully.[30]

Freeport, unlike Bre-X and even Barrick, was not in the business of spectacular accumulation, the economy of appearances. Freeport worked with its own cultural logic of investment and development, which, at least at this period, differed from that of Bre-X. Freeport was no mining junior, amassing capital to finance further exploration. Instead, it had established itself as a big, solid outpost of "American civilization" in Indonesia. As CEO Jim Bob Moffett put it, "We are thrusting a spear of economic development into the heartland of Irian Jaya [West Papua]" (Marr 1993: 71). Freeport built residential neighborhoods in West Papua reminiscent of US suburbs; Moffett performed Elvis Presley imitations during Christmas visits. Freeport's culture of business, then, offered Americanization rather than "frontier discovery" as a model of profitability.

Freeport had long since gained its miracle deal from the Suharto regime. Its personal Contract of Work far exceeded the benefits of all other investors. In turn, Freeport was the largest source of investor tax revenue for the Indonesian government. It had spent an enormous amount of money developing its Grasberg mine in West Papua, where it depended on the army to keep local residents in line. In 1995, however, riots closed the mine; in 1996, West Papuan tribal leaders sued the company for environmental destruc-tion and human rights abuses, and the Overseas Private Investment Corporation (an agency of the US government) cancelled the company's risk insurance because of its environmental policies. In 1997, then, Freeport was busy hiving down international accusations of environmental and social irresponsibility in West Papua. It needed a green profile and solid production results, not an economic miracle.[31] In this spirit, Freeport sent in a sober team to assess the gold at Busang. There was nothing there. "It makes me sick every time I think about it," said Jim Bob Moffett, Freeport's CEO (Behar 1997: 128). After a few most impressive last gasps, the spectacle wound down and collapsed. Said Bre-X President David Walsh, "Four and a half years of hard work and the pot at the end of the rainbow is a bucket of slop" (*Calgary Sun*, October 12, 1997).[32]

On Spectacular Accumulation

What does this story allow us to learn about transnational finance and its globalist aspirations? In the midst of their dramatic roles, the major players usefully remind us of the stage they have laid. Like Bob Hasan, I am struck by the North American character of the dreams and schemes of investment that swirled around Bre-X. With Bre-X stockholders, I marvel at the ability of Indonesian nation makers to usurp an economic process that has been imagined as so independent from national controls. And as for the Kalimantan landscape, it is hard not to mourn: The pot at the end of the rainbow is a bucket of eroding mud, damaged forests, and mercury-poisoned rivers. Slop indeed.

It was the Canadian imagination of the combined frontier of investment and mining that made this drama possible. The mining industry has been historically important to Canada's economy and identity. By the 1980s, its locus had shifted from mining *in* Canada to mining *for* Canada. It represented opportunity, initiative, and the potential prosperity in national character. Bre-X's run from the bottom of the Alberta stock exchange to the top of the Toronto exchange and into the world was a source of pride for many Canadians. As much as for profits, Canadians invested for reasons of national pride.[33]

Yet the national specificity of attraction to investments disappears in the excitement of commitments to globalism in the financial world. When one thinks about finance in the Bre-X case, there was nothing worldwide about it at all; it was Canadian and US investment in Indonesia. Yet it was easy to assimilate this specific trajectory of investment to an imagined globalism to the extent at the global is defined as the opening-up process in which remote places submit to foreign finance. Every time finance finds a new site of engagement, we think that the world is getting more global. In this act of conjuring, *global* becomes the process of finding new sites. In the force field of this particular globalism, Canadian national dreams are reimagined as transcendent, circulating, beyond culture.

Despite the enormous coercions and seductions of financiers, which aim to make the whole world ready for investment, there is great particularity not only in the reasons a Canadian might want to invest but also in places where he or she can invest. In the 1990s, when the dreams of the Indonesian elite linked with those of Canadians to jointly conjure the promise of gold, Indonesia became one of those places. Images of remote wild places that could make independent-minded Canadians rich and free touched Indonesian visions of a miracle nation, a nation that could come into being in the arms of foreign finance. Flying in the face of financiers' fantasies of making the nation disappear for the greater mobility of capital, the magic of the miracle nation, waving its CoWs, asserted itself as the only door to North American investment. CoWs, as I have argued, are not merely mechanical adjustments of economic affairs. They are fetish objects, charged with conjuring the miracle nation in the face of competing alternative visions, which unless warded off might come to control the apparatus of the state. From investors' perspectives, they are charged, too, with the security of profit and property. As a gift, they remake the identities of both giver and receiver, vitalizing the miracle nation and its globalist speculators.

For the aspirations of international investors and national elites to emerge as more than a moment's daydream, however, they must be made tangible on a regional landscape. They must engage people, places, and environments. The anti-local culture of Kalimantan frontier regionalism nurtured and raised up both the miracle nation and Canadian speculation. Here is a truly cosmopolitan scene, where varied dreams are jumbled together, naming and renaming creeks, valleys, routes, and towns. The dreamers jostle, fight bitterly, and patronize each other. As they make their own new places, these too are knocked away. Old residents become aliens as the familiar landscape is transformed by trauma, danger, and the anxiety of the unknown. Here mystery can flourish, and unexpected discoveries can be made. Unimagined riches can be found because the layout of wealth and poverty is unsettled, un-imagined. Impossible promises cannot be ignored. On this landscape, the economy of appearances seems so real that it must be true.

When the spectacle passes on, what is left is rubble and mud, the residues of success and failure. People with other stakes and stories will have to pick up the pieces.

At the intersection of projects for making globes, nations, and regions, new kinds of economies can emerge. In the Bre-X drama, globalist commitments to opening up fresh sites for Canadian mining investments enabled Indonesian visions of a miracle nation at the same time as they stimulated the search for mining frontiers. The program of the miracle nation offered speculators security as it also forced potential frontier regions into lawless violence and abolished customary tenure. When Kalimantan responded by developing a wild frontier, its regional reformation confirmed the proprietary rights of the miracle nation. The Kalimantan frontier could then appeal to globalist speculation, offering a landscape where both discovery and loss were possible. Three scale-making projects came into conjunction here: the globe-making aspirations of finance capital; the nation-making coercions of franchise cronyism; and the region-making claims of frontier culture (see figure 77.1). Globalist, nationalist, and regionalist dreams linked to enunciate a distinctive economic program, the program of spectacular accumulation.

Spectacular accumulation occurs when investors speculate on a product that may or may not exist. Investors are looking for the appearance of success. They cannot afford to find out if the product is solid; by then their chances for profit will be gone. To invest in software development requires this kind of leap: Software developers sell their potential, not their product. Biotechnology requires a related if distinctive leap of faith to trust the processes of innovation and patenting to yield as-yet-unknown property rights and royalties. Real estate development requires an assessment of desirability and growth, not demonstrated occupancy; it sells investors attractiveness. In each of these cases, economic performance is conjured dramatically.[34]

I use the term *spectacular accumulation* mainly to argue with evolutionary assumptions in popular theories of the ever-changing world economy. According to regulation theorists, "flexible accumulation" is the latest stage of capitalism. Flexible accumulation follows Fordist production as barbarism follows savagery, that is, up a singular political-economic ladder. David Harvey's writing (1989) has made this conceptualization influential among anthropologists, who suggest correlated changes in culture, spatiality, and scale to go along with this evolutionary progression. Thus, too, scholars imagine evolutionary changes in the making of space and time. Theories of globalization have us imagine a worldwide condensation of space and time in which spaces grow smaller and times more instantaneous and effortless. Consider, however, the space-time requirements of Bre-X's spectacular accumulation: Space is hugely enlarged; far from miniature and easy, it becomes expansive, labored, and wild, spreading muddy, malarial frontiers.

Time is quickened but into the rush of acceleration, not the efficiency of quick transfers. It is not effortless; if you can't feel the rush and the intensity, you are missing the point, and you'll keep your money at home. Moreover, this spectacular accumulation does not call out to be imagined as new. It is self-consciously old, drawing us back to the South Sea bubble and every gold rush in history. In contrast with flexible accumulation, its power is not its rejection of the past, but its ability to keep this old legacy untarnished.

This is more than yet another classificatory device in the annals of capitalism. My point is to show the heterogeneity of capitalism at every moment in time. Capitalist forms and processes are continually made and unmade; if we offer singular predictions we allow ourselves to be caught by them as ideologies. This seems especially pressing in considering the analysis of scale. Since the 1990s, every ambitious world-making project has wanted to show itself able to forge new scales. Nongovernmental organizations, ethnic groups and coalitions, initiatives for human rights and social justice: We all want to be creative and self-conscious about our scale-making. We want to claim the globe as ours. In this context, rather than ally myself with globalist financiers to tell of *their* globe, I trace how that globe comes into being both as a culturally specific set of commitments and as a set of practices. The investment drama of the Bre-X story shows how articulations among globalist, nationalist, and regionalist projects bring each project to life. [. . .] The particularity of globalist projects, I am arguing, is best seen in the contingent articulations that make them possible and bring them to life: These are "aphids," Articulations among Partially Hegemonic Imagined Different Scales.

Often we turn to capitalism to understand how what seem to be surface developments form part of an underlying pattern of exploitation and class formation. Yet before we succumb to the capitalist monolith called up in these analyses, it is useful to look at the continual emergence of new capitalist niches, cultures, and forms of agency. For this task, Stuart Hall's idea about the role of articulation in the formation of new political subjects is helpful (1996). New political subjects form, he argues, as pre-existing groups link and, through linking, enunciate new identities and interests. Social processes and categories also can develop in this way. I have used this insight to trace the spectacular accumulation brought into being by the articulation of finance capital, franchise cronyism, and frontier culture. While each of these linked projects achieved only a moment of partial hegemony, this was also a moment of dramatic success.

Soon after the story I have told, Indonesia precipitously collapsed as a celebrated site for investment; the miracle nation was discredited, and the articulation fell apart. Afterward, analysts scrambled to tell the difference between good and bad investments. They recognized that the Busang saga had contributed in a small way to the Indonesian crash. But they ignored or refused its allegorical quality: Bre-X offered a dramatic rendition of the promises and perils of the economic miracle attributed, in Indonesia and beyond, to globalization.[35]

How might scholars take on the challenge of freeing critical imaginations from the specter of neoliberal conquest – singular, universal, global? Attention to the frictions of contingent articulation can help us describe the effectiveness, and the fragility, of emergent capitalist – and globalist – forms. In this shifting heterogeneity there are new sources of hope, and, of course, new nightmares.

Notes

1. *Oxford English Dictionary*, 2d ed. s.v. "scale."
2. As much as any place in the world, Indonesia rode high on the wave of enthusiasm for mobile, finance-driven international investment in the 1980s and early 1990s. Between the late 1980s and 1997, economic growth averaged about 8 percent per year, and in early 1997, for economists, "there was little sign of the turmoil that was to emerge" when the economy crashed and the Suharto regime followed in 1998 (McLeod 1999: 209). Looking back, many once-enthusiastic analysts blamed the crisis on "cronyism," residual protectionism, and bad national regulatory practices. See, e.g., Jackson (1999).
3. From the first, the Bre-X story caught the popular imagination, especially in Canada, and thousands of articles have been written about it. Most major Canadian newspapers covered the story in detail; *The Calgary Sun, The Calgary Herald*, and the *Ottawa Citizen* have had many installments of Bre-X news. Only rather late in the game did US newspapers cover the Bre-X story regularly, but at the height of its fame and infamy, much of the media across North America covered the story. Indonesian newspapers and news magazines also offered considerable coverage. Indonesian nongovernmental organizations added their perspectives in flyers and newsletters. Several books have been published about Bre-X, mainly by journalists. Francis (1997) and Goold and Willis (1997) tell the story with lively excitement. Danielson and Whyte (editor and staff writer, respectively, for *The Northern Miner*) offer their expertise on the people and politics of the mining scene (1997). Bondan Winarno's (1997) account includes useful detail on Indonesian politics and texts of a number of Bre-X documents. Jennifer Well's coverage for the Canadian news magazine *Macleans* and John McBeth's coverage for the *Far Eastern Economic Review* have also been very informative. John Behar (1997) offers a useful description of Bre-X's operations. Internet investor chat lines with Bre-X "threads" offer a wealth of both technical information and personal views on the drama.
4. For discussion of these issues, see *CFRA News Talk Radio*, August 20, 1998.
5. Bre-X lawsuits had their own website, the Bre-X/Bresea Shareholder Class Action Information Website. Key issues involved the liability of stock exchanges as well as Bre-X officials (Francis 1999); the ability of Canadians to participate in US class-action lawsuits (*Daily Mining News*, March 31, 1999); and the nationwide (vs. provincial) scope of Canadian class action lawsuits (Rubin 1999).
6. The Bre-Xscam.com website peddled jokes, news, and art about the Bre-X saga on their "Bungle in the Jungle" web page. A Canadian stockholder named Ross Graham recorded a song called "The Bre-X Blues" and made the CD available for sale on the *Red Deer Advocate* web page. He claims to have made back his losses on Bre-X investment through selling these CDs (*Breaking News*, December 22, 1998).

7. Junior companies prospecting for gold in Kalimantan with "post-Bre-X" advertising of their claims include Kalimantan Gold Corporation (Vancouver); Twin Gold Corporation (Toronto); and Nevada Manhattan Mining Inc. (Calabasas, CA). See *GFRA News Talk Radio*, March 20, 1999.

8. See, e.g., Behar (1997: 121).

9. To "conjure" is both to call forth spirits and to perform magical tricks; in each case, the term highlights the intentionality of the performance, the studied charisma of the performer, and the hope of moving the audience beyond the limits of rational calculation. These features characterize the economic strategies I discuss here, in which everyday performance requirements – for contracts, marketing, reports, and the like – are made into dramatic shows of potential.

10. This version of the much-told story is taken from Goold and Willis (1997).

11. *The Privateer Gold Pages* (www.the-privateer.com/gold.html) reviews the recent history of government, interstate, and private uses and prices of gold.

12. The importance of Filipino geologists in Indonesian mining highlights the national and regional cultural demands of the industry, which, like other industries, operates through stereotypes about the appropriate cultural specifications of labor power. Goold and Willis (1997: 170) write, "The Filipinos have their own culture in the mining world. They are well-educated and often trained at big US-owned mines in the Philippines. They are fun-loving, attuned to Western tastes and sensibilities, yet Asian." Meanwhile, the resentment of Indonesian professionals toward the access of Filipinos to Indonesian projects makes them easy scapegoats when things go wrong. Bondan Winarno says Indonesian geologists use the term "Filipino Mafiosi" (1997: 164).

13. This version draws on Goold and Willis (1997).

14. Wives: Waldman and Solomon (1997); parachute rumors: *The Ottawa Citizen* March 25, 1997. The autopsy results are discussed in *The Ottawa Citizen*, April 10, 1997; Platt (1997a, 1997b, 1997c, 1997d, 1997e). Winarno (1997: 134–35) discusses the theory that de Guzman wore false teeth while the corpse had natural teeth.

15. Bob Hasan rumors: Warmington 1997a, 1997b; New York investors: Warmington 1997c. April 2 trading: Jala 1997.

16. Strathcona Mineral Services conducted the independent technical audit. In the words of the report: "We very much regret having to express the firm opinion that an economic gold deposit has not been identified in the Southeast zone of the Busang property, and is unlikely to be. We realize that the conclusions reached in this interim report will be a great disappointment to the many investors, employees, suppliers, and the joint-venture partners associated with Bre-X, to the Government of Indonesia, and to the mining industry elsewhere. However, the magnitude of the tampering with core samples that we believe has occurred and resulting falsification of assay values at Busang, is of a scale and over a period of time and with a precision that, to our knowledge, is without precedent in the history of mining anywhere in the world" (Farquarson 1997: 27).

17. McLeod (1999) gives considerable weight to the Bre-X affair in bringing on the Indonesian financial crisis by undermining investor confidence. He writes, "Perhaps the most significant recent event to crystallize attitudes on the part of the general public, the intellectual and business elite, and the foreign investment community regarding the direction in which government had been heading was the so-called Busang saga" (215). In my view, the Bre-X saga became important because it *dramatized* issues of what came to be called, following Philippine precedent from the 1980s, "crony capitalism."

18. Rumble: Wells 1997a; bungle: Bre-Xscam.com; jumble: Platt 1997f.

19. Goold and Willis (1997: 207) write about the Canadian scene: "Because so many small investors held Bre-X stock, virtually everyone knew someone who had won or lost money. Their stories, often exaggerated, played out across the country. In this environment, any rumour had legs."

20. "On Silicon's popular net forum Techstox, Bre-X dominated for months. More than 4,000 new people a day were searching for Bre-X information, and more than 700 items were being posted about the company for all to read" (Francis 1997: 153).

21. Personal narratives of frontier gold discovery often give more clues to the interdependence of company miners and independent gold seekers than official discovery tales. Bre-X geologists were quite willing to admit, informally, that they chose their prospecting sites through the advice of small-scale Kalimantan miners, who led them to gold-rich sites. Consider, for example, the narrative Bre-X chief geologist Felderhof told reporters about how he first found Busang: "Felderhof had first heard of Busang in the early 1980s, when he and his Australian colleague Mike Bird were exploring the logging roads of Borneo on rented motorcycles. They roared from village to village, asking the locals to point out where they had found gold nuggets in stream beds" (Goold & Willis 1997: 36). Indeed, one of the earliest clouds of suspicion about the rich "southeast zone" of Busang was generated by the fact that small-scale miners did not pan for gold in this area (Danielson & Whyte 1997: 197). Despite acknowledging this interdependence, it never occurred to the geologists that it might interfere with their personal rights – or their official stories – of "discovery."

22. In April 1967, Freeport Indonesia was granted a tax holiday, concessions on normal levies, exemption from royalties, freedom in the use of foreign personnel and goods, and exemption from the requirement for Indonesian equity. The terms were changed slightly in 1976, cancelling the remaining 18 months of the tax holiday and allowing the Indonesian government to purchase an 8.5 percent share (Soesastro & Sudarsono 1988).

23. More restrictive second-generation and less restrictive third-generation CoWs were introduced in 1968 and 1976, respectively. 1986–7 marked the Australian "gold rush" in Indonesia and introduced fourth-generation CoWs, with "one year of general survey ending with 25% relinquishment of concession area; three years of exploration with 75% relinquishment by the end of the fourth year; an Indonesian partner in the CoW; and equity divestment after five years of operation so that ideally after 10 years of production the local partner holds 51%" (Marr 1993: 16). Fifth-generation contracts began in 1990, with tax incentives and low tariff property taxes. A 1992 law required foreign investors in frontier areas to reduce their equity shares to a maximum of 95 percent within five years and to 80 percent within 20 years (Marr 1993: 17). Sixth-generation CoWs, requiring environmental impact assessments, were offered in 1997 (Winarno 1997: 28).

24. Dr. Soetaryo Sigit, ex-Director General of Mines, "Current Mining Developments in Indonesia," quoted in Marr (1993: 26).

25. Rachman Wiriosudarmo, quoted by Wells (1997a: 41).

26. US ex-president Bush wrote Suharto to express his "highly favorable" impression of Barrick (Wells 1997c).

27. By this time, it was clear to all the players that the Indonesian government was calling the shots. Placer Domne sent their bid directly to the president (McBeth & Solomon 1997).

28. Hasan's perspective was developed in a context in which other Indonesians were calling for greater national control of Busang. Amien Rais, for example, argued that the gold "should be kept for our grandchildren in the 21st century" (cited in Francis 1997: 130). Winarno (1997: 84–94) details nationalist claims.

29. Hasan's investments during is period are detailed in McBeth and Solomon (1997).

30. Bre-X President David Walsh said he was setting with an arrangement that reflected "Indonesia's political, economic, and social environment" (Borsuk 1997).

31. The history of Freeport McMoran is the subject of a forthcoming book by journalist Robert Bryce and anthropologist Steven Feld. For issues above, see Francis (1997: 129); Goold and Willis (1997: 113–14). Marr (1993) details Freeport's West Papuan operations, with special attention to the mine's history of environmental problems and human rights abuses.

32. David Walsh died of a stroke on June 4, 1998. He had spent the last months of his life fighting class action suits and trying to clear his name (Rubin 1998).

33. The importance of small, popular investment in Bre-X highlights the importance of this national agenda. "At its peak in May 1996, 70 percent of Bre-X's 240 million shares were in the hands of individual investors" (Goold & Willis 1997: 239). This compares to a more ordinary Canadian company, which might have 30 percent of its shares owned by individuals. In 1996, according to Goold and Willis (1997: 105), Bre-X had 13,000 shareholders, including pension funds and insurance companies. According to Francis (1997: 199), about 5 percent of Bre-X trading was from outside Canada. 90 percent of all Bre-X trading was conducted on the Toronto Stock Exchange (Francis 1997: 197).

34. It is possible to make a great deal of money from speculation even if the product comes to nothing. Bre-X shareholders made money merely by selling their shares while the price was still high. The outspoken investors Greg and Kathy Chorny, for example, sold two-thirds of their stock for C$40 million and lost a comparatively minor sum on remaining shares (Francis 1997: 196). At the end, smart investors made money by "short selling," that is, borrowing Bre-X shares from brokers, selling them, and returning them by buying them back at a lower price. Goold and Willis (1997: 221) report that 5.5 million Bre-X shares were sold short; Francis (1997: 203) reports that the investment bank Oppenheimer and Co. made C$100 million shorting Bre-X stock. Meanwhile, other firms and individuals, including Quebec's public pension fund and the Ontario Teachers Pension Plan Board, lost major amounts of money (Goold and Willis 1997: 248).

35. Other Bre-X allegories have been suggested, for example, that greed blinds everyone's eyes (Goold & Willis 1997: 267), or that the international flow of money means business must deal with "exotic and troublesome regimes" (Francis 1997: 232). Outside of Canada, the allegorical reading arose that this was just the way of Canadian business, where stock exchanges are a "regulatory Wild West" (quotation attributed to the US mass media in Winarno 1997: 208). My reading refuses the distinction between the seeing and the blind to point to the money being made even in a scam. I emphasize the exotic and troublesome nature of capitalism itself – both in and beyond Canada and Indonesia.

References

Behar, John (1997). Jungle Fever. *Fortune*, June 9, pp. 116–28.

Borsuk, Richard (1997). Bre-X Minerals Defends Pact with Indonesia. *Wall Street Journal*, February 2, p. B3A.

"Breaking News" (1998). Bre-X Investor Gets Last Laugh with Song. December 22. CANOE website www.canoe.ca/moneyBreXSaga/dec22_brexblues.html

Bre-X/Bresea Shareholder Class Action Information website www.Brexclass.com (site now discontinued).

Bre-Xscam.com website. The Bungle in the Jungle. www.Bre-xscam.com (site now discontinued).

"Calgary Sun" (1997). Ultimate Betrayal: Bre-X Boss Says Pair Ruined Dream. October 12. CANOE website www.calgarysun.com

CFRA News Talk Radio website (1998). TSE Raises Listing Standards for Mining and Exploration Companies; and TSE Tightens Rules for Junior Miners. August 20. www.cfra. com

"Daily Mining News" (1999). Will Canadians Be Allowed in American Bre-X Suit? March 31.

Danielson, Vivian & James Whyte (1997). *Bre-X: Gold Today, Gone Tomorrow*. Toronto: The Northern Miner.

DePalma, Anthony (1997). At End of a Miner's Rainbow, a Cloud of Confusion Lingers. *New York Times*, March 31, pp. A1, D10.

Eisler, Dale (1997). Sorrow in St. Paul. *MacLean's* 110(7, April 14), p. 55.

Farquarson, G. (1997). Busang Technical Audit: Interim Report. *Gatra* 17(May), p. 27.

Francis, Diane (1997). *Bre-X: The Inside Story*. Toronto: Key Porter Books.

Francis, Diane (1999). Brokers Must Pay for Their Role in Bre-X. *National Post Online*, May 20, at www.nationalpost.com

Goold, Douglas & Andrew Willis (1997). *The Bre-X Fraud*. Toronto: McClelland and Stewart Inc.

Hajari, Nisid (1997). Is the Pot at the End of the Rainbow Empty? *Time* 149(14, April 7), online version at www.time.com/

Hall, Stuart (1996). On Postmodernism and Articulation: An Interview with Stuart Hall, edited by Lawrence Grossberg. In: David Morley & Kuan-Hsing Chen (eds.), *Stuart Hall: Critical Dialogues in Cultural Studies*, pp. 131–50. London: Routledge.

Harvey, David (1989). *The Condition of Postmodernity*. Oxford: Basil Blackwell.

Jackson, Karl (ed.) (1999). Introduction: The Roots of the Crisis. In: Karl Jackson (ed.), *Asian Contagion*, pp. 1–27. Boulder, CO: Westview Press.

Jala, David (1997). Frenzy Stuns Market. *Calgary Sun*, April 2, at www.calgarysun.com

Lundin, Brien (1998). International Pursuit: Turning World-Class Potential into World-Class Reality. *Gold Newsletter's Mining Share Focus* 2(1), p. 4.

Marr, Carolyn (1993). *Digging Deep: The Hidden Costs of Mining in Indonesia*. London: Down to Earth.

McBeth, John (1997). The Golden Boys. *Far Eastern Economic Review* 160(10, March 6), pp. 42–4.

McBeth, John & Jay Solomon (1997). First Friend. *Far Eastern Economic Review* 160(8, February 20), pp. 52–4.

McLeod, Ross (1999). Indonesia's Crisis and Future Prospects. In: Karl Jackson (ed.), *Asian Contagion*, pp. 209–40. Boulder, CO: Westview Press.

Newman, Peter (1996). Peter Munk: A Dreamer Who Became a King. *Maclean's* 109(50, December 9), p. 42.

"Ottawa Citizen" (1997). Rumors Swirl Around Bre-X, March 25, at www.ottawacitizen.com

"Ottawa Citizen" (1997). Buried Body not Geologist: Report, April 10, at www.ottawacitizen. com

Platt, Michael (1997a). ID Challenged. *Calgary Sun*, April 5, at www.calgarysun.com

Platt, Michael (1997b). Dead or Alive? *Calgary Sun*, April 11, at www.calgarysun.com

Platt, Michael (1997c). Foul Play Fears Haunt Geologist. *Calgary Sun*, April 19, at www. calgarysun.com

Platt, Michael (1997d). Family Accepts Autopsy. *Calgary Sun*, April 21, at www.calgarysun. com

Platt, Michael (1997e). Print Identified as De Guzman's. *Calgary Sun*, April 24, at www. calgarysun.com

Platt, Michael (1997f). Rush Hour in the Jungle. *Calgary Sun*, May 23, at www.calgarysun. com

Rubin, Sandra (1998). Obituary: David Walsh. *Financial Post*, June 5. CANOE website, http://acmi.canoe.ca/MoneyBreXSaga/jun5_obituaryda.html

Rubin, Sandra (1999). Let All Canadian Bre-X Shareholders in Class-Action Suit, Court Urged. *Financial Post*, February 11. CANOE website, http://acmi.canoe.ca/MoneyBreXSaga/feb2_letallbrex.html

Soesastro, Hadi & Budi Sudarsono (1988). Mineral and Energy Development in Indonesia. In: Bruce McKern & Praipol Koomnsup (eds.), *The Minerals Industries of ASEAN and Australia*, pp. 161–208. Sydney: Allen & Unwin.

Waldman, Peter & Jay Solomon (1997). Geologist's Death May Lie at Heart of Busang Mystery. *Wall Street Journal*, April 9, p. A10.

Warmington, Joe (1997a). Bre-X Takeover Claim. *Calgary Sun*, April 6, at www.calgarysun. com

Warmington, Joe (1997b). Bank on More Intrigue. *Calgary Sun*, April 8, at www.calgarysun. com

Warmington, Joe (1997c). Yanks Waiting: Americans Ready to Gobble Up Bre-X Shares. *Calgary Sun*, April 13, at www.calgarysun.com

Wells, Jennifer (1996). King of Gold. *Maclean's* 109(50, December 9), pp. 39–40.

Wells, Jennifer (1997a). Rumble in the Jungle. *Maclean's* 110(5, February 3), pp. 38–9.

Wells, Jennifer (1997b). Gunning for Gold. *Maclean's* 110(7, February 17), p. 52.

Wells, Jennifer (1997c). Greed, Graft, Gold. *Maclean's* 110(9, March 3), pp. 38–45.

Winarno, Bondan (1997). *Bre-X: Sebungkah Emas Di Kaki Pelangi*. Jakarta: Penerit Inspirasi Indonesia.

Zgodzinski, David (1997). Bre-X: The Battle between Bulls and Bears on SI. May 4. Silicon Investor website www.siliconinvestor.com/

78

Francophonie and the National Airwaves: A History of Television in Senegal

*Jo Ellen Fair**

The growth and content of television programming in Africa since the 1960s could be read as a story of media imperialism. The flood of Western programming into Africa alone makes this reading credible. Television's rapid transmission of distant words and pictures has challenged cultural practices that once emerged from particular geographic spaces. Indeed, as audiences view television, they now claim membership in several communities at once: the group of family and friends seated in the room; the entire community of nationals filtering televised images in ways unique to that national culture; and the international community of media cognoscenti, people around the world bound together in their knowledge of the language, rhetoric, and quirks of this or that program or program genre. Globalized media create this cognoscenti in Africa as they do every-where, encouraging cosmopolitanism as they introduce and even impose attitudes that are, by all evidence, at least at the outset, foreign.

Media imperialism is too simple a concept, however. We know that local conditions check and modulate the flow of cultural products into Africa from the West. Neither state nor public waits impassively for the arrival of imported culture. The range of media products that become available in a country and the preferences that develop over time depend on an interplay of politics and taste on the national scene and the world at large.

This chapter explores the political and cultural history of television in Senegal. Its purpose is to show how the personalities of powerful figures, political calculations at a range of scales, the state's structure and regulation of media, and the preferences and tastes of diverse national populations have shaped the growth of television and the content of programming there. Television was introduced to Senegal in the mid-1960s, soon after independence from France, but it has never been a strong force for cultural nationalism. In fact, television has been important in creating a new urban culture in Senegal, and a sense in that culture of belonging to a larger francophone community, which France purports to lead ("Francophonie par satellite," *Jeune Afrique* 5–11 December 1990; Tudesq 1992, 197–213; Silla 1994; Ager 1996, 44–62). Despite the constant

*Pp. 189–210 from *Planet TV: A Global Television Reader*, ed. L. Parks and S. Kumar (New York: New York University Press). © 2003 by New York University. Reprinted with permission of the author and New York University Press.

flow of French cultural products through the airwaves into Senegal and their partial absorption into daily life, especially in the cities, Senegalese cultures, urban and rural, will always stand apart from the French and the global *francophonie* France seeks to create. An additional purpose of this chapter, therefore, is to recount the history of French television in Senegal and to show how it has shaped urban Senegalese discourse around regional, national, and international cultural identities.

Senegal's Colonial Past

Senegal long has had a unique relationship with France. For example, during the colonial period, which extended from 1885 to 1960, Senegal was the only colony in sub-Saharan Africa where France fully applied its ideas of colonial assimilation, whereby Senegal was granted its own governmental assemblies and municipal councils, and whereby a small class of assimilated elites (*evolués*) could qualify for French citizenship (Gellar 1995, 5–19). For some, the connection between Senegal's colonial history and its contemporary environment, especially in relation to the emergence and development of television, may seem remote and even tenuous. But as many observers of Senegal have noted, the country's colonial experiences have influenced its present-day political, economic, and social organization, as well as its cultural life profoundly (Gellar 1995, 8; Martin 1995; Schraeder 1997; see also Coulon 1988; Diop & Diouf 1990, 251–81; Boone 1992, 344–49; McNamara 1989, 95–141).

Through the colonial policy of *la mission civilsatrice*, France sought to consolidate its power by spreading French language and culture. When Senegal became independent, France abandoned its formal civilizing mission. Instead, government officials and diplomats embarked on policies for a new period of decolonization, which centered discursively on notions of cooperation among French-speaking countries (Martin 1995; Ager 1996; Schraeder 1997). Replacing the colonial mission of "Frenchifying" the Senegalese was *francophonie*, which in its most literal sense means the community of those having the ability to speak French. But in a more political sense it invokes a global French-speaking partnership led by France and concerted efforts (particularly by states) to keep this cultural-political alliance intact (Miller 1990, 182–201; Hargreaves & McKinney 1997, 3–6; Léger 1987; Schraeder 1997; Tétu 1987).

The first two presidents of Senegal, Léopold Sédar Senghor (1960–1980) and Abdou Diouf (1981–2000), have been keen to maintain the country's participation in the francophone community and reinforce Senegal's special relationship with France (Chipman 1989, 227–55; Diop & Diouf 1990, 251–81; Gellar 1995, 83–107; Schraeder 1997). However, it is difficult to understand fully *francophonie's* cultural and political force without exploring its modes of operation (Hargreaves & McKinney 1997, 3–6; Miller 1990, 182). In many ways, the French presence and its ties to *francophonie* in Senegal have been developed and maintained first through the development of a national television service in the 1960s and then through the introduction of primarily French television in the early 1990s (McNamara 1989, 133; Silla 1994). Yet the French cultural intrusion never has been complete and always has been complicated by national (Senegalese) cultural groups who have appropriated, reformed, and come up with new or hybridized uses, meanings, and understandings of television and its programming.

The remainder of this chapter addresses television in Senegal in relationship to its development by the French and more recent trends in terms of the introduction of French and other international television channels. The discussion is organized around the institutional history of television in Senegal and the country's contemporary broadcast landscape. Throughout, the discussion explores the interplay among stakeholders – state, capital, market, and the public – that combine to shape Senegalese television.

The *Sénégalisation* of Television

By nearly any measure, Africa remains the least connected, the least wired, and the least developed of all the world's media environments. As access to television has expanded rapidly and widely in other regions, Africans generally still see little of the medium. According to UN statistics, in 1965 there were 192 million TV receivers in the world, of which 600,000 receivers were in Africa (compared with 84 million in North America). By the mid-1990s, there were 1.3 billion receivers, of which 37 million were in Africa (compared with 338 million in North America). As of 1996, there are some 320,000 receivers in Senegal, a country of nearly 10 million people.

Senegalese television first began its operations in Dakar, the capital city, in 1964. At the outset, the government declared the mission of telecasting to be purely educational and developmental. In an address to officials of his party, the Union Progressiste Sénégalaise, President Senghor noted that television's mission was to serve as a base of "knowledge and training for the masses," which ultimately would facilitate "our march toward progress" (Congrès de l'Union 1969).[1] Funded by UNESCO, the UN Development Program, and the French and Canadian governments, the television service provided viewers in Dakar with information and training to improve farming, nutrition, health, and entrepreneurial skills.[2] The six-year experiment was modest in scale. Some offices at Radio Sénégal were converted for television production, producers and technicians were sent to France for training, a dozen or so television receivers were imported, and programs were aired for an hour or two in the evenings. In the early part of the experiment, from 1964 to 1966, programming on housekeeping, nutrition, and hygiene was targeted to five hundred women. These women were organized into groups or *télé-clubs* so that they could watch and discuss programs together. Later, from 1966, the experiment focused on general adult literacy training (Fougeyrollas 1967; Head 1974, 302; Katz & Wedell 1977, 84–9; Carlos 1985).

The emphasis of Senegalese television on education is not at all surprising, given the era in which the experiment was launched. Broadcast media – both radio and television – were hypothesized to be capable not only of transforming "traditional" societies into "modern" ones but also of fending off communism (Lerner 1958; Schramm 1964; Simpson 1994). These objectives made UN agencies, as well as Western governments such as the French, keen to fund them. Moreover, the French, ever influential in Senegal, transferred their state-dominated, noncommercial, public service model of broadcasting to former colonies through the training of broadcasters, in the assistance of program production, and through technology imports. For its part, the Senegalese government recognized the poor state of general education, a legacy left by the French in many of its former colonies, and sought a remedy through broadcasting (Head 1974, 302; Cruise O'Brien 1985; Tudesq 1992, 47–59).

For Senghor, both radio and television broadcasting contributed to Senegalese society by providing information, knowledge, and culture that would elevate average Senegalese citizens, transform them qualitatively, and stave off "subversive attempts" (Congrès de l'Union 1969). What is somewhat unusual about the experiment's development-oriented programming was that it was exclusively in Wolof, the largest national (but not official) language. Most television services of newly decolonized countries in the early 1960s used former colonial languages with the intent of building them as lingua francas. The president himself widely promoted French language use as a means by which Senegalese society could remain a part of a global francophone community. He saw French as central to the "convergence of [French-speaking] civilizations," as well as to the "consciousness of a society marching toward modernity" (Allocution de M. le Président 1968). In particular, he pushed for the use of French in print media (Allocution de M. le Président 1968). Yet he supported Wolof, rather than French, as the language of television. Interestingly, Senghor's nuanced position on media language allowed him to achieve various political aims. Television in Wolof allowed the government to appear to reach out to the masses in an attempt to transform society and to resist continued French cultural influence by promoting a national language. At the same time, promoting French as the language of print media allowed Senghor and his government to stay "engaged in the project of *francophonie*. . . . our cultural reality," a long and important obsession of Senghor's (Allocution de M. le Président 1968).

When funding for the television experiment was exhausted in 1969, television in Senegal simply ended. At the time, there was no intention of developing a general service, though wealthy expatriate French, Lebanese, Moroccan, and Portuguese communities could and perhaps would have given substantial support to telecasting that emphasized entertainment programming over development (Head 1974; Carlos 1985). Nonetheless, Senghor opposed the continuation of television broadcasting as too expensive for the country, which was faced with mounting debt and declining living standards (Congrès de l'Union 1969; see also Gellar 1995).

Soon after the end of the experiment, rich expatriates and Senegalese elites began to exert pressure on the Senghor government to relaunch television as a conventional entertainment medium. By 1972, television in Senegal was reintroduced, despite the opposition of many government ministers, including the president. In fact, one minister called television "a jewel for the tired and spent bourgeoisie" (Katz & Wedell 1977, 87). In considering whether to have any television at all, the government began by revisiting its experimental model from the 1960s. One government report suggested that using existing equipment and facilities from the earlier experiment would keep down the cost of reintroduction. The report also raised the question of how the government might "facilitate individual reception through the acquisition of television sets" when in the earlier experimental phase all viewing occurred communally (Compte rendu du Conseil interministériel 1971). In the end, the government's decision to relaunch television was made easier by an offer from Thomson–CSF, a French manufacturer, to donate the necessary equipment. In an arrangement negotiated through the French Ministry of Cooperation, Thomson–CFS gave a number of television sets to be used for communal viewing around Dakar, which was the only viewing area. But more important, the French company became the sole supplier of television sets bought by elites and imported into Senegal.

After a ground station was installed in Gandiol (just south of Saint-Louis), Senegal's second try with television began just in time for the 1972 Olympics. Innumerable newspaper ads for Thomson–CSF television sets promoted sales so that Senegalese could join the rest of the world watching the Olympics live and in color. But as letters and columns to various local newspapers suggest, many potential Senegalese television viewers were frustrated by the sets' prohibitive cost. Television remained a medium for elites. As one man asked rhetorically in a letter to the government newspaper, *Le Soleil*,

> "For us, a developing country, with still limited means, having just recently obtained television, the provider of information, education, and entertainment, . . . what kind of television should we have? And also, for whom? The elite or the masses?" ("Télé – des émissions pour qui?" 13 August 1972).

This frustration also was recorded in a person-on-the-street poll conducted by *Le Soleil*. One man queried in the poll worried that television sets would become mandatory in dowries given when daughters married. Another man said he wondered why the government made receivers so expensive when they were supposed to be used by all for development purposes. A woman ventured that the government should make businesses sell sets on credit. Still another man interviewed thought that buying a television was ridiculous if the government did not have plans to continue broadcasting entertainment programs after the end of the Olympics ("L'enquête," *Le Soleil* 29 August 1972). Indeed, letters and columns indicate widespread concern about who would have access to television. In an article published in a small opposition newspaper, the writer complained that telecasting was intended not for the people but for elites:

> We have learned that the government has "ordered" the installation of some 100 television sets. "In the homes of all the ministers; all members of the cabinet; the secretaries general; and some of the members of the National Assembly, the Supreme Court, the Economic and Social Counsel, and the governor of Cap-Vert." This information sounds a little overstated. . . . Nonetheless, only about 50 televisions were installed for the entire UNESCO project [of the 1960s]. ("Télé-Munich 'Ministériel'?" *La Lettre Fermée* 11–24 August 1972)

Though the government initially planned to have broadcasts only for the three weeks of the Olympic Games, demand for television's continuation, especially among buyers of sets, was strong enough that the Senghor government decided not to pull the plug. In a report recommending the formation of a broadcast policy committee, the secretary general's office noted that television would continue because it had become an "irreversible part of modern life" (Projet de décret portant création 1972). In fact, the government went so far as to encourage further sales of receivers when it decided against adopting license fees and dropped the 105 percent import tax ("Baisse effectivement des prix," *Le Soleil* 15 March 1973).

In December 1973 with the passage of Law 73–51, the government formed a new broadcast structure, the Office de Radiodiffusion-Télévision Sénégalaise (ORTS). Administratively, ORTS was modeled on the French broadcasting authority (ORTF). Established as a public corporation with oversight from the Ministry of Communication, ORTS expanded its mandate from purely educational objectives to include entertainment ("La télé continue," *Le Soleil* 14 September 1972; Projet de loi abrogeant 1977). Newly conceived, the medium was no longer "only educational, but a television of the masses at the same time informative, cultural, and entertaining" ("Décisions hier au Conseil," *Le Soleil* 5 October 1971). Senghor recognized, though apparently with reluctance, the powerful draw of television. In a speech given at a ribbon-cutting ceremony of a transmitter in Thiès (seventy kilometers northeast of Dakar), the president said,

> why all this passion for television? Why, every day, under the stars, do men, women, young and old, poor and rich, commune, immobile and silent, as with a ritual, in the front of the little screen? It's because television fulfills mankind's dream permitting him to witness the world: to live in the universe and share the feeling of being a citizen of the planet. (Allocution de M. le Président 1976)

Part of being this global citizen meant speaking French and participating in the francophone community. Unlike the UNESCO television experiment in which broadcasts were in Wolof, the new service used French almost exclusively ("L'ORTS est né," *Le Soleil* 23 November 1973). At the time, the French government, through ORTF, was responsible for most of the new service's technology, training of technicians and producers, and programs (Compte rendu du Conseil national 1976). In the mid-1970s, about 75 percent of programs aired on Senegalese television were imported (Katz and Wedell 1977, 157). Though ORTS broadcast some literacy and development-oriented shows in national languages, the program schedule had taken a decidedly entertainment turn, with most shows being action-adventure, family-situation dramas, soap operas, and films. Programs originated most often in France and the United States (which were then dubbed) (Katz & Wedell 1977, 156–66; Carlos 1985, 166–88; Ly Diop 1989, 23–4). French feature films and series such as *Animals of the World* and European soccer were popular among viewers. American shows such as *Mannix*, *Columbo*, and *Gunsmoke* also attracted audiences. Despite the movement of ORTS into entertainment, Senghor still thought of television as playing a grander role in Senegalese society than mere "distraction":

> Our television is not a commercial one whose chief objective would be the conditioning of viewers to make themselves into commodity consumers. We have deliberately opted for a different solution, because it is the best way to assure consideration of the general concerns and interests of all Senegalese, and especially to stay rooted in our place, while at the same time to be open to all civilizations of the world. (Allocution de M. le Président 1976)

As the president continued, television was "to serve 'Homosénégalensis,' to assist him in development, to enrich his personality, that is the task of 'Télésenégalaise'" (Allocution de M. le Président 1976). To fulfill that role, Senegalese television had to be both outward and inward looking: It had to connect Senegalese citizens outward to the francophone world and to provide programs that were thought to be culturally relevant by the government. In the same speech, Senghor begins to make use of the terms *sénégaliser* (infinitive) and *sénégalisation* (noun) to suggest that television, though primarily in French, must be made to feel Senegalese and imbue Senegalese values.

The challenge to the *sénégalisation* of television was that ORTS lacked the funds to create programs that were of the technical quality of the imports. While attention was being paid to the quality of the French language used in broadcasts ("L'ORTS est né," *Le Soleil* 23 November 1973), shows were being produced in the same poorly equipped television studio, once converted from a radio office, used for the UNESCO project ("Quand le petit écran," *Le Soeil* 28 May 1973). *Sénégalisation* came to mean, in government mandates to ORTS, expansion of television diffusion beyond Dakar, an increase in locally produced programs in national languages and French, diversification of programming, better-quality programs, collaborative work between film and television producers, and a decrease, between 25 to 30 percent, of imported programs (see, e.g., Conseil national de l'audio-visuel 1978; Allocution de M. Cherif Thiam, l'ORTS 1985).

Making Senegalese television more Senegalese was going to be expensive. While the president talked about ORTS's importance to *francophonie* and to nation building, the government – like many other newly decolonized countries – found it had to reconcile demands for the *sénégalisation* of television with the budgetary realities of a failing economy. Some critics, such as Abdou Rahman Cissé, acting commissioner of the Ministry of Information from 1962 to 1964, have suggested that television was intentionally underfunded so it could remain a toy for the amusement of elites rather than a tool of social change (personal interview 14 July 1996). Because the government's attentions were turned toward Senegal's high rates of unemployment and inflation, funding for television seriously stagnated and plans for *sénégalisation* stalled from the mid-1970s through the 1980s ("Conseil interministériel," *Le Soleil* 26 October 1983). Though some 80 percent of ORTS's operating budget came from the government during this period, ORTS still had to seek ways of keeping itself afloat. The governments of France and Germany were courted and gave financial and technical support ("Plan d'urgence," *Le Soleil* 2 November 1979; "300 millions," *Le Soleil* 28 April 1981). The government, now led by President Abdou Diouf, also tried tinkering with ORTS's mandate as a way to make the service revenue-generating. According to a revision of the law that created ORTS as purely a public corporation, ORTS was redefined as a "public corporation with industrial and commercial features," freeing the service to pursue advertising, corporate, and other nongovernmental revenue (Projet de loi 1977; Secrétariat du Conseil des Ministrès 1985).

RTS and Canal Horizons in the 1990s

Throughout the 1970s and 1980s, ORTS hobbled along on its tight budget. But political, economic, and social currents in Senegal were undergoing change. In the early

1990s, Diouf began to suggest the need to open Senegal's media landscape. Scrapping the language of *sénégalisation*, Diouf set out a new course:

> our country, engaged in a battle of image and sound on a global level, must find appropriate responses that affirm Senegal's spirit and preserve its cultural identity. Today, the proliferation of television signals that crisscross the world and the development of direct satellite television have brought about a competition, a conquest of audiences not only national but transnational. The African continent can no longer be sheltered from these upheavals of the global broadcast landscape. The risks of cultural erosion and the fragmentation of our national audiences are real. But this situation can and must be for us, a developing country, an opportunity to transform ourselves, to evolve qualitatively, and to renew our imagination. (Allocution de M. le Président 1990)

With this statement Diouf then announced two key changes in government broadcast policy: the restructuring of ORTS into a new entity, Radiodiffusion-Télévision Sénégalaise (RTS), and the approval of the French satellite subscription channel, Canal Horizons, to begin operation in 1991. The purpose of the reorganization of ORTS into RTS was to permit the service to pursue revenue generation further. Passed by Law 92–02 in January 1992, RTS remained a state-run entity but was defined as a "national company" rather than a public corporation. Though it retained its educational, development, and nation-building mandates, it also was newly charged with creating programs of sufficient quality that they could be exchanged internationally. To fulfill these objectives, the government intended for RTS to become more efficient and financially self-sustaining by handing over day-to-day management to a "dynamic cadre capable of improving [RTS's] production potential" (Projet de loi portant approbation 1992; see also "La RTS passe société nationale," *Le Soleil* 30 January 1992).

Despite the restructuring of ORTS into RTS, the Senegalese television authority faced intense public criticism. As one viewer commented, "RTS translated by the young people of Podor [a town just south of the Mauritanian border] means 'nothing on every night'" (a play on words: "Rien Tous les Soirs" [RTS]) ("Podor sans télé," *Sud Quotidien* 5 August 1993). Many letters to the editor in newspapers such as *Le Soleil*, *Sud Quotidien*, and *Wal Fadjri* described RTS programming as "dull," "poor quality," "silly," and as involving "too much talking." Wrote one columnist, "In brief, we have not a public service television but a state television, and with that, inertia, controls, and heavy handedness" ("Le télé unique, un mal unique," *Sud Quotidien* 31 December 1993).

The president's calls for RTS's programming "to contribute to civil society," "to reflect the political, cultural, religious diversity of the Senegalese people," and "to prompt a national democratic dialogue" ("Edifier un paysage," *Le Soleil* 2 November 1990) were met with skepticism by many. Opposition party members began to argue that there could be no democratic debate if RTS was the sole television outlet. As one guest columnist, showing his frustration, wrote to the government newspaper, *Le Soleil*, "Democratic dialogue can only take place when ideas compete. It's necessary at minimum to open the media of the state not only to the opposition, but also to civil society" ("Recentrer le débat," 2 November 1990).

By the late 1980s and early 1990s, Diouf's government had been dogged by a number of political crises – university strikes, conflict with Mauritania, rioting in the capital, and charges of corruption of elections. He was very much in need of regaining his political authority (Coulon 1988; Diop & Diouf 1990; Diouf 1996; Gellar 1995). When he first announced in his 1990 speech the creation of RTS and the launching of the French Canal Horizons, he suggested that both would "improve and diversify programming, and stimulate national production" (Allocution de M. le Président 1990). Certainly, improving and diversifying programming at the national level would help to satisfy domestic critics and perhaps to deflect some of the political heat focused on him. Seemingly responding to criticism that RTS could not foster and sustain democratic dialogue, pluralism, and civil society, the government created the Haut Conseil de la Radio Télévision (HCRT) in 1991 (Law 92–57). The task of the High Council was (and is) to provide opposition parties with some access to RTS. It was described as an independent structure that would guard pluralism and guarantee freedom of information by allowing Senegalese political parties to have broadcast time to present their platforms ("L'ère de responsabilité," *Le Soleil* 27–28 July 1991). Still, many found the government's opening of Senegalese airwaves to be little more than an empty gesture. As one Ministry of Communication official, who later became a High Council member, said,

> I would like to think the Council will work. But the problem of television in Senegal is that the opposition doesn't have access to RTS. Even with the electoral code [which set out airtime allocations], the opposition doesn't have the same access, what with the president and ministers shown day in and day out. (personal interview with Moussa Paye 5 July 1994)

In fact, several parties complained that their time on RTS was too limited or that they received broadcast time only when there would be few viewers (Ly 1993, 98; "L'opposition boycotte," *Le Soleil* 15 March 1992; "Dialogue sur l'utilisation des mediats d'état," *Le Soleil* 22 January 1993). The government argued that the High Council was necessary to ensure access to RTS at a time when the government saw itself as undergoing a "change of direction toward deregulation" ("L'ère de responsabilité," *Le Soleil* 27–28 July 1991; see also, "Respecter les principes du pluralism," *Le Soleil* 10 December 1992). Some media professionals fretted about the potential chilling effect that government broadcasting directives might have on actual political debate (Paye 1992; "Parlez, il en restera," *Wal Fadjri* 8–14 January 1993; personal interview with Mame Less Camara 12 July 1996). Yet others, such as journalist and playwright Boubacar Boris Diop, defended the HCRT, suggesting it was a show of "good will on the part of the state to encourage greater pluralism" ("L'HCRT vu par les professionels," *Le Soleil* 4 September 1991; see also "Les objections du RND," *Le Soleil* 19 September 1991). The reorganization of RTS, which brought about the subsequent creation of the HCRT, was an important element in the government's rehabilitation of its political image. By embracing discourses of democracy and pluralism, the Diouf government could point to RTS as the domestic forum that would "contribute to the enrichment of national political debate" (Haut Conseil de la Radio-Télévision 1994, 25).

But Diouf also had a second communications strategy for improving his political fortunes by opening the broadcast environment: the introduction of international broadcasting into Senegal. Given the long and sometimes vitriolic debate about the impact of Western media on "developing" societies seen in the discussions of the New World Information and Communication Order, it seems almost counterintuitive that the Senegalese government would invite a major French communications corporation to broadcast within its borders. Earlier in his presidency, Diouf expressed concerns about the impact of global informational and entertainment imbalances (Allocution de M. le Président 1986). But just months after his 1990 speech, Diouf announced the introduction of Canal Horizons. Serge Adda, Canal Horizons' director general, soon arrived in Dakar to help set up shop. Canal Horizons is a subsidiary of Canal Plus and a French public broadcast agency (Société Financière de Radiodiffusion, SOFIRAD) that manages international broadcast operations. Adda, touting the Canal venture and appealing to national pride, noted that the country would "play a pioneering role in Africa" with the opening of the service in Senegal, Tunisia, and Gabon ("CH montre ses grilles," *Le Soleil* 19 October 1990; see also "La France multiplie les médias," *Jeune Afrique* 11 December 1990). Furthermore, using some of the language of the president, he told Diouf that Canal programs would support "pluralism, dialogues of cultures, and equal relations between North–South." Adda also promised to help fund Senegalese programming on the station ("CH montre ses grilles," *Le Soleil* 19 October 1990).

Diouf liked what he heard. A month later, he said that Canal Horizons would be "an axis of cultural development, a lever for the creation and production of Senegalese television, and a melting pot of cultural dialogue, notably North–South, but otherwise too" ("CH en vue," *Le Soleil* 21 November 1990). What Diouf and his government had in mind by allowing Canal Horizons to broadcast in Senegal is not exactly clear. At home, he allowed a slight opening of RTS to the opposition. With Canal Horizons, he could engage in a ruse: He could tell opponents that they could voice their issues on Senegal-produced programs airing on Canal Horizons, though he probably suspected (correctly) that there would be none. Either way – with the reorganization of RTS and the introduction of Canal Horizons – Diouf could look like a proponent of free, pluralistic, democratic dialogue.

The Canal Horizons deal also afforded the Senegalese government another payoff. Via RTS and SONATEL, the then parastatal telephone service, the government received 15 percent of Canal Horizons earnings in Senegal. The private Senegalese investors, two former ministers (one of whom was restored to office in late 1991), a prominent Muslim cleric, and six businessmen, took a total of 70 percent (the other 15 percent presumably went to France; figures vary according to source; "Sénégal; Images très privées," *Jeune Afrique* 25 July–1 August 1990; "CH en vue," *Le Soleil* 21 November 1990; personal interview with Anne Marie Senghor Boissy 7 July 1994). Additionally, Fara N'Diaye, former deputy and closely affiliated with Abdoulaye Wade, who was Diouf's chief opposition in the 1988 and 2000 elections, was appointed president of the Senegalese franchise.

Certainly, media groups such as Canal Horizons did not enter African countries because they thought they would be hugely profitable. African media markets were and remain the smallest and poorest in the world. In many instances, the French government, through a host of agencies, urged French media corporations to enter Africa. Maintaining a French presence in Africa was as much a goal as turning a profit was ("Un paysage audiovisuel," *Jeune Afrique* 18 December 1991–8 January 1992; "Les chaînes d'Afrique," *Jeune Afrique* 3–9 February 1994). The introduction of Canal Horizons into Senegal permitted the notion of *francophonie*, and Senegal's connection to the rest of the French-speaking world, to continue shaping the country's broadcast landscape. The francophone connection was vital enough that three years later, in 1994, another service, this one explicitly devoted to preserving the French language and protecting francophone cultures, entered the Senegalese market at the request of the Diouf government. Negotiations began at the 1989 Francophonie Summit, held in Dakar, where Diouf pleaded with delegates to help create an African television channel. Such a channel was seen as too costly, so Diouf seized the idea of expanding TV5, a television consortium of French-speaking countries, into francophone Africa ("Une chaîne pour l'Afrique," *Jeune Afrique* 9–15 July 1992; Silla 1994; "Les chaînes d'Afrique," *Jeune Afrique* 3–9 February 1994). Planning of this expansion was facilitated through the French Ministry of Francophonie. Senegalese Mactar Silla, who became the president of the TV5 Afrique, described the service as "the channel for cross-cultural meeting and diversity, the channel of francophones and francophiles" ("L'apport de TV5," *Le Soleil* 1 October 1992), TV5 began in 1984 with five member groups: three French channels (TF1, Atenne 2, FR3), one Belgian (RTBF), and one Swiss (TSR). Later, a Québec channel (CTQR) joined TV5, with each participating channel contributing French-language programming.

By 1994, some thirty years after television in Senegal was first launched, broadcasting had evolved in ways that Senghor would not have anticipated. The introduction of French and francophone television into Senegal also came at a time when radio broadcasting was undergoing great change. As it did with television, by the early 1990s the government began to allow international radio broadcasters into Senegal. The first of these were Radio France Internationale (RFI) and Afrique No. 1. Then, on July 1, 1994, Sud FM became Senegal's first private commercial radio station. The station's owner, Babacar Touré of the newspaper *Sud Quotidien*, had negotiated with the government for seven years, and at various points his production equipment had been seized (personal interview with Touré, 27 June 1994). Sud FM was soon followed by other privately owned Senegalese radio stations, such as Duniya and Nostalgie. A Ministry of Communication official, Moussa Paye, suggested that the government had to privatize radio if its stated "commitment to opening all forms of communication was not to be a charade" (personal interview 5 July 1994; see also "L'antenne ne sera pas à tous," *Wal Fadjri* 23 November 1993). Indeed, the private radio stations carried many call-in and talk show programs that frequently turned political. Despite the fact that radio reaches far more Senegalese than television does, the government did not acquiesce to pressures from business and religious sectors to permit private Senegalese-owned and operated television. There was too much potential that such stations could become venues for domestic political challenge. Instead, the government preferred the appearance of openness that international television services afforded.

Though the government continued to discuss broadcasting for rural development purposes, that line of discourse all but disappeared in the context of major urban areas such as Dakar and Saint-Louis (see, e.g., "Quelles programmes pour l'Afrique" and "Les antennes diaboliques," both *Jeune Afrique* 17–23 November 1994). While TV5 itself was largely devoted to news, information, documentaries, talk shows, and some films, the service provided a "bouquet" of other channels, including Canal France Internationale (CFI), CNN (which the French opposed because it operates in English and is US-based), MCM, a French music video channel, and Portuguese and Moroccan television. Canal Horizons continued to be devoted, as ever, to entertainment: movies, many of which were American and dubbed into French; sports, particularly soccer but also Worldwide Wrestling Federation events; cartoons, such as *Tintin*; and music, especially jazz. RTS, which rightly surmised that it could not compete on a technical level with TV5 or Canal Horizons, continued to show largely imported entertainment programs (around 75 percent, according to the RTS journalist Adrienne Diop, personal interview 7 July 1994) but also found a niche in game shows, religious programs, Senegalese wrestling (*bëre* or *làmb* in Wolof), regional news, theater, storytelling, and music in Wolof and other national languages ("Les programmes de la nouvelle grille," *Le Soleil* 2, November 1990; "TV: La grille du changement?" *Le Soleil* 8 October 1992).

Because of all the publicity surrounding Canal Horizons and TV5, demand for these services grew. But access to these channels was limited to major cities and to those who could afford the start-up costs and/or monthly fees for special equipment. For example, viewers of TV5 needed a special (MMDS) antenna, which, in 1994, cost 100,000 CFA or about $182. Likewise, to receive Canal Horizons, viewers needed a decoder box, which was bought (not rented) for 50,000 CFA or about $91, with an additional monthly subscriber fee of 17,000 CFA or about $31. A television set itself cost about 300,000 CFA or $545 in 1994. These prices were steep for many Senegalese, who had seen their French-backed currency, the CFA franc, devalued by 50 percent in January 1994. Responding to the economic situation while trying to build their audience base, Canal Horizons and TV5 offered subscribers special breaks in prices (personal interviews with Wahab Touré of TV5 5 July 1994; and Boissy of Canal Horizons 7 July 1994). Particularly around major holidays and special events – Ramadan, Christmas, the Africa Cup, the Olympics – ads in newspapers and on radio and television (including RTS) publicized price reductions for services. Even particular groups, such as civil servants and teachers who were just on the fringe of being able to afford Canal Horizons and TV5, were targeted in campaigns.

The relations among the three television services were largely noncompetitive. Each had its own market niche and saw itself as complementing or supplementing the others (personal interviews with W. Touré 5 July 1994; Diop and Boissy 7 July 1994). RTS saw itself as appealing to viewers who wanted Senegalese programs. Of course, the tight budget for programming was a constant issue as RTS tried to create new shows to generate new ad revenue (personal interview with Diop 7 July 1994). As Babacar Diagne, RTS's director for television, noted, "My ambition is not to compete with Canal Horizons in the international domain. We haven't the means. I will invest in another area: national life" ("Les programmes de la nouvelle grille," *Le Soleil* 2 November 1990). For its part, Canal Horizons saw itself as a provider of international entertainment. Its marketing research revealed that in Dakar and its environs (about two million people in and around a thirty five-Kilometer perimeter of Dakar, Rufisque, and Bargny), there were some 65,000 households with television sets. Of those 65,000, Canal Horizons sought to subscribe 25,000. By 1994 the service had reached into 11,000 homes. An additional 3,500 households subscribed periodically when they could scrape together enough to pay the monthly fee. Of Canal Horizons' subscribers, 70 percent were Senegalese (personal interview with Boissy 7 July 1994). Because its service had only recently been introduced, TV5 had the smallest audience share in 1994. According to a TV5 marketing survey of 525 Dakar residents, the service had somewhat less than half of Canal Horizons' subscribers. TV5's Wahab Touré put the figure at about 5,000.[3] He also suggested that because TV5 was more affordable than Canal Horizons and because of the channel's emphasis on informational programming, the service was reaching largely well-educated Senegalese (personal interview 5 July 1994). To help build an audience base by stabilizing the cost of the services, Canal Horizons began to distribute the TV5 "bouquet" of channels in late 1994, offering various kinds of price packages for basic and premium services, which included TV5.

Though all three television services had worked out their appeals to various segments of Senegalese viewers, Canal Horizons and TV5 at their launchings had promised to facilitate North-South dialogues. In practice, for Canal Horizons that meant little more than increasing the number of films from the "South" to about 12 percent ("Les chaînes d'Afrique," *Jeune Afrique* 3–9 February 1994). By contrast, TV5 had vowed to help African producers create new programs for broadcast. At the 1993 Francophonie Summit, promises were made, in particular through the French government's Agence de Coopération Culturelle et Technique (ACCT), to coproduce five African programs that would air two hours a day. The funds for this level of coproduction never materialized. But there have been attempts at some coproduction. The first was a soap-style show set in Senegal called *Fann Océan* and described as "le 'Dallas' sénégalais." The program – six fifty-minute shows – was created through efforts of RTS, the Belgian TV5 partner, and the French ACCT, and it aired in 1992 on RTS. While some viewers wrote to newspapers to say that as Senegalese they were proud that *Fann Océan* had been produced, press reviews of the program were fairly harsh ("Le Fann," *Sud Quotidien* 7 January 1992; "Les bons and les méchants," *Sud Quotidien* 8 October 1993). One avid television viewer said of the show, "Just thinking about it gives me a headache."[4]

Whether *Fann Océan* was bad may matter little. One of the outcomes of the program was that it served as an opportunity to train Senegalese producers and helped them land positions on other coproductions. The letters, reviews, and reactions to *Fann Océan* also are all examples of a larger debate about the role Senegalese audiences think television should play in the national discourse. For many viewers, programs such as *Fann Océan* evoked a national pride. Others whom I interviewed or corresponded with said that television helped them to think about Senegal's relation to the rest of world, particularly outside francophone regions. For these respondents, Paris was no longer the single metropole to which they looked for knowledge and inspiration concerning economics, politics, education, immigration, and even fashion. The anglophone world was in, and many shifted their sights toward New York and Washington, DC. For example, the arrest of O. J. Simpson, with all the accompanying discussions of *Miranda* rights and due process, allowed many Senegalese viewers both to question the legal code inherited from the French and to consider in a new light the government's harassment of political opponents.

By no means are domestic and international television services accepted uncritically. The impact of television, particularly Western programs, on the values and attitudes of young people has been the source of much public discussion. Columnists in the press have argued that Western programs on any of the channels carry values that are not compatible with those of Senegal, influencing, for example, the manner in which children address parents, how young girls dress, sexuality, and life expectations ("Un mal nécessaire?" *Le Soleil* 4 February 1992; "Une autre télévision pour les riches," *Wal Fadjri* 7 July 1993; "A consommer avec modération," *Wal Fadjri* 29 September 1993; "Promiscuité familiale," *Sud Quotidien* 1 October 1993; "Des jeunes africains," *Le Soleil* 9 July 1996; see also "Doit-on interdire à nos enfants," *Sudonline* 16 February 1999). In both interviews and questionnaires, many Senegalese viewers suggested that television did not have any effect on their lives. As several Senegalese described television's impact: "I'm autonomous in my thinking"; "I'm independent in what I believe"; and "I think for myself, then talk with family and friends." Perhaps summarizing this view best, a student at the Université Gaston Berger said, "I know Westerners think Africans aren't very smart and so will think TV will have a big influence on us, but it's not true. We know what is real and what is not real on TV. I can judge." But while many regular viewers of television claimed that television did not affect them, they argued that it influenced others. Notably, male viewers often said that television shaped the attitudes and behaviors of young women too much, and women said that television swayed children too much. Many pointed toward changes in fashion – preference for Western clothes, length of dresses, emphasis put on slimness, wearing of dreadlocks, and the use of rap/hip hop language and posturing – as examples of how television influences young people for the worse.

Others argued that television has divided Senegal further into "haves" and "have nots," especially in terms of class but also region ("Une autre télévision pour les riches," *Wal Fadjri* 7 July 1993; "Ma télé? Il n'en a pas," *Sad Quotidien* 19 July 1993; "Télévision: Les paraboles des riches," *Sud Quotidien* 27 September 1993). Because of the cost associated with obtaining Canal Horizons and TV5, those services in particular have been criticized for their elitism. Both Moussa Paye of the Communication Ministry and Babacar Touré of *Sud* (personal interviews 5 July 1994 and 27 June 1994) have suggested that the Senegalese government allowed Canal Horizons and TV5 to enter the country to meet elites' demands for the trappings of "modern" society. Many of my respondents echoed this view and added that they felt the French and francophone channels helped the Senegalese government divert viewers' attention away from local reporting on domestic issues. Many Senegalese I talked with said they did not want to be swamped by imported television programming; they valued Senegalese shows, though they wished they were of higher technical quality. Some viewers suggested that they wanted the government to intervene to ensure greater educational or cultural content, but many more said that the government should have no interest in RTS or the other international channels because such involvement was undemocratic.

Conclusion

While there has been a good deal of research that has explored how older and/or traditional forms and functions of popular art in Africa have been transformed through interaction with foreign cultures (see, e.g., Arnoldi et al. 1996; Barber 1997a, 1997b), there has not been a corresponding interest in media. In the past thirty years, television has become part of the Senegalese popular imagination, with images and ideas about television making their way into songs, *sous verre* (under glass) painting, cartoons, postcards, wood carvings, magazines, and radio talk shows. The entry of television into Senegalese thought and national discourse and the form that television in Senegal has taken are closely tied to a uniquely Senegalese postcolonial history. Senegal has not been simply inundated since independence by a larger flood of images and programming coming from the West. Rather, the attenuated introduction of television to the country and the array of programming made incrementally available to different segments of Senegalese society suggest a nation and its leaders trying, largely unsuccessfully, to manage cultural life according to their own designs. Government decisions have set parameters for television growth and content, but the overall effect of policy has been to contribute to the eclecticism of Senegalese airwaves, rather than shape television content. Television, like the rest of Senegalese cultural life, is variously parochial and cosmopolitan, but distinctly Senegalese in its combination of values.

Central to the emergence of this eclecticism have been the idiosyncratic thought and careful political positioning of key leaders such as Senghor and Diouf, navigating through decades of political and cultural change in their country. As shown here, they have needed at various times to appeal to particular ethnic and class constituencies, and these appeals have led to ad hoc and therefore often inconsistent decisions about media, especially television. The increasing cosmopolitanism of the Senegalese population at large, partly a function of world travels of Senegalese citizens from a surprising variety of ethnic and class backgrounds, is a major cultural condition that leaders are navigating now (Perry 1997). Openings to world television during the 1990s have only partly satisfied the demand for variety and quality. The trend toward media openness and a free market of cultural ideas is likely to continue because large segments of the Senegalese population demand it. State oversight has a long tradition in Senegal, however, and the continued opening of media markets is likely to be a state-managed process until such time as available technology has overridden the capacity of the state to control it.

Notes

1. All translations from French to English are by the author. Texts of speeches, government documents, and news clippings were gathered at the Senegalese National Archives in Dakar. The newspaper *Le Soleil*, which is government-owned, is treated as part of official government discourse. *Le Soleil* calls itself the "Official newspaper of Senegal." Stories used from other private (often opposition) newspapers, such as *Sud Quotidien* and *Wal Fadjri*, were gathered at the newspapers' libraries in Dakar.

2.   With a 0.05-kilowatt transmitter, broadcasts did not reach beyond thirty kilometers, roughly the city limits.

3.   Finding just how many people watch television or have access to television is quite difficult. For instance, though a single household may subscribe to Canal Horizons, viewing usually occurs in groups, with neighbors, friends, and family, and sometimes interested passersby who are invited to watch. People also watch television in bars, restaurants, and appliance shops, especially during soccer championships, when large groups assemble. According to both Boissy and W. Touré, women usually made the decision as to whether a household subscribed to the television services. Boissy also noted that women were more likely than men to complain about Canal Horizons programming, saying that the channel had too many sporting events.

4.   During the summers of 1994 and 1996, I conducted a series of informal interviews with Senegalese television viewers in Dakar and Saint-Louis. Additionally, I asked other television viewers to complete a questionnaire about their television habits (when and how often they watched, what programs they liked best, what they thought of RTS, Canal Horizons, and TV5, who they watched with, where they watched, etc.), My research assistant, Papa Demba Sarr, and I collected some eighty-eight completed questionnaires in 1994 and another forty-six in 1996. Any quoted material is anonymous. Though the results have not been systematized and were part of a convenience sample, there were a variety (age, gender, ethnicity) of respondents. However, I do not try to generalize but only report some anecdotes and apparent patterns.

References

Books and Journal Articles

Ager, D. (1996). *"Francophonie" in the 1990s: Problems and Opportunities*. Clevedon, England: Multilingual Matters.

Arnoldi, M. J., C. M. Geary & K. L. Hardin (eds.) (1996). *African Material Culture*. Bloomington: Indiana University Press.

Barber, K., (ed.) (1997a). *Readings in African Popular Culture*. Oxford: James Currey Press.

Barber, K., guest (ed.) (1997b). Audiences in Action. *Africa* 67(3), pp. 347–490.

Boone, C. (1992). *Merchant Capital and the Roots of State Power in Senegal, 1930–1985*. Cambridge: Cambridge University Press.

Carlos, J. (1985). La Radio et la Télévision en Faveur de la Participation à la vie Culturelle: Le cas du Sénégal. In: J. G. Sorgho (ed.), *La Fonction Culturelle de l'information en Afrique*, pp. 157–90. Dakar: Les Nouvelles Editions Africaines.

Chipman, J. (1989). *French Power in Africa*. Oxford: Basil Blackwell.

Coulon, C. (1988). Senegal: The Development and Fragility of Semidemocracy. In: Diamond, L., J. Linz & S. Lipset (ed.), *Democracy in Developing Countries: Africa*, vol. 2, pp. 141–78. Boulder, CO: Lynne Rienner.

Cruise O'Brien, R. (1985). Broadcast Professionalism in Senegal. In: F. O. Ugboajah (ed.), *Mass Communication, Culture and Society in West Africa*, pp. 187–99. Munich: Hans Zell.

Diop, M. & M. Diouf (1990). *Le Sénégal sous Abdou Diouf*. Paris: Editions Karthala.

Diouf, M. (1996). Urban Youth and Senegalese Politics: Dakar, 1988–1994. *Public Culture* 8, pp. 225–49.

Fougeyrollas, P. (1967). *L'education des adultes au Sénégal*. Paris: UNESCO.

Gellar, S. (1995). *Senegal: An African Nation Between Islam and the West*. 2d ed. Boulder CT: Westview.

Hargreaves, A. & M. McKinney (1997). *Post-Colonial Cultures in France*. London: Routledge.

Head, S. W. (1974). *Broadcasting in Africa: A Continental Survey of Radio and TV*. Philadelphia: Temple University Press.

Katz, E. & G. Wedell (1977). *Broadcasting in the Third World*. Cambridge MA: Harvard University Press.

Léger, J.-M. (1987). *La Francophonie: Grand Dessein, Grande Ambiguité*. Québec: Hurtubise HMH.

Lerner, D. (1958). *The Passing of Traditional Society*. Glencoe, IL: Free Press.

Ly, S. (1993). Senegal: Pluralism in Radio Broadcasting. In: Lena Senghor (ed.), *Radio Pluralism in West Africa*, vol. 3, pp. 91–118. Paris: PANOS.

Ly Diop, F. (1989). *Communication, audio-visuel et education: Etude de l'impact des émissions de télévision sur les enfants*. Projet de recherche dans le cadre du diplôme d'études approfondies d'anthropologie. Dakar: Chiekh Anta Diop.

Martin, G. (1995). Continuity and Change in Franco-African Relations. *Journal of Modern African Studies* 33, pp. 1–20.

McNamara, F. T. (1989). *France in Black Africa*. Washington, DC: National Defense University.

Miller, C. (1990). *Theories of Africans: Francophone Literature and Anthropology in Africa*. Chicago: University of Chicago Press.

Paye, M. (1992). La presse et le pouvoir. In: M. C. Diop (ed.), *Sénégal: Trajectoires d'un état*, pp. 331–77. Dakar: CODESRIA.

Perry, Donna L. (1997). Rural Ideologies and Urban Imaginings: Wolof Immigrants in New York City. *Africa Today* 44(2), pp. 229–60.

Schraeder, P. (1997). Senegal's Foreign Policy: Challenges of Democratization and Marginalization. *African Affairs* 96, pp. 485–508.

Schramm, W. (1964). *Mass Media and National Development: The Role of Information in the Developing Countries*. Stanford: Stanford University Press.

Silla, M. (1994). *Le paria du village planetaire our l'Afrique de la télévision mondiale*. Dakar: Les Nouvelles Editions Africaines du Sénégal.

Simpson, C. (1994). *The Science of Coercion: Communication Research and Psychological Warfare, 1945–1960*. New York: Oxford University Press.

Tétu, M. (1987). *La Francophonie: Histoire, Problématique et Perspectives*. Montréal: Guérin.

Tudesq, A.-J. (1992). *L'Afrique noire et ses télévisions*. Paris: Anthropos/INA.

Government Documents and Records

Allocution de M. (1968). le Président de la République [Senghor] à l'occasion de l'inauguration de l'exposition de la presse de langue française, December 10.

Allocution de M. (1976). le Président de la République [Senghor] à l'occasion de l'inauguration du centre émetteur de télévision de Thiès, July 21.

Allocution de M. (1986).le Président de la République [Diouf] au Conseil intergouvernemental des ministrès de l'information des pays non-alignés, January 9.

Allocution de M. (1990). le Président de la République [Diouf] au Conseil national, *La corrélation entre la communication et le développement est évidente*, May 28.

Allocution de M. (1985). Cherif Thiam, ORTS, *L'ORTS et la télévision en milieu rural. Première semaine nationale de l'audiovisuel et de l'ORTS*, May 7.

Compte rendu du Conseil interministériel (1971). Secrétariat général du gouvernement, October 25, no. 5493.

Compte rendu du Conseil nation de l'audio-visuel (1976). Secrétariat général du gouvernement, January 30.

Congrès (VIIe) de l'Union Progressiste Sénégalaise (Maison de Parti) (1969). *Résolution sur la Presse*, December 27–30.

Conseil national de l'audio-visuel (1978). Ministère de l'Information et des Télécommunications changé des rélations avec les Assemblées, Jean Pierre Bondi, July 3.

Haut Conseil de la Radio-Télévision (1994 and 1995). *Rapport annuel au président de la république*, Dakar: Tandian and TECNOEDIT.

Projet de décret portant création du Comité National de l'action culturelle et des moyens audio-visuel (1972). Secrétariat général du gouvernement, September 13, no. 04258.

Projet de loi abrogeant et remplacant le 2 alinea de l'article premier de la loi, no. 73–51, du 4 déc (1973). transformant la radiodiffusion nationale en Office de Radiodiffusion-télévision au Sénégal (ORTS) (1977). Secrétariat général du gouvernement, January 13.

Projet de loi portant approbation des statuts de la radiodiffusion télévision sénégalaise (1992). République du Sénégal. Ministère de la Communication, February 12.

Secrétariat du Conseil des Ministrès (1985). *Rapport de présentation du projet de decret fixant les règles d'organisation et de fonctionnement de l'Office de la Radiodiffusion-télévision*, January 14.

Newspaper Articles

Le Soleil:

L'apport de TV5-Afrique (1992). October 1, by Moudo M. Faye.

Baisse effectivement des prix, mais les vendeurs ne font pas de crédit sur les téléviseurs (1973). March 15.

CH en vue (1990). November 21, by Lassana Cissokho.

CH montre ses grilles (1990). October 19.

Conseil interministériel sur les objectifs et les moyens de la communication audio-visuel: Réhabilitation des stations régionals (1983). October 26, by Abdallah Faye.

Décisions hier au Conseil interministériel, augmentation de la subvention à la radio; misc à l'étude d'un projet de télé (1971). October 5 .

Dialogue sur l'utilisation des médiats d'état (1993). January 22.

Edifier un paysage a-v national, credible, et compétitive (1990). November 2, by Amadou Mbaye.

L'enquête (1972). August 29, by M. Touré.

L'ère de responsabiité (1991). July 27–28, by Seeyni Ndiaye.

L'HCRT vu par les professionals (1991). September 4.

Des jeunes Africains face à la culture "mediatique" transnationale (1996). July 9, by Moustapha Gueye.

Les objections du RND (1991). September 19.

L'opposition boycotte (1992). March 15.

L'ORTS est né (1973). November 23, by Ibrahim Mansour M'Boup. Plan d'urgence pour ORTS (1979). November 2.

Les programmes de la nouvelle grille (1990). November 2, by Amadou Mbaye.

Quand le petit écran fait relanche (1973). May 28.

Recentrer le débat (1990). November 2, by Mouhamadou Dia.

Respecter les principes du pluralism (1992). December 10, by Papa Boubacar Samb.

La RTS passe société nationale (1992). January 30, by Abdoulaye Elimane Kane.

Télé – Des émissions pour qui? (1972). August 13.

La télé continue (1972). September 14.

300 millions d'Allemagne fédérale pour ORTS (1981). April 28.

TV: La grille au changement? (1992). October 8, by El Hadj Amadou Mbaye.
Un mal nécessaire? (1992). February 4, by A. F. Bodian.

Sud Quotidien:
Les bons et les méchants (1993). October 8, by Boucar Niang.
Le Fann (1992). January 7.
Ma télé? Il n'en a pas (1993). July 19, by Oumar Ndao.
Podor sans télé (1993). August 5, by Ahmed Sy.
Promiscuité familiale (1993). October 1.
La télé unique, un mal unique (1993). December 31, by Boucar Niang.
Télévision: Les paraboles des riches (1993). September 27, by M. T. Talla.

Wal Fadjri:
A consommer avec moderation (1993). September 29, by Valérie Gas.
L'antenne ne sera pas à tous (1993). November 23, by Jean Meïssa Diop.
Parlez, il en restera quelque chose (1993). January 8–14, by Jean Meïssa Diop.
Une autre télévision pour les riches (1993). July 7, by Jean Meïssa Diop.

Jeune Afrique:
Les antennes diaboliques (1994). November 17–23. 1767: 56–7, by Assou Massou.
Les chaînes d'Afrique se déchaînes (1994). February 3–9. 1726: 60–3, by Jean-Luc Eyguesier.
La France multiplie les medias (1990). December 11. 1562: 78–80, by Pierre Huster.
Francophonie par satellite (1990). December 5–11. 1562: 85–7, by Yves Gallard.
Un paysage audiovisuel en pleine mutation (1991–8). December 18 January 1992. 1616–1617: 59, 61–3, by Phillipe Tranchard.
Quelles programmes pour l'Afrique? (1994) November 17–23. 1767: 47–8, 51, by Bernard Duhamel.
Sénégal: Images très privées (1990). July 1 August 25. 1543: 27–30, by Ariane Poissonnier.
Une chaîne pour l'Afrique (1992). July 9–15. 1644: 34–5, by Frédéric Dorce.

Other:
Télé Munich 'Ministériel'? (1972) *La Lettre Fermée*. August 11–24, by Abdou Rahman Cissé.

Personal Interviews

Boissy, Anne Marie Senghor, assistant director general, Canal Horizons (1994). July 7, Dakar.
Camara, Maine Less, secretary general, SYNPICS (Syndicat des professionnels de l'information et de la communication du Sénégal) (1996). July 12, Dakar.
Cissé, Abdou Rahman, acting commissioner of the Ministry of Information from 1962 to 1964 and former publisher of *La Lettre Fermée* (1996). July 14, Dakar.
Diop, Adrienne, journalist and programmer at RTS (1994). July 7, Dakar.
Paye, Moussa, official at the Ministry of Communication (1994). July 5, Dakar.
Touré, Babacar, publisher of *Sud Quotidien* and owner of *Sud FM* (1994). June 27, Dakar.
Touré, Wahab, director general, TV5 (1994). July 5, Dakar.

Websites

Doit-on interdire à nos enfants de regarder la television? (1999). February 16, by Arame Gaye Diop. http://sudonline.com/Rubriques%20infos/opinion2.htm (February 20 1999).
RTS, www.primature.sn/rts.

79

Discrepant Intimacy: Popular Culture Flows in East Asia

*Koichi Iwabuchi**

The development of communications technologies has facilitated the simultaneous circulation of media information, images, and texts on a global level. In this process, various (national) markets are being penetrated and integrated by powerful global media giants such as News Corp and Disney. However, media globalization does not just mean the spread of the same products of Western (mostly American) origin all over the world through these media conglomerates. Non-Western players also actively collaborate in the production and circulation of global media products. For transnational corporations to maximize the profit, the imperatives are the global selection of new cultural products with an international appeal as well as the establishment of a business tie-up with partners at each level – whether in the form of buy-out or tie-up – to enter simultaneously such various market domains as global, supranational regional, national, and local. In this context of increasing integration, networking, and cooperation among transnational cultural industries, we are witnessing the global circulation of Japanese animation and video games, Hong Kong stars and directors' inroads into Hollywood, and the involvement of Japanese corporations such as Sony in global media conglomeration.

These developments testify to a decentering of capitalist modernity from the West and of the global cultural power structure from the US (Tomlinson, 1997). The unambiguous dominance of Western cultural, political, economic, and military power has constructed a modern world-system covering the whole globe. However, the historical process of globalization has not simply produced a Westernization of the world. Its impact on the constitution of the world is much more heterogeneous and contradictory. The experience of "the forced appropriation of modernity" in the non-West has also produced polymorphic vernacular modernities (Ang & Stratton, 1996). This testifies to the ample incorporation of the Western mode of capitalist modernity into non-Western contexts (Dirlik, 1994). Yet, this ongoing asymmetrical cultural encounter in the course of the spread of Western modernity sheds light on various kinds of similar *and* different experiences of urbanization and modernization in many parts of the world. As Ang and Stratton (1996: 22–4) argue, we have come to live in "a world where all cultures are both (like) 'us' and (not like) 'us,'" one where familiar difference and bizarre sameness

* Taken from pp. 19–36 in *Asian Media Studies*, ed. J. Erni and S. H. Chua (Malden, MA: Blackwell). First appeared as "Becoming Culturally Proximate: A/scent of Japanese Idol Dramas in Taiwan," pp. 54–74 from *Asian Media Productions*, ed. B. Moeran (London, Curzon, 2001) and as "Nostalgia for Asian Modernities: Media Consumption of 'Asia'," in *Japan Positions: East Asia Cultures Critique*, vol. 10, no. 3 (2002). The chapter is also a condensed version of some chapters from (2002) *Recentring Globalization: Popular Culture and Japanese Transnationalism* (Durham, NC: Duke University Press). © 2005 by Blackwell Publishing Ltd. Reprinted with permission from Blackwell Publishing.

are simultaneously articulated in multiple ways through the unpredictable dynamic of uneven global cultural encounters.

The proliferation of modernities in the world does not just construct a milieu in which "the Rest" plays a significant role in media globalization. It has also facilitated the capitalization on intraregional cultural resonances with the emergence of regional media and cultural centers such as Brazil, Egypt, Hong Kong, and Japan (e.g., Straubhaar, 1991; Sinclair et al., 1996). In east Asia, intraregional media flows particularly among Japan, Taiwan, Hong Kong, and South Korea are gradually becoming active and constant more than ever. Popular culture circulating in east Asia in most cases unavoidably embodies American origin. Nevertheless, preferred cultural products in the region are not without east Asian flavor, as those are reworked in Asian context by hybridizing various latest fads all over the world; they are inescapably global and (East) Asian at the same time, lucidly representing intertwined composition of global homogenization and heterogenization in east Asian context.

Popular culture flows might promote dialogue as well as asymmetry in Asian regions. This chapter explores how the unevenness of transnational media flows is embedded in the perception of cultural distance, which is in a state of flux under globalization processes. Non-Western countries have tended to face the West to interpret their position and understand the distance from Modernity. The encounter has always been based upon the expectation of difference and time lag. The perception of cultural distance among non-Western nations has tended to be swayed by their relative temporal proximity to Western modernity, the standard by which the developmental ranking of the non-West has been determined (cf. Fabian, 1983). As an apt illustration, such a developmental yardstick was earlier exploited by Japanese imperialist ideology to confirm Japan's superiority to other racially and culturally similar Asian nations and justify the Japanese mission to civilize Asia.

The intensification of media and popular culture flows in east Asia suggests a possibility that the diminishing temporal lag, thanks to shared experience of industrialization, global spread of consumerist lifestyles, and the (simultaneous) transnational circulation of media images and information, (re)activates the sense of spatial affiliation and resonance in the region. While in this context some non-Western modern nations are now facing each other to find their neighbors experiencing and feeling similar things, such as the temporality of east Asian vernacular modernities through media and popular culture flows, the careful analysis of intraregional cultural flows will also underline the newly articulated time–space configurations and asymmetrical cultural power relations. In the following, I will examine how the perception of cultural intimacy and "familiar difference" of cultural neighbors is experienced differently and unevenly as media industries increasingly capitalize on the regional cultural resonance in east Asia through the promotion and consumption of Japanese TV dramas in Taiwan and of Hong Kong stars in Japan.[1]

Japanese TV Dramas in Taiwan

Animation, comics, characters, computer games, fashion, pop music, and TV dramas – a variety of Japanese popular culture has been so well received in east and southeast

Asia. Particularly noticeable are Japanese TV dramas attracting young audiences in the regions. According to a 1997 Communication White Paper published by the Japanese Ministry of Posts and Telecommunication, the number of TV programs exported to Asian markets in 1995 amounted to 47 percent of the total export and TV dramas occupied 53 percent of the export to Asia.

The most receptive market to Japanese TV drama is Taiwan, in which there are four cable TV channels solely broadcasting Japanese programs. The Taiwanese government banned the broadcasting of Japanese-language programs when the Japanese government officially reestablished diplomatic relations with China in 1972, but Japanese TV programs have been widely watched through pirated videos/VCDs (video compact disks) and illegal cable channels in Taiwan. After the government removed its ban on broadcasting Japanese-language TV programs and songs around the end of 1993, the spread of Japanese TV dramas in east Asia has come to rest on a far broader consumer base. The increasing presence of Japanese popular culture in Taiwan is not mostly initiated by Japanese cultural industries. Rather, there has been a strong local initiative as local companies have grabbed business opportunities to sell Japanese TV programs during the process of media globalization in Taiwan (see Iwabuchi, 1998). Along with political and economic liberalization, the expansion of the entertainment industry and market in Taiwan has facilitated the influx of Japanese popular culture in Taiwan. This development has exposed the audience in Taiwan to more information about Japanese pop icons, through newspapers, magazines, and television, and given the local industries an incentive to exploit the commercial value of Japanese popular music, encouraging them to invest a large amount of money in promoting it in Taiwan.

In Taiwan, the recent surge of Japanese cultural influence is inevitably discussed in relation to the history of colonial rule. In 1997, a leading weekly newsmagazine in Taiwan had feature articles on Japanese popular culture in Taiwan titled "Watch Out! Your Kids are Becoming Japanese." The journal coined a new Taiwanese phrase, 哈日族 [*harizhu*], to describe young people who adore things Japanese (*Journalist*, April 13–19, 1997). While Japan was not strongly condemned for "cultural invasion," the spread of Japanese popular culture was associated with the colonial habit of mimicking, which is thought to be sedimented deeply in Taiwanese society (see also *China Times*, March 17, 1997).[2] Undeniably, the historical legacy of Japanese colonization has over-determined the recent influx of Japanese popular culture. From food and housing to language, examples can easily be found of a lingering Japanese cultural influence in Taiwan. Besides Korea, the number of people speaking Japanese that can be found in Taiwan is by far the largest in the world and many Japanese words and cultural meanings have become indigenized. Older people who were educated during the Japanese occupation still speak fluent Japanese and enjoy Japanese-language books, songs, and TV programs. Many also regard their former colonizers in a relatively positive light, the bitter memories of their rule having diminished by contrast with the repressive and authoritarian rule of the KMT government which moved from mainland China to the island after the Second World War (see Liao, 1997). These conditions surely make Japanese TV programs much more accessible than in other parts of Asia, particularly in stark contrast to South Korea.

Yet avid young consumers of Japanese popular culture hold quite different views of and affinity with Japan. The meaning "Japan" possesses for young Taiwanese, most of whom do not understand Japanese language, is undoubtedly different from that which it holds for their forebears. It is often argued that the younger generations have no special affection for Japanese culture, and the symbolic meaning of "Japan" articulated through Japanese popular culture in Taiwan is marked by superficiality.[3] There is some truth in this postmodernist claim of image consumption in the age of global mass culture (Hall, 1991). Nevertheless this does not sufficiently address the issue of why Japanese popular culture is preferred to those from other parts of the world and what cultural resonances are evoked for east Asians by it. In the next section, focusing on the reception of TV dramas, I will consider if and how the ascent of Japanese popular culture is associated with the ascent of transnational regional modernity in Taiwan.

East Asian Modernities and Japanese TV Dramas

One of the most popular daily newspapers, *The China Times*, started an interactive column on Japanese dramas in February 1996. A reporter writing on Japanese dramas for a newspaper informed me that: "Most high school and university students who watch Japanese dramas discuss the storyline with their friends. It is the most common topic for them just as Taiwan prime-time dramas [8 p.m. in the evening] used to be." Japanese dramas have become indispensable for everyday gossip in the younger generation.

There are many things that the audience wants to talk about in watching Japanese dramas. One of the main reasons why people watch Japanese drama in Taiwan is that they feature good-looking Japanese idols. Food, fashion, consumer goods, and music are also popular topics. However, Taiwanese audiences talk most eagerly about the story and the characters in the drama. Japanese dramas are diverse in terms of storylines, setting, and topics, but the dramas that become popular in Taiwan are stories featuring younger people's love affairs and lives in an urban setting. According to my interview with undergraduate students in Taiwan, one of the attractions of Japanese TV drama is its new style of portraying love, work, and women's position in society. These are all issues which young people are facing in urban areas in Taiwan, but which Taiwan TV dramas until recently did not offer to audiences. It seems to be this void that makes Japanese dramas popular texts to be talked about in everyday life.

For example, the popularity of *Tokyo Love Story*, the story of a couple in their early twenties, which sparked off the popularity and recognition of the quality of Japanese dramas in Taiwan and Hong Kong in the early 1990s, has much to do with (female) audiences' identification with the story and the heroine, Akana Rika. Rika is an unusually expressive and positive Japanese woman. A famous phrase uttered to her boyfriend which characterizes Rika symbolically is "Kanchi, let's have a sex!" Rika's single-minded pursuit of love and her frank expression of feelings is the object of admiration and emulation. My interviewees often expressed two seemingly contradictory statements about her. While on the one hand they would observe that "I have a strong feeling that she is exactly what I want to be," they would also remark that "I would not be able to become as brave and open as Rika." It was thus Rika's role as an ideal model that many women considered particularly appealing: she is what one could never quite become but someone one wants to be. Satomi, in contrast, served as Rika's foil. She was the embodiment of the traditional woman – dependent, submissive, domestic, and passive. It may be the case that audiences find Satomi more empirically realistic in the Taiwanese context. As such she was an object of aversion for all of my interviewees. The juxtaposition of Rika and Satomi brings Rika's attractiveness into sharp relief.

The attractiveness of *Tokyo Love Story* does not reside simply in making audiences feel that something different from the present can be imagined and dreamed of. Emotional involvement in the drama is facilitated by its depiction of a sentiment that the audience thinks and feels desirable but not unrealistic. It is not just a dream of tomorrow but a (possible) picture of today. Things happening in *Tokyo Love Story* also seem to be realistic or at least accessible to most of its young audiences. The same things could happen in their own everyday lives. On his home page, a young Hong Kong man explained why he liked the drama in these terms: "The twenty-something urban professionals of the series face a tightrope of coping that young people in many Asian cities have faced, but rarely more sympathetically. The major attraction of *Tokyo Love Story* to me is that it is not a story about somebody else. It is a story about our generation, about us, about myself. I can easily identify shadows of Rika or Kanchi among my peer group, even in myself" ("Kevin's Home," http://home.ust. hk/~kwtse).

This sense of the series being a "story about us" was strongly shared by the Taiwanese fans. More than 60 percent of 61 university students surveyed by Li et al. (1995) – and 75 percent of the female subjects – replied that love affairs such as those portrayed in *Tokyo Love Story* could happen around them. However, like the realism of Rika's character discussed before, this should not be straightforwardly read as evidence of the objective, empirical realism of *Tokyo Love Story*, with which audiences identify. As Ang (1985: 44–5) argues concerning audiences' identification with *Dallas*, "the concrete situations and complications are rather regarded as symbolic representations of more general experiences: rows, intrigues, problems, happiness and misery. And it is precisely in this sense that these letter-writers find *Dallas* realistic. In other words, at a connotative level they ascribe mainly emotional meanings to Dallas." What audiences find "realistic" in viewing *Tokyo Love Story* is thus not that an identical love affair would actually happen or that anyone can become like Rika. Li et al. (1995) suggest that one of the attractions of *Tokyo Love Story* for university students in Taiwan is its new style of portraying love, work, and women's position in society. These are all issues which young people are actually facing in urban areas in Taiwan, but which American or Taiwanese TV dramas have never sympathetically dealt with. It is at this more generalized level of meaning concerning love affairs and human relations represented in *Tokyo Love Story* that audiences in Taiwan perceive it as "our" story.

In my research in Taiwan, I often heard Taiwanese young viewers say that Japanese dramas represent favorable realism that cannot be gained from Western/American dramas or from Taiwan dramas. An early twenties informant told me that the lifestyle and love affairs in an American drama such as *Beverley Hills 90210* are something she enjoys watching, but she found Japanese love stories more realistic and easier to relate to. A 17-year-old high school student also told me that "Japanese dramas better reflect our reality. Yeah, *Beverley Hills 90210* is too exciting [to be realistic]. Boy always meets girl. But it is neither our reality nor dream."

Many people tended to associate Japanese drama's "realism" with cultural similarities between Taiwan and Japan. Japanese dramas are consciously watched as foreign, but Japanese culture is perceived as closer to Taiwan while physical appearance and skin color are quite similar to the American counterpart. "Japan is not quite but much like us," as two early twenties females said, "the distance we feel to Japan is comfortable, while Americans are complete strangers"; "I've never seen such dramas which perfectly express my feeling . . . the West is so far away from us, so I cannot relate to American dramas." They said that the ways of expressing love in Japanese dramas which were delicate and elegant were much more culturally acceptable than those of American dramas, and human relations between family and lovers also looked culturally closer to Taiwan, so much so that Taiwanese audiences could relate to Japanese dramas more easily.

This seems to correspond with a finding that audiences tend to prefer watching TV programs from countries which are supposed to be culturally proximate to their own (cf. Straubhaar, 1991; Sinclair et al., 1996). Yet the perception of "cultural proximity" here should not be conceived in an essentialist manner. There might be some similar cultural values concerning family and individualism between Taiwan and Japan, but the attractiveness of such values is newly articulated by particular programs under a specific historical context. Rika's forward-looking and independent attitude depicted in *Tokyo Love Story*, for example, was perceived as a desirable image of "modern" or "new age" woman in Taiwan. Taiwanese viewers told me that Rika's attitude to love in *Tokyo Love Story* is different both from that of the characters of American dramas like *Beverley Hills 90210* which is too open and not single-minded, and from that of Taiwan dramas which are very passive and submissive. Taiwanese dramas often emphasize a traditional value: "fidelity" of women (Chan, 1996). Young audiences do not relate to it, but they favorably identify Rika's active and "modern" single-mindedness. Conversely, Rika may be too open to emulate, but her single-mindedness is different from American openness. It still represents "our" (Asian) reality and is therefore something to which the audience in Taiwan can emotionally relate. However, what is at stake here is not fidelity or single-mindedness in general or essentialized terms but a specific kind of single-mindedness as it is represented in *Tokyo Love Story*. In other words, this single-mindedness has been articulated through a Japanese (at the site of production) and Taiwanese (at the site of consumption) reworking of cultural modernity in the particular media text. Only through these dynamic processes has it come to embody an attractive single-mindedness, which is perceived to illustrate "New Age woman" in that it is at once implicated in the global (in the sense of "American" in this instance) and situated in east Asian contexts. To engage with the complexity of audience identification with Rika's attractive character in Taiwan, we thus need to consider it in a wider sociocultural context of the 1990s in which cultural modernity is reworked in east Asia.

Becoming Culturally Proximate

In non-Western countries, America has long been closely associated with images of being modern. Whenever American popular culture is consumed, people also enjoy a yearning for the American way of life. As Mike Featherstone (1996: 8) argues regarding the symbolic power of McDonald's, "It is a product from a superior global center, which has long represented itself as the center. For those on the periphery it offers the possibility of the psychological benefits of identifying with the powerful." Indeed, I clearly remember that I ate Kentucky Fried Chicken in the late 1970s in Tokyo, feeling that I was becoming an American. But such a stage is over. In Japan in 1995 I saw a 7-year-old boy express his amazement at seeing a Kentucky Fried Chicken shop in the United States on TV: "Wow there is a Kentucky in America as well." "American dreams" have been indigenized in some modernized non-Western countries (cf. Watson, 1997).

To some Taiwanese audiences for whom modernity is no longer just dreams, images, and yearnings of affluence, but reality, that is, the material conditions in which people live, Japanese popular culture offers what can be called an "operational realism"; American dreams are concretized into something ready for use. A manager of a Japanese cable channel explains this astutely.

> When Taiwan was still a poor country, we had just a dream of a modern lifestyle. It was an American dream. But now that we have become rich, we no longer have a dream but it is time to put the dream into practice. Not American dream but Japanese reality is a good object to emulate for this practical purpose.

It should be noted here that even for those who delight in watching Japanese TV dramas, "Japan" does not attain the status as an object of yearning that "America" once did. Although the recent influx of Japanese popular culture in Taiwan is undoubtedly overdetermined by the legacy of Japanese colonial rule, and the cultural flows between Japan and Taiwan are unambiguously uneven, the popularity of Japanese television dramas in Taiwan does not suggest that the relationship between Japan and Taiwan is straightforwardly conceived to be one of center–periphery. It is not the pleasure of "identifying with the powerful" but rather a sense of living in the same temporality, a sense of being equal, that sustains Japanese cultural presence in Taiwan. As Fabian (1983: 23) argues in his discussion of how the Western denial of recognizing the sharing of the same temporality with non-Western cultural others has been institutionalized in anthropological research, the term "coevalness" connotes two interrelated meanings: synchronicity and contemporaneity. The development of global communication technologies and networks may further the denial of "contemporaneity" of the periphery through the facilitation of "synchronicity." To illustrate, Mark Liechty (1995: 194) elucidated the Nepalese experience of modernity as "the ever growing gap between imagination and reality, becoming and being." The disappearance of a time lag in the distribution of cultural products in many parts of the world has left wide political, economic, and cultural gaps intact, so much so that they facilitate the feeling in non-Western countries that "'catching up' is never really possible" (Morley & Robins, 1995: 226–7).

In Taiwan, as the gap in terms of material conditions narrows or even is disappearing, the meaning of "becoming" also changes from abstract to practical. An early twenties female who has long been a fan of Japanese popular culture said that:

> Taiwan used to follow Japan, always be a "Japan" of ten years ago. But now we are living in the same age. There is no time lag between Taiwan and Japan. I think since this sense of living in the same age emerged three or four years ago, more people have become interested in things in Japan.

Seen in this way, cultural proximity should not be conceived in terms of a static attribute of "being" but a dynamic process of "becoming." Cultural proximity in the consumption of media texts is thus being articulated and made conscious under homogenizing forces of "modernization" and "globalization." There is an ever-narrowing gap between Japan and Taiwan in terms of material conditions, the urban consumerism of an expanding middle class, the changing role of women in society, the development of communication technologies and media industries, the reworking of local cultural values, and the reterritorialization of images diffused by American popular culture. Historically overdetermined by Japanese colonization, under simultaneously homogenizing and heterogenizing forces of modernization, Americanization, and globalization, all elements complicatedly interact to articulate Japanese cultural power in the form of the cultural resonance of Japanese TV dramas for some Taiwanese viewers who synchronously and contemporaneously experience "Asian modernity" in mid-1990s east Asia, which American popular culture could never have presented.

Consuming Hong Kong Popular Culture in Japan

In Japan, however, popular culture from other Asian nations does not necessarily signify the same perception of cultural similarity and of living in the synchronous temporality as for Taiwanese viewers of Japanese TV dramas. Japanese consumption of Asian popular music and culture displays a rather different time–space configuration. The ever-increasing intraregional cultural flows within Asia and the narrowing economic gap between Japan and some Asian countries have activated a nostalgic longing for modernized/modernizing Asia, which strongly reflects Japan's colonial legacy in the region.

Since the early 1990s, as the Japanese media industry extended their activities to other (mainly east) Asian markets (Iwabuchi, 1998), the lively east Asian music scenes have captured wide media attention in Japanese male magazines. Particularly conspicuous in the mid-1990s was the heavy promotion of Hong Kong popular culture by the Japanese media industry (see *Nikke Entertainment*, Dec. 1997: 50–7). On the one hand, the main strategy of Japanese media industries is to sell "modern" and "fashionable" images of Hong Kong to a public more used to viewing the city as backward and dowdy. An example of a firm that pursued this tactic was Purénon H, a small film-distribution company. To improve the image of Hong Kong films, Purénon H organized a Hong Kong film fan club, Honkon Yamucha Kurabu, and established a Hong Kong film shop,

"Cine City Hong Kong," in a trendy spot in Tokyo, where many young people enjoy window-shopping in an elegantly decorated space. Purénon H distributed Wong Karwai's *Chungking Express* in Japan in 1995, which became a phenomenal hit. It was admired because it was the first Asian movie that refrained from playing upon Hong Kong's alleged exoticism and, instead, made it look like any other major European city (say, Paris) (Edagawa, 1997). Apart from this quality of the film, the director of Purénon H has striven to overcome Hong Kong film's dominant image of kung fu or (vulgar) slapstick comedy. The company chose the Japanese title *Koisuru Wakusei* ('A Loving Planet'), totally unrelated to the original title, *Chungking Express*, from more than 2,000 possibilities, so that the film could sound modern and accessible to wider audiences (*Nikkei Entertainment*, Dec. 1997: 53).

The success of Wong Kar-wai's stylish collage films, as well as the upsurge of Japanese media industries' promotion in the lead-up to the return of Hong Kong to China in July 1997, further fanned the flames of interest in "modern" Hong Kong popular culture in Japan. Especially keenly promoted by Japanese media industries are Hong Kong male stars such as Jacky Cheung, Andy Lau, Leslie Cheung, and Kaneshiro Takeshi,[4] all of whom have performed in Wong Kar-wai's films. Japanese production companies have contracted those stars for media appearances in Japan (*Nikkei Trendy*, June 1997: 97–104). Since December 1995, Hong Kong's "four heavenly kings" have held concerts in Japan and increased their appearances in the Japanese media.[5]

Nevertheless, the growing interest in Asia is never free from Japan's historically constituted haughty conception of "behind-the-times Asia." This is readily discerned in the representation of "Asia" in Japanese media texts in the 1990s, which were marked by nostalgia for Asia. Here, modernizing Asian nations are nostalgically seen to embody a social vigor and optimism for the future which Japan allegedly is losing or has lost. The appreciation of cultural modernity of other parts of Asia tends to be discussed and judged via economic developmental terms. This perception, revealing as it does Japan's disavowal of any possibility of it sharing the same temporality as other Asian nations, displays the asymmetrical flow of intraregional cultural consumption in east Asia.

Similarly, the consumption of Hong Kong popular culture also smacks of the nostalgic yearning for Asia's modern vigor, which is eled by a deep sense of disillusionment and discontent with Japanese society. The attraction of the films and performers, again, tends to be linked to the loss of energy and power of Japanese society in general, as women in their late twenties and late thirties told me: "Japanese TV dramas do not have dreams or passions. I sometimes enjoy watching them, but still feel [compared with Hong Kong actors] Japanese young actors lack a basic power and hunger for life"; "Wong Kar-wai's films always tell me how human beings are wonderful creatures and how love and affection for others are important for us to live. All of those are, I think, what Japan has lost and forgotten." The consumption of Hong Kong popular culture in Japan has made Japanese fans feel like regaining the vigor and hope they have lost in their daily lives. As a woman in her mid-twenties remarked: "I think people in Hong Kong really have a positive attitude to life. My image is that even if they know they are dying soon, they would not be pessimistic. This is in sharp contrast to present-day Japan. I can become vigorous when watching Hong Kong films and pop stars on video. Hong Kong and its films are the source of my vitality."

Ambivalent Nostalgia for Asian Modernity

The associations of present-day Hong Kong with Japan's loss, it can be argued, testify to the effortless consumption of an idealized Asian other which smacks of refusal to consider it as dwelling in the same temporality. However, as I listened carefully to these fans, I came to think that the sense of longing for vanished popular-cultural styles and social vigor does not exclusively attest to the perception of a time lag. It also manifests the Japanese fans' appreciation for the difference between Japanese and Hong Kong cultural modernity. Here we can see an ambivalence in Japan's nostalgia for a different Asian modernity: the conflation of a nostalgic longing for "what Japan has lost" and a longing for "what Japanese modernity has never achieved." What matters is Japan's lack as well as Japan's loss.

Here, the ever-increasing intraregional cultural flows within east Asia and the narrowing economic gap between Japan and Hong Kong display a rather different time–space configuration in the consumption of Hong Kong popular culture in Japan. Almost all Japanese interviewees also told me that they, like Taiwanese audiences of Japanese TV dramas, can more easily relate to Hong Kong stars and films than to Western ones due to perceived cultural and physical similarities. Western popular culture looks too remote from their everyday lives. However, unlike Taiwanese audiences of Japanese TV dramas, the sense of cultural and bodily proximity tends to simultaneously strengthen the Japanese fans' perception of cultural difference between Japan and Hong Kong. What is crucial here is that such perception is facilitated by recognition of the disappearance of temporal distance between Japan and Hong Kong. As a female in her late twenties told me: "I think that Hong Kong films are powerful and energetic. Hong Kong is apparently similar to Japan in terms of physical appearances, but I realized that its culture is actually completely different from us. [This is clearly shown by the fact that] Hong Kong has also achieved a high economic development, but still retains the vitality that Japan has lost." Although acknowledging Japanese economic superiority to Hong Kong, this Japanese female fan does not assume that Hong Kong is also losing something important, becoming like "us," precisely because Hong Kong has already achieved the same degree of economic growth and modernization as "ours." What sets Hong Kong apart is neither solely attributed to some primordial cultural difference nor to some developmental difference. Rather, the difference between Hong Kong and Japan has become evident in the course of modernization, especially through the way in which Western cultural influence is negotiated.

The Japanese representation and consumption of Hong Kong in the 1990s shows that many Japanese are attempting to recuperate something they think their country allegedly either is losing or has lost. Whether Japan ever had the social vigor projected on Asian popular culture is highly debatable – and ultimately irrelevant. The object of nostalgia is not necessarily some "real" past – the things that used to be[6]; the important point is that nostalgia arises out of a sense of insecurity and anguish in the present and of the present.

In the face of rapid modernization and globalization, nostalgia has played a significant role in the imagining of Japan's cultural authenticity and identity. These processes have intensified the country's cultural encounters with the West, and these, in turn, have generated a nostalgic desire in Japan, "a longing for a pre-modernity, a time before the West, before the catastrophic imprint of westernization" (Ivy, 1995: 241). A similar longing for the purity and authenticity of primordial life underpins Japanese media representations of, and backpacking trips to, "premodern" Asia. However, in the Japanese reception of Hong Kong popular culture, nostalgia is projected onto a more recent past, not before but after the West, or, more precisely, one in conjunction with the West. This nostalgia for a modern Asia is not fed by a nationalistic impulse to get rid of Western influence or to recuperate an "authentic" Japan. Rather, the issue at stake is how to live with Western-induced capitalist modernity, how to make life in actual, modern Japan more promising and humane.

This sense of urgency explains, if partly, why the object of nostalgia is directed to Asia's present. Japan's newly imagined "Asia" serves as a contraposition to their own society – one which is commonly regarded as suffocating, closed, and rigidly structured as well as worn down by a pessimism about the future, instilled by a prolonged economic recession. Here, "Asia" is not simply idealized as the way things were in Japan. Some people in Japan also appreciate it, for the purpose of self-reformation, as representing an alternative, more uplifting cultural modernity.

While it shows the possibility of transcending Japan's denial of coevalness with Hong Kong, the Japanese appreciation of Hong Kong's cultural modernity at the same time reproduces a "backward" Asia. Being critical of the Japanese mode of negotiation with the West nonetheless affirms Western-dominated capitalist modernity. As Morris-Suzuki (1998: 20) argues, the new Asianism in Japan "no longer implies rejection of material wealth and economic success, but rather represents a yearning for a wealth and success which will be somehow *different*" (emphasis in original). The fans' armchair engagement with "Hong Kong" modernity depends crucially on its imagined capitalist sophistication as opposed to the lack thereof in "Asia."

Many Japanese fans of Hong Kong popular culture emphasize the difference between "Hong Kong" and "Asia." This, on the one hand, looks a promising corrective to the construction of an abstract, totalizing conception of "Asia." These Japanese fans reject the dominant media's tendency to use the term "Asia" to refer to Hong Kong male stars.[7] It is in their encounter with a concretized Asia (e.g., appreciating Wong Kar-wai or Leslie Cheung, not Asian film or music in general) that we can detect self-reflexive voices and the realization that Japanese must meet other Asians on equal terms. However, in such a conception, other Asian nations are still reduced to entities that are undifferentiatedly represented by urban middle-class strata, the main players of consumerism. Moreover, the demarcation between Hong Kong and Asia is imperative for many fans, as the latter is predominantly associated with the image of backwardness. I have often heard interviewees remark that premodern China would corrupt Hong Kong's charm: "I am afraid that Hong Kong might be more Sinicized after the return to China. Hong Kong is losing a liberal atmosphere of 'anything goes' by political selfrestriction and is influenced by more traditional mainland Chinese culture which is definitely old-fashioned"; "The British presence has made Hong Kong sophisticated and something special. But I think Hong Kong is becoming dirtier and losing its vigor after its return to China."

China is threatening to destroy the cosmopolitan attraction of Hong Kong not only because of its rigid communist policy, as pointed out by Japanese commentators (e.g., Edagawa, 1997), but because of its "premodern" Chineseness. The imagining of a modern, intimate Asian identity is still based upon the reconstruction of an oriental Orientalism. As observed in the depiction of Asian male stars in *Elle Japon*, "Asian guys are becoming more and more stunning and beautiful with economic development in the region." A certain degree of economic development is thus a minimum condition for other Asian cultures to enter "our" realm of modernity. "Premodern" Asia never occupies a coeval space with capitalist Asia but represents a place and a time that some Japanese fans of Hong Kong popular culture have no desire to identify with. It is not temporally proximate enough to evoke a nostalgic longing for a (different) Asian modernity.

Unevenness Embedded in Intraregional Cultural Flows in East Asia

As we enter the new century, intraregional media and popular culture flows have been increasingly activated. We are observing more co-production and mutual promotion, and the rise of a new player – the popularity of Korean TV dramas and pop music in east Asian markets. My brief research in Taiwan in March 2002 showed that Taiwanese viewers now perceive Korean TV dramas, which subtly depict youth's love affairs in connection with family matters, as "ours" even more than Japanese TV dramas. Popular culture is connecting people at a great distance in east Asia; however, as I have shown in this chapter, the cultural immediacy which the intensifying cultural flows in east Asia evoke does not necessarily lead to cultural dialogue on equal terms. A close look at intraregional cultural flows and consumption highlights the newly articulated asymmetrical power relations in the region, not just in terms of quantity of media import/export, but also in terms of the perception of temporality manifest in the consumption of the media products of cultural neighbors.

Neither should we uncritically deal with the transnational regional flow of a highly commercialized materialistic consumer culture. The connections forged by media and popular culture is mostly between urban areas, especially between Tokyo, Hong Kong, Taipei, Seoul, Singapore, Shanghai, Bangkok, etc.; and many economically deprived people in these areas are still excluded from the shared experience of feeling vernacular modernities in the region. The active construction of meanings takes place under the system of global capitalism in which Japan has a major role. This point became acute at the beginning of the twenty-first century, especially after September 11, 2001, as we were compelled to recognize, through sudden, massive media attention on a hitherto forgotten country, Afghanistan, how the disparity between the haves and have-nots had been greatly widening, and how the disparity itself had been left out of global concern. The development of communication technologies and the intensification of media and cultural flows that simultaneously interconnect many parts of the world have also brought forward global indifference towards many deprived people and regions.

A series of events since September 11 has highlighted anew American economic and military supremacy, and a view that equates globalization with Americanization has accordingly regained momentum. However, I would suggest that such a view is misleading, as it conceals the fact that the unevenness in transnational connections is intensified not solely by the American command but by the various kinds of collusive alliances among the developed countries under the patronage of the dominant American military power. It cannot be emphasized enough that the decentering process of globalization has not dissolved global power structures: the latter has been subtly diffused and even solidified, unceasingly producing asymmetry and indifference on a global scale.

To be critically engaged with those issues, we should take intraregional dynamics in east Asia seriously. No armchair speculation – be it optimistic or pessimistic – would be able to fully capture the contradictory and unforeseeable processes. Empirically and rigorously attending to the way in which transnational popular culture flows connect east Asia is imperative in the study of the globalization of culture, which has heretofore been highly biased towards the ubiquity of Western media and popular culture and has tended to neglect intraregional interactions.

Notes

1. This chapter is a condensed version of some chapters of my book, *Recentering Globalization: Popular Culture and Japanese Transnationalism* (Durham, NC: Duke University Press, 2002). Some parts also appeared in "Becoming Culturally Proximate: A/Scent of Japanese Idol Dramas in Taiwan," in B. Moeran, ed., *Asian Media Productions* (London: Curzon, 2001, 54–74) and "Nostalgia for Asian Modernities: Media Consumption of 'Asia' in Japan," *Positions: East Asia Cultures Critique* 10(3) (2002). Field research was conducted in Tokyo in mid-January to late February in 1997 and from mid-March to late April 1998, and in Taipei from mid-December 1996 to mid-January and late May in 1997. I conducted informal depth interviews with 18 young female and 3 male viewers (age ranging from 17 to late twenties) of Japanese TV dramas in Taipei, and with 24 female "fans" (age ranging from early twenties to fifties) of Hong Kong film and pop singers in Tokyo.
2. In May 1997 I witnessed the occurrence of two incidents in Taiwan which, when juxtaposed, nicely illustrate that country's complicated relationship with Japan. The first was an anti-Japanese demonstration over the issue of Japan's possession of the Diaoyu Islands. The other was a rock concert by popular Japanese artists such as Globe and Amuro Namie which attracted much media attention as well as young audiences (see also *The Journalist*, June 1–7, 1997). This juxtaposition of "anti-" and "pro-" Japanese sentiment articulates a new generational divide.
3. Wu Nianzhen, the film director of *Dosan: A Borrowed Life* (1994), comments on the popularity of Japanese culture among the younger generation in Taiwan, "[m]y generation and my father's generation have a deep love-and-hate feeling towards Japan, though in quite different ways. But the younger generations have no special affection for Japanese culture, as there is no difference between Japan, America and Europe for them. Japan is just one option among many. I think the relationship between Taiwan and Japan will be more superficial in terms of affective feelings while deepened materially" (quoted in *Views*, Feb. 1996: 42). Like other Asian nations, Wu suggests, the symbolic meaning of "Japan" articulated through Japanese popular culture in Taiwan is marked by a waning affection for it.

4. Kaneshiro is Taiwanese-Japanese, but Hong Kong film has been his main field of activities.
5. Following the successful concerts in Japan of Jacky Cheung in 1995 and Andy Lau in 1996, Leslie Cheung and Aaron Kwok also held concerts in 1997.
6. Stewart (1988: 26) argues: "Nostalgia, like any form of narrative, is always ideological: the past it seeks has never existed except as narrative, and hence, always absent, that past continually threatens to reproduce itself as a felt lack."
7. E.g. *Nikkei Entertainment* (Dec. 1997); *Elle Japon* (Nov. 1997).

References

Ang, Ien (1985). Watching Dallas: Soap Opera and the Melodramatic Imagination. London: Methuen.

Ang, Ien & Jon Stratton (1996). Asianizing Australia: Notes toward a Critical Transnationalism in Cultural Studies. *Cultural Studies* 10(1), pp. 16–36.

Chan, Joseph Man (1996). Television in Greater China: Structure, Exports, and Market Formation. In: J. Sinclair, et al. (eds.), *New Patterns in Global Television: Peripheral Vision*, pp. 126–60. New York: Oxford University Press.

Dirlik, Arlif (1994). After the Revolution: Waking to Global Capitalism. Hanover: Wesleyan University Press.

Edagawa, Koichi (1997). HongKong 24:00 [Honkon 24ji: Konton toshi no shitataka na hitobito]. Tokyo: Magazin Hausu.

Fabian, Johannes (1983). Time and the Other: How Anthropology Makes Its Object. New York: Columbia University Press.

Featherstone, Mike (1996). Undoing Culture: Globalization, Postmodernism and Identity. London: Sage.

Hall, Stuart (1991). The Local and the Global. Globalization and Ethnicity. In: A. King (ed.), *Culture, Globalization, and the World-System*. pp. 19–39. London: Macmillan.

Ivy, Marilyn (1995). Discourses of the Vanishing: Modernity, Phantasm, Japan. Chicago: University of Chicago Press.

Iwabuchi, Koichi (1998). Marketing "Japan": Japanese Cultural Presence under a Global Gaze. *Japanese Studies* 18(2), pp. 165–80.

Iwabuchi, Koichi (2001). Uses of Japanese Popular Culture: Media Globalization and Postcolonial Desire for "Asia." *Emergences: Journal of Media and Composite Cultures* 11(2), pp. 197–220.

Li, Zhen-Yi, Zhen-Ling Peng, Qing Li & Jia-Qi Zhang (1995). Tokyo Love Story: A Study on the Reason of the Popularity and Audience Motivations in Taiwan. Unpublished undergraduate research paper of National University of Politics, Taiwan (In Chinese).

Liao, Chaoyang (1997). Borrowed Modernity: History and the Subject in A Borrowed Life. Boundary 2 24(3), pp. 225–45.

Liechty, Mark (1995). Media, Markets and Modernization: Youth Identities and the Experience of Modernity in Katmandu, Nepal. In: V. Amit-Talai & H. Wulff (eds.), *Youth Culture: A Cross-Cultural Perspective*, pp. 166–201. London: Routledge.

Morley, David & Kevin Robins (1995). Spaces of Identities: Global Media, Electronic Landscapes and Cultural Boundaries. London: Routledge.

Morris-Suzuki, Tessa (1998). Invisible Countries: Japan and the Asian Dream. *Asian Studies Review* 22(1), pp. 5–22.

Sinclair, John, Elizabeth Jacka & Stuart Cunningham (eds.) (1996). New Patterns in Global Television: Peripheral Vision. Oxford: Oxford University Press.

Stewart, Kathleen (1988). *Nostalgia: A Polemic. Cultural Anthropology* 3(3), August, pp. 227–41. Collection published by Duke University Press.

Straubhaar, J. (1991). Beyond Media Imperialism: Asymmetrical Interdependence and Cultural Proximity. *Critical Studies in Mass Communication* 8(1), 39–59.

Tomlinson, John (1997). Cultural Globalization and Cultural Imperialism. In: A. Mohammadi (ed.), International Communication and Globalization: *A Critical Introduction*, pp. 170–90. London: Sage.

Watson, James L. (ed.) (1997). Golden Arches East: McDonald's in East Asia. Stanford: Stanford University Press.

80

Contemporary Approaches to the Arts

Greg Dimitriadis and Cameron McCarthy*

Contemporary critical thinking on art and aesthetics, we argue, tends to take one of three approaches. Each of these approaches has contributed enormously to our understanding of the role of art in contemporary life, influencing a generation of first world critics in profound ways. Yet a major – indeed debilitating – constraint common to all three is that they cannot account for the specific circumstances of colonized people in the Third World and on the periphery of the first. Contemporary critical theories of art tend to disavow or silence the historical specificity and productivity of postcolonial artistic and cultural practices, a crucial and paralyzing elision.

The first approach has its roots in the work of Frankfurt School theorists such as Theodor Adorno, Max Horkheimer, and more recently Jurgen Habermas. This approach can be described as *anti-populist*. Proponents of anti-populism argue that the modern aesthetic object is little more than a work of capitalist wish fulfillment. The modern art object is located squarely in the metropolitan center, its elaboration of capitalism and its sinuous culture industry. Modern art, in the anti-populist view, is so compromised by the routinization and mass mediation of the culture industry that it has lost its unique capacity to critique or instruct (Adorno, 1980; Held, 1980).

The second approach in contemporary critical studies of art is linked to a more charitable view of art. This discursive move is *pro-populist* (McGuigan, 1992) and can be genealogically traced to the alternative wing of the Frankfurt School in treatises such as Walter Benjamin's "The Work of Art in the Age of Mechanical Reproduction" (1968) and more recently to Cultural Studies of the Birmingham School in England and its analogous traditions in Australia, Canada, the United States, and elsewhere. This approach sees contemporary art as participating in processes of political resistance, offering the masses a way out of the pitiless and inexorable logic of capitalism.

The third approach distinguishes itself from the previous two by suggesting a temporal shift in human sensibilities, the nature of capitalism, and alas, art itself, toward a contemporary condition in which the connection between art and society is severed, releasing new radical energies of multiplicity, irony, and destabilization. This approach to contemporary art goes under the banner of *postmodernism*. Postmodern cultural critics

such as Charles Jencks argue that we have entered a new millennium in which all hierarchies, from social organization to international relations to aesthetics, are being
replaced by loose, non-hierarchical structures whose omnivorousness is aided by a
computerization of all areas of life. In the postmodern world art does not imitate life;
life is aestheticized, and art is the genetic code for the new forms of existence and the
care of the self.

At best, anti-populist, pro-populist and postmodern criticism are capable of understanding aesthetic creations of the Third World only as some kind of Baudrillardian
counterfeit, the (Third World) copy that desires the place of the (first world) original,
but has no real aesthetic or intellectual home of its own. Postcolonial art is thought to
arise, via what Homi Bhabha (1994) calls a "time lag," in the tracks of the more dominant art discourses of the West. It is considered a harlequin patched together from
borrowed robes, a figure caught in the undertow of Western art and wrestling anxiously
to the surface for air. By contrast, in this chapter we will offer some thoughts toward a
new understanding of postcolonial art, attending to its historical specificity and productivity in careful and, we hope, richly suggestive ways.

In what follows in this chapter, we discuss some critical features of postcolonial art
by analyzing the work of a number of artists from the Third World and from the
periphery of the metropole. In so doing, we highlight the social and imaginative space
these artists share, the themes and tropes that run across these art forms and mark them
as historically and politically distinct. However, we offer no new theory here, nor do
we wish to subsume the work of these artists within a new, overarching "meta-narrative." The work of these artists, we found, has consistently exceeded the explanatory
frameworks we have brought to bear upon them. We thus look for specificity in this art
as we are continually alerted to its variability – a tension that will propel us through
ensuing chapters in which we explore in more detail what these artists have to offer the
field of education today.

We want to highlight, in particular, three important motifs and directions of the
work of art in the postcolonial imagination and draw a few conclusions. These three
motifs – *counterhegemonic representation*, *double or triple coding*, and *emancipatory or utopic
visions* – help define an emergent postcolonial aesthetic.

First, we consider postcolonial art's vigorous challenge of Western models of classical
realism and technologies of truth, which preserve the unity of the Western subject.
Second, we suggest that the work of art in the postcolonial imagination effectively
rewrites the binary logic of modernity that privileges the place of the West and empire
by creating oppositions of "center" and "periphery," "developed" and "underdeveloped," and "civilized" and "primitive." Third, we look at the way in which the work
of postcolonial artists foregrounds an emancipatory critical reflexivity and thoughtful-
ness that allow the artist to look upon his or her own traditions with the dispassion of
what Walter Benjamin calls "melancholy" (1977). By melancholy, we do not mean a
state of self-absorbed sadness or depression, but the whole process of historical alienation from received tradition understood as eternal truth. The melancholic artist therefore questions and problematizes inherited cultures and tradition using this approach
to explore the full complexity of the human condition as a whole. These practices of

"melancholic" skepticism and self-vigilance serve as critical elements in the aesthetic attempts of postcolonial artists to visualize a utopian community in which criteria for membership are not given *a priori*, in an inherited set of characteristics or a political platform.

We will now discuss each motif, bringing in illustrative examples from the works of a representative number of artists. We turn now to the postcolonial scrutiny of the theme of hegemonic representation.

The Critique of Hegemonic Representation

Traditions of European aesthetics – for example, in the art of the novel or perspectival oil painting – construct a freestanding subject at the heart of aesthetic work and address an equally coherent and fully integrated subject in the implied reader or viewer (Belsey, 1980; Berger, 1972). Both colonialism and perspectival imaging trace the emergence of a unified subject in Europe and European colonies. As Gayatri Spivak (1988) argues, even when the work of antimodernist/postmodernist writers foregrounds narrative collapse, what collapses is still a singular overmastering voice (see, for example, François Lyotard's *The Postmodern Condition* [1984] or Michel Foucault's *The Care of the Self* [1988]). In contrast, what we find in the work of the postcolonial artist – in the installations of Mona Hatoum or Young Soon Min, in painters such as Gordon Bennett, the Guyanese Aubrey Williams, or Indrani Gaul from India, in writings such as Wilson Harris's *The Palace of the Peacock* (1960), Isabel Allende's *The House of the Spirits* (1985), Wole Soyinka's *The Interpreters* (1965), Ayi Armah's *The Beautyful Ones are not yet Born* (1968), or Toni Morrison's *Song of Solomon* (1977) – is the effort to visualize community, a new community of fragile and polyglot souls. In contrast to the postmodern position, in postcolonial art the self is embedded in communal – though hybrid and multiple – trajectories. There is always an effort to link individual will and fortune to collective possibility.

Thus, postcolonial African writers like the Nigerian Wole Soyinka directly challenge the nineteenth-century novel's hierarchical arrangement of character and its insistence on a rational interiority or persona and verisimilitude of context and situation. In novels such as *Season of Anomy* (1974) and *The Interpreters* (1965), Soyinka offers up a set of characters who exist as principles or forces. They are parabolic characters or types. Their sense of interiority is diminished as they function as the carriers or vehicles of a Yoruba tradition engaged in a struggle with Western hegemony. The urbanized Lagos of *The Interpreters* exists as a cultural melting pot for all types of people and situations – a polyglot world populated by characters that we can hardly separate from one another. Our moral guides are Egbo, a Foreign Office diplomatic clerk; Sagoe, a journalist; Sekoni, an engineer and sculptor; Kola, an artist and Bandele University lecturer; and Lasunwon, a lawyer. These are "the interpreters," idealistic but hopelessly incorporated, even as they struggle against the corruption of European values and cultural forms that dominate modern Nigerian life. These characters collectively form a center of resistance alienated from the teeming, pretentious, and crassly materialistic world of post-independence Lagos.

Soyinka weaves into this social cauldron the brooding presence of the gods of Yoruba mythology and ritual. Time and space are altered, and events proceed within an unfolding ledger of fantasy and the constant subversion of reality. To transcend the spiritual wasteland of the city of Lagos, the interpreters must experience symbolic or real deaths, epitomized by Sekoni's passing. Narrated as the fulfillment of a ritual sacrifice to the god Obtala, Sekoni's death is compared to that of the dying bull in a Spanish bullfight (even death does not escape the narrator's satire and deep suspicion of the technological gifts of Westernness):

> The rains of May become in July arteries of the sacrificial bull, a million bleeding punctures of the sky-bull hidden in convulsive cloud humps. ... The blood of earth dwellers mingles with blanched streams of the mocking bull, and flows into currents eternally below the earth. The dome cracked above Sekoni's short sighted head one messy night. Too late the insanity of a lorry parked right in his path, a swerve turned into a skid and a cruel arabesque of tires. A futile heap of metal, and Sekoni's body lay surprised across the open door, showers of laminated glass around him, his beard one fastness of wet blood. (Soyinka, 1965, p. 155)

Soyinka's critique of imperialism is delivered in a novel in which men double up as gods and struggle to reconcile the ridiculousness of their world with fantasy, ritual, and tradition.

One is reminded here of the fiction of other African novelists such as Ayi Armah (*The Beautyful Ones are not yet Born*), Bessie Head (*A Question of Power* and *When Rain Clouds Gather*), and Ngũgĩ wa Thiang'o (*Devil on the Cross*) – a fiction that offers, like Soyinka's, a withering critique of the excesses of Europeans in Africa while at the same time exposing the ambivalence of cultural heritage that defines modern African identity. Like their creators, characters in the African postcolonial novel struggle with their colonial intimacy as illustrated by the protagonist of Ngũgĩ's *Devil on the Cross*, Wariinga, whose tormented dreams are the revelation of a divided personality as well as the staging ground for an ideological struggle over cultural imperialism:

> Instead of Jesus on the cross, she would see the devil, with skin as white as that of a very fat European she once saw near *The Rift Valley Sports Club*, being crucified by people in tattered clothes – like the ones she used to see in Bondeni – and after three days, when he was in the throes of death, he would be taken down from the cross by black suits and ties, and, thus restored to life, he would mock Wariinga. (Ngũgĩ, 1982, p. 139)

Like Soyinka and Ngũgĩ, the Puerto Rican painter Arnaldo Roche-Rabell uses his work to problematize contemporary existence on his island, dominated as it is by the impositions of the United States. Roche-Rabell also challenges the hegemony of the Western aesthetic norms in which he was schooled while showing their contradictory impact on the modern Puerto Rican subject. His deliberately oversized oil paintings, published in the catalogue *Arnaldo Roche-Rabell: The Uncommonwealth* (Hobbs, 1996), are particularly illustrative of Puerto Rico's struggle to construct identity and subjectivity from the fragments of an agonizing and tragic history. Roche-Rabell prosecutes his concern with the politics of identity and anti-colonialism in the creation of larger-than-life figures that often seem buried or interred in some kind of deeper structure. These figures are denied corporeal completeness or unity. And like Soyinka's characters, Roche-Rabell's figures are principles or parabolic types – protean sources of ambiguity or hybridity. In the canvas mural *Poor Devil* (1988), to give one example, the face of the devil seems thickly and densely overlaid, applied with multiple levels of red paint, on the head of a blue-eyed man. Roche-Rabell gives form to the repressed demons and monsters produced in Puerto Rico's history of colonization. His concern with the twinness or doubleness of personality and flawed subjectivity connects the themes of anti-colonialism and the themes of refusal of coherent subjectivity.

The devil folk mythology of the French Caribbean humanizes the powers of extreme evil in Derek Walcott's (1970) plays *Ti Jean and His Brothers* and *Dream on Monkey Mountain*. The devil as a trope of folk rejection of capitalism is also present in the lore of many plantation cultures throughout the Caribbean and Latin America, as Michael Taussig (1980) tells us in *The Devil and Commodity Fetishism in South America*. But Roche-Rabell adds a twist to this set of observations: the devil is in all of us. The postcolonial soul is damaged, but in its double or multiple personality, a new community is waiting to be born.

The utopian construction of community recurs across a range of traditions and historical contexts, including in the work of postcolonial African American novelists such as Toni Morrison. Morrison's novels mine a broad range of literary and vernacular traditions – from the Judeo-Christian Bible to the work of Shakespeare to African American spirituals to African folklore to blues and jazz and beyond. In this polyglot, alchemical manner, Morrison forges a vision of black communities that are both fragile and highly resilient, communities girded by traditions that are always open and subject to multiple manifestations. Her characters enter the fictive world as partial, fragmented selves ceaselessly reconstructing the past in the present, always in an open ended and protean fashion.

For example, the novel *Jazz* (Morrison, 1992) places us in the middle of a culturally brimming Harlem Renaissance following a murderous love triangle that plays itself out by way of the rhythms and tempos of that most protean and improvisational of musical idioms, jazz. Indeed, *Jazz* does not unfold in traditional narrative form (however melodramatic the "plot" might seem). Like jazz itself, the text layers multiple voices on top of one another, blurring the line between what has been composed in the past and what is realized in the moment, making linear narrative progression seem entirely anomalous.

Jazz is an appropriate and telling metaphor for the processes of community construction at the heart of this novel. Displaced Southerners in black Harlem must forge selves – improvisatory voices, so to speak – by way of a contingent group identity. This is delicate business. Ralph Ellison explores this connection between jazz improvisation and the constructed nature of marginalized identities in his essay on jazz, "The Charlie Christian Story" (1972). In an often-quoted passage, he notes:

> There is a cruel contradiction implicit in the art form itself. For true jazz is an art of indi-
> vidual assertion within and against the group. Each true jazz moment . . . springs from a
> contest in which each artist challenges all the rest; each solo flight, or improvisation, rep-
> resents (like the successive canvases of a painter) a definition of his identity: as individual,
> as member of the collectivity and as a link in the chain of tradition. Thus, because jazz
> finds its very life in an endless improvisation upon traditional materials, the jazzman must
> lose his identity even as he finds it. (p. 234)

This tension of finding, losing, and finding oneself in and through dynamic, traditional
group processes is on every page of *Jazz* and the rhythms and cultural practices on
which it draws.

The search for identity is thus a search for a collective self that connects the disenfranchised to multiple traditions, both global and local. This hybridity of culture, so
evident in the work of such artists as Gordon Bennett, Toni Morrison, and Nicholas
Guillen, transforms the binary oppositions privileged in the brutal colonial imagination:
West versus East, North versus South, the high versus the low, the civilized versus the
primitive. Transcending these binary oppositions allows these artists to rework the
center-versus-periphery distinction that has so undergirded the iconography and social
sciences of Western intellectuals, in order to look beyond its strictures to new histories,
new discourses, new ways of being.

We offer one last example of the plurality and multiplicity that one finds in the work
of Third World artists: the celebration of epic Indian ritual in everyday life in a distant
corner of the Caribbean, in the work of the St. Lucian Derek Walcott. In his 1993 Nobel
lecture, "The Antilles: Fragments of Epic Memory," Walcott talks about taking some
American friends to a peasant performance of the ancient Hindu epic of Ramayana
in a forgotten corner of the Caroni Plain in Trinidad. The name of this tiny village
is the happily agreeable – and English – "Felicity." The actors who spin this immortal
web of memory, ancientness, and modernity are the plain-as-day East Indian villagers.
Walcott is "surprised by sin" as the simple native world unfurls in its utter
flamboyance:

> Felicity is a village in Trinidad on the edge of the Caroni Plain, the wide central plain that
> still grows sugar and to which indentured cane cutters were brought after emancipation,
> so the small population of Felicity is East Indian, and on the afternoon that I visited it
> with friends from America, all the faces along its road were Indian, which as I hope to
> show was a moving, beautiful thing, because this Saturday afternoon Ramleela, the epic
> dramatization of the Hindu epic of Ramayana, was going to be performed, and the cos-
> tumed actors from the village were assembling on a field strung with different-colored
> flags, like a new gas station, and beautiful Indian Boys in red and black were aiming arrows
> haphazardly into the afternoon light. Low blue mountains on the horizon, bright grass,
> clouds that would gather colour before the light went. Felicity! What a gentle Anglo-Saxon
> name for an epical memory. (p. 1)

The world on the Caroni Plain integrates the ancient and modern, as Indian peasants
historically displaced to the Caribbean create in their daily lives a re-memory of their
past before modern colonialism. In so doing, they add an extraordinary ritual and

threnodic nuance to the folk culture of the Caribbean as a whole. In the art of living, these East Indian peasants triumph over the imposed history of marginalization and the Middle Passage history of indentureship.

Ultimately, these artists all wrestle with the question of hegemonic representation, with how to look past ways of ordering the world that rely on the kinds of binaries discussed above. These artists encourage us to look toward new and less prefigured terms of identification and association. They offer unique resources for educators struggling to speak with young people who are negotiating identities that often exceed easy predictive categories.

The Strategy of Double Coding

A second mode of meaning construction in works of art in the postcolonial imagination is the strategy of double coding. By *double coding* we mean the tendency of the postcolonial artist to mobilize two or more fields of reference or idiom in any given work, or what Wilson Harris (1989) calls "the wedding of opposites." The postcolonial artist may therefore quote or combine the vernacular and the classical, the tradition and the modern, the cultural reservoir of images of the East and the West, the first world and the Third, the colonial master and the slave. Again, we want to distinguish this strategy from the type of double coding that postmodernist critics such as Charles Jencks (1996) talk about when defining postmodernism. Instead of foregrounding the collapse of master narratives through the individualistic deployment of competing codes, we are pointing to the use of double coding to serve the collective purposes, collective history, and visualization of community that constitute the central issues in the postcolonial artistic project.

The filiation of such strategies, as Paul Gilroy notes in *The Black Atlantic* (1993) and in his essay "Cruciality and the Frog's Perspective" (1988–9), can be traced to the historical practices of marginalized groups. For example, the code switching and multiple articulations or revisions of Christian hymns by African slaves allowed them to circulate meaning around and beyond the gaze of plantation owners. Similarly, the Africanesque revision of Catholicism in the Voudun Candomble religions of Haiti and Brazil, respectively, represents a popular expression of the subaltern subject's use of double and triple register.

The strategy of double coding is powerfully foregrounded in the work of the Aboriginal painter Gordon Bennett (McLean & Bennett, 1996). As we will discuss more fully in Chapter 5, one of his pivotal paintings, *The Outsider* (1988), combines the methods of Aboriginal pointillism and Western perspectival painting to stunning effect. This painting ironically quotes Vincent van Gogh's *Starry Night* (1888) and *Vincent's Bedroom in Arles* (1889), replacing their tense, disturbing calmness, perhaps expressions of van Gogh's imminent madness and suicide, with an atmosphere of brusque, startling anxiety. Bennett's double coding of European and native traditions exposes an unsettling environment of cultural hegemony, highlighting the incompleteness of the modern Aboriginal search for identity. To be homeless in one's home – to inherit both the wealth and violence of the encounter between indigenous and European cultures – is the fundamental postcolonial condition.

One is reminded here of the video installation work of the London-based Lebanese Palestinian artist Mona Hatoum, recently on exhibit at the London Tate Modern Museum. In an intensely personal, multilayered, fifteen-minute video entitled *Measures of Distance* (2000), Hatoum explores the gendered dimensions of Palestinian life under Israeli occupation. This experimental video depicts Hatoum's mother taking a shower. The video has no "plot" as such, but it relays a series of letters that were exchanged between Hatoum and her mother during the 1982 Israeli military offensive in Lebanon. The letters, written in Arabic calligraphy, are superimposed on the image of Hatoum's middle-aged mother bathing – a matter of everyday life in the context of this incongruous, surreal war. The effect of the superimposition of Arabic calligraphy over the nude body of this middle-aged Palestinian woman is that of barbed wire. The nude figure is muted, and viewers are prevented from having clear access to her body by the Arabic text that is superimposed on her image.

These images are accompanied by a multilayered soundtrack that features Hatoum's melancholy and monotone reading of the letters as well as a recording of the animated conversation between Hatoum and her mother in Arabic. Fading in and out of this audio text is the voice-over of a narrator translating the Arabic conversation into English (Archer, Brett, & De Zegher, 1997; Ritsma, 2000). This multifaceted video installation works to distance us from any coherent sense of the subject and from prescriptive standards of beauty. The Western nude aesthetic is imbued with powerful ideological critique. And the installation activates multiple cultural registers and schemes of reference. Above all, we are reminded of the precariousness of modern Third World subjectivity and the multiple constraints imposed on the subjectivity of diasporic women in particular.

The deconstruction of the fantasy of authentic origins, the clear-cut hierarchy of "high" and "low," is realized most explicitly in the work of Jean-Michel Basquiat (Marshall, 1995). Basquiat's early career was as a graffiti artist in New York City, painting SAMO – "Same Old Shit" – on myriad public spots throughout Manhattan. (Interestingly, this early alter ego took shape in New York City's alternative City-as-School, where Basquiat attended high school and wrote for the school newspaper [Hoban, 1998].) Basquiat was part of the burgeoning and (then) vibrantly multiethnic hip-hop cultural movement in New York City, a movement that integrated in equal measure rap music, break dancing, and graffiti writing (in fact, Basquiat produced a single featuring rapper Rammellzee). While his work contains numerous references to these and other cultural signifiers, Basquiat's work draws, most interestingly and with great complexity, on the jazz idiom. Its artists and their themes pepper his works, from bop drummer Max Roach to singer Billie Holiday to (especially) saxophonist Charlie Parker.

This should not be surprising. The entire history of black diasporic art in the United States would be inconceivable without the jazz idiom – it is fundamental, for example, to the paintings of Romare Bearden. Basquiat, however, separates his work on jazz from the idiom's modernist tendencies, which can be heard in the extended compositions of Duke Ellington. His paintings are not driven by modernist concerns with coherent textuality, nor do they uphold the kinds of stable cultural identities traditionally celebrated in Afrocentrism. One need only look at *Charles the First* (1982), a composition

Robert Farris Thompson calls "pivotal," to understand this (Thompson, 1995, p. 37). *Charles the First*, a tribute to jazz great Charlie Parker, has no narrative core. Like many of his works, its energy comes from the apt juxtaposition of radically divergent cultural signifiers (e.g., jazz, opera, comic book superheroes). *Charles the First*, in short, does not tell a simple story, nor does it have a singular theme.

As Thompson points out, this is the first of many triptychs (compositions of three panels) that Basquiat would produce. The evocation of the number *3* has played an important role in jazz, most especially in the work of composer Charles Mingus. Mingus opens his 1971 autobiography *Beneath the Underdog* by stating, "In other words, I am three." One is reminded, as well, of his album titles, which include *Mingus, Ah, Um* and *Me, Myself, an Eye*. The word play on Latin conjugation in the former and referentiality in the latter point to the strategies of "triple coding" so much a part of jazz, a music that thrives not as much on original compositions as on "riffs" on the standards. Jazz, as Henry Louis Gates points out, is a music of signifying, a music that explicitly rejects the "original" in favor of constant intertextuality. In fact, Gates links these concerns to the entire history of African American literature in his now-canonical text, *The Signifying Monkey* (1988).

It is this condition of multiple heritages and their open possibilities that the Guyanese novelist Wilson Harris similarly mines in novels such as *The Palace of the Peacock* (1960), *Companions of the Day and Night* (1975), and *Carnival* (1985). The fusion of the colonized and colonizer subject is at the epicenter of *The Palace of the Peacock*, a novel about the psychological reintegration of opposites in the conquistadorial search for the mythical colony of Mariella, located in the hinterland of Guyana. As the principal character, Donne, and his ill-fated polyglot crew sail up the Cuyuni River in their tortuous journey to reclaim this colony, they discover the subtle and abiding links and associations between each other and the world:

> Cameron's great-grandfather had been a dour Scot, and his great-grand-mother an African slave mistress. Cameron was related to Schomburgh (whom he addressed as Uncle with the other members of the crew) and it was well-known that Schomburgh's great-grandfather had come from Germany, and his great-grandmother was an Arawak American Indian. The whole crew was a spiritual family living and dying together in the common grave out of which they had sprung from again from the same soul and womb as it were. They were all knotted and bound together in the enormous bruised head of Cameron's ancestry and nature as in the white unshaved head of Schomburgh's age and presence. (Harris, 1960, p. 39)

Harris's complex genealogy undermines the myth of original subjectivity, the clarity of classical realism as well as the bureaucratic deployment of characterization, and associated traditions of the 19th-century novel. An array of double-coded figures – Harris's "Idiot Nameless" in his *Companions of the Day and Night* (1975), Jorge Luis Borges's Cartographers of the Empire, and the Cuban novelist Reinaldo Arenas's twisted characters who, in the middle of his *Graveyard of the Angels* (1987), announce their dissatisfaction with their lives and ask the author for different roles – all offer alternatives to the bureaucratic deployment of characterization in the European novelistic tradition.

The ultimate argument these authors make is that modern humanity and modern life are necessarily interdependent and deeply hybrid. The underside of modernity and modernization is a quilt, a patchwork of associations, repressed in the philosophies of reason associated with Enlightenment discourses and best exposed through strategies of ambiguity and double or triple play. These strategies – so central to the work of postcolonial artists – offer educators rich and generative resources to think through contemporary questions about culture. Strategies of double and triple play treat culture less as a sealed-off property than as a ground of possibility and use.

Among others, Derek Walcott has theorized the implications of double and triple coding for educational practice. Reflecting on his own colonial education, he notes, "There was absolutely no problem in reciting a passage from *Henry V* in class and going outside of class and relaxing; there was no tension in the recitation of the passage from *Henry V* and going outside and making jokes in patois or relaxing in a kind of combination patois of English and French." There was, he says, "an excitement that could be shared in both languages at the same time" (as quoted in Baer, 1996, pp. 126–7). We see this excitement reflected in Walcott's work – including his powerful *Omeros* (1990), which reworks Homer's *Odyssey* – *as* he struggles toward a language that speaks beyond an easy referent to stable identity.

So far, we have looked at both the critique of hegemonic representation and the strategies of double coding that are a central part of the postcolonial aesthetic. These motifs, we argue, are unique to the postcolonial imagination and cannot be subsumed by the three critical traditions with which we opened. We want to look now, more specifically, at how histories of oppression have informed these motifs and how a brutal history of colonialism has necessitated the proliferation of utopian visions that also mark this art.

Utopic Visions

The third and final theme of the postcolonial imagination we pursue in this chapter is the link between art and emancipatory vision. Postcolonial art is engaged in what C. L. R. James calls in *American Civilization* (1993) "the struggle for happiness" (p. 166). By this James meant the struggle of postcolonial peoples to overcome oppression and glean from everyday life a sense of possibility in a Calibanesque reordering of contemporary social and cultural arrangements. Postcolonial artists link the techniques of aesthetic persuasion to the struggle of Third World people for better lives. They are committed to imagining possibility even when faced with impossible barriers.

In this regard, the paintings of Arnaldo Roche-Rabell, such as *I Want to Die as a Negro* (1993), reclaim and reintegrate the repressed identity of Africa in the Caribbean space. Also worthy of note is Roche-Rabell's *Under the Total Eclipse of the Sun* (1991), in which body parts and human faces seem to rise from the shadowed landscape of the city acropolis. Here we see foregrounded the temporary eclipsing of the power of the United States Congress, which refuses to listen to the voices of the Puerto Rican people.

In a similar manner, Korean artist Yong Soon Min offers viewers a strikingly multilayered installation, "The Bridge of No Return" (1997), in which she explores the parallel realities of the separated peoples of Korea (North and South) and their desires for reintegration across the divides of perspectives and territory (Min, 1997, p. 11). Min foregrounds the deliberately ambiguous nature of her *Bridge* installation as a statement of relationality and interconnectedness but also of inbetweenness and alterity:

> A bridge is, by definition, a connection, fostering relationship between the two otherwise separate sites at either end. A bridge also exists as its own entity, as an interstitial space to be traversed, presumably in both directions. A bridge of one-way passage, of no return, with no connection, no exchange, no continuity, defies the logic of a bridge like an oxymoron. (Min, 1997, p. 11)

The bridge offers a metaphor for the latent connection that courses through the divisions of all races and peoples at the beginning of the 21st century. This latency is also foregrounded in Gordon Bennett's painting *Terra Nullius* (1989), in which he projects the footsteps of the Australian Aboriginal people high above the implanting of the British Union Jack on the Aboriginal landscape in the creation of Australia.

Postcolonial art does not offer the viewer clear solutions to complex problems. Unlike many nationalist art movements (e.g., African American neorealist filmmakers in the US and earlier proponents of Negritude movements, such as Léopold Senghor and Aimé Césaire, in Africa and the Caribbean), this work is marked by contingency, raising questions more than it offers firm solutions. Following Walter Benjamin (1977), these artists forge visions that can sustain and nurture a communal consciousness, if only in qualified and contingent ways. These artists work hard for their momentary victories but are sober enough to realize that struggle is not simple, nor will victory come in one fell swoop. One is reminded of Gordon Bennett's *Prologue: They Sailed Slowly Nearer* (1988), in which the history of colonial oppression is configured in popstyle pointillism, with British colonizers and aboriginal figures juxtaposed, one on top of the other, complete with comic book – like speech bubbles. Bennett evokes in his style the contingency of historical formations and the possibility of new and different futures.

These works persistently remind us that emancipation has to be built from the bottom up. There is no predictable flow of effects from artistic wish fulfillment, vanguard theory, or even politics to the fruition of social solidarity and the realization of a new community. Writers like Wilson Harris maintain that the new community must be built in the everyday production of difference, cobbled together piece by reluctant piece – only then can the process of dialogue and reintegration of opposites take place. The Palace of the Peacock is Harris's mythical place for the radical encounter between opposites – and it can come into view only in the imaginative work of artists, not in the edicts and *a priori* declarations of theorists and pundits.

Indeed, like the characters in Harris's *The Palace of the Peacock*, we must all give something up, allow our self-interests and crass identities to be scrutinized and perhaps even wrecked in the process of transformation. This is the path of revision and reconciliation that Donne, the rambunctious colonizer and cattle rancher, must go through in the ante-room of the Palace:

> Every movement and glance and expression was a chiseling touch, the divine alienation and translation of flesh and blood into everything and anything on earth. The chisel was

as old as life, old as a fingernail. The saw was the teeth of bone. Donne felt himself sliced with this skeleton-saw by the craftsman of God in the window pane of his eye. The swallow flew in and out like a picture on the wall framed by the carpenter to breathe perfection. He began hammering again louder than ever to draw the carpenter's intimate attention. He had never felt before such terrible desire and frustration all mingled. He knew the chisel and the saw in the room had touched him and done something in the wind and the sun to make him anew. Finger nail and bone were the secret panes of glass in the stone of blood through which spiritual eyes were being opened. (Harris, 1960, pp. 102–3)

Donne's turmoil is the turmoil of the contemporary world. It is the turmoil of the colonizer and the colonized, both of whom must endure painful transformation in the search of new possibility, a new home.

One also finds this insistence on the labor of emancipation and the incompleteness of the process of transformation foregrounded in the work of the Barbadian author George Lamming, in novels such as *Season of Adventure* (1960) and *Natives of My Person* (1971). In the latter novel, Lamming reverses the Middle Passage story and tells it through the tortured minds of a colonizer ship captain and his crew, who search for redemption by founding a new, more egalitarian and equitable colony. Lamming adds a further twist to this allegory, however, as the ship, *Reconnaissance*, which is making the triangular trade journey, is mysteriously stalled outside the chosen site of the community, the Island of San Cristobal. In this scenario, the men can only inhabit the island after a rapprochement with their women. Though imagined, emancipation and egalitarian relations are not given. The work of change is where the practice of transformation must truly begin.

As the wife of one of the crew explains, in a somewhat ironic tone, men like her husband must work at collaboration even as they consider altering the fate of others:

> Surgeon's Wife: They would come in the evening. His company. All of the same learning and skill. My husband's house was like a school. Sometimes I would forget the indignities done to me when I saw them in such close collaboration. Discussing prescriptions for every sickness the Kingdom might suffer. ... I felt they had a wholesome purpose. To heal whatever sickness the Kingdom was suffering. To build a group of New World men. (Lamming, 1971, p. 336)

Emancipation, her monologue suggests, begins not with the creation of a utopian community but with redress to the indignities inflicted within the home space itself.

We point briefly now to a utopian theme raised in the writings of Cornel West (1992) and Gina Dent (1992), namely the link between the work of the imagination and the realization of change. Both West and Dent distinguish between the individualized celebration of incorporated aesthetic work and the vital dynamic of visualizing community. They summarize this distinction in the tension between artistic "pleasure" and communal "joy," a distinction that holds for much postcolonial art. Pleasure is a personal and atomized kind of enjoyment, one that has been explicitly linked to certain kinds of psychoanalytic and filmic cultural criticism. Yet, as noted, postcolonial artists have always seen the self as interwoven with community, making such atomized models entirely untenable.

One recalls here the Kenyan poet Christopher Okigbo's dynamic use of the tension between the private and the public, the individual and the collective, in his collection of poems *Labyrinths* (1971). There is, for instance, an oscillation between anxiety and celebration, desolation and triumph, that produces a cathartic feeling of uncluttered joy at the end of Okigbo's poem "Limits – Fragments out of the Deluge," where he proclaims, "The sun bird sings again." Here the poet links the personal and spiritual triumph over European intrusion to a national and collective African rebirth.

Like Okigbo's poetic narrator, then, postcolonial artists have struggled for "joy," the experience of pleasure in and through collective contexts. Such art takes joy in envisioning new ways for collective struggle, new politic possibilities, new ways of being and acting. Artists like Roche-Rabell, Bennett, and Basquiat and writers like Harris, Morrison, and Lamming suggest that this work is not complete. For them the means of struggle is as important, if not more so, than the ends. Transformation cannot be dictated, but is a process in which people work together to build change without the false security of guarantees.

We close with the reflections of Gordon Bennett as he excavates the pedagogical impulses at the heart of his own work:

If I were to choose a single word to describe my art practice it would be the word *question*. If I were to choose a single word to describe my underlying drive it would be *freedom*. This should not be regarded as an heroic proclamation. Freedom is a practice. It is a way of thinking in other ways to those we have become accustomed to. Freedom is never assumed by the laws and institutions that are intended to guarantee it. To be free is to be able to question the way power is exercised, disputing claims to domination. (quoted in McLean & Bennett, 1996, pp. 10–11)

Bennett clearly evokes a transformative pedagogy here, one that encourages a constant questioning, one that looks beyond laws and institutions and their *a priori* dictates, one rooted in everyday practice. Art is a ground of democratic possibility here.

Conclusion

The great effort of the artists whose work we have reviewed is to find the elements that link them and their work to larger communal, national, and global ecumenical orders. This expansive enterprise, however, is threatened by several pressing dangers.

Specifically, these art forms co-exist with a global culture industry that seeks to commodify them in debilitating ways. Walter Benjamin made this tension exceedingly clear in his classic essay "The Work of Art in the Age of Mechanical Reproduction" (1968), in which he argues that the advent of "mechanical reproduction" both opened art up to wider audiences and used and robbed it of its particular "aura" or air of authenticity. The global circulation of postcolonial art – these novels, paintings, video installations, poems, and songs – has opened up the possibility of unique and compelling dialogues across multiple communities and constituencies.

However, as a parallel phenomenon, many of these artists and their works are being rapidly incorporated into an ever-expanding culture industry. These works thus run the risk of being domesticated, robbed of their emancipatory potential, as they come to serve the imperatives of industry first and foremost. In this regard, we draw attention to the recent film adaptation of Basquiat's life (*Basquiat*, 1996, by Julian Schnabel) as well as Jonathan Demme's 1998 adaptation of Morrison's *Beloved*. Both films dulled the radicalism of the artists and their works by reinstating the same unified subject that Basquiat and Morrison were at pains to critique. We draw attention as well to a growing academic enterprise that would neatly herd these artists into stable disciplines and theoretical paradigms such as multiculturalism and certain kinds of literaiy postcolonialism.

The rapid circulation of art and aesthetics around the globe thus necessitates a pedagogical intervention. As we have noted, wrestling with the work of art in the postcolonial imagination reveals much that can be useful for pedagogues as they attempt to understand and act upon an increasingly fraught social, material, and cultural landscape.

References

Adorno, T. (1980). *Prisms*. Cambridge, MA: MIT Press.

Allende, I. (1985). *The House of the Spirits*, trans. M. Bogin. New York: A. A. Knopf.

Archer, M., G. Brett & C. De Zegher (1997). *Mona Hatoum*. London: Phaidon.

Arenas, R. (1987). *Graveyard of the Angels*. New York: Avon.

Armah, A. (1968). *The Beautiful Ones Are not Yet Born*. Boston: Houghton Mifllin.

Baer, W. (ed.). (1996). *Conversations with Derek Walcott*. Jackson: University Press of Mississippi.

Belsey, C. (1980). *Critical Practice*. London: Methuen.

Benjamin, W. (1968). The Work of Art in the Age of Mechanical Reproduction. In: H. Zohn (ed.), *Illuminations: Essays and Reflections*, trans. pp. 217–42. New York: Schocken Books.

Benjamin, W. (1977). *The Origin of German Tragic Drama*, trans. J. Osbourne. London: New Left Books.

Berger, J. (1972). *Ways of Seeing*. London: Penguin.

Bhabha, H. K. (1994). *The Location of Culture: Literature Related to Politics*. London: Routledge.

Dent, G. (1992). Black Pleasure, Black Joy: An Introduction. In: G. Dent (ed.), *Black Popular Culture*, pp. 1–20. Seattle: Bay Press.

Ellison, R. (1972). *Shadow and Act*. New York: Vintage.

Foucault, M. (1988). *The Care of the Self: The History of Sexuality, Volume III*, trans. R. Hurley. New York: Vintage.

Gates, H. L. (1988). *The Signifying Monkey: A Theory of Afro American Literary Criticism*. New York: Oxford University Press.

Gilroy, P. (1988–9). Cruciality and the Frog's Perspective. *Third Text* 5, pp. 33–4.

Gilroy, P. (1993). *The Black Atlantic*. Cambridge, MA: Harvard University Press.

Harris, W. (1960). *The Palace of the Peacock*. London: Faber.

Harris, W. (1975). *Companions of the Day and Night*. London: Faber.

Harris, W. (1985). *Carnival*. London: Faber.

Harris, W. (1989). Literacy and the Imagination. In: M. Gilkes (ed.), *The Literate Imagination*, pp. 13–30. London: MacMillan.

Hatoum, M. (2000). *Measures of Distance*. London: London Tate Modern.

Head, B. (1968). *When rain Clouds Gather*. New York: Simon & Schuster.

Head, B. (1974). *A Question of Power*. London: Heinemann Educational.

Held, D. (1980). *Introduction to Critical Theory*. Berkeley: University of California Press.

Hoban, P. (1998). *Basquiat: A Quick Killing in Art*. New York: Viking.

Hobbs, R. (1996). *Arnaldo Roche-Rabell: The Uncommonwealth*. Seattle: University of Washington Press.

James, C. L. R. (1993). *America Civilization*. London: Blackwell.

Jencks, C. (1996). *What Is Postmodernism?* London: Academy Editions.

Lamming, L. (1960). *Season of Adventure*. London: Allison & Busby.

Lamming, G. (1971). *Natives of My Person*. London: Allison & Busby.

Lyotard, F. (1984). *The Postmodern Condition: A Report on Knowledge*, trans. G. Bennington & B. Massumi. Minneapolis, MN: University of Minnesota Press.

McGuigan, J. (1992). *Cultural Populism*. London: Routledge.

McLean, I. & G. Bennett (1996). *The Art of Gordon Bennett*. Roseville East, New South Waks, Australia: Craftsman House.

Marshall, R. (1995). *Jean-Michel Basquiat*. New York: Whitney/Abrams.

Min, Y. S. (1997). Bridge of No Return. In: *Krannert Art Museum Fall 1997 Catalogue*, p. 11. Champaign, IL: Krannert Art Museum.

Mingus, C. (1971). *Beneath the Underdog*. New York: Vintage.

Morrison, T. (1977). *Song of Solomon*. New York: Signet.

Morrison, T. (1992). *Jazz*. New York: Knopf.

Ngũgĩ wa Thiang'o. (1982). *Devil on the Cross*. London: Heinemann.

Okigbo, C. (1971). *Labrinths*. London: Heinemann.

Ritsma, N. (2000). *Mona Hatoum*. Unpublished paper, Urbana, IL: Department of Art History, University of Illinois.

Soyinka, W. (1965). *The Interpreters*. London: Andre Deutsch.

Soyinka, W. (1974). *Season of Anomy*. New York: Third Press.

Spivak, G. (1988). Can the Subaltern Speak? In: C. Nelson & L. Grossberg (eds.), *Marxism and the Interpretation of Culture*, pp. 271–313. Chicago: University of Illinois Press.

Taussig, M. (1980). *The Devil and Commodity Fetishism in South America*. Chapel Hill: University of North Carolina.

Thompson, R. F. (1995). Royalty, Heroism, and the Streets: The Art of Jean Basquiat. In: R. Marshall (ed.), *Jean-Michel Basquiat*, pp. 28–42. New York: Whitney/Abrams.

Walcott, D. (1970). Dream *on Monkey Mountain and Other Plays*. New York: Farrar, Strauss and Giroux.

Walcott, D. (1990). *Omeros*. New York: Farrar, Straus, & Giroux.

Walcott, D. (1993). *The Antilles: Fragments of Epic Memory*. New York: Farrar, Strauss and Giroux.

West, C. (1992). Nihilism in Black America. In: C. Dent (ed.), *Black Popular Culture*, pp. 37–47. Seattle: Bay Press.

81

Conceptualizing an East Asian
Popular Culture[1]

*Chua Beng Huat**

No one would ever suggest conceptualizing Asia as a culturally homogeneous space. The adjective 'Asian' is complicated by a multitude of possible cultural references, from relatively culturally homogeneous countries in East Asian, such as Japan and Korea[2] to multiethnic/multiracial/multicultural/multireligious/multilingual postcolonial nations in Southeast and South Asia. For this occasion, I would risk this complexity and talk about East Asia plus one, namely Singapore, because of its overwhelming majority population of ethnic Chinese. The imaginary coherence of this grouping lies in the relatively imaginable possibility of constructing an 'East Asian' identity. Such a project of constructing a coherent and stable East Asian identity is a project that has a rather long standing. Most recently, in the early 1990s, in the triumphant days of the rise of capital in these countries, this group of countries was designated as a relatively coherent 'cultural' unit under the label of the 'dragon' economies. The symbol of the 'dragon', the sign of imperial China, obviously refers to their allegedly common Confucian heritage, which points beyond the Chinese population and enabled the inclusion of Japanese and Korean populations. This alleged presence of Confucianism in the ways of life of the huge, aggregated population of these countries provided for both the reason and its 'discovery' of Confucianism as an explanation for the rise of capitalism in East Asia, parallel to the affinity of Protestantism in the emergence of capitalism in the West (Tu 1991a). After the 1997 Asian financial crisis, this Confucian project has been displaced. Against this displacement, I am attempting to delineate an object of analysis, calling it 'East Asia Popular Culture', to designate the development, production, exchange, flow and consumption of popular cultural products between the People's Republic of China (PRC), Japan, South Korea, Taiwan, Hong Kong and Singapore.

Confucian East Asia Displaced

First, let me briefly review the idea of a Confucian East Asia. During those triumphal days, from about the mid-1980s till 1997, continuous domestic economic growth in

*Pp. 200–221 from *Inter-Asia Cultural Studies*, vol. 5, no. 2. © 2004 by Taylor & Francis Ltd. Reprinted with permission from the publisher (Taylor & Francis Ltd, http://www.tandf.co.uk/journals).

Korea, Taiwan, Hong Kong and Singapore, with Japan as the forerunner and model, coupled with the economic opening-up of the PRC, spawned several ideologically significant gestures in East Asia. The economic condition had spawned the search for an explanation of the rapid expansion of capitalism in East Asia in Confucian philosophy as everyday life (MacFarquar 1980).[3] More specifically, the visible expansion of overseas Chinese capital in Asia finessed a new confidence in the so-called Chinese 'culture', which supposedly unites and provides cultural continuities exemplified by, among other allegedly 'ethnic-cultural' characters, the apparent positive disposition to engage in business activities, among the overseas Chinese across their geographical dispersion; a suggestion that disregards the historical colonial economic social structure that left the immigrant Chinese with few opportunities other than to trade.[4] Nevertheless, the diasporic ethnic Chinese business communities and their intellectual promoters, perhaps the most euphoric about what appeared to be sustainable miraculous economic growth, convened international conferences on Chinese businesses, Chinese communities and Chinese identities.

The new confidence gave rise to the idea of a 'cultural China', spearheaded by the neo-Confucianist, Tu Weiming, and circulated through his editorial introduction, 'Cultural China: the periphery as the center', in the special issue of *Daedelus, The Living Tree: the Changing Meaning of being Chinese Today* (Tu 1991b). With the rise of the ethnic Chinese economies in Asia outside the PRC, Tu surmised that these 'peripheral' locations 'will come to set the economic and cultural agenda for the center [PRC]'. The desire behind the concept of 'cultural China' was not the political displacement of the Communist Party in the now marketized PRC, but more importantly, the possibility of a resurrection of a neo-Confucianism that will unite not only the dispersed Chinese population, by extension the larger population of East Asia.

In this construction of a Confucian East Asia, the countries included are organized in a relatively fixed configuration: the ethnic Chinese dominant locations, such as Hong Kong, Taiwan and Singapore are the exemplary 'periphery' and the PRC as the economic laggard because of its very recent entry into global market capitalism but it is also the economic future of the grouping because of its massive consumption power. Beyond the immediate Chinese dominant locations, Japan is the economic leader and often the model, although culturally suspect because of memories of the Second World War and, finally, South Korea is economically at similar structural level as Hong Kong, Taiwan and Singapore but culturally, arguably, formally more Confucian than these locations.

Even before the 1997 Asian regional financial crisis cast a pall on the euphoria and the Cultural China project, sceptics abounded. Detractors saw the search for Confucian values as no more than an ideological gloss over political authoritarianism in the less than democratic nations in the region. The actual might and reach of the economic power of the overseas Chinese communities in the region had also been a constant source of disagreements. The 'uniqueness' of the Chinese family firm has been frequently exposed as, among other things, an institution of exploitation of family, particularly women and child labour (Yao 2002). However, critics were kept baying at the margins until the financial crisis. With the crisis, half-hearted espousers of things 'Confucian' had quickly scurried off the stage. Only the staunchly ideologically committed are willing to continue to fly the flag, such as the Senior Minister of Singapore, Lee Kuan Yew. Pestered by international journalists for his view on the so-called 'Asian values' in the face of the economic crisis, he suggests,

> [There] has been a debasement of what I call Confucian value; I mean duty to friends and family. You're supposed to look after your family and your extended family, and to be loyal and supportive of your friends. And you should do it from your private purse and not from the public treasury. Now when you have weak governments and corruption seeps in, then this private obligation is often fulfilled at the public expense, and that's wrong. (*Straits Times*, 28 May 1998)

The ideological and emotional desire for a Confucian East Asia lives off a simple assumption that Confucianism constitutes the foundational culture of everyday life of East Asians. Empirically, any cursory observation of the Southeast Asian ethnic Chinese population will suggest that this is a flimsy assumption. Take, for example, Singapore, where the learning of Mandarin is compulsory for all primary and secondary ethnic Chinese students. Here, few individuals below the age of 30, or even 40, have ever read any Confucian texts. The shallowness of Confucianism in the everyday life of Singaporeans was further reflected in the failure to institute it as a part of the curriculum in moral education among the Chinese students. In the late 1980s, in an attempt to supposedly shore-up moral values against the supposedly corrupting cultural influences from the West, religious education, without God, was introduced as compulsory moral education to primary and secondary school students. Confucian ethics were offered as an option for Chinese students who professed no religion; the teaching material was developed by foreign experts, including Tu. The moral education curriculum, including Confucian ethics, was quickly abandoned when local social scientists discovered that students were becoming more religious as a result of the lessons and this may potentially give rise to greater divisiveness among the multiracial and multireligious population. The evidence would suggest that any presumption of cultural 'depth' in the grand Chinese philosophical traditions among Singaporean Chinese is dubious.[5] This shallowness in Singapore is at one extreme of the highly uneven inscription of Confucianism in the everyday life among the six East Asian locations with, perhaps, the Korean society at the other end of the continuum; indeed, Korean scholars are among the most active East Asian intellects who are engaged in the ongoing attempt to square Confucianism with contemporary social theories and contemporary democratic politics.

The Idea of an East Asian Pop Culture

In contrast to the very uneven and abstract presence of Confucianism, since the 1980s popular cultural products have criss-crossed the national borders of the East Asian countries and constituted part of the culture of consumption that defines a very large part of everyday life of the population throughout the region. This empirically highly visible cultural traffic allows for the discursive construction of an 'East Asian Popular Culture' as an object of analysis.

American music, movie and television industries loom large globally, penetrating all locations where local income levels have reached a standard that can pay the price. Consequently, in economically developed parts of Asia, the predominant cultural/ moral interests in popular culture and its consumption are often focused on American imports. Public discussions are often ideologically directed at the generalized liberal attitudes that are portrayed in American popular cultural products. This cultural liberalism is seen by some people as pushing the conservatism of Asians and is thus desired. Others cast it as culturally and morally 'corrosive' of 'wholesome' Asian values.[6] Significantly, side by side with the American popular culture, in every major urban centre in East Asia – Hong Kong, Taipei, Singapore, Shanghai, Seoul and Tokyo – there are dense flows of cultural products from the same centres into one another, albeit the directions and volumes of flows vary unevenly between them.

Popular cultural products and personalities from these East Asian urban centres criss-cross as daily features of all major newspapers in these cities. The trials and tribulations of the pop stars and celebrities make up part of the daily gossip by fans in different locations. Music, movies and television reviewers often face barrages of complaints from fans of the stars – singers and actors of big and small screens – if they penned negative reviews of the fans' pop 'idols'; the term 'idols' has become an adjective that characterizes a specific segment of the popular culture products, as in 'idol-drama'. Some of the artists, such as the so-called 'fifth generation' of the PRC film directors or individual Hong Kong directors, such as Wong Kar Wai, have received focused analysis because they have reached international 'artiste' status. So too, have the Japanese 'trendy dramas' whose popularity has declined since the end of the 1990s. They are but part of a larger regional phenomenon.

As popular culture is unavoidably a sphere of capitalist activities, the economics of this larger phenomenon are most concretely observable. Marketing, distribution, promotion and circulation of popular cultural products throughout the geographic East Asia are now part of the planning of all product producers, from financiers to directors, producers and the artistes, wherever these individuals might be located geographically. For example, a space like Singapore is inundated with television shows, movies, popular music, fashion and food from all parts of East Asia. At the same time, Singaporean television companies are cooperating in joint ventures with production companies and/or engaging artistes from elsewhere in East Asia in local productions, so as to expand their own market and enterprise. These flows of finance, production personnel and consumers across linguistic and national boundaries in East Asian locations give substance to the concept of East Asia Popular Culture.[7] This thick and intensifying traffic between locations – the economics of this trans-location cultural industry, the boundary crossings of pop cultural products, of artistes and the variable modes of consumption of audiences of different median different locations – as a cultural phenomenon in its own right has received relatively scant analytic interest.

Nevertheless, there is some pioneering work and more is coming on stream. The most notable is Iwabuchi's (2002) analysis of the penetration of Japanese popular

cultural products in East and Southeast Asia, although he is well aware of the larger
East Asian regional context for the production, circulation and consumption of popular
culture as an 'underdeveloped area in the study of cultural globalization' (Iwabuchi
2002: 50). This work provides important insights into the industrial strategies adopted
by Japanese popular cultural industries in their attempts to penetrate the Asian regional
market since the early 1990s. He came to the conclusion that, at least for the popular
music industry, 'Japanese ventures for cultivating pan-Asian pop idols have only been,
at best, partially successful' (Iwabuchi 2002: 107); and since the record company, Pony
Canyon, 'retreated from Asian markets in late 1997' (Iwabuchi 2002: 107), even 'partially successful' may be an overly optimistic conclusion. In contrast, Japanese television
dramas of romance among urban young were very popularly received by young audiences throughout the region during the later half of the 1990s.[8] Iwabuchi found that
popular reception in Taiwan was based on a sense of 'coevalness' between the Taiwanese
audience and the Japanese represented in the dramas – 'the feeling that Taiwanese share
a modern temporality with the Japanese. This 'coevalness' constitutes the dynamic
vector in generating and sustaining 'cultural proximity' between the audience and the
drama-mediated representation of Japanese (Iwabuchi 2002: 122). Finally, Iwabuchi
also examined Japanese audiences' reception of popular culture products imported from
elsewhere in Asia. Here, he found that, diametrically opposite the Taiwanese reception
of Japanese television dramas, the Japanese audience's reception of imported Asian
popular culture was based on a 'refusal to accept that it [Japan] shares the same temporality as other Asian nations' (Iwabuchi 2002: 159) and that reception of the imported
products was mediated by a sense of nostalgia of Japan's own past that is the present of
elsewhere in Asia.[9] The analysis of these two empirical instances and their explanations
provides us with insights into the differences between local audiences watching imported
popular culture products; insights that have implications on methodological issues in
cross-cultural reception research.

   Although Japanese television dramas constituted the bulk of the total export of
Japanese television programmes, the success of these dramas in the region was somewhat serendipitous because the television industry was not very interested in the export
market as the financial returns were paltry relative to the costs of production. By the
early 2000s, the regional space of Japanese television drama faced increased competition
from the aggressive export of similar products from Korea, where the government had
targeted the export of Korean popular culture as a new economic initiative, after the
1997 Asian regional financial crisis. In the popular music industry, the opening up of
the Peoples' Republic of China as a huge consumer market provided a much needed
infusion of motivation energy in reviving the Chinese popular music industry in the
1990s. The ailing Cantonese pop music (Cantopop) became progressively displaced by
Mandarin popular music, which in turn created a space for Taiwan as a centre for
Mandarin-Chinese music production. Thus, at the beginning of the 21st century, the
above mentioned dense traffic of popular culture products across the national/cultural
boundaries in East Asia has far exceeded the analytic boundaries that are determined
by any focus on a specific location. It is this empirical reality's conceptual and analytic
shape and contour that cultural studies in Asia must now work out, and the present
attempt is a preliminary step.[10]

Methodological Note

As I have suggested elsewhere,

> The life of a consumer product is very short. It is meant to be so in order to keep the factory that produces it working, the workers employed, its consumers happy but not for long, and the economy moving. This brevity of existence is a constraint on critical analysis of any consumer object, singularly or in constellation as a trend or a lifestyle. The problem is that by the time the analyst figures out the critical angle for commentary, the object in question would have already been consumed and committed to the trash-heap. Consumed and rejected, or unsold and rejected, either way it is discarded . . . the brevity of Life of a consumer object and of a consumer trend makes it unavoidable that all published materials on consumer products and trends are by definition 'historical'. (Chua, 2003: vii)

The same is true of popular culture products of course. Film, television programmes, popular music and musicians — in short, the data one is working with – are often already off the screen way before any analysis is completed. Secondly, many of the readers/ audiences have not seen the films nor heard the music; that is, they are not familiar with the products the analyst is engaged with. For these reasons, analytic interest should not be in the products themselves, although as they constitute the empirical material of the analysis it is unavoidable to analyse and comment on them. The larger analytic interest should be oriented towards the structures and modalities through which the products partake in the social and economic material relations within the different locations where the products are produced, circulated and consumed.

The most generalized outline of East Asian popular culture as an object of analysis may be delineated by its three constitutive elements: production, distribution and consumption. Each East Asian location participates in different and unequal levels in the production and consumption of the circulating popular cultural materials. Here, the structural configuration that was noted in the displaced Confucian East Asia project appears to be serviceable: Japan as the financial leader is also a production site that leads and indeed, shows the way in many aspects of the popular culture. Ethnic-Chinese dominant locations constitute a subset that produces and consumes cultural products of different Chinese languages – Mandarin, Cantonese and Minan, also known as Hokkien (*Fujian*) which, for the Taiwan independentists, is Taiwanese – with a written script that is comprehensible to most individuals literate in any Chinese language, in spite of the two different written scripts and local innovations, such as Cantonese or *Fujian* words. The written script enables access to material across different spoken Chinese languages, which explains the curious phenomenon that Chinese audiences are often found watching Chinese movies and television programmes with Chinese subtitles. In this ethnic Chinese subset, the PRC remains at the margin of production because of the lingering effects of its socialist ideology and politics, which I will discuss in greater detail later. There is an emergent popular cultural traffic between South Korea and Japan, after 1989, when the very porous 'ban' on the importation of the Japanese cultural products into Korea was formally lifted (Han 2000). Meanwhile, South Korea is beginning to export its own products into all the other East Asian locations, creating a so-called 'Korean Wave' in these locations. Given the uneven presence of the different locations in production, distribution and consumption, these processes need to be examined at every East Asian location. Collaborative research efforts are therefore essential to comprehensively analyse the object, East Asian Popular Culture. The following are tentative steps in teasing out the constitute elements of both the production, distribution and consumption processes to facilitate comparative studies across the region.

Production and Export/Distribution

The production of a popular cultural product – writings, all technical skills from acting, singing, filming and recording and financing arrangements – can either be entirely located in a single geographic location or, alternatively, with contemporary technology and globalized economy, each of the necessary constituent processes can be executed from different locations. In the case of the East Asian popular culture industry, preference for either arrangement tends to reflect the relative dominance of the production location in exporting its finished products. At one end of the dominance is the case of Japan in television drama and popular music. The ability to finance expensive television drama productions and staged expensive concerts and promotions has given the Japanese popular culture industry a dominant exporting position, giving rise to an ubiquitous impression that there is a 'Japanese invasion' or 'Japanization' of popular culture throughout the region, in spite of, according to Iwabuchi (2002: 85–120), the Japanese popular culture industries tentativeness about expanding into the rest of Asia.

The high quality of Japanese television is captured, in a rather essentialist manner, by an American critique:

> The most positive aspect of the primacy of form and the perfection of role is the creation of excellent images. The Japanese concern with the visual, in combination with their advanced technology, ensures that Japanese television is often very pleasing to the eye. Sets are technically well designed and the photography is excellent. . . . If television is used as a means of relaxation and escape, as opposed to education and enlightenment, it may be very enjoyable to lose oneself among the images without having to bother with the search for ideas. (Stronach 1989: 155)

The most illustrative examples are Japanese television urban drama series. These series are also known as 'trendy drama' for obvious reasons: the story line is generally about romance among urban young professionals. The visual pleasure comes from the fact that, on the set and scenes, the characters, major and minor, are very well-dressed in designer clothes, live in cosy small apartments, eat in expensive – usually Western – restaurants in the entertainment districts of the city but, above all, all the actors and actresses are beautiful men and women; of this last element, more will be discussed later. According to the producer of the very first of these dramas, *Tokyo Love Story*, when he was given the task as a producer, at age 28, Japanese television was filled with programmes for middle-aged individuals and he would not watch any of them. He asked himself, and people like him, what would he/they like to watch on television and came up with a simple list: beautiful people, beautiful clothes, good food and good entertainment, the plot is secondary.[11] Although the production cost per episode was phenomenally expensive, with about 50% going to pay the beautiful cast, the local Japanese market, in the euphoric days of the bubble economy, was able to support the cost. No considerations were given to a potential export market. The subsequent popularity of these series was possibly a surprise to the Japanese producers and came as surplus profit when it happened.

Successes throughout East Asia did not go unnoticed; they spawned an explicit ambition to address directly the enlarged audience population in order to consolidate it. In 2000, the drama series, *Romance 2000*, was simultaneously broadcast in Tokyo, Taiwan, Hong Kong and Singapore. Conceptually, with the desire to capture directly the expanded audience, the plot of the series incorporated elements of generalized 'pan Asian' interest. It went beyond the formulaic simple story line of such dramas to include Cold War politics, which is still very much alive in East Asia today. The plot understandably became very complex, with the beautiful lovers cursed by political ideologies. Briefly summarized: as an unnamed government had kidnapped and threatened to kill his mother and sister if he did not carried out its orders, a young Korean was forced to become an assassin in Japan. As fate would have it, a young Japanese woman found him when he was hurt, she harboured and nursed him back to health and, of course, fell in love with him. She became involved in his affairs, leading eventually to her own death – she sacrificed her life to save a multitude of people in an amusement park from a bomb explosion. One could say the complex plot, incorporating a generalized regional political anxiety, ultimately destroyed the fantasy that sustained such a drama of romance. In addition, it sank the series. In contrast to the serendipitous success of the drama created for Japanese audience, ironically, this conscious attempt to transnationalize the content, presumably to be 'more relevant' to the enlarged East Asian audience, failed. Conceptually, this 'noble' failure poses some interesting issues. Are the audiences of the East Asian popular culture ready for the mixing of cultural and political themes that are hewed from different locations? Does the failure suggests an absence of a possibility of an emergence of what might be called an 'East Asian identity' from emerging through popular culture, in this instance television drama? The answers to these and other questions will, of course, have serious implications on the development of the contents of the products and on any idea of an East Asia as culturally, relatively coherent entity.

Such failures aside, the popularity of the Japanese 'trendy dramas' across East Asia from the mid to late 1990s was without doubt. This was reflected not only in media attention but also attracted much academic analysis, both in Japan and elsewhere in East Asia.[12] An international conference on such dramas, held at the International Christian University in Tokyo, drew participants from every location in East Asia, including young East Asian scholars studying in the US.[13] Within the television drama industry, the quality of Japanese production clearly sets the industry standard; producers elsewhere in East Asian tend to take the Japanese as industry leader. Perhaps, the very high standard of production, and thus the elevated demands of a Japanese audience, has contributed to the relative absence of imports from other East Asian locations into the

Japanese market. Iwabuchi, however, provides an ideological explanation for the unequal flow of products in and out of Japan; he argues that this is the result of 'Japan's refusal to accept that it shares the same temporality as other Asian nations' (Iwabuchi 2002: 159). Nevertheless, some breaks in the boundaries are taking place; for example, Japanese pop singers have sung duets with those from the region, partly in efforts to expand their market reach into the huge Chinese audience, and even globally, through singing in English.[14] In any case, the relative impermeability of the Japanese pop cultural sphere to imports from other East Asian locations is a question that requires further research.

Korean popular culture industry appears to be the most influenced by the standards of Japanese production. Dare one suggest that this is part of the postcolonial connection? At the political level, there was a formal ban on Japanese cultural products since its decolonization from Japanese imperialism, immediately after the Second World War. This formal ban was not lifted until October 1998, with the Joint Declaration of the New 21st Century Korea – Japan Partnership. However, the ban did not make Korea impermeable to Japanese popular cultural products; even the government-owned Korean Broadcasting Station was guilty of illegal importation (Han 2000: 14–15). In the words of one Korean cultural commentator: 'We firmly lock and bar front doors but leave our back doors wide open. With our left hands we indignantly slap away any offers but we are busy snatching at any opportunities with our right. This has been our society's attitude toward popular Japanese culture during the last 30 years' (Do Jung Il quoted in Kim Hyun-Mee 2002: 1).[15] In addition to this constant stream of underground importation, Japanese popular cultural products have also been 'copied', 'partially integrated', 'plagiarized' and 'mixed' and 'reproduced' into Korean products. Little wonder that Korean fans of Japanese popular music suggest, 'When we listened to Korean songs it is easy to recognize similar or same parts from Japanese songs' (quoted in Kim Hyun-Mee 2002: 4). Kim further concludes that 'in the case of TV animations and comics, most [Korean products] are adaptations of Japanese products so Japanese culture in Korea has already set its roots deep into the emotional structure of Koreans' (Kim Hyun-Mee 2002: 4). After the lifting of the ban, Japanese cultural products now flow smoothly into Korean popular cultural spaces. And in 2002, the first Japanese and South Korean co-produced television drama series, *Friends* – a drama series about the relationship between a Korean man and a Japanese woman – was broadcast in both locations simultaneously, marking not only a pop culture event but also a 'political' event in Korean–Japanese relations.

Significantly, production of Japanese 'trendy drama' has lapsed and the exports slowed by late 1990s. The media space in Hong Kong, Taiwan and Singapore has been, in a sense, replaced and occupied by Korean imports; the influence of Japanese trendy drama on the Korean product is unmistakable. The importance of Korean export can be seen from its effects in Singapore. In 1999, the local monopoly that publishes all the major newspapers in all four official languages of the city-state, ventured into commercial television with two free-to-air stations, one in English (I Channel) and the other in Mandarin (U Channel), under a new company called, *Mediawork*. Of the two channels, the English-channel local programmes have been an abject failure and the studio effectively shut down within less than two years of its establishment. The local English programming is reduced to daily news programmes; all the other programmes are imported, largely from the US. On the other hand, the Mandarin channel was able to carve out and take away a significant size of the audience population from the already established state-owned station, *MediaCorp*, through a combination of broadcasting Korean drama series and local variety shows which look and feel like the similar shows in Taiwan, which in turn are very similar to those in Japan. MediaCorp has since also imported Korean drama series; such that, by late 2003, there is at least one Korean drama series on Singaporean television stations every night, after the daily news. The drama series has brought Korean artistes not only onto Singaporean television screens but also into the entertainment pages of the print media, particularly Mandarin publications. Korean drama series have thus become a site for local media competition, which perhaps, justifies these exports as part of the so-called 'Korean Wave', which includes Korean movies and Korean popular music exports.

Korean movies made their debut in East Asia, as perhaps elsewhere, through the Hollywood style blockbuster *Shiri*, followed by *Joint Security Area*, in late 1990s. Both films translated the Cold War tension of North–South Korea into personalized relations. The first is a romance between secret agents from both side of the divide, a female agent from the North being involved with a male counterpart from the South. The second film thematized 'illicit' friendship and camaraderie between North and South Korean soldiers who police the demilitarized zones. A second category of Korean films that were popular in their time is what may be labelled 'gangster comedies', where criminals are let off all accusations, guilt and punishment and humanized by their ineptness or goofiness in other aspects of their daily lives.[16] Since then Korean films have had a constant but not particularly dense presence in East Asian market. Again, it should be noted that this Korean presence came at a time when Japanese films had been all but absence in the export market. However, the success of the Japanese horror movie, *The Ring*, in late 1990s, sparked off a string of 'horror/ghost' movies from Korea, Hong Kong, Singapore and Thailand, which is still coming on stream in 2003.

In terms of production and export capacity, Hong Kong and Taiwan may be said to occupy the same in-between position as South Korean popular cultural industry. However, they occupy prominent, if not dominating, positions in the pan ethic-Chinese segment of East Asian Popular Culture. In addition to their own domestic audiences, which still constitute the first market, television programmes, films and music from Hong Kong and Taiwan have always had a constant presence in the other locations where there are significant ethnic Chinese populations, such as Singapore and Malaysia and, of course, the PRC, especially after its economic liberalization. Hong Kong had been the major production site of Chinese movies from the 1950s to the late 1980s, and although the production rate slowed down considerably in the 1990s, it remains the major production location of Chinese movies, predominantly in Cantonese and increasingly also in Mandarin. However, its television drama programmes have grown as a result of film producers, such as the Shaw Brothers, switching to the small screen. Taiwan has a continuing presence in exporting 'traditional' family dramas in which the much maligned and oppressed daughter-in-law eventually triumphs when her moral righteousness survives her long suffering. However, since the success of the young adult romance drama, *Meteor Garden* (discussed below), it has also begun to export contemporary drama series, including the 'updating' of traditional family dramas by dressing the characters in contemporary clothes, without altering the plots and themes.

In popular music, Hong Kong was without rival in the 1970s and 1980s, with the invention of Cantopop. However, in the 1990s, with the impending and final 'incorporation' as a Special Authority Region of the People's Republic of China, Cantopop has waned and all major popular music performers have switched over to singing in Mandarin in order to catch the huge mainland market. This switch in language has enabled Taiwan to emerge as a major recording location for Mandarin-pop. It features much more prominently as a place to train, record and market music for all ethnic-Chinese singers who are not hewn from Hong Kong, particularly those from Southeast Asia, especially Singapore and Malaysia.[17]

The presence of the PRC as a production location for East Asian popular culture can be said to be very marginal, in contrast to its huge consumer market for imports from other East Asia locations. (Since the absorption of HK as an SAR, HK television companies have been quick to capitalize on the huge market by making television series that are directed specifically at the mainland audience.)[18] This is due in part to the underdevelopment of such industries under socialism, and economic marketization is still in its early days. As consumerism is a new phenomenon in PRC, its mass cultural products are still far behind in quality and style for them to be picked up by the more advanced consumers in the other affluent Asian locations; there is a sense of what is commonly labelled 'country feel' (*tu qi*).

However, there are two divergent, deeper 'cultural' problems that constrain its cultural products for the export market. First, ironically, the PRC is tied to being the root-site of 'traditional' Chinese culture. Secondly, the popular cultural products from the PRC, from rock music to television, films and other visual art forms, are deeply inscribed and haunted by the revolutionary politics of the past, particularly the Communist revolution, and its antagonists, 'tradition' and authoritarianism, both traditional arid contemporary. As the origin of Chinese history, PRC producers are often compelled to translate into screen historical dramas and/or transform literary classics of either historical or mythic pasts, such as the famous historical/mythical huge novels, *Water Margin* and the *Three Kingdom*, which were very well produced long running television drama series. As long narratives of heroic acts of mythic figures in ancient Chinese history, these series speak little to the young consumers of popular culture; the length of the series only emphasizes its tedium. In terms of contemporary popular culture, the deep inscription of revolutionary politics and its discontents is most observable in the case of rock music from PRC. The lyrics are so heavily laden with local politics (Do Kloet 2000) that they are difficult to understand by consumers who are not part of the local scene; consequently, their presence in the other ethnic-Chinese predominant locations in East Asia is limited to the margins of 'alternative' music. Similarly, PRC television programmes are ideologically overdetermined and regularly play up the themes of involuntary exile or voluntary migration against the social and political conditions in the mainland itself (Sun 2002).

These two divergent ideological constraints are reflected in the works of no less an internationally acclaimed director than Zhang Yimou. Along with his critique of the oppressiveness of the 'Chinese traditions' in such films as *Raise the Red Lantern* and his depiction of the rural poverty of contemporary China in films such as *Not One Less*, he also did the monumental film *Hero*, which narrates a version of the failed assassination of the brutal Emperor Qin, the first man to unify what was then China.

Zhang's movies, like those of the other directors from the PRC, are unable to avoid political inscription and reading by foreign audiences. The reading by audiences in the West or West-educated in East Asia is very succinctly put by Chen Xiaoming:

> once his films enter the world film market, politics inevitably captures the spotlight. Hence, in the eyes of a Western beholder, Zhang Yimou's *Judou* (1991) is interpreted as an innuendo against the gerontocracy, and *Raise the Red Lantern* (1992) is seen as a political power struggle. Political readings of these Chinese films are not necessarily farfetched misreadings insofar as the cultural imaginary of Oriental culture has always already inculcated an invisible, but omnipresent, nexus of absolute power and totalitarianism, which overshadows Zhang Yimou's, and other's, films. It does not matter whether such a power nexus refers to ancient feudalism or despotism, or to the 'proletariat dictatorship' of modern China, for the cultural imaginary of Oriental culture is fundamentally timeless – the present is all but a reappearance of the past. Politics is thus a determinant situation in the cultural imaginary of China. (Chen 2000: 229)

Such complex political inscriptions are too taxing for mass audiences of popular culture and the films are, consequently, delegated to the international, art-house and film festival circuits with their sophisticated audiences.[19]

The other essentially consumer location is Singapore. With its very limited domestic market, Singapore has no film and music industries and a relatively new television industry.[20] However, it is cash rich. Here, the decomposition of the production process, with each input coming from different locations is most observable. From its very beginning (and it continues to be true), the Singaporean television industry depended on imports of professionals from Hong Kong. Until recently, the Hong Kong professionals worked behind the screen. However, since early 2000, Hong Kong television actors and actresses have been appearing in leading roles in situation comedies and other productions; two notable examples are Lydia Sum who leads in *Living with Lydia* and Carol Cheng in *Oh! Carol*, both programmes have survived the first season and have become weekly features. In these instances, the 'lesser' position of Singapore is clearly reflected, as Singaporean actors are placed in supporting roles, one might say as 'apprentices' to the Hong Kong stars.[21] Similar arrangement is also found in Singapore financed movies.[22] The other television company, Mediawork, has also launched, in 2004, its first collaborative productions with Taiwan company, *Sanlih e-tv*, in a teenage drama series featuring the members of an all-male singers/actors group, *5566*, entitled *Westside Story*, making reference to Taipei's teenage shopping area, Simenting (West Gate Square), with one of the popular Singaporean female actress in its stable acting as the mother of the lead character. At this point in the development of Singapore's television industry, such joint productions must be seen as a way of introducing Singaporean artistes into the ethnic-Chinese segment of the East Asia Popular Culture, as the products are often sold to Taiwan and PRC stations.[23]

In recent years, joint ventures, co-productions or direct financing of films have picked up pace. Reflecting the government's ambition in establishing a 'creative industry' in the knowledge-based economy, the government has set up a film commission to help finance film projects. As part of this industrial strategy, the film company, *Raintree Pictures*, was established within the state-owned television company, *MediaCorp*. So far, interests in production financing are restricted to collaboration with participants in the pan-ethnic Chinese segment, particularly with Hong Kong; in addition, there are collaborations with individual artiste in other Southeast Asian countries. A successful co-production effort is the three-part film series, *Infernal Affairs*, in 2003–04, a detective story set entirely in Hong Kong with Hong Kong actors, where Singapore does not feature at all, either in setting or actors on screen. A central non-Hong Kong character was played by the Mainland Chinese actor, Chen Daoming. And, it must be mentioned that the producer of this film series is a Hong Kong person working in Singapore for *Raintree*.

From a methodological angle, a location like Singapore, being at the other extreme end of the production continuum and an essentially consumption location, is very advantageous in observing and researching the relative placing of all these production locations. Singapore's radio waves, television screens and movies theatres constitute sites in which Japanese, Korean, Hong Kong and Taiwanese films, television drama and variety shows and popular music compete for space, reflecting their relative market position in the different media and genres. This will be discussed in tile next section.

Obviously, the linearity of the written text and its reading on this occasion is a clumsy structure for the depiction of the complexity of flows of popular cultural products, and thus the porosity of the 'national' boundaries, throughout East Asia. These flows take place routinely on a synchronous plane within these spaces through a variety of media, including *manga*, films, television, music and fashion. To give a sense of the fluidity of these flows, I will take the example of the latest sensation in East Asian popular culture, the F4 phenomenon.

In 2000, a Taiwanese producer reproduced a Japanese *manga* story into a television series, *Meteor Gardens*. The college-students drama series featured four complete unknown young men (of the same height) as the principal actors, collectively introduced to the media world as F4. The series was an instant success throughout East Asia. It was screened in Hong Kong and Singapore and subsequently in Korea in 2002, whereas in the PRC they were watched on DVDs.[24] It transformed F4 from complete obscurity to the hottest boy-band in the past two years; their television appearance had finessed their entry into popular music, although their singing skills are noticeably limited. Every public appearance by F4 throughout the region draws huge crowds of screaming fans; for example, their appearance in a Shanghai shopping centre had to be cut to 10 minutes because of the crushing crowd, and their scheduled concert was cancelled by the local government. Their success in East Asia has, of course, spawned other Taiwanese boy bands and individual male singers who are marketed throughout an especially ethnic-Chinese predominant East Asia, usurping popular attention at a time when Hong Kong singers and Cantopop are in relative decline.

Before proceeding with consumption issues, the current structural arrangement of the production and export of East Asian cultural products can be summarized thus:

Japan is the leader that sets the industry quality standard and is the prime production and export location, with relatively little importation from the rest of the constituent regional locations. South Korea has made a very conscious effort to export its popular culture products as part of its export-oriented economy, especially after the 1997 Asian regional financial crisis. Hong Kong and Taiwan play central roles in the production of Chinese language popular culture products, with an apparently skewed division of labour, movies and television programmes in Hong Kong and popular music in Taiwan. PRC and Singapore remain largely locations of consumption of East Asian popular culture, each with its own problems of trying to elevate itself into a serious production location. The PRC appears unable at this point to shake off its ideological baggage, both traditional/historical and contemporary/political, for its popular culture products to have mass appeal, while Singapore is trying to get into the business through its investment power, without apparently any other ideological interests.

Audience Position as Methodological Constraint

If the production processes of popular cultural products can be disaggregated and organized transnationally, consumption is, however, thoroughly grounded in specific locations. Consumers are geographically located within cultural spaces in which they are embedded and meanings and viewing pleasures are generated within the local cultures of a specific audience. Of course, the 'local' cultural space is not to be conceived as a hermetically sealed entity but one that is porous and actively engaged, appropriate and absorbing cultural elements and fragments from all the directions with which the 'local' has contact. Without this openness, there would be no such discursive object as East Asian Popular Culture. Nevertheless, local cultural proclivities continue to work their effects in the ongoing movements and boundary shaping of the local cultural sphere.

Conceptually, there are three possible audience or consumption positions in consuming popular culture programmes. The first and least complicated position is an audience watching a locally produced programme. Here, the audience is embedded in the very culture of the location of production as his/her own. Identification with the themes and characters may be said to come 'naturally' – as in phenomenologically the 'natural attitude of everyday life' – and references can be readily made to events, individuals and other activities that are 'similar' to those on screen. The audience may be said to 'know' the filmic or lyrical representations of events, issues and characters from the 'inside'. There is an excess of knowledge that is then used to judge the 'accuracy', 'truth' and 'critical reflections' of the content of the cultural programme. In this sense, the program may be used as a 'critical' mirror to one's own life and community. An exemplary instance is Kim Soyoung's analysis of the eclipse of 'Korean women' in recent big budget Korean films, such as *Joint Security Area*, as indicative of a generalized shrinking of the 'women's sphere' and the elevation of male-bonding in post 1997 financial crisis Korea (Kim Soyoung 2003).

Second, the audience could be a diasporic subject watching or listening to a programme that is thematically concerned with one's homeland. The programme may be produced either by homeland or foreign producers. Here, the audience position and relation with the content is once removed, that is, less immediate than the first position. Nevertheless, the audience is still being interpellated, voluntarily or otherwise, into the programme. The same knowingness as the first position will be brought to bear on the content. However, the judgements made are likely to be with hesitancy, due to, and dependent on, the distance of both space and time away from home. An additional 'nationalist' element may arise if the programme is foreign produced; the audience may protest and charge the foreign producer with politically motivated misrepresentation or, if one were in political exile, affirm the representation as a reasonable critique of conditions in the 'homeland'; a critique or misrepresentation lays obviously not in the substance of the content but in the viewing position of the audience. For detailed analysis of the diasporic subject position on East Asian popular culture, see Sun's (2002) insightful analysis of various films and television programmes, produced for the PRC audience, with either local or foreign or co-funding.

The third position is an audience watching an imported programme. Here, the audience is not embedded in the culture of the production location. The audience is thus distanced from the detailed knowledge of the first and second position; what knowledge he or she has is derived from outside the programme itself. It is in this viewing position that the differences between the cultures of the location of consumption and that of the production location become most apparent. The 'meaningfulness' of the programme is now relocated into the horizon of relevance of the audience's own cultural context. The audience has now brought his or her own cultural context to bear on the content and to read accordingly; here, the earlier mentioned empirical studies, by Iwabuchi (2002), of Taiwanese audiences of Japanese dramas and Japanese consumers of popular culture products imported from elsewhere in Asia are illustrative and instructive. It is in this sense that the cultural product may be said to have crossed a 'cultural' boundary, beyond the simple fact of having it means it has been exported/imported into a different location as an economic activity.

Each of these stances may involve different investment of the self in identification with the characters and themes on screen or in music. The effects of the consumption of the imported cultural products will, of course, differ from those derived from consuming a product which represents the culture in which one is embedded. The intensity of self-investment is likely to decrease in proportion to the immediacy of 'home/national' self-identification, with the third viewing position coming closest to an idea of 'mere' entertainment. Each of these positions is, of course, a field of analysis in its own right and each would illuminate different aspects of audience-ship.

In this particular instance, in the delineation of the discursive concept and object of an East Asian Popular Culture, the central analytic focus is on how products criss-cross the cultural boundaries within the region to reach non-home-audiences. Consequently, the analytic starting point would have to be that of the third audience or consumption position of a local audience watching foreign imports. This is a necessary methodologically constraint in the analysis of cultural border crossing of popular culture material. The East Asian Popular Culture must therefore be conceptualized as a complex discursive object that incorporates, and is constituted by, the popular culture of each regional location as both culture of production and culture of consumption. The ever-changing contours, shapes and substance of this discursive object are, therefore, necessarily a collaborative collective enterprise of analysts across the region.

Being a Singaporean and living in Singapore, I am therefore methodologically constrained to confine myself to sketching out some, by no means exhaustive, characteristics of a Singaporean audience as part of this East Asian popular cultural sphere.[25] This exercise is therefore largely an illustrative instance, as the same constraint would apply to local analysts elsewhere throughout the region with different outcomes. Furthermore, I shall restrict myself to the discussion of television and film products rather than music, both for ease of presentation and reception, because they are much less abstract than music.[26]

How a Singaporean Watches Imported Television

Urban stories

Singapore as a city-state has no rural hinterland. Singaporeans in general have little or no contact with things and sentiments rural. 'Rural' is ideologically often reduced to 'backward', 'underdeveloped' and lacking in urban amenities, thus inconvenient; at its most generous, 'rural' appears as nostalgia, a place to escape the urban stress. Consequently, imported drama series that are popularly received are almost all urban romance stories featuring young, single professionals, either living on their own or with their families of origin; in general, the Japanese series tend to have young professionals in their own well appointed apartments, while the Korean series appear yet to have shaken off the yoke of family. Historical period dramas of work from Japan and Korea – and there are plenty of such drama series in both countries – do not travel well to Singapore and thus are never seen on local television. However, programmes that are set in imperial Chinese dynasties are common because there is a vague (fake) sense among the ethnic-Chinese Singaporean audience of knowing Chinese history.

The trials and tribulations of urban living are of course intimately familiar to Singaporeans. Familiarity makes the urban stories accessible, audience friendly. A Singapore consumer can readily identify with the themes and characters as representations of 'urban' people and phenomena that are familiar, if not similar, to themselves; that is, if desired, a Singapore audience can allow itself to identify completely with the representation of the urban characters on screen. However, 'foreignness', nevertheless, remains a feature desired by the same audience. First, local programmes generally deal with issues of Singaporean everyday life, with messages that are relevant and didactic but, precisely because of these features, can become 'tiresome' rather than 'entertaining'. So, foreignness, and the 'exoticism', of imported products is part of the local audience's desire and viewing pleasure. However, of greater conceptual significance is that the 'imported' status of the programme can be used by a Singapore audience to limit the degree of identification, that is the degree of interpellation of self, with the themes and characters on screen. That the product is a foreign import enables a Singaporean audience to maintain a stance of 'watching', in a voyeuristic manner, the lives of others, elsewhere in East Asia. It enables a difference between self and other East Asians to be maintained, in spite of sharing similar urban and familial dispositions. Thus, foreignness must remain recognizably foreign in the programme. The most immediately foreign difference should be, of course, language; however, as discussed below, this is most easily erased through dubbing. Two other markers are retained, background music and outdoor scenery.

Background music, particularly the programme's theme songs, is generally left untouched, preserving the foreignness. However, this is increasingly unreliable as a marker of the location of production. First, the visual and the audio contents of a programme can be produced separately at the point of production. The importing location is free to supply both dialogue and music to the video material; the 'imported/foreign' features are thus suppressed for the local audience. Second, the background music can be intentionally foreign at the point of production; for example, Taiwan drama series often come with background music sung in Japanese – in the interest of 'exoticizing' local products and/or exporting the product to foreign locations. In a location such as Singapore, where both Taiwan and Japan are foreign, such mixing leaves the 'foreignness' undisrupted but locating the 'origin' of the product is made problematic.

Scenery is a more stable marker of foreignness as it is built into the visuals of the story. Scenery transports a localized audience into a foreign space and place; it constitutes a mode of visual tourism. Thus, avid fans of television dramas can become so enamoured by the sceneries that the locations become 'must visit' places when the fan gets a chance to be an actual tourist to the country in question and, upon arrival, feel completely familiar with the environment, with a sense of *deja vu*. Screened sights have become tourist sites. At their peak of popularity, Singaporean tour promoters did organize tours of the 'trendy drama' sites in Tokyo for the fans; similarly for Singaporean fans of Korean television drama.[27]

An extension of scenery and a marker of foreignness to the Singapore audience is the seasons. Seasons are completely foreign to Singaporeans who live permanently in hot tropical weather. Autumn, with its changing colours of the trees, and winter, with its cold and snow, are quintessentially romantic – enhancing the romantic themes intrinsic to the programmes – for Singaporeans.[28] Along with cold weather is fashion. The hot, humid tropical climate is a bane of the fashionable because it denies them the seasonal changes of fashion. The fashionable Singaporean is thus jealous of the layers upon layers of warm clothes that enables the making of fashion statements; (s)he is denied the 'layering' effects of fashion.

Chinese languages

There are four 'official' languages in Singapore; of which English and Mandarin are two that are used in dubbing and subtitling of imported television programmes and films from East Asia.[29] All imported films and television programmes, no matter whether the products are in Korean, Japanese or other Chinese languages, such as Cantonese from Hong Kong and *Minan* from Taiwan, are dubbed into Mandarin; as we will see, this practice has great significance in the consumption of East Asian popular culture. English subtitles are often provided, reflecting the primacy of the language in Singapore. There have been instances when a television series was particularly popular and

English subtitles were not provided, which led to public complaints from those Chinese who do not understand Mandarin that they were being denied the pleasure of watching the series.[30] Obviously, dubbing of foreign languages makes the cultural products accessible to a Singaporean audience. Japanese and Korean popular music have a far lesser presence in Singapore than popular television programmes and films, largely because of the language barrier. However, with duo-sound technology in television, a Singapore audience can watch Korean and Japanese programmes in the original languages if they so choose.

Elsewhere in Chinese-dominant East Asian locations, Mandarin is not always the official or even the primary language of the Chinese. In Hong Kong, the official language is Cantonese, with Mandarin making an increasing appearance. In Taiwan, a mixture of Mandarin and *Minan* or *Fujian* language is the common practice. All these Chinese languages and more were, until not too long ago, living languages among the Singaporean Chinese population. In the early 1970s, they were labelled derogatorily as 'dialects' and since then banned from all mass media. In their place, the government, ostensibly with the desire to unify the multi-tongued Chinese population through a single, standard, formal language, adopted Mandarin as the one language – both phonologically and written – for all Singaporean-Chinese; thus, there is dubbing of Chinese programmes other than those in Mandarin.

Technically, Chinese languages can be phonologically strange to each other, although a relatively common written language facilitates communications among all literate Chinese. Consequently, Chinese films and television programmes will very often have the dialogue and lyrics of songs in one of the Chinese languages, with Chinese written scripts as subtitles. These subtitles are different from conventional subtitles that translate the film's language into a completely different language, such as from Japanese to English. Although the Chinese subtitles may have the same translation function, they translate from one Chinese language to another Chinese language.

Although it is often assumed that the written script provides the common language for all literate Chinese, the meaning of a written word is nevertheless not always assured. This is because a written word may be used only phonologically as a transliteration of spoken sound, with the meaning of the word completely discarded; then, it would be completely meaningless if read literally. For example, in Cantonese, the common sound for 'yes' is 'hai' and a Chinese character with similar sound is used in the written script of Cantonese newspapers or Cantonese subtitles. The written word means 'category' in Mandarin, which is completely different from 'yes', which in Mandarin, would be written as 'si'. The multiple Chinese languages situation sometimes creates an interesting disjuncture when a Chinese audience is watching a film or a television programme that is dubbed in one Chinese language while carrying scripted Chinese subtitles in another, when one simultaneously listens to and reads the dialogue.

One disjuncture that significantly reflects the localness of consumption is illustrative. As noted earlier, the ethnic Chinese population in Singapore was, before the 1970s, very Chinese-multilingual. However, this multilingualism has been progressively reduced by the official policy of banning the use of all Chinese 'dialects' except Mandarin. Nevertheless, the presence of the suppressed languages was never entirely erased. A socially and culturally severe consequence is that, other than Mandarin, all Chinese languages have come to mark their users as the poorly educated, the uncouth and the rude – generally, the lower social class. These other Chinese languages can no longer be entrusted with carrying a serious communicative substance. The appearances of speakers of non-Mandarin Chinese languages on television programmes and films have thus become 'laughable' and are, accordingly, used by local producers to get the desired 'comedy' effects (Chua & Yeo 2003). Significantly, this 'comedy' effect has been put to critical use recently in locally produced films, in which dialect-speaking Chinese characters use their self-deprecation as a mode of marking their marginalization in Singapore society, particularly English-speaking Singapore society, thus raising indirectly the marginalization of 'Chineseness' in spite of being a demographically Chinese predominant society.

The marginalization of other Chinese languages also has its effect on the boundary crossing of films and television programmes from other Chinese–East Asian locations. For example, in Taiwan, for those who are politically committed to independence from the PRC, there is a preference to speak exclusively *Fujian*; this language has been politically elevated to the status of 'Taiwanese' and is spoken with pride. The mismatch of the political status of the *Fujian* in Singapore and Taiwan results in a Singaporean audience laughing at the wrong nuances in the dialogue, and it completely misses the political intention of the insistence of the use of the language in Taiwan television, films and music.[31] The result is not only a miscommunication but also a political misreading when a Singaporean who still knows the remnants of *Fujian* watches a Taiwanese film (Chua & Yeo 2003). A similar effect often holds in the way Chinese-Singaporeans watch Cantonese programmes from Hong Kong.

Beyond the specificity of one Chinese language other than Mandarin, a different kind of disjuncture occurs when two Chinese languages are used simultaneously, one in dialogue and in subtitles. On one occasion, I was watching a Korean gangster comedy in which the dialogue was in Mandarin and the subtitles in Cantonese.[32] Questions of the migratory path of the film arose: given the Chinese linguistic conditions, the film was likely subtitled in Hong Kong and re-dubbed in Singapore, otherwise the dialogue would be in Cantonese.[33] If this was so, then the film is first exported from Korea to Hong Kong and then re-exported to Singapore. Or could it have been dubbed and subtitled in Hong Kong in two different languages in the first place, in order to capture both Mandarin and Cantonese speaking audience in Hong Kong itself, since there is a significant, and increasing, size of only Mandarin-speaking audience? And was the film then re-exported to Singapore? Finally, could it have first been imported to Singapore and intentionally dubbed and subtitled in the two languages with the view of re-exporting it to Hong Kong? The path of circulation of this particular film is an interesting puzzle. This latter issue is, perhaps, not specific to a Singapore–Chinese audience but all Chinese audiences as such.

The above elements are constitutive of the audience position of Singaporean consumers of East Asian popular culture. They may or may not be shared by audiences elsewhere in the region. Indeed, it is conceivable the localized audience of each of the constituent locations of East Asia will have its own set of specific characteristics grounded and derived from their respective everyday life. However, it is not inconceivable that the audiences of all the constituent locations would also share certain characters by virtue of being consumers of the same products in circulation. These questions remain empirical issues that can be answered only through collaborative comparative analysis across the region. The possibility of a set of shared features raises, perhaps, the most contested question that underlies this conceptual exercise and its implied research programme.

Effects of Viewing: a Pan East Asian Identity?

Finally, to the most controversial issue that needs to be considered in the conceptualization of East Asian Popular Culture, the question of an East Asian identity as an ideological effect of the production and consumption of the popular culture. This is, no doubt, the most elusive and the most contentious question. An Initial step must be to identify how the cultural products may work in unison to create a discursive and imaginative space for the emergence of such an identity.

First, it should be noted that the border-crossing popular urban television dramas and films have displaced, if not erased, references to East Asia as a space of 'traditional' in relation to a sense of the 'rural'. The struggle of rural migrants into urban areas in search of better living is a theme that is almost exclusively still used because of its continuing social relevance for PRC products (Sun 2002). The image of the rest of East Asia is urban and modern. Occasionally, the 'rural' will be evoked as a nostalgic reference to a mythic time and place when life was simpler and people less cunning than the urban present, an imaginary escape but not a place to live in the present.[34] The emphasis of the urban facilitates culture-border crossing; in contrast to the idea of 'tradition' that specifies 'uniqueness' and 'boundedness' of a culture, the urban increasingly lacks specificity, it is 'anywhere', 'anyplace' and 'anyone', the urban thus passes through cultural boundaries through its insistence on 'sameness' – the most extreme of this urban sameness is, of course, the banking district of every city, and then come the shopping complexes of imported goods, each differentiated only by landmark buildings of famous designer-architects, that is if one even knows who these star-architects are in the first place.

Second, the focus on the urban, young and single professionals has a tendency to displace the central place of the family; an urban consumer oriented culture is evoked to displace the tradition-soaked Confucianism. However, unlike the American series – such as *Friends* and *Sex in the City* – in which the family has all but disappeared, in East Asian urban television dramas and films, the family still has a presence. The family appears to alternate between an obstacle and a refuge to romance and the city. The presence of family and its influence varies across the locations of production and is accordingly inscribed into the culture products. As noted earlier, references to family as an institution have largely disappeared in Japanese 'trendy' drama, but continue to have a very significant presence in Korean urban drama series, and strong versions of Confucian filial piety are still often scripted into such series. The presence/absence of the traditional family is, in part, determined by the 'age' of the screen characters; it can be completely absent in series that feature urban, adult professionals in their late 20s or older but has to be present in teenage or school drama series, even if vaguely. For example, in a number of recent Taiwanese series centred on college youth, the family is referred to in dialogue but parents are distinctively absent, enabling the children to do things contrary to parental desires.[35] Furthermore, in these instances, the screen characters have sympathy and form coalitions with each other against their parents. Within the context of the popular culture programmes, Confucian familialism appears to be largely a working class ideology in contemporary East Asia. Dramas with working class themes and characters continue to be inclined to use the family as the foil to dramatize its members' struggle for upward mobility, while the middle class turns increasingly urban, inscribed with competitive consumer-based Individualism dictated by global capitalism.

Third, the emphasis on urban lifestyles enables the screen-visual images of middle-classness to transcend the relativities of real incomes in different East Asian locations. Although the income of an accountant, for example, in Taiwan and Korea is much lower than in Tokyo and Singapore, so too are the relative costs of living in these cities; consequently, while each urban middle-class stratum is embedded in their different spatial locations, a comparable level of lifestyle consumption is available to most, if not all. With the emphasis on lifestyles, urban middle-class Asians are given interchangeable bodies on screen, despite income differences and geographical location dispersion. Young professionals throughout East Asia will be able to identify with their screen representations in a 'clear, direct, and seemingly transparent' manner, through the 'immediate and efficacious' media that is television and films (Chow 1995: 10). To put it more categorically, urban dramas are imaginable, realistic, and foster identification among those who are willing to interpellate themselves into the screen, by temporarily or permanently suppressing their national/ethnic identities; again, Iwabuchi's empirical study of the Taiwanese audience's reception of Japanese trendy dramas and his conceptualization of this reception as based on 'coevalness' testifies to this (Iwabuchi 2002: 85–120).

Fourth, East Asian popular culture, following the lead of Japanese popular culture, consciously cultivates a genre of 'beautiful' youth; particularly noticeable are the leading men who are boyish, have brown-tinted, full, fluffed-up long hair and are earnest, if not innocent – a mode of 'beautiful masculinity'.[36] The lead women are beautiful, of course, self-confident with very non-revealing clothing, commonly in formal office wear, showing very little explicit sexuality. The packaging is so similar that only the trained eyes of aficionados who can recognize the actors and actresses are able to distinguish one country's product from that of another, particularly television drama, on screen; an indoor shot of a Korean drama looks very much like one from Taiwan or Japan or, increasingly, from Hong Kong.[37] The beautiful look is arguably more important than acting or other performing talents, including singing. The similarity of packaging and the indistinguishable sameness creates visual and discursive room for the insertion and projection of an idea of 'Asian-ness', with nationalities suppressed.

Finally, unlike the Confucian identity that is supposed to seep quietly, through years of implicit socialization, into the identity formation of East Asians, the construction of a pan East Asian identity is a conscious ideological project for the producers of East Asian cultural products, based on the commercial desire of capturing a larger audience and market. Apart from co-financing, producers increasingly feature and mix artistes from different East Asian locations in the same television programmes and films, in the hope that audience from the different locations will identify with the artistes that are hewn from their own space and place, thus expanding aggregate consumption. At its most extreme, a film may even be divided into 'filmlets', each coming from a different location, with its own directors and artistes.[38]

Obviously, there are no linear effects of consumption of popular culture on such a film's audience, ranging from completely without resonance to a strong sense of identification. However, the displacement of the 'traditional', the emphasis on the similarities of young, urban, middle-class consumer lifestyles and a projection of 'Asian-ness' are the building blocks to facilitate audience identification across East Asia with the personas on screens, large and small. One could say that the discursive and conceptual spaces for the possible emergence and formation of a pan-East Asian identity have been laid. It is here that the strategic methodological insistence of the audience position is consequential. It has to be a local audience, watching imported products, which is potentially able to transcend their grounded nationalities to forge abstract identification with the foreign characters on screen, a foreignness that is in turn potentially reabsorbed into an idea of (East) 'Asia'.

The expansion of East Asian popular culture is still a nascent phenomenon. It is also a new phenomenon in generational terms, for it has emerged in the current generation of youth below 30 years, who can or have moved beyond, or embrace only much diluted emotions towards the histories of the Japanese colonization of Korea and Taiwan, Japanese incursions in China before the Second World War and Japanese occupation of Singapore during the War. The place of this nascent phenomenon in the process of East Asian identity formation will obviously be long and circuitous. Although there are signs of its emergence, they come, ironically, from instances of attempts to suppress it by national political interest. A good example is the case of Chang Huei Mei, more popularly known as 'Ah Mei', the Taiwanese popular singer, who was banned by from all appearances in the PRC, and all her appearances in screen and print ads selling soft drinks were removed from the media, when she performed at the inauguration ceremony that celebrated Chen Shui Bian's election to the Presidency of Taiwan. Nevertheless, Chang's popularity among her PRC fans continued unabated and she was finally allowed to return to perform in the PRC after having performed during the 2001 government supported trade union May Day celebration in Singapore and a charity show in Hong Kong in August the same year. The singer, buoyed by her fans across the ethnic Chinese dominant locations in East Asia, appeared to be beyond the clutches of the state and, in fact, able to bring the latter to capitulation. Whatever may be one's political sentiment about the desirability of such an emergent identity, its possibility is nevertheless an issue that cannot be analytically avoided, without intellectual dishonesty.

Conclusion

Popular cultural products criss-cross cultural borders everyday in East Asia. East Asian popular culture has been able to carve out a significant segment of the regional consumption economy, although the US popular culture industry still dominates the airwaves and the large and small screens, and is unlikely to be displaced anytime soon. Furthermore, players in the US media industry are not sitting by waiting to lose part of their global empire but have formed a partnership with East Asian producers to produce East Asian popular culture.[39] There are, of course, many worthy researches to be done on the economies of these transnational product chains and product flows; similarly for researches into the organizations of the media industries in different specific locations and transnationally. The possibility and realization of a transnational East Asian identity, facilitated by the production and consumption of popular culture, remain empirical questions in each of the East Asian locations. The mapping of the manifest forms and contents of the pan-East Asian identities will require the collaboration of researchers in different locations, as the identities take shape and change. I only hope that I have delineated here, a conceptual boundary within which such empirical research may find a starting point.

Notes

1. An earlier version of this essay, entitled 'The making of an East Asia popular culture', was delivered as the Inaugural Distinguished Visiting Scholar Lecture, Carolina Asia Center, University of North Carolina, Chapel Hill, 28 February 2003.
2. Throughout this essay, Korea refers only to South Korea.
3. This later morphed into the search for 'Asian Values' in multiracial societies in Southeast Asia, such as Singapore and Malaysia.
4. The literature on diasporic Chinese businesses abound, covering the entire range of praises and critiques; a selection of which is Redding (1990), Ong & Nonini (1997), Ong (1999) and Yao (2002). Similarly for the issue of pan-Chinese identities, see Ang (2001); Chun (1996).
5. This attempted inscription of Confucianism to the ethnic Chinese Singaporeans further ignored the historical fact that the local Chinese educated community was heavily influenced by the 4 May Cultural Movements of the early 1990s and had since then adopted the use of the so-called 'common language' rather than classical texts in the local Chinese school curriculum.
6. While the generalized term of 'Western' influence is often evoked, Europe is largely absence in the popular cultural sphere.
7. In a consumption space like Singapore, where there are substantive quantities of South Asian population and Malays, Bollywood products also feature prominently in the popular cultural sphere.
8. The popularity of Japanese television drama led Iwabuchi to organize the International Conference on Japanese Drama, International Christian University, Tokyo, 2001. The book of edited essays is published as *Feeling Asian Modernities*: Transnational Consumption of Japanese Television Dramas (Hong Kong: Hong Kong University Press, 2004).
9. This finding about the Japanese audience's reception of other Asian popular culture as 'nostalgia' for Japan's past is, as noted by Chin (2000: 250) also found in another Japanese critic's, Tsubouchi Takahiko's, 'explanation' of the popularity of the television drama Oshin, in Asia during the 1980s. Chin himself, instead of criticizing such a simplistic reductionist reading of the reception by Asian audiences, proceeded to use these Japanese

readings as the evidence for the presence of 'Asian regionalism', 'Asianism' or 'Asian consciousness'. Without empirical evidence of the basis for a popular reception of audiences
in different locations in Asia, the best that could be said of Takahiko's reading is the critic's
own desire 'to Japanize Asia' and 'Asianize Japan', 'a desire both to see Japan as the embodiment of Asia and to construct Asia as a reflection of Japan's past' (Chin 2002: 254). Such
Japanese 'superiority' is, if anything, a sure way of alienating other Asians rather than a
basis for an Asian regionalism.

10. The very sketchy and preliminary manner of this unfinished piece of conceptual work is
    presented as the inaugural lecture of the Carolina Asia Center, and is, I hope, consistent
    with the spirit of the opening of the new research centre where the definition of its character
    lies in the work that has yet to be done.

11. This was a statement given by the producer of *Tokyo Love Story* in a talk given at the
    International Conference on Japanese Drama, International Christian University, Tokyo,
    2001. Up until that time, and in contrast to the 'trendy dramas' that feature urban, beauti-
    ful, independent and unmarried working youth, the Japanese television series were largely
    about family problems (Gossmann 2000).

12. Eva Tsai (2003) gives a fascinating reflective biographical account as a researcher of such
    dramas.

13. International Conference, 'Feeling "Asian" Modernities: TV drama consumption in East
    and Southeast Asia', International Christian University, Tokyo, 2001. During this confer-
    ence, analysts from Southeast Asia countries, with the exception of the paper from Singa-
    pore, worked on non-Japanese drama series.

14. During a trip to Kyoto in February 2004, I saw a Korean television drama being broadcast
    into two languages. This and one news event channel were the only non-Japanese pro-
    grammes in 12 channels.

15. As the Japanese pop cultural products were 'illegal', this generated additional pleasures of
    illicit consumption, see Kim Hyun-Mee (2002).

16. The first category includes the films *Shiri* and *Joint Security Area*, the second includes the
    films *My Wife is a Gangster* and *Guns and Talk*. In the last film, mid to late 20s assassins
    who could design elaborate plots of murder are shown to be completely at the mercy of
    women, as clients and as potential victims.

17. The most outstanding example of a Singaporean singer who had achieved star status is
    Stefanie Sun Yanzi. The Taiwanese, I am told, claim her as one of their own.

18. Eric Ma of Chinese University of Hong Kong reported research on such productions
    during the 'Feeling Asia' conference at ICU, 2000.

19. For example, the most recent US financed *wuxia* blockbuster film, *Hero* by Zhang Yimou
    was immediately subjected to debates of whether the director, known for having his films
    banned in the PRC because of their critical political stance, has 'sold' out to the Party when
    his film was released without event, and was a huge commercial success.

20. In the 1950s, there were two film studios that produced Malay films.

21. The latest joint production television series, for 2002–3, is *'innocently Guilty'*, an oxymo-
    ronic translation of the Chinese title *'There Are Fair Weather Days in the Law'* (*Fa nei you
    qiang tian*), a reference to the generalized Chinese belief that the court is to be avoided at
    all cost. It stars, the Hong Kong actress, Anita Yuen.

22. One such instance is the 'ghost story', *The Tree*, which features Singaporean leading actress,
    Zoe Tay, next to Hong Kong actor, Wu Zhenyu (Francis Ng).

23. One Singaporean actress that has achieved some success through this mode of entry is Fann
    Wong, who played the Little Dragon Girl in a popular *wuxia* series and, in 2003, starred
    in Jackie Chan's blockbuster, Hollywood produced movie, *Shanghai Knights*.

24. It was also the very first popular Mandarin television series to be screened in Indonesia after the lifting of the official ban on Chinese culture. It was alleged that the '*Meteor Garden* has turned many Indonesians on to anything Chinese' (*Straits Times*, 21 July 2002).

25. Significantly, if the idea of 'Asian-ness' is absent, identification is also absent. For example, Sun (2002:100) notes that PRC audiences consistently report that they do not identify (*rentong*) with Taiwanese or Hong Kong televisual cultural products.

26. I am concerned in this chapter with only the ethnic-Chinese audience. The two other constituent racial groups in the population, Indians and Malays have their own viewing preferences in Hindi movies, and thus, in spite of geographic and national location, do not partake significantly in the East Asian popular cultural sphere.

27. Tour companies in Singapore organize tours to these televised sites for the fans. In a recent instance (December 2002), a group of Singapore tourists to Korea for winter holidays were persuaded by one of the members of the tour to change their designated ski resort to one that was featured in the popular drama series, *Winter Sonata* (*Straits Times*, 4 January 2003).

28. Singaporeans never fail to mention their first encounter with snow in their correspondence and Memories. For example, a friend who is a foreign correspondent wrote this in January 2003: 'It is very cold here in New York and temperatures fall below zero daily. But I was lucky enough to see amazing snow fall in the city, which drives New Yorkers crazy but had me with a big smile on my face for the entire day.'

29. The other two are Malay and Tamil, a southern Indian language of the majority of the resident Indian population.

30. English subtitles make it, in principle, accessible to South Asian and Malay audiences, although as noted in note 25, few Malays and Indians seldom consume East Asian popular culture, preferring Hindi films and locally produced Malay programmes.

31. The association of low social class status with *Fujian* language is most pronounced in popular music, where popular songs imported from Taiwan *Fujian* are sung almost exclusively by working class men in karaoke lounges.

32. In the late 1990s and early 2000s, there was a spate of Korean movies that were well received in Singapore, that featured 'emotionally sensitive' male or female gangsters who may be social misfits or inept, but deadly sophisticated in their execution of murder and other violence. This mismatch of character is used as the foil for comedy; such as *Guns and Talks* and *My Wife is a Gangster* in contrast to the more serious gangster film, *Friends*.

33. For a Singaporean Chinese who does not realize that Cantonese can be phonologically transcribed with Chinese written words, the subtitle would be incomprehensible. Nevertheless, he or she would still understand dialogue.

34. In most newly industrialized countries that have undergone very rapid urbanization, nostalgic imagination of the simplicity of pre-industrialized and urbanized life is often evoked as a lament and a criticism of the high stresses of life in the city in pursuit of better material life (Chua 1995).

35. This is especially true in the depiction of absent parents who are fabulously successful entrepreneurs but thoroughly negligent of their families, especially teenage children; for example, the series, *MVP Lover* and the earlier mentioned, *Westend Youth*.

36. For example, the four members of Taiwanese F4 (*Meteor Garden*), the Taiwan born Japanese actor, Takashi Kaneshiro and Korean actors, Bae yong Jun (*Winter Sonata*) and Won Bin (*Friends*).

37. In one instance, in Hanoi, I was not able to identify where in East Asia the on-screen drama programme was from until Mandarin could be heard beneath the local quality voiceover of Vietnamese narration; in Vietnam, due to lack of funds, there is a tendency for a narrator

to tell the story that is unfolding in a voiceover rather than dubbing the original dialogue.

38. The most recent offering in this 'filmlet' structure is a film called *'Three'*, which contains three ghost stories, one each from South Korea, Thailand and Hong Kong, produced by a company that is consciously aiming to be pan-Asia.

39. Indeed, all the major record companies – Polymer, EMI, Bertelsmann, Warner and Sony – are already here, with East Asia accounting for up to a quarter of their global earnings since the mid 1990s. In addition, Warner Brothers have entered into joint production, with Singapore's Raintree Pictures and Hong Kong's Milkway Image, of a new film adaptation of popular Taiwan romance novel, *Turn Left, Turn Right*, in 2003 (*Straits Times*, 17 December 2002).

References

Ang, Ien (2001). *On Not Speaking Chinese*. London: Routledge.

Chen, Xiaoming (2000). The Mysterious Other: Postpolitics in Chinese Films. In: Arif Dirlik & Xudog Zhang (eds.), *Postmodernism and China*, pp. 222–38. Durham, US: Duke University Press.

Chin, Leo (2000). Globalizing the Regional, Regionalizing the Global: Mass Culture and Asianism in the Age of Late Capitalism. *Public Culture* 12(1), pp. 233–58.

Chow, Rey (1995). *Primitive Passions: Visuality, Sexuality, Ethnography and Contemporary Chinese Cinema*. New York: Columbia University Press.

Chua, Beng-Huat (1995). That Imagined Space: Nostalgia for the *Kampungs*. In: Brenda S. A. Yeoh & Lily Kong (eds.), *Portrait of Places: History, Community and Identity in Singapore*, pp. 222–41. Singapore: Times Editions.

Chua, Beng-Huat (2003). *Life Is Not Complete without Shopping*. Singapore: Singapore University Press.

Chua, Beng-Huat & Wei Wei Yeo (2003). Singapore Cinema: Eric Khoo and Jack Neo – Critique from the Margin and Mainstream. *Inter-Asia Cultural Studies* 4(1), pp. 117–25.

Chun, Allen (1996). Fuck Chineseness: On the Ambiguities of Ethnicity as Culture as Identity. *Boundary* 2(23), pp. 111–38.

De Kloet, Jeroen (2000). "Let Him Fucking See the Green Smoke beneath My Groin": The Mythology of Chinese Rock. In: Arif Dirlik & Xudong Zhang (eds.), *Postmodernism and China*, pp. 239–74. Durham, NC: Duke University Press.

Gossmann, Hilaria M. (2000). New Role Models for Men and Women? Gender in Japanese TV Drama. In: Timothy J. Graig (ed.), *Japan Pop: Inside the World of Japanese Pop Culture*, pp. 207–21. Armonk, NY: M. E. Sharpe.

Han, Seung-Mi (2000). Consuming the Modern: Globalization, Things Japanese, and the Politics of Cultural Identity in Korea. *Journal of Pacific Asia* 6, pp. 7–26.

Iwabuchi, Koichi (2002). *Recentering Globalization: Popular Culture and Japanese Transnationalism*. Durham, NC: Duke University Press.

Kim, Hyun-Mee (2002). The Inflow of Japanese Culture and the Historical Construction of "Fandom" in South Korea. Paper presented at the International Conference on Culture in the Age of Informatization: East Asia into 21st Century, Institute of East and West Studies, Yonsei University, November 16.

Kim, Soyoung (2003). The Birth of the Local Feminist Sphere in the Global Era: Trans-cinema and *Yosongjang*. *Inter-Asia Cultural Studies* 4(1), pp. 10–24.

MacFarquar, Roderick (1980). The Post-Confucian Challenge. *Economist*, February 9.

Ong, Aihwa (1999). *Flexible Citizenship: The Cultural Logic of Transnationalism*. Durham, NC: Duke University Press.

Ong, Aihwa & Donald M. Nonini (1997). *Ungrouded Empires: The Cultural Politics of Modern Chinese Transnationalism*. London: Routledge.

Redding, S. G. (1990). *The Spirit of Chinese Capitalism*. Berlin/New York: W. de Gruyter.

Stronach, Bruce (1989). Japanese Television. In: Richard G. Powers & Hidetoshi Kato (eds.), *Handbook of Japanese Popular Culture*, pp. 127–66. New York: Greenwood Press.

Sun, Wanning (2002). *Leaving China: Media, Migration and Transnational Imagination*. Lanham, MD: Rowan & Littlefield.

Tsai, Eva (2003). Decolonizing Japanese TV Drama: Syncopated Notes from a "Sixth Grader" Researcher Relocated in Taiwan. *Inter-Asia Cultural Studies* 4(3), pp. 503–12.

Tu, Wei-Ming (1991a). *The Triadic Chord: Confucian Ethics, Industrial East Asia and Max Weber*. Singapore: Institute of East Asia Philosophy.

Tu, Wei-Ming (1991b). *The Living Tree: The Changing Meaning of Being Chinese Today*. Special issue, *Daedelus, Annals of the American Academy of Arts and Science*.

Tu, Wei-Ming (1991c). The Search for Roots in East Asia: The Case of the Confucian Revival. In: Martin E. Marty & R. Scott Appleby (eds.), *Fundamentalism Observed*. Chicago: Chicago University Press.

Yao, Souchou (2002). *Confucian Capitalism*. London: Routledge.

82

Introduction to the Study of Popular Cultures

*Néstor García Canclini**

Definition of the Popular: Romanticism, Positivism, and the Gramscian Tendency

How can we formulate a concept of popular culture? First of all, popular culture must not be taken as the "expression" of the personality of a particular people, as idealism does, because such a personality does not exist as a metaphysical a priori entity, and comes into being as a result of the interaction of social relations. Nor is it a set of ideal traditions or essences, ethereally preserved: cultural production, as we have seen, emerges from material living conditions and is rooted in them. This is very clearly shown in the case of popular classes, where songs, beliefs, and *fiestas* are more closely linked on a daily basis to those material tasks that consume virtually all of their time. For that very reason, it does not seem useful, in order to account for popular cultural processes, to conceptualize them either as empty forms universally found, as functionalism does, or as mental logical processes that will adopt particular types in different contexts, as structuralism does.

Popular cultures (rather than popular culture) are formed through a process of unequal appropriation of the economic and cultural property of a nation or ethnic group by some of its subordinate sectors, and through both a symbolic and real understanding, reproduction, and transformation of general as well as particular living and working conditions.

We have already discussed relations between economic and cultural capital, as well as the fact that ownership or otherwise of economic capital gives rise to unequal participation in educational capital and therefore in the appropriation of cultural property available in a particular society. However, the peculiarity of popular cultures does not derive solely from the fact that the appropriation of what society has is smaller and different; it also derives from the fact that the people create at work, and in their lives in general, specific forms of representation, reproduction, and symbolic reelaboration of their social relations. In the previous chapter, we examined the sense in which culture is representation, production, reproduction, and symbolic reelaboration. At this point, we must add that the people carry out these processes while participating in the general

*Pp. 21–35 and 116 (notes) from N. García Canclini, *Transforming Modernity: Popular Culture in Mexico*, trans. Lidia Lozano (Austin: University of Texas Press). © 1993 by the University of Texas Press. Reprinted with permission from the University of Texas Press.

conditions of production, circulation, and consumption of the system in which they live (e.g., a dependent social formation) and at the same time by creating their own structures. Therefore, popular cultures are constituted within two spaces: (1) labor, familial, communication, and all other kinds of practices through which the capitalist system organizes the life of all its members; and (2) practices and forms of thought that popular sectors create for themselves, to conceptualize and express their own reality, their own subordinate role in the spheres of production, circulation, and consumption. In a sense, what owner and worker have in common is their participation in the same job in the same factory, the fact that they watch the same television channels (though, of course, from distinct positions that generate different decodifications); but at the same time, there are economic and cultural options that differentiate them, as well as separate jargons and channels of communication peculiar to each class. Both spaces, that of hegemonic culture and that of popular culture, interpenetrate each other, such that the particular language of workers or peasants is partly original construction, partly reformulation of the language of the mass media and political power, or a specific mode of referring to social conditions shared by all (e.g., jokes on inflation). A similar interaction exists in the opposite direction too: the hegemonic language of the mass media or politicians will incorporate popular forms of expression to the extent that it wants to reach the entire population.

In short, popular cultures are the product of *unequal appropriation* of cultural capital, the *people's own reflections* about their living conditions, and *conflict-ridden interaction* with hegemonic sectors. Thus understood, their analysis can move away from the two positions that have prevailed until now: immanent interpretations, formulated in Europe by romantic populism and in Latin America by conservative nationalism and *indigenismo*, on the one hand, and positivism, which, concerned with scientific precision, ignored the political meaning of symbolic production among the people, on the other.

Romantics regarded the people as a homogeneous and autonomous whole, whose spontaneous creativity represented the highest expression of human values and the way of life to which humanity should return. Belief in popular culture as the authentic repository of human nature and the true essence of the nation, set apart from the artificial meaning of a "civilization" that denied its existence, was somewhat useful to vindicate popular thought and customs, to stimulate its study and protection after a long absence from academic learning. However, such exaltation was based on sentimental enthusiasm, which could not be kept up when positivist philology showed that what the people produced – it was referring particularly to the case of poetry – came out of both the direct experience of popular classes and their contact with "high" art and thought, that their existence derived to a considerable degree from a "degraded absorption" of the dominant culture.[1]

Romantic idealization, into which hardly any scholar dares fall any longer, still attracts many folklorists and *indigenistas* in Latin America, and it continues to be used within nationalist political discourse. Though not always influenced by European romanticism, they fall back onto many of its hypotheses. This metaphysical vision of the people imagines them as the place where virtues of a biological (appertaining to race) and irrational character (love for the land, religion, and ancestral beliefs) would be preserved untouched. Overvaluing biological and telluric components, characteristic of right-wing thinking, helps bourgeois nationalist populism identify its interests with those of the nation, and conceal its dependence on imperialism and, internally, any class conflicts that threaten its privileges. The historical dynamic that formed the concept and sense of nationhood is neutralized and diluted in "tradition." From this concept of folklore as a fossilized and apolitical archive, a populist policy is promoted that, under the pretext of "giving the people what they like," avoids worrying itself with whether popular culture develops by being offered canned goods or the right to choose and create. Nor is the question posed as to who does the giving, or who, through centuries of domination, shaped their taste.

For many university scholars, the scientific alternative to this idealization is empiricism, more or less positivistic. They urge direct contact with reality, careful and detailed study of objects and customs, and their classification by ethnic origin and immediately observable differences. This alternative form of passion, governed by analytical precision but fascinated by the neglected worth of oppressed ethnic enclaves to the point of spending many years in a small village to record even the most minute detail, has produced monographs and books of great value for understanding myths, legends, ceremonies, crafts, customs, and institutions. However, we have to ask ourselves why there is an imbalance in most of these works between the data gathered and the conclusions that have been reached. It seems that this results from a narrow focus on the object studied – they look only at crafts or at the local community – and its misconceived role within the process of development of capitalism.

The drawbacks of this approach did not disappear as attempts were made to account for changes in the identity of traditional societies through a theory of "culture contact." Such studies, launched in the thirties with the early works on acculturation by the American Social Science Research Council[2] and the publication in the United Kingdom of *Methods of Study of Culture Contact in Africa in 1938*,[3] were not able to overcome the neutral character of the concepts of acculturation and cultural contact and their inability to explain those conflicts and processes of domination they usually involve. With meticulous kindheartedness, they called the exploiters "givers of values" and the reaction of the oppressed "assimilation." Linton introduced a significant variation when he talked of "guided change" to account for cases in which "a contact group interferes actively or intentionally with the culture of another."[4] But he also failed to situate such interference properly in relation to its socioeconomic causes.

Psychologistic and culturalist interpretations with which anthropologists in the metropolis sought to account for cultural change and local resistance found a mild echo among Latin American anthropologists, particularly those who had had Redfield, Beals, and other ideologues of the theory of "modernization of primitive societies" as teachers. Perhaps Aguirre Beltrán stands out among those who follow this tendency because of his somewhat original reformulation of acculturation phenomena and his influence on *indigenista* policies. Although his works consider forms of domination and the productive foundations of intercultural contacts, they do not assign sufficient weight to material determinations. They overrate ethnicity, which is seen in isolation, and their theoretical and empirical problematic fits the objectives of integration and conciliation that permeate their political project, that is, to construct a "doctrine which guides and explains the methods and goals pursued by *indigenista* action."[5]

We believe that the analysis of intercultural conflicts cannot be guided by a concern either to exalt popular culture or to attach oneself conservatively to the immediate appearance and meaning that the community itself attributes to these facts, nor can it be guided by an interest in making it ready for modernization. The critical issue is to understand popular cultures in relation to conflicts between social classes and to the conditions of exploitation under which those sectors produce and consume.

In fact, when ways of approaching intercultural relations are placed within their political and historical context, their controversial nature becomes clearer. Concern with what has been called cultural contact or acculturation *between different societies* emerged during the imperialist expansion of capitalism and the need to widen the world market at the end of the nineteenth century and beginning of the twentieth. On the other hand, rapid industrialization and urbanization since the forties, with consequent massive migrations and the creation of slums (*ciudades perdidas, villas miserias, favelas*) in large urban centers and capitalist reorganization of the peasant economy and culture, intensified existing contradictions in the countryside, in the city, and between them: out of this process came the concern to understand intercultural conflicts within individual societies and between their different classes and ethnic groups.

However, the failure to explain these processes is not unique to anthropological trends. Marxism, which offers a theory with greater explanatory power regarding such conflicts under capitalism, has not generated much research on the subject either: it has tended to favor the analysis of economic aspects, and on the issue of culture it has concerned itself almost exclusively with the ideology of the dominant classes. Since Gramsci, the popular has gained a new scientific and political place of its own, but only in recent years have some anthropologists, particularly Italian ones, applied his laconic intuitions from prison to empirical research. A first conclusion of these reflections is that the most promising framework for the study of popular cultures can be found at the crossroads of Marxist accounts of the dynamics of capitalism and empirical, and in part methodological, contributions of anthropology and sociology.

It is necessary, in order to define more precisely our own ideas, to mention briefly those aspects in the texts by Gramsci and his followers (Cirese, Lombardi Satriani) that we consider most valuable as well as those that in our view are problematic. One Gramscian contribution that we regard as most fruitful is the connection made between culture and hegemony. His notes were edited and further elaborated by Alberto M. Cirese in a study that constitutes perhaps the most valuable European theoretical contribution on this subject. Cirese rejects those who define popular culture according to some intrinsic qualities or set of characteristics peculiar to it, and denotes it instead in relation to those cultures that oppose it. The popular element in any phenomenon must be established by its use rather than by its origin, "as fact rather than essence, as relational position rather than substance." What constitutes the popular aspect of a cultural fact, he goes on to say, "is the historical relationship, one of difference or contrast, with other cultural facts."[6] However, this *dialectical* conception of social relations is contradicted by his further suggestion of "imbalances" between cultures. He distinguishes two kinds: "external imbalances," that is, those that exist between European societies and "ethnological or primitive" ones, and "internal imbalances" within Western societies, between dominant and subordinate strata in a single social formation. To talk of *levels* at various heights seems too static, implying a concept that can scarcely encompass those *inequalities* and *conflicts* that constantly link popular and hegemonic cultures. The use of terms like these leads him to call those processes involving messages and products as they pass from one level to another "downward" and "upward processes," something which – despite many caveats – connotes an unacceptable hierarchy.

If we look seriously at the "reciprocal exchanges, diffusion and conditionings" beween popular cultures and others to which Cirese himself refers,[7] the concept of imbalance does not seem the most suitable to describe them. On the contrary, compart-mentalizing culture into parallel processes, as in some kind of geological stratification, implies giving in to those static classifications so characteristic of classical folklore and against which both Gramsci and Cirese in his most Gramscian texts set up a critical and dynamic analytical strategy. Research cannot focus on imbalance; it must look at inequalities and conflicts between symbolic manifestations of classes that are prevented from becoming autonomous by their joint participation in the same system.

All studies influenced by a Gramscian analytical framework share one problem: the strong emphasis placed on both the opposition between subordinate and hegemonic cultures and the political need to protect the independence of the former leads them to regard both as systems foreign to each other. This is even more clear in the works of Lombardi Satriani, particularly in the way they have been interpreted in Latin America. Hegemonic and subordinate cultures are set in contrast to each other in such a Manichean fashion that "anesthetizing" or "challenging" qualities are too easily attrib-uted to cultural phenomena that are neither one nor the other, but a combination of experiences and representations whose ambiguities correspond to the unresolved nature of contradictions among popular sectors. One cannot deny the value of Lombardi Satriani's thought-provoking analyses of the structure of popular cultures, including their interaction with the dominant culture (e.g., the chapter on "folkmarkets" in *Apro-piación y destrucción de la cultura de las clases subalternas*),[8] but his approach is dominated by a categorical opposition between hegemonic and subordinate, which are seen as intrinsic qualities of certain messages rather than forms – ambiguous and temporary – of conflicts binding them together.

For Satriani, the opposition between domination and cultural resistance has an inceptive nature, as if we were dealing with two phenomena foreign to each other, whose existence came before both cultures became part of a single social system. This model might fit the initial processes of colonization, when capitalist expansion brought its own standards in from abroad and Indian communities confronted this imposition as a mass. It is useful to explain the conquest of America by Spaniards and Portuguese, as well as later stages when the reduction of conflict gave rise to a certain degree of relative autonomy of subjected and dominant cultures. But it cannot be applied to the present development of monopoly capitalism that brings under its control every society it dominates, thus building a dense system in which socioeconomic and cultural conflict *precedes* policies of domination and resistance, and which combines the anesthetizing, challenging, or other uses that products may undergo.

Instead of considering "questioning" and "anesthetizing" phenomena, then, the study should focus on the structure of conflict, which does indeed include the former phenomena, as well as others of integration, interpenetration, concealment,

dissimulation, and cushioning of social contradictions. We still lack a typology of interactions between popular and dominant cultures, and the only way to construct one is
to carry out research on various processes, as long as such studies include the diversity
of existing links between cultures without hastening to classify them according to positive or negative effects.

Finally, why talk of popular cultures? We prefer this term to others used in anthropology, sociology, and folklore – oral, traditional, or subordinate culture – which assume
to some extent the possibility of reducing the popular to an essential characteristic.
While we might occasionally use the term *traditional* to refer to a certain aspect or type
of popular culture that comes into being through opposition to *modernity*, such words
must be read in quotation marks (though we may have left them out in order to simplify
the text), as formulas used for their functional value, to identify *phenomena*, not essences,
that exist and need to be given a name, though they are not determinant. Equally, we
will use *subordinate culture* when we wish to emphasize popular culture's opposition to
the dominant one. But, in fact, there is no such thing as *an* oral, traditional, or subordinate culture. We agree with Giovanni Battista Bronzini when he writes that

> oral culture, traditionalism, illiteracy, subordination, are phenomena of communication
> and/or of an economic and social nature, inherent to the structure of society and the
> system of production . . . As phenomena they do not produce culture, nor do they create
> sufficient conditions for its production, but they become cultural channels and means of
> production in given times and places and in certain social situations. Subordination itself
> is historically differentiated: as socioeconomic condition it smothers culture, as class con-
> sciousness it stimulates it. The constant factor in cultural production is the work done by
> popular classes during phases of oppression and liberation.[9]

Why Crafts and *Fiestas*

I have chosen these two manifestations to examine changes in popular culture under
capitalism because artisanal *objects* and the *event* of the *fiesta* are not only fundamental
but also reflect, in Indian as well as many mestizo villages, the major conflicts that result
from their integration into capitalism to modernization. Through the production, circulation, and consumption of crafts and through changes undergone by *fiestas,* we can
study the *economic* function of cultural facts (instruments for social reproduction), their
political function (fighting for hegemony), and their *psychosocial* functions (to create
consensus and identity and to neutralize or work out contradictions at the symbolic
level). The complex composition of crafts and *fiestas* and the diversity of social phenomena included in them helps the simultaneous study of culture as it manifests itself
in three main areas: *texts, social practices or relations*, and *organization of space*. To talk
of crafts requires much more than descriptions of design and methods of production;
their meaning can be fully comprehended only when they are considered in relation to
texts that predict and promote them (myths and decrees, tourist brochures and conditions for contests), to the social practices of the people who produce and trade them,
who look at them or buy them (in a village, a peasant or urban market, a boutique, or

a museum), and to the place they occupy together with other objects in the social organization of space (vegetables or antiques, on a dirt floor or behind the seductive cunning of shop windows).

What gives crafts their character: the fact that they are produced by Indians or peasants, by hand and anonymously, their elementary nature, or their traditional iconography? Establishing their identity and boundaries has become more difficult in recent years, because goods considered to be crafts change as they come into contact with the capitalist market, tourism, "cultural industry," "modern" forms of art, communication, and recreation. But it is not just a question of changes in the meaning and function of crafts; this problem is part of a widespread identity crisis felt in contemporary societies. The homogenization of cultural patterns and the grave nature of conflicts between symbolic systems challenges a whole series of assumptions and differences that until now have reassured us: whites on one side, blacks on the other; Westerners over here, Indians over there; art in urban galleries and museums, crafts in the countryside.

Aesthetic stereotypes such as those that distinguished between "high" art and "mass" and popular art have also succumbed. These three systems of representation functioned fairly independently of each other and each one reflected different social classes: high art reflected the interests and tastes of the bourgeoisie and cultured sectors of the petite bourgeoisie, mass art – more accurately described as art for the masses – reflected those of urban middle and proletarian sectors, and crafts reflected those of the peasantry. The distance between elitist aesthetic standards and the artistic prowess of subordinate classes expressed, and reaffirmed, the separation between social classes. The dominant sectors had exclusive control over codes of "good taste," as established by themselves, and this served as a status symbol against cultural massification. Art for the masses and folklore both conveyed to popular classes a worldview that legitimized their oppression and vindicated their traditions and customs within a distinct space, where ignorance of "great culture" and inability to understand and enjoy it validated the distance between people and elites. Both came together formally in official speeches and in calls for national unity, but were neatly separated when it came to setting up different organisms for their management, awarding prizes, or representing their country abroad: crafts were entered in competitions of popular art; works of art were sent to exhibitions.

This is still going on to some extent. But many factors conspire against such a rigorous distinction between symbolic systems. Certain factories resort to native designs in their industrial production, and there are artisans who introduce the iconography of high art or the mass media in their works, as is the case of the Zapotec artisans from Teotitlan del Valle, in Oaxaca, who weave *sarapes* (colorful woolen shawls) with images by Klee and Picasso. In urban stores and rural markets, there are both crafts and industrial goods. Multinational record corporations distribute traditional music in metropolises, while the dances with which small peasant villages celebrate their ancient *fiestas* take place to the music of rock groups. We could cite pop art, satirical verses put to commercial music, and the use of peasant images in advertising to suggest the "natural" character of a recently created product, plastic decorations in rural households and hand looms present in modern apartments, as further examples of the way in which aesthetic systems encounter each other and seem to break up into mixed forms of representation and organization of space.[10]

Popular culture, then, cannot be defined, as we have already said, according to some a priori essence; neither can arts and crafts nor *fiestas*: there is no intrinsic element – for example, the fact that they are handmade – that is sufficient, nor can the problem be solved by an accumulation of several such elements.

Recent studies have attempted to define the specificity of crafts from the perspective of economic analysis, taking into account only the labor process (not the meaning that develops through consumption) or the type of economic subordination to capitalism (without considering, however, the role of cultural factors in such characterization).

Nor is it possible to define popular art or culture only in contrast to high or mass art; the starting point must be the system that gives rise to them all, which ascribes a particular place to each one of them, and reorganizes and combines them, in order to fulfill economic, political, and psychosocial functions necessary for its reproduction. Therefore, we need to look at arts and crafts as process rather than outcome,[11] as products that echo social relations rather than self-contained objects.

However, which concept of crafts will we use to make ourselves clear? If we consider the various uses of the term – in official texts and store signs, in colloquial language and tourist guides – we would have to include virtually everything made by hand, in a rudimentary fashion, by Indians and others, with forms that evoke pre-Columbian iconography or simply suggest "oldness" or "primitivism": rush baskets and hats, domestic ceramics and clay sculptures, expensive and rustic silver articles, objects carved by young urban hippies, and others, made and used by peasants, whose aesthetic value is unimportant (*huaraches,* hammocks, etc.).

These articles differ from each other in terms of labor processes, channels of circulation, market value, consumers, and uses and meanings attributed to them by different recipients. It does not seem desirable to confine the term *crafts* to one area of this cosmos before we have set out on our intended theoretical and empirical study. We will provisionally adopt this diversity of meaning and include in our research very different situations when the term is used in ways not immediately compatible: raising questions about this semantic and pragmatic confusion will help us understand the extent and change of their social functions.

We will not talk about *fiestas*, as phenomenologists of religion (Otto, Eliade) and some anthropologists (Duvignaud) do, as a break from routine, a change from the profane to the sacred, a search for a primordial time when "the sacred dimension of life is fully encountered, the sanctity of human existence as divine creation is experienced."[12] On the contrary, I realized through my fieldwork that the *fiesta* reflects the entire life of each community, its economic organization and cultural structures, its political relations and any projects to change them. In a phenomenal sense, it is true that the *fiesta* involves a degree of discontinuity and exceptionality: Indians interrupt regular work (though this is done in order to perform other tasks, sometimes longer and more intense), wear special clothes, and make unusual meals and decorations. However, I do not feel that all these factors together place the *fiesta* in a time and place set against everyday life.

Peasant *fiestas*, with Indian and colonial roots, and even religious ones of more recent origin, are movements of communal unification to celebrate events or beliefs that *originate* from their daily experience with nature and other individuals (when they are the product of popular initiative) or are *imposed* (by the church or cultural power) to guide the representation of their material living conditions. Often associated with the productive cycle and the rhythm of sowing and harvesting, they are a way to do at the symbolic level, and sometimes to appropriate materially, what a hostile nature or an unjust society denies them, to celebrate that gift, to remember and relive the manner in which they received it in the past, and to search and prepare for its future arrival. Whether they celebrate a recent event (a plentiful harvest) or commemorate distant and mythical ones (the crucifixion and resurrection of Christ), the reason behind the *fiesta* is related to the communal life of the village. Instead of seeing it, as Duvignaud does, as a moment when "society comes out of itself, escapes from its own definition,"[13] we will regard it as an occasion when society goes into its deepest self, that part that normally escapes it, in order to understand and restore itself. The cause of the distance between routine and *fiesta* lies in everyday history, in what they lack or do not understand at work, in their family life, and in their powerless dealings with death.

We can understand the difference of the *fiesta*, its excesses, waste, and widespread decorations, if we relate them to everyday needs. From a materialist approach, they can be interpreted as ideal or symbolic compensation for economic shortfalls. Behind the wantonness and sublimation of the *fiesta*, a dynamic (psychoanalytic) interpretation reveals the outburst or hidden realization of desires repressed in social life. In both instances, discontinuity represents one manner of talking about what is left behind, another way to keep it going. I do not agree that the essence of the *fiesta* is escape from the social order, the pursuit of a place "without structure or codes, the world of nature where only the forces of the 'it' are at work, the great instances of subversion."[14] On the contrary, it is through the ritual of the *fiesta* that the village imposes a certain order over powers it feels are beyond control; it seeks to transcend the coercion or frustration of limiting structures through their ceremonial reorganization, and it visualizes alternative social practices, which sometimes are enforced during the permissive period of celebration. These practices are not always liberating (they might be evasive when misfortune is construed in a resigned or guilty fashion), but they are structured, both by their own internal order and by the confined space they take up in the routine that comes before and after them and defines them.

The *fiesta* prolongs daily existence to such an extent that its development reproduces society's contradictions. It cannot become a place for subversion or egalitarian free expression, or if it does it is with reluctance, because it is not just a movement of collective unification; it duplicates social and economic differences. Thus, I do not share the view that recreational and monetary expenditure for the *fiesta* is a mechanism of economic redistribution or leveling: communal pressure for wealthy members to take up *cargos* and *mayordomías* is regarded by authors like Castile as a means to force them to reinvest their profits on celebrations, thus reducing income inequality.[15] I have occasionally found this process of coercion at work, and I believe it is legitimate to regard it as one way of making sure that the surplus is reinvested within the village, thus preventing greater exchange with the outside world from destroying internal cohesion. However, apart from the fact that there is no redistribution because wealthy individuals do not transfer part of the profits to the poor but spend them instead on the celebrations, this "loss" is often compensated by other earnings: they are also the ones who sell beer and food, who run the entertainment. By benefiting those who are already better off and enabling them to earn even more through increased consumption, the *fiesta* reasserts social differences and offers another opportunity of internal and external exploitation of the village. While it includes elements of collective solidarity, the *fiesta* displays those inequalities and differences that stop us from idealizing Indian "communities" and make us use this term with certain reservation when it is applied to such villages. (We cannot speak of communities as if they constituted homogeneous blocks; the term can be used to refer to groupings where collective factors are stronger than in "modern" societies, as long as we point out their internal contradictions.)

Having considered the fiesta as a *structure*, homologous or opposite to the social structure, we can now understand those elements in it that represent occurrence, transgression, and reinvention of everyday life and those that transcend social control and awaken desire. But tension between structure and occurrence does not manifest itself equally in every class and situation, hence the significance of first knowing both social structures and the structure of the *fiesta*, instead of speculating on the *fiesta* in general, and distinguishing between civic, religious, familial, rural, and urban ones. I will try to justify this theoretical approach with at look at three religious *fiestas* in Michoacán, namely, those of Saint Peter and Saint Paul in Ocumicho, of Christ the King in Patamban, and of the dead in the area around Lake Pátzcuaro.

Changing Popular Cultures: The Tarascan Case

Tarascans or *purépechas* have been and are still one of the major ethnic enclaves in Mexico. When the Spaniards arrived, they occupied the present-day state of Michoacán and parts of Guerrero, Guanajuato, and Querétaro, a total area of 27.6 thousand square miles, home to a million and a half people. This number included other ethnic groups, primarily Nahuatls, Toltecs, and *chichimecas*, but Tarascans constituted the dominant group. The few documents that tell about their pre-Columbian life, the *Relaciones de Michoacán y Tancítaro*, in which Sahagún echoes the respect Aztecs felt for them, are sufficient to give us an idea of their customs and power, their artisanal skills and luxury items, and their importance before the Conquest.

Colonized by the Spaniards, they lost land and independence and had to give up their customs to some degree, though many withdrew to the *sierra*. Through their stubborn resistance and the social action of Vasco de Quiroga, who took part in the process of colonization but became interested in developing certain Indian institutions, the Tarascan heritage was able to survive better than in other areas of Mexico. The overexploitation of the colony, fighting during the period of Independence and the Revolution, struggles between *agraristas* and *sinarquistas* – which upset and changed their cultural continuity – did not entirely destroy communal experience in the exploitation of land and forests, local organizations of government, artisanal methods, and some rituals and *fiestas*. These changes in past centuries have been widely discussed in several works, particularly those by Carrasco and Van Zantwijk.

Arriving in Patamban by day: after traveling for an hour and a quarter on a dirt road, we can see semiarid plots of land, some cracked, and during the best months, a few fields of corn, beans, and squash. Despite the lack of rain, vast pine woods surround the village. The inhabitants seem used to the cold characteristic of an altitude of 12,000 feet, and they leave very early, men and youths, on horses and mules, carrying axes and saws, in search of wood and resin. Around the houses – most of them built from large logs, others made of adobe – women, children, and a few men look after animals, tend small plots, and make green earthenware with ornate designs, which is taken to the *plaza* or displayed at their door during *fiestas*. They also go to the *plaza*, along dirt or half-paved streets, to fetch water that sometimes is rationed and to buy what they do not get from their fields. The older people speak Tarascan, the young ones understand it, and the children learn only Spanish at school. Since the rate of migration is the same as that of demographic growth, their number has been stable at some six thousand for some time.

Arriving in Patamban on Saturday night, the eve of the *fiesta* of Christ the King: 1.8 miles before the actual village, we know we are near because the wheel of fortune, as high as the church tower and lit with neon lights, can be seen in the distance. Through uneven streets, unaccustomed to cars and trucks of state agencies and private traders who come to collect crafts from the competition, we keep close to houses to let vehicles by, and we listen to the remarks of villagers who turn the doors of their houses into theater seats. In the *plaza* and surrounding streets, the younger ones gather to watch how stalls with manufactured goods and arcade and chance games are set up. As in other peasant villages, we notice that one way of "dressing for the *fiesta*" is to wear T-shirts and jackets with designs of American sports teams, bought during their work stay on the other side of the border; kids prefer to wear television images, such as Charlie's Angels and Bionic Woman. On the platform above the fountain, a representative of the delegation from the Office of Tourism announces that the *pirekua* (old Tarascan songs) contest is about to start. The first group is ready to sing, and men (only men), some forty of them, approach them with tape recorders raised for the best position to record the music. After each song, there is applause and the sound of the "off" buttons. During a break in the show, they answer my questions by telling me that the recorders were bought in Morelia or in the Federal District, others in the United States, when they worked as *braceros*, and that they want to record the music to be able to listen to it when the *fiesta* is over and they have to leave again. The break is over and they go back to their places, next to the platform or kneeling down to form a circle, around a large loudspeaker: in their attitude of concentration vis-à-vis electronic gadgets, in their slow and careful motions as they move the controls, covered by their large *jorongos* (blankets) that protect them from the cold, we can see that the tape recorders are part of the *fiesta* ritual. Like so many ceremonial objects, they represent one way of appropriating and preserving symbols of their identity. It is apparent that what they use, where it comes from, and where they take it reveal how identity is changing.

The other area studied, that of Lake Pátzcuaro, particularly the town that bears that name, seems to indicate the direction in which the process is headed that we saw in its beginnings in Patamban and other *sierra* villages. Besides its better farming, cattle, and fishing resources, the lake region, due to its key role in the economy, politics, and culture of the region since pre-Hispanic times to the present day, also includes archaeological and colonial centers (churches, convents, cities untouched after four centuries), arts and crafts, and tourist services. An excellent road system makes it easy for Pátzcuaro's twenty-four thousand inhabitants to travel often and to get manufactured goods, magazines, *fotonovelas*, and newspapers. For these same reasons, the activities of many official agencies were also concentrated in this area: the Secretary of Human Settlements and Public Works, which builds, among others, workshops and stores to sell crafts; the Indigenista National Institute, which sets up schools and shelters and offers technical and commercial advice to farmers and artisans; and the Office of Tourism and its advertising campaigns. There is also an international agency, the Regional Center for Basic Education in Latin America (Centro Regional de Educación Fundamental para América Latina, CREFAL), until recently under the control of UNESCO: it devotes itself to communal organization and peasant education, and, in the decade of the sixties, it influenced artisanal production through studies, courses, technical assistance, and proposals submitted to governmental organizations.

However, differences among villages bordering on the lake – for example, two of equal political and religious importance since the Conquest, Ihuatzio and Tzintzuntzan – do not allow us to resort to evolutionary simplifications that would characterize this area as an example of what will happen in the *sierra*. Tzintzuntzan is a mestizo town that no longer speaks the Indian language and is economically and culturally integrated into the national society. Nearby, Ihuatzio – which is also only a short distance from Janitzio, opposite the island that is the biggest center of commercialization of the *fiesta* of the dead in Mexico – preserves Tarascan customs, language, and forms of social organization. This process cannot be conceived as a progressive and inevitable incorporation of traditional cultures into the capitalist system. It is more complex, with comings and goings, disconcerting coexistences, and multiple combinations.

I have not outlined all the theoretical and methodological bases necessary to pursue research within the historical and social framework of the region. I prefer to interweave data and remarks throughout the text, allowing the description of phenomena revealed during my fieldwork to be guided by a conceptual explanation, and comparing and contrasting time and time again the theoretical work against the empirical basis.

Notes

1. Alberto M. Cirese, *Ensayo sobre las culturas subalternas*, pp. 55–6, 68–70.
2. Edward H. Spicer, "Acculturation," pp. 21–7.
3. Memorandum 15, International Institute of African Languages and Culture. Quoted in George Pierre Castile, *Cherán*, p. 14.
4. Ralph Linton, *Acculturation in Seven American Indian Tribes*. Quoted in Castile, *Cherán*, p. 16.
5. Gonzalo Aguirre Beltrán, *El proceso de acuhturación*.
6. Cirese, *Ensayo*, p. 51.
7. Ibid., p. 54.
8. L. M. Lombardi Satriani, *Apropiación y destrucción de la cultura de las clases subalternas*, pp. 77–119.
9. Giovanni Battista Bronzini, *Cultura popolare – dialettica e contestualitá*, p. 15.
10. In a later book, *Culturas híbridas*, I analyze this process in detail.

11. Novelo, *Artesanías*, p. 7.
12. Mircea Eliade, *Lo sagrado y lo profano*, p. 80.
13. Jean Duvignaud, *Fêtes et civilizations*, p. 46.
14. Ibid., p. 41.
15. Eric Wolf is among those who hold the "redistribution" thesis; Aguirre Beltrán has criticized their position and has talked instead of "leveling." Castile developed both aspects in his study of Tarascans quoted above (*Cherán*, pp. 62–6).

References

Aguirre Beltran, Gonzalo (1957). *El proceso de aculturación*. Mexico City: Universidad Nacional Autonoma de México (UNAM).

Bronzini, Giovanni Battista (1980). *Cultura popolare – dialettica e contestualitá*. Bari: Dedalo Libri.

Castile, George Pierre (1974). *Cherán: la adaptación de una comuniad tradicional de Michoacán*. Mexico City: Instituto Nacional Indigenista (INI).

Cirese, Alberto M. (1979). *Ensayo sobre las culturas subalternas*. Mexico City: Centro de Investigaciones Superiores del INAH, Cuadernos de la Casa Chata, no. 24.

Dubignaud, Jean (1973). *Fêtes et civilizations*. Geneva: Librarie Weber.

Eliade, Mircea (1967). *Lo sagrado y lo profano*. Madrid: Ediciones Guadarrama.

Linton, Ralph (1941). *Acculturation in Seven American Indian Tribes*. New York: D. Appleton-Century.

Lombardi Satriani, L. M. (1975) *Anthropologia cultural – análisis de la cultura subalterna*. Buenos Aires: Galerna.

Novelo, Victoria (1976). *Artesanías y capitalismo en México*. Mexico City: SEP-INAH.

Spicer, Edward (1968). Acculturation. In: *International Encyclopedia of Social Sciences*, vol. 1, pp. 21–7. New York: Macmillan.

83

Brazilian Culture: Nationalism by Elimination

Roberto Schwarz*

We Brazilians and other Latin Americans constantly experience the artificial, inauthentic and imitative nature of our cultural life. An essential element in our critical thought since independence, it has been variously interpreted from romantic, naturalist, modernist, right-wing, left-wing, cosmopolitan and nationalist points of view, so we may suppose that the problem is enduring and deeply rooted. Before attempting another explanation, let us assume that this malaise is a fact. Its everyday manifestations range from the inoffensive to the horrifying. Examples of inappropriateness include Father Christmas sporting an eskimo outfit in a tropical climate and, for traditionalists, the electric guitar in the land of samba. Representatives of the 1964 dictatorship often used to say that Brazil was not ready for democracy, that it would be out of place here. In the nineteenth century people spoke of the gulf between the empire's liberal façade, copied from the British parliamentary system, and the actual reality of the system of labour, which was slavery. In his 'Lundu do Escritor Difícil' Mário de Andrade[1] ridiculed his fellow countrymen whose knowledge spanned only foreign matters. Recently, when the São Paulo state government extended its human rights policy to the prisons, there were demonstrations of popular discontent at the idea that such guarantees should be introduced inside prisons when so many people did not enjoy them outside. In this perspective even human rights seem spurious in Brazil. These examples, taken from unrelated spheres and presupposing incompatible points of view, show how widespread the problem is. They all involve the same sense of contradiction between the real Brazil and the ideological prestige of the countries used as models.[2]

Let us examine the problem from a literary point of view. In twenty years of teaching the subject I have witnessed a transition in literary criticism from impressionism, through positivist historiography, American New Criticism, stylistics, Marxism, phenomenology, structuralism, post-structuralism, and now Reception theories. The list is impressive and demonstrates our university's efforts to overcome provincialism. But it is easy to see that the change from one school of thought to another rarely arises from the exhaustion of a particular project; usually it expresses the high regard that Brazilians feel for the newest doctrine from America or Europe. The disappointing impression

*Pp. 1–18 & 121–29 (relevant refs) from *Misplaced Ideas: Essays on Brazilian Culture*, ed. J. Gledson (London, Verso). © 1992 by Roberto Schwartz.

created, therefore, is one of change and development with no inner necessity and therefore no value. The thirst for terminological and doctrinal novelty prevails over the labour of extending knowledge and is another illustration of the imitative nature of our cultural life. We shall see that the problem has not been correctly posed, although we may start by accepting its relative validity.

In Brazil intellectual life seems to start from scratch with each generation.[3] The hankering for the advanced countries' latest products nearly always has as its reverse side a lack of interest in the work of the previous generation of Brazilian writers, and results in a lack of intellectual continuity. As Machado de Assis noted in 1879: 'A foreign impetus determines the direction of movement.' What is the meaning of this passing over of the internal impulse, which is in any case much less inevitable than it was then? You do not have to be a traditionalist or believe in an impossible intellectual autarky to recognize the difficulties. There is a lack of conviction, both in the constantly changing theories and in their relationship to the movement of society as a whole. As a result little importance is attached to work itself or to the object of investigation. Outstanding analyses and research on the country's culture are periodically cut short and problems that have been identified and tackled with great difficulty are not developed as they deserve. This bias is negatively confirmed by the stature of such few outstanding writers as Machado de Assis,[4] Mário de Andrade and now Antonio Candido. None of them lacked information or an openness to contemporary trends, but they all knew how to make broad and critical use of their predecessors' work, which they regarded not as dead weight but as a dynamic and unfinished element underlying present day contradictions.

It is not a question of continuity for the sake of it. We have to identify a set of real, specific problems – with their own historical insertion and duration – which can draw together existing forces and allow fresh advances to be made. With all due respect to the theoreticians we study in our faculties, I believe we would do better to devote ourselves to a critical assessment of the ideas put forward by Silvio Romero,[5] Oswald and Mário de Andrade, Antonio Candido, the concretists and the CPCs.[6] A certain degree of cultural density arises out of alliances or disagreements between scientific disciplines, artistic, social and political groups, without which the idea of breaking away in pursuit of the new becomes meaningless. We should bear in mind that to many Latin Americans Brazil's intellectual life appears to have an enviably organic character, and however incredible it may seem, there may be some relative truth in this view.

Little remains of the conceptions and methods that we have passed under review, since the rhythm of change has not allowed them to attain a mature expression. There is a real problem here, part of that feeling of inappropriateness from which we started out. Nothing seems more reasonable, for those who are aware of the damage, than to steer in the opposite direction and think it is enough to avoid copying metropolitan trends in order to achieve an intellectual life with greater substance. This conclusion is illusory, as we shall see, but has strong intuitive support. For a time it was taken up by both right and left nationalists, in a convergence that boded ill for the left and, through its wide diffusion, contributed to a low intellectual level and a high estimation of ideological crudities.

The search for genuine (i.e. unadulterated) national roots leads us to ask: What would popular culture be like if it were possible to isolate it from commercial interests and particularly from the mass media? What would a national economy be like if there were no admixture? Since 1964 the internationalization of capital, the commodification of social relations, and the presence of the mass media have developed so rapidly that these very questions have come to seem implausible. Yet barely twenty years ago they still excited intellectuals and figured on their agenda. A combative frame of mind still prevailed – for which progress would result from a kind of *reconquista*, or rather from the expulsion of the invaders. Once imperialism had been pushed back, its commercial and industrial forms of culture neutralized, and its allied, anti-national section of the bourgeoisie isolated, the way would be clear for the flowering of national culture, which had been *distorted by these elements as by an alien body*. This correct emphasis on the mechanisms of US domination served to mythologize the Brazilian community as object of patriotic fervour, whereas a class analysis would have made this much more problematic. Here a qualification is necessary: such ideas reached their height in the period of the Goulart government, when extraordinary events, which brought about experimentation and democratic realignments on a large scale, were taking place. The period cannot be reduced to the inconsistencies of its self-image – indicative though they are of the illusion inherent in populist nationalism that the outside world is the source of all evil.

In 1964 the right-wing nationalists branded Marxism as an alien influence, perhaps imagining that fascism was a Brazilian invention. But over and above their differences, the two nationalist tendencies were alike in hoping to find their goal by eliminating anything that was not indigenous. The residue would be the essence of Brazil. The same illusion was popular in the last century, but at that time the new national culture owed more to diversification of the European models than to exclusion of the Portuguese. Opponents of the romantic liberal distortion of Brazilian society did not arrive at the authentic country, since once French and English imports had been rooted out, the colonial order was restored. And that was a Portuguese creation. The paradox of this kind of purism is apparent in the person of Policarpo Quaresma, whose quest for authenticity led him to write in Tupi, a language foreign to him.[7] The same goes for Antonio Callado's *Quarup*, in which the real Brazil is found not in the colonial past – as suggested by Lima Barreto's hero – but in the heart of the interior, far from the Atlantic coast with its overseas contacts. A group of characters mark the centre of the country on a map and go off in search of it. After innumerable adventures they reach their destination, where they find . . . an ants' nest.

The standard US models that arrived with the new communications networks were regarded by the nationalists as an unwelcome foreign presence. The next generation, however, already breathing naturally in this air, considered nationalism to be archaic and provincial. For the first time, as far as I know, the idea spread that it was a worthless enterprise to defend national characteristics against imperialist uniformity. The culture industry would cure the sickness of Brazilian culture – at least for those who were willing to delude themselves.

In the 1960s nationalism also came under fire from those who thought of themselves as politically and artistically more advanced. Their views are now being taken up in the context of international mass media, only this time without the elements of class struggle and anti-imperialism. In this 'world' environment of uniform mythology, the struggle to establish an 'authentic' culture appears as a relic from the past. Its illusory nature becomes evident, and it seems a provincial phenomenon associated with archaic forms of oppression. The argument is irrefutable, but it must be said that in the new context an emphasis on the international dimension of culture becomes no more than a legitimation of the existing mass media. Just as nationalists used to condemn imperialism and hush up bourgeois oppression, so the anti-nationalists invoke the authoritarianism and backwardness of their opponents, with good reason, while suggesting that the reign of mass communication is either emancipatory or aesthetically acceptable. A modern, critical position, perhaps, but fundamentally conformist. There is another imaginary reversal of roles: although the 'globalists' operate within the dominant ideology of our time, they defend their positions as if they were being hunted down, or as if they were par of the heroic vanguard, aesthetic or libertarian, of the early twentieth century; they line up with the authorities in the manner of one who is starting a revolution.

In the same order of paradox, we can see that the imposition of foreign ideology and the cultural expropriation of the people are realities which do not cease to exist just because there is mystification in the nationalists' theories about them. Whether they are right or wrong, the nationalists become involved in actual conflicts, imparting to them a certain degree of visibility. The mass media modernists, though right in their criticisms, imagine a universalist world which does not exist. It is a question of choosing between the old and the new error, both upheld in the name of progress. The sight of the Avenida Paulista is a fine illustration of what I mean: ugly mansions, once used by the rich to flaunt their wealth, now seem perversely tolerable at the foot of modern skyscrapers, both for reasons of proportion and because of that poetry which emanates from any historically superseded power.

Recent French philosophy has been another factor in the discrediting of cultural nationalism. Its anti-totalizing tendency, its preference for levels of historicity alien to the national milieu, its dismantling of conventional literary scaffolding such as authorship, 'the work', influence, originality, etc. – all these destroy, or at least discredit, that romantic correspondence between individual heroism, masterly execution and collective redemption which imbues the nationalist schemas with their undeniable knowledge-value and potential for mystification. To attack these coordinates can be exciting and partially convincing, besides appeasing national sensibility in an area where one would least expect this to be possible.

A commonplace idea suggests that the copy is secondary with regard to the original, depends upon it, is worth less, and so on. Such a view attaches a negative sign to the totality of cultural forces in Latin America and is at the root of the intellectual malaise that we are discussing. Now, contemporary French philosophers such as Foucault and Derrida have made it their speciality to show that such hierarchies have no basis. Why should the prior be worth more than the posterior, the model more than the imitation, the central more than the peripheral, the economic infrastructure more than cultural life, and so forth? According to the French philosophers, it is a question of conditioning processes (but are they all of the same order?) – prejudices which do not express the life of the spirit in its real movement but reflect the orientation inherent in the traditional human sciences. In their view, it would be more accurate and unbiased to think in terms of an infinite sequence of transformations, with no beginning or end, no first or last, no worse or better. One can easily appreciate how this would enhance the self-esteem and relieve the anxiety of the underdeveloped world, which is seen as tributary to the central countries. We would pass from being a backward to an advanced part of the world, from a deviation to a paradigm, from inferior to superior lands (although the analysis set out to suppress just such superiority). All this because countries which live in the humiliation of having to imitate are more willing than the metropolitan countries to give up the illusion of an original source, even though the theory originated there and not here. Above all, the problem of mirror-culture would no longer be ours alone, and instead of setting our sights on the Europeanization or Americanization of Latin America we would, in a certain sense, be participating in the Latin Americanization of the central cultures.[8]

It remains to be seen whether this conceptual break with the primacy of origins would enable us to balance out or combat relations of actual subordination. Would the innovations of the advanced world suddenly become dispensable once they had lost the distinction of originality? In order to use them in a free and non-imitative manner, it is not enough simply to divest them of their sacred aura. Contrary to what the above analysis might lead us to believe, the breaking down of cultural dazzlement in the under-developed countries does not go to the heart of a problem which is essentially practical in character. Solutions are reproduced from the advanced world in response to cultural, economic and political needs, and the notion of copying, with its psychologistic connotations, throws no light whatsoever on this reality. If theory remains at this level, it will continue to suffer from the same limitations, and the radicalism of an analysis that passes over efficient causes will become in its turn largely delusive. The inevitability of cultural imitation is bound up with a specific set of historical imperatives over which abstract philosophical critiques can exercise no power. Even here nationalism is the weak part of the argument, and its supersession at the level of philosophy has no purchase on the realities to which it owes its strength. It should be noted that while nationalism has recently been almost absent from serious intellectual debate, it has a growing presence in the administration of culture, where, for better or worse, it is impossible to escape from the national dimension. Now that economic, though not political, space has become international – which is not the same as homogeneous – this return of nationalism by the back door reflects the insuperable paradox of the present day.

In the 1920s Oswald de Andrade's 'anthropophagous' Pau-Brazil programme also tried to give a triumphalist interpretation of our backwardness.[9] The disharmony between bourgeois models and the realities of rural patriarchy is at the very heart of his poetry – the first of these two elements appearing in the role of absurd caprice ('Rui Barbosa[10]: A Top Hat in Senegambia'). Its true novelty lies in the fact that the lack of accord is a source not of distress but of optimism, evidence of the country's innocence and the possibility of an alternative, non-bourgeois historical development. This *sui generis* cult of progress is rounded out with a technological wager: Brazil's innocence (the result of Christianization and *embourgeoisement* barely scraping the surface) plus technology equals utopia; modern material progress will make possible a direct leap from pre-bourgeois society to paradise. Marx himself, in his famous letter of 1881 to Vera Zasulich, came up with a similar hypothesis that the Russian peasant commune would achieve socialism without a capitalist interregnum, thanks to the means made available by progress in the West. Similarly, albeit in a register combining jokes, provocation, philosophy of history and prophecy (as, later, in the films of Glauber Rocha), Anthropophagy set itself the aim of leaping a whole stage.

Returning once more to the idea that Western culture has been inappropriately copied in Brazil, we can see that Oswald's programme introduced a change of tone. Local primitivism would give back a modern sense to tired European culture, liberating it from Christian mortification and capitalist utilitarianism. Brazil's experience would be a differentiated cornerstone, with utopian powers, on the map of contemporary history. (The poems of Mário de Andrade and Raúl Bopp[11] on Amazonian slothfulness contain a similar idea.) Modernism therefore brought about a profound change in values: for the first time the processes under way in Brazil were weighed in the context of the present-day world, as having something to offer in that larger context. Oswald de Andrade advocated cultural irreverence in place of subaltern obfuscation, using the metaphor of 'swallowing up' the alien: a copy, to be sure, but with regenerative effect. Historical distance allows us to see the ingenuousness and jingoism contained in these propositions.

The new vogue for Oswald's manifestoes in the 1960s and particularly the 1970s appeared in the very different context of a military dictatorship which, for all its belief in technological progress and its alliance with big capital both national and international, was less repressive than expected in regard to everyday habits and morality. In the other camp, the attempt to overthrow capitalism through revolutionary war also changed the accepted view of what could be termed 'radical'. This now had no connection with the provincial narrowness of the 1920s, when the Antropófago rebellion assumed a highly libertarian and enlightening role. In the new circumstances technological optimism no longer held water, while the brazen cultural irreverence of Oswald's 'swallowing up' acquired a sense of exasperation close to the mentality of direct action (although often with good artistic results). Oswald's clarity of construction, penetrating vision and sense of discovery all suffered as greater value was attached to his primal, 'de-moralizing' literary practices. One example of this evolution is the guiltlessness of the act of swallowing up. What was then freedom against Catholicism, the bourgeoisie and the glare of Europe has become in the eighties an awkward excuse to handle uncritically those ambiguities of mass culture that stand in need of elucidation. How can one fail to notice that the *Antropófagos* – like the nationalists – take as their subject the abstract Brazilian, with no class specification; or that the analogy with the digestive process throws absolutely no light on the politics and aesthetics of contemporary cultural life?

Since the last century educated Brazilians – the concept is not meant as a compliment but refers to a social category – have had the sense of living among ideas and institutions copied from abroad that do not reflect local reality. It is not sufficient, however, to give up loans in order to think and live more authentically. Besides, one cannot so much as conceive of giving them up. Nor is the problem eliminated by a philosophical deconstruction of the concept of copy. The programmatic innocence of the Antropófagos, which allows them to ignore the malaise, does not prevent it from emerging anew. 'Tupi or not Tupi, that is the question!' Oswald's famous saying, with its contradictory use of the English language, a classical line and a play on words to pursue the search for national identity, itself says a great deal about the nature of the impasse.

The problem may appear simpler in historical perspective. Silvio Romero, despite many absurdities, made a number of excellent remarks on the matter. The following extract is taken from a work on Machado de Assis, written in 1897 to prove that this greatest Brazilian writer produced nothing but a literature of Anglomania, incompetent, unattuned, slavish, etc.

> Meanwhile a kind of absurdity developed . . . a tiny intellectual elite separated itself off from the mass of the population, and while the majority remained almost entirely uneducated, this elite, being particularly gifted in the art of learning and copying, threw itself into political and literary imitation of everything it found in the Old World. So now we have an exotic literature and politics, which live and procreate in a hothouse that has no relationship to the outside temperature and environment. This is the bad side of our feeble, illusory skill of mestizo southerners, passionate, given to fantasy, capable of imitation but organically unsuited to create, invent or produce things of our own that spring from the immediate or remote depths of our life and history.
>
> In colonial times, a skilful policy of segregation cut us off from foreigners and kept within us a certain sense of cohesion. This is what gave us Basilio,[12] Durào, Gonzaga, Alvarenga Peixoto, Claudio and Silva Alvarenga, who all worked in a milieu of exclusively Portuguese and Brazilian ideas.
>
> With the first emperor and the Regency, the first breach [opened] in our wall of isolation by Dom Joào VI grew wider, and we began to copy the political and literary romanticism of the French.
>
> We aped the Charter of 1814 and transplanted the fantasies of Benjamin Constant; we mimicked the parliamentarism and constitutional politics of the author of *Adolphe*, intermingled with the poetry and dreams of the author of *René* and *Atala*.
>
> The people . . . remained illiterate.
>
> The Second Reign[13], whose policy was for fifty years vacillating, uncertain and incompetent, gradually opened all the gates in a chaotic manner lacking any criteria or sense of discrimination. Imitation, mimicking of everything – customs, laws, codes, verse, theatre, novel – was the general rule.
>
> Regular sailings assured direct communication with the old continent and swelled the inflow of imitation and servile copying. . . .
>
> This is why, in terms of copying, mimickry and pastiches to impress the gringos, no people has a better Constitution on paper . . . , everything is better . . . on paper. The reality is appalling.[14]

Silvio Romero's account and analysis are uneven, sometimes incompatible. In some instances it is the argument that is interesting, in others the ideology, so that the modern reader will want to examine them separately. The basic schema is as follows: a tiny elite devotes itself to copying Old World culture, separating itself off from the mass of the population, which remains uneducated. As a result, literature and politics come to occupy an exotic position, and we become incapable of *creating things of our own that spring from the depths of our life and history*. Implicit in this demand is the norm of an organic, reasonably homogeneous national culture with popular roots – a norm that cannot be reduced to a mere illusion of literary history or of romanticism, since in some measure it expresses the conditions of modern citizenship. It is in its opposition to this norm that the Brazilian configuration – Europeanized minority, uneducated majority – constitutes an *absurdity*. On the other hand, in order to make the picture more realistic, we should remember that the organic requirement arose at the same time as the expansion of imperialism and organized science – two tendencies which rendered obsolete the idea of a harmonious and auto-centred national culture.

The original sin, responsible for the severing of connections, was the copy. Its negative effects already made themselves felt in the social fissure between *culture* (unrelated to its surroundings) and *production* (not springing from the depths of our life). However, the disproportion between cause and effects is such that it raises some doubts about the cause itself, and Silvio Romero's own remarks are an invitation to follow a different line of argument from the one he pursues. Let us also note in passing that it is in the nature of an absurdity to be avoidable, and that Romero's argument and invective actually suggest that the elite had an obligation to correct the error that had separated it from the people. His critique was seeking to make the class gulf intolerable for *educated people*, since in a country recently emancipated from slavery the weakness of the popular camp inhibited the emergence of other solutions.

It would seem, then, that the origins of our cultural absurdity are to be found in the imitative talent of mestizo southerners who have few creative capacities. The *petitio principii* is quite transparent: imitativeness is explained by a (racial) tendency to that very imitativeness which is supposed to be explained. (The author's argument, we should note, itself imitated the scientific naturalism then in vogue in Europe.) Today such explanations can hardly be taken seriously, although it is worth examining them as an ideological mechanism and an expression of their times. If the Brazilians' propensity for copying is racial in origin, why should the elite have been alone in indulging it? If everyone had copied, all the effects of 'exoticism' (lack of relation to the environment) and 'absurdity' (separation between elite and people) would have vanished as if by magic, and with them the whole problem. It is not copying in general but *the copying of one class* that constitutes the problem. The explanation must lie not in race but in class.

Silvio Romero goes on to sketch how the vice of imitation developed in Brazil. Absolute zero was in the colonial period, when writers 'worked in a milieu of exclusively Portuguese and Brazilian ideas.' Could it be that the distance between elite and people was smaller in that epoch? Or the fondness for copying less strong? Surely not – and anyway that is not what the text says. The 'cohesion' to which it refers is of a different order, the result of a 'skilful policy of segregation' (!) that separated Brazil from everything non-Portuguese. In other words, the comparison between stages lacks an object: the demand for homogeneity points, in one case, to a social structure remarkable for its inequality, and in the other case to the banning of foreign ideas. Still, if the explanation does not convince us, the observation that it seeks to clarify is accurate enough. Before the nineteenth century, the copying of the European model and the distance between educated people and the mass did not constitute an 'absurdity'. In highly schematic terms, we could say that educated people, in the colonial period, felt solidarity towards the metropolis, Western tradition and their own colleagues, but not towards the local population. To base oneself on a foreign model, in cultural estrangement from the local surroundings, did not appear as a defect – quite the contrary! We should not forget that neoclassical aesthetics was itself universalist and greatly appreciated respect for canonical forms, while the theory of art current at that time set a positive value on imitation. As Antonio Candido acutely observed, the Arcadian poet who placed a nymph in the waters of the Carmo was not lacking in originality; he incorporated Minas Gerais into the traditions of the West and, quite laudably, cultivated those traditions in a remote corner of the earth.[15]

The act of copying, then, did not begin with independence and the opening of the ports[16], as Silvio Romero would have it. But it is true that only then did it become the insoluble problem which is still discussed today, and which calls forth such terms as 'mimickry', 'apeing' or 'pastiche'. How did imitation acquire these pejorative connotations?

It is well known that Brazil's gaining of independence did not involve a revolution. Apart from changes in external relations and a reorganization of the top administration, the socio-economic structure created by colonial exploitation remained intact, though now for the benefit of local dominant classes. It was thus inevitable that modern forms of civilization entailing freedom and citizenship, which arrived together with the wave of political emancipation, should have appeared foreign and artificial, 'anti-national', 'borrowed', 'absurd' or however else critics cared to describe them. The strength of the epithets indicates the acrobatics which the self-esteem of the Brazilian elite was forced into, since it faced the depressing alternative of deprecating the bases of its social pre-eminence in the name of progress, or deprecating progress in the name of its social preeminence. On the one hand, there were the slave trade, the latifundia and clientelism – that is to say, a set of relations with their own rules, consolidated in colonial times and impervious to the universalism of bourgeois civilization; on the other hand, stymied by these relations, but also stymying them, there was the Law before which everyone was equal, the separation between public and private, civil liberties, parliament, romantic patriotism, and so on. The ensuring of the stable coexistence of these two conceptions, in principle so incompatible, was at the centre of ideological and moral preoccupations in Brazil in the nineteenth century. For some, the colonial heritage was a relic to be superseded in the march of progress; for others, it was the real Brazil, to be preserved against absurd imitations. Some wanted to harmonize progress and slave labour, so as not to have to give up either, while still others believed that such a reconciliation already existed, with deleterious moral results. Silvio Romero, for his part, used conservative arguments with a progressive intent, focusing on the 'real' Brazil as the continuation of colonial authoritarianism, but doing so in order to attack its foundations. He scorned as ineffectual the 'illusory' country of laws, lawyers and imported culture: 'No people has a better Constitution on paper . . . ; the reality is appalling.'

Silvio Romero's list of 'imitations', not to be allowed through customs, included fashions, patterns of behaviour, laws, codes, poetry, drama and novels. Judged separately against the social reality of Brazil, these articles were indeed superfluous imports which would serve to obscure the real state of impoverishment and create an illusion of progress. In their combination, however, they entered into the formation and equipping of the new nation-state, as well as laying the ground for the participation of new elites in contemporary culture. This modernizing force – whatever its imitative appearance and its distance from the daily course of things – became more inseparably bound up with the reality of Brazil than the institution of slave labour, which was later replaced by other forms of forced labour equally incompatible with the aspiration to enlightenment. As time passed, the ubiquitous stamp of 'inauthenticity' came to be seen as the most authentic part of the national drama, its very mark of identity. Grafted from nineteenth-century Europe on to a colonial social being, the various perfections of civilization began to follow different rules from those operating in the hegemonic countries. This led to a widespread sense of the indigenous pastiche. Only a great figure like Machado de Assis had the impartiality to see a peculiar mode of ideological functioning where other critics could distinguish no more than a lack of consistency. Sérgio Buarque de Holanda remarked: 'The speed at which the "new ideas" spread in the old colony, and the fervour with which they were adopted in many circles on the eve of independence, show quite unequivocally that they had the potential to satisfy an impatient desire for change and that the people were ripe for such change. But it is also clear that the social order expressed in these ideas was far from having an exact equivalent in Brazil, particularly outside the cities. The articulation of society, the basic criteria of economic exploitation and the distribution of privileges were so different here that the "new ideas" could not have the same meaning that was attached to them in parts of Europe or ex-English America.'[17]

When Brazil became an independent state, a permanent collaboration was established between the forms of life characteristic of colonial oppression and the innovations of bourgeois progress. The new stage of capitalism broke up the exclusive relationship with the metropolis, converting local property-owners and administrators into a national ruling class (effectively part of the emergent world bourgeoisie), and yet retained the old forms of labour exploitation which have not been fully modernized up to the present day. In other words, the discrepancy between the 'two Brazils' was not due to an imitative tendency, as Silvio Romero and many others thought; nor did it correspond to a brief period of transition. It was the lasting result of the creation of a nation-state on the basis of slave labour – which, if the reader will forgive the shorthand, arose in turn out of the English industrial revolution and the consequent crisis of the old colonial system. That is to say, *it arose out of contemporary history*.[18] Thus Brazil's backward deformation belongs to the same order of things as the progress of the advanced countries. Silvio Romero's 'absurdities' – in reality, the Cyclopean discords of world capitalism – are not a historical deviation. They are linked to the finality of a single process which, in the case of Brazil, requires the continuation of forced or semi-forced labour and a corresponding cultural separation of the poor. With certain modifications, much of it has survived to this day. The panorama now seems to be changing, thanks to the desegregationist impulse of mass consumption and mass communications. These new terms of cultural oppression and expropriation have not yet been much studied.

The thesis of cultural copying thus involves an ideology in the Marxist sense of the term – that is, an illusion supported by appearances. The well-known coexistence of bourgeois principles with those of the ancien régime is here explained in accordance with a plausible and wide-ranging schema, essentially individualist in nature, in which effects and causes are systematically inverted.

For Silvio Romero imitation results in the lack of a common denominator between popular and elite culture, and in the elite's low level of permeation by the national. But why not reverse the argument? Why should the imitative character of our life not stem from forms of inequality so brutal that they lack the minimal reciprocity ('common denominator') without which modern society can only appear artificial and 'imported'? At a time when the idea of the nation had become the norm, the dominant class's *unpatriotic* disregard for the lives it exploited gave it the feeling of being alien. The origins of this situation in colonialism and slavery are immediately apparent.

The defects normally associated with imitation can be explained in the same way. We can agree with its detractors that the copy is at the opposite pole from originality, from national creativity, from independent and well-adapted judgements, and so on. Absolute domination entails that culture expresses nothing of the conditions that gave it life, except for that intrinsic sense of futility on which a number of writers have been able to work artistically. Hence the 'exotic' literature and politics unrelated to the 'immediate or remote depths of our life and history'; hence, too, the lack of 'discrimination' or 'criteria' and, above all, the intense conviction that all is mere paper. In other words, the painfulness of an imitative civilization is produced not by imitation – which is present at any event – but by the social structure of the country. It is this which places culture in an untenable position, contradicting its very concept of itself, and which nevertheless was not as sterile, at that time, as Silvio Romero would have us believe. Nor did the segregated section of society remain unproductive. Its modes of expression would later acquire, for educated intellectuals, the value of a non-bourgeois component of national life, an element serving to fix Brazilian identity (with all the evident ambiguities).

The exposure of cultural transplantation has become the axis of a naive yet widespread critical perspective. Let us conclude by summarizing some of its defects.

1. It suggests that imitation is avoidable, thereby locking the reader into a false problem.
2. It presents as a national characteristic what is actually a malaise of the dominant class, bound up with the difficulty of morally reconciling the advantages of progress with those of slavery or its surrogates.
3. It implies that the elites could conduct themselves in some other way which is tantamount to claiming that the beneficiary of a given situation will put an end to it.
4. The argument obscures the essential point, since it concentrates its fire on the relationship between elite and model whereas the real crux is the exclusion of the poor from the universe of contemporary culture.
5. Its implicit solution is that the dominant class should reform itself and give up imitation. We have argued, on the contrary, that the answer lies in the workers gaining access to the terms of contemporary life, so that they can re-define them through their own initiative. This, indeed, would be in this context a concrete definition of democracy in Brazil.
6. A copy refers to a prior original exiting elsewhere, of which it is an inferior reflection. Such deprecation often corresponds to the self-consciousness of Latin

American elites, who attach mythical solidity – in the form of regional intellectual specialization – to the economic, technological and political inequalities of the international order. The authentic and the creative are to the imitative what the advanced countries are to the backward. But one cannot solve the problem by going to the opposite extreme. As we have seen, philosophical objections to the concept of originality tend to regard as non-existent a real problem that it is absurd to dismiss. Cultural history has to be set in the world perspective of the economics and culture of the left, which attempt to explain our 'backwardness' as part of the contemporary history of capital and *its advances*.[19] Seen in terms of the copy, the anachronistic juxtaposition of forms of modern civilization and realities originating in the colonial period is a mode of nonbeing or even a humiliatingly imperfect realization of a model situated elsewhere. Dialectical criticism, on the other hand, investigates the same anachronism and seeks to draw out a figure of the modern world, set on a course that is either full of promise, grotesque or catastrophic.

7. The file idea of the copy that we have been discussing counterposes national and foreign, original and imitative. These are unreal oppositions which do not allow us to see the share of the foreign in the nationally specific, of the imitative in the original and of the original in the imitative. (In a key study, Paulo Emilio Salles Comes refers to our 'creative lack of competence in copying'.)[20] If I am not mistaken, the theory presupposes three elements – a Brazilian subject, reality of the country, civilization of the advanced nations – such that the third helps the first to forget the second. This schema is also unreal, and it obscures the organized, cumulative nature of the process, the potent strength even of bad tradition, and the power relations, both national and international, that are in play. Whatever its unacceptable aspects – unacceptable for whom? – Brazilian cultural life has elements of dynamism which display both originality and lack of originality. Copying is not a false problem, so long as we treat it pragmatically, from an aesthetic and political point of view freed from the mythical requirement of creation *ex nihilo*.

Notes

1. *Mário de Andrade* (1893–1945), novelist, poet and critic, was the acknowledged leader of the modernist movement in Brazil and bore the brunt of the initial scandal that it caused. The language of his *Macunaima: The Hero without Any Character* (1928) synthesizes idioms and dialects from all the regions of Brazil. [*Trs.*]

2. For a balanced and considered opinion on the subject, see Antonio Candido, 'Literatura e subdesenvolvimento', *Argumento* No. 1, São Paulo, October 1973.

3. This observation was made by Vinicius Dantas.

4. *Joaquim Maria Machado de Assis* (1839–1908) is regarded as the greatest of all Portuguese-language novelists. He wrote nine novels and two hundred short stories, including *Epitaph of a Small Winner* (1880), *Dom Casmurro* (1990) and *Esau and Jacob* (1904), which are considered to be far ahead of their time. [*Trs.*]

5. *Sílvio Romero* (1851–1914) wrote the first modern history of Brazilian literature, a work which is still of interest today, despite the scientistic language of the period. [*Trs.*]

6. The *Centro Popular de Cultura* (CPC) was established in 1961 at the start of the social ferment that ended with the military coup in 1964. The movement was created under the auspices of the National Union of Students, which wanted to fuse together artistic irreverence, political teaching and the people. It produced surprisingly inventive cinema, theatre and other stage performances. Several of its members became major artistic figures: Glauber Rocha, Joaquim Pedro de Andrade and Ferreira Gullar among others. The convergence of the student and popular movements gave rise to completely new artistic possibilities. [*Note supplied by Ana McMac*].

7. Policarpo Quaresma is the hero of the novel *Triste fim de Policarpo Quaresma* (1915) (translated as *The Patriot* [London: Peter Owen, 1978], by Afonso Henriques de Lima Barreto [1881–1922]. The hero is a caricature patriot, if a sympathetic character, who gradually becomes disillusioned with the state of Brazil.

8. See Silviano Santiago, 'O Entre-lugar do discurso latino-americano', in *Uma literatura nos trópicos*, São Paulo 1978; and Haroldo de Campos, 'Da razão antropofágica: diálogo e diferença na cultura brasileira', *Boletim Bibliográfico Biblioteca Mário de Andrade*, vol 44, January–December 1983.

9. *Oswald de Andrade* introduced European avant-garde ideas into Brazil. He espoused extreme primitivism (anthropophagy) and his *Manifesto da Poesia Pau-Brasil* (1924) and *Manifesto Antropofágo* (1928) are the most daring writings of the 'modern movement' which emerged in 1922, attacking academic values and respectability and seeking poetry written in the Brazilian vernacular. [*Trs.*]

10. *Rui Barbosa* (1849–1923) was a prominent liberal politician, and regarded as a model of culture, linguistic purity and erudition in the early twentieth century: he achieved an almost mythical status, known as 'The Eagle of the Hague' for his diplomacy at an International Conference there in 1906. In this phrase, obviously, it is the incongruity of such false representatives of high culture in Brazil which is underlined.

11. The greatest achievement of *Raúl Bopp* (b. 1898) was his 'cannibalist' poem 'Cobra Norato' (1921), an exploration of the Amazon jungle. [*Trs.*]

12. The names of a group of the so-called Minas group of Arcadian poets who flourished in the interior, gold-mining area of the country in the latter half of the eighteenth century.

13. That of the Emperor Pedro II, which lasted from 1840 to 1889.

14. Sílvio Romero, *Machado de Assis*, Rio de Janeiro 1897, pp. 121–3.

15. Antonio Candido, *Formação da literatura brasileira*, São Paulo 1969, vol. 1, p. 74.

16. In the wake of his flight to Brazil, to escape Napoleon's invasion of Portugal in 1807–8, in which he was escorted by the British fleet, King João VI opened the ports of the colony for the first time to non-Portuguese (largely British) shipping.

17. Sergio Buarque de Holanda, *Do império à republica*, II, São Paulo 1977, pp. 77–78.

18. Emília Viotti da Costa, *Da monarquia à república: Momentos decisivos*, São Paulo 1977, Chapter I; Luis Felipe de Alencastro, 'La traite negrière et l'unité nationale brésilienne', *Revue Française de l'Histoire de l'Outre-Mer*, vol. 46, 1979; Fernando Novais, 'Passagens para o Novo Mundo', *Novos Estudos Cebrap 9*, July 1984.

19. See Celso Furtado, *A Pre-Revolução Brasileira*, Rio de Janeiro 1962, and Fernando H. Cardoso, *Empresario industrial e desenvolvimento económico no Brasil*, São Paulo 1964.

20. Paulo Emílio Salles Gomes, 'Cinema: trajetória no subdesenvolvimento', *Argumento* No. 1, October 1973.

Index